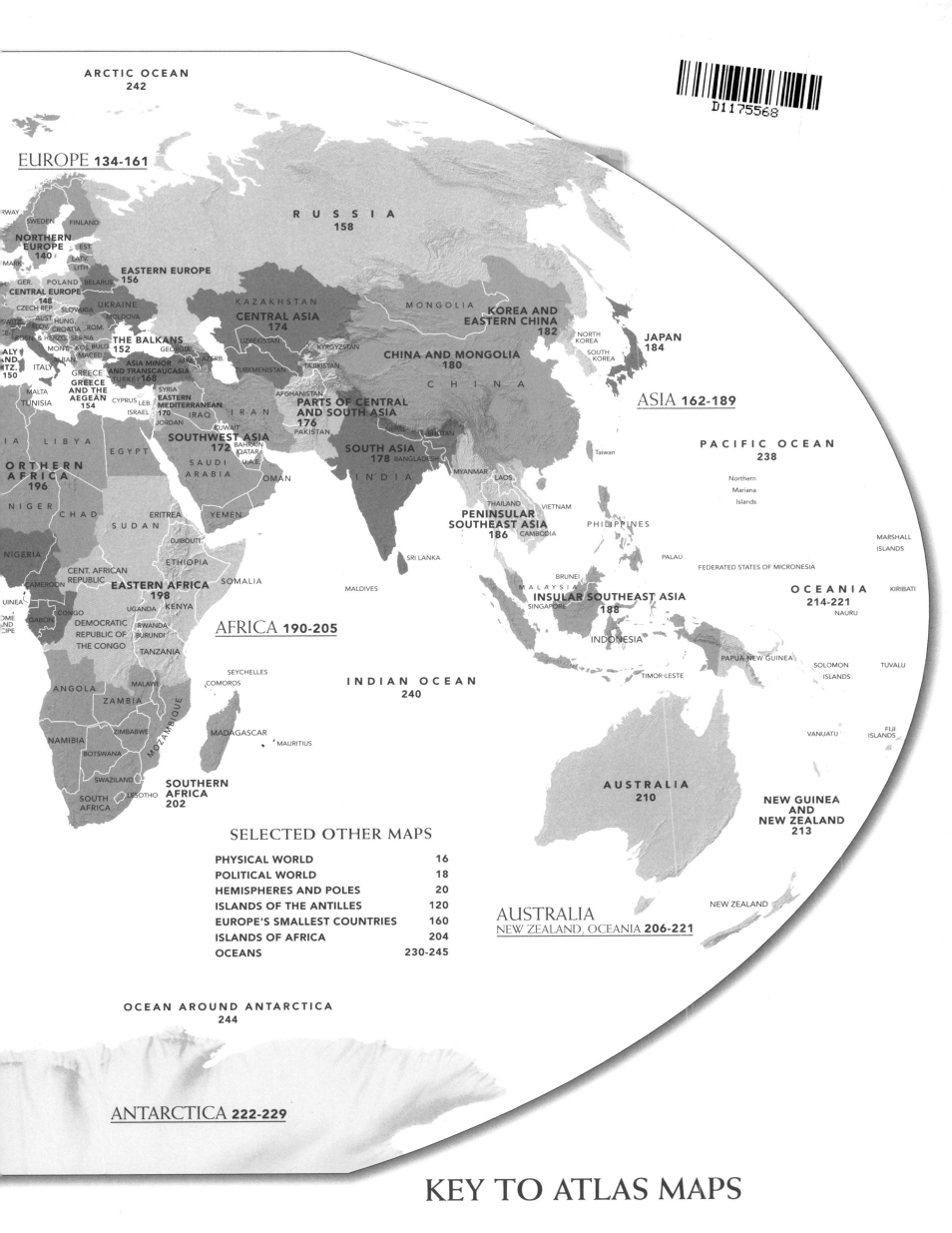

ARCTIC OCEAN
242

EUROPE **134-161**

R U S S I A
158

NORWAY
SWEDEN   FINLAND

NORTHERN
EUROPE
140
EST.
DENMARK   LATV.
LITH.

EASTERN EUROPE
156
GER.   POLAND   BELARUS

CENTRAL EUROPE
148
CZECH REP.
SLOVAKIA   UKRAINE
SWITZ.   AUST.   HUNG.   MOLDOVA
SLOV.   CROATIA   ROM.

KAZAKHSTAN

CENTRAL ASIA
174

MONGOLIA

KOREA AND
EASTERN CHINA
182

NORTH
KOREA

JAPAN
184

SOUTH
KOREA

BOSN. & HERZG.   SERBIA
ITALY   MONT.   KOS.   BULG.
AND   ALBAN.   MACED.
SWITZ.   ITALY
150

THE BALKANS
152
GEORGIA
ASIA MINOR
AND TRANSCAUCASIA
TURKEY 168
ARM.   AZERB.

UZBEKISTAN

KYRGYZSTAN

TAJIKISTAN

TURKMENISTAN

CHINA AND MONGOLIA
180

C H I N A

ASIA **162-189**

MALTA
GREECE
AND THE
AEGEAN
154
TUNISIA
CYPRUS   LEB.
ISRAEL
SYRIA
EASTERN
MEDITERRANEAN
170
JORDAN
IRAQ
I R A N

AFGHANISTAN

PARTS OF CENTRAL
AND SOUTH ASIA
176
PAKISTAN

NEPAL   BHUTAN

SOUTH ASIA
178   BANGLADESH

Taiwan

PACIFIC OCEAN
238

Northern
Mariana
Islands

LIBYA
EGYPT

SOUTHWEST ASIA
172
BAHRAIN
QATAR
KUWAIT
SAUDI
ARABIA   U.A.E.
OMAN

I N D I A

MYANMAR
LAOS

MARSHALL
ISLANDS

NORTHERN
AFRICA
196
NIGER   CHAD
SUDAN
ERITREA
YEMEN

THAILAND   VIETNAM

PENINSULAR
SOUTHEAST ASIA
186   CAMBODIA

PHILIPPINES

PALAU

FEDERATED STATES OF MICRONESIA

NIGERIA
DJIBOUTI
ETHIOPIA
SOMALIA

SRI LANKA

BRUNEI

M A L A Y S I A

OCEANIA
214-221

KIRIBATI

CENT. AFRICAN
REPUBLIC
CAMEROON
EASTERN AFRICA
198
UGANDA   KENYA

MALDIVES

INSULAR SOUTHEAST ASIA
188

SINGAPORE

NAURU

GUINEA
SÃO TOMÉ
AND
PRÍNCIPE
GABON   CONGO
DEMOCRATIC
REPUBLIC OF
THE CONGO
RWANDA
BURUNDI
TANZANIA

AFRICA **190-205**

INDONESIA

PAPUA NEW GUINEA

SOLOMON
ISLANDS

TUVALU

INDIAN OCEAN
240

TIMOR-LESTE

ANGOLA
ZAMBIA
MALAWI
SEYCHELLES
COMOROS

FIJI
ISLANDS

NAMIBIA
ZIMBABWE
BOTSWANA
MOZAMBIQUE
MADAGASCAR
MAURITIUS

VANUATU

AUSTRALIA
210

NEW GUINEA
AND
NEW ZEALAND
213

SOUTH
AFRICA
SWAZILAND
LESOTHO
SOUTHERN
AFRICA
202

NEW ZEALAND

AUSTRALIA
NEW ZEALAND, OCEANIA **206-221**

OCEAN AROUND ANTARCTICA
244

ANTARCTICA **222-229**

KEY TO ATLAS MAPS

NATIONAL GEOGRAPHIC

Family REFERENCE Atlas WORLD OF THE

THIRD EDITION

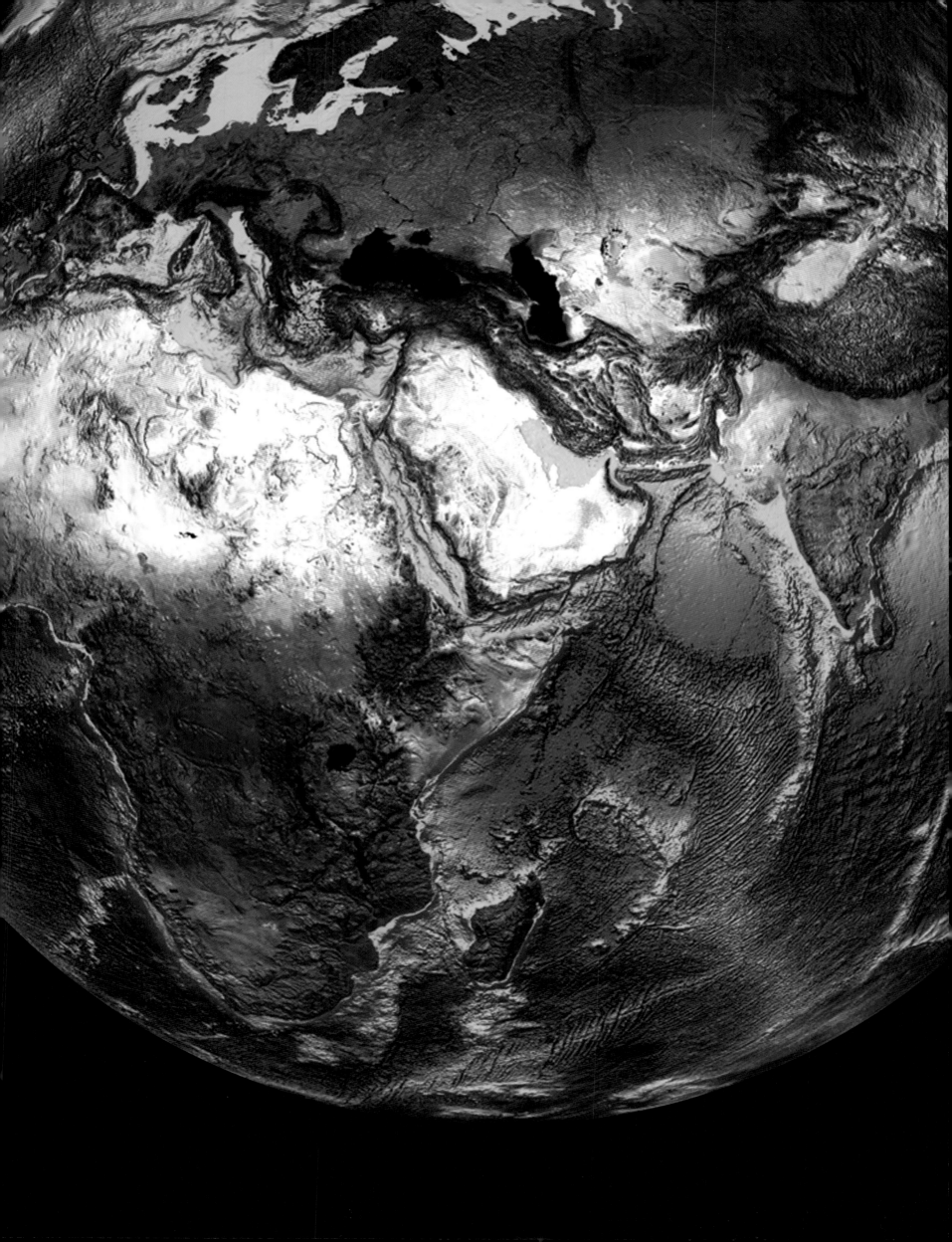

NATIONAL GEOGRAPHIC

Family
REFERENCE
Atlas
OF THE
WORLD

THIRD EDITION

NATIONAL GEOGRAPHIC
WASHINGTON, D.C.

The National Geographic Society is one of the world's largest nonprofit scientific and educational organizations. Founded in 1888 to "increase and diffuse geographic knowledge," the Society works to inspire people to care about the planet. It reaches more than 325 million people worldwide each month through its official journal, *National Geographic*, and other magazines; National Geographic Channel; television documentaries; music; radio; films; books; DVDs; maps; exhibitions; school publishing programs; interactive media; and merchandise. National Geographic has funded more than 9,000 scientific research, conservation and exploration projects and supports an education program combating geographic illiteracy.

For more information, please call
1-800-NGS LINE (647-5463)
or write to the following address:

National Geographic Society
1145 17th Street N.W.
Washington, D.C. 20036-4688 U.S.A.

Visit us online at www.nationalgeographic.com

For information about special discounts
for bulk purchases, please contact
National Geographic Books Special Sales:
ngspecsales@ngs.org

For rights or permissions inquiries, please contact
National Geographic Books Subsidiary Rights:
ngbookrights@ngs.org

For more information about our award-winning
National Geographic atlases, please visit:
www.shopng.com/atlases

ISBN: 978-1-4262-0543-9

Printed in Italy
09/MV/1

This atlas was made possible by the contributions of numerous experts and organizations around the world, including the following:

Center for International Earth Science Information
  Network (CIESIN), Columbia University

Central Intelligence Agency (CIA)

Conservation International (CI)

Cooperative Association for Internet Data Analysis (CAIDA)

Earth Science System Education Program,
  Michigan State University

Global Land Cover Group, University of Maryland

International Monetary Fund (IMF)

International Union for the Conservation of Nature and
  Natural Resources (IUCN)

Lunar and Planetary Institute (LPI)

National Aeronautics and Space Administration (NASA)
  NASA Ames Research Center, NASA Goddard Space
  Flight Center, NASA Jet Propulsion Laboratory (JPL),
  NASA Marshall Space Flight Center

National Geospatial-Intelligence Agency (NGA)

National Oceanic and Atmospheric Administration (NOAA)
  National Climatic Data Center (NCDC), National
  Environmental Satellite, Data, and Information Service
  (NESDIS), National Geophysical Data Center (NGDC),
  National Ocean Service (NOS)

National Science Foundation (NSF)

Population Reference Bureau (PRB)

Scripps Institution of Oceanography

Smithsonian Institution

United Nations (UN)
  UN Conference on Trade and Development (UNCTAD),
  UN Development Programme (UNDP), UN Educational,
  Scientific, and Cultural Organization (UNESCO),
  UN Environment Programme (UNEP), UN Millennium
  Project, UN Population Division, UN Refugee Agency
  (UNHCR), UN Statistics Division (UNSD), Food and
  Agriculture Organization of the United Nations (FAO),
  International Telecommunication Union (ITU), World
  Conservation Monitoring Centre (WCMC)

U.S. Board on Geographic Names (BGN)

U.S. Bureau of the Census

U.S. Department of Agriculture (USDA)

U.S. Department of Energy (DOE)

U.S. Department of the Interior
  Bureau of Land Management (BLM), National Park
  Service (NPS), U.S. Geological Survey (USGS)

U.S. Department of State: Office of the Geographer

World Bank

World Health Organization (WHO)
  Pan American Health Organization (PAHO)

World Resources Institute (WRI)

World Trade Organization (WTO)

Worldwatch Institute

World Wildlife Fund (WWF)

For a complete listing of contributors, see page 380.

Introduction

EARTH HAS ALWAYS BEEN dynamic and changeable. Today, though, the human imprint on the planet is causing global shifts at an unprecedented rate. Almost before our eyes, the world is morphing politically, climatically, and physically, as countries redefine themselves, populations grow, rivers and lakes contract, ice caps shrink, and the oceans expand. Maps are the ultimate key to understanding this increasingly complicated world. They track the more elusive boundaries that result in cultural and religious divides and the borderless, global community created by technological advances. They record changes in the physical world and predict future trends. In this Third Edition of our *Family Reference Atlas* maps become pictures that tell stories of natural phenomena and of human hopes, desires, disasters, and accomplishments.

National Geographic has been at the forefront of cartographic innovation for nearly a century, but the mapmaking technologies we now use surpass the wildest imaginings of our predecessors. Those master craftsmen made maps by the traditional pen-and-ink method; today, satellites and computer systems allow us to acquire, combine, and overlay data in moments. By marrying the artistry of mapmaking with science and technology, we can track how the growing trend toward urbanization in many countries is depleting resources, affecting weather patterns, and encouraging poverty and disease worldwide; and how shrinking populations in other countries are impacting economic growth and future opportunity. This single volume offers a quick understanding of these and other permutations and what their implications are for regions, continents, the planet, and humankind.

In order to bring you a more detailed picture of critical parts of the globe, we've completely revised the Middle East section to provide the most up-to-date information on this nexus of geopolitical concern. And we've enhanced world thematic maps on globalization, technology and communication, hot spots of conflicts—even the Internet and Internet-spread viruses. We've also updated the Space section, which addresses Pluto, now one of several newly designated "dwarf planets" in our solar system.

Large questions loom in our future: What will the continued growth of India and China mean for the planet? How will melting glaciers, rising sea levels, and an ever more volatile climate impact us all? Can we find workable solutions to global warming, the continued threat of international terrorism, or the rise of pandemics in an increasingly interconnected world? And perhaps most important, how can we, in our daily lives, add to the quality of life on Earth? We hope this atlas will serve to inspire and inform you, giving you and your family the knowledge you need to be engaged global citizens.

JOHN M. FAHEY, JR.
PRESIDENT AND
CHIEF EXECUTIVE OFFICER

Table of Contents

10 USING THIS ATLAS   MAP POLICIES • PHYSICAL MAPS • POLITICAL MAPS •
WORLD THEMATIC MAPS • REGIONAL MAPS • MAP SYMBOLS

14 WORLD

14 Introduction

16 Physical World

18 Political World

20 Hemispheres and Poles

22 Structure of the Earth
Continents Adrift in Time • Geologic Time • Geologic Forces
Change the Face of the Planet • Plate Tectonics

24 Earth's Rocky Exterior
Rock Classes • The Rock Cycle • Global Distribution of Rock Types •
Reading Earth History from Rocks

26 Landforms
Major Landform Types • Endogenic Landforms • Exogenic Landforms •
Other Landforms • Landforms Created by Wind • Landforms Created
by Water • Landforms Created by Ice

30 Surface of the Earth
Distribution of Earth's Elevations and Depths (Hypsometry) • Surface by
the Numbers • A Slice of Earth • Earth Surface Elevations and Depths

32 Land Cover
Global Land Cover Composition

34 Climate
January and July: Solar Energy, Average Temperature, Cloud Cover,
Precipitation • Major Factors that Influence Climate • Temperature
Change over Time • Climate Zones • Climographs

38 Weather
Major Factors that Influence Weather • Cloud Types • Tropical Cyclones •
Lightning • El Niño and La Niña

40 Biosphere
The Biosphere from Space • Biosphere Dynamics • Earth System
Dynamics • Size of the Biosphere • The Biosphere over Time

42 Biodiversity
The Natural World • Species Diversity • Threatened Ecoregions •
Threatened Species • Projected Biodiversity Status

44 Population
Lights of the World • Population Pyramids • Population Growth •
Population Density • Regional Population Growth Disparities • Fertility •
Urban Population Densities • Urban Population Growth • Life Expectancy •
Migration • Most Populous Places • Most Crowded Places •
Demographic Extremes

48 Languages
Voices of the World • Vanishing Languages • Evolution of Languages •
How Many Speak What? • Major Language Families Today

50 Religions
Dominant Religion • Sacred Places • Adherents Worldwide • Adherents
by Continent • Adherents by Country

52 Health and Education
Health Care Availability • Income Levels: Indicators of Health and
Literacy • Access to Improved Sanitation • Nutrition • HIV • Global
Disease Burden • Causes of Death • Under-Five Mortality • Maternal
Mortality • Education and Literacy • School Enrollment for Girls •
Developing Human Capital

54 Conflicts
Political Violence • State Fragility • Change in Magnitude of Ongoing
Conflicts • Global Regimes by Type • Genocides and Politicides Since
1955 • Refugees • Terrorist Attacks • Weapons Possessions

56 Economy
Global Economic Activity • Labor Migration • Top GDP Growth Rates •
The World's Richest and Poorest Countries • Gross Domestic Product •
Gross Domestic Product: Purchasing Power Parity (PPP) • Major
Exporters

58 Trade
World Merchandise Trade • Growth of World Trade • Merchandise
Exports • Main Trading Nations • World Debt • Trade Blocs • Trade Flow:
Fuels • Trade Flow: Agricultural Products • Top Merchandise Exporters
and Importers • Top Commercial Services Exporters and Importers

60 Food
Croplands of the World • Fishing and Aquaculture • World Agricultural
Production • Undernourishment in the Developing World •
Caloric Supply • Distribution of Major Crops and Livestock

62 Energy
Annual Energy Consumption • Energy Production • Fossil Fuel Extraction •
Biomass, Hydroelectric, and Geothermal Power • Wind and Solar Power •
Renewable Resources

64 Minerals
World Mineral Production • World Minerals by Economic Value

66 Environmental Stresses
Global Climate Change • Depletion of the Ozone Layer • Pollution •
Water Scarcity • Land Degradation and Desertification • Deforestation

68 Protected Areas
World Heritage Sites • Designated Protected Areas • The World
Heritage Site System • Endemism

70 Globalization
Globalization Status • Transnational Corporations • Extremes of
Globalization • Economic Integration • Personal Contact • Technological
Connectivity • Political Engagement • International Outsourcing

72 Technology and Communication
Centers of Technological Innovation • Milestones in Technology •
The Digital Divide

74 Internet
Mapping the Spread of a Computer Virus • Internet Users Worldwide
(estimated), 1995-2007 • Global Internet Connectivity • Worldwide
Distribution of Internet Resources

76 NORTH AMERICA

76 Introduction

80 North America: Physical and Political

82 Canada
Canada • Greenland • St.-Pierre and Miquelon

84 United States: Physical

86 United States: Political

88 United States
Temperature and Precipitation • Land Use, Agriculture, and Fishing • Population • Industry and Mining

90 United States: Major Highways

92 United States: Federal Lands

NORTHEAST **94**
Connecticut • Maine • Massachusetts • New Hampshire • New Jersey • New York • Pennsylvania • Rhode Island • Vermont

SOUTH ATLANTIC **96**
Delaware • District of Columbia • Florida • Georgia • Maryland • North Carolina • South Carolina • Virginia • West Virginia

GREAT LAKES **98**
Illinois • Indiana • Michigan • Ohio • Wisconsin

MIDDLE SOUTH **100**
Alabama • Arkansas • Kentucky • Louisiana • Mississippi • Tennessee

TEXAS AND OKLAHOMA **102**

NORTHERN PLAINS **104**
Iowa • Kansas • Minnesota • Missouri • Nebraska • North Dakota • South Dakota

ROCKY MOUNTAINS **106**
Arizona • Colorado • Idaho • Montana • New Mexico • Utah • Wyoming

WEST COAST **108**
California • Nevada • Oregon • Washington

ALASKA **110**

HAWAI'I **112**

114 Mexico and Central America
Belize • Costa Rica • El Salvador • Guatemala • Honduras • Mexico • Nicaragua • Panama

116 Bahamas and Greater Antilles
Bahamas • Bermuda • Cayman Islands • Cuba • Dominican Republic • Haiti • Jamaica • Puerto Rico • Turks and Caicos Islands

118 Lesser Antilles
Anguilla • Antigua and Barbuda • Aruba • Barbados • British Virgin Islands • Dominica • Grenada • Guadeloupe • Martinique • Montserrat • Netherlands Antilles • St. Kitts and Nevis • St. Lucia • St. Vincent and the Grenadines • Trinidad and Tobago • U.S. Virgin Islands

120 Islands of the Antilles
Abaco Islands • Anguilla • Antigua • Aruba • Barbados • Bermuda Islands • Bimini Islands • Bonaire • Curacao • Dominica • Eleuthera • Exuma • Grand Bahama Island • Grand Cayman • Grenada • Guadeloupe • Jamaica • Martinique • Montserrat • New Providence • Puerto Rico • San Salvador • St. Croix • St. Kitts and Nevis • St. Lucia • St. Martin (St. Maarten) • St. Thomas and St. John • St. Vincent • Tobago • Tortola • Trinidad • Virgin Gorda

122 SOUTH AMERICA

122 Introduction

126 South America: Physical and Political

128 Northern South America
Colombia • Ecuador • French Guiana • Guyana • Suriname • Venezuela

130 Central South America
Bolivia • Brazil • Paraguay • Peru

132 Southern South America
Argentina • Chile • Falkland Islands • Uruguay

134 EUROPE

134 Introduction

138 Europe: Physical and Political

140 Northern Europe
Denmark • Estonia • Finland • Iceland • Latvia • Lithuania • Norway • Sweden • Faroe Islands

142 Britain and Ireland
Ireland • United Kingdom

144 Iberian Peninsula
Portugal • Spain

146 France and the Low Countries
Belgium • France • Luxembourg • Netherlands

148 Central Europe
Austria • Czech Republic • Germany • Hungary • Poland • Slovakia

150 Italy and Switzerland

152 The Balkans
Albania • Bosnia and Herzegovina • Bulgaria • Croatia • Kosovo • Macedonia • Montenegro • Romania • Serbia • Slovenia

154 Greece and the Aegean

156 Eastern Europe
Belarus • Moldova • Ukraine • Western Russia

158 Russia

160 Europe's Smallest Countries
Andorra • Cyprus • Liechtenstein • Luxembourg • Malta • Monaco • San Marino • Vatican City • Gibraltar

CONTINUES NEXT PAGE >

Table of Contents

162 ASIA

162 Introduction

166 Asia: Physical and Political

168 Asia Minor and Transcaucasia
Armenia • Azerbaijan • Georgia • Turkey

170 Eastern Mediterranean
Israel • Jordan • Lebanon • Syria

172 Southwest Asia
Bahrain • Iran • Iraq • Kuwait • Oman • Qatar • Saudi Arabia •
United Arab Emirates • Yemen

174 Central Asia
Kazakhstan • Turkmenistan • Uzbekistan

176 Parts of Central and South Asia
Afghanistan • Kyrgyzstan • Pakistan • Tajikistan

178 South Asia
Bangladesh • Bhutan • India • Maldives • Nepal • Sri Lanka

180 China and Mongolia

182 Korea and Eastern China
Eastern China • North Korea • South Korea

184 Japan

186 Peninsular Southeast Asia
Cambodia • Laos • Myanmar • Thailand • Vietnam

188 Insular Southeast Asia
Brunei • Indonesia • Malaysia • Philippines • Singapore • Timor-Leste

190 AFRICA

190 Introduction

194 Africa: Physical and Political

196 Northern Africa
Algeria • Chad • Egypt • Gambia • Libya • Mali • Mauritania • Morocco •
Niger • Senegal • Tunisia • Western Sahara

198 Eastern Africa
Burundi • Central African Republic • Democratic Republic of the
Congo • Djibouti • Eritrea • Ethiopia • Kenya • Rwanda • Somalia •
Sudan • Tanzania • Uganda

200 West-Central Africa
Benin • Burkina Faso • Cameroon • Congo • Côte d'Ivoire • Equatorial
Guinea • Gabon • Ghana • Guinea • Guinea-Bissau • Liberia • Nigeria •
Sao Tome and Principe • Sierra Leone • Togo

202 Southern Africa
Angola • Botswana • Cabinda • Comoros • Lesotho • Madagascar •
Malawi • Mozambique • Namibia • Seychelles • South Africa •
Swaziland • Zambia • Zimbabwe

204 Islands of Africa
Bioko • Canary Islands • Cape Verde • Comoros • Madiera Islands •
Mauritius • Mayotte • Réunion • Rodrigues • Sao Tome and Principe •
Seychelles

206 AUSTRALIA • NEW ZEALAND • OCEANIA

206 Introduction

210 Australia: Physical and Political

212 Australia
Temperature and Precipitation • Land Use, Agriculture, and Fishing •
Population • Industry and Mining

213 New Guinea and New Zealand
New Zealand • Papua New Guinea

214 Islands of Oceania

216 Oceania
Inset Maps • Flags and Facts

222 ANTARCTICA

222 Introduction

226 Antarctica: Physical

228 Antarctica
Elevation of the Ice Sheet • Measurements of a Paradox • Ice on the
Move • Ultimate Winds • Antarctic Treaty • Antarctic Convergence

230 OCEANS

230 World Bathymetry

232 Oceanography
The Ocean Floor • Major Surface Currents • Ocean Conveyor Belt

234 Limits of the Oceans and Seas

236 Atlantic Ocean

238 Pacific Ocean

240 Indian Ocean

242 Arctic Ocean

244 Ocean Around Antarctica

246 SPACE

246 Introduction

248 The Moon: Near Side

250 The Moon: Far Side

252 The Solar System

254 The Planets
Sun • Mercury • Venus • Earth • Mars • Jupiter • Saturn •
Uranus • Neptune

256 Mars

258 The Universe

260 Space Exploration Time Line

262 APPENDIX

262 Airline Distances, Abbreviations, Metric Conversions

264 Geographic Comparisons

266 Political Entities and Status
Independent States of the World • Dependencies of the World •
Areas of Special Status • Areas Geographically Separated from
Mainland Countries

270 Special Flags
Development of the Stars and Stripes • International Flags •
Regional Flags • Religious Flags • Ethnic Flags • Specialized Flags

272 Foreign Terms

274 World Time Zones

276 World Temperature and Rainfall

280 Major Cities of the World

282 Glossary of Geographic Terms

285 INDEX

285 Place-name Index

378 Moon Index

380 Acknowledgments
Consultants • Physical and Political Maps • Principal Reference Sources •
Satellite Images • Photographs • Key to Flags and Facts

A long belt of land and mostly sea—reaching ten degrees north and ten degrees south of the Equator—wraps around the globe to form a complete circle of elevation coverage (top and previous spread).

The round—azimuthal—projection (bottom) represents a view from atop the world. The geographic North Pole at 90 degrees north latitude is located at the center of the image. Shown in its entirety, the Northern Hemisphere radiates from the Pole to the periphery of the map, aligning with the Equator at zero degrees latitude.

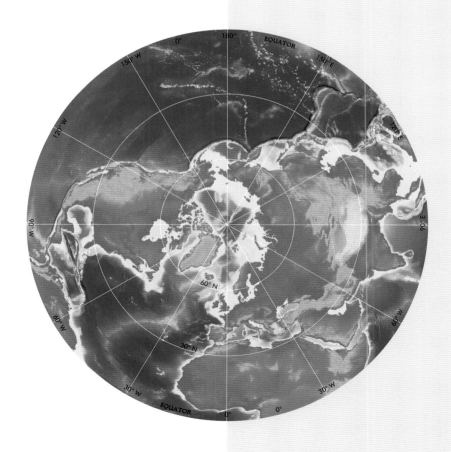

Using this Atlas

MAP POLICIES Maps are a rich, useful, and—to the extent humanly possible—accurate means of depicting the world. Yet maps inevitably make the world seem a little simpler than it really is. A neatly drawn boundary may in reality be a hotly contested war zone. The government-sanctioned, "official" name of a provincial city in an ethnically diverse region may bear little resemblance to the name its citizens routinely use. These cartographic issues often seem obscure and academic. But maps arouse passions. Despite our carefully reasoned map policies, users of National Geographic maps write us strongly worded letters when our maps are at odds with their worldviews.

How do National Geographic cartographers deal with these realities? With constant scrutiny, considerable discussion, and help from many outside experts. Examples:

Nations: Issues of national sovereignty and contested borders often boil down to "de facto versus de jure" discussions. Governments and international agencies frequently make official rulings about contested regions.

These de jure decisions, no matter how legitimate, are often at odds with the wishes of individuals and groups, and they often stand in stark contrast to real-world situations. The inevitable conclusion: It is simplest and best to show the world as it is—de facto—rather than as we or others wish it to be.

Africa's Western Sahara, for example, was divided by Morocco and Mauritania after the Spanish government withdrew in 1976. Although Morocco now controls the entire territory, the United Nations does not recognize Morocco's sovereignty over this still-disputed area. This atlas shows the de facto Moroccan rule but includes an explanatory note.

Place-names: Ride a barge down the Danube, and you'll hear the river called *Donau, Duna, Dunaj, Dunărea, Dunav, Dunay*. These are local names. This atlas uses the conventional name, "Danube," on physical maps. On political maps, local names are used, with the conventional name in parentheses where space permits. Usage conventions for both foreign and domestic place-names are established by the U.S. Board on Geographic Names, a group with representatives from several federal agencies.

Physical Maps

Physical maps of the world, the continents, and the ocean floor reveal landforms and vegetation in stunning detail. Painted by relief artists John Bonner and Tibor Tóth, the maps have been edited for accuracy. Although painted maps are human interpretations, these depictions can emphasize subtle features that are sometimes invisible in satellite imagery.

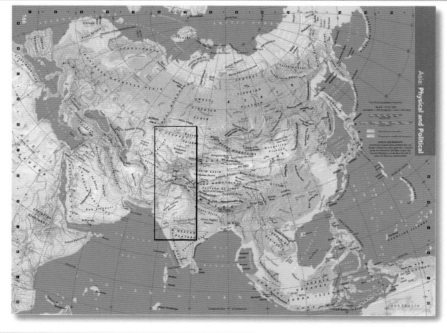

PHYSICAL FEATURES: Colors and shading illustrate variations in elevation, landforms, and vegetation. Patterns indicate specific landscape features, such as sand, glaciers, and swamps.

WATER FEATURES: Blue lines indicate rivers; other water bodies are shown as areas of blue. Lighter shading reflects a depth of 200 meters or less.

BOUNDARIES AND POLITICAL DIVISIONS are shown in red. Dotted lines indicate disputed or uncertain boundaries.

Political Maps

Political maps portray features such as international boundaries, the locations of cities, road networks, and other important elements of the world's human geography. Most index entries are keyed to the political maps, listing the page numbers and then the specific locations on the pages. (See page 285 for details on how to use the index.)

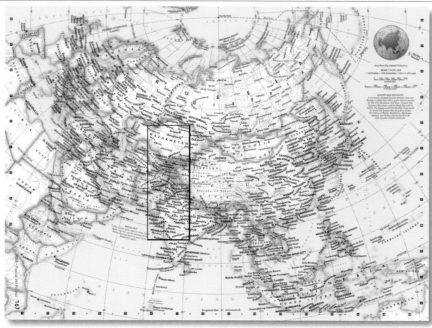

PHYSICAL FEATURES: Gray relief shading depicts surface features such as mountains, hills, and valleys.

WATER FEATURES are shown in blue. Solid lines and filled-in areas indicate perennial water features; dashed lines and patterns indicate intermittent features.

BOUNDARIES AND POLITICAL DIVISIONS are defined with both lines and colored bands; they vary according to whether a boundary is internal or international (for details, see map symbols key at right).

CITIES: The regional political maps that form the bulk of this atlas depict four categories of cities or towns. The largest cities are shown in all capital letters (e.g., LONDON).

World Thematic Maps

Thematic maps reveal the rich patchwork and infinite interrelationships of our changing planet. The thematic section at the beginning of the atlas focuses on physical and biological topics such as geology, landforms, land cover, and biodiversity. It also charts human patterns, with information on population, languages, religions, and the world economy. Two-page spreads on energy and minerals illustrate how people have learned to use Earth's resources, while spreads devoted to environmental stresses and protected lands focus on the far-reaching effects of human activities and the need for resource conservation. Throughout this section of the atlas, maps are coupled with satellite imagery, charts, diagrams, photographs, and tabular information; together, they create a very useful framework for studying geographic patterns.

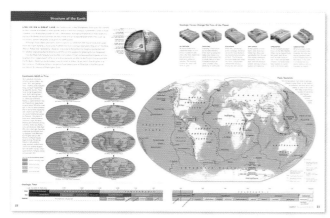

Structure of the Earth

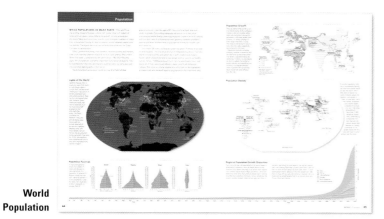

World Population

Regional Maps

This atlas divides the continents into several subregions, each displayed on a two-page spread. Large-scale maps capture the political divisions and major surface features, whereas accompanying regional thematic maps lend insight into natural and human factors that give character to a region. Fact boxes, which include flag designs and information on populations, languages, religions, and economies, appear alongside the maps as practical reference tools.

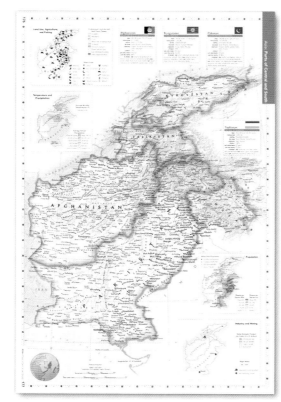

For more details on the regional map spreads, see pages 12–13.

Map Symbols

BOUNDARIES

	Defined
	Undefined or disputed
	Offshore line of separation
	International boundary (Physical Maps)
	Disputed or undefined boundary (Physical Maps)

CITIES

⊛ ★ ◉ ◎ Capitals

● ● ● · Towns

TRANSPORTATION

	Superhighway
	Highway
	Road
	Ferry
	Highway tunnel
INTERSTATE · STATE · FEDERAL	Highway numbers

WATER FEATURES

	Drainage
	Intermittent drainage
	Intermittent lake
	Dry salt lake
	Swamp
	Bank or shoal
	Coral reef
200	Depth curves in meters
51	Water surface elevation in meters
	Falls or rapids
	Aqueduct

PHYSICAL FEATURES

	Relief
⊙	Crater
	Lava and volcanic debris
+8850 (29035 ft)	Elevation in meters (feet in United States)
·-86	Elevation in meters below sea level
⊱	Pass
	Sand
	Salt desert
	Below sea level
	Ice shelf
	Glacier

CULTURAL FEATURES

⌙	Oil field
	Canal
I	Dam
	Wall
	U.S. National Park
▫	Site
∴	Ruin

Using this Atlas

LOCATORS:
Each regional spread contains a locator map showing where the featured region lies within a continent. The region of interest is highlighted in the continental section's color (in this case, purple, for Europe). Surrounding areas on the same continent appear in gray; other land areas are brown.

Spain
KINGDOM OF SPAIN
AREA 505,988 sq km (195,363 sq mi)
POPULATION 46,501,000
CAPITAL Madrid 5,567,000
RELIGION Roman Catholic
LANGUAGE Castilian Spanish, Catalan, Galician, Basque
LITERACY 98%
LIFE EXPECTANCY 80 years
GDP PER CAPITA $30,800
ECONOMY IND: textiles and apparel (including footwear), food and beverages, metals and metal manufactures, chemicals AGR: grain, vegetables, olives, wine grapes; beef; fish EXP: machinery, motor vehicles, foodstuffs, pharmaceuticals

FLAGS AND FACTS:
This atlas recognizes 194 independent nations. All of these countries, along with dependencies and U.S. states, are profiled in the continental regional sections of the atlas. Accompanying each entry are highlights of geographic, demographic, and economic data. These details provide a brief overview of each country, state, or territory; they are not intended to be comprehensive. A detailed description of the sources and policies used in compiling the listings is included in the Key to Flags and Facts on page 383.

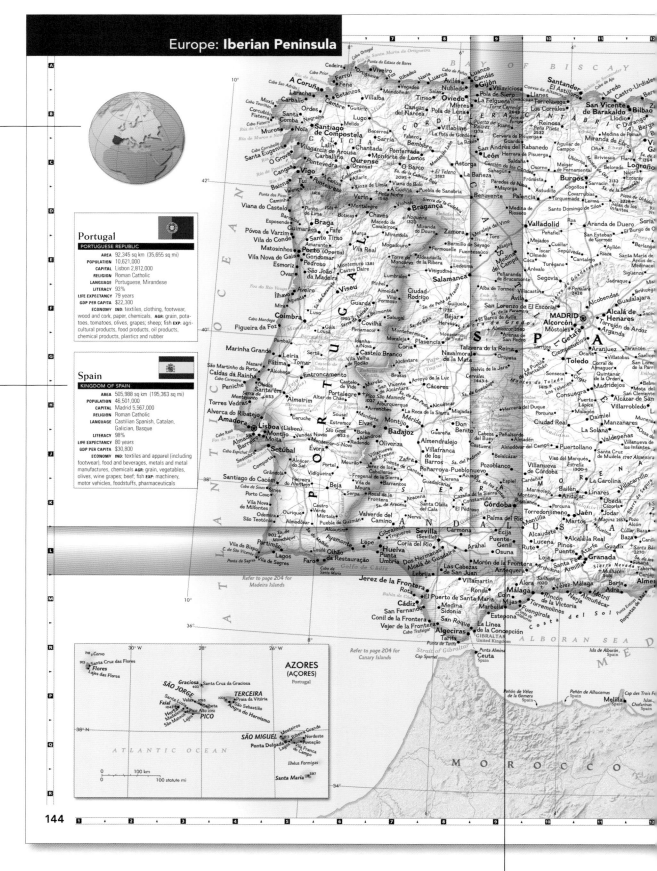

INDEX AND GRID:
Beginning on page 285 is a full index of place-names found in this atlas. The edge of each map is marked with letters (in rows) and numbers (in columns), to which the index entries are referenced. As an example, "Osuna, *Sp.* **144** L9" (see inset section, right) refers to the grid section on page 144 where row L and column 9 meet. More examples and additional details about the index are included on page 285.

Ostrów Wielkopolski, *Pol.* **149** EI4
O'Sullivan Dam, *Wash., U.S.* **108** D7
Osŭm, river, *Bulg.* **153** HI4
Ōsumi Kaikyō, *Japan* **185** U4
Ōsumi Shotō, *Japan* **185** U4
Osuna, *Sp.* 144 L9
Oswego, *N.Y., U.S.* **94** H8
Oswestry, *Eng., U.K.* **143** TIO
Ōta, *Japan* **185** NI2
Otaki, *N.Z.* **213** MI9
Otar, *Kaz.* **175** HI6

MAP PROJECTIONS:
Map projections determine how land shapes are distorted when transferred from a sphere (the Earth) to a flat piece of paper. Many different projections are used in this atlas—each carefully chosen for a map's particular coverage area and purpose.

MAP SCALES:
Scale information indicates the distance on Earth represented by a given length on the map. Here, map scale is expressed in three ways: 1) as a representative fraction where scale is shown as a fraction or ratio as in 1:3,290,000. This means that one centimeter or one inch on the map represents 3,290,000 centimeters or inches on Earth's surface. 2) as a verbal statement: one centimeter equals 118 kilometers or one inch equals 187 miles and 3) as a bar scale, a linear graph symbol subdivided to show map lengths in kilometers and miles in the real world.

THEMATIC MAPS:
In combination, the four thematic maps on each regional spread—Temperature and Precipitation; Population; Land Use, Agriculture, and Fishing; and Industry and Mining—provide a fascinating overview of the area's physical and cultural geography. Temperature and Precipitation maps show which areas receive the most rain, and what the average temperatures are at different times during the year. Population maps allow one to see, at a glance, which areas are the least and most crowded, and where the major urban centers are located. Land Use, Agriculture, and Fishing maps paint a general picture of the ways humans use land resources. And Industry and Mining maps indicate the relative economic well-being of countries (expressed in GDP per capita) and show major centers of mining, mineral processing, and manufacturing. Interesting relationships can be observed: For example, although mines can be located anywhere that mineral deposits occur, processing centers are only feasible in areas with inexpensive electricity and adequate access to transportation.

INDUSTRY AND MINING MAPS:
On these maps, major manufacturing centers, mines, and processing plants are shown with symbols; countries are colored according to gross domestic product (GDP) per capita. The GDP per-capita key breakdowns are consistent among all regions of a continent. For example, Northern Europe, Britain and Ireland, and the remaining regional maps of Europe match this key for the Iberian Peninsula.

TEMPERATURE AND PRECIPITATION MAPS:
These maps show climatic averages over time. Colors represent precipitation information; point symbols show average January and July temperatures for selected cities and towns.

POPULATION MAPS:
Colors indicate relative population density, with the most crowded areas shown in the darkest red-orange color. Geometric point symbols indicate the sizes of selected major cities and national capitals and their urban areas.

LAND USE, AGRICULTURE, AND FISHING MAPS:
The colors on these maps indicate predominant land use and land-cover types—showing, for example, whether an area comprises mainly cropland or forest. Symbols for major crops give a general picture of each region's agricultural activity.

NORTH AMERICA

EUROPE

AFRICA

SOUTH AMERICA

The rapid worldwide decline in the diversity of plant and animal life ("biodiversity"), an unfortunate result of human activity, is catching the growing attention of scientists. Increasingly, conservationists realize that to protect the planet's biodiversity they must look past political boundaries to work with nature's own organization. The many hundreds of terrestrial and coastal marine areas shown on this map represent ecoregions defined by the World Wildlife Fund (WWF) and The Nature Conservancy. Each ecoregion has unique species and communities, many found nowhere else on Earth. For detailed information on each region, see the online maps at: www.worldwildlife.org/science/ecoregions/item1267.html and www.worldwildlife.org/MEOW.

The World

Some 93 million miles from the sun, Earth whirls in space, its exact origins shrouded in time. According to scientists, our planet and every other object in the solar system descend from a great cloud of interstellar gas and dust that condensed to form the sun about 4.6 billion years ago. Life is known to have found a foothold only on Earth—more than 3.5 billion years ago—but in recent years researchers have made intriguing discoveries about potential habitats for life on other planets or their moons.

Scientists continue to study habitats here at home as well. Using the very latest technologies, they are gaining a much better understanding of the natural processes that support life, shape landscapes, and keep the currents of the air and sea always in motion. They are learning, too, how we humans, relative newcomers among life-forms, are affecting our world, for better or worse.

The image at left represents one way to see and under-stand the diversity of life on Earth. It portrays more than a thousand "ecoregions," charted according to climate, oceanography, plant and animal communities, and other ecological features, rather than political bound-aries. Maps such as this can be an invaluable learning tool for scientists and laypeople alike.

The following pages present a wide array of other maps, tables, graphs, images, and text, covering all aspects of physical and cultural geography. Together, they reveal the state of our world, this complex, dynamic realm we call Earth.

ASIA

AUSTRALIA

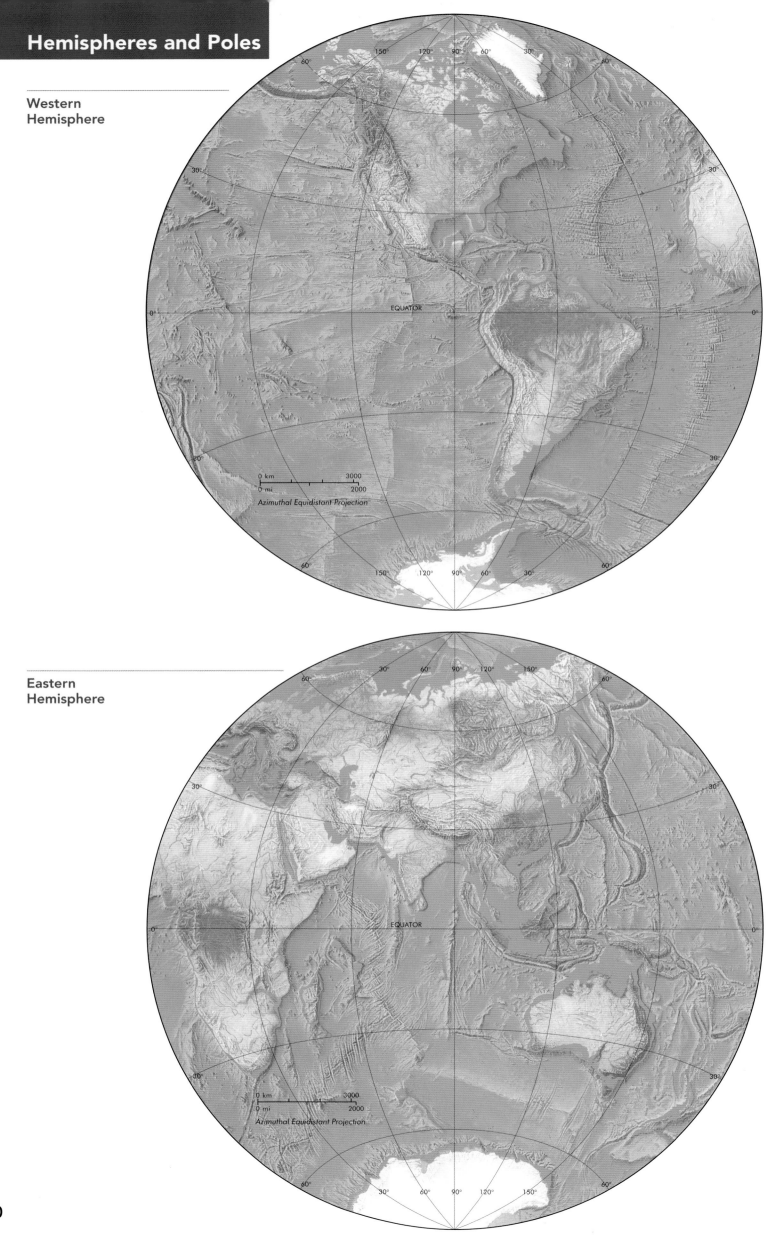

Western Hemisphere

EQUATOR

0 km 3000
0 mi 2000

Azimuthal Equidistant Projection

Eastern Hemisphere

EQUATOR

0 km 3000
0 mi 2000

Azimuthal Equidistant Projection

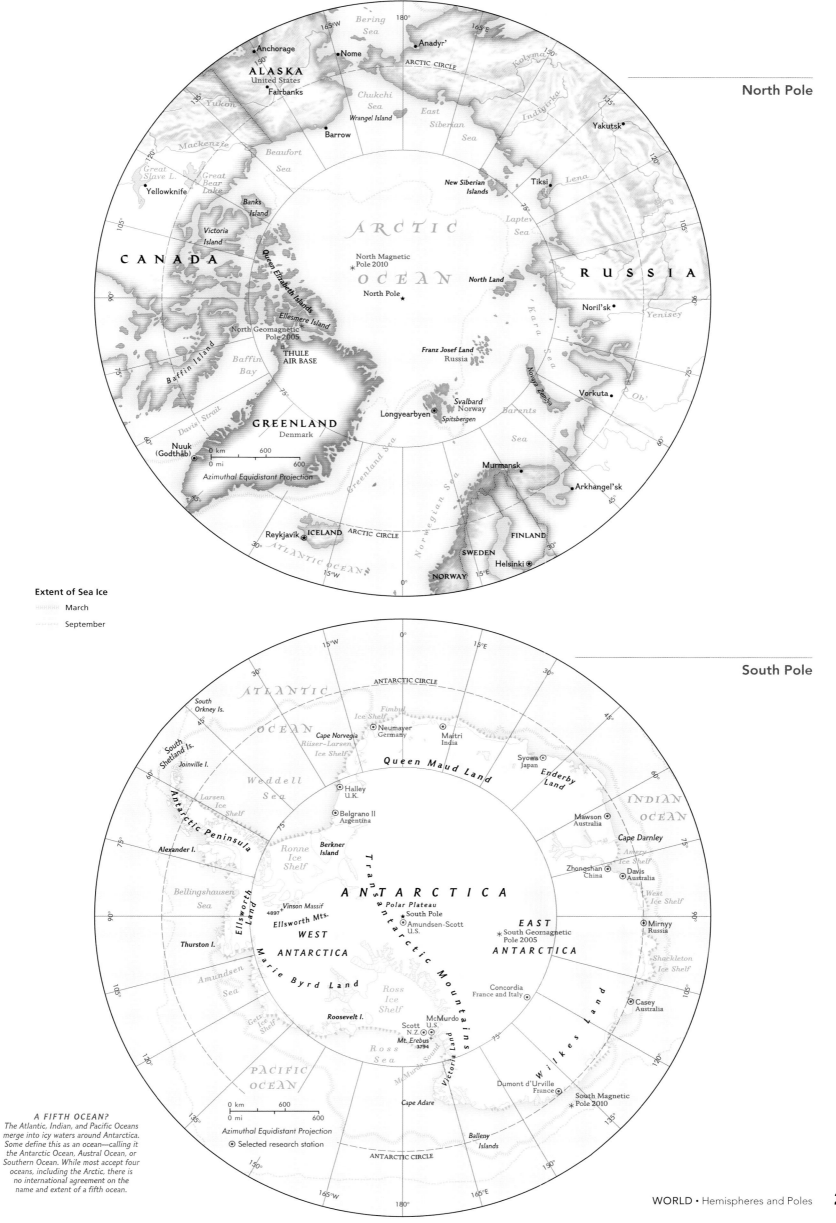

North Pole Map

Anchorage
Nome
Anadyr'
ALASKA
United States
Fairbanks
ARCTIC CIRCLE
Yakutsk
Barrow
Wrangel Island
Chukchi
Sea
East
Siberian
Sea
Kolyma
Indigirka
Yukon
Mackenzie
Beaufort
Sea
Great
Slave L.
Great
Bear
Lake
Yellowknife
Banks
Island
Tiksi
Lena
Laptev
Sea
New Siberian
Islands
Victoria
Island
ARCTIC
CANADA
Queen Elizabeth Islands
OCEAN
RUSSIA
North Magnetic
Pole 2010
North Pole
North Land
Noril'sk
Yenisey
Ellesmere Island
North Geomagnetic
Pole 2005
Franz Josef Land
Russia
Kara
Sea
Baffin Island
Baffin
Bay
THULE
AIR BASE
Novaya Zemlya
Vorkuta
Davis Strait
GREENLAND
Denmark
Svalbard
Norway
Spitsbergen
Barents
Sea
Ob'
Longyearbyen
Greenland Sea
Nuuk
(Godthåb)
0 km   600
0 mi   600
Azimuthal Equidistant Projection
Murmansk
Arkhangel'sk
Norwegian Sea
Reykjavík ICELAND ARCTIC CIRCLE
FINLAND
SWEDEN
ATLANTIC OCEAN
Helsinki
NORWAY

Extent of Sea Ice
March
September

South Pole Map

ANTARCTIC CIRCLE
South
Orkney Is.
ATLANTIC
OCEAN
Fimbul
Ice Shelf
Cape Norvegia
Neumayer
Germany
Maitri
India
Queen Maud Land
Syowa
Japan
Enderby
Land
INDIAN
OCEAN
South
Shetland Is.
Joinville I.
Riiser-Larsen
Ice Shelf
Weddell
Sea
Antarctic Peninsula
Larsen
Ice
Shelf
Halley
U.K.
Belgrano II
Argentina
Mawson
Australia
Cape Darnley
Amery
Ice Shelf
Alexander I.
Ronne
Ice
Shelf
Berkner
Island
Zhongshan
China
Davis
Australia
West
Ice Shelf
Bellingshausen
Sea
Ellsworth Land
ANTARCTICA
Transantarctic Mountains
Vinson Massif
4897
Ellsworth Mts.
WEST
ANTARCTICA
Polar Plateau
South Pole
Amundsen-Scott
U.S.
EAST
ANTARCTICA
South Geomagnetic
Pole 2005
Mirnyy
Russia
Thurston I.
Amundsen
Sea
Marie Byrd Land
Ross
Ice
Shelf
Concordia
France and Italy
Shackleton
Ice Shelf
Getz Ice Shelf
Roosevelt I.
McMurdo
U.S.
Scott
N.Z.
Mt. Erebus
3794
Victoria Land
Wilkes Land
Casey
Australia
PACIFIC
OCEAN
0 km   600
0 mi   600
Azimuthal Equidistant Projection
Selected research station
McMurdo Sound
Ross
Sea
Cape Adare
Dumont d'Urville
France
South Magnetic
Pole 2010
Balleny
Islands
ANTARCTIC CIRCLE

A FIFTH OCEAN?
The Atlantic, Indian, and Pacific Oceans merge into icy waters around Antarctica. Some define this as an ocean—calling it the Antarctic Ocean, Austral Ocean, or Southern Ocean. While most accept four oceans, including the Arctic, there is no international agreement on the name and extent of a fifth ocean.

LIKE ICE ON A GREAT LAKE, the Earth's crust, or the lithosphere, floats over the planet's molten innards, is cracked in many places, and is in slow but constant movement. Earth's surface is broken into 16 enormous slabs of rock, called plates, averaging thousands of miles wide and having a thickness of several miles. As they move and grind against each other, they push up mountains, spawn volcanoes, and generate earthquakes.

Although these often cataclysmic events capture our attention, the movements that cause them are imperceptible, a slow waltz of rafted rock that continues over eons. How slow? The Mid-Atlantic Ridge (see "spreading" diagram, opposite) is being built by magma oozing between two plates, separating North America and Africa at the speed of a growing human fingernail.

The dividing lines between plates often mark areas of high volcanic and earthquake activity as plates strain against each other or one dives beneath another. In the Ring of Fire around the Pacific Basin, disastrous earthquakes have occurred in Kobe, Japan, and in Los Angeles and San Francisco, California. Volcanic eruptions have taken place at Pinatubo in the Philippines and Mount St. Helens in Washington State.

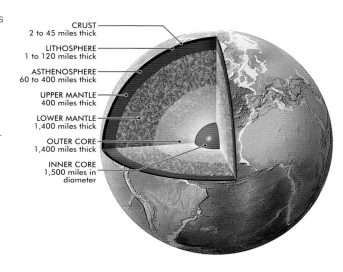

CRUST
2 to 45 miles thick

LITHOSPHERE
1 to 120 miles thick

ASTHENOSPHERE
60 to 400 miles thick

UPPER MANTLE
400 miles thick

LOWER MANTLE
1,400 miles thick

OUTER CORE
1,400 miles thick

INNER CORE
1,500 miles in diameter

Continents Adrift in Time

With unceasing movement of Earth's tectonic plates, continents "drift" over geologic time—breaking apart, reassembling, and again fragmenting to repeat the process. Three times during the past billion years, Earth's drifting landmasses have merged to form so-called supercontinents. Rodinia, a supercontinent in the late Precambrian, began breaking apart about 750 million years ago. In time, its pieces reassembled to form another supercontinent, which in turn later split into smaller landmasses during the Paleozoic. The largest of these were called Euramerica (ancestral Europe and North America) and Gondwana (ancestral Africa, Antarctica, Arabia, India, and Australia). More than 250 million years ago, these two landmasses recombined, forming Pangaea. In the Mesozoic era, Pangaea split and the Atlantic and Indian Oceans began forming. Though the Atlantic is still widening today, scientists predict it will close as the seafloor recycles back into Earth's mantle. A new supercontinent, Pangaea Ultima, will eventually form.

650 Million Years Ago (Late Proterozoic)

250 Million Years in the Future

390 Million Years Ago (Early Devonian)

150 Million Years in the Future

237 Million Years Ago (Early Triassic)

50 Million Years in the Future

KEY TO PALEO-GEOGRAPHIC MAPS

Seafloor spreading ridge

Subduction zone

Ancient landmass

Continental shelf

94 Million Years Ago (Late Cretaceous)

Present

Geologic Time

EON	PRISCOAN	ARCHAEAN				PROTEROZOIC		
ERA	EOARCHEAN	PALEOARCHEAN	MESOARCHEAN	NEOARCHEAN	PALEOPROTEROZOIC		MESOPROTEROZOIC	
PERIOD	No subdivision into periods				SIDERIAN / RHYACIAN / OROSIRIAN / STATHERIAN		CALYMMIAN / ECTASIAN / STENIAN / TONIAN / CRYOGENIAN	

4,500 MILLIONS OF YEARS AGO — 3,500 — 3,000 — 2,500 — 2000 — 1500 — 1000

Geologic Forces Change the Face of the Planet

ACCRETION
As ocean plates move toward the edges of continents or island arcs and slide under them, seamounts are skimmed off and piled up in submarine trenches. The resulting buildup can cause continents to grow.

FAULTING
Enormous crustal plates do not slide smoothly. Strain built up along their edges may release in a series of small jumps, felt as minor tremors on land. Extended buildup can cause a sudden jump, producing an earthquake.

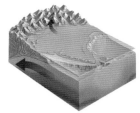

COLLISION
When two continental plates converge, the result can be the most dramatic mountain-building process on Earth. The Himalaya mountain range rose when the Indian subcontinent collided with Eurasia, driving the land upward.

HOT SPOTS
In the cauldron of inner Earth, some areas burn hotter than others and periodically blast through their crustal covering as volcanoes. Such a "hot spot" built the Hawaiian Islands, leaving a string of oceanic protuberances.

SPREADING
At the divergent boundary known as the Mid-Atlantic Ridge, oozing magma forces two plates apart by as much as eight inches a year. If that rate had been constant, the ocean could have reached its current width in 30 million years.

SUBDUCTION
When an oceanic plate and a continental plate converge, the older and heavier sea plate takes a dive. Plunging back into the interior of the Earth, it is transformed into molten material, only to rise again as magma.

Plate Tectonics

Tectonic boundaries mark areas of geologic change in ocean floors, on the margins of continents, and even within continents, as seen in the Great Rift Valley of East Africa. Clusters of volcanoes and frequent earthquakes indicate unstable areas.

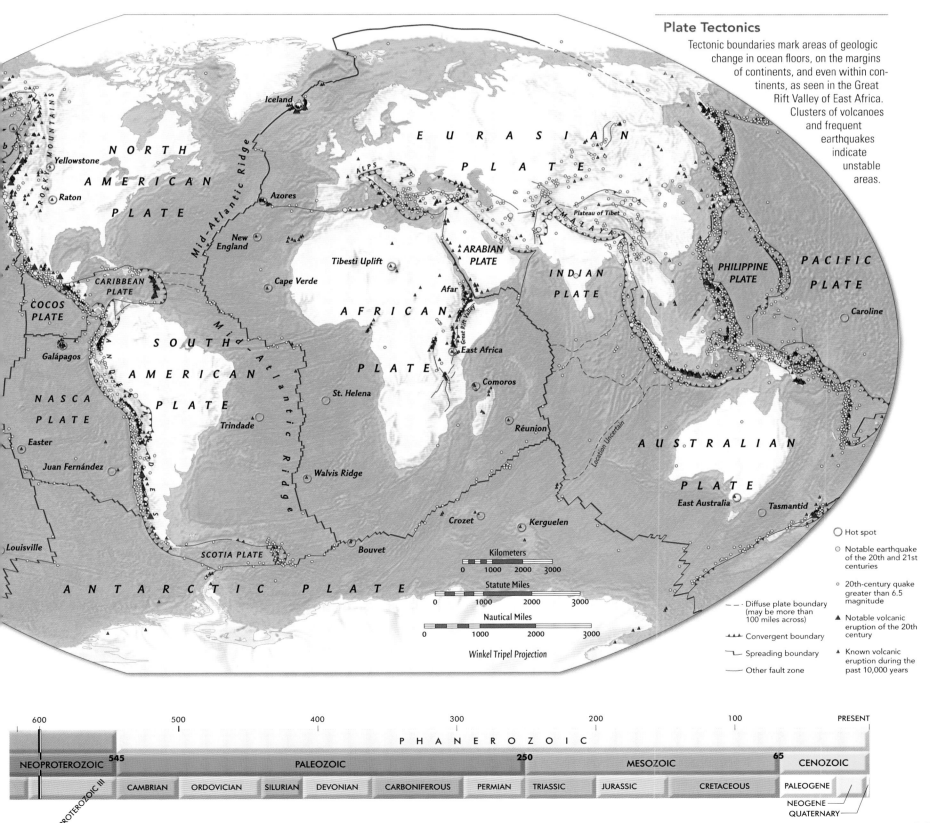

Kilometers
0 1000 2000 3000

Statute Miles
0 1000 2000 3000

Nautical Miles
0 1000 2000 3000

Winkel Tripel Projection

○ Hot spot
◎ Notable earthquake of the 20th and 21st centuries
○ 20th-century quake greater than 6.5 magnitude
⊶ Diffuse plate boundary (may be more than 100 miles across)
▲ Notable volcanic eruption of the 20th century
⊶⊶ Convergent boundary
⊐ Spreading boundary
▲ Known volcanic eruption during the past 10,000 years
— Other fault zone

| 600 | 500 | 400 | 300 | 200 | 100 | PRESENT |

P H A N E R O Z O I C

| NEOPROTEROZOIC | 545 | PALEOZOIC | 250 | MESOZOIC | 65 | CENOZOIC |

NEOPROTEROZOIC III

| CAMBRIAN | ORDOVICIAN | SILURIAN | DEVONIAN | CARBONIFEROUS | PERMIAN | TRIASSIC | JURASSIC | CRETACEOUS | PALEOGENE |

NEOGENE
QUATERNARY

EARTH'S OUTERMOST LAYER, the crust, ranges from 2 to 45 miles (3 to 70 km) thick and comprises a large variety of rocks that are aggregates of one or more types of minerals.

Scientists recognize three main classes of rock. Igneous rock forms when molten material cools and solidifies, either rapidly at the Earth's surface—as perhaps a lava flow—or more slowly underground, as an intrusion. Sedimentary rocks form from mineral or rock fragments, or from organic material that is eroded or dissolved, then deposited at Earth's surface. Metamorphic rocks form when rocks of any origin (igneous, sedimentary, or metamorphic) are subjected to very high temperature and pressure; this type also forms as rocks react with fluids deep within the crust. Igneous and metamorphic rocks make up 95 percent of the crust's volume. Sedimentary rocks make up only about 5 percent; even so, they cover a large percentage of Earth's surface.

As a result of plate tectonics, the crust is in constant slow motion; thus, rocks change positions over time. Their compositions also change as they are gradually modified by metamorphism and melting. Rocks form and re-form in a sequence known as the rock cycle (see below). Understanding their nature and origin is important because rocks contain materials that sustain modern civilization. For example, steel requires the processing of iron—mainly from ancient sedimentary rocks; copper is mined principally from slowly cooled igneous rocks called plutons; and fossil fuels (e.g., coal, oil, natural gas) derive from organic material trapped ages ago in relatively young sedimentary rocks.

Rock Classes

IGNEOUS

Igneous rocks form when molten rock (magma) originating from deep within the Earth solidifies. The chemical composition of the magma and its cooling rate determine the final rock type.

Intrusive (Plutonic)

Intrusive igneous rocks are formed from magma that cools and solidifies deep beneath the Earth's surface. The insulating effect of the surrounding rock allows the magma to solidify very slowly. Slow cooling means the individual mineral grains have a long time to grow, so they grow to a relatively large size. Intrusive rocks typically are coarser grained than volcanic rocks.

Examples: gabbro, diorite, granite

Extrusive (Volcanic)

Extrusive igneous rocks are formed from magma that cools and solidifies at or near the Earth's surface. Exposure to the relatively cool temperature of the atmosphere or water makes the erupted magma solidify very quickly. Rapid cooling means the individual mineral grains have only a short time to grow, so their final size is very tiny, or fine-grained. Sometimes the magma is quenched so rapidly that individual minerals have no time to grow. This is how volcanic glass forms.

Examples: basalt, andesite, and rhyolite

SEDIMENTARY

Sedimentary rocks are formed from preexisting rocks or pieces of once living organisms. They form deposits that accumulate on the Earth's surface, generally with distinctive layering or bedding.

Clastic

Clastic sedimentary rocks are made up of pieces (clasts) of preexisting rocks. Pieces of rock are loosened by weathering, then transported to a basin or depression where sediment is trapped. If the sediment is buried deeply, it becomes compacted and cemented, forming sedimentary rock. Clastic sedimentary rocks may have particles ranging in size from microscopic clay to huge boulders. Their names are based on their grain size.

Examples: sandstone, mudstone, conglomerate

Chemical

Chemical sedimentary rocks are formed by chemical precipitation. This process begins when water traveling through rock dissolves some of the minerals, carrying them away from their source. Eventually these minerals are redeposited when the water evaporates.

Examples: evaporite, dolomite

Biologic

Biologic sedimentary rocks form from once living organisms. They may comprise accumulated carbon-rich plant material or deposits of animal shells.

Examples: coal, chalk, limestone, chert

METAMORPHIC

Metamorphic rocks are those rocks that have been substantially changed from their original igneous, sedimentary, or earlier metamorphic form. They form when rocks are subjected to high heat; high pressure; hot, mineral-rich fluids; or, more commonly, some combination of these.

Foliated

Foliated rocks form when pressure deforms tabular minerals within a rock so they become aligned. These rocks develop a platy or sheetlike structure that reflects the directions from which pressure was applied.

Examples: schist, gneiss, slate

Massive (Nonfoliated)

Nonfoliated metamorphic rocks do not have a platy or sheetlike structure. There are several ways that nonfoliated rocks can be produced. Some rocks, such as limestone, are made of minerals that are not flat or elongated; no matter how much pressure is applied, the grains will not align despite recrystallization. Contact metamorphism occurs when hot igneous rock intrudes into preexisting rock. The preexisting rock is essentially baked by the heat, which changes mineral composition and texture primarily from heating rather than pressure effects.

Examples: marble, quartzite, hornfels

The Rock Cycle

To learn the origin and history of rocks, geologists study their mineralogy, texture, and fabric—characteristics that result from dynamic Earth-shaping processes driven by internal and external energy.

Internal energy is heat contained within the Earth. This intense heat creates convection currents in the mantle, which in turn cause tectonic plate movements and volcanism. External energy comes from the sun, which drives atmospheric processes that produce rain, snow, ice, and wind—powerful agents of weathering and erosion.

As internal energy builds and rebuilds Earth's rocky exterior, the forces of weathering and erosion break down surface materials and wear them away.

Ultimately, soil particles and rock fragments, called sediments, are carried by rivers into the oceans, where they may lithify, or harden into solid rock. In time, these sedimentary rocks may be subjected to heat and pressure at great depth. Mineral and structural changes occur as the rocks break and fold; they are transformed into metamorphic rocks.

Solid rocks subject to high heat and pressure during metamorphism can melt to form magma, which later can form igneous rocks, either intrusive or extrusive. The subsurface intrusive rocks (i.e., plutons) can later be uplifted by tectonic forces and (or) exposed by erosion. At the surface, the cycle continues as weathering and erosion break it down and wear it away.

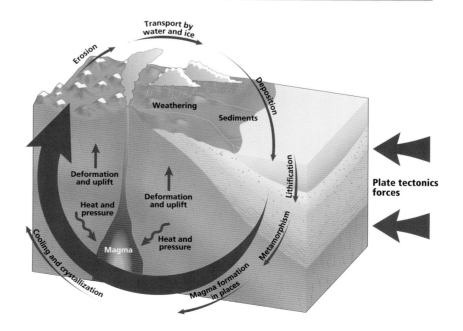

Global Distribution of Rock Types

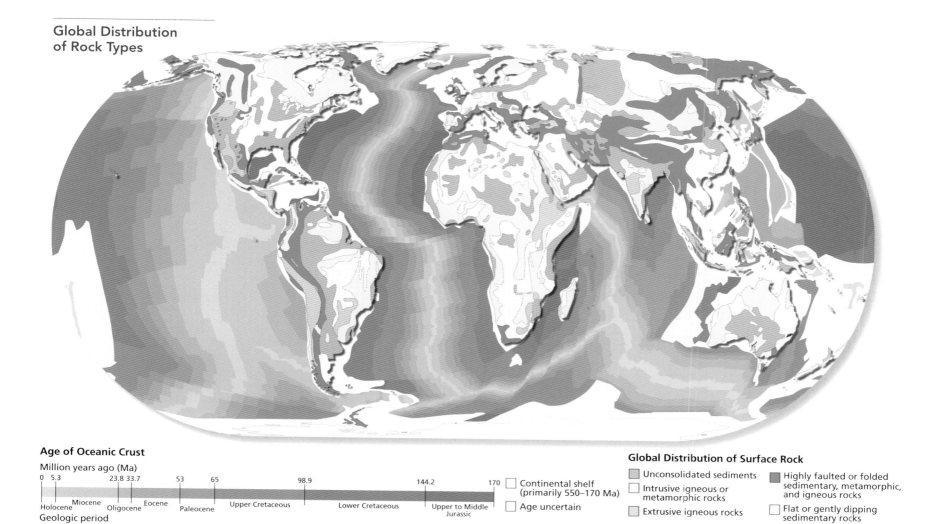

Age of Oceanic Crust

Million years ago (Ma)

0 5.3   23.8 33.7   53   65   98.9   144.2   170

Holocene | Miocene | Oligocene | Eocene | Paleocene | Upper Cretaceous | Lower Cretaceous | Upper to Middle Jurassic

Geologic period

In general, oceanic crust is much younger than surface rock.

☐ Continental shelf (primarily 550–170 Ma)
☐ Age uncertain

Global Distribution of Surface Rock

▨ Unconsolidated sediments
▨ Intrusive igneous or metamorphic rocks
▨ Extrusive igneous rocks
▨ Highly faulted or folded sedimentary, metamorphic, and igneous rocks
☐ Flat or gently dipping sedimentary rocks

Reading Earth History from Rocks

The Earth is 4.6 billion years old, with a long, complex history written in layers of rock.* By reading sequences of sedimentary rock, we can discover information about past environments and processes. The principle of superposition states that, provided rocks are not turned upside down by deformation, the oldest rocks are at the bottom of a sequence and younger rocks are found at the top. Unconformities tell us that uplift and erosion occurred before the deposition of younger sediments resumed. As an example, the rock sequence exposed in the Grand Canyon of Arizona indicates from oldest to youngest, the following major events:

DURING PRECAMBRIAN TIME:
1. Deposition of Vishnu sediment (about 2 billion years ago)
2. Mountain building, metamorphism of Vishnu sediment into Vishnu schist, and intrusion of Zoroaster granite (1.8 to 1.4 billion years ago)
3. Uplift and erosion resulting in an unconformity (1.4 to 1.2 billion years ago)
4. Deposition of Unkar Group sediments (1.2 to 1 billion years ago)
5. Tilting (1 billion years ago)
6. Erosion resulting in angular unconformity (1 billion to 543 million years ago)

DURING THE PHANEROZOIC (CAMBRIAN-RECENT) EON:
7. Deposition of Cambrian to Permian (and younger rocks not shown) sediments (543 to 520 million years ago), with disconformities indicating erosion and "missing" time where noted
8. Uplift and erosion of the Grand Canyon (20 million years ago to present)

The ages for these events are broadly defined by the radioisotopic dating of minerals in the metamorphic and igneous rocks, and by fossils and correlation to other rocks for the sedimentary rocks that are younger than the Precambrian-Cambrian boundary (543 million years ago).

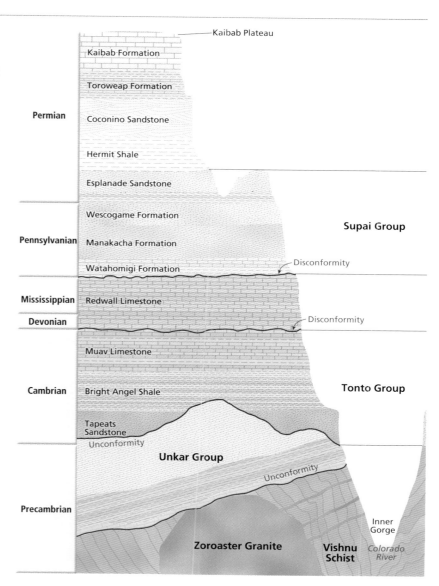

Yavapai Point, Grand Canyon

The oldest known, dated rocks on Earth go back to 4 billion years ago; geologic records of older rocks have been destroyed by more recent geologic events.

SEVEN MAJOR LANDFORM types are found on Earth's surface (see map); except for ice caps, all result from tectonic movements and denudational forces.

The loftiest landforms, mountains, often define the edges of tectonic plates. In places where continental plates converge, Earth's crust crumples into high ranges such as the Himalaya. Where oceanic plates dive beneath continental ones, volcanic mountains can rise. Volcanoes are common along the west coast of South America, which is part of the so-called Pacific Ring of Fire, the world's most active mountain-building zone.

Widely spaced mountains are another type, and examples of this landform are seen in the Basin and Range province of the western United States. These features are actually the tops of heavily eroded, faulted mountains. The eroded material filled adjacent valleys, giving these old summits the look of widely spaced mountains.

Extensive, relatively flat lands that are higher than surrounding areas are called plateaus. Formed by uplift, they include the Guiana Highlands of South America. Hills and low plateaus are rounded natural elevations of land with some local relief. The Canadian Shield and Ozarks of North America provide good examples. Depressions are large basins delimited by higher lands, an example of which is the Tarim Basin in western China. Plains are extensive areas of level or rolling treeless country. Examples include the steppes of Eurasia, the Ganges River plains, and the outback of Australia.

Major Landform Types
- Mountains
- Widely spaced mountains
- High plateaus
- Hills and low plateaus
- Depressions
- Plains
- Ice caps

Endogenic Landforms

LANDFORMS THAT RESULT FROM "INTERNAL" PROCESSES

Forces deep within the Earth give rise to mountains and other endogenic landforms. Some mountains (e.g., the Himalaya) were born when continental plates collided. Others rose in the form of volcanoes (the Cascades of North America, Mount Fuji of Japan) as sea plates subducted beneath continental plates or as plates moved over hot spots in Earth's mantle (Hawai'i). Still others were thrust up by tectonic uplift (parts of the western United States). Rifting and faulting, which occur along plate boundaries and sometimes within the plates themselves, also generate vertical tectonic landforms; these can be seen in Africa's Rift Valley and along the San Andreas Fault of California.

Clockwise from above: The Wasatch Range in Utah, uplifted by tectonic forces; the San Andreas Fault in California, a fracture in Earth's crust marking a plate boundary; Mount Fuji in Japan, a volcanic peak; Crater Lake in Oregon, a deep lake inside the caldera of Mount Mazama.

EUROPE
Alps
Northern European Plain
Ural Mts.
Western Siberian Plain
Central Siberian Plateau
ASIA
Caucasus Mts.
Tian Shan
Tarim Basin
Hindu Kush
Kunlun Mts.
Fuji
PACIFIC OCEAN
Atlas Mts.
Zagros Mts.
Himalaya
AFRICA
Ethiopian Highlands
Deccan Plateau
Western Ghats
Congo Basin
Great Rift Valley
INDIAN OCEAN
AUSTRALIA
Great Dividing Ra.
ANTARCTICA

Exogenic Landforms

LANDFORMS THAT RESULT FROM "EXTERNAL" PROCESSES

External agents create exogenic landforms. Weathering by rain, groundwater, and other natural elements slowly breaks down rocks, such as the limestone in karst land-scapes or the granite in an exfoliation dome (Yosemite's Half Dome). Erosion removes weathered material and transports it from place to place. In the American South-west, erosion continues to shape the spires of Bryce Canyon and the walls of slot canyons.

Other Landforms

Some landforms are the impact sites (or craters) of asteroids, comets, and meteorites. The most readily observable are Meteor Crater in Arizona and New Quebec Crater in eastern Canada. Other landforms include man-made dams and open-pit mines, as well as biogenic features such as coral reefs made by coral polyps and giant mounds built by termites.

Meteor Crater, Arizona

Termite mound, Cape York Peninsula, Australia

Clockwise from above: tower karst in Thailand, weathered limestone in humid climate; Bryce Canyon in Utah, eroded sedimentary rocks in arid climate; slot canyon in the American Southwest, sedimentary rock eroded by water; Half Dome in Yosemite, California, weathered granite batholith.

Landforms

All of Earth's features are created and continually reshaped by such factors as wind, water, ice, tectonics, and humans. This painting brings together 34 natural and man-made features to show typical locations and relationships of landforms; it does not depict an actual region. Definitions of most landforms can be found in the glossary.

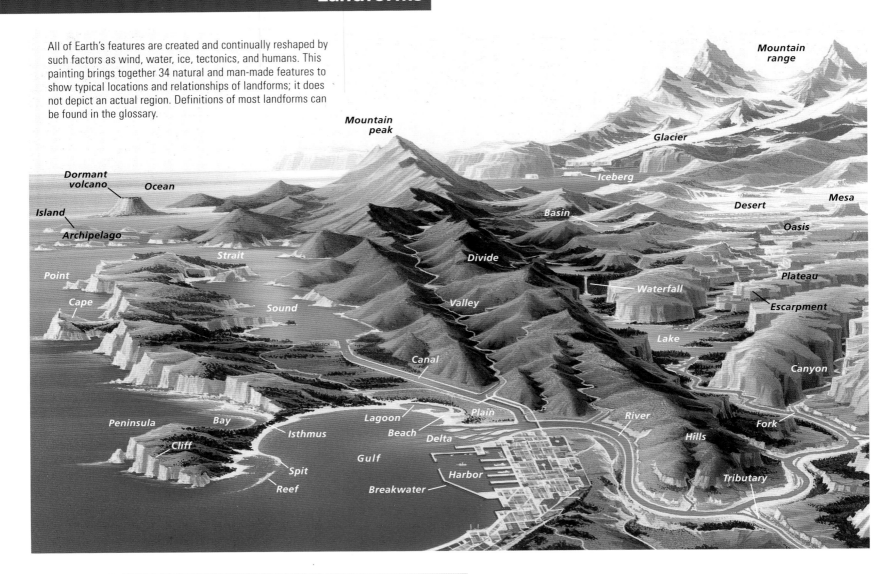

Landforms Created by Wind

The term "eolian" (from Aeolus, the Greek god of the winds) describes landforms shaped by the wind. The erosive action of wind is characterized by deflation, or the removal of dust and sand from dry soil; sandblasting, the erosion of rock by wind-borne sand; and deposition, the laying down of sediments. The effects of wind erosion are evident in many parts of the world (see map), particularly where there are large deposits of sand or loess (dust and silt dropped by wind). Among desert landforms, sand dunes may be the most spectacular. They come in several types (below): **Barchan dunes** are crescents with arms pointing downwind; **transverse dunes** are "waves," with crests perpendicular to the wind; **star dunes** have curving ridges radiating from their centers; **parabolic dunes** are crescents with arms that point upwind; and **longitudinal dunes** lie parallel to the wind.

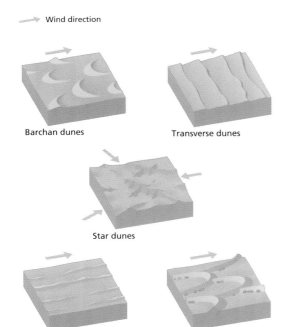

Wind direction

Barchan dunes

Transverse dunes

Star dunes

Longitudinal (seif) dunes

Parabolic dunes

Desert
Loess deposit
See Land Cover pp. 32-33

EOLIAN LANDFORMS
Desert dunes, which actually cover only a small portion of desert areas, range in height from just a few feet to more than a thousand feet. Coastal dunes form when wind and waves deposit sediments along the shores of oceans and other large bodies of water. Loess hills are large deposits of wind-borne silt, the most extensive of which are found in North America and Asia.

Desert dunes: Death Valley National Park, California

Coastal dunes: Dune du Nord, Quebec

Loess deposits: Palouse Hills, Washington

Landforms Created by Water

Highlighted on the map at right are Earth's major watersheds. These are drainage basins for rivers, which create fluvial (from a Latin word meaning "river") landforms. Wave action and ground-water also produce characteristic landforms.

RIVERS

Some rivers form broad loops called meanders (below) as faster currents erode their outer banks and slower currents deposit materials along inner banks. When a river breaks through the narrow neck of a meander, the abandoned curve becomes an oxbow lake.

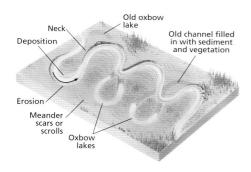

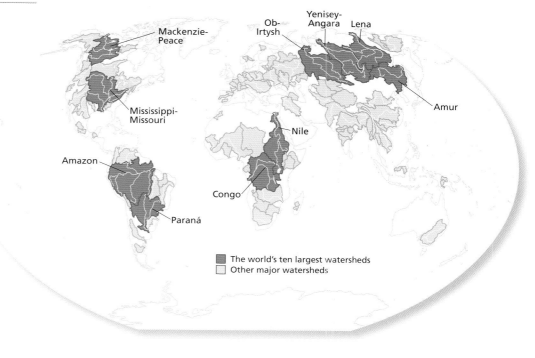

The world's ten largest watersheds
Other major watersheds

RIVER DELTAS

Sediment deposited at a river's mouth builds a delta, a term first used by the ancient Greeks to describe the Nile Delta; its triangular shape resembles the fourth letter of the Greek alphabet. Not all deltas have that classic shape: The Mississippi River forms a bird's-foot delta.

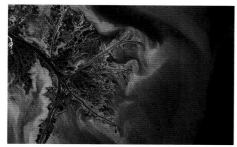

Mississippi River Delta

COASTAL AREAS

Through erosion and deposition, tides and wave action continually reshape the coastlines of the world. Ocean currents transport sand and gravel from one part of a shore to another, sometimes building beach extensions called spits, long ridges that project into open water. Relentless waves undercut coastal cliffs, eroding volumes of material and leaving behind sea stacks and sea arches, remnants made of more resistant rock. As ocean levels rise, narrow arms of the sea (fjords) may reach inland for miles, filling deep valleys once occupied by glaciers flowing to the sea.

Sea stacks: Victoria, Australia

GROUNDWATER

Water in the ground slowly dissolves lime-stone, a highly soluble rock. Over time, caves form and underground streams flow through the rock; sinkholes develop at the surface as underlying rock gives way. Karst landscapes, named for the rugged Karst region of the for-mer Yugoslavia, are large areas of unusual landforms created by weathered and eroded limestone.

Karst cave: Kickapoo Cave, Texas

Landforms Created by Ice

Among the legacies of Earth's most recent ice age (see map) are landforms shaped by glaciers. There are two kinds of glaciers: valley, or alpine, and continental ice sheets. These large, slow-moving masses of ice can crush or topple anything in their paths; they even stop rivers in their tracks, creating ice-dammed lakes. Glaciers are also powerful agents of erosion, grinding against the ground and picking up and carrying huge amounts of rock and soil, which they deposit at their margins when they begin to melt; these deposits are called lateral and terminal moraines. The paintings below show how an ice sheet (upper) leaves a lasting imprint on the land (lower).

BEFORE AND AFTER (LEFT)

Meltwater deposits mate-rial in long, nar-row ridges (eskers). Ice embedded in the ground melts and forms lakes (kettles). Ice overruns unconsolidated materials and shapes them into hills (drumlins).

Greatest extent of ice during last ice age

POSTGLACIAL LANDFORMS

As they move, alpine glaciers widen their V-shaped valleys, often leaving behind U-shaped ones when they withdraw (left). Ice sheets leave an even larger legacy simply because they cover more territory. Among their cre-ations are drumlin fields (right) and lake basins, including the ones now filled by the Great Lakes of North America.

Glacial valley: Sierra Nevada, California

Drumlins: Kejimkujik Lake, Nova Scotia

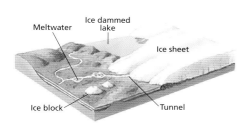

Surface of the Earth

EARTH'S LARGEST FEATURES—oceans and continents—can be seen from thousands of miles out in space. So can some of its relatively smaller ones: vast plains and long mountain chains, huge lakes and great ice sheets. The sizes, shapes, locations, and interrelationships of these and innumerable other features, large and small, give Earth its unique appearance.

Mountains, plateaus, and plains give texture to the land. In North and South America, the Rockies and Andes rise above great basins and plains, while in Asia the Himalaya and Plateau of Tibet form the rugged core of Earth's largest continent. All are the result of powerful forces within the planet pushing up the land. Other features, such as valleys and canyons, were created when weathering and erosion wore down parts of the surface. Landmasses are not the only places with dramatic features: Lying beneath the oceans are enormous mountains and towering volcanoes, high plateaus and seemingly bottomless trenches.

Around most continents are shallow seas concealing gently sloping continental shelves. From the margins of these shelves, steeper continental slopes lead ever deeper into the abyss. Although scientists use different terms to describe their studies of the ocean depths (bathymetry) and the lay of the land (topography), Earth's surface is a continuum, with similar features giving texture to lands both above and below the sea level.

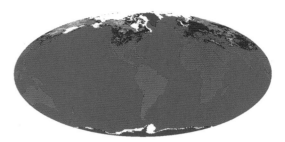

SNOW AND ICE Just over 2 percent of Earth's water is locked in ice, snow, and glaciers. Ice and snow reflect solar energy back into space, thus regulating the temperature. Ocean levels can also be affected, rising or falling as polar ice sheets shrink or grow.

Distribution of Earth's Elevations and Depths (Hypsometry)

Hypsometry measures the distribution of elevation and depth as a function of the area covered. At right, the "Raw %" curve shows two concentrations of average elevation: about 4,000 meters (13,000 ft) below sea level and about 800 meters (2,600 ft) above sea level. The "peaks" in the curve reflect the large, nearly flat areas of ocean floor, and vast land areas of Asia, Greenland, and Antarctica. The "Cumulative %" curve shows that about 72 percent of Earth's surface is below sea level, based on a worldwide two-minute (latitude-longitude) grid and a 200-meter (650-ft) grouping of vertical data.

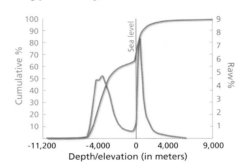

Earth Surface Elevations and Depths

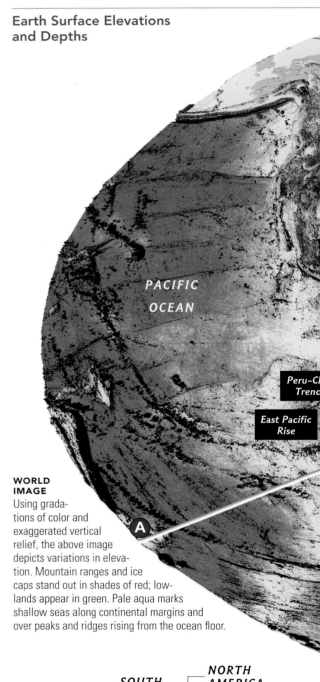

WORLD IMAGE
Using gradations of color and exaggerated vertical relief, the above image depicts variations in elevation. Mountain ranges and ice caps stand out in shades of red; lowlands appear in green. Pale aqua marks shallow seas along continental margins and over peaks and ridges rising from the ocean floor.

Surface by the Numbers

AREA
TOTAL SURFACE AREA: 196,938,000 square miles (510,066,000 sq km)
LAND AREA: 57,393,000 square miles (148,647,000 sq km), 29.1 percent of total surface area
WATER AREA: 139,545,000 square miles (361,419,000 sq km), 70.9 percent of total surface area

SURFACE FEATURES
HIGHEST LAND: Mount Everest, 29,035 feet (8,850 m) above sea level
LOWEST LAND: shore of Dead Sea, 1,380 feet (421 m) below sea level

OCEAN DEPTHS
DEEPEST PART OF OCEAN: Challenger Deep, in the Pacific Ocean southwest of Guam, 35,827 feet (10,920 m) below the surface
AVERAGE OCEAN DEPTH: 12,205 feet (3,720 m)

CHEMICAL MAKEUP OF EARTH'S CRUST
As a percentage of the crust's weight: oxygen 46.6, silicon 27.7, aluminum 8.1, iron 5.0, calcium 3.6, sodium 2.8, potassium 2.6, magnesium 2.1, and other elements totaling 1.5.

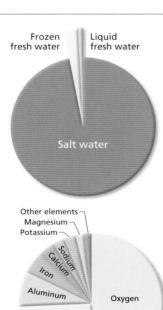

A Slice of Earth

Combining bathymetric and topographic data, this profile shows details of the Earth's crust—from the western Pacific Basin (A) to the Atlantic Basin; across Africa, the Himalaya, and the Japan Trench; then back to the western Pacific margin (B).

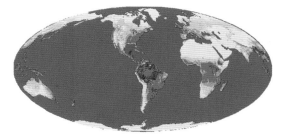

VEGETATIVE COVER Forests and woodlands cover 28 percent of Earth's land areas, helping those regions retain heat and thus playing a major role in the shaping of climate. Vast grasslands hold grains that are an important element in the world food supply.

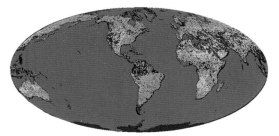

DAY AND NIGHT TEMPERATURE DIFFERENCES Vegetative cover influences variations between day and night temperatures in an area. Rain forests and other heavily vegetated regions retain heat well and experience relatively small changes, whereas deserts (in red) are subject to extreme variations.

CLOUD COVER This composite image shows the regions with the heaviest cloud cover (red) on a typical June day. The gradation to blue signifies decreasing cover. Clouds contain moisture, affect temperatures, and on any given day cover 50 to 70 percent of Earth's surface.

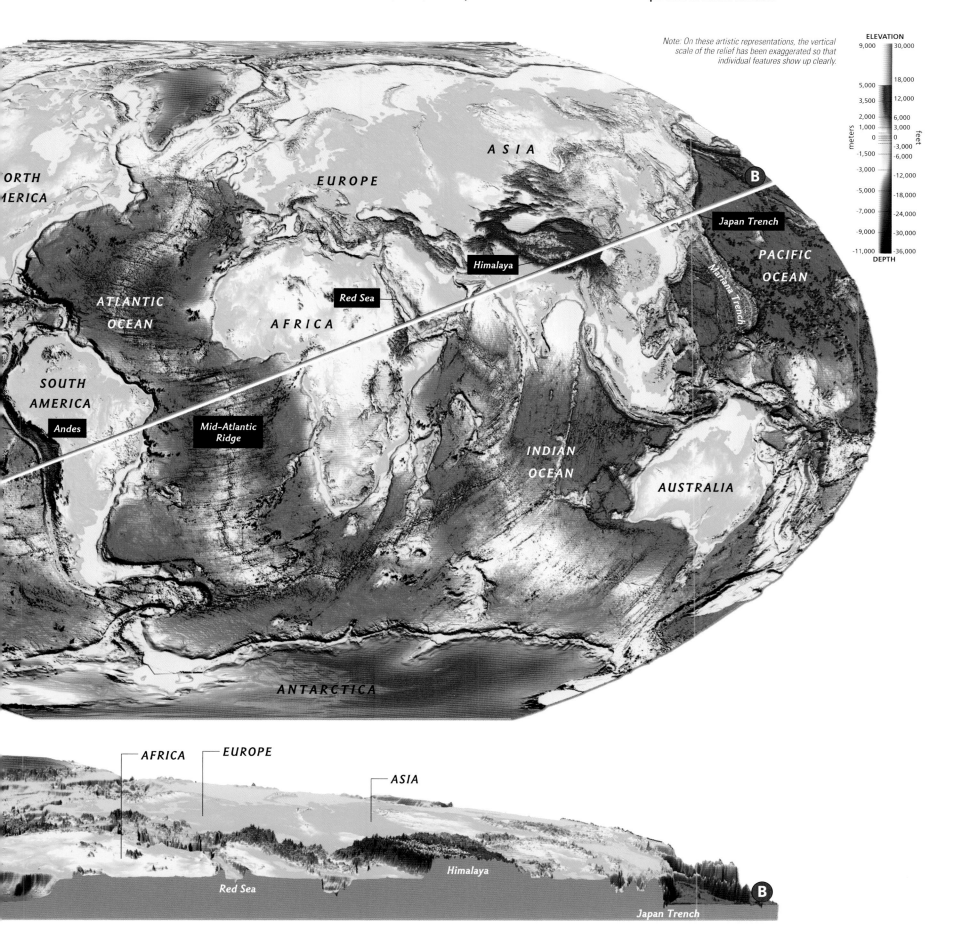

Note: On these artistic representations, the vertical scale of the relief has been exaggerated so that individual features show up clearly.

ELEVATION

meters	feet
9,000	30,000
5,000	18,000
3,500	12,000
2,000	6,000
1,000	3,000
0	0
-1,500	-3,000
	-6,000
-3,000	-12,000
-5,000	-18,000
-7,000	-24,000
-9,000	-30,000
-11,000	-36,000

DEPTH

RELIABLE INFORMATION on global vegetative cover is an important requirement for many Earth-system studies, and the best source for an overall view of the planet is satellite data. Such data allow for the creation of internally consistent, reproducible, and accurate land cover maps like the one at right, which is based on a year of global satellite imagery from the Advanced Very High Resolution Radiometer (AVHRR) at a spatial resolution of one kilometer.

The change of vegetation through time, or its phenology, is captured in the satellite record and used to differentiate classes of vegetative cover. By recording the data at different wavelengths of the electromagnetic spectrum, scientists can derive land cover types through spectral variation. Maps made from this information help identify places undergoing changes. Descriptions of the various land cover types are provided below.

Global Land Cover Composition

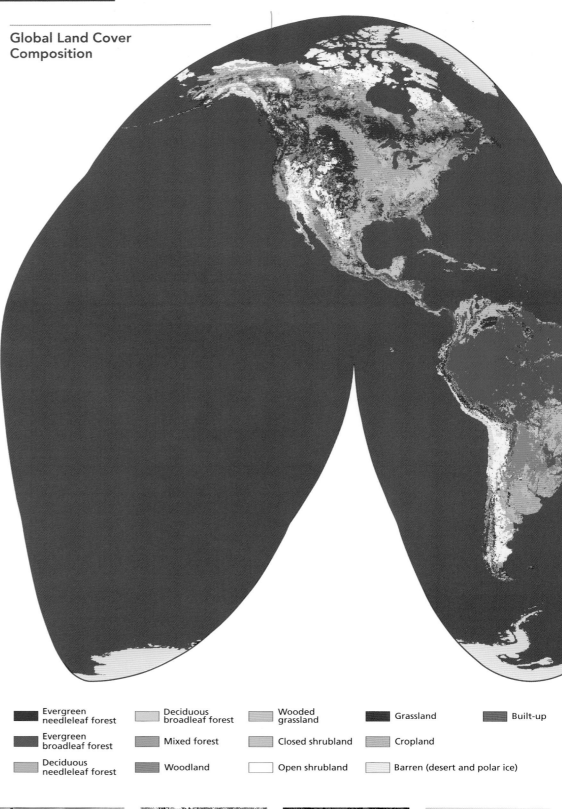

Legend:
- Evergreen needleleaf forest
- Evergreen broadleaf forest
- Deciduous needleleaf forest
- Deciduous broadleaf forest
- Mixed forest
- Woodland
- Wooded grassland
- Closed shrubland
- Open shrubland
- Grassland
- Cropland
- Barren (desert and polar ice)
- Built-up

EVERGREEN NEEDLE-LEAF FOREST
In this land cover type, more than 60 percent of the land is covered by a forest canopy; tree height exceeds 5 meters. Evergreen needleleaf forests are typical of the boreal (northern subarctic) region. In many of these areas, trees are grown on plantations and logged for the making of paper and building products.

EVERGREEN BROAD-LEAF FOREST
More than 60 percent of the land is covered by a forest canopy; tree height exceeds 5 meters. Such forests, which include tropical rain forests, dominate in the tropics and contain the greatest concentrations of biodiversity. In many areas, mechanized farms, ranches, and tree plantations are replacing this land cover.

DECIDUOUS NEEDLE-LEAF FOREST
More than 60 percent of the land is covered by a forest canopy; tree height exceeds 5 meters. Trees respond to cold seasons by shedding their leaves simultaneously. This class is dominant only in Siberia, taking the form of larch forests with a short June-to-August growing season.

DECIDUOUS BROAD-LEAF FOREST
More than 60 percent of the land is covered by a forest canopy; tree height exceeds 5 meters. In dry or cold seasons, trees shed their leaves simultaneously. Much of this forest has been converted to cropland in temperate regions, with large remnants found only on steep slopes.

MIXED FOREST
More than 60 percent of the land is covered by a forest canopy; tree height exceeds 5 meters. Both needleleaf and deciduous types appear, with neither having coverage of less than 25 percent or more than 75 percent. This type is largely found between temperate deciduous and boreal evergreen forests.

WOODLAND
Land has herbaceous or woody understories and tree canopy cover of 40 to 60 percent; trees exceed 5 meters and may be evergreen or deciduous. This type is common in the tropics and is most highly degraded in areas with long histories of human habitation, such as West Africa.

WOODED GRASSLAND
Land has herbaceous or woody understories and tree canopy cover of 10 to 40 percent; trees exceed 5 meters and may be evergreen or deciduous. This type includes classic African savanna, as well as open boreal woodlands that demarcate tree lines and the beginning of tundra ecosystems.

CLOSED SHRUBLAND
Bushes or shrubs dominate, with a canopy coverage of more than 40 percent. Bushes do not exceed 5 meters in height; shrubs or bushes can be evergreen or deciduous. Tree canopy is less than 10 percent. This land cover can be found where prolonged cold or dry seasons limit plant growth.

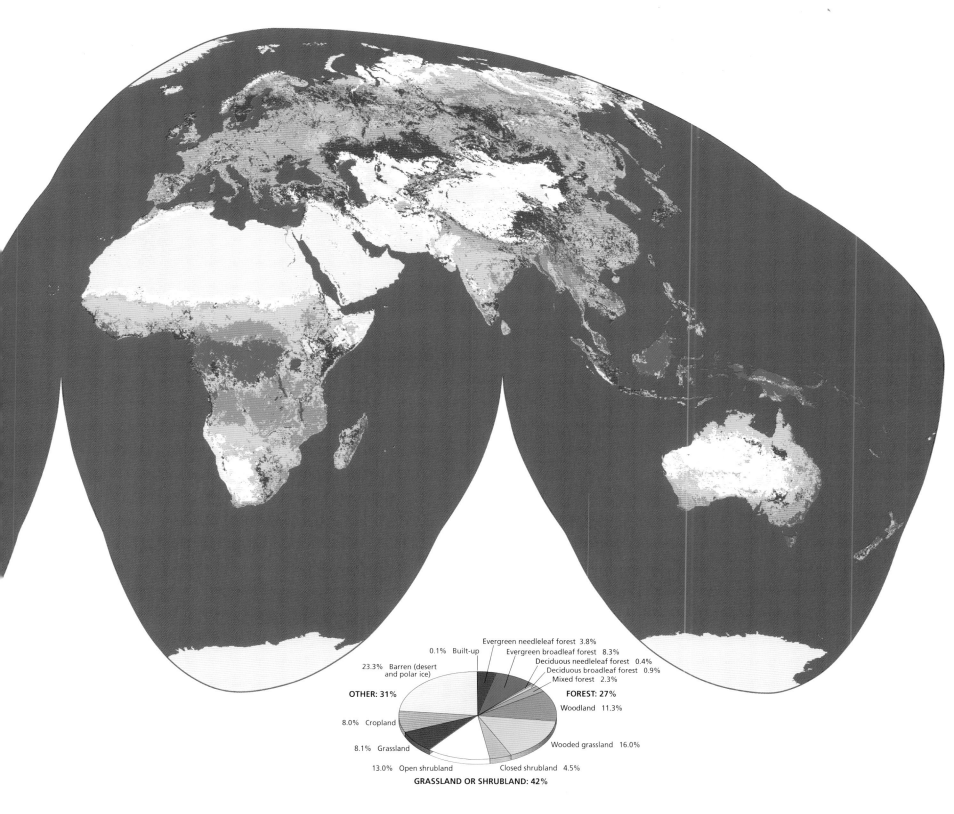

Evergreen needleleaf forest 3.8%
Evergreen broadleaf forest 8.3%
Deciduous needleleaf forest 0.4%
Deciduous broadleaf forest 0.9%
Mixed forest 2.3%

0.1% Built-up

23.3% Barren (desert and polar ice)

OTHER: 31%

8.0% Cropland

8.1% Grassland

13.0% Open shrubland

FOREST: 27%

Woodland 11.3%

Wooded grassland 16.0%

Closed shrubland 4.5%

GRASSLAND OR SHRUBLAND: 42%

OPEN SHRUBLAND
Shrubs are dominant, with a canopy cover between 10 and 40 percent; they do not exceed 2 meters in height and can be evergreen or deciduous. The remaining land is either barren or characterized by annual herbaceous cover. This land cover type occurs in semiarid or severely cold regions.

GRASSLAND
Land has continuous herbaceous cover and less than 10 percent tree or shrub canopy cover. This type occurs in a wide range of habitats. Perennial grasslands in the central United States and Russia, for example, are the most extensive and mark a line of decreased precipitation that limits agriculture.

CROPLAND
Crop-producing fields make up more than 80 percent of the landscape. Areas of high-intensity agriculture, including mechanized farming, stretch across temperate regions. Much agriculture in the developing world is fragmented, however, and occurs on small plots of land.

BARREN AND DESERT
Exposed soil, sand, or rocks are typical; the land never has more than 10 percent vegetated cover during any time of year. This class includes true deserts, such as the Sahara in Africa. Desertification, the expansion of deserts due to land degradation or climate change, is a problem in areas.

URBAN AND BUILT-UP
Land cover includes buildings and other man-made structures. This class was mapped using the populated places layer that is part of the "Digital Chart of the World" (Danko, 1992). Urban and built-up cover represents the most densely developed areas of human habitation.

SNOW AND ICE
Land has permanent snow and ice; it never has more than 10 percent vegetated cover at any time of year. The greatest expanses of this class can be seen in Greenland, on other Arctic islands, and in Antarctica. Glaciers at high elevations form significant examples in Alaska, the Himalaya, and Iceland.

THE TERM "CLIMATE" describes the average "weather" conditions, as measured over many years, that prevail at any given point around the world at a given time of the year. Daily weather may differ dramatically from that expected on the basis of climatic statistics.

Energy from the sun drives the global climate system. Much of this incoming energy is absorbed in the tropics. Outgoing heat radiation, much of which exits at high latitudes, balances the absorbed incoming solar energy. To achieve a balance across the globe, huge amounts of heat are moved from the tropics to polar regions by both the atmosphere and the oceans.

The tilt of Earth's axis leads to shifting patterns of incoming solar energy throughout the year. More energy is transported to higher latitudes in winter than in summer, and hence the contrast in temperatures between the tropics and polar regions is greatest at this time of year—especially in the Northern Hemisphere.

Scientists present this data in many ways, using climographs (see page 36), which show information about specific places. Alternatively, they produce maps, which show regional and worldwide data.

The effects of the climatic contrasts are seen in the distribution of Earth's lifeforms. Temperature, precipitation, and the amount of sunlight all determine what plants can grow in a region and the animals that live there. People are more adaptable, but climate exerts powerful constraints on where we live.

Climatic conditions define planning decisions, such as how much heating oil we need for the winter, and the necessary rainfall for agriculture in the summer. Fluctuations from year to year (e.g., cold winters or summer droughts) make planning more difficult.

In the longer term, continued global warming may change climatic conditions around the world, which could dramatically alter temperature and precipitation patterns and lead to more frequent heat waves, floods, and droughts.

JANUARY SOLAR ENERGY*

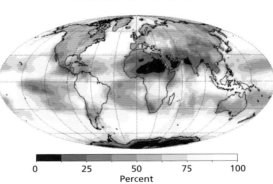

Watts per square yard

| 0 | 115.0 | 230.0 | 344.9 | 459.9 |

| 0 | 137.5 | 275 | 412.5 | 550 |

Watts per square meter

JULY SOLAR ENERGY*

Watts per square yard

| 0 | 115.0 | 230.0 | 344.9 | 459.9 |

| 0 | 137.5 | 275 | 412.5 | 550 |

Watts per square meter

Amount of solar energy reaching the upper atmosphere.

JANUARY AVERAGE TEMPERATURE

°Fahrenheit

| -40 | 32 | 104 |
| -40 | 0 | 40 |

°Celsius

JULY AVERAGE TEMPERATURE

°Fahrenheit

| -40 | 32 | 104 |
| -40 | 0 | 40 |

°Celsius

JANUARY CLOUD COVER

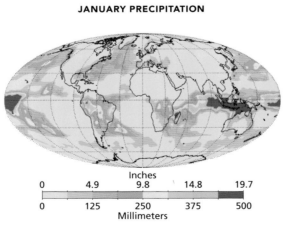

| 0 | 25 | 50 | 75 | 100 |

Percent

JULY CLOUD COVER

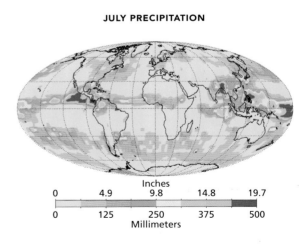

| 0 | 25 | 50 | 75 | 100 |

Percent

JANUARY PRECIPITATION

Inches

| 0 | 4.9 | 9.8 | 14.8 | 19.7 |

| 0 | 125 | 250 | 375 | 500 |

Millimeters

JULY PRECIPITATION

Inches

| 0 | 4.9 | 9.8 | 14.8 | 19.7 |

| 0 | 125 | 250 | 375 | 500 |

Millimeters

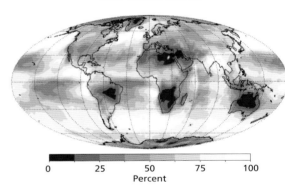

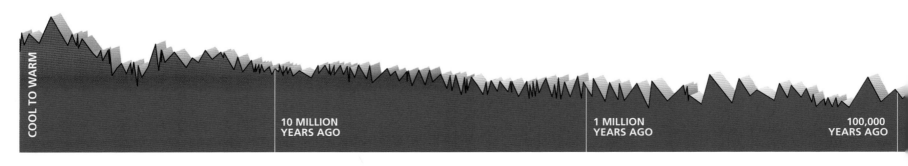

COOL TO WARM

10 MILLION YEARS AGO

1 MILLION YEARS AGO

100,000 YEARS AGO

Major Factors that Influence Climate

LATITUDE AND ANGLE OF THE SUN'S RAYS

As Earth circles the sun, the tilt of its axis causes changes in the angle of the sun's rays and in the periods of daylight at different latitudes. Polar regions experience the greatest variation, with long periods of limited or no sunlight in winter and sometimes 24 hours of daylight in the summer.

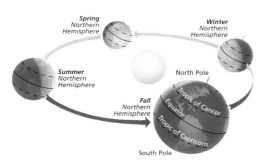

ELEVATION (ALTITUDE)

In general, climatic conditions become colder as elevation increases, just as they do when latitude increases. "Life zones" on a high mountain reflect the changes: Plants at the base are the same as those in surrounding countryside. Farther up, treed vegetation distinctly ends at the tree line; at the highest elevations, snow covers the mountain.

Mount Shasta, California

TOPOGRAPHY

Mountain ranges are natural barriers to air movement. In California (see diagram at right), winds off the Pacific carry moisture-laden air toward the coast. The Coast Ranges allow for some condensation and light precipitation. Inland, the taller Sierra Nevada range wrings more significant precipitation from the air. On the leeward slopes of the Sierra Nevada, sinking air warms from compression, clouds evaporate, and dry conditions prevail.

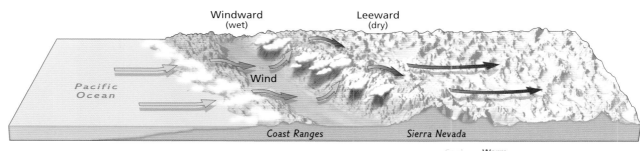

Temperature variations as air moves over mountains

EFFECTS OF GEOGRAPHY

The location of a place and its distance from mountains and bodies of water help determine its prevailing wind patterns and what types of air masses affect it. Coastal areas may enjoy refreshing breezes in summer, when cooler ocean air moves ashore. Places south and east of the Great Lakes can expect "lake effect" snow in winter, when cold air travels over relatively warmer waters. In spring and summer, people living in "Tornado Alley" in the central United States watch for thunderstorms. Here, three types of air masses often converge: cold and dry from the north, warm and dry from the southwest, and warm and moist from the Gulf of Mexico. The colliding air masses often spawn tornadic storms.

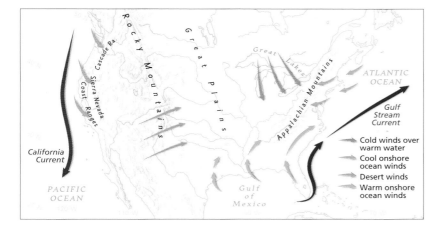

PREVAILING GLOBAL WIND PATTERNS

As shown at right, three large-scale wind patterns are found in the Northern Hemisphere and three are found in the Southern Hemisphere. These are average conditions and do not necessarily reflect conditions on a particular day. As seasons change, the wind patterns shift north or south. So does the intertropical convergence zone, which moves back and forth across the Equator. Sailors called this zone the doldrums because its winds are typically weak.

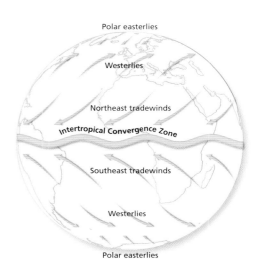

SURFACE OF THE EARTH

Just look at any globe or a world map showing land cover, and you will see another important influence on climate: Earth's surface. The amount of sunlight that is absorbed or reflected by the surface determines how much atmospheric heating occurs. Darker areas, such as heavily vegetated regions, tend to be good absorbers; lighter areas, such as snow- and ice-covered regions, tend to be good reflectors. Oceans absorb a high proportion of the solar energy falling upon them, but release it more slowly. Both the oceans and the atmosphere distribute heat around the globe.

Temperature Change over Time

Cold and warm periods punctuate Earth's long history. Some were fairly short (perhaps hundreds of years); others spanned hundreds of thousands of years. In some cold periods, glaciers grew and spread over large regions. In subsequent warm periods, the ice retreated. Each period profoundly affected plant and animal life. The most recent cool period, often called the little ice age, ended in western Europe around the year 1850.

Since the turn of the 20th century, temperatures have been rising steadily throughout the world. But it is not yet clear how much of this warming is due to natural causes and how much derives from human activities, such as the burning of fossil fuels and the clearing of forests.

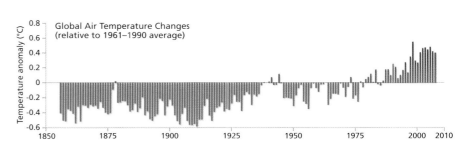

CLIMATE ZONES ARE PRIMARILY CONTROLLED by latitude—which governs the prevailing winds, the angle of the sun's rays, and the length of day throughout the year—and by geographical location with respect to mountains and oceans. Elevation, surface attributes, and other variables modify the primary controlling factors. Latitudinal banding of climate zones is most pronounced over Africa and Asia, where fewer north-south mountain ranges mean less disruption of prevailing winds. In the Western Hemisphere, the high, almost continuous mountain range that extends from western Canada to southern South America helps create dry regions on its leeward slopes. Over the United States, where westerly winds prevail, areas to the east of the range lie in a "rain shadow" and are therefore drier. In northern parts of South America, where easterly trade winds prevail, the rain shadow lies west of the mountains. Ocean effects dominate much of western Europe and southern parts of Australia.

Climographs

The map at right shows the global distribution of climate zones, while the following 12 climographs (graphs of monthly temperature and precipitation) provide snapshots of the climate at specific places. Each place has a different climate type, which is described in general terms. Rainfall is shown in a bar graph format (scale on right side of the graph); temperature is expressed with a line graph (scale on left side). Places with highland and upland climates were not included because local changes in elevation can produce significant variations in local conditions.

TROPICAL WET

This climate type has the most predictable conditions. Warm and rainy year-round, regions with a tropical wet climate experience little variation from month to month. This type is mainly found within a zone extending about 10 degrees on either side of the Equator. With as much as 60 inches (152 cm) of rain each year, the tropical wet climate supports lush vegetation.

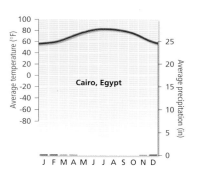

TROPICAL WET AND DRY

Because of seasonal reversals in wind direction (monsoons), this climate type is characterized by a slightly cooler dry season and a warmer, very moist wet season. The highest temperatures usually occur just before the wet season. Although average annual conditions may be similar to a tropical wet climate, the rainy season brings much more rain.

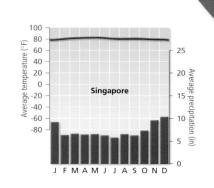

ARID

Centered between 20° and 30° north and south latitude, this climate type is the result of a persistent high-pressure area and, along the western margins of continents, a cold ocean current. Rainfall amounts in regions with this climate type are negligible, and there is some seasonal variation in temperature. Desert vegetation is typically sparse.

SEMIARID

Regions with a semiarid climate lie poleward of areas with a desert (arid) climate; they have a much greater range in monthly temperatures and receive significantly more rainfall than deserts. This climate type is often found in inland regions, in the rain shadow of mountain ranges. Annual rainfall amounts support mainly grasses and small shrubs.

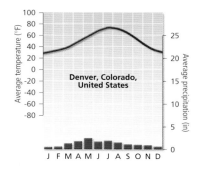

MARINE WEST COAST

This climate type is primarily found between 40 and 60 degrees latitude; it occurs on the west coasts of continents and across much of Europe. Prevailing westerly winds bring milder ocean air ashore, but sunny days are limited and precipitation is frequent. Except in the highest elevations, most precipitation falls as rain. This climate supports extensive forests.

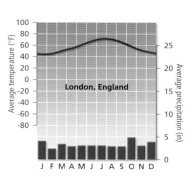

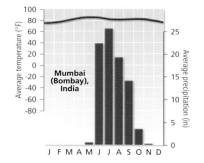

Climate Zones
(based on modified Köppen system)

Tropical
- Tropical wet
- Tropical wet & dry

Dry
- Semiarid
- Arid

Mild
- Marine west coast
- Mediterranean
- Humid subtropical

Continental
- Warm summer
- Cool summer
- Subarctic

Polar
- Tundra
- Ice sheet

High elevations
- Highlands
- Uplands

— Warm ocean current
— Cool ocean current

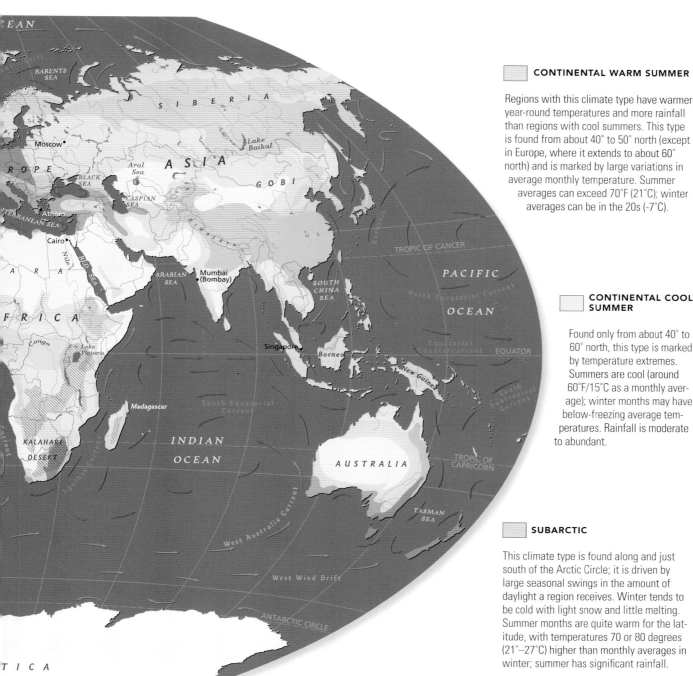

CONTINENTAL WARM SUMMER

Regions with this climate type have warmer year-round temperatures and more rainfall than regions with cool summers. This type is found from about 40° to 50° north (except in Europe, where it extends to about 60° north) and is marked by large variations in average monthly temperature. Summer averages can exceed 70°F (21°C); winter averages can be in the 20s (-7°C).

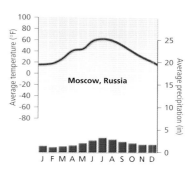
Chicago, Illinois, United States

CONTINENTAL COOL SUMMER

Found only from about 40° to 60° north, this type is marked by temperature extremes. Summers are cool (around 60°F/15°C as a monthly average); winter months may have below-freezing average temperatures. Rainfall is moderate to abundant.

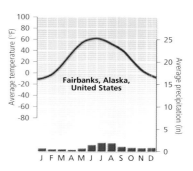
Moscow, Russia

SUBARCTIC

This climate type is found along and just south of the Arctic Circle; it is driven by large seasonal swings in the amount of daylight a region receives. Winter tends to be cold with light snow and little melting. Summer months are quite warm for the latitude, with temperatures 70 or 80 degrees (21°–27°C) higher than monthly averages in winter; summer has significant rainfall.

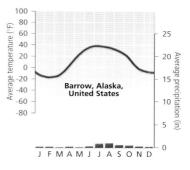
Fairbanks, Alaska, United States

MEDITERRANEAN

This term describes the climate of much of the Mediterranean region. Such a climate is also found in narrow bands along the west coasts of continents that lie around 30 to 35 degrees poleward from the Equator. Summer months are typically warm to hot with dry conditions, while winter months are cool (but not cold) and provide modest precipitation.

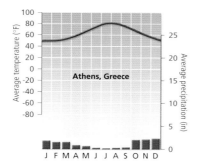
Athens, Greece

TUNDRA

Along the southern boundary of this climatic zone, ground-hugging plants meet the northernmost trees (the tree line). Here, the warmest average monthly temperature is below 50°F (10°C), with only one to four months having an average monthly temperature that is above freezing. Precipitation amounts are low, typically about 10 inches (25 cm) or less annually.

Barrow, Alaska, United States

HUMID SUBTROPICAL

This climate type dominates eastern regions of continents at 30 to 35 degrees latitude. Here, warm ocean waters lead to warm and humid summers. Rainfall is greatest near the coast, supporting forest growth; precipitation is less farther west, supporting grasslands. Winter can bring cold waves and snowy periods, except in areas right on the coast.

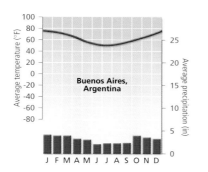
Buenos Aires, Argentina

ICE SHEET

This climate type is found at high latitudes in interior Greenland and across most of Antarctica; average monthly temperatures are around zero degrees Fahrenheit (-18°C) and below. Snow defines the landscape, but precipitation is only about 5 inches (13 cm) or less annually. The combined effects of cold and dryness produce desert-like conditions.

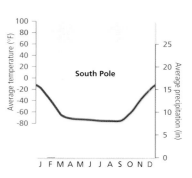
South Pole

STEP OUTSIDE AND YOU EXPERIENCE many facets of weather. Humidity, air temperature and pressure, wind speed and direction, cloud cover and type, and the amount and form of precipitation are all atmospheric characteristics of the momentary conditions we call weather.

The sun is ultimately responsible for the weather. Its rays are absorbed differently by land and water surfaces (equal amounts of solar radiation heat the ground more quickly than they heat water). Differential warming, in turn, causes variations in the temperature and pressure of overlying air masses.

As an air mass warms, it becomes lighter and rises higher into the atmosphere. As an air mass cools, it becomes heavier and sinks. Pressure differences between masses of air generate winds, which tend to blow from high-pressure areas to areas of low pressure. Fast-moving, upper-atmosphere winds known as jet streams help move weather systems around the world.

Large weather systems called cyclones rotate counterclockwise in the Northern Hemisphere (clockwise in the Southern Hemisphere); they are also called "lows," because their centers are low-pressure areas. Clouds and precipitation are usually associated with these systems. Anticyclones, or "highs," rotate in the opposite direction and are high-pressure areas. They usually bring clearer skies and more settled weather.

The boundary between two air masses is called a front. Here, wind, temperature, and humidity change abruptly, producing atmospheric instability. When things get "out of balance" in the atmosphere, storms may develop, bringing rain or snow and sometimes thunder and lightning as well. Storms are among nature's great equalizers.

The weather you experience is influenced by many factors, including your location's latitude, elevation, and proximity to water bodies. Even the degree of urban development, which creates "heat islands," and the amount of snow cover, which chills an overlying air mass, play important roles. The next time you watch a weather report on television, think about the many factors, some thousands of miles away, that help make the weather what it is.

The swirling cloud pattern and well-formed eye of Hurricane Katrina stand out in this NOAA satellite image from late morning on August 29, 2005. At the time, Katrina was making its third landfall near the Louisiana-Mississippi border, and was by now a weakening Category Two storm. (The other two landfalls were near Miami, Florida, as a strong tropical storm, and just south of New Orleans as a hurricane.) Its storm surge, flooding, and high winds caused incredible destruction from Louisiana eastward to Alabama, and Katrina ranks as the costliest—and also one of the deadliest—hurricanes ever to strike the U.S.

Hurricanes (defined as tropical low-pressure systems with sustained winds of at least 74 miles an hour) can also be prolific rainmakers. In 1972, Agnes dropped torrents of rain on the northeast U.S., causing severe flooding in several states. Despite the dramatic rainfall sometimes brought by hurricanes, nontropical (or extratropical) low-pressure systems actually bring most of the precipitation that falls in the middle latitudes (30° to 60° latitude).

Major Factors that Influence Weather

THE WATER CYCLE

As the sun warms the surface of Earth, water rises in the form of water vapor from lakes, rivers, oceans, plants, the ground, and other sources. This process is called evaporation. Water vapor provides the moisture that forms clouds; it eventually returns to Earth in the form of precipitation, and the cycle continues.

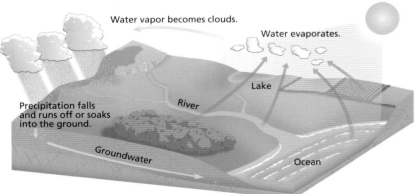

AIR MASSES

When air hovers for a while over a surface area with uniform humidity and temperature, it takes on the characteristics of the area below. For example, an air mass over the tropical Atlantic Ocean would become warm and humid; an air mass over the winter snow and ice of northern Canada would become cold and dry. These massive volumes of air often cover thousands of miles and reach to the stratosphere. Over time, mid-latitude cyclonic storms and global wind patterns move them to locations far from their source regions.

JET STREAM

A meandering current of high-speed wind, a jet stream is usually found around five to ten miles above Earth's surface. It generally flows west to east, often in a noncontinuous wavy fashion, with cold, Equatorward dips (called troughs) and warm, Poleward bulges (called ridges). The polar jet separates cold and warm masses of air; the subtropical jet is less likely to be related to temperature differences. Fronts and low-pressure areas are typically located near a jet stream.

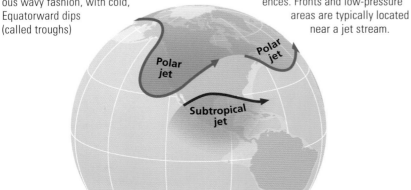

WEATHER FRONTS

The transition zone between two air masses of different humidity and temperature is called a front. Along a cold front, cold air displaces warm air; along a warm front, warm air displaces cold air. When neither air mass displaces the other, a stationary front develops. Towering clouds and intense storms may form along cold fronts, while widespread clouds and rain, snow, sleet, or drizzle may accompany warm fronts.

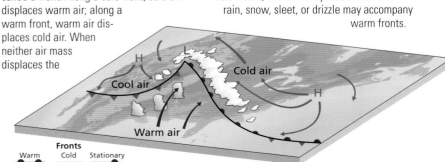

Cloud Types

Clouds are the visible collections of water droplets or ice particles in the atmosphere. Meteorologists classify them according to shape and altitude.

Stratus are low-level clouds that are flat or layered; they are much longer and wider than they are tall. Fog is a stratus cloud that touches the ground. Altostratus (alto means "high") is a stratus cloud about two miles above Earth. When these clouds rain or snow, they are called nimbostratus. Cirrostratus clouds lie at an altitude of about four miles.

Cumulus clouds have flat bottoms and puffy tops. The flat bottoms mark the altitude at which rising air reaches its condensation level (typically about a mile above Earth's surface); the puffy tops show how the cloud "bubbles up." Cumulus often develop as sunlight heats the ground and the ground, in turn, heats the air. If cumulus tower, they can transform into cumulonimbus (thunderstorm) clouds, with their tops reaching an altitude of seven miles or more.

Cumulus clouds can also develop in layers. Stratocumulus is a layered cumulus cloud about a mile above the ground. Altocumulus is a similar cloud at an altitude of two miles. Its greater distance from the ground makes the cumulus puffs appear smaller than those of stratocumulus clouds. The cirrocumulus type (with still smaller puffs) is found about four to five miles higher.

Cirrus clouds occur at an altitude of four miles or more, where the temperature is always below freezing; hence, these clouds are always filled with ice crystals.

As a general forecasting rule, dry weather is most likely when cumulus clouds remain flat and/or when mid-level (altocumulus) clouds are not present. Precipitation is most likely when two or more clouds occur at the same time, and/or when cumulus clouds tower to great heights or turn into cumulonimbus clouds.

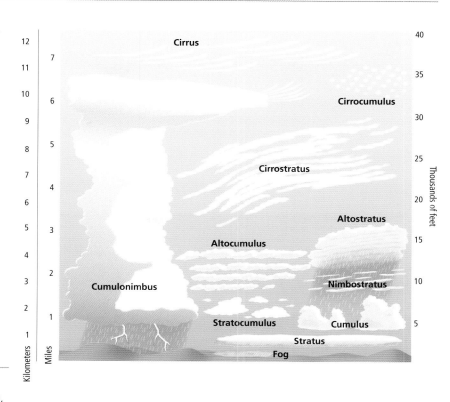

Tropical Cyclones

Hurricanes and their counterparts in other places (typhoons near Japan and cyclones off India and Australia) are moderately large low-pressure systems that form most often during the warmer months of the year. They occur mainly near the Equator, in regions with prevailing easterly winds. These systems develop winds between 75 and 150 miles an hour and, on some rare occasions, even stronger winds. As the storms move toward the middle latitudes, where the prevailing winds are mainly westerly, they can "recurve" (move toward the east). Some hurricanes have stayed nearly stationary at times, while others have made loops and spirals along their paths.

Lightning

In order to estimate the mean annual distribution of lightning (more than 1.2 billion intracloud and cloud-to-ground flashes), NASA scientists used five years of data taken from a satellite orbiting 460 miles above Earth. Lightning distribution is directly linked to climate, with maximal occurrence in areas that see frequent thunderstorms (the red areas on the map below).

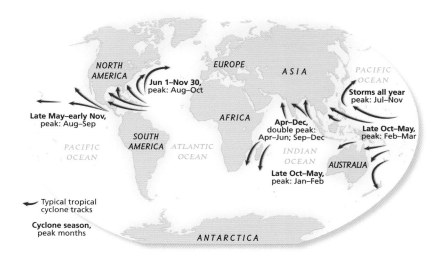

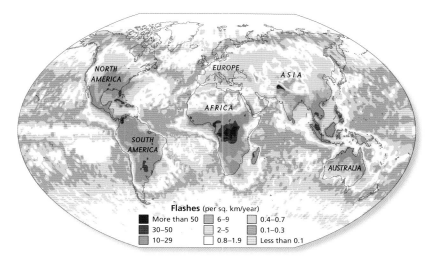

El Niño and La Niña

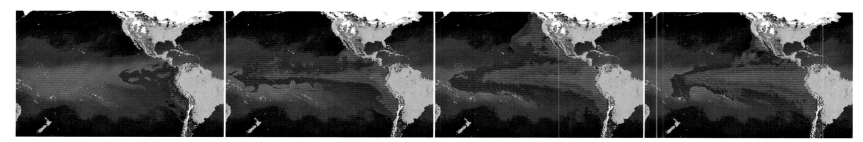

Periodic shifts in wind speed and direction in the tropical eastern Pacific can lead to changes in sea-surface temperatures. In what scientists call El Niño events, prevailing easterly winds weaken or give way to westerly winds, and the normal upwelling process, which brings cool, nutrient-rich waters up from lower levels of the ocean, stops. This stoppage causes sea-surface temperatures to rise, providing an unfavorable habitat for many fish. The warmer ocean conditions can also lead to more rainfall and floods along the west coast of the Americas. A stronger easterly wind flow, on the other hand, can increase upwelling and make the sea-surface tempera-tures even colder, producing La Niña. Both phenomena can have far-reaching weather effects. For example, strong El Niño events often result in a weak Atlantic Ocean hurricane season but produce plentiful precipita-tion in the normally dry southwestern United States. La Niña events favor more Atlantic hurricanes, but can spell drought in the southwestern U.S., even for normally dry southern California.

From left to right, the above image sequence shows how temperatures in the Pacific Ocean changed as the 1997 to 1998 El Niño event evolved. The first image, from March 10, 1997, shows a mostly cool ocean (blue shades). By mid-June, sea-surface temperatures (red shades) were above average from South America across much of the tropical Pacific. By mid-September, the warmth had extended from California southward to Chile and west-ward across most of the tropical Pacific. The final image, from late December 1997, shows a major El Niño, with sea-surface temperatures measuring six to eight degrees above average on the Fahrenheit scale.

To learn about weather extremes, see Geographic Comparisons on page 264.

Biosphere

HOME TO ALL LIVING THINGS, the biosphere is an intricate system made up of constantly interacting realms that support life: parts of the atmosphere (air), lithosphere (land), and hydrosphere (water in the ground, at the surface, and in the air).

As a result of the interaction between realms of the biosphere and changes in the distance of Earth's revolution around the sun, Earth's flora and fauna have changed over the eons, sometimes slowly and sometimes rapidly. Some species have continued to evolve; others, like the dinosaurs, have become extinct.

Life, of course, interacts with the land, water, and air, playing a significant role in shaping Earth's face and influencing its natural processes. Billions of years ago one of the smallest life-forms, photosynthetic bacteria (organisms that produce oxygen as a by-product of their metabolism), helped provide the oxygen in the air we breathe.

Human beings are currently Earth's dominant life-form. Through the ages, we have evolved the means to affect the planet in ways both positive and negative. At present, we are introducing changes to the biosphere at greater rates than natural processes may be able to accommodate, as societies make ever increasing demands on Earth's resources.

It is now clear that human beings are able to greatly influence the fate of the biosphere. It is also clear that developing a better understanding of how the biosphere functions, and how its realms interact, is fundamental to sustaining it. This requires a multi- and interdisciplinary perspective that brings together different worldviews from each of the physical, biological, and social sciences.

The Biosphere from Space

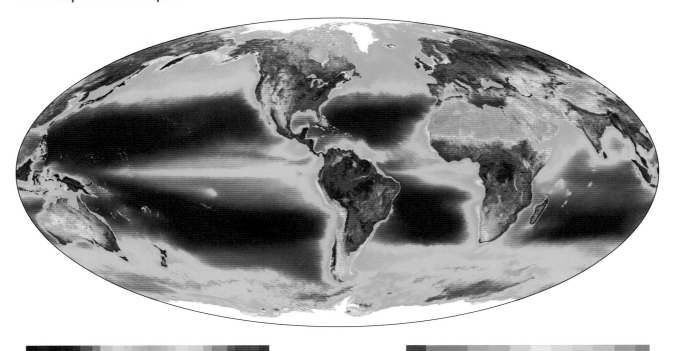

Satellite technology enables us to monitor life on Earth. For example, satellite sensors help us measure the amount of chlorophyll—the green pigment used by plants during photosynthesis—on land and in masses of water. Satellite measurements can also provide an estimate of the distribution and abundance of both terrestrial vegetation and aquatic phytoplankton. By color-coding data (see the color scales for the world map), we can actually quantify changes in vegetation on land and in the oceans from season to season and from year to year. The map reveals an unequal distribution of life for the June-to-August period. Most of the Northern Hemisphere has become green, except in areas of low rainfall or poor soil. Spectacular phytoplankton blooms are evident in the equatorial Pacific. Vegetation has lightened in the southern winter, as the rays of the sun provide less energy.

>.01   .05   .2   1   2   5   20   50
OCEAN: CHLOROPHYLL *a* CONCENTRATION (mg/m³)

Maximum   Minimum
LAND: NORMALIZED DIFFERENCE VEGETATION INDEX

Biosphere Dynamics

A fundamental characteristic of the biosphere is the interconnectivity among all of its components. Known as holoceonosis, this interrelationship means that when one part of the biosphere changes, so will others. The biosphere is a dynamic system where interactions are occurring all the time between and within living and non-living components.

The main fuel that keeps the biosphere dynamic is the sun's energy, which is captured by Earth's surface and later harvested by plants and other photosynthetic organisms. The energy flows from these organisms through a living web that includes herbivores (plant feeders), carnivores (flesh feeders), and decomposers (detritus feeders). Energy from the sun also drives the recycling of water and all chemical elements necessary for life. The flow of energy and the continuous recycling of matter are two key processes of the biosphere.

Humans are part of this web of life. We have evolved, we interact with other living organisms, and we may become extinct. We have also developed large-scale organizations (societies, for example) that constitute the "sociosphere." Human interactions within this sphere occur through a diverse array of technologies and cultural frameworks and include activities such as fishing, agriculture, forestry, mining, and urban development. All are resource-utilization processes that can affect the biosphere on a global scale.

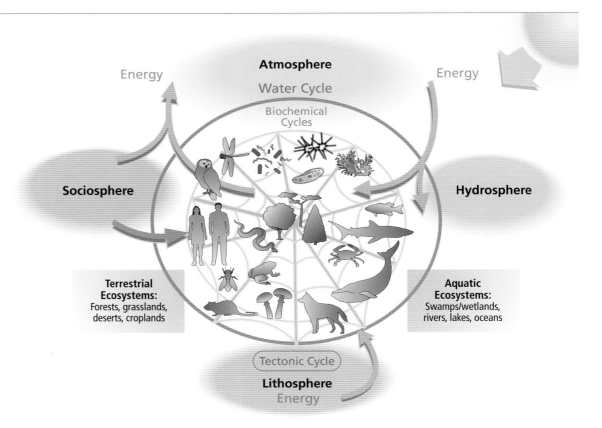

Earth System Dynamics

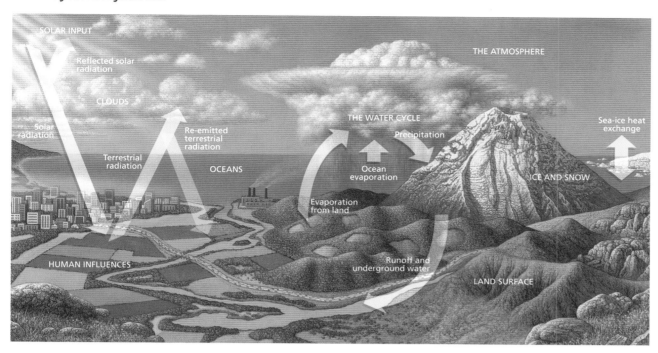

Earth is a dynamic system driven by energy flow from the sun and the planet's interior. Electromagnetic energy from the sun is converted to heat energy in the atmosphere (the greenhouse effect). Energy imbalances cause atmospheric and oceanic currents and drive the water cycle—a result of which is the wearing down of landscapes. Energy flow from Earth's interior drives the tectonic cycle, which builds landscapes. The cycles vary because they derive from independent forces that operate on different time scales and with changing intensities. Variations in these cycles keep the complex interactions among the biosphere, lithosphere, hydrosphere, and atmosphere from reaching a balance; the tendency of Earth processes to reach a balance causes natural global change. People can influence these interactions: By modifying the chemical composition of the atmosphere, for example, humans can cause changes in the greenhouse effect.

Size of the Biosphere

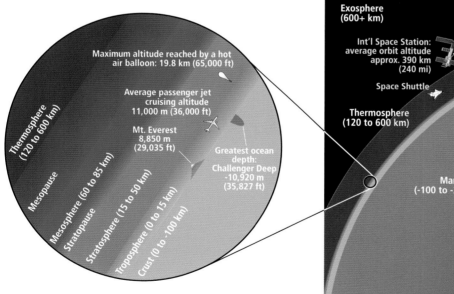

The biosphere reaches from the ocean floor to more than 10,000 meters (33,000 ft) above sea level. Most life, however, occurs in a zone extending from about 200 meters (650 ft) below the surface of the ocean to 6,000 meters (20,000 ft) above sea level. Humans can occupy much of the biosphere and exert influence on all of its regions.

Organisms that make up the biosphere vary greatly in size and number. Small life-forms generally reach very high numbers, while large ones may be relatively rare. Mycoplasmas, which are very small parasitic bacteria, can measure 0.2 to 0.3 micrometers (one micrometer is one-millionth of a meter, or three-millionths of a foot). Other organisms can be very large: Blue whales weigh about 110,000 kilograms (240,000 lbs) and reach a length of more than 25 meters (80 ft); they are the largest animals on Earth. Dinosaurs weighed as much as 80,000 kilograms (175,000 lbs) and measured up to 33 meters (108 ft) long.

The Biosphere over Time

Ever since life arose on Earth more than three billion years ago, the biosphere has gone through many changes (see time line at right). These have been driven, in part, by drifting continents, ice ages, shifting sea levels, and the consequences of activities in the biosphere itself. Over millions of years, the addition of oxygen to the atmosphere allowed for the development of terrestrial ecosystems. But in fairly rapid fashion, humans have had a significant effect on the world's ecosystems; our ability to modify species through gene manipulation will further increase our impact.

Thousand Years Ago	
2	First transgenic organisms Industrial metabolism begins
4	
6	
8	
10	First domestication of wild species

Million Years Ago	
	First humans
	First grasslands Dinosaurs become extinct
100	First flowering plants
	First birds
200	First mammals First dinosaurs
300	
	First amphibians First forests
400	Oxygen reaches present level in atmosphere First land plants
500	First fish
600	
700	First multicellular animal

Billion Years Ago	
2.6	Free oxygen in the atmosphere
3.6	Oldest fossils
4.6	Ocean formation Earth formation

BIODIVERSITY REFERS TO THREE MEASURES of Earth's intricate web of life: the number of different species, the genetic diversity within a species, and the variety of ecosystems in which species live. Greatest in the wet tropics, biodiversity is important for many reasons, including helping to provide food and medicine, breathable air, drinkable water, livable climates, protection from pests and diseases, and ecosystem stability.

Humankind is only one species in a vast array of life-forms. It is, however, an especially influential and increasingly disruptive actor in the huge cast of characters on the stage of planet Earth. Estimates of the total number of plant and animal species range from ten million to a hundred million; of these, fewer than two million have been described. Yet a substantial number of those species may be gone before we even have a chance to understand their value.

For most of human history, people have often looked at plants and animals simply as resources for meeting their own basic needs. Scientists today count more than a quarter million plant species, of which just nine provide three-quarters of all our food; in that respect, biodiversity has been an unimaginable luxury. It is ironic that as humankind's power to destroy other species grows, so does our ingenuity in finding new and beneficial uses for them.

Sometimes the benefits of preserving a species may have nothing to do with food or medicine. Before a worldwide ban on exports of elephant ivory, the estimated value of such exports was 40 million dollars a year for all of Africa. Now, in Kenya alone, the viewing value of elephants by tourists is thought to be 25 million dollars a year.

The Natural World
Labeled for their natural vegetation, biomes are defined by their distinctive mix of plants and animals.

1. Tundra
2. Northern coniferous forest (also called boreal forest or taiga)
3. Temperate coniferous forest
4. Temperate broadleaf forest (includes rain forest)
5. Temperate grassland
6. Desert and dry shrub
7. Mediterranean shrub
8. Mountain grassland
9. Flooded grassland and savanna
10. Tropical grassland and savanna
11. Tropical dry forest
12. Tropical coniferous forest
13. Tropical moist broadleaf (includes rain forest)
14. Mangrove
15. Permanent ice cover

Species Diversity

Among fauna and flora, insects make up the largest classification in terms of sheer number of species, with fungi ranked a distant second. At the other extreme, the categories with the smallest numbers—mammals, birds, and mollusks—also happen to be the classes with the greatest percentage of threatened species (see middle graph, below). This is not just a matter of proportion: These groups include the most at-risk species in terms of absolute numbers as well.

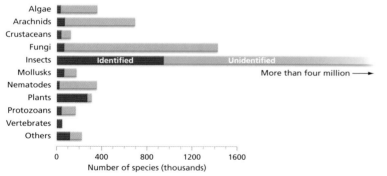

Number of species (thousands)

Threatened Ecoregions

British ecologist Norman Myers defined the "biodiversity hotspot" concept in 1988 to help address the dilemma of identifying conservation priorities. The biodiversity hotspots hold especially high numbers of endemic species, yet their combined area of remaining habitat covers only 2.3 percent of the Earth's land surface. Each hotspot faces extreme threats and has already lost at least 70 percent of its original natural vegetation. Of particular concern to scientists is that 75 percent of all threatened terrestrial vertebrates occur only in the hotspots.

Biodiversity "Hotspots"
◯ Hotspot region

Threatened Species

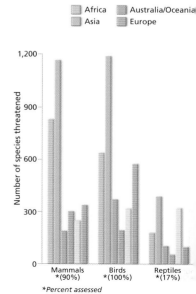

Africa — Australia/Oceania
Asia — Europe

Number of species threatened

Mammals *(90%)   Birds *(100%)   Reptiles *(17%)

*Percent assessed

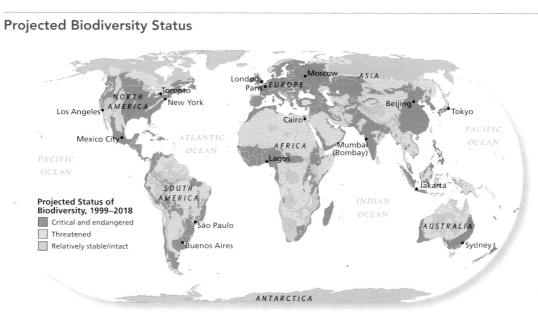
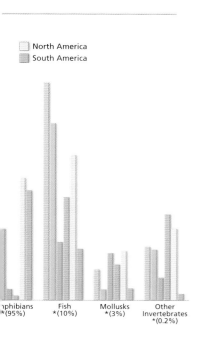

SIBERIAN TAIGA

Wood wasp
Urocerus gigas

Pacific golden plover
Pluvialis fulva

Sable
Martes zibellina

Mazarine blue butterfly
Cyaniris semiargus

Pacific diver
Gavia pacifica

Ross's gull
Rhodostethia rosea

Orange stump mushroom
Naematoloma capnoides

Short-billed dowitcher
Limnodromus griseus

Caesar's mushroom
Amanita caesarea

Reindeer
Rangifer tarandus

Lichen

Yellow-brown boletus
Suillus luteus

Radiola sp.

Goshawk
Accipiter gentilis

Siberian crane
Grus leucogeranus

Peacock butterfly
Inachis io

King bird of paradise
Cicinnurus regius

NEW GUINEA FORESTS

Victoria crowned pigeon
Goura victoria

Rhododendron alticolum

Tree frog
Litoria sp.

Goodfellow's tree-kangaroo
Dendrolagus goodfellowi

D'Albert's python
Liasis albertisii

Spotted cuscus
Spilocuscus maculatus

Papuan tiger orchid
Grammatophyllum papuanum

Common birdwing
Ornithoptera priamus

Spectacled warbler
Sylvia conspicillata

Cedar of Lebanon
Cedrus libani

Hermann's tortoise
Testudo hermanni

European mouflon
Ovis orientalis musimon

Petromarula
Petromarula pinnata

Spiny mullein
Verbascum spinosum

Moussier's redstart
Phoenicurus moussieri

Corsican red deer
Cervus elaphus corsicanus

Scarab (beetle)
Scarabaeus laticollis

MEDITERRANEAN REGION

Ruin lizard
Lacerta sicula

Cork oak
Quercus suber

Great pied hornbill
Buceros bicornis

Asian elephant
Elephas maximus

Lion-tailed macaque
Macaca silenus

Orchid
Dendrobium nanum

Nilgiri tahr (wild goat)
Hemitragus hylocrius

Mugger crocodile
Crocodylus palustris

Dragonfly
Trithemis aurora

Rhodomyrtus sp.

WESTERN GHATS

Tiger
Panthera tigris

Gaur
Bos gaurus

Jumping spider
Chrysilla sp.

Madagascar

SOUTH AMERICA

BRAZIL

Black hawk-eagle
Spizaetus tyrannus

Butterfly
Dismorphia amphione

ATLANTIC FORESTS

Maned sloth
Bradypus torquatus

Jequitiranabóia
Fulgora laternaria

Emerald pit viper
Bothriopsis bilineata

Black Jacobin
Melanotrochilus fuscus

Common tegu
Tupinambis teguixin

Golden lion tamarin
Leontopithecus rosalia

Tree fern
Alsophila armata

Seven-colored tanager
Tangara fastuosa

Orchid
Cattleya forbesii

Vriesea sp.

Table Mountain ghost frog
Heleophryne rosei

Chacma baboon
Papio cynocephalus

Geometric tortoise
Psammobates geometricus

CAPE FLORISTIC REGION

KALAHARI DESERT

SOUTH AFRICA

Cape mountain zebra
Equus zebra zebra

Cape grysbok
Raphicerus melanotis

Silver tree
Leucadendron argenteum

King protea
Protea cynaroides

King cricket
Maxentius sp.

NEW ZEALAND

Southern rata
Metrosideros umbellata

Flax weevil
Anagotus fairburni

Fiordland crested penguin
Eudyptes pachyrhynchus

Snail
Paryphanta lignaria

Kakapo (parrot)
Strigops habroptilus

Tree weta
Hemideina sp.

Lancewood
Pseudopanax crassifolius

Wild spaniard
Aciphylla sp.

Takahe
Porphyrio mantelli

Snowberry
Gaultheria sp.

strap penguin
celis antarctica

efish
agetopsis macropterus

arctic krill
hausia superba

ANTARCTIC PENINSULA

Projected Biodiversity Status

Projected Status of Biodiversity, 1999–2018
- Critical and endangered
- Threatened
- Relatively stable/intact

North America
South America

mphibians *(95%)* · Fish *(10%)* · Mollusks *(3%)* · Other Invertebrates *(0.2%)*

Biodiversity is decreasing at a rapidly increasing rate. According to scientists, current extinction rates are a hundred to a thousand times greater than the normal rate of extinction; furthermore, the number of species threatened with extinction continues to increase (with, for example, one in three amphibians and one in four mammals at risk in the wild). Species are not being killed off directly: The two leading causes of extinction are loss of habitats and the impact of invasive species, although other threats include overexploitation, pollution, disease, and climate change.

WHILE POPULATIONS IN MANY PARTS of the world are expanding, those of Europe—along with some other rich industrial areas such as Japan—show little to no growth, or may actually be shrinking. Many such countries must bring in immigrant workers to keep their economies thriving. A clear correlation exists between wealth and low fertility: the higher the incomes and educational levels, the lower the rates of reproduction.

Many governments keep vital statistics, recording births and deaths, and count their populations regularly to try to plan ahead. The United States has taken a census every ten years since 1790, recording the ages, the occupations, and other important facts about its people. The United Nations helps less developed countries carry out censuses and improve their demographic information.

Governments of some poor countries may find that half their populations are under the age of 20. They are faced with the overwhelming tasks of providing adequate education and jobs while encouraging better family-planning programs. Governments of nations with low birthrates find themselves with growing numbers of elderly people but fewer workers able to provide tax money for health care and pensions.

In a mere 150 years, world population has grown fivefold, at an ever increasing pace. The industrial revolution helped bring about improvements in food supplies and advances in both medicine and public health, which allowed people to live longer and to have more healthy babies. Today, 15,000 people are born into the world every hour, and nearly all of them are in poor African, Asian, and South American nations. This situation concerns planners, who look to demographers (professionals who study all aspects of population) for important data.

Lights of the World

Satellite imagery offers a surprising view of the world at night. Bright lights in Europe, Asia, and the United States give a clear picture of densely populated areas with ample electricity. Reading this map requires great care, however. Some totally dark areas, like most of Australia, do in fact have very small populations, but other light-free areas—in China and Africa, for example—may simply hide dense populations with not enough electricity to be seen by a satellite. Wealthy areas with fewer people, such as Florida, may be using their energy wastefully. Ever since the 1970s, demographers have supplemented census data with information from satellite imagery.

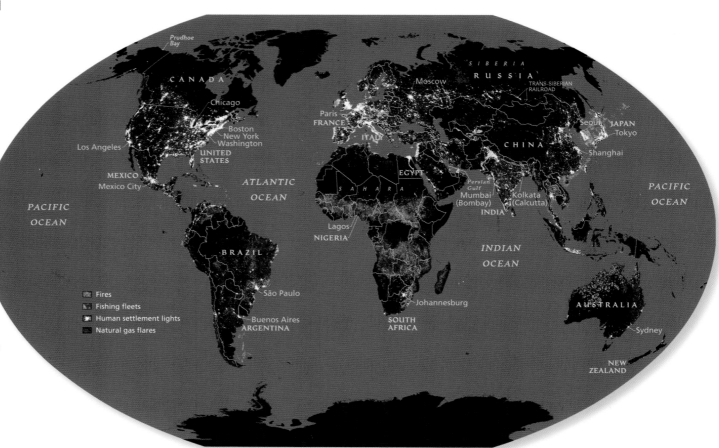

Fires
Fishing fleets
Human settlement lights
Natural gas flares

Population Pyramids

A population pyramid shows the number of males and females in every age group of a population. A pyramid for Nigeria reveals that over half—about 55 percent—of the population is under 20, while only 19 percent of Italy's population is younger than 20.

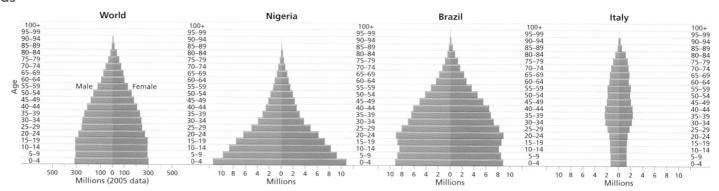

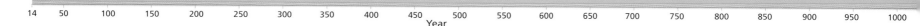

Population Growth

The population of the world is not distributed evenly. In this cartogram Canada is almost invisible, while India looks enormous because its population is 34 times greater than Canada's. In reality, Canada is 3 times larger than India, in size. The shape of almost every country looks distorted when populations are compared in this way.

Population sizes are constantly changing, however. In countries that are experiencing many more births than deaths, population totals are ballooning. In others, too few babies are born to replace the number of people who die, and populations are shrinking. A cartogram devoted solely to growth rates around the world would look quite different from this one.

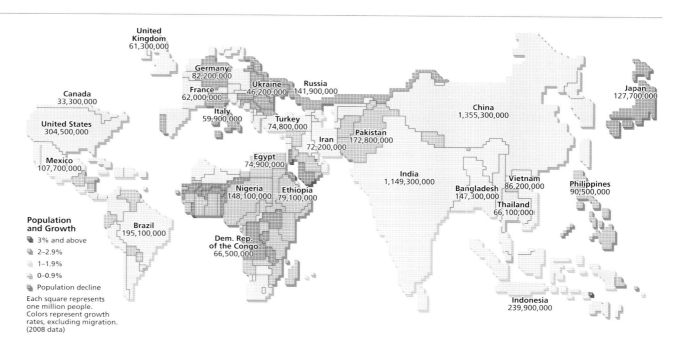

Population and Growth
- 3% and above
- 2–2.9%
- 1–1.9%
- 0–0.9%
- Population decline

Each square represents one million people. Colors represent growth rates, excluding migration. (2008 data)

United Kingdom 61,300,000
Germany 82,200,000
France 62,000,000
Ukraine 46,200,000
Russia 141,900,000
Canada 33,300,000
United States 304,500,000
Italy 59,900,000
Turkey 74,800,000
Iran 72,200,000
Pakistan 172,800,000
China 1,355,300,000
Japan 127,700,000
Mexico 107,700,000
Egypt 74,900,000
India 1,149,300,000
Vietnam 86,200,000
Philippines 90,500,000
Nigeria 148,100,000
Ethiopia 79,100,000
Bangladesh 147,300,000
Thailand 66,100,000
Brazil 195,100,000
Dem. Rep. of the Congo 66,500,000
Indonesia 239,900,000

Population Density

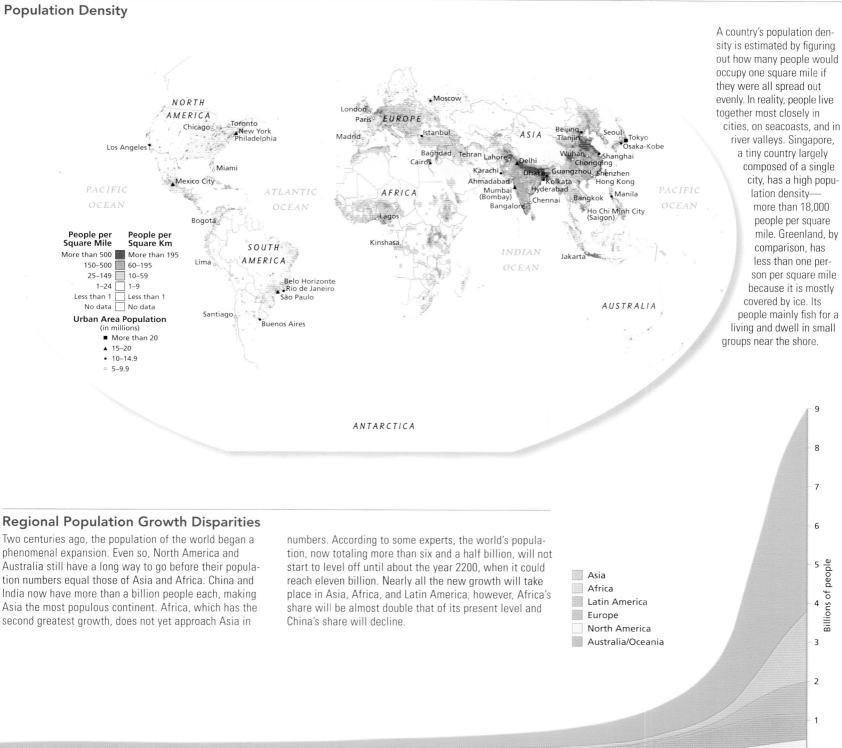

A country's population density is estimated by figuring out how many people would occupy one square mile if they were all spread out evenly. In reality, people live together most closely in cities, on seacoasts, and in river valleys. Singapore, a tiny country largely composed of a single city, has a high population density—more than 18,000 people per square mile. Greenland, by comparison, has less than one person per square mile because it is mostly covered by ice. Its people mainly fish for a living and dwell in small groups near the shore.

People per Square Mile	People per Square Km
More than 500	More than 195
150–500	60–195
25–149	10–59
1–24	1–9
Less than 1	Less than 1
No data	No data

Urban Area Population (in millions)
- ■ More than 20
- ▲ 15–20
- ● 10–14.9
- ○ 5–9.9

Regional Population Growth Disparities

Two centuries ago, the population of the world began a phenomenal expansion. Even so, North America and Australia still have a long way to go before their population numbers equal those of Asia and Africa. China and India now have more than a billion people each, making Asia the most populous continent. Africa, which has the second greatest growth, does not yet approach Asia in numbers. According to some experts, the world's population, now totaling more than six and a half billion, will not start to level off until about the year 2200, when it could reach eleven billion. Nearly all the new growth will take place in Asia, Africa, and Latin America; however, Africa's share will be almost double that of its present level and China's share will decline.

- Asia
- Africa
- Latin America
- Europe
- North America
- Australia/Oceania

Fertility

Fertility, or birthrate, measures the average number of children born to women in a given population. It can also be expressed as the number of live births per thousand people in a population per year. In low-income countries with limited educational opportunities for girls and women, fertility is often highest.

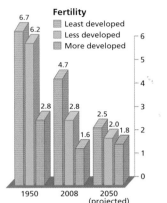

Fertility
- Least developed
- Less developed
- More developed

6.7 6.2 2.8 (1950)
4.7 2.8 1.6 (2008)
2.5 2.0 1.8 (2050 projected)

Fertility
- 6.0 and above
- 4.0–5.9
- 2.2–3.9
- 1.6–2.1
- Less than 1.6

Fertility is the average number of children born to women in a given population.

The highest and lowest values for each continent are labeled individually.

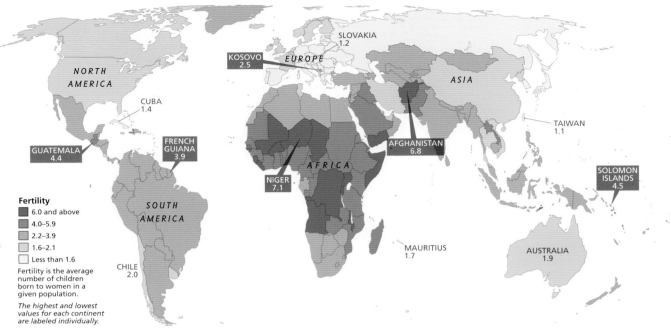

NORTH AMERICA

SOUTH AMERICA

EUROPE

ASIA

AFRICA

AUSTRALIA

SLOVAKIA 1.2
KOSOVO 2.5
CUBA 1.4
GUATEMALA 4.4
FRENCH GUIANA 3.9
AFGHANISTAN 6.8
TAIWAN 1.1
SOLOMON ISLANDS 4.5
NIGER 7.1
MAURITIUS 1.7
AUSTRALIA 1.9
CHILE 2.0

Urban Population Densities

People around the world are leaving farms and moving to cities, where jobs and opportunities are better. In 2008, half the world's people lived in towns or cities. The shift of population from the countryside to urban centers will probably continue in less developed countries for many years to come.

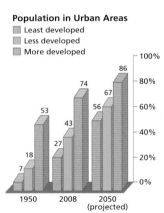

Population in Urban Areas
- Least developed
- Less developed
- More developed

7 18 53 (1950)
27 43 74 (2008)
56 67 86 (2050 projected)

Population in Urban Areas (as a percentage of total population)
- 75 and above
- 50–74
- 25–49
- 0–24

Urban Agglomeration (5 million people and above)
- • 2007
- ○ 2025 (projected)

The highest and lowest values for each continent are labeled individually.

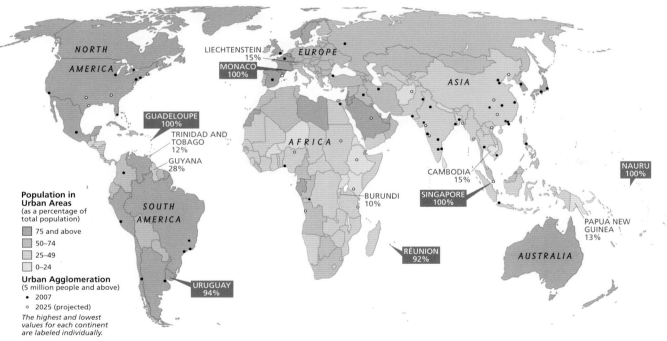

NORTH AMERICA

SOUTH AMERICA

EUROPE

ASIA

AFRICA

AUSTRALIA

LIECHTENSTEIN 15%
MONACO 100%
GUADELOUPE 100%
TRINIDAD AND TOBAGO 12%
GUYANA 28%
BURUNDI 10%
CAMBODIA 15%
SINGAPORE 100%
NAURU 100%
PAPUA NEW GUINEA 13%
RÉUNION 92%
URUGUAY 94%

Urban Population Growth

Urban populations are growing more than twice as fast as populations as a whole. The world's city dwellers now outnumber its rural inhabitants as towns have become cities and cities have merged into megacities with more than ten million people. Globalization speeds the process. Although cities generate wealth and provide better health care along with electricity, clean water, sewage treatment, and other benefits, they can also cause great ecological damage. Squatter settlements and slums may develop if cities cannot keep up with millions of new arrivals. Smog, congestion, pollution, and crime are other dangers. Good city management is a key to future prosperity.

Urban Population Growth, 1950–2005 (in millions)
- Over 100
- 50–100
- 10–49
- Under 10

Population growth for largest cities in 2025 (populations shown for years 1950, 2005, and 2025)
- 1950
- 2005
- 2025 (projected)

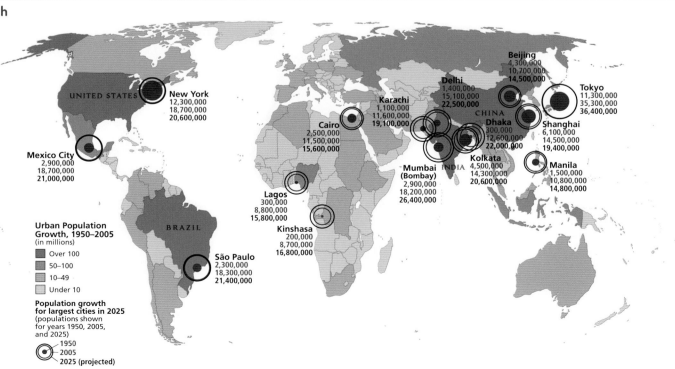

UNITED STATES

BRAZIL

CHINA

INDIA

New York
12,300,000
18,700,000
20,600,000

Mexico City
2,900,000
18,700,000
21,000,000

São Paulo
2,300,000
18,300,000
21,400,000

Lagos
300,000
8,800,000
15,800,000

Kinshasa
200,000
8,700,000
16,800,000

Cairo
2,500,000
11,500,000
15,600,000

Karachi
1,100,000
11,600,000
19,100,000

Beijing
4,300,000
10,700,000
14,500,000

Delhi
1,400,000
15,100,000
22,500,000

Dhaka
300,000
12,600,000
22,000,000

Shanghai
6,100,000
14,500,000
19,400,000

Tokyo
11,300,000
35,300,000
36,400,000

Mumbai (Bombay)
2,900,000
18,200,000
26,400,000

Kolkata
4,500,000
14,300,000
20,600,000

Manila
1,500,000
10,800,000
14,800,000

Life Expectancy

Life expectancy for population groups does not mean that all people die by a certain age. It is an average of death statistics. High infant mortality results in low life expectancy: People who live to adulthood will probably reach old age; there are just fewer of them.

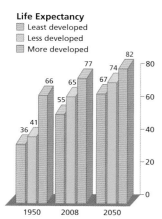

Life Expectancy
- Least developed
- Less developed
- More developed

1950 · 1950: 36, 41
2008 · 55, 66, 65, 77
2050 · 67, 74, 82

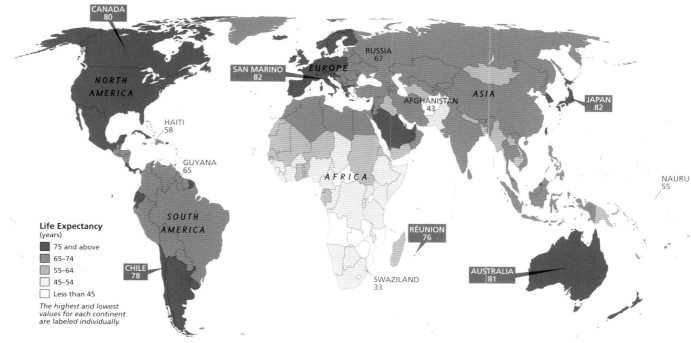

Life Expectancy (years)
- 75 and above
- 65–74
- 55–64
- 45–54
- Less than 45

The highest and lowest values for each continent are labeled individually.

Map labels: CANADA 80, SAN MARINO 82, RUSSIA 67, EUROPE, ASIA, AFGHANISTAN 43, JAPAN 82, NORTH AMERICA, HAITI 58, GUYANA 65, AFRICA, NAURU 55, SOUTH AMERICA, RÉUNION 76, AUSTRALIA 81, SWAZILAND 33, CHILE 78

Migration

International migration has reached its highest level, with foreign workers now providing the labor in several Middle Eastern countries and immigrant workers proving essential to rich countries with low birthrates. Refugees continue to escape grim political and environmental conditions, while businesspeople and tourists keep many economies spinning.

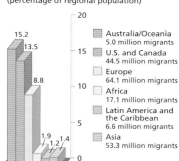

Migrant Population (percentage of regional population)

15.2, 13.5, 8.8, 1.9, 1.2, 1.4

- Australia/Oceania 5.0 million migrants
- U.S. and Canada 44.5 million migrants
- Europe 64.1 million migrants
- Africa 17.1 million migrants
- Latin America and the Caribbean 6.6 million migrants
- Asia 53.3 million migrants

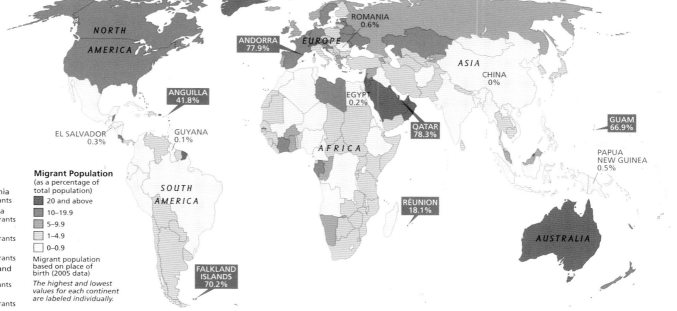

Migrant Population (as a percentage of total population)
- 20 and above
- 10–19.9
- 5–9.9
- 1–4.9
- 0–0.9

Migrant population based on place of birth (2005 data)

The highest and lowest values for each continent are labeled individually.

Map labels: NORTH AMERICA, ROMANIA 0.6%, ANDORRA 77.9%, EUROPE, ASIA, CHINA 0%, ANGUILLA 41.8%, EGYPT 0.2%, QATAR 78.3%, GUAM 66.9%, EL SALVADOR 0.3%, GUYANA 0.1%, AFRICA, PAPUA NEW GUINEA 0.5%, SOUTH AMERICA, RÉUNION 18.1%, AUSTRALIA, FALKLAND ISLANDS 70.2%

Most Populous Places

(MID-2008 DATA)

1. China 1,355,300,000
2. India 1,149,300,000
3. United States 304,500,000
4. Indonesia 239,900,000
5. Brazil 195,100,000
6. Pakistan 172,800,000
7. Nigeria 148,100,000
8. Bangladesh 147,300,000
9. Russia 141,900,000
10. Japan 127,700,000
11. Mexico 107,700,000
12. Philippines 90,500,000
13. Vietnam 86,200,000
14. Germany 82,200,000
15. Ethiopia 79,100,000
16. Egypt 74,900,000
17. Turkey 74,800,000
18. Iran 72,200,000
19. Dem. Rep. of Congo 66,500,000
20. Thailand 66,100,000

Most Crowded Places

POPULATION DENSITY (POP/SQ. MI.)

1. Monaco 45,333
2. Singapore 18,784
3. Gibraltar (U.K.) 11,600
4. Vatican City 4,000
5. Malta 3,377
6. Bermuda (U.K.) 3,048
7. Bahrain 2,816
8. Maldives 2,696
9. Bangladesh 2,585
10. Channel Islands (U.K.) 2,031
11. Occupied Palestinian Territory 1,787
12. Barbados 1,687
13. Taiwan (China) 1,655
14. Mauritius 1,609
15. Aruba (Neth.) 1,400
16. Mayotte (France) 1,299
17. San Marino 1,292
18. South Korea 1,268
19. Nauru 1,250
20. Puerto Rico (U.S.) 1,128

Demographic Extremes

LIFE EXPECTANCY
LOWEST (FEMALE, IN YEARS):
34 Swaziland
36 Lesotho
37 Zambia
40 Zimbabwe

LOWEST (MALE, IN YEARS):
33 Swaziland
35 Lesotho
38 Zambia
40 Zimbabwe

POPULATION AGE STRUCTURE
HIGHEST % POPULATION UNDER AGE 15
49% Niger, Uganda
48% Guinea-Bissau, Mali
47% Dem. Rep. of Congo, Liberia
46% Angola, Burkina Faso, Chad, Guinea, Malawi, Occupied Palestinian Territory, Zambia

HIGHEST (FEMALE, IN YEARS):
86 Japan
85 France, San Marino
84 Australia, Italy, Switzerland

HIGHEST (MALE, IN YEARS):
80 San Marino
79 Australia, Iceland, Israel, Italy, Japan, Liechtenstein, Sweden, Switzerland
78 Canada, France, Luxembourg, Netherlands, New Zealand, Norway, Singapore

HIGHEST % POPULATION OVER AGE 65
22% Japan, Monaco
20% Italy
19% Germany, Greece
18% Sweden

A PERSON'S NATIONALITY AND LANGUAGE are often assumed to be the same: A German speaks German, for example. The ability to use a specific language has often been viewed as a defining characteristic of a citizen. But there are only about 200 countries, while there are some 5,000 living languages. In a quarter of all nations, no single language is spoken by a majority of the inhabitants. Canada is legally bilingual; India has 23 officially-recognized languages; and French, Spanish, English, Portuguese, and German are each the official language of at least two nations.

Most languages are spoken by only a few hundred or a few thousand people. Over 200 languages are spoken by more than a million people; 23 languages have 50 million or more speakers.

How we define language makes it difficult to determine the exact number of languages. A dialect, for instance, is a variety of language used by a specific group of persons, with its own rules of grammar or pronunciation. Other linguistic systems that fail to attain the full status of languages are pidgins (contact languages used by groups with different native languages to communicate) and creoles (what pidgins are called when they are adopted as native languages).

Vanishing Languages

Some 10,000 languages—or more—are thought to have once existed (see graph at right). This is an estimate; unlike extinct animals, dead languages rarely left traces, as most lacked a written form. About 5,000 still exist, but linguists fear that the rate of loss is quickening.

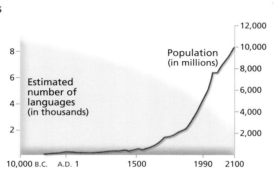

Evolution of Languages

Even as many languages have disappeared, a few dominant linguistic groups have spawned numerous related tongues. Thus, the Germanic language, which derived from Proto-Indo-European and was spoken by tribes that settled in northern and western Europe, has diversified into several major languages today.

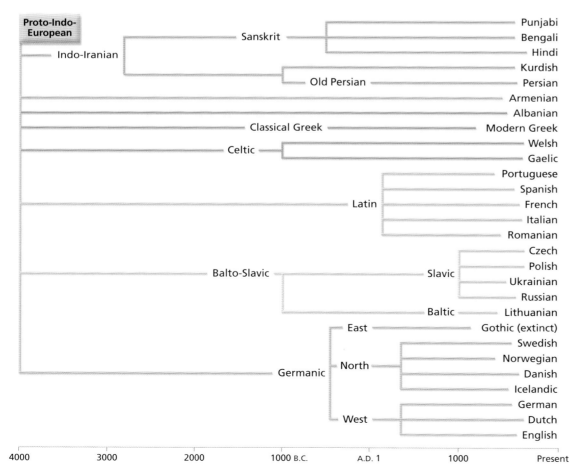

Voices of the World

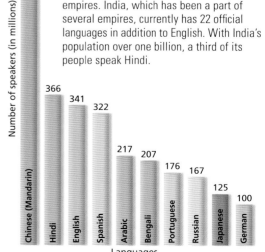

ESKIMO-ALEUT
Of this family's dozen languages in Asia and North America, only Greenlandic, Greenland's official language, may outlive this century.

AMERICAN INDIAN (NORTH)
More than 300 native languages were once spoken in the United States and Canada. Two-thirds survive, but the few speakers left are aging. Even as native languages fade, their sounds echo in place-names such as Chicago and Massachusetts.

1	Algonquian-Ritwan	8	Penutian
2	Caddoan	9	Salishan
3	Hokan	10	Siouan
4	Iroquoian	11	Uto-Aztecan
5	Kiowa-Tanoan	12	Wakashan
6	Muskogean	13	Undetermined
7	Nadene		

AMERICAN INDIAN (MESO-)
Quiché and Yucatec, Mayan languages, are the region's strongest indigenous tongues. Most languages faded after European contact, but a few were documented by missionaries. Alonso de Molina recorded Nahuatl, the Aztec language, in the mid-1500s.

1	Macro-Chibchan	4	Oto-Manguean
2	Mayan	5	Totonacan
3	Mixe-Zoquean	6	Uto-Aztecan

AFRO-ASIATIC
The languages of ancient Babylon, Assyria, Egypt, and Palestine belonged to this family. Still thriving, the largest living Afro-Asiatic language, Arabic, spreads in tandem with Islam.

1	Berber	4	Omotic
2	Chadic	5	Semitic
3	Cushitic		

ISOLATES
Dozens of rare languages—such as Basque in Spain and France, Burushaski in Pakistan—persist as linguistic islands. Despite decades of research, links to known language groups have yet to be verified. Chukchi, spoken in Siberia, is an example of a member of an isolated small language family.

■ Isolates and isolated small families

AMERICAN INDIAN (SOUTH)
Perhaps a thousand Indian languages that once had a voice here have disappeared. Two modest success stories: Quechua, the language of the Inca, has ten million speakers; Guaraní is the major language of Paraguay.

1	Arawakan	6	Quechumaran
2	Kariban	7	Tukánoan
3	Macro-Chibchan	8	Tupian
4	Macro-Ge	9	Other
5	Pano-Takanan	10	Undetermined

PACIFIC OCEAN

How Many Speak What?

Languages can paint vivid historical pictures of migration and colonization. English, Spanish, and Portuguese, for example, originated in parts of Europe with only a tenth of China's population and area; yet they rival Mandarin Chinese in total number of speakers. They spread because England, Spain, and Portugal built large overseas empires. India, which has been a part of several empires, currently has 22 official languages in addition to English. With India's population over one billion, a third of its people speak Hindi.

Language	Number of speakers (in millions)
Chinese (Mandarin)	874
Hindi	366
English	341
Spanish	322
Arabic	217
Bengali	207
Portuguese	176
Russian	167
Japanese	125
German	100

CAUCASIAN FAMILIES

Ancient Arab geographers called the Caucasus the "mountain of tongues." In an area the size of California, some 40 Caucasian languages survive.

1 Northeast   3 South
2 Northwest

URALIC

Finnish, Hungarian, and Estonian are safeguarded by their status as national languages. Other Uralic languages have declined in this century, many crowded out by Russian.

1 Finno-Ugric   2 Samoyed

ALTAIC

Some linguists think Mongolian, Tungusic, and Turkic languages are linked by kinship. Others attribute similarities to linguistic borrowing between traditionally nomadic peoples.

1 Mongolian   3 Turkic
2 Tungusic

JAPANESE/KOREAN

Japanese and Korean may be related. Both were influenced by Chinese: Many words are Chinese loans, and Japanese writing still uses Chinese characters.

1 Japanese-   2 Korean
Ryukyuan

SINO-TIBETAN

This family includes around eight mutually unintelligible Chinese languages, often mistakenly called dialects. China pushes the standard use of Beijing-based Mandarin.

1 Sinitic   2 Tibeto-Burman

INDO-EUROPEAN

...d around the world by ...ialism, the Indo-European ...ages sprang from a ...ue spoken on the Russian ...es perhaps 6,000 years ...Their influence continues ...w with the widespread ...ion of English as a second ...age.

...banian   5 Germanic
...rmenian   6 Greek
...alto-Slavic 7 Indo-Iranian
...eltic   8 Romance

HMONG-MIEN

Most of the speakers of these three dozen languages live in China's mountainous south, where use of native tongues has been declining.

AUSTRONESIAN

Island-hopping seafarers spread Austronesian languages across the Pacific and Indian Oceans from Hawai'i to Madagascar. More than 1,200 languages remain—about a hundred on the tiny Pacific islands of Vanuatu alone.

1 Formosan   2 Malayo-Polynesian

DRAVIDIAN

Pockets of Dravidian language speakers live in Pakistan and Sri Lanka, but most are found in southern India, where linguistic independence movements in the 1950s led to the birth of several language-based states—such as Andhra Pradesh, home of Telugu.

1 Central   3 South Central
2 Northern   4 Southern

KAM-TAI

Now mostly spoken by Thai and Laotians, the Tai languages may have come from southwest China.

1 Kadai   3 Tai
2 Kam-Sui

NILO-SAHARAN

About 200 Nilo-Saharan languages are spoken by ethnic minorities in their home countries. Only Dongolawi, a Nubian language of the southern Nile in Sudan, has a long written record.

1 Chari-Nile   4 Maban
2 Fur   5 Saharan
3 Komuz   6 Songhai

NIGER-CONGO

With more than 1,400 languages—almost one-fourth of the world's total—Niger-Congo is one of the largest language families. It includes Swahili, used by 35 million East Africans as a lingua franca.

1 Adamawan   6 Kordofanian
2 Benue-Congo   7 Kru
3 Dogon   8 Kwa
4 Gur   9 Mande
5 Ijo   10 West Atlantic

KHOISAN

Famous for complex click consonants, the Khoisan languages may be Africa's oldest. Several have vanished; most have fewer than a thousand speakers.

1 Central   4 Sandawe
2 Hadza   5 Southern
3 Northern

AUSTRO-ASIATIC

Now distributed from Vietnam to India, the Austro-Asiatic languages may once have dominated most of Southeast Asia.

1 Mon-Khmer   2 Munda

AUSTRALIAN FAMILIES

As many as 250 of Australia's Aboriginal languages may have slipped into extinction since Europeans arrived. Only five of the remaining 250 languages have more than a thousand speakers.

Pama-Nyungan   1-17 Other
Undetermined

1 Burarran, Djeebbana, Nakkara
2 Daly
3 Djamindjungan
4 Enindhilyagwa
5 Gungaragany
6 Gunwinyguan
7 Laragiyan
8 Mangarayi
9 Mangerrian
10 Maran
11 Murrinhpatha
12 Nunggubuyu
13 Tiwi
14 Waray
15 Yanyuwa
16 Yiwaidjan
17 Unclassified

PAPUAN FAMILIES

When linguists came to New Guinea, they found languages unlike nearby Austronesian tongues. More than 750 Papuan languages have been counted; isolation keeps them relatively healthy.

Major Language Families Today

Many of the world's languages belong to the Indo-European language group, which is thought to have ancient roots in the Russian Steppes. The map at right illustrates how far members of this group—and others—have spread over the millennia. The map locates languages by territory; it does not indicate the number of speakers. For example, the Altaic group covers a vast area, but it has only about 145 million speakers. Austronesian, on the other hand, is spoken within a much smaller area, but it has 312 million speakers.

Major Language Families Today
- Afro-Asiatic
- Altaic
- Austro-Asiatic
- Austronesian
- Dravidian
- Indo-European
- Japanese/Korean
- Kam-Tai
- Niger-Congo
- Nilo-Saharan
- Sino-Tibetan
- Uralic
- Other

Religions

THE GREAT POWER OF RELIGION comes from its ability to speak to the heart of individuals and societies. Since earliest human times, honoring nature spirits or the belief in a supreme being has brought comfort and security in the face of fundamental questions of life and death.

Billions of people are now adherents of Hinduism, Buddhism, Judaism, Christianity, and Islam, all of which began in Asia or the Middle East. Universal elements of these faiths include worship, sacred sites, saints and martyrs, ritual clothing, dietary laws and fasting, festivals and holy days, and special ceremonies for life's major moments. Each of these religions gives its followers ways to relate to the spiritual realm, as well as moral guidelines that attempt to make life better on Earth as well. Their tenets and goals are taught not only at the church, synagogue, mosque, or temple, but also through schools, storytelling, and artistic creations.

The world's major religions blossomed from the teachings and revelations of individuals who transmitted the voice of God or discovered a way to salvation that could be understood by others. Abraham and Moses for Jews, the Buddha for Buddhists, Jesus Christ for Christians, and Prophet Muhammad for Muslims fulfilled the roles of divine teachers who experienced essential truths of existence.

Throughout history, priests, rabbis, ministers, and imams have proclaimed the words of sacred texts to the faithful. The great religions have responded to a deep longing within the human mind for a sense of purpose in the universe. Today the world's religions, with their guidance here on Earth and hopes and promises for the afterlife, continue to exert an extraordinary force on billions of people.

Dominant Religion

80% and above
50%–79.9%
Below 50%
not affiliated

Buddhism · Christianity · Hinduism · Islam · Judaism · Ethno-religionism

BUDDHISM
Founded about 2,500 years ago by Shakyamuni Buddha (or Gautama Buddha), Buddhism teaches liberation from suffering through the threefold cultivation of morality, meditation, and wisdom. Buddhists revere the Three Jewels: Buddha (the Awakened One), Dharma (the Truth), and Sangha (the community of monks and nuns).

CHRISTIANITY
Christian belief in eternal life is based on the example of Jesus Christ, a Jew born some 2,000 years ago. The New Testament tells of his teaching, persecution, Crucifixion, and resurrection. Today Christianity is found around the world in three main forms: Roman Catholicism, Eastern Orthodoxy, and Protestantism.

HINDUISM
Hinduism began in India more than 4,000 years ago and is still flourishing. Sacred texts known as the Vedas form the basis of Hindu faith and ritual.

Adherents Worldwide

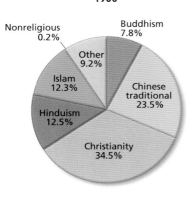

1900

- Nonreligious 0.2%
- Buddhism 7.8%
- Other 9.2%
- Islam 12.3%
- Hinduism 12.5%
- Christianity 34.5%
- Chinese traditional 23.5%

2010

- Other 6.0%
- Buddhism 6.8%
- Chinese traditional 6.6%
- Nonreligious 11.3%
- Islam 22.4%
- Christianity 33.2%
- Hinduism 13.7%

The growth of Islam and the decline of Chinese traditional religion stand out as significant changes over the past hundred and ten years. Christianity, the largest of the world's main faiths, has remained fairly stable in its number of adherents. Today more than one in nine people claim to be atheistic or nonreligious.

Adherents by Continent

In terms of the total number of religious adherents, Asia ranks first. This is not only because half the world's people live on that continent, but also because three of the five major faiths are practiced there: Hinduism in South Asia; Buddhism in East and Southeast Asia; and Islam from Indonesia to the Central Asian republics to Turkey. Oceania, Europe, North America, and South America are overwhelmingly Christian. Africa, with many millions of Muslims and Christians, also retains large numbers of animists.

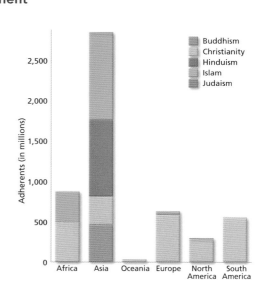

Legend: Buddhism, Christianity, Hinduism, Islam, Judaism

Adherents (in millions): 0, 500, 1,000, 1,500, 2,000, 2,500

Continents: Africa, Asia, Oceania, Europe, North America, South America

Sacred Places

BUDDHISM
1. Bodhgaya: Where Buddha attained awakening
2. Kusinagara: Where Buddha entered nirvana
3. Lumbini: Place of Buddha's last human birth
4. Sarnath: Place where Buddha delivered his first sermon
5. Sanchi: Location of famous stupa containing relics of Buddha

CHRISTIANITY
1. Jerusalem: Church of the Holy Sepulchre, Jesus' Crucifixion
2. Bethlehem: Jesus' birthplace
3. Nazareth: Hometown of Jesus Christ
4. Shore of the Sea of Galilee: Where Jesus gave the Sermon on the Mount
5. Rome and the Vatican: Tombs of St. Peter and St. Paul
6. Mount Sinai: Site of God's manifestation to Moses and the revelation of the Ten Commandments given to him by God

HINDUISM
1. Varanasi (Banaras): Most holy Hindu site, home of Shiva
2. Vrindavan: Krishna's birthplace
3. Allahabad: At confluence of Ganges and Yamuna Rivers, purest place to bathe
4. Madurai: Temple of Minakshi, great goddess of the south
5. Badrinath: Vishnu's shrine

ISLAM
1. Mecca: The Prophet Muhammad's birthplace; destination of the pilgrimage, or hajj; houses the Kaaba
2. Medina: Burial place of the Prophet Muhammad; contains the tombs of the 2nd, 4th, 5th, and 6th Shiite imams
3. Jerusalem: The first Qibla before replaced by Mecca; site of nightlong ascension of the Prophet Muhammad to the heavens
4. Najaf (Shiite): Tomb of the first imam, Ali; ancient center of Shiite learning; known as the "Vatican City" of Shiism
5. Karbala (Shiite): Tomb of the 3rd imam and martyr, Hussein

JUDAISM
1. Jerusalem: Location of the Western Wall and First and Second Temples; City of David; the ancient and modern capital of Israel
2. Hebron: Burial spot of patriarchs and matriarchs
3. Safed: Where Kabbalah (Jewish mysticism) flourished
4. Tiberias: Where Talmud (source of Jewish law) first composed
5. Bethlehem: Site of Rachel's tomb
6. Mount Sinai: Site of God's revelation, where God appeared to Moses and gave him the Ten Commandments

The main trinity of gods comprises Brahma the creator, Vishnu the preserver, and Shiva the destroyer. Hindus believe in reincarnation.

ISLAM
Muslims believe that the Koran, Islam's sacred book, accurately records the spoken word of God (Allah) as revealed to the Prophet Muhammad, born in Mecca around A.D. 570. Strict adherents pray five times a day, fast during the holy month of Ramadan, and make at least one pilgrimage to Mecca, Islam's holiest city.

JUDAISM
The 4,000-year-old religion of the Jews stands as the oldest of the major faiths that believe in a single god. Judaism's traditions, customs, laws, and beliefs date back to Abraham, the founder, and to the Torah, the first five books of the Old Testament, believed to have been handed down to Moses on Mount Sinai.

Adherents by Country

COUNTRIES WITH THE MOST BUDDHISTS		COUNTRIES WITH THE MOST CHRISTIANS		COUNTRIES WITH THE MOST HINDUS		COUNTRIES WITH THE MOST MUSLIMS		COUNTRIES WITH THE MOST JEWS	
COUNTRY	**BUDDHISTS**	**COUNTRY**	**CHRISTIANS**	**COUNTRY**	**HINDUS**	**COUNTRY**	**MUSLIMS**	**COUNTRY**	**JEWS**
1. China	190,000,000	1. United States	257,311,000	1. India	891,520,000	1. Indonesia	188,164,000	1. Israel	5,295,000
2. Japan	71,562,000	2. Brazil	180,932,000	2. Nepal	20,630,000	2. India	168,250,000	2. United States	5,220,000
3. Thailand	56,497,000	3. Russia	115,120,000	3. Bangladesh	15,600,000	3. Pakistan	166,576,000	3. France	610,000
4. Vietnam	44,383,000	4. China	115,009,000	4. Indonesia	4,550,000	4. Bangladesh	148,078,000	4. Palestinian Areas*	510,000
5. Myanmar	36,851,000	5. Mexico	105,583,000	5. Sri Lanka	2,550,000	5. Turkey	75,670,000	5. Argentina	494,000
6. Sri Lanka	13,315,000	6. Philippines	83,151,000	6. Pakistan	2,260,000	6. Iran	73,276,000	6. Canada	435,000
7. Cambodia	12,930,000	7. Nigeria	72,302,000	7. Malaysia	1,750,000	7. Nigeria	72,306,000	7. United Kingdom	280,000
8. India	8,500,000	8. Congo, Dem. Rep.	65,803,000	8. United States	1,445,000	8. Egypt	68,804,000	8. Germany	230,000
9. South Korea	7,325,000	9. India	58,367,000	9. South Africa	1,175,000	9. Algeria	34,712,000	9. Russia	180,000
10. Taiwan*	6,250,000	10. Germany	58,123,000	10. Myanmar	855,000	10. Morocco	31,845,000	10. Ukraine	175,000

*Non-sovereign nation

All figures are estimates based on data for the year 2010.

Countries with the highest reported nonreligious populations include China, Russia, United States, Germany, India, Japan, North Korea, South Korea, Vietnam, France, and Italy.

IN THE PAST 50 YEARS, health conditions have improved dramatically. With better economic and living conditions and access to immunization and other basic health services, global life expectancy has risen from 40 to 65 years; the death rate for children under five years old has fallen by half; and many infectious and parasitic diseases that once killed and disabled millions have been eradicated, eliminated, or greatly reduced in impact. Today, fully three-quarters of the world's children benefit from protection against six infectious diseases that were responsible in the past for many millions of infant and child deaths.

Despite major strides, however, infant and child mortality from infectious diseases remains relatively high in many of the poorest countries. Each year, nearly ten million children under five years old die—about four out of every ten of those deaths occur in sub-Saharan Africa and three in South Asia. Undernutrition is a major contributor to a third of child deaths, hitting poor families the hardest.

The age-old link between social inequality and ill health is also manifested in the emergence of new health threats. The HIV/AIDS pandemic has erased decades of steady improvements in sub-Saharan Africa. The death toll in southern African countries, where adult prevalence exceeds 15 percent, is contributing to reversals in life expectancy—just 47 years instead of the estimated 62 years without AIDS. Because of both biological and social factors, adolescent girls are the most vulnerable: Three out of every four HIV-positive individuals ages 10 to 24 in southern Africa are female.

Increasingly, lifestyle diseases are also afflicting low-income countries, coming with demographic changes, urbanization, changes in eating habits and physical activity, and environmental degradation. Traffic accidents account for more than a million deaths and upward of 50 million injuries annually; with the rapid increase of automobile use, observers expect that by 2020 the number of traffic deaths will have increased by more than 80 percent in developing countries.

While many international leaders focus on high-profile infectious diseases, the looming challenges of chronic diseases may be even greater. In many high- and middle-income countries, chronic, lifestyle-related diseases such as cardiovascular disease, diabetes, and others are becoming the predominant cause of disability and death. In developed countries, smoking is the cause of more than one-third of male deaths in middle age, and about one in eight female deaths. Because the focus of policymakers has been on treatment rather than prevention, the costs of dealing with these ailments contributes to high (and increasing) health care spending.

Health Care Availability

Regional differences in health care resources are striking. While countries in Europe and the Americas have relatively large numbers of physicians and nurses, nations with far higher burdens of disease (particularly African countries) are experiencing severe deficits in both health workers and health facilities.

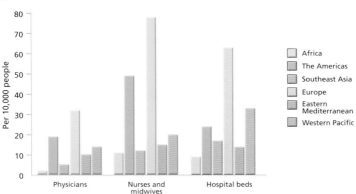

Income Levels: Indicators of Health and Literacy

Personal Income
- High income
- Upper middle income
- Lower middle income
- Low income
- No data

Access to Improved Sanitation

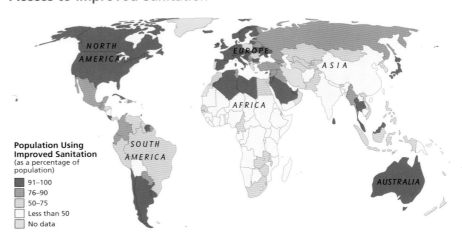

Population Using Improved Sanitation (as a percentage of population)
- 91–100
- 76–90
- 50–75
- Less than 50
- No data

Nutrition

Undernourishment (as a percentage of population)
- 50–100
- 30–49
- 15–29
- 5–14
- 0–4
- No data

HIV

HIV (percentage of adults, ages 15–49, living with HIV)
- 20–29
- 10–19
- 5–9
- 2–4
- 0–1
- No data

Global Disease Burden

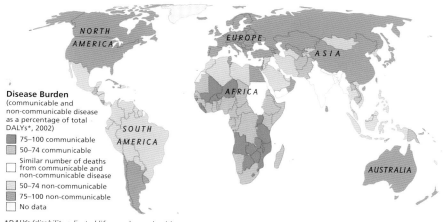

Disease Burden
(communicable and non-communicable disease as a percentage of total DALYs*, 2002)

- 75–100 communicable
- 50–74 communicable
- Similar number of deaths from communicable and non-communicable disease
- 50–74 non-communicable
- 75–100 non-communicable
- No data

*DALYs (disability adjusted life years) are a health gap measure used to quantify potential years of life lost to illness or premature death. One DALY can be thought of as one lost year of "healthy" life.

While infectious and parasitic diseases account for nearly one-quarter of total deaths in developing countries, they result in relatively few deaths in wealthier countries. In contrast, cardiovascular diseases and cancer are more significant causes of death in industrialized countries.

Over time, as fertility rates fall, social and living conditions improve, the population ages, and further advances are made against infectious diseases in poorer countries, the differences in causes of death between high-income and low-income countries may converge.

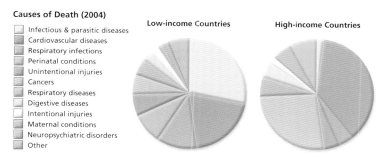

Causes of Death (2004)

- Infectious & parasitic diseases
- Cardiovascular diseases
- Respiratory infections
- Perinatal conditions
- Unintentional injuries
- Cancers
- Respiratory diseases
- Digestive diseases
- Intentional injuries
- Maternal conditions
- Neuropsychiatric disorders
- Other

Low-income Countries

High-income Countries

Under-Five Mortality

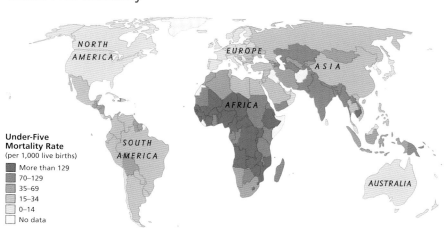

Under-Five Mortality Rate
(per 1,000 live births)

- More than 129
- 70–129
- 35–69
- 15–34
- 0–14
- No data

Maternal Mortality

MATERNAL MORTALITY RATIO PER 100,000 LIVE BIRTHS*

COUNTRIES WITH THE HIGHEST MATERNAL MORTALITY RATES:		COUNTRIES WITH THE LOWEST MATERNAL MORTALITY RATES:	
1. Sierra Leone	2,100	1. Ireland	1
2. Niger	1,800	2. Sweden	3
3. Chad	1,500	3. Denmark	3
4. Angola	1,400	4. Italy	3
5. Rwanda	1,300	5. Greece	3
6. Guinea-Bissau	1,100	6. Bosnia and Herzegovina	3
7. Dem. Rep. of the Congo	1,100	7. Iceland	4
8. Burundi	1,100	8. Australia	4
9. Malawi	1,100	9. Spain	4
10. Nigeria	1,100	10. Germany	4

*Adjusted for underreporting and misclassification

Education and Literacy

Adult Literacy
(as a percentage of population)

- 95–100
- 85–94
- 70–84
- 50–69
- 0–49
- No data

Basic education is an investment for the long-term prosperity of a country, generating individual, household, and social benefits. Some countries (e.g., Eastern and Western Europe, the U.S.) have long traditions of high educational attainment among both genders, and now have well-educated populations of all ages. In contrast, many low-income countries have only recently expanded access to primary education; girls still lag behind boys in enrollment and completion of primary school, and then in making the transition to secondary school. These countries will have to wait many years before most individuals in the productive ages have even minimal levels of reading, writing, and basic arithmetic skills.

The expansion of secondary schooling tends to lag even further behind, so countries with low educational attainment will likely be at a disadvantage for at least a generation. While no one doubts that the key to long-term economic growth and poverty reduction lies in greater education opportunities for all, many poor countries face the tremendous challenge of paying for schools and teachers today, while having to wait 20 years for the economic returns to those investments.

School Enrollment for Girls

Primary Education Enrollment of Girls
(as a percentage of primary school-age girls)

- 96–100
- 90–95
- 80–89
- 60–79
- 0–59
- No data

Developing Human Capital

In the pyramids below, more red and blue in the bars indicates a higher level of educational attainment, or "human capital," which contributes greatly to a country's ability for future economic growth. These two countries are similar in population size, but their human capital measures are significantly different.

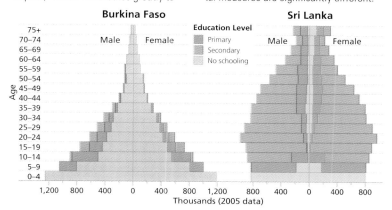

Burkina Faso

Sri Lanka

Education Level
- Primary
- Secondary
- No schooling

Thousands (2005 data)

POLITICAL VIOLENCE, WAR, AND TERROR

continue to plague many areas of the world in the early 21st century, despite dramatic decreases in major armed conflict since 1991. The 20th century is often described as the century of "total war" as modern weapons technologies made every facet of society a potential target in warfare. The globe was rocked by two world wars, self-determination wars in developing countries, and the threat of nuclear annihilation during the Cold War. Whereas the first half of the century was torn by interstate wars among the most powerful states, the latter half was consumed by protracted civil wars in the weakest states. The end of the Cold War emboldened international engagement, and concerted efforts toward peace had reduced armed conflicts more than half by early 2009.

While wars still smolder in Africa and Asia in the early 21st century, global apprehension is riveted on super-powerful states, super-empowered individuals, and the proliferation of "weapons of mass disruption." Globalization is both bringing people closer together and making us ever more vulnerable. Though violence is generally subsiding and democracy spreading, tensions appear to be increasing across the world's oil-producing regions. A little-understood "war on terror" punctuates the hard-won peace and prods us toward an uncertain future. Prospects for an ever more peaceful world are good, yet much work remains to be done.

Political Violence

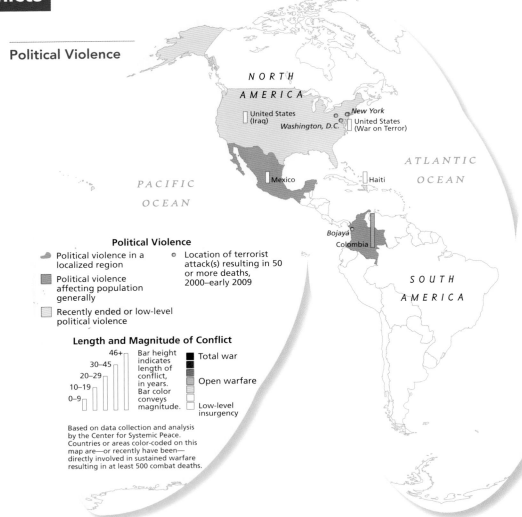

Political Violence

- Political violence in a localized region
- Political violence affecting population generally
- Recently ended or low-level political violence
- ○ Location of terrorist attack(s) resulting in 50 or more deaths, 2000–early 2009

Length and Magnitude of Conflict

46+
30–45
20–29
10–19
0–9

Bar height indicates length of conflict, in years. Bar color conveys magnitude.

- Total war
- Open warfare
- Low-level insurgency

Based on data collection and analysis by the Center for Systemic Peace. Countries or areas color-coded on this map are—or recently have been—directly involved in sustained warfare resulting in at least 500 combat deaths.

State Fragility

The quality of a government's response to rising tensions is the most crucial factor in the management of political conflict. State fragility gauges a country's vulnerability to civil disorder and political violence by evaluating government effectiveness and legitimacy in its four functions: security, political, economic, and social. Fragility is most serious when a government cannot provide reasonable levels of security; engages in brutal repression; lacks political accountability and responsiveness; excludes or marginalizes social groups; suffers from poverty and inadequate development; fails to manage growth or reinvest; and neglects the well-being and key aspirations of its citizens. State fragility is an especially serious challenge in many African and Muslim countries.

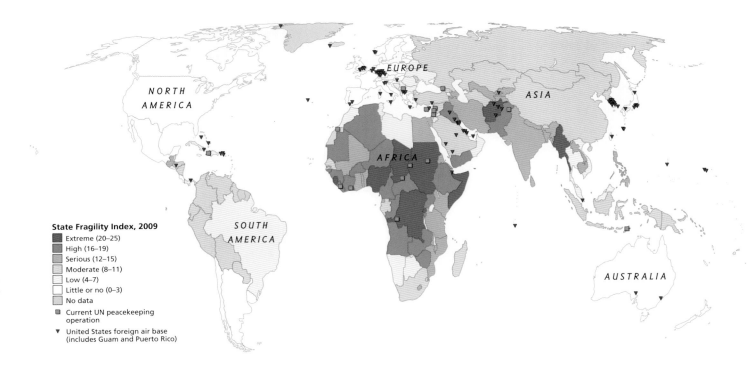

State Fragility Index, 2009
- Extreme (20–25)
- High (16–19)
- Serious (12–15)
- Moderate (8–11)
- Low (4–7)
- Little or no (0–3)
- No data
- ◼ Current UN peacekeeping operation
- ▼ United States foreign air base (includes Guam and Puerto Rico)

Change in Magnitude of Ongoing Conflicts

Individual wars are scored in a ten-point magnitude scale and summed annually to chart warfare trends over time. The UN system was designed to control interstate wars and has been fairly successful. Societal wars, mainly in new and fragile states, increased during the Cold War but have fallen sharply since 1992.

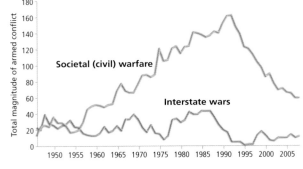

Societal (civil) warfare

Interstate wars

Global Regimes by Type

Autocracy and democracy are two distinct and fairly stable forms of governance. Weakly autocratic or democratic regimes, and those with mixed forms of rule, are less able to provide basic needs and manage political conflict. The end of the Cold War is marked by dramatic changes in the nature of governance.

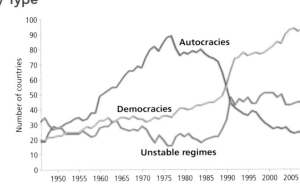

Autocracies

Democracies

Unstable regimes

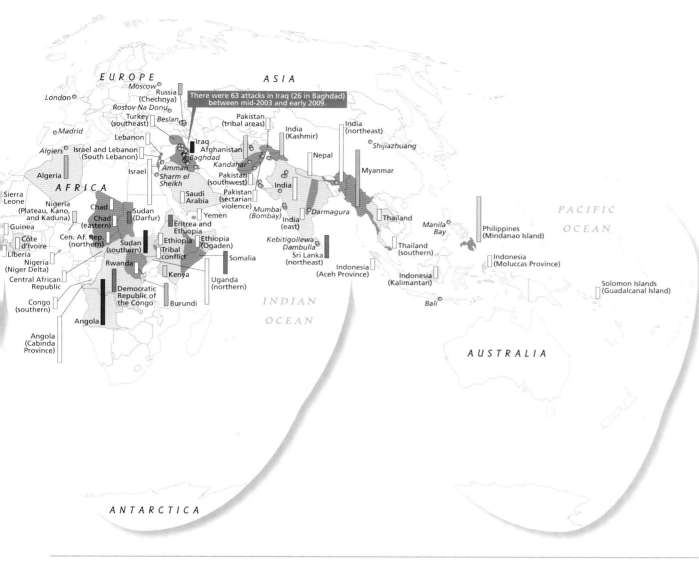

There were 63 attacks in Iraq (26 in Baghdad) between mid-2003 and early 2009.

Terrorist Attacks

Terrorism has a special connotation with violent attacks on civilians. The vast majority of such attacks are domestic; both state and non-state actors can engage in terror tactics. International terrorism is a special subset of attacks linked to globalization in which militants go abroad to strike their targets, select domestic targets linked to a foreign state, or attack international transports such as planes or ships. The intentional bombing of civilian targets has become a common tactic in the wars of the early 21st century.

Deaths from International Terrorist Attacks

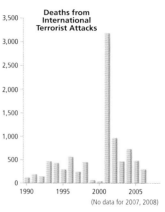

(No data for 2007, 2008)

High-Casualty Terrorist Bombings

- Attacks in Muslim countries
- Attacks by Muslim groups, in non-Muslim countries
- Other attacks in non-Muslim countries

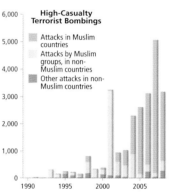

Genocides and Politicides Since 1955

Our worst fears are realized when governments are directly involved in killing their own, unarmed citizens. Lethal repression is most often associated with autocratic regimes; its most extreme forms are termed genocide and politicide. These policies involve the intentional destruction, in whole or in part, of a communal or ethnic group (genocide) or opposition group (politicide). Death squads and ethnic cleansing have brutalized populations in 29 countries at various times since 1955. Humanitarian crises increase human suffering in the world's most fragile states.

Genocides and Politicides
(number of deaths since 1955)
- More than 500,000
- 100,000–500,000
- 50,000–99,999
- 10,000–49,999
- 1,000–9,999

Weapons Possessions

	Nuclear			Chemical	Biological
	Declared stockpile	Suspected or undeclared program	Declared stockpile now being destroyed	Undeclared stockpile or development program	Suspected offensive development program
Albania			●		
China	●			●	●
Egypt				●	●
France	●				
India	●		●		●
Iran		○		●	●
Israel	●			●	
Libya			●		
North Korea		○		●	●
Pakistan	●				
Russia	●		●		●
South Korea			●		
Syria				●	●
United Kingdom	●				
United States	●		●		●

The proliferation of weapons of mass destruction (WMD) is a principal concern in the 21st century. State weakness and official corruption increase the possibilities that these modern technologies might fall into the wrong hands and be a source of terror, extortion, or war.

Refugees

Refugees are persons who have fled their country of origin due to fear of persecution for reasons of, for example, race, religion, or political opinion. IDPs are often displaced for the same reasons as refugees, but they still reside in their country of origin. By the end of 2007, there were nearly 10 million refugees, with Asia hosting 53%, followed by Africa (25%), Europe (16%), North America (5%), Latin America-Caribbean (0.4%), and Oceania (0.4%). Iraq and Afghanistan were the top two countries of origin, with an estimated 2.3 and 1.9 million refugees, respectively.

Refugee Population
(by country of asylum)
- More than 200,000
- 50,000–200,000
- 10,000–49,999
- 1,000–9,999
- Less than 1,000
- No data

Internally Displaced Persons (IDPs)
(countries with at least 300,000 IDPs)
- More than 2 million
- 1 to 2 million
- 500,000 to 999,999
- 300,000 to 499,999

A GLOBAL ECONOMIC ACTIVITY MAP (right) reveals striking differences in the composition of output in advanced economies (such as the United States, Japan, and Western Europe) compared with less developed countries (such as Nigeria and China). Advanced economies tend to have high proportions of their GDP in services, while developing economies have relatively high proportions in agriculture and industry.

There are different ways of looking at the distribution of manufacturing industry activity. When examined by country, the United States leads in production in many industries, but Western European countries are also a major manufacturing force. Western Europe outpaces the U.S. in the production of cars, chemicals, and food.

The world's sixth largest economy is found in China, and it has been growing quite rapidly. Chinese workers take home only a fraction of the cash pocketed each week by their economic rivals in the West, but are quickly catching up to the global economy with their purchase of cell phones and motor vehicles—two basic consumer products of the modern age.

The Middle East—a number of whose countries enjoy relatively high per capita GDP values—produces more fuel than any other region, but it has virtually no other economic output besides that single commodity.

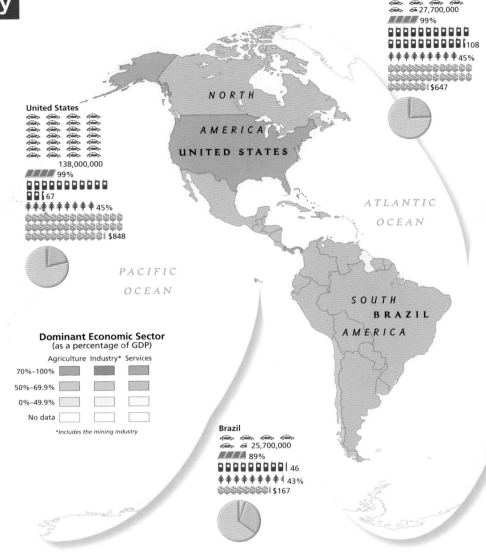

Dominant Economic Sector
(as a percentage of GDP)

	Agriculture	Industry*	Services
70%–100%			
50%–69.9%			
0%–49.9%			
No data			

*Includes the mining industry

Labor Migration

People in search of jobs gravitate toward the higher-income economies, unless immigration policies prevent them from doing so. Japan, for instance, has one of the world's most restrictive immigration policies and a population that is more than 99 percent Japanese. Some nations are "labor importers," while others are "labor exporters." In the mid-1990s, Malaysia was the largest Asian importer (close to a million workers) and the Philippines was the largest Asian exporter (4.2 million). The largest share of foreign workers in domestic employment is found in the Persian Gulf region and in Singapore.

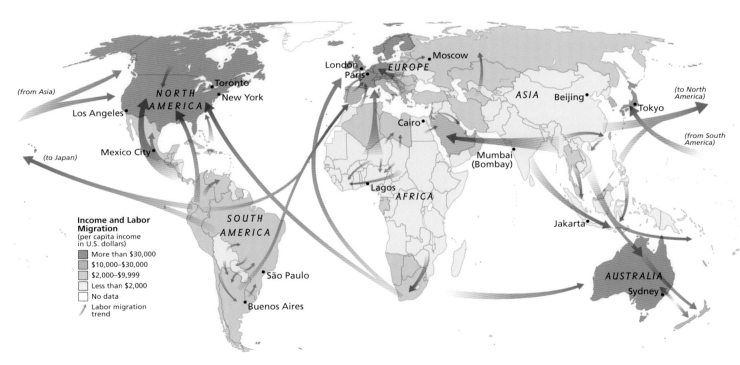

Income and Labor Migration
(per capita income in U.S. dollars)

- More than $30,000
- $10,000–$30,000
- $2,000–$9,999
- Less than $2,000
- No data
- Labor migration trend

Top GDP Growth Rates
(based on PPP, or purchasing power parity)*

(2000–2008 AVERAGE)

1.	Equatorial Guinea	23.8%
2.	Azerbaijan	19.0%
3.	Turkmenistan	16.7%
4.	Angola	15.2%
5.	Armenia	15.1%
6.	Qatar	13.9%
7.	Sierra Leone	13.7%
8.	Myanmar	13.4%
9.	China	12.8%
10.	Kazakhstan	12.2%

The World's Richest and Poorest Countries

RICHEST		GDP PER CAPITA (PPP) (2008)	POOREST		GDP PER CAPITA (PPP) (2008)
1.	Qatar	$86,700	1.	Democratic Republic of the Congo	$340
2.	Luxembourg	$81,700	2.	Liberia	$378
3.	Norway	$55,200	3.	Burundi	$389
4.	Singapore	$51,600	4.	Guinea-Bissau	$497
5.	Brunei	$50,600	5.	Niger	$691
6.	United States	$47,000	6.	Sierra Leone	$728
7.	Switzerland	$42,840	7.	Eritrea	$748
8.	Ireland	$42,780	8.	Central African Republic	$754
9.	Kuwait	$40,900	9.	Afghanistan	$783
10.	Netherlands	$40,430	10.	Togo	$824

Source: International Monetary Fund (IMF)

Source: International Monetary Fund (IMF)

*For more information on PPP, please see map on page 57.

Figures are listed in U.S. dollars.

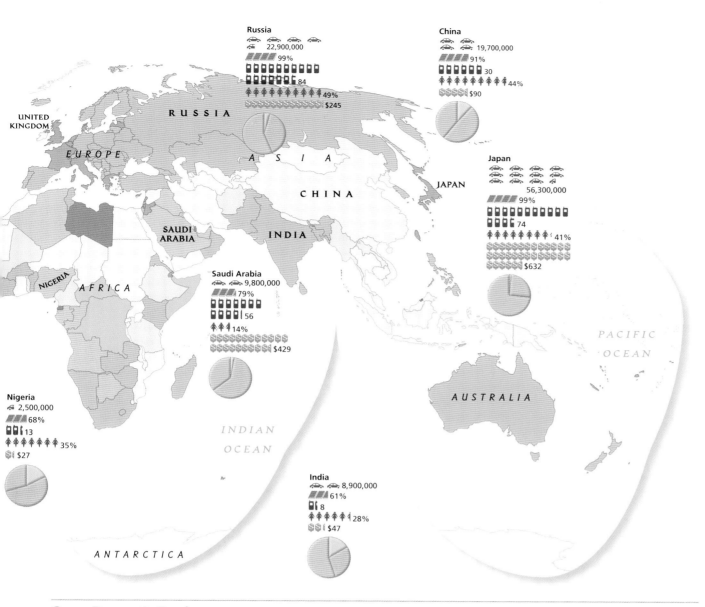

Russia
🚗🚗🚗🚗 22,900,000
99%
84
49%
$245

China
🚗🚗 19,700,000
91%
30
44%
$90

Japan
56,300,000
99%
74
41%
$632

Saudi Arabia
9,800,000
79%
56
14%
$429

Nigeria
2,500,000
68%
13
35%
$27

India
8,900,000
61%
8
28%
$47

UNITED KINGDOM
EUROPE
RUSSIA
ASIA
CHINA
INDIA
SAUDI ARABIA
JAPAN
NIGERIA
AFRICA
PACIFIC OCEAN
AUSTRALIA
INDIAN OCEAN
ANTARCTICA

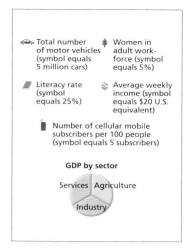

🚗 Total number of motor vehicles (symbol equals 5 million cars)

🧍 Women in adult work-force (symbol equals 5%)

▰ Literacy rate (symbol equals 25%)

💵 Average weekly income (symbol equals $20 U.S. equivalent)

📱 Number of cellular mobile subscribers per 100 people (symbol equals 5 subscribers)

GDP by sector
Services / Agriculture / Industry

Major Exporters

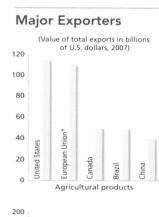

(Value of total exports in billions of U.S. dollars, 2007)

Agricultural products
United States, European Union*, Canada, Brazil, China

Automotive products
European Union*, Japan, United States, Canada, South Korea

Chemicals
European Union*, United States, Japan, China, Switzerland

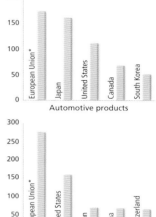

Iron and steel
European Union*, China, Japan, Russia, Ukraine

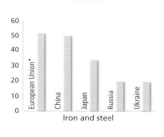

Office and telecom equipment
China, Hong Kong (China), United States, Singapore, European Union*

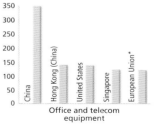

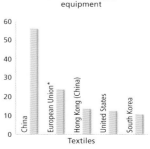

Textiles
China, European Union*, Hong Kong (China), United States, South Korea

*European Union exports to non-European Union members.

Gross Domestic Product

The gross domestic product (GDP) is the total market value of goods and services produced by a nation's economy in a given year using global currency exchange rates. It is a convenient way of calculating the level of a nation's international purchasing power and economic strength, but it does not show average wealth of individuals or measure standard of living. For example, a country could have high exports in products but still have a low standard of living.

Gross Domestic Product Per Capita
(currency in U.S. dollars)
- More than $25,000
- $10,000–$25,000
- $5,000–$9,999
- $1,500–$4,999
- Less than $1,500
- No data

Source: International Monetary Fund (IMF)

NORTH AMERICA, Toronto, New York, Los Angeles, Mexico City, London, Paris, EUROPE, Moscow, ASIA, Beijing, Tokyo, Cairo, Mumbai (Bombay), Lagos, AFRICA, SOUTH AMERICA, São Paulo, Buenos Aires, Jakarta, AUSTRALIA, Sydney

Gross Domestic Product: Purchasing Power Parity (PPP)

The PPP method calculates the relative value of currencies based on what each currency will buy in its country of origin—providing a good comparison between national economies. Per capita GDP at PPP is a very good but not perfect indicator of living standards. For instance, although workers in China earn only a fraction of the wage of American workers, (measured at current dollar rates) they also spend it in a lower-cost environment.

Gross Domestic Product Per Capita
(PPP in U.S. dollars)
- More than $25,000
- $10,000–$25,000
- $5,000–$9,999
- $1,500–$4,999
- Less than $1,500
- No data

Source: International Monetary Fund (IMF)

NORTH AMERICA, Toronto, New York, Los Angeles, Mexico City, London, Paris, EUROPE, Moscow, ASIA, Beijing, Tokyo, Cairo, Mumbai (Bombay), Lagos, AFRICA, SOUTH AMERICA, São Paulo, Buenos Aires, Jakarta, AUSTRALIA, Sydney

WORLD TRADE HAS EXPANDED at a dizzying pace in the decades following World War II. The dollar value of world merchandise exports rose from $61 billion in 1950 to $10.1 trillion in 2005. Adjusted for price changes, world trade grew 30 times over the last 55 years, much faster than world output. Trade in manufactures expanded much faster than that of mining products (including fuels) and agricultural products. In the last decades many developing countries (e.g., China, South Korea, Mexico) have become important exporters of manufactures. However, there are still many less developed countries—primarily in Africa and the Middle East—that are dependent on a few primary commodities for their export earnings. Commercial services exports have expanded rapidly over the past two decades, and amounted to

$2.4 trillion in 2005. While developed countries account for more than two-thirds of world services trade, some developing countries now gain most of their export earnings from services exports. Earnings from tourism in the Caribbean and that from software exports in India are prominent examples of developing countries' dynamic services exports.

Capital flows and worker remittances have gained in importance worldwide and are another important aspect of globalization. The stock of worldwide foreign direct investment was estimated to be close to $9 trillion at the end of 2004, $2.2 trillion of which was invested in developing countries. Capital markets in many developing countries remain small, fragile, and underdeveloped, which hampers household savings and the funding of local enterprises.

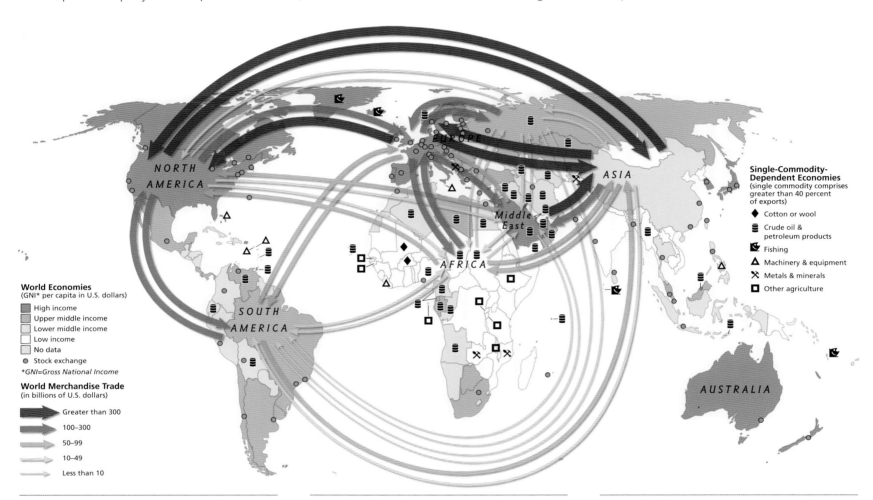

Single-Commodity-Dependent Economies
(single commodity comprises greater than 40 percent of exports)

- ◆ Cotton or wool
- ▤ Crude oil & petroleum products
- ◤ Fishing
- △ Machinery & equipment
- ✕ Metals & minerals
- ☐ Other agriculture

World Economies
(GNI* per capita in U.S. dollars)

- High income
- Upper middle income
- Lower middle income
- Low income
- No data
- ○ Stock exchange

*GNI=Gross National Income

World Merchandise Trade
(in billions of U.S. dollars)

- Greater than 300
- 100–300
- 50–99
- 10–49
- Less than 10

Growth of World Trade

After World War II the export growth of manufactured goods greatly outstripped other exports. This graph shows the volume growth on a semi-log scale (a straight line represents constant growth) rather than a standard scale (a straight line indicates a constant increase in the absolute values in each year).

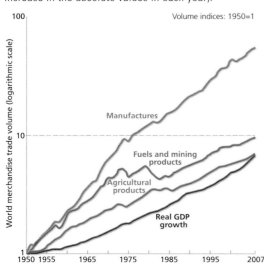

Volume indices: 1950=1

World merchandise trade volume (logarithmic scale)

Manufactures
Fuels and mining products
Agricultural products
Real GDP growth

1950 1955 1965 1975 1985 1995 2007

Merchandise Exports

Fuels, due to their heavy concentration in relatively few areas, are the leading category of exports. Manufactured goods, however, account for three-quarters of world merchandise exports. Export values of two subtypes—machinery and office/telecom equipment—exceed the total export value of mining products.

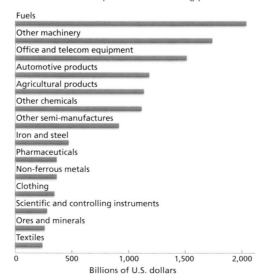

Fuels
Other machinery
Office and telecom equipment
Automotive products
Agricultural products
Other chemicals
Other semi-manufactures
Iron and steel
Pharmaceuticals
Non-ferrous metals
Clothing
Scientific and controlling instruments
Ores and minerals
Textiles

0   500   1,000   1,500   2,000
Billions of U.S. dollars

Main Trading Nations

The U.S., Germany, and China account for nearly 30 percent of total world merchandise trade. Ongoing negotiations among the 153 member nations of the World Trade Organization are tackling market-access barriers in agriculture, textiles, and clothing—areas where many developing countries hope to compete.

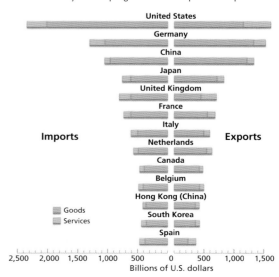

United States
Germany
China
Japan
United Kingdom
France
Italy
Netherlands
Canada
Belgium
Hong Kong (China)
South Korea
Spain

Imports / **Exports**

Goods
Services

2,500 2,000 1,500 1,000 500   0   500   1,000 1,500
Billions of U.S. dollars

World Debt

Measuring a country's outstanding foreign debt in relation to its GDP indicates the size of future income needed to pay back the debt; it also shows how much a country has relied in the past on foreign savings to finance investment and consumption expenditures. A high external debt ratio can pose a financial risk if debt service payments are not assured.

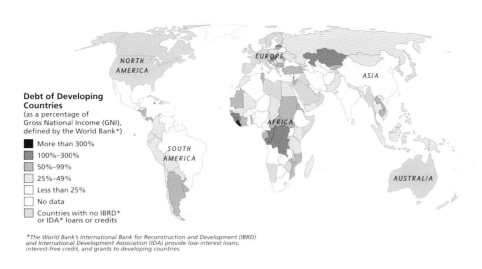

Debt of Developing Countries
(as a percentage of Gross National Income (GNI), defined by the World Bank*)

- More than 300%
- 100%–300%
- 50%–99%
- 25%–49%
- Less than 25%
- No data
- Countries with no IBRD* or IDA* loans or credits

The World Bank's International Bank for Reconstruction and Development (IBRD) and International Development Association (IDA) provide low-interest loans, interest-free credit, and grants to developing countries.

Trade Blocs

Regional trade is on the rise. Agreements between neighboring countries to offer each other trade benefits can create larger markets and improve the economy of the region as a whole. But they can also lead to discrimination, especially when more efficient suppliers outside the regional agreements are prevented from supplying their goods and services.

Major Regional Trade Agreements
- **APEC** - Asia-Pacific Economic Cooperation
- **ASEAN** - Association of Southeast Asian Nations
- **APEC & ASEAN**
- **COMESA** - Common Market for Eastern and Southern Africa
- **ECOWAS** - Economic Community of West African States
- **EU** - European Union
- **MERCOSUR** - Southern Common Market
- **NAFTA & APEC** - North American Free Trade Agreement
- **SAPTA** - South Asian Preferential Trade Arrangement

Trade Flow: Fuels

The leading exporters of fuel products are countries in the Middle East, Africa, Russia, and central and western Asia; all export more fuel than they consume. But intra-regional energy trade is growing, with some of the key producers—Canada, Indonesia, Norway, and the United Kingdom, for example—located in regions that are net energy importers.

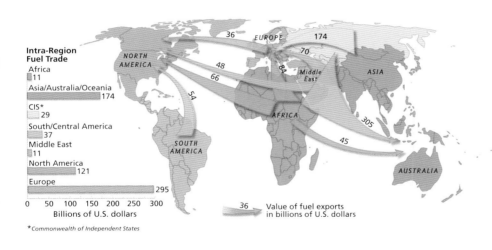

Intra-Region Fuel Trade
- Africa — 11
- Asia/Australia/Oceania — 174
- CIS* — 29
- South/Central America — 37
- Middle East — 11
- North America — 121
- Europe — 295

0 50 100 150 200 250 300
Billions of U.S. dollars

36 — Value of fuel exports in billions of U.S. dollars

*Commonwealth of Independent States

Trade Flow: Agricultural Products

The world trade in agricultural products is less concentrated than trade in fuels, with processed goods making up the majority. Agricultural products encounter high export barriers, which limit the opportunities for some exporters to expand into foreign markets. Reducing such barriers is a major challenge for governments that are engaged in agricultural trade negotiations.

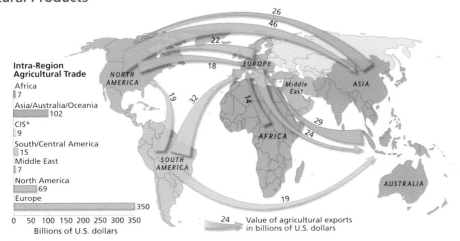

Intra-Region Agricultural Trade
- Africa — 7
- Asia/Australia/Oceania — 102
- CIS* — 9
- South/Central America — 15
- Middle East — 7
- North America — 69
- Europe — 350

0 50 100 150 200 250 300 350
Billions of U.S. dollars

24 — Value of agricultural exports in billions of U.S. dollars

*Commonwealth of Independent States

Top Merchandise Exporters and Importers

	PERCENTAGE OF WORLD TOTAL	VALUE (BILLIONS)
TOP EXPORTERS		
Germany	9.5	$1,326
China	8.7	$1,218
United States	8.3	$1,163
Japan	5.1	$713
France	4.0	$553
Netherlands	4.0	$551
Italy	3.5	$492
United Kingdom	3.1	$438
Belgium	3.1	$431
Canada	3.0	$419
South Korea	2.7	$372
Russia	2.5	$355
Hong Kong (China)	2.5	$349
Singapore	2.1	$299
Mexico	2.0	$272
TOP IMPORTERS		
United States	14.2	$2,020
Germany	7.4	$1,059
China	6.7	$956
Japan	4.4	$621
United Kingdom	4.4	$620
France	4.3	$615
Italy	3.5	$505
Netherlands	3.5	$492
Belgium	2.9	$413
Canada	2.7	$390
Spain	2.6	$373
Hong Kong (China)	2.6	$370
South Korea	2.5	$357
Mexico	2.1	$296
Singapore	1.8	$263

Top Commercial Services Exporters and Importers

(includes transportation, travel, and other services)

	PERCENTAGE OF WORLD TOTAL	VALUE (BILLIONS)
TOP EXPORTERS		
United States	13.9	$456
United Kingdom	8.3	$273
Germany	6.3	$206
France	4.2	$137
Spain	3.9	$128
Japan	3.9	$127
China	3.7	$122
Italy	3.4	$111
India	2.7	$90
Ireland	2.7	$89
Netherlands	2.7	$88
Hong Kong (China)	2.5	$83
Belgium	2.3	$76
Singapore	2.0	$67
Sweden	1.9	$64
TOP IMPORTERS		
United States	10.9	$336
Germany	8.1	$251
United Kingdom	6.3	$194
Japan	4.8	$149
China	4.2	$129
France	4.0	$124
Italy	3.8	$118
Spain	3.2	$98
Ireland	3.1	$95
Netherlands	2.8	$87
South Korea	2.7	$83
Canada	2.6	$80
India	2.5	$77
Belgium	2.3	$71
Singapore	2.3	$70

Food

THE POPULATION OF THE PLANET, which already tops six and a half billion, continues to increase by 220,000 mouths a day. What will they eat? Where will the additional food come from?

Worldwide, agricultural production also continues to grow, but the food-producing regions are unevenly distributed around the globe. Though efforts to raise the levels of production even more (while relying less on chemical applications that damage the environment) are vitally important, they can go only so far in solving a great dilemma: How can we get more food to the millions of people who do not have enough to eat? Invariably, it is the economic situation of countries—which ones

have food surpluses to sell; which ones need food and have or don't have enough money to buy it—that determines who goes hungry.

For people in the world's poorest regions, the situation is grim. The United Nations Food and Agriculture Organization reports that every night 815 million people in the developing world go to bed hungry and that malnourishment contributes to at least one-third of all child deaths. It also says that 13 million people in southern Africa face famine. Most cases of malnutrition are found in the developing countries of the tropics, where rapid population growth and other factors are depleting agricultural and financial resources.

Croplands of the World

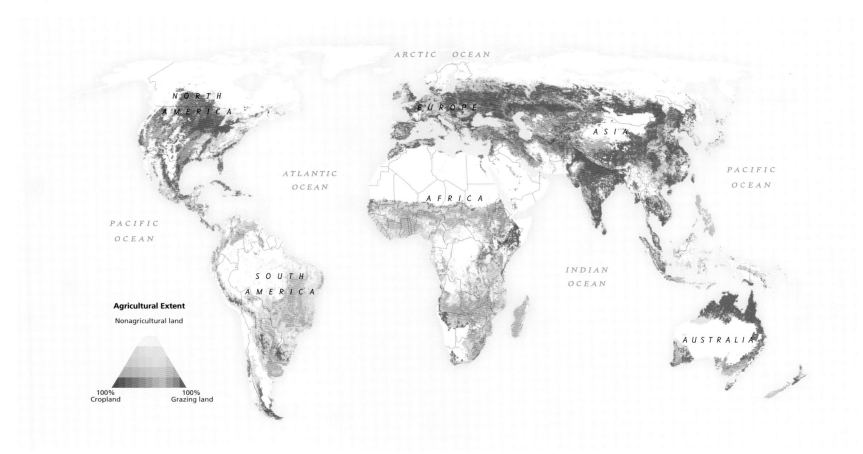

Agricultural Extent

Nonagricultural land

100% Cropland — 100% Grazing land

Fishing and Aquaculture

Marine fisheries are vital for food security in developing countries, and are a heavily subsidized industry in developed countries. Today, no parts of the world's oceans are unaffected. Most fish are caught in coastal waters, with the most intense fishing in northern Europe, and off China and Southeast Asia. The world's reported catch has more than quadrupled since 1950, but peaked in the late 1980s and has leveled off since. Fish farming, called aquaculture, is one of the fastest growing areas of food production. The bulk of marine aquaculture occurs in developing countries, with China accounting for around two-thirds of the total output.

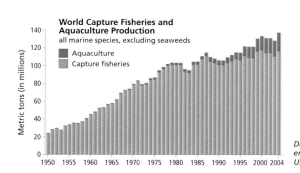

World Capture Fisheries and Aquaculture Production
all marine species, excluding seaweeds
- Aquaculture
- Capture fisheries

Data for fish landings, capture fisheries, and aquaculture: Sea Around Us Project, www.seaaroundus.org.

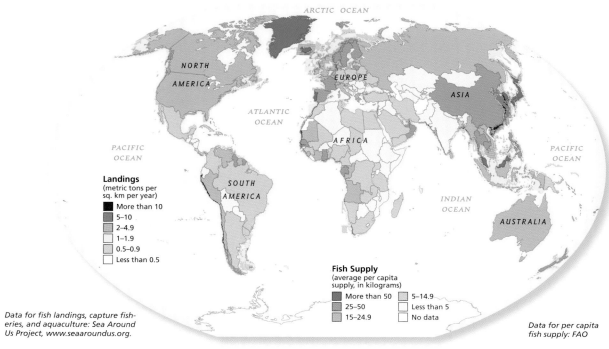

Landings (metric tons per sq. km per year)
- More than 10
- 5–10
- 2–4.9
- 1–1.9
- 0.5–0.9
- Less than 0.5

Fish Supply (average per capita supply, in kilograms)
- More than 50
- 25–50
- 15–24.9
- 5–14.9
- Less than 5
- No data

Data for per capita fish supply: FAO

World Agricultural Production

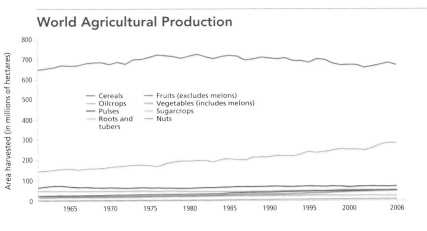

In the past few decades, world food production has more than kept pace with the burgeoning global population. Meat and cereals account for the most dramatic increases. New high-yield crops, additional irrigated land, and fertilizers have contributed to the rise in production. But there are related problems: Scientists warn that overuse of fertilizers causes nitrogen overload in Earth's waters, and insufficient use, in particular in Africa, has long-term adverse consequences for food security.

Undernourishment in the Developing World

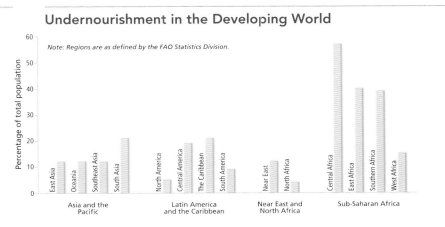

More food than ever is produced, but its distribution is uneven. Africa, in particular, is a continent of contrasts: Almost half the people in central, eastern, and southern Africa are undernourished, while a much lower percentage of people in the north and west are undernourished. The United Nations estimates that more than three-quarters of a billion people suffer from persistent malnourishment. Without access to adequate food, these populations cannot lead healthy, productive lives.

Caloric Supply

As shown at right, cereals (grains) dominate the caloric supply of people in Africa and Asia. Sugars, oils, and proteins compose a much higher portion in other parts of the world, and the increasing consumption rates of these foods leads to obesity problems in many countries.

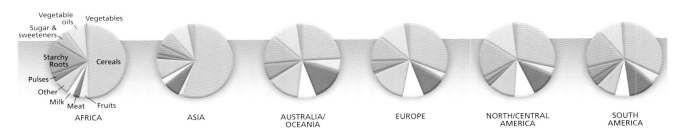

Divisions indicate breakdown of per-capita calorie supply.

Distribution of Major Crops and Livestock

Humans rely on plant sources for carbohydrates, with grains (the edible parts of cereal plants) providing 80 percent of the food energy (calorie) supply. This means that the major grains—corn, wheat, and rice—are the foods that fuel humanity. Most cereal grains are grown in the Northern Hemisphere, with the United States and France producing enough to be the largest exporters.

In many parts of the world, cereal grains cannot be grown, due to the lack of productive farmland or the necessary technology. Again and again throughout history, the actions of countries have been shaped by disparities in the supply and demand of grains, and by the knowledge that grains equal survival. Waverley Root, a food historian, once wrote: "[P]ossession of wheat or lack of it sways the destinies of nations; nor is it rare to find wheat being used as a political weapon.... [I]t is difficult to foresee any future in which it will not still exert a powerful influence on human history."

Recently, rising standards of living in developing countries have increased the worldwide demand for meat and other animal products, further widening demand for grains as a result of the increased need for livestock feed. The rapidly expanding livestock sector will soon provide about half of the global agricultural GDP.

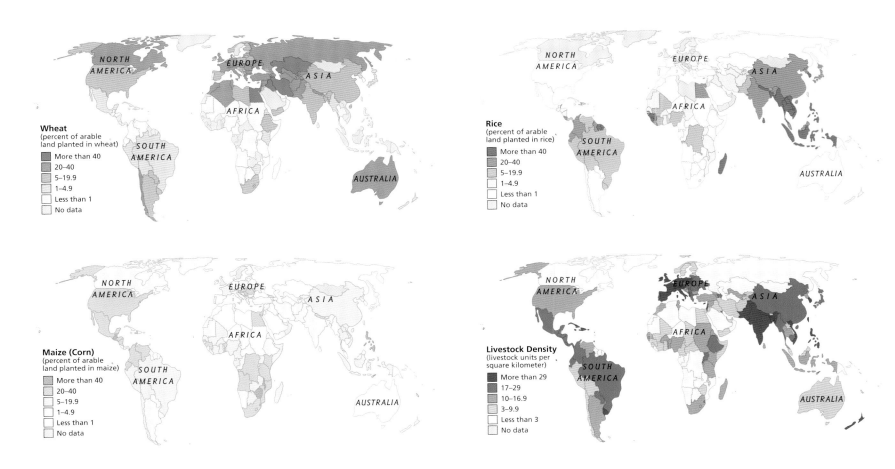

PRIMARY ENERGY comes in many different forms. Some fuels, such as animal dung and fuelwood, have a low energy content, while coal, natural gas, and oil contain much more. By adopting a common measurement that takes these differences into account, we can compare energy usage around the world. Today, the international standard is the "metric ton of oil equivalent" (toe), which translates all forms of energy (solid, liquid, or gas) to a common baseline. On this basis, global energy consumption is currently about 11.4 billion metric tons of oil equivalent a year.

The world's chief sources of energy are oil, coal, and natural gas. In each case, however, the major consuming countries are becoming increasingly dependent on imports. While oil has been shipped from producing countries to consumers for many years, increasing amounts of coal—mainly used for generating electricity—are on the move. Western Europe and countries like the United States and Japan are also importing more liquified natural gas, adding to their reliance on energy from elsewhere.

Production and consumption patterns show major differences worldwide. North America, with less than one-tenth of the world's population, uses about one-quarter of its energy. Countries with rapidly developing economies, like China and India, need more. As demand for energy grows, prices rise and alternative sources become more attractive.

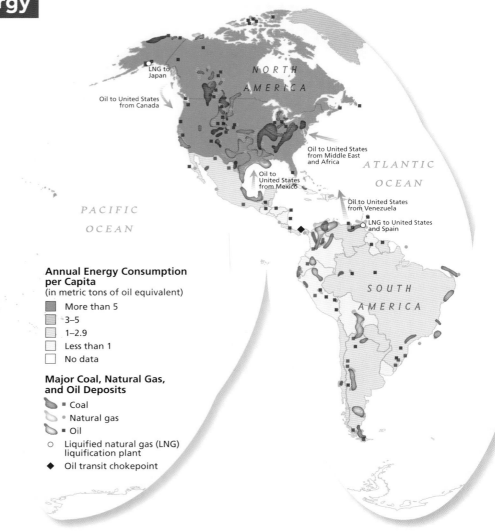

Annual Energy Consumption per Capita
(in metric tons of oil equivalent)
- More than 5
- 3–5
- 1–2.9
- Less than 1
- No data

Major Coal, Natural Gas, and Oil Deposits
- ■ Coal
- ■ Natural gas
- ■ Oil
- ○ Liquified natural gas (LNG) liquification plant
- ◆ Oil transit chokepoint

Energy Production

WORLD ENERGY PRODUCTION BY TYPE

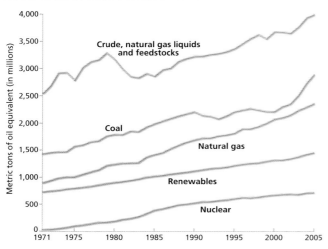

WORLD ENERGY PRODUCTION BY REGION

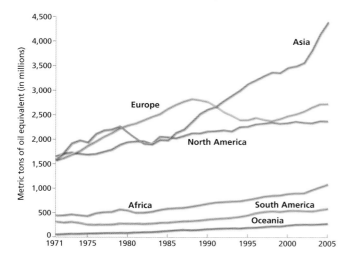

Fossil Fuel Extraction

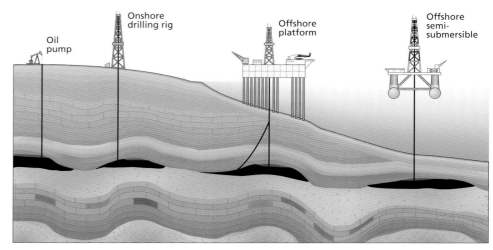

OIL EXTRACTION
Drilling-operation types depend on whether oil is in the ground or under the ocean. An onshore drilling rig uses a basic derrick; offshore drilling is done with platform or semisubmersible designs (as shown above).

GAS EXTRACTION
Natural gas occurs in many of the same types of geologic structures as oil, and it is generally thought to have the same organic origins as oil. Gas-drilling and oil-drilling operations are essentially the same.

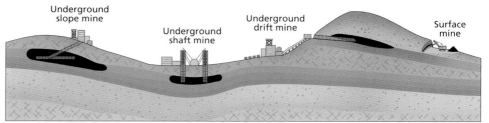

COAL MINING
The mining of coal made the industrial revolution possible, and coal still provides a major energy source. Once a labor-intensive process, coal mining is now heavily mechanized. An underground slope mine allows coal to be transported to the surface by a conveyor rather than an elevator. Underground drift mines and surface mines allow the easiest use of coal-cutting machinery.

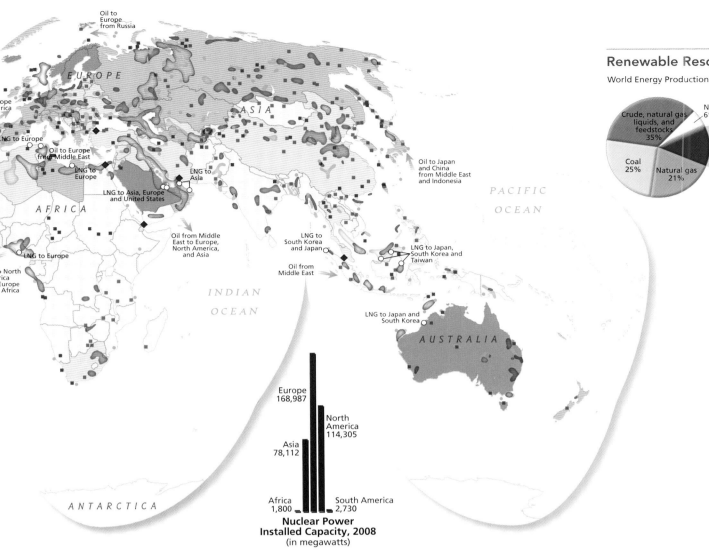

Oil to Europe from Russia

Oil to Europe from Middle East

LNG to Europe

LNG to Asia, Europe and United States

LNG to Europe

Oil from Middle East to Europe, North America, and Asia

Oil from Middle East

LNG to Asia

LNG to South Korea and Japan

LNG to Japan, South Korea and Taiwan

LNG to Japan and South Korea

EUROPE

ASIA

AFRICA

PACIFIC OCEAN

INDIAN OCEAN

AUSTRALIA

ANTARCTICA

Renewable Resources

World Energy Production

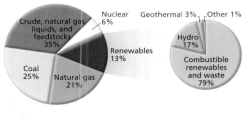

Crude, natural gas liquids, and feedstocks 35%

Coal 25%

Natural gas 21%

Renewables 13%

Nuclear 6%

Geothermal 3%

Other 1%

Hydro 17%

Combustible renewables and waste 79%

Nuclear Power Installed Capacity, 2008 (in megawatts)

- Europe 168,987
- North America 114,305
- Asia 78,112
- Africa 1,800
- South America 2,730

HYDROELECTRIC POWER
Hydroelectric plants in South America and the United States (Hoover Dam, on the Arizona-Nevada border) are among the largest in the world. China has the greatest hydroelectric potential.

GEOTHERMAL POWER
Geothermal power plants pipe steam and hot water from the ground to make electricity. The world's largest installation— The Geysers—is in California.

SOLAR POWER
Concentrated solar thermal (above), and solar photovoltaic are two of the most common types of solar power plants currently in operation.

WIND POWER
Harnessing the wind is the goal of the fastest-growing energy technology. Germany, the United States, and Spain lead the world in wind-power capacity, accounting for over half the world's total.

Biomass, Hydroelectric, and Geothermal Power

Burning biomass to release energy is a carbon-neutral process (i.e., it does not cause a net increase in carbon dioxide); the carbon is already part of the cycle. Biomass would require extensive conversion, however. Hydroelectric power is potentially the major renewable energy source, and more than 30 percent of the potential sites around the world have not yet been developed. In many geothermal sites it is possible to drill wells for a steady supply of steam, which can then be used to run turbines to generate electricity.

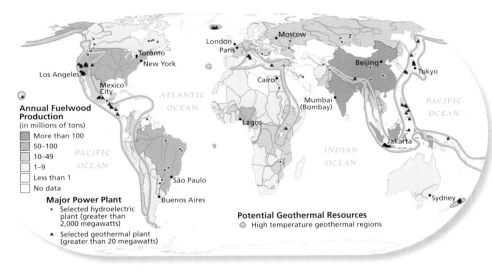

Annual Fuelwood Production (in millions of tons)
- More than 100
- 50–100
- 10–49
- 1–9
- Less than 1
- No data

Major Power Plant
- Selected hydroelectric plant (greater than 2,000 megawatts)
- ▲ Selected geothermal plant (greater than 20 megawatts)

Potential Geothermal Resources
- High temperature geothermal regions

Toronto, New York, London, Paris, Moscow, Beijing, Tokyo, Cairo, Mumbai (Bombay), Lagos, Jakarta, Los Angeles, Mexico City, São Paulo, Buenos Aires, Sydney

ATLANTIC OCEAN, PACIFIC OCEAN, INDIAN OCEAN

Wind and Solar Power

Wind, solar, tidal, wave, and other technologies are promising sources of natural, renewable energy. As the technology and economics of wind power improve, certain regions of the world could become "Saudi Arabias of wind." Solar radiation received on Earth each year corresponds to 3,000 times global energy consumption, but the problem with solar energy, just as with many other renewable energy resources, is their intermittent nature and the lack of storage technologies.

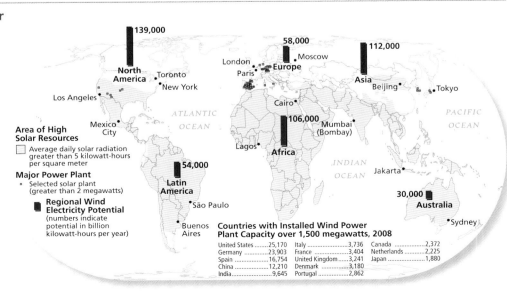

Area of High Solar Resources
- Average daily solar radiation greater than 5 kilowatt-hours per square meter

Major Power Plant
- Selected solar plant (greater than 2 megawatts)

Regional Wind Electricity Potential (numbers indicate potential in billion kilowatt-hours per year)

- North America 139,000
- Europe 58,000
- Asia 112,000
- Africa 106,000
- Latin America 54,000
- Australia 30,000

London, Paris, Moscow, Toronto, New York, Beijing, Tokyo, Cairo, Mumbai (Bombay), Lagos, Jakarta, Los Angeles, Mexico City, São Paulo, Buenos Aires, Sydney

Countries with Installed Wind Power Plant Capacity over 1,500 megawatts, 2008

United States 25,170	Italy 3,736	Canada 2,372
Germany 23,903	France 3,404	Netherlands 2,225
Spain 16,754	United Kingdom.....3,241	Japan 1,880
China 12,210	Denmark 3,180	
India......................9,645	Portugal 2,862	

THE SPATIAL PATTERN of world mineral production is the result of several factors: geology, climate, economic systems, and social preferences. This pattern can be seen on the map at right, which locates major production and processing sites for various mineral commodities (see below for profiles on 18 important minerals).

Plate movements, volcanism, and sedimentation are geologic processes that form valuable concentrations of minerals. The same geologic forces that formed the Andes, for example, are responsible for the porphyry copper deposits along South America's Pacific coast. Other processes concentrate copper in sedimentary basins and in volcanic arcs. Climatic factors, such as the tropical conditions that contribute to bauxite formation, are also important.

Mineral consumption by industries is positively correlated with income and differs greatly among countries. Developed nations use larger volumes of materials and a wider variety of mineral commodities than less developed countries. In developed nations, annual copper use is typically 5 to 10 kilograms per person; for less developed ones, usage is only a few kilograms per person. Recent economic growth has led to greater demand for many mineral resources. Meeting that need without causing harm to the environment will be one of the major challenges for societies in the 21st century.

World Mineral Production

Gross Domestic Product per Capita (PPP)
(in U.S. dollars)

- More than 20,000
- 5,000–20,000
- 2,500–4,999
- 1,000–2,499
- Less than 1,000
- No data

Industry and Mining

- ▽ Diamonds
- ◣ Phosphate
- ◆ Potash
- ▲ Processing plant
- ⊞ Rare earth elements
- Steel manufacturing

Major Mines

Al	Aluminum	Mn	Manganese
Sb	Antimony	Mo	Molybdenum
Bi	Bismuth	Ni	Nickel
Cr	Chromium	Pt	Platinum
Co	Cobalt	Ag	Silver
Cu	Copper	Sn	Tin
Au	Gold	Ti	Titanium
Fe	Iron ore	W	Tungsten
Pb	Lead	Zn	Zinc

 Aluminum (Al) Bauxite, the principal ore of aluminum, is an aggregate of millimeter- to centimeter-size oval structures, composed of aluminum hydroxide, that form in areas of deep and prolonged tropical weathering of aluminum-rich parent materials. World production of bauxite was 156 million tons in 2004. Australia was the largest producer (56 million), followed by Brazil, Guinea, and China. Alumina (Al$_2$O$_3$), an intermediate product, is made by refining bauxite and then smelting to make aluminum metal; both of these steps are very energy intensive. China, the United States, and Russia have the largest aluminum smelting capacities. In 2004, the world production of aluminum was estimated at 28.9 million tons.

 Chromium (Cr) Chromite (FeCr$_2$O$_4$) is the principal ore mineral of chromium. Black chromite forms in layered, iron- and magnesium-rich igneous deposits (as in this photo), which contributed nearly half the world's 2004 production, estimated at more than 17 million tons. South Africa has long been the largest producer on the planet. Kazakhstan and India together produced another 33 percent. The main use of chromium is in the manufacture of stainless and heat-resistant steels. Chromite is also used in the production of chromium chemicals and in acid-resistant refractories.

 Copper (Cu) Chalcopyrite (CuFeS$_2$), the principal ore of copper, occurs as veins and disseminations in igneous and sedimentary host rocks. Copper is also mined as other sulfides, the native metal, and oxides. In 2004, world mine production of copper metal was 14.5 million tons. Chile was the leading producer (5.4 million tons), followed by the U.S. (1.2 million), and Peru (1 million). Copper is used for electric and electronic products, in construction of buildings, and as an alloy metal.

 Diamond (gem and industrial) Diamonds are used both as gems and as materials to increase the hardness of cutting tools. Natural diamonds are generally brought to the Earth's surface by unusual volcanic eruptions, gas-charged igneous melts that originate at depths of 150+ km in the Earth. The map locates the major producers of natural gems and industrial diamonds. Diamonds can also be produced synthetically, and about 88 percent of industrial diamonds now have this origin. Industrial diamond mining produced 70 million carats in 2004, more than 90 percent of which came from the Congo, Australia, Russia, Botswana, and South Africa.

 Gold (Au) Native gold and electrum, an alloy with silver, are the most common forms and precipitate from hot, water-rich fluids in the Earth. Historically, gold was used as money or as a backup for paper money. Today, no major country backs its currency with gold, but private investors may hold gold as a hedge against economic uncertainty. Gold is also used in jewelry, as a dental material, and in electronic equipment. South Africa was the largest producer of mined gold in 2004 (344 tons), followed by the U.S., Australia, and China. Total world production in 2004 was estimated at 2,470 tons.

 Iron Ore and Steel Iron (Fe) is the 4th most abundant element in the Earth's crust and occurs in a wide variety of oxide (magnetite and hematite), hydroxide (goethite), sulfide (pyrite, pyrrhotite), carbonate (siderite), and silicate minerals found in sedimentary rocks. Nearly all the 2004 world production of 1.25 billion tons came from iron oxide and hydroxide deposits. The largest producers were China, Brazil, and Australia. In 2004, world crude steel production was over one billion tons. China, the EU countries, and Japan were the main producers.

 Lead (Pb) Galena (PbS) is the principal ore mineral of lead. In 2004, world mine production of lead was 3.1 million tons. China was the largest producer (950,000 tons), followed by Australia and the United States. Due to lead's toxicity, the number of lead-containing products has been reduced in recent years, and automobile lead-acid batteries are effectively recycled. This effort has reduced the consumption of primary (new) lead in the United States and Europe, but China's use continues to expand. Lead is also used in ammunition, solder, in television glass, and in the radiation shields for x-ray equipment.

 Manganese (Mn) This element is essential to steel making as an additive to remove sulfur and excess oxygen. It is also employed as an alloying element and is used in dry-cell batteries. Mn geochemistry is similar to iron's; however, it is never mined from the same deposits. World production was 11 million tons in 2004. The largest producers are South Africa and Gabon. Australia comes in third, followed by Brazil, Ghana, and India. China does not produce much, and must import manganese.

 Nickel (Ni) Two very different types of deposits are the sources for nickel. In sulfide deposits found in ultramafic rock complexes, nickel occurs primarily in the mineral pentlandite ((Fe,Ni)$_9$S$_8$). It is also produced from oxide and silicate minerals in thick soils that form over certain rock types in tropical environments. World mine production was 1.4 million tons in 2004. Russia (the top producer, at 315,000 tons) and Canada produce nickel from sulfide ores; Australia, Indonesia, and New Caledonia rely on the deeply weathered soils. Nickel is used to make stainless steel and in electroplating.

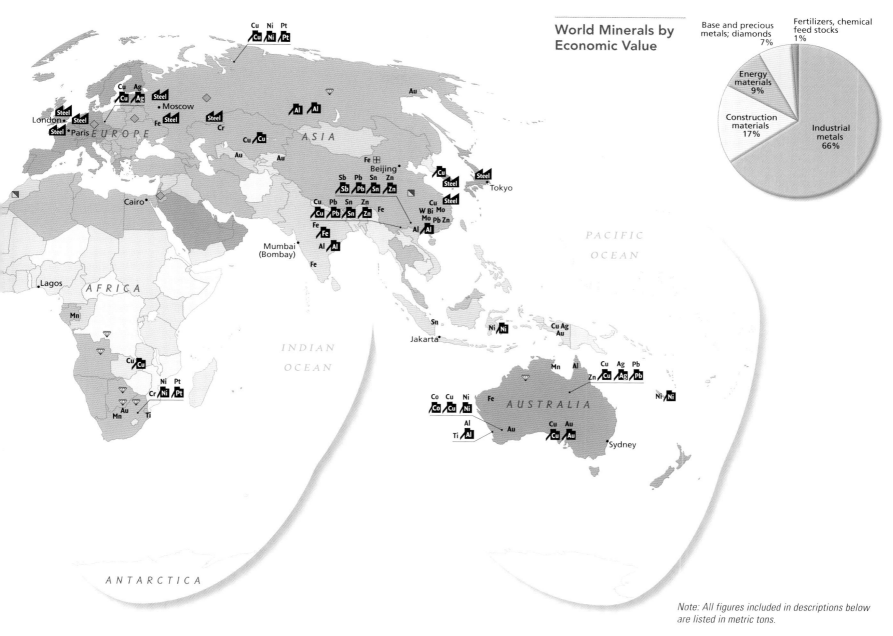

Cu Ni Pt

Cu Ag
Steel
Cu Ag
London•
Steel Steel
Steel •Paris E U R O P E
•Moscow
Fe Steel Steel
Cr
Al Al
Au

Cairo•

A S I A

Cu Cu

Au Au

Fe
Beijing•
Sb Pb Sn Zn
Sb Pb Sn Zn
Cu Pb Sn Zn
Cu Pb Sn Zn Fe
W Bi Mo
Mo Pb Zn
Al Al

Cu
Steel
Steel
Cu Steel
Steel Tokyo

Au

Mumbai
(Bombay)
Fe
Fe
Al Al
Fe

Lagos•
A F R I C A

Mn

Cu Cu

Ni Pt
Cr Ni Pt

Au
Mn Ti

P A C I F I C

O C E A N

Sn•

Ni Ni

Cu Ag
Au

Jakarta•
I N D I A N
O C E A N

Mn Al
Cu Ag Pb
Zn Cu Ag Pb

Co Cu Ni
Co Cu Ni
Fe A U S T R A L I A

Ni Ni

Al
Ti Al
Au
Cu Au
Cu Au
•Sydney

A N T A R C T I C A

World Minerals by Economic Value

Base and precious metals; diamonds 7%

Fertilizers, chemical feed stocks 1%

Energy materials 9%

Construction materials 17%

Industrial metals 66%

Note: All figures included in descriptions below are listed in metric tons.

 Phosphate Rock (P) This substance is the primary ore needed to make phosphoric acid, which is used in the production of certain fertilizers. Most phosphate deposits initially formed when phosphorus-rich deep-ocean waters upwelled onto tropical continental shelves, and phosphate-rich sediments were deposited through biologic activity. In 2004, the world production of phosphate rock was 138 million tons; the United States was the leading producer (37 million tons). China (25 million) was second, while Morocco and Western Sahara together accounted for 23 million tons.

 Platinum-Group Metals (Pt, Pd, Ru, Rh, Ir, Os) These substances are used in catalytic converters that clean the exhaust from cars; they are also used in jewelry and in chemotherapy for cancer. World mine production of platinum and palladium in 2004 was 218 tons and 190 tons, respectively, and came from mafic igneous rock complexes, usually of Precambrian age. South Africa was the leading producer of platinum (163 tons), followed by Russia (36 tons). Russia produced 74 tons of palladium, while South Africa mined 78 tons. Other important producers of platinum-group metals are the U.S. and Canada.

 Potash (K) This term is the industrial name for a group of water-soluble salts that contain potassium. The main sources are deposits that include mixtures of the minerals halite (NaCl), sylvite (KCl), and carnallite (KMgCl3•6H2O), along with other potassium-, magnesium-, and bromine-bearing minerals and saline brines. Most is used in fertilizer, while the remainder is employed in the production of chemicals. Total 2004 production of 30 million tons came mainly from Canada (9.5), Russia (4.7), Belarus (4.65), and Germany (3.67 million). Israel and Jordan produce significant amounts of potash from the Dead Sea.

 Rare Earths (REE) This group of 17 metals ranges from lanthanum (La) to lutetium (Lu) in the periodic table of elements. Rare earth metals are used in the making of a wide variety of products, including chemical catalysts for petroleum refining, rechargeable batteries, phosphors for TV and computer screens, and superalloys. These elements are indeed "rare," and concentrated only in unusual igneous bodies. World mine production of rare earth oxides was 102,000 tons in 2004 with China producing the great majority (95,000) of these.

 Silver (Ag) This substance has the highest electrical conductivity of all elements. It occurs in native form; mixed with native gold in electrum; as simple sulfides (argentite, Ag_2S); as complex antimony- and arsenic-bearing minerals; and as a trace constituent in galena. Silver is used for coins, electrical and electronic components, jewelry, tableware, and in film photography (digital cameras are causing a reduced demand). In 2004, world mine production was 19,500 tons. Mexico, which mined 2,850 tons of silver, was the largest producer; it was followed by Peru (2,800 tons) and China (2,600 tons).

 Tin (Sn) The most common use of tin is as a coating to prevent oxidation of a covered metal, such as steel in "tin cans." When alloyed with other metals, tin makes solder, pewter, and bronze. Window glass is manufactured by floating molten glass on molten tin. Organo-tin chemicals are used as pesticides, fungicides, and wood preservatives. The major ore mineral of tin is cassiterite (SnO_2). China, which mined 100,000 tons in 2004, was the world's largest producer that year. Indonesia (70,000 tons) and Peru (40,000 tons) were the second and third largest producers. Total world production in 2004 was 250,000 tons.

 Titanium (Ti) More than 95 percent of titanium is consumed as TiO_2 pigment; the rest is processed to make titanium metal or sponge. Because titanium metal is light, has high strength, and resists corrosion, it is used in aerospace, marine, medical, and military applications. Russia, Japan, and Kazakhstan were the largest makers of titanium sponge in 2004. The titanium-bearing minerals ilmenite ($FeTiO_3$) and rutile (TiO_2), originally formed in igneous rocks, are common components in beach and dune sands and are processed into TiO_2 pigment used in paints and plastics. Australia (1.1 million tons) and South Africa (also 1.1 million) were the largest producers of titanium-bearing mineral concentrates in 2004.

 Tungsten (formerly wolfram) (W) The main use of tungsten is in tungsten-carbide cutting tools. Because of its high melting point, this substance is added to certain steels to give them strength at high temperatures. It is also used in light-bulb filaments. Tungsten mainly occurs in two types of deposits—either in skarns than contain scheelite (CaWO4), or in veins that contain wolframite ($Fe,Mn(WO_4)$). In 2004, China produced 53,000 tons of tungsten, followed by Russia, with 3,500 tons. World production was 60,000 tons.

 Zinc (Zn) The largest use of zinc is as a coating for steel; zinc-coated, "galvanized" steel resists rust and corrosion. Zinc is also used to make brass, solder, and batteries, and it is added to soil, rubber, and cosmetics. In 2004, world mine production was 9.1 million tons. The largest producers were China (2 million), Peru (1.4 million), and Australia (1.3 million). Canada and the United States were also significant producers, with 90 percent of U.S. production coming from a single mine in Alaska. Sphalerite (ZnS) is the principal ore mineral of zinc.

MOST ENVIRONMENTAL DAMAGE
is due to human activity. Some harmful actions are inadvertent—the release, for example, of chlorofluorocarbons (CFCs), once thought to be inert gases, into the atmosphere. Others are deliberate and include such acts as the disposal of sewage into rivers.

Among the root causes of human-induced damage are excessive consumption (mainly in industrialized countries) and rapid population growth (primarily in the developing countries). So, even though scientists may develop products and technologies that have no adverse effects on the environment, their efforts will be muted if both population and consumption continue to increase worldwide.

Socioeconomic and environmental indicators can reveal much about long-term trends; unfortunately, such data are not collected routinely in many countries. With respect to stresses from urban areas, suitable indicators would include electricity consumption, numbers of automobiles, and rates of land conversion from rural to urban. The rapid conversion of countryside to built-up areas during the last 25 to 50 years is a strong indicator that change is occurring at an ever quickening pace.

Many types of environmental stress are interrelated and may have far-reaching consequences. Global warming, for one, will likely increase water scarcity, desertification, deforestation, and coastal flooding (due to rising sea level)—all of which can have a significant impact on human populations.

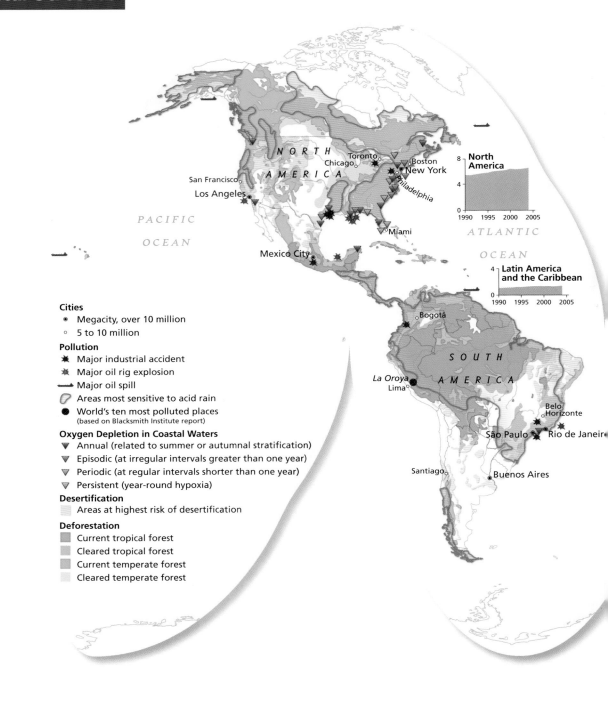

Cities
- ● Megacity, over 10 million
- ○ 5 to 10 million

Pollution
- ✳ Major industrial accident
- ✴ Major oil rig explosion
- ➔ Major oil spill
- ⬭ Areas most sensitive to acid rain
- ● World's ten most polluted places
  (based on Blacksmith Institute report)

Oxygen Depletion in Coastal Waters
- ▼ Annual (related to summer or autumnal stratification)
- ▼ Episodic (at irregular intervals greater than one year)
- ▼ Periodic (at regular intervals shorter than one year)
- ▼ Persistent (year-round hypoxia)

Desertification
- ▨ Areas at highest risk of desertification

Deforestation
- ▨ Current tropical forest
- ▨ Cleared tropical forest
- ▨ Current temperate forest
- ▨ Cleared temperate forest

Global Climate Change

The world's climate is constantly changing—over decades, centuries, and millennia. Currently, several lines of reasoning support the idea that we are likely to live in a much warmer world by the end of this century. Atmospheric concentrations of carbon dioxide and other greenhouse gases are now well above historical levels, and emissions from human activities are the main drivers of change. Simulation models predict that these gases will result in a warming of the lower atmosphere (particularly in polar regions) but a cooling of the stratosphere. Experimental evidence supports these predictions.

Indeed, throughout the last decade the globally averaged annual surface temperature was higher than the hundred-year average. Model simulations of the impacts of this warming—and studies indicating reductions already occurring in polar permafrost and sea ice cover—are so alarming that most scientists and many policy people believe that immediate action must be taken to curb emissions and adapt to change.

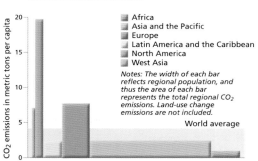

Carbon Dioxide Emissions

Legend:
- Africa
- Asia and the Pacific
- Europe
- Latin America and the Caribbean
- North America
- West Asia

Notes: The width of each bar reflects regional population, and thus the area of each bar represents the total regional CO_2 emissions. Land-use change emissions are not included.

World average

CO_2 emissions in metric tons per capita

Depletion of the Ozone Layer

The ozone layer in the stratosphere has long shielded the biosphere from harmful solar ultraviolet radiation. Since the 1970s, however, the layer has been thinning over Antarctica—and more recently elsewhere. If the process continues, there will be significant effects on human health, including more cases of skin cancer and eye cataracts, and on biological systems. Fortunately, scientific understanding of the phenomenon came rather quickly.

Beginning in the 1950s, increasing amounts of CFCs (and other gases with similar properties) were released into the atmosphere. CFCs are chemically inert in the lower atmosphere but decompose in the stratosphere, subsequently destroying ozone. This understanding provided the basis for successful United Nations actions (Vienna Convention, 1985; Montréal Protocol, 1987) to phase out these gases.

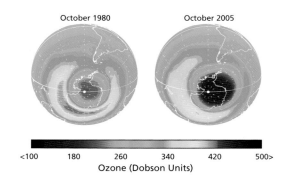

October 1980   October 2005

<100   180   260   340   420   500>
Ozone (Dobson Units)

Pollution

Examples of water and soil pollution include the contamination of groundwater, salinization of irrigated lands in semiarid regions, and the so-called chemical time bomb issue, where accumulated toxins are suddenly mobilized following a change in external conditions. Oceans and estuaries are also increasingly polluted. A growing problem is the creation of "dead zones" (areas of oxygen depletion), mostly due to agricultural runoff and municipal effluents. Addressing the problem requires prevention or reduction at the source; safely disposing of and cleaning up pollution should be strategies of last resort. The modernization of industrial plants, more staff training, a better understanding of the problems, effective policies, and greater public support are needed.

Urban air quality remains a serious problem, particularly in developing countries. One of the main reasons is the rapid increase in passenger cars. In some developed countries, successful control measures have improved air quality over the past 50 years; in others, trends have actually reversed, with brown haze often hanging over metropolitan areas.

Solid and hazardous waste disposal is a universal urban strain, and the issue is on many political agendas. In the world's poorest countries, "garbage pickers" (usually women and children) are symbols of abject poverty. In North America, toxic wastes are frequently transported long distances; this introduces the risk of ocean, highway, and rail accidents, causing serious local contamination.

Pollution also often occurs as a result of armed conflict. Lebanon, for example, suffered extensive environmental damage after its oil depots were hit by Israeli bombers in 2006.

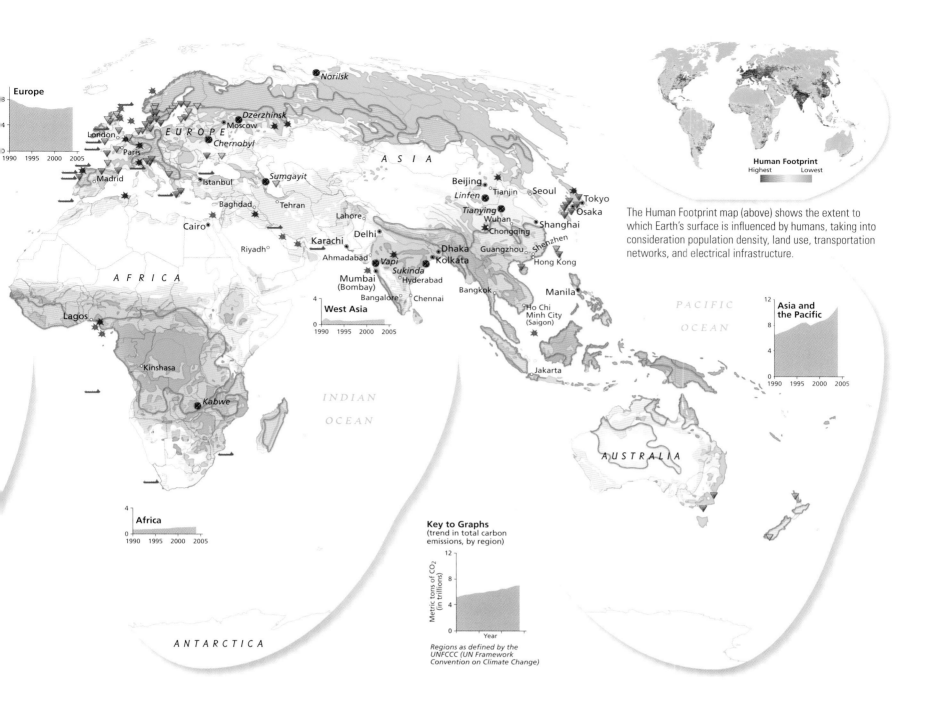

Europe
1990 1995 2000 2005

Norilsk

Dzerzhinsk
Moscow
Chernobyl

London
E U R O P E
Paris
Madrid
Istanbul
Sumgayit
Baghdad
Tehran
Cairo
Riyadh

A S I A

Beijing
Linfen Tianjin   Seoul
Tianying   Tokyo
Wuhan   Osaka
Chongqing   Shanghai
Lahore
Delhi
Karachi
Ahmadabad
Vapi
Sukinda
Mumbai (Bombay)
Bangalore
Hyderabad
Chennai
Dhaka
Kolkata
Guangzhou
Shenzhen
Hong Kong
Bangkok

A F R I C A

Lagos

Kinshasa

Kabwe

INDIAN OCEAN

West Asia
1990 1995 2000 2005

Manila

Ho Chi Minh City (Saigon)

Jakarta

PACIFIC OCEAN

Asia and the Pacific
1990 1995 2000 2005

A U S T R A L I A

ANTARCTICA

Africa
1990 1995 2000 2005

Key to Graphs
(trend in total carbon emissions, by region)

Metric tons of CO$_2$ (in trillions)

Year

Regions as defined by the UNFCCC (UN Framework Convention on Climate Change)

Human Footprint
Highest   Lowest

The Human Footprint map (above) shows the extent to which Earth's surface is influenced by humans, taking into consideration population density, land use, transportation networks, and electrical infrastructure.

Water Scarcity

Shortages of drinking water are increasing in many parts of the world, and the United Nations' Global Environment Outlook (GEO-4) predicts that by 2025, if present trends continue, 1.8 billion people will be living in countries or regions with absolute water scarcity and that two-thirds of the world population could be subject to water stress.

Water is essential for health, hygiene, agriculture, power generation, industry, and transportation, as well as for maintaining healthy freshwater habitats. With increasing pressures from population growth, industrialization, higher standards of living, and climate change, the situation can only worsen. Scarcity of this critical resource will continue to be a major obstacle to economic development in many of the world's poorest regions, from Asia through Central and South America and across most of Africa.

Some countries are pumping groundwater more rapidly than it can be replaced, an activity that will lead to even greater water shortages. In river basins where water is shared among jurisdictions, political tensions are likely to increase. This is particularly so in the Middle East, North Africa, and East Africa, where the availability of fresh water is less than 1,300 cubic yards (1,000 cubic meters) per person per year; water-rich countries such as Iceland, New Zealand, and Canada enjoy more than a hundred times as much.

Irrigation can be a particularly wasteful use, with up to 70 percent of the water being lost through leaky pipes. In many of the world's cities, aging distribution systems are also a problem, with losses from leakages exceeding 40 percent in cities across North America and Europe.

Land Degradation and Desertification

Deserts exist where rainfall is too little and too erratic to support life except in a few favored localities. Even in these "oases," occasional sandstorms may inhibit agricultural activity. In semiarid zones, lands can easily become degraded or desert-like if they are overused or subject to long or frequent drought. The Sahel of Africa faced this situation in the 1970s and early 1980s, but rainfall subsequently returned to normal, and some of the land recovered.

Often, an extended drought over a wide area can trigger desertification if the land has already been degraded by human actions. Causes of degradation include overgrazing, deforestation, overcultivation, overconsumption of groundwater, and the salinization/waterlogging of irrigated lands.

An emerging issue is the effect of climate warming on desertification: Warming will probably lead to more drought in more parts of the world. As glaciers begin to disappear, the meltwater flowing through semiarid downstream areas diminishes as a consequence.

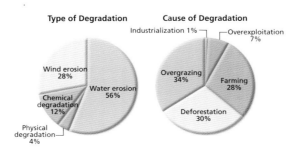

Type of Degradation

Wind erosion 28%
Water erosion 56%
Chemical degradation 12%
Physical degradation 4%

Cause of Degradation

Industrialization 1%
Overexploitation 7%
Overgrazing 34%
Farming 28%
Deforestation 30%

Deforestation

Widespread deforestation in the wet tropics is largely the result of short-term and unsustainable uses. In Mexico, Brazil, and Peru, only 30, 42, and 45 percent (respectively) of the total land area still has a closed forest cover. International agencies such as FAO, UNEP, UNESCO, WWF/IUCN, and others are working to improve the situation through education, restoration, and land protection. Venezuela enjoys a very high level of forest protection (63 percent); by comparison, Russia protects just 2 percent.

Forest loss has contributed to the atmospheric buildup of carbon dioxide (a greenhouse gas; see sidebar opposite), changes in rainfall patterns (in Brazil at least), soil erosion, and soil nutrient losses. Deforestation in the wet tropics, where more than half of the world's species and millions of forest people live, is the main cause of biodiversity loss. In contrast, forest cover in temperate zones has increased slightly in the last 50 years because of the adoption of conservation practices and because forests have replaced some abandoned farmlands.

Million hectares

20
10
0
-10
-20
-30
-40
-50
-60
-70

Europe
Australia/Oceania
North/Central America
Asia
Africa
South America

Changes in Forest Area (1990–2005)

IN RECENT YEARS, environmental groups and world organizations have identified certain sites and land areas whose value is so great, and status so critical, that they require special protection.

This protection takes various forms. UNESCO's World Heritage Committee has identified more than 875 sites that are of great cultural or natural value. Some are very famous: Stonehenge, the Great Wall of China, the Taj Mahal, the Great Barrier Reef, and the Grand Canyon, for example. Others are monuments to important and sometimes tragic chapters in history: Auschwitz in Poland and the Senegalese island of Gorée, which was for 400 years the largest slaving station on the African coast. Some sites are threatened natural features of great value: the Danube Delta in Romania, for instance, and Lake Baikal in Russia.

Conservationists have identified 34 "biodiversity hotspots" (see World Biodiversity, pp. 42-43) that make up less than 2.5 percent of Earth's land surface but are the only remaining habitats for 50 percent of all plant species and 42 percent of all nonfish vertebrates. Currently, the average protected area coverage of hotspots is 10 percent of their original extent.

Though "protected areas" vary greatly in their objectives, the extent to which they are integrated into the wider landscape, and the effectiveness with which they are managed, provide powerful evidence of a nation's commitment to conservation.

World Heritage Sites
- Cultural
- Natural
- Mixed site (site with both cultural and natural value)

Designated Protected Areas

An array of overlapping conventions designed to preserve everything from wetlands, seas, and wilderness to birds and biogenetic reserves protects approximately 11.5 percent of Earth's land area. In contrast, less than one percent of the total ocean area is protected.

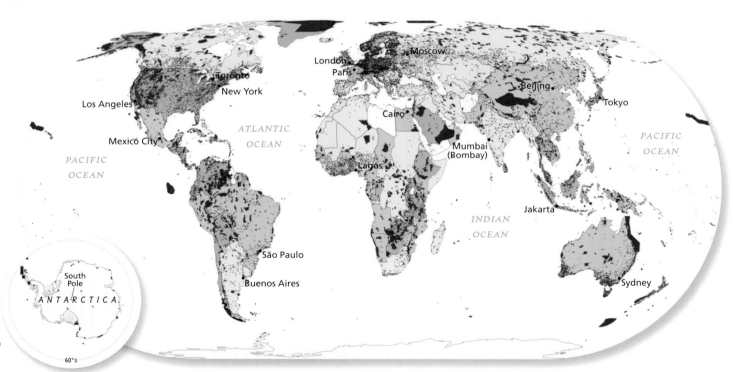

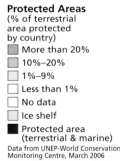

Protected Areas
(% of terrestrial area protected by country)
- More than 20%
- 10%–20%
- 1%–9%
- Less than 1%
- No data
- Ice shelf
- Protected area (terrestrial & marine)

Data from UNEP-World Conservation Monitoring Centre, March 2006

COUNTRY (WITH TOTAL AREA >11,000 SQ. MI.)	PERCENTAGE OF LAND PROTECTED	GDP PER CAPITA (U.S. $)	POP. DENSITY (SQ. MI.)
COUNTRIES WITH HIGHEST % PROTECTED AREA			
Venezuela	70.3	12,900	79
Zambia	41.5	1,400	42
Tanzania	39.7	1,400	110
Saudi Arabia	38.5	24,100	37
Panama	37.2	11,300	116
Guatemala	32.6	4,900	325
Colombia	32.6	8,300	101
New Zealand	32.1	27,000	41
Germany	31.5	35,600	596
Estonia	31.4	20,800	77

COUNTRY (WITH TOTAL AREA >11,000 SQ. MI.)	PERCENTAGE OF LAND PROTECTED	GDP PER CAPITA (U.S. $)	POP. DENSITY (SQ. MI.)
COUNTRIES WITH LOWEST % PROTECTED AREA			
Iraq	0.0	4,000	175
Yemen	0.0	2,400	107
Libya	0.1	14,600	9
Lesotho	0.2	1,400	154
Haiti	0.3	1,300	850
Afghanistan	0.3	800	130
Uruguay	0.4	12,700	49
Bosnia and Herzegovina	0.5	7,600	195
Somalia	0.8	600	36
Mauritania	1.1	2,100	8

CONTINENT OR REGION	SQUARE MILES PROTECTED	AS PERCENTAGE OF TOTAL LAND AREA
PROTECTED LAND AREAS BY REGION		
North America	1,249,049	16.5
South America	1,370,046	19.8
Europe	877,583	9.0
Africa	1,187,394	10.2
Asia	1,193,905	12.0
Australia/Oceania	382,786	12.3
Antarctica	1,749	0.03
WORLD	**6,653,720**	**11.5**

London
Paris
Moscow
EUROPE
ASIA
Cairo
AFRICA
Lagos
Beijing
Tokyo
Mumbai (Bombay)
INDIAN OCEAN
Jakarta
PACIFIC OCEAN
AUSTRALIA
Sydney
ANTARCTICA

Endemism

Regional Share of Plant Endemism

South America 24%
Africa 10%
North America 17%
Europe 2%
Australia/Oceania 12%
Asia 35%

Endemism—the presence of species found nowhere else—is a key criterion for determining conservation priorities, as areas with high levels of endemism are the most vulnerable to biodiversity loss. The highest levels of endemism occur on oceanic islands and in montane regions.

Ouratea dependens is one of thousands of plants unique to Madagascar.

The World Heritage Site System

NATURAL HERITAGE SITE
Canada's Tatshenshini-Alsek Provincial Wilderness holds a portion of the largest nonpolar ice cap and hundreds of valley glaciers; it is the last major stronghold for North America's grizzly bears. The park designation averted what would have been an enormous open-pit mine.

CULTURAL HERITAGE SITE
Site of some of the most important monuments of ancient Greece, the Acropolis illustrates the civilizations, myths, and religions that flourished there for a period of over a thousand years. Europe claims about half of the world's cultural heritage sites, with over 300.

MIXED HERITAGE SITE
The town of Ohrid, on the shores of Lake Ohrid in the former Yugoslav Republic of Macedonia, exemplifies a mixed heritage site. The ten-million-year-old lake may be the oldest in Europe, and the town is one of the continent's oldest continuously inhabited sites.

WORLD HERITAGE LIST

The World Heritage List was established under the terms of the 1972 UNESCO "Convention Concerning the Protection of the World Cultural and Natural Heritage."

The first 12 World Heritage Sites were named in 1978; among them were L'Anse aux Meadows in Canada, the site of the first Viking settlement in North America; the Galápagos Islands; the cathedral of Aachen, Germany; the historic city center of Krakow, Poland; the island of Gorée,

off Senegal; and Mesa Verde and Yellowstone National Parks in the United States.

New sites are added annually. At the time of publication, the list comprised 878 sites, with 679 cultural, 174 natural, and 25 mixed sites, located in 145 countries. On average, 30 newly designated sites are added to the list each year, but 2000 must have been considered an auspicious time for listings; 61 sites were added that year, the largest number ever.

MOST VISITED NATURAL HERITAGE SITES

NAME	SIZE OF SITE (SQ. MI.)	COUNTRY	VISITORS PER YEAR
Great Smoky Mountains National Park	805	United States	9,205,037
Wet Tropics of Queensland	3,453	Australia	5,000,000
Canadian Rocky Mountain Parks	8,907	Canada	6,017,221
Grand Canyon National Park	1,880	United States	4,308,549
Yosemite National Park	1,176	United States	3,272,155
Olympic National Park	1,425	United States	3,047,234
Yellowstone National Park	3,428	United States	2,866,785
Glacier/Waterton National Park	1,767	U.S./Canada	2,399,161
Great Barrier Reef	134,633	Australia	1,971,945

THERE IS A GROWING CONSENSUS that globalization is defined by increasing levels of interdependence over vast distances, not just in the economic dimension, but along the lines of person-to-person contact, technological connectivity, and political ties. In many important ways, global integration is continuing to deepen over the years—and ties between countries have continued to strengthen, despite deterrents such as acts of terror, stalling of trade talks, and divisions over international peace and security issues.

The A.T. Kearney/*Foreign Policy* magazine Globalization Index "reverse engineers" the globalization phenomenon and quantifies its most important component indicators—spanning trade, finance, political engagement, information technology, and personal contact—to determine the rankings of 72 places. Together, they account for 97 percent of the world's gross domestic product (GDP) and 88 percent of the world's population. The index measures 12 variables, which are divided into four "baskets": economic integration, technological connectivity, personal contact, and political engagement.

In years past, Western European countries have claimed many of the top spots as engaged participants in the international system. Small trading countries like Singapore have tended to take top places in the index due in part to their particular reliance on other countries for trade, investment, and tourism.

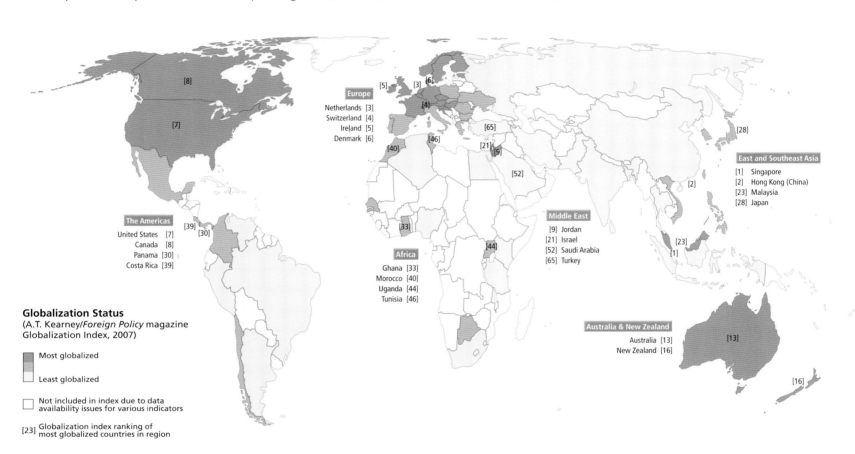

Europe
Netherlands [3]
Switzerland [4]
Ireland [5]
Denmark [6]

East and Southeast Asia
[1] Singapore
[2] Hong Kong (China)
[23] Malaysia
[28] Japan

The Americas
United States [7]
Canada [8]
Panama [30]
Costa Rica [39]

Middle East
[9] Jordan
[21] Israel
[52] Saudi Arabia
[65] Turkey

Africa
Ghana [33]
Morocco [40]
Uganda [44]
Tunisia [46]

Australia & New Zealand
Australia [13]
New Zealand [16]

Globalization Status
(A.T. Kearney/*Foreign Policy* magazine Globalization Index, 2007)

- Most globalized
- Least globalized
- Not included in index due to data availability issues for various indicators
- [23] Globalization index ranking of most globalized countries in region

Transnational Corporations

Transnational corporations have played an important role in global economic integration, through sales, investments, and operations in countries around the world. In fact, a number of them have assets equivalent to or larger than the nominal GDPs of some countries. Many of these companies have also made their non-economic influence felt as their products and services shape consumption habits, business practices, and local cultures.

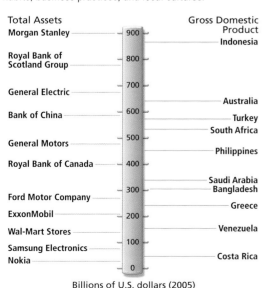

Total Assets
Morgan Stanley
Royal Bank of Scotland Group
General Electric
Bank of China
General Motors
Royal Bank of Canada
Ford Motor Company
ExxonMobil
Wal-Mart Stores
Samsung Electronics
Nokia

Gross Domestic Product
Indonesia
Australia
Turkey
South Africa
Philippines
Saudi Arabia
Bangladesh
Greece
Venezuela
Costa Rica

Billions of U.S. dollars (2005)

Extremes of Globalization

For the fourth time in seven years, Singapore topped the Globalization Index as the most globalized country in the world. Hong Kong debuted in the 2007 index in second place and distinguished itself with the highest scores in both the economic and the personal contact dimensions. Smaller countries tend to be more globalized. Eight of the index's top ten places have land areas smaller than the U.S. state of Indiana, and seven have fewer than eight million citizens. Countries such as Singapore and the Netherlands lack natural resources while some others, like Denmark and Ireland, have limited domestic markets and no choice but to open up and attract trade and foreign investment.

Those who seek to expand globalization's benefits have their work cut out for them. The bottom ten are home to more than three billion people. Many indicators are measured on a per-capita basis, and gains from globalization may be slow to reach the massive populations of these countries.

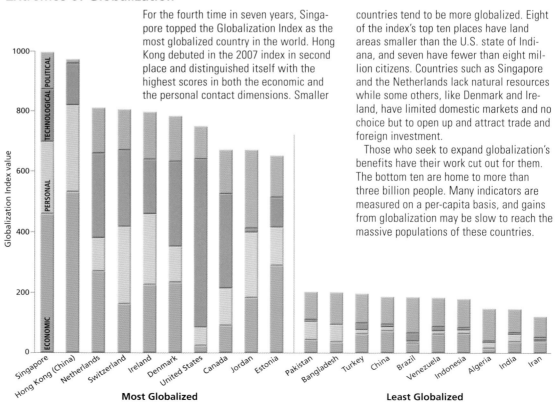

Most Globalized

Least Globalized

Economic Integration

Economic integration combines data on trade and foreign direct investment. Measured as a percentage of gross domestic product (GDP), foreign direct investment flows include investments in physical assets, such as plant and equipment, both into and out of a country. These measures reflect a country's dependence on global trade and investment; however, they do not necessarily reflect economic strength.

Foreign Direct Investment (combined inflow and outflow as a percentage of Gross Domestic Product, 2005)
- More than 10%
- 5%–10%
- 2.5%–4.9%
- 1.0%–2.4%
- Less than 1%
- No data

Personal Contact

Personal contact tracks international travel and tourism, international telephone traffic, and cross-border remittances and personal transfers (including worker remittances, compensation to employees, and other person-to-person and non-governmental transfers). International telephone calls sum up the total number of minutes of telephone traffic into and out of a country on a per-capita basis.

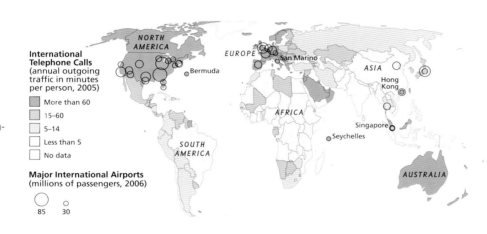

International Telephone Calls (annual outgoing traffic in minutes per person, 2005)
- More than 60
- 15–60
- 5–14
- Less than 5
- No data

Major International Airports (millions of passengers, 2006)
- 85
- 30

Technological Connectivity

Technological connectivity counts the number of Internet users, hosts, and secure servers through which transactions are carried out. These indicators measure penetration—that is, how many users there are, as well as how widespread the infrastructure is, for each country. The Internet has broken down physical borders, bridging continents and multiplying networks between businesses, governments, and citizens at a faster pace than ever.

Internet Use (users per 100 inhabitants, 2005)
- More than 60
- 30–60
- 15–29
- 5–14
- Less than 5
- No data

Political Engagement

Political engagement includes each country's memberships in a variety of representative international organizations, personnel and financial contributions to UN peacekeeping missions, ratification of selected multilateral treaties, and amounts of governmental transfer payments and receipts. The measures provide an indication of how various countries rank as participants of international arrangements relative to their economic and population sizes.

Government Contributions to International Aid (in millions of U.S. dollars, 2005)
- More than 5,000
- 1,000–5,000
- 100–999
- 10–99
- Less than 10
- No data

International Outsourcing

Improvements in communication technologies, such as the Internet and digital telephone lines, are making it increasingly possible for firms to source their service inputs from suppliers abroad. Recent examples include call centers and computer software development services provided by India to the rest of the world. Until recently, global production networks mostly involved the offshoring of manufactured intermediate inputs, whereas now many services as well can be produced in one country and utilized in another.

TRENDS IN OUTSOURCING

International outsourcing of services has been steadily increasing but it is still at relatively low levels. Although U.S. business service imports have roughly doubled in each of the past several decades, they remained at less than one percent of total GDP in 2007. India, reported to be the recipient of significant outsourcing, itself outsources a large amount of services.

Imports in Business Services as a Share of GDP
- China
- India
- United Kingdom
- United States

As shown in the graph below, the U.K. and the U.S. have significant net surpluses in business services. But this is not true for all industrialized countries. The data reveal no clear pattern of developing or industrial countries either being net exporters or net importers. For example, in addition to the U.K. and the U.S. having a net surplus in business services, India also does. Yet, Indonesia has a large net deficit in business services, as do Germany and Ireland.

Balance of Trade in Business Services

TOP OUTSOURCERS OF BUSINESS SERVICES

VALUE (BILLIONS OF U.S. DOLLARS)

United States	52
Germany	46
France	34
Italy	32
Netherlands	31
United Kingdom	31
Japan	26
Ireland	26

In dollar value terms, the U.S. ranks highest in outsourcing of business services, but as a share of the country's overall GDP, its value is comparatively low (0.53 percent in 2007). In smaller countries, trade generally accounts for a larger percentage of GDP. Among the top relative outsourcers of business services are several small developing countries, such as Angola (16 percent of GDP), Lebanon (12 percent), Congo (10 percent), Azerbaijan (9 percent), and the Seychelles (8 percent).

THE TECHNOLOGICAL REVOLUTION that began in the 1950s has given rise to a new Information Age in which global communications networks underpin virtually every facet of modern life. Each day, trillions of dollars worth of goods and services are traded worldwide in the form of bits and bytes, zipping through space, under the seas, beneath our feet, and in the air around us. Information has never been so plentiful, or so cheap. The first mass-produced book, the Gutenberg Bible, took up to two years to print and was beyond the means of all but a wealthy few. Today, a copy of the Bible can be downloaded over the Internet for free in seconds.

The Net itself has quickly evolved into a ubiquitous "network of networks" carrying everything from financial data to phone calls, entertainment to e-shopping, messaging to multimedia. Now the stage is set for a paradigm shift that will see inanimate objects around us become part of an intelligent "Internet of things," exchanging information spontaneously without the need for human intervention.

Already, tiny radio-frequency tags track goods from manufacturer to consumer; soon they could be providing information about a person's identity, buying habits, medical history, and more. Work is also underway on networks of miniscule wireless sensors capable of measuring a huge range of environmental variables, from temperature, pressure, and movement to whether a refrigerator needs restocking.

Centers of Technological Innovation

With access to information technology (IT) now a major determinant of economic growth and social development, researchers are working on ways to measure and map the distribution of technology.

The Technological Achievement Index aims to provide a country-by-country snapshot of IT penetration by measuring local levels of innovation, access to newer technologies like the Internet, the availability of old technology (e.g., telephones and electricity), and the potential for future skills development via schools and training.

The Technological Innovation Index, meanwhile, shines a spotlight on the centers of innovation that are driving today's technological revolution. Each country is assigned an innovation score based on the number of patents generated by its residents, which is then weighted against national population figures to provide a global perspective. The results can be surprising, with some of the world's smaller nations easily outstripping the industrial giants.

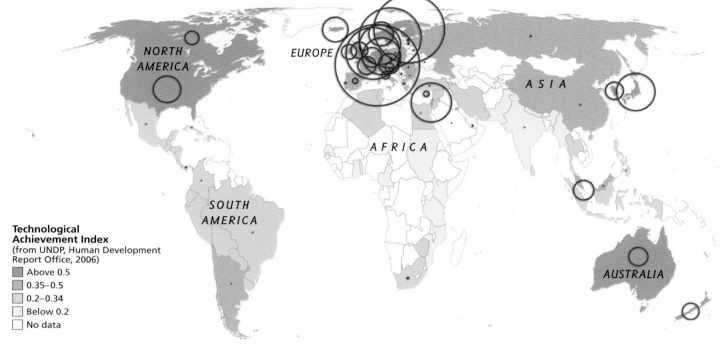

Technological Achievement Index
(from UNDP, Human Development Report Office, 2006)
- Above 0.5
- 0.35–0.5
- 0.2–0.34
- Below 0.2
- No data

Technological Innovation Index
(international patent applications per 1 million people)

424.1 (maximum)

29.3 (average)
0.3 (minimum)

Data from World Intellectual Property Organization, 2006

424.1	Switzerland	100.9	Belgium	10.5	Czech Republic	2.3	Belarus
354.4	Finland	95.8	Australia	9.7	Estonia	1.9	China
311.4	Sweden	90.9	South Korea	7.6	South Africa	1.4	Malaysia
269.6	Netherlands	90.9	France	6.5	Latvia	1.4	Brazil
229.8	Luxembourg	85.0	New Zealand	5.9	Slovakia	1.3	Saudi Arabia
204.9	Denmark	84.4	United Kingdom	5.0	Portugal	1.3	Mexico
202.1	Israel	76.6	Ireland	5.0	Greece	1.1	Ukraine
193.7	Japan	70.1	Canada	5.0	United Arab Emirates	1.0	Cuba
191.6	Germany	43.0	Slovenia	4.0	Panama	0.7	Egypt
138.4	United States	39.4	Italy	3.8	Russia	0.6	Romania
128.8	Iceland	28.0	Cyprus	3.3	former Serb. & Mont.	0.6	India
124.5	Norway	25.4	Spain	2.7	Bulgaria	0.5	Colombia
103.8	Austria	16.0	Croatia	2.5	Poland	0.5	Argentina
101.0	Singapore	15.6	Hungary	2.3	Turkey	0.3	Philippines

Milestones in Technology

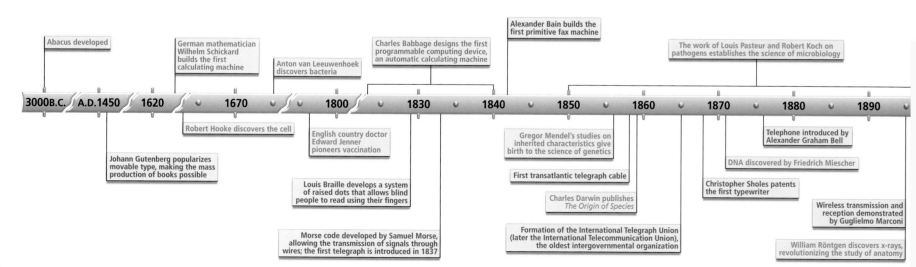

Abacus developed

German mathematician Wilhelm Schickard builds the first calculating machine

Anton van Leeuwenhoek discovers bacteria

Charles Babbage designs the first programmable computing device, an automatic calculating machine

Alexander Bain builds the first primitive fax machine

The work of Louis Pasteur and Robert Koch on pathogens establishes the science of microbiology

3000 B.C. | A.D. 1450 | 1620 | 1670 | 1800 | 1830 | 1840 | 1850 | 1860 | 1870 | 1880 | 1890

Robert Hooke discovers the cell

English country doctor Edward Jenner pioneers vaccination

Gregor Mendel's studies on inherited characteristics give birth to the science of genetics

Telephone introduced by Alexander Graham Bell

Johann Gutenberg popularizes movable type, making the mass production of books possible

Louis Braille develops a system of raised dots that allows blind people to read using their fingers

First transatlantic telegraph cable

DNA discovered by Friedrich Miescher

Christopher Sholes patents the first typewriter

Charles Darwin publishes The Origin of Species

Wireless transmission and reception demonstrated by Guglielmo Marconi

Morse code developed by Samuel Morse, allowing the transmission of signals through wires; the first telegraph is introduced in 1837

Formation of the International Telegraph Union (later the International Telecommunication Union), the oldest intergovernmental organization

William Röntgen discovers x-rays, revolutionizing the study of anatomy

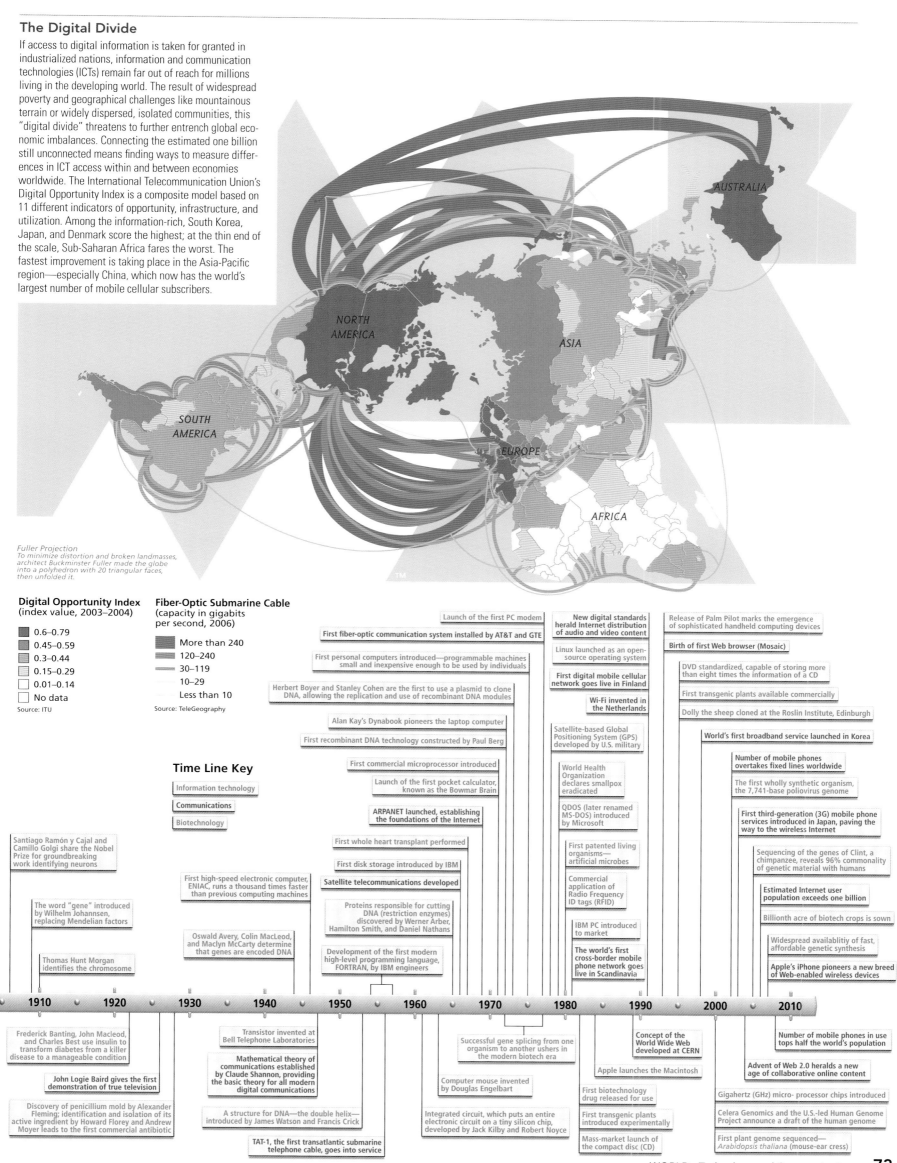

The Digital Divide

If access to digital information is taken for granted in industrialized nations, information and communication technologies (ICTs) remain far out of reach for millions living in the developing world. The result of widespread poverty and geographical challenges like mountainous terrain or widely dispersed, isolated communities, this "digital divide" threatens to further entrench global economic imbalances. Connecting the estimated one billion still unconnected means finding ways to measure differences in ICT access within and between economies worldwide. The International Telecommunication Union's Digital Opportunity Index is a composite model based on 11 different indicators of opportunity, infrastructure, and utilization. Among the information-rich, South Korea, Japan, and Denmark score the highest; at the thin end of the scale, Sub-Saharan Africa fares the worst. The fastest improvement is taking place in the Asia-Pacific region—especially China, which now has the world's largest number of mobile cellular subscribers.

AUSTRALIA

NORTH
AMERICA

ASIA

SOUTH
AMERICA

EUROPE

AFRICA

Fuller Projection
To minimize distortion and broken landmasses, architect Buckminster Fuller made the globe into a polyhedron with 20 triangular faces, then unfolded it.

Digital Opportunity Index
(index value, 2003–2004)

- 0.6–0.79
- 0.45–0.59
- 0.3–0.44
- 0.15–0.29
- 0.01–0.14
- No data

Source: ITU

Fiber-Optic Submarine Cable
(capacity in gigabits per second, 2006)

- More than 240
- 120–240
- 30–119
- 10–29
- Less than 10

Source: TeleGeography

Time Line Key

- Information technology
- Communications
- Biotechnology

Launch of the first PC modem

First fiber-optic communication system installed by AT&T and GTE

First personal computers introduced—programmable machines small and inexpensive enough to be used by individuals

Herbert Boyer and Stanley Cohen are the first to use a plasmid to clone DNA, allowing the replication and use of recombinant DNA modules

Alan Kay's Dynabook pioneers the laptop computer

First recombinant DNA technology constructed by Paul Berg

First commercial microprocessor introduced

Launch of the first pocket calculator, known as the Bowmar Brain

ARPANET launched, establishing the foundations of the Internet

First whole heart transplant performed

First disk storage introduced by IBM

Satellite telecommunications developed

Proteins responsible for cutting DNA (restriction enzymes) discovered by Werner Arber, Hamilton Smith, and Daniel Nathans

Development of the first modern high-level programming language, FORTRAN, by IBM engineers

New digital standards herald Internet distribution of audio and video content

Linux launched as an open-source operating system

First digital mobile cellular network goes live in Finland

Wi-Fi invented in the Netherlands

Satellite-based Global Positioning System (GPS) developed by U.S. military

World Health Organization declares smallpox eradicated

QDOS (later renamed MS-DOS) introduced by Microsoft

First patented living organisms—artificial microbes

Commercial application of Radio Frequency ID tags (RFID)

IBM PC introduced to market

The world's first cross-border mobile phone network goes live in Scandinavia

Release of Palm Pilot marks the emergence of sophisticated handheld computing devices

Birth of first Web browser (Mosaic)

DVD standardized, capable of storing more than eight times the information of a CD

First transgenic plants available commercially

Dolly the sheep cloned at the Roslin Institute, Edinburgh

World's first broadband service launched in Korea

Number of mobile phones overtakes fixed lines worldwide

The first wholly synthetic organism, the 7,741-base poliovirus genome

First third-generation (3G) mobile phone services introduced in Japan, paving the way to the wireless Internet

Sequencing of the genes of Clint, a chimpanzee, reveals 96% commonality of genetic material with humans

Estimated Internet user population exceeds one billion

Billionth acre of biotech crops is sown

Widespread availablitiy of fast, affordable genetic synthesis

Apple's iPhone pioneers a new breed of Web-enabled wireless devices

Santiago Ramón y Cajal and Camillo Golgi share the Nobel Prize for groundbreaking work identifying neurons

The word "gene" introduced by Wilhelm Johannsen, replacing Mendelian factors

Thomas Hunt Morgan identifies the chromosome

First high-speed electronic computer, ENIAC, runs a thousand times faster than previous computing machines

Oswald Avery, Colin MacLeod, and Maclyn McCarty determine that genes are encoded DNA

| 00 | 1910 | 1920 | 1930 | 1940 | 1950 | 1960 | 1970 | 1980 | 1990 | 2000 | 2010 |

Frederick Banting, John Macleod, and Charles Best use insulin to transform diabetes from a killer disease to a manageable condition

John Logie Baird gives the first demonstration of true television

Discovery of penicillin mold by Alexander Fleming; identification and isolation of its active ingredient by Howard Florey and Andrew Moyer leads to the first commercial antibiotic

Transistor invented at Bell Telephone Laboratories

Mathematical theory of communications established by Claude Shannon, providing the basic theory for all modern digital communications

A structure for DNA—the double helix—introduced by James Watson and Francis Crick

TAT-1, the first transatlantic submarine telephone cable, goes into service

Successful gene splicing from one organism to another ushers in the modern biotech era

Computer mouse invented by Douglas Engelbart

Integrated circuit, which puts an entire electronic circuit on a tiny silicon chip, developed by Jack Kilby and Robert Noyce

Concept of the World Wide Web developed at CERN

Apple launches the Macintosh

First biotechnology drug released for use

First transgenic plants introduced experimentally

Mass-market launch of the compact disc (CD)

Number of mobile phones in use tops half the world's population

Advent of Web 2.0 heralds a new age of collaborative online content

Gigahertz (GHz) micro- processor chips introduced

Celera Genomics and the U.S.-led Human Genome Project announce a draft of the human genome

First plant genome sequenced— *Arabidopsis thaliana* (mouse-ear cress)

THE "COOPERATIVE ANARCHY"

of the global Internet, a vast collection of interconnected computer networks communicating through specific protocols (information exchange rules), defies easy characterization or measurement of its behavior. Still, a lack of understanding has not stalled development of technologies that enable and support Internet growth.

Old behavior models for telephone networks no longer apply to packet delivery (data sent over a network) and to application support over multiple links, routers, and Internet Service Providers (ISPs). The sheer volume of traffic and the high capacity of electronic pathways have made Internet monitoring and analysis a more challenging endeavor. Users and providers both benefit from measurements that detect and isolate problems, but watching every link is not practical or particularly effective.

Each ISP monitors its own infrastructure and quality of service; however, business and policy concerns often keep ISPs from sharing such information. Common sense supports creation of a measurement infrastructure that would yield maximal Internet coverage for a reasonable price. But dynamically changing network configurations, as well as complex business and geopolitical concerns, make it difficult to acquire a worldwide view of the Internet.

A BRIEF HISTORY

1960s: ARPANET, a system designed to promote the sharing of supercomputers by researchers in the United States, is commissioned by the Department of Defense.

1970s: People begin to use ARPANET to collaborate on research projects and discuss common interests. In **1974**, a commercial version goes online for the first time.

1980s: Corporations begin to use the Internet for e-mail. As the Internet grows in importance, viruses start to create concerns about online privacy and security. New terms such as "hacker" come into use.

1990s: After the introduction of browsers for navigating the World Wide Web, Internet use expands rapidly (see graph below). By the late 1990s, 200 million people are connected, with online consumer spending totaling in the tens of billions of dollars. During this time, Internet-related companies attract enormous amounts of money from investors.

EARLY 2000s: Internet stock values take a deep plunge following the "dotcom" crash of April 2000. But rapid Internet growth continues, with more than 100 million new users each year. Satellite communications technology allows people to easily access the Internet with handheld devices.

Mapping the Spread of a Computer Virus

The graphics below detail the spread of the Nyxem E-mail Virus during early 2006. This virus operates in much the same way other viruses do, running as an e-mail attachment that attempts to disable antivirus software and harvest e-mail addresses to automatically spread itself. However, the Nyxem virus stands out because it exhibits the rare behavior of reporting its progress to a single web site, thus allowing researchers to undertake a detailed analysis of its activity.

These images, generated with a geographic visualization tool called Cuttlefish, highlight the correlation between human activity at certain times of the day (e.g., booting computers and reading e-mail), the spread of the virus, and the corresponding geographical locations of the infected computers.

The image at upper left includes a key that maps colors to the number of infected hosts. Circles of varying diameter and color depict the number of infected hosts in each region. At top right is a histogram showing the number of infected hosts over the roughly two-week period of analysis.

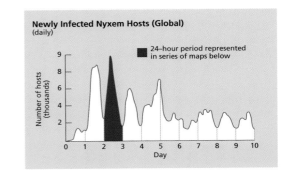

Newly Infected Nyxem Hosts
(per location, in thousands)

329–1,399	5–17	
77–328	2–4	
18–76	1	

Circle diameter represents a logarithmic scale of the number of hosts affected per location at a given time.

Coordinated Universal Time (UTC) is the international time standard. It is the current term for what was commonly referred to as Greenwich Meridian Time (GMT). Zero (0) hours UTC is midnight in Greenwich England, which lies on the zero longitudinal meridian. Universal Time is based on a 24-hour clock; therefore, afternoon hours such as 5 pm UTC are expressed as 17:00 UTC (seventeen hours, zero minutes).

Newly Infected Nyxem Hosts (Global)
(daily)

24-hour period represented in series of maps below

00:00 UTC

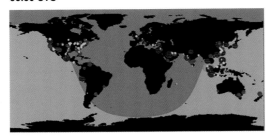

12:00 UTC

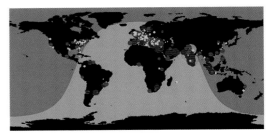

03:00 UTC

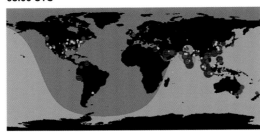

15:00 UTC

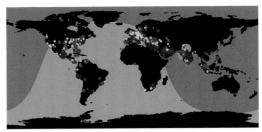

06:00 UTC

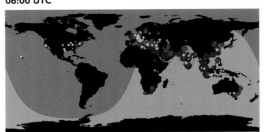

18:00 UTC

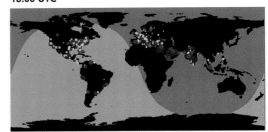

09:00 UTC

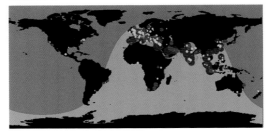

21:00 UTC

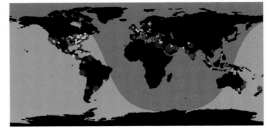

Internet Users Worldwide (estimated), 1995–2007

December 1995: 40 million

December 2000: 393 million

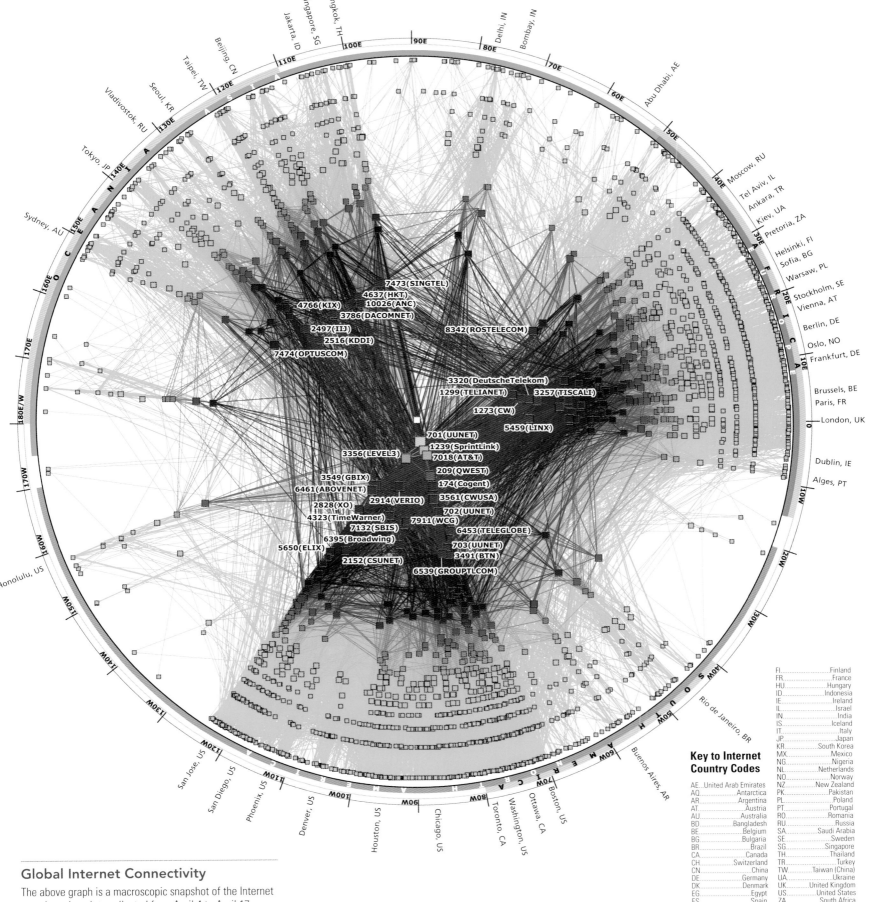

7473 (SINGTEL)
4637 (HKT)
10026 (ANC)
4766 (KIX)
3786 (DACOMNET)
2497 (IIJ)
2516 (KDDI)
7474 (OPTUSCOM)
8342 (ROSTELECOM)

3320 (DeutscheTelekom)
1299 (TELIANET)
3257 (TISCALI)
1273 (CW)
5459 (LINX)
701 (UUNET)
1239 (SprintLink)
3356 (LEVEL3)
7018 (AT&T)
209 (QWEST)
3549 (GBIX)
174 (Cogent)
6461 (ABOVENET)
2914 (VERIO)
3561 (CWUSA)
2828 (XO)
702 (UUNET)
4323 (TimeWarner)
7911 (WCG)
7132 (SBIS)
6453 (TELEGLOBE)
6395 (Broadwing)
5650 (ELIX)
703 (UUNET)
3491 (BTN)
2152 (CSUNET)
6539 (GROUPTLCOM)

Global Internet Connectivity

The above graph is a macroscopic snapshot of the Internet core, based on data collected from April 4 to April 17, 2005. Internet Service Providers (ISPs) are represented by squares, with better-connected ISPs found toward the center. The colors indicate "outdegree" (the number of "next-hop" systems that were observed accepting traffic from a link), from lowest (blue) to highest (yellow).

The top 11 network nodes observed in this data set are based in the United States, and one of the European ISPs in the top 15 observed networks is the European branch of an American company. While ISPs in Europe and Asia have many links with ISPs in the United States, there are few direct links between ISPs in Asia and Europe. Both technical (cabling and router placement and management) and policy factors (business and cost models, geopolitical considerations) contribute to the ISP associations represented in this graph.

Key to Internet Country Codes

AE	United Arab Emirates
AQ	Antarctica
AR	Argentina
AT	Austria
AU	Australia
BD	Bangladesh
BE	Belgium
BG	Bulgaria
BR	Brazil
CA	Canada
CH	Switzerland
CN	China
DE	Germany
DK	Denmark
EG	Egypt
ES	Spain
FI	Finland
FR	France
HU	Hungary
ID	Indonesia
IE	Ireland
IL	Israel
IS	Iceland
IT	Italy
JP	Japan
KR	South Korea
MX	Mexico
NG	Nigeria
NL	Netherlands
NO	Norway
NZ	New Zealand
PK	Pakistan
PL	Poland
PT	Portugal
RO	Romania
RU	Russia
SA	Saudi Arabia
SE	Sweden
SG	Singapore
TH	Thailand
TR	Turkey
TW	Taiwan (China)
UA	Ukraine
UK	United Kingdom
US	United States
ZA	South Africa

Worldwide Distribution of Internet Resources

The worldwide distribution of Internet resources—ISPs, Autonomous System (AS) routers, address space—is highly non-uniform and is unrelated to a region's size or population. For this graph, Internet addresses of routable paths announced on March 21, 2006, were mapped to physical locations and compared with public demographic data.

Legend: Africa · Antarctica · Asia · Australia and Oceania · Europe · Middle East · North America · South America

Area — AQ 9% · RU 11% · CN 6% · IN · AU · US 6% · CA 6% · BR 5% · Africa 20% · Asia 28%

Population — NG · BD · JP · RU · CN 20% · PK · IN 17% · ID · US 4% · BR · Africa 14% · Asia 59% · Europe 9%

Gross Domestic Product — JP 12% · RU · CN 5% · IN · DE 7% · FR 5% · IT 4% · US 30% · BR · Asia 25% · Europe 30% · North America 35%

Address space — JP · RU · KR · UK · DE · NL 4% · US 57% · CA · Asia 12% · Europe 19% · North America 61%

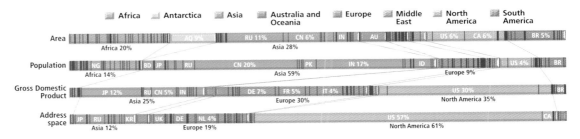

December 2005: 1.05 billion

December 2007: 1.38 billion

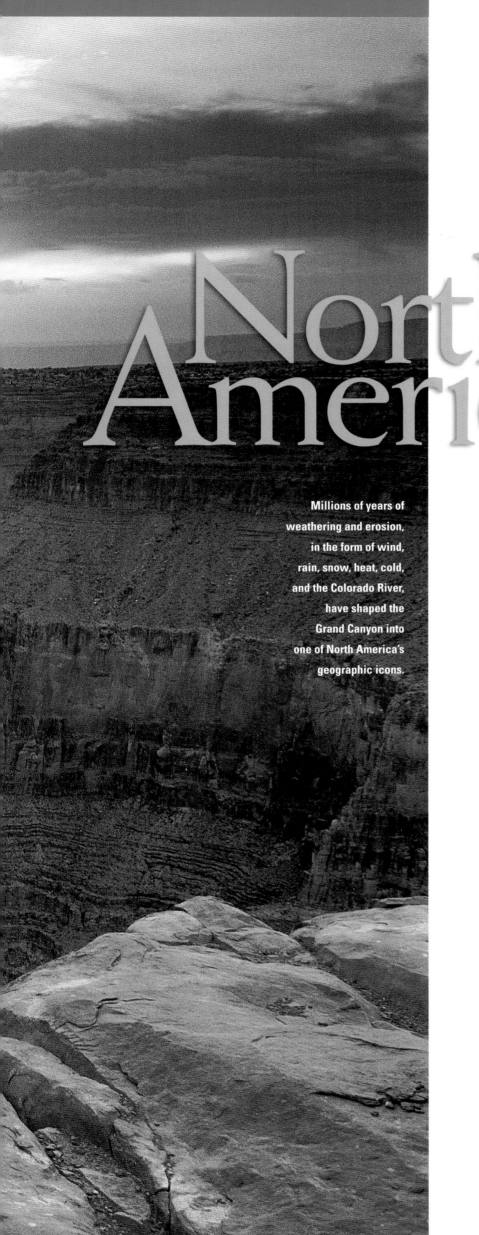

North America

Millions of years of weathering and erosion, in the form of wind, rain, snow, heat, cold, and the Colorado River, have shaped the Grand Canyon into one of North America's geographic icons.

North America is both incredibly old, geologically speaking, and relatively young, when viewed in terms of its human history.

About 200 million years ago, North America separated from Africa when the supercontinent Pangaea began to break apart. For a while, it was attached to Europe, but in time that connection was broken and the North American landmass began roughly assuming its current shape and size. Meanwhile, the other continents were still separating from one another and jockeying for position on the face of the planet.

Some of the oldest stones in the world are found in North America. Dating from nearly four billion years ago, they form the stout underbelly of Canada's frozen tundra. In the east, an ancient mountain system—the Appalachians—runs from the United States into Canada. But not everything is so utterly ancient: North America's human history is only

thousands of years old, while that of Africa, the birthplace of humankind, dates back millions of years. Just in the past couple of centuries, North America has experienced dramatic changes in its population, landscapes, and environment, an incredible transformation brought about by waves of immigration, booming economies, and relentless development.

PHYSICAL GEOGRAPHY From the world's largest island (Greenland) and greatest concentration of fresh water (the Great Lakes) to such spectacular features as the Grand Canyon and Niagara Falls, North America holds a wealth of superlatives. It is also home to Earth's largest and tallest trees (the redwoods of California) and many of its biggest animals (grizzly bears, moose, and bison). The continent is known as well for dramatic extremes of climate—from the sauna-like 134°F (57°C) recorded in California's Death Valley to the brutally cold minus 87°F (-66°C) logged on Greenland's windswept ice cap.

Third largest of the continents, after Asia and Africa, North America encompasses 9.45 million square miles (24.5 million sq km); its northernmost tip is in Greenland (Cape Morris Jesup), and its southernmost point is in Panama (Península de Azuero).

Deeply indented with inlets and bays, North America claims the longest coastline when compared with other continents. Its land is surrounded by vast oceans and sizable seas: the Atlantic in the east, the Pacific in the west, the Arctic in the north, and the Gulf of Mexico and Caribbean Sea in the south. This geographic circumstance kept the continent isolated for millions of years, greatly influencing the development of its flora and fauna, as well as its human history. Into North America's coastal waters pour a number of mighty rivers, including the Saint Lawrence, Rio Grande, Yukon, Columbia, and Mississippi.

Three significant geologic features dominate the continental landmass: the Canadian (Laurentian) Shield; the great Western Cordillera, which includes the Rocky Mountains, Sierra Nevada, and Sierra Madre; and a colossal flatland that embraces the Great Plains, the Mississippi-Missouri River basin, and most of the Great Lakes region. Other major components include the ancient Appalachian Mountains and the predominantly volcanic islands of the Caribbean Sea. The continent peaks out at 20,320 feet (6,194 m) on the summit of Mount McKinley (Denali), in Alaska, and drops to 282 feet (86 m) below sea level in Death Valley.

The climates of North America range from the frigid conditions of the Arctic ice cap to the steamy tropics of Central America (considered part of North America) and the Caribbean; in between are variations of dry, mild, and continental climes.

The continent has an equally diverse biological heritage, ranging from seemingly endless tundra and coniferous forests in the north to vast deserts and dense rain forests in the south. North America once held huge herds of bison, antelope, elk, and other large wildlife, but such populations declined as the human population grew and spread across the continent.

HISTORY Although the exact date will probably never be determined, North America's human history began sometime between 14,000 and 24,000 years ago, when Asiatic nomads crossed the Bering Strait into Alaska. The descendants of these people spread throughout the continent, evolving into distinct tribes with their own lifestyles and more than 550 different languages.

Most of these original Americans were still hunting and gathering when Europeans arrived in North America; however, several groups had already developed sophisticated cultures. By 1200 B.C., the Olmec of Mexico had created what is generally deemed the first "civilization" in the Western Hemisphere; theirs was a highly advanced society with a calendar, writing system, and stonework architecture. About a hundred years later, the Maya took root in Mexico and Central America, reaching an apex around A.D. 700 with the creation of an elaborate religion and sprawling temple cities. In central Mexico, the highly militaristic Toltec and Aztec forged sprawling empires that drew cultural inspiration from both the Olmec and Maya.

One of the most significant moments for North America—indeed, it was among the most influential events in world history—came in 1492, when a Spanish expedition under Christopher Columbus set foot on an island in the Bahamas. This initial landing ushered in an era of European exploration and settlement that would alter the social fabric of the entire continent. In the next few decades, Hernán Cortés vanquished the Aztec, and Spain claimed virtually the whole Caribbean region and Central America. Other Europeans soon followed—English, French, Dutch, Russians, and even Danes—the leading edge of a migration that would become one of the greatest in human history (more than 70 million people and still counting).

The Native American cultures were unable to compete: They were plagued by European diseases, against which they had little or no resistance; unable to counter the superior firepower of the invaders; and relentlessly driven from their lands. The continent's rich tribal mosaic gradually melted away, replaced by myriad European colonies. By the end of the 19th century, these colonies had been superseded by autonomous nation-states, such as Canada, Mexico, and the United States. Since 1960, many of the Caribbean isles have gained independence, yet quite a few remain colonial possessions under the British, French, Dutch, and U.S. flags.

During the past century, both the U.S. and Canada managed to propel themselves into the ranks of the world's richest nations. But the rest of the continent failed to keep pace, plagued by poverty, despotic governments, and social unrest. In the decades since World War II, many of the Spanish-speaking nations—Cuba, the Dominican

The ceremonial core of Tikal, a major Maya cultural and population center in Guatemala's Petén region, covers approximately one square mile (2.5 sq km). From its early beginnings as a small village (900–300 B.C.), Tikal grew in stature and size to house some 50,000 people at its peak (A.D. 600–800). Even in ruins, its massive Temple I (left) and Temple II (right) remain impressive structures amid myriad palaces, plazas, and ball courts.

Republic, Nicaragua, El Salvador, and Guatemala—have been racked by bloody revolution. The U.S., on the other hand, ended the 20th century as the only true superpower, with a military presence and political, economic, and cultural influences that extend around the globe.

CULTURE North America's cultural landscape has changed profoundly over the past 500 years. Before the 16th century, the continent was fragmented into hundreds of different cultures developed along tribal lines. From the Inuit people of the Arctic to the Cuña Indians of the Panama jungle, a majority of North America's people had barely risen above Stone Age cultural levels. Noteworthy exceptions included the great civilizations of Mexico and Central America, the pueblo builders of the southwestern U.S., and the highly organized cultivators of the Great Lakes region and the Mississippi Valley. But for the most part, the average North American was migratory, had no concept of written language, and used stone or wooden tools.

The arrival of the Europeans brought permanent settlements, metal tools (and weapons), and written languages. The newcomers founded towns based on Old World models, some of which would evolve into world-class cities—New York, Los Angeles, Chicago, Toronto, and Mexico City among them. Native tongues gave way to a trio of European languages—English, Spanish, and French— now spoken by most of North America's 529 million people. And ancient beliefs yielded to new religions, like Roman Catholicism and Protestantism, which now dominate the continent's spiritual life. The Europeans brought ideas—concepts like democracy, capitalism, religious choice, and free speech—that continue to shape political, intellectual, and economic life.

Despite common historical threads, the coat that comprises today's North America is one of many colors. Mexico and Central America are dominated by Hispano-Indian culture and tend to have more in common with South America than with their neighbors north of the Rio Grande. Although Anglo-Saxon ways still hold sway in the U.S. and Canada, a surge of immigration from Latin America, Asia, and Pacific islands has introduced new cultural traditions. From the Rastafarians of Jamaica to the Creoles of Martinique, the Caribbean islands have fostered myriad microcultures that blend European, African, and Latin traditions.

ECONOMY When it comes to business and industry, North America— and especially the U.S.—is the envy of the world. No other continent produces such an abundance of merchandise or profusion of crops, and no other major region comes close to North America's per capita resource and product consumption. From the high-tech citadels of Silicon Valley to the dream factories of Hollywood, the continent is a world leader in dozens of fields and industries, including computers, entertainment, aerospace, finance, medicine, defense, and agriculture.

The quest for monetary and material success can be traced all the way back to early European immigrants and the tireless work ethic they brought with them. These people, and their cultural descendants,

sought to improve their standard of living by exploiting the natural wealth of the land. North America's forests, minerals, and farmlands stoked an industrial revolution that by the end of the 19th century had propelled the U.S. into the ranks of the richest and most powerful nations. Indeed, the continent has an abundance of natural resources: vast petroleum reserves in Alaska and around the Gulf of Mexico, huge coal deposits in the Appalachian and Rocky Mountains, swift-flowing rivers to produce hydropower, and fertile soils that lead to copious harvests.

But the most important product has always been ideas—the ability of its inhabitants to imagine. Next is the ability to transform those ideas into reality through experimentation and hard work. Many of the innovations that revolutionized modern life—the telephone, electric lighting, motor vehicles, airplanes, computers, shopping malls, television, the Internet—were either invented or first mass-produced in the U.S.

Globalization has spread U.S. goods—and by extension, American ideas and culture—around the planet. To a large extent this has been facilitated by thousands of miles of open coastline, which allow for numerous major ports and harbors, as well as ready trading partners to the north and south. The creation of the North American Free Trade Association (NAFTA) in 1994 drew Canada and Mexico into the same economic web. But success has brought a host of concerns, not the least of which involves the continued exploitation of natural resources. North America is home to only roughly 8 percent of the planet's people, yet its per capita consumption of energy is almost six times as great as the average for all other continents. Its appetite for timber, metals, and water resources is just as voracious.

Other parts of the continent continue to lag in terms of economic vitality. Most Caribbean nations—along with Costa Rica and Belize— now rely on the tourist industry to generate the bulk of their gross national product, while most Central American countries continue to bank on agricultural commodities such as bananas and coffee. Poverty has spurred millions of Mexicans, Central Americans, and Caribbean islanders to migrate northward (legally and illegally) in search of better lives. Finding ways to integrate these disenfranchised masses into the continent's economic fabric is one of the greatest challenges facing North America in the 21st century.

NORTH AMERICA • Physical and Political

81

Temperature and Precipitation

Average Annual Precipitation

Over 80 inches		Over 200 cm
55–80 inches		140–200 cm
40–54 inches		100–139 cm
25–39 inches		60–99 cm
8–24 inches		20–49 cm
Under 8 inches		Under 20 cm

Resolute (-26°/40°)
Inuvik (-20°/57°)
Cambridge Bay (-28°/46°)
Whitehorse (-1°/57°)
Yellowknife (-18°/61°)
Iqaluit (-15°/46°)
C A N A D A
Edmonton (7°/62°)
Churchill (-17°/54°)
Sept-Îles (6°/59°)
St. John's (24°/59°)
Victoria (40°/60°)
Vancouver (37°/63°)
Calgary (14°/62°)
Winnipeg (-2°/67°)
Québec (10°/67°)
St.-Pierre and Miquelon Fr.
Thunder Bay (5°/64°)
Ottawa (12°/69°)
Montréal (15°/70°)
Halifax (22°/65°)
Toronto (23°/70°)

Average Monthly Temperatures (°F)
(January/July)

Population

People per Square Mile	People per Square Km
Over 500	Over 195
50–500	20–195
10–49	5–19
1–9	1–4
Under 1	Under 1

C A N A D A
Vancouver
Edmonton
Calgary
Montréal
Ottawa
Toronto
St.-Pierre and Miquelon Fr.

Urban Area Population
- ■ 5 million and greater
- ● 750,000–999,999
- ▲ 1 million–4,999,999
- ○ Under 750,000

Azimuthal Equidistant Projection

SCALE 1:14,903,000
1 CENTIMETER = 149 KILOMETERS; 1 INCH = 235 MILES

0 200 400 600 800
KILOMETERS

0 200 400 600 800
STATUTE MILES

Land Use, Agriculture, and Fishing

Major Crops
- Barley
- Beet sugar
- Cattle
- Corn
- Deciduous fruit
- Fish
- Flaxseed
- Forest products
- Oats
- Potatoes
- Rye
- Sheep
- Soybeans
- Swine
- Tobacco
- Wheat

C A N A D A

Predominant Land Use and Land Cover Classes
- Grassland
- Woodland
- Forest
- Mixed-use, including crops
- Cropland
- Wetland
- Desert, barren land
- Ice, cold desert, tundra
- Urban agglomeration

Canada
CANADA

AREA	9,984,670 sq km (3,855,103 sq mi)
POPULATION	33,304,000
CAPITAL	Ottawa 1,145,000
RELIGION	Roman Catholic, Protestant
LANGUAGE	English, French
LITERACY	99%
LIFE EXPECTANCY	80 years
GDP PER CAPITA	$39,300
ECONOMY	**IND:** transportation equipment, chemicals, processed and unprocessed minerals, food products **AGR:** wheat, barley, oilseed, tobacco; dairy products; forest products; fish **EXP:** motor vehicles and parts, industrial machinery, aircraft, telecommunications equipment

Greenland (Denmark)
GREENLAND

SOVEREIGN   LOCAL

AREA	2,166,086 sq km (836,330 sq mi)
POPULATION	58,000
CAPITAL	Nuuk (Godthåb) 15,000
RELIGION	Evangelical Lutheran
LANGUAGE	Greenlandic, Danish, English
LITERACY	100%
LIFE EXPECTANCY	67 years
GDP PER CAPITA	$20,000
ECONOMY	**IND:** fish processing (shrimp, halibut), mining, handicrafts, hides and skins **AGR:** forage crops, garden and greenhouse vegetables; sheep; fish **EXP:** fish and fish products, prawns

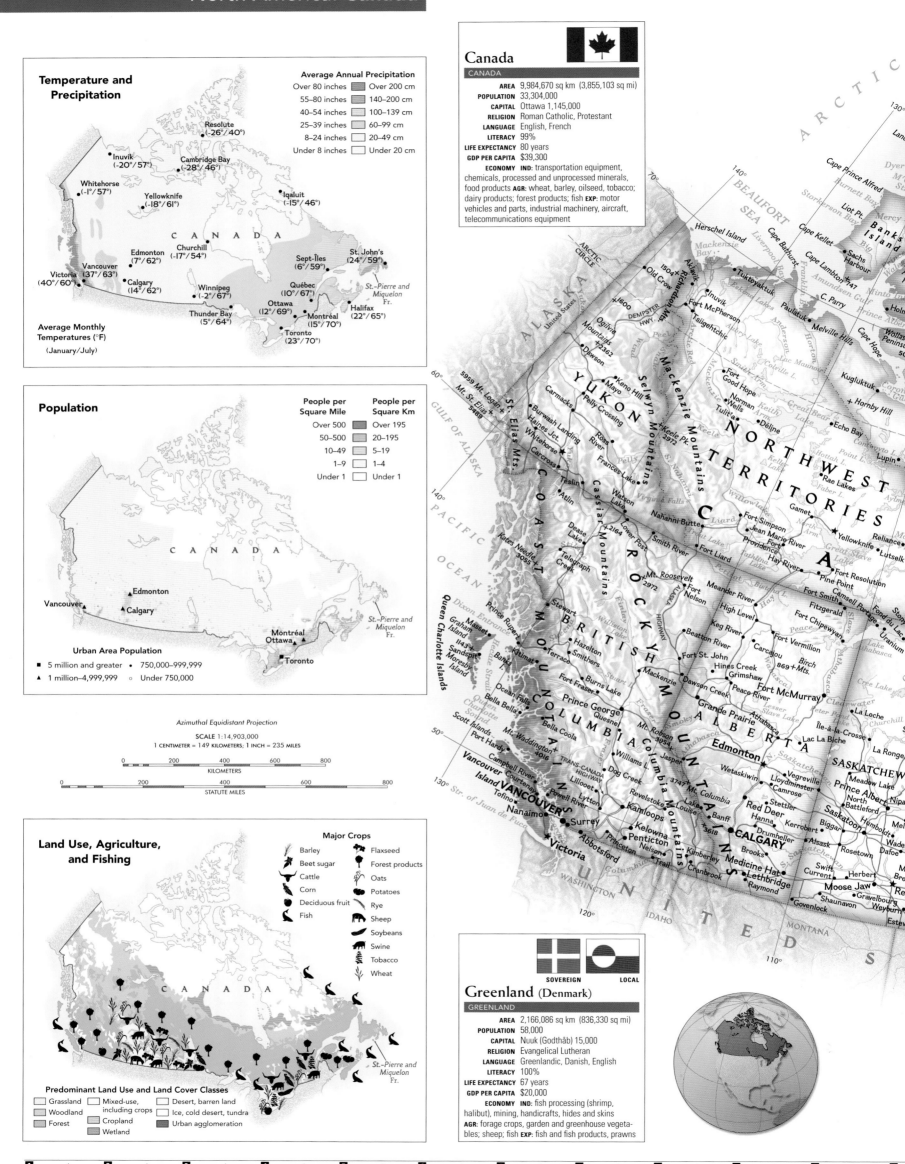

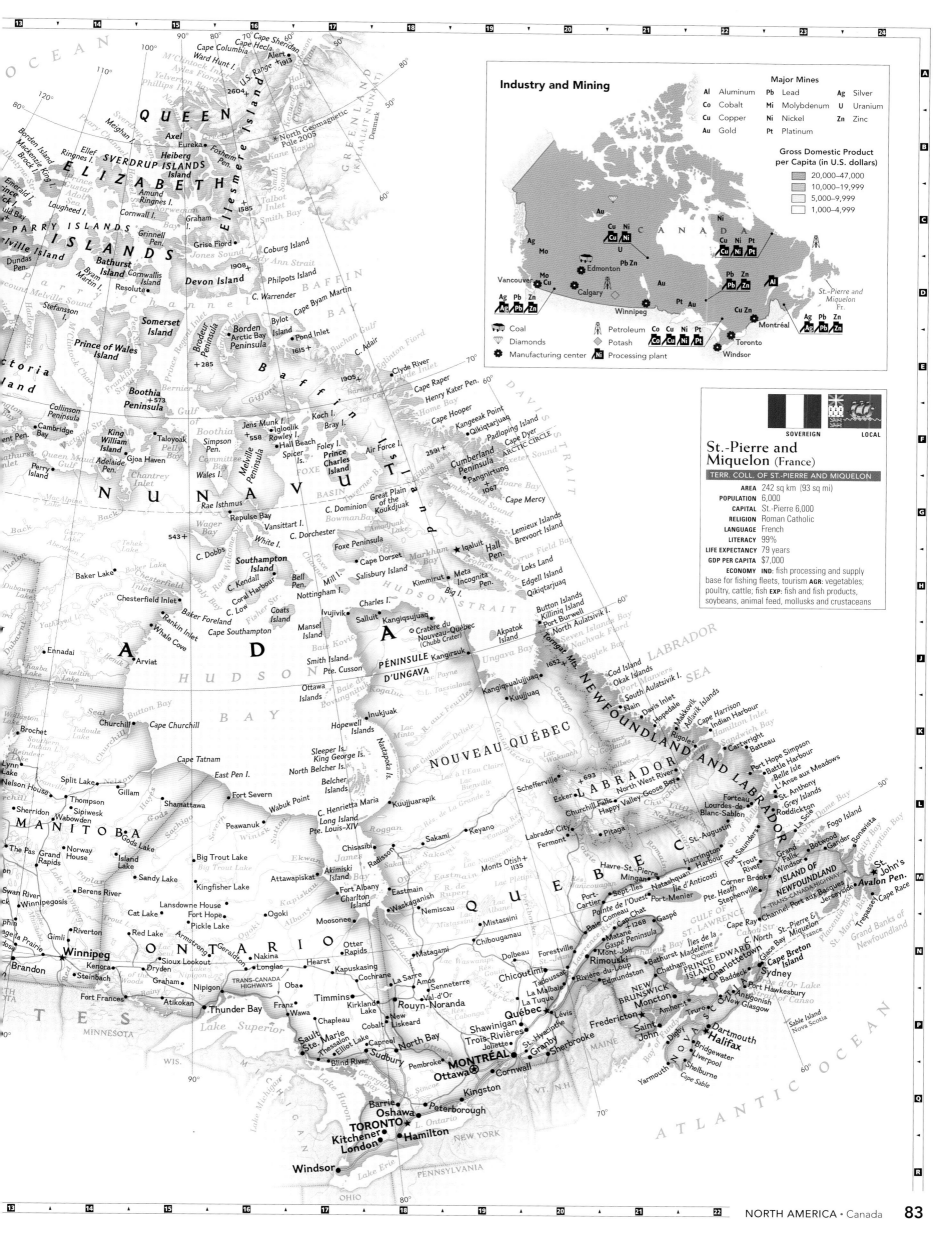

PACIFIC OCEAN

R O C K Y   M O U N T A I N S

GREAT PLAINS

COLUMBIA PLATEAU

GREAT BASIN

COLORADO PLATEAU

SIERRA NEVADA

CASCADE RANGE

COAST RANGE

Str. of Juan de Fuca
Cape Flattery
Cape Disappointment
Cape Blanco
Cape Mendocino
Point Arena
Point Reyes
Farallon Is.
San Francisco Bay
Monterey Bay
Point Sur
Santa Lucia Ra.
Point Buchon
Point Conception
Santa Barbara Channel
San Miguel
Santa Rosa
Santa Cruz
San Nicolas
Santa Catalina
San Clemente
Channel Islands
Gulf of Santa Catalina

+ Mt. Baker 10778
+ Mt. Olympus 7980
Mt. Rainier + 14411
Mt. St. Helens 8366
+ Mt. Adams 12307
Mt. Hood + 11239
+ Mt. Shasta 14162
Klamath Mountains
+ Lassen Peak 10457
Eagle Pk. + 9892
Black Rock Desert
Donner Pass 7088
Pyramid L.
Warner Mts.
Steens Mt. 9733
Goose L.
Harney Basin
Great Sandy Desert
Carson Sink
Mono L.
Tahoe
Tuolumne
+ Boundary Peak 13140
Mt. Whitney 14494 (4418 m)
Death Valley -282 (-86 m)
Mojave Desert
+ Mt. San Antonio 10064
Palomar Mt. 6140 + Salton Sea -232
Imperial Valley
Sacramento Valley
San Joaquin Valley
San Diablo Range
San Joaquin Range

Columbia
Snake
John Day
Willamette
Blue Mountains
Wallowa Mts.
Buffalo Hump 8924
Clearwater Mts.
Illinois Pk. + 7690
Bitterroot Range
Continental Divide
Salmon River Mountains
+ Borah Pk. 12662
Salmon
Snake River Plain
Shoshone Falls
Great Salt Lake Desert
Great Salt Lake
Ruby Dome 11387
Ruby Mts.
Humboldt
Shoshone Mts.
Toiyabe Ra.
Monitor Ra.
Schell Cr. Ra.
Troy Pk. + 11298
Mt. Moriah + 12050
Wheeler Pk. 13063
Bald Mt. 9380
Spring Mts.
Lake Mead
Mount Trumbull 8029
Kaibab Plateau
Grand Canyon
Painted Desert
Black Mts.
Humphreys Peak + 12633
Mogollon Rim
Baldy Peak + 11403
Colorado
Gila
Salt
Sonoran Desert

Penrille Oreille L.
Flathead Lake
Yellowstone
Jackson L.
Yellowstone L.
Grand Teton 13770
Absaroka Range
Snake
Teton
American Falls Res.
Sherman Pk. + 9682
Bear River Ra.
Wind River Ra.
Gannett Pk. 13804
Kings Pk. + 13528
Uinta Mts.
Utah Lake
Wasatch Ra.
Roan Cliffs
Sevier Lake
Sevier
Colorado
Uncompahgre Plateau
Uncompahgre Pk. + 14309
Lake Powell
Chuska Mts.
Matthews Pk. 9512
Continental Divide

Missouri
Milk
Bear Paw Mts.
Fort Peck Lake
Musselshell
Yellowstone
Tongue
Powder
Bighorn
Bighorn Mts.
Cloud Pk. 13165
Belle Fourche
Cheyenne
Laramie Mts.
Laramie Pk. + 10272
Medicine Bow Mts.
Front Range
Longs Peak + 14255
Mt. Elbert + 14433
Pikes Peak 14110
Sangre de Cristo Mts.
Blanca Pk. 14345
Rio Grande
San Juan Mts.
Wheeler Pk. + 13161
Elephant Butte Res.
Sierra Blanca Pk. 11973
San Andres Mts.
Sacramento Mts.
Guadalupe Pk. + 8749
Guadalupe Mts.
Caballo Res.
Black Range
Gila
Rio Grande
Pecos

Souris
Lake Sakakawea
Sheyenne
L. Ashtabula
Heart
Badlands
White Butte + 3506
Little Missouri
Moreau
Grand
Lake Oahe
L. Sharpe
Cheyenne
White
Lake Francis Case
James
Missouri
Niobrara
Sand Hills
N. Platte
Panorama Point + 5423
S. Platte
Platte
Loup
Elkhorn
Republican
Solomon
Smoky Hills + 1654
Smokey Hill
Arkansas
Mt. Sunflower 4039
L. Meredith
Canadian
N. Canadian
Washita
Red Hills
2265 +
Wichita Mts. 2479 +
Llano Estacado
Cap Rock Escarpment
Red
L. Texo
Brazos
Cimarron
Keystone

Geographical Center of the 50 United States
Geographical Center of the 48 Contiguous United States
Great Divide Basin
Flaming Gorge Reservoir

Black Hills
+ Harney Pk. 7242

M E X I C O

Edwards Plateau 2487 +
Hill Country
Amistad Reservoir
Rio Grande
Guadalupe
Nueces
San Antonio
Matagor
Corpus Christi Bay
Baffin Bay
Falcon Lake
Padre Island
TROPIC OF CANCER

ALASKA

CHUKCHI SEA
BEAUFORT SEA
ARCTIC CIRCLE
RUSSIA
Point Barrow
Dease Inlet
Smith Bay
Icy Cape
Teshekpuk Lake
Harrison Bay
Prudhoe Bay
Camden Bay
Demarcation Point
North Slope
Cape Lisburne
Point Hope
Tingmerkpuk Mt. 3787 +
De Long Mountains
Mt. Isto 9060
Davidson Mts.
British Mts.
Philip Smith Mts.
Endicott Mts.
B R O O K S   R A N G E
Baird Mountains
Bering Str.
Diomede Is.
Kotzebue Sd.
C. Prince of Wales
SEWARD PENINSULA
Kobuk
Selawik Lake
Natak
Porcupine
CANADA
U.S.
Yukon Flats
White Mts.
Ray Mts.
Yukon
Konukuk
St. Lawrence Island 2207 +
Norton Sound
Stuart I.
Kaiyuh Mts.
A L A S K A
Tanana
Kuskokwim Mountains
A L A S K A   R A N G E
+ Mt. McKinley (Denali) 20320 (6194 m)
Susitna
Talkeetna Mts.
Mt. Gerdine 11258
Copper
Wrangell Mts.
+ Mt. Blackburn 16390
Chugach Mountains
St. Elias Mountains
Mt. St. Elias 18008
Yukon
KENAI PENINSULA
Cook Inlet
Prince William Sd.
Montague I.
Yakutat Bay
Mt. Fairweather 15300
Cross Sound
Admiralty Island
Chichagof Island
Baranof Island
Kruzof I.
Kupreanof Island
Prince of Wales I.
Revillagigedo Island
ALEXANDER ARCHIPELAGO
C O A S T   M O U N T A I N S
Nunivak I.
Cape Romanzof
Yukon Delta
Yukon
Roberts Mt. + 1675
Kuskokwim Bay
Cape Newenham
Bristol Bay
Iliamna Lake
Kennedy Entrance
GULF OF ALASKA
+ Mt. Katmai 6715
Afognak I.
Kodiak Island
4470 +
Trinity Is.
ALASKA PENINSULA
ALEUTIAN RANGE
+ Mt. Veniaminof 8225
KILBUCK MTS.
BERING SEA
C. Prince of Wales
St. Matthew
Norton Bay

0   100   200   300 km
0   50   100   150 statute mi

Temperature and Precipitation

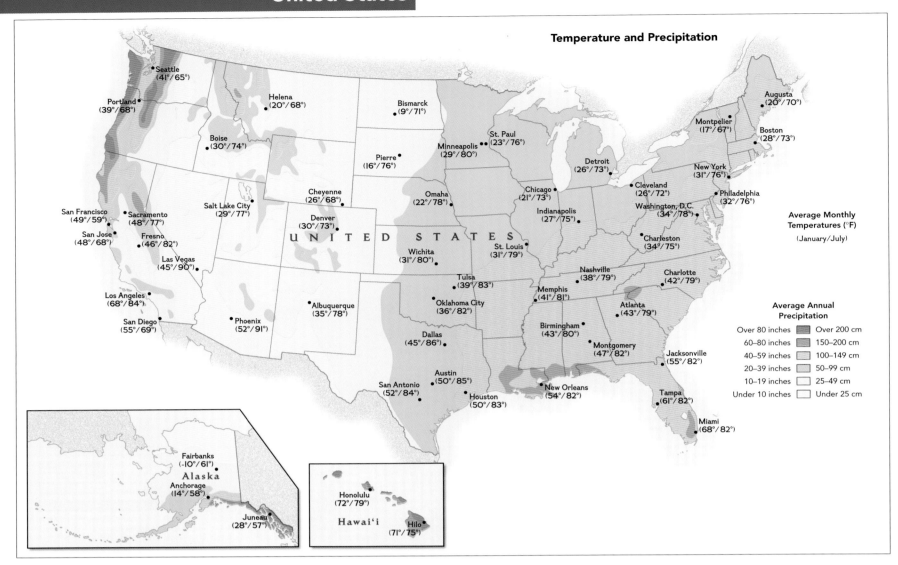

Seattle (41°/65°)
Portland (39°/68°)
Helena (20°/68°)
Bismarck (9°/71°)
Augusta (20°/70°)
Montpelier (17°/67°)
Boston (28°/73°)
Boise (30°/74°)
Pierre (16°/76°)
Minneapolis (29°/80°)
St. Paul (23°/76°)
Detroit (26°/73°)
New York (31°/76°)
San Francisco (49°/59°)
Sacramento (48°/77°)
Salt Lake City (29°/77°)
Cheyenne (26°/68°)
Omaha (22°/78°)
Chicago (21°/73°)
Cleveland (26°/72°)
Philadelphia (32°/76°)
Washington, D.C. (34°/78°)
San Jose (48°/68°)
Fresno (46°/82°)
Denver (30°/73°)
Indianapolis (27°/75°)
Las Vegas (45°/90°)
Wichita (31°/80°)
St. Louis (31°/79°)
Charleston (34°/75°)
Nashville (38°/79°)
Charlotte (42°/79°)
Los Angeles (68°/84°)
Albuquerque (35°/78°)
Tulsa (39°/83°)
Oklahoma City (36°/82°)
Memphis (41°/81°)
Atlanta (43°/79°)
San Diego (55°/69°)
Phoenix (52°/91°)
Dallas (45°/86°)
Birmingham (43°/80°)
Montgomery (47°/82°)
Jacksonville (55°/82°)
Austin (50°/85°)
San Antonio (52°/84°)
Houston (50°/83°)
New Orleans (54°/82°)
Tampa (61°/82°)
Miami (68°/82°)

Fairbanks (-10°/61°)
Alaska
Anchorage (14°/58°)
Juneau (28°/57°)
Honolulu (72°/79°)
Hawai'i
Hilo (71°/75°)

Average Monthly Temperatures (°F)
(January/July)

Average Annual Precipitation

Over 80 inches	Over 200 cm
60–80 inches	150–200 cm
40–59 inches	100–149 cm
20–39 inches	50–99 cm
10–19 inches	25–49 cm
Under 10 inches	Under 25 cm

Land Use, Agriculture, and Fishing

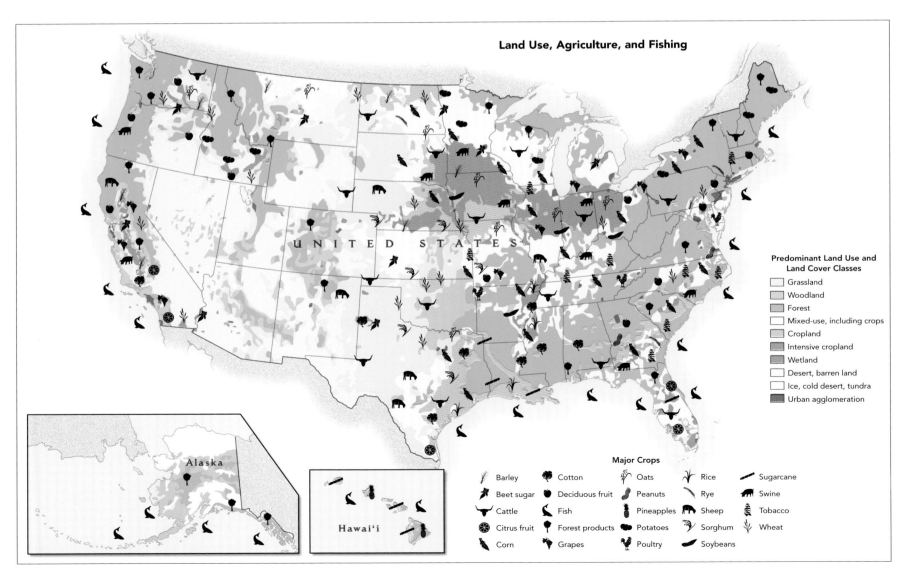

Alaska

Hawai'i

Predominant Land Use and Land Cover Classes

- Grassland
- Woodland
- Forest
- Mixed-use, including crops
- Cropland
- Intensive cropland
- Wetland
- Desert, barren land
- Ice, cold desert, tundra
- Urban agglomeration

Major Crops

Barley	Cotton	Oats	Rice	Sugarcane
Beet sugar	Deciduous fruit	Peanuts	Rye	Swine
Cattle	Fish	Pineapples	Sheep	Tobacco
Citrus fruit	Forest products	Potatoes	Sorghum	Wheat
Corn	Grapes	Poultry	Soybeans	

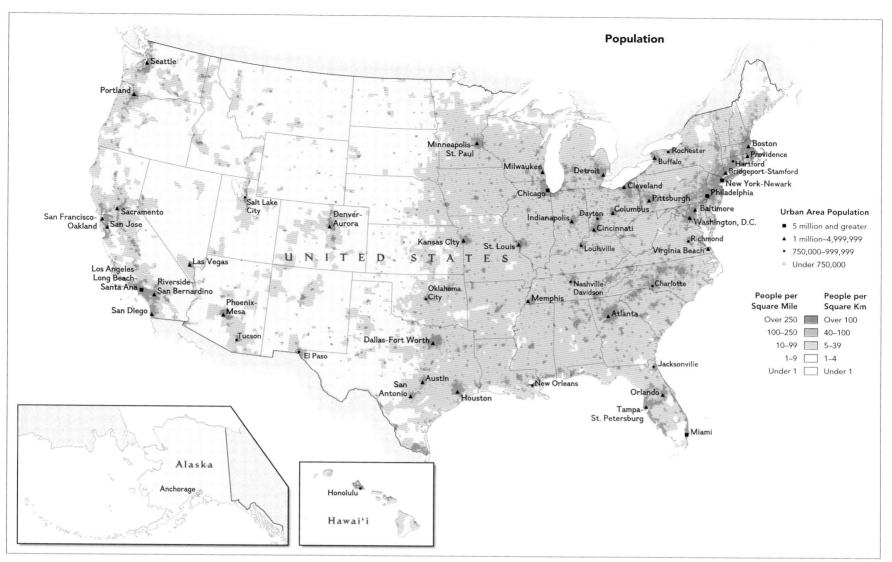

Population

Seattle

Portland

San Francisco-Oakland
Sacramento
San Jose

Los Angeles-
Long Beach-
Santa Ana
Riverside-
San Bernardino

San Diego

Phoenix-
Mesa

Tucson

Las Vegas

Salt Lake
City

Denver-
Aurora

U N I T E D   S T A T E S

El Paso

San
Antonio

Austin

Dallas-Fort Worth

Houston

New Orleans

Oklahoma
City

Kansas City

St. Louis

Memphis

Minneapolis-
St. Paul

Milwaukee

Chicago

Indianapolis

Detroit

Dayton

Cincinnati

Louisville

Nashville-
Davidson

Atlanta

Columbus

Cleveland

Pittsburgh

Rochester

Buffalo

Boston
Providence
Hartford
Bridgeport-Stamford
New York-Newark
Philadelphia

Baltimore

Washington, D.C.

Richmond

Virginia Beach

Charlotte

Jacksonville

Orlando

Tampa-
St. Petersburg

Miami

Urban Area Population
■ 5 million and greater
▲ 1 million–4,999,999
• 750,000–999,999
○ Under 750,000

People per Square Mile	People per Square Km
Over 250	Over 100
100–250	40–100
10–99	5–39
1–9	1–4
Under 1	Under 1

Alaska

Anchorage

Honolulu

Hawai'i

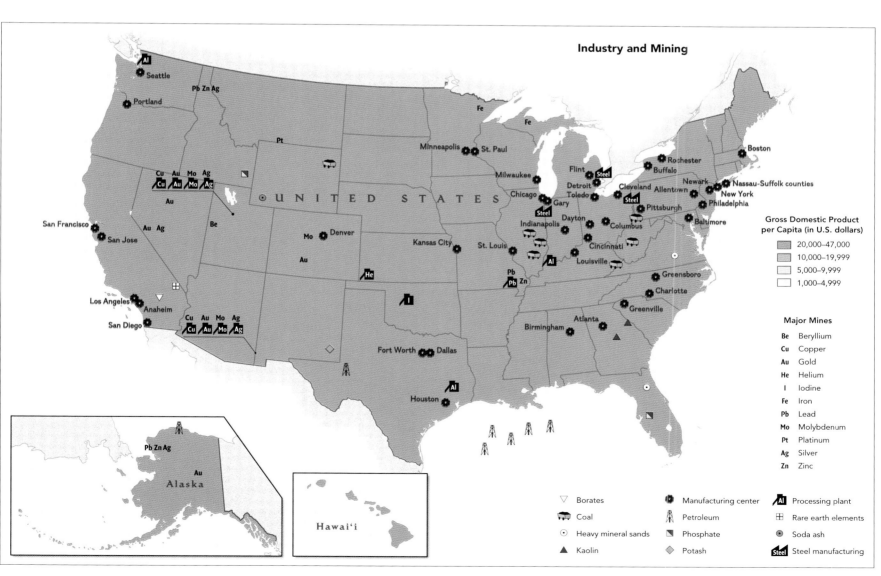

Industry and Mining

Al Seattle

Portland

Pb Zn Ag

Fe

Fe

Pt

Cu Au Mo Ag
Cu Au Mo Ag

Au

San Francisco
San Jose

Au Ag

Be

Mo Denver

Au

He

I

Minneapolis   St. Paul

Milwaukee

Flint   Steel

Chicago   Gary   Steel   Detroit   Toledo

Indianapolis   Dayton   Columbus

St. Louis   Cincinnati

Kansas City

Pb   Louisville
Pb Zn   Al

Boston

Rochester   Buffalo

Cleveland   Allentown   Newark   Nassau-Suffolk counties
Steel   Pittsburgh   New York
Philadelphia
Baltimore

Greensboro

Charlotte

U N I T E D   S T A T E S

Los Angeles
Anaheim

San Diego

Cu Au Mo Ag
Cu Au Mo Ag

Fort Worth   Dallas

Houston   Al

Birmingham   Atlanta

Greenville

Gross Domestic Product per Capita (in U.S. dollars)
	20,000–47,000
	10,000–19,999
	5,000–9,999
	1,000–4,999

Major Mines
Be	Beryllium
Cu	Copper
Au	Gold
He	Helium
I	Iodine
Fe	Iron
Pb	Lead
Mo	Molybdenum
Pt	Platinum
Ag	Silver
Zn	Zinc

Pb Zn Ag

Au

Alaska

Hawai'i

▽ Borates
🚍 Coal
⊙ Heavy mineral sands
▲ Kaolin

✹ Manufacturing center
🛢 Petroleum
◩ Phosphate
◇ Potash

Al Processing plant
⊞ Rare earth elements
◉ Soda ash
Steel Steel manufacturing

OLYMPIC COAST
NATIONAL MARINE
SANCTUARY

NORTH
CASCADES
N.P.

OLYMPIC N.P.

GLACIER
N.P.

WASHINGTON

MT.
RAINIER
N.P.

PACIFIC

OCEAN

Snake

Columbia

MONTANA

Missouri

Yellowstone

NORTH DAKOTA

THEODORE
ROOSEVELT
N.P.

OREGON

CRATER LAKE
N.P.

IDAHO

SOUTH DAKOTA

Snake

YELLOWSTONE
N.P.

GRAND
TETON
N.P.

WIND CAVE
N.P.

BADLANDS
N.P.

REDWOOD
N.P.

LASSEN
VOLCANIC
N.P.

NEVADA

Great
Salt
Lake

WYOMING

NEBRASKA

Platte

CORDELL BANK
N.M.S.

GULF OF THE
FARALLONES
N.M.S.

MONTEREY BAY
N.M.S.

CALIFORNIA

YOSEMITE
N.P.

KINGS
CANYON
N.P.

SEQUOIA N.P.

DEATH VALLEY N.P.

GREAT BASIN
N.P.

UTAH

ARCHES N.P.

CAPITOL REEF
N.P.

BRYCE CANYON N.P.

CANYONLANDS
N.P.

ZION N.P.

Colorado

GRAND
CANYON
N.P.

ROCKY MOUNTAIN
N.P.

COLORADO

BLACK CANYON
OF THE GUNNISON
N.P.

MESA VERDE
N.P.

GREAT SAND
DUNES N.P.

KANS

Arkansas

CHANNEL ISLANDS
N.M.S.

CHANNEL
ISLANDS
N.P.

ARIZONA

JOSHUA TREE N.P.

PETRIFIED
FOREST
N.P.

NEW MEXICO

OKL

SAGUARO
N.P.

CARLSBAD
CAVERNS
N.P.

GUADALUPE
MOUNTAINS
N.P.

TEX

Rio Grande

Pecos

Red

MEXICO

BIG BEND
N.P.

ARCTIC   OCEAN

RUSSIA

GATES OF THE
ARCTIC
N.P. AND
PRESERVE

KOBUK VALLEY
N.P.

Noatak

ALASKA

CANADA

DENALI
N.P. AND
PRESERVE

WRANGELL-ST. ELIAS
N.P. AND PRESERVE

LAKE CLARK
N.P. AND
PRESERVE

KENAI
FJORDS
N.P.

GLACIER BAY
N.P. AND PRESERVE

KATMAI
N.P. AND
PRESERVE

BERING SEA

GULF OF ALASKA

ALASKA

0   200 km
0   200 statute mi

MAP KEY

National Park System

National Forest

National Wildlife Refuge

National Grassland

Bureau of Land Management

Indian Reservation

Military Reservation

Department of Energy

National Marine Sanctuary

*Only national parks and marine
sanctuaries are labeled.*

92

Lambert Conformal Conic Projection, Standard Parallels 33° And 45°

SCALE 1:3,102,000
1 CENTIMETER = 31 KILOMETERS; 1 INCH = 49 MILES

50   100   150
KILOMETERS

50   100   150
STATUTE MILES

Elevations in feet

75°

45°

ONTARIO CA

St. Lawrence

• Massena   Rouses Point
Norwood   Malone   Plattsburgh
• Potsdam   Dannemora
Ogdensburg   • Canton
ST. LAWRENCE   Lake
ISLANDS N.P.   • Morristown   Champlain   • Burlington
Alexandria   • Gouverneur
Bay   • Saranac Lake
• Clayton   • Tupper Lake   • Lake Placid
• Cape   ADIRONDACK   Mt. Marcy+
Vincent   Sackets   Cranberry   5344   Port Henry
Harbor   • Watertown   • Carthage   Lake   • Ticonderoga
Raquette L.   MOUNTAINS
• Lowville   Snowy Mt.+   Lake
Ellisburg   3899   George
78°   • Port Ontario   FT. STANWIX   • Whitehall
Lycoming   • Pulaski   • Boonville   NAT. MON.   Great Sacandaga   • Fair
LAKE ONTARIO   Oswego   Camden   • Rome   Lake   Haven
Fulton   • Oneida   • Gloversville   • Saratoga
Niagara R.   Albion   Canastota   Utica   • Johnstown   Springs
• Kendall   • Brockport • Greece   Solvay • Oneida   Little Falls • Ilion Herkimer   • Amsterdam
Lockport • Medina   • Irondequoit   Baldwinsville   • Syracuse   Mohawk
Niagara Falls   • Palmyra • Newark   • Schenectady
• N. Tonawanda   Rochester   • Fairport • Lyons   Auburn   Cooperstown   • Cohoes   • Troy
Grand   • Batavia   • Canandaigua   • Geneva   Seneca Falls   • Hamilton   Albany ★ Mt. Greylock+
Island Amherst   • Le Roy   Geneseo   • Penn   • Homer   • Oneonta   • Ravena   • Chatham   3491
Buffalo • Cheektowaga   NEW   Yan • Cortland Norwich   Delhi Stamford
Lackawanna • E. Aurora   YORK   • Oneonta   +2817   • Catskill   • Hudson
• Hamburg   • Springville   Dansville Watkins Glen   Sidney   CATSKILL
Farnham   I-390   • Hornell • Ithaca   Walton   MTS.+   • Kingston
• Dunkirk • Gowanda   Franklinville   • Bath   Cayuga L.   Johnson City   Liberty   Slide Mt.
Fredonia   Springville Hornell   Canisteo   Corning Horseheads Endicott Binghamton   4180   • Hyde Park
Westfield +2115 • Franklinville I-219   Wellsville   2548 Elmira • Owego Deposit   I-17   • Poughkeepsie
North East   Salamanca   I-86   • Olean   417   Waverly   Susquehanna   +2289   +Mt. Frissel
42° Erie • Wesleyville • Falconer   • Tioga   • Sayre   2380
N. Springfield • Girard • Jamestown   Elkland   Towanda   Elk Mt.   Honesdale   • Middletown Newburgh
Corry • Warren   Bradford Coudersport Galeton • Mansfield   • Canton   +2693   Carbondale   • West Point Danbury
Cambridge Springs   Union Smethport   • Wellsboro   PENN   Archbald   Middletown   • Peekskill
Pymatuning City   • Titusville   Port Allegany   S Scranton   Dickson City Port Jervis   West Point
Res.   • Meadville   Kane Mt. Emporium • Austin   Y   • Dunmore   • New City Bridgeport
Greenville   • Oil City   Johnsonburg Jewett   Renovo   • Montoursville L • Old Forge   High Point White Plains Norwalk
Sharon • Polk • Franklin Ridgway • St. Marys 120 Williamsport V Kingston   Pittston   1803   • Peekskill   Stamford
• Farrell   Clarion   Brookville • Brockway   Lock Haven   Jersey Shore A Plymouth Wilkes- Pocono Mts. Paterson New Rochelle
Slippery Rock   Grove City   Du Bois   Clearfield   • Muncy   N Barre Nanticoke   DELAWARE Morristown Mount Vernon
New • Brookville PENNSYLVANIA • Philipsburg Milton   I-11   I-80   WATER GAP   E. Orange NEW
Castle Butler   • Indiana   • Bellefonte   • Sunbury Hazleton N.R.A. Stroudsburg Newark YORK
Aliquippa   Kittanning • Punxsutawney • Tyrone State College • Shamokin Mt. Carmel • Easton Elizabeth CITY
McKees Rocks I-76   119   220   Altoona   Lewistown • Shenandoah Bethlehem Plainfield Jersey
Pittsburgh Penn Hills Indiana Huntingdon • Hollidaysburg Mechanicsburg Pottsville I-81 Allentown NEW
Upper St. Clair Duquesne Greensburg +3136 Carlisle • Lebanon Emmaus New Brunswick JERSEY
Canonsburg McKeesport Windber FLIGHT 93   Harrisburg ★ Reading Quakertown Doylestown Princeton Long Branch
Washington Clairton Somerset NAT. MEM. Steelton I-76 New Holland Freehold • Asbury Park
Monessen I-70   I-99   • Bedford Shippensburg Lancaster Columbia Norristown Lansdale Trenton Lakewood
I-79   I-40   Uniontown Breezewood Chambersburg York PHILADELPHIA Levittown Point Pleasant
WEST   Waynesburg Masontown Bedford Greencastle Gettysburg • Hanover Oxford Upper Darby Camden Seaside Park
VIRGINIA Mt. Davis+ I-70 • Waynesboro Chester W. Chester NEW Barnegat
3213   MARYLAND DELAWARE Woodbury JERSEY Barnegat Light
Glassboro Hammonton
Woodstown Pleasantville Beach Haven
Bridgeton Vineland Tuckerton Great Bay
Millville Atlantic City
Port Norris Ventnor City
Ocean City
39° Delaware Wildwood 39°
Bay Cape May
75°

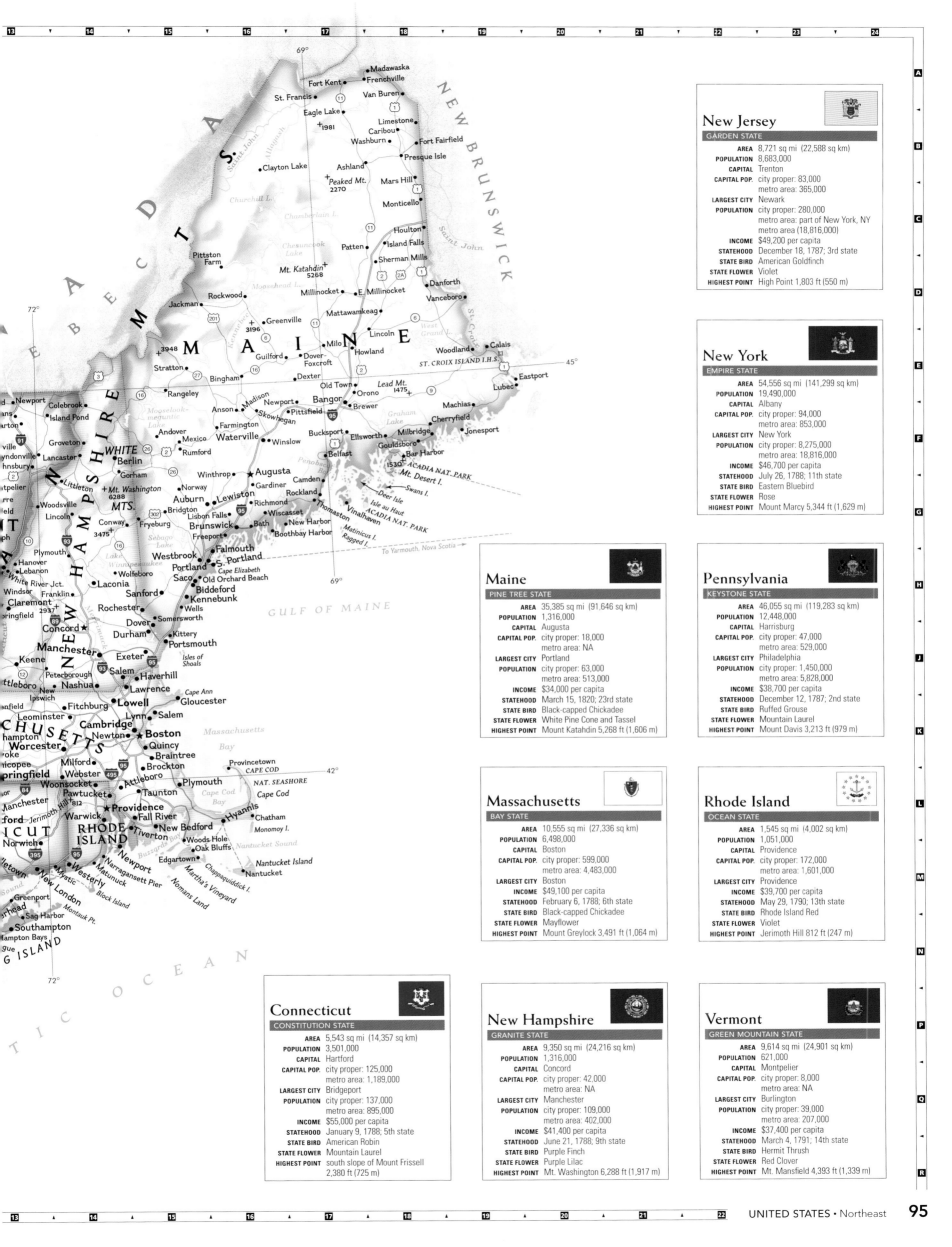

New Jersey
GARDEN STATE

AREA	8,721 sq mi (22,588 sq km)
POPULATION	8,683,000
CAPITAL	Trenton
CAPITAL POP.	city proper: 83,000
	metro area: 365,000
LARGEST CITY	Newark
POPULATION	city proper: 280,000
	metro area: part of New York, NY
	metro area (18,816,000)
INCOME	$49,200 per capita
STATEHOOD	December 18, 1787; 3rd state
STATE BIRD	American Goldfinch
STATE FLOWER	Violet
HIGHEST POINT	High Point 1,803 ft (550 m)

New York
EMPIRE STATE

AREA	54,556 sq mi (141,299 sq km)
POPULATION	19,490,000
CAPITAL	Albany
CAPITAL POP.	city proper: 94,000
	metro area: 853,000
LARGEST CITY	New York
POPULATION	city proper: 8,275,000
	metro area: 18,816,000
INCOME	$46,700 per capita
STATEHOOD	July 26, 1788; 11th state
STATE BIRD	Eastern Bluebird
STATE FLOWER	Rose
HIGHEST POINT	Mount Marcy 5,344 ft (1,629 m)

Maine
PINE TREE STATE

AREA	35,385 sq mi (91,646 sq km)
POPULATION	1,316,000
CAPITAL	Augusta
CAPITAL POP.	city proper: 18,000
	metro area: NA
LARGEST CITY	Portland
POPULATION	city proper: 63,000
	metro area: 513,000
INCOME	$34,000 per capita
STATEHOOD	March 15, 1820; 23rd state
STATE BIRD	Black-capped Chickadee
STATE FLOWER	White Pine Cone and Tassel
HIGHEST POINT	Mount Katahdin 5,268 ft (1,606 m)

Pennsylvania
KEYSTONE STATE

AREA	46,055 sq mi (119,283 sq km)
POPULATION	12,448,000
CAPITAL	Harrisburg
CAPITAL POP.	city proper: 47,000
	metro area: 529,000
LARGEST CITY	Philadelphia
POPULATION	city proper: 1,450,000
	metro area: 5,828,000
INCOME	$38,700 per capita
STATEHOOD	December 12, 1787; 2nd state
STATE BIRD	Ruffed Grouse
STATE FLOWER	Mountain Laurel
HIGHEST POINT	Mount Davis 3,213 ft (979 m)

Massachusetts
BAY STATE

AREA	10,555 sq mi (27,336 sq km)
POPULATION	6,498,000
CAPITAL	Boston
CAPITAL POP.	city proper: 599,000
	metro area: 4,483,000
LARGEST CITY	Boston
INCOME	$49,100 per capita
STATEHOOD	February 6, 1788; 6th state
STATE BIRD	Black-capped Chickadee
STATE FLOWER	Mayflower
HIGHEST POINT	Mount Greylock 3,491 ft (1,064 m)

Rhode Island
OCEAN STATE

AREA	1,545 sq mi (4,002 sq km)
POPULATION	1,051,000
CAPITAL	Providence
CAPITAL POP.	city proper: 172,000
	metro area: 1,601,000
LARGEST CITY	Providence
INCOME	$39,700 per capita
STATEHOOD	May 29, 1790; 13th state
STATE BIRD	Rhode Island Red
STATE FLOWER	Violet
HIGHEST POINT	Jerimoth Hill 812 ft (247 m)

Connecticut
CONSTITUTION STATE

AREA	5,543 sq mi (14,357 sq km)
POPULATION	3,501,000
CAPITAL	Hartford
CAPITAL POP.	city proper: 125,000
	metro area: 1,189,000
LARGEST CITY	Bridgeport
POPULATION	city proper: 137,000
	metro area: 895,000
INCOME	$55,000 per capita
STATEHOOD	January 9, 1788; 5th state
STATE BIRD	American Robin
STATE FLOWER	Mountain Laurel
HIGHEST POINT	south slope of Mount Frissell 2,380 ft (725 m)

New Hampshire
GRANITE STATE

AREA	9,350 sq mi (24,216 sq km)
POPULATION	1,316,000
CAPITAL	Concord
CAPITAL POP.	city proper: 42,000
	metro area: NA
LARGEST CITY	Manchester
POPULATION	city proper: 109,000
	metro area: 402,000
INCOME	$41,400 per capita
STATEHOOD	June 21, 1788; 9th state
STATE BIRD	Purple Finch
STATE FLOWER	Purple Lilac
HIGHEST POINT	Mt. Washington 6,288 ft (1,917 m)

Vermont
GREEN MOUNTAIN STATE

AREA	9,614 sq mi (24,901 sq km)
POPULATION	621,000
CAPITAL	Montpelier
CAPITAL POP.	city proper: 8,000
	metro area: NA
LARGEST CITY	Burlington
POPULATION	city proper: 39,000
	metro area: 207,000
INCOME	$37,400 per capita
STATEHOOD	March 4, 1791; 14th state
STATE BIRD	Hermit Thrush
STATE FLOWER	Red Clover
HIGHEST POINT	Mt. Mansfield 4,393 ft (1,339 m)

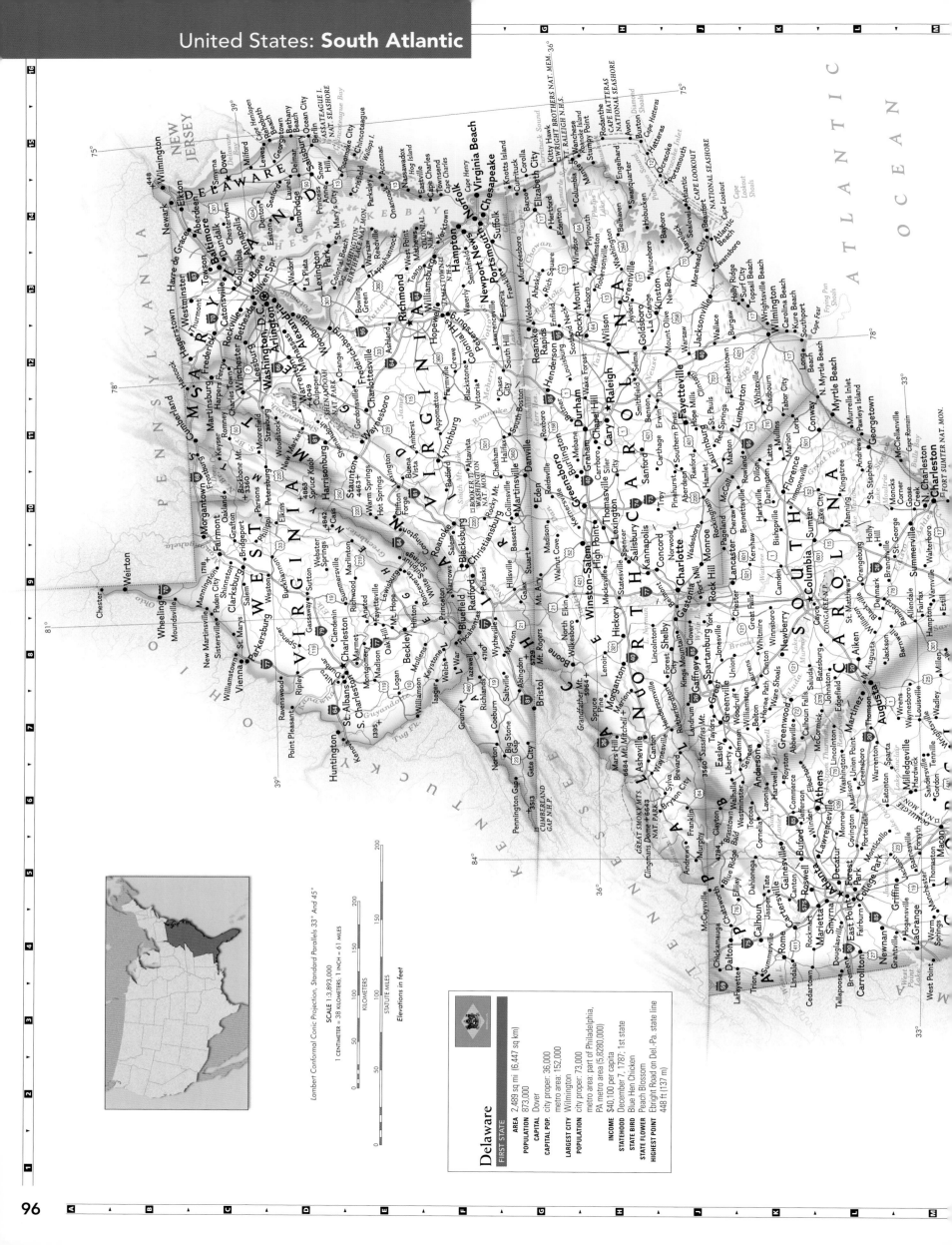

Lambert Conformal Conic Projection, Standard Parallels 33° And 45°

SCALE 1:3,893,000

1 CENTIMETER = 38 KILOMETERS; 1 INCH = 61 MILES

KILOMETERS

STATUTE MILES

Elevations in feet

Delaware

FIRST STATE

AREA	2,489 sq mi (6,447 sq km)
POPULATION	873,000
CAPITAL	Dover
CAPITAL POP.	city proper: 36,000
	metro area: 152,000
LARGEST CITY	Wilmington
POPULATION	city proper: 73,000
	metro area: part of Philadelphia, PA metro area (5,8280,000)
INCOME	$40,100 per capita
STATEHOOD	December 7, 1787; 1st state
STATE BIRD	Blue Hen Chicken
STATE FLOWER	Peach Blossom
HIGHEST POINT	Ebright Road on Del.-Pa. state line 448 ft (137 m)

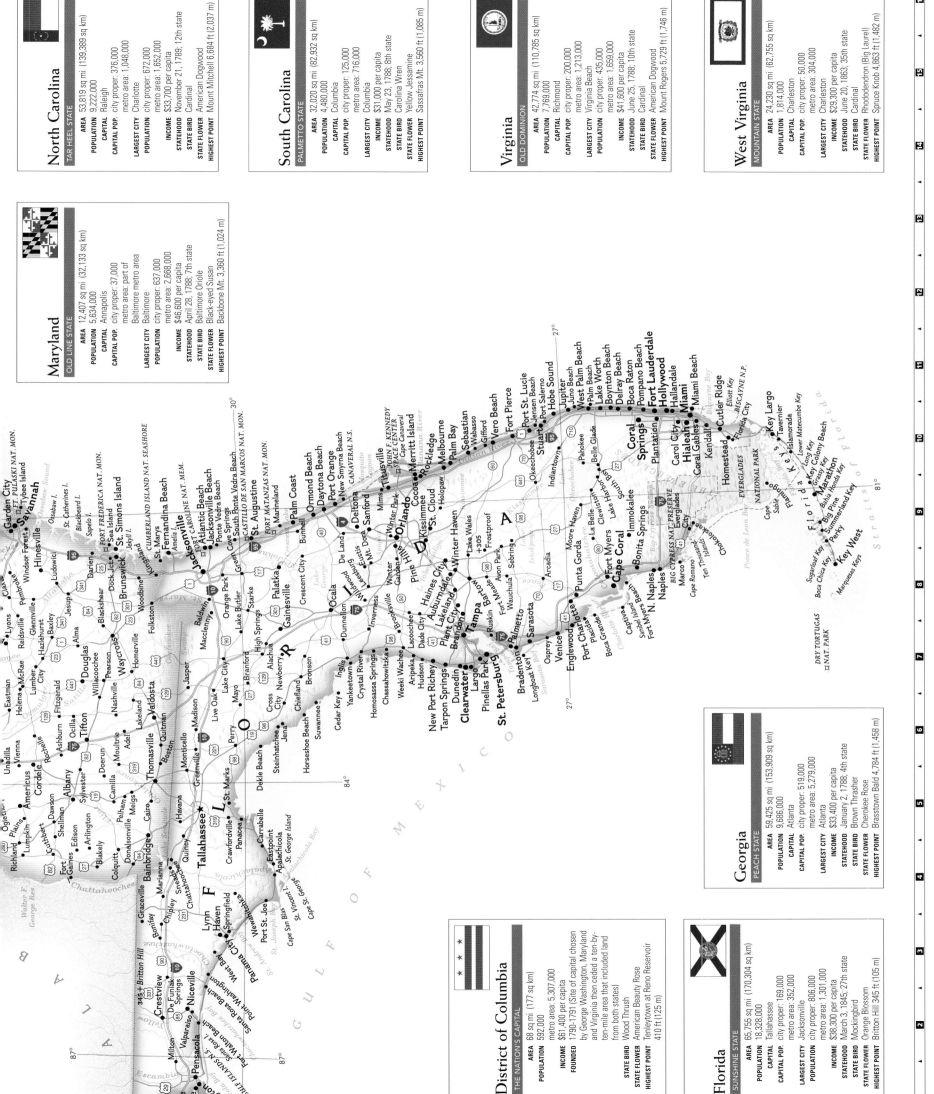

North Carolina
TAR HEEL STATE
AREA 53,819 sq mi (139,389 sq km)
POPULATION 9,222,000
CAPITAL Raleigh
CAPITAL POP. city proper: 376,000
metro area: 1,048,000
LARGEST CITY Charlotte
POPULATION city proper: 672,000
metro area: 1,652,000
INCOME $33,700 per capita
STATEHOOD November 21, 1789; 12th state
STATE BIRD Cardinal
STATE FLOWER American Dogwood
HIGHEST POINT Mount Mitchell 6,684 ft (2,037 m)

South Carolina
PALMETTO STATE
AREA 32,020 sq mi (82,932 sq km)
POPULATION 4,480,000
CAPITAL Columbia
CAPITAL POP. city proper: 125,000
metro area: 716,000
LARGEST CITY Columbia
INCOME $31,000 per capita
STATEHOOD May 23, 1788; 8th state
STATE BIRD Carolina Wren
STATE FLOWER Yellow Jessamine
HIGHEST POINT Sassafras Mt. 3,560 ft (1,085 m)

Virginia
OLD DOMINION
AREA 42,774 sq mi (110,785 sq km)
POPULATION 7,769,000
CAPITAL Richmond
CAPITAL POP. city proper: 200,000
metro area: 1,213,000
LARGEST CITY Virginia Beach
POPULATION city proper: 435,000
metro area: 1,659,000
INCOME $41,600 per capita
STATEHOOD June 25, 1788; 10th state
STATE BIRD Cardinal
STATE FLOWER American Dogwood
HIGHEST POINT Mount Rogers 5,729 ft (1,746 m)

West Virginia
MOUNTAIN STATE
AREA 24,230 sq mi (62,755 sq km)
POPULATION 1,814,000
CAPITAL Charleston
CAPITAL POP. city proper: 50,000
metro area: 304,000
LARGEST CITY Charleston
INCOME $29,300 per capita
STATEHOOD June 20, 1863; 35th state
STATE BIRD Cardinal
STATE FLOWER Rhododendron (Big Laurel)
HIGHEST POINT Spruce Knob 4,863 ft (1,482 m)

Maryland
OLD LINE STATE
AREA 12,407 sq mi (32,133 sq km)
POPULATION 5,634,000
CAPITAL Annapolis
CAPITAL POP. city proper: 37,000
metro area: part of
Baltimore metro area
LARGEST CITY Baltimore
POPULATION city proper: 637,000
metro area: 2,668,000
INCOME $46,600 per capita
STATEHOOD April 28, 1788; 7th state
STATE BIRD Baltimore Oriole
STATE FLOWER Black-eyed Susan
HIGHEST POINT Backbone Mt. 3,360 ft (1,024 m)

District of Columbia
THE NATION'S CAPITAL
AREA 68 sq mi (177 sq km)
POPULATION 592,000
metro area: 5,307,000
INCOME $61,400 per capita
FOUNDED 1790-1791 (Site of capital chosen
by George Washington; Maryland
and Virginia then ceded a ten-by-
ten-mile area that included land
from both states)
STATE BIRD Wood Thrush
STATE FLOWER American Beauty Rose
HIGHEST POINT Tenleytown at Reno Reservoir
410 ft (125 m)

Georgia
PEACH STATE
AREA 59,425 sq mi (153,909 sq km)
POPULATION 9,686,000
CAPITAL Atlanta
CAPITAL POP. city proper: 519,000
metro area: 5,279,000
LARGEST CITY Atlanta
INCOME $33,400 per capita
STATEHOOD January 2, 1788; 4th state
STATE BIRD Brown Thrasher
STATE FLOWER Cherokee Rose
HIGHEST POINT Brasstown Bald 4,784 ft (1,458 m)

Florida
SUNSHINE STATE
AREA 65,755 sq mi (170,304 sq km)
POPULATION 18,328,000
CAPITAL Tallahassee
CAPITAL POP. city proper: 169,000
metro area: 352,000
LARGEST CITY Jacksonville
POPULATION city proper: 806,000
metro area: 1,301,000
INCOME $38,300 per capita
STATEHOOD March 3, 1845; 27th state
STATE BIRD Mockingbird
STATE FLOWER Orange Blossom
HIGHEST POINT Britton Hill 345 ft (105 m)

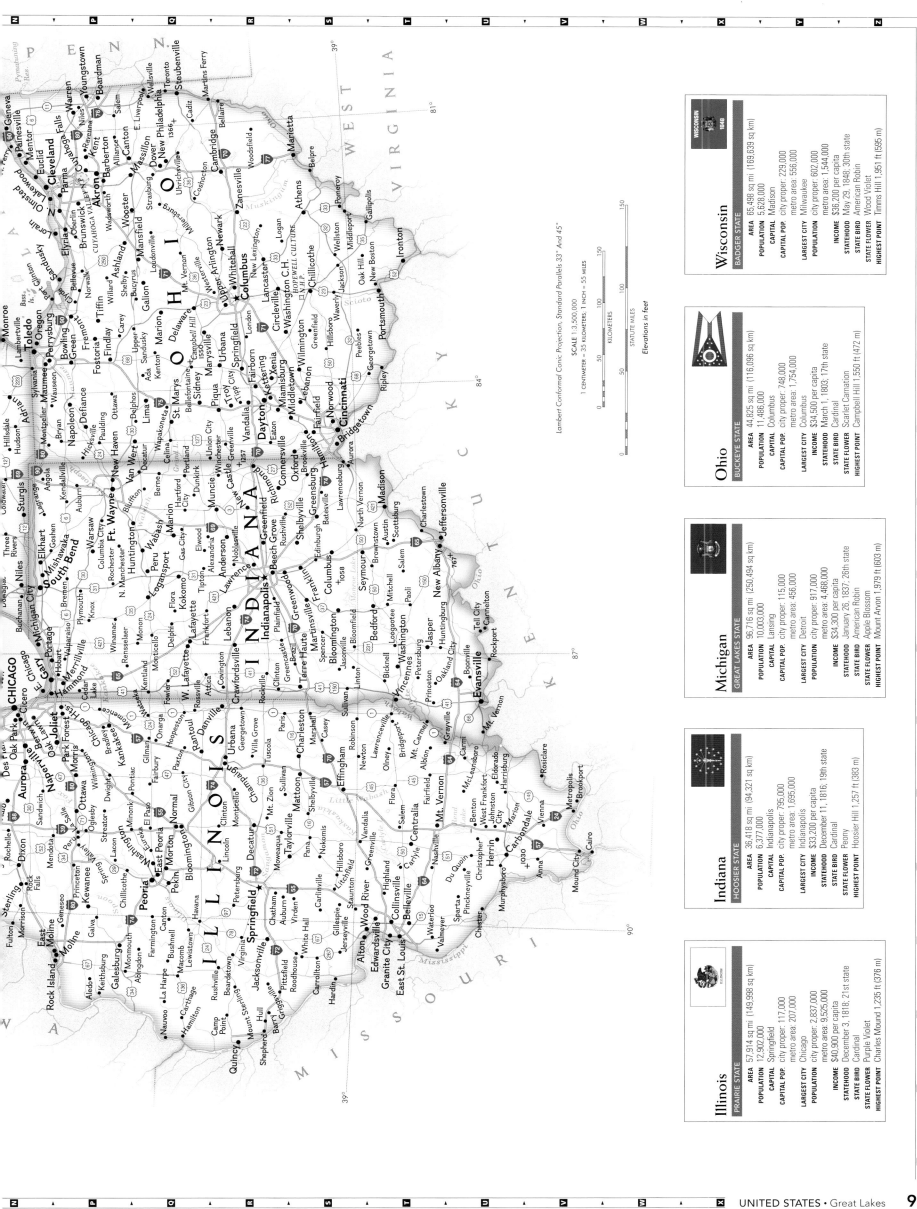

Illinois

PRAIRIE STATE

AREA	57,914 sq mi (149,998 sq km)
POPULATION	12,902,000
CAPITAL	Springfield
CAPITAL POP.	city proper: 117,000
	metro area: 207,000
LARGEST CITY	Chicago
POPULATION	city proper: 2,837,000
	metro area: 9,525,000
INCOME	$40,900 per capita
STATEHOOD	December 3, 1818; 21st state
STATE BIRD	Cardinal
STATE FLOWER	Purple Violet
HIGHEST POINT	Charles Mound 1,235 ft (376 m)

Indiana

HOOSIER STATE

AREA	36,418 sq mi (94,321 sq km)
POPULATION	6,377,000
CAPITAL	Indianapolis
CAPITAL POP.	city proper: 795,000
	metro area: 1,695,000
LARGEST CITY	Indianapolis
INCOME	$33,200 per capita
STATEHOOD	December 11, 1816; 19th state
STATE BIRD	Cardinal
STATE FLOWER	Peony
HIGHEST POINT	Hoosier Hill 1,257 ft (383 m)

Michigan

GREAT LAKES STATE

AREA	96,716 sq mi (250,494 sq km)
POPULATION	10,003,000
CAPITAL	Lansing
CAPITAL POP.	city proper: 115,000
	metro area: 456,000
LARGEST CITY	Detroit
POPULATION	city proper: 917,000
	metro area: 4,468,000
INCOME	$34,300 per capita
STATEHOOD	January 26, 1837; 26th state
STATE BIRD	American Robin
STATE FLOWER	Apple Blossom
HIGHEST POINT	Mount Arvon 1,979 ft (603 m)

Ohio

BUCKEYE STATE

AREA	44,825 sq mi (116,096 sq km)
POPULATION	11,486,000
CAPITAL	Columbus
CAPITAL POP.	city proper: 748,000
	metro area: 1,754,000
LARGEST CITY	Columbus
INCOME	$34,500 per capita
STATEHOOD	March 1, 1803; 17th state
STATE BIRD	Cardinal
STATE FLOWER	Scarlet Carnation
HIGHEST POINT	Campbell Hill 1,550 ft (472 m)

Wisconsin

BADGER STATE

AREA	65,498 sq mi (169,639 sq km)
POPULATION	5,628,000
CAPITAL	Madison
CAPITAL POP.	city proper: 229,000
	metro area: 556,000
LARGEST CITY	Milwaukee
POPULATION	city proper: 602,000
	metro area: 1,544,000
INCOME	$36,200 per capita
STATEHOOD	May 29, 1848; 30th state
STATE BIRD	American Robin
STATE FLOWER	Wood Violet
HIGHEST POINT	Timms Hill 1,951 ft (595 m)

SCALE 1:3,500,000

Lambert Conformal Conic Projection, Standard Parallels 33° And 45°

1 CENTIMETER = 35 KILOMETERS, 1 INCH = 55 MILES

STATUTE MILES

KILOMETERS

Elevations in feet

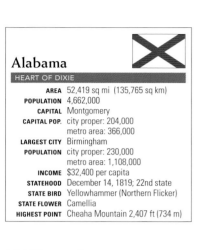

Alabama
HEART OF DIXIE

AREA	52,419 sq mi (135,765 sq km)
POPULATION	4,662,000
CAPITAL	Montgomery
CAPITAL POP.	city proper: 204,000
	metro area: 366,000
LARGEST CITY	Birmingham
POPULATION	city proper: 230,000
	metro area: 1,108,000
INCOME	$32,400 per capita
STATEHOOD	December 14, 1819; 22nd state
STATE BIRD	Yellowhammer (Northern Flicker)
STATE FLOWER	Camellia
HIGHEST POINT	Cheaha Mountain 2,407 ft (734 m)

Arkansas
NATURAL STATE

AREA	53,179 sq mi (137,732 sq km)
POPULATION	2,855,000
CAPITAL	Little Rock
CAPITAL POP.	city proper: 187,000
	metro area: 666,000
LARGEST CITY	Little Rock
INCOME	$30,100 per capita
STATEHOOD	June 15, 1836; 25th state
STATE BIRD	Mockingbird
STATE FLOWER	Apple Blossom
HIGHEST POINT	Magazine Mt. 2,753 ft (839 m)

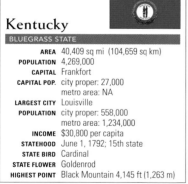

Kentucky
BLUEGRASS STATE

AREA	40,409 sq mi (104,659 sq km)
POPULATION	4,269,000
CAPITAL	Frankfort
CAPITAL POP.	city proper: 27,000
	metro area: NA
LARGEST CITY	Louisville
POPULATION	city proper: 558,000
	metro area: 1,234,000
INCOME	$30,800 per capita
STATEHOOD	June 1, 1792; 15th state
STATE BIRD	Cardinal
STATE FLOWER	Goldenrod
HIGHEST POINT	Black Mountain 4,145 ft (1,263 m)

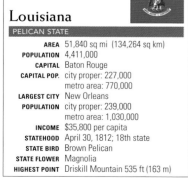

Louisiana
PELICAN STATE

AREA	51,840 sq mi (134,264 sq km)
POPULATION	4,411,000
CAPITAL	Baton Rouge
CAPITAL POP.	city proper: 227,000
	metro area: 770,000
LARGEST CITY	New Orleans
POPULATION	city proper: 239,000
	metro area: 1,030,000
INCOME	$35,800 per capita
STATEHOOD	April 30, 1812; 18th state
STATE BIRD	Brown Pelican
STATE FLOWER	Magnolia
HIGHEST POINT	Driskill Mountain 535 ft (163 m)

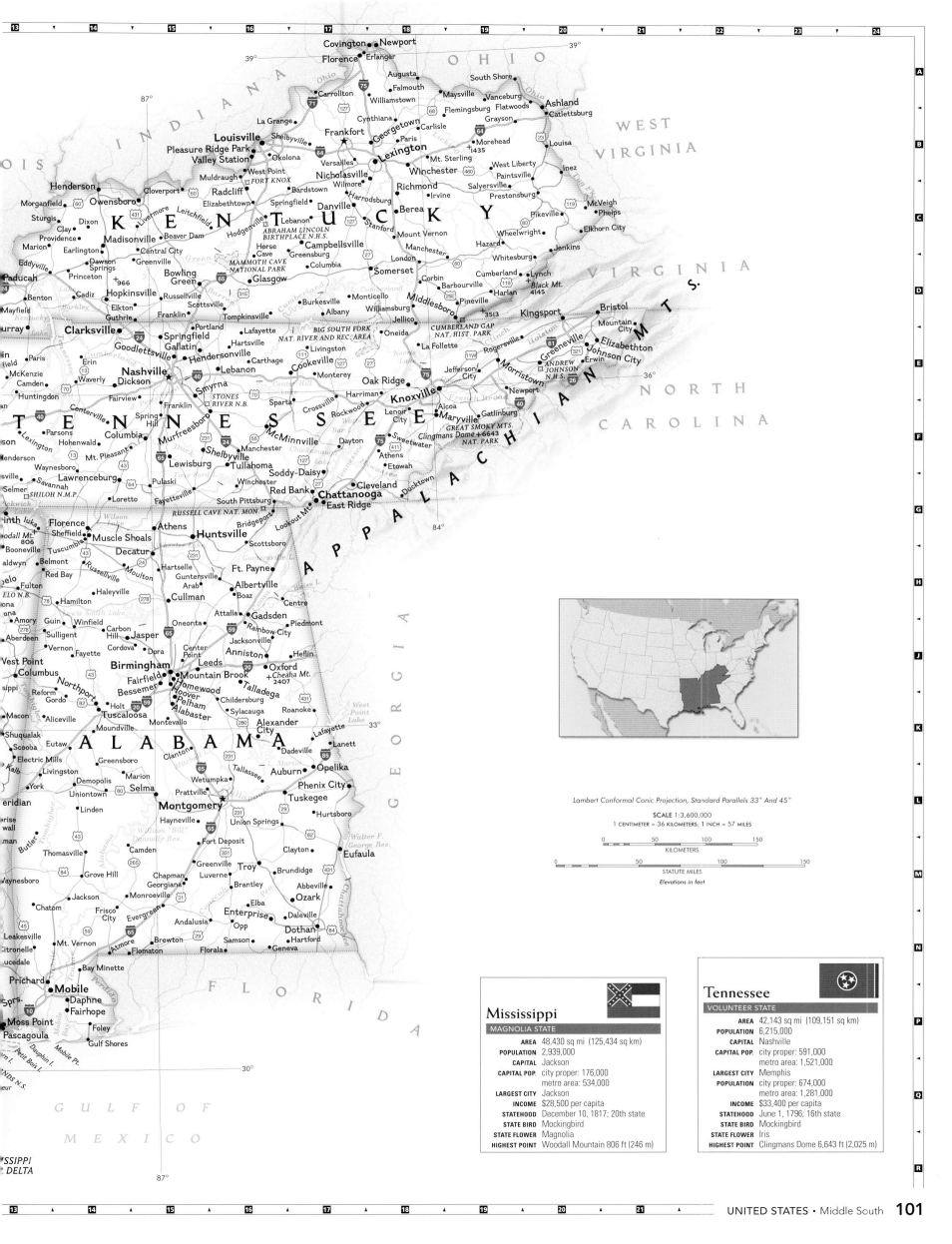

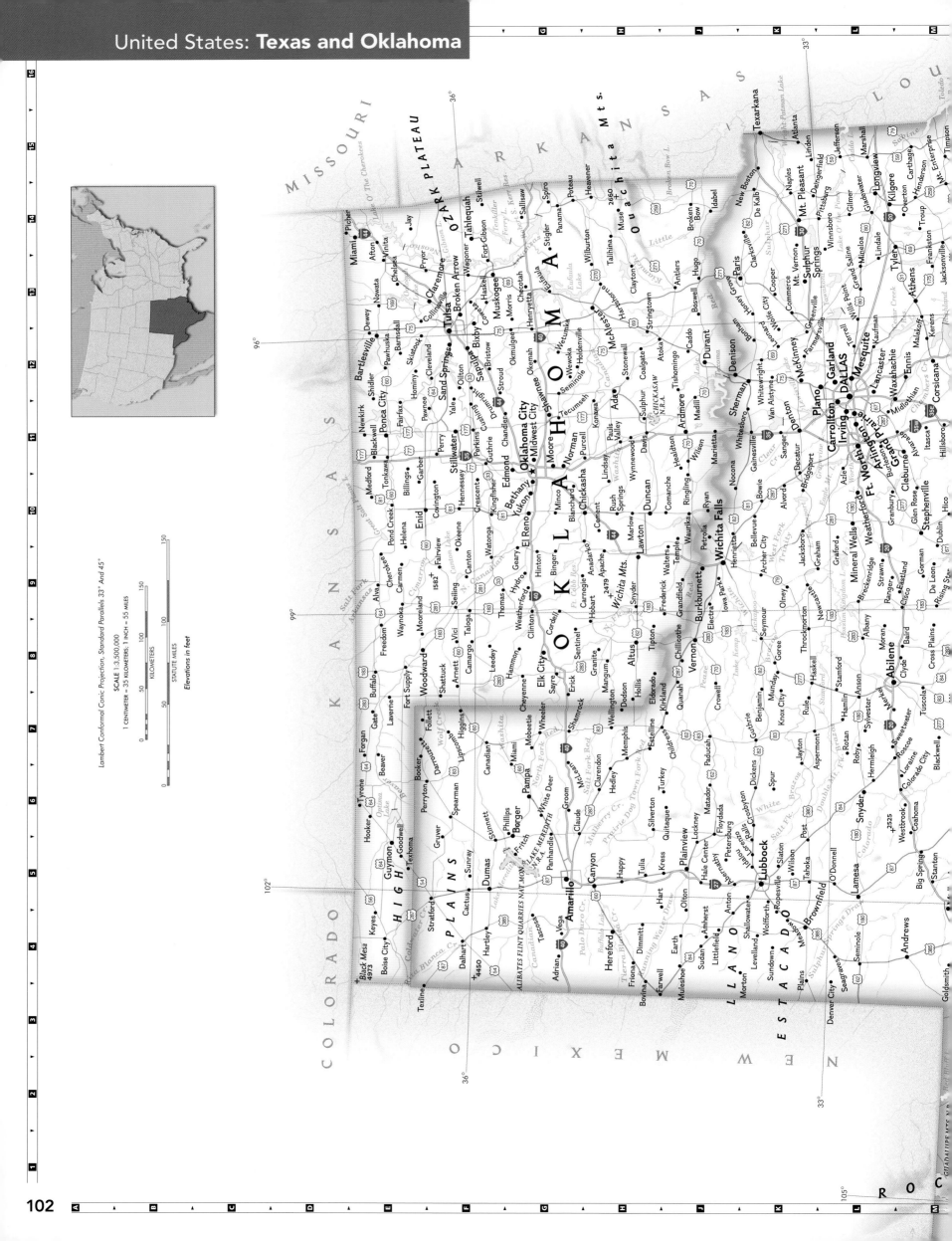

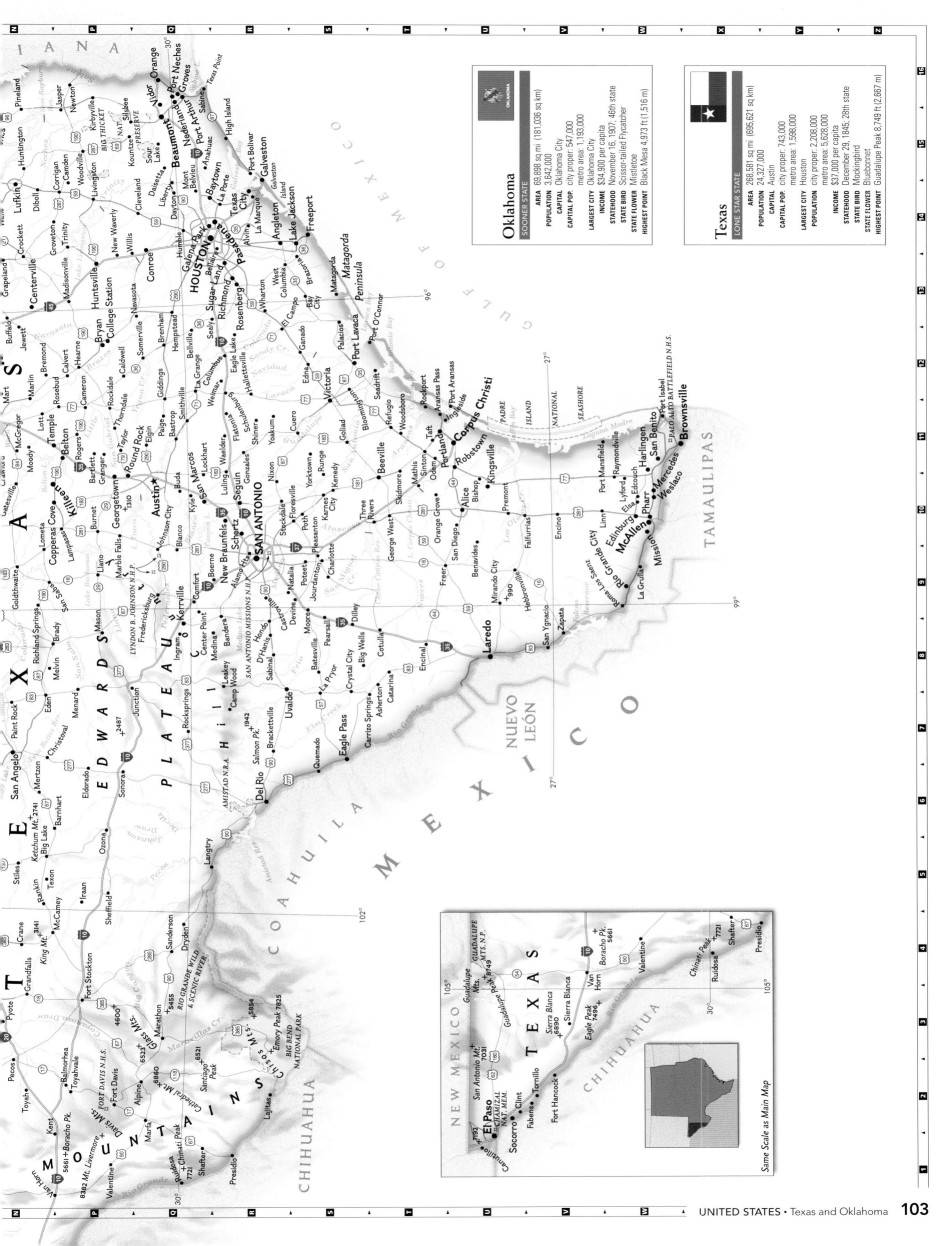

Oklahoma
SOONER STATE

AREA	69,898 sq mi (181,036 sq km)
POPULATION	3,642,000
CAPITAL	Oklahoma City
CAPITAL POP.	city proper: 547,000
	metro area: 1,193,000
LARGEST CITY	Oklahoma City
INCOME	$34,900 per capita
STATEHOOD	November 16, 1907; 46th state
STATE BIRD	Scissor-tailed Flycatcher
STATE FLOWER	Mistletoe
HIGHEST POINT	Black Mesa 4,973 ft (1,516 m)

Texas
LONE STAR STATE

AREA	268,581 sq mi (695,621 sq km)
POPULATION	24,327,000
CAPITAL	Austin
CAPITAL POP.	city proper: 743,000
	metro area: 1,598,000
LARGEST CITY	Houston
POPULATION	city proper: 2,208,000
	metro area: 5,628,000
INCOME	$37,000 per capita
STATEHOOD	December 29, 1845; 28th state
STATE BIRD	Mockingbird
STATE FLOWER	Bluebonnet
HIGHEST POINT	Guadalupe Peak 8,749 ft (2,667 m)

Same Scale as Main Map

Iowa

HAWKEYE STATE

AREA	56,272 sq mi (145,743 sq km)
POPULATION	3,003,000
CAPITAL	Des Moines
CAPITAL POP.	city proper: 197,000 metro area: 547,000
LARGEST CITY	Des Moines
INCOME	$34,800 per capita
STATEHOOD	December 28, 1846; 29th state
STATE BIRD	American Goldfinch
STATE FLOWER	Wild Prairie Rose
HIGHEST POINT	Hawkeye Point 1,670 ft (509 m)

Kansas

SUNFLOWER STATE

AREA	82,277 sq mi (213,096 sq km)
POPULATION	2,802,000
CAPITAL	Topeka
CAPITAL POP.	city proper: 123,000 metro area: 229,000
LARGEST CITY	Wichita
POPULATION	city proper: 361,000 metro area: 596,000
INCOME	$36,500 per capita
STATEHOOD	January 29, 1861; 34th state
STATE BIRD	Western Meadowlark
STATE FLOWER	Sunflower
HIGHEST POINT	Mt. Sunflower 4,039 ft (1,231 m)

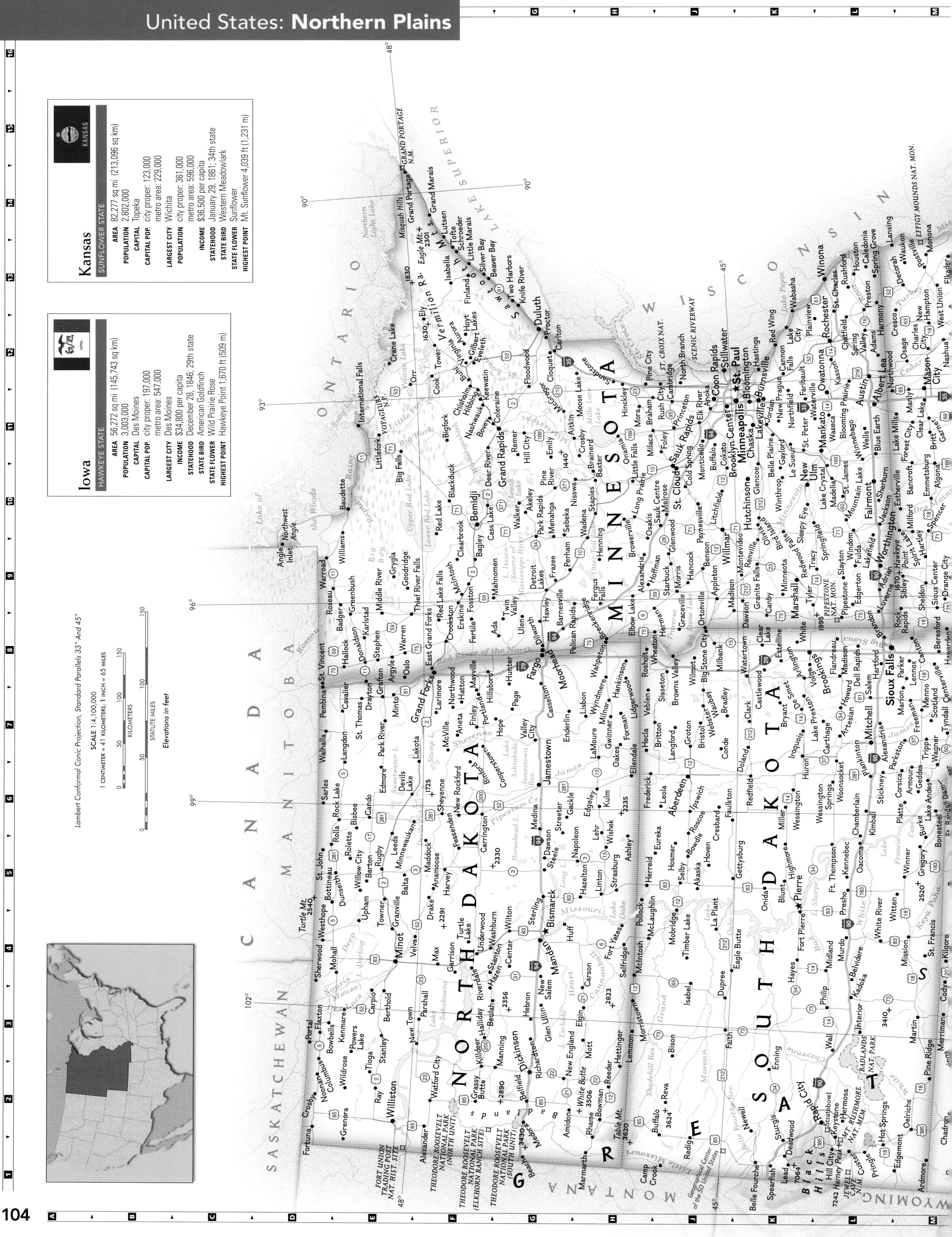

Lambert Conformal Conic Projection, Standard Parallels 33° And 45°
SCALE 1:4,100,000
1 CENTIMETER = 41 KILOMETERS; 1 INCH = 65 MILES
KILOMETERS
STATUTE MILES
Elevations in feet
CANADA
SASKATCHEWAN
MANITOBA
ONTARIO
NORTH DAKOTA
SOUTH DAKOTA
MINNESOTA
WISCONSIN
MONTANA
WYOMING
LAKE SUPERIOR
Bismarck
Pierre
St. Paul
Minneapolis
Fargo
Sioux Falls
Duluth
Rapid City
Grand Forks
Minot
Black Hills

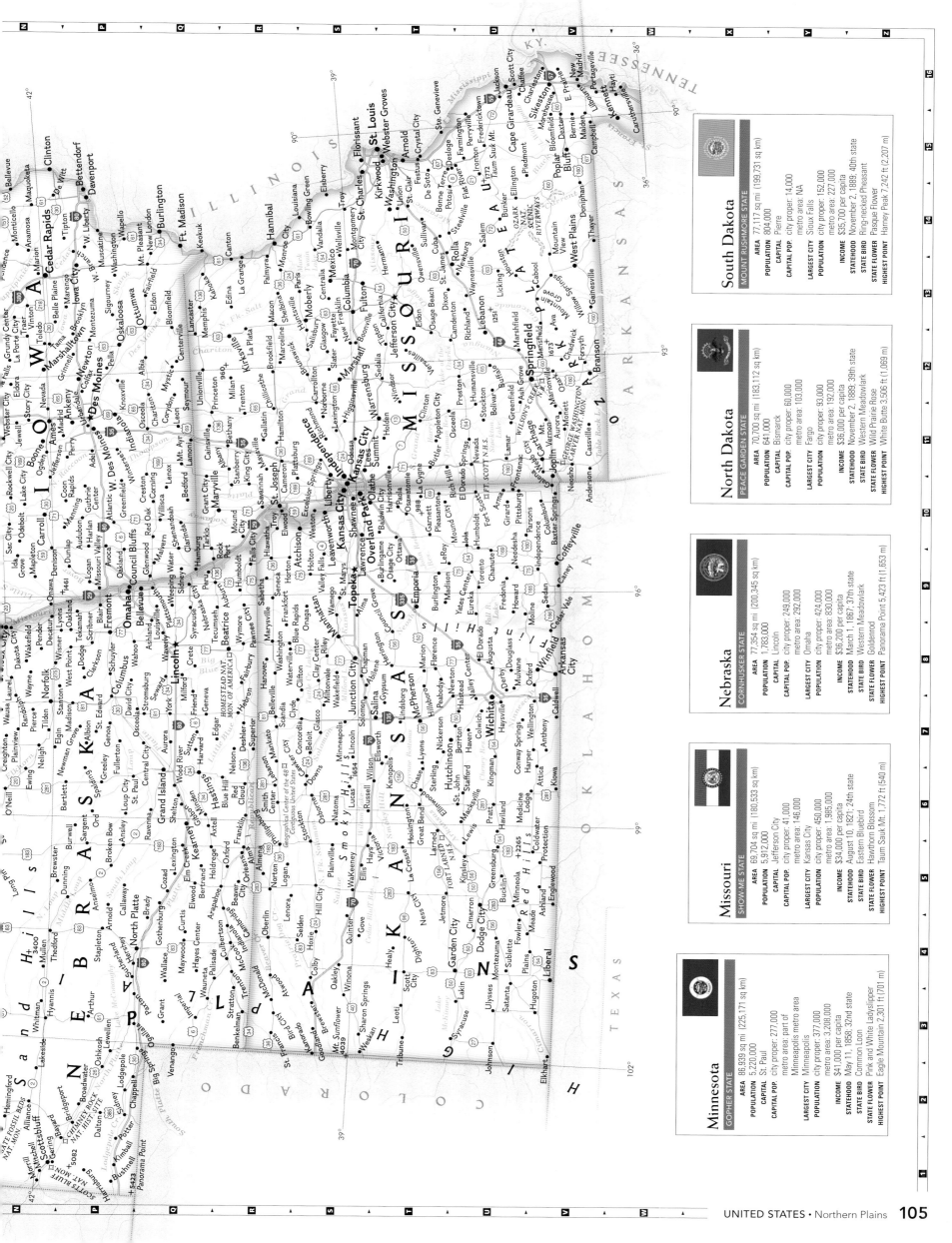

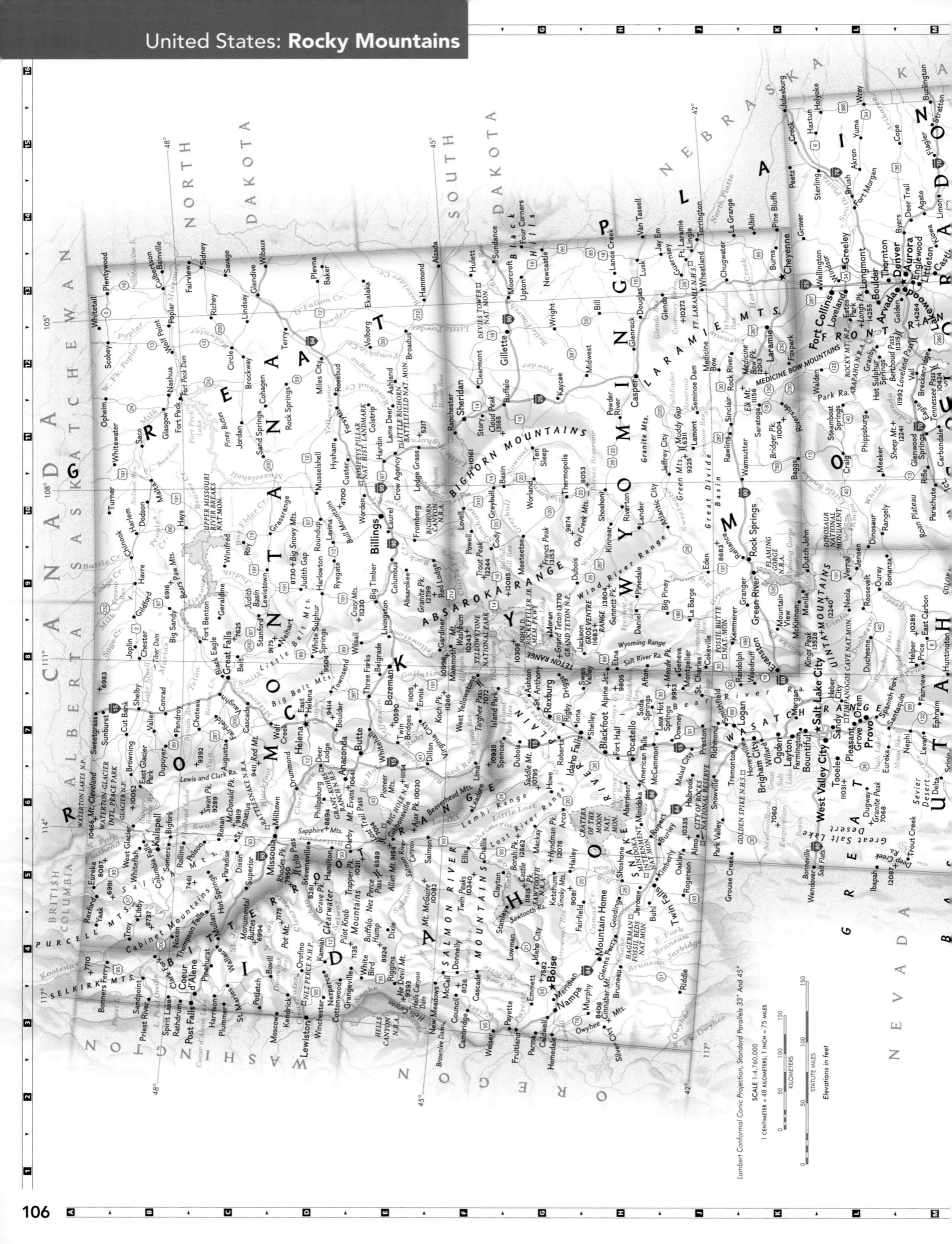

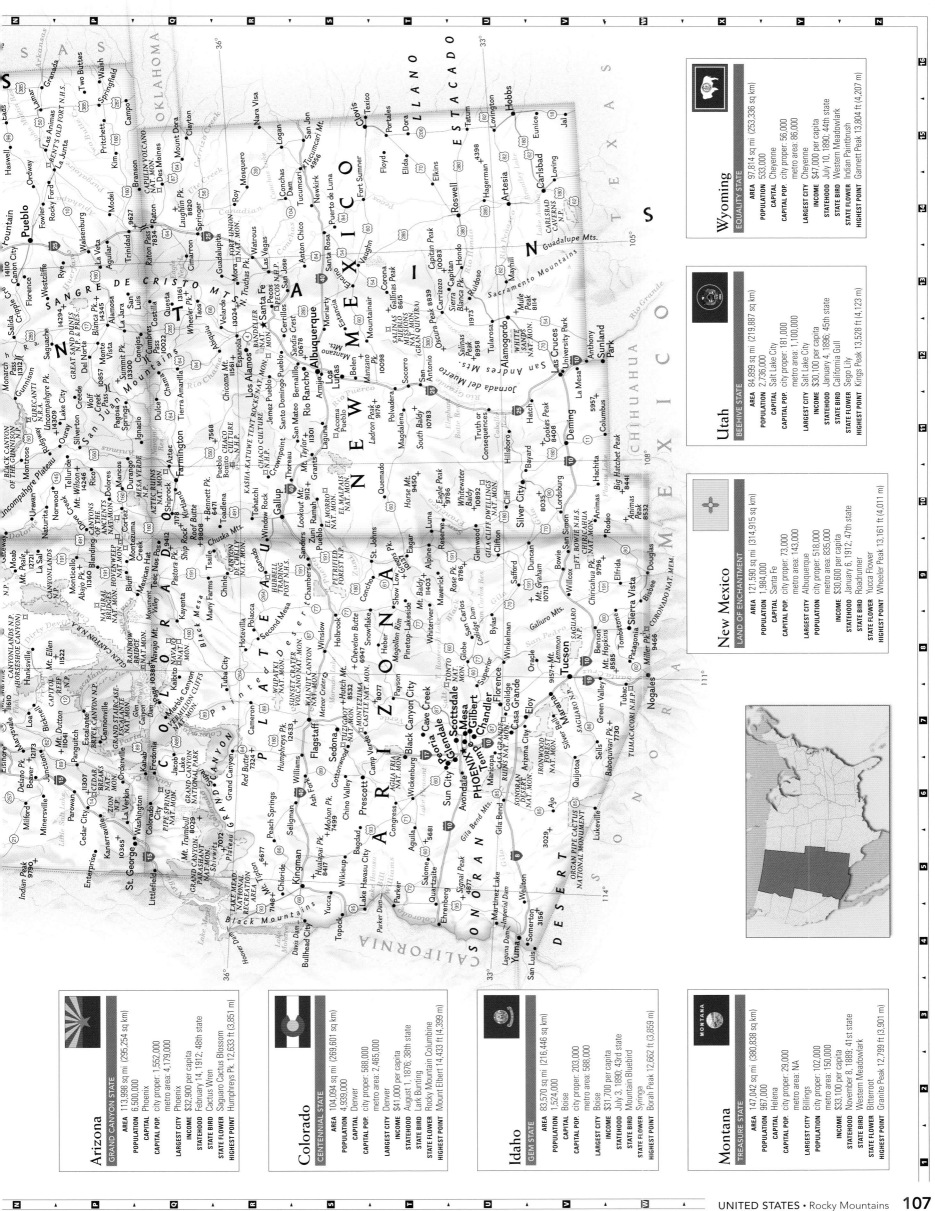

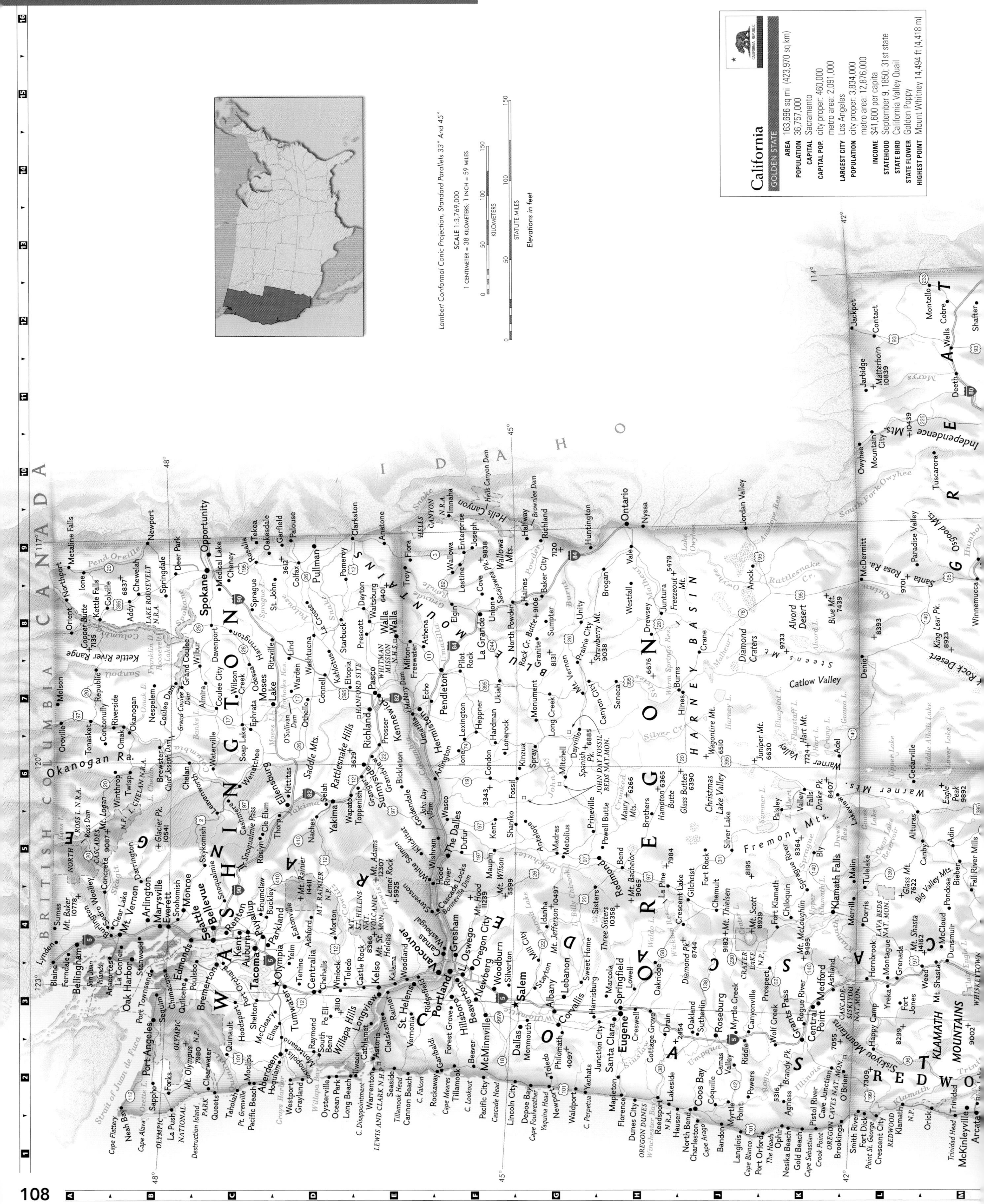

California
GOLDEN STATE

AREA	163,696 sq mi (423,970 sq km)
POPULATION	36,757,000
CAPITAL	Sacramento
CAPITAL POP.	city proper: 460,000
	metro area: 2,091,000
LARGEST CITY	Los Angeles
POPULATION	city proper: 3,834,000
	metro area: 12,876,000
INCOME	$41,600 per capita
STATEHOOD	September 9, 1850; 31st state
STATE BIRD	California Valley Quail
STATE FLOWER	Golden Poppy
HIGHEST POINT	Mount Whitney 14,494 ft (4,418 m)

Lambert Conformal Conic Projection, Standard Parallels 33° And 45°

SCALE 1:3,769,000
1 CENTIMETER = 38 KILOMETERS; 1 INCH = 59 MILES

KILOMETERS

STATUTE MILES

Elevations in feet

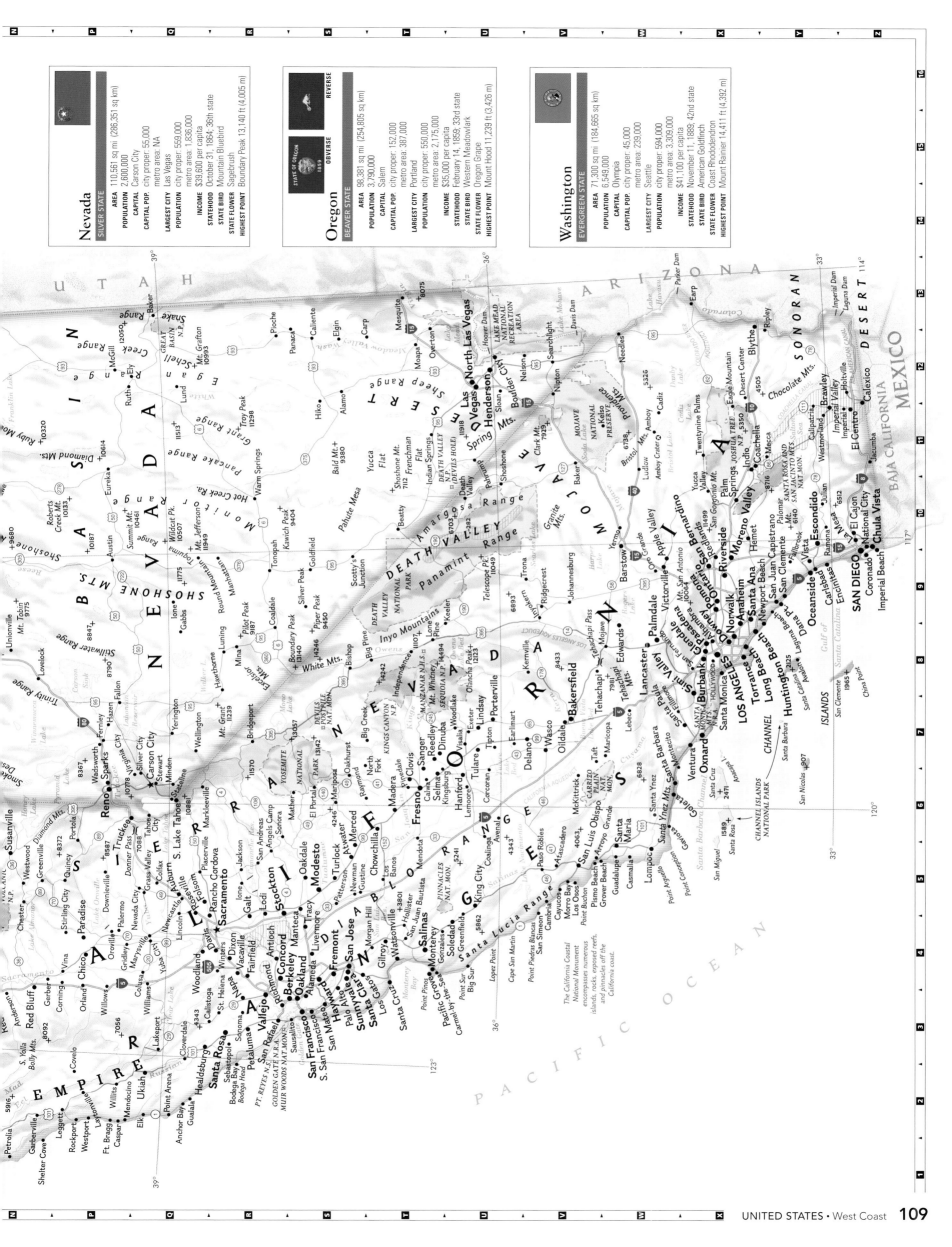

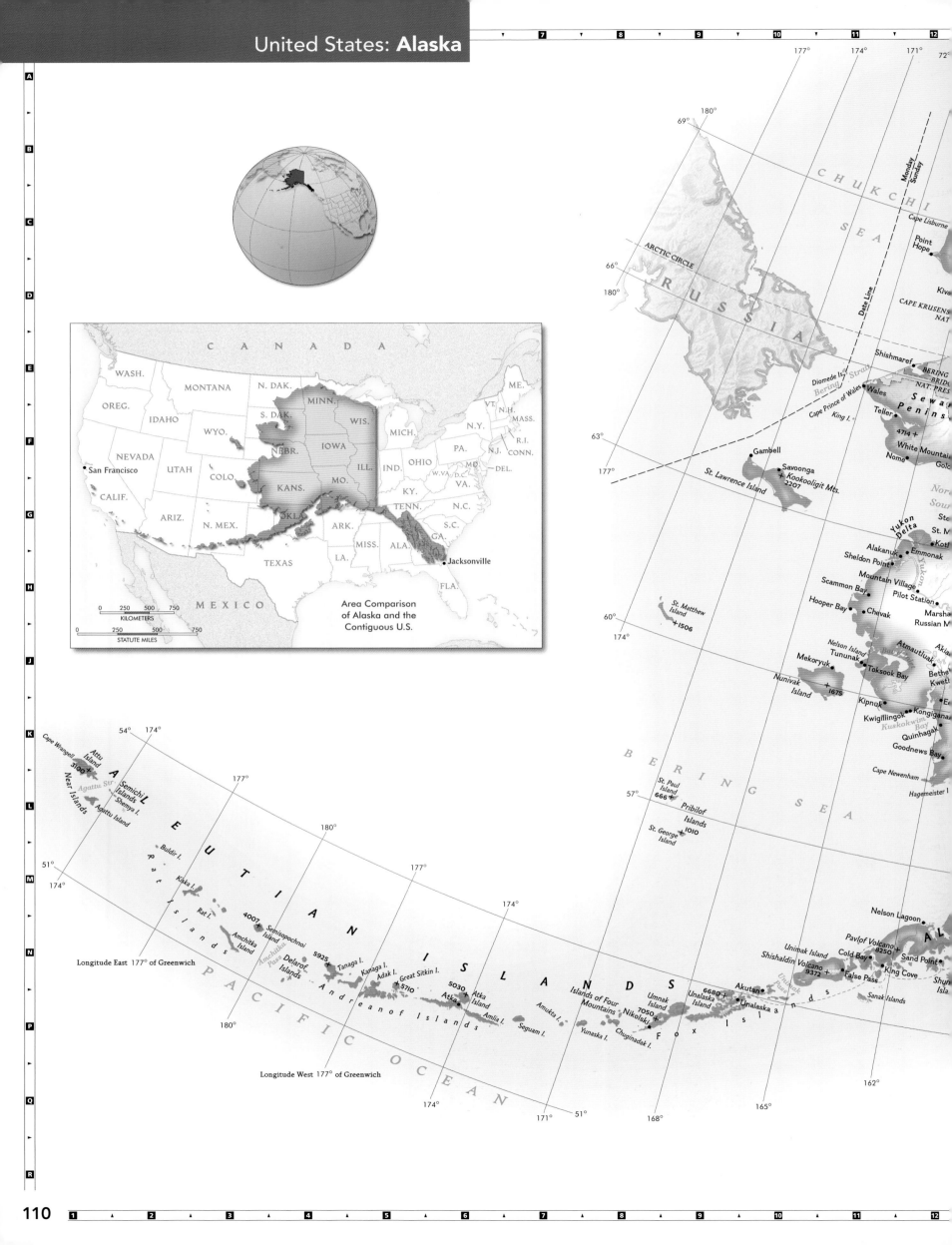

CANADA

WASH.
MONTANA
N. DAK.
OREG.
IDAHO
WYO.
S. DAK.
MINN.
WIS.
ME.
VT.
N.H.
MASS.
NEVADA
UTAH
NEBR.
IOWA
MICH.
N.Y.
R.I.
CONN.
San Francisco
COLO.
KANS.
MO.
ILL.
IND.
OHIO
PA.
N.J.
W.VA.
D.C.
DEL.
MD.
CALIF.
ARIZ.
N. MEX.
OKLA.
ARK.
KY.
VA.
TENN.
N.C.
S.C.
MISS.
ALA.
GA.
TEXAS
LA.
Jacksonville
FLA.

MEXICO

Area Comparison of Alaska and the Contiguous U.S.

0 250 500 750
KILOMETERS

0 250 500 750
STATUTE MILES

CHUKCHI SEA

RUSSIA

ARCTIC CIRCLE

Cape Lisburne

Point Hope

Monday Sunday

Date Line

66°
180°

CAPE KRUSENS NAT.

Shishmaref

Kiva

BERING BRIDG NAT. PRES.

Diomede Is

Bering Strait

Cape Prince of Wales   Wales
King I.

Sewa Penins

Teller

4714 +

63°
177°

Gambell

St. Lawrence Island

Savoonga
Kookooligit Mts.
+ 2207

White Mountain

Nome

Gold

Nor Sou

Yukon Delta

Ste

St. M

Alakanuk   Emmonak   Kotl

Sheldon Point

Mountain Village   Yukon

Scammon Bay

Pilot Station

60°
174°

St. Matthew Island

+ 1506

Hooper Bay   Chevak

Marsha
Russian M

Nelson Island   Atmautluat
Tununak
Mekoryuk   Toksook Bay

Akia

Bethe
Kweth

Nunivak Island   + 1675
Kipnuk

Ee

Kwigillingok   Kongigana
Kuskokwim Bay
Quinhaga

Goodnews Bay

54°   174°

Cape Wrangell   Attu Island
3100 +
Agattu Str.   Semichi Islands
Near Islands   Shemya I.
Agattu Island

A L

E U T I A N

B E R I N G   S E A

Cape Newenham

Hagemeister I

St. Paul Island
57°
666 +
Pribilof Islands

St. George Island   1010 +

177°

51°
174°

Buldir I.

Rat Islands

Kiska I.

4007 +   Semisopochnoi Island

Longitude East 177° of Greenwich

180°

177°

174°

5925 +   Tanaga I.

Delarof Islands

Amchitka Island   Amchitka Pass

Andreanof Islands

Kanaga I.

Adak I.

Great Sitkin I.

5710 +

5030 +   Atka Island
Atka

Amlia I.

Amukta I.

Islands of Four Mountains

Seguam I.

Yunaska I.

Chuginadak I.

PACIFIC OCEAN

Longitude West 177° of Greenwich

Nelson Lagoon

AL

Pavlof Volcano
8250 +
Unimak Island
Shishaldin Volcano
9372 +
Cold Bay
Sand Point
False Pass
King Cove
Shun
Isla

6680 +   Akutan
7050 +
Umnak Island   Unalaska Island
Nikolski   Unalaska
Fox Islands
Unimak Pass

Sanak Islands

162°

165°

168°

171°
51°

174°

I S L A N D S

N D S

180°

174°

177°

180°

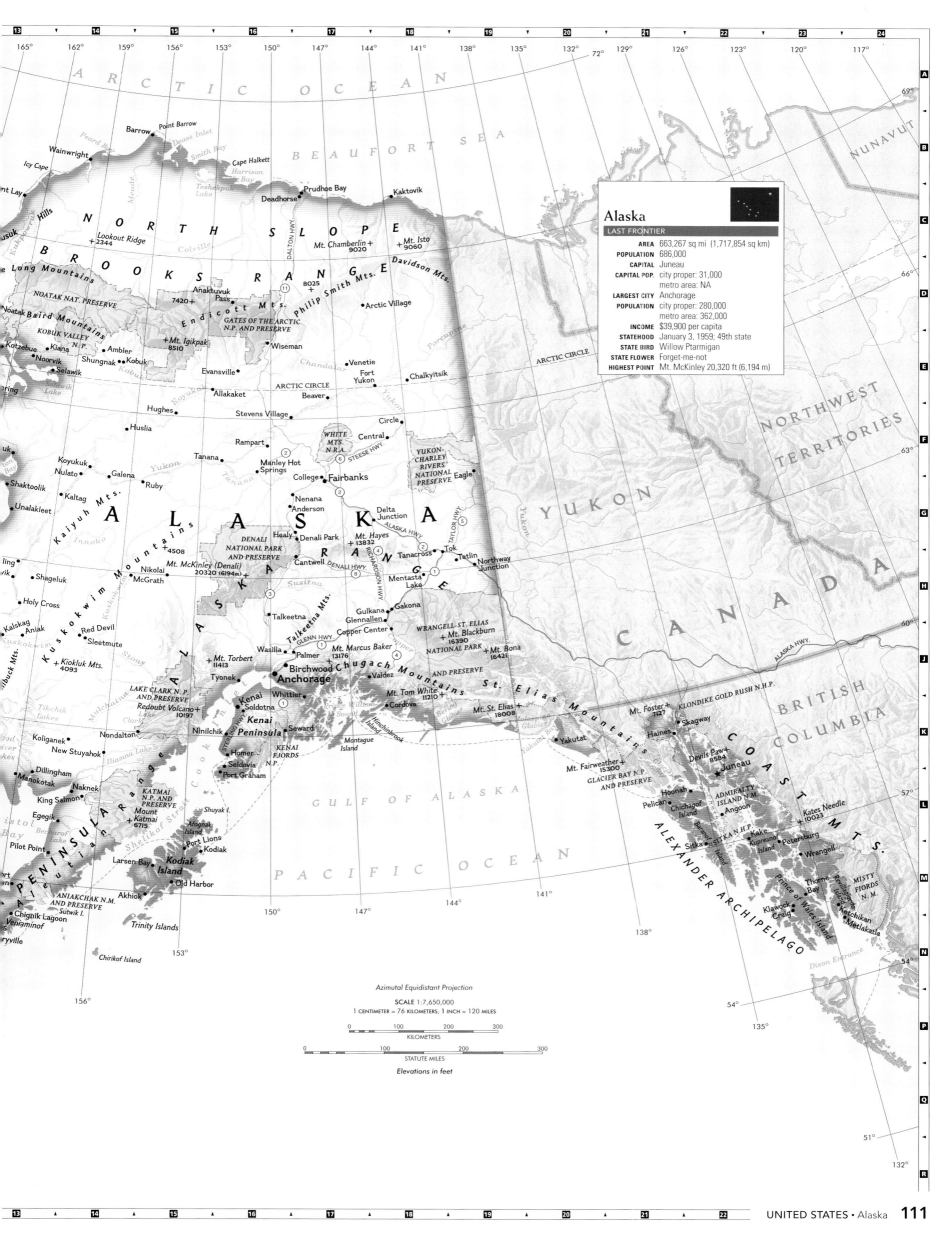

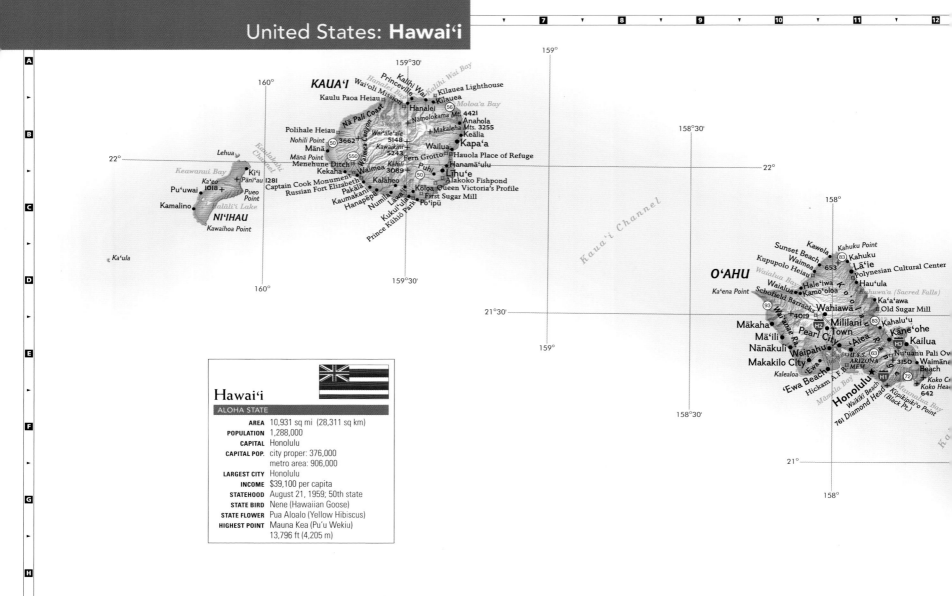

KAUA'I

Kalihi Wai
Princeville
Wai'oli Mission
Kaulu Paoa Heiau
Kilauea Lighthouse
Kilauea
Nā Pali Coast
Hanalei
Nāmolokama Mt. 4421
Anahola
Polihale Heiau
Makaleha Mts. 3255
Kapa'a
Nohili Point
Wai'ale'ale 5148
Keālia
Māna
Kawaikini 5243
Wailua
Fern Grotto
Hauola Place of Refuge
Māna Point
3662
Menehune Ditch
Kāhili 3089
Hanamā'ulu
Kekaha
Waimea
Puhi
Līhu'e
Captain Cook Monument
Kalāheo
Alakoko Fishpond
Russian Fort Elizabeth
Numila
Queen Victoria's Profile
Pakala
Lāwa'i
First Sugar Mill
Kaumakani
Kōloa
Hanapēpē
Kukui'ula
Po'ipū
Prince Kūhiō Park

NI'IHAU

Lehua
Ki'i
Pāni'au 1281
Pu'uwai
Ka'eo 1018
Pueo Point
Kamalino
Kawaihoa Point

'Ka'ula

O'AHU

Sunset Beach
Kawela
Kahuku Point
Waimea
653
Kahuku
Kupupolo Heiau
Lā'ie
Polynesian Cultural Center
Hale'iwa
Hau'ula
Ka'ena Point
Waialua
Kamo'oloa
Sacred Falls
Schofield Barracks
Wahiawā
Ka'a'awa
4019
Old Sugar Mill
Mililani Town
Mākaha
Pearl City
Kahalu'u
Mā'ili
Kāne'ohe
Nānākuli
'Aiea
Kailua
Waipahu
Nu'uanu Pali Ov
Makakilo City
3150
Waimāna Beach
Kalealoa
'Ewa Beach
Koko Cr
'Ewa
Koko Hea
Hickam A.F.B.
642
Honolulu
Waikīkī Beach
Diamond Head (Black Pt.)
Kūpikipiki'o Point

Hawai'i
ALOHA STATE

AREA	10,931 sq mi (28,311 sq km)
POPULATION	1,288,000
CAPITAL	Honolulu
CAPITAL POP.	city proper: 376,000
	metro area: 906,000
LARGEST CITY	Honolulu
INCOME	$39,100 per capita
STATEHOOD	August 21, 1959; 50th state
STATE BIRD	Nene (Hawaiian Goose)
STATE FLOWER	Pua Aloalo (Yellow Hibiscus)
HIGHEST POINT	Mauna Kea (Pu'u Wekiu)
	13,796 ft (4,205 m)

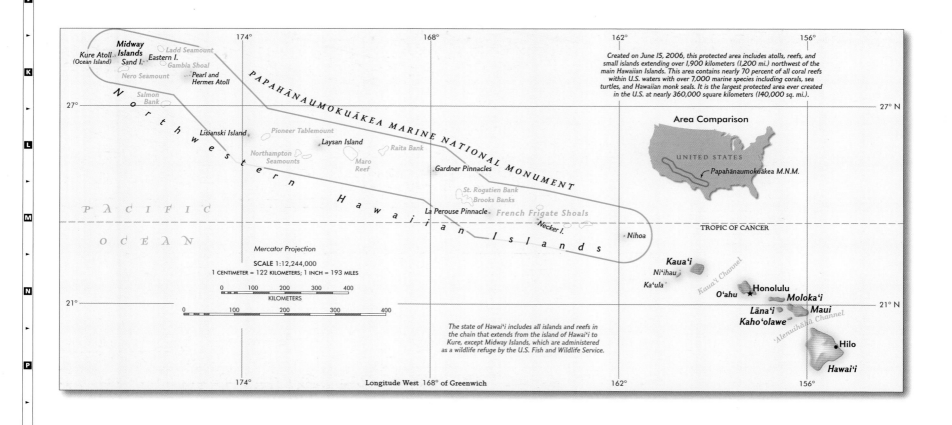

Kure Atoll (Ocean Island)
Midway Islands
Sand I.
Eastern I.
Ladd Seamount
Gambia Shoal
Nero Seamount
Pearl and Hermes Atoll

Salmon Bank

PAPAHĀNAUMOKUĀKEA MARINE NATIONAL MONUMENT

Created on June 15, 2006, this protected area includes atolls, reefs, and small islands extending over 1,900 kilometers (1,200 mi.) northwest of the main Hawaiian Islands. This area contains nearly 70 percent of all coral reefs within U.S. waters with over 7,000 marine species including corals, sea turtles, and Hawaiian monk seals. It is the largest protected area ever created in the U.S. at nearly 360,000 square kilometers (140,000 sq. mi.).

Northwestern Hawaiian Islands

Lisianski Island
Pioneer Tablemount
Laysan Island
Northampton Seamounts
Maro Reef
Raita Bank
Gardner Pinnacles

PACIFIC OCEAN

St. Rogatien Bank
Brooks Banks
La Perouse Pinnacle
French Frigate Shoals
Necker I.
Nihoa

Area Comparison

UNITED STATES
Papahānaumokuākea M.N.M.

TROPIC OF CANCER

Kaua'i
Ni'ihau
Ka'ula
Kaua'i Channel
O'ahu
★ Honolulu
Moloka'i
Lāna'i
Maui
Kaho'olawe
'Alenuihāhā Channel
Hilo
Hawai'i

Mercator Projection

SCALE 1:12,244,000

1 CENTIMETER = 122 KILOMETERS; 1 INCH = 193 MILES

KILOMETERS
0 100 200 300 400

0 100 200 300 400

The state of Hawai'i includes all islands and reefs in the chain that extends from the island of Hawai'i to Kure, except Midway Islands, which are administered as a wildlife refuge by the U.S. Fish and Wildlife Service.

Longitude West 168° of Greenwich

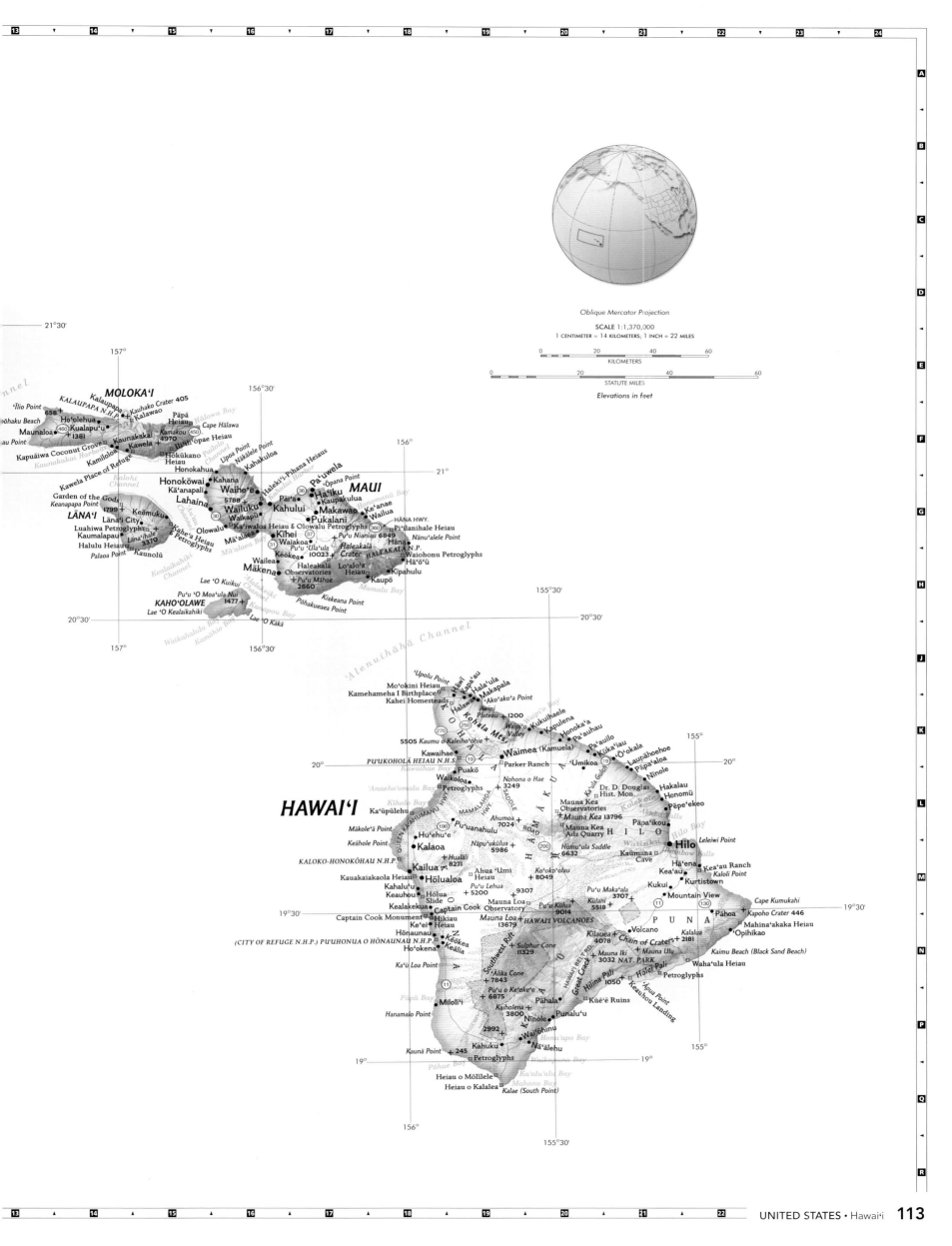

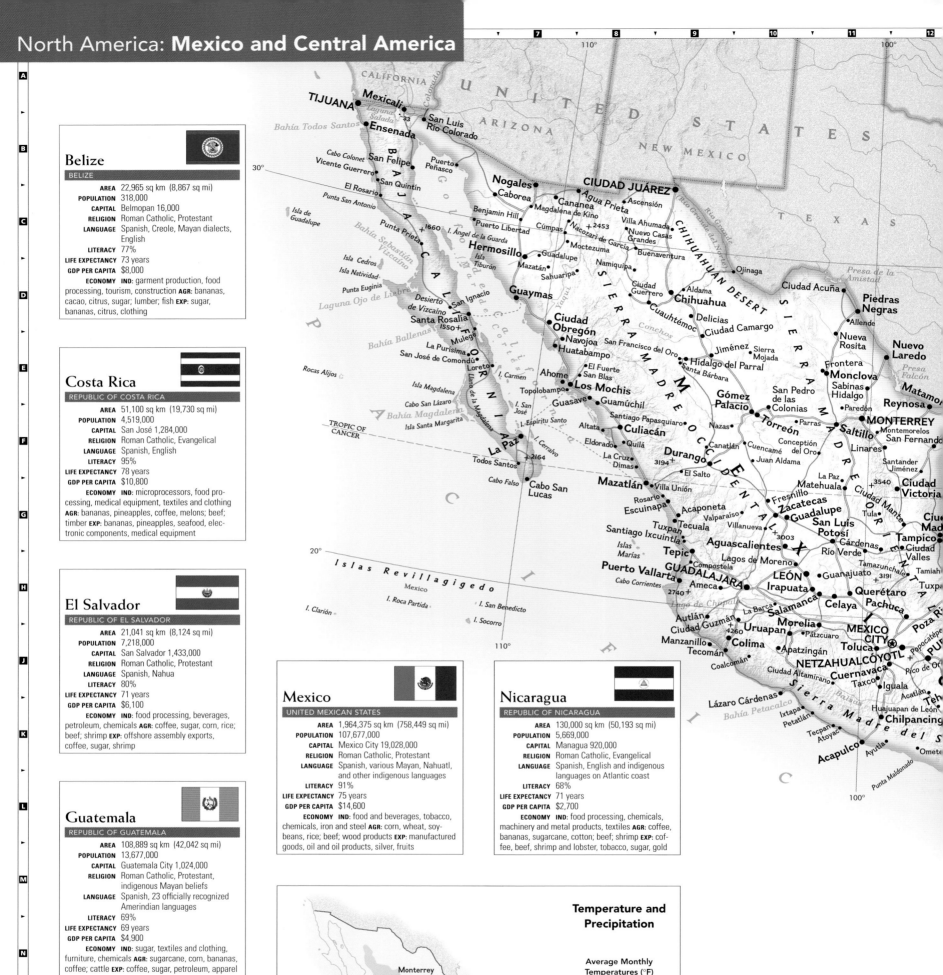

Belize
BELIZE

AREA	22,965 sq km (8,867 sq mi)
POPULATION	318,000
CAPITAL	Belmopan 16,000
RELIGION	Roman Catholic, Protestant
LANGUAGE	Spanish, Creole, Mayan dialects, English
LITERACY	77%
LIFE EXPECTANCY	73 years
GDP PER CAPITA	$8,000

ECONOMY IND: garment production, food processing, tourism, construction **AGR:** bananas, cacao, citrus, sugar; lumber; fish **EXP:** sugar, bananas, citrus, clothing

Costa Rica
REPUBLIC OF COSTA RICA

AREA	51,100 sq km (19,730 sq mi)
POPULATION	4,519,000
CAPITAL	San José 1,284,000
RELIGION	Roman Catholic, Evangelical
LANGUAGE	Spanish, English
LITERACY	95%
LIFE EXPECTANCY	78 years
GDP PER CAPITA	$10,800

ECONOMY IND: microprocessors, food processing, medical equipment, textiles and clothing **AGR:** bananas, pineapples, coffee, melons; beef; timber **EXP:** bananas, pineapples, seafood, electronic components, medical equipment

El Salvador
REPUBLIC OF EL SALVADOR

AREA	21,041 sq km (8,124 sq mi)
POPULATION	7,218,000
CAPITAL	San Salvador 1,433,000
RELIGION	Roman Catholic, Protestant
LANGUAGE	Spanish, Nahua
LITERACY	80%
LIFE EXPECTANCY	71 years
GDP PER CAPITA	$6,100

ECONOMY IND: food processing, beverages, petroleum, chemicals **AGR:** coffee, sugar, corn, rice; beef; shrimp **EXP:** offshore assembly exports, coffee, sugar, shrimp

Guatemala
REPUBLIC OF GUATEMALA

AREA	108,889 sq km (42,042 sq mi)
POPULATION	13,677,000
CAPITAL	Guatemala City 1,024,000
RELIGION	Roman Catholic, Protestant, indigenous Mayan beliefs
LANGUAGE	Spanish, 23 officially recognized Amerindian languages
LITERACY	69%
LIFE EXPECTANCY	69 years
GDP PER CAPITA	$4,900

ECONOMY IND: sugar, textiles and clothing, furniture, chemicals **AGR:** sugarcane, corn, bananas, coffee; cattle **EXP:** coffee, sugar, petroleum, apparel

Honduras
REPUBLIC OF HONDURAS

AREA	112,492 sq km (43,433 sq mi)
POPULATION	7,322,000
CAPITAL	Tegucigalpa 946,000
RELIGION	Roman Catholic
LANGUAGE	Spanish, Amerindian dialects
LITERACY	80%
LIFE EXPECTANCY	72 years
GDP PER CAPITA	$4,300

ECONOMY IND: sugar, coffee, textiles, clothing **AGR:** bananas, coffee, citrus; beef; timber; shrimp **EXP:** coffee, shrimp, bananas, gold

Mexico
UNITED MEXICAN STATES

AREA	1,964,375 sq km (758,449 sq mi)
POPULATION	107,677,000
CAPITAL	Mexico City 19,028,000
RELIGION	Roman Catholic, Protestant
LANGUAGE	Spanish, various Mayan, Nahuatl, and other indigenous languages
LITERACY	91%
LIFE EXPECTANCY	75 years
GDP PER CAPITA	$14,600

ECONOMY IND: food and beverages, tobacco, chemicals, iron and steel **AGR:** corn, wheat, soybeans, rice; beef; wood products **EXP:** manufactured goods, oil and oil products, silver, fruits

Nicaragua
REPUBLIC OF NICARAGUA

AREA	130,000 sq km (50,193 sq mi)
POPULATION	5,669,000
CAPITAL	Managua 920,000
RELIGION	Roman Catholic, Evangelical
LANGUAGE	Spanish, English and indigenous languages on Atlantic coast
LITERACY	68%
LIFE EXPECTANCY	71 years
GDP PER CAPITA	$2,700

ECONOMY IND: food processing, chemicals, machinery and metal products, textiles **AGR:** coffee, bananas, sugarcane, cotton; beef; shrimp **EXP:** coffee, beef, shrimp and lobster, tobacco, sugar, gold

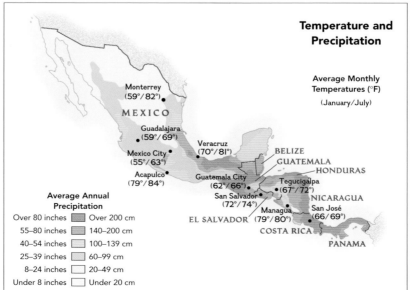

Temperature and Precipitation

Average Monthly Temperatures (°F)

(January/July)

Monterrey (59°/82°)
Guadalajara (59°/69°)
Veracruz (70°/81°)
Mexico City (55°/63°)
Acapulco (79°/84°)
Guatemala City (62°/66°)
Tegucigalpa (67°/72°)
San Salvador (72°/74°)
Managua (79°/80°)
San José (66°/69°)

Average Annual Precipitation

Over 80 inches	Over 200 cm
55–80 inches	140–200 cm
40–54 inches	100–139 cm
25–39 inches	60–99 cm
8–24 inches	20–49 cm
Under 8 inches	Under 20 cm

Panama
REPUBLIC OF PANAMA

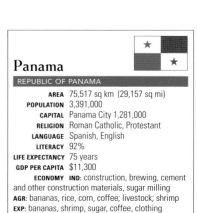

AREA	75,517 sq km (29,157 sq mi)
POPULATION	3,391,000
CAPITAL	Panama City 1,281,000
RELIGION	Roman Catholic, Protestant
LANGUAGE	Spanish, English
LITERACY	92%
LIFE EXPECTANCY	75 years
GDP PER CAPITA	$11,300

ECONOMY IND: construction, brewing, cement and other construction materials, sugar milling **AGR:** bananas, rice, corn, coffee; livestock; shrimp **EXP:** bananas, shrimp, sugar, coffee, clothing

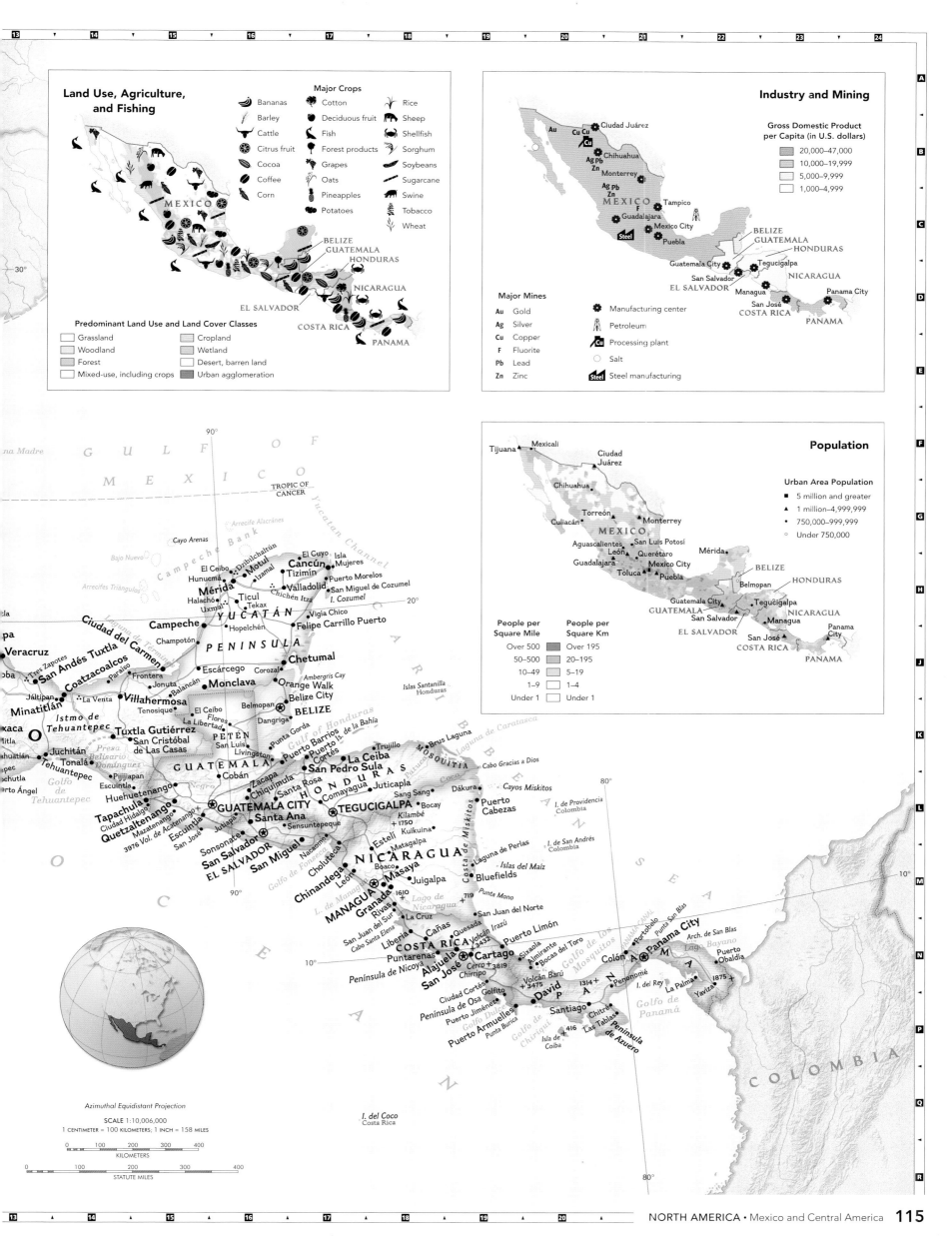

Land Use, Agriculture, and Fishing

Major Crops

- Bananas
- Barley
- Cattle
- Citrus fruit
- Cocoa
- Coffee
- Corn
- Cotton
- Deciduous fruit
- Fish
- Forest products
- Grapes
- Oats
- Pineapples
- Potatoes
- Rice
- Sheep
- Shellfish
- Sorghum
- Soybeans
- Sugarcane
- Swine
- Tobacco
- Wheat

Predominant Land Use and Land Cover Classes

- Grassland
- Woodland
- Forest
- Mixed-use, including crops
- Cropland
- Wetland
- Desert, barren land
- Urban agglomeration

Industry and Mining

Gross Domestic Product per Capita (in U.S. dollars)

- 20,000–47,000
- 10,000–19,999
- 5,000–9,999
- 1,000–4,999

Major Mines

- Au Gold
- Ag Silver
- Cu Copper
- F Fluorite
- Pb Lead
- Zn Zinc
- Manufacturing center
- Petroleum
- Cu Processing plant
- Salt
- Steel Steel manufacturing

Population

Urban Area Population

- ■ 5 million and greater
- ▲ 1 million–4,999,999
- ● 750,000–999,999
- ○ Under 750,000

People per Square Mile	People per Square Km
Over 500	Over 195
50–500	20–195
10–49	5–19
1–9	1–4
Under 1	Under 1

Azimuthal Equidistant Projection

SCALE 1:10,006,000
1 CENTIMETER = 100 KILOMETERS; 1 INCH = 158 MILES

KILOMETERS
STATUTE MILES

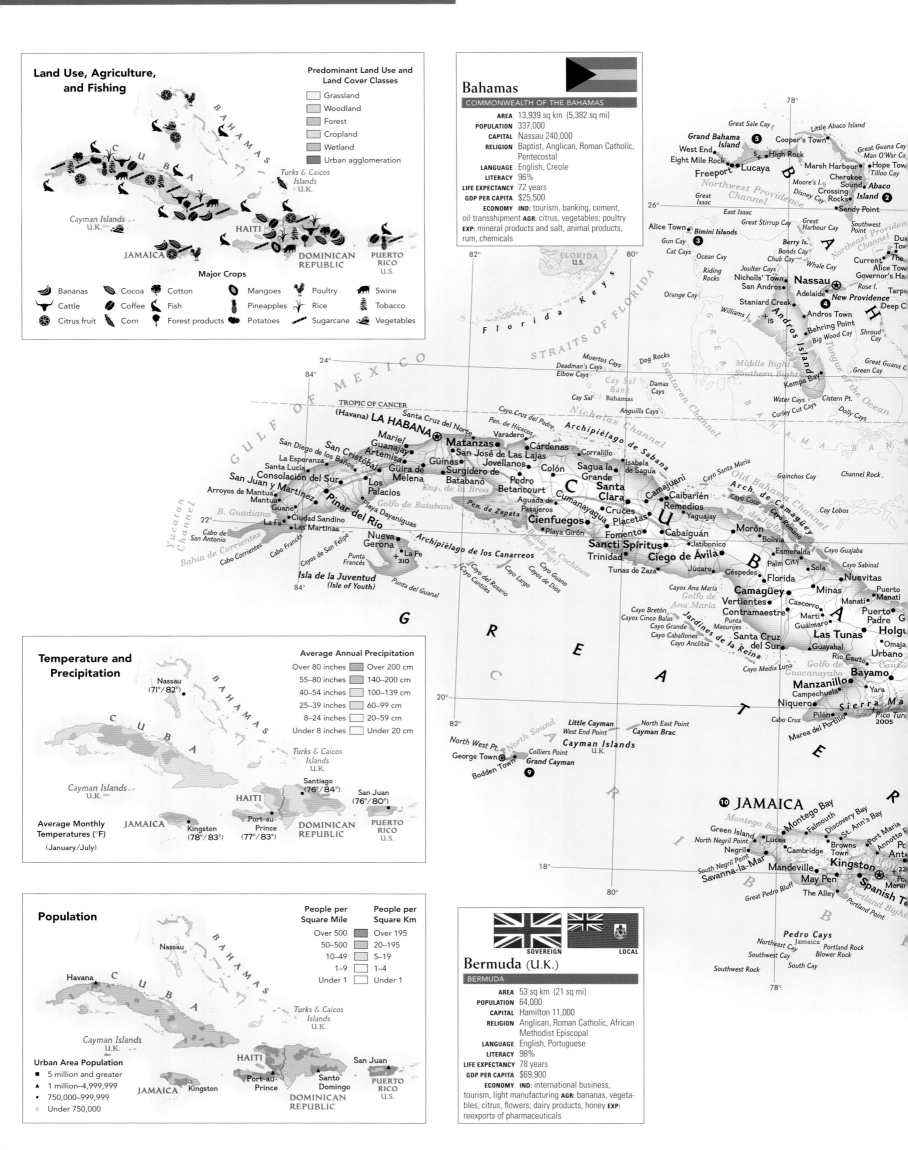

Land Use, Agriculture, and Fishing

Predominant Land Use and Land Cover Classes
- Grassland
- Woodland
- Forest
- Cropland
- Wetland
- Urban agglomeration

Major Crops
- Bananas
- Cattle
- Citrus fruit
- Cocoa
- Coffee
- Corn
- Cotton
- Fish
- Forest products
- Mangoes
- Pineapples
- Potatoes
- Poultry
- Rice
- Sugarcane
- Swine
- Tobacco
- Vegetables

Bahamas
COMMONWEALTH OF THE BAHAMAS

AREA	13,939 sq km (5,382 sq mi)
POPULATION	337,000
CAPITAL	Nassau 240,000
RELIGION	Baptist, Anglican, Roman Catholic, Pentecostal
LANGUAGE	English, Creole
LITERACY	96%
LIFE EXPECTANCY	72 years
GDP PER CAPITA	$25,500

ECONOMY IND: tourism, banking, cement, oil transshipment AGR: citrus, vegetables; poultry EXP: mineral products and salt, animal products, rum, chemicals

Temperature and Precipitation

Average Annual Precipitation

Over 80 inches	Over 200 cm
55–80 inches	140–200 cm
40–54 inches	100–139 cm
25–39 inches	60–99 cm
8–24 inches	20–59 cm
Under 8 inches	Under 20 cm

Average Monthly Temperatures (°F) (January/July)

Nassau (71°/82°)
Santiago (76°/84°)
San Juan (76°/80°)
Kingston (78°/83°)
Port-au-Prince (77°/83°)

Population

	People per Square Mile	People per Square Km
	Over 500	Over 195
	50–500	20–195
	10–49	5–19
	1–9	1–4
	Under 1	Under 1

Urban Area Population
- 5 million and greater
- 1 million–4,999,999
- 750,000–999,999
- Under 750,000

Bermuda (U.K.)

SOVEREIGN   LOCAL

BERMUDA

AREA	53 sq km (21 sq mi)
POPULATION	64,000
CAPITAL	Hamilton 11,000
RELIGION	Anglican, Roman Catholic, African Methodist Episcopal
LANGUAGE	English, Portuguese
LITERACY	98%
LIFE EXPECTANCY	78 years
GDP PER CAPITA	$69,900

ECONOMY IND: international business, tourism, light manufacturing AGR: bananas, vegetables, citrus, flowers; dairy products, honey EXP: reexports of pharmaceuticals

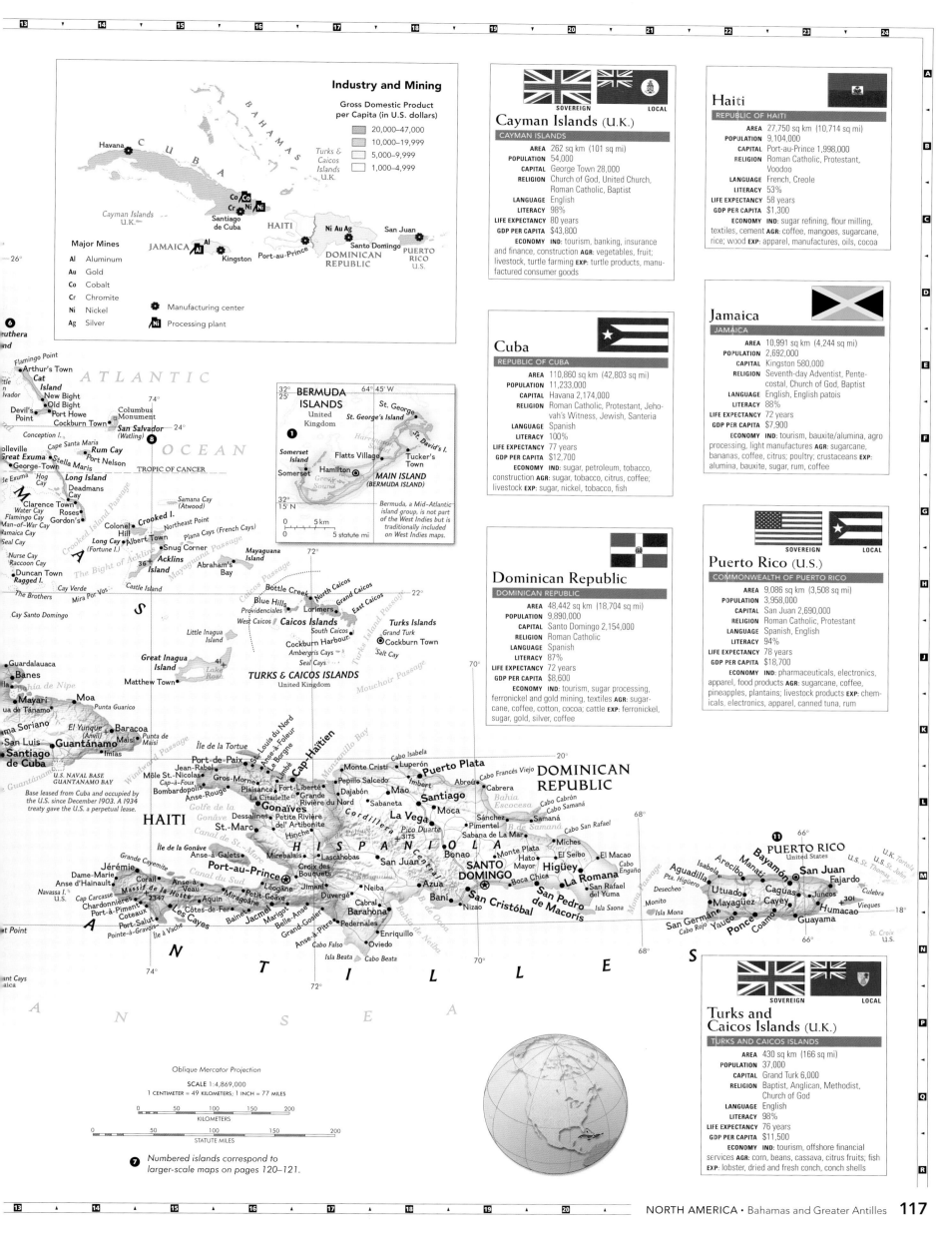

Industry and Mining

Gross Domestic Product per Capita (in U.S. dollars)
- 20,000–47,000
- 10,000–19,999
- 5,000–9,999
- 1,000–4,999

Major Mines
- **Al** Aluminum
- **Au** Gold
- **Co** Cobalt
- **Cr** Chromite
- **Ni** Nickel
- **Ag** Silver

- Manufacturing center
- **Ni** Processing plant

Cayman Islands (U.K.)
SOVEREIGN   LOCAL

CAYMAN ISLANDS

- **AREA** 262 sq km (101 sq mi)
- **POPULATION** 54,000
- **CAPITAL** George Town 28,000
- **RELIGION** Church of God, United Church, Roman Catholic, Baptist
- **LANGUAGE** English
- **LITERACY** 98%
- **LIFE EXPECTANCY** 80 years
- **GDP PER CAPITA** $43,800
- **ECONOMY IND:** tourism, banking, insurance and finance, construction **AGR:** vegetables, fruit; livestock, turtle farming **EXP:** turtle products, manufactured consumer goods

---

Cuba

REPUBLIC OF CUBA

- **AREA** 110,860 sq km (42,803 sq mi)
- **POPULATION** 11,233,000
- **CAPITAL** Havana 2,174,000
- **RELIGION** Roman Catholic, Protestant, Jehovah's Witness, Jewish, Santeria
- **LANGUAGE** Spanish
- **LITERACY** 100%
- **LIFE EXPECTANCY** 77 years
- **GDP PER CAPITA** $12,700
- **ECONOMY IND:** sugar, petroleum, tobacco, construction **AGR:** sugar, tobacco, citrus, coffee; livestock **EXP:** sugar, nickel, tobacco, fish

---

Dominican Republic

DOMINICAN REPUBLIC

- **AREA** 48,442 sq km (18,704 sq mi)
- **POPULATION** 9,890,000
- **CAPITAL** Santo Domingo 2,154,000
- **RELIGION** Roman Catholic
- **LANGUAGE** Spanish
- **LITERACY** 87%
- **LIFE EXPECTANCY** 72 years
- **GDP PER CAPITA** $8,600
- **ECONOMY IND:** tourism, sugar processing, ferronickel and gold mining, textiles **AGR:** sugarcane, coffee, cotton, cocoa; cattle **EXP:** ferronickel, sugar, gold, silver, coffee

---

Haiti

REPUBLIC OF HAITI

- **AREA** 27,750 sq km (10,714 sq mi)
- **POPULATION** 9,104,000
- **CAPITAL** Port-au-Prince 1,998,000
- **RELIGION** Roman Catholic, Protestant, Voodoo
- **LANGUAGE** French, Creole
- **LITERACY** 53%
- **LIFE EXPECTANCY** 58 years
- **GDP PER CAPITA** $1,300
- **ECONOMY IND:** sugar refining, flour milling, textiles, cement **AGR:** coffee, mangoes, sugarcane, rice; wood **EXP:** apparel, manufactures, oils, cocoa

---

Jamaica

JAMAICA

- **AREA** 10,991 sq km (4,244 sq mi)
- **POPULATION** 2,692,000
- **CAPITAL** Kingston 580,000
- **RELIGION** Seventh-day Adventist, Pentecostal, Church of God, Baptist
- **LANGUAGE** English, English patois
- **LITERACY** 88%
- **LIFE EXPECTANCY** 72 years
- **GDP PER CAPITA** $7,900
- **ECONOMY IND:** tourism, bauxite/alumina, agro processing, light manufactures **AGR:** sugarcane, bananas, coffee, citrus; poultry; crustaceans **EXP:** alumina, bauxite, sugar, rum, coffee

---

Puerto Rico (U.S.)
SOVEREIGN   LOCAL

COMMONWEALTH OF PUERTO RICO

- **AREA** 9,086 sq km (3,508 sq mi)
- **POPULATION** 3,958,000
- **CAPITAL** San Juan 2,690,000
- **RELIGION** Roman Catholic, Protestant
- **LANGUAGE** Spanish, English
- **LITERACY** 94%
- **LIFE EXPECTANCY** 78 years
- **GDP PER CAPITA** $18,700
- **ECONOMY IND:** pharmaceuticals, electronics, apparel, food products **AGR:** sugarcane, coffee, pineapples, plantains; livestock products **EXP:** chemicals, electronics, apparel, canned tuna, rum

---

Turks and Caicos Islands (U.K.)
SOVEREIGN   LOCAL

TURKS AND CAICOS ISLANDS

- **AREA** 430 sq km (166 sq mi)
- **POPULATION** 37,000
- **CAPITAL** Grand Turk 6,000
- **RELIGION** Baptist, Anglican, Methodist, Church of God
- **LANGUAGE** English
- **LITERACY** 98%
- **LIFE EXPECTANCY** 76 years
- **GDP PER CAPITA** $11,500
- **ECONOMY IND:** tourism, offshore financial services **AGR:** corn, beans, cassava, citrus fruits; fish **EXP:** lobster, dried and fresh conch, conch shells

---

BERMUDA ISLANDS
United Kingdom

Bermuda, a Mid-Atlantic island group, is not part of the West Indies but is traditionally included on West Indies maps.

Oblique Mercator Projection

SCALE 1:4,869,000
1 CENTIMETER = 49 KILOMETERS; 1 INCH = 77 MILES

KILOMETERS
STATUTE MILES

Numbered islands correspond to larger-scale maps on pages 120–121.

Anguilla (U.K.)
ANGUILLA
AREA 96 sq km (37 sq mi)
POPULATION 15,000
CAPITAL The Valley 1,500
RELIGION Anglican, Methodist, other Protestant, Roman Catholic
LANGUAGE English
LITERACY 95%
LIFE EXPECTANCY 79 years
GDP PER CAPITA $8,800
ECONOMY IND: tourism, boat building, off-shore financial services **AGR:** small quantities of tobacco, vegetables; cattle raising **EXP:** lobster, fish, livestock, salt, concrete blocks

Antigua and Barbuda
ANTIGUA AND BARBUDA
AREA 442 sq km (171 sq mi)
POPULATION 86,000
CAPITAL St. John's 26,000
RELIGION Anglican, other Protestant, Roman Catholic
LANGUAGE English, local dialects
LITERACY 86%
LIFE EXPECTANCY 73 years
GDP PER CAPITA $18,900
ECONOMY IND: tourism, construction, light manufacturing (clothing, alcohol, household appliances) **AGR:** cotton, bananas, coconuts, cucumbers, mangoes; livestock **EXP:** petroleum products, bedding, handicrafts, electronic components, transport equipment

Aruba (Netherlands)
ARUBA
AREA 193 sq km (75 sq mi)
POPULATION 105,000
CAPITAL Oranjestad 32,000
RELIGION Roman Catholic, Protestant
LANGUAGE Papiamento, Spanish, English, Dutch
LITERACY 97%
LIFE EXPECTANCY 73 years
GDP PER CAPITA $21,800
ECONOMY IND: tourism, transshipment facilities, oil refining **AGR:** aloes; livestock; fish **EXP:** live animals and animal products, art and collectibles, machinery and electrical equipment, transport equipment

Barbados
BARBADOS
AREA 430 sq km (166 sq mi)
POPULATION 280,000
CAPITAL Bridgetown 116,000
RELIGION Anglican, Pentecostal, Methodist
LANGUAGE English
LITERACY 100%
LIFE EXPECTANCY 76 years
GDP PER CAPITA $19,200
ECONOMY IND: tourism, sugar, light manufacturing, component assembly for export **AGR:** sugarcane, vegetables, cotton **EXP:** manufactures, sugar and molasses, rum, foods and beverages, chemicals

British Virgin Islands (U.K.)
BRITISH VIRGIN ISLANDS
AREA 153 sq km (59 sq mi)
POPULATION 23,000
CAPITAL Road Town 9,000
RELIGION Protestant, Roman Catholic
LANGUAGE English
LITERACY 98%
LIFE EXPECTANCY 74 years
GDP PER CAPITA $38,500
ECONOMY IND: tourism, light industry, construction, rum **AGR:** fruits, vegetables; livestock; fish **EXP:** rum, fresh fish, fruits, animals, gravel, sand

Dominica
COMMONWEALTH OF DOMINICA
AREA 751 sq km (290 sq mi)
POPULATION 73,000
CAPITAL Roseau 14,000
RELIGION Roman Catholic, Protestant
LANGUAGE English, French patois
LITERACY 94%
LIFE EXPECTANCY 75 years
GDP PER CAPITA $10,000
ECONOMY IND: soap, coconut oil, tourism, copra, furniture **AGR:** bananas, citrus, mangoes, root crops, coconuts **EXP:** bananas, soap, bay oil, vegetables, grapefruit

Grenada
GRENADA
AREA 344 sq km (133 sq mi)
POPULATION 106,000
CAPITAL St. George's 32,000
RELIGION Roman Catholic, Anglican, other Protestant
LANGUAGE English, French patois
LITERACY 96%
LIFE EXPECTANCY 68 years
GDP PER CAPITA $11,200
ECONOMY IND: food and beverages, textiles, light assembly operations, tourism **AGR:** bananas, cocoa, nutmeg, mace, citrus **EXP:** bananas, cocoa, nutmeg, fruits and vegetables, clothing

Guadeloupe (France)
OVERSEAS DEPARTMENT OF FRANCE
AREA 1,705 sq km (658 sq mi)
POPULATION 420,000
CAPITAL Basse-Terre 12,000
RELIGION Roman Catholic
LANGUAGE French
LITERACY 90%
LIFE EXPECTANCY 79 years
GDP PER CAPITA $7,900
ECONOMY IND: construction, cement, rum, sugar **AGR:** bananas, sugarcane, tropical fruits and vegetables; cattle **EXP:** bananas, sugar, rum

Martinique (France)
OVERSEAS DEPARTMENT OF FRANCE
AREA 1,100 sq km (425 sq mi)
POPULATION 405,000
CAPITAL Fort-de-France 93,000
RELIGION Roman Catholic, Protestant
LANGUAGE French, Creole patois
LITERACY 98%
LIFE EXPECTANCY 80 years
GDP PER CAPITA $14,400
ECONOMY IND: construction, rum, cement, oil refining **AGR:** pineapples, avocados, bananas, flowers **EXP:** refined petroleum products, bananas, rum, pineapples

Montserrat (U.K.)
MONTSERRAT
AREA 102 sq km (39 sq mi)
POPULATION 10,000
CAPITAL Brades (administrative) 700; Plymouth (abandoned)
RELIGION Anglican, Methodist, Roman Catholic, Pentecostal, Seventh-day Adventist, other Christian
LANGUAGE English
LITERACY 97%
LIFE EXPECTANCY 78 years
GDP PER CAPITA $3,400
ECONOMY IND: tourism, rum, textiles, electronic appliances **AGR:** cabbages, carrots, cucumbers, tomatoes; livestock products **EXP:** electronic components, plastic bags, apparel, hot peppers

Netherlands Antilles (Neth.)
NETHERLANDS ANTILLES
AREA 800 sq km (309 sq mi)
POPULATION 199,000
CAPITAL Willemstad 120,000
RELIGION Roman Catholic, Pentecostal
LANGUAGE Papiamento, English, Dutch, Spanish
LITERACY 97%
LIFE EXPECTANCY 75 years
GDP PER CAPITA $16,000
ECONOMY IND: tourism, petroleum refining, petroleum transshipment facilities, light manufacturing **AGR:** aloes, sorghum, peanuts, vegetables, tropical fruits **EXP:** petroleum products

St. Kitts and Nevis
FEDERATION OF SAINT KITTS AND NEVIS
AREA 269 sq km (104 sq mi)
POPULATION 48,000
CAPITAL Basseterre 13,000
RELIGION Anglican, other Protestant, Roman Catholic
LANGUAGE English
LITERACY 98%
LIFE EXPECTANCY 70 years
GDP PER CAPITA $14,400
ECONOMY IND: tourism, cotton, salt, copra **AGR:** sugarcane, rice, yams, vegetables; fish **EXP:** machinery, food, electronics, beverages, tobacco

St. Lucia
SAINT LUCIA
AREA 616 sq km (238 sq mi)
POPULATION 171,000
CAPITAL Castries 14,000
RELIGION Roman Catholic, Seventh-day Adventist, Pentecostal
LANGUAGE English, French patois
LITERACY 90%
LIFE EXPECTANCY 73 years
GDP PER CAPITA $10,900
ECONOMY IND: clothing, assembly of electronic components, beverages, corrugated cardboard boxes **AGR:** bananas, coconuts, vegetables, citrus **EXP:** bananas, clothing, cocoa, vegetables

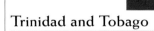

St. Vincent and the Grenadines
SAINT VINCENT AND THE GRENADINES
AREA 389 sq km (150 sq mi)
POPULATION 110,000
CAPITAL Kingstown 26,000
RELIGION Anglican, Methodist, Roman Catholic
LANGUAGE English, French patois
LITERACY 96%
LIFE EXPECTANCY 72 years
GDP PER CAPITA $10,500
ECONOMY IND: food processing, cement, furniture, clothing **AGR:** bananas, coconuts, sweet potatoes, spices; cattle; fish **EXP:** bananas, eddoes, dasheen (taro), arrowroot starch, tennis racquets

Trinidad and Tobago
REPUBLIC OF TRINIDAD AND TOBAGO
AREA 5,128 sq km (1,980 sq mi)
POPULATION 1,338,000
CAPITAL Port-of-Spain 54,000
RELIGION Roman Catholic, Hindu, Anglican, Baptist, Pentecostal, Muslim
LANGUAGE English, Caribbean Hindustani, French, Spanish, Chinese
LITERACY 99%
LIFE EXPECTANCY 69 years
GDP PER CAPITA $19,700
ECONOMY IND: petroleum, chemicals, tourism, food processing **AGR:** cocoa, rice, citrus, coffee; poultry **EXP:** petroleum and petroleum products, liquefied natural gas (LNG), methanol, ammonia

Virgin Islands (U.S.)
UNITED STATES VIRGIN ISLANDS
AREA 386 sq km (149 sq mi)
POPULATION 108,000
CAPITAL Charlotte Amalie 53,000
RELIGION Baptist, Roman Catholic, Episcopalian
LANGUAGE English, Spanish or Spanish Creole, French or French Creole
LITERACY 90-95%
LIFE EXPECTANCY 79 years
GDP PER CAPITA $14,500
ECONOMY IND: tourism, petroleum refining, watch assembly, rum distilling **AGR:** fruit, vegetables, sorghum; Senepol cattle **EXP:** refined petroleum products

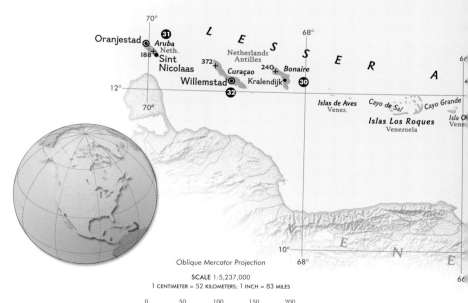

Oblique Mercator Projection

SCALE 1:5,237,000
1 CENTIMETER = 52 KILOMETERS; 1 INCH = 83 MILES

KILOMETERS

STATUTE MILES

21 *Numbered islands correspond to larger-scale maps on pages 120–121.*

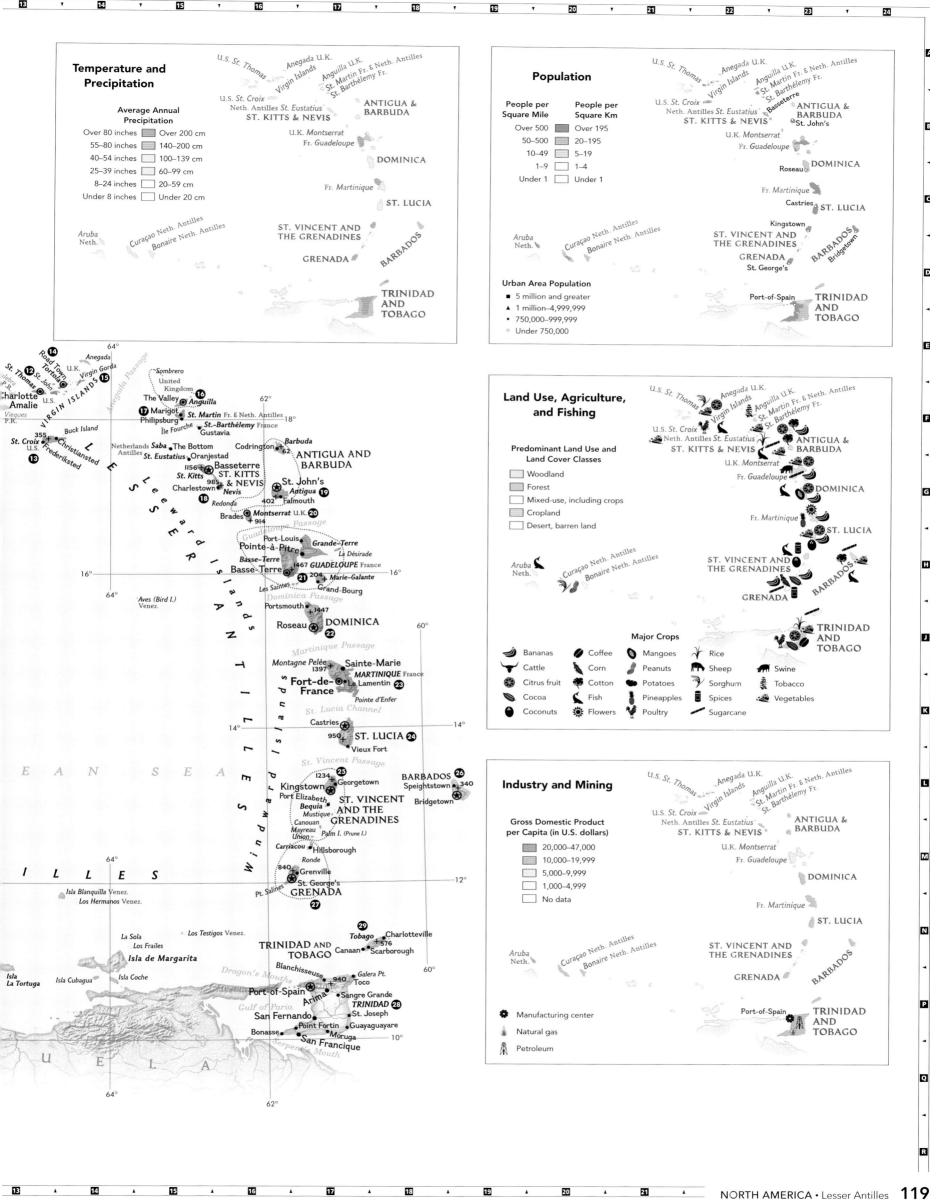

Temperature and Precipitation

Average Annual Precipitation

Over 80 inches		Over 200 cm
55–80 inches		140–200 cm
40–54 inches		100–139 cm
25–39 inches		60–99 cm
8–24 inches		20–59 cm
Under 8 inches		Under 20 cm

Population

People per Square Mile	People per Square Km
Over 500	Over 195
50–500	20–195
10–49	5–19
1–9	1–4
Under 1	Under 1

Urban Area Population
- ■ 5 million and greater
- ▲ 1 million–4,999,999
- • 750,000–999,999
- ○ Under 750,000

Land Use, Agriculture, and Fishing

Predominant Land Use and Land Cover Classes
- Woodland
- Forest
- Mixed-use, including crops
- Cropland
- Desert, barren land

Major Crops

Bananas	Coffee	Mangoes	Rice	
Cattle	Corn	Peanuts	Sheep	Swine
Citrus fruit	Cotton	Potatoes	Sorghum	Tobacco
Cocoa	Fish	Pineapples	Spices	Vegetables
Coconuts	Flowers	Poultry	Sugarcane	

Industry and Mining

Gross Domestic Product per Capita (in U.S. dollars)
- 20,000–47,000
- 10,000–19,999
- 5,000–9,999
- 1,000–4,999
- No data

- ✦ Manufacturing center
- Natural gas
- Petroleum

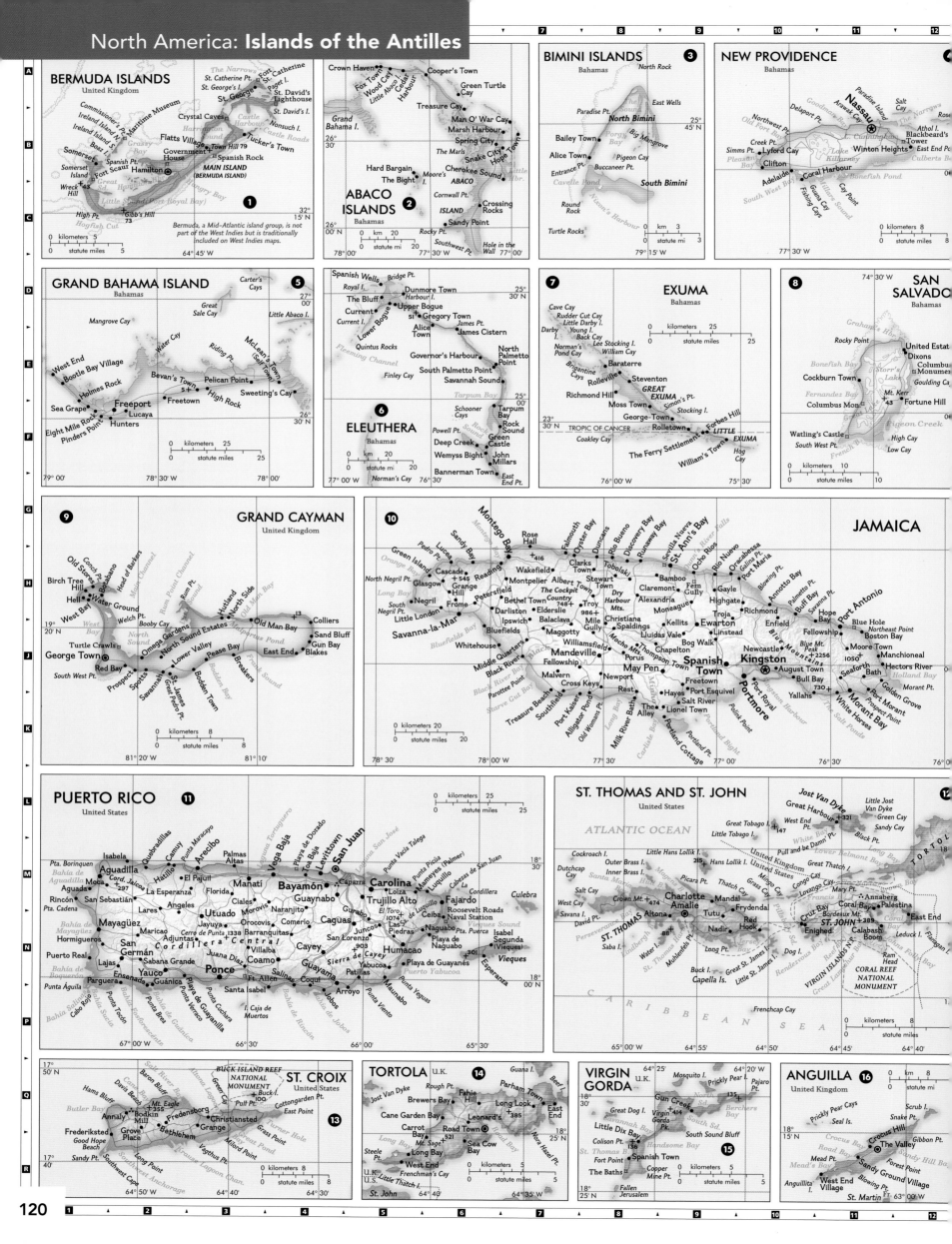

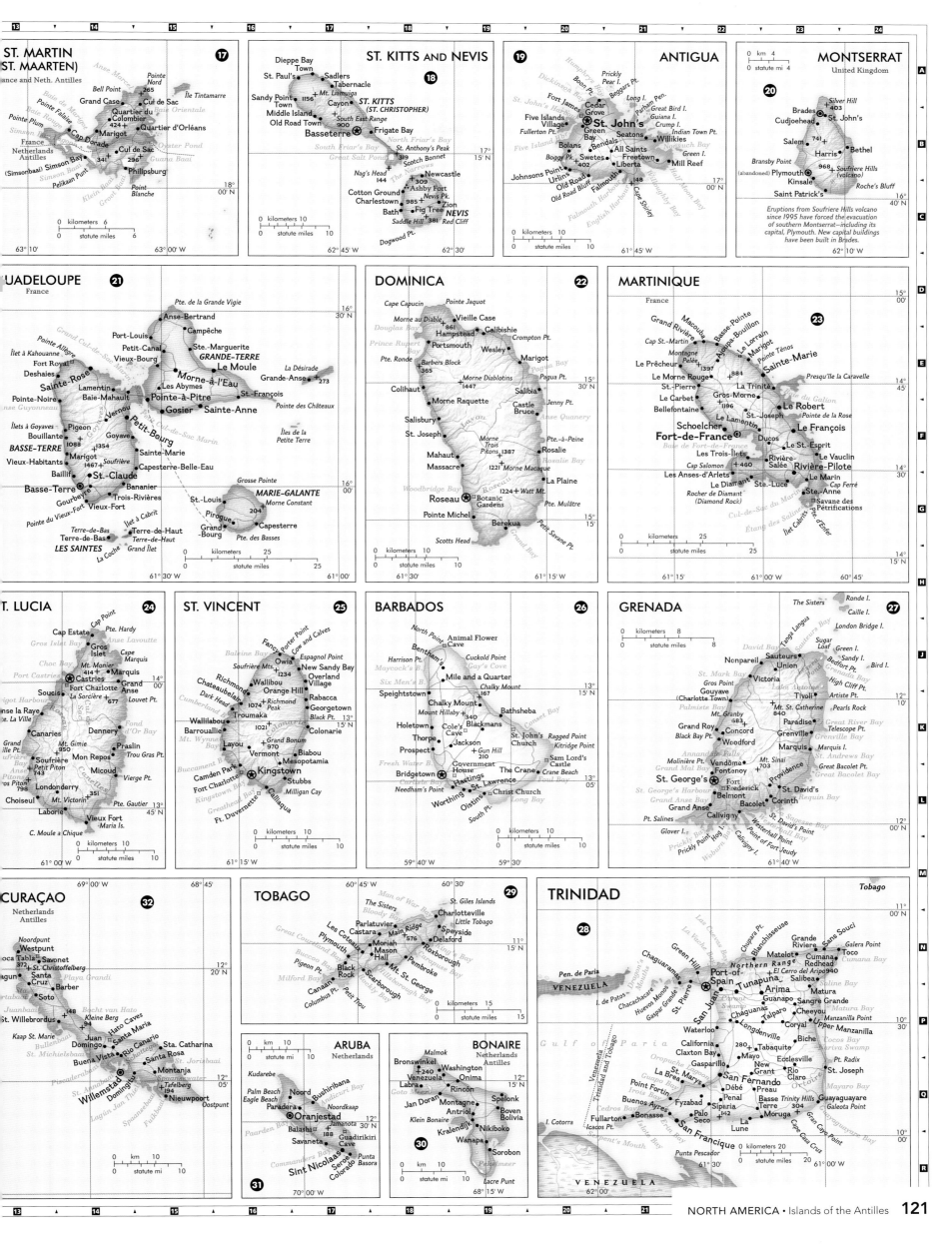

South America

South America is a place of remarkable extremes—sweltering jungle heat and face-numbing cold, endless towering mountains and dense tropical forests that seem to stretch forever, the world's mightiest river and the planet's driest spot. While the region's coastal areas are highly developed, the heart of the continent remains largely vacant, a rugged expanse of mountains, desert, grassland, and forest that constitutes one of the world's last great wilderness treasures.

Although much of the continent remains wild and untamed, South America has its refined side. It provided a cradle for several ancient civilizations and in modern times has given birth to some of the world's biggest metropolises. Yet indigenous communities, though only a small percentage of the population, still exist—high in the mountains of Ecuador, deep in the Amazon jungle of Brazil, scattered in the forested hinterlands of Suriname, and elsewhere.

The ice-shrouded Torres del Paine Mountains take pride of place in Chile's harsh Patagonia region. Home to indigenous populations and endemic flora and fauna, Patagonia, which also encompasses a large swath of Argentina, has often been described as "the last place on Earth."

South America has also afforded us some of the great cultural highlights of the past hundred years—the astonishing discovery of the lost city of Machu Picchu in the Peruvian Andes, Evita Perón rousing crowds in Argentina, the alluring "Girl from Ipanema" on the beach in Brazil, and Pele's magic with a soccer ball.

PHYSICAL GEOGRAPHY With a base along the Caribbean coast and an apex at Cape Horn, South America is shaped rather like an elongated triangle. Embracing a total area of nearly 6.9 million square miles (17.8 million sq km), it's the fourth largest continent, bounded by the Atlantic Ocean in the east, the Pacific Ocean in the west, and the Caribbean Sea in the north. Its only connection to another landmass (North America) is the narrow Isthmus of Panama between Colombia and Panama. In the deep south, only the stormy Drake Passage separates South America from the Antarctic continent.

Despite its hefty size, South America has a relatively short coastline and few islands. However its offshore elements are distinctive: frigid Tierra del Fuego, the battle-torn Falklands (Malvinas), the biologically wondrous Galápagos, the spectacular fiord country of southern Chile, and untamed Marajó Island in the Amazon delta.

Three huge physical features dominate the South American mainland: the Andes mountains, the Amazon Basin, and a wide southern plain that encompasses the Pampas, the Gran Chaco, and much of Patagonia. The Andes cordillera, which runs all the way from northern Colombia to southern Chile and Argentina, is the world's longest mountain range. It's also one of the highest—more than 50 peaks over 20,000 feet (6,100 m)—and one of the most active in terms of volcanism and earthquakes.

South America's hydrology is perhaps the most astounding of any continent. Rainwater spilling off the Andes creates the mighty Amazon River and its thousand-plus tributaries, which in turn sustain the world's largest rain forest and greatest diversity of flora and fauna. Although the Amazon itself is not the planet's longest watercourse, it carries more liquid than the next ten biggest rivers combined. Spilling off a tabletop mountain in the northern Amazon is Angel Falls, the world's highest cascade at 3,212 feet (979 m), and tumbling off an ancient lava cliff between Brazil and Argentina is thunderous Iguazú Falls.

Among the continent's other geographic oddities are windswept Patagonia at the continent's southern tip and the extremely arid Atacama Desert, which often goes without rain for hundreds of years. The endless Pampas prairie of Argentina and Uruguay was the birthplace of gaucho culture, while the Pantanal region of southern Brazil is among the Earth's great wetlands.

HISTORY Like its continental cousin to the north, South America was first inhabited by nomads whose Asiatic ancestors crossed the Bering Strait during the last great ice age, sometime between 14,000 and 24,000 years ago. After crossing the Isthmus of Panama, they diffused throughout the continent and evolved into hundreds of different tribal groups with their own languages, customs, and traditions.

Starting around 3000 B.C., Amerindians living in the Andes region began to cultivate beans, squash, cotton, and potatoes. By 1000 B.C., villages along Peru's northern coastal plain had evolved into the Chavin culture, the continent's first true civilization. With a religion based on worship of the jaguar god, the Chavin built great ceremonial centers with mud-brick temples and pyramids. They also developed polychrome pottery, intricate weaving, and South America's first metallurgy. By the sixth century A.D., the Chavin had been eclipsed by other sophisticated Peruvian cultures such as the Moche, Nasca, and Tiwanaku. The last of the region's great Amerindian cultures was the Inca; master stonemasons and soldiers, the Inca forged an empire that stretched from present-day southern Colombia to northern Chile and Argentina.

Christopher Columbus "discovered" South America in 1498 on his third voyage to the New World, but the landmass (and adjacent North America) didn't receive its current name until Italian mariner Amerigo Vespucci explored its coast (1499–1502) and first postulated that it was a continent unto itself rather than part of Asia. In their quest for riches, the Spanish conquistadors came into violent contact with local Amerindian groups, climaxing in Francisco Pizarro's invasion of the Andes and bloody triumph over the Inca Empire in the 1530s. While the Spaniards were busy conquering the west coast, the Portuguese were claiming the continent's eastern shore, an area they called Brazil after a local dyewood tree. Driven off their land, decimated by disease, and pressed into slavery, South America's native population quickly declined in all but the most remote regions. Within half a century of first contact, European hegemony over the entire continent was assured.

Three distinct groups—the military, wealthy families, and the Roman Catholic Church—came to dominate South America's new Iberian colonies by the end of the 16th century. Using Indian labor and millions of slaves imported from Africa, they developed a society based on sprawling ranches and European-style cities such as Lima and Bogotá. Missions under the direction of the Jesuits and Franciscans were used to convert and control Indians in frontier areas. By the dawn of the 19th century—inspired by popular uprisings in the United States and France—South America's colonies had hatched their own revolutions. Between 1810 and 1824, Simón Bolívar and José de San Martín liberated all of the region's Spanish-speaking lands. Brazil declared its independence from Portugal in 1822.

Despite impressive economic gains in some countries—most notably Argentina—most of South America's independent states were stagnant by the early 20th century, struggling beneath a twin yoke of brutal military rule and neocolonial economic exploitation. This status quo endured until the late 1990s, when democracy flowered across the continent.

One of the most dramatic ruins in South America, the Inca ceremonial center of Machu Picchu hovers 2,000 feet (610 m) above the Urubamba River in the Peruvian Andes. It was built in the mid- to late 1400s at the behest of Pachacuti, the ruler who greatly enlarged the Inca Empire through conquest and colonization.

CULTURE A rich blend of Iberian, African, and Amerindian traditions, South America has some of the world's most lively and distinctive cultures. These cultures are also among the most urban. Despite romantic images of the Amazon and Machu Picchu, the vast majority of South Americans live in cities rather than the rain forest or mountains. A massive rural exodus since the 1950s has transformed South America into the most urbanized continent after Australia, a region that now boasts three of the world's 15 largest cities: São Paulo (19 million), Buenos Aires (13 million), and Rio de Janeiro (12 million). Ninety percent of these people live within 200 miles (320 km) of the coast, leaving huge expanses of the interior virtually unpopulated.

Several common threads bind the continent's more than 386 million people. Iberian languages dominate, with about half speaking Spanish and the other half Portuguese. There are several linguistic anomalies—French, Dutch, and English in the Guianas, and Amerindian dialects in the remote Amazon and Andes—but most South Americans don't need a translator when talking to one another. And despite recent inroads by Protestant missionaries—especially among remote Indian tribes and the urban poor—nearly 85 percent of South Americans adhere to the Roman Catholic faith.

Yet the continent also flaunts an amazing ethnic diversity. Although the majority of people can still trace their ancestors back to Spain or Portugal, waves of immigration have transformed South America into an ethnic smorgasbord. Amerindians and mixed-blood mestizos make up more than 80 percent of the population in Bolivia, Ecuador, and Peru. More than one-third of Argentines can boast Italian roots. Blond-haired, blue-eyed Germans populate many parts of Chile, Uruguay, and southern Brazil. Almost 40 percent of Brazilians and a high percentage of the residents of coastal Colombia and Venezuela are the descendants of African slaves. Asian Indians comprise the largest ethnic groups in both Suriname and Guyana.

This blend has produced a vibrant modern culture with influence far beyond the bounds of its South American cradle. Argentina's beloved tango—music, lyrics, and dance steps born of the Buenos Aires ghettos—is now an icon of romance all around the world. Brazil's steamy port cities hatched sensual Afro-Latino rhythms such as samba and bossa nova, Peruvian pipe music has become synonymous with the Andes, while Colombia has produced a rousing Latino rock. South America's rich literary map includes everything from the magical realism of Gabriel García Márquez and Mario Vargas Llosa to the sensual poems of Pablo Neruda and the poignant prose of Jorge Luis Borges. A similar passion flows through soccer, the region's favorite game, where the likes of Pele and Maradona have led their respective national teams (Brazil and Argentina) to multiple World Cup titles.

ECONOMICS Even though South America's colonies gained their independence at a relatively early stage, they were not able to achieve economic autonomy to any large extent. By the early 20th century, nearly all of them were dependent on commodity exports to Europe or the United States: bananas, rubber, sugar, coffee, timber, emeralds, copper, oil, and beef. In the short term some countries did very well with exports, especially Argentina, which counted itself among the world's richest nations until the 1950s. But failure to make a full transition from resource extraction into modern business and industry spelled economic doom for the entire continent.

By the 1960s, most of South America was mired in negative or neutral economic growth, increasingly dependent on overseas aid, and plagued by unemployment and poverty. Corruption, military rule, and mismanagement augmented an already dire situation. Hyperinflation of several hundred percent per annum battered Brazil and Argentina in the 1980s, nearly crippling the continent's two largest economies. During the same era, narcotics became one of South America's most important money spinners—cocaine exported in great quantities from Colombia, Bolivia, and Peru. Yet by the 1990s, most countries saw light at the end of their dim economic tunnels. In the early years of the 21st century, although fundamental problems remain—like huge foreign debt—the region's nouvelle democracy spurred an era of relative prosperity, raising the GDP per capita in many countries.

South America still relies, to a large extent, on commodity exports: oil from Venezuela, coffee from Colombia, and copper from Chile. But recent decades have seen a dramatic shift toward manufacturing and niche agriculture. Brazil now earns more money from making automobiles and aircraft than from shipping rubber overseas. Chile has earned a worldwide market for its wine, fruit, and salmon.

Despite protests from indigenous tribes and environmental groups, South American governments have tried to spur even more growth by opening up the Amazon region to economic exploitation—the extraction of oil and timber and the transformation of rain forest into cattle ranches. But this practice is already wreaking widespread ecological havoc. The Amazon could very well be the key to the region's economic future—not by the decimation of the world's richest forest, but by the sustainable management and commercial development of its largely untapped biodiversity into medical, chemical, and nutritional products. Many researchers believe that potential treatments for cancer and other ailments may lie hidden in South America's shadowy rain forest.

CARIBBEAN SEA
Guajira Peninsula
Gulf of Venezuela
Paraguaná Pen.
LESSER ANTILLES
Tortuga I.
Margarita I.
Paria Pen.
Trinidad
Tobago
Sierra Nevada de Santa Marta +5775
Lake Valencia
L. Valencia
2660
Orinoco River Delta
Gulf of Morrosquillo
Coast Range
Shell Beach
Longitude West 55° of Greenwich
Isthmus of Panama
PANAMA CANAL
Maracaibo Basin
Cordillera de Mérida
Apure
Orinoco
Angel Falls Total drop 979 meters World's highest waterfall
Pakaraima Mts.
Mt. Roraima 2772
Wilhelmina Mts.
Devil's Island
Gulf of Urabá
Gulf of Panama
Serranía de Baudó
4080
+5493
Cordillera Central
Cordillera Oriental
Tomo
GUIANA HIGHLANDS
Serra Pacaraima
Kanuku Mts. 854
Serra de Tumucumaque
Cape Orange
Malpelo Island
Cerro Otare 910
Source of the Orinoco
Maracá Island
Galera Point
Pico da Neblina 3014
Branco
Balbina Reservoir
Gurupá I.
Marajó Island
Marajó Bay
Cape Gurupi
Mouths of the Amazon
EQUATOR
Santa Elena Peninsula
Chimborazo 6310
Napo
Amazon
AMAZON
Amazon (Solimões)
São Marcos Bay
Pt. Jericoacoara
Gulf of Guayaquil
Pongo de Manseriche
Marañón
Juruá
Purus
Madeira
Tapajós
Xingu
Tocantins
Serra do Tiracambu
Parnaíba
Sa. da Ibiapaba 725
Atol das Rocas
Fernando de Noronha
Aguja Point
Sechura Desert
Cordillera Central
Cordillera Oriental
Ucayali
Purus
Selvas
BASIN
Serra dos Parecis
Caatinga
Anaguaia
Tocantins
Cape São Roque
Lobos Islands
Nevado Huascarán 6768
MONTAÑA
Beni
Mamoré
Guaporé
Serra do Tombador
Serra Formosa
670
Serra Dourada
Espigão Mestre
Borborema Plateau 1123
Mãnguinho Point
Chincha Is.
Source of the Amazon
Jiparaná
Juruena
Serra do Roncador 640
BRAZILIAN
São Francisco
Todos os Santos Bay
Paracas Peninsula
Lake Titicaca
Illampú 6362
Yungas
Cord. Oriental
Secure
Grande
Pantanal
Sertão
Source of the Amazon 3810
Illimani 6462
Cordillera Central 5453
Altiplano
Bañados del Izozog
HIGHLANDS
Serra Dourada 1349
Serra do Espinhaço 2040
Baleia Point
Madrid Point
Salar de Uyuni
Chaco Boreal
Pilcomayo
Serra de Maracaju
Grande
Source of the Paraná
Pico de la Bandeira 2890
Angamos Point
Puna de Atacama
Cerro Galán 6600
Gran Chaco
Chaco Austral
Serra Geral 558
Paraná
Paranaíba
1340
Serra da Mantiqueira
Cape São Tomé
Cape Frio
São Sebastião I.
TROPIC OF CAPRICORN
Isla San Félix
Isla San Ambrosio
Cerro Bonete 6872
Salado
Salinas Grandes
Salinas de Ambargasta
Uruguay
Sete Quedas Falls
Iguaçu Falls
Paranaguá Bay
Cape Bascuñán
Lengua de Vaca Pt.
Cerro Mercedario 6770
Sierra de Córdoba 2790
Laguna Mar Chiquita
Entre Ríos
Patos Lagoon
Cape Santa Marta Grande
Highest point in South America
Cerro Aconcagua + 6960 (22834 ft)
Cerro Tupungato 6800
Paraná
Negro
Lake Rincón del Bonete 299
Cuchilla Grande
Islas Juan Fernández
Isla Róbinson Crusoe
Maipo Volcano 5323
River Plate
Punta del Este
PAMPAS
Samborombón Bay
Cape San Antonio
Sierra del Tandil 524
Mogotes Point
Arauco Gulf
Colorado
Colorado
Llaima Volcano 3060
Capulhue Pass 2101
Negro
Blanca Bay
Arco Pass 1401
Embalse Ezequiel Ramos Mexía
Negro
Rasa Point
San Matías Gulf
Meseta de Somuncurá
Valdés Peninsula -40
Isla Grande de Chiloé
Chubut
Meseta de Montemayor
Chonos Archipelago
Lake Buenos Aires
Gulf of San Jorge
Cape Tres Puntas
Tres Montes Peninsula
PATAGONIA
Deseado
Cerro Puntudo 1000
San Julián Bay
Wellington Island
Laguna del Carbón Lowest point in South America -105 (-344 ft)
Lake Viedma
Grande Bay
FALKLAND ISLANDS
Lake Argentino
Cape Vírgenes
West Falkland
East Falkland
Queen Adelaida Archipelago
Strait of Magellan
TIERRA DEL FUEGO
Staten Island
Shag Rocks
Cape Horn
Black Rock
South Georgia

PACIFIC OCEAN

ATLANTIC OCEAN

ANDES

LLANOS

Orinoco

Negro

Tocantins

SCALE 1:22,838,000
1 CENTIMETER = 228 KILOMETERS; 1 INCH = 360 MILES

Azimuthal Equidistant Projection

0   200   400   600   800
KILOMETERS

0   200   400   600   800
STATUTE MILES

International boundary

126

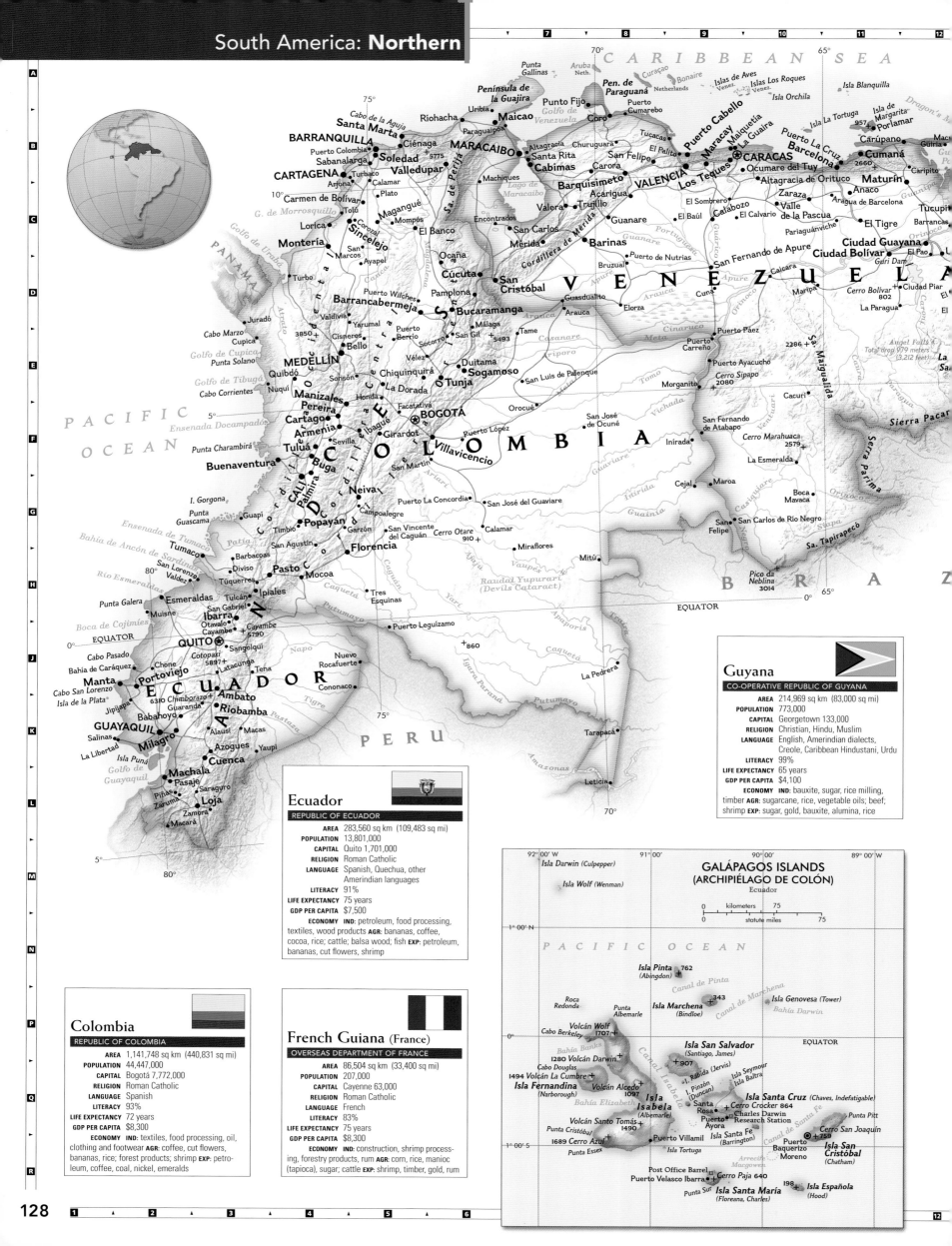

Ecuador
REPUBLIC OF ECUADOR

AREA 283,560 sq km (109,483 sq mi)
POPULATION 13,801,000
CAPITAL Quito 1,701,000
RELIGION Roman Catholic
LANGUAGE Spanish, Quechua, other Amerindian languages
LITERACY 91%
LIFE EXPECTANCY 75 years
GDP PER CAPITA $7,500
ECONOMY **IND:** petroleum, food processing, textiles, wood products **AGR:** bananas, coffee, cocoa, rice; cattle; balsa wood; fish **EXP:** petroleum, bananas, cut flowers, shrimp

Guyana
CO-OPERATIVE REPUBLIC OF GUYANA

AREA 214,969 sq km (83,000 sq mi)
POPULATION 773,000
CAPITAL Georgetown 133,000
RELIGION Christian, Hindu, Muslim
LANGUAGE English, Amerindian dialects, Creole, Caribbean Hindustani, Urdu
LITERACY 99%
LIFE EXPECTANCY 65 years
GDP PER CAPITA $4,100
ECONOMY **IND:** bauxite, sugar, rice milling, timber **AGR:** sugarcane, rice, vegetable oils; beef; shrimp **EXP:** sugar, gold, bauxite, alumina, rice

Colombia
REPUBLIC OF COLOMBIA

AREA 1,141,748 sq km (440,831 sq mi)
POPULATION 44,447,000
CAPITAL Bogotá 7,772,000
RELIGION Roman Catholic
LANGUAGE Spanish
LITERACY 93%
LIFE EXPECTANCY 72 years
GDP PER CAPITA $8,300
ECONOMY **IND:** textiles, food processing, oil, clothing and footwear **AGR:** coffee, cut flowers, bananas, rice; forest products; shrimp **EXP:** petroleum, coffee, coal, nickel, emeralds

French Guiana (France)
OVERSEAS DEPARTMENT OF FRANCE

AREA 86,504 sq km (33,400 sq mi)
POPULATION 207,000
CAPITAL Cayenne 63,000
RELIGION Roman Catholic
LANGUAGE French
LITERACY 83%
LIFE EXPECTANCY 75 years
GDP PER CAPITA $8,300
ECONOMY **IND:** construction, shrimp processing, forestry products, rum **AGR:** corn, rice, manioc (tapioca), sugar; cattle **EXP:** shrimp, timber, gold, rum

GALÁPAGOS ISLANDS
(ARCHIPIÉLAGO DE COLÓN)
Ecuador

Tobago
TRINIDAD AND TOBAGO
TRINIDAD
60°
nt's Mouth
10°
Boca Grande
San José de Amacuro
Morawhanna
po
Shell Beach
Mabaruma
Port Kaituma
atthew's
Ridge
emo
Charity
Suddie
Parika
Georgetown
Buxton
New Amsterdam
Bartica
Mara
Corriverton
Linden
Issano
Nieuw Nickerie
Totness
Mahdia
Ituni
Mt. Roraima
2772
Avanavero
Apoteri
Orinduik
anta Elena
Lethem
Kanuku
Mts.
Serra de Tumucumaque

ATLANTIC OCEAN
55°
Paramaribo
Nieuw Amsterdam
Pointe Isère
Mana
Moengo
Iracoubo
Sinnamary
Zanderij
St. Laurent
Brokopondo
du Maroni
Kourou
Brownsweg
Afobaka
Île du Diable
(Devil's I.)
Cayenne
Rémire
Roura
5°
Régina
FRENCH
GUIANA
France
SURINAME
Wilhelmina Gebergte
1230
Kayser
Gebergte
861
Mont Saint-Marcel
635
Boundary
claimed
by Suriname
Boundary
claimed by Suriname
Acarai Mts.
1177
55°
60°
I   L

Azimuthal Equidistant Projection
SCALE 1:9,550,000
1 CENTIMETER = 96 KILOMETERS; 1 INCH = 151 MILES
0   100   200   300   400
KILOMETERS
0   100   200   300   400
STATUTE MILES

Suriname
REPUBLIC OF SURINAME
AREA 163,265 sq km (63,037 sq mi)
POPULATION 500,000
CAPITAL Paramaribo 252,000
RELIGION Hindu, Protestant, Roman Catholic, Muslim
LANGUAGE Dutch, English, Sranang Tongo, Hindustani, Javanese
LITERACY 90%
LIFE EXPECTANCY 69 years
GDP PER CAPITA $8,300
ECONOMY IND: bauxite and gold mining, alumina production, oil, lumbering **AGR:** paddy rice, bananas, palm kernels, coconuts; beef; forest products; shrimp **EXP:** alumina, gold, crude oil, lumber, shrimp and fish

Venezuela
BOLIVARIAN REPUBLIC OF VENEZUELA
AREA 912,050 sq km (352,144 sq mi)
POPULATION 27,935,000
CAPITAL Caracas 2,985,000
RELIGION Roman Catholic
LANGUAGE Spanish, numerous indigenous dialects
LITERACY 93%
LIFE EXPECTANCY 73 years
GDP PER CAPITA $12,900
ECONOMY IND: petroleum, construction materials, food processing, textiles **AGR:** corn, sorghum, sugarcane, rice; beef; fish **EXP:** petroleum, bauxite and aluminum, steel, chemicals

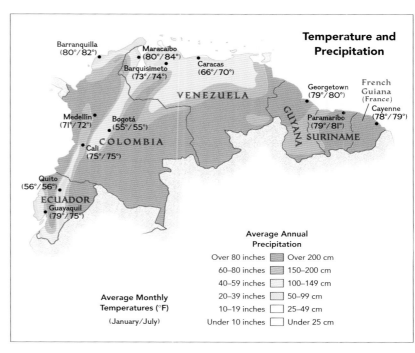

Temperature and Precipitation

Barranquilla (80°/82°)
Maracaibo (80°/84°)
Caracas (66°/70°)
Barquisimeto (73°/74°)
VENEZUELA
Georgetown (79°/80°)
French Guiana (France)
Medellín (71°/72°)
Bogotá (55°/55°)
COLOMBIA
Paramaribo (79°/81°)
Cayenne (78°/79°)
GUYANA
SURINAME
Cali (75°/75°)
Quito (56°/56°)
ECUADOR
Guayaquil (79°/75°)

Average Annual Precipitation

Over 80 inches		Over 200 cm	
60–80 inches		150–200 cm	
40–59 inches		100–149 cm	
20–39 inches		50–99 cm	
10–19 inches		25–49 cm	
Under 10 inches		Under 25 cm	

Average Monthly Temperatures (°F)
(January/July)

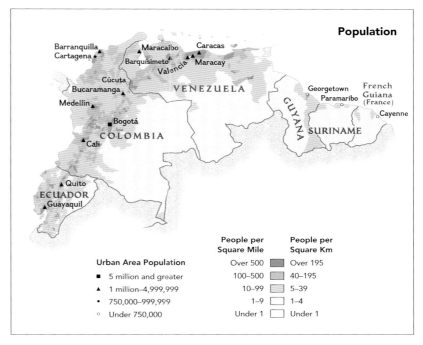

Population

Barranquilla
Cartagena
Maracaibo
Caracas
Barquisimeto
Maracay
Valencia
Cúcuta
VENEZUELA
Georgetown
French Guiana (France)
Bucaramanga
Paramaribo
Medellín
GUYANA
SURINAME
Cayenne
Bogotá
COLOMBIA
Cali
Quito
ECUADOR
Guayaquil

Urban Area Population
- ■ 5 million and greater
- ▲ 1 million–4,999,999
- • 750,000–999,999
- ○ Under 750,000

People per Square Mile	People per Square Km
Over 500	Over 195
100–500	40–195
10–99	5–39
1–9	1–4
Under 1	Under 1

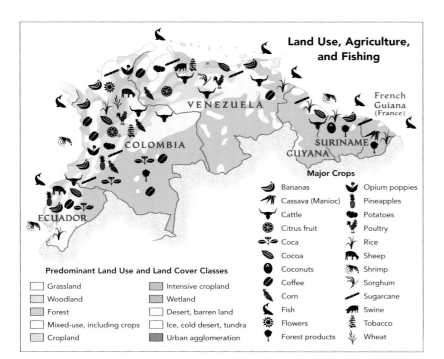

Land Use, Agriculture, and Fishing

VENEZUELA
French Guiana (France)
COLOMBIA
SURINAME
GUYANA
ECUADOR

Major Crops
- Bananas
- Cassava (Manioc)
- Cattle
- Citrus fruit
- Coca
- Cocoa
- Coconuts
- Coffee
- Corn
- Fish
- Flowers
- Opium poppies
- Pineapples
- Potatoes
- Poultry
- Rice
- Sheep
- Shrimp
- Sorghum
- Sugarcane
- Swine
- Tobacco
- Forest products
- Wheat

Predominant Land Use and Land Cover Classes
- Grassland
- Woodland
- Forest
- Mixed-use, including crops
- Cropland
- Intensive cropland
- Wetland
- Desert, barren land
- Ice, cold desert, tundra
- Urban agglomeration

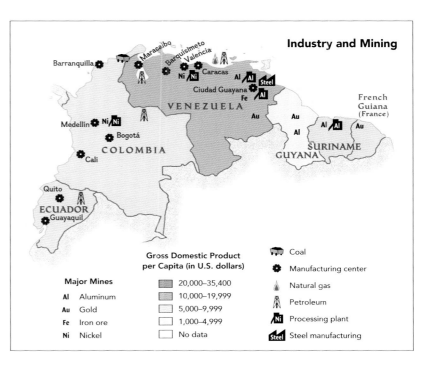

Industry and Mining

Barranquilla
Maracaibo
Barquisimeto
Valencia
Ni Ni Caracas
Al Al
Ciudad Guayana Steel
Fe Al
VENEZUELA
French Guiana (France)
Medellín Ni Ni
Au
Au
Al Al
Bogotá
COLOMBIA
Au
SURINAME
Al
GUYANA
Cali
Quito
ECUADOR
Guayaquil

Major Mines
- **Al** Aluminum
- **Au** Gold
- **Fe** Iron ore
- **Ni** Nickel

Gross Domestic Product per Capita (in U.S. dollars)
- 20,000–35,400
- 10,000–19,999
- 5,000–9,999
- 1,000–4,999
- No data

- Coal
- Manufacturing center
- Natural gas
- Petroleum
- Processing plant
- Steel manufacturing

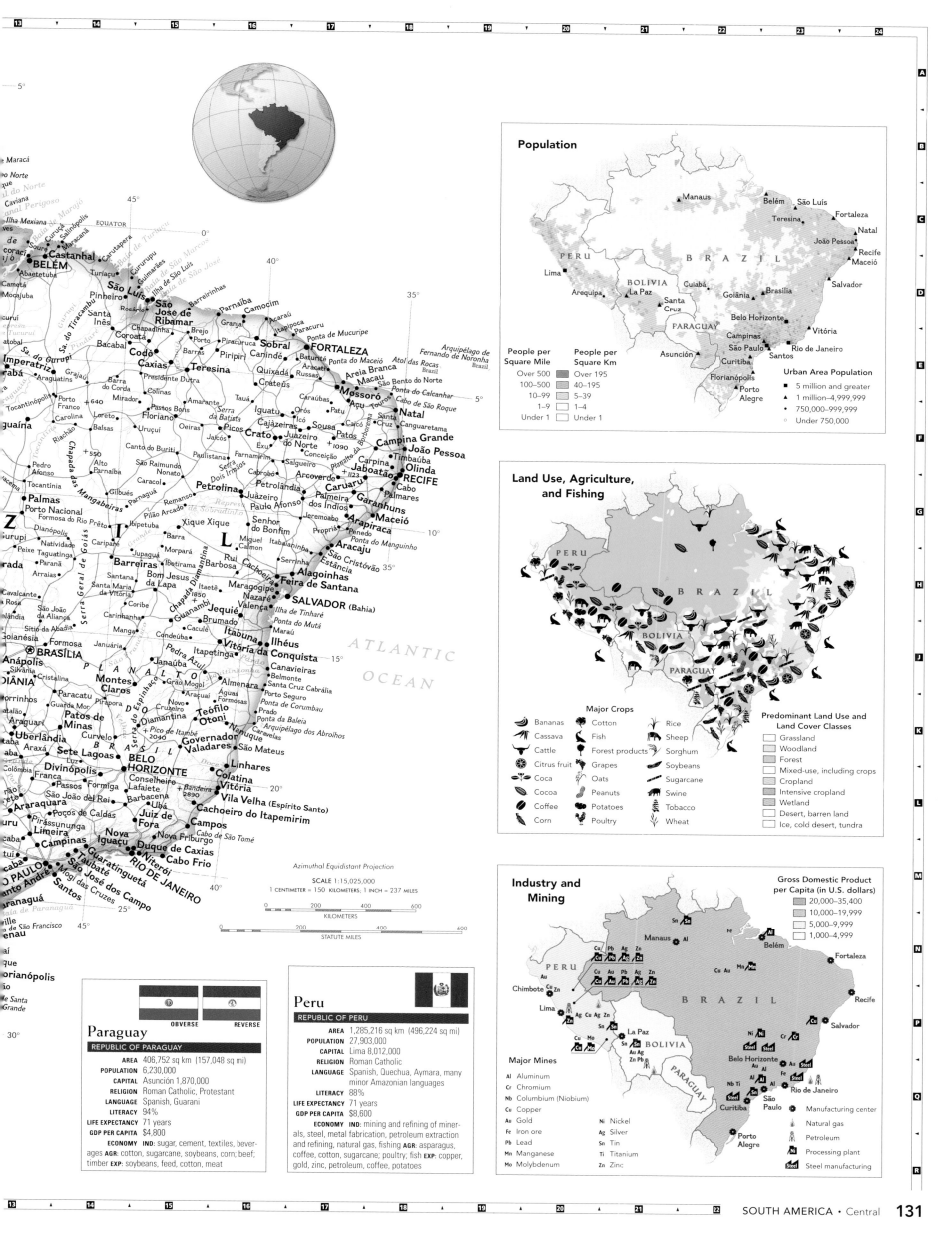

Population

People per Square Mile / People per Square Km
- Over 500 / Over 195
- 100–500 / 40–195
- 10–99 / 5–39
- 1–9 / 1–4
- Under 1 / Under 1

Urban Area Population
- ■ 5 million and greater
- ▲ 1 million–4,999,999
- • 750,000–999,999
- ○ Under 750,000

Land Use, Agriculture, and Fishing

Major Crops
- Bananas
- Cassava
- Cattle
- Citrus fruit
- Coca
- Cocoa
- Coffee
- Corn
- Cotton
- Fish
- Forest products
- Grapes
- Oats
- Peanuts
- Potatoes
- Poultry
- Rice
- Sheep
- Sorghum
- Soybeans
- Sugarcane
- Swine
- Tobacco
- Wheat

Predominant Land Use and Land Cover Classes
- Grassland
- Woodland
- Forest
- Mixed-use, including crops
- Cropland
- Intensive cropland
- Wetland
- Desert, barren land
- Ice, cold desert, tundra

Industry and Mining

Gross Domestic Product per Capita (in U.S. dollars)
- 20,000–35,400
- 10,000–19,999
- 5,000–9,999
- 1,000–4,999

Major Mines
- Al Aluminum
- Cr Chromium
- Nb Columbium (Niobium)
- Cu Copper
- Au Gold
- Fe Iron ore
- Pb Lead
- Mn Manganese
- Mo Molybdenum
- Ni Nickel
- Ag Silver
- Sn Tin
- Ti Titanium
- Zn Zinc

- ✦ Manufacturing center
- Natural gas
- Petroleum
- Ni Processing plant
- Steel Steel manufacturing

Paraguay
REPUBLIC OF PARAGUAY

OBVERSE · REVERSE

AREA 406,752 sq km (157,048 sq mi)
POPULATION 6,230,000
CAPITAL Asunción 1,870,000
RELIGION Roman Catholic, Protestant
LANGUAGE Spanish, Guarani
LITERACY 94%
LIFE EXPECTANCY 71 years
GDP PER CAPITA $4,800
ECONOMY IND: sugar, cement, textiles, beverages AGR: cotton, sugarcane, soybeans, corn; beef; timber EXP: soybeans, feed, cotton, meat

Peru
REPUBLIC OF PERU

AREA 1,285,216 sq km (496,224 sq mi)
POPULATION 27,903,000
CAPITAL Lima 8,012,000
RELIGION Roman Catholic
LANGUAGE Spanish, Quechua, Aymara, many minor Amazonian languages
LITERACY 88%
LIFE EXPECTANCY 71 years
GDP PER CAPITA $8,600
ECONOMY IND: mining and refining of minerals, steel, metal fabrication, petroleum extraction and refining, natural gas, fishing AGR: asparagus, coffee, cotton, sugarcane; poultry; fish EXP: copper, gold, zinc, petroleum, coffee, potatoes

Azimuthal Equidistant Projection

SCALE 1:15,025,000
1 CENTIMETER = 150 KILOMETERS; 1 INCH = 237 MILES

KILOMETERS
STATUTE MILES

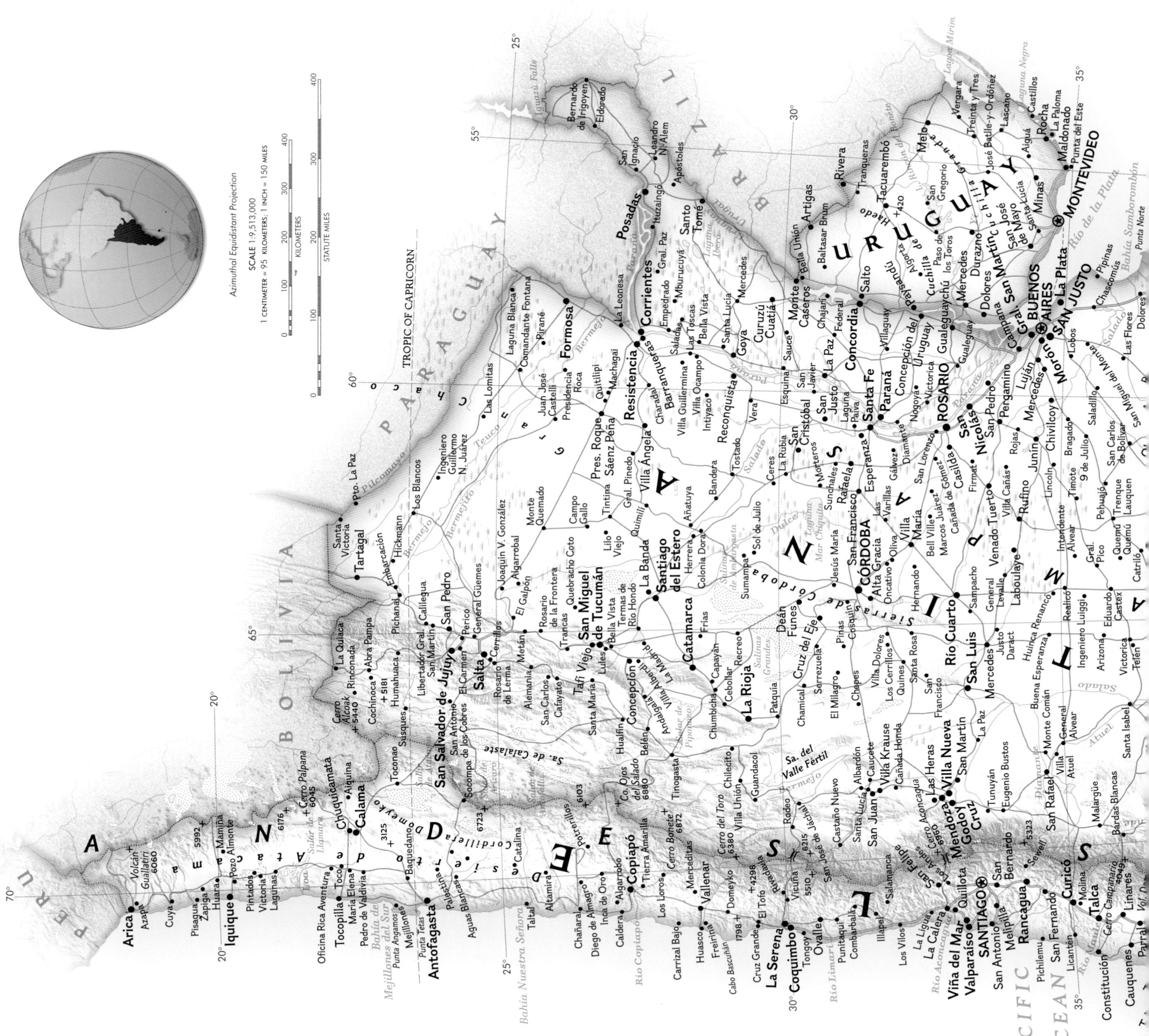

Azimuthal Equidistant Projection

SCALE 1:9,513,000

1 CENTIMETER = 95 KILOMETERS; 1 INCH = 150 MILES

KILOMETERS
STATUTE MILES

TROPIC OF CAPRICORN

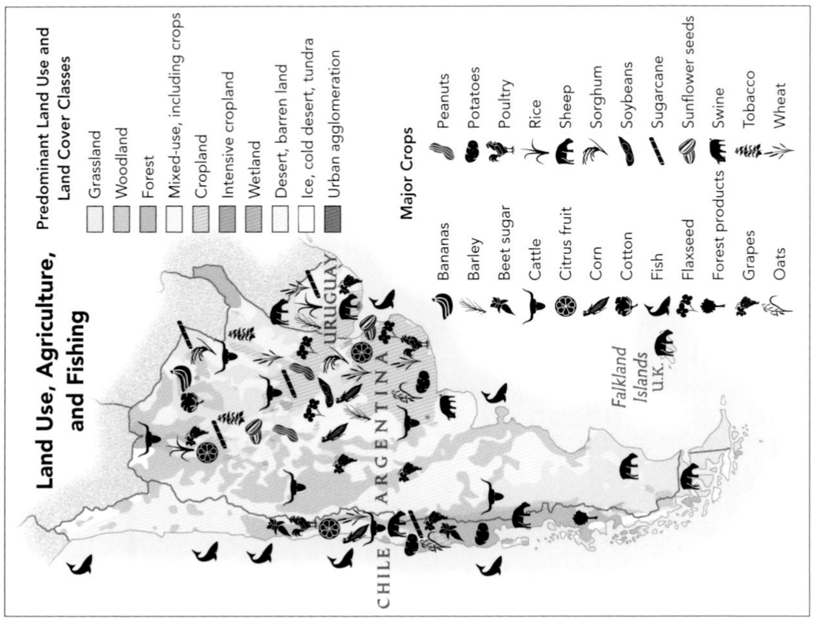

Land Use, Agriculture, and Fishing

Predominant Land Use and Land Cover Classes

- Grassland
- Woodland
- Forest
- Mixed-use, including crops
- Cropland
- Intensive cropland
- Wetland
- Desert, barren land
- Ice, cold desert, tundra
- Urban agglomeration

Major Crops

Bananas	Peanuts
Barley	Potatoes
Beet sugar	Poultry
Cattle	Rice
Citrus fruit	Sheep
Corn	Sorghum
Cotton	Soybeans
Fish	Sugarcane
Flaxseed	Sunflower seeds
Forest products	Swine
Grapes	Tobacco
Oats	Wheat

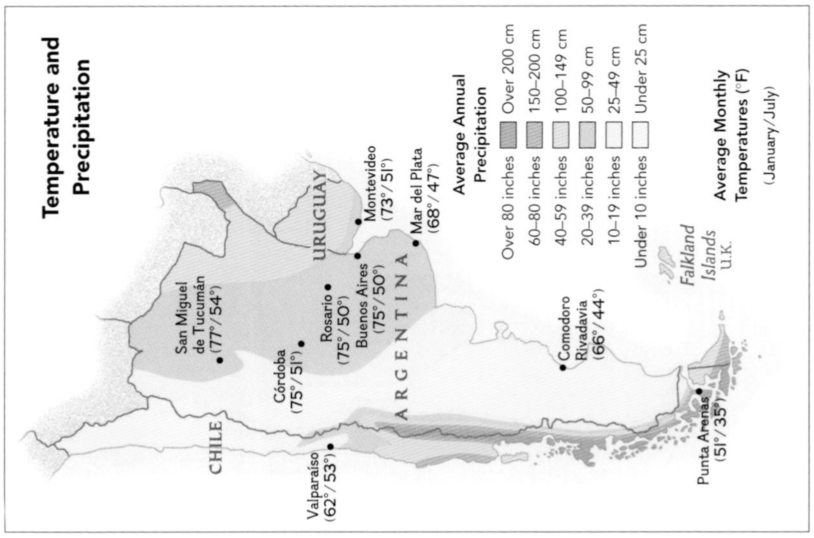

Temperature and Precipitation

Average Annual Precipitation

- Over 80 inches — Over 200 cm
- 60–80 inches — 150–200 cm
- 40–59 inches — 100–149 cm
- 20–39 inches — 50–99 cm
- 10–19 inches — 25–49 cm
- Under 10 inches — Under 25 cm

Average Monthly Temperatures (°F)
(January/July)

San Miguel de Tucumán (77°/54°)
Córdoba (75°/51°)
Rosario (75°/50°)
Buenos Aires (75°/50°)
Comodoro Rivadavia (66°/44°)
Valparaíso (62°/53°)
Punta Arenas (51°/35°)
Montevideo (73°/51°)
Mar del Plata (68°/47°)

PERU
BOLIVIA
PARAGUAY
BRAZIL
URUGUAY
ARGENTINA
CHILE

ANDES
Cordillera

Falkland Islands U.K.

PACIFIC OCEAN

MONTEVIDEO
BUENOS AIRES
CÓRDOBA
ROSARIO
SANTIAGO
Mendoza
Corrientes
Resistencia
Formosa
Posadas
Salta
San Salvador de Jujuy
San Miguel de Tucumán
Santiago del Estero
Catamarca
La Rioja
San Luis
Río Cuarto
Santa Fe
Paraná
Antofagasta
Calama
Iquique
Arica
Copiapó
La Serena
Coquimbo
Valparaíso
Viña del Mar

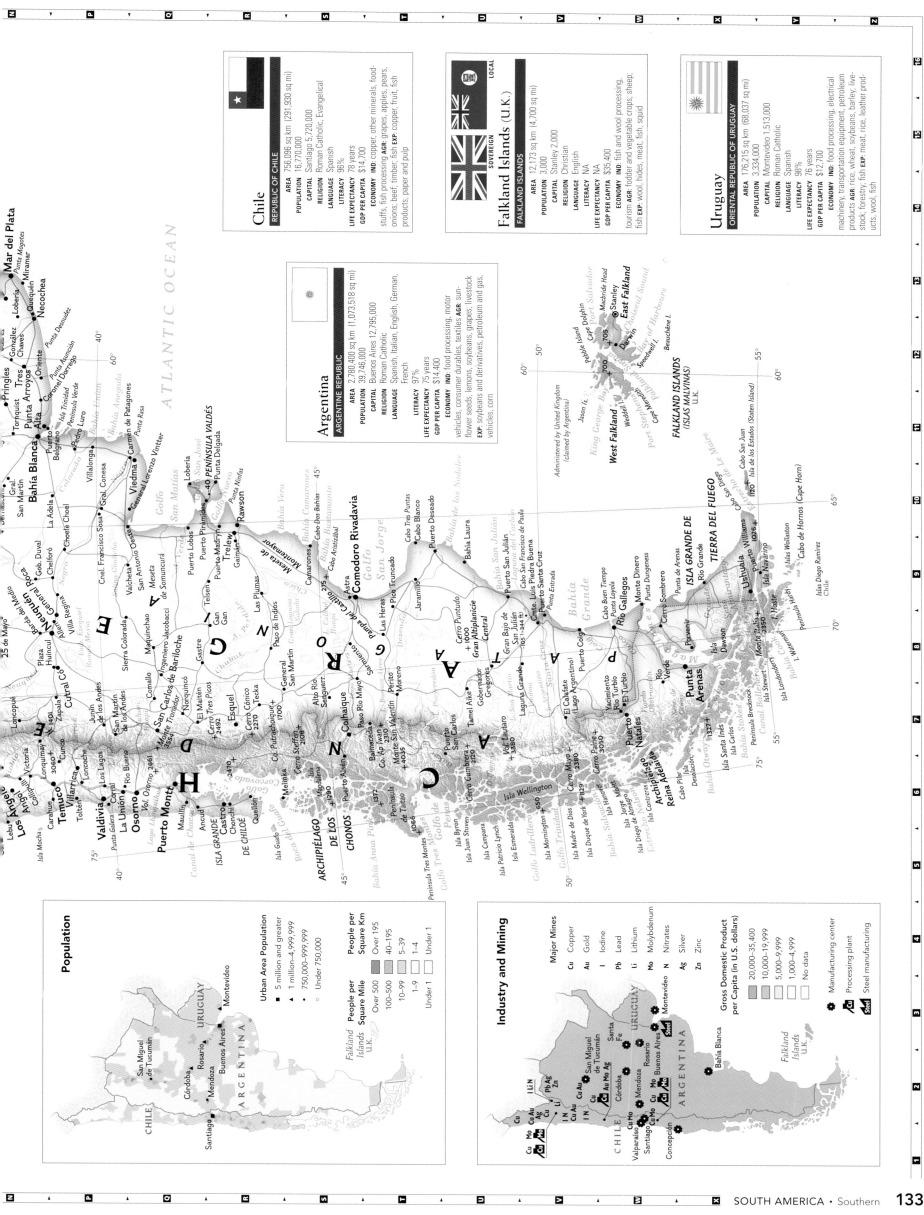

Chile
REPUBLIC OF CHILE
AREA 756,096 sq km (291,930 sq mi)
POPULATION 16,770,000
CAPITAL Santiago 5,720,000
RELIGION Roman Catholic, Evangelical
LANGUAGE Spanish
LITERACY 96%
LIFE EXPECTANCY 78 years
GDP PER CAPITA $14,700
ECONOMY IND: copper, other minerals, foodstuffs, fish processing, iron and steel, wood and wood products, transport equipment, cement, textiles. **AGR:** grapes, apples, pears, onions, beef; timber; fish. **EXP:** copper, fruit, fish products, paper and pulp

Falkland Islands (U.K.)
FALKLAND ISLANDS
AREA 12,173 sq km (4,700 sq mi)
POPULATION 3,000
CAPITAL Stanley 2,000
RELIGION Christian
LANGUAGE English
LITERACY NA
LIFE EXPECTANCY NA
GDP PER CAPITA $35,400
ECONOMY IND: fish and wool processing, tourism. **AGR:** fodder and vegetable crops; sheep; fish. **EXP:** wool, hides, meat, fish, squid

Uruguay
ORIENTAL REPUBLIC OF URUGUAY
AREA 176,215 sq km (68,037 sq mi)
POPULATION 3,334,000
CAPITAL Montevideo 1,513,000
RELIGION Roman Catholic
LANGUAGE Spanish
LITERACY 98%
LIFE EXPECTANCY 76 years
GDP PER CAPITA $12,700
ECONOMY IND: food processing, electrical machinery, transportation equipment, petroleum products. **AGR:** rice, wheat, soybeans, barley, livestock; forestry; fish. **EXP:** meat, rice, leather products, wool, fish

Argentina
ARGENTINE REPUBLIC
AREA 2,780,400 sq km (1,073,518 sq mi)
POPULATION 39,746,000
CAPITAL Buenos Aires 12,795,000
RELIGION Roman Catholic
LANGUAGE Spanish, Italian, English, German, French
LITERACY 97%
LIFE EXPECTANCY 75 years
GDP PER CAPITA $14,400
ECONOMY IND: food processing, motor vehicles, consumer durables, textiles. **AGR:** sunflower seeds, lemons, soybeans, grapes; livestock. **EXP:** soybeans and derivatives, petroleum and gas, vehicles, corn

Population
Urban Area Population
- ■ 5 million and greater
- ▲ 1 million–4,999,999
- ▲ 750,000–999,999
- ○ Under 750,000

People per Square Mile / People per Square Km
Over 500	Over 195
100–500	40–195
10–99	5–39
1–9	1–4
Under 1	Under 1

Industry and Mining
Major Mines
- Cu Copper
- Au Gold
- I Iodine
- Pb Lead
- Li Lithium
- Mo Molybdenum
- N Nitrates
- Ag Silver
- Zn Zinc

Gross Domestic Product per Capita (in U.S. dollars)
- 20,000–35,400
- 10,000–19,999
- 5,000–9,999
- 1,000–4,999
- No data

- Manufacturing center
- Processing plant
- Steel manufacturing

ATLANTIC OCEAN

Europe

The fantastical Neuschwanstein Castle, built in the late 1800s and later the model for Disneyland's iconic fairy-tale castle, sits high above the Alpsee in the Bavarian Alps. Although "Mad King Ludwig" intended his creation to be a paean to medieval architecture, he actually incorporated running water, automatic flush toilets, and other revolutionary conveniences of the day.

Europe is the world's second smallest continent, after Australia. A cluster of peninsulas and islands extending from northwestern Asia, Europe comprises 46 countries. Despite its northern location, most of its population enjoys a mild climate tempered by warm ocean currents such as the Gulf Stream.

Europe has been inhabited for some 40,000 years. During the past millennium Europeans explored the planet and established far-flung empires. Europe led the world in science and invention, and launched the industrial revolution. By the end of the 19th century, it dominated world commerce, spreading European ideas, languages, legal systems, and political patterns around the globe.

The 20th century brought unprecedented changes. Germany and its neighbors ignited two world wars. The Russian Revolution introduced communism. And Europe, weakened by war, lost its dominant position in the world along with its empires.

In 1947, the United States and the Soviet Union entered into a Cold War, pitting capitalism and democracy against communism and state control. Western Europe, backed by the U.S., prospered with market economies, democracy, and free speech; Eastern and Central European countries, their centrally planned economies closely tied to the Soviet Union's, fell behind and, despite full employment and social benefits, people suffered the lack of personal freedom.

In Western Europe, age-old enemies started cooperating. In 1952 six countries founded a common market for coal and steel; it soon included more countries and more commodities until, in 1991, the European Union was formed. Border controls were eliminated between 15 member countries (in 1999, 12 members introduced a common European currency). Also in 1991, the Soviet Union collapsed. Germany, which had been split by the Cold War, was reunified. Eastern and Central Europe started the difficult transition toward Western-style democracy and privatization.

When chaos overtook the Balkans, Yugoslavia shattered into seven countries. But other forces are working toward a cohesive Europe. People move freely throughout the continent; they share the same pop culture, pursue similar urban lifestyles, and rely heavily on cell phones and the Internet.

Environmental problems are often international. Acid rain from England kills life in Swedish lakes. A nuclear accident in Ukraine damages dozens of countries. The Danube and Rhine Rivers spread industrial pollution downstream. Wherever possible, regional solutions hold the most promise, like the projected cleanup of the Baltic Sea involving nine surrounding countries.

Although the European Union enforces strict environmental laws, Eastern Europe understood little about the environment until the 1990s. Some countries still contain toxic waste dumps, untreated sewage, and other hazards, but they have insufficient funds to meet the high costs of cleanup.

A political United States of Europe will probably never happen, but the economic advantages of the European Union have greatly benefitted its member countries (currently numbering 27, with 3 more waiting for membership) as they enter a new era of history.

PHYSICAL GEOGRAPHY Europe is bounded by the Arctic Ocean in the north, the Atlantic Ocean in the west, the Mediterranean and Black Seas in the south, and the Caspian Sea in the southeast. The traditional land boundary is a line following the Ural Mountains south across Russia from the Arctic Ocean, via the Ural River to the Caspian Sea. The line then continues west along the crest of the Caucasus Mountains between the Caspian and Black Seas, making Mount El'brus (18,510 ft; 5,642 m), on the northern side, the highest mountain in Europe. Waterways linking the Black Sea to the Mediterranean place a small part of Turkey in Europe.

Two mountain systems lie between icy tundra and boreal forest in the far north and the warm, dry, hilly Mediterranean coast in the south. Ancient, rugged highlands, worn down by successive Ice Age glaciers, arc southwestward from Scandinavia, through the British Isles, to the Iberian Peninsula, while an active Alpine system spreads east to west across southern Europe. Still rising from a collision of tectonic plates, these mountains include the Carpathians, the Alps, the Pyrenees, and their many spurs. The high point is Mont Blanc (15,781 ft; 4,810 m), shared by France and Italy. Three major navigable rivers—the Danube, the Rhine, and the Rhône—rise in the Alps. Europe's longest river, however, is the Volga, flowing southeast across Russia to the Caspian Sea. Movements in Earth's crust cause earthquakes and volcanic eruptions in southern Europe and in Iceland. The best known volcanoes are Vesuvius, Etna, and Stromboli, all three in Italy.

Between Europe's two mountain systems, a rolling, fertile plain stretches across the continent from the Pyrenees to the Urals, well drained by several rivers. Some of the world's greatest cities are located here, including Paris, Berlin, and Moscow. Huge industrial areas on this plain are home to much of Europe's dense population.

HISTORY Named for King Minos, the first civilization in Europe appeared in Crete about 2000 B.C. Minoans traded with Egypt and western Asia, produced impressive art and architecture, and developed a unique form of writing. Around 1450 B.C., their culture disappeared, probably after a major volcanic eruption or an invasion by warlike Mycenaeans. Homer's *Iliad* and *Odyssey* describe the Mycenaean era that followed.

Classical Greek civilization began in the eighth century B.C. The great achievements of the Greeks in philosophy, mathematics, natural sciences, political thought, and the arts have influenced European civilization ever since. Greece bequeathed its legacy to Rome, known for its builders, engineers, military strategists, and lawmakers. The Roman Empire eventually reached from Britain to Persia and lasted roughly 500 years, until invasions by Germanic tribes from the north destroyed it.

During Roman times a new religion, Christianity, entered Europe from western Asia. As Rome declined, the Christian Church became the common thread binding Europeans together. It maintained schools and learning in its monasteries through the Middle Ages. In the 11th century, theological differences split Christianity into Orthodoxy in the east, led by patriarchs, and Roman Catholicism in the west, under popes.

Ottoman Turks introduced Islam to the Balkans through conquest during the 14th and 15th centuries. A hundred years later, the Protestant Reformation in northern Europe broke the unity of the Roman Catholic Church and provoked a century of wars.

Rome's greatest landmark, the Colosseum, was completed in A.D. 80; it held 50,000 spectators during gladiator fights and other events. Four stories high, this structure combines Greek esthetics with Roman building techniques.

In the 15th and 16th centuries, the Renaissance—a rebirth of arts, science, and culture—spread northward throughout the continent. Political power shifted to Western Europe, where strong nations emerged, notably England, France, Spain, and Portugal. Under powerful kings, worldwide explorations created mercantile empires, even as ideas of democracy and equality started circulating.

In the 18th century, Britain's American colonies became independent and, in the wake of the French Revolution that toppled the monarchy, Napoleon tried, but failed, to seize all of Europe. In 1815, a balance of power was reestablished among European countries until the forces of nationalism, socialism, and democracy exploded into two world wars a century later.

Following World War II, the Cold War between the U.S. and the Soviet Union replaced the old balance of power with a deadly balance of nuclear armaments, reducing Europe to lesser status. But by the time the Cold War came to an end in the 1990s, Western Europe had coalesced into the European Union. A large number of countries were also allied with the North Atlantic Treaty Organization (NATO), and Europe was embarking on a new era of economic and military cooperation.

CULTURE Next to Asia, Europe has the world's densest population. Scores of distinct ethnic groups, speaking some 40 languages, inhabit more than 40 countries, which vary in size from vast European Russia to tiny Vatican City, each with its own history and traditions. Yet Europe has a more uniform culture than any other continent. Its population is overwhelmingly of one race, Caucasian, despite the recent arrival of immigrants from Africa and Asia. Most of its languages fall into three groups with Indo-European roots: Germanic, Romance, or Slavic. One religion, Christianity, predominates in various forms, and social structures nearly everywhere are based on economic classes.

Great periods of creativity in the arts have occurred at various times all over the continent and shape its collective culture. Classical Greek sculpture and architecture are widely seen as paradigms of beauty. Gothic cathedrals of medieval France still inspire awe. Renaissance works of art, from paintings by Leonardo da Vinci in Florence to plays by Shakespeare in England, are famous worldwide. Music composed by Mozart of Austria, Beethoven of Germany, and Tchaikovsky of Russia has passed far beyond Europe. Spanish artist Pablo Picasso transformed the Western world's concept of art. By the 20th century, European culture had penetrated everywhere.

The success of America's multibillion-dollar entertainment industry makes some Europeans feel culturally threatened. American movies flood the continent; American products and lifestyles are aggressively marketed. English is becoming the preferred second language for students all over Europe. Others see the blending of cultures as an inevitable aspect of globalization and a chance to export their own pop music, plays, architecture, fashions, and gourmet foods to other countries. A more imminent worry focuses on immigrant groups established as legitimate and illegal workers, refugees, and asylum seekers, who cling to their own habits, religions, and languages. Every European society is becoming multicultural, with political as well as cultural consequences.

ECONOMY Europe is fortunate in having fertile soil, a temperate climate, ample natural resources, and a long, irregular coastline that gives most countries access to the sea and foreign trade. Navigable rivers often help the 15 landlocked countries.

Europe is currently undertaking two of the most far-reaching economic experiments in its history. While some countries in Eastern and Central Europe are still converting centrally planned, communist-style economies to the democratic market system, 16 highly developed European nations have created a powerful "eurozone" by replacing their national money with the euro, a shared currency.

The progress of many ex-Soviet bloc countries has been slower than anticipated due, in part, to a need for laws preventing corruption and abuse of the new system, and for institutions to assure sound financial management. Poland and Slovenia have been among the most successful. Russia and Belarus, on the other hand, have slipped into worsening poverty, causing some people to clamor for a return to the safety nets of communism.

The eurozone countries did not have a totally smooth transition to the single currency. The new European Central Bank could not keep the euro from losing a quarter of its value against the U.S. dollar in its first three years; however, in recent years, the euro has strengthened considerably and the advantages of a shared currency are increasingly tangible: Banking has become faster and easier, and the newly enlarged bond market has led to many corporate reforms and important mergers. A majority of voters in Britain, Sweden, and Denmark, called "euroskeptics," refused to adopt the euro in 1999 like other European Union members. But they will probably vote to do so as the eurozone grows in strength and influence.

Meanwhile, the advantages offered by the European Union encourage outside countries to practice the tough economic and fiscal policies that are prerequisites for membership. Ten countries were admitted in 2004: Estonia, Latvia, Lithuania, Cyprus, Malta, the Czech Republic, Hungary, Poland, Slovakia, and Slovenia. With the addition of Bulgaria and Romania in 2007, the European Union now has a population of nearly half a billion, firmly cementing it as one of the largest economies in the world. Many Europeans speculate that in time the euro may rival the U.S. dollar as the principal global currency.

Denmark
KINGDOM OF DENMARK
AREA	43,098 sq km (16,640 sq mi)
POPULATION	5,490,000
CAPITAL	Copenhagen 1,085,000
RELIGION	Evangelical Lutheran, other Protestant, Roman Catholic
LANGUAGE	Danish, German
LITERACY	99%
LIFE EXPECTANCY	78 years
GDP PER CAPITA	$38,200
ECONOMY	**IND:** iron, steel, nonferrous metals, chemicals **AGR:** barley, wheat, potatoes, sugar beets; pork; fish **EXP:** machinery and instruments, meat and meat products, dairy products, fish

Latvia
REPUBLIC OF LATVIA
AREA	64,589 sq km (24,938 sq mi)
POPULATION	2,266,000
CAPITAL	Riga 722,000
RELIGION	Lutheran, Orthodox
LANGUAGE	Latvian, Russian, Lithuanian
LITERACY	100%
LIFE EXPECTANCY	72 years
GDP PER CAPITA	$17,800
ECONOMY	**IND:** buses, vans, street and railroad cars, synthetic fibers, agricultural machinery **AGR:** grain, sugar beets, potatoes, vegetables; beef; fish **EXP:** wood and wood products, machinery and equipment, metals, textiles

Norway
KINGDOM OF NORWAY
AREA	323,758 sq km (125,004 sq mi)
POPULATION	4,765,000
CAPITAL	Oslo 835,000
RELIGION	Church of Norway (Lutheran)
LANGUAGE	Norwegian, Sami
LITERACY	100%
LIFE EXPECTANCY	80 years
GDP PER CAPITA	$55,200
ECONOMY	**IND:** petroleum and gas, food processing, shipbuilding, pulp and paper products **AGR:** barley, wheat, potatoes; pork; fish **EXP:** petroleum and petroleum products, machinery and equipment, metals, chemicals, ships, fish

Sweden
KINGDOM OF SWEDEN
AREA	449,964 sq km (173,732 sq mi)
POPULATION	9,214,000
CAPITAL	Stockholm 1,264,000
RELIGION	Lutheran
LANGUAGE	Swedish, Sami, Finnish
LITERACY	99%
LIFE EXPECTANCY	81 years
GDP PER CAPITA	$37,500
ECONOMY	**IND:** iron and steel, precision equipment, wood pulp and paper products, processed foods **AGR:** barley, wheat, sugar beets; meat, milk **EXP:** machinery, motor vehicles, paper products, pulp and wood, iron and steel products

Estonia
REPUBLIC OF ESTONIA
AREA	45,227 sq km (17,462 sq mi)
POPULATION	1,340,000
CAPITAL	Tallinn 397,000
RELIGION	Evangelical Lutheran, Orthodox
LANGUAGE	Estonian, Russian
LITERACY	100%
LIFE EXPECTANCY	73 years
GDP PER CAPITA	$20,800
ECONOMY	**IND:** engineering, electronics, wood and wood products, textiles **AGR:** potatoes, vegetables; livestock and dairy products; fish **EXP:** machinery and equipment, wood and paper, textiles, food products, furniture

Lithuania
REPUBLIC OF LITHUANIA
AREA	65,300 sq km (25,212 sq mi)
POPULATION	3,357,000
CAPITAL	Vilnius 543,000
RELIGION	Roman Catholic, Russian Orthodox
LANGUAGE	Lithuanian, Russian, Polish
LITERACY	100%
LIFE EXPECTANCY	71 years
GDP PER CAPITA	$18,900
ECONOMY	**IND:** metal-cutting machine tools, electric motors, television sets, refrigerators and freezers **AGR:** grain, potatoes, sugar beets, flax; beef; fish **EXP:** mineral products, textiles and clothing, machinery and equipment, chemicals

Finland
REPUBLIC OF FINLAND
AREA	338,145 sq km (130,558 sq mi)
POPULATION	5,312,000
CAPITAL	Helsinki 1,115,000
RELIGION	Lutheran Church of Finland
LANGUAGE	Finnish, Swedish
LITERACY	100%
LIFE EXPECTANCY	79 years
GDP PER CAPITA	$36,800
ECONOMY	**IND:** metals and metal products, electronics, machinery and scientific instruments, shipbuilding **AGR:** barley, wheat, sugar beets, potatoes; dairy cattle; fish **EXP:** machinery and equipment, chemicals, metals, timber, paper, pulp

Iceland
REPUBLIC OF ICELAND
AREA	103,000 sq km (39,769 sq mi)
POPULATION	319,000
CAPITAL	Reykjavík 192,000
RELIGION	Lutheran Church of Iceland
LANGUAGE	Icelandic, English, Nordic languages, German
LITERACY	99%
LIFE EXPECTANCY	81 years
GDP PER CAPITA	$39,700
ECONOMY	**IND:** fish processing, aluminum smelting, ferrosilicon production, geothermal power **AGR:** potatoes, green vegetables; mutton, dairy products; fish **EXP:** fish and fish products, aluminum, animal products, ferrosilicon, diatomite

Temperature and Precipitation

Average Monthly Temperatures (°F)
(January/July)

Reykjavik (32°/52°) ICELAND

Oslo (19°/60°)
Stockholm (26°/63°)
Helsinki (21°/62°)
Tallinn (23°/62°)
Göteborg (27°/60°)
Riga (23°/64°)
Copenhagen (31°/63°)
Vilnius (22°/65°)

Average Annual Precipitation

Over 80 inches	Over 200 cm
60–80 inches	150–200 cm
40–59 inches	100–149 cm
20–39 inches	50–99 cm
10–19 inches	25–49 cm
Under 10 inches	Under 25 cm

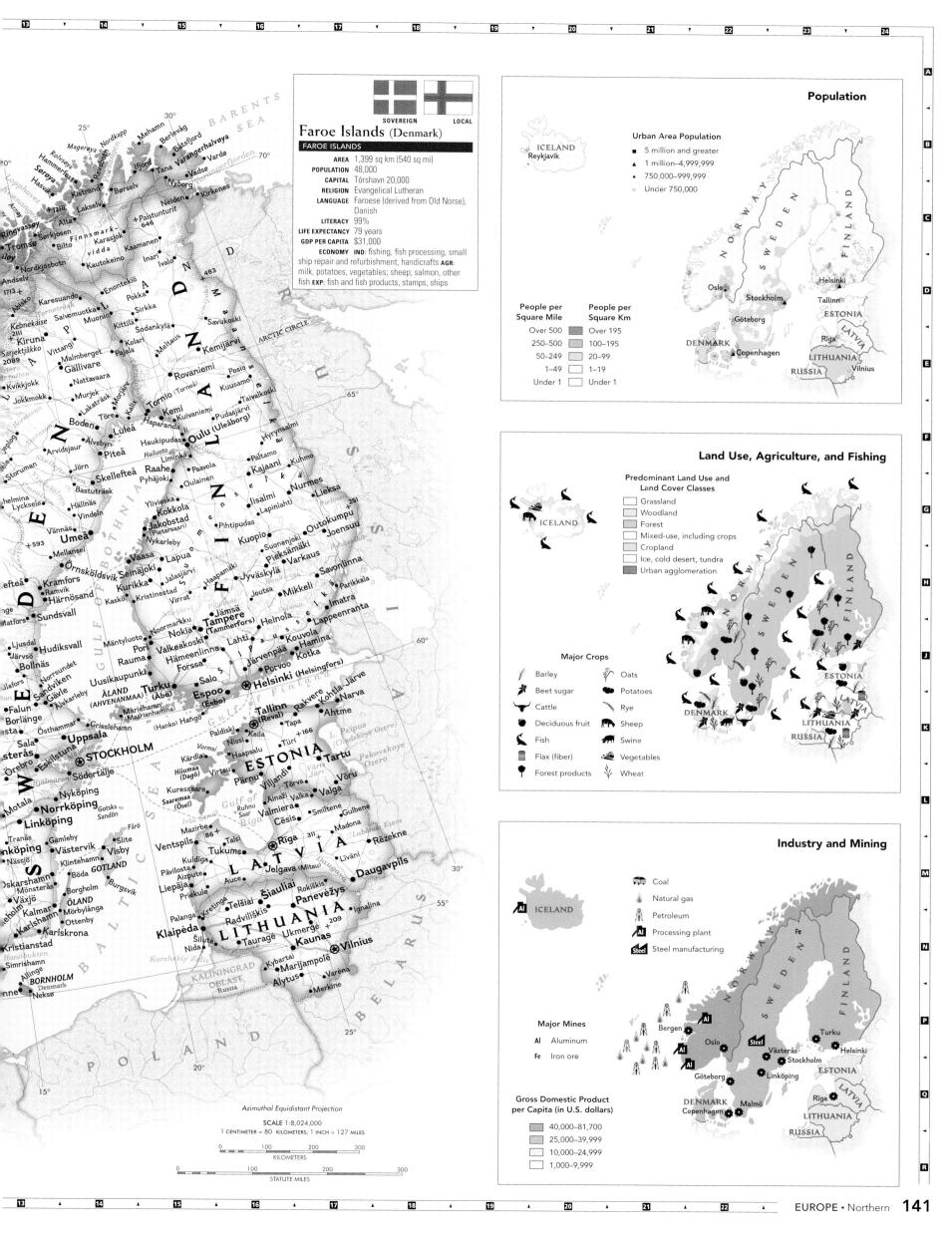

Faroe Islands (Denmark)

FAROE ISLANDS

SOVEREIGN / LOCAL

AREA 1,399 sq km (540 sq mi)
POPULATION 48,000
CAPITAL Tórshavn 20,000
RELIGION Evangelical Lutheran
LANGUAGE Faroese (derived from Old Norse), Danish
LITERACY 99%
LIFE EXPECTANCY 79 years
GDP PER CAPITA $31,000
ECONOMY IND: fishing, fish processing, small ship repair and refurbishment, handicrafts AGR: milk, potatoes, vegetables; sheep; salmon, other fish EXP: fish and fish products, stamps, ships

Population

ICELAND
Reykjavik

Urban Area Population
- ■ 5 million and greater
- ▲ 1 million–4,999,999
- ▲ 750,000–999,999
- ○ Under 750,000

People per Square Mile	People per Square Km
Over 500	Over 195
250–500	100–195
50–249	20–99
1–49	1–19
Under 1	Under 1

Land Use, Agriculture, and Fishing

Predominant Land Use and Land Cover Classes
- Grassland
- Woodland
- Forest
- Mixed-use, including crops
- Cropland
- Ice, cold desert, tundra
- Urban agglomeration

ICELAND

Major Crops
- Barley
- Beet sugar
- Cattle
- Deciduous fruit
- Fish
- Flax (fiber)
- Forest products
- Oats
- Potatoes
- Rye
- Sheep
- Swine
- Vegetables
- Wheat

Industry and Mining

ICELAND

- Coal
- Natural gas
- Petroleum
- Al Processing plant
- Steel Steel manufacturing

Major Mines
- Al Aluminum
- Fe Iron ore

Gross Domestic Product per Capita (in U.S. dollars)
- 40,000–81,700
- 25,000–39,999
- 10,000–24,999
- 1,000–9,999

Azimuthal Equidistant Projection

SCALE 1:8,024,000
1 CENTIMETER = 80 KILOMETERS; 1 INCH = 127 MILES

KILOMETERS
0 100 200 300

STATUTE MILES
0 100 200 300

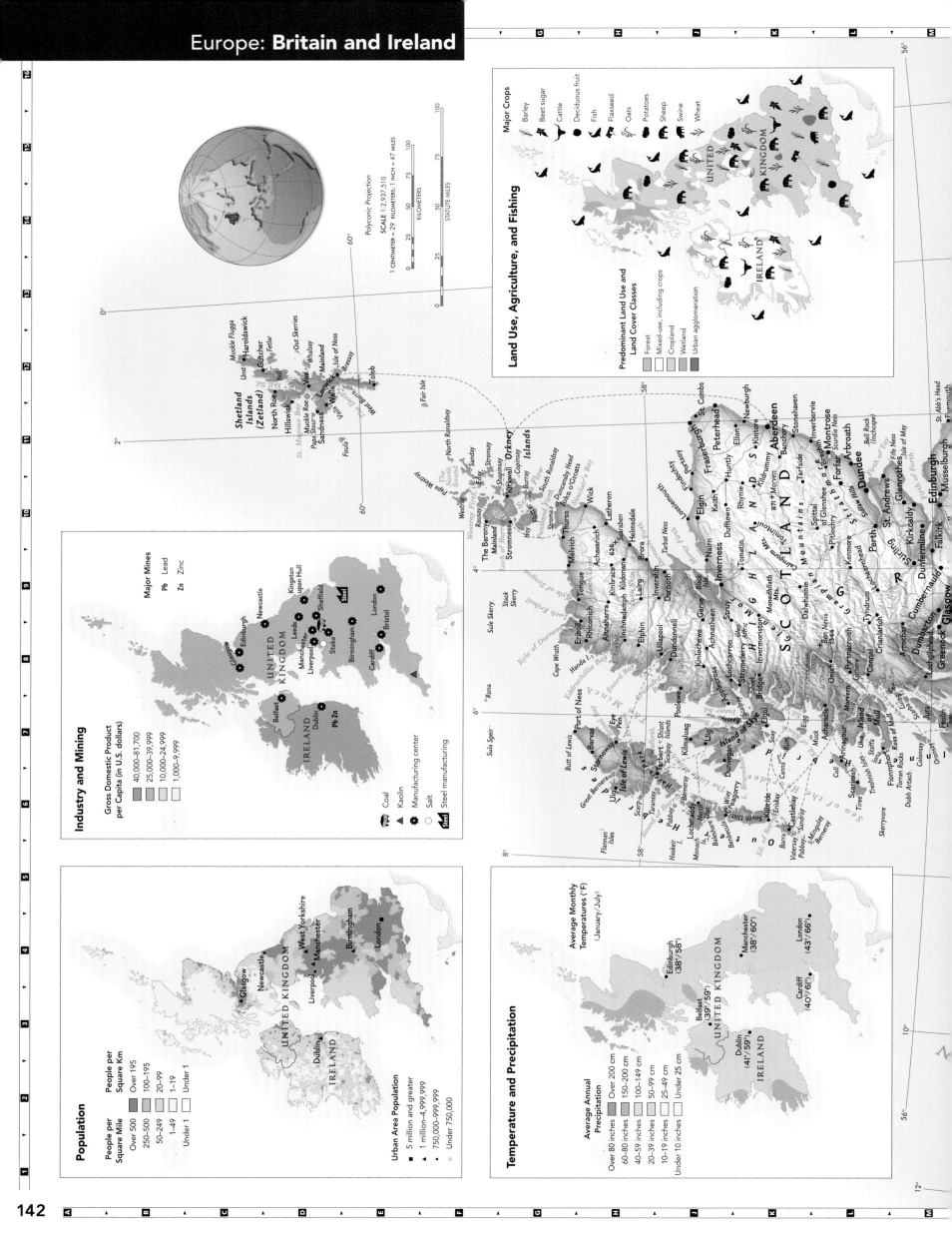

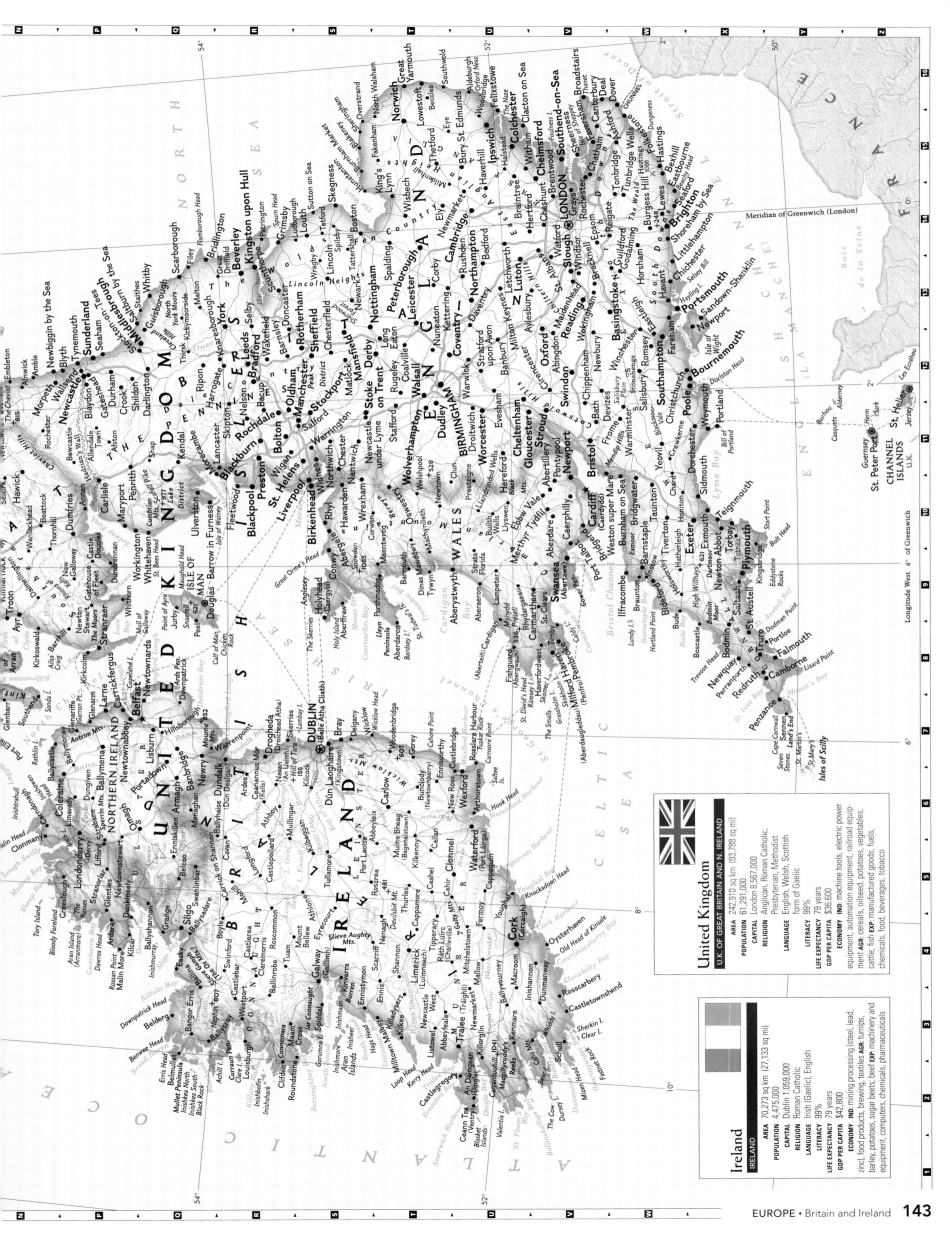

United Kingdom

U.K. OF GREAT BRITAIN AND N. IRELAND

AREA	242,910 sq km (93,788 sq mi)
POPULATION	61,291,000
CAPITAL	London 8,567,000
RELIGION	Anglican, Roman Catholic, Presbyterian, Methodist
LANGUAGE	English, Welsh, Scottish form of Gaelic
LITERACY	99%
LIFE EXPECTANCY	79 years
GDP PER CAPITA	$36,600
ECONOMY	**IND:** machine tools, electric power equipment, automation equipment, railroad equipment **AGR:** cereals, oilseed, potatoes, vegetables; cattle; fish **EXP:** manufactured goods, fuels, chemicals, food, beverages, tobacco

Ireland

IRELAND

AREA	70,273 sq km (27,133 sq mi)
POPULATION	4,475,000
CAPITAL	Dublin 1,059,000
RELIGION	Roman Catholic
LANGUAGE	Irish (Gaelic), English
LITERACY	99%
LIFE EXPECTANCY	79 years
GDP PER CAPITA	$42,800
ECONOMY	**IND:** mining processing (steel, lead, zinc), food products, brewing, textiles **AGR:** turnips, barley, potatoes, sugar beets; beef **EXP:** machinery and equipment, computers, chemicals, pharmaceuticals

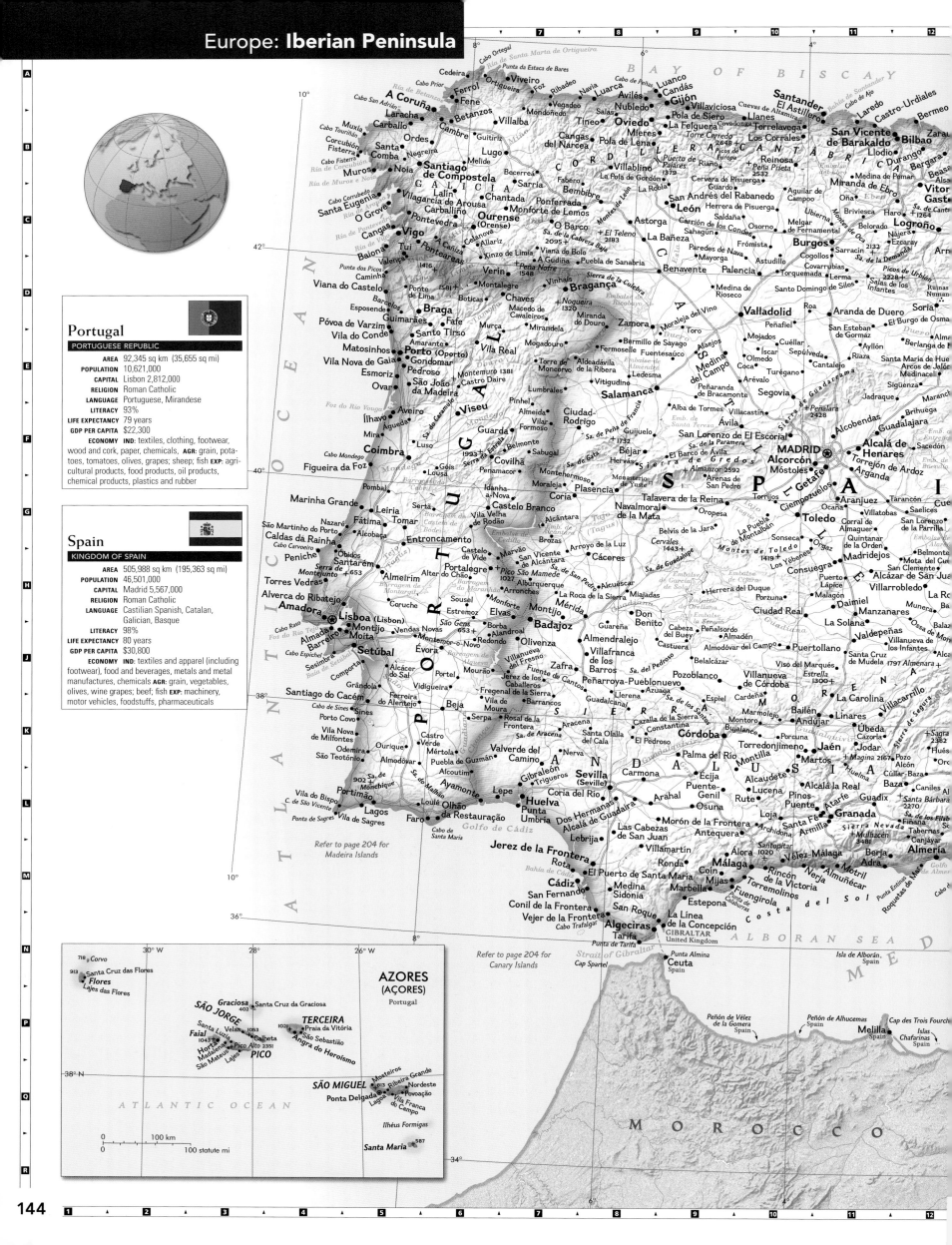

Portugal
PORTUGUESE REPUBLIC

AREA	92,345 sq km (35,655 sq mi)
POPULATION	10,621,000
CAPITAL	Lisbon 2,812,000
RELIGION	Roman Catholic
LANGUAGE	Portuguese, Mirandese
LITERACY	93%
LIFE EXPECTANCY	79 years
GDP PER CAPITA	$22,300
ECONOMY	**IND:** textiles, clothing, footwear, wood and cork, paper, chemicals. **AGR:** grain, potatoes, tomatoes, olives, grapes; sheep; fish **EXP:** agricultural products, food products, oil products, chemical products, plastics and rubber

Spain
KINGDOM OF SPAIN

AREA	505,988 sq km (195,363 sq mi)
POPULATION	46,501,000
CAPITAL	Madrid 5,567,000
RELIGION	Roman Catholic
LANGUAGE	Castilian Spanish, Catalan, Galician, Basque
LITERACY	98%
LIFE EXPECTANCY	80 years
GDP PER CAPITA	$30,800
ECONOMY	**IND:** textiles and apparel (including footwear), food and beverages, metals and metal manufactures, chemicals **AGR:** grain, vegetables, olives, wine grapes; beef; fish **EXP:** machinery, motor vehicles, foodstuffs, pharmaceuticals

Refer to page 204 for Madeira Islands

Refer to page 204 for Canary Islands

AZORES (AÇORES) Portugal

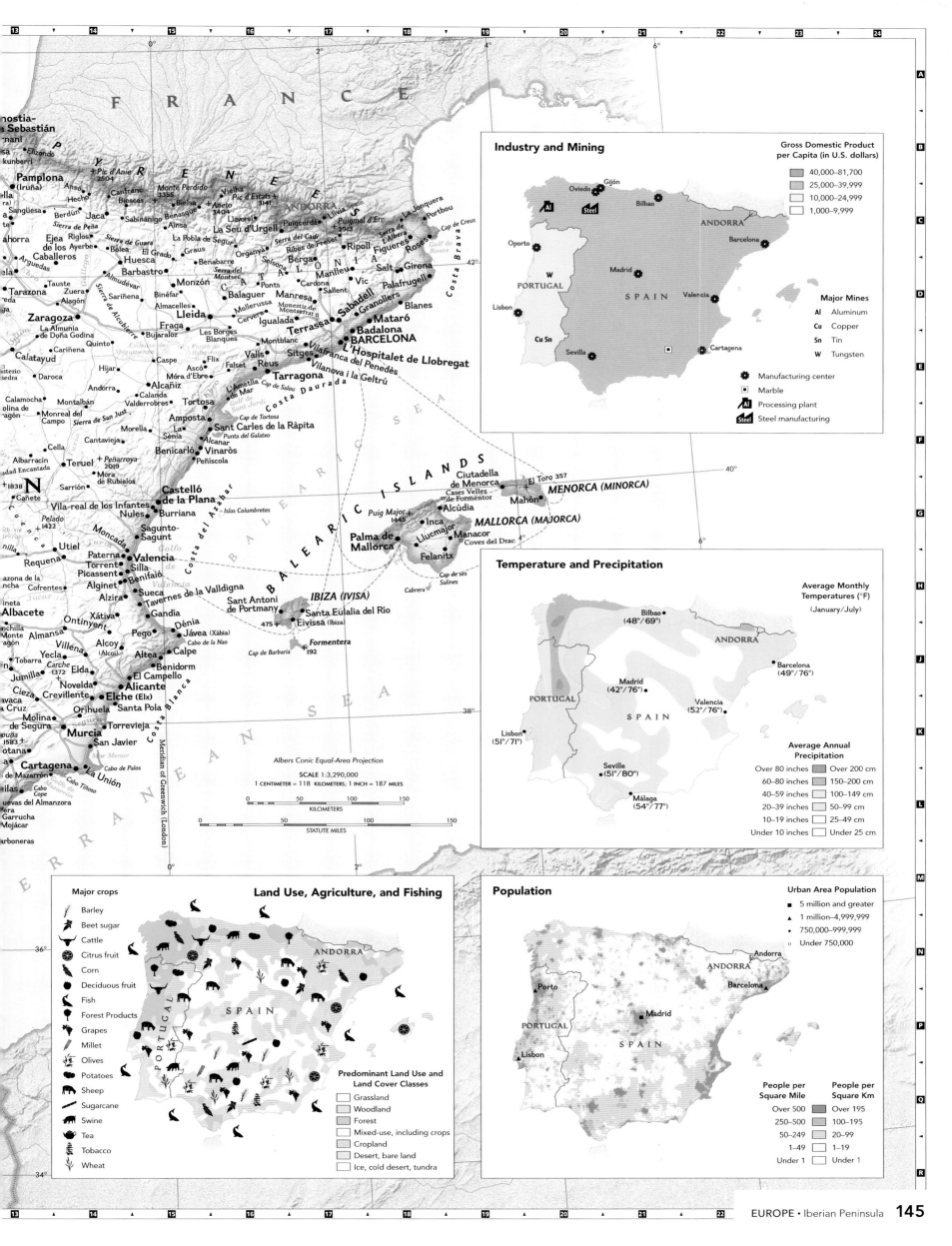

Main Map (Iberian Peninsula - East)

FRANCE

PYRENEES

ANDORRA

CATALONIA

BALEARIC ISLANDS

MEDITERRANEAN SEA

Major cities and places:

Donostia-San Sebastián, Irun, Elizondo, Pamplona (Iruña), Anso, Heche, Berdún, Jaca, Sangüesa, Canfranc, Biescas, Sabiñánigo, Bénasque, Bielsa, Ainsa, Llavorsí, Puigcerdà, Llívia, Puigmal d'Err 2913, La Jonquera, Portbou, Cap de Creus

Pic d'Anie 2504, Monte Perdido 3355, Pic d'Estats 3141, Aneto 3404

La Pobla de Segur, La Seu d'Urgell, Organyà, Ribes de Freser, Ripoll, Figueres, Roses, Golf de Roses, Costa Brava

Ejea de los Caballeros, Riglos, El Grado, Graus, Benabarre, Serra del Cadí, Solsona, Berga, Manlleu, Salt, Girona

Tauste, Zuera, Alagón, Huesca, Barbastro, Monzón, Binéfar, Almacelles, Cervera, Cardona, Vic, Palafrugell, Blanes

Zaragoza, La Almunia de Doña Godina, Cariñena, Quinto, Sariñena, Balaguer, Manresa, Sallent, Granollers, Mataró

Calatayud, Daroca, Bujaraloz, Lleida, Fraga, Les Borges Blanques, Igualada, Terrassa, Sabadell, Badalona

Calamocha, Montalbán, Caspe, Móra d'Ebre, Flix, Montblanc, Vilafranca del Penedès, BARCELONA, L'Hospitalet de Llobregat

Teruel, Peñarroya 2019, Valderrobres, Alcañiz, Calanda, Ascó, Falset, Valls, Reus, Sitges, Vilanova i la Geltrú

Albarracín, Sarrión, Morella, Cantavieja, La Sènia, Alcanar, Benicarló, Vinaròs, Tarragona, L'Ametlla de Mar, Cap de Salou, Costa Daurada

Cañete, Móra de Rubielos, Peñíscola, Tortosa, Amposta, Sant Carles de la Ràpita, Cap de Tortosa, Golf de Sant Jordi

Castelló de la Plana, Vila-real de los Infantes, Nules, Burriana, Islas Columbretes, Punta del Galatxo

Utiel, Sagunto-Sagunt, Moncada, Paterna, Silla, Benifaió, Picassent, Alginet, Sueca, Tavernes de la Valldigna, Gandía

Requena, VALENCIA, Torrent, Alzira, Cullera, Golfo de Valencia, Costa del Azahar

Albacete, Xàtiva, Ontinyent, Pego, Dénia, Jávea (Xàbia), Cabo de la Nao

Almansa, Villena, Alcoy (Alcoi), Calpe, Altea, Benidorm

Yecla, Elda, Novelda, El Campello, Carche 1372

Jumilla, Cieza, Crevillente, ALICANTE, Elche (Elx), Santa Pola

Molina de Segura, Orihuela, Torrevieja, Costa Blanca

Murcia, San Javier, Mar Menor, Cabo de Palos

Cartagena, La Unión, Cabo de Mazarrón, Cabo Tiñoso, Cabo Cope, Garrucha, Mojácar, Cuevas del Almanzora

BALEARIC ISLANDS:
Ciutadella de Menorca, Cases Velles de Formentor, Mahón, El Toro 357, MENORCA (MINORCA)
Puig Major 1445, Alcúdia, Inca, Manacor, Coves del Drac, MALLORCA (MAJORCA)
Palma de Mallorca, Llucmajor, Felanitx, Cap de ses Salines, Cabrera
Sant Antoni de Portmany, Santa Eulalia del Río, Eivissa (Ibiza), IBIZA (IVISA), Cap de Barbaria 192, Formentera

N (compass)

Scale:
Albers Conic Equal-Area Projection
SCALE 1:3,290,000
1 CENTIMETER = 118 KILOMETERS; 1 INCH = 187 MILES
KILOMETERS 0 50 100 150
STATUTE MILES 0 50 100 150

Industry and Mining

Gross Domestic Product per Capita (in U.S. dollars)
- 40,000–81,700
- 25,000–39,999
- 10,000–24,999
- 1,000–9,999

PORTUGAL, SPAIN, ANDORRA
Oviedo, Gijón, Bilbao, Oporto, Barcelona, Madrid, Valencia, Lisbon, Sevilla, Cartagena
W, Al, Steel, Cu Sn

Major Mines:
- Al Aluminum
- Cu Copper
- Sn Tin
- W Tungsten

- Manufacturing center
- Marble
- Al Processing plant
- Steel Steel manufacturing

Temperature and Precipitation

Average Monthly Temperatures (°F) (January/July)

PORTUGAL, SPAIN, ANDORRA
Bilbao (48°/69°)
Barcelona (49°/76°)
Madrid (42°/76°)
Valencia (52°/76°)
Lisbon (51°/71°)
Seville (51°/80°)
Málaga (54°/77°)

Average Annual Precipitation:
Over 80 inches	Over 200 cm
60–80 inches	150–200 cm
40–59 inches	100–149 cm
20–39 inches	50–99 cm
10–19 inches	25–49 cm
Under 10 inches	Under 25 cm

Land Use, Agriculture, and Fishing

Major crops:
- Barley
- Beet sugar
- Cattle
- Citrus fruit
- Corn
- Deciduous fruit
- Fish
- Forest Products
- Grapes
- Millet
- Olives
- Potatoes
- Sheep
- Sugarcane
- Swine
- Tea
- Tobacco
- Wheat

PORTUGAL, SPAIN, ANDORRA

Predominant Land Use and Land Cover Classes:
- Grassland
- Woodland
- Forest
- Mixed-use, including crops
- Cropland
- Desert, bare land
- Ice, cold desert, tundra

Population

Urban Area Population
- 5 million and greater
- 1 million–4,999,999
- 750,000–999,999
- Under 750,000

PORTUGAL, SPAIN, ANDORRA
Porto, Lisbon, Madrid, Barcelona, Andorra

People per Square Mile	People per Square Km
Over 500	Over 195
250–500	100–195
50–249	20–99
1–49	1–19
Under 1	Under 1

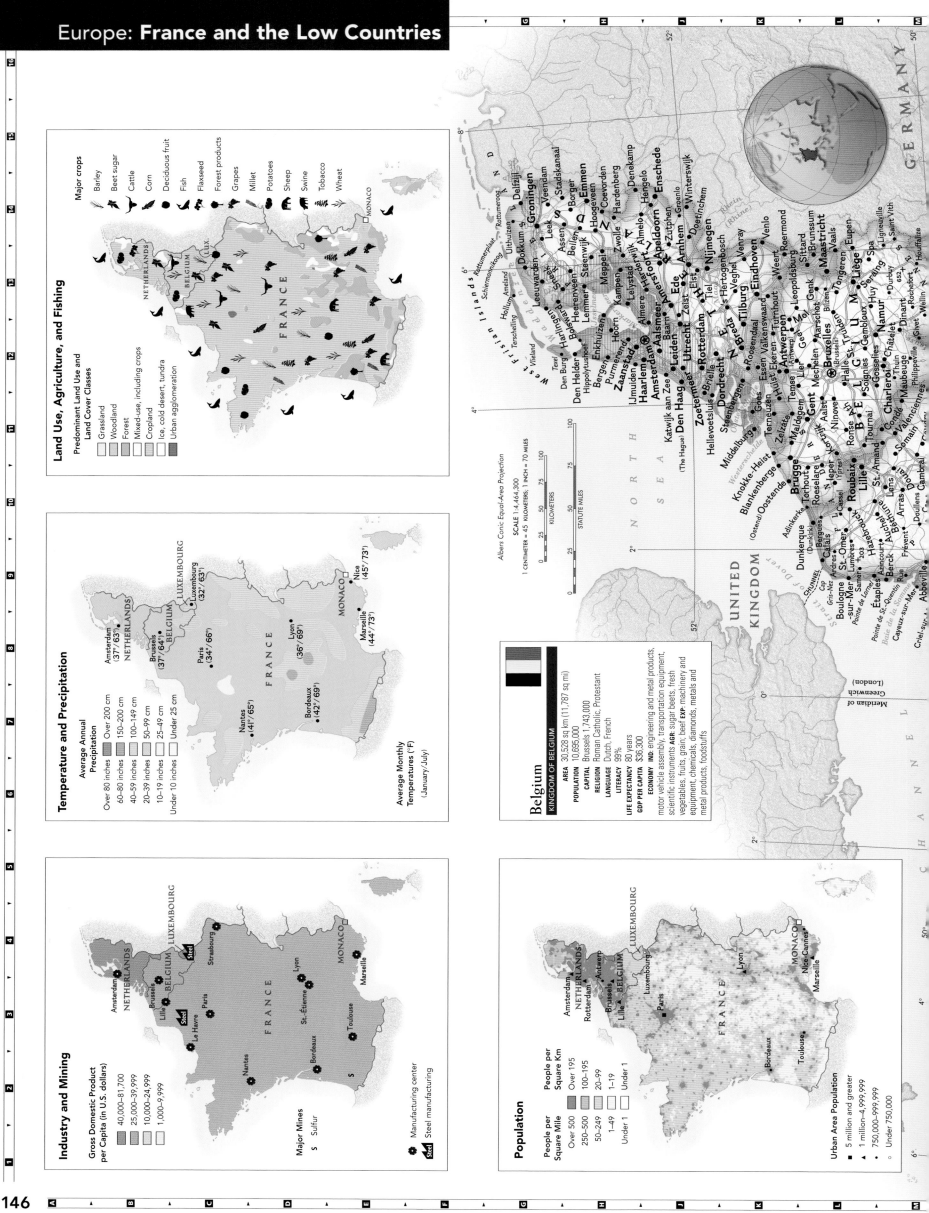

Industry and Mining

Gross Domestic Product per Capita (in U.S. dollars)

- 40,000–81,700
- 25,000–39,999
- 10,000–24,999
- 1,000–9,999

Major Mines

S   Sulfur

● Manufacturing center

Steel   Steel manufacturing

Temperature and Precipitation

Average Annual Precipitation

- Over 80 inches · Over 200 cm
- 60–80 inches · 150–200 cm
- 40–59 inches · 100–149 cm
- 20–39 inches · 50–99 cm
- 10–19 inches · 25–49 cm
- Under 10 inches · Under 25 cm

Average Monthly Temperatures (°F)

(January/July)

Amsterdam (37°/63°)
Brussels (37°/64°)
Luxembourg (32°/63°)
Paris (34°/66°)
Nantes (41°/65°)
Bordeaux (42°/69°)
Lyon (36°/69°)
Marseille (44°/73°)
Nice (45°/73°)

Land Use, Agriculture, and Fishing

Predominant Land Use and Land Cover Classes

- Grassland
- Woodland
- Forest
- Mixed-use, including crops
- Cropland
- Ice, cold desert, tundra
- Urban agglomeration

Major crops

- Barley
- Beet sugar
- Cattle
- Corn
- Deciduous fruit
- Fish
- Flaxseed
- Forest products
- Grapes
- Millet
- Potatoes
- Sheep
- Swine
- Tobacco
- Wheat

Population

People per Square Mile · **People per Square Km**

- Over 500 · Over 195
- 250–500 · 100–195
- 50–249 · 20–99
- 1–49 · 1–19
- Under 1 · Under 1

Urban Area Population

- ■ 5 million and greater
- ■ 1 million–4,999,999
- ● 750,000–999,999
- ○ Under 750,000

Belgium

KINGDOM OF BELGIUM

AREA 30,528 sq km (11,787 sq mi)
POPULATION 10,695,000
CAPITAL Brussels 1,743,000
RELIGION Roman Catholic, Protestant
LANGUAGE Dutch, French
LITERACY 99%
LIFE EXPECTANCY 80 years
GDP PER CAPITA $36,300
ECONOMY IND: engineering and metal products, motor vehicle assembly, transportation equipment, scientific instruments **AGR:** sugar beets, fresh vegetables, fruits, grain; beef **EXP:** machinery and equipment, chemicals, diamonds, metals and metal products, foodstuffs

Albers Conic Equal-Area Projection

SCALE 1:4,464,300
1 CENTIMETER = 45 KILOMETERS; 1 INCH = 70 MILES

KILOMETERS
STATUTE MILES

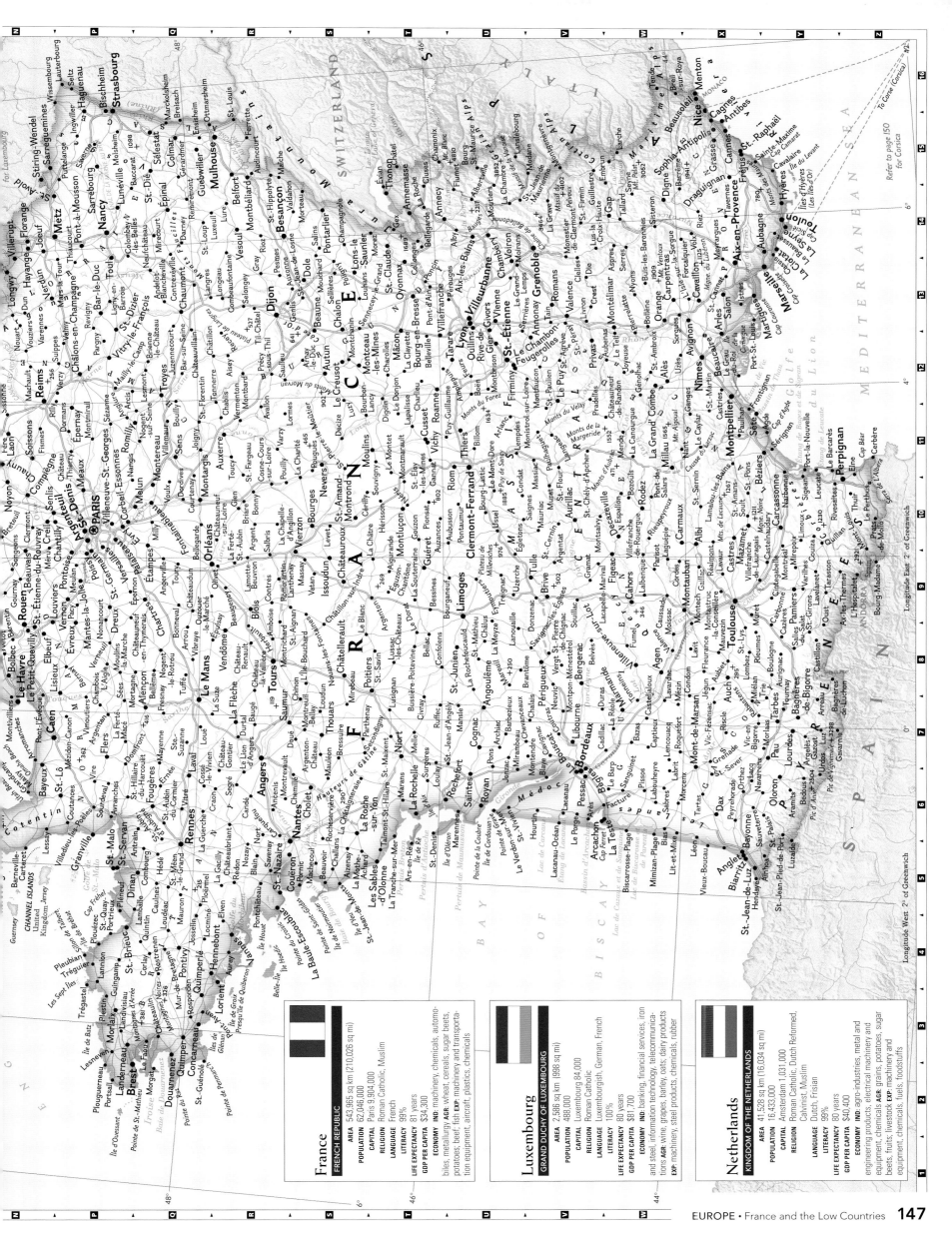

France
FRENCH REPUBLIC

AREA 543,965 sq km (210,026 sq mi)
POPULATION 62,046,000
CAPITAL Paris 9,904,000
RELIGION Roman Catholic, Muslim
LANGUAGE French
LITERACY 99%
LIFE EXPECTANCY 81 years
GDP PER CAPITA $34,300
ECONOMY **IND:** machinery, chemicals, automobiles, metallurgy, aircraft, electronics; textiles, food processing; tourism. **AGR:** wheat, cereals, sugar beets, potatoes; beef. **EXP:** machinery and transportation equipment, aircraft, plastics, chemicals

Luxembourg
GRAND DUCHY OF LUXEMBOURG

AREA 2,586 sq km (998 sq mi)
POPULATION 488,000
CAPITAL Luxembourg 84,000
RELIGION Roman Catholic
LANGUAGE Luxembourgish, German, French
LITERACY 100%
LIFE EXPECTANCY 80 years
GDP PER CAPITA $81,700
ECONOMY **IND:** banking, financial services, iron and steel, information technology, telecommunications. **AGR:** wine, grapes, barley, oats; dairy products. **EXP:** machinery, steel products, chemicals, rubber

Netherlands
KINGDOM OF THE NETHERLANDS

AREA 41,528 sq km (16,034 sq mi)
POPULATION 16,433,000
CAPITAL Amsterdam 1,031,000
RELIGION Roman Catholic, Dutch Reformed, Calvinist, Muslim
LANGUAGE Dutch, Frisian
LITERACY 99%
LIFE EXPECTANCY 80 years
GDP PER CAPITA $40,400
ECONOMY **IND:** agro-industries, metal and engineering products, electrical machinery and equipment, chemicals. **AGR:** grains, potatoes, sugar beets, fruits; livestock. **EXP:** machinery and equipment, chemicals, fuels, foodstuffs

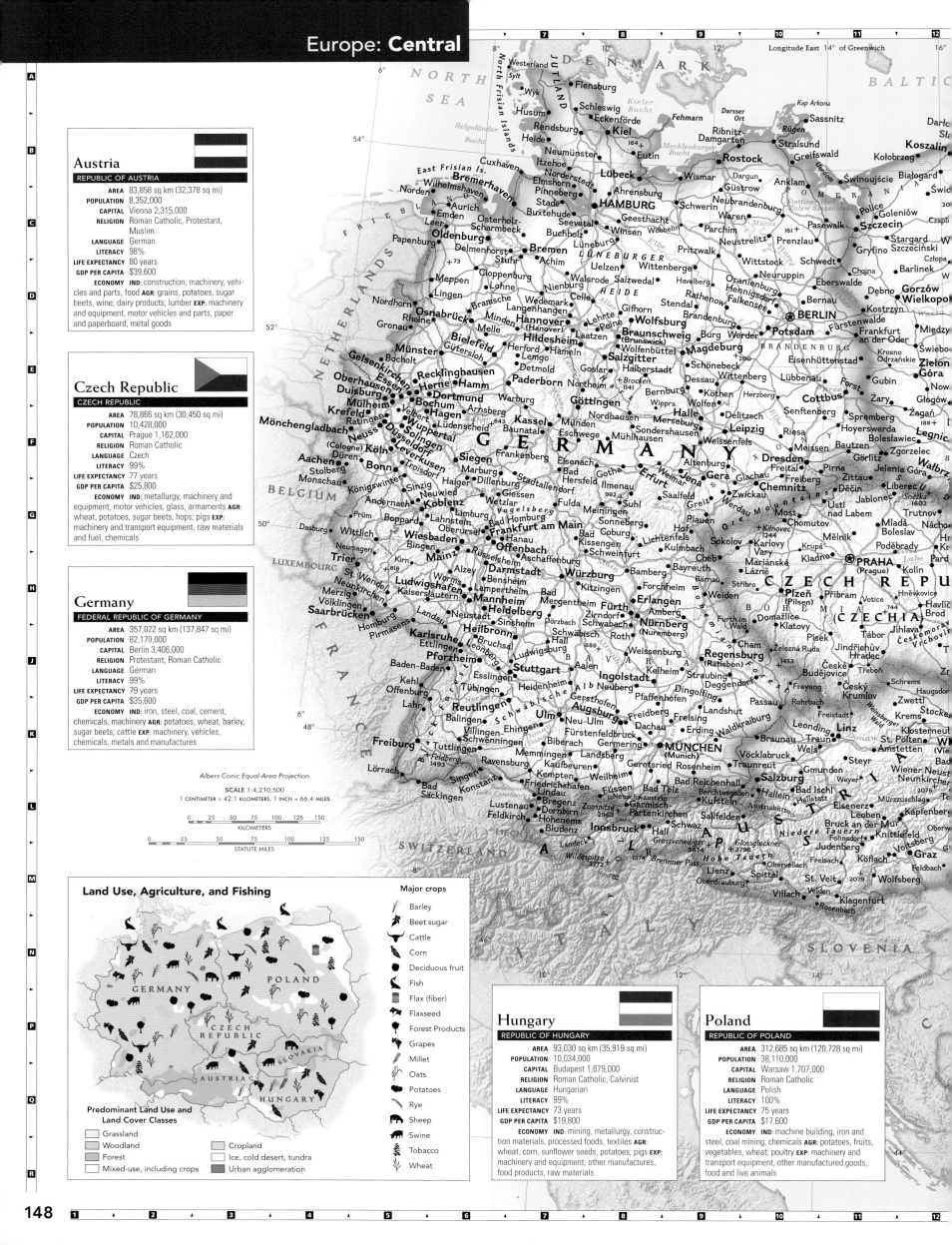

Austria
REPUBLIC OF AUSTRIA
AREA 83,858 sq km (32,378 sq mi)
POPULATION 8,352,000
CAPITAL Vienna 2,315,000
RELIGION Roman Catholic, Protestant, Muslim
LANGUAGE German
LITERACY 98%
LIFE EXPECTANCY 80 years
GDP PER CAPITA $39,600
ECONOMY IND: construction, machinery, vehicles and parts, food **AGR:** grains, potatoes, sugar beets, wine; dairy products; lumber **EXP:** machinery and equipment, motor vehicles and parts, paper and paperboard, metal goods

Czech Republic
CZECH REPUBLIC
AREA 78,866 sq km (30,450 sq mi)
POPULATION 10,428,000
CAPITAL Prague 1,162,000
RELIGION Roman Catholic
LANGUAGE Czech
LITERACY 99%
LIFE EXPECTANCY 77 years
GDP PER CAPITA $25,800
ECONOMY IND: metallurgy, machinery and equipment, motor vehicles, glass, armaments **AGR:** wheat, potatoes, sugar beets, hops; pigs **EXP:** machinery and transport equipment, raw materials and fuel, chemicals

Germany
FEDERAL REPUBLIC OF GERMANY
AREA 357,022 sq km (137,847 sq mi)
POPULATION 82,170,000
CAPITAL Berlin 3,406,000
RELIGION Protestant, Roman Catholic
LANGUAGE German
LITERACY 99%
LIFE EXPECTANCY 79 years
GDP PER CAPITA $35,600
ECONOMY IND: iron, steel, coal, cement, chemicals, machinery **AGR:** potatoes, wheat, barley, sugar beets; cattle **EXP:** machinery, vehicles, chemicals, metals and manufactures

Albers Conic Equal-Area Projection

SCALE 1:4,210,500
1 CENTIMETER = 42.1 KILOMETERS; 1 INCH = 66.4 MILES

KILOMETERS
0 25 50 75 100 125 150

STATUTE MILES
0 25 50 75 100 125 150

Land Use, Agriculture, and Fishing

Major crops
- Barley
- Beet sugar
- Cattle
- Corn
- Deciduous fruit
- Fish
- Flax (fiber)
- Flaxseed
- Forest Products
- Grapes
- Millet
- Oats
- Potatoes
- Rye
- Sheep
- Swine
- Tobacco
- Wheat

Predominant Land Use and Land Cover Classes
- Grassland
- Woodland
- Forest
- Mixed-use, including crops
- Cropland
- Ice, cold desert, tundra
- Urban agglomeration

Hungary
REPUBLIC OF HUNGARY
AREA 93,030 sq km (35,919 sq mi)
POPULATION 10,034,000
CAPITAL Budapest 1,679,000
RELIGION Roman Catholic, Calvinist
LANGUAGE Hungarian
LITERACY 99%
LIFE EXPECTANCY 73 years
GDP PER CAPITA $19,800
ECONOMY IND: mining, metallurgy, construction materials, processed foods, textiles **AGR:** wheat, corn, sunflower seeds, potatoes; pigs **EXP:** machinery and equipment, other manufactures, food products, raw materials

Poland
REPUBLIC OF POLAND
AREA 312,685 sq km (120,728 sq mi)
POPULATION 38,110,000
CAPITAL Warsaw 1,707,000
RELIGION Roman Catholic
LANGUAGE Polish
LITERACY 100%
LIFE EXPECTANCY 75 years
GDP PER CAPITA $17,600
ECONOMY IND: machine building, iron and steel, coal mining, chemicals **AGR:** potatoes, fruits, vegetables, wheat; poultry **EXP:** machinery and transport equipment, other manufactured goods, food and live animals

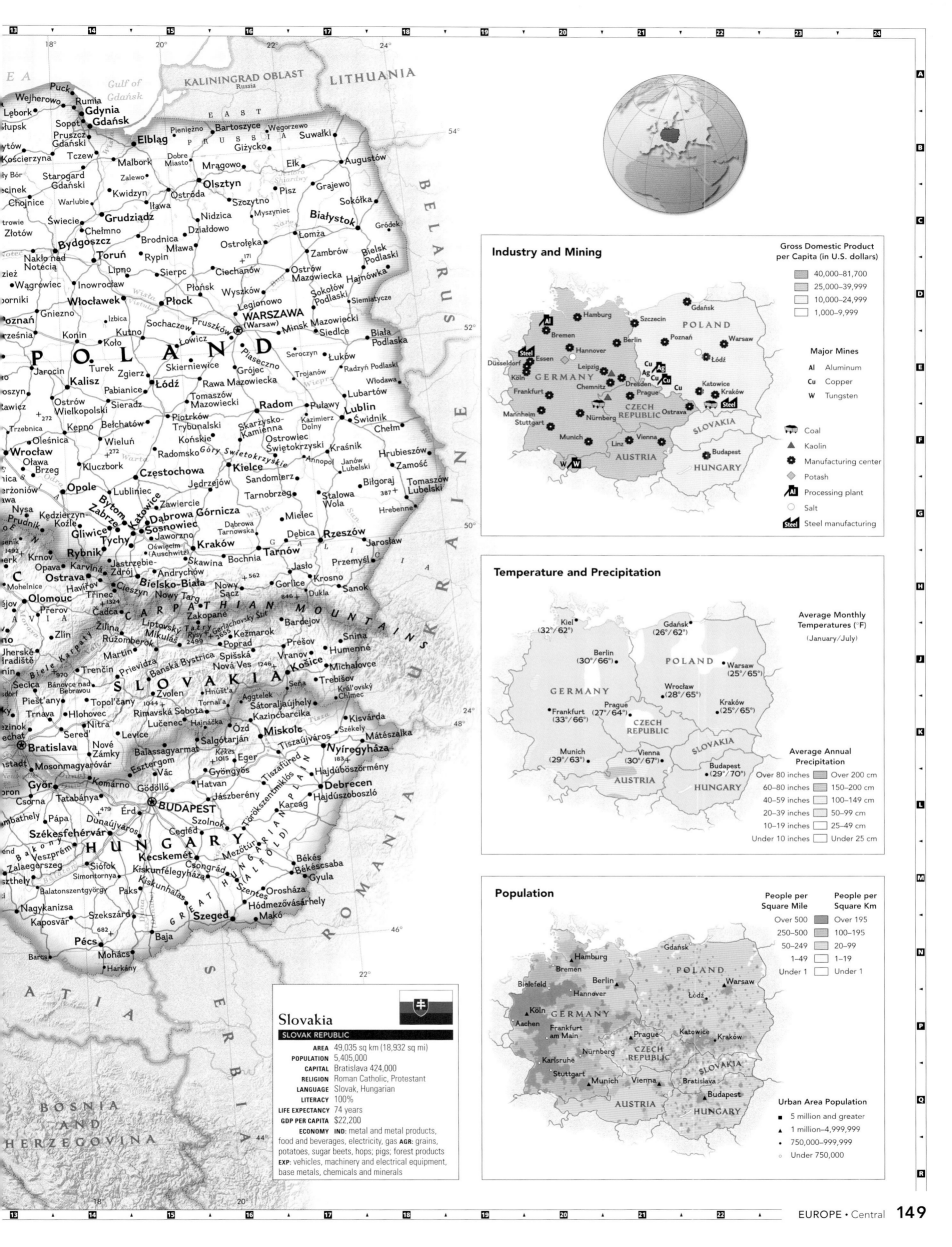

Map labels (Poland, Slovakia, Hungary region)

KALININGRAD OBLAST
Russia
LITHUANIA
Gulf of Gdańsk
EAST PRUSSIA
BELARUS
UKRAINE
ROMANIA
SERBIA
BOSNIA AND HERZEGOVINA

POLAND
Puck, Wejherowo, Rumia, Gdynia, Gdańsk, Sopot, Pruszcz Gdański, Elbląg, Tczew, Malbork, Kwidzyn, Starogard Gdański, Chojnice, Świecie, Grudziądz, Bydgoszcz, Toruń, Włocławek, Płock, WARSZAWA (Warsaw), Łódź, Kalisz, Wrocław, Opole, Częstochowa, Katowice, Kraków, Tarnów, Rzeszów, Lublin, Białystok, Olsztyn, Suwałki, Ełk, Augustów

SLOVAKIA
Bratislava, Žilina, Martin, Košice, Prešov, Poprad, Nitra

HUNGARY
BUDAPEST, Győr, Miskolc, Debrecen, Szeged, Pécs, Kecskemét, Nyíregyháza, Székesfehérvár

CARPATHIAN MOUNTAINS

Industry and Mining

Gross Domestic Product per Capita (in U.S. dollars)
- 40,000–81,700
- 25,000–39,999
- 10,000–24,999
- 1,000–9,999

Major Mines
- Al — Aluminum
- Cu — Copper
- W — Tungsten
- Coal
- Kaolin
- Manufacturing center
- Potash
- Processing plant
- Salt
- Steel manufacturing

Temperature and Precipitation

Average Monthly Temperatures (°F) (January/July)
- Kiel (32°/62°)
- Gdańsk (26°/62°)
- Berlin (30°/66°)
- Warsaw (25°/65°)
- Wrocław (28°/65°)
- Frankfurt (33°/66°)
- Prague (27°/64°)
- Kraków (25°/65°)
- Munich (29°/63°)
- Vienna (30°/67°)
- Budapest (29°/70°)

Average Annual Precipitation
Over 80 inches	Over 200 cm
60–80 inches	150–200 cm
40–59 inches	100–149 cm
20–39 inches	50–99 cm
10–19 inches	25–49 cm
Under 10 inches	Under 25 cm

Population

People per Square Mile	People per Square Km
Over 500	Over 195
250–500	100–195
50–249	20–99
1–49	1–19
Under 1	Under 1

Urban Area Population
- 5 million and greater
- 1 million–4,999,999
- 750,000–999,999
- Under 750,000

Slovakia
SLOVAK REPUBLIC
- **AREA** 49,035 sq km (18,932 sq mi)
- **POPULATION** 5,405,000
- **CAPITAL** Bratislava 424,000
- **RELIGION** Roman Catholic, Protestant
- **LANGUAGE** Slovak, Hungarian
- **LITERACY** 100%
- **LIFE EXPECTANCY** 74 years
- **GDP PER CAPITA** $22,200
- **ECONOMY IND:** metal and metal products, food and beverages, electricity, gas **AGR:** grains, potatoes, sugar beets, hops; pigs; forest products **EXP:** vehicles, machinery and electrical equipment, base metals, chemicals and minerals

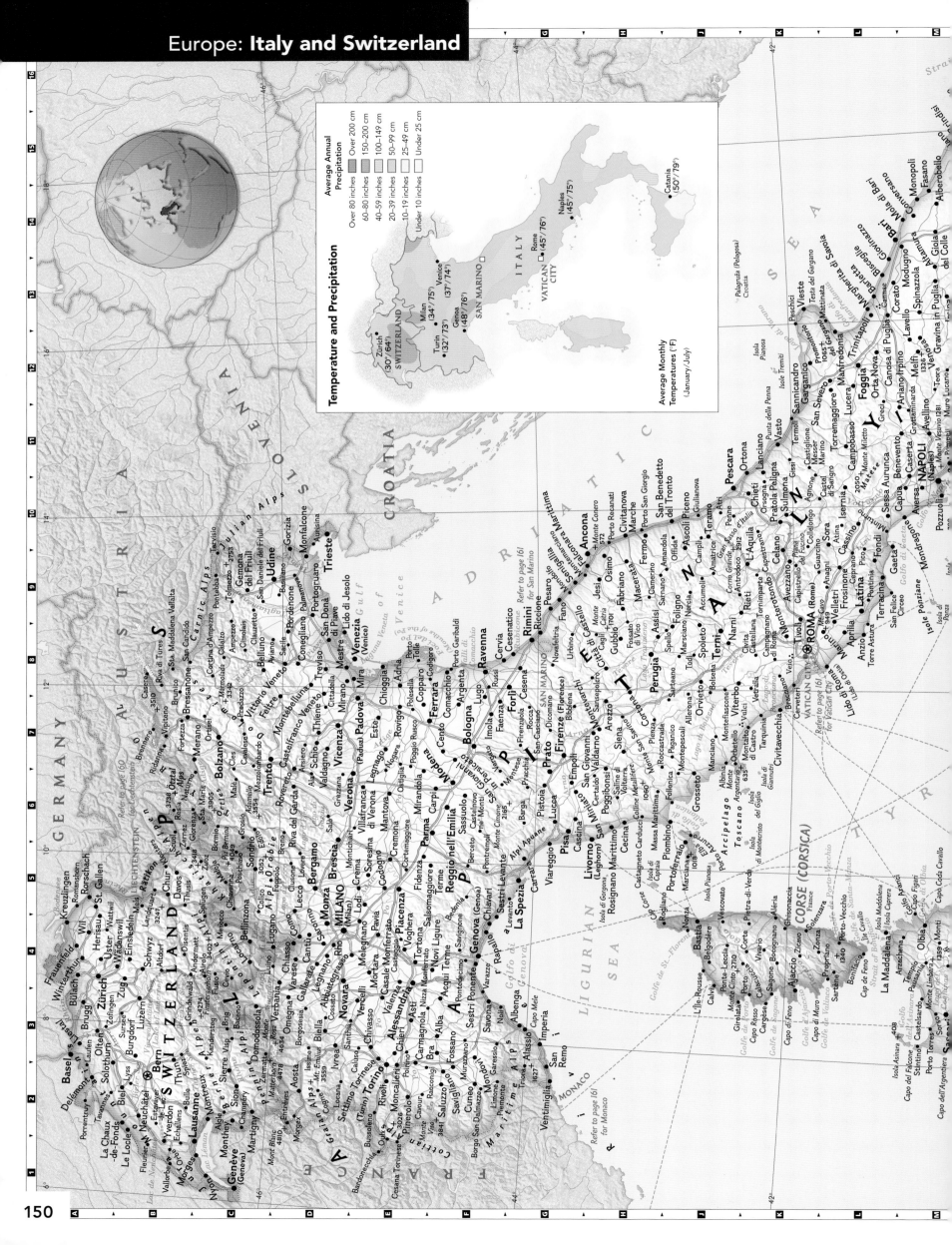

Temperature and Precipitation

Average Annual Precipitation

Over 80 inches	Over 200 cm
60–80 inches	150–200 cm
40–59 inches	100–149 cm
20–39 inches	50–99 cm
10–19 inches	25–49 cm
Under 10 inches	Under 25 cm

Average Monthly Temperatures (°F) (January / July)

Zürich (30°/64°)
Turin (32°/73°)
Milan (34°/75°)
Venice (37°/74°)
Genoa (48°/76°)
Rome (45°/76°)
Naples (45°/75°)
Catania (50°/79°)

SWITZERLAND
ITALY
SAN MARINO
VATICAN CITY

Palagruža (Pelagosa) Croatia

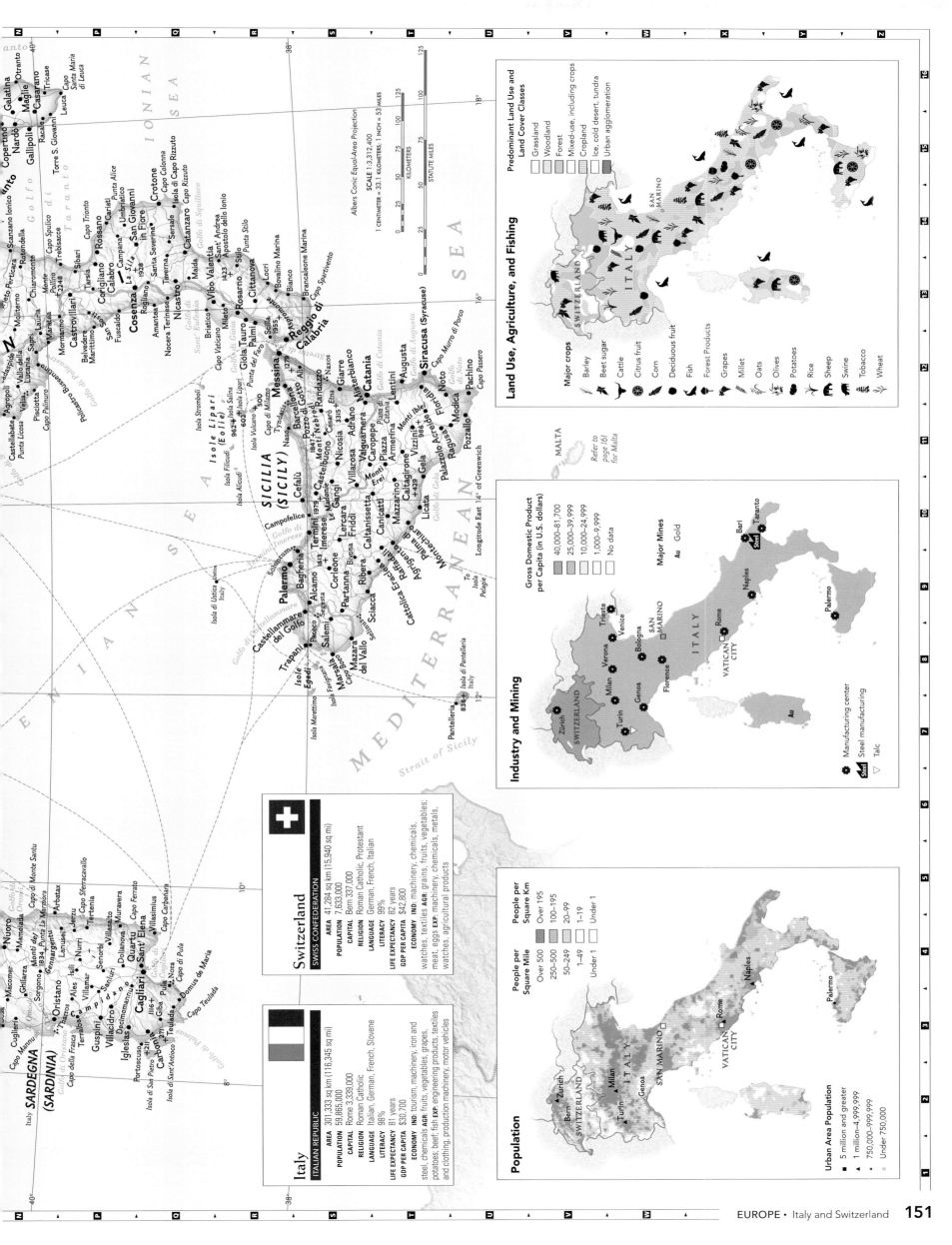

Italy

ITALIAN REPUBLIC

AREA 301,333 sq km (116,345 sq mi)
POPULATION 59,865,000
CAPITAL Rome 3,339,000
RELIGION Roman Catholic
LANGUAGE Italian, German, French, Slovene
LITERACY 98%
LIFE EXPECTANCY 81 years
GDP PER CAPITA $30,700
ECONOMY IND: tourism, machinery, iron and steel, chemicals **AGR:** fruits, vegetables, grapes, potatoes; beef; fish **EXP:** engineering products, textiles and clothing, production machinery, motor vehicles

Switzerland

SWISS CONFEDERATION

AREA 41,284 sq km (15,940 sq mi)
POPULATION 7,633,000
CAPITAL Bern 337,000
RELIGION Roman Catholic, Protestant
LANGUAGE German, French, Italian
LITERACY 99%
LIFE EXPECTANCY 82 years
GDP PER CAPITA $42,800
ECONOMY IND: machinery, chemicals, watches, textiles **AGR:** grains, fruits, vegetables; meat, eggs **EXP:** machinery, chemicals, metals, watches, agricultural products

Land Use, Agriculture, and Fishing

Predominant Land Use and Land Cover Classes
- Grassland
- Woodland
- Forest
- Mixed-use, including crops
- Cropland
- Ice, cold desert, tundra
- Urban agglomeration

Major crops
- Barley
- Beet sugar
- Cattle
- Citrus fruit
- Corn
- Deciduous fruit
- Fish
- Forest Products
- Grapes
- Millet
- Oats
- Olives
- Potatoes
- Rice
- Sheep
- Swine
- Tobacco
- Wheat

Industry and Mining

Gross Domestic Product per Capita (in U.S. dollars)
- 40,000–81,700
- 25,000–39,999
- 10,000–24,999
- 1,000–9,999
- No data

Major Mines
- Au Gold

- Manufacturing center
- Steel manufacturing
- Talc

Population

People per Square Mile / **People per Square Km**
- Over 500 / Over 195
- 250–500 / 100–195
- 50–249 / 20–99
- 1–49 / 1–19
- Under 1 / Under 1

Urban Area Population
- 5 million and greater
- 1 million–4,999,999
- 750,000–999,999
- Under 750,000

SCALE 1:3,312,400
1 CENTIMETER = 33.1 KILOMETERS; 1 INCH = 53 MILES
Albers Conic Equal-Area Projection

Albania

REPUBLIC OF ALBANIA

AREA	28,748 sq km (11,100 sq mi)
POPULATION	3,241,000
CAPITAL	Tirana 406,000
RELIGION	Muslim, Albanian Orthodox, Roman Catholic
LANGUAGE	Albanian, Greek, Vlach, Romani, Slavic dialects
LITERACY	99%
LIFE EXPECTANCY	75 years
GDP PER CAPITA	$6,800

ECONOMY IND: food processing, textiles and clothing, lumber, oil AGR: wheat, corn, potatoes, vegetables; meat EXP: textiles and footwear, asphalt, metals and metallic ores, crude oil

Bosnia and Herzegovina

BOSNIA AND HERZEGOVINA

AREA	51,129 sq km (19,741 sq mi)
POPULATION	3,843,000
CAPITAL	Sarajevo 376,000
RELIGION	Muslim, Orthodox, Roman Catholic
LANGUAGE	Bosnian, Croatian, Serbian
LITERACY	97%
LIFE EXPECTANCY	74 years
GDP PER CAPITA	$7,600

ECONOMY IND: steel, coal, iron ore, vehicle assembly, textiles AGR: wheat, corn, fruits, vegetables; livestock EXP: metals, clothing, wood products

Bulgaria

REPUBLIC OF BULGARIA

AREA	110,994 sq km (42,855 sq mi)
POPULATION	7,621,000
CAPITAL	Sofia 1,185,000
RELIGION	Bulgarian Orthodox, Muslim
LANGUAGE	Bulgarian, Turkish, Roma
LITERACY	98%
LIFE EXPECTANCY	73 years
GDP PER CAPITA	$12,400

ECONOMY IND: electricity, gas, food and beverages, machinery and equipment AGR: vegetables, fruits, tobacco, wine; livestock EXP: clothing, footwear, iron, steel, machinery and equipment, fuels

Croatia

REPUBLIC OF CROATIA

AREA	56,542 sq km (21,831 sq mi)
POPULATION	4,433,000
CAPITAL	Zagreb 690,000
RELIGION	Roman Catholic, Orthodox
LANGUAGE	Croatian
LITERACY	98%
LIFE EXPECTANCY	76 years
GDP PER CAPITA	$16,500

ECONOMY IND: chemicals and plastics, machine tools, fabricated metal, electronics, iron and steel products AGR: wheat, corn, sugar beets, sunflower seeds; livestock EXP: transport equipment, textiles, chemicals, foodstuffs, fuels

Romania

ROMANIA

AREA	238,391 sq km (92,043 sq mi)
POPULATION	21,498,000
CAPITAL	Bucharest 1,942,000
RELIGION	Eastern Orthodox, Protestant, Roman Catholic
LANGUAGE	Romanian, Hungarian
LITERACY	97%
LIFE EXPECTANCY	71 years
GDP PER CAPITA	$12,700

ECONOMY IND: electric machinery and equipment, textiles, footwear, auto assembly, mining AGR: wheat, corn, barley, sugar beets; eggs EXP: machinery, textiles, footwear, metals, minerals

Macedonia

REPUBLIC OF MACEDONIA

AREA	25,713 sq km (9,928 sq mi)
POPULATION	2,049,000
CAPITAL	Skopje 480,000
RELIGION	Macedonian Orthodox, Muslim
LANGUAGE	Macedonian, Albanian, Turkish
LITERACY	96%
LIFE EXPECTANCY	74 years
GDP PER CAPITA	$9,100

ECONOMY IND: food processing, beverages, textiles, chemicals AGR: grapes, wine, tobacco, vegetables; milk EXP: food, tobacco, textiles, iron, steel

Kosovo

REPUBLIC OF KOSOVO

AREA	10,887 sq km (4,203 sq mi)
POPULATION	2,191,000
CAPITAL	Prishtina (Pristina) 600,000
RELIGION	Muslim, Serbian Orthodox, Roman Catholic
LANGUAGE	Albanian, Serbian, Bosnian, Turkish
LITERACY	NA
LIFE EXPECTANCY	69 years
GDP PER CAPITA	$1,800

ECONOMY IND: mineral mining, construction materials, base metals, leather AGR: wheat, corn, grapes EXP: mining and processed metal products, scrap metals, leather products, machinery

Montenegro

MONTENEGRO

AREA	14,026 sq km (5,415 sq mi)
POPULATION	627,000
CAPITAL	Podgorica 142,000
RELIGION	Orthodox, Muslim, Roman Catholic
LANGUAGE	Serbian, Montenegrin, Bosnian, Albanian
LITERACY	NA
LIFE EXPECTANCY	73 years
GDP PER CAPITA	$10,600

ECONOMY IND: steelmaking, aluminum, agricultural processing, consumer goods, tourism AGR: grains, tobacco, potatoes, citrus fruits, olives, grapes; sheepherding EXP: NA

Serbia

REPUBLIC OF SERBIA

AREA	77,474 sq km (29,913 sq mi)
POPULATION	7,354,000
CAPITAL	Belgrade 1,099,000
RELIGION	Serbian Orthodox, Roman Catholic, Muslim
LANGUAGE	Serbian, Hungarian, Albanian
LITERACY	96%
LIFE EXPECTANCY	73 years
GDP PER CAPITA	$10,900

ECONOMY IND: sugar, agricultural machinery, electrical and communications equipment, paper and pulp AGR: wheat, maize, sugar beets, sunflower seeds; beef EXP: manufactured goods, food and live animals, machinery and transport equipment

Slovenia

REPUBLIC OF SLOVENIA

AREA	20,273 sq km (7,827 sq mi)
POPULATION	2,034,000
CAPITAL	Ljubljana 244,000
RELIGION	Roman Catholic
LANGUAGE	Slovene, Serbian, Croatian
LITERACY	100%
LIFE EXPECTANCY	78 years
GDP PER CAPITA	$28,900

ECONOMY IND: ferrous metallurgy and aluminum products, lead and zinc smelting, electronics, trucks AGR: potatoes, hops, wheat, sugar beets; cattle EXP: manufactured goods, machinery and transport equipment, chemicals, food

KOSOVO
On February 17, 2008, Kosovo declared its independence. Serbia still claims it as a province.

Albers Conic Equal-Area Projection

SCALE 1:4,013,000
1 CENTIMETER = 40 KILOMETERS, 1 INCH = 63 MILES

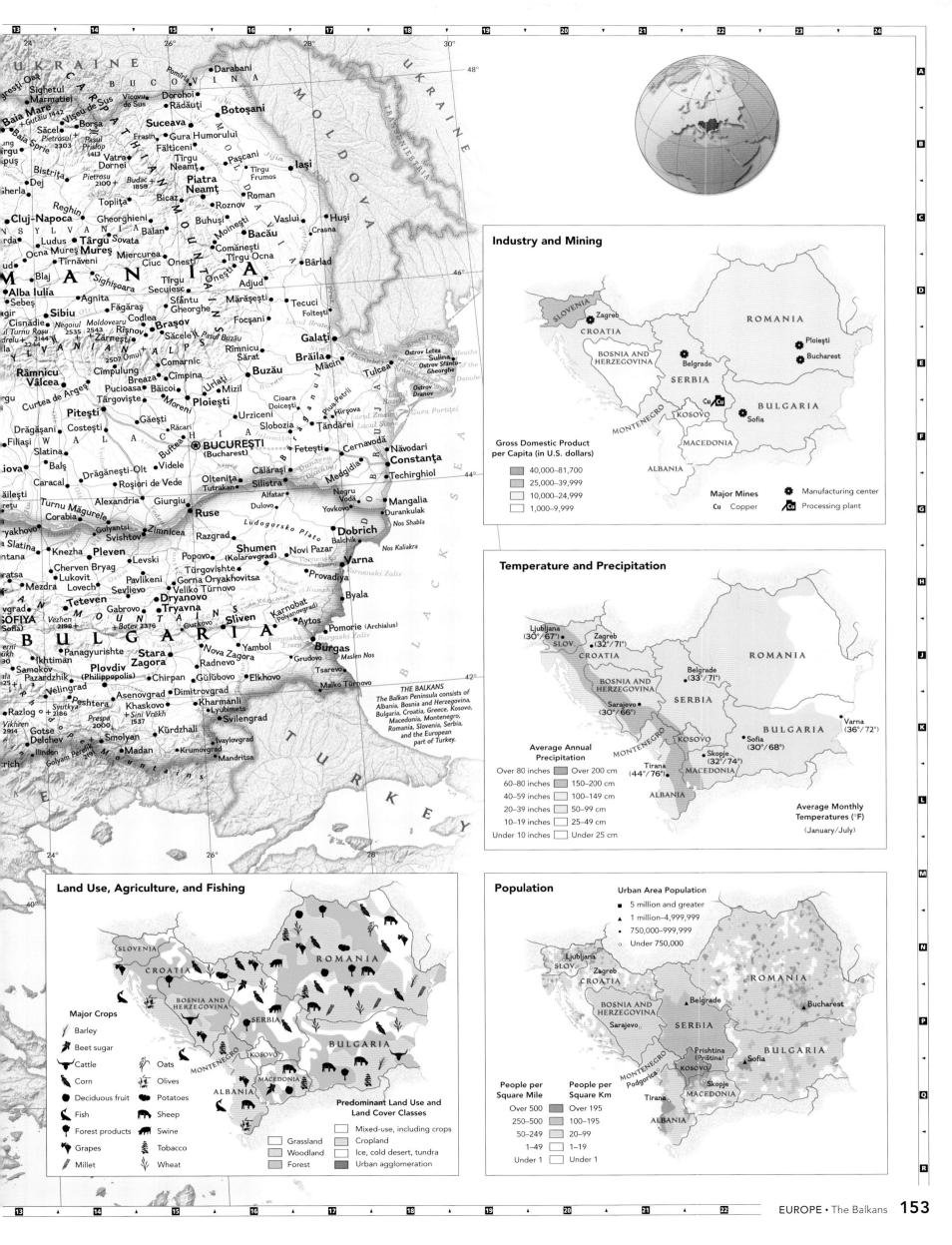

Industry and Mining

Gross Domestic Product per Capita (in U.S. dollars)
- 40,000–81,700
- 25,000–39,999
- 10,000–24,999
- 1,000–9,999

Major Mines
- Cu Copper

- ✹ Manufacturing center
- Cu Processing plant

Temperature and Precipitation

Ljubljana (30°/67°)
Zagreb (32°/71°)
Belgrade (33°/71°)
Sarajevo (30°/66°)
Tirana (44°/76°)
Skopje (32°/74°)
Sofia (30°/68°)
Varna (36°/72°)

Average Annual Precipitation
Over 80 inches	Over 200 cm
60–80 inches	150–200 cm
40–59 inches	100–149 cm
20–39 inches	50–99 cm
10–19 inches	25–49 cm
Under 10 inches	Under 25 cm

Average Monthly Temperatures (°F)
(January/July)

Land Use, Agriculture, and Fishing

Major Crops
- Barley
- Beet sugar
- Cattle
- Corn
- Deciduous fruit
- Fish
- Forest products
- Grapes
- Millet
- Oats
- Olives
- Potatoes
- Sheep
- Swine
- Tobacco
- Wheat

Predominant Land Use and Land Cover Classes
- Grassland
- Woodland
- Forest
- Mixed-use, including crops
- Cropland
- Ice, cold desert, tundra
- Urban agglomeration

Population

Urban Area Population
- ■ 5 million and greater
- ▲ 1 million–4,999,999
- ● 750,000–999,999
- ○ Under 750,000

People per Square Mile
- Over 500
- 250–500
- 50–249
- 1–49
- Under 1

People per Square Km
- Over 195
- 100–195
- 20–99
- 1–19
- Under 1

THE BALKANS
The Balkan Peninsula consists of Albania, Bosnia and Herzegovina, Bulgaria, Croatia, Greece, Kosovo, Macedonia, Montenegro, Romania, Slovenia, Serbia, and the European part of Turkey.

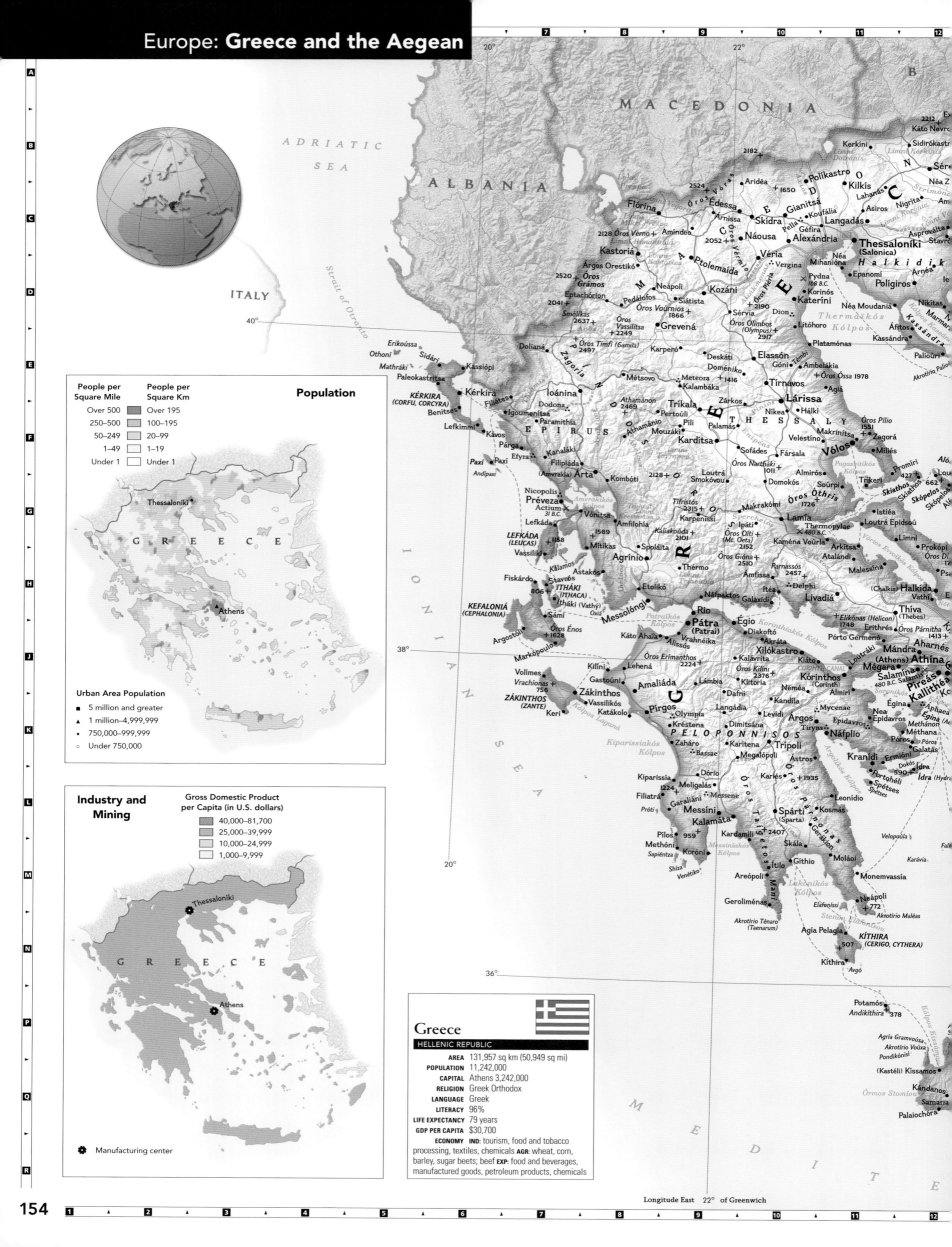

ADRIATIC SEA

ITALY

Strait of Otranto

Population

People per Square Mile	People per Square Km
Over 500	Over 195
250–500	100–195
50–249	20–99
1–49	1–19
Under 1	Under 1

Thessaloníki

G R E E C E

Athens

Urban Area Population

- ■ 5 million and greater
- ▲ 1 million–4,999,999
- • 750,000–999,999
- ○ Under 750,000

Industry and Mining

Gross Domestic Product per Capita (in U.S. dollars)

	40,000–81,700
	25,000–39,999
	10,000–24,999
	1,000–9,999

Thessaloníki

G R E E C E

Athens

✿ Manufacturing center

Greece
HELLENIC REPUBLIC

AREA	131,957 sq km (50,949 sq mi)
POPULATION	11,242,000
CAPITAL	Athens 3,242,000
RELIGION	Greek Orthodox
LANGUAGE	Greek
LITERACY	96%
LIFE EXPECTANCY	79 years
GDP PER CAPITA	$30,700
ECONOMY	**IND:** tourism, food and tobacco processing, textiles, chemicals **AGR:** wheat, corn, barley, sugar beets; beef **EXP:** food and beverages, manufactured goods, petroleum products, chemicals

Longitude East 22° of Greenwich

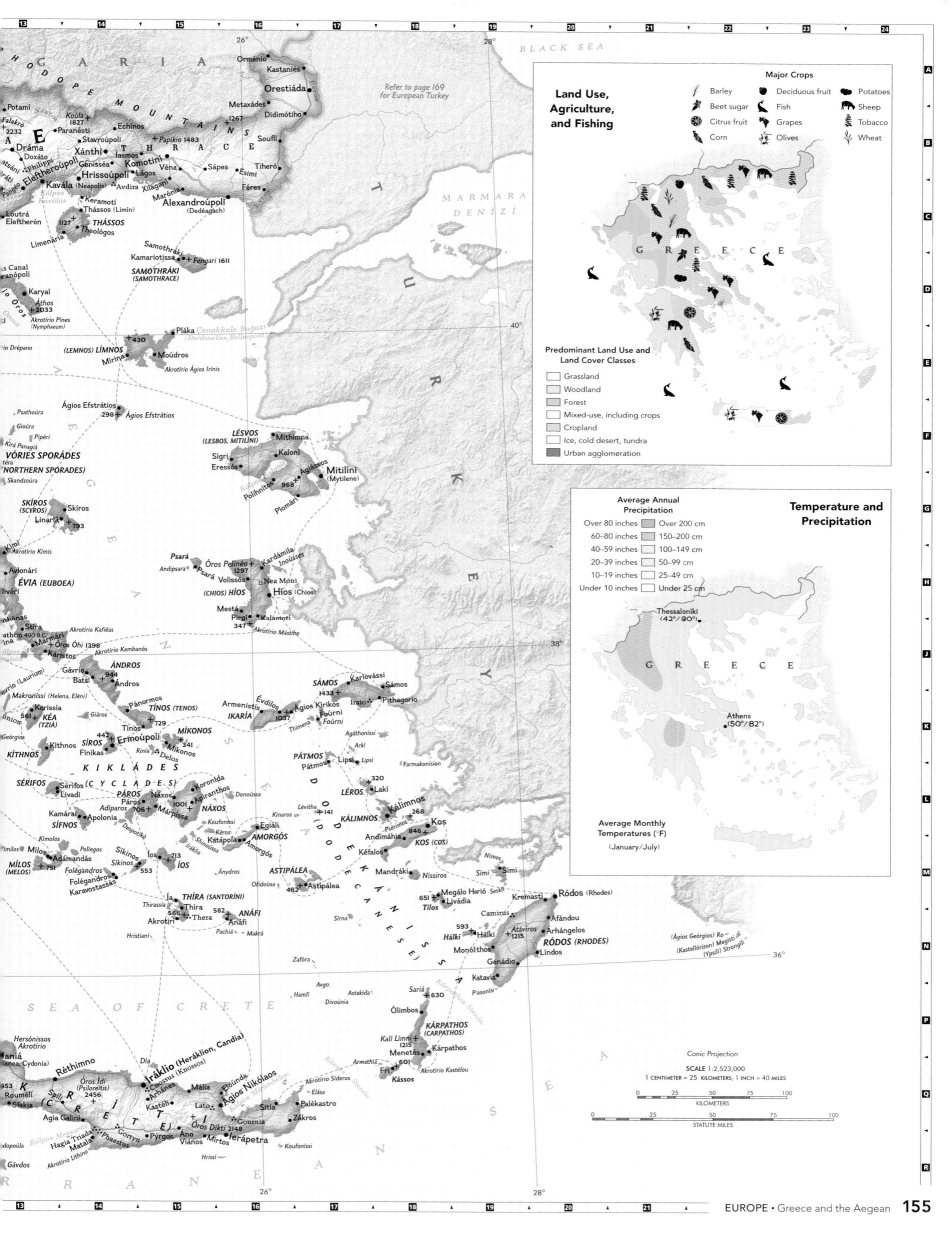

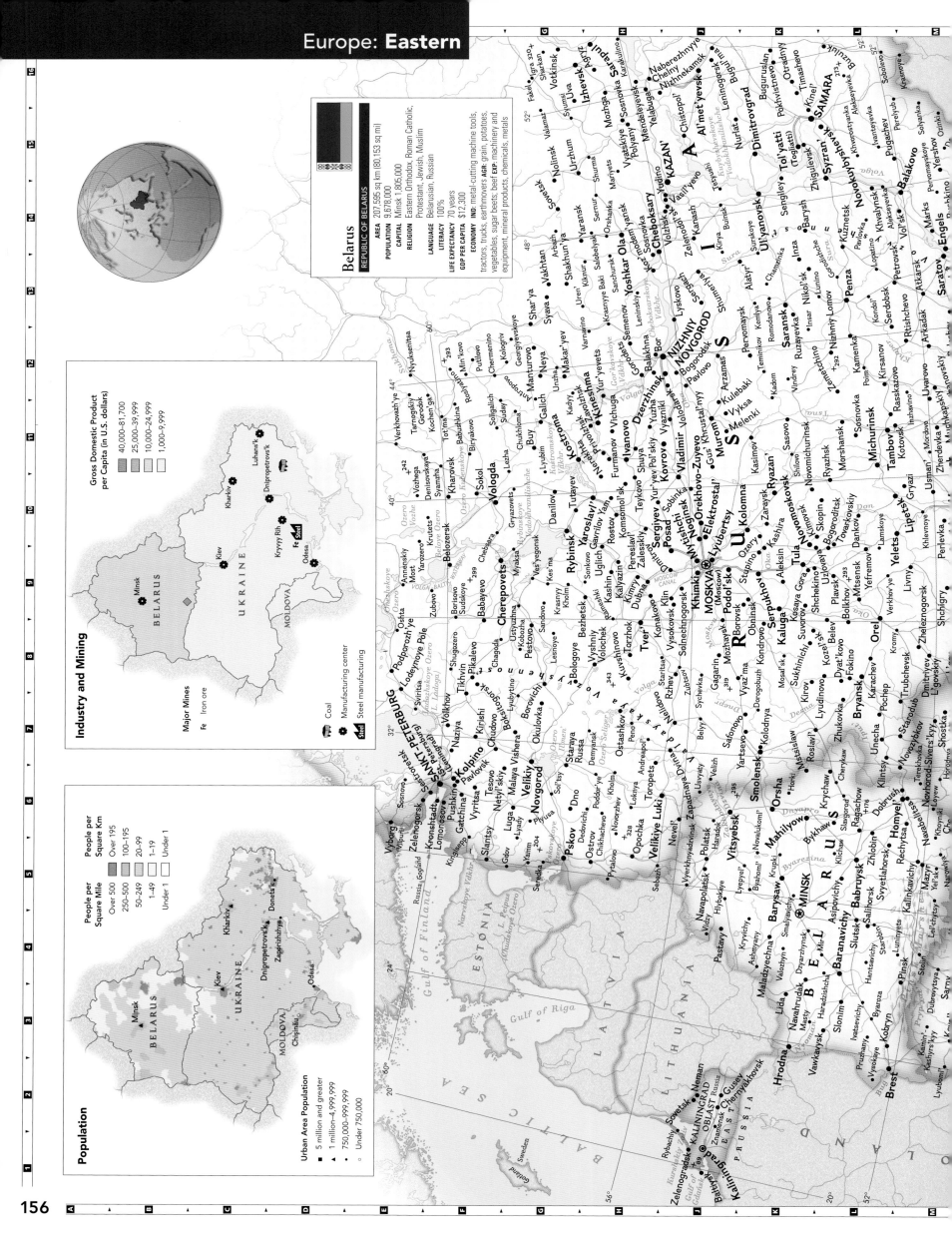

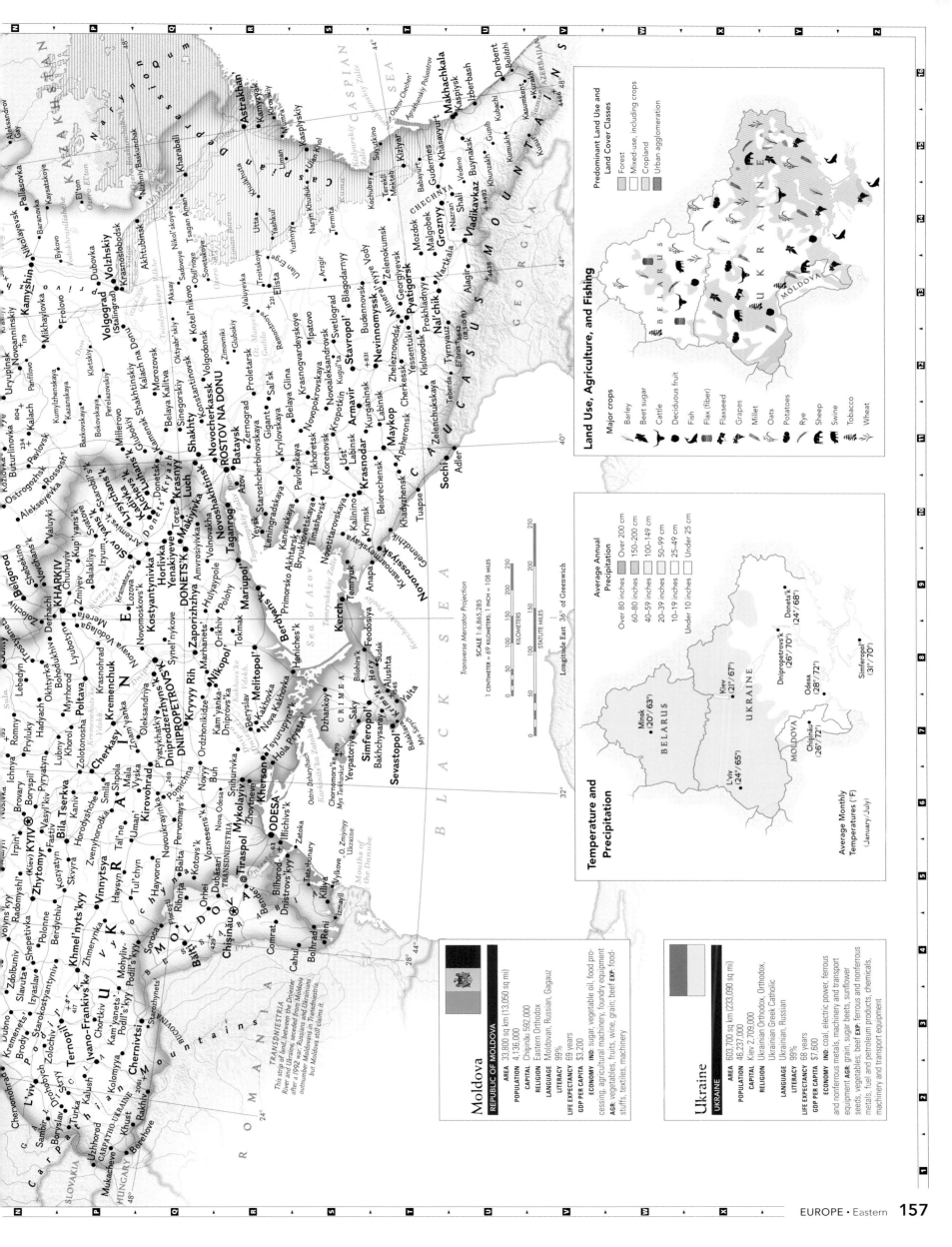

Moldova
REPUBLIC OF MOLDOVA

AREA 33,800 sq km (13,050 sq mi)
POPULATION 4,136,000
CAPITAL Chişinău 592,000
RELIGION Eastern Orthodox
LANGUAGE Moldovan, Russian, Gagauz
LITERACY 99%
LIFE EXPECTANCY 69 years
GDP PER CAPITA $3,200
ECONOMY IND: sugar, vegetable oil, food processing, agricultural machinery, foundry equipment
AGR: vegetables, fruits, wine, grain; beef EXP: foodstuffs, textiles, machinery

This strip of land, between the Dniester River and Ukraine, seceded from Moldova after a 1992 war. Russians and Ukrainians outnumber Moldovans in Transdniestria, but Moldova still claims it.

Ukraine
UKRAINE

AREA 603,700 sq km (233,090 sq mi)
POPULATION 46,237,000
CAPITAL Kiev 2,709,000
RELIGION Ukrainian Orthodox, Orthodox, Ukrainian Greek Catholic
LANGUAGE Ukrainian, Russian
LITERACY 99%
LIFE EXPECTANCY 68 years
GDP PER CAPITA $7,600
ECONOMY IND: coal, electric power, ferrous and nonferrous metals, machinery and transport equipment AGR: grain, sugar beets, sunflower seeds, vegetables, beef EXP: ferrous and nonferrous metals, fuel and petroleum products, chemicals, machinery and transport equipment

Temperature and Precipitation

Average Monthly Temperatures (F)
(January/July)

Average Annual Precipitation

- Over 200 cm — Over 80 inches
- 150–200 cm — 60–80 inches
- 100–149 cm — 40–59 inches
- 50–99 cm — 20–39 inches
- 25–49 cm — 10–19 inches
- Under 25 cm — Under 10 inches

Minsk (20°/63°)
Kiev (21°/67°)
L'viv (24°/65°)
Chişinău (26°/72°)
Odesa (28°/72°)
Dnipropetrovs'k (26°/70°)
Donets'k (24°/68°)
Simferopol' (31°/70°)

Land Use, Agriculture, and Fishing

Predominant Land Use and Land Cover Classes
- Forest
- Mixed-use, including crops
- Cropland
- Urban agglomeration

Major crops
- Barley
- Beet sugar
- Cattle
- Deciduous fruit
- Fish
- Flax (fiber)
- Flaxseed
- Grapes
- Millet
- Oats
- Potatoes
- Rye
- Sheep
- Swine
- Tobacco
- Wheat

Transverse Mercator Projection

SCALE 1:6,865,285
1 CENTIMETER = 69 KILOMETERS; 1 INCH = 108 MILES

KILOMETERS
STATUTE MILES

Longitude East 36° of Greenwich

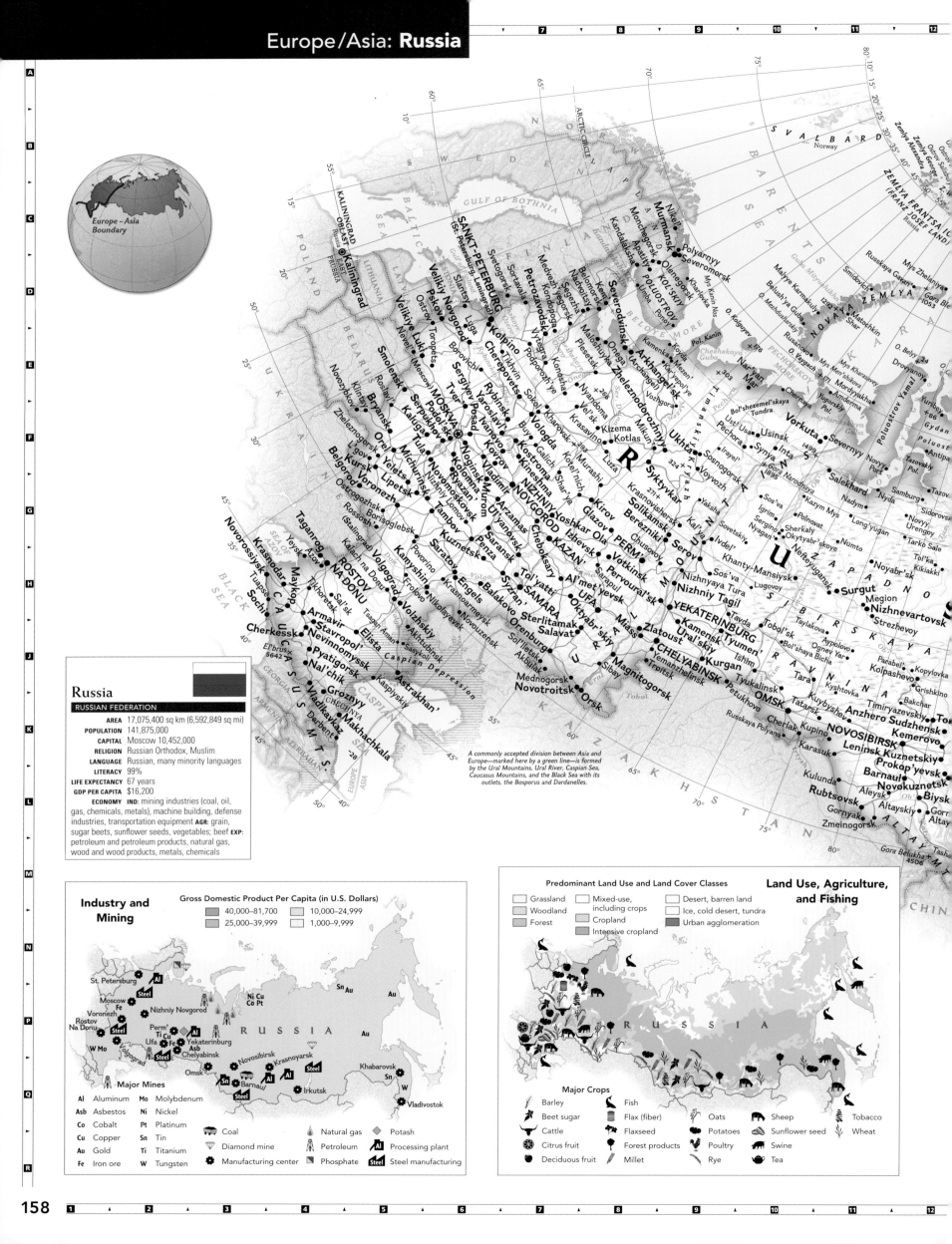

Europe – Asia Boundary

Russia
RUSSIAN FEDERATION

AREA	17,075,400 sq km (6,592,849 sq mi)
POPULATION	141,875,000
CAPITAL	Moscow 10,452,000
RELIGION	Russian Orthodox, Muslim
LANGUAGE	Russian, many minority languages
LITERACY	99%
LIFE EXPECTANCY	67 years
GDP PER CAPITA	$16,200
ECONOMY	IND: mining industries (coal, oil, gas, chemicals, metals), machine building, defense industries, transportation equipment AGR: grain, sugar beets, sunflower seeds, vegetables; beef EXP: petroleum and petroleum products, natural gas, wood and wood products, metals, chemicals

A commonly accepted division between Asia and Europe—marked here by a green line—is formed by the Ural Mountains, Ural River, Caspian Sea, Caucasus Mountains, and the Black Sea with its outlets, the Bosporus and Dardanelles.

Industry and Mining

Gross Domestic Product Per Capita (in U.S. Dollars)
- 40,000–81,700
- 25,000–39,999
- 10,000–24,999
- 1,000–9,999

Major Mines

Al	Aluminum	Mo	Molybdenum
Asb	Asbestos	Ni	Nickel
Co	Cobalt	Pt	Platinum
Cu	Copper	Sn	Tin
Au	Gold	Ti	Titanium
Fe	Iron ore	W	Tungsten

- Coal
- Diamond mine
- Manufacturing center
- Natural gas
- Petroleum
- Phosphate
- Potash
- Al Processing plant
- Steel Steel manufacturing

Land Use, Agriculture, and Fishing

Predominant Land Use and Land Cover Classes
- Grassland
- Woodland
- Forest
- Mixed-use, including crops
- Cropland
- Intensive cropland
- Desert, barren land
- Ice, cold desert, tundra
- Urban agglomeration

Major Crops

- Barley
- Beet sugar
- Cattle
- Citrus fruit
- Deciduous fruit
- Fish
- Flax (fiber)
- Flaxseed
- Forest products
- Millet
- Oats
- Potatoes
- Poultry
- Rye
- Tea
- Sheep
- Sunflower seed
- Swine
- Tobacco
- Wheat

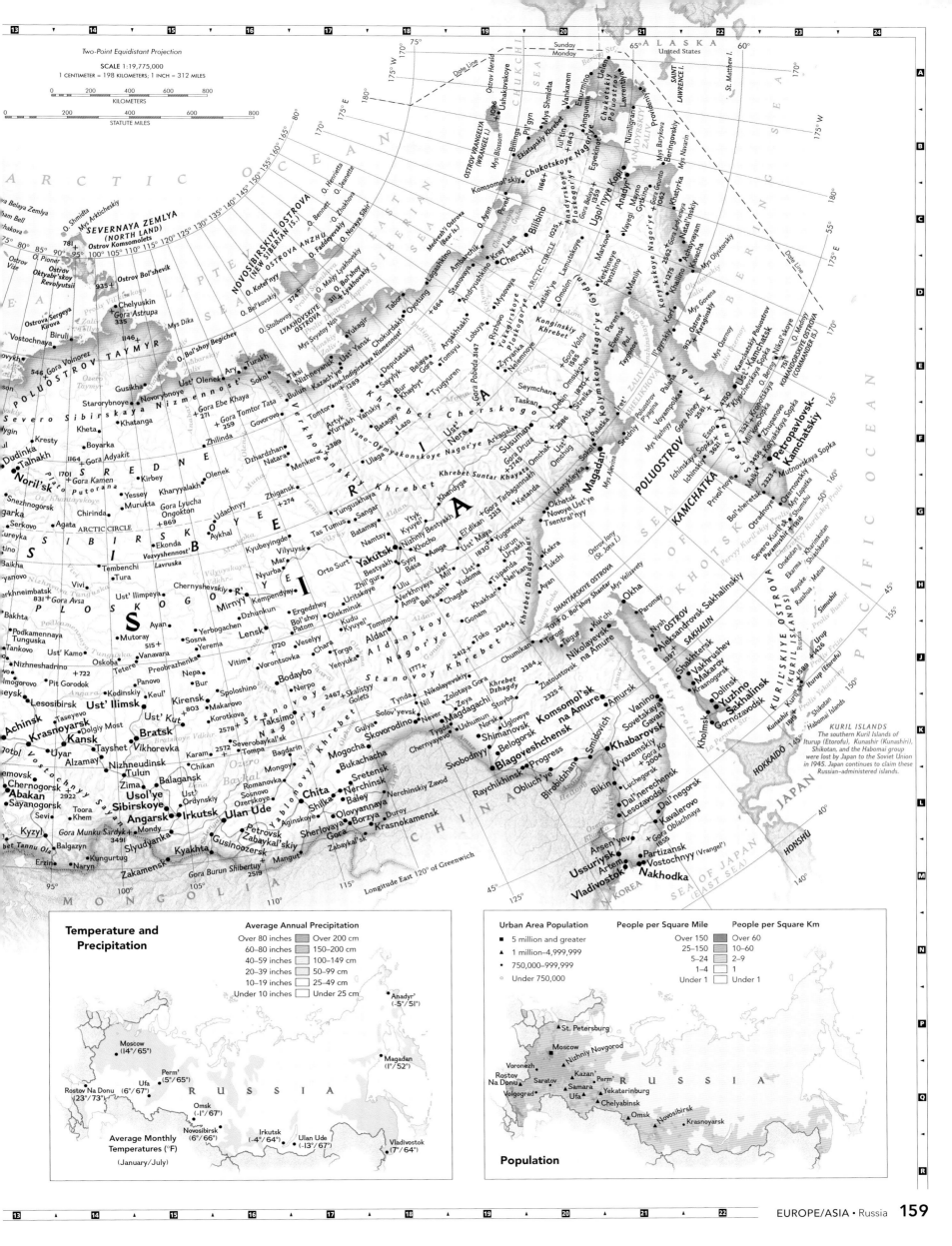

Independent Nations

Andorra

PRINCIPALITY OF ANDORRA

AREA	468 sq km (181 sq mi)
POPULATION	85,000
CAPITAL	Andorra la Vella 24,000
RELIGION	Roman Catholic
LANGUAGE	Catalan, French, Castilian Spanish, Portuguese
LITERACY	100%
LIFE EXPECTANCY	83 years
GDP PER CAPITA	$38,800

ECONOMY IND: tourism (particularly skiing), cattle raising, timber, banking **AGR:** rye, wheat, barley, oats; sheep **EXP:** tobacco products, furniture

Cyprus

REPUBLIC OF CYPRUS

AREA	9,251 sq km (3,572 sq mi)
POPULATION	1,060,000
CAPITAL	Nicosia 233,000
RELIGION	Greek Orthodox, Muslim
LANGUAGE	Greek, Turkish, English
LITERACY	98%
LIFE EXPECTANCY	78 years
GDP PER CAPITA	$28,400

ECONOMY IND: tourism, food and beverage processing, cement and gypsum production, ship repair **AGR:** citrus, vegetables, barley, grapes; poultry **EXP:** citrus, potatoes, pharmaceuticals, cement

Liechtenstein

PRINCIPALITY OF LIECHTENSTEIN

AREA	160 sq km (62 sq mi)
POPULATION	36,000
CAPITAL	Vaduz 5,000
RELIGION	Roman Catholic, Protestant
LANGUAGE	German, Alemannic dialect
LITERACY	100%
LIFE EXPECTANCY	80 years
GDP PER CAPITA	$118,000

ECONOMY IND: electronics, metal manufacturing, dental products **AGR:** wheat, barley, corn; livestock **EXP:** small machinery, audio/video connectors

Luxembourg

GRAND DUCHY OF LUXEMBOURG

AREA	2,586 sq km (998 sq mi)
POPULATION	488,000
CAPITAL	Luxembourg 84,000
RELIGION	Roman Catholic
LANGUAGE	Luxembourgish, German, French
LITERACY	100%
LIFE EXPECTANCY	80 years
GDP PER CAPITA	$81,700

ECONOMY IND: banking, iron, steel, information technology **AGR:** wine, grapes, barley, oats; dairy **EXP:** machinery, steel products, chemicals, rubber

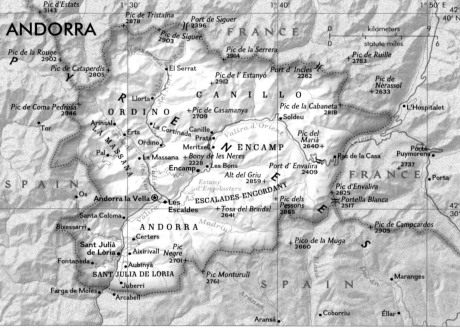

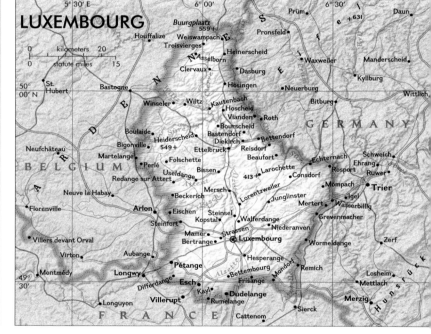

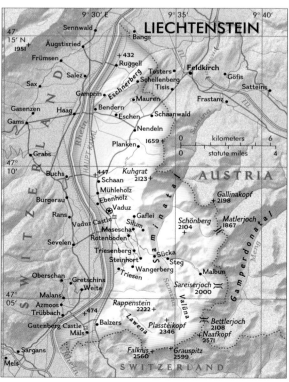

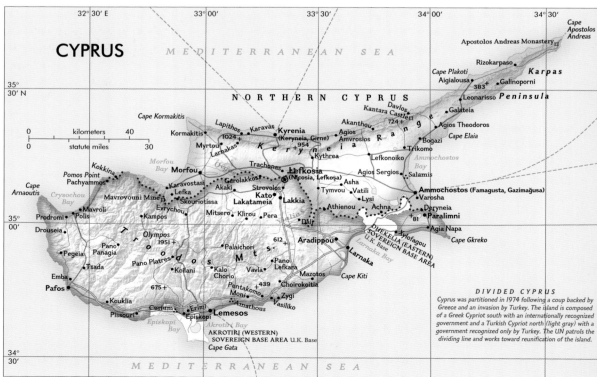

DIVIDED CYPRUS
Cyprus was partitioned in 1974 following a coup backed by Greece and an invasion by Turkey. The island is composed of a Greek Cypriot south with an internationally recognized government and a Turkish Cypriot north (light gray) with a government recognized only by Turkey. The UN patrols the dividing line and works toward reunification of the island.

Malta
REPUBLIC OF MALTA

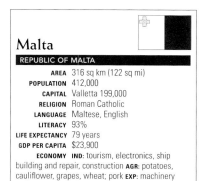

AREA	316 sq km (122 sq mi)
POPULATION	412,000
CAPITAL	Valletta 199,000
RELIGION	Roman Catholic
LANGUAGE	Maltese, English
LITERACY	93%
LIFE EXPECTANCY	79 years
GDP PER CAPITA	$23,900

ECONOMY IND: tourism, electronics, ship building and repair, construction **AGR:** potatoes, cauliflower, grapes, wheat; pork **EXP:** machinery and transport equipment, manufactures

Monaco
PRINCIPALITY OF MONACO

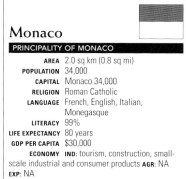

AREA	2.0 sq km (0.8 sq mi)
POPULATION	34,000
CAPITAL	Monaco 34,000
RELIGION	Roman Catholic
LANGUAGE	French, English, Italian, Monegasque
LITERACY	99%
LIFE EXPECTANCY	80 years
GDP PER CAPITA	$30,000

ECONOMY IND: tourism, construction, small-scale industrial and consumer products **AGR:** NA **EXP:** NA

San Marino
REPUBLIC OF SAN MARINO

AREA	61 sq km (24 sq mi)
POPULATION	31,000
CAPITAL	San Marino 4,000
RELIGION	Roman Catholic
LANGUAGE	Italian
LITERACY	96%
LIFE EXPECTANCY	82 years
GDP PER CAPITA	$46,100

ECONOMY IND: tourism, banking, textiles, electronics **AGR:** wheat, grapes, corn, olives; cattle **EXP:** building stone, lime, wood, chestnuts

Vatican City
THE HOLY SEE (STATE OF THE VATICAN CITY)

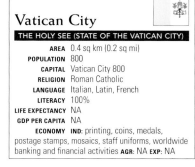

AREA	0.4 sq km (0.2 sq mi)
POPULATION	800
CAPITAL	Vatican City 800
RELIGION	Roman Catholic
LANGUAGE	Italian, Latin, French
LITERACY	100%
LIFE EXPECTANCY	NA
GDP PER CAPITA	NA

ECONOMY IND: printing, coins, medals, postage stamps, mosaics, staff uniforms, worldwide banking and financial activities **AGR:** NA **EXP:** NA

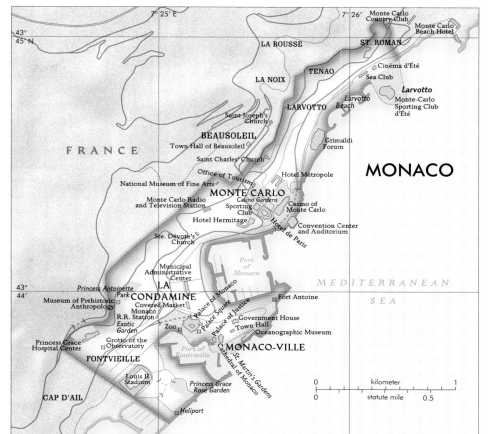

MONACO

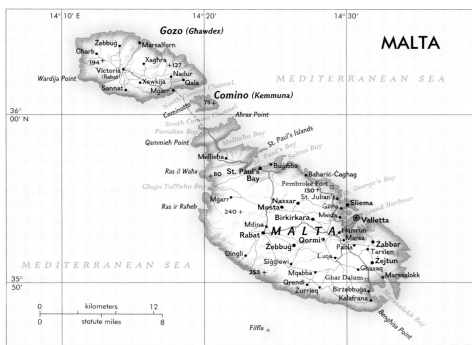

MALTA

SAN MARINO

VATICAN CITY

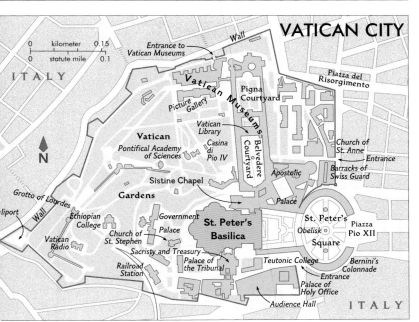

Dependency

SOVEREIGN	LOCAL

Gibraltar (U.K.)
GIBRALTAR

AREA	6.5 sq km (2.5 sq mi)
POPULATION	29,000
CAPITAL	Gibraltar 29,000
RELIGION	Roman Catholic, Church of England
LANGUAGE	English, Spanish, Italian, Portuguese
LITERACY	above 80%
LIFE EXPECTANCY	81 years
GDP PER CAPITA	$38,200

ECONOMY IND: tourism, banking and finance, ship repairing, tobacco **AGR:** NA **EXP:** reexports of petroleum and manufactured goods

GIBRALTAR

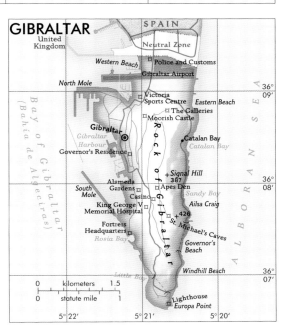

Immortalized in art and verse, the beautiful Li River in southern China meanders 105 miles (169 km) through a landscape of towering limestone peaks clad with verdant bamboo forests, rushing waterfalls, and precariously perched villages, where traditional ways of life such as night fishing still hold sway.

Asia

The continent of Asia, occupying four-fifths of the giant Eurasian landmass, stretches across ten time zones from the Pacific Ocean in the east to the Ural Mountains and Black Sea in the west. It is the largest of continents, with dazzling geographic diversity and 30 percent of the Earth's land surface. Asia includes numerous island nations, such as Japan, the Philippines, Indonesia, and Sri Lanka, as well as many of the world's major islands: Borneo, Sumatra, Honshu, Celebes, Java, and half of New Guinea.

Siberia, the huge Asian section of Russia, reaches deep inside the Arctic Circle and fills the continent's northern quarter. To its south lie the large countries of Kazakhstan, Mongolia, and China. In all, Asia contains 46 nations, accounting for 60 percent of the Earth's population—more than 4.1 billion people—yet deserts, mountains, jungles, and other inhospitable zones render much of Asia empty or underpopulated.

For millennia, people have lived near the seas and along great rivers. Early civilizations arose in China along the Yellow River, in South Asia on the Indus, and in the Middle East along the Tigris and Euphrates. Today, Asia's large populations continue to thrive near inland waterways and coastal regions.

India and China, historically isolated from each other by the Himalaya Mountains and Myanmar's jungles, developed rich, vibrant cultures with art, literature, and philosophy of the highest order. China's 1.3 billion people and India's billion make up nearly two-thirds of Asia's population. These countries stand as rivals, each trying to modernize and assert itself while struggling with formidable problems of poverty, pollution, urbanization, and illiteracy.

Breakup of the Soviet Union in 1991 allowed for the creation of eight new Asian countries, five in Central Asia—Kazakhstan, Kyrgyzstan, Uzbekistan, Turkmenistan, and Tajikistan—and three in the Caucasus region—Georgia, Armenia, and Azerbaijan.

Asia's few democracies, including Israel, India, and Japan, contrast with much more authoritarian governments or military regimes, which are numerous and widespread. Monarchies in Bhutan, Nepal, Jordan, Saudi Arabia, and Brunei (a sultanate) pass rulership through family lines.

Events at the start of the 21st century have put new focus on the Middle East, the role of Islam, and control of religious extremism. More than half of Asia's countries are Muslim, yet they possess very different languages, climates, economies, and ethnic groups. But all share emotional links with their co-religionists and care deeply about the development of Islam in the decades ahead.

PHYSICAL GEOGRAPHY Asia, the planet's youngest continent, displays continuing geologic activity. Volcanoes form a chain known as the Ring of Fire along the entire Pacific edge, from Siberia's Kamchatka Peninsula to the islands of the Philippines and Indonesia. The Indian subcontinent pushes into the heart of Asia, raising and contorting the towering Karakoram and Himalaya ranges. Earthquakes rattle China, Japan, and West Asia.

Geographic extremes allow Asia to claim many world records. Mount Everest, monarch of the Himalaya, is the planet's highest point at 29,035 feet (8,850 m). The super-salty Dead Sea lies 1,380 feet (421 m) below sea level—the lowest point. A site in Assam, India, receives an astonishing 39 feet (12 m) of rain each year, making it the wettest spot on Earth, and Siberia's ancient Lake Baikal, arcing 395 miles (636 km), plunges over a mile (5,371 ft; 1,637 m) as the world's deepest lake. It harbors many unique plant and animal species, including tens of thousands of freshwater seals.

The Caspian Sea, salty and isolated on the border of Europe and Asia, is the largest lake, measuring more than four times the area of Lake Superior. A 39,000-mile (62,800 km) coastline, longest of any continent's, allows all but 12 Asian nations direct access to the sea.

These landlocked countries, mostly in Central Asia (excepting Laos), form part of a great band across the middle latitudes comprised of deserts, mountains, and arid plateaus. The vast Tibetan Plateau, home to the yak, snow leopard, wild ass, and migrating antelope, gives rise to Asia's vital rivers: the Huang (Yellow), Yangtze, Indus, Ganges, Salween, and Mekong. At the heart of the continent exists a convergence of the world's mighty mountains: Himalaya, Karakoram, Hindu Kush, Pamir, and Kunlun.

Flowing sand dunes of the Arabian Peninsula contrast with steppes that extend for thousands of grassy miles from Europe to Mongolia. To the north, girdling Asia's northern latitudes, grow boreal forests made up of conifers—the taiga—largest unbroken woodlands in the world. Beyond the taiga lie frozen expanses of tundra.

Far to the south, monsoon winds bring annual rains to thickly populated regions of South and Southeast Asia. These wet, green domains support some of the world's last rain forests and amazing numbers of plants. Human impact through agriculture, animal grazing, and forestry has altered much of Asia's landscape and continues to threaten the natural realm.

HISTORY Asia's great historical breadth encompasses thousands of years, vast distances, and a kaleidoscope of peoples. From China to Lebanon, from Siberia to Sri Lanka, Asia has more ethnic and national groups than any other continent. Their histories have evolved through peaceful growth and migration, but more often through military conquest.

The Fertile Crescent region of the Middle East saw the emergence of agriculture and early settlements some 10,000 years ago. Later, successful irrigation helped bring forth the first civilization in Sumer, today's southern Iraq; Sumerians invented the first wheeled vehicles, the potter's wheel, the first system of writing—cuneiform—and codes of law.

During the second millennium B.C., a pastoral people called Aryans, or Indo-Iranians, pushed into present-day Afghanistan and eastern Iran, then steadily occupied much of India, Western, and Central Asia.

Central Asia has always been a historic melting pot of flourishing cultures. More than 2,000 years ago a braid of ancient caravan tracks—the Silk Road—carried precious goods between East Asia and the rest of the world: sleek horses, exotic foods, medicines, jewels, birds, and perfume. More practical were gunpowder, the magnetic compass, the printing press, mathematics, ceramics, and silk. Trade flourished especially during China's Han dynasty (206 B.C.–A.D. 220), Tang dynasty (A.D. 618–907), and the Mongol period (13th and 14th centuries). Mongols at their height came closer than any other people to conquering all of Asia, threatening Europe in the west and twice trying to invade Japan.

Another great expansion was the conquest and settlement of Siberia and Central Asia by Russians. The Trans-Siberian Railway, built between 1891 and 1905, opened up Siberia for settlement. During the 19th century, Russian armies and colonizers spread through Central

In 1791, King Bodawapaya of Myanmar commissioned an enormous Buddhist pagoda in Mingun. Although construction stopped upon the king's death in 1819, the building still measures an astounding 256 feet square (78 m sq) at its base and is 150 feet (45.7 m) tall. Subsequent earthquakes cracked the structure.

Asia as well, claiming the khanates for an expanding Russian empire. Great Britain, France, and other European countries also laid claim to parts of Asia.

Today, colonial empires have ended and a seemingly stable community of nations with defined borders exists in Asia. Yet rivalries, threats, and war dominate many regions. Indochina is only now healing after decades of violence. The Korean Peninsula remains divided. Nuclear-armed India and Pakistan have fought three wars since independence in 1947. Religious and ethnic hostilities inflame many areas, nowhere more so than in the Middle East. Troubled Afghanistan, victim of almost continuous warfare since 1979, saw a U.S.-led invasion in 2001 to oust the Taliban government and destroy terrorist groups. Many claim peace will come to these areas only after economic stability, steps towards democracy, and recognition of human rights are achieved.

CULTURE   Numerous cultural forces, each linked to broad geographic areas, have formed and influenced Asia's rich civilizations and hundreds of ethnic groups. The two oldest are the cultural milieus of India and China.

India's culture still reverberates throughout countries as varied as Sri Lanka, Pakistan, Afghanistan, Nepal, Bangladesh, Myanmar (Burma), and across seas to Thailand, Cambodia, Singapore, and Indonesia. The world religions of Hinduism and Buddhism originated in India and spread as traders, scholars, and priests sought distant footholds. The island of Bali in predominantly Muslim Indonesia remains Hindu today. Many regions of Asia first encountered writing in the form of Sanskrit, the holy script of Hinduism.

China's civilization, more than four thousand years old, has profoundly influenced the development of all of East Asia, much of Southeast Asia, and parts of Central Asia. Chinese institutions such as government, warfare, architecture, the arts and sciences, and even chopsticks reached to the heart of other lands and peoples. Most important of all were the Chinese written language, a complex script with thousands of characters, and Confucianism, an ethical world view that affected philosophy, politics, and relations within society. Japan, Korea, and Vietnam especially absorbed these cultural gifts.

Today, most Chinese call themselves "Han," a term that embraces more than 90 percent of the population—a billion plus people—and thus makes them the world's largest ethnic group. In addition, China's government recognizes 55 other ethnic minorities within its borders.

Islam, a third great cultural influence in Asia, proved formidable in its energy and creative genius. Arabs from the seventh century onward, spurred on by faith, moved rapidly into Southwest Asia. Their religion and culture, particularly Arabic writing, spread through Iran and Afghanistan to the Indian subcontinent. In time, shipping, commerce, and missionaries carried Islam on to the Malay Peninsula and Indonesian archipelago. Indonesia, the largest Muslim country with more than 200 million believers, and Pakistan and Bangladesh, each with more than 100 million Muslims, attest to Islam's success.

Europeans, too, have affected Asia's cultures, from the conquests of Alexander the Great to today's multinational corporations. Colonial powers, especially Britain in India, France in Indochina, Holland in the Indonesian archipelago, and numerous countries in China, left a lasting mark even after nationalist movements forced them out in the late 1940s and early 1950s.

ECONOMY   Blessed with resources and teeming with energetic people, Asia still suffers from great disparities between rich and poor. The livelihood of most Asians rests on agriculture and age-old methods of production. Vietnamese women turn waterwheels by foot-power. Iranian farmers plow using buffaloes. Indian villagers, bent at the waist, plant rice seedlings by hand. Bangladeshi fishermen cast circular nets, hoping for a few small fish. Burmese lacquerwork, Chinese embroidery, Middle Eastern brassware, and Indonesian batik cloth represent local crafts.

Wet-rice cultivation from Japan southward has shaped life for hundreds of millions of Asians. To the west, across north China, Central Asia, and beyond to the Middle East, wheat growing has dominated. Plantation and cash crops, too, such as rubber, tea, palm oil, coconuts, sugarcane, and tobacco continue to sustain regional economies.

Across Asia, country dwellers have flocked in the millions to the cities, seeking jobs and a better life. From Jakarta to Baghdad, the growth of megacities represents a dramatic change over the past 50 years. In China, as many as 100 million people form a floating population, seeking work wherever it can be found.

The emergence of postwar Japan as Asia's strongest economy set a model for newly industrialized centers such as South Korea, Hong Kong, Singapore, and Taiwan. Japan, with few natural resources, imports oil, foodstuffs, and textiles, but succeeds by exporting cars, chemicals, and electronics. Central Asian nations of the former Soviet Union have industrialized but require further diversification to rise above poverty. Lands in the Persian Gulf region have flourished from petroleum, and many countries now use light industry as a motor for growth. Tourism, too, plays its part and has helped Thailand, Nepal, and parts of Indonesia and China, including Hong Kong.

India's liberalized economy has encouraged a large, growing middle class, and China—an economic dynamo with plentiful resources—may become the world's largest economy in 25 years.

Yet hunger for minerals, water, agricultural land, fuelwood, housing, and animal products poses great challenges for Asia as every nation tries to raise the standard of living of its people.

Asia: Physical and Political

Two-Point Equidistant Projection
SCALE 1:39,821,000
1 CENTIMETER = 398 KILOMETERS; 1 INCH = 629 MILES

KILOMETERS

STATUTE MILES

International boundary

Disputed or undefined boundary

EUROPE-ASIA BOUNDARY
A commonly accepted division between Asia and Europe—marked here with a green line—is formed by the Ural Mountains, Ural River, Caspian Sea, Caucasus Mountains, and the Black Sea with its outlets, the Bosporus and Dardanelles.

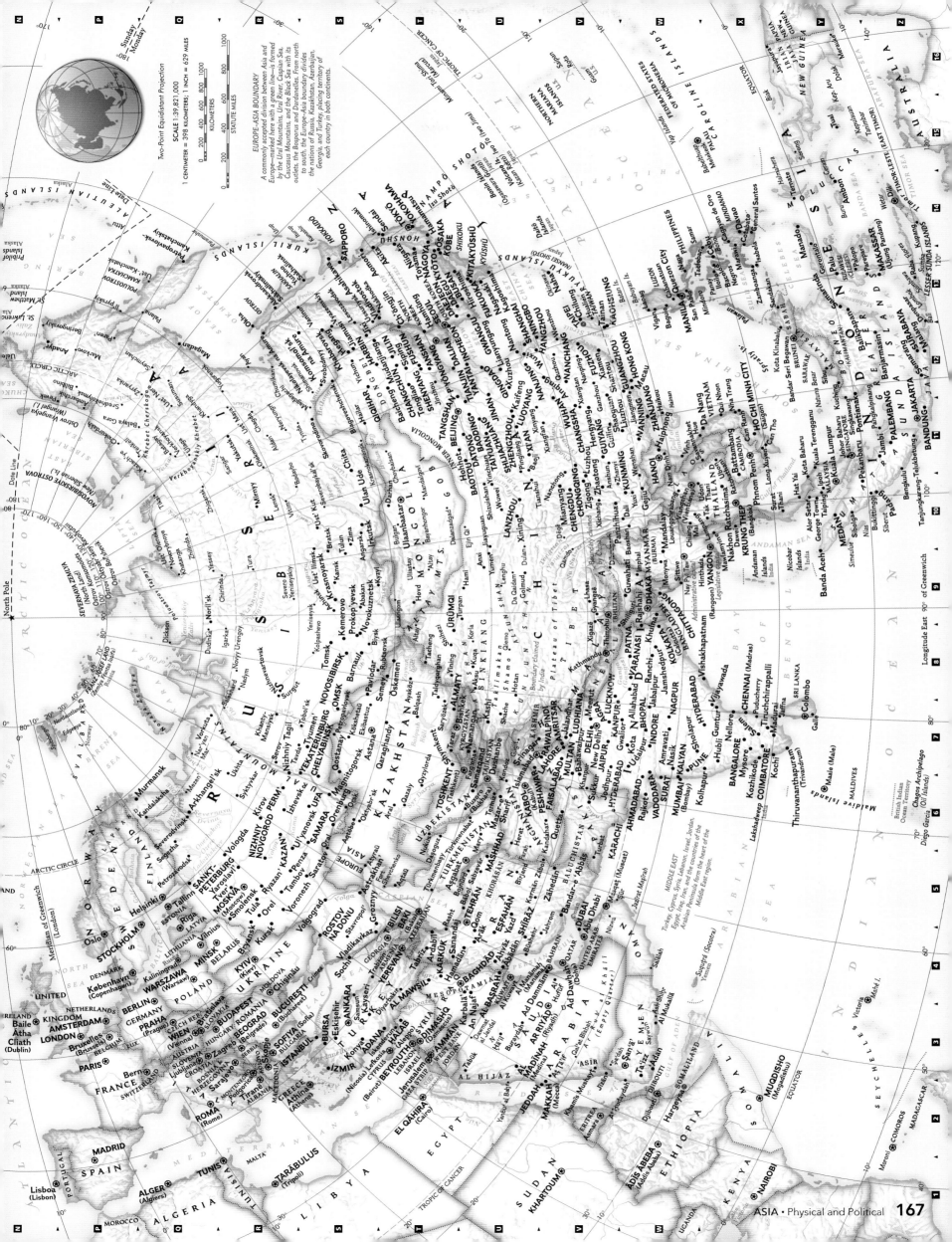

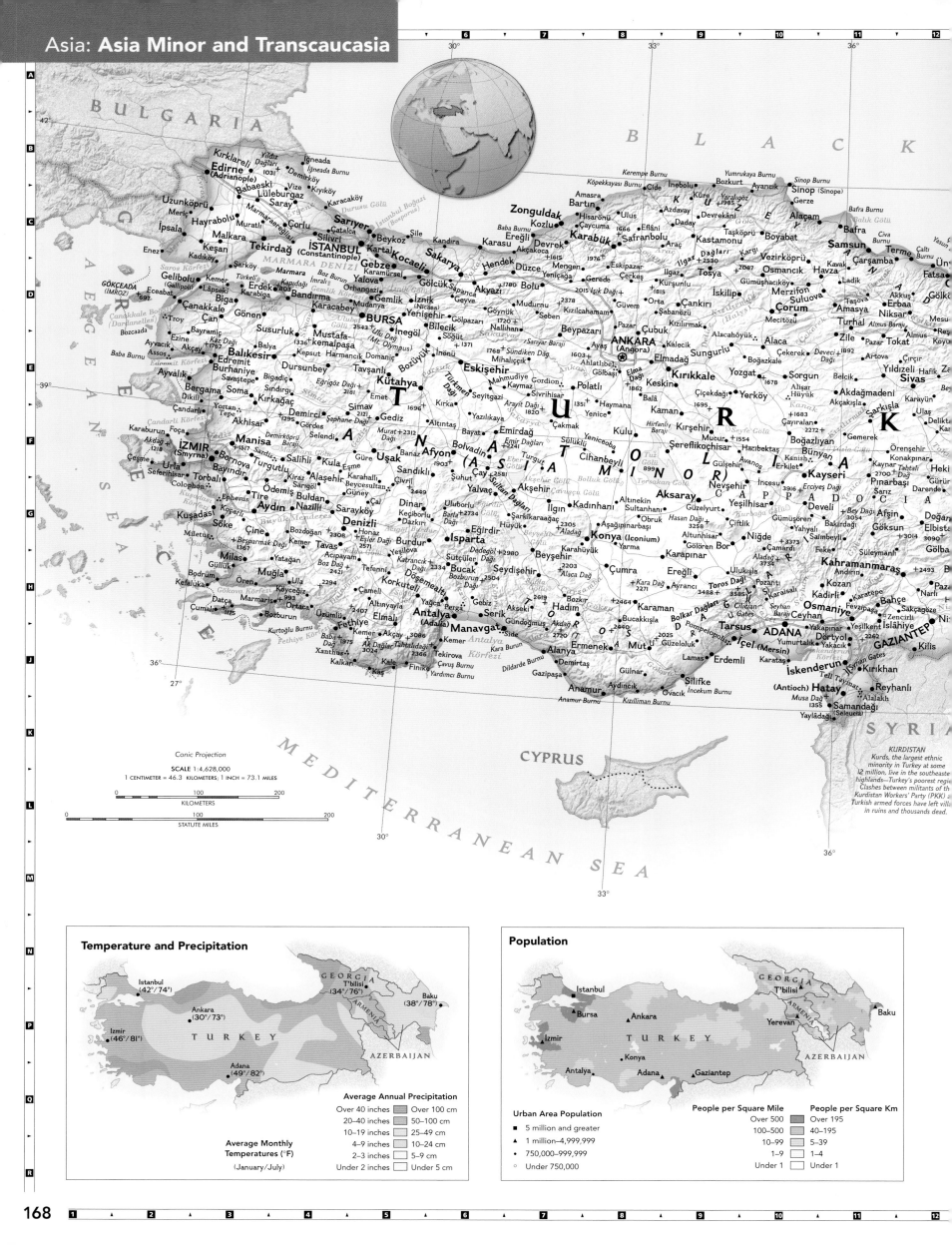

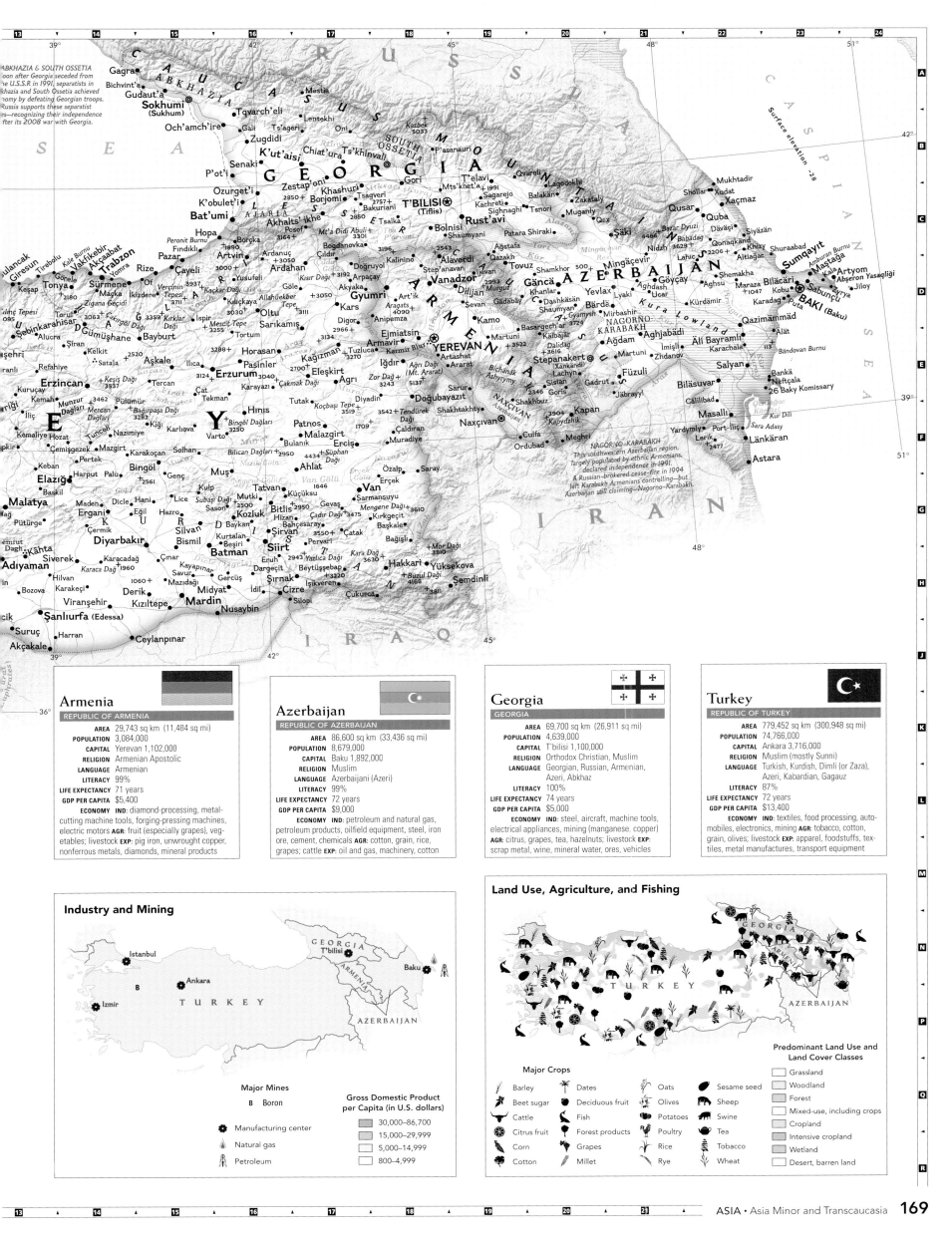

ABKHAZIA & SOUTH OSSETIA
...oon after Georgia seceded from the U.S.S.R in 1991, separatists in ...khazia and South Ossetia achieved ...nomy by defeating Georgian troops. ...Russia supports these separatist ...s—recognizing their independence ...fter its 2008 war with Georgia.

Surface elevation -28

Armenia

REPUBLIC OF ARMENIA

AREA 29,743 sq km (11,484 sq mi)
POPULATION 3,084,000
CAPITAL Yerevan 1,102,000
RELIGION Armenian Apostolic
LANGUAGE Armenian
LITERACY 99%
LIFE EXPECTANCY 71 years
GDP PER CAPITA $5,400
ECONOMY IND: diamond-processing, metal-cutting machine tools, forging-pressing machines, electric motors **AGR:** fruit (especially grapes), vegetables; livestock **EXP:** pig iron, unwrought copper, nonferrous metals, diamonds, mineral products

Azerbaijan

REPUBLIC OF AZERBAIJAN

AREA 86,600 sq km (33,436 sq mi)
POPULATION 8,679,000
CAPITAL Baku 1,892,000
RELIGION Muslim
LANGUAGE Azerbaijani (Azeri)
LITERACY 99%
LIFE EXPECTANCY 72 years
GDP PER CAPITA $9,000
ECONOMY IND: petroleum and natural gas, petroleum products, oilfield equipment, steel, iron ore, cement, chemicals **AGR:** cotton, grain, rice, grapes; cattle **EXP:** oil and gas, machinery, cotton

Georgia

GEORGIA

AREA 69,700 sq km (26,911 sq mi)
POPULATION 4,639,000
CAPITAL T'bilisi 1,100,000
RELIGION Orthodox Christian, Muslim
LANGUAGE Georgian, Russian, Armenian, Azeri, Abkhaz
LITERACY 100%
LIFE EXPECTANCY 74 years
GDP PER CAPITA $5,000
ECONOMY IND: steel, aircraft, machine tools, electrical appliances, mining (manganese, copper) **AGR:** citrus, grapes, tea, hazelnuts; livestock **EXP:** scrap metal, wine, mineral water, ores, vehicles

Turkey

REPUBLIC OF TURKEY

AREA 779,452 sq km (300,948 sq mi)
POPULATION 74,766,000
CAPITAL Ankara 3,716,000
RELIGION Muslim (mostly Sunni)
LANGUAGE Turkish, Kurdish, Dimli (or Zaza), Azeri, Kabardian, Gagauz
LITERACY 87%
LIFE EXPECTANCY 72 years
GDP PER CAPITA $13,400
ECONOMY IND: textiles, food processing, automobiles, electronics, mining **AGR:** tobacco, cotton, grain, olives; livestock **EXP:** apparel, foodstuffs, textiles, metal manufactures, transport equipment

Industry and Mining

Major Mines
B Boron

⚙ Manufacturing center
△ Natural gas
🛢 Petroleum

Gross Domestic Product per Capita (in U.S. dollars)
30,000–86,700
15,000–29,999
5,000–14,999
800–4,999

Land Use, Agriculture, and Fishing

Major Crops

Barley | Dates | Oats | Sesame seed
Beet sugar | Deciduous fruit | Olives | Sheep
Cattle | Fish | Potatoes | Swine
Citrus fruit | Forest products | Poultry | Tea
Corn | Grapes | Rice | Tobacco
Cotton | Millet | Rye | Wheat

Predominant Land Use and Land Cover Classes
Grassland
Woodland
Forest
Mixed-use, including crops
Cropland
Intensive cropland
Wetland
Desert, barren land

NAGORNO-KARABAKH
This southwestern Azerbaijan region, largely populated by ethnic Armenians, declared independence in 1991. A Russian-brokered cease-fire in 1994 left Karabakh Armenians controlling—but Azerbaijan still claiming—Nagorno-Karabakh.

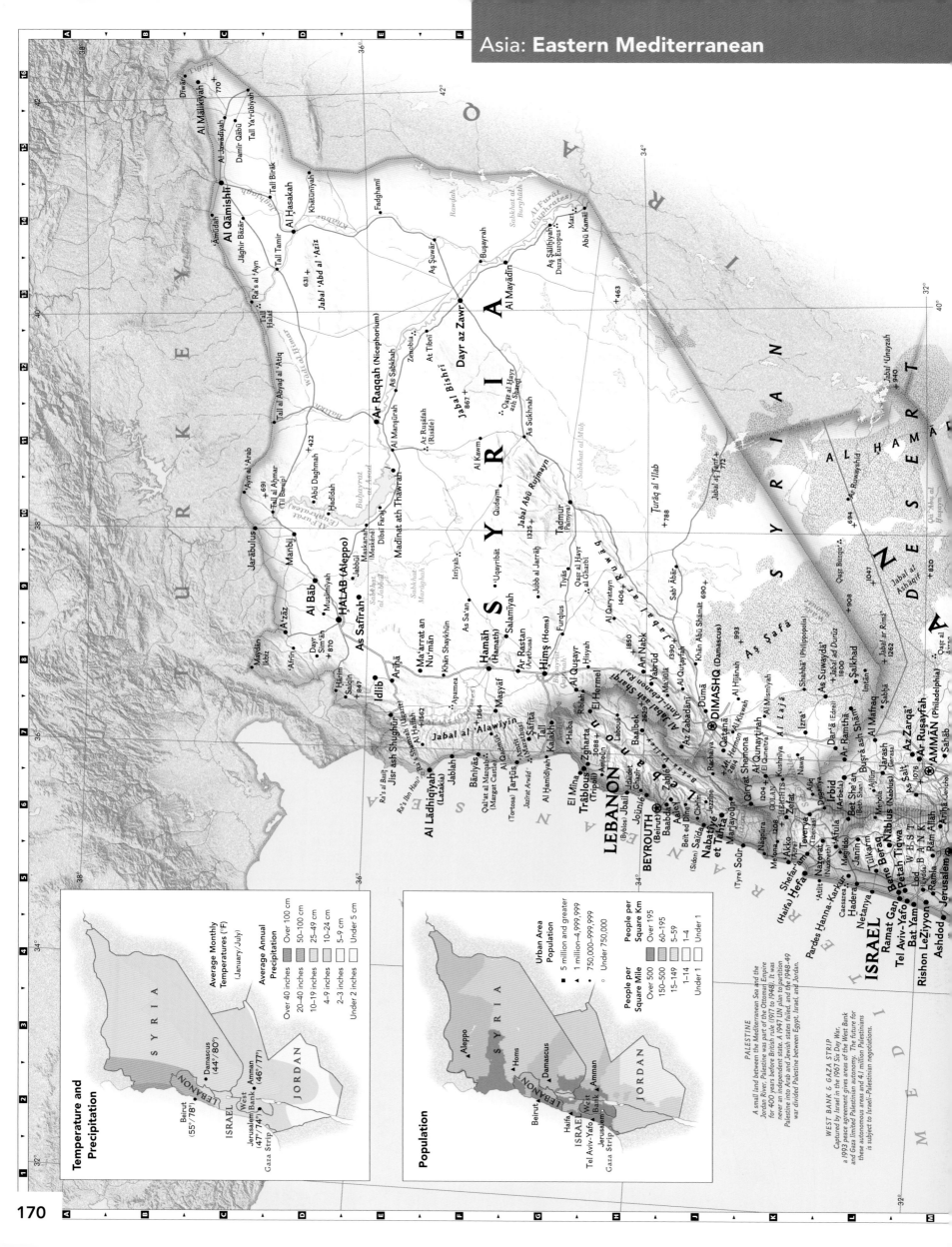

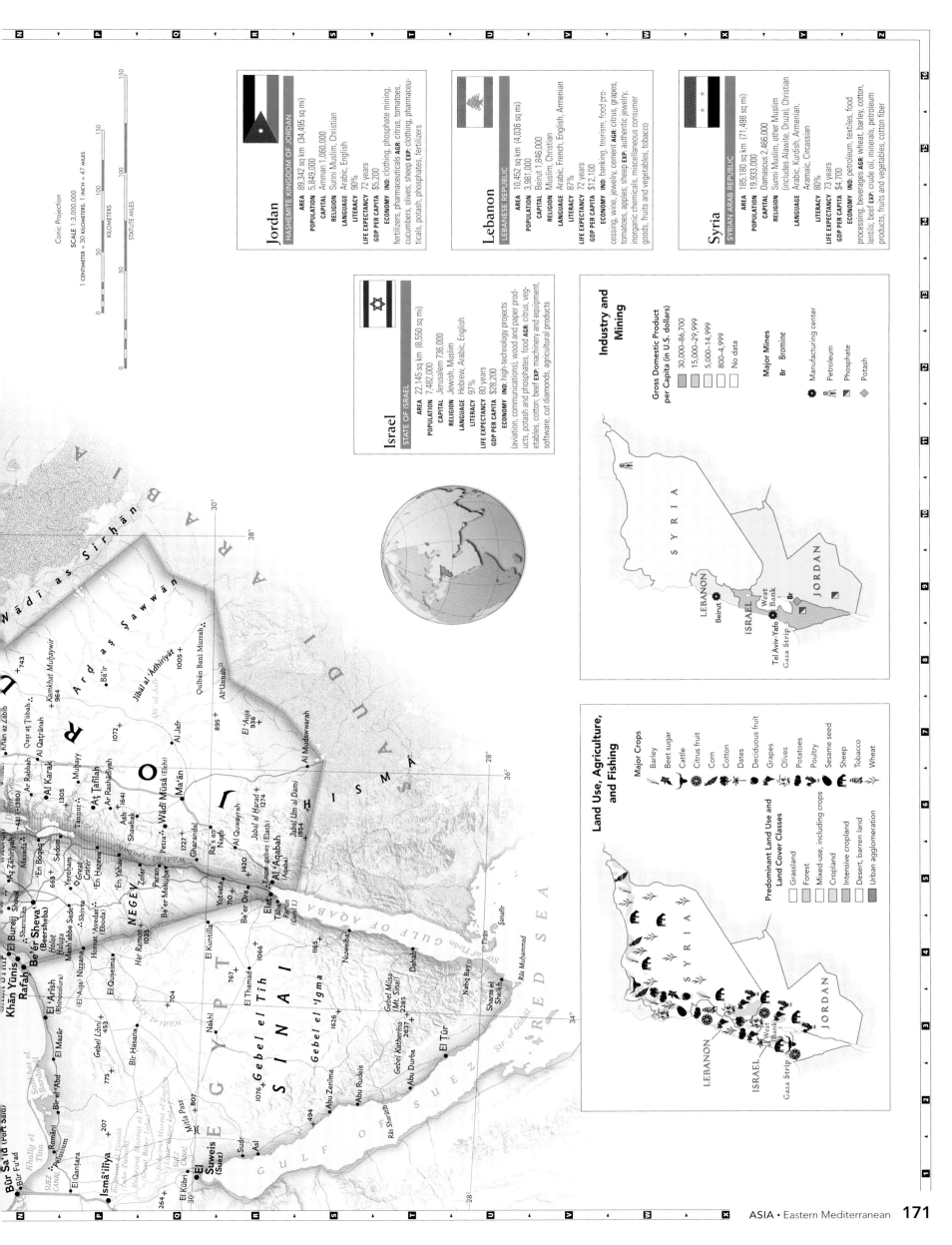

Jordan
HASHEMITE KINGDOM OF JORDAN

AREA 89,342 sq km (34,495 sq mi)
POPULATION 5,849,000
CAPITAL Amman 1,060,000
RELIGION Sunni Muslim, Christian
LANGUAGE Arabic, English
LITERACY 90%
LIFE EXPECTANCY 72 years
GDP PER CAPITA $5,200
ECONOMY IND: clothing, phosphate mining, fertilizers, pharmaceuticals **AGR:** citrus, tomatoes, cucumbers, olives; sheep **EXP:** clothing, pharmaceuticals, potash, phosphates, fertilizers

Lebanon
LEBANESE REPUBLIC

AREA 10,452 sq km (4,036 sq mi)
POPULATION 3,981,000
CAPITAL Beirut 1,846,000
RELIGION Muslim, Christian
LANGUAGE Arabic, French, English, Armenian
LITERACY 87%
LIFE EXPECTANCY 72 years
GDP PER CAPITA $12,100
ECONOMY IND: banking, tourism, food processing, wine, jewelry, cement **AGR:** citrus, grapes, tomatoes, apples; sheep **EXP:** authentic jewelry, inorganic chemicals, miscellaneous consumer goods, fruits and vegetables, tobacco

Syria
SYRIAN ARAB REPUBLIC

AREA 185,180 sq km (71,498 sq mi)
POPULATION 19,933,000
CAPITAL Damascus 2,466,000
RELIGION Sunni Muslim, other Muslim (includes Alawite, Druze), Christian
LANGUAGE Arabic, Kurdish, Armenian, Aramaic, Circassian
LITERACY 80%
LIFE EXPECTANCY 73 years
GDP PER CAPITA $4,700
ECONOMY IND: petroleum, textiles, food processing, beverages **AGR:** wheat, barley, cotton, lentils; beef **EXP:** crude oil, minerals, petroleum products, fruits and vegetables, cotton fiber

Israel
STATE OF ISRAEL

AREA 22,145 sq km (8,550 sq mi)
POPULATION 7,482,000
CAPITAL Jerusalem 736,000
RELIGION Jewish, Muslim
LANGUAGE Hebrew, Arabic, English
LITERACY 97%
LIFE EXPECTANCY 80 years
GDP PER CAPITA $28,200
ECONOMY IND: high-technology projects (aviation, communications), wood and paper products, potash and phosphates, food **AGR:** citrus, vegetables, cotton; beef **EXP:** machinery and equipment, software, cut diamonds, agricultural products

Conic Projection

SCALE 1:3,000,000
1 CENTIMETER = 30 KILOMETERS; 1 INCH = 47 MILES

Industry and Mining

Gross Domestic Product per Capita (in U.S. dollars)
- 30,000–86,700
- 15,000–29,999
- 5,000–14,999
- 800–4,999
- No data

Major Mines
Br Bromine

- Manufacturing center
- Petroleum
- Phosphate
- Potash

Land Use, Agriculture, and Fishing

Major Crops
- Barley
- Beet sugar
- Cattle
- Citrus fruit
- Corn
- Cotton
- Dates
- Deciduous fruit
- Grapes
- Olives
- Potatoes
- Poultry
- Sesame seed
- Sheep
- Tobacco
- Wheat

Predominant Land Use and Land Cover Classes
- Grassland
- Forest
- Mixed-use, including crops
- Cropland
- Intensive cropland
- Desert, barren land
- Urban agglomeration

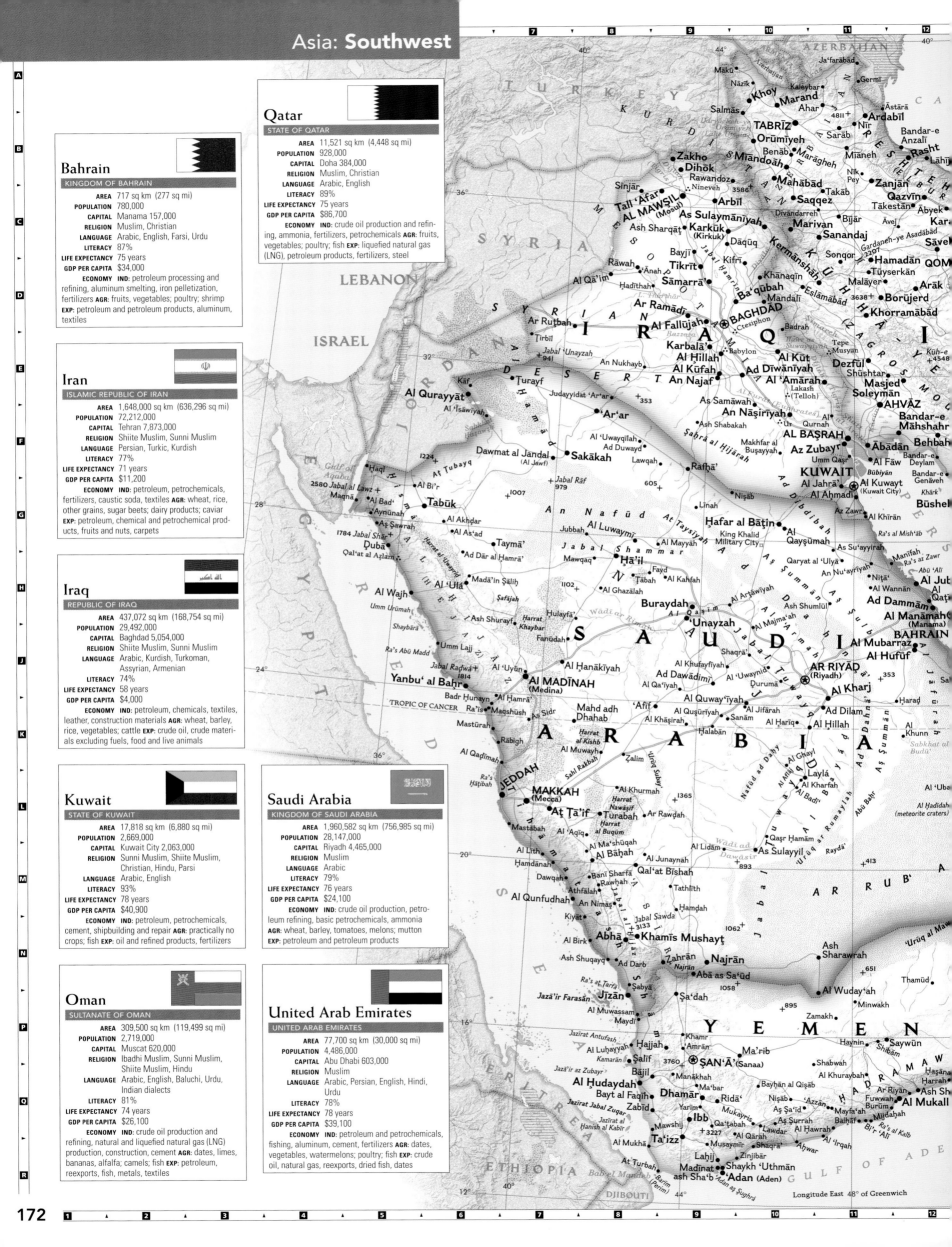

Qatar

STATE OF QATAR

AREA 11,521 sq km (4,448 sq mi)
POPULATION 928,000
CAPITAL Doha 384,000
RELIGION Muslim, Christian
LANGUAGE Arabic, English
LITERACY 89%
LIFE EXPECTANCY 75 years
GDP PER CAPITA $86,700
ECONOMY **IND:** crude oil production and refining, ammonia, fertilizers, petrochemicals **AGR:** fruits, vegetables; poultry; fish **EXP:** liquefied natural gas (LNG), petroleum products, fertilizers, steel

Bahrain

KINGDOM OF BAHRAIN

AREA 717 sq km (277 sq mi)
POPULATION 780,000
CAPITAL Manama 157,000
RELIGION Muslim, Christian
LANGUAGE Arabic, English, Farsi, Urdu
LITERACY 87%
LIFE EXPECTANCY 75 years
GDP PER CAPITA $34,000
ECONOMY **IND:** petroleum processing and refining, aluminum smelting, iron pelletization, fertilizers **AGR:** fruits, vegetables; poultry; shrimp **EXP:** petroleum and petroleum products, aluminum, textiles

Iran

ISLAMIC REPUBLIC OF IRAN

AREA 1,648,000 sq km (636,296 sq mi)
POPULATION 72,212,000
CAPITAL Tehran 7,873,000
RELIGION Shiite Muslim, Sunni Muslim
LANGUAGE Persian, Turkic, Kurdish
LITERACY 77%
LIFE EXPECTANCY 71 years
GDP PER CAPITA $11,200
ECONOMY **IND:** petroleum, petrochemicals, fertilizers, caustic soda, textiles **AGR:** wheat, rice, other grains, sugar beets; dairy products; caviar **EXP:** petroleum, chemical and petrochemical products, fruits and nuts, carpets

Iraq

REPUBLIC OF IRAQ

AREA 437,072 sq km (168,754 sq mi)
POPULATION 29,492,000
CAPITAL Baghdad 5,054,000
RELIGION Shiite Muslim, Sunni Muslim
LANGUAGE Arabic, Kurdish, Turkoman, Assyrian, Armenian
LITERACY 74%
LIFE EXPECTANCY 58 years
GDP PER CAPITA $4,000
ECONOMY **IND:** petroleum, chemicals, textiles, leather, construction materials **AGR:** wheat, barley, rice, vegetables; cattle **EXP:** crude oil, crude materials excluding fuels, food and live animals

Kuwait

STATE OF KUWAIT

AREA 17,818 sq km (6,880 sq mi)
POPULATION 2,669,000
CAPITAL Kuwait City 2,063,000
RELIGION Sunni Muslim, Shiite Muslim, Christian, Hindu, Parsi
LANGUAGE Arabic, English
LITERACY 93%
LIFE EXPECTANCY 78 years
GDP PER CAPITA $40,900
ECONOMY **IND:** petroleum, petrochemicals, cement, shipbuilding and repair **AGR:** practically no crops; fish **EXP:** oil and refined products, fertilizers

Saudi Arabia

KINGDOM OF SAUDI ARABIA

AREA 1,960,582 sq km (756,985 sq mi)
POPULATION 28,147,000
CAPITAL Riyadh 4,465,000
RELIGION Muslim
LANGUAGE Arabic
LITERACY 79%
LIFE EXPECTANCY 76 years
GDP PER CAPITA $24,100
ECONOMY **IND:** crude oil production, petroleum refining, basic petrochemicals, ammonia **AGR:** wheat, barley, tomatoes, melons; mutton **EXP:** petroleum and petroleum products

Oman

SULTANATE OF OMAN

AREA 309,500 sq km (119,499 sq mi)
POPULATION 2,719,000
CAPITAL Muscat 620,000
RELIGION Ibadhi Muslim, Sunni Muslim, Shiite Muslim, Hindu
LANGUAGE Arabic, English, Baluchi, Urdu, Indian dialects
LITERACY 81%
LIFE EXPECTANCY 74 years
GDP PER CAPITA $26,100
ECONOMY **IND:** crude oil production and refining, natural and liquefied natural gas (LNG) production, construction, cement **AGR:** dates, limes, bananas, alfalfa; camels; fish **EXP:** petroleum, reexports, fish, metals, textiles

United Arab Emirates

UNITED ARAB EMIRATES

AREA 77,700 sq km (30,000 sq mi)
POPULATION 4,486,000
CAPITAL Abu Dhabi 603,000
RELIGION Muslim
LANGUAGE Arabic, Persian, English, Hindi, Urdu
LITERACY 78%
LIFE EXPECTANCY 78 years
GDP PER CAPITA $39,100
ECONOMY **IND:** petroleum and petrochemicals, fishing, aluminum, cement, fertilizers **AGR:** dates, vegetables, watermelons; poultry; fish **EXP:** crude oil, natural gas, reexports, dried fish, dates

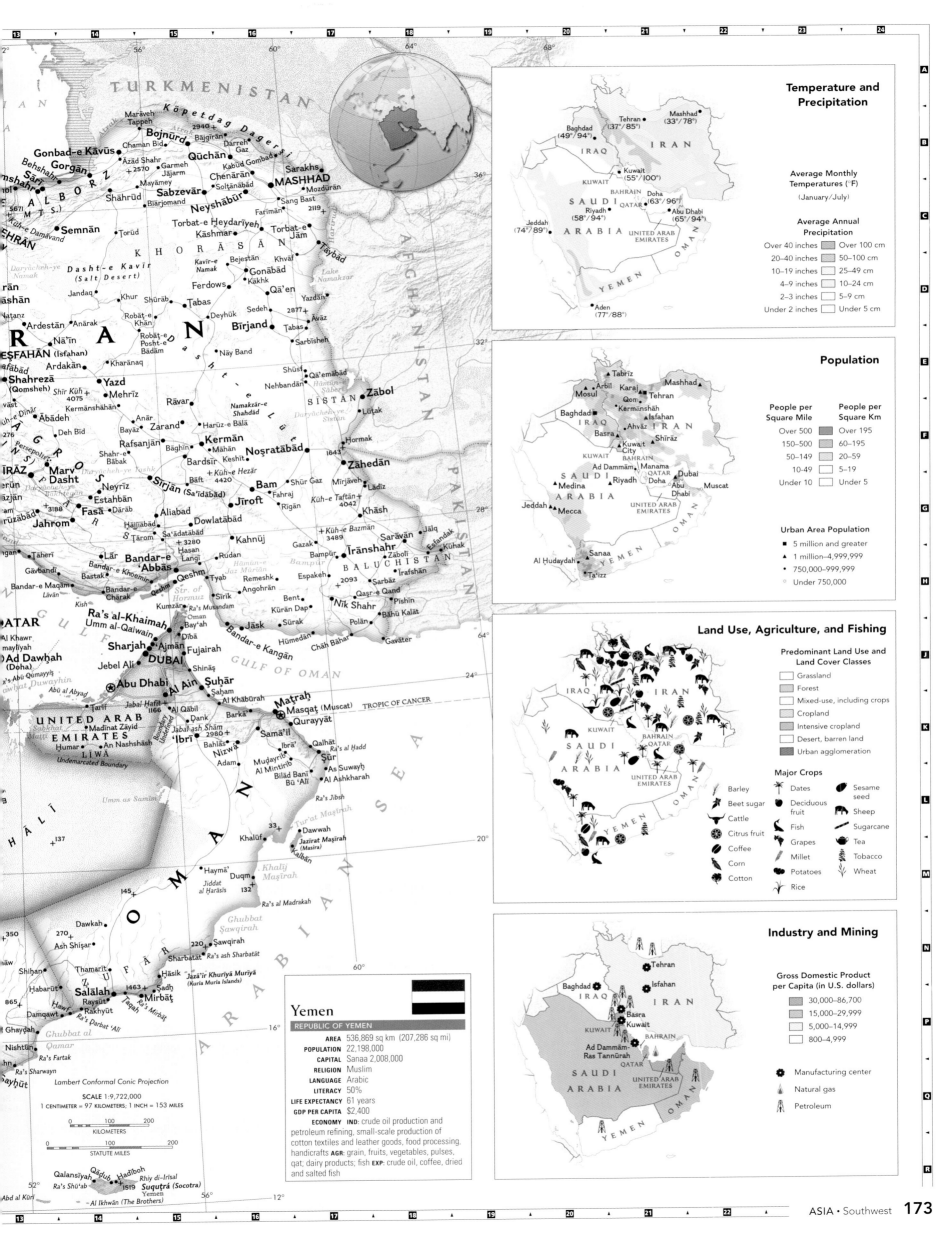

Temperature and Precipitation

Average Monthly Temperatures (°F)
(January/July)

Baghdad (49°/94°)
Tehran (37°/85°)
Mashhad (33°/78°)
Kuwait (55°/100°)
Doha (63°/96°)
Riyadh (58°/94°)
Abu Dhabi (65°/94°)
Jeddah (74°/89°)
Aden (77°/88°)

Average Annual Precipitation

Over 40 inches	Over 100 cm
20–40 inches	50–100 cm
10–19 inches	25–49 cm
4–9 inches	10–24 cm
2–3 inches	5–9 cm
Under 2 inches	Under 5 cm

Population

People per Square Mile	People per Square Km
Over 500	Over 195
150–500	60–195
50–149	20–59
10–49	5–19
Under 10	Under 5

Urban Area Population
■ 5 million and greater
▲ 1 million–4,999,999
● 750,000–999,999
○ Under 750,000

Land Use, Agriculture, and Fishing

Predominant Land Use and Land Cover Classes
- Grassland
- Forest
- Mixed-use, including crops
- Cropland
- Intensive cropland
- Desert, barren land
- Urban agglomeration

Major Crops
- Barley
- Beet sugar
- Cattle
- Citrus fruit
- Coffee
- Corn
- Cotton
- Dates
- Deciduous fruit
- Fish
- Grapes
- Millet
- Potatoes
- Rice
- Sesame seed
- Sheep
- Sugarcane
- Tea
- Tobacco
- Wheat

Industry and Mining

Gross Domestic Product per Capita (in U.S. dollars)
| 30,000–86,700 |
| 15,000–29,999 |
| 5,000–14,999 |
| 800–4,999 |

✿ Manufacturing center
Natural gas
Petroleum

Yemen
REPUBLIC OF YEMEN
AREA 536,869 sq km (207,286 sq mi)
POPULATION 22,198,000
CAPITAL Sanaa 2,008,000
RELIGION Muslim
LANGUAGE Arabic
LITERACY 50%
LIFE EXPECTANCY 61 years
GDP PER CAPITA $2,400
ECONOMY IND: crude oil production and petroleum refining, small-scale production of cotton textiles and leather goods, food processing, handicrafts AGR: grain, fruits, vegetables, pulses, qat; dairy products; fish EXP: crude oil, coffee, dried and salted fish

Lambert Conformal Conic Projection
SCALE 1:9,722,000
1 CENTIMETER = 97 KILOMETERS; 1 INCH = 153 MILES

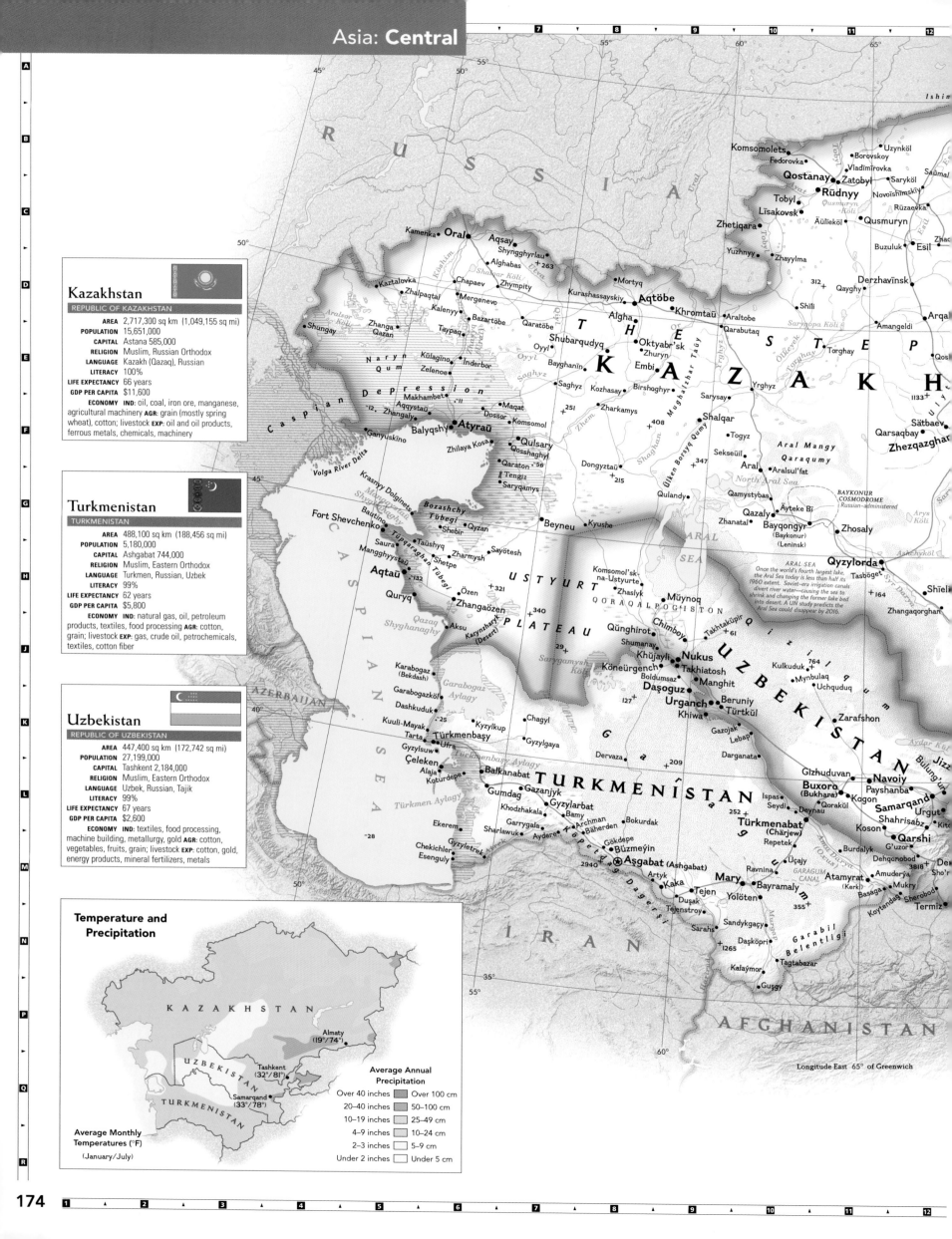

Kazakhstan
REPUBLIC OF KAZAKHSTAN

AREA 2,717,300 sq km (1,049,155 sq mi)
POPULATION 15,651,000
CAPITAL Astana 585,000
RELIGION Muslim, Russian Orthodox
LANGUAGE Kazakh (Qazaq), Russian
LITERACY 100%
LIFE EXPECTANCY 66 years
GDP PER CAPITA $11,600
ECONOMY **IND:** oil, coal, iron ore, manganese, agricultural machinery **AGR:** grain (mostly spring wheat), cotton; livestock **EXP:** oil and oil products, ferrous metals, chemicals, machinery

Turkmenistan
TURKMENISTAN

AREA 488,100 sq km (188,456 sq mi)
POPULATION 5,180,000
CAPITAL Ashgabat 744,000
RELIGION Muslim, Eastern Orthodox
LANGUAGE Turkmen, Russian, Uzbek
LITERACY 99%
LIFE EXPECTANCY 62 years
GDP PER CAPITA $5,800
ECONOMY **IND:** natural gas, oil, petroleum products, textiles, food processing **AGR:** cotton, grain; livestock **EXP:** gas, crude oil, petrochemicals, textiles, cotton fiber

Uzbekistan
REPUBLIC OF UZBEKISTAN

AREA 447,400 sq km (172,742 sq mi)
POPULATION 27,199,000
CAPITAL Tashkent 2,184,000
RELIGION Muslim, Eastern Orthodox
LANGUAGE Uzbek, Russian, Tajik
LITERACY 99%
LIFE EXPECTANCY 67 years
GDP PER CAPITA $2,600
ECONOMY **IND:** textiles, food processing, machine building, metallurgy, gold **AGR:** cotton, vegetables, fruits, grain; livestock **EXP:** cotton, gold, energy products, mineral fertilizers, metals

Temperature and Precipitation

Almaty (19°/74°)
Tashkent (32°/81°)
Samarqand (33°/78°)

Average Monthly Temperatures (°F)
(January/July)

Average Annual Precipitation

Over 40 inches	Over 100 cm
20–40 inches	50–100 cm
10–19 inches	25–49 cm
4–9 inches	10–24 cm
2–3 inches	5–9 cm
Under 2 inches	Under 5 cm

ARAL SEA
Once the world's fourth largest lake, the Aral Sea today is less than half its 1960 extent. Soviet-era irrigation canals divert river water—causing the sea to shrink and changing the former lake bed into desert. A UN study predicts the Aral Sea could disappear by 2016.

Longitude East 65° of Greenwich

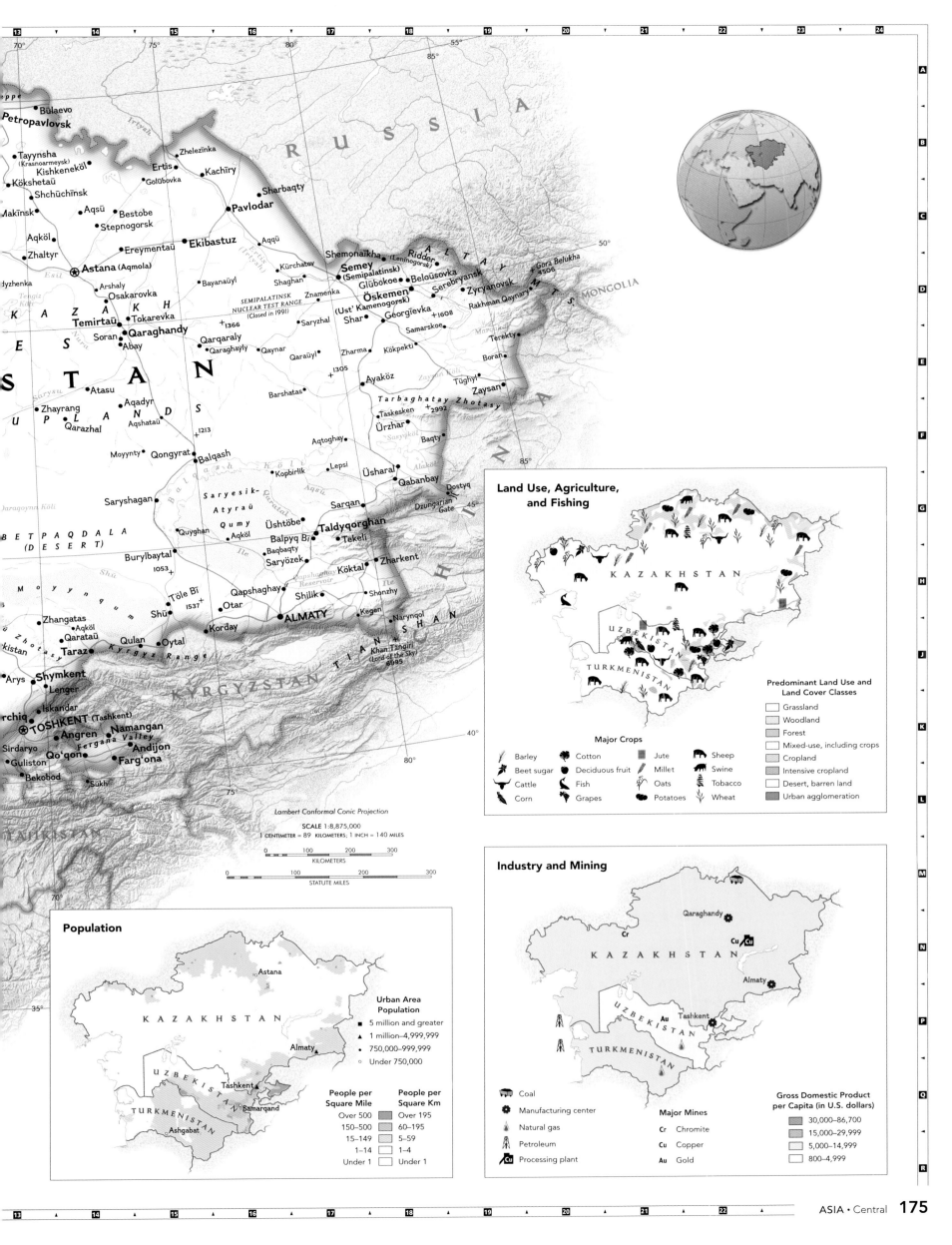

Land Use, Agriculture, and Fishing

Major Crops

Barley
Beet sugar
Cattle
Corn

Cotton
Deciduous fruit
Fish
Grapes

Jute
Millet
Oats
Potatoes

Sheep
Swine
Tobacco
Wheat

Predominant Land Use and Land Cover Classes

Grassland
Woodland
Forest
Mixed-use, including crops
Cropland
Intensive cropland
Desert, barren land
Urban agglomeration

Lambert Conformal Conic Projection

SCALE 1:8,875,000
1 CENTIMETER = 89 KILOMETERS; 1 INCH = 140 MILES

| 0 | 100 | 200 | 300 |
KILOMETERS

| 0 | 100 | 200 | 300 |
STATUTE MILES

Population

Urban Area Population

■ 5 million and greater
▲ 1 million–4,999,999
● 750,000–999,999
○ Under 750,000

People per Square Mile	People per Square Km
Over 500	Over 195
150–500	60–195
15–149	5–59
1–14	1–4
Under 1	Under 1

Industry and Mining

Coal
Manufacturing center
Natural gas
Petroleum
Processing plant

Major Mines

Cr Chromite
Cu Copper
Au Gold

Gross Domestic Product per Capita (in U.S. dollars)

30,000–86,700
15,000–29,999
5,000–14,999
800–4,999

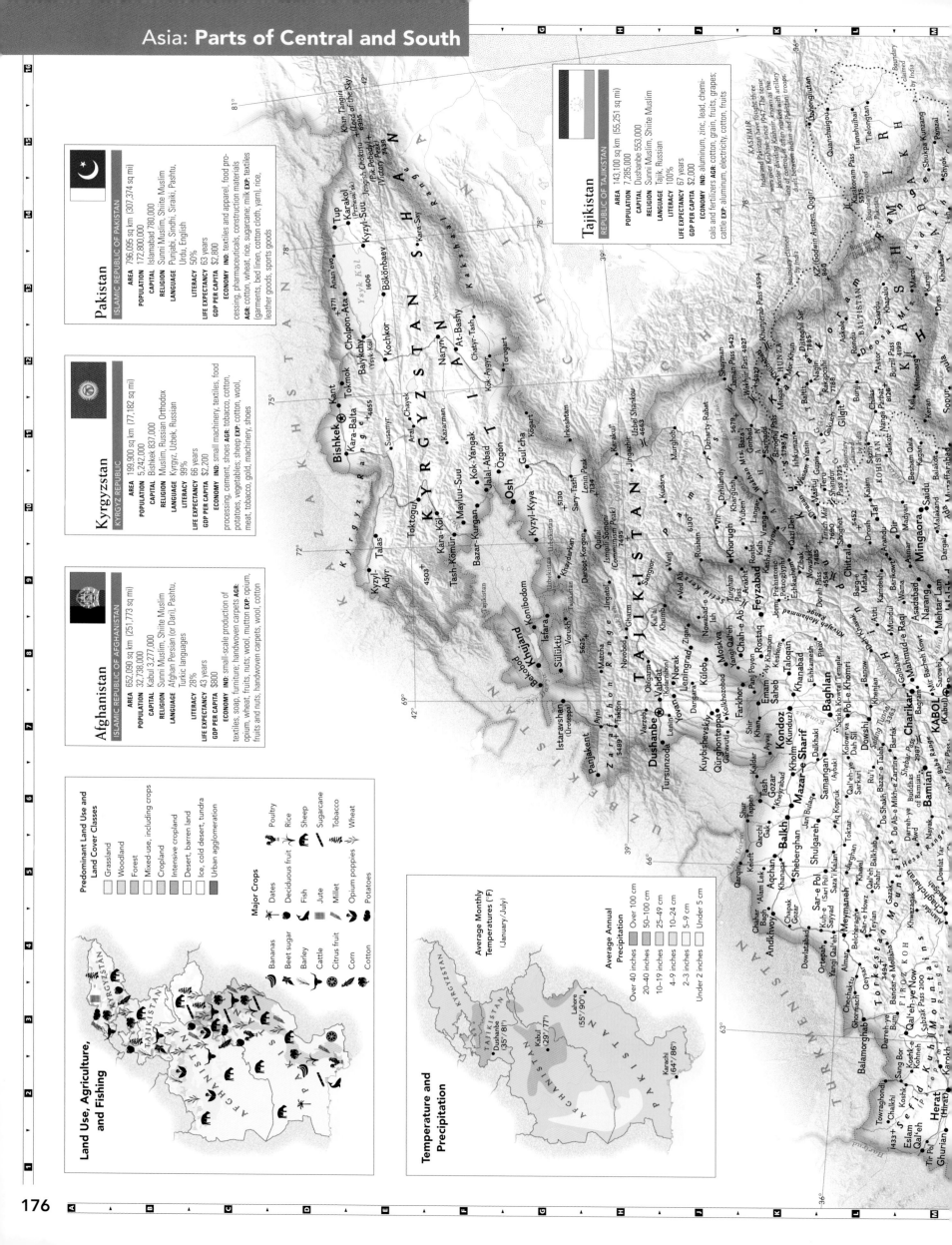

Pakistan
ISLAMIC REPUBLIC OF PAKISTAN
AREA 796,095 sq km (307,374 sq mi)
POPULATION 172,800,000
CAPITAL Islamabad 780,000
RELIGION Sunni Muslim, Shiite Muslim
LANGUAGE Punjabi, Sindhi, Siraiki, Pashtu, Urdu, English
LITERACY 50%
LIFE EXPECTANCY 63 years
GDP PER CAPITA $2,800
ECONOMY IND: textiles and apparel, food processing, pharmaceuticals, construction materials **AGR:** cotton, wheat, rice, sugarcane; milk **EXP:** textiles (garments, bed linen, cotton cloth, yarn), rice, leather goods, sports goods

Kyrgyzstan
KYRGYZ REPUBLIC
AREA 199,900 sq km (77,182 sq mi)
POPULATION 5,242,000
CAPITAL Bishkek 837,000
RELIGION Muslim, Russian Orthodox
LANGUAGE Kyrgyz, Uzbek, Russian
LITERACY 99%
LIFE EXPECTANCY 66 years
GDP PER CAPITA $2,200
ECONOMY IND: small machinery, textiles, food processing, cement, shoes **AGR:** tobacco, cotton, potatoes, vegetables; sheep **EXP:** cotton, wool, meat, tobacco, gold, machinery, shoes

Afghanistan
ISLAMIC REPUBLIC OF AFGHANISTAN
AREA 652,090 sq km (251,773 sq mi)
POPULATION 32,738,000
CAPITAL Kabul 3,277,000
RELIGION Sunni Muslim, Shiite Muslim
LANGUAGE Afghan Persian (or Dari), Pashtu, Turkic languages
LITERACY 28%
LIFE EXPECTANCY 43 years
GDP PER CAPITA $800
ECONOMY IND: small-scale production of textiles, soap, furniture; handwoven carpets **AGR:** opium, wheat, fruits, nuts; wool; mutton **EXP:** opium, fruits and nuts, handwoven carpets, wool, cotton

Tajikistan
REPUBLIC OF TAJIKISTAN
AREA 143,100 sq km (55,251 sq mi)
POPULATION 7,285,000
CAPITAL Dushanbe 553,000
LANGUAGE Tajik, Russian
LITERACY 100%
LIFE EXPECTANCY 67 years
GDP PER CAPITA $2,000
ECONOMY IND: aluminum, zinc, lead, chemicals and fertilizers **AGR:** cotton, grain, fruits, grapes; cattle **EXP:** aluminum, electricity, cotton, fruits

Land Use, Agriculture, and Fishing

Predominant Land Use and Land Cover Classes
Grassland
Woodland
Forest
Mixed-use, including crops
Cropland
Intensive cropland
Desert, barren land
Ice, cold desert, tundra
Urban agglomeration

Major Crops
Bananas
Beet sugar
Barley
Cattle
Citrus fruit
Corn
Cotton
Dates
Deciduous fruit
Fish
Jute
Millet
Opium poppies
Potatoes
Poultry
Rice
Sheep
Sugarcane
Tobacco
Wheat

Temperature and Precipitation

Average Monthly Temperatures (°F) (January/July)

Average Annual Precipitation
Over 40 inches — Over 100 cm
20–40 inches — 50–100 cm
10–19 inches — 25–49 cm
4–9 inches — 10–24 cm
2–3 inches — 5–9 cm
Under 2 inches — Under 5 cm

Dushanbe (35°/81°)
Kabul (29°/77°)
Lahore (55°/90°)
Karachi (64°/86°)

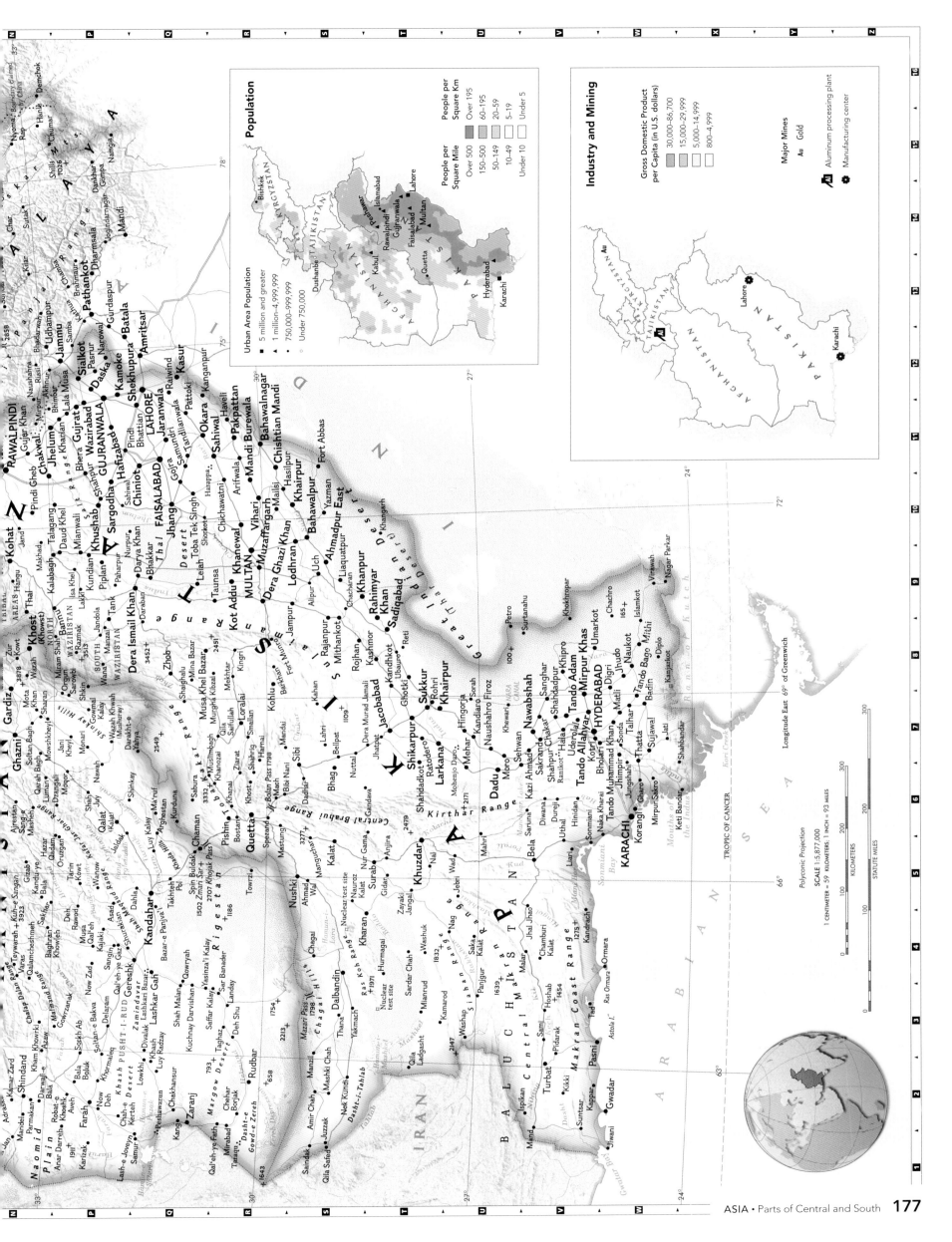

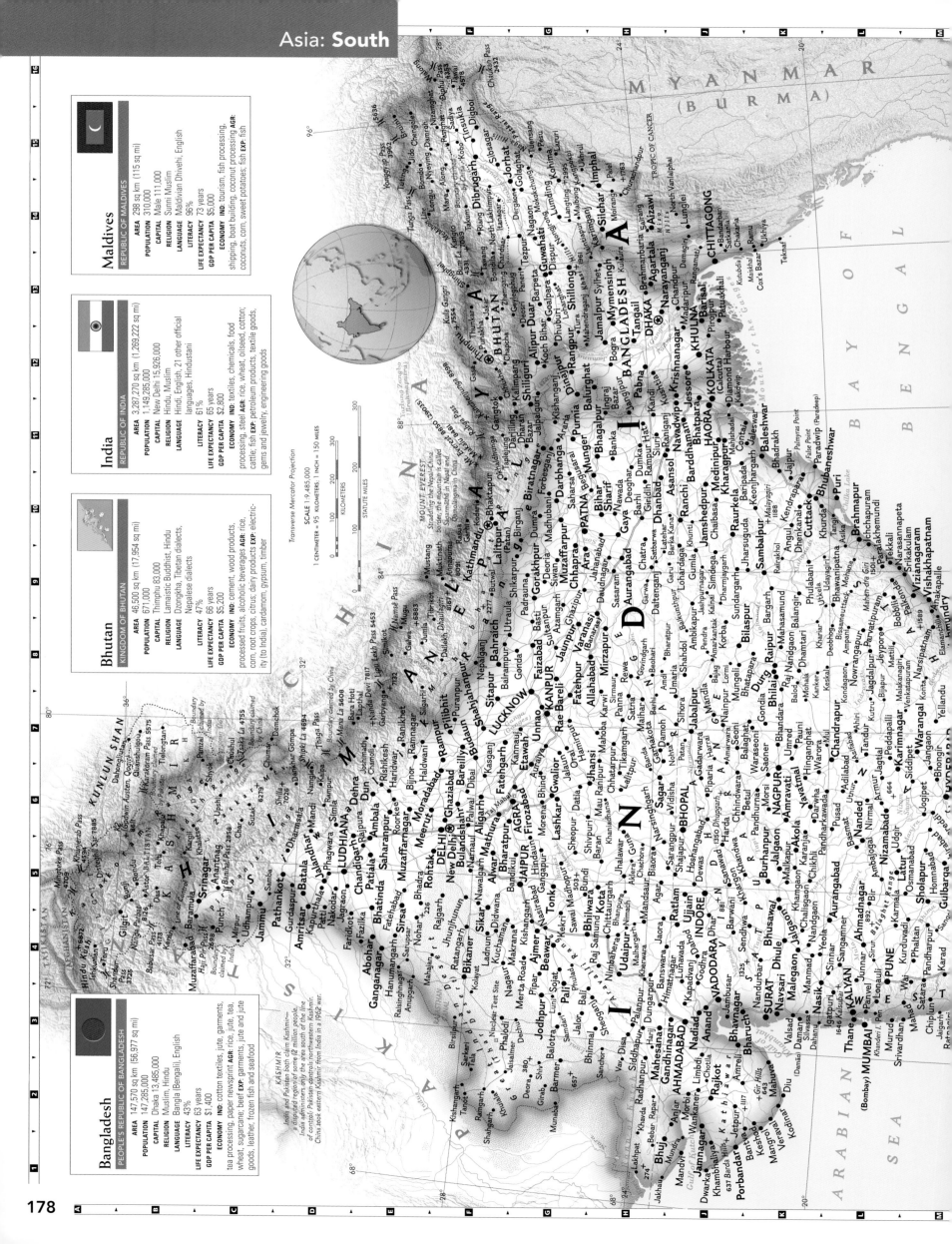

Bangladesh
PEOPLE'S REPUBLIC OF BANGLADESH
AREA 147,570 sq km (56,977 sq mi)
POPULATION 147,285,000
CAPITAL Dhaka 13,485,000
RELIGION Muslim, Hindu
LANGUAGE Bangla (Bengali), English
LITERACY 43%
LIFE EXPECTANCY 63 years
GDP PER CAPITA $1,400
ECONOMY IND: cotton textiles, jute, garments, tea processing, paper newsprint **AGR:** rice, jute, tea, wheat, sugarcane; beef **EXP:** garments, jute and jute goods, leather, frozen fish and seafood

Bhutan
KINGDOM OF BHUTAN
AREA 46,500 sq km (17,954 sq mi)
POPULATION 671,000
CAPITAL Thimphu 83,000
RELIGION Lamaistic Buddhist, Hindu
LANGUAGE Dzongkha, Tibetan dialects, Nepalese dialects
LITERACY 47%
LIFE EXPECTANCY 66 years
GDP PER CAPITA $5,200
ECONOMY IND: cement, wood products, processed fruits, alcoholic beverages **AGR:** rice, corn, root crops, citrus; dairy products **EXP:** electricity (to India), cardamom, gypsum, timber

India
REPUBLIC OF INDIA
AREA 3,287,270 sq km (1,269,222 sq mi)
POPULATION 1,149,285,000
CAPITAL New Delhi 15,926,000
RELIGION Hindu, Muslim
LANGUAGE Hindi, English, 21 other official languages, Hindustani
LITERACY 61%
LIFE EXPECTANCY 65 years
GDP PER CAPITA $2,800
ECONOMY IND: textiles, chemicals, food processing, steel **AGR:** rice, wheat, oilseed, cotton; cattle, fish **EXP:** petroleum products, textile goods, gems and jewelry, engineering goods

Maldives
REPUBLIC OF MALDIVES
AREA 298 sq km (115 sq mi)
POPULATION 310,000
CAPITAL Male 111,000
RELIGION Sunni Muslim
LANGUAGE Maldivian Dhivehi, English
LITERACY 96%
LIFE EXPECTANCY 73 years
GDP PER CAPITA $5,000
ECONOMY IND: tourism, fish processing, shipping, boat building, coconut processing **AGR:** coconuts, corn, sweet potatoes; fish **EXP:** fish

KASHMIR
India and Pakistan both claim Kashmir—a disputed region of some 12 million people. India administers only the area south of the line of control. Pakistan controls northwestern Kashmir. China took over eastern Kashmir from India in a 1962 war.

Transverse Mercator Projection
SCALE 1:9,485,000
1 CENTIMETER = 95 KILOMETERS; 1 INCH = 150 MILES

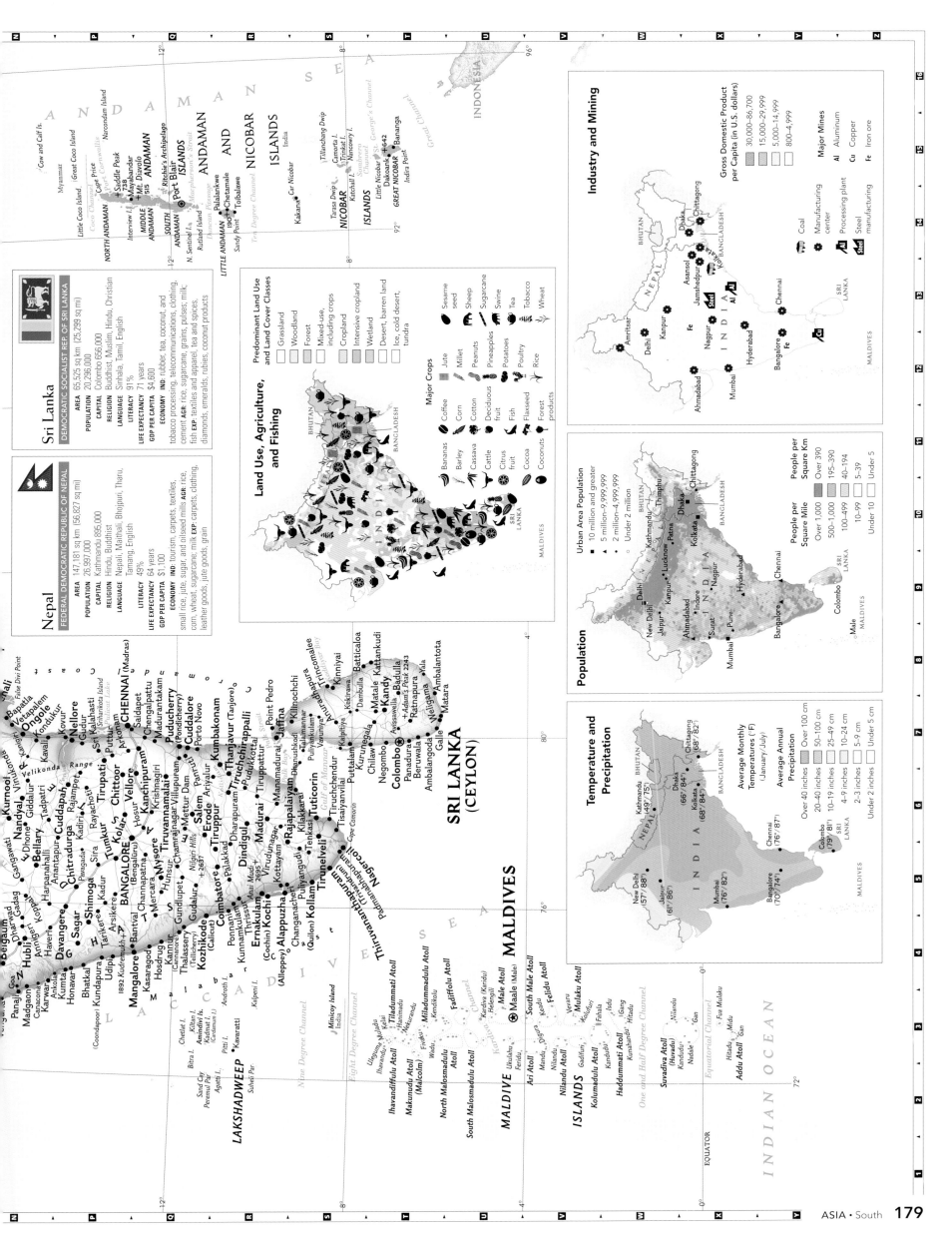

Nepal

FEDERAL DEMOCRATIC REPUBLIC OF NEPAL

AREA	147,181 sq km (56,827 sq mi)
POPULATION	26,997,000
CAPITAL	Kathmandu 895,000
RELIGION	Hindu, Buddhist
LANGUAGE	Nepali, Maithali, Bhojpuri, Tharu, Tamang, English
LITERACY	49%
LIFE EXPECTANCY	64 years
GDP PER CAPITA	$1,100
ECONOMY	**IND:** tourism, carpets, textiles, small rice, jute, sugar, and oilseed mills **AGR:** rice, corn, wheat, sugarcane, milk **EXP:** carpets, clothing, leather goods, jute goods, grain

Sri Lanka

DEMOCRATIC SOCIALIST REP. OF SRI LANKA

AREA	65,525 sq km (25,299 sq mi)
POPULATION	20,296,000
CAPITAL	Colombo 656,000
RELIGION	Buddhist, Muslim, Hindu, Christian
LANGUAGE	Sinhala, Tamil, English
LITERACY	91%
LIFE EXPECTANCY	71 years
GDP PER CAPITA	$4,600
ECONOMY	**IND:** rubber, tea, coconut, and tobacco processing, telecommunications, clothing, cement **AGR:** rice, sugarcane, grains, pulses; milk; fish **EXP:** textiles and apparel, tea and spices, diamonds, emeralds, rubies, coconut products

Land Use, Agriculture, and Fishing

Predominant Land Use and Land Cover Classes
- Grassland
- Woodland
- Forest
- Mixed-use, including crops
- Cropland
- Intensive cropland
- Wetland
- Desert, barren land
- Ice, cold desert, tundra

Major Crops
- Bananas
- Barley
- Cassava
- Cattle
- Citrus fruit
- Cocoa
- Coconuts
- Coffee
- Corn
- Cotton
- Deciduous fruit
- Fish
- Flaxseed
- Forest products
- Jute
- Millet
- Peanuts
- Pineapples
- Potatoes
- Poultry
- Rice
- Sesame seed
- Sheep
- Sugarcane
- Swine
- Tea
- Tobacco
- Wheat

Population

Urban Area Population
- 10 million and greater
- 5 million–9,999,999
- 2 million–4,999,999
- Under 2 million

People per Square Mile / People per Square Km
People per Square Mile	People per Square Km
Over 1,000	Over 390
500–1,000	195–390
100–499	40–194
10–99	5–39
Under 10	Under 5

Temperature and Precipitation

Average Monthly Temperatures (°F) (January/July)
- Over 40 inches / Over 100 cm
- 20–40 inches / 50–100 cm
- 10–19 inches / 25–49 cm
- 4–9 inches / 10–24 cm
- 2–3 inches / 5–9 cm
- Under 2 inches / Under 5 cm

Average Annual Precipitation

Industry and Mining

Gross Domestic Product per Capita (in U.S. dollars)
- 30,000–86,700
- 15,000–29,999
- 5,000–14,999
- 800–4,999

Major Mines
- Al Aluminum
- Cu Copper
- Fe Iron ore

- Coal
- Manufacturing center
- Processing plant
- Steel manufacturing

Mongolia

MONGOLIA

AREA 1,564,116 sq km (603,909 sq mi)
POPULATION 2,655,000
CAPITAL Ulaanbaatar 885,000
RELIGION Buddhist Lamaist, Shamanist, Christian
LANGUAGE Khalkha Mongol, Turkic, Russian
LITERACY 98%
LIFE EXPECTANCY 64 years
GDP PER CAPITA $3,500
ECONOMY **IND:** construction and construction materials, mining (coal, copper), oil, food and beverages **AGR:** wheat, barley, vegetables, forage crops; sheep **EXP:** copper, apparel, livestock, animal products

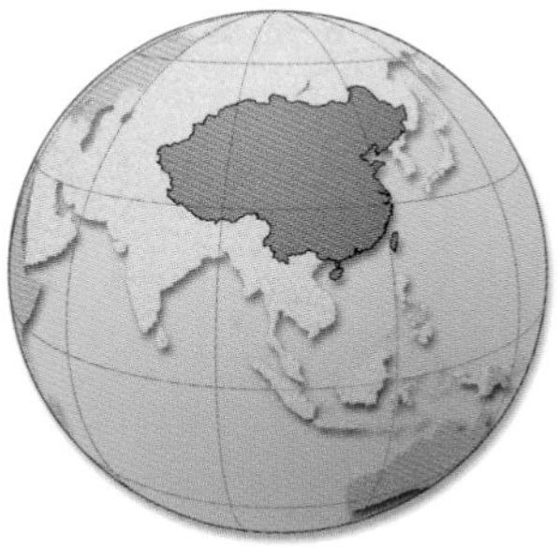

Longitude East 100° of Greenwich
RUSSIA
KAZAKHSTAN
KYRGYZSTAN
TAJIKISTAN
AFGHAN.
PAKISTAN
KASHMIR
AKSAI CHIN
Boundary claimed by India
INDIA
NEPAL
BHUTAN
MYANMAR (BURMA)
LAOS
VIETNAM
MONGOLIA
CHINA
TIAN SHAN
ALTAY MTS.
HANGAYN NURUU
GOBI ALTAY MTS.
Junggar Pendi (Dzungarian Basin)
TARIM PENDI
TAKLIMAKAN SHAMO
KUNLUN SHAN
ALTUN SHAN
QILIAN SHAN
Qaidam Pendi
PLATEAU OF TIBET
TIBET
HIMALAYA
Tanggula Shan
Gangdisê Shan
Hengduan Shan
Bayan Har Shan
Badain Jaran Shamo
ÜRÜMQI
Ulaanbaatar (Ulan Bator)
Lhasa
Kashi (Kashgar)
Hotan
Aksu
Korla
Turpan (Turfan)
Hami (Kumul)
Golmud
Xining
LANZHOU
CHENGDU
CHONGQING
KUNMING
Dunhuang
Jiayuguan
Jiuquan Satellite Launch Center
Mount Everest 8850 m (29035 ft)
K2 8611
Turpan Pendi -154
Source of the Yangtze
MOUNT EVEREST
Straddling the Nepal-China border, the mountain is called Sagarmāthā in Nepal and Qomolangma in China.
TROPIC OF CANCER
Oblique Parabolic Equal-Area Projection
SCALE 1:15,013,000
1 CENTIMETER = 150 KILOMETERS; 1 INCH = 237 MILES
KILOMETERS
STATUTE MILES

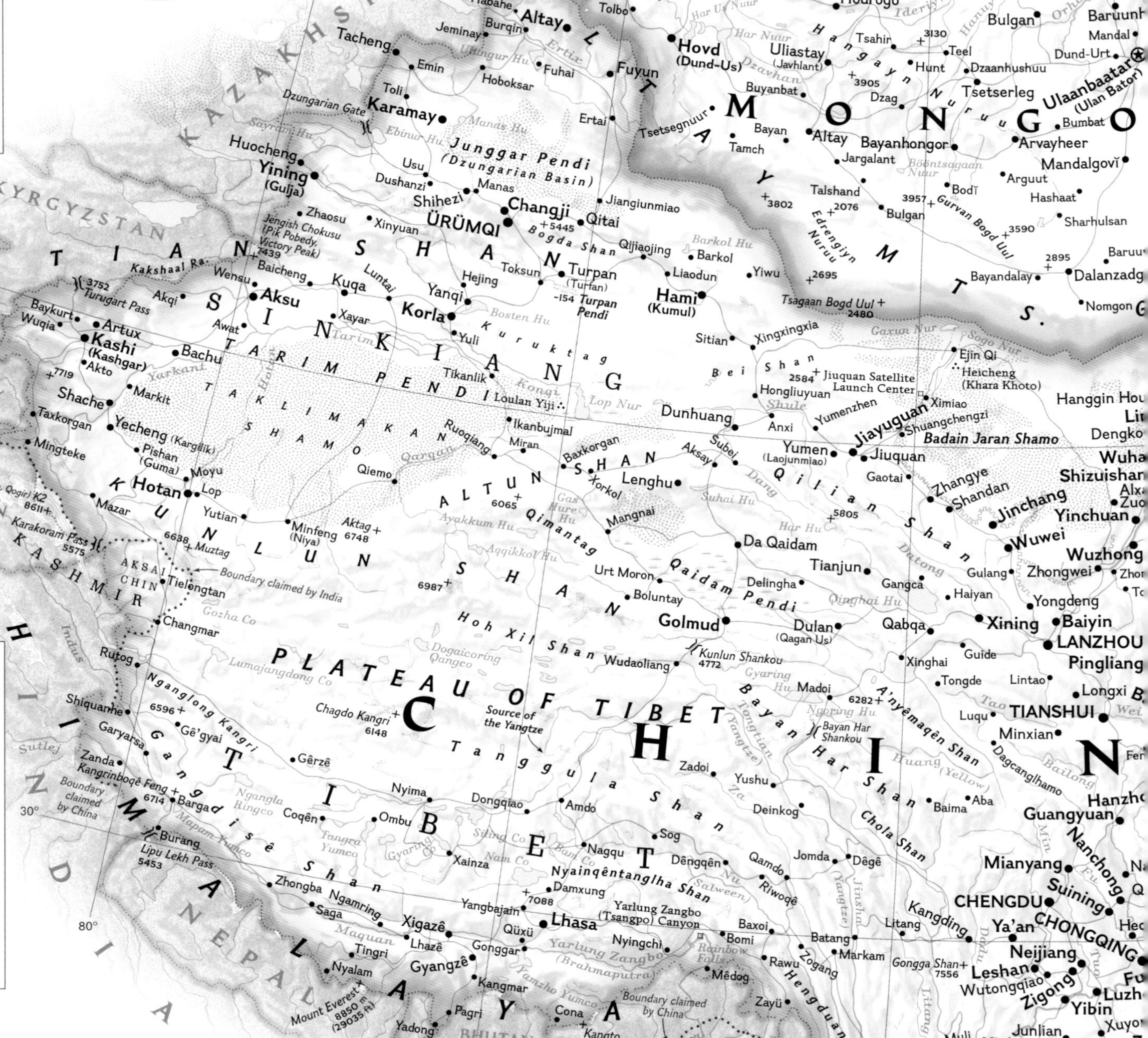

China

PEOPLE'S REPUBLIC OF CHINA

AREA 9,596,960 sq km (3,705,407 sq mi)
POPULATION 1,355,251,000
CAPITAL Beijing 11,106,000
RELIGION Daoist (Taoist), Buddhist
LANGUAGE Standard Chinese or Mandarin, Yue, Wu, Minbei, local dialects and languages
LITERACY 91%
LIFE EXPECTANCY 73 years
GDP PER CAPITA $5,900
ECONOMY **IND:** mining, ore processing, iron, steel, aluminum, coal, machine building, armaments, textiles **AGR:** rice, wheat, potatoes, corn; pork; fish **EXP:** electrical and other machinery, data processing equipment, apparel, textiles, iron, steel

Temperature and Precipitation

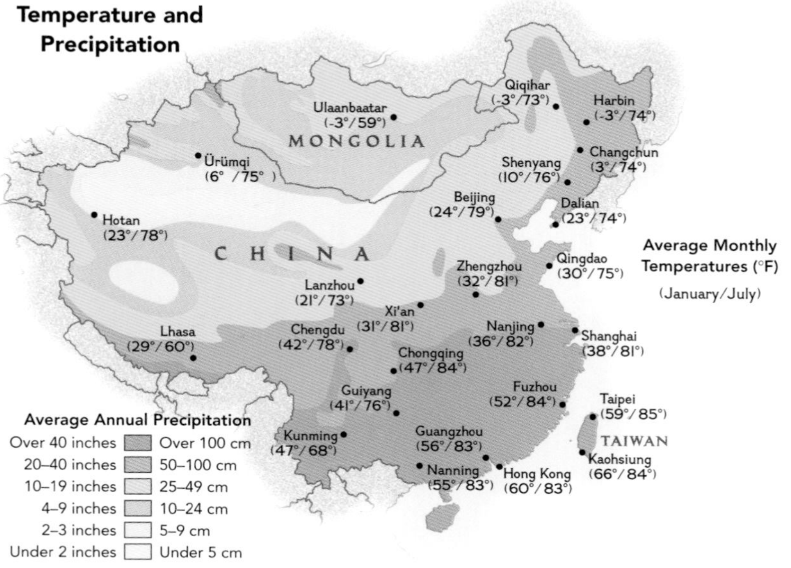

MONGOLIA
CHINA
TAIWAN
Ulaanbaatar (-3°/59°)
Ürümqi (6°/75°)
Hotan (23°/78°)
Lhasa (29°/60°)
Lanzhou (21°/73°)
Chengdu (42°/78°)
Xi'an (31°/81°)
Chongqing (47°/84°)
Kunming (47°/68°)
Guiyang (41°/76°)
Qiqihar (-3°/73°)
Harbin (-3°/74°)
Changchun (3°/74°)
Shenyang (10°/76°)
Beijing (24°/79°)
Dalian (23°/74°)
Qingdao (30°/75°)
Zhengzhou (32°/81°)
Nanjing (36°/82°)
Shanghai (38°/81°)
Fuzhou (52°/84°)
Taipei (59°/85°)
Kaohsiung (66°/84°)
Guangzhou (56°/83°)
Nanning (55°/83°)
Hong Kong (60°/83°)
Average Monthly Temperatures (°F) (January/July)
Average Annual Precipitation
Over 40 inches | Over 100 cm
20–40 inches | 50–100 cm
10–19 inches | 25–49 cm
4–9 inches | 10–24 cm
2–3 inches | 5–9 cm
Under 2 inches | Under 5 cm

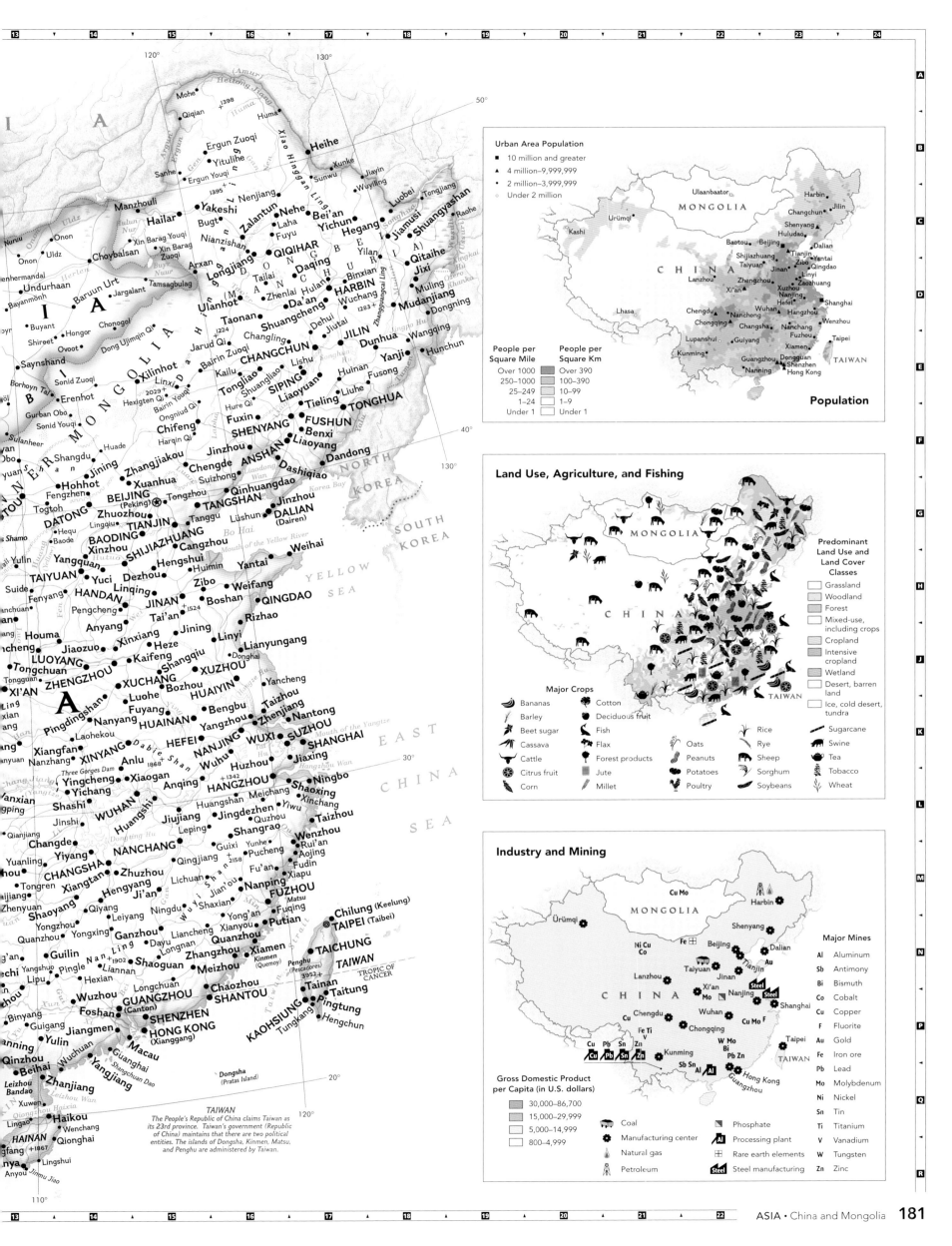

Population

Urban Area Population
- ■ 10 million and greater
- ▲ 4 million–9,999,999
- ▲ 2 million–3,999,999
- ○ Under 2 million

People per Square Mile	People per Square Km
Over 1000	Over 390
250–1000	100–390
25–249	10–99
1–24	1–9
Under 1	Under 1

MONGOLIA — Ulaanbaatar, Ürümqi, Kashi

CHINA — Baotou, Beijing, Shijiazhuang, Taiyuan, Lanzhou, Zhengzhou, Xi'an, Jinan, Xuzhou, Nanjing, Hefei, Wuhan, Nanchong, Chengdu, Chongqing, Changsha, Nanchang, Hangzhou, Shanghai, Wenzhou, Lhasa, Guiyang, Xiamen, Fuzhou, Kunming, Lupanshui, Guangzhou, Dongguan, Shenzhen, Nanning, Hong Kong, Harbin, Changchun, Jilin, Shenyang, Huludao, Dalian, Yantai, Zibo, Qingdao, Linyi, Zaozhuang, Taipei, TAIWAN

Land Use, Agriculture, and Fishing

Predominant Land Use and Land Cover Classes
- Grassland
- Woodland
- Forest
- Mixed-use, including crops
- Cropland
- Intensive cropland
- Wetland
- Desert, barren land
- Ice, cold desert, tundra

Major Crops
- Bananas
- Barley
- Beet sugar
- Cassava
- Cattle
- Citrus fruit
- Corn
- Cotton
- Deciduous fruit
- Fish
- Flax
- Forest products
- Jute
- Millet
- Oats
- Peanuts
- Potatoes
- Poultry
- Rice
- Rye
- Sheep
- Sorghum
- Soybeans
- Sugarcane
- Swine
- Tea
- Tobacco
- Wheat

Industry and Mining

Gross Domestic Product per Capita (in U.S. dollars)
- 30,000–86,700
- 15,000–29,999
- 5,000–14,999
- 800–4,999

- Coal
- Manufacturing center
- Natural gas
- Petroleum
- Phosphate
- Processing plant
- Rare earth elements
- Steel manufacturing

Major Mines
Al	Aluminum
Sb	Antimony
Bi	Bismuth
Co	Cobalt
Cu	Copper
F	Fluorite
Au	Gold
Fe	Iron ore
Pb	Lead
Mo	Molybdenum
Ni	Nickel
Sn	Tin
Ti	Titanium
V	Vanadium
W	Tungsten
Zn	Zinc

TAIWAN — The People's Republic of China claims Taiwan as its 23rd province. Taiwan's government (Republic of China) maintains that there are two political entities. The islands of Dongsha, Kinmen, Matsu, and Penghu are administered by Taiwan.

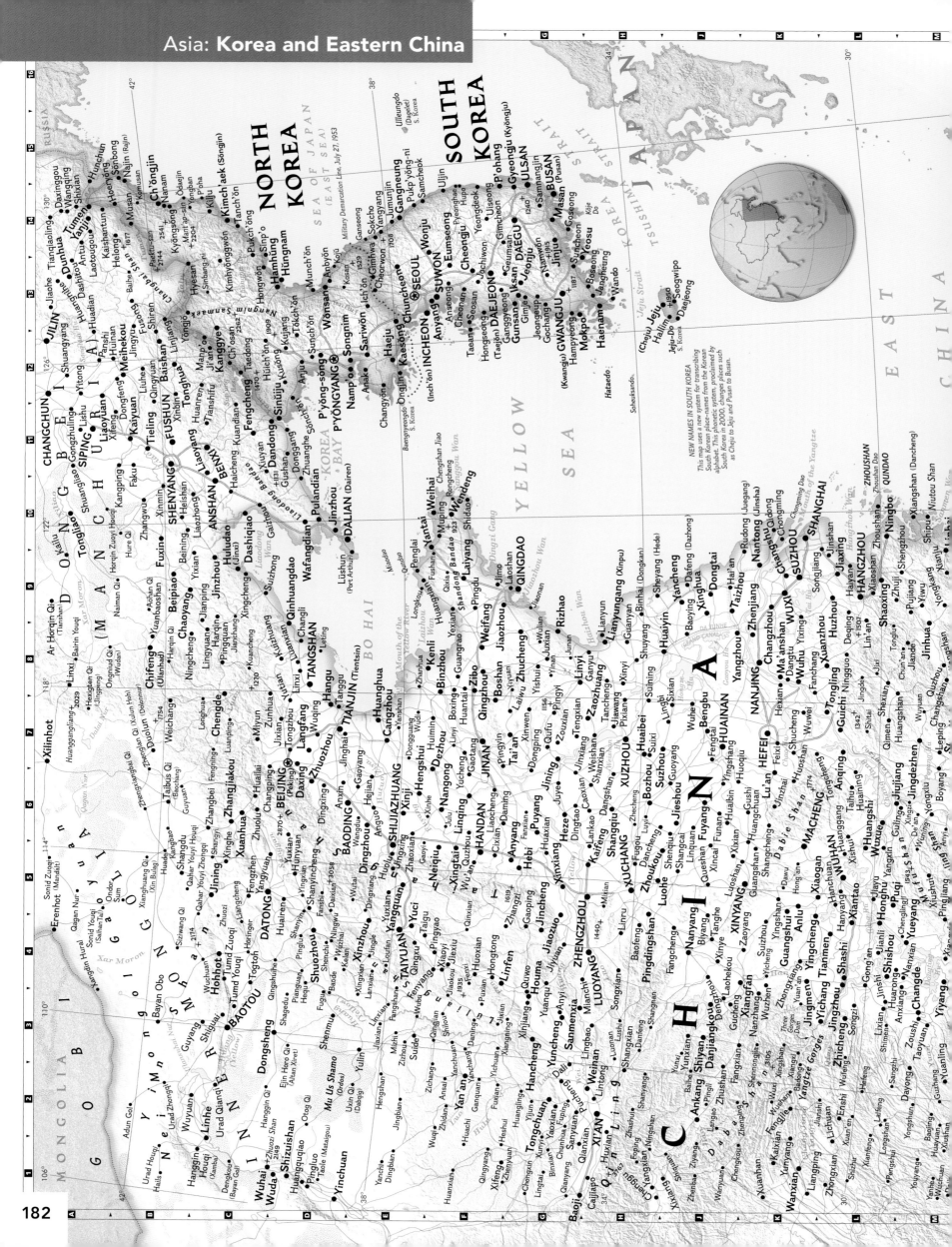

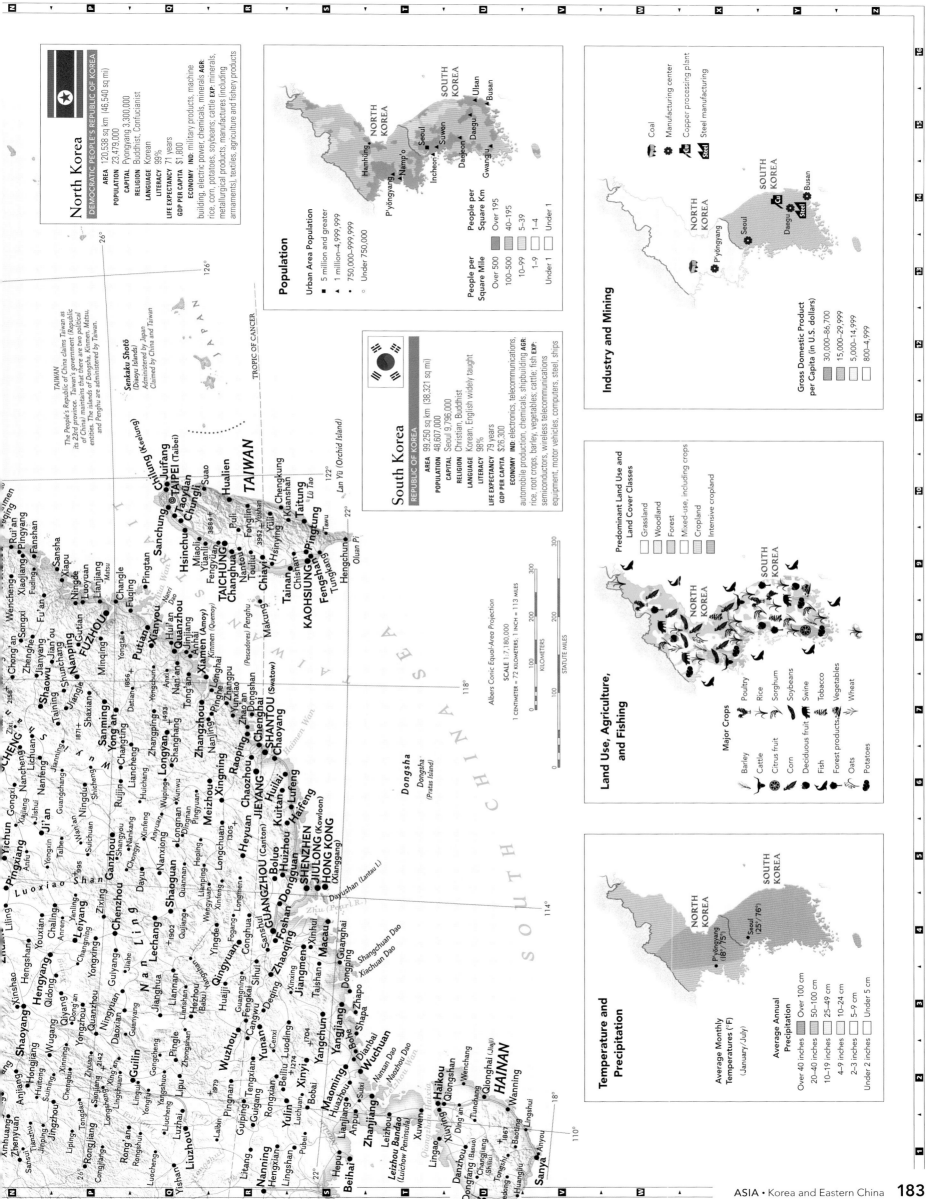

North Korea
DEMOCRATIC PEOPLE'S REPUBLIC OF KOREA

AREA 120,538 sq km (46,540 sq mi)
POPULATION 23,479,000
CAPITAL Pyongyang 3,300,000
RELIGION Buddhist, Confucianist
LANGUAGE Korean
LITERACY 99%
LIFE EXPECTANCY 71 years
GDP PER CAPITA $1,800
ECONOMY IND: military products, machine building, electric power, chemicals, minerals **AGR:** rice, corn, potatoes, soybeans; cattle **EXP:** minerals, metallurgical products, manufactures (including armaments), textiles, agriculture and fishery products

South Korea
REPUBLIC OF KOREA

AREA 99,250 sq km (38,321 sq mi)
POPULATION 48,607,000
CAPITAL Seoul 9,796,000
RELIGION Christian, Buddhist
LANGUAGE Korean; English widely taught
LITERACY 98%
LIFE EXPECTANCY 79 years
GDP PER CAPITA $26,300
ECONOMY IND: electronics, telecommunications, automobile production, chemicals, shipbuilding **AGR:** rice, root crops, barley, vegetables; cattle; fish **EXP:** semiconductors, wireless telecommunications equipment, motor vehicles, computers, steel, ships

TAIWAN
The People's Republic of China claims Taiwan as its 23rd province. Taiwan's government (Republic of China) maintains that there are two political entities. The islands of Dongsha, Kinmen, Matsu, and Penghu are administered by Taiwan.

Senkaku Shotō
(Diaoyu Islands)
Administered by Japan
Claimed by China and Taiwan

TROPIC OF CANCER

Population

Urban Area Population
- ■ 5 million and greater
- ■ 1 million–4,999,999
- ▲ 750,000–999,999
- ○ Under 750,000

People per Square Mile
- Over 500
- 100–500
- 10–99
- 1–9
- Under 1

People per Square Km
- Over 195
- 40–195
- 5–39
- 1–4
- Under 1

Industry and Mining

- Coal
- Manufacturing center
- Copper processing plant
- Steel manufacturing

Gross Domestic Product per Capita (in U.S. dollars)
- 30,000–86,700
- 15,000–29,999
- 5,000–14,999
- 800–4,999

Land Use, Agriculture, and Fishing

Predominant Land Use and Land Cover Classes
- Grassland
- Woodland
- Forest
- Mixed-use, including crops
- Cropland
- Intensive cropland

Major Crops
- Barley
- Cattle
- Citrus fruit
- Corn
- Deciduous fruit
- Fish
- Forest products
- Oats
- Potatoes
- Poultry
- Rice
- Sorghum
- Soybeans
- Swine
- Tobacco
- Vegetables
- Wheat

Temperature and Precipitation

Average Monthly Temperatures (°F)
(January/July)

Average Annual Precipitation
- Over 40 inches — Over 100 cm
- 20–40 inches — 50–100 cm
- 10–19 inches — 25–49 cm
- 4–9 inches — 10–24 cm
- 2–3 inches — 5–9 cm
- Under 2 inches — Under 5 cm

SCALE 1:7,180,000
Albers Conic Equal-Area Projection
1 CENTIMETER = 72 KILOMETERS; 1 INCH = 113 MILES

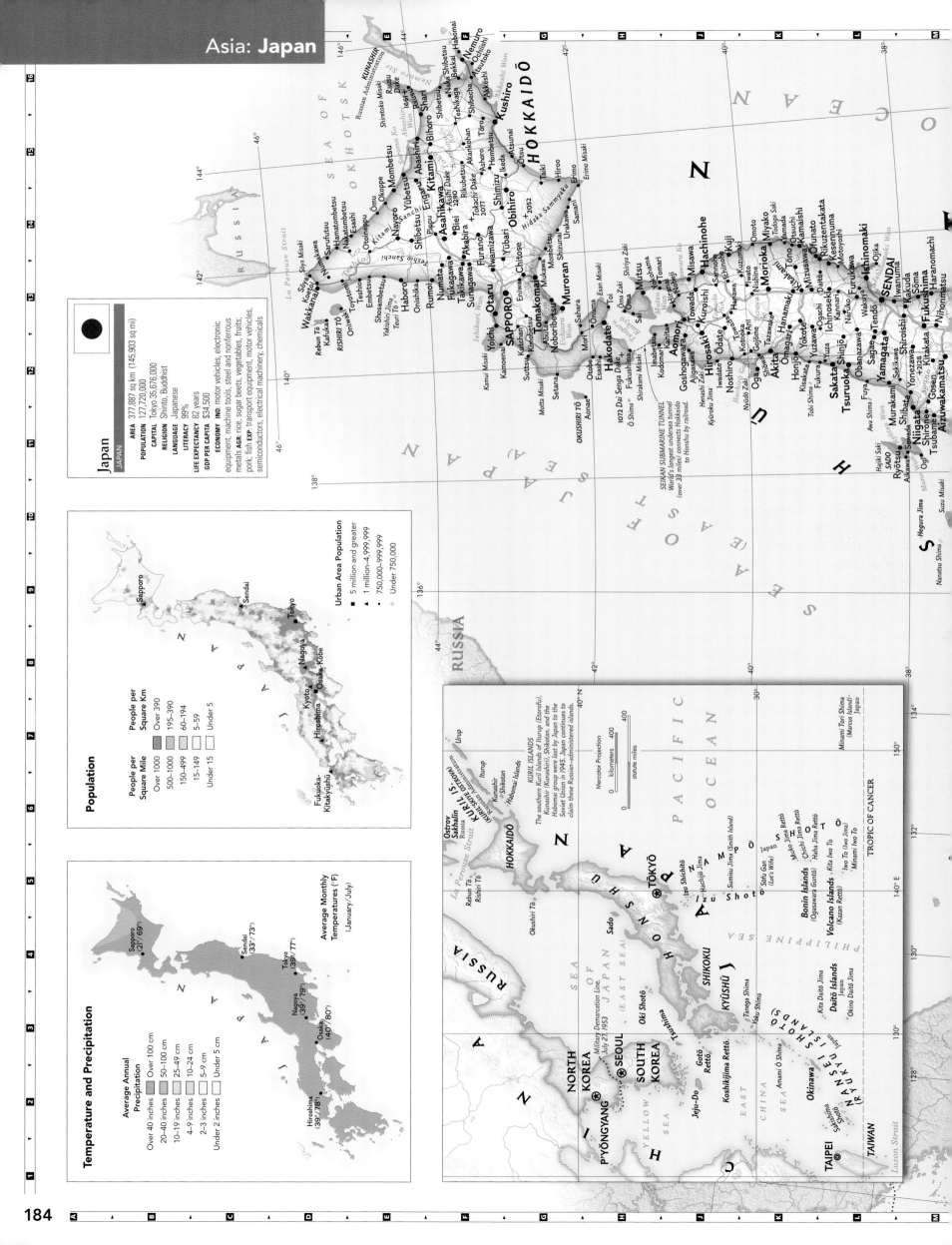

Japan

JAPAN

AREA 377,887 sq km (145,903 sq mi)
POPULATION 127,720,000
CAPITAL Tokyo 35,676,000
RELIGION Shinto, Buddhist
LANGUAGE Japanese
LITERACY 99%
LIFE EXPECTANCY 82 years
GDP PER CAPITA $34,500
ECONOMY IND: motor vehicles, electronic equipment, machine tools, steel and nonferrous metals **AGR:** rice, sugar beets, vegetables, fruits; pork; fish **EXP:** transport equipment, motor vehicles, semiconductors, electrical machinery, chemicals

Population

People per Square Mile / **People per Square Km**
- Over 1000 / Over 390
- 500–1000 / 195–390
- 150–499 / 60–194
- 15–149 / 5–59
- Under 15 / Under 5

Urban Area Population
- ■ 5 million and greater
- ▲ 1 million–4,999,999
- ● 750,000–999,999
- ○ Under 750,000

Temperature and Precipitation

Average Annual Precipitation
- Over 40 inches / Over 100 cm
- 20–40 inches / 50–100 cm
- 10–19 inches / 25–49 cm
- 4–9 inches / 10–24 cm
- 2–3 inches / 5–9 cm
- Under 2 inches / Under 5 cm

Average Monthly Temperatures (F) (January/July)

Sapporo (21°/69°)
Sendai (33°/73°)
Tokyo (39°/77°)
Nagoya (39°/79°)
Osaka (40°/80°)
Hiroshima (39°/78°)

SEIKAN SUBMARINE TUNNEL World's longest undersea tunnel (over 33 miles) connects Hokkaido to Honshu by railroad.

KURIL ISLANDS The southern Kuril Islands of Iturup (Etorofu), Kunashir (Kunashiri), Shikotan, and the Habomai group were lost by Japan to the Soviet Union in 1945. Japan continues to claim these Russian-administered islands.

Mercator Projection

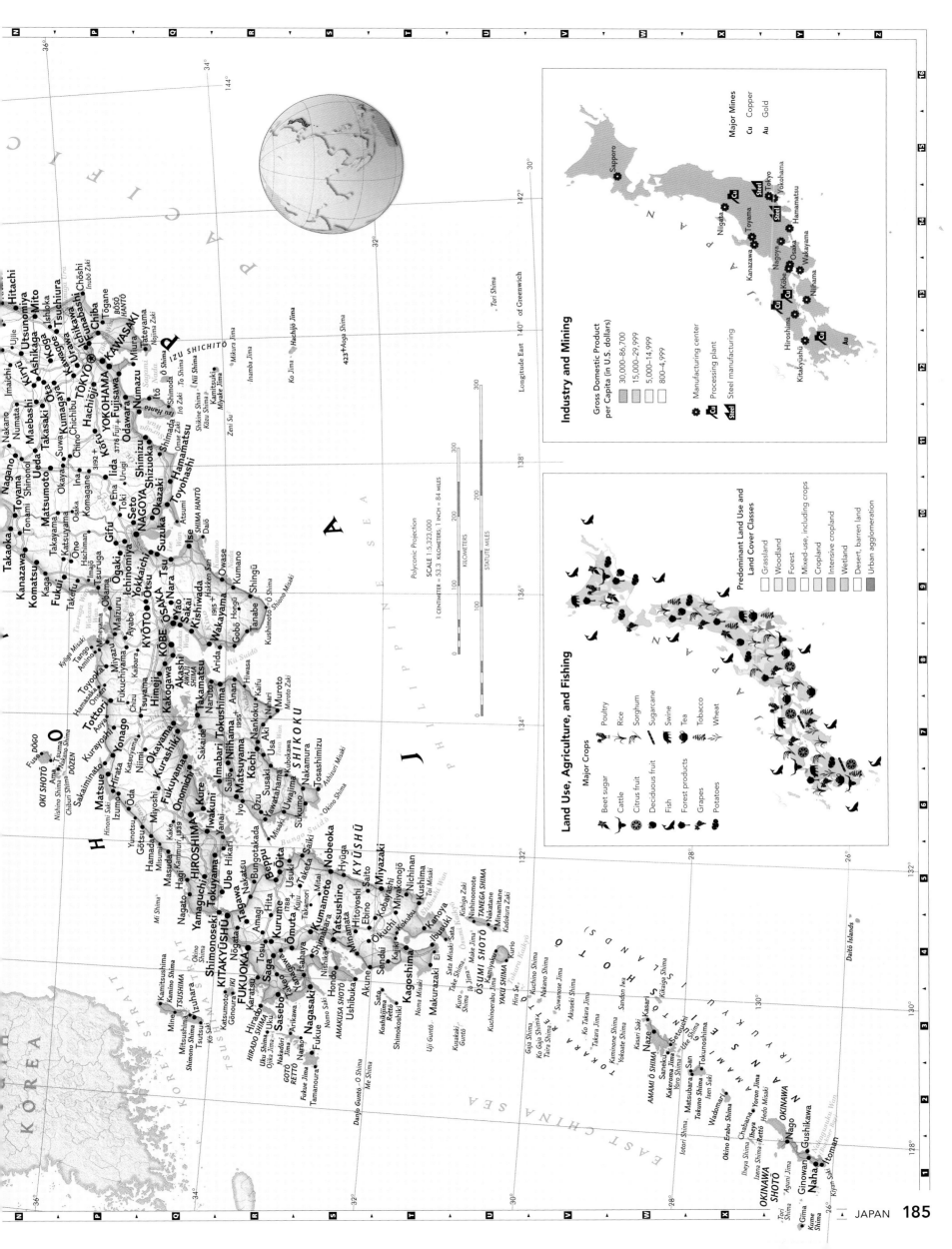

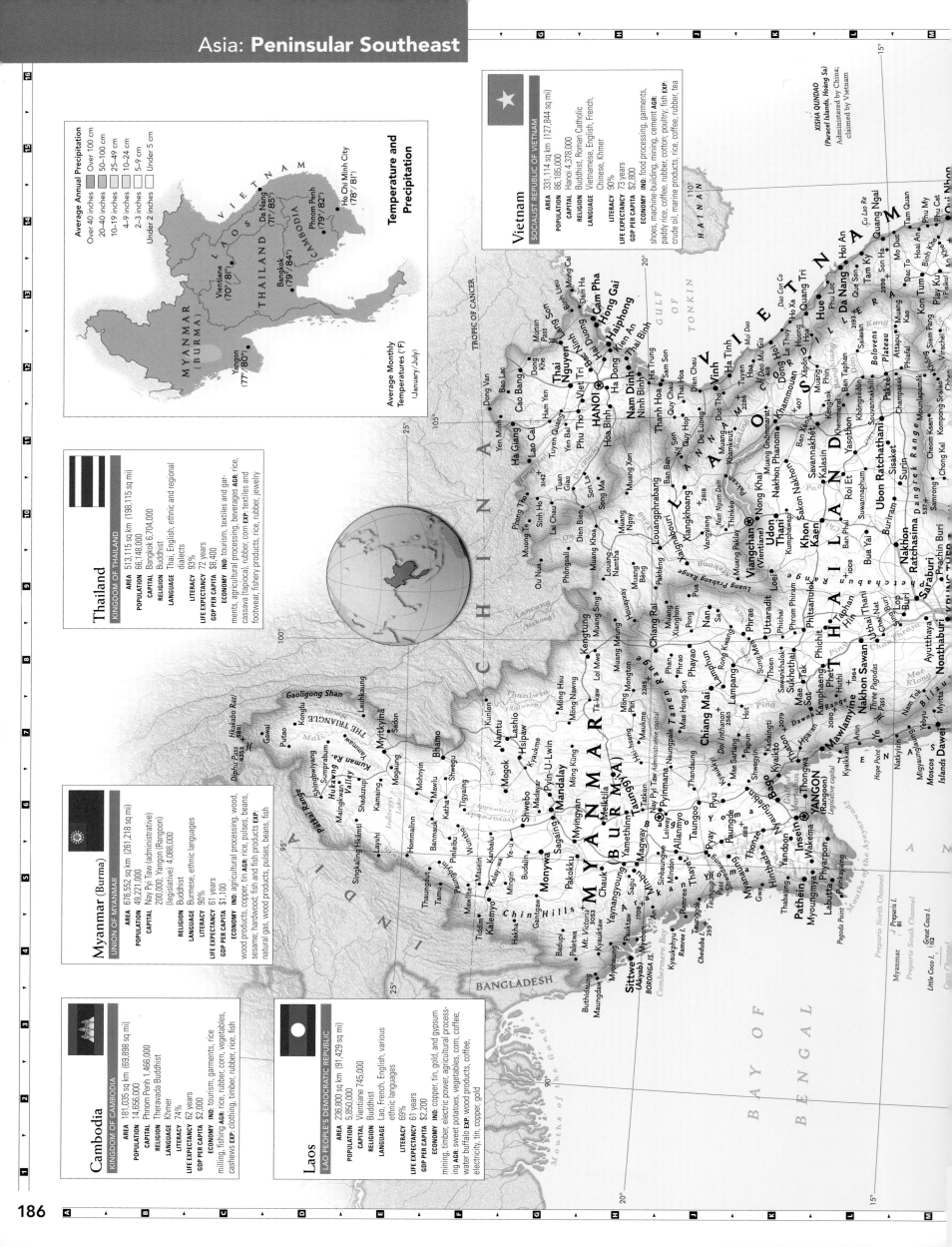

Vietnam

SOCIALIST REPUBLIC OF VIETNAM

AREA 331,114 sq km (127,844 sq mi)
POPULATION 86,185,000
CAPITAL Hanoi 4,378,000
RELIGION Buddhist, Roman Catholic
LANGUAGE Vietnamese, English, French, Chinese, Khmer
LITERACY 90%
LIFE EXPECTANCY 73 years
GDP PER CAPITA $2,800
ECONOMY IND: food processing, garments, shoes, machine-building, mining, cement **AGR:** paddy rice, coffee, rubber, cotton; poultry; fish **EXP:** crude oil, marine products, rice, coffee, rubber, tea

Thailand

KINGDOM OF THAILAND

AREA 513,115 sq km (198,115 sq mi)
POPULATION 66,148,000
CAPITAL Bangkok 6,704,000
RELIGION Buddhist
LANGUAGE Thai, English, ethnic and regional dialects
LITERACY 93%
LIFE EXPECTANCY 72 years
GDP PER CAPITA $8,400
ECONOMY IND: tourism, textiles and garments, agricultural processing, beverages **AGR:** rice, cassava (tapioca), rubber, corn **EXP:** textiles and footwear, fishery products, rice, rubber, jewelry

Myanmar (Burma)

UNION OF MYANMAR

AREA 676,552 sq km (261,218 sq mi)
POPULATION 49,221,000
CAPITAL Nay Pyi Taw (administrative) 200,000; Yangon (Rangoon) (legislative) 4,088,000
RELIGION Buddhist
LANGUAGE Burmese, ethnic languages
LITERACY 90%
LIFE EXPECTANCY 61 years
GDP PER CAPITA $1,100
ECONOMY IND: agricultural processing, wood, wood products, copper, tin **AGR:** rice, pulses, beans, sesame; hardwood; fish and fish products **EXP:** natural gas, wood products, pulses, beans, fish

Cambodia

KINGDOM OF CAMBODIA

AREA 181,035 sq km (69,898 sq mi)
POPULATION 14,656,000
CAPITAL Phnom Penh 1,466,000
RELIGION Theravada Buddhist
LANGUAGE Khmer
LITERACY 74%
LIFE EXPECTANCY 62 years
GDP PER CAPITA $2,000
ECONOMY IND: tourism, garments, rice milling, fishing **AGR:** rice, rubber, corn, vegetables, cashews **EXP:** clothing, timber, rubber, rice, fish

Laos

LAO PEOPLE'S DEMOCRATIC REPUBLIC

AREA 236,800 sq km (91,429 sq mi)
POPULATION 5,850,000
CAPITAL Vientiane 745,000
RELIGION Buddhist
LANGUAGE Lao, French, English, various ethnic languages
LITERACY 69%
LIFE EXPECTANCY 61 years
GDP PER CAPITA $2,200
ECONOMY IND: copper, tin, gold, and gypsum mining, timber, electric power, agricultural processing **AGR:** sweet potatoes, vegetables, corn, coffee; water buffalo **EXP:** wood products, coffee, electricity, tin, copper, gold

Average Annual Precipitation

Over 40 inches	Over 100 cm
20–40 inches	50–100 cm
10–19 inches	25–49 cm
4–9 inches	10–24 cm
2–3 inches	5–9 cm
Under 2 inches	Under 5 cm

Temperature and Precipitation

Average Monthly Temperatures (°F) (January/July)

Vientiane (70°/81°)
Yangon (77°/80°)
Bangkok (79°/84°)
Phnom Penh (79°/82°)
Da Nang (71°/85°)
Ho Chi Minh City (78°/81°)

XISHA QUNDAO (Paracel Islands, Hoang Sa) Administered by China; claimed by Vietnam

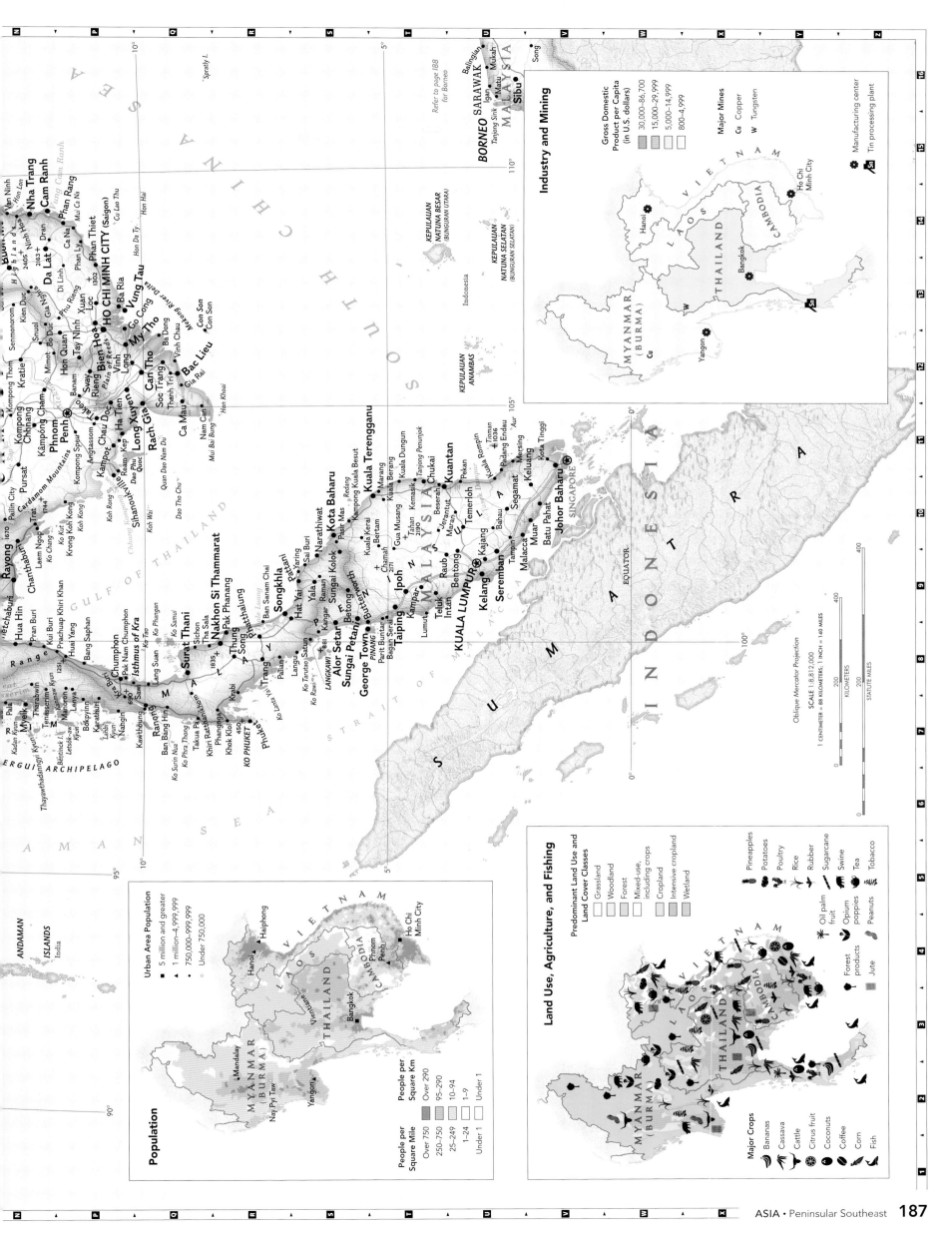

Industry and Mining

Gross Domestic Product per Capita (in U.S. dollars)
- 30,000–86,700
- 15,000–29,999
- 5,000–14,999
- 800–4,999

Major Mines
- Cu Copper
- W Tungsten

- Manufacturing center
- Tin processing plant

Population

Urban Area Population
- ■ 5 million and greater
- ■ 1 million–4,999,999
- ▲ 750,000–999,999
- ○ Under 750,000

People per Square Mile
- Over 750
- 250–750
- 25–249
- 1–24
- Under 1

People per Square Km
- Over 290
- 95–290
- 10–94
- 1–9
- Under 1

Land Use, Agriculture, and Fishing

Predominant Land Use and Land Cover Classes
- Grassland
- Woodland
- Forest
- Mixed-use, including crops
- Cropland
- Intensive cropland
- Wetland

Major Crops
- Bananas
- Cassava
- Cattle
- Citrus fruit
- Coconuts
- Coffee
- Corn
- Fish
- Forest products
- Jute
- Oil palm fruit
- Opium poppies
- Peanuts
- Pineapples
- Potatoes
- Poultry
- Rice
- Rubber
- Sugarcane
- Swine
- Tea
- Tobacco

SCALE 1:8,812,000
1 CENTIMETER = 88 KILOMETERS; 1 INCH = 140 MILES
Oblique Mercator Projection

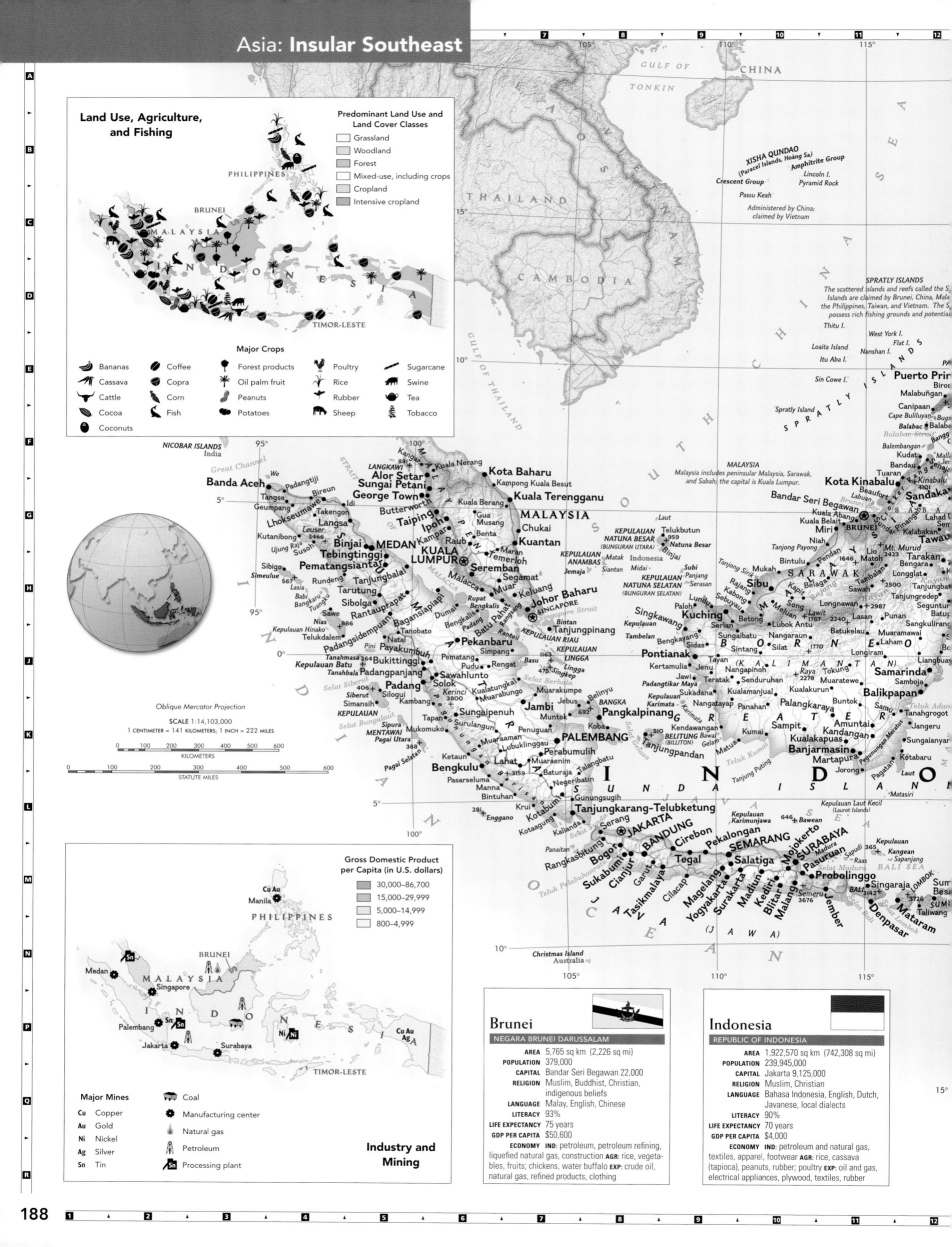

Land Use, Agriculture, and Fishing

Predominant Land Use and Land Cover Classes
- Grassland
- Woodland
- Forest
- Mixed-use, including crops
- Cropland
- Intensive cropland

Major Crops
- Bananas
- Cassava
- Cattle
- Cocoa
- Coconuts
- Coffee
- Copra
- Corn
- Fish
- Forest products
- Oil palm fruit
- Peanuts
- Potatoes
- Poultry
- Rice
- Rubber
- Sheep
- Swine
- Sugarcane
- Tea
- Tobacco

Oblique Mercator Projection

SCALE 1:14,103,000
1 CENTIMETER = 141 KILOMETERS; 1 INCH = 222 MILES

KILOMETERS
0 100 200 300 400 500 600

STATUTE MILES
0 100 200 300 400 500 600

Gross Domestic Product per Capita (in U.S. dollars)
- 30,000–86,700
- 15,000–29,999
- 5,000–14,999
- 800–4,999

Major Mines
- Cu Copper
- Au Gold
- Ni Nickel
- Ag Silver
- Sn Tin

- Coal
- Manufacturing center
- Natural gas
- Petroleum
- Sn Processing plant

Industry and Mining

Brunei
NEGARA BRUNEI DARUSSALAM
- **AREA** 5,765 sq km (2,226 sq mi)
- **POPULATION** 379,000
- **CAPITAL** Bandar Seri Begawan 22,000
- **RELIGION** Muslim, Buddhist, Christian, indigenous beliefs
- **LANGUAGE** Malay, English, Chinese
- **LITERACY** 93%
- **LIFE EXPECTANCY** 75 years
- **GDP PER CAPITA** $50,600
- **ECONOMY IND:** petroleum, petroleum refining, liquefied natural gas, construction **AGR:** rice, vegetables, fruits; chickens, water buffalo **EXP:** crude oil, natural gas, refined products, clothing

Indonesia
REPUBLIC OF INDONESIA
- **AREA** 1,922,570 sq km (742,308 sq mi)
- **POPULATION** 239,945,000
- **CAPITAL** Jakarta 9,125,000
- **RELIGION** Muslim, Christian
- **LANGUAGE** Bahasa Indonesia, English, Dutch, Javanese, local dialects
- **LITERACY** 90%
- **LIFE EXPECTANCY** 70 years
- **GDP PER CAPITA** $4,000
- **ECONOMY IND:** petroleum and natural gas, textiles, apparel, footwear **AGR:** rice, cassava (tapioca), peanuts, rubber; poultry **EXP:** oil and gas, electrical appliances, plywood, textiles, rubber

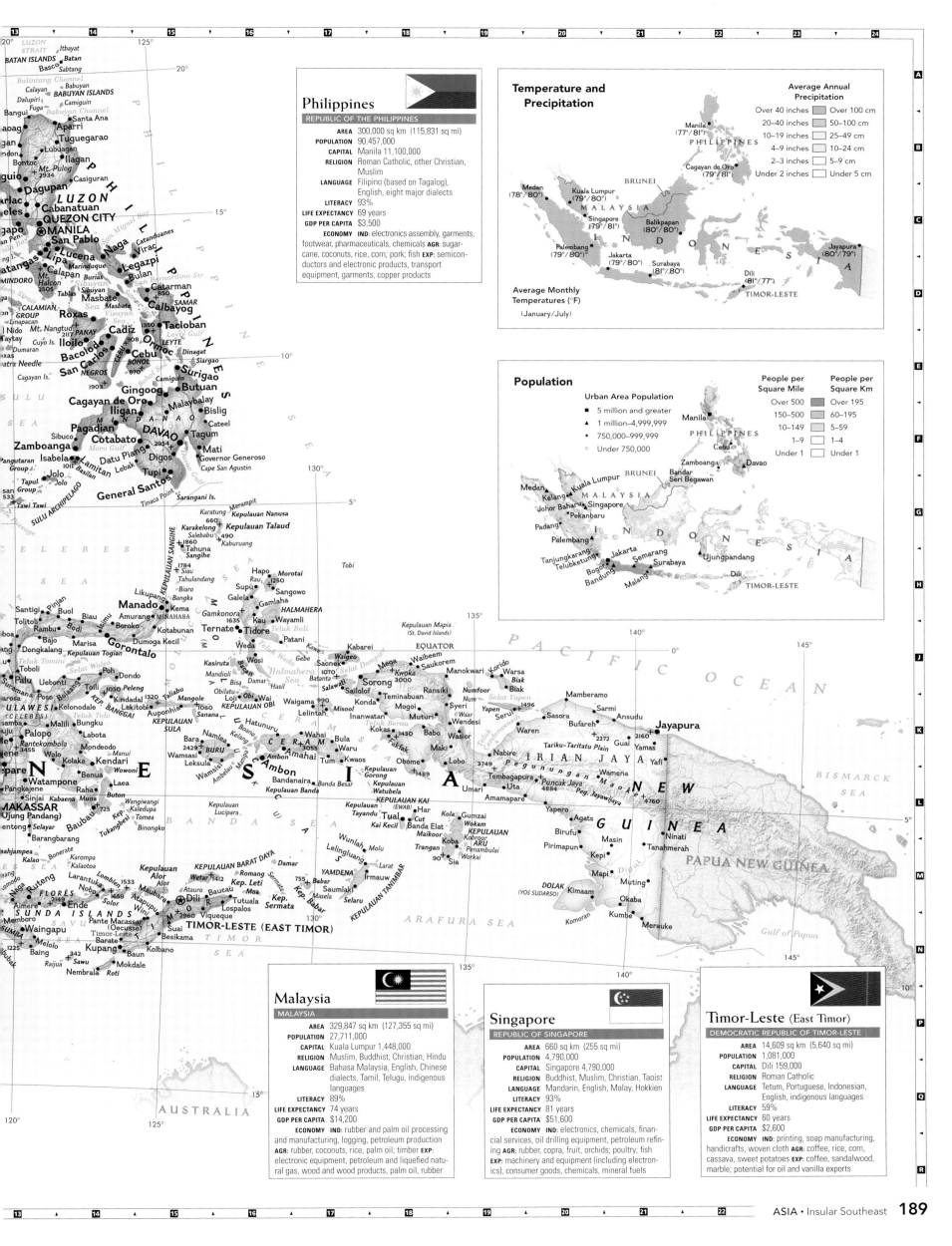

Philippines
REPUBLIC OF THE PHILIPPINES

AREA	300,000 sq km (115,831 sq mi)
POPULATION	90,457,000
CAPITAL	Manila 11,100,000
RELIGION	Roman Catholic, other Christian, Muslim
LANGUAGE	Filipino (based on Tagalog), English, eight major dialects
LITERACY	93%
LIFE EXPECTANCY	69 years
GDP PER CAPITA	$3,500
ECONOMY	**IND**: electronics assembly, garments, footwear, pharmaceuticals, chemicals **AGR**: sugarcane, coconuts, rice, corn; pork; fish **EXP**: semiconductors and electronic products, transport equipment, garments, copper products

Temperature and Precipitation

Average Monthly Temperatures (°F)
(January/July)

Average Annual Precipitation

Over 40 inches	Over 100 cm
20–40 inches	50–100 cm
10–19 inches	25–49 cm
4–9 inches	10–24 cm
2–3 inches	5–9 cm
Under 2 inches	Under 5 cm

Manila (77°/81°)
Medan (78°/80°)
Kuala Lumpur (79°/80°)
Cagayan de Oro (79°/81°)
Singapore (79°/81°)
Balikpapan (80°/80°)
Palembang (79°/80°)
Jayapura (80°/79°)
Jakarta (79°/80°)
Surabaya (81°/80°)
Dili (81°/77°)

Population

Urban Area Population
- ■ 5 million and greater
- ▲ 1 million–4,999,999
- ● 750,000–999,999
- ○ Under 750,000

People per Square Mile	People per Square Km
Over 500	Over 195
150–500	60–195
10–149	5–59
1–9	1–4
Under 1	Under 1

Malaysia
MALAYSIA

AREA	329,847 sq km (127,355 sq mi)
POPULATION	27,711,000
CAPITAL	Kuala Lumpur 1,448,000
RELIGION	Muslim, Buddhist, Christian, Hindu
LANGUAGE	Bahasa Malaysia, English, Chinese dialects, Tamil, Telugu, indigenous languages
LITERACY	89%
LIFE EXPECTANCY	74 years
GDP PER CAPITA	$14,200
ECONOMY	**IND**: rubber and palm oil processing and manufacturing, logging, petroleum production **AGR**: rubber, coconuts, rice, palm oil; timber **EXP**: electronic equipment, petroleum and liquefied natural gas, wood and wood products, palm oil, rubber

Singapore
REPUBLIC OF SINGAPORE

AREA	660 sq km (255 sq mi)
POPULATION	4,790,000
CAPITAL	Singapore 4,790,000
RELIGION	Buddhist, Muslim, Christian, Taoist
LANGUAGE	Mandarin, English, Malay, Hokkien
LITERACY	93%
LIFE EXPECTANCY	81 years
GDP PER CAPITA	$51,600
ECONOMY	**IND**: electronics, chemicals, financial services, oil drilling equipment, petroleum refining **AGR**: rubber, copra, fruit, orchids; poultry; fish **EXP**: machinery and equipment (including electronics), consumer goods, chemicals, mineral fuels

Timor-Leste (East Timor)
DEMOCRATIC REPUBLIC OF TIMOR-LESTE

AREA	14,609 sq km (5,640 sq mi)
POPULATION	1,081,000
CAPITAL	Dili 159,000
RELIGION	Roman Catholic
LANGUAGE	Tetum, Portuguese, Indonesian, English, indigenous languages
LITERACY	59%
LIFE EXPECTANCY	60 years
GDP PER CAPITA	$2,600
ECONOMY	**IND**: printing, soap manufacturing, handicrafts, woven cloth **AGR**: coffee, rice, corn, cassava, sweet potatoes **EXP**: coffee, sandalwood, marble; potential for oil and vanilla exports

Africa

A lone African elephant drinks at a water hole in Chobe National Park, Botswana, where protected enclaves help support some 120,000 of the continent's 400,000 to 660,000 elephants. In the late 1970s, there were 1.3 million elephants in Africa; poaching and habitat loss contributed to the decline.

Africa is often called the continent of beginnings. Fossil and bone records of the earliest humans go back more than 4 million years, and perhaps 1.8 million years ago our early upright ancestor, *Homo erectus*, departed Africa on the long journey that eventually peopled the Earth. It now seems likely that every person today comes from a lineage that leads back to an ancient African. Innumerable cave paintings and petroglyphs, from the Sahara to South Africa, provide clues to the beliefs and way of life of these age-old hominids.

Second largest continent after Asia, Africa accounts for a fifth of the world's land surface. Its unforgettable form, bulging to the west, lies surrounded by oceans and seas and can be considered underpopulated because only slightly more than 14 percent of the world's population lives here. Yet Africa's 53 countries now contain more than 967 million people, two-thirds living in the countryside, mostly in coastal regions, near lakes, and along river courses.

The mighty Sahara, largest hot desert in the world, covers more than a quarter of Africa's surface and divides the continent. Desert zones—Sahara, Kalahari, Namib—contrast with immense tropical rain forests. Watered regions of lakes and rivers lie beyond the Sahel, a vast semiarid zone of short grasses that spans the continent south of the Sahara. Most of Africa is made up of savanna—high, rolling, grassy plains.

These savannas have been home since earliest times to people often called Bantu, a reference to both social groupings and their languages. Other distinct physical types exist around the continent as well: BaMbuti (Pygmies), San (Bushmen), Nilo-Saharans, and Hamito-Semitics (Berbers and Cushites). Africa's astonishing number of spoken languages—1,600, more than any other continent—reflect the great diversity of ethnic and social groups.

Near the Equator, perpetual ice and snow crown Mount Kilimanjaro, the continent's highest point at 19,340 feet (5,895 m). The Nile, longest river in the world at 4,241 miles (6,825 km), originates in mountains south of the Equator and flows north-northeast before finally delivering its life-giving waters into the Mediterranean Sea.

Africa, blessed with wondrous deserts, rivers, grasslands, forests, and multihued earth, and possessing huge reserves of mineral wealth and biodiversity, waits expectantly for a prosperous future.

Many obstacles, however, complicate the way forward. African countries experience great gaps in wealth between city and country, such as between Lagos and Nigeria and Cairo and Egypt.

Nearly 50 African cities have populations numbering more than a million. Lack of clean water and the spread of diseases—malaria, tuberculosis, cholera, and AIDS among them—undermine people's health. In addition, war and huge concentrations of refugees displaced by fighting, persecution, and famine deter any chance of growth and stability. Africa today seems to stand between hope and hopelessness.

PHYSICAL Africa stretches an astounding 5,000 miles (8,047 km) from north to south and 4,600 miles (7,403 km) from east to west. The continent rises from generally narrow coastal strips to form a gigantic plateau, with portions over 2,000 feet (610 m) in height. It has limited harbors and a coastline with few bays and inlets. Though formed by a series of expansive uplands, Africa has few true mountain chains. Main ranges in the north are the Atlas in Morocco and the Ahaggar in the Sahara. To the southeast, the Ethiopian Highlands form a broad area of high topography. The massive volcanic peaks of Mount Kilimanjaro and Mount Kenya rise in dramatic isolation from surrounding plains. Between Uganda and Democratic Republic of the Congo, the Ruwenzori Range runs north to south and falls steeply in the west to the Rift Valley.

The East African Rift System is the continent's most dramatic geologic feature. This great rent actually begins in the Red Sea, then cuts southward to form the stunning landscape of lakes, volcanoes, and deep valleys that finally ends near the mouth of the Zambezi River. The Rift Valley, a region of active plate tectonics, marks the divide where East Africa is steadily being pulled away, eventually to become a mini-continent.

The Great Escarpment in southern Africa, a plateau edge that falls off to the coastal strip, is best represented by the stark, highly eroded Drakensberg Range, which reaches altitudes over 11,400 feet (3,482 m).

Madagascar, fourth largest island in the world, lies east of the main continent and is remarkable for its flora and fauna, including medicinal plants and lemur species.

Africa's great rivers include the Niger, Congo, and Zambezi, each regionally important for internal transport and fishing. The Nile drains 6 percent of the continent; its two main branches, the Blue Nile and the White Nile, meet at Khartoum, in Sudan.

Wildlife still abounds in eastern and southern Africa and supports ecotourism, but hundreds of plant and animal species live precariously close to extinction.

HISTORY After millions of years of human evolution, there arose along the Nile River the brilliant civilization of Egypt. Mastery of agriculture and the river's annual flooding led to a series of dynasties that lasted for some 3,000 years, creating an astounding legacy of tombs, statuary, pyramids, temples, and hieroglyphic writing.

The long-standing power of Carthage ruled the western Mediterranean, but was conquered by the Roman Empire in 146 B.C. Rome and Byzantium henceforth controlled all of North Africa's coastal strip until the Arab influx from the seventh century onward. The Arabs quickly took all of North Africa and spread their language and religion. Arabic and Islam have been unifying forces ever since. Trans-Sahara trade and contact converted many sub-Saharan people, such as the Hausa of Nigeria, to Islam.

Indigenous kingdoms have punctuated Africa's history. Finds from Great Zimbabwe, a massive fortress-city and inland empire that flourished from the 11th to 15th centuries, show contacts with places as far away as India and China.

Along the Niger River, regional empires rose and fell between A.D. 800 and 1600. Slaves, ivory, gold, and kola nuts, used for flavoring and medicine, formed the basis of trade. In the Niger Delta area, Yoruba, Ashanti, and Hausa states also had their periods of grandness. Longest lasting of all was Benin, a major African kingdom that survived from the 13th to 19th centuries.

The Swahili (literally, "coastal plain") culture arose from a mix of Arabs, local people, and others who from A.D. 900 onward spread to towns and cities of the east coast, along the Indian Ocean, from Somalia to Zanzibar. The Swahili language remains a major lingua franca in east, central, and southern Africa.

The magnificent Temple of Ramses II (circa 1279–1213 B.C.) at Abu Simbel is so revered that when the damming of the Nile at Aswan promised to submerge it, both it and the Temple of Nefertari (not shown) were meticulously dismantled and reassembled (1964–68) on higher ground 600 feet (184 m) to the west.

Colonialism's long period of domination, during which Portugal, Great Britain, France, Belgium, Germany, and Italy ruled the continent, spans from the mid-1500s to the mid-1900s. The Portuguese arrived first in search of riches and the sea route to India. In time, commerce and Christianity pushed Europe into Africa.

The terrible slave trade shipped millions of Africans to North and South America and Arab regions. European presence encouraged exploration to find the sources of Africa's main rivers and to fill in blank spots on the map.

In the late 19th century, Europe's powers embarked on a "scramble for Africa," which led to a partitioning of the entire continent by 1914. After the two World Wars colonialism weakened. Independence for some countries began in the 1950s and came to most in the 1960s, in power transfers ranging from peaceful (Ghana, Senegal) to bloody (Kenya, Algeria). Freedom arrived in Rhodesia, with the new name Zimbabwe, in 1980, and in Namibia in 1990. The end of white rule in South Africa culminated with the election of Nelson Mandela in 1994.

CULTURE Hunting, fishing, and gathering supported Africa's early humans. In time, agriculture led to permanent settlements and diversity in society, first along the Nile River and then in the south.

Village-based communities, resilient and lasting in their institutions, have formed the core of African life for thousands of years. With crop cultivation came domestication of animals—cattle, sheep, and goats. Ironworking reached sub-Saharan Africa from the north by about the fourth century B.C., allowing for new tools and weapons that accelerated change.

Kingdoms grew from the soil of village life. Kings and their courts resembled village elders in their roles as judges, mediators of disputes, and masters of trade. Early kingdoms in Mali, Ghana, and elsewhere conducted long-distance trade in gold, ivory, hides, jewels, feathers, and salt.

In some places, religious leaders became kings. Seen as divine, they assumed rights over land and cattle herds and in return took responsibility for the people's well-being.

Settled life allowed time and energy for arts, crafts, and other creative activities. In West Africa, artists, carvers, and bronze casters of the Ife (12th and 13th centuries) and Benin (16th and 17th centuries) kingdoms produced masterpieces in different mediums, culminating in terra-cotta heads and bronze statues and bas-reliefs of exquisite craftsmanship and naturalism. African art, especially sculpture, continues to hold a high place in world culture.

Rich traditions of oral narrative survive to preserve the history and collective memories of different tribes and groups. Bards known as griots tell tales and sing epic songs while accompanied by their instruments.

Traditional religion and ritual still have a powerful place in Africa, for health, wealth, good harvests, and to honor the forces of nature. The Dogon people retain a complex cosmology and perform a great ceremony every 60 years to mark the appearance of the star Sirius between two mountains.

Most major world religions are represented in Africa: Islam, Christianity, Judaism, even Hinduism. Islam predominates in the north, and south of the Sahara Christianity claims multitudes of followers—Islam and Christianity claim respectively 350 million and 400 million followers.

European languages and schooling, legacies of colonialism, have had lasting effects on modern Africa. Yet far from the cities one can still find blue-turbanned Tuareg wandering the Sahara, slender Masai on the savannas of East Africa, Pygmies in the rain forests, and San (Bushmen) adapted to the Kalahari Desert's harsh conditions. Color, exuberance, and diversity manage to shine through the clouds of trouble that beset the nations of Africa.

ECONOMY Africa ranks among the richest regions in the world in natural resources; it contains vast reserves of fossil fuels, precious metals, ores, and gems, including almost all of the world's chromium, much uranium, copper, tremendous underground gold reserves, and diamonds. West Africa exports major amounts of iron ore.

Yet Africa, the poorest continent, accounts for a mere one percent of world economic output. South Africa's economy alone nearly equals that of all other sub-Saharan countries combined.

With little history of refining and manufacturing (limited to parts of North and South Africa), small-scale agriculture dominates the activities of more than 60 percent of Africans: Main crops are corn, wheat, rice, yams, potatoes, and cassava. Economic life revolves around farmsteads and village markets. Important cash crops include cacao, coffee, tea, fruit, and palm and vegetable oils.

Even though food production is increasing, agriculture takes place on only 6 percent of Africa's land and fails to keep pace with population growth—six children is the average for every woman, and in many countries nearly half the people are under 15. Most countries rely on imported food and loans. A cycle of crushing debt repayment, unemployment, and instability repels much-needed foreign investment.

Tourism, while offering hope to numerous countries, mostly in north, east, and southern Africa, highlights the need for conservation and interdependence between humans and the varied ecosystems that support Africa's plants and wildlife. Stresses today include poaching, overgrazing, and deforestation.

The African Union (AU)—formerly the Organization of African Unity (OAU)—and numerous regional trading blocks try to encourage economic cooperation and political stability, essential for sustained growth. After decades of corruption, ruinous to many economies, Africans now realize that any hope for development lies with themselves and their leaders.

Africa: Physical and Political

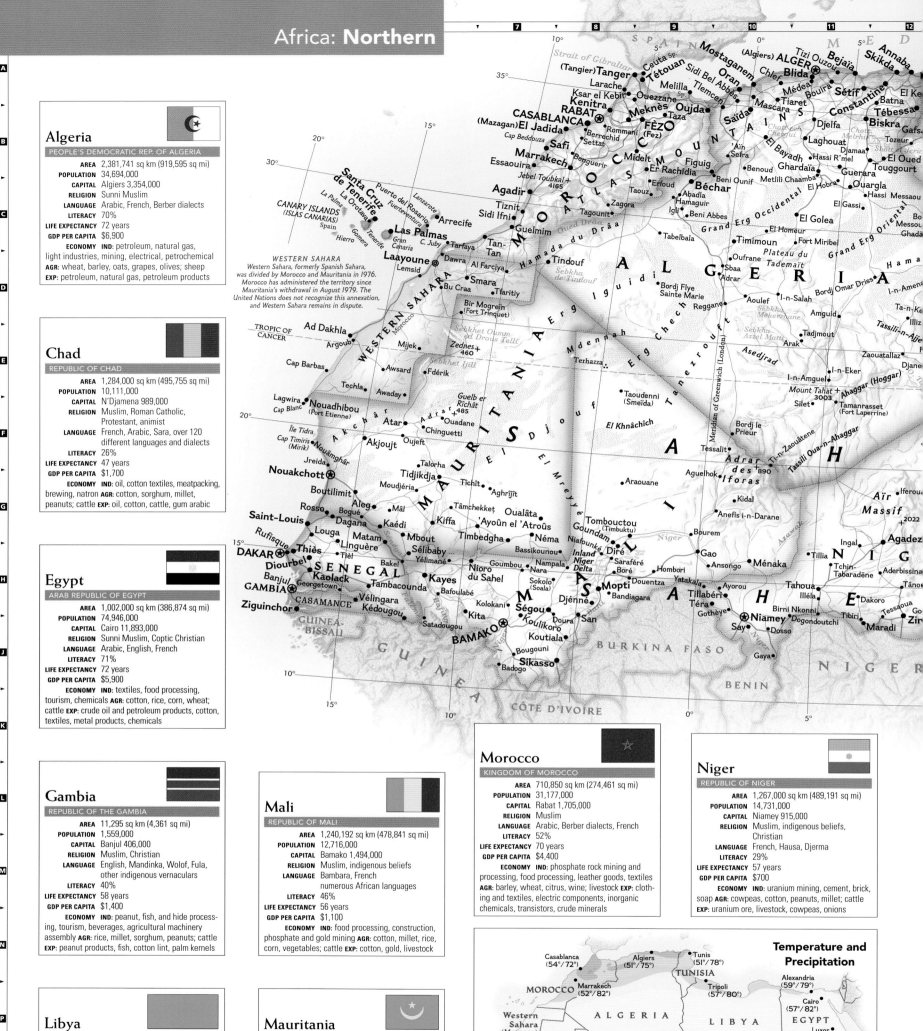

Algeria

PEOPLE'S DEMOCRATIC REP. OF ALGERIA

AREA	2,381,741 sq km (919,595 sq mi)
POPULATION	34,694,000
CAPITAL	Algiers 3,354,000
RELIGION	Sunni Muslim
LANGUAGE	Arabic, French, Berber dialects
LITERACY	70%
LIFE EXPECTANCY	72 years
GDP PER CAPITA	$6,900

ECONOMY IND: petroleum, natural gas, light industries, mining, electrical, petrochemical **AGR:** wheat, barley, oats, grapes, olives; sheep **EXP:** petroleum, natural gas, petroleum products

Chad

REPUBLIC OF CHAD

AREA	1,284,000 sq km (495,755 sq mi)
POPULATION	10,111,000
CAPITAL	N'Djamena 989,000
RELIGION	Muslim, Roman Catholic, Protestant, animist
LANGUAGE	French, Arabic, Sara, over 120 different languages and dialects
LITERACY	26%
LIFE EXPECTANCY	47 years
GDP PER CAPITA	$1,700

ECONOMY IND: oil, cotton textiles, meatpacking, brewing, natron **AGR:** cotton, sorghum, millet, peanuts; cattle **EXP:** oil, cotton, cattle, gum arabic

Egypt

ARAB REPUBLIC OF EGYPT

AREA	1,002,000 sq km (386,874 sq mi)
POPULATION	74,946,000
CAPITAL	Cairo 11,893,000
RELIGION	Sunni Muslim, Coptic Christian
LANGUAGE	Arabic, English, French
LITERACY	71%
LIFE EXPECTANCY	72 years
GDP PER CAPITA	$5,900

ECONOMY IND: textiles, food processing, tourism, chemicals **AGR:** cotton, rice, corn, wheat; cattle **EXP:** crude oil and petroleum products, cotton, textiles, metal products, chemicals

Gambia

REPUBLIC OF THE GAMBIA

AREA	11,295 sq km (4,361 sq mi)
POPULATION	1,559,000
CAPITAL	Banjul 406,000
RELIGION	Muslim, Christian
LANGUAGE	English, Mandinka, Wolof, Fula, other indigenous vernaculars
LITERACY	40%
LIFE EXPECTANCY	58 years
GDP PER CAPITA	$1,400

ECONOMY IND: peanut, fish, and hide processing, tourism, beverages, agricultural machinery assembly **AGR:** rice, millet, sorghum, peanuts; cattle **EXP:** peanut products, fish, cotton lint, palm kernels

Mali

REPUBLIC OF MALI

AREA	1,240,192 sq km (478,841 sq mi)
POPULATION	12,716,000
CAPITAL	Bamako 1,494,000
RELIGION	Muslim, indigenous beliefs
LANGUAGE	Bambara, French numerous African languages
LITERACY	46%
LIFE EXPECTANCY	56 years
GDP PER CAPITA	$1,100

ECONOMY IND: food processing, construction, phosphate and gold mining **AGR:** cotton, millet, rice, corn, vegetables; cattle **EXP:** cotton, gold, livestock

Morocco

KINGDOM OF MOROCCO

AREA	710,850 sq km (274,461 sq mi)
POPULATION	31,177,000
CAPITAL	Rabat 1,705,000
RELIGION	Muslim
LANGUAGE	Arabic, Berber dialects, French
LITERACY	52%
LIFE EXPECTANCY	70 years
GDP PER CAPITA	$4,400

ECONOMY IND: phosphate rock mining and processing, food processing, leather goods, textiles **AGR:** barley, wheat, citrus, wine; livestock **EXP:** clothing and textiles, electric components, inorganic chemicals, transistors, crude minerals

Niger

REPUBLIC OF NIGER

AREA	1,267,000 sq km (489,191 sq mi)
POPULATION	14,731,000
CAPITAL	Niamey 915,000
RELIGION	Muslim, indigenous beliefs, Christian
LANGUAGE	French, Hausa, Djerma
LITERACY	29%
LIFE EXPECTANCY	57 years
GDP PER CAPITA	$700

ECONOMY IND: uranium mining, cement, brick, soap **AGR:** cowpeas, cotton, peanuts, millet; cattle **EXP:** uranium ore, livestock, cowpeas, onions

Libya

GR. SOC. PEOPLE'S LIBYAN ARAB JAMAHIRIYA

AREA	1,759,540 sq km (679,362 sq mi)
POPULATION	6,283,000
CAPITAL	Tripoli 2,189,000
RELIGION	Sunni Muslim
LANGUAGE	Arabic, Italian, English
LITERACY	83%
LIFE EXPECTANCY	73 years
GDP PER CAPITA	$14,600

ECONOMY IND: petroleum, iron and steel, food processing, textiles, handicrafts **AGR:** wheat, barley, olives, dates; cattle **EXP:** crude oil, refined petroleum products, natural gas, chemicals

Mauritania

ISLAMIC REPUBLIC OF MAURITANIA

AREA	1,030,700 sq km (397,955 sq mi)
POPULATION	3,204,000
CAPITAL	Nouakchott 673,000
RELIGION	Muslim
LANGUAGE	Arabic, Pulaar, Soninke, Wolof, French, Hassaniya
LITERACY	51%
LIFE EXPECTANCY	60 years
GDP PER CAPITA	$2,100

ECONOMY IND: fish processing, mining of iron ore and gypsum **AGR:** dates, millet, sorghum, rice; cattle **EXP:** iron ore, fish and fish products, gold

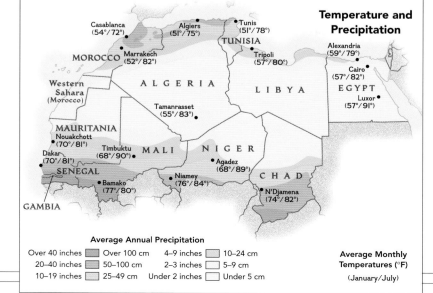

Temperature and Precipitation

Average Annual Precipitation

Over 40 inches	Over 100 cm	4–9 inches	10–24 cm
20–40 inches	50–100 cm	2–3 inches	5–9 cm
10–19 inches	25–49 cm	Under 2 inches	Under 5 cm

Average Monthly Temperatures (°F)

(January/July)

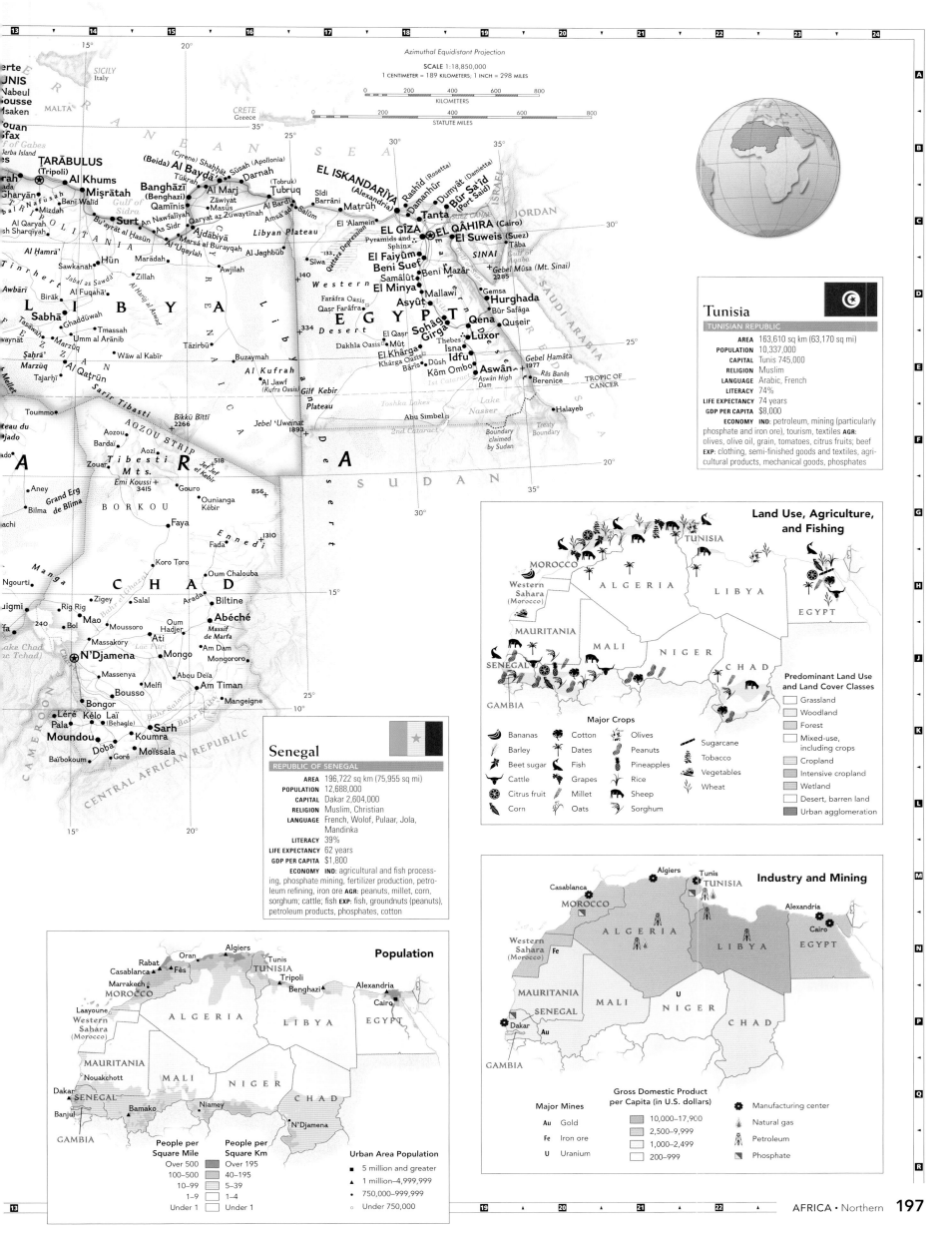

Azimuthal Equidistant Projection

SCALE 1:18,850,000
1 CENTIMETER = 189 KILOMETERS; 1 INCH = 298 MILES

Tunisia
TUNISIAN REPUBLIC
AREA 163,610 sq km (63,170 sq mi)
POPULATION 10,337,000
CAPITAL Tunis 745,000
RELIGION Muslim
LANGUAGE Arabic, French
LITERACY 74%
LIFE EXPECTANCY 74 years
GDP PER CAPITA $8,000
ECONOMY IND: petroleum, mining (particularly phosphate and iron ore), tourism, textiles AGR: olives, olive oil, grain, tomatoes, citrus fruits; beef EXP: clothing, semi-finished goods and textiles, agricultural products, mechanical goods, phosphates

Senegal
REPUBLIC OF SENEGAL
AREA 196,722 sq km (75,955 sq mi)
POPULATION 12,688,000
CAPITAL Dakar 2,604,000
RELIGION Muslim, Christian
LANGUAGE French, Wolof, Pulaar, Jola, Mandinka
LITERACY 39%
LIFE EXPECTANCY 62 years
GDP PER CAPITA $1,800
ECONOMY IND: agricultural and fish processing, phosphate mining, fertilizer production, petroleum refining, iron ore AGR: peanuts, millet, corn, sorghum; cattle; fish EXP: fish, groundnuts (peanuts), petroleum products, phosphates, cotton

Land Use, Agriculture, and Fishing

Major Crops

Bananas	Cotton	Olives
Barley	Dates	Peanuts
Beet sugar	Fish	Pineapples
Cattle	Grapes	Rice
Citrus fruit	Millet	Sheep
Corn	Oats	Sorghum

Sugarcane
Tobacco
Vegetables
Wheat

Predominant Land Use and Land Cover Classes

Grassland
Woodland
Forest
Mixed-use, including crops
Cropland
Intensive cropland
Wetland
Desert, barren land
Urban agglomeration

Population

People per Square Mile / **People per Square Km**

People per Square Mile	People per Square Km
Over 500	Over 195
100–500	40–195
10–99	5–39
1–9	1–4
Under 1	Under 1

Urban Area Population

- 5 million and greater
- 1 million–4,999,999
- 750,000–999,999
- Under 750,000

Industry and Mining

Major Mines

Au Gold
Fe Iron ore
U Uranium

Gross Domestic Product per Capita (in U.S. dollars)

10,000–17,900
2,500–9,999
1,000–2,499
200–999

Manufacturing center
Natural gas
Petroleum
Phosphate

Burundi
REPUBLIC OF BURUNDI

AREA	27,834 sq km (10,747 sq mi)
POPULATION	8,856,000
CAPITAL	Bujumbura 429,000
RELIGION	Roman Catholic, indigenous beliefs, Muslim, Protestant
LANGUAGE	Kirundi, French, Swahili
LITERACY	59%
LIFE EXPECTANCY	49 years
GDP PER CAPITA	$400

ECONOMY IND: light consumer goods such as blankets, shoes, soap; assembly of imported components, public works construction, food processing **AGR:** coffee, cotton, tea, corn, sorghum; beef, milk **EXP:** coffee, tea, sugar, cotton, hides

Central African Republic
CENTRAL AFRICAN REPUBLIC

AREA	622,984 sq km (240,535 sq mi)
POPULATION	4,435,000
CAPITAL	Bangui 672,000
RELIGION	indigenous beliefs, Protestant, Roman Catholic, Muslim
LANGUAGE	French, Sangho, tribal languages
LITERACY	49%
LIFE EXPECTANCY	43 years
GDP PER CAPITA	$800

ECONOMY IND: gold and diamond mining, logging, brewing, textiles, footwear **AGR:** cotton, coffee, tobacco, manioc (tapioca); timber **EXP:** diamonds, timber, cotton, coffee, tobacco

Congo,
Democratic Republic of the
DEMOCRATIC REPUBLIC OF THE CONGO

AREA	2,344,885 sq km (905,365 sq mi)
POPULATION	66,515,000
CAPITAL	Kinshasa 7,843,000
RELIGION	Roman Catholic, Protestant, Kimbanguist, Muslim
LANGUAGE	French, Lingala, Kingwana, Kikongo, Tshiluba
LITERACY	67%
LIFE EXPECTANCY	53 years
GDP PER CAPITA	$300

ECONOMY IND: mining (diamonds, gold, copper, cobalt), mineral processing, consumer products, cement **AGR:** coffee, sugar, palm oil, rubber; wood products **EXP:** diamonds, copper, crude oil, coffee

Djibouti
REPUBLIC OF DJIBOUTI

AREA	23,200 sq km (8,958 sq mi)
POPULATION	848,000
CAPITAL	Djibouti 583,000
RELIGION	Muslim, Christian
LANGUAGE	French, Arabic, Somali, Afar
LITERACY	68%
LIFE EXPECTANCY	54 years
GDP PER CAPITA	$2,400

ECONOMY IND: construction, agricultural processing, **AGR:** fruits, vegetables; goats, sheep, camels, animal hides **EXP:** reexports, hides and skins, coffee (in transit)

Eritrea
STATE OF ERITREA

AREA	121,144 sq km (46,774 sq mi)
POPULATION	5,006,000
CAPITAL	Asmara 601,000
RELIGION	Muslim, Coptic Christian, Roman Catholic, Protestant
LANGUAGE	Afar, Arabic, Tigre, Kunama, Tigrinya, other Cushitic languages
LITERACY	59%
LIFE EXPECTANCY	57 years
GDP PER CAPITA	$700

ECONOMY IND: food processing, beverages, clothing and textiles, light manufacturing, salt **AGR:** sorghum, lentils, vegetables, corn; livestock; fish **EXP:** livestock, sorghum, textiles, food

Ethiopia
FEDERAL DEMOCRATIC REP. OF ETHIOPIA

AREA	1,133,380 sq km (437,600 sq mi)
POPULATION	79,087,000
CAPITAL	Addis Ababa 3,100,000
RELIGION	Christian (Orthodox, Protestant), Muslim
LANGUAGE	Amharic, Oromigna, Tigrinya, Guaragigna, Somali
LITERACY	43%
LIFE EXPECTANCY	49 years
GDP PER CAPITA	$900

ECONOMY IND: food processing, beverages, textiles, leather, chemicals **AGR:** cereals, pulses, coffee, oilseeds; hides; fish **EXP:** coffee, qat, gold, leather products, live animals, oilseeds

Kenya
REPUBLIC OF KENYA

AREA	580,367 sq km (224,081 sq mi)
POPULATION	37,954,000
CAPITAL	Nairobi 3,010,000
RELIGION	Protestant, Roman Catholic, Muslim, indigenous beliefs
LANGUAGE	English, Kiswahili, many indigenous languages
LITERACY	85%
LIFE EXPECTANCY	53 years
GDP PER CAPITA	$1,700

ECONOMY IND: small-scale consumer goods (plastic, furniture), agricultural products, horticulture, oil refining, aluminum **AGR:** tea, coffee, corn, wheat; dairy products **EXP:** tea, horticultural products, coffee, petroleum products, fish, cement

Temperature and Precipitation

Average Monthly Temperatures (°F)
(January/July)

Average Annual Precipitation

Over 40 inches	Over 100 cm
20–40 inches	50–100 cm
10–19 inches	25–49 cm
4–9 inches	10–24 cm
2–3 inches	5–9 cm
Under 2 inches	Under 5 cm

Khartoum (73°/89°)
Asmara (57°/62°)
Djibouti (77°/95°)
Addis Ababa (61°/60°)
Bangui (78°/77°)
Kisangani (77°/75°)
Kampala (72°/68°)
Mogadishu (80°/79°)
Nairobi (67°/62°)
Bujumbura (74°/73°)
Kinshasa (77°/71°)
Dar es Salaam (81°/74°)
Lubumbashi (69°/64°)

SUDAN
ERITREA
DJIBOUTI
CENTRAL AFRICAN REPUBLIC
ETHIOPIA
SOMALIA
UGANDA
KENYA
RWANDA
DEM. REPUBLIC OF THE CONGO
BURUNDI
TANZANIA

Azimuthal Equidistant Projection
SCALE 1:18,454,000
1 CENTIMETER = 185 KILOMETERS; 1 INCH = 291 MILES

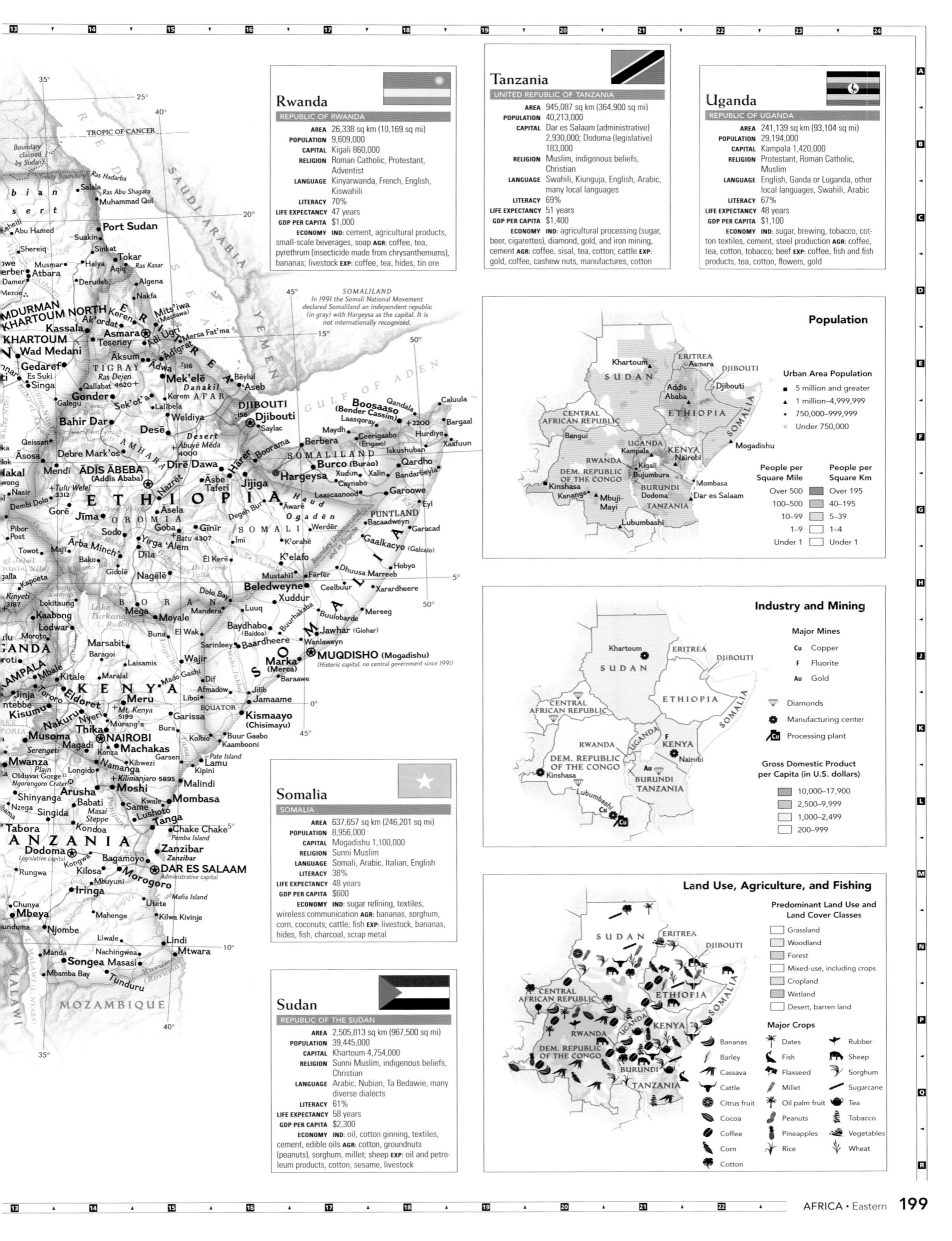

Rwanda
REPUBLIC OF RWANDA
AREA 26,338 sq km (10,169 sq mi)
POPULATION 9,609,000
CAPITAL Kigali 860,000
RELIGION Roman Catholic, Protestant, Adventist
LANGUAGE Kinyarwanda, French, English, Kiswahili
LITERACY 70%
LIFE EXPECTANCY 47 years
GDP PER CAPITA $1,000
ECONOMY IND: cement, agricultural products, small-scale beverages, soap **AGR:** coffee, tea, pyrethrum (insecticide made from chrysanthemums), bananas; livestock **EXP:** coffee, tea, hides, tin ore

Tanzania
UNITED REPUBLIC OF TANZANIA
AREA 945,087 sq km (364,900 sq mi)
POPULATION 40,213,000
CAPITAL Dar es Salaam (administrative) 2,930,000; Dodoma (legislative) 183,000
RELIGION Muslim, indigenous beliefs, Christian
LANGUAGE Swahili, Kiunguja, English, Arabic, many local languages
LITERACY 69%
LIFE EXPECTANCY 51 years
GDP PER CAPITA $1,400
ECONOMY IND: agricultural processing (sugar, beer, cigarettes), diamond, gold, and iron mining, cement **AGR:** coffee, sisal, tea, cotton; cattle **EXP:** gold, coffee, cashew nuts, manufactures, cotton

Uganda
REPUBLIC OF UGANDA
AREA 241,139 sq km (93,104 sq mi)
POPULATION 29,194,000
CAPITAL Kampala 1,420,000
RELIGION Protestant, Roman Catholic, Muslim
LANGUAGE English, Ganda or Luganda, other local languages, Swahili, Arabic
LITERACY 67%
LIFE EXPECTANCY 48 years
GDP PER CAPITA $1,100
ECONOMY IND: sugar, brewing, tobacco, cotton textiles, cement, steel production **AGR:** coffee, tea, cotton, tobacco; beef **EXP:** coffee, fish and fish products, tea, cotton, flowers, gold

SOMALILAND
In 1991 the Somali National Movement declared Somaliland an independent republic (in gray) with Hargeysa as the capital. It is not internationally recognized.

Somalia
SOMALIA
AREA 637,657 sq km (246,201 sq mi)
POPULATION 8,956,000
CAPITAL Mogadishu 1,100,000
RELIGION Sunni Muslim
LANGUAGE Somali, Arabic, Italian, English
LITERACY 38%
LIFE EXPECTANCY 48 years
GDP PER CAPITA $600
ECONOMY IND: sugar refining, textiles, wireless communication **AGR:** bananas, sorghum, corn, coconuts; cattle; fish **EXP:** livestock, bananas, hides, fish, charcoal, scrap metal

Sudan
REPUBLIC OF THE SUDAN
AREA 2,505,813 sq km (967,500 sq mi)
POPULATION 39,445,000
CAPITAL Khartoum 4,754,000
RELIGION Sunni Muslim, indigenous beliefs, Christian
LANGUAGE Arabic, Nubian, Ta Bedawie, many diverse dialects
LITERACY 61%
LIFE EXPECTANCY 58 years
GDP PER CAPITA $2,300
ECONOMY IND: oil, cotton ginning, textiles, cement, edible oils **AGR:** cotton, groundnuts (peanuts), sorghum, millet; sheep **EXP:** oil and petroleum products, cotton, sesame, livestock

Population
Urban Area Population
- 5 million and greater
- 1 million–4,999,999
- 750,000–999,999
- Under 750,000

People per Square Mile	People per Square Km
Over 500	Over 195
100–500	40–195
10–99	5–39
1–9	1–4
Under 1	Under 1

Industry and Mining
Major Mines
Cu Copper
F Fluorite
Au Gold

Diamonds
Manufacturing center
Cu Processing plant

Gross Domestic Product per Capita (in U.S. dollars)
- 10,000–17,900
- 2,500–9,999
- 1,000–2,499
- 200–999

Land Use, Agriculture, and Fishing
Predominant Land Use and Land Cover Classes
- Grassland
- Woodland
- Forest
- Mixed-use, including crops
- Cropland
- Wetland
- Desert, barren land

Major Crops
Bananas	Dates	Rubber
Barley	Fish	Sheep
Cassava	Flaxseed	Sorghum
Cattle	Millet	Sugarcane
Citrus fruit	Oil palm fruit	Tea
Cocoa	Peanuts	Tobacco
Coffee	Pineapples	Vegetables
Corn	Rice	Wheat
Cotton		

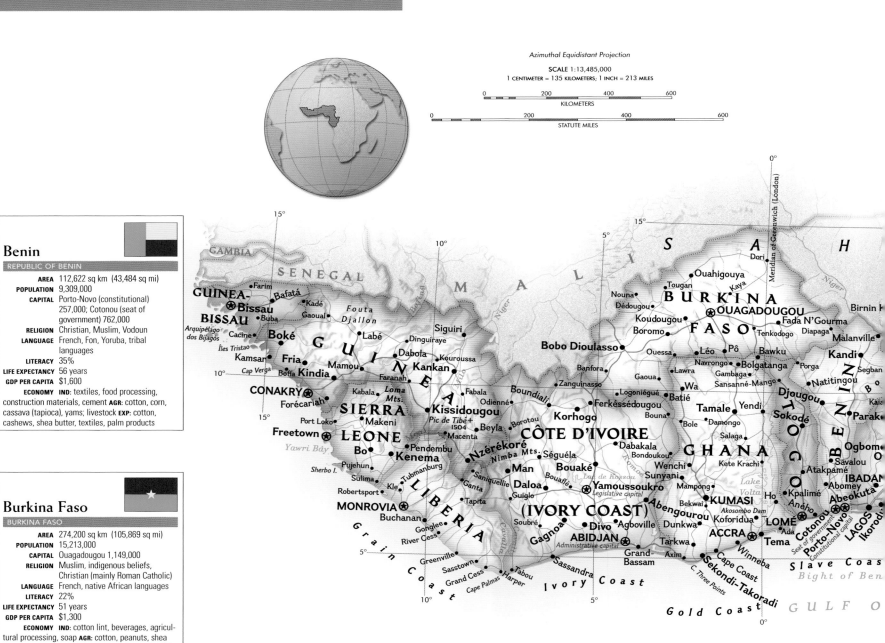

Azimuthal Equidistant Projection
SCALE 1:13,485,000
1 CENTIMETER = 135 KILOMETERS; 1 INCH = 213 MILES

KILOMETERS

STATUTE MILES

Benin
REPUBLIC OF BENIN

AREA 112,622 sq km (43,484 sq mi)
POPULATION 9,309,000
CAPITAL Porto-Novo (constitutional) 257,000; Cotonou (seat of government) 762,000
RELIGION Christian, Muslim, Vodoun
LANGUAGE French, Fon, Yoruba, tribal languages
LITERACY 35%
LIFE EXPECTANCY 56 years
GDP PER CAPITA $1,600
ECONOMY **IND**: textiles, food processing, construction materials, cement **AGR**: cotton, corn, cassava (tapioca), yams; livestock **EXP**: cotton, cashews, shea butter, textiles, palm products

Burkina Faso
BURKINA FASO

AREA 274,200 sq km (105,869 sq mi)
POPULATION 15,213,000
CAPITAL Ouagadougou 1,149,000
RELIGION Muslim, indigenous beliefs, Christian (mainly Roman Catholic)
LANGUAGE French, native African languages
LITERACY 22%
LIFE EXPECTANCY 51 years
GDP PER CAPITA $1,300
ECONOMY **IND**: cotton lint, beverages, agricultural processing, soap **AGR**: cotton, peanuts, shea nuts, sesame; livestock **EXP**: cotton, livestock, gold

Cameroon
REPUBLIC OF CAMEROON

AREA 475,442 sq km (183,569 sq mi)
POPULATION 18,468,000
CAPITAL Yaoundé 1,611,000
RELIGION indigenous beliefs, Christian, Muslim
LANGUAGE 24 major African language groups, English, French
LITERACY 68%
LIFE EXPECTANCY 52 years
GDP PER CAPITA $2,200
ECONOMY **IND**: petroleum production and refining, aluminum production, food processing, light consumer goods **AGR**: coffee, cocoa, cotton, rubber; livestock; timber **EXP**: crude oil and petroleum products, lumber, cocoa beans, aluminum

Côte d'Ivoire (Ivory Coast)
REPUBLIC OF CÔTE D'IVOIRE

AREA 322,462 sq km (124,503 sq mi)
POPULATION 20,677,000
CAPITAL Abidjan (administrative) 3,802,000; Yamoussoukro (legislative) 668,000
RELIGION Muslim, Christian, indigenous beliefs
LANGUAGE French, 60 native dialects with Dioula the most widely spoken
LITERACY 49%
LIFE EXPECTANCY 52 years
GDP PER CAPITA $1,800
ECONOMY **IND**: foodstuffs, beverages, wood products, oil refining, truck and bus assembly **AGR**: coffee, cocoa beans, bananas, palm kernels; timber **EXP**: cocoa, coffee, timber, petroleum, cotton

Gabon
GABONESE REPUBLIC

AREA 267,667 sq km (103,347 sq mi)
POPULATION 1,350,000
CAPITAL Libreville 576,000
RELIGION Christian, animist
LANGUAGE French, Fang, Myene, Nzebi, Bapounou/Eschira, Bandjabi
LITERACY 63%
LIFE EXPECTANCY 57 years
GDP PER CAPITA $14,700
ECONOMY **IND**: petroleum extraction and refining, manganese, gold, chemicals, ship repair **AGR**: cocoa, coffee, sugar, palm oil; cattle; okoume (a tropical softwood); fish **EXP**: crude oil, timber, manganese, uranium

Guinea
REPUBLIC OF GUINEA

AREA 245,857 sq km (94,926 sq mi)
POPULATION 10,302,000
CAPITAL Conakry 1,494,000
RELIGION Muslim, Christian, indigenous beliefs
LANGUAGE French, ethnic languages
LITERACY 30%
LIFE EXPECTANCY 54 years
GDP PER CAPITA $1,000
ECONOMY **IND**: bauxite, gold, diamonds, iron, alumina refining, light manufacturing **AGR**: rice, coffee, pineapples, palm kernels; cattle; timber **EXP**: bauxite, alumina, gold, diamonds, coffee, fish

Congo
REPUBLIC OF THE CONGO

AREA 342,000 sq km (132,047 sq mi)
POPULATION 3,847,000
CAPITAL Brazzaville 1,355,000
RELIGION Christian, animist
LANGUAGE French, Lingala, Monokutuba, local languages
LITERACY 84%
LIFE EXPECTANCY 53 years
GDP PER CAPITA $4,000
ECONOMY **IND**: petroleum extraction, cement, lumber, brewing **AGR**: cassava (tapioca), sugar, rice, corn; forest products **EXP**: petroleum, lumber, plywood, sugar, cocoa

Equatorial Guinea
REPUBLIC OF EQUATORIAL GUINEA

AREA 28,051 sq km (10,831 sq mi)
POPULATION 617,000
CAPITAL Malabo 96,000
RELIGION Christian (predominantly Roman Catholic), pagan practices
LANGUAGE Spanish, French, Fang, Bubi
LITERACY 87%
LIFE EXPECTANCY 59 years
GDP PER CAPITA $17,400
ECONOMY **IND**: petroleum, fishing, sawmilling, natural gas **AGR**: coffee, cocoa, rice, yams; livestock; timber **EXP**: petroleum, methanol, timber, cocoa

Ghana
REPUBLIC OF GHANA

AREA 238,537 sq km (92,100 sq mi)
POPULATION 23,947,000
CAPITAL Accra 2,121,000
RELIGION Christian, Muslim, traditional beliefs
LANGUAGE Asante, Ewe, Fante, other African languages, English
LITERACY 58%
LIFE EXPECTANCY 59 years
GDP PER CAPITA $1,500
ECONOMY **IND**: mining, lumbering, light manufacturing, aluminum smelting, food processing **AGR**: cocoa, rice, cassava (tapioca), peanuts; timber **EXP**: gold, cocoa, timber, tuna, bauxite, aluminum

Guinea-Bissau
REPUBLIC OF GUINEA-BISSAU

AREA 36,125 sq km (13,948 sq mi)
POPULATION 1,746,000
CAPITAL Bissau 330,000
RELIGION Muslim, indigenous beliefs, Christian
LANGUAGE Portuguese, Crioulo, African languages
LITERACY 42%
LIFE EXPECTANCY 45 years
GDP PER CAPITA $500
ECONOMY **IND**: agricultural products processing, beer, soft drinks **AGR**: rice, corn, beans, cassava (tapioca); timber; fish **EXP**: cashew nuts, shrimp, peanuts, palm kernels, sawn lumber

Liberia

REPUBLIC OF LIBERIA

AREA	111,370 sq km (43,000 sq mi)
POPULATION	3,942,000
CAPITAL	Monrovia 1,041,000
RELIGION	Christian, indigenous beliefs, Muslim
LANGUAGE	English, some 20 ethnic group languages
LITERACY	58%
LIFE EXPECTANCY	46 years
GDP PER CAPITA	$400
ECONOMY	**IND:** rubber processing, palm oil processing, timber, diamonds **AGR:** rubber, coffee, cocoa, rice; sheep; timber **EXP:** rubber, timber, iron, diamonds, cocoa, coffee

Sierra Leone

REPUBLIC OF SIERRA LEONE

AREA	71,740 sq km (27,699 sq mi)
POPULATION	5,450,000
CAPITAL	Freetown 827,000
RELIGION	Muslim, indigenous beliefs, Christian
LANGUAGE	English, Mende, Temne, Krio
LITERACY	35%
LIFE EXPECTANCY	48 years
GDP PER CAPITA	$700
ECONOMY	**IND:** diamond mining, small-scale manufacturing (beverages, textiles, cigarettes), petroleum refining, small ship repair **AGR:** rice, coffee, cocoa, palm kernels; poultry; fish **EXP:** diamonds, rutile, cocoa, coffee, fish

Nigeria

FEDERAL REPUBLIC OF NIGERIA

AREA	923,768 sq km (356,669 sq mi)
POPULATION	148,071,000
CAPITAL	Abuja 1,576,000
RELIGION	Muslim, Christian, indigenous beliefs
LANGUAGE	English, Hausa, Yoruba, Igbo (Ibo), Fulani
LITERACY	68%
LIFE EXPECTANCY	47 years
GDP PER CAPITA	$2,100
ECONOMY	**IND:** crude oil, coal, tin, palm oil, peanuts, hides and skins, textiles **AGR:** cocoa, peanuts, palm oil, corn; cattle; timber; fish **EXP:** petroleum and petroleum products, cocoa, rubber

Togo

TOGOLESE REPUBLIC

AREA	56,785 sq km (21,925 sq mi)
POPULATION	6,761,000
CAPITAL	Lomé 1,452,000
RELIGION	indigenous beliefs, Christian, Muslim
LANGUAGE	French, Ewe, Mina, Kabye, Dagomba
LITERACY	61%
LIFE EXPECTANCY	58 years
GDP PER CAPITA	$800
ECONOMY	**IND:** phosphate mining, agricultural processing, cement, handicrafts, textiles **AGR:** coffee, cocoa, cotton, yams; livestock; fish **EXP:** reexports, cotton, phosphates, coffee, cocoa

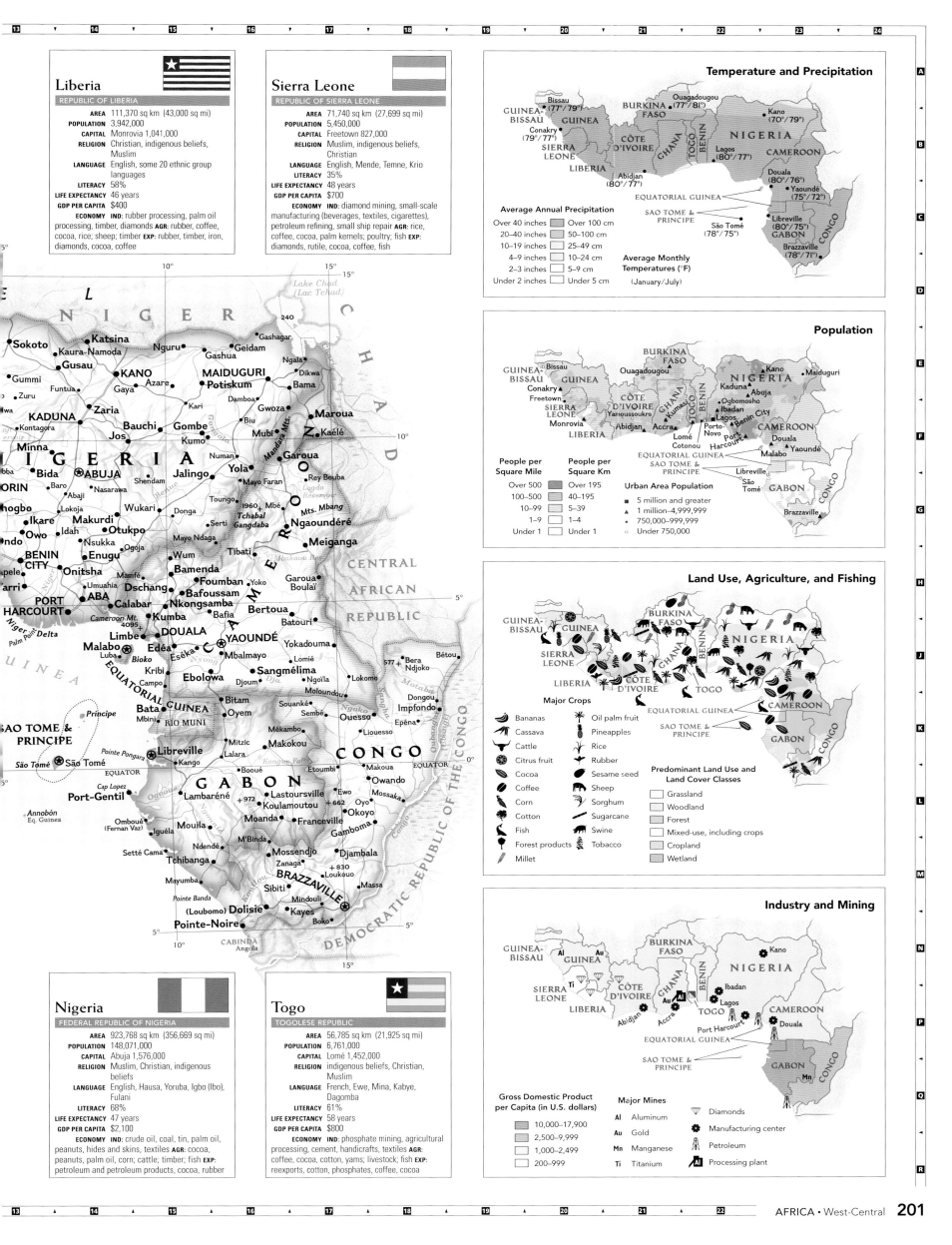

Temperature and Precipitation

Average Annual Precipitation

Over 40 inches	Over 100 cm
20–40 inches	50–100 cm
10–19 inches	25–49 cm
4–9 inches	10–24 cm
2–3 inches	5–9 cm
Under 2 inches	Under 5 cm

Average Monthly Temperatures (°F)
(January/July)

Population

People per Square Mile	People per Square Km
Over 500	Over 195
100–500	40–195
10–99	5–39
1–9	1–4
Under 1	Under 1

Urban Area Population
- ■ 5 million and greater
- ▲ 1 million–4,999,999
- ● 750,000–999,999
- ○ Under 750,000

Land Use, Agriculture, and Fishing

Major Crops

- Bananas
- Cassava
- Cattle
- Citrus fruit
- Cocoa
- Coffee
- Corn
- Cotton
- Fish
- Forest products
- Millet
- Oil palm fruit
- Pineapples
- Rice
- Rubber
- Sesame seed
- Sheep
- Sorghum
- Sugarcane
- Swine
- Tobacco

Predominant Land Use and Land Cover Classes

- Grassland
- Woodland
- Forest
- Mixed-use, including crops
- Cropland
- Wetland

Industry and Mining

Gross Domestic Product per Capita (in U.S. dollars)

10,000–17,900	
2,500–9,999	
1,000–2,499	
200–999	

Major Mines

- Al Aluminum
- Au Gold
- Mn Manganese
- Ti Titanium
- Diamonds
- Manufacturing center
- Petroleum
- Processing plant

Angola
REPUBLIC OF ANGOLA
AREA	1,246,700 sq km (481,354 sq mi)
POPULATION	16,752,000
CAPITAL	Luanda 4,000,000
RELIGION	indigenous beliefs, Roman Catholic, Protestant
LANGUAGE	Portuguese, Bantu and other African languages
LITERACY	67%
LIFE EXPECTANCY	43 years
GDP PER CAPITA	$6,400

ECONOMY IND: petroleum, diamonds, iron ore, phosphates **AGR:** bananas, sugarcane, coffee, sisal; livestock; forest products; fish **EXP:** crude oil, diamonds, refined petroleum products, gas

Botswana
REPUBLIC OF BOTSWANA
AREA	581,730 sq km (224,607 sq mi)
POPULATION	1,842,000
CAPITAL	Gaborone 224,000
RELIGION	Christian, Badimo
LANGUAGE	Setswana, Kalanga
LITERACY	81%
LIFE EXPECTANCY	49 years
GDP PER CAPITA	$17,900

ECONOMY IND: diamonds, copper, nickel, salt, soda ash, livestock processing, textiles **AGR:** livestock, sorghum, maize, millet, beans **EXP:** diamonds, copper, nickel, soda ash, meat, textiles

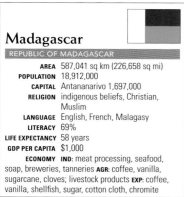

Lesotho
KINGDOM OF LESOTHO
AREA	30,355 sq km (11,720 sq mi)
POPULATION	1,801,000
CAPITAL	Maseru 210,000
RELIGION	Christian, indigenous beliefs
LANGUAGE	Sesotho, English, Zulu, Xhosa
LITERACY	85%
LIFE EXPECTANCY	36 years
GDP PER CAPITA	$1,400

ECONOMY IND: food, beverages, textiles, apparel assembly, handicrafts, construction, tourism **AGR:** corn, wheat, pulses, sorghum; livestock **EXP:** clothing, footwear, road vehicles, wool and mohair, food and live animals

Madagascar
REPUBLIC OF MADAGASCAR
AREA	587,041 sq km (226,658 sq mi)
POPULATION	18,912,000
CAPITAL	Antananarivo 1,697,000
RELIGION	indigenous beliefs, Christian, Muslim
LANGUAGE	English, French, Malagasy
LITERACY	69%
LIFE EXPECTANCY	58 years
GDP PER CAPITA	$1,000

ECONOMY IND: meat processing, seafood, soap, breweries, tanneries **AGR:** coffee, vanilla, sugarcane, cloves; livestock products **EXP:** coffee, vanilla, shellfish, sugar, cotton cloth, chromite

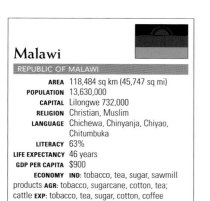

Malawi
REPUBLIC OF MALAWI
AREA	118,484 sq km (45,747 sq mi)
POPULATION	13,630,000
CAPITAL	Lilongwe 732,000
RELIGION	Christian, Muslim
LANGUAGE	Chichewa, Chinyanja, Chiyao, Chitumbuka
LITERACY	63%
LIFE EXPECTANCY	46 years
GDP PER CAPITA	$900

ECONOMY IND: tobacco, tea, sugar, sawmill products **AGR:** tobacco, sugarcane, cotton, tea; cattle **EXP:** tobacco, tea, sugar, cotton, coffee

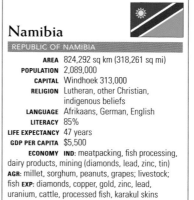

Mozambique
REPUBLIC OF MOZAMBIQUE
AREA	799,380 sq km (308,642 sq mi)
POPULATION	20,387,000
CAPITAL	Maputo 1,446,000
RELIGION	Roman Catholic, Muslim, Zionist Christian
LANGUAGE	Emakhuwa, Xichangana, Portuguese, Elomwe, Cisena, Echuwabo, other local languages
LITERACY	48%
LIFE EXPECTANCY	43 years
GDP PER CAPITA	$900

ECONOMY IND: food, beverages, chemicals (fertilizer, soap, paints), aluminum **AGR:** cotton, cashew nuts, sugarcane, tea; beef **EXP:** aluminum, prawns, cashews, cotton, sugar

Namibia
REPUBLIC OF NAMIBIA
AREA	824,292 sq km (318,261 sq mi)
POPULATION	2,089,000
CAPITAL	Windhoek 313,000
RELIGION	Lutheran, other Christian, indigenous beliefs
LANGUAGE	Afrikaans, German, English
LITERACY	85%
LIFE EXPECTANCY	47 years
GDP PER CAPITA	$5,500

ECONOMY IND: meatpacking, fish processing, dairy products, mining (diamonds, lead, zinc, tin) **AGR:** millet, sorghum, peanuts, grapes; livestock; fish **EXP:** diamonds, copper, gold, zinc, lead, uranium, cattle, processed fish, karakul skins

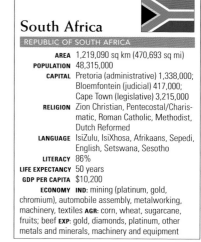

South Africa
REPUBLIC OF SOUTH AFRICA
AREA	1,219,090 sq km (470,693 sq mi)
POPULATION	48,315,000
CAPITAL	Pretoria (administrative) 1,338,000; Bloemfontein (judicial) 417,000; Cape Town (legislative) 3,215,000
RELIGION	Zion Christian, Pentecostal/Charismatic, Roman Catholic, Methodist, Dutch Reformed
LANGUAGE	IsiZulu, IsiXhosa, Afrikaans, Sepedi, English, Setswana, Sesotho
LITERACY	86%
LIFE EXPECTANCY	50 years
GDP PER CAPITA	$10,200

ECONOMY IND: mining (platinum, gold, chromium), automobile assembly, metalworking, machinery, textiles **AGR:** corn, wheat, sugarcane, fruits; beef **EXP:** gold, diamonds, platinum, other metals and minerals, machinery and equipment

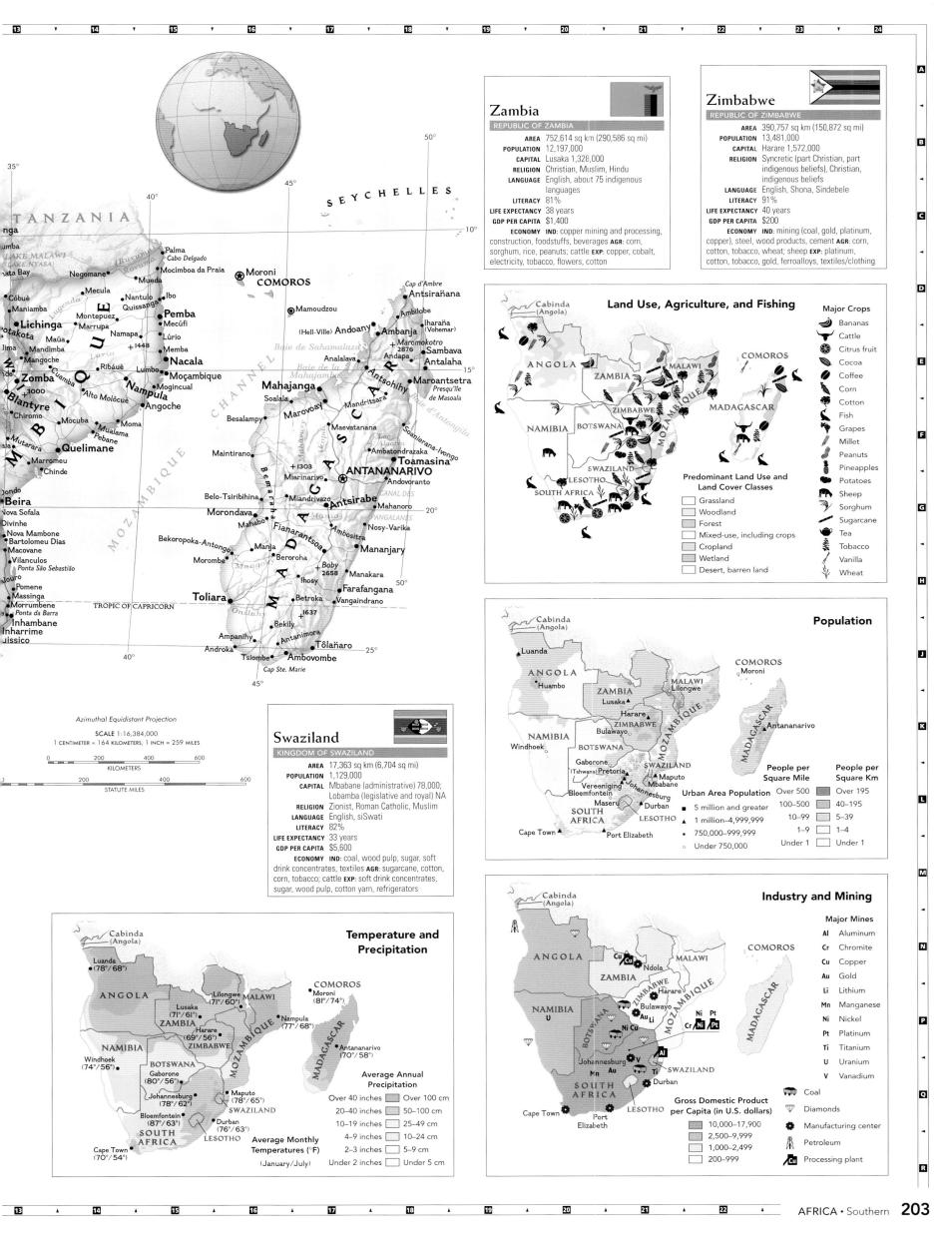

Zambia

REPUBLIC OF ZAMBIA

AREA 752,614 sq km (290,586 sq mi)
POPULATION 12,197,000
CAPITAL Lusaka 1,328,000
RELIGION Christian, Muslim, Hindu
LANGUAGE English, about 75 indigenous languages
LITERACY 81%
LIFE EXPECTANCY 38 years
GDP PER CAPITA $1,400
ECONOMY **IND:** copper mining and processing, construction, foodstuffs, beverages **AGR:** corn, sorghum, rice, peanuts; cattle **EXP:** copper, cobalt, electricity, tobacco, flowers, cotton

Zimbabwe

REPUBLIC OF ZIMBABWE

AREA 390,757 sq km (150,872 sq mi)
POPULATION 13,481,000
CAPITAL Harare 1,572,000
RELIGION Syncretic (part Christian, part indigenous beliefs), Christian, indigenous beliefs
LANGUAGE English, Shona, Sindebele
LITERACY 91%
LIFE EXPECTANCY 40 years
GDP PER CAPITA $200
ECONOMY **IND:** mining (coal, gold, platinum, copper), steel, wood products, cement **AGR:** corn, cotton, tobacco, wheat; sheep **EXP:** platinum, cotton, tobacco, gold, ferroalloys, textiles/clothing

Land Use, Agriculture, and Fishing

Major Crops

- Bananas
- Cattle
- Citrus fruit
- Cocoa
- Coffee
- Corn
- Cotton
- Fish
- Grapes
- Millet
- Peanuts
- Pineapples
- Potatoes
- Sheep
- Sorghum
- Sugarcane
- Tea
- Tobacco
- Vanilla
- Wheat

Predominant Land Use and Land Cover Classes

- Grassland
- Woodland
- Forest
- Mixed-use, including crops
- Cropland
- Wetland
- Desert, barren land

Population

People per Square Mile / **People per Square Km**

- Over 500 / Over 195
- 100–500 / 40–195
- 10–99 / 5–39
- 1–9 / 1–4
- Under 1 / Under 1

Urban Area Population

- ■ 5 million and greater
- ■ 1 million–4,999,999
- • 750,000–999,999
- ○ Under 750,000

Swaziland

KINGDOM OF SWAZILAND

AREA 17,363 sq km (6,704 sq mi)
POPULATION 1,129,000
CAPITAL Mbabane (administrative) 78,000; Lobamba (legislative and royal) NA
RELIGION Zionist, Roman Catholic, Muslim
LANGUAGE English, siSwati
LITERACY 82%
LIFE EXPECTANCY 33 years
GDP PER CAPITA $5,600
ECONOMY **IND:** coal, wood pulp, sugar, soft drink concentrates, textiles **AGR:** sugarcane, cotton, corn, tobacco; cattle **EXP:** soft drink concentrates, sugar, wood pulp, cotton yarn, refrigerators

Temperature and Precipitation

Luanda (78°/68°)
Lusaka (71°/61°)
Lilongwe (71°/60°)
Moroni (81°/74°)
Nampula (77°/68°)
Harare (69°/56°)
Antananarivo (70°/58°)
Windhoek (74°/56°)
Gaborone (80°/56°)
Johannesburg (78°/62°)
Maputo (78°/65°)
Bloemfontein (87°/63°)
Durban (76°/63°)
Cape Town (70°/54°)

Average Annual Precipitation

- Over 40 inches / Over 100 cm
- 20–40 inches / 50–100 cm
- 10–19 inches / 25–49 cm
- 4–9 inches / 10–24 cm
- 2–3 inches / 5–9 cm
- Under 2 inches / Under 5 cm

Average Monthly Temperatures (°F)

(January/July)

Industry and Mining

Major Mines

- Al Aluminum
- Cr Chromite
- Cu Copper
- Au Gold
- Li Lithium
- Mn Manganese
- Ni Nickel
- Pt Platinum
- Ti Titanium
- U Uranium
- V Vanadium

Gross Domestic Product per Capita (in U.S. dollars)

- 10,000–17,900
- 2,500–9,999
- 1,000–2,499
- 200–999

- Coal
- Diamonds
- Manufacturing center
- Petroleum
- Processing plant

Azimuthal Equidistant Projection

SCALE 1:16,384,000
1 CENTIMETER = 164 KILOMETERS; 1 INCH = 259 MILES

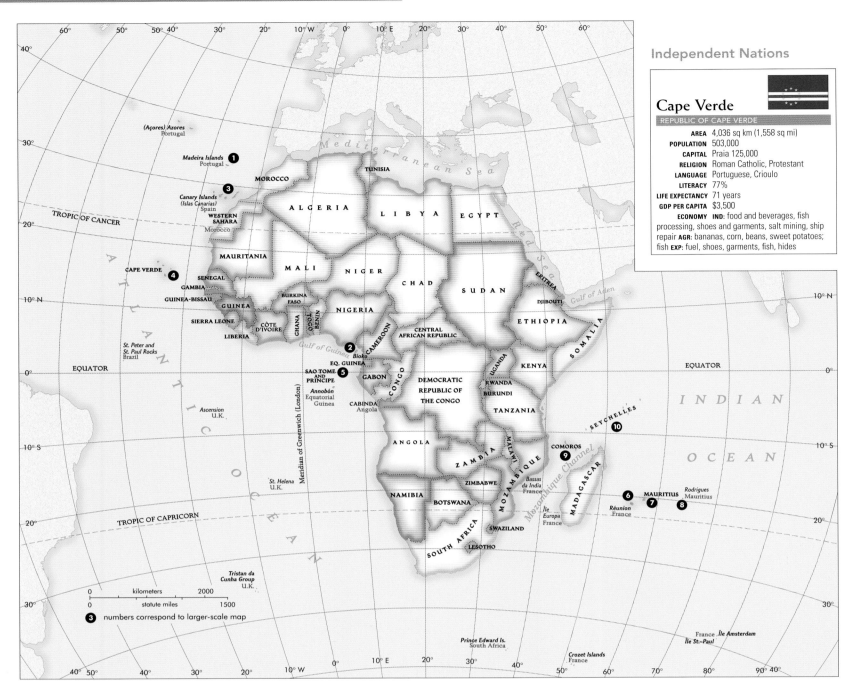

(Açores) Azores
Portugal

Mediterranean Sea

Madeira Islands ❶
Portugal

MOROCCO

TUNISIA

Canary Islands ❸
(Islas Canarias)
Spain

TROPIC OF CANCER

WESTERN
SAHARA
Morocco

ALGERIA

LIBYA

EGYPT

Red Sea

MAURITANIA

MALI

NIGER

CHAD

SUDAN

ERITREA

Gulf of Aden

CAPE VERDE ❹

SENEGAL

GAMBIA

GUINEA-BISSAU

GUINEA

BURKINA
FASO

NIGERIA

DJIBOUTI

ETHIOPIA

SOMALIA

SIERRA LEONE

CÔTE
D'IVOIRE

GHANA

TOGO
BENIN

CENTRAL
AFRICAN REPUBLIC

LIBERIA

Gulf of Guinea

CAMEROON

Bioko

UGANDA

KENYA

St. Peter and
St. Paul Rocks
Brazil

EQUATOR

SAO TOME
AND
PRINCIPE ❺

EQ. GUINEA

GABON

CONGO

DEMOCRATIC
REPUBLIC
OF
THE CONGO

RWANDA

BURUNDI

TANZANIA

INDIAN

Ascension
U.K.

Annobón
Equatorial
Guinea

CABINDA
Angola

SEYCHELLES ❿

EQUATOR

OCEAN

St. Helena
U.K.

ANGOLA

ZAMBIA

MALAWI

COMOROS ❾

St. Helena
U.K.

MADAGASCAR

Rodrigues
Mauritius

NAMIBIA

ZIMBABWE

Bassas
da India
France

MAURITIUS ❻
❼ Réunion
France
❽

BOTSWANA

Île
Europa
France

TROPIC OF CAPRICORN

SWAZILAND

SOUTH AFRICA

LESOTHO

Tristan da
Cunha Group
U.K.

kilometers 2000

statute miles 1500

❸ numbers correspond to larger-scale map

Prince Edward Is.
South Africa

France Île Amsterdam
Île St.~Paul

Crozet Islands
France

ATLANTIC OCEAN

Meridian of Greenwich (London)

Mozambique Channel

Independent Nations

Cape Verde
REPUBLIC OF CAPE VERDE

AREA	4,036 sq km (1,558 sq mi)
POPULATION	503,000
CAPITAL	Praia 125,000
RELIGION	Roman Catholic, Protestant
LANGUAGE	Portuguese, Crioulo
LITERACY	77%
LIFE EXPECTANCY	71 years
GDP PER CAPITA	$3,500

ECONOMY IND: food and beverages, fish processing, shoes and garments, salt mining, ship repair **AGR:** bananas, corn, beans, sweet potatoes; fish **EXP:** fuel, shoes, garments, fish, hides

---

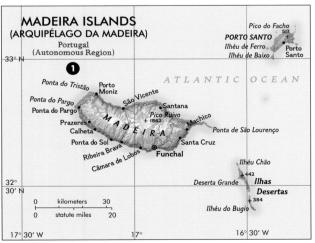

MADEIRA ISLANDS
(ARQUIPÉLAGO DA MADEIRA)
Portugal
(Autonomous Region)

❶

ATLANTIC OCEAN

Pico do Facho
517

PORTO SANTO
Ilhéu de Ferro
Ilhéu de Baixo

Porto
Santo

33° N

Ponta do Tristão
Porto
Moniz

Ponta do Pargo

São Vicente

Santana

Ponta do Pargo

Pico Ruivo
+1862

Ponta do Sol

Prazeres

Machico

Calheta

MADEIRA

Ponta de São Lourenço

Ponta do Sol

+442

Santa Cruz

Ilhéu Chão

Ribeira Brava

Câmara de Lobos

Funchal

Deserta Grande

Ilhas
Desertas

32°
30' N

+384

Ilhéu do Bugio

kilometers 30

statute miles 20

17° 30' W   17°   16° 30' W

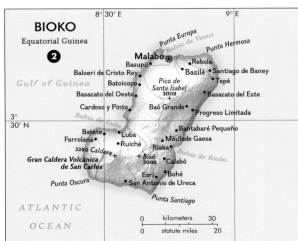

BIOKO
Equatorial Guinea

❷

8° 30' E   9° E

Gulf of Guinea

Punta Europa
Bahia de Venus

Malabo ✪

Rebola

Punta Hermosa

Basupú

Basilé

Santiago de Baney

Baloeri de Cristo Rey

Batoicopo

Tepé

Basacato del Oeste

Pico de
Santa Isabel
3008

Basacato del Este

Cardoso y Pinto

Baó Grande

Progreso Limitada

3°
30' N

Bahia de Tutú

Batete

Luba

Bantabaré Pequeño

Ferrolana

Ruiché

Moulele Gaesa

2260 Caldera

Riaba

Gran Caldera Volcánica
de San Carlos

Biaó
+2009

Calabó

Eori

Bohé

Punta Oscura

San Antonio de Ureca

Bahia de Riaba

Punta Santiago

*ATLANTIC
OCEAN*

kilometers 30

statute miles 20

Comoros
UNION OF THE COMOROS

AREA	1,862 sq km (719 sq mi)
POPULATION	732,000
CAPITAL	Moroni 46,000
RELIGION	Sunni Muslim
LANGUAGE	Arabic, French, Shikomoro
LITERACY	57%
LIFE EXPECTANCY	64 years
GDP PER CAPITA	$1,100

ECONOMY IND: fishing, tourism, perfume distillation **AGR:** vanilla, cloves, ylang-ylang (perfume essence), copra, coconuts, bananas **EXP:** vanilla, ylang-ylang, cloves, copra

---

CANARY ISLANDS
(ISLAS CANARIAS)
Spain
(Autonomous Community)

❸

29° N

18° W   17°   16°   15°   14°   Alegranza 13° W

ATLANTIC OCEAN

Graciosa
Punta Fariones

671 Peñas del Cache

LANZAROTE

Haría

Roque de los Muchachos
2426

Caldera de Taburiente

Tinajo

Teguise

Los Llanos

Santa Cruz de la Palma

608 Atalaya de Femés

Arrecife

LA PALMA

Fuencaliente

Playa Blanca

Puerto Honda

TENERIFE

Puerto del Carmen

Punta de Fuencaliente

Solyplayas

La Oliva

Puerto de la Cruz

La Laguna

Punta de Anaga

689 Muda

Antigua

Santa Cruz de Tenerife

Guía de Isora

La Orotava

+ Pico de Teide

Puerto del Rosario

Vallehermoso

3718

Granadilla

Agaete

Arucas

FUERTEVENTURA

1487 Garajonay +

La Isleta

GOMERA

Los Cristianos

Costa
del Silencio

Pico de las Nieves
+1949

Gáldar

Las Palmas

Jandia
807

Gran Tarajal

(FERRO) HIERRO

Mogán

Telde

Punta de Jandia

Cape Juby

Tarfaya

Valverde

GRAN CANARIA

Sabinosa

Malpaso 1501

Maspalomas

MOROCCO

Punta Restinga

28° N

19° W

Morocco WESTERN SAHARA

kilometers 100

statute miles 75

Mauritius
REPUBLIC OF MAURITIUS

AREA	2,040 sq km (788 sq mi)
POPULATION	1,268,000
CAPITAL	Port Louis 150,000
RELIGION	Hindu, Roman Catholic, Muslim, other Christian
LANGUAGE	Creole, Bhojpuri, French
LITERACY	84%
LIFE EXPECTANCY	72 years
GDP PER CAPITA	$12,000

ECONOMY IND: food processing (largely sugar milling), textiles, clothing, mining **AGR:** sugarcane, tea, corn, potatoes; cattle; fish **EXP:** clothing and textiles, sugar, cut flowers, molasses, fish

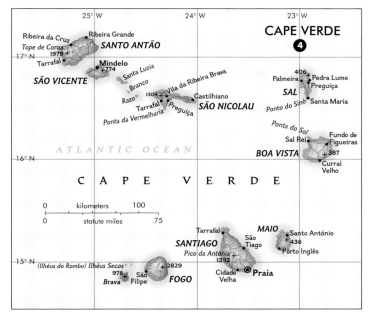

CAPE VERDE ❹

Ribeira da Cruz · Ribeira Grande
Tope de Coroa · *SANTO ANTÃO*
1979 +
17°N · Tarrafal
Mindelo +774 · Santa Luzia
SÃO VICENTE · Branco
Razo · 1304 · Vila da Ribeira Brava
Tarrafal + · Preguiça · *SÃO NICOLAU*
Ponta da Vermelharia
Palmeira · 406 · Pedra Lume
Preguiça
SAL
Castilhiano
Ponto do Sinó · Santa Maria

Ponta do Sol
Sal Rei · Fundo de Figueiras
BOA VISTA · +387
16°N · Curral Velho

A T L A N T I C   O C E A N

C A P E   V E R D E

kilometers 100
statute miles 75

MAIO
Tarrafal · Santo António
+436
SANTIAGO · São Tiago · Pôrto Inglês
Pico da Antónia +
1392
15°N · (Ilhéus do Rombo) Ilhéus Secos · +2829
976 + · São
Brava · Filipe · *FOGO* · Cidade Velha · ⊛ Praia

25°W · 24°W · 23°W

SAO TOME AND PRINCIPE ❺

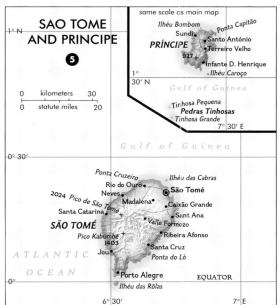

same scale as main map
Ilhéu Bombom
Sundi · Ponta Capitão
PRÍNCIPE · Santo António
927 · Terreiro Velho
Infante D. Henrique
· Ilhéu Caroço
1°N
30'N · *Gulf of Guinea*
kilometers 30
statute miles 20
Tinhosa Pequena
Pedras Tinhosas
Tinhosa Grande
7°30'E

Gulf of Guinea
0°30'

Ponta Cruzeiro · Ilhéu das Cabras
Rio do Ouro · ⊛ São Tomé
Neves
2024 · Pico de São Tomé · Caixão Grande
Santa Catarina · Madalena · Sant Ana
SÃO TOMÉ · Valle Formoso
Pico Kabumbé · Ribeira Afonso
1403 · Santa Cruz
Jou · Ponta do Ló

A T L A N T I C   O C E A N
Porto Alegre
Ilhéu das Rôlas
0° · EQUATOR
6°30' · 7°E

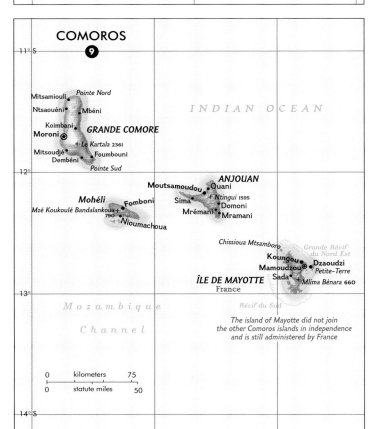

RÉUNION
France ❻

Pointe des Galets · Sainte-Marie
Saint-Denis ⊛
Le Port · La Possession · Sainte-Suzanna
Saint-Paul · **Saint-André**
St.-Gilles-les-Bains · 2277 + · Salazie · Bras-Panon
Hell-Bourg · **Saint-Benoît**
Trois-Bassins · +941
2896 + · + Piton des Neiges
Cilaos · 3069 · 1685 · La Plaine
Saint-Leu · Sainte-Rose
Entre- · La Plaine
Les Avirons · Deux · des Cafres · Piton de la Fournaise
Étang-Salé · La Rivière · + 2631
Saint-Louis
Saint-Pierre · Le Tampon · Petite Île · 281
· Pointe de la Table
Saint-Joseph · Saint-Philippe

I N D I A N   O C E A N

55°00'E · 55°30' · 56°00'E
21°S
21°30'S

kilometers 30
statute miles 20

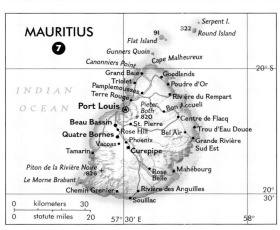

MAURITIUS ❼

Serpent I.
91 · 322 · Round Island
Flat Island
Gunners Quoin
Canonniers Point · Cape Malheureux
Grand Baie · Goodlands
Triolet · Poudre d'Or
INDIAN · Pamplemousses
OCEAN · Terre Rouge · Rivière du Rempart
Port Louis ⊛ · Pieter · Bon Accueil
Both
+820 · Centre de Flacq
Beau Bassin · St. Pierre
Quatre Bornes · Rose Hill · Trou d'Eau Douce
· Bel Air
Phoenix · Grande Rivière
Tamarin · **Curepipe** · Sud Est
Vacoas
Piton de la Rivière Noire · Rose · Mahébourg
Le Morne Brabant · 826 · Belle
· Rivière des Anguilles
Chemin Grenier · Souillac

20°S
20°30'

kilometers 30
statute miles 20
57°E · 57°30'E · 58°

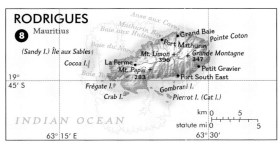

RODRIGUES ❽
Mauritius

Anse aux Cayes
Mathurin · Baie aux Huîtres · Pointe Coton
Baie du Nord · **Grand Baie**
(Sandy I.) Île aux Sables · Port Mathurin
Cocoa I. · Mt. Limon + · Grande Montagne
396 · 347
La Ferme · Petit Gravier
Mt. Papai + · Port South East
19° · 283
45'S · Frégate I. · Gombrani I.
Crab I. · Pierrot I. (Cat I.)

INDIAN OCEAN

km 0 · 5
statute mi 0 · 5
63°15'E · 63°30'

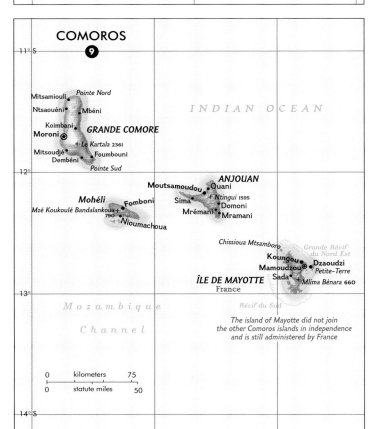

COMOROS ❾

Mitsamiouli · Pointe Nord
Ntsaouéni · Mbéni
Koimbani
Moroni ⊛ · *GRANDE COMORE*
Mitsoudjé · + Le Kartala 2361
Dembéni · Foumbouni
Pointe Sud

INDIAN OCEAN

Moutsamoudou · *ANJOUAN*
Mohéli · Ouani
Mohéli · Sima · + Ntingui 1595
Mzé Koukoulé Bandalankoua · Domoni
790 · Mrémani · Mramani
Nioumachoua

Chissioua Mtsamboro
Grande Récif du Nord Est
Koungou
Mamoudzou ⊛ · Dzaoudzi
Sada · Petite-Terre
ÎLE DE MAYOTTE · Mlima Bénara 660
France

Mozambique Channel · Récif du Sud

The island of Mayotte did not join the other Comoros islands in independence and is still administered by France.

kilometers 75
statute miles 50
43°E · 44° · 45°E
11°S · 12° · 13° · 14°S

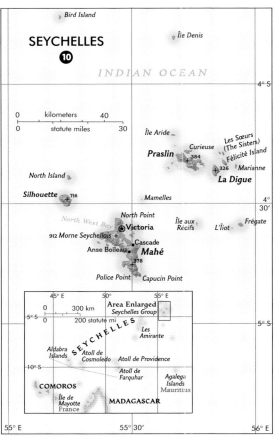

SEYCHELLES ❿

Bird Island
Île Denis
INDIAN OCEAN
4°S
kilometers 40
statute miles 30
Île Aride
Curieuse · Les Sœurs (The Sisters)
North Island · **Praslin** · 384 · Félicité Island
Silhouette · +716 · +326 · Marianne
· **La Digue**
4°30'
Mamelles
North West Bay · North Point
912 Morne Seychellois + · Île aux
· Victoria · Récifs · L'Îlot · Frégate
Anse Boileau · Cascade
Mahé
378
Police Point · Capucin Point

45°E · 50° · 55°E
5°S · Area Enlarged · Seychelles Group
0 · 300 km
0 · 200 statute mi
SEYCHELLES
Aldabra · Les Amirantes
Islands
10°S · Atoll de Cosmoledo · Atoll de Providence
COMOROS · Atoll de Farquhar
Île de Mayotte · Agalega Islands Mauritius
France · *MADAGASCAR*

55°E · 55°30' · 56°E

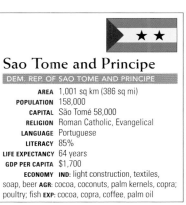

Sao Tome and Principe
DEM. REP. OF SAO TOME AND PRINCIPE

AREA 1,001 sq km (386 sq mi)
POPULATION 158,000
CAPITAL São Tomé 58,000
RELIGION Roman Catholic, Evangelical
LANGUAGE Portuguese
LITERACY 85%
LIFE EXPECTANCY 64 years
GDP PER CAPITA $1,700
ECONOMY IND: light construction, textiles, soap, beer **AGR:** cocoa, coconuts, palm kernels, copra; poultry; fish **EXP:** cocoa, copra, coffee, palm oil

---

Seychelles
REPUBLIC OF SEYCHELLES

AREA 455 sq km (176 sq mi)
POPULATION 87,000
CAPITAL Victoria 26,000
RELIGION Roman Catholic, Anglican
LANGUAGE Creole, English
LITERACY 92%
LIFE EXPECTANCY 72 years
GDP PER CAPITA $17,600
ECONOMY IND: fishing, tourism, processing of coconuts and vanilla, coir (coconut fiber) rope **AGR:** coconuts, cinnamon, vanilla, sweet potatoes; poultry; tuna **EXP:** canned tuna, frozen fish, cinnamon bark, copra, petroleum products (reexports)

Dependencies

Mayotte (France)
TERRITORIAL COLLECTIVITY OF MAYOTTE

AREA 374 sq km (144 sq mi)
POPULATION 187,000
CAPITAL Mamoudzou NA
RELIGION Muslim
LANGUAGE Mahorian (a Swahili dialect), French
LITERACY NA
LIFE EXPECTANCY 74 years
GDP PER CAPITA $4,900
ECONOMY IND: newly created lobster and shrimp industry, construction **AGR:** vanilla, ylang-ylang (perfume essence), coffee, copra; livestock; fish **EXP:** ylang-ylang (perfume essence), vanilla, copra, coconuts, coffee

Réunion (France)
OVERSEAS DEPARTMENT OF FRANCE

AREA 2,507 sq km (968 sq mi)
POPULATION 812,000
CAPITAL St.-Denis 143,000
RELIGION Roman Catholic, Hindu, Muslim, Buddhist
LANGUAGE French, Creole patois
LITERACY 89%
LIFE EXPECTANCY 76 years
GDP PER CAPITA $6,200
ECONOMY IND: sugar, rum, cigarettes, handicraft items **AGR:** sugarcane, vanilla, tobacco, tropical fruits **EXP:** sugar, rum and molasses, perfume essences, lobster

SOVEREIGN · LOCAL

St. Helena (U.K.)
SAINT HELENA

AREA 411 sq km (159 sq mi)
POPULATION 6,000
CAPITAL Jamestown 1,000
RELIGION Anglican, Baptist, Seventh-day Adventist, Roman Catholic
LANGUAGE English
LITERACY 97%
LIFE EXPECTANCY 77 years
GDP PER CAPITA $2,500
ECONOMY IND: construction, crafts (furniture, lacework, fancy woodwork), fishing, philatelic sales **AGR:** coffee, corn, potatoes, vegetables; livestock; timber; fish **EXP:** fish (frozen, canned, and salt-dried skipjack, tuna), coffee, handicrafts

Australia
New Zealand and Oceania

The largest structure ever built by living creatures, the Great Barrier Reef lies off Australia's northeast coast. Some 400 coral species and 1,500 species of fish inhabit its warm, shallow waters.

Smallest of continents and sixth largest country in the world, Australia is the lowest, flattest, and, apart from Antarctica, the driest continent.

The Australian landmass is relatively arid, but varied climatic zones give it surprising diversity and a rich ecology. Unlike Europe and North America, where much of the landscape dates back 20,000 years to when great ice sheets retreated, Australia's land is many millions of years old; it retains an ancient feeling and distinctive geography and endures extremes of droughts, floods, tropical cyclones, severe storms, and bushfires.

Off the coast of northeast Queensland lies the Great Barrier Reef, the world's largest coral reef, which extends about 1,429 miles (2,300 km). The reef was formed and expanded over millions of years as tiny marine animals deposited their skeletons. Coral reefs, and the Great Barrier Reef especially, are considered the rain forests of the ocean for their complex life forms and multilayered biodiversity.

The island of Tasmania lies off Australia's southeast coast. East from there, across the Tasman Sea, is the island nation of New Zealand, composed of South Island and North Island, respectively the 12th and 14th largest islands on Earth. North Island, unlike its southern neighbor, is riddled with geothermic activity.

Extending into the massive Pacific Ocean north and east of Australia and New Zealand are the thousands of islands—which include 12 independent nations and more than 20 territories—that make up greater Oceania. The term Oceania normally designates all the islands of the Central and South Pacific, including Australia, New Zealand, and specifically the islands of Melanesia, Micronesia, and Polynesia, including Hawai'i. Eons of isolation have allowed outstanding and bizarre life-forms to evolve, such as the duck-billed platypus—a monotreme, or egg-laying mammal native to Australia and Tasmania—and New Zealand's kiwi, a timid, nocturnal, wingless bird.

Oceania has many ethnic groups and layers and types of society, from sophisticated cosmopolitan cities to near-Stone Age people in the New Guinea highlands. Many became Christian converts in the 19th century; as a result, Christianity is widespread and dominant in many countries today. Excluding Australia, some 14 million people live in Oceania, three-fourths of whom are found in Papua New Guinea and New Zealand.

Polynesia, which means "many islands," is the most extensive of the ocean realms. It can be seen as a huge triangle in the central-south Pacific, with the points being New Zealand in the southwest, Easter Island in the southeast, and Hawai'i as the northern point. Other island groups include Tuvalu, Tokelau, Wallis and Futuna, Samoa, Tonga, Cook Islands, and French Polynesia.

Micronesia, north and west of Polynesia, includes the islands and island groups of Nauru, Marshall Islands, Palau, Mariana Islands, Kiribati, and Guam.

Melanesia, one of the three main divisions of Oceania, includes the Solomon Islands, Vanuatu, New Caledonia, the Bismarck Archipelago, and Fiji, and sometimes takes in Papua New Guinea, where more than 750 of the giant region's 1,200 languages are spoken.

PHYSICAL GEOGRAPHY The continent of Australia can be divided into three parts: the Western Plateau, Central Lowlands, and Eastern Highlands. The Western Plateau consists of very old rocks, some more than three billion years old. Much of the center of Australia is flat, but some ranges and the famous landmark Ayers Rock (Uluru) still rise up, everything around them having eroded away.

Much variety exists within the general context of a red, dusty, dry, flat continent, of which a third is desert and a third scrub and steppe. Sand dunes, mostly fixed and running north to south, and stony deserts mark the great tableland.

Many of Australia's rivers drain inland; though they erode their valleys near the highland sources, their lower courses are filling up with alluvium, and the rivers often end in salt lakes, dry for much of each year, when they become beds of salt and caked mud. Yet occasional spring rains in the outback can bring spectacular wildflowers.

Sparsely populated, Australia has nearly all its 21 million people along the east and southeast coasts, and of these about 40 percent live in the two cities of Sydney and Melbourne. Along the coasts are some fine harbors and long beaches and rocky headlands.

The Eastern Highlands rise gently from central Australia toward a series of high plateaus, the highest part around Mount Kosciuszko (7,310 ft; 2,228 m). The Great Escarpment runs from northern Queensland to the Victoria border in the south. Australia's highest waterfalls occur where rivers flow over the Great Escarpment.

The longest of all Australian river systems, the Murray River and its tributaries, including the long Darling River, drain part of Queensland, the major part of New South Wales, and a large part of Victoria before finally flowing into the Indian Ocean just east of Adelaide.

Most of the Great Dividing Range that separates rivers flowing to Central Australia from those flowing to the Pacific runs across remarkably flat country dotted with lakes and airstrips. In ancient times volcanoes erupted in eastern Australia, and lava plains covered large areas.

Australia is blessed with a fascinating mix of native flora and fauna. Its distinctive plants include the ubiquitous eucalyptus, sometimes called a gum tree, and acacia, which Australians call wattle, each with several hundred species. Other common plants include bottlebrushes, paperbarks, and tea trees. Animals include the iconic kangaroo, koala, wallaby, wombat, and dog-like dingo, also the echidna—a spiny anteater—and numerous beloved birds, such as parrots, cockatoos, and kookaburras, and the emu, second largest of all birds after the ostrich.

Foreign animals have been introduced. The rabbit and fox have proven to be particularly noxious pests, overgrazing the land and killing and driving out native species. A fence built in 1907, still maintained, runs a thousand miles from the north coast to the south to prevent rabbits from invading Western Australia.

New Zealand is mountainous compared to Australia; it has peaks over 10,000 feet in the Southern Alps and considerably more rain, making the climate cooler and more temperate. Among New Zealand's oddities is a fossil lizard species, the tuatara; individuals can live up to a hundred years.

The atolls, mountains, volcanoes, and sandy isles of greater Oceania, with limited land and small populations, have for most of history been isolated from the more settled parts of the world.

Peaks and promontories of the many islands of Polynesia form clouds and capture rain, making these islands very wet.

HISTORY Australia's first inhabitants, the Aborigines, migrated there some 50,000 or more years ago from Asia. Until the arrival of Europeans, the Aborigines had remained isolated from outside influences except for occasional trading in the north with Indonesian islanders.

Aboriginal pictographs, some repainted generation upon generation, grace the rock shelters and escarpment walls of Kakadu National Park in Australia's Northern Territory. Some paintings are considered *andjamun,* sacred and dangerous, and only may be viewed by tribal elders, while others may be looked upon by everyone.

In 1688 Englishman William Dampier landed on the northwest coast. Little interest was aroused, however, until Capt. James Cook noted the fertile east coast during his 1770 voyage, which stopped at Botany Bay, just south of today's Sydney. He claimed the entire continent for the British Empire and named it New South Wales.

Australia's formative moment came when Britain began colonizing the east coast in 1788 as a penal colony, so as to relieve overcrowded prisons in England. Altogether, 161,000 English, Irish, and other convicts were forced to settle there. Prison transports ended in 1868, and by that time regular emigrants had already begun settling down under, as Australia was called for being so far south of the Equator. By the mid-1800s systematic, permanent colonization had completely replaced the old penal settlements.

Introduction of sheep proved vital, and the wool industry flourished. A gold strike in Victoria in 1851 attracted prospectors from all over the world. Other strikes followed, and with minerals, sheep, and grain forming the base of the economy, Australia developed rapidly, expanding across the whole continent.

By 1861, Australians had established the straight-line boundaries between the colonies, and the Commonwealth of Australia was born January 1, 1901, relying on British parliamentary and U.S. federal traditions. Australia and New Zealand share a common British heritage and many similar characteristics, and both are democracies that continue to honor the British monarch.

The great seafaring navigators of Polynesia and Micronesia took part in the last phase of mankind's settlement of the globe, into the widely dispersed islands of the great Pacific. Their particular genius and contribution was the development of seafaring and navigation skills and canoe technology, which let them sail back and forth among islands across great distances. The more diverse, land-based Melanesians fished along the coasts and practiced horticulture farther inland.

CULTURE Australia's Aborigines were hunters and gatherers moving with the seasons, taking with them only those possessions necessary for hunting and preparing food. Perhaps 500 or more tribes lived in Australia at the time of Captain Cook in 1770.

Aboriginal society was based on a complex network of intricate kinship relationships. No formal government or authority existed, but social control was maintained by a system of beliefs called the Dreaming. These beliefs found expression in song, art, and dance. A rich oral tradition existed in which stories of the Dreamtime, the time of creation, or recent history were passed down. Aboriginal rock carvings and paintings date back at least 30,000 years.

Australia's Aborigines have faced two centuries and more of lost land, brutalization, and discrimination. In the 1960s an Aboriginal movement grew to press for full citizenship and improved education. Modern Aboriginal art has undergone a revival as Aboriginal artists have preserved their ancient values while learning from the contemporary world.

Most Australians are of British and Irish ancestry and the majority live in urban areas. The population has more than doubled since the end of World War II, spurred by an ambitious postwar immigration program, with many coming from Greece, Turkey, Italy, and Lebanon. In the 1970s Australia officially ended discriminatory immigration policies, and substantial Asian immigration followed. Today Asians make up some 7 percent of the population.

The largest church groups are the Anglican and Roman Catholic, though some say sport is the national religion; Australians are famous in cricket, rugby, and swimming.

The Maori—indigenous Polynesian people of New Zealand—arrived in different migrations starting around 1150, and a "great fleet" arrived in the 14th century, probably from Tahiti. Maori art is characterized by beautiful wood carvings that adorn houses and fish hooks carved out of whale bone. In the 1840 Treaty of Waitangi, the Maori gave formal control of their land to the British, though they kept all other rights of livelihood.

ECONOMY Australia dominates all of Oceania economically. Its connection to Asia grows more important as a supplier of raw material to other Pacific Rim countries and an importer of finished manufactured products. Japan is Australia's leading trade partner and thousands of children learn Japanese in Australian schools. The standard of living is high and people have considerable leisure time, a sign for Australians of a good life.

Most of the rich farmland and good ports are in the east, particularly the southeast, and the areas around Perth, in Western Australia. Melbourne, Sydney, Brisbane, and Adelaide are the leading industrial and commercial cities.

Australia is highly industrialized. Its chief industries include mining, food processing, and the manufacture of industrial and transportation equipment, chemicals, iron and steel, textiles, machinery, and motor vehicles. Some lumbering is done in the east and southeast. Tropical and subtropical produce are also important, as are vineyards, dairy farms, and tobacco farms.

Chief export commodities are coal, gold, beef, mutton, wool, minerals, cereals, and manufactured products. Australia's economic ties with Asia and the Pacific Rim are increasingly important. Air transport and modern communications have shrunk distances, with landing strips on isolated atolls, in the desert outback, and in Papuan jungles.

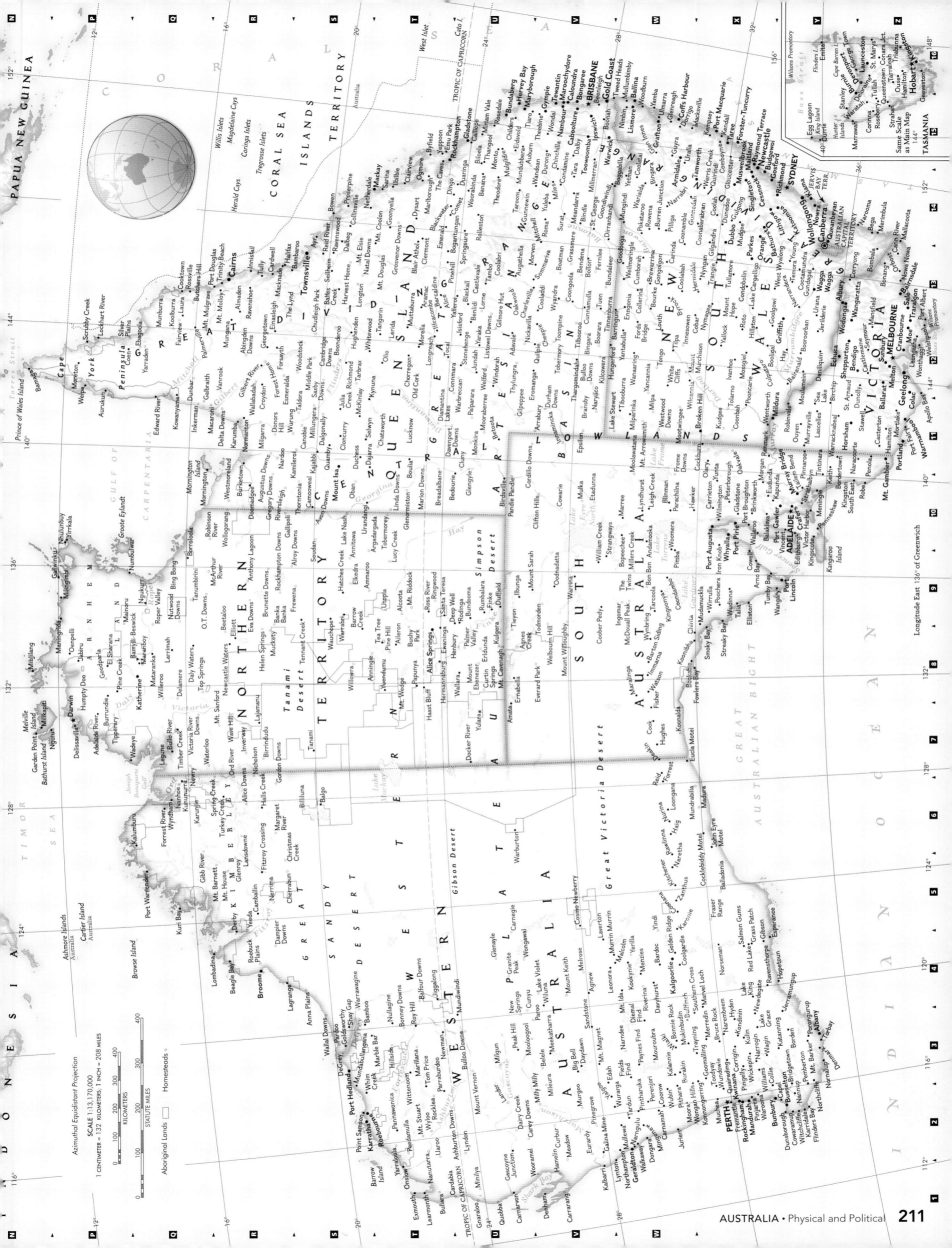

AUSTRALIA • Physical and Political

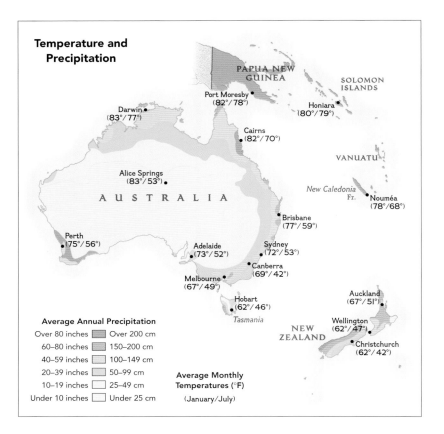

Temperature and Precipitation

Port Moresby (82°/78°)

Darwin (83°/77°)

Honiara (80°/79°)

Cairns (82°/70°)

Alice Springs (83°/53°)

AUSTRALIA

PAPUA NEW GUINEA

SOLOMON ISLANDS

VANUATU

New Caledonia Fr.

Nouméa (78°/68°)

Perth (75°/56°)

Brisbane (77°/59°)

Adelaide (73°/52°)

Sydney (72°/53°)

Canberra (69°/42°)

Melbourne (67°/49°)

Auckland (67°/51°)

Hobart (62°/46°)

Wellington (62°/47°)

Tasmania

NEW ZEALAND

Christchurch (62°/42°)

Average Annual Precipitation

Over 80 inches	Over 200 cm
60–80 inches	150–200 cm
40–59 inches	100–149 cm
20–39 inches	50–99 cm
10–19 inches	25–49 cm
Under 10 inches	Under 25 cm

Average Monthly Temperatures (°F)

(January/July)

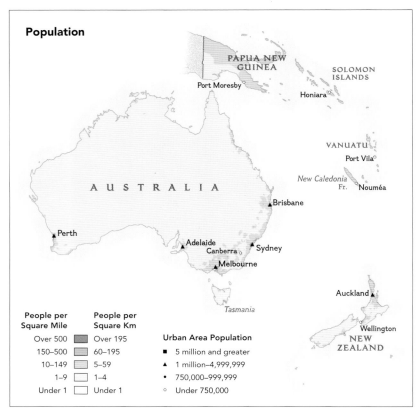

Population

PAPUA NEW GUINEA

Port Moresby

SOLOMON ISLANDS

Honiara

VANUATU

Port Vila

AUSTRALIA

New Caledonia Fr.

Nouméa

Brisbane

Perth

Adelaide

Canberra

Sydney

Melbourne

Tasmania

Auckland

Wellington

NEW ZEALAND

People per Square Mile	People per Square Km
Over 500	Over 195
150–500	60–195
10–149	5–59
1–9	1–4
Under 1	Under 1

Urban Area Population

- ■ 5 million and greater
- ▲ 1 million–4,999,999
- ● 750,000–999,999
- ○ Under 750,000

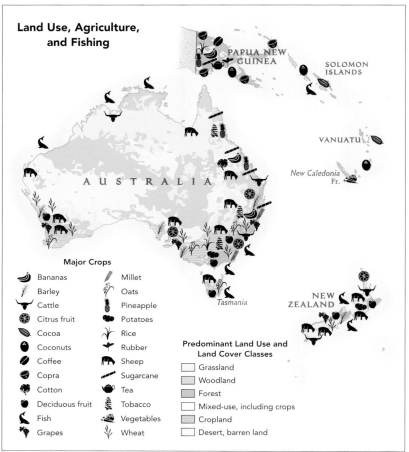

Land Use, Agriculture, and Fishing

PAPUA NEW GUINEA

SOLOMON ISLANDS

VANUATU

New Caledonia Fr.

AUSTRALIA

Tasmania

NEW ZEALAND

Major Crops

Bananas		Millet	
Barley		Oats	
Cattle		Pineapple	
Citrus fruit		Potatoes	
Cocoa		Rice	
Coconuts		Rubber	
Coffee		Sheep	
Copra		Sugarcane	
Cotton		Tea	
Deciduous fruit		Tobacco	
Fish		Vegetables	
Grapes		Wheat	

Predominant Land Use and Land Cover Classes

- Grassland
- Woodland
- Forest
- Mixed-use, including crops
- Cropland
- Desert, barren land

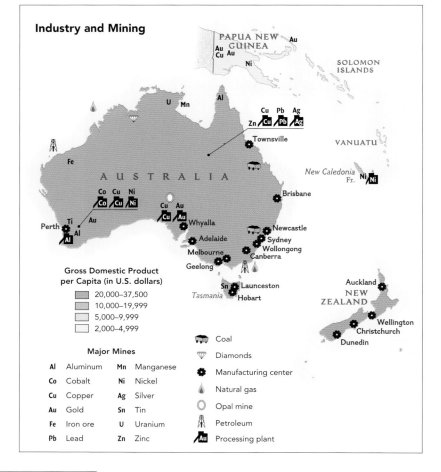

Industry and Mining

PAPUA NEW GUINEA

Au Au Cu Au

Ni

SOLOMON ISLANDS

U Mn Al

Cu Pb Ag Zn Cu Pb Ag

Townsville

VANUATU

Fe

AUSTRALIA

New Caledonia Fr.

Ni Ni

Co Cu Ni Co Cu Ni

Cu Au

Brisbane

Ti Au Al

Cu Au

Perth Al

Whyalla

Adelaide

Newcastle

Sydney

Melbourne

Wollongong Canberra

Geelong

Sn Launceston

Tasmania

Hobart

Auckland

NEW ZEALAND

Wellington

Christchurch

Dunedin

Gross Domestic Product per Capita (in U.S. dollars)

20,000–37,500
10,000–19,999
5,000–9,999
2,000–4,999

Major Mines

Al	Aluminum	Mn	Manganese
Co	Cobalt	Ni	Nickel
Cu	Copper	Ag	Silver
Au	Gold	Sn	Tin
Fe	Iron ore	U	Uranium
Pb	Lead	Zn	Zinc

- Coal
- Diamonds
- Manufacturing center
- Natural gas
- Opal mine
- Petroleum
- Processing plant

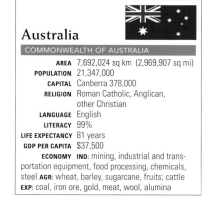

Australia

COMMONWEALTH OF AUSTRALIA

AREA	7,692,024 sq km (2,969,907 sq mi)
POPULATION	21,347,000
CAPITAL	Canberra 378,000
RELIGION	Roman Catholic, Anglican, other Christian
LANGUAGE	English
LITERACY	99%
LIFE EXPECTANCY	81 years
GDP PER CAPITA	$37,500
ECONOMY	**IND:** mining, industrial and transportation equipment, food processing, chemicals, steel **AGR:** wheat, barley, sugarcane, fruits; cattle **EXP:** coal, iron ore, gold, meat, wool, alumina

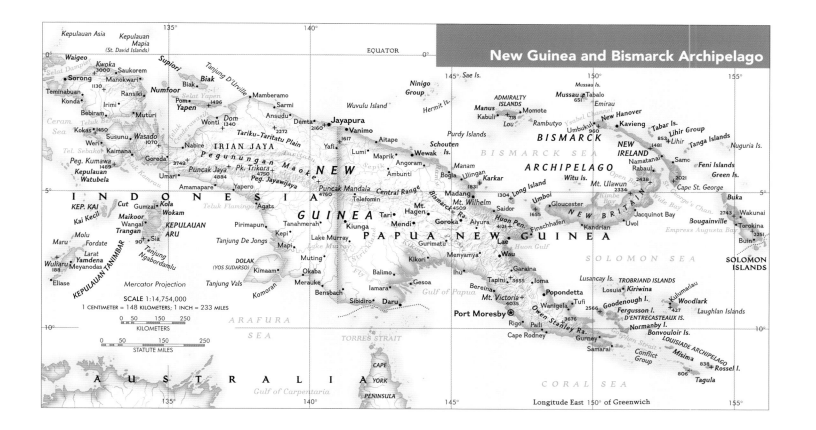

New Guinea and Bismarck Archipelago

SCALE 1:14,754,000
1 CENTIMETER = 148 KILOMETERS; 1 INCH = 233 MILES

Mercator Projection

KILOMETERS 0 50 150 250
STATUTE MILES 0 50 150 250

Longitude East 150° of Greenwich

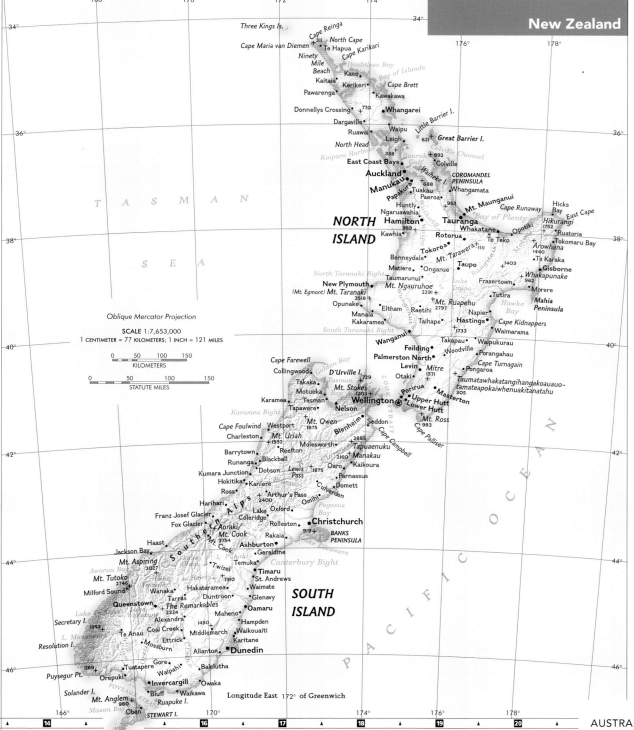

New Zealand

NORTH ISLAND

SOUTH ISLAND

Oblique Mercator Projection

SCALE 1:7,653,000
1 CENTIMETER = 77 KILOMETERS; 1 INCH = 121 MILES

KILOMETERS 0 50 100 150
STATUTE MILES 0 50 100 150

Longitude East 172° of Greenwich

New Zealand
NEW ZEALAND
AREA	270,534 sq km (104,454 sq mi)
POPULATION	4,272,000
CAPITAL	Wellington 366,000
RELIGION	Anglican, Roman Catholic, Presbyterian, other Christian
LANGUAGE	English, Maori
LITERACY	99%
LIFE EXPECTANCY	80 years
GDP PER CAPITA	$27,000
ECONOMY	**IND:** food processing, wood and paper products, textiles, machinery **AGR:** wheat, barley, potatoes, pulses; dairy, wool; fish **EXP:** dairy products, meat, wood and wood products, fish

Papua New Guinea
IND. STATE OF PAPUA NEW GUINEA
AREA	462,840 sq km (178,703 sq mi)
POPULATION	6,458,000
CAPITAL	Port Moresby 299,000
RELIGION	Roman Catholic, Evangelical Lutheran, United Church, Seventh-day Adventist, other Protestant
LANGUAGE	Melanesian Pidgin, Motu, 820 indigenous languages
LITERACY	57%
LIFE EXPECTANCY	57 years
GDP PER CAPITA	$2,100
ECONOMY	**IND:** copra crushing, palm oil processing, plywood production, mining, crude oil **AGR:** coffee, cocoa, copra, palm kernels; poultry; shellfish **EXP:** oil, gold, copper ore, logs, palm oil

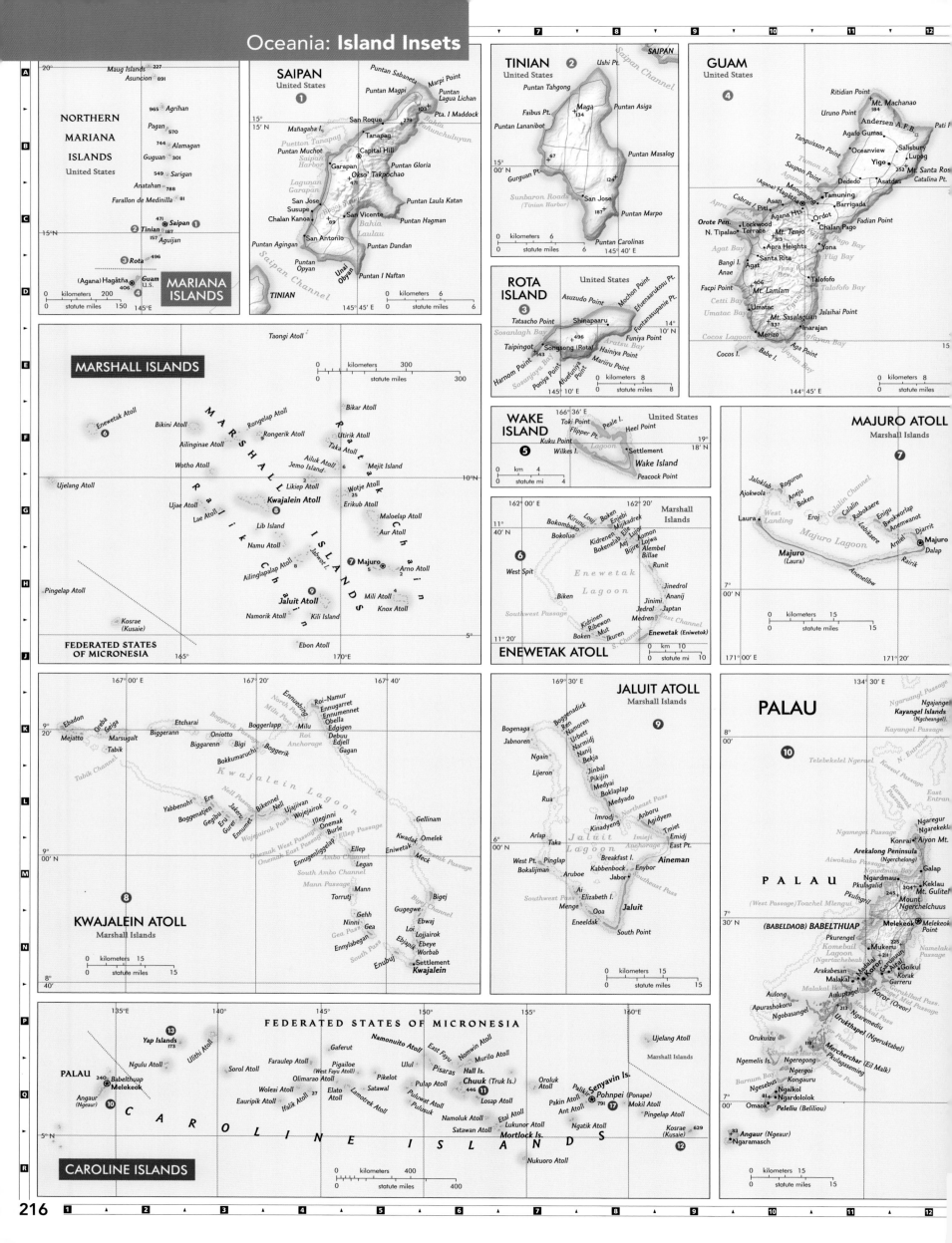

NORTHERN MARIANA ISLANDS
United States

Maug Islands 227
Asuncion 891
Agrihan 965
Pagan 570
Alamagan 744
Guguan 301
Sarigan 549
Anatahan 788
Farallon de Medinilla 81
Saipan 471
Tinian 157 187
Aguijan
Rota 496
(Agana) Hagåtña 406
Guam U.S.

MARIANA ISLANDS

SAIPAN
United States

Maug Islands 227
Puntan Sabaneta
Marpi Point
Puntan Magpi
Puntan Lagua Lichan
Pta. I Maddock
103
San Roque 279
Mañagaha I.
Tanapag
Puntan Muchot
Capital Hill
Saipan Harbor
Garapan
Puntan Gloria
Lagunan Garapan
Okso' Takpochao 471
Puntan Laula Katan
San Jose
Susupe
Chalan Kanoa
San Vicente
89
Puntan Hagman
Bahia Laulau
San Antonio
Puntan Agingan
Puntan Dandan
Puntan Opyan
Unai Obyan
Puntan I Naftan
Saipan Channel
TINIAN

TINIAN
United States

Ushi Pt.
SAIPAN
Saipan Channel
Puntan Tahgong
Faibus Pt.
Maga 134
Puntan Asiga
Puntan Lananibot
67
Puntan Masalog
Gurguan Pt.
124
San Jose 187
Puntan Marpo
Sunbaron Roads (Tinian Harbor)
Puntan Carolinas

GUAM
United States

Ritidian Point
Mt. Machanao 184
Uruno Point
Andersen A.F.B.
Pati Pt
Agafo Gumas
Tuman Bay
Tanguisson Point
Oceanview
Salisbury
Lupeg
Yigo
252 Mt. Santa Ros
Dededo
Asatdas
Catalina Pt.
Cabras I Piti
Asan
Tamuning
Barrigada
Agana Hts.
Mongmong
Ordot
Fadian Point
Orote Pen.
Lockwood
N. Tipalao
Terrace
Mt. Tenjo 313
Chalan Pago
Pago Bay
Apra Heights
Santa Rita
Yona
Ylig Bay
Bangi I.
406
Mt. Lamlam
Talofofo
Anae
Talofofo Bay
Facpi Point
Umatac
Mt. Sasalaguan
Jalaihai Point
Cetti Bay
Merizo
Inarajan
Umatac Bay
Aga Point
Ajayan Bay
Cocos Lagoon
Cocos I.
Babe I.

ROTA ISLAND
United States

Tataacho Point
Mochon Point
Asuzudo Point
Efuenaarukosu Pt.
Shinapaaru
Funtansupanie Pt.
Taipingot
Songsong (Rota) 143 496
Funiya Point
Harnom Point
Hainiya Point
Sosanlagh Bay
Mariiru Point
Poniya Point
Afuefunya Point

WAKE ISLAND
United States

166° 36' E
Toki Point
Peale I.
Heel Point
Flipper Pt.
Kuku Point
Lagoon
Settlement
Wilkes I.
Wake Island
Peacock Point

ENEWETAK ATOLL
Marshall Islands

162° 00' E
162° 20'
Kirunu
Louji
Boken
Enjebi
Bokombako
Mijikadrek
Bokoluo
Kidrenen
Elle
Aomon
West Spit
Bokenelab
Aej
Lujor
Alembel
Bijire
Lojwa
Billae
Enewetak Lagoon
Runit
West Spit
Biken
Jinedrol
Jinimi
Ananij
Southwest Passage
Jedrol
Japtan
Kidrinen
Medren
East Channel
Boken
Ribewon
Mut
Ikuren
Enewetak (Eniwetok)

MAJURO ATOLL
Marshall Islands

Jalokiab
Roguron
Ajokwola
Aneju
Boken
Calalin Channel
Laura
Eroj
Calalin
Enigu
Robokaere
Bwokworlap
West Landing
Kobikaere
Anemwanet
Majuro Lagoon
Ariel
Djarrit
Majuro (Laura)
Majuro
Dalap
Anenelibw
Rairik

MARSHALL ISLANDS
FEDERATED STATES OF MICRONESIA

Taongi Atoll
Bikar Atoll
Enewetak Atoll
Bikini Atoll
Rongelap Atoll
Utirik Atoll
Ailinginae Atoll
Rongerik Atoll
Taka Atoll
Wotho Atoll
Ailuk Atoll
Jemo Island
Mejit Island
Ujelang Atoll
Likiep Atoll
Wotje Atoll
Ujae Atoll
Kwajalein Atoll
Erikub Atoll
Lae Atoll
Lib Island
Maloelap Atoll
Namu Atoll
Aur Atoll
Ailinglapalap Atoll
Jabwot I.
Majuro
Arno Atoll
Pingelap Atoll
Jaluit Atoll
Mili Atoll
Knox Atoll
Kosrae (Kusaie)
Namorik Atoll
Kili Island
Ebon Atoll

KWAJALEIN ATOLL
Marshall Islands

Ebadon
Oreba
Geiga
Roi-Namur
Mejatto
Marsugalt
Biggerann
Ennuebing
Ennugarret
Ennummennet
Obella
Tabik
Biggarenn
Bokkumaruch
Boggerik
Edgigen
Debuu
Edjell
Gagan
Tabik Channel
Kwajalein Lagoon
Yabbenohr
Ere
Ujajiivan
Boggenatjen
Jakenu
Wojejairok
Gegbu
Illeginni
Omelek
Guret
Onemak
Kwadak
Burle
Ennugengiggelap
Ellep
Eniwetak
Meck
Legan
Mann
Torrutj
Bigej
Gugegwe
Gehh
Ebwaj
Ninni
Loi
Lojjairok
Gea
Ennylabegan
Ebeye
Worbab
Enubuj
Settlement
Kwajalein

JALUIT ATOLL
Marshall Islands

169° 30' E
Bogenadick
Ren
Namoren
Bogenaga
Urbett
Jabnoren
Narmidj
Nanij
Ngain
Bekja
Jinbal
Lijeron
Pikijin
Medyai
Rua
Boklaplap
Medyado
Imrodj
Anboru
Kinadyenb
Agidyem
Arlap
Taka
Tmiet
West Pt.
Pinglap
Emidj
Bokalijman
Breakfast I.
East Pt.
Aineman
Aruboe
Enybor
Ai
Jabor
Elizabeth I.
Menge
Ooa
Jaluit
Eneeldak
South Point

PALAU

134° 30' E
Ngajangel
Ngarumgl Islands
Kayangel Islands (Ngcheangel)
Kayangel Passage
Telebekelel Ngerael
Kossol Passage
N Entrance
East Entran
Ngaregur
Ngarekekla
Ngamegei Passage
Konrai
Aiyon Mt.
Arekalong Peninsula (Ngerchelong)
Galap
Ngardmau 3047
Keklau
Mount Ngerchelchuus
(BABELDAOB) BABELTHUAP
Melekeok
Melekeok Point
Pkurengel
Mukeru
Komebail Lagoon (Ngertachebesab)
Malakal
Ngaraard
Arakabesan
Goikul
Korak
Garreru
Aulong
Auluptagel
Koror (Oreor)
Apurashokoru
Ngarmediu
Ngabasangel
Urukthapel (Ngeruktabel)
Orukuizu
Mercherchar (Eil Malk)
Ngemelis Is.
Ngeregong
Peleliu (Beliliou)
Ngesebus
Ngalkol
Angaur (Ngeaur)
Omaok
Ngaramasch

PALAU
CAROLINE ISLANDS

135° E
140°
145°
150°
155°
160° E
FEDERATED STATES OF MICRONESIA
Yap Islands 173
Ulithi Atoll
Namonuito Atoll
East Fayu
Nomwin Atoll
Ujelang Atoll
Ngulu Atoll
Gaferut
Murilo Atoll
PALAU
Faraulep Atoll
Pigailoe (West Fayu Atoll)
Ulul
Pikelot
Marshall Islands
Babelthuap 240
Sorol Atoll
Pisaras
Hall Is.
Melekeok
Olimarao Atoll
Satawal
Chuuk (Truk Is.) 446
Oroluk Atoll
Senyavin Is.
Woleai Atoll
Elato Atoll
Lamotrek Atoll
Puluwat Atoll
Pulap Atoll
Pakin Atoll
Pohnpei (Ponape) 791
Angaur (Ngeaur)
Eauripik Atoll
Ifalik Atoll
Puluwat
Losap Atoll
Ant Atoll
Mokil Atoll
Namoluk Atoll
Pingelap Atoll
Kosrae (Kusaie) 629
Mortlock Is.
Satawan Atoll
Ngatik Atoll
Lukunor Atoll
Nukuoro Atoll

CAROLINE ISLANDS

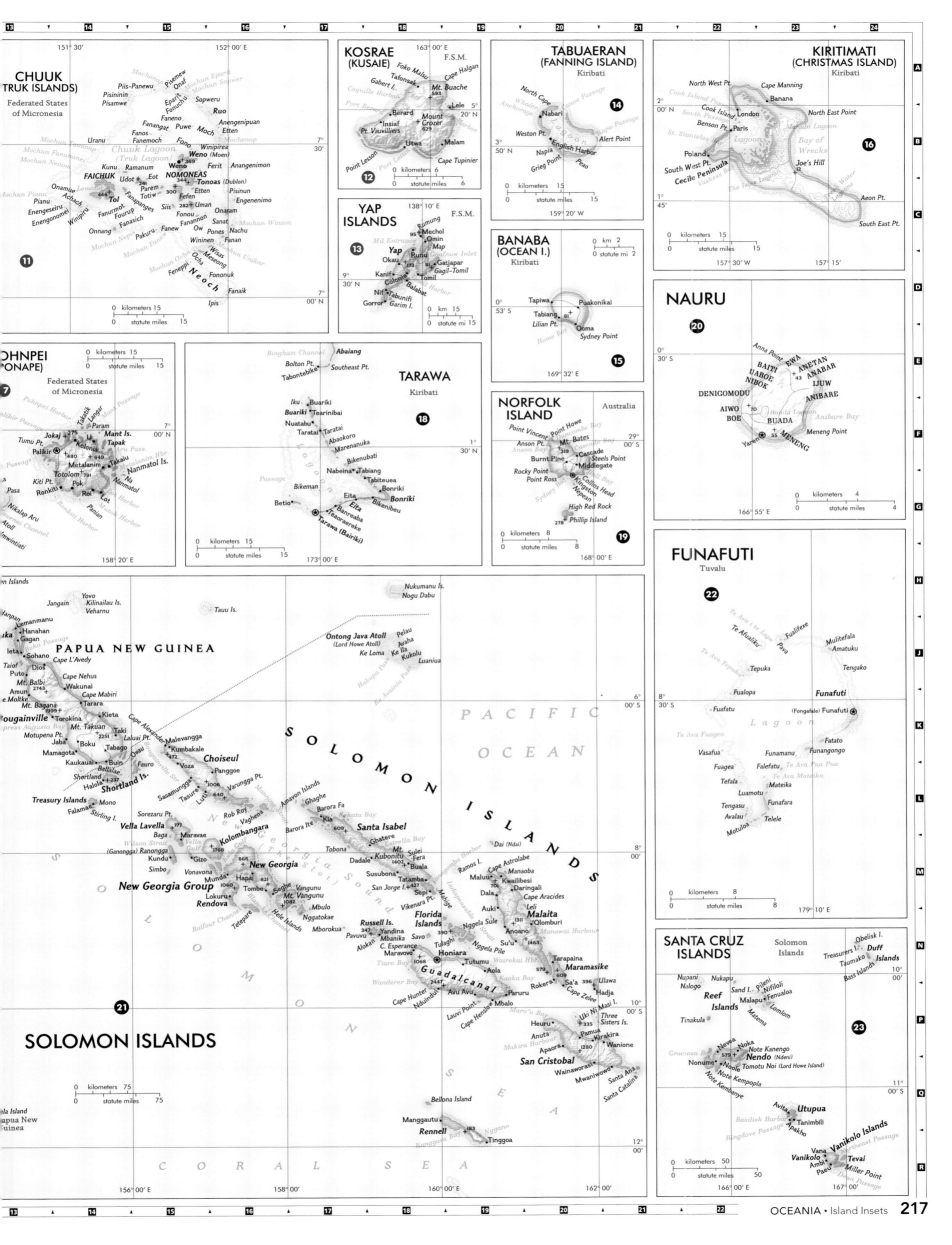

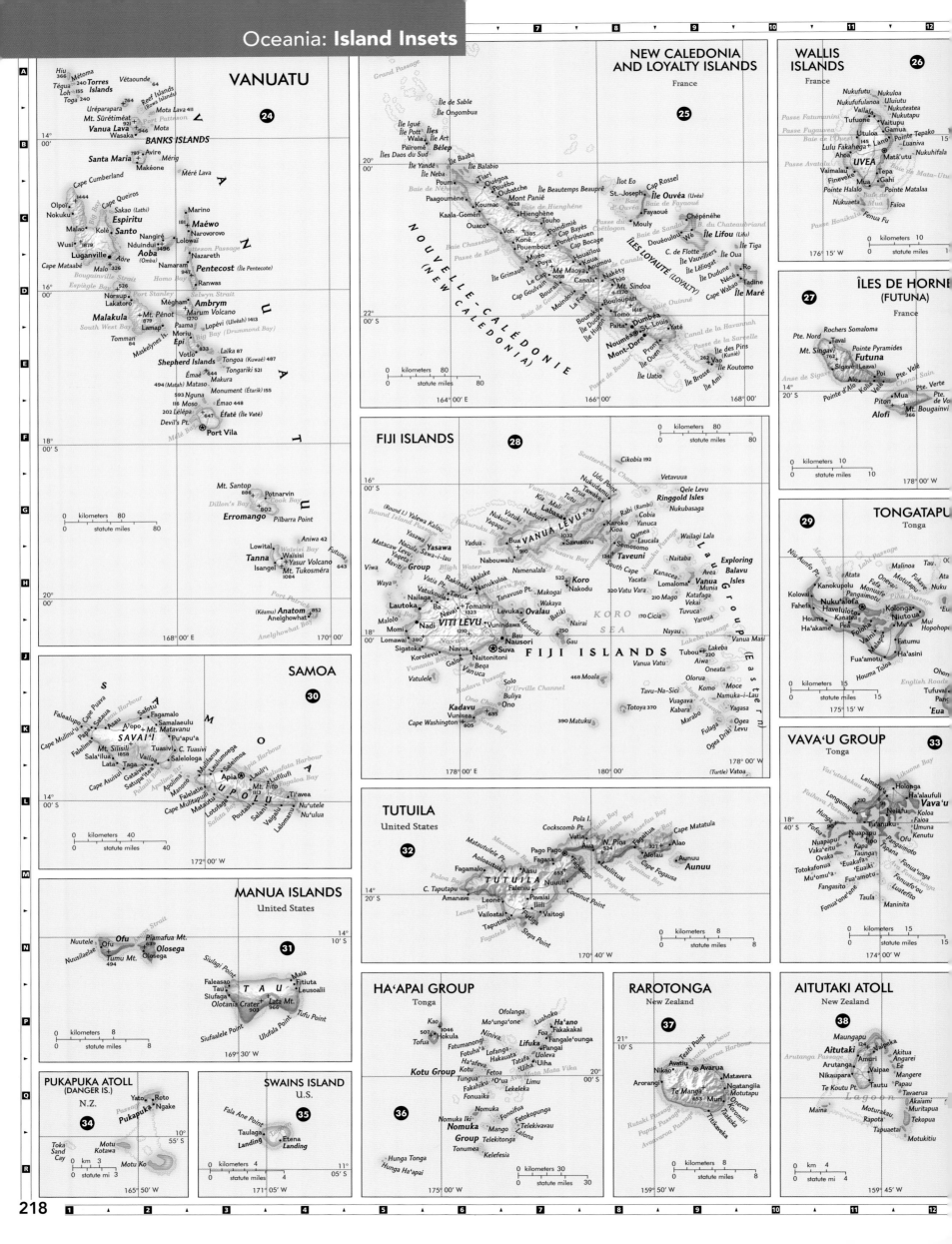

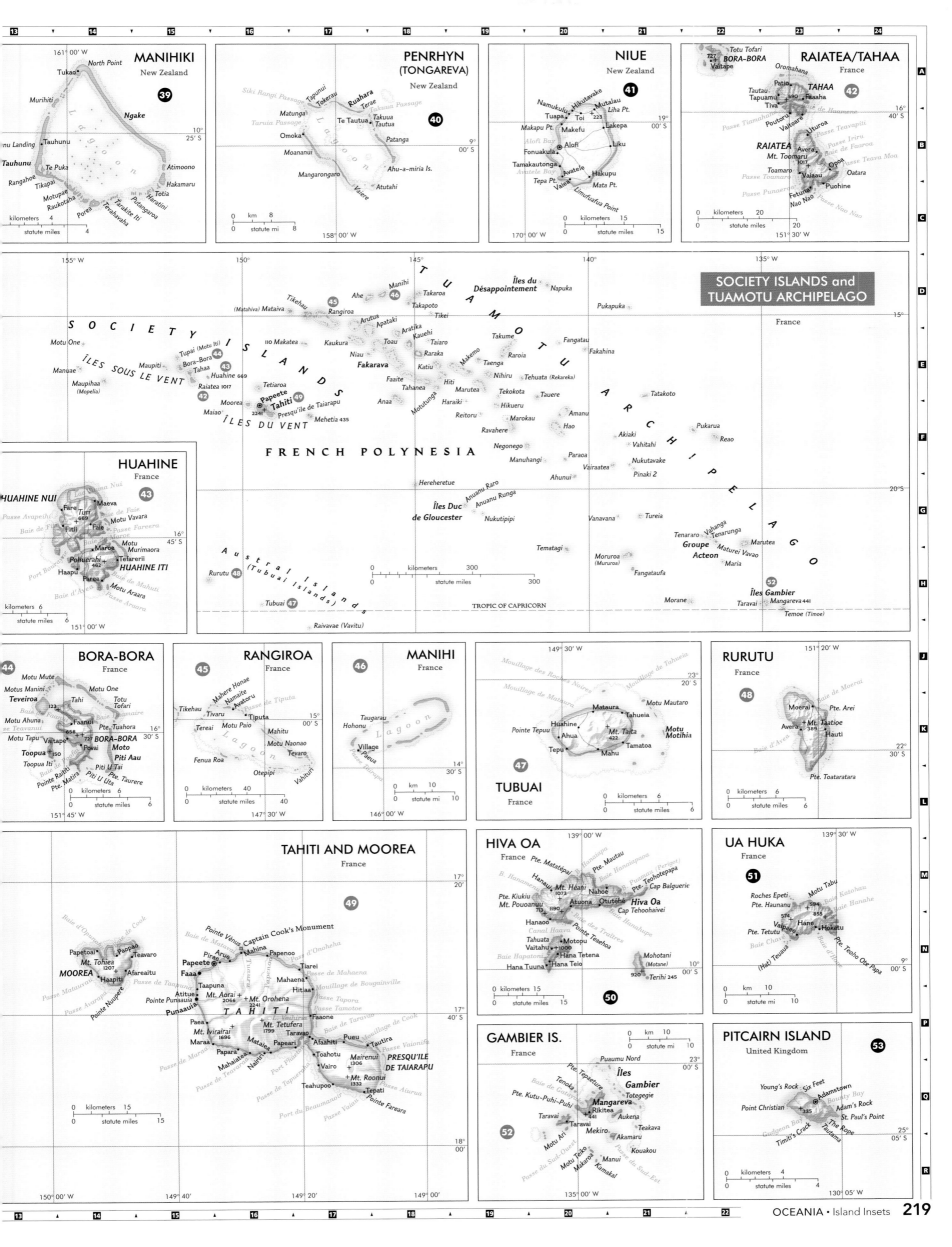

Independent Nations

Fiji Islands
REPUBLIC OF THE FIJI ISLANDS

AREA	18,376 sq km (7,095 sq mi)
POPULATION	864,000
CAPITAL	Suva 224,000
RELIGION	Christian, Hindu, Muslim
LANGUAGE	English, Fijian, Hindustani
LITERACY	94%
LIFE EXPECTANCY	68 years
GDP PER CAPITA	$4,400

ECONOMY IND: tourism, sugar, clothing, copra **AGR:** sugarcane, coconuts, cassava (tapioca), rice; cattle; fish **EXP:** sugar, garments, gold, timber, fish

Kiribati
REPUBLIC OF KIRIBATI

AREA	811 sq km (313 sq mi)
POPULATION	98,000
CAPITAL	Tarawa 42,000
RELIGION	Roman Catholic, Protestant
LANGUAGE	I-Kiribati, English
LITERACY	NA
LIFE EXPECTANCY	61 years
GDP PER CAPITA	$3,700

ECONOMY IND: fishing, handicrafts **AGR:** copra, taro, breadfruit, sweet potatoes, vegetables; fish **EXP:** copra, coconuts, seaweed, fish

Marshall Islands
REPUBLIC OF THE MARSHALL ISLANDS

AREA	181 sq km (70 sq mi)
POPULATION	53,000
CAPITAL	Majuro 28,000
RELIGION	Protestant, Assembly of God, Roman Catholic
LANGUAGE	Marshallese, English
LITERACY	94%
LIFE EXPECTANCY	66 years
GDP PER CAPITA	$2,900

ECONOMY IND: copra, tuna processing, tourism, craft items (from seashells, wood, and pearls) **AGR:** coconuts, tomatoes, melons, taro; pigs **EXP:** copra cake, coconut oil, handicrafts, fish

Micronesia
FEDERATED STATES OF MICRONESIA

AREA	702 sq km (271 sq mi)
POPULATION	108,000
CAPITAL	Palikir 7,000
RELIGION	Roman Catholic, Protestant
LANGUAGE	English, Chuukese, Kosrean, Pohnpeian, other indigenous languages
LITERACY	89%
LIFE EXPECTANCY	67 years
GDP PER CAPITA	$2,300

ECONOMY IND: tourism, construction, fish processing, specialized aquaculture **AGR:** black pepper, tropical fruits and vegetables, coconuts; pigs; fish **EXP:** fish, garments, bananas, black pepper

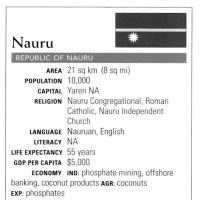

Nauru
REPUBLIC OF NAURU

AREA	21 sq km (8 sq mi)
POPULATION	10,000
CAPITAL	Yaren NA
RELIGION	Nauru Congregational, Roman Catholic, Nauru Independent Church
LANGUAGE	Nauruan, English
LITERACY	NA
LIFE EXPECTANCY	55 years
GDP PER CAPITA	$5,000

ECONOMY IND: phosphate mining, offshore banking, coconut products **AGR:** coconuts **EXP:** phosphates

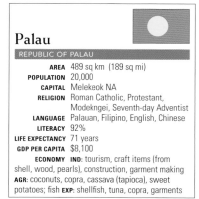

Palau
REPUBLIC OF PALAU

AREA	489 sq km (189 sq mi)
POPULATION	20,000
CAPITAL	Melekeok NA
RELIGION	Roman Catholic, Protestant, Modekngei, Seventh-day Adventist
LANGUAGE	Palauan, Filipino, English, Chinese
LITERACY	92%
LIFE EXPECTANCY	71 years
GDP PER CAPITA	$8,100

ECONOMY IND: tourism, craft items (from shell, wood, pearls), construction, garment making **AGR:** coconuts, copra, cassava (tapioca), sweet potatoes; fish **EXP:** shellfish, tuna, copra, garments

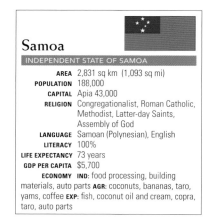

Samoa
INDEPENDENT STATE OF SAMOA

AREA	2,831 sq km (1,093 sq mi)
POPULATION	188,000
CAPITAL	Apia 43,000
RELIGION	Congregationalist, Roman Catholic, Methodist, Latter-day Saints, Assembly of God
LANGUAGE	Samoan (Polynesian), English
LITERACY	100%
LIFE EXPECTANCY	73 years
GDP PER CAPITA	$5,700

ECONOMY IND: food processing, building materials, auto parts **AGR:** coconuts, bananas, taro, yams, coffee **EXP:** fish, coconut oil and cream, copra, taro, auto parts

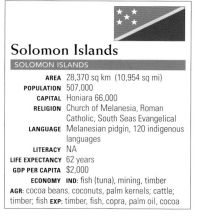

Solomon Islands
SOLOMON ISLANDS

AREA	28,370 sq km (10,954 sq mi)
POPULATION	507,000
CAPITAL	Honiara 66,000
RELIGION	Church of Melanesia, Roman Catholic, South Seas Evangelical
LANGUAGE	Melanesian pidgin, 120 indigenous languages
LITERACY	NA
LIFE EXPECTANCY	62 years
GDP PER CAPITA	$2,000

ECONOMY IND: fish (tuna), mining, timber **AGR:** cocoa beans, coconuts, palm kernels; cattle; timber; fish **EXP:** timber, fish, copra, palm oil, cocoa

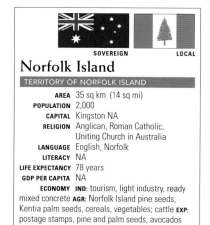

Tonga
KINGDOM OF TONGA

AREA	748 sq km (289 sq mi)
POPULATION	102,000
CAPITAL	Nuku'alofa 25,000
RELIGION	Free Wesleyan Church, other Christian
LANGUAGE	Tongan, English
LITERACY	99%
LIFE EXPECTANCY	71 years
GDP PER CAPITA	$5,400

ECONOMY IND: tourism, construction, fishing **AGR:** squash, coconuts, copra, bananas; fish **EXP:** squash, fish, vanilla beans, root crops

Tuvalu
TUVALU

AREA	26 sq km (10 sq mi)
POPULATION	10,000
CAPITAL	Funafuti 5,000
RELIGION	Church of Tuvalu (Congregationalist)
LANGUAGE	Tuvaluan, English, Samoan, Kiribati
LITERACY	NA
LIFE EXPECTANCY	64 years
GDP PER CAPITA	$1,600

ECONOMY IND: fishing, tourism, copra **AGR:** coconuts; fish **EXP:** copra, fish

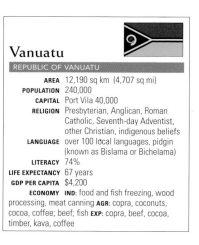

Vanuatu
REPUBLIC OF VANUATU

AREA	12,190 sq km (4,707 sq mi)
POPULATION	240,000
CAPITAL	Port Vila 40,000
RELIGION	Presbyterian, Anglican, Roman Catholic, Seventh-day Adventist, other Christian, indigenous beliefs
LANGUAGE	over 100 local languages, pidgin (known as Bislama or Bichelama)
LITERACY	74%
LIFE EXPECTANCY	67 years
GDP PER CAPITA	$4,200

ECONOMY IND: food and fish freezing, wood processing, meat canning **AGR:** copra, coconuts, cocoa, coffee; beef; fish **EXP:** copra, beef, cocoa, timber, kava, coffee

Dependencies

AUSTRALIA

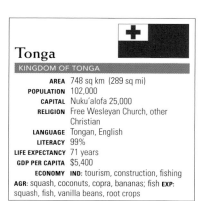

SOVEREIGN   LOCAL

Norfolk Island
TERRITORY OF NORFOLK ISLAND

AREA	35 sq km (14 sq mi)
POPULATION	2,000
CAPITAL	Kingston NA
RELIGION	Anglican, Roman Catholic, Uniting Church in Australia
LANGUAGE	English, Norfolk
LITERACY	NA
LIFE EXPECTANCY	78 years
GDP PER CAPITA	NA

ECONOMY IND: tourism, light industry, ready mixed concrete **AGR:** Norfolk Island pine seeds, Kentia palm seeds, cereals, vegetables; cattle **EXP:** postage stamps, pine and palm seeds, avocados

Coral Sea Islands
CORAL SEA ISLANDS TERRITORY

AREA	Less than 3 sq km (1 sq mi)
POPULATION	none

UNITED KINGDOM

SOVEREIGN   LOCAL

Pitcairn Islands
PITCAIRN, HENDERSON, DUCIE, & OENO IS.

AREA	47 sq km (18 sq mi)
POPULATION	45
CAPITAL	Adamstown 45
RELIGION	Seventh-day Adventist
LANGUAGE	English, Pitkern
LITERACY	NA
LIFE EXPECTANCY	NA
GDP PER CAPITA	NA

ECONOMY IND: postage stamps, handicrafts, beekeeping, honey **AGR:** honey, fruits, vegetables; goats; fish **EXP:** fruits, vegetables, curios, stamps

Dependencies

FRANCE

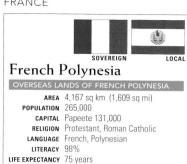

French Polynesia
OVERSEAS LANDS OF FRENCH POLYNESIA

AREA 4,167 sq km (1,609 sq mi)
POPULATION 265,000
CAPITAL Papeete 131,000
RELIGION Protestant, Roman Catholic
LANGUAGE French, Polynesian
LITERACY 98%
LIFE EXPECTANCY 75 years
GDP PER CAPITA $17,500
ECONOMY **IND:** tourism, pearls, agricultural processing, handicrafts, phosphates **AGR:** coconuts, vanilla, vegetables, fruits, coffee; poultry; fish **EXP:** cultured pearls, coconut products, mother-of-pearl, vanilla, shark meat

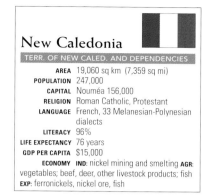

New Caledonia
TERR. OF NEW CALED. AND DEPENDENCIES

AREA 19,060 sq km (7,359 sq mi)
POPULATION 247,000
CAPITAL Nouméa 156,000
RELIGION Roman Catholic, Protestant
LANGUAGE French, 33 Melanesian-Polynesian dialects
LITERACY 96%
LIFE EXPECTANCY 76 years
GDP PER CAPITA $15,000
ECONOMY **IND:** nickel mining and smelting **AGR:** vegetables; beef, deer, other livestock products; fish **EXP:** ferronickels, nickel ore, fish

Wallis and Futuna
TERR. OF THE WALLIS AND FUTUNA ISLANDS

AREA 161 sq km (62 sq mi)
POPULATION 16,000
CAPITAL Matâ'utu 1,000
RELIGION Roman Catholic
LANGUAGE Wallisian (indigenous Polynesian language), Futunian, French
LITERACY 50%
LIFE EXPECTANCY 74 years
GDP PER CAPITA $3,800
ECONOMY **IND:** copra, handicrafts, fishing, lumber **AGR:** breadfruit, yams, taro, bananas; pigs; fish **EXP:** copra, chemicals, construction materials

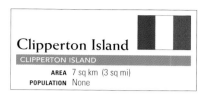

Clipperton Island
CLIPPERTON ISLAND

AREA 7 sq km (3 sq mi)
POPULATION None

NEW ZEALAND

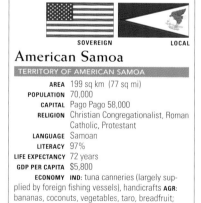

Cook Islands
COOK ISLANDS

AREA 240 sq km (93 sq mi)
POPULATION 11,000
CAPITAL Avarua 10,000
RELIGION Cook Islands Christian Church, Roman Catholic, Seventh-day Adventist
LANGUAGE English, Maori
LITERACY 95%
LIFE EXPECTANCY 70 years
GDP PER CAPITA $9,100
ECONOMY **IND:** fruit processing, tourism, fishing, clothing, handicrafts **AGR:** copra, citrus, pineapples, tomatoes; pigs **EXP:** copra, papayas, fresh and canned citrus fruits, coffee, fish, pearls, clothing

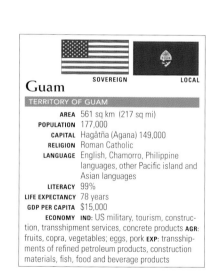

Niue
NIUE

AREA 263 sq km (102 sq mi)
POPULATION 1,300
CAPITAL Alofi 600
RELIGION Ekalesia Niue, Latter-day Saints, Roman Catholic
LANGUAGE Niuean, English
LITERACY 95%
LIFE EXPECTANCY 70 years
GDP PER CAPITA $5,800
ECONOMY **IND:** tourism, handicrafts, food processing **AGR:** coconuts, passion fruit, honey, limes; pigs **EXP:** canned coconut cream, copra, honey, vanilla, passion fruit products, pawpaws

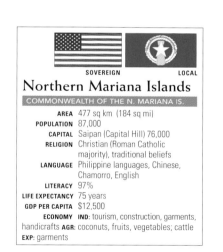

Tokelau
TOKELAU

AREA 12 sq km (5 sq mi)
POPULATION 1,500
CAPITAL none
RELIGION Congregational Christian Church, Roman Catholic
LANGUAGE Tokelauan (a Polynesian language), English
LITERACY NA
LIFE EXPECTANCY 69 years
GDP PER CAPITA $1,000
ECONOMY **IND:** small-scale copra production, woodworking, plaited craft goods, stamps, coins, fishing **AGR:** coconuts, copra, breadfruit, papayas; pigs; fish **EXP:** stamps, copra, handicrafts

UNITED STATES

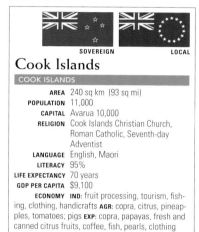

American Samoa
TERRITORY OF AMERICAN SAMOA

AREA 199 sq km (77 sq mi)
POPULATION 70,000
CAPITAL Pago Pago 58,000
RELIGION Christian Congregationalist, Roman Catholic, Protestant
LANGUAGE Samoan
LITERACY 97%
LIFE EXPECTANCY 72 years
GDP PER CAPITA $5,800
ECONOMY **IND:** tuna canneries (largely supplied by foreign fishing vessels), handicrafts **AGR:** bananas, coconuts, vegetables, taro, breadfruit; dairy products **EXP:** canned tuna

Guam
TERRITORY OF GUAM

AREA 561 sq km (217 sq mi)
POPULATION 177,000
CAPITAL Hagåtña (Agana) 149,000
RELIGION Roman Catholic
LANGUAGE English, Chamorro, Philippine languages, other Pacific island and Asian languages
LITERACY 99%
LIFE EXPECTANCY 78 years
GDP PER CAPITA $15,000
ECONOMY **IND:** US military, tourism, construction, transshipment services, concrete products **AGR:** fruits, copra, vegetables; eggs, pork **EXP:** transshipments of refined petroleum products, construction materials, fish, food and beverage products

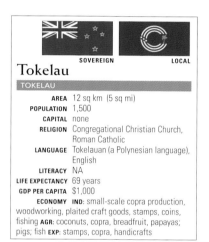

Northern Mariana Islands
COMMONWEALTH OF THE N. MARIANA IS.

AREA 477 sq km (184 sq mi)
POPULATION 87,000
CAPITAL Saipan (Capital Hill) 76,000
RELIGION Christian (Roman Catholic majority), traditional beliefs
LANGUAGE Philippine languages, Chinese, Chamorro, English
LITERACY 97%
LIFE EXPECTANCY 75 years
GDP PER CAPITA $12,500
ECONOMY **IND:** tourism, construction, garments, handicrafts **AGR:** coconuts, fruits, vegetables; cattle **EXP:** garments

Baker Island
BAKER ISLAND

AREA 1.4 sq km (0.5 sq mi)
POPULATION None

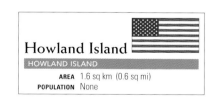

Howland Island
HOWLAND ISLAND

AREA 1.6 sq km (0.6 sq mi)
POPULATION None

Jarvis Island
JARVIS ISLAND

AREA 4.5 sq km (1.7 sq mi)
POPULATION None

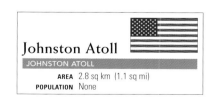

Johnston Atoll
JOHNSTON ATOLL

AREA 2.8 sq km (1.1 sq mi)
POPULATION None

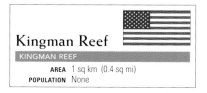

Kingman Reef
KINGMAN REEF

AREA 1 sq km (0.4 sq mi)
POPULATION None

Midway Islands
MIDWAY ISLANDS

AREA 6.2 sq km (2.4 sq mi)
POPULATION None

Palmyra Atoll
PALMYRA ATOLL

AREA 11.9 sq km (4.6 sq mi)
POPULATION None

Wake Island
WAKE ISLAND

AREA 6.5 sq km (2.5 sq mi)
POPULATION None

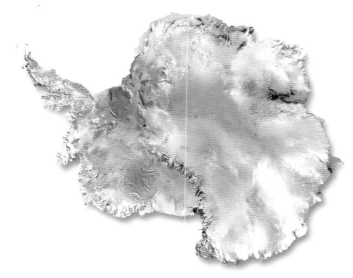

Antarctica

A tabular iceberg drifts in the Bransfield Strait near the tip of the Antarctic Peninsula. These types of icebergs, which break off of ice shelves, can be very large. B-15, which calved from the Ross Ice Shelf in March 2000, measured nearly 4,244 square miles (10,990 sq km), the size of Jamaica, before it broke into relatively smaller bergs.

Often called the last wilderness on Earth, Antarctica's unspoiled expanses of austere frozen beauty remain largely untouched by humans. Antarctica is the driest, coldest, windiest, and least populated of Earth's seven continents, and an average elevation of 8,000 ft (2,438 m) makes it the highest as well. It is larger than Europe or Australia; its 5.1 million square miles (13.2 million sq km) of ice-shrouded land sit at the bottom of the world.

Antarctica's ice cap, the greatest body of ice in the world, holds some 70 percent of Earth's fresh water. Yet despite all this ice and water, the Antarctic interior averages only two inches of precipitation per year, making it the largest ice desert in the world; the little snow that does fall, however, almost never melts.

The immensely heavy ice sheet, averaging over a mile (1.6 km) thick and reaching almost three miles (4.8 km) thick in places, compresses much of the continent's surface to below sea level. The weight actually deforms the South Pole, creating a slightly pear-shaped Earth.

Beneath the ice exists a continent of valleys, lakes, islands, and mountains, little dreamed of until the compilation of more than 2.5 million ice-thickness measurements revealed startling topography below. Less than 2 percent of Antarctica actually breaks through the ice cover to reveal stretches of coastline, islands, and features such as the outstanding Transantarctic Mountains, which extend for 1,800 miles (2,898 km) and separate East and West Antarctica.

In spite of perpetual light during the Antarctic summer (December to March), little heat accumulates because the white, snowy landscape reflects as much as 90 percent of the sun's incoming rays. During the half year of darkness, terrible cold and storms buffet the continent. The winter of 1983 saw the lowest temperature ever recorded on Earth—minus 128.6°F (-89.2°C).

Annual winter temperatures over the elevated central plateau average minus 80°F (-62.2°C), and this cold season causes the ice around Antarctica to grow quickly. Sea ice averaging six feet (2 m) deep more than doubles the size of the continent, extending outward to create a belt ranging from 300 miles to more than 1,000 miles (483–1,610 km) wide.

In spring, melting ice coincides with calving of huge white and blue-green icebergs from the Antarctic glaciers. The largest iceberg ever spotted, in 1956, measured 208 miles (335 km) long by 60 miles (97 km) wide, slightly larger than Belgium.

Antarctica's southern ocean, which holds 10 percent of the world's seawater, swirls in rhythm with the Antarctic Circumpolar Current, the largest, fastest current in the world, which sweeps clockwise around the globe unimpeded by any land. These high southern latitudes experience extremes of wind and weather. At around 60° south latitude, a remarkable interface of relatively warm waters from the southern Atlantic, Indian, and Pacific Oceans and the cold southern ocean creates conditions for an eruption of rich nutrients, phytoplankton, and zooplankton. These form the base for a flourishing marine ecosystem. Though limited in numbers of species—for example, only about 120 kinds of the world's 20,000 fish swim here—Antarctica's animal life has adapted extremely well to so harsh a climate. Seasonal feeding and energy storage in fats exemplify this specialization. Well-known animals of the far south include seals, whales, and distinctive birds such as flightless penguins, albatrosses, terns, and petrels.

PHYSICAL GEOGRAPHY Every summer thousands of scientists travel to Antarctica to obtain vital information about Earth's weather and ecology and the state of the southernmost continent. This interest attests to the region's role as a pristine laboratory, where measurements and rates of change in numerous scientific fields can point to larger issues of the world's environmental health.

Antarctica's oceanic and atmospheric system—indicator and element of climate change—is a main area of focus. Oceanographers attempt to understand more fully the global exchange of heat, sea-ice dynamics, salt and trace elements, and the entire marine biosphere. Other important research has included the 1985 discovery of a hole in Earth's

protective ozone layer by scientists at the British Halley research station. This find brought to prominence a major ecological threat.

Ice and sediment cores provide insight into the world's ancient climate and allow for comparison with conditions today. Studies of the Antarctic ice sheet help predict future sea levels, important news for the three billion people who live in coastal areas. If the Antarctic ice sheet were to melt, global seas would rise by an estimated 200 feet, inundating many oceanic islands and gravely altering the world's coastlines.

Three basic water masses comprise the southern ocean: Antarctic Surface Water, Circumpolar Deep Water, and Antarctic Bottom Water. Sharp boundaries separate the water masses, each with its own characteristics. These differences drive circulation around the continent and contribute to the global heat engine and overall transfer of energy around the world.

Prominent physical features include the Vinson Massif, Antarctica's highest mountain at 16,067 feet (4,897 m). Discovered only in 1958 by U.S. Navy aircraft, it was first climbed by an American team in 1966.

The Antarctic Peninsula, reaching like a long arm 800 miles (1,288 km) into the Southern Ocean toward the tip of South America, is made up of a mountain range and many islands linked together by ice. Seals, penguins, and other sea birds find it particularly suitable, and the peninsula's relative accessibility makes it the Antarctic area most visited by humans.

The continent's only sizable river, the Onyx, arises from a coastal glacier near McMurdo Sound. Every summer its waters flow inland for some 20 miles (32 km), replenishing and raising the surface level of Lake Vanda, one of several lakes in the Dry Valleys. These valleys, free of snow and ice unlike the rest of Antarctica, were created by ancient glaciers. They stretch to the coast from the Transantarctic Mountains, a range high enough here to prevent the great Polar Plateau ice sheet from flowing down to the sea through the Dry Valleys, perhaps the driest places on Earth.

Immense ice shelves, produced by the main plateau disgorging masses of ice, rim much of the continent's coast and extend far into the sea. Largest are the Ross Ice Shelf, the size of France, and the Ronne Ice Shelf.

Special names exist for the many different types of ice: frazil ice, an early stage of sea-ice growth in which crystals below the surface form an unstructured slush; nilas, a thin sheen of ice on the sea surface that bends but does not break with wave action; pancake ice, named for its flattened circular shape; pack ice, frozen sea water and floating ice driven together to form a continuous mass; and fast ice, that part of the sea-ice cover attached to land.

Scientists seeking to understand sea ice are suspended above the icescape. Pancake ice forms when a thin surface film of ice crystals breaks up and thickens into irregular disks. These disks can measure from 1 to 10 feet (0.3–3 m) in diameter. Constant battering of the disks against one another causes the turned-up rims.

CULTURE, HISTORY, AND EXPLORATION The search for Antarctica represented the last great adventure of global exploration. British Capt. James Cook crossed three times into Antarctic waters between 1772 and 1775 and was probably the first to cross the Antarctic Circle. Though he never saw the continent, he believed in "a tract of land at the Pole that is the source of all the ice that is spread over this vast southern ocean."

His observations of marine mammals in great numbers lured whalers and sealers into the freezing southern waters in search of skins and oil. First sightings of the continent then followed in 1820.

Scientists seeking the south magnetic pole included British naval officer James Clark Ross, who between 1839–43 charted unknown territory, including a giant ice shelf later named after him, and located the approximate position of the south magnetic pole—the point toward which a compass needle points from any direction throughout surrounding areas.

In 1895 Norwegian whalers landed on the continent beyond the Antarctic Peninsula for the first time, and in 1898 a major Belgian scientific expedition overwintered in the Antarctic when their ship became stuck in pack ice for almost 13 months.

Douglas Mawson reached the south magnetic pole as part of Ernest Shackleton's 1907 Nimrod expedition. Later, Mawson led the Australasian Antarctic Expedition (1911–14), which produced observations in magnetism, geology, biology, and meteorology.

A race to reach the South Geographic Pole came to a climax in 1911–12. Norwegian Roald Amundsen's expedition reached the South Pole on December 14, 1911, after 97 days on the move, relying on husky dogs to pull their sleds. Simultaneously, the British team of Robert Falcon Scott and four companions set off unaware of Amundsen's swifter, better-managed effort. Scott's use of Manchurian ponies proved a mistake; his team reached the Pole 34 days later, only to find the Norwegian flag flying. The five men began the bitter return trip, but succumbed to cold, hunger, exhaustion, and bad weather, just 11 miles (18 km) from supplies. All died.

Another epic adventure involved Ernest Shackleton, whose British expedition aimed to traverse the entire continent. In 1915 Shackleton's main party of 28 men became stranded when sea ice trapped and crushed their ship. After more than a year on drifting ice, they sailed in lifeboats to Elephant Island at the tip of the Antarctic Peninsula. Shackleton and five others then embarked on an astonishing 800-mile (1,288 km) journey in a small boat to South Georgia, from where he eventually rescued his other men.

In 1935 Caroline Mikkelsen, wife of a Norwegian whaling captain, became the first woman to stand on Antarctica. Almost a dozen years later the U.S. Navy brought 4,700 men, 13 ships, and 23 aircraft to the continent, using icebreakers for the first time. The vast enterprise mapped large areas of the coastline and interior and took 70,000 aerial photographs.

The modern scientific era arrived with the 18-month-long International Geophysical Year (IGY, 1957–58), when many nations advanced knowledge of the continent. The Antarctic Treaty, signed in 1959 by 12 leading IGY participants, has done much to protect Antarctica.

Today around 45 research stations stand at many sites around Antarctica, and an ever shifting population, including tourists, can reach as high as 23,000 people in the summer. Tourism brings its own troubles. Recently, species of non-native grasses, presumably carried on visitors' clothing, have been found on the continent. Further unintentional aliens, such as algae, crustaceans, and parasites arrive on floating plastic bottles and other man-made debris.

MINERALS AND ECONOMY Many believe Antarctica has great resource wealth, but the harsh climate, short work season, and need to drill through thick ice make the recovery of these resources difficult.

Minerals under the ice include gold, uranium, cobalt, chromium, nickel, copper, iron, and platinum, as well as potentially large deposits of diamonds. Oil probably exists below the ocean floor, and coal deposits have been detected along the coast and throughout the Transantarctic Mountains.

A pressing reason to limit mineral exploration and drilling is Antarctica's extreme fragility. Sensitive plants, including rare moss beds on the Antarctic Peninsula, take three to four hundred years to grow, and a single human boot can cause tremendous damage.

In January 1998 an addition to the Antarctic Treaty, known as the Madrid Protocol, went into force, deeming Antarctica a natural reserve devoted to peace and science. It specifically banned mining and mineral exploitation of any kind until 2048.

But pressure builds yearly to find new mineral and petroleum deposits. Despite the ban, Russia and other countries appear to be actively exploring Antarctic oil, gas, and mineral resources. Also significant is the growing commercialization of southern ocean fisheries. Particularly vulnerable are the tiny shrimp-like krill that form a vital part of Antarctica's food chain. The collapse of fish and krill species might be analogous to the wholesale slaughter of fur seal populations in the late 1700s and early 1800s and the near destruction of the southern ocean's whales in the 20th century.

Antarctica already witnesses vehicle pollution; dumping of plastics, solid wastes, food, and batteries; burning of fossil fuels; and construction of roads and airstrips at the many scientific bases.

Even the most obvious resource of all—ice—may one day serve to relieve thirsty nations. Ships towing icebergs from Antarctica to all parts of the world could deliver this huge potential of fresh water, but at present such a project is simply too expensive.

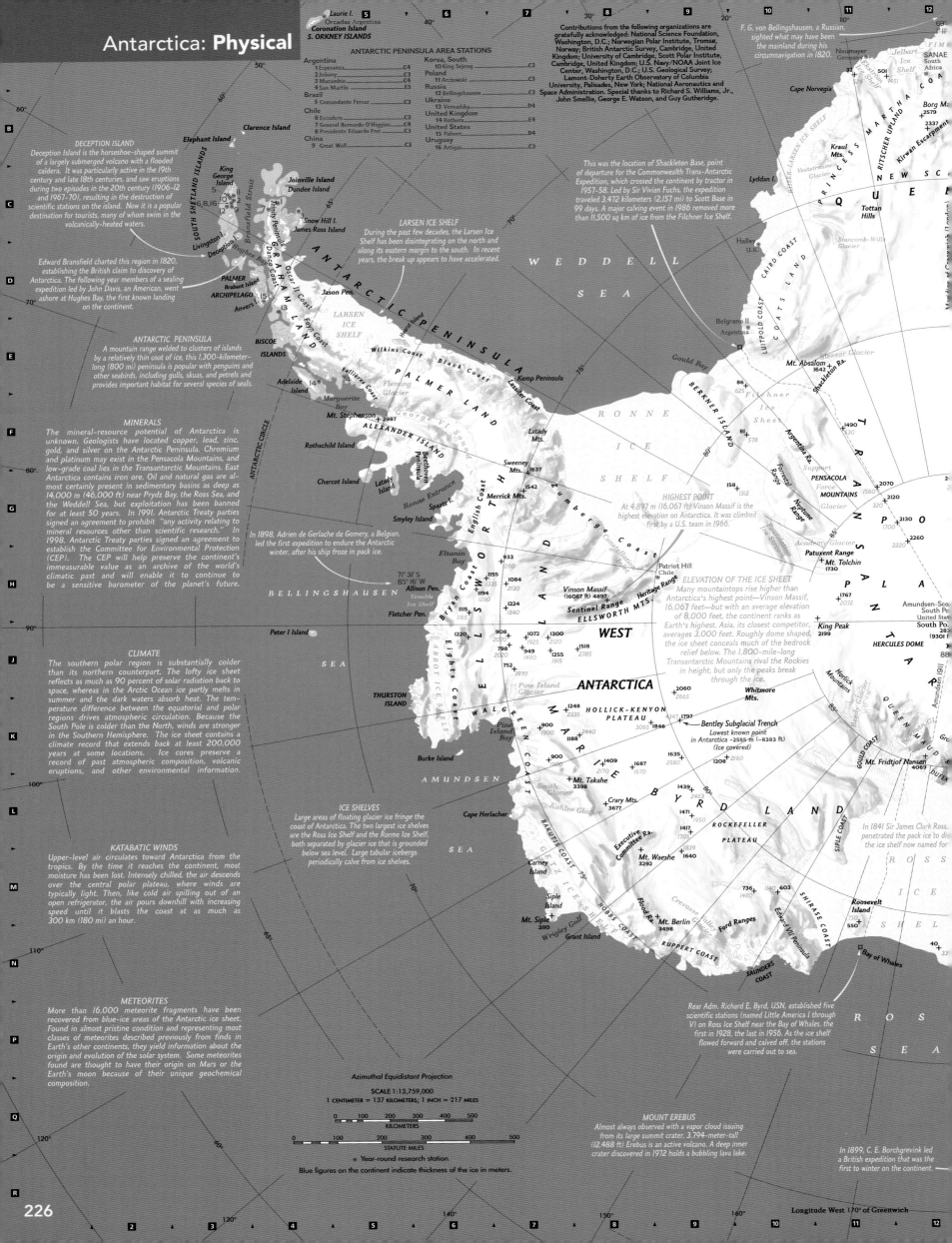

Antarctica: Physical

Contributions from the following organizations are gratefully acknowledged: National Science Foundation, Washington, D.C.; Norwegian Polar Institute, Tromsø, Norway; British Antarctic Survey, Cambridge, United Kingdom; University of Cambridge, Scott Polar Institute, Cambridge, United Kingdom; U.S. Navy/NOAA Joint Ice Center, Washington, D.C.; U.S. Geological Survey; Lamont-Doherty Earth Observatory of Columbia University, Palisades, New York; National Aeronautics and Space Administration. Special thanks to Richard S. Williams, Jr., John Smellie, George E. Watson, and Guy Gutheridge.

ANTARCTIC PENINSULA AREA STATIONS

Argentina
1 Esperanza C4
2 Jubany C4
3 Marambio C4
4 San Martín E5

Brazil
5 Comandante Ferraz C4

Chile
6 Escudero C3
7 General Bernardo O'Higgins C4
8 Presidente Eduardo Frei ... C3

China
9 Great Wall C3

Korea, South
10 King Sejong C3

Poland
11 Arctowski C4

Russia
12 Bellingshausen C3

Ukraine
13 Vernadsky D4

United Kingdom
14 Rothera E4

United States
15 Palmer D4

Uruguay
16 Artigas C3

DECEPTION ISLAND
Deception Island is the horseshoe-shaped summit of a largely submerged volcano with a flooded caldera. It was particularly active in the 19th century and late 18th centuries, and saw eruptions during two episodes in the 20th century (1906-12 and 1967-70), resulting in the destruction of scientific stations on the island. Now it is a popular destination for tourists, many of whom swim in the volcanically-heated waters.

Edward Bransfield charted this region in 1820, establishing the British claim to discovery of Antarctica. The following year members of a sealing expedition led by John Davis, an American, went ashore at Hughes Bay, the first known landing on the continent.

ANTARCTIC PENINSULA
A mountain range welded to clusters of islands by a relatively thin coat of ice, this 1,300-kilometer-long (800 mi) peninsula is popular with penguins and other seabirds, including gulls, skuas, and petrels and provides important habitat for several species of seals.

MINERALS
The mineral-resource potential of Antarctica is unknown. Geologists have located copper, lead, zinc, gold, and silver on the Antarctic Peninsula. Chromium and platinum may exist in the Pensacola Mountains, and low-grade coal lies in the Transantarctic Mountains. East Antarctica contains iron ore. Oil and natural gas are almost certainly present in sedimentary basins as deep as 14,000 m (46,000 ft) near Prydz Bay, the Ross Sea, and the Weddell Sea, but exploitation has been banned for at least 50 years. In 1991, Antarctic Treaty parties signed an agreement to prohibit "any activity relating to mineral resources other than scientific research." In 1998, Antarctic Treaty parties signed an agreement to establish the Committee for Environmental Protection (CEP). The CEP will help preserve the continent's immeasurable value as an archive of the world's climatic past and will enable it to continue to be a sensitive barometer of the planet's future.

CLIMATE
The southern polar region is substantially colder than its northern counterpart. The lofty ice sheet reflects as much as 90 percent of solar radiation back to space, whereas in the Arctic Ocean ice partly melts in summer and the dark waters absorb heat. The temperature difference between the equatorial and polar regions drives atmospheric circulation. Because the South Pole is colder than the North, winds are stronger in the Southern Hemisphere. The ice sheet contains a climate record that extends back at least 200,000 years at some locations. Ice cores preserve a record of past atmospheric composition, volcanic eruptions, and other environmental information.

KATABATIC WINDS
Upper-level air circulates toward Antarctica from the tropics. By the time it reaches the continent, most moisture has been lost. Intensely chilled, the air descends over the central polar plateau, where winds are typically light. Then, like cold air spilling out of an open refrigerator, the air pours downhill with increasing speed until it blasts the coast at as much as 300 km (180 mi) an hour.

METEORITES
More than 16,000 meteorite fragments have been recovered from blue-ice areas of the Antarctic ice sheet. Found in almost pristine condition and representing most classes of meteorites described previously from finds on Earth's other continents, they yield information about the origin and evolution of the solar system. Some meteorites found are thought to have their origin on Mars or the Earth's moon because of their unique geochemical composition.

LARSEN ICE SHELF
During the past few decades, the Larsen Ice Shelf has been disintegrating on the north and along its eastern margin to the south. In recent years, the break up appears to have accelerated.

This was the location of Shackleton Base, point of departure for the Commonwealth Trans-Antarctic Expedition, which crossed the continent by tractor in 1957-58. Led by Sir Vivian Fuchs, the expedition traveled 3,472 kilometers (2,157 mi) to Scott Base in 99 days. A major calving event in 1986 removed more than 11,500 sq km of ice from the Filchner Ice Shelf.

F. G. von Bellingshausen, a Russian, sighted what may have been the mainland during his circumnavigation in 1820.

HIGHEST POINT
At 4,897 m (16,067 ft) Vinson Massif is the highest elevation on Antarctica. It was climbed first by a U.S. team in 1966.

ELEVATION OF THE ICE SHEET
Many mountaintops rise higher than Antarctica's highest point—Vinson Massif, 16,067 feet—but with an average elevation of 8,000 feet, the continent ranks as Earth's highest. Asia, its closest competitor, averages 3,000 feet. Roughly dome shaped, the ice sheet conceals much of the bedrock relief below. The 1,800-mile-long Transantarctic Mountains rival the Rockies in height, but only the peaks break through the ice.

Bentley Subglacial Trench
Lowest known point in Antarctica -2555 m (-8383 ft) (Ice covered)

ICE SHELVES
Large areas of floating glacier ice fringe the coast of Antarctica. The two largest ice shelves are the Ross Ice Shelf and the Ronne Ice Shelf, both separated by glacier ice that is grounded below sea level. Large tabular icebergs periodically calve from ice shelves.

Rear Adm. Richard E. Byrd, USN, established five scientific stations (named Little America I through V) on Ross Ice Shelf near the Bay of Whales, the first in 1928, the last in 1956. As the ice shelf flowed forward and calved off, the stations were carried out to sea.

In 1841 Sir James Clark Ross penetrated the pack ice to discover the ice shelf now named for him.

In 1899, C. E. Borchgrevink led a British expedition that was the first to winter on the continent.

MOUNT EREBUS
Almost always observed with a vapor cloud issuing from its large summit crater, 3,794-meter-tall (12,448 ft) Erebus is an active volcano. A deep inner crater discovered in 1972 holds a bubbling lava lake.

Azimuthal Equidistant Projection

SCALE 1:13,759,000
1 CENTIMETER = 137 KILOMETERS; 1 INCH = 217 MILES

0 100 200 300 400 500
KILOMETERS

0 100 200 300 400 500
STATUTE MILES

● Year-round research station

Blue figures on the continent indicate thickness of the ice in meters.

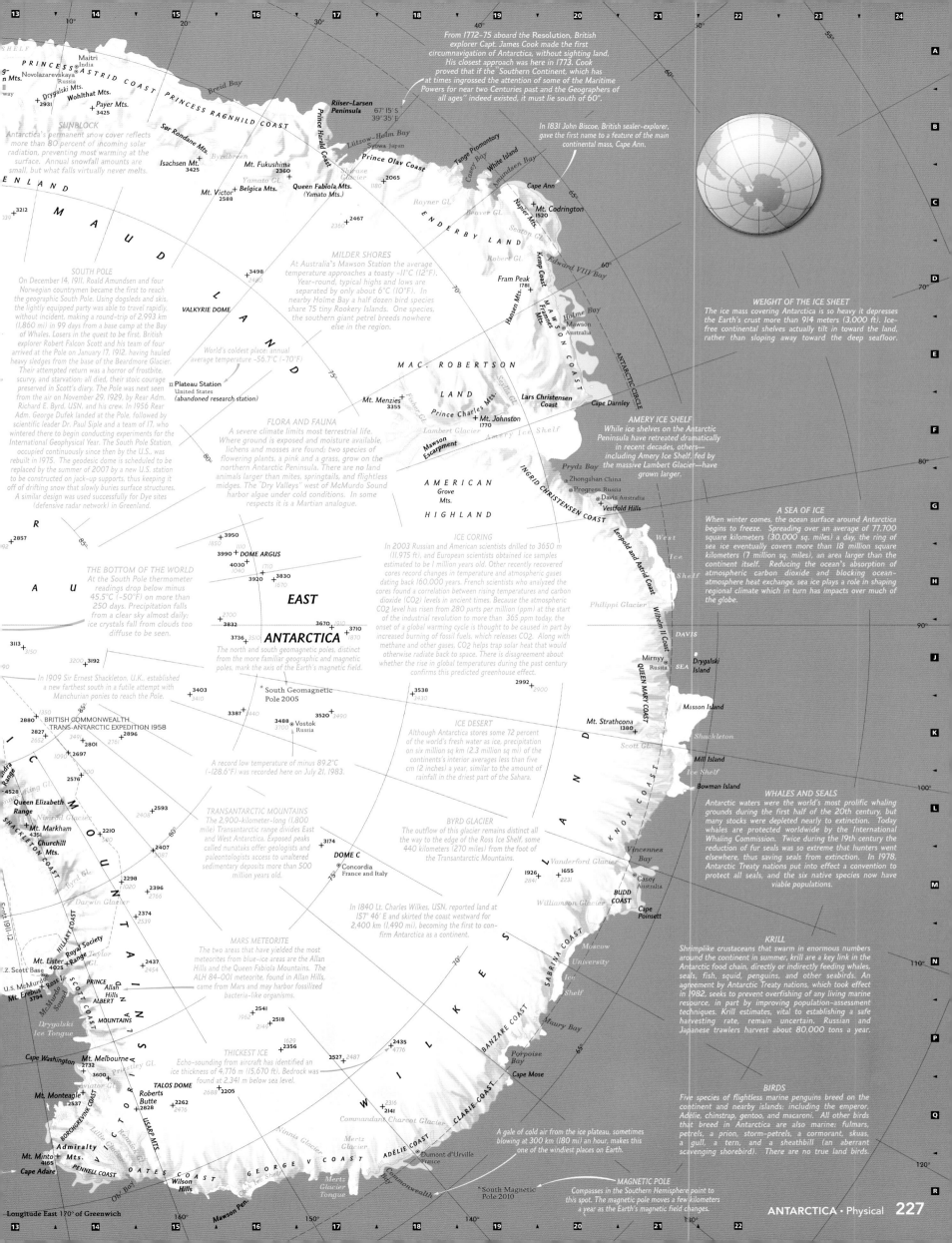

PRINCESS ASTRID COAST   PRINCESS RAGNHILD COAST

SUNBLOCK
Antarctica's permanent snow cover reflects more than 80 percent of incoming solar radiation, preventing most warming at the surface. Annual snowfall amounts are small, but what falls virtually never melts.

From 1772–75 aboard the Resolution, British explorer Capt. James Cook made the first circumnavigation of Antarctica, without sighting land. His closest approach was here in 1773. Cook proved that if the "Southern Continent, which has at times ingrossed the attention of some of the Maritime Powers for near two Centuries past and the Geographers of all ages" indeed existed, it must lie south of 60°.

In 1831 John Biscoe, British sealer-explorer, gave the first name to a feature of the main continental mass, Cape Ann.

WEIGHT OF THE ICE SHEET
The ice mass covering Antarctica is so heavy it depresses the Earth's crust more than 914 meters (3,000 ft). Ice-free continental shelves actually tilt in toward the land, rather than sloping away toward the deep seafloor.

SOUTH POLE
On December 14, 1911, Roald Amundsen and four Norwegian countrymen became the first to reach the geographic South Pole. Using dogsleds and skis, the lightly equipped party was able to travel rapidly, without incident, making a round-trip of 2,993 km (1,860 mi) in 99 days from a base camp at the Bay of Whales. Losers in the quest to be first, British explorer Robert Falcon Scott and his team of four arrived at the Pole on January 17, 1912, having hauled heavy sledges from the base of the Beardmore Glacier. Their attempted return was a horror of frostbite, scurvy, and starvation; all died, their stoic courage preserved in Scott's diary. The Pole was next seen from the air on November 29, 1929, by Rear Adm. Richard E. Byrd, USN, and his crew. In 1956 Rear Adm. George Dufek landed at the Pole, followed by scientific leader Dr. Paul Siple and a team of 17, who wintered there to begin conducting experiments for the International Geophysical Year. The South Pole Station, occupied continuously since then by the U.S., was rebuilt in 1975. The geodesic dome is scheduled to be replaced by the summer of 2007 by a new U.S. station to be constructed on jack-up supports, thus keeping it off of drifting snow that slowly buries surface structures. A similar design was used successfully for Dye sites (defensive radar network) in Greenland.

MILDER SHORES
At Australia's Mawson Station the average temperature approaches a toasty –11°C (12°F). Year-round, typical highs and lows are separated by only about 6°C (10°F). In nearby Holme Bay a half dozen bird species share 75 tiny Rookery Islands. One species, the southern giant petrel breeds nowhere else in the region.

World's coldest place; annual average temperature –56.7°C (–70°F)

Plateau Station United States (abandoned research station)

FLORA AND FAUNA
A severe climate limits most terrestrial life. Where ground is exposed and moisture available, lichens and mosses are found; two species of flowering plants, a pink and a grass, grow on the northern Antarctic Peninsula. There are no land animals larger than mites, springtails, and flightless midges. The "Dry Valleys" west of McMurdo Sound harbor algae under cold conditions. In some respects it is a Martian analogue.

AMERY ICE SHELF
While ice shelves on the Antarctic Peninsula have retreated dramatically in recent decades, others—including Amery Ice Shelf, fed by the massive Lambert Glacier—have grown larger.

A SEA OF ICE
When winter comes, the ocean surface around Antarctica begins to freeze. Spreading over an average of 77,700 square kilometers (30,000 sq. miles) a day, the ring of sea ice eventually covers more than 18 million square kilometers (7 million sq. miles), an area larger than the continent itself. Reducing the ocean's absorption of atmospheric carbon dioxide and blocking ocean-atmosphere heat exchange, sea ice plays a role in shaping regional climate which in turn has impacts over much of the globe.

ICE CORING
In 2003 Russian and American scientists drilled to 3650 m (11,975 ft), and European scientists obtained ice samples estimated to be 1 million years old. Other recently recovered cores record changes in temperature and atmospheric gases dating back 160,000 years. French scientists who analyzed the cores found a correlation between rising temperatures and carbon dioxide (CO2) levels in ancient times. Because the atmospheric CO2 level has risen from 280 parts per million (ppm) at the start of the industrial revolution to more than 365 ppm today, the onset of a global warming cycle is thought to be caused in part by increased burning of fossil fuels, which releases CO2. Along with methane and other gases, CO2 helps trap solar heat that would otherwise radiate back to space. There is disagreement about whether the rise in global temperatures during the past century confirms this predicted greenhouse effect.

EAST ANTARCTICA
The north and south geomagnetic poles, distinct from the more familiar geographic and magnetic poles, mark the axis of the Earth's magnetic field.

THE BOTTOM OF THE WORLD
At the South Pole thermometer readings drop below minus 45.5°C (–50°F) on more than 250 days. Precipitation falls from a clear sky almost daily; ice crystals fall from clouds too diffuse to be seen.

In 1909 Sir Ernest Shackleton, U.K., established a new farthest south in a futile attempt with Manchurian ponies to reach the Pole.

BRITISH COMMONWEALTH TRANS-ANTARCTIC EXPEDITION 1958

South Geomagnetic Pole 2005

A record low temperature of minus 89.2°C (–128.6°F) was recorded here on July 21, 1983.

Vostok Russia

ICE DESERT
Although Antarctica stores some 72 percent of the world's fresh water as ice, precipitation on six million sq km (2.3 million sq mi) of the continents's interior averages less than five cm (2 inches) a year, similar to the amount of rainfall in the driest part of the Sahara.

WHALES AND SEALS
Antarctic waters were the world's most prolific whaling grounds during the first half of the 20th century, but many stocks were depleted nearly to extinction. Today whales are protected worldwide by the International Whaling Commission. Twice during the 19th century the reduction of fur seals was so extreme that hunters went elsewhere, thus saving seals from extinction. In 1978, Antarctic Treaty nations put into effect a convention to protect all seals, and the six native species now have viable populations.

TRANSANTARCTIC MOUNTAINS
The 2,900-kilometer-long (1,800 mile) Transantarctic range divides East and West Antarctica. Exposed peaks called nunataks offer geologists and paleontologists access to unaltered sedimentary deposits more than 500 million years old.

BYRD GLACIER
The outflow of this glacier remains distinct all the way to the edge of the Ross Ice Shelf, some 440 kilometers (270 miles) from the foot of the Transantarctic Mountains.

DOME C
Concordia France and Italy

KRILL
Shrimplike crustaceans that swarm in enormous numbers around the continent in summer, krill are a key link in the Antarctic food chain, directly or indirectly feeding whales, seals, fish, squid, penguins, and other seabirds. An agreement by Antarctic Treaty nations, which took effect in 1982, seeks to prevent overfishing of any living marine resource, in part by improving population-assessment techniques. Krill estimates, vital to establishing a safe harvesting rate, remain uncertain. Russian and Japanese trawlers harvest about 80,000 tons a year.

In 1840 Lt. Charles Wilkes, USN, reported land at 157° 46' E and skirted the coast westward for 2,400 km (1,490 mi), becoming the first to confirm Antarctica as a continent.

MARS METEORITE
The two areas that have yielded the most meteorites from blue-ice areas are the Allan Hills and the Queen Fabiola Mountains. The ALH 84-001 meteorite, found in Allan Hills, came from Mars and may harbor fossilized bacteria-like organisms.

BIRDS
Five species of flightless marine penguins breed on the continent and nearby islands; including the emperor, Adélie, chinstrap, gentoo, and macaroni. All other birds that breed in Antarctica are also marine: fulmars, petrels, a prion, storm-petrels, a cormorant, skuas, a gull, a tern, and a sheathbill (an aberrant scavenging shorebird). There are no true land birds.

THICKEST ICE
Echo-sounding from aircraft has identified an ice thickness of 4,776 m (15,670 ft). Bedrock was found at 2,341 m below sea level.

A gale of cold air from the ice plateau, sometimes blowing at 300 km (180 mi) an hour, makes this one of the windiest places on Earth.

MAGNETIC POLE
Compasses in the Southern Hemisphere point to this spot. The magnetic pole moves a few kilometers a year as the Earth's magnetic field changes.

South Magnetic Pole 2010

Longitude East 170° of Greenwich

ANTARCTICA · Physical   **227**

Elevation of the Ice Sheet

Antarctica is Earth's coldest, driest, and on average highest continent (about 8,000 ft; 2,438 m). The continent is covered by a vast ice sheet that blankets over 96 percent of the land mass. The highest point, located in East Antarctica, rises to 13,222 feet (4,030 m). The ice sheet is interrupted only by occasional mountain peaks that pierce the ice. One such peak is the Vinson Massif, Antarctica's highest point, which reaches an elevation of 16,067 feet (4,897 m) and is located in West Antarctica. Otherwise the icy surface is smooth (surface slopes rarely exceed more than 1 or 2 degrees). The shape of the ice sheet is determined in part by the weight of the ice itself, which causes the ice to flow outward. It is also determined in part by forces acting at the base of the ice sheet that tend to restrain it. The balance of these forces leads to a characteristically parabola-like shape.

Departures from this simple shape occur as the ice from the interior domes spreads slowly over hills and valleys in the rocky base and where coastal mountain ranges channel the flow into outlet glaciers. Ice shelves form where there is sufficient ice to spread over the ocean. Ice shelves are the lowest and flattest parts of the ice sheet and are the source of the huge tabular icebergs that intermittently calve into the coastal ocean.

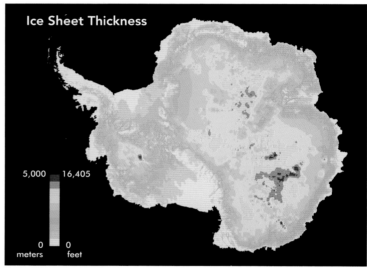

Surface Elevation

Vinson Massif 4897 m (16,067 ft) Highest elevation on Antarctica

5,000 — 16,405

0 — 0
meters — feet

Measurements of a Paradox

Ninety percent of the world's ice and 70 percent of the world's fresh water are found here, yet most of Antarctica is truly a desert. The snow equivalent of less than three inches of rain falls over the high interior of the continent each year. But snow and ice have been slowly accumulating on Antarctica for millions of years. More than 15,600 feet (4,755 m) deep at its thickest, the mean depth of the ice exceeds 6,600 feet (2,012 m). Ice is generally much thicker on the interior of the ice sheet than at edges. This is because ice flows from the interior to edges, where it eventually returns to the ocean either in the form of icebergs or by melting directly into the ocean. The few areas of thin ice on the interior lie over chains of subglacial mountains. Glaciologists measure ice thickness with either a downward-pointing radar or by seismic sounding, which records the echo from an explosive shot buried just beneath the surface of the ice sheet. The thickness measurements used for this map were collected by scientists from 15 nations over the last 50 years. Although in theory the amount of ice in the ice sheet is sufficient to raise global sea levels by approximately 187 feet (57 m), it is extremely unlikely that the entire ice sheet could be lost in the foreseeable future.

Ice Sheet Thickness

5,000 — 16,405

0 — 0
meters — feet

Ice on the Move

Glaciologists once thought that ice motion in Antarctica's interior was slow and relatively uniform, with just a few fast-moving outlet glaciers and some ice streams (in West Antarctica) drawing ice from the interior down to the ice shelves and the sea. A computer model of ice flow, based on new satellite elevation measurements, suggests a more intricate ice-movement pattern. Like rivers, coastal ice flows appear to be fed by complex systems of tributaries that penetrate hundreds of miles into major drainage basins, and the major streams identified in East Antarctica dwarf those of the West. New satellite-based radar images agree with this more dynamic view. Ice velocities in the streams can be ten times greater than the flow of the adjacent slow-moving ice, and the resulting stream boundaries are often heavily crevassed and detectable from space. The computer model combines measurements of surface elevation, ice sheet thickness, and snowfall to calculate the pattern of ice flow that would keep Antarctica in balance at its present shape. The resulting continent-wide baseline picture of this "balanced" flow generally resembles the actual situation, and detailed observations can be compared against it to uncover any changes occurring in the size and shape of the ice sheet.

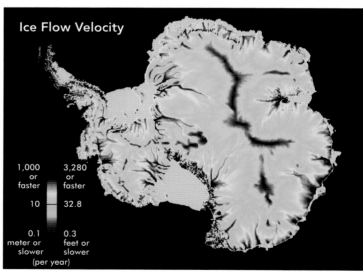

Ice Flow Velocity

1,000 or faster — 3,280 or faster

10 — 32.8

0.1 meter or slower — 0.3 feet or slower
(per year)

Ultimate Winds

Katabatic winds—cold air pouring down glacial slopes—often blow at 80 miles (129 km) per hour and can exceed 180 miles (290 km) per hour. These winds, which drain cold air masses from central Antarctica under the influence of gravity, are funnelled down valleys outward towards the coast, as indicated by the streamline arrows (right) on the white background of the Antarctic continent. When katabatic winds reach the coastline they often turn westward to blow counterclockwise around the continent. Offshore, circumpolar winds and currents push against the sea ice that grows to surround Antarctica each winter, leading to drift distances of up to several miles per day. The resulting near-shore movement of the sea ice is known as the East Wind drift, due to the dominant winds from the east. In some locations, such as the Weddell Sea, the drift is forced northward along the Antarctic Peninsula. In this case, and in the Bellingshausen, Amundsen, and Ross Seas, the combination of winds, currents, bathymetry, and topography leads to clockwise circulations known as gyres. In this image, the average sea-ice drift was determined from meteorological satellites. It illustrates the monthly average drift during the austral mid-winter, when sea-ice cover is at its maximum extent.

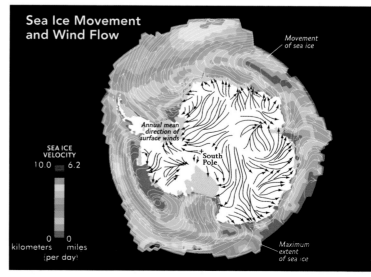

Sea Ice Movement and Wind Flow

Movement of sea ice

Annual mean direction of surface winds

+ South Pole

SEA ICE VELOCITY
10.0 — 6.2

0 — 0
kilometers — miles
(per day)

Maximum extent of sea ice

Antarctic Treaty

On December 1, 1959, after a decade of secret meetings, 12 nations—Argentina, Australia, Belgium, Chile, France, Japan, New Zealand, Norway, South Africa, the Soviet Union (Russia), the United Kingdom, and the United States—signed the Antarctic Treaty to preserve the frozen continent for peaceful scientific use only, a major feat during the height of Cold War rivalries. Since then, 32 other nations have joined.

The treaty includes all land, islands, and ice shelves south of 60° south latitude and enshrines the principles of peace, freedom of scientific research and exchange, and total banning of all military activity, nuclear testing, or disposal of radioactive waste. In addition, research stations are fully open to inspection, scientists may travel anywhere on the continent at any time, and countries can carry out aerial observations over any area.

A 1991 meeting prohibited mining in Antarctica. Other gatherings have asserted the importance of protecting wildlife, such as the Ross and fur seals, conserving unique biological habitats, and limiting human impact on sensitive ecological zones. The Antarctic Treaty made static all territorial claims held by 7 of the original 12 countries and prohibits any new claims. The treaty affirms that no country "rules the continent." For more than four decades it has proven to be an unprecedented example of international cooperation.

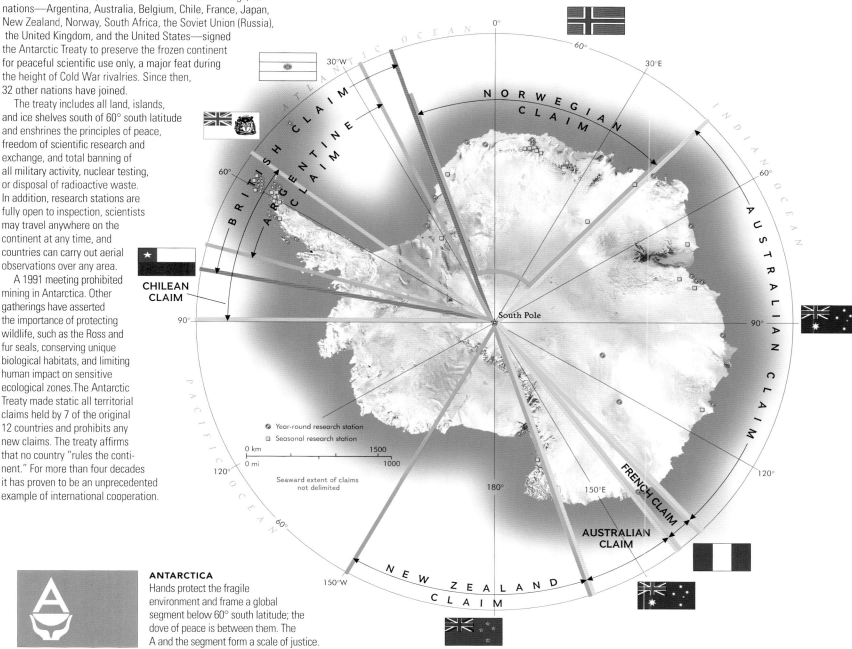

ANTARCTICA
Hands protect the fragile environment and frame a global segment below 60° south latitude; the dove of peace is between them. The A and the segment form a scale of justice.

Antarctic Convergence

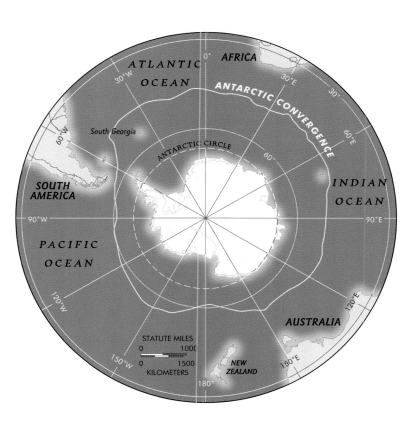

The Antarctic Convergence refers to an undulating boundary in the seas that rings Antarctica roughly 950 miles (1,529 km) off the continental coast, between 50° and 60° south latitude. This narrow zone marks the meeting place of relatively warm waters from the southern Atlantic, Indian, and Pacific Oceans and the cold Antarctic Circumpolar Current. Because cold water sinks, it slips under the more buoyant warmer water and acts to power the great oceanic conveyor belt that affects life and weather around the world. The Antarctic Convergence also generates one of Earth's richest marine ecosystems. Mist and fog often rise at the interface of blended warm and cold waters. Immediately air becomes brisker and marine life alters. Water temperatures can plummet a dozen degrees (Fahrenheit) or more upon entering the Southern Ocean. The Antarctic Convergence functions as a barrier and forms Antarctica's biological extent. It delimits the Southern Ocean, which holds 10 percent of the world's seawater, and thus creates a largely closed ecosystem and isolates the continent from warmer waters. Deep, cold waters permit the proliferation of diatoms—single-celled algae—that in turn support krill, shrimp-like organisms that exist in enormous numbers. Krill form a vital part of the food chain, directly or indirectly providing nutrition for Antarctica's amazing wildlife, particularly fish, seals, whales, and birds, including five species of flightless penguins. Losses of this food source through over-harvesting by humans would seriously affect marine life. As one travels north into warmer regions beyond the Antarctic Convergence, krill—the basis of Antarctica's life—perish and disappear. The Southern Ocean's rich waters, full of plant and animal life, stand apart from the continent itself, frozen and incredibly harsh, where vegetation is limited to lichens, mosses, and a mere two species of flowering plants. A small insect known as the wingless midge represents the largest land animal. In contrast, large body size and slow growth mark many marine animals, all of which have adapted magnificently to the cold environment.

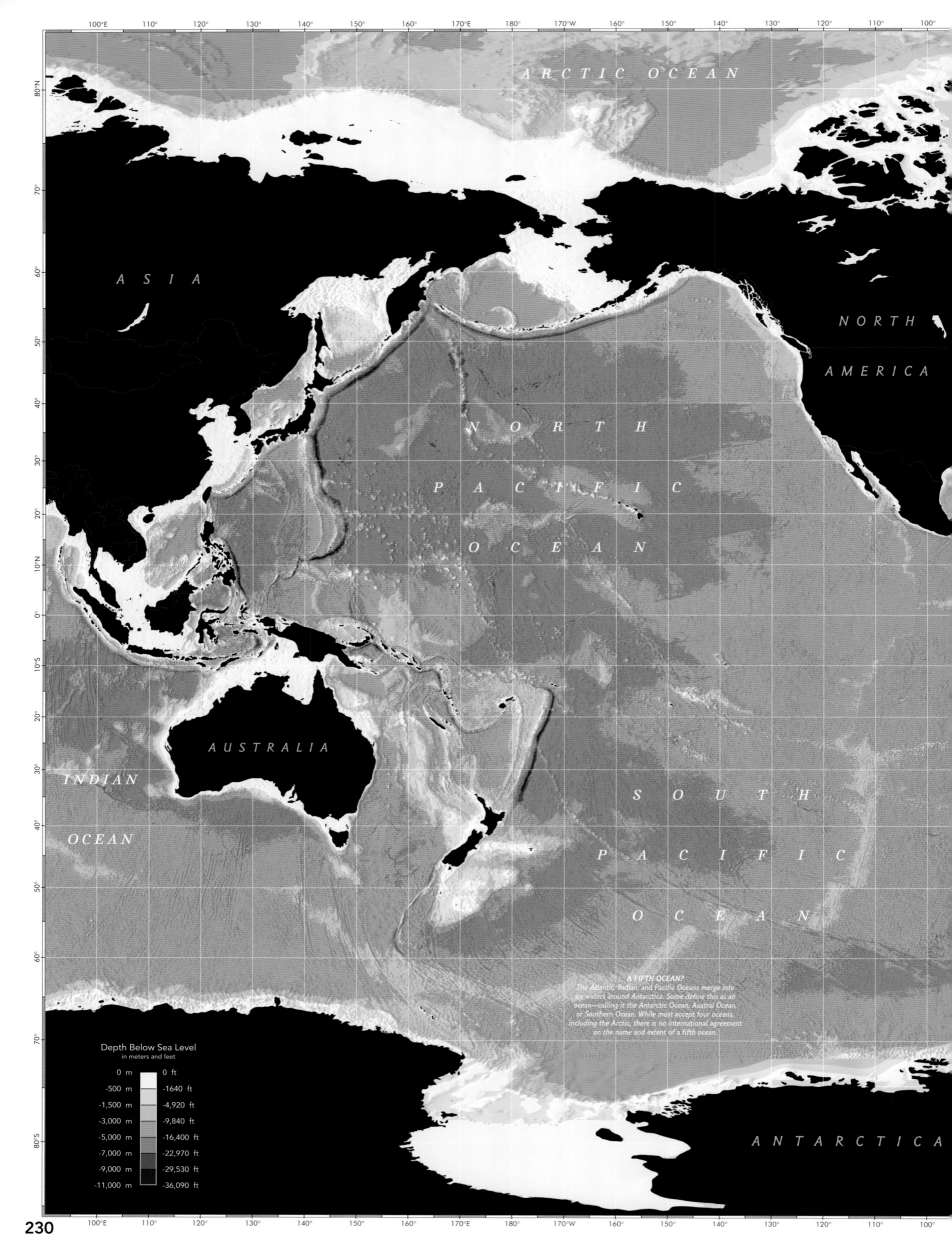

ARCTIC OCEAN

ASIA

NORTH

AMERICA

NORTH

PACIFIC

OCEAN

INDIAN

OCEAN

AUSTRALIA

SOUTH

PACIFIC

OCEAN

A FIFTH OCEAN?
The Atlantic, Indian, and Pacific Oceans merge into
icy waters around Antarctica. Some define this as an
ocean—calling it the Antarctic Ocean, Austral Ocean,
or Southern Ocean. While most accept four oceans,
including the Arctic, there is no international agreement
on the name and extent of a fifth ocean.

Depth Below Sea Level
in meters and feet

0 m	0 ft
-500 m	-1640 ft
-1,500 m	-4,920 ft
-3,000 m	-9,840 ft
-5,000 m	-16,400 ft
-7,000 m	-22,970 ft
-9,000 m	-29,530 ft
-11,000 m	-36,090 ft

ANTARCTICA

ARCTIC OCEAN

Greenland

EUROPE

ASIA

NORTH

ATLANTIC

OCEAN

Oceans

AFRICA

SOUTH
AMERICA

SOUTH

ATLANTIC

OCEAN

INDIAN

OCEAN

World Bathymetry

Kilometers

| 0 | 1,000 | 2,000 | 3,000 |

Statute Miles

| 0 | 1,000 | 2,000 | 3,000 |

Nautical Miles

| 0 | 1,000 | 2,000 | 3,000 |

Scale at the Equator
Miller Cylindrical Projection

EARTH IS A WATERY PLANET: More than 70 percent of its surface is covered by interconnected bodies of salt water that together make up a continuous, global ocean. Over the centuries, people have created artificial boundaries that divide this great water body into smaller oceans with numerous seas, gulfs, bays, straits, and channels.

The global ocean is a dynamic participant in Earth's physical, chemical, and biological processes. Millions of years ago, life itself most likely evolved in its waters. These are restless waters, always in motion. Tidal movement—the regular rise and fall of the ocean surface—results from gravitational forces exerted by the sun and the moon. The spin of Earth on its axis, coupled with wind, generates surface currents that redistribute warm and cold water around the planet. Variations in the temperature and salinity of water keep the thermohaline circulation system moving; this enormous system of interconnected currents, at the surface and deep in the ocean, influences climate patterns and circulates nutrients.

Where marine and terrestrial realms meet, one may find reefs built by tiny coral polyps or see cliffs and sea stacks shaped by countless waves. Many coastal zones are threatened, however, by overdevelopment, pollution, and overfishing. Farther out, in the deep ocean, lie vast untouched plains, high mountains and ridges, and valleys with floors lying as much as seven miles (11 km) below the sea surface. Teeming with life, the ocean includes "rain forests of the sea" and a host of marine species—even creatures who dwell in superhot waters near hydrothermal vents.

New technology is helping scientists to explore ever deeper and farther and to create more accurate maps of the ocean. Some of this underwater world has been explored with diving vessels and satellite imagery, but so much more remains to be discovered.

The Ocean Floor

The ocean floor is dynamic and varied. From the edge of the continental shelf (the shelf break), the continental slope plunges to the continental rise, which reaches to the abyssal plain. Periodically, terrestrial rocks and sediment flow through submarine canyons and form alluvial fans. The Mid-Ocean Ridge builds new seafloor; erosion and subsidence create atolls and guyots; and subducting tectonic plates form deep trenches in the ocean floor.

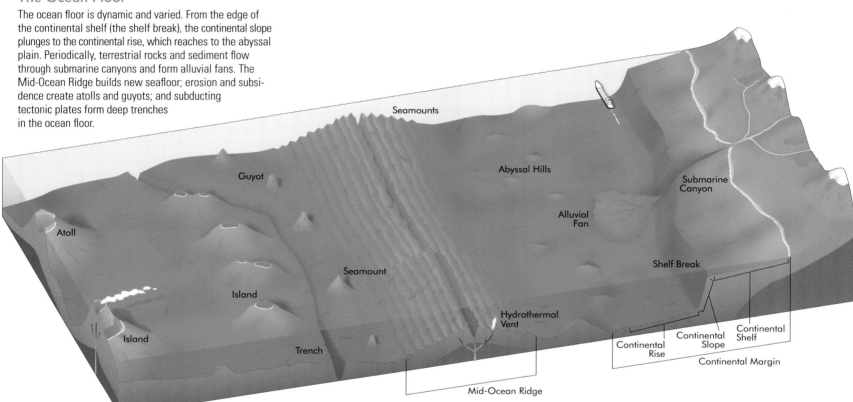

OCEAN WAVES

Waves may be born thousands of miles from shore, a result of large storms churning over the ocean. Wind pushing on the sea surface forms unorganized groups of waves that travel in all directions. In time, they organize into swell—groups of waves that can carry energy over thousands of miles of ocean. As the waves approach a surf zone, they steepen until their crests curl forward and break upon the beach.

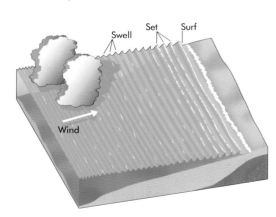

CORAL MORPHOLOGY

Coral reefs—Earth's largest structures with biological origins—form primarily in the tropics, where water is clear and warm. They begin as fringing reefs, colonies built along coastlines by tiny organisms known as coral polyps. As a coastal area subsides, a fringing reef becomes a barrier reef enclosing a protected lagoon. Corals on a reef's seaward side rely on spur and groove formations to withstand powerful waves.

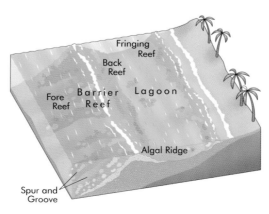

COASTAL MORPHOLOGY

The contours of a coast determine how approaching ocean waves release their energy. In bays, wave energy is dispersed; at headlands, it is concentrated. Waves approaching at an angle produce longshore currents, which flow parallel to shore and transport sediment. Rip currents, generated by wind and the return flow of water, move outward. Over time, waves and currents reshape the coastlines of the world.

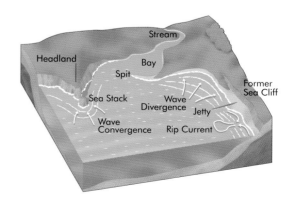

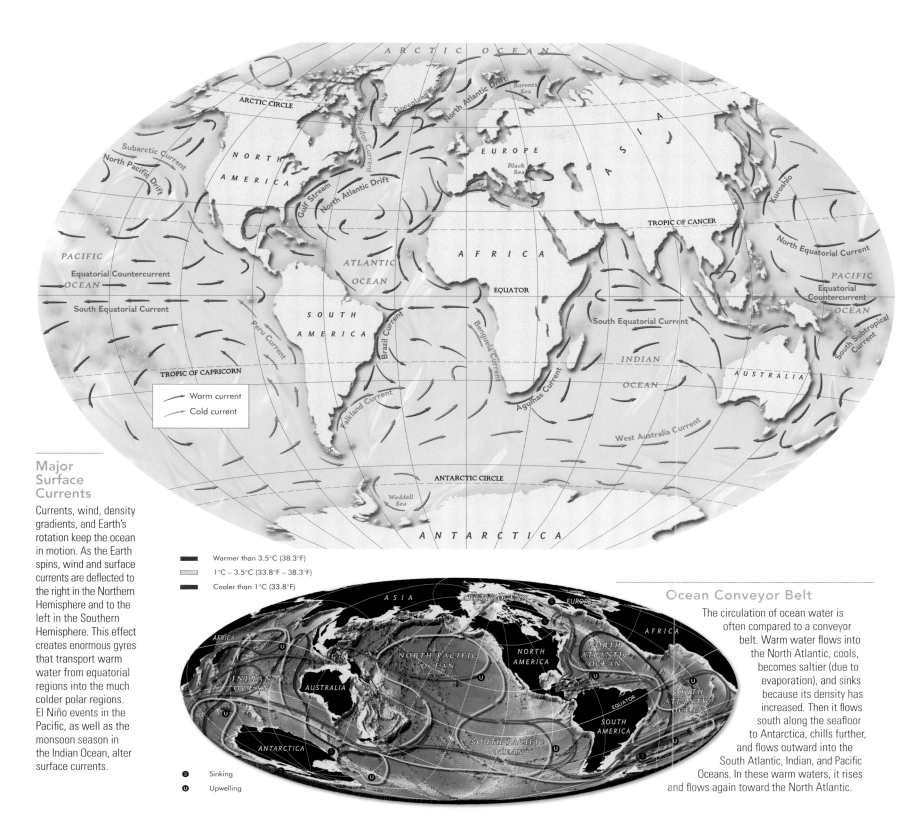

Major Surface Currents

Currents, wind, density gradients, and Earth's rotation keep the ocean in motion. As the Earth spins, wind and surface currents are deflected to the right in the Northern Hemisphere and to the left in the Southern Hemisphere. This effect creates enormous gyres that transport warm water from equatorial regions into the much colder polar regions. El Niño events in the Pacific, as well as the monsoon season in the Indian Ocean, alter surface currents.

Warmer than 3.5°C (38.3°F)

1°C – 3.5°C (33.8°F – 38.3°F)

Cooler than 1°C (33.8°F)

● Sinking

● Upwelling

Ocean Conveyor Belt

The circulation of ocean water is often compared to a conveyor belt. Warm water flows into the North Atlantic, cools, becomes saltier (due to evaporation), and sinks because its density has increased. Then it flows south along the seafloor to Antarctica, chills further, and flows outward into the South Atlantic, Indian, and Pacific Oceans. In these warm waters, it rises and flows again toward the North Atlantic.

TIDES

Both the sun and moon exert gravitational force on the Earth's ocean, creating tides. But because the moon is closer, its tug is much greater. During spring tides, when the moon is new or full, the combined pull of the sun and moon causes very high and low tides. Neap tides occur during the first and third quarters of the moon; at those times, the difference between tides is much smaller.

MAPPING THE OCEAN

Mapping the ocean requires myriad devices. In space, some satellites carry microwave radars to record data on wind speed and sea height; others use visible and infrared radiometers to collect biological productivity data. Radar altimetry and scatterometry are also used to record wind speed and direction. Out in the ocean, profiling floats collect temperature and salinity data. Ships use acoustics to map the sea floor.

THERMOHALINE CIRCULATION SYSTEM

Differences in the relative densities of volumes of water—determined by temperature (thermo) and salinity (haline)—drive thermohaline circulation. In polar regions, density increases as water cools and as evaporation makes it saltier; the mass of water sinks and flows along the ocean floor. Near the Equator, water warms and rises to the surface. If this system shut down, significant climate effects could occur.

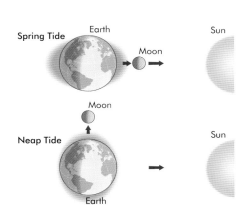

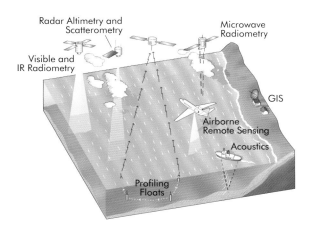

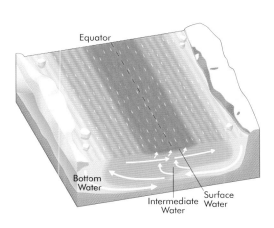

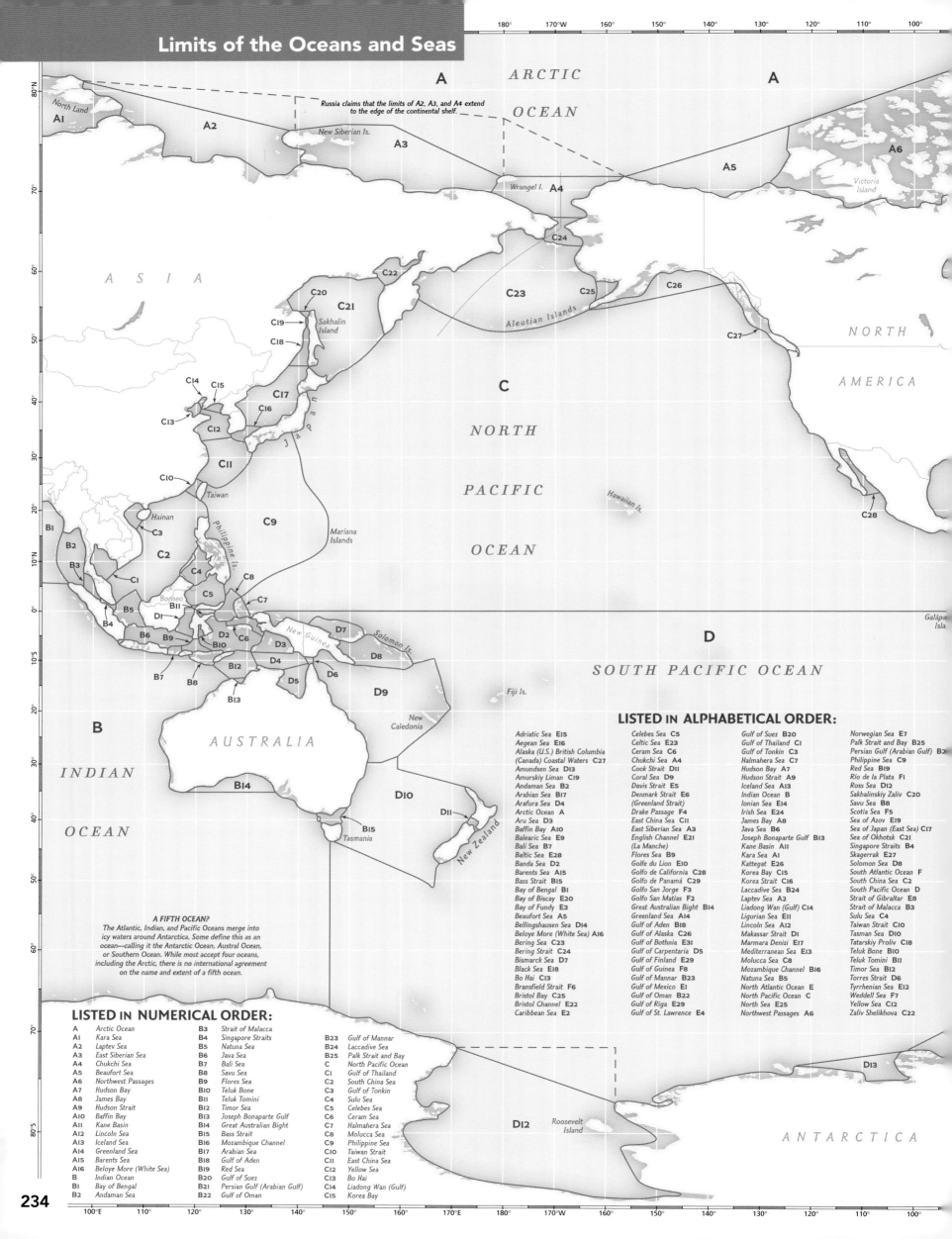

A FIFTH OCEAN?
The Atlantic, Indian, and Pacific Oceans merge into icy waters around Antarctica. Some define this as an ocean—calling it the Antarctic Ocean, Austral Ocean, or Southern Ocean. While most accept four oceans, including the Arctic, there is no international agreement on the name and extent of a fifth ocean.

Russia claims that the limits of A2, A3, and A4 extend to the edge of the continental shelf.

LISTED IN ALPHABETICAL ORDER:

Adriatic Sea E15	Celebes Sea C5	Gulf of Suez B20	Norwegian Sea E7
Aegean Sea E16	Celtic Sea E23	Gulf of Thailand C1	Palk Strait and Bay B25
Alaska (U.S.) British Columbia	Chukchi Sea A4	Gulf of Tonkin C3	Persian Gulf (Arabian Gulf) B21
(Canada) Coastal Waters C27	Ceram Sea C6	Halmahera Sea C7	Philippine Sea C9
Amundsen Sea D13	Cook Strait D11	Hudson Bay A7	Red Sea B19
Amurskiy Liman C19	Coral Sea D9	Hudson Strait A9	Río de la Plata F1
Andaman Sea B2	Davis Strait E5	Iceland Sea A13	Ross Sea D12
Arabian Sea B17	Denmark Strait E6	Indian Ocean B	Sakhalinskiy Zaliv C20
Arafura Sea D4	(Greenland Strait)	Ionian Sea E14	Savu Sea B8
Arctic Ocean A	Drake Passage F4	Irish Sea E24	Scotia Sea F5
Aru Sea D3	East China Sea C11	James Bay A8	Sea of Azov E19
Baffin Bay A10	East Siberian Sea A3	Java Sea B6	Sea of Japan (East Sea) C17
Balearic Sea E9	English Channel E21	Joseph Bonaparte Gulf B13	Sea of Okhotsk C21
Bali Sea B7	(La Manche)	Kane Basin A11	Singapore Straits B4
Baltic Sea E28	Flores Sea B9	Kara Sea A1	Skagerrak E27
Banda Sea D2	Golfe du Lion E10	Kattegat E26	Solomon Sea D8
Barents Sea A15	Golfo de California C28	Korea Bay C15	South Atlantic Ocean F
Bass Strait B15	Golfo de Panamá C29	Korea Strait C16	South China Sea C2
Bay of Bengal B1	Golfo San Jorge F3	Laccadive Sea B24	South Pacific Ocean D
Bay of Biscay E20	Golfo San Matías F2	Laptev Sea A2	Strait of Gibraltar E8
Bay of Fundy E3	Great Australian Bight B14	Ligurian Sea E11	Strait of Malacca B3
Beaufort Sea A5	Greenland Sea A14	Lincoln Sea A12	Sulu Sea C4
Bellingshausen Sea D14	Gulf of Aden B18	Makassar Strait D1	Taiwan Strait C10
Beloye More (White Sea) A16	Gulf of Alaska C26	Marmara Denizi E17	Tasman Sea D10
Bering Sea C23	Gulf of Bothnia E31	Mediterranean Sea E13	Tatarskiy Proliv C18
Bering Strait C24	Gulf of Carpentaria D5	Molucca Sea C8	Teluk Bone B10
Bismarck Sea D7	Gulf of Finland E29	Mozambique Channel B16	Teluk Tomini B11
Black Sea E18	Gulf of Guinea F8	Natuna Sea B5	Timor Sea B12
Bo Hai C13	Gulf of Mannar B23	North Atlantic Ocean E	Torres Strait D6
Bransfield Strait F6	Gulf of Mexico E1	North Pacific Ocean C	Tyrrhenian Sea E12
Bristol Bay C25	Gulf of Oman B22	North Sea E25	Weddell Sea F7
Bristol Channel E22	Gulf of Riga E29	Northwest Passages A6	Yellow Sea C12
Caribbean Sea E2	Gulf of St. Lawrence E4		Zaliv Shelikhova C22

LISTED IN NUMERICAL ORDER:

A	Arctic Ocean	B3	Strait of Malacca	B23	Gulf of Mannar
A1	Kara Sea	B4	Singapore Straits	B24	Laccadive Sea
A2	Laptev Sea	B5	Natuna Sea	B25	Palk Strait and Bay
A3	East Siberian Sea	B6	Java Sea	C	North Pacific Ocean
A4	Chukchi Sea	B7	Bali Sea	C1	Gulf of Thailand
A5	Beaufort Sea	B8	Savu Sea	C2	South China Sea
A6	Northwest Passages	B9	Flores Sea	C3	Gulf of Tonkin
A7	Hudson Bay	B10	Teluk Bone	C4	Sulu Sea
A8	James Bay	B11	Teluk Tomini	C5	Celebes Sea
A9	Hudson Strait	B12	Timor Sea	C6	Ceram Sea
A10	Baffin Bay	B13	Joseph Bonaparte Gulf	C7	Halmahera Sea
A11	Kane Basin	B14	Great Australian Bight	C8	Molucca Sea
A12	Lincoln Sea	B15	Bass Strait	C9	Philippine Sea
A13	Iceland Sea	B16	Mozambique Channel	C10	Taiwan Strait
A14	Greenland Sea	B17	Arabian Sea	C11	East China Sea
A15	Barents Sea	B18	Gulf of Aden	C12	Yellow Sea
A16	Beloye More (White Sea)	B19	Red Sea	C13	Bo Hai
B	Indian Ocean	B20	Gulf of Suez	C14	Liadong Wan (Gulf)
B1	Bay of Bengal	B21	Persian Gulf (Arabian Gulf)	C15	Korea Bay
B2	Andaman Sea	B22	Gulf of Oman		

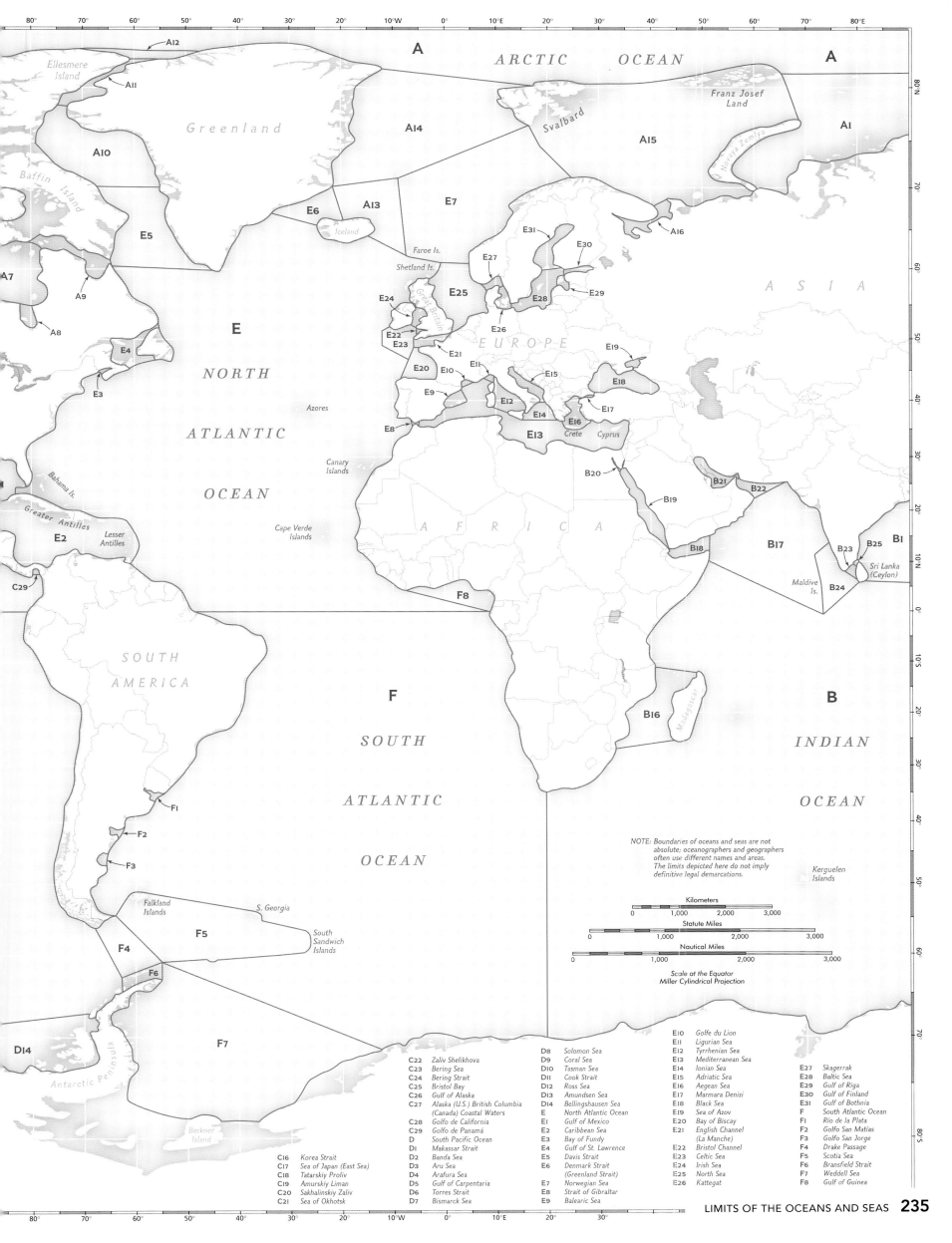

NOTE: Boundaries of oceans and seas are not absolute; oceanographers and geographers often use different names and areas. The limits depicted here do not imply definitive legal demarcations.

Kilometers
0 1,000 2,000 3,000

Statute Miles
0 1,000 2,000 3,000

Nautical Miles
0 1,000 2,000 3,000

Scale at the Equator
Miller Cylindrical Projection

C16 Korea Strait	E10 Golfe du Lion
C17 Sea of Japan (East Sea)	E11 Ligurian Sea
C18 Tatarskiy Proliv	E12 Tyrrhenian Sea
C19 Amurskiy Liman	E13 Mediterranean Sea
C20 Sakhalinskiy Zaliv	E14 Ionian Sea
C21 Sea of Okhotsk	E15 Adriatic Sea
C22 Zaliv Shelikhova	E16 Aegean Sea
C23 Bering Sea	E17 Marmara Denizi
C24 Bering Strait	E18 Black Sea
C25 Bristol Bay	E19 Sea of Azov
C26 Gulf of Alaska	E20 Bay of Biscay
C27 Alaska (U.S.) British Columbia (Canada) Coastal Waters	E21 English Channel (La Manche)
C28 Golfo de California	E22 Bristol Channel
C29 Golfo de Panamá	E23 Celtic Sea
D South Pacific Ocean	E24 Irish Sea
D1 Makassar Strait	E25 North Sea
D2 Banda Sea	E26 Kattegat
D3 Aru Sea	E27 Skagerrak
D4 Arafura Sea	E28 Baltic Sea
D5 Gulf of Carpentaria	E29 Gulf of Riga
D6 Torres Strait	E30 Gulf of Finland
D7 Bismarck Sea	E31 Gulf of Bothnia
D8 Solomon Sea	F South Atlantic Ocean
D9 Coral Sea	F1 Río de la Plata
D10 Tasman Sea	F2 Golfo San Matías
D11 Cook Strait	F3 Golfo San Jorge
D12 Ross Sea	F4 Drake Passage
D13 Amundsen Sea	F5 Scotia Sea
D14 Bellingshausen Sea	F6 Bransfield Strait
E North Atlantic Ocean	F7 Weddell Sea
E1 Gulf of Mexico	F8 Gulf of Guinea
E2 Caribbean Sea	
E3 Bay of Fundy	
E4 Gulf of St. Lawrence	
E5 Davis Strait	
E6 Denmark Strait (Greenland Strait)	
E7 Norwegian Sea	
E8 Strait of Gibraltar	
E9 Balearic Sea	

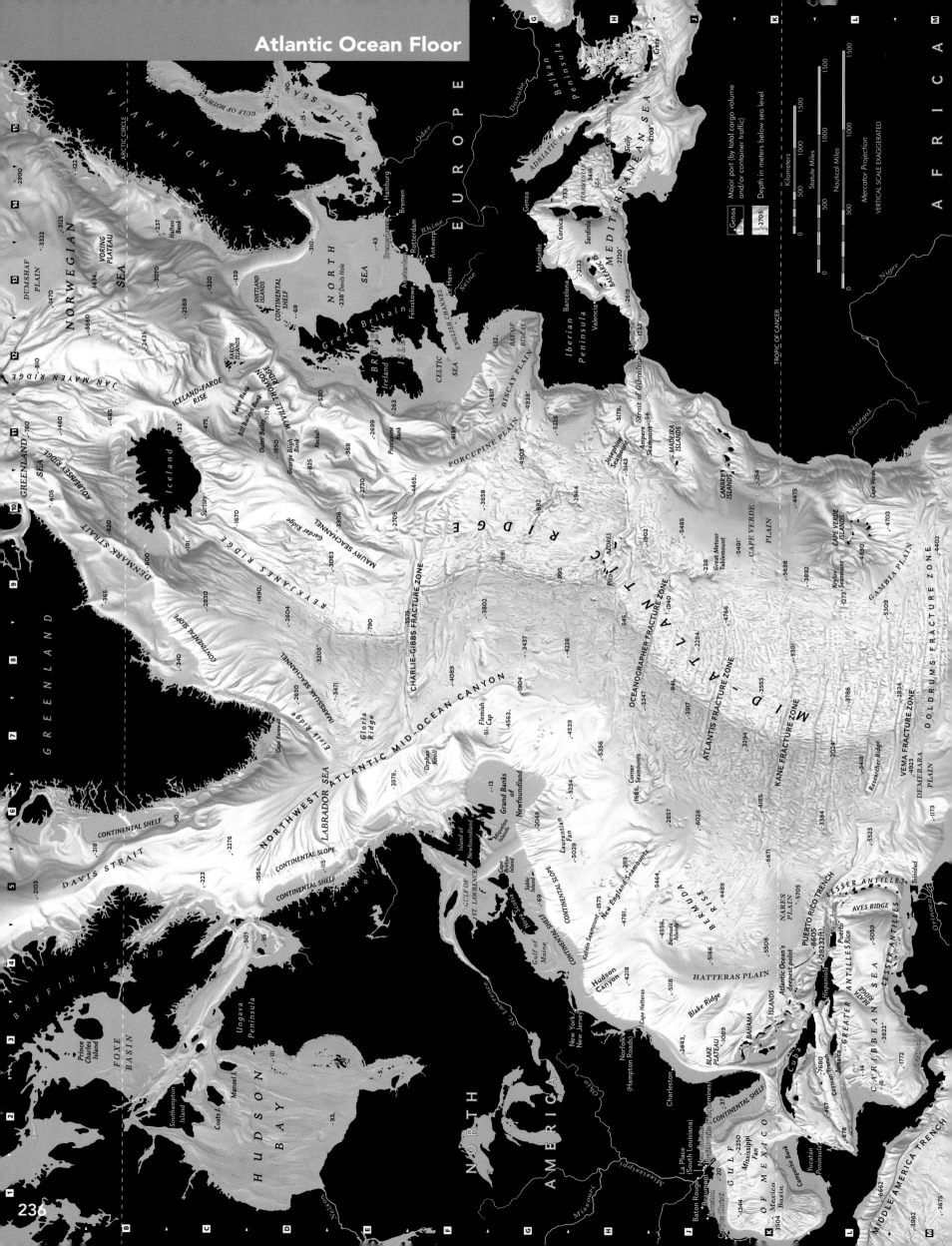

The ragged spine of the Mid-Atlantic Ridge fills the center of the Atlantic Ocean Basin from north to south. This prominent spreading ridge was not discovered until the middle of the 20th century.

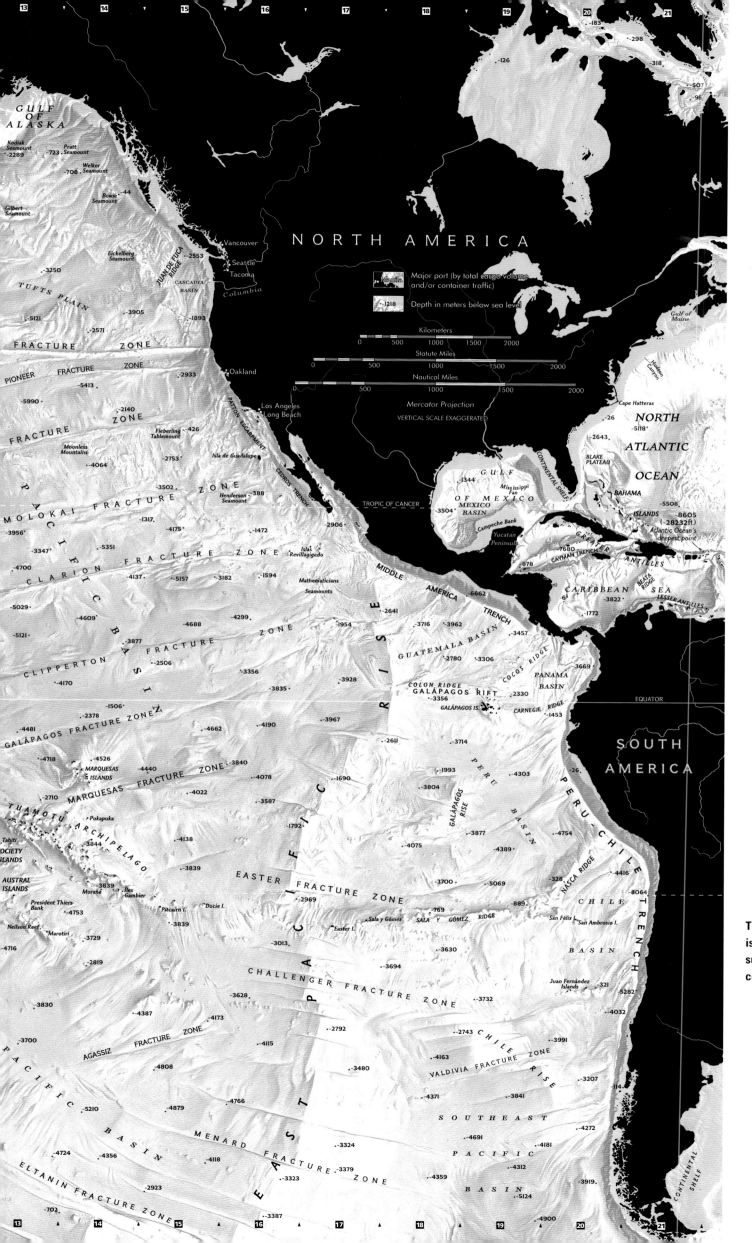

The Pacific Ocean Basin is shrinking as it is subsumed under surrounding continents on all sides.

Dead Sea -421 (-1380 ft) World's lowest point

Mt. Everest + (29035 ft) 8850 World's highest point

TROPIC OF CANCER

Dubai ▮ Major port (by total cargo volume and/or container traffic)

-2548 ▮ Depth in meters below sea level

Kilometers
0 200 400 600 800 1000 1200

Statute Miles
0 200 400 600 800 1000 1200

Nautical Miles
0 200 400 600 800 1000 1200

Mercator Projection
VERTICAL SCALE EXAGGERATED

EQUATOR

TROPIC OF CAPRICORN

A S I

I N D I A

BAY OF BENGAL
Ganges Fan

ARABIAN SEA
ARABIAN BASIN

PERSIAN GULF

GULF OF OMAN

ARABIA

PENINSULA

S A H A R A

A F R I C A

RED SEA

GULF OF ADEN

OWEN FRACTURE ZONE

CARLSBERG RIDGE

SOMALI BASIN

MASCARENE PLATEAU

MID-INDIAN RIDGE

CHAGOS-LACCADIVE RIDGE

MID-INDIAN BASIN

NINETYEAST RIDGE

Sri Lanka (Ceylon)

ANDAMAN

Andaman Islands

Nicobar Islands

Maldive Islands

Lakshadweep

Chagos Archipelago

Diego Garcia

VEMA FRACTURE ZONE

CHAGOS TRENCH

Seychelles

Amirante Isles

AMIRANTE TRENCH

Farquhar Group

Aldabra Is.

Comoro Islands

Zanzibar I.

Agalega Islands

Saya de Malha Bank

Nazareth Bank

Cargados Carajos Bank

Tromelin

MASCARENE BASIN

MASCARENE PLAIN

Mauritius

Réunion

MAURITIUS TRENCH

RODRIGUES FRACTURE ZONE

Rodrigues

EGERIA FRACTURE ZONE

OSBORN PLATEAU

Nikitin Seamount

Socotra

Error Tablemount

COCO-DE-MER SEAMOUNTS

Indus Fan

CONTINENTAL SHELF

Nile

Euphrates

Tigris

Indus

Ganges

Brahmaputra

Lake Victoria

Lake Malawi

Zambezi

Shire

Limpopo

Madagascar

Bassas da India

Europa

MADAGASCAR PLATEAU

MADAGASCAR BASIN

MOZAMBIQUE BASIN

MOZAMBIQUE ESCARPMENT

CONTINENTAL SHELF

Richards Bay

Cape of Good Hope

Cape Agulhas

Agulhas Bank

CONTINENTAL SLOPE

AGULHAS PLATEAU

AGULHAS BASIN

Walters Shoal

SOUTHWEST INDIAN RIDGE

PRINCE EDWARD FRACTURE ZONE

INDOMED FRACTURE ZONE

ATLANTIS-II FRACTURE ZONE

CROZET BASIN

CROZET PLATEAU

Crozet Islands

Prince Edward Islands

Amsterdam

St. Paul

Kerguelen Islands

KERGUELEN PLATEAU

SOUTHEAST

BROKEN

ATLANTIC-INDIAN RIDGE

Ob' Tablemount

240

Ra's al Hadd

Colombo

Dubai

-2266
-5278
Socotra -1706
-368
-2758
-4160
-4652
-5106
-1534
-1906
-3096
-3343
-4962
-3932
-4609
-5273
-3674
-3511
-3619
-338
-3621
-1584
-3292
-4654
-1916
-1555
-1216
-5077
-4574
-6291
-2590
-5536
-5371
-772
-3943
-5819
-1244
-2911
-3049
-4571
-4473
-3327
-247
-254
-4270
-4438
-4590
-4199
-2700
-638
-283
-2946
-1372
-205
-6110
-516
-4459
-4634
-5340
-1916
-5194
-1525
-16
-38
-10
-13
-13
-7
-3372
-2643
-291
-3345
-82
-2769
-2284
-1940
-73
-4738
-2805
-1682
-2919
-3583
-2780
-4179
-4025
-4442
-4735
-5406
-1906
-6402
-799
-1240
-5183
-5421
-5166
-4993
-1517
-4983
-4270
-3996
-3919
-3429
-5967
-1922
-4521
-2619
-2599
-927
-3974
-4305
-847
-4321
-6035
-2548
-2067
-3784
-3131
-3540
-3745
-4680
-4920
-5195
-4000
-4945
-451
-1976
-4080
-3540
-3261
-2315
-2529
-4181
-366
-1710
-450
-1124
-1423
-2577
-2821
-3173
-3602
-4267
-1842
-2302
-4547
-1549
-59
-6291
-2595
-772

The Ninetyeast Ridge, the longest linear feature in the world, formed as ocean crust moved north over a hot spot deep in the Earth.

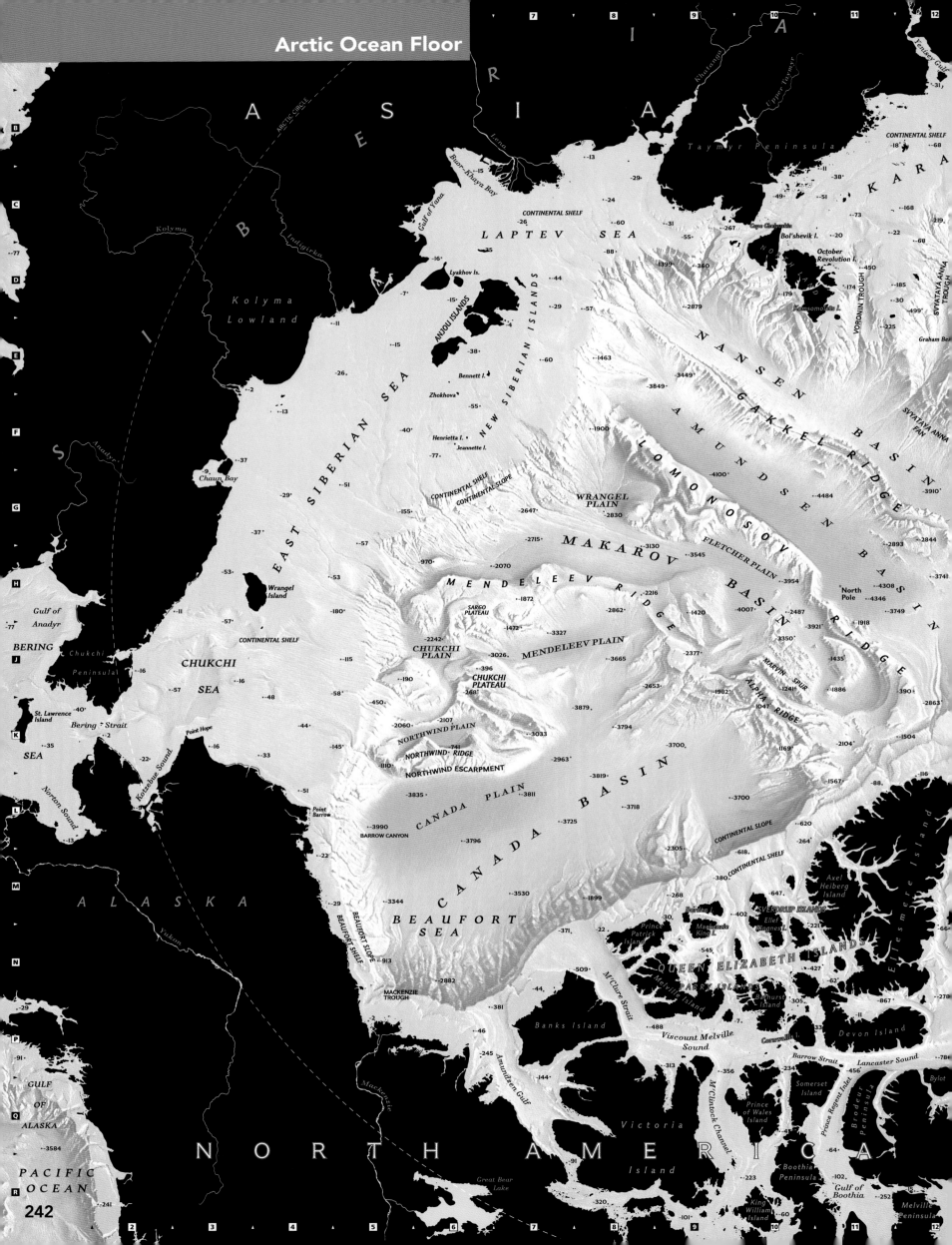

EUROPE

Northern Dvina

Top margin grid: 14 15 16 17 18 19 20 21

Gulf of Ob

Yamal Peninsula

Boydaraia Bay
-33

-14
Pechora Bay

-11
-5
Chesha Bay

-139
-199
-29
-91

-84
-60
-90
-41
WHITE SEA
-90
-19

S E A
-260
-380
-86
-235
Kola Peninsula

-115
EAST NOVAYA ZEMLYA TROUGH
-97
-90
-240
-53
GULF OF BOTHNIA
-100

390
Novaya Zemlya
-121
-124
-294
-12

CONTINENTAL SHELF
Gusinaya Bank
-249
-289
-375
-119
-98

-174
-179
-183
-271
MURMANSK RISE
-184

-90
-230
-183
-100
North Cape

-170
-280
-419
-53
-307
-155
-172
-400
-16
-58
-137
CONTINENTAL SHELF
-235
-75
-220

FRANZ JOSEF LAND
-119
OLGA BASIN
-155
-30
-90
-480
-319
-85
-405
-124
Røst Bank
-222
Halten Bank
-91

George Land
Alexandra Land
-57
Spitsbergen Bank
-745
-1929
-170
CONTINENTAL SHELF
-94

SVALBARD
-79
-322
Bjørnøya
-1955
-2953
CONTINENTAL SLOPE

North East Land
-143
-150
-2260
-2695
-1250

-5122
Spitsbergen
-615
-3170
N O R W E G I A N
-3322
VORING PLATEAU
-1275
-1460
-1770

Arctic Ocean's deepest point
-147
-1622
-3272
DUMSHAF PLAIN
-3235

YERMAK PLATEAU
Molloy Hole
-5669
(-18599 ft)
-2571
-1769
S E A
-1156
-2447
-3906
-3403

-3749
G *Boreas Plain*
-2899
-3888
-2734
-160
AEGIR RIDGE
-2476

LENA TROUGH
-375
GREENLAND FRACTURE ZONE
-3541
-1360
FAROE ISLANDS

-4038
-53
Ob' Bank
CONTINENTAL SHELF
-382
-2939
-163
Jan Mayen
-894
-854

MORRIS JESUP RISE
-1144
-369
-55
-2196
JAN MAYEN RIDGE
-2176
-1233
-402
-290
ICELAND-FAROE RISE

-1196
-33
ICELAND PLATEAU
-1875
KOLBEINSEY RIDGE
-168
-7
-1440

GREENLAND PLAIN
MOHNS RIDGE
JAN MAYEN FRACTURE ZONE
-271
-613

| -1955 | Depth in meters below sea level |

-1650
-519
-369
Iceland
-98
-1830

Kilometers
0 100 200 300 400 500

-146
-106
-1100
-2380

Statute Miles
0 100 200 300 400 500

Surtsey

Nautical Miles
0 100 200 300 400 500

-128
DENMARK STRAIT
-1103
-64
-183
REYKJANES RIDGE

Azimuthal Equidistant Projection
VERTICAL SCALE EXAGGERATED

-549
-152
-949
-1938

G R E E N L A N D

-902

-58

B A F F I N
-384

-102

169
-2377
-475
CONTINENTAL SLOPE
-1825
-2840
-722

Qeqertarsuaq (Disko)
ARCTIC CIRCLE
-607
A T L A N T I C
-2410

B A Y
-64
-155
-165
-3360

Baffin Island
-2149
-1326
-256
-59
O C E A N

-1800
-46
-2890

DAVIS STRAIT
-214
-1125
-90
-340
-2918

Cape Farewell

Water depths in the Arctic Ocean must often be measured from submarines under the ice. They discovered three almost parallel ridges crossing the Arctic Basin.

Bottom margin grid: 13 14 15 16 17 18 19 20 21

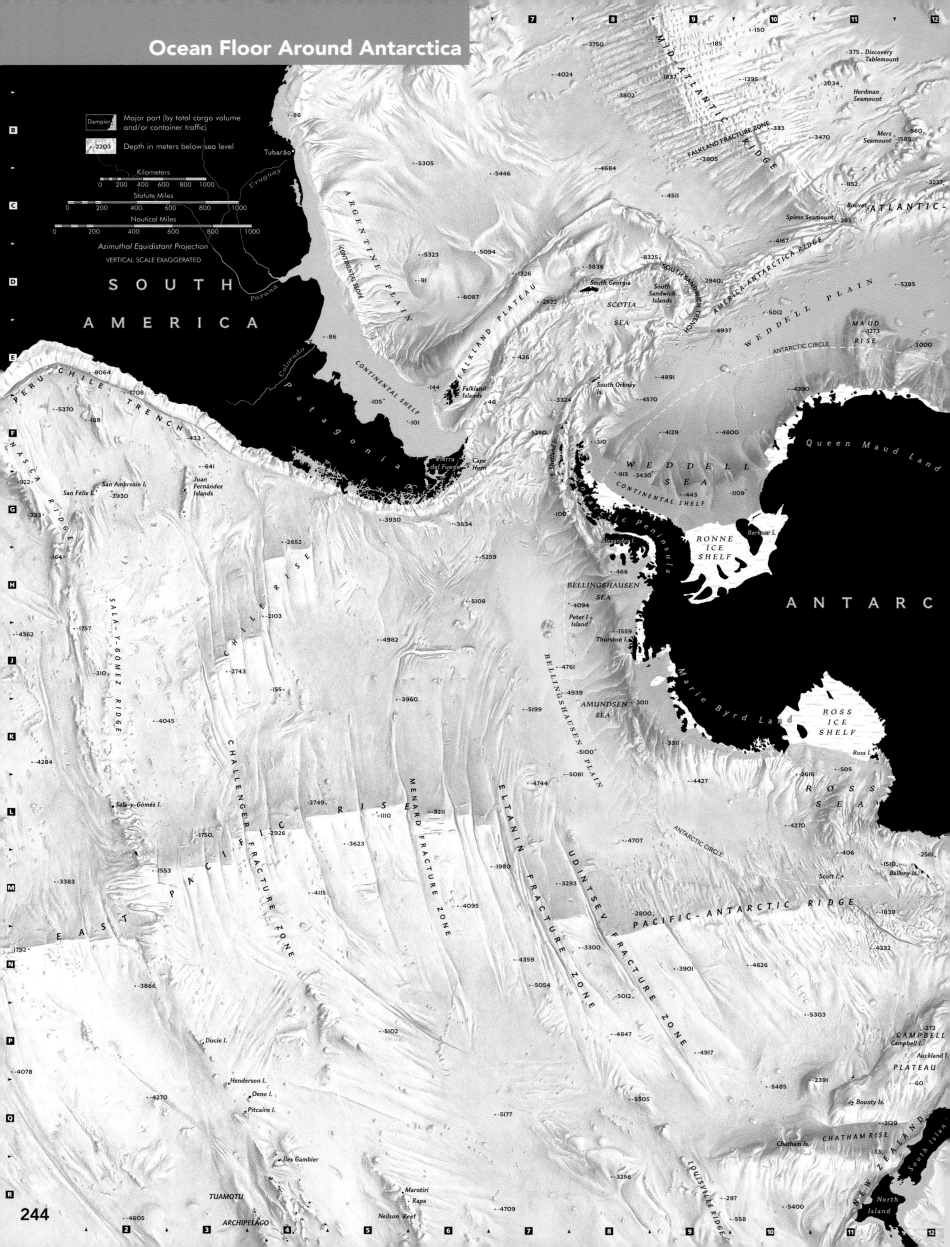

Dampier ▪ Major port (by total cargo volume and/or container traffic)

-2203 Depth in meters below sea level

Kilometers
0 200 400 600 800 1000

Statute Miles
0 200 400 600 800 1000

Nautical Miles
0 200 400 600 800 1000

Azimuthal Equidistant Projection
VERTICAL SCALE EXAGGERATED

SOUTH

AMERICA

Uruguay
Tubarão
Paraná
Colorado
Patagonia
Argentine Plain
Continental Slope
Continental Shelf
Tierra del Fuego
Cape Horn

PERU–CHILE TRENCH
NASCA RIDGE
San Félix I.
San Ambrosio I.
Juan Fernández Islands
SALA-Y-GÓMEZ RIDGE
CHILE RISE
Sala-y-Gómez I.
CHALLENGER FRACTURE ZONE
EAST PACIFIC RISE
Ducie I.
Henderson I.
Oeno I.
Pitcairn I.
Îles Gambier
TUAMOTU ARCHIPELAGO
Marotiri
Rapa
Neilson Reef

MENARD FRACTURE ZONE

FALKLAND PLATEAU
Falkland Islands
SCOTIA SEA
South Georgia
South Sandwich Islands
S. Shetland Is.
South Orkney Is.
Antarctic Peninsula
Alexander I.
BELLINGSHAUSEN SEA
Peter I Island
Thurston I.
BELLINGSHAUSEN PLAIN
AMUNDSEN SEA
ELTANIN FRACTURE ZONE
UDINTSEV FRACTURE ZONE
PACIFIC–ANTARCTIC RIDGE
LOUISVILLE RIDGE

MID ATLANTIC RIDGE
FALKLAND FRACTURE ZONE
Discovery Tablemount
Herdman Seamount
Merz Seamount
Bouvet
Spiess Seamount
ATLANTIC
SOUTH SANDWICH TRENCH
AMERICA–ANTARCTICA RIDGE
WEDDELL PLAIN
ANTARCTIC CIRCLE
MAUD RISE
WEDDELL SEA
CONTINENTAL SHELF
Queen Maud Land
RONNE ICE SHELF
Berkner I.
ANTARCTICA
Marie Byrd Land
ROSS ICE SHELF
Ross I.
ROSS SEA
ANTARCTIC CIRCLE
Scott I.
Balleny Is.
CAMPBELL PLATEAU
Campbell I.
Auckland I.
Bounty Is.
CHATHAM RISE
Chatham Is.
NEW ZEALAND
North Island
South Island

-86 -4024 -3750 -185 -150 -375 -1837 -3802 -1395 -2034 -5305 -5446 -4684 -333 -3470 -560 -1585 -5323 -5094 -4511 -3805 -1152 -3227 -285 -4167 -91 -1326 -3836 -8325 -2940 -5285 -6087 -2522 -5012 -1273 -3000 -426 -4937 -4891 -144 -46 -3324 -4570 -4390 -105 -101 -5250 -310 -4129 -4800 -915 -3430 -443 -1109 -3930 -3634 -100 -466 -2652 -5259 -4094 -2103 -5108 -1559 -4362 -1757 -4982 -4761 -310 -2743 -4939 -3011 -155 -3960 -5199 -4045 -5100 -3311 -4284 -5081 -4744 -4427 -2616 -505 -2749 -3211 -1110 -4707 -4270 -406 -1750 -3623 -1980 -3293 -406 -1510 -2561 -1553 -4115 -2926 -4095 -2800 -1839 -3383 -4359 -3300 -4626 -4332 -1792 -5054 -3901 -3866 -5012 -5303 -5102 -4847 -272 -4917 -5485 -2391 -60 -4078 -5505 -4270 -5177 -2129 -4709 -4605 -3256 -297 -5400 -558

244

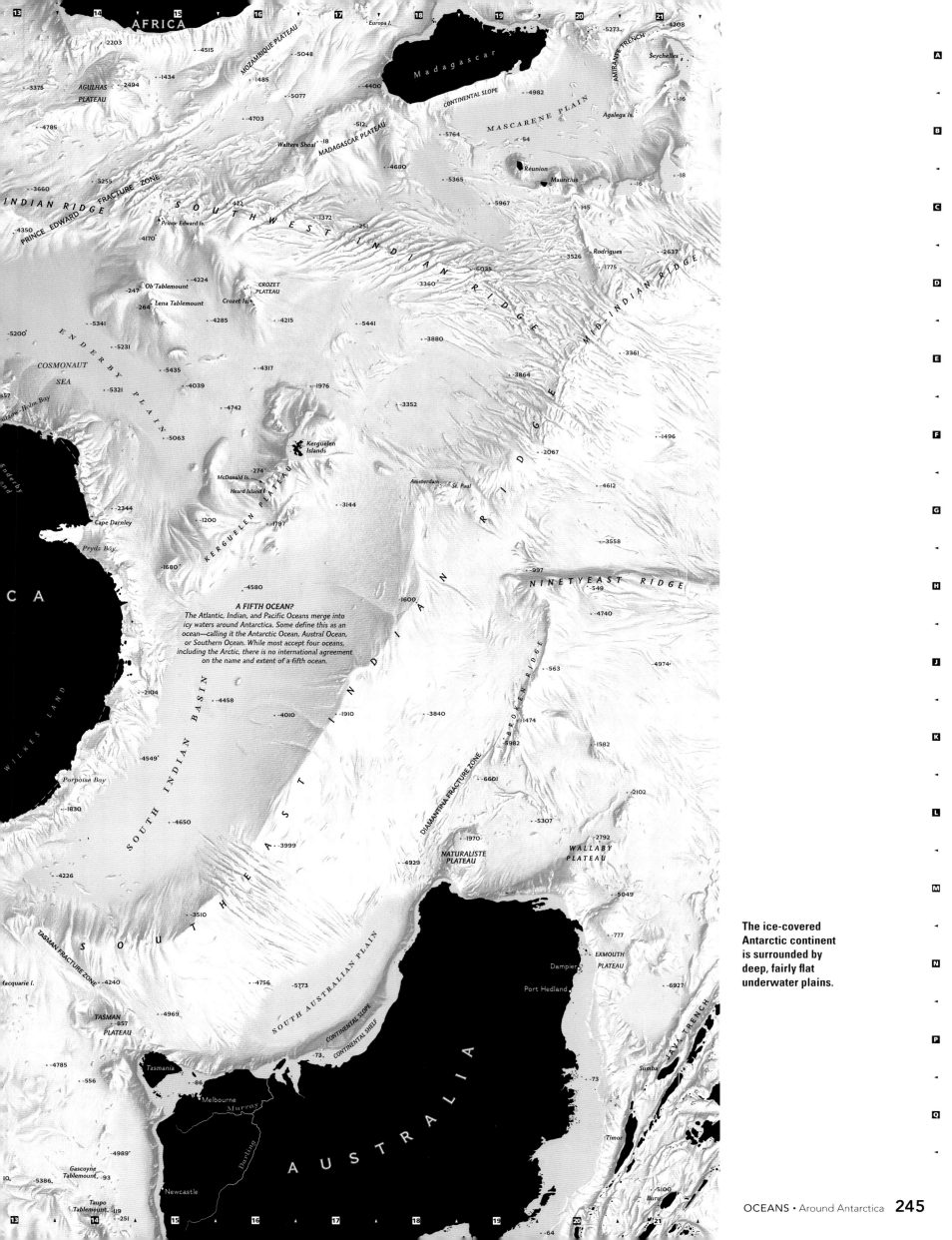

A FIFTH OCEAN?
The Atlantic, Indian, and Pacific Oceans merge into icy waters around Antarctica. Some define this as an ocean—calling it the Antarctic Ocean, Austral Ocean, or Southern Ocean. While most accept four oceans, including the Arctic, there is no international agreement on the name and extent of a fifth ocean.

The ice-covered Antarctic continent is surrounded by deep, fairly flat underwater plains.

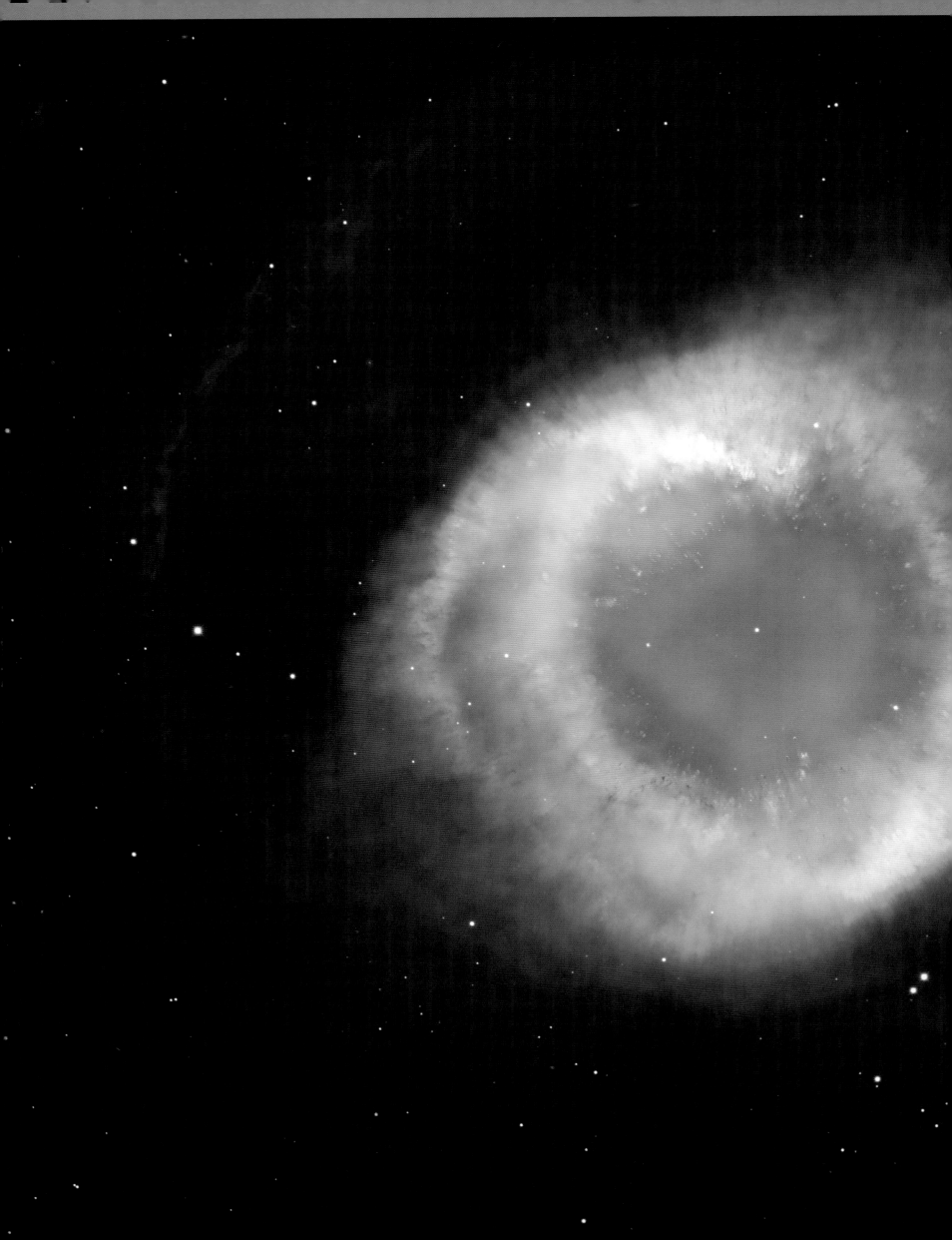

Space

In the first decade of the new millennium, astronomers are conducting extensive surveys of new frontiers in space, registering millions of galaxies, each composed of billions of stars. New orbiters and surface rovers explored Mars, confirming the presence of liquid water in its distant past and detecting methane in its atmosphere. A probe descended through the atmosphere of Titan, a moon of Saturn, and returned the first pictures from its surface, showing a strange, cold new world. A capsule traveling through space returned samples of the sun, and another spacecraft is now en route to Pluto. Meanwhile, a copper "cannonball" deployed from a spacecraft created the first man-made impact crater on a comet while another returned comet dust to Earth.

Wherever we look, we see evidence of cataclysmic events, indicating that we live in a 13-billion-year-old universe that is still evolving. Some suns, their atmospheres curiously enriched with telltale elements, may be "death stars" that swallowed whole planets long ago. Our own Milky Way is gradually devouring a small galaxy in the constellation Sagittarius, and elsewhere larger galaxies collide and distort each other. The universe began with a big bang and has been expanding ever since. A mysterious "dark energy" that exceeds all known forms of energy is thought to cause this expansion; space is also pervaded by unseen "dark matter," the dominant component of the universe. In laboratories on Earth and on the drawing boards of aerospace engineers, we are preparing to explore the next frontier of astronomical observation, looking for gravitational waves that may disturb the very fabric of space and time.

A composite view of two images, one taken from the WIYN Telescope in Arizona and the other from the Hubble Space Telescope, shows in amazing detail the outbursts in the Helix Nebula, a glowing gaseous shell of a dying sun-like star. Closest planetary nebula to the Earth, Helix Nebula is estimated to be approximately 650 light-years away from our planet. High-resolution images from Hubble and other telescopes are showing new details that enable us to understand the evolution of stars and other mysteries of the universe.

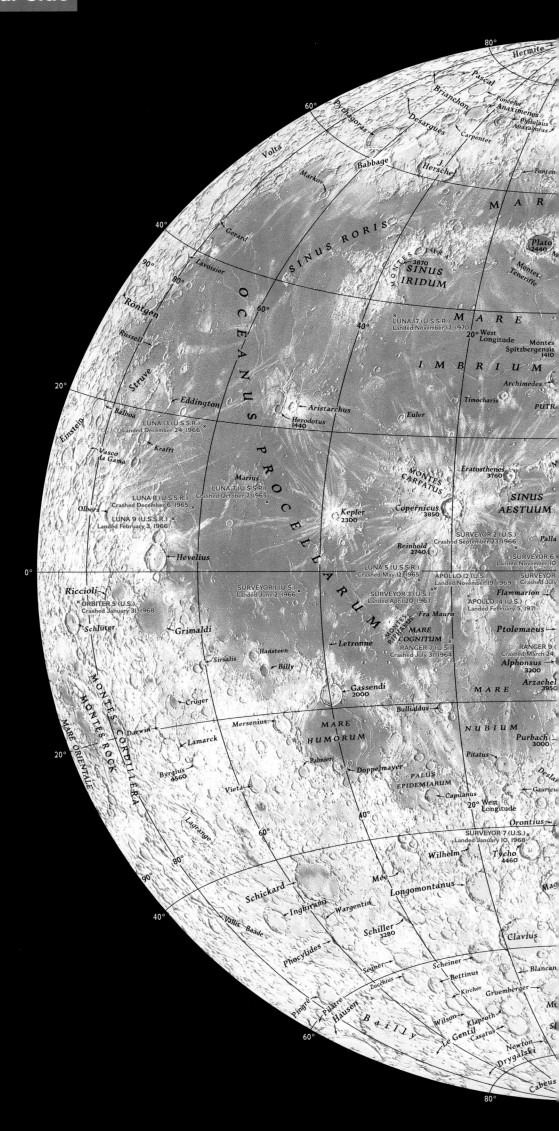

YOUNG EARTH HAD NO MOON.

At some point in Earth's early history (certainly within the first 100 million years), an object roughly the size of Mars struck Earth a great, glancing blow. Instantly, most of the rogue body and a sizable chunk of Earth were vaporized. The ensuing cloud rose to above 14,000 miles (22,500 km) altitude, where it condensed into innumerable solid particles that orbited Earth as they aggregated into ever larger moonlets, eventually combining to form the moon. This "giant impact" hypothesis of the moon's origin is based on computer simulations and on laboratory analyses of lunar rocks gathered by six teams of Apollo astronauts. It also fits with data on the lunar topography and environment recorded by the United States' Clementine and Lunar Prospector spacecraft.

The airless lunar surface bakes in the sun at up to 243°F (117°C) for two weeks at a time. All the while, it is sprayed with the solar wind of subatomic particles. Then, for an equal period, the same spot is in the dark, cooling to about minus 272°F (-169°C) when the sun sets. Day and night, the moon is bombarded by micrometeoroids and larger space rocks. Orbiting at an average distance of 239,000 miles (385,000 km), the moon's rotation is synchronized with its orbital period in such a way that it is gravitationally locked, meaning it always shows the same face, the near side, to Earth. The far side can never be seen from Earth and has been photographed only from spacecraft.

Recently, NASA scientists used Earth-based radio telescopes to produce very detailed radar maps of the southern polar region, revealing that the terrain is much more rugged than had previously been thought. The south pole, specifically the area near the Shackleton Crater, has been considered as a possible landing site for a future manned mission to the moon. It remains attractive because the bottoms of deep craters in this region may contain water ice, deposited there by previous comet impacts. The ice is a potential source of liquid water for drinking, as well as hydrogen and oxygen for fuel. If future missions to the moon and Mars are able to use local resources, they will not be as reliant on new supplies from Earth.

(Continued on page 250)

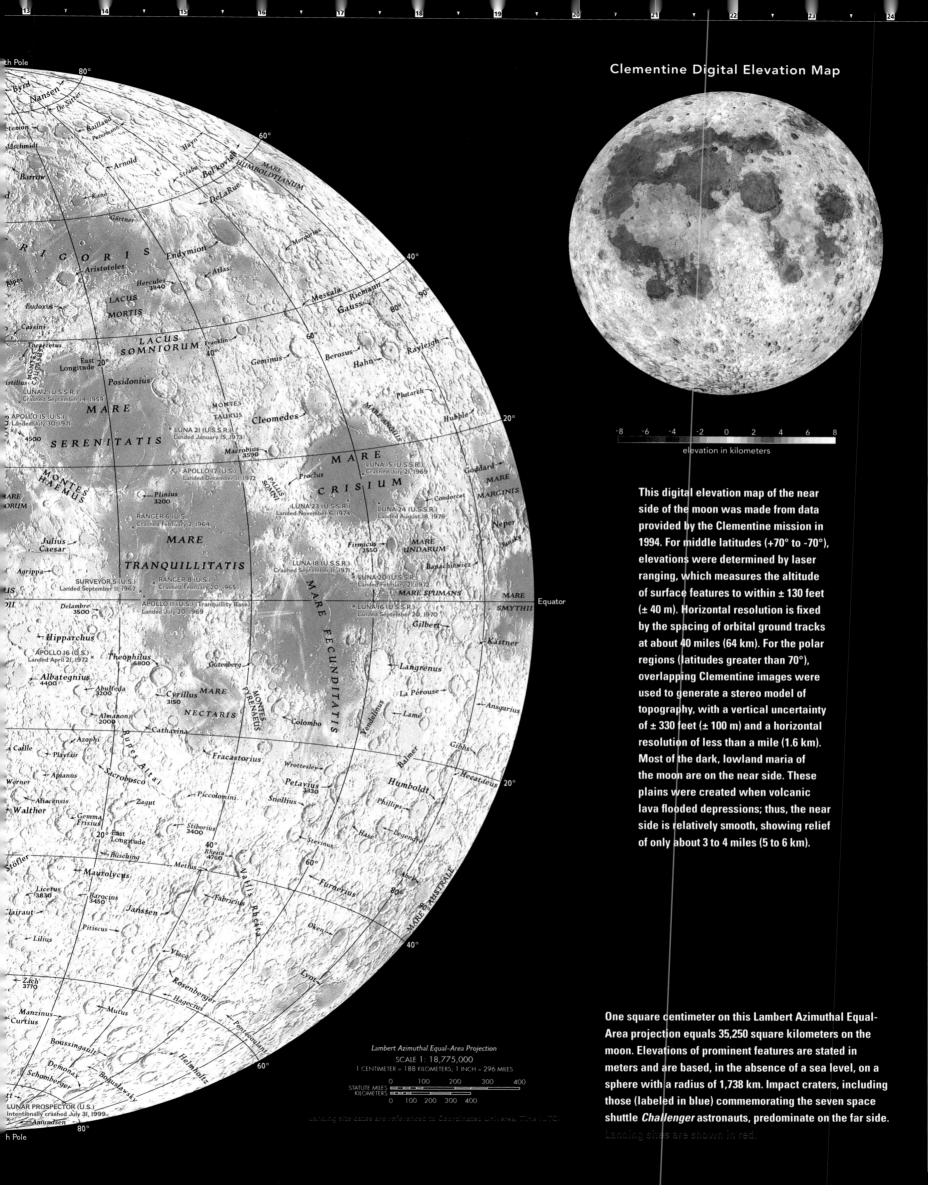

Clementine Digital Elevation Map

-8 -6 -4 -2 0 2 4 6 8
elevation in kilometers

This digital elevation map of the near side of the moon was made from data provided by the Clementine mission in 1994. For middle latitudes (+70° to -70°), elevations were determined by laser ranging, which measures the altitude of surface features to within ± 130 feet (± 40 m). Horizontal resolution is fixed by the spacing of orbital ground tracks at about 40 miles (64 km). For the polar regions (latitudes greater than 70°), overlapping Clementine images were used to generate a stereo model of topography, with a vertical uncertainty of ± 330 feet (± 100 m) and a horizontal resolution of less than a mile (1.6 km). Most of the dark, lowland maria of the moon are on the near side. These plains were created when volcanic lava flooded depressions; thus, the near side is relatively smooth, showing relief of only about 3 to 4 miles (5 to 6 km).

One square centimeter on this Lambert Azimuthal Equal-Area projection equals 35,250 square kilometers on the moon. Elevations of prominent features are stated in meters and are based, in the absence of a sea level, on a sphere with a radius of 1,738 km. Impact craters, including those (labeled in blue) commemorating the seven space shuttle *Challenger* astronauts, predominate on the far side. Landing sites are shown in red.

Lambert Azimuthal Equal-Area Projection
SCALE 1: 18,775,000
1 CENTIMETER = 188 KILOMETERS; 1 INCH = 296 MILES
STATUTE MILES   0   100   200   300   400
KILOMETERS   0   100   200   300   400

Landing site dates are referenced to Coordinated Universal Time (UTC).

Continued from page 248)

The rocks and materials brought back by the Apollo missions are extremely dry; the moon has no indigenous water. However, it is bombarded by water-rich comets and meteoroids. Most of this water is lost to space, but some is trapped and frozen in permanently shadowed areas near the Moon's poles.

To the unaided eye, the bright lunar highlands and the dark maria (Latin for "seas") make up the "man in the moon." A telescope shows that they consist of a great variety of round impact features, scars left by objects that struck the moon long ago. In the highlands, craters are closely packed together. In the maria, they are fewer. The largest scars are the impact basins, ranging up to about 1,500 miles (2,400 km) across. The basin floors were flooded with lava some time after the titanic collisions that formed them. The dark lava flows are what the eye discerns as maria. Wrinkled ridges, domed hills, and fissures mark the maria, all familiar aspects of volcanic landscapes. Young craters are centers of radial patterns of bright ejecta, material thrown from the impacts that made them. Because the force of gravity is weaker on the Moon (only about one-sixth that on Earth), blocks of rock hurled from impacts travel farther than they would on Earth.

The moon has no mountains like the Himalaya, produced by one tectonic plate bumping into another. There is no continental drift. Everywhere, the lunar surface is sheathed in regolith, a rocky rubble created by the constant bombardment of meteoroids, asteroids, and comets. Lunar mountains consist of volcanic domes, as well as the central peaks and rims of impact craters.

The Lunar Reconnaissance Orbiter, scheduled for a 2009 launch, should provide exceptionally clear images of the moon's surface, including three-dimensional information and polar illumination observations. It will also perform detailed measurements of the temperature and radiation environment. These data will help scientists choose intersting, yet safe, locations for future manned missions to the moon, planned to commence around 2020. Members of the general public were invited to submit their names for inclusion in an electronic roster that will travel aboard the Orbiter.

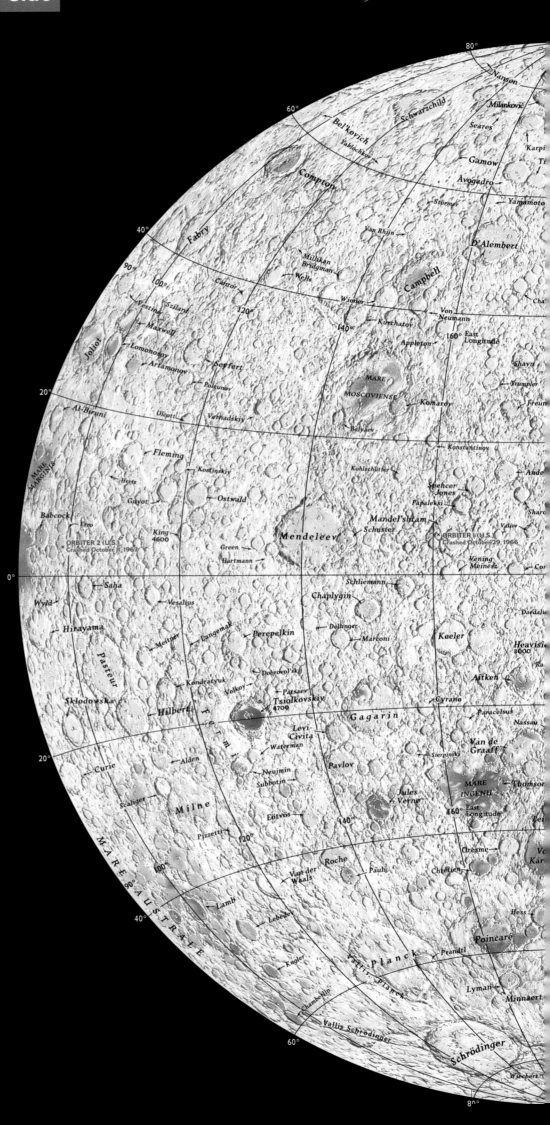

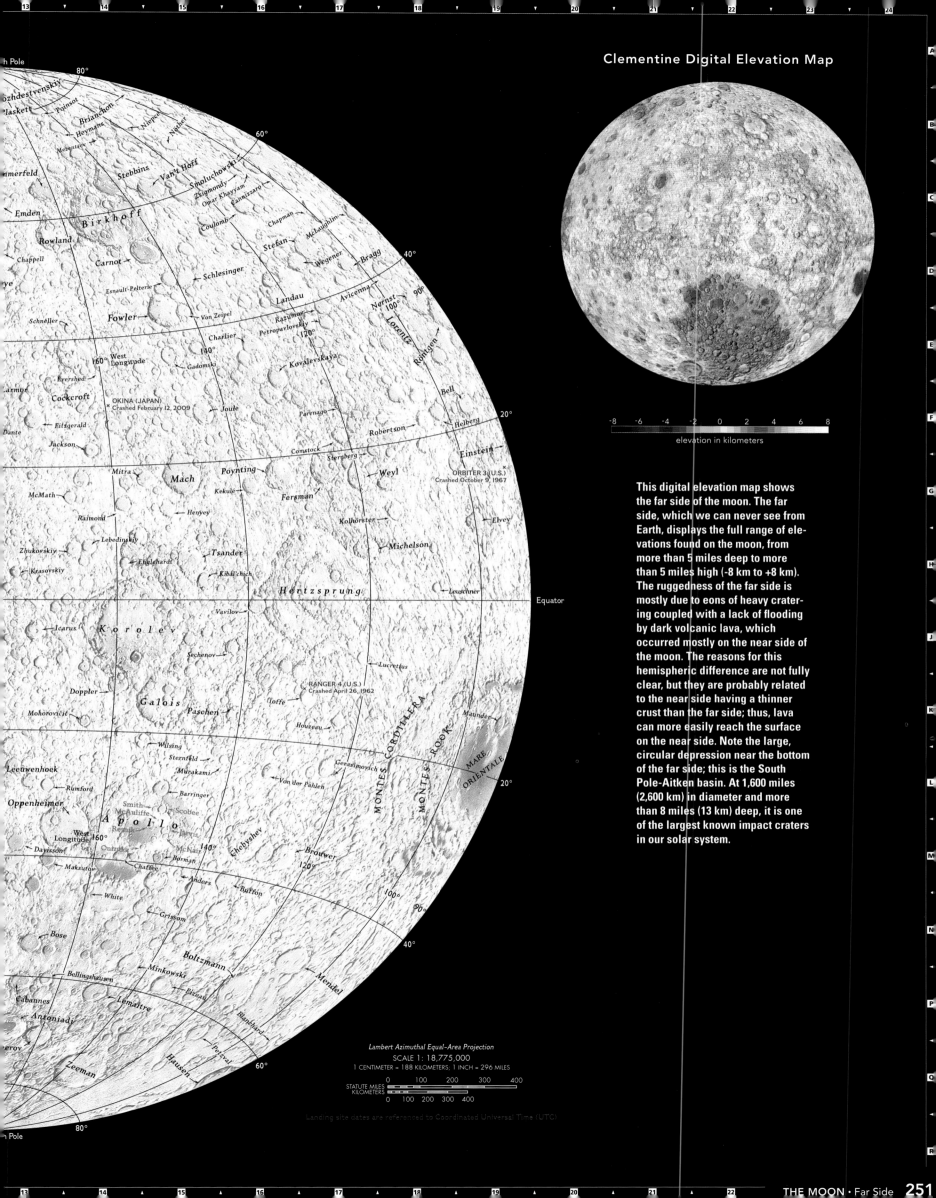

elevation in kilometers

This digital elevation map shows the far side of the moon. The far side, which we can never see from Earth, displays the full range of elevations found on the moon, from more than 5 miles deep to more than 5 miles high (-8 km to +8 km). The ruggedness of the far side is mostly due to eons of heavy cratering coupled with a lack of flooding by dark volcanic lava, which occurred mostly on the near side of the moon. The reasons for this hemispheric difference are not fully clear, but they are probably related to the near side having a thinner crust than the far side; thus, lava can more easily reach the surface on the near side. Note the large, circular depression near the bottom of the far side; this is the South Pole-Aitken basin. At 1,600 miles (2,600 km) in diameter and more than 8 miles (13 km) deep, it is one of the largest known impact craters in our solar system.

Lambert Azimuthal Equal-Area Projection
SCALE 1: 18,775,000
1 CENTIMETER = 188 KILOMETERS; 1 INCH = 296 MILES

STATUTE MILES
KILOMETERS
0   100   200   300   400

Landing site dates are referenced to Coordinated Universal Time (UTC)

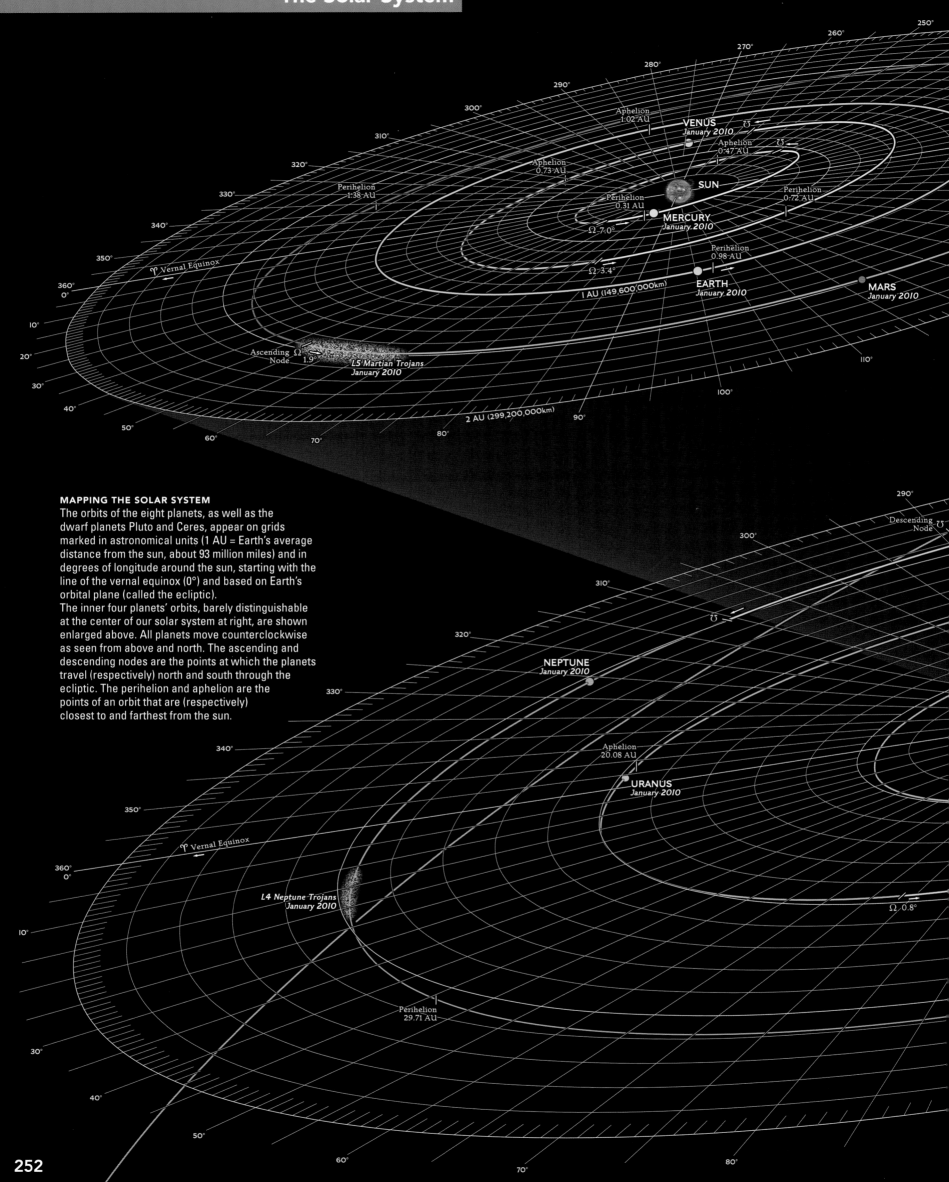

Aphelion
1.02 AU

VENUS
January 2010

Aphelion
0.47 AU

Aphelion
0.73 AU

SUN

Perihelion
1.38 AU

Perihelion
0.31 AU

Perihelion
0.72 AU

MERCURY
January 2010

Ω 7.0°

Perihelion
0.98 AU

Ω 3.4°

EARTH
January 2010

MARS
January 2010

1 AU (149,600,000km)

♈ Vernal Equinox

Ascending Ω
Node 1.9°

L5 Martian Trojans
January 2010

2 AU (299,200,000km)

MAPPING THE SOLAR SYSTEM
The orbits of the eight planets, as well as the
dwarf planets Pluto and Ceres, appear on grids
marked in astronomical units (1 AU = Earth's average
distance from the sun, about 93 million miles) and in
degrees of longitude around the sun, starting with the
line of the vernal equinox (0°) and based on Earth's
orbital plane (called the ecliptic).
The inner four planets' orbits, barely distinguishable
at the center of our solar system at right, are shown
enlarged above. All planets move counterclockwise
as seen from above and north. The ascending and
descending nodes are the points at which the planets
travel (respectively) north and south through the
ecliptic. The perihelion and aphelion are the
points of an orbit that are (respectively)
closest to and farthest from the sun.

Descending
Node

NEPTUNE
January 2010

Aphelion
20.08 AU

URANUS
January 2010

♈ Vernal Equinox

Ω 0.8°

L4 Neptune Trojans
January 2010

Perihelion
29.71 AU

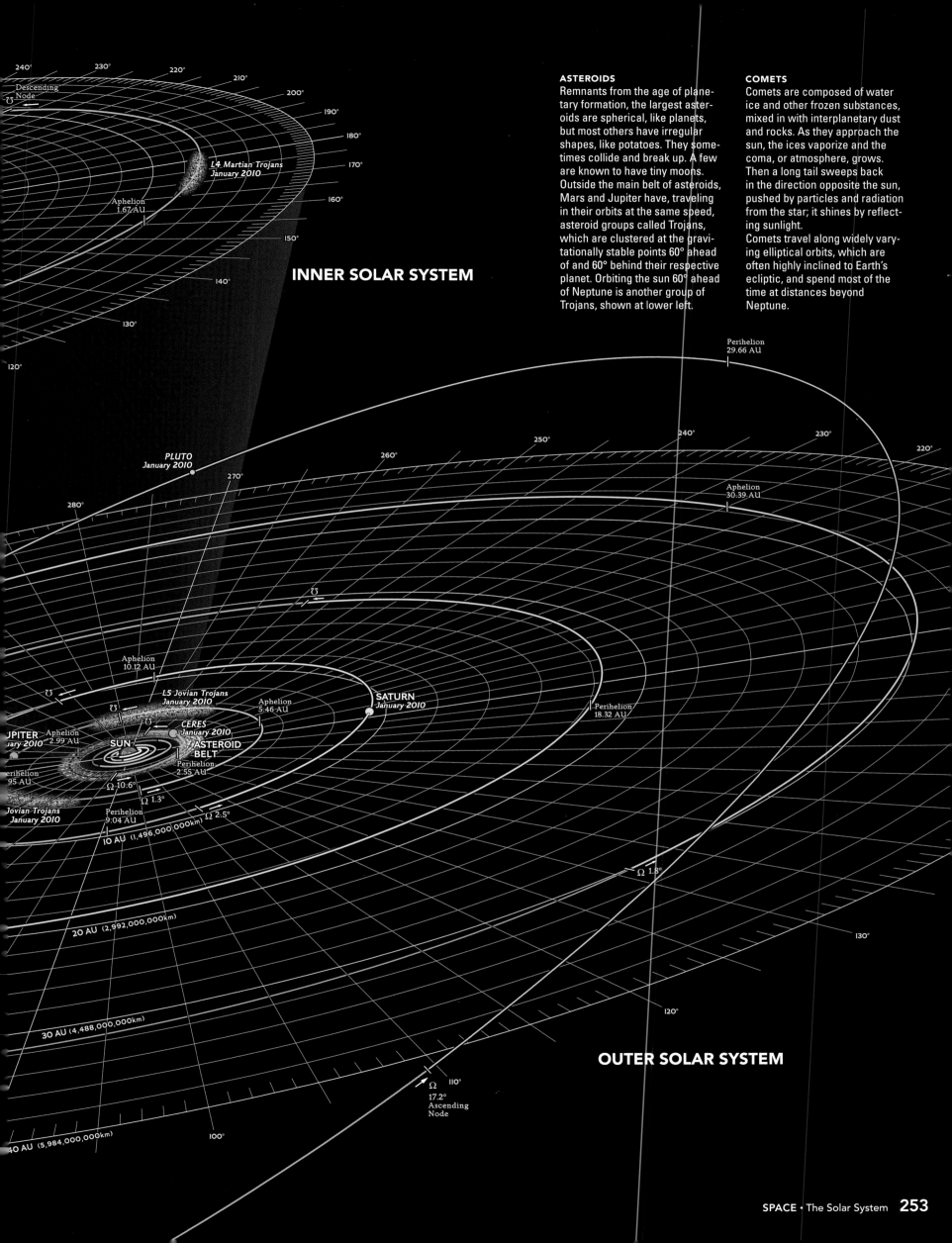

INNER SOLAR SYSTEM

240° 230° 220° 210° 200° 190° 180° 170° 160° 150° 140° 130° 120°

Descending Node ☊ ←

L4 Martian Trojans January 2010

Aphelion 1.67 AU

ASTEROIDS
Remnants from the age of planetary formation, the largest asteroids are spherical, like planets, but most others have irregular shapes, like potatoes. They sometimes collide and break up. A few are known to have tiny moons. Outside the main belt of asteroids, Mars and Jupiter have, traveling in their orbits at the same speed, asteroid groups called Trojans, which are clustered at the gravitationally stable points 60° ahead of and 60° behind their respective planet. Orbiting the sun 60° ahead of Neptune is another group of Trojans, shown at lower left.

COMETS
Comets are composed of water ice and other frozen substances, mixed in with interplanetary dust and rocks. As they approach the sun, the ices vaporize and the coma, or atmosphere, grows. Then a long tail sweeps back in the direction opposite the sun, pushed by particles and radiation from the star; it shines by reflecting sunlight.
Comets travel along widely varying elliptical orbits, which are often highly inclined to Earth's ecliptic, and spend most of the time at distances beyond Neptune.

Perihelion 29.66 AU

250° 260° 270° 280° 240° 230° 220°

PLUTO January 2010

Aphelion 30.39 AU

Aphelion 10.12 AU

L5 Jovian Trojans January 2010

Aphelion 5.46 AU

SATURN January 2010

Perihelion 18.32 AU

JPITER January 2010

Aphelion 2.99 AU

CERES January 2010

SUN

ASTEROID BELT

Perihelion 2.55 AU

Perihelion 95 AU

Jovian Trojans January 2010

Perihelion 9.04 AU

Ω 10.6°

Ω 1.3°

Ω 2.5°

10 AU (1,496,000,000km)

Ω 1.8°

20 AU (2,992,000,000km)

130°

30 AU (4,488,000,000km)

120°

OUTER SOLAR SYSTEM

☊ 110°
17.2° Ascending Node

40 AU (5,984,000,000km)

100°

JUPITER

SATURN

URANUS

NEPTUNE

RELATIVE SCALE

The planets are shown here in proportionate size to one another and the sun, whose edge is shown across the top. The dwarf planets are less than 3,000 km in diameter – much smaller than Mercury.

See the Planetary Orbits diagram in the upper right of this plate for their proper relationship to the sun.

 EARTH

 VENUS

 MARS

 MERCURY

WHAT IS A PLANET?

Our solar system has two classes of planets whose origins can be partially explained or understood. The terrestrial, or inner planets (Mercury, Venus, Earth, and Mars), are small and have solid surfaces and mean densities that suggest an iron core surrounded by a rocky, partially molten mantle. The jovian, or outer planets (Jupiter, Saturn, Uranus, and Neptune), are very large bodies consisting primarily of hydrogen and helium in gas and liquid forms; thus, they have much lower average densities than the terrestrial planets. Planets within our solar system vary widely in other ways as well: For example, in whether they have moons, rings,or internal heat sources, and whether they rotate rapidly or slowly.

In the past two decades, a large number of rocky, icy bodies have been discovered beyond the orbit of Neptune, in the general vicinity of Pluto, in a region known as the Kuiper belt. A few of these Kuiper belt objects are not much smaller than Pluto. One of them, Eris, is slightly larger than Pluto and has a moon, Dysnomia. The Kuiper belt can thus be considered an icy, distant analog of the asteroid belt between Mars and Jupiter, which contains many small, rocky bodies, the largest of which is Ceres. Astronomers hope to learn more about Pluto and the Kuiper belt when the New Horizons spacecraft (launched in 2006) reaches Pluto in 2015. This should provide new clues to the origin of the solar system.

The exact definition of a planet is still being debated. So, although our solar system is now said to have only eight planets, the consensus could change in the future.

Also, improvements in telescopic observation have led astronomers to detect evidence of large bodies orbiting other stars than our sun. Of the more than 300 such "exoplanets" or "extrasolar planets" discovered in the past two decades, many have strange, unexpected properties, such as giant planets orbiting very close to stars ("hot Jupiters"), planets with highly eccentric (elliptical) orbits, bloated planets, and planets with ferocious winds. There are even three small "planets" known to orbit a neutron star—a tiny, ultra-dense stellar remnant that formed when the massive star exploded at the end of its life.

MERCURY

Average distance from the sun:	57,900,000 km
Perihelion:	46,000,000 km
Aphelion:	69,820,000 km
Revolution period:	88 days
Average orbital speed:	47.9 km/s
Average temperature:	167°C
Rotation period:	58.9 days
Equatorial diameter:	4,879 km
Mass (Earth=1):	0.055
Density:	5.43 g/cm³
Surface gravity (Earth=1):	0.38
Known satellites:	none

Image by: Mariner 10

INNER PLANETS ▶

In 2006, the International Astronomical Union (IAU), an organization of professional astronomers, decided to reclassify Pluto as a "dwarf planet" rather than a genuine planet. Eris and Ceres are also now considered to be dwarf planets; they orbit the sun, and they are large enough to be roughly spherical, but they are not large enough to clear most other, smaller bodies out of their orbital regions. All of the other, smaller objects are now known as "small solar-system bodies," although some of them will probably become reclassified as dwarf planets if they are sufficiently large to be roughly spherical. In 2008 those dwarf planets outside Neptune's orbit were subclassified as plutoids, which currently are known to include Pluto and Eris. However, not all astronomers agree with the IAU demotion of Pluto from planetary status.

Perihelion and aphelion define the orbit's closest and farthest points from the sun. Mass and surface gravity data for each planet are expressed in proportional relation to Earth. Approximate values for Earth are given in both categories, allowing comparison between planets.

JUPITER

Average distance from the sun:	778,600,000 km
Perihelion:	740,520,000 km
Aphelion:	816,620,000 km
Revolution period:	11.87 years
Average orbital speed:	13.1 km/s
Average temperature:	-110°C
Rotation period:	9.9 hours
Equatorial diameter:	142,984 km
Mass (Earth=1):	317.8
Density:	1.33 g/cm³
Surface gravity (Earth=1):	2.36
Known satellites:	63
Largest satellites:	Ganymede, Callisto, Io, Europa

Image by: Cassini Orbiter

OUTER PLANETS ▶

SUN

Average surface temperature:	5,505°C
Average core temperature:	16,000,000°C
Rotation period:	25 days
Equatorial diameter:	1,392,000 km
Mass (Earth=1):	332,950
Density:	1.41 g/cm³
Surface gravity (Earth=1):	28.0

PLANETARY ORBITS
(see also page 252)

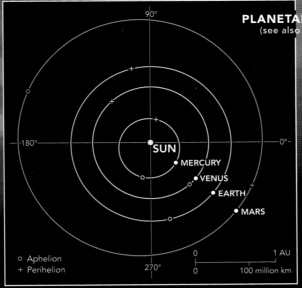

INNER PLANETS

o Aphelion
+ Perihelion

SUN
MERCURY
VENUS
EARTH
MARS

0	1 AU
0	100 million km

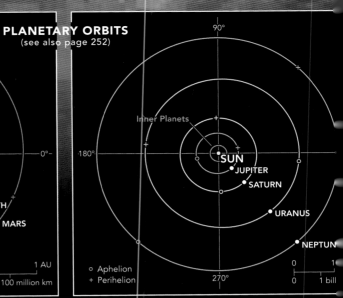

OUTER PLANETS

Inner Planets

o Aphelion
+ Perihelion

SUN
JUPITER
SATURN
URANUS
NEPTUN

0	1
0	1 bill

VENUS

Average distance from the sun:	108,200,000 km
Perihelion:	107,480,000 km
Aphelion:	108,940,000 km
Revolution period:	224.7 days
Average orbital speed:	35 km/s
Average temperature:	464°C
Rotation period:	244 days
Equatorial diameter:	12,104 km
Mass (Earth=1):	0.816
Density:	5.24 g/cm³
Surface gravity (Earth=1):	0.91
Known satellites:	none

Image by: Magellan

EARTH

Average distance from the sun:	149,600,000 km
Perihelion:	147,090,000 km
Aphelion:	152,100,000 km
Revolution period:	365.2 days
Average orbital speed:	29.8 km/s
Average temperature:	15°C
Rotation period:	23.9 hours
Equatorial diameter:	12,756 km
Mass:	5,974,000,000,000,000,000,000 metric tons
Density:	5.52 g/cm³
Surface gravity	9.81 m/s²
Known satellites:	1
Largest satellite:	Earth's moon

Image by: Galileo Orbiter

MARS

Average distance from the sun:	227,900,000 km
Perihelion:	206,620,000 km
Aphelion:	249,230,000 km
Revolution period:	687 days
Average orbital speed:	24.1 km/s
Average temperature:	-65°C
Rotation period:	24.6 hours
Equatorial diameter:	6,794 km
Mass (Earth=1):	0.107
Density:	3.93 g/cm³
Surface gravity (Earth=1):	0.38
Known satellites:	2
Largest satellites:	Phobos, Deimos

Image by: Mars Global Surveyor

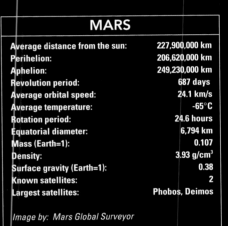

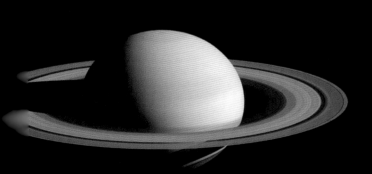

SATURN

Average distance from the sun:	1,433,500,000 km
Perihelion:	1,352,550,000 km
Aphelion:	1,514,500,000 km
Revolution period:	29.44 years
Average orbital speed:	9.7 km/s
Average temperature:	-140°C
Rotation period:	10.7 hours
Equatorial diameter:	120,536 km
Mass (Earth=1):	95.2
Density:	0.69 g/cm³
Surface gravity (Earth=1):	0.92
Known satellites:	47
Largest satellites:	Titan, Rhea, Iapetus, Dione, Tethys

Image by: Cassini Orbiter

URANUS

Average distance from the sun:	2,872,500,000 km
Perihelion:	2,741,300,000 km
Aphelion:	3,003,620,000 km
Revolution period:	83.81 years
Average orbital speed:	6.8 km/s
Average temperature:	-195°C
Rotation period:	17.2 hours
Equatorial diameter:	51,118 km
Mass (Earth=1):	14.5
Density:	1.27 g/cm³
Surface gravity (Earth=1):	0.89
Known satellites:	27
Largest satellites:	Titania, Oberon, Umbriel, Ariel

Image by: Hubble Space Telescope

NEPTUNE

Average distance from the sun:	4,495,100,000 km
Perihelion:	4,444,450,000 km
Aphelion:	4,545,670,000 km
Revolution period:	163.84 years
Average orbital speed:	5.4 km/s
Average temperature:	-200°C
Rotation period:	16.1 hours
Equatorial diameter:	49,528 km
Mass (Earth=1):	17.1
Density:	1.64 g/cm³
Surface gravity (Earth=1):	1.12
Known satellites:	13
Largest satellite:	Triton

Image by: Voyager II

THE MARTIAN LANDSCAPE is both familiar and alien. All of its features, from rugged riverbeds to shifting sand dunes, are also found on Earth. Yet Mars, with its lower gravity and much thinner atmosphere, imprints its own character on these features: The volcanoes are taller, the canyons wider, the ice caps more ephemeral than on Earth.

Compiled from NASA spacecraft data, the map at right depicts the remarkable terrain of the orange-red planet. Mars's polar caps have frozen water, like our Arctic and Antarctic, but during the winters frozen carbon dioxide also coats the poles. The huge crater at far left is a caldera atop Olympus Mons, a Missouri-size volcano more than two times the height of Earth's Mount Everest. Three more large calderas, to the right of Olympus Mons, mark the peaks of three other volcanoes along the Tharsis rise. To the right of Tharsis, the dark canyons of the Valles Marineris (Mariner Valleys) extend more than 2,500 miles (4,000 kilometers), nearly the entire width of the contiguous United States. To the right of center, the dark patch running north-south is Syrtis Major, often the easiest feature to spot with a small telescope.

Studies of Mars continue in earnest. For example, in June 2008, the Phoenix Mars lander conducted several analyses of soil in the Martian arctic, finding some water-soluble elements and compounds that are necessary for life. Similarly, the Mars Odyssey orbiter recently found regions in the southern highlands where salt deposits appear to be present, revealing where water was once abundant. NASA's Mars Science Laboratory, scheduled to launch in the fall of 2011, might assist in determining the origin of recently identified methane gas – is it geological, or biological?

MARS RECONNAISSANCE ORBITER

The best maps of Mars already show greater detail than maps of some regions of Earth. The latest Mars mission, Mars Reconnaissance Orbiter, will make the maps even better by snapping pictures that show details as small as a card table. Scientists will combine the pictures with elevation readings to produce perspective views like this one showing the contours of Martian mountains and canyons. Images like these help to plan future missions that will search for signs of past life.

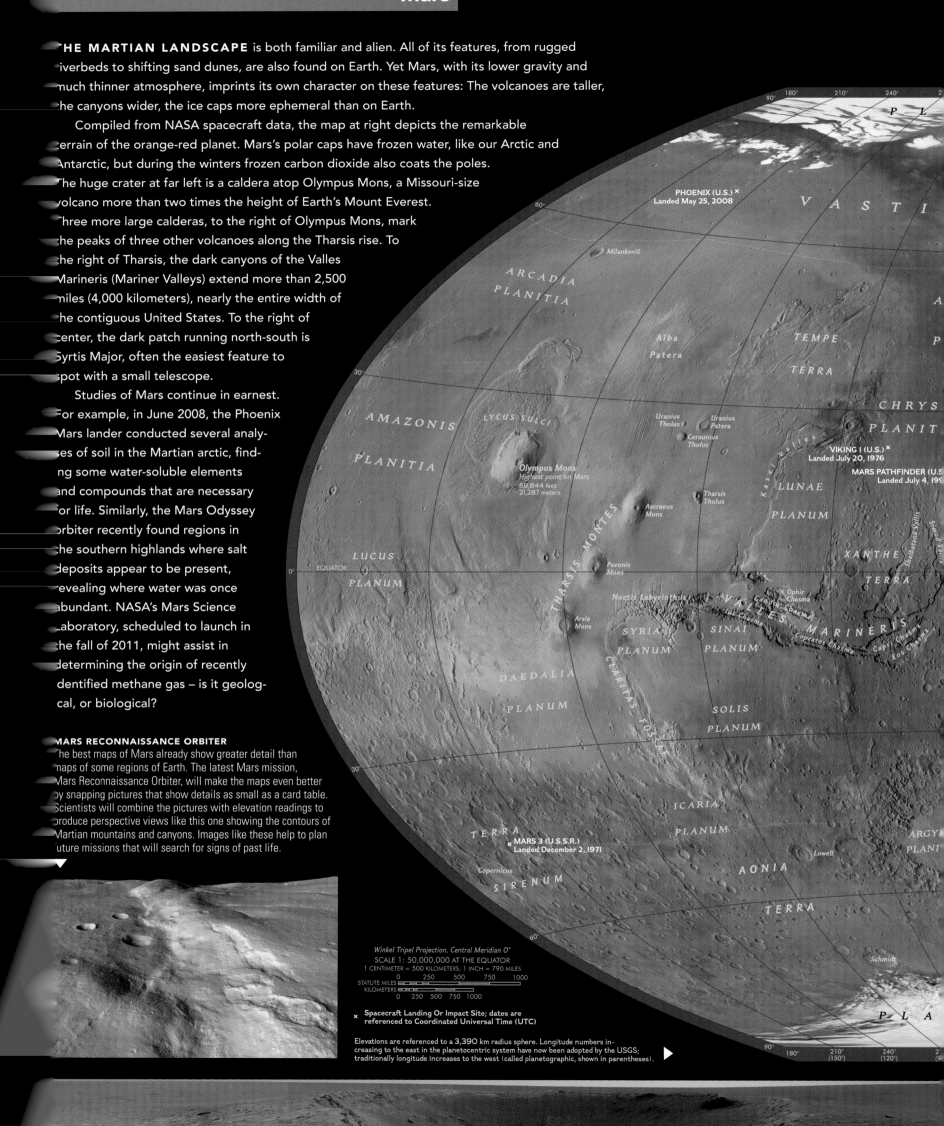

Winkel Tripel Projection, Central Meridian 0°
SCALE 1: 50,000,000 AT THE EQUATOR
1 CENTIMETER = 500 KILOMETERS; 1 INCH = 790 MILES
0   250   500   750   1000
STATUTE MILES
KILOMETERS
0   250   500 750 1000

× Spacecraft Landing Or Impact Site; dates are referenced to Coordinated Universal Time (UTC)

Elevations are referenced to a 3,390 km radius sphere. Longitude numbers increasing to the east in the planetocentric system have now been adopted by the USGS; traditionally longitude increases to the west (called planetographic, shown in parentheses).

PHOENIX (U.S.) ×
Landed May 25, 2008

VIKING I (U.S.) ×
Landed July 20, 1976

MARS PATHFINDER (U.S.
Landed July 4, 199

MARS 3 (U.S.S.R.)
Landed December 2, 1971

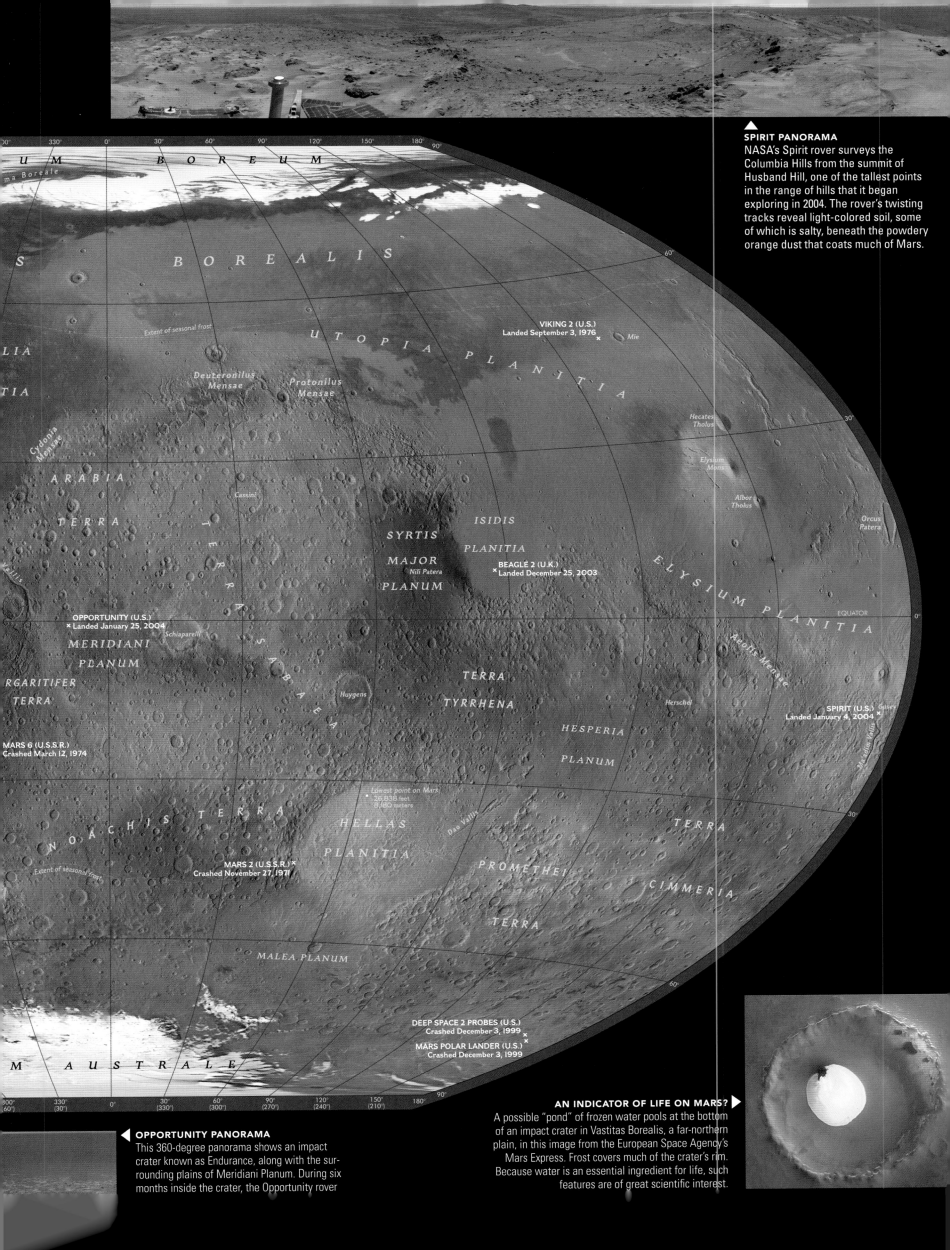

SPIRIT PANORAMA
NASA's Spirit rover surveys the Columbia Hills from the summit of Husband Hill, one of the tallest points in the range of hills that it began exploring in 2004. The rover's twisting tracks reveal light-colored soil, some of which is salty, beneath the powdery orange dust that coats much of Mars.

UM BOREUM

ma Boreale

S B O R E A L I S

LIA

TIA

Extent of seasonal frost

U T O P I A   P L A N I T I A

VIKING 2 (U.S.)
Landed September 3, 1976   ×   Mie

Deuteronilus
Mensae

Protonilus
Mensae

Cydonia
Mensae

Hecates
Tholus

ARABIA

Cassini

ISIDIS

Elysium
Mons

Albor
Tholus

Orcus
Patera

TERRA

SYRTIS

PLANITIA

MAJOR

Nili Patera

BEAGLE 2 (U.K.)
× Landed December 25, 2003

E L Y S I U M   P L A N I T I A

PLANUM

EQUATOR   0°

OPPORTUNITY (U.S.)
× Landed January 25, 2004

Schiaparelli

Aeolis Mensae

MERIDIANI

PLANUM

TERRA

RGARITIFER

Huygens

TYRRHENA

Herschel

SPIRIT (U.S.) ×
Landed January 4, 2004

TERRA

HESPERIA

MARS 6 (U.S.S.R.)
Crashed March 12, 1974

PLANUM

Lowest point on Mars
26,838 feet
8,180 meters

TERRA

N O A C H I S   T E R R A

HELLAS

Dao Vallis

PLANITIA

CIMMERIA

MARS 2 (U.S.S.R.) ×
Crashed November 27, 1971

PROMETHEI

Extent of seasonal frost

TERRA

MALEA PLANUM

DEEP SPACE 2 PROBES (U.S.)
Crashed December 3, 1999   ×
MARS POLAR LANDER (U.S.)   ×
Crashed December 3, 1999

M A U S T R A L E

330°
(30°)   0°   30°
(330°)   60°
(300°)   90°
(270°)   120°
(240°)   150°
(210°)   180°
90°

◄ **OPPORTUNITY PANORAMA**
This 360-degree panorama shows an impact crater known as Endurance, along with the surrounding plains of Meridiani Planum. During six months inside the crater, the Opportunity rover

AN INDICATOR OF LIFE ON MARS? ▶
A possible "pond" of frozen water pools at the bottom of an impact crater in Vastitas Borealis, a far-northern plain, in this image from the European Space Agency's Mars Express. Frost covers much of the crater's rim. Because water is an essential ingredient for life, such features are of great scientific interest.

LOOKING BACK IN TIME FOR ORIGINS

Supercomputer calculations simulate the structure of the early universe. The formation of great chains of protogalaxies was probably triggered by seed concentrations of as yet unidentified dark matter. The first stars in the 13.7 billion-year-old universe may have formed as early as 200 to 300 million years after the dawn of time, and a total of only 500 to 800 million years elapsed until the first galaxies formed. Hydrogen and helium from the big bang were transformed by nuclear reactions in stars and supernova explosions into all the other chemical elements found on Earth.

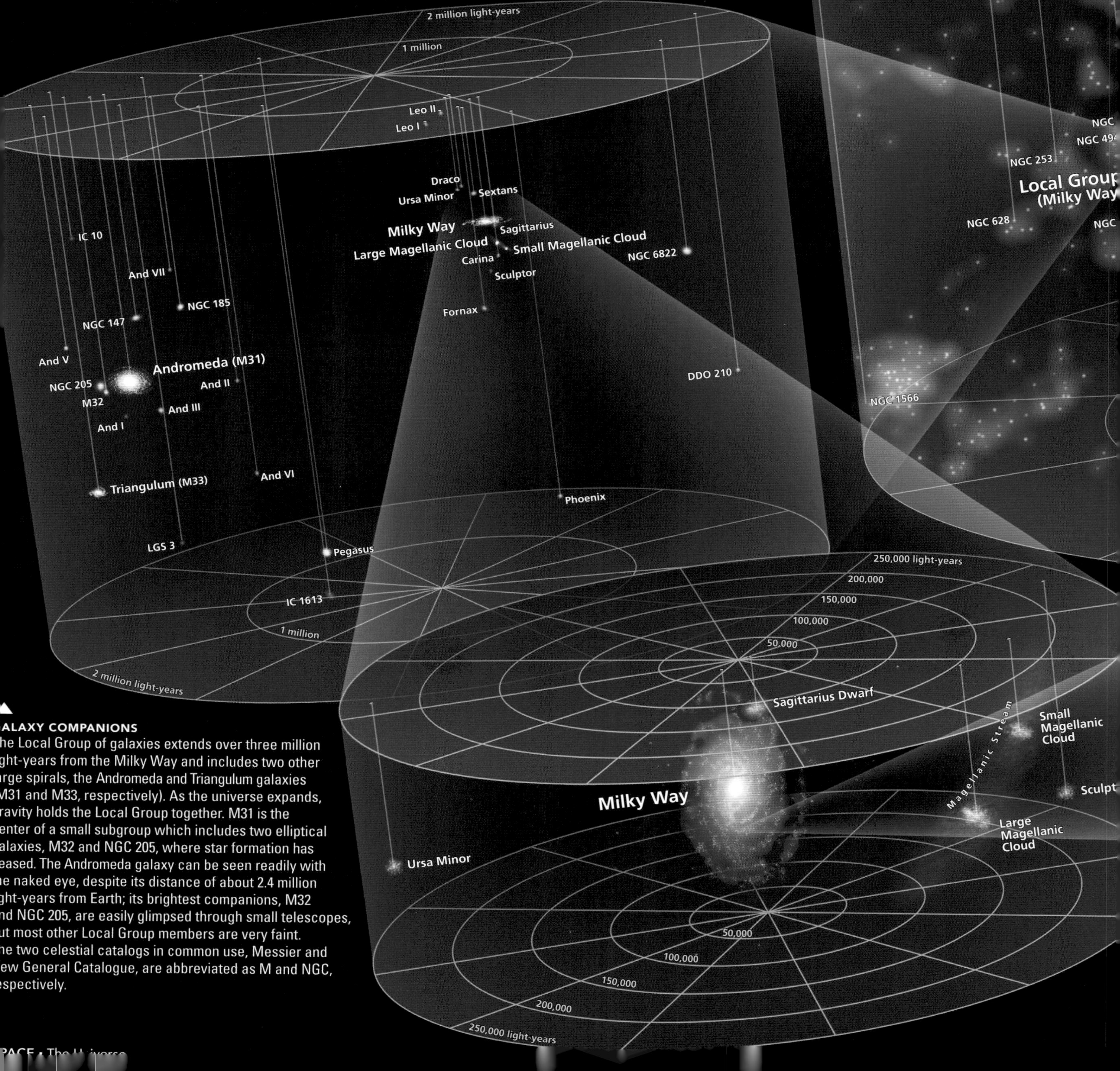

GALAXY COMPANIONS

The Local Group of galaxies extends over three million light-years from the Milky Way and includes two other large spirals, the Andromeda and Triangulum galaxies (M31 and M33, respectively). As the universe expands, gravity holds the Local Group together. M31 is the center of a small subgroup which includes two elliptical galaxies, M32 and NGC 205, where star formation has ceased. The Andromeda galaxy can be seen readily with the naked eye, despite its distance of about 2.4 million light-years from Earth; its brightest companions, M32 and NGC 205, are easily glimpsed through small telescopes, but most other Local Group members are very faint. The two celestial catalogs in common use, Messier and New General Catalogue, are abbreviated as M and NGC, respectively.

2 million light-years

1 million

Leo II
Leo I

Draco
Ursa Minor
Sextans

IC 10

Milky Way
Sagittarius

Large Magellanic Cloud
Small Magellanic Cloud

And VII
Carina

Sculptor
NGC 6822

NGC 185
Fornax

NGC 147

And V
Andromeda (M31)

NGC 205
And II

M32
And III

And I

DDO 210

Triangulum (M33)
And VI

Phoenix

LGS 3

Pegasus

IC 1613

1 million

2 million light-years

NGC
NGC 494

NGC 253

Local Group
(Milky Way

NGC 628
NGC

Local Group
(Milky Way

NGC 1566

250,000 light-years
200,000
150,000
100,000
50,000

Sagittarius Dwarf

Magellanic Stream

Small Magellanic Cloud

Milky Way

Sculpt

Ursa Minor

Large Magellanic Cloud

50,000

100,000

150,000

200,000

250,000 light-years

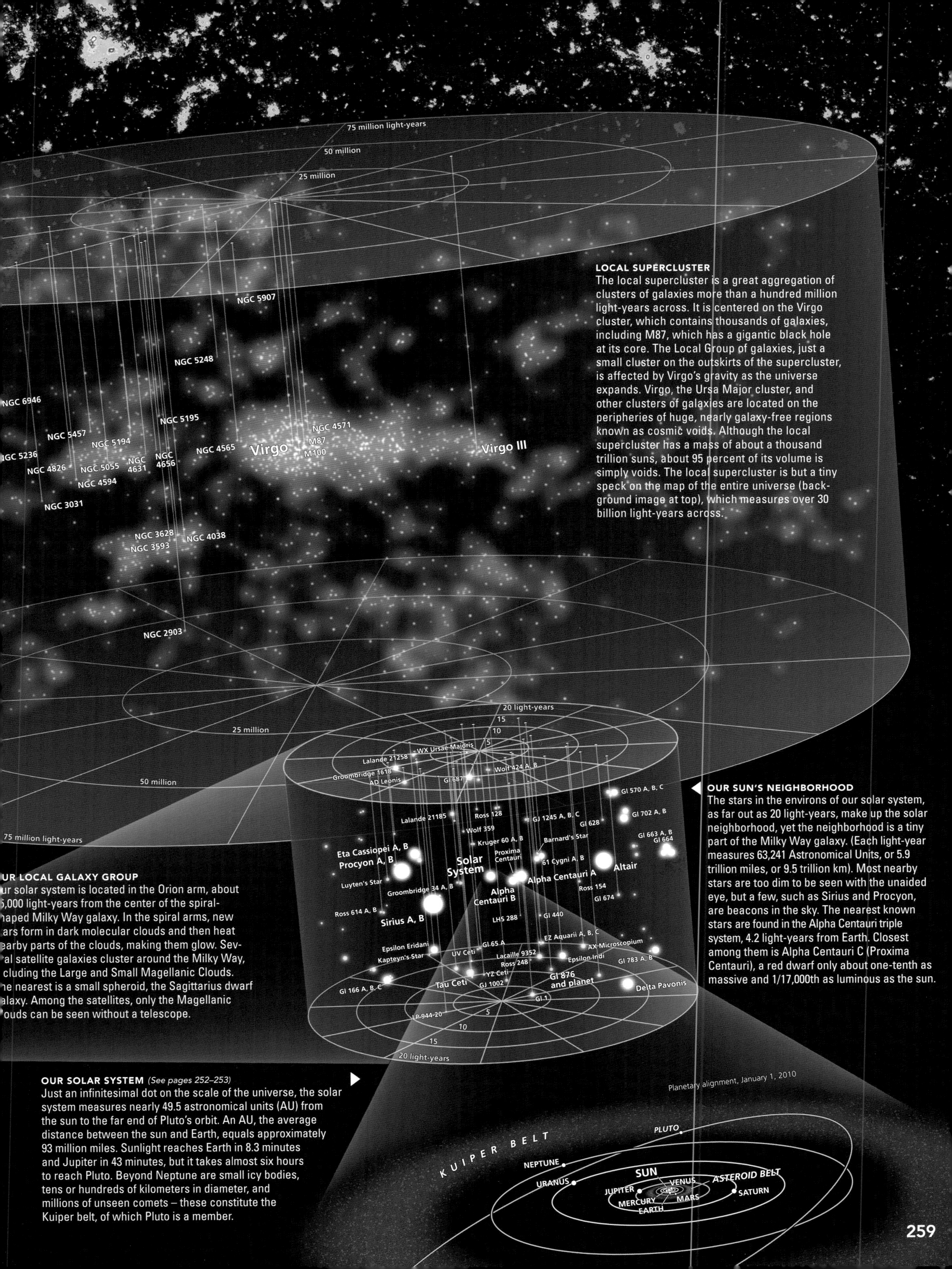

LOCAL SUPERCLUSTER

The local supercluster is a great aggregation of clusters of galaxies more than a hundred million light-years across. It is centered on the Virgo cluster, which contains thousands of galaxies, including M87, which has a gigantic black hole at its core. The Local Group of galaxies, just a small cluster on the outskirts of the supercluster, is affected by Virgo's gravity as the universe expands. Virgo, the Ursa Major cluster, and other clusters of galaxies are located on the peripheries of huge, nearly galaxy-free regions known as cosmic voids. Although the local supercluster has a mass of about a thousand trillion suns, about 95 percent of its volume is simply voids. The local supercluster is but a tiny speck on the map of the entire universe (background image at top), which measures over 30 billion light-years across.

(Local Supercluster labels)

75 million light-years
50 million
25 million

NGC 5907
NGC 5248
NGC 6946
NGC 5457
NGC 5194
NGC 5195
NGC 5236
NGC 4826
NGC 5055
NGC 4631
NGC 4594
NGC 4565
NGC 4656
NGC 4571
M87
M100
Virgo
Virgo III
NGC 3031
NGC 3628
NGC 3593
NGC 4038
NGC 2903

25 million
50 million
75 million light-years

OUR SUN'S NEIGHBORHOOD

The stars in the environs of our solar system, as far out as 20 light-years, make up the solar neighborhood, yet the neighborhood is a tiny part of the Milky Way galaxy. (Each light-year measures 63,241 Astronomical Units, or 5.9 trillion miles, or 9.5 trillion km). Most nearby stars are too dim to be seen with the unaided eye, but a few, such as Sirius and Procyon, are beacons in the sky. The nearest known stars are found in the Alpha Centauri triple system, 4.2 light-years from Earth. Closest among them is Alpha Centauri C (Proxima Centauri), a red dwarf only about one-tenth as massive and 1/17,000th as luminous as the sun.

(Sun's Neighborhood labels)

20 light-years
15
10
5

WX Ursae Majoris
Lalande 21258
Groombridge 1618
AD Leonis
Wolf 424 A, B
GI 687
GI 570 A, B, C
Lalande 21185
Ross 128
GJ 1245 A, B, C
GI 702 A, B
GI 628
Wolf 359
Kruger 60 A, B
Barnard's Star
GI 663 A, B
GI 664
Eta Cassiopei A, B
Procyon A, B
Proxima Centauri
61 Cygni A, B
Altair
Solar System
Alpha Centauri A
Luyten's Star
Groombridge 34 A, B
Alpha Centauri B
Ross 154
GI 674
Ross 614 A, B
Sirius A, B
LHS 288
GI 440
Epsilon Eridani
GI 65 A
EZ Aquarii A, B, C
AX Microscopium
Kapteyn's Star
UV Ceti
Lacaille 9352
Epsilon Indi
Ross 248
GI 783 A, B
GI 166 A, B, C
YZ Ceti
GI 876 and planet
Tau Ceti
GJ 1002
Delta Pavonis
GI.1
LP-944-20
5
10
15
20 light-years

OUR LOCAL GALAXY GROUP

Our solar system is located in the Orion arm, about 5,000 light-years from the center of the spiral-shaped Milky Way galaxy. In the spiral arms, new stars form in dark molecular clouds and then heat nearby parts of the clouds, making them glow. Several satellite galaxies cluster around the Milky Way, including the Large and Small Magellanic Clouds. The nearest is a small spheroid, the Sagittarius dwarf galaxy. Among the satellites, only the Magellanic Clouds can be seen without a telescope.

OUR SOLAR SYSTEM (See pages 252–253)

Just an infinitesimal dot on the scale of the universe, the solar system measures nearly 49.5 astronomical units (AU) from the sun to the far end of Pluto's orbit. An AU, the average distance between the sun and Earth, equals approximately 93 million miles. Sunlight reaches Earth in 8.3 minutes and Jupiter in 43 minutes, but it takes almost six hours to reach Pluto. Beyond Neptune are small icy bodies, tens or hundreds of kilometers in diameter, and millions of unseen comets – these constitute the Kuiper belt, of which Pluto is a member.

Planetary alignment, January 1, 2010

(Solar System labels)

KUIPER BELT
PLUTO
NEPTUNE
URANUS
SUN
JUPITER
VENUS
ASTEROID BELT
MERCURY
MARS
EARTH
SATURN

Space Exploration Time Line

● Mercury mission　○ Venus mission　○ Earth mission　○ Moon mission

1957

First Artificial Satellite

U.S.S.R.
Oct. 4, 1957

Sputnik 1 was launched; it transmitted radio signals back to Earth for a short time.

First Live Animal in Space

U.S.S.R.
Nov. 3, 1957

A dog named Laika lived eight days in space aboard *Sputnik 2.*

1958

First American Satellite

U.S.
Jan. 31, 1958

Explorer 1 discovered radiation belts around Earth.

Creation of NASA

U.S.
Oct. 1, 1958

National Aeronautics and Space Administration (NASA) was established.

1959

First Man-made Object to Achieve Solar Orbit

U.S.S.R.
Jan. 4, 1959

Luna 1 was launched on Jan. 2; its orbit lies between those of Earth and Mars.

First Spacecraft to Impact on the Moon

U.S.S.R.
Sept. 14, 1959

Launched Sept. 12, *Luna 2* confirmed detection of solar wind before impact.

First View of Moon's Far Side

U.S.S.R.
Oct. 7, 1959

Launched Oct. 4, *Luna 3* photographed 70 percent of the far side of the moon.

1960

First Weather Satellite

U.S.
Apr. 1, 1960

Tiros 1 established satellites as useful tools for studying weather conditions.

1961

First Man in Space

U.S.S.R.
Apr. 12, 1961

Yuri Gagarin orbited Earth once in *Vostok 1,* completing the trip in 108 minutes.

First American in Space

U.S.
May 5, 1961

Alan Shepard's *Freedom 7* flight lasted 15 minutes and did not reach orbit.

1962

First American in Orbit

U.S.
Feb. 20, 1962

John Glenn orbited Earth three times on *Friendship 7.*

1963

First Probe to Reach Another Planet

U.S.
Dec. 14, 1962

Launched Aug. 27, 1962, *Mariner 2* flew past Venus and transmitted data back to Earth.

1970

Apollo 13 Launch

U.S.
Apr. 11, 1970

After oxygen tanks exploded, the 3 astronauts were nearly killed; Mission Control coordinated their dramatic rescue.

First Automated Return of Lunar Soil

U.S.S.R.
Sept. 24, 1970

Launched Sept. 12, automated spacecraft *Luna 16* returned lunar soil samples to Earth.

First Remote-controlled Lunar Rover

U.S.S.R.
Nov. 17, 1970

Orbiter *Luna 17* lands rover *Lunokhod 1* on the moon; controlled from Earth.

1971

First Landing on Venus

U.S.S.R.
Dec. 15, 1970

Launched Aug. 17, *Venera 7* (first spacecraft to land on another planet) transmitted data from Venus's surface for about an hour.

First Space Station

U.S.S.R.
Apr. 19, 1971

Salyut 1 orbited for 175 days, and fell back to Earth on Oct. 11, 1971.

First Occupation of Space Station

U.S.S.R.
June 7, 1971

Three cosmonauts occupied *Salyut 1* for several weeks.

1972

First Manned Lunar Rover

U.S.
July 31, 1971

Apollo 15's astronauts explored the moon's surface in an electric vehicle.

First Spacecraft to Orbit Another Planet

U.S.
Nov. 13, 1971

Launched May 30, *Mariner 9* orbited Mars and mapped the surface.

1973

First Black Hole Candidate

U.S.
Dec. 1972

Observed from the satellite *Uhuru,* Cygnus X-1 was designated as a probable black hole.

First U.S. Space Station

U.S.
May 14, 1973

Skylab was launched for science experiments.

First *Skylab* Crew

U.S.
May 25, 1973

A crew repaired damage to *Skylab* sustained during launch.

1974

Close-up View of Jupiter

U.S.
Dec. 4, 1974

Launched April 6, 1973, space probe *Pioneer 11* passes Jupiter and moves on toward Saturn.

1980

Passing of Saturn by *Voyager 1*

U.S.
Nov. 12, 1980

Voyager 1 (launched Sept. 5, 1977) transmitted data of the planet, its rings, and its largest moon, Titan.

1981

First Space Shuttle Launch

U.S.
Apr. 12, 1981

The re-usable orbiter *Columbia* launched as the first mission of the Space Transportation System (STS-1), or space shuttle.

Passing of Saturn by *Voyager 2*

U.S.
Aug. 26, 1981

Voyager 2 (launched Aug. 20, 1977) transmitted close-up images of the planet and its moons, as well as temperature data.

1982

First Venus Soil Samples

U.S.S.R.
Mar. 1, 1982

Launched Oct. 30, 1981, *Venera 13* transmitted data for 2 hours, including the first color images from Venus's surface.

First Operational Space Shuttle Mission

U.S.
Nov. 11, 1982

On mission STS-5, Space shuttle *Columbia* deployed two satellites.

1983

New Space Endurance Record

U.S.S.R.
Dec. 10, 1982

Two Soviet cosmonauts inhabited space station *Salyut 7* for 211 days.

Maiden Voyage of *Challenger*

U.S.
Apr. 4, 1983

America's second space shuttle debuted with mission STS-6.

First American Woman in Space

U.S.
June 18, 1983

Sally Ride traveled on *Challenger* mission STS-7.

1984

First Untethered Space Walk

U.S.
Feb. 3, 1984

During *Challenger*'s mission STS-41-B, astronaut Bruce McCandless used the Manned Maneuvering Unit.

Maiden Voyage of *Discovery*

U.S.
Aug. 30, 1984

America's third space shuttle debuted with mission STS-41-D.

1990

Passing of Venus by *Galileo*

U.S.
Feb. 10, 1990

Launched from space shuttle *Atlantis*' mission STS-34 on Oct. 18, 1989, *Galileo* flew by Venus on the way to its ultimate goal of Jupiter.

Launch of Hubble Space Telescope

U.S.
Apr. 24, 1990

The HST was successfully deployed, but a flawed mirror resulted in fuzzy images.

1991

Arrival of *Magellan* at Venus

U.S.
Aug. 10, 1990

Launched from space shuttle *Atlantis*' mission STS-30 on May 4, 1989, *Magellan* used radar to map the Venusian surface.

First Flyby of an Asteroid

U.S.
Oct. 29, 1991

Launched from space shuttle *Atlantis* on Oct. 18, 1989, *Galileo* flew by the asteroid Gaspra on its way to Jupiter.

1992

Maiden Voyage of *Endeavour*

U.S.
May 7, 1992

Launch of mission STS-49 brought the number of orbiters in the shuttle fleet back to four.

50th Space Shuttle Mission

U.S.
Sept. 12, 1992

STS-47, the second *Endeavour* mission, was the 50th space shuttle mission.

1993

Flyby of an Asteroid and Its Moon

U.S.
Aug. 28, 1993

On its way to Jupiter, *Galileo* flew by the asteroid Ida and discovered its moon, named Dactyl.

First HST Servicing Mission

U.S.
Dec. 2, 1993

Endeavour began the first servicing mission of the Hubble Space Telescope.

1994

First Russian Cosmonaut Aboard Shuttle

U.S.–Russia
Feb. 3, 1994

Sergei Krikalev flew aboard *Discovery* on mission STS-60.

2000

100th Space Shuttle Mission

U.S.
Oct. 11, 2000

STS-92, the 28th *Discovery* mission, was the 100th space shuttle mission.

2001

First Craft Landing on an Asteroid

U.S.
Feb. 12, 2001

Launched Feb. 17, 1996, and flown past asteroid Mathilde June 27, 1997, *NEAR Shoemaker* landed on asteroid Eros and sent back data.

100th U.S. Space Walk

U.S.
Feb. 14, 2001

A space walk was necessary to install a new module for the ISS.

New Space Walk Record

U.S.
Mar. 11, 2001

Susan Helms and Jim Voss spent 8 hours and 56 minutes installing a new ISS module.

2002

First Tourist in Space

U.S.–Russia
Apr. 28, 2001

Dennis Tito paid $20 million to fly in a Russian *Soyuz* space capsule and board the ISS.

Launch of *Shenzhou 4*

China
Dec. 30, 2002

China launched its *Shenzhou 4* spacecraft in a test launch to prepare for manned space voyages.

2003

Space Shuttle *Columbia* Tragedy

U.S.
Feb. 1, 2003

Mission STS-107's shuttle *Columbia* broke up during its descent, killing all seven crew members.

Successful Chinese Orbit

China
Oct. 15, 2003

China launched a human into space, who returned safely after orbiting Earth for two days.

Mars Rover *Spirit*

U.S.
Jan. 4, 2004

Launched June 10, 2003, NASA's rover *Spirit* landed on Mars and rolled onto the surface nearly two weeks later, collecting data.

2004

Mars Rover *Opportunity*

U.S.
Jan. 25, 2004

Launched July 8, 2003, NASA's rover *Opportunity* landed on Mars and proceeded to collect data.

First Orbit of Saturn

U.S.–Europe
July 1, 2004

Launched Oct. 15, 1997, NASA's spacecraft *Cassini* achieved Saturn orbit, carrying the European Space Agency's probe *Huygens.*

1964

First Woman in Space

U.S.S.R.
June 16, 1963

Valentina Tereshkova orbited Earth 48 times in Vostok 6.

1965

First Space Walk

U.S.S.R.
Mar. 18, 1965

Alexei Leonov's tethered space walk lasted 12 minutes.

First Images of Mars from Deep Space

U.S.
July 14, 1965

Launched Nov. 28, 1964, Mariner 4 transmitted the first pictures taken of another planet.

1966

First Spacecraft to Land on the Moon

U.S.S.R.
Feb. 3, 1966

Launched Jan. 31, Luna 9 demonstrated the moon's surface is strong enough to support large spacecraft.

First American Spacecraft on the Moon

U.S.
June 2, 1966

Launched May 30, Surveyor 1 soft-landed on the moon and transmitted photographs.

1967

First U.S. Space Tragedy

U.S.
Jan. 27, 1967

Three astronauts were killed in a fire during a test for the Apollo 1 mission.

First Spaceflight Casualty

U.S.S.R.
Apr. 24, 1967

Soyuz 1 crashed the day after launch, killing its cosmonaut.

First Venus Probe Launched

U.S.S.R.
June 12, 1967

Venera 4 compiled data on Venusian atmosphere, arriving there Oct. 18.

1968

First Lunar Orbit and Recovery

U.S.S.R.
Sept. 18, 1968

Launched Sept. 15 from an orbiting Sputnik, Zond 5 orbited the moon once and returned to Earth.

First Manned Apollo Mission

U.S.
Oct. 11, 1968

NASA launched Apollo 7 with 3 astronauts, and orbited Earth 163 times.

1969

First Manned Moon Orbit

U.S.
Dec. 24, 1968

Launched Dec. 21, Apollo 8 made 10 lunar orbits on its 6-day mission.

First Manned Moon Landing

U.S.
July 20, 1969

Launched July 16, Apollo 11's Neil Armstrong and Edwin Aldrin, Jr., were first to set foot on the moon.

1975

First International Space Rendezvous

U.S.–U.S.S.R.
July 17, 1975

American and Soviet spacecraft docked together in orbit for the Apollo-Soyuz Test Project.

First Surface Images of Venus

U.S.S.R.
Oct. 22, 1975

Venera 9, launched June 8, landed on Venus Oct. 22 and returned the first surface photos of another planet.

1976

First Surface Images of Mars

U.S.
July 20, 1976

With Viking 1, launched Aug. 20, 1975, the U.S. succeeded in its first attempt at landing on another planet.

1977

Discovery of Water Ice on Mars

U.S.
Sept. 1976

Launched Sept. 9, 1975, Viking 2 found water (in the form of ice), the possible requirement for past or present life.

Launch of Voyager Missions

U.S.
Aug.–Sept. 1977

Voyager 1 and 2 traveled to Jupiter and Saturn; they were the first spacecraft sent to explore these planets.

1978

Arrival of U.S. Craft Pioneer Venus 1

U.S.
Dec. 4, 1978

Launched May 20, Pioneer Venus 1 entered orbit, obtained data on the atmosphere, and mapped Venus's surface.

Arrival of U.S. Craft Pioneer Venus 2

U.S.
Dec. 9, 1978

Launched Aug. 8, Pioneer Venus 2 entered orbit Nov. 16 and released 4 probes into Venus's atmosphere.

1979

Passing of Jupiter by Voyager 1

U.S.
Mar. 5, 1979

Voyager 1 (launched Sept. 5, 1977) transmitted close-up images of the planet and its moons.

Passing of Jupiter by Voyager 2

U.S.
July 9, 1979

Voyager 2 (launched Aug. 20, 1977) discovered volcanism on Jupiter's moon Io, and discovered a few rings.

First Images of Saturn

U.S.
Sept. 1, 1979

Launched April 6, 1973, space probe Pioneer 11 passed Jupiter before encountering Saturn.

1985

Maiden Voyage of Atlantis

U.S.
Oct. 3, 1985

America's fourth space shuttle debuted with mission STS-51-J.

1986

Passing of Uranus by Voyager 2

U.S.
Jan. 24, 1986

Launched Aug. 20, 1977, Voyager 2 transmitted the first close-up images of Uranus and its moons and rings.

Challenger Tragedy

U.S.
Jan. 28, 1986

Challenger's crew of seven was killed in an explosion when a leak ignited the fuel tank shortly after liftoff for mission STS-51-L.

1987

Launch of Mir Space Station

U.S.S.R.
Feb. 20, 1986

Mir's first module was successfully launched into orbit.

1988

New Space Endurance Record

U.S.S.R.
Dec. 29, 1987

Yuri Romanenko inhabited Mir for 326 days.

1989

Passing of Neptune by Voyager 2

U.S.
Aug. 25, 1989

Launched Aug. 20, 1977, Voyager 2 transmitted the first close-up images of Neptune and its moon Triton.

1995

First Female Shuttle Pilot

U.S.
Feb. 3, 1995

Eileen M. Collins piloted Discovery on mission STS-63.

New Space Endurance Record

Russia
Mar. 22, 1995

Valeriy Polyakov spent 438 days aboard Mir.

1996

First Shuttle Docking with Mir

U.S.–Russia
June 29, 1995

During mission STS-71, the American space shuttle Atlantis rendezvoused with the Russian space station.

Arrival of Galileo at Jupiter

U.S.
Dec. 7, 1995

Launched from space shuttle Atlantis on Oct. 18, 1989, Galileo conducted studies of the planet and its moons.

1997

75th Space Shuttle Mission

U.S.
Feb. 22, 1996

STS-75, the 19th Columbia mission, was the 75th space shuttle mission.

Return of Shannon Lucid From Mir

U.S.–Russia
Sept. 26, 1996

Lucid set a U.S. space endurance record of 188 days, with 179 days aboard Mir.

1998

First Landing of a Rover on Another Planet

U.S.
July 4, 1997

Launched Dec. 4, 1996, NASA's Mars Pathfinder examined terrain and returned images of the planet's surface.

Return of John Glenn to Space

U.S.
Oct. 29, 1998

Aboard Discovery for mission STS-95, John Glenn returned to space for the first time in 36 years.

Launch of First Module of ISS (International Space Station)

Russia
Nov. 20, 1998

A Russian rocket launched Zarya, the first component of the ISS.

1999

First American ISS Module

U.S.
Dec. 4, 1998

The Unity module was attached to the Zarya module.

2005

Data from Saturn's Moon Titan

U.S.–Europe
Jan. 14, 2005

ESA's Huygens made a parachute-assisted descent through the atmosphere of Titan (Saturn's largest moon), collecting data.

2006

First Probe into a Comet

U.S.
July 4, 2005

Launched Jan. 12, 2005, Deep Impact became the first space mission to probe inside the surface of a comet (Tempel 1).

Japanese Craft Visits an Asteroid

Japan
Nov. 19, 2005

Japan's Hayabusa gathered dust samples from the asteroid Itokawa, and is scheduled to return to Earth in June 2010.

First Sample of Comet Dust

U.S.
Jan. 15, 2006

Launched Feb. 7, 1999, NASA's Stardust capsule returned to Earth, bringing samples of comet Wild 2.

2007

Mission to Pluto

U.S.
Jan. 19, 2006

NASA's New Horizons launched, passed Jupiter Feb. 28, 2007, and is scheduled to reach Pluto July 14, 2015.

ESA Venus Express

Europe
Apr. 11, 2006

Launched Nov. 9, 2005, from Baikonur, Kazakhstan, European Space Agency's (ESA) Venus Express went into orbit around Venus.

2008

Japanese Moon Orbiter

Japan
Oct. 3, 2007

Launched Sept. 14, the unmanned Kaguya reached the moon and deployed two micro-satellites, Ouna and Okina (Okina crashed Feb. 12, 2009).

Chinese Moon Orbiter

China
Nov. 5, 2007

Launched Oct. 24, 2007, unmanned Chang'e 1 reached lunar orbit and relayed images of the moon's surface.

Mars Phoenix Lander

U.S.
May 25, 2008

Launched Aug. 4, 2007, Phoenix landed and analyzed soil near the Martian north pole, where water ice was presumed to exist.

2009

Indian Moon Orbiter

India
Nov. 8, 2008

Launched Oct. 22, 2008, unmanned Chandrayaan 1 reached lunar orbit and released an impact probe onto the moon on Nov. 14.

Search for Extrasolar Terrestrial Planets

U.S.
Mar. 7, 2009

NASA launched Kepler to survey Earth's vicinity of the Milky Way for the existence of Earthlike planets orbiting other stars.

FUTURE

NASA plans many more missions to the moon, Mars, Jupiter, and the sun, as well as asteroids Vesta and Ceres, while Japan targets Venus in 2010, and in collaboration with the ESA, launch a mission in 2013 that would arrive in 2019.

Appendix

Airline Distances in Kilometers

	BEIJING	CAIRO	CAPE TOWN	CARACAS	HONG KONG	HONOLULU	LONDON	MELBOURNE	MEXICO CITY	MONTRÉAL	MOSCOW	NEW DELHI	NEW YORK	PARIS	RIO DE JANEIRO	ROME	SAN FRANCISCO	SINGAPORE	STOCKHOLM	TOKYO
BEIJING		7557	12947	14411	1972	8171	8160	9093	12478	10490	5809	3788	11012	8236	17325	8144	9524	4465	6725	2104
CAIRO	7557		7208	10209	8158	14239	3513	13966	12392	8733	2899	4436	9042	3215	9882	2135	12015	8270	3404	9587
CAPE TOWN	12947	7208		10232	11867	18562	9635	10338	13703	12744	10101	9284	12551	9307	6075	8417	16487	9671	10334	14737
CARACAS	14411	10209	10232		16380	9694	7500	15624	3598	3932	9940	14221	3419	7621	4508	8363	6286	18361	8724	14179
HONG KONG	1972	8158	11867	16380		8945	9646	7392	14155	12462	7158	3770	12984	9650	17710	9300	11121	2575	8243	2893
HONOLULU	8171	14239	18562	9694	8945		11653	8862	6098	7915	11342	11930	7996	11988	13343	12936	3857	10824	11059	6208
LONDON	8160	3513	9635	7500	9646	11653		16902	8947	5240	2506	6724	5586	341	9254	1434	8640	10860	1436	9585
MELBOURNE	9093	13966	10338	15624	7392	8862	16902		13557	16730	14418	10192	16671	16793	13227	15987	12644	6050	15593	8159
MEXICO CITY	12478	12392	13703	3598	14155	6098	8947	13557		3728	10740	14679	3362	9213	7669	10260	3038	16623	9603	11319
MONTRÉAL	10490	8733	12744	3932	12462	7915	5240	16730	3728		7077	11286	533	5522	8175	6601	4092	14816	5900	10409
MOSCOW	5809	2899	10101	9940	7158	11342	2506	14418	10740	7077		4349	7530	2492	11529	2378	9469	8426	1231	7502
NEW DELHI	3788	4436	9284	14221	3770	11930	6724	10192	14679	11286	4349		11779	6601	14080	5929	12380	4142	5579	5857
NEW YORK	11012	9042	12551	3419	12984	7996	5586	16671	3362	533	7530	11779		5851	7729	6907	4140	15349	6336	10870
PARIS	8236	3215	9307	7621	9650	11988	341	16793	9213	5522	2492	6601	5851		9146	1108	8975	10743	1546	9738
RIO DE JANEIRO	17325	9882	6075	4508	17710	13343	9254	13227	7669	8175	11529	14080	7729	9146		9181	10647	15740	10682	18557
ROME	8144	2135	8417	8363	9300	12936	1434	15987	10260	6601	2378	5929	6907	1108	9181		10071	10030	1977	9881
SAN FRANCISCO	9524	12015	16487	6286	11121	3857	8640	12644	3038	4092	9469	12380	4140	8975	10647	10071		13598	8644	8284
SINGAPORE	4465	8270	9671	18361	2575	10824	10860	6050	16623	14816	8426	4142	15349	10743	15740	10030	13598		9646	5317
STOCKHOLM	6725	3404	10334	8724	8243	11059	1436	15593	9603	5900	1231	5579	6336	1546	10682	1977	8644	9646		8193
TOKYO	2104	9587	14737	14179	2893	6208	9585	8159	11319	10409	7502	5857	10870	9738	18557	9881	8284	5317	8193	

Abbreviations

Adm. Administrative
Af. Africa
Afghan. Afghanistan
Agr. Agriculture
Ala. Alabama
Alas. Alaska
Alban. Albania
Alg. Algeria
Alta. Alberta
Ant. Antilles
Arch. Archipelago, Archipiélago
Arg. Argentina
Ariz. Arizona
Ark. Arkansas
Arm. Armenia
Atl. Oc. Atlantic Ocean
Aust. Austria
Austral. Australia
Azerb. Azerbaijan
B. Baai, Baía, Baie, Bahía, Bay, Buḩayrat
B.C. British Columbia
Belg. Belgium
Bol. Bolivia
Bosn. & Herzg. Bosnia and Herzegovina
Braz. Brazil
Bulg. Bulgaria
C. Cabo, Cap, Cape, Capo
Calif. California
Can. Canada
Cen. Af. Rep. Central African Republic
C.H. Court House
Chan. Channel
Chap. Chapada
Cmte. Comandante
Cnel. Coronel
Co.-s. Cerro-s
Col. Colombia
Colo. Colorado
Conn. Connecticut
Cord. Cordillera
C.R. Costa Rica
Cr. Creek, Crique
C.S.I. Terr. Coral Sea Islands Territory
D.C. District of Columbia
Del. Delaware
Den. Denmark
Dom. Rep. Dominican Republic

D.R.C. Democratic Republic of the Congo
E. East-ern
Ecua. Ecuador
El Salv. El Salvador
Eng. England
Ens. Ensenada
Eq. Equatorial
Est. Estonia
Eth. Ethiopia
Exp. Exports
Falk. Is. Falkland Islands
Fd. Fiord, Fiordo, Fjord
Fin. Finland
Fk. Fork
Fla. Florida
Fn. Fortín
Fr. France, French
F.S.M. Federated States of Micronesia
ft feet
Ft. Fort
G. Golfe, Golfo, Gulf
Ga. Georgia
Ger. Germany
Gl. Glacier
Gr. Greece
Gral. General
Hbr. Harbor, Harbour
Hist. Historic, -al
Hond. Honduras
Hts. Heights
Hung. Hungary
Hwy. Highway
I.-s. Île-s, Ilha-s, Isla-s, Island-s, Isle, Isol-a, -e
Ice. Iceland
I.H.S. International Historic Site
Ill. Illinois
Ind. Indiana
Ind. Industry
Ind. Oc. Indian Ocean
Intl. International
Ire. Ireland
It. Italy
Jap. Japan
Jct. Jonction, Junction
Kans. Kansas
Kaz. Kazakhstan
Kep. Kepulauan
Kos. Kosovo
Ky. Kentucky

Kyrg. Kyrgyzstan
L. Lac, Lago, Lake, Límni, Loch, Lough
La. Louisiana
Lab. Labrador
Lag. Laguna
Latv. Latvia
Leb. Lebanon
Lib. Libya
Liech. Liechtenstein
Lith. Lithuania
Lux. Luxembourg
m meters
Maced. Macedonia
Madag. Madagascar
Maurit. Mauritius
Mass. Massachusetts
Md. Maryland
Me. Maine
Medit. Sea Mediterranean Sea
Mex. Mexico
Mgne. Montagne
Mich. Michigan
Minn. Minnesota
Miss. Mississippi
M.N.M. Marine National Monument
Mo. Missouri
Mon. Monument
Mont. Montana
Mont. Montenegro
Mor. Morocco
Mt.-s. Mont-s, Mount-ain-s
N. North-ern
NA Not available, Not applicable
Nat. National
Nat. Mem. National Memorial
Nat. Mon. National Monument
N.B. National Battlefield
N.B. New Brunswick
N.C. North Carolina
N. Dak. North Dakota
N.E. Northeast
Nebr. Nebraska
Neth. Netherlands
Nev. Nevada
Nfld. Newfoundland
N.H. New Hampshire
Nicar. Nicaragua
Nig. Nigeria
N. Ire. Northern Ireland

N.J. New Jersey
N. Mex. New Mexico
N.M.P. National Military Park
N.M.S. National Marine Sanctuary
Nor. Norway
N.P. National Park
N.S. Nova Scotia
N.S.W. New South Wales
N.V.M. National Volcanic Monument
N.W.T. Northwest Territories
N.Y. New York
N.Z. New Zealand
O. Ostrov, Oued
Oc. Ocean
Okla. Oklahoma
Ont. Ontario
Oreg. Oregon
Oz. Ozero
Pa. Pennsylvania
Pac. Oc. Pacific Ocean
Pak. Pakistan
Pan. Panama
Para. Paraguay
Pass. Passage
Peg. Pegunungan
P.E.I. Prince Edward Island
Pen. Peninsula, Péninsule
Pk. Peak
P.N.G. Papua New Guinea
Pol. Poland
Pol. Poluostrov
Port. Portugal, Portuguese
P.R. Puerto Rico
Prov. Province, Provincial
Pt.-e. Point-e
Pta. Ponta, Punta
Qnsld. Queensland
Que. Quebec
R. Río, River, Rivière
Ra.-s. Range-s
Rec. Recreation
Rep. Republic
Res. Reservoir, Reserve, Reservatório
R.I. Rhode Island
Rom. Romania
Russ. Russia
S. South-ern
Sa.-s. Serra, Sierra-s
S. Af. South Africa

Sask. Saskatchewan
S.C. South Carolina
Scot. Scotland
Sd. Sound
S. Dak. South Dakota
Serb. Serbia
Sev. Severn-yy, -aya, -oye
Sk. Shankou
Slov. Slovenia
Sp. Spain, Spanish
Spr.-s. Spring-s
Sta. Santa
St.-e. Saint-e, Sankt, Sint
Str.-s. Straat, Strait-s
Switz. Switzerland
Syr. Syria
Taj. Tajikistan
Tas. Tasmania
Tenn. Tennessee
Terr. Territory
Tex. Texas
Tg. Tanjung
Thai. Thailand
Trin. Trinidad
Tun. Tunisia
Turk. Turkey
Turkm. Turkmenistan
U.A.E. United Arab Emirates
U.K. United Kingdom
Ukr. Ukraine
U.N. United Nations
Uru. Uruguay
U.S. United States
Uzb. Uzbekistan
Va. Virginia
Vdkhr. Vodokhranilishche
Vdskh. Vodoskhovyshche
Venez. Venezuela
V.I. Virgin Islands
Vic. Victoria
Viet. Vietnam
Vol. Volcán, Volcano
Vt. Vermont
W. Wadi, Wādī, Webi
W. West-ern
Wash. Washington
Wis. Wisconsin
W. Va. West Virginia
Wyo. Wyoming
Yug. Yugoslavia
Zakh. Zakhod-ni, -nyaya, -nye
Zimb. Zimbabwe

QUICK REFERENCE CHART FOR METRIC TO ENGLISH CONVERSION

1 METER	1 METER = 100 CENTIMETERS
1 FOOT	1 FOOT = 12 INCHES
1 KILOMETER	1 KILOMETER = 1,000 METERS
1 MILE	1 MILE = 5,280 FEET

METERS	1	10	20	50	100	200	500	1,000	2,000	5,000	10,000
FEET	3.281	32.81	65.62	164.04	328.1	656.2	1,640.4	3,280.8	6,561.7	16,404.2	32,808.4
KILOMETERS	1	10	20	50	100	200	500	1,000	2,000	5,000	10,000
MILES	0.621	6.21	12.43	31.07	62.1	124.3	310.7	621.4	1,242.7	3,106.9	6,213.7

CONVERSION FROM METRIC MEASURES

SYMBOL	WHEN YOU KNOW	MULTIPLY BY	TO FIND	SYMBOL
LENGTH				
cm	centimeters	0.39	inches	in
m	meters	3.28	feet	ft
m	meters	1.09	yards	yd
km	kilometers	0.62	miles	mi
AREA				
cm^2	square centimeters	0.16	square inches	in^2
m^2	square meters	10.76	square feet	ft^2
m^2	square meters	1.20	square yards	yd^2
km^2	square kilometers	0.39	square miles	mi^2
ha	hectares	2.47	acres	—
MASS				
g	grams	0.04	ounces	oz
kg	kilograms	2.20	pounds	lb
t	metric tons	1.10	short tons	—
VOLUME				
mL	milliliters	0.06	cubic inches	in^3
mL	milliliters	0.03	liquid ounces	liq oz
L	liters	2.11	pints	pt
L	liters	1.06	quarts	qt
L	liters	0.26	gallons	gal
m^3	cubic meters	35.31	cubic feet	ft^3
m^3	cubic meters	1.31	cubic yards	yd^3
TEMPERATURE				
°C	degrees Celsius (centigrade)	9/5 then add 32	degrees Fahrenheit	°F

CONVERSION TO METRIC MEASURES

SYMBOL	WHEN YOU KNOW	MULTIPLY BY	TO FIND	SYMBOL
LENGTH				
in	inches	2.54	centimeters	cm
ft	feet	0.30	meters	m
yd	yards	0.91	meters	m
mi	miles	1.61	kilometers	km
AREA				
in^2	square inches	6.45	square centimeters	cm^2
ft^2	square feet	0.09	square meters	m^2
yd^2	square yards	0.84	square meters	m^2
mi^2	square miles	2.59	square kilometers	km^2
—	acres	0.40	hectares	ha
MASS				
oz	ounces	28.35	grams	g
lb	pounds	0.45	kilograms	kg
—	short tons	0.91	metric tons	t
VOLUME				
in^3	cubic inches	16.39	milliliters	mL
liq oz	liquid ounces	29.57	milliliters	mL
pt	pints	0.47	liters	L
qt	quarts	0.95	liters	L
gal	gallons	3.79	liters	L
ft^3	cubic feet	0.03	cubic meters	m^3
yd^3	cubic yards	0.76	cubic meters	m^3
TEMPERATURE				
°F	degrees Fahrenheit	5/9 after subtracting 32	degrees Celsius (centigrade)	°C

THE EARTH

Mass: 5,973,600,000,000,000,000,000 (5.9736 sextillion) metric tons

Total Area: 510,066,000 sq km (196,938,000 sq mi)

Land Area: 148,647,000 sq km (57,393,000 sq mi), 29.1% of total

Water Area: 361,419,000 sq km (139,545,000 sq mi), 70.9% of total

Diameter (polar): 12,714 km (7,900 mi)

Diameter (equatorial): 12,756 km (7,926 mi)

Circumference (polar): 40,008 km (24,860 mi)

Circumference (equatorial): 40,075 km (24,902 mi)

Population: 6,705,327,000

THE EARTH'S EXTREMES

Hottest Place: Dalol, Danakil Desert, Ethiopia, annual average temperature 34°C (93°F)

Coldest Place: Plateau Station, Antarctica, annual average temperature -56.7°C (-70°F)

Hottest Recorded Temperature: Al Aziziyah, Libya 58°C (136.4°F), September 3, 1922

Coldest Recorded Temperature: Vostok, Antarctica -89.2°C (-128.6°F), July 21, 1983

Wettest Place: Mawsynram, Assam, India, annual average rainfall 1,187 cm (467 in)

Driest Place: Arica, Atacama Desert, Chile, rainfall barely measurable

Highest Waterfall: Angel Falls, Venezuela 979 m (3,212 ft)

Largest Hot Desert: Sahara, Africa 9,000,000 sq km (3,475,000 sq mi)

Largest Ice Desert: Antarctica 13,209,000 sq km (5,100,000 sq mi)

Largest Canyon: Grand Canyon, Colorado River, Arizona 446 km (277 mi) long along river, 180 m (600 ft) to 29 km (18 mi) wide, about 1.8 km (1.1 mi) deep

Largest Cave Chamber: Sarawak Cave, Gunung Mulu National Park, Malaysia 16 hectares and 79 meters high (40.2 acres and 260 feet)

Largest Cave System: Mammoth Cave, Kentucky, over 530 km (330 mi) of passageways mapped

Most Predictable Geyser: Old Faithful, Wyoming, annual average interval 66 to 80 minutes

Longest Reef: Great Barrier Reef, Australia 2,300 km (1,429 mi)

Greatest Tides: Bay of Fundy, Canadian Atlantic Coast 16 m (52 ft)

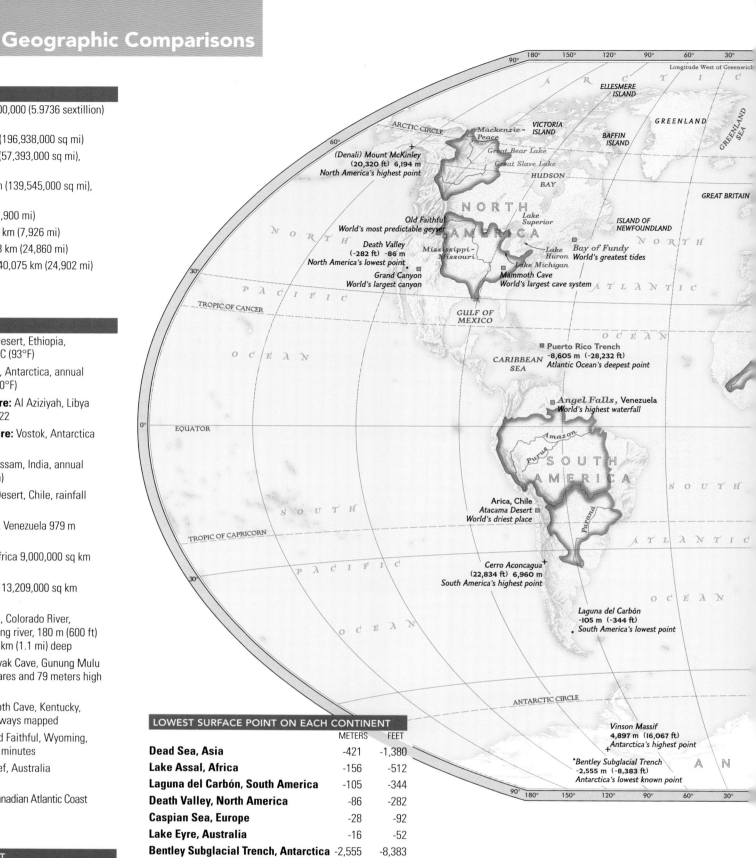

AREA OF EACH CONTINENT

	SQ KM	SQ MI	PERCENT OF EARTH'S LAND
Asia	44,570,000	17,208,000	30.0
Africa	30,065,000	11,608,000	20.2
North America	24,474,000	9,449,000	16.5
South America	17,819,000	6,880,000	12.0
Antarctica	13,209,000	5,100,000	8.9
Europe	9,947,000	3,841,000	6.7
Australia	7,692,000	2,970,000	5.2

HIGHEST POINT ON EACH CONTINENT

	METERS	FEET
Mount Everest, Asia	8,850	29,035
Cerro Aconcagua, South America	6,960	22,834
Mount McKinley (Denali), N. America	6,194	20,320
Kilimanjaro, Africa	5,895	19,340
El'brus, Europe	5,642	18,510
Vinson Massif, Antarctica	4,897	16,067
Mount Kosciuszko, Australia	2,228	7,310

LOWEST SURFACE POINT ON EACH CONTINENT

	METERS	FEET
Dead Sea, Asia	-421	-1,380
Lake Assal, Africa	-156	-512
Laguna del Carbón, South America	-105	-344
Death Valley, North America	-86	-282
Caspian Sea, Europe	-28	-92
Lake Eyre, Australia	-16	-52
Bentley Subglacial Trench, Antarctica	-2,555	-8,383

LARGEST ISLANDS

		AREA SQ KM	SQ MI
1	**Greenland**	2,166,000	836,000
2	**New Guinea**	792,500	306,000
3	**Borneo**	725,500	280,100
4	**Madagascar**	587,000	226,600
5	**Baffin Island**	507,500	196,000
6	**Sumatra**	427,300	165,000
7	**Honshu**	227,400	87,800
8	**Great Britain**	218,100	84,200
9	**Victoria Island**	217,300	83,900
10	**Ellesmere Island**	196,200	75,800
11	**Sulawesi (Celebes)**	178,700	69,000
12	**South Island (New Zealand)**	150,400	58,100
13	**Java**	126,700	48,900
14	**North Island (New Zealand)**	113,700	43,900
15	**Island of Newfoundland**	108,900	42,000

LARGEST DRAINAGE BASINS

		AREA SQ KM	SQ MI
1	**Amazon, South America**	7,050,000	2,721,000
2	**Congo, Africa**	3,700,000	1,428,000
3	**Mississippi-Missouri, North America**	3,250,000	1,255,000
4	**Paraná, South America**	3,100,000	1,197,000
5	**Yenisey-Angara, Asia**	2,700,000	1,042,000
6	**Ob-Irtysh, Asia**	2,430,000	938,000
7	**Lena, Asia**	2,420,000	934,000
8	**Nile, Africa**	1,900,000	733,400
9	**Amur, Asia**	1,840,000	710,000
10	**Mackenzie-Peace, North America**	1,765,000	681,000
11	**Ganges-Brahmaputra, Asia**	1,730,000	668,000
12	**Volga, Europe**	1,380,000	533,000
13	**Zambezi, Africa**	1,330,000	513,000
14	**Niger, Africa**	1,200,000	463,000
15	**Chang Jiang (Yangtze), Asia**	1,175,000	454,000

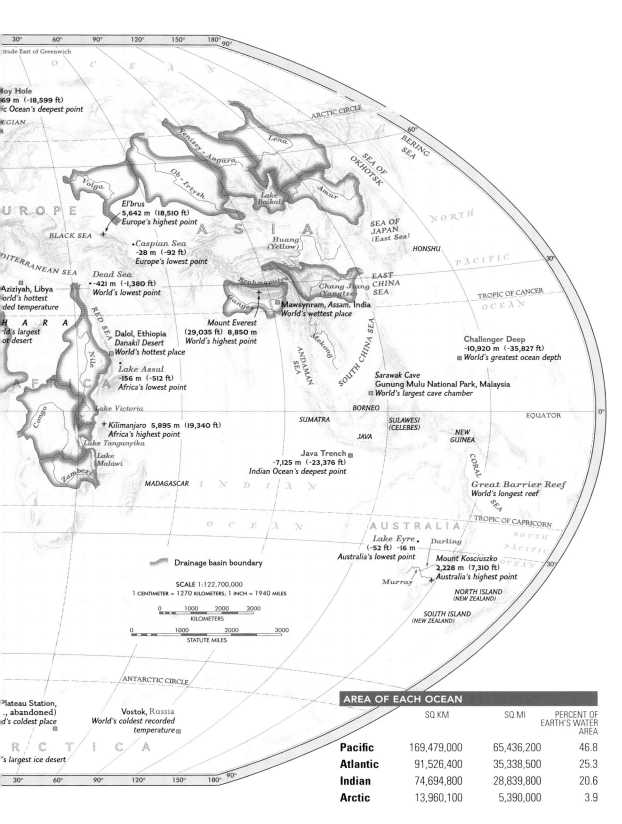

Map labels (clockwise/by region):

30° 60° 90° 120° 150° 180° 90°

itude East of Greenwich

O C E A N

loy Hole
69 m (-18,599 ft)
ic Ocean's deepest point

EGIAN

ARCTIC CIRCLE

BERING
SEA

SEA OF
OKHOTSK

Yenisey-Angara   Lena

Ob-Irtysh   Amur

Volga   Lake
Baikal

NORTH

EUROPE

El'brus
5,642 m (18,510 ft)
Europe's highest point

A S I A

SEA OF
JAPAN
(East Sea)

BLACK SEA

Caspian Sea
-28 m (-92 ft)
Europe's lowest point

Huang
(Yellow)

HONSHU

PACIFIC

DITERRANEAN SEA

Dead Sea
-421 m (-1,380 ft)
World's lowest point

Brahmaputra

Chang Jiang
(Yangtze)

EAST
CHINA
SEA

TROPIC OF CANCER

OCEAN

Aziziyah, Libya
orld's hottest
ded temperature

Ganges

Mawsynram, Assam, India
World's wettest place

Challenger Deep
-10,920 m (-35,827 ft)
World's greatest ocean depth

HARA
ld's largest
ot desert

Dalol, Ethiopia
Danakil Desert
World's hottest place

Mount Everest
(29,035 ft) 8,850 m
World's highest point

Mekong

ANDAMAN
SEA

Nile

Lake Assal
-156 m (-512 ft)
Africa's lowest point

Sarawak Cave
Gunung Mulu National Park, Malaysia
World's largest cave chamber

RED SEA

Lake Victoria

SOUTH CHINA SEA

BORNEO

EQUATOR   0°

AFRICA

Congo

Kilimanjaro 5,895 m (19,340 ft)
Africa's highest point

SUMATRA

JAVA

SULAWESI
(CELEBES)

NEW
GUINEA

Lake Tanganyika

Lake
Malawi

Zambezi

Java Trench
-7,125 m (-23,376 ft)
Indian Ocean's deepest point

CORAL

MADAGASCAR

I N D I A N

Great Barrier Reef
World's longest reef

SEA

O C E A N

AUSTRALIA

TROPIC OF CAPRICORN

SOUTH
PACIFIC

Drainage basin boundary

Lake Eyre
(-52 ft) -16 m
Australia's lowest point

Darling

Mount Kosciuszko
2,228 m (7,310 ft)
Australia's highest point

OCEAN   30°

SCALE 1:122,700,000
1 CENTIMETER = 1270 KILOMETERS; 1 INCH = 1940 MILES

Murray

0   1000   2000   3000
KILOMETERS

0   1000   2000   3000
STATUTE MILES

NORTH ISLAND
(NEW ZEALAND)

SOUTH ISLAND
(NEW ZEALAND)

ANTARCTIC CIRCLE

Plateau Station
., abandoned)
d's coldest place

Vostok, Russia
World's coldest recorded
temperature

RCTICA

's largest ice desert

30° 60° 90° 120° 150° 180° 90°

Largest Country: Russia 17,075,400 sq km
(6,592,849 sq mi)

Smallest Country: Vatican City 0.4 sq km (0.2 sq mi)

Most Populous Country: China 1,355,251,000 people

Least Populous Country: Vatican City 800 people

Most Crowded Country: Monaco 17,400 per sq km
(45,300 per sq mi)

Least Crowded Country: Mongolia 1.7 per sq km
(4.4 per sq mi)

Largest Metropolitan Area: Tokyo 35,676,000 people

Country with the Greatest Number of Bordering Countries: China 14, Russia 14

ENGINEERING WONDERS

Tallest Manmade Structure and Tallest Building (under construction): Burj Dubai, United Arab Emirates 818 m (2,684 ft)

Tallest Building (in current use): Taipei 101, Taipei, Taiwan 509 m (1,671 ft) to top of spire

Longest Wall: Great Wall of China, approx. 3,460 km (2,150 mi)

Longest Road: Pan-American Highway (not including gap in Panama and Colombia), more than 24,140 km (15,000 mi)

Longest Railroad: Trans-Siberian Railroad, Russia 9,288 km (5,772 mi)

Longest Road Tunnel: Laerdal Tunnel, Laerdal, Norway 24.5 km (15.2 mi)

Longest Rail Tunnel: Seikan submarine rail tunnel, Honshu to Hokkaido, Japan 53.9 km (33.5 mi)

Largest Subway System: London Underground, United Kingdom, total length of network 402 km (250 mi)

Highest Bridge (over water): Millau Viaduct, France 343 m (1,125 ft) above water

Longest Highway Bridge: Lake Pontchartrain Causeway, Louisiana 38.4 km (23.9 mi)

Longest Suspension Bridge: Akashi-Kaikyo Bridge, Japan 3,911 m (12,831 ft)

Longest Boat Canal: Grand Canal, China, over 1,770 km (1,100 mi)

Longest Irrigation Canal: Garagum Canal, Turkmenistan, nearly 1,100 km (700 mi)

Largest Artificial Lake: Lake Volta, Volta River, Ghana 9,065 sq km (3,500 sq mi)

Tallest Dam: Rogun Dam, Vakhsh River, Tajikistan 335 m (1,099 ft)

Tallest Pyramid: Great Pyramid of Khufu, Egypt 137 m (450 ft)

Deepest Mine: Tau Tona Mine, South Africa 3,902 m (12,802 ft) deep

Longest Submarine Cable: Sea-Me-We 3 cable, connects 33 countries on four continents, 39,000 km (24,200 mi) long

AREA OF EACH OCEAN

	SQ KM	SQ MI	PERCENT OF EARTH'S WATER AREA
Pacific	169,479,000	65,436,200	46.8
Atlantic	91,526,400	35,338,500	25.3
Indian	74,694,800	28,839,800	20.6
Arctic	13,960,100	5,390,000	3.9

LONGEST RIVERS

		KM	MI
1	**Nile, Africa**	6,825	4,241
2	**Amazon, South America**	6,437	4,000
3	**Chang Jiang (Yangtze), Asia**	6,380	3,964
4	**Mississippi-Missouri, North America**	5,971	3,710
5	**Yenisey-Angara, Asia**	5,536	3,440
6	**Huang (Yellow), Asia**	5,464	3,395
7	**Ob-Irtysh, Asia**	5,410	3,362
8	**Amur, Asia**	4,416	2,744
9	**Lena, Asia**	4,400	2,734
10	**Congo, Africa**	4,370	2,715
11	**Mackenzie-Peace, North America**	4,241	2,635
12	**Mekong, Asia**	4,184	2,600
13	**Niger, Africa**	4,170	2,591
14	**Paraná-Río de la Plata, S. America**	4,000	2,485
15	**Murray-Darling, Australia**	3,718	2,310
16	**Volga, Europe**	3,685	2,290
17	**Purus, South America**	3,380	2,100

DEEPEST POINT IN EACH OCEAN

	METERS	FEET
Challenger Deep, Pacific Ocean	-10,920	-35,827
Puerto Rico Trench, Atlantic Ocean	-8,605	-28,232
Java Trench, Indian Ocean	-7,125	-23,376
Molloy Hole, Arctic Ocean	-5,669	-18,599

LARGEST LAKES BY AREA

		AREA SQ KM	SQ MI	MAXIMUM DEPTH METERS	FEET
1	**Caspian Sea**	371,000	143,200	1,025	3,363
2	**Lake Superior**	82,100	31,700	406	1,332
3	**Lake Victoria**	69,500	26,800	82	269
4	**Lake Huron**	59,600	23,000	229	751
5	**Lake Michigan**	57,800	22,300	281	922
6	**Lake Tanganyika**	32,600	12,600	1,470	4,823
7	**Lake Baikal**	31,500	12,200	1,637	5,371
8	**Great Bear Lake**	31,300	12,100	446	1,463
9	**Lake Malawi**	28,900	11,200	695	2,280
10	**Great Slave Lake**	28,600	11,000	614	2,014

LARGEST SEAS BY AREA

		AREA SQ KM	SQ MI	AVERAGE DEPTH METERS	FEET
1	**Coral Sea**	4,183,510	1,615,260	2,471	8,107
2	**South China Sea**	3,596,390	1,388,570	1,180	3,871
3	**Caribbean Sea**	2,834,290	1,094,330	2,596	8,517
4	**Bering Sea**	2,519,580	972,810	1,832	6,010
5	**Mediterranean Sea**	2,469,100	953,320	1,572	5,157
6	**Sea of Okhotsk**	1,625,190	627,490	814	2,671
7	**Gulf of Mexico**	1,531,810	591,430	1,544	5,066
8	**Norwegian Sea**	1,425,280	550,300	1,768	5,801
9	**Greenland Sea**	1,157,850	447,050	1,443	4,734
10	**Sea of Japan**	1,008,260	389,290	1,647	5,404
11	**Hudson Bay**	1,005,510	388,230	119	390
12	**East China Sea**	785,990	303,470	374	1,227
13	**Andaman Sea**	605,760	233,890	1,061	3,481
14	**Red Sea**	436,280	168,450	494	1,621
15	**Black Sea**	410,150	158,360	1,336	4,383

ALL OF THE EARTH'S LANDS are grouped into four categories on pages 266 through 269: independent states, dependencies, areas of special status, and areas geographically separated from their mainland countries. At right, a world map uses different colors to show the distribution of lands within each category.

Each of the 194 countries listed in the independent states category (below) is a recognized territory whose government is the highest legal authority over the land and people within its boundaries.

A dependency, on the other hand, is a region whose territory is controlled by another, often very distant, country; it is not, however, considered an inherent part of the controlling country. Most dependencies are inhabited and have some form of local government with limited autonomy.

An area of special status is a region of ambiguous political status. Most of these areas can be described as disputed territory, territory not recognized as independent by other countries, or territory leased by one government to another. In the fourth category are populated lands considered integral parts of independent states, but they are separated from the rest of their countries by a significant distance.

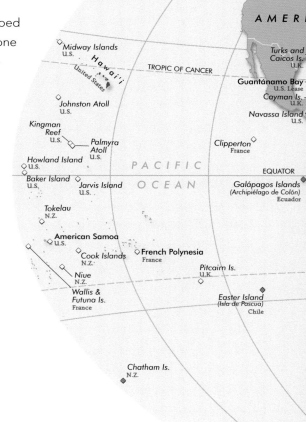

INDEPENDENT STATES OF THE WORLD

COUNTRY	CAPITAL	2008 POPULATION	DATE OF INDEPENDENCE
AFGHANISTAN	Kabul	32,738,000	Aug. 19, 1919
ALBANIA	Tirana	3,241,000	Nov. 28, 1912
ALGERIA	Algiers	34,694,000	July 5, 1962
ANDORRA	Andorra la Vella	85,000	1278
ANGOLA	Luanda	16,752,000	Nov. 11, 1975
ANTIGUA AND BARBUDA	St. John's	86,000	Nov. 1, 1981
ARGENTINA	Buenos Aires	39,746,000	July 9, 1816
ARMENIA	Yerevan	3,084,000	Sept. 21, 1991
AUSTRALIA	Canberra	21,347,000	Jan. 1, 1901
AUSTRIA	Vienna	8,352,000	1156
AZERBAIJAN	Baku	8,679,000	Aug. 30, 1991
BAHAMAS	Nassau	337,000	July 10, 1973
BAHRAIN	Manama	780,000	Aug. 15, 1971
BANGLADESH	Dhaka	147,285,000	Dec. 16, 1971
BARBADOS	Bridgetown	280,000	Nov. 30, 1966
BELARUS	Minsk	9,678,000	Aug. 25, 1991
BELGIUM	Brussels	10,695,000	July 21, 1831
BELIZE	Belmopan	318,000	Sept. 21, 1981
BENIN	Cotonou, Porto-Novo	9,309,000	Aug. 1, 1960
BHUTAN	Thimphu	671,000	Aug. 8, 1949
BOLIVIA	La Paz, Sucre	10,028,000	Aug. 6, 1825
BOSNIA AND HERZEGOVINA	Sarajevo	3,843,000	Mar. 1, 1992
BOTSWANA	Gaborone	1,842,000	Sept. 30, 1966
BRAZIL	Brasília	195,138,000	Sept. 7, 1822
BRUNEI	Bandar Seri Begawan	379,000	Jan. 1, 1984
BULGARIA	Sofia	7,621,000	Mar. 3, 1878
BURKINA FASO	Ouagadougou	15,213,000	Aug. 5, 1960
BURUNDI	Bujumbura	8,856,000	July 1, 1962
CAMBODIA	Phnom Penh	14,656,000	Nov. 9, 1953
CAMEROON	Yaoundé	18,468,000	Jan. 1, 1960
CANADA	Ottawa	33,304,000	Dec. 11, 1931
CAPE VERDE	Praia	503,000	July 5, 1975
CENTRAL AFRICAN REPUBLIC	Bangui	4,435,000	Aug. 13, 1960
CHAD	N'Djamena	10,111,000	Aug. 11, 1960
CHILE	Santiago	16,770,000	Sept. 18, 1810
CHINA	Beijing	1,355,251,000	221 B.C.
COLOMBIA	Bogotá	44,447,000	July 20, 1810
COMOROS	Moroni	732,000	July 6, 1975
CONGO	Brazzaville	3,847,000	Aug. 15, 1960
CONGO, DEMOCRATIC REPUBLIC OF THE	Kinshasa	66,515,000	June 30, 1960
COSTA RICA	San José	4,519,000	Sept. 15, 1821
CÔTE D'IVOIRE	Abidjan, Yamoussoukro	20,677,000	Aug. 7, 1960
CROATIA	Zagreb	4,433,000	June 25, 1991
CUBA	Havana	11,233,000	May 20, 1902
CYPRUS	Nicosia	1,060,000	Aug. 16, 1960
CZECH REPUBLIC (CZECHIA)	Prague	10,428,000	Jan. 1, 1993
DENMARK	Copenhagen	5,490,000	10th century

COUNTRY	CAPITAL	2008 POPULATION	DATE OF INDEPENDENCE
DJIBOUTI	Djibouti	848,000	June 27, 1977
DOMINICA	Roseau	73,000	Nov. 3, 1978
DOMINICAN REPUBLIC	Santo Domingo	9,890,000	Feb. 27, 1844
ECUADOR	Quito	13,801,000	May 24, 1822
EGYPT	Cairo	74,946,000	Feb. 28, 1922
EL SALVADOR	San Salvador	7,218,000	Sept. 15, 1821
EQUATORIAL GUINEA	Malabo	617,000	Oct. 12, 1968
ERITREA	Asmara	5,006,000	May 24, 1993
ESTONIA	Tallinn	1,340,000	May 1919
ETHIOPIA	Addis Ababa	79,087,000	circa 1 A.D.
FIJI ISLANDS	Suva	864,000	Oct. 10, 1970
FINLAND	Helsinki	5,312,000	Dec. 6, 1917
FRANCE	Paris	62,046,000	486
GABON	Libreville	1,350,000	Aug. 17, 1960
GAMBIA	Banjul	1,559,000	Feb. 18, 1965
GEORGIA	T'bilisi	4,639,000	April 9, 1991
GERMANY	Berlin	82,170,000	Jan. 18, 1871
GHANA	Accra	23,947,000	Mar. 6, 1957
GREECE	Athens	11,242,000	1829
GRENADA	St. George's	106,000	Feb. 7, 1974
GUATEMALA	Guatemala City	13,677,000	Sept. 15, 1821
GUINEA	Conakry	10,302,000	Oct. 2, 1958
GUINEA-BISSAU	Bissau	1,746,000	Sept. 24, 1973
GUYANA	Georgetown	773,000	May 26, 1966
HAITI	Port-au-Prince	9,104,000	Jan. 1, 1804
HONDURAS	Tegucigalpa	7,322,000	Sept. 15, 1821
HUNGARY	Budapest	10,034,000	1001
ICELAND	Reykjavík	319,000	June 17, 1944
INDIA	New Delhi	1,149,285,000	Aug. 15, 1947
INDONESIA	Jakarta	239,945,000	Aug. 17, 1945
IRAN	Tehran	72,212,000	Apr. 1, 1979
IRAQ	Baghdad	29,492,000	Oct. 3, 1932
IRELAND	Dublin	4,475,000	Dec. 6, 1921
ISRAEL	Jerusalem	7,482,000	May 14, 1948
ITALY	Rome	59,865,000	Mar. 17, 1861
JAMAICA	Kingston	2,692,000	Aug. 6, 1962
JAPAN	Tokyo	127,720,000	660 B.C.
JORDAN	Amman	5,849,000	May 25, 1946
KAZAKHSTAN	Astana	15,651,000	Dec. 16, 1991
KENYA	Nairobi	37,954,000	Dec. 12, 1963
KIRIBATI	Tarawa	98,000	July 12, 1979
KOREA, NORTH	Pyongyang	23,479,000	Aug. 15, 1945
KOREA, SOUTH	Seoul	48,607,000	Aug. 15, 1945
KOSOVO	Prishtina	2,191,000	Feb. 17, 2008
KUWAIT	Kuwait City	2,669,000	June 19, 1961
KYRGYZSTAN	Bishkek	5,242,000	Aug. 31, 1991
LAOS	Vientiane	5,850,000	July 19, 1949
LATVIA	Riga	2,266,000	Dec. 1919
LEBANON	Beirut	3,981,000	Nov. 22, 1943
LESOTHO	Maseru	1,801,000	Oct. 4, 1966
LIBERIA	Monrovia	3,942,000	July 26, 1847
LIBYA	Tripoli	6,283,000	Dec. 24, 1951

COUNTRY	CAPITAL	2008 POPULATION	DATE OF INDEPENDENCE
LIECHTENSTEIN	Vaduz	36,000	Jan. 23, 1719
LITHUANIA	Vilnius	3,357,000	April 1919
LUXEMBOURG	Luxembourg	488,000	1839
MACEDONIA	Skopje	2,049,000	Sept. 17, 1991
MADAGASCAR	Antananarivo	18,912,000	June 26, 1960
MALAWI	Lilongwe	13,630,000	July 6, 1964
MALAYSIA	Kuala Lumpur	27,711,000	Aug. 31, 1957
MALDIVES	Male	310,000	July 26, 1965
MALI	Bamako	12,716,000	Sept. 22, 1960
MALTA	Valletta	412,000	Sept. 21, 1964
MARSHALL ISLANDS	Majuro	53,000	Oct. 21, 1986
MAURITANIA	Nouakchott	3,204,000	Nov. 28, 1960
MAURITIUS	Port Louis	1,268,000	Mar. 12, 1968
MEXICO	Mexico City	107,677,000	Sept. 16, 1810
MICRONESIA, FEDERATED STATES OF	Palikir	108,000	Nov. 3, 1986
MOLDOVA	Chisinau	4,136,000	Aug. 27, 1991
MONACO	Monaco	34,000	1419
MONGOLIA	Ulaanbaatar	2,655,000	July 11, 1921
MONTENEGRO	Podgorica	627,000	June 3, 2006
MOROCCO	Rabat	31,177,000	Mar. 2, 1956
MOZAMBIQUE	Maputo	20,387,000	June 25, 1975
MYANMAR (BURMA)	Nay Pyi Taw, Yangon (Rangoon)	49,221,000	Jan. 4, 1948
NAMIBIA	Windhoek	2,089,000	Mar. 21, 1990
NAURU	Yaren	10,000	Jan. 31, 1968
NEPAL	Kathmandu	26,997,000	1768
NETHERLANDS	Amsterdam	16,433,000	1579

266

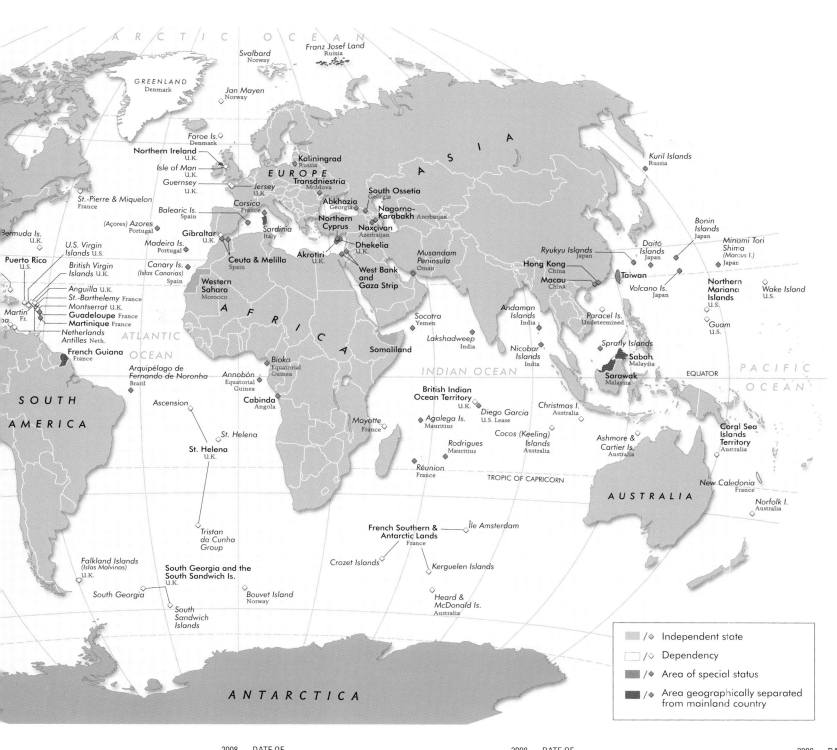

Independent state
Dependency
Area of special status
Area geographically separated from mainland country

COUNTRY	CAPITAL	2008 POPULATION	DATE OF INDEPENDENCE
NEW ZEALAND	Wellington	4,272,000	Sept. 26, 1907
NICARAGUA	Managua	5,669,000	Sept. 15, 1821
NIGER	Niamey	14,731,000	Aug. 3, 1960
NIGERIA	Abuja	148,071,000	Oct. 1, 1960
NORWAY	Oslo	4,765,000	June 7, 1905
OMAN	Muscat	2,719,000	1650
PAKISTAN	Islamabad	172,800,000	Aug. 14, 1947
PALAU	Melekeok	20,000	Oct. 1, 1994
PANAMA	Panama City	3,391,000	Nov. 3, 1903
PAPUA NEW GUINEA	Port Moresby	6,458,000	Sept. 16, 1975
PARAGUAY	Asunción	6,230,000	May 14, 1811
PERU	Lima	27,903,000	July 28, 1821
PHILIPPINES	Manila	90,457,000	July 4, 1946
POLAND	Warsaw	38,110,000	Nov. 11, 1918
PORTUGAL	Lisbon	10,621,000	1140
QATAR	Doha	928,000	Sept. 3, 1971
ROMANIA	Bucharest	21,498,000	Mar. 26, 1881
RUSSIA	Moscow	141,875,000	Aug. 24, 1991
RWANDA	Kigali	9,609,000	July 1, 1962
ST. KITTS AND NEVIS	Basseterre	48,000	Sept. 19, 1983
ST. LUCIA	Castries	171,000	Feb. 22, 1979
ST. VINCENT AND THE GRENADINES	Kingstown	110,000	Oct. 27, 1979
SAMOA	Apia	188,000	Jan. 1, 1962
SAN MARINO	San Marino	31,000	Sept. 3, 301
SAO TOME AND PRINCIPE	São Tomé	158,000	July 12, 1975
SAUDI ARABIA	Riyadh	28,147,000	Sept. 23, 1932
SENEGAL	Dakar	12,688,000	Aug. 20, 1960
SERBIA	Belgrade	7,354,000	Apr. 27, 1992
SEYCHELLES	Victoria	87,000	June 29, 1976
SIERRA LEONE	Freetown	5,450,000	Apr. 27, 1961
SINGAPORE	Singapore	4,790,000	Aug. 9, 1965
SLOVAKIA	Bratislava	5,405,000	Jan. 1, 1993
SLOVENIA	Ljubljana	2,034,000	June 25, 1991
SOLOMON ISLANDS	Honiara	507,000	July 7, 1978
SOMALIA	Mogadishu	8,956,000	July 1, 1960
SOUTH AFRICA	Pretoria, Cape Town, Bloemfontein	48,315,000	May 31, 1910
SPAIN	Madrid	46,501,000	1492
SRI LANKA	Colombo	20,296,000	Feb. 4, 1948
SUDAN	Khartoum	39,445,000	Jan. 1, 1956
SURINAME	Paramaribo	500,000	Nov. 25, 1975
SWAZILAND	Mbabane, Lobamba	1,129,000	Sept. 6, 1968
SWEDEN	Stockholm	9,214,000	June 6, 1523
SWITZERLAND	Bern	7,633,000	Aug. 1, 1291
SYRIA	Damascus	19,933,000	Apr. 17, 1946
TAJIKISTAN	Dushanbe	7,285,000	Sept. 9, 1991
TANZANIA	Dar es Salaam, Dodoma	40,213,000	Apr. 26, 1964
THAILAND	Bangkok	66,148,000	1238
TIMOR-LESTE (EAST TIMOR)	Dili	1,081,000	May 20, 2002
TOGO	Lomé	6,761,000	Apr. 27, 1960
TONGA	Nuku'alofa	102,000	June 4, 1970
TRINIDAD AND TOBAGO	Port-of-Spain	1,338,000	Aug. 31, 1962
TUNISIA	Tunis	10,337,000	Mar. 20, 1956
TURKEY	Ankara	74,766,000	Oct. 29, 1923
TURKMENISTAN	Ashgabat	5,180,000	Oct. 27, 1991
TUVALU	Funafuti	10,000	Oct. 1, 1978
UGANDA	Kampala	29,194,000	Oct. 9, 1962
UKRAINE	Kiev	46,237,000	Aug. 24, 1991
UNITED ARAB EMIRATES	Abu Dhabi	4,486,000	Dec. 2, 1971
UNITED KINGDOM	London	61,291,000	10th century
UNITED STATES	Washington, D.C.	304,486,000	July 4, 1776
URUGUAY	Montevideo	3,334,000	Aug. 25, 1825
UZBEKISTAN	Tashkent	27,199,000	Sept. 1, 1991
VANUATU	Port Vila	240,000	July 30, 1980
VATICAN CITY	Vatican City	800	Feb. 11, 1929
VENEZUELA	Caracas	27,935,000	July 5, 1811
VIETNAM	Hanoi	86,185,000	Sept. 2, 1945
YEMEN	Sanaa	22,198,000	May 22, 1990
ZAMBIA	Lusaka	12,197,000	Oct. 24, 1964
ZIMBABWE	Harare	13,481,000	Apr. 18, 1980

DEPENDENCIES OF THE WORLD

DEPENDENCY	POPULATION	LOCATION	CAPITAL OR CHIEF CITY	DEPENDENCY OF	POLITICAL STATUS (SYSTEM)*
AMERICAN SAMOA	70,000	South Pacific Ocean	Pago Pago	United States	Unincorporated territory
ANGUILLA	15,000	Caribbean Sea	The Valley	United Kingdom	Overseas territory
ARUBA	105,000	Caribbean Sea	Oranjestad	Netherlands	Part of the Netherlands (parliamentary democracy)
ASHMORE AND CARTIER ISLANDS	no indigenous inhabitants	Indian Ocean	Administered from Canberra	Australia	Territory
BAKER ISLAND	uninhabited	North Pacific Ocean	Administered from Washington, D.C.	United States	Unincorporated territory
BERMUDA	64,000	North Atlantic Ocean	Hamilton	United Kingdom	Overseas territory (parliamentary government)
BOUVET ISLAND	uninhabited	South Atlantic Ocean	Administered from Oslo	Norway	Territory
BRITISH INDIAN OCEAN TERRITORY[1]	no indigenous inhabitants	Indian Ocean	Administered from London	United Kingdom	Overseas territory
BRITISH VIRGIN ISLANDS	23,000	Caribbean Sea	Road Town	United Kingdom	Overseas territory
CAYMAN ISLANDS	54,000	Caribbean Sea	George Town	United Kingdom	Overseas territory (British crown colony)
CHRISTMAS ISLAND	500	Indian Ocean	The Settlement	Australia	Territory
CLIPPERTON	uninhabited	North Pacific Ocean	Administered from Paris	France	Possession of France
COCOS (KEELING) ISLANDS	600	Indian Ocean	West Island	Australia	Territory
COOK ISLANDS	11,000	South Pacific Ocean	Avarua	New Zealand	Free association with New Zealand (parliamentary democracy)
CORAL SEA ISLANDS TERRITORY	no indigenous inhabitants	South Pacific Ocean	Administered from Canberra	Australia	Territory
FALKLAND ISLANDS[2]	3,000	South Atlantic Ocean	Stanley	United Kingdom	Overseas territory
FAROE ISLANDS	48,000	North Atlantic Ocean	Tórshavn	Denmark	Part of Denmark (self-governing overseas division)
FRENCH POLYNESIA	265,000	South Pacific Ocean	Papeete	France	Overseas territory
FRENCH SOUTHERN AND ANTARCTIC LANDS[3]	no indigenous inhabitants	Indian Ocean	Administered from Paris	France	Overseas territory
GIBRALTAR	29,000	Europe	Gibraltar	United Kingdom	Overseas territory
GREENLAND (KALAALLIT NUNAAT)	58,000	North Atlantic Ocean	Nuuk (Godthåb)	Denmark	Part of Denmark (self-governing overseas division)
GUAM	177,000	North Pacific Ocean	Hagåtña (Agana)	United States	Unincorporated territory
GUERNSEY (Channel Islands)[4]	66,000	English Channel	St. Peter Port	United Kingdom	British crown dependency
HEARD AND MCDONALD ISLANDS	uninhabited	Indian Ocean	Administered from Canberra	Australia	Territory
HOWLAND ISLAND	uninhabited	North Pacific Ocean	Administered from Washington, D.C.	United States	Unincorporated territory
ISLE OF MAN	82,000	Irish Sea	Douglas	United Kingdom	British crown dependency (parliamentary democracy)
JAN MAYEN[5]	no indigenous inhabitants	Norwegian Sea	Administered from Oslo	Norway	Territory
JARVIS ISLAND	uninhabited	South Pacific Ocean	Administered from Washington, D.C.	United States	Unincorporated territory
JERSEY (Channel Islands)	92,000	English Channel	St. Helier	United Kingdom	British crown dependency
JOHNSTON ATOLL	uninhabited	North Pacific Ocean	Administered from Washington, D.C.	United States	Unincorporated territory
KINGMAN REEF	uninhabited	North Pacific Ocean	Administered from Washington, D.C.	United States	Unincorporated territory
MAYOTTE	187,000	Mozambique Channel	Mamoudzou	France	Territorial collectivity
MIDWAY ISLANDS	no indigenous inhabitants	North Pacific Ocean	Administered from Washington, D.C.	United States	Unincorporated territory
MONTSERRAT	10,000	Caribbean Sea	Brades, Plymouth (abandoned)	United Kingdom	Overseas territory
NAVASSA ISLAND	uninhabited	Caribbean Sea	Administered from Washington, D.C.	United States	Unincorporated territory
NETHERLANDS ANTILLES[6]	199,000	Caribbean Sea	Willemstad	Netherlands	Part of the Netherlands (parliamentary government)
NEW CALEDONIA	247,000	South Pacific Ocean	Nouméa	France	Overseas territory
NIUE	1,300	South Pacific Ocean	Alofi	New Zealand	Free association with New Zealand (parliamentary democracy)
NORFOLK ISLAND	2,000	South Pacific Ocean	Kingston	Australia	Territory
NORTHERN MARIANA ISLANDS	87,000	North Pacific Ocean	Saipan	United States	Commonwealth in political union with the U.S. (commonwealth government)
PALMYRA ATOLL	no indigenous inhabitants	North Pacific Ocean	Administered from Washington, D.C.	United States	Incorporated territory
PARACEL ISLANDS[7]	no indigenous inhabitants	South China Sea	Administered from China	undetermined	NA
PITCAIRN ISLANDS	45	South Pacific Ocean	Adamstown	United Kingdom	Overseas territory
PUERTO RICO	3,958,000	Caribbean Sea	San Juan	United States	Commonwealth associated with the U.S. (commonwealth government)
ST.-BARTHELEMY	7,000	Caribbean Sea	Gustavia	France	Overseas collectivity
ST. HELENA[8]	6,000	South Atlantic Ocean	Jamestown	United Kingdom	Overseas territory
ST. MARTIN	29,000	Caribbean Sea	Marigot	France	Overseas collectivity
ST.-PIERRE AND MIQUELON	6,000	North Atlantic Ocean	St.-Pierre	France	Self-governing territorial overseas collectivity
SOUTH GEORGIA AND THE SOUTH SANDWICH ISLANDS[2]	no indigenous inhabitants	South Atlantic Ocean	Administered from Stanley	United Kingdom	Overseas territory
SVALBARD	2,100	Arctic Ocean	Longyearbyen	Norway	Territory
TOKELAU	1,500	South Pacific Ocean	Administered from Wellington	New Zealand	Territory
TURKS AND CAICOS ISLANDS	37,000	North Atlantic Ocean	Grand Turk	United Kingdom	Overseas territory
U.S. VIRGIN ISLANDS	108,000	Caribbean Sea	Charlotte Amalie	United States	Unincorporated territory
WAKE ISLAND	no indigenous inhabitants	North Pacific Ocean	Administered from Washington	United States	Unincorporated territory
WALLIS AND FUTUNA ISLANDS	16,000	South Pacific Ocean	Matâ'utu	France	Overseas territory

NOTES TO DEPENDENCIES OF THE WORLD

* The political status of dependencies is based on the designation provided by the administering country. The variety of political designations reflects the diverse nature of the relationship dependencies have with their controlling countries.

[1] Chagos Archipelago

[2] Dependent territory of the United Kingdom (also claimed by Argentina).

[3] The French Southern and Antarctic Lands dependency includes Île Amsterdam, Île Saint-Paul, the Crozet Islands, and the Kerguelen Islands in the southern Indian Ocean. It also includes Terre Adélie, the French-claimed sector of Antarctica; the French claim to this region is not internationally recognized, however (see "Areas of Special Status," opposite, for information on claims to Antarctica).

[4] The Bailiwick of Guernsey includes the islands of Alderney, Guernsey, Herm, and Sark, as well as smaller islands nearby.

[5] Jan Mayen is administered from Oslo, Norway, through a governor resident in Longyearbyen, Svalbard.

[6] Netherlands Antilles comprises two groupings of islands: Curaçao and Bonaire are located off the coast of Venezuela; Saba, Sint Eustatius, and Sint Maarten (the Dutch two-fifths of the island of Saint Martin) lie 500 miles (800 km) to the northeast.

[7] South China Sea islands are occupied by China but claimed by Vietnam.

[8] The territory of Saint Helena includes the island group of Tristan da Cunha, far to the southwest. Saint Helena also administers Ascension Island, lying to the northwest.

AREA	POPULATION	LOCATION
ABKHAZIA	180,000	Part of Georgia

In 1991, following the fall of the Soviet Union and Georgia's declaration of independence, tensions grew between Abkhazia's ethnic Abkhaz and Georgians. Georgian troops were sent to Abkhazia in 1992 but were expelled from most of the region by 1993, with Abkhazia and Georgia signing a cease-fire agreement in 1994. Abkhazia voted overwhelmingly for independence in 1999, this coincided with a growth in aid from neighboring Russia. In 2008, Russia recognized Abkhazian independence; however, Georgia continues to claim Abkhazia.

ANTARCTICA	no indigenous inhabitants	Territory south of 60 degrees south latitude

Seven countries claim Antarctic territory, but these claims are not legally recognized by the Antarctic Treaty of 1959. This treaty prohibits military activities and dedicates Antarctica to peaceful use and free exchange of scientific information. Nations maintain research stations, and the projects they support typically involve collaborators from many countries.

DIEGO GARCIA	military base	Indian Ocean

The largest and southernmost island of the British Indian Ocean Territory, Diego Garcia is a United Kingdom dependency. In 1966, the United States leased Diego Garcia for 50 years and established a joint military base with Great Britain on the island. The U.S. lease will expire in 2016. Diego Garcia, along with the Chagos Archipelago, is claimed by Mauritius.

GUANTANAMO BAY	military base	Cuba

After helping Cuba gain independence in 1902, the United States leased 45 square miles (116 sq km) of territory around Guantanamo Bay. This lease was reaffirmed in a 1934 treaty - stipulating that the return of Guantanamo Bay to Cuba could only be arranged through the mutual consent of the U.S. and Cuba. Though Guantanamo Bay remains sovereign Cuban territory, the American lease does not have a termination date.

HONG KONG	6,990,000	Part of China

Hong Kong became a Special Administrative Region (SAR) of China on July 1, 1997. China has promised that under its "one country, two systems" formula, China's socialist economic system will not be practiced in Hong Kong and that Hong Kong will enjoy a high degree of autonomy in all matters, except foreign and defense affairs, for the next 50 years.

MACAU	551,000	Part of China

After more than 400 years as a Portuguese outpost, Macau reverted to China in December 1999 as a Special Administrative Region, a status it will maintain for 50 years. Like Hong Kong, it enjoys a high degree of autonomy in all matters except foreign and defense affairs.

NAGORNO-KARABAKH	138,000	Part of Azerbaijan

A predominantly ethnic Armenian enclave within Azerbaijan, Nagorno-Karabakh sought to unite with Armenia in 1988. Nagorno-Karabakh declared independence in 1991, and hostilities between Azeris and Armenians led to war in 1992. More than 30,000 have died and over a million people have been displaced as a result of the fighting. The war left Armenian and Karabakhi forces in control of most of the region. A cease-fire, brokered by Russia, was signed in 1994, and international efforts for a political settlement are ongoing.

NORTHERN CYPRUS	257,000	Eastern Mediterranean Sea

Following a Greek-led coup and the landing of Turkish forces on the island in 1974, Cyprus split into two hostile territories. The internationally recognized Greek Cypriot government controls the southern portion of the island whereas Turkish Cypriots, bolstered by a Turkish military force, control the northern portion. Turkish Cypriots unilaterally declared independence in 1983, but their claims have not been recognized by any nation other than Turkey. Only the Greek Cypriot south (Republic of Cyprus) benefits from joining the European Union in 2004.

SOMALILAND	3,500,000	Part of Somalia

The government of Somalia collapsed in 1991, after a bloody civil war. Somaliland claims independence and governs some three million people in the north—an area that roughly corresponds to the former British Somaliland.

SOUTH OSSETIA	70,000	Part of Georgia

In 1990 South Ossetia, wishing to unite with North Ossetia in the Russian Federation, declared independence from Georgia. Armed conflict broke out between Georgian and Ossetian forces in 1991; Russia brokered a cease-fire in 1992, creating a peacekeeping force made up of Georgians, Ossetians, and Russians. Tension between Russia and Georgia over South Ossetia escalated into war in August 2008, with Russian forces bombing and occupying parts of Georgia. Shortly after the war, Russia recognized South Ossetia's independence, but Georgia maintains its claim to the region.

SPRATLY ISLANDS	no indigenous inhabitants	South China Sea

The scattered islands and reefs known as the Spratly Islands are claimed in part by Brunei, Malaysia, the Philippines, and entirely by China, Taiwan, and Vietnam. The Spratlys possess rich fishing grounds and potential oil.

TAIWAN	23,002,000	Part of China

The People's Republic of China claims the island of Taiwan as its 23rd province. The government of Taiwan (Republic of China) maintains that there are two political entities.

TRANSDNIESTRIA	555,000	Part of Moldova

In 1992 separatist forces, made up largely of Ukrainian and Russian minorities, declared a "Dniester Republic" between the east bank of the Dniester River and the Ukrainian border. Armed conflict occurred between Moldovan government forces and Transdniestrian separatists. Negotiations to resolve the conflict continue, and a cease-fire is still in effect.

WEST BANK AND GAZA STRIP	4,154,000	Adjacent to Israel

The West Bank and Gaza Strip were captured by Israel in the 1967 Six Day War. A peace agreement was signed in 1993, which gave areas of the West Bank and Gaza Strip limited Palestinian autonomy. In August 2005 Israel evacuated the Gaza Strip, removing settlers and military personnel. The future of the autonomous regions, and more than 4.1 million Palestinians, is subject to Israeli-Palestinian negotiations.

WESTERN SAHARA	497,000	Southwest of Morocco

Formerly Spanish Sahara, Western Sahara was annexed by Morocco in the late 1970s and brought under Moroccan administration. The Polisario Front, a resistance group that repudiated Moroccan sovereignty, fought a guerrilla war that ended in a 1991 cease-fire administered by the United Nations. A referendum on the final status of Western Sahara has repeatedly been postponed. New rounds of UN-led talks began in mid-2007 with no resolution in sight.

REGION	POPULATION	COUNTRY	LOCATION
AGALEGA ISLANDS	300	Mauritius	Indian Ocean
AKROTIRI	military base	United Kingdom	Cyprus
ALASKA	686,000	United States	North America
ANDAMAN ISLANDS	314,000	India	Indian Ocean
ANNOBÓN	5,000	Equatorial Guinea	Gulf of Guinea
ARQUIPÉLAGO DE FERNANDO DE NORONHA	2,800	Brazil	South Atlantic Ocean
AZORES	244,000	Portugal	North Atlantic Ocean
BALEARIC ISLANDS	1,073,000	Spain	Mediterranean Sea
BIOKO	260,000	Equatorial Guinea	Gulf of Guinea
BONIN ISLANDS	2,700	Japan	North Pacific Ocean
CABINDA	265,000	Angola	Africa
CANARY ISLANDS	2,076,000	Spain	North Atlantic Ocean
CEUTA AND MELILLA	149,000	Spain	North Africa
CHATHAM ISLANDS	600	New Zealand	South Pacific Ocean
CORSICA	281,000	France	Mediterranean Sea
DAITO ISLANDS	2,100	Japan	North Pacific Ocean
DHEKELIA	military base	United Kingdom	Cyprus
EASTER ISLAND	4,000	Chile	South Pacific Ocean
FRANZ JOSEF LAND	not permanently inhabited	Russia	Arctic Ocean
FRENCH GUIANA	207,000	France	South America
GALÁPAGOS ISLANDS	19,000	Ecuador	Pacific Ocean
GUADELOUPE	420,000	France	Caribbean Sea
HAWAI'I	1,288,000	United States	North Pacific Ocean
KALININGRAD	937,000	Russia	Europe
KURIL ISLANDS	17,000	Russia	North Pacific Ocean
LAKSHADWEEP	69,000	India	Indian Ocean
MADEIRA ISLANDS	247,000	Portugal	North Atlantic Ocean
MARTINIQUE	405,000	France	Caribbean Sea
MUSANDAM PENINSULA	28,000	Oman	Arabian Peninsula
NAXÇIVAN	384,000	Azerbaijan	Asia
NICOBAR ISLANDS	42,000	India	Indian Ocean
NORTHERN IRELAND	1,759,000	United Kingdom	Ireland
RÉUNION	812,000	France	Indian Ocean
RODRIGUES	38,000	Mauritius	Indian Ocean
RYUKYU ISLANDS	1,533,000	Japan	North Pacific Ocean
SABAH AND SARAWAK	4,675,000	Malaysia	Borneo
SARDINIA	1,670,000	Italy	Mediterranean Sea
SOCOTRA	50,000	Yemen	Indian Ocean
VOLCANO ISLANDS	no indigenous inhabitants	Japan	North Pacific Ocean

DISCLAIMER

The list of geographically separate areas includes places that do not fit conveniently into any of the three previous categories. Politically, these areas are integral parts of independent countries; thus, they are not dependencies. Nor are they areas of special status. They warrant inclusion in this category simply because they lie a significant distance, across either land or water, from the rest of their countries' land areas. In compiling this list, we chose to include only the areas that are populated at least part of the year. This means that we have not listed myriad uninhabited islands. Determining exactly what constitutes sufficient geographical separation to justify inclusion involves a certain degree of subjectivity. For this reason, the fourth category of Earth's lands should not be considered an official grouping. Instead, it should be viewed only as one way of classifying areas that do not fall neatly into the three other categories—but which are significant enough to deserve special attention.

IF WE COULD BRING A SNAPSHOT back from the future, few images would tell us more about what lies ahead than a flag chart showing the banners of all countries. The independence of new nations, the breakup of empires, even changing political and religious currents—all would be reflected in the symbols and colors of the national flags. This is dramatically evident in the changing flag of the United States (below), but similar visual statements could be made for most countries.

Germany provides another example. In the Middle Ages a gold banner with a black eagle proclaimed its Holy Roman Emperor a successor to the Caesars. A united 19th-century German Empire adopted a black-white-red tricolor for Bismarck's "blood and iron" policies. The liberal Weimar and Federal Republics (1919-1933 and since 1949) hailed a black-red-gold tricolor. The dark years from 1933 to 1945 were under the swastika flag of the Nazi regime. These and similar flags in other countries are more than visual aids to history: Their development and use are a fundamental part of the political and social life of a community.

Like maps, flags are ways to communicate information in condensed form. The study of geography is paralleled by the study of flags, known as vexillology (from the Latin word vexillum, for "small sail" or flag). Books, journals, Web sites, and other sources convey information on vexillology; there are also organizations and institutions around the world linked by the International Federation of Vexillological Associations. Even very young students can gain understanding of countries, populations, political changes, religious movements, and historical events by learning about flags.

All flags embody myths and historical facts, whether they are displayed at the Olympic Games, carried by protesters, placed at a roadside shrine, or arrayed at a ceremony of national significance, such as a presidential inauguration. Flags are powerful symbols, attractive to groups of all kinds; hence their once prominent display by Nazis and Communists to manipulate the masses, their waving by the East Timorese after a successful struggle for independence, and their spontaneous use by people in the United States after September 11, 2001.

Flags of nations may be the most significant flags today, but they are far from the only ones. Sport teams, business enterprises, religious groups, ethnic groups, schools, and international organizations frequently rally, reward, and inspire people through the use of flags. An observant person will also notice advertising banners, nautical signals, warning flags, decorative pennants, the rank flags of important individuals, and many related symbols such as coats of arms and logos. Examples of flags, as presented on these two pages, only hint at the rich possibilities of design, usage, and symbolism. The vexillophile (flag hobbyist) can easily and inexpensively acquire a substantial collection of flags and flag-related items. The vexillographer (flag designer) can create flags for self or family, club or team, or even for a city or county. The vexillologist (flag scholar) will find endless connections between flags and history, political science, communications theory, social behavior, and other areas. As with geography, the knowledge gained by a study of flags can be a richly rewarding personal experience.

Development of the Stars and Stripes

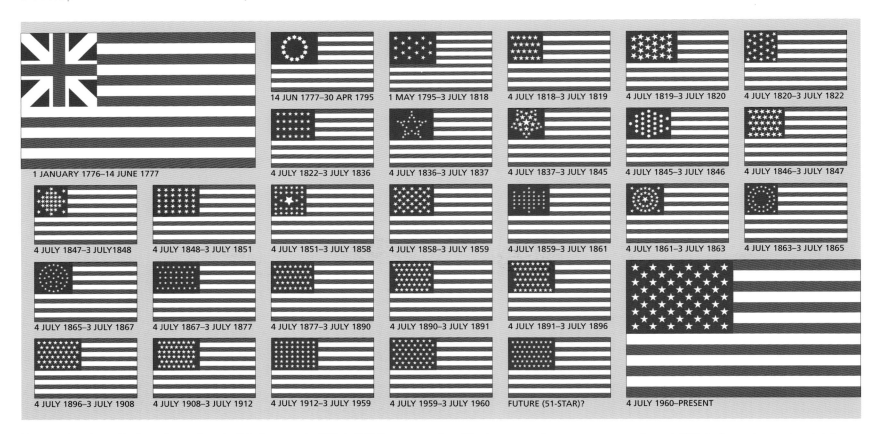

No country has changed its flag as frequently as the United States. The Continental Colors (top left) represented the Colonies during the early years of the American Revolution. Its British Union Jack, which signified loyalty to the crown, was replaced on June 14, 1777, by "13 stars...representing a new constellation." Congressman Francis Hopkinson was the designer.

The number of stars and stripes was increased to 15 in 1795. In 1817 Congressman Peter Wendover wrote the current flag law. The number of stripes was permanently limited to 13; the stars were to correspond to the number of states, with new stars added to the flag the following Fourth of July.

Star arrangement was not specified, however, and throughout the 19th century a variety of exuberant star designs—"great luminaries," rings, ovals, and diamonds—

were actually used. With the increasing number of states, the modern alternating rows of stars became standard. Finally, in 1912, President Taft set forth exact regulations for all flag details.

If a new state joins the Union, a 51-star flag will be needed. There is a logical design for it: alternating rows of nine and eight stars, as shown above.

MOURNING
The black flag signals death, piracy, protest, and danger. It is also a symbol of mourning for the dead.

OLYMPIC GAMES
The colors refer to those in the national flags of participating countries. The Olympic flag was created in 1913.

RED CRESCENT
In Muslim nations, Geneva Convention organizations rejected the red cross in favor of a red crescent, officially recognized in 1906.

RED CROSS
The Geneva Convention chose its symbol and flag in 1864 to identify people, vehicles, and buildings protected during wartime.

TRUCE/PEACE
For a thousand years a white flag has served as a symbol of truce, surrender, noncombatant status, neutrality, and peace.

UNITED NATIONS
Olive branches of peace and a world map form the symbol adopted by the United Nations in 1946. The flag dates from 1947.

ARAB LEAGUE
The color green and the crescent are often symbols in member countries of the League of Arab States, founded in 1945.

ASEAN
A stylized bundle of rice, the principal local crop, appears on the flag of the Association of South East Asian Nations (ASEAN).

COMMONWEALTH
Once the British Empire, the modern Commonwealth under this flag informally links countries with common goals.

EUROPEAN UNION
The number of stars for this flag, adopted in 1955, is permanently set at 12. The ring is a symbol for unity.

OAS
Flags of member nations appear on the flag of the Organization of American States; each new member prompts a flag change.

PACIFIC COMMISSION
The palm tree, surf, and sailboat are found in all of the member nations; each star on the flag represents a country.

BUDDHISM
Designed in 1885 by Henry Olcott of the United States, the Buddhist flag features the auras associated with the Buddha.

CHRISTIANITY
The sacrifice of Christ on the Cross is heralded in this 1897 flag, which features a white field for purity.

ISLAM
"There Is No God But Allah and Muhammad Is the Prophet of Allah" is written on this widely used but unofficial flag.

LA RAZA
Crosses for the ships of Columbus and a golden Inca sun recall the Spanish and Indian heritage of Latin Americans.

PALESTINIANS
Since 1922 Palestinians have used this flag, with traditional Arab dynastic colors, as a symbol of the statehood they desire.

ROMA (GYPSIES)
Against a background of blue sky and green grass, a wheel represents the vehicles (and homes) of the nomadic Roma people.

ANARCHISTS
Opposition to all forms of authority is hinted at in the "hand-drawn" rendition of an encircled A in the anarchist flag.

BLUE FLAG
The campaign for the improvement of the environment presents this flag as an award for success.

BOY SCOUTS
Created in 1961, this flag shows the traditional Boy Scout fleur-de-lis within a rope tied with a reef knot.

CIRCLE CROSS
This ancient religious symbol, related to the swastika, is widely used as a neo-Nazi symbol in Europe and North America.

DIVERS FLAG
As a warning signal to other boats, this flag flies wherever divers are underwater nearby—and at divers' clubhouses.

ESPERANTO
On the flag promoting Esperanto as a world language, a star signifies unity; green, traditionally, is a symbol of hope.

FRANCOPHONIE
French speakers share their common language and culture in periodic conferences and activities held under this flag.

GAY PRIDE
The Rainbow Flag, in various configurations, has been flown since 1978 by the gay and lesbian community and their families.

GIRL SCOUTS
The trefoil with a compass needle adorns the World Flag of Girl Guides and Girl Scouts, which was adopted in May 1991.

GREEN CROSS
Organizations that display this flag promote public safety in natural disasters, transportation, and the workplace.

MASONS
The unofficial flag of the Masons displays their traditional logo with symbolic square and compass.

POW-MIA
Aside from Old Glory, no U.S. flag is as popular as the one saluting war prisoners and the missing in action. It recalls those lost but not forgotten.

A aglet — well
Aain — spring
Aauinat — spring
Āb — river, water
Ache — stream
Açude — reservoir
Ada,-si — island
Adrar — mountain-s, plateau
Aguada — dry lake bed
Aguelt — water hole, well
'Ain, Aïn — spring, well
Aïoun-et — spring-s, well
Aivi — mountain
Ákra, Akrotírion — cape, promontory
Alb — mountain, ridge
Alföld — plain
Alin' — mountain range
Alpe-n — mountain-s
Altiplanicie — high-plain, plateau
Alto — hill-s, mountain-s, ridge
Älv-en — river
Āmba — hill, mountain
Anou — well
Anse — bay, inlet
Ao — bay, cove, estuary
Ap — cape, point
Archipel, Archipiélago — archipelago
Arcipelago, Arkhipelag — archipelago
Arquipélago — archipelago
Arrecife-s — reef-s
Arroio, Arroyo — brook, gully, rivulet, stream
Ås — ridge
Ava — channel
Aylagy — gulf
'Ayn — spring, well

B a — intermittent stream, river
Baai — bay, cove, lagoon
Bāb — gate, strait
Badia — bay
Bælt — strait
Bagh — bay
Bahar — drainage basin
Bahía — bay
Bahr, Baḥr — bay, lake, river, sea, wadi
Baía, Baie — bay
Bajo-s — shoal-s
Ban — village
Bañado-s — flooded area, swamp-s
Banc, Banco-s — bank-s, sandbank-s, shoal-s
Band — lake
Bandao — peninsula
Baño-s — hot spring-s, spa
Baraj-ı — dam, reservoir
Barra — bar, sandbank
Barrage, Barragem — dam, lake, reservoir
Barranca — gorge, ravine
Bazar — marketplace
Ben, Benin — mountain
Belt — strait
Bereg — bank, coast, shore
Berg-e — mountain-s
Bil — lake
Biq'at — plain, valley
Bir, Bîr, Bi'r — spring, well
Birket — lake, pool, swamp
Bjerg-e — mountain-s, range
Boca, Bocca — channel, river, mouth
Bocht — bay
Bodden — bay
Boğaz, -i — strait
Bögeni — reservoir
Boka — gulf, mouth
Bol'sh-oy, -aya, -oye — big
Bolsón — inland basin
Boubairet — lagoon, lake
Bras — arm, branch of a stream
Braṭ, -ul — arm, branch of a stream

Bre, -en — glacier, ice cap
Bredning — bay, broad water
Bruch — marsh
Bucht — bay
Bugt-en — bay
Buḥayrat, Buheirat — lagoon, lake, marsh
Bukhta, Bukta, Bukt-en — bay
Bulak, Bulaq — spring
Bum — hill, mountain
Burnu, Burun — cape, point
Busen — gulf
Buuraha — hill-s, mountain-s
Buyuk — big, large

C abeza-s — head-s, summit-s
Cabo — cape
Cachoeira — rapids, waterfall
Cal — hill, peak
Caleta — cove, inlet
Campo-s — field-s, flat country
Canal — canal, channel, strait
Caño — channel, stream
Cao Nguyen — mountain, plateau
Cap, Capo — cape
Capitán — captain
Càrn — mountain
Castillo — castle, fort
Catarata-s — cataract-s, waterfall-s
Causse — upland
Çay — brook, stream
Cay-s, Cayo-s — island-s, key-s, shoal-s
Cerro-s — hill-s, peak-s
Chaîne, Chaînons — mountain chain, range
Chapada-s — plateau, upland-s
Chedo — archipelago
Chenal — river channel
Chersónisos — peninsula
Chhung — bay
Chi — lake
Chiang — bay
Chiao — cape, point, rock
Ch'ih — lake
Chink — escarpment
Chott — intermittent salt lake, salt marsh
Chou — island
Ch'ü — canal
Ch'üntao — archipelago, islands
Chute-s — cataract-s, waterfall-s
Chyrvony — red
Cima — mountain, peak, summit
Ciudad — city
Co — lake
Col — pass
Collina, Colline — hill, mountains
Con — island
Cordillera — mountain chain
Corno — mountain, peak
Coronel — colonel
Corredeira — cascade, rapids
Costa — coast
Côte — coast, slope
Coxilha, Cuchilla — range of low hills
Crique — creek, stream
Csatorna — canal, channel
Cul de Sac — bay, inlet

D a — great, greater
Daban — pass
Dağ, -ı, Dagh — mountain
Dağlar, -ı — mountains
Dahr — cliff, mesa
Dake — mountain, peak
Dal-en — valley
Dala — steppe
Dan — cape, point
Danau — lake
Dao — island
Dar'ya — lake, river
Daryācheh — lake, marshy lake
Dasht — desert, plain

Dawan — pass
Dawḥat — bay, cove, inlet
Deniz, -i — sea
Dent-s — peak-s
Deo — pass
Desēt — hummock, island, land-tied island
Desierto — desert
Détroit — channel, strait
Dhar — hills, ridge, tableland
Ding — mountain
Distrito — district
Djebel — mountain, range
Do — island-s, rock-s
Doi — hill, mountain
Dome — ice dome
Dong — village
Dooxo — floodplain
Dzong — castle, fortress

E iland-en — island-s
Eilean — island
Ejland — island
Elv — river
Embalse — lake, reservoir
Emi — mountain, rock
Enseada, Ensenada — bay, cove
Ér — rivulet, stream
Erg — sand dune region
Est — east
Estación — railroad station
Estany — lagoon, lake
Estero — estuary, inlet, lagoon, marsh
Estrecho — strait
Étang — lake, pond
Eylandt — island
Ežeras — lake
Ezers — lake

F alaise — cliff, escarpment
Farvand-et — channel, sound
Fell — mountain
Feng — mount, peak
Fiord-o — inlet, sound
Fiume — river
Fjäll-et — mountain
Fjällen — mountains
Fjärd-en — fjord
Fjardar, Fjördur — fjord
Fjeld — mountain
Fjell-ene — mountain-s
Fjöll — mountain-s
Fjord-en — inlet, fjord
Fleuve — river
Fljót — large river
Flói — bay, marshland
Foci — river mouths
Fõcsatorna — principal canal
Förde — fjord, gulf, inlet
Forsen — rapids, waterfall
Fortaleza — fort, fortress
Fortín — fortified post
Foss-en — waterfall
Foum — pass, passage
Foz — mouth of a river
Fuerte — fort, fortress
Fwafwate — waterfalls

G acan-ka — hill, peak
Gal — pond, spring, water hole, well
Gang — harbor
Gangri — peak, range
Gaoyuan — plateau
Garaet, Gara'et — lake, lake bed, salt lake
Gardaneh — pass
Garet — hill, mountain
Gat — channel
Gata — bay, inlet, lake
Gattet — channel, strait
Gaud — depression, saline tract
Gave — mountain stream

Gebel — mountain-s, range
Gebergte — mountain range
Gebirge — mountains, range
Geçidi — mountain pass, passage
Geçit — mountain pass, passage
Gezâir — islands
Gezîra-t, Gezîret — island, peninsula
Ghats — mountain range
Ghubb-at, -et — bay, gulf
Giri — mountain
Gletscher — glacier
Gobernador — governor
Gobi — desert
Gol — river, stream
Göl, -ü — lake
Golets — mountain, peak
Golf, -e, -o — gulf
Gor-a, -y, Gór-a, -y — mountain, -s
Got — point
Gowd — depression
Goz — sand ridge
Gran, -de — great, large
Gryada — mountains, ridge
Guan — pass
Guba — bay, gulf
Guelta — well
Gum — desert
Guntō — archipelago
Gunung — mountain
Gura — mouth, passage
Guyot — table mount

H ̣adabat — plateau
Haehyŏp — strait
Haff — lagoon
Hai — lake, sea
Haihsia — strait
Haixia — channel, strait
Hakau — reef, rock
Hakuchi — anchorage
Halvø, Halvøy-a — peninsula
Hama — beach
Hamada, Ḥammādah — rocky desert
Hamn — harbor, port
Hāmūn, Hamun — depression, lake
Hana — cape, point
Hantō — peninsula
Har — hill, mound, mountain
Ḥarrat — lava field
Hasi, Hassi — spring, well
Hauteur — elevation, height
Hav-et — sea
Havn, Havre — harbor, port
Hawr — lake, marsh
Hāyk' — lake, reservoir
Hegy, -ség — mountain, -s, range
Heiau — temple
Ho — canal, lake, river
Hoek — hook, point
Hög-en — high, hill
Höhe, -n — height, high
Høj — height, hill
Holm, -e, Holmene — island-s, islet -s
Ḥolot — dunes
Hon — island-s
Hor-a, -y — mountain, -s
Horn — horn, peak
Houma — point
Hoved — headland, peninsula, point
Hraun — lava field
Hsü — island
Hu — lake, reservoir
Huk — cape, point
Hüyük — hill, mound

I dehan — sand dunes
Île-s, Ilha-s, Illa-s, Îlot-s — island-s, islet-s
Îlet, Ilhéu-s — islet, -s
Irhil — mountain-s
'Irq — sand dune-s
Isblink — glacier, ice field
Is-en — glacier

Isla-s, Islote — island-s, islet
Isol-a, -e — island, -s
Istmo — isthmus
Iwa — island, islet, rock

J abal, Jebel — mountain-s, range
Järv, -i, Jaure, Javrre — lake
Jazā'ir, Jazīrat, Jazīreh — island-s
Jehīl — lake
Jezero, Jezioro — lake
Jiang — river, stream
Jiao — cape
Jibāl — hill, mountain, ridge
Jima — island-s, rock-s
Jøkel, Jökull — glacier, ice cap
Joki, Jokka — river
Jökulsá — river from a glacier
Jūn — bay

K aap — cape
Kafr — village
Kaikyō — channel, strait
Kaise — mountain
Kaiwan — bay, gulf, sea
Kanal — canal, channel
Kangri — mountain, peak
Kap, Kapp — cape
Kavīr — salt desert
Kefar — village
Kënet' — lagoon, lake
Kep — cape, point
Kepulauan — archipelago, islands
Khalīg, Khalīj — bay, gulf
Khirb-at, -et — ancient site, ruins
Khrebet — mountain range
Kinh — canal
Klint — bluff, cliff
Kō — bay, cove, harbor
Ko — island, lake
Koh — island, mountain, range
Köl-i — lake
Kólpos — gulf
Kong — mountain
Körfez, -i — bay, gulf
Kosa — spit of land
Kou — estuary, river mouth
Kowtal-e — pass
Krasn-yy, -aya, -oye — red
Kryazh — mountain range, ridge
Kuala — estuary, river mouth
Kuan — mountain pass
Kūh, Kūhhā — mountain-s, range
Kul', Kuli — lake
Kum — sandy desert
Kundo — archipelago
Kuppe — hill-s, mountain-s
Kust — coast, shore
Kyst — coast
Kyun — island

L a — pass
Lac, Lac-ul, -us — lake
Lae — cape, point
Lago, -a — lagoon, lake
Lagoen, Lagune — lagoon
Laguna-s — lagoon-s, lake-s
Laht — bay, gulf, harbor
Laje — reef, rock ledge
Laut — sea
Lednik — glacier
Leida — channel
Lhari — mountain
Li — village
Liedao — archipelago, islands
Liehtao — archipelago, islands
Liman-ı — bay, estuary
Límni — lake
Ling — mountain-s, range
Linn — pool, waterfall
Lintasan — passage
Liqen — lake
Llano-s — plain-s
Loch, Lough — lake, arm of the sea
Loma-s — hill-s, knoll-s

Mal — mountain, range
Mal-yy, -aya, -oye — little, small
Mamarr — pass, path
Man — bay
Mar, Mare — large lake, sea
Marsa, Marsá — bay, inlet
Masabb — mouth of river
Massif — mountain-s
Mauna — mountain
Mēda — plain
Meer — lake, sea
Melkosopochnik — undulating plain
Mesa, Meseta — plateau, tableland
Mierzeja — sandspit
Minami — south
Mios — island
Misaki — cape, peninsula, point
Mochun — passage
Mong — town, village
Mont-e, -i, -s — mount, –ain, –s
Montagne, -s — mount, –ain, –s
Montaña, -s — mountain, –s
More — sea
Morne — hill, peak
Morro — bluff, headland, hill
Motu, -s — islands
Mouïet — well
Mouillage — anchorage
Muang — town, village
Mui — cape, point
Mull — headland, promontory
Munkhafad — depression
Munte — mountain
Munţi-i — mountains
Muong — town, village
Mynydd — mountain
Mys — cape

Nacional — national
Nada — gulf, sea
Næs, Näs — cape, point
Nafūd — area of dunes, desert
Nagor'ye — mountain range, plateau
Nahar, Nahr — river, stream
Nakhon — town
Namakzār — salt waste
Ne — island, reef, rock–s
Neem — cape, point, promontory
Nes, Ness — peninsula, point
Nevado-s — snow-capped mountain-s
Nez — cape, promontory
Ni — village
Nísi, Nísia, Nisís, Nísoi — island-s, islet-s
Nisídhes — islets
Nizhn-iy, -yaya, -eye — lower
Nizmennost' — low country
Noord — north
Nord-re — north-ern
Nørre — north-ern
Nos — cape, nose, point
Nosy — island, reef, rock
Nov-yy, -aya, -oye — new
Nudo — mountain
Numa — lake
Nunatak, -s, -ker — peak-s surrounded by ice cap
Nur — lake, salt lake
Nuruu — mountain range, ridge
Nut-en — peak
Nuur — lake

Ö-n, Ø-er — island-s
Oblast' — administrative division, province, region
Oceanus — ocean
Odde-n — cape, point
Øer-ne — islands
Oglat — group of wells
Oguilet — well
Ór-os, -i — mountain, –s
Órmos — bay, port

Ort — place, point
Øst-er — east
Ostrov, -a, Ostrv-o, -a — island, –s
Otoci, Otok — islands, island
Ouadi, Oued — river, watercourse
Øy-a — island
Øyane — islands
Ozer-o, -a — lake, –s

Pää — mountain, point
Palus — marsh
Pampa-s — grassy plain-s
Pantà — lake, reservoir
Pantanal — marsh, swamp
Pao, P'ao — lake
Parbat — mountain
Parque — park
Pas, -ul — pass
Paso, Passo — pass
Passe — channel, pass
Pasul — pass
Pedra — rock
Pegunungan — mountain range
Pellg — bay, bight
Peña — cliff, rock
Pendi — basin
Penedo-s — rock-s
Péninsule — peninsula
Peñón — point, rock
Pereval — mountain pass
Pertuis — strait
Peski — sands, sandy region
Phnom — hill, mountain, range
Phou — mountain range
Phu — mountain
Piana-o — plain
Pic, Pik, Piz — peak
Picacho — mountain, peak
Pico-s — peak-s
Pistyll — waterfall
Piton-s — peak-s
Pivdennyy — southern
Plaja, Playa — beach, inlet, shore
Planalto, Plato — plateau
Planina — mountain, plateau
Plassen — lake
Ploskogor'ye — plateau, upland
Pointe — point
Polder — reclaimed land
Poluostrov — peninsula
Pongo — water gap
Ponta, -l — cape, point
Ponte — bridge
Poolsaar — peninsula
Portezuelo — pass
Porto — port
Poulo — island
Praia — beach, seashore
Presa — reservoir
Presidente — president
Presqu'île — peninsula
Prokhod — pass
Proliv — strait
Promontorio — promontory
Průsmyk — mountain pass
Przylądek — cape
Puerto — bay, pass, port
Pulao — island-s
Pulau, Pulo — island
Puncak — peak, summit, top
Punt, Punta, -n — point, -s
Pun — peak
Puu — hill, mountain
Puy — peak

Qal'eh — castle, fort
Qā' — depression, marsh, mud flat
Qal'at — fort
Qanâ — canal
Qārat — hill-s, mountain-s
Qaşr — castle, fort, hill
Qila — fort
Qiryat — settlement, suburb

Qolleh — peak
Qooriga — anchorage, bay
Qoz — dunes, sand ridge
Qu — canal
Quebrada — ravine, stream
Qullai — peak, summit
Qum — desert, sand
Qundao — archipelago, islands
Qurayyāt — hills

Raas — cape, point
Rabt — hill
Rada — roadstead
Rade — anchorage, roadstead
Rags — point
Ramat — hill, mountain
Rand — ridge of hills
Rann — swamp
Raqaba — wadi, watercourse
Ras, Râs, Ra's — cape
Ravnina — plain
Récif-s — reef-s
Regreg — marsh
Represa — reservoir
Reservatório — reservoir
Restinga — barrier, sand area
Rettō — chain of islands
Ri — mountain range, village
Ría — estuary
Ribeirão — stream
Río, Rio — river
Rivière — river
Roca-s — cliff, rock-s
Roche-r, -s — rock-s
Rosh — mountain, point
Rt — cape, point
Rubha — headland
Rupes — scarp

Saar — island
Saari, Sar — island
Sabkha-t, Sabkhet — lagoon, marsh, salt lake
Sagar — lake, sea
Sahara, Şaḩrā' — desert
Sahl — plain
Saki — cape, point
Salar — salt flat
Salina — salt pan
Salin-as, -es — salt flat-s, salt marsh-es
Salto — waterfall
Sammyaku — mountain range
San — hill, mountain
San, -ta, -to — saint
Sandur — sandy area
Sankt — saint
Sanmaek — mountain range
São — saint
Sarīr — gravel desert
Sasso — mountain, stone
Savane — savanna
Scoglio — reef, rock
Se — reef, rock-s, shoal-s
Sebjet — salt lake, salt marsh
Sebkha — salt lake, salt marsh
Sebkhet — lagoon, salt lake
See — lake, sea
Selat — strait
Selkä — lake, ridge
Semenanjung — peninsula
Sen — mountain
Seno — bay, gulf
Serra, Serranía — range of hills or mountains
Severn-yy, -aya, -oye — northern
Sgùrr — peak
Sha — island, shoal
Sha'ib — ravine, watercourse
Shamo — desert
Shan — island-s, mountain-s, range
Shankou — mountain pass
Shanmo — mountain range

Sharm — cove, creek, harbor
Shaṭṭ — large river
Shi — administrative division, municipality
Shima — island-s, rock-s
Shō — island, reef, rock
Shotō — archipelago
Shott — intermittent salt lake
Shuiku — reservoir
Shuitao — channel
Shyghanaghy — bay, gulf
Sierra — mountain range
Silsilesi — mountain chain, ridge
Sint — saint
Sinus — bay, sea
Sjö-n — lake
Skarv-et — barren mountain
Skerry — rock
Slieve — mountain
Sø — lake
Sopka — conical mountain, volcano
Sor — lake, salt lake
Sør, Sör — south-ern
Sory — salt lake, salt marsh
Spitz-e — peak, point, top
Sredn-iy, -yaya, -eye — central, middle
Stagno — lake, pond
Stantsiya — station
Stausee — reservoir
Stenón — channel, strait
Step'-i — steppe-s
Štít — summit, top
Stor-e — big, great
Straat — strait
Straum-en — current-s
Strelka — spit of land
Stretet, Stretto — strait
Su — reef, river, rock, stream
Sud — south
Sudo — channel, strait
Suidō — channel, strait
Şummān — rocky desert
Sund — sound, strait
Sunden — channel, inlet, sound
Svyat-oy, -aya, -oye — holy, saint
Sziget — island

Tagh — mountain-s
Tall — hill, mound
T'an — lake
Tanezrouft — desert
Tang — plain, steppe
Tangi — peninsula, point
Tanjong, Tanjung — cape, point
Tao — island-s
Tarso — hill-s, mountain-s
Tassili — plateau, upland
Tau — mountain-s, range
Taūy — hills, mountains
Tchabal — mountain-s
Te Ava — tidal flat
Tel-l — hill, mound
Telok, Teluk — bay
Tepe, -si — hill, peak
Tepuí — mesa, mountain
Terara — hill, mountain, peak
Testa — bluff, head
Thale — lake
Thang — plain, steppe
Tien — lake
Tierra — land, region
Ting — hill, mountain
Tir'at — canal
Tó — lake, pool
To, Tō — island-s, rock-s
Tonle — lake
Tope — hill, mountain, peak
Top-pen — peak-s
Träsk — bog, lake
Tso — lake
Tsui — cape, point

Tūbegi — peninsula
Tulu — hill, mountain
Tunturi-t — hill-s, mountain-s

Uad — wadi, watercourse
Udde-m — point
Ujong, Ujung — cape, point
Umi — bay, lagoon, lake
Ura — bay, inlet, lake
'Urūq — dune area
Uul, Uula — mountain, range
'Uyûn — springs

Vaara — mountain
Vaart — canal
Vær — fishing station
Vaïn — channel, strait
Valle, Vallée — valley, wadi
Vallen — waterfall
Valli — lagoon, lake
Vallis — valley
Vanua — land
Varre — mountain
Vatn, Vatten, Vatnet — lake, water
Veld — grassland, plain
Verkhn-iy, -yaya, -eye — higher, upper
Vesi — lake, water
Vest-er — west
Via — road
Vidda — plateau
Vig, Vík, Vik, -en — bay, cove
Vinh — bay, gulf
Vodokhranilishche — reservoir
Vodoskhovyshche — reservoir
Volcan, Volcán — volcano
Vostochn-yy, -aya, -oye — eastern
Vötn — stream
Vozvyshennost' — plateau, upland
Vozyera — lake-s
Vrchovina — mountains
Vrch-y — mountain-s
Vrh — hill, mountain
Vrükh — mountain
Vyaliki — big, large
Vysočina — highland

Wabē — stream
Wadi, Wâdi, Wādī — valley, watercourse
Wâhât, Wāḩat — oasis
Wald — forest, wood
Wan — bay, gulf
Water — harbor
Webi — stream
Wiek — cove, inlet

Xia — gorge, strait
Xiao — lesser, little

Yanchi — salt lake
Yang — ocean
Yarymadasy — peninsula
Yazovir — reservoir
Yŏlto — island group
Yoma — mountain range
Yü — island
Yumco — lake
Yunhe — canal
Yuzhn-yy, -aya, -oye — southern

Zaki — cape, point
Zaliv — bay, gulf
Zan — mountain, ridge
Zangbo — river, stream
Zapadn-yy, -aya, -oye — western
Zatoka — bay, gulf
Zee — bay, sea
Zemlya — land
Zhotasy — mountains

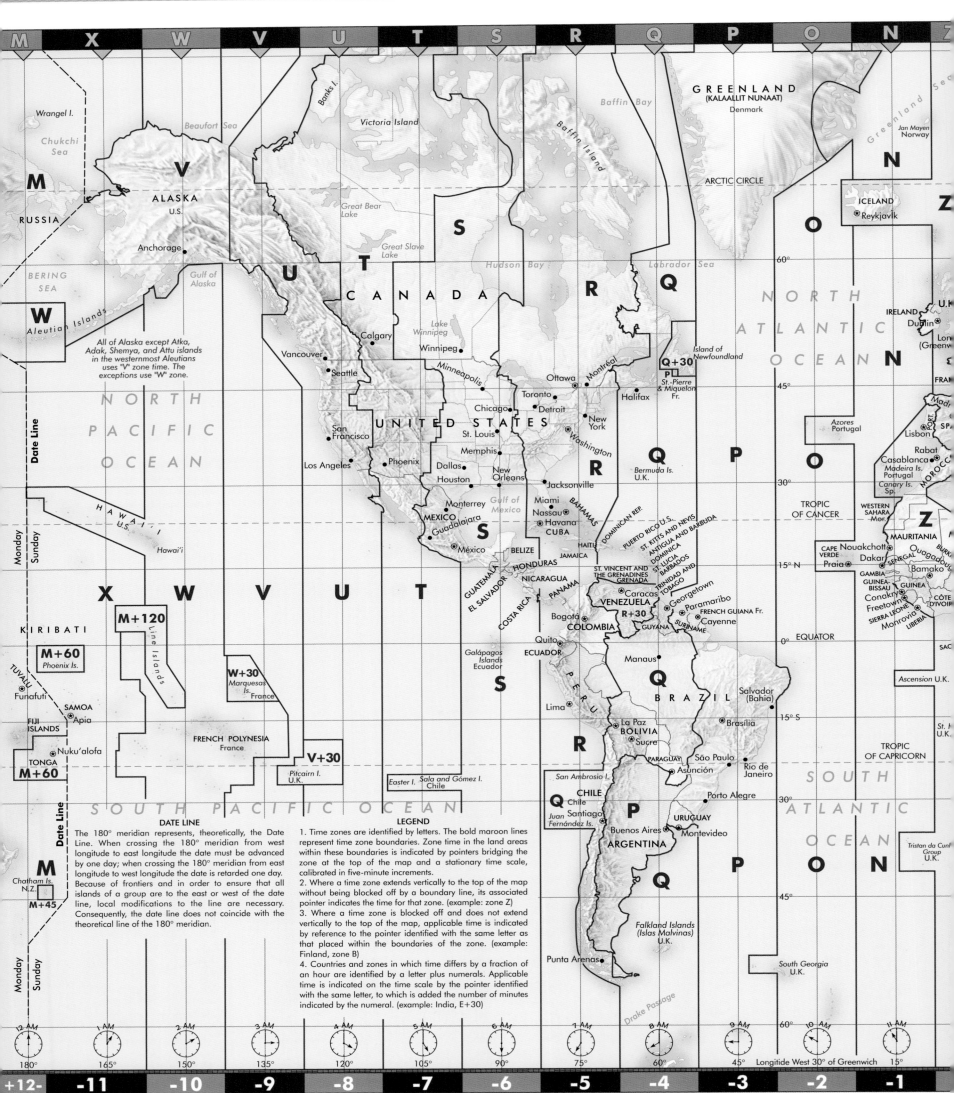

M X W V U T S R Q P O N

V
ALASKA
U.S.

RUSSIA

Wrangel I.

Chukchi Sea

M

Anchorage

BERING SEA

W
Aleutian Islands

All of Alaska except Atka, Adak, Shemya, and Attu islands in the westernmost Aleutians uses "V" zone time. The exceptions use "W" zone.

Banks I.

Beaufort Sea

Victoria Island

Baffin Bay

GREENLAND
(KALAALLIT NUNAAT)
Denmark

Greenland Sea

Jan Mayen Norway

ARCTIC CIRCLE

N

ICELAND
Reykjavík

Z

Great Bear Lake

Great Slave Lake

Hudson Bay

Labrador Sea

U T S

C A N A D A

R

Q

60°

IRELAND
Dublin

U.K.

U.K.
(Green

N

Vancouver
Seattle

Calgary

Winnipeg

Lake Winnipeg

Minneapolis

Ottawa
Montréal

Q+30
P
St.-Pierre & Miquelon Fr.

Halifax

Island of Newfoundland

45°

NORTH

ATLANTIC

OCEAN

Azores Portugal

Lisbon

SPA

Mad

NORTH PACIFIC OCEAN

Date Line

San Francisco

Los Angeles

U N I T E D   S T A T E S

Chicago
Toronto
Detroit

St. Louis

New York

Washington

R
Q

P

Bermuda Is. U.K.

O

30°

Rabat
Casablanca
Madeira Is. Portugal

MOROCCO

Phoenix

Dallas

Memphis

New Orleans

Houston

Jacksonville

Canary Is. Sp.

TROPIC OF CANCER

WESTERN SAHARA Mor.

Z

H A W A I I
U.S.

Hawai'i

Monday
Sunday

Monterrey

MEXICO
Guadalajara

México

S

Gulf of Mexico

Miami
Nassau
Havana
CUBA

BAHAMAS

BELIZE

HAITI
DOMINICAN REP.
PUERTO RICO U.S.
ST. KITTS AND NEVIS
ANTIGUA AND BARBUDA
DOMINICA
ST. LUCIA
BARBADOS

15° N

MAURITANIA

Nouakchott
CAPE VERDE
Dakar
Praia

SENEGAL

Ouagadoug

BURK

GAMBIA
GUINEA-BISSAU
Conakry
Freetown
SIERRA LEONE
Monrovia
LIBERIA

GUINEA
CÔTE D'IVOIR

X

W

V

U

T

KIRIBATI

M+120

M+60
Phoenix Is.

TUVALU
Funafuti

SAMOA
Apia

FIJI ISLANDS

Nuku'alofa

TONGA
M+60

W+30
Marquesas Is. France

FRENCH POLYNESIA
France

V+30

Pitcairn I. U.K.

Line Islands

GUATEMALA
EL SALVADOR

HONDURAS

NICARAGUA

COSTA RICA

PANAMA

Galápagos Islands Ecuador

S

Easter I. *Sala and Gómez I. Chile*

ST. VINCENT AND THE GRENADINES
GRENADA

VENEZUELA
Caracas
R+30

Bogotá
COLOMBIA

Quito
ECUADOR

Lima

PERU

La Paz
BOLIVIA
Sucre

TRINIDAD AND TOBAGO
Georgetown
Paramaribo
GUYANA
Cayenne
FRENCH GUIANA Fr.
SURINAME

Manaus

Q
BRAZIL

Brasília

EQUATOR

ASCENSION U.K.

SAO

0°

15° S

Salvador (Bahia)

St. M
U.K.

TROPIC OF CAPRICORN

R

PARAGUAY

São Paulo
Rio de Janeiro

Asunción

San Ambrosio I.

CHILE

Q

Juan Fernández Is.

Santiago

Chile

Porto Alegre

30°

Montevideo

SOUTH

ATLANTIC

OCEAN

P
URUGUAY

Buenos Aires

ARGENTINA

Tristan da Cunh Group U.K.

M

Chatham Is. N.Z.

M+45

Monday
Sunday

Date Line

Q

Q

P

O

N

45°

Falkland Islands (Islas Malvinas) U.K.

Punta Arenas

Drake Passage

South Georgia U.K.

60°

DATE LINE

The 180° meridian represents, theoretically, the Date Line. When crossing the 180° meridian from west longitude to east longitude the date must be advanced by one day; when crossing the 180° meridian from east longitude to west longitude the date is retarded one day. Because of frontiers and in order to ensure that all islands of a group are to the east or west of the date line, local modifications to the line are necessary. Consequently, the date line does not coincide with the theoretical line of the 180° meridian.

LEGEND

1. Time zones are identified by letters. The bold maroon lines represent time zone boundaries. Zone time in the land areas within these boundaries is indicated by pointers bridging the zone at the top of the map and a stationary time scale, calibrated in five-minute increments.
2. Where a time zone extends vertically to the top of the map without being blocked off by a boundary line, its associated pointer indicates the time for that zone. (example: zone Z)
3. Where a time zone is blocked off and does not extend vertically to the top of the map, applicable time is indicated by reference to the pointer identified with the same letter as that placed within the boundaries of the zone. (example: Finland, zone B)
4. Countries and zones in which time differs by a fraction of an hour are identified by a letter plus numerals. Applicable time is indicated on the time scale by the pointer identified with the same letter, to which is added the number of minutes indicated by the numeral. (example: India, E+30)

12 AM 180° | 1 AM 165° | 2 AM 150° | 3 AM 135° | 4 AM 120° | 5 AM 105° | 6 AM 90° | 7 AM 75° | 8 AM 60° | 9 AM 45° | 10 AM 30° | 11 AM 15°

Longitide West 30° of Greenwich

+12- | -11 | -10 | -9 | -8 | -7 | -6 | -5 | -4 | -3 | -2 | -1

The numeral in each tab directly above shows the number of hours to be added to, or subtracted from, Coordinated Universal Time (UTC), formerly Greenwich Mean Time (GMT).

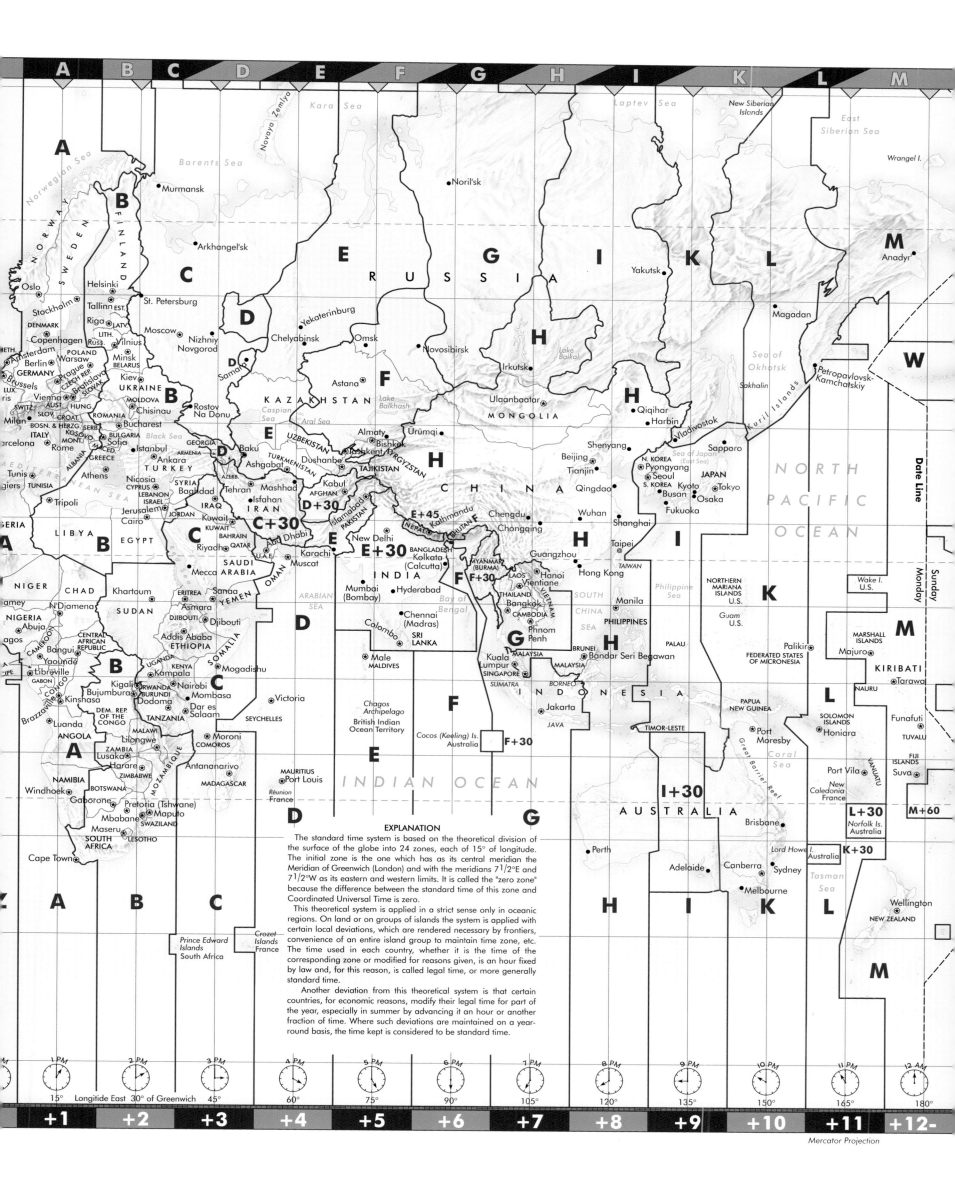

EXPLANATION

The standard time system is based on the theoretical division of the surface of the globe into 24 zones, each of 15° of longitude. The initial zone is the one which has as its central meridian the Meridian of Greenwich (London) and with the meridians 7¹/₂°E and 7¹/₂°W as its eastern and western limits. It is called the "zero zone" because the difference between the standard time of this zone and Coordinated Universal Time is zero.

This theoretical system is applied in a strict sense only in oceanic regions. On land or on groups of islands the system is applied with certain local deviations, which are rendered necessary by frontiers, convenience of an entire island group to maintain time zone, etc. The time used in each country, whether it is the time of the corresponding zone or modified for reasons given, is an hour fixed by law and, for this reason, is called legal time, or more generally standard time.

Another deviation from this theoretical system is that certain countries, for economic reasons, modify their legal time for part of the year, especially in summer by advancing it an hour or another fraction of time. Where such deviations are maintained on a year-round basis, the time kept is considered to be standard time.

Mercator Projection

World Temperature and Rainfall

Average daily high and low temperatures and monthly rainfall for selected world locations:

CANADA	JAN.			FEB.			MARCH			APRIL			MAY			JUNE			JULY			AUG.			SEPT.			OCT.			NOV.			DEC.		
CALGARY, *Alberta*	-4	-16	14	-2	-14	15	3	-9	20	11	-3	27	17	3	54	20	7	82	24	9	65	23	8	57	18	3	40	12	-1	18	3	-9	16	-2	-13	14
CHARLOTTETOWN, *P.E.I.*	-3	-11	100	-3	-12	83	1	-7	83	7	-1	77	14	4	79	20	10	75	24	14	78	23	14	86	18	10	91	13	5	106	6	0	106	0	-7	111
CHURCHILL, *Manitoba*	-23	-31	15	-22	-30	12	-15	-25	18	-6	-15	23	2	-5	27	11	1	43	17	7	55	16	7	62	9	2	53	2	-4	44	-9	-16	31	-18	-26	18
EDMONTON, *Alberta*	-9	-18	23	-5	-15	18	0	-9	19	10	-1	24	17	5	45	21	9	79	23	12	87	22	10	64	17	5	36	11	0	20	0	-8	18	-6	-15	22
FORT NELSON, *B.C.*	-18	-27	23	-11	-23	21	-2	-15	21	8	-4	20	16	3	44	21	8	65	23	10	76	21	8	58	15	3	39	6	-4	28	-9	-17	26	-16	-24	23
GOOSE BAY, *Nfld. & Lab.*	-12	-22	1	-10	-21	4	-4	-15	4	3	-7	15	10	0	46	17	5	97	21	10	119	19	9	98	14	4	87	6	-2	58	0	-8	21	-9	-18	7
HALIFAX, *Nova Scotia*	0	-8	139	0	-9	121	3	-5	123	8	0	109	14	5	110	18	9	96	22	13	93	22	14	103	19	10	93	13	5	127	8	1	142	2	-5	141
MONTRÉAL, *Quebec*	-6	-15	71	-4	-13	66	2	-7	71	11	1	74	18	8	69	24	13	84	26	16	87	25	14	91	20	10	84	13	4	76	5	-2	90	-3	-11	85
MOOSONEE, *Ontario*	-14	-27	39	-12	-25	32	-5	-19	37	3	-8	36	11	0	55	18	5	72	22	9	79	20	8	78	15	5	77	8	0	66	-1	-9	53	-11	-21	41
OTTAWA, *Ontario*	-6	-16	67	-5	-15	59	1	-8	67	11	0	60	19	7	72	24	12	82	27	15	86	25	13	80	20	9	77	13	3	69	4	-3	70	-4	-12	74
PRINCE RUPERT, *B.C.*	4	-3	237	6	-1	198	7	0	202	9	2	179	12	5	133	14	8	110	16	10	115	16	10	149	15	8	218	11	5	345	7	1	297	5	-1	275
QUÉBEC, *Quebec*	-7	-17	85	-6	-16	75	0	-9	79	8	-1	76	17	5	93	22	10	108	25	13	112	23	12	109	18	7	113	11	2	89	3	-4	100	-5	-13	104
REGINA, *Saskatchewan*	-12	-23	17	-9	-21	13	-2	-13	18	10	-3	20	18	3	45	23	9	77	26	11	59	25	10	44	19	4	35	11	-2	20	0	-11	16	-8	-19	14
SAINT JOHN, *N.B.*	-3	-14	141	-2	-14	115	3	-7	111	10	-1	111	17	4	116	22	9	103	25	12	100	24	11	100	19	7	108	14	2	118	6	-3	149	-1	-10	157
ST. JOHN'S, *Nfld. & Lab.*	-1	-8	69	-1	-9	69	1	-6	74	5	-2	80	10	1	91	16	6	95	20	11	78	20	11	122	16	8	125	11	3	147	6	0	122	2	-5	91
TORONTO, *Ontario*	-1	-8	68	-1	-9	60	3	-4	66	11	2	65	17	7	71	23	13	68	26	16	77	25	15	70	21	11	73	14	5	62	7	0	70	1	-6	67
VANCOUVER, *B.C.*	5	0	146	8	1	121	10	2	102	13	5	69	17	8	56	19	11	47	22	13	31	22	13	37	19	10	60	14	6	116	9	3	155	6	1	172
WHITEHORSE, *Yukon*	-14	-23	17	-9	-18	13	-2	-13	13	5	-5	9	13	1	14	18	5	30	20	8	37	18	6	39	12	3	31	4	-3	21	-6	-13	20	-12	-20	19
WINNIPEG, *Manitoba*	-13	-23	21	-10	-21	19	-2	-13	26	9	-2	34	18	5	55	23	10	81	26	14	74	25	12	66	19	6	55	12	1	35	-1	-9	26	-9	-18	22
YELLOWKNIFE, *N.W.T.*	-24	-32	14	-20	-30	12	-12	-24	11	-1	-13	10	10	0	16	18	8	20	21	12	35	18	10	39	10	4	29	1	-4	32	-10	-18	23	-20	-28	17
UNITED STATES																																				
ALBANY, *New York*	-1	-12	61	1	-10	59	7	-4	76	14	2	77	21	7	86	26	13	83	29	15	80	27	14	87	23	10	78	17	4	77	9	-1	80	2	-8	74
AMARILLO, *Texas*	9	-6	13	12	-4	14	16	0	23	22	6	28	26	11	71	31	16	88	33	19	70	32	18	74	28	14	50	23	7	35	15	0	15	10	-5	15
ANCHORAGE, *Alaska*	-6	-13	20	-3	-11	21	1	-8	17	6	-2	15	12	4	17	16	8	26	18	11	47	17	10	62	13	5	66	5	-2	47	-3	-9	29	-5	-12	28
ASPEN, *Colorado*	0	-18	32	2	-16	26	5	-11	35	10	-6	28	16	-2	39	22	1	34	26	5	44	25	4	45	21	0	34	15	-5	36	6	-10	31	1	-15	32
ATLANTA, *Georgia*	10	0	117	13	1	117	18	6	139	23	10	103	26	15	100	30	19	92	31	21	134	31	21	93	28	18	91	23	11	77	17	6	95	12	2	105
ATLANTIC CITY, *New Jersey*	5	-6	83	6	-5	78	11	0	98	16	4	86	22	10	82	27	15	63	29	18	103	29	18	103	25	13	78	19	7	72	13	2	84	7	-3	81
AUGUSTA, *Maine*	-2	-11	76	0	-10	71	4	-5	84	11	1	92	19	7	95	23	12	85	26	16	85	25	15	84	20	10	80	14	4	92	7	-1	114	0	-8	93
BIRMINGHAM, *Alabama*	11	0	128	14	1	114	19	6	150	24	10	114	27	14	112	31	18	97	32	21	132	32	20	95	29	17	105	24	10	75	18	5	103	13	2	120
BISMARCK, *North Dakota*	-7	-19	12	-3	-15	11	4	-8	20	13	-1	37	20	6	56	25	11	74	29	14	59	28	12	44	22	6	38	15	0	21	4	-8	14	-4	-16	12
BOISE, *Idaho*	2	-6	38	7	-3	28	12	0	32	16	3	31	22	7	31	27	11	22	32	14	8	31	14	9	25	9	16	18	4	18	9	-1	35	3	-5	35
BOSTON, *Massachusetts*	2	-6	95	3	-5	91	8	0	100	13	5	93	19	10	84	25	15	79	28	18	73	27	18	92	23	14	82	17	8	87	11	4	110	5	-3	105
BROWNSVILLE, *Texas*	21	10	37	22	11	36	26	15	16	29	19	41	31	22	64	33	24	74	34	24	39	34	24	69	32	23	134	30	19	89	26	15	41	22	11	30
BURLINGTON, *Vermont*	-4	-14	46	-3	-13	44	4	-6	55	12	1	71	20	7	78	24	13	85	27	15	90	26	14	101	21	9	85	14	4	77	7	-1	76	-1	-9	59
CHARLESTON, *South Carolina*	14	3	88	16	4	80	20	9	114	24	12	71	28	17	97	31	21	155	32	23	180	32	22	176	29	20	135	25	14	77	21	8	63	16	5	82
CHARLESTON, *West Virginia*	5	-5	87	7	-4	82	14	2	100	19	6	85	24	11	99	28	15	92	30	18	126	29	17	102	26	14	81	20	7	67	14	2	85	8	-2	85
CHEYENNE, *Wyoming*	3	-9	10	5	-8	11	7	-6	26	13	-1	35	18	4	64	24	9	56	28	13	51	27	12	42	22	7	31	16	1	19	8	-5	15	4	-9	10
CHICAGO, *Illinois*	-1	-10	48	1	-7	42	8	-1	72	15	5	97	22	10	83	27	16	103	29	19	103	28	18	89	24	14	79	18	7	70	9	1	73	2	-6	65
CINCINNATI, *Ohio*	3	-6	89	5	-4	67	12	1	97	18	7	94	24	12	101	28	17	99	30	19	102	30	18	86	26	14	75	19	8	62	12	3	81	5	-3	75
CLEVELAND, *Ohio*	1	-7	62	2	-6	58	8	-2	78	15	4	85	21	9	90	26	14	89	28	17	88	27	16	86	23	12	86	17	7	65	10	2	80	3	-4	70
DALLAS, *Texas*	13	1	47	15	4	58	20	8	74	25	13	105	29	18	125	33	22	86	35	24	56	35	24	60	31	20	82	26	14	100	19	8	64	14	3	60
DENVER, *Colorado*	6	-9	14	8	-7	16	11	-3	34	17	1	45	22	6	63	27	11	43	31	15	47	30	14	38	25	9	28	19	2	26	11	-4	23	7	-8	15
DES MOINES, *Iowa*	-2	-12	26	1	-9	30	8	-2	57	17	4	85	23	11	103	28	16	108	30	19	97	29	18	105	24	13	80	18	6	58	9	-1	46	0	-9	31
DETROIT, *Michigan*	-1	-7	42	1	-7	43	7	-2	62	14	4	75	21	10	69	26	15	85	29	18	86	27	18	87	23	14	78	16	7	55	9	2	67	2	-4	67
DULUTH, *Minnesota*	-9	-19	31	-6	-16	21	1	-9	49	9	-2	59	17	4	84	22	9	105	25	13	102	23	12	101	18	7	95	11	2	62	2	-6	48	-6	-15	32
EL PASO, *Texas*	13	-1	11	17	1	11	21	5	8	26	9	7	31	14	9	36	18	17	36	20	38	34	19	39	31	16	34	26	10	20	19	4	11	14	-1	14
FAIRBANKS, *Alaska*	-19	-28	14	-14	-26	11	-5	-19	9	5	-6	7	15	3	15	21	10	35	22	11	45	19	8	46	13	2	28	0	-8	21	-12	-21	18	-17	-26	19
HARTFORD, *Connecticut*	1	-9	83	2	-7	79	8	-2	97	16	3	97	22	9	95	27	14	85	29	17	86	28	16	104	24	11	101	18	5	96	11	0	105	3	-6	99
HELENA, *Montana*	-1	-12	15	3	-9	12	7	-5	18	13	-1	24	19	4	45	24	9	53	29	12	28	28	11	27	21	5	28	15	0	19	6	-6	14	0	-12	16
HONOLULU, *Hawai'i*	27	19	80	27	19	68	28	20	72	28	20	32	29	21	25	30	22	10	31	23	15	32	23	14	31	23	18	31	22	53	29	21	67	27	19	89
HOUSTON, *Texas*	16	4	98	19	6	75	22	10	88	26	15	91	29	18	142	32	21	133	34	22	85	34	22	95	31	20	106	28	14	120	22	10	97	18	6	91
INDIANAPOLIS, *Indiana*	1	-8	69	4	-6	61	11	0	92	17	5	94	23	11	98	28	16	98	30	18	111	29	17	88	25	13	74	19	6	69	11	1	89	4	-5	77
JACKSONVILLE, *Florida*	18	5	83	19	6	89	23	10	100	26	13	77	29	17	92	32	21	140	33	22	164	33	22	186	31	21	199	27	15	99	23	10	52	19	6	65
JUNEAU, *Alaska*	-1	-7	139	1	-5	116	4	-3	113	8	0	105	13	4	109	16	7	88	18	9	120	17	8	160	13	6	217	8	3	255	3	-2	186	0	-5	153
KANSAS CITY, *Missouri*	2	-9	30	5	-6	32	12	0	67	18	7	88	24	12	138	29	17	102	32	20	115	30	19	99	26	14	120	20	8	83	11	1	56	4	-6	43
LAS VEGAS, *Nevada*	14	0	14	17	4	12	20	7	13	25	10	5	31	16	5	38	21	3	41	25	9	40	23	13	35	19	7	28	12	6	20	6	11	14	1	10
LITTLE ROCK, *Arkansas*	9	-1	85	12	1	88	17	6	120	23	11	134	26	15	141	31	20	84	33	22	83	32	21	80	28	18	85	23	11	102	16	6	153	10	1	123
LOS ANGELES, *California*	19	9	70	19	10	61	19	10	51	20	12	20	21	14	3	22	15	1	24	17	1	25	18	2	25	17	5	24	15	7	21	12	38	19	9	43
LOUISVILLE, *Kentucky*	5	-5	85	7	-3	88	14	2	113	20	7	101	24	13	114	29	17	90	31	20	106	30	19	84	27	15	76	21	8	68	14	3	92	7	-2	89
MEMPHIS, *Tennessee*	9	-1	118	12	2	114	17	6	136	23	11	142	27	16	126	32	21	98	34	23	101	33	22	87	29	18	83	24	11	74	17	6	124	11	2	135
MIAMI, *Florida*	24	15	52	25	16	53	26	18	63	28	20	82	30	22	150	31	24	227	32	25	152	32	25	198	31	24	215	29	22	178	27	19	80	25	16	47
MILWAUKEE, *Wisconsin*	-3	-11	32	-1	-8	31	5	-3	54	12	2	87	18	7	73	24	13	87	27	17	85	26	16	94	22	12	95	15	6	66	7	-1	65	0	-7	53
MINNEAPOLIS, *Minnesota*	-6	-16	21	-3	-13	22	4	-5	45	14	2	58	21	9	80	26	14	103	29	17	97	27	16	95	22	10	70	15	4	49	5	-4	37	-4	-12	24
NASHVILLE, *Tennessee*	8	-3	108	10	-1	100	16	4	127	22	9	104	26	14	118	30	18	99	32	21	99	31	20	85	28	16	89	23	9	67	16	4	101	10	-1	112
NEW ORLEANS, *Louisiana*	16	5	136	18	7	147	22	11	124	26	15	119	29	18	135	32	22	147	33	23	167	32	23	157	30	21	138	26	15	76	22	11	101	18	7	132
NEW YORK, *New York*	3	-4	80	4	-3	76	9	1	99	15	7	94	21	12	93	26	17	80	29	21	101	28	20	107	24	16	85	18	10	81	12	5	96	6	-1	90
OKLAHOMA CITY, *Oklahoma*	8	-4	28	11	-1	36	17	4	61	22	9	76	26	14	145	31	19	107	34	21	74	34	21	65	29	17	97	23	10	80	16	4	43	10	-2	37
OMAHA, *Nebraska*	-1	-12	18	2	-9	21	9	-2	61	17	5	73	23	11	118	28	16	105	30	19	96	29	18	95	24	13	90	18	6	60	9	-1	35	1	-9	23
PENSACOLA, *Florida*	15	5	109	17	7	126	21	11	150	25	15	112	28	19	105	32	22	168	32	23	187	32	23	176	30	21	166	26	15	102	21	11	91	17	7	105
PHILADELPHIA, *Pennsylvania*	3	-5	82	5	-4	70	11	1	95	17	6	88	23	12	94	28	17	87	30	20	108	29	19	97	25	15	86	19	8	67	13	3	85	6	-2	86
PHOENIX, *Arizona*	19	3	21	22	5	21	25	7	30	29	9	7	33	13	5	38	18	3	39	23	21	38	22	30	36	18	23	30	12	14	23	7	18	19	3	28
PITTSBURGH, *Pennsylvania*	1	-8	66	3	-7	60	9	-1	85	16	4	80	21	9	92	26	14	91	28	16	98	27	16	83	24	12	74	17	6	61	10	1	69	4	-4	71
PORTLAND, *Oregon*	7	1	133	11	2	105	13	4	92	16	5	61	20	8	53	23	12	38	27	14	15	27	14	23	24	11	41	18	7	76	11	4	135	8	2	149
PROVIDENCE, *Rhode Island*	3	-7	101	4	-6	91	8	-2	111	14	3	102	20	9	89	25	14	77	28	17	77	27	17	102	24	12	88	18	6	93	12	2	117	5	-4	110
RALEIGH, *North Carolina*	9	-2	89	11	0	88	17	4	94	22	8	70	26	13	96	29	18	91	31	20	111	30	20	110	27	16	79	22	9	77	17	4	76	12	0	79
RAPID CITY, *South Dakota*	2	-12	10	4	-10	12	8	-6	26	14	0	52	20	6	84	25	12	89	30	15	63	29	13	43	23	7	32	17	1	26	8	-5	12	3	-11	10
RENO, *Nevada*	7	-6	28	11	-4	24	14	-2	20	18	1	11	23	5	17	28	8	11	33	11	7	32	10	6	26	5	9	20	1	10	12	-3	19	8	-7	27
ST. LOUIS, *Missouri*	3	-6	50	6	-4	54	13	2	84	19	8	97	25	13	100	30	19	103	32	21	92	31	20	76	27	16	73	20	9	70	13	3	78	5	-3	64
SALT LAKE CITY, *Utah*	2	-7	32	6	-4	30	11	0	45	16	3	52	22	8	46	28	13	23	33	18	18	32	17	21	26	11	27	19	5	34	10	-1	34	3	-6	34
SAN DIEGO, *California*	19	9	56	19	10	41	19	12	50	20	13	20	21	15	5	22	17	2	25	19	1	25	20	2	25	19	5	24	16	9	21	12	30	19	9	35
SAN FRANCISCO, *California*	14	8	112	16	9	77	16	9	78	17	10	34	17	10	10	18	11	4	18	12	1	19	13	2	20	13	7	20	13	28	17	11	73	14	8	91

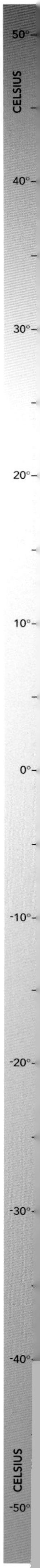

50°
CELSIUS
40°
30°
20°
10°
0°
-10°
-20°
-30°
-40°
CELSIUS
-50°

RED FIGURES: Average daily high temperature (°C) **BLUE FIGURES:** Average daily low temperature (°C) **BLACK FIGURES:** Average monthly rainfall (mm)
1 millimeter = 0.039 inches

	JAN.	FEB.	MARCH	APRIL	MAY	JUNE	JULY	AUG.	SEPT.	OCT.	NOV.	DEC.
UNITED STATES												
SANTA FE, *New Mexico*	6 -10 11	9 -7 9	13 -5 12	18 -1 13	24 4 23	29 9 31	31 12 52	29 11 64	25 7 38	20 1 32	13 -5 14	7 -9 12
SEATTLE, *Washington*	7 2 141	10 3 107	12 4 94	14 5 64	18 4 42	21 11 38	24 13 20	24 13 27	21 11 47	15 8 89	10 5 149	7 2 149
SPOKANE, *Washington*	1 -6 52	5 -3 39	9 -1 37	14 2 28	19 6 35	24 10 33	28 12 15	28 12 16	22 8 20	15 2 31	5 -2 51	1 -6 57
TAMPA, *Florida*	21 10 54	22 11 73	25 14 90	28 16 44	31 20 76	32 23 143	32 24 189	32 24 196	32 23 160	29 18 60	25 14 46	22 11 54
VICKSBURG, *Mississippi*	14 2 155	16 3 131	21 8 160	25 12 147	29 16 130	32 20 88	33 22 106	33 21 80	30 18 85	26 12 106	20 8 126	16 4 168
WASHINGTON, *D.C.*	6 -3 71	8 -2 66	14 3 90	19 8 72	25 14 94	29 19 80	31 22 97	31 21 104	27 17 84	21 10 78	15 5 76	8 0 79
WICHITA, *Kansas*	4 -7 19	8 -5 23	14 1 57	20 7 57	25 12 99	30 18 105	34 21 82	33 20 78	27 15 85	21 8 62	13 1 37	6 -5 29
MIDDLE AMERICA												
ACAPULCO, *Mexico*	29 21 8	31 21 1	31 21 0	31 22 1	32 23 36	32 24 325	32 24 231	32 24 236	31 24 353	31 23 170	31 22 30	31 21 10
BALBOA, *Panama*	31 22 34	32 22 16	32 22 14	32 23 73	31 23 198	30 23 203	31 23 176	31 23 200	30 23 197	29 23 271	29 23 260	31 23 133
CHARLOTTE AMALIE, *Virgin Is.*	28 23 50	27 22 41	28 23 49	28 23 63	29 24 105	30 25 67	31 26 71	31 26 112	31 26 132	31 25 139	29 24 131	28 23 69
GUATEMALA CITY, *Guatemala*	23 12 4	25 12 5	27 14 10	28 14 32	29 16 110	27 16 257	26 16 197	26 16 193	26 16 235	24 16 98	23 14 33	22 13 13
GUAYMAS, *Mexico*	23 13 17	24 14 6	26 16 5	29 18 1	31 21 2	34 24 1	34 27 46	35 27 71	35 26 28	32 22 17	28 18 8	23 13 18
HAVANA, *Cuba*	26 18 71	26 18 46	27 19 46	29 21 58	30 22 119	31 23 165	32 24 124	32 24 135	31 24 150	29 23 173	27 21 79	26 19 58
KINGSTON, *Jamaica*	30 19 29	30 19 24	30 20 23	31 21 39	31 22 104	32 23 96	32 23 46	32 23 107	32 23 127	31 23 181	31 22 95	31 21 41
MANAGUA, *Nicaragua*	33 21 2	33 21 3	35 22 4	36 23 3	35 24 136	32 23 237	32 23 132	32 23 121	33 23 213	32 23 315	32 22 42	32 22 10
MÉRIDA, *Mexico*	28 17 30	29 17 23	32 19 18	33 21 20	34 22 81	33 23 142	33 23 132	33 23 142	32 23 173	31 22 97	29 19 33	28 18 33
MEXICO CITY, *Mexico*	19 6 8	21 6 5	24 8 11	25 11 19	26 12 49	24 13 106	23 12 129	23 12 121	23 12 110	21 10 44	20 8 15	19 6 7
MONTERREY, *Mexico*	20 9 18	22 11 23	24 14 16	29 17 29	31 20 40	33 22 68	32 22 62	33 22 76	30 21 151	27 18 78	22 13 26	18 10 20
NASSAU, *Bahamas*	25 18 48	25 18 43	26 19 41	27 21 65	29 22 132	31 23 178	31 24 153	32 24 170	31 24 180	29 23 171	27 21 71	26 19 43
PORT-AU-PRINCE, *Haiti*	31 20 32	31 20 50	32 21 79	32 22 156	32 22 218	33 23 96	34 23 73	34 23 139	33 23 166	32 22 164	31 22 84	31 21 35
PORT-OF-SPAIN, *Trinidad*	29 19 69	30 19 41	31 19 46	31 21 53	32 21 94	31 22 193	31 21 218	31 22 246	31 22 193	31 22 170	31 21 183	30 21 124
SAN JOSÉ, *Costa Rica*	24 14 11	24 14 5	26 15 14	26 17 46	27 17 224	26 17 276	25 17 215	26 16 243	26 16 326	25 16 323	25 16 148	24 14 42
SAN JUAN, *Puerto Rico*	27 21 75	27 21 56	27 21 59	28 22 95	29 23 156	29 24 112	29 24 115	29 24 133	30 24 136	29 24 140	29 23 148	27 22 118
SAN SALVADOR, *El Salvador*	32 16 7	33 16 7	34 17 13	34 18 53	33 19 179	31 19 315	32 18 312	32 19 307	31 19 317	31 18 230	31 17 40	32 16 12
SANTO DOMINGO, *Dom. Rep.*	29 19 57	29 19 43	29 19 49	29 21 77	30 22 179	31 22 154	31 22 155	31 23 162	31 22 173	31 22 164	30 21 111	29 19 63
TEGUCIGALPA, *Honduras*	25 13 9	27 14 4	29 14 8	30 17 32	29 18 151	28 18 159	28 17 82	28 17 87	28 17 185	27 17 135	26 16 38	25 15 12
SOUTH AMERICA												
ANTOFAGASTA, *Chile*	24 17 0	24 17 0	23 16 0	21 14 0	19 13 0	18 11 1	17 11 1	17 11 1	18 12 0	19 13 0	21 14 0	22 16 0
ASUNCIÓN, *Paraguay*	35 22 150	34 22 133	33 21 142	29 18 145	25 14 120	22 12 73	23 12 51	26 14 48	28 16 83	30 17 136	32 18 144	34 21 142
BELÉM, *Brazil*	31 22 351	30 22 412	31 23 441	31 23 370	31 23 282	31 22 164	31 22 154	31 22 122	32 22 129	32 22 105	32 22 101	32 22 202
BOGOTÁ, *Colombia*	19 9 48	20 9 52	19 10 81	19 11 119	19 11 103	18 11 61	18 10 47	18 10 48	19 9 58	19 10 142	19 10 115	19 9 67
BRASÍLIA, *Brazil*	27 18 262	27 18 213	28 18 202	28 17 103	26 13 20	25 11 4	26 11 4	28 13 6	31 16 35	28 18 140	28 19 238	26 18 329
BUENOS AIRES, *Argentina*	29 17 93	28 17 81	26 16 117	22 12 90	18 8 77	14 5 64	14 6 59	16 6 65	18 8 78	21 10 97	24 13 89	28 16 96
CARACAS, *Venezuela*	24 13 41	25 13 27	26 14 22	27 16 20	27 17 36	26 17 52	26 16 53	26 16 53	27 16 48	26 16 47	25 16 50	26 14 58
COM. RIVADAVIA, *Argentina*	26 13 16	25 13 11	22 11 21	18 8 21	13 6 34	11 3 21	11 3 25	12 3 22	14 5 13	19 9 13	22 10 13	24 12 15
CÓRDOBA, *Argentina*	31 16 110	30 16 102	28 14 96	24 11 45	21 7 25	18 3 10	18 3 10	21 4 13	23 7 27	25 11 69	28 13 97	30 16 118
GUAYAQUIL, *Ecuador*	31 21 224	31 22 278	31 22 287	32 22 180	31 20 53	31 20 17	29 19 2	30 18 0	31 19 2	30 20 3	31 20 3	31 21 30
LA PAZ, *Bolivia*	17 6 130	17 6 105	18 6 72	18 4 47	18 3 13	17 1 6	17 1 9	17 2 14	18 3 29	19 4 40	19 6 50	18 6 93
LIMA, *Peru*	28 19 1	28 19 1	28 19 1	27 17 0	23 16 1	20 14 2	19 14 4	19 13 3	20 14 3	22 14 2	23 16 1	26 17 1
MANAUS, *Brazil*	31 24 264	31 24 262	31 24 298	31 24 283	31 24 204	31 24 103	32 24 67	33 24 46	33 24 63	33 24 111	33 24 161	32 24 220
MARACAIBO, *Venezuela*	32 23 5	32 23 5	33 23 6	33 24 39	33 25 65	34 25 55	34 24 25	34 25 53	34 25 76	33 24 119	33 24 55	33 24 22
MONTEVIDEO, *Uruguay*	28 17 95	28 16 100	26 15 111	22 12 83	18 9 76	15 6 74	14 6 86	15 6 84	17 8 90	20 9 98	23 12 78	26 15 84
PARAMARIBO, *Suriname*	29 22 209	29 22 149	29 22 168	30 23 219	30 23 307	30 23 302	31 23 227	32 23 163	33 23 80	33 23 82	32 23 117	30 22 204
PUNTA ARENAS, *Chile*	14 7 35	14 7 28	12 5 39	10 4 41	7 2 42	5 1 32	4 -1 34	6 1 33	8 2 28	11 3 24	12 4 29	14 6 32
QUITO, *Ecuador*	22 8 113	22 8 128	22 8 154	21 8 176	21 8 124	22 7 48	22 7 20	23 7 24	23 7 78	22 8 127	22 7 109	22 8 103
RECIFE, *Brazil*	30 25 62	30 25 102	30 24 197	29 24 252	28 23 301	28 23 302	27 22 254	27 22 156	28 23 78	29 24 36	29 24 29	29 25 40
RIO DE JANEIRO, *Brazil*	29 23 135	29 23 124	28 22 134	27 21 109	25 19 78	24 18 52	24 17 45	24 18 46	24 18 62	25 19 82	26 20 100	28 22 137
SANTIAGO, *Chile*	29 12 3	29 11 3	27 9 5	23 7 13	18 5 64	14 3 84	15 3 76	17 4 56	19 6 30	22 7 15	26 9 8	28 11 5
SÃO PAULO, *Brazil*	27 17 225	28 18 208	27 17 160	26 14 71	23 12 67	22 11 54	22 9 35	23 11 48	23 12 77	24 14 117	26 15 139	27 16 185
VALPARAÍSO, *Chile*	22 13 0	22 13 0	21 12 0	19 11 22	17 10 38	16 9 100	16 8 111	16 8 42	17 9 27	18 10 15	21 11 15	22 12 1
EUROPE												
AJACCIO, *Corsica, France*	13 3 76	14 4 58	16 5 66	18 7 56	21 10 41	25 14 23	27 16 71	28 16 18	26 15 43	22 11 97	18 7 112	15 4 79
AMSTERDAM, *Netherlands*	4 1 79	5 1 44	8 3 89	11 6 39	16 10 50	18 13 60	21 15 73	20 15 60	18 13 80	13 9 104	8 5 76	5 2 72
ATHENS, *Greece*	13 6 48	14 7 41	16 8 41	20 11 23	25 16 18	30 20 7	33 23 5	33 23 8	29 19 10	24 15 53	19 12 55	15 8 62
BARCELONA, *Spain*	13 6 38	14 7 38	16 9 47	18 11 47	21 14 44	25 18 38	28 21 28	28 21 44	25 19 76	21 15 96	16 11 51	13 8 44
BELFAST, *N. Ireland, U.K.*	6 2 83	7 2 55	9 3 59	12 4 51	15 6 56	18 9 65	18 11 79	18 11 78	16 9 82	13 7 85	9 4 75	7 3 84
BELGRADE, *Serbia*	3 -3 42	5 -2 39	11 2 43	18 7 57	23 12 73	26 15 84	28 17 63	28 17 53	24 13 47	18 8 50	11 4 55	5 0 52
BERLIN, *Germany*	2 -3 43	3 -3 38	8 0 38	13 4 41	19 8 49	22 12 64	24 14 71	23 13 62	20 10 44	13 6 44	7 2 46	3 -1 48
BIARRITZ, *France*	11 4 106	12 4 93	15 6 92	16 8 95	18 11 97	22 14 93	23 16 64	24 16 74	22 15 102	19 11 129	15 7 135	12 5 134
BORDEAUX, *France*	9 2 76	11 2 65	15 4 66	17 6 65	20 9 71	24 12 65	25 14 52	26 14 59	23 12 70	18 8 87	13 5 88	9 3 86
BRINDISI, *Italy*	12 6 57	13 7 61	15 8 67	18 11 35	22 14 26	26 18 20	29 21 9	29 21 25	26 18 47	22 15 71	18 11 72	14 8 65
BRUSSELS, *Belgium*	4 -1 82	7 0 51	10 2 81	14 5 53	18 8 74	22 11 74	23 12 58	22 12 42	21 11 69	15 7 85	9 3 61	6 0 68
BUCHAREST, *Romania*	1 -7 44	4 -5 37	10 -1 35	18 5 46	23 10 65	27 14 86	30 16 56	30 15 56	25 11 35	18 6 28	10 2 45	4 -3 42
BUDAPEST, *Hungary*	1 -4 41	4 -2 36	10 2 41	17 7 49	22 11 69	26 15 71	28 16 53	27 16 53	23 12 45	16 7 52	8 3 58	4 -1 49
CAGLIARI, *Sardinia, Italy*	14 7 53	15 7 52	17 9 45	19 11 35	23 14 27	27 18 10	30 21 3	30 21 10	27 19 29	23 15 57	19 11 56	16 9 55
CANDIA, *Crete, Greece*	16 9 94	16 9 76	17 10 41	20 12 23	23 15 18	27 19 3	29 21 1	29 22 3	27 19 18	24 17 43	21 14 69	18 11 102
COPENHAGEN, *Denmark*	2 -2 42	2 -3 25	5 -1 35	10 3 40	16 8 42	19 11 52	22 14 67	21 14 75	18 11 51	12 7 53	7 3 52	4 1 51
DUBLIN, *Ireland*	7 2 64	8 2 51	10 3 52	12 5 49	14 7 56	18 9 55	19 11 65	19 11 77	17 10 62	14 7 73	10 4 69	8 3 69
DURAZZO, *Albania*	11 6 76	12 6 84	13 8 99	17 13 56	22 17 41	25 21 48	28 23 13	28 22 48	24 18 43	20 14 180	14 11 216	12 8 185
EDINBURGH, *Scotland, U.K.*	6 1 55	6 1 41	8 2 47	11 4 39	14 6 50	17 9 50	18 11 64	18 11 69	16 9 63	12 7 62	9 4 63	7 2 61
FLORENCE, *Italy*	9 2 64	11 3 62	14 5 69	19 8 71	23 12 73	27 15 56	30 18 34	30 17 47	26 15 83	20 11 99	14 7 103	11 4 79
GENEVA, *Switzerland*	4 -2 55	6 -1 53	10 2 60	15 5 63	19 9 76	23 13 81	25 15 72	24 14 90	21 12 90	14 7 91	8 3 81	4 0 66
HAMBURG, *Germany*	2 -2 61	3 -2 40	7 -1 52	13 3 47	18 7 55	21 11 74	22 13 81	22 12 79	19 10 68	13 6 62	7 3 65	4 0 71
HELSINKI, *Finland*	-3 -9 46	-4 -9 37	0 -7 35	6 -1 37	14 4 42	19 9 46	22 13 62	20 12 75	15 8 67	8 3 69	3 -1 66	-1 -5 55
LISBON, *Portugal*	14 8 95	15 8 87	17 10 85	20 12 60	21 13 44	25 15 18	27 17 4	28 17 5	26 17 33	22 14 75	17 11 100	15 9 97
LIVERPOOL, *England, U.K.*	7 2 69	7 2 48	9 3 38	11 5 41	14 8 56	17 11 51	19 13 71	18 13 79	16 11 66	13 8 76	9 5 76	7 3 64
LONDON, *England, U.K.*	7 2 62	7 2 36	11 8 50	13 4 43	17 7 45	21 11 46	23 13 46	22 12 44	19 11 43	14 7 73	9 4 45	7 2 59
LUXEMBOURG, *Luxembourg*	3 -1 66	4 -1 54	10 1 55	14 4 53	18 8 66	21 11 65	23 13 70	22 12 69	19 10 62	13 6 70	7 3 71	4 0 74
MADRID, *Spain*	9 2 45	11 2 43	15 5 37	18 7 45	21 10 40	27 15 25	31 17 9	30 17 10	25 14 29	19 10 46	13 5 64	9 2 47
MARSEILLE, *France*	10 2 49	12 2 40	15 5 45	18 8 46	22 11 46	26 15 26	29 17 15	28 17 24	25 15 63	20 10 94	15 6 76	11 3 59

World Temperature and Rainfall

Average daily high and low temperatures and monthly rainfall for selected world locations:

EUROPE	JAN.			FEB.			MARCH			APRIL			MAY			JUNE		
MILAN, *Italy*	5	0	61	8	2	58	13	6	72	18	10	85	23	14	98	27	17	81
MUNICH, *Germany*	1	-5	49	3	-5	43	9	-1	52	14	3	70	18	7	101	21	11	123
NANTES, *France*	8	2	79	9	2	62	13	4	62	15	6	54	19	9	61	22	12	55
NAPLES, *Italy*	12	4	94	13	5	81	15	6	76	18	9	66	22	12	46	26	16	46
NICE, *France*	13	4	77	13	5	73	15	7	73	17	9	64	20	13	49	24	16	37
OSLO, *Norway*	-2	-7	41	-1	-7	31	4	-4	34	10	1	36	16	6	45	20	10	59
PALERMO, *Sicily, Italy*	16	8	44	16	8	35	17	9	30	20	11	29	24	14	14	27	18	9
PALMA DE MALLORCA, *Spain*	14	6	39	15	6	35	17	8	37	19	10	35	22	13	34	26	17	20
PARIS, *France*	6	1	46	7	1	39	12	4	41	16	6	44	20	10	56	23	13	57
PRAGUE, *Czech Rep.*	1	-4	21	3	-2	19	7	1	26	13	4	36	18	9	59	22	13	68
RIGA, *Latvia*	-4	-10	32	-3	-10	24	2	-7	26	10	1	35	16	6	42	21	9	58
ROME, *Italy*	11	5	80	13	5	71	15	7	69	19	10	67	23	13	52	28	17	34
SEVILLE, *Spain*	15	6	56	17	7	74	20	9	84	24	11	58	27	13	33	32	17	23
SOFIA, *Bulgaria*	2	-4	34	4	-3	34	10	1	38	16	5	54	21	10	69	24	14	78
SPLIT, *Croatia*	10	5	80	11	5	65	14	7	65	18	11	62	23	16	62	27	19	48
STOCKHOLM, *Sweden*	-1	-5	31	-1	-5	25	3	-4	26	8	1	29	14	6	34	19	11	44
VALENCIA, *Spain*	15	6	23	16	6	38	18	8	23	20	10	30	23	13	28	26	17	33
VALETTA, *Malta*	14	10	84	15	10	58	16	11	38	18	13	20	22	16	10	26	19	3
VENICE, *Italy*	6	1	51	8	2	53	12	5	61	17	10	71	21	14	81	25	17	84
VIENNA, *Austria*	1	-4	38	3	-3	36	8	1	46	15	6	51	19	10	71	23	14	69
WARSAW, *Poland*	0	-6	28	0	-6	26	6	-2	31	12	3	37	20	9	50	23	12	66
ZÜRICH, *Switzerland*	2	-3	61	5	-2	61	10	1	68	15	4	85	19	8	101	23	12	127
ASIA																		
ADEN, *Yemen*	27	23	8	27	23	7	29	24	8	31	26	4	34	28	3	35	29	1
ALMATY, *Kazakhstan*	-5	-14	33	-3	13	23	4	-6	56	13	3	102	20	10	94	24	14	66
ANKARA, *Turkey*	4	-4	49	6	-3	52	11	-1	45	17	4	44	23	9	56	26	12	37
ARKHANGEL'SK, *Russia*	-12	-20	30	-10	-18	28	-4	-13	28	5	-4	18	12	2	33	17	6	48
BAGHDAD, *Iraq*	16	4	27	18	6	28	22	9	27	29	14	19	36	19	7	41	23	0
BALIKPAPAN, *Indonesia*	29	23	243	30	23	221	30	23	249	29	23	226	29	23	258	29	23	252
BANGKOK, *Thailand*	32	20	11	33	22	28	34	24	31	35	25	72	34	25	189	33	24	152
BEIJING, *China*	2	-9	4	5	-7	5	12	-1	8	20	7	18	27	13	33	31	18	78
BEIRUT, *Lebanon*	17	11	187	17	11	151	19	12	96	22	14	51	26	18	19	28	21	2
BRUNEI	30	24	371	30	24	193	31	24	198	32	24	249	32	24	277	31	24	241
CHENNAI (MADRAS), *India*	29	19	29	31	20	9	33	22	9	35	26	17	38	28	44	38	27	52
CHONGQING, *China*	9	5	18	13	7	21	18	11	38	23	16	94	27	19	148	29	22	174
COLOMBO, *Sri Lanka*	30	22	84	31	22	64	31	23	114	31	24	255	31	26	335	29	25	190
DAMASCUS, *Syria*	12	2	39	14	4	32	18	6	23	24	9	13	29	13	5	33	16	1
DAVAO, *Philippines*	31	22	117	32	22	110	32	22	109	33	22	149	32	23	223	31	23	205
DHAKA, *Bangladesh*	26	13	8	28	15	21	32	20	58	33	23	116	33	24	267	32	26	358
HANOI, *Vietnam*	20	13	20	21	14	30	23	17	64	28	21	91	32	23	104	33	26	284
HO CHI MINH CITY, *Vietnam*	32	21	14	33	22	4	34	23	9	35	24	51	33	24	213	32	24	309
HONG KONG, *China*	18	13	27	17	13	44	19	16	75	24	19	140	28	23	298	29	26	399
IRKUTSK, *Russia*	-16	-26	13	-12	-25	10	-4	-17	8	6	-7	15	13	1	33	20	7	56
ISTANBUL, *Turkey*	8	3	91	9	2	69	11	3	62	16	7	42	21	12	30	25	16	28
JAKARTA, *Indonesia*	29	23	342	29	23	302	30	23	210	31	24	135	31	24	108	31	23	90
JEDDAH, *Saudi Arabia*	29	19	5	29	18	1	29	19	1	33	21	1	35	23	1	36	24	0
JERUSALEM, *Israel*	13	5	140	13	6	111	18	8	116	23	10	17	27	14	6	29	16	0
KABUL, *Afghanistan*	2	-8	33	4	-6	54	12	1	70	19	6	66	26	11	21	31	13	1
KARACHI, *Pakistan*	25	13	7	26	14	10	29	19	10	32	23	3	34	26	0	34	28	10
KATHMANDU, *Nepal*	18	2	17	19	4	15	25	7	30	28	12	37	30	16	102	29	19	201
KOLKATA (CALCUTTA), *India*	27	13	12	29	15	25	34	21	32	36	24	53	36	25	129	33	26	291
KUNMING, *China*	16	3	11	18	4	14	21	7	17	24	11	20	26	14	90	25	17	175
LAHORE, *Pakistan*	21	4	25	22	7	24	28	12	27	35	17	15	40	22	17	41	26	39
LHASA, *China*	7	-10	0	9	-7	3	12	-2	4	16	1	6	19	5	24	24	9	72
MANAMA, *Bahrain*	30	14	14	21	15	16	24	17	11	29	21	8	33	26	1	36	28	0
MANDALAY, *Myanmar*	28	13	2	31	15	13	36	19	7	38	25	35	37	26	142	34	26	124
MANILA, *Philippines*	30	21	21	31	21	10	33	22	15	34	23	30	34	24	123	33	24	262
MOSCOW, *Russia*	-9	-16	38	-6	-14	36	0	-8	28	10	1	46	19	8	56	21	11	74
MUMBAI (BOMBAY), *India*	28	19	3	28	19	1	30	22	1	32	24	2	33	27	14	32	26	518
MUSCAT, *Oman*	25	19	28	25	19	18	28	22	10	32	26	10	37	30	1	38	31	3
NAGASAKI, *Japan*	9	2	75	10	2	87	14	5	124	19	10	190	23	14	191	26	18	326
NEW DELHI, *India*	21	7	23	24	9	20	31	14	15	36	20	10	41	26	15	39	28	68
NICOSIA, *Cyprus*	15	5	70	16	5	50	19	7	35	24	10	21	29	14	26	34	18	9
ODESA, *Ukraine*	0	-6	25	2	-4	18	5	-1	18	12	6	28	19	12	28	23	16	48
PHNOM PENH, *Cambodia*	31	21	7	32	22	9	34	23	32	34	24	73	33	24	149	33	24	149
PONTIANAK, *Indonesia*	31	23	275	32	23	213	32	23	242	33	23	280	33	23	279	32	23	228
RIYADH, *Saudi Arabia*	21	8	14	23	9	10	28	13	30	32	18	30	38	22	13	42	25	0
ST. PETERSBURG, *Russia*	-7	-13	25	-5	-12	23	0	-8	23	8	4	25	15	6	41	20	11	51
SANDAKAN, *Malaysia*	29	23	454	29	23	271	30	23	200	31	23	118	32	23	153	32	23	196
SAPPORO, *Japan*	-2	-12	100	-1	-11	79	2	-7	70	11	0	61	16	4	59	21	10	65
SEOUL, *South Korea*	0	-9	21	3	-7	28	8	-2	49	17	5	105	22	11	88	27	16	151
SHANGHAI, *China*	8	1	47	8	1	61	13	4	85	19	10	95	25	15	104	28	19	174
SINGAPORE, *Singapore*	30	23	239	31	23	165	31	24	174	31	24	166	32	24	171	31	24	163
TAIPEI, *China*	19	12	95	18	12	141	21	14	162	25	17	167	28	21	209	32	23	280
T'BILISI, *Georgia*	6	-2	16	7	-1	21	12	2	30	18	7	52	23	12	83	27	16	73
TEHRAN, *Iran*	7	-3	42	10	0	37	15	4	39	22	9	33	28	14	15	34	19	3
TEL AVIV-YAFO, *Israel*	17	9	165	18	9	64	19	10	58	23	12	13	27	16	3	29	18	0
TOKYO, *Japan*	8	-2	50	9	-1	72	12	2	106	17	8	129	22	12	144	24	17	176
ULAANBAATAR, *Mongolia*	-19	-32	1	-13	-29	1	-4	-22	3	7	-8	5	13	-2	8	21	7	25
VIENTIANE, *Laos*	28	14	7	30	17	18	33	19	41	34	23	88	32	23	212	32	24	216
VLADIVOSTOK, *Russia*	-11	-18	8	-6	-14	10	1	-7	18	8	1	30	13	6	53	17	11	74

EUROPE	JULY			AUG.			SEPT.			OCT.			NOV.			DEC.		
MILAN, *Italy*	29	20	68	28	19	81	24	16	82	17	11	116	10	6	106	6	2	75
MUNICH, *Germany*	23	13	127	23	12	112	20	9	83	13	4	62	7	0	54	2	-4	51
NANTES, *France*	24	14	50	24	13	54	21	12	70	16	8	89	11	5	91	8	3	86
NAPLES, *Italy*	29	18	15	29	18	18	26	16	71	22	12	130	17	9	114	14	6	137
NICE, *France*	27	18	19	27	18	32	25	16	65	21	12	111	17	8	117	13	5	88
OSLO, *Norway*	22	13	75	21	12	86	16	8	72	9	3	71	3	-1	57	0	-4	49
PALERMO, *Sicily, Italy*	30	21	2	30	21	8	28	19	28	25	16	59	21	12	66	18	10	68
PALMA DE MALLORCA, *Spain*	29	20	8	29	20	18	27	18	52	23	14	77	18	10	54	15	8	54
PARIS, *France*	25	15	57	24	14	55	21	12	53	16	8	57	10	5	54	7	2	49
PRAGUE, *Czech Rep.*	23	14	67	23	14	62	18	11	41	12	7	30	5	2	27	1	-2	23
RIGA, *Latvia*	22	11	72	21	11	68	17	8	66	11	4	54	4	-1	52	-2	-7	39
ROME, *Italy*	30	20	16	30	19	24	26	17	69	22	13	113	16	9	111	13	6	97
SEVILLE, *Spain*	36	20	3	36	20	3	32	18	28	26	14	66	20	10	94	16	7	71
SOFIA, *Bulgaria*	27	16	56	26	15	43	22	11	40	17	8	35	9	3	52	4	-2	44
SPLIT, *Croatia*	30	22	28	30	22	43	26	19	66	20	14	87	15	10	111	12	7	113
STOCKHOLM, *Sweden*	22	14	64	20	13	66	15	9	49	9	5	51	5	1	44	2	-2	39
VALENCIA, *Spain*	29	20	10	29	20	13	27	18	56	23	13	41	19	10	64	16	7	33
VALETTA, *Malta*	29	22	1	29	23	5	27	22	33	24	19	69	20	16	91	16	12	99
VENICE, *Italy*	27	19	66	27	18	66	24	16	66	19	11	94	12	7	89	8	3	66
VIENNA, *Austria*	25	15	76	24	15	69	20	11	51	14	7	25	7	3	48	3	-1	46
WARSAW, *Poland*	24	15	77	23	14	72	19	10	47	13	5	41	6	1	38	2	-3	35
ZÜRICH, *Switzerland*	25	14	128	24	13	124	20	11	98	14	6	83	7	2	71	3	-2	72
ASIA																		
ADEN, *Yemen*	34	28	2	33	27	3	34	28	4	32	26	2	29	24	2	27	23	4
ALMATY, *Kazakhstan*	27	16	36	27	14	30	22	8	25	13	2	51	4	-5	48	-2	-9	33
ANKARA, *Turkey*	30	15	13	31	15	8	26	11	28	21	7	21	14	3	28	6	-2	63
ARKHANGEL'SK, *Russia*	20	10	66	19	10	69	12	5	56	4	-1	48	-2	-7	41	-8	-15	33
BAGHDAD, *Iraq*	43	24	0	43	24	0	40	21	0	33	16	3	25	11	20	18	6	26
BALIKPAPAN, *Indonesia*	28	23	259	29	23	257	29	23	201	29	23	186	29	23	176	29	23	245
BANGKOK, *Thailand*	32	24	158	32	24	187	32	24	320	31	24	231	31	22	57	31	20	9
BEIJING, *China*	32	22	224	31	21	170	27	14	58	21	7	18	10	-1	9	3	-7	3
BEIRUT, *Lebanon*	31	23	0	32	23	0	30	23	6	27	21	48	23	16	119	18	13	176
BRUNEI	31	25	229	31	24	185	31	24	300	31	24	368	31	24	386	30	24	330
CHENNAI (MADRAS), *India*	36	26	99	35	26	124	34	25	125	32	24	285	29	22	345	29	21	138
CHONGQING, *China*	34	24	151	35	25	128	28	22	144	22	16	103	16	12	49	13	8	23
COLOMBO, *Sri Lanka*	29	25	129	29	25	96	29	25	158	29	24	353	29	23	308	29	22	152
DAMASCUS, *Syria*	36	18	0	37	18	0	33	16	0	27	12	9	19	8	26	13	4	42
DAVAO, *Philippines*	31	22	171	31	22	161	32	22	177	32	22	184	32	22	139	31	22	139
DHAKA, *Bangladesh*	31	26	399	31	26	317	32	26	256	31	24	164	29	19	30	26	14	6
HANOI, *Vietnam*	33	26	302	32	26	386	31	24	254	29	22	89	26	18	66	22	15	71
HO CHI MINH CITY, *Vietnam*	31	24	295	31	24	271	31	23	342	31	23	261	31	23	119	31	22	47
HONG KONG, *China*	31	26	371	31	26	377	29	25	297	27	23	119	23	18	38	20	15	25
IRKUTSK, *Russia*	21	10	79	20	9	71	14	2	43	5	-6	18	-7	-17	15	-16	-24	15
ISTANBUL, *Turkey*	28	18	24	28	19	31	24	16	48	20	13	66	15	9	92	11	5	114
JAKARTA, *Indonesia*	31	23	59	31	23	48	31	23	69	31	23	106	30	23	139	29	23	208
JEDDAH, *Saudi Arabia*	37	23	1	37	27	1	36	25	1	35	23	1	33	22	25	30	19	30
JERUSALEM, *Israel*	31	17	0	31	18	0	29	17	0	27	15	11	21	12	68	15	7	129
KABUL, *Afghanistan*	33	16	5	33	15	1	29	11	2	23	6	4	17	1	11	8	-3	21
KARACHI, *Pakistan*	33	27	90	31	26	58	31	25	27	33	22	3	31	18	3	27	14	5
KATHMANDU, *Nepal*	29	20	375	28	20	325	28	19	189	27	13	56	23	7	2	19	3	10
KOLKATA (CALCUTTA), *India*	32	26	329	32	26	338	32	26	266	32	23	131	29	18	21	26	13	7
KUNMING, *China*	25	17	205	25	17	203	24	15	126	21	12	78	18	7	40	17	3	13
LAHORE, *Pakistan*	38	27	155	36	26	135	36	23	63	35	15	10	28	8	3	23	4	14
LHASA, *China*	23	9	132	22	9	128	21	7	58	17	1	9	13	-5	1	9	-9	1
MANAMA, *Bahrain*	37	29	0	38	29	0	36	27	0	32	24	0	28	21	7	22	16	17
MANDALAY, *Myanmar*	34	26	83	33	25	113	33	24	155	32	23	125	29	19	45	27	14	10
MANILA, *Philippines*	31	24	423	31	24	421	31	24	353	31	23	197	31	22	135	30	21	65
MOSCOW, *Russia*	23	13	76	22	12	74	16	7	48	9	3	69	2	-3	43	-5	-10	41
MUMBAI (BOMBAY), *India*	29	25	647	29	24	384	29	24	276	32	24	55	32	23	15	31	21	2
MUSCAT, *Oman*	36	31	1	33	29	1	34	28	0	34	27	3	30	23	10	26	20	18
NAGASAKI, *Japan*	29	23	284	31	23	187	27	20	236	22	14	108	17	9	89	12	4	80
NEW DELHI, *India*	36	27	200	34	26	200	34	24	123	34	18	19	29	11	3	23	8	10
NICOSIA, *Cyprus*	37	21	1	37	21	2	33	18	6	28	14	23	22	10	41	17	7	74
ODESA, *Ukraine*	26	18	41	26	18	36	21	14	28	16	9	36	10	4	28	4	-2	28
PHNOM PENH, *Cambodia*	32	24	151	32	24	157	31	24	231	31	24	259	30	23	129	30	22	38
PONTIANAK, *Indonesia*	32	23	178	32	23	206	32	23	245	32	23	356	31	23	385	31	23	321
RIYADH, *Saudi Arabia*	42	26	0	42	24	0	39	22	0	34	16	1	29	13	5	21	9	11
ST. PETERSBURG, *Russia*	21	13	64	20	13	71	15	9	53	9	4	46	2	-2	36	-3	-8	30
SANDAKAN, *Malaysia*	32	23	185	32	23	205	32	23	240	31	23	263	31	23	356	30	23	470
SAPPORO, *Japan*	24	14	86	26	16	117	22	11	136	16	4	114	8	-2	106	1	-8	102
SEOUL, *South Korea*	29	21	384	31	22	263	26	15	160	19	7	49	11	0	43	3	-7	24
SHANGHAI, *China*	32	23	145	32	23	137	28	19	138	23	14	69	17	7	52	12	2	37
SINGAPORE, *Singapore*	31	24	150	31	24	171	31	24	164	31	23	191	31	23	250	31	23	269
TAIPEI, *China*	33	24	248	33	24	277	31	23	201	27	19	112	24	17	76	21	14	76
T'BILISI, *Georgia*	31	19	49	31	19	40	26	15	44	20	9	39	13	4	32	8	0	21
TEHRAN, *Iran*	37	22	2	36	22	2	32	18	2	24	12	9	17	6	24	11	1	32
TEL AVIV-YAFO, *Israel*	31	21	0	31	21	0	30	20	1	29	18	14	25	15	85	19	11	144
TOKYO, *Japan*	28	21	136	30	22	149	26	19	216	21	13	194	16	6	96	11	1	54
ULAANBAATAR, *Mongolia*	22	11	74	21	8	48	14	2	20	6	-8	5	-6	-20	5	-16	-28	3
VIENTIANE, *Laos*	31	24	209	31	24	254	31	24	244	31	21	81	29	18	16	28	16	5
VLADIVOSTOK, *Russia*	22	16	84	24	18	119	20	13	109	13	5	48	2	-4	30	-7	-13	15

RED FIGURES: Average daily high temperature (°C)

BLUE FIGURES: Average daily low temperature (°C)

BLACK FIGURES: Average monthly rainfall (mm)
1 millimeter = 0.039 inches

	JAN.			FEB.			MARCH			APRIL			MAY			JUNE			JULY			AUG.			SEPT.			OCT.			NOV.			DEC.		
ASIA																																				
WUHAN, *China*	8	1	41	9	2	57	14	6	92	21	13	136	26	18	165	31	23	212	34	26	165	34	26	114	29	21	73	23	16	74	17	9	49	11	3	30
YAKUTSK, *Russia*	-43	-47	8	-33	-40	5	-18	-29	3	-3	-14	8	9	-1	10	19	9	28	23	12	41	19	9	33	10	1	28	-5	-12	13	-26	-31	10	-39	-43	8
YANGON (RANGOON), *Myanmar*	32	18	4	33	19	4	36	22	17	36	24	47	33	25	307	30	24	478	29	24	535	29	24	511	30	24	368	31	24	183	31	23	62	31	19	11
YEKATERINBURG, *Russia*	-14	-21	8	-10	-17	10	-4	-12	5	6	-3	8	14	4	15	18	9	48	21	12	38	18	10	53	12	5	46	3	-2	23	-7	-12	10	-12	-18	8
AFRICA																																				
ABIDJAN, *Côte d'Ivoire*	31	23	22	32	24	47	32	24	110	32	24	142	31	24	309	29	23	543	28	23	238	28	22	36	28	23	74	29	23	172	31	23	168	31	23	85
ACCRA, *Ghana*	31	23	15	31	24	29	31	24	57	31	24	90	31	24	136	29	23	199	27	23	50	27	22	19	27	23	43	29	23	64	31	24	34	31	24	20
ADDIS ABABA, *Ethiopia*	24	6	17	24	8	38	25	9	68	25	10	86	25	10	86	23	9	132	21	10	268	21	10	281	22	9	186	24	7	28	23	6	11	23	5	10
ALEXANDRIA, *Egypt*	18	11	52	19	11	28	21	13	13	23	15	4	26	18	1	28	21	0	29	23	0	31	23	0	30	23	1	28	20	8	25	17	35	21	13	55
ALGIERS, *Algeria*	15	9	93	16	9	73	17	11	67	20	13	52	23	15	34	26	18	14	28	21	2	29	22	5	27	21	33	23	17	77	19	13	96	16	11	114
ANTANANARIVO, *Madagascar*	26	16	287	26	16	262	26	16	194	24	14	57	23	12	18	21	10	9	20	9	8	21	9	10	23	11	16	27	12	61	27	14	153	27	16	290
ASMARA, *Eritrea*	23	7	0	24	8	0	25	9	1	26	11	7	26	12	23	26	12	48	22	12	114	22	12	123	23	13	49	22	12	4	22	10	3	22	9	0
BAMAKO, *Mali*	33	16	0	36	19	0	39	22	3	39	24	19	39	24	59	34	23	131	32	22	229	31	22	307	32	22	198	34	22	63	34	18	7	33	17	0
BANGUI, *Central African Rep.*	32	20	20	34	21	39	33	22	107	33	22	133	32	21	163	31	21	143	29	21	181	29	21	225	31	21	190	31	21	202	31	20	93	32	19	29
BEIRA, *Mozambique*	32	24	267	32	24	259	31	23	263	30	22	117	28	18	67	26	16	40	25	16	34	26	17	33	28	18	25	31	22	34	31	22	121	31	23	243
BENGHAZI, *Libya*	17	10	66	18	11	41	21	12	20	23	14	5	26	17	3	28	20	1	29	22	1	29	22	1	28	21	3	27	19	18	23	16	46	19	12	66
BUJUMBURA, *Burundi*	29	20	97	29	20	97	29	20	126	29	20	129	29	20	64	29	19	11	30	19	3	30	19	17	31	20	43	31	20	62	29	20	98	29	20	100
CAIRO, *Egypt*	18	8	5	21	9	4	24	11	4	28	14	2	33	17	1	35	20	0	36	21	0	35	22	0	32	20	0	30	18	1	26	14	3	20	10	6
CAPE TOWN, *South Africa*	26	16	16	26	16	15	25	14	22	22	12	50	19	9	92	18	8	105	17	7	91	18	8	83	18	9	54	21	11	40	23	13	24	24	14	19
CASABLANCA, *Morocco*	17	7	57	18	8	53	19	9	51	21	11	38	22	13	21	24	16	6	26	18	0	27	19	1	26	17	6	24	14	34	21	11	65	18	8	73
CONAKRY, *Guinea*	31	22	1	31	23	1	32	23	6	32	23	21	32	24	141	30	23	503	28	22	1210	28	22	1016	29	23	664	31	23	318	31	24	106	31	23	14
DAKAR, *Senegal*	26	18	1	27	17	1	27	18	0	27	18	0	29	20	1	31	23	15	31	24	75	31	24	215	32	24	146	32	24	42	30	23	3	27	19	4
DAR ES SALAAM, *Tanzania*	31	25	66	31	25	66	31	24	130	30	23	290	29	22	188	29	20	33	28	19	31	28	19	30	28	19	30	29	21	41	30	22	74	31	24	91
DURBAN, *South Africa*	27	21	119	27	21	126	27	20	132	26	18	84	24	14	56	23	12	34	22	11	35	22	13	49	23	15	73	24	17	110	25	18	118	26	19	120
HARARE, *Zimbabwe*	26	16	190	26	16	177	26	14	107	26	13	33	23	9	10	21	7	3	21	7	1	23	8	2	26	12	7	28	14	32	27	16	93	26	16	173
JOHANNESBURG, *South Africa*	26	14	150	25	14	129	24	13	110	22	10	48	19	6	24	17	4	6	17	4	10	20	6	10	23	9	25	25	12	65	25	13	126	26	14	141
KAMPALA, *Uganda*	28	18	58	28	18	68	27	18	128	26	18	185	26	17	134	25	17	71	25	17	55	26	16	87	27	17	100	27	17	119	27	17	142	27	17	95
KHARTOUM, *Sudan*	32	15	0	34	16	0	38	19	0	41	22	0	42	25	4	41	26	7	38	25	49	37	24	69	39	25	21	40	24	5	36	20	0	33	17	0
KINSHASA, *D.R.C.*	31	21	138	31	22	148	32	22	184	32	22	220	31	22	145	29	19	5	27	18	3	29	18	4	31	20	40	31	21	133	31	22	235	30	21	156
KISANGANI, *D.R.C.*	31	21	97	31	21	107	31	21	172	31	21	190	31	21	162	30	21	128	29	19	114	28	20	178	29	20	164	30	20	233	29	20	207	30	20	105
LAGOS, *Nigeria*	31	23	27	32	25	44	32	26	98	32	25	146	31	24	252	29	23	414	28	23	253	28	23	69	28	23	153	29	23	197	31	24	66	31	24	25
LIBREVILLE, *Gabon*	31	23	164	31	22	137	32	23	248	32	23	232	31	22	181	29	21	24	28	20	3	29	21	6	29	22	69	30	22	332	30	22	378	31	22	197
LIVINGSTONE, *Zambia*	29	19	175	29	19	160	29	18	95	30	15	25	28	11	5	25	7	1	25	7	0	28	10	0	32	15	2	34	19	26	33	19	78	31	19	176
LUANDA, *Angola*	28	23	34	29	24	35	30	24	90	29	24	127	28	23	18	25	20	0	23	18	0	23	18	1	24	19	2	26	22	6	28	23	32	28	23	23
LUBUMBASHI, *D.R.C.*	28	16	253	28	17	256	28	16	210	28	14	51	27	10	4	26	7	1	26	6	0	28	8	0	32	11	6	33	14	31	31	16	150	28	17	272
LUSAKA, *Zambia*	26	17	213	26	17	172	26	17	104	26	15	22	25	12	3	23	10	0	23	9	0	25	12	0	29	15	1	31	18	14	29	18	86	27	17	200
LUXOR, *Egypt*	23	6	0	26	7	0	30	10	0	35	15	0	40	21	0	41	21	0	42	23	0	41	23	0	39	22	0	37	18	1	31	12	0	26	7	0
MAPUTO, *Mozambique*	30	22	153	31	22	134	29	21	99	28	19	52	27	16	29	25	13	18	24	13	15	26	14	13	27	16	32	28	18	51	28	19	78	29	21	94
MARRAKECH, *Morocco*	18	4	27	20	6	31	23	9	36	26	11	32	29	14	17	33	17	7	38	19	2	38	20	3	33	17	7	28	14	20	23	9	37	19	6	28
MOGADISHU, *Somalia*	30	23	0	30	23	0	31	24	8	32	26	58	32	25	59	29	23	78	28	23	67	28	23	42	29	23	21	30	24	30	31	24	40	30	24	9
MONROVIA, *Liberia*	30	23	5	29	23	3	31	23	112	31	23	297	30	22	340	27	23	917	27	22	615	27	23	472	27	22	759	28	22	640	29	23	208	30	23	74
NAIROBI, *Kenya*	25	12	45	26	13	43	25	14	73	24	14	160	22	13	119	21	12	30	21	11	13	21	11	13	24	11	26	24	13	42	23	13	121	23	13	77
N'DJAMENA, *Chad*	34	14	0	37	16	0	40	21	0	42	23	8	40	25	31	38	24	62	33	22	150	31	22	215	33	22	91	36	21	22	36	17	0	33	14	0
NIAMEY, *Niger*	34	14	0	37	18	0	41	22	3	42	25	6	41	27	35	38	25	75	34	23	143	32	23	187	34	23	90	38	23	16	38	18	1	34	15	0
NOUAKCHOTT, *Mauritania*	29	14	1	31	15	3	32	17	1	32	18	1	34	21	1	33	23	3	32	23	13	32	24	104	34	24	23	33	22	10	32	18	3	28	13	1
TIMBUKTU, *Mali*	31	13	0	34	14	0	38	19	0	42	22	1	43	26	4	43	27	19	39	25	62	36	24	79	39	24	33	40	23	3	37	18	0	32	13	0
TRIPOLI, *Libya*	16	8	69	17	9	40	19	11	27	22	14	13	24	16	5	27	19	1	29	22	0	30	22	1	29	22	11	27	18	38	23	14	60	18	9	81
TUNIS, *Tunisia*	14	6	62	16	7	52	18	8	46	21	11	38	24	13	22	29	17	10	32	20	3	33	21	7	31	19	32	25	15	55	20	11	54	16	7	63
WADI HALFA, *Sudan*	24	9	0	27	10	0	31	14	0	36	18	0	40	22	1	41	24	0	41	25	1	41	25	0	40	24	0	37	21	0	30	15	0	25	11	0
YAOUNDÉ, *Cameroon*	29	19	26	29	19	55	29	19	140	29	19	193	28	19	216	27	19	163	27	19	62	27	18	80	27	19	216	27	18	292	28	19	120	28	19	28
ZANZIBAR, *Tanzania*	32	24	75	33	24	61	33	25	150	30	25	350	29	24	251	28	23	54	28	22	44	28	22	39	29	22	48	30	23	86	32	24	201	32	24	145
ZOMBA, *Malawi*	27	18	299	27	18	269	26	18	230	26	17	85	24	14	23	22	12	13	22	12	8	24	13	8	27	15	8	29	18	29	29	19	124	27	18	281
ATLANTIC ISLANDS																																				
ASCENSION ISLAND	29	23	4	31	23	8	31	24	23	31	24	27	31	23	10	29	23	14	29	22	12	28	22	10	28	22	8	28	22	7	28	22	4	29	22	3
FALKLAND ISLANDS	13	6	71	13	5	58	12	4	64	9	3	66	7	1	66	5	-1	53	4	-1	51	5	-1	51	7	1	38	9	2	41	11	3	51	12	4	71
FUNCHAL, *Madeira Is.*	19	13	87	18	13	88	19	13	79	19	14	43	21	16	22	22	17	9	24	19	2	24	19	3	24	19	27	23	18	85	22	16	106	19	14	87
HAMILTON, *Bermuda Is.*	20	14	112	20	14	119	20	14	122	22	15	104	24	18	117	27	21	112	29	23	114	30	23	137	29	22	132	26	21	147	23	17	127	21	16	119
LAS PALMAS, *Canary Is.*	21	14	28	22	14	21	22	15	15	22	16	10	23	17	3	24	18	1	25	19	1	26	21	0	26	21	6	26	19	18	24	18	37	22	16	32
NUUK, *Greenland*	-7	-12	36	-7	-13	43	-4	-11	41	-1	-7	30	4	-2	43	8	1	36	11	3	56	11	3	79	6	1	84	2	-3	64	-2	-7	48	-5	-10	38
PONTA DELGADA, *Azores*	17	12	105	17	11	91	17	12	87	18	12	62	20	13	57	22	15	36	25	17	25	26	18	34	25	17	75	22	16	97	20	14	108	18	12	98
PRAIA, *Cape Verde*	25	20	1	25	19	2	26	20	0	26	21	0	27	21	0	28	22	0	28	24	7	29	24	63	29	25	88	29	24	44	28	23	15	26	22	5
REYKJAVÍK, *Iceland*	2	-2	86	3	-2	75	4	-1	76	6	1	56	10	4	42	12	7	45	14	9	51	14	8	62	11	6	71	7	3	88	4	0	83	2	-2	84
THULE, *Greenland*	-17	-27	7	-20	-29	8	-19	-28	4	-13	-23	4	-2	-9	5	5	-1	6	8	2	14	6	1	17	1	-6	13	-5	-13	11	-11	-19	11	-18	-27	5
TRISTAN DA CUNHA	19	15	103	20	16	110	19	14	133	18	14	137	16	12	153	14	11	153	14	10	54	13	9	162	13	9	157	15	11	148	16	12	124	18	14	131
AUSTRALIA and PACIFIC ISLANDS																																				
APIA, *Samoa*	30	24	437	29	24	360	30	23	356	30	24	236	29	23	174	29	23	135	29	23	100	29	24	111	29	23	144	29	24	206	30	23	259	29	23	374
AUCKLAND, *New Zealand*	23	16	70	23	16	86	22	15	77	19	13	96	17	11	115	14	9	126	13	8	131	14	8	112	16	9	94	17	11	93	19	12	82	21	14	78
DARWIN, *Australia*	32	25	396	32	25	331	33	25	282	33	24	97	33	23	18	31	21	3	31	19	1	32	21	4	33	23	15	34	25	60	34	26	130	33	26	239
DUNEDIN, *New Zealand*	19	10	81	19	10	70	17	9	78	15	7	75	12	5	78	9	4	78	9	3	70	11	3	61	13	5	61	15	6	70	17	7	79	18	9	81
GALÁPAGOS IS., *Ecuador*	30	22	20	30	24	36	31	24	28	31	24	18	30	23	1	28	22	1	27	21	1	27	19	1	27	19	1	27	19	1	27	20	1	28	21	1
GUAM, *Mariana Is.*	29	24	138	29	23	116	29	24	121	31	24	108	31	25	164	31	25	150	30	24	274	30	24	368	30	24	374	30	24	334	30	25	231	29	24	160
HOBART, *Tasmania*	22	12	51	22	12	38	20	11	46	17	9	51	14	7	46	12	5	51	11	4	51	13	5	49	15	6	47	17	8	60	19	9	52	21	11	57
MELBOURNE, *Australia*	26	14	48	26	14	47	24	13	52	20	11	57	17	8	58	14	7	49	13	6	49	15	6	50	17	8	59	19	9	67	22	11	60	24	12	59
NAHA, *Okinawa*	19	13	125	19	13	126	21	15	159	24	18	165	27	20	252	29	24	280	32	25	178	31	25	270	31	24	175	27	21	165	24	18	133	21	14	111
NOUMÉA, *New Caledonia*	30	22	111	29	23	130	29	22	155	28	21	121	26	19	106	25	18	107	24	17	91	24	16	73	26	17	56	27	18	53	28	20	55	30	21	77
PAPEETE, *Tahiti*	32	22	335	32	22	292	32	22	165	32	22	173	31	21	124	30	21	81	30	20	66	30	20	48	30	21	58	31	21	86	31	22	165	31	22	302
PERTH, *Australia*	29	17	9	29	17	13	27	16	19	24	14	45	21	12	122	18	10	182	17	9	174	18	9	136	19	10	80	21	12	53	24	14	21	27	16	13
PORT MORESBY, *P.N.G.*	32	24	179	31	24	196	31	24	190	31	24	120	30	24	65	29	23	39	28	23	27	28	23	26	29	23	33	30	24	35	31	24	56	32	24	121
SUVA, *Fiji Islands*	30	23	305	30	23	293	30	23	367	29	23	342	28	22	261	27	21	166	26	20	142	26	20	184	27	21	200	27	21	217	28	22	266	29	23	296
SYDNEY, *Australia*	26	18	103	26	18	111	24	17	131	22	14	130	19	11	123	16	9	129	16	8	103	17	9	80	19	11	69	22	13	83	23	16	81	25	17	78
WELLINGTON, *New Zealand*	21	13	79	21	13	80	19	12	85	17	11	98	14	8	121	13	7	124	12	6	139	12	6	121	14	8	99	16	9	105	17	10	88	19	12	90

NOTES ON MAJOR CITY DATA

The population figures in the following list are from *World Urbanization Prospects: the 2007 Revision*, prepared by the United Nations. All figures are rounded to the nearest thousand. The list shows urban agglomerations with at least 1,000,000 inhabitants in the year 2007. An "urban agglomeration" is a contiguous territory with an urban level of population density; it includes one or more cities or towns and adjacent thickly settled areas. Thus, its geographic extent roughly coincides with the limits of a built-up urban area as seen from on high. Since an urban agglomeration is basically a metropolitan area, the population figure given for each area on the list will naturally be greater than the city-proper population figure cited in many other publications.

It is difficult to compare city populations because definitions of cities and metropolitan areas, as well as the availability of statistics, vary widely among countries. Also, the names given to metropolitan areas and the regions that comprise them may vary. As a result, some

of the urban agglomeration names and population figures used in this atlas differ from names and figures given for the same general areas included on lists in other publications.

Spellings may vary, too. The UN list sometimes uses spellings that do not agree with ones used on National Geographic maps. In such cases, we have listed the place-names as they appear in the *Family Reference Atlas*. We did not change a UN spelling if we included it in the atlas as a parenthetical name or used it as a conventional name on world or physical maps.

Some of the Chinese city names in the following list do not appear on maps in this atlas because of space limitations due to the combination of map scale and the high density of large cities in that country. Populations used to classify the cities as shown on the maps in this atlas are city-proper population figures, which may be much smaller than the urban agglomeration figure.

CITY	COUNTRY	POPULATION
ABIDJAN	Côte d'Ivoire	3,802,000
ABUJA	Nigeria	1,576,000
ACCRA	Ghana	2,121,000
ADANA	Turkey	1,293,000
ADDIS ABABA	Ethiopia	3,100,000
ADELAIDE	Australia	1,145,000
AGRA	India	1,592,000
AHMADABAD	India	5,375,000
ALEXANDRIA	Egypt	4,165,000
ALGIERS	Algeria	3,354,000
ALLAHABAD	India	1,201,000
ALMATY	Kazakhstan	1,209,000
AMMAN	Jordan	1,060,000
AMRITSAR	India	1,212,000
AMSTERDAM	Netherlands	1,031,000
ANKARA	Turkey	3,716,000
ANSHAN	China	1,639,000
ANTANANARIVO	Madagascar	1,697,000
ASANSOL	India	1,328,000
ASUNCIÓN	Paraguay	1,870,000
ATHENS	Greece	3,242,000
ATLANTA	United States	4,506,000
AUCKLAND	New Zealand	1,245,000
AURANGABAD	India	1,113,000
AUSTIN	United States	1,161,000
BAGHDAD	Iraq	5,054,000
BAKU	Azerbaijan	1,892,000
BALTIMORE	United States	2,255,000
BAMAKO	Mali	1,494,000
BANDUNG	Indonesia	2,394,000
BANGALORE	India	6,787,000
BANGKOK	Thailand	6,704,000
BAODING	China	1,107,000
BAOTOU	China	2,036,000
BARCELONA	Spain	4,920,000
BARQUISIMETO	Venezuela	1,116,000
BARRANQUILLA	Colombia	1,798,000
BEIJING (PEKING)	China	11,106,000
BEIRUT	Lebanon	1,846,000
BELÉM	Brazil	2,167,000
BELGRADE	Serbia	1,099,000
BELO HORIZONTE	Brazil	5,575,000
BENGHAZI	Libya	1,180,000
BENIN CITY	Nigeria	1,190,000
BENXI	China	1,012,000
BERLIN	Germany	3,406,000
BHOPAL	India	1,727,000
BIRMINGHAM	United Kingdom	2,285,000
BOGOTÁ	Colombia	7,772,000
BOSTON	United States	4,467,000
BRASÍLIA	Brazil	3,599,000
BRAZZAVILLE	Congo	1,355,000
BRIDGEPORT	United States	1,018,000
BRISBANE	Australia	1,860,000
BRUSSELS	Belgium	1,743,000
BUCARAMANGA	Colombia	1,009,000
BUCHAREST	Romania	1,942,000
BUDAPEST	Hungary	1,679,000
BUENOS AIRES	Argentina	12,795,000
BUFFALO	United States	1,016,000
BURSA	Turkey	1,492,000
BUSAN (PUSAN)	South Korea	3,480,000
CAIRO	Egypt	11,893,000
CALGARY	Canada	1,110,000
CALI	Colombia	2,254,000
CAMPINAS	Brazil	2,791,000
CAPE TOWN	South Africa	3,215,000

CITY	COUNTRY	POPULATION
CARACAS	Venezuela	2,985,000
CASABLANCA	Morocco	3,181,000
CHANGCHUN	China	3,183,000
CHANGDE	China	1,469,000
CHANGSHA	China	2,604,000
CHANGZHOU	Russia	1,327,000
CHELYABINSK	Russia	1,091,000
CHENGDU	China	4,123,000
CHENNAI (MADRAS)	India	7,163,000
CHICAGO	United States	8,990,000
CHIFENG (ULANHAD)	China	1,277,000
CHITTAGONG	Bangladesh	4,529,000
CHONGQING	China	6,461,000
CINCINNATI	United States	1,636,000
CIUDAD JUÁREZ	Mexico	1,343,000
CLEVELAND	United States	1,890,000
COIMBATORE	India	1,696,000
COLOGNE	Germany	1,004,000
COLUMBUS	United States	1,270,000
CONAKRY	Guinea	1,494,000
COPENHAGEN	Denmark	1,085,000
CÓRDOBA	Argentina	1,452,000
CURITIBA	Brazil	3,084,000
DAEGU	South Korea	2,460,000
DAEJEON (TAEJON)	South Korea	1,468,000
DAKAR	Senegal	2,604,000
DALIAN (DAIREN)	China	3,167,000
DALLAS-FORT WORTH	United States	4,798,000
DAMASCUS	Syria	2,466,000
DAQING	China	1,693,000
DAR ES SALAAM	Tanzania	2,930,000
DATONG	China	1,873,000
DAVAO	Philippines	1,402,000
DELHI	India	15,926,000
DENVER	United States	2,313,000
DETROIT	United States	4,101,000
DHAKA	Bangladesh	13,485,000
DHANBAD	India	1,246,000
DNIPROPETROVSK	Ukraine	1,050,000
DONGGUAN	China	4,528,000
DOUALA	Cameroon	1,906,000
DUBAI	U. A. E.	1,379,000
DUBLIN	Ireland	1,059,000
DURBAN	South Africa	2,729,000
DURG-BHILAI	India	1,097,000
EAST RAND	South Africa	2,986,000
EDMONTON	Canada	1,058,000
ESFAHAN	Iran	1,628,000
FAISALABAD	Pakistan	2,617,000
FARIDABAD	India	1,394,000
FEZ	Morocco	1,002,000
FLORIANÓPOLIS	Brazil	1,023,000
FORTALEZA	Brazil	3,389,000
FUSHUN	China	1,470,000
FUZHOU	China	2,606,000
GAZIANTEP	Turkey	1,044,000
GHAZIABAD	India	1,341,000
GLASGOW	United Kingdom	1,160,000
GOIÂNIA	Brazil	2,022,000
GRANDE VITÓRIA	Brazil	1,704,000
GUADALAJARA	Mexico	4,198,000
GUANGZHOU (CANTON)	China	8,829,000
GUATEMALA CITY	Guatemala	1,024,000
GUAYAQUIL	Ecuador	2,514,000
GUIYANG	China	3,662,000

CITY	COUNTRY	POPULATION
GUJRANWALA	Pakistan	1,513,000
GWANGJU (KWANGJU)	South Korea	1,440,000
HAIFA	Israel	1,011,000
HAIPHONG	Vietnam	1,969,000
HALAB (ALEPPO)	Syria	2,738,000
HAMBURG	Germany	1,757,000
HANDAN	China	1,631,000
HANGZHOU	China	3,007,000
HANOI	Vietnam	4,378,000
HARARE	Zimbabwe	1,572,000
HARBIN	China	3,621,000
HAVANA	Cuba	2,174,000
HEFEI	China	2,035,000
HELSINKI	Finland	1,115,000
HENGYANG	China	1,016,000
HEZE	China	1,338,000
HIROSHIMA	Japan	2,045,000
HO CHI MINH CITY (SAIGON)	Vietnam	5,314,000
HOHHOT	China	1,726,000
HOMS	Syria	1,005,000
HONG KONG	China	7,206,000
HOUSTON	United States	4,459,000
HUAINAN	China	1,451,000
HUAIYIN	China	1,264,000
HUZHOU	China	1,231,000
HYDERABAD	India	6,376,000
HYDERABAD	Pakistan	1,459,000
IBADAN	Nigeria	2,628,000
INCHEON	South Korea	2,550,000
INDIANAPOLIS	United States	1,436,000
INDORE	India	2,026,000
ISTANBUL	Turkey	10,061,000
IZMIR	Turkey	2,587,000
JABALPUR	India	1,285,000
JAIPUR	India	2,917,000
JAKARTA	Indonesia	9,125,000
JAMSHEDPUR	India	1,300,000
JEDDAH	Saudi Arabia	3,012,000
JIAMUSI	China	1,020,000
JILIN	China	2,396,000
JINAN	China	2,798,000
JINING	China	1,186,000
JINXI	China	2,426,000
JOHANNESBURG	South Africa	3,435,000
KABUL	Afghanistan	3,277,000
KADUNA	Nigeria	1,442,000
KAMPALA	Uganda	1,420,000
KANO	Nigeria	3,140,000
KANPUR	India	3,162,000
KANSAS CITY	United States	1,469,000
KAOHSIUNG	China	1,538,000
KARACHI	Pakistan	12,130,000
KARAJ	Iran	1,423,000
KAZAN	Russia	1,115,000
KHARKIV	Ukraine	1,461,000
KHARTOUM	Sudan	4,754,000
KHULNA	Bangladesh	1,553,000
KIEV	Ukraine	2,709,000
KINSHASA	D. R. C.	7,843,000
KITAKYUSHU	Japan	2,792,000
KOCHI (COCHIN)	India	1,519,000
KOLKATA (CALCUTTA)	India	14,787,000
KUALA LUMPUR	Malaysia	1,448,000
KUMASI	Ghana	1,646,000

CITY	COUNTRY	POPULATION
KUNMING	China	2,931,000
KUWAIT CITY	Kuwait	2,063,000
KYOTO	Japan	1,805,000
LA PAZ	Bolivia	1,590,000
LAGOS	Nigeria	9,466,000
LAHORE	Pakistan	6,577,000
LANZHOU	China	2,561,000
LAS VEGAS	United States	1,823,000
LEÓN	Mexico	1,488,000
LESHAN	China	1,157,000
LILLE	France	1,044,000
LIMA	Peru	8,012,000
LINYI	China	2,082,000
LISBON	Portugal	2,812,000
LIUZHOU	China	1,497,000
LOMÉ	Togo	1,452,000
LONDON	United Kingdom	8,567,000
LOS ANGELES	United States	12,500,000
LU'AN	China	1,690,000
LUANDA	Angola	4,000,000
LUBUMBASHI	D. R. C.	1,352,000
LUCKNOW	India	2,695,000
LUDHIANA	India	1,649,000
LUOYANG	China	1,715,000
LUPANSHUI	China	1,221,000
LUSAKA	Zambia	1,328,000
LUZHOU	China	1,537,000
LYON	France	1,423,000
MACEIÓ	Brazil	1,186,000
MADRID	Spain	5,567,000
MADURAI	India	1,294,000
MAKASSAR	Indonesia	1,262,000
MANAUS	Brazil	1,753,000
MANCHESTER	United Kingdom	2,230,000
MANILA	Philippines	11,100,000
MAPUTO	Mozambique	1,446,000
MARACAIBO	Venezuela	2,072,000
MARACAY	Venezuela	1,007,000
MARSEILLE	France	1,400,000
MASHHAD	Iran	2,469,000
MBUJI-MAYI	D. R. C.	1,295,000
MECCA	Saudi Arabia	1,385,000
MEDAN	Indonesia	2,115,000
MEDELLÍN	Colombia	3,297,000
MEDINA	Saudi Arabia	1,010,000
MEERUT	India	1,398,000
MELBOURNE	Australia	3,728,000
MEMPHIS	United States	1,081,000
MEXICO CITY	Mexico	19,028,000
MIAMI	United States	5,585,000
MIANYANG	China	1,396,000
MILAN	Italy	2,945,000
MILWAUKEE	United States	1,388,000
MINNEAPOLIS-ST. PAUL	United States	2,616,000
MINSK	Belarus	1,805,000
MOGADISHU	Somalia	1,100,000
MONROVIA	Liberia	1,041,000
MONTERREY	Mexico	3,712,000
MONTEVIDEO	Uruguay	1,513,000
MONTRÉAL	Canada	3,678,000
MOSCOW	Russia	10,452,000
MOSUL	Iraq	1,316,000
MUDANJIANG	China	1,244,000
MULTAN	Pakistan	1,522,000
MUMBAI (BOMBAY)	India	18,978,000
MUNICH	Germany	1,275,000
NAGOYA	Japan	3,230,000
NAGPUR	India	2,454,000
NAIROBI	Kenya	3,010,000
NAMPO	North Korea	1,127,000
NANCHANG	China	2,350,000
NANCHONG	China	2,174,000
NANJING	China	3,679,000
NANNING	China	2,167,000
NANYANG	China	1,944,000
NAPLES	Italy	2,250,000
NASIK	India	1,473,000
NATAL	Brazil	1,088,000
NEIJIANG	China	1,466,000
NEW YORK	United States	19,040,000
NINGBO	China	1,923,000
NIZHNIY NOVGOROD	Russia	1,278,000

CITY	COUNTRY	POPULATION
NOVOSIBIRSK	Russia	1,389,000
OMSK	Russia	1,135,000
ORLANDO	United States	1,350,000
OSAKA	Japan	11,294,000
OTTAWA	Canada	1,145,000
OUAGADOUGOU	Burkina Faso	1,149,000
PALEMBANG	Indonesia	1,749,000
PANAMA CITY	Panama	1,281,000
PARIS	France	9,904,000
PATNA	India	2,158,000
PERTH	Australia	1,532,000
PESHAWAR	Pakistan	1,303,000
PHILADELPHIA	United States	5,492,000
PHNOM PENH	Cambodia	1,466,000
PHOENIX	United States	3,551,000
PITTSBURGH	United States	1,838,000
PORT ELIZABETH	South Africa	1,021,000
PORT HARCOURT	Nigeria	1,020,000
PORT-AU-PRINCE	Haiti	1,998,000
PORTLAND-VANCOUVER	United States	1,875,000
PORTO	Portugal	1,337,000
PORTO ALEGRE	Brazil	3,917,000
PRAGUE	Czech Republic	1,162,000
PRETORIA	South Africa	1,338,000
PROVIDENCE-PAWTUCKET	United States	1,277,000
PUEBLA	Mexico	2,195,000
PUNE	India	4,672,000
P'YONGYANG	North Korea	3,300,000
QINGDAO	China	2,866,000
QINHUANGDAO	China	1,003,000
QIQIHAR	China	1,641,000
QUANZHOU	China	1,463,000
QUITO	Ecuador	1,701,000
RABAT	Morocco	1,705,000
RAJKOT	India	1,260,000
RANCHI	India	1,044,000
RAWALPINDI	Pakistan	1,858,000
RECIFE	Brazil	3,651,000
RIO DE JANEIRO	Brazil	11,748,000
RIVERSIDE-SAN BERNARDINO	United States	1,745,000
RIYADH	Saudi Arabia	4,465,000
ROME	Italy	3,339,000
ROSARIO	Argentina	1,203,000
ROSTOV NA DONU	Russia	1,052,000
ROTTERDAM	Netherlands	1,005,000
SACRAMENTO	United States	1,604,000
ST. LOUIS	United States	2,199,000
ST. PETERSBURG	Russia	4,553,000
SALVADOR	Brazil	3,484,000
SAMARA	Russia	1,137,000
SAN ANTONIO	United States	1,473,000
SAN DIEGO	United States	2,916,000
SAN FRANCISCO-OAKLAND	United States	3,450,000
SAN JOSÉ	Costa Rica	1,284,000
SAN JOSE	United States	1,668,000
SAN JUAN	Puerto Rico	2,690,000
SAN SALVADOR	El Salvador	1,433,000
SANAA	Yemen	2,008,000
SANTA CRUZ	Bolivia	1,422,000
SANTIAGO	Chile	5,720,000
SANTO DOMINGO	Dominican Republic	2,154,000
SANTOS	Brazil	1,709,000
SÃO LUÍS	Brazil	1,038,000
SÃO PAULO	Brazil	18,845,000
SAPPORO	Japan	2,544,000
SEATTLE	United States	3,074,000
SEMARANG	Indonesia	1,396,000
SENDAI	Japan	2,250,000
SEOUL	South Korea	9,796,000
SHANGHAI	China	14,987,000
SHANGQIU	China	1,753,000
SHANTOU (SWATOW)	China	1,601,000
SHENYANG	China	4,787,000
SHENZHEN	China	7,581,000
SHIJIAZHUANG	China	2,417,000
SHIRAZ	Iran	1,240,000

CITY	COUNTRY	POPULATION
SHOLAPUR	India	1,057,000
SINGAPORE	Singapore	4,436,000
SOFIA	Bulgaria	1,185,000
SRINAGAR	India	1,140,000
STOCKHOLM	Sweden	1,264,000
SUINING	China	1,425,000
SURABAYA	Indonesia	2,845,000
SURAT	India	3,842,000
SUWON	South Korea	1,078,000
SUZHOU, ANHUI	China	1,964,000
SUZHOU, JIANGSU	China	1,650,000
SYDNEY	Australia	4,327,000
TABRIZ	Iran	1,413,000
TAIAN	China	1,629,000
TAICHUNG	China	1,078,000
TAIPEI	China	2,603,000
TAIYUAN	China	2,913,000
TAMPA-ST. PETERSBURG-CLEARWATER	United States	2,314,000
TANGSHAN	China	1,879,000
TASHKENT	Uzbekistan	2,184,000
T'BILISI	Georgia	1,100,000
TEHRAN	Iran	7,873,000
TEL AVIV-YAFO	Israel	3,112,000
TIANJIN (TIENTSIN)	China	7,180,000
TIANMEN	China	1,708,000
TIANSHUI	China	1,225,000
TIJUANA	Mexico	1,553,000
TOKYO	Japan	35,676,000
TOLUCA	Mexico	1,531,000
TORONTO	Canada	5,213,000
TORREÓN	Mexico	1,144,000
TRIPOLI	Libya	2,189,000
TURIN	Italy	1,652,000
UFA	Russia	1,018,000
ULSAN	South Korea	1,061,000
URUMQI	China	2,151,000
VADODARA	India	1,756,000
VALENCIA	Venezuela	1,770,000
VANCOUVER	Canada	2,146,000
VARANASI (BANARES)	India	1,352,000
VEREENIGING	South Africa	1,074,000
VIENNA	Austria	2,315,000
VIJAYAWADA	India	1,137,000
VIRGINIA BEACH	United States	1,491,000
VISHAKHAPATNAM	India	1,529,000
WARSAW	Poland	1,707,000
WASHINGTON, D.C.	United States	4,338,000
WEIFANG	China	1,553,000
WENZHOU	China	2,350,000
WEST YORKSHIRE	United Kingdom	1,529,000
WUHAN	China	7,243,000
WUXI	China	1,749,000
XIAMEN	China	2,519,000
XI'AN	China	4,009,000
XIANGFAN	China	1,069,000
XIANTAO	China	1,556,000
XIANYANG	China	1,126,000
XINING	China	1,048,000
XINYANG	China	1,541,000
XUZHOU	China	2,091,000
YANGON (RANGOON)	Myanmar	4,088,000
YANTAI	China	2,116,000
YAOUNDÉ	Cameroon	1,611,000
YEKATERINBURG	Russia	1,313,000
YEREVAN	Armenia	1,102,000
YIYANG	China	1,352,000
YONGZHOU	China	1,000,000
YULIN	China	1,127,000
ZAOZHUANG	China	2,145,000
ZHANGJIAKOU	China	1,046,000
ZHANJIANG	China	1,590,000
ZHENGZHOU	China	2,636,000
ZHUHAI	China	1,023,000
ZHUZHOU	China	1,080,000
ZIBO	China	3,061,000
ZIGONG	China	1,105,000
ZURICH	Switzerland	1,108,000

A

abyssal plain a flat, relatively featureless region of the deep ocean floor extending from the mid-ocean ridge to a continental rise or deep-sea trench

acculturation the process of losing the traits of one cultural group while assimilating with another cultural group

alloy a substance that is a mixture of two metals or a metal and a nonmetal

alluvial fan a depositional, fan-shaped feature found where a stream or channel gradient levels out at the base of a mountain

antipode a point that lies diametrically opposite any given point on the surface of the Earth

Archaean (Archean) eon the second eon of Earth's geologic history, ending around 2,500 million years ago

archipelago an associated group of scattered islands in a large body of water

asthenosphere the uppermost zone of Earth's mantle; it consists of rocks in a "plastic" state, immediately below the lithosphere

atmosphere the thin envelope of gases surrounding the solid Earth and comprising mostly nitrogen, oxygen, and various trace gases

atoll a circular coral reef enclosing a lagoon

B

barrier island a low-lying, sandy island parallel to a shoreline but separated from the mainland by a lagoon

basin a low-lying depression in the Earth's surface; some basins are filled with water and sediment, while others are dry most of the time

bathymetry the measurement of depth within bodies of water or the information gathered from such measurements

bay an area of a sea or other body of water bordered on three sides by a curved stretch of coastline but usually smaller than a gulf

biodiversity a broad concept that refers to the variety and range of species (flora and fauna) present in an ecosystem

biogeography the study of the distribution patterns of plants and animals and the processes that produce those patterns

biological weapon a weapon that uses an organism or toxin, such as a bacteria or virus, to harm individuals

biome a very large ecosystem made up of specific plant and animal communities interacting with the physical environment (climate and soil)

biosphere the realm of Earth that includes all plant and animal life-forms

bluff a steep slope or wall of consolidated sediment adjacent to a river or its floodplain

bog soft, spongy, waterlogged ground consisting chiefly of partially decayed plant matter (peat)

breakwater a stone or concrete structure built near a shore to prevent damage to watercraft or construction

butte a tall, steep-sided, flat-topped tower of rock that is a remnant of extensive erosional processes

C

caldera a large, crater-like feature with steep, circular walls and a central depression resulting from the explosion and collapse of a volcano

canal an artificially made channel of water used for navigation or irrigation

canopy the ceiling-like layer of branches and leaves that forms the uppermost layer of a forest

capitalism an economic system characterized by resource allocation primarily through market mechanisms; means of production are privately owned (by either individuals or corporations), and production is organized around profit maximization

capture fishery all of the variables involved in the activities to harvest a given fish (e.g., location, target resource, technology used, social characteristic, purpose, season)

carbon cycle one of the several geochemical cycles by which matter is recirculated through the lithosphere, hydrosphere, atmosphere, and biosphere

carbon neutral process a process resulting in zero net change in the balance between emission and absorption of carbon

carrying capacity the maximum number of animals and/or people a given area can support at a given time under specified levels of consumption

cartogram a map designed to present statistical information in a diagrammatic way, usually not to scale

cartographer a person who interprets, designs, and creates maps and other modes of geographic representation

chemical weapon a weapon that uses toxic properties of chemical substances to harm individuals

chlorofluorocarbon a molecule of industrial origin containing chlorine, fluorine, and carbon atoms; causes severe ozone destruction

civilization a cultural concept suggesting substantial development in the form of agriculture, cities, food and labor surplus, labor specialization, social stratification, and state organization

climate the long-term behavior of the atmosphere; it includes measures of average weather conditions (e.g., temperature, humidity, precipitation, and pressure), as well as trends, cycles, and extremes

colonialism the political, social, or economic domination of a state over another state or people

commodity an economic good or product that can be traded, bought, or sold

composite image a product of combining two or more images

coniferous trees and shrubs with thin leaves and producing cones; also a forest or wood composed of these trees

continental drift a theory that suggests the continents were at one time all part of a prehistoric supercontinent that broke apart; according to the theory, the continents slowly "drifted" across the Earth's surface to their present positions

continental shelf the submerged, offshore extension of a continent

continental slope the steeply graded sea floor connecting the edge of the continental shelf to the deep-ocean floor

convection the transfer of heat within a gas or solid of nonuniform temperature from mass movement or circulatory motion due to gravity and uneven density within the substance

convergent boundary where tectonic plates move toward each other along their common boundary, causing subduction

core the dense, innermost layer of Earth; the outer core is liquid, while the inner core is solid

Coriolis effect the deflection of wind systems and ocean currents (as well as freely moving objects not in contact with the solid Earth) to the right in the Northern Hemisphere and to the left in the Southern Hemisphere as a consequence of the Earth's rotation

crust the rocky, relatively low density, outermost layer of Earth

cultural diffusion the spread of cultural elements from one group to another

culture the "way of life" for a group; it is transmitted from generation to generation and involves a shared system of meanings, beliefs, values, and social relations; it also includes language, religion, clothing, music, laws, and entertainment

D

dead zone oxygen-starved areas in oceans and lakes where marine life cannot be supported, often linked to runoff of excess nutrients

deciduous trees and shrubs that shed their leaves seasonally; also a forest or wood mostly composed of these trees

deformation general term for folding and faulting of rocks due to natural shearing, compression, and extension forces

delta a flat, low-lying, often fan-shaped region at the mouth of a river; it is composed of sediment deposited by a river entering a lake, an ocean, or another large body of water

demography the study of population statistics, changes, and trends based on various measures of fertility, mortality, and migration

denudation the overall effect of weathering, mass wasting, and erosion, which ultimately wears down and lowers the continental surface

desert a region that has little or no vegetation and averages less than 10 inches of precipitation a year

desertification the spread of desert conditions in arid and semiarid regions; desertification results from a combination of climatic changes and increasing human pressures in the form of overgrazing, removal of natural vegetation, and cultivation of marginal land

developed country general term for an industrialized country with a diversified and self-sustaining economy, strong infrastructure, and high standard of living

developing country general term for a non-industrialized country with a weak economy, little modern infrastructure, and low standard of living

dialect a regional variation of one language, with differences in vocabulary, accent, pronunciation, and syntax

diffuse plate boundary a zone of faulting and earthquakes extending to either side of a plate boundary

digital elevation model (DEM) a digital representation of Earth's topography in which data points representing altitude are assigned coordinates and viewed spatially; sometimes called a digital terrain model (DTM)

disconformity a discontinuity in sedimentary rocks in which the rock beds remain parallel

divide a ridge separating watersheds

dormant volcano an active volcano that is temporarily in repose, but expected to erupt in the future

E

earthquake vibrations and shock waves caused by volcanic eruptions or the sudden movement of Earth's crustal rocks along fracture zones called faults

easterlies a regular wind that blows from the east

ecosystem a group of organisms and the environment with which they interact

elevation the height of a point or place above an established datum, sometimes mean sea level

El Niño a pronounced warming of the surface waters along the coast of Peru and the equatorial region of the east Pacific Ocean; it is caused by weakening (sometimes reversal) of the trade winds, with accompanying changes in ocean circulation (including cessation of upwelling in coastal waters)

emigrant a person migrating away from a country or area; an out-migrant

endangered species a species at immediate risk of extinction

endemic typical to or native of a particular area, people, or environment

endogeneous introduced from or originating within a given organism or system

environment the sum of the conditions and stimuli that influence an organism

eon the largest time unit on the geologic time scale; consists of several shorter units called eras

Equator latitude 0°; an imaginary line running east and west around Earth and dividing it into two equal parts known as the Northern and Southern Hemispheres; the Equator always has approximately 12 hours of daylight and 12 hours of darkness

equinox the time of year (usually September 22-23 and March 21-22) when the length of night and day are about equal, and the sun is directly overhead at the Equator

era a major subdivision of time on the geologic time scale; consists of several shorter units called periods

erosion the general term for the removal of surface rocks and sediment by the action of water, air, ice, or gravity

escarpment a cliff or steep rock face that separates two comparatively level land surfaces

estuary a broadened seaward end or extension of a river (usually a drowned river mouth), characterized by tidal influences and the mixing of fresh and saline water

ethnic group minority group with a collective self-identity within a larger host population

ethnocentrism a belief in the inherent superiority of one's own ethnic group and culture; a tendency to view all other groups or cultures in terms of one's own

eutrophication the process that occurs when large amounts of nutrients from fertilizers or animal wastes enter a water body and bacteria break down the nutrients; the bacterial action causes depletion of dissolved oxygen

Exclusive Economic Zone (EEZ) an oceanic zone extending up to 200 nautical miles (370 km) from a shoreline, within which a coastal state claims jurisdiction over fishing, mineral exploration, and other economically important activities

exogenous introduced from or originating outside a given organism or system

external debt debt owed to non-residents; repayable in foreign currency, goods, or services

F

fault a fracture or break in rock where the opposite sides are displaced relative to each other

fjord a coastal inlet that is narrow and deep and reaches far inland; it is usually formed by the sea filling in a glacially scoured valley or trough

flood basalt a huge lava flow that produces thick accumulations of basalt layers over a large area

floodplain a wide, relatively flat area adjacent to a stream or river and subject to flooding and sedimentation; it is the most preferred land area for human settlement and agriculture

food chain the feeding pattern of organisms in an ecosystem, through which energy from food passes from one level to the next in a sequence

fork the place where a river separates into branches; also may refer to one of those branches

fossil fuel fuel in the form of coal, petroleum, or natural gas derived from the remains of ancient plants and animals trapped and preserved in sedimentary rocks

G

galaxy a collection of stars, gas, and dust bound together by gravity; there are billions of galaxies in the universe, and the Earth is in the Milky Way galaxy

genocide the intentional destruction, in whole or in part, of a national, ethnic, racial, or religious group

genome the complete set of genetic material of an organism

geochemistry a branch of geology focusing on the chemical composition of earth materials

geographic information system (GIS) an integrated hardware-software system used to store, organize, analyze, manipulate, model, and display geographic information or data

geography literally means "Earth description"; as a modern academic discipline, geography is concerned with the explanation of the physical and human characteristics and patterns of Earth's surface

geomorphology the study of planetary surface features, especially the processes of landform evolution on Earth

geopolitics the study of how factors such as geography, economics, and demography affect the power and foreign policy of a state

glaciation a period of glacial advancement through the growth of continental ice sheets and/or mountain glaciers

glacier a large, natural accumulation of ice that spreads outward on the land or moves slowly down a slope or valley

global positioning system (GPS) a system of artificial satellites that provides information on three-dimensional position and velocity to users at or near the Earth's surface

global warming the warming of Earth's average global temperature due to a buildup of "greenhouse gases" (e.g., carbon dioxide and methane) released by human activities; increased levels of these gases cause enhanced heat absorption by the atmosphere

globe a scale model of the Earth that correctly represents not only the area, relative size, and shape of physical features but also the distance between points and true compass directions

great circle the largest circle that can be drawn around a sphere such as a globe; a great circle route is the shortest route between two points on the surface of a sphere

greenhouse effect an enhanced near-surface warming that is due to certain atmospheric gases absorbing and re-radiating long-wave radiation that might otherwise have escaped to space had those gases not been present in the atmosphere

gross domestic product (GDP) the total market value of goods and services produced by a nation's economy in a given year using global currency exchange rates

gross national income (GNI) the income derived from the capital and income belonging to nationals employed domestically or abroad

gravitational waves ripples in the fabric of space and time, usually caused by the interaction of two or more large masses

gulf a very large area of an ocean or a sea bordered by coastline on three sides

gyre a large, semicontinuous system of major ocean currents flowing around the outer margins of every major ocean basin

H

habitat the natural environment (including controlling physical factors) in which a plant or animal is usually found or prefers to exist

hemisphere half a sphere; cartographers and geographers, by convention, divide the Earth into the Northern and Southern Hemispheres at the Equator and the Eastern and Western Hemispheres at the prime meridian (longitude 0°) and 180° meridian

herbaceous a type of plant lacking woody tissue, and usually with a life of just one growing season

hot spot a localized and intensely hot region or mantle plume beneath the lithosphere; it tends to stay relatively fixed geographically as a lithospheric plate migrates over it

human geography one of the two major divisions of systematic geography; it is concerned with the spatial analysis of human population, cultures, and social, political, and economic activities

hurricane a large, rotating storm system that forms over tropical waters, with very low atmospheric pressure in the central region and winds in excess of 74 mph (119 km/h); it is called a typhoon over the western Pacific Ocean and a cyclone over the northern Indian Ocean

hydrologic cycle the continuous recirculation of water from the oceans, through the atmosphere, to the continents, through the biosphere and lithosphere, and back to the sea

hydrosphere all of the water found on, under, or over Earth's surface

hypsometry the measurement of contours and elevation of land above sea level

I

ice age a period of pronounced glaciation usually associated with worldwide cooling, a greater proportion of global precipitation falling as snow, and a shorter snowmelt period

igneous the rock type formed from solidified molten rock (magma) that originates deep within Earth; the chemical composition of the magma and its cooling rate determine the final rock type

immigrant a person migrating into a particular country or area; an in-migrant

impact crater a circular depression on the surface of a planet or moon caused by the collision of another body, such as an asteroid or comet

indigenous native to or occurring naturally in a specific area or environment

industrial metabolism a concept that describes the process of converting raw materials into a final product and waste through energy and labor

infrastructure transportation and communications networks that allow goods, people, and information to flow across space

inorganic not relating to or being derived from living things

interdependence mutual reliance among beings or processes

internally displaced person a person who flees his/her home, to escape danger or persecution, but does not leave the country

International Date Line an imaginary line that roughly follows the 180° meridian in the Pacific Ocean; immediately west of the date line the calendar date is one day ahead of the calendar date east of the line; people crossing the date line in a westward direction lose one calendar day, while those crossing eastward gain one calendar day

intertropical convergence zone (ITCZ) a zone of low atmospheric pressure created by intense solar heating, thereby leading to rising air and horizontal convergence of northeast and southeast trade winds; over the oceans, the ITCZ is usually found between 10° N and 10° S, and over continents the seasonal excursion of the ITCZ is much greater

isthmus a relatively narrow strip of land with water on both sides and connecting two larger land areas

J

jet stream a high-speed west-to-east wind current; jet streams flow in narrow corridors within upper-air westerlies, usually at the interface of polar and tropical air

K

karst a region underlain by limestone and characterized by extensive solution features such as sinkholes, underground streams, and caves

L

lagoon a shallow, narrow water body located between a barrier island and the mainland, with freshwater contributions from streams and saltwater exchange through tidal inlets or breaches throughout the barrier system

La Niña the pronounced cooling of equatorial waters in the eastern Pacific Ocean

latitude the distance north or south of the Equator; lines of latitude, called parallels, are evenly spaced from the Equator to the North and South Poles (from 0° to 90° N and S latitude); latitude and longitude (see below) are measured in terms of the 360 degrees of a circle and are expressed in degrees, minutes, and seconds

leeward the side away from or sheltered by the wind

lingua franca a language used beyond its native speaker population as a common or commercial language

lithosphere the rigid outer layer of the Earth, located above the asthenosphere and comprising the outer crust and the upper, rigid portion of the mantle

longitude the distance measured in degrees east or west of the prime meridian (0° longitude) up to 180°; lines of longitude are called meridians (compare with latitude, above)

M

macroscopic concerned with or considered in large units

magma molten, pressurized rock in the mantle that is occasionally intruded into the lithosphere or extruded to the surface of the Earth by volcanic activity

magnetic pole the points at Earth's surface at which the geomagnetic field is vertical; the location of these points constantly changes

mantle the dense layer of Earth below the crust; the upper mantle is solid and with the crust, forms the lithosphere, the zone containing tectonic plates; the lower mantle is partially molten, making it the pliable base upon which the lithosphere "floats"

map projection the geometric system of transferring information about a round object, such as a globe, to a flat piece of paper or other surface for the purpose of producing a map with known properties and quantifiable distortion

maria volcanic plains on the moon's surface that appear to the naked eye as smooth, dark areas

meridian a north-south line of longitude used to reference distance east or west of the prime meridian (longitude 0°)

mesa a broad, flat-topped hill or mountain with marginal cliffs and/or steep slopes formed by progressive erosion of horizontally bedded sedimentary rocks

metamorphic the rock type formed from preexisting rocks that have been substantially changed from their original igneous, sedimentary, or earlier metamorphic form; catalysts of this change include high heat, high pressure, hot and mineral-rich fluids, or, more commonly, some combination of these

metric ton (tonne) unit of weight equal to 1,000 kilograms or 2,205 pounds

micrometeoroids a tiny particle of rock or dust in space, usually weighing less than a gram

microscopic considered in or concerned with small units

migration the movement of people across a specified boundary for the purpose of establishing a new place of residence

mineral an inorganic solid with a distinctive chemical composition and a specific crystal structure that affect its physical characteristics

moment magnitude scale a measure of the total energy released by an earthquake; preferred to the Richter scale because it more accurately measures strong earthquakes and can be used with data for distant earthquakes

monsoon a seasonal reversal of prevailing wind patterns, often associated with pronounced changes in moisture

N

nation a cultural concept for a group of people bound together by a strong sense of shared values and cultural characteristics, including language, religion, and common history

nebula a cloud of interstellar gas and dust

node a point where distinct lines or objects intersect

Normalized Difference Vegetation Index (NDVI) a measurement of plant growth density over the Earth's surface, measured on a scale of 0.1 to 0.8 (low to high vegetation)

North Pole the most northerly geographic point on the Earth; the northern end of the Earth's axis of rotation; 90° N

nuclear weapon a weapon which uses nuclear reactions to derive destructive force

O

oasis a fertile area with water and vegetation in a desert

ocean current the regular and persistent flow of water in the oceans, usually driven by atmospheric wind and pressure systems or by regional differences in water density (temperature, salinity)

offshoring relocating business processes to another country, where they are performed by either another branch of the parent company or an external contractor (international outsourcing)

organic relating to or derived from living things

oxbow lake a crescent-shaped lake or swamp occupying a channel abandoned by a meandering river

outsourcing delegating non-core processes from within a business to an external entity such as a subcontractor

ozone a bluish gas composed of three oxygen atoms and harmful to breathe

ozone layer region of Earth's atmosphere where ozone concentration is relatively high; the ozone layer absorbs harmful ultraviolet rays from the sun

P

paleo-geographic map a map depicting the past positions of the continents, developed from historic magnetic, biological, climatological, and geologic evidence

Pangaea the supercontinent from which today's continents are thought to have originated

peninsula a long piece of land jutting out from a larger piece of land into a body of water

period a basic unit of time on the geologic time scale, generally 35 to 70 million years in duration; a subdivision of an era

Phanerozoic eon an eon of Earth's geologic history that comprises the Paleozoic, Mesozoic, and Cenozoic eras

photosynthesis process by which plants convert carbon dioxide and water to oxygen and carbohydrates

physical geography one of the two major divisions of systematic geography; the spatial analysis of the structure, process, and location of Earth's natural phenomena, such as climate, soil, plants, animals, water, and topography

pilgrimage a typically long and difficult journey to a special place, often of religious importance

plain an extensive, flat-lying area characterized generally by the absence of local relief features

planetary nebula an interstellar cloud of gas and dust formed when a star runs out of central nuclear fuel, finally ejecting its outer layers in a gaseous shell

plate tectonics the theory that Earth's lithospheric plates slide or shift slowly over the asthenosphere and that their interactions cause earthquakes, volcanic eruptions, movement of landmasses, and other geologic events

plateau a landform feature characterized by high elevation and gentle upland slopes

politicide the intentional destruction, in whole or in part, of a group of people based on their political or ideological beliefs

point a sharp prominence or headland on the coast that juts out into a body of water

pollution a direct or indirect process resulting from human activity; part of the environment is made potentially or actually unsafe or hazardous to the welfare of the organisms that live in it

porphyry an igneous rock characterized by large crystals within a matrix of much finer crystals

primary energy energy sources as they are found naturally—i.e., before they have been processed or transformed into secondary sources

prime meridian the line of 0° longitude that runs through Greenwich, England, and separates the Eastern and Western Hemispheres

Priscoan eon the earliest eon of Earth's geologic history; also known as the Hadean eon

proliferation the process of growing rapidly and suddenly

Proterozoic eon the eon of geologic time that includes the interval between the Archean and Phanerozoic eons and is marked by rocks that contain fossils indicating the first appearance of eukaryotic organisms (as algae)

protogalaxy a cloud of gas, possibly consisting of dark matter, hydrogen, and helium, that is forming into a galaxy

purchasing power parity (PPP) a method of measuring gross domestic product that compares the relative value of currencies based on what each currency will buy in its country of origin; PPP provides a good comparison between national economies and is a decent indicator of living standards

R

rain shadow the dry region on the downwind (leeward) side of a mountain range

raster data spatial data represented as a unified grid of equal-area cells, each with a single numerical value; best-suited for contiguous data such as elevation

red dwarf a relatively small, cool, and faint star with a very long estimated lifespan; the most common type of star

reef a strip of rocks or sand either at or just below the surface of water

refugee a person who flees his/her country of origin to escape danger or persecution for reasons of, for example, race, religion, or political opinion

regolith a layer of disintegrated or partly decomposed rock overlying unweathered parent materials; regolith is usually found in areas of low relief where the physical transport of debris is weak

remote sensing the measurement of some property of an object by means other than direct contact, usually from aircraft or satellites

renewable resource a resource that can be regenerated or maintained if used at rates that do not exceed natural replenishment

Richter scale a logarithmic scale devised to represent the relative amount of energy released by an earthquake; moment magnitude has superceded the Richter scale as the preferred measurement of earthquake magnitude

rift a long, narrow trough created by plate movement at a divergent boundary

rift valley a long, structural valley formed by the lowering of a block between two parallel faults

Ring of Fire (also Rim of Fire) an arc of volcanoes and tectonic activity along the perimeter of the Pacific Ocean

S

salinization the accumulation of salts in soil

satellite data information collected by a vehicle orbiting a celestial body

savanna a tropical grassland with widely spaced trees; it experiences distinct wet and dry seasons

seamount a submerged volcano rising from the ocean floor

sedimentary the rock type formed from preexisting rocks or pieces of once-living organisms; deposits accumulate on Earth's surface, generally with distinctive layering or bedding

solar radiation energy emitted by the sun

solar wind the stream of atoms and ions moving outward from the solar corona at 300 to 500 kilometers per second

solstice a celestial event that occurs twice a year (usually June 20-21 and December 21-22), when the sun appears directly overhead to observers at the Tropic of Cancer or the Tropic of Capricorn

sound a broad channel or passage of water connecting two larger bodies of water or separating an island from the mainland

South Pole the most southerly geographic point on the Earth; the southern end of the Earth's axis of rotation; 90° S

spatial resolution a measure of the smallest distinguishable separation between two objects

spectral resolution a measure of the ability of a sensing system to distinguish electromagnetic radiation of different frequencies

spit beach extension that forms along a shoreline with bays and other indentations

spreading boundary where plates move apart along their common boundary, creating a crack in the Earth's crust (typically at the mid-ocean ridge), which is then filled with upwelling molten rock; also called a divergent boundary

steppe semiarid, relatively flat, treeless region that receives between 10 and 20 inches of precipitation yearly

state an area with defined and internationally acknowledged boundaries; a political unit

strait a narrow passage of water that connects two larger bodies of water

subduction the tectonic process by which the down-bent edge of one lithospheric plate is forced underneath another plate

subatomic particle a part of an atom, such as a proton, neutron, or electron

T

tariff a surcharge on imports levied by a state; a form of protectionism designed to increase imports' market price and thus inhibit their consumption

tectonic plate (also lithospheric or crustal plate) a section of the Earth's rigid outer layer that moves as a distinct unit upon the plastic-like mantle materials in the asthenosphere

temperate mild or moderate

temporal resolution a measure of the frequency with which a sensing system gathers data

terrestrial radiation natural sources of radiation found in earth materials

threatened species species at some, but not immediate, risk of extinction

tide the regular rise and fall of the ocean, caused by the mutual gravitational attraction between the Earth, moon, and sun, as well as the rotation of the Earth-moon system around its center of gravity

ton a unit of weight equal to 2,000 pounds in the U.S. or 2,240 pounds in the U.K.

tonne (see metric ton)

topography the relief features that are evident on a planetary surface

tornado a violently rotating, funnel-shaped column of air characterized by extremely low atmospheric pressures and exceptional wind speeds generated within intense thunderstorms

tradewind a wind blowing persistently from the same direction; particularly from the subtropical high-pressure centers toward the equatorial low-pressure zone

transgenic an organism artificially or naturally containing one or more genes from a different type of organism

tributary a river or stream flowing into a larger river or stream

tropical warm and moist; occuring in or characteristic of the Tropics

Tropic of Cancer latitude 23.5° N; the farthest northerly excursion of the sun when it is directly overhead

Tropic of Capricorn latitude 23.5° S; the farthest southerly excursion of the sun when it is directly overhead

tsunami a series of ocean waves, often very destructive along coasts, caused by the vertical displacement of the seafloor during an earthquake, submarine landslide, or volcanic eruption

tundra a zone in cold, polar regions (mostly in the Northern Hemisphere) that is transitional between the zone of polar ice and the limit of tree growth; it is usually characterized by low-lying vegetation, with extensive permafrost and waterlogged soils

U

unconformity a discontinuity in sedimentary rocks caused by erosion or nondeposition

uplift the slow, upward movement of Earth's crust

upwelling the process by which water rich in nutrients rises from depth toward the ocean surface; it is usually the result of diverging surface waters

urban agglomeration a group of several cities and/or towns and their suburbs

urbanization a process in which there is an increase in the percentage of people living and working in urban places as compared to rural places; a process of change from a rural to urban lifestyle

V

vector data spatial data represented as as nodes and connectors identified by geographic coordinates, and related to one another to symbolize geographic features; best-suited for geographic features that can be represented as points, lines, or polygons

volcanism the upward movement and expulsion of molten (melted) material and gases from within the Earth's mantle onto the surface where it cools and hardens, producing characteristic terrain

W

watershed the drainage area of a river and its tributaries

weathering the processes or actions that cause the physical disintegration and chemical decomposition of rock and minerals

westerlies a regular wind that blows from the west

wetland an area of land covered by water or saturated by water sufficiently enough to support vegetation adapted to wet conditions

wilderness a natural environment that has remained essentially undisturbed by human activities and, increasingly, is protected by government or nongovernment organizations

windward the side toward or unsheltered from the wind

X

xerophyte a plant that thrives in a dry environment

Y

yazoo a tributary stream that runs parallel to the main river for some distance

Z

zenith the point in the sky that is immediately overhead; also the highest point above the observer's horizon obtained by a celestial body

zoning the process of subdividing urban areas as a basis for land-use planning and policy

Place-Name Index

THE FOLLOWING SYSTEM is used to locate a place on a map in the National Geographic Family Reference Atlas of the World. The boldface type after an entry refers to the plate on which the map is found. The letter-number combination refers to the grid on which the particular place-name is located. The edge of each map is marked horizontally with numbers and vertically with letters. In between, at equally spaced intervals, are index ticks (▲). If these ticks were connected with lines, each page would be divided into a 12- by 16-square grid. Take Abilene, Kansas, for example. The index entry reads "Abilene, *Kans., U.S.* **105** S8." On page 105, Abilene is located within the grid square where row S and column 8 intersect.

A place-name may appear on several maps, but the index lists only the best presentation. Usually, this means that a feature is indexed to the largest-scale map on which it appears in its entirety. (Note: Rivers are often labeled multiple times even on a single map. In such cases, the rivers are indexed to labels that are closest to their mouths.) The name of the country or continent in which a feature lies is shown in italic type and is usually abbreviated. (A full list of abbreviations appears on page 262.)

The index lists more than proper names. Some entries include a description, as in "Elba, *island, It.* **150** J5" and "Urubamba, *river, Peru* **130** H5." In languages other than English, the description of a physical feature may be part of the name; e.g., the "Berg" in "Kleine Berg, *Neth. Antilles, Neth.* **121** P14" means "mountain." The Glossary of Foreign Terms on page 272 translates such terms into English.

When a feature or place can be referred to by more than one name, both may appear in the index with cross-references. These are especially useful for finding major cities in China, where the phonetic Pinyin system has replaced the Wade-Giles system for the romanization of the Chinese language. For example, the entry for Canton reads "Canton *see* Guangzhou, *China* **183** R4." That entry is "Guangzhou (Canton), *China* **183** R4."

A

Aachen, *Ger.* **148** F4
Aalen, *Ger.* **148** J7
Aaley, *Leb.* **170** J6
Aalsmeer, *Neth.* **146** J12
Aalst, *Belg.* **146** L11
Aansluit, *S. Af.* **202** J9
Aare, *river, Switz.* **150** A3
Aarschot, *Belg.* **146** L12
Aasu, *Amer. Samoa, U.S.* **218** M7
Aba, *China* **180** K11
Aba, *Dem. Rep. of the Congo* **198** H12
Aba, *Nigeria* **201** H14
Abā as Sa'ūd, *Saudi Arabia* **172** N9
Abaco Island, *Bahamas* **120** C6
Ābādān, *Iran* **172** F11
Ābādeh, *Iran* **173** F13
Abadla, *Alg.* **196** C9
Abaetetuba, *Braz.* **131** D13
Abaiang, *island, Kiribati* **214** G8
Abaji, *Nigeria* **201** G14
Abajo Peak, *Utah, U.S.* **107** P9
Abakan, *Russ.* **159** L13
Abancay, *Peru* **130** H5
Abaokoro, *island, Kiribati* **217** F17
Abashiri, *Japan* **184** E15
Abashiri Wan, *Japan* **184** E15
Abay, *Kaz.* **175** E14
Ābaya Hāyk', *Eth.* **199** H14
Abbaye, Point, *Mich., U.S.* **98** E7
Abbeville, *Ala., U.S.* **101** M17
Abbeville, *Fr.* **146** M9
Abbeville, *La., U.S.* **100** Q8
Abbeville, *S.C., U.S.* **96** K7

Abbeyfeale, *Ire.* **143** T3
Abbeyleix, *Ire.* **143** T5
Abbiategrasso, *It.* **150** E4
Abbot Ice Shelf, *Antarctica* **226** J6
Abbotsford, *B.C., Can.* **82** M8
Abbotsford, *Wis., U.S.* **98** H4
Abbottabad, *Pak.* **176** M11
'Abd al 'Azīz, Jabal, *Syr.* **170** D13
'Abd al Kūrī, *island, Yemen* **173** R13
Abéché, *Chad* **197** H16
Ab-e Istadeh-ye Moqor, *lake, Afghan.* **177** P7
Abemama, *island, Kiribati* **214** G8
Abengourou, *Côte d'Ivoire* **200** H9
Åbenrå, *Den.* **140** P11
Abeokuta, *Nigeria* **200** G12
Aberaeron, *Wales, U.K.* **143** U9
Aberdare, *Wales, U.K.* **143** V10
Aberdaron, *Wales, U.K.* **143** T8
Aberdaugleddau *see* Milford Haven, *Wales, U.K.* **143** V8
Aberdeen, *Idaho, U.S.* **106** H6
Aberdeen, *Md., U.S.* **96** C14
Aberdeen, *Miss., U.S.* **101** J13
Aberdeen, *N.C., U.S.* **96** J11
Aberdeen, *S. Dak., U.S.* **104** J6
Aberdeen, *Scot., U.K.* **142** K11
Aberdeen, *Wash., U.S.* **108** D2
Aberdeen Lake, *Nunavut, Can.* **83** H14
Aberffraw, *Wales, U.K.* **143** S9
Abergele, *Wales, U.K.* **143** S10
Abergwaun *see* Fishguard, *Wales, U.K.* **143** U8
Abernathy, *Tex., U.S.* **102** J5
Abert, Lake, *Oreg., U.S.* **108** K6

Abertawe *see* Swansea, *Wales, U.K.* **143** V9
Aberteifi *see* Cardigan, *Wales, U.K.* **143** U9
Abertillery, *Wales, U.K.* **143** V10
Aberystwyth, *Wales, U.K.* **143** U9
Abhā, *Saudi Arabia* **172** N8
Abidjan, *Côte d'Ivoire* **200** H9
Abilene, *Kans., U.S.* **105** S8
Abilene, *Tex., U.S.* **102** L8
Abingden Downs, *Qnsld., Austral.* **211** R12
Abingdon *see* Pinta, Isla, *island, Ecua.* **128** N9
Abingdon, *Eng., U.K.* **143** V12
Abingdon, *Ill., U.S.* **99** Q4
Abingdon, *Va., U.S.* **96** G8
Abiquiu, *N. Mex., U.S.* **107** R12
Abisko, *Sw.* **141** D13
Abitibi, *river, N. Amer.* **80** H8
Abitibi, Lake, *N. Amer.* **80** H8
Abkhazia, *Rep. of Georgia* **169** A15
Åbo *see* Turku, *Fin.* **141** K15
Abohar, *India* **178** E4
Abomey, *Benin* **200** G11
Abraham Lincoln Birthplace National Historic Site, *Ky., U.S.* **101** C16
Abraham's Bay, *Bahamas* **117** H16
Abra Pampa, *Arg.* **132** D9
Abreú, *Dom. Rep.* **117** L19
Abrolhos, Arquipélago dos, *Braz.* **131** K16
Absalom, Mount, *Antarctica* **226** E11
Absaroka Range, *Wyo., U.S.* **106** F9
Absarokee, *Mont., U.S.* **106** E9
Abşeron Yasaqlıği, *peninsula, Azerb.* **169** D23
Abū al Abyaḍ, *island, U.A.E.* **173** J14

Abu al Ḥuṣayn, Qā', *Jordan* **170** M10
Abū 'Alī, *island, Saudi Arabia* **172** H12
Abū Baḥr, *plain, Saudi Arabia* **172** L11
Abu Ballâs, *peak, Egypt* **194** E8
Abū Daghmah, *Syr.* **170** D10
Abu Dhabi, *U.A.E.* **173** J14
Abu Durba, *Egypt* **171** T2
Abu Hamed, *Sudan* **199** C13
Abuja, *Nigeria* **201** F14
Abū Kamāl, *Syr.* **170** H14
Abū Madd, Ra's, *Saudi Arabia* **172** J6
Abu Matariq, *Sudan* **198** F11
Abunã, *river, Bol., Braz.* **130** G7
Abunã, *Braz.* **130** G7
Abū Qumayyiṣ, Ra's, *Saudi Arabia* **173** J13
Abu Rudeis, *Egypt* **171** S2
Abū Rujmayn, Jabal, *Syr.* **170** G10
Abu Shagara, Ras, *Sudan* **199** C14
Abu Simbel, *site, Egypt* **197** F19
Abuta, *Japan* **184** G13
Ābuyē Mēda, *peak, Eth.* **199** F15
Abu Zabad, *Sudan* **198** F12
Abu Zenîma, *Egypt* **171** S2
Abwong, *Sudan* **199** G13
Abyad, El Bahr el (White Nile), *Sudan* **199** F13
Ābyek, *Iran* **172** C12
Academy Glacier, *Antarctica* **226** H10
Acadia National Park, *Me., U.S.* **95** F18
A Cañiza, *Sp.* **144** C6
Acaponeta, *Mex.* **114** G9
Acapulco, *Mex.* **114** K11
Acarai Mountains, *Guyana* **129** G14
Acaraú, *Braz.* **131** D16
Acarigua, *Venez.* **128** C8
Acatenango, Volcán de, *Guatemala* **115** L15
Acatlán, *Mex.* **114** J12
Accomac, *Va., U.S.* **96** E15
Accra, *Ghana* **200** H11
Accumoli, *It.* **150** J9
Achach, *island, F.S.M.* **217** C14
Acharacle, *Scot., U.K.* **142** L7
Achavanich, *Scot., U.K.* **142** H10
Achayvayam, *Russ.* **159** D21
Achill Island, *Ire.* **143** R3
Achim, *Ger.* **148** C7
Achinsk, *Russ.* **159** K13
Achna, *Cyprus* **160** P9
Achnasheen, *Scot., U.K.* **142** J8
Acıgöl, *lake, Turk.* **168** G5
Acıpayam, *Turk.* **168** H5
Ackerman, *Miss., U.S.* **100** K12
Ackley, *Iowa, U.S.* **105** N12
Acklins, The Bight of, *Bahamas* **117** H15
Acklins Island, *Bahamas* **117** H15
Acoma Pueblo, *N. Mex., U.S.* **107** S11
Aconcagua, Cerro, *Arg.* **132** K7
Aconcagua, Río, *Chile* **132** K6
Açores *see* Azores, *islands, Atl. Oc.* **204** C3
A Coruña, *Sp.* **144** A6
Acquaviva, *San Marino* **161** J14
Acqui Terme, *It.* **150** F3
Acraman, Lake, *Austral.* **210** J9
Acre, *river, Braz., Peru* **130** G6
Acre *see* 'Akko, *Israel* **170** K5
Acteon, Groupe, *Fr. Polynesia, Fr.* **219** G22
Actium, *battle, Gr.* **154** G7
Açu, *Braz.* **131** F17
Ada, *Ghana* **200** H11
Ada, *Minn., U.S.* **104** G8
Ada, *Ohio, U.S.* **99** Q12
Ada, *Okla., U.S.* **102** H12
Ada, *Serb.* **152** D10
Adair, Cape, *Nunavut, Can.* **83** E17
Adak Island, *Alas., U.S.* **110** N5
Adalia *see* Antalya, *Turk.* **168** H6
Adam, *Oman* **173** K16
Adámandás, *Gr.* **155** M13
Adamello, *peak, It.* **150** C6
Adams, *Minn., U.S.* **104** L12
Adams, *Wis., U.S.* **98** K5
Adams, Mount, *Wash., U.S.* **108** E5
Adam's Peak, *Sri Lanka* **179** T7
Adam's Rock, *Pitcairn I., U.K.* **219** Q23
Adamstown, *Pitcairn I., U.K.* **219** Q23
Adamsville, *Tenn., U.S.* **101** G13
'Adan (Aden), *Yemen* **172** R9
Adana, *Turk.* **168** J10
'Adan aş Şughrá, *cape, Yemen* **172** R9
Adang, Teluk, *Indonesia* **188** K12
Adare, Cape, *Antarctica* **227** R13
Adavale, *Qnsld., Austral.* **211** U12

Adda, *river, It.* **150** E5
Ad Dahnā', *desert, Saudi Arabia* **172** H10
Ad Dakhla, *W. Sahara, Mor.* **196** E5
Ad Dammām, *Saudi Arabia* **172** H12
Ad Dār al Ḥamrā', *Saudi Arabia* **172** H6
Ad Darb, *Saudi Arabia* **172** N8
Ad Dawādimī, *Saudi Arabia* **172** J9
Ad Dawḥah (Doha), *Qatar* **173** J13
Ad Dibdibah, *region, Iraq, Kuwait, Saudi Arabia* **172** G10
Ad Dilam, *Saudi Arabia* **172** K11
Addis Ababa *see* Ādīs Ābeba, *Eth.* **199** G15
Ad Dīwānīyah, *Iraq* **172** E10
Addu Atoll, *Maldives* **179** X3
Ad Duwayd, *Saudi Arabia* **172** F8
Addy, *Wash., U.S.* **108** B8
Adel, *Ga., U.S.* **97** P6
Adel, *Iowa, U.S.* **105** P11
Adel, *Oreg., U.S.* **108** L6
Adelaide, *Bahamas* **120** B10
Adelaide, *S. Aust., Austral.* **211** Y10
Adelaide Island, *Antarctica* **226** E4
Adelaide Peninsula, *Nunavut, Can.* **83** F14
Adelaide River, *N. Terr., Austral.* **211** P7
Adelfi, *island, Gr.* **155** G13
Adélie Coast, *Antarctica* **227** Q18
Aden *see* 'Adan, *Yemen* **172** R9
Aden, Gulf of, *Ind. Oc.* **240** E5
Aderbissinat, *Niger* **196** H12
'Adhirīyāt, Jibāl al, *peak, Jordan* **171** P8
Adieu, Cape, *Austral.* **210** J8
Adige, *river, It.* **150** E7
Ādigrat, *Eth.* **199** E15
Adilabad, *India* **178** L6
Adímilos, *island, Gr.* **155** M13
Adin, *Calif., U.S.* **108** M5
Adinkerke, *Belg.* **146** L10
Adíparos, *island, Gr.* **155** L14
Adirondack Mountains, *N.Y., U.S.* **94** G11
Ādīs Ābeba (Addis Ababa), *Eth.* **199** G15
Adi Ugri, *Eritrea* **199** E15
Adıyaman, *Turk.* **169** H13
Adjud, *Rom.* **153** D16
Adjuntas, *P.R., U.S.* **120** N3
Adlavik Islands, *Nfld. & Lab., Can.* **83** K22
Adler, *Russ.* **157** U11
Admiralty Inlet, *Nunavut, Can.* **83** E16
Admiralty Inlet, *Wash., U.S.* **108** B4
Admiralty Island, *Alas., U.S.* **84** Q7
Admiralty Island National Monument, *Alas., U.S.* **111** L22
Admiralty Islands, *P.N.G.* **213** B19
Admiralty Mountains, *Antarctica* **227** Q14
Abou Deïa, *Chad* **197** J15
Adour, *river, Fr.* **147** X7
Adra, *Sp.* **144** M11
Adrano, *It.* **151** S11
Adrar, *Alg.* **196** D10
Adrar, *region, Mauritania* **196** F6
Adrar des Iforas, *range, Mali* **196** F10
Adraskan, *Afghan.* **177** N2
Adria, *It.* **150** E8
Adrian, *Mich., U.S.* **99** N11
Adrian, *Minn., U.S.* **104** L9
Adrian, *Tex., U.S.* **102** G4
Adrianople *see* Edirne, *Turk.* **168** B3
Adriatic Sea, *Eur.* **138** J7
Adun Gol, *China* **182** B2
Ādwa, *Eth.* **199** E15
Adyakit, Gora, *Russ.* **159** F14
Aegean Sea, *Eur.* **138** K9
Aegina *see* Égina, *island, Gr.* **154** K12
Aegir Ridge, *Arctic Oc.* **243** J20
Aej, *island, Marshall Is.* **216** G8
Aeon Point, *Kiribati* **217** C24
Afaahiti, *Fr. Polynesia, Fr.* **219** P17
Afándou, *Gr.* **155** N20
Afar, *region, Eth.* **199** E16
Afareaitu, *Fr. Polynesia, Fr.* **219** N14
Affric, Glen, *Scot., U.K.* **142** K8
Afghanistan, *Asia* **167** U6
'Afīf, *Saudi Arabia* **172** K8
Afiq, *Israel* **170** K6
Afitos, *Gr.* **154** D12
Afmadow, *Somalia* **199** J16
Afobaka, *Suriname* **129** E16
Afognak Island, *Alas., U.S.* **111** L15
Afono Bay, *Amer. Samoa, U.S.* **218** L8
'Afrīn, *Syr.* **170** D8

Afşin, *Turk.* 168 GI2
Afton, *Okla., U.S.* 102 EI4
Afton, *Wyo., U.S.* 106 H8
Afuefuniya Point, *N. Mariana Is., U.S.* 216 E8
'Afula, *Israel* 170 L5
Afyon, *Turk.* 168 F6
Agadez, *Niger* 196 GI2
Agadir, *Mor.* 196 C7
Agaete, *Canary Is.* 204 Q5
Agafo Gumas, *Guam, U.S.* 216 BII
Agalega Islands, *Seychelles* 205 Q2O
Agana *see* Hagåtña, *Guam, U.S.* 216 CIO
Agana Bay, *Guam, U.S.* 216 CII
Agana Heights, *Guam, U.S.* 216 CIO
Agano, river, *Japan* 184 MI2
Aga Point, *Guam, U.S.* 216 EIO
Agar, *India* 178 H5
Agartala, *India* 178 HI3
Agassiz Fracture Zone, *Pac. Oc.* 239 PI4
Agat, *Guam, U.S.* 216 DIO
Agata, *Russ.* 159 GI4
Agat Bay, *Guam, U.S.* 216 CIO
Agate, *Colo., U.S.* 106 MI4
Agate Fossile Beds National Monument, *Nebr., U.S.* 105 NI
Agathoníssi, island, *Gr.* 155 KI8
Agats, *Indonesia* 189 L2O
Agatti Island, *India* 179 R2
Agattu Island, *Alas., U.S.* IIO LI
Agattu Strait, *Alas., U.S.* IIO LI
Agboville, *Côte d'Ivoire* 200 H9
Ağdam, *Azerb.* 169 E2O
Agde, *Fr.* 147 YII
Agde, Cap d', *Fr.* 147 YII
Agen, *Fr.* 147 W8
Agfayan Bay, *Guam, U.S.* 216 EIO
Aggtelek, *Hung.* 149 KI6
Aghdash, *Azerb.* 169 D2I
Aghjabädi, *Azerb.* 169 E2I
Aghrïjït, *Mauritania* 196 G7
Aghsu, *Azerb.* 169 D22
Agiá, *Gr.* 154 EII
Agia Galini, *Gr.* 155 QI4
Agia Napa, *Cyprus* 160 PIO
Agía Pelagía, *Gr.* 154 NII
Agía Rouméli, *Gr.* 155 QI3
Agiássos, *Gr.* 155 GI7
Agidyem, island, *Marshall Is.* 216 L8
Agingan, Puntan, *N. Mariana Is., U.S.* 216 C4
Aginskoye, *Russ.* 159 LI7
Ágio Óros, peninsula, *Gr.* 155 DI3
Agios Amvrosios, *Cyprus* 160 N9
Agios Efstrátios, *Gr.* 155 FI4
Ágios Irínis, Akrotírio, *Gr.* 155 EI5
Ágios Kírikos, *Gr.* 155 KI6
Ágios Nikólaos, *Gr.* 155 QI6
Agios Sergios, *Cyprus* 160 NIO
Agios Theodoros, *Cyprus* 160 NIO
Agiou Orous, Kólpos, *Gr.* 154 DI2
Agnes Creek, *S. Aust., Austral.* 211 U8
Agness, *Oreg., U.S.* 108 K2
Agnew, *W. Aust., Austral.* 211 V4
Agnita, *Rom.* 153 DI4
Agnone, *It.* 150 KII
Agra, *India* 178 G6
Agrakhanskiy Poluostrov, *Russ.* 157 TI5
Agrakhanskiy Zaliv, *Russ.* 157 TI5
Ágreda, *Sp.* 145 DI3
Agri, *Turk.* 169 EI7
Agría Gramvoúsa, *Gr.* 154 PI2
Ağrı Dağı (Mount Ararat), *Turk.* 169 EI8
Agrigento, *It.* 151 TIO
Agrihan, island, *N. Mariana Is., U.S.* 216 A2
Agrópoli, *It.* 151 NII
Agrínio, *Gr.* 154 H8
Agryz, *Russ.* 156 HI6
Ağstafa, *Azerb.* 169 CI9
Aguada, *P.R., U.S.* 120 MI
Aguada de Pasajeros, *Cuba* 116 H8
Aguadilla, *P.R., U.S.* 120 MI
Aguadilla, Bahía de, *P.R., U.S.* 120 MI
Agua Fria National Monument, *Ariz., U.S.* 107 T7
Aguán, river, *N. Amer.* 80 P7
Aguapeí, *Braz.* 130 J9
Agua Prieta, *Mex.* 114 C8
Aguas Blancas, *Chile* 132 E7
Aguascalientes, *Mex.* 114 GIO
Águas Formosas, *Braz.* 131 KI6
A Gudiña, *Sp.* 144 D7

Águeda, *Port.* 144 F5
Aguelhok, *Mali* 196 GIO
Aguijan, island, *N. Mariana Is., U.S.* 216 C2
Águila, Punta, *P.R., U.S.* 120 PI
Aguila, *Ariz., U.S.* 107 T6
Aguilar, *Colo., U.S.* 107 PI4
Aguilar de Campoo, *Sp.* 144 CIO
Aguilas, *Sp.* 145 LI3
Aguja, Cabo de la, *Col.* 128 B5
Agulhas, Cape, *S. Af.* 202 M8
Agulhas Bank, *Ind. Oc.* 240 NI
Agulhas Basin, *Ind. Oc.* 240 QI
Agulhas Plateau, *Ind. Oc.* 240 N2
Aguni Jima, *Japan* 185 YI
Ahaggar (Hoggar), range, *Alg.* 196 EII
Ahar, *Iran* 172 AII
Aharnés, *Gr.* 154 JI2
Ahe, island, *Fr. Polynesia, Fr.* 219 DI7
Ahelóos, river, *Gr.* 154 H8
Ahiri, *India* 178 L7
Ahlat, *Turk.* 169 FI7
Ahlatlıbel, ruin, *Turk.* 168 E8
Ahmadabad, *India* 178 J3
Ahmadnagar, *India* 178 L4
Ahmadpur East, *Pak.* 177 S9
Ahmad Wal, *Pak.* 177 S5
Ahoa, *Wallis & Futuna, Fr.* 218 BII
Ahome, *Mex.* 114 E7
Ahoskie, *N.C., U.S.* 96 GI3
Ahram, *Iran* 173 DI2
Ahrax Point, *Malta* 161 J2I
Ahrensburg, *Ger.* 148 C8
Ahtme, *Est.* 141 KI7
Ahua, *Fr. Polynesia, Fr.* 219 K2O
Ahu-a-miria Islands, *Cook Is., N.Z.* 219 BI8
Ahua 'Umi Heiau, *Hawaii, U.S.* 113 MI9
Ahumoa, peak, *Hawaii, U.S.* 113 LI9
Ahuna, Motu, *Fr. Polynesia, Fr.* 219 KI3
Ahunui, island, *Fr. Polynesia, Fr.* 219 G2O
Ahvāz, *Iran* 172 FII
Ahvenanmaa *see* Åland, island, *Fin.* 141 KI4
Ahwar, *Yemen* 172 RIO
Ai, island, *Marshall Is.* 216 M7
'Aiea, *Hawai'i, U.S.* 112 EII
Aigialousa, *Cyprus* 160 MII
Aigle, *Switz.* 150 C2
Aigoual, Mont, *Fr.* 147 WII
Aiguá, *Uru.* 132 LI4
Aigurande, *Fr.* 147 T9
Aikawa, *Japan* 184 MII
Aiken, *S.C., U.S.* 96 L8
Aileron, *N. Terr., Austral.* 211 T8
Ailinginae Atoll, *Marshall Is.* 216 F3
Ailinglapalap Atoll, *Marshall Is.* 216 H4
Ailsa Craig, *Gibraltar, U.K.* 161 Q23
Ailsa Craig, island, *Scot., U.K.* 143 N8
Ailuk Atoll, *Marshall Is.* 216 F4
Aimere, *Indonesia* 189 MI3
Ainaži, *Latv.* 141 LI6
Aineman, island, *Marshall Is.* 216 M9
Aïnhoa, *Fr.* 147 Y5
Aínsa, *Sp.* 145 CI5
'Aïn Sefra, *Alg.* 196 BIO
Ainsworth, *Nebr., U.S.* 105 N5
Aiquile, *Bol.* 130 K7
Aiquina, *Chile* 132 D8
Airai, *Palau* 216 NI2
Airão, *Braz.* 130 D9
Air Force Island, *Nunavut, Can.* 83 FI7
Aïr Massif, *Niger* 196 GI2
Airolo, *Switz.* 150 C4
Aisey, *Fr.* 147 RI2
Aitape, *P.N.G.* 213 CI8
Aitkin, *Minn., U.S.* 104 GII
Aitutaki, island, *Cook Is., N.Z.* 218 PII
Aitutaki Atoll, *Cook Is., N.Z.* 214 KI2
Aiud, *Rom.* 153 DI3
Aiurua, Passe, *Fr. Polynesia, Fr.* 219 QI8
Aiwa, island, *Fiji Is.* 218 J9
Aiwo, region, *Nauru* 217 F22
Aiwokako Passage, *Palau* 216 MII
Aix, Île d', *Fr.* 147 T6
Aix-en-Provence, *Fr.* 147 XI3
Aixirivall, *Andorra* 160 K2
Aix-les-Bains, *Fr.* 147 UI4
Aiyon Mountain, *Palau* 216 LI2
Aiyura, *P.N.G.* 213 DI9
Aizawl, *India* 178 HI4
Aizenay, *Fr.* 147 S5
Aizpute, *Latv.* 141 MI5

Aizuwakamatsu, *Japan* 184 MI2
Ajaccio, *Fr.* 150 K3
Ajaccio, Golfe d', *Fr.* 150 K3
Ajajú, river, *Col.* 128 H6
Ajaria, *Rep. of Georgia* 169 CI6
Ajax Peak, *Idaho, U.S.* 106 E6
Ajayan Bay, *Guam, U.S.* 216 EIO
Ajdābiyā, *Lib.* 197 CI5
Ajigasawa, *Japan* 184 JI2
'Ajlūn, *Jordan* 170 L6
'Ajman, *U.A.E.* 173 JI5
Ajmer, *India* 178 G4
Ajo, *Ariz., U.S.* 107 V6
Ajo, Cabo de, *Sp.* 144 BII
Ajokwola, island, *Marshall Is.* 216 GIO
Ajoupa-Bouillon, *Martinique, Fr.* 121 E22
Ajrestan, *Afghan.* 177 N6
Akabira, *Japan* 184 FI4
Akaiami, island, *Cook Is., N.Z.* 218 QI2
Akaka Falls, *Hawai'i, U.S.* 113 L2I
Akaki, *Cyprus* 160 P8
Akamaru, island, *Fr. Polynesia, Fr.* 219 R2I
Akankohan, *Japan* 184 FI5
Akanthou, *Cyprus* 160 N9
Akashi, *Japan* 185 Q8
Akaska, *S. Dak., U.S.* 104 J5
Akbulak, *Russ.* 158 J7
Akçaabat, *Turk.* 169 DI4
Akçadağ, *Turk.* 169 GI3
Akçakale, *Turk.* 169 JI3
Akçakışla, *Turk.* 168 EII
Akçakoca, *Turk.* 168 C7
Akçay, *Turk.* 168 E3
Akçay, *Turk.* 168 J5
Akchâr, region, *Mauritania* 196 F5
Akdağ, peak, *Turk.* 168 F2
Akdağ, peak, *Turk.* 168 J7
Ak Dağlar, *Turk.* 168 J5
Akdağmadeni, *Turk.* 168 EII
Akeley, *Minn., U.S.* 104 GIO
Akera, river, *Azerb.* 169 E2O
Aketi, *Dem. Rep. of the Congo* 198 JIO
Akhalts'ikhe, *Rep. of Georgia* 169 CI7
Akhḍar, Jabal al, *Lib.* 194 D7
Akhiok, *Alas., U.S.* III MI5
Akhisar, *Turk.* 168 F3
Akhnur, *India* 177 NI2
Akhtuba, river, *Russ.* 174 E4
Akhtubinsk, *Russ.* 157 QI4
Aki, *Japan* 185 R7
Akiachak, *Alas., U.S.* IIO JI2
Akiaki, island, *Fr. Polynesia, Fr.* 219 F2I
Akimiski Island, *Nunavut, Can.* 83 MI7
Akita, *Japan* 184 KI2
Akitua, island, *Cook Is., N.Z.* 218 PII
Akjoujt, *Mauritania* 196 F5
Akkeshi, *Japan* 184 FI6
Akkeshi Wan, *Japan* 184 FI6
'Akko (Acre), *Israel* 170 K5
Akkuş, *Turk.* 168 DI2
Aklavik, *N.W.T., Can.* 82 E9
Aklera, *India* 178 H5
'Ako'ako'a Point, *Hawai'i, U.S.* 113 KI9
Akobo, *Sudan* 199 GI3
Akobo, river, *Eth.* 199 GI3
Akola, *India* 178 K5
Ak'ordat, *Eritrea* 199 DI4
Akosombo Dam, *Ghana* 200 HII
Akpatok Island, *Nunavut, Can.* 83 JI9
Akqi, *China* 180 F5
Akranes, *Ice.* 140 F2
Akráta, *Gr.* 154 JIO
Akron, *Colo., U.S.* 106 LI5
Akron, *Iowa, U.S.* 104 M8
Akron, *Ohio, U.S.* 99 PI4
Akrotiri, *Gr.* 155 NI5
Akrotiri Bay, *Cyprus* 160 Q7
Akrotiri (Western) Sovereign Base Area, *Cyprus* 160 Q7
Aksai Chin, *China* 180 H4
Aksaray, *Turk.* 168 G9
Aksay, *China* 180 G9
Aksay, *Russ.* 157 QI3
Akşehir, *Turk.* 168 G7
Akşehir Gölü, *Turk.* 168 G7
Akseki, *Turk.* 168 H7
Aksu, *China* 180 F5
Aksu, *Kaz.* 174 J6
Aksu, river, *Turk.* 168 H6
Āksum, *Eth.* 199 EI5
Aktag, peak, *China* 180 H6
Akto, *China* 180 F4

Akune, *Japan* 185 S4
Akureyri, *Ice.* 140 E3
Akuseki Shima, *Japan* 185 V3
Akutan, *Alas., U.S.* IIO NIO
Akyab *see* Sittwe, *Myanmar* 186 H4
Akyaka, *Turk.* 169 DI7
Akyazı, *Turk.* 168 D6
Alà, Monti di, *It.* 150 M4
Ala, *It.* 150 D6
Alabama, river, *Ala., U.S.* 101 MI4
Alabama, *U.S.* 101 KI4
Alabaster, *Ala., U.S.* 101 KI5
Alaca, *Turk.* 168 EIO
Alaçam, *Turk.* 168 CII
Alacahöyük, ruin, *Turk.* 168 EIO
Alachua, *Fla., U.S.* 97 R7
Alacránes, Arrecife, *Mex.* 115 GI6
Aladağ, peak, *Turk.* 168 G7
Aladağ, peak, *Turk.* 168 HIO
Alaejos, *Sp.* 144 E9
Al Aflāj, region, *Saudi Arabia* 172 LIO
Alagir, *Russ.* 157 UI3
Alagoinhas, *Braz.* 131 HI7
Alagón, *Sp.* 145 DI4
Al Aḥmadī, *Kuwait* 172 GII
Al Ain, *U.A.E.* 173 JI5
Alaja, *Turkm.* 174 L6
Alajuela, *Costa Rica* 115 NI9
Alaka'i Swamp, *Hawai'i, U.S.* 112 B5
Alakanuk, *Alas., U.S.* IIO HI2
Al Akhḍar, *Saudi Arabia* 172 G6
Alakoko Fishpond, *Hawai'i, U.S.* 112 C6
Alaköl, lake, *Kaz.* 175 FI8
'Alalakeiki Channel, *Hawai'i, U.S.* 113 HI6
Alalakh, ruin, *Turk.* 168 JII
Alamagan, island, *N. Mariana Is., U.S.* 216 B2
Al 'Amārah, *Iraq* 172 EII
Alameda, *Calif., U.S.* 109 S3
Alameda Gardens, *Gibraltar, U.K.* 161 P22
Al Amārah *see* ... Alamosa, *Colo., U.S.* 107 PI2
Alamo, *Nev., U.S.* 109 SI2
Alamo, *Tenn., U.S.* 100 FI2
Alamogordo, *N. Mex., U.S.* 107 UI3
Alamo Heights, *Tex., U.S.* 103 R9
Alamosa, *Colo., U.S.* 107 PI2
Åland (Ahvenanmaa), island, *Fin.* 141 KI4
Alandar, *Afghan.* 176 M4
Alandroal, *Port.* 144 J6
Alanya, *Turk.* 168 J7
Alao, *Amer. Samoa, U.S.* 218 M9
Alaotra, Lac, *Madagascar* 203 FI8
Alappuzha (Alleppey), *India* 179 R5
Al 'Aqabah (Aqaba), *Jordan* 171 R5
Al 'Aqīq, *Saudi Arabia* 172 L8
Alara, river, *Turk.* 168 J7
Alarcón, Embalse de, *Sp.* 144 GI2
Al 'Armah, plateau, *Saudi Arabia* 172 HIO
Al Arṭāwīyah, *Saudi Arabia* 172 HIO
Al 'Āṣ (Orontes), river, *Syr.* 170 F7
Al As'ad, *Saudi Arabia* 172 G6
Alaşehir, *Turk.* 168 F4
Al Ashkharah, *Oman* 173 LI7
Alaska, *U.S.* III GI4
Alaska, Gulf of, *Alas., U.S.* III LI8
Alaska Highway, *Alas., U.S.* III GI8
Alaska Peninsula, *Alas., U.S.* IIO MI3
Alaska Range, *Alas., U.S.* III JI5
Alassio, *It.* 150 G3
Alāt, *Azerb.* 169 E23
Alatyr', *Russ.* 156 KI3
Alausí, *Ecua.* 128 K3
Alava, Cape, *Wash., U.S.* 108 BI
Alaverdi, *Arm.* 169 DI8
'Alawīyīn, Jabal al, *Syr.* 170 F7
Alazani, river, *Azerb., Rep. of Georgia* 169 C2O
Alba, *It.* 150 F3
Al Bāb, *Syr.* 170 D9
Albac, *Rom.* 152 CI2
Albacete, *Sp.* 145 HI3
Al Bad', *Saudi Arabia* 172 G5
Alba de Tormes, *Sp.* 144 F9
Al Badī', *Saudi Arabia* 172 LIO
Al Bāḥah, *Saudi Arabia* 172 M8
Alba Iulia, *Rom.* 153 DI3
Albania, *Eur.* 139 X8
Albany, *Ga., U.S.* 97 P5
Albany, *Ky., U.S.* 101 DI7

Albany, *Mo., U.S.* 105 RII
Albany, *N.Y., U.S.* 94 KII
Albany, river, *Ont., Can.* 83 NI7
Albany, *Oreg., U.S.* 108 G3
Albany, *Tex., U.S.* 102 L8
Albany, *W. Aust., Austral.* 211 Y3
Al Bardī, *Lib.* 197 CI7
Albardón, *Arg.* 132 J8
Albarracín, *Sp.* 145 FI3
Al Baṣrah, *Iraq* 172 FII
Albatross Bay, *Austral.* 210 BI2
Al Bayāḍ, plain, *Saudi Arabia* 172 LII
Al Bayḍā' (Beida), *Lib.* 197 BI6
Albemarle *see* Isabela, Isla, island, *Ecua.* 128 Q8
Albemarle, Punta, *Ecua.* 128 P8
Albemarle Sound, *N.C., U.S.* 96 GI4
Albenga, *It.* 150 G3
Albera, Serra de l', *Fr.* 147 ZIO
Albereto, *It.* 161 KI7
Alberobello, *It.* 150 MI4
Albert, Lake, *Austral.* 210 LIO
Albert, Lake, *Dem. Rep. of the Congo, Uganda* 198 JI2
Alberta, *Can.* 82 LIO
Albert Lea, *Minn., U.S.* 104 LII
Albert Nile, river, *Uganda* 199 JI3
Albert Town, *Bahamas* 117 GI4
Albert Town, *Jam.* 120 H8
Albertville, *Ala., U.S.* 101 HI6
Albertville, *Fr.* 147 UI4
Albi, *Fr.* 147 XIO
Albia, *Iowa, U.S.* 105 QI2
Albin, *Wyo., U.S.* 106 KI4
Albina Point, *Angola* 194 M6
Albini, river, *It.* 161 HI4
Albinia, *It.* 150 J7
Albion, *Ill., U.S.* 99 SII
Albion, *Mich., U.S.* 98 MII
Albion, *N.Y., U.S.* 94 H6
Albion, *Nebr., U.S.* 105 P7
Al Bi'r, *Saudi Arabia* 172 G5
Al Birk, *Saudi Arabia* 172 N8
Alborán, Isla de, *Sp.* 144 NII
Alboran Sea, *Sp.* 144 NIO
Ålborg, *Den.* 140 NII
Alborz, Reshteh-ye (Elburz Mountains), *Iran* 172 BII
Albox, *Sp.* 144 LI2
Albuquerque, *N. Mex., U.S.* 107 SI2
Alburquerque, *Sp.* 144 H7
Albury, *N.S.W., Austral.* 211 YI3
Alby, *Fr.* 147 UI4
Alcácer do Sal, *Port.* 144 J5
Alcalá de Guadaira, *Sp.* 144 L8
Alcalá de Henares, *Sp.* 144 FII
Alcalá la Real, *Sp.* 144 LIO
Alcamo, *It.* 151 S9
Alcanar, *Sp.* 145 FI5
Alcañiz, *Sp.* 145 EI5
Alcántara, *Sp.* 144 G7
Alcántara, Embalse de, *Sp.* 144 G7
Alcaraz, *Sp.* 144 JI2
Alcaudete, *Sp.* 144 LIO
Alcázar de San Juan, *Sp.* 144 HII
Alcedo, Volcán, *Ecua.* 128 Q8
Alchevs'k, *Ukr.* 157 QIO
Alcoa, *Tenn., U.S.* 101 FI8
Alcoak, Cerro, *Arg.* 132 D8
Alcobaça, *Port.* 144 G5
Alcobendas, *Sp.* 144 FII
Alcoi *see* Alcoy, *Sp.* 145 JI4
Alcoota, *N. Terr., Austral.* 211 T9
Alcorcón, *Sp.* 144 FII
Alcoutim, *Port.* 144 L6
Alcoy (Alcoi), *Sp.* 145 JI4
Alcubierre, Sierra de, *Sp.* 145 DI4
Alcúdia, *Sp.* 145 GI8
Alcuéscar, *Sp.* 144 H8
Aldabra Islands, *Seychelles* 203 CI7
Aldama, *Mex.* 114 D9
Aldan, river, *Russ.* 159 GI8
Aldan, *Russ.* 159 JI8
Aldanskoye Nagor'ye, *Russ.* 159 JI8
Aldeadávila de la Ribera, *Sp.* 144 E7
Aldeburgh, *Eng., U.K.* 143 UI6
Alderney, island, *Ch. Is.* 143 YII
Aledo, *Ill., U.S.* 99 P3
Aleg, *Mauritania* 196 G5
Alegranza, island, *Canary Is.* 204 P8
Alegrete, *Braz.* 130 PIO
Aleksandrov Gay, *Russ.* 157 NI5
Aleksandrovsk Sakhalinskiy, *Russ.* 159 J2I
Alekseyevka, *Russ.* 156 LI4

Alekseyevka, *Russ.* 156 LI6
Alekseyevka, *Russ.* 157 NIO
Aleksin, *Russ.* 156 K9
Aleksinac, *Serb.* 152 HII
Alemania, *Arg.* 132 F9
Alembel, island, *Marshall Is.* 216 H8
Alençon, *Fr.* 147 Q7
Alenquer, *Braz.* 130 DII
'Alenuihāhā Channel, *Hawai'i, U.S.*
  113 JI8
Aleppo see Ḥalab, *Syr.* 170 D9
Aléria, *Fr.* 150 K4
Alert, *Nunavut, Can.* 83 AI6
Alert Point, *Kiribati* 217 B2O
Alès, *Fr.* 147 WI2
Ales, *It.* 151 P3
Alessandria, *It.* 150 E4
Ålesund, *Nor.* 140 JIO
Aleutian Basin, *Pac. Oc.* 238 B9
Aleutian Islands, *Alas., U.S.* III L2
Aleutian Range, *Alas., U.S.* III MI3
Aleutian Trench, *Pac. Oc.* 238 C9
Alevina, Mys, *Russ.* 159 F2I
Alexander, *N. Dak., U.S.* 104 F2
Alexander, Cape, *Solomon Is.* 217 KI5
Alexander Archipelago, *Alas., U.S.*
  III M22
Alexander Bay, *S. Af.* 202 K6
Alexander City, *Ala., U.S.* 101 KI6
Alexander Island, *Antarctica* 226 F5
Alexandra, *N.Z.* 213 QI6
Alexandra, Zemlya, *Russ.* 158 BI2
Alexándria, *Gr.* 154 CIO
Alexandria see El Iskandarîya, *Egypt*
  197 CI8
Alexandria, *Ind., U.S.* 99 Q9
Alexandria, *Jam.* 120 H8
Alexandria, *La., U.S.* 100 N8
Alexandria, *Minn., U.S.* 104 H9
Alexandria, *Rom.* 153 CI5
Alexandria, *S. Dak., U.S.* 104 L7
Alexandria, *Va., U.S.* 96 DI3
Alexandria Bay, *N.Y., U.S.* 94 G9
Alexandrina, Lake, *Austral.* 210 LIO
Alexandroúpoli (Dedéagach), *Gr.*
  155 CI6
Aleysk, *Russ.* 158 LII
Al Fallūjah, *Iraq* 172 D9
Al Farciya, *W. Sahara, Mor.* 196 D7
Alfaro, *Sp.* 145 DI3
Alfatar, *Bulg.* 153 GI6
Al Fāw, *Iraq* 172 FII
Alföld see Great Hungarian Plain, plain,
  Hung., Serb. 149 MI6
Al Fuqahā', *Lib.* 197 DI4
Al Furāt (Euphrates), river, *Iraq*
  172 FIO
Algarrobal, *Arg.* 132 FIO
Algarrobo, *Chile* 132 G7
Algeciras, *Sp.* 144 N8
Algeciras, Bahía de see Gibraltar, Bay of,
  Gibraltar, U.K. 161 P2I
Algena, *Eritrea* 199 DI5
Alger (Algiers), *Alg.* 196 AII
Algeria, *Af.* 195 EI6
Algha, *Kaz.* 174 D8
Alghabas, *Kaz.* 174 D6
Al Ghaydah, *Yemen* 173 PI3
Al Ghayl, *Saudi Arabia* 172 KIO
Al Ghazālah, *Saudi Arabia* 172 H8
Alghero, *It.* 150 M3
Algiers see Alger, *Alg.* 196 AII
Alginet, *Sp.* 145 HI4
Algoa Bay, *S. Af.* 194 R8
Algoma, *Wis., U.S.* 98 J7
Algona, *Iowa, U.S.* 104 MII
Algorta, *Uru.* 132 KI3
Al Ḥadīdah, crater, *Saudi Arabia*
  172 LI2
Al Ḥaffah, *Syr.* 170 F7
Al Ḥamād, desert, *Jordan, Saudi Arabia*
  172 E7
Alhambra, *Calif., U.S.* 109 X8
Al Ḥamīdīyah, *Syr.* 170 G7
Al Ḥamrā', *Saudi Arabia* 172 K6
Al Ḥamrā', region, *Lib.* 197 CI3
Al Ḥanākīyah, *Saudi Arabia* 172 J7
Al Ḥarīq, *Saudi Arabia* 172 KIO
Al Ḥarūj al Aswad, range, *Lib.* 197 DI5
Al Ḥasakah, *Syr.* 170 DI4
Al Ḥawrah, *Yemen* 172 QII
Al Hījānah, *Syr.* 170 K7
Al Ḥijāz (Hejaz), region, *Saudi Arabia*
  172 H6
Al Ḥillah, *Iraq* 172 E9

Al Ḥillah, *Saudi Arabia* 172 KIO
Alhucemas, Peñón de, *Sp.* 144 PIO
Al Ḥudaydah, *Yemen* 172 Q8
Al Hufūf, *Saudi Arabia* 172 JI2
Ali, *It.* 151 SI2
Aliabad, *Iran* 173 GI5
Aliákmonas, river, *Gr.* 154 DIO
Alibates Flint Quarries National
  Monument, *Tex., U.S.* 102 G5
Äli Bayramlı, *Azerb.* 169 E22
Alicante, *Sp.* 145 JI4
Alice, *Qnsld., Austral.* 211 TI3
Alice, *Tex., U.S.* 103 UIO
Alice, Punta, *It.* 151 PI4
Alice Downs, *W. Aust., Austral.* 211 R6
Alice Springs, *N. Terr., Austral.* 211 T8
Alice Town, *Bahamas* 120 B8
Alice Town, *Bahamas* 120 D6
Aliceville, *Ala., U.S.* 101 KI3
Alicudi, Isola, *It.* 151 RII
Aligarh, *India* 178 F6
Alijos, Rocas, *Mex.* 114 E4
Alijos Rocks see Alijos, Rocas, *N. Amer.*
  80 M2
Al Ikhwān (The Brothers), islands,
  Yemen 173 RI4
Alindau, *Indonesia* 189 JI3
Alingsås, *Sw.* 140 MI2
Alipur, *Pak.* 177 S9
Alipur Duar, *India* 178 GI2
Aliquippa, *Pa., U.S.* 94 N3
Al 'Irqah, *Yemen* 172 RII
Alişar Hüyük, ruin, *Turk.* 168 EIO
Al 'Īsāwīyah, *Saudi Arabia* 172 F6
Alissós, *Gr.* 154 J9
Alistráti, *Gr.* 155 BI3
Alivéri, *Gr.* 155 HI3
Aliwal North, *S. Af.* 202 LIO
Al Jafr, *Jordan* 171 Q7
Al Jāfūrah, desert, *Saudi Arabia* 172 JI2
Al Jaghbūb, *Lib.* 197 CI6
Al Jahrah, *Kuwait* 172 GII
Al Jawādīyah, *Syr.* 170 CI5
Al Jawf see Dawmat al Jandal, *Saudi
  Arabia* 172 F7
Al Jawf (Kufra Oasis), *Lib.* 197 EI6
Al Jifārah, *Saudi Arabia* 172 KIO
Al Jīzah, *Jordan* 170 M7
Al Jubayl, *Saudi Arabia* 172 HI2
Al Jumaylīyah, *Qatar* 173 JI3
Al Junaynah, *Saudi Arabia* 172 M8
Al Junaynah see Geneina, *Sudan*
  198 EIO
Al Kahfah, *Saudi Arabia* 172 H9
Al Karak, *Jordan* 171 N6
Al Kawm, *Syr.* 170 FII
Al Khābūrah, *Oman* 173 KI6
Al Khalīl (Hebron), *W. Bank* 171 N5
Al Kharfah, *Saudi Arabia* 172 LIO
Al Kharj, *Saudi Arabia* 172 KII
Al Khāṣirah, *Saudi Arabia* 172 K9
Al Khawr, *Qatar* 173 JI3
Al Khīrān, *Kuwait* 172 GII
Al Khufayfīyah, *Saudi Arabia* 172 J9
Al Khums, *Lib.* 197 BI4
Al Khunn, *Saudi Arabia* 172 KI2
Al Khuraybah, *Yemen* 172 QII
Al Khurmah, *Saudi Arabia* 172 L8
Al Kiswah, *Syr.* 170 J7
Al Kūfah, *Iraq* 172 E9
Al Kufrah, region, *Lib.* 197 EI6
Al Kūt, *Iraq* 172 EIO
Al Lādhiqīyah (Latakia), *Syr.* 170 F6
Allagash, river, *Me., U.S.* 95 BI6
Allahüekber Tepe, *Turk.* 169 DI7
Allahabad, *India* 178 H8
Al Lajā, desert, *Syr.* 170 K7
Allakaket, *Alas., U.S.* III EI6
All American Canal, *Calif., U.S.* 109 ZI2
Allan Hills, *Antarctica* 227 NI4
Allan Mountain, *Idaho, U.S.* 106 E5
Allanmyo, *Myanmar* 186 J5
Allanton, *N.Z.* 213 RI6
Allaríz, *Sp.* 144 C6
Allegan, *Mich., U.S.* 98 M9
Allegheny, river, *Pa., U.S.* 94 N4
Allegheny Mountains, *U.S.* 85 HI8
Allegheny Reservoir, *Pa.* 94 L5
Allègre, Pointe, *Guadeloupe, Fr.* 121 EI4
Allen, *Arg.* 133 P8
Allen, Bog of, *Ire.* 143 S6
Allen, Lough, *Ire.* 143 Q5
Allendale, *S.C., U.S.* 96 M8
Allendale Town, *Eng., U.K.* 143 PII

Allende, *Mex.* 114 DII
Allentown, *Pa., U.S.* 94 N9
Alleppey see Alappuzha, *India* 179 R5
Aller, river, *Ger.* 148 D8
Allerona, *It.* 150 J8
Alliance, *Nebr., U.S.* 105 N2
Alliance, *Ohio, U.S.* 99 PI5
Al Lidām, *Saudi Arabia* 172 M9
Alligator Pond, *Jam.* 120 J8
Allinge, *Den.* 141 PI3
Allison Peninsula, *Antarctica* 226 H6
Al Līth, *Saudi Arabia* 172 M7
All Saints, *Antigua & Barbuda* 121 B2I
Al Luḥayyah, *Yemen* 172 P8
Al Luwaymī, *Saudi Arabia* 172 G8
Alma, *Ark., U.S.* 100 F6
Alma, *Ga., U.S.* 97 P7
Alma, *Kans., U.S.* 105 S9
Alma, *Mich., U.S.* 98 LII
Alma, *Nebr., U.S.* 105 R5
Almacelles, *Sp.* 145 DI5
Almada, *Port.* 144 J4
Almadén, *Sp.* 144 J9
Almaden, *Qnsld., Austral.* 211 RI3
Al Madīnah (Medina), *Saudi Arabia*
  172 J7
Al Mafraq, *Jordan* 170 L7
Al Majma'ah, *Saudi Arabia* 172 JIO
Al Mālikīyah, *Syr.* 170 CI6
Al Manāmah (Manama), *Bahrain*
  172 HI2
Al Mansūrah, *Syr.* 170 EII
Almanzor, peak, *Sp.* 144 F9
Al Marj, *Lib.* 197 CI5
Al Ma'shūqah, *Saudi Arabia* 172 M8
Al Mawṣil (Mosul), *Iraq* 172 C9
Al Mayādīn, *Syr.* 170 GI3
Al Mayyāh, *Saudi Arabia* 172 G9
Almazán, *Sp.* 144 F7
Almeida, *Port.* 144 F7
Almeirim, *Port.* 144 H5
Almeirim, *Braz.* 130 DI2
Almelo, *Neth.* 146 HI4
Almena, *Kans., U.S.* 105 R5
Almenara, peak, *Sp.* 144 JI2
Almenara, *Braz.* 131 JI6
Almendra, Embalse de, *Sp.* 144 E8
Almendralejo, *Sp.* 144 J8
Almere, *Neth.* 146 JI2
Almería, *Sp.* 144 MI2
Almería, Golfo de, *Sp.* 144 MI2
Al'met'yevsk, *Russ.* 156 JI6
Almina, Punta, *Sp.* 144 N9
Al Mintirib, *Oman* 173 KI6
Almira, *Wash., U.S.* 108 C7
Almirantazgo, Seno, *Chile* 133 X8
Almirante, *Pan.* 115 N2O
Almirí, *Gr.* 154 JII
Almirós, *Gr.* 154 FII
Al Mismīyah, *Syr.* 170 K7
Almo, *Idaho, U.S.* 106 J6
Almodôvar, *Port.* 144 K5
Almodóvar del Campo, *Sp.* 144 JIO
Al Mubarraz, *Saudi Arabia* 172 JI2
Al Mudawwarah, *Jordan* 171 S7
Almudévar, *Sp.* 145 DI4
Al Mukallā, *Yemen* 172 QI2
Al Mukhā, *Yemen* 172 R8
Almus, *Turk.* 168 DI2
Almus Barajı, *Turk.* 168 DI2
Al Muwassam, *Saudi Arabia* 172 P8
Al Muwayh, *Saudi Arabia* 172 K8
Alney, Gora, *Russ.* 159 F22
Alnwick, *Eng., U.K.* 143 NI2
Alo, *Wallis & Futuna, Fr.* 218 EII
Alo, Pointe d', *Wallis & Futuna, Fr.*
  218 EII
Alofau, *Amer. Samoa, U.S.* 218 M8
Alofi, *Niue, N.Z.* 219 B2O
Alofi, island, *Wallis & Futuna, Fr.* 218 FII
Alofi Bay, *Niue, N.Z.* 219 B2O
Alokan, island, *Solomon Is.* 217 NI8
Along, *India* 178 FI5
Alónissos, island, *Gr.* 154 FI2
Alónissos, *Gr.* 154 GI2
Alor, island, *Indonesia* 189 MI5
Alor, Kepulauan, *Indonesia* 189 MI5
Alora, *Sp.* 144 M9
Alor Setar, *Malaysia* 187 S8
Aloysius, Mount, *Austral.* 210 G7

Alpena, *Mich., U.S.* 98 HI2
Alpha Ridge, *Arctic Oc.* 242 KIO
Alpine, *Ariz., U.S.* 107 T9
Alpine, *Tex., U.S.* 103 Q2
Alpine Junction, *Wyo., U.S.* 106 H8
Alps, range, *Eur.* 138 H6
Al Qābil, *Oman* 173 KI5
Al Qaḍīmah, *Saudi Arabia* 172 K7
Al Qadmūs, *Syr.* 170 F7
Al Qā'im, *Iraq* 172 D8
Al Qa'īyah, *Saudi Arabia* 172 J9
Al Qāmishlī, *Syr.* 170 CI5
Al Qārah, *Yemen* 172 QI5
Al Qaryah ash Sharqīyah, *Lib.* 197 CI3
Al Qaryatayn, *Syr.* 170 H9
Al Qaṣīm, region, *Saudi Arabia* 172 H9
Al Qaṭīf, *Saudi Arabia* 172 HI2
Al Qaṭrānah, *Jordan* 171 N7
Al Qaṭrūn, *Lib.* 197 EI4
Al Qayṣūmah, *Saudi Arabia* 172 GIO
Alqueva, Barragem de, *Port.* 144 J6
Al Qunayṭirah (El Quneitra), *Syr.*
  170 K6
Al Qunfudhah, *Saudi Arabia* 172 M7
Al Qurayyāt, *Saudi Arabia* 172 E6
Al Qurnah, *Iraq* 172 FII
Al Quṣayr, *Syr.* 170 G8
Al Qusūrīyah, *Saudi Arabia* 172 K9
Al Quṭayfah, *Syr.* 170 J8
Al Quway'īyah, *Saudi Arabia* 172 KIO
Al Quwayrah, *Jordan* 171 R5
Alroy Downs, *N. Terr., Austral.* 211 R9
Alsace, region, *Fr.* 147 QI5
Alsask, *Sask., Can.* 82 MII
Alsasua, *Sp.* 144 BI2
Alsek, river, *Can.* 80 L3
Alsta, *Nor.* 141 CI4
Alston, *Eng., U.K.* 143 PII
Alta, *Iowa, U.S.* 105 N9
Alta, *Nor.* 141 CI4
Alta Floresta, *Braz.* 130 GIO
Alta Gracia, *Arg.* 132 JIO
Altagracia, *Venez.* 128 B7
Altagracia de Orituco, *Venez.* 128 BIO
Altamaha, river, *Ga., U.S.* 97 P8
Altamira, *Chile* 132 F7
Altamira, *Braz.* 130 DI2
Altamura, *It.* 150 MI3
Altan Xiret see Ejin Horo Qi, *China*
  182 D3
Altar Desert, *N. Amer.* 80 L3
Altata, *Mex.* 114 F8
Altavista, *Va., U.S.* 96 FII
Altay, *China* 180 D8
Altay, *Mongolia* 180 DIO
Altay Mountains, *Russ.* 158 MI2
Altayskiy, *Russ.* 158 LI2
Alt del Griu, *Andorra* 160 J4
Altdorf, *Switz.* 150 B4
Altea, *Sp.* 145 JI5
Altenburg, *Ger.* 148 F9
Alter do Chão, *Port.* 144 H6
Altiağac, *Azerb.* 169 C22
Altınekin, *Turk.* 168 G8
Altıntaş, *Turk.* 168 F6
Altınyayla, *Turk.* 168 H5
Altiplano, region, *S. Amer.* 126 H4
Altmühl, river, *Ger.* 148 J8
Altnaharra, *Scot., U.K.* 142 H9
Alto, *Tex., U.S.* 103 NI4
Alto, Pico, *Azores* 144 P3
Alto Araguaia, *Braz.* 130 JII
Alto Garças, *Braz.* 130 JII
Alto Molócuè, *Mozambique* 203 EI4
Alton, *Ill., U.S.* 99 S4
Altona, *Virgin Islands, U.S.* 120 N9
Altona Lagoon, *Virgin Islands, U.S.*
  120 Q3
Altoona, *Pa., U.S.* 94 N5
Alto Paraguai, *Braz.* 130 HIO
Alto Parnaíba, *Braz.* 131 GI4
Alto Purús, river, *Peru* 130 G5
Alto Río Senguerr, *Arg.* 133 S7
Altunhisar, *Turk.* 168 G9
Altun Shan, *China* 180 G7
Alturas, *Calif., U.S.* 108 L5
Altus, *Okla., U.S.* 102 H8
Al 'Ubaylah, *Saudi Arabia* 172 LI2
Alucra, *Turk.* 169 EI3
Al 'Ulá, *Saudi Arabia* 172 H6
Al 'Unnāb, site, *Jordan* 171 R8
Al Uqaylah, *Lib.* 197 CI5
Alushta, *Ukr.* 157 T8
Aluta, *Dem. Rep. of the Congo* 198 KII
Al 'Uwaynāt, *Lib.* 197 EI3
Al 'Uwaynid, *Saudi Arabia* 172 JIO
Al 'Uwayqīlah, *Saudi Arabia* 172 F8

Al 'Uyūn, *Saudi Arabia* 172 J7
Alva, *Okla., U.S.* 102 E9
Alvarado, *Tex., U.S.* 102 MII
Ålvdalen, *Sw.* 140 JI2
Alverca do Ribatejo, *Port.* 144 H4
Alvesta, *Sw.* 141 MI3
Alvin, *Tex., U.S.* 103 RI4
Älvkarleby, *Sw.* 141 KI3
Alvorada, *Braz.* 131 HI3
Alvord, *Tex., U.S.* 102 KIO
Alvord Desert, *Oreg., U.S.* 108 K8
Alvord Lake, *Oreg., U.S.* 108 K8
Al Wajh, *Saudi Arabia* 172 H5
Al Wannān, *Saudi Arabia* 172 HII
Alwar, *India* 178 F5
Al Wuday'ah, *Saudi Arabia* 172 PII
Alxa Zuoqi, *China* 180 HI2
Alytus, *Lith.* 141 NI7
Alzada, *Mont., U.S.* 106 FI3
Alzamay, *Russ.* 159 KI4
Alzette, river, *Lux.* 160 JIO
Alzey, *Ger.* 148 H6
Alzira, *Sp.* 145 HI4
Ama, *Japan* 185 P6
Amadeus, Lake, *Austral.* 210 F7
Amadeus Depression, *Austral.* 210 F7
Amadi, *Sudan* 198 HI2
Amadjuak Lake, *Nunavut, Can.* 83 GI8
Amadora, *Port.* 144 H4
Amagi, *Japan* 185 R4
Amahai, *Indonesia* 189 KI6
Amakusa Shotō, *Japan* 185 S4
Åmål, *Sw.* 140 LI2
Amalfi, *It.* 150 MII
Amaliáda, *Gr.* 154 J8
Amamapare, *Indonesia* 189 L2O
Amambaí, *Braz.* 130 MII
Amami Guntō, *Japan* 185 X3
Amami Ō Shima, *Japan* 185 W3
Amanave, *Amer. Samoa, U.S.* 218 M6
Amandola, *It.* 150 J9
Amangeldi, *Kaz.* 174 DII
Amantea, *It.* 151 QI3
Amanu, island, *Fr. Polynesia, Fr.* 219 F2O
Amapá, *Braz.* 130 BI2
Amarante, *Port.* 144 E6
Amarante, *Braz.* 131 FI5
Amargosa Range, *Calif., U.S.* 109 UIO
Amarillo, *Tex., U.S.* 102 G5
Amarkantak, *India* 178 J8
Amarwara, *India* 178 J7
Amasa, *Mich., U.S.* 98 F6
Amasra, *Turk.* 168 C8
Amasya, *Turk.* 168 DII
Amata, *S. Aust., Austral.* 211 U7
Amatari, *Braz.* 130 D9
Amathous, ruin, *Cyprus* 160 Q8
Amatrice, *It.* 150 J9
Amatuku, island, *Tuvalu* 217 J23
Amatusuk Hills, *Alas., U.S.* III CI3
Amavon Islands, *Solomon Is.* 217 LI6
Amazon (Solimões), river, *S. Amer.*
  126 D8
Amazon, Mouths of the, *S. Amer.*
  126 C8
Amazon, Source of the, *S. Amer.*
  126 G3
Amazonas, river, *S. Amer.* 126 D8
Amazon Basin, *S. Amer.* 126 D4
Ambajogai, *India* 178 L5
Ambala, *India* 178 E6
Ambalangoda, *Sri Lanka* 179 T7
Ambalantota, *Sri Lanka* 179 T8
Ambanja, *Madagascar* 203 EI8
Ambarchik, *Russ.* 159 CI9
Ambargasta, Salinas de, *Arg.* 132 HIO
Ambato, *Ecua.* 128 J3
Ambatondrazaka, *Madagascar* 203 FI8
Ambelákia, *Gr.* 154 EIO
Ambelau, island, *Indonesia* 189 KI6
Amberg, *Ger.* 148 H9
Ambergris Cay, *Belize* 115 JI7
Ambergris Cays, *Turks & Caicos Is., U.K.*
  117 JI7
Ambi, *Solomon Is.* 217 R23
Ambikapur, *India* 178 J9
Ambilobe, *Madagascar* 203 DI8
Amble, *Eng., U.K.* 143 NI2
Ambler, *Alas., U.S.* III EI4
Ambo, *Peru* 130 G3
Ambo Channel, *Marshall Is.* 216 M5
Amboise, *Fr.* 147 R8
Ambon, island, *Indonesia* 189 KI6
Ambon, *Indonesia* 189 KI6
Ambositra, *Madagascar* 203 GI7

Ambovombe, *Madagascar* **203** J16
Amboy, *Calif., U.S.* **109** W11
Amboy Crater, *Calif., U.S.* **109** W11
Ambre, Cap d', *Madagascar* **203** D18
Ambriz, *Angola* **202** C5
Ambrym, island, *Vanuatu* **218** D3
Ambunti, *P.N.G.* **213** C18
Amburan Burnu, *Azerb.* **169** D23
Am Dam, *Chad* **197** J15
Amderma, *Russ.* **158** E11
Amdi, *India* **178** H8
Amdo, *China* **180** K8
Ameca, *Mex.* **114** H9
Ameland, island, *Neth.* **146** G13
Amelia Island, *Fla., U.S.* **97** Q8
America-Antarctica Ridge, *Antarctic Oc.* **244** D10
American Falls, *Idaho, U.S.* **106** H6
American Falls Reservoir, *Idaho, U.S.* **106** H6
American Highland, *Antarctica* **227** G19
American Samoa, *U.S., Pac. Oc.* **214** J10
Americus, *Ga., U.S.* **97** N5
Amersfoort, *Neth.* **146** J13
Amery, *Wis., U.S.* **98** H2
Amery Ice Shelf, *Antarctica* **227** F19
Ames, *Iowa, U.S.* **105** N11
Amfilohía, *Gr.* **154** G8
Amfípoli, *Gr.* **154** C12
Amfissa, *Gr.* **154** H10
Amga, river, *Russ.* **159** H18
Amga, *Russ.* **159** H18
Amguema, *Russ.* **159** B20
Amguid, *Alg.* **196** D11
Amhara, region, *Eth.* **199** F15
Amherst, *N.S., Can.* **83** P22
Amherst, *N.Y., U.S.* **94** J5
Amherst, *Tex., U.S.* **102** J4
Amherst, *Va., U.S.* **96** E11
Ami, Île, *New Caledonia, Fr.* **218** E9
Amidon, *N. Dak., U.S.* **104** G2
Amiens, *Fr.* **146** M10
Amik Gölü, *Turk.* **168** J11
Amíndeo, *Gr.* **154** C9
Amindivi Islands, *India* **179** Q3
Amino, *Japan* **185** P8
Aminuis, *Namibia* **202** H7
Amioûn, *Leb.* **170** H6
Amir, river, *Afghan.* **176** L6
Amir Chah, *Pak.* **177** S2
Amistad, Presa de la, *Mex.* **114** D11
Amistad National Recreation Area, *Tex., U.S.* **103** R6
Amistad Reservoir, *Tex., U.S.* **103** R5
Amite, *La., U.S.* **100** N10
Amity, *Ark., U.S.* **100** H7
Åmli, *Nor.* **140** L11
Amlia Island, *Alas., U.S.* **110** P6
'Ammān (Philadelphia), *Jordan* **170** M7
Ammaroo, *N. Terr., Austral.* **211** S9
Ammochostos (Famagusta, Gazimağusa), *Cyprus* **160** P10
Ammochostos Bay, *Cyprus* **160** N10
Āmol, *Iran* **173** C13
Amolar, *Braz.* **130** K10
Amorgós, island, *Gr.* **155** M16
Amorgós, *Gr.* **155** M16
Amory, *Miss., U.S.* **101** J13
Amos, *Que., Can.* **83** P18
Amoy see Xiamen, *China* **183** Q7
Ampani, *India* **178** L8
Ampanihy, *Madagascar* **203** J16
Ampere Seamount, *Atl. Oc.* **236** H11
Ampezzo, *It.* **150** C9
Amplepuis, *Fr.* **147** T12
Amposta, *Sp.* **145** F15
'Amrān, *Yemen* **172** P9
Amravati, *India* **178** K6
Amreli, *India* **178** J2
'Amrīt (Marathus), ruin, *Syr.* **170** G7
Amritsar, *India* **177** Q12
Amsā'ad, *Lib.* **197** C17
Amsterdam, island, *Ind. Oc.* **240** N10
Amsterdam, *N.Y., U.S.* **94** J11
Amsterdam, *Neth.* **146** J12
Amsterdam, Île, *Ind. Oc.* **204** J10
Amstetten, *Aust.* **148** K11
Am Timan, *Chad* **197** J15
'Āmūdah, *Syr.* **170** C14
Amu Darya (Oxus), river, *Turkm.* **174** M11

Amuderýa, *Turkm.* **174** M11
Amukta Island, *Alas., U.S.* **110** P7
Amun, *P.N.G.* **217** K13
Amund Ringnes Island, *Nunavut, Can.* **83** C15
Amundsen Basin, *Arctic Oc.* **242** G10
Amundsen Bay, *Antarctica* **227** C19
Amundsen Gulf, *N.W.T., Can.* **82** E11
Amundsen-Scott South Pole, station, *Antarctica* **226** J12
Amundsen Sea, *Antarctica* **226** L6
Amuntai, *Indonesia* **188** K11
Amur, river, *Asia* **166** D12
Amurang, *Indonesia* **189** H15
Amuri, *Cook Is., N.Z.* **218** P11
Amur-Onon, Source of the, *Mongolia* **166** F10
Amursk, *Russ.* **159** K21
Amvrakía see Árta, *Gr.* **154** F8
Amvrakikós Kolpos, *Gr.* **154** G8
Amvrosiyivka, *Ukr.* **157** Q10
An, *Myanmar* **186** H5
Anaa, island, *Fr. Polynesia, Fr.* **219** E18
Anabar, region, *Nauru* **217** E23
Anabar, river, *Russ.* **159** F15
Anabarskiy Zaliv, *Russ.* **159** E15
Anacapa Island, *Calif., U.S.* **109** X7
Anaco, *Venez.* **128** C11
Anacoco, *La., U.S.* **100** N7
Anaconda, *Mont., U.S.* **106** E6
Anacortes, *Wash., U.S.* **108** B4
Anadarko, *Okla., U.S.* **102** H10
Anadyr, Gulf of, *Russ.* **166** A12
Anadyr', river, *Russ.* **166** B12
Anadyr', *Russ.* **159** B21
Anadyrskiy Zaliv, *Russ.* **159** B21
Anadyrskoye Ploskogor'ye, *Russ.* **159** C20
Anae, island, *Guam, U.S.* **216** D10
'Anaeho'omalu Bay, *Hawaii, U.S.* **113** L18
Anáfi, island, *Gr.* **155** N16
Anáfi, *Gr.* **155** N16
Anaga, Punta de, *Canary Is.* **204** Q5
Anagni, *It.* **150** L9
'Ānah, *Iraq* **172** D8
Anaheim, *Calif., U.S.* **109** X9
Anahola, *Hawaii, U.S.* **113** L11
Anahuac, *Tex., U.S.* **103** Q15
Anai Mudi, peak, *India* **179** R5
Anak, *N. Korea* **182** E12
Anakapalle, *India* **178** M9
Anaktuvuk Pass, *Alas., U.S.* **111** D16
Analalava, *Madagascar* **203** E17
Anamã, *Braz.* **130** D8
Ana María, Cayos, *Cuba* **116** J10
Ana María, Golfo de, *Cuba* **116** J10
Anambas, Kepulauan, *Indonesia* **188** H8
Anamoose, *N. Dak., U.S.* **104** F5
Anamosa, *Iowa, U.S.* **105** N14
Anamur, *Turk.* **168** J8
Anamur Burnu, *Turk.* **168** K8
Anan, *Japan* **185** R8
Anand, *India* **178** J3
Anan'evo, *Kyrg.* **176** D13
Anangenimon, island, *F.S.M.* **217** B16
Ananij, island, *Marshall Is.* **216** H9
Anantapur, *India* **179** P6
Anantnag (Islamabad), *India* **177** N12
Anapa, *Russ.* **157** T9
Anápolis, *Braz.* **131** J13
Anār, *Iran* **173** F14
Anārak, *Iran* **173** D14
Anar Darreh, *Afghan.* **177** P2
Anatahan, island, *N. Mariana Is., U.S.* **216** C2
Anatolia (Asia Minor), region, *Turk.* **168** F5
Anatom (Kéamu), island, *Vanuatu* **218** H4
Anatone, *Wash., U.S.* **108** E9
Añatuya, *Arg.* **132** H11
Anboru, island, *Marshall Is.* **216** L8
Anbyŏn, *N. Korea* **182** D13
Ancenis, *Fr.* **147** R6
Anchorage, *Alas., U.S.* **111** J16
Anchor Bay, *Calif., U.S.* **109** Q2
Anclitas, Cayo, *Cuba* **116** K10
Ancón de Sardinas, Bahía de, *Col., Ecua.* **128** H3
Ancud, *Chile* **133** Q6
Andacollo, *Arg.* **133** N7
An Daingean (Dingle), *Ire.* **143** U2
Andalgalá, *Arg.* **132** G9
Åndalsnes, *Nor.* **140** J10
Andalusia, *Ala., U.S.* **101** N16
Andalusia, region, *Sp.* **144** K9

Andaman and Nicobar Islands, *India* **179** Q15
Andaman Basin, *Ind. Oc.* **240** E12
Andaman Islands, *India* **179** Q15
Andaman Sea, *Ind. Oc.* **166** K10
Andamooka, *S. Aust., Austral.* **211** W10
Andapa, *Madagascar* **203** E18
Andelot-Blancheville, *Fr.* **147** Q13
Andenes, *Nor.* **140** D12
Andermatt, *Switz.* **150** B4
Andernach, *Ger.* **148** G5
Andersen Air Force Base, *Guam, U.S.* **216** B12
Anderson, *Alas., U.S.* **111** G16
Anderson, *Calif., U.S.* **109** N3
Anderson, *Ind., U.S.* **99** R9
Anderson, *Mo., U.S.* **105** V11
Anderson, river, *N.W.T., Can.* **82** E11
Anderson, *S.C., U.S.* **96** K7
Andes, range, *S. Amer.* **126** D2
Andfjorden, bay, *Nor.* **140** D12
Andicuri Bay, *Aruba, Neth.* **121** Q17
Andijon, *Uzb.* **175** K14
Andikíthira, island, *Gr.* **154** P11
Andimáhia, *Gr.* **155** M18
Andípaxi, island, *Gr.* **154** F6
Andipsara, island, *Gr.* **155** H15
Andırın, *Turk.* **168** H11
Andkhvoy, *Afghan.* **176** K4
Andoany (Hell-Ville), *Madagascar* **203** D18
Andoas, *Peru* **130** D3
Andorra, region, *Andorra* **160** K3
Andorra, *Eur.* **160** D2
Andorra, *Sp.* **145** E14
Andorra la Vella, *Andorra* **160** J3
Andover, *Me., U.S.* **95** F15
Andovoranto, *Madagascar* **203** G18
Andøya, island, *Nor.* **140** D12
Andradina, *Braz.* **130** L12
Andreanof Islands, *Alas., U.S.* **110** P5
Andreapol', *Russ.* **156** H7
Andrew Johnson National Historic Site, *Tenn., U.S.* **101** E20
Andrews, *N.C., U.S.* **96** J5
Andrews, *S.C., U.S.* **96** L11
Andrews, *Tex., U.S.* **102** M4
Andrijevica, *Mont.* **152** J9
Androka, *Madagascar* **203** J16
Ándros, island, *Gr.* **155** J14
Andros, *Gr.* **155** J14
Andros Island, *Bahamas* **116** E11
Andros Town, *Bahamas* **116** E11
Androth Island, *India* **179** R3
Andrychów, *Pol.* **149** H15
Andryushkino, *Russ.* **159** D19
Andselv, *Nor.* **141** D13
Andújar, *Sp.* **144** K10
Anefis i-n-Darane, *Mali* **196** G10
Anegada, island, *Virgin Islands, U.K.* **119** E14
Anegada, Bahía, *Arg.* **133** P11
Anegada Passage, *Lesser Antilles* **119** F14
Aného, *Togo* **200** H11
Aneju, island, *Marshall Is.* **216** G10
Anelghowhat, *Vanuatu* **218** H4
Anelghowhat Bay, *Vanuatu* **218** H4
Anemwanot, island, *Marshall Is.* **216** G11
Anenelibw, island, *Marshall Is.* **216** H11
Anengenipuan, island, *F.S.M.* **217** B16
Aneta, *N. Dak., U.S.* **104** F7
Anetan, region, *Nauru* **217** E23
Aneto, peak, *Sp.* **145** C15
Aney, *Niger* **197** G13
Anfu, *China* **183** N5
Angamos, Punta, *Chile* **132** E6
Angara, river, *Russ.* **166** E9
Angarei, island, *Cook Is., N.Z.* **218** Q11
Angarsk, *Russ.* **159** L15
Angaur (Ngeaur), island, *Palau* **216** R10
Ånge, *Sw.* **141** J13
Ángel de la Guarda, Isla, *Mex.* **114** C6
Angeles, *P.R., U.S.* **120** N2
Angeles, *Philippines* **189** C13
Angel Falls, *Venez.* **128** E12
Angels Camp, *Calif., U.S.* **109** R5
Angelina, river, *Tex., U.S.* **103** N14
Angels Camp, *Calif., U.S.* **109** R5
Ångermanälven, river, *Sw.* **141** G13
Angers, *Fr.* **147** R7
Angerville, *Fr.* **147** Q9
Angkor, ruin, *Cambodia* **186** M11
Angle Inlet, *Minn., U.S.* **104** D9
Anglem, Mount, *N.Z.* **213** R15
Anglesey, island, *Wales, U.K.* **143** S9
Anglet, *Fr.* **147** X5

Angleton, *Tex., U.S.* **103** R14
Anglure, *Fr.* **147** P11
Ango, *Dem. Rep. of the Congo* **198** H11
Angoche, *Mozambique* **203** F15
Angoche, Ilha, *Mozambique* **203** F15
Angohrān, *Iran* **173** H16
Angol, *Chile* **133** N6
Angola, *Af.* **195** M19
Angola, *Ind., U.S.* **99** N10
Angola Plain, *Atl. Oc.* **237** Q13
Angora see Ankara, *Turk.* **168** E8
Angoram, *P.N.G.* **213** C18
Angoulême, *Fr.* **147** U7
Angra do Heroísmo, *Azores* **144** P4
Angren, *Uzb.* **175** K14
Angtassom, *Cambodia* **187** P11
Anguilla, island, *U.K., Lesser Antilles* **119** F15
Anguilla Cays, *Bahamas* **116** F9
Anguillita Island, *Anguilla, U.K.* **120** R10
Angul, *India* **178** K10
Anguo, *China* **182** E6
Angvik, *Nor.* **140** J10
Anhai, *China* **183** Q8
Anhua, *China* **182** M3
Anholt, island, *Den.* **140** N12
Anhui, *China* **182** L7
Ani, *Japan* **184** K12
Aniak, *Alas., U.S.* **111** J13
Aniakchak National Monument and Preserve, *Alas., U.S.* **111** M13
Anibare, region, *Nauru* **217** F23
Anibare Bay, *Nauru* **217** F23
Anie, Pic d', *Fr., Sp.* **145** B14
Animal Flower Cave, *Barbados* **121** J18
Animas, river, *Colo., U.S.* **107** P11
Animas, *N. Mex., U.S.* **107** V10
Animas Peak, *N. Mex., U.S.* **107** W10
Anin, *Myanmar* **186** L7
Anina, *Rom.* **152** E11
Anipemza, *Arm.* **169** D18
Anixab, *Namibia* **202** G6
Anjar, *India* **178** J2
Anjiang, *China* **183** N2
Anjira, *Pak.* **177** T5
Anjouan, island, *Comoros* **205** N16
Anjou Islands, *Russ.* **242** E6
Anju, *N. Korea* **182** D12
Ankang, *China* **182** J2
Ankara, river, *Turk.* **168** E7
Ankara (Angora), *Turk.* **168** E8
Ankeny, *Iowa, U.S.* **105** P11
An Khe, *Vietnam* **186** M14
Anklam, *Ger.* **148** C10
Ankola, *India* **179** P4
Anlu, *China* **182** K5
Ann, Cape, *Antarctica* **227** C19
Ann, Cape, *Mass., U.S.* **95** J15
Anna, *Ill., U.S.* **99** V5
Anna, Lake, *Va., U.S.* **96** E12
Annaba, *Alg.* **196** A12
Annaberg, ruin, *Virgin Islands, U.S.* **120** M11
An Nabk, *Syr.* **170** H8
An Nafūd, desert, *Saudi Arabia* **172** G7
An Najaf, *Iraq* **172** E9
Annaly, *Virgin Islands, U.S.* **120** Q2
Annam Cordillera, *Laos, Vietnam* **186** K12
Annan, *Scot., U.K.* **143** P10
Annandale Falls, *Grenada* **121** K22
Anna Plains, *W. Aust., Austral.* **211** S4
Anna Point, *Nauru* **217** E23
Annapolis, *Md., U.S.* **96** C13
Annapurna, peak, *Nepal* **178** F9
Ann Arbor, *Mich., U.S.* **98** M12
An Nashshāsh, *U.A.E.* **173** K14
An Nāşirīyah, *Iraq* **172** F10
An Nawfalīyah, *Lib.* **197** C15
Annean, Lake, *Austral.* **210** H3
Annecy, *Fr.* **147** T14
Annecy, Lac d', *Fr.* **147** U14
Annemasse, *Fr.* **147** T14
Annenskiy Most, *Russ.* **156** E9
Annigeri, *India* **179** N4
An Nimāş, *Saudi Arabia* **172** M8
Anningie, *N. Terr., Austral.* **211** S8
Anniston, *Ala., U.S.* **101** J16
Annitowa, *N. Terr., Austral.* **211** S9
Annobón, island, *Eq. Guinea* **201** L13
Annonay, *Fr.* **147** V12
Annopol, *Pol.* **149** F17
Annotto Bay, *Jam.* **120** H10
An Nu'ayrīyah, *Saudi Arabia* **172** H11

An Nukhayb, *Iraq* **172** E8
Annunziata, *It.* **150** M11
Anoano, *Solomon Is.* **217** N19
Anoka, *Minn., U.S.* **104** J11
Ano Viános, *Gr.* **155** R15
Anpu, *China* **183** S2
Anqing, *China* **182** L7
Anren, *China* **183** P4
Ansai, *China* **182** F2
Anse-à-Foleur, *Haiti* **117** L16
Anse-à-Galets, *Haiti* **117** M16
Anse-à-Pitre, *Haiti* **117** N17
Anse-à-Veau, *Haiti* **117** M15
Anse-Bertrand, *Guadeloupe, Fr.* **121** D15
Anse Boileau, *Seychelles* **205** P20
Anse d'Hainault, *Haiti* **117** M14
Anse la Raye, *St. Lucia* **121** K13
Anselmo, *Nebr., U.S.* **105** P5
Anseong, *S. Korea* **182** F13
Anse-Rouge, *Haiti* **117** L16
Anshan, *China* **182** C10
Ansley, *Nebr., U.S.* **105** P5
Ansó, *Sp.* **145** C14
Anson, *Me., U.S.* **95** F16
Anson, *Tex., U.S.* **102** L7
Anson Bay, *Austral.* **210** B7
Anson Bay, *Norfolk I., Austral.* **217** F20
Ansongo, *Mali* **196** H9
Anson Point, *Norfolk I., Austral.* **217** F20
Ansted, *W. Va., U.S.* **96** E8
Ansudu, *Indonesia* **189** K21
Antalaha, *Madagascar* **203** E18
Antalya (Adalia), *Turk.* **168** H6
Antalya Körfezi, *Turk.* **168** J6
Antananarivo, *Madagascar* **203** G17
Antanimora, *Madagascar* **203** J16
Antarctic Peninsula, *Antarctica* **226** D5
Ant Atoll, *F.S.M.* **216** Q8
Antelope, *Oreg., U.S.* **108** G5
Antelope Reservoir, *Oreg., U.S.* **108** K9
Antequera, *Sp.* **144** L10
Anthony, *Kans., U.S.* **105** V7
Anthony, *N. Mex., U.S.* **107** V12
Anthony Lagoon, *N. Terr., Austral.* **211** R9
Antibes, *Fr.* **147** X15
Anticosti, Île d', *Que., Can.* **83** M21
Anticosti Island, *N. Amer.* **80** G10
Antifer, Cap d', *Fr.* **147** N7
Antigo, *Wis., U.S.* **98** H6
Antigonish, *N.S., Can.* **83** P22
Antigua, island, *Antigua & Barbuda* **119** G16
Antigua, *Canary Is.* **204** Q7
Antigua and Barbuda, *N. Amer.* **81** N24
Anti-Lebanon see Sharqī, Al Jabal ash, range, *Leb., Syr.* **170** H7
Antilla, *Cuba* **117** J13
Antioch, *Calif., U.S.* **109** R4
Antioch see Hatay, *Turk.* **168** J11
Antioche, Pertuis d', *Fr.* **147** T5
Antipayuta, *Russ.* **158** F12
Antipodes Islands, *N.Z.* **214** Q9
Antlers, *Okla., U.S.* **102** J13
Antofagasta, *Chile* **132** E7
Antofalla, Salar de, *Arg.* **132** F8
Antoine, Lake, *Grenada* **121** J23
Anton, *Tex., U.S.* **102** J4
Anton Chico, *N. Mex., U.S.* **107** S13
Antongila, Baie d', *Madagascar* **203** E18
Antónia, Pico da, *Cape Verde* **205** D16
Antrain, *Fr.* **147** Q6
Antrim Mountains, *N. Ire., U.K.* **143** P7
Antriol, *Neth. Antilles, Neth.* **121** Q19
Antrodoco, *It.* **150** J9
Antropovo, *Russ.* **156** G12
Antsirabe, *Madagascar* **203** G17
Antsirañana, *Madagascar* **203** D18
Antsohihy, *Madagascar* **203** E17
Antu, *China* **182** A14
Antufash, Jazīrat, *Yemen* **172** P8
Antwerp see Antwerpen, *Belg.* **146** K12
Antwerpen (Antwerp), *Belg.* **146** K12
An Uaimh see Navan, *Ire.* **143** R6
Anuanu Raro, island, *Fr. Polynesia, Fr.* **219** G19
Anuanu Runga, island, *Fr. Polynesia, Fr.* **219** G19
Anupgarh, *India* **178** E4
Anuradhapura, *Sri Lanka* **179** S7
Anuta, *Solomon Is.* **217** P20
Anuta (Cherry Island), island, *Solomon Is.* **214** J7
Anvers Island, *Antarctica* **226** D4
Anvik, *Alas., U.S.* **111** H13
Anvil see El Yunque, peak, *Cuba* **117** K14

Anxi, China 183 Q8
Anxi, China 180 G9
Anxiang, China 182 M4
Anxin, China 182 D6
Anyang, China 182 G5
Anyang, S. Korea 182 F13
Ánydros, island, Gr. 155 MI5
A'nyêmaqên Shan, China 180 JIO
Anyi, China 182 G3
Anyi, China 182 M6
Anyou, China 183 VI
Anyuan, China 183 Q6
Anzhero Sudzhensk, Russ. 158 KI2
Anzhu, Ostrova, Russ. 159 DI7
Anzio, It. 150 L8
Aoa Bay, Amer. Samoa, U.S. 218 M8
Aoba (Omba), island, Vanuatu 218 C2
Ao Ban Don, bay, Thai. 187 Q8
Aoga Shima, Japan 185 SI2
Aohan Qi, China 182 B9
Aojing, China 181 MI7
Aola, Solomon Is. 217 NI9
Aoloautuai, Amer. Samoa, U.S. 218 M7
Aomon, island, Marshall Is. 216 G8
Aomori, Japan 184 JI3
Aonae, Japan 184 HI2
Aóös, river, Gr. 154 E8
A'opo, Samoa 218 K2
Aorai, Mont, Fr. Polynesia, Fr. 219 PI6
Aoraki, peak, N.Z. 213 PI6
Aóre, island, Vanuatu 218 D2
Aosta, It. 150 D2
Aoulef, Alg. 196 DIO
Aoumou, New Caledonia, Fr. 218 D8
Aoya, Japan 185 P7
Aozi, Chad 197 FI5
Aozou, Chad 197 FI4
Aozou Strip, region, Chad 197 FI5
Apa, river, Braz., Parag. 130 LIO
Apache, Okla., U.S. 102 HI9
Apakho, Solomon Is. 217 Q23
Apalachee Bay, Fla., U.S. 85 MI8
Apalachicola, river, Fla., U.S. 97 R4
Apalachicola, Fla., U.S. 97 R4
Apalachicola Bay, Fla., U.S. 97 R4
Apamea, ruin, Syr. 170 F7
Apaora, Solomon Is. 217 P2O
Apaporis, river, Col. 128 E7
Aparri, Philippines 189 BI4
Apataki, island, Fr. Polynesia, Fr. 219 DI8
Apatin, Serb. 152 E9
Apatity, Russ. 158 D8
Apatzingán, Mex. 114 JIO
Apeldoorn, Neth. 146 JI3
A. Perdido, river, Arg. 133 R8
Apes Den, Gibraltar, U.K. 161 P23
Áphaea, ruin, Gr. 154 KI2
Apia, Samoa 218 L3
Apia, Samoa 214 JIO
Apia Harbour, Samoa 218 L3
Apíranthos, Gr. 155 LI5
Apishapa, river, Colo., U.S. 107 PI4
Ap Iwan, Cerro, Chile 133 T7
Apolima, island, Samoa 218 L2
Apolima Strait, Samoa 218 L2
Apollo Bay, Vic., Austral. 211 ZI2
Apollonia, ruin, Albania 152 L9
Apollonia, ruin, Lib. 197 BI6
Apolo, Bol. 130 J6
Apolonia, Gr. 155 LI4
Apopka, Lake, Fla., U.S. 97 T8
Aporema, Braz. 130 CI2
Apostle Islands, Wis., U.S. 98 E4
Apostle Islands National Lakeshore,
  Wis., U.S. 98 E4
Apóstoles, Arg. 132 GI4
Apostolic Palace, Vatican City 161 PI6
Apostolos Andreas, Cape, Cyprus 160 LI2
Apostolos Andreas Monastery, Cyprus
  160 MI2
Apoteri, Guyana 129 FI4
Appalachian Mountains, U.S. 85 JI7
Appalachian Plateau, U.S. 85 JI7
Appennini, It. 150 F3
Applecross, Scot., U.K. 142 J7
Appleton, Minn., U.S. 104 J9
Appleton, Wis., U.S. 98 J6
Appleton City, Mo., U.S. 105 TII
Apple Valley, Calif., U.S. 109 W9
Appomattox, Va., U.S. 96 FII
Apra Harbor, Guam, U.S. 216 CIO
Apra Heights, Guam, U.S. 216 CIO
Aprilia, It. 150 L8
Apsheronsk, Russ. 157 TII
Apuane, Alpi, It. 150 G5

'Āpua Point, Hawai'i, U.S. 113 N2I
Apucarana, Braz. 130 MI2
Apurashokoru, island, Palau 216 PIO
Apure, river, Venez. 128 D9
Apurímac, river, Peru 130 H4
Apuseni Mountains, Rom. 152 CI2
Aqaba see Al 'Aqabah, Jordan 171 R5
Aqaba, Gulf of, Asia 166 F2
Aqadyr, Kaz. 175 FI4
Aqchan, Afghan. 176 K5
Aqiq, Sudan 199 DI4
Aqköl, Kaz. 175 CI3
Aqköl, Kaz. 175 GI6
Aqköl, Kaz. 175 JI4
Aq Kopruk, Afghan. 176 L6
Aqmola see Astana, Kaz. 175 DI4
Aqqikkol Hu, China 180 H7
Aqqū, Kaz. 175 CI6
Aqqystaū, Kaz. 174 F6
Aqsay, Kaz. 174 C7
Aqshataū, Kaz. 175 FI5
Aqsū, river, Kaz. 175 GI7
Aqsū, Kaz. 175 CI4
Aqtaū, Kaz. 174 H5
Aqtöbe, Kaz. 174 D8
Aqtoghay, Kaz. 175 FI7
Aqtaū, Kaz. 174 H5
Aquidauana, Braz. 130 LIO
Aquin, Haiti 117 MI5
Aquitaine Basin, Fr. 138 H4
Ara, India 178 G9
Araara, Motu, Fr. Polynesia, Fr. 219 HI4
Araara, Passe, Fr. Polynesia, Fr. 219 HI4
Arab, Ala., U.S. 101 HI5
'Arab, Bahr el, Sudan 194 H8
'Arabah, Wādī al, Israel, Jordan 171 Q5
Arabian Basin, Ind. Oc. 240 E8
Arabian Peninsula, Asia 166 G3
Arabian Sea, Ind. Oc. 166 J5
Arabs Gulf, Egypt 194 D8
Araç, river, Turk. 168 C9
Araç, Turk. 168 C9
Aracaju, Braz. 131 HI7
Aracati, Braz. 131 EI7
Araçatuba, Braz. 130 LI2
Aracena, Sp. 144 K7
Aracena, Sierra de, Sp. 144 K7
Aracides, Cape, Solomon Is. 217 M2O
Araçuaí, Braz. 131 KI5
Arad, Rom. 152 DII
Arada, Chad 197 HI5
Aradippou, Cyprus 160 P9
Aragarças, Braz. 130 JI2
Aragats, peak, Arm. 169 DI8
Arago, Cape, Oreg., U.S. 108 JI
Araguacema, Braz. 131 FI3
Aragua de Barcelona, Venez. 128 CII
Araguaia, river, Braz. 131 EI3
Araguaína, Braz. 131 FI3
Araguari, Braz. 131 KI3
Araguatins, Braz. 131 EI3
Arahal, Sp. 144 L8
Árahthos, river, Gr. 154 F8
Arai, Japan 185 NII
Arak, Alg. 196 EII
Arāk, Iran 172 D7
Arakabesan, island, Palau 216 NII
Arakan Yoma, range, Myanmar 186 J5
Arakht, Afghan. 176 K9
Aral, Kaz. 174 FIO
Aral, Kyrg. 176 EII
Aral Mangy Qaraqumy, desert, Kaz.
  174 FIO
Aral Sea, Kaz., Uzb. 174 G9
Aralsor, Lake, Kaz. 138 FI3
Aralsor Köli, Kaz. 174 D5
Aralsul'fat, Kaz. 174 FIO
Araltobe, Kaz. 174 G9
Aramac, Qnsld., Austral. 211 TI3
Aramits, Fr. 147 Y6
Ārān, Iran 173 DI3
Aranda de Duero, Sp. 144 DII
Aranđelovac, Serb. 152 FIO
Arandu, Pak. 176 L9
Aran Island (Arranmore), Ire. 143 P4
Aran Islands, Ire. 143 S3
Aranjuez, Sp. 144 GII
Aransá, river, Sp. 160 K4
Aransá, Sp. 160 L4
Aransas, river, Tex., U.S. 103 TII
Aransas Pass, Tex., U.S. 103 TII
Araouane, Mali 196 G8
Arapahoe, Nebr., U.S. 105 R5
Arapaho National Recreation Area,
  Colo., U.S. 106 LI2

Arapiraca, Braz. 131 GI7
Arapkir, Turk. 169 FI3
'Ar'ar, Saudi Arabia 172 F8
Araraquara, Braz. 131 LI3
Ararat, Arm. 169 EI9
Ararat, Mount see Ağrı Dağı, Turk.
  169 EI8
Araria, India 178 GII
Aras (Araxes), river, Turk. 169 EI7
Aratika, island, Fr. Polynesia, Fr. 219 EI8
Aratsu Bay, N. Mariana Is., U.S. 216 E8
Arauá, river, Braz. 130 E7
Arauca, Col. 128 D7
Arauca, river, Col., Venez. 128 D8
Arauco Gulf, S. Amer. 126 M3
Araxá, Braz. 131 KI3
Araxes see Aras, river, Turk. 169 EI7
Arbatax, It. 151 N5
Arbazh, Russ. 156 GI4
Arbela see Irbid, Jordan 170 L6
Arbīl, Iraq 172 C9
Arbīl, Iraq 172 C9
Arbroath, Scot., U.K. 142 LII
Arcabell, Sp. 160 K2
Arcachon, Fr. 147 V6
Arcachon, Bassin d', Fr. 147 V6
Arcadia, Fla., U.S. 97 V8
Arcadia, La., U.S. 100 L7
Arcadia, Mich., U.S. 98 J9
Arcadia, Wis., U.S. 98 J3
Arcata, Calif., U.S. 108 M2
Archangel see Arkhangel'sk, Russ. 158 E8
Archbald, Pa., U.S. 94 M9
Archer City, Tex., U.S. 102 K9
Arches National Park, Utah, U.S. 107 N9
Archiac, Fr. 147 U7
Archialus see Pomorie, Bulg. 153 JI7
Archidona, Sp. 144 LIO
Archman, Turkm. 174 L7
Arcis, Fr. 147 PI2
Arco, Idaho, U.S. 106 G6
Arco Pass, S. Amer. 126 N4
Arcos de Jalón, Sp. 144 EI2
Arcoverde, Braz. 131 GI7
Arctic Bay, Nunavut, Can. 83 EI6
Arctic Red, river, N.W.T., Can. 82 E9
Arctic Village, Alas., U.S. III DI7
Arctowski, station, Antarctica 226 C3
Arda, river, Bulg. 153 KI5
Ardabīl, Iran 172 BII
Ardahan, Turk. 169 DI7
Ardakān, Iran 173 EI4
Ardanuç, Turk. 169 DI6
Ardara, Ire. 143 P4
Arḍ aş Şawwān, region, Jordan 171 P8
Ardee, Ire. 143 R6
Ardennes, region, Belg., Fr. 146 MI3
Ardennes, Canal des, Fr. 147 NI2
Ardestān, Iran 173 DI3
Ardmore, Okla., U.S. 102 JII
Ardmore, S. Dak., U.S. 104 MI
Ardres, Fr. 146 L9
Ards Peninsula, N. Ire., U.K. 143 Q8
Åre, Sw. 140 HI2
Arecibo, P.R., U.S. 120 M3
Arei, Pointe, Fr. Polynesia, Fr. 219 K23
Areia Branca, Braz. 131 EI7
Arekalong Peninsula (Ngerchelong),
  Palau 216 MI2
Arena, Point, Calif., U.S. 84 F2
Arenápolis, Braz. 130 HIO
Arenas, Cayo, Mex. 115 GI5
Arenas, Punta de, Arg. 133 W9
Arenas de San Pedro, Sp. 144 G9
Arendal, Nor. 140 MII
Areópoli, Gr. 154 MIO
Arequipa, Peru 130 J5
Arere, Fr. 147 V6
Arethusa see Ar Rastan, Syr. 170 G8
Arévalo, Sp. 144 EIO
Arezzo, It. 150 H7
Argadargada, N. Terr., Austral. 211 SIO
Argakhtakh, Russ. 159 DI9
Arganda, Sp. 144 FII
Argelès-Gazost, Fr. 147 Y7
Argent, Fr. 147 RIO
Argenta, It. 150 F7
Argentan, Fr. 147 P7
Argentario, Monte, It. 150 J7
Argentat, Fr. 147 V9
Argenteuil, Fr. 147 PIO

Argentiera, Capo dell', It. 150 M3
Argentina, S. Amer. 127 PI7
Argentina Range, Antarctica 226 FIO
Argentine Plain, Atl. Oc. 237 V6
Argentino, Lago, Arg. 133 V7
Argenton, Fr. 147 T9
Argenton-Château, Fr. 147 S7
Argeş, river, Rom. 153 FI5
Arghandab, river, Afghan. 177 P6
Arghandab, Band-e, Afghan. 177 Q5
Arghastan, river, Afghan. 177 Q5
Arghestan, Afghan. 177 Q6
Argo, Sudan 198 CI2
Argolikós Kólpos, Gr. 154 KII
Argonne, range, Fr. 147 NI3
Argos, Gr. 154 KIO
Argos Orestikó, Gr. 154 D8
Argostóli, Gr. 154 J7
Argoub, W. Sahara, Mor. 196 E5
Arguedas, Sp. 145 DI3
Arguello, Point, Calif., U.S. 109 W5
Argun, river, China, Russ. 166 EII
Argus, Dome, Antarctica 227 HI6
Arguut, Mongolia 180 EII
Argyle, Minn., U.S. 104 E8
Argyle, Lake, Austral. 210 C7
Argyrus see Gjirokastër, Albania 152 M9
Arhánes, Gr. 155 QI5
Arhángelos, Gr. 155 N2O
Ar Horqin Qi (Tianshan), China 182 A9
Århus, Den. 140 NII
Ari, Motu, Fr. Polynesia, Fr. 219 Q2O
Ari Atoll, Maldives 179 V3
Ariano Irpino, It. 150 MII
Ariari, river, Col. 128 F6
Arica, Chile 130 L6
Arica, Col. 128 B6
Arid, Cape, Austral. 210 K5
Arida, Japan 185 R8
Aride, Île, Seychelles 205 M2O
Aridéa, Gr. 154 BIO
Ariège, river, Fr. 160 H5
Arīḥā, Syr. 170 E8
Arīḥā (Jericho), W. Bank 170 M6
Arikaree, river, Colo., U.S. 106 LI5
Arikawa, Japan 185 R3
Arimã, Braz. 130 E8
Arima, Trinidad & Tobago 121 P22
Arinagour, Scot., U.K. 142 L7
Arinos, river, Braz. 130 HIO
Arinsal, river, Andorra 160 H2
Arinsal, Andorra 160 H2
Aripeka, Fla., U.S. 97 T7
Aripo, El Cerro del, Trinidad & Tobago
  121 N23
Ariporo, river, Col. 128 E7
Aripuanã, river, Braz. 130 F9
Aripuanã, Braz. 130 G9
Ariquemes, Braz. 130 G8
'Arīsh, Wādi el, Egypt 171 Q3
Aristizábal, Cabo, Arg. 133 S9
Ariyalur, India 179 R6
Arizaro, Salar de, Arg. 132 F8
Arizona, Arg. 132 M9
Arizona, U.S. 107 T5
Arizona City, Ariz., U.S. 107 U7
Arjeplog, Sw. 141 FI3
Arjona, Col. 128 B5
Arkadak, Russ. 156 MI2
Arkadelphia, Ark., U.S. 100 H7
Arkagala, Russ. 159 FI9
Arkaig, Loch, Scot., U.K. 142 K8
Arkansas, river, U.S. 85 KI4
Arkansas, U.S. 100 G7
Arkansas City, Ark., U.S. 100 JIO
Arkansas City, Kans., U.S. 105 V8
Arkansas Post National Memorial, Ark.,
  U.S. 100 H9
Arkhangel'sk (Archangel), Russ. 158 E8
Arkhangel'skoye, Russ. 156 MII
Arkí, island, Gr. 155 KI7
Arkítsa, Gr. 154 GII
Arkona, Kap, Ger. 148 AIO
Arkonam, India 179 P7
Arkticheskiy, Mys, Russ. 159 CI4
Arlanc, Fr. 147 UII
Arlap, island, Marshall Is. 216 L7
Arles, Fr. 147 XI2
Arlington, Ga., U.S. 97 P4
Arlington, Oreg., U.S. 108 F6
Arlington, S. Dak., U.S. 104 K8
Arlington, Tex., U.S. 102 LII
Arlington, Va., U.S. 96 CI3
Arlington, Wash., U.S. 108 B4
Arlington Heights, Ill., U.S. 99 N7

Arlon, Belg. 147 NI3
Arma, Kans., U.S. 105 UIO
Armagh, N. Ire., U.K. 143 Q6
Armathiá, island, Gr. 155 QI8
Armavir, Arm. 169 EI8
Armavir, Russ. 157 SII
Armenia, Asia 167 T4
Armenia, Col. 128 F4
Armenistís, Gr. 155 KI6
Armidale, N.S.W., Austral. 211 WI5
Armijo, N. Mex., U.S. 107 SI2
Armilla, Sp. 144 LII
Armorican Massif, Fr. 138 G4
Armour, S. Dak., U.S. 104 M6
Armstrong, Ont., Can. 83 NI5
Armur, India 178 L6
Arnaoutis, Cape, Cyprus 160 P5
Arnay-le-Duc, Fr. 147 SI2
Arnéa, Gr. 154 DI2
Arnedo, Sp. 144 CI2
Årnes, Nor. 140 HII
Arnett, Okla., U.S. 102 F8
Arnhem, Neth. 146 JI3
Arnhem, Cape, Austral. 210 BIO
Arnhem Land, N. Terr., Austral. 211 P9
Arniel, island, Marshall Is. 216 GI2
Árnissa, Gr. 154 C9
Arno, river, It. 150 G6
Arno Atoll, Marshall Is. 216 H5
Arno Bay, S. Aust., Austral. 211 X9
Arnold, Mo., U.S. 105 TI5
Arnold, Nebr., U.S. 105 P5
Arnøy, island, Nor. 141 CI3
Arnsberg, Ger. 148 F6
Aroab, Namibia 202 K8
Arock, Oreg., U.S. 108 J9
Arorae, island, Kiribati 214 G8
Arorangi, Cook Is., N.Z. 218 Q9
Arousa, Ría de, Sp. 144 C5
Arowhana, peak, N.Z. 213 K2O
Arpa, river, Arm., Turk. 169 DI8
Arpaçay, Turk. 169 DI7
Arqalyq, Kaz. 174 DI2
Ar Rabbah, Jordan 171 N6
Arrabury, Qnsld., Austral. 211 VII
Arraias, Braz. 131 HI4
Ar Ramādī, Iraq 172 D9
Ar Ramthā, Jordan 170 L7
Arran, Island of, Scot., U.K. 143 N8
Arranmore see Aran Island, island, Ire.
  143 P4
Ar Raqqah (Nicephorium), Syr. 170 EII
Arras, Fr. 146 MIO
Ar Rashādīyah, Jordan 171 P6
Ar Rastan (Arethusa), Syr. 170 G8
Ar Rawḍah, Saudi Arabia 172 L8
Arreau, Fr. 147 Y7
Arrecife, Canary Is. 204 P7
Arrée, Montagnes d', Fr. 147 Q3
Ar Riyāḍ (Riyadh), Saudi Arabia 172 JIO
Ar Riyān, Yemen 172 QI2
Arrochar, Scot., U.K. 142 M8
Arromanches, Fr. 147 N7
Arronches, Port. 144 H7
Arrou, Fr. 147 Q8
Arrow, Lough, Ire. 143 Q4
Arrowrock Reservoir, Idaho, U.S. 106 G4
Arroyo, P.R., U.S. 120 P5
Arroyo de la Luz, Sp. 144 H7
Arroyo Grande, Calif., U.S. 109 V5
Arroyos de Mantua, Cuba 116 H4
Arroyos y Esteros, Parag. 130 MIO
Ar Rub' Al Khālī, desert, Saudi Arabia
  172 LI2
Ar Ruşāfah (Risāfe), ruin, Syr. 170 FII
Ar Ruşayfah, Jordan 170 M7
Ar Ruţbah, Iraq 172 D7
Ar Ruwayshid, Jordan 170 LIO
Ars-en-Ré, Fr. 147 T5
Arsen'yev, Russ. 159 L2I
Arshaly, Kaz. 175 DI4
Arsiero, It. 150 D7
Arsikere, India 179 P5
Arsuk, Greenland, Den. 81 D22
Art, Île, New Caledonia, Fr. 218 B6
Árta (Amvrakía), Gr. 154 F8
Artashat, Arm. 169 EI8
Artem, Russ. 159 M2I
Artemisa, Cuba 116 G6
Artemivs'k, Ukr. 157 QIO
Artemovsk, Russ. 159 LI3
Artesia, N. Mex., U.S. 107 UI4
Artesia, S. Dak., U.S. 104 L7
Arthur, Nebr., U.S. 105 P3
Arthur's Pass, N.Z. 213 NI7

Arthur's Town, *Bahamas* 117 E13
Arthurstown, *Ire.* 143 U6
Artigas, *station, Antarctica* 226 C3
Artigas, *Uru.* 132 J14
Art'ik, *Arm.* 169 D18
Artiste Point, *Grenada* 121 K23
Artova, *Turk.* 168 E11
Artux, *China* 180 F4
Artvin, *Turk.* 169 D16
Artyk, *Turkm.* 174 M8
Artyk Yuryakh, *Russ.* 159 F17
Artyom, *Azerb.* 169 D23
Aru, Kepulauan, *Indonesia* 213 D15
Arua, *Uganda* 198 J12
Aruanã, *Braz.* 130 J12
Aruba, *island, Neth., Lesser Antilles* 118 M8
Aruboe, *island, Marshall Is.* 216 M7
Arucas, *Canary Is.* 204 Q6
Arue, *Fr. Polynesia, Fr.* 219 N16
Aru Islands, *Indonesia* 166 L15
Arumã, *Braz.* 130 E8
Aru Passage, *F.S.M.* 217 F14
Arusha, *Tanzania* 199 L14
Arutanga, *Cook Is., N.Z.* 218 Q11
Arutanga Passage, *Cook Is., N.Z.* 218 Q11
Arutua, *island, Fr. Polynesia, Fr.* 219 D17
Aruwimi, *river, Dem. Rep. of the Congo* 198 J11
Arvada, *Colo., U.S.* 106 M13
Arvayheer, *Mongolia* 180 E11
Arviat, *Nunavut, Can.* 83 J15
Arvidsjaur, *Sw.* 141 F13
Arvika, *Sw.* 140 L12
Arvon, Mount, *Mich., U.S.* 98 F7
Arwād, Jazīrat, *Syr.* 170 G2
Arxan, *China* 181 D15
Ary, *Russ.* 159 E16
Arys, *Kaz.* 175 J13
Arys Köli, *Kaz.* 174 G12
Arzachena, *It.* 150 M4
Arzamas, *Russ.* 156 J12
Arzgir, *Russ.* 157 S13
Asad, *Afghan.* 177 P5
Asad, Buḩayrat al, *Syr.* 170 E10
Asadābād, Gardaneh-ye, *Iran* 172 D11
Asadabad, *Afghan.* 176 M9
Asaga Strait, *Amer. Samoa, U.S.* 218 N2
Aşağıpınarbaşı, *Turk.* 168 G8
Asahi, *river, Japan* 185 Q7
Asahi Dake, *Japan* 184 F14
Asahikawa, *Japan* 184 F14
Asan, *Guam, U.S.* 216 C10
Asansol, *India* 178 J11
Asatdas, *Guam, U.S.* 216 B11
Asau, *Samoa* 218 K1
Asau Harbour, *Samoa* 218 K1
Āsbe Taferī, *Eth.* 199 G15
Asbury Park, *N.J., U.S.* 94 P11
Ascención, *Bol.* 130 J8
Ascensión, *Mex.* 114 C8
Ascension, *island, Atl. Oc.* 204 G4
Ascension Fracture Zone, *Atl. Oc.* 237 P11
Aschaffenburg, *Ger.* 148 H7
Ascó, *Sp.* 145 E15
Ascoli Piceno, *It.* 150 J10
'Aseb, *Eritrea* 199 E16
Asedjrad, *range, Alg.* 196 E10
Āsela, *Eth.* 199 G15
Asenovgrad, *Bulg.* 153 K14
Aşgabat (Ashgabat), *Turkm.* 174 M8
Asha, *Cyprus* 160 N9
Ashāqif, Jabal al, *Jordan* 170 M9
Ashburn, *Ga., U.S.* 97 P6
Ashburton, *river, W. Aust., Austral.* 211 T2
Ashburton, *N.Z.* 213 P17
Ashburton Downs, *W. Aust., Austral.* 211 T2
Ashby Fort, *ruin, St. Kitts & Nevis* 121 C18
Ashchyköl, *lake, Kaz.* 174 H12
Ashdod, *Israel* 170 M5
Ashdown, *Ark., U.S.* 100 J6
Asherton, *Tex., U.S.* 103 T8
Asheville, *N.C., U.S.* 96 H7
Ashford, *Eng., U.K.* 143 W15
Ashford, *Wash., U.S.* 108 D4
Ash Fork, *Ariz., U.S.* 107 S6
Ashgabat *see* Aşgabat, *Turkm.* 174 M8
Ash Grove, *Mo., U.S.* 105 U11
Ashikaga, *Japan* 185 N12
Ashizuri Misaki, *Japan* 185 S6
Ashland, *Kans., U.S.* 105 V5
Ashland, *Ky., U.S.* 101 A20
Ashland, *Me., U.S.* 95 B18
Ashland, *Mont., U.S.* 106 E12
Ashland, *Nebr., U.S.* 105 Q8

Ashland, *Ohio, U.S.* 99 P14
Ashland, *Oreg., U.S.* 108 K3
Ashland, *Va., U.S.* 96 E13
Ashland, *Wis., U.S.* 98 F4
Ashley, *N. Dak., U.S.* 104 H6
Ashley, *river, S.C., U.S.* 96 M10
Ashmore Islands, *W. Aust., Austral.* 211 P4
Ashmyany, *Belarus* 156 K4
Ashoro, *Japan* 184 F15
Ashqelon, *Israel* 170 M4
Ash Shabakah, *Iraq* 172 F9
Ash Sharawrah, *Saudi Arabia* 172 N11
Ash Sharqāţ, *Iraq* 172 C9
Ash Shawbak, *Jordan* 171 P6
Ash Shiḩr, *Yemen* 172 Q12
Ash Shiṣar, *Oman* 173 N14
Ash Shumlūl, *Saudi Arabia* 172 H11
Ash Shuqayq, *Saudi Arabia* 172 N8
Ash Shurayf, *Saudi Arabia* 172 J7
Ashtabula, *Ohio, U.S.* 99 N15
Ashtabula, Lake, *N. Dak., U.S.* 104 G7
Ashton, *Idaho, U.S.* 106 G7
Asia, Kepulauan, *Indonesia* 213 A14
Asia Minor *see* Anatolia, *region, Turk.* 168 F6
Asifabad, *India* 178 L7
Asiga, Puntan, *N. Mariana Is., U.S.* 216 B8
Asika, *India* 178 M11
'Asīr, *region, Saudi Arabia* 172 M8
Asinara, Golfo dell', *It.* 150 M3
Asinara, Isola, *It.* 150 M3
Asipovichy, *Belarus* 156 L5
Asiros, *Gr.* 154 C11
Aşkale, *Turk.* 169 E15
Askenderun Körfezi, *Turk.* 168 J11
Askole, *Pak.* 176 L13
Asl, *Egypt* 171 R1
Asmar, *Afghan.* 176 M9
Asmara, *Eritrea* 199 E15
Āsosa, *Eth.* 199 F13
Aspen, *Colo., U.S.* 106 M11
Aspermont, *Tex., U.S.* 102 K7
Aspiring, Mount, *N.Z.* 213 P15
Aspres, *Fr.* 147 W14
Aspromonte, *range, It.* 151 R13
Asproválta, *Gr.* 154 C12
As Sa'an, *Syr.* 170 F9
As Sabkhah, *Syr.* 170 E12
Aş Şafā, *desert, Syr.* 170 K8
As Safīrah, *Syr.* 170 E9
Aş Ṣa'īd, *Yemen* 172 Q10
Assal, Lake, *Djibouti* 199 F16
Aş Ṣāliḩiyah, *Syr.* 170 G14
As Salţ, *Jordan* 170 M6
As Samāwah, *Iraq* 172 F10
As Sanām, *desert, Saudi Arabia* 173 K13
Assateague Island National Seashore, *Md., U.S.* 96 D15
Aş Şawrah, *Saudi Arabia* 172 G5
Asselborn, *Lux.* 160 G9
Assen, *Neth.* 146 G14
As Sidr, *Lib.* 197 C15
As Sidr, *Saudi Arabia* 172 K7
Assis, *Braz.* 130 L12
Assisi, *It.* 150 H8
Assos, *ruin, Turk.* 168 E2
As Su'ayyirah, *Saudi Arabia* 172 H11
As Sukhnah, *Syr.* 170 G11
As Sulaymānīyah, *Iraq* 172 C10
As Sulayyil, *Saudi Arabia* 172 M10
Aş Şulb, *region, Saudi Arabia* 172 H11
Aş Şummān, *plateau, Saudi Arabia* 172 H10
Assumption Island, *Seychelles* 203 C17
Aş Şurrah, *Saudi Arabia* 172 Q10
Aş Şuwār, *Syr.* 170 F14
As Suwaydā', *Syr.* 170 L8
As Suwayḩ, *Oman* 173 K17
Assynt, Loch, *Scot., U.K.* 142 H8
Astakída, *island, Gr.* 155 P17
Astakós, *Gr.* 154 H8
Astana (Aqmola), *Kaz.* 175 D14
Astara, *Azerb.* 169 F22
Āstārā, *Iran* 172 B11
Asti, *It.* 150 E3
Astipálea, *island, Gr.* 155 M17
Astipálea, *Gr.* 155 M17
Astola Island, *Pak.* 177 W3
Astor, *Pak.* 176 L12
Astorga, *Sp.* 144 C8
Astoria, *Oreg., U.S.* 108 E2
Astra, *Arg.* 133 S9
Astrakhan', *Russ.* 157 R15
Astrolabe, Cape, *Solomon Is.* 217 M19

Astros, *Gr.* 154 K10
Astrupa, Gora, *Russ.* 159 D14
Astudillo, *Sp.* 144 C10
Asuisui, Cape, *Samoa* 218 L2
Asunción, *Parag.* 130 M10
Asunción, Punta, *Arg.* 133 N12
Asuncion, *island, N. Mariana Is., U.S.* 216 A2
Asuzudo Point, *N. Mariana Is., U.S.* 216 D8
Aswân, *Egypt* 197 E19
Aswân High Dam, *Egypt* 197 E19
Asyûţ, *Egypt* 197 D18
Ata, *island, Tonga* 214 K9
Ata, *island, Tonga* 218 H12
Atafu, *island, Tokelau, N.Z.* 214 H10
Atakpamé, *Togo* 200 G11
Atalándi, *Gr.* 154 H11
Atalaya de Femés, *peak, Canary Is.* 204 P7
Atamyrat (Kerki), *Turkm.* 174 M11
Atapupu, *Indonesia* 189 M15
Atar, *Mauritania* 196 F6
Atarfe, *Sp.* 144 L11
Atascadero, *Calif., U.S.* 109 V5
Atascosa, *river, Tex., U.S.* 103 S10
Atasu, *Kaz.* 175 E14
Atata, *island, Tonga* 218 H11
Atauro, *island, Timor-Leste* 189 M15
Atáviros, *peak, Gr.* 155 N19
Atbara, *river, Sudan* 199 D13
Atbara, *Sudan* 199 D13
At-Bashy, *Kyrg.* 176 F12
Atchafalaya, *river, La., U.S.* 100 P9
Atchafalaya Bay, *La., U.S.* 100 Q9
Atchison, *Kans., U.S.* 105 S10
Ateca, *Sp.* 145 E13
Ath, *Belg.* 146 L11
Athabasca, *river, Alta., Can.* 82 K11
Athabasca, *Alta., Can.* 82 L10
Athabasca, Lake, *Alta., Sask., Can.* 82 J12
Athamánio, *Gr.* 154 F8
Athamánon, *peak, Gr.* 154 F8
Athboy, *Ire.* 143 R6
Athena, *Oreg., U.S.* 108 E8
Athens, *Ala., U.S.* 101 G15
Athens, *Ga., U.S.* 96 L6
Athens *see* Athína, *Gr.* 154 J12
Athens, *Ohio, U.S.* 99 S14
Athens, *Tenn., U.S.* 101 F18
Athens, *Tex., U.S.* 102 M13
Atherton Tableland, *Austral.* 210 D13
Athfālah, *Saudi Arabia* 172 M8
Athienou, *Cyprus* 160 P9
Athienou, *Cyprus* 160 P9
Athína (Athens), *Gr.* 154 J12
Athlone, *Ire.* 143 S5
Athol Island, *Bahamas* 120 B12
Athos, *peak, Gr.* 155 D13
Ati, *Chad* 197 J15
Atico, *Peru* 130 J4
Atikokan, *Ont., Can.* 83 P15
Atimoono, *island, Cook Is., N.Z.* 219 B15
Atina, *It.* 150 L10
Atiti, *Afghan.* 176 L8
Atitue, *Fr. Polynesia, Fr.* 219 P15
Atiu, *island, Cook Is., N.Z.* 214 K12
Atka, *Alas., U.S.* 110 P6
Atka, *Russ.* 159 F20
Atka Island, *Alas., U.S.* 110 P6
Atkarsk, *Russ.* 156 M13
Atkins, *Ark., U.S.* 100 F8
Atkinson, *Nebr., U.S.* 105 N6
Atlanta, *Ga., U.S.* 96 L5
Atlanta, *Mich., U.S.* 98 H11
Atlanta, *Tex., U.S.* 102 K15
Atlantic, *Iowa, U.S.* 105 P10
Atlantic, *N.C., U.S.* 96 J14
Atlantic Beach, *Fla., U.S.* 97 Q9
Atlantic Beach, *N.C., U.S.* 96 J14
Atlantic City, *N.J., U.S.* 94 Q10
Atlantic City, *Wyo., U.S.* 106 J10
Atlantic-Indian Ridge, *Ind. Oc.* 240 R1
Atlantis Fracture Zone, *Atl. Oc.* 236 J7
Atlantis II Fracture Zone, *Ind. Oc.* 240 N6
Atlas Mountains, *Alg., Mor.* 196 B9
Atlin, *B.C., Can.* 82 G8
'Atlit, *Israel* 170 L5
Atmautluak, *Alas., U.S.* 110 J12
Atmore, *Ala., U.S.* 101 N14
Atoka, *Okla., U.S.* 102 H12
Atoyac, *Mex.* 114 K11

Atrak, *river, Iran* 173 B14
Atrato, *river, Col.* 128 D4
Atrek, *river, Turkm.* 174 M6
Atri, *It.* 150 J10
Atsumi, *Japan* 185 Q10
Atsunai, *Japan* 184 G15
Atsutoko, *Japan* 184 F16
Aţ Ţafīlah, *Jordan* 171 P6
Aţ Ţā'if, *Saudi Arabia* 172 L7
Attalla, *Ala., U.S.* 101 H16
Attapu, *Laos* 186 M12
Attawapiskat, *river, Can.* 80 G7
Attawapiskat, *Ont., Can.* 83 M17
At Taysīyah, *plateau, Saudi Arabia* 172 G9
Attent, *river, Lux.* 160 J9
At Tibnī, *Syr.* 170 F12
Attica, *Ind., U.S.* 99 Q8
Attica, *Kans., U.S.* 105 V6
Attleboro, *Mass., U.S.* 95 L14
Attu, *Greenland, Den.* 81 D21
At Tubayq, *region, Saudi Arabia* 172 F6
Attu Island, *Alas., U.S.* 110 K1
At Turbah, *Yemen* 172 R8
Atuel, *river, Arg.* 132 M8
Atuona, *Fr. Polynesia, Fr.* 219 M20
Atutahi, *island, Cook Is., N.Z.* 219 C18
Atwater, *Calif., U.S.* 109 S5
Atwood *see* Samana Cay, *island, Bahamas* 117 G15
Atwood, *Kans., U.S.* 105 R4
Atwood, Lake, *Ohio, U.S.* 99 P14
Atyraū, *Kaz.* 174 F6
Aua, *Amer. Samoa, U.S.* 218 M8
Auas Mountains, *Namibia* 194 P7
'Au'au Channel, *Hawai'i, U.S.* 113 G15
Aubagne, *Fr.* 147 Y14
Aubange, *Belg.* 160 K9
Aubenas, *Fr.* 147 W12
Aubiet, *Fr.* 147 X8
Aubinyà, *Andorra* 160 K2
Aubrac, Monts d', *Fr.* 147 W11
Aubry Lake, *N.W.T., Can.* 82 E10
Auburn, *Ala., U.S.* 101 L17
Auburn, *Calif., U.S.* 109 Q5
Auburn, *Ill., U.S.* 99 R5
Auburn, *Ind., U.S.* 99 P10
Auburn, *Me., U.S.* 95 G15
Auburn, *N.Y., U.S.* 94 J8
Auburn, *Nebr., U.S.* 105 R9
Auburn, *Qnsld., Austral.* 211 U15
Auburn, *Wash., U.S.* 108 C4
Auburndale, *Fla., U.S.* 97 U8
Aubusson, *Fr.* 147 U10
Auce, *Latv.* 141 M16
Auch, *Fr.* 147 X8
Auchel, *Fr.* 146 L10
Auckland, *N.Z.* 213 J19
Auckland Islands, *N.Z.* 214 Q7
Audience Hall, *Vatican City* 161 R16
Audincourt, *Fr.* 147 R15
Audubon, *Iowa, U.S.* 105 P10
Augathella, *Qnsld., Austral.* 211 U13
Augrabies Falls, *S. Af.* 202 K8
Augsburg, *Ger.* 148 K8
Augstsried, *Switz.* 160 M2
Augusta, *Ark., U.S.* 100 F10
Augusta, *Ga., U.S.* 96 L8
Augusta, *Kans., U.S.* 105 U8
Augusta, *Ky., U.S.* 101 A18
Augusta, *Me., U.S.* 95 F16
Augusta, *Mont., U.S.* 106 C7
Augusta, *Wis., U.S.* 98 J3
Augusta, Golfo di, *It.* 151 T12
Augustów, *Pol.* 149 B17
August Town, *Jam.* 120 J10
Augustus, Mount, *Austral.* 210 F2
Augustus Downs, *Qnsld., Austral.* 211 R11
Aukena, *island, Fr. Polynesia, Fr.* 219 Q21
Auki, *Solomon Is.* 217 M19
Auld, Lake, *Austral.* 210 F5
Auletta, *It.* 150 M12
Aulong, *island, Palau* 216 P10
Auluptagel, *island, Palau* 216 P11
Aunuu, *island, Amer. Samoa, U.S.* 218 M9
Aunuu, *Amer. Samoa, U.S.* 218 M9
Auob, *river, Namibia* 202 J8
Auponhia, *Indonesia* 189 K15
Aur, *island, Malaysia* 187 U11
Auraiya, *India* 178 G7
Aurangabad, *India* 178 H9
Aurangabad, *India* 178 L4
Aur Atoll, *Marshall Is.* 216 G5
Auray, *Fr.* 147 R4
Aurich, *Ger.* 148 C6

Aurignac, *Fr.* 147 Y8
Aurillac, *Fr.* 147 V10
Aurisina, *It.* 150 D10
Aurora, *Colo., U.S.* 106 M13
Aurora, *Ill., U.S.* 99 N6
Aurora, *Ind., U.S.* 99 S10
Aurora, *Minn., U.S.* 104 F12
Aurora, *Mo., U.S.* 105 V11
Aurora, *Nebr., U.S.* 105 Q7
Aurukun, *Qnsld., Austral.* 211 P12
Aus, *Namibia* 202 J6
Ausa, *river, It., San Marino* 161 G18
Au Sable, *river, Mich., U.S.* 98 J11
Au Sable, *Mich., U.S.* 98 J12
Au Sable Point, *Mich., U.S.* 98 F9
Auschwitz *see* Oświęcim, *Pol.* 149 H15
Austin, *Ind., U.S.* 99 T9
Austin, *Minn., U.S.* 104 L12
Austin, *Nev., U.S.* 109 P9
Austin, *Pa., U.S.* 94 L6
Austin, *Tex., U.S.* 103 Q10
Austin, Lake, *Austral.* 210 H3
Australia 210
Australian Alps, *Austral.* 210 M13
Australian Capital Territory, *Austral.* 211 Y13
Austral Islands (Tubuai Islands), *Fr. Polynesia, Fr.* 219 H16
Austria, *Eur.* 139 V6
Austriahütte, *site, Aust.* 148 L10
Austvågøy, *island, Nor.* 140 E12
Autazes, *Braz.* 130 D9
Autlán, *Mex.* 114 H9
Autun, *Fr.* 147 S12
Aux Barques, Pointe, *Mich., U.S.* 98 K13
Auxerre, *Fr.* 147 R11
Auxonne, *Fr.* 147 S13
Auzances, *Fr.* 147 T10
Ava, *Mo., U.S.* 105 V12
Avaavaroa Passage, *Cook Is., N.Z.* 218 Q9
Ava Fonua'unga, *bay, Tonga* 218 M12
Avaha, *island, Solomon Is.* 217 J18
Avala, *peak, Serb.* 152 F10
Avalau, *island, Tuvalu* 217 L22
Avallon, *Fr.* 147 R11
Avalon, *Calif., U.S.* 109 Y8
Avalon, Lake, *N. Mex., U.S.* 107 V14
Avalon Peninsula, *Nfld. & Lab., Can.* 83 M24
Ava Mata Mata Vika, *bay, Tonga* 218 Q7
Avanavero, *Suriname* 129 E15
Avanos, *Turk.* 168 F10
Avapeihi, Passe, *Fr. Polynesia, Fr.* 219 G13
Avarapa, Passe, *Fr. Polynesia, Fr.* 219 P14
Avarua, *Cook Is., N.Z.* 218 Q9
Avarua Harbour, *Cook Is., N.Z.* 218 Q9
Avatele, *Niue, N.Z.* 219 B20
Avatele Bay, *Niue, N.Z.* 219 B20
Avatiu, *Cook Is., N.Z.* 218 Q9
Avatiu Harbour, *Cook Is., N.Z.* 218 Q9
Avatolu, *Passe, Wallis & Futuna, Fr.* 218 B11
Avatoru, *Fr. Polynesia, Fr.* 219 K16
Āvāz, *Iran* 173 D17
Avdira, *ruin, Gr.* 155 C14
Avea, *island, Fiji Is.* 218 H9
Avea, Baie d', *Fr. Polynesia, Fr.* 219 H14
Avea, Baie d', *Fr. Polynesia, Fr.* 219 K23
Aveiro, *Port.* 144 F5
Aveiro, *Braz.* 130 D11
Āvej, *Iran* 172 C12
Avellino, *It.* 150 M11
Avenal, *Calif., U.S.* 109 U6
Avera, *Fr. Polynesia, Fr.* 219 B23
Avera, *Fr. Polynesia, Fr.* 219 K23
A. Verde, *river, Arg.* 133 Q9
Aversa, *It.* 150 M10
Avesnes, *Fr.* 147 N11
Avesta, *Sw.* 141 K13
Avezzano, *It.* 150 K9
Avgó, *island, Gr.* 154 N11
Avgo, *island, Gr.* 155 P17
Aviano, *It.* 150 D8
Aviator Glacier, *Antarctica* 227 Q14
Avignon, *Fr.* 147 X13
Avila, *Sp.* 144 F10
Avilés, *Sp.* 144 A8
Avire, *Vanuatu* 218 B2
Avissawella, *Sri Lanka* 179 T7
Avita, *Solomon Is.* 217 Q23
Avlonári, *Gr.* 155 H13
Avoca, *Iowa, U.S.* 105 P9
Avon, *river, Eng., U.K.* 143 U12

Avon, river, Eng., U.K. 143 VII
Avon, N.C., U.S. 96 HI5
Avondale, Ariz., U.S. 107 U6
Avon Downs, N. Terr., Austral. 211 SIO
Avon Park, Fla., U.S. 97 U9
Avranches, Fr. 147 P6
Avsa, Gora, Russ. 159 HI3
Åvsbyn, Sw. 141 FI4
Avu Avu, Solomon Is. 217 PI9
Awaday, W. Sahara, Mor. 196 E6
Awaji Shima, Japan 185 Q8
Āwarē, Eth. 199 GI6
Awarua Bay, N.Z. 213 PI5
Awa Shima, Japan 184 LI2
Awat, China 180 F5
Awbārī, Şaḥrā', Lib. 197 DI3
Awe, Loch, Scot., U.K. 142 L8
Aweil, Sudan 198 GII
Awini Plateau, Hawai'i, U.S. 113 KI9
Awjilah, Lib. 197 DI6
Awsard, W. Sahara, Mor. 196 E5
Axel Heiberg Island, Nunavut, Can. 83 BI5
Axim, Ghana 200 HIO
Axinim, Braz. 130 E9
Axiós, river, Gr. 154 BIO
Ax-les-Thermes, Fr. 147 Z9
Axtell, Nebr., U.S. 105 Q6
Ayabe, Japan 185 P8
Ayacucho, Arg. 133 NI3
Ayacucho, Peru 130 H4
Ayakkum Hu, China 180 H7
Ayaköz, Kaz. 175 EI7
Ayamonte, Sp. 144 L6
Ayan, Russ. 159 H2O
Ayan, Russ. 159 JI5
Ayancık, Turk. 168 CIO
Ayapel, Col. 128 D5
Ayaş, Turk. 168 E8
Ayat, river, Kaz. 174 CIO
Ayaviri, Peru 130 J5
Aybak see Samangan, Afghan. 176 L7
Aydar Kŭl, Kaz., Uzb. 174 KI2
Ayden, N.C., U.S. 96 HI3
Aydere, Turkm. 174 L7
Aydın, Turk. 168 G3
Aydıncık, Turk. 168 J8
Ayerbe, Sp. 145 CI4
Ayers Rock (Uluru), Austral. 210 G7
Ayeyarwady (Irrawaddy), river, Myanmar
    186 F6
Ayeyarwady, Mouths of the, Myanmar
    186 L5
Aykhal, Russ. 159 GI5
Ay Khanom, ruin, Afghan. 176 K8
Aylesbury, Eng., U.K. 143 VI3
Ayles Fiord, Nunavut, Can. 83 AI6
Ayllón, Sp. 144 EII
'Ayn al 'Arab, Syr. 170 CIO
Ayní, Taj. 176 H7
'Aynūnah, Saudi Arabia 172 G5
Ayon, Ostrov, Russ. 159 CI9
Ayorou, Niger 196 HIO
'Ayoûn el 'Atroûs, Mauritania 196 G7
Aypolovo, Russ. 158 JII
Ayr, Qnsld., Austral. 211 SI4
Ayr, Scot., U.K. 143 N9
Ayranci, Turk. 168 H9
Äyteke Bī, Kaz. 174 GIO
Aytos, Bulg. 153 JI7
Ayutla, Mex. 114 KII
Ayutthaya, Thai. 186 M9
Ayvacık, Turk. 168 E2
Ayvaj, Taj. 176 K7
Ayvalık, Turk. 168 E2
Āzād Shahr, Iran 173 BI4
Azahar, Costa del, Sp. 145 GI5
Azamgarh, India 178 G9
Azapa, Chile 132 B7
Azare, Nigeria 201 EI5
Azaw, Afghan. 177 N3
Azawak, river, Mali, Nigeria 196 GII
A'zāz, Syr. 170 D8
Azdavay, Turk. 168 C9
Azerbaijan, Asia 167 T4
Azerbaijan, region, Iran 172 CIO
Azincourt, Fr. 146 M9
Azle, Tex., U.S. 102 LII
Azmoos, Switz. 160 Q2
Azogues, Ecua. 128 K3
Azores (Açores), islands, Atl. Oc. 204 C3
Azov, Russ. 157 RIO
Azov, Sea of, Russ., Ukr. 157 S9
Azov Upland, Ukr. 138 GII

Azraq, El Bahr el (Blue Nile), Sudan
    199 FI3
Azraq, Qaşr al, Jordan 170 M8
Aztec, N. Mex., U.S. 107 QII
Aztec Ruins National Monument, N. Mex.,
    U.S. 107 QIO
Azua, Dom. Rep. 117 MI8
Azuaga, Sp. 144 J8
Azuero, Península de, Pan. 115 P2I
Azuero Peninsula see Azuero, Península
    de, N. Amer. 80 Q9
Azul, Arg. 132 MI2
Azul, Cerro, Ecua. 128 R8
Azurduy, Bol. 130 K8
Az Zabadānī, Syr. 170 J7
Az̧ Z̧āhirīyah, W. Bank 171 N5
'Azzān, Yemen 172 QII
Az Zarqā', Jordan 170 M7
Az Zawr, Kuwait 172 GII
Azzel Matti, Sebkha, Alg. 196 EIO
Az Zilfī, Saudi Arabia 172 HIO
Az Zubayr, Iraq 172 FII

B

Ba, Fiji Is. 218 H6
Baaba, Île, New Caledonia, Fr. 218 B6
Baabda, Leb. 170 J6
Baalbek, Leb. 170 H7
Baardheere, Somalia 199 JI6
Baarn, Neth. 146 JI3
Baba Burnu, Turk. 168 C7
Baba Burnu, Turk. 168 E2
Baba Dağ, Turk. 168 J4
Babadag, peak, Azerb. 169 C22
Babaeski, Turk. 168 C3
Babahoyo, Ecua. 128 K2
Babanüsah, Sudan 198 FII
Babar, island, Indonesia 189 MI7
Babar, Kepulauan, Indonesia 189 MI7
Babati, Tanzania 199 LI4
Babayevo, Russ. 156 F9
Babayurt, Russ. 157 TI5
Babe Island, Guam, U.S. 216 EIO
Babeldaob see Babelthuap, island, Palau
    216 NII
Babelthuap (Babeldaob), island, Palau
    216 NII
Babi, island, Indonesia 188 H4
Babin Nos, Bulg., Serb. 152 GI2
Babo, Indonesia 189 KI8
Baboquivari Peak, Ariz., U.S. 107 W7
Babruysk, Belarus 156 L5
Babu see Hezhou, China 183 Q3
Babusar Pass, Pak. 178 B4
Babushkina, Russ. 156 FII
Babuyan, island, Philippines 189 AI4
Babuyan Channel, Philippines 189 BI4
Babuyan Islands, Philippines 189 AI3
Babylon, ruin, Iraq 172 E9
Bacaadweyn, Somalia 199 GI7
Bacabal, Braz. 131 EI4
Bacan, island, Indonesia 189 JI6
Bacău, Rom. 153 CI6
Baccarat, Fr. 147 PI4
Baceno, It. 150 C3
Bachelor, Mount, Oreg., U.S. 108 H4
Bachu, China 180 F5
Back, river, Nunavut, Can. 83 GI4
Bačka, region, Serb. 152 E9
Bačka Palanka, Serb. 152 E9
Bačka Topola, Serb. 152 D9
Backbone Mountain, Md., U.S. 96 CIO
Back Cay, Bahamas 120 E7
Bac Lieu, Vietnam 187 QI2
Bac Ninh, Vietnam 186 HI2
Bacolet, Grenada 121 L23
Bacolod, Philippines 189 EI4
Bacup, Eng., U.K. 143 RII
Bad, river, S. Dak., U.S. 104 L4
Badain Jaran Shamo, China 180 GII
Badajoz, Sp. 144 H7
Badalona, Sp. 145 DI6
Bad Axe, Mich., U.S. 98 KI3
Baddeck, N.S., Can. 83 N22
Baddo, river, Pak. 177 T4
Baden, Aust. 148 K9
Baden-Baden, Ger. 148 J6
Baderna, Croatia 152 E4
Badgah, Afghan. 176 M5
Badger, Minn., U.S. 104 E9
Bad Hersfeld, Ger. 148 F7
Bad Homburg, Ger. 148 G6

Badin, Pak. 177 W7
Bad Ischl, Aust. 148 LIO
Bad Kissengen, Ger. 148 G7
Badlands, region, N. Dak., U.S. 104 G2
Badlands National Park, S. Dak., U.S.
    104 L2
Bad Mergentheim, Ger. 148 H7
Badogo, Mali 196 J7
Ba Dong, Vietnam 187 QI2
Badong, China 182 K3
Badrah, Iraq 172 EIO
Bad Reichenhall, Ger. 148 LIO
Badr Ḥunayn, Saudi Arabia 172 K6
Bad Säckingen, Ger. 148 L5
Bad Tölz, Ger. 148 L8
Badulla, Sri Lanka 179 T8
Badupi, Myanmar 186 G4
Baengnyeongdo, island, S. Korea 182 EII
Baetic Mountains, Sp. 138 K2
Bafa Gölü, Turk. 168 G3
Bafatá, Guinea-Bissau 200 E4
Baffin Bay, Nunavut, Can. 83 DI7
Baffin Bay, Tex., U.S. 103 UII
Baffin Island, Nunavut, Can. 83 EI6
Bafia, Cameroon 201 HI5
Bafing, river, Guinea, Mali 194 G2
Bafoulabé, Mali 196 H6
Bafoussam, Cameroon 201 HI5
Bafra, Turk. 168 CII
Bafra Burnu, Turk. 168 CII
Bāft, Iran 173 GI5
Baga, island, Solomon Is. 217 LI5
Bagamoyo, Tanzania 199 MI5
Bagan, Mount, P.N.G. 217 KI4
Bagan Serai, Malaysia 187 T9
Bagansiapiapi, Indonesia 188 H6
Bagdad, Ariz., U.S. 107 S6
Bagdarin, Russ. 159 KI6
Bagé, Braz. 130 QII
Bagenalstown see Muine Bheag, Ire.
    143 T6
Bages et de Sigean, Étang de, Fr. 147 YII
Baggs, Wyo., U.S. 106 KII
Baghdād, Iraq 172 D9
Bagheria, It. 151 S9
Bāghīn, Iran 173 FI5
Baghlan, Afghan. 176 L7
Baghran Khowleh, Afghan. 177 N4
Bağırpaşa Dağı, Turk. 169 FI4
Bağışlı, Turk. 169 GI8
Bago, Myanmar 186 K6
Bago Yoma, Myanmar 186 J6
Bagram, Afghan. 176 M8
Bagrimi, Afghan. 176 M8
Baguio, Philippines 189 BI3
Bagzane, Mount, Niger 194 F5
Bahama Islands, N. Amer. 80 M9
Bahamas, N. Amer. 81 M2I
Baharic̆-C̆aghag, Malta 161 J22
Bahau, Malaysia 187 UIO
Bahawalnagar, Pak. 177 RII
Bahawalpur, Pak. 177 SIO
Bahçe, Turk. 168 HII
Bahçesaray, Turk. 169 GI7
Bäherden, Turkm. 174 L8
Bahia see Salvador, Braz. 117 HI7
Bahía, Isla de la, Hond. 115 KI7
Bahía Blanca, Arg. 133 NII
Bahía de Caráquez, Ecua. 128 J2
Bahía Honda Key, Fla., U.S. 97 Y9
Bahía Laura, Arg. 133 U9
Bahir Dar, Eth. 199 FI4
Bahlās, Oman 173 KI6
Bahraich, India 178 G8
Bahrain, Asia 167 V4
Bāhū Kalāt, Iran 173 HI8
Baia de Aramă, Rom. 152 FI2
Baía dos Tigres, Angola 202 F5
Baia Mare, Rom. 153 BI3
Baia Sprie, Rom. 153 BI3
Baïbokoum, Chad 197 KI4
Bai Bung, Mui, Vietnam 187 QII
Baicheng, China 180 F6
Băicoi, Rom. 153 EI5
Baidoa see Baydhabo, Somalia 199 JI6
Baie-Comeau, Que., Can. 83 N2O
Baie-Mahault, Guadeloupe, Fr. 121 EI4
Baihe, China 182 BI3
Baihe, China 182 J2
Baikal, Lake, Russ. 166 EIO
Baikha, Russ. 159 HI3
Baikunthpur, India 178 J8

Baile Átha Cliath see Dublin, Ire. 143 S7
Bailén, Sp. 144 KII
Băileşti, Rom. 153 GI3
Baileys Harbor, Wis., U.S. 98 H8
Bailey Town, Bahamas 120 B8
Bailique, Braz. 131 CI3
Baillif, Guadeloupe, Fr. 121 GI4
Bailong, river, China 180 KI2
Bailundo, Angola 202 D6
Baima, China 180 KII
Bainbridge, Ga., U.S. 97 Q5
Bainet, Haiti 117 NI6
Baing, Indonesia 189 NI3
Bainville, Mont., U.S. 106 BI3
Baiona, Sp. 144 C5
Baird, Tex., U.S. 102 M8
Baird Inlet, Alas., U.S. 110 JI2
Baird Mountains, Alas., U.S. III DI4
Bairiki see Tarawa, Kiribati 217 GI7
Bairin Youqi, China 180 E4
Bairin Zuoqi, China 181 EI5
Bairnsdale, Vic., Austral. 211 ZI3
Baishan, China 182 BI2
Baiti, region, Nauru 217 E23
Baixo, Ilhéu da, Madeira 204 L5
Baiyin, China 180 JII
Baja, Hung. 149 NI5
Baja California, peninsula, Mex. 114 B5
Bajag, India 178 J8
Bäjgīrān, Iran 173 BI6
Bājil, Yemen 172 Q8
Bajo, Indonesia 189 JI3
Bajmok, Serb. 152 D9
Bajo, Indonesia 189 QI3
Bakchar, Russ. 158 KI2
Bakel, Senegal 196 H6
Baker, Calif., U.S. 109 VII
Baker, river, Chile 133 U6
Baker, Mont., U.S. 106 DI3
Baker, Nev., U.S. 109 SI3
Baker, Mount, Wash., U.S. 108 A4
Baker City, Oreg., U.S. 108 G8
Baker Foreland, Nunavut, Can. 83 HI5
Baker Island, Pac. Oc. 214 G9
Baker Lake, Austral. 210 G6
Baker Lake, Nunavut, Can. 83 HI4
Baker Lake, Nunavut, Can. 83 HI4
Bakersfield, Calif., U.S. 109 V7
Bakhchysaray, Ukr. 157 T7
Bakhmach, Ukr. 157 N7
Bakhta, Russ. 159 HI3
Bakhtegān, Daryācheh-ye, Iran 173 GI4
Baki (Baku), Azerb. 169 D23
Bakırdağı, Turk. 168 GII
Bakkafjördur, Ice. 140 F4
Bakkagerđi, Ice. 140 F4
Bako, Eth. 199 HI4
Bakony, range, Hung. 149 MI3
Baku see Baki, Azerb. 169 D23
Bakuriani, Rep. of Georgia 169 CI7
Bakutis Coast, Antarctica 226 L7
Balā, Turk. 168 E8
Balabac, island, Philippines 188 FI2
Balabac, Philippines 188 FI2
Balabac Strait, Malaysia, Philippines
    188 FI2
Balabat, F.S.M. 217 DI8
Balabio, Île, New Caledonia, Fr. 218 B6
Bala Boluk, Afghan. 177 P2
Balaclava, Jam. 120 J7
Balagansk, Russ. 159 LI5
Balaghat, India 178 K7
Balaghat Range, India 178 L5
Balaguer, Sp. 145 DI6
Balakän, Azerb. 169 C2O
Balakhna, Russ. 156 HI2
Balaklava, S. Aust., Austral. 211 XIO
Balaklava, Ukr. 157 T7
Balakliya, Ukr. 157 P9
Balakot, Pak. 176 MII
Balakovo, Russ. 156 MI4
Balamorghab, Afghan. 176 L3
Balan, Rom. 153 CI5
Balancán, Mex. 115 JI5
Balangir, India 178 K9
Balaözen, river, Kaz., Russ. 174 D5
Balashi, site, Aruba, Neth. 121 QI7
Balashov, Russ. 156 MI2
Balassagyarmat, Hung. 149 KI5
Balaton, lake, Hung. 149 MI4
Balatonszentgyörgy, Hung. 149 MI3
Balazote, Sp. 144 JI2
Balbi, Mount, P.N.G. 217 JI3
Balbina Reservoir, S. Amer. 126 D6
Balcarce, Arg. 133 NI3

Balchik, Bulg. 153 GI7
Balclutha, N.Z. 213 RI6
Bald Knob, Ark., U.S. 100 F9
Bald Mountain, Nev., U.S. 109 SII
Baldwin, Fla., U.S. 97 Q8
Baldwin City, Kans., U.S. 105 TIO
Baldwinsville, N.Y., U.S. 94 J8
Baldwyn, Miss., U.S. 101 HI3
Baldy, Mount, Ariz., U.S. 107 T9
Baldy Peak see Baldy, Mount, Ariz., U.S.
    84 K7
Balearic Islands, Sp. 145 HI6
Balearic Sea, Sp. 145 GI6
Baleia, Ponta da, Braz. 131 KI6
Baleine Bay, St. Vincent & the Grenadines
    121 JI6
Balembangan, island, Malaysia 188 FI2
Baleshare, island, Scot., U.K. 142 J6
Baleshwar, India 178 KII
Baley, Russ. 159 LI7
Balfes Creek, Qnsld., Austral. 211 SI3
Balfour Channel, Solomon Is. 217 MI6
Balfour Downs, W. Aust., Austral. 211 T4
Balgazyn, Russ. 159 MI4
Balgo, W. Aust., Austral. 211 S6
Balguerie, Cap, Fr. Polynesia, Fr. 219 M2I
Balḥāf, Yemen 172 QII
Bali, India 178 H3
Bali, island, Indonesia 188 MII
Bali, Selat, Indonesia 188 MII
Balıkesir, Turk. 168 E4
Balık Gölü, Turk. 168 CII
Balīkh, river, Syr. 170 DII
Balikpapan, Indonesia 188 JI2
Balimo, P.N.G. 213 DI8
Balingen, Ger. 148 K6
Balingian, Malaysia 187 UI6
Balintang Channel, Philippines 189 AI4
Bali Sea, Indonesia 188 MII
Balkanabat, Turkm. 174 L6
Balkan Mountains, Bulg. 152 HI2
Balkan Peninsula, Eur. 138 J9
Balkh, Afghan. 176 K6
Balkhab, Afghan. 176 L6
Balkhash, Lake, Kaz. 166 F7
Balladonia, W. Aust., Austral. 211 X5
Ballalae, island, Solomon Is. 217 LI4
Ballarat, Vic., Austral. 211 ZI2
Ballard, Lake, Austral. 210 J4
Ball Bay, Norfolk I., Austral. 217 G2O
Ballenas, Bahía, Mex. 114 D6
Ballenero, Canal, Chile 133 Y8
Ballina, Ire. 143 Q4
Ballina, N.S.W., Austral. 211 WI5
Ballinger, Tex., U.S. 103 N7
Ballinrobe, Ire. 143 R3
Ballinskelligs Bay, Ire. 143 U2
Ballinger, Tex., U.S. 103 N7
Ball's Pyramid, island, Austral. 214 M6
Ballycastle, N. Ire., U.K. 143 N7
Ballycroy, Ire. 143 Q3
Ballyhaise, Ire. 143 R6
Ballymena, N. Ire., U.K. 143 P7
Ballymoney, N. Ire., U.K. 143 P7
Ballysadare, Ire. 143 Q4
Ballyshannon, Ire. 143 Q5
Ballyvourney, Ire. 143 U3
Balmaceda, Chile 133 T7
Balmorhea, Tex., U.S. 103 P2
Balod, India 178 K8
Baloeri de Cristo Rey, Eq. Guinea 204 L7
Balonne, river, Qnsld., Austral. 211 VI4
Balotra, India 178 G3
Balpyq Bī, Kaz. 175 GI7
Balqash, Kaz. 175 FI5
Balqash Köli, Kaz. 175 GI5
Balrampur, India 178 F8
Balranald, N.S.W., Austral. 211 YI2
Balş, Rom. 153 FI3
Balsas, river, Mex. 114 JII
Balsas, Braz. 131 F4
Balta, N. Dak., U.S. 104 E5
Balta, Ukr. 157 Q5
Baltasar Brum, Uru. 132 JI3
Bălţi, Mold. 157 Q4
Baltic Plains, Eur. 138 E8
Baltic Sea, Eur. 138 E8
Baltimore, Md., U.S. 96 CI3
Baltistan, region, Pak. 176 LI3
Baltit, Pak. 176 KI2
Baltiysk, Russ. 156 JI
Baltra, Isla, Ecua. 128 Q9
Baluchistan, region, Iran, Pak. 177 U2
Balurghat, India 178 HI2
Balya, Turk. 168 E3

Balykchy (Ysyk-Köl), *Kyrg.* 176 E12
Balyqshy, *Kaz.* 174 F6
Balzers, *Liech.* 160 Q2
Bam, *Iran* 173 G16
Bama, *Nigeria* 201 E17
Bamaga, *Qnsld., Austral.* 211 N12
Bamako, *Mali* 196 J7
Bambari, *Cen. Af. Rep.* 198 H9
Bambaroo, *Qnsld., Austral.* 211 R13
Bamberg, *Ger.* 148 H8
Bamberg, *S.C., U.S.* 96 L9
Bamboo, *Jam.* 120 H8
Bamboo, *W. Aust., Austral.* 211 S3
Bam Co, *China* 180 K8
Bamenda, *Cameroon* 201 H15
Bamian (Bamiyan), *Afghan.* 176 M6
Bamingui, *Cen. Af. Rep.* 198 G9
Bamiyan see Bamian, *Afghan.* 176 M6
Bampūr, river, *Iran* 173 H17
Bampūr, *Iran* 173 H17
Bamy, *Turkm.* 174 L7
Bamyili-Beswick, *N. Terr., Austral.*
  211 Q8
Banaba (Ocean Island), *Kiribati* 214 G7
Banalia, *Dem. Rep. of the Congo* 198 J11
Banam, *Cambodia* 187 P12
Banana, river, *Fla., U.S.* 97 T10
Banana, *Kiribati* 217 A23
Banana, *Qnsld., Austral.* 211 U14
Bananal, Ilha do, *Braz.* 130 G12
Bananga, *India* 179 T15
Bananier, *Guadeloupe, Fr.* 121 G14
Banaras see Varanasi, *India* 178 H9
Banâs, Râs, *Egypt* 197 E20
Banas, river, *India* 178 G5
Banat, region, *Rom., Serb.* 152 D10
Banaz, *Turk.* 168 F5
Ban Ban, *Laos* 186 J10
Ban Bang Hin, *Thai.* 187 Q7
Banbridge, *N. Ire., U.K.* 143 Q7
Banbury, *Eng., U.K.* 143 U12
Banchory, *Scot., U.K.* 142 K11
Bancroft, *Iowa, U.S.* 104 M11
Banda, *India* 178 H6
Banda, Kepulauan, *Indonesia* 189 L17
Banda, Pointe, *Gabon* 201 M15
Banda Aceh, *Indonesia* 188 G3
Banda Besar, island, *Indonesia* 189 L17
Banda Elat, *Indonesia* 189 L18
Bandanaira, *Indonesia* 189 L17
Bandar see Machilipatnam, *India* 179 N8
Bandarban, *Bangladesh* 178 J14
Bandarbeyla, *Somalia* 199 F18
Bandar-e 'Abbās, *Iran* 173 H15
Bandar-e Anzalī, *Iran* 172 B12
Bandar-e Chārak, *Iran* 173 H14
Bandar-e Deylam, *Iran* 172 F12
Bandar-e Genāveh, *Iran* 173 H14
Bandar-e Kangān, *Iran* 173 H16
Bandar-e Khoemir, *Iran* 173 H15
Bandar-e Māh Shahr, *Iran* 172 F12
Bandar-e Maqām, *Iran* 173 H14
Bandar-e Mollaha, *Afghan.* 176 L4
Bandar Seri Begawan, *Brunei* 188 G11
Banda Sea, *Ind. Oc.* 241 H17
Banda Sea, *Indonesia* 189 L16
Bandau, *Malaysia* 188 F12
Bandeira, peak, *Braz.* 131 L15
Bandeirante, *Braz.* 130 H12
Bandelier National Monument, *N. Mex.,*
  U.S. 107 R12
Bandera, *Arg.* 132 H11
Bandera, *Tex., U.S.* 103 R9
Banderas Bay, *N. Amer.* 80 N4
Bandiagara, *Mali* 196 H8
Bandikui, *India* 178 G5
Bandırma, *Turk.* 168 D4
Ban Don, *Vietnam* 187 N13
Bandon, *Oreg., U.S.* 108 J1
Bāndovan Burnu, *Azerb.* 169 E23
Bandundu, *Dem. Rep. of the Congo*
  198 L8
Bandung, *Indonesia* 188 M8
Banes, *Cuba* 117 J13
Banff, *Alta., Can.* 82 M10
Banfora, *Burkina Faso* 200 F9
Bangalore (Bengalūru), *India* 179 P6
Bangassou, *Cen. Af. Rep.* 198 H10
Banggai, Kepulauan, *Indonesia* 189 K14
Banggi, island, *Malaysia* 188 F12
Banggong Co, *China, India* 178 C7
Banghāzī (Benghazi), *Lib.* 197 C15
Banghiang, river, *Laos* 186 L12
Bangi Island, *Guam, U.S.* 216 D10
Bangka, island, *Indonesia* 189 H15

Bangka, island, *Indonesia* 188 K8
Bangkaru, island, *Indonesia* 188 H4
Bangkok see Krung Thep, *Thai.* 186 M9
Bangladesh, *Asia* 167 W9
Bangor, *Me., U.S.* 95 E17
Bangor Erris, *Ire.* 143 Q3
Bangs, *Aust.* 160 L2
Bangs, *Tex., U.S.* 103 N8
Bang Saphan, *Thai.* 187 P8
Bangui, *Cen. Af. Rep.* 198 H8
Bangui, *Philippines* 189 B13
Bangweulu, Lake, *Zambia* 202 D11
Bani, river, *Mali* 196 H8
Baní, *Dom. Rep.* 117 M19
Banihal Pass, *India* 177 N12
Banī Sharfā, *Saudi Arabia* 172 M8
Banī Walīd, *Lib.* 197 C14
Bāniyās, *Syr.* 170 F7
Banja Luka, *Bosn. & Herzg.* 152 F7
Banjarmasin, *Indonesia* 188 K11
Banjul, *Gambia* 196 H4
Bankä, *Azerb.* 169 E23
Banka, *India* 178 H11
Banka Banka, *N. Terr., Austral.* 211 R9
Banks Island, *B.C., Can.* 82 K7
Banks Island, *N.W.T., Can.* 82 D12
Banks Islands, *Vanuatu* 218 B2
Banks Lake, *Wash., U.S.* 108 C7
Banks Peninsula, *N.Z.* 213 P18
Banmauk, *Myanmar* 186 F6
Bann, river, *N. Ire., U.K.* 143 P7
Bannerman Town, *Bahamas* 120 F6
Bannu, *Pak.* 177 P9
Bánovce nad Bebravou, *Slovakia* 149 J14
Banow, *Afghan.* 176 L8
Ban Phai, *Thai.* 186 L10
Banreaba, *Kiribati* 217 G17
Ban Sanam Chai, *Thai.* 187 R9
Banská Bystrica, *Slovakia* 149 J15
Banswara, *India* 178 J4
Bantaberá Pequeño, *Eq. Guinea* 204 M7
Ban Taphan, *Laos* 186 L12
Bantry Bay, *Ire.* 143 V3
Bantva, *India* 178 K2
Bantval, *India* 179 Q4
Ban Xénô, *Laos* 186 K11
Banzare Coast, *Antarctica* 227 P19
Baochang see Taibus Qi, *China* 182 B6
Baode, *China* 182 D3
Baoding, *China* 182 D6
Baofeng, *China* 182 H4
Baó Grande, *Eq. Guinea* 204 M8
Baoji, *China* 182 G1
Baojing, *China* 182 M2
Bao Lac, *Vietnam* 186 G12
Baoro, *Cen. Af. Rep.* 198 H8
Baoshan, *China* 180 N10
Baoting, *China* 183 U1
Baotou, *China* 182 C3
Baoying, *China* 182 J8
Bapatla, *India* 179 N7
Baqbaqty, *Kaz.* 175 H16
Baqty, *Kaz.* 175 F18
Ba'qūbah, *Iraq* 172 D10
Baquedano, *Chile* 132 E7
Bar, *Mont.* 152 J8
Bara, *Indonesia* 189 K15
Bara, *Sudan* 198 E12
Baraawe, *Somalia* 199 J16
Baraboo, *Wis., U.S.* 98 L5
Baracoa, *Cuba* 117 K14
Baraga, *Mich., U.S.* 98 F6
Bărăganul, plain, *Rom.* 153 F17
Baragoi, *Kenya* 199 J14
Barahona, *Dom. Rep.* 117 M18
Bara Hoti, *India* 178 E7
Barak, *Turk.* 168 J12
Baraki, *Afghan.* 177 N7
Baramula, *India* 176 M12
Baran, *India* 178 H5
Baranavichy, *Belarus* 156 L4
Barangbarang, *Indonesia* 189 L13
Baranof Island, *Alas., U.S.* 111 M22
Baranovka, *Russ.* 157 N14
Barão de Melgaço, *Braz.* 130 J10
Barataria Bay, *La., U.S.* 100 R11
Barat Daya, Kepulauan, *Indonesia*
  189 M16
Barate, *Indonesia* 189 N14
Bar-aterre, *Bahamas* 120 E8
Barbacena, *Braz.* 131 L14
Barbacoas, *Col.* 128 H3
Barbados, *N. Amer.* 81 P24
Barbados, island, *N. Amer.* 80 P12

Barbaria, Cap de, *Sp.* 145 J17
Barbastro, *Sp.* 145 D15
Barber, *Neth. Antilles, Neth.* 121 P13
Barbers Block, peak, *Dominica* 121 E18
Barberton, *Ohio, U.S.* 99 P14
Barbezieux, *Fr.* 147 U7
Barbourville, *Ky., U.S.* 101 D18
Barbuda, island, *Antigua & Barbuda*
  119 F16
Barcaldine, *Qnsld., Austral.* 211 T13
Barcellona Pozzo di Gotto, *It.* 151 R12
Barcelona, *Sp.* 145 E17
Barcelona, *Venez.* 128 B11
Barcelos, *Port.* 144 D5
Barcelos, *Braz.* 130 C8
Barco, *N.C., U.S.* 96 G14
Barcoo, river, *Austral.* 210 G12
Barcs, *Hung.* 149 N13
Bārda, *Azerb.* 169 D21
Barda del Medio, *Arg.* 133 N8
Barda Hills, *India* 178 J1
Bardaï, *Chad* 197 F14
Bardas Blancas, *Arg.* 132 M7
Bardawīl, Sabkhet el, *Egypt* 171 N2
Barddhaman, *India* 178 J11
Bardejov, *Slovakia* 149 H16
Bardoc, *W. Aust., Austral.* 211 W4
Bardonecchia, *It.* 150 E1
Bardsey Island, *Wales, U.K.* 143 T8
Bardsīr, *Iran* 173 F15
Bardstown, *Ky., U.S.* 101 C17
Bardwell, *Ky., U.S.* 100 D12
Bareilly, *India* 178 F7
Barentin, *Fr.* 147 N8
Barents Plain, *Arctic Oc.* 243 G13
Barents Sea, *Arctic Oc.* 243 D15
Barfak, *Afghan.* 176 L7
Barfleur, *Fr.* 147 N6
Barfleur, Pointe de, *Fr.* 147 N6
Barga, *China* 180 K5
Barga, *It.* 150 G6
Bargaal, *Somalia* 199 F18
Bargarh, *India* 178 K9
Barg-e Matal, *Afghan.* 176 L9
Barh, *India* 178 H10
Barhi, *India* 178 H7
Bari, *It.* 150 L14
Ba Ria, *Vietnam* 187 P13
Barigello, river, *It.* 161 G16
Barikowt, *Afghan.* 176 L9
Barīm (Perim), island, *Yemen* 172 R8
Barima, river, *Guyana* 129 D14
Barinas, *Venez.* 128 C7
Baripada, *India* 178 J11
Barisal, *Bangladesh* 178 J13
Barisan, Pegunungan, *Indonesia* 188 K6
Barisan Mountains see Barisan, Pegu-
  nungan, *Indonesia* 166 M11
Barka', *Oman* 173 K16
Barka Kana, *India* 178 J10
Barkana, *Pak.* 177 R8
Barkley, Lake, *Ky., U.S.* 101 D14
Barkly Tableland, *Austral.* 210 D9
Barkol, *China* 180 E9
Barkol Hu, *China* 180 E9
Barla Dağı, *Turk.* 168 G6
Bar-le-Duc, *Fr.* 147 P13
Barlee, Lake, *Austral.* 210 J3
Barletta, *It.* 150 L13
Barlinek, *Pol.* 148 D11
Barmer, *India* 178 H3
Barmouth, *Wales, U.K.* 143 T9
Barnaul, *Russ.* 158 L12
Barnegat, *N.J., U.S.* 94 Q11
Barnegat Light, *N.J., U.S.* 94 Q11
Barnes Ice Cap, *Nunavut, Can.* 83 E17
Barnesville, *Ga., U.S.* 96 M5
Barnesville, *Minn., U.S.* 104 G8
Barneville-Carteret, *Fr.* 147 N5
Barnhart, *Tex., U.S.* 103 P6
Barn Hill, *Austral.* 210 D4
Barnsdall, *Okla., U.S.* 102 E12
Barnsley, *Eng., U.K.* 143 R12
Barnstaple, *Eng., U.K.* 143 W9
Barnstaple Bay, *Eng., U.K.* 143 W9
Barnum Bay, *Palau* 216 Q10
Barnwell, *S.C., U.S.* 96 L8
Baro, *Nigeria* 201 G13
Baroghil Pass, *Afghan., Pak.* 176 K11
Baron Bluff, *Virgin Islands, U.S.* 120 Q2
Barora Fa, island, *Solomon Is.* 217 L17

Barora Ite, island, *Solomon Is.* 217 L17
Barpeta, *India* 178 G13
Barquisimeto, *Venez.* 128 B8
Barra, island, *Scot., U.K.* 142 K6
Barra, *Braz.* 131 G15
Barra, Ponta da, *Mozambique* 203 H13
Barra, Sound of, *Scot., U.K.* 142 K6
Barra do Bugres, *Braz.* 130 J10
Barra do Corda, *Braz.* 131 E14
Barra do São Manuel, *Braz.* 130 F10
Barrancabermeja, *Col.* 128 D5
Barrancas, *Venez.* 128 C12
Barrancos, *Port.* 144 K7
Barranqueras, *Arg.* 132 G13
Barranquilla, *Col.* 128 B5
Barranquitas, *P.R., U.S.* 120 N4
Barras, *Braz.* 131 E15
Barrax, *Sp.* 144 H12
Barre, *Vt., U.S.* 95 G13
Barre, *Vt., U.S.* 95 G13
Barreiras, *Braz.* 131 H14
Barreirinha, *Braz.* 130 D10
Barreirinhas, *Braz.* 131 D15
Barreiro, *Port.* 144 J4
Barrême, *Fr.* 147 W14
Barren, river, *Ky., U.S.* 101 D16
Barren, Nosy, *Madagascar* 203 F16
Barrhill, *Scot., U.K.* 143 P8
Barrie, *Ont., Can.* 83 Q18
Barrigada, *Guam, U.S.* 216 C11
Barrington see Santa Fe, Isla, island,
  Ecua. 128 Q10
Barringun, *N.S.W., Austral.* 211 W13
Barron, *Wis., U.S.* 98 H3
Barrouallie, *St. Vincent & the Grenadines*
  121 K16
Barrow, *Alas., U.S.* 111 B15
Barrow, river, *Ire.* 143 T6
Barrow, Point, *Alas., U.S.* 111 B15
Barrow Canyon, *Arctic Oc.* 242 L5
Barrow Creek, *N. Terr., Austral.* 211 S8
Barrow in Furness, *Eng., U.K.* 143 Q10
Barrow Island, *W. Aust., Austral.* 211 S1
Barrow Strait, *Arctic Oc.* 242 P10
Barry, *Ill., U.S.* 99 R3
Barrytown, *N.Z.* 213 N17
Barshatas, *Kaz.* 175 E17
Barstow, *Calif., U.S.* 109 W10
Bar-sur-Seine, *Fr.* 147 Q12
Bartholomew, Bayou, *Ark., La., U.S.*
  100 K9
Bartica, *Guyana* 129 D14
Bartın, *Turk.* 168 C8
Bartle Frere, peak, *Austral.* 210 D13
Bartlesville, *Okla., U.S.* 102 E12
Bartlett, *Nebr., U.S.* 105 P6
Bartlett, *Tex., U.S.* 103 P11
Barton, *N. Dak., U.S.* 104 E5
Barton, *Vt., U.S.* 95 F13
Barton Siding, *S. Aust., Austral.* 211 W8
Bartoszyce, *Pol.* 149 B16
Bartow, *Fla., U.S.* 97 U8
Barú, Volcán, *Pan.* 115 N20
Baruunharaa, *Mongolia* 180 C12
Baruunsuu, *Mongolia* 180 F12
Baruun Urt, *Mongolia* 181 D14
Barvas, *Scot., U.K.* 142 H7
Barwon, river, *N.S.W., Austral.* 211 W14
Barykova, Mys, *Russ.* 159 B21
Barysaw, *Belarus* 156 K5
Barysh, *Russ.* 156 K14
Basacato del Este, *Eq. Guinea* 204 M8
Basacato del Oeste, *Eq. Guinea* 204 M7
Basaga, *Turkm.* 174 M11
Basankusu, *Dem. Rep. of the Congo*
  198 J9
Basargech'ar, *Arm.* 169 D19
Basaseachic Falls, *N. Amer.* 80 M4
Basco, *Philippines* 189 A14
Bascuñán, Cabo, *Chile* 132 H6
Basel, *Switz.* 150 A3
Basilan, island, *Philippines* 189 F14
Basilé, *Eq. Guinea* 204 L8
Basile, *La., U.S.* 100 P8
Basiliano, *It.* 150 D9
Basilisk Harbor, *Solomon Is.* 217 Q23
Basin, *Wyo., U.S.* 106 G10
Basingstoke, *Eng., U.K.* 143 W13
Basīt, Ra's al, *Syr.* 170 E7
Başkale, *Turk.* 169 G18
Baskil, *Turk.* 169 G13
Baskunchak, Ozero, *Russ.* 157 Q14

Basmat, *India* 178 L5
Basoko, *Dem. Rep. of the Congo* 198 J10
Basora, Punta, *Aruba, Neth.* 121 R17
Bass, Îlots de see Marotiri, *Fr. Polynesia,*
  Fr. 215 L14
Bassae, ruin, *Gr.* 154 K9
Bassas da India, islands, *Mozambique Ch.*
  203 H14
Basse-Pointe, *Martinique, Fr.* 121 E22
Basses, Pointe des, *Guadeloupe, Fr.*
  121 G16
Basse Terre, *Trinidad & Tobago* 121 Q22
Basseterre, *St. Kitts & Nevis* 121 B17
Basse-Terre, island, *Guadeloupe, Fr.*
  121 F14
Basse-Terre, *Guadeloupe, Fr.* 121 G14
Bassett, *Nebr., U.S.* 105 N5
Bassett, *Va., U.S.* 96 G10
Bassikounou, *Mauritania* 196 H8
Bass Islands, *Ohio, U.S.* 99 N13
Bass Islands, *Solomon Is.* 217 N24
Bass Strait, *Vic., Austral.* 211 Z12
Bastak, *Iran* 173 H14
Bastendorf, *Lux.* 160 H10
Basti, *India* 178 G8
Bastia, *Fr.* 150 J4
Bastogne, *Belg.* 146 M13
Bastrop, *La., U.S.* 100 K9
Bastrop, *Tex., U.S.* 103 Q11
Basutsuträsk, *Sw.* 141 G14
Basu, island, *Indonesia* 188 J7
Basuo see Dongfang, *China* 183 U1
Basupú, *Eq. Guinea* 204 L7
Bata, *Eq. Guinea* 201 K15
Bataan Peninsula, *Philippines* 189 C13
Batabanó, Golfo de, *Cuba* 116 H6
Batagay, *Russ.* 159 F18
Batala, *India* 178 P12
Batamay, *Russ.* 159 G18
Batan, island, *Philippines* 189 A14
Batang, *China* 180 L10
Batangafo, *Cen. Af. Rep.* 198 G8
Batangas, *Philippines* 189 C13
Batan Islands, *Philippines* 189 A14
Batanta, island, *Indonesia* 189 J17
Batavia, *N.Y., U.S.* 94 J6
Bataysk, *Russ.* 157 R11
Bates, Mount, *Norfolk I., Austral.* 217 F20
Batesburg, *S.C., U.S.* 96 L8
Batesville, *Ark., U.S.* 100 F9
Batesville, *Ind., U.S.* 99 S10
Batesville, *Miss., U.S.* 100 H11
Batesville, *Tex., U.S.* 103 S8
Batete, *Eq. Guinea* 204 M7
Bath, *Eng., U.K.* 143 V11
Bath, *Jam.* 120 J11
Bath, *Me., U.S.* 95 G16
Bath, *N.Y., U.S.* 94 K7
Bath, *St. Kitts & Nevis* 121 C18
Bathsheba, *Barbados* 121 K19
Bathurst, *N.B., Can.* 83 N21
Bathurst, *N.S.W., Austral.* 211 X14
Bathurst, Cape, *N.W.T., Can.* 82 D11
Bathurst Inlet, *Nunavut, Can.* 83 F13
Bathurst Island, *N. Terr., Austral.* 211 N7
Bathurst Island, *Nunavut, Can.* 83 D14
Batié, *Burkina Faso* 200 F9
Batiki, island, *Fiji Is.* 218 J7
Batista, Serra da, *Braz.* 131 F16
Batman, *Turk.* 169 G15
Batna, *Alg.* 196 A12
Batoicopo, *Eq. Guinea* 204 L7
Baton Rouge, *La., U.S.* 100 P10
Batouri, *Cameroon* 201 H17
Båtsfjord, *Nor.* 141 B15
Batsí, *Gr.* 155 J14
Battambang, *Cambodia* 187 N10
Batteau, *Nfld. & Lab., Can.* 83 K22
Batticaloa, *Sri Lanka* 179 S8
Battle Creek, *Mich., U.S.* 98 M10
Battle Creek, *Mont., U.S.* 106 A9
Battle Harbour, *Nfld. & Lab., Can.* 83 L23
Battle Mountain, *Nev., U.S.* 109 N9
Batu, peak, *Eth.* 199 G15
Batu, Kepulauan, *Indonesia* 188 J5
Batukelau, *Indonesia* 188 J11
Bat'umi, *Rep. of Georgia* 169 C16
Batu Pahat, *Malaysia* 187 V10
Batuputih, *Indonesia* 188 H12
Baturaja, *Indonesia* 188 L7
Baturité, *Braz.* 131 E17
Bat Yam, *Israel* 170 M5
Batz, Île de, *Fr.* 147 P3
Bau, island, *Fiji Is.* 218 J7
Baubau, *Indonesia* 189 L14

Baucau, *Timor-Leste* **189** MI5
Bauchi, *Nigeria* **201** FI5
Baudette, *Minn., U.S.* **104** EIO
Baudó, Serranía de, *S. Amer.* **126** B2
Baugé, *Fr.* **147** R7
Bauges, range, *Fr.* **147** UI4
Baun, *Indonesia* **189** NI4
Baunatal, *Ger.* **148** F7
Baures, river, *Bol.* **130** H8
Bauru, *Braz.* **131** LI3
Baús, *Braz.* **130** KII
Bautino, *Kaz.* **174** G5
Bautzen, *Ger.* **148** FII
Bavaria, region, *Ger.* **148** J8
Bawal, island, *Indonesia* **188** K9
Bawean, island, *Indonesia* **188** LIO
Bawku, *Ghana* **200** FII
Baxkorgan, *China* **180** G8
Baxley, *Ga., U.S.* **97** N7
Baxoi, *China* **180** L9
Baxter, *Minn., U.S.* **104** HIO
Baxter Springs, *Kans., U.S.* **105** VIO
Bay'ah, *Oman* **173** JI5
Bayamo, *Cuba* **116** KI2
Bayamón, *P.R., U.S.* **120** M4
Bayan, *Mongolia* **180** E9
Bayanaūyl, *Kaz.* **175** DI5
Bayandalay, *Mongolia* **180** FII
Bayanga, *Cen. Af. Rep.* **198** J8
Bayan Gol *see* Dengkou, *China* **182** CI
Bayan Har Shan, *China* **180** J9
Bayan Har Shankou, *China* **180** JIO
Bayanhongor, *Mongolia* **180** EII
Bayanmönh, *Mongolia* **181** DI3
Bayano, Lago, *Pan.* **115** N22
Bayan Obo, *China* **182** B3
Bayan Range, *Afghan.* **176** M5
Bayard, *N. Mex., U.S.* **107** VIO
Bayard, *Nebr., U.S.* **105** PI
Bayat, *Turk.* **168** F6
Bayāz, *Iran* **173** FI5
Bayboro, *N.C., U.S.* **96** JI4
Bayburt, *Turk.* **169** EI5
Bay City, *Mich., U.S.* **98** KI2
Bay City, *Tex., U.S.* **103** SI3
Baydarata Bay, *Arctic Oc.* **243** AI4
Baydaratskaya Guba, *Russ.* **158** FII
Baydhabo (Baidoa), *Somalia* **199** JI6
Bayès, Cap, *New Caledonia, Fr.* **218** C7
Bayeux, *Fr.* **147** N7
Bayfield, *Wis., U.S.* **98** E4
Bayghanīn, *Kaz.* **174** E8
Bayḩān al Qişāb, *Yemen* **172** QIO
Bayındır, *Turk.* **168** G3
Bay Islands, *N. Amer.* **80** P7
Bayjī, *Iraq* **172** C9
Baykal, Ozero, *Russ.* **159** LI6
Baykan, *Turk.* **169** GI6
Baykonur *see* Bayqongyr, *Kaz.* **174** GIO
Baykonur Cosmodrome, *Kaz.* **174** GII
Baykurt, *China* **180** F4
Bay Minette, *Ala., U.S.* **101** NI4
Bay of Whales, station, *Antarctica* **226** NII
Bayonne, *Fr.* **147** X5
Bayqongyr (Baykonur, Leninsk), *Kaz.* **174** GIO
Bayramaly, *Turkm.* **174** MIO
Bayramiç, *Turk.* **168** E2
Bayreuth, *Ger.* **148** H9
Bay St. Louis, *Miss., U.S.* **100** PI2
Bay Springs, *Miss., U.S.* **100** MI2
Bayt al Faqīh, *Yemen* **172** Q8
Bayt Laḩm (Bethlehem), *W. Bank* **170** M5
Baytown, *Tex., U.S.* **103** QI4
Baza, *Sp.* **144** LI2
Baza'i Gonbad, *Afghan.* **176** KII
Bazar Dyuzi, peak, *Azerb.* **169** C2I
Bazar-e Panjva'i, *Afghan.* **177** Q5
Bazar-e Taleh, *Afghan.* **176** L7
Bazar-Kurgan, *Kyrg.* **176** FIO
Bazartöbe, *Kaz.* **174** D6
Bazas, *Fr.* **147** W7
Bazkovskaya, *Russ.* **157** PII
Bazmān, Kūh-e, *Iran* **173** GI7
Be, Nosy, *Madagascar* **203** DI8
Beach, *N. Dak., U.S.* **104** GI
Beach Haven, *N.J., U.S.* **94** QII
Beachy Head, *Eng., U.K.* **143** WI4
Beagle Bay, *W. Aust., Austral.* **211** R4
Béar, Cap, *Fr.* **147** ZII
Bearden, *Ark., U.S.* **100** J8
Beardmore Glacier, *Antarctica* **227** LI3
Beardstown, *Ill., U.S.* **99** R4
Bear Island, *Ire.* **143** V2

Bear Islands *see* Medvezh'i Ostrova, *Russ.* **159** CI9
Bear Lake, *Idaho, Utah, U.S.* **106** J8
Bear Paw Mountains, *Mont., U.S.* **84** C8
Bear River Range, *Idaho, Utah, U.S.* **106** J7
Bears Paw Mountains, *Mont., U.S.* **106** B9
Beasain, *Sp.* **144** BI2
Beata, Cabo, *Dom. Rep.* **117** NI7
Beata, Isla, *Dom. Rep.* **117** NI7
Beata Ridge, *Atl. Oc.* **236** L4
Beatrice, *Nebr., U.S.* **105** R8
Beatrice, Cape, *Austral.* **210** BIO
Beattock, *Scot., U.K.* **143** NIO
Beatton River, *B.C., Can.* **82** J9
Beatty, *Nev., U.S.* **109** TIO
Beau Bassin, *Mauritius* **205** GI9
Beaucaire, *Fr.* **147** XI2
Beauchêne Island, *Falkland Is., U.K.* **133** WI2
Beaufort, *Lux.* **160** JIO
Beaufort, *Malaysia* **188** GII
Beaufort, *N.C., U.S.* **96** JI4
Beaufort, *S.C., U.S.* **96** M9
Beaufort Sea, *Arctic Oc.* **242** M5
Beaufort Shelf, *Arctic Oc.* **242** N5
Beaufort Slope, *Arctic Oc.* **242** N5
Beaufort West, *S. Af.* **202** L9
Beaugency, *Fr.* **147** R9
Beaumanoir, Port du, *Fr. Polynesia, Fr.* **219** QI7
Beaumont, *Tex., U.S.* **103** QI5
Beaune, *Fr.* **147** SI3
Beausoleil, *Fr.* **147** XI6
Beausoleil, Town Hall of, *Fr.* **161** C2I
Beautemps Beaupré, Île, *New Caledonia, Fr.* **218** C8
Beauvais, *Fr.* **147** N9
Beauvoir, *Fr.* **147** S5
Beaver, *Alas., U.S.* **111** EI7
Beaver, river, *Okla., U.S.* **102** E6
Beaver, *Okla., U.S.* **102** E7
Beaver, *Oreg., U.S.* **108** F2
Beaver, *Utah, U.S.* **107** N6
Beaver Bay, *Minn., U.S.* **104** FI3
Beaver City, *Nebr., U.S.* **105** R5
Beaver Creek, *Kans., U.S.* **105** S4
Beaver Creek, *Mont., U.S.* **106** BIO
Beaver Dam, *Ky., U.S.* **101** CI5
Beaver Dam, *Wis., U.S.* **98** L6
Beaver Falls, *Pa., U.S.* **94** N3
Beaver Glacier, *Antarctica* **227** CI9
Beaverhead, river, *Mont., U.S.* **106** F6
Beaverhead Mountains, *Mont., U.S.* **106** F6
Beaver Island, *Mich., U.S.* **98** G9
Beaver Lake, *Ark., U.S.* **100** E6
Beaverton, *Oreg., U.S.* **108** F3
Beawar, *India* **178** G4
Bebar, *India* **178** HI
Bebiram, *Indonesia* **213** BI4
Beccles, *Eng., U.K.* **143** TI6
Bečej, *Serb.* **152** EIO
Becerreá, *Sp.* **144** B7
Béchar, *Alg.* **196** C9
Becharof Lake, *Alas., U.S.* **111** LI4
Beckerich, *Lux.* **160** J9
Beckley, *W. Va., U.S.* **96** E8
Beddouza, Cap, *Mor.* **196** B7
Bedford, *Eng., U.K.* **143** UI3
Bedford, *Ind., U.S.* **99** T9
Bedford, *Iowa, U.S.* **105** QIO
Bedford, *Pa., U.S.* **94** P5
Bedford, *Va., U.S.* **96** FIO
Bedford, Cape, *Austral.* **210** CI3
Bedfort Point, *Grenada* **121** J23
Bedonia, *It.* **150** F5
Bedourie, *Qnsld., Austral.* **211** UIO
Bedous, *Fr.* **147** Y6
Beebe, *Ark., U.S.* **100** G9
Beech Grove, *Ind., U.S.* **99** R9
Beechworth, *Vic., Austral.* —
Beef Island, *Virgin Islands, U.K.* **120** Q7
Beenleigh, *Qnsld., Austral.* **211** VI5
Be'er Menuḩa, *Israel* **171** Q5
Be'er Ora, *Israel* **171** R5
Beersheba *see* Be'er Sheva', *Israel* **171** N5
Be'ér Sheva' (Beersheba), *Israel* **171** N5
Beetaloo, *N. Terr., Austral.* **211** R8
Bega, *N.S.W., Austral.* **211** ZI4
Bega, river, *Rom.* **152** DI2
Bega, Canalul, *Rom.* **152** EIO

Begejski Kanal, *Serb.* **152** EIO
Beggars Point, *Antigua & Barbuda* **121** A2I
Begusarai, *India* **178** HIO
Behagle *see* Laï, *Chad* **197** KI4
Behbahān, *Iran* **172** FI2
Behring Point, *Bahamas* **116** EII
Behshahr, *Iran* **173** BI4
Bei, river, *China* **181** NI4
Bei'an, *China* **181** CI7
Beida *see* Al Bayḑā', *Lib.* **197** BI6
Beihai, *China* **183** SI
Beijing (Peking), *China* **182** D7
Beilen, *Neth.* **146** HI4
Beiliu, *China* **183** R2
Beining, *China* **182** BIO
Beipiao, *China* **182** B9
Beira, *Mozambique* **203** GI3
Beirut *see* Beyrouth, *Leb.* **170** H6
Bei Shan, *China* **180** F9
Beitbridge, *Zimb.* **202** HII
Beït ed Dîne, *Leb.* **170** J6
Beiuş, *Rom.* **152** CI2
Beja, *Port.* **144** K6
Beja, *Tun.* **196** AI2
Bejaïa, *Alg.* **196** AII
Béjar, *Sp.* **144** F8
Bejestān, *Iran* **173** DI6
Bekaa Valley, *Leb.* **170** J7
Bekdash *see* Karabogaz, *Turkm.* **174** J6
Békés, *Hung.* **149** MI7
Békéscsaba, *Hung.* **149** MI7
Bekily, *Madagascar* **203** JI6
Bekja, island, *Marshall Is.* **216** K8
Bekkai, *Japan* **184** FI6
Bekobod, *Taj.* **176** G8
Bekobod, *Uzb.* **175** LI3
Bekoropoka-Antongo, *Madagascar* **203** HI6
Bekwai, *Ghana* **200** HIO
Bela, *Pak.* **177** V5
Belaga, *Malaysia* **188** HII
Bel Air, *Mauritius* **205** G2O
Belalcázar, *Sp.* **144** J9
Belarus, *Eur.* **139** T9
Bela Vista, *Braz.* **130** LIO
Belaya, river, *Russ.* **138** DI4
Belaya, Gora, *Russ.* **159** C2O
Belaya Glina, *Russ.* **157** SII
Belaya Gora, *Russ.* **159** EI8
Belaya Kalitva, *Russ.* **157** QII
Belaya Zemlya, Ostrova, *Russ.* **159** CI3
Bełchatów, *Pol.* **149** FI5
Belcheragh, *Afghan.* **176** L5
Belcher Islands, *Nunavut, Can.* **83** LI7
Belcik, *Turk.* **168** EII
Belcoo, *N. Ire., U.K.* **143** Q5
Belderg, *Ire.* **143** Q3
Belding, *Mich., U.S.* **98** LIO
Beledweyne, *Somalia* **199** HI7
Belele, *W. Aust., Austral.* **211** V3
Belém, *Braz.* **131** DI3
Belén, *Arg.* **132** G8
Belen, *N. Mex., U.S.* **107** SI2
Bélep, Îles, *New Caledonia, Fr.* **218** B6
Bélep, Îles, *New Caledonia, Fr.* **214** K7
Belev, *Russ.* **156** L9
Belfast, *Me., U.S.* **95** FI7
Belfast, *N. Ire., U.K.* **143** Q7
Belfast Lough, *N. Ire., U.K.* **143** P7
Belfield, *N. Dak., U.S.* **104** G2
Belfort, *Fr.* **147** RI5
Belgaum, *India* **179** N4
Belgica Bank, *Arctic Oc.* **243** JI5
Belgica Mountains, *Antarctica* **227** CI6
Belgium, *Eur.* **139** T5
Belgodère, *Fr.* **150** J4
Belgorod, *Russ.* **157** N9
Belgrade, *Mont., U.S.* **106** E8
Belgrade *see* Beograd, *Serb.* **152** FIO
Belgrano II, station, *Antarctica* **226** EIO
Belhaven, *N.C., U.S.* **96** HI4
Belidzhi, *Russ.* **157** UI6
Belilou *see* Peleliu, island, *Palau* **216** QIO
Belinyu, *Indonesia* **188** K8
Belisario Domínguez, *Mex.* **115** KI4
Belitung (Billiton), island, *Indonesia* **188** K9
Belize, *N. Amer.* **81** PI9
Belize City, *Belize* **115** KI6
Bel'kachi, *Russ.* **159** HI9
Bel'kovskiy, Ostrov, *Russ.* **159** DI6
Bella Bella, *B.C., Can.* **82** K7

Bellac, *Fr.* **147** T8
Bella Coola, *B.C., Can.* **82** K8
Bellaire, *Mich., U.S.* **98** HIO
Bellaire, *Ohio, U.S.* **99** RI5
Bellaire, *Tex., U.S.* **103** RI4
Bellary, *India* **179** N5
Bella Unión, *Uru.* **132** JI3
Bella Vista, *Arg.* **132** G9
Bella Vista, *Arg.* **132** HI3
Bellavista, *Peru* **130** F2
Belle-Anse, *Haiti* **117** MI7
Belledonne, Chaîne de, *Fr.* **147** UI4
Bellefontaine, *Martinique, Fr.* **121** F22
Bellefontaine, *Ohio, U.S.* **99** QI2
Bellefonte, *Pa., U.S.* **94** N6
Belle Fourche, *S. Dak., U.S.* **104** KI
Belle Fourche, river, *Wyo., U.S.* **106** GI3
Belle Fourche Reservoir, *S. Dak., U.S.* **104** KI
Bellegarde, *Fr.* **147** QIO
Bellegarde, *Fr.* **147** TI4
Belle Glade, *Fla., U.S.* **97** VIO
Belle-Île, *Fr.* **147** R4
Belle Isle, *Nfld. & Lab., Can.* **83** L23
Belle Isle, Strait of, *Nfld. & Lab., Can.* **83** L22
Bellême, *Fr.* **147** Q8
Belle Plaine, *Iowa, U.S.* **105** NI3
Belle Plaine, *Minn., U.S.* **104** KII
Belleville, *Fr.* **147** TI2
Belleville, *Ill., U.S.* **99** T4
Belleville, *Kans., U.S.* **105** R7
Bellevue, *Iowa, U.S.* **105** NI4
Bellevue, *Nebr., U.S.* **105** Q9
Bellevue, *Ohio, U.S.* **99** PI3
Bellevue, *Tex., U.S.* **102** KIO
Bellevue, *Wash., U.S.* **108** C4
Bellingham, *Wash., U.S.* **108** A4
Bellingshausen, station, *Antarctica* **226** C3
Bellingshausen Plain, *Antarctic Oc.* **244** J7
Bellingshausen Sea, *Antarctica* **226** H4
Bellinzona, *Switz.* **150** C4
Bello, *Col.* **128** E4
Bellona Island, *Solomon Is.* **217** QI8
Bellows Falls, *Vt., U.S.* **95** JI3
Bellpat, *Pak.* **177** S7
Bell Peninsula, *Nunavut, Can.* **83** HI7
Bell Point, *St. Martin, Fr.* **121** AI4
Bell Rock (Inchcape), *Scot., U.K.* **142** LII
Bells, *Tenn., U.S.* **100** FI2
Belluno, *It.* **150** D8
Bell Ville, *Arg.* **132** KII
Bellville, *Tex., U.S.* **103** QI2
Belmond, *Iowa, U.S.* **104** MII
Belmont, *Grenada* **121** L22
Belmont, *Miss., U.S.* **101** HI3
Belmont, *N.C., U.S.* **96** J9
Belmonte, *Port.* **144** F7
Belmonte, *Sp.* **144** HI2
Belmonte, *Braz.* **131** JI6
Belmopan, *Belize* **115** KI6
Belmullet, *Ire.* **143** Q3
Belogorsk, *Russ.* **159** KI9
Belo Horizonte, *Braz.* **131** LI4
Beloit, *Kans., U.S.* **105** S7
Beloit, *Wis., U.S.* **98** M6
Belomorsk, *Russ.* **158** D8
Belorado, *Sp.* **144** CII
Belorechensk, *Russ.* **157** TII
Belo-Tsiribihina, *Madagascar* **203** GI6
Beloūsovka, *Kaz.* **175** DI8
Beloye, Lake *see* Beloye, Ozero, *Russ.* **138** CIO
Beloye More, *Russ.* **158** D8
Beloye Ozero, *Russ.* **156** F9
Belozersk, *Russ.* **156** F9
Belpre, *Ohio, U.S.* **99** SI5
Belt, *Mont., U.S.* **106** C8
Belterra, *Braz.* **130** DII
Belton, *S.C., U.S.* **96** K7
Belton, *Tex., U.S.* **103** PII
Belton Lake, *Tex., U.S.* **103** NII
Belukha, peak, *Russ.* **166** F8
Belukha, Gora, *Russ.* **158** MI2
Belush'ya Guba, *Russ.* **158** DIO
Belvedere Courtyard, *Vatican City* **161** PI6
Belvedere Marittimo, *It.* **151** PI3
Belvès, *Fr.* **147** V8
Belvidere, *Ill., U.S.* **98** M6
Belvidere, *S. Dak., U.S.* **104** L4
Belvís de la Jara, *Sp.* **144** G9
Belyando, river, *Austral.* **210** FI3

Belyy, *Russ.* **156** J7
Belyy, Ostrov, *Russ.* **158** EI2
Belzoni, *Miss., U.S.* **100** KIO
Bemaraha, plateau, *Madagascar* **203** GI6
Bembe, *Angola* **202** B6
Bembibre, *Sp.* **144** C8
Bemidji, *Minn., U.S.* **104** FIO
Benāb, *Iran* **172** BIO
Benabarre, *Sp.* **145** DI5
Benadir, region, *Somalia* **194** KII
Benasque, *Sp.* **145** CI5
Benavente, *Sp.* **144** D9
Benavides, *Tex., U.S.* **103** UIO
Benbecula, island, *Scot., U.K.* **142** J6
Bend, *Oreg., U.S.* **108** H5
Bendals, *Antigua & Barbuda* **121** B2O
Bendena, *Qnsld., Austral.* **211** VI3
Bender, *Mold.* **157** R5
Bender Cassim *see* Boosaaso, *Somalia* **199** FI8
Bendern, *Liech.* **160** M2
Bendigo, *Vic., Austral.* **211** ZI2
Bene Beraq, *Israel* **170** M5
Benetutti, *It.* **151** N4
Benevento, *It.* **150** MII
Bengal, Bay of, *Ind. Oc.* **166** K8
Bengalūru *see* Bangalore, *India* **179** P6
Bengara, *Indonesia* **188** HI2
Bengbu, *China* **182** J7
Benghazi *see* Banghāzī, *Lib.* **197** CI5
Benghisa Point, *Malta* **161** L23
Bengkalis, island, *Indonesia* **188** H6
Bengkalis, *Indonesia* **188** H6
Bengkayang, *Indonesia* **188** J9
Bengkulu, *Indonesia* **188** K6
Bengo, Baía do, *Angola* **202** C5
Benguela, *Angola* **202** D5
Benguerir, *Mor.* **196** B8
Beni, river, *Bol.* **130** H7
Beni Abbes, *Alg.* **196** C9
Benicarló, *Sp.* **145** FI5
Benidorm, *Sp.* **145** JI5
Benifaió, *Sp.* **145** HI4
Beni Mazâr, *Egypt* **197** DI8
Benin, *Af.* **195** HI6
Benin, Bight of, *Af.* **194** J4
Benin City, *Nigeria* **201** HI3
Beni Ounif, *Alg.* **196** BIO
Beni Suef, *Egypt* **197** DI8
Benitses, *Gr.* **154** F6
Benjamin, *Tex., U.S.* **102** K8
Benjamin Constant, *Braz.* **130** E5
Benjamin Hill, *Mex.* **114** C7
Benkelman, *Nebr., U.S.* **105** R3
Benlidi, *Qnsld., Austral.* **211** UI3
Bennett, Ostrov, *Russ.* **159** CI7
Bennett Peak, *N. Mex., U.S.* **107** QIO
Bennettsville, *S.C., U.S.* **96** JIO
Ben Nevis, peak, *Scot., U.K.* **142** L8
Benneydale, *N.Z.* **213** KI9
Bennington, *Vt., U.S.* **94** JI2
Benoud, *Alg.* **196** BIO
Bensbach, *P.N.G.* **213** EI7
Bensheim, *Ger.* **148** H6
Benson, *Ariz., U.S.* **107** V8
Benson, *Minn., U.S.* **104** J9
Benson, *N.C., U.S.* **96** HI2
Benson Point, *Kiribati* **217** B22
Bent, *Iran* **173** HI7
Benta, *Malaysia* **188** G6
Bentham's, *Barbados* **121** JI8
Bentinck Island, *Myanmar* **187** P7
Bentiu, *Sudan* **198** GI2
Bentley Subglacial Trench, *Antarctica* **226** KIO
Benton, *Ark., U.S.* **100** H8
Benton, *Ill., U.S.* **99** U6
Benton, *Ky., U.S.* **101** DI3
Benton, *La., U.S.* **100** K6
Bentong, *Indonesia* **189** LI3
Bentong, *Malaysia* **187** U9
Benton Harbor, *Mich., U.S.* **99** N9
Benton Lake, *Mont., U.S.* **106** C8
Bentonville, *Ark., U.S.* **100** E6
Bent's Old Fort National Historic Site, *Colo., U.S.* **107** NI5
Benua, *Indonesia* **189** LI4
Benue, river, *Nigeria* **201** GI5
Benwee Head, *Ire.* **143** Q3
Benxi, *China* **182** CII
Beograd (Belgrade), *Serb.* **152** FIO
Beohari, *India* **178** H8
Beowawe, *Nev., U.S.* **109** NIO
Beppu, *Japan* **185** R5
Beqa, island, *Fiji Is.* **218** J6

Bequia, island, *St. Vincent & the Grenadines* 119 LI7
Bera Ndjoko, *Congo* 201 JI8
Berane, *Mont.* 152 H9
Berard, *F.S.M.* 217 BI8
Berard, Port, *F.S.M.* 217 BI8
Berat, *Albania* 152 L9
Berau, Teluk, *Indonesia* 189 KI8
Berber, *Sudan* 199 DI3
Berbera, *Somalia* 199 FI7
Berbérati, *Cen. Af. Rep.* 198 H8
Berbice, river, *Guyana* 129 EI5
Berceto, *It.* 150 F5
Berchers Bay, *Virgin Islands, U.K.* 120 Q9
Berchtesgaden, *Ger.* 148 LIO
Berck, *Fr.* 146 M9
Berdún, *Sp.* 145 CI4
Berdyans'k, *Ukr.* 157 R9
Berdychiv, *Ukr.* 157 N5
Berea, *Ky., U.S.* 101 CI8
Berehove, *Ukr.* 157 PI
Bereina, *P.N.G.* 213 EI9
Berekua, *Dominica* 121 GI9
Berenice, *Egypt* 197 E2O
Berens River, *Man., Can.* 83 MI4
Beresford, *S. Dak., U.S.* 104 M8
Beretău, river, *Rom.* 152 BI2
Berezniki, *Russ.* 158 G9
Berga, *Sp.* 145 DI7
Bergama, *Turk.* 168 E3
Bergamo, *It.* 150 D5
Bergara, *Sp.* 144 BI2
Bergen, *Neth.* 146 HI2
Bergen, *Nor.* 140 K9
Bergerac, *Fr.* 147 V8
Bergues, *Fr.* 146 LIO
Berhala, Selat, *Indonesia* 188 J7
Bering, Ostrov, *Russ.* 159 E23
Bering Glacier, *Alas., U.S.* 111 KI8
Bering Land Bridge National Preserve, *Alas., U.S.* 110 EI2
Beringovskiy, *Russ.* 159 B2I
Bering Sea, *Pac. Oc.* 238 BIO
Bering Strait, *Asia, N. Amer.* 166 AI2
Berja, *Sp.* 144 MII
Berkeley, *Calif., U.S.* 109 S3
Berkeley, Cabo, *Ecua.* 128 P7
Berkner Island, *Antarctica* 226 F9
Berlanga de Duero, *Sp.* 144 EI2
Berlevåg, *Nor.* 141 BI5
Berlin, *Ger.* 148 DIO
Berlin, *Md., U.S.* 96 DI5
Berlin, *N.H., U.S.* 95 FI4
Berlin, *Wis., U.S.* 98 K6
Berlin, Mount, *Antarctica* 226 M9
Bermejito, river, *Arg.* 132 EII
Bermejo, river, *Arg.* 132 GI3
Bermejo, river, *Arg.* 132 J8
Bermeo, *Sp.* 144 BI2
Bermillo de Sayago, *Sp.* 144 E8
Bermuda Island *see* Main Island, *Bermuda, U.K.* 120 B3
Bermuda Islands, *U.K., N. Amer.* 80 KII
Bermuda Rise, *Atl. Oc.* 236 J5
Bern, *Switz.* 150 B2
Bernalda, *It.* 151 NI4
Bernalillo, *N. Mex., U.S.* 107 SI2
Bernardo de Irigoyen, *Arg.* 132 GI5
Bernasconi, *Arg.* 133 NIO
Bernau, *Ger.* 148 DIO
Bernay, *Fr.* 147 P8
Bernburg, *Ger.* 148 E9
Berne, *Ind., U.S.* 99 QIO
Berner Alpen, *Switz.* 150 C2
Berneray, island, *Scot., U.K.* 142 J6
Berneray, island, *Scot., U.K.* 142 L5
Bernice, *La., U.S.* 100 K8
Bernie, *Mo., U.S.* 105 VI5
Bernier Bay, *Nunavut, Can.* 83 EI5
Bernina, Piz, *It., Switz.* 150 C5
Bernini's Colonnade, *Vatican City* 161 QI7
Beroroha, *Madagascar* 203 HI6
Berre, Étang de, *Fr.* 147 XI3
Berrechid, *Mor.* 196 B8
Berry Islands, *Bahamas* 116 DII
Berryville, *Ark., U.S.* 100 E7
Bertam, *Malaysia* 187 TIO
Berthold, *N. Dak., U.S.* 104 E3
Bertholet, Cape, *Austral.* 210 D4
Berthoud Pass, *Colo., U.S.* 106 MI2
Bertoua, *Cameroon* 201 HI7
Bertraghboy Bay, *Ire.* 143 S3
Bertrand, *Nebr., U.S.* 105 Q5

Bertrange, *Lux.* 160 K9
Beru, island, *Kiribati* 214 G8
Beruniy, *Uzb.* 174 K9
Beruri, *Braz.* 130 E9
Beruwala, *Sri Lanka* 179 T7
Berwick, *La., U.S.* 100 Q9
Berwick upon Tweed, *Eng., U.K.* 142 MII
Berwyn, *Ill., U.S.* 99 N7
Berwyn, region, *Wales, U.K.* 143 TIO
Beryslav, *Ukr.* 157 R7
Besalampy, *Madagascar* 203 FI6
Besançon, *Fr.* 147 RI4
Beseral, *Malaysia* 187 TIO
Besham Qala, *Pak.* 176 MIO
Besikama, *Indonesia* 189 NI5
Beşiri, *Turk.* 169 GI6
Besni, *Turk.* 168 HI2
Beşparmak Dağı, *Turk.* 168 G3
Bessarabia, region, *Mold., Ukr.* 157 Q4
Bessemer, *Ala., U.S.* 101 JI5
Bessemer, *Mich., U.S.* 98 F5
Bessines, *Fr.* 147 T9
Bestobe, *Kaz.* 175 CI4
Bestyakh, *Russ.* 159 HI8
Betanzos, *Sp.* 144 B6
Betanzos, Ría de, *Sp.* 144 A6
Bethanie, *Namibia* 202 J7
Bethany, *Mo., U.S.* 105 RII
Bethany, *Okla., U.S.* 102 GIO
Bethany Beach, *Del., U.S.* 96 DI5
Bethel, *Alas., U.S.* 110 JI2
Bethel, *Montserrat, U.K.* 121 B24
Bethel Town, *Jam.* 120 H6
Bethesda, *Md., U.S.* 96 CI3
Bethlehem, *Pa., U.S.* 94 N9
Bethlehem, *S. Af.* 202 KIO
Bethlehem, *Virgin Islands, U.S.* 120 Q2
Bethlehem *see* Bayt Laḥm, *W. Bank* 170 M5
Beth Shan *see* Bet She'an, *Israel* 170 L6
Béthune, *Fr.* 146 LIO
Betio, *Kiribati* 217 GI7
Betong, *Malaysia* 188 HIO
Betong, *Thai.* 187 S9
Betoota, *Qnsld., Austral.* 211 UII
Bétou, *Congo* 201 JI9
Betpaqdala, desert, *Kaz.* 175 GI3
Betroka, *Madagascar* 203 HI7
Betsiboka, river, *Madagascar* 194 MII
Bettembourg, *Lux.* 160 KIO
Bettendorf, Iowa, *U.S.* 105 PI4
Bettendorf, *Lux.* 160 HIO
Bettlerjoch, pass, *Aust., Liech.* 160 Q3
Betul, *India* 178 J6
Beulah, *N. Dak., U.S.* 104 F3
Bevan's Town, *Bahamas* 120 E3
Beverley, *Eng., U.K.* 143 RI3
Bewcastle, *Eng., U.K.* 143 PII
Bexhill, *Eng., U.K.* 143 WI5
Beycesultan, ruin, *Turk.* 168 G5
Bey Dağı, *Turk.* 168 EI2
Bey Dağı, *Turk.* 168 GII
Beykoz, *Turk.* 168 C5
Beyla, *Guinea* 200 G7
Bēylul, *Eritrea* 199 EI6
Beyneu, *Kaz.* 174 G7
Beypazarı, *Turk.* 168 E7
Beyrouth (Beirut), *Leb.* 170 H6
Beyşehir, *Turk.* 168 H7
Beyşehir Gölü, *Turk.* 168 G7
Beytüşşebap, *Turk.* 169 HI7
Bezhetsk, *Russ.* 156 H9
Béziers, *Fr.* 147 YII
Bhadarwah, *India* 177 NI3
Bhadra, *India* 178 E5
Bhadrakh, *India* 178 KII
Bhag, *Pak.* 177 S6
Bhagalpur, *India* 178 HII
Bhakkar, *Pak.* 177 Q9
Bhaktapur, *Nepal* 178 FIO
Bhamo, *Myanmar* 186 F7
Bhandara, *India* 178 K7
Bhanpura, *India* 178 H5
Bharatpur, *India* 178 F6
Bharatpur, *India* 178 H8
Bharuch, *India* 178 K3
Bhatapara, *India* 178 K8
Bhatinda, *India* 178 E5
Bhatkal, *India* 179 P4
Bhatpara, *India* 178 JI2
Bhavnagar, *India* 178 J3
Bhawanipatna, *India* 178 L9
Bhera, *Pak.* 177 PII
Bhilai, *India* 178 K8

Bhilwara, *India* 178 H4
Bhima, river, *India* 178 M5
Bhimbar, *Pak.* 177 NII
Bhind, *India* 178 G6
Bhinmal, *India* 178 H3
Bhisho, *S. Af.* 202 MIO
Bholari, *Pak.* 177 W7
Bhongir, *India* 178 M6
Bhopal, *India* 178 J6
Bhubaneshwar, *India* 178 KIO
Bhuj, *India* 178 HI
Bhusawal, *India* 178 K5
Bhutan, *Asia* 167 V9
Biabou, *St. Vincent & the Grenadines* 121 KI7
Biak, island, *Indonesia* 189 JI9
Biak, *Indonesia* 189 JI9
Biała Podlaska, *Pol.* 149 EI8
Białogard, *Pol.* 148 BI2
Biały Bór, *Pol.* 149 BI3
Białystok, *Pol.* 149 CI7
Bianco, *It.* 151 RI3
Biaó, peak, *Eq. Guinea* 204 M7
Biaora, *India* 178 H5
Biāro, island, *Indonesia* 189 HI5
Biarritz, *Fr.* 147 X5
Bias, *Fr.* 147 W6
Biau, *Indonesia* 189 HI4
Bibala, *Angola* 202 E5
Bibbiena, *It.* 150 G7
Biberach, *Ger.* 148 K7
Bibi Nani, *Pak.* 177 R6
Bicaz, *Rom.* 153 CI5
Bichänäk Ashyrymy, range, *Arm.* 169 EI9
Biche, *Trinidad & Tobago* 121 P23
Bichvint'a, *Abkhazia* 169 AI5
Bickleton, *Wash., U.S.* 108 E6
Bicknell, *Ind., U.S.* 99 T8
Bicknell, *Utah, U.S.* 107 N7
Bida, *Nigeria* 201 FI3
Bideford, *Eng., U.K.* 143 W9
Bié Plateau, *Angola* 194 M6
Biebrach, *Fla., U.S.* 97 W9
Big, river, *N.W.T., Can.* 82 DI2
Biga, *Turk.* 168 D3
Bigadiç, *Turk.* 168 E4
Big Bay, *Mich., U.S.* 98 F7
Big Bay, *Vanuatu* 218 CI
Big Bay (Drummond Bay), *Vanuatu* 218 E3
Big Bell, *W. Aust., Austral.* 211 V3
Big Belt Mountains, *Mont., U.S.* 106 D8
Big Bend National Park, *Tex., U.S.* 103 R3
Big Blue, river, *Nebr., U.S.* 105 Q8
Big Bog, *Minn., U.S.* 104 E9
Big Canyon, river, *Tex., U.S.* 103 Q4
Big Creek, *Calif., U.S.* 109 T7
Big Cypress National Preserve, *Fla., U.S.* 97 W9
Big Cypress Swamp, *Fla., U.S.* 97 W9
Bigej, island, *Marshall Is.* 216 M6
Bigej Channel, *Marshall Is.* 216 M6
Big Falls, *Minn., U.S.* 104 EII
Big Fork, *Minn., U.S.* 104 EII
Bigfork, *Minn., U.S.* 104 FII
Bigfork, *Mont., U.S.* 106 B6
Biggar, *Sask., Can.* 82 MII
Biggarenn, island, *Marshall Is.* 216 K3
Biggerann, island, *Marshall Is.* 216 K2
Big Hatchet Peak, *N. Mex., U.S.* 107 WIO
Big Hole, river, *Mont., U.S.* 106 E6
Big Hole National Battlefield, *Mont., U.S.* 106 E6
Bighorn, river, *Wyo., U.S.* 106 GIO
Bighorn Canyon National Recreation Area, *Mont., U.S.* 106 FIO
Bighorn Lake, *Mont., U.S.* 106 FIO

Bighorn Mountains, *Wyo., U.S.* 106 FII
Bigi, island, *Marshall Is.* 216 K3
Big Island, *Nunavut, Can.* 83 HI8
Big Lake, *Tex., U.S.* 103 N5
Big Mangrove, *Bahamas* 120 B8
Big Pine, *Calif., U.S.* 109 T8
Big Pine, *Fla., U.S.* 97 Y9
Big Piney, *Wyo., U.S.* 106 J9
Big Rapids, *Mich., U.S.* 98 KIO
Big Sandy, *Mont., U.S.* 106 B9
Big Sandy, river, *Wyo., U.S.* 106 J9
Big Sioux, river, *S. Dak., U.S.* 104 L8
Big Snowy Mountains, *Mont., U.S.* 106 D9
Big South Fork National River and Recreation Area, *Ky., Tenn., U.S.* 101 EI7
Big Spring, *Tex., U.S.* 102 M5
Big Springs, *Nebr., U.S.* 105 Q3
Big Stone City, *S. Dak., U.S.* 104 J8
Big Stone Gap, *Va., U.S.* 96 G7
Big Stone Lake, *Minn., S. Dak., U.S.* 104 J8
Big Sur, *Calif., U.S.* 109 U4
Big Thicket National Preserve, *Tex., U.S.* 103 PI5
Big Timber, *Mont., U.S.* 106 E9
Big Trout Lake, *Ont., Can.* 83 MI5
Big Valley Mountains, *Calif., U.S.* 108 M5
Big Wells, *Tex., U.S.* 103 S8
Big Wood, river, *Idaho, U.S.* 106 H5
Big Wood Cay, *Bahamas* 116 EII
Bihać, *Bosn. & Herzg.* 152 F6
Bihar Sharif, *India* 178 HIO
Bihoro, *Japan* 184 FI5
Bijagós, Arquipélago dos, *Guinea-Bissau* 200 E4
Bijapur, *India* 178 L7
Bijapur, *India* 178 M5
Bījār, *Iran* 172 CII
Bijeljina, *Bosn. & Herzg.* 152 F9
Bijie, *China* 180 MI2
Bijire, island, *Marshall Is.* 216 G8
Bijnor, *India* 178 E6
Bikaner, *India* 178 F4
Bikar Atoll, *Marshall Is.* 216 F5
Bikeman, island, *Kiribati* 217 GI7
Biken, island, *Marshall Is.* 216 H7
Bikenibeu, *Kiribati* 217 GI8
Bikennel, island, *Marshall Is.* 216 L3
Bikenubati, island, *Kiribati* 217 FI7
Bikin, *Russ.* 159 L2I
Bikini Atoll, *Marshall Is.* 216 F3
Bīkkū Bīttī, peak, *Lib.* 197 FI5
Bikoro, *Dem. Rep. of the Congo* 198 K8
Bilācāri, *Azerb.* 169 D23
Bilād Banī Bū 'Alī, *Oman* 173 LI7
Bilaspur, *India* 178 J8
Bilāsuvar, *Azerb.* 169 E22
Bila Tserkva, *Ukr.* 157 P5
Bilauktaung Range, *Myanmar, Thai.* 186 M8
Bilbao, *Sp.* 144 BI2
Bileća, *Bosn. & Herzg.* 152 H8
Bilecik, *Turk.* 168 D5
Bilġoraj, *Pol.* 149 GI7
Bilhorod-Dnistrovs'kyy, *Ukr.* 157 R5
Bilibino, *Russ.* 159 C2O
Bilican Dağları, *Turk.* 169 FI6
Bilin, *Myanmar* 186 K7
Billae, island, *Marshall Is.* 216 H8
Bill Baileys Bank, *Atl. Oc.* 236 DII
Billiluna, *W. Aust., Austral.* 211 S6
Billings, *Mont., U.S.* 106 EIO
Billings, *Okla., U.S.* 102 EII
Billings, *Russ.* 159 BI9
Billiton *see* Belitung, island, *Indonesia* 188 K9
Billom, *Fr.* 147 UII
Bill Williams, river, *Ariz., U.S.* 107 T5
Billy Chinook, Lake, *Oreg., U.S.* 108 G5
Bilma, *Niger* 197 GI3
Biloela, *Qnsld., Austral.* 211 UI5
Bilohirs'k, *Ukr.* 157 S8
Bilopillya, *Ukr.* 157 N8
Biloxi, *Miss., U.S.* 100 PI2
Biltine, *Chad* 197 HI6
Bilto, *Nor.* 141 CI3
Bilüü, *Mongolia* 180 C8
Bilzen, *Belg.* 146 LI3
Bimini Islands, *Bahamas* 116 D9

Bindle, *Qnsld., Austral.* 211 VI4
Bindloe *see* Marchena, Isla, island, *Ecua.* 128 P9
Bindura, *Zimb.* 202 FI2
Binéfar, *Sp.* 145 DI5
Binford, *N. Dak., U.S.* 104 F7
Bingara, *N.S.W., Austral.* 211 WI4
Bingara, *Qnsld., Austral.* 211 VI2
Bing Bong, *N. Terr., Austral.* 211 Q9
Bingen, *Ger.* 148 G6
Binger, *Okla., U.S.* 102 G9
Bingham, *Me., U.S.* 95 EI6
Bingham Channel, *Kiribati* 217 EI7
Binghamton, *N.Y., U.S.* 94 K9
Bingöl, *Turk.* 169 FI5
Bingöl Dağları, *Turk.* 169 FI6
Binhai (Dongkan), *China* 182 H9
Binh Khe, *Vietnam* 186 MI4
Binh Lieu, *Vietnam* 186 GI3
Binjai, *Indonesia* 188 G5
Binjai, *Indonesia* 188 G9
Binongko, island, *Indonesia* 189 LI5
Bintan, island, *Indonesia* 188 H7
Bintuhan, *Indonesia* 188 L7
Bintulu, *Malaysia* 188 HIO
Binxian, *China* 182 GI
Binxian, *China* 181 DI7
Binyang, *China* 181 PI3
Binzhou, *China* 182 F8
Biobío, river, *Chile* 133 N6
Bioč, peak, *Mont.* 152 H8
Bioko, island, *Eq. Guinea* 204 F5
Biokovo, peak, *Croatia* 152 H7
Bir, *India* 178 L5
Birāk, *Lib.* 197 DI4
Bi'r 'Alī, *Yemen* 172 QII
Birao, *Cen. Af. Rep.* 198 FIO
Biratnagar, *Nepal* 178 GII
Birchip, *Vic., Austral.* 211 YII
Birch Mountains, *Alta., Can.* 82 KII
Birch Tree Hill, *Cayman Is., U.K.* 120 HI
Birchwood, *Alas., U.S.* 111 JI6
Bird City, *Kans., U.S.* 105 R3
Bird Island, *Grenada* 121 J24
Bird Island, *Minn., U.S.* 104 KIO
Bird Island, *Seychelles* 205 KI9
Bird Island *see* Aves, *Venez.* 119 JI5
Birdsville, *Qnsld., Austral.* 211 UIO
Birecik, *Turk.* 169 HI3
Bîr el 'Abd, *Egypt* 171 N2
Bireun, *Indonesia* 188 G4
Birganj, *Nepal* 178 GIO
Bîr Ḩasana, *Egypt* 171 P3
Bīrjand, *Iran* 173 DI6
Birkenhead, *Eng., U.K.* 143 SIO
Birkirkara, *Malta* 161 K22
Bîrlad, river, *Rom.* 153 CI7
Bîrlad, *Rom.* 153 DI7
Birmingham, *Ala., U.S.* 101 JI5
Birmingham, *Eng., U.K.* 143 TI2
Bir Mogreïn (Fort Trinquet), *Mauritania* 196 D6
Birnie Island, *Kiribati* 214 HIO
Birnin Kebbi, *Nigeria* 200 EI2
Birni Nkonni, *Niger* 196 HII
Birobidzhan, *Russ.* 159 K2O
Birong, *Philippines* 188 EI2
Birrindudu, *N. Terr., Austral.* 211 R7
Birshoghyr, *Kaz.* 174 K9
Birsilpur, *India* 178 F3
Birtin, *Rom.* 152 CI2
Birufu, *Indonesia* 189 L2O
Biruli, *Russ.* 159 EI4
Biryakovo, *Russ.* 156 FII
Biržebbuġa, *Malta* 161 L23
Bisa, island, *Indonesia* 189 JI6
Bisbee, *Ariz., U.S.* 107 W9
Bisbee, *N. Dak., U.S.* 104 E6
Biscarosse et de Parentis, Lac de, *Fr.* 147 W6
Biscarrosse-Plage, *Fr.* 147 W6
Biscay, Bay of, *Eur.* 138 G3
Biscayne Bay, *Fla., U.S.* 97 XIO
Biscayne National Park, *Fla., U.S.* 97 XIO
Biscay Plain, *Atl. Oc.* 236 GI2
Bisceglie, *It.* 150 LI3
Bischheim, *Fr.* 147 PI5
Biscoe Islands, *Antarctica* 226 E4
Biševo, island, *Croatia* 152 H6
Bishkek, *Kyrg.* 176 DII
Bishop, *Calif., U.S.* 109 S8
Bishop, *Tex., U.S.* 103 UIO
Bishopville, *S.C., U.S.* 96 KIO
Bishrī, Jabal, *Syr.* 170 FI2

Biskra, *Alg.* **196** B11
Bislig, *Philippines* **189** F15
Bismarck, *N. Dak., U.S.* **104** G4
Bismarck Archipelago, *P.N.G.* **213** C20
Bismarck Range, *P.N.G.* **213** C19
Bismarck Sea, *P.N.G.* **213** C20
Bismil, *Turk.* **169** G15
Bison, *S. Dak., U.S.* **104** J3
Bissagos Islands see Bijagós, Arquipélago dos, *Guinea-Bissau* **194** G1
Bissameuttack, *India* **178** L9
Bissau, *Guinea-Bissau* **200** E4
Bissen, *Lux.* **160** J10
Bistcho Lake, *Alta., Can.* **82** J10
Bistineau, Lake, *La., U.S.* **100** L7
Bistreţu, *Rom.* **153** G13
Bistriţa, river, *Rom.* **153** C15
Bistriţa, *Rom.* **153** B14
Bitam, *Gabon* **201** K16
Bitburg, *Ger.* **160** H11
Bitlis, *Turk.* **169** G16
Bitola, *Maced.* **152** L11
Bitra Island, *India* **179** Q2
Bitterfontein, *S. Af.* **202** L7
Bitterroot, river, *Mont., U.S.* **106** D5
Bitterroot Range, *Idaho, Mont., U.S.* **106** E5
Biu, *Nigeria* **201** F16
Bivona, *It.* **151** S9
Biwa Ko, *Japan* **185** P9
Bixby, *Okla., U.S.* **102** F13
Bixessarri, *Andorra* **160** K2
Biyang, *China* **182** J5
Biysk, *Russ.* **158** L12
Bizerte, *Tun.* **197** A13
Bjelolasica, peak, *Croatia* **152** E5
Bjelovar, *Croatia* **152** D7
Bjøllånes, *Nor.* **140** F12
Bjørnafjorden, bay, *Nor.* **140** K9
Bjørnøya, island, *Arctic Oc.* **243** F17
Black, river, *Ariz., U.S.* **107** U9
Black, river, *Ark., U.S.* **100** F10
Black, river, *Jam.* **120** J7
Black, river, *Mo., U.S.* **105** V15
Black, river, *N.Y., U.S.* **94** H9
Black see Da, river, *Vietnam* **186** H11
Black, river, *Wis., U.S.* **98** J4
Blackall, *Qnsld., Austral.* **211** U13
Blackball, *N.Z.* **213** N17
Black Bay Point, *Grenada* **121** K22
Blackbeard Island, *Ga., U.S.* **97** P9
Blackbeard's Tower, *Bahamas* **120** B12
Black Belt, region, *Ala., U.S.* **85** L16
Blackburn, *Eng., U.K.* **143** R11
Blackburn, Mount, *Alas., U.S.* **111** J18
Black Canyon City, *Ariz., U.S.* **107** T7
Black Canyon of the Gunnison National Park, *Colo., U.S.* **107** N11
Black Coast, *Antarctica* **226** E6
Blackduck, *Minn., U.S.* **104** F10
Black Eagle, *Mont., U.S.* **106** C8
Blackfoot, *Idaho, U.S.* **106** H7
Blackfoot, river, *Mont., U.S.* **106** D6
Blackfoot Reservoir, *Idaho, U.S.* **106** H7
Black Forest, *Ger.* **148** K6
Black Hills, *S. Dak., Wyo., U.S.* **84** E10
Black Irtysh, river, *China, Kaz.* **166** F8
Black Isle, *Scot., U.K.* **142** J9
Black Lake, *Mich., U.S.* **98** H11
Blackmans, *Barbados* **121** K19
Black Mesa, *Ariz., U.S.* **107** Q8
Black Mesa, *Okla., U.S.* **102** E4
Blackmoor Vale, *Eng., U.K.* **143** W11
Black Mountain, *Ky., U.S.* **101** D20
Black Mountains, *Ariz., U.S.* **107** R4
Black Mountains, *Wales, U.K.* **143** U10
Black Point, *Virgin Islands, U.K.* **120** L11
Black Point see Kūpikipiki'o Point, *Hawai'i, U.S.* **112** E11
Black Point, *St. Vincent & the Grenadines* **121** K17
Blackpool, *Eng., U.K.* **143** R10
Black Range, *N. Mex., U.S.* **84** K8
Black River, *Jam.* **120** J7
Black River Bay, *Jam.* **120** J7
Black River Falls, *Wis., U.S.* **98** J4
Black Rock, *Ire.* **143** Q2
Black Rock, *S. Amer.* **126** R9
Black Rock, *Trinidad & Tobago* **121** N17
Black Rock Desert, *Nev., U.S.* **108** M7
Black Sand Beach see Kaimu Beach, *Hawai'i, U.S.* **113** N22
Blacksburg, *Va., U.S.* **96** F9
Black Sea, *Asia* **166** E4
Black Sea, *Asia, Eur.* **138** H11

Black Sea Lowland, *Ukr.* **138** H10
Blacks Fork, *Wyo., U.S.* **106** K8
Blackshear, *Ga., U.S.* **97** P7
Blacksod Bay, *Ire.* **143** Q3
Blackstone, *Va., U.S.* **96** F12
Blackville, *S.C., U.S.* **96** L9
Black Volta, river, *Af.* **194** H3
Blackwater, river, *Ire.* **143** U4
Blackwater, *Qnsld., Austral.* **211** T14
Blackwell, *Okla., U.S.* **102** E11
Blackwell, *Tex., U.S.* **102** M7
Blagodarnyy, *Russ.* **157** S13
Blagoevgrad, *Bulg.* **152** K12
Blagoveshchensk, *Russ.* **159** K19
Blain, *Fr.* **147** R5
Blaine, *Wash., U.S.* **108** A3
Blair, *Nebr., U.S.* **105** P9
Blair Athol, *Qnsld., Austral.* **211** T14
Blaj, *Rom.* **153** D13
Blakely, *Ga., U.S.* **97** P4
Blake Plateau, *Atl. Oc.* **236** J3
Blake Point, *Mich., U.S.* **98** C6
Blake Ridge, *Atl. Oc.* **236** J3
Blakes, *Cayman Is., U.K.* **120** J4
Blanc, Cap, *Mauritania* **196** F4
Blanc, Cape, *Tun.* **194** C5
Blanc, Mont, *Fr., It.* **147** U15
Blanca, Bahía, *Arg.* **127** M18
Blanca, Costa, *Sp.* **145** K15
Blanca, Portella, *Andorra, Fr.* **160** J5
Blanca, Sierra, *Tex., U.S.* **103** V3
Blanca Peak, *Colo., U.S.* **107** P13
Blanchard, *Okla., U.S.* **102** G10
Blanche, Lake, *Austral.* **210** H11
Blanche, Pointe, *Neth. Antilles, Neth.* **121** C14
Blanche Channel, *Solomon Is.* **217** M16
Blanchisseuse, *Trinidad & Tobago* **121** N22
Blanchisseuse, *Trinidad & Tobago* **119** P17
Blanco, river, *Bol.* **130** J8
Blanco, river, *Tex., U.S.* **103** Q10
Blanco, *Tex., U.S.* **103** Q9
Blanco, Cape, *Oreg., U.S.* **108** J1
Blanding, *Utah, U.S.* **107** P9
Blanes, *Sp.* **145** D18
Blangy, *Fr.* **146** M9
Blankenberge, *Belg.* **146** K10
Blanquilla, Isla, *Venez.* **128** A11
Blantyre, *Malawi* **203** E13
Blasket Islands, *Ire.* **143** U2
Blaydon, *Eng., U.K.* **143** P12
Blaye, *Fr.* **147** V6
Blaze, Point, *Austral.* **210** B7
Blednaya, Gora, *Russ.* **158** D12
Blenheim, *N.Z.* **213** M18
Blida, *Alg.* **196** A11
Blidinje Jezero, *Bosn. & Herzg.* **152** G7
Bligh Water, *Fiji Is.* **218** H6
Blima, Grand Erg de, *Niger* **197** G14
Blind River, *Ont., Can.* **83** Q17
Blinman, *S. Aust., Austral.* **211** W10
Blitar, *Indonesia* **188** M10
Block Island, *R.I., U.S.* **95** M14
Bloemfontein, *S. Af.* **202** K10
Bloemhof, *S. Af.* **202** K10
Blois, *Fr.* **147** R9
Blönduós, *Ice.* **140** E3
Bloody Bay, *Trinidad & Tobago* **121** N18
Bloody Foreland, *Ire.* **143** N5
Bloomer, *Wis., U.S.* **98** H3
Bloomfield, *Ind., U.S.* **99** S8
Bloomfield, *Iowa, U.S.* **105** Q12
Bloomfield, *Mo., U.S.* **105** V15
Bloomfield, *Nebr., U.S.* **105** N7
Blooming Prairie, *Minn., U.S.* **104** L12
Bloomington, *Ill., U.S.* **99** Q6
Bloomington, *Ind., U.S.* **99** S8
Bloomington, *Minn., U.S.* **104** K11
Bloomington, *Tex., U.S.* **103** S12
Bloomsburg, *Pa., U.S.* **94** M8
Blossom, Mys, *Russ.* **159** B19
Blouberg, peak, *S. Af.* **194** P9
Blower Rock, *Jam.* **116** P11
Blowing Point, *Anguilla, U.K.* **120** R11
Blowing Point, *Jam.* **120** H10
Bludenz, *Aust.* **148** L7
Blue Earth, *Minn., U.S.* **104** L11
Bluefield, *W. Va., U.S.* **96** F8
Bluefields, *Jam.* **120** J6
Bluefields, *Nicar.* **115** M19
Bluefields Bay, *Jam.* **120** J6

Blue Hill, *Nebr., U.S.* **105** R6
Blue Hills, *Turks & Caicos Is., U.K.* **117** H16
Blue Hole, site, *Jam.* **120** J11
Bluejoint Lake, *Oreg., U.S.* **108** K7
Blue Lake, *Calif., U.S.* **108** M2
Blue Mountain, *Ark., U.S.* **100** G6
Blue Mountain, *Oreg., U.S.* **108** K8
Blue Mountain Peak, *Jam.* **120** J10
Blue Mountains, *Jam.* **120** J10
Blue Mountains, *Oreg., Wash., U.S.* **108** G7
Blue Nile see Azraq, El Bahr el, river, *Sudan* **199** F13
Blue Nile Falls see T'is Isat Fwafwatē, *Eth.* **199** F14
Blue Rapids, *Kans., U.S.* **105** R8
Blue Ridge, *Ga., U.S.* **96** J5
Blue Ridge, *Va., N.C., U.S.* **85** J18
Bluff, *N.Z.* **213** R15
Bluff, *Utah, U.S.* **107** P9
Bluff Knoll, *Austral.* **210** L3
Bluff Point, *Austral.* **210** H1
Bluffton, *Ind., U.S.* **99** Q10
Blumenau, *Braz.* **131** N13
Blunt, *S. Dak., U.S.* **104** K5
Bly, *Oreg., U.S.* **108** K5
Blyth, *Eng., U.K.* **143** P12
Blythe, *Calif., U.S.* **109** X13
Blytheville, *Ark., U.S.* **100** F11
Bø, *Nor.* **140** D12
Bø, *Nor.* **140** K9
Bo, *Sierra Leone* **200** G6
Boaco, *Nicar.* **115** M18
Boano, island, *Indonesia* **189** K16
Boardman, *Ohio, U.S.* **99** P16
Boatman, *Qnsld., Austral.* **211** V13
Boa Vista, island, *Cape Verde* **205** C17
Boa Vista, *Braz.* **130** B9
Boaz, *Ala., U.S.* **101** H16
Boaz Island, *Bermuda, U.K.* **120** B1
Bobai, *China* **183** S2
Bobbili, *India* **178** L9
Bobo Dioulasso, *Burkina Faso* **200** E9
Bobovdol, *Bulg.* **152** J12
Boby, peak, *Madagascar* **203** H17
Boca Chica, *Dom. Rep.* **117** M19
Boca Chica Key, *Fla., U.S.* **97** Y8
Boca do Acre, *Braz.* **130** F6
Bôca do Jari, *Braz.* **130** D12
Bocage, Cap, *New Caledonia, Fr.* **218** C7
Boca Grande, *Fla., U.S.* **97** V8
Boca Mavaca, *Venez.* **128** G10
Boca Raton, *Fla., U.S.* **97** W10
Bocas del Toro, *Pan.* **115** N20
Boca Tabla, site, *Neth. Antilles, Neth.* **121** N13
Bocay, *Nicar.* **115** L18
Bochnia, *Pol.* **149** H16
Bocholt, *Ger.* **148** E5
Bocht van Hato, bay, *Neth. Antilles, Neth.* **121** P14
Bochum, *Ger.* **148** E5
Bocognano, *Fr.* **150** K4
Bocşa, *Rom.* **152** E11
Böda, *Sw.* **141** M14
Bodaybo, *Russ.* **159** J16
Bodden Bay, *Cayman Is., U.K.* **120** J4
Bodden Town, *Cayman Is., U.K.* **120** J3
Bodega Bay, *Calif., U.S.* **109** R2
Bodega Head, *Calif., U.S.* **109** R2
Bodele Depression, *Chad* **194** G6
Boden, *Sw.* **141** F14
Bodensee (Lake Constance), *Aust., Ger., Switz.* **148** L7
Bodï, *Mongolia* **180** E11
Bodi, *Indonesia* **189** H14
Bodkin Mill, ruin, *Virgin Islands, U.S.* **120** Q2
Bodmin, *Eng., U.K.* **143** X8
Bodmin Moor, *Eng., U.K.* **143** X9
Bodø, *Nor.* **140** E12
Bodrum, *Turk.* **168** H3
Bo Duc, *Vietnam* **187** N13
Boe, region, *Nauru* **217** F22
Boën, *Fr.* **147** U12
Boende, *Dem. Rep. of the Congo* **198** K9
Boeo, Capo, *It.* **151** S8
Boerne, *Tex., U.S.* **103** R9
Boeuf, river, *La., U.S.* **100** L9
Boffa, *Guinea* **200** F5
Bogalusa, *La., U.S.* **100** N11
Bogan, river, *Austral.* **210** J13
Bogantungan, *Qnsld., Austral.* **211** T13
Bogazi, *Cyprus* **160** N10

Boğazkale, *Turk.* **168** E10
Boğazlıyan, *Turk.* **168** F10
Bogdanovka, *Rep. of Georgia* **169** C17
Bogda Shan, *China* **180** E8
Bogenaga, island, *Marshall Is.* **216** K7
Boggabilla, *N.S.W., Austral.* **211** V14
Boggenadick, island, *Marshall Is.* **216** L3
Boggenatjen, island, *Marshall Is.* **216** L3
Boggerik, island, *Marshall Is.* **216** K3
Boggerik Passage, *Marshall Is.* **216** K3
Boggerlapp, island, *Marshall Is.* **216** K4
Boggy Peak, *Antigua & Barbuda* **121** B20
Bogia, *P.N.G.* **213** C19
Bogor, *Indonesia* **188** M8
Bogoroditsk, *Russ.* **156** L10
Bogorodsk, *Russ.* **156** J12
Bogotá, *Col.* **128** F5
Bogotol, *Russ.* **159** K13
Bogra, *Bangladesh* **178** H12
Bogué, *Mauritania* **196** G5
Bog Walk, *Jam.* **120** J9
Bo Hai, bay, *China* **182** E8
Bohé, *Eq. Guinea* **204** N7
Bohe, *China* **183** S2
Bohemia, region, *Czech Rep.* **148** H10
Bohemian Forest, *Ger.* **148** J9
Bohodukhiv, *Ukr.* **157** N8
Bohol, island, *Philippines* **189** E15
Bohol Sea, *Philippines* **189** E15
Boiaçu, *Braz.* **130** C8
Boim, *Braz.* **130** D11
Bois Blanc Island, *Mich., U.S.* **98** G11
Boisé, Port, *New Caledonia, Fr.* **218** E9
Boise, *Idaho, U.S.* **106** G4
Boise City, *Okla., U.S.* **102** E4
Bojnūrd, *Iran* **173** B15
Boka Kotorska, *Mont.* **152** J8
Bokalijman, island, *Marshall Is.* **216** M7
Boké, *Guinea* **200** E5
Boken, island, *Marshall Is.* **216** G8
Boken, island, *Marshall Is.* **216** J8
Boken, island, *Marshall Is.* **216** G10
Bokenelab, island, *Marshall Is.* **216** G8
Bokkumaruchi, island, *Marshall Is.* **216** K3
Boklaplap, island, *Marshall Is.* **216** L8
Boknafjorden, bay, *Nor.* **140** L9
Boko, *Congo* **201** N17
Bokoluo, island, *Marshall Is.* **216** G7
Bokombako, island, *Marshall Is.* **216** G8
Bökönbaev, *Kyrg.* **176** E13
Bokovskaya, *Russ.* **157** P12
Bokpyinn, *Myanmar* **187** P7
Boksitogorsk, *Russ.* **156** F8
Boku, *P.N.G.* **217** K14
Bokungu, *Dem. Rep. of the Congo* **198** K10
Bokurdak, *Turkm.* **174** L8
Bol, *Chad* **197** J14
Bolaang, *Indonesia* **189** J14
Bolan Pass, *Pak.* **177** R6
Bolans, *Antigua & Barbuda* **121** B20
Bolbec, *Fr.* **147** N8
Bole, *Ghana* **200** F10
Bolea, *Sp.* **145** C14
Bolesławiec, *Pol.* **148** F12
Bolgatanga, *Ghana* **200** F10
Bolhrad, *Ukr.* **157** S4
Bolivar, *Mo., U.S.* **105** U12
Bolivar, *Tenn., U.S.* **100** G12
Bolívar, Cerro, *Venez.* **128** D11
Bolivia, *Cuba* **116** H10
Bolivia, *S. Amer.* **127** G17
Bolkar Dağları, *Turk.* **168** H9
Bolkhov, *Russ.* **156** L8
Bollène, *Fr.* **147** W13
Bollnäs, *Sw.* **141** J13
Bollon, *Qnsld., Austral.* **211** V13
Bollons Tablemount, *Pac. Oc.* **238** R10
Bolluk Gölü, *Turk.* **168** G8
Bolnisi, *Rep. of Georgia* **169** C18
Bolobo, *Dem. Rep. of the Congo* **198** K8
Bologna, *It.* **150** F7
Bolognesi, *Peru* **130** G4
Bologoye, *Russ.* **156** G8
Bolovens Plateau, *Laos* **186** L12
Bolsena, *It.* **150** J8
Bolsena, Lago di, *It.* **150** J7
Bol'shaya Bicha, *Russ.* **158** J12
Bol'sheretsk, *Russ.* **159** G23
Bol'shevik, Ostrov, *Russ.* **159** D14
Bol'shevik Island, *Russ.* **166** B9
Bol'shezemel'skaya Tundra, *Russ.* **138** A12

Bol'shoy Begichev, Ostrov, *Russ.* **159** E15
Bol'shoy Lyakhovskiy, Ostrov, *Russ.* **159** D17
Bol'shoy Patom, *Russ.* **159** J17
Bol'shoy Shantar, Ostrov, *Russ.* **159** H20
Bolsward, *Neth.* **146** G13
Bolt Head, *Eng., U.K.* **143** Y10
Bolton, *Eng., U.K.* **143** R11
Bolton Point, *Kiribati* **217** E17
Bolu, *Turk.* **168** D7
Boluntay, *China* **180** H8
Boluo, *China* **183** R5
Bolvadin, *Turk.* **168** F6
Bolzano, *It.* **150** C7
Boma, *Dem. Rep. of the Congo* **198** L7
Bomba, Gulf of, *Lib.* **194** D7
Bombala, *N.S.W., Austral.* **211** Z13
Bombardopolis, *Haiti* **117** L15
Bombay see Mumbai, *India* **178** L3
Bombom, Ilhéu, *Sao Tome and Principe* **205** A21
Bomdila, *India* **178** F14
Bomdo, *India* **178** E15
Bomi, *China* **180** L9
Bom Jesus da Lapa, *Braz.* **131** H15
Bomongo, *Dem. Rep. of the Congo* **198** J8
Bomu, river, *Cen. Af. Rep., Dem. Rep. of the Congo* **198** H10
Bona, Mount, *Alas., U.S.* **111** J19
Bon Accueil, *Mauritius* **205** G20
Bonaire, island, *Neth. Antilles, Neth.* **118** M10
Bonang, *Vic., Austral.* **211** Z13
Bonanza, *Utah, U.S.* **106** L9
Bonao, *Dom. Rep.* **117** M18
Bonaparte Archipelago, *Austral.* **210** B5
Bonasse, *Trinidad & Tobago* **121** Q21
Bonavista, *Nfld. & Lab., Can.* **83** M24
Bonavista Bay, *N. Amer.* **80** G11
Bon Bon, *S. Aust., Austral.* **211** W9
Bondo, *Dem. Rep. of the Congo* **198** H10
Bondoukou, *Côte d'Ivoire* **200** G9
Bonds Cay, *Bahamas* **116** D11
Bonefish Bay, *Bahamas* **120** E11
Bonefish Pond, *Bahamas* **120** B11
Bonerate, island, *Indonesia* **189** M13
Bonesteel, *S. Dak., U.S.* **104** M6
Bonete, Cerro, *Arg.* **132** K7
Bongandanga, *Dem. Rep. of the Congo* **198** J9
Bongaree, *Qnsld., Austral.* **211** V15
Bongo Lava, region, *Madagascar* **194** N11
Bongor, *Chad* **197** K14
Bongos, Chaîne des, *Cen. Af. Rep.* **198** G9
Bonham, *Tex., U.S.* **102** K12
Bonifacio, *Fr.* **150** L4
Bonifacio, Strait of, *Fr., It.* **150** L4
Bonifay, *Fla., U.S.* **97** Q3
Bonin Islands (Ogasawara Guntō), *Japan* **184** K5
Bonin Trench, *Pac. Oc.* **238** G6
Bonita Springs, *Fla., U.S.* **97** W8
Bonito, *Braz.* **130** L10
Bonn, *Ger.* **148** F5
Bonners Ferry, *Idaho, U.S.* **106** A4
Bonne Terre, *Mo., U.S.* **105** T15
Bonneval, *Fr.* **147** Q9
Bonneville Dam, *Oreg., U.S., Wash., U.S.* **108** F4
Bonneville Salt Flats, *Utah, U.S.* **106** K5
Bonney Downs, *W. Aust., Austral.* **211** T3
Bonnie Rock, *W. Aust., Austral.* **211** W3
Bonny, *Fr.* **147** R10
Bonorva, *It.* **151** N3
Bonriki, island, *Kiribati* **217** G18
Bonriki, *Kiribati* **217** G18
Bontang, *Indonesia* **188** J12
Bontoc, *Philippines* **189** B13
Bonvouloir Islands, *P.N.G.* **213** E21
Bony de les Neres, *Andorra* **160** J3
Booby Cay, *Cayman Is., U.K.* **120** J2
Bookabie, *S. Aust., Austral.* **211** W8
Booker, *Tex., U.S.* **102** E7
Booker T. Washington National Monument, *Va., U.S.* **96** F10
Booligal, *N.S.W., Austral.* **211** X12
Boomi, *Qnsld., Austral.* **211** V13
Boonah, *Qnsld., Austral.* **211** V15
Boonderoo, *Qnsld., Austral.* **211** S12
Boone, *Iowa, U.S.* **105** N11
Boone, *N.C., U.S.* **96** G8
Booneville, *Ark., U.S.* **100** G6

Booneville, *Miss., U.S.* 101 H13
Boon Point, *Antigua & Barbuda* 121 A20
Bööntsagaan Nuur, *Mongolia* 180 E10
Boonville, *Ind., U.S.* 99 U8
Boonville, *Mo., U.S.* 105 S12
Boonville, *N.Y., U.S.* 94 H9
Boorama, *Somalia* 199 F16
Boorara, *Qnsld., Austral.* 211 V12
Booroorban, *N.S.W., Austral.* 211 Y12
Boosaaso (Bender Cassim), *Somalia* 199 F18
Boothbay Harbor, *Me., U.S.* 95 G16
Boothia, Gulf of, *Nunavut, Can.* 83 F15
Boothia Peninsula, *Nunavut, Can.* 83 F15
Bootle Bay Village, *Bahamas* 120 E1
Booué, *Gabon* 201 L16
Bopeechee, *S. Aust., Austral.* 211 W10
Boppard, *Ger.* 148 G5
Boquerón, Bahía de, *P.R., U.S.* 120 N1
Bor, *Russ.* 156 H12
Bor, *Serb.* 152 G11
Bor, *Turk.* 168 G9
Bora-Bora, island, *Fr. Polynesia, Fr.* 219 E15
Boracho Peak, *Tex., U.S.* 103 P1
Borah Peak, *Idaho, U.S.* 106 G6
Boran, region, *Eth.* 199 H15
Boran, *Kaz.* 175 E19
Borås, *Sw.* 140 M12
Borāzjān, *Iran* 173 G13
Borba, *Port.* 144 J6
Borba, *Braz.* 130 E9
Borborema, Planalto da, *Braz.* 131 F17
Borchgrevink Coast, *Antarctica* 227 Q14
Borçka, *Turk.* 169 C16
Bordeaux, *Fr.* 147 V6
Bordeaux Mountain, *Virgin Islands, U.S.* 120 N11
Borden, *W. Aust., Austral.* 211 Y3
Borden Island, *N.W.T., Nunavut, Can.* 83 B13
Borden Peninsula, *Nunavut, Can.* 83 E16
Bordertown, *S. Aust., Austral.* 211 Y11
Bordeyri, *Ice.* 140 E2
Bordj Flye Sainte Marie, *Alg.* 196 D9
Bordj le Prieur, *Alg.* 196 F10
Bordj Messouda, *Alg.* 196 C12
Bordj Omar Driss, *Alg.* 196 D12
Boré, *Mali* 196 H8
Boreas Plain, *Arctic Oc.* 243 H16
Borgarnes, *Ice.* 140 F2
Borger, *Neth.* 146 H14
Borger, *Tex., U.S.* 102 G6
Borgholm, *Sw.* 141 M14
Borg Massif, *Antarctica* 226 B12
Borgne, Lake, *La., U.S.* 100 Q11
Borgo Maggiore, *San Marino* 161 J15
Borgo San Dalmazzo, *It.* 150 F2
Borgosesia, *It.* 150 D3
Borgou, range, *Benin, Nigeria* 200 F12
Borhoyn Tal, *Mongolia* 181 E13
Borinquen, Punta, *P.R., U.S.* 120 M1
Borisoglebsk, *Russ.* 156 M12
Borisovo Sudskoye, *Russ.* 156 F9
Borjomi, *Rep. of Georgia* 169 C17
Borkou, region, *Chad* 197 G15
Borlänge, *Sw.* 141 K13
Bormio, *It.* 150 C6
Borneo (Kalimantan), island, *Indonesia* 188 J10
Bornholm, island, *Den.* 141 P13
Bornova, *Turk.* 168 F3
Boro, river, *Sudan* 198 G11
Boroko, *Indonesia* 189 J14
Boromo, *Burkina Faso* 200 E9
Boronga Islands, *Myanmar* 186 H4
Borotou, *Côte d'Ivoire* 200 G7
Borovichi, *Russ.* 156 G8
Borovo, *Croatia* 152 E9
Borovsk, *Russ.* 156 K9
Borovskoy, *Kaz.* 174 B11
Borroloola, *N. Terr., Austral.* 211 Q9
Borşa, *Rom.* 153 B14
Børselv, *Nor.* 141 C14
Borūjerd, *Iran* 172 D11
Boryslav, *Ukr.* 157 P2
Boryspil', *Ukr.* 157 N6
Borzya, *Russ.* 159 L17
Bosa, *It.* 151 N3
Bosanska Gradiška, *Bosn. & Herzg.* 152 E7
Bosanski Brod, *Bosn. & Herzg.* 152 E8
Bosanski Petrovac, *Bosn. & Herzg.* 152 F6
Boscastle, *Eng., U.K.* 143 X8

Boscobel, *Wis., U.S.* 98 L4
Bose, *China* 180 P12
Boseong, *S. Korea* 182 H13
Boshan, *China* 182 F7
Bosilegrad, *Serb.* 152 J12
Bosna, river, *Bosn. & Herzg.* 152 F8
Bosnia and Herzegovina, *Eur.* 139 W7
Bosobolo, *Dem. Rep. of the Congo* 198 H9
Bōsō Hantō, *Japan* 185 P13
Bosporus see İstanbul Boğazi, strait, *Turk.* 168 C5
Bossangoa, *Cen. Af. Rep.* 198 G8
Bossembélé, *Cen. Af. Rep.* 198 H8
Bossier City, *La., U.S.* 100 L6
Bossut, Cape, *Austral.* 210 D4
Bostan, *Pak.* 177 R6
Bosten Hu, *China* 180 F7
Boston, *Eng., U.K.* 143 S14
Boston, *Ga., U.S.* 97 Q6
Boston, *Mass., U.S.* 95 K15
Boston Bay, *Jam.* 120 J11
Boston Mountains, *Ark., U.S.* 100 F7
Boswell, *Okla., U.S.* 102 J13
Botabano, *Cayman Is., U.K.* 120 H1
Botanic Gardens, *Dominica* 121 G19
Botany Bay, *Austral.* 210 L14
Botev, peak, *Bulg.* 153 J14
Botevgrad, *Bulg.* 153 H13
Bothnia, Gulf of, *Fin., Sw.* 141 H14
Boticas, *Port.* 144 D6
Botoşani, *Rom.* 153 B16
Botswana, *Af.* 195 P20
Bottineau, *N. Dak., U.S.* 104 D5
Bottle Creek, *Turks & Caicos Is., U.K.* 117 H17
Botwood, *Nfld. & Lab., Can.* 83 M23
Bouaflé, *Côte d'Ivoire* 200 G8
Bouaké, *Côte d'Ivoire* 200 G9
Bouar, *Cen. Af. Rep.* 198 H8
Bougainville, island, *P.N.G.* 217 K13
Bougainville, Cape, *Austral.* 210 B5
Bougainville, Mont, *Wallis & Futuna, Fr.* 218 F12
Bougainville, Mouillage de, *Fr. Polynesia, Fr.* 219 N17
Bougainville Strait, *Solomon Is.* 217 K15
Bougainville Strait, *Vanuatu* 218 D2
Bougouni, *Mali* 196 J7
Bouillante, *Guadeloupe, Fr.* 121 F14
Bouillon, *Belg.* 147 N13
Bouilly, *Fr.* 147 Q12
Bouira, *Alg.* 196 A11
Boujdour, Cape, *W. Sahara, Mor.* 194 E1
Boulaide, *Lux.* 160 H9
Boulari, Passe de, *New Caledonia, Fr.* 218 E8
Boulder, *Colo., U.S.* 106 L13
Boulder, *Mont., U.S.* 106 D7
Boulder City, *Nev., U.S.* 109 U12
Boulia, *Qnsld., Austral.* 211 T11
Boulogne, *Fr.* 147 Y8
Boulogne-sur-Mer, *Fr.* 146 L9
Bouloupari, *New Caledonia, Fr.* 218 D8
Bouna, *Côte d'Ivoire* 200 F9
Boundary Peak, *Nev., U.S.* 109 S8
Boundiali, *Côte d'Ivoire* 200 F8
Bountiful, *Utah, U.S.* 106 K7
Bounty Bay, *Pitcairn I., U.K.* 219 Q23
Bounty Islands, *N.Z.* 214 Q9
Bounty Trough, *Pac. Oc.* 238 Q9
Bourail, *New Caledonia, Fr.* 218 D7
Bouraké, *New Caledonia, Fr.* 218 D8
Bourayne, Port, *Fr. Polynesia, Fr.* 219 H14
Bourbon-Lancy, *Fr.* 147 S11
Bourem, *Mali* 196 G9
Bourganeuf, *Fr.* 147 U9
Bourg-en-Bresse, *Fr.* 147 T13
Bourges, *Fr.* 147 S10
Bourget, Lac du, *Fr.* 147 U14
Bourg-Lastic, *Fr.* 147 U10
Bourg-Madame, *Fr.* 147 Z9
Bourgneuf, Baie de, *Fr.* 147 S5
Bourg-St. Maurice, *Fr.* 147 U15
Bourke, *N.S.W., Austral.* 211 W13
Bournemouth, *Eng., U.K.* 143 X12
Bourscheid, *Lux.* 160 H10
Bousso, *Chad* 197 K14
Boutilimit, *Mauritania* 196 G5
Bouvard, Cape, *Austral.* 210 K2
Bovalino Marina, *It.* 151 R13
Boven Bolivia, *Neth. Antilles, Neth.* 121 Q19
Bovey, *Minn., U.S.* 104 F11

Bovill, *Idaho, U.S.* 106 D4
Bovina, *Tex., U.S.* 102 H4
Bowbells, *N. Dak., U.S.* 104 D3
Bowdle, *S. Dak., U.S.* 104 J5
Bowdoin, Lake, *Mont., U.S.* 106 B11
Bowen, *Qnsld., Austral.* 211 S14
Bowers Ridge, *Pac. Oc.* 238 C10
Bowie, *Ariz., U.S.* 107 V9
Bowie, *Md., U.S.* 96 C13
Bowie, *Tex., U.S.* 102 K10
Bowie Seamount, *Pac. Oc.* 239 C14
Bowling Green, *Ky., U.S.* 101 D15
Bowling Green, *Mo., U.S.* 105 S14
Bowling Green, *Ohio, U.S.* 99 P12
Bowling Green, *Va., U.S.* 96 E13
Bowman, *N. Dak., U.S.* 104 H2
Bowman Bay, *Nunavut, Can.* 83 G18
Bowman Glacier, *Antarctica* 226 K12
Bowman Island, *Antarctica* 227 L22
Box Butte Reservoir, *Nebr., U.S.* 105 N2
Box Elder Creek, *Mont., U.S.* 106 C10
Boxelder Creek, *Mont., U.S.* 106 E13
Boxing, *China* 182 F8
Boyabat, *Turk.* 168 C10
Boyang, *China* 182 M7
Boyarka, *Russ.* 159 F14
Boyce, *La., U.S.* 100 M8
Boyer, river, *Iowa, U.S.* 105 P9
Boyle, *Ire.* 143 R4
Boyne, river, *Ire.* 143 R6
Boyne City, *Mich., U.S.* 98 H10
Boynton Beach, *Fla., U.S.* 97 W10
Boyoma Falls, *Dem. Rep. of the Congo* 198 J11
Boysen Reservoir, *Wyo., U.S.* 106 H10
Bozashchy Tübegi, *Kaz.* 174 G6
Boz Burun, *Turk.* 168 D4
Bozburun, *Turk.* 168 H3
Bozburun Dağı, *Turk.* 168 H6
Bozcaada, island, *Turk.* 168 D2
Boz Dağ, *Turk.* 168 H4
Bozdoğan, *Turk.* 168 G4
Bozeman, *Mont., U.S.* 106 E8
Bozhou, *China* 182 H6
Bozkır, *Turk.* 168 H7
Bozkurt, *Turk.* 168 B9
Bozouls, *Fr.* 147 W10
Bozoum, *Cen. Af. Rep.* 198 G8
Bozova, *Turk.* 169 H13
Bozüyük, *Turk.* 168 E6
Bra, *It.* 150 F3
Brabant Island, *Antarctica* 226 D4
Brač, island, *Croatia* 152 H6
Bracadale, Loch, *Scot., U.K.* 142 K7
Bracciano, *It.* 150 K8
Bracciano, Lago di, *It.* 150 K8
Brackettville, *Tex., U.S.* 103 R7
Brački Kanal, *Croatia* 152 H6
Bracknell, *Eng., U.K.* 143 V13
Brad, *Rom.* 152 D12
Bradenton, *Fla., U.S.* 97 U7
Brades, *Montserrat, U.K.* 121 B23
Bradford, *Eng., U.K.* 143 R12
Bradford, *Pa., U.S.* 94 L5
Bradley, *Ill., U.S.* 99 P7
Bradley, *S. Dak., U.S.* 104 J7
Brady, *Nebr., U.S.* 105 Q4
Brady, *Tex., U.S.* 103 P8
Braga, *Port.* 144 D5
Bragado, *Arg.* 132 L12
Bragança, *Port.* 144 D7
Braham, *Minn., U.S.* 104 H11
Brahmanbaria, *Bangladesh* 178 H13
Brahmapur, *India* 178 L10
Brahmaputra, river, *Asia* 166 H9
Brahmaur, *India* 177 P13
Brăila, *Rom.* 153 E17
Brainerd, *Minn., U.S.* 104 H10
Braintree, *Eng., U.K.* 143 V14
Braintree, *Mass., U.S.* 95 K15
Bramsche, *Ger.* 148 D6
Brancaleone Marina, *It.* 151 S13
Branchville, *S.C., U.S.* 96 L9
Branco, island, *Cape Verde* 205 B15
Branco, river, *Braz.* 130 C8
Brandberg, peak, *Namibia* 194 N6
Brandenburg, region, *Ger.* 148 E10
Brandenburg, *Ger.* 148 D9
Brandfort, *S. Af.* 202 K10
Brandon, *Fla., U.S.* 97 U8
Brandon, *Man., Can.* 83 N13
Brandon, *Miss., U.S.* 100 L11
Brandon, *S. Dak., U.S.* 104 L8
Brandon Bay, *Ire.* 143 U2
Brandvlei, *S. Af.* 202 L8

Brandy Peak, *Oreg., U.S.* 108 K2
Branford, *Fla., U.S.* 97 R7
Bransby, *Qnsld., Austral.* 211 V11
Bransby Point, *Montserrat, U.K.* 121 B23
Bransfield Strait, *Antarctica* 226 C4
Branson, *Colo., U.S.* 107 Q14
Branson, *Mo., U.S.* 105 V12
Brantley, *Ala., U.S.* 101 M16
Brantley Lake, *N. Mex., U.S.* 107 V14
Brantôme, *Fr.* 147 U8
Bras d'Or Lake, *N.S., Can.* 83 N22
Brasil, Planalto do, *Braz.* 131 J14
Brasília, *Braz.* 131 J13
Brasília Legal, *Braz.* 130 E11
Braşov, *Rom.* 153 E15
Bras-Panon, *Reunion, Fr.* 205 G17
Brasstown Bald, peak, *Ga., U.S.* 96 J5
Brateş, Lacul, *Rom.* 153 E17
Bratislava, *Slovakia* 149 K13
Bratsk, *Russ.* 159 K15
Bratskoye Vodokhranilishche, *Russ.* 159 K15
Bratsk Reservoir, *Russ.* 166 E9
Brattleboro, *Vt., U.S.* 95 J13
Braţul Chilia, river, *Rom.* 153 E18
Braţul Sfântu-Gheorghe, river, *Rom.* 153 E18
Braunau, *Aust.* 148 K10
Braunschweig (Brunswick), *Ger.* 148 E8
Braunton, *Eng., U.K.* 143 W9
Brava, island, *Cape Verde* 205 E15
Brava, Costa, *Sp.* 145 D19
Brawley, *Calif., U.S.* 109 Y11
Bray, *Ire.* 143 S7
Bray Island, *Nunavut, Can.* 83 F17
Brazil, *Ind., U.S.* 99 S8
Brazil, *S. Amer.* 127 F19
Brazilian Highlands, *S. Amer.* 126 F9
Brazoria, *Tex., U.S.* 103 S13
Brazos, river, *Tex., U.S.* 103 P12
Brazzaville, *Congo* 201 M17
Brčko, *Bosn. & Herzg.* 152 F8
Brea, Punta, *P.R., U.S.* 120 P2
Breadalbane, *Qnsld., Austral.* 211 T11
Breakers, *Cayman Is., U.K.* 120 J3
Breakfast Island, *Marshall Is.* 216 M8
Breaux Bridge, *La., U.S.* 100 P9
Breaza, *Rom.* 153 E15
Brechin, *Scot., U.K.* 142 L11
Breckenridge, *Colo., U.S.* 106 M12
Breckenridge, *Minn., U.S.* 104 H8
Breckenridge, *Tex., U.S.* 102 L9
Brecknock, Península, *Chile* 133 X7
Brecon, *Wales, U.K.* 143 V10
Breda, *Neth.* 146 K12
Bredasdorp, *S. Af.* 202 M8
Breezewood, *Pa., U.S.* 94 P5
Bregalnica, river, *Maced.* 152 K12
Bregenz, *Aust.* 148 L7
Bréhat, Île de, *Fr.* 147 P4
Breidafjördur, bay, *Ice.* 140 E2
Breid Bay, *Antarctica* 227 B15
Breil-sur-Roya, *Fr.* 147 W16
Breisach, *Fr.* 147 Q15
Brejo, *Braz.* 131 E15
Bremen, *Ga., U.S.* 96 L4
Bremen, *Ger.* 148 C7
Bremen, *Ind., U.S.* 99 P9
Bremerhaven, *Ger.* 148 C7
Bremerton, *Wash., U.S.* 108 C3
Bremond, *Tex., U.S.* 103 N12
Brenham, *Tex., U.S.* 103 Q12
Brennero, *It.* 150 B7
Brenner Pass, *Aust.* 148 M8
Breno, *It.* 150 D6
Brentwood, *Eng., U.K.* 143 V14
Brentwood, *N.Y., U.S.* 94 N12
Brescia, *It.* 150 D6
Bressanone, *It.* 150 B7
Bressay, island, *Scot., U.K.* 142 D12
Bressuire, *Fr.* 147 S7
Brest, *Belarus* 156 L2
Brest, *Fr.* 147 Q2
Breteuil, *Fr.* 147 N10
Bretón, Cayo, *Cuba* 116 J9
Breton, Pertuis, *Fr.* 147 T5
Breton Islands, *La., U.S.* 100 Q12
Breton Sound, *La., U.S.* 100 Q12
Brett, Cape, *N.Z.* 213 H18
Breu, river, *Braz., Peru* 130 G5
Brevard, *N.C., U.S.* 96 J7
Breves, *Braz.* 130 D12
Brevoort Island, *Nunavut, Can.* 83 G19
Brewarrina, *N.S.W., Austral.* 211 W13
Brewer, *Me., U.S.* 95 F17
Brewers Bay, *Virgin Islands, U.K.* 120 Q6

Brewster, *Kans., U.S.* 105 S3
Brewster, *Nebr., U.S.* 105 N5
Brewster, *Wash., U.S.* 108 B6
Brewton, *Ala., U.S.* 101 N15
Bria, *Cen. Af. Rep.* 198 G10
Briare, *Fr.* 147 R10
Briatico, *It.* 151 Q13
Bridgend, *Wales, U.K.* 143 V10
Bridge Point, *Bahamas* 120 D5
Bridgeport, *Ala., U.S.* 101 G16
Bridgeport, *Calif., U.S.* 109 R7
Bridgeport, *Conn., U.S.* 94 M12
Bridgeport, *Ill., U.S.* 99 T7
Bridgeport, *Nebr., U.S.* 105 P2
Bridgeport, *Tex., U.S.* 102 K10
Bridgeport, *W. Va., U.S.* 96 C9
Bridgeport, Lake, *Tex., U.S.* 102 K10
Bridger Peak, *Wyo., U.S.* 106 K11
Bridgeton, *N.J., U.S.* 94 Q9
Bridgetown, *Barbados* 121 L18
Bridgetown, *Ohio, U.S.* 99 S11
Bridgetown, *W. Aust., Austral.* 211 Y3
Bridgewater, *N.S., Can.* 83 P22
Bridgton, *Me., U.S.* 95 G15
Bridgwater, *Eng., U.K.* 143 W10
Bridlington, *Eng., U.K.* 143 Q13
Brielle, *Neth.* 146 J11
Brienne-le-Château, *Fr.* 147 Q12
Brienza, *It.* 151 N12
Brienzer See, *Switz.* 150 B3
Brig, *Switz.* 150 C3
Brigantine Cays, *Bahamas* 120 E7
Brigham City, *Utah, U.S.* 106 K7
Brighton, *Eng., U.K.* 143 W14
Brihuega, *Sp.* 144 F12
Brijuni Otoci, *Croatia* 152 E4
Brindisi, *It.* 150 M15
Brinkley, *Ark., U.S.* 100 G10
Brinkworth, *S. Aust., Austral.* 211 X10
Brisbane, *Qnsld., Austral.* 211 V15
Bristol, *Conn., U.S.* 94 L12
Bristol, *Eng., U.K.* 143 V11
Bristol, *Pa., U.S.* 94 P10
Bristol, *S. Dak., U.S.* 104 J7
Bristol, *Tenn., U.S.* 101 D20
Bristol, *Va., U.S.* 96 G7
Bristol Bay, *Alas., U.S.* 111 L13
Bristol Channel, *Eng., Wales, U.K.* 143 W9
Bristol Lake, *Calif., U.S.* 109 W11
Bristol Mountains, *Calif., U.S.* 109 W11
Bristow, *Okla., U.S.* 102 F12
British Columbia, *Can.* 82 J8
British Isles, *Ire., U.K.* 143 R4
British Mountains, *U.S., Can.* 84 M5
British Virgin Islands, *U.K., Lesser Antilles* 119 E14
British Virgin Islands, *U.K., Lesser Antilles* 119 E14
Britstown, *S. Af.* 202 L9
Britt, *Iowa, U.S.* 104 M11
Brittany, region, *Fr.* 147 Q4
Britton, *S. Dak., U.S.* 104 J7
Britton Hill, *Fla., U.S.* 97 Q3
Brive, *Fr.* 147 V9
Briviesca, *Sp.* 144 C11
Brno, *Czech Rep.* 149 J13
Broa, Ensenada de la, *Cuba* 116 G7
Broad, river, *S.C., U.S.* 96 J8
Broad Bay, *Scot., U.K.* 142 H7
Broad Haven, *Ire.* 143 Q3
Broadstairs, *Eng., U.K.* 143 V16
Broadus, *Mont., U.S.* 106 E12
Broadview, *Sask., Can.* 82 N12
Broadwater, *Nebr., U.S.* 105 P2
Brochet, *Man., Can.* 83 K13
Brocken, peak, *Ger.* 148 E8
Brock Island, *N.W.T., Can.* 83 B13
Brockport, *N.Y., U.S.* 94 H6
Brockton, *Mass., U.S.* 95 K15
Brockway, *Mont., U.S.* 106 C12
Brockway, *Pa., U.S.* 94 M5
Brodeur Peninsula, *Nunavut, Can.* 83 E15
Brodnica, *Pol.* 149 C15
Brody, *Ukr.* 157 N3
Brogan, *Oreg., U.S.* 108 H9
Broken Arrow, *Okla., U.S.* 102 F13
Broken Bow, *Nebr., U.S.* 105 P5
Broken Bow, *Okla., U.S.* 102 J14
Broken Bow Lake, *Okla., U.S.* 102 J14
Broken Hill, *N.S.W., Austral.* 211 X11
Broken Ridge, *Ind. Oc.* 240 M12
Brokopondo, *Suriname* 129 E16
Brønnøysund, *Nor.* 140 G11
Bronson, *Fla., U.S.* 97 S7

Bronswinkel, *Neth. Antilles, Neth.* 121 Q18
Bronte, *Tex., U.S.* 102 M7
Brookfield, *Mo., U.S.* 105 R12
Brookfield, *Wis., U.S.* 98 L7
Brookhaven, *Miss., U.S.* 100 M10
Brookings, *Oreg., U.S.* 108 L1
Brookings, *S. Dak., U.S.* 104 K8
Brooklyn, *Iowa, U.S.* 105 P12
Brooklyn Center, *Minn., U.S.* 104 J11
Brookport, *Ill., U.S.* 99 V6
Brooks, *Alta., Can.* 82 M10
Brooks Banks, *Hawai'i, U.S.* 112 M6
Brooks Range, *Alas., U.S.* 111 D14
Brooksville, *Fla., U.S.* 97 T7
Brookville, *Ind., U.S.* 99 S10
Brookville, *Pa., U.S.* 94 M4
Broome, *W. Aust., Austral.* 211 R4
Brora, *Scot., U.K.* 142 H9
Brosse, Île, *New Caledonia, Fr.* 218 E9
Brothers, *Oreg., U.S.* 108 H5
Broughton Islands, *Austral.* 210 K15
Brovary, *Ukr.* 157 N6
Browerville, *Minn., U.S.* 104 H10
Brown, Point, *Austral.* 210 J8
Brown Bay, *Virgin Islands, U.S.* 120 M11
Brownfield, *Tex., U.S.* 102 K4
Browning, *Mont., U.S.* 106 B6
Brownlee Dam, *Idaho, Oreg., U.S.* 108 G9
Browns Town, *Jam.* 116 M11
Brownstown, *Ind., U.S.* 99 T9
Browns Valley, *Minn., U.S.* 104 J8
Brownsville, *Tenn., U.S.* 100 F12
Brownsville, *Tex., U.S.* 103 X11
Brownsweg, *Suriname* 129 E16
Brownwood, *Tex., U.S.* 103 N9
Brownwood, Lake, *Tex., U.S.* 102 M9
Browse Island, *W. Aust., Austral.* 211 Q4
Brozas, *Sp.* 144 G7
Bruce, *Miss., U.S.* 100 J12
Bruce Rock, *W. Aust., Austral.* 211 X3
Bruchsal, *Ger.* 148 J6
Bruciate, river, *San Marino* 161 K16
Bruciato, *It.* 161 H14
Bruck an der Mur, *Aust.* 148 L12
Brugg, *Switz.* 150 A3
Brugge, *Belg.* 146 K11
Bruini, *India* 178 E15
Brule, river, *Wis., U.S.* 98 G6
Brumado, *Braz.* 131 J15
Brundidge, *Ala., U.S.* 101 M16
Bruneau, river, *Idaho, U.S.* 106 H4
Bruneau, *Idaho, U.S.* 106 H4
Brunei, *Asia* 167 Y12
Brunei Bay, *Brunei, Malaysia* 188 G11
Brunette Downs, *N. Terr., Austral.* 211 R9
Brunico, *It.* 150 B8
Brunner, Lake, *N.Z.* 213 N17
Brunssum, *Neth.* 146 L13
Brunswick, *Ga., U.S.* 97 P8
Brunswick see Braunschweig, *Ger.* 148 E8
Brunswick, *Me., U.S.* 95 G16
Brunswick, *Mo., U.S.* 105 S12
Brunswick, *Ohio, U.S.* 99 P14
Brunswick Bay, *Austral.* 210 C5
Brush, *Colo., U.S.* 106 L14
Brus Laguna, *Hond.* 115 K18
Brusque, *Braz.* 131 N13
Brussels see Bruxelles, *Belg.* 146 L12
Bruxelles (Brussels), *Belg.* 146 L12
Bruzual, *Venez.* 128 D8
Bryan, *Ohio, U.S.* 99 P11
Bryan, *Tex., U.S.* 103 P12
Bryan Coast, *Antarctica* 226 H6
Bryansk, *Russ.* 156 L8
Bryant, *Ark., U.S.* 100 G8
Bryant, *S. Dak., U.S.* 104 K7
Bryce Canyon National Park, *Utah, U.S.* 107 P7
Bryson City, *N.C., U.S.* 96 J6
Bryukhovetskaya, *Russ.* 157 S10
Brzeg, *Pol.* 149 F13
Brzeg Dolny, *Pol.* 149 F13
Bua, *Fiji Is.* 218 G7
Bua Bay, *Fiji Is.* 218 H7
Buache, Mount, *F.S.M.* 217 A18
Buada, region, *Nauru* 217 F23
Buada Lagoon, *Nauru* 217 F23
Buala, *Solomon Is.* 217 M18
Buariki, island, *Kiribati* 217 F17
Buariki, *Kiribati* 217 F17
Bua Yai, *Thai.* 186 L10

Bu'ayrāt al Ḥasūn, *Lib.* 197 C14
Buba, *Guinea-Bissau* 200 E4
Būbiyān, island, *Kuwait* 172 F11
Bucak, *Turk.* 168 H6
Bucakkışla, *Turk.* 168 H8
Bucaramanga, *Col.* 128 D6
Buccament Bay, *St. Vincent & the Grenadines* 121 K16
Buccaneer Archipelago, *Austral.* 210 C4
Buccaneer Point, *Bahamas* 120 B8
Buccoo Bay, *Trinidad & Tobago* 121 N17
Buchanan, *Liberia* 200 H6
Buchanan, *Mich., U.S.* 99 N9
Buchanan, Lake, *Tex., U.S.* 103 P9
Buchan Gulf, *Nunavut, Can.* 83 E17
Bucharest see Bucureşti, *Rom.* 153 F15
Buchholz, *Ger.* 148 C8
Buchon, Point, *Calif., U.S.* 109 V5
Buchs, *Switz.* 160 N2
Buckhannon, *W. Va., U.S.* 96 D9
Buck Island, *Virgin Islands, U.S.* 120 N9
Buck Island, *Virgin Islands, U.S.* 120 Q3
Buck Island Reef National Monument, *Virgin Islands, U.S.* 120 Q3
Buckland Tableland, *Austral.* 210 G13
Buckley, *Wash., U.S.* 108 C4
Bucklin, *Kans., U.S.* 105 U5
Buckner Bay see Nakagusuku Wan, *Japan* 185 Y1
Bucksport, *Me., U.S.* 95 F17
Bucovina, region, *Rom., Ukr.* 153 A15
Buco Zau, *Angola* 202 A5
Bu Craa, *W. Sahara, Mor.* 196 D6
Bucureşti (Bucharest), *Rom.* 153 F15
Bucyrus, *Ohio, U.S.* 99 Q13
Bud, *Nor.* 140 J10
Buda, *Tex., U.S.* 103 Q10
Budac, region, *Rom.* 153 C15
Budalin, *Myanmar* 186 G5
Budapest, *Hung.* 149 L15
Búdardalur, *Ice.* 140 F3
Budaun, *India* 178 F7
Budd Coast, *Antarctica* 227 M21
Buddhas of Bamian, ruin, *Afghan.* 176 M6
Buddusò, *It.* 150 M4
Bude, *Eng., U.K.* 143 W9
Bude, *Miss., U.S.* 100 M10
Bude Bay, *Eng., U.K.* 143 W9
Budennovsk, *Russ.* 157 S13
Búdir, *Ice.* 140 F4
Budjala, *Dem. Rep. of the Congo* 198 J9
Budū', Sabkhat al, *Saudi Arabia* 172 K12
Buena Esperanza, *Arg.* 132 L9
Buenaventura, *Col.* 128 F4
Buenaventura, *Mex.* 114 C8
Buenaventura Bay, *S. Amer.* 126 C2
Buena Vista, *Colo., U.S.* 107 N12
Buena Vista, *Neth. Antilles, Neth.* 121 P14
Buena Vista, *Ga., U.S.* 97 N5
Buena Vista, *Va., U.S.* 96 E10
Buena Vista Lake Bed, *Calif., U.S.* 109 V7
Buendía, Embalse de, *Sp.* 144 F12
Buenos Aires, *Arg.* 132 L13
Buenos Aires, Lago, *Arg.* 133 T7
Buenos Ayres, *Trinidad & Tobago* 121 Q21
Buen Tiempo, Cabo, *Arg.* 133 W8
Bufareh, *Indonesia* 189 K20
Buffalo, river, *Ark., U.S.* 100 E8
Buffalo, *Minn., U.S.* 104 J11
Buffalo, *Mo., U.S.* 105 U12
Buffalo, *N.Y., U.S.* 94 J5
Buffalo, *Okla., U.S.* 102 E8
Buffalo, *S. Dak., U.S.* 104 J2
Buffalo, *Tex., U.S.* 103 N13
Buffalo, *Wyo., U.S.* 106 G11
Buffalo Bill Reservoir, *Wyo., U.S.* 106 F9
Buffalo Hump, peak, *Idaho, U.S.* 106 E4
Buffalo Lake, *Tex., U.S.* 102 H5
Buffalo National River, *Ark., U.S.* 100 E8
Buff Bay, *Jam.* 120 H10
Buford, *Ga., U.S.* 96 K5
Buftea, *Rom.* 153 F15
Bug, river, *Belarus, Pol.* 138 F8
Buga, *Col.* 128 F4
Buġibba, *Malta* 161 J22
Bugio, Ilhéu do, *Madeira* 204 N4
Bugsuk, island, *Philippines* 188 F12
Bugt, *China* 181 C16
Burg, *Ger.* 148 E9

Bugul'ma, *Russ.* 156 J16
Buguruslan, *Russ.* 156 K16
Buhl, *Idaho, U.S.* 106 H5
Buhl, *Minn., U.S.* 104 F12
Buhuşi, *Rom.* 153 C16
Builth Wells, *Wales, U.K.* 143 U10
Buin, *P.N.G.* 217 K14
Buinsk, *Russ.* 156 J14
Buis-les-Baronnies, *Fr.* 147 W13
Bujalance, *Sp.* 144 K10
Bujanovac, *Serb.* 152 J11
Bujaraloz, *Sp.* 145 E15
Bujumbura, *Burundi* 198 L12
Buka, island, *P.N.G.* 217 J13
Bukachacha, *Russ.* 159 L17
Bukama, *Dem. Rep. of the Congo* 198 N11
Bukanik, Maja, *Albania* 152 L10
Buka Passage, *P.N.G.* 217 J13
Bukavu, *Dem. Rep. of the Congo* 198 K12
Bukhara see Buxoro, *Uzb.* 174 L11
Bukittinggi, *Indonesia* 188 J5
Bukoba, *Tanzania* 199 K13
Bula, *Indonesia* 189 K17
Bülach, *Switz.* 150 A4
Bülaevo, *Kaz.* 175 A13
Bulan, *Philippines* 189 D14
Bulanash, *Russ.* 156 G11
Bulancak, *Turk.* 169 D13
Bulandshahr, *India* 178 F6
Bulanık, *Turk.* 169 F16
Bulawayo, *Zimb.* 202 G11
Buldan, *Turk.* 168 G4
Buldir Island, *Alas., U.S.* 111 M2
Bulgan, *Mongolia* 180 C11
Bulgan, *Mongolia* 180 C11
Bulgan, *Mongolia* 180 E10
Bulgaria, *Eur.* 139 W9
Buli, Teluk, *Indonesia* 189 J16
Buliluyan, Cape, *Philippines* 188 F12
Buliya, island, *Fiji Is.* 218 K7
Bullara, *W. Aust., Austral.* 211 T1
Bull Bay, *Jam.* 120 J10
Bulle, *Switz.* 150 B2
Bullenbaai, bay, *Neth. Antilles, Neth.* 121 P14
Bullfinch, *W. Aust., Austral.* 211 W3
Bullhead City, *Ariz., U.S.* 107 S4
Bull Mountains, *Mont., U.S.* 106 D10
Bulloo Downs, *Qnsld., Austral.* 211 V12
Bulloo Downs, *W. Aust., Austral.* 211 U3
Bullo River, *N. Terr., Austral.* 211 Q7
Bulls Bay, *S.C., U.S.* 96 M11
Bull Shoals Lake, *Ark., U.S.* 100 E8
Bulun, *Russ.* 159 E16
Bulung'ur, *Uzb.* 174 L12
Bumba, *Dem. Rep. of the Congo* 198 J10
Bumbat, *Mongolia* 180 D12
Bum La, *China, India* 178 F13
Buna, *Kenya* 199 J15
Bunbury, *W. Aust., Austral.* 211 X2
Bunclody (Newtownbarry), *Ire.* 143 T6
Bundaberg, *Qnsld., Austral.* 211 U15
Bundaleer, *Qnsld., Austral.* 211 V13
Bundi, *India* 178 G5
Bundooma, *N. Terr., Austral.* 211 U9
Bungalaut, Selat, *Indonesia* 188 K5
Bungku, *Indonesia* 189 K14
Bungo Suidō, *Japan* 185 S6
Bungotakada, *Japan* 185 R5
Bunia, *Dem. Rep. of the Congo* 198 J12
Bunji, *Pak.* 176 M12
Bunker, *Mo., U.S.* 105 U14
Bunkie, *La., U.S.* 100 N8
Bunnell, *Fla., U.S.* 97 S9
Buntok, *Indonesia* 188 K11
Bunyu, island, *Indonesia* 188 H12
Buol, *Indonesia* 189 H14
Buon Me Thuot, *Vietnam* 187 N13
Buor-Khaya Bay, *Arctic Oc.* 242 B6
Buqūm, Ḥarrat al, *Saudi Arabia* 172 L8
Bur, *Russ.* 159 J15
Bura, *Kenya* 199 K15
Burakin, *W. Aust., Austral.* 211 W3
Burang, *China* 180 K4
Burao see Burco, *Somalia* 199 F17
Buras, *La., U.S.* 100 R12
Buraydah, *Saudi Arabia* 172 H9
Burbank, *Calif., U.S.* 109 X8
Burco (Burao), *Somalia* 199 F17
Burdalyk, *Turkm.* 174 M11
Burdekin, river, *Austral.* 210 E13
Burdur, *Turk.* 168 G6
Burdur Gölü, *Turk.* 168 G6
Bûr Fu'ad, *Egypt* 171 N1

Burgas, *Bulg.* 153 J17
Burgaski Zaliv, *Bulg.* 153 J17
Burgasko Ezero, *Bulg.* 153 J17
Burgaw, *N.C., U.S.* 96 J12
Burgdorf, *Switz.* 150 B3
Burgerau, *Switz.* 160 P2
Burgess Hill, *Eng., U.K.* 143 W14
Burghūth, Sabkhat al, *Syr.* 170 G14
Burgos, *Sp.* 144 C11
Burgsvik, *Sw.* 141 M14
Burgundy, region, *Fr.* 147 S12
Burhaniye, *Turk.* 168 E3
Burhanpur, *India* 178 K5
Burhou, island, *Ch. Is.* 143 Y11
Burias, island, *Philippines* 189 D14
Burica, Punta, *Costa Rica, Pan.* 115 P19
Burica Point, *N. Amer.* 80 R8
Buriram, *Thai.* 186 M10
Burkburnett, *Tex., U.S.* 102 J9
Burke, *S. Dak., U.S.* 104 M6
Burke Island, *Antarctica* 226 K6
Burkesville, *Ky., U.S.* 101 D17
Burketown, *Qnsld., Austral.* 211 R11
Burkina Faso, *Af.* 195 G15
Burle, island, *Marshall Is.* 216 L4
Burleson, *Tex., U.S.* 102 L11
Burley, *Idaho, U.S.* 106 H5
Burlingame, *Kans., U.S.* 105 T9
Burlington, *Colo., U.S.* 106 M16
Burlington, *Iowa, U.S.* 105 Q14
Burlington, *Kans., U.S.* 105 T9
Burlington, *N.C., U.S.* 96 G10
Burlington, *Vt., U.S.* 94 F12
Burlington, *Wash., U.S.* 108 B4
Burlington, *Wis., U.S.* 98 M6
Burma see Myanmar, *Asia* 167 W9
Burma Road, *China* 180 N10
Burnet, *Tex., U.S.* 103 P10
Burnett Bay, *N.W.T., Can.* 82 C12
Burney, *Calif., U.S.* 108 M4
Burnham Market, *Eng., U.K.* 143 S15
Burnham on Sea, *Eng., U.K.* 143 W10
Burnie, *Tas., Austral.* 211 Y16
Burns, *Oreg., U.S.* 108 J7
Burns, *Wyo., U.S.* 106 K14
Burnside, Lake, *Austral.* 210 G5
Burns Lake, *B.C., Can.* 82 K8
Burnsville, *Minn., U.S.* 104 K11
Burnt, river, *Oreg., U.S.* 108 G8
Burnt Pine, *Norfolk I., Austral.* 217 F20
Burqin, *China* 180 D7
Burqu', Qaşr, *Jordan* 170 L10
Burray, island, *Scot., U.K.* 142 G10
Burren, region, *Ire.* 143 S3
Burrendong Reservoir, *Austral.* 210 K14
Burren Junction, *N.S.W., Austral.* 211 W14
Burriana, *Sp.* 145 G15
Burrton, *Kans., U.S.* 105 U7
Burrundie, *N. Terr., Austral.* 211 P8
Burrwood, *La., U.S.* 100 R12
Bursa, *Turk.* 168 D5
Bûr Safâga, *Egypt* 197 D19
Bûr Sa'îd (Port Said), *Egypt* 171 N1
Burt Lake, *Mich., U.S.* 98 H11
Burton, *Mich., U.S.* 98 L7
Burton, *Nebr., U.S.* 104 M5
Buru, island, *Indonesia* 189 K16
Burūm, *Yemen* 172 Q11
Burundi, *Af.* 195 K21
Burun Shibertuy, Gora, *Russ.* 159 M16
Bururi, *Burundi* 198 L12
Burwash Landing, *Yukon, Can.* 82 F7
Burwell, *Nebr., U.S.* 105 P6
Burylbaytal, *Kaz.* 175 H15
Bury St. Edmunds, *Eng., U.K.* 143 U15
Burzil Pass, *Pak.* 176 M12
Busan (Pusan), *S. Korea* 182 G14
Busanga Swamp, *Zambia* 202 E10
Buşayrah, *Syr.* 170 F13
Büshehr, *Iran* 172 G12
Bushiribana, *Aruba, Neth.* 121 Q17
Bushnell, *Ill., U.S.* 99 Q4
Bushnell, *Nebr., U.S.* 105 P1
Bushy Park, *N. Terr., Austral.* 211 T8
Businga, *Dem. Rep. of the Congo* 198 H9
Bušk Blato, *Bosn. & Herzg.* 152 G7
Buşrá ash Shām, *Syr.* 170 L7
Busselton, *W. Aust., Austral.* 211 Y2
Bussière-Poitevine, *Fr.* 147 T8
Bussol', Proliv, *Russ.* 159 J23
Bussoleno, *It.* 150 E2
Bustamante, Bahía, *Arg.* 133 S9
Busuanga, island, *Philippines* 189 D13

Busu-Djanoa, *Dem. Rep. of the Congo* 198 J9
Buta, *Dem. Rep. of the Congo* 198 J10
Butare, *Rwanda* 198 K12
Butaritari, island, *Kiribati* 214 G8
Butchers Hill, *Qnsld., Austral.* 211 Q13
Bute, Island of, *Scot., U.K.* 142 M8
Butembo, *Dem. Rep. of the Congo* 198 J12
Buthidaung, *Myanmar* 186 H4
Butler, *Ala., U.S.* 101 L13
Butler, *Ga., U.S.* 96 M5
Butler, *Mo., U.S.* 105 T11
Butler, *Pa., U.S.* 94 N3
Butler Bay, *Virgin Islands, U.S.* 120 Q1
Butner, *N.C., U.S.* 96 G11
Buton, island, *Indonesia* 189 L14
Butrint, *Albania* 152 N9
Butte, *Mont., U.S.* 106 E7
Butte, *Nebr., U.S.* 104 M6
Butterworth, *Malaysia* 187 S9
Butt of Lewis, *Scot., U.K.* 142 G7
Button Bay, *Man., Can.* 83 K15
Button Islands, *Nunavut, Can.* 83 H20
Butuan, *Philippines* 189 E15
Buturlinovka, *Russ.* 157 N11
Butwal, *Nepal* 178 F9
Buulobarde, *Somalia* 199 H17
Buur Gaabo, *Somalia* 199 K16
Buurhakaba, *Somalia* 199 J16
Buxoro (Bukhara), *Uzb.* 174 L11
Buxtehude, *Ger.* 148 C7
Buxton, *Guyana* 129 D15
Buxton, *N.C., U.S.* 96 H15
Buy, *Russ.* 156 G11
Buyanbat, *Mongolia* 180 D10
Buyant, *Mongolia* 181 D13
Buynaksk, *Russ.* 157 U15
Buyr Nuur, *Mongolia* 181 D15
Büyük Menderes, river, *Turk.* 168 G4
Buzău, river, *Rom.* 153 E16
Buzău, *Rom.* 153 E16
Buzău, Pasul, *Rom.* 153 E15
Buzaymah, *Lib.* 197 E16
Búzi, river, *Mozambique* 202 G12
Büzmeýin, *Turkm.* 174 M8
Buzul Daği, *Turk.* 169 H18
Buzuluk, *Kaz.* 174 C12
Buzuluk, *Russ.* 156 L16
Buzzards Bay, *Mass., U.S.* 95 L15
Bwokworlap, island, *Marshall Is.* 216 G11
Byahoml', *Belarus* 156 K5
Byala, *Bulg.* 153 H17
Byala Slatina, *Bulg.* 153 H13
Byam Martin, Cape, *Nunavut, Can.* 83 D17
Byam Martin Island, *Nunavut, Can.* 83 D14
Byarezina, river, *Belarus* 156 K5
Byaroza, *Belarus* 156 L3
Byblos see Jbail, *Leb.* 170 H6
Bydgoszcz, *Pol.* 149 C13
Byers, *Colo., U.S.* 106 M14
Byfield, *Qnsld., Austral.* 211 T15
Bykhaw, *Belarus* 156 L6
Bykovo, *Russ.* 157 P13
Bylas, *Ariz., U.S.* 107 U8
Bylot Island, *Nunavut, Can.* 83 D16
Bynum Reservoir, *Mont., U.S.* 106 B7
Byrdbreen, glacier, *Antarctica* 227 B16
Byrd Glacier, *Antarctica* 227 M14
Byrock, *N.S.W., Austral.* 211 W13
Byron, Cape, *Austral.* 210 H15
Byron, Isla, *Chile* 133 U6
Bytom, *Pol.* 149 G14
Bytów, *Pol.* 149 B13

C

C, Dome, *Antarctica* 227 M17
Caála, *Angola* 202 D6
Caazapá, *Parag.* 130 N10
Cabaiguán, *Cuba* 116 H9
Caballones, Cayo, *Cuba* 116 J10
Caballo Reservoir, *N. Mex., U.S.* 107 U11
Cabanatuan, *Philippines* 189 C13
Cabaneta, Pic de la, *Andorra, Fr.* 160 H5
Cabeza del Buey, *Sp.* 144 J9
Cabezas, *Bol.* 130 K8
Cabimas, *Venez.* 128 B7
Cabinda, region, *Angola* 202 B5
Cabinda, *Angola* 202 B5

Cabinet Mountains, *Mont., U.S.* 106 B4
Cable, *Wis., U.S.* 98 F3
Cabo, *Braz.* 131 GI8
Cabo Blanco, *Arg.* 133 T9
Cabo Frio, *Braz.* 131 MI5
Cabonga, Réservoir, *Que., Can.* 83 PI9
Cabool, *Mo., U.S.* 105 VI3
Caboolture, *Qnsld., Austral.* 211 VI5
Caborea, *Mex.* 114 C6
Cabo San Lucas, *Mex.* 114 G7
Cabot, *Ark., U.S.* 100 G9
Cabot Strait, *Nfld. & Lab., N.S., Can.* 83 N22
Cabral, *Dom. Rep.* 117 MI8
Cabras, Ilhéu das, *Sao Tome and Principe* 205 C2O
Cabras Island, *Guam, U.S.* 216 CIO
Cabrera, *Dom. Rep.* 117 LI9
Cabrera, island, *Sp.* 145 HI8
Cabrera Baja, Sierra de la, *Sp.* 144 C7
Cabrit, Îlet à, *Guadeloupe, Fr.* 121 GI4
Cabrits, Îlet, *Martinique, Fr.* 121 G23
Cabrobó, *Braz.* 131 GI6
Cabrón, Cabo, *Dom. Rep.* 117 L2O
Čačak, *Serb.* 152 GIO
Caccia, Capo, *It.* 150 M3
Cáceres, *Sp.* 144 H8
Cáceres, *Braz.* 130 JIO
Cache, river, *Ark., U.S.* 100 EIO
Ca'Chiavello, river, *San Marino* 161 KI6
Cachimbo, *Braz.* 130 GII
Cachoeira, *Braz.* 131 HI6
Cachoeira do Sul, *Braz.* 130 PII
Cachoeiro do Itapemirim, *Braz.* 131 LI5
Cacine, *Guinea-Bissau* 200 E4
Cacolo, *Angola* 202 C7
Cactus, *Tex., U.S.* 102 F5
Caçu, *Braz.* 130 KI2
Caculé, *Braz.* 131 JI5
Cacuri, *Venez.* 128 EIO
Čadca, *Slovakia* 149 HI4
Caddo, *Okla., U.S.* 102 JI2
Caddo Lake, *La., Tex., U.S.* 100 K6
Cadena, Punta, *P.R., U.S.* 120 MI
Cadí, Serra del, *Sp.* 145 CI7
Cadillac, *Fr.* 147 W7
Cadillac, *Mich., U.S.* 98 JIO
Çadır Dağı, *Turk.* 169 GI7
Cádiz, *Sp.* 144 M7
Cádiz, Bahía de, *Sp.* 144 M7
Cádiz, Golfo de, *Port., Sp.* 144 L6
Cadiz, *Calif., U.S.* 109 WII
Cadiz, *Ky., U.S.* 101 DI4
Cadiz, *Ohio, U.S.* 99 QI5
Cadiz, *Philippines* 189 EI4
Cadiz Lake, *Calif., U.S.* 109 XI2
Caen, *Fr.* 147 N7
Caerdydd see Cardiff, *Wales, U.K.* 143 VIO
Caergybi see Holyhead, *Wales, U.K.* 143 S9
Caernarfon Bay, *Wales, U.K.* 143 S9
Caerphilly, *Wales, U.K.* 143 VIO
Caesarea, ruin, *Israel* 170 L5
Cafayate, *Arg.* 132 F9
Cagayan de Oro, *Philippines* 189 FI5
Cagayan Islands, *Philippines* 189 EI3
Cagayan Sulu Island, *Philippines* 188 FI2
Cagli, *It.* 150 H8
Cagliari, *It.* 151 Q4
Cagliari, Golfo di, *It.* 151 Q4
Cagnes, *Fr.* 147 XI5
Caguán, river, *Col.* 128 H5
Caguas, *P.R., U.S.* 120 N5
Caha Mountains, *Ire.* 143 V3
Cahir, *Ire.* 143 U5
Cahora Bassa, Lago de, *Mozambique* 202 EI2
Cahore Point, *Ire.* 143 T7
Cahors, *Fr.* 147 W9
Cahul, *Mold.* 157 S4
Caia, *Mozambique* 203 FI3
Caiapônia, *Braz.* 130 JI2
Caibarién, *Cuba* 116 H9
Caicara, *Venez.* 128 DIO
Caicó, *Braz.* 131 FI7
Caicos Islands, *Turks & Caicos Is., U.K.* 117 JI7
Caicos Passage, *Bahamas, Turks & Caicos Is., U.K.* 117 HI6
Caijiao, *China* 182 HI
Caille Island, *Grenada* 121 H24
Cailungo, *San Marino* 161 JI5
Cainsville, *Mo., U.S.* 105 QII
Caird Coast, *Antarctica* 226 DIO

Cairngorm Mountains, *Scot., U.K.* 142 K9
Cairns, *Qnsld., Austral.* 211 RI3
Cairo see El Qâhira, *Egypt* 197 CI8
Cairo, *Ga., U.S.* 97 Q5
Cairo, *Ill., U.S.* 99 V5
Caixão Grande, *Sao Tome and Principe* 205 D2O
Caja de Muertos, Isla, *P.R., U.S.* 120 P3
Cajamarca, *Peru* 130 F2
Cajàzeiras, *Braz.* 131 FI7
Çakırgöl Dağı, *Turk.* 169 DI4
Cakit, river, *Turk.* 168 HIO
Çakmak, *Turk.* 168 F7
Çakmak Dağı, *Turk.* 169 EI6
Cakovec, *Croatia* 152 C6
Çal, *Turk.* 168 G5
Calabar, *Nigeria* 201 HI4
Calabash Boom, *Virgin Islands, U.S.* 120 NII
Calabó, *Eq. Guinea* 204 M7
Calabozo, *Venez.* 128 C9
Calabria, region, *It.* 138 K7
Calaburras, Punta de, *Sp.* 144 M9
Calacuccia, *Fr.* 150 K4
Calafat, *Bulg.* 152 GI2
Calafat, *Rom.* 152 GI2
Calahorra, *Sp.* 145 CI3
Calais, *Fr.* 146 L9
Calais, *Me., U.S.* 95 EI9
Calalaste, Sierra de, *Arg.* 132 F8
Calalin, island, *Marshall Is.* 216 GII
Calalin Channel, *Marshall Is.* 216 GII
Calalzo, *It.* 150 C8
Calama, *Chile* 132 D7
Calama, *Braz.* 130 F8
Calamar, *Col.* 128 B5
Calamar, *Col.* 128 G6
Calamian Group, *Philippines* 189 DI3
Calamocha, *Sp.* 145 EI3
Cǎlan, *Rom.* 152 DI2
Calanda, *Sp.* 145 EI5
Calanscio, Sand Sea of, *Lib.* 194 E7
Calanscio, Sarīr, *Lib.* 194 E7
Calapan, *Philippines* 189 DI3
Calatafimi, *It.* 151 PI2
Cǎlǎraşi, *Rom.* 153 FI6
Calatayud, *Sp.* 145 EI3
Calayan, island, *Philippines* 189 AI3
Calbayog, *Philippines* 189 DI5
Calcanhar, Ponta do, *Braz.* 131 EI8
Calcasieu, river, *La., U.S.* 100 N7
Calcasieu Lake, *La., U.S.* 100 Q7
Calçoene, *Braz.* 130 BI2
Calcutta see Kolkata, *India* 178 JI2
Caldas da Rainha, *Port.* 144 G4
Caldera, *Chile* 132 G6
Caldera, peak, *Eq. Guinea* 204 M7
Çaldıran, *Turk.* 169 FI8
Caldwell, *Idaho, U.S.* 106 G3
Caldwell, *Kans., U.S.* 105 V7
Caldwell, *Tex., U.S.* 103 PI2
Caldy Island, *Wales, U.K.* 143 V8
Caledonia, *Minn., U.S.* 104 LI3
Caledonian Canal, *Scot., U.K.* 142 K8
Calexico, *Calif., U.S.* 109 ZI2
Calf of Man, cape, *Isle of Man, U.K.* 143 R8
Calgary, *Alta., Can.* 82 MIO
Calheta, *Azores* 144 P3
Calheta, *Madeira* 204 M2
Calhoun, *Ga., U.S.* 96 K4
Calhoun City, *Miss., U.S.* 100 JI2
Calhoun Falls, *S.C., U.S.* 96 K7
Cali, *Col.* 128 G4
Calibishie, *Dominica* 121 EI9
Calico Rock, *Ark., U.S.* 100 E9
Calicut see Kozhikode, *India* 179 Q5
Caliente, *Nev., U.S.* 109 SI2
California, *Mo., U.S.* 105 TI3
California, *Trinidad & Tobago* 121 P22
California, *U.S.* 109 N4
California, Golfo de (Mar de Cortés), *Mex.* 114 C6
California, Gulf of see California, Golfo de, *N. Amer.* 80 L3
California Aqueduct, *Calif., U.S.* 109 V6
Calilegua, *Arg.* 132 EIO
Cǎlilibad, *Azerb.* 169 E22
Calipatria, *Calif., U.S.* 109 YII
Calistoga, *Calif., U.S.* 109 R3
Calivigny, *Grenada* 121 L22
Calivigny Island, *Grenada* 121 L22
Callabonna, Lake, *Austral.* 210 HII
Callan, *Ire.* 143 T5
Callao, *Peru* 130 H3

Callaway, *Nebr., U.S.* 105 P5
Calliaqua, *St. Vincent & the Grenadines* 121 LI6
Calliope, *Qnsld., Austral.* 211 UI5
Calliope Range, *Austral.* 210 GI5
Caloosahatchee, river, *Fla., U.S.* 97 V8
Caloundra, *Qnsld., Austral.* 211 VI5
Calpe, *Sp.* 145 JI5
Caltagirone, *It.* 151 TII
Caltanissetta, *It.* 151 TIO
Çaltı Burnu, *Turk.* 168 CI2
Calulo, *Angola* 202 C6
Calumet, *Mich., U.S.* 98 E6
Caluso, *It.* 150 E3
Caluula, *Somalia* 199 FI8
Calvert, *Tex., U.S.* 103 PI2
Calvi, *Fr.* 150 J4
Calvinia, *S. Af.* 202 L8
Calw, *Calif., U.S.* 109 T6
Calwa, *Calif., U.S.* 109 T6
Camabatela, *Angola* 202 C6
Camacupa, *Angola* 202 D7
Camagüey, *Cuba* 116 JII
Camagüey, Archipiélago de, *Cuba* 116 GIO
Camajuaní, *Cuba* 116 H9
Camaná, *Peru* 130 J5
Camanche Reservoir, *Calif., U.S.* 109 R5
Camapuã, *Braz.* 130 KII
Câmara de Lobos, *Madeira* 204 M3
Camarat, Cap, *Fr.* 147 YI5
Çamardı, *Turk.* 168 GIO
Camargo, *Bol.* 130 L7
Camargo, *Okla., U.S.* 102 F8
Camargue, Île de la, *Fr.* 147 XI2
Camarón, Cape, *N. Amer.* 80 P8
Camarones, *Arg.* 133 S9
Camarones, Bahía, *Arg.* 133 S9
Camas, *Wash., U.S.* 108 F4
Camas Creek, *Idaho, U.S.* 106 H4
Camas Valley, *Oreg., U.S.* 108 J2
Ca Mau, *Vietnam* 187 QI2
Camballin, *W. Aust., Austral.* 211 R5
Cambodia, *Asia* 167 XII
Camborne, *Eng., U.K.* 143 Y8
Cambrai, *Fr.* 146 MII
Cambre, *Sp.* 144 B6
Cambria, *Calif., U.S.* 109 V5
Cambrian Mountains, *Wales, U.K.* 143 UIO
Cambridge, *Eng., U.K.* 143 UI4
Cambridge, *Idaho, U.S.* 106 F3
Cambridge, *Jam.* 116 MII
Cambridge, *Mass., U.S.* 95 KI5
Cambridge, *Md., U.S.* 96 DI4
Cambridge, *Minn., U.S.* 104 JII
Cambridge, *Nebr., U.S.* 105 R5
Cambridge, *Ohio, U.S.* 99 RI4
Cambridge Bay, *Nunavut, Can.* 83 FI3
Cambridge Downs, *Qnsld., Austral.* 211 SI2
Cambridge Springs, *Pa., U.S.* 94 L3
Cambundi-Catembo, *Angola* 202 C7
Çam Burnu, *Turk.* 168 DI2
Camden, *Ala., U.S.* 101 MI4
Camden, *Ark., U.S.* 100 J8
Camden, *Me., U.S.* 95 GI7
Camden, *N.J., U.S.* 94 P9
Camden, *N.Y., U.S.* 94 HI9
Camden, *S.C., U.S.* 96 K9
Camden, *Tenn., U.S.* 101 EI3
Camden, *Tex., U.S.* 103 PI4
Camden Bay, *Alas., U.S.* 84 L4
Camden Park, *St. Vincent & the Grenadines* 121 LI6
Camdenton, *Mo., U.S.* 105 TI2
Çameli, *Turk.* 168 H5
Camerino, *It.* 150 H9
Cameron, *Ariz., U.S.* 107 R7
Cameron, *La., U.S.* 100 Q7
Cameron, *Mo., U.S.* 105 RII
Cameron, *Tex., U.S.* 103 PII
Cameroon, *Af.* 195 JI8
Cameroon Mountain, *Cameroon* 201 JI5
Cancún, *Mex.* 115 HI7
Cametá, *Braz.* 131 DI3
Camiguin, island, *Philippines* 189 AI4
Camiguin, island, *Philippines* 189 EI5
Camilla, *Ga., U.S.* 97 P5
Caminha, *Port.* 144 D5
Camiri, *Bol.* 130 L8
Camirus, ruin, *Gr.* 155 NI9
Camissombo, *Angola* 202 C8
Camocim, *Braz.* 131 DI6
Camooweal, *Qnsld., Austral.* 211 SIO
Camopi, river, *Fr. Guiana, Fr.* 129 FI8
Camorta Island, *India* 179 SI5

Campagnano di Roma, *It.* 150 K8
Campana, *Arg.* 132 LI2
Campana, *It.* 151 PI4
Campana, Isla, *Chile* 133 U6
Campanario, Cerro, *Arg., Chile* 132 M7
Campbell, *Mo., U.S.* 105 VI5
Campbell, Cape, *N.Z.* 213 NI8
Campbell Hill, *Ohio, U.S.* 99 QI2
Campbell Island, *N.Z.* 214 R7
Campbell Plateau, *Pac. Oc.* 238 R9
Campbell River, *B.C., Can.* 82 L7
Campbellsville, *Ky., U.S.* 101 CI7
Campcardos, Pic de, *Fr., Sp.* 160 J6
Camp Crook, *S. Dak., U.S.* 104 JI
Campêche, *Guadeloupe, Fr.* 121 EI5
Campeche, *Mex.* 115 HI5
Campeche Bank, *Atl. Oc.* 236 KI
Campeche Bank, *Mex.* 115 HI5
Campechuela, *Cuba* 116 KII
Cam Pha, *Vietnam* 186 HI3
Campidano, plain, *It.* 151 P3
Campina Grande, *Braz.* 131 FI8
Campinas, *Braz.* 131 MI3
Campli, *It.* 150 JIO
Campo, *Cameroon* 201 JI5
Campo, *Colo., U.S.* 107 PI5
Campoalegre, *Col.* 128 G5
Campobasso, *It.* 150 LII
Campofelice, *It.* 151 SIO
Campo Gallo, *Arg.* 132 GII
Campo Grande, *Braz.* 130 LII
Campo Mourão, *Braz.* 130 MI2
Campos, region, *S. Amer.* 126 G9
Campos, *Braz.* 131 LI5
Camp Point, *Ill., U.S.* 99 R3
Campti, *La., U.S.* 100 M7
Camp Verde, *Ariz., U.S.* 107 S7
Camp Wood, *Tex., U.S.* 103 R7
Cam Ranh, *Vietnam* 187 NI4
Cam Ranh, Vung, *Vietnam* 187 NI4
Camrose, *Alta., Can.* 82 LIO
Camsell Portage, *Sask., Can.* 82 JI2
Camuy, *P.R., U.S.* 120 M2
Cambodia, *Asia* 167 XII
Cambrai, *Fr.* 146 MII
Ca Na, *Vietnam* 187 PI4
Ca Na, Mui, *Vietnam* 187 PI4
Canaan, *Trinidad & Tobago* 121 NI7
Canacona, *India* 179 N4
Canada, *N. Amer.* 81 FI8
Canada Basin, *Arctic Oc.* 242 M6
Cañada de Gómez, *Arg.* 132 KII
Cañada Honda, *Arg.* 132 K8
Canada Plain, *Arctic Oc.* 242 L6
Canadian, river, *N. Mex., U.S.* 107 RI4
Canadian, river, *Okla., Tex., U.S.* 102 HI2
Canadian, *Tex., U.S.* 102 F7
Canadian Shield, *N. Amer.* 80 E5
Çanakkale, *Turk.* 168 D2
Çanakkale Boğazı (Dardanelles), *Turk.* 168 D2
Canala, Baie de, *New Caledonia, Fr.* 218 D8
Canala, *New Caledonia, Fr.* 218 D8
Canandaigua, *N.Y., U.S.* 94 J7
Cananea, *Mex.* 114 C7
Canarias, Islas see Canary Islands, *Atl. Oc.* 204 C4
Canaries, *St. Lucia* 121 KI3
Canarreos, Archipiélago de los, *Cuba* 116 H6
Canary Islands (Islas Canarias), *Atl. Oc.* 204 C4
Cañas, *Costa Rica* 115 NI8
Canastota, *N.Y., U.S.* 94 J9
Canatlán, *Mex.* 114 F9
Canaveral, Cape, *Fla., U.S.* 97 TIO
Canaveral National Seashore, *Fla., U.S.* 97 S9
Canavieiras, *Braz.* 131 JI6
Canberra, *A.C.T., Austral.* 211 YI4
Canby, *Calif., U.S.* 108 M5
Canby, *Minn., U.S.* 104 K9
Cancún, *Mex.* 115 HI7
Çandarlı, *Turk.* 168 F3
Candás, *Sp.* 144 A9
Candé, *Fr.* 147 R6
Candia see Iráklio, *Gr.* 155 QI5
Cando, *N. Dak., U.S.* 104 E6
Candon, *Philippines* 189 BI3
Canea see Haniá, *Gr.* 155 QI3
Cane Bay, *Virgin Islands, U.S.* 120 Q2
Cane Garden Bay, *Virgin Islands, U.K.* 120 Q6
Canelles, river, *St. Lucia* 121 LI4

Cañete, *Sp.* 145 GI3
Caney, *Kans., U.S.* 105 V9
Canfranc, *Sp.* 145 CI4
Cangamba, *Angola* 202 E8
Cangas, *Sp.* 144 C5
Cangas del Narcea, *Sp.* 144 B8
Canguaretama, *Braz.* 131 FI8
Cangwu, *China* 183 R3
Cangzhou, *China* 182 E7
Caniapiscau, river, *Que., Can.* 83 KI9
Caniapiscau, Réservoir, *Que., Can.* 83 LI9
Canicattì, *It.* 151 TIO
Caniles, *Sp.* 144 LI2
Canillo, region, *Andorra* 160 H4
Canillo, *Andorra* 160 H4
Canindé, *Braz.* 131 EI6
Canipaan, *Philippines* 188 FI2
Canisteo, *N.Y., U.S.* 94 K6
Canjáyar, *Sp.* 144 LI2
Çankırı, *Turk.* 168 D9
Canna, island, *Scot., U.K.* 142 K7
Cannae, ruin, *It.* 150 LI3
Cannanore see Kannur, *India* 179 Q4
Cannelton, *Ind., U.S.* 99 U8
Cannes, *Fr.* 147 XI5
Canning Hill, *Austral.* 210 H3
Cannonball, river, *N. Dak., U.S.* 104 H4
Cannon Beach, *Oreg., U.S.* 108 E2
Cannon Falls, *Minn., U.S.* 104 KI2
Cannonville, *Utah, U.S.* 107 P7
Cann River, *Vic., Austral.* 211 ZI3
Canoas, *Braz.* 130 PI2
Canobie, *Qnsld., Austral.* 211 SII
Canoe Passage, *Kiribati* 217 B2O
Canon City, *Colo., U.S.* 107 NI3
Canonniers Point, *Mauritius* 205 F2O
Canonsburg, *Pa., U.S.* 94 P3
Canosa di Puglia, *It.* 150 LI3
Canouan, island, *St. Vincent & the Grenadines* 119 MI7
Canso, Strait of, *N.S., Can.* 83 P22
Cantabria, Sierra de, *Sp.* 144 CI2
Cantabrian Mountains see Cantabrica, Cordillera, *Sp.* 138 H2
Cantabrica, Cordillera, *Sp.* 144 B7
Cantalejo, *Sp.* 144 EIO
Cantavieja, *Sp.* 145 FI4
Canterbury, *Eng., U.K.* 143 VI5
Canterbury Bight, *N.Z.* 213 PI7
Can Tho, *Vietnam* 187 QI2
Cantiles, Cayo, *Cuba* 116 H7
Canto do Buriti, *Braz.* 131 FI5
Canton see Guangzhou, *China* 183 R4
Canton, *Ga., U.S.* 96 K5
Canton, *Ill., U.S.* 99 Q4
Canton, *Miss., U.S.* 100 LII
Canton, *Mo., U.S.* 105 RI3
Canton, *N.C., U.S.* 96 H7
Canton, *N.Y., U.S.* 94 F9
Canton, *Ohio, U.S.* 99 PI5
Canton, *Okla., U.S.* 102 F9
Canton, *Pa., U.S.* 94 L7
Canton, *S. Dak., U.S.* 104 M8
Canton Lake, *Okla., U.S.* 102 F9
Cantù, *It.* 150 D4
Cantwell, *Alas., U.S.* 111 HI7
Canumã, *Braz.* 130 E9
Canutama, *Braz.* 130 F7
Canutillo, *Tex., U.S.* 103 UI
Cany-Barville, *Fr.* 147 N8
Canyon, *Tex., U.S.* 102 H5
Canyon City, *Oreg., U.S.* 108 G7
Canyon de Chelly National Monument, *Ariz., U.S.* 107 R9
Canyon Ferry Lake, *Mont., U.S.* 106 D7
Canyon Lake, *Tex., U.S.* 103 QIO
Canyonlands National Park, *Utah, U.S.* 107 N9
Canyons of the Ancients National Monument, *Colo., U.S.* 107 PIO
Canyonville, *Oreg., U.S.* 108 J3
Cao Bang, *Vietnam* 186 GI2
Caoxian, *China* 182 H6
Caparra, ruin, *P.R., U.S.* 120 M4
Capayán, *Arg.* 132 H9
Cap Barbas, *W. Sahara, Mor.* 196 E5
Cap-Chat, *Que., Can.* 83 N2I
Cap d'Ail, *Fr.* 161 FI9
Cap Dorade, *St. Martin, Fr.* 121 BI4
Cape Barren Island, *Tas., Austral.* 211 YI6
Cape Breton Island, *N.S., Can.* 83 N23
Cape Charles, *Va., U.S.* 96 FI4
Cape Coast, *Ghana* 200 HIO
Cape Cod Bay, *Mass., U.S.* 95 LI6

Cape Cod National Seashore, Mass., U.S. **95** LI6
Cape Coral, Fla., U.S. **97** W8
Cape Dorset, Nunavut, Can. **83** HI7
Cape Fear, river, N.C., U.S. **96** KI2
Cape Girardeau, Mo., U.S. **105** UI6
Cape Hatteras National Seashore, N.C., U.S. **96** HI5
Cape Krusenstern National Monument, Alas., U.S. **110** DI2
Capel, W. Aust., Austral. **211** Y2
Capella Islands, Virgin Islands, U.S. **120** N9
Cape Lookout National Seashore, N.C., U.S. **96** JI4
Cape Lookout Shoals, N.C., U.S. **96** JI4
Cape May, N.J., U.S. **94** RIO
Capenda-Camulembu, Angola **202** C7
Cape Palmas, Liberia **200** J7
Cape Plain, Atl. Oc. **237** TI4
Cape Rodney, P.N.G. **213** E2O
Cap Estate, St. Lucia **121** JI4
Capesterre, Guadeloupe, Fr. **121** GI6
Capesterre-Belle-Eau, Guadeloupe, Fr. **121** FI5
Capestrano, It. **150** KIO
Cape Town, S. Af. **202** M7
Cape Verde, Atl. Oc. **204** D3
Cape Verde Plain, Atl. Oc. **236** KIO
Cape Vincent, N.Y., U.S. **94** G8
Cape York Peninsula, Qnsld., Austral. **211** PI2
Cap-Haïtien, Haiti **117** LI7
Capistrello, It. **150** K9
Cappoquin, Ire. **143** U5
Capital Hill, N. Mariana Is., U.S. **216** B5
Capitán Pablo Lagerenza, Parag. **130** K9
Capitan Peak, N. Mex., U.S. **107** TI3
Capitão, Ponta, Sao Tome and Principe **205** A2I
Capitol Reef National Park, Utah, U.S. **107** P8
Capodistria see Koper, Slov. **152** D4
Capoeira, Corredeira, Braz. **130** FIO
Cappadocia, region, Turk. **168** G9
Cappamore, Ire. **143** T4
Cap Point, St. Lucia **121** JI4
Cappoquin, Ire. **143** U5
Capraia, Isola di, It. **150** H5
Caprera, Isola, It. **150** L4
Capri, Isola di, It. **151** NIO
Capricorn Channel, Austral. **210** FI5
Capricorn Group, Austral. **210** FI5
Caprivi Strip, region, Namibia **202** F9
Cap Rock Escarpment, Tex., U.S. **84** KII
Captain Cook, Hawai'i, U.S. **113** MI8
Captain Cook Monument, Hawai'i, U.S. **112** C5
Captain Cook Monument, Hawai'i, U.S. **113** NI8
Captain Cook's Monument, Fr. Polynesia, Fr. **219** NI6
Captieux, Fr. **147** W7
Captiva, Fla., U.S. **97** W8
Capua, It. **150** MIO
Capucin, Cape, Dominica **121** DI8
Capucin Point, Seychelles **205** P2O
Capulin Volcano National Monument, N. Mex., U.S. **107** QI4
Caquetá, river, Col. **128** J7
Caracal, Rom. **153** GI4
Caracaraí, Braz. **130** B9
Caracas, Venez. **128** B9
Caracol, Braz. **131** GI5
Carahue, Chile **133** P6
Carajás, Serra dos, Braz. **130** EI2
Caramulo, Serra do, Port. **144** F6
Caransebeş, Rom. **152** EI2
Carapuse Bay, Trinidad & Tobago **121** NI8
Caratasca, Laguna de, Hond. **115** KI9
Caratasca Lagoon, N. Amer. **80** P8
Carauari, Braz. **130** E7
Caraúbas, Braz. **131** FI7
Caravaca de la Cruz, Sp. **145** KI3
Caravelas, Braz. **131** KI6
Caravelle, Presqu'île la, Martinique, Fr. **121** E23
Carballiño, Sp. **144** C6
Carballo, Sp. **144** B5
Carbón, Laguna del, Arg. **133** V8
Carbonara, Capo, It. **151** Q4
Carbondale, Colo., U.S. **106** MII
Carbondale, Ill., U.S. **99** U5

Carbondale, Pa., U.S. **94** L9
Carboneras, Sp. **145** LI3
Carbon Hill, Ala., U.S. **101** JI4
Carbonia, It. **151** Q3
Carbonne, Fr. **147** Y8
Carcajou, Alta., Can. **82** JIO
Carcans, Lac de, Fr. **147** V6
Carcasse, Cap, Haiti **117** MI4
Carcassonne, Fr. **147** YIO
Carche, peak, Sp. **145** JI4
Carcross, Yukon, Can. **82** G8
Cardabia, W. Aust., Austral. **211** TI
Cardamom Mountains, Cambodia **187** NIO
Cardamum Island see Kadmat Island, India **179** Q3
Cardeña, Sp. **144** JIO
Cárdenas, Cuba **116** G7
Cárdenas, Mex. **114** GII
Cardiff (Caerdydd), Wales, U.K. **143** VIO
Cardigan (Aberteifi), Wales, U.K. **143** U9
Cardigan Bay, Wales, U.K. **143** T9
Cardona, Sp. **145** DI7
Cardoso y Pinto, Eq. Guinea **204** M7
Cardwell, Qnsld., Austral. **211** RI3
Carei, Rom. **152** BI2
Careiro da Várzea, Braz. **130** D9
Carey, Ohio, U.S. **99** PI2
Carey, Lake, Austral. **210** H4
Carey Downs, W. Aust., Austral. **211** U2
Cargados Carajos Bank, Ind. Oc. **240** J7
Cargèse, Fr. **150** K3
Carhué, Arg. **132** MII
Cariati, It. **151** PI4
Caribbean Sea, Atl. Oc. **236** L3
Caribou, Me., U.S. **95** BI8
Caribou Mountains, N. Amer. **80** F4
Carinda, N.S.W., Austral. **211** WI3
Cariñena, Sp. **145** EI3
Carinhanha, Braz. **131** JI5
Cariparé, Braz. **131** HI4
Caripito, Venez. **128** BI2
Carlin, Nev., U.S. **109** NIO
Carlingford Lough, Ire., U.K. **143** R7
Carlinville, Ill., U.S. **99** S4
Carlisle, Ark., U.S. **100** G9
Carlisle, Eng., U.K. **143** PIO
Carlisle, Ky., U.S. **101** BI8
Carlisle, Pa., U.S. **94** P7
Carlisle Bay, Barbados **121** LI8
Carlisle Bay, Jam. **120** K8
Carlos, Isla, Chile **133** X7
Carlow, Ire. **143** T6
Carlsbad, Calif., U.S. **109** Y9
Carlsbad, N. Mex., U.S. **107** VI4
Carlsbad, Tex., U.S. **103** N6
Carlsbad Caverns National Park, N. Mex., U.S. **107** VI4
Carlsberg Ridge, Ind. Oc. **240** F7
Carlton, Minn., U.S. **104** GI2
Carlyle, Ill., U.S. **99** T5
Carlyle Lake, Ill., U.S. **99** T5
Carmacks, Yukon, Can. **82** F8
Carmagnola, It. **150** E2
Carmarthen, Wales, U.K. **143** V9
Carmarthen Bay, Wales, U.K. **143** V9
Carmaux, Fr. **147** WIO
Carmel-by-the-Sea, Calif., U.S. **109** T4
Carmen, Okla., U.S. **102** E9
Carmen, Isla, Mex. **114** E6
Carmen de Bolívar, Col. **128** C5
Carmen de Patagones, Arg. **133** QII
Carmi, Ill., U.S. **99** U6
Carmona, Sp. **144** L8
Carnamah, W. Aust., Austral. **211** W2
Carnarvon, S. Af. **202** L8
Carnarvon, W. Aust., Austral. **211** UI
Carndonagh, Ire. **143** N6
Carnegie, Okla., U.S. **102** G9
Carnegie, W. Aust., Austral. **211** U5
Carnegie, Lake, Austral. **210** G4
Carnegie Ridge, Pac. Oc. **239** KI9
Carney Island, Antarctica **226** M7
Carnic Alps, It. **150** C9
Car Nicobar, island, India **179** SI4
Carnot, Cen. Af. Rep. **198** H8
Carnot, Cape, Austral. **210** K9
Carnsore Point, Ire. **143** U7
Caro, Mich., U.S. **98** KI2
Caroço, Ilhéu, Sao Tome and Principe **205** B2I
Carol City, Fla., U.S. **97** WIO
Carolina, P.R., U.S. **120** M5
Carolina, Braz. **131** FI3
Carolina Beach, N.C., U.S. **96** KI2

Carolinas, Puntan, N. Mariana Is., U.S. **216** C8
Caroline Island (Millennium Island), Kiribati **215** HI3
Caroline Islands, F.S.M. **214** F3
Caroní, river, Venez. **128** DI2
Caroni Swamp, Trinidad & Tobago **121** P22
Carora, Venez. **128** B8
Carp, Nev., U.S. **109** TI2
Carpathian Mountains, Eur. **138** G8
Carpentaria, Gulf of, Austral. **210** BIO
Carpentras, Fr. **147** WI3
Carpi, It. **150** F6
Carpina, Braz. **131** FI8
Carpio, N. Dak., U.S. **104** E3
Carquefou, Fr. **147** R6
Carrabelle, Fla., U.S. **97** R4
Carrantuohill, peak, Ire. **143** U3
Carrara, It. **150** G5
Carrarang, W. Aust., Austral. **211** VI
Carrboro, N.C., U.S. **96** HII
Carriacou, island, Grenada **119** MI7
Carrickfergus, N. Ire., U.K. **143** P7
Carrick on Shannon, Ire. **143** R5
Carrieton, S. Aust., Austral. **211** XIO
Carrington, N. Dak., U.S. **104** F6
Carrión de los Condes, Sp. **144** CIO
Carrizal Bajo, Chile **132** G6
Carrizo Creek, river, N. Mex., U.S. **107** QI5
Carrizo Plain National Monument, Calif., U.S. **109** V6
Carrizo Springs, Tex., U.S. **103** T7
Carrizozo, N. Mex., U.S. **107** TI3
Carroll, Iowa, U.S. **105** NIO
Carrollton, Ga., U.S. **96** L4
Carrollton, Ill., U.S. **99** S4
Carrollton, Ky., U.S. **101** AI7
Carrollton, Mo., U.S. **105** SII
Carrollton, Tex., U.S. **102** LII
Carrot Bay, Virgin Islands, U.K. **120** R6
Carrowmore Lough, Ire. **143** Q3
Çarşamba, river, Turk. **168** H8
Çarşamba, Turk. **168** DII
Carson, N. Dak., U.S. **104** H4
Carson City, Nev., U.S. **109** Q6
Carson Sink, Nev., U.S. **109** P8
Carsonville, Mich., U.S. **98** LI3
Cartagena, Col. **128** B4
Cartagena, Sp. **145** LI4
Cartago, Col. **128** F4
Cartago, Costa Rica **115** NI9
Carter's Cays, Bahamas **120** D3
Cartersville, Ga., U.S. **96** K4
Carthage, Ark., U.S. **100** H8
Carthage, Ill., U.S. **99** Q3
Carthage, Miss., U.S. **100** KI2
Carthage, Mo., U.S. **105** VII
Carthage, N.C., U.S. **96** HII
Carthage, N.Y., U.S. **94** G9
Carthage, S. Dak., U.S. **104** L7
Carthage, Tenn., U.S. **101** EI6
Carthage, Tex., U.S. **102** MI5
Cartier Island, W. Aust., Austral. **211** P4
Cartwright, Nfld. & Lab., Can. **83** K22
Caruaru, Braz. **131** GI7
Carúpano, Venez. **128** BI2
Carutapera, Braz. **131** DI4
Caruthersville, Mo., U.S. **105** WI6
Carvoeiro, Braz. **130** D8
Carvoeiro, Cabo, Port. **144** G4
Cary, N.C., U.S. **96** HII
Caryapundy Swamp, Austral. **210** HII
Casablanca, Mor. **196** B8
Casa Cruz, Cape, Trinidad & Tobago **121** Q23
Casa Grande, Ariz., U.S. **107** U7
Casa Grande Ruins National Monument, Ariz., U.S. **107** U7
Casale Monferrato, It. **150** E3
Casamance, region, Senegal **196** H5
Casamanya, Pic de, Andorra **160** H3
Casanare, river, Col. **128** E7
Casarano, It. **151** NI5
Cascade, Idaho, U.S. **106** F4
Cascade, Jam. **120** H6
Cascade, Mont., U.S. **106** C7
Cascade, Norfolk I., Austral. **217** F2O
Cascade, Seychelles **205** P2O
Cascade Bay, Norfolk I., Austral. **217** F2O
Cascade Head, Oreg., U.S. **108** F2

Cascade Locks, Oreg., U.S. **108** F4
Cascade Range, U.S. **84** E3
Cascade Reservoir, Idaho, U.S. **106** F4
Cascade-Siskiyou National Monument, Oreg., U.S. **108** L3
Cascadia Basin, Pac. Oc. **239** DI5
Cascavel, Braz. **130** MII
Cascina, It. **150** G6
Cascorro, Cuba **116** JII
Casere, It. **150** B8
Caserta, It. **150** MII
Casey, station, Antarctica **227** M2I
Casey, Ill., U.S. **99** S7
Casey Bay, Antarctica **227** CI9
Cashel, Ire. **143** T5
Cashmere, Wash., U.S. **108** C6
Casigran, Philippines **189** BI4
Casilda, Arg. **132** KII
Casina di Pio IV, Vatican City **161** PI6
Casino Gardens, Monaco **161** D22
Casino of Monte Carlo, Monaco **161** D22
Casiquiare, river, Venez. **128** GIO
Casma, Peru **130** G3
Casmalia, Calif., U.S. **109** W5
Caspar, Calif., U.S. **109** P2
Caspe, Sp. **145** EI5
Casper, Wyo., U.S. **106** HI2
Caspian Depression, Kaz., Russ. **166** E5
Caspian Sea, Asia **166** F5
Casquets, island, Ch. Is. **143** YII
Cass, W. Va., U.S. **96** DIO
Cass City, Mich., U.S. **98** KI2
Cassel, Fr. **146** LIO
Casselton, N. Dak., U.S. **104** G8
Cassiar Mountains, B.C., Can. **82** H8
Cassino, It. **150** LIO
Cassis, Fr. **147** YI4
Cass Lake, Minn., U.S. **104** FIO
Cassville, Mo., U.S. **105** VII
Cassville, Wis., U.S. **98** M3
Castagneto Carducci, It. **150** H6
Castanhal, Braz. **131** DI3
Castaño Nuevo, Arg. **132** J7
Castara, Trinidad & Tobago **121** NI8
Casteggio, It. **150** E4
Castela de Bode, Barragem do, Port. **144** G6
Castelbuono, It. **151** SIO
Castel di Sangro, It. **150** LIO
Castelfranco Veneto, It. **150** D8
Casteljaloux, Fr. **147** W7
Castellabate, It. **151** NII
Castellaccio, peak, San Marino **161** KI5
Castellammare, Golfo di, It. **151** S9
Castellammare del Golfo, It. **151** S9
Castellaneta, It. **150** MI4
Castello, It. **161** LI5
Castelló de la Plana, Sp. **145** GI5
Castello di Montemaggio, It. **161** KI3
Castelnaudary, Fr. **147** Y9
Castelnovo ne'Monti, It. **150** F6
Castelo Branco, Port. **144** G6
Castelo de Vide, Port. **144** H6
Castelsardo, It. **150** M3
Casterton, Vic., Austral. **211** ZII
Castiglione Messer Marino, It. **150** KII
Castilhiano, Cape, Cape Verde **205** BI6
Castille, region, Sp. **144** FIO
Castillo de San Marcos National Monument, Fla., U.S. **97** R9
Castillon, Fr. **147** Y8
Castillos, Uru. **132** LI5
Castlebar, Braz. **143** R3
Castlebay, Scot., U.K. **142** K6
Castlebridge, Ire. **143** U6
Castle Bruce, Dominica **121** F2O
Castle Dale, Utah, U.S. **106** M8
Castle Douglas, Scot., U.K. **143** P9
Castlegregory, Ire. **143** U2
Castle Harbour, Bermuda, U.K. **120** B3
Castle Island, Bahamas **117** HI4
Castlemaine, Vic., Austral. **211** ZI2
Castlepollard, Ire. **143** R6
Castlerea, Ire. **143** R4
Castlereagh, river, Austral. **210** JI4
Castle Roads, Bermuda, U.K. **120** B3
Castle Rock, Colo., U.S. **106** MI3
Castle Rock, Wash., U.S. **108** E3
Castres, Fr. **147** XIO
Castries, Fr. **147** XI2

Castries, St. Lucia **121** JI4
Castries, Port, St. Lucia **121** JI4
Castro, Chile **133** R6
Castro Daire, Port. **144** E6
Castro-Urdiales, Sp. **144** BII
Castro Verde, Port. **144** K5
Castrovillari, It. **151** PI3
Castroville, Tex., U.S. **103** R9
Castuera, Sp. **144** J9
Çat, Turk. **169** EI5
Catahoula Lake, La., U.S. **100** M8
Çatak, Turk. **169** GI7
Catalan Bay, Gibraltar, U.K. **161** P23
Catalão, Braz. **131** KI3
Çatalca, Turk. **168** C4
Catalina, Chile **132** F7
Catalina Point, Guam, U.S. **216** BI2
Catalonia, region, Sp. **145** DI7
Catamarca, Arg. **132** H9
Catanduanes, island, Philippines **189** CI5
Catania, It. **151** SI2
Catania, Golfo di, It. **151** TI2
Catania, Piana di, It. **151** TII
Catanzaro, It. **151** QI4
Cataperdís, Pic de, Andorra, Fr. **160** G2
Catarina, Tex., U.S. **103** T8
Cataman, Philippines **189** DI5
Catawba, river, N.C., S.C., U.S. **85** JI8
Cat Cays, Bahamas **116** D9
Cateel, Philippines **189** FI5
Catete, Angola **202** C5
Cathedral Mountain, Tex., U.S. **103** Q2
Cathedral of Monaco, Monaco **161** F2I
Cathlamet, Wash., U.S. **108** E3
Catingas, region, S. Amer. **126** E7
Cat Island, Bahamas **117** EI3
Cat Island see Pierrot Island, Mauritius **205** K2O
Cat Island, Miss., U.S. **100** PI2
Cat Lake, Ont., Can. **83** NI5
Catlettsburg, Ky., U.S. **101** B2O
Catlow Valley, Oreg., U.S. **108** K7
Catoche, Cape, N. Amer. **80** N7
Cato Island, Coral Sea Is. Terr., Austral. **211** UI6
Catonsville, Md., U.S. **96** CI3
Catria, Monte, It. **150** H8
Catriló, Arg. **132** MIO
Catrimani, river, Braz. **130** C8
Catrimani, Braz. **130** C8
Catskill, N.Y., U.S. **94** KII
Catskill Mountains, N.Y., U.S. **94** KIO
Cattenom, Fr. **160** LIO
Cattolica Eraclea, It. **151** T9
Cauca, river, Col. **128** D5
Caucasus Mountains, Asia, Eur. **138** HI3
Caucete, Arg. **132** J8
Caudry, Fr. **146** MII
Caulnes, Fr. **147** Q5
Caungula, Angola **202** C7
Cauquenes, Chile **132** M6
Caura, river, Venez. **128** EII
Caussade, Fr. **147** W9
Causse du Larzac, range, Fr. **147** XII
Cauto, river, Cuba **116** KI2
Cavaillon, Fr. **147** XI3
Cavalaire, Fr. **147** YI5
Cavalcante, Braz. **131** HI3
Cavalese, It. **150** C7
Cavalier, N. Dak., U.S. **104** E7
Cavalla see Cavally, river, Liberia **200** H7
Cavallo, Île, Fr. **150** L4
Cavally see Cavalla, river, Côte d'Ivoire **200** H7
Cavan, Ire. **143** R6
Cave Cay, Bahamas **120** D7
Cave Creek, Ariz., U.S. **107** T7
Cave Junction, Oreg., U.S. **108** K2
Cavelle Pond, Bahamas **120** C8
Caves, Anse aux, Mauritius **205** J2O
Caviana, Ilha, Braz. **131** CI3
Cavignac, Fr. **147** V7
Cavo, Mount, It. **150** L8
Cavour, It. **150** E2
Çavuş Burnu, Turk. **168** J6
Çavuşçu Gölü, Turk. **168** G7
Cawker City, Kans., U.S. **105** S6
Caxias, Braz. **131** EI5
Caxias, Braz. **130** E5
Caxias do Sul, Braz. **130** PI2
Caxito, Angola **202** C5
Çay, Turk. **168** F6
Cayambe, peak, Ecua. **128** J3
Cayambe, Ecua. **128** J3
Cayce, S.C., U.S. **96** K9

Çaycuma, *Turk.* 168 C7
Çayeli, *Turk.* 169 D15
Cayenne, *Fr. Guiana, Fr.* 129 E18
Cayeux-sur-Mer, *Fr.* 146 M9
Cayey, *P.R., U.S.* 120 N4
Cayey, Sierra de, *P.R.* 120 N5
Çayıralan, *Turk.* 168 F10
Cayman Brac, *Cayman Is., U.K.* 116 L9
Cayman Islands, *U.K., Greater Antilles* 116 L8
Cayman Trench, *Atl. Oc.* 236 L3
Caynabo, *Somalia* 199 G17
Cayon, *St. Kitts & Nevis* 121 A17
Cay Point, *Bahamas* 120 C11
Cay Sal Bank, *Bahamas* 116 F9
Cayucos, *Calif., U.S.* 109 V5
Cayuga Lake, *N.Y., U.S.* 94 K8
Cazalla de la Sierra, *Sp.* 144 K8
Cazaux et de Sanguinet, Lac de, *Fr.* 147 W6
Cazères, *Fr.* 147 Y8
Cazombo, *Angola* 202 D9
Cazorla, *Sp.* 144 K11
Ceanannus Mór (Kells), *Ire.* 143 R6
Ceann Tra (Ventry), *Ire.* 143 U2
Ceara Plain, *Atl. Oc.* 237 N8
Cebollar, *Arg.* 132 H9
Cebu, island, *Philippines* 189 E14
Cebu, *Philippines* 189 E14
Cecile Peninsula, *Kiribati* 217 B22
Cecina, *It.* 150 H6
Cedar, river, *Iowa, U.S.* 105 N13
Cedar Bluff Reservoir, *Kans., U.S.* 105 T5
Cedar Breaks National Monument, *Utah, U.S.* 107 P6
Cedar City, *Utah, U.S.* 107 P6
Cedar Creek Reservoir, *Tex., U.S.* 102 M12
Cedar Falls, *Iowa, U.S.* 105 N12
Cedar Grove, *Antigua & Barbuda* 121 A20
Cedar Harbour, *Bahamas* 120 A5
Cedar Key, *Fla., U.S.* 97 S6
Cedar Lake, *Ind., U.S.* 99 P7
Cedar Rapids, *Iowa, U.S.* 105 N13
Cedar River, *Mich., U.S.* 98 H8
Cedartown, *Ga., U.S.* 96 K4
Cedar Vale, *Kans., U.S.* 105 V8
Cedarville, *Calif., U.S.* 108 L6
Cedarville, *Mich., U.S.* 98 G11
Cedeira, *Sp.* 144 A6
Cedillo, Embalse de, *Port., Sp.* 144 G7
Cedros, Isla, *Mex.* 114 D5
Cedros Bay, *Trinidad & Tobago* 121 Q21
Cedros Trench, *Pac. Oc.* 239 G16
Ceelbuur, *Somalia* 199 H17
Ceerigaabo (Erigavo), *Somalia* 199 F17
Cefalù, *It.* 151 S10
Cegléd, *Hung.* 149 L15
Cehotina, river, *Bosn. & Herzg., Mont.* 152 H9
Ceiba, *P.R., U.S.* 120 N6
Cejal, *Col.* 128 G9
Çekerek, river, *Turk.* 168 D10
Çekerek, *Turk.* 168 E10
Celano, *It.* 150 K9
Celanova, *Sp.* 144 C6
Celaya, *Mex.* 114 H11
Celebes *see* Sulawesi, island, *Indonesia* 189 K13
Celebes Basin, *Ind. Oc.* 241 F16
Celebes Sea, *Indonesia* 189 H14
Çeleken, *Turkm.* 174 L6
Celina, *Ohio, U.S.* 99 Q11
Celje, *Slov.* 152 D5
Cella, *Sp.* 145 F13
Celle, *Ger.* 148 D8
Celtic Sea, *Ire., U.K.* 143 W6
Cement, *Okla., U.S.* 102 H10
Çemişgezek, *Turk.* 169 F13
Cenderawasih, Teluk, *Indonesia* 189 K19
Center, *N. Dak., U.S.* 104 G4
Center, *Tex., U.S.* 102 M15
Center Hill Lake, *Tenn., U.S.* 101 E16
Center Point, *Ala., U.S.* 101 J15
Center Point, *Tex., U.S.* 103 Q9
Centerville, *Iowa, U.S.* 105 Q12
Centerville, *S. Dak., U.S.* 104 M8
Centerville, *Tenn., U.S.* 101 F14
Centerville, *Tex., U.S.* 103 N13
Cento, *It.* 150 F7
Central, *Alas., U.S.* 111 F18
Central, Cordillera, *Dom. Rep.* 117 L18
Central, Cordillera, *P.R.* 120 N3
Central, Cordillera, *S. Amer.* 126 C2
Central, Massif, *Fr.* 147 U10

Central African Republic, *Af.* 195 H19
Central America, *N. Amer.* 80 P7
Central Brahui Range, *Pak.* 177 S6
Central City, *Ky., U.S.* 101 C15
Central City, *Nebr., U.S.* 105 Q7
Central Highlands, *Vietnam* 186 M13
Centralia, *Ill., U.S.* 99 T5
Centralia, *Mo., U.S.* 105 S13
Centralia, *Wash., U.S.* 108 D3
Central Lowland, *U.S.* 85 F14
Central Lowlands, *Austral.* 210 E10
Central Makran Range, *Pak.* 177 U4
Central Pacific Basin, *Pac. Oc.* 238 J9
Central Point, *Oreg., U.S.* 108 K3
Central Range, *P.N.G.* 213 C18
Central Range, *Russ.* 166 C13
Central Russian Upland, *Russ.* 138 E11
Central Siberian Plateau, *Russ.* 166 C9
Central Valley, *Calif., U.S.* 109 N3
Centre, *Ala., U.S.* 101 H16
Centre de Flacq, *Mauritius* 205 G20
Centreville, *Miss., U.S.* 100 N10
Cenxi, *China* 183 R2
Cephalonia *see* Kefaloniá, *Gr.* 154 H7
Ceprano, *It.* 150 L9
Ceram, island, *Indonesia* 189 K17
Ceram Sea, *Indonesia* 189 K17
Cerasolo, *It.* 161 G18
Cerbère, *Fr.* 147 Z11
Ceres, *Arg.* 132 H11
Ceres, *Braz.* 131 J13
Cerf Island, *Seychelles* 203 C19
Ceriano, *It.* 161 G16
Cérilly, *Fr.* 147 S10
Çerkeş, *Turk.* 168 D8
Çermik, *Turk.* 169 G14
Cernavodă, *Rom.* 153 F17
Cerralvo, Isla, *Mex.* 114 F7
Cerredo, Torre, *Sp.* 144 B9
Cerreto, Monte, *San Marino* 161 J14
Cerrillos, *It.* 132 F9
Cerrillos, *N. Mex., U.S.* 107 R12
Cerro de Pasco, *Peru* 130 G3
Cerro Sombrero, *Chile* 133 W8
Certaldo, *It.* 150 H6
Certers, *Andorra* 160 K3
Cervales, peak, *Sp.* 144 G9
Cervera, *Sp.* 145 D16
Cervera de Pisuerga, *Sp.* 144 B10
Cerveteri, *It.* 150 K8
Cervia, *It.* 150 F8
Cesana Torinese, *It.* 150 E1
Cesar, river, *Col.* 128 B6
Cesena, *It.* 150 G8
Cesenatico, *It.* 150 G8
Cēsis, *Latv.* 141 L17
České Budějovice, *Czech Rep.* 148 J11
Českomoravská Vrchovina, *Czech Rep.* 148 J12
Český Krumlov, *Czech Rep.* 148 J11
Çeşme, *Turk.* 168 F2
Céspedes, *Cuba* 116 J10
Cessnock, *N.S.W., Austral.* 211 X14
Cetinje, *Mont.* 152 J8
Cetti Bay, *Guam, U.S.* 216 D10
Ceuta, *Sp.* 144 N9
Cévennes, range, *Fr.* 147 W12
Cevio, *Switz.* 150 C4
Ceyhan, river, *Turk.* 168 H11
Ceyhan, *Turk.* 168 H11
Ceylanpınar, *Turk.* 169 J14
Ceylon *see* Sri Lanka, *Asia* 179 T7
Chabana, *Japan* 185 X2
Chablis, *Fr.* 147 R11
Chacachacare, island, *Trinidad & Tobago* 121 P21
Chacao, Canal de, *Chile* 133 Q6
Chachapoyas, *Peru* 130 F3
Chacharan, *Pak.* 177 S9
Chachora, *India* 178 H7
Chachro, *Pak.* 177 W9
Chaco Austral, region, *S. Amer.* 126 K6
Chaco Boreal, region, *S. Amer.* 126 H6
Chaco Culture National Historic Park, *N. Mex., U.S.* 107 R11
Chad, *Af.* 195 G19
Chad, Lake (Lac Tchad), *Af.* 194 G6
Chadan, *Russ.* 159 L13
Chadbourn, *N.C., U.S.* 96 K11
Chadron, *Nebr., U.S.* 104 M2
Chadwick, *Mo., U.S.* 105 V12
Chafarinas, Islas, *Sp.* 144 P12
Chaffee, *Mo., U.S.* 105 U16

Chagai, *Pak.* 177 S4
Chagai Hills, *Pak.* 177 S3
Chagda, *Russ.* 159 H18
Chaghcharan, *Afghan.* 176 M5
Chagoda, *Russ.* 156 F8
Chagos Archipelago, *Ind. Oc.* 166 M6
Chagos-Laccadive Ridge, *Ind. Oc.* 240 F9
Chagos Trench, *Ind. Oc.* 240 H9
Chaguanas, *Trinidad & Tobago* 121 P22
Chaguaramas, *Trinidad & Tobago* 121 N21
Chagyl, *Turkm.* 174 K7
Chahar Bagh, *Afghan.* 176 K5
Chahar Borj, *Afghan.* 176 M2
Chah Bāhar, *Iran* 173 J17
Chah-e Ab, *Afghan.* 176 K8
Chah-e Kerteh, *Afghan.* 177 P2
Chaibasa, *India* 178 J10
Chai-Nat, *Thai.* 186 L8
Chain Fracture Zone, *Atl. Oc.* 237 N10
Chain of Craters, *Hawai'i, U.S.* 113 N21
Chajarí, *Arg.* 132 J13
Chakar, river, *Pak.* 177 S7
Chakaria, *Bangladesh* 178 J14
Chake Chake, *Tanzania* 199 L15
Chakhansur, *Afghan.* 177 Q2
Chakwal, *Pak.* 177 N11
Chalais, *Fr.* 147 V7
Chalan Kanoa, *N. Mariana Is., U.S.* 216 C4
Chalan Pago, *Guam, U.S.* 216 C11
Chalap Dalan Range, *Afghan.* 177 N3
Chalbi Desert, *Kenya* 194 J10
Chalhuanca, *Peru* 130 J4
Chaling, *China* 183 P4
Chalisgaon, *India* 178 K4
Chalkhi, *Afghan.* 176 L2
Chalkis *see* Halkída, *Gr.* 154 H12
Chalkyitsik, *Alas., U.S.* 111 E18
Chalky Mount, *Barbados* 121 K19
Chalky Mount, *Barbados* 121 K19
Challans, *Fr.* 147 S5
Challenger Deep, *Pac. Oc.* 238 H6
Challenger Fracture Zone, *Pac. Oc.* 239 N16
Challis, *Idaho, U.S.* 106 F5
Chalon, *Fr.* 147 S13
Châlons-sur-Marne, *Fr.* 147 P12
Châlus, *Fr.* 147 U8
Cham, *Ger.* 148 J9
Chama, *N. Mex., U.S.* 107 Q12
Chamah, peak, *Malaysia* 187 T9
Chaman, *Pak.* 177 Q5
Chaman Bid, *Iran* 173 B15
Chamatang, *India* 177 N15
Chamba, *India* 177 P13
Chambal, river, *India* 178 G5
Chamberlain, *S. Dak., U.S.* 104 L6
Chamberlain Lake, *Me., U.S.* 95 C16
Chamberlin, Mount, *Alas., U.S.* 111 C17
Chambers, *Ariz., U.S.* 107 S9
Chambersburg, *Pa., U.S.* 94 P6
Chambers Creek, *Tex., U.S.* 102 M12
Chambéry, *Fr.* 147 U14
Chambeshi, river, *Zambia* 194 M9
Chambois, *Fr.* 147 P7
Chamburi Kalat, *Pak.* 177 V4
Chamical, *Arg.* 132 J9
Chamizal National Memorial, *Tex., U.S.* 103 U2
Chamkani, *Afghan.* 177 N8
Ch'amo Hāyk, *Eth.* 199 H14
Chamoli, *India* 178 E7
Chamonix, *Fr.* 147 T15
Champagne, region, *Fr.* 147 Q12
Champagnole, *Fr.* 147 S14
Champaign, *Ill., U.S.* 99 R6
Champasak, *Laos* 186 M12
Champéry, *Switz.* 150 C2
Champlain, Lake, *N.Y., Vt., U.S.* 94 F12
Champotón, *Mex.* 115 J15
Chamrajnagar, *India* 179 Q5
Chamzinka, *Russ.* 156 K13
Chañaral, *Chile* 132 F6
Chança, river, *Port., Sp.* 144 K6
Chandalar, river, *Alas., U.S.* 111 E17
Chandeleur Islands, *La., U.S.* 101 Q13
Chandeleur Sound, *La., U.S.* 100 Q12
Chandigarh, *India* 178 E6
Chandler, *Ariz., U.S.* 107 U7
Chandler, *Okla., U.S.* 102 G11
Chandless, river, *Braz., Peru* 130 G5
Chandpur, *Bangladesh* 178 J13

Chandrapur, *India* 178 L7
Chang, Ko, *Thai.* 187 N10
Changanacheri, *India* 179 R5
Changane, river, *Mozambique* 202 H12
Changbai Shan, *China* 182 B13
Chang Chenmo Range, *China, India* 176 M15
Changchun, *China* 182 A12
Changde, *China* 182 M3
Changhua, *Taiwan, China* 183 R9
Changji, *China* 180 E7
Chang Jiang (Yangtze), river, *China* 181 J13
Changjiang (Shiliu), *China* 183 U1
Changjin Reservoir, *N. Korea* 182 C13
Changle, *China* 183 P8
Changli, *China* 182 D8
Changling, *China* 181 E16
Changmar, *China* 180 J4
Changning, *China* 183 P4
Changping, *China* 182 D7
Changsha, *China* 182 M4
Changshan, *China* 182 M8
Changshu, *China* 182 K9
Changting, *China* 183 P6
Changyŏn, *N. Korea* 182 E12
Changzhou, *China* 182 K9
Chanion, Kólpos, *Gr.* 154 P12
Channapatna, *India* 179 Q5
Channel Country, *Austral.* 210 G11
Channel Islands, *Calif., U.S.* 109 Y7
Channel Islands, *U.K.* 143 Z11
Channel Islands National Park, *Calif., U.S.* 109 X6
Channel-Port aux Basques, *Nfld. & Lab., Can.* 83 N23
Channel Rock, *Bahamas* 116 G12
Chanthaburi, *Thai.* 187 N10
Chantilly, *Fr.* 147 P10
Chantrey Inlet, *Nunavut, Can.* 83 G14
Chanute, *Kans., U.S.* 105 U9
Chão, Ilhéu, *Madeira* 204 N4
Chao Hu, *China* 182 K7
Chao Phraya, river, *Thai.* 186 L8
Chaoyang, *China* 182 B9
Chaoyang, *China* 183 R6
Chaozhou, *China* 183 R6
Chapadinha, *Braz.* 131 E15
Chapaev, *Kaz.* 174 D6
Chapak Gozar, *Afghan.* 176 K4
Chapala, Lago de, *Mex.* 114 H10
Chapala, Lake *see* Chapala, Lago de, *N. Amer.* 80 N4
Chapcha, *Bhutan* 178 F12
Chapecó, *Braz.* 130 N11
Chapel Hill, *N.C., U.S.* 96 H11
Chapelton, *Jam.* 120 J8
Chapleau, *Ont., Can.* 83 P17
Chapman, *Ala., U.S.* 101 M15
Chapman, *Kans., U.S.* 105 S8
Chappaquiddick Island, *Mass., U.S.* 95 M15
Chappell, *Nebr., U.S.* 105 P2
Char, *India* 177 N14
Chara, river, *Russ.* 159 J17
Chara, *Russ.* 159 J17
Charadai, *Arg.* 132 G12
Charagua, *Bol.* 130 K8
Charambirá, Punta, *Col.* 128 F3
Charcot Island, *Antarctica* 226 G5
Chard, *Eng., U.K.* 143 W11
Chardonnières, *Haiti* 117 M14
Charduar, *India* 178 F14
Chari, river, *Chad* 194 H6
Charikar, *Afghan.* 176 M8
Chariton, *Iowa, U.S.* 105 Q12
Chariton, river, *Mo., U.S.* 105 Q12
Charity, *Guyana* 129 D14
Chärjew *see* Türkmenabat, *Turkm.* 174 L10
Charleroi, *Belg.* 146 M12
Charles *see* Santa María, Isla, island, *Ecua.* 128 R9
Charles, Cape, *Va., U.S.* 96 F14
Charles City, *Iowa, U.S.* 104 M12
Charles Darwin Research Station, *Ecua.* 128 Q9
Charles Island, *Nunavut, Can.* 83 H18
Charles Mound, *Ill., U.S.* 98 M4
Charles Point, *Austral.* 210 B7
Charleston, *Ill., U.S.* 99 S7
Charleston, *Miss., U.S.* 100 H11
Charleston, *Mo., U.S.* 105 V16
Charleston, *N.Z.* 213 N17

Charleston, *Oreg., U.S.* 108 J1
Charleston, *S.C., U.S.* 96 M10
Charleston, *W. Va., U.S.* 96 D8
Charlestown, *Ind., U.S.* 99 T10
Charlestown, *St. Kitts & Nevis* 121 C18
Charleville *see* Ráth Luirc, *Ire.* 143 U4
Charleville, *Qnsld., Austral.* 211 U13
Charleville-Mézières, *Fr.* 147 N12
Charlevoix, *Mich., U.S.* 98 H10
Charlie-Gibbs Fracture Zone, *Atl. Oc.* 236 F8
Charlieu, *Fr.* 147 T12
Charlotte, *Mich., U.S.* 98 M10
Charlotte, *N.C., U.S.* 96 J9
Charlotte, *Tex., U.S.* 103 S9
Charlotte Amalie, *Virgin Islands, U.S.* 120 M9
Charlotte Harbor, *Fla., U.S.* 97 V8
Charlottenberg, *Sw.* 140 K12
Charlottesville, *Va., U.S.* 96 E11
Charlotte Town *see* Gouyave, *Grenada* 121 K22
Charlottetown, *P.E.I., Can.* 83 N22
Charlotteville, *Trinidad & Tobago* 121 N18
Charlton Island, *Nunavut, Can.* 83 M18
Charolles, *Fr.* 147 T12
Charsadda, *Pak.* 176 M10
Chartres, *Fr.* 147 Q9
Chascomús, *Arg.* 132 M13
Chase, *Kans., U.S.* 105 T6
Chase City, *Va., U.S.* 96 F12
Chaska, *Minn., U.S.* 104 K11
Chassahowitzka, *Fla., U.S.* 97 T7
Chasseloup, Baie, *New Caledonia, Fr.* 218 C7
Chateaubelair, *St. Vincent & the Grenadines* 121 K16
Chateaubriand, Baie du, *New Caledonia, Fr.* 218 C9
Châteaubriant, *Fr.* 147 R6
Châteaudun, *Fr.* 147 Q9
Château-Gontier, *Fr.* 147 R6
Château-la-Vallière, *Fr.* 147 R8
Châteaulin, *Fr.* 147 Q3
Châteauneuf-de-Randon, *Fr.* 147 W11
Châteauneuf-en-Thymerais, *Fr.* 147 P9
Châteauneuf-sur-Loire, *Fr.* 147 R10
Château-Renault, *Fr.* 147 R8
Châteauroux, *Fr.* 147 S9
Château-Thierry, *Fr.* 147 P11
Châteauvillain, *Fr.* 147 Q12
Châteaux, Pointe des, *Guadeloupe, Fr.* 121 F16
Châtel, *Fr.* 147 T15
Châtelet, *Belg.* 146 M12
Châtellerault, *Fr.* 147 S8
Chatfield, *Minn., U.S.* 104 L12
Chatham *see* San Cristóbal, Isla, island, *Ecua.* 128 Q9
Chatham, *Eng., U.K.* 143 V15
Chatham, *Ill., U.S.* 99 R5
Chatham, *Mass., U.S.* 95 L16
Chatham, *N.B., Can.* 83 N21
Chatham, *N.Y., U.S.* 94 K11
Chatham, *Va., U.S.* 96 F11
Chatham Island, *N.Z.* 214 P9
Chatham Islands, *N.Z.* 214 P9
Chatham Rise, *Pac. Oc.* 238 Q9
Chatham Strait, *Alas., U.S.* 111 L22
Châtillon, *Fr.* 147 R12
Châtillon-sur-Indre, *Fr.* 147 S8
Chatom, *Ala., U.S.* 101 M13
Chatra, *India* 178 H10
Chatsworth, *Ga., U.S.* 96 J4
Chatsworth, *Qnsld., Austral.* 211 T11
Chattahoochee, river, *Ala., Ga., U.S.* 97 P4
Chattahoochee, *Fla., U.S.* 97 Q4
Chattanooga, *Tenn., U.S.* 101 G17
Chatyr-Tash, *Kyrg.* 176 F13
Chau Doc, *Vietnam* 187 P11
Chauk, *Myanmar* 186 H5
Chaukan Pass, *India, Myanmar* 178 F16
Chaumont, *Fr.* 147 Q13
Chaun Bay, *Arctic Oc.* 242 G3
Chaunskaya Guba, *Russ.* 159 C19
Chauny, *Fr.* 147 N11
Chavé, Baie, *Fr. Polynesia, Fr.* 219 N23
Chaves *see* Santa Cruz, Isla, island, *Ecua.* 128 Q9
Chaves, *Port.* 144 D7
Chaves, *Braz.* 131 C13
Chayek, *Kyrg.* 176 E11

Cheaha Mountain, *Ala., U.S.* **101** J16
Cheb, *Czech Rep.* **148** H9
Cheboksarskoye Vodokhranilishche, *Russ.* **156** H13
Cheboksary, *Russ.* **156** H14
Cheboygan, *Mich., U.S.* **98** G11
Chebsara, *Russ.* **156** F10
Chech, Erg, *Alg., Mali* **196** E9
Chechaktu, *Afghan.* **176** L4
Chechen', Ostrov, *Russ.* **157** T15
Chechnya, region, *Russ.* **157** T14
Checotah, *Okla., U.S.* **102** G13
Cheduba Island, *Myanmar* **186** J4
Cheektowaga, *N.Y., U.S.* **94** J5
Cheepie, *Qnsld., Austral.* **211** V12
Cheeyou, *Trinidad & Tobago* **121** P23
Chehalis, *Wash., U.S.* **108** D3
Chehar Borjak, *Afghan.* **177** R2
Cheju see Jeju, *S. Korea* **182** J13
Chekichler, *Turkm.* **174** M6
Chelan, *Wash., U.S.* **108** B6
Chelan, Lake, *Wash., U.S.* **108** B6
Chelforó, *Arg.* **133** P9
Chełm, *Pol.* **149** F18
Chełmno, *Pol.* **149** C14
Chelmsford, *Eng., U.K.* **143** V15
Chelsea, *Okla., U.S.* **102** E13
Cheltenham, *Eng., U.K.* **143** U12
Chelyabinsk, *Russ.* **158** J8
Chelyuskin, *Russ.* **159** D14
Chemillé, *Fr.* **147** S6
Chemin Grenier, *Mauritius* **205** H19
Chemnitz, *Ger.* **148** G10
Chemult, *Oreg., U.S.* **108** J4
Chemung, river, *N.Y., U.S.* **94** L7
Chenāb, river, *India, Pak.* **177** R10
Chenārān, *Iran* **173** B16
Cheney, *Wash., U.S.* **108** C9
Cheney Reservoir, *Kans., U.S.* **105** U7
Chengalpattu, *India* **179** Q7
Chengbu, *China* **183** P2
Chengde, *China* **182** C8
Chengdu, *China* **180** L11
Chengele, *India* **178** E15
Chenggu, *China* **182** H1
Chenghai, *China* **183** R7
Chengkou, *China* **182** J1
Chengkung, *Taiwan, China* **183** R10
Chenglingji, *China* **182** M4
Chengshan Jiao, cape, *China* **182** F10
Chennai (Madras), *India* **179** P7
Chenxi, *China* **182** M2
Chenzhou, *China* **183** P4
Cheom Ksan, *Cambodia* **186** M11
Cheonan, *S. Korea* **182** F13
Cheongju, *S. Korea* **182** F13
Cheorwon, *S. Korea* **182** E13
Chepén, *Peru* **130** F2
Chépénéhe, *New Caledonia, Fr.* **218** C9
Chepes, *Arg.* **132** J9
Chequamegon Bay, *Wis., U.S.* **98** F4
Cheraw, *S.C., U.S.* **96** J10
Cherbourg-Octeville, *Fr.* **147** N6
Cherepovets, *Russ.* **156** F9
Chergui, Chott ech, *Alg.* **196** B10
Cherkasy, *Ukr.* **157** P6
Cherkessk, *Russ.* **157** T12
Cherlak, *Russ.* **158** K10
Chermenino, *Russ.* **156** F12
Chernaya, *Russ.* **158** E10
Chernihiv, *Ukr.* **156** M6
Chernivtsi, *Ukr.* **157** Q3
Chernobyl' see Chornobyl', *Ukr.* **156** M6
Chernogorsk, *Russ.* **159** L13
Chernyakhovsk, *Russ.* **156** J2
Chernyayevo, *Russ.* **159** K19
Chernyshevskiy, *Russ.* **159** H16
Cherokee, *Iowa, U.S.* **104** M9
Cherokee, *Okla., U.S.* **102** E9
Cherokees, Lake O' The, *Okla., U.S.* **102** E14
Cherokee Sound, *Bahamas* **120** B6
Cherrabun, *W. Aust., Austral.* **211** R5
Cherryfield, *Me., U.S.* **95** F18
Cherry Island see Anuta, *Solomon Is.* **214** J7
Cherskiy, *Russ.* **159** D19
Cherskiy Range, *Russ.* **166** C11
Cherskogo, Khrebet, *Russ.* **159** F18
Cherven Bryag, *Bulg.* **153** H13
Chervonohrad, *Ukr.* **157** N2
Cherykaw, *Belarus* **156** L6
Chesaning, *Mich., U.S.* **98** L11
Chesapeake, *Va., U.S.* **96** F14

Chesapeake Bay, *Md., Va., U.S.* **96** D14
Chesha Bay, *Arctic Oc.* **243** A17
Chesha Bay, *Russ.* **138** A11
Cheshskaya Guba, *Russ.* **158** E9
Cheshunt, *Eng., U.K.* **143** V14
Chesht-e Sharif, *Afghan.* **176** M3
Chester, *Calif., U.S.* **109** N5
Chester, *Eng., U.K.* **143** S11
Chester, *Ill., U.S.* **99** U4
Chester, *Mont., U.S.* **106** B8
Chester, *Pa., U.S.* **94** Q9
Chester, *S.C., U.S.* **96** J9
Chester, *W. Va., U.S.* **96** A9
Chesterfield, *Eng., U.K.* **143** S12
Chesterfield, Îles, *New Caledonia, Fr.* **214** K6
Chesterfield Inlet, *Nunavut, Can.* **83** H15
Chesterfield Inlet, *Nunavut, Can.* **83** H15
Chestertown, *Md., U.S.* **96** C14
Chesuncook Lake, *Me., U.S.* **95** C16
Chetamale, *India* **179** R14
Chetek, *Wis., U.S.* **98** H3
Chetlat Island, *India* **179** Q3
Chetumal, *Mex.* **115** J16
Chetumal Bay, *N. Amer.* **80** P7
Chetvertyy Kuril'skiy Proliv, *Russ.* **159** G23
Chevak, *Alas., U.S.* **110** H11
Chevanceaux, *Fr.* **147** V7
Chevelon Butte, *Ariz., U.S.* **107** S8
Cheviot Hills, *Scot., U.K.* **143** N11
Ch'ew Bahir, lake, *Eth., Kenya* **199** H14
Chewelah, *Wash., U.S.* **108** B8
Cheyenne, *Okla., U.S.* **102** G8
Cheyenne, river, *S. Dak., U.S.* **104** K3
Cheyenne, *Wyo., U.S.* **106** K13
Cheyenne Bottoms, *Kans., U.S.* **105** T6
Cheyenne Wells, *Colo., U.S.* **107** N16
Chhapra, *India* **178** G10
Chhatarpur, *India* **178** H7
Chhep, *Cambodia* **186** M12
Chhim, *Leb.* **170** J6
Chhindwara, *India* **178** J6
Chhukha, *Bhutan* **178** F12
Chhung Kompong Saom, bay, *Cambodia* **187** P10
Chi, river, *Thai.* **186** L11
Chiang Mai, *Thai.* **186** J8
Chiang Rai, *Thai.* **186** H8
Chiaromonte, *It.* **151** N13
Chiasso, *Switz.* **150** D4
Chiat'ura, *Rep. of Georgia* **169** B17
Chiavari, *It.* **150** F4
Chiavenna, *It.* **150** C5
Chiayi, *Taiwan, China* **183** R9
Chiba, *Japan* **185** P12
Chibemba, *Angola* **202** E6
Chibia, *Angola* **202** E5
Chibougamau, *Que., Can.* **83** N19
Chiburi Shima, *Japan* **185** P6
Chicago, *Ill., U.S.* **99** N7
Chicago Heights, *Ill., U.S.* **99** P7
Chicapa, river, *Angola* **202** C8
Chichagof Island, *Alas., U.S.* **111** L22
Chichawatni, *Pak.* **177** R10
Chichén Itzá, ruin, *Mex.* **115** H16
Chichester, *Eng., U.K.* **143** W13
Chichester Range, *Austral.* **210** F3
Chichibu, *Japan* **185** P12
Chichi Jima Rettō, *Japan* **184** K5
Chickamauga, *Ga., U.S.* **96** J4
Chickamauga Lake, *Tenn., U.S.* **101** F17
Chickasaw National Recreation Area, *Okla., U.S.* **102** H11
Chickasha, *Okla., U.S.* **102** H10
Chicken Rock, *Isle of Man, U.K.* **143** R8
Chiclayo, *Peru* **130** F2
Chico, river, *Arg.* **133** S9
Chico, river, *Arg.* **133** W8
Chico, *Calif., U.S.* **109** P4
Chico, river, *Chile* **133** W8
Chicoma Mountain, *N. Mex., U.S.* **107** R12
Chicomo, *Mozambique* **202** J12
Chicopee, *Mass., U.S.* **95** K13
Chicoutimi, *Que., Can.* **83** N20
Chief Joseph Dam, *Wash., U.S.* **108** B6
Chiefland, *Fla., U.S.* **97** S7
Chieri, *It.* **150** E3
Chiesanuova, *San Marino* **161** L14
Chieti, *It.* **150** K10
Chifeng (Ulanhad), *China* **182** B8
Chignik Lagoon, *Alas., U.S.* **111** M13
Chihuahua, *Mex.* **114** D9
Chihuahuan Desert, *Mex.* **114** D9

Chikan, *Russ.* **159** K15
Chikhachevo, *Russ.* **156** H6
Chikhli, *India* **178** K5
Chilas, *Pak.* **176** L11
Chilaw, *Sri Lanka* **179** T7
Chilca, *Peru* **130** H3
Childers, *Qnsld., Austral.* **211** U15
Childersburg, *Ala., U.S.* **101** K16
Childress, *Tex., U.S.* **102** J7
Chile, *S. Amer.* **127** P16
Chile Basin, *Pac. Oc.* **239** M20
Chilecito, *Arg.* **132** H8
Chile Rise, *Pac. Oc.* **239** P19
Chililabombwe, *Zambia* **202** D10
Chilka Lake, *India* **178** L10
Chillán, *Chile* **132** M6
Chillicothe, *Ill., U.S.* **99** P5
Chillicothe, *Mo., U.S.* **105** R11
Chillicothe, *Ohio, U.S.* **99** S13
Chillicothe, *Tex., U.S.* **102** J8
Chiloé, Isla Grande de, *Chile* **133** R6
Chiloquin, *Oreg., U.S.* **108** K4
Chilpancingo, *Mex.* **114** K11
Chiltern Hills, *Eng., U.K.* **143** V13
Chilton, *Wis., U.S.* **98** K7
Chilumba, *Malawi* **203** C13
Chilwa, Lake, *Malawi, Mozambique* **194** M10
Chimacum, *Wash., U.S.* **108** B3
Chimborazo, peak, *Ecua.* **128** K3
Chimbote, *Peru* **130** G2
Chimboy, *Uzb.* **174** J9
Chimney Rock National Historic Site, *Nebr., U.S.* **105** P1
Chimoio, *Mozambique* **202** G12
China, *Asia* **167** U9
China Point, *Calif., U.S.* **109** Z8
Chinandega, *Nicar.* **115** M17
China, river, *S. Amer.* **126** G2
Chincha Alta, *Peru* **130** H3
Chincha Islands, *S. Amer.* **126** G2
Chinchilla, *Qnsld., Austral.* **211** V14
Chinchilla de Monte Aragón, *Sp.* **145** J13
Chincoteague, *Va., U.S.* **96** E15
Chincoteague Bay, *Md., U.S.* **96** D15
Chinde, *Mozambique* **203** F13
Chindwin, river, *Myanmar* **186** E5
Chingola, *Zambia* **202** D10
Chinguetti, *Mauritania* **196** F6
Chin Hills, *Myanmar* **186** G5
Chinhoyi, *Zimb.* **202** F11
Chiniot, *Pak.* **177** Q11
Chinle, *Ariz., U.S.* **107** R9
Chino, *Japan* **185** P11
Chinon, *Fr.* **147** S7
Chinook, *Mont., U.S.* **106** B9
Chinook Trough, *Pac. Oc.* **238** E10
Chino Valley, *Ariz., U.S.* **107** S6
Chinsali, *Zambia* **202** C12
Chinta, *S. Aust., Austral.* **211** W8
Chioggia, *It.* **150** E8
Chios see Híos, island, *Gr.* **155** H16
Chios see Híos, *Gr.* **155** H16
Chipata, *Zambia* **202** E12
Chipley, *Fla., U.S.* **97** Q3
Chiplun, *India* **178** M3
Chippenham, *Eng., U.K.* **143** V11
Chippewa, river, *Wis., U.S.* **98** G3
Chippewa, Lake, *Wis., U.S.* **98** G3
Chippewa Falls, *Wis., U.S.* **98** H3
Chiquián, *Peru* **130** G3
Chiquimula, *Guatemala* **115** L16
Chiquinquirá, *Col.* **128** E5
Chirchiq, *Uzb.* **175** K13
Chiredzi, *Zimb.* **202** G12
Chiricahua National Monument, *Ariz., U.S.* **107** V9
Chiricahua Peak, *Ariz., U.S.* **107** V9
Chirikof Island, *Alas., U.S.* **111** N14
Chirinda, *Russ.* **159** G14
Chiriquí, Golfo de, *Pan.* **115** P20
Chiromo, *Malawi* **203** F13
Chirpan, *Bulg.* **153** J15
Chirripó, Cerro, *Costa Rica* **115** N19
Chisamba, *Que., Can.* **83** M18
Chishan, *Taiwan, China* **183** S9
Chisholm, *Minn., U.S.* **104** F12
Chishtian Mandi, *Pak.* **177** R11
Chisimayu see Kismaayo, *Somalia* **199** K16
Chişinău, *Mold.* **157** R4
Chişineu Criş, *Rom.* **152** C11
Chisos Mountains, *Tex., U.S.* **103** R3

Chissioua Mtsamboro, island, *Mayotte, Fr.* **205** N17
Chistopol', *Russ.* **156** J15
Chita, *Russ.* **159** L17
Chitado, *Angola* **202** F6
Chitato, *Angola* **202** B8
Chitembo, *Angola* **202** E7
Chitipa, *Malawi* **202** C12
Chitose, *Japan* **184** G13
Chitradurga, *India* **179** P5
Chitral, *Pak.* **176** L10
Chitré, *Pan.* **115** P21
Chittagong, *Bangladesh* **178** J13
Chittaurgarh, *India* **178** H4
Chittoor, *India* **179** P6
Chitungwiza, *Zimb.* **202** F11
Chiumbe, river, *Angola* **202** C8
Chivasso, *It.* **150** E3
Chivilcoy, *Arg.* **132** L12
Chizu, *Japan* **185** P7
Chlef, *Alg.* **196** A10
Chloride, *Ariz., U.S.* **107** R5
Chobe, river, *Namibia, Zimb.* **194** N8
Chocolate Mountains, *Calif., U.S.* **109** Y12
Choc Bay, *St. Lucia* **121** J14
Choctawhatchee, river, *Fla., U.S.* **97** Q3
Choctawhatchee Bay, *Fla., U.S.* **97** Q2
Chodzież, *Pol.* **149** D13
Choele Choel, *Arg.* **133** P9
Choirokoitia, *Cyprus* **160** Q8
Choiseul, island, *Solomon Is.* **217** K15
Choiseul, *St. Lucia* **121** L13
Choiseul Sound, *Falkland Is., U.K.* **133** W12
Chojna, *Pol.* **148** D11
Chojnice, *Pol.* **149** C13
Choke Canyon Reservoir, *Tex., U.S.* **103** T10
Chokoloskee, *Fla., U.S.* **97** X9
Chokurdakh, *Russ.* **159** D18
Chola Shan, *China* **180** K10
Cholet, *Fr.* **147** S6
Cholpon-Ata, *Kyrg.* **176** D13
Choluteca, *Hond.* **115** L17
Choma, *Zambia* **202** F10
Chomutov, *Czech Rep.* **148** G10
Chon Buri, *Thai.* **187** N9
Chonchi, *Chile* **133** R6
Chone, *Ecua.* **128** J2
Chong'an, *China* **183** N7
Ch'ŏngjin, *N. Korea* **182** B14
Chong Kal, *Cambodia* **186** M10
Chongming, *China* **182** K10
Chongming Dao, *China* **182** K10
Chongqing, *China* **180** L12
Chongxin, *China* **182** G1
Chongyi, *China* **183** P5
Chonogol, *Mongolia* **181** D14
Chonos, Archipiélago de los, *Chile* **133** S6
Chornobyl' (Chernobyl'), *Ukr.* **156** M6
Chornomors'ke, *Ukr.* **157** S7
Chorregon, *Qnsld., Austral.* **211** T12
Chorrillos, *Peru* **130** H3
Chortkiv, *Ukr.* **157** P3
Ch'osan, *N. Korea* **182** C12
Chōshi, *Japan* **185** P13
Chos Malal, *Arg.* **133** N7
Chota Nagpur Plateau, *India* **166** J8
Choteau, *Mont., U.S.* **106** C7
Chotila, *India* **178** J2
Chowan, river, *N.C., U.S.* **96** G14
Chowchilla, *Calif., U.S.* **109** T6
Choybalsan, *Mongolia* **181** D14
Choyr, *Mongolia* **181** D13
Christ Church, *Barbados* **121** L19
Christchurch, *Eng., U.K.* **143** X12
Christchurch, *N.Z.* **213** P17
Christian, Point, *Pitcairn I., U.K.* **219** Q23
Christiana, *Jam.* **120** J8
Christiansburg, *Va., U.S.* **96** F9
Christiansted, *Virgin Islands, U.S.* **120** Q3
Christmas Creek, *W. Aust., Austral.* **211** R5
Christmas Island, *Austral.* **188** N8
Christmas Island see Kiritimati, *Kiribati* **214** G12
Christmas Lake Valley, *Oreg., U.S.* **108** J6
Christopher, *Ill., U.S.* **99** U5
Christoval, *Tex., U.S.* **103** N7
Chubb Crater see Nouveau-Québec, Cratère du, *Que., Can.* **83** J18
Chub Cay, *Bahamas* **116** D11

Chubut, river, *Arg.* **133** R8
Chudleigh Park, *Qnsld., Austral.* **211** S12
Chudovo, *Russ.* **156** F7
Chudskoye Ozero see Peipus, Lake, *Est., Russ.* **141** K17
Chugach Mountains, *Alas., U.S.* **111** J18
Chuginadak Island, *Alas., U.S.* **110** P8
Chugwater, *Wyo., U.S.* **106** J13
Chuhuyiv, *Ukr.* **157** P9
Chuí, *Braz.* **130** R11
Chukai, *Malaysia* **187** T10
Chukchi Peninsula, *Russ.* **166** A12
Chukchi Plain, *Arctic Oc.* **242** J6
Chukchi Plateau, *Arctic Oc.* **242** J6
Chukchi Range, *Russ.* **166** A12
Chukchi Sea, *Arctic Oc.* **242** J3
Chukhloma, *Russ.* **156** G11
Chukotskiy Poluostrov, *Russ.* **159** A21
Chukotskoye Nagor'ye, *Russ.* **159** B20
Chula Vista, *Calif., U.S.* **109** Z10
Chumar, *India* **177** N15
Chumbicha, *Arg.* **132** H9
Chumikan, *Russ.* **159** J20
Chumphon, *Thai.* **187** P8
Chun'an, *China* **182** M8
Chuncheon, *S. Korea* **182** E13
Chungli, *Taiwan, China* **183** Q10
Chunhua, *China* **182** G2
Chunnel, tunnel, *Eng., U.K., Fr.* **143** W16
Chunya, *Tanzania* **199** M13
Chupara Point, *Trinidad & Tobago* **121** N22
Chuquibamba, *Peru* **130** J5
Chuquicamata, *Chile* **132** D7
Chur, *Switz.* **150** B5
Churachandpur, *India* **178** H14
Churchill, river, *Man., Can.* **83** K14
Churchill, *Man., Can.* **83** K15
Churchill, river, *Nfld. & Lab., Can.* **83** L21
Churchill, river, *Sask., Can.* **83** L13
Churchill, Cape, *Man., Can.* **83** K15
Churchill Falls, *Nfld. & Lab., Can.* **83** L21
Churchill Lake, *Me., U.S.* **95** C16
Churchill Lake, *Sask., Can.* **82** L12
Churchill Mountains, *Antarctica* **227** L13
Church of St. Anne, *Vatican City* **161** P17
Church of St. Stephen, *Vatican City* **161** Q15
Church Point, *La., U.S.* **100** P8
Churuguara, *Venez.* **128** B8
Chushul, *India* **177** N15
Chuska Mountains, *Ariz., N. Mex., U.S.* **107** R10
Chusovoy, *Russ.* **158** H9
Chuuk (Truk Islands), *F.S.M.* **216** Q6
Chuuk Lagoon (Truk Lagoon), *F.S.M.* **217** B15
Chuxiong, *China* **180** N11
Ciales, *P.R., U.S.* **120** M3
Cianjur, *Indonesia* **188** M8
Çiçekdağı, *Turk.* **168** E9
Cicero, *Ill., U.S.* **99** N7
Cicia, island, *Fiji Is.* **218** H9
Cidade Velha, *Cape Verde* **205** E16
Cide, *Turk.* **168** C8
Ciechanów, *Pol.* **149** D16
Ciego de Ávila, *Cuba* **116** H10
Ciempozuelos, *Sp.* **144** G11
Ciénaga, *Col.* **128** B5
Cienfuegos, *Cuba* **116** H8
Cieszyn, *Pol.* **149** H14
Cieza, *Sp.* **145** K13
Çiftlik, *Turk.* **168** G9
Cihanbeyli, *Turk.* **168** F8
Cijara, Embalse de, *Sp.* **144** H9
Çikës, Maja e, *Albania* **152** M9
Cikobia, island, *Fiji Is.* **218** F8
Cilacap, *Indonesia* **188** M9
Cilaos, *Reunion, Fr.* **205** G16
Çıldır, *Turk.* **169** D17
Çıldır Gölü, *Turk.* **169** D17
Cilician Gates, *Turk.* **168** H10
Cimarron, *Kans., U.S.* **105** U4
Cimarron, river, *Kans., Okla., U.S.* **84** J12
Cimarron, *N. Mex., U.S.* **107** Q13
Cimolais, *It.* **150** C8
Cimone, Monte, *It.* **150** G6
Cîmpina, *Rom.* **153** E15
Cîmpulung, *Rom.* **153** E14
Çınar, *Turk.* **169** H15
Cinaruco, river, *Venez.* **128** D9
Cincinnati, *Ohio, U.S.* **99** S11
Cinco Balas, Cayos, *Cuba* **116** H9
Cîndrelu, peak, *Rom.* **153** E13
Çine, *Turk.* **168** G3

Cinéma d'Eté, *Monaco* 161 B23
Cinnabar Mountain, *Idaho, U.S.* 106 H3
Cintegabelle, *Fr.* 147 Y9
Cinto, Monte, *Fr.* 150 J4
Cioara Doiceşti, *Rom.* 153 F17
Čiovo, island, *Croatia* 152 G6
Çırçır, *Turk.* 168 E12
Circle, *Alas., U.S.* III F18
Circle, *Mont., U.S.* 106 C12
Circleville, *Ohio, U.S.* 99 R13
Cirebon, *Indonesia* 188 M9
Cirencester, *Eng., U.K.* 143 V12
Ciscaucasia, region, *Russ.* 138 G12
Cisco, *Tex., U.S.* 102 M9
Cisco, *Utah, U.S.* 107 N9
Cisnădie, *Rom.* 153 D13
Cisneros, *Col.* 128 E5
Cistern Point, *Bahamas* 116 F11
Citronelle, *Ala., U.S.* 101 N13
Cittadella, *It.* 150 D7
Città di Castello, *It.* 150 H8
Cittanova, *It.* 151 R13
City of Refuge National Historic Park
  see Pu'uhonua o Hōnaunau National
  Historic Park, *Hawai'i, U.S.* 113 N18
City of Rocks National Reserve, *Idaho,*
  U.S. 106 J5
Ciucea, *Rom.* 152 C12
Ciudad Acuña, *Mex.* 114 D11
Ciudad Altamirano, *Mex.* 114 J11
Ciudad Bolívar, *Venez.* 128 C11
Ciudad Camargo, *Mex.* 114 E9
Ciudad Cortés, *Costa Rica* 115 N19
Ciudad del Carmen, *Mex.* 115 J15
Ciudad del Este, *Parag.* 130 N11
Ciudad Guayana, *Venez.* 128 C12
Ciudad Guerrero, *Mex.* 114 D8
Ciudad Guzmán, *Mex.* 114 H10
Ciudad Hidalgo, *Mex.* 115 L15
Ciudad Juárez, *Mex.* 114 C9
Ciudad Madero, *Mex.* 114 G12
Ciudad Mante, *Mex.* 114 G12
Ciudad Obregón, *Mex.* 114 D7
Ciudad Piar, *Venez.* 128 D12
Ciudad Real, *Sp.* 144 H10
Ciudad-Rodrigo, *Sp.* 144 F7
Ciudad Sandino, *Cuba* 116 H4
Ciudad Valles, *Mex.* 114 G12
Ciudad Victoria, *Mex.* 114 G12
Ciutadella de Menorca, *Sp.* 145 G19
Civa Burnu, *Turk.* 168 C11
Civita Castellana, *It.* 150 K8
Civitanova Marche, *It.* 150 H10
Civitavecchia, *It.* 150 K7
Civray, *Fr.* 147 T7
Çivril, *Turk.* 168 G5
Cixian, *China* 182 F5
Cizre, *Turk.* 169 H16
Clacton on Sea, *Eng., U.K.* 143 U15
Clair Engle Lake, *Calif., U.S.* 108 M3
Clairton, *Pa., U.S.* 94 P3
Clairview, *Qnsld., Austral.* 211 T14
Clam Lake, *Wis., U.S.* 98 F4
Clanton, *Ala., U.S.* 101 K15
Clare, *Mich., U.S.* 98 K10
Clare Island, *Ire.* 143 R3
Claremont, *Jam.* 120 H4
Claremont, *N.H., U.S.* 95 H13
Claremore, *Okla., U.S.* 102 F13
Claremorris, *Ire.* 143 R4
Clarence, river, *N.Z.* 213 N18
Clarence Island, *Antarctica* 226 B3
Clarence Strait, *Austral.* 210 A7
Clarence Town, *Bahamas* 117 G14
Clarendon, *Ark., U.S.* 100 G10
Clarendon, *Tex., U.S.* 102 H6
Clarie Coast, *Antarctica* 227 Q19
Clarinda, *Iowa, U.S.* 105 Q10
Clarión, Isla, *Mex.* 114 H4
Clarion, *Iowa, U.S.* 104 M11
Clarion, *Pa., U.S.* 94 M4
Clarion Fracture Zone, *Pac. Oc.* 239 H13
Clarión Island, *N. Amer.* 80 N2
Clark, *S. Dak., U.S.* 104 K7
Clark, Lake, *Alas., U.S.* III K15
Clarke Range, *Austral.* 210 E14
Clark Fork, *Idaho, U.S.* 106 B4
Clark Fork, *Mont., U.S.* 106 D6
Clark Mountain, *Calif., U.S.* 109 V11
Clarks, *La., U.S.* 100 L8
Clarksburg, *W. Va., U.S.* 96 C9
Clarksdale, *Miss., U.S.* 100 H10
Clarks Fork, *Wyo., U.S.* 106 F9
Clarkson, *Nebr., U.S.* 105 P8
Clarkston, *Wash., U.S.* 108 E9

Clarks Town, *Jam.* 120 H8
Clarksville, *Ark., U.S.* 100 F7
Clarksville, *Tenn., U.S.* 101 E14
Clarksville, *Tex., U.S.* 102 K14
Clatskanie, *Oreg., U.S.* 108 E3
Claude, *Tex., U.S.* 102 G6
Claxton, *Ga., U.S.* 97 N8
Claxton Bay, *Trinidad & Tobago* 121 P22
Clay, *Ky., U.S.* 101 C14
Clay Center, *Kans., U.S.* 105 S8
Clayton, *Ala., U.S.* 101 M17
Clayton, *Ga., U.S.* 96 J6
Clayton, *Idaho, U.S.* 106 F5
Clayton, *La., U.S.* 100 M9
Clayton, *N. Mex., U.S.* 107 Q15
Clayton, *N.Y., U.S.* 94 G8
Clayton, *Okla., U.S.* 102 H13
Clayton Lake, *Me., U.S.* 95 B16
Clearbrook, *Minn., U.S.* 104 F9
Clear Creek, *Tex., U.S.* 102 K12
Clear Island, *Ire.* 143 V3
Clear Lake, *Calif., U.S.* 109 Q3
Clear Lake, *Iowa, U.S.* 104 M11
Clear Lake, *S. Dak., U.S.* 104 K8
Clear Lake, *Wash., U.S.* 108 B4
Clear Lake, *Wis., U.S.* 98 H2
Clear Lake Reservoir, *Calif., U.S.* 108 L5
Clearmont, *Wyo., U.S.* 106 F12
Clearwater, river, *Alta., Sask., Can.*
  82 K11
Clearwater, *Fla., U.S.* 97 U7
Clearwater, river, *Idaho, U.S.* 106 D3
Clearwater, *Wash., U.S.* 108 C2
Clearwater Mountains, *Idaho, U.S.*
  106 D5
Cleburne, *Tex., U.S.* 102 M11
Cle Elum, *Wash., U.S.* 108 C5
Clelles, *Fr.* 147 V13
Clemson, *S.C., U.S.* 96 K7
Clendenin, *W. Va., U.S.* 96 D8
Cleopatra Needle, peak, *Philippines*
  189 E13
Clermont, *Fr.* 147 N10
Clermont, *Qnsld., Austral.* 211 T14
Clermont-Ferrand, *Fr.* 147 U11
Clervaux, *Lux.* 160 G9
Clervé, river, *Lux.* 160 H9
Cles, *It.* 150 C7
Cleveland, *Miss., U.S.* 100 J10
Cleveland, *Ohio, U.S.* 99 N14
Cleveland, *Okla., U.S.* 102 F12
Cleveland, *Tenn., U.S.* 101 G14
Cleveland, *Tex., U.S.* 103 Q14
Cleveland, *Wis., U.S.* 98 K7
Cleveland, Mount, *Mont., U.S.* 106 A6
Cleveland Hills, *Eng., U.K.* 143 Q12
Clew Bay, *Ire.* 143 R3
Clewiston, *Fla., U.S.* 97 V9
Clifden, *Ire.* 143 R3
Cliff, *N. Mex., U.S.* 107 U10
Clifton, *Ariz., U.S.* 107 U9
Clifton, *Kans., U.S.* 105 S8
Clifton, *Bahamas* 120 B10
Clifton, *Tex., U.S.* 103 N11
Clifton Forge, *Va., U.S.* 96 E10
Clifton Hills, *S. Aust., Austral.* 211 V10
Clinch, river, *Tenn., U.S.* 101 E19
Clingmans Dome, *N.C., Tenn., U.S.* 85 J17
Clint, *Tex., U.S.* 103 U2
Clinton, *Ark., U.S.* 100 F8
Clinton, *Ill., U.S.* 99 R6
Clinton, *Ind., U.S.* 99 R7
Clinton, *Iowa, U.S.* 105 N15
Clinton, *Ky., U.S.* 100 D12
Clinton, *Miss., U.S.* 100 L11
Clinton, *Mo., U.S.* 105 T11
Clinton, *N.C., U.S.* 96 J12
Clinton, *Okla., U.S.* 102 G9
Clinton, *S.C., U.S.* 96 K8
Clintonville, *Wis., U.S.* 98 J6
Clipperton, island, *Pac. Oc.* 215 F19
Clipperton Fracture Zone, *Pac. Oc.*
  239 J13
Cliza, *Bol.* 130 K7
Cloates, Point, *Austral.* 210 F1
Clonakilty Bay, *Ire.* 143 V4
Cloncurry, river, *Austral.* 210 D11
Cloncurry, *Qnsld., Austral.* 211 S11
Cloncurry Plateau, *Austral.* 210 E11
Clonmany, *Ire.* 143 N6
Clonmel, *Ire.* 143 U5
Cloppenburg, *Ger.* 148 D6
Cloquet, *Minn., U.S.* 104 G12

Cloud Peak, *Wyo., U.S.* 106 F11
Clover, *S.C., U.S.* 96 J8
Cloverdale, *Calif., U.S.* 109 Q3
Cloverport, *Ky., U.S.* 101 C15
Clovis, *Calif., U.S.* 109 T6
Clovis, *N. Mex., U.S.* 107 S15
Clun, *Eng., U.K.* 143 U10
Cluny, *Qnsld., Austral.* 211 U11
Cluses, *Fr.* 147 T14
Clusone, *It.* 150 D5
Clutha, river, *N.Z.* 213 R16
Clyde, *Kans., U.S.* 105 S7
Clyde, *Ohio, U.S.* 99 P13
Clyde, *Tex., U.S.* 102 M8
Clyde, Firth of, *Scot., U.K.* 143 N8
Clyde Inlet, *Nunavut, Can.* 83 E18
Clyde River, *Nunavut, Can.* 83 E18
Cnossus (Knossos), ruin, *Gr.* 155 Q15
Coachella, *Calif., U.S.* 109 X11
Coachella Canal, *Calif., U.S.* 109 Y12
Coahoma, *Tex., U.S.* 102 M6
Coakley Cay, *Bahamas* 120 F8
Coalcomán, *Mex.* 114 J10
Coal Creek, *N.Z.* 213 Q16
Coaldale, *Nev., U.S.* 109 R8
Coalgate, *Okla., U.S.* 102 H12
Coalinga, *Calif., U.S.* 109 U6
Coalville, *Eng., U.K.* 143 T12
Coamo, *P.R., U.S.* 120 N4
Coari, river, *Braz.* 130 E8
Coari, *Braz.* 130 E8
Coastal Plain, *U.S.* 85 N12
Coast Mountains, *Alas., U.S.* III L23
Coast Mountains, *B.C., Can.* 82 H7
Coast Range, *S. Amer.* 126 A4
Coast Ranges, *Calif., Oreg., U.S.* 84 C3
Coats Island, *Nunavut, Can.* 83 H16
Coats Land, *Antarctica* 226 E10
Coatzacoalcos, *Mex.* 115 J14
Cobalt, *Ont., Can.* 83 P18
Cobán, *Guatemala* 115 L16
Cobar, *N.S.W., Austral.* 211 W13
Cobia, island, *Fiji Is.* 218 G8
Cobija, *Bol.* 130 G6
Coborriu, *Sp.* 160 L5
Cobourg, *Ger.* 148 G8
Cobourg Peninsula, *Austral.* 210 A8
Cobre, *Nev., U.S.* 108 M12
Cóbuè, *Mozambique* 203 D13
Coburg, *Ger.* 148 G8
Coburg Island, *Nunavut, Can.* 83 D16
Coca, *Sp.* 144 E10
Cocanada *see* Kakinada, *India* 178 M8
Cochabamba, *Bol.* 130 K7
Coche, Isla, *Venez.* 119 P14
Cochin *see* Kochi, *India* 179 R5
Cochinoca, *Arg.* 132 D9
Cochinos, Bahía de (Bay of Pigs), *Cuba*
  116 H7
Cochran, *Ga., U.S.* 97 N6
Cochrane, *Ont., Can.* 83 N17
Cockburn, *S. Aust., Austral.* 211 X11
Cockburn Harbour, *Turks & Caicos Is.,*
  U.K. 117 J17
Cockburn Town, *Bahamas* 120 E11
Cockburn Town, *Turks & Caicos Is., U.K.*
  117 J18
Cocklebiddy Motel, *W. Aust., Austral.*
  211 X6
Cockroach Island, *Virgin Islands, U.S.*
  120 M7
Cockscomb Point, *Amer. Samoa, U.S.*
  218 L8
Coco, river, *Hond., Nicar.* 115 L19
Coco, Cayo, *Cuba* 116 H10
Coco, Isla del, *Costa Rica* 115 Q17
Cocoa, *Fla., U.S.* 97 T9
Cocoa Island, *Mauritius* 205 J19
Coco Channel, *India* 179 P14
Coco-de-Mer Seamounts, *Ind. Oc.*
  240 G6
Coconut Point, *Amer. Samoa, U.S.* 218 M7
Cocos Bay, *Trinidad & Tobago* 121 P23
Cocos Island, *Guam, U.S.* 216 J7
Cocos Island, *N. Amer.* 80 R7
Cocos (Keeling) Islands, *Austral., Ind. Oc.*
  241 H13
Cocos Lagoon, *Guam, U.S.* 216 E10
Cocos Ridge, *Pac. Oc.* 239 J19
Cod, Cape, *Mass., U.S.* 95 L16
Coda Cavallo, Capo, *It.* 150 M5
Codajás, *Braz.* 130 D8
Codigoro, *It.* 150 F8
Cod Island, *Nfld. & Lab., Can.* 83 J21
Codlea, *Rom.* 153 D15

Codó, *Braz.* 131 E15
Codogno, *It.* 150 E5
Codrington, *Antigua & Barbuda* 119 F16
Codrington, Mount, *Antarctica* 227 C19
Cody, *Nebr., U.S.* 104 M4
Cody, *Wyo., U.S.* 106 F9
Coeburn, *Va., U.S.* 96 F7
Coen, *Qnsld., Austral.* 211 P12
Coëtlogon, Passe du, *New Caledonia, Fr.*
  218 C8
Coeur d'Alene, *Idaho, U.S.* 106 C3
Coeur d'Alene Lake, *Idaho, U.S.* 106 C3
Coevorden, *Neth.* 146 H14
Coffeyville, *Kans., U.S.* 105 V9
Coffs Harbour, *N.S.W., Austral.* 211 W15
Cofrentes, *Sp.* 145 H14
Coghinas, Lago del, *It.* 150 M4
Cognac, *Fr.* 147 U7
Cogne, *It.* 150 D2
Cogollos, *Sp.* 144 D11
Cohagen, *Mont., U.S.* 106 C11
Cohoes, *N.Y., U.S.* 94 J11
Coiba, Isla de, *Pan.* 115 P20
Coiba Island, *N. Amer.* 80 R8
Coig, river, *Arg.* 133 V8
Coihaique, *Chile* 133 S7
Coimbatore, *India* 179 R5
Coimbra, *Port.* 144 F5
Coín, *Sp.* 144 M9
Coipasa, Salar de, *Bol.* 130 K6
Cojimíes, Boca de, *Ecua.* 128 J2
Cokato, *Minn., U.S.* 104 J10
Cokeville, *Wyo., U.S.* 106 J8
Colac, *Vic., Austral.* 211 Z12
Colatina, *Braz.* 131 L16
Colby, *Kans., U.S.* 105 S4
Colchester, *Eng., U.K.* 143 U15
Cold Bay, *Alas., U.S.* 110 N11
Cold Spring, *Minn., U.S.* 104 J10
Coldwater, *Kans., U.S.* 105 V5
Coldwater, *Mich., U.S.* 99 N10
Coldwater Creek, *Tex., U.S.* 102 E4
Colebrook, *N.H., U.S.* 95 F14
Coleman, *Mich., U.S.* 98 K11
Coleman, *Tex., U.S.* 102 M8
Coleraine, *Minn., U.S.* 104 F11
Coleraine, *N. Ire., U.K.* 143 P6
Colesberg, *S. Af.* 202 L9
Cole's Cave, *Barbados* 121 K19
Colfax, *Calif., U.S.* 109 Q5
Colfax, *Iowa, U.S.* 105 P12
Colfax, *La., U.S.* 100 M8
Colfax, *Wash., U.S.* 108 D9
Colhué Huapí, Lago, *Arg.* 133 S8
Colico, *It.* 150 C5
Colídor, *Braz.* 130 G11
Colihaut, *Dominica* 121 E18
Colima, *Mex.* 114 J9
Colinas, *Braz.* 131 E15
Colison Point, *Virgin Islands, U.K.* 120 R8
Coll, island, *Scot., U.K.* 142 L7
Colle, river, *It.* 161 L15
College, *Alas., U.S.* III G17
College Park, *Ga., U.S.* 96 L5
College Station, *Tex., U.S.* 103 P12
Collelongo, *It.* 150 K10
Collerina, *N.S.W., Austral.* 211 W13
Collie, *W. Aust., Austral.* 211 X2
Collier Bay, *Austral.* 210 C5
Collier Range, *Austral.* 210 G3
Colliers, *Cayman Is., U.K.* 120 J4
Colliers Point, *Cayman Is., U.K.* 116 L7
Collierville, *Tenn., U.S.* 100 G12
Collingwood, *N.Z.* 213 M17
Collins, *Miss., U.S.* 100 M12
Collins Head, *Norfolk I., Austral.*
  217 G20
Collinson Peninsula, *Nunavut, Can.*
  83 F14
Collinsville, *Ill., U.S.* 99 T4
Collinsville, *Okla., U.S.* 102 E13
Collinsville, *Qnsld., Austral.* 211 S14
Collinsville, *Va., U.S.* 96 G10
Collipulli, *Chile* 133 N6
Collonges, *Fr.* 147 T14
Colmar, *Fr.* 147 Q15
Cologne *see* Köln, *Ger.* 148 F5
Colombey-les-Belles, *Fr.* 147 P14
Colômbia, *Braz.* 131 L13
Colombia, *S. Amer.* 127 C15
Colombo, *Sri Lanka* 179 T7
Colón, *Cuba* 116 G8
Colón, *Pan.* 115 N21
Colonarie, river, *St. Vincent & the*
  Grenadines 121 K16

Colonarie, *St. Vincent & the Grenadines*
  121 K17
Colonel Bogado, *Parag.* 130 N10
Colonel Hill, *Bahamas* 117 G14
Colonel Oviedo, *Parag.* 130 M10
Colonet, Cabo, *Mex.* 114 B5
Colonia, *F.S.M.* 217 D18
Colonia Dora, *Arg.* 132 H10
Colonial Beach, *Va., U.S.* 96 D13
Colonial Heights, *Va., U.S.* 96 F13
Colonial National Historic Park, *Va., U.S.*
  96 F14
Colonna, Capo, *It.* 151 Q14
Colon Ridge, *Pac. Oc.* 239 J18
Colonsay, island, *Scot., U.K.* 142 M7
Colophon, ruin, *Turk.* 168 G3
Colorado, river, *Arg.* 133 P10
Colorado, river, *Tex., U.S.* 103 R12
Colorado, river, *U.S.* 84 K5
Colorado, *U.S.* 106 M11
Colorado City, *Ariz., U.S.* 107 Q6
Colorado City, *Tex., U.S.* 102 M6
Colorado National Monument, *Colo.,*
  U.S. 106 M10
Colorado Plateau, *Ariz., U.S.* 107 Q7
Colorado River Aqueduct, *Calif., U.S.*
  109 X12
Colorado Springs, *Colo., U.S.* 107 N13
Colotepec, *Mex.* 115 L13
Colquitt, *Ga., U.S.* 97 P4
Colstrip, *Mont., U.S.* 106 E11
Columbia, *Ky., U.S.* 101 D17
Columbia, *La., U.S.* 100 L8
Columbia, *Md., U.S.* 96 C13
Columbia, *Miss., U.S.* 100 N11
Columbia, *Mo., U.S.* 105 S13
Columbia, *N.C., U.S.* 96 G14
Columbia, *Pa., U.S.* 94 P8
Columbia, *S.C., U.S.* 96 K9
Columbia, *Tenn., U.S.* 101 F15
Columbia, river, *U.S.* 84 C4
Columbia, Cape, *Nunavut, Can.* 83 A16
Columbia, District of, *U.S.* 96 C13
Columbia, Mount, *Alta., B.C., Can.* 82 L9
Columbia City, *Ind., U.S.* 99 P10
Columbia Falls, *Mont., U.S.* 106 B5
Columbia Mountains, *B.C., Can.* 82 L9
Columbia Plateau, *U.S.* 84 C5
Columbia Seamount, *Atl. Oc.* 237 R9
Columbine, Cape, *S. Af.* 202 M7
Columbretes, Islas, *Sp.* 145 G16
Columbus, *Ga., U.S.* 97 N4
Columbus, *Ind., U.S.* 99 S9
Columbus, *Kans., U.S.* 105 V10
Columbus, *Miss., U.S.* 101 J13
Columbus, *Mont., U.S.* 106 E9
Columbus, *N. Dak., U.S.* 104 D3
Columbus, *N. Mex., U.S.* 107 W11
Columbus, *Nebr., U.S.* 105 P7
Columbus, *Ohio, U.S.* 99 R13
Columbus, *Tex., U.S.* 103 R12
Columbus, *Wis., U.S.* 98 L6
Columbus Monument, *Bahamas* 120 E12
Columbus Monument, *Bahamas* 120 F11
Columbus Point, *Trinidad & Tobago*
  121 P17
Colusa, *Calif., U.S.* 109 Q4
Colville, river, *Alas., U.S.* III C15
Colville, *N.Z.* 213 J19
Colville, *Wash., U.S.* 108 A8
Colville Channel, *N.Z.* 213 J19
Colville Lake, *N.W.T., Can.* 82 F10
Colwich, *Kans., U.S.* 105 U7
Comacchio, *It.* 150 F8
Comacchio, Valli di, *It.* 150 F8
Comallo, *Arg.* 133 Q7
Comanche, *Okla., U.S.* 102 J10
Comanche, *Tex., U.S.* 102 M9
Comandante Ferraz, station, *Antarctica*
  226 C3
Comandante Fontana, *Arg.* 132 F12
Comandante Luis Piedra Buena, *Arg.*
  133 V8
Comăneşti, *Rom.* 153 C16
Coma Pedrosa, Pic de, *Andorra, Sp.*
  160 H2
Comarnic, *Rom.* 153 E15
Comayagua, *Hond.* 115 L17
Combarbalá, *Chile* 132 J6
Combeaufontaine, *Fr.* 147 R14
Combermere Bay, *Myanmar* 186 J4
Combles, *Fr.* 146 M10
Combourg, *Fr.* 147 Q5
Comboyne, *N.S.W., Austral.* 211 X15
Comerío, *P.R., U.S.* 120 N4

Comet, *Qnsld., Austral.* **211** T14
Comfort, *Tex., U.S.* **103** Q9
Comino (Kemmuna), island, *Malta* **161** H21
Cominotto, island, *Malta* **161** H21
Commandant Charcot Glacier, *Antarctica* **227** Q17
Commander Islands see Komandorskiye Ostrova, *Russ.* **159** E23
Commanders Bay, *Aruba, Neth.* **121** R17
Commerce, *Ga., U.S.* **96** K6
Commerce, *Tex., U.S.* **102** K13
Commissioner's Point, *Bermuda, U.K.* **120** B2
Committee Bay, *Nunavut, Can.* **83** F16
Commonwealth Bay, *Antarctica* **227** R18
Communism Peak see Qullai Ismoili Somoni, *Taj.* **176** H10
Como, *It.* **150** D4
Como, Lago di, *It., Switz.* **150** C4
Comodoro Rivadavia, *Arg.* **133** S9
Comorin, Cape, *India* **179** S6
Comoro Islands, *Mozambique Chan.* **194** M11
Comoros, *Af.* **204** G8
Compiègne, *Fr.* **147** N10
Comporta, *Port.* **144** J5
Compostela, *Mex.* **114** H9
Comrat, *Mold.* **157** R4
Comstock Seamount, *Pac. Oc.* **238** D12
Cona, *China* **180** M8
Conakry, *Guinea* **200** F5
Conara Junction, *Tas., Austral.* **211** Z16
Conca, river, *It.* **161** L18
Concarneau, *Fr.* **147** Q3
Conceição, *Braz.* **131** F17
Conceição do Maú, *Braz.* **130** B9
Concepción, *Arg.* **132** G9
Concepción, *Bol.* **130** J8
Concepción, *Chile* **133** N6
Concepción del Uruguay, *Arg.* **132** K13
Conception, Point, *Calif., U.S.* **109** W5
Conception Bay, *Nfld. & Lab., Can.* **83** M24
Concepción del Oro, *Mex.* **114** F11
Conception Island, *Bahamas* **117** F14
Conchas, river, *N. Mex., U.S.* **107** R14
Conchas Dam, *N. Mex., U.S.* **107** R14
Conchas Lake, *N. Mex., U.S.* **107** R14
Concho, *Ariz., U.S.* **107** T9
Concho, river, *Tex., U.S.* **103** N7
Conchos, river, *Mex.* **114** E9
Conch Point, *Cayman Is., U.K.* **120** H1
Conconully, *Wash., U.S.* **108** A6
Concord, *Calif., U.S.* **109** R4
Concord, *Grenada* **121** K22
Concord, *N.C., U.S.* **96** H9
Concord, *N.H., U.S.* **95** J14
Concordia, *Arg.* **132** J13
Concordia, *Kans., U.S.* **105** S7
Concrete, *Wash., U.S.* **108** A4
Condamine, *Qnsld., Austral.* **211** V14
Condat, *Fr.* **147** U10
Condé, *Fr.* **146** M11
Conde, *S. Dak., U.S.* **104** J7
Condeúba, *Braz.* **131** J15
Condobolin, *N.S.W., Austral.* **211** X13
Condom, *Fr.* **147** X8
Condon, *Oreg., U.S.* **108** F6
Concordia, station, *Antarctica* **227** M17
Conecuh, river, *Ala., U.S.* **101** M16
Conegliano, *It.* **150** D8
Conejos, *Colo., U.S.* **107** Q12
Conero, Monte, *It.* **150** H10
Conflict Group, *P.N.G.* **213** E21
Confolens, *Fr.* **147** T8
Congaree National Park, *S.C., U.S.* **96** L9
Conghua, *China* **183** R4
Congjiang, *China* **183** P1
Congo, *Af.* **195** K18
Congo, river, *Af.* **194** K6
Congo, Source of the, *Dem. Rep. of the Congo* **194** M8
Congo Basin, *Dem. Rep. of the Congo* **194** J7
Congo Canyon, *Atl. Oc.* **237** P14
Congo Cay, *Virgin Islands, U.S.* **120** M10
Congress, *Ariz., U.S.* **107** T6
Cónico, Cerro, *Arg.* **133** R7
Conil de la Frontera, *Sp.* **144** M8
Conn, Lough, *Ire.* **143** Q3
Connaught, region, *Ire.* **143** R4
Conneaut, *Ohio, U.S.* **99** N15

Connecticut, river, *U.S.* **95** J13
Connecticut, *U.S.* **94** L12
Connel, *Scot., U.K.* **142** L8
Connell, *Wash., U.S.* **108** D7
Connellsville, *Pa., U.S.* **94** P4
Connemara, region, *Ire.* **143** R3
Connersville, *Ind., U.S.* **99** R10
Connmara, *Qnsld., Austral.* **211** T12
Connors Range, *Austral.* **210** F14
Cononaco, *Ecua.* **128** J5
Conrad, *Mont., U.S.* **106** B7
Conroe, *Tex., U.S.* **103** Q14
Consdorf, *Lux.* **160** J10
Conselheiro Lafaiete, *Braz.* **131** L14
Conset Bay, *Barbados* **121** K20
Consolación del Sur, *Cuba* **116** G5
Con Son, island, *Vietnam* **187** Q12
Con Son, *Vietnam* **187** Q12
Constance, Lake see Bodensee, *Aust., Ger.* **148** L7
Constância dos Baetas, *Braz.* **130** E8
Constant, Morne, *Guadeloupe, Fr.* **121** G16
Constanţa, *Rom.* **153** F18
Constantina, *Sp.* **144** K8
Constantine, *Alg.* **196** A12
Constantinople see İstanbul, *Turk.* **168** C5
Constellation Inlet, *Antarctica* **226** H8
Constitución, *Chile* **132** M6
Consuegra, *Sp.* **144** H11
Contact, *Nev., U.S.* **108** L12
Contai, *India* **178** K11
Contamana, *Peru* **130** F4
Contramaestre, *Cuba* **116** J11
Contreras, Embalse de, *Sp.* **145** G13
Contreras, Isla, *Chile* **133** W6
Contres, *Fr.* **147** R9
Contrexéville, *Fr.* **147** Q14
Contwoyto Lake, *Nunavut, Can.* **82** G12
Convention Center and Auditorium, *Monaco* **161** D22
Conversano, *It.* **150** M14
Conway, *Ark., U.S.* **100** G8
Conway, *N.H., U.S.* **95** G14
Conway, *S.C., U.S.* **96** K11
Conway Springs, *Kans., U.S.* **105** U7
Conwy, *Wales, U.K.* **143** S9
Coober Pedy, *S. Aust., Austral.* **211** V9
Cook, *Minn., U.S.* **104** F12
Cook, *S. Aust., Austral.* **211** W7
Cook, Bahía, *Chile* **133** Y8
Cook, Baie de, *Fr. Polynesia, Fr.* **219** N14
Cook, Mouillage de, *Fr. Polynesia, Fr.* **219** P17
Cook, Mount see Aoraki, *N.Z.* **213** P16
Cook Bay, *Vanuatu* **218** G4
Cookes Peak, *N. Mex., U.S.* **107** V11
Cookeville, *Tenn., U.S.* **101** E17
Cook Ice Shelf, *Antarctica* **227** R16
Cook Inlet, *Alas., U.S.* **111** L15
Cook Island, *Kiribati* **217** B22
Cook Island Passage, *Kiribati* **217** B22
Cook Islands, *N.Z., Pac. Oc.* **214** J11
Cook Strait, *N.Z.* **213** M18
Cooktown, *Qnsld., Austral.* **211** Q13
Coolabah, *N.S.W., Austral.* **211** W13
Coolabri, *Qnsld., Austral.* **211** U13
Cooladdi, *Qnsld., Austral.* **211** V13
Coolah, *N.S.W., Austral.* **211** X14
Coolatai, *N.S.W., Austral.* **211** W14
Coolgardie, *W. Aust., Austral.* **211** W4
Coolidge, *Ariz., U.S.* **107** U7
Coolidge, *Tex., U.S.* **103** N12
Coolidge Dam, *Ariz., U.S.* **107** U8
Coonabarabran, *N.S.W., Austral.* **211** X14
Coonamble, *N.S.W., Austral.* **211** W14
Coonana, *W. Aust., Austral.* **211** W5
Coonbah, *N.S.W., Austral.* **211** X11
Coondambo, *S. Aust., Austral.* **211** W9
Coondapoor see Kundapura, *India* **179** P4
Coongoola, *Qnsld., Austral.* **211** V13
Coon Rapids, *Iowa, U.S.* **105** P10
Coon Rapids, *Minn., U.S.* **104** J11
Cooper, *Tex., U.S.* **102** K13
Cooper Creek, *Austral.* **210** H10
Cooper's Town, *Bahamas* **120** A6
Cooperstown, *N. Dak., U.S.* **104** F7
Cooperstown, *N.Y., U.S.* **94** J10
Coorow, *W. Aust., Austral.* **211** W2
Coosa, river, *Ala., U.S.* **101** H16
Cootamundra, *N.S.W., Austral.* **211** Y13
Copano Bay, *Tex., U.S.* **103** T11

Cope, *Colo., U.S.* **106** M15
Cope, Cabo, *Sp.* **145** L13
Copeland Island, *N. Ire., U.K.* **143** P8
Copeland Island, *N. Ire., U.K.* **143** P8
Copenhagen see København, *Den.* **140** N12
Copertino, *It.* **151** N15
Copiapó, *Chile* **132** G7
Copiapó, Río, *Chile* **132** G6
Copinsay, island, *Scot., U.K.* **142** G11
Copparo, *It.* **150** E7
Copper, river, *Alas., U.S.* **111** J18
Copperas Cove, *Tex., U.S.* **103** P10
Copper Butte, *Wash., U.S.* **108** A8
Copper Center, *Alas., U.S.* **111** J18
Copper Harbor, *Mich., U.S.* **98** E7
Copper Mine Point, *Virgin Islands, U.K.* **120** R8
Copulhue Pass, *S. Amer.* **126** M4
Coqên, *China* **180** K6
Coquí, *P.R., U.S.* **120** N4
Coquille, *Oreg., U.S.* **108** J2
Coquille Harbor, *F.S.M.* **217** A18
Coquimbo, *Chile* **132** J6
Corabia, *Rom.* **153** G14
Coracora, *Peru* **130** J4
Corail, *Haiti* **117** M15
Coral Bay, *Virgin Islands, U.S.* **120** N11
Coral Bay, *Virgin Islands, U.S.* **120** M11
Coral Gables, *Fla., U.S.* **97** X10
Coral Harbour, *Bahamas* **120** B10
Coral Harbour, *Nunavut, Can.* **83** H16
Coral Island see Far'ūn, *Egypt* **171** R5
Coral Reef National Monument, *Virgin Islands, U.S.* **120** N11
Coral Sea, *Pac. Oc.* **238** M7
Coral Sea Basin, *Pac. Oc.* **238** L7
Coral Sea Islands Territory, *Austral.* **211** R15
Coral Springs, *Fla., U.S.* **97** W10
Corangamite, Lake, *Austral.* **210** M12
Corantijn, river, *Suriname* **129** E15
Corato, *It.* **150** L13
Corbeil-Essonnes, *Fr.* **147** P10
Corbières, range, *Fr.* **147** Y10
Corbin, *Ky., U.S.* **101** D18
Corby, *Eng., U.K.* **143** T13
Corcaigh see Cork, *Ire.* **143** U4
Corcoran, *Calif., U.S.* **109** U6
Corcovado, Golfo, *Chile* **133** R6
Corcubión, *Sp.* **144** B5
Corcyra see Kérkira, island, *Gr.* **154** E6
Cordele, *Ga., U.S.* **97** N6
Cordell, *Okla., U.S.* **102** G9
Cordes, *Fr.* **147** W9
Cordillo Downs, *S. Aust., Austral.* **211** U11
Córdoba, *Arg.* **132** J10
Córdoba, *Mex.* **115** J13
Córdoba, *Sp.* **144** K9
Córdoba, Sierras de, *Arg.* **132** J10
Cordouan, Île de, *Fr.* **147** U6
Cordova, *Ala., U.S.* **101** J15
Cordova, *Alas., U.S.* **111** K18
Corentyne, river, *Guyana* **129** E15
Corfu see Kérkira, island, *Gr.* **154** E6
Corguinho, *Braz.* **130** K11
Coria, *Sp.* **144** G7
Coria del Río, *Sp.* **144** L8
Corianino, *San Marino* **161** J16
Coribe, *Braz.* **131** H14
Corigliano Calabro, *It.* **151** P13
Coringa Islets, *Coral Sea Is. Terr., Austral.* **211** R15
Corinna, *Tas., Austral.* **211** Z15
Corinth see Kórinthos, *Gr.* **154** J11
Corinth, *Grenada* **121** L23
Corinth, *Miss., U.S.* **101** G13
Corinth, *N.Y., U.S.* **94** J11
Corinth Canal, *Gr.* **154** J11
Cork (Corcaigh), *Ire.* **143** U4
Cork Harbour, *Ire.* **143** V4
Corlay, *Fr.* **147** Q4
Corleone, *It.* **151** S9
Corleto Perticara, *It.* **151** N13
Çorlu, *Turk.* **168** C4
Cornelia, *Ga., U.S.* **96** K6
Cornell, *Wis., U.S.* **98** H3
Corner Brook, *Nfld. & Lab., Can.* **83** M23
Corner Seamounts, *Atl. Oc.* **236** H6
Corning, *Ark., U.S.* **100** E10
Corning, *Calif., U.S.* **109** P4
Corning, *Iowa, U.S.* **105** Q10
Corning, *N.Y., U.S.* **94** K7
Corno Grande, *It.* **150** J9
Cornwall, region, *Eng., U.K.* **143** X8
Cornwall, *Ont., Can.* **83** Q19

Cornwall, Cape, *Eng., U.K.* **143** Y7
Cornwallis, Port, *India* **179** P14
Cornwallis Island, *Nunavut, Can.* **83** D15
Cornwall Island, *Nunavut, Can.* **83** C15
Cornwall Point, *Bahamas* **120** C6
Coro, *Venez.* **128** B8
Coroatá, *Braz.* **131** E15
Corocoro, *Bol.* **130** K6
Coroico, *Bol.* **130** J6
Corolla, *N.C., U.S.* **96** G15
Coromandel Coast, *India* **179** Q8
Coromandel Peninsula, *N.Z.* **213** J19
Corona, *N. Mex., U.S.* **107** T13
Coronado, *Calif., U.S.* **109** Z9
Coronado Bay, *N. Amer.* **80** Q8
Coronado National Memorial, *Ariz., U.S.* **107** W8
Coronation Gulf, *Nunavut, Can.* **82** F12
Coronation Island, *Antarctica* **226** A4
Coronel, *Chile* **133** N6
Coronel Dorrego, *Arg.* **133** N11
Coronel Francisco Sosa, *Arg.* **133** P10
Coronel Pringles, *Arg.* **133** N11
Coronel Suárez, *Arg.* **133** N11
Coropuna, Nevado, *Peru* **130** J5
Corozal, *Belize* **115** J16
Corozal, *Col.* **128** C5
Corpus Christi, *Tex., U.S.* **103** U11
Corpus Christi, Lake, *Tex., U.S.* **103** T10
Corpus Christi Bay, *Tex., U.S.* **84** N12
Corral, *Chile* **133** P6
Corral de Almaguer, *Sp.* **144** G11
Corralillo, *Cuba* **116** G8
Corrib, Lough, *Ire.* **143** R3
Corrientes, *Arg.* **132** G13
Corrientes, Bahia de, *Cuba* **116** H4
Corrientes, Cabo, *Col.* **128** E3
Corrientes, Cabo, *Cuba* **116** H4
Corrientes, Cabo, *Mex.* **114** H9
Corrigan, *Tex., U.S.* **103** P14
Corrigin, *W. Aust., Austral.* **211** X3
Corriverton, *Guyana* **129** E15
Corrubedo, Cabo, *Sp.* **144** C5
Corry, *Pa., U.S.* **94** L4
Corryong, *Vic., Austral.* **211** Y13
Corse (Corsica), island, *Fr.* **150** K4
Corse, Cap, *Fr.* **150** H4
Corsica see Corse, island, *Fr.* **150** K4
Corsica, *S. Dak., U.S.* **104** M6
Corsicana, *Tex., U.S.* **102** M12
Corte, *Fr.* **150** K4
Cortemaggiore, *It.* **150** E5
Cortés, Mar de see California, Golfo de, *Mex.* **114** C6
Cortez, *Colo., U.S.* **107** P10
Cortina d'Ampezzo, *It.* **150** C8
Cortland, *N.Y., U.S.* **94** K8
Cortona, *It.* **150** H8
Corubal, river, *Gui.-Bissau* **144** B5
Coruche, *Port.* **144** H5
Çoruh, river, *Turk.* **169** D15
Çorum, *Turk.* **168** D10
Corumbá, *Braz.* **130** K10
Corumbau, Ponta de, *Braz.* **131** K16
Corvallis, *Oreg., U.S.* **108** G3
Corvo, island, *Azores* **144** N1
Corwen, *Wales, U.K.* **143** T10
Coryal, *Trinidad & Tobago* **121** P23
Corydon, *Iowa, U.S.* **105** Q12
Cos see Kos, island, *Gr.* **155** M18
Cosenza, *It.* **151** P13
Coshocton, *Ohio, U.S.* **99** Q14
Cosmoledo, Atoll de, *Seychelles* **203** C17
Cosmoledo Group, *Seychelles* **194** L12
Cosmonaut Sea, *Antarctic Oc.* **245** E13
Cosmo Newberry, *W. Aust., Austral.* **211** V5
Cosmopolis, *Wash., U.S.* **108** D2
Cosne-Cours-sur-Loire, *Fr.* **147** R10
Cosquín, *Arg.* **132** J10
Cossato, *It.* **150** D3
Cossé-le-Vivien, *Fr.* **147** Q6
Costa del Silencio, *Canary Is.* **204** R4
Costa Rica, *N. Amer.* **81** Q20
Costeşti, *Rom.* **153** F14
Costilla, *N. Mex., U.S.* **107** Q13
Cotabato, *Philippines* **189** F15
Cotagaita, *Bol.* **130** L7
Coteaux, *Haiti* **117** N15
Côte d'Ivoire, *Af.* **195** H15
Côte d'Or, range, *Fr.* **147** S12
Côtes-de-Fer, *Haiti* **117** M16
Coton, Pointe, *Mauritius* **205** J21
Cotonou, *Benin* **200** H12

Cotopaxi, peak, *Ecua.* **128** J3
Cotorra, Isla, *Venez.* **121** Q20
Cotswold Hills, *Eng., U.K.* **143** V11
Cottage Grove, *Oreg., U.S.* **108** H3
Cottbus, *Ger.* **148** E11
Cotter, *Ark., U.S.* **100** E8
Cottian Alps, *Fr., It.* **147** V15
Cottongarden Point, *Virgin Islands, U.S.* **120** Q4
Cotton Ground, *St. Kitts & Nevis* **121** C18
Cotton Plant, *Ark., U.S.* **100** G10
Cotton Valley, *La., U.S.* **100** K7
Cottonwood, *Ariz., U.S.* **107** S7
Cottonwood, *Idaho, U.S.* **106** D4
Cotulla, *Tex., U.S.* **103** T8
Coubre, Pointe de la, *Fr.* **147** U6
Coudersport, *Pa., U.S.* **94** L6
Couëron, *Fr.* **147** S5
Couiza, *Fr.* **147** Y10
Coulee City, *Wash., U.S.* **108** C7
Coulee Dam, *Wash., U.S.* **108** B7
Council, *Idaho, U.S.* **106** F3
Council Bluffs, *Iowa, U.S.* **105** P9
Council Grove, *Kans., U.S.* **105** T8
Couronne, Cap, *Fr.* **147** Y13
Courtenay, *B.C., Can.* **82** L7
Courtenay, *Fr.* **147** Q10
Courtmacsherry Bay, *Ire.* **143** V4
Coushatta, *La., U.S.* **100** L7
Coutances, *Fr.* **147** P6
Coutras, *Fr.* **147** V7
Covadonga, site, *Sp.* **144** B9
Covarrubias, *Sp.* **144** D11
Cove, *Oreg., U.S.* **108** F8
Covelo, *Calif., U.S.* **109** P2
Coventry, *Eng., U.K.* **143** T12
Covered Market, *Monaco* **161** E20
Coves del Drac, *Sp.* **145** G19
Covilhã, *Port.* **144** F6
Covington, *Ga., U.S.* **96** L5
Covington, *Ind., U.S.* **99** R7
Covington, *Ky., U.S.* **101** A18
Covington, *La., U.S.* **100** P11
Covington, *Okla., U.S.* **102** F10
Covington, *Tenn., U.S.* **100** F12
Covington, *Va., U.S.* **96** E10
Cowal, Lake, *Austral.* **210** K13
Cowan, Cerro, *Ecua.* **128** P9
Cowan, Lake, *Austral.* **210** J4
Cow and Calf Islands, *Myanmar* **179** N15
Cow and Calves, islands, *St. Vincent & the Grenadines* **121** J17
Cowaramup, *W. Aust., Austral.* **211** Y2
Cowarie, *S. Aust., Austral.* **211** V10
Cowell, *S. Aust., Austral.* **211** X9
Coweta, *Okla., U.S.* **102** F13
Cowlitz, river, *Wash., U.S.* **108** D4
Coxim, river, *Braz.* **130** K11
Coxim, *Braz.* **130** K11
Cox's Bazar, *Bangladesh* **178** K14
Coyanosa Draw, *Tex., U.S.* **103** P3
Cozad, *Nebr., U.S.* **105** Q5
Cozumel, Isla, *Mex.* **115** H17
Cozumel Island see Cozumel, Isla, *N. Amer.* **80** N7
Crab Island, *Mauritius* **205** J20
Cradock, *S. Af.* **202** L10
Crafers, *S. Aust., Austral.* **211** Y10
Craig, *Alas., U.S.* **111** M23
Craig, *Colo., U.S.* **106** L11
Craiova, *Rom.* **153** F13
Cranberry Lake, *N.Y., U.S.* **94** G10
Cranbourne, *Vic., Austral.* **211** Z12
Cranbrook, *B.C., Can.* **82** M9
Crandon, *Wis., U.S.* **98** G6
Crane, *Oreg., U.S.* **108** J8
Crane, *Tex., U.S.* **103** N4
Crane Beach, *Barbados* **121** L20
Crane Lake, *Minn., U.S.* **104** E12
Craon, *Fr.* **147** R6
Crary Mountains, *Antarctica* **226** L8
Crasna, river, *Rom.* **152** B12
Crasna, *Rom.* **153** C17
Crater Lake, *Oreg., U.S.* **108** J4
Crater Lake National Park, *Oreg., U.S.* **108** J4
Craters of the Moon National Monument, *Idaho, U.S.* **106** H6
Crateús, *Braz.* **131** E16
Crato, *Braz.* **131** F16
Crawford, *Nebr., U.S.* **104** M1
Crawford, *Tex., U.S.* **103** N11
Crawfordsville, *Ind., U.S.* **99** R8
Crawfordville, *Fla., U.S.* **97** R5
Crazy Mountains, *Mont., U.S.* **106** E9

Creagorry, Scot., U.K. 142 J6
Crécy, Fr. 147 N11
Cree, river, Sask., Can. 82 K12
Creede, Colo., U.S. 107 P11
Creek Point, Bahamas 120 B10
Cree Lake, Sask., Can. 82 K12
Creeslough, Ire. 143 P5
Creighton, Nebr., U.S. 105 N7
Creil, Fr. 147 N10
Crema, It. 150 E5
Cremona, It. 150 E5
Cres, island, Croatia 152 E4
Cresbard, S. Dak., U.S. 104 J6
Crescent, Okla., U.S. 102 F10
Crescent City, Calif., U.S. 108 L1
Crescent City, Fla., U.S. 97 S8
Crescent Group, China 188 B10
Crescent Junction, Utah, U.S. 107 N9
Crescent Lake, Fla., U.S. 97 S8
Crescent Lake, Oreg., U.S. 108 J4
Cresco, Iowa, U.S. 104 M13
Crest, Fr. 147 V13
Creston, Iowa, U.S. 105 Q10
Crestview, Fla., U.S. 97 Q2
Creswell, Oreg., U.S. 108 H3
Crete see Kríti, island, Gr. 155 Q14
Crete, Nebr., U.S. 105 Q8
Crete, Sea of, Gr. 155 P13
Creus, Cap de, Sp. 145 C18
Crevasse Valley Glacier, Antarctica 226 N9
Crevillente, Sp. 145 K14
Crewe, Va., U.S. 96 F12
Crewkerne, Eng., U.K. 143 W11
Crianlarich, Scot., U.K. 142 L9
Criciúma, Braz. 130 P12
Criel-sur-Mer, Fr. 146 M9
Crimea, region, Ukr. 157 S7
Crimean Mountains see Krims'ke Hory, Ukr. 138 H11
Crinan Canal, Scot., U.K. 142 M8
Cripple Creek, Colo., U.S. 107 N13
Crisfield, Md., U.S. 96 E14
Cristalina, Braz. 131 J13
Cristóbal, Punta, Ecua. 128 Q8
Crişul Alb, river, Rom. 152 D12
Crişul Negra, river, Rom. 152 C11
Crişul Repede, river, Rom. 152 C12
Crna, river, Maced. 152 L11
Croatia, Eur. 139 V7
Crocker, Cerro, Ecua. 128 Q9
Crocker Range, Malaysia 188 G11
Crockett, Tex., U.S. 103 N13
Crocus Bay, Anguilla, U.K. 120 R11
Crocus Hill, Anguilla, U.K. 120 R11
Crofton, Nebr., U.S. 104 M7
Croisette, Cap, Fr. 147 Y13
Croisic, Pointe du, Fr. 147 R4
Croix des Bouquets, Haiti 117 M17
Croker Island, Austral. 210 A8
Cromarty Firth, Scot., U.K. 142 J9
Crompton Point, Dominica 121 E19
Crook, Colo., U.S. 106 K15
Crook, Eng., U.K. 143 P12
Crooked, river, Oreg., U.S. 108 H6
Crooked Island, Bahamas 117 G15
Crooked Island Passage, Bahamas 117 G14
Crook Point, Oreg., U.S. 108 K1
Crookston, Minn., U.S. 104 F8
Crosby, Minn., U.S. 104 H11
Crosby, N. Dak., U.S. 104 D2
Crosbyton, Tex., U.S. 102 K6
Cross City, Fla., U.S. 97 R6
Crossett, Ark., U.S. 100 K9
Crossing Rocks, Bahamas 120 C6
Cross Keys, Jam. 120 J8
Cross Plains, Tex., U.S. 102 M8
Cross Sound, Alas., U.S. 111 K21
Crossville, Tenn., U.S. 101 E17
Croswell, Mich., U.S. 98 L13
Crotone, It. 151 Q14
Crow Agency, Mont., U.S. 106 E11
Crowell, Tex., U.S. 102 J8
Crowley, La., U.S. 100 P8
Crown Haven, Bahamas 120 A5
Crown Mountain, Virgin Islands, U.S. 120 M8
Crownpoint, N. Mex., U.S. 107 R10
Crown Prince Christian Land, N. Amer. 80 A8
Croydon, Qnsld., Austral. 211 R12
Crozer, Mount, F.S.M. 217 B18
Crozet Basin, Ind. Oc. 240 N7
Crozet Islands, Ind. Oc. 204 K8
Crozet Plateau, Ind. Oc. 240 Q5
Cruces, Cuba 116 H8
Crump Island, Antigua & Barbuda 121 B21
Crump Lake, Oreg., U.S. 108 K6
Cruz, Cabo, Cuba 116 L11
Cruz Alta, Braz. 130 P11
Cruz Bay, Virgin Islands, U.S. 120 N10
Cruz del Eje, Arg. 132 J10
Cruz del Padre, Cayo, Cuba 116 G8
Cruzeiro, Ponta, Sao Tome and Principe 205 C20
Cruzeiro do Sul, Braz. 130 F4
Cruz Grande, Chile 132 H6
Crysochou Bay, Cyprus 160 P5
Crystal Caves, Bermuda, U.K. 120 B3
Crystal City, Mo., U.S. 105 T15
Crystal City, Tex., U.S. 103 S8
Crystal Falls, Mich., U.S. 98 G6
Crystal Lake, Ill., U.S. 98 M6
Crystal Mountains, Af. 194 K6
Crystal River, Fla., U.S. 97 S7
Crystal Springs, Miss., U.S. 100 M11
Csongrád, Hung. 149 M16
Csorna, Hung. 149 L13
Ctesiphon, ruin, Iraq 172 E10
Cuamba, Mozambique 203 E13
Cuando, river, Angola 202 E8
Cuangar, Angola 202 F7
Cuango, river, Angola 202 C7
Cuanza, river, Angola 202 C6
Cuauhtémoc, Mex. 114 D8
Cuba, Mo., U.S. 105 T14
Cuba, N. Amer. 81 N21
Cuba, island, N. Amer. 80 N9
Cubagua, Isla, Venez. 119 P14
Cubal, Angola 202 D6
Cubango, river, Angola 202 F7
Çubuk, Turk. 168 E8
Cuchara, Punta, P.R., U.S. 120 P3
Cuchilla de Haedo, range, Uru. 132 K13
Cuchilla Grande, range, Uru. 132 L14
Cuckold Point, Barbados 121 J19
Cucuí, Braz. 130 C7
Cúcuta, Col. 128 D6
Cudahy, Wis., U.S. 98 L7
Cuddalore, India 179 Q7
Cuddapah, India 179 P6
Cudjoehead, Montserrat, U.K. 121 B23
Cuéllar, Sp. 144 E10
Cuenca, Ecua. 128 K3
Cuenca, Sp. 144 G12
Cuenca, Serranía de, Sp. 144 F12
Cuencamé, Mex. 114 F10
Cuernavaca, Mex. 114 J11
Cuero, Tex., U.S. 103 S11
Cuevas de Altamira, Sp. 144 B10
Cuevas del Almanzora, Sp. 145 L13
Cuevo, Bol. 130 L8
Cugir, Rom. 153 D13
Cuglieri, It. 151 N3
Cuiabá, Braz. 130 J10
Cuito, river, Angola 202 F7
Cuito Cuanavale, Angola 202 E7
Çukurca, Turk. 169 H18
Cu Lao Re, island, Vietnam 186 L14
Cu Lao Thu, island, Vietnam 187 P14
Culberts Bay, Bahamas 120 B12
Culbertson, Mont., U.S. 106 B13
Culbertson, Nebr., U.S. 105 R4
Cul de Sac, river, St. Lucia 121 K14
Cul de Sac, Neth. Antilles, Neth. 121 B14
Cul de Sac, St. Martin, Fr. 121 A15
Cul-de-Sac du Marin, bay, Martinique, Fr. 121 G23
Culebra, island, P.R., U.S. 120 M7
Culebra, Sierra de la, Sp. 144 D8
Culfa, Azerb. 169 F19
Culiacán, Mex. 114 F8
Culion, island, Philippines 189 D13
Cúllar-Baza, Sp. 144 L12
Cullman, Ala., U.S. 101 H15
Culpataro, N.S.W., Austral. 211 X12
Culpeper, Va., U.S. 96 D12
Culpepper see Darwin, Isla, island, Ecua. 128 M7
Culuene, river, Braz. 130 H11
Culver, Point, Austral. 210 K5
Culverden, N.Z. 213 N17
Cumalı, Turk. 168 H3
Cumaná, Venez. 128 B11
Cumana Bay, Trinidad & Tobago 121 N23
Cumana Redhead, Trinidad & Tobago 121 N23
Cumanayagua, Cuba 116 H8
Cumberland, Ky., U.S. 101 D19
Cumberland, river, Ky., Tenn., U.S. 85 J16
Cumberland, Md., U.S. 96 C11
Cumberland, Wis., U.S. 98 G2
Cumberland, Cape, Vanuatu 218 C1
Cumberland, Lake, Ky., U.S. 101 D17
Cumberland Bay, St. Vincent & the Grenadines 121 K16
Cumberland Gap National Historic Park, Ky., Va., Tenn., U.S. 101 D19
Cumberland Island National Seashore, Ga., U.S. 97 Q8
Cumberland Islands, Austral. 210 E14
Cumberland Peninsula, Nunavut, Can. 83 F19
Cumberland Plateau, Ala., Ky., Tenn., U.S. 85 J17
Cumberland Sound, Nunavut, Can. 83 G19
Cumbernauld, Scot., U.K. 142 M9
Cumborah, N.S.W., Austral. 211 W13
Cumbrera, Cerro, Chile 133 U7
Cumbres Pass, Colo., U.S. 107 Q12
Cumbrian Mountains, Eng., U.K. 143 Q10
Cuminá, Braz. 130 D10
Cumina see Paru de Oeste, river, Braz. 130 C11
Cúmpas, Mex. 114 C7
Çumra, Turk. 168 H8
Cuna, Venez. 128 D9
Cunco, Chile 133 P6
Cunene see Kunene, river, Angola 202 F5
Cuneo, It. 150 F2
Cunnamulla, Qnsld., Austral. 211 V13
Cunningham, Lake, Bahamas 120 B11
Cunyu, W. Aust., Austral. 211 U3
Cupica, Col. 128 E3
Cupica, Golfo de, Col. 128 E3
Curaçao, island, Neth. Antilles, Neth. 119 M9
Curanilahue, Chile 133 N6
Curbur, W. Aust., Austral. 211 V2
Curcubăta, peak, Rom. 152 C12
Curecanti National Recreation Area, Colo., U.S. 107 N11
Curepipe, Mauritius 205 G20
Curiapo, Venez. 129 C13
Curicó, Chile 132 L7
Curieuse, island, Seychelles 205 M20
Curitiba, Braz. 130 N13
Curium, ruin, Cyprus 160 Q7
Curley Cut Cays, Bahamas 116 F11
Curral Velho, Cape Verde 205 C17
Curraun Peninsula, Ire. 143 R3
Current, Bahamas 120 D5
Current, river, Mo., U.S. 105 V14
Current Island, Bahamas 120 D5
Currie, Tas., Austral. 211 Y15
Currituck, N.C., U.S. 96 G14
Currituck Sound, N.C., U.S. 96 G15
Curtea de Argeş, Rom. 153 E14
Curtici, Rom. 152 D11
Curtin Springs, N. Terr., Austral. 211 U8
Curtis, Nebr., U.S. 105 Q4
Curtis Island, Kermadec Is., N.Z. 214 L9
Curuá, river, Braz. 130 F11
Curuaés, river, Braz. 130 F11
Curuçá, river, Braz. 130 E5
Curuçá, Braz. 131 C13
Cururupu, Braz. 131 D14
Curuzú Cuatiá, Arg. 132 H13
Curvelo, Braz. 131 K14
Cusco, Peru 130 H5
Cushing, Okla., U.S. 102 F11
Cusset, Fr. 147 T11
Cusson, Pointe, Que., Can. 83 J17
Custer, Mont., U.S. 106 E11
Custer, S. Dak., U.S. 104 L1
Cut, island, Indonesia 189 L18
Cut Bank, Mont., U.S. 106 B7
Cuthbert, Ga., U.S. 97 P4
Cutler Ridge, Fla., U.S. 97 X10
Cutral Có, Arg. 133 P8
Cuttack, India 178 K10
Cuvier, Cape, Austral. 210 G1
Cuvier Plateau, Ind. Oc. 241 L14
Cuxhaven, Ger. 148 B7
Cuya, Chile 132 B7
Cuyahoga Falls, Ohio, U.S. 99 P15
Cuyahoga Valley National Park, Ohio, U.S. 99 P14
Cuyama, river, Calif., U.S. 109 W7
Cuyo Islands, Philippines 189 E13
Cuyuni, river, Guyana 129 D13
Cyclades see Kikládes, Gr. 155 L14
Cydonia see Haniá, Gr. 155 Q13
Cynthiana, Ky., U.S. 101 B18
Cyprus, Eur. 160 E6
Cyrenaica, region, Lib. 197 C16
Cyrene see Shaḩḩāt, Lib. 197 B16
Cyrus Field Bay, Nunavut, Can. 83 H19
Cythera see Kíthira, island, Gr. 154 N11
Czaplinek, Pol. 148 C12
Czech Republic (Czechia), Eur. 139 U7
Częstochowa, Pol. 149 G15
Człopa, Pol. 148 D12

D

Da (Black), river, Vietnam 186 H11
Da'an, China 181 D16
Ḑab'ah, Jordan 171 N7
Dabakala, Côte d'Ivoire 200 G9
Daba Shan, China 182 J2
Dabie Shan, China 182 K6
Dabola, Guinea 200 F6
Dabqig see Uxin Qi, China 182 E2
Dąbrowa Górnicza, Pol. 149 G15
Dąbrowa Tarnowska, Pol. 149 G16
Dachau, Ger. 148 K8
Dac To, Vietnam 186 M13
Dadale, Solomon Is. 217 M18
Daday, Turk. 168 C9
Dade City, Fla., U.S. 97 T8
Dadeville, Ala., U.S. 101 K16
Dadhar, Pak. 177 S6
Dadu, river, China 180 L11
Dadu, Pak. 177 U6
Daegu, S. Korea 182 G14
Daejeon (Taejŏn), S. Korea 182 F13
Daejeong, S. Korea 182 J13
Dafeng (Dazhong), China 182 J9
Dafní, Gr. 154 J9
Dafoe, Sask., Can. 82 M12
Dagana, Senegal 196 G5
Dagcanglhamo, China 180 K11
Dagelet see Ulleungdo, island, S. Korea 182 E15
Dagerşi, Köpetdag, Iran 173 B16
Dagö see Hiiumaa, island, Est. 141 L15
Dagupan, Philippines 189 C13
Dahab, Egypt 171 T4
Dahanu, India 178 K3
Da Hinggan Ling, China 181 E15
Dahla, Afghan. 177 Q5
Dahlak Archipelago, Eritrea 194 G10
Dahlonega, Ga., U.S. 96 K5
Dahod, India 178 J4
Dahongliutan, China 176 K15
Dai (Ndai), island, Solomon Is. 217 M19
Daigo, Japan 185 N13
Dailekh, Nepal 178 F8
Daimiel, Sp. 144 H11
Daingerfield, Tex., U.S. 102 K14
Daiō, Japan 185 Q10
Dair, Jebel ed, Sudan 194 G9
Dairen see Dalian, China 182 E10
Dairy Creek, W. Aust., Austral. 211 U2
Dai Senga Dake, Japan 184 H12
Daisetta, Tex., U.S. 103 Q15
Daitō, Japan 184 L13
Daitō Islands, Japan 184 L3
Daixian, China 182 D5
Dajabón, Dom. Rep. 117 L17
Dajarra, Qnsld., Austral. 211 S11
Dajt, Mal, Albania 152 L9
Dakar, Senegal 196 H4
Dakhla Oasis, Egypt 197 E18
Dakoank, India 179 T15
Dakoro, Niger 196 H11
Dakota City, Nebr., U.S. 105 N8
Đakovica see Gjakova, Kos. 152 J10
Đakovo, Croatia 152 E8
Dákura, Nicar. 115 L19
Dala, Solomon Is. 217 M19
Dalai Nur, China 182 A7
Dalaman, river, Turk. 168 H4
Dalanzadgad, Mongolia 180 F12
Dalap, island, Marshall Is. 216 H12
Da Lat, Vietnam 187 N14
Dalbandin, Pak. 177 S4
Dalbeg, Qnsld., Austral. 211 S14
Dalby, Qnsld., Austral. 211 V15
Dale, Nor. 140 K10
Dale Country, Eng., U.K. 143 R12
Daleville, Ala., U.S. 101 N16
Dalgonally, Qnsld., Austral. 211 S11
Dalhart, Tex., U.S. 102 F4
Dali, China 182 G3
Dali, China 180 N10
Dali, Cyprus 160 P8
Dalian (Dairen), China 182 E10
Dalidag, peak, Azerb. 169 E20
Dalkhaki, Afghan. 176 L7
Dallas, Oreg., U.S. 108 G3
Dallas, Tex., U.S. 102 L12
Dall Island, Alas., U.S. 84 R7
Dalmatia, region, Croatia 152 G6
Dalmellington, Scot., U.K. 143 N9
Dal'negorsk, Russ. 159 L21
Dal'nerechensk, Russ. 159 L21
Daloa, Côte d'Ivoire 200 G8
Daltenganj, India 178 H9
Dalton, Ga., U.S. 96 J4
Dalton, Nebr., U.S. 105 P2
Dalton Highway, Alas., U.S. 111 C17
Dalupiri, island, Philippines 189 A13
Dalwhinnie, Scot., U.K. 142 K9
Daly, river, N. Terr., Austral. 211 P7
Daly Bay, Nunavut, Can. 83 H15
Daly Waters, N. Terr., Austral. 211 Q8
Daman (Damão), India 178 K3
Damanhûr, Egypt 197 C18
Damão see Daman, India 178 K3
Damar, island, Indonesia 189 J16
Damar, island, Indonesia 189 M16
Damas Cays, Bahamas 116 F9
Damascus see Dimashq, Syr. 170 J7
Damāvand, Kūh-e, Iran 173 C13
Damboa, Nigeria 201 E16
Dambulla, Sri Lanka 179 S7
Dame-Marie, Haiti 117 M14
Dam Ha, Vietnam 186 H13
Damietta see Dumyât, Egypt 197 C18
Daming, China 182 F6
Damīr Qābū, Syr. 170 C15
Damoh, India 178 H7
Damongo, Ghana 200 F10
Dampier, Selat, Indonesia 189 J17
Dampier Archipelago, Austral. 210 E2
Dampier Downs, W. Aust., Austral. 211 R4
Dampier Land, Austral. 210 D4
Damqawt, Yemen 173 P14
Damroh, India 178 F15
Damxung, China 180 L8
Dan, river, N.C., U.S. 96 G10
Danakil Desert, Eth. 199 E15
Da Nang, Vietnam 186 L13
Dana Point, Calif., U.S. 109 Y9
Danbury, Conn., U.S. 94 M12
Danby Lake, Calif., U.S. 109 X12
Dancheng, China 182 H6
Dancheng see Xiangshan, China 182 M10
Danco Coast, Antarctica 226 D4
Dandan, Puntan, N. Mariana Is., U.S. 216 C5
Dandong, China 182 D11
Daneborg, Greenland, Den. 81 A21
Danfeng, China 182 H3
Danforth, Me., U.S. 95 D18
Dang, river, China 180 G9
Dangara, Taj. 176 J8
Danger Islands see Pukapuka Atoll, Cook Is., N.Z. 214 J11
Dangrek Range, Thai. 186 M11
Dangriga, Belize 115 K17
Dangshan, China 182 H6
Dangtu, China 182 K8
Daniel, Wyo., U.S. 106 H9
Danilov, Russ. 156 G10
Daning, China 182 F3
Danjiangkou, China 182 J3
Danjo Guntō, Japan 185 S2
Ḑank, Oman 173 K15
Dankhar Gömpa, India 177 P15
Dankov, Russ. 156 L10
Danmark Havn, Greenland, Den. 81 A21
Dannemora, N.Y., U.S. 94 F11
Dansville, N.Y., U.S. 94 K6
Danube see Donau, Duna, Dunaj, Dunărea, Dunav, Dunay, river, Eur. 138 H9
Danube, Mouths of the, Rom. 153 E19
Danube, Source of the, Ger. 138 G6
Danube River Delta, Rom. 138 H10
Danville, Ill., U.S. 99 R7
Danville, Ky., U.S. 101 C17
Danville, Va., U.S. 96 G10
Danzhou, China 183 U1

Dao, Mui, *Vietnam* **186** KI2
Daos du Sud, Îles, *New Caledonia, Fr.* **218** B6
Daoxian, *China* **183** P3
Daphne, *Ala., U.S.* **101** PI4
Da Qaidam, *China* **180** H9
Daqing, *China* **181** DI7
Dāqūq, *Iraq* **172** C9
Dar'ā (Edrei), *Syr.* **170** L7
Dārāb, *Iran* **173** GI4
Daraban, *Pak.* **177** Q9
Darabani, *Rom.* **153** AI5
Darakht-e Yahya, *Afghan.* **177** Q7
Ḍarbat 'Alī, Ra's, *Oman* **173** PI4
Darbhanga, *India* **178** GIO
Darby, *Mont., U.S.* **106** E5
Darby Island, *Bahamas* **120** D7
Dardanelle, *Ark., U.S.* **100** G7
Dardanelle, Lake, *Ark., U.S.* **100** F7
Dardanelles *see* Çanakkale Boğazı, strait, *Turk.* **168** D2
Darende, *Turk.* **168** GI2
Dar es Salaam, *Tanzania* **199** MI5
Darfur, region, *Sudan* **198** EIO
Dargai, *Pak.* **176** MIO
Darganata, *Turkm.* **174** KIO
Dargaville, *N.Z.* **213** HI8
Dargeçit, *Turk.* **169** HI6
Dargun, *Ger.* **148** BIO
Darhan, *Mongolia* **180** CI2
Darien, *Ga., U.S.* **97** P8
Daringali, *Solomon Is.* **217** MI9
Darjiling, *India* **178** GII
Dark Head, *St. Vincent & the Grenadines* **121** KI6
Darling, river, *N.S.W., Austral.* **211** XI2
Darling, Lake, *N. Dak., U.S.* **104** E4
Darling, Source of the, *Austral.* **210** HI5
Darling Downs, *Austral.* **210** HI4
Darling Range, *Austral.* **210** K3
Darlington, *Eng., U.K.* **143** QI2
Darlington, *S.C., U.S.* **96** KIO
Darliston, *Jam.* **120** H6
Darlot, Lake, *Austral.* **210** H4
Darłowo, *Pol.* **148** BI2
Darmstadt, *Ger.* **148** H6
Darnah, *Lib.* **197** BI6
Darney, *Fr.* **147** QI4
Darnley, Cape, *Antarctica* **227** F2O
Daroca, *Sp.* **145** EI3
Daroot-Korgon, *Kyrg.* **176** HIO
Darregueira, *Arg.* **133** NIO
Darreh Gaz, *Iran* **173** BI6
Darreh-ye Awd, *Afghan.* **176** M5
Darreh-ye Bum, *Afghan.* **176** M3
Darrington, *Wash., U.S.* **108** B5
Dar Rounga, region, *Cen. Af. Rep.* **194** H7
Darrouzett, *Tex., U.S.* **102** E7
Darsser Ort, island, *Ger.* **148** BIO
Dartmoor, plateau, *Eng., U.K.* **143** X9
Dartmouth, *N.S., Can.* **83** P22
Daru, *P.N.G.* **213** EI8
Darwaji-e Bala, *Afghan.* **177** N2
Darwha, *India* **178** K6
Darwin, *Falkland Is., U.K.* **133** WI2
Darwin, *N. Terr., Austral.* **211** P7
Darwin, Bahía, *Ecua.* **128** PIO
Darwin, Isla (Culpepper), *Ecua.* **128** M7
Darwin, Volcán, *Ecua.* **128** P8
Darwin Glacier, *Antarctica* **227** MI4
Darya Khan, *Pak.* **177** Q9
Das, *Pak.* **178** B5
Dasburg, *Ger.* **148** G4
Dashiqiao, *China* **182** CIO
Dashitou, *China* **182** AI3
Dashkäsän, *Azerb.* **169** D2O
Dashkuduk, *Turkm.* **174** K6
Dasht, river, *Pak.* **177** V2
Daska, *Pak.* **177** PI2
Daşköpri, *Turkm.* **174** NIO
Daşoguz, *Turkm.* **174** J9
Datça, *Turk.* **168** H3
Datia, *India* **178** G6
Datian, *China* **183** Q7
Datong, river, *China* **180** HIO
Datong, *China* **182** C5
Datu Piang, *Philippines* **189** FI5
Da Ty, Hon, *Vietnam* **187** QI4
Daud Khel, *Pak.* **177** P9
Daudnagar, *India* **178** H9
Daugava, river, *Latv.* **141** MI7
Daugavpils, *Latv.* **141** MI7
Daun, *Ger.* **160** GI2
Dauphin, *Man., Can.* **83** NI3
Dauphin Island, *Ala., U.S.* **101** PI3

Daurada, Costa, *Sp.* **145** FI6
Däväçi, *Azerb.* **169** C22
Davangere, *India* **179** P5
Davao, *Philippines* **189** FI5
Davao Gulf, *Philippines* **189** FI5
Davenport, *Iowa, U.S.* **105** PI4
Davenport, *Wash., U.S.* **108** C8
Davenport Downs, *Qnsld., Austral.* **211** TII
Davenport Range, *Austral.* **210** E9
Daventry, *Eng., U.K.* **143** UI3
David, *Pan.* **115** P2O
David Bay, *Grenada* **121** J23
David City, *Nebr., U.S.* **105** P8
David Point, *Virgin Islands, U.S.* **120** N8
Davidson Mountains, *Alas., U.S.* **III** DI8
Davis, station, *Antarctica* **227** G2O
Davis, *Calif., U.S.* **109** R4
Davis, *Okla., U.S.* **102** HII
Davis, Mount, *Pa., U.S.* **94** Q4
Davis Beach, *Virgin Islands, U.S.* **120** Q2
Davis Dam, *Ariz., Nev., U.S.* **109** U9
Davis Inlet, *Nfld. & Lab., Can.* **83** K2I
Davis Mountains, *Tex., U.S.* **103** P2
Davis Sea, *Antarctica* **227** J2I
Davis Strait, *Arctic Oc.* **243** RI6
Davlos, *Cyprus* **160** NIO
Davos, *Switz.* **150** B5
Davyhurst, *W. Aust., Austral.* **211** W4
Dawa, river, *Eth., Kenya* **194** JII
Dawāsir, Wādī ad, *Saudi Arabia* **172** M9
Dawei, *Myanmar* **186** M7
Dawkah, *Oman* **173** LI7
Dawmat al Jandal (Al Jawf), *Saudi Arabia* **172** F7
Dawna Range, *Myanmar, Thai.* **186** L7
Dawqah, *Saudi Arabia* **172** M7
Dawra, *W. Sahara, Mor.* **196** D6
Dawros Head, *Ire.* **143** P4
Dawson, river, *Austral.* **210** GI4
Dawson, *Ga., U.S.* **97** P5
Dawson, *Minn., U.S.* **104** K9
Dawson, *N. Dak., U.S.* **104** G5
Dawson, *Tex., U.S.* **102** MI2
Dawson, *Yukon, Can.* **82** E8
Dawson, Isla, *Chile* **133** X8
Dawson Creek, *B.C., Can.* **82** K9
Dawson Springs, *Ky., U.S.* **101** DI4
Dawu, *China* **182** K5
Dawwah, *Oman* **173** LI7
Dax, *Fr.* **147** X6
Daxing, *China* **182** D7
Daxinggou, *China* **182** AI4
Daxue Mountains, *China* **166** HIO
Daydawn, *W. Aust., Austral.* **211** V3
Dayong, *China* **182** M2
Dayr az Zawr, *Syr.* **170** FI3
Dayr Sim'ān, *Syr.* **170** D8
Dayton, *Ohio, U.S.* **99** RII
Dayton, *Tenn., U.S.* **101** FI7
Dayton, *Tex., U.S.* **103** QI4
Dayton, *Wash., U.S.* **108** E8
Daytona Beach, *Fla., U.S.* **97** S9
Dayu, *China* **183** Q5
Da Yunhe (Grand Canal), *China* **182** J8
Dayushan (Lantau Island), *China* **183** S4
Dayville, *Oreg., U.S.* **108** G7
Dazhong *see* Dafeng, *China* **182** J9
Dazkırı, *Turk.* **168** G5
De Aar, *S. Af.* **202** L9
Deadhorse, *Alas., U.S.* **III** CI7
Deadmans Cay, *Bahamas* **117** GI4
Deadman's Cays, *Bahamas* **116** F8
Dead Sea, *Israel, Jordan, W. Bank* **171** N6
Deadwood, *S. Dak., U.S.* **104** KI
Deakin, *W. Aust., Austral.* **211** W7
Deal, *Eng., U.K.* **143** VI6
De'an, *China* **182** M6
Deán Funes, *Arg.* **132** JIO
Dean Passage, *Solomon Is.* **217** R23
Dearborn, *Mich., U.S.* **98** MI2
Dease Inlet, *Alas., U.S.* **III** BI5
Dease Lake, *B.C., Can.* **82** H8
Dease Strait, *Nunavut, Can.* **83** FI3
Death Valley, *Calif., U.S.* **109** UIO
Death Valley, *Calif., U.S.* **109** T9
Death Valley National Park, *Calif., U.S.* **109** T9
Debar, *Maced.* **152** KIO
Débé, *Trinidad & Tobago* **121** Q22
Dębica, *Pol.* **149** GI6
Debin, *Russ.* **159** F2O
Debir, ruin, *Israel* **171** N5
Dębno, *Pol.* **148** DII
Débo, Lake, *Niger* **194** G3

Debrecen, *Hung.* **149** LI7
Debre Mark'os, *Eth.* **199** FI4
Debuu, island, *Marshall Is.* **216** K4
Decatur, *Ala., U.S.* **101** HI5
Decatur, *Ga., U.S.* **96** L5
Decatur, *Ill., U.S.* **99** R6
Decatur, *Ind., U.S.* **99** QIO
Decatur, *Nebr., U.S.* **105** N9
Decatur, *Tex., U.S.* **102** KII
Decazeville, *Fr.* **147** WIO
Deccan, plateau, *India* **179** P5
Deception Island, *Antarctica* **226** C3
Dechu, *India* **178** G3
Decimomannu, *It.* **151** P4
Děčín, *Czech Rep.* **148** GII
Decize, *Fr.* **147** SII
Decorah, *Iowa, U.S.* **104** MI3
Dedéagach *see* Alexandroúpoli, *Gr.* **155** CI6
Dededo, *Guam, U.S.* **216** BII
Dedegöl Dağı, *Turk.* **168** H6
Dédougou, *Burkina Faso* **200** E9
Dedovichi, *Russ.* **156** H6
Deep, river, *N. Dak., U.S.* **104** E4
Deep Creek, *Bahamas* **120** F6
Deep Creek Lake, *Md., U.S.* **96** CIO
Deep Creek Range, *Utah, U.S.* **106** L5
Deep Well, *N. Terr., Austral.* **211** U9
Deering, *Alas., U.S.* **III** EI3
Deer Isle, *Me., U.S.* **95** GI7
Deer Lodge, *Mont., U.S.* **106** D7
Deer Park, *Wash., U.S.* **108** B9
Deer River, *Minn., U.S.* **104** FII
Deerton, *Mich., U.S.* **98** F8
Deer Trail, *Colo., U.S.* **106** MI4
Deeth, *Nev., U.S.* **108** MII
Defiance, *Ohio, U.S.* **99** PII
De Funiak Springs, *Fla., U.S.* **97** Q3
Deganya, *Israel* **170** L6
Dêgê, *China* **180** KIO
Degeh Bur, *Eth.* **199** GI6
Deggendorf, *Ger.* **148** JIO
DeGrey, *W. Aust., Austral.* **211** S3
DeGrey, river, *W. Aust., Austral.* **211** S3
Deh Bīd, *Iran* **173** FI4
Deh Khavak, *Afghan.* **176** L8
Dehqonobod, *Uzb.* **174** MI2
Dehra Dun, *India* **178** E6
Deh Rawod, *Afghan.* **177** P5
Deh Shu, *Afghan.* **177** R3
Dehui, *China* **181** DI7
Deim Zubeir, *Sudan* **198** GII
Deinkog, *China* **180** K9
Dej, *Rom.* **153** CI3
Dejen, Ras, *Eth.* **199** EI5
Dejiang, *China* **182** MI
De Jongs, Tanjung, *Indonesia* **213** DI6
De Kalb, *Miss., U.S.* **101** KI3
De Kalb, *Tex., U.S.* **102** KI4
DeKalb, *Ill., U.S.* **99** N6
Dekese, *Dem. Rep. of the Congo* **198** L9
Dekle Beach, *Fla., U.S.* **97** R6
Delaford, *Trinidad & Tobago* **121** NI8
Delamere, *N. Terr., Austral.* **211** Q8
De Land, *Fla., U.S.* **97** S9
Delano, *Calif., U.S.* **109** V7
Delano Peak, *Utah, U.S.* **107** N6
Delaport Point, *Bahamas* **120** BII
Delaram, *Afghan.* **177** P3
Delarof Islands, *Alas., U.S.* **110** N4
Delavan, *Wis., U.S.* **98** M6
Delaware, *Ohio, U.S.* **99** QI3
Delaware, river, *U.S.* **94** L9
Delaware, *S.C., U.S.* **96** CI4
Delaware Bay, *Del., N.J., U.S.* **85** G2O
Delaware Water Gap National Recreation Area, *N.J., Pa., U.S.* **94** MIO
De Leon, *Tex., U.S.* **102** M9
Delfzijl, *Neth.* **146** GI4
Delgado, Cabo, *Mozambique* **203** DI5
Delgany, *Ire.* **143** S7
Delgo, *Sudan* **198** CI2
Delhi, *India* **178** F6
Delhi, *La., U.S.* **100** L9
Delhi, *N.Y., U.S.* **94** KIO
Delice, river, *Turk.* **168** E9
Delicias, *Mex.* **114** D9
Deliktaş, *Turk.* **168** FI2
Délįne, *N.W.T., Can.* **82** FIO
Delingha, *China* **180** H9
Delissaville, *N. Terr., Austral.* **211** P7
Delitzsch, *Ger.* **148** F9
Dell Rapids, *S. Dak., U.S.* **104** L8
Delmar, *Del., Md., U.S.* **96** DI5

Delmenhorst, *Ger.* **148** C7
Del Norte, *Colo., U.S.* **107** PI2
De Long Mountains, *Alas., U.S.* **III** DI3
Deloraine, *Tas., Austral.* **211** ZI6
Delos, ruin, *Gr.* **155** KI5
Delphi, ruin, *Gr.* **154** HIO
Delphi, *Ind., U.S.* **99** Q8
Delphos, *Ohio, U.S.* **99** QII
Delray Beach, *Fla., U.S.* **97** WIO
Del Rio, *Tex., U.S.* **103** R6
Delta, *Colo., U.S.* **107** NIO
Delta, *Utah, U.S.* **106** M6
Delta Downs, *Qnsld., Austral.* **211** RII
Delta Junction, *Alas., U.S.* **III** GI8
Deltona, *Fla., U.S.* **97** S9
Del Verme Falls, *Eth.* **199** HI5
Demagiri, *India* **178** JI4
Demanda, Sierra de la, *Sp.* **144** DII
Demarcation Point, *Alas., U.S.* **84** M5
Demba, *Dem. Rep. of the Congo* **198** LIO
Dembéni, *Comoros* **205** MI4
Dembi Dolo, *Eth.* **199** GI3
Demchok, *India* **177** NI6
Demerara Plain, *Atl. Oc.* **236** M7
Deming, *N. Mex., U.S.* **107** VII
Demini, river, *Braz.* **130** C8
Demirci, *Turk.* **168** F4
Demirköprü Baraji, *Turk.* **168** F4
Demirköy, *Turk.* **168** B4
Demirtaş, *Turk.* **168** J7
Democratic Republic of the Congo, *Af.* **195** K2O
Demopolis, *Ala., U.S.* **101** LI4
Dempster Highway, *Yukon, Can.* **82** E9
Demta, *Indonesia* **213** BI7
Demyansk, *Russ.* **156** H7
Denali *see* McKinley, Mount, peak, *Alas., U.S.* **III** HI4
Denali Highway, *Alas., U.S.* **III** HI7
Denali National Park and Preserve, *Alas., U.S.* **III** HI6
Denali Park, *Alas., U.S.* **III** GI7
Den Burg, *Neth.* **146** GI2
Denekamp, *Neth.* **146** HI4
Denges Passage, *Palau* **216** QII
Dengkou (Bayan Gol), *China* **182** CI
Dêngqên, *China* **180** L9
Dengzhou, *China* **182** J4
Denham, *W. Aust., Austral.* **211** VI
Denham Springs, *La., U.S.* **100** PIO
Den Helder, *Neth.* **146** HI2
Dénia, *Sp.* **145** JI5
Denigomodu, region, *Nauru* **217** E22
Deniliquin, *N.S.W., Austral.* **211** YI2
Denio, *Nev., U.S.* **108** L8
Denis, Île, *Seychelles* **205** L2O
Denison, *Iowa, U.S.* **105** N9
Denison, *Tex., U.S.* **102** JI2
Denisovskaya, *Russ.* **156** EII
Denizli, *Turk.* **168** G4
Denmark, *Eur.* **139** S6
Denmark, *S.C., U.S.* **96** L9
Denmark, *W. Aust., Austral.* **211** Y3
Denmark Strait, *Arctic Oc.* **243** LI9
Dennery, *St. Lucia* **121** KI4
Denov, *Uzb.* **174** MI2
Denpasar, *Indonesia* **188** MII
Denton, *Md., U.S.* **96** CI4
Denton, *Tex., U.S.* **102** KII
D'Entrecasteaux, Point, *Austral.* **210** L3
D'Entrecasteaux Islands, *P.N.G.* **213** E2I
Denver, *Colo., U.S.* **106** MI3
Denver City, *Tex., U.S.* **102** L4
Deobhog, *India* **178** L8
Deoghar, *India* **178** HII
Deo Mu Gia, pass, *Laos, Vietnam* **186** KI2
Deora, *India* **178** G2
Deoria, *India* **178** G9
Deosai Mountains, *Pak.* **176** LI2
Deosri, *India* **178** GI3
De Pere, *Wis., U.S.* **98** J7
Depoe Bay, *Oreg., U.S.* **108** G2
Deposit, *N.Y., U.S.* **94** L9
Depósito, *Braz.* **130** B9
Deputatskiy, *Russ.* **159** EI8
Deqing, *China* **182** L9
Deqing, *China* **183** R3
De Queen, *Ark., U.S.* **100** H6
De Quincy, *La., U.S.* **100** P7
Dera Ghazi Khan, *Pak.* **177** R9
Dera Ismail Khan, *Pak.* **177** Q9
Dera Murad Jamali, *Pak.* **177** T7
Derbent, *Russ.* **157** UI6
Derby, *Eng., U.K.* **143** TI2
Derby, *Kans., U.S.* **105** U8

Derby, *W. Aust., Austral.* **211** R5
Derg, Lough, *Ire.* **143** P5
Derg, Lough, *Ire.* **143** S4
Dergachi, *Russ.* **156** MI5
Dergaon, *India* **178** GI4
Derhachi, *Ukr.* **157** N9
De Ridder, *La., U.S.* **100** N7
Derik, *Turk.* **169** HI5
Dermott, *Ark., U.S.* **100** J9
Dernberg, Cape, *Namibia* **202** K6
Dernieres, Isles, *La., U.S.* **100** RIO
Derravaragh, Lough, *Ire.* **143** R6
Derry *see* Londonderry, *N. Ire., U.K.* **143** P6
Derudeb, *Sudan* **199** DI4
Dervaza, *Turkm.* **174** K8
Derventa, *Bosn. & Herzg.* **152** E7
Deryneia, *Cyprus* **160** PIO
Derzhavīnsk, *Kaz.* **174** DI2
Désappointement, Îles du, *Fr. Polynesia, Fr.* **219** D2O
Des Arc, *Ark., U.S.* **100** G9
Deschutes, river, *Oreg., U.S.* **108** G5
Desē, *Eth.* **199** FI5
Deseado, river, *Arg.* **133** T8
Desecheo Island, *P.R., U.S.* **117** M2I
Deserta Grande, island, *Madeira* **204** N4
Desertas, Ilhas, *Madeira* **204** N4
Desert Center, *Calif., U.S.* **109** XI2
Deshaies, *Guadeloupe, Fr.* **121** EI4
Deshler, *Nebr., U.S.* **105** R7
Deskáti, *Gr.* **154** E9
Des Lacs, river, *N. Dak., U.S.* **104** E3
Desloge, *Mo., U.S.* **105** TI5
De Smet, *S. Dak., U.S.* **104** K7
Des Moines, river, *Iowa, U.S.* **85** FI3
Des Moines, *Iowa, U.S.* **105** PII
Des Moines, *N. Mex., U.S.* **107** QI4
Desna, river, *Russ.* **156** K7
Desnudez, Punta, *Arg.* **133** NI2
Desolación, Isla, *Chile* **133** X6
De Soto, *Mo., U.S.* **105** TI5
Des Plaines, *Ill., U.S.* **99** N7
Despotikó, island, *Gr.* **155** LI4
Dessalines, *Haiti* **117** LI6
Dessau, *Ger.* **148** E9
Destruction Island, *Wash., U.S.* **108** C2
Detmold, *Ger.* **148** E7
De Tour Village, *Mich., U.S.* **98** GII
Detroit, *Mich., U.S.* **98** MI3
Detroit Lake, *Oreg., U.S.* **108** G4
Detroit Lakes, *Minn., U.S.* **104** GIO
Detroit Seamount, *Pac. Oc.* **238** C8
Deva, *Rom.* **152** DI2
Deveci Dağı, *Turk.* **168** EII
Develi, *Turk.* **168** GIO
Devils, river, *Tex., U.S.* **103** Q6
Devilsbit Mountain, *Ire.* **143** T5
Devils Cataract *see* Raudal Yupurari, *Col.* **128** H7
Devils Hole, *Atl. Oc.* **236** EI3
Devils Hole, *Nev., U.S.* **109** UIO
Devil's Island *see* Diable, Île du, *Fr. Guiana, Fr.* **129** EI8
Devils Lake, *N. Dak., U.S.* **104** F6
Devils Lake, *N. Dak., U.S.* **104** F6
Devils Paw, peak, *Alas., U.S.* **III** K22
Devil's Point, *Bahamas* **117** FI3
Devil's Point, *Vanuatu* **218** F3
Devils Postpile National Monument, *Calif., U.S.* **109** S7
Devils Tower National Monument, *Wyo., U.S.* **106** FI3
Devine, *Tex., U.S.* **103** S9
Devizes, *Eng., U.K.* **143** VI2
Devon Island, *Nunavut, Can.* **83** DI6
Devonport, *Tas., Austral.* **211** ZI6
Devrek, *Turk.* **168** C7
Devrekâni, *Turk.* **168** C9
Devrukh, *India* **178** M3
Dewas, *India* **178** J5
Dewey, *Okla., U.S.* **102** EI2
De Witt, *Ark., U.S.* **100** H9
De Witt, *Iowa, U.S.* **105** NI4
Dexter, *Me., U.S.* **95** FI7
Dexter, *Mo., U.S.* **105** VI5
Dey Dey, Lake, *Austral.* **210** H7
Deyhūk, *Iran* **173** DI5
Deynau, *Turkm.* **174** LIO
Dezfūl, *Iran* **172** EII
Dezhou, *China* **182** F7
Dhaka, *Bangladesh* **178** HI3
Dhamār, *Yemen* **172** Q9
Dhamtari, *India* **178** K8
Dhanbad, *India* **178** HIO

D'Hanis, *Tex., U.S.* 103 R8
Dhanushkodi, *India* 179 S7
Dhar, *India* 178 J4
Dharan Bazar, *Nepal* 178 G11
Dharapuram, *India* 179 R6
Dharmjaygarh, *India* 178 J9
Dharmsala, *India* 177 P13
Dharwad, *India* 179 N4
Dhaulagiri, peak, *Nepal* 178 F9
Dhekelia (Eastern) Sovereign Base
  Area, *Cyprus* 160 P9
Dhenkanal, *India* 178 K10
Dhībān, *Jordan* 171 N6
Dhone, *India* 179 N6
Dhuburi, *India* 178 G12
Dhule, *India* 178 K4
Dhupgarh, peak, *India* 178 J6
Dhuusa Marreeb, *Somalia* 199 H17
Día, island, *Gr.* 155 Q15
Diable, Morne au, *Dominica* 121 D18
Diable, Île du (Devil's Island), *Fr. Guiana,
  Fr.* 129 E18
Diablo Range, *Calif., U.S.* 109 S4
Diablotins, Morne, *Dominica* 121 E19
Diakoftó, *Gr.* 154 J10
Diamant, Rocher de (Diamond Rock),
  Martinique, Fr. 121 G22
Diamante, river, *Arg.* 132 L8
Diamante, *Arg.* 132 K12
Diamantina, river, *Qnsld., Austral.* 211 T11
Diamantina, *Braz.* 131 K15
Diamantina, Chapada, *Braz.* 131 H15
Diamantina Fracture Zone, *Ind. Oc.*
  241 M13
Diamantina Lakes, *Qnsld., Austral.* 211 T11
Diamantino, *Braz.* 130 H10
Diamond Craters, *Oreg., U.S.* 108 J7
Diamond Harbour, *India* 178 J11
Diamond Head, *Hawai'i, U.S.* 112 E11
Diamond Mountains, *Calif., U.S.* 109 N6
Diamond Mountains, *Nev., U.S.* 109 P11
Diamond Peak, *Oreg., U.S.* 108 J4
Diamond Rock *see* Diamant, Rocher de,
  Martinique, Fr. 121 G22
Diamond Shoals, *N.C., U.S.* 96 H15
Dianbai, *China* 183 S2
Dian Chi, lake, *China* 180 N11
Dianópolis, *Braz.* 131 G14
Diaoyu Islands *see* Senkaku Shotō, *China*
  183 P11
Diapaga, *Burkina Faso* 200 E12
Diavolo, Mount, *India* 179 Q14
Dībā, *U.A.E.* 173 J15
Dibai, *India* 178 F6
Diboll, *Tex., U.S.* 103 N14
Dibrugarh, *India* 178 F15
Dibsī Faraj, *Syr.* 170 E10
Dickens, *Tex., U.S.* 102 K6
Dickinson, *N. Dak., U.S.* 104 G2
Dickinson Bay, *Antigua & Barbuda*
  121 A20
Dickson, *Russ.* 159 E13
Dickson, *Tenn., U.S.* 101 E14
Dickson City, *Pa., U.S.* 94 M9
Dicle, *Turk.* 169 G14
Dicle (Tigris), river, *Turk.* 169 H16
Dicomano, *It.* 150 G7
Didimótiho, *Gr.* 155 B17
Didwana, *India* 178 F4
Die, *Fr.* 147 V13
Diego de Almagro, *Chile* 132 G7
Diego de Almagro, Isla, *Chile* 133 W6
Diego Ramírez, Islas, *Chile* 133 Y9
Diekirch, *Lux.* 160 H10
Diemal Find, *W. Aust., Austral.* 211 W3
Dien Bien, *Vietnam* 186 H10
Dien Chau, *Vietnam* 186 J12
Dieppe, *Fr.* 146 M4
Dieppe Bay Town, *St. Kitts & Nevis*
  121 A17
Dierks, *Ark., U.S.* 100 H6
Dif, *Kenya* 199 J15
Diffa, *Niger* 197 J13
Differdange, *Lux.* 160 K9
Digboi, *India* 178 F15
Digby, *N.S., Can.* 83 P21
Dighton, *Kans., U.S.* 105 T4
Digne, *Fr.* 147 W14
Digoin, *Fr.* 147 T12
Digor, *Turk.* 169 D17
Digos, *Philippines* 189 F15
Digri, *Pak.* 177 W8
Digul, river, *Indonesia* 189 M21
Digura, island, *Maldives* 179 V3
Dihōk, *Iraq* 172 B9

Dijlah (Tigris), river, *Iraq* 172 E11
Dijon, *Fr.* 147 R13
Dika, Mys, *Russ.* 159 D15
Dikili, *Turk.* 168 E3
Díkti, Óros, *Gr.* 155 Q15
Dikwa, *Nigeria* 201 E17
Dīla, *Eth.* 199 H15
Dildarde Burnu, *Turk.* 168 J7
Dili, *Timor-Leste* 189 M15
Dilijan, *Arm.* 169 D19
Di Linh, *Vietnam* 187 P13
Dillenburg, *Ger.* 148 G6
Dilley, *Tex., U.S.* 103 S8
Dilling, *Sudan* 198 F12
Dillingham, *Alas., U.S.* 111 L13
Dillon, *Mont., U.S.* 106 F7
Dillon, *S.C., U.S.* 96 K11
Dillon's Bay, *Vanuatu* 218 G3
Dilolo, *Dem. Rep. of the Congo* 198 N9
Dilworth, *Minn., U.S.* 104 G8
Dimas, *Mex.* 114 F8
Dimashq (Damascus), *Syr.* 170 J7
Dimitrovgrad, *Bulg.* 153 K15
Dimitrovgrad, *Russ.* 156 K15
Dimitsána, *Gr.* 154 K9
Dimmitt, *Tex., U.S.* 102 H4
Dinagat, *Philippines* 189 E15
Dinajpur, *Bangladesh* 178 G12
Dinan, *Fr.* 147 Q5
Dinant, *Belg.* 146 M12
Dinar, *Turk.* 168 G5
Dīnār, Kūh-e, *Iran* 173 F13
Dinara, peak, *Bosn. & Herzg., Croatia*
  152 G6
Dinara, range, *Bosn. & Herzg., Croatia*
  152 G6
Dinaric Alps, *Eur.* 152 D5
Dinas Mawddwy, *Wales, U.K.* 143 T10
Ding'an, *China* 183 U2
Dingbian, *China* 182 E1
Dingle *see* An Daingean, *Ire.* 143 U2
Dingle Bay, *Ire.* 143 U2
Dingli, *Malta* 161 L21
Dingnan, *China* 183 Q5
Dingo, *Qnsld., Austral.* 211 T14
Dingolfing, *Ger.* 148 K9
Dingtao, *China* 182 G6
Dinguiraye, *Guinea* 200 E6
Dingxiang, *China* 182 E5
Dingxing, *China* 182 D6
Dingzhou, *China* 182 E6
Dingzi Gang, bay, *China* 182 F9
Dinosaur, *Colo., U.S.* 106 L10
Dinosaur National Monument, *Colo.,
  U.S.* 106 L10
Dinuba, *Calif., U.S.* 109 T7
Diomede Islands, *Russ., U.S.* 110 E11
Dion, ruin, *Gr.* 154 D10
Dios, *P.N.G.* 217 J13
Dios, Cayos de, *Cuba* 116 H7
Diourbel, *Senegal* 196 H4
Diphu Pass, *India, Myanmar* 186 C7
Diplo, *Pak.* 177 W8
Dir, *Pak.* 176 M10
Diré, *Mali* 196 H8
Dire Dawa, *Eth.* 199 H16
Dírfis, Óros, *Gr.* 154 H12
Dirico, *Angola* 202 F8
Dirj, *Lib.* 197 C13
Dirk Hartog Island, *Austral.* 210 H1
Dirranbandi, *Qnsld., Austral.* 211 V14
Dirty Devil, river, *Utah, U.S.* 107 N8
Disa, *India* 178 H3
Disappointment, Cape, *Wash., U.S.*
  108 E2
Disappointment, Lake, *Austral.* 210 F4
Discovery Bay, *Austral.* 210 M11
Discovery Bay, *Jam.* 120 H8
Discovery Tablemount, *Atl. Oc.* 237 U13
Disentis, *Switz.* 150 B4
Disney Cay, *Bahamas* 116 D11
Dispur, *India* 178 G13
Disteghil Sar, peak, *Pak.* 176 K12
Diu, *India* 178 K2
Divalak, *Afghan.* 177 Q3
Dīvāndarreh, *Iran* 172 C11
Divinhe, *Mozambique* 203 G13
Divinópolis, *Braz.* 131 L14
Diviso, *Col.* 128 H3
Divo, *Côte d'Ivoire* 200 H8
Divoúnia, island, *Gr.* 155 P17
Divriği, *Turk.* 169 F11
Diwana, *Pak.* 177 V6
Dīwār, *Syr.* 170 C16

Dixie, *Idaho, U.S.* 106 E4
Dixon, *Calif., U.S.* 109 R4
Dixon, *Ill., U.S.* 99 N5
Dixon, *Ky., U.S.* 101 C14
Dixon, *Mo., U.S.* 105 T13
Dixon, *Mont., U.S.* 106 C5
Dixon Entrance, *Alas., U.S., B.C., Can.*
  111 N23
Dixons, *Bahamas* 120 E12
Diyadin, *Turk.* 169 E18
Diyālā, river, *Iraq* 172 D10
Diyarbakır, *Turk.* 169 G15
Dja, river, *Cameroon* 201 J16
Djado, *Niger* 197 F13
Djado, Plateau du, *Niger* 197 F13
Djamaa, *Alg.* 196 B11
Djambala, *Congo* 201 M17
Djanet, *Alg.* 196 E12
Djarrit, island, *Marshall Is.* 216 G12
Djelfa, *Alg.* 196 B11
Djénné, *Mali* 196 H8
Djibouti, *Af.* 195 G23
Djibouti, *Djibouti* 199 F16
Djougou, *Benin* 200 F11
Djoum, *Cameroon* 201 J16
Djúpavík, *Ice.* 140 E2
Djúpivogur, *Ice.* 140 F4
Dmitriya Lapteva, Proliv, *Russ.* 159 D17
Dmitriyev L'govskiy, *Russ.* 156 M8
Dmitrov, *Russ.* 156 J9
Dnepr, river, *Russ.* 156 J7
Dnieper *see* Dnipro, river, *Ukr.* 157 R7
Dnieper, Source of the, *Russ.* 138 E10
Dnieper Lowland, *Belarus, Ukr.* 138 F10
Dnieper Upland, *Ukr.* 138 G10
Dniester, river, *Mold., Ukr.* 157 R5
Dnipro (Dnieper), river, *Ukr.* 157 R7
Dniprodzerzhyns'k, *Ukr.* 157 Q8
Dnipropetrovs'k, *Ukr.* 157 Q8
Dno, *Russ.* 156 G6
Dnyapro, river, *Belarus* 156 K6
Do Ab-e Mikh-e Zarrin, *Afghan.* 176 L7
Doba, *Chad* 197 K14
Dobane, *Cen. Af. Rep.* 198 H10
Dobbs, *Cape, Nunavut, Can.* 83 H16
Doboj, *Bosn. & Herzg.* 152 F8
Dobre Miasto, *Pol.* 149 B15
Dobrich, *Bulg.* 153 G17
Dobruja, region, *Bulg., Rom.* 153 F18
Dobrush, *Belarus* 156 M6
Dobson, *N.Z.* 213 N17
Docampadó, Ensenada, *Col.* 128 F3
Doce, river, *Braz.* 131 L16
Docker River, *N. Terr., Austral.* 211 U7
Dock Junction, *Ga., U.S.* 97 P8
Doctor David Douglas Historic Monu-
  ment, *Hawai'i, U.S.* 113 L20
Dodecanese *see* Dodekánissa, *Gr.* 155 M17
Dodekánissa (Dodecanese), *Gr.* 155 M17
Dodge, *Nebr., U.S.* 105 P8
Dodge City, *Kans., U.S.* 105 U5
Dodgeville, *Wis., U.S.* 98 L4
Dodman Point, *Eng., U.K.* 143 Y8
Dodoma, *Tanzania* 199 M14
Dodona, ruin, *Gr.* 154 F7
Dodson, *Mont., U.S.* 106 B10
Dodson, *Tex., U.S.* 102 H7
Doerun, *Ga., U.S.* 97 P5
Doetinchem, *Neth.* 146 J14
Dogaicoring Qangco, lake, *China* 180 J7
Doğanşehir, *Turk.* 168 G12
Dog Creek, *B.C., Can.* 82 L8
Dog Island, *Virgin Islands, U.S.* 120 N10
Dōgo, island, *Japan* 185 N7
Dogondoutchi, *Niger* 196 H10
Dog Rocks, *Bahamas* 116 F9
Doğruyol, *Turk.* 169 D17
Doğubayazıt, *Turk.* 169 E18
Dogwood Point, *St. Kitts & Nevis* 121 C18
Doha *see* Ad Dawḩah, *Qatar* 173 J13
Doi Inthanon, peak, *Thai.* 186 J7
Doïran, Lake *see* Dojransko Ezero,
  Maced. 152 L12
Doïránis, Límni, *Gr.* 154 B11
Dois Irmãos, Serra, *Braz.* 131 G16
Dojransko Ezero (Lake Doïran), *Maced.*
  152 L12
Dokdo (Takeshima, Liancourt Rocks),
  Japan 184 M6
Dokós, island, *Gr.* 154 K12
Dolak (Yos Sudarso), island, *Indonesia*
  189 N20
Doland, *S. Dak., U.S.* 104 K7
Dolbeau, *Que., Can.* 83 N19

Doldrums Fracture Zone, *Atl. Oc.*
  236 M8
Dole, *Fr.* 147 S13
Dolgiy Most, *Russ.* 159 K14
Doliana, *Gr.* 154 E7
Dolianova, *It.* 151 P4
Dolinsk, *Russ.* 159 K22
Dolisie (Loubomo), *Congo* 201 M16
Dolly Cays, *Bahamas* 116 F11
Dolo Bay, *Eth.* 199 H16
Dolomites, range, *It.* 150 C7
Dolonnur *see* Duolun, *China* 182 B7
Dolores, *Arg.* 132 M13
Dolores, river, *Colo., U.S.* 107 N10
Dolores, *Colo., U.S.* 107 P10
Dolores, *Uru.* 132 L13
Dolphin, Cape, *Falkland Is., U.K.* 133 V12
Dom, peak, *Indonesia* 213 B16
Domagnano, *San Marino* 161 J16
Domaniç, *Turk.* 168 E5
Domažlice, *Czech Rep.* 148 H10
Dombås, *Nor.* 140 J11
Doméniko, *Gr.* 154 E10
Domett, *N.Z.* 213 N18
Domeyko, *Chile* 132 H6
Domeyko, Cordillera, *Chile* 132 E7
Domfront, *Fr.* 147 P7
Domingitu, *Neth. Antilles, Neth.* 121 Q14
Dominica, *N. Amer.* 81 N24
Dominica, island, *N. Amer.* 80 N12
Dominican Republic, *N. Amer.* 81 N22
Dominica Passage, *Lesser Antilles*
  119 H17
Dominion, Cape, *Nunavut, Can.* 83 G17
Domodossola, *It.* 150 C3
Domokós, *Gr.* 154 G10
Domoni, *Comoros* 205 N16
Domus de Maria, *It.* 151 Q3
Domuyo, Volcán, *Arg.* 132 M7
Dôn, river, *Laos* 186 L12
Don, river, *Russ.* 157 R10
Donaldson, *Minn., U.S.* 104 E8
Donaldsonville, *La., U.S.* 100 P10
Donalsonville, *Ga., U.S.* 97 Q4
Donau (Danube), river, *Ger.* 148 K7
Don Benito, *Sp.* 144 H8
Doncaster, *Eng., U.K.* 143 R12
Dondo, *Angola* 202 C6
Dondo, *Indonesia* 189 J14
Dondo, *Mozambique* 203 G13
Donegal Bay, *Ire.* 143 Q5
Donets, *Ukr.* 157 Q9
Donets'k, *Ukr.* 157 Q11
Donets' Kryazh, *Russ., Ukr.* 157 Q10
Donets Ridge *see* Donets' Kryazh, *Russ.,
  Ukr.* 138 G12
Donga, *Nigeria* 201 G15
Dong'an, *China* 183 P3
Dongara, *W. Aust., Austral.* 211 W2
Dongbei (Manchuria), region, *China*
  181 D16
Dongfang (Basuo), *China* 183 U1
Dongfeng, *China* 182 B12
Donggang, *China* 182 D11
Dongguan, *China* 183 R5
Dongguang, *China* 182 E7
Donghai, *China* 181 J16
Dong Hoi, *Vietnam* 186 K12
Dongkalang, *Indonesia* 189 J13
Dongkan *see* Binhai, *China* 182 H9
Dong Khe, *Vietnam* 186 G12
Dongning, *China* 181 D18
Dongo, *Dem. Rep. of the Congo* 198 J8
Dongola, *Sudan* 198 C12
Dongou, *Congo* 201 K18
Dongping, *China* 182 G7
Dongping, *China* 183 S3
Dongqiao, *China* 180 K7
Dongsha, islands, *Taiwan, China* 183 T6
Dongsha (Pratas Island), *Taiwan, China*
  183 T6
Dongshan, *China* 183 R7
Dongsheng, *China* 182 D3
Dongtai, *China* 182 J9
Dongting Hu, *China* 182 M4
Dong Ujimqin Qi, *China* 181 D15
Dong Van, *Vietnam* 186 F11
Dongxiang, *China* 183 N6
Dongyztaū, *Kaz.* 174 F8

Donors Hill, *Qnsld., Austral.* 211 R11
Donostia-San Sebastián, *Sp.* 145 B13
Donoússa, island, *Gr.* 155 L16
Donzenac, *Fr.* 147 V9
Doomadgee, *Qnsld., Austral.* 211 R10
Doon, Loch, *Scot., U.K.* 143 N9
Door Peninsula, *Wis., U.S.* 98 H8
Dora, *Ala., U.S.* 101 K15
Dora, *N. Mex., U.S.* 107 T15
Dora, Lake, *Austral.* 210 F4
Dorado, Playa de, *P.R., U.S.* 120 M4
Dorah Pass, *Afghan.* 176 L9
Dorchester, *Eng., U.K.* 143 X11
Dorchester, Cape, *Nunavut, Can.* 83 G17
Dordives, *Fr.* 147 Q10
Dordogne, river, *Fr.* 147 V8
Dordogne, river, *Fr.* 147 Q2
Dordrecht, *Neth.* 146 J12
Dori, *Burkina Faso* 200 D11
Dório, *Gr.* 154 L9
Dormans, *Fr.* 147 P11
Dornbirn, *Aust.* 148 L7
Dornoch, *Scot., U.K.* 142 J9
Dornoch Firth, *Scot., U.K.* 142 J9
Dorogobuzh, *Russ.* 156 K7
Dorohoi, *Rom.* 153 A15
Dorrigo, *N.S.W., Austral.* 211 W15
Dorris, *Calif., U.S.* 108 L4
Dortmund, *Ger.* 148 E6
Dörtyol, *Turk.* 168 J11
Dörzbach, *Ger.* 148 H7
Dos Bahías, Cabo, *Arg.* 133 S9
Döşemealtı, *Turk.* 168 H6
Do Shakh, *Afghan.* 176 L6
Dos Hermanas, *Sp.* 144 L8
Dosso, *Niger* 196 H10
Dossor, *Kaz.* 174 F6
Dostyq, *Kaz.* 175 G19
Dothan, *Ala., U.S.* 101 N17
Douai, *Fr.* 146 M10
Douala, *Cameroon* 201 J15
Douarnenez, *Fr.* 147 Q3
Douarnenez, Baie de, *Fr.* 147 Q2
Double Island Point, *Austral.* 210 G15
Double Mountain Fork Brazos, river,
  Tex., U.S. 102 L6
Double Point, *Austral.* 210 D13
Doubtless Bay, *N.Z.* 213 H18
Doué, *Fr.* 147 S7
Douentza, *Mali* 196 H8
Douéoulou, *New Caledonia, Fr.* 218 C9
Douglas, *Ariz., U.S.* 107 W9
Douglas, *Ga., U.S.* 97 P7
Douglas, *Isle of Man, U.K.* 143 Q9
Douglas, *Mich., U.S.* 98 M9
Douglas, *Wyo., U.S.* 106 H13
Douglas, *Cabo, Ecua.* 128 Q7
Douglas Bay, *Dominica* 121 E18
Douglas Lake, *Tenn., U.S.* 101 E19
Douglass, *Kans., U.S.* 105 U8
Douglasville, *Ga., U.S.* 96 L4
Doullens, *Fr.* 146 M10
Doura, *Mali* 196 H7
Dourada, Serra, *S. Amer.* 126 G8
Dourados, *Braz.* 130 L11
Douro, river, *Port., Sp.* 144 E6
Dove Creek, *Colo., U.S.* 107 P10
Dover, *Del., U.S.* 96 C15
Dover, *Eng., U.K.* 143 W16
Dover, *N.H., U.S.* 95 J15
Dover, *Ohio, U.S.* 99 Q15
Dover, Strait of, *Fr., U.K.* 143 W16
Dover-Foxcroft, *Me., U.S.* 95 E17
Dowagiac, *Mich., U.S.* 99 N9
Dowlatabad, *Afghan.* 176 K4
Dowlatābād, *Iran* 173 G15
Dowlat Yar, *Afghan.* 176 M5
Downey, *Calif., U.S.* 109 X8
Downey, *Idaho, U.S.* 106 J7
Downieville, *Calif., U.S.* 109 P5
Downpatrick, *N. Ire., U.K.* 143 Q7
Downpatrick Head, *Ire.* 143 Q3
Downs, *Kans., U.S.* 105 S6
Dowshi, *Afghan.* 176 L7
Doxáto, *Gr.* 155 B13
Doylestown, *Pa., U.S.* 94 P10
Dōzen, island, *Japan* 185 P6
Drâa, Hamada du, *Alg., Mor.* 196 D7
Drâa, Oued, *Alg., Mor.* 196 C8
Drăgăneşti-Olt, *Rom.* 153 G14
Drăgăşani, *Rom.* 153 F14
Dragon's Mouths, strait, *Trinidad &
  Tobago* 121 N21
Draguignan, *Fr.* 147 X15
Drain, *Oreg., U.S.* 108 H3
Drake, *N. Dak., U.S.* 104 F5

Drakensberg, range, *S. Af.* 202 L12
Drake Peak, *Oreg., U.S.* 108 K6
Dráma, *Gr.* 155 B13
Drammen, *Nor.* 140 L12
Dran, *Vietnam* 187 N14
Dranov, Ostrov, *Rom.* 153 E18
Dras, *India* 176 M13
Drasan, *Pak.* 176 K10
Drau, *river, Aust.* 148 M10
Drava, *river, Croatia, Hung., Slov.* 138 H7
Dravograd, *Slov.* 152 C5
Drayton, *N. Dak., U.S.* 104 E8
Drépano, Akrotírio, *Gr.* 155 E13
Dresden, *Ger.* 148 F10
Dreux, *Fr.* 147 P9
Drevsjø, *Nor.* 140 J12
Drew, *Miss., U.S.* 100 J10
Drewsey, *Oreg., U.S.* 108 H8
Drews Reservoir, *Oreg., U.S.* 108 L5
Driggs, *Idaho, U.S.* 106 G8
Drin, *river, Albania* 152 K9
Drina, *river, Bosn. & Herzg., Serb.* 152 F9
Drinit, Gjiri i, *Albania* 152 K9
Driskill Mountain, *La., U.S.* 100 L7
Drøbak, *Nor.* 140 L12
Drobeta-Turnu Severin, *Rom.* 152 F12
Drogheda (Droichead Átha), *Ire.* 143 R7
Drohobych, *Ukr.* 157 P2
Droichead Átha *see* Drogheda, *Ire.* 143 R7
Droitwich, *Eng., U.K.* 143 U11
Drosh, *Pak.* 176 L10
Drouseia, *Cyprus* 160 P5
Drovyanoy, *Russ.* 158 E12
Drua, *island, Fiji* 218 G8
Drumheller, *Alta., Can.* 82 M10
Drummond, *Mont., U.S.* 106 D6
Drummond Bay *see* Big Bay, *Vanuatu* 218 E3
Drummond Island, *Mich., U.S.* 98 G12
Drummond Range, *Austral.* 210 F13
Drumright, *Okla., U.S.* 102 F12
Druza, Gora, *Russ.* 159 F19
Dryanovo, *Bulg.* 153 H15
Dryden, *Ont., Can.* 83 N15
Dryden, *Tex., U.S.* 103 Q4
Drygalski Ice Tongue, *Antarctica* 227 P13
Drygalski Island, *Antarctica* 227 J21
Drygalski Mountains, *Antarctica* 227 B14
Dry Harbour Mountains, *Jam.* 120 H8
Drysdale, *river, Austral.* 210 C6
Dry Tortugas, *islands, Fla., U.S.* 85 P18
Dry Tortugas National Park, *Fla., U.S.* 97 Y7
Dschang, *Cameroon* 201 H15
Duaringa, *Qnsld., Austral.* 211 U14
Duarte, Pico, *Dom. Rep.* 117 M18
Ḍubā, *Saudi Arabia* 172 G5
Dubai, *U.A.E.* 173 J15
Dubăsari, *Mold.* 157 R5
Dubawnt, *river, N.W.T., Can.* 83 J13
Dubawnt Lake, *Nunavut, Can.* 83 H13
Dubbo, *N.S.W., Austral.* 211 X14
Dubh Artach, *Scot., U.K.* 142 M6
Dublin, *Ga., U.S.* 96 M7
Dublin, *Tex., U.S.* 102 M10
Dublin (Baile Átha Cliath), *Ire.* 143 S7
Dublon *see* Tonoas, *island, F.S.M.* 217 C15
Dubna, *Russ.* 156 H9
Dubno, *Ukr.* 157 N3
Du Bois, *Pa., U.S.* 94 M5
Dubois, *Idaho, U.S.* 106 G7
Dubois, *Wyo., U.S.* 106 G9
Dubovka, *Russ.* 157 P13
Dubrovnik (Ragusa), *Croatia* 152 J8
Dubrovytsya, *Ukr.* 156 M4
Dubuque, *Iowa, U.S.* 105 N14
Duc de Gloucester, Îles, *Fr. Polynesia, Fr.* 219 G19
Duchesne, *river, Utah, U.S.* 106 L8
Duchesne, *Utah, U.S.* 106 L8
Duchess, *Qnsld., Austral.* 211 S11
Ducie Island, *Pac. Oc.* 215 L16
Duck, *river, Tenn., U.S.* 101 F15
Duck Hill, *Miss., U.S.* 100 J11
Ducktown, *Tenn., U.S.* 101 G18
Ducos, *Martinique, Fr.* 121 F23
Ducos, Île, *New Caledonia, Fr.* 218 D8
Duc Tho, *Vietnam* 186 J12
Dudelange, *Lux.* 160 K10
Dudinka, *Russ.* 159 F13
Dudley, *Eng., U.K.* 143 T11
Dudune, Île, *New Caledonia, Fr.* 218 D9
Duero, *river, Sp.* 144 E9

Dufek Coast, *Antarctica* 226 L12
Duffield, *N. Terr., Austral.* 211 U9
Duff Islands, *Solomon Is.* 217 N24
Dufftown, *Scot., U.K.* 142 J10
Dufur, *Oreg., U.S.* 108 F5
Dugi Otok, *island, Croatia* 152 G5
Dugway, *Utah, U.S.* 106 L6
Duifken Point, *Austral.* 210 B12
Duisburg, *Ger.* 148 E5
Duitama, *Col.* 128 E6
Dukla, *Pol.* 149 H17
Dulan (Qagan Us), *China* 180 J10
Dulce, *river, Arg.* 132 J11
Dulce, *N. Mex., U.S.* 107 Q11
Dulce, Golfo, *Costa Rica* 115 P19
Dulovo, *Bulg.* 153 G16
Duluth, *Minn., U.S.* 104 G12
Dūmā, *Syr.* 170 J7
Dumai, *Indonesia* 188 H6
Dumaran, *island, Philippines* 189 E13
Dumas, *Ark., U.S.* 100 J9
Dumas, *Tex., U.S.* 102 F5
Dumbarton, *Scot., U.K.* 142 M9
Dumbéa, *New Caledonia, Fr.* 218 E8
Dumfries, *Scot., U.K.* 143 P10
Dumka, *India* 178 H11
Dumoga Kecil, *Indonesia* 189 J15
Dumont d'Urville, *station, Antarctica* 227 Q18
Dumra, *India* 178 G10
Dumshaf Plain, *Arctic Oc.* 243 H19
Dumyât (Damietta), *Egypt* 197 C18
Dun, *Fr.* 147 N13
Duna (Danube), *river, Hung.* 149 M15
Dunaj (Danube), *river, Slovakia* 149 L14
Dunărea (Danube), *river, Rom., Serb. & Mont.* 153 F17
Dunaújváros, *Hung.* 149 L15
Dunav (Danube), *river, Bulg., Rom., Serb.* 153 G15
Dunay (Danube), *river, Rom.* 153 E17
Durrës, *Albania* 152 L9
Dunbar, *Qnsld., Austral.* 211 Q12
Dunbar, *W. Va., U.S.* 96 D8
Duncan, *Ariz., U.S.* 107 V9
Duncan de Pinzón, Isla, *island, Ecua.* 128 Q9
Duncan, *Okla., U.S.* 102 H10
Duncan Passage, *India* 179 Q14
Duncans, *Jam.* 120 H8
Duncansby Head, *Scot., U.K.* 142 G10
Duncan Town, *Bahamas* 117 H13
Duncombe Bay, *Norfolk I., Austral.* 217 F20
Dundalk, *Md., U.S.* 96 C13
Dundalk (Dún Dealgan), *Ire.* 143 R7
Dundalk Bay, *Ire.* 143 R7
Dundas, Lake, *Austral.* 210 K4
Dún Dealgan *see* Dundalk, *Ire.* 143 R7
Dundee, *Scot., U.K.* 142 L10
Dundee, *Scot., U.K.* 142 L10
Dundee Island, *Antarctica* 226 C4
Dundonnell, *Scot., U.K.* 142 J8
Dundrennan, *Scot., U.K.* 143 P9
Dundrum Bay, *N. Ire., U.K.* 143 Q7
Dund-Urt, *Mongolia* 180 D12
Dund-Us *see* Hovd, *Mongolia* 180 D9
Dunedin, *Fla., U.S.* 97 U7
Dunedin, *N.Z.* 213 R16
Dunedoo, *N.S.W., Austral.* 211 X14
Dunes City, *Oreg., U.S.* 108 H2
Dunfermline, *Scot., U.K.* 142 M10
Dungarpur, *India* 178 H4
Dungarvan Harbour, *Ire.* 143 U5
Dungeness, *Eng., U.K.* 143 W15
Dungeness, Punta, *Arg.* 133 W9
Dungiven, *N. Ire., U.K.* 143 P6
Dunhua, *China* 182 A13
Dunhuang, *China* 180 G9
Dunkerque (Dunkirk), *Fr.* 146 L10
Dunkineely, *Ire.* 143 P4
Dunkirk *see* Dunkerque, *Fr.* 146 L10
Dunkirk, *Ind., U.S.* 99 Q10
Dunkirk, *N.Y., U.S.* 94 K4
Dunkwa, *Ghana* 200 H10
Dún Laoghaire (Kingstown), *Ire.* 143 S7
Dunlap, *Iowa, U.S.* 105 P9
Dunmanus Bay, *Ire.* 143 V3
Dunmanway, *Ire.* 143 V3
Dunmore, *Pa., U.S.* 94 M9
Dunmore Town, *Bahamas* 120 D5
Dunn, *N.C., U.S.* 96 H11
Dunnellon, *Fla., U.S.* 97 S7
Dunning, *Nebr., U.S.* 105 P5
Dunn's River Falls, *Jam.* 120 H9
Dunolly, *Vic., Austral.* 211 Z12

Dunsborough, *W. Aust., Austral.* 211 Y2
Dunseith, *N. Dak., U.S.* 104 E5
Dunsmuir, *Calif., U.S.* 108 M4
Duntroon, *N.Z.* 213 Q16
Dunvegan, *Scot., U.K.* 142 J7
Dunvegan Head, *Scot., U.K.* 142 J7
Duolun (Dolonnur), *China* 182 B7
Dupree, *S. Dak., U.S.* 104 J3
Dupuyer, *Mont., U.S.* 106 B7
Duqm, *Oman* 173 M16
Duque de Caxias, *Braz.* 131 M15
Duque de York, Isla, *Chile* 133 V6
Duquesne, *Pa., U.S.* 94 N3
Du Quoin, *Ill., U.S.* 99 U5
Dura Europus, *ruin, Syr.* 170 G14
Durán, *river, Sp.* 160 K6
Durance, *river, Fr.* 147 W14
Durand, *Wis., U.S.* 98 J2
Durango, *Colo., U.S.* 107 P11
Durango, *Mex.* 114 F9
Durango, *Sp.* 144 B12
Durankulak, *Bulg.* 153 G18
Durant, *Miss., U.S.* 100 K11
Durant, *Okla., U.S.* 102 J12
Duras, *Fr.* 147 V7
Durazno, *Uru.* 132 K14
Durban, *S. Af.* 202 L12
Durbuy, *Belg.* 146 M13
Ðurđevac, *Croatia* 152 D7
Dureji, *Pak.* 177 V6
Düren, *Ger.* 148 F5
Durg, *India* 178 K8
Durham, *Eng., U.K.* 143 P12
Durham, *N.C., U.S.* 96 H11
Durham, *N.H., U.S.* 95 J14
Durham Downs, *Qnsld., Austral.* 211 V11
Durlston Head, *Eng., U.K.* 143 X12
Durmitor, *peak, Serb. & Mont.* 138 J8
Durness, Kyle of, *Scot., U.K.* 142 G8
Durong, *Qnsld., Austral.* 211 V15
Duroy, *Russ.* 159 L18
Durrës, *Albania* 152 L9
Durrësit, Gjiri i, *Albania* 152 L9
Dursey Island, *Ire.* 143 V2
Dursunbey, *Turk.* 168 E4
Durtal, *Fr.* 147 R7
Ḍurūz, Jabal ad, *Syr.* 170 L8
Duşak, *Turkm.* 174 M9
Dûsh, *Egypt* 197 E18
Dushanbe, *Taj.* 176 H7
Dushanzi, *China* 180 E7
Düsseldorf, *Ger.* 148 F5
Dutchcap Cay, *Virgin Islands, U.S.* 120 M7
Dutch John, *Utah, U.S.* 106 K9
Dutton, *Mont., U.S.* 106 C7
Duvergé, *Dom. Rep.* 117 M17
Duwayhin, Dawḩat, *Saudi Arabia* 173 J13
Duyun, *China* 180 N12
Düzce, *Turk.* 168 D7
Dvina Bay, *Russ.* 138 B10
Dwarka, *India* 178 J1
Dwight, *Ill., U.S.* 99 P6
Dworshak Reservoir, *Idaho, U.S.* 106 D4
Dyat'kovo, *Russ.* 156 L8
Dyer, Cape, *Nunavut, Can.* 83 F19
Dyer Bay, *N.W.T., Can.* 82 C12
Dyersburg, *Tenn., U.S.* 100 E12
Dysart, *Qnsld., Austral.* 211 T14
Dzaanhushuu, *Mongolia* 180 D11
Dzag, *Mongolia* 180 D10
Dzangali, *Afghan.* 177 P6
Dzaoudzi, *Mayotte, Fr.* 205 P17
Dzavhan, *river, Mongolia* 180 D9
Dzerzhinsk, *Russ.* 156 J12
Dzhagdy, Khrebet, *Russ.* 159 J19
Dzhagdy Range *see* Dzhagdy, Khrebet, *Russ.* 166 D12
Dzhankoy, *Ukr.* 157 S8
Dzhardzhan, *Russ.* 159 F16
Dzharty-Rabat, *Taj.* 176 J11
Dzharylhach, Ostriv, *Ukr.* 157 S7
Dzhilandy, *Taj.* 176 J10
Dzhugdzhur, Khrebet, *Russ.* 159 H20
Dzhugdzhur Range *see* Dzhugdzhur, Khrebet, *Russ.* 166 D12
Dzhunkun, *Russ.* 159 H16
Działdowo, *Pol.* 149 C15
Dzibilchaltún, *ruin, Mex.* 115 H16
Dzibilchaltún, *ruin, Mex.* 115 H16
Dzierżoniów, *Pol.* 149 G13

Dzöölön, *Mongolia* 180 B10
Dzungarian Basin *see* Junggar Pendi, *China* 180 E7
Dzungarian Gate, *China, Kaz.* 175 G19
Dzvina, *river, Belarus* 156 J6
Dzyarzhynsk, *Belarus* 156 K4

E

Eads, *Colo., U.S.* 107 N15
Eagar, *Ariz., U.S.* 107 T9
Eagle, *Alas., U.S.* 111 F19
Eagle, *Colo., U.S.* 106 M11
Eagle, Mount, *Virgin Islands, U.S.* 120 Q2
Eagle Beach, *Aruba, Neth.* 121 Q16
Eagle Butte, *S. Dak., U.S.* 104 J4
Eagle Grove, *Iowa, U.S.* 105 N11
Eagle Harbor, *Mich., U.S.* 98 E7
Eagle Lake, *Calif., U.S.* 109 N5
Eagle Lake, *Me., U.S.* 95 B17
Eagle Lake, *Tex., U.S.* 103 R12
Eagle Mountain, *Calif., U.S.* 109 X11
Eagle Mountain, *Minn., U.S.* 104 F14
Eagle Mountain Lake, *Tex., U.S.* 102 L12
Eagle Nest Lake, *N. Mex., U.S.* 107 Q13
Eagle Pass, *Tex., U.S.* 103 S7
Eagle Peak, *Calif., U.S.* 108 M6
Eagle Peak, *N. Mex., U.S.* 107 T10
Eagle Peak, *Tex., U.S.* 103 V3
Eagle River, *Mich., U.S.* 98 E7
Eagle River, *Wis., U.S.* 98 G5
Eagles Mere, *Pa., U.S.* 94 M8
Earle, *Ark., U.S.* 100 G11
Earlimart, *Calif., U.S.* 109 U7
Earlington, *Ky., U.S.* 101 C14
Earp, *Calif., U.S.* 109 X13
Earth, *Tex., U.S.* 102 J4
Easky, *Ire.* 143 Q4
Easley, *S.C., U.S.* 96 J7
East Anglia, *region, Eng., U.K.* 143 U15
East Anglian Heights, *Eng., U.K.* 143 U14
East Antarctica, *region, Antarctica* 227 H17
East Aurora, *N.Y., U.S.* 94 J5
East Bay, *La., U.S.* 100 R12
Eastbourne, *Eng., U.K.* 143 W14
East Caicos, *island, Turks & Caicos Is., U.K.* 117 H17
East Cape, *N.Z.* 213 K21
East Cape, *Russ.* 166 A12
East Carbon, *Utah, U.S.* 106 M8
East Channel, *Marshall Is.* 216 H9
East Chicago, *Ind., U.S.* 99 N7
East China Sea, *Pac. Oc.* 238 F4
East Coast Bays, *N.Z.* 213 J19
East Cote Blanche Bay, *La., U.S.* 100 Q9
East Dubuque, *Ill., U.S.* 98 M4
East End, *Virgin Islands, U.K.* 120 Q7
East End, *Cayman Is., U.K.* 120 J4
East End, *Virgin Islands, U.S.* 120 M12
East End Point, *Bahamas* 120 G6
East End Point, *Bahamas* 120 B12
East Entrance, *Palau* 216 L12
Easter Fracture Zone, *Pac. Oc.* 239 M16
Easter Island *see* Pascua, Isla de, *Chile* 215 L19
Eastern Beach, *Gibraltar, U.K.* 161 N23
Eastern Channel, *Japan* 185 Q3
Eastern Desert, *Egypt* 197 D19
Eastern Ghats, *range, India* 179 Q6
Eastern Island, *Hawai'i, U.S.* 112 K2
Eastern Sayan Mountains, *Russ.* 166 E9
Eastern Sovereign Base Area *see* Dhekelia Sovereign Base Area, *Cyprus* 160 P9
East Falkland, *island, Falkland Is., U.K.* 133 W12
East Fayu, *island, F.S.M.* 216 Q6
East Fork Bruneau, *river, Idaho, U.S.* 106 J4
East Fork White, *river, Ind., U.S.* 85 G16
East Frisian Islands, *Ger.* 148 B6
East Glacier Park, *Mont., U.S.* 106 B6
East Grand Forks, *Minn., U.S.* 104 F8
East Helena, *Mont., U.S.* 106 D7
East Indiaman Ridge, *Ind. Oc.* 241 L13
East Isaac, *island, Bahamas* 116 D10
East Jordan, *Mich., U.S.* 98 H10
East Lake, *Mich., U.S.* 98 J9
Eastland, *Tex., U.S.* 102 M9
East Lansing, *Mich., U.S.* 98 M11
Eastleigh, *Eng., U.K.* 143 W12

East Liverpool, *Ohio, U.S.* 99 Q16
East London, *S. Af.* 202 M10
Eastmain, *river, Que., Can.* 83 M19
Eastmain, *Que., Can.* 83 M18
Eastman, *Ga., U.S.* 97 N6
East Mariana Basin, *Pac. Oc.* 238 H7
East Millinocket, *Me., U.S.* 95 D17
East Moline, *Ill., U.S.* 99 P4
East Novaya Zemlya Trough, *Arctic Oc.* 243 C14
Easton, *Md., U.S.* 96 C14
Easton, *Pa., U.S.* 94 N9
East Orange, *N.J., U.S.* 94 N11
East Pacific Rise, *Pac. Oc.* 239 R16
East Pen Island, *Ont., Can.* 83 L16
East Peoria, *Ill., U.S.* 99 Q5
East Point, *Ga., U.S.* 96 L5
East Point, *Marshall Is.* 216 M9
East Point, *Virgin Islands, U.S.* 120 Q4
Eastpoint, *Fla., U.S.* 97 R4
Eastport, *Me., U.S.* 95 E19
East Prairie, *Mo., U.S.* 105 V16
East Prussia, *region, Pol., Russ.* 149 B16
East Ridge, *Tenn., U.S.* 101 G17
East St. Louis, *Ill., U.S.* 99 T4
East Sea *see* Japan, Sea of, *Pac. Oc.* 238 E5
East Siberian Sea, *Arctic Oc.* 242 G4
East Tawas, *Mich., U.S.* 98 J12
East Timor *see* Timor-Leste, *Asia* 167 Z14
Eastville, *Va., U.S.* 96 E14
East Wells, *Bahamas* 120 A8
Eaton, *Ohio, U.S.* 99 R11
Eaton Rapids, *Mich., U.S.* 98 M11
Eatonton, *Ga., U.S.* 96 L6
Eatonville, *Wash., U.S.* 108 D4
Eau Claire, *Wis., U.S.* 98 H3
Eau Claire, Lac à l', *Que., Can.* 83 L18
Eauripik Atoll, *F.S.M.* 216 Q4
Eauripik Rise, *Pac. Oc.* 238 J6
Ebadon, *island, Marshall Is.* 216 K1
Ebagoola, *Qnsld., Austral.* 211 Q12
Ebbw Vale, *Wales, U.K.* 143 V10
Ebe Khaya, Gora, *Russ.* 159 F15
Ebenholz, *Liech.* 160 P2
Eber Gölü, *Turk.* 168 F7
Eberswalde, *Ger.* 148 D10
Ebeye, *island, Marshall Is.* 216 N5
Ebino, *Japan* 185 S4
Ebinur Hu, *China* 180 D6
Ebjapik, *island, Marshall Is.* 216 N5
Eboda *see* Horvat 'Avedat, *ruin, Israel* 171 P5
Eboli, *It.* 150 M11
Ebolowa, *Cameroon* 201 J16
Ebon Atoll, *Marshall Is.* 216 J4
Ebro, *river, Sp.* 145 E15
Ebro, Embalse del, *Sp.* 144 B11
Ebwaj, *island, Marshall Is.* 216 N5
Ecclesville, *Trinidad & Tobago* 121 Q23
Eceabat, *Turk.* 168 D2
Echallens, *Switz.* 150 B1
Echínos, *Gr.* 155 B14
Echo, *Oreg., U.S.* 108 E7
Echo Bay, *N.W.T., Can.* 82 F11
Echternach, *Lux.* 160 J11
Echuca, *N.S.W., Austral.* 211 Y12
Ecija, *Sp.* 144 L9
Eckenförde, *Ger.* 148 B8
Ecuador, *S. Amer.* 127 D14
Edah, *W. Aust., Austral.* 211 V3
Edcouch, *Tex., U.S.* 103 W10
Ed Damer, *Sudan* 199 D13
Ed Debba, *Sudan* 198 D12
Eddrachillis Bay, *Scot., U.K.* 142 H8
Eddystone Rocks, *Eng., U.K.* 143 Y9
Eddyville, *Ky., U.S.* 101 D13
Ede, *Neth.* 146 J13
Edéa, *Cameroon* 201 J15
Eden, *N.C., U.S.* 96 G10
Eden, *Tex., U.S.* 103 N7
Eden, *Wyo., U.S.* 106 J9
Edenburg, *S. Af.* 202 L10
Edenton, *N.C., U.S.* 96 G14
Édessa, *Gr.* 154 C9
Edessa *see* Şanlıurfa, *Turk.* 169 H13
Edgar, *Nebr., U.S.* 105 R7
Edgartown, *Mass., U.S.* 95 M15
Edgefield, *S.C., U.S.* 96 L8
Edgeley, *N. Dak., U.S.* 104 H6
Edgell Island, *Nunavut, Can.* 83 H19
Edgemont, *S. Dak., U.S.* 104 M1
Edgeøya, *island, Norway* 167 P7
Edgerton, *Minn., U.S.* 104 L9

Edgerton, *Wis., U.S.* 98 M6
Edgigen, island, *Marshall Is.* 216 K4
Edina, *Mo., U.S.* 105 K13
Edinburg, *Tex., U.S.* 103 W10
Edinburgh, *Ind., U.S.* 99 S9
Edinburgh, *Scot., U.K.* 142 M10
Edirne (Adrianople), *Turk.* 168 B3
Edison, *Ga., U.S.* 97 P4
Edison, *N.J., U.S.* 94 N10
Edisto, river, *S.C., U.S.* 96 M9
Edisto Island, *S.C., U.S.* 96 M10
Edithburgh, *S. Aust., Austral.* 211 Y10
Edjell, island, *Marshall Is.* 216 K4
Edmond, *Okla., U.S.* 102 G11
Edmonds, *Wash., U.S.* 108 B4
Edmonton, *Alta., Can.* 82 L10
Edmore, *N. Dak., U.S.* 104 E6
Edmundston, *N.B., Can.* 83 N20
Edna, *Tex., U.S.* 103 S12
Edolo, *It.* 150 C6
Edrei *see* Darʿā, *Syr.* 170 L7
Edremit, *Turk.* 168 E3
Edremit Körfezi, *Turk.* 168 E3
Edrengiyn Nuruu, range, *Mongolia* 180 E10
Eduardo Castex, *Arg.* 132 M10
Edward, river, *Austral.* 210 L12
Edward, Lake, *Dem. Rep. of the Congo, Uganda* 198 K12
Edward River, *Qnsld., Austral.* 211 Q11
Edwards, *Calif., U.S.* 109 W8
Edwards Plateau, *Tex., U.S.* 103 P7
Edwardsville, *Ill., U.S.* 99 T4
Edward VIII Bay, *Antarctica* 227 D20
Edward VII Peninsula, *Antarctica* 226 M10
Ee, island, *Cook Is., N.Z.* 218 Q12
Eek, *Alas., U.S.* 110 K12
Eel, river, *Calif., U.S.* 109 N2
Éfaté (Île Vaté), *Vanuatu* 218 F3
Effigy Mounds National Monument, *Iowa, U.S.* 104 M14
Effingham, *Ill., U.S.* 99 S6
Eflâni, *Turk.* 168 C8
Efstrátios, Ágios, *Gr.* 155 F14
Efuenaarukosu Point, *N. Mariana Is., U.S.* 216 D8
Efyra, ruin, *Gr.* 154 F7
Egadi, Isole, *It.* 151 S8
Egan Range, *Nev., U.S.* 109 Q12
Egegik, *Alas., U.S.* 111 L13
Eger, *Hung.* 149 K16
Egeria Fracture Zone, *Ind. Oc.* 240 K8
Egersund, *Nor.* 140 M10
Egg Lagoon, *Tas., Austral.* 211 Y15
Egiáli, *Gr.* 155 L16
Eğil, *Turk.* 169 G14
Egilsstaðir, *Ice.* 140 F4
Égina (Aegina), island, *Gr.* 154 K12
Egina, *Gr.* 154 K12
Egio, *Gr.* 154 H9
Eğirdir, *Turk.* 168 G6
Eğirdir Gölü, *Turk.* 168 G6
Egiyn, river, *Mongolia* 180 C11
Égletons, *Fr.* 147 U9
Eglinton Fiord, *Nunavut, Can.* 83 E18
Egmont, Mount *see* Taranaki, Mount, *N.Z.* 213 L18
Eğrigöz Dağı, *Turk.* 168 E5
Éguzon-Chantôme, *Fr.* 147 T9
Egvekinot, *Russ.* 159 B20
Egypt, *Af.* 195 E21
Ehingen, *Ger.* 148 K7
Ehrang, *Ger.* 160 J12
Ehrenberg, *Ariz., U.S.* 107 T4
Ei, *Japan* 185 T4
Eiao, island, *Fr. Polynesia, Fr.* 215 H14
Eickelberg Seamount, *Pac. Oc.* 239 D14
Eidsvold, *Qnsld., Austral.* 211 U15
Eifel, range, *Ger.* 160 G11
Eigg, island, *Scot., U.K.* 142 K7
Eight Degree Channel, *Maldives* 179 S3
Eight Mile Rock, *Bahamas* 120 F1
Eights Coast, *Antarctica* 226 J6
Eighty Mile Beach, *Austral.* 210 E4
Eildon, *Vic., Austral.* 211 M12
Eil Malk *see* Mercherchar, island, *Palau* 216 P11
Einasleigh, *Qnsld., Austral.* 211 R12
Eindhoven, *Neth.* 146 K13
Einsiedeln, *Switz.* 150 B4
Eirik Ridge, *Atl. Oc.* 236 D7
Eirunepé, *Braz.* 130 F5
Eisch, river, *Lux.* 160 J9
Eischen, *Lux.* 160 J9

Eisenach, *Ger.* 148 F8
Eisenerz, *Aust.* 148 L11
Eisenhüttenstad, *Ger.* 148 E11
Eisenstadt, *Aust.* 149 L13
Eita, island, *Kiribati* 217 G17
Eita, *Kiribati* 217 G17
Eivissa (Ibiza), *Sp.* 145 H17
Ejea de los Caballeros, *Sp.* 145 D14
Ejin Horo Qi (Altan Xiret), *China* 182 D3
Ejin Qi, *China* 180 F11
Ejmiatsin, *Arm.* 169 E18
Ekalaka, *Mont., U.S.* 106 E13
Ekarma, island, *Russ.* 159 H23
Ekerem, *Turkm.* 174 L6
Ekeren, *Belg.* 146 K12
Ekiatapskiy Khrebet, *Russ.* 159 B20
Ekibastuz, *Kaz.* 175 C15
Ekonda, *Russ.* 159 G15
Ekström Ice Shelf, *Antarctica* 226 A11
Ekwan, river, *Ont., Can.* 83 M17
Elafonísou, Stenón, *Gr.* 154 N11
Elafonísi, island, *Gr.* 154 M11
Elaia, Cape, *Cyprus* 160 N10
El ʿAlamein, *Egypt* 197 C18
Elamanchili, *India* 178 M9
El ʿArîsh (Rhinocolura), *Egypt* 171 N3
Elása, island, *Gr.* 155 Q17
Elassón, *Gr.* 154 F10
El Astillero, *Sp.* 144 B11
Elat, *Israel* 171 R5
Elath *see* Ezion-geber, ruin, *Jordan* 171 R5
Elato Atoll, *F.S.M.* 216 Q5
El ʿAuja *see* Nizzana, *Israel* 171 P4
El ʿAuja, peak, *Jordan* 171 R7
Elazığ, *Turk.* 169 G14
Elba, *Ala., U.S.* 101 M16
Elba, island, *It.* 150 J5
Elba, Cape (Ras Hadarba), *Egypt* 194 F10
El Banco, *Col.* 128 C5
El Barco de Ávila, *Sp.* 144 F9
Elbasan, *Albania* 152 L9
El Baúl, *Venez.* 128 C9
El Bayadh, *Alg.* 196 B10
Elbe, river, *Ger.* 148 C8
Elbert, Mount, *Colo., U.S.* 106 M12
Elberta, *Mich., U.S.* 98 J9
Elberton, *Ga., U.S.* 96 K7
Elbeuf, *Fr.* 147 N8
Elbistan, *Turk.* 168 G12
Elblag, *Pol.* 149 B15
Elbow Cays, *Bahamas* 116 F8
Elbow Lake, *Minn., U.S.* 104 H9
El'brus, peak, *Russ.* 157 U12
El Bureij, *Gaza Strip* 171 N4
El Burgo de Osma, *Sp.* 144 D11
Elburz Mountains *see* Alborz, Reshteh-ye, *Iran* 172 B12
El Cajon, *Calif., U.S.* 109 Z10
El Calafate (Lago Argentino), *Arg.* 133 V7
El Callao, *Venez.* 128 D12
El Calvario, *Venez.* 128 C9
El Campello, *Sp.* 145 J14
El Campo, *Tex., U.S.* 103 R12
El Carmen, *Arg.* 132 E9
El Ceibo, *Guatemala* 115 K15
El Ceibo, *Mex.* 115 H16
El Centro, *Calif., U.S.* 109 Z11
El Cerro, *Bol.* 130 K9
Elche (Elx), *Sp.* 145 K14
Elchi *see* Wādī Mūsá, *Jordan* 171 Q6
El Cuyo, *Mex.* 115 H17
Elda, *Sp.* 145 J14
Elderslie, *Jam.* 120 H7
El'dikan, *Russ.* 159 G19
El Djouf, region, *Mali, Mauritania* 196 F7
Eldon, *Iowa, U.S.* 105 Q13
Eldon, *Mo., U.S.* 105 T12
Eldora, *Iowa, U.S.* 105 N12
El Dorado, *Ark., U.S.* 100 K8
El Dorado, *Kans., U.S.* 105 U8
El Dorado, *Venez.* 128 D12
Eldorado, *Arg.* 132 G15
Eldorado, *Ill., U.S.* 99 U6
Eldorado, *Mex.* 114 F8
Eldorado, *Okla., U.S.* 102 H8
Eldorado, *Tex., U.S.* 103 P6
El Dorado Springs, *Mo., U.S.* 105 U11
Eldoret, *Kenya* 199 J14
Electra, *Tex., U.S.* 102 J9
Electric Mills, *Miss., U.S.* 101 K13
Eleftheroúpoli, *Gr.* 155 C13
Elektrostal', *Russ.* 156 J10

Eléni *see* Makroníssi, island, *Gr.* 155 K13
Elephant Butte Reservoir, *N. Mex., U.S.* 107 U11
Elephant Island, *Antarctica* 226 B3
Eleşkirt, *Turk.* 169 E17
Eleuthera Island, *Bahamas* 117 E13
El Faiyûm, *Egypt* 197 C18
El Fasher, *Sudan* 198 E11
El Fifi, *Sudan* 198 F10
Elfrida, *Ariz., U.S.* 107 W9
El Fuerte, *Mex.* 114 E8
El Galpón, *Arg.* 132 F10
El Gassi, *Alg.* 196 C11
El Gezira, region, *Sudan* 194 G9
Elgin, *Ill., U.S.* 99 N6
Elgin, *N. Dak., U.S.* 104 H3
Elgin, *Nebr., U.S.* 105 N7
Elgin, *Nev., U.S.* 109 S12
Elgin, *Oreg., U.S.* 108 F8
Elgin, *Scot., U.K.* 142 J10
Elgin, *Tex., U.S.* 103 Q11
El Gîza, *Egypt* 197 C18
Elgol, *Scot., U.K.* 142 K7
El Golea, *Alg.* 196 C11
Elgon, Mount, *Kenya, Uganda* 194 J9
El Grado, *Sp.* 145 D15
El Hermel, *Leb.* 170 H7
El Hobra, *Alg.* 196 C11
El Homeur, *Alg.* 196 C10
Eliase, *Indonesia* 213 D14
Elida, *N. Mex., U.S.* 107 T15
Elikónas (Helicon), peak, *Gr.* 154 H11
Elím, *Alas., U.S.* 111 F13
Elisabethville, *Dem. Rep. of the Congo* 198 N11
El Iskandarîya (Alexandria), *Egypt* 197 C18
Elista, *Russ.* 157 R13
Elizabeth, *La., U.S.* 100 N7
Elizabeth, *N.J., U.S.* 94 N11
Elizabeth, Bahía, *Ecua.* 128 Q8
Elizabeth, Cape, *Me., U.S.* 95 H16
Elizabeth City, *N.C., U.S.* 96 G14
Elizabeth Island, *Marshall Is.* 216 M8
Elizabethton, *Tenn., U.S.* 101 E20
Elizabethtown, *Ky., U.S.* 101 C16
Elizabethtown, *N.C., U.S.* 96 J12
Elizondo, *Sp.* 145 B13
El Jadida (Mazagan), *Mor.* 196 B8
Elk, *Pol.* 149 B17
Elk, *Calif., U.S.* 109 Q2
Elk, river, *W. Va., U.S.* 96 D9
Elkader, *Iowa, U.S.* 104 M13
Elk City, *Okla., U.S.* 102 G8
Elkedra, *N. Terr., Austral.* 211 S9
El Kef, *Tun.* 196 A12
Ẽ Kerê, *Eth.* 199 H16
El Khandaq, *Sudan* 198 D12
El Khârga, *Egypt* 197 E18
Elkhart, *Ind., U.S.* 99 N9
Elkhart, *Kans., U.S.* 105 V3
El Khnâchîch, region, *Mali* 196 F8
Elkhorn, river, *Nebr., U.S.* 105 N6
Elkhorn City, *Ky., U.S.* 101 C20
Elkhovo, *Bulg.* 153 J16
Elkin, *N.C., U.S.* 96 G9
Elkins, *N. Mex., U.S.* 107 T14
Elkins, *W. Va., U.S.* 96 D10
Elkland, *Pa., U.S.* 94 L7
Elk Mountain, *Pa., U.S.* 94 L9
Elk Mountain, *Wyo., U.S.* 106 K12
Elko, *Nev., U.S.* 108 M11
Elk Point, *S. Dak., U.S.* 104 N8
Elk River, *Minn., U.S.* 104 J11
Elkton, *Ky., U.S.* 101 D15
Elkton, *Md., U.S.* 96 B14
El Kûbri, *Egypt* 171 Q1
El Kuntilla, *Egypt* 171 Q4
Ellar, *Sp.* 160 L6
Elle, island, *Marshall Is.* 216 G8
Ellef Ringnes Island, *Nunavut, Can.* 83 B14
Ellen, Mount, *Utah, U.S.* 107 P8
Ellendale, *N. Dak., U.S.* 104 H6
Ellensburg, *Wash., U.S.* 108 D6
Ellep, island, *Marshall Is.* 216 M10
Ellep Passage, *Marshall Is.* 216 L4
Ellesmere, Lake, *N.Z.* 213 P17
Ellesmere Island, *Nunavut, Can.* 83 B16
Ellijay, *Ga., U.S.* 96 J5
Ellington, *Mo., U.S.* 105 U14
Ellinwood, *Kans., U.S.* 105 T6
Elliot Lake, *Ont., Can.* 83 P17
Elliott, *N. Terr., Austral.* 211 R8
Elliott Key, *Fla., U.S.* 97 X10

Ellis, *Idaho, U.S.* 106 F5
Ellis, *Kans., U.S.* 105 S5
Ellisburg, *N.Y., U.S.* 94 H8
Elliston, *S. Aust., Austral.* 211 X9
Ellisville, *Miss., U.S.* 100 M12
Ellon, *Scot., U.K.* 142 K11
Ellsworth, *Kans., U.S.* 105 T7
Ellsworth, *Me., U.S.* 95 F18
Ellsworth Land, *Antarctica* 226 J6
Ellsworth Mountains, *Antarctica* 226 H8
Elma, *Wash., U.S.* 108 D3
El Macao, *Dom. Rep.* 117 M20
Elmadağ, *Turk.* 168 E8
Elma Dağı, *Turk.* 168 E8
El Maitén, *Arg.* 133 Q7
Elmalı, *Turk.* 168 H5
El Malpais National Monument, *N. Mex., U.S.* 107 S10
El Mazâr, *Egypt* 171 N3
Elm Creek, *Nebr., U.S.* 105 Q5
Elm Creek, *Tex., U.S.* 103 S7
El Milagro, *Arg.* 132 J9
El Mîna, *Leb.* 170 H6
El Minya, *Egypt* 197 D18
Elmira, *N.Y., U.S.* 94 L7
El Morro National Monument, *N. Mex., U.S.* 107 S10
El Mreyyé, region, *Mali, Mauritania* 196 F7
Elmshorn, *Ger.* 148 B7
Elne, *Fr.* 147 Z11
El Nido, *Philippines* 189 E13
El Obeid, *Sudan* 198 E12
El Odaiya, *Sudan* 198 F11
Elorza, *Venez.* 128 D8
El Oued, *Alg.* 196 B12
Eloúnda, *Gr.* 155 Q16
Eloy, *Ariz., U.S.* 107 U7
El Pajuil, *P.R., U.S.* 120 M2
El Palito, *Venez.* 128 B9
El Pao, *Venez.* 128 C12
El Paso, *Ill., U.S.* 99 Q6
El Paso, *Tex., U.S.* 103 U1
El Pedroso, *Sp.* 144 K8
Elphin, *Scot., U.K.* 142 H8
El Portal, *Calif., U.S.* 109 S6
El Puerto de Santa María, *Sp.* 144 M8
El Qâhira (Cairo), *Egypt* 197 C18
El Qantara, *Egypt* 171 P1
El Qasr, *Egypt* 197 E18
El Quneitra *see* Al Qunaytirah, *Syr.* 170 K6
El Quseima, *Egypt* 171 P4
El Reno, *Okla., U.S.* 102 G10
El Rosario, *Mex.* 114 C5
Elroy, *Wis., U.S.* 98 K4
Elsa, *Tex., U.S.* 103 W10
El Salto, *Mex.* 114 F9
El Salvador, *N. Amer.* 81 Q19
Elsberry, *Mo., U.S.* 105 S14
El Seibo, *Dom. Rep.* 117 M20
El Serrat, *Andorra* 160 G3
El Sharana, *N. Terr., Austral.* 211 P8
Elsinore, *Utah, U.S.* 107 N7
El Sombrero, *Venez.* 128 C9
Elst, *Neth.* 146 J13
El Suweis (Suez), *Egypt* 171 Q1
Eltanin Bay, *Antarctica* 226 H6
Eltanin Fracture Zone, *Pac. Oc.* 239 R14
El Teleno, peak, *Sp.* 144 C8
Eltham, *N.Z.* 213 L18
El Thamad, *Egypt* 171 R4
El Tigre, *Venez.* 128 C11
El Tofo, *Chile* 132 H6
El'ton, *Russ.* 157 P14
El'ton, Ozero, *Russ.* 157 P14
Eltopia, *Wash., U.S.* 108 D7
El Toro, peak, *P.R., U.S.* 120 N5
El Toro, peak, *Sp.* 145 G20
El Ţûr, *Egypt* 171 T3
El Turbio, *Arg.* 133 W7
Eluru, *India* 178 M8
Elvas, *Port.* 144 H7
Elven, *Fr.* 147 R4
Elverum, *Nor.* 140 K11
El Wak, *Kenya* 199 J15
Elwell, Lake, *Mont., U.S.* 106 B8
Elwood, *Ind., U.S.* 99 Q9
Elwood, *Kans., U.S.* 105 R10
Elwood, *Nebr., U.S.* 105 Q5
Elx *see* Elche, *Sp.* 145 K14
Ely, *Eng., U.K.* 143 T14
Ely, *Minn., U.S.* 104 F12
Ely, *Nev., U.S.* 109 Q12

Elyria, *Ohio, U.S.* 99 P14
El Yunque (Anvil), peak, *Cuba* 117 K14
Émaé, island, *Vanuatu* 218 E3
Emam Saheb, *Afghan.* 176 K7
Émao, island, *Vanuatu* 218 F3
Emba, *Cyprus* 160 Q5
Embarcación, *Arg.* 132 E10
Embetsu, *Japan* 184 E13
Embi, *Kaz.* 174 E9
Embleton, *Eng., U.K.* 143 N12
Emden, *Ger.* 148 C6
Emerald, *Qnsld., Austral.* 211 T14
Emerald Basin, *Pac. Oc.* 238 R8
Emerald Island, *N.W.T., Can.* 83 C13
Emery, *Utah, U.S.* 107 N8
Emet, *Turk.* 168 E5
Emidj, island, *Marshall Is.* 216 L9
Emigrant Pass, *Nev., U.S.* 109 N10
Emi Koussi, peak, *Chad* 197 G15
Emilius, Mount, *It.* 150 D2
Emily, *Minn., U.S.* 104 G11
Emin, *China* 180 D6
Emirau, island, *P.N.G.* 213 B20
Emirdağ, *Turk.* 168 F6
Emir Dağları, *Turk.* 168 F7
Emita, *Tas., Austral.* 211 Y16
Emmaus, *Pa., U.S.* 94 N9
Emmen, *Neth.* 146 H14
Emmetsburg, *Iowa, U.S.* 104 M10
Emmett, *Idaho, U.S.* 106 G3
Emmonak, *Alas., U.S.* 110 H12
Emory Peak, *Tex., U.S.* 103 R3
Empedrado, *Arg.* 132 G13
Emperor Seamounts, *Pac. Oc.* 238 D8
Emperor Trough, *Pac. Oc.* 238 D9
Empire, *Mich., U.S.* 98 J9
Empoli, *It.* 150 G6
Emporia, *Kans., U.S.* 105 T9
Emporia, *Va., U.S.* 96 F13
Emporium, *Pa., U.S.* 94 L5
Empress Augusta Bay, *P.N.G.* 217 K14
Ems, river, *Ger.* 148 C6
Emu Park, *Qnsld., Austral.* 211 T15
Ena, *Japan* 185 P10
Enard Bay, *Scot., U.K.* 142 H8
'En Boqeq, *Israel* 171 N6
Encamp, region, *Andorra* 160 H4
Encamp, *Andorra* 160 J3
Encarnación, *Parag.* 130 N10
Encinal, *Tex., U.S.* 103 T8
Encinitas, *Calif., U.S.* 109 Y9
Encino, *N. Mex., U.S.* 107 S13
Encino, *Tex., U.S.* 103 V10
Encontrados, *Venez.* 128 C6
Encounter Bay, *Austral.* 210 L10
Ende, *Indonesia* 189 M14
Endeavour Hill, *Austral.* 210 C7
Endeavour Strait, *Austral.* 210 A12
Enderbury Island, *Kiribati* 214 G10
Enderby Land, *Antarctica* 227 C18
Enderby Plain, *Antarctic Oc.* 245 E14
Enderlin, *N. Dak., U.S.* 104 G7
Endicott, *N.Y., U.S.* 94 M8
Endicott Mountains, *Alas., U.S.* 111 D15
Eneeldak, island, *Marshall Is.* 216 N8
Enengeseiru, island, *F.S.M.* 217 C14
Enengonomei, island, *F.S.M.* 217 C14
Enewetak (Eniwetok), island, *Marshall Is.* 216 J8
Enewetak Atoll, *Marshall Is.* 216 F1
Enewetak Lagoon, *Marshall Is.* 216 H8
Enez, *Turk.* 168 C2
Enfer, Pointe d', *Martinique, Fr.* 121 G23
Enfield, *Jam.* 120 H10
Enfield, *N.C., U.S.* 96 G13
Engaño, Cabo, *Dom. Rep.* 117 M21
Engaru, *Japan* 184 E15
Engelhard, *N.C., U.S.* 96 H14
Engels, *Russ.* 156 M14
Engenenimo, island, *F.S.M.* 217 C16
Enggano, island, *Indonesia* 188 L6
England, *Ark., U.S.* 100 H9
England, *U.K.* 143 T12
Englewood, *Colo., U.S.* 106 M13
Englewood, *Fla., U.S.* 97 V7
Englewood, *Kans., U.S.* 105 V5
English Channel (La Manche), *Eur.* 143 X13
English Coast, *Antarctica* 226 G6
English Harbor, *Kiribati* 217 B20
English Harbour, *Antigua & Barbuda* 121 C21
English Roads, *Tonga* 218 J12

'En Ḥazeva, *Israel* 171 P5
Enid, *Okla., U.S.* 102 EIO
Enighed, *Virgin Islands, U.S.* 120 NIO
Enigu, island, *Marshall Is.* 216 GII
Enipéas, river, *Gr.* 154 FIO
Eniwa, *Japan* 184 GI3
Eniwetak, island, *Marshall Is.* 216 M5
Eniwetak Passage, *Marshall Is.* 216 M5
Eniwetok see Enewetak, island, *Marshall Is.* 216 J8
Enjebi, island, *Marshall Is.* 216 G8
Enkhuizen, *Neth.* 146 HI3
Ennadai, *Nunavut, Can.* 83 JI3
En Nahud, *Sudan* 198 EII
Ennedi, range, *Chad* 197 GI6
Ennell, Lough, *Ire.* 143 S5
Enngonia, *N.S.W., Austral.* 211 WI3
Enning, *S. Dak., U.S.* 104 K2
Ennis, *Ire.* 143 T4
Ennis, *Mont., U.S.* 106 E7
Ennis, *Tex., U.S.* 102 MI2
Enniscorthy, *Ire.* 143 T6
Enniskillen, *N. Ire., U.K.* 143 Q5
Ennistymon, *Ire.* 143 S3
Ennuebing, island, *Marshall Is.* 216 K4
Ennugarret, island, *Marshall Is.* 216 K4
Ennugenliggelap, island, *Marshall Is.* 216 M4
Ennumennet, island, *Marshall Is.* 216 K4
Ennumet, island, *Marshall Is.* 216 L3
Ennylabegan, island, *Marshall Is.* 216 N5
Enontekiö, *Fin.* 141 DI4
Énos, Óros, *Gr.* 154 J7
Enriquillo, *Dom. Rep.* 117 NI8
Enriquillo, Lago, *Dom. Rep.* 117 MI7
Enschede, *Neth.* 146 JI4
Ensenada, *Mex.* 114 B5
Ensenada, *P.R., U.S.* 120 N2
Enshi, *China* 182 L2
Ensisheim, *Fr.* 147 QI5
Entebbe, *Uganda* 199 KI3
Enterprise, *Ala., U.S.* 101 NI6
Enterprise, *Miss., U.S.* 101 LI3
Enterprise, *Oreg., U.S.* 108 F9
Enterprise, *Utah, U.S.* 107 P5
Entinas, Punta, *Sp.* 144 MI2
Entrada, Punta, *Arg.* 133 V8
Entrance Point, *Bahamas* 120 B8
Entre-Deux, *Reunion, Fr.* 205 HI6
Entrepeñas, Embalse de, *Sp.* 144 FI2
Entre Ríos, region, *S. Amer.* 126 L6
Entrèves, *It.* 150 D2
Entroncamento, *Port.* 144 G5
Enubuj, island, *Marshall Is.* 216 N5
Enugu, *Nigeria* 201 HI4
Enumclaw, *Wash., U.S.* 108 C4
Enurmino, *Russ.* 159 A2O
Envalira, Pic d', *Andorra, Fr.* 160 J5
Envalira, Port d', *Andorra* 160 J5
Envira, *Braz.* 130 F5
'En Yahav, *Israel* 171 P5
Enybor, island, *Marshall Is.* 216 M8
Eo, Îlot, *New Caledonia, Fr.* 218 C8
Eolie see Lipari, Isole, *It.* 151 RII
Eori, *Eq. Guinea* 204 N7
Eot, island, *F.S.M.* 217 CI5
Epanomí, *Gr.* 154 DII
Eparit, island, *F.S.M.* 217 AI5
Eparit, Mochun, *F.S.M.* 217 AI5
Epéna, *Congo* 201 KI8
Épernay, *Fr.* 147 PII
Épernon, *Fr.* 147 P9
Epeti, Roches, *Fr. Polynesia, Fr.* 219 M23
Ephesus, ruin, *Turk.* 168 G3
Ephraim, *Utah, U.S.* 106 MIO
Ephrata, *Wash., U.S.* 108 C7
Epi, island, *Vanuatu* 218 E3
Epidavros, ruin, *Gr.* 154 KII
Épinal, *Fr.* 147 QI4
Epirus, region, *Albania, Gr.* 154 F7
Episkopi, *Cyprus* 160 Q7
Episkopi Bay, *Cyprus* 160 Q7
Epsilon, *Qnsld., Austral.* 211 VII
Epsom, *Eng., U.K.* 143 VI4
Eptachórion, *Gr.* 154 D8
Épuisay, *Fr.* 147 R8
Epukiro, *Namibia* 202 H7
Epu Pel, *Arg.* 133 NIO
Equatorial Channel, *Maldives* 179 X3
Equatorial Guinea, *Af.* 195 JI7
Erbaa, *Turk.* 168 DII
Erçek, *Turk.* 169 GI8
Erçek Gölü, *Turk.* 169 FI8
Erciş, *Turk.* 169 FI7
Erciyeş Dağı, *Turk.* 168 GIO

Érd, *Hung.* 149 LI5
Erdek, *Turk.* 168 D4
Erdemli, *Turk.* 168 J9
Erding, *Ger.* 148 K9
Ere, island, *Marshall Is.* 216 L3
Erebus, Mount, *Antarctica* 227 NI3
Erechim, *Braz.* 130 NI2
Ereğli, *Turk.* 168 C7
Ereğli, *Turk.* 168 H9
Erei, Monti, *It.* 151 TII
Erenhot, *China* 182 A4
Eressós, *Gr.* 155 FI6
Erétria, *Gr.* 154 HI2
Ereymentaū, *Kaz.* 175 CI4
Erfoud, *Mor.* 196 C9
Erfurt, *Ger.* 148 F8
Ergani, *Turk.* 169 GI4
Ergedzhey, *Russ.* 159 HI7
Ergene, river, *Turk.* 168 C4
Ergun see Argun', river, *China* 181 BI5
Ergun Youqi, *China* 181 BI5
Ergun Zuoqi, *China* 181 BI5
Er Hai, lake, *China* 180 NIO
Eriboll, *Scot., U.K.* 142 H9
Eriboll, Loch, *Scot., U.K.* 142 G9
Ericht, Loch, *Scot., U.K.* 142 L9
Erick, *Okla., U.S.* 102 G7
Erie, *Pa., U.S.* 94 K3
Erie, Lake, *Can., U.S.* 85 FI8
Erie Canal, *N.Y., U.S.* 94 J5
Erigavo see Ceerigaabo, *Somalia* 199 FI7
Erikoússa, island, *Gr.* 154 E5
Erikub Atoll, *Marshall Is.* 216 G5
Erímanthos, Óros, *Gr.* 154 J9
Erimi, *Cyprus* 160 Q7
Erimo, *Japan* 184 GI5
Erimo Misaki, *Japan* 184 GI5
Erin, *Tenn., U.S.* 101 EI4
Erin Bay, *Trinidad & Tobago* 121 Q2I
Eriskay, island, *Scot., U.K.* 142 K6
Erisort, Loch, *Scot., U.K.* 142 H7
Erithrés, *Gr.* 154 JII
Eritrea, *Af.* 195 G22
Erkilet, *Turk.* 168 FIO
Erlangen, *Ger.* 148 H8
Erlanger, *Ky., U.S.* 101 AI7
Erldunda, *N. Terr., Austral.* 211 U8
Erling, Lake, *Ark., U.S.* 100 K7
Ermenek, *Turk.* 168 J8
Ermióni, *Gr.* 154 KII
Ermoúpoli, *Gr.* 155 KI4
Ernabella, *S. Aust., Austral.* 211 U8
Ernakulam, *India* 179 R5
Ernée, *Fr.* 147 Q6
Erode, *India* 179 Q6
Eroj, island, *Marshall Is.* 216 GII
Eromanga, *Qnsld., Austral.* 211 UI2
Er Rachidia, *Mor.* 196 B9
Er Rahad, *Sudan* 198 EI2
Er Rif, range, *Mor.* 194 C3
Erris Head, *Ire.* 143 Q3
Erromango, island, *Vanuatu* 218 G3
Error Tablemount, *Ind. Oc.* 240 E6
Erskine, *Minn., U.S.* 104 F9
Ertai, *China* 180 D8
Ertis, *Kaz.* 175 BI5
Ertis (Irtysh), river, *Kaz.* 175 CI6
Ertix, river, *China* 180 D8
Erts, *Andorra* 160 H2
Eru, island, *Marshall Is.* 216 L3
Eruh, *Turk.* 169 HI6
Erwin, *N.C., U.S.* 96 HII
Erwin, *Tenn., U.S.* 101 E2O
Erzin, *Russ.* 159 MI3
Erzincan, *Turk.* 169 EI4
Erzin, *Turk.* 168 H9
Erzurum, *Turk.* 169 EI6
Esan Misaki, *Japan* 184 HI3
Esashi, *Japan* 184 EI4
Esashi, *Japan* 184 HI2
Esbjerg, *Den.* 140 PII
Esbo see Espoo, *Fin.* 141 KI6
Escalades-Engordany, region, *Andorra* 160 J4
Escalante, river, *Utah, U.S.* 107 P8
Escalante, *Utah, U.S.* 107 P7
Escambia, river, *Fla., U.S.* 97 QI
Escanaba, river, *Mich., U.S.* 98 G8
Escanaba, *Mich., U.S.* 98 G8
Escárcega, *Mex.* 115 JI5
Esch, *Lux.* 160 K9
Eschen, *Liech.* 160 N2
Eschnerberg, range, *Liech.* 160 M2
Eschwege, *Ger.* 148 F7
Escocesa, Bahía, *Dom. Rep.* 117 LI9
Escondido, *Calif., U.S.* 109 YIO

Escudero, station, *Antarctica* 226 C3
Escuinapa, *Mex.* 114 G9
Escuintla, *Guatemala* 115 LI5
Escuintla, *Mex.* 115 LI5
Eséka, *Cameroon* 201 JI5
Esenguly, *Turkm.* 174 M6
Eşfahan (Isfahan), *Iran* 173 EI3
Esfandak, *Iran* 173 HI8
Eshkamesh, *Afghan.* 176 K8
Eshkashem, *Afghan.* 176 K9
Esil, river, *Kaz.* 174 BI2
Esil, *Kaz.* 174 CI2
Esimi, *Gr.* 155 BI6
Eskifjördur, *Ice.* 140 F4
Eskilstuna, *Sw.* 141 LI3
Eskimo Lakes, *N.W.T., Can.* 82 EIO
Eskipazar, *Turk.* 168 D8
Eskişehir, *Turk.* 168 E6
Esla, river, *Sp.* 144 C9
Eslāmābād, *Iran* 172 DIO
Eslam Qal'eh, *Afghan.* 176 MI
Eşler Dağı, *Turk.* 168 G5
Eşme, *Turk.* 168 F4
Esmeralda, *Cuba* 116 HIO
Esmeralda, *Qnsld., Austral.* 211 RI2
Esmeralda, Isla, *Chile* 133 U6
Esmeraldas, *Ecua.* 128 H2
Esmeraldas, Río, *Ecua.* 128 H2
Esmoriz, *Port.* 144 E5
Espagnol Point, *St. Vincent & the Grenadines* 121 JI7
Espakeh, *Iran* 173 HI7
Espalion, *Fr.* 147 WIO
Española, Isla (Hood), *Ecua.* 128 RIO
Espanola, *N. Mex., U.S.* 107 RI2
Esperance, *W. Aust., Austral.* 211 X4
Esperance, Cape, *Solomon Is.* 217 NI8
Esperanza, station, *Antarctica* 226 C4
Esperanza, *Arg.* 132 JII
Esperanza, *P.R., U.S.* 120 N6
Esperanza, *Peru* 130 G4
Espichel, Cabo, *Port.* 144 J4
Espiègle Bay, *Vanuatu* 218 D2
Espiel, *Sp.* 144 K9
Espigão Mestre, range, *S. Amer.* 126 G9
Espinhaço, Serra do, *Braz.* 131 KI5
Espírito Santo see Vila Velha, *Braz.* 131 LI6
Espiritu Santo, island, *Vanuatu* 218 C2
Espíritu Santo, Isla, *Mex.* 114 F7
Espoo (Esbo), *Fin.* 141 KI6
Esposende, *Port.* 144 D5
Espuña, peak, *Sp.* 145 KI3
Espungabera, *Mozambique* 202 GI2
Esquel, *Arg.* 133 R7
Esquina, *Arg.* 132 JI2
Essaouira, *Mor.* 196 B7
Essen, *Belg.* 146 KI2
Essen, *Ger.* 148 E5
Essendon, Mount, *Austral.* 210 G4
Essequibo, river, *Guyana* 129 EI4
Essex, Punta, *Ecua.* 128 R8
Essex Junction, *Vt., U.S.* 94 FI2
Essexville, *Mich., U.S.* 98 KI2
Essington, Port, *Austral.* 210 A8
Esslingen, *Ger.* 148 J7
Esso, *Russ.* 159 F22
Es Suki, *Sudan* 199 EI3
Estaca de Bares, Punta da, *Sp.* 144 A7
Estacado, Llano, *N. Mex., Tex., U.S.* 84 KIO
Estados, Isla de los (Staten Island), *Arg.* 133 XIO
Estahbān, *Iran* 173 GI4
Estância, *Braz.* 131 HI7
Estancia, *N. Mex., U.S.* 107 SI2
Estany d'Engolasters, lake, *Andorra* 160 J3
Estanyó, Pic de l', *Andorra* 160 H4
Estats, Pic d', *Sp.* 145 CI6
Estavayer-le-Lac, *Switz.* 150 B2
Este, *It.* 150 E7
Este, Punta del, *S. Amer.* 126 M7
Estelí, *Nicar.* 115 MI8
Estella (Lizarra), *Sp.* 145 CI3
Estelline, *S. Dak., U.S.* 104 K8
Estelline, *Tex., U.S.* 102 H7
Estepona, *Sp.* 144 M9
Estes Park, *Colo., U.S.* 106 LI3
Estevan, *Sask., Can.* 82 NI2
Estherville, *Iowa, U.S.* 104 MIO
Estill, *S.C., U.S.* 96 M9
Estonia, *Eur.* 139 R9
Estrela, Serra da, *Port.* 144 F6

Estrella, peak, *Sp.* 144 JII
Estrella Bay, *Solomon Is.* 217 MI8
Estremoz, *Port.* 144 H6
Esztergom, *Hung.* 149 LI4
Etadunna, *S. Aust., Austral.* 211 VIO
Etal Atoll, *F.S.M.* 216 Q7
Étampes, *Fr.* 147 QIO
Étang-Sale, *Reunion, Fr.* 205 HI5
Étaples, *Fr.* 146 L9
Étarik see Monument, island, *Vanuatu* 218 E3
Etawah, *India* 178 G7
Etcharai, island, *Marshall Is.* 216 K2
Etena, *Amer. Samoa, U.S.* 218 R4
Ethiopia, *Af.* 195 H23
Ethiopian College, *Vatican City* 161 QI4
Ethiopian Highlands, *Eth.* 194 HIO
Etive, Loch, *Scot., U.K.* 142 L8
Etna, peak, *It.* 151 SII
Etna, *Wyo., U.S.* 106 H8
Etolikó, *Gr.* 154 H8
Etorofu see Iturup, island, *Russ.* 159 J23
Etosha Pan, *Namibia* 202 G6
Etoumbi, *Congo* 201 LI7
Etowah, *Tenn., U.S.* 101 FI8
Etrek see Atrak, river, *Iran* 173 BI4
Ettelbruck, *Lux.* 160 HIO
Etten, island, *F.S.M.* 217 BI6
Etten, island, *F.S.M.* 217 CI5
Ettlingen, *Ger.* 148 J6
Ettrick, *N.Z.* 213 QI6
Eu, *Fr.* 146 M9
'Eua, island, *Tonga* 214 KIO
'Euaiki, island, *Tonga* 218 HI2
'Euaiki, island, *Tonga* 218 MII
'Euakafa, island, *Tonga* 218 MII
Euboea see Évia, island, *Gr.* 155 HI3
Eucla Basin, *Austral.* 210 J6
Eucla Motel, *W. Aust., Austral.* 211 W7
Euclid, *Ohio, U.S.* 99 NI4
Eucumbene, Lake, *Austral.* 210 LI3
Eudora, *Ark., U.S.* 100 K9
Eudunda, *S. Aust., Austral.* 211 XIO
Eufaula, *Ala., U.S.* 101 MI7
Eufaula, *Okla., U.S.* 102 GI3
Eufaula Lake, *Okla., U.S.* 102 GI3
Eugene, *Oreg., U.S.* 108 H3
Eugenia Point, *N. Amer.* 80 L3
Eugenio Bustos, *Arg.* 132 L8
Euginia, Punta, *Mex.* 114 D5
Eumseong, *S. Korea* 182 FI3
Eunice, *La., U.S.* 100 P8
Eunice, *N. Mex., U.S.* 107 VI5
Eupen, *Belg.* 146 LI3
Euphrates, river, *Asia* 166 F3
Eupora, *Miss., U.S.* 100 JI2
Eurardy, *W. Aust., Austral.* 211 V2
Eureka, *Calif., U.S.* 108 MI
Eureka, *Ill., U.S.* 99 Q5
Eureka, *Kans., U.S.* 105 U9
Eureka, *Mont., U.S.* 106 A5
Eureka, *Nev., U.S.* 109 PII
Eureka, *Nunavut, Can.* 83 BI5
Eureka, *S. Dak., U.S.* 104 J5
Eureka, *Utah, U.S.* 106 L7
Eureka Springs, *Ark., U.S.* 100 E7
Europa, Île, *Mozambique Ch.* 203 HI5
Europa, Picos de, *Sp.* 144 B9
Europa, Punta, *Eq. Guinea* 204 L7
Europa Point, *Gibraltar, U.K.* 161 R23
Eustis, *Fla., U.S.* 97 S8
Eutaw, *Ala., U.S.* 101 KI4
Eutin, *Ger.* 148 B8
Eva Downs, *N. Terr., Austral.* 211 R9
Evans, Mount, *Mont., U.S.* 106 E6
Evanston, *Ill., U.S.* 99 N7
Evanston, *Wyo., U.S.* 106 K8
Evansville, *Alas., U.S.* 111 EI6
Evansville, *Ind., U.S.* 99 U7
Evart, *Mich., U.S.* 98 KIO
Eveleth, *Minn., U.S.* 104 FI2
Everard, Lake, *Austral.* 210 J9
Everard Park, *S. Aust., Austral.* 211 V8
Everest, Mount, *China, Nepal* 178 FII
Everett, *Wash., U.S.* 108 B4
Everglades City, *Fla., U.S.* 97 X9
Everglades National Park, *Fla., U.S.* 97 X9
Evergreen, *Ala., U.S.* 101 MI5
Evesham, *Eng., U.K.* 143 UI2
Évia (Euboea), island, *Gr.* 155 HI3
Évian, *Fr.* 147 TI4
Evora, *Port.* 144 J6

Évreux, *Fr.* 147 P8
Évros, river, *Gr.* 155 CI6
Évros, river, *Turk.* 168 C3
Evrótas, river, *Gr.* 154 LIO
Évry, *Fr.* 147 PIO
Evrychou, *Cyprus* 160 P7
'Ewa, *Hawai'i, U.S.* 112 EII
Ewab see Kai, Kepulauan, islands, *Indonesia* 189 LI3
'Ewa Beach, *Hawai'i, U.S.* 112 EII
Ewaninga, *N. Terr., Austral.* 211 T8
Ewarton, *Jam.* 120 J9
Ewing, *Nebr., U.S.* 105 N6
Ewo, *Congo* 201 LI7
Excelsior Mountains, *Nev., U.S.* 109 R8
Excelsior Springs, *Mo., U.S.* 105 SII
Executive Committee Range, *Antarctica* 226 L8
Exeter, *Calif., U.S.* 109 U7
Exeter, *Eng., U.K.* 143 XIO
Exeter, *N.H., U.S.* 95 JI5
Exeter Sound, *Nunavut, Can.* 83 FI9
Exmoor, plateau, *Eng., U.K.* 143 WIO
Exmouth, *Eng., U.K.* 143 XIO
Exmouth, *W. Aust., Austral.* 211 TI
Exmouth Gulf, *Austral.* 210 FI
Exmouth Plateau, *Ind. Oc.* 241 KI5
Exohí, *Gr.* 154 BI2
Exotic Garden, *Monaco* 161 E2O
Exploring Balavu Isles, *Fiji Is.* 218 H9
Exu, *Braz.* 131 HI6
Exuma Sound, *Bahamas* 116 EI2
Eye, *Eng., U.K.* 143 TI5
Eyemouth, *Scot., U.K.* 142 MII
Eye Peninsula, *Scot., U.K.* 142 H7
Eyl, river, *Somalia* 199 GI8
Eyl, *Somalia* 199 GI8
Eymoutiers, *Fr.* 147 U9
Eyrarbakki, *Ice.* 140 F2
Eyre, Lake, *Austral.* 210 HIO
Eyre North, Lake, *S. Aust., Austral.* 211 VIO
Eyre Peninsula, *Austral.* 210 K9
Eyre South, Lake, *Austral.* 210 HIO
Eysturoy, island, *Faroe Is., Den.* 140 J6
Ezcaray, *Sp.* 144 CII
Ezequiel Ramos Mexia, Embalse, *Arg.* 133 P8
Ezine, *Turk.* 168 E2
Ezion-geber (Elath), ruin, *Jordan* 171 R5

F

Faaa, *Fr. Polynesia, Fr.* 219 NI5
Faaaha, *Fr. Polynesia, Fr.* 219 A23
Faaite, island, *Fr. Polynesia, Fr.* 219 EI8
Faanui, *Fr. Polynesia, Fr.* 219 KI4
Faanui, Baie de, *Fr. Polynesia, Fr.* 219 KI4
Faaone, *Fr. Polynesia, Fr.* 219 PI7
Faaroa, Baie de, *Fr. Polynesia, Fr.* 219 B23
Fabala, *Guinea* 200 F7
Fabens, *Tex., U.S.* 103 V2
Faber Lake, *N.W.T., Can.* 82 GII
Fabero, *Sp.* 144 C8
Fabriano, *It.* 150 H9
Facatativá, *Col.* 128 F5
Fachi, *Niger* 197 GI3
Facho, Pico do, *Madeira* 204 L5
Facpi Point, *Guam, U.S.* 216 D9
Facture, *Fr.* 147 W6
Fada, *Chad* 197 GI6
Fada N'Gourma, *Burkina Faso* 200 EII
Faddeyevskiy, Ostrov, *Russ.* 159 DI7
Fadghamī, *Syr.* 170 EI4
Fadian Point, *Guam, U.S.* 216 CII
Fadiffolu Atoll, *Maldives* 179 U3
Faenza, *It.* 150 F7
Faetano, *San Marino* 161 KI7
Fafa, island, *Tonga* 218 HII
Fafe, *Port.* 144 D6
Fagaitua, *Amer. Samoa, U.S.* 218 M8
Fagaitua Bay, *Amer. Samoa, U.S.* 218 M8
Fagaloa Bay, *Samoa* 218 L4
Fagamalo, *Samoa* 218 K3
Fagamalo, *Amer. Samoa, U.S.* 218 M6
Făgăraş, *Rom.* 153 DI4
Fagasa, *Amer. Samoa, U.S.* 218 M7
Fagatele Bay, *Amer. Samoa, U.S.* 218 N7
Fagatogo, *Amer. Samoa, U.S.* 218 M7

Fagernes, *Nor.* **140** KII
Fagnano, Lago, *Chile* **133** X9
Faguibine, Lake, *Niger* **194** G3
Fagurhólsmýri, *Ice.* **140** G3
Fahala, island, *Maldives* **179** V3
Fahefa, *Tonga* **218** HIO
Fahie Hill, *Virgin Islands, U.K.* **120** Q6
Fahraj, *Iran* **173** GI6
Faial, island, *Azores* **144** P3
Faibus Point, *N. Mariana Is., U.S.* **216** B7
Faichuk, island, *F.S.M.* **217** CI4
Faie, *Fr. Polynesia, Fr.* **219** GI4
Faie, Baie de, *Fr. Polynesia, Fr.* **219** GI4
Faihava Passage, *Tonga* **218** LII
Faioa, island, *Tonga* **218** LI2
Faïoa, island, *Wallis & Futuna, Fr.* **218** CII
Fairbanks, *Alas., U.S.* **III** GI7
Fairborn, *Ohio, U.S.* **99** RI2
Fairburn, *Ga., U.S.* **96** L5
Fairbury, *Ill., U.S.* **99** Q6
Fairbury, *Nebr., U.S.* **105** R8
Fairfax, *Okla., U.S.* **102** EII
Fairfax, *S.C., U.S.* **96** M9
Fairfield, *Ala., U.S.* **101** JI5
Fairfield, *Calif., U.S.* **109** R4
Fairfield, *Idaho, U.S.* **106** H5
Fairfield, *Ill., U.S.* **99** T6
Fairfield, *Iowa, U.S.* **105** QI3
Fairfield, *Mont., U.S.* **106** C7
Fairfield, *Ohio, U.S.* **99** SII
Fairfield, *Tex., U.S.* **103** NI2
Fair Haven, *Vt., U.S.* **94** HI2
Fairhope, *Ala., U.S.* **101** PI4
Fair Isle, *Scot., U.K.* **142** FII
Fairmont, *Minn., U.S.* **104** LIO
Fairmont, *W. Va., U.S.* **96** C9
Fairport, *Mich., U.S.* **98** G8
Fairport, *N.Y., U.S.* **94** J7
Fairview, *Mont., U.S.* **106** CI3
Fairview, *Okla., U.S.* **102** F9
Fairview, *Qnsld., Austral.* **211** QI2
Fairview, *Tenn., U.S.* **101** EI5
Fairview, *Utah, U.S.* **106** M7
Fairweather, Mount, *Alas., U.S.* **III** K2I
Fais, island, *F.S.M.* **214** F3
Faisalabad, *Pak.* **177** QII
Faith, *S. Dak., U.S.* **104** J3
Faizabad, *India* **178** G8
Fajardo, *P.R., U.S.* **120** M6
Fajardo, *P.R., U.S.* **117** M23
Fakahiku, island, *Tonga* **218** Q6
Fakahina, island, *Fr. Polynesia, Fr.* **219** E2O
Fakakakai, *Tonga* **218** P7
Fakaofo, island, *Tokelau, N.Z.* **214** HIO
Fakarava, island, *Fr. Polynesia, Fr.* **219** EI8
Fakel, *Russ.* **156** GI6
Fakenham, *Eng., U.K.* **143** TI5
Fakfak, *Indonesia* **189** KI8
Faku, *China* **182** BII
Fala Ane Point, *Amer. Samoa, U.S.* **218** Q3
Falaise, Pointe, *St. Martin, Fr.* **121** BI4
Falakró, Óros, *Gr.* **155** BI3
Falamae, *Solomon Is.* **217** LI4
Falciano, *San Marino* **161** GI7
Falcon, Cape, *Oreg., U.S.* **108** E2
Falcón, Presa, *Mex.* **114** EI2
Falconara Marittima, *It.* **150** H9
Falcone, Capo del, *It.* **150** M3
Falconer, *N.Y., U.S.* **94** K4
Falcon Reservoir, *Tex., U.S.* **103** V8
Falealupo, *Samoa* **218** KI
Faleasao, *Amer. Samoa, U.S.* **218** P3
Falefatu, island, *Tuvalu* **217** L23
Falelatie, *Samoa* **218** L3
Falelima, *Samoa* **218** KI
Falémé, river, *Mali, Senegal* **196** H6
Faleniu, *Amer. Samoa, U.S.* **218** M7
Falfurrias, *Tex., U.S.* **103** VIO
Falkenberg, *Sw.* **140** NI2
Falkensee, *Ger.* **148** DIO
Falkirk, *Scot., U.K.* **142** M9
Falkland Escarpment, *Atl. Oc.* **237** V6
Falkland Fracture Zone, *Antarctic Oc.* **244** B9
Falkland Islands (Islas Malvinas), *Falkland Is., U.K.* **133** WI2
Falkland Plateau, *Atl. Oc.* **237** V6
Falkland Sound, *Falkland Is., U.K.* **133** WI2
Falknis, peak, *Liech., Switz.* **160** R3
Falkonéra, island, *Gr.* **154** MI2
Falköping, *Sw.* **140** MI2

Fallbrook, *Calif., U.S.* **109** Y9
Fallen Jerusalem, island, *Virgin Islands, U.K.* **120** R8
Fallières Coast, *Antarctica* **226** E5
Fallon, *Nev., U.S.* **109** P7
Fall River, *Mass., U.S.* **95** LI5
Fall River Lake, *Kans., U.S.* **105** U9
Fall River Mills, *Calif., U.S.* **108** M4
Falls City, *Nebr., U.S.* **105** R9
Falmouth, *Antigua & Barbuda* **121** B2I
Falmouth, *Eng., U.K.* **143** Y8
Falmouth, *Jam.* **120** H7
Falmouth, *Ky., U.S.* **101** AI8
Falmouth, *Me., U.S.* **95** HI6
Falmouth Harbour, *Antigua & Barbuda* **121** B2I
False Bay, *S. Af.* **194** R7
False Cape, *N. Amer.* **80** N3
False Divi Point, *India* **179** N8
False Pass, *Alas., U.S.* **110** NII
False Point, *India* **178** KII
Falset, *Sp.* **145** EI6
Falso, Cabo, *Dom. Rep.* **117** NI7
Falso, Cabo, *Mex.* **114** G7
Falster, island, *Den.* **140** PI2
Fălticeni, *Rom.* **153** BI5
Falun, *Sw.* **141** KI3
Famagusta *see* Ammochostos, *Cyprus* **160** PIO
Fanaik, island, *F.S.M.* **217** DI6
Fanan, island, *F.S.M.* **217** CI6
Fanananei, Mochun, *F.S.M.* **217** BI4
Fanangat, island, *F.S.M.* **217** BI5
Fanannon, island, *F.S.M.* **217** CI5
Fanapanges, island, *F.S.M.* **217** CI4
Fanasich, island, *F.S.M.* **217** CI4
Fanchang, *China* **182** K8
Fancy, *St. Vincent & the Grenadines* **121** JI6
Fanemoch, island, *F.S.M.* **217** BI5
Faneno, island, *F.S.M.* **217** BI5
Fanew, island, *F.S.M.* **217** CI5
Fanew, Mochun, *F.S.M.* **217** CI5
Fangak, *Sudan* **198** GI2
Fangale'ounga, *Tonga* **218** P7
Fangasito, island, *Tonga* **218** MII
Fangatau, island, *Fr. Polynesia, Fr.* **219** E2O
Fangataufa, island, *Fr. Polynesia, Fr.* **219** H2I
Fangcheng, *China* **182** J4
Fangshan, *China* **182** E4
Fangxian, *China* **182** J3
Fanning Island *see* Tabuaeran, *Kiribati* **214** FI2
Fano, *It.* **150** G9
Fanos, island, *F.S.M.* **217** BI5
Fanshan, *China* **183** N9
Fanshi, *China* **182** D5
Fanūdah, *Saudi Arabia* **172** J7
Fañunchuluyan, Bahia, *N. Mariana Is., U.S.* **216** B6
Fanurmot, island, *F.S.M.* **217** CI4
Fanxian, *China* **182** G6
Farafangana, *Madagascar* **203** HI7
Farâfra Oasis, *Egypt* **197** DI8
Farah, river, *Afghan.* **177** P2
Farah, *Afghan.* **177** P2
Farallon de Medinilla, island, *N. Mariana Is., U.S.* **216** C2
Farallon de Pajaros, island, *N. Mariana Is., U.S.* **214** D4
Farallon Islands, *Calif., U.S.* **84** G2
Faranah, *Guinea* **200** F6
Farasān, Jazā'ir, *Saudi Arabia* **172** P8
Faraulep Atoll, *F.S.M.* **216** Q4
Fare, *Fr. Polynesia, Fr.* **219** GI4
Fareara, Pointe, *Fr. Polynesia, Fr.* **219** QI7
Fareara, Passe, *Fr. Polynesia, Fr.* **219** GI4
Fareham, *Eng., U.K.* **143** WI3
Farewell, Cape *see* Nunap Isua, *Greenland, Den.* **81** D22
Farewell, Cape, *N.Z.* **213** MI7
Farga de Moles, *Sp.* **160** K2
Fargo, *N. Dak., U.S.* **104** G8
Farg'ona, *Uzb.* **175** KI4
Faribault, *Minn., U.S.* **104** KII
Faridkot, *India* **178** D4
Farim, *Guinea-Bissau* **200** E4
Farīmān, *Iran* **173** CI6
Fariones, Punta, *Canary Is.* **204** P8
Farkhor, *Taj.* **176** K8
Farmakonísion, *Gr.* **155** LI8

Farmersville, *Tex., U.S.* **102** KI2
Farmerville, *La., U.S.* **100** K8
Farmington, *Ill., U.S.* **99** Q4
Farmington, *Me., U.S.* **95** FI6
Farmington, *Mo., U.S.* **105** UI5
Farmington, *N. Mex., U.S.* **107** QIO
Farmington, *Utah, U.S.* **106** K7
Farmville, *Va., U.S.* **96** FI2
Farnham, *N.Y., U.S.* **94** K4
Fårö, island, *Sw.* **141** LI4
Faro, *Port.* **144** L6
Faro, Punta del, *It.* **151** RI2
Faroe Bank, *Atl. Oc.* **236** CI2
Faroe Islands (Føroyar), *Den.* **140** J5
Farquhar, Atoll de, *Seychelles* **203** CI9
Farrell, *Pa., U.S.* **94** M3
Fārs, region, *Iran* **173** GI4
Fársala, *Gr.* **154** FIO
Farsund, *Nor.* **140** MIO
Fartak, Ra's, *Yemen* **173** PI3
Far'ûn (Coral Island), *Egypt* **171** R5
Farwell, *Tex., U.S.* **102** H3
Fasā, *Iran* **173** GI4
Fasano, *It.* **150** MI4
Fastiv, *Ukr.* **157** N5
Fastnet Rock, *Ire.* **143** V3
Fataka (Mitre Island), *Solomon Is.* **214** J8
Fatato, island, *Tuvalu* **217** K23
Fatehabad, *India* **178** E5
Fatehgarh, *India* **178** F7
Fatehpur, *India* **178** G7
Fátima, *Port.* **144** G5
Fatsa, *Turk.* **168** DI2
Fatu Hiva, island, *Fr. Polynesia, Fr.* **215** HI5
Fatumanini, Passe, *Wallis & Futuna, Fr.* **218** BII
Fatumanongi, island, *Tonga* **218** P6
Fatumu, *Tonga* **218** JI2
Faucilles, Monts, *Fr.* **147** QI4
Faulkton, *S. Dak., U.S.* **104** J6
Fauna Nui, Lac, *Fr. Polynesia, Fr.* **219** GI4
Fauro, island, *Solomon Is.* **217** KI5
Fauske, *Nor.* **140** EI2
Faversham, *Eng., U.K.* **143** VI5
Favignana, Isola, *It.* **151** S8
Faxaflói, bay, *Ice.* **140** F2
Faya, *Chad* **197** GI5
Fayaoué, *New Caledonia, Fr.* **218** C8
Fayaoué, Baie de, *New Caledonia, Fr.* **218** C8
Fayd, *Saudi Arabia* **172** H8
Fayette, *Ala., U.S.* **101** JI4
Fayette, *Miss., U.S.* **100** MIO
Fayette, *Mo., U.S.* **105** SI2
Fayetteville, *Ark., U.S.* **100** E6
Fayetteville, *N.C., U.S.* **96** JII
Fayetteville, *Tenn., U.S.* **101** GI5
Fayetteville, *W. Va., U.S.* **96** E8
Fazilka, *India* **178** E4
Fdérik, *Mauritania* **196** E6
Fear, Cape, *N.C., U.S.* **96** KI2
Fécamp, *Fr.* **147** N8
Federal, *Arg.* **132** JI3
Federated States of Micronesia, *Pac. Oc.* **214** F4
Fedorovka, *Kaz.* **174** BIO
Fefen, island, *F.S.M.* **217** CI5
Fehmarn, island, *Ger.* **148** B9
Feijó, *Braz.* **130** F5
Feilding, *N.Z.* **213** LI9
Feira de Santana, *Braz.* **131** HI6
Feixi, *China* **182** K7
Feke, *Turk.* **168** GII
Felanitx, *Sp.* **145** HI8
Feldbach, *Aust.* **148** MI2
Feldberg, peak, *Ger.* **148** K6
Feldkirch, *Aust.* **148** L7
Feldkirch, *Aust.* **160** M3
Félicité Island, *Seychelles* **205** M2I
Felidu Atoll, *Maldives* **179** V3
Felipe Carrillo Puerto, *Mex.* **115** HI7
Felixstowe, *Eng., U.K.* **143** UI5
Fellowship, *Jam.* **120** JII
Fellowship, *Jam.* **120** J7
Feltre, *It.* **150** D7
Femund, lake, *Nor.* **140** JII
Fena Valley Reservoir, *Guam, U.S.* **216** DIO
Fen Country, *Eng., U.K.* **143** TI4
Fene, *Sp.* **144** A6

Feneppi, island, *F.S.M.* **217** DI5
Fengari, peak, *Gr.* **155** DI5
Fengcheng, *China* **182** CII
Fengcheng, *China* **183** N6
Fenghuang, *China* **183** N2
Fengjie, *China* **182** K2
Fengkai, *China* **183** R3
Fenglin, *Taiwan, China* **183** RIO
Fengning, *China* **182** C7
Fengshan, *Taiwan, China* **183** S9
Fengtai, *China* **182** J7
Fengxian, *China* **180** KI2
Fengyüan, *Taiwan, China* **183** R9
Fengzhen, *China* **182** C5
Feni Islands, *P.N.G.* **213** C22
Feno, Cap de, *Fr.* **150** L4
Feno, Capo di, *Fr.* **150** K3
Fenua Fu, island, *Wallis & Futuna, Fr.* **218** CII
Fenualoa, island, *Solomon Is.* **217** P23
Fenua Roa, island, *Fr. Polynesia, Fr.* **219** KI6
Fenxi, *China* **182** F4
Fenyang, *China* **182** F4
Feodosiya, *Ukr.* **157** S8
Feolin Ferry, *Scot., U.K.* **142** M7
Fer, Point au, *La., U.S.* **100** R9
Fera, island, *Solomon Is.* **217** MI8
Ferdows, *Iran* **173** DI6
Féres, *Gr.* **155** CI6
Fergana Valley, *Uzb.* **175** KI4
Fergus Falls, *Minn., U.S.* **104** H9
Ferguson Seamount, *Pac. Oc.* **238** F9
Fergusson Island, *P.N.G.* **213** E2I
Feridu, island, *Maldives* **179** U3
Ferit, island, *F.S.M.* **217** BI6
Ferizaj (Uroševac), *Kos.* **152** JIO
Ferkéssédougou, *Côte d'Ivoire* **200** F8
Fermo, *It.* **150** HIO
Fermont, *Que., Can.* **83** L2O
Fermoselle, *Sp.* **144** E8
Fermoy, *Ire.* **143** U4
Fernandez Bay, *Bahamas* **120** EII
Fernandina, Isla (Narborough), *Ecua.* **128** Q7
Fernandina Beach, *Fla., U.S.* **97** Q8
Fernando de Noronha, *S. Amer.* **126** EI2
Fernando de Noronha, Arquipélago de, *Braz.* **131** EI9
Fernan Vaz *see* Omboué, *Gabon* **201** LI5
Ferndale, *Calif., U.S.* **109** NI
Ferndale, *Wash., U.S.* **108** A4
Fern Grotto, *Hawai'i, U.S.* **112** B6
Fern Gully, *Jam.* **120** H9
Fernlee, *Qnsld., Austral.* **211** VI3
Fernley, *Nev., U.S.* **109** P7
Ferrara, *It.* **150** F7
Ferrato, Capo, *It.* **151** P4
Ferré, Cap, *Martinique, Fr.* **121** G23
Ferreira do Alentejo, *Port.* **144** K5
Ferreira Gomes, *Braz.* **130** CI2
Ferreñafe, *Peru* **130** F2
Ferret, Cap, *Fr.* **147** W6
Ferrette, *Fr.* **147** RI5
Ferriday, *La., U.S.* **100** M9
Ferro *see* Hierro, island, *Canary Is.* **204** R3
Ferro, Ilhéu de, *Madeira* **204** L5
Ferrol, *Sp.* **144** A6
Ferrolana, *Eq. Guinea* **204** M6
Ferrysburg, *Mich., U.S.* **98** JII
Fertile, *Minn., U.S.* **104** F8
Feshi, *Dem. Rep. of the Congo* **198** M8
Fessenden, *N. Dak., U.S.* **104** F5
Festus, *Mo., U.S.* **105** TI5
Feteşti, *Rom.* **153** FI7
Fethiye, *Turk.* **168** J4
Fethiye Körfezi, *Turk.* **168** J4
Fetlar, island, *Scot., U.K.* **142** DI2
Fetoa, island, *Tonga* **218** Q6
Fetokopunga, island, *Tonga* **218** Q7
Fetuna, *Fr. Polynesia, Fr.* **219** C23
Feuet, *Lib.* **196** EI2
Feuilles, Rivière aux, *Que., Can.* **83** KI9
Feurs, *Fr.* **147** UI2
Fevzipaşa, *Turk.* **168** HII
Feyzabad, *Afghan.* **176** K9
Fez *see* Fès, *Mor.* **196** B9
Fezzan, region, *Lib.* **197** EI3
Fianarantsoa, *Madagascar* **203** HI7
Fichtelberg, peak, *Czech Rep.* **148** GIO
Fidenza, *It.* **150** E5
Fieberling Tablemount, *Pac. Oc.* **239** FI5

Fields Find, *W. Aust., Austral.* **211** W3
Fier, *Albania* **152** L9
Fier-Shegan, *Albania* **152** L9
Fife Lake, *Mich., U.S.* **98** JIO
Fife Ness, *Scot., U.K.* **142** MII
Fifth Cataract, *Sudan* **199** DI3
Figari, Capo, *It.* **150** M5
Figeac, *Fr.* **147** W9
Fig Tree, *St. Kitts & Nevis* **121** CI8
Figueira da Foz, *Port.* **144** F5
Figueres, *Sp.* **145** CI8
Figuig, *Mor.* **196** B9
Fiji Islands, *Pac. Oc.* **214** J9
Fiji Islands Plateau, *Pac. Oc.* **238** LIO
Filabres, Sierra de los, *Sp.* **144** LI2
Filadelfia, *Parag.* **130** L9
Filchner Ice Sheet, *Antarctica* **226** FIO
Filey, *Eng., U.K.* **143** QI3
Filfla, island, *Malta* **161** M22
Filiaşi, *Rom.* **153** FI3
Filiátes, *Gr.* **154** E7
Filiatrá, *Gr.* **154** L9
Filicudi, Isola, *It.* **151** RII
Filiourí, river, *Gr.* **155** BI5
Filipiáda, *Gr.* **154** F7
Filipstad, *Sw.* **140** KI2
Fillmore, *Calif., U.S.* **109** W7
Fillmore, *Utah, U.S.* **107** N7
Filyos, river, *Turk.* **168** C8
Fimbul Ice Shelf, *Antarctica* **226** AI2
Fimi, river, *Dem. Rep. of the Congo* **198** K8
Fiñana, *Sp.* **144** LI2
Fındıklı, *Turk.* **169** CI5
Findlay, *Ohio, U.S.* **99** PI2
Findochty, *Scot., U.K.* **142** JIO
Fineveke, *Wallis & Futuna, Fr.* **218** BII
Finger Lakes, *N.Y., U.S.* **94** K7
Fingoè, *Mozambique* **202** EI2
Finikas, *Gr.* **155** KI4
Finike, *Turk.* **168** J5
Finisterre, Cape, *Sp.* **138** H2
Finke, river, *N. Terr., Austral.* **211** U9
Finke, *N. Terr., Austral.* **211** U9
Finland, *Eur.* **139** Q9
Finland, *Minn., U.S.* **104** FI3
Finland, Gulf of, *Est., Fin.* **141** KI6
Finlay, river, *B.C., Can.* **82** J9
Finley, *N. Dak., U.S.* **104** F7
Finley Cay, *Bahamas* **120** E5
Finnmark Plateau, *Nor.* **138** A8
Finnmark-vidda, region, *Nor.* **141** CI4
Finschhafen, *P.N.G.* **213** D2O
Finsteraarhorn, peak, *Switz.* **150** C3
Fionn Loch, *Scot., U.K.* **142** J8
Fionnphort, *Scot., U.K.* **142** L7
Fiorentino, *San Marino* **161** KI5
Fiorina, river, *San Marino* **161** HI6
Fiorina, *San Marino* **161** HI6
Frías, *Arg.* **132** H9
Firat (Euphrates), river, *Turk.* **169** EI5
Fire Island National Seashore, *N.Y., U.S.* **94** NI2
Firenze (Florence), *It.* **150** G7
Firenzuola, *It.* **150** G7
Firmat, *Arg.* **132** KII
Firminy, *Fr.* **147** UI2
Firozabad, *India* **178** G6
Firoz Koh, region, *Afghan.* **176** M4
First Cataract, *Egypt* **197** EI9
First Sugar Mill, *Hawai'i, U.S.* **112** C5
Fish, river, *Namibia* **202** J7
Fisher, river, *Mont., U.S.* **106** B5
Fisher, S. Aust., Austral.* **211** W7
Fisher Glacier, *Antarctica* **227** FI8
Fisher Strait, *Nunavut, Can.* **83** HI6
Fishguard (Abergwaun), *Wales, U.K.* **143** U8
Fishing Cays, *Bahamas* **120** CIO
Fish Lake, *Utah, U.S.* **107** N7
Fiskárdo, *Gr.* **154** H7
Fismes, *Fr.* **147** NII
Fisterra, *Sp.* **144** B5
Fisterra, Cabo, *Sp.* **144** B5
Fitchburg, *Mass., U.S.* **95** KI4
Fitii, *Fr. Polynesia, Fr.* **219** GI4
Fitii, Baie de, *Fr. Polynesia, Fr.* **219** GI4
Fitiuta, *Amer. Samoa, U.S.* **218** N4
Fito, Mount, *Samoa* **218** L3
Fitri, Lac, *Chad* **197** JI5
Fitzgerald, *Alta., Can.* **82** JII
Fitzgerald, *Ga., U.S.* **97** P6
Fitzroy, river, *Qnsld., Austral.* **210** FI5
Fitzroy, river, *W. Aust., Austral.* **211** R5

Fitzroy Crossing, *W. Aust., Austral.* **211** R5
Fiume *see* Rijeka, *Croatia* **152** E4
Fiumicello, river, *San Marino* **161** J16
Fivaku, island, *Maldives* **179** T3
Five Island Harbour, *Antigua & Barbuda* **121** B2O
Five Islands Village, *Antigua & Barbuda* **121** B2O
Flagler, *Colo., U.S.* **106** M15
Flagstaff, *Ariz., U.S.* **107** S7
Flagstaff Lake, *Oreg., U.S.* **108** K6
Flåm, *Nor.* **140** K1O
Flambeau, river, *Wis., U.S.* **98** G4
Flamborough Head, *Eng., U.K.* **143** Q14
Flaming Gorge National Recreation Area, *Wyo., U.S.* **106** K9
Flaming Gorge Reservoir, *Utah, Wyo., U.S.* **106** K9
Flamingo, *Fla., U.S.* **97** Y9
Flamingo, Teluk, *Indonesia* **213** C16
Flamingo Cay, *Bahamas* **117** G13
Flamingo Point, *Bahamas* **117** E13
Flanagan Island, *Virgin Islands, U.S.* **120** N12
Flanders, region, *Belg., Fr.* **146** L1O
Flandreau, *S. Dak., U.S.* **104** L8
Flannan Isles, *Scot., U.K.* **142** H6
Flathead Lake, *Mont., U.S.* **106** B6
Flat Island, *Mauritius* **205** F2O
Flat Island, *Spratly Is.* **188** E11
Flatonia, *Tex., U.S.* **103** R11
Flat River, *Mo., U.S.* **105** U15
Flattery, Cape, *Austral.* **210** C13
Flattery, Cape, *Wash., U.S.* **108** B1
Flatts Village, *Bermuda, U.K.* **120** B3
Flatwoods, *Ky., U.S.* **101** A2O
Flaxton, *N. Dak., U.S.* **104** D3
Fleeming Channel, *Bahamas* **120** E5
Fleetwood, *Eng., U.K.* **143** R1O
Flekkefjord, *Nor.* **140** M1O
Fleming Glacier, *Antarctica* **226** E5
Flemingsburg, *Ky., U.S.* **101** B18
Flemish Cap, *Atl. Oc.* **236** F7
Flensburg, *Ger.* **148** A7
Flers, *Fr.* **147** P7
Fletcher Peninsula, *Antarctica* **226** H5
Fletcher Plain, *Arctic Oc.* **242** H9
Fleurance, *Fr.* **147** X8
Fleurier, *Switz.* **150** B1
Flight 93 National Memorial, *Pa., U.S.* **94** P4
Flinders, river, *Qnsld., Austral.* **211** S12
Flinders Bay, *W. Aust., Austral.* **211** Y2
Flinders Island, *Tas., Austral.* **211** Y16
Flinders Ranges, *Austral.* **210** J1O
Flin Flon, *Man., Can.* **83** L13
Flint, river, *Ga., U.S.* **97** P5
Flint, *Mich., U.S.* **98** L12
Flint Hills, *Kans., U.S.* **105** U8
Flint Island, *Kiribati* **215** J13
Flipper Point, *Wake I., U.S.* **216** F8
Flisa, *Nor.* **140** K12
Flix, *Sp.* **145** E15
Flixecourt, *Fr.* **146** M9
Flocca, river, *San Marino* **161** H15
Flomaton, *Ala., U.S.* **101** N14
Flood Range, *Antarctica* **226** M8
Floodwood, *Minn., U.S.* **104** G12
Flora, *Ill., U.S.* **99** T6
Flora, *Ind., U.S.* **99** Q9
Flora, *Oreg., U.S.* **108** E9
Florala, *Ala., U.S.* **101** N16
Florange, *Fr.* **147** N14
Floreana *see* Santa María, Isla, island, *Ecua.* **128** R9
Florence, *Ala., U.S.* **101** G14
Florence, *Ariz., U.S.* **107** U7
Florence, *Colo., U.S.* **107** N13
Florence *see* Firenze, *It.* **150** G7
Florence, *Kans., U.S.* **105** T8
Florence, *Ky., U.S.* **101** A17
Florence, *Oreg., U.S.* **108** H2
Florence, *S.C., U.S.* **96** K1O
Florence, *Wis., U.S.* **98** G7
Florencia, *Col.* **128** H4
Florenville, *Belg.* **160** J7
Flores, island, *Azores* **144** N1
Flores, *Guatemala* **115** K16
Flores, island, *Indonesia* **189** M14
Flores Sea, *Indonesia* **189** M13
Floreşti, *Mold.* **157** Q4
Floresville, *Tex., U.S.* **103** S1O
Floriano, *Braz.* **131** F15
Floriano Peixoto, *Braz.* **130** G6

Florianópolis, *Braz.* **131** N13
Florida, *Cuba* **116** J1O
Florida, peninsula, *N. Amer.* **80** M8
Florida, *P.R., U.S.* **120** M3
Florida, *U.S.* **97** R4
Florida, Straits of, *Bahamas, U.S.* **80** M8
Florida Bay, *Fla., U.S.* **97** Y1O
Florida City, *Fla., U.S.* **97** X1O
Florida Islands, *Solomon Is.* **217** N18
Florida Keys, *Fla., U.S.* **97** Y9
Floridia, *It.* **151** T12
Flórina, *Gr.* **154** C8
Florissant, *Mo., U.S.* **105** S15
Florissant Fossil Beds National Monument, *Colo., U.S.* **107** N13
Florø, *Nor.* **140** J9
Flotta, island, *Scot., U.K.* **142** G1O
Flotte, Cap de, *New Caledonia, Fr.* **218** D9
Floyd, *N. Mex., U.S.* **107** T15
Floydada, *Tex., U.S.* **102** J6
Flumet, *Fr.* **147** U14
Fly, river, *P.N.G.* **213** D17
Foa, island, *Tonga* **218** P7
Foça, *Turk.* **168** F2
Foča, *Bosn. & Herzg.* **152** H8
Focşani, *Rom.* **153** D16
Fofoa, island, *Tonga* **218** L11
Fogang, *China* **183** R4
Fogausa, Cape, *Amer. Samoa, U.S.* **218** M8
Foggia, *It.* **150** L12
Fogo, island, *Cape Verde* **205** E15
Fogo Island, *Nfld. & Lab., Can.* **83** L23
Fohnsdorf, *Aust.* **148** L11
Fokino, *Russ.* **156** L8
Foko Malsu, cape, *F.S.M.* **217** A18
Folda, bay, *Nor.* **140** G11
Folégandros, *Gr.* **155** M14
Folégandros, island, *Gr.* **155** M14
Foley, *Ala., U.S.* **101** P14
Foley, *Minn., U.S.* **104** J11
Foley Island, *Nunavut, Can.* **83** F17
Foligno, *It.* **150** H9
Folkestone, *Eng., U.K.* **143** W15
Folkston, *Ga., U.S.* **97** Q8
Follett, *Tex., U.S.* **102** E7
Follonica, *It.* **150** J6
Follonica, Golfo di, *It.* **150** J6
Folly Beach, *S.C., U.S.* **96** M1O
Foloha, *Tonga* **218** J11
Folschette, *Lux.* **160** J9
Folsom, *Calif., U.S.* **109** Q5
Folteşti, *Rom.* **153** D17
Fomboni, *Comoros* **205** N15
Fomento, *Cuba* **116** H9
Fond d'Or Bay, *St. Lucia* **121** J14
Fond du Lac, *Sask., Can.* **82** J12
Fond du Lac, *Wis., U.S.* **98** K6
Fondi, *It.* **150** L9
Fongafale *see* Funafuti, *Tuvalu* **217** K24
Fono, island, *F.S.M.* **217** B15
Fonoifua, island, *Tonga* **218** Q6
Fononuk, island, *F.S.M.* **217** D16
Fonou, island, *F.S.M.* **217** C15
Fonseca, Golfo de, *Hond.* **115** M17
Fonseca, Gulf of *see* Fonseca, Golfo de, *N. Amer.* **80** Q7
Fontainebleau, *Fr.* **147** Q1O
Fontana Lake, *N.C., U.S.* **96** J6
Fontaneda, *Andorra* **160** K2
Fonte Boa, *Braz.* **130** D7
Fontenelle Reservoir, *Wyo., U.S.* **106** J9
Fontenoy, *Grenada* **121** L22
Fontvieille, *Monaco* **161** F2O
Fontvieille, Port of, *Monaco* **161** F21
Fonuafo'ou, island, *Tonga* **218** M12
Fonuaika, island, *Tonga* **218** Q6
Fonuakula, *Niue, N.Z.* **219** B2O
Fonua'one'one, island, *Tonga* **218** M11
Fonua'unga, island, *Tonga* **218** M12
Fonuchu, island, *F.S.M.* **217** A15
Foping, *China* **182** H1
Foppolo, *It.* **150** D5
Forbesganj, *India* **178** G11
Forbes Hill, *Bahamas* **120** F9
Forcalquier, *Fr.* **147** W14
Forchheim, *Ger.* **148** H8
Ford, Cape, *Austral.* **210** B7
Fordate, island, *Indonesia* **213** D14
Førde, *Nor.* **140** K1O
Ford Ranges, *Antarctica* **226** N9
Fords Bridge, *N.S.W., Austral.* **211** W12
Fordyce, *Ark., U.S.* **100** J8
Forécariah, *Guinea* **200** F5

Forel, Mont, *N. Amer.* **80** C1O
Foreman, *Ark., U.S.* **100** J6
Forest, *Miss., U.S.* **100** L12
Forest City, *Iowa, U.S.* **104** M11
Forest City, *N.C., U.S.* **96** J8
Forest Grove, *Oreg., U.S.* **108** F3
Forest Home, *Qnsld., Austral.* **211** R12
Forest Park, *Ga., U.S.* **96** L5
Forest Point, *Anguilla, U.K.* **120** R11
Forestville, *Mich., U.S.* **98** K13
Forestville, *Que., Can.* **83** N2O
Forez, Monts du, *Fr.* **147** U12
Forfar, *Scot., U.K.* **142** L1O
Forgan, *Okla., U.S.* **102** E7
Forges-les-Eaux, *Fr.* **147** N9
Forks, *Wash., U.S.* **108** B2
Forlì, *It.* **150** G8
Forman, *N. Dak., U.S.* **104** H7
Formentera, island, *Sp.* **145** J17
Formiga, *Braz.* **131** L14
Formigas, Ilhéus, *Azores* **144** Q6
Formosa, *Arg.* **132** F13
Formosa, *Braz.* **131** J13
Formosa, Serra, *Braz.* **130** G11
Formosa do Rio Prêto, *Braz.* **131** G14
Føroyar *see* Faroe Islands, *Den.* **140** J5
Forrest, *W. Aust., Austral.* **211** W6
Forrestal Range, *Antarctica* **226** G1O
Forrest City, *Ark., U.S.* **100** G1O
Forrest River, *W. Aust., Austral.* **211** Q6
Forsayth, *Qnsld., Austral.* **211** R12
Forssa, *Fin.* **141** J15
Forst, *Ger.* **148** E11
Forster-Tuncurry, *N.S.W., Austral.* **211** X15
Forsyth, *Ga., U.S.* **96** M5
Forsyth, *Mo., U.S.* **105** V12
Forsyth, *Mont., U.S.* **106** D11
Fort Abbas, *Pak.* **177** S11
Fort Albany, *Ont., Can.* **83** M17
Fortaleza, *Braz.* **131** E17
Fort Allen, *P.R., U.S.* **120** N3
Fort Antoine, *Monaco* **161** E22
Fort Atkinson, *Wis., U.S.* **98** L6
Fort Benton, *Mont., U.S.* **106** C8
Fort Bowie National Historic Site, *Ariz., U.S.* **107** V9
Fort Bragg, *Calif., U.S.* **109** P2
Fort Caroline National Memorial, *Fla., U.S.* **97** Q8
Fort Charlotte, *St. Lucia* **121** J14
Fort Charlotte, *St. Vincent & the Grenadines* **121** L16
Fort Chipewyan, *Alta., Can.* **82** J11
Fort Cobb Reservoir, *Okla., U.S.* **102** G9
Fort Collins, *Colo., U.S.* **106** L13
Fort Davis, *Tex., U.S.* **103** P2
Fort Davis National Historic Site, *Tex., U.S.* **103** P2
Fort-de-France, *Martinique, Fr.* **121** F22
Fort-de-France, Baie de, *Martinique, Fr.* **121** F22
Fort Deposit, *Ala., U.S.* **101** M15
Fort Dick, *Calif., U.S.* **108** L2
Fort Dodge, *Iowa, U.S.* **105** N11
Fort Duvernette, *St. Vincent & the Grenadines* **121** L16
Forteau, *Nfld. & Lab., Can.* **83** L22
Forteau, *Que., Can.* **83** L22
Fortescue, river, *W. Aust., Austral.* **211** T3
Fortezza, *It.* **150** B7
Fort Fairfield, *Me., U.S.* **95** B18
Fort Frances, *Ont., Can.* **83** P14
Fort Fraser, *B.C., Can.* **82** K8
Fort Frederica National Monument, *Ga., U.S.* **97** P8
Fort Frederick, *Grenada* **121** L22
Fort Gaines, *Ga., U.S.* **97** P4
Fort Gibson, *Okla., U.S.* **102** F13
Fort Gibson Lake, *Okla., U.S.* **102** F13
Fort Good Hope, *N.W.T., Can.* **82** F1O
Forth, Firth of, *Scot., U.K.* **142** M1O
Fort Hall, *Idaho, U.S.* **106** H7
Fort Hancock, *Tex., U.S.* **103** V2
Fort Hope, *Ont., Can.* **83** N16
Fortín General Díaz, *Parag.* **130** M9
Fortín Infante Rivarola, *Parag.* **130** L8
Fortín Madrejón, *Parag.* **130** L8
Fortín Mayor Alberto Gardel, *Parag.* **130** L8
Fortín Presidente Ayala, *Parag.* **130** M9
Fortín Suárez Arana, *Bol.* **130** K9
Fort James, *Antigua & Barbuda* **121** B2O
Fort Jeudy, Point of, *Grenada* **121** L22

Fort Jones, *Calif., U.S.* **108** L3
Fort Kent, *Me., U.S.* **95** A17
Fort Klamath, *Oreg., U.S.* **108** K4
Fort Knox, *Ky., U.S.* **101** C16
Fort Laperrine *see* Tamanrasset, *Alg.* **196** F11
Fort Laramie, *Wyo., U.S.* **106** J13
Fort Laramie National Historic Site, *Wyo., U.S.* **106** J13
Fort Larned National Historic Site, *Kans., U.S.* **105** T5
Fort Lauderdale, *Fla., U.S.* **97** W1O
Fort Liard, *N.W.T., Can.* **82** H1O
Fort-Liberté, *Haiti* **117** L17
Fort Madison, *Iowa, U.S.* **105** Q14
Fort Matanzas National Monument, *Fla., U.S.* **97** R9
Fort McMurray, *Alta., Can.* **82** K11
Fort McPherson, *N.W.T., Can.* **82** E9
Fort Meade, *Fla., U.S.* **97** U8
Fort Mill, *S.C., U.S.* **96** J9
Fort Miribel, *Alg.* **196** C11
Fort Morgan, *Colo., U.S.* **106** L14
Fort Munro, *Pak.* **177** R8
Fort Myers, *Fla., U.S.* **97** W8
Fort Myers Beach, *Fla., U.S.* **97** W8
Fort Nelson, *B.C., Can.* **82** J9
Fort Payne, *Ala., U.S.* **101** H16
Fort Peck, *Mont., U.S.* **106** B11
Fort Peck Dam, *Mont., U.S.* **106** B12
Fort Peck Lake, *Mont., U.S.* **106** C11
Fort Pierce, *Fla., U.S.* **97** U1O
Fort Pierre, *S. Dak., U.S.* **104** K5
Fort Point, *Virgin Islands, U.K.* **120** R8
Fort Portal, *Uganda* **198** J12
Fort Providence, *N.W.T., Can.* **82** H11
Fort Pulaski National Monument, *Ga., U.S.* **97** N9
Fort Raleigh National Historic Site, *N.C., U.S.* **96** G15
Fort Randall Dam, *S. Dak., U.S.* **104** M6
Fort Resolution, *N.W.T., Can.* **82** H11
Fortress Headquarters, *Gibraltar, U.K.* **161** Q22
Fort Rock, *Oreg., U.S.* **108** J5
Fort Royal, *Guadeloupe, Fr.* **121** E14
Fort St. Catherine, *Bermuda, U.K.* **120** A3
Fort St. John, *B.C., Can.* **82** K9
Fort Scaur, *Bermuda, U.K.* **120** B1
Fort Scott, *Kans., U.S.* **105** U1O
Fort Scott National Historic Site, *Kans., U.S.* **105** U1O
Fort Severn, *Ont., Can.* **83** L16
Fort Shevchenko, *Kaz.* **174** G5
Fort Simpson, *N.W.T., Can.* **82** H1O
Fort Smith, *Ark., U.S.* **100** F6
Fort Smith, *N.W.T., Can.* **82** J11
Fort Stanwix National Monument, *N.Y., U.S.* **94** J9
Fort Stockton, *Tex., U.S.* **103** P3
Fort Sumner, *N. Mex., U.S.* **107** S14
Fort Sumter National Monument, *S.C., U.S.* **96** M1O
Fort Supply, *Okla., U.S.* **102** E8
Fort Thompson, *S. Dak., U.S.* **104** L5
Fort Trinquet *see* Bir Mogreïn, *Mauritania* **196** D6
Fortuna, *Calif., U.S.* **109** N1
Fortuna, *N. Dak., U.S.* **104** D2
Fortune Hill, *Bahamas* **120** E12
Fortune Island *see* Long Cay, *Bahamas* **117** H14
Fort Union National Monument, *N. Mex., U.S.* **107** R13
Fort Union Trading Post National Historic Site, *N. Dak., U.S.* **104** E1
Fort Valley, *Ga., U.S.* **96** M5
Fort Vermilion, *Alta., Can.* **82** J1O
Fort Walton Beach, *Fla., U.S.* **97** Q2
Fort Wayne, *Ind., U.S.* **99** P1O
Fort Worth, *Tex., U.S.* **102** L11
Fort Yates, *N. Dak., U.S.* **104** H4
Fort Yukon, *Alas., U.S.* **111** E18
Fosforescénte, Bahía, *P.R., U.S.* **120** P2
Foshan, *China* **183** R4
Fosheim Peninsula, *Nunavut, Can.* **83** B11
Fossano, *It.* **150** F2
Fossil, *Oreg., U.S.* **108** G6
Fossil Butte National Monument, *Wyo., U.S.* **106** J9
Fosston, *Minn., U.S.* **104** F9
Foster, Mount, *Alas., U.S.* **111** K21

Fostoria, *Ohio, U.S.* **99** P12
Fotuha'a, island, *Tonga* **218** P6
Fougères, *Fr.* **147** Q6
Foula, island, *Scot., U.K.* **142** D11
Foul Bay, *Barbados* **121** L2O
Foulness Island, *Eng., U.K.* **143** V15
Foulweather, Cape, *Oreg., U.S.* **108** G2
Foulwind, Cape, *N.Z.* **213** N17
Foumban, *Cameroon* **201** H15
Foumbouni, *Comoros* **205** M14
Foundation Ice Stream, *Antarctica* **226** G1O
Fountain, *Colo., U.S.* **107** N13
Fountain City, *Wis., U.S.* **98** J3
Fourche, Île, *Lesser Antilles* **119** F15
Four Corners, *Wyo., U.S.* **106** G14
Fourcroy, Cape, *Austral.* **210** A7
Fourmies, *Fr.* **146** M11
Four Mountains, Islands of, *Alas., U.S.* **110** P8
Fournaise, Piton de la, *Reunion, Fr.* **205** H17
Foúrni, island, *Gr.* **155** K17
Foúrni, *Gr.* **155** K17
Fourth Cataract, *Sudan* **199** D13
Fourup, island, *F.S.M.* **217** C15
Fouta Djallon, region, *Guinea* **200** E6
Foux, Cap-à-, *Haiti* **117** L15
Foveaux Strait, *N.Z.* **213** R15
Fowler, *Colo., U.S.* **107** N14
Fowler, *Ind., U.S.* **99** Q8
Fowler, *Kans., U.S.* **105** U4
Fowlers Bay, *S. Aust., Austral.* **211** W8
Fox, river, *Ill., U.S.* **99** P6
Fox, river, *Wis., U.S.* **98** J7
Foxe Basin, *Nunavut, Can.* **83** G17
Foxe Channel, *Nunavut, Can.* **83** H17
Foxe Peninsula, *Nunavut, Can.* **83** H17
Fox Glacier, *N.Z.* **213** P16
Fox Islands, *Alas., U.S.* **110** P1O
Foxpark, *Wyo., U.S.* **106** K12
Fox Town, *Bahamas* **120** A5
Foyle, Lough, *N. Ire., U.K.* **143** P6
Foyn Coast, *Antarctica* **226** E4
Foz, *Sp.* **144** A7
Foz do Cunene, *Angola* **202** F5
Foz do Iguaçu, *Braz.* **130** M11
Fraga, *Sp.* **145** D15
Framnes Mountains, *Antarctica* **227** E2O
Fram Peak, *Antarctica* **227** D19
Franca, *Braz.* **131** L13
France, *Eur.* **139** U4
Francés, Cabo, *Cuba* **116** H4
Francés, Punta, *Cuba* **116** H5
Frances Lake, *Yukon, Can.* **82** G9
Francés Viejo, Cabo, *Dom. Rep.* **117** L19
Franceville, *Gabon* **201** L17
Francis Bay, *Virgin Islands, U.S.* **120** M11
Francis Case, Lake, *S. Dak., U.S.* **104** M6
Francistown, *Botswana* **202** G1O
Francs Peak, *Wyo., U.S.* **106** G9
Frankenberg, *Ger.* **148** F7
Frankfort, *Ind., U.S.* **99** Q8
Frankfort, *Kans., U.S.* **105** R8
Frankfort, *Ky., U.S.* **101** B17
Frankfort, *Mich., U.S.* **98** J9
Frankfurt am Main, *Ger.* **148** G6
Frankfurt an der Oder, *Ger.* **148** E11
Franklin, *Ind., U.S.* **99** S9
Franklin, *Ky., U.S.* **101** D15
Franklin, *La., U.S.* **100** Q9
Franklin, *N.C., U.S.* **96** J6
Franklin, *N.H., U.S.* **95** H14
Franklin, *Nebr., U.S.* **105** R6
Franklin, *Pa., U.S.* **94** M3
Franklin, *Tenn., U.S.* **101** F15
Franklin, *Va., U.S.* **96** F13
Franklin Bay, *N.W.T., Can.* **82** E11
Franklin D. Roosevelt Lake, *Wash., U.S.* **108** B8
Franklin Lake, *Nev., U.S.* **109** N11
Franklin Mountains, *N. Amer.* **80** D4
Franklin Strait, *Nunavut, Can.* **83** E14
Franklinton, *La., U.S.* **100** N11
Franklinville, *N.Y., U.S.* **94** K5
Frank Sound, *Cayman Is., U.K.* **120** J3
Frankston, *Tex., U.S.* **102** M13
Frantsa Iosifa, Zemlya (Franz Josef Land), *Russ.* **158** C12
Franz, *Ont., Can.* **83** P17
Franz Josef Glacier, *N.Z.* **213** P16
Franz Josef Land *see* Frantsa Iosifa, Zemlya, *Russ.* **158** C12

Frasca, Capo della, *It.* 151 P3
Fraser, river, *B.C., Can.* 82 L8
Fraserburg, *S. Af.* 202 L8
Fraserburgh, *Scot., U.K.* 142 J11
Fraser Island (Great Sandy Island), *Austral.* 210 G16
Fraser Range, *W. Aust., Austral.* 211 X5
Frasertown, *N.Z.* 213 L20
Frasin, *Rom.* 153 B15
Frastanz, *Aust.* 160 M4
Fratta, river, *San Marino* 161 K14
Frauenfeld, *Switz.* 150 A4
Frazee, *Minn., U.S.* 104 G9
Fredensborg, *Virgin Islands, U.S.* 120 Q2
Frederick, *Md., U.S.* 96 C12
Frederick, *Okla., U.S.* 102 J9
Frederick, *S. Dak., U.S.* 104 H6
Frederick, Mount, *Austral.* 210 D7
Fredericksburg, *Tex., U.S.* 103 Q9
Fredericksburg, *Va., U.S.* 96 D12
Fredericktown, *Mo., U.S.* 105 U15
Fredericton, *N.B., Can.* 83 P21
Frederikshavn, *Den.* 140 M11
Frederiksted, *Virgin Islands, U.S.* 120 R2
Fredonia, *Ariz., U.S.* 107 Q6
Fredonia, *Kans., U.S.* 105 U9
Fredonia, *N.Y., U.S.* 94 K4
Fredrikstad, *Nor.* 140 L11
Freedom, *Okla., U.S.* 102 E8
Freehold, *N.J., U.S.* 94 P11
Freeman, *S. Dak., U.S.* 104 M7
Freeport, *Bahamas* 120 F2
Freeport, *Ill., U.S.* 98 M5
Freeport, *Me., U.S.* 95 G16
Freeport, *N.Y., U.S.* 94 N11
Freeport, *Tex., U.S.* 103 S14
Freer, *Tex., U.S.* 103 T9
Freetown, *Antigua & Barbuda* 121 B21
Freetown, *Bahamas* 120 E2
Freetown, *Jam.* 120 J9
Freetown, *Sierra Leone* 200 G5
Freezeout Mountain, *Oreg., U.S.* 108 H9
Frégate, island, *Seychelles* 205 N21
Frégate Island, *Mauritius* 205 J19
Fregenal de la Sierra, *Sp.* 144 K7
Fréhel, Cap, *Fr.* 147 P5
Freiberg, *Ger.* 148 F10
Freiburg, *Ger.* 148 K5
Freidberg, *Ger.* 148 K8
Freirina, *Chile* 132 H6
Freisach, *Aust.* 148 M11
Freising, *Ger.* 148 K9
Freistadt, *Aust.* 148 K11
Freital, *Ger.* 148 F10
Fréjus, *Fr.* 147 X15
Fremantle, *W. Aust., Austral.* 211 X2
Fremont, *Calif., U.S.* 109 S4
Fremont, *Mich., U.S.* 98 L9
Fremont, *Nebr., U.S.* 105 P8
Fremont, *Ohio, U.S.* 99 P12
Fremont, river, *Utah, U.S.* 107 N8
Fremont Lake, *Wyo., U.S.* 106 H9
Fremont Mountains, *Oreg., U.S.* 108 J5
French Bay, *Bahamas* 120 F11
French Broad, river, *Tenn., U.S.* 101 E19
Frenchcap Cay, *Virgin Islands, U.S.* 120 P10
French Cays *see* Plana Cays, *Bahamas* 117 H15
French Frigate Shoals, *Hawai'i, U.S.* 112 M7
French Guiana, *S. Amer.* 127 B20
Frenchman Creek, *Nebr., U.S.* 105 Q3
Frenchman Flat, *Nev., U.S.* 109 T11
Frenchman's Cay, *Virgin Islands, U.K.* 120 R5
French Polynesia, *Pac. Oc.* 215 K14
Frenchville, *Me., U.S.* 95 A18
Fresh Water Bay, *Barbados* 121 K18
Fresh Water Lagoons, *Kiribati* 217 C23
Fresnay, *Fr.* 147 Q7
Fresnillo, *Mex.* 114 G10
Fresno, *Calif., U.S.* 109 T6
Fresno Reservoir, *Mont., U.S.* 106 B9
Frévent, *Fr.* 146 M10
Frewena, *N. Terr., Austral.* 211 S9
Freyung, *Ger.* 148 J10
Fri, *Gr.* 155 Q18
Fria, *Guinea* 200 F5
Friars Point, *Miss., U.S.* 100 H10
Fridtjof Nansen, Mount, *Antarctica* 226 K12
Friedrichshafen, *Ger.* 148 L7
Friend, *Nebr., U.S.* 105 Q7
Friesland, region, *Ger., Neth.* 146 G14

Frigate Bay, *St. Kitts & Nevis* 121 B18
Frio, river, *Tex., U.S.* 103 S8
Frio, Cape, *S. Amer.* 126 J10
Friona, *Tex., U.S.* 102 H4
Frisange, *Lux.* 160 K10
Frisco City, *Ala., U.S.* 101 M14
Frisian Islands, *Eur.* 138 E5
Frissell, Mount, *Conn., U.S.* 94 L12
Fritch, *Tex., U.S.* 102 G5
Friza, Proliv, *Russ.* 159 J23
Frobisher Bay, *Nunavut, Can.* 83 H19
Frolovo, *Russ.* 157 P12
Fromberg, *Mont., U.S.* 106 E10
Frome, *Eng., U.K.* 143 W11
Frome, *Jam.* 120 H6
Frome, Lake, *S. Aust., Austral.* 211 W11
Frome Downs, *S. Aust., Austral.* 211 W11
Frómista, *Sp.* 144 C10
Frontenac, *Kans., U.S.* 105 U10
Frontera, *Mex.* 114 E11
Frontera, *Mex.* 115 J14
Frontignan, *Fr.* 147 X11
Front Range, *Colo., U.S.* 106 L12
Frosinone, *It.* 150 L9
Frostburg, *Md., U.S.* 96 C11
Frostproof, *Fla., U.S.* 97 U8
Frøya, island, *Nor.* 140 H10
Fruita, *Colo., U.S.* 106 M10
Fruitland, *Idaho, U.S.* 106 G3
Frümsen, *Switz.* 160 M2
Frydendal, *Virgin Islands, U.S.* 120 M9
Fryeburg, *Me., U.S.* 95 G15
Frying Pan Shoals, *N.C., U.S.* 96 L13
Fu, river, *China* 183 N6
Fu, river, *China* 180 L12
Fua'amotu, *Tonga* 218 J11
Fua'amotu, island, *Tonga* 218 M11
Fuafatu, island, *Tuvalu* 217 K22
Fuagea, island, *Tuvalu* 217 L22
Fuagea, Te Ava, *Tuvalu* 217 K22
Fualifexe, island, *Tuvalu* 217 J23
Fualopa, island, *Tuvalu* 217 K22
Fua Mulaku, island, *Maldives* 179 X3
Fu'an, *China* 183 N9
Fucino, Piana del, *It.* 150 K10
Fudin, *China* 181 M17
Fuding, *China* 183 N9
Fuencaliente, *Canary Is.* 204 Q3
Fuencaliente, Punta de, *Canary Is.* 204 Q3
Fuengirola, *Sp.* 144 M9
Fuente de Cantos, *Sp.* 144 J8
Fuentesaúco, *Sp.* 144 E9
Fuerte Olimpo, *Parag.* 130 L10
Fuerteventura, island, *Canary Is.* 204 Q7
Fuga, island, *Philippines* 189 A13
Fugauvea, Passe, *Wallis & Futuna, Fr.* 218 B11
Fugou, *China* 182 H5
Fugu, *China* 182 D3
Fuhai, *China* 180 D7
Fuikbaai, bay, *Neth. Antilles, Neth.* 121 Q15
Fujairah, *U.A.E.* 173 J15
Fuji, peak, *Japan* 185 P11
Fujisawa, *Japan* 185 P11
Fukagawa, *Japan* 184 F14
Fukave, island, *Tonga* 218 H12
Fukuchiyama, *Japan* 185 P8
Fukue, *Japan* 185 S3
Fukue Jima, *Japan* 185 S2
Fukui, *Japan* 185 P9
Fukuoka, *Japan* 185 R4
Fukura, *Japan* 184 L12
Fukushima, *Japan* 184 H12
Fukushima, *Japan* 184 M13
Fukushima, Mount, *Antarctica* 227 C16
Fukuyama, *Japan* 185 Q7
Fulaga, island, *Fiji Is.* 218 K9
Fulaga Passage, *Fiji Is.* 218 K9
Fulda, *Ger.* 148 G7
Fulda, *Minn., U.S.* 104 L9
Fuling, *China* 180 L12
Fullarton, *Trinidad & Tobago* 121 Q21
Fullerton, *Nebr., U.S.* 105 P7
Fullerton Point, *Antigua & Barbuda* 121 B20
Fulton, *Ill., U.S.* 99 N4
Fulton, *Ky., U.S.* 100 E12
Fulton, *Miss., U.S.* 101 H13
Fulton, *Mo., U.S.* 105 S13
Fulton, *N.Y., U.S.* 94 H8
Fumay, *Fr.* 146 M12
Fumel, *Fr.* 147 W8
Funabashi, *Japan* 185 P12
Funafara, island, *Tuvalu* 217 L23

Funafuti, island, *Tuvalu* 217 K24
Funafuti (Fongafale), *Tuvalu* 217 K24
Funamanu, island, *Tuvalu* 217 K23
Funan, *China* 182 J6
Funangongo, island, *Tuvalu* 217 K23
Funchal, *Madeira* 204 M3
Fundo de Figueiras, *Cape Verde* 205 C17
Fundy, Bay of, *N.B., Can., N.S.* 83 P21
Funhalouro, *Mozambique* 203 H13
Funiya Point, *N. Mariana Is., U.S.* 216 E8
Funtanasupanie Point, *N. Mariana Is., U.S.* 216 E8
Funtua, *Nigeria* 201 E14
Fuping, *China* 182 G2
Fuqing, *China* 183 Q8
Furano, *Japan* 184 F14
Furmanov, *Russ.* 156 H11
Furneaux Group, *Austral.* 210 L16
Furqlus, *Syr.* 170 G8
Fürstenfeldbruck, *Ger.* 148 K8
Fürstenwalde, *Ger.* 148 E11
Fürth, *Ger.* 148 H8
Furth im Wald, *Ger.* 148 J10
Füssen, *Ger.* 148 L8
Futiga, *Amer. Samoa, U.S.* 218 M7
Futuna, island, *Wallis & Futuna, Fr.* 218 E11
Futuna, island, *Vanuatu* 218 H5
Fuwwah, *Yemen* 172 Q12
Fuxian, *China* 182 F2
Fuxin, *China* 182 B10
Fuya, *Japan* 184 L12
Fuyang, river, *China* 182 E6
Fuyang, *China* 182 J6
Fuyu, *China* 181 C16
Fuyun, *China* 180 D8
Fuzhou, *China* 183 P8
Füzuli, *Azerb.* 169 E21
Fyn, island, *Den.* 140 P11
Fyne, Loch, *Scot., U.K.* 142 M8
Fyzabad, *Trinidad & Tobago* 121 Q22

G

Gaalkacyo (Galcaio), *Somalia* 199 G17
Gabbs, *Nev., U.S.* 109 Q8
Gabela, *Angola* 202 D6
Gabert Island, *F.S.M.* 217 A18
Gabes, *Tun.* 197 B13
Gabes, Gulf of, *Tun.* 197 B13
Gabon, *Af.* 195 K18
Gaborone, *Botswana* 202 J10
Gabras, *Sudan* 198 F11
Gabriel Vera, *Bol.* 130 K7
Gabrovo, *Bulg.* 153 H15
Gackle, *N. Dak., U.S.* 104 G6
Gädäbäy, *Azerb.* 169 D19
Gadag, *India* 179 N5
Gadarwara, *India* 178 J6
Gäddede, *Sw.* 140 G12
Gadifuri, island, *Maldives* 179 V3
Gadrut, *Azerb.* 169 E21
Gadwal, *India* 179 N6
Gǎeşti, *Rom.* 153 F15
Gaeta, *It.* 150 L10
Gaeta, Golfo di, *It.* 150 M10
Gaferut, island, *F.S.M.* 216 P4
Gaffney, *S.C., U.S.* 96 J8
Gaflei, *Liech.* 160 P2
Gafsa, *Tun.* 196 B12
Gagan, island, *Marshall Is.* 216 K4
Gagan, *P.N.G.* 217 J13
Gagarin, *Russ.* 156 J8
Gagil-Tomil, peak, *F.S.M.* 217 D18
Gagnoa, *Côte d'Ivoire* 200 H8
Gagra, *Abkhazia* 169 A15
Gahi, *Wallis & Futuna, Fr.* 218 C11
Gaiano, river, *It.* 161 L17
Gaillac, *Fr.* 147 X9
Gaillimh *see* Galway, *Ire.* 143 S4
Gaimán, *Arg.* 133 R9
Gainesville, *Fla., U.S.* 97 R7
Gainesville, *Ga., U.S.* 96 K5
Gainesville, *Mo., U.S.* 105 V13
Gainesville, *Tex., U.S.* 102 K11

Gairdner, Lake, *Austral.* 210 J9
Gaizhou, *China* 182 C10
Gaja Shima, *Japan* 185 V3
Gakkel Ridge, *Arctic Oc.* 242 F10
Gakona, *Alas., U.S.* III H18
Gakuch, *Pak.* 176 L11
Galan, Cerro, *S. Amer.* 126 J5
Galanado, *Ariz., U.S.* 107 R9
Ganado, *Tex., U.S.* 103 S12
Galápagos Fracture Zone, *Pac. Oc.* 239 K14
Galápagos Islands, *Pac. Oc.* 215 G21
Galápagos Rift, *Pac. Oc.* 239 J18
Galápagos Rise, *Pac. Oc.* 239 L18
Galashiels, *Scot., U.K.* 143 N11
Galatás, *Gr.* 154 K12
Galateia, *Cyprus* 160 M10
Galați, *Rom.* 153 E17
Galatina, *It.* 151 N15
Galatxo, Punta del, *Sp.* 145 F16
Galax, *Va., U.S.* 96 G9
Galaxidi, *Gr.* 154 H10
Galbraith, *Qnsld., Austral.* 211 Q11
Galcaio *see* Gaalkacyo, *Somalia* 199 G17
Gáldar, *Canary Is.* 204 Q5
Galdhøpiggen, *Nor.* 140 J10
Galegu, *Sudan* 199 E14
Galela, *Indonesia* 189 H16
Galena, *Alas., U.S.* III G14
Galena, *Ill., U.S.* 98 M4
Galena, *Kans., U.S.* 105 V10
Galena Park, *Tex., U.S.* 103 Q14
Galera, Punta, *Chile* 133 P6
Galera, Punta, *Ecua.* 128 H2
Galeota Point, *Trinidad & Tobago* 121 Q23
Galera, Punta, *Chile* 133 P6
Galera Point, *Trinidad & Tobago* 121 N24
Galesburg, *Ill., U.S.* 99 P4
Galeton, *Pa., U.S.* 94 L6
Galesville, *Wis., U.S.* 98 K3
Galeton, *Pa., U.S.* 94 L6
Gali, *Abkhazia* 169 B16
Galich, *Russ.* 156 G11
Galicia, region, *Pol., Ukr.* 149 G17
Galicia, region, *Sp.* 144 C6
Galilee, Lake, *Austral.* 210 F13
Galilee, Sea of, *Israel* 170 K6
Galina Mine, *W. Aust., Austral.* 211 V2
Galina Point, *Jam.* 120 H10
Galinoporni, *Cyprus* 160 M11
Galion, *Ohio, U.S.* 99 Q13
Galion, Baie du, *Martinique, Fr.* 121 E23
Galiuro Mountains, *Ariz., U.S.* 107 V8
Galiwinku, *N. Terr., Austral.* 211 P9
Gallarate, *It.* 150 D4
Gallatin, *Mo., U.S.* 105 R11
Gallatin, river, *Mont., U.S.* 106 E8
Gallatin, *Tenn., U.S.* 101 E15
Galle, *Sri Lanka* 179 T7
Gállego, river, *Sp.* 145 D14
Gallinakopf, peak, *Aust., Liech.* 160 P3
Gallinas, Punta, *Col.* 128 A7
Gallinas Peak, *N. Mex., U.S.* 107 T13
Gallipoli, *It.* 151 N15
Gallipoli, *N. Terr., Austral.* 211 R10
Gallipoli *see* Gelibolu, *Turk.* 168 D3
Gallipolis, *Ohio, U.S.* 99 S14
Gällivare, *Sw.* 141 E13
Gallup, *N. Mex., U.S.* 107 R10
Galoa, *Fiji Is.* 218 J6
Galt, *Calif., U.S.* 109 R5
Galty Mountains, *Ire.* 143 U5
Galva, *Ill., U.S.* 99 P4
Galveston, *Tex., U.S.* 103 R15
Galveston Bay, *Tex., U.S.* 103 R14
Galveston Island, *Tex., U.S.* 103 R14
Gálvez, *Arg.* 132 K11
Galwa, *Nepal* 178 E8
Galway (Gaillimh), *Ire.* 143 S4
Galway Bay, *Ire.* 143 S3
Gambaga, *Ghana* 200 F10
Gambell, *Alas., U.S.* 110 F10
Gambia, *Af.* 195 G13
Gambia, river, *Gambia, Senegal* 194 G1
Gambia Plain, *Atl. Oc.* 236 L9
Gambia Shoal, *Hawai'i, U.S.* 112 K2
Gambier, Îles, *Fr. Polynesia, Fr.* 219 Q21
Gamboma, *Congo* 201 L18

Gamua, *Wallis & Futuna, Fr.* 218 B11
Gan, river, *China* 183 P5
Gan, river, *China* 181 B16
Gan, island, *Maldives* 179 X3
Gan, island, *Maldives* 179 X3
Gana, river, *Nigeria* 194 H5
Ganado, *Ariz., U.S.* 107 R9
Ganado, *Tex., U.S.* 103 S12
Ganäveh, *Iran* 172 G12
Gäncä, *Azerb.* 169 D20
Gandajika, *Dem. Rep. of the Congo* 198 M10
Gandava, *Pak.* 177 T6
Gander, *Nfld. & Lab., Can.* 83 M23
Gandhinagar, *India* 178 J3
Gandía, *Sp.* 145 H15
Gang, island, *Maldives* 179 W3
Ganga (Ganges), river, *India* 178 G7
Gan Gan, *Arg.* 133 R8
Ganganagar, *India* 178 E4
Gangapur, *India* 178 G5
Gangawati, *India* 179 N5
Gangca, *China* 180 H10
Gangdise Range, *China* 166 H8
Gangdisê Shan, *China* 180 K5
Ganges, river, *Bangladesh, India* 166 J8
Ganges, *Fr.* 147 X11
Ganges, Mouths of the, *Bangladesh, India* 178 K12
Ganges Fan, *Ind. Oc.* 240 D11
Ganges Plain, *India* 166 H8
Ganggyeong, *S. Korea* 182 F13
Gangi, *It.* 151 S10
Gangneung, *S. Korea* 182 E14
Gangtok, *India* 178 F12
Gannat, *Fr.* 147 T11
Gannett Peak, *Wyo., U.S.* 106 H9
Ganongga *see* Ranongga, island, *Solomon Is.* 217 M15
Ganquan, *China* 182 F2
Ganseong, *S. Korea* 182 E14
Ganta, *Guinea* 200 G7
Gantgaw, *Myanmar* 186 G5
Ganysukīno, *Kaz.* 174 F5
Ganyu, *China* 182 H8
Ganzhou, *China* 183 P5
Gao, *Mali* 196 H9
Gaoligong Shan, *Myanmar* 186 D8
Gaoping, *China* 182 G4
Gaotai, *China* 180 G10
Gaotang, *China* 182 F6
Gaoua, *Burkina Faso* 200 F9
Gaoual, *Guinea* 200 E5
Gaoyang, *China* 182 E5
Gaoyi, *China* 182 E5
Gaoyou Hu, *China* 182 J8
Gap, *Fr.* 147 W14
Garabil Belentligi, *Turkm.* 174 N11
Garabogaz Bay, *Turkm.* 166 F5
Garabogazköl, *Turkm.* 174 K6
Garacad, *Somalia* 199 G18
Garagum, desert, *Turkm.* 174 K8
Garagum Canal, *Turkm.* 174 M10
Garaina, *P.N.G.* 213 D19
Garajonay, peak, *Canary Is.* 204 Q4
Garaliáni, *Gr.* 154 L9
Garanhuns, *Braz.* 131 G17
Garapan, *N. Mariana Is., U.S.* 216 B4
Garapan, Lagunan, *N. Mariana Is., U.S.* 216 C4
Garavuti, *Taj.* 176 J7
Garber, *Okla., U.S.* 102 E10
Garberville, *Calif., U.S.* 109 N2
Garbyang, *India* 178 E8
García de Sola, Embalse de, *Sp.* 144 H9
Garda, Lago di, *It.* 150 D6
Gardar Ridge, *Atl. Oc.* 236 D10
Garden City, *Ga., U.S.* 97 N9
Garden City, *Kans., U.S.* 105 U4
Garden Island Bay, *La., U.S.* 100 R12
Garden of the Gods, *Hawai'i, U.S.* 113 G14
Garden Point, *N. Terr., Austral.* 211 N7
Gardiner, *Me., U.S.* 95 G16
Gardiner, *Mont., U.S.* 106 F8
Gardiner, Lake, *S. Aust., Austral.* 211 W9
Gardiz, *Afghan.* 177 N8
Gardner Pinnacles, *Hawai'i, U.S.* 112 L6
Garessio, *It.* 150 F3
Garfield, *Wash., U.S.* 108 D9
Gargano, Promontorio del, *It.* 150 K12
Garhakota, *India* 178 H7
Garibaldi, *Oreg., U.S.* 108 F2
Garies, *S. Af.* 202 L7
Garim Island, *F.S.M.* 217 D18
Garissa, *Kenya* 199 K15

Garland, *Tex., U.S.* 102 L12
Garm Ab, *Afghan.* 177 N4
Garmeh Jājarm, *Iran* 173 B15
Garmisch-Partenkirchen, *Ger.* 148 L8
Garner, *Iowa, U.S.* 104 M11
Garnett, *Kans., U.S.* 105 T10
Garonne, *river, Fr.* 147 W7
Garoowe, *Somalia* 199 G18
Garoua, *Cameroon* 201 F16
Garoua Boulaï, *Cameroon* 201 H17
Garreru, *island, Palau* 216 N12
Garrison, *N. Dak., U.S.* 104 F4
Garrison, *Utah, U.S.* 107 N5
Garron Point, *N. Ire., U.K.* 143 P7
Garrucha, *Sp.* 145 L13
Garrygala, *Turkm.* 174 L7
Garry Lake, *Nunavut, Can.* 83 G14
Garsen, *Kenya* 199 K15
Garu, *India* 178 J9
Garub, *Namibia* 202 J6
Garusuun, *Palau* 216 N11
Garut, *Indonesia* 188 M8
Garve, *Scot., U.K.* 142 J9
Garwa, *India* 178 H9
Gary, *Ind., U.S.* 99 N8
Garyarsa, *China* 180 K4
Garzón, *Col.* 128 G4
Gasa, *Bhutan* 178 F12
Gas City, *Ind., U.S.* 99 Q10
Gasconade, *river, Mo., U.S.* 105 U13
Gascony, *region, Fr.* 147 X7
Gascoyne, *river, W. Aust., Austral.* 211 U3
Gascoyne Junction, *W. Aust., Austral.* 211 U2
Gascoyne Tablemount, *Pac. Oc.* 238 P7
Gasenzen, *Switz.* 160 N1
Gashagar, *Nigeria* 201 E16
Gashua, *Nigeria* 201 E15
Gas Hure Hu, *China* 180 H8
Gaspar Grande, *island, Trinidad & Tobago* 121 P21
Gasparillo, *Trinidad & Tobago* 121 Q22
Gaspé, *Que., Can.* 83 N21
Gaspé Peninsula, *Que., Can.* 83 N21
Gassaway, *W. Va., U.S.* 96 D9
Gaston, Lake, *N.C., Va., U.S.* 96 G12
Gastonia, *N.C., U.S.* 96 J9
Gastoúni, *Gr.* 154 J8
Gastre, *Arg.* 133 Q8
Gata, Cabo de, *Sp.* 144 M12
Gata, Cape, *Cyprus* 160 R7
Gata, Sierra de, *Sp.* 144 F8
Gataivai, *Samoa* 218 L2
Gatayake, Baie de, *Fr. Polynesia, Fr.* 219 Q2O
Gatchina, *Russ.* 156 F6
Gate, *Okla., U.S.* 102 E7
Gate City, *Va., U.S.* 96 G7
Gatehouse of Fleet, *Scot., U.K.* 143 P9
Gateshead, *Eng., U.K.* 143 P12
Gates of the Arctic National Park and Preserve, *Alas., U.S.* 111 D16
Gatesville, *Tex., U.S.* 103 N10
Gateway, *Colo., U.S.* 107 N10
Gatjapar, *F.S.M.* 217 D18
Gatlinburg, *Tenn., U.S.* 101 F19
Gau, *island, Fiji Is.* 218 J7
Gausta, *peak, Nor.* 140 L10
Gautier, Pointe, *St. Lucia* 121 L14
Gavarnie, *Fr.* 147 Y7
Gavāter, *Iran* 173 J18
Gāvbandī, *Iran* 173 H14
Gavdopoúla, *island, Gr.* 155 R13
Gávdos, *island, Gr.* 155 R13
Gaviota, *Calif., U.S.* 109 W6
Gävle, *Sw.* 141 K13
Gavrilov Yam, *Russ.* 156 H10
Gávrio, *Gr.* 155 J14
Gawachab, *Namibia* 202 K7
Gawai, *Myanmar* 186 C7
Gawler, *S. Aust., Austral.* 211 Y10
Gawler Ranges, *Austral.* 210 J9
Gaxun Nur, *China* 180 F11
Gaya, *India* 178 H10
Gaya, *Niger* 196 J10
Gaya, *Nigeria* 201 E15
Gayle, *Jam.* 120 H9
Gaylord, *Mich., U.S.* 98 H11
Gaylord, *Minn., U.S.* 104 K10
Gay's Cove, *Barbados* 121 J19
Gaza City *see* Ghazzah, *Gaza Strip* 171 N4
Gazak, *Afghan.* 176 L5
Gazak, *Iran* 173 G17
Gazanjyk, *Turkm.* 174 L7

Gaza Strip, *occupied territory, Asia* 171 N4
Gaziantep, *Turk.* 168 H12
Gazimağusa *see* Ammochostos, *Cyprus* 160 P10
Gazipaşa, *Turk.* 168 J7
Gazojak, *Turkm.* 174 K10
Gbadolite, *Dem. Rep. of the Congo* 198 H9
Gcuwa, *S. Af.* 202 L10
Gdańsk, *Pol.* 149 B14
Gdańsk, Gulf of, *Pol.* 138 E7
Gdov, *Russ.* 156 G5
Gdynia, *Pol.* 149 B14
Gea, *island, Marshall Is.* 216 N5
Gea Pass, *Marshall Is.* 216 N5
Geary, *Okla., U.S.* 102 G9
Gebe, *island, Indonesia* 189 J17
Gebiz, *Turk.* 168 H6
Gebze, *Turk.* 168 D5
Gedaref, *Sudan* 199 E14
Geddes, *S. Dak., U.S.* 104 M6
Gediz, *river, Turk.* 168 F3
Gediz, *Turk.* 168 F5
Gedser, *Den.* 140 P12
Geel, *Belg.* 146 K12
Geelong, *Vic., Austral.* 211 Z12
Geelvink Channel, *Austral.* 210 H1
Geesthacht, *Ger.* 148 C8
Geeveston, *Tas., Austral.* 211 Z16
Gefara, *region, Lib., Tun.* 194 D6
Géfira, *Gr.* 154 C11
Gegibu, *island, Marshall Is.* 216 L3
Gê'gyai, *China* 180 J5
Gehh, *island, Marshall Is.* 216 N5
Geidam, *Nigeria* 201 E16
Geiga, *island, Marshall Is.* 216 K1
Geilo, *Nor.* 140 K10
Geita, *Tanzania* 199 L13
Gejiu, *China* 180 P11
Gela, *It.* 151 T11
Gela, Golfo di, *It.* 151 T11
Gelam, *island, Indonesia* 188 K9
Gelasa, Selat, *Indonesia* 188 K8
Gelendzhik, *Russ.* 157 T10
Gelibolu (Gallipoli), *Turk.* 168 D3
Gellinam, *island, Marshall Is.* 216 L5
Gelsenkirchen, *Ger.* 148 E5
Gembloux, *Belg.* 146 L12
Gemena, *Dem. Rep. of the Congo* 198 J9
Gemerek, *Turk.* 168 F11
Gemlik, *Turk.* 168 D5
Gemlik Körfezi, *Turk.* 168 D5
Gemona del Friuli, *It.* 150 C9
Gemsa, *Egypt* 197 D19
Gen, *river, China* 181 B15
Genádio, *Gr.* 155 N19
Genalē, *river, Eth.* 199 H15
Genç, *Turk.* 169 F15
Geneina (Al Junaynah), *Sudan* 198 E10
General Acha, *Arg.* 133 N10
General Alvear, *Arg.* 132 L8
General Bernardo O'Higgins, *station, Antarctica* 226 C4
General Carrera, Lago, *Chile* 133 T7
General Conesa, *Arg.* 133 P10
General Eugenio A. Garay, *Parag.* 130 L8
General Güemes, *Arg.* 132 E9
General Guido, *Arg.* 132 M13
General Juan Madariaga, *Arg.* 132 M13
General La Madrid, *Arg.* 133 N11
General Levalle, *Arg.* 132 L10
General Lorenzo Vintter, *Arg.* 133 Q10
General Paz, *Arg.* 132 G13
General Pico, *Arg.* 132 M10
General Pinedo, *Arg.* 132 G11
General Roca, *Arg.* 133 P8
General San Martín, *Arg.* 132 L13
General San Martín, *Arg.* 133 N10
General San Martín, *Arg.* 133 R7
General Santos, *Philippines* 189 F15
Genesee, *river, N.Y., U.S.* 94 K6
Geneseo, *Ill., U.S.* 99 P14
Geneseo, *N.Y., U.S.* 94 J6
Geneva, *Ala., U.S.* 101 N16
Geneva, *Ill., U.S.* 99 N16
Geneva, *Idaho, U.S.* 106 J8
Geneva, *N.Y., U.S.* 94 J7
Geneva, *Nebr., U.S.* 105 Q7
Geneva, *Ohio, U.S.* 99 N15
Geneva *see* Genève, *Switz.* 150 C1
Geneva, Lake of *see* Léman, Lac, *Fr.* 147 T15
Genève (Geneva), *Switz.* 150 C1
Genil, *river, Sp.* 144 K9
Genisséa, *Gr.* 155 B14

Genk, *Belg.* 146 L13
Genlis, *Fr.* 147 R13
Gennargentu, Monti del, *It.* 151 N4
Genoa *see* Genova, *It.* 150 F4
Genoa, *Nebr., U.S.* 105 P7
Génolhac, *Fr.* 147 W12
Genova (Genoa), *It.* 150 F4
Genova, Golfo di, *It.* 150 G4
Genovesa, Isla (Tower), *Ecua.* 128 P10
Gent, *Belg.* 146 L11
Geographe Bay, *Austral.* 210 K2
Geographe Channel, *Austral.* 210 G1
George, *river, Que., Can.* 83 K20
George, *S. Af.* 202 M8
George, Lake, *Austral.* 210 L14
George, Lake, *Fla., U.S.* 97 S8
George, Lake, *N.Y., U.S.* 94 H11
George, Zemlya, *Russ.* 158 B12
George Bligh Bank, *Atl. Oc.* 236 D11
George Town, *Cayman Is., U.K.* 120 J1
George Town, *Malaysia* 187 S8
George Town, *Tas., Austral.* 211 Y16
Georgetown, *Del., U.S.* 96 D15
Georgetown, *Gambia* 196 H5
Georgetown, *Guyana* 129 D14
Georgetown, *Ill., U.S.* 99 R8
Georgetown, *Ky., U.S.* 101 B18
Georgetown, *Ohio, U.S.* 99 T12
Georgetown, *Qnsld., Austral.* 211 R12
Georgetown, *S.C., U.S.* 96 L11
Georgetown, *St. Vincent & the Grenadines* 121 K17
Georgetown, *Tex., U.S.* 103 P10
George-Town, *Bahamas* 120 F9
George V Coast, *Antarctica* 227 R16-R17
George VI Sound, *Antarctica* 226 F6
George Washington Birthplace National Monument, *Va., U.S.* 96 D13
George Washington Carver National Monument, *Mo., U.S.* 105 V11
George West, *Tex., U.S.* 103 T10
Georgia, *U.S.* 96 M4
Georgia, Republic of, *Asia* 167 S4
Georgia, Strait of, *B.C., Can.* 82 M8
Georgiana, *Ala., U.S.* 101 M15
Georgian Bay, *Ont., Can.* 83 Q18
Georgíevka, *Kaz.* 175 D18
Georgína, *river, Qnsld., Austral.* 211 S10
Geórgios, Ágios, *Gr.* 155 K13
Geórgios, Ágios *see* Ro, *Gr.* 155 N22
Georgiyevsk, *Russ.* 157 T13
Georgiyevskoye, *Russ.* 156 G12
Gera, *Ger.* 148 F9
Gerákion, *Gr.* 154 L10
Geral, Serra, *S. Amer.* 126 J8
Geral de Goiás, Serra, *Braz.* 131 H14
Geraldine, *Mont., U.S.* 106 C9
Geraldine, *N.Z.* 213 P17
Geraldton, *Ont., Can.* 83 N16
Geraldton, *W. Aust., Austral.* 211 W2
Gérardmer, *Fr.* 147 Q15
Gerasa *see* Jarash, *Jordan* 170 L6
Gerber, *Calif., U.S.* 109 N4
Gercüş, *Turk.* 169 H16
Gerdine, Mount, *Alas., U.S.* 84 P4
Gerede, *Turk.* 168 D8
Gereshk, *Afghan.* 177 Q4
Geretsried, *Ger.* 148 K8
Gering, *Nebr., U.S.* 105 N1
Gerlach, *Nev., U.S.* 109 N7
Gerlach, peak, *Slovakia* 138 G8
Gerlachovsky Štit, *Slovakia* 149 J16
Germantown, *Tenn., U.S.* 100 G11
Germany, *Eur.* 139 T6
Germering, *Ger.* 148 K8
Germfask, *Mich., U.S.* 98 F9
Germī, *Iran* 172 A11
Gerolakkos, *Cyprus* 160 N8
Geroliménas, *Gr.* 154 M10
Gersthofen, *Ger.* 148 K8
Gêrzê, *China* 180 K6
Gerze, *Turk.* 168 C10
Gesoa, *P.N.G.* 213 D18
Gesso, *It.* 161 L17
Getafe, *Sp.* 144 F11
Gettysburg, *Pa., U.S.* 94 Q7
Gettysburg, *S. Dak., U.S.* 104 K5
Getz Ice Shelf, *Antarctica* 226 M7
Geumpang, *Indonesia* 188 G4
Geumsan, *S. Korea* 182 G13
Geunto, Gora, *Russ.* 159 C21
Gevaş, *Turk.* 169 G17
Gex, *Fr.* 147 T14
Geylegphug, *Bhutan* 178 G13
Geyve, *Turk.* 168 D6

Ghadāmis, *Lib.* 196 C12
Ghaddūwah, *Lib.* 197 D14
Ghaghe, *island, Solomon Is.* 217 L17
Ghajn Tuffieħa Bay, *Malta* 161 K21
Ghana, *Af.* 195 H16
Ghanzi, *Botswana* 202 H8
Gharandal, *Jordan* 171 Q5
Gharb, *Malta* 161 H19
Gharb, *Pak.* 177 W6
Ghardaïa, *Alg.* 196 B11
Ghar Dalam, *site, Malta* 161 L23
Gharm, *Taj.* 176 H8
Gharo, *Pak.* 177 W6
Gharyān, *Lib.* 197 C13
Ghatere, *Solomon Is.* 217 M18
Ghawdex *see* Gozo, *island, Malta* 161 H20
Ghaxaq, *Malta* 161 L23
Ghazal, Bahr el, *Chad* 197 H14
Ghaziabad, *India* 178 F6
Ghazipur, *India* 178 G9
Ghazni, *Afghan.* 177 N7
Ghazzah (Gaza City), *Gaza Strip* 171 N4
Gheorghieni, *Rom.* 153 C15
Gherla, *Rom.* 153 C13
Ghilarza, *It.* 151 N3
Ghisonaccia, *Fr.* 150 K4
Ghormach, *Afghan.* 176 L3
Ghotki, *Pak.* 177 T8
Ghow Gardan Pass, *Afghan.* 176 M6
Ghurian, *Afghan.* 176 M2
Gia Nghia, *Vietnam* 187 N13
Gianitsá, *Gr.* 154 C10
Giannutri, Isola di, *It.* 150 K6
Gia Rai, *Vietnam* 187 Q12
Giáros, *island, Gr.* 155 K14
Giarre, *It.* 151 S12
Giba, *It.* 151 Q3
Gibara, *Cuba* 116 J12
Gibbon, *Nebr., U.S.* 105 Q6
Gibbon Point, *Anguilla, U.K.* 120 R12
Gibbonsville, *Idaho, U.S.* 106 E6
Gibb River, *W. Aust., Austral.* 211 Q6
Gibb's Hill, *Bermuda, U.K.* 120 C2
Gibeon, *Namibia* 202 J7
Gibraleón, *Sp.* 144 L7
Gibraltar, *Eur.* 160 E1
Gibraltar, *Gibraltar, U.K.* 161 P22
Gibraltar, Bay of (Bahía de Algeciras), *Gibraltar, U.K.* 161 P21
Gibraltar, Rock of, *Gibraltar, U.K.* 161 P23
Gibraltar, Strait of, *Af., Eur.* 196 A8
Gibraltar Airport, *Gibraltar, U.K.* 161 N23
Gibraltar Harbour, *Gibraltar, U.K.* 161 P22
Gibsland, *La., U.S.* 100 L7
Gibson, *W. Aust., Austral.* 211 X4
Gibson City, *Ill., U.S.* 99 Q6
Gibson Desert, *W. Aust., Austral.* 211 U5
Gidar, *Pak.* 177 T5
Giddalur, *India* 179 N6
Giddings, *Tex., U.S.* 103 Q12
Gīdolē, *Eth.* 199 H14
Gien, *Fr.* 147 R10
Giessen, *Ger.* 148 G6
Gifford, *Fla., U.S.* 97 U10
Gifford, *river, Nunavut, Can.* 83 E16
Gifhorn, *Ger.* 148 D8
Gifu, *Japan* 185 P9
Gigant, *Russ.* 157 R11
Gigha Island, *Scot., U.K.* 143 N7
Giglio, Isola del, *It.* 150 K6
Gijón, *Sp.* 144 A9
Gila, *river, Ariz., U.S.* 107 U5
Gila Bend, *Ariz., U.S.* 107 U6
Gila Bend Mountains, *Ariz., U.S.* 107 U6
Gila Cliff Dwellings National Monument, *N. Mex., U.S.* 107 U10
Gilbert, *Ariz., U.S.* 107 U7
Gilbert, *Minn., U.S.* 104 F12
Gilbert, *river, Qnsld., Austral.* 211 R12
Gilbert Islands, *Kiribati* 214 G8
Gilbert River, *Qnsld., Austral.* 211 R12
Gilbert Seamount, *Pac. Oc.* 239 C13
Gilbués, *Braz.* 131 G14
Gilchrist, *Oreg., U.S.* 108 J4
Gildford, *Mont., U.S.* 106 B9
Gilf Kebir Plateau, *Egypt* 197 E17
Gilgandra, *N.S.W., Austral.* 211 X14
Gilgit, *region, Pak.* 176 L11
Gilgit, *river, Pak.* 176 L11
Gilgit, *Pak.* 176 L11
Gill, Lough, *Ire.* 143 Q4
Gillam, *Man., Can.* 83 L14
Gillen, Lake, *Austral.* 210 G5
Gilles, Lake, *Austral.* 210 K9
Gillespie, *Ill., U.S.* 99 S4

Gillett, *Ark., U.S.* 100 H9
Gillette, *Wyo., U.S.* 106 G12
Gills Rock, *Wis., U.S.* 98 H8
Gilman, *Ill., U.S.* 99 Q7
Gilmer, *Tex., U.S.* 102 L14
Gilmore Hut, *Qnsld., Austral.* 211 U12
Gilpeppee, *Qnsld., Austral.* 211 U11
Gilroy, *Calif., U.S.* 109 T4
Gima, *Japan* 185 Y1
Gimcheon, *S. Korea* 182 F14
Gimhwa, *S. Korea* 182 E13
Gimie, Mount, *St. Lucia* 121 K14
Gimje, *S. Korea* 182 G13
Gimli, *Man., Can.* 83 N14
Gingoog, *Philippines* 189 E15
Gīnīr, *Eth.* 199 G15
Ginowan, *Japan* 185 Y1
Giohar *see* Jawhar, *Somalia* 199 J17
Gioia, Golfo di, *It.* 151 R13
Gioia del Colle, *It.* 150 M14
Gioia Tauro, *It.* 151 R13
Gióna, Óros, *Gr.* 154 H10
Gioúra, *island, Gr.* 155 F13
Giovinazzo, *It.* 150 L13
Gippsland, *region, Austral.* 210 M13
Girab, *India* 178 G2
Girard, *Kans., U.S.* 105 U10
Girard, *Pa., U.S.* 94 K3
Girardot, *Col.* 128 F5
Giresun, *Turk.* 169 D13
Girga, *Egypt* 197 D19
Gir Hills, *India* 178 K2
Giridih, *India* 178 H10
Girne *see* Kyrenia, *Cyprus* 160 N8
Girolata, *Fr.* 150 J3
Girona, *Sp.* 145 D18
Gironde, *river, Fr.* 147 U6
Gisborne, *N.Z.* 213 K20
Gissi, *It.* 150 K11
Gitega, *Burundi* 198 L12
Githio, *Gr.* 154 M10
Giulianova, *It.* 150 J10
Giurgiu, *Rom.* 153 G15
Givet, *Fr.* 146 M12
Givors, *Fr.* 147 U13
Gizab, *Afghan.* 177 N5
Gizhuduvan, *Uzb.* 174 L11
Gizo, *Solomon Is.* 217 M15
Giżycko, *Pol.* 149 B16
Gjakova (Đakovica), *Kos.* 152 J10
Gjeravica, *peak, Kos.* 152 J10
Gjilan (Gnjilane), *Kos.* 152 J11
Gjirokastër (Argyrus), *Albania* 152 M9
Gjoa Haven, *Nunavut, Can.* 83 F14
Gjøvik, *Nor.* 140 K11
Gkreko, Cape, *Cyprus* 160 P10
Glachau, *Ger.* 148 G9
Glacier Bay, *Alas., U.S.* 111 L21
Glacier Bay National Park and Preserve, *Alas., U.S.* 111 L21
Glacier National Park, *Mont., U.S.* 106 B6
Glacier Peak, *Wash., U.S.* 108 B5
Gladewater, *Tex., U.S.* 102 L14
Gladstone, *Mich., U.S.* 98 G8
Gladstone, *Qnsld., Austral.* 211 U15
Gladstone, *S. Aust., Austral.* 211 X10
Gladwin, *Mich., U.S.* 98 K11
Glåma, *river, Nor.* 140 J11
Glasco, *Kans., U.S.* 105 S7
Glasgow, *Jam.* 120 H6
Glasgow, *Ky., U.S.* 101 D16
Glasgow, *Mo., U.S.* 105 S12
Glasgow, *Mont., U.S.* 106 B11
Glasgow, *Scot., U.K.* 142 M9
Glassboro, *N.J., U.S.* 94 Q9
Glass Buttes, *Oreg., U.S.* 108 J6
Glass Mountain, *Calif., U.S.* 108 L4
Glass Mountains, *Tex., U.S.* 103 Q3
Glazov, *Russ.* 158 G8
Glénan, Îles de, *Fr.* 147 R3
Glen Arbor, *Mich., U.S.* 98 H9
Glenariffe, *N. Ire., U.K.* 143 P7
Glenarm, *N. Ire., U.K.* 143 P7
Glenavy, *N.Z.* 213 Q17
Glenayle, *W. Aust., Austral.* 211 U4
Glenbarr, *Scot., U.K.* 143 N7
Glen Canyon Dam, *Ariz., U.S.* 107 Q7
Glen Canyon National Recreation Area, *Utah, U.S.* 107 P8
Glencoe, *Minn., U.S.* 104 K10
Glendale, *Ariz., U.S.* 107 U6
Glendale, *Calif., U.S.* 109 X8
Glendive, *Mont., U.S.* 106 C13
Glendo, *Wyo., U.S.* 106 J13

Glendo Reservoir, Wyo., U.S. 106 H13
Glengyle, Qnsld., Austral. 211 U11
Glen Innes, N.S.W., Austral. 211 W15
Glenmora, La., U.S. 100 N8
Glennallen, Alas., U.S. 111 H18
Glenn Highway, Alas., U.S. 111 J17
Glenns Ferry, Idaho, U.S. 106 H4
Glennville, Ga., U.S. 97 N8
Glenormiston, Qnsld., Austral. 211 T10
Glenreagh, N.S.W., Austral. 211 W15
Glenrock, Wyo., U.S. 106 H12
Glen Rose, Tex., U.S. 102 M10
Glenrothes, Scot., U.K. 142 M10
Glenroy, W. Aust., Austral. 211 R5
Glens Falls, N.Y., U.S. 94 H11
Glenties, Ire. 143 P5
Glen Ullin, N. Dak., U.S. 104 G3
Glenwood, Ark., U.S. 100 H7
Glenwood, Iowa, U.S. 105 Q9
Glenwood, Minn., U.S. 104 J9
Glenwood, N. Mex., U.S. 107 U10
Glenwood Springs, Colo., U.S. 106 M11
Glidden, Wis., U.S. 98 F4
Glina, Croatia 152 E6
Gliwice, Pol. 149 G14
Globe, Ariz., U.S. 107 U8
Głogów, Pol. 148 E12
Glorenza, It. 150 C6
Gloria, Puntan, N. Mariana Is., U.S. 216 B5
Gloria Ridge, Atl. Oc. 236 E7
Glorieuses, Îles, Mozambique Ch. 203 D17
Glossglockner, peak, Aust. 148 M9
Gloster, Miss., U.S. 100 N10
Gloucester, Eng., U.K. 143 V11
Gloucester, Mass., U.S. 95 K15
Gloucester, N.S.W., Austral. 211 X15
Gloucester, P.N.G. 213 C20
Glover Island, Grenada 121 L22
Gloversville, N.Y., U.S. 94 J10
Glubokiy, Russ. 157 Q11
Glubokiy, Russ. 157 R12
Glūbokoe, Kaz. 175 D18
Gmunden, Aust. 148 L10
Gnaraloo, W. Aust., Austral. 211 U1
Gniezno, Pol. 149 D13
Gnjilane see Gjilan, Kos. 152 J11
Goa, India 179 N4
Goalpara, India 178 G13
Goba, Eth. 199 G15
Gobabis, Namibia 202 H7
Gobernador Duval, Arg. 133 N9
Gobernador Gregores, Arg. 133 U8
Gobi, desert, China, Mongolia 181 F13
Gobō, Japan 185 R9
Gochang, S. Korea 182 G13
Go Cong, Vietnam 187 P13
Godalming, Eng., U.K. 143 W13
Godavari, river, India 178 M8
Godavari, Mouths of the, India 179 N8
Goderville, Fr. 147 N8
Godhavn see Qeqertarsuaq, Greenland, Den. 81 C21
Godhra, India 178 J4
Gödöllő, Hung. 149 L15
Godoy Cruz, Arg. 132 K8
Gods, river, Man., Can. 83 L15
Gods Lake, Man., Can. 83 L14
Godthåb see Nuuk, Greenland, Den. 81 D21
Godwin Austen see K2, peak, China, Pak. 176 L13
Goes, Neth. 146 K11
Göfis, Aust. 160 M4
Gogebic, Lake, Mich., U.S. 98 F5
Gogebic Range, Mich., Wis., U.S. 85 D15
Gogland, island, Russ. 156 E5
Gogrial, Sudan 198 G11
Goianésia, Braz. 131 J13
Goiânia, Braz. 131 J13
Goikul, Palau 216 N12
Góis, Port. 144 F6
Gojōme, Japan 184 K12
Gojra, Pak. 177 Q10
Gök, river, Turk. 168 C10
Gokak, India 179 N4
Gökçeada (İmroz), island, Turk. 168 D2
Gökdepe, Turkm. 174 M8
Gökova Körfezi, Turk. 168 H3
Göksu, river, Turk. 168 G11
Göksu, river, Turk. 168 J9
Göksun, Turk. 168 G11
Golaghat, India 178 G14
Golan Heights, region, Israel 170 K6
Golbahar, Afghan. 176 M8
Gölbaşı, Turk. 168 E8
Gölbaşı, Turk. 168 H12
Golconda, Nev., U.S. 108 M9
Gölcük, Turk. 168 D5
Gold Beach, Oreg., U.S. 108 K1
Gold Coast, Ghana 194 J3
Gold Coast, Qnsld., Austral. 211 V15
Golden, Colo., U.S. 106 M13
Golden Bay, N.Z. 213 M17
Goldendale, Wash., U.S. 108 E5
Golden Gate, Calif., U.S. 109 S3
Golden Gate National Recreation Area, Calif., U.S. 109 R3
Golden Grove, Jam. 120 J11
Golden Meadow, La., U.S. 100 R11
Golden Ridge, W. Aust., Austral. 211 W4
Golden Spike National Historic Site, Utah, U.S. 106 K6
Goldfield, Nev., U.S. 109 S9
Goldsboro, N.C., U.S. 96 H12
Goldsmith, Tex., U.S. 102 M4
Goldsworthy, W. Aust., Austral. 211 S3
Goldthwaite, Tex., U.S. 103 N9
Göle, Turk. 169 D17
Golela, S. Af. 202 K12
Goleniów, Pol. 148 C11
Goleta, Calif., U.S. 109 W6
Golfito, Costa Rica 115 P19
Golfo Aranci, It. 150 M5
Goliad, Tex., U.S. 103 S11
Gölköy, Turk. 168 D12
Golmud, China 180 J9
Golo, river, Fr. 150 J4
Gölören, Turk. 168 G9
Golovin, Alas., U.S. 110 F12
Gölpazarı, Turk. 168 D6
Golūbovka, Kaz. 175 B15
Golyama Kamchiya, river, Bulg. 153 H16
Golyam Perelik, peak, Bulg. 153 K14
Goma, Dem. Rep. of the Congo 198 K12
Gombe, Nigeria 201 F15
Gombrani Island, Mauritius 205 J20
Gomera, island, Canary Is. 204 Q4
Gómez Palacio, Mex. 114 F10
Gonābād, Iran 173 D16
Gonaïves, Haiti 117 L16
Gonam, river, Russ. 159 J18
Gonam, Russ. 159 H19
Gonâve, Golfe de la, Haiti 117 L15
Gonâve, Gulf of see Gonâve, Golfo de la, N. Amer. 80 N10
Gonâve, Île de la, Haiti 117 M15
Gonbad-e Kāvūs, Iran 173 B14
Gonda, India 178 G8
Gonder, Eth. 199 E14
Gondia, India 178 K7
Gondomar, Port. 144 E5
Gönen, Turk. 168 D3
Gong'an, China 182 L4
Gongcheng, China 183 Q2
Gonggar, China 180 L7
Gongga Shan, China 166 H10
Gongga Shan, China 180 L11
Gonglee, Liberia 200 H7
Gongola, river, Nigeria 201 F16
Gongolgon, N.S.W., Austral. 211 W13
Gongxi, China 183 N6
Gongzhuling, China 182 A11
Góni, Gr. 154 E10
Gōno, river, Japan 185 Q6
Gōnoura, Japan 185 R3
Gonzales, Calif., U.S. 109 T4
Gonzales, Tex., U.S. 103 R11
González Chaves, Arg. 133 N12
Goodenough Island, P.N.G. 213 E21
Good Hope, Cape of, S. Af. 202 M7
Good Hope Beach, Virgin Islands, U.S. 120 R1
Goodhouse, S. Af. 202 K7
Gooding, Idaho, U.S. 106 H5
Goodland, Kans., U.S. 105 S3
Goodlands, Mauritius 205 F20
Goodlettsville, Tenn., U.S. 101 E15
Goodman, Miss., U.S. 100 K11
Goodman, Wis., U.S. 98 G6
Goodman Bay, Bahamas 120 B11
Goodnews Bay, Alas., U.S. 110 K12
Goodooga, N.S.W., Austral. 211 W13
Goodparla, N. Terr., Austral. 211 P8
Goodridge, Minn., U.S. 104 E9
Goodwell, Okla., U.S. 102 E5
Goofnuw Inlet, F.S.M. 217 D18
Goolgowi, N.S.W., Austral. 211 X12
Goomalling, W. Aust., Austral. 211 X3
Goondiwindi, Qnsld., Austral. 211 V14
Goongarrie, Lake, Austral. 210 J4
Goonyella, Qnsld., Austral. 211 T14
Goose Creek, S.C., U.S. 96 M10
Goose Lake, Calif., Oreg., U.S. 108 L6
Gora, Russ. 159 L17
Gora Belukha, peak, Kaz. 175 D20
Gorakhpur, India 178 G9
Goraklbad Passage, Palau 216 P12
Gördes, Turk. 168 F4
Gordion, ruin, Turk. 168 E7
Gordo, Ala., U.S. 101 K14
Gordon, Ga., U.S. 96 M6
Gordon, Nebr., U.S. 104 M3
Gordon, Wis., U.S. 98 F3
Gordon, Lake, Austral. 210 M16
Gordon Downs, W. Aust., Austral. 211 R6
Gordon's, Bahamas 117 G14
Gordonsville, Va., U.S. 96 E12
Goré, Chad 197 K14
Gore, N.Z. 213 R16
Gorē, Eth. 199 G14
Goreda, Indonesia 213 C15
Goree, Tex., U.S. 102 K8
Görele, Turk. 169 D13
Gorey, Ire. 143 T7
Gorgān, Iran 173 B14
Gorgona, Isla, Col. 128 G3
Gorgona, Isola di, It. 150 H5
Gorham, N.H., U.S. 95 F14
Gori, Rep. of Georgia 169 B18
Goris, Arm. 169 E20
Gorizia, It. 150 D10
Gor'kiy Reservoir see Gor'kovskoye Vodokhranilishche, Russ. 138 D11
Gor'kovskoye Vodokhranilishche, Russ. 156 H12
Gorlice, Pol. 149 H16
Görlitz, Ger. 148 F11
Gorman, Tex., U.S. 102 M9
Gorna Oryakhovitsa, Bulg. 153 H15
Gornja Radgona, Slov. 152 C6
Gornji Milanovac, Serb. 152 G10
Gorno Altaysk, Russ. 158 L12
Gornozavodsk, Russ. 159 K22
Gornyak, Russ. 158 L11
Gorodets, Russ. 156 H12
Gorodishche, Russ. 156 L13
Goroka, P.N.G. 213 D19
Gorong, Kepulauan, Indonesia 189 L17
Gorongosa, Serra da, Mozambique 194 N9
Gorontalo, Indonesia 189 J14
Gorror, F.S.M. 217 D18
Gros-Morne, Haiti 117 L16
Gortyn, ruin, Gr. 155 Q14
Gorumna Island, Ire. 143 S3
Góry Swietokrzyskie, Pol. 149 F16
Gorzów Wielkopolski, Pol. 148 D11
Goschen Strait, P.N.G. 213 E21
Gosen, Japan 184 M12
Goseong, S. Korea 182 G14
Gosford, N.S.W., Austral. 211 X14
Goshen, Ind., U.S. 99 N9
Goshogawara, Japan 184 J12
Gosier, Guadeloupe, Fr. 121 F15
Goslar, Ger. 148 E8
Gosnel, Ark., U.S. 100 E11
Gospić, Croatia 152 F5
Gosselies, Belg. 146 L12
Gostivar, Maced. 152 K10
Göteborg, Sw. 140 M12
Gotha, Ger. 148 F8
Gothenburg, Nebr., U.S. 105 Q5
Gothèye, Niger 196 H10
Gotland, island, Sw. 141 M14
Goto Meer, Neth. Antilles, Neth. 121 Q18
Gotō Rettō, Japan 185 R2
Gotse Delchev, Bulg. 153 K13
Gotska Sandön, island, Sw. 141 L14
Gōtsu, Japan 185 Q6
Göttingen, Ger. 148 F7
Gouaro, Baie de, New Caledonia, Fr. 218 D7
Gouin, Réservoir, Que., Can. 83 N19
Gould, Ark., U.S. 100 H9
Gould Bay, Antarctica 226 E9
Gould Coast, Antarctica 226 K11
Goulding Cay, Bahamas 120 E12
Gouldsboro, Me., U.S. 95 F18
Goulvain, Cap, New Caledonia, Fr. 218 D7
Goumbou, Mali 196 H7
Goundam, Mali 196 G8
Gourbeyre, Guadeloupe, Fr. 121 G14
Gouré, Niger 196 H12
Gournay, Fr. 147 N9
Gournia, ruin, Gr. 155 Q16
Gouro, Chad 197 G15
Gouverneur, N.Y., U.S. 94 G9
Gouyave (Charlotte Town), Grenada 121 K22
Gouzon, Fr. 147 T10
Gove, Kans., U.S. 105 S4
Govena, Mys, Russ. 159 D22
Govenlock, Sask., Can. 82 N11
Gove Peninsula, Austral. 210 B9
Governador Valadares, Braz. 131 K15
Government House, Barbados 121 L19
Government House, Bermuda, U.K. 120 B2
Government House, Monaco 161 E21
Government Palace, Vatican City 161 Q15
Governor Generoso, Philippines 189 F15
Governor's Beach, Gibraltar, U.K. 161 Q23
Governor's Harbour, Bahamas 120 E6
Governor's Residence, Gibraltar, U.K. 161 P22
Govindgarh, India 178 H8
Govorovo, Russ. 159 F16
Gowanda, N.Y., U.S. 94 K5
Gowd-e Zereh, Dasht-e, Afghan. 177 R2
Gower Peninsula, Wales, U.K. 143 V9
Gowmal Kalay, Afghan. 177 P7
Gowrzanak, Afghan. 177 P3
Goya, Arg. 132 H12
Goyave, Guadeloupe, Fr. 121 F14
Goyaves, river, Guadeloupe, Fr. 121 F14
Goyaves, Îlets à, Guadeloupe, Fr. 121 F14
Göyçay, Azerb. 169 D21
Göynük, Turk. 168 D6
Gozha Co, China 180 H5
Gozo (Ghawdex), island, Malta 161 H20
Goz Sassulko, region, Cen. Af. Rep., Sudan 198 F10
Graaff-Reinet, S. Af. 202 L9
Grabs, Switz. 160 N1
Gračac, Croatia 152 F5
Gračanica, Bosn. & Herzg. 152 F8
Graceville, Fla., U.S. 97 Q3
Graceville, Minn., U.S. 104 J8
Gracias a Dios, Cabo, Nicar. 115 K19
Graciosa, island, Azores 144 P3
Graciosa, island, Canary Is. 204 P8
Graciosa Bay, Solomon Is. 217 P22
Gradaús, Braz. 130 F12
Graford, Tex., U.S. 102 L10
Grafton, N. Dak., U.S. 104 E7
Grafton, N.S.W., Austral. 211 W15
Grafton, W. Va., U.S. 96 C10
Grafton, Wis., U.S. 98 L7
Grafton, Mount, Nev., U.S. 109 Q12
Graham, N.C., U.S. 96 G11
Graham, Ont., Can. 83 N15
Graham, Tex., U.S. 102 K9
Graham, Mount, Ariz., U.S. 107 V9
Graham Bell, Ostrov, Russ. 159 C13
Graham Island, B.C., Can. 82 J7
Graham Island, Nunavut, Can. 83 C15
Graham Lake, Me., U.S. 95 F18
Graham Land, Antarctica 226 D4
Graham's Harbor, Bahamas 120 E11
Grahamstown, S. Af. 202 M10
Graian Alps, Fr., It. 147 U15
Grain Coast, Liberia 194 J2
Grajaú, Braz. 131 E14
Grajewo, Pol. 149 C17
Gramat, Fr. 147 V9
Grámos, Óros, Gr. 154 D8
Grampian Mountains, Scot., U.K. 142 L9
Granada, Colo., U.S. 107 N16
Granada, Nicar. 115 M18
Granada, Sp. 144 L11
Granadilla, Canary Is. 204 Q5
Gran Altiplanicie Central, plateau, Arg. 133 U8
Granbury, Tex., U.S. 102 L10
Granby, Colo., U.S. 106 L12
Granby, Que., Can. 83 P20
Granby, Mount, Grenada 121 K22
Gran Canaria, island, Canary Is. 204 R6
Gran Cayo Point, Trinidad & Tobago 121 Q23
Gran Chaco, region, S. Amer. 126 J6
Grand, river, Mich., U.S. 98 L10
Grand, river, Mo., U.S. 105 R12
Grand, river, S. Dak., U.S. 104 J3
Grand Anse, Grenada 121 L22
Grand Anse, St. Lucia 121 J14
Grand Anse Bay, Grenada 121 L22
Grand Bahama Island, Bahamas 116 C10
Grand Baie, Mauritius 205 F20
Grand Baie, Mauritius 205 J20
Grand Banks of Newfoundland, Nfld. & Lab., Can. 83 N24
Grand-Bassam, Côte d'Ivoire 200 H9
Grand Bay, Dominica 121 G19
Grand Bonum, peak, St. Vincent & the Grenadines 121 K16
Grand-Bourg, Guadeloupe, Fr. 121 G16
Grand Caicos, island, Turks & Caicos Is., U.K. 117 H17
Grand Caille Point, St. Lucia 121 K13
Grandcamp-Maisy, Fr. 147 N6
Grand Canal see Da Yunhe, China 182 J8
Grand Canal, Ire. 143 S6
Grand Canyon, Ariz., U.S. 107 R6
Grand Canyon, Ariz., U.S. 107 R7
Grand Canyon National Park, Ariz., U.S. 107 Q6
Grand Canyon-Parashant National Monument, Ariz., U.S. 107 Q5
Grand Case, St. Martin, Fr. 121 A14
Grand Cayman, island, Cayman Is., U.K. 116 L7
Grand Cess, Liberia 200 H7
Grand Coulee, Wash., U.S. 108 B7
Grand Coulee Dam, Wash., U.S. 108 B7
Grand Cul-de-Sac Marin, Guadeloupe, Fr. 121 E14
Grande, river, Arg. 132 M7
Grande, river, Arg., Chile 133 X9
Grande, river, Bol. 130 J8
Grande, river, Braz. 131 G15
Grande, river, Braz. 131 L13
Grande, Bahía, Arg. 133 V8
Grande, Boca, Venez. 129 C13
Grande, Cayo, Cuba 116 J9
Grande, Cayo, Venez. 118 N12
Grande, Rio, N. Amer. 80 M5
Grande, Salina, Arg. 133 N8
Grande-Anse, Guadeloupe, Fr. 121 E17
Grande Cayemite, island, Haiti 117 M15
Grande Comore, island, Comoros 205 M14
Grande del Norte, Río see Grande, Rio, Mex. 114 C9
Grande Montagne, Mauritius 205 J20
Grande Prairie, Alta., Can. 82 K10
Grande Riviere, Trinidad & Tobago 121 N23
Grande Rivière du Nord, Haiti 117 L17
Grande Rivière Sud Est, Mauritius 205 G20
Grande Ronde, river, Oreg., U.S. 108 E8
Grandes, Salinas, Arg. 132 H9
Grande-Terre, island, Guadeloupe, Fr. 121 E15
Grande Vigie, Pointe de la, Guadeloupe, Fr. 121 D15
Grandfalls, Tex., U.S. 103 N3
Grand Falls-Windsor, Nfld. & Lab., Can. 83 M23
Grandfather Mountain, N.C., U.S. 96 H8
Grandfield, Okla., U.S. 102 J9
Grand Forks, N. Dak., U.S. 104 F8
Grand-Gosier, Haiti 117 M17
Grand Harbour, Malta 161 K23
Grand Haven, Mich., U.S. 98 L9
Grand Îlet, Guadeloupe, Fr. 121 G14
Grand Island, Mich., U.S. 98 F8
Grand Island, N.Y., U.S. 94 J5
Grand Island, Nebr., U.S. 105 Q6
Grand Isle, La., U.S. 100 R11
Grand Junction, Colo., U.S. 106 M10
Grand Lake, La., U.S. 100 Q7
Grand Lake, Ohio, U.S. 99 Q11
Grand Ledge, Mich., U.S. 98 M11
Grand Lieu, Lac de, Fr. 147 S5
Grand Mal Bay, Grenada 121 L22
Grand Marais, Mich., U.S. 98 F9
Grand Marais, Minn., U.S. 104 F14
Grândola, Port. 144 J5
Grand Passage, New Caledonia, Fr. 218 A5
Grand Portage, Minn., U.S. 104 E14
Grand Portage National Monument, Minn., U.S. 104 E14
Grand Prairie, Tex., U.S. 102 L11
Grand Rapids, Man., Can. 83 M13
Grand Rapids, Mich., U.S. 98 L10
Grand Rapids, Minn., U.S. 104 G11
Grand Rivière, Martinique, Fr. 121 E22
Grand Roy, Grenada 121 K22

Grand Saline, *Tex., U.S.* **102** LI3
Grand Staircase-Escalante National Monument, *Utah, U.S.* **107** P7
Grand Teton, *Wyo., U.S.* **106** G8
Grand Teton National Park, *Wyo., U.S.* **106** G8
Grand Traverse Bay, *Mich., U.S.* **98** HIO
Grand Turk, island, *Turks & Caicos Is., U.K.* **117** JI8
Grandview, *Wash., U.S.* **108** E6
Grandvilliers, *Fr.* **147** N9
Grange, *Ire.* **143** Q4
Grange, *Virgin Islands, U.S.* **120** Q3
Grange Hill, *Jam.* **120** H6
Granger, *Tex., U.S.* **103** PII
Granger, *Wash., U.S.* **108** E6
Granger, *Wyo., U.S.* **106** K9
Grangeville, *Idaho, U.S.* **106** E4
Granite, *Okla., U.S.* **102** H8
Granite, *Oreg., U.S.* **108** G8
Granite City, *Ill., U.S.* **99** T4
Granite Falls, *Minn., U.S.* **104** K9
Granite Mountains, *Calif., U.S.* **109** VIO
Granite Mountains, *Wyo., U.S.* **106** HII
Granite Peak, *Mont., U.S.* **106** F9
Granite Peak, *Nev., U.S.* **108** M7
Granite Peak, *Utah, U.S.* **106** L6
Granite Peak, *W. Aust., Austral.* **211** U4
Granja, *Braz.* **131** EI6
Gran Laguna Salada, *Arg.* **133** S9
Granollers, *Sp.* **145** DI7
Gran Quivira *see* Salinas Pueblo Missions National Monument, site, *N. Mex., U.S.* **107** TI2
Gran Sasso d'Italia, *It.* **150** JIO
Grant, *Nebr., U.S.* **105** Q3
Grant, Mount, *Nev., U.S.* **109** R7
Gran Tarajal, *Canary Is.* **204** Q7
Grant City, *Mo., U.S.* **105** QIO
Grant Island, *Antarctica* **226** N8
Grant-Kohrs Ranch National Historic Site, *Mont., U.S.* **106** D6
Grant Range, *Nev., U.S.* **109** RII
Grants, *N. Mex., U.S.* **107** SII
Grantsburg, *Wis., U.S.* **98** G2
Grants Pass, *Oreg., U.S.* **108** K2
Grantville, *Ga., U.S.* **96** M4
Granville, *Fr.* **147** P6
Granville, *N. Dak., U.S.* **104** E4
Granville, *N.Y., U.S.* **94** HI2
Granville Lake, *Man., Can.* **83** LI3
Grão Mogol, *Braz.* **131** JI5
Grapeland, *Tex., U.S.* **103** NI3
Grapevine Lake, *Tex., U.S.* **102** LI2
Grasse, *Fr.* **147** XI5
Grassholm Island, *Wales, U.K.* **143** V8
Grassmere, *Qnsld., Austral.* **211** VI3
Grass Patch, *W. Aust., Austral.* **211** X4
Grass Point, *Virgin Islands, U.S.* **120** Q3
Grassrange, *Mont., U.S.* **106** DIO
Grass Valley, *Calif., U.S.* **109** Q5
Grassy Bay, *Bermuda, U.K.* **120** B2
Grassy Butte, *N. Dak., U.S.* **104** F2
Grassy Key, *Fla., U.S.* **97** Y9
Graus, *Sp.* **145** CI5
Grauspitz, peak, *Liech., Switz.* **160** R3
Grave, Pointe de, *Fr.* **147** U6
Gravelbourg, *Sask., Can.* **82** NI2
Grave Peak, *Idaho, U.S.* **106** D5
Gravette, *Ark., U.S.* **100** E6
Gravina in Puglia, *It.* **150** MI3
Gravois, Pointe-à-, *Haiti* **117** NI5
Gray, *Fr.* **147** RI3
Grayland, *Wash., U.S.* **108** D2
Grayling, *Alas., U.S.* **111** HI3
Grayling, *Mich., U.S.* **98** JII
Grays, *Eng., U.K.* **143** VI4
Grays Harbor, *Wash., U.S.* **108** D2
Grays Lake, *Idaho, U.S.* **106** H7
Grayson, *Ky., U.S.* **101** BI9
Grayville, *Ill., U.S.* **99** T7
Graz, *Aust.* **148** MI2
Great Artesian Basin, *Austral.* **210** GI2
Great Australian Bight, *Austral.* **210** K7
Great Bacolet Bay, *Grenada* **121** L23
Great Bacolet Point, *Grenada* **121** L23
Great Bahama Bank, *Bahamas* **116** EIO
Great Barrier Island, *N.Z.* **213** DI6
Great Barrier Reef, *Austral.* **210** EI5
Great Basin, *Nev., Utah, U.S.* **84** G5
Great Basin National Park, *Nev., U.S.* **109** QI3
Great Bay, *N.J., U.S.* **94** QIO
Great Bear Lake, *N.W.T., Can.* **82** FII

Great Bend, *Kans., U.S.* **105** T6
Great Bernera, island, *Scot., U.K.* **142** H6
Great Bird Island, *Antigua & Barbuda* **121** B2I
Great Bitter Lake *see* Murrat el Kubra, Buheirat, *Egypt* **171** QI
Great Britain, island, *U.K.* **142** M9
Great Channel, *India, Indonesia* **179** TI5
Great Coco Island, *Myanmar* **186** M4
Great Courtland Bay, *Trinidad & Tobago* **121** NI7
Great Crack, crater, *Hawai'i, U.S.* **113** N2O
Great Crater, *Israel* **171** P5
Great Dismal Swamp, *N.C., U.S.* **96** GI4
Great Divide Basin, *Wyo., U.S.* **106** JIO
Great Dividing Range, *Austral.* **210** CI2
Great Dog Island, *Virgin Islands, U.K.* **120** Q8
Great Driffield, *Eng., U.K.* **143** RI3
Great Eastern Dunes, *Alg., Tun.* **194** D5
Greater Antilles, islands, *N. Amer.* **80** NIO
Greater Khingan Range, *China* **166** EII
Greater Sunda Islands, *Indonesia* **188** K9
Great Exuma, island, *Bahamas* **120** E8
Great Fall, *Guyana* **129** EI3
Great Falls, *Mont., U.S.* **106** C8
Great Falls, *S.C., U.S.* **96** K9
Great Guana Cay, *Bahamas* **116** CI2
Great Guana Cay, *Bahamas* **116** FI2
Great Harbour, *Virgin Islands, U.K.* **120** LII
Great Harbour Cay, *Bahamas* **116** DII
Greathead Bay, *St. Vincent & the Grenadines* **121** LI6
Great Hungarian Plain (Alföld), *Hung., Serb.* **149** MI6
Great Inagua Island, *Bahamas* **117** JI5
Great Indian Desert (Thar Desert), *India, Pak.* **177** T9
Great Isaac, island, *Bahamas* **116** DIO
Great Karroo, region, *S. Af.* **194** Q7
Great Lake, *Bahamas* **120** FII
Great Lameshur Bay, *Virgin Islands, U.S.* **120** NII
Great Meteor Tablemount, *Atl. Oc.* **236** J9
Great Miami, river, *Ohio, U.S.* **85** GI7
Great Namaland, region, *Namibia* **202** J7
Great Nicobar, island, *India* **179** TI5
Great Orme's Head, *Wales, U.K.* **143** S9
Great Pedro Bluff, *Jam.* **116** NII
Great Pedro Point, *Cayman Is., U.K.* **120** J2
Great Pee Dee, river, *S.C., U.S.* **96** LII
Great Plains, *U.S.* **84** C9
Great Pond Bay, *Virgin Islands, U.S.* **120** Q3
Great Rift Valley, *Af.* **194** L9
Great River Bay, *Grenada* **121** K23
Great Ruaha, river, *Tanzania* **199** MI4
Great Sacandaga Lake, *N.Y., U.S.* **94** JII
Great St. James Island, *Virgin Islands, U.S.* **120** NIO
Great Sale Cay, *Bahamas* **120** D3
Great Salt Lake, *Utah, U.S.* **106** K6
Great Salt Lake Desert, *Utah, U.S.* **106** L6
Great Salt Plains Lake, *Okla., U.S.* **102** EIO
Great Salt Pond, *St. Kitts & Nevis* **121** BI8
Great Sand Dunes National Park, *Colo., U.S.* **107** PI3
Great Sandy Desert, *Austral.* **210** E5
Great Sandy Desert, *Oreg., U.S.* **84** D4
Great Sandy Island *see* Fraser Island, *Austral.* **210** GI6
Great Sitkin Island, *Alas., U.S.* **110** N5
Great Slave Lake, *N.W.T., Can.* **82** HII
Great Smoky Mountains, *N.C., Tenn., U.S.* **85** JI8
Great Smoky Mountains National Park, *N.C., Tenn., U.S.* **96** H6
Great Sound, *Bermuda, U.K.* **120** CI
Great Stirrup Cay, *Bahamas* **116** DII
Great Tenasserim, river, *Myanmar* **187** N8
Great Thatch Island, *Virgin Islands, U.K.* **120** MII
Great Tobago Island, *Virgin Islands, U.K.* **120** LIO
Great Victoria Desert, *Austral.* **210** H6

Great Wall, station, *Antarctica* **226** C3
Great Wall, *China* **181** HI3
Great Western Dunes, *Alg.* **194** D4
Great Western Tiers, *Austral.* **210** LI6
Great Yarmouth, *Eng., U.K.* **143** TI6
Great Zab, river, *Turk.* **169** GI8
Great Zimbabwe, ruin, *Zimb.* **202** GII
Greci, *It.* **150** LI2
Gredos, Sierra de, *Sp.* **144** F9
Greece, *Eur.* **139** X8
Greece, *N.Y., U.S.* **94** H6
Greeley, *Colo., U.S.* **106** LI3
Greeley, *Nebr., U.S.* **105** P6
Greely Fiord, *Nunavut, Can.* **83** BI6
Green, river, *Ky., U.S.* **101** DI5
Green, river, *Utah, U.S.* **106** L9
Green Bay, *Antigua & Barbuda* **121** B2O
Green Bay, *Wis., U.S.* **98** H7
Green Bay, *Wis., U.S.* **98** J7
Greenbrier, river, *W. Va., U.S.* **96** EIO
Greenbush, *Mich., U.S.* **98** JI2
Greenbush, *Minn., U.S.* **104** E9
Green Castle, *Bahamas* **120** F6
Greencastle, *Ind., U.S.* **99** R8
Greencastle, *Pa., U.S.* **94** Q6
Green Cay, *Bahamas* **116** FII
Green Cay, *Virgin Islands, U.K.* **120** LII
Green Cay, *Virgin Islands, U.S.* **120** Q3
Green Cove Springs, *Fla., U.S.* **97** R8
Greeneville, *Tenn., U.S.* **101** E2O
Greenfield, *Calif., U.S.* **109** U5
Greenfield, *Ind., U.S.* **99** R9
Greenfield, *Iowa, U.S.* **105** PIO
Greenfield, *Mass., U.S.* **94** KI2
Greenfield, *Mo., U.S.* **105** UII
Greenfield, *Ohio, U.S.* **99** SI2
Greenfield, *Tenn., U.S.* **101** EI3
Greenfield, *Wis., U.S.* **98** L7
Green Head, *Austral.* **210** J2
Green Hill, *Trinidad & Tobago* **121** N22
Green Island, *Antigua & Barbuda* **121** B2I
Green Island, *Grenada* **121** J23
Green Island, *Jam.* **120** H6
Green Islands, *P.N.G.* **213** C22
Greenland, island, *N. Amer.* **80** C9
Greenland (Kalaallit Nunaat), *N. Amer.* **81** B2O
Greenland Fracture Zone, *Arctic Oc.* **243** HI6
Greenland Plain, *Arctic Oc.* **243** JI7
Greenland Sea, *Arctic Oc.* **243** HI5
Green Mountains, *Vt., U.S.* **94** JI2
Green Mountains, *Wyo., U.S.* **106** JII
Greenock, *Scot., U.K.* **142** M8
Greenport, *N.Y., U.S.* **95** MI3
Green River, *Utah, U.S.* **106** M9
Green River, *Wyo., U.S.* **106** K9
Greensboro, *Ala., U.S.* **101** LI4
Greensboro, *Ga., U.S.* **96** L6
Greensboro, *N.C., U.S.* **96** HI3
Greensburg, *Ind., U.S.* **99** SIO
Greensburg, *Kans., U.S.* **105** U5
Greensburg, *Ky., U.S.* **101** CI7
Greensburg, *Pa., U.S.* **94** P4
Greens Peak, *Ariz., U.S.* **107** T9
Green Turtle Cay, *Bahamas* **120** A6
Green Valley, *Ariz., U.S.* **107** V8
Greenville, *Ala., U.S.* **101** MI5
Greenville, *Calif., U.S.* **109** N5
Greenville, *Fla., U.S.* **97** Q6
Greenville, *Ill., U.S.* **99** T5
Greenville, *Ky., U.S.* **101** DI5
Greenville, *Liberia* **200** H7
Greenville, *Me., U.S.* **95** DI6
Greenville, *Miss., U.S.* **98** LIO
Greenville, *Miss., U.S.* **100** JIO
Greenville, *N.C., U.S.* **96** HI3
Greenville, *Ohio, U.S.* **99** RII
Greenville, *Pa., U.S.* **94** M3
Greenville, *S.C., U.S.* **96** J7
Greenville, *Tex., U.S.* **102** KI2
Greenwood, *Ark., U.S.* **100** F6
Greenwood, *Ind., U.S.* **99** R9
Greenwood, *Miss., U.S.* **100** JII
Greenwood, *S.C., U.S.* **96** K7
Greer, *S.C., U.S.* **96** J7
Greers Ferry Lake, *Ark., U.S.* **100** F8
Gregory, river, *Austral.* **210** DII
Gregory, *S. Dak., U.S.* **104** M5
Gregory, Lake, *Austral.* **210** HIO
Gregory Downs, *Qnsld., Austral.* **211** RIO
Gregory Range, *Austral.* **210** DI2
Gregory Town, *Bahamas* **120** D5
Greifswald, *Ger.* **148** BIO
Greiz, *Ger.* **148** G9

Grenada, *Calif., U.S.* **108** L3
Grenada, *Miss., U.S.* **100** JII
Grenada, *N. Amer.* **81** P24
Grenada, island, *N. Amer.* **80** PI2
Grenada Bay, *Grenada* **121** J23
Grenade, *Fr.* **147** X7
Grenoble, *Fr.* **147** VI4
Grenora, *N. Dak., U.S.* **104** E2
Grenville, *Grenada* **121** K23
Grenville, Cape, *Austral.* **210** AI2
Grenville, Point, *Wash., U.S.* **108** C2
Grenville Bay, *Grenada* **121** K23
Gresham, *Oreg., U.S.* **108** F4
Gretna, *La., U.S.* **100** QII
Gretschins, *Switz.* **160** Q2
Grevená, *Gr.* **154** D8
Grevenmacher, *Lux.* **160** JII
Grey, Mount, *Austral.* **210** J3
Greybull, river, *Wyo., U.S.* **106** GIO
Greybull, *Wyo., U.S.* **106** FIO
Grey Islands, *Nfld. & Lab., Can.* **83** L23
Greylock, Mount, *Mass., U.S.* **94** KI2
Grey Range, *Austral.* **210** HI2
Grezzana, *It.* **150** D6
Gribanovskiy, *Russ.* **156** MII
Gridley, *Calif., U.S.* **109** P4
Grieg Point, *Kiribati* **217** B2O
Griffin, Ga., U.S. **96** M5
Griffith, *N.S.W., Austral.* **211** YI3
Griggsville, *Ill., U.S.* **99** R3
Grimaldi Forum, *Monaco* **161** C22
Grimault, Île, *New Caledonia, Fr.* **218** D7
Grimsby, *Eng., U.K.* **143** RI4
Grímsey, island, *Ice.* **140** E3
Grimshaw, *Alta., Can.* **82** KIO
Grimstad, *Nor.* **140** MII
Grindelwald, *Switz.* **150** B3
Grinnell, *Iowa, U.S.* **105** PI2
Grinnell Peninsula, *Nunavut, Can.* **83** CI5
Grintavec, peak, *Slov.* **152** C4
Griquatown, *S. Af.* **202** K9
Grise Fiord, *Nunavut, Can.* **83** CI6
Grishkino, *Russ.* **158** JI2
Gris-Nez, Cap, *Fr.* **146** L9
Grisslehamn, *Sw.* **141** KI4
Gródek, *Pol.* **149** CI8
Groenlo, *Neth.* **146** JI4
Groesbeck, *Tex., U.S.* **103** NI2
Groix, Île de, *Fr.* **147** R3
Grójec, *Pol.* **149** EI6
Gronau, *Ger.* **148** D5
Groningen, *Neth.* **146** GI4
Groom, *Tex., U.S.* **102** G6
Groot Baai, *Neth. Antilles, Neth.* **121** BI4
Groote Eylandt, *N. Terr., Austral.* **211** PIO
Grootfontein, *Namibia* **202** G7
Grosio, *It.* **150** C6
Gros Islet, *St. Lucia* **121** JI4
Gros Islet Bay, *St. Lucia* **121** JI4
Gros-Morne, *Martinique, Fr.* **121** E22
Gros Piton, peak, *St. Lucia* **121** LI3
Gros Point, *Grenada* **121** J22
Grosse Pointe, *Guadeloupe, Fr.* **121** GI6
Grosseto, *It.* **150** J6
Grossvenediger, peak, *Aust.* **148** M9
Grosvenor Downs, *Qnsld., Austral.* **211** TI4
Grosvenor Mountains, *Antarctica* **226** KI2
Grosvenor Seamount, *Pac. Oc.* **238** G8
Gros Ventre Range, *Wyo., U.S.* **106** H8
Grotli, *Nor.* **140** JIO
Groton, *S. Dak., U.S.* **104** J7
Grottaminarda, *It.* **150** MII
Grotto of Lourdes, *Vatican City* **161** QI4
Grotto of the Observatory, *Monaco* **161** FI9
Grouse Creek, *Utah, U.S.* **106** J5
Grove, *Mo., U.S.* **105** VI3
Grove City, *Pa., U.S.* **94** M3
Grove Hill, *Ala., U.S.* **101** MI4
Grove Mountains, *Antarctica* **227** GI8
Grove Place, *Virgin Islands, U.S.* **120** Q2
Grover, *Colo., U.S.* **106** KI4
Grover Beach, *Calif., U.S.* **109** V5
Groves, *Tex., U.S.* **103** QI6
Groveton, *N.H., U.S.* **95** FI4
Groveton, *Tex., U.S.* **103** PI4
Groznyy, *Russ.* **157** TI4
Grudovo, *Bulg.* **153** JI7
Grudziądz, *Pol.* **149** CI4
Gruinard Bay, *Scot., U.K.* **142** J8
Grundy, *Va., U.S.* **96** F7
Grundy Center, *Iowa, U.S.* **105** NI2

Gruver, *Tex., U.S.* **102** F5
Gryazi, *Russ.* **156** MIO
Gryazovets, *Russ.* **156** GIO
Gryfino, *Pol.* **148** CII
Grygla, *Minn., U.S.* **104** E9
Guacanayabo, Golfo de, *Cuba* **116** KII
Guadalajara, *Mex.* **114** HIO
Guadalajara, *Sp.* **144** FII
Guadalcanal, island, *Solomon Is.* **217** NI9
Guadalcanal, *Sp.* **144** K8
Guadalquivir, river, *Sp.* **144** K9
Guadalupe, *Calif., U.S.* **109** W5
Guadalupe, *Mex.* **114** C7
Guadalupe, *Mex.* **114** GIO
Guadalupe, river, *Tex., U.S.* **103** SII
Guadalupe, Isla de, *Mex.* **114** C4
Guadalupe, Sierra de, *Sp.* **144** H9
Guadalupe Island *see* Guadalupe, Isla de, *N. Amer.* **80** L2
Guadalupe Mountains, *N. Mex., U.S.* **107** VI4
Guadalupe Mountains National Park, *Tex., U.S.* **102** MI
Guadalupe Peak, *Tex., U.S.* **102** MI
Guadalupita, *N. Mex., U.S.* **107** RI3
Guadarrama, Sierra de, *Sp.* **144** FIO
Guadeloupe, island, *Lesser Antilles* **119** HI7
Guadeloupe Passage, *Lesser Antilles* **119** HI6
Guadiana, river, *Port.* **144** K6
Guadiana, river, *Sp.* **144** H8
Guadiana, Bahía, *Cuba* **116** H4
Guadirikiri Cave, *Aruba, Neth.* **121** RI7
Guadix, *Sp.* **144** LII
Guafo, Boca del, *Chile* **133** R6
Guafo, Isla, *Chile* **133** R5
Guai, *Indonesia* **189** K2I
Guáimaro, *Cuba* **116** JII
Guainía, river, *Col.* **128** G8
Guaíra, *Braz.* **130** MII
Guajaba, Cayo, *Cuba* **116** HII
Guajará-Mirim, *Braz.* **130** G7
Guajira, Península de la, *Col.* **128** A7
Gualala, *Calif., U.S.* **109** Q2
Gualdicciolo, *San Marino* **161** JI4
Gualeguay, *Arg.* **132** KI2
Gualeguaychú, *Arg.* **132** KI3
Gualicho, Salina, *Arg.* **133** P9
Guallatiri, Volcán, *Chile* **132** B7
Guam, island, *Pac. Oc.* **214** E4
Guamúchil, *Mex.* **114** E8
Gua Musang, *Malaysia* **187** TIO
Guanal, Punta del, *Cuba* **116** J6
Guana Baai, *Neth. Antilles, Neth.* **121** BI5
Guana Cay, *Bahamas* **120** CIO
Guana Island, *Virgin Islands, U.K.* **120** Q7
Guanajay, *Cuba* **116** G6
Guanajuato, *Mex.* **114** HII
Guanambi, *Braz.* **131** JI5
Guanapo, *Trinidad & Tobago* **121** P23
Guanare, river, *Venez.* **128** C8
Guanare, *Venez.* **128** C8
Guandacol, *Arg.* **132** H8
Guane, *Cuba* **116** H4
Guangchang, *China* **183** P6
Guangfeng, *China* **183** N8
Guanghai, *China* **183** S4
Guangning, *China* **183** R3
Guangrao, *China* **182** F8
Guangshan, *China* **182** K5
Guangshui, *China* **182** K5
Guangyuan, *China* **180** KI2
Guangzhou (Canton), *China* **183** R4
Guánica, P.R., U.S. **120** P2
Guánica, Bahía de, *P.R., U.S.* **120** P2
Guanipa, river, *Venez.* **128** CI2
Guano, Cayo, *Cuba* **116** H8
Guano Lake, *Oreg., U.S.* **108** L7
Guantánamo, *Cuba* **117** KI3
Guantánamo, Bahía de, *Cuba* **117** LI3
Guantánamo Bay, U.S. Naval Base, *Cuba* **117** LI4
Guanyan, *China* **182** H8
Guanyang, *China* **183** P3
Guapí, *Col.* **128** G3
Guapo Bay, *Trinidad & Tobago* **121** Q2I
Guaporé, river, *Bol., Braz.* **130** H9
Guara, Sierra de, *Sp.* **145** CI4
Guaranda, *Ecua.* **128** K3
Guarapuava, *Braz.* **130** MI2
Guaratinguetá, *Braz.* **131** MI4
Guarcino, *It.* **150** K9
Guarda, *Port.* **144** F7
Guardalavaca, *Cuba* **117** JI3

Guarda Mor, Braz. 131 K13
Guardo, Sp. 144 C9
Guareña, Sp. 144 J8
Guárico, river, Venez. 128 C9
Guarico, Punta, Cuba 117 K14
Guasave, Mex. 114 E8
Guascama, Punta, Col. 128 G3
Guasdualito, Venez. 128 D7
Guatemala City, Guatemala 115 L16
Guatemala, N. Amer. 81 P19
Guatemala Basin, Pac. Oc. 239 J18
Guaviare, river, Col. 128 F8
Guaviare, river, S. Amer. 126 C4
Guayabal, Cuba 116 K11
Guayaguayare, Trinidad & Tobago 121 Q23
Guayaguayare Bay, Trinidad & Tobago 121 Q23
Guayama, P.R., U.S. 120 N4
Guayaquil, Ecua. 128 K2
Guayaquil, Gulf of, S. Amer. 126 D1
Guaymas, Mex. 114 D7
Guaynabo, P.R., U.S. 120 M4
Gûbâl, Strait of, Egypt 171 U3
Gubbio, It. 150 H8
Gubin, Pol. 148 E11
Gubkin, Russ. 157 N9
Gucheng, China 182 J3
Gudalur, India 179 Q5
Gudaut'a, Abkhazia 169 A15
Gudermes, Russ. 157 T14
Gudgeon Bay, Pitcairn I., U.K. 219 Q23
Gudur, India 179 P7
Guebwiller, Fr. 147 Q15
Guelb er Rîchât, peak, Mauritania 196 F6
Guelmim, Mor. 196 C7
Güeppí, Peru 130 C3
Guéra Massif, Chad 194 G7
Guerara, Alg. 196 B11
Guéret, Fr. 147 T9
Guernsey, island, Ch. Is. 143 Z11
Guernsey, Wyo., U.S. 106 J13
Guernsey Reservoir, Wyo., U.S. 106 J13
Gueydan, La., U.S. 100 P8
Gugegwe, island, Marshall Is. 216 M6
Guguan, island, N. Mariana Is., U.S. 216 B2
Gui, river, China 183 R2
Guía de Isora, Canary Is. 204 Q4
Guiana Highlands, S. Amer. 126 B6
Guiana Island, Antigua & Barbuda 121 B21
Guichi, China 182 L7
Guide, China 180 J11
Guienne, region, Fr. 147 W7
Guigang, China 183 R1
Guiglo, Côte d'Ivoire 200 G7
Guijá, Mozambique 202 J12
Guijuelo, Sp. 144 F8
Guildford, Eng., U.K. 143 W13
Guilford, Me., U.S. 95 E16
Guilin, China 183 Q2
Guillaume-Delisle, Lac, Que., Can. 83 L18
Guillestre, Fr. 147 V15
Guimarães, Port. 144 D6
Guimarães, Braz. 131 D15
Guin, Ala., U.S. 101 J14
Guinchos Cay, Cuba 116 G11
Guinea, Af. 195 H14
Guinea, Gulf of, Af. 194 J4
Guinea-Bissau, Af. 195 G13
Güines, Cuba 116 G6
Guingamp, Fr. 147 P4
Guiping, China 183 R2
Güira de Melena, Cuba 116 G6
Güiria, Venez. 128 B12
Guisborough, Eng., U.K. 143 Q12
Guitiriz, Sp. 144 B6
Guixi, China 183 N7
Guiyang, China 183 P4
Guiyang, China 180 N12
Gujar Khan, Pak. 177 N11
Gujranwala, Pak. 177 P12
Gujrat, Pak. 177 P11
Gulang, China 180 H11
Gulbarga, India 178 M5
Gulbene, Latv. 141 L17
Gul'cha, Kyrg. 176 G11
Gulf Islands National Seashore, Fla., U.S. 97 Q2
Gulf Islands National Seashore, Miss., U.S. 101 P13
Gulfport, Miss., U.S. 100 P12
Gulf Shores, Ala., U.S. 101 P14
Gulgong, N.S.W., Austral. 211 X14
Guling, China 182 M6
Guliston, Uzb. 175 K13
Gulitel, Mount, Palau 216 M12
Gulja see Yining, China 180 E6
Gulkana, Alas., U.S. 111 H18
Güllük, Turk. 168 H3
Gülnar, Turk. 168 J8
Gülşehir, Turk. 168 F10
Gulu, Uganda 199 J13
Gŭlŭbovo, Bulg. 153 J15
Gulya, Russ. 159 K18
Gulyantsi, Bulg. 153 G14
Guma see Pishan, China 180 G4
Gumdag, Turkm. 174 L6
Gumla, India 178 J9
Gummi, Nigeria 201 E13
Gümüşhacıköy, Turk. 168 D10
Gümüşhane, Turk. 169 D14
Gümüşören, Turk. 168 G10
Gumzai, Indonesia 189 L19
Guna, India 178 H6
Gun Bay, Cayman Is., U.K. 120 J4
Gun Cay, Bahamas 116 D9
Gun Creek, Virgin Islands, U.K. 120 Q9
Gundagai, N.S.W., Austral. 211 Y13
Gundlupet, India 179 Q5
Gündoğmuş, Turk. 168 J7
Güney, Turk. 168 G4
Gungu, Dem. Rep. of the Congo 198 L9
Gun Hill, Barbados 121 K19
Gunib, Russ. 157 U15
Gunnbjørn, peak, N. Amer. 80 B10
Gunnedah, N.S.W., Austral. 211 W14
Gunners Quoin, island, Mauritius 205 F20
Gunnewin, Qnsld., Austral. 211 U14
Gunnison, Colo., U.S. 107 N11
Gunnison, Utah, U.S. 106 M7
Gunsan, S. Korea 182 G13
Gunt, river, Taj. 176 J10
Guntersville, Ala., U.S. 101 H16
Guntersville Lake, Ala., U.S. 101 H16
Guntur, India 179 N7
Gunungsugih, Indonesia 188 L7
Guoyang, China 182 J6
Gupis, Pak. 176 L11
Gurabo, P.R., U.S. 120 N5
Gurage, peak, Eth. 194 H10
Gura Humorului, Rom. 153 B15
Gura Portiıei, strait, Rom. 153 F18
Gurban Obo, China 181 F14
Gurdaspur, India 177 P13
Gurdon, Ark., U.S. 100 J7
Güre, Turk. 168 F5
Gurer, island, Marshall Is. 216 L3
Gurguan Point, N. Mariana Is., U.S. 216 B7
Guri Dam, Venez. 128 D12
Guri i Topit, peak, Albania 152 L10
Gurimatu, P.N.G. 213 D19
Gurkovo, Bulg. 153 J15
Gurney, P.N.G. 213 E21
Gürün, Turk. 168 F12
Gurupá, Braz. 130 D12
Gurupá Island, S. Amer. 126 D8
Gurupi, river, Braz. 131 D14
Gurupi, Braz. 131 G13
Gurupi, Cape, S. Amer. 126 D9
Gurupi, Serra do, Braz. 131 E13
Gurvan Bogd Uul, range, Mongolia 180 E11
Gusau, Nigeria 201 E14
Gusev, Russ. 156 J2
Guşgy, Turkm. 174 P10
Gushan, China 182 D11
Gushi, China 182 K6
Gushikawa, Japan 185 Y1
Gusikha, Russ. 159 E15
Gusinaya Bank, Arctic Oc. 243 C16
Gusinoozersk, Russ. 159 L16
Gus' Khrustal'nyy, Russ. 156 J11
Guspini, It. 151 P3
Güssing, Aust. 148 M12
Gustavia, St.-Barthélemy 119 F15
Gustine, Calif., U.S. 109 S5
Güstrow, Ger. 148 C9
Gutăiu, peak, Rom. 153 B13
Gutcher, Scot., U.K. 142 C12
Gutenberg Castle, Liech. 160 Q2
Gütersloh, Ger. 148 E6
Guthrie, Ky., U.S. 101 D15
Guthrie, Okla., U.S. 102 F11
Guthrie, Tex., U.S. 102 K7
Guthrie Center, Iowa, U.S. 105 P10
Gutian, China 183 P8
Guttenberg, Iowa, U.S. 104 M14
Güvem, Turk. 168 D8
Guwahati, India 178 G13
Guyana, S. Amer. 127 B18
Guyandotte, river, W. Va., U.S. 96 E7
Guyang, China 182 C3
Guymon, Okla., U.S. 102 E5
Guyonneau, Anse, Guadeloupe, Fr. 121 F14
Guyra, N.S.W., Austral. 211 W15
Guyuan, China 182 B6
Güzeloluk, Turk. 168 J9
Güzelyurt, Turk. 168 G9
Guzhang, China 182 M2
G'uzor, Uzb. 174 M12
Gwa, Myanmar 186 K5
Gwadar, Pak. 177 W2
Gwai, Zimb. 202 G10
Gwalior, India 178 G6
Gwanda, Zimb. 202 G11
Gwangju (Kwangju), S. Korea 182 G13
Gwardafuy, Cape, Somalia 194 G12
Gwatar Bay, Pak. 177 W1
Gweebarra Bay, Ire. 143 P4
Gweru, Zimb. 202 G11
Gwinn, Mich., U.S. 98 F7
Gwinner, N. Dak., U.S. 104 H7
Gwoza, Nigeria 201 F16
Gwydir, river, Austral. 210 J14
Gyamysh, peak, Azerb. 169 D20
Gyangzê, China 180 L7
Gyaring Co, China 180 K7
Gyaring Hu, China 180 J9
Gydan see Kolymskoye Nagor'ye, range, Russ. 159 D20
Gydanskiy Poluostrov, Russ. 158 F12
Gyda Peninsula, Russ. 166 C8
Gyeongju (Kyŏngju), S. Korea 182 G15
Gympie, Qnsld., Austral. 211 V15
Gyöngyös, Hung. 149 L15
Győr, Hung. 149 L14
Gypsum, Kans., U.S. 105 T7
Gyula, Hung. 149 M17
Gyumri, Arm. 169 D18
Gyzylarbat, Turkm. 174 L7
Gyzyletrek, Turkm. 174 M6
Gyzylgaya, Turkm. 174 K7
Gyzylsuw, Turkm. 174 K6
Għira, Malta 161 K23

H

Ha'afeva, island, Tonga 218 Q6
Haag, Switz. 160 N2
Ha'akame, Tonga 218 J11
Ha'alaufuli, Tonga 218 L12
Haamaire, Baie, Fr. Polynesia, Fr. 219 K14
Haamene, Baie de, Fr. Polynesia, Fr. 219 A23
Ha'ano, island, Tonga 218 P7
Ha'apai Group, Tonga 214 K10
Haapamäki, Fin. 141 H15
Haapiti, Fr. Polynesia, Fr. 219 N14
Haapsalu, Est. 141 K16
Haapu, Fr. Polynesia, Fr. 219 H14
Haarlem, Neth. 146 J12
Ha'asini, Tonga 218 J12
Haast, N.Z. 213 P15
Haast Bluff, N. Terr., Austral. 211 T8
Haava, Canal, Fr. Polynesia, Fr. 219 N20
Hab, river, Pak. 177 V6
Habahe, China 180 C7
Ḩabarūt, Oman 173 N14
Habomai, Japan 184 F16
Habomai Islands, Russ. 184 G6
Haboro, Japan 184 E13
Hachijō Jima, Japan 185 S12
Hachiman, Japan 185 P10
Hachinohe, Japan 184 J13
Hachiōji, Japan 185 P12
Hachirō Gata, Japan 184 K12
Hachita, N. Mex., U.S. 107 V10
Hacıbektaş, Turk. 168 F9
Hadarba, Ras, Sudan 199 B14
Ḩadd, Ra's al, Oman 173 K17
Haddummati Atoll, Maldives 179 W3
Hadejia, river, Nigeria 194 G5
Ḩadera, Israel 170 L5
Hadhramaut see Ḩaḑramawt, region, Yemen 166 J3
Hadiboh, Yemen 173 R14
Ḩadīdah, Syr. 170 D10
Hadım, Turk. 168 H7
Ḩadīthah, Iraq 172 D8
Hadja, Solomon Is. 217 P20
Hadley Bay, Nunavut, Can. 83 E13
Ha Dong, Vietnam 186 H12
Ḩaḑramawt, region, Yemen 172 Q11
Hadrian's Wall, Eng., U.K. 143 P11
Hadyach, Ukr. 157 N7
Haeju, N. Korea 182 E12
Hā'ena, Hawai'i, U.S. 113 M22
Haenam, S. Korea 182 H13
Ḩafar al Bāţin, Saudi Arabia 172 G10
Hafik, Turk. 168 E12
Ḩafīt, Jabal, U.A.E. 173 K15
Hafizabad, Pak. 177 P11
Hagåtña (Agana), Guam, U.S. 216 C10
Hagemeister Island, Alas., U.S. 110 L12
Hagen, Ger. 148 F6
Hagerman, N. Mex., U.S. 107 U14
Hagerman Fossil Beds National Monument, Idaho, U.S. 106 H4
Hagerstown, Md., U.S. 96 B12
Häggenås, Sw. 140 H12
Hagi, Japan 185 Q5
Ha Giang, Vietnam 186 G11
Hagia Triada, ruin, Gr. 155 R14
Hagman, Puntan, N. Mariana Is., U.S. 216 C5
Hagoi Susupe, lake, N. Mariana Is., U.S. 216 C4
Hags Head, Ire. 143 S3
Hague, Cap de la, Fr. 147 N5
Haguenau, Fr. 147 P15
Haha Jima Rettō, Japan 184 K5
Hai, Hon, Vietnam 187 Q14
Hai'an, China 182 J9
Haicheng, China 182 C10
Hai Duong, Vietnam 186 H12
Haifa see Ḩefa, Israel 170 K5
Haifeng, China 183 S5
Haig, W. Aust., Austral. 211 W6
Haiger, Ger. 148 G6
Haikou, China 183 T2
Ha'iku, Hawai'i, U.S. 113 G17
Ḩā'il, Saudi Arabia 172 H8
Hailar, China 181 C15
Hailey, Idaho, U.S. 106 G5
Hails, China 182 B1
Hailuoto, island, Fin. 141 F15
Haimen see Taizhou, China 182 M10
Haimen Wan, China 183 R6
Hainan, island, China 183 U2
Haines, Alas., U.S. 111 K21
Haines, Oreg., U.S. 108 G8
Haines City, Fla., U.S. 97 U8
Haines Junction, Yukon, Can. 82 G7
Hainiya Point, N. Mariana Is., U.S. 216 E8
Haiphong, Vietnam 186 H12
Haiti, N. Amer. 81 N22
Haiya, Sudan 199 D14
Haiyan, China 182 L9
Haiyan, China 180 H11
Haizhou Wan, China 182 H8
Hajdúböszörmény, Hung. 149 L17
Hajdúszoboszló, Hung. 149 L17
Hajiki Saki, Japan 184 L11
Haji Pir Pass, India, Pak. 177 N11
Ḩajjah, Yemen 172 P9
Ḩājjīābād, Iran 173 G15
Hajnáčka, Slovakia 149 K15
Hajnówka, Pol. 149 D18
Hakalau, Hawai'i, U.S. 113 L21
Hakamaru, island, Cook Is., N.Z. 219 B15
Hakataramea, N.Z. 213 Q16
Hakauata, island, Tonga 218 P7
Hakha, Myanmar 186 G4
Hakkari, Turk. 169 H18
Hakken San, Japan 185 Q9
Hakodate, Japan 184 H13
Hakui, Japan 185 N10
Hakupa Pass, Solomon Is. 217 J18
Hakupu, Niue, N.Z. 219 B20
Hala, Pak. 177 V7
Ḩalab (Aleppo), Syr. 170 D9
Ḩalabān, Saudi Arabia 172 K9
Halachó, Mex. 115 H16
Halāli'i Lake, Hawai'i, U.S. 112 C3
Halalo, Pointe, Wallis & Futuna, Fr. 218 C11
Hala'ula, Hawai'i, U.S. 113 K19
Halawa, Hawai'i, U.S. 113 K19
Hālawa, Cape, Hawai'i, U.S. 113 F15
Hālawa Bay, Hawai'i, U.S. 113 F15
Halayeb, Egypt 197 F20
Halba, Leb. 170 G7
Halban, Mongolia 180 C10
Halberstadt, Ger. 148 E8
Halcon, Mount, Philippines 189 D13
Haldwani, India 178 E7
Hale, Mich., U.S. 98 J12
Haleakalā Crater, Hawai'i, U.S. 113 H17
Haleakalā National Park, Hawai'i, U.S. 113 H18
Haleakalā Observatories, Hawai'i, U.S. 113 H17
Hale Center, Tex., U.S. 102 J5
Hale'iwa, Hawai'i, U.S. 112 D10
Haleki'i-Pihana Heiaus, Hawai'i, U.S. 113 G16
Haleyville, Ala., U.S. 101 H14
Halfeti, Turk. 168 H12
Half Moon Bay, Antigua & Barbuda 121 B21
Halfway, Oreg., U.S. 108 G9
Halgan, Cape, F.S.M. 217 A19
Halifax, N.S., Can. 83 P22
Halifax, Qnsld., Austral. 211 R13
Halifax, Va., U.S. 96 F11
Halkett, Cape, Alas., U.S. 111 B16
Hálki, island, Gr. 155 N19
Hálki, island, Gr. 155 N19
Hálki, Gr. 154 F10
Halkída (Chalkis), Gr. 154 H12
Halkidikí, peninsula, Gr. 154 D12
Hall, Aust. 148 L8
Hallandale, Fla., U.S. 97 W10
Hall Basin, Nunavut, Can. 83 A17
Hall Beach, Nunavut, Can. 83 F16
Halle, Belg. 146 L12
Halle, Ger. 148 F9
Hallein, Aust. 148 L10
Hallettsville, Tex., U.S. 103 R12
Halley, station, Antarctica 226 D10
Halliday, N. Dak., U.S. 104 F3
Hallim, S. Korea 182 J13
Hall Islands, F.S.M. 216 Q6
Hällnäs, Sw. 141 G14
Hallock, Minn., U.S. 104 E8
Hall Peninsula, Nunavut, Can. 83 H19
Halls, Tenn., U.S. 100 F12
Halls Creek, W. Aust., Austral. 211 R6
Hallstatt, Aust. 148 L10
Halmahera, island, Indonesia 189 H16
Halmahera Sea, Indonesia 189 J17
Halmeu, Rom. 152 A12
Halmstad, Sw. 140 N12
Halola, Solomon Is. 217 L14
Halsa, Nor. 140 H10
Halstead, Eng., U.K. 143 U15
Halstead, Kans., U.S. 105 U7
Haltdalen, Nor. 140 H11
Halten Bank, Atl. Oc. 236 C14
Halulu Heiau, Hawai'i, U.S. 113 G14
Halys see Kızılırmak, river, Turk. 168 D9
Ham, Fr. 147 N10
Hamada, Japan 185 Q6
Hamadān, Iran 172 D11
Hamaguir, Alg. 196 C9
Ḩamāh (Hamath), Syr. 170 F8
Hāmākua, region, Hawai'i, U.S. 113 L20
Hamamatsu, Japan 185 Q10
Hamamet, Gulf of, Tun. 194 C6
Hamar, Nor. 140 K11
Hamasaka, Japan 185 P8
Ḩamâta, Gebel, Egypt 197 E20
Hamath see Ḩamāh, Syr. 170 F8
Hamatombetsu, Japan 184 D14
Hamburg, Ark., U.S. 100 K9
Hamburg, Ger. 148 C8
Hamburg, Iowa, U.S. 105 Q9
Hamburg, Mo., U.S. 105 Q9
Hamburg, N.Y., U.S. 94 J5
Ḩamḑah, Saudi Arabia 172 M9
Ḩamdānah, Saudi Arabia 172 M7
Hamden, Conn., U.S. 94 M12
Hämeenlinna, Fin. 141 J16
Hamelin, W. Aust., Austral. 211 V1
Hameln, Ger. 148 E7
Hamersley Range, Austral. 210 F3
Hamhŭng, N. Korea 182 D13
Hami (Kumul), China 180 F9
Hamilton, Ala., U.S. 101 H14
Hamilton, Bermuda, U.K. 120 B2
Hamilton, Ill., U.S. 99 Q3
Hamilton, Mo., U.S. 105 R11
Hamilton, Mont., U.S. 106 D5
Hamilton, N.Y., U.S. 94 J9
Hamilton, N.Z. 213 K19
Hamilton, Ohio, U.S. 99 S11
Hamilton, Ont., Can. 83 R18
Hamilton, Scot., U.K. 142 M9

Hamilton, *Tas., Austral.* 211 Z16
Hamilton, *Tex., U.S.* 103 N10
Hamilton, *Vic., Austral.* 211 Z11
Hamilton, Lake, *Ark., U.S.* 100 H7
Hamilton Harbour, *Bermuda, U.K.*
  120 B2
Hamilton Inlet, *Nfld. & Lab., Can.*
  83 K22
Hamina, *Fin.* 141 J17
Hamirpur, *India* 178 G7
Hamlet, *N.C., U.S.* 96 J10
Hamlí, island, *Gr.* 155 P16
Hamlin, *Tex., U.S.* 102 L7
Hamm, *Ger.* 148 E6
Ḩammār, Hawr al, *Iraq* 166 G4
Hammerfest, *Nor.* 141 C14
Hammon, *Okla., U.S.* 102 G8
Hammond, *Ind., U.S.* 99 N7
Hammond, *La., U.S.* 100 P10
Hammond, *Mont., U.S.* 106 F13
Hammonton, *N.J., U.S.* 94 Q10
Hampden, *N.Z.* 213 Q16
Hampstead, *Dominica* 121 E19
Hampton, *Ark., U.S.* 100 J8
Hampton, *Iowa, U.S.* 104 M12
Hampton, *S.C., U.S.* 96 M9
Hampton, *Va., U.S.* 96 F14
Hampton Bays, *N.Y., U.S.* 95 N13
Hampton Butte, *Oreg., U.S.* 108 H6
Hampton Tableland, *Austral.* 210 J6
Hampyeong, *S. Korea* 182 G13
Ḩamrīn, Jabal, *Iraq* 172 D9
Hamrun, *Malta* 161 K23
Hams Bluff, *Virgin Islands, U.S.* 120 Q2
Ham Yen, *Vietnam* 186 G11
Han, river, *China* 182 K4
Hāna, *Hawai'i, U.S.* 113 G18
Hanahan, *P.N.G.* 217 J13
Hanahe, Baie, *Fr. Polynesia, Fr.* 219 M23
Hāna Highway, *Hawai'i, U.S.* 113 G18
Hanahupe, Baie, *Fr. Polynesia, Fr.*
  219 M21
Hanaiapa, Baie, *Fr. Polynesia, Fr.*
  219 M20
Hanaiapaoa, Baie, *Fr. Polynesia, Fr.*
  219 M20
Hanalei, *Hawai'i, U.S.* 112 B5
Hanalei Bay, *Hawai'i, U.S.* 112 B5
Hanamaki, *Japan* 184 M13
Hanamalo Point, *Hawai'i, U.S.* 113 P18
Hanamā'ulu, *Hawai'i, U.S.* 112 B6
Hanamenu, Baie, *Fr. Polynesia, Fr.*
  219 M20
Hanaoo, *Fr. Polynesia, Fr.* 219 N20
Hanapēpē, *Hawai'i, U.S.* 112 C5
Hana Teio, *Fr. Polynesia, Fr.* 219 N20
Hana Tetena, *Fr. Polynesia, Fr.* 219 N20
Hana Tuuna, *Fr. Polynesia, Fr.* 219 N20
Hanau, *Ger.* 148 G6
Hanaui, *Fr. Polynesia, Fr.* 219 M20
Hanawa, *Japan* 184 J13
Hancheng, *China* 182 G3
Hanchuan, *China* 182 L5
Hancock, *Md., U.S.* 96 B12
Hancock, *Mich., U.S.* 98 E6
Hancock, *Minn., U.S.* 104 J9
Handa Island, *Scot., U.K.* 142 H8
Handan, *China* 182 F5
Handsome Bay, *Virgin Islands, U.K.*
  120 R8
Hane, *Fr. Polynesia, Fr.* 219 N23
Hane, Baie d', *Fr. Polynesia, Fr.*
  219 N23
Hanford, *Calif., U.S.* 109 U6
Hanford Site, *Wash., U.S.* 108 E7
Hangayn Nuruu, range, *Mongolia*
  180 D10
Hanggin Houqi (Xamba), *China* 182 C1
Hanggin Qi, *China* 182 C2
Hangö (Hanko), *Fin.* 141 K15
Hangu, *China* 182 D7
Hangu, *Pak.* 177 N9
Hangzhou, *China* 182 L9
Hangzhou Wan, *China* 182 L10
Hani, *Turk.* 169 G15
Haniá (Canea, Cydonia), *Gr.* 155 Q13
Hanimadu, island, *Maldives* 179 T3
Ḩanish al Kabīr, Jazīrat al, *Yemen*
  172 Q8
Hankinson, *N. Dak., U.S.* 104 H8
Hanko *see* Hangö, *Fin.* 141 K15
Hanksville, *Utah, U.S.* 107 N8
Hanle, *India* 177 N15
Hanna, *Alta., Can.* 82 M10
Hannibal, *Mo., U.S.* 105 R14

Hannover (Hanover), *Ger.* 148 D7
Hanöbukten, *Sw.* 141 N13
Hanoi, *Vietnam* 186 H12
Hanover *see* Hannover, *Ger.* 148 D7
Hanover, *Kans., U.S.* 105 R8
Hanover, *N.H., U.S.* 95 H13
Hanover, *Pa., U.S.* 94 Q7
Hanover, Isla, *Chile* 133 V6
Hanpan, Cape, *P.N.G.* 217 J13
Hansen Mountains, *Antarctica* 227 D19
Hans Lollik Island, *Virgin Islands, U.S.*
  120 M9
Hantsavichy, *Belarus* 156 L4
Hanumangarh, *India* 178 E4
Hanuy, river, *Mongolia* 180 C11
Hanyang, *China* 182 L5
Hanzhong, *China* 180 K12
Hao, island, *Fr. Polynesia, Fr.* 219 F20
Haora, *India* 178 J11
Hā'ō'ū, *Hawai'i, U.S.* 113 H18
Hapai, *Solomon Is.* 217 M16
Haparanda, *Sw.* 141 F15
Hapatoni, Baie, *Fr. Polynesia, Fr.*
  219 N20
Hapo, *Indonesia* 189 H16
Happy, *Tex., U.S.* 102 H5
Happy Camp, *Calif., U.S.* 108 L2
Happy Valley-Goose Bay, *Nfld. & Lab.,*
  Can. 83 L21
Ḩaql, *Saudi Arabia* 172 F5
Har, *Indonesia* 189 L18
Ḩaraḍ, *Saudi Arabia* 172 K12
Ḩarad, Jabal al, *Jordan* 171 R6
Haradok, *Belarus* 156 J6
Haradzishcha, *Belarus* 156 L4
Haraiki, island, *Fr. Polynesia, Fr.* 219 E19
Haranomachi, *Japan* 184 M13
Harappa, ruin, *Pak.* 177 R11
Harare, *Zimb.* 202 F11
Haratini, island, *Cook Is., N.Z.* 219 C15
Har Ayrag, *Mongolia* 181 E13
Harbin, *China* 181 D17
Harbor Beach, *Mich., U.S.* 98 K13
Harbor Springs, *Mich., U.S.* 98 H10
Harbour Island, *Bahamas* 120 D5
Harbours, Bay of, *Falkland Is., U.K.*
  133 W12
Harda, *India* 178 J5
Hardangerfjorden, bay, *Nor.* 140 K10
Hard Bargain, *Bahamas* 120 B5
Hardenberg, *Neth.* 146 H14
Harderwijk, *Neth.* 146 J13
Hardin, *Ill., U.S.* 99 S3
Hardin, *Mont., U.S.* 106 E11
Harding, *S. Af.* 202 L11
Hardman, *Oreg., U.S.* 108 F6
Hardwick, *Ga., U.S.* 96 M6
Hardy, *Ark., U.S.* 100 E9
Hardy, Península, *Chile* 133 Y9
Hardy, Pointe, *St. Lucia* 121 J14
Härer, *Eth.* 199 G16
Hargeysa, *Somalia* 199 G16
Har Hu, *China* 180 H10
Haría, *Canary Is.* 204 P8
Haridwar, *India* 178 E6
Harihari, *N.Z.* 213 P16
Harij, *India* 178 H3
Ḩarīm, *Syr.* 170 D8
Haripur, *Pak.* 177 N11
Harirud, river, *Asia* 173 C17
Harkány, *Hung.* 149 N14
Harlan, *Iowa, U.S.* 105 P9
Harlan, *Ky., U.S.* 101 D19
Harlem, *Mont., U.S.* 106 B10
Harlingen, *Neth.* 146 G13
Harlingen, *Tex., U.S.* 103 W11
Harlowton, *Mont., U.S.* 106 D9
Harmancık, *Turk.* 168 E5
Harmony, *Minn., U.S.* 104 L13
Harnai, *Pak.* 177 R7
Harney Basin, *Oreg., U.S.* 108 J7
Harney Lake, *Oreg., U.S.* 108 J7
Harney Peak, *S. Dak., U.S.* 104 L1
Harnom Point, *N. Mariana Is., U.S.*
  216 E7
Härnösand, *Sw.* 141 H13
Har Nuur, *Mongolia* 180 D9
Haro, *Sp.* 144 C12
Haroldswick, *Scot., U.K.* 142 C12
Harpanahalli, *India* 179 N5
Harper, *Kans., U.S.* 105 V7
Harper, *Liberia* 200 J7
Harper Lake, *Calif., U.S.* 109 W9
Harpers Ferry, *W. Va., U.S.* 96 C12
Harput, *Turk.* 169 G14

Harqin, *China* 182 C9
Harqin Qi, *China* 182 B8
Ḩarrah, *Yemen* 172 Q12
Harrai, *India* 178 J7
Har Ramon, peak, *Israel* 171 Q4
Harran, *Turk.* 169 J13
Harray, Loch of, *Scot., U.K.* 142 G10
Harricana, river, *Que., Can.* 83 N18
Harriman, *Tenn., U.S.* 101 E18
Harrington, *Wash., U.S.* 108 C8
Harrington Harbour, *Que., Can.* 83 M22
Harrington Sound, *Bermuda, U.K.*
  120 B3
Harris, *Montserrat, U.K.* 121 B24
Harris, Lake, *Austral.* 210 J9
Harris, Sound of, *Scot., U.K.* 142 J6
Harrisburg, *Ark., U.S.* 100 F10
Harrisburg, *Ill., U.S.* 99 U6
Harrisburg, *Nebr., U.S.* 105 P1
Harrisburg, *Oreg., U.S.* 108 G3
Harrisburg, *Pa., U.S.* 94 P7
Harrison, *Ark., U.S.* 100 E7
Harrison, *Idaho, U.S.* 106 C3
Harrison, *Mich., U.S.* 98 K10
Harrison, *Nebr., U.S.* 104 M1
Harrison, Cape, *Nfld. & Lab., Can.*
  83 K22
Harrison Bay, *Alas., U.S.* 111 B16
Harrisonburg, *La., U.S.* 100 M9
Harrisonburg, *Va., U.S.* 96 D11
Harrison Point, *Barbados* 121 J18
Harrisonville, *Mo., U.S.* 105 T11
Harris Park, *Scot., U.K.* 142 J6
Harris Seamount, *Pac. Oc.* 238 D12
Harrisville, *Mich., U.S.* 98 J12
Harrodsburg, *Ky., U.S.* 101 C17
Harrogate, *Eng., U.K.* 143 R12
Harry S Truman Reservoir, *Mo., U.S.*
  105 T11
Harşit, river, *Turk.* 169 D13
Harstad, *Nor.* 140 D12
Hart, *Mich., U.S.* 98 K9
Hart, *Tex., U.S.* 102 H5
Hartford, *Ala., U.S.* 101 N17
Hartford, *Ark., U.S.* 100 G6
Hartford, *Conn., U.S.* 95 L13
Hartford, *Mich., U.S.* 99 N9
Hartford, *S. Dak., U.S.* 104 L8
Hartford, *Vt., U.S.* 95 H13
Hartford, *Wis., U.S.* 98 L6
Hartford City, *Ind., U.S.* 99 Q10
Hartington, *Nebr., U.S.* 105 N8
Hart Lake, *Oreg., U.S.* 108 K6
Hartland Point, *Eng., U.K.* 143 W9
Hartley, *Iowa, U.S.* 104 M9
Hartley, *Tex., U.S.* 102 F4
Hart Mountain, *Oreg., U.S.* 108 K6
Hartselle, *Ala., U.S.* 101 H15
Hartshorne, *Okla., U.S.* 102 H13
Hartsville, *S.C., U.S.* 96 K10
Hartsville, *Tenn., U.S.* 101 E16
Hartwell, *Ga., U.S.* 96 K6
Hartwell Lake, *Rep. of Georgia, S.C., U.S.*
  96 K7
Har Us Nuur, *Mongolia* 180 D9
Harut, river, *Afghan.* 177 P1
Harūz-e Bālā, *Iran* 173 F15
Harvard, *Ill., U.S.* 98 M6
Harvard, *Nebr., U.S.* 105 Q7
Harvest Home, *Qnsld., Austral.* 211 S13
Harvey, *N. Dak., U.S.* 104 F5
Harz, range, *Ger.* 148 E8
Ḩaşānah, *Yemen* 172 Q12
Hasan Dağı, *Turk.* 168 G9
Ḩasan Langī, *Iran* 173 H15
Hasa Plain, *Saudi Arabia* 166 H4
Hashaat, *Mongolia* 180 E12
Ḩāsik, *Oman* 173 N15
Hasil, island, *Indonesia* 189 J16
Hasilpur, *Pak.* 177 R10
Haskeir Island, *Scot., U.K.* 142 J6
Haskell, *Okla., U.S.* 102 F13
Haskell, *Tex., U.S.* 102 K8
Hassel Sound, *Nunavut, Can.* 83 C14
Hassi Messaoud, *Alg.* 196 C11
Hassi R'mel, *Alg.* 196 B11
Hässleholm, *Sw.* 141 N13
Hastings, *Barbados* 121 L19
Hastings, battlefield, *Eng., U.K.* 143 W15
Hastings, *Eng., U.K.* 143 W15
Hastings, *Mich., U.S.* 98 M10
Hastings, *Minn., U.S.* 104 K12
Hastings, *N.Z.* 213 L20
Hastings, *Nebr., U.S.* 105 Q6
Hasvik, *Nor.* 141 C13

Haswell, *Colo., U.S.* 107 N15
Hat *see* Teuaua, island, *Fr. Polynesia, Fr.*
  219 N23
Hataedo, islands, *S. Korea* 182 H12
Hatay (Antioch), *Turk.* 168 J11
Hatch, *N. Mex., U.S.* 107 V11
Hatches Creek, *N. Terr., Austral.* 211 S9
Hatchie, river, *Tenn., U.S.* 100 F12
Ḩaţeg, *Rom.* 152 E12
Hatgal, *Mongolia* 180 C11
Hatherleigh, *Eng., U.K.* 143 W9
Ḩāţibah, Ra's, *Saudi Arabia* 172 L6
Ha Tien, *Vietnam* 187 P11
Hatillo, *P.R., U.S.* 120 M2
Ha Tinh, *Vietnam* 186 J12
Hato Caves, *Neth. Antilles, Neth.* 121 P14
Hato Mayor, *Dom. Rep.* 117 M20
Ha Trung, *Vietnam* 186 H12
Hatteras, *N.C., U.S.* 96 H15
Hatteras, Cape, *N.C., U.S.* 96 H15
Hatteras Plain, *Atl. Oc.* 236 J4
Hattiesburg, *Miss., U.S.* 100 N12
Hatton, *N. Dak., U.S.* 104 F7
Hatunuru, *Indonesia* 189 K16
Hatutu, island, *Fr. Polynesia, Fr.* 215 H14
Hatvan, *Hung.* 149 L15
Haud, plateau, *Eth.* 199 G17
Haugesund, *Nor.* 140 L9
Haugsdorf, *Aust.* 148 J12
Haukeligrend, *Nor.* 140 L10
Haukipudas, *Fin.* 141 F15
Haukivesi, *Fin.* 141 H17
Haunanu, Pointe, *Fr. Polynesia, Fr.*
  219 M23
Hauola Place of Refuge, *Hawai'i, U.S.*
  112 B6
Haupt Kanal, *Liech.* 160 N2
Hauraki Gulf, *N.Z.* 213 J19
Hauser, *Oreg., U.S.* 108 J2
Haut, Isle au, *Me., U.S.* 95 G18
Hauteurs de Gâtine, *Fr.* 147 S6
Hauti, *Fr. Polynesia, Fr.* 219 K23
Hau'ula, *Hawai'i, U.S.* 112 D11
Havana *see* La Habana, *Cuba* 116 G6
Havana, *Fla., U.S.* 97 Q5
Havana, *Ill., U.S.* 99 Q4
Havannah, Canal de la, *New Caledonia,*
  Fr. 218 E9
Havant, *Eng., U.K.* 143 W13
Havasu, Lake, *Ariz., Calif., U.S.* 109 W13
Havel, river, *Ger.* 148 C10
Havelberg, *Ger.* 148 D9
Haveli, *Pak.* 177 R11
Havelock, *N.C., U.S.* 96 J14
Haveluloto, *Tonga* 218 H11
Haven, *Kans., U.S.* 105 U7
Haverfordwest, *Wales, U.K.* 143 V8
Haverhill, *Eng., U.K.* 143 U14
Haverhill, *Mass., U.S.* 95 J15
Haveri, *India* 179 N4
Haviland, *Kans., U.S.* 105 U6
Havířov, *Czech Rep.* 149 H14
Havlíčkův Brod, *Czech Rep.* 148 H12
Havre, *Mont., U.S.* 106 B9
Havre de Grace, *Md., U.S.* 96 B14
Havre-St.-Pierre, *Que., Can.* 83 M21
Havza, *Turk.* 168 D11
Hawai'i, island, *Hawai'i, U.S.* 113 L18
Hawai'i, *U.S.* 113 L17
Hawaiian Ridge, *Pac. Oc.* 238 G11
Hawai'i Belt Road, *Hawai'i, U.S.* 113 N20
Hawai'i Volcanoes National Park,
  Hawai'i, U.S. 113 N20
Hawarden, *Iowa, U.S.* 104 M8
Hawarden, *Wales, U.K.* 143 S10
Hawea, Lake, *N.Z.* 213 Q16
Hawera, *N.Z.* 213 L20
Hawesville, *Ky., U.S.* 101 C16
Hawick, *Scot., U.K.* 143 N11
Hawke Bay, *N.Z.* 213 L20
Hawker, *S. Aust., Austral.* 211 W10
Hawkeye Point, *Iowa, U.S.* 104 M9
Hawkinsville, *Ga., U.S.* 97 N6
Hawley, *Minn., U.S.* 104 G8
Hawthorne, *Nev., U.S.* 109 R8
Haxtun, *Colo., U.S.* 106 K15
Hay, river, *Alta., Can.* 82 J10
Hay, river, *N. Terr., Austral.* 211 U10
Hay, *N.S.W., Austral.* 211 Y12
Hayange, *Fr.* 147 N14
Hayes, *Jam.* 120 J9
Hayes, river, *Man., Can.* 83 L15
Hayes, *S. Dak., U.S.* 104 K4
Hayes, Mount, *Alas., U.S.* 111 G17

Hayes Center, *Nebr., U.S.* 105 Q4
Hayes Peninsula, *N. Amer.* 80 B7
Hayfork, *Calif., U.S.* 109 N3
Hayling Island, *Eng., U.K.* 143 W13
Haymā', *Oman* 173 M15
Haymana, *Turk.* 168 E8
Haynesville, *La., U.S.* 100 K7
Hayneville, *Ala., U.S.* 101 L15
Haynin, *Yemen* 172 P11
Hayrabolu, *Turk.* 168 C3
Ḩayr al Gharbī, Qaşr al, *Syr.* 170 H9
Ḩayr ash Sharqī, Qaşr al, *Syr.* 170 G11
Hay River, *N.W.T., Can.* 82 H11
Hays, *Kans., U.S.* 105 S5
Hays, *Mont., U.S.* 106 B10
Hay Springs, *Nebr., U.S.* 104 M2
Haysville, *Kans., U.S.* 105 U7
Haysyn, *Ukr.* 157 P5
Hayti, *Mo., U.S.* 105 W16
Hayvoron, *Ukr.* 157 Q5
Hayward, *Calif., U.S.* 109 S4
Hayward, *Wis., U.S.* 98 G3
Hazarajat, region, *Afghan.* 177 N6
Hazard, *Ky., U.S.* 101 C19
Hazar Gölü, *Turk.* 169 G14
Hazar Qadam, *Afghan.* 177 P6
Ḩazawzā', Sabkhat, *Saudi Arabia* 172 F6
Hazebrouck, *Fr.* 146 L10
Hazelton, *B.C., Can.* 82 J8
Hazelton, *N. Dak., U.S.* 104 H5
Hazen, *Ark., U.S.* 100 G9
Hazen, *N. Dak., U.S.* 104 F4
Hazen, *Nev., U.S.* 109 P7
Hazlehurst, *Ga., U.S.* 97 N7
Hazlehurst, *Miss., U.S.* 100 M11
Hazleton, *Pa., U.S.* 94 N8
Hazro, *Turk.* 169 G15
Healdsburg, *Calif., U.S.* 109 Q3
Healdton, *Okla., U.S.* 102 J11
Healy, *Alas., U.S.* 111 G17
Healy, *Kans., U.S.* 105 T4
Héani, Mont, *Fr. Polynesia, Fr.* 219 M20
Heard Island, *Antarctic Oc.* 245 G16
Hearne, *Tex., U.S.* 103 P12
Hearst, *Ont., Can.* 83 N17
Hearst Island, *Antarctica* 226 E5
Heart, river, *N. Dak., U.S.* 104 G4
Herat (Hirat), *Afghan.* 176 M2
Heath, Pointe, *Que., Can.* 83 M22
Heavener, *Okla., U.S.* 102 H14
Hebbronville, *Tex., U.S.* 103 U9
Heber, *Ariz., U.S.* 107 T8
Heber City, *Utah, U.S.* 106 L7
Heber Springs, *Ark., U.S.* 100 F9
Hebgen Lake, *Mont., U.S.* 106 F8
Hebi, *China* 182 G5
Hebrides, Sea of the, *Scot., U.K.* 142 L6
Hebron, *N. Dak., U.S.* 104 G3
Hebron, *Nebr., U.S.* 105 R7
Hebron *see* Al Khalīl, *W. Bank* 171 N5
Hecate Strait, *B.C., Can.* 82 K7
Hechi, *China* 181 N13
Hecho, *Sp.* 145 C14
Hechuan, *China* 180 L12
Hecla, *S. Dak., U.S.* 104 H7
Hecla, Cape, *Nunavut, Can.* 83 A16
Hectors River, *Jam.* 120 J11
Heddal, *Nor.* 140 L11
Hédé, *Fr.* 147 Q5
Hede *see* Sheyang, *China* 182 H9
Hede, *Sw.* 140 J12
He Devil Mountain, *Idaho, U.S.* 106 E3
Hedley, *Tex., U.S.* 102 H6
Hedo Misaki, *Japan* 185 Y2
Heel Point, *Wake I., U.S.* 216 F8
Heerenveen, *Neth.* 146 H13
Ḩefa (Haifa), *Israel* 170 K5
Hefei, *China* 182 K7
Hefeng, *China* 182 L2
Heflin, *Ala., U.S.* 101 J17
Hegang, *China* 181 C18
Hegura Jima, *Japan* 184 M10
Heicheng (Khara Khoto), ruin, *China*
  180 F11
Heide, *Ger.* 148 B7
Heidelberg, *Ger.* 148 H6
Heidelberg, *Miss., U.S.* 100 M12
Heidenheim, *Ger.* 148 J7
Heiderscheid, *Lux.* 160 H9
Heihe, *China* 181 B17
Heilbronn, *Ger.* 148 J7
Heilong Jiang (Amur), river, *China*
  181 A16
Heimaey, island, *Ice.* 140 G2
Heinerscheid, *Lux.* 160 G10

Heinola, *Fin.* 141 J16
Heishan, *China* 182 B10
Hejaz *see* Al Ḥijāz, region, *Saudi Arabia* 172 H6
Hejian, *China* 182 E6
Hejing, *China* 180 F7
Hekimhan, *Turk.* 168 F12
Hekla, peak, *Ice.* 140 F2
Hekou, *China* 180 P11
Helagsfjället, peak, *Sw.* 140 H12
Hele Islands, *Solomon Is.* 217 M16
Helena, *Ark., U.S.* 100 H10
Helena, *Ga., U.S.* 97 N7
Helena *see* Makroníssi, island, *Gr.* 155 K13
Helena, *Mont., U.S.* 106 D7
Helena, *Okla., U.S.* 102 E9
Helengili, island, *Maldives* 179 U3
Helen Island, *Palau* 214 G2
Helen Springs, *N. Terr., Austral.* 211 R8
Helgoländer Bucht, *Ger.* 148 B6
Helicon *see* Elikónas, peak, *Gr.* 154 H11
Hell, *Cayman Is., U.K.* 120 H1
Hell, *Nor.* 140 H11
Hell-Bourg, *Reunion, Fr.* 205 G16
Hellespont *see* Çanakkale Boğazı, strait, *Gr.* 155 E16
Hellevoetsluis, *Neth.* 146 J11
Hellín, *Sp.* 145 J13
Hellissandur, *Ice.* 140 E1
Hells Canyon, *Idaho, Oreg., U.S.* 108 F9
Hells Canyon Dam, *Idaho, Oreg., U.S.* 108 F10
Hells Canyon National Recreation Area, *Idaho, Oreg., U.S.* 108 E9
Hell-Ville *see* Andoany, *Madagascar* 203 D18
Helmand, river, *Afghan.* 177 P5
Helmand, river, *Afghan.* 177 R2
Helmsdale, *Scot., U.K.* 142 H10
Helong, *China* 182 B14
Helper, *Utah, U.S.* 106 M8
Helsingborg, *Sw.* 140 N12
Helsingfors *see* Helsinki, *Fin.* 141 J16
Helsinki (Helsingfors), *Fin.* 141 J16
Hemet, *Calif., U.S.* 109 X10
Hemingford, *Nebr., U.S.* 105 N2
Hempstead, *N.Y., U.S.* 94 N11
Hempstead, *Tex., U.S.* 103 Q13
Henashi Zaki, *Japan* 184 J12
Henbury, *N. Terr., Austral.* 211 U8
Hendaye, *Fr.* 147 X5
Hendek, *Turk.* 168 D6
Henderson, *Ky., U.S.* 101 C14
Henderson, *N.C., U.S.* 96 G12
Henderson, *Nev., U.S.* 109 U12
Henderson, *Tenn., U.S.* 101 F13
Henderson, *Tex., U.S.* 102 M14
Henderson Island, *Pac. Oc.* 215 L16
Henderson Seamount, *Pac. Oc.* 239 G16
Hendersonville, *N.C., U.S.* 96 J7
Hendersonville, *Tenn., U.S.* 101 E15
Hengchun, *Taiwan, China* 183 S9
Hengduan Shan, *China* 180 M10
Hengelo, *Neth.* 146 J14
Hengshan, *China* 182 E2
Hengshan, *China* 183 N4
Hengshui, *China* 182 E6
Hengxian, *China* 183 R1
Hengyang, *China* 183 N4
Heniches'k, *Ukr.* 157 S8
Henlopen, Cape, *Del., U.S.* 96 C15
Hennebont, *Fr.* 147 R4
Hennessey, *Okla., U.S.* 102 F10
Hennigsdorf, *Ger.* 148 D10
Henning, *Minn., U.S.* 104 H9
Henrietta, *Tex., U.S.* 102 J10
Henrietta, Ostrov, *Russ.* 159 C17
Henrietta Maria, Cape, *Ont., Can.* 83 L17
Henry, Cape, *Va., U.S.* 96 F14
Henryetta, *Okla., U.S.* 102 G12
Henry Kater Peninsula, *Nunavut, Can.* 83 F18
Henrys Fork, *Idaho, U.S.* 106 G7
Henslow, Cape, *Solomon Is.* 217 P19
Hentiyn Nuruu, range, *Mongolia* 181 C13
Heping, *China* 183 Q5
Heppner, *Oreg., U.S.* 108 F7
Hepu, *China* 183 S1
Hequ, *China* 182 D4
Heráklion *see* Iráklio, *Gr.* 155 Q15
Herald, Ostrov, *Russ.* 159 A19

Herald Cays, *Coral Sea Is. Terr., Austral.* 211 R14
Herbault, *Fr.* 147 R8
Herbert, river, *Austral.* 210 D13
Herbert, *Sask., Can.* 82 N11
Hercules Dome, *Antarctica* 226 J11
Herdman Seamount, *Atl. Oc.* 237 U13
Hereford, *Eng., U.K.* 143 U11
Hereford, *Tex., U.S.* 102 H4
Hereheretue, island, *Fr. Polynesia, Fr.* 219 G18
Herford, *Ger.* 148 E7
Herington, *Kans., U.S.* 105 T8
Herisau, *Switz.* 150 A4
Hérisson, *Fr.* 147 T10
Heritage Range, *Antarctica* 226 H8
Herkimer, *N.Y., U.S.* 94 J10
Herlacher, Cape, *Antarctica* 226 L6
Herlen, river, *Mongolia* 181 D14
Herm, island, *Ch. Is.* 143 Z11
Herman, *Minn., U.S.* 104 J9
Hermann, *Mo., U.S.* 105 T14
Hermannsburg, *N. Terr., Austral.* 211 T8
Hermansville, *Mich., U.S.* 98 G7
Hermanus, *S. Af.* 202 M7
Hermidale, *N.S.W., Austral.* 211 X13
Hermiston, *Oreg., U.S.* 108 E7
Hermit Islands, *P.N.G.* 213 B19
Hermleigh, *Tex., U.S.* 102 L6
Hermon, Mount, *Leb., Syr.* 170 J6
Hermosa, *S. Dak., U.S.* 104 L2
Hermosa, Punta, *Eq. Guinea* 204 L8
Hermosillo, *Mex.* 114 C7
Hernando, *Arg.* 132 K10
Hernando, *Miss., U.S.* 100 G11
Hernani, *Sp.* 145 B13
Herne, *Ger.* 148 E5
Herreid, *S. Dak., U.S.* 104 H5
Herrera, *Arg.* 132 H10
Herrera del Duque, *Sp.* 144 H9
Herrera de Pisuerga, *Sp.* 144 C10
Herrin, *Ill., U.S.* 99 U5
Herschel Island, *Yukon, Can.* 82 D9
Hershey, *Nebr., U.S.* 105 P4
Hersónissos Akrotírio, *Gr.* 155 P13
Hertford, *Eng., U.K.* 143 V14
Hertford, *N.C., U.S.* 96 G14
Hervás, *Sp.* 144 F8
Hervey Bay, *Austral.* 210 G15
Hervey Bay, *Qnsld., Austral.* 211 U15
Hervey Islands, *Cook Is., N.Z.* 214 K12
Herzberg, *Ger.* 148 E10
Herzberg, *Ger.* 148 E10
Hesar Range, *Afghan.* 176 M5
Heshui, *China* 182 F1
Hesperange, *Lux.* 160 K10
Hess Rise, *Pac. Oc.* 238 E9
Hettinger, *N. Dak., U.S.* 104 H2
Heuru, *Solomon Is.* 217 P20
Hexian, *China* 182 K8
Hexigten Qi (Jingpeng), *China* 182 A7
Heyuan, *China* 183 R5
Hezār, Kuh-e, *Iran* 173 F15
Heze, *China* 182 G6
Hezhou (Babu), *China* 183 Q3
Hialeah, *Fla., U.S.* 97 X10
Hiawatha, *Kans., U.S.* 105 R9
Hibbing, *Minn., U.S.* 104 F11
Hicacos, Peninsula de, *Cuba* 116 G7
Hickam Air Force Base, *Hawai'i, U.S.* 112 E11
Hickman, *Ky., U.S.* 100 E12
Hickman, *Arg.* 132 E10
Hickory, *N.C., U.S.* 96 H8
Hicks Bay, *N.Z.* 213 K20
Hicksville, *Ohio, U.S.* 99 P11
Hico, *Tex., U.S.* 102 M10
Hidaka Sammyaku, range, *Japan* 184 G14
Hidalgo del Parral, *Mex.* 114 E9
Hienghène, *New Caledonia, Fr.* 218 C7
Hienghène, Baie de, *New Caledonia, Fr.* 218 C7
Hierro (Ferro), island, *Canary Is.* 204 R3
Higgins, *Tex., U.S.* 102 F7
Higgins Lake, *Mich., U.S.* 98 J10
Higginsville, *Mo., U.S.* 105 S11
High Atlas, range, *Mor.* 194 D3
High Cay, *Bahamas* 120 F11
High Cliff Point, *Grenada* 121 J23
Highgate, *Jam.* 120 H10
High Island, *Tex., U.S.* 103 R15
Highland, *Ill., U.S.* 99 T5
Highland Park, *Ill., U.S.* 99 N7
Highlands, plateau, *Scot., U.K.* 142 K8
High Level, *Alta., Can.* 82 J10
Highmore, *S. Dak., U.S.* 104 K5

High Plains, *U.S.* 84 J10
High Point, *Bermuda, U.K.* 120 C1
High Point, *N.C., U.S.* 96 H10
High Point, *N.J., U.S.* 94 M10
High Red Rock, *Norfolk I., Austral.* 217 G20
High Rock, *Bahamas* 116 C10
High Rock, *Bahamas* 120 E3
High Springs, *Fla., U.S.* 97 R8
High Willhays, peak, *Eng., U.K.* 143 X9
Higüero, Punta, *P.R., U.S.* 117 M22
Higüey, *Dom. Rep.* 117 M20
Hiiumaa, island, *Est.* 141 L15
Híjar, *Sp.* 145 E14
Ḥijārah, Ṣaḥrā al, *Iraq* 172 F9
Hijāz, Jabal al, *Saudi Arabia* 172 M8
Hikari, *Japan* 185 R5
Hikiau Heiau, *Hawai'i, U.S.* 113 N18
Hiko, *Nev., U.S.* 109 S12
Hikueru, island, *Fr. Polynesia, Fr.* 219 F19
Hikurangi, peak, *N.Z.* 213 K20
Hikutavake, *Niue, N.Z.* 219 B20
Hilāl, Ras al, *Lib.* 194 D7
Hildesheim, *Ger.* 148 E7
Hilina Pali, *Hawai'i, U.S.* 113 N20
Hillaby, Mount, *Barbados* 121 K19
Hillary Coast, *Antarctica* 227 N14
Hill City, *Kans., U.S.* 105 S5
Hill City, *Minn., U.S.* 104 G11
Hill City, *S. Dak., U.S.* 104 L1
Hill Country, *Tex., U.S.* 103 Q8
Hillman, *Mich., U.S.* 98 H11
Hillsboro, *Ill., U.S.* 99 S5
Hillsboro, *Kans., U.S.* 105 T8
Hillsboro, *N. Dak., U.S.* 104 F8
Hillsboro, *N. Mex., U.S.* 107 U11
Hillsboro, *Ohio, U.S.* 99 S12
Hillsboro, *Oreg., U.S.* 108 F3
Hillsboro, *Tex., U.S.* 102 M11
Hillsborough, *Grenada* 119 M17
Hillsborough, *N. Ire., U.K.* 143 Q7
Hillsborough Bay, *Trinidad & Tobago* 121 N18
Hillsdale, *Mich., U.S.* 99 N11
Hillside, *W. Aust., Austral.* 211 T3
Hillston, *N.S.W., Austral.* 211 X12
Hillsville, *Va., U.S.* 96 G9
Hillswick, *Scot., U.K.* 142 D11
Hilo, region, *Hawai'i, U.S.* 113 L21
Hilo, *Hawai'i, U.S.* 113 M21
Hilo Bay, *Hawai'i, U.S.* 113 L21
Hilton Head Island, *S.C., U.S.* 97 N9
Hilvan, *Turk.* 169 H13
Himadítida, Límni, *Gr.* 154 C9
Himalaya, range, *Asia* 166 H8
Ḥimar, Wādī al, *Syr.* 170 D12
Himatnagar, *India* 178 H3
Himeji, *Japan* 185 Q8
Ḥimṣ (Homs), *Syr.* 170 G8
Hinako, Kepulauan, *Indonesia* 188 J4
Hinche, *Haiti* 117 L17
Hinchinbrook Island, *Alas., U.S.* 111 K18
Hinchinbrook Island, *Austral.* 210 D13
Hinckley, *Minn., U.S.* 104 H12
Hindaun, *India* 178 G6
Hindmarsh, Lake, *Austral.* 210 L11
Hindu Kush, range, *Afghan., Pak.* 176 L8
Hines, *Oreg., U.S.* 108 J7
Hines Creek, *Alta., Can.* 82 K10
Hinesville, *Ga., U.S.* 97 N8
Hinganghat, *India* 178 K6
Hingol, river, *Pak.* 177 V4
Hingorja, *Pak.* 177 U7
Hinidan, *Pak.* 177 V6
Hınıs, *Turk.* 169 F16
Hinnøya, island, *Nor.* 140 D12
Hinoemata, *Japan* 185 N12
Hinomi Saki, *Japan* 185 P6
Hinthada, *Myanmar* 186 K5
Hinton, *Okla., U.S.* 102 G9
Hinton, *W. Va., U.S.* 96 E9
Híos (Chios), island, *Gr.* 155 H16
Híos (Chios), *Gr.* 155 H16
Hippolytushoef, *Neth.* 146 H12
Hirado, *Japan* 185 R3
Hirado Shima, *Japan* 185 R3
Hiranai, *Japan* 184 J13
Hira Se, island, *Japan* 185 U4
Hirat *see* Heart, *Afghan.* 176 M2
Hirata, *Japan* 185 P6
Hirfanlı Baraji, *Turk.* 168 F9
Hiroo, *Japan* 184 G15
Hirosaki, *Japan* 184 J12
Hiroshima, *Japan* 185 Q6

Hirson, *Fr.* 146 M12
Hîrṣova, *Rom.* 153 F17
Hisarönü, *Turk.* 168 C7
Ḥismá, desert, *Jordan, Saudi Arabia* 171 S6
Ḥismá, region, *Saudi Arabia* 172 G5
Hispaniola, island, *N. Amer.* 80 N10
Ḥisyah, *Syr.* 170 H8
Hita, *Japan* 185 R5
Hitachi, *Japan* 185 N13
Hitadu, island, *Maldives* 179 W3
Hitadu, island, *Maldives* 179 X3
Hiti, island, *Fr. Polynesia, Fr.* 219 E18
Hitiaa, *Fr. Polynesia, Fr.* 219 N17
Hitoyoshi, *Japan* 185 S4
Hitra, island, *Nor.* 140 H10
Hiu, island, *Vanuatu* 218 A1
Hiva Oa, island, *Fr. Polynesia, Fr.* 215 H15
Hiwasa, *Japan* 185 R8
Hiwassee, river, *Tenn., U.S.* 101 G18
Hizan, *Turk.* 169 G17
Hjälmaren, lake, *Sw.* 141 L13
Hjørring, *Den.* 140 M11
Hkakabo Razi, peak, *Myanmar* 186 C7
Hlohovec, *Slovakia* 149 K14
Hlukhiv, *Ukr.* 156 M7
Hlybokaye, *Belarus* 156 J5
Hněvkovice, *Czech Rep.* 148 H11
Hnúšt'a, *Slovakia* 149 J15
Hoàng Sa *see* Xisha Qundao, islands, *China* 188 B10
Hoa Binh, *Vietnam* 186 H11
Hoai An, *Vietnam* 186 M14
Ho, *China* 183 R5
Hoanib, river, *Namibia* 202 G5
Hoare Bay, *Nunavut, Can.* 83 G19
Hobart, *Ind., U.S.* 99 P8
Hobart, *Okla., U.S.* 102 H8
Hobart, *Tas., Austral.* 211 Z16
Hobbs, *N. Mex., U.S.* 107 U15
Hobbs, Mount, *Austral.* 210 M16
Hobbs Coast, *Antarctica* 226 M8
Hobe Sound, *Fla., U.S.* 97 V10
Hoboksar, *China* 180 D7
Hobro, *Den.* 140 N11
Hobucken, *N.C., U.S.* 96 H14
Hobyo, *Somalia* 199 H18
Ho Chi Minh City (Saigon), *Vietnam* 187 P12
Hodge, *La., U.S.* 100 L8
Hodgenville, *Ky., U.S.* 101 C16
Hodgson, river, *Austral.* 210 C9
Hodh, region, *Mauritania* 194 G2
Hódmezővásárhely, *Hung.* 149 M16
Hodonín, *Czech Rep.* 149 J13
Hödrögö, *Mongolia* 180 C10
Hoedic, Île, *Fr.* 147 R4
Hoedspruit, *S. Af.* 202 J11
Hoeryŏng, *N. Korea* 182 B14
Hof, *Ger.* 148 G9
Höfðakaupstaður, *Ice.* 140 E3
Hoffman, *Minn., U.S.* 104 H9
Höfn, *Ice.* 140 G4
Hofsjökull, glacier, *Ice.* 140 F3
Hogansville, *Ga., U.S.* 96 M4
Hog Cay, *Bahamas* 120 F10
Hogfish Cut, *Bermuda, U.K.* 120 C1
Hoggar *see* Ahaggar, range, *Alg.* 196 E11
Hog Island, *Grenada* 121 L22
Hog Island, *Va., U.S.* 96 E15
Hohenems, *Aust.* 148 L7
Hohenwald, *Tenn., U.S.* 101 F14
Hohe Tauern, *Aust.* 148 M9
Hohhot, *China* 182 C4
Hohonu, island, *Fr. Polynesia, Fr.* 219 K17
Hoh Xil Shan, *China* 180 J7
Hoi An, *Vietnam* 186 L13
Hoisington, *Kans., U.S.* 105 T6
Hokatu, *Fr. Polynesia, Fr.* 219 N23
Hokitika, *N.Z.* 213 N16
Hokkaidō, island, *Japan* 184 G15
Hōkūkano Heiau, *Hawai'i, U.S.* 113 F15
Hokula, *Tonga* 218 P6
Hola Prystan', *Ukr.* 157 R7
Holbrook, *Ariz., U.S.* 107 S8
Holbrook, *Idaho, U.S.* 106 J6
Holden, *Mo., U.S.* 105 T11
Holden, *Utah, U.S.* 106 M7
Holdenville, *Okla., U.S.* 102 G12
Holdrege, *Nebr., U.S.* 105 Q5
Hole in the Wall, cape, *Bahamas* 120 C6
Hōlei Pali, *Hawai'i, U.S.* 113 N21
Holetown, *Barbados* 121 K18
Holguín, *Cuba* 116 J12

Holland, *Mich., U.S.* 98 M9
Hollandale, *Miss., U.S.* 100 K10
Holland Bay, *Jam.* 120 J11
Hollandsbird Island, *Namibia* 202 J6
Hollick-Kenyon Plateau, *Antarctica* 226 K8
Hollidaysburg, *Pa., U.S.* 94 N5
Hollis, *Okla., U.S.* 102 H7
Hollister, *Calif., U.S.* 109 T4
Hollum, *Neth.* 146 G13
Holly Hill, *S.C., U.S.* 96 L10
Holly Ridge, *N.C., U.S.* 96 J13
Holly Springs, *Miss., U.S.* 100 G12
Hollywood, *Calif., U.S.* 109 X8
Hollywood, *Fla., U.S.* 97 W10
Holman, *N.W.T., Can.* 82 E12
Hólmavík, *Ice.* 140 E2
Holme Bay, *Antarctica* 227 E20
Holmes Rock, *Bahamas* 120 E1
Holonga, *Tonga* 218 L12
Holopaw, *Fla., U.S.* 97 T9
Ḥolot Ḥaluza, desert, *Israel* 171 N4
Holstebro, *Den.* 140 N11
Holstein, *Iowa, U.S.* 105 N9
Holston, river, *Tenn., U.S.* 101 E20
Holsworthy, *Eng., U.K.* 143 W9
Holt, *Ala., U.S.* 101 K14
Holton, *Kans., U.S.* 105 S9
Holtville, *Calif., U.S.* 109 Z12
Hōlualoa, *Hawai'i, U.S.* 113 M18
Hōlua Slide, *Hawai'i, U.S.* 113 M18
Holy Cross, *Alas., U.S.* 111 H13
Holyhead (Caergybi), *Wales, U.K.* 143 S9
Holy Island, *Wales, U.K.* 143 S9
Holy Island (Lindisfarne), *Eng., U.K.* 143 N12
Holyoke, *Colo., U.S.* 106 L15
Holyoke, *Mass., U.S.* 95 K13
Hombetsu, *Japan* 184 F15
Hombori, *Mali* 196 H5
Homburg, *Ger.* 148 H5
Home Bay, *Banaba, Kiribati* 217 E20
Home Bay, *Nunavut, Can.* 83 F18
Homedale, *Idaho, U.S.* 106 G3
Homer, *Alas., U.S.* 111 K16
Homer, *La., U.S.* 100 K7
Homer, *Mich., U.S.* 99 N11
Homer, *N.Y., U.S.* 94 K8
Homerville, *Ga., U.S.* 97 Q7
Homestead, *Fla., U.S.* 97 X10
Homestead National Monument of America, *Nebr., U.S.* 105 R8
Homewood, *Ala., U.S.* 101 J15
Hominy, *Okla., U.S.* 102 E12
Hommalinn, *Myanmar* 186 E5
Homnabad, *India* 178 M5
Homo Bay, *Vanuatu* 218 D3
Homosassa Springs, *Fla., U.S.* 97 T7
Homs *see* Ḥimṣ, *Syr.* 170 G8
Homyel', *Belarus* 156 M6
Hōnaunau, *Hawai'i, U.S.* 113 N18
Honavar, *India* 179 P4
Honaz, *Turk.* 168 G5
Honda, *Col.* 128 E5
Hondo, *Japan* 185 S4
Hondo, *N. Mex., U.S.* 107 U13
Hondo, *Tex., U.S.* 103 R8
Honduras, *N. Amer.* 81 P20
Honduras, Gulf of, *Belize, Guatemala* 115 K17
Honea Path, *S.C., U.S.* 96 K7
Hønefoss, *Nor.* 140 K11
Honesdale, *Pa., U.S.* 94 L9
Honey Grove, *Tex., U.S.* 102 K13
Honey Lake, *Calif., U.S.* 109 N6
Honeyville, *Utah, U.S.* 106 K7
Hong (Red), river, *Vietnam* 186 G11
Hong'an, *China* 182 K5
Hong Gai, *Vietnam* 186 H13
Hong Hu, *China* 182 L4
Honghu, *China* 182 L4
Hongjiang, *China* 183 N2
Hong Kong (Xianggang), *China* 183 S5
Hongliuyuan, *China* 180 G9
Hongor, *Mongolia* 181 E14
Hongseong, *S. Korea* 182 F13
Hongshui, river, *China* 183 Q1
Hongtong, *China* 182 F4
Hongū, *Japan* 185 R9
Hongwŏn, *N. Korea* 182 C13
Hongze Hu, *China* 182 J8
Honiara, *Solomon Is.* 217 N18
Honiara, *Solomon Is.* 214 H6
Honikulu, Passe, *Wallis & Futuna, Fr.* 218 C11

Honiton, *Eng., U.K.* **143** W10
Honjō, *Japan* **184** K12
Honokaʻa, *Hawaiʻi, U.S.* **113** K20
Honokahua, *Hawaiʻi, U.S.* **113** F16
Honokōwai, *Hawaiʻi, U.S.* **113** G15
Honolulu, *Hawaiʻi, U.S.* **112** E11
Honomanū Bay, *Hawaiʻi, U.S.* **113** G17
Honomū, *Hawaiʻi, U.S.* **113** L21
Hon Quan, *Vietnam* **187** P12
Honshū, *island, Japan* **185** P5
Honuʻapo Bay, *Hawaiʻi, U.S.* **113** P20
Hood *see* Española, Isla, *island, Ecua.*
  128 R10
Hood, Mount, *Oreg., U.S.* **108** F4
Hood River, *Oreg., U.S.* **108** E5
Hoodsport, *Wash., U.S.* **108** C3
Hoogeveen, *Neth.* **146** H14
Hoʻokena, *Hawaiʻi, U.S.* **113** N18
Hooker, *Okla., U.S.* **102** E6
Hook Head, *Ire.* **143** U6
Hoʻolehua, *Hawaiʻi, U.S.* **113** F14
Hoonah, *Alas., U.S.* **111** L22
Hooper, *Cape, Nunavut, Can.* **83** F18
Hooper Bay, *Alas., U.S.* **110** H11
Hoopeston, *Ill., U.S.* **99** Q7
Hoorn, *Neth.* **146** H12
Hoover, *Ala., U.S.* **101** J15
Hoover Dam, *Ariz., Nev., U.S.* **109** U12
Hopa, *Turk.* **169** C16
Hope, *Ark., U.S.* **100** J7
Hope, *N. Dak., U.S.* **104** G7
Hope, Cape, *Nunavut, Can.* **82** F12
Hope, Lake, *Austral.* **210** K4
Hope, Point, *Alas., U.S.* **84** M2
Hope Bay, *Jam.* **120** H10
Hopedale, *Nfld. & Lab., Can.* **83** K21
Hopelchén, *Mex.* **115** J16
Hope Mills, *N.C., U.S.* **96** J11
Hope Point, *Myanmar* **186** L7
Hopetoun, *W. Aust., Austral.* **211** Y4
Hope Town, *Bahamas* **120** B7
Hopetown, *S. Af.* **202** L9
Hopewell, *Va., U.S.* **96** F13
Hopewell Culture National Historic
  Park, *Ohio, U.S.* **99** S13
Hopewell Islands, *Nunavut, Can.* **83** K17
Hopkins, Mount, *Ariz., U.S.* **107** W8
Hopkinsville, *Ky., U.S.* **101** D14
Hoquiam, *Wash., U.S.* **108** D2
Horasan, *Turk.* **169** E16
Horgos, *Serb. & Mont.* **152** D9
Horicon, *Wis., U.S.* **98** L6
Horinger, *China* **182** C4
Horki, *Belarus* **156** K6
Horlick Mountains, *Antarctica* **226** J11
Horlivka, *Ukr.* **157** Q10
Ḥormak, *Iran* **173** F17
Hormigueros, *P.R., U.S.* **120** N1
Hormuz, Strait of, *Iran, Oman* **173** H15
Horn, Cape *see* Hornos, Cabo de, *Chile*
  133 Y9
Hornavan, *lake, Sw.* **141** F13
Hornbeck, *La., U.S.* **100** M7
Hornbrook, *Calif., U.S.* **108** L3
Hornby Hill, *Nunavut, Can.* **82** F11
Horne, Îles de, *Pac. Oc.* **214** J9
Hornell, *N.Y., U.S.* **94** K6
Horn Island, *Miss., U.S.* **101** P13
Hornos, Cabo de (Cape Horn), *Chile*
  133 Y9
Horodnya, *Ukr.* **156** M6
Horodyshche, *Ukr.* **157** P6
Horqin Zuoyi Houqi, *China* **182** A10
Horqueta, *Parag.* **132** M10
Horse Cave, *Ky., U.S.* **101** D16
Horse Creek, *Wyo., U.S.* **106** K13
Horsehead Lake, *N. Dak., U.S.* **104** G5
Horseheads, *N.Y., U.S.* **94** K7
Horse Mountain, *N. Mex., U.S.* **107** T10
Horseshoe Beach, *Fla., U.S.* **97** S6
Horseshoe Bend, *Ark., U.S.* **100** E9
Horseshoe Canyon, *Utah, U.S.* **107** N8
Horsham, *Eng., U.K.* **143** W14
Horsham, *Vic., Austral.* **211** Y11
Horta, *Azores* **144** P3
Horten, *Nor.* **140** L11
Horton, *Kans., U.S.* **105** R9
Horton, *river, N.W.T., Can.* **82** E11
Horvat ʻAvedat (Eboda), *Israel* **171** P5
Hoscheid, *Lux.* **160** H10
Hosdrug, *India* **179** Q4
Hoshab, *Pak.* **177** V3
Hoshangabad, *India* **178** J6
Hosingen, *Lux.* **160** H10
Hosmer, *S. Dak., U.S.* **104** J5

Hoste, Isla, *Chile* **133** Y9
Hosur, *India* **179** Q6
Hot, *Thai.* **186** K7
Hotan, *river, China* **180** F5
Hotan, *China* **180** G5
Hotchkiss, *Colo., U.S.* **107** N11
Hotel de Paris, *Monaco* **161** D22
Hotel Hermitage, *Monaco* **161** D21
Hotel Métropole, *Monaco* **161** C22
Hotevilla, *Ariz., U.S.* **107** R8
Hot Springs, *Ark., U.S.* **100** H7
Hot Springs, *Mont., U.S.* **106** C5
Hot Springs, *S. Dak., U.S.* **104** L1
Hot Springs, *Va., U.S.* **96** E10
Hot Springs National Park, *Ark., U.S.*
  100 H7
Hotspur Seamount, *Atl. Oc.* **237** Q8
Hot Sulphur Springs, *Colo., U.S.* **106** L12
Hottah Lake, *N.W.T., Can.* **82** G11
Hotte, Massif de la, *Haiti* **117** M15
Hottentot Bay, *Namibia* **202** J6
Houaïlou, *New Caledonia, Fr.* **218** D7
Houat, Île, *Fr.* **147** R4
Houayxay, *Laos* **186** H9
Houffalize, *Belg.* **146** M13
Houghton, *Mich., U.S.* **98** E6
Houlton, *Me., U.S.* **95** C18
Houma, *China* **182** G3
Houma, *La., U.S.* **100** Q10
Houma, *Tonga* **218** J11
Houma Toloa, *cape, Tonga* **218** J11
Hourtin, *Fr.* **147** V6
Houston, *Minn., U.S.* **104** L13
Houston, *Miss., U.S.* **100** J12
Houston, *Mo., U.S.* **105** U13
Houston, *Tex., U.S.* **103** Q14
Houtman Abrolhos, *islands, Austral.*
  210 J1
Hovd (Dund-Us), *Mongolia* **180** D9
Hoven, *S. Dak., U.S.* **104** J5
Hovenweep National Monument, *Utah,*
  U.S. **107** P9
Hövsgöl, *Mongolia* **181** E13
Hövsgöl Nuur, *Mongolia* **180** C11
Howar, Wadi, *Sudan* **198** D11
Howard, *Kans., U.S.* **105** U9
Howard, *S. Dak., U.S.* **104** L7
Howard City, *Mich., U.S.* **98** L10
Howard Lake, *N.W.T., Can.* **82** H13
Howe, *Idaho, U.S.* **106** G6
Howe, Cape, *Austral.* **210** M14
Howe, Point, *Norfolk I., Austral.* **217** F20
Howland, *Me., U.S.* **95** E17
Howland Island, *Pac. Oc.* **214** G9
Ho Xa, *Vietnam* **186** M11
Hoxie, *Ark., U.S.* **100** E10
Hoxie, *Kans., U.S.* **105** S4
Hoy, *island, Scot., U.K.* **142** G10
Høyanger, *Nor.* **140** K10
Hoyerswerda, *Ger.* **148** F11
Hoyt Lakes, *Minn., U.S.* **104** F12
Hozat, *Turk.* **169** F14
Hpa-an, *Myanmar* **186** K7
Hradec Králové, *Czech Rep.* **148** G12
Hrazdan, *river, Arm.* **169** D18
Hrebenne, *Pol.* **149** G18
Hríssi, *island, Gr.* **155** R16
Hrissoúpoli, *Gr.* **155** C14
Hristianí, *island, Gr.* **155** N15
Hrodna, *Belarus* **156** K3
Hron, *river, Slovakia* **149** J15
Hrubieszów, *Pol.* **149** F18
Hsi-hseng, *Myanmar* **186** H7
Hsinchu, *Taiwan, China* **183** Q9
Hsinying, *Taiwan, China* **183** R9
Hsipaw, *Myanmar* **186** G7
Huachi, *China* **182** F1
Huacho, *Peru* **130** H3
Huade, *China* **182** B5
Huadian, *China* **182** A13
Hua Hin, *Thai.* **187** N8
Huahine, *island, Fr. Polynesia, Fr.*
  219 E15
Huahine, *island, Fr. Polynesia, Fr.*
  215 J13
Huahine, *Fr. Polynesia, Fr.* **219** K20
Huahine Iti, *island, Fr. Polynesia, Fr.*
  219 H14
Huahine Nui, *island, Fr. Polynesia, Fr.*
  219 G14
Huaibei, *China* **182** H7
Huaibin, *China* **181** D17
Huaiji, *China* **183** R3
Huailai, *China* **182** C6

Huainan, *China* **182** J7
Huaining, *China* **182** L7
Huairen, *China* **182** D5
Huai Yang, *Thai.* **187** P8
Huaiyin, *China* **182** J8
Huajuapan de León, *Mex.* **114** K12
Hualāli, *peak, Hawaiʻi, U.S.* **113** M18
Hualapai Peak, *Ariz., U.S.* **107** S5
Hualfín, *Arg.* **132** G8
Hualien, *Taiwan, China* **183** R10
Huallaga, *river, Peru* **130** F3
Huambo, *Angola* **202** E2
Huancané, *Peru* **130** J6
Huancavelica, *Peru* **130** H4
Huancayo, *Peru* **130** H4
Huang (Yellow), *river, China* **181** G13
Huangchuan, *China* **182** K6
Huanggang, *China* **182** L5
Huanggangliang, *peak, China* **182** A7
Huanghua, *China* **182** E7
Huangling, *China* **182** G2
Huangliu, *China* **183** U1
Huangnihe, *China* **182** A13
Huangquqiao, *China* **182** D1
Huangshan, *China* **182** M8
Huangshi, *China* **182** L5
Huangxian, *China* **182** E9
Huangyan, *China* **182** M10
Huanren, *China* **182** C12
Huanta, *Peru* **130** H4
Huantai, *China* **182** F8
Huánuco, *Peru* **130** G3
Huanxian, *China* **182** F1
Huara, *Chile* **132** K4
Huaral, *Peru* **130** H3
Huaraz, *Peru* **130** G3
Huarmey, *Peru* **130** G3
Huarong, *China* **182** L4
Huascarán, *Nevado, S. Amer.* **126** F2
Huasco, *Chile* **132** H6
Huatabampo, *Mex.* **114** E7
Huaura, *Peru* **130** H3
Huaxian, *China* **182** G5
Huayuan, *China* **182** M2
Huazhou, *China* **183** S2
Hubbard, *Tex., U.S.* **102** M12
Hubbard Lake, *Mich., U.S.* **98** J12
Hubbell Trading Post National Historic
  Site, *Ariz., U.S.* **107** R9
Hubli, *India* **179** N4
Hudiksvall, *Sw.* **141** J13
Hudson, *Fla., U.S.* **97** T7
Hudson, *Mich., U.S.* **99** N11
Hudson, *river, N.Y., U.S.* **94** L12
Hudson, *N.Y., U.S.* **94** K11
Hudson Bay, *Can.* **83** J14
Hudson Bay, *Sask., Can.* **83** M13
Hudson Canyon, *Atl. Oc.* **236** H4
Hudson Strait, *Nunavut, Can.* **83** H18
Hue, *Vietnam* **186** L13
Huʻehuʻe, *Hawaiʻi, U.S.* **113** L18
Huehuetenango, *Guatemala* **115** L15
Huelma, *Sp.* **144** K11
Huelva, *Sp.* **144** L7
Huerfano, *river, Colo., U.S.* **107** P13
Huesca, *Sp.* **145** D14
Huéscar, *Sp.* **144** K12
Huevos Monos, *island, Trinidad &*
  Tobago **121** P21
Huff, *N. Dak., U.S.* **104** G4
Hughenden, *Qnsld., Austral.* **211** S12
Hughes, *Alas., U.S.* **111** F15
Hughes, *Ark., U.S.* **100** G11
Hughes, *S. Aust., Austral.* **211** W7
Hughes Bay, *Antarctica* **226** D4
Hugli, *river, India* **178** J11
Hugo, *Okla., U.S.* **102** J13
Hugon, Île, *New Caledonia, Fr.* **218** D8
Hugoton, *Kans., U.S.* **105** V3
Huiʻan, *China* **183** Q8
Huichang, *China* **183** Q6
Hŭich'ŏn, *N. Korea* **182** C12
Huilai, *China* **183** R6
Huíla Plateau, *Angola* **194** M6
Huimin, *China* **182** F7
Huinan, *China* **182** B12
Huinca Renancó, *Arg.* **132** L10
Huitong, *China* **183** N2
Huîtres, Baie aux, *Mauritius* **205** J20
Huize, *China* **180** N11
Huizhou, *China* **183** R5
Hukawng Valley, *Myanmar* **186** D6
Hulan, *China* **181** D17
Ḥulayfāʼ, *Saudi Arabia* **172** H7
Hulbert, *Mich., U.S.* **98** F10

Hulett, *Wyo., U.S.* **106** F13
Hull, *Ill., U.S.* **99** R3
Hull Bay, *Virgin Islands, U.S.* **120** M9
Hulst, *Neth.* **146** K11
Hulu, *river, China* **182** F2
Huludao (Jinxi), *China* **182** C9
Hulun Nur, *China* **181** C15
Hulyaypole, *Ukr.* **157** Q9
Huma, *river, China* **181** A16
Huma, *China* **181** A16
Humacao, *P.R., U.S.* **120** N5
Humahuaca, *Arg.* **132** E9
Humaitá, *Braz.* **130** F8
Humansdorp, *S. Af.* **202** M9
Humansville, *Mo., U.S.* **105** U11
Ḥumar, *U.A.E.* **173** K14
Humber, *river, Eng., U.K.* **143** R13
Humble, *Tex., U.S.* **103** Q14
Humboldt, *Iowa, U.S.* **104** M11
Humboldt, *Kans., U.S.* **105** U10
Humboldt, *Nebr., U.S.* **105** R9
Humboldt, *river, Nev., U.S.* **108** M9
Humboldt, *Sask., Can.* **82** M12
Humboldt, *Tenn., U.S.* **100** F12
Humboldt Bay, *Calif., U.S.* **108** M1
Hümedān, *Iran* **173** J14
Humenné, *Slovakia* **149** J17
Humphreys Peak, *Ariz., U.S.* **107** S7
Humphrys Bay, *Antigua & Barbuda*
  121 A20
Humpty Doo, *N. Terr., Austral.* **211** P7
Humuʻula Saddle, *Hawaiʻi, U.S.* **113** M20
Hūn, *Lib.* **197** D14
Húnaflói, *bay, Ice.* **140** E2
Hunchun, *China* **182** A15
Hunedoara, *Rom.* **152** D12
Hunga, *island, Tonga* **218** L11
Hunga Haʻapai, *island, Tonga* **218** R5
Hunga Tonga, *island, Tonga* **218** R5
Hungary, *Eur.* **139** V8
Hungerford, *N.S.W., Austral.* **211** V12
Hŭngnam, *N. Korea* **182** D13
Hungry Bay, *Bermuda, U.K.* **120** B2
Hungry Horse Reservoir, *Mont., U.S.*
  106 B6
Hungund, *India* **179** N5
Huns Mountains, *Namibia* **194** Q6
Hunsrück, *range, Ger.* **160** K12
Hunstanton, *Eng., U.K.* **143** S14
Hunsur, *India* **179** Q5
Hunt, *Mongolia* **180** D10
Hunter, *N. Dak., U.S.* **104** G8
Hunter, *island, Vanuatu* **214** K8
Hunter, Cape, *Solomon Is.* **217** P18
Hunter Islands, *Tas., Austral.* **211** Y15
Hunters, *Bahamas* **120** F2
Huntingburg, *Ind., U.S.* **99** T8
Huntingdon, *Pa., U.S.* **94** N6
Huntingdon, *Tenn., U.S.* **101** E13
Huntington, *Ind., U.S.* **99** Q10
Huntington, *Oreg., U.S.* **108** G9
Huntington, *Tex., U.S.* **103** N15
Huntington, *Utah, U.S.* **106** M8
Huntington, *W. Va., U.S.* **96** D7
Huntington Beach, *Calif., U.S.* **109** X8
Huntly, *N.Z.* **213** K19
Huntly, *Scot., U.K.* **142** J10
Huntsville, *Ala., U.S.* **101** G15
Huntsville, *Ark., U.S.* **100** E7
Huntsville, *Mo., U.S.* **105** S12
Huntsville, *Tex., U.S.* **103** P13
Hunucmá, *Mex.* **115** H16
Hunyuan, *China* **182** D5
Hunza, *region, Pak.* **176** K12
Huocheng, *China* **180** E6
Huolu, *China* **182** E5
Huoqiu, *China* **182** J6
Huoshan, *China* **182** K6
Huoxian, *China* **182** F4
Hupo, *S. Korea* **182** F14
Hurdiyo, *Somalia* **199** F18
Hure Qi, *China* **182** B10
Hurghada, *Egypt* **197** D19
Hurley, *Wis., U.S.* **98** F4
Hurley, *N. Mex., U.S.* **107** T4
Huron, *S. Dak., U.S.* **104** K7
Huron, Lake, *Can., U.S.* **85** D17
Huron Mountain, *Mich., U.S.* **98** E7
Hurtsboro, *Ala., U.S.* **101** L17
Húsavík, *Ice.* **140** E3

Huşi, *Rom.* **153** C17
Huslia, *Alas., U.S.* **111** F14
Husum, *Ger.* **148** B7
Hutag, *Mongolia* **180** C11
Hutchinson, *Kans., U.S.* **105** U7
Hutchinson, *Minn., U.S.* **104** K10
Hutch Mountain, *Ariz., U.S.* **107** S7
Huthi, *Myanmar* **186** L8
Hutland, *Cayman Is., U.K.* **120** H3
Huttig, *Ark., U.S.* **100** K8
Hutuo Ziya, *river, China* **182** E6
Huvadu *see* Suvadiva Atoll, *island,*
  Maldives **179** W3
Huxian, *China* **182** H2
Huy, *Belg.* **146** L13
Hüyük, *Turk.* **168** G7
Huzhou, *China* **182** L9
Hvammstangi, *Ice.* **140** E2
Hvannadalshnúkur, *peak, Ice.* **138** A3
Hvar (Pharus), *island, Croatia* **152** H6
Hvarski Kanal, *Croatia* **152** H6
Hveragerdi, *Ice.* **140** F2
Hvítá, *river, Ice.* **140** F2
Hwange, *Zimb.* **202** F10
Hyannis, *Mass., U.S.* **95** L16
Hyannis, *Nebr., U.S.* **105** N3
Hyargas Nuur, *Mongolia* **180** C9
Hyden, *W. Aust., Austral.* **211** X3
Hyde Park, *N.Y., U.S.* **94** L11
Hyderabad, *India* **178** M6
Hyderabad, *Pak.* **177** V7
Hydra *see* Ídra, *island, Gr.* **154** L12
Hydro, *Okla., U.S.* **102** G9
Hyères, *Fr.* **147** Y14
Hyères, Îles de (Les Îles d'Or), *Fr.*
  147 Y14
Hyesan, *N. Korea* **182** B13
Hyndman Peak, *Idaho, U.S.* **106** G5
Hyrra Banda, *Cen. Af. Rep.* **198** H10
Hyrynsalmi, *Fin.* **141** F16
Hysham, *Mont., U.S.* **106** D11
Hyūga, *Japan* **185** S5

I

Ía, *Gr.* **155** M15
Iaco, *river, Braz.* **130** G6
Iaeger, *W. Va., U.S.* **96** F8
Ialomiţa, *river, Rom.* **153** F16
Iamara, *P.N.G.* **213** E18
Iar Connaught, *region, Ire.* **143** S3
Iaşi, *Rom.* **153** B17
Íasmos, *Gr.* **155** B15
Iauaretê, *Braz.* **130** C6
Ibadan, *Nigeria* **200** G12
Ibagué, *Col.* **128** F5
Ibapah, *Utah, U.S.* **106** L5
Ibarra, *Ecua.* **128** H3
Ibb, *Yemen* **172** Q9
Iberá, *Laguna, Arg.* **132** H13
Iberia, *Peru* **130** G6
Iberian Mountains, *Sp.* **138** J3
Iberian Peninsula, *Eur.* **138** H2
Ibiapaba, *Serra da, S. Amer.* **126** E10
Ibipetuba, *Braz.* **131** G14
Ibiza *see* Eivissa, *Sp.* **145** H17
Ibiza (Ivisa), *island, Sp.* **145** H17
Iblei, Monti, *It.* **151** T11
Ibn Hani', Ra's, *Syr.* **170** F6
Ibo, *Mozambique* **203** D15
Iboperenda, *Bol.* **130** K8
Ibotirama, *Braz.* **131** H15
Ibra, Wadi, *Sudan* **198** F10
Ibrāʼ, *Oman* **173** K16
ʻIbrī, *Oman* **173** K15
Ibusuki, *Japan* **185** T4
Içá, *river, Braz.* **130** D6
Ica, *river, Peru* **130** J4
Ica, *Peru* **130** J4
Icacos Point, *Trinidad & Tobago* **121** Q21
Içana, *river, Braz.* **130** C6
Içana, *Braz.* **130** C6
İçel (Mersin), *Turk.* **168** J9
Iceland, *Eur.* **139** N3
Iceland-Faroe Rise, *Atl. Oc.* **236** C11
Iceland Plateau, *Arctic Oc.* **243** K19
Ichchapuram, *India* **178** L10
Ichikawa, *Japan* **185** P12
Ichinohe, *Japan* **184** J13
Ichinomiya, *Japan* **185** P10
Ichinoseki, *Japan* **184** L13
Ichinskaya Sopka, *Russ.* **159** F22
Ichinskiy, *Russ.* **159** F22

Ichnya, *Ukr.* **157** N7
Ich'ŏn, *N. Korea* **182** EI3
Icó, *Braz.* **131** FI7
Iconium *see* Konya, *Turk.* **168** G8
Icoraci, *Braz.* **131** DI4
Icy Cape, *Alas., U.S.* **III** BI3
Idabel, *Okla., U.S.* **102** JI4
Ida Grove, *Iowa, U.S.* **105** N9
Idah, *Nigeria* **201** GI4
Idaho, *U.S.* **106** C4
Idaho City, *Idaho, U.S.* **106** G4
Idaho Falls, *Idaho, U.S.* **106** G7
Idalou, *Tex., U.S.* **102** K5
Idanha, *Oreg., U.S.* **108** G4
Idanha-a-Nova, *Port.* **144** G7
'Idd el Ghanam, *Sudan* **198** FIO
Ideriyn, river, *Mongolia* **180** CIO
Idfu, *Egypt* **197** EI9
Idi, *Indonesia* **188** G4
Ídi, Óros (Psiloreítis), *Gr.* **155** QI4
İdil, *Turk.* **169** HI6
Idiofa, *Dem. Rep. of the Congo* **198** L9
Idlib, *Syr.* **170** E8
Ídra (Hydra), *Gr.* **154** LI2
Ídra, *Gr.* **154** KI2
Ieper (Ypres), *Belg.* **146** LIO
Ierápetra, *Gr.* **155** RI6
Ierissós, *Gr.* **154** DI2
Ieta, *P.N.G.* **217** JI3
Ifalik Atoll, *F.S.M.* **216** Q4
Ife, *Nigeria* **201** GI3
Iferouâne, *Niger* **196** GI2
Ifjord, *Nor.* **141** BI4
Igan, *Malaysia* **187** UI6
Igara Paraná, river, *Col.* **128** J6
Igarka, *Russ.* **159** GI3
Igatpuri, *India* **178** L3
Iğdır, *Turk.* **169** EI8
Igel, *Ger.* **160** JII
Igikpak, Mount, *Alas., U.S.* **III** EI5
Iglesias, *It.* **151** P3
Igli, *Alg.* **196** C9
Igloolik, *Nunavut, Can.* **83** FI6
'Igma, Gebel el, *Egypt* **171** S3
Ignacio, *Colo., U.S.* **107** QII
Ignalina, *Lith.* **141** NI7
İğneada, *Turk.* **168** B4
İğneada Burnu, *Turk.* **168** B4
Igoumenítsa, *Gr.* **154** F7
Igra, *Russ.* **156** GI6
Igrim, *Russ.* **158** GIO
Iguaçu, Cataratas do, *Braz.* **130** NII
Iguala, *Mex.* **114** JII
Igualada, *Sp.* **145** DI7
Iguatu, *Braz.* **131** FI6
Iguazú Falls, *Arg.* **132** FI5
Igué, Île, *New Caledonia, Fr.* **218** B6
Iguéla, *Gabon* **201** LI5
Iguidi, Erg, *Alg., Mauritania* **196** D8
Iharaña (Vohemar), *Madagascar* **203** DI8
Ihavandiffulu Atoll, *Maldives* **179** T3
Ihavandu, island, *Maldives* **179** T3
Iheya Rettō, *Japan* **185** XI
Iheya Shima, *Japan* **185** XI
Ihosy, *Madagascar* **203** HI7
Ihu, *P.N.G.* **213** DI9
Ii, *Fin.* **141** FI5
Iida, *Japan* **185** PII
Iisalmi, *Fin.* **141** GI6
Iittuarmiit, *Greenland, Den.* **81** D22
Ijevan, *Arm.* **169** DI9
Ijill, Sebkhet, *Mauritania* **196** E6
IJmuiden, *Neth.* **146** HI2
IJsselmeer, bay, *Neth.* **146** HI3
Ijuí, *Braz.* **130** PII
Ijuw, region, *Nauru* **217** E23
Ikanbujmal, *China* **180** G7
Ikare, *Nigeria* **201** GI3
Ikaría, island, *Gr.* **155** KI6
Ikeda, *Japan* **184** GI5
Ikela, *Dem. Rep. of the Congo* **198** KIO
Ikhtiman, *Bulg.* **153** JI3
Iki, island, *Japan* **185** R4
İkizdere, *Turk.* **169** DI5
Ikopa, river, *Madagascar* **203** FI7
Ikorodu, *Nigeria* **200** HI2
Iksan, *S. Korea* **182** GI3
Iku, island, *Kiribati* **217** FI7
Ikuren, island, *Marshall Is.* **216** J8
Ilagan, *Philippines* **189** BI4
Ilave, *Peru* **130** J6
Iława, *Pol.* **149** CI5
Ilbilbie, *Qnsld., Austral.* **211** TI4
Ilbunga, *S. Aust., Austral.* **211** U9

Ile, river, *Kaz.* **175** HI6
Île-à-la-Crosse, *Sask., Can.* **82** LI2
Ilebo, *Dem. Rep. of the Congo* **198** L9
Ilek, river, *Kaz., Russ.* **138** EI4
Ilfracombe, *Eng., U.K.* **143** W9
Ilfracombe, *Qnsld., Austral.* **211** TI2
Ilgaz, *Turk.* **168** D9
Ilgaz Dağları, *Turk.* **168** C9
Ilgın, *Turk.* **168** G7
Ílhavo, *Port.* **144** F5
Ilhéus, *Braz.* **131** JI6
Ili, river, *China, Kaz.* **166** F7
Iliamna Lake, *Alas., U.S.* **III** KI4
İliç, *Turk.* **169** FI3
Ilıca, *Turk.* **169** EI5
Iligan, *Philippines* **189** FI5
Iliili, *Amer. Samoa, U.S.* **218** M7
Ili'ili'ōpae Heiau, *Hawai'i, U.S.* **113** FI5
Ilinden, *Bulg.* **153** KI3
Ilion, *N.Y., U.S.* **94** JIO
'Īlio Point, *Hawai'i, U.S.* **113** FI3
Ill, river, *Aust.* **160** M3
Illampu, peak, *S. Amer.* **126** G4
Illapel, *Chile* **132** J6
Illeginni, island, *Marshall Is.* **216** L4
Illéla, *Niger* **196** HII
Illichivs'k, *Ukr.* **157** R5
Illimani, peak, *S. Amer.* **126** G4
Illinois, river, *Ill., U.S.* **99** Q4
Illinois, river, *Oreg., U.S.* **108** K2
Illinois, *U.S.* **99** R4
Illinois Peak, *Idaho, Mont., U.S.* **84** C6
Illizi, *Alg.* **196** DI2
Il'men', Ozero, *Russ.* **156** G7
Ilmenau, *Ger.* **148** G8
Ilo, *Peru* **130** K5
Iloilo, *Philippines* **189** EI4
Ilorin, *Nigeria* **201** GI3
Ilovik, island, *Croatia* **152** F4
Il'pyrskiy, *Russ.* **159** E2I
Ilulissat, *Greenland, Den.* **81** C2I
Ilwaco, *Wash., U.S.* **108** E2
Imabari, *Japan* **185** R6
Imabetsu, *Japan* **184** HI2
Imaichi, *Japan* **185** NI2
Imajō, *Japan* **185** P9
Imandra, Lake, *Russ.* **138** A9
Imarssuak Seachannel, *Atl. Oc.* **236** D8
Imatra, *Fin.* **141** HI7
Imbert, *Dom. Rep.* **117** LI8
Imese, *Dem. Rep. of the Congo* **198** J8
Īmī, *Eth.* **199** GI6
Imías, *Cuba* **117** KI4
Imieji Anchorage, *Marshall Is.* **216** M8
İmişli, *Azerb.* **169** E2I
Imjun, river, *N. Korea* **182** DI3
Imlay, *Nev., U.S.* **109** N8
Imlay City, *Mich., U.S.* **98** LI2
Immarna, *S. Aust., Austral.* **211** W8
Immokalee, *Fla., U.S.* **97** W9
Imnaha, *Oreg., U.S.* **108** F9
Imola, *It.* **150** F7
Imotski, *Croatia* **152** H7
Imperatriz, *Braz.* **131** EI3
Imperia, *It.* **150** G3
Imperial, *Calif., U.S.* **109** ZII
Imperial, *Nebr., U.S.* **105** Q3
Imperial Beach, *Calif., U.S.* **109** Z9
Imperial Dam, *Ariz., Calif., U.S.* **109** YI3
Imperial Valley, *Calif., U.S.* **109** YII
Impfondo, *Congo* **201** KI8
Imphal, *India* **178** HI4
İmralı, island, *Turk.* **168** D4
İmranlı, *Turk.* **169** EI3
Imrodj, island, *Marshall Is.* **216** L8
İmroz *see* Gökçeada, island, *Turk.* **168** D2
Imtān, *Syr.* **170** L8
Ina, *Japan* **185** PII
Inaccessible, island, *Tristan da Cunha Is., U.K.* **194** R2
I Naftan, Puntan, *N. Mariana Is., U.S.* **216** D5
Inamba Jima, *Japan* **185** RI2
I-n-Amenas, *Alg.* **196** DI2
I-n-Amguel, *Alg.* **196** EII
Inanwatan, *Indonesia* **189** KI8
Inarajan, *Guam, U.S.* **216** DIO
Inari, lake, *Fin.* **141** CI5
Inari, *Fin.* **141** DI5
Inca, *Sp.* **145** GI8
Inca de Oro, *Chile* **132** G7
İncekum Burnu, *Turk.* **168** J9

İncesu, *Turk.* **168** GIO
Inchcape *see* Bell Rock, island, *Scot., U.K.* **142** LII
Incheon (Inch'on), *S. Korea* **182** FI3
Inch Island, *Ire.* **143** P5
Inchnadamph, *Scot., U.K.* **142** H8
Inch'on *see* Incheon, *S. Korea* **182** FI3
Incles, Port d', *Andorra, Fr.* **160** G5
Indalsälven, river, *Sw.* **138** C7
Indawgyi Lake, *Myanmar* **186** E6
Indefatigable *see* Santa Cruz, Isla, island, *Ecua.* **128** Q9
Independence, *Calif., U.S.* **109** T8
Independence, *Iowa, U.S.* **105** NI3
Independence, *Kans., U.S.* **105** V9
Independence, *Mo., U.S.* **105** SIO
Independence Mountains, *Nev., U.S.* **108** MIO
India, *Asia* **167** W7
Indian, river, *Fla., U.S.* **97** UIO
Indiana, *Pa., U.S.* **94** N4
Indiana, *U.S.* **99** R9
Indianapolis, *Ind., U.S.* **99** R9
Indian Harbour, *Nfld. & Lab., Can.* **83** K22
Indianola, *Iowa, U.S.* **105** PII
Indianola, *Miss., U.S.* **100** JIO
Indianola, *Nebr., U.S.* **105** R4
Indian Peak, *Utah, U.S.* **107** N5
Indian Springs, *Nev., U.S.* **109** TII
Indiantown, *Fla., U.S.* **97** VIO
Indian Town Point, *Antigua & Barbuda* **121** B2I
Indigirka, river, *Russ.* **166** CII
Indija, *Serb.* **152** EIO
Indio, *Calif., U.S.* **109** XII
Indira Point, *India* **179** TI5
Indispensable Strait, *Solomon Is.* **217** NI9
Indochina Peninsula, *Asia* **166** JII
Indomed Fracture Zone, *Ind. Oc.* **240** P5
Indonesia, *Asia* **167** ZII
Indore, *India* **178** J5
Indravati, river, *India* **178** L8
Indus, river, *India, Pak.* **177** W6
Indus, Mouths of the, *Pak.* **177** W6
Indus Fan, *Ind. Oc.* **240** D8
Inebolu, *Turk.* **168** B9
İnegöl, *Turk.* **168** D5
I-n-Eker, *Alg.* **196** EII
Ineu, *Rom.* **152** DII
Inez, *Ky., U.S.* **101** B2O
Infante D. Henrique, *Sao Tome and Principe* **205** B2I
Ingal, *Niger* **196** HII
Ingende, *Dem. Rep. of the Congo* **198** K9
Ingeniero Guillermo N. Juárez, *Arg.* **132** EII
Ingeniero Jacobacci, *Arg.* **133** Q8
Ingeniero Luiggi, *Arg.* **132** MIO
Ingettolgoy, *Mongolia* **180** CII
Ingleside, *Tex., U.S.* **103** UII
Inglewood, *Tex., U.S.* **102** J9
Inglis, *Fla., U.S.* **97** S7
Ingolstadt, *Ger.* **148** J8
Ingomar, *S. Aust., Austral.* **211** W9
Ingraj Bazar, *India* **178** HII
Ingram, *Tex., U.S.* **103** Q8
Ingrid Christensen Coast, *Antarctica* **227** GI9
Ingwiller, *Fr.* **147** PI5
Inhambane, *Mozambique* **203** HI3
Inharrime, *Mozambique* **203** JI3
Inírida, *Col.* **128** F9
Inírida, river, *Col.* **128** G8
Inishannon, *Ire.* **143** V4
Inishbofin, island, *Ire.* **143** R2
Inisheer, island, *Ire.* **143** S3
Inishkea North, island, *Ire.* **143** Q2
Inishkea South, island, *Ire.* **143** Q2
Inishmaan, island, *Ire.* **143** S3
Inishmore, island, *Ire.* **143** S3
Inishmurray, island, *Ire.* **143** Q4
Inishowen Head, *Ire.* **143** N6
Inishshark, island, *Ire.* **143** R2
Inishtrahull, island, *Ire.* **143** N6
Inkerman, *Qnsld., Austral.* **211** QII
Inland Niger Delta, *Mali* **196** H8
Inland Sea, *Japan* **185** Q6
Inn, river, *Aust., Ger.* **148** KIO
Innamincka, *S. Aust., Austral.* **211** VII
Inner Brass Island, *Virgin Islands, U.S.* **120** M8
Inner Hebrides, *Scot., U.K.* **142** L7
Inner Mongolia, region, *China* **181** GI3

Inner Sound, *Scot., U.K.* **142** J7
Innesowen, *N.S.W., Austral.* **211** WI2
Innisfail, *Qnsld., Austral.* **211** RI3
Innoko, river, *Alas., U.S.* **III** GI4
Innsbruck, *Aust.* **148** L8
Inongo, *Dem. Rep. of the Congo* **198** K8
İnönü, *Turk.* **168** E6
Inoússes, island, *Gr.* **155** HI6
Inowrocław, *Pol.* **149** DI4
I-n-Salah, *Alg.* **196** DIO
Insar, *Russ.* **156** KI2
Inscription, Cape, *Austral.* **210** GI
Insein, *Myanmar* **186** K6
Insiaf, *F.S.M.* **217** BI8
Instow, *Eng., U.K.* **143** W9
Inta, *Russ.* **158** FIO
Intendente Alvear, *Arg.* **132** LIO
Interior, *S. Dak., U.S.* **104** L3
International Falls, *Minn., U.S.* **104** EII
Interview Island, *India* **179** PI4
Intiyaco, *Arg.* **132** HI2
Inubō Zaki, *Japan* **185** PI3
Inukjuak, *Que., Can.* **83** KI8
Inuvik, *N.W.T., Can.* **82** EIO
Inuya, river, *Peru* **130** G4
Inverbervie, *Scot., U.K.* **142** KII
Invercargill, *N.Z.* **213** RI5
Invermoriston, *Scot., U.K.* **142** K9
Inverness, *Fla., U.S.* **97** T7
Inverness, *Scot., U.K.* **142** J9
Invershin, *Scot., U.K.* **142** J9
Inverway, *N. Terr., Austral.* **211** R7
Investigator Ridge, *Ind. Oc.* **241** HI3
Investigator Strait, *Austral.* **210** LIO
Inyokern, *Calif., U.S.* **109** V9
Inyo Mountains, *Calif., U.S.* **109** T8
Inza, *Russ.* **156** KI3
Inzhavino, *Russ.* **156** MI2
Inzia, river, *Dem. Rep. of the Congo* **198** M8
Ioánina, *Gr.* **154** E7
Iō Jima, *Japan* **185** U4
Iola, *Kans., U.S.* **105** UIO
Ioma, *P.N.G.* **213** D2O
Iona, *Idaho, U.S.* **106** G7
Iona, island, *Scot., U.K.* **142** M2
Ione, *Calif., U.S.* **109** R5
Ione, *Nev., U.S.* **109** Q9
Ione, *Oreg., U.S.* **108** F6
Ione, *Wash., U.S.* **108** A9
Ionia, *Mich., U.S.* **98** LIO
Ionian Islands, *Gr.* **138** K8
Ionian Sea, *Eur.* **138** K8
Iony, Ostrov (St. Jona Island), *Russ.* **159** H2O
Iori, river, *Azerb., Rep. of Georgia* **169** C2O
Íos, island, *Gr.* **155** MI5
Íos, *Gr.* **155** MI5
Iotori Shima, *Japan* **185** X2
Iowa, river, *Iowa, U.S.* **105** PI3
Iowa, *U.S.* **105** NIO
Iowa City, *Iowa, U.S.* **105** PI3
Iowa Falls, *Iowa, U.S.* **105** NI2
Iowa Park, *Tex., U.S.* **102** J9
Ipáti, *Gr.* **154** GIO
Ipatovo, *Russ.* **157** SI2
Ipiales, *Col.* **128** H3
Ipis, island, *F.S.M.* **217** DI6
Ipixuna, river, *Braz.* **130** F4
Ipixuna, *Braz.* **130** F5
Ipoh, *Malaysia* **187** T9
Iporá, *Braz.* **130** JI2
Ipsala, *Turk.* **168** C2
Ipswich, *Eng., U.K.* **143** UI5
Ipswich, *Jam.* **120** H7
Ipswich, *Qnsld., Austral.* **211** VI5
Ipswich, *S. Dak., U.S.* **104** J6
Iput', river, *Russ.* **156** L7
Iqaluit, *Nunavut, Can.* **83** HI9
Iquique, *Chile* **132** C7
Iquitos, *Peru* **130** E4
Iraan, *Tex., U.S.* **103** P5
Iracoubo, *Fr. Guiana, Fr.* **129** EI7
Īrafshān, *Iran* **173** HI8
Iraio, ruin, *Gr.* **155** KI7
Irákleia, island, *Gr.* **155** MI5
Iráklio (Candia, Heráklion), *Gr.* **155** QI5
Iran, *Asia* **167** U5
Īrānshahr, *Iran* **173** HI7
Irapuato, *Mex.* **114** HIO
Iraq, *Asia* **167** T4
Irayel', *Russ.* **158** F9
Irazú, Volcán, *Costa Rica* **115** NI9
Irbe Strait, *Est., Latv.* **141** LI5

Irbid (Arbela), *Jordan* **170** L6
Ireland, *Eur.* **139** S3
Ireland, island, *Ire., U.K.* **143** T4
Ireland Island North, *Bermuda, U.K.* **120** B2
Ireland Island South, *Bermuda, U.K.* **120** B2
Iret', *Russ.* **159** F2I
Irian Jaya, region, *Indonesia* **213** CI6
Irimi, *Indonesia* **213** BI4
Iringa, *Tanzania* **199** MI4
Iriri, river, *Braz.* **130** EII
Iriru, Passe, *Fr. Polynesia, Fr.* **219** B23
Irish Sea, *Ire., U.K.* **143** S8
Irkeshtam, *Kyrg.* **176** GII
Irkutsk, *Russ.* **159** LI5
Irmauw, *Indonesia* **189** MI7
Irois Bay, *Trinidad & Tobago* **121** Q2I
Iroise, *Fr.* **147** Q2
Irondequoit, *N.Y., U.S.* **94** H6
Iron Gate, *Rom., Serb. & Mont.* **138** H8
Iron Gate Dam, *Rom., Serb. & Mont.* **152** FI2
Iron Knob, *S. Aust., Austral.* **211** XIO
Iron Mountain, *Mich., U.S.* **98** G7
Iron River, *Mich., U.S.* **98** G6
Iron River, *Wis., U.S.* **98** F3
Ironton, *Mo., U.S.* **105** UI5
Ironton, *Ohio, U.S.* **99** TI3
Ironwood, *Mich., U.S.* **98** F5
Ironwood Forest National Monument, *Ariz., U.S.* **107** V7
Iroquois, *S. Dak., U.S.* **104** K7
Irō Zaki, *Japan* **185** QII
Irpin', *Ukr.* **157** N6
Irrawaddy *see* Ayeyarwady, river, *Myanmar* **186** F6
Iruña *see* Pamplona, *Sp.* **145** CI3
Irvine, *Ky., U.S.* **101** CI8
Irvine, *Scot., U.K.* **143** N9
Irving, *Tex., U.S.* **102** LII
Isabel, *S. Dak., U.S.* **104** J4
Isabela, P., *U.S.* **120** M2
Isabela, *Philippines* **189** FI4
Isabela, Cabo, *Dom. Rep.* **117** KI8
Isabela, Canal, *Ecua.* **128** Q9
Isabela, Isla (Albemarle), *Ecua.* **128** Q8
Isabela de Sagua, *Cuba* **116** G9
Isabella, *Minn., U.S.* **104** FI3
Isabelle, Point, *Mich., U.S.* **98** E7
Isabel Segunda (Vieques), *P.R., U.S.* **120** N6
Isachsen Mountain, *Antarctica* **227** BI5
Ísafjörður, *Ice.* **140** E2
Isahaya, *Japan* **185** S4
Isa Khel, *Pak.* **177** P9
Isangel, *Vanuatu* **218** H4
Isar, river, *Ger.* **148** K9
Íscar, *Sp.* **144** EIO
Ischia, Isola d', *It.* **150** MIO
Isdu, island, *Maldives* **179** W3
Ise, *Japan* **185** QIO
Isen Saki, *Japan* **185** X2
Iseo, Lago d', *It.* **150** D5
Isère, Pointe, *Fr. Guiana, Fr.* **129** EI7
Isernia, *It.* **150** LIO
Ise Wan, *Japan* **185** QIO
Isfahan *see* Eşfahan, *Iran* **173** EI3
Isfara, *Taj.* **176** G9
Ishikari Wan, *Japan* **184** FI3
Ishim, river, *Russ.* **158** JIO
Ishim, *Russ.* **158** JIO
Ishim Steppe, *Kaz., Russ.* **174** AI2
Ishinomaki, *Japan* **184** LI3
Ishinomaki Wan, *Japan* **184** LI3
Ishioka, *Japan* **185** NI3
Ishkuman, *Pak.* **176** KII
Ishpeming, *Mich., U.S.* **98** F7
Işık Dağı, *Turk.* **168** D8
Işıkveren, *Turk.* **169** HI7
Isili, *It.* **151** P4
Isimu, *Indonesia* **189** JI4
Isiro, *Dem. Rep. of the Congo* **198** JII
Isisford, *Qnsld., Austral.* **211** UI2
Iskandar, *Uzb.* **175** KI3
İskenderun, *Turk.* **168** JII
İskilip, *Turk.* **168** D9
Iskŭr, river, *Bulg.* **153** GI4
Iskushuban, *Somalia* **199** FI8
İslâhiye, *Turk.* **168** HII
Islamabad *see* Anantnag, *India* **177** NI2
Islamabad, *Pak.* **177** NII
Islamkot, *Pak.* **177** W9

Islamorada, *Fla., U.S.* **97** YlO
Isla Mujeres, *Mex.* **115** Hl7
Island Falls, *Me., U.S.* **95** Cl8
Island Lagoon, *Austral.* **210** J9
Island Lake, *Man., Can.* **83** Ml4
Island Park, *Idaho, U.S.* **106** F8
Island Park Reservoir, *Idaho, U.S.* **106** F7
Island Pond, *Vt., U.S.* **95** Fl3
Islands, Bay of, *N.Z.* **213** Hl8
Islas Orcadas Rise, *Atl. Oc.* **237** V9
Islay, island, *Scot., U.K.* **142** M7
Isle of Man, *U.K.*
Isle of Man, island, *U.K.* **143** Q9
Isle Royale National Park, *Mich., U.S.*
98 D6
Islote Bay, *Trinidad & Tobago* **121** Q2l
Ismā'īlīya, *Egypt* **171** Pl
Isna, *Egypt* **197** El9
Isoka, *Zambia* **202** Cl2
Isola di Capo Rizzuto, *It.* **151** Ql4
Isonzo, river, *It., Slov.* **150** D9
Isparta, *Turk.* **168** G6
Ispas, *Turkm.* **174** LlO
Ispikan, *Pak.* **177** V2
İspir, *Turk.* **169** Dl5
Israel, *Asia* **167** T3
Isrīyah, ruin, *Syr.* **170** F9
Issano, *Guyana* **129** El4
Issime, *It.* **150** D3
Issoudun, *Fr.* **147** S9
Ist, island, *Croatia* **152** F4
İstanbul (Constantinople), *Turk.* **168** C5
İstanbul Boğazi (Bosporus), *Turk.* **168** C5
Istaravshan (Ŭroteppa), *Taj.* **176** G7
Istiéa, *Gr.* **154** Gll
Isto, Mount, *Alas., U.S.* **111** Cl8
Istokpoga, Lake, *Fla., U.S.* **97** V9
Istres, *Fr.* **147** Xl3
Istria, peninsula, *Croatia* **152** E4
Itabaianinha, *Braz.* **131** Hl7
Itabuna, *Braz.* **131** Jl6
Itacoatiara, *Braz.* **130** DlO
Itaetê, *Braz.* **131** Hl6
Itaipú Dam, *Braz., Parag.* **130** Mll
Itaituba, *Braz.* **130** ElO
Itajaí, *Braz.* **131** Nl3
Italia, Monte, *Chile* **133** Y8
Italy, *Eur.* **139** W7
Itamarat, *Braz.* **130** F6
Itambé, Pico de, *Braz.* **131** Kl5
Itanagar, *India* **178** Fl4
Itapetinga, *Braz.* **131** Jl6
Itapipoca, *Braz.* **131** El6
Itapiranga, *Braz.* **130** DlO
Itasca, *Tex., U.S.* **102** Mll
Itasca, Lake *see* Mississippi, Source of
the, *Minn., U.S.* **104** G9
Itatupã, *Braz.* **130** Cl2
Itbayat, island, *Philippines* **189** Al4
Itéa, *Gr.* **154** HlO
Iténez, river, *Bol., Braz.* **130** H9
Itezhi-Tezhi, Lake, *Zambia* **202** ElO
Ithaca *see* Itháki, island, *Gr.* **154** H7
Ithaca, *Mich., U.S.* **98** Lll
Ithaca, *N.Y., U.S.* **94** K8
Itháki (Ithaca), island, *Gr.* **154** H7
Itháki (Vathý), *Gr.* **154** H7
Ítilo, *Gr.* **154** MlO
Itimbiri, river, *Dem. Rep. of the Congo*
194 J7
Itiquira, river, *Braz.* **130** JlO
Itō, *Japan* **185** Ql2
Itoman, *Japan* **185** Yl
Itta Bena, *Miss., U.S.* **100** Jll
Ittiri, *It.* **150** M3
Ittoqqortoormiit, *Greenland, Den.* **81** B22
Itu Aba Island, *Spratly Is.* **188** Ell
Ituí, river, *Braz.* **130** E5
Ituiutaba, *Braz.* **131** Kl3
Ituni, *Guyana* **129** El4
Iturama, *Braz.* **130** Kl2
Iturup (Etorofu), island, *Russ.* **159** J23
Ituxi, river, *Braz.* **130** F7
Ituzaingó, *Arg.* **132** Gl4
Itzehoe, *Ger.* **148** B7
Iuka, *Miss., U.S.* **101** Gl3
Iul'tin, *Russ.* **159** B2O
Ivaí, river, *Braz.* **130** Mll
Ivalo, *Fin.* **141** Dl5
Ivangrad, *Serb. & Mont.* **152** H9
Ivanhoe, *N.S.W., Austral.* **211** Xl2
Ivanhoe, *W. Aust., Austral.* **211** Q6
Ivanić Grad, *Croatia* **152** D6
Ivanjica, *Serb.* **152** GlO
Ivano-Frankivs'k, *Ukr.* **157** P2
Ivanovo, *Russ.* **156** Hll

Ivanteyevka, *Russ.* **156** Ll5
Ivatsevichy, *Belarus* **156** L3
Ivaylovgrad, *Bulg.* **153** Kl5
Ivdel', *Russ.* **158** G9
Ivirairai, Mont, *Fr. Polynesia, Fr.* **219** Pl6
Ivisa *see* Ibiza, island, *Sp.* **145** Hl7
Ivory Coast, *Cote dIvoire* **194** J2
Ivrea, *It.* **150** D3
Ivujivik, *Que., Can.* **83** Hl7
Iwadate, *Japan* **184** Jl2
Iwaki, *Japan* **185** Nl3
Iwakuni, *Japan* **185** Q6
Iwamizawa, *Japan* **184** Fl3
Iwanuma, *Japan* **184** Ll3
Iwate, *Japan* **184** Kl3
Iwembere Steppe, *Tanzania* **194** K9
Iwo, *Nigeria* **200** Gl2
Iwo Jima *see* Iwo To, island, *Japan* **184** L5
Iwo To (Iwo Jima), island, *Japan* **184** L5
Ixtapa, *Mex.* **114** KlO
Iyo, *Japan* **185** R6
Iž, island, *Croatia* **152** G5
Īzadkhvāst, *Iran* **173** El3
Izamal, *Mex.* **115** Hl6
Izberbash, *Russ.* **157** Ul6
Izbica, *Pol.* **149** Dl4
Izena Shima, *Japan* **185** Xl
Izhevsk, *Russ.* **156** Gl6
Izhevsk, *Russ.* **158** H8
Izhma, river, *Russ.* **138** Bl2
Izmayil, *Ukr.* **157** S4
İzmir (Smyrna), *Turk.* **168** F3
İznik (Nicaea), *Turk.* **168** D5
İznik Gölü, *Turk.* **168** D5
Izozog, Bañados del, *S. Amer.* **126** H5
Izra', *Syr.* **170** K7
Izu Hantō, *Japan* **185** Qll
Izuhara, *Japan* **185** Q3
Izu Islands, *Japan* **166** Fl4
Izumo, *Japan* **185** P6
Izu Shichitō, *Japan* **185** Ql2
Izu Shotō, *Japan* **184** J5
Izu Trench, *Pac. Oc.* **238** F6
Izyaslav, *Ukr.* **157** N4
Izyum, *Ukr.* **157** P9

Jaba, *P.N.G.* **217** Kl4
Jabalpur, *India* **178** J7
Jabal Zuqar, Jazīrat, *Yemen* **172** Q8
Jabbūl, *Syr.* **170** E9
Jabbūl, Sabkhat al, *Syr.* **170** E9
Jabel Abyad Plateau, *Sudan* **194** F8
Jabiru, *N. Terr., Austral.* **211** P8
Jablah, *Syr.* **170** F7
Jablaničko Jezero, *Bosn. & Herzg.* **152** G7
Jablonec, *Czech Rep.* **148** Gll
Jabnoren, island, *Marshall Is.* **216** K7
Jaboatão, *Braz.* **131** Gl8
Jabor, *Marshall Is.* **216** M8
Jabuka, island, *Croatia* **152** H5
Jabwot Island, *Marshall Is.* **216** H4
Jaca, *Sp.* **145** Cl4
Jacareacanga, *Braz.* **130** ElO
Jaciparaná, *Braz.* **130** G7
Jackman, *Me., U.S.* **95** Dl5
Jackpot, *Nev., U.S.* **108** Ll2
Jacksboro, *Tex., U.S.* **102** KlO
Jackson, *Ala., U.S.* **101** Ml4
Jackson, *Barbados* **121** Kl9
Jackson, *Calif., U.S.* **109** R5
Jackson, *Ga., U.S.* **96** L5
Jackson, *La., U.S.* **100** N9
Jackson, *Mich., U.S.* **98** Mll
Jackson, *Minn., U.S.* **104** Ll0
Jackson, *Miss., U.S.* **100** Lll
Jackson, *Mo., U.S.* **105** Ul6
Jackson, *Ohio, U.S.* **99** Sl3
Jackson, *S.C., U.S.* **96** L8
Jackson, *Tenn., U.S.* **101** Fl3
Jackson, *Wyo., U.S.* **106** H8
Jackson, Ostrov, *Russ.* **158** Cl2
Jackson Bay, *N.Z.* **213** Pl5
Jackson Lake, *Ga., U.S.* **96** L5
Jackson Lake, *Wyo., U.S.* **106** G8
Jacksonport, *Wis., U.S.* **98** H8
Jacksonville, *Ala., U.S.* **101** Jl6
Jacksonville, *Ark., U.S.* **100** G9
Jacksonville, *Fla., U.S.* **97** Q8
Jacksonville, *Ill., U.S.* **99** R4
Jacksonville, *N.C., U.S.* **96** Jl3

Jacksonville, *Tex., U.S.* **102** Ml4
Jacksonville Beach, *Fla., U.S.* **97** R9
Jacmel, *Haiti* **117** Ml6
Jacobabad, *Pak.* **177** T7
Jacob Lake, *Ariz., U.S.* **107** Q7
Jacquinot Bay, *P.N.G.* **213** C2l
Jacumba, *Calif., U.S.* **109** Zll
J.A.D. Jensen Nunatakker, peak, *N.*
Amer. **80** DlO
Jadraque, *Sp.* **144** El2
Jaén, *Peru* **130** F2
Jaén, *Sp.* **144** Kll
Ja'farābād, *Iran* **172** All
Jaffa, Cape, *Austral.* **210** LlO
Jaffna, *Sri Lanka* **179** R7
Jafr, Qā' al, *Jordan* **171** Q7
Jagdalpur, *India* **178** L8
Jāghīr Bāzār, *Syr.* **170** Cl4
Jaghjagh, river, *Syr.* **170** Cl4
Jagodina, *Serb.* **152** Gll
Jagraon, *India* **178** D5
Jagtial, *India* **178** L6
Jaguarão, *Braz.* **130** Qll
Jahanabad, *India* **178** HlO
Jahorina, peak, *Bosn. & Herzg.* **152** G8
Jahrom, *Iran* **173** Gl4
Jaicoa, Cordillera, *P.R., U.S.* **120** M2
Jaigarh, *India* **178** M3
Jaintiapur, *Bangladesh* **178** Hl3
Jaipur, *India* **178** G5
Jaisalmer, *India* **178** F2
Jajpur, *India* **178** KlO
Jajce, *Bhutan* **178** Fl3
Jakar, *Bhutan* **178** Fl3
Jakarta, *Indonesia* **188** L8
Jakeru, island, *Marshall Is.* **216** L3
Jakhau, *India* **178** Hl
Jakobstad (Pietarsaari), *Fin.* **141** Gl5
Jal, *N. Mex., U.S.* **107** Vl5
Jalaihai Point, *Guam, U.S.* **216** Dll
Jalalabad, *Afghan.* **176** M9
Jalal-Abad, *Kyrg.* **176** FlO
Jalandhar, *India* **178** D5
Jalasjärvi, *Fin.* **141** Hl5
Jalaun, *India* **178** G7
Jaldak, *Afghan.* **177** P6
Jaleswar, *India* **178** Kll
Jalgaon, *India* **178** K5
Jalgaon, *India* **178** K5
Jalingo, *Nigeria* **201** Gl6
Jalkot, *Pak.* **176** Lll
Jaloklab, island, *Marshall Is.* **216** GlO
Jalón, river, *Sp.* **145** El3
Jalor, *India* **178** G3
Jalpaiguri, *India* **178** Gl2
Jālq, *Iran* **173** Gl8
Jáltipan, *Mex.* **115** Kl4
Jaluit, island, *Marshall Is.* **216** M8
Jaluit Atoll, *Marshall Is.* **216** H4
Jaluit Lagoon, *Marshall Is.* **216** M8
Jamaame, *Somalia* **199** Kl6
Jamaica, *N. Amer.* **81** P2l
Jamaica, island, *N. Amer.* **80** N9
Jamaica Cay, *Bahamas* **117** Gl3
Jamalpur, *Bangladesh* **178** Hl2
Jamanota, peak, *Aruba, Neth.* **121** Ql7
Jaman Pass, *Afghan., Taj.* **176** Jl2
Jambi, *Indonesia* **188** K7
Jambusar, *India* **178** J3
James *see* San Salvador, Isla, island,
Ecua. **128** P9
James, river, *N. Dak., U.S.* **104** G6
James, river, *S. Dak., U.S.* **104** M7
James, river, *Va., U.S.* **96** Ell
James Bay, *N. Amer.* **80** G4
James Cistern, *Bahamas* **120** E6
James Point, *Bahamas* **120** D6
James Range, *Austral.* **210** F8
James Ross Island, *Antarctica* **226** C4
Jamestown, *N. Dak., U.S.* **104** G6
Jamestown, *N.Y., U.S.* **94** K4
Jamestown National Historic Site, *Va.,*
U.S. **96** Fl3
Jamestown Reservoir, *N. Dak., U.S.*
104 G6
Jammu, *India* **177** Pl2
Jamnagar, *India* **178** J2
Jampur, *Pak.* **177** S9
Jämsä, *Fin.* **141** Jl5
Jamshedpur, *India* **178** JlO
Jamuna, river, *Bangladesh* **178** Hl2
Janaúba, *Braz.* **131** Jl5
Jan Bulaq, *Afghan.* **176** K6
Jand, *Pak.* **177** NlO
Jandaq, *Iran* **173** Dl4

Jandia, peak, *Canary Is.* **204** Q7
Jandia, Punta de, *Canary Is.* **204** Q7
Jandiatuba, river, *Braz.* **130** E6
Jandola, *Pak.* **177** P8
Jan Doran, Neth. Antilles, *Neth.* **121** Ql8
Janesville, *Wis., U.S.* **98** M6
Jangain, island, *P.N.G.* **217** Hl4
Jangaon, *India* **178** M7
Jangeru, *Indonesia* **188** Kl2
Jangheung, *S. Korea* **182** Hl3
Jangipur, *India* **178** Hll
Jani Kheyl, *Afghan.* **177** P7
Janīn, *W. Bank* **170** L6
Jan Mayen, island, *Nor.* **81** A22
Jan Mayen Fracture Zone, *Arctic Oc.*
243 Jl3
Jan Mayen Ridge, *Arctic Oc.* **243** Jl9
Janów Lubelski, *Pol.* **149** Fl7
Jansenville, *S. Af.* **202** M9
Jan Thiel, Lagún, Neth. Antilles, *Neth.*
121 Ql5
Januária, *Braz.* **131** Jl4
Jaora, *India* **178** H4
Japan, *Asia* **167** Tl4
Japan, Sea of (East Sea), *Asia* **166** Fl3
Japan Trench, *Pac. Oc.* **238** E6
Japtan, island, *Marshall Is.* **216** H9
Japurá, *Braz.* **130** D7
Jaquot, Pointe, *Dominica* **121** Dl8
Jarābulus, *Syr.* **170** ClO
Jaramillo, *Arg.* **133** T9
Jaranwala, *Pak.* **177** Qll
Jarash (Gerasa), *Jordan* **170** L6
Jarbidge, river, *Idaho, U.S.* **106** J4
Jarbidge, *Nev., U.S.* **108** Lll
Jardim, *Braz.* **130** LlO
Jardines de la Reina, islands, *Cuba*
116 JlO
Jargalant, *Mongolia* **181** Dl4
Jargalant, *Mongolia* **180** ElO
Jarghan, *Afghan.* **176** L5
Jari, river, *Braz.* **130** Cl2
Jarocin, *Pol.* **149** El3
Jarosław, *Pol.* **149** Gl7
Jarud Qi, *China* **181** El6
Järvenpää, *Fin.* **141** Jl6
Järvsö, *Sw.* **141** Jl3
Jarvis Island, *Pac. Oc.* **214** Gl2
Jāsk, *Iran* **173** Jl6
Jashpurnagar, *India* **178** J9
Jāsk, *Iran* **173** Jl6
Jasło, *Pol.* **149** Hl7
Jason Islands, *Falkland Is., U.K.* **133** Vll
Jason Peninsula, *Antarctica* **226** D5
Jasonville, *Ind., U.S.* **99** S8
Jasper, *Ala., U.S.* **101** Jl4
Jasper, *Alta., Can.* **82** L9
Jasper, *Ark., U.S.* **100** E7
Jasper, *Fla., U.S.* **97** Q7
Jasper, *Ga., U.S.* **96** K5
Jasper, *Ind., U.S.* **99** T8
Jasper, *Tex., U.S.* **103** Pl5
Jastrowie, *Pol.* **149** Cl3
Jastrzębie-Zdrój, *Pol.* **149** Hl4
Jászberény, *Hung.* **149** Ll5
Jataí, *Braz.* **130** Kl2
Jatibonico, *Cuba* **116** H9
Jatobal, *Braz.* **131** El3
Jaú, river, *Braz.* **130** D8
Jauaperi, river, *Braz.* **130** C9
Jaunpur, *India* **178** G8
Java (Jawa), island, *Indonesia* **188** M9
Javari, river, *Braz., Peru* **130** E4
Java Ridge, *Ind. Oc.* **241** Hl5
Java Sea, *Indonesia* **188** LlO
Java Trench, *Ind. Oc.* **241** Hl4
Jávea (Xàbia), *Sp.* **145** Jl5
Javhlant *see* Uliastay, *Mongolia* **180** DlO
Jawa *see* Java, island, *Indonesia* **188** M9
Jawhar (Giohar), *Somalia* **199** Jl7
Jawhar, *Indonesia* **188** J9
Jawi, *Indonesia* **188** J9
Jaworzno, *Pol.* **149** Gl5
Jay, *Okla., U.S.* **102** El4
Jaya, Puncak, *Indonesia* **213** Cl6
Jaya Peak, *Indonesia* **166** Ll6
Jayapura, *Indonesia* **189** K2l
Jayawijaya, Pegunungan, *Indonesia*
189 L2O
Jay Em, *Wyo., U.S.* **106** Jl3
Jayton, *Tex., U.S.* **102** K7
Jayuya, *P.R., U.S.* **120** N3
Jaz Mūrīān, Hāmūn-e, *Iran* **173** Hl6
Jbail (Byblos), *Leb.* **170** H6
Jdaïdet Ghazîr, *Leb.* **170** H6
Jeanerette, *La., U.S.* **100** Q9

Jeanette, Ostrov, *Russ.* **159** Cl7
Jean Marie River, *N.W.T., Can.* **82** HlO
Jean-Rabel, *Haiti* **117** Ll6
Jebba, *Nigeria* **201** Fl3
Jebel, Bahr el (Mountain Nile), *Sudan*
199 Hl3
Jebel Ali, *U.A.E.* **173** Jl5
Jebri, *Pak.* **177** U5
Jebus, *Indonesia* **188** K7
Jeddah, *Saudi Arabia* **172** L7
Jedrol, island, *Marshall Is.* **216** H8
Jędrzejów, *Pol.* **149** Gl6
Jefferson, *Ga., U.S.* **96** K6
Jefferson, *Iowa, U.S.* **105** NlO
Jefferson, river, *Mont., U.S.* **106** E7
Jefferson, *Tex., U.S.* **102** Ll5
Jefferson, *Wis., U.S.* **98** L6
Jefferson, Mount, *Nev., U.S.* **109** QlO
Jefferson, Mount, *Oreg., U.S.* **108** G4
Jefferson City, *Mo., U.S.* **105** Tl3
Jefferson City, *Tenn., U.S.* **101** El9
Jeffersonville, *Ind., U.S.* **99** TlO
Jeffrey City, *Wyo., U.S.* **106** Jll
Jega, *Nigeria* **201** El3
Jégun, *Fr.* **147** X8
Jeju (Cheju), *S. Korea* **182** Jl3
Jeju-Do, *S. Korea* **182** Jl3
Jeju Strait, *S. Korea* **182** Hl3
Jekyll Island, *Ga., U.S.* **97** P8
Jelbart Ice Shelf, *Antarctica* **226** Al2
Jelenia Góra, *Pol.* **148** Fl2
Jelgava (Mitau), *Latv.* **141** Ml6
Jellico, *Tenn., U.S.* **101** Dl8
Jemaja, island, *Indonesia* **188** H8
Jember, *Indonesia* **188** Mll
Jembongan, island, *Malaysia* **188** Fl2
Jemez Pueblo, *N. Mex., U.S.* **107** Rl2
Jeminay, *China* **180** D7
Jemo Island, *Marshall Is.* **216** F4
Jena, *Fla., U.S.* **97** R6
Jena, *Ger.* **148** F9
Jena, *La., U.S.* **100** M8
Jengish Chokusu (Pik Pobedy, Victory
Peak), *China, Kyrg.* **176** El5
Jenkins, *Ky., U.S.* **101** C2O
Jennings, *La., U.S.* **100** P8
Jenny Point, *Dominica* **121** F2O
Jensen, *Utah, U.S.* **106** L9
Jensen Beach, *Fla., U.S.* **97** VlO
Jens Munk Island, *Nunavut, Can.* **83** Fl6
Jenu, *Indonesia* **188** J9
Jeongeup, *S. Korea* **182** Gl3
Jeonju, *S. Korea* **182** Gl3
Jequié, *Braz.* **131** Hl6
Jequitinhonha, river, *Braz.* **131** Jl6
Jerantut, *Malaysia* **187** TlO
Jerba Island, *Tun.* **197** Bl3
Jérémie, *Haiti* **117** Ml5
Jeremoabo, *Braz.* **131** Gl7
Jerez de la Frontera, *Sp.* **144** M8
Jerez de los Caballeros, *Sp.* **144** J7
Jericho *see* Arīḥā, *W. Bank* **170** M6
Jericoacoara, Point, *S. Amer.* **126** DlO
Jerid, Shott el, *Tun.* **196** Bl2
Jerilderie, *N.S.W., Austral.* **211** Yl2
Jerimoth Hill, *R.I., U.S.* **95** Ll4
Jerome, *Idaho, U.S.* **106** H5
Jerramungup, *W. Aust., Austral.* **211** Y3
Jersey, island, *Ch. Is.* **143** Zll
Jersey Bay, *Virgin Islands, U.S.* **120** NlO
Jersey City, *N.J., U.S.* **94** Nll
Jersey Shore, *Pa., U.S.* **94** M7
Jerseyside, *Nfld. & Lab., Can.* **83** M24
Jerseyville, *Ill., U.S.* **99** S4
Jerusalem, *Israel* **170** M5
Jervis *see* Rábida, Isla, island, *Ecua.*
128 Q9
Jervis Bay, *Austral.* **210** Ll4
Jervis Bay Territory, *Austral.* **211** Yl4
Jerzu, *It.* **151** P4
Jesenice, *Slov.* **152** C4
Jeseník, *Czech Rep.* **149** Gl3
Jesi, *It.* **150** H9
Jessore, *Bangladesh* **178** Jl2
Jesup, *Ga., U.S.* **97** P8
Jesús María, *Arg.* **132** JlO
Jetmore, *Kans., U.S.* **105** T5
Jetpur, *India* **178** J2
Jewel Cave National Monument, *S. Dak.,*
U.S. **104** Ll
Jewell, *Iowa, U.S.* **105** Nll
Jewett, *Tex., U.S.* **103** Nl2
Jeypore, *India* **178** L8
Jezercë, Maja, *Albania* **152** J9

Jezioro Shiardwy, *Pol.* 149 B16
Jezzîne, *Leb.* 170 J6
Jhalawar, *India* 178 H5
Jhal Jhao, *Pak.* 177 V5
Jhang, *Pak.* 177 Q10
Jhansi, *India* 178 H6
Jharsuguda, *India* 178 K9
Jhatpat, *Pak.* 177 T7
Jhelum, *Pak.* 177 Q10
Jhelum, *S. Korea* 182 G14
Jhelum, *Pak.* 177 P11
Jhimpir, *Pak.* 177 W7
Jhal Jhao, *Pak.* 177 V5
Jhang, *Pak.* 177 Q10
Jhansi, *India* 178 H6
Jharsuguda, *India* 178 K9
Jhatpat, *Pak.* 177 T7
Jhelum, river, *Pak.* 177 Q10
Jhelum, *Pak.* 177 P11
Jhimpir, *Pak.* 177 W7
Jhudo, *Pak.* 177 W8
Jhunjhunun, *India* 178 F5
Jiahe, *China* 183 P3
Jiaji see Qionghai, *China* 183 U2
Jiamusi, *China* 181 C18
Ji'an, *China* 182 C12
Ji'an, *China* 183 N5
Jianchang, *China* 182 C9
Jianchuan, *China* 180 N10
Jiande, *China* 182 M8
Jianghua, *China* 183 Q3
Jiangiunmiao, *China* 180 E8
Jiangle, *China* 183 P7
Jiangling, *China* 182 L4
Jiangmen, *China* 183 S4
Jiangshan, *China* 182 M8
Jianli, *China* 182 L4
Jianning, *China* 183 P7
Jian'ou, *China* 183 P7
Jianping, *China* 182 C9
Jianshi, *China* 182 L2
Jianyang, *China* 183 N7
Jiaohe, *China* 182 A13
Jiaojiang see Taizhou, *China* 182 M10
Jiaokou, *China* 182 F3
Jiaonan, *China* 182 G9
Jiaozhou, *China* 182 F9
Jiaozhou Wan, *China* 182 G9
Jiaozuo, *China* 182 G5
Jiawang, *China* 182 H7
Jiaxian, *China* 182 E3
Jiaxing, *China* 182 L9
Jiayin, *China* 181 B17
Jiayu, *China* 182 L5
Jiayuguan, *China* 180 G10
Jibsh, Ra's, *Oman* 173 L17
Jiddat al Ḥarāsīs, desert, *Oman* 173 M15
Jido, *India* 178 E15
Jieshou, *China* 182 J6
Jiesjavrre, *Nor.* 141 C14
Jiexiu, *China* 182 F4
Jieyang, *China* 183 R6
Jiggalong, *W. Aust., Austral.* 211 T4
Jigüey, Bahía de, *Cuba* 116 H10
Jihlava, *Czech Rep.* 148 J12
Jijia, river, *Rom.* 153 B16
Jijiga, *Eth.* 199 G16
Jilib, *Somalia* 199 J16
Jilin, *China* 182 A12
Jiloy, *Azerb.* 169 D24
Jīma, *Eth.* 199 G14
Jimaní, *Dom. Rep.* 117 M17
Jimbolia, *Rom.* 152 D10
Jiménez, *Mex.* 114 E9
Jimo, *China* 182 F9
Jinan, *China* 182 F7
Jinbal, island, *Marshall Is.* 216 L8
Jinchang, *China* 180 H11
Jincheng, *China* 182 G4
Jindřichův Hradec, *Czech Rep.* 148 J11
Jinedrol, island, *Marshall Is.* 216 H9
Jingazhiri, *Taj.* 176 H11
Jingbian, *China* 182 E2
Jingde, *China* 182 L8
Jingdezhen, *China* 182 M7
Jinggu, *China* 180 P10
Jinghai, *China* 182 D7
Jinghong, *China* 180 Q10
Jingle, *China* 182 E4
Jingmen, *China* 182 K4
Jingpeng see Hexigten Qi, *China* 182 A7
Jingpo Hu, *China* 181 D18
Jingxi, *China* 180 P12
Jingxing, *China* 182 E5
Jingyu, *China* 182 B13

Jingzhou, *China* 182 L4
Jingzhou, *China* 183 P2
Jinhua, *China* 182 M9
Jinimi, island, *Marshall Is.* 216 H9
Jining, *China* 182 C5
Jining, *China* 182 G7
Jinja, *Uganda* 199 K13
Jinjiang, *China* 183 Q8
Jinju, *S. Korea* 182 G14
Jinmu Jiao, *China* 181 R13
Jinping, *China* 183 N1
Jinsha see Nantong, *China* 182 K9
Jinsha (Yangtze), river, *China* 180 N11
Jinshan, *China* 182 L9
Jinshi, *China* 182 L3
Jinxi see Huludao, *China* 182 C9
Jinxiang, *China* 182 G6
Jinzhai, *China* 182 K6
Jinzhou, *China* 182 C9
Jinzhou, *China* 182 D10
Jiparaná, river, *Braz.* 130 F8
Ji-Paraná (Rondônia), *Braz.* 130 G8
Jipijapa, *Ecua.* 128 K2
Jirgatol, *Taj.* 176 H9
Jiroft, *Iran* 173 G16
Jishou, *China* 182 M2
Jishui, *China* 183 N5
Jisr ash Shughūr, *Syr.* 170 E7
Jiu, river, *Rom.* 153 G13
Jiujiang, *China* 182 M6
Jiuling Shan, *China* 182 M5
Jiulong (Kowloon) *China* 183 S5
Jiuquan, *China* 180 G10
Jiuquan Satellite Launch Center, *China* 180 G10
Jiutai, *China* 181 E17
Jiwani, *Pak.* 177 W1
Jixi, *China* 182 L8
Jixi, *China* 181 D18
Jixian, *China* 182 D7
Jixian, *China* 182 F3
Jiyuan, *China* 182 G4
Jīzān, *Saudi Arabia* 172 P8
Jizzax, *Uzb.* 174 L12
Joaçaba, *Braz.* 130 N12
João Pessoa, *Braz.* 131 F18
Joaquín V. González, *Arg.* 132 F10
Jobos, *P.R., U.S.* 120 P4
Jobos, Bahía de, *P.R., U.S.* 120 P4
Jochiwon, *S. Korea* 182 F13
Jodar, *Sp.* 144 K11
Jodhpur, *India* 178 G3
Joensuu, *Fin.* 141 G17
Joe's Hill, *Kiribati* 217 B23
Jōetsu, *Japan* 184 M11
Joeuf, *Fr.* 147 N14
Jogindarnagar, *India* 177 P14
Jogipet, *India* 178 M6
Johannesburg, *Calif., U.S.* 109 V9
Johannesburg, *S. Af.* 202 J10
John Day, river, *Oreg., U.S.* 108 G6
John Day Dam, *Oreg., U.S., Wash., U.S.* 108 E5
John Day Fossil Beds National Monument, *Oreg., U.S.* 108 G6
John D. Rockefeller Jr. Memorial Parkway, *Wyo., U.S.* 106 G8
John Eyre Motel, *W. Aust., Austral.* 211 X6
John F. Kennedy Space Center, *Fla., U.S.* 97 T10
John H. Kerr Reservoir, *N.C., Va., U.S.* 96 G12
John Martin Reservoir, *Colo., U.S.* 107 N15
John Millars, *Bahamas* 120 F6
John o'Groats, site, *Scot., U.K.* 142 G10
John Redmond Reservoir, *Kans., U.S.* 105 T9
Johns Folly Bay, *Virgin Islands, U.S.* 120 N11
Johnson, *Kans., U.S.* 105 U3
Johnsonburg, *Pa., U.S.* 94 M5
Johnson City, *N.Y., U.S.* 94 K8
Johnson City, *Tenn., U.S.* 101 E20
Johnson City, *Tex., U.S.* 103 Q9
Johnson Draw, *Tex., U.S.* 103 Q6
Johnsons Point, *Antigua & Barbuda* 121 B20
Johnston, *S.C., U.S.* 96 L8
Johnston, Lake, *Austral.* 210 K4
Johnston, Mount, *Antarctica* 227 F19
Johnston Atoll, *Pac. Oc.* 214 E10
Johnston City, *Ill., U.S.* 99 U6
Johnstone, *Scot., U.K.* 142 M9

Johnstown, *N.Y., U.S.* 94 J10
Johnstown, *Pa., U.S.* 94 P4
Johor Baharu, *Malaysia* 187 VII
Joigny, *Fr.* 147 Q11
Joinville, *Braz.* 131 N13
Joinville Island, *Antarctica* 226 C4
Jokaj, island, *F.S.M.* 217 F14
Jokkmokk, *Sw.* 141 F13
Jolo, island, *Philippines* 189 G14
Jolo, *Philippines* 189 G13
Jomda, *China* 180 L10
Jonesboro, *Ark., U.S.* 100 F10
Jonesboro, *La., U.S.* 100 L8
Jonesport, *Me., U.S.* 95 F19
Jonesville, *La., U.S.* 100 M9
Jonesville, *S.C., U.S.* 96 J8
Jönköping, *Sw.* 141 M13
Jonuta, *Mex.* 115 J15
Jonzac, *Fr.* 147 U7
Joplin, *Mo., U.S.* 105 V10
Joplin, *Mont., U.S.* 106 B8
Jordan, *Asia* 167 T3
Jordan, river, *Jordan, W. Bank* 170 M6
Jordan, *Minn., U.S.* 104 K11
Jordan, *Mont., U.S.* 106 C11
Jordan Valley, *Oreg., U.S.* 108 J9
Jorge Montt, Isla, *Chile* 133 W6
Jorhat, *India* 178 G15
Jorm, *Afghan.* 176 K9
Jormá , *Afghan.* 176 K9
Jörn, *Sw.* 141 G14
Jornada del Muerto, desert, *N. Mex., U.S.* 107 U12
Jorong, *Indonesia* 188 K11
Jørpeland, *Nor.* 140 L10
Jos, *Nigeria* 201 F14
José Batlle-y-Ordóñez, *Uru.* 132 L14
Joseph, *Oreg., U.S.* 108 F9
Joseph Bonaparte Gulf, *Austral.* 210 B6
Josephine Seamount, *Atl. Oc.* 236 H11
José Rodrigues, *Braz.* 130 E12
Joshimath, *India* 178 E7
Joshua Tree National Park, *Calif., U.S.* 109 X11
Josipdol, *Croatia* 152 E5
Jos Plateau, *Nigeria* 194 H5
Josselin, *Fr.* 147 Q4
Jost Van Dyke, island, *Virgin Islands, U.K.* 120 L11
Jotunheimen, range, *Nor.* 140 K10
Jou, *Sao Tome and Principe* 205 D19
Joulter Cays, *Bahamas* 116 D11
Joûnié, *Leb.* 170 H6
Jourdanton, *Tex., U.S.* 103 S9
Joutsa, *Fin.* 141 H16
Joux, Lac de, *Switz.* 147 S14
Jovellanos, *Cuba* 116 G7
Joyeuse, *Fr.* 147 W12
J. Percy Priest Lake, *Tenn., U.S.* 101 E15
Jreida, *Mauritania* 196 F5
J. Strom Thurmond Reservoir, *Ga., S.C., U.S.* 96 L7
Ju, river, *China* 182 K3
Juana Díaz, *P.R., U.S.* 120 N3
Juan Aldama, *Mex.* 114 F10
Juan de Fuca, Strait of, *Can., U.S.* 84 A3
Juan de Fuca Ridge, *Pac. Oc.* 239 D15
Juan de Nova, Île, *Mozambique Ch.* 203 D12
Juan Domingo, *Neth. Antilles, Neth.* 121 P14
Juan Fernández, Islas, *S. Amer.* 126 M2
Juan José Castelli, *Arg.* 132 F12
Juanjuí, *Peru* 130 F3
Juan Stuven, Isla, *Chile* 133 U6
Juárez, *Arg.* 133 N12
Juàzeiro, *Braz.* 131 G16
Juazeiro do Norte, *Braz.* 131 F16
Juba, *Sudan* 199 H13
Jubany, station, *Antarctica* 226 C3
Jubba, Webi, *Somalia* 199 J16
Jubbah, *Saudi Arabia* 172 G8
Jubb al Jarrāḥ, *Syr.* 170 G9
Juberri, *Andorra* 160 K2
Juby, Cape, *Mor.* 196 C6
Júcar, river, *Sp.* 145 H13
Júcaro, *Cuba* 116 J10
Juchitán, *Mex.* 115 K13

Judith Gap, *Mont., U.S.* 106 D9
Judsonia, *Ark., U.S.* 100 F9
Juegang see Rudong, *China* 182 K10
Juifang, *Taiwan, China* 183 Q10
Juigalpa, *Nicar.* 115 M18
Juiz de Fora, *Braz.* 131 L15
Jokaj, island, *F.S.M.* 217 F14
Julesburg, *Colo., U.S.* 106 K15
Juliaca, *Peru* 130 J6
Julia Creek, *Qnsld., Austral.* 211 S11
Julian, *Calif., U.S.* 109 Y10
Julian Alps, *It., Slov.* 150 C10
Julu, *China* 182 F6
Jumilla, *Sp.* 145 J13
Jumla, *Nepal* 178 E8
Jumunjin, *S. Korea* 182 E14
Junan, *China* 182 G8
Juncos, *P.R., U.S.* 120 N5
Junction, *Tex., U.S.* 103 Q8
Junction, *Utah, U.S.* 107 N7
Junction City, *Ark., U.S.* 100 K8
Junction City, *Kans., U.S.* 105 S8
Junction City, *Oreg., U.S.* 108 H3
Jundah, *Qnsld., Austral.* 211 U12
Juneau, *Alas., U.S.* 113 L22
Junggar Pendi (Dzungarian Basin), *China* 180 E7
Junglinster, *Lux.* 160 J10
Jungshahi, *Pak.* 177 W7
Juniata, river, *Pa., U.S.* 94 N7
Junín, *Arg.* 132 L11
Junín, *Peru* 130 H3
Junín de los Andes, *Arg.* 133 P7
Juniper Mountain, *Oreg., U.S.* 108 J6
Junlian, *China* 180 M12
Junnar, *India* 178 L4
Juno Beach, *Fla., U.S.* 97 V10
Juntura, *Oreg., U.S.* 108 H8
Jupaguá, *Braz.* 131 H14
Jupiter, *Fla., U.S.* 97 V10
Jura, island, *Scot., U.K.* 142 M7
Jura, Sound of, *Scot., U.K.* 142 M7
Jurado, *Col.* 128 D3
Jura Mountains, *Fr., Switz.* 138 G5
Jurby, *Isle of Man, U.K.* 143 Q9
Jurien, *W. Aust., Austral.* 211 W2
Juruá, river, *Braz.* 130 E7
Juruá, *Braz.* 130 D7
Juruena, river, *Braz.* 130 F10
Juruti, *Braz.* 130 D10
Justo Daract, *Arg.* 132 L9
Jutaí, river, *Braz.* 130 E6
Jutaí, *Braz.* 130 E6
Jutiapa, *Guatemala* 115 L16
Juticalpa, *Hond.* 115 L18
Jutland see Jylland, region, *Den., Ger.* 140 N11
Juventud, Isla de la (Isle of Youth), *Cuba* 116 J5
Juxian, *China* 182 G8
Juye, *China* 182 G6
Juzennecourt, *Fr.* 147 Q13
Juzzak, *Pak.* 177 S1
Jylland (Jutland), region, *Den., Ger.* 140 N11
Jyväskylä, *Fin.* 141 H16

K

K2 (Godwin Austen, Qogir), peak, *China, Pak.* 176 L13
Ka'a'awa, *Hawai'i, U.S.* 112 D11
Kaabong, *Uganda* 199 H13
Kaala-Gomén, *New Caledonia, Fr.* 218 C6
Ka'alu'alu Bay, *Hawai'i, U.S.* 113 Q19
Kaamanen, *Fin.* 141 C15
Kaamboni, *Somalia* 199 K16
Kaam, booni, Raas, *Kenya, Somalia* 194 K11
Kā'anapali, *Hawai'i, U.S.* 113 G15
Kaap Plateau, *S. Af.* 194 Q8
Kabaena, island, *Indonesia* 189 L14
Kabala, *Sierra Leone* 200 F6
Kabale, *Uganda* 198 K12
Kabalo, *Dem. Rep. of the Congo* 198 M11
Kabambare, *Dem. Rep. of the Congo* 198 L12
Kabara, island, *Fiji Is.* 218 K9
Kabarei, *Indonesia* 189 J17
Kabbenbock, island, *Marshall Is.* 216 M8
Kabinda, *Dem. Rep. of the Congo* 198 M10
Kabīr, river, *Leb., Syr.* 170 G7
Kabol (Kabul), *Afghan.* 176 M8

Kabong, *Malaysia* 188 H10
Kabongo, *Dem. Rep. of the Congo* 198 M11
Kabūd Gombad, *Iran* 173 B16
Kabul, river, *Afghan.* 176 M8
Kabul see Kabol, *Afghan.* 176 M8
Kabuli, *P.N.G.* 213 B19
Kabumbé, Pico, *Sao Tome and Principe* 205 D20
Kaburuang, island, *Indonesia* 189 G16
Kabwe, *Zambia* 202 E11
Kachīry, *Kaz.* 175 D13
Kachreti, *Rep. of Georgia* 169 C19
Kaçkar Dağı, *Turk.* 169 D15
Kadaingti, *Myanmar* 186 K7
Kadan Kyun, *Myanmar* 187 N7
Kadavu, island, *Fiji Is.* 218 K6
Kadavu Passage, *Fiji Is.* 218 J6
Kadé, *Guinea* 200 E5
Kadıköy, *Turk.* 168 D3
Kading, river, *Laos* 186 K11
Kadınhanı, *Turk.* 168 G7
Kadiri, *India* 179 P6
Kadirli, *Turk.* 168 H11
Kadivka, *Ukr.* 157 Q10
Kadmat Island (Cardamum Island), *India* 179 Q3
Kadoka, *S. Dak., U.S.* 104 L3
Kadokura Zaki, *Japan* 185 U4
Kadom, *Russ.* 156 K12
Kadoma, *Zimb.* 202 F11
Kadugli, *Sudan* 198 F12
Kaduna, *Nigeria* 201 F14
Kadur, *India* 179 P5
Kadyy, *Russ.* 156 G12
Kaédi, *Mauritania* 196 G5
Kaélé, *Cameroon* 201 F17
Ka'ena Point, *Hawai'i, U.S.* 112 D10
Ka'eo, peak, *Hawai'i, U.S.* 112 C3
Kaeo, *N.Z.* 213 H18
Kaesŏng, *N. Korea* 182 E13
Kāf, *Saudi Arabia* 172 E6
Kafar Jar Ghar Range, *Afghan.* 177 P6
Kafia Kingi, *Sudan* 198 G10
Kafiéas, Akrotírio, *Gr.* 155 J14
Kafue, river, *Zambia* 202 E10
Kafue, *Zambia* 202 E10
Kafuka, *Japan* 184 D13
Kaga, *Japan* 185 N9
Kaga Bandoro, *Cen. Af. Rep.* 198 G9
Kagan, *Pak.* 176 M11
Kağızman, *Turk.* 169 E17
Kagmar, *Sudan* 198 E12
Kagoshima, *Japan* 185 T4
Kahakuloa, *Hawai'i, U.S.* 113 F16
Kahalu'u, *Hawai'i, U.S.* 112 E11
Kahalu'u, *Hawai'i, U.S.* 113 M18
Kahama, *Tanzania* 199 L13
Kahan, *Pak.* 177 S7
Kahana, *Hawai'i, U.S.* 113 G15
Kahe'a Heiau and Petroglyphs, *Hawai'i, U.S.* 113 G15
Kahei Homesteads, *Hawai'i, U.S.* 113 K19
Kahemba, *Dem. Rep. of the Congo* 198 M8
Kāhili, peak, *Hawai'i, U.S.* 112 B5
Kahlotus, *Wash., U.S.* 108 D8
Kahnūj, *Iran* 173 G16
Kahoka, *Mo., U.S.* 105 Q13
Kaho'olawe, island, *Hawai'i, U.S.* 113 H15
Kahouanne, Îlet à, *Guadeloupe, Fr.* 121 E14
Kahramanmaraş, *Turk.* 168 H12
Kâhta, *Turk.* 169 H13
Kahuku, *Hawai'i, U.S.* 112 D11
Kahuku, *Hawai'i, U.S.* 113 P19
Kahuku Point, *Hawai'i, U.S.* 112 D11
Kahului, *Hawai'i, U.S.* 113 G16
Kahului Harbor, *Hawai'i, U.S.* 113 G16
Kahuwa'a (Sacred Falls), *Hawai'i, U.S.* 112 D11
Kai, Kepulauan (Ewab), *Indonesia* 189 L18
Kaiama, *Nigeria* 200 F12
Kaibab Plateau, *Ariz., U.S.* 84 H6
Kaibara, *Japan* 185 Q8
Kaibito, *Ariz., U.S.* 107 Q8
Kaieteur Fall, *Guyana* 129 E14
Kaifeng, *China* 182 H5
Kaijin, *Japan* 185 R7
Kaiholena, peak, *Hawai'i, U.S.* 113 P20
Kai Kecil, island, *Indonesia* 189 L18
Kaikoura, *N.Z.* 213 N18
Kailu, *China* 182 A9
Kailua, *Hawai'i, U.S.* 112 E12

Kailua, *Hawai'i, U.S.* 113 M18
Kaimana, *Indonesia* 213 C15
Kaimu Beach (Black Sand Beach), *Hawai'i, U.S.* 113 N22
Kainji Reservoir, *Nigeria* 201 F13
Kaipara Harbour, *N.Z.* 213 J18
Kaiserslautern, *Ger.* 148 H6
Kaishantun, *China* 182 A14
Kaitaia, *N.Z.* 213 H18
Ka'iwaloa Heiau and Olowalu Petroglyphs, *Hawai'i, U.S.* 113 G16
Kaiwi Channel, *Hawai'i, U.S.* 112 F12
Kaixian, *China* 182 K1
Kaiyuan, *China* 182 B11
Kaiyuan, *China* 180 P11
Kaiyuh Mountains, *Alas., U.S.* 111 G14
Kajaani, *Fin.* 141 G16
Kajabbi, *Qnsld., Austral.* 211 S11
Kajaki, *Afghan.* 177 P4
Kajaki, Band-e, *Afghan.* 177 P4
Kajang, *Malaysia* 187 U9
Kajiki, *Japan* 185 T4
Kaka, *Sudan* 199 F13
Kaka, *Turkm.* 174 M9
Kākā, Lae 'O, *Hawai'i, U.S.* 113 H16
Kakamas, *S. Af.* 202 K8
Kakana, *India* 179 S14
Kakaramea, *N.Z.* 213 L18
Kakdwip, *India* 178 J11
Kake, *Alas., U.S.* 111 L22
Kake, *Japan* 185 Q6
Kakeroma Jima, *Japan* 185 W3
Kākhk, *Iran* 173 D16
Kakhovka, *Ukr.* 157 R7
Kakhovka Reservoir, *Ukr.* 138 G11
Kakhovs'ke Vodoskhovyshche, *Ukr.* 157 R7
Kakinada (Cocanada), *India* 178 M8
Kakogawa, *Japan* 185 Q8
Kakshaal Range, *China, Kyrg.* 176 F14
Kaktovik, *Alas., U.S.* 111 C18
Kakuda, *Japan* 184 M13
Kala, *Azerb.* 169 D23
Kalaallit Nunaat *see* Greenland, *N. Amer.* 81 C21
Kalabagh, *Pak.* 177 P9
Kalabakan, *Malaysia* 188 G12
Kalabo, *Zambia* 202 E9
Kalach, *Russ.* 157 N11
Kalach na Donu, *Russ.* 157 P12
Kalae (South Point), *Hawai'i, U.S.* 113 Q19
Kalafrana, *Malta* 161 L23
Kalahari Desert, *Botswana, Namibia* 202 H8
Kalāheo, *Hawai'i, U.S.* 112 C5
Kal'ai Khumb, *Taj.* 176 J9
Kalalea, Heiau o, *Hawai'i, U.S.* 113 Q19
Kalalua, peak, *Hawai'i, U.S.* 113 N21
Kalam, *Pak.* 176 L10
Kalama, *Wash., U.S.* 108 E3
Kalamáta, *Gr.* 154 L9
Kalamazoo, river, *Mich., U.S.* 98 M9
Kalamazoo, *Mich., U.S.* 98 M10
Kalambáka, *Gr.* 154 E9
Kálamos, island, *Gr.* 154 H7
Kalamotí, *Gr.* 155 J14
Kalannie, *W. Aust., Austral.* 211 W3
Kalao, island, *Indonesia* 189 M13
Kalaoa, *Hawai'i, U.S.* 113 M18
Kalaotoa, island, *Indonesia* 189 M14
Kalasin, *Thai.* 186 L10
Kalat *see* Qalat, *Afghan.* 177 P6
Kalat, *Pak.* 177 S5
Kalaupapa, *Hawai'i, U.S.* 113 F14
Kalaupapa National Historic Park, *Hawai'i, U.S.* 113 F14
Kalávrita, *Gr.* 154 J9
Kalawao, site, *Hawai'i, U.S.* 113 F15
Kalaýmor, *Turkm.* 174 N10
Kalay-wa, *Myanmar* 186 F5
Kalb, Ra's al, *Yemen* 172 Q11
Kälbäjär, *Azerb.* 169 E20
Kalbān, *Oman* 173 M17
Kaldar, *Afghan.* 176 K6
Kale, *Turk.* 168 J5
Kalealoa, cape, *Hawai'i, U.S.* 112 E10
Kale Burnu, *Turk.* 169 D14
Kalecik, *Turk.* 168 E9
Kaledupa, island, *Indonesia* 189 L14
Kalemie, *Dem. Rep. of the Congo* 198 M12
Kalemyo, *Myanmar* 186 F5
Kalenyy, *Kaz.* 174 D6
Kaleybar, *Iran* 172 A11

Kalgoorlie, *W. Aust., Austral.* 211 W4
Kaliakoúda, peak, *Gr.* 154 G9
Kaliakra, Nos, *Bulg.* 153 H18
Kalianda, *Indonesia* 188 L8
Kalihi Wai, *Hawai'i, U.S.* 112 B5
Kalihi Wai Bay, *Hawai'i, U.S.* 112 A6
Kalí Límni, *Gr.* 155 P18
Kálimnos, island, *Gr.* 155 L18
Kálimnos, *Gr.* 155 L18
Kalimpang, *India* 178 G11
Kaliningrad, *Russ.* 156 J1
Kaliningrad Oblast, *Russ.* 156 J2
Kalinino, *Arm.* 169 C18
Kalinino, *Russ.* 157 S10
Kalininsk, *Russ.* 156 M13
Kalinkavichy, *Belarus* 156 M5
Kalísz, *Pol.* 149 E14
Kalix, *Sw.* 141 E14
Kalkan, *Turk.* 168 J5
Kalkaska, *Mich., U.S.* 98 J10
Kallithéa, *Gr.* 154 J12
Kallsjön, lake, *Sw.* 140 H12
Kalmar, *Sw.* 141 N13
Kalnai, *India* 178 J9
Kalnik, peak, *Croatia* 152 D6
Kalo Chorio, *Cyprus* 160 Q7
Kalohi Channel, *Hawai'i, U.S.* 113 G14
Kaloko-Honokōhau National Historic Park, *Hawai'i, U.S.* 113 M18
Kaloli Point, *Hawai'i, U.S.* 113 M22
Kaloní, *Gr.* 155 F16
Kalonís, Kólpos, *Gr.* 155 G16
Kalpa, *India* 178 G7
Kalpeni Island, *India* 179 R3
Kalpitiya, *Sri Lanka* 179 S7
Kalskag, *Alas., U.S.* 111 J13
Kalsubai, peak, *India* 178 L4
Kaltag, *Alas., U.S.* 111 G14
Kaluga, *Russ.* 156 K9
Kalumburu, *W. Aust., Austral.* 211 Q6
Kalush, *Ukr.* 157 P2
Kal'ya, *Russ.* 158 G9
Kalyan, *India* 178 L3
Kalyazin, *Russ.* 156 H9
Kama, river, *Russ.* 158 H8
Kamaing, *Myanmar* 186 E6
Kamaishi, *Japan* 184 K14
Kamakal, island, *Fr. Polynesia, Fr.* 219 R20
Kamakou, peak, *Hawai'i, U.S.* 113 F15
Kamalino, *Hawai'i, U.S.* 112 C3
Kaman, *Turk.* 168 F9
Kamárai, *Gr.* 155 L14
Kamarān, island, *Yemen* 172 P8
Kama Reservoir, *Russ.* 138 C13
Kamariotissa, *Gr.* 155 D15
Kamarod, *Pak.* 177 T3
Kamar Zard, *Afghan.* 177 N2
Kambang, *Indonesia* 188 K6
Kambanós, Akrotírio, *Gr.* 155 J14
Kambove, *Dem. Rep. of the Congo* 198 N11
Kamchatka, Poluostrov, *Russ.* 159 F22
Kamchatka Peninsula *see* Kamchatskiy Poluostrov, *Russ.* 166 C13
Kamchatskiy Poluostrov, *Russ.* 159 E22
Kamchiya, river, *Bulg.* 153 H17
Kamdesh, *Afghan.* 176 L9
Kamehameha I Birthplace, *Hawai'i, U.S.* 113 J18
Kamen, Gora, *Russ.* 159 G14
Kaména Voúrla, *Gr.* 154 G11
Kamenka, *Kaz.* 174 C6
Kamenka, *Russ.* 156 L12
Kamenka, *Russ.* 158 E9
Kamenskiy, *Russ.* 157 N13
Kamensk Shakhtinskiy, *Russ.* 157 Q11
Kamensk Ural'skiy, *Russ.* 158 J3
Kamiah, *Idaho, U.S.* 106 D4
Kamieskroon, *S. Af.* 202 L7
Kamileroi, *Qnsld., Austral.* 211 S11
Kamiloloa, *Hawai'i, U.S.* 113 F14
Kamina, *Dem. Rep. of the Congo* 198 M10
Kamin'-Kashyrs'kyy, *Ukr.* 156 M3
Kaminone Shima, *Japan* 185 W3
Kamino Shima, *Japan* 185 Q3
Kamitsuki, *Japan* 185 R12
Kamitsushima, *Japan* 185 Q3
Kamiyaku, *Japan* 185 U4
Kamkhat Muḩaywir, ruin, *Jordan* 171 N7
Kamloops, *B.C., Can.* 82 M9

Kammuri, peak, *Japan* 185 Q6
Kamo, *Arm.* 169 D19
Kamoenai, *Japan* 184 F12
Kamōhio Bay, *Hawai'i, U.S.* 113 H16
Kamoke, *Pak.* 177 P12
Kamo'oloa, *Hawai'i, U.S.* 112 D10
Kampala, *Uganda* 199 K13
Kampar, *Malaysia* 187 T9
Kampen, *Neth.* 146 H13
Kamphaeng Phet, *Thai.* 186 L8
Kâmpóng Cham, *Cambodia* 187 N12
Kampong Kuala Besut, *Malaysia* 187 S10
Kampos, *Cyprus* 160 P6
Kampot, *Cambodia* 187 P11
Kamrau, Teluk, *Indonesia* 213 C15
Kamsack, *Sask., Can.* 83 M13
Kamsar, *Guinea* 200 F4
Kamuela *see* Waimea, *Hawai'i, U.S.* 113 K19
Kamui Misaki, *Japan* 184 F12
Kam'yanets'-Podil's'kyy, *Ukr.* 157 P3
Kam'yanka-Dniprovs'ka, *Ukr.* 157 R8
Kamyshin, *Russ.* 157 N13
Kamyzyak, *Russ.* 157 R15
Kanab, *Utah, U.S.* 107 Q6
Kanab Creek, *Ariz., Utah, U.S.* 107 Q6
Kanacea, island, *Fiji Is.* 218 H9
Kanaga Island, *Alas., U.S.* 110 N5
Kanak, river, *Turk.* 168 E10
Kanaláki, *Gr.* 154 F7
Kananga, *Dem. Rep. of the Congo* 198 L10
Kanapou Bay, *Hawai'i, U.S.* 113 H16
Kanarraville, *Utah, U.S.* 107 P6
Kanash, *Russ.* 156 J14
Kanatea, island, *Tonga* 218 J11
Kanawha, river, *W. Va., U.S.* 96 D7
Kanazawa, *Japan* 185 N9
Kanbalu, *Myanmar* 186 F6
Kanchenjunga, peak, *India, Nepal* 178 F11
Kanchipuram, *India* 179 Q7
Kandahar, *Afghan.* 177 Q5
Kandalaksha, *Russ.* 158 D8
Kandalakshskiy Zaliv, *Russ.* 158 D8
Kandangan, *Indonesia* 188 K11
Kándanos, *Gr.* 154 Q12
Kandersteg, *Switz.* 150 C3
Kandhkot, *Pak.* 177 T8
Kandi, *Benin* 200 F12
Kandi, *India* 178 H11
Kandiaro, *Pak.* 177 U7
Kandíla, *Gr.* 154 K10
Kandıra, *Turk.* 168 C6
Kandrach, *Pak.* 177 V5
Kandrian, *P.N.G.* 213 D20
Kandudu, island, *Maldives* 179 W3
Kandudu, island, *Maldives* 179 X3
Kandu-ye Bala, *Afghan.* 177 N5
Kandy, *Sri Lanka* 179 T7
Kane, *Pa., U.S.* 94 L5
Kane Basin, *Nunavut, Can.* 83 B16
Kane Fracture Zone, *Atl. Oc.* 236 K7
Kanengo, Note, *Solomon Is.* 217 P22
Kāne'ohe, *Hawai'i, U.S.* 112 E11
Kanevskaya, *Russ.* 157 S10
Kang, *Afghan.* 177 Q2
Kangaamiut, *Greenland, Den.* 81 D21
Kangal, *Turk.* 168 F12
Kangan, *Iran* 173 G13
Kanganpur, *Pak.* 177 Q12
Kangar, *Malaysia* 187 S8
Kangaroo Island, *S. Aust., Austral.* 211 Y10
Kangbao, *China* 182 B6
Kangding, *China* 180 L11
Kangean, Kepulauan, *Indonesia* 188 M11
Kangeeak Point, *Nunavut, Can.* 83 F19
Kangerlussuaq, *Greenland, Den.* 81 D21
Kangertittivaq, bay, *N. Amer.* 80 B10
Kanggava Bay, *Solomon Is.* 217 Q19
Kanggye, *N. Korea* 182 D13
Kangiqsualujjuaq, *Que., Can.* 83 J20
Kangiqsujuaq, *Que., Can.* 83 J18
Kangirsuk, *Que., Can.* 83 J19
Kangmar, *China* 180 M7
Kango, *Gabon* 201 K15
Kangping, *China* 182 B11
Kangpokpi, *India* 178 G14
Kangrinboqê Feng, peak, *China* 180 K5
Kangto, peak, *China, India* 178 F14
Kaniama, *Dem. Rep. of the Congo* 198 M10
Kaniere, *N.Z.* 213 N17
Kanif, *F.S.M.* 217 D18
Kanigiri, *India* 179 N7

Kanin, Poluostrov, *Russ.* 158 E9
Kanin Nos, Mys, *Russ.* 158 D9
Kanin Peninsula *see* Kanin, Poluostrov, *Russ.* 138 A11
Kanish, ruin, *Turk.* 168 F10
Kanita, *Japan* 184 J13
Kaniv, *Ukr.* 157 P6
Kanjarkot, site, *Pak.* 177 W8
Kanjiža, *Serb.* 152 D10
Kankakee, *Ill., U.S.* 99 P7
Kankakee, river, *Ill., Ind., U.S.* 99 P8
Kankan, *Guinea* 200 F7
Kanker, *India* 178 K8
Kanmaw Kyun, *Myanmar* 187 P7
Kanmen, *China* 183 N10
Kannapolis, *N.C., U.S.* 96 H9
Kannari, *Japan* 184 L13
Kannauj, *India* 178 G7
Kannur (Cannanore), *India* 179 Q4
Kano, *Nigeria* 201 E14
Kanokupolu, *Tonga* 218 H11
Kanopolis, *Kans., U.S.* 105 T7
Kanorado, *Kans., U.S.* 105 S3
Kanosh, *Utah, U.S.* 107 N6
Kanoya, *Japan* 185 T4
Kanpur, *India* 178 G7
Kansas, river, *Kans., U.S.* 105 S8
Kansas, *U.S.* 105 T4
Kansas City, *Kans., U.S.* 105 S10
Kansas City, *Mo., U.S.* 105 S10
Kansk, *Russ.* 159 K14
Kant, *Kyrg.* 176 D11
Kantara Castle, *Cyprus* 160 N10
Kanton, island, *Kiribati* 214 G10
Kanuku Mountains, *Guyana* 129 F14
Kanye, *Botswana* 202 J9
Kao, island, *Tonga* 218 P6
Kaohsiung, *Taiwan, China* 183 S9
Kaoka Bay, *Solomon Is.* 217 N19
Kaokoland, region, *Namibia* 202 G5
Kaolack, *Senegal* 196 H4
Kaoma, *Zambia* 202 E9
Kapa, island, *Tonga* 218 M11
Kapa'a, *Hawai'i, U.S.* 112 B6
Kapa'au, *Hawai'i, U.S.* 113 K19
Kapadvanj, *India* 178 J3
Kapan, *Arm.* 169 F20
Kapanga, *Dem. Rep. of the Congo* 198 M10
Kapela, range, *Croatia* 152 E5
Kapfenberg, *Aust.* 148 L12
Kapıdağı, peak, *Turk.* 168 D4
Kapingamarangi Atoll, *F.S.M.* 214 G5
Kapiri Mposhi, *Zambia* 202 E11
Kapisillit, *Greenland, Den.* 81 D22
Kapiskau, river, *Ont., Can.* 83 M17
Kapit, *Malaysia* 188 H10
Kaplan, *La., U.S.* 100 Q8
Kapoeta, *Sudan* 199 H13
Kapoho Crater, *Hawai'i, U.S.* 113 M22
Kaposvár, *Hung.* 149 N14
Kappar, *Pak.* 177 V2
Kapūaiwa Coconut Grove, *Hawai'i, U.S.* 113 F14
Kapulena, *Hawai'i, U.S.* 113 K20
Kapunda, *S. Aust., Austral.* 211 X10
Kapurthala, *India* 178 D5
Kapuskasing, *Ont., Can.* 83 N17
Kapydzhik, peak, *Arm.* 169 F20
Kara-Balta, *Kyrg.* 176 E11
Karabiga, *Turk.* 168 D3
Karabogaz (Bekdash), *Turkm.* 174 J6
Karabük, *Turk.* 168 C8
Kara Burun, *Turk.* 168 J7
Karaburun, peninsula, *Albania* 152 M9
Karaburun, *Turk.* 168 F2
Karacabey, *Turk.* 168 D4
Karaca Dağ, *Turk.* 169 H14
Karacadağ, *Turk.* 169 H14
Karacaköy, *Turk.* 168 C4
Karachala, *Azerb.* 169 E22
Karachay, *Russ.* 156 L8
Karachi, *Pak.* 177 W6
Karad, *India* 178 M4
Kara Dağ, *Turk.* 169 H18
Kara Dağ, *Turk.* 168 H8
Karadag, *Azerb.* 169 D23
Karaginskiy, Ostrov, *Russ.* 159 E22
Karahallı, *Turk.* 168 G5
Karahüyük, *Turk.* 168 G7
Karaisalı, *Turk.* 168 H10
Karaj, *Iran* 172 C12
Karakeçi, *Turk.* 169 H14
Karakelong, island, *Indonesia* 189 G16
Karakoçan, *Turk.* 169 F14

Kara-Köl, *Kyrg.* 176 F10
Karakol (Przheval'sk), *Kyrg.* 176 E14
Karakoram Pass, *China, India* 176 L14
Karakoram Range, *India, Pak.* 176 K12
Karakul', *Taj.* 176 H11
Karakulino, *Russ.* 156 H16
Karakuwisa, *Namibia* 202 G8
Karam, *Russ.* 159 K15
Karaman, *Turk.* 168 H8
Karamay, *China* 180 D7
Karamea, *N.Z.* 213 M17
Karamea Bight, *N.Z.* 213 M17
Karamürsel, *Turk.* 168 D5
Karanja, *India* 178 K6
Karapınar, *Turk.* 168 H9
Kara-Say, *Kyrg.* 176 E14
Karasburg, *Namibia* 202 K7
Kara Sea, *Arctic Oc.* 242 C11
Karasjok, *Nor.* 141 C14
Karas Mountains, *Namibia* 194 Q7
Karasu, river, *Turk.* 169 E15
Karasu, river, *Turk.* 169 F18
Karasu, *Turk.* 168 C6
Karasuk, *Russ.* 158 K11
Karataş, *Turk.* 168 J10
Karatepe, *Turk.* 168 H11
Karathuri, *Myanmar* 187 P7
Karatsu, *Japan* 185 R4
Karatung, island, *Indonesia* 189 G16
Karaul, *Russ.* 159 F13
Karavas, *Cyprus* 160 N8
Karávia, island, *Gr.* 154 M12
Karavostasi, *Cyprus* 160 P7
Karavostassás, *Gr.* 155 M14
Karawanken, range, *Slov.* 152 C4
Karayazı, *Turk.* 169 E16
Karayün, *Turk.* 168 E12
Karbalā', *Iraq* 172 E9
Karcag, *Hung.* 149 L16
Kardámila, *Gr.* 155 H16
Kardámili, *Gr.* 154 L10
Kardítsa, *Gr.* 154 F9
Kardiva (Karidu), island, *Maldives* 179 U3
Kardiva Channel, *Maldives* 179 U3
Kärdla, *Est.* 141 K15
Karesuando, *Sw.* 141 D14
Kargı, *Turk.* 168 D10
Kargil, *India* 176 M13
Kargilik *see* Yecheng, *China* 180 G4
Kari, *Nigeria* 201 F15
Kariba, *Zimb.* 202 F11
Kariba, Lake, *Zambia, Zimb.* 202 F10
Karidu *see* Kardiva, island, *Maldives* 179 U3
Kariés, *Gr.* 154 L10
Karikari, Cape, *N.Z.* 213 H18
Karimata, island, *Indonesia* 188 K9
Karimata, Kepulauan, *Indonesia* 188 K9
Karimganj, *India* 178 H14
Karimnagar, *India* 178 L7
Karimunjawa, Kepulauan, *Indonesia* 188 L9
Káristos, *Gr.* 155 J13
Karitane, *N.Z.* 213 Q16
Karítena, *Gr.* 154 K9
Karizak, *Afghan.* 177 P1
Karkar, island, *P.N.G.* 213 C19
Karkinits'ka Zatoka, *Ukr.* 157 S7
Karkūk (Kirkuk), *Iraq* 172 C9
Karlıova, *Turk.* 169 F15
Karlovac, *Croatia* 152 E5
Karlovássi, *Gr.* 155 J17
Karlovy Vary, *Czech Rep.* 148 G10
Karlshamn, *Sw.* 141 N13
Karlskrona, *Sw.* 141 N13
Karlsruhe, *Ger.* 148 J6
Karlstad, *Minn., U.S.* 104 E8
Karlstad, *Sw.* 140 L12
Karmala, *India* 178 L4
Karmir Blur, ruin, *Arm.* 169 E18
Karnali, river, *Nepal* 178 E8
Karnaphuli Reservoir, *Bangladesh* 178 J14
Karnes City, *Tex., U.S.* 103 S10
Karnobat (Polyanovgrad), *Bulg.* 153 J16
Karoi, *Zimb.* 202 F11
Karokh, *Afghan.* 176 M2
Karoko, *Fiji Is.* 218 G8
Karompa, island, *Indonesia* 189 M14
Karonga, *Malawi* 203 C13
Karonie, *W. Aust., Austral.* 211 W5
Karosa, *Indonesia* 189 K13
Karpas Peninsula, *Cyprus* 160 M11
Kárpathos, *Gr.* 155 P18

Kárpathos (Carpathos), island, *Gr.* **155** P18
Kárpathos Stenón, *Gr.* **155** P19
Karpeníssi, *Gr.* **154** G9
Karperó, *Gr.* **154** E9
Karratha, *W. Aust., Austral.* **211** S2
Karre Mountains, *Cen. Af. Rep.* **194** H6
Karridale, *W. Aust., Austral.* **211** Y2
Kars, *Turk.* **169** D17
Kartal, *Turk.* **168** C5
Karumba, *Qnsld., Austral.* **211** R11
Kārūn, river, *Iran* **172** F11
Karunjie, *W. Aust., Austral.* **211** Q6
Karviná, *Czech Rep.* **149** H14
Karwar, *India* **179** N4
Karwi, *India* **178** H8
Karyaí, *Gr.* **155** D13
Kar'yepol'ye, *Russ.* **158** E9
Karynzharyk, desert, *Kaz.* **174** J6
Kaş, *Turk.* **168** J5
Kas, *Sudan* **198** E10
Kasai, river, *Angola, Dem. Rep. of the Congo* **194** K7
Kasaji, *Dem. Rep. of the Congo* **198** N10
Kasama, *Zambia* **202** C12
Kasane, *Botswana* **202** F9
Kasar, Ras, *Eritrea* **199** D15
Kasaragod, *India* **179** Q4
Kasari, *Japan* **185** W3
Kasari Saki, *Japan* **185** W3
Kasba Lake, *N.W.T., Nunavut, Can.* **82** J13
Kasempa, *Zambia* **202** E10
Kasenga, *Dem. Rep. of the Congo* **198** N11
Kasese, *Dem. Rep. of the Congo* **198** K11
Kasganj, *India* **178** F6
Kasha-Katuwe Tent Rocks National Monument, *N. Mex., U.S.* **107** R12
Kāshān, *Iran* **173** D13
Kashgar see Kashi, *China* **180** F4
Kashi (Kashgar), *China* **180** F4
Kashin, *Russ.* **156** H9
Kashira, *Russ.* **156** K9
Kashiwazaki, *Japan* **184** M11
Kashkandyow, *Afghan.* **176** K10
Kāshmar, *Iran* **173** C16
Kashmir, region, *China, India, Pak.* **176** M12
Kashmir, Vale of, *India* **176** M12
Kashmor, *Pak.* **177** T8
Kasimov, *Russ.* **156** K11
Kasiruta, island, *Indonesia* **189** J16
Kaskaskia, river, *Ill., U.S.* **99** S6
Kaskö, *Fin.* **141** H14
Kasongo, *Dem. Rep. of the Congo* **198** L12
Kasongo-Lunda, *Dem. Rep. of the Congo* **198** M8
Kaspiysk, *Russ.* **157** U15
Kaspiyskiy, *Russ.* **157** S15
Kassala, *Sudan* **199** E14
Kassándra, peninsula, *Gr.* **154** E12
Kassándra, *Gr.* **154** E12
Kassándras, Kólpos, *Gr.* **154** D12
Kassel, *Ger.* **148** F7
Kassiópi, *Gr.* **154** E6
Kasson, *Minn., U.S.* **104** L12
Kássos, island, *Gr.* **155** Q18
Kássos Stenón, *Gr.* **155** Q17
Kastamonu, *Turk.* **168** C9
Kastaniés, *Gr.* **155** A17
Kastéli see Kíssamos, *Gr.* **154** Q12
Kastéli, *Gr.* **155** Q15
Kastellórizon see Megísti, island, *Gr.* **155** N22
Kastélou, Akrotírio, *Gr.* **155** Q18
Kastoriá, *Gr.* **154** C8
Kastorías, Límni, *Gr.* **154** D8
Kasumiga Ura, lake, *Japan* **185** P13
Kasumkent, *Russ.* **157** V16
Kasur, *Pak.* **177** Q12
Katafaga, island, *Fiji Is.* **218** H9
Katahdin, Mount, *Me., U.S.* **95** D17
Katákolo, *Gr.* **154** K8
Katanga, region, *Dem. Rep. of the Congo* **198** N11
Katanga Plateau, *Dem. Rep. of the Congo, Zambia* **194** M8
Katanning, *W. Aust., Austral.* **211** Y3
Katápola, *Gr.* **155** M16
Kata Tjuta see Olga, Mount, peak, *Austral.* **210** G7
Katavía, *Gr.* **155** N19
Katchall Island, *India* **179** S15
Kateríni, *Gr.* **154** D10

Kates Needle, peak, *Alas., U.S., B.C., Can.* **111** L23
Katha, *Myanmar* **186** F6
Katherîna, Gebel, *Egypt* **171** T3
Katherine, river, *Austral.* **210** B8
Katherine, *N. Terr., Austral.* **211** Q8
Kathiawar, region, *India* **178** J2
Kathmandu, *Nepal* **178** F10
Kathua, *India* **177** P13
Katiu, island, *Fr. Polynesia, Fr.* **219** E18
Katlanovo, *Maced.* **152** K11
Katmai, Mount, *Alas., U.S.* **111** L14
Katmai National Park and Preserve, *Alas., U.S.* **111** L15
Káto Ahaïa, *Gr.* **154** J8
Katohau, Baie, *Fr. Polynesia, Fr.* **219** M23
Kato Lakatameia, *Cyprus* **160** P8
Káto Nevrokópi, *Gr.* **154** B12
Katoomba, *N.S.W., Austral.* **211** Y14
Katowice, *Pol.* **149** G15
Katrancık Dağı, *Turk.* **168** H6
Katrine, Loch, *Scot., U.K.* **142** M9
Katsina, *Nigeria* **201** E14
Katsumoto, *Japan* **185** R3
Katsuyama, *Japan* **185** P9
Katsuyama, *Japan* **185** Q7
Kattankudi, *Sri Lanka* **179** T8
Kattegat, strait, *Den., Sw.* **140** N12
Katun', river, *Russ.* **158** L12
Katwe, *Uganda* **198** K12
Katwijk aan Zee, *Neth.* **146** J12
Ka'ū, region, *Hawai'i, U.S.* **113** P20
Kau, *Indonesia* **189** H16
Kaua'i, island, *Hawai'i, U.S.* **112** B5
Kaua'i Channel, *Hawai'i, U.S.* **112** C8
Kauakaiakaola Heiau, *Hawai'i, U.S.* **113** M18
Kauehi, island, *Fr. Polynesia, Fr.* **219** E18
Kaufbeuren, *Ger.* **148** K8
Kaufman, *Tex., U.S.* **102** L12
Kauhako Crater, *Hawai'i, U.S.* **113** F14
Kaukauai, *P.N.G.* **217** K14
Kaukauna, *Wis., U.S.* **98** J6
Kaukura, island, *Fr. Polynesia, Fr.* **219** E17
Ka'ula, island, *Hawai'i, U.S.* **112** D1
Ka'ula Gulch, *Hawai'i, U.S.* **113** L20
Kaulakahi Channel, *Hawai'i, U.S.* **112** B3
Ka'ū Loa Point, *Hawai'i, U.S.* **113** N18
Kaulu Paoa Heiau, *Hawai'i, U.S.* **112** B5
Kaumakani, *Hawai'i, U.S.* **112** C5
Kaumalapau, *Hawai'i, U.S.* **113** G14
Kaūmana Cave, *Hawai'i, U.S.* **113** M21
Kaumu o Kaleiho'ohie, peak, *Hawai'i, U.S.* **113** K19
Kaunakahi, *Hawai'i, U.S.* **113** F14
Kaunakakai Harbour, *Hawai'i, U.S.* **113** F14
Kaunā Point, *Hawai'i, U.S.* **113** P18
Kaunas, *Lith.* **141** N16
Kaunolū, site, *Hawai'i, U.S.* **113** H14
Kaupakulua, *Hawai'i, U.S.* **113** G17
Kaupō, *Hawai'i, U.S.* **113** H18
Ka'ūpūlehu, site, *Hawai'i, U.S.* **113** L18
Kaura-Namoda, *Nigeria* **201** E14
Kautenbach, *Lux.* **160** H9
Kautokeino, *Nor.* **141** D14
Kavacha, *Russ.* **159** D22
Kavadarci, *Maced.* **152** K11
Kavajë, *Albania* **152** L9
Kavak, *Turk.* **168** D11
Kavála (Neapolis), *Gr.* **155** C13
Kaválas, Kólpos, *Gr.* **155** C13
Kavalerovo, *Russ.* **159** L21
Kavali, *India* **179** N7
Kavaratti, *India* **179** R3
Kavieng, *P.N.G.* **213** B21
Kavīr, Dasht-e (Salt Desert), *Iran* **173** D14
Kavīr-e Namak, desert, *Iran* **173** D15
Kávos, *Gr.* **154** F6
Kawagoe, *Japan* **185** P12
Kawaihae, *Hawai'i, U.S.* **113** K19
Kawaihae Bay, *Hawai'i, U.S.* **113** L19
Kawaihoa Point, *Hawai'i, U.S.* **112** C3
Kawaikini, peak, *Hawai'i, U.S.* **112** B5
Kawakawa, *N.Z.* **213** H18
Kawambwa, *Zambia* **202** C11
Kawasaki, *Japan* **185** P12
Kawasak Passage, *Palau* **216** L12
Kawe, island, *Indonesia* **189** J17
Kawela, *Hawai'i, U.S.* **112** D11
Kawela, *Hawai'i, U.S.* **113** F14
Kawela Place of Refuge, *Hawai'i, U.S.* **113** F14

Kawhia, *N.Z.* **213** K19
Kawich Peak, *Nev., U.S.* **109** R10
Kawthoung, *Myanmar* **187** Q7
Kaya, *Burkina Faso* **200** E10
Kaya, *Indonesia* **188** H12
Kayan, river, *Indonesia* **188** H12
Kayangel Islands (Ngcheangel), *Palau* **216** K12
Kayangel Passage, *Palau* **216** K12
Kayapınar, *Turk.* **169** H15
Kaycee, *Wyo., U.S.* **106** G12
Kayenta, *Ariz., U.S.* **107** Q8
Kayes, *Congo* **201** M16
Kayes, *Mali* **196** H6
Kayl, *Lux.* **160** K9
Kaymaz, *Turk.* **168** E6
Kaynar, *Turk.* **168** F11
Kaysatskoye, *Russ.* **157** N14
Kayser Gebergte, peak, *Suriname* **129** F15
Kayseri, *Turk.* **168** F10
Kazach'ye, *Russ.* **159** E17
Kazakhstan, *Asia* **167** T6
Kazakh Uplands, *Kaz.* **175** D14
Kazakh Uplands, *Kaz.* **109** W11
Kazan, river, *Nunavut, Can.* **83** H14
Kazan', *Russ.* **156** J14
Kazan Rettō see Volcano Islands, *Japan* **184** L5
Kazanskaya, *Russ.* **157** P11
Kazarman, *Kyrg.* **176** F11
Kazbek, peak, *Rep. of Georgia* **169** B18
Kaz Dağı, *Turk.* **168** E3
Kāzerūn, *Iran* **173** G13
Kazi Ahmad, *Pak.* **177** V7
Kazimierz Dolny, *Pol.* **149** F17
Kazincbarcika, *Hung.* **149** K16
Kaztalovka, *Kaz.* **174** D5
Kazym Mys, *Russ.* **158** G10
Kéa (Tziá), island, *Gr.* **155** K13
Kea'au, *Hawai'i, U.S.* **113** M22
Kea'au Ranch, *Hawai'i, U.S.* **113** M22
Keadu, island, *Maldives* **179** V3
Keāhole Point, *Hawai'i, U.S.* **113** M18
Kealaikahiki, Lae 'O, *Hawai'i, U.S.* **113** H15
Kealaikahiki Channel, *Hawai'i, U.S.* **113** H15
Kealakekua, *Hawai'i, U.S.* **113** M18
Keālia, *Hawai'i, U.S.* **112** B6
Keālia, *Hawai'i, U.S.* **113** N18
Kéamu see Anatom, island, *Vanuatu* **218** H4
Ke'anae, *Hawai'i, U.S.* **113** G17
Keanapapa Point, *Hawai'i, U.S.* **113** G14
Kearney, *Nebr., U.S.* **105** Q6
Keauhou, *Hawai'i, U.S.* **113** M18
Keauhou Landing, *Hawai'i, U.S.* **113** N21
Ke Avainiu Pass, *Solomon Is.* **217** J18
Keawanui Bay, *Hawai'i, U.S.* **112** C3
Keban, *Turk.* **169** F13
Kebnekaise, peak, *Sw.* **141** E13
Kech, river, *Pak.* **177** V3
Keçiborlu, *Turk.* **168** G6
Kecskemét, *Hung.* **149** M15
Kediri, *Indonesia* **188** M10
Kédougou, *Senegal* **196** J6
Ke'ei, *Hawai'i, U.S.* **113** N18
Keele, river, *N.W.T., Can.* **82** G10
Keele Peak, *N.W.T., Yukon, Can.* **82** G9
Keeler, *Calif., U.S.* **109** U8
Keelung see Chilung, *Taiwan, China* **183** Q10
Keene, *N.H., U.S.* **95** J13
Keer-weer, Cape, *Austral.* **210** B11
Keetmanshoop, *Namibia* **202** J7
Keewatin, *Minn., U.S.* **104** F11
Kefaloniá (Cephalonia), island, *Gr.* **154** H7
Kéfalos, *Gr.* **155** M18
Kefaluka, *Turk.* **168** H3
Keflavík, *Ice.* **140** F1
Kegen, *Kaz.* **175** H17
Keg River, *Alta., Can.* **82** J10
Keheili, *Sudan* **199** C13
Kehl, *Ger.* **148** J5
Keila, *Est.* **141** K16
Kéita, Bahr, *Chad* **197** K15
Keitele, lake, *Fin.* **141** H16
Keith, *S. Aust., Austral.* **211** Y11
Keith, *Scot., U.K.* **142** J10
Keith Arm, *N.W.T., Can.* **82** F10
Keithsburg, *Ill., U.S.* **99** P3
Kekaha, *Hawai'i, U.S.* **112** C4
Kékes, peak, *Hung.* **149** K16
Kekirawa, *Sri Lanka* **179** S7

Keklau, *Palau* **216** M12
Kekra, *Russ.* **159** H20
Kekri, *India* **178** G4
Kel, *Pak.* **176** M12
K'elafo, *Eth.* **199** H16
Kelai, island, *Maldives* **179** T3
Kelan, *China* **182** D4
Kelang, island, *Indonesia* **189** K16
Kelang, *Malaysia* **187** U9
Këlcyrë, *Albania* **152** M10
Kelefesia, island, *Tonga* **218** R6
Keleft, *Afghan.* **176** K5
Kelheim, *Ger.* **148** J9
Kelkit, river, *Turk.* **168** D12
Kelkit, *Turk.* **169** E14
Kellet, Cape, *N.W.T., Can.* **82** D11
Keller Lake, *N.W.T., Can.* **82** G10
Kellits, *Jam.* **120** J9
Kells see Ceanannus Mór, *Ire.* **143** R6
Kélo, *Chad* **197** K14
Ke Loma, island, *Solomon Is.* **217** J18
Kelowna, *B.C., Can.* **82** M9
Kelso, *Calif., U.S.* **109** W11
Kelso, *Wash., U.S.* **108** E3
Keluang, *Malaysia* **187** V10
Kelvin Seamount Cap, *Atl. Oc.* **236** H5
Kem', *Russ.* **158** D8
Kema, *Indonesia* **189** H15
Kemah, *Turk.* **169** E13
Kemaliye, *Turk.* **169** F13
Kemasik, *Malaysia* **187** T10
Kembanye, Note, *Solomon Is.* **217** Q22
Kemer, *Turk.* **168** D3
Kemer, *Turk.* **168** G4
Kemer, *Turk.* **168** J5
Kemer, *Turk.* **168** J6
Kemerovo, *Russ.* **158** K12
Kemi, river, *Fin.* **138** B8
Kemi, *Fin.* **141** F15
Kemijärvi, lake, *Fin.* **141** E15
Kemijärvi, *Fin.* **141** E15
Kemijoki, river, *Fin.* **141** D15
Kemlya, *Russ.* **156** K13
Kemmerer, *Wyo., U.S.* **106** J8
Kemmuna see Comino, island, *Malta* **161** H21
Kemp, Lake, *Tex., U.S.* **102** J8
Kemp Coast, *Antarctica* **227** D20
Kempendyay, *Russ.* **159** H17
Kempopla, Note, *Solomon Is.* **217** Q22
Kemp Peninsula, *Antarctica* **226** E7
Kemps Bay, *Bahamas* **116** F11
Kempsey, *N.S.W., Austral.* **211** X15
Kempten, *Ger.* **148** L7
Kenai, *Alas., U.S.* **111** K16
Kenai Fjords National Park, *Alas., U.S.* **111** K16
Kenai Peninsula, *Alas., U.S.* **111** K16
Kenansville, *Fla., U.S.* **97** X10
Kendal, *Eng., U.K.* **143** Q11
Kendall, *Fla., U.S.* **97** X10
Kendall, *N.S.W., Austral.* **211** X15
Kendall, *N.Y., U.S.* **94** H6
Kendall, Cape, *Nunavut, Can.* **83** H16
Kendallville, *Ind., U.S.* **99** P10
Kendari, *Indonesia* **189** K14
Kendawangan, *Indonesia* **188** K9
Kendikolu, island, *Maldives* **179** T3
Kendrapara, *India* **178** K12
Kendrick, *Idaho, U.S.* **106** D3
Kenedy, *Tex., U.S.* **103** S10
Kenema, *Sierra Leone* **200** G6
Kèngkok, *Laos* **186** L11
Kengtung, *Myanmar* **186** H8
Kenhardt, *S. Af.* **202** K8
Kenitra, *Mor.* **196** B8
Kenli, *China* **182** F8
Kenmare, *Ire.* **143** U3
Kenmare, *N. Dak., U.S.* **104** E3
Kenmore, *Scot., U.K.* **142** L9
Kennebec, river, *Me., U.S.* **95** D16
Kennebec, *S. Dak., U.S.* **104** L5
Kennebunk, *Me., U.S.* **95** H15
Kennedy, Cape see Canaveral, Cape, *N. Amer.* **80** M8
Kennedy Channel, *Nunavut, Can.* **83** B16
Kennedy Entrance, *Alas., U.S.* **84** Q4
Kenner, *La., U.S.* **100** Q11
Kennett, *Mo., U.S.* **105** W15
Kennewick, *Wash., U.S.* **108** E7
Keno Hill, *Yukon, Can.* **82** F8
Kenora, *Ont., Can.* **83** N14
Kenosha, *Wis., U.S.* **98** M7
Kenova, *W. Va., U.S.* **96** D7

Kent, *Ohio, U.S.* **99** P15
Kent, *Oreg., U.S.* **108** F5
Kent, *Tex., U.S.* **103** N2
Kent, *Wash., U.S.* **108** C4
Kentland, *Ind., U.S.* **99** Q7
Kenton, *Ohio, U.S.* **99** Q12
Kent Peninsula, *Nunavut, Can.* **83** F13
Kentucky, river, *Ky., U.S.* **85** H17
Kentucky, *U.S.* **101** C14
Kentucky Lake, *Ky., U.S.* **101** D13
Kentwood, *La., U.S.* **100** N10
Kentwood, *Mich., U.S.* **98** L10
Kenutu, island, *Tonga* **218** L12
Kenya, *Af.* **195** J22
Kenya, Mount, *Kenya* **199** K14
Kenya Highlands, *Kenya* **194** K10
Keōkea, *Hawai'i, U.S.* **113** H17
Keōkea, *Hawai'i, U.S.* **113** N18
Ke'oke'o, Pu'u o, *Hawai'i, U.S.* **113** P19
Keokuk, *Iowa, U.S.* **105** Q14
Keōmuku, *Hawai'i, U.S.* **113** G15
Keonjhargarh, *India* **178** K10
Kep, *Cambodia* **187** P11
Kepi, *Indonesia* **189** M21
Kepi i Rodonit, *Albania* **152** K9
Kępno, *Pol.* **149** F14
Kepsut, *Turk.* **168** E4
Keramotí, *Gr.* **155** C14
Keran, *Pak.* **176** M11
Kerch, *Ukr.* **157** S9
Kerchenskiy Proliv, *Russ., Ukr.* **157** S9
Kerempe Burnu, *Turk.* **168** B9
Keren, *Eritrea* **199** D15
Kerens, *Tex., U.S.* **102** M12
Kerguelen Islands, *Ind. Oc.* **240** Q8
Kerguelen Plateau, *Ind. Oc.* **240** R9
Keri, *Gr.* **154** K7
Kerikeri, *N.Z.* **213** H18
Kerinci, peak, *Indonesia* **188** K6
Kerki see Atamyrat, *Turkm.* **174** M11
Kerkíni, *Gr.* **154** B11
Kerkínis, Límni, *Gr.* **154** B11
Kérkira, *Gr.* **154** E6
Kérkira (Corfu, Corcyra), island, *Gr.* **154** E6
Kermadec Islands, *N.Z.* **214** L9
Kermadec Trench, *Pac. Oc.* **238** P10
Kermān, *Iran* **173** F15
Kermānshāh, *Iran* **172** D11
Kermānshāhān, *Iran* **173** F14
Kermit, *Tex., U.S.* **102** M3
Kern, river, *Calif., U.S.* **109** V7
Kernersville, *N.C., U.S.* **96** G10
Kernville, *Calif., U.S.* **109** V8
Kéros, island, *Gr.* **155** L15
Kerr, Mount, *Bahamas* **120** E11
Kerrobert, *Sask., Can.* **82** M11
Kerrville, *Tex., U.S.* **103** Q8
Kerry Head, *Ire.* **143** T2
Kershaw, *S.C., U.S.* **96** K9
Kertamulia, *Indonesia* **188** J9
Keryneia see Kyrenia, *Cyprus* **160** N9
Keryneia Range, *Cyprus* **160** N9
Keşan, *Turk.* **168** C3
Keşap, *Turk.* **169** D13
Kesennuma, *Japan* **184** L13
Keshem, *Afghan.* **176** K8
Keshod, *India* **178** K2
Keşiş Dağı, *Turk.* **169** E14
Keskal, *India* **178** L8
Keskin, *Turk.* **168** E9
Kes'ma, *Russ.* **156** G9
Keszthely, *Hung.* **149** M13
Ketanda, *Russ.* **159** G19
Ketaun, *Indonesia* **188** K6
Ketchikan, *Alas., U.S.* **111** M23
Ketchum, *Idaho, U.S.* **106** G5
Ketchum Mountain, *Tex., U.S.* **103** N6
Kete Krachi, *Ghana* **200** G11
Keti Bandar, *Pak.* **177** X6
Kettering, *Eng., U.K.* **143** T13
Kettering, *Ohio, U.S.* **99** R11
Kettle Falls, *Wash., U.S.* **108** A8
Kettle River Range, *Wash., U.S.* **108** A8
Keul', *Russ.* **159** K15
Kewanee, *Ill., U.S.* **99** P4
Kewaunee, *Wis., U.S.* **98** J7
Keweenaw Bay, *Mich., U.S.* **98** E6
Keweenaw National Historic Park, *Mich., U.S.* **98** E6
Keweenaw Peninsula, *Mich., U.S.* **98** E7
Keweenaw Point, *Mich., U.S.* **98** E7
Key, Lough, *Ire.* **143** R5
Keyano, *Que., Can.* **83** L19

Keya Paha, river, *S. Dak., U.S.* **104** M5
Key Colony Beach, *Fla., U.S.* **97** Y9
Keyes, *Okla., U.S.* **102** E4
Keyhole Reservoir, *Wyo., U.S.* **106** FI3
Key Largo, *Fla., U.S.* **97** YIO
Keyser, *W. Va., U.S.* **96** CII
Keystone, *S. Dak., U.S.* **104** L2
Keystone, *W. Va., U.S.* **96** F8
Keystone Lake, *Okla., U.S.* **84** JI2
Key West, *Fla., U.S.* **97** Y8
Kežmarok, *Slovakia* **149** JI6
Khabarovsk, *Russ.* **159** K2I
Khābūr, river, *Syr.* **170** DI4
Khada Hills, *Afghan.* **177** Q5
Khadyzhensk, *Russ.* **157** TII
Khailino, *Russ.* **159** D2I
Khairpur, *Pak.* **177** SIO
Khairpur, *Pak.* **177** T7
Khakhar', *Russ.* **159** HI9
Khalatse, *India* **176** MI4
Khalūf, *Oman* **173** LI6
Khambhaliya, *India* **178** JI
Khambhat, Gulf of, *India* **178** K3
Khamgaon, *India* **178** K5
Khamīs Mushayţ, *Saudi Arabia* **172** N8
Kham Khowrki, *Afghan.* **177** N3
Khammouan, *Laos* **186** KII
Khamr, *Yemen* **172** P9
Khanabad, *Afghan.* **176** K8
Khān Abū Shāmāt, *Syr.* **170** J8
Khanai, *Pak.* **177** R6
Khanaqa, *Afghan.* **176** K5
Khānaqīn, *Iraq* **172** DIO
Khān az Zābīb, *Jordan* **171** N7
Khanderi Island, *India* **178** L3
Khandwa, *India* **178** K5
Khandyga, *Russ.* **159** GI8
Khanewal, *Pak.* **177** RIO
Khangarh, *Pak.* **177** TIO
Khaniadhana, *India* **178** H6
Khanka, Lake *see* Khanka, Ozero, *China, Russ.* **166** EI2
Khanka, Ozero *see* Xingkai Hu, *China, Russ.* **181** DI9
Khanlar, *Azerb.* **169** D2O
Khanozai, *Pak.* **177** R6
Khanpur, *Pak.* **177** S9
Khān Shaykhūn, *Syr.* **170** F8
Khan Tängiri (Lord of the Sky), peak, *Kaz., Kyrg.* **176** EI5
Khantayskoye, Ozero, *Russ.* **159** GI3
Khanty-Mansiysk, *Russ.* **158** HIO
Khān Yūnis, *Gaza Strip* **171** N4
Khapalu, *Pak.* **176** LI3
Kharabali, *Russ.* **157** QI5
Kharagpur, *India* **178** JII
Khara Khoto *see* Heicheng, ruin, *China* **180** FII
Kharan, *Pak.* **177** T4
Kharānaq, *Iran* **173** EI4
Kharasavey, Mys, *Russ.* **158** EII
Khârga Oasis, *Egypt* **197** EI8
Khargon, *India* **178** K5
Khargūsh, *Taj.* **176** JIO
Kharian, *Pak.* **177** PII
Khariar, *India* **178** K9
Kharimkotan, island, *Russ.* **159** H23
Khārk, island, *Iran* **172** GI2
Kharkiv, *Ukr.* **157** P9
Kharlovka, *Russ.* **158** D9
Kharmanli, *Russ.* **153** KI5
Kharovsk, *Russ.* **156** FIO
Khartoum, *Sudan* **199** EI3
Khartoum North, *Sudan* **199** EI3
Kharyyalakh, *Russ.* **159** GI5
Khasavyurt, *Russ.* **157** TI5
Khash, river, *Afghan.* **177** P4
Khash, *Afghan.* **177** Q3
Khāsh, *Iran* **173** GI7
Khash Desert, *Afghan.* **177** P2
Khashuri, *Rep. of Georgia* **169** CI7
Khasi Hills, *India* **178** GI3
Khaskovo, *Bulg.* **153** KI5
Khatanga, *Russ.* **159** FI4
Khatangskiy Zaliv, *Russ.* **159** EI5
Khatisch Alpen, *Switz.* **150** C5
Khātūnīyah, *Syr.* **170** DI5
Khatyrka, *Russ.* **159** C2I
Khaval, *Afghan.* **176** L5
Khavda, *India* **178** H2
Khaybar, Ḩarrat, *Saudi Arabia* **172** J7
Khaydarkan, *Kyrg.* **176** G9
Khemmarat, *Thai.* **186** LII
Khenjan, *Afghan.* **176** L7
Kherson, *Ukr.* **157** R7

Kherwara, *India* **178** H4
Kheta, *Russ.* **159** FI4
Khewari, *Pak.* **177** U7
Kheyrabad, *Afghan.* **176** K6
Khimki, *Russ.* **156** J9
Khipro, *Pak.* **177** V8
Khiri Ratthanikhom, *Thai.* **187** Q8
Khiwa, *Uzb.* **174** K9
Khizy, *Azerb.* **169** C22
Khlevnoye, *Russ.* **156** MIO
Khmel'nyts'kyy, *Ukr.* **157** P4
Khoai, Hon, *Vietnam* **187** RII
Khocho, *Russ.* **159** HI8
Khodzhakala, *Turkm.* **174** L7
Khojak Pass, *Pak.* **177** Q5
Khokhol'skiy, *Russ.* **156** MIO
Khokhropar, *Pak.* **177** V9
Khok Kloi, *Thai.* **187** R7
Kholm, *Afghan.* **176** K6
Kholm, *Russ.* **156** H6
Kholmsk, *Russ.* **159** K22
Không, *Laos* **186** MI2
Khôngxédôn, *Laos* **186** LI2
Khon Kaen, *Thai.* **186** LIO
Khoper, river, *Russ.* **156** MI2
Khorāsān, region, *Iran* **173** CI5
Khormaleq, *Afghan.* **177** P2
Khorol, *Ukr.* **157** P7
Khorramābād, *Iran* **172** DII
Khorugh, *Taj.* **176** J9
Khost, *Pak.* **177** R6
Khost (Khowst), *Afghan.* **177** N8
Khowst *see* Khost, *Afghan.* **177** N8
Khoy, *Iran* **172** AIO
Khoyniki, *Belarus* **156** M6
Khrenovoye, *Russ.* **157** NII
Khromtaū, *Kaz.* **174** D9
Khudabad, *Pak.* **176** KI2
Khuiala, *India* **178** F2
Khujand, *Taj.* **176** G8
Khūjayli, *Uzb.* **174** J9
Khulkhuta, *Russ.* **157** RI4
Khulna, *Bangladesh* **178** JI2
Khunjerab Pass, *China, Pak.* **176** KI2
Khunti, *India* **178** JIO
Khunzakh, *Russ.* **157** UI5
Khur, *Iran* **173** DI4
Khurda, *India* **178** KIO
Khūrīyā Murīyā, Jazā'ir (Kuria Muria Islands), *Oman* **173** NI5
Khushab, *Pak.* **177** PIO
Khust, *Ukr.* **157** P2
Khuzdar, *Pak.* **177** T5
Khvāf, *Iran* **173** CI7
Khvajeh Mohammad Range, *Afghan.* **176** K9
Khvalynsk, *Russ.* **156** LI4
Khvorostyanka, *Russ.* **156** LI5
Khwazagak, *Afghan.* **176** M5
Khyber Pass, *Afghan., Pak.* **176** M9
Kia, island, *Fiji Is.* **218** G7
Kia, *Solomon Is.* **217** LI7
Kiakeana Point, *Hawai'i, U.S.* **113** HI7
Kiama, *N.S.W., Austral.* **211** YI4
Kiamichi, river, *Okla., U.S.* **102** HI3
Kiana, *Alas., U.S.* **III** EI3
Kiáto, *Gr.* **154** JIO
Kibombo, *Dem. Rep. of the Congo* **198** LII
Kibwezi, *Kenya* **199** KI4
Kičevo, *Maced.* **152** KIO
Kickapoo, Lake, *Tex., U.S.* **102** K9
Kidal, *Mali* **196** GIO
Kidnappers, Cape, *N.Z.* **213** L2O
Kidrenen, island, *Marshall Is.* **216** G8
Kidrinen, island, *Marshall Is.* **216** J8
Kiel, *Ger.* **148** B8
Kiel, *Wis., U.S.* **98** K7
Kielce, *Pol.* **149** HI4
Kieler Bucht, *Ger.* **148** A8
Kien An, *Vietnam* **186** HI2
Kien Duc, *Vietnam* **187** NI3
Kieta, *P.N.G.* **217** KI4
Kiev *see* Kyiv, *Ukr.* **157** N6
Kiffa, *Mauritania* **196** G6
Kifissiá, *Gr.* **154** JI2
Kifissos, river, *Gr.* **154** HIO
Kifrī, *Iraq* **172** DIO
Kigali, *Rwanda* **198** KI2
Kiği, *Turk.* **169** FI5
Kigoma, *Tanzania* **198** LI2
Kīhei, *Hawai'i, U.S.* **113** GI6
Kīholo Bay, *Hawai'i, U.S.* **113** LI8
Ki'i, *Hawai'i, U.S.* **112** B3
Kii Suidō, *Japan* **185** R8
Kikaiga Shima, *Japan* **185** W3

Kikiakki, *Russ.* **158** HI2
Kikinda, *Serb. & Mont.* **152** DIO
Kikki, *Pak.* **177** V2
Kikládes (Cyclades), *Gr.* **155** LI4
Kiknur, *Russ.* **156** HI3
Kikori, river, *P.N.G.* **213** DI8
Kikori, *P.N.G.* **213** DI8
Kikwit, *Dem. Rep. of the Congo* **198** L8
Kil, river, *Pak.* **177** V3
Kilafors, *Sw.* **141** JI3
Kilakkarai, *India* **179** S6
Kilambé, river, *Nicar.* **115** LI8
Kilar, *India* **177** NI3
Kīlauea, peak, *Hawai'i, U.S.* **113** N2I
Kīlauea, *Hawai'i, U.S.* **112** B6
Kīlauea Lighthouse, *Hawai'i, U.S.* **112** A6
Kilbeggan, *Ire.* **143** S5
Kilbrannan Sound, *Scot., U.K.* **143** N8
Kilbride, *Scot., U.K.* **142** K6
Kilbuck Mountains, *Alas., U.S.* **III** JI3
Kilcar, *Ire.* **143** P4
Kilchoman, *Scot., U.K.* **142** M7
Kilcock, *Ire.* **143** S6
Kilcowera, *Qnsld., Austral.* **211** VI2
Kildonan, *Scot., U.K.* **142** H9
Kildrummy, *Scot., U.K.* **142** KIO
Kilgore, *Nebr., U.S.* **104** M4
Kilgore, *Tex., U.S.* **102** LI4
Kılıçkaya, *Turk.* **169** DI6
Kilíni, *Gr.* **154** J8
Kilíni, Óros, *Gr.* **154** JIO
Kilinochchi, *Sri Lanka* **179** S7
Kilis, *Turk.* **168** JI2
Kiliya, *Ukr.* **157** S5
Kilju, *N. Korea* **182** CI4
Kilkee, *Ire.* **143** T3
Kilkenny, *Ire.* **143** T6
Kilkís, *Gr.* **154** CII
Killadysert, *Ire.* **143** T3
Killala Bay, *Ire.* **143** Q4
Killarney, Lake, *Bahamas* **120** BII
Killary Harbour, *Ire.* **143** R3
Killdeer, *N. Dak., U.S.* **104** F2
Killeen, *Tex., U.S.* **103** PIO
Killiniq Island, *Nunavut, Can.* **83** J2O
Killorglin, *Ire.* **143** U3
Kilmaluag, *Scot., U.K.* **142** J7
Kilmarnock, *Scot., U.K.* **143** N9
Kilombero, river, *Tanzania* **199** MI4
Kilosa, *Tanzania* **199** MI4
Kiltan Island, *India* **179** Q3
Kilwa Kivinje, *Tanzania* **199** NI5
Kim, *Colo., U.S.* **107** PI5
Kimaam, *Indonesia* **189** M2O
Kimball, *Nebr., U.S.* **105** PI
Kimball, *S. Dak., U.S.* **104** L6
Kimbe Bay, *P.N.G.* **213** C2I
Kimberley, *B.C., Can.* **82** M9
Kimberley, *S. Af.* **202** K9
Kimberley, region, *W. Aust., Austral.* **211** R6
Kimberley, Cape, *Austral.* **210** CI3
Kimberley Plateau, *Austral.* **210** C6
Kimberly, *Idaho, U.S.* **106** H5
Kimch'aek (Sŏngjin), *N. Korea* **182** CI4
Kimhyŏnggwŏn, *N. Korea* **182** CI3
Kími, *Gr.* **155** HI3
Kímis, Akrotírio, *Gr.* **155** HI3
Kimmirut, *Nunavut, Can.* **83** HI9
Kimobetsu, *Japan* **184** GI3
Kimolos, island, *Gr.* **155** MI4
Kimovsk, *Russ.* **156** KIO
Kimry, *Russ.* **156** H9
Kinabalu, peak, *Malaysia* **188** GI2
Kinadyeng, island, *Marshall Is.* **216** L8
Kínaros, island, *Gr.* **155** LI6
Kinbrace, *Scot., U.K.* **142** H9
Kindadal, *Indonesia* **189** KI4
Kinder, *La., U.S.* **100** P7
Kindia, *Guinea* **200** F5
Kindu, *Dem. Rep. of the Congo* **198** LII
Kinel', *Russ.* **156** KI5
Kineshma, *Russ.* **156** HII
King Christian IX Land, *N. Amer.* **80** CIO
King Christian X Land, *N. Amer.* **80** B9
King City, *Calif., U.S.* **109** U5
King City, *Mo., U.S.* **105** RIO
King Cove, *Alas., U.S.* **110** NII
Kingfisher, *Okla., U.S.* **102** FIO
Kingfisher Lake, *Ont., Can.* **83** MI5

King Frederik VI Coast, *N. Amer.* **80** DIO
King Frederik VIII Land, *N. Amer.* **80** A8
King George Bay, *Falkland Is., U.K.* **133** WI2
King George Island, *Antarctica* **226** C3
King George Islands, *Nunavut, Can.* **83** KI7
King George Sound, *Austral.* **210** L3
King George V Memorial Hospital, *Gibraltar, U.K.* **161** Q23
Kingisepp, *Russ.* **156** F6
King Island, *Alas., U.S.* **110** FII
King Island, *Tas., Austral.* **211** YI5
King Khalid Military City, *Saudi Arabia* **172** GIO
King Lear Peak, *Nev., U.S.* **108** M8
King Leopold Ranges, *Austral.* **210** D5
Kingman, *Ariz., U.S.* **107** S5
Kingman, *Kans., U.S.* **105** U7
King Mountain, *Tex., U.S.* **103** N4
Kingoonya, *S. Aust., Austral.* **211** W9
King Peak, *Antarctica* **226** JII
Kingri, *Pak.* **177** R8
Kings, river, *Calif., U.S.* **109** T7
King Salmon, *Alas., U.S.* **III** LI4
King's Bay, *Trinidad & Tobago* **121** NI8
Kingsbridge, *Eng., U.K.* **143** XIO
Kingsburg, *Calif., U.S.* **109** T6
Kings Canyon National Park, *Calif., U.S.* **109** T7
Kingscote, *S. Aust., Austral.* **211** YIO
Kingsford, *Mich., U.S.* **98** G7
Kingsland, *Ga., U.S.* **97** Q8
King's Lynn, *Eng., U.K.* **143** TI4
Kings Mountain, *N.C., U.S.* **96** J8
King Sound, *Austral.* **210** C4
Kings Peak, *Utah, U.S.* **106** L8
Kingsport, *Tenn., U.S.* **101** D2O
Kingston, *Jam.* **120** JIO
Kingston, *N.Y., U.S.* **94** LII
Kingston, *Norfolk I., Austral.* **217** G2O
Kingston, *Ont., Can.* **83** QI9
Kingston, *Pa., U.S.* **94** M8
Kingston, *Tas., Austral.* **211** ZI6
Kingston Harbour, *Jam.* **120** JIO
Kingston South East, *S. Aust., Austral.* **211** YIO
Kingston upon Hull, *Eng., U.K.* **143** RI3
Kingstown *see* Dún Laoghaire, *Ire.* **143** S7
Kingstown, *St. Vincent & the Grenadines* **121** LI6
Kingstown Bay, *St. Vincent & the Grenadines* **121** LI6
Kingstree, *S.C., U.S.* **96** LIO
Kingsville, *Tex., U.S.* **103** UIO
King Wilhelm Land, *N. Amer.* **80** A9
King William Island, *Nunavut, Can.* **83** FI4
Kiniama, *Dem. Rep. of the Congo* **198** NII
Kinlochewe, *Scot., U.K.* **142** J8
Kinmen (Quemoy), island, *Taiwan, China* **183** R8
Kinnear, *Wyo., U.S.* **106** HIO
Kinniyai, *Sri Lanka* **179** S8
Kino, river, *Japan* **185** Q8
Kinsale, *Montserrat, U.K.* **121** B23
Kinsale, Old Head of, *Ire.* **143** V4
Kinshasa (Léopoldville), *Dem. Rep. of the Congo* **198** L7
Kinsley, *Kans., U.S.* **105** U5
Kinston, *N.C., U.S.* **96** HI3
Kintore, *Scot., U.K.* **142** KII
Kintyre, peninsula, *Scot., U.K.* **143** N8
Kinvarra, *Ire.* **143** S4
Kinyeti, peak, *Sudan* **199** HI3
Kinzua, *Oreg., U.S.* **108** G6
Kioa, island, *Fiji Is.* **218** G8
Kiokluk Mountains, *Alas., U.S.* **III** JI4
Kiowa, *Colo., U.S.* **106** MI4
Kiowa, *Kans., U.S.* **105** V6

Kirbyville, *Tex., U.S.* **103** PI6
Kirensk, *Russ.* **159** KI5
Kiri, *Dem. Rep. of the Congo* **198** K9
Kiribati, *Pac. Oc.* **214** GIO
Kırıkhan, *Turk.* **168** JII
Kırıkkale, *Turk.* **168** E9
Kirishi, *Russ.* **156** F7
Kiritimati (Christmas Island), *Kiribati* **214** GI2
Kiriwina, island, *P.N.G.* **213** E2I
Kırka, *Turk.* **168** E6
Kırkağaç, *Turk.* **168** E3
Kirkcaldy, *Scot., U.K.* **142** MIO
Kirkcolm, *Scot., U.K.* **143** P8
Kirkenes, *Nor.* **141** CI5
Kırkgeçit, *Turk.* **169** GI8
Kirkjub jarklaustur, *Ice.* **140** G3
Kirkland, *Tex., U.S.* **102** J7
Kirkland Lake, *Ont., Can.* **83** PI8
Kırklar Dağı, *Iran* **169** DI5
Kırklareli, *Turk.* **168** B3
Kirkoswald, *Scot., U.K.* **143** N8
Kirksville, *Mo., U.S.* **105** RI2
Kirkuk *see* Karkūk, *Iraq* **172** C9
Kirkwall, *Scot., U.K.* **142** GIO
Kirkwood, *Mo., U.S.* **105** TI5
Kirn, *Ger.* **148** H5
Kirov, *Russ.* **156** K8
Kirov, *Russ.* **158** G8
Kirovohrad, *Ukr.* **157** Q6
Kirovskiy, *Russ.* **157** RI5
Kirsanov, *Russ.* **156** LI2
Kırşehir, *Turk.* **168** F9
Kirthar Range, *Pak.* **177** U6
Kirtland, *N. Mex., U.S.* **107** QIO
Kiruna, *Sw.* **141** EI3
Kirunu, island, *Marshall Is.* **216** G8
Kirwan Escarpment, *Antarctica* **226** BI2
Kirya, *Russ.* **156** JI4
Kiryū, *Japan* **185** NI2
Kisakata, *Japan* **184** KI2
Kisangani (Stanleyville), *Dem. Rep. of the Congo* **198** JIO
Kish, island, *Iran* **173** HI4
Kishanganj, *India* **178** GII
Kishangarh, *India* **178** F2
Kishangarh, *India* **178** G4
Kishb, Ḩarrat al, *Saudi Arabia* **172** K8
Kishiga Zaki, *Japan* **185** U4
Kishiwada, *Japan* **185** Q8
Kishkeneköl, *Kaz.* **175** BI4
Kisigo, river, *Tanzania* **194** LIO
Kiska Island, *Alas., U.S.* **110** M3
Kiskunfélegyháza, *Hung.* **149** MI5
Kiskunhalas, *Hung.* **149** MI5
Kislovodsk, *Russ.* **157** TI2
Kismaayo (Chisimayu), *Somalia* **199** KI6
Kiso, river, *Japan* **185** PIO
Kíssamos (Kastéli), *Gr.* **154** QI2
Kissámou, Kólpos, *Gr.* **154** PI2
Kissidougou, *Guinea* **200** F6
Kissimmee, river, *Fla., U.S.* **97** V9
Kissimmee, *Fla., U.S.* **97** T9
Kissimmee, Lake, *Fla., U.S.* **97** U9
Kistrand, *Nor.* **141** CI4
Kisumu, *Kenya* **199** KI3
Kisvárda, *Hung.* **149** KI7
Kita, *Mali* **196** H6
Kita Daitō Jima, *Japan* **184** L3
Kitaibaraki, *Japan* **185** NI3
Kita Iwo To, island, *Japan* **184** L5
Kitakami, *Japan* **184** KI3
Kitakata, *Japan* **184** MI2
Kitakyūshū, *Japan* **185** R4
Kitale, *Kenya* **199** JI4
Kitami, *Japan* **184** FI5
Kitami Sanchi, range, *Japan* **184** EI4
Kit Carson, *Colo., U.S.* **107** NI5
Kitchener, *Ont., Can.* **83** RI8
Kitchener, *W. Aust., Austral.* **211** W5
Kithira, *Gr.* **154** NII
Kithira (Cerigo, Cythera), island, *Gr.* **154** NII
Kíthnos, island, *Gr.* **155** KI3
Kíthnos, *Gr.* **155** KI3
Kiti, Cape, *Cyprus* **160** Q9
Kitimat, *B.C., Can.* **82** K7
Kiti Point, *F.S.M.* **217** GI4
Kitob, *Uzb.* **176** J9
Kitridge Point, *Barbados* **121** K2O
Kittanning, *Pa., U.S.* **94** N4
Kittery, *Me., U.S.* **95** JI5
Kittilä, *Fin.* **141** DI4
Kittitas, *Wash., U.S.* **108** D6

Kitty Hawk, *N.C., U.S.* 96 GI5
Kitwe, *Zambia* 202 DIO
Kitzingen, *Ger.* 148 H7
Kiukiu, Pointe, *Fr. Polynesia, Fr.* 219 M20
Kiunga, *P.N.G.* 213 DI7
Kivalina, *Alas., U.S.* 110 DI2
Kivu, Lac, *Dem. Rep. of the Congo, Rwanda* 198 KI2
Kiyan Saki, *Japan* 185 YI
Kiyāt, *Saudi Arabia* 172 N8
Kıyıköy, *Turk.* 168 C4
Kizema, *Russ.* 158 F8
Kızılcahamam, *Turk.* 168 D8
Kızılin, *Turk.* 169 HI3
Kızılırmak, *Turk.* 168 D9
Kızılırmak (Halys), river, *Turk.* 168 D9
Kızılliman Burnu, *Turk.* 168 K8
Kızıltepe, *Turk.* 169 HI5
Kizlyar, *Russ.* 157 TI5
Kizlyarskiy Zaliv, *Russ.* 157 SI5
Kladno, *Czech Rep.* 148 HII
Klagenfurt, *Aust.* 148 MII
Klaipėda, *Lith.* 141 NI5
Klaksvík, *Faroe Is., Den.* 140 J6
Klamath, *Calif., U.S.* 108 L2
Klamath, river, *Calif., Oreg., U.S.* 108 L2
Klamath Falls, *Oreg., U.S.* 108 K4
Klamath Mountains, *Calif., U.S.* 108 M3
Klarälven, river, *Sw.* 140 KI2
Klatovy, *Czech Rep.* 148 JIO
Klawer, *S. Af.* 202 L7
Klawock, *Alas., U.S.* III M23
Kle, *Liberia* 200 G6
Klein Baai, *Neth. Antilles, Neth.* 121 BI4
Klein Bonaire, island, *Neth. Antilles, Neth.* 121 QI9
Kleine Berg, *Neth. Antilles, Neth.* 121 PI4
Klekovača, *Bosn. & Herzg.* 152 F6
Klerksdorp, *S. Af.* 202 KIO
Klesiv, *Ukr.* 156 M4
Kletskiy, *Russ.* 157 PI2
Klichaw, *Belarus* 156 L5
Klickitat, *Wash., U.S.* 108 E5
Klin, *Russ.* 156 J9
Klintehamn, *Sw.* 141 MI4
Klintsy, *Russ.* 156 L7
Klirou, *Cyprus* 160 P8
Klitoría, *Gr.* 154 J9
Klondike Gold Rush National Historic Park, *Alas., U.S.* III K2I
Klosterneuburg, *Aust.* 148 KI2
Klosters, *Switz.* 150 B5
Kluczbork, *Pol.* 149 FI4
Klyaz'ma, river, *Russ.* 138 DII
Klyuchevskaya Sopka, peak, *Russ.* 166 CI3
Knaresborough, *Eng., U.K.* 143 RI2
Knezha, *Bulg.* 153 HI3
Knife River, *Minn., U.S.* 104 GI3
Knin, *Croatia* 152 G6
Knittlefeld, *Aust.* 148 LII
Knjaževac, *Serb.* 152 GI2
Knob, Cape, *Austral.* 210 L4
Knockadoon Head, *Ire.* 143 U5
Knokke-Heist, *Belg.* 146 KII
Knossos *see* Cnossus, ruin, *Gr.* 155 QI5
Knotts Island, *N.C., U.S.* 96 GI4
Knox, *Ind., U.S.* 99 P8
Knox Atoll, *Marshall Is.* 216 H5
Knox City, *Tex., U.S.* 102 L9
Knox Coast, *Antarctica* 227 L2I
Knoxville, *Iowa, U.S.* 105 PI2
Knoxville, *Tenn., U.S.* 101 EI8
Knud Rasmussen Land, *Greenland, Den.* 81 B2O
Knysna, *S. Af.* 202 M9
Ko, Gora, *Russ.* 159 K2I
Koba, *Indonesia* 188 K8
Koba, *Indonesia* 189 MI9
Kobarid, *Slov.* 152 C4
Kobayashi, *Japan* 185 T4
Kōbe, *Japan* 185 Q8
København (Copenhagen), *Den.* 140 NI2
Koblenz, *Ger.* 148 G5
Kobo, *Indonesia* 188 FI5
Kobozha, *Russ.* 156 G8
Kobroor, island, *Indonesia* 189 LI9
Kobryn, *Belarus* 156 L3
Kobu, *Azerb.* 169 D23
Kobuk, river, *Alas., U.S.* III EI4
Kobuk, *Alas., U.S.* III EI4
Kobuk Valley National Park, *Alas., U.S.* III EI4
K'obulet'i, *Rep. of Georgia* 169 CI6

Kocaeli, *Turk.* 168 D5
Kočani, *Maced.* 152 KI2
Koçarlı, *Turk.* 168 G3
Koçbaşı Tepe, *Turk.* 169 FI7
Koch Bihar, *India* 178 GI2
Kochen'ga, *Russ.* 156 FI2
Kochi (Cochin), *India* 179 R5
Kōchi, *Japan* 185 R7
Koch Island, *Nunavut, Can.* 83 FI7
Kochkor, *Kyrg.* 176 EI2
Koch Peak, *Mont., U.S.* 106 F7
Kochubey, *Russ.* 157 TI5
Kodari, *Nepal* 178 FIO
Koddiyar Bay, *Sri Lanka* 179 S8
Kodiak, *Alas., U.S.* III MI5
Kodiak Island, *Alas., U.S.* III MI5
Kodiak Seamount, *Pac. Oc.* 239 BI3
Kodinar, *India* 178 K2
Kodinskiy, *Russ.* 159 JI4
Kodok, *Sudan* 199 FI3
Kodomari, *Japan* 184 HI2
Köes, *Namibia* 202 J7
Koetoi, *Japan* 184 DI3
Ko Gaja Shima, *Japan* 185 V3
Kogaluc, river, *Que., Can.* 83 JI8
Kögart, *Kyrg.* 176 GII
Kogon, *Uzb.* 174 LII
Kohala, region, *Hawai'i, U.S.* 113 KI9
Kohala Mountains, *Hawai'i, U.S.* 113 KI9
Kohat, *Pak.* 177 N9
Koh-e Baba Range, *Afghan.* 176 M6
Kohistan, region, *Pak.* 176 LII
Kohler Glacier, *Antarctica* 226 L7
Kohlu, *Pak.* 177 R8
Kohnieh, *Cambodia* 187 NI3
Kohtla-Järve, *Est.* 141 KI7
Koilani, *Cyprus* 160 Q7
Koimbani, *Comoros* 205 MI4
Kōje Do, *S. Korea* 182 GI4
Ko Jima, *Japan* 185 SI2
Kojŭ, *N. Korea* 182 DI3
Kokas, *Indonesia* 189 KI8
Kök-Aygyr, *Kyrg.* 176 FI2
Kokina, *Cyprus* 160 N6
Kokkola, *Fin.* 141 GI5
Koko, *Nigeria* 201 EI3
Koko Crater, *Hawai'i, U.S.* 112 EI2
Koko Head, *Hawai'i, U.S.* 112 EI2
Kokomo, *Ind., U.S.* 99 Q9
Kok-Yangak, *Kyrg.* 176 FIO
Kokubu, *Japan* 185 T4
Kökpekti, *Kaz.* 175 EI8
Kökshetaū, *Kaz.* 175 CI3
Köktal, *Kaz.* 175 HI7
Kokubu, *Japan* 185 T4
Kola, island, *Indonesia* 189 LI9
Kolachi, river, *Pak.* 177 T6
Kolaka, *Indonesia* 189 KI4
Kola Peninsula, *Russ.* 138 AIO
Kolar, *India* 179 P6
Kolari, *Fin.* 141 EI4
Kolarovgrad *see* Shumen, *Bulg.* 153 HI6
Kolayat, *India* 178 F3
Kolbano, *Indonesia* 189 NI5
Kolbeinsey Ridge, *Arctic Oc.* 243 KI8
Kolbio, *Kenya* 199 LI5
Kolding, *Den.* 140 PII
Kolé, *Vanuatu* 218 C2
Kole, *Dem. Rep. of the Congo* 198 JII
Kole, *Dem. Rep. of the Congo* 198 LIO
Kolekole, river, *Hawai'i, U.S.* 113 L2I
Kolguyev, Ostrov, *Russ.* 158 EIO
Kolguyev Island, *Russ.* 138 AII
Kolhapur, *India* 178 M4
Kolia, *Wallis & Futuna, Fr.* 218 EII
Koliganek, *Alas., U.S.* III KI4
Kolín, *Czech Rep.* 148 HI2
Kolkata (Calcutta), *India* 178 JI2
Kolkhozobod, *Taj.* 176 J7
Kollam (Quilon), *India* 179 S5
Kollidam, river, *India* 179 R6
Kolmogorovo, *Russ.* 159 JI3
Köln (Cologne), *Ger.* 148 F5
Koło, *Pol.* 149 EI4
Koloa, island, *Tonga* 218 LI2
Kōloa, *Hawai'i, U.S.* 112 C5
Kołobrzeg, *Pol.* 148 BI2
Kolodnya, *Russ.* 156 K7
Kologriv, *Russ.* 156 GI2
Kolokani, *Mali* 196 H7

Kolombangara, island, *Solomon Is.* 217 MI6
Kolomna, *Russ.* 156 KIO
Kolomyya, *Ukr.* 157 P3
Kolonga, *Tonga* 218 HI2
Kolonia, *F.S.M.* 217 FI4
Kolonodale, *Indonesia* 189 KI4
Kolosovykh, *Russ.* 159 EI3
Kolovai, *Tonga* 218 HIO
Kolowr va Dah Sil, *Afghan.* 176 L7
Kolpashevo, *Russ.* 158 JI2
Kolpino, *Russ.* 156 F6
Kol'skiy Poluostrov, *Russ.* 158 D9
Kolufuri, island, *Maldives* 179 V3
Kolumadulu Atoll, *Maldives* 179 V3
Kolwezi, *Dem. Rep. of the Congo* 198 NIO
Kolyma, river, *Russ.* 166 BII
Kolyma Lowland, *Russ.* 166 BII
Kolyma Range, *Russ.* 166 BI2
Kolymskoye Nagor'ye (Gydan), *Russ.* 159 E2O
Kom, peak, *Bulg.* 152 HI2
Komagane, *Japan* 185 PII
Komandorskiye Ostrova (Commander Islands), *Russ.* 159 E23
Komárno, *Slovakia* 149 LI4
Komatsu, *Japan* 185 N9
Kombóti, *Gr.* 154 G8
Komebail Lagoon (Ngertachebeab), *Palau* 216 NII
Komo, island, *Fiji Is.* 218 J9
Komoé, river, *Côte d'Ivoire* 200 G9
Komodo, island, *Indonesia* 189 MI3
Kôm Ombo, *Egypt* 197 EI9
Komoran, island, *Indonesia* 189 M2O
Komotiní, *Gr.* 155 BI5
Komovi, peak, *Mont.* 152 J9
Kompong Chhnang, *Cambodia* 187 NII
Kompong Speu, *Cambodia* 187 PII
Kompong Sralao, *Cambodia* 186 MI2
Kompong Thom, *Cambodia* 187 NII
Komsomol, *Kaz.* 174 F7
Komsomolets, *Kaz.* 174 BIO
Komsomolets, Ostrov, *Russ.* 159 CI4
Komsomolets Island *see* Komsomolets, Ostrov, *Russ.* 166 B9
Komsomol'sk, *Russ.* 156 HIO
Komsomol'skiy, *Russ.* 159 BI9
Komsomol'sk na Amure, *Russ.* 159 K2O
Komsomol'sk-na-Ustyurte, *Uzb.* 174 H8
Komusan, *N. Korea* 182 BI4
Kona, region, *Hawai'i, U.S.* 113 MI9
Konakovo, *Russ.* 156 H9
Konakpınar, *Turk.* 168 FI2
Konawa, *Okla., U.S.* 102 HII
Konda, *Indonesia* 189 KI8
Kondagaon, *India* 178 L8
Kondinin, *W. Aust., Austral.* 211 X3
Kondoa, *Tanzania* 199 LI4
Kondol', *Russ.* 156 LI3
Kondopoga, *Russ.* 158 E7
Kondoz (Kunduz), *Afghan.* 176 K7
Kondrovo, *Russ.* 156 K8
Kondukur, *India* 179 N7
Konduz, river, *Afghan.* 176 K7
Koné, *New Caledonia, Fr.* 218 C7
Koné, Passe de, *New Caledonia, Fr.* 218 C7
Köneürgench, *Turkm.* 174 J9
Kong, river, *Laos* 186 LI3
Kong, Koh, *Cambodia* 187 PIO
Kongauru, island, *Palau* 216 QIO
Kongiganak, *Alas., U.S.* 110 KI2
Konginskiy Khrebet, *Russ.* 159 D2O
Konglu, *Myanmar* 186 D7
Kongolo, *Dem. Rep. of the Congo* 198 LII
Kongor, *Sudan* 198 GI2
Kongsberg, *Nor.* 140 LII
Kongsvinger, *Nor.* 140 KI2
Kongue Falls, *Gabon* 201 KI6
Kongwa, *Tanzania* 199 MI4
Konibodom, *Taj.* 176 G8
Königswinter, *Ger.* 148 F5
Konin, *Pol.* 149 EI4
Konispol, *Albania* 152 N9
Konjuh, peak, *Bosn. & Herzg.* 152 F8
Konnongorring, *W. Aust., Austral.* 211 X3
Konosha, *Russ.* 158 E7
Konotop, *Ukr.* 157 N7
Konqi, river, *China* 180 G7
Konrai, *Palau* 216 MI2
Końskie, *Pol.* 149 FI6
Konstantinovsk, *Russ.* 157 QII
Konstanz, *Ger.* 148 L6

Konta, *India* 178 M8
Kontagora, *Nigeria* 201 FI3
Kon Tum, *Vietnam* 186 MI3
Konya (Iconium), *Turk.* 168 G8
Konza, *Kenya* 199 KI4
Ko'oko'olau, peak, *Hawai'i, U.S.* 113 M2O
Kookooligit Mountains, *Alas., U.S.* 110 FIO
Kookynie, *W. Aust., Austral.* 211 W4
Ko'olau Range, *Hawai'i, U.S.* 112 DII
Koolburra, *Qnsld., Austral.* 211 QI2
Koonalda, *S. Aust., Austral.* 211 W7
Koonibba, *S. Aust., Austral.* 211 W8
Kootenay, river, *B.C., Can.* 106 A4
Kopaonik, range, *Kos., Serb.* 152 HIO
Kópasker, *Ice.* 140 E4
Köpbirlik, *Kaz.* 175 FI6
Koper (Capodistria), *Slov.* 152 D4
Kopervik, *Nor.* 140 L9
Köpetdag Dagerşi, mountains, *Turkm.* 174 M8
Kopet Mountains, *Iran, Turkm.* 166 G5
Köprü, river, *Turk.* 168 H6
Kopstal, *Lux.* 160 JIO
Kopylovka, *Russ.* 158 JI2
Korab, Mal, *Albania, Maced.* 152 KIO
K'orahē, *Eth.* 199 GI6
Korak, island, *Palau* 216 NI2
Korangi, *Pak.* 177 W6
Korba, *India* 178 J8
Korça, *Albania* 152 MIO
Korčula, island, *Croatia* 152 H6
Korčulanski Kanal, *Croatia* 152 H6
Korday, *Kaz.* 175 JI5
Korea, peninsula, *Asia* 166 FI2
Korea Bay, *N. Korea, China* 182 DII
Korea Strait, *S. Korea* 182 HI4
Korem, *Eth.* 199 EI4
Korenovsk, *Russ.* 157 SIO
Korf, *Russ.* 159 D2I
Korhogo, *Côte d'Ivoire* 200 F8
Kori Creek, *India* 177 X7
Korido, *Indonesia* 189 JI9
Korinós, *Gr.* 154 DIO
Korinthiakós Kólpos, *Gr.* 154 JIO
Kórinthos (Corinth), *Gr.* 154 JII
Korissía, *Gr.* 155 KI3
Kōriyama, *Japan* 184 MI3
Korkuteli, *Turk.* 168 H5
Korla, *China* 180 F7
Kormakitis, *Cyprus* 160 N7
Kormakitis, Cape, *Cyprus* 160 N7
Körmend, *Hung.* 149 MI3
Kornat, island, *Croatia* 152 G5
Koro, island, *Fiji Is.* 218 H7
Korolevu, *Fiji Is.* 218 J6
Koromiri, island, *Cook Is., N.Z.* 218 Q9
Koróni, *Gr.* 154 M9
Korónia, Límni, *Gr.* 154 CII
Koronída, *Gr.* 155 LI5
Koropí, *Gr.* 154 JI2
Koror, *Palau* 216 NII
Koror (Oreor), island, *Palau* 216 NII
Koro Sea, *Fiji Is.* 218 J8
Korosten', *Ukr.* 157 N5
Korotkova, *Russ.* 159 KI5
Koro Toro, *Chad* 197 HI5
Korotoyak, *Russ.* 157 NIO
Korsnes, *Nor.* 140 EI2
Korti, *Sudan* 198 DI2
Kortrijk, *Belg.* 146 LII
Koryak Range, *Russ.* 166 BI2
Koryakskaya Sopka, *Russ.* 159 F23
Koryakskoye Nagor'ye, *Russ.* 159 D2I
Kos, *Gr.* 155 LI8
Kos (Cos), island, *Gr.* 155 MI8
Kō Saki, *Japan* 185 Q3
Kosan, *N. Korea* 182 DI3
Kosaya Gora, *Russ.* 156 K9
Kościerzyna, *Pol.* 149 BI3
Kosciusko, *Miss., U.S.* 100 KI2
Kosciuszko, Mount, *Austral.* 210 LI3
Koshikijima Rettō, *Japan* 185 T3
Kōshim, river, *Kaz.* 174 D6
Koshk, *Afghan.* 176 M2
Koshk-e Kohneh, *Afghan.* 176 M2
Košice, *Slovakia* 149 JI7
Kosmás, *Gr.* 154 LIO
Koson, *Uzb.* 174 LII
Kosovo, *Eur.* 139 W8
Kosrae (Kusaie), island, *F.S.M.* 216 Q9

Kossol Passage, *Palau* 216 LI2
Kossou, Lac de, *Côte d'Ivoire* 200 G8
Kosti, *Sudan* 199 FI3
Kostino, *Russ.* 159 HI3
Kostopil', *Ukr.* 157 N4
Kostroma, *Russ.* 156 GII
Kostromskoye Vodokhranilishche, *Russ.* 156 GII
Kostrzyn, *Pol.* 148 DII
Kostyantynivka, *Ukr.* 157 Q9
Koszalin, *Pol.* 148 BI2
Kota, *India* 178 H5
Kotaagung, *Indonesia* 188 L7
Kota Baharu, *Malaysia* 187 SIO
Kotabaru, *Indonesia* 188 KI2
Kotabumi, *Indonesia* 188 L7
Kotabunan, *Indonesia* 189 JI5
Kot Addu, *Pak.* 177 R9
Ko Takara Jima, *Japan* 185 V3
Kota Kinabalu, *Malaysia* 188 GII
Kota Tinggi, *Malaysia* 187 VII
Kotel'nich, *Russ.* 158 G7
Kotel'nikovo, *Russ.* 157 QI2
Kotel'nyy, Ostrov, *Russ.* 159 DI6
Kotel'nyy Island, *Russ.* 166 BIO
Köthen, *Ger.* 148 E9
Kotka, *Fin.* 141 JI6
Kotlas, *Russ.* 158 F8
Kotlik, *Alas., U.S.* 110 GI2
Kotooka, *Japan* 184 KI2
Kotovs'k, *Ukr.* 157 Q5
Kotovsk, *Russ.* 156 LII
Kotri, *Pak.* 177 V7
Kottayam, *India* 179 R5
Kotto, river, *Cen. Af. Rep.* 198 GIO
Kotu, island, *Tonga* 218 Q6
Kotu Group, *Tonga* 218 Q6
Koturdepe, *Turkm.* 174 L6
Kotzebue, *Alas., U.S.* III EI3
Kotzebue Sound, *Alas., U.S.* III EI3
Koua, *New Caledonia, Fr.* 218 D8
Kouakou, island, *Fr. Polynesia, Fr.* 219 R2I
Kouango, *Cen. Af. Rep.* 198 H9
Koudougou, *Burkina Faso* 200 EIO
Koufália, *Gr.* 154 CIO
Koufoníssi, island, *Gr.* 155 LI5
Koufoníssi, island, *Gr.* 155 RI6
Koufós, *Gr.* 154 EI2
Kouilou, river, *Congo* 201 MI6
Koukdjuak, Great Plain of the, *Nunavut, Can.* 83 GI8
Kouklia, *Cyprus* 160 Q6
Koúla, peak, *Gr.* 155 BI4
Koulamoutou, *Gabon* 201 LI6
Koulen, *Cambodia* 186 MII
Koulikoro, *Mali* 196 H7
Koumac, *New Caledonia, Fr.* 218 C6
Koumra, *Chad* 197 KI5
Koungou, *Mayotte, Fr.* 205 PI7
Kountze, *Tex., U.S.* 103 PI5
Kourou, *Fr. Guiana, Fr.* 129 EI8
Kouroussa, *Guinea* 200 F7
Koutiala, *Mali* 196 J8
Koutomo, Île, *New Caledonia, Fr.* 218 E9
Kouvola, *Fin.* 141 JI6
Kovel', *Ukr.* 156 M3
Kovic, Baie, *Que., Can.* 83 JI7
Kovin, *Serb.* 152 FIO
Kovrov, *Russ.* 156 JII
Kovur, *India* 179 P7
Kowanyama, *Qnsld., Austral.* 211 QI2
Kowloon *see* Jiulong, *China* 183 S5
Köyceğiz, *Turk.* 168 H4
Koyda, *Russ.* 158 D9
Koytendag, *Turkm.* 174 MI2
Koyuk, *Alas., U.S.* III FI3
Koyukuk, river, *Alas., U.S.* III EI5
Koyukuk, *Alas., U.S.* III FI4
Koyulhisar, *Turk.* 168 EI2
Kozan, *Turk.* 168 HII
Kozáni, *Gr.* 154 D9
Kozel'sk, *Russ.* 156 K8
Kozhasay, *Kaz.* 174 E8
Kozhikode (Calicut), *India* 179 Q5
Kozjak, peak, *Maced.* 152 KII
Kozlovka, *Russ.* 157 NII
Kozlu, *Turk.* 168 C7
Kozluk, *Turk.* 169 GI6
Koz'modem'yansk, *Russ.* 156 HI3
Kōzu Shima, *Japan* 185 QI2
Kozyatyn, *Ukr.* 157 P5
Kpalimé, *Togo* 200 GII
Kra, Isthmus of, *Thai.* 187 Q8
Krabi, *Thai.* 187 R8

Kra Buri, *Thai.* **187** P7
Kragerø, *Nor.* **140** LII
Kragujevac, *Serb.* **152** GIO
Kraków, *Pol.* **149** GI5
Kralendijk, *Neth. Antilles, Neth.* **121** QI9
Kraljevo, *Serb.* **152** GIO
Král'ovský Chlmec, *Slovakia* **149** KI7
Kramators'k, *Ukr.* **157** Q9
Kramfors, *Sw.* **141** HI3
Kranídi, *Gr.* **154** KII
Kranj, *Slov.* **152** C4
Krasavino, *Russ.* **158** F8
Kraśnik, *Pol.* **149** FI7
Krasnoarmeysk, *Kaz.* **175** BI3
Krasnoarmeysk, *Russ.* **158** H6
Krasnoarmeyskaya, *Russ.* **157** SIO
Krasnodar, *Russ.* **157** SIO
Krasnogorsk, *Russ.* **159** J22
Krasnogvardeyskoye, *Russ.* **157** SI2
Krasnohrad, *Ukr.* **157** P8
Krasnokamensk, *Russ.* **159** LI8
Krasnoslobodsk, *Russ.* **157** PI3
Krasnovishersk, *Russ.* **158** G9
Krasnoye, *Russ.* **156** MI6
Krasnoyarsk, *Russ.* **159** KI3
Krasnyy Dolginets, *Kaz.* **174** G5
Krasnyye Baki, *Russ.* **156** HI3
Krasnyy Kholm, *Russ.* **156** G9
Krasnyy Luch, *Ukr.* **157** QIO
Krasnyy Yar, *Russ.* **157** NI3
Kratie, *Cambodia* **187** NI2
Kraul Mountains, *Antarctica* **226** BII
Krause Lagoon Channel, *Virgin Islands, U.S.* **120** R2
Kray Lesa, *Russ.* **159** DI9
Krefeld, *Ger.* **148** F5
Kremastí, *Gr.* **155** M2O
Kremen, peak, *Croatia* **152** F6
Kremenchuk, *Ukr.* **157** P7
Kremenchuk Reservoir *see* Kremenchuts'ke Vodoskhovyshche, *Ukr.* **138** GIO
Kremenchuts'ke Vodoskhovyshche, *Ukr.* **157** P7
Kremenets', *Ukr.* **157** N3
Krems, *Aust.* **148** KI2
Kress, *Tex., U.S.* **102** J5
Kréstena, *Gr.* **154** K9
Kresty, *Russ.* **159** FI3
Kretinga, *Lith.* **141** NI5
Kreuzlingen, *Switz.* **150** A4
Kribi, *Cameroon* **201** JI5
Krim, peak, *Slov.* **152** D4
Krims'ke Hory, *Ukr.* **157** T7
Krishna, river, *India* **179** N5
Krishnagiri, *India* **179** Q6
Krishnanagar, *India* **178** JI2
Kristiansand, *Nor.* **140** MIO
Kristianstad, *Sw.* **141** NI3
Kristiansund, *Nor.* **140** HIO
Kristinestad, *Fin.* **141** HI4
Kríti (Crete), island, *Gr.* **155** QI4
Krk, island, *Croatia* **152** E4
Krnov, *Czech Rep.* **149** HI3
Kroken, *Nor.* **140** GI2
Krolevets', *Ukr.* **156** M7
Kromy, *Russ.* **156** M8
Krong Koh Kong, *Cambodia* **187** PIO
Kronotskaya Sopka, *Russ.* **159** F22
Kronshtadt, *Russ.* **156** F6
Kroonstad, *S. Af.* **202** KIO
Kropotkin, *Russ.* **157** SII
Krosno, *Pol.* **149** HI7
Krosno Odrzańskie, *Pol.* **148** EII
Krotoszyn, *Pol.* **149** EI3
Krstača, peak, *Mont.* **152** HIO
Krui, *Indonesia* **188** L7
Krumovgrad, *Bulg.* **153** KI5
Krung Thep (Bangkok), *Thai.* **186** M9
Krupá, *Czech Rep.* **148** GIO
Krupište, *Maced.* **152** KI2
Krupki, *Belarus* **156** K5
Kruševac, *Serb.* **152** GII
Krutets, *Russ.* **156** FIO
Kruzof Island, *Alas., U.S.* **84** R6
Krychaw, *Belarus* **156** L6
Krylov Seamount, *Atl. Oc.* **236** L9
Krylovskaya, *Russ.* **157** RII
Krymsk, *Russ.* **157** TIO
Kryvychi, *Belarus* **156** K4
Kryvyy Rih, *Ukr.* **157** Q7
Ksar el Kebir, *Mor.* **196** A8
Kuala Abang, *Brunei* **188** GII
Kuala Belait, *Brunei* **188** GII
Kuala Berang, *Malaysia* **187** TIO
Kuala Dungun, *Malaysia* **187** TIO

Kualakapuas, *Indonesia* **188** KII
Kuala Kerai, *Malaysia* **187** SIO
Kualakurun, *Indonesia* **188** JII
Kuala Lumpur, *Malaysia* **187** U9
Kualamanjual, *Indonesia* **188** JIO
Kuala Nerang, *Malaysia* **188** F6
Kualapu'u, *Hawai'i, U.S.* **113** FI4
Kuala Rompin, *Malaysia* **187** UIO
Kuala Terengganu, *Malaysia* **187** TIO
Kualatungkal, *Indonesia* **188** J7
Kuancheng, *China* **182** C8
Kuandian, *China* **182** CII
Kuanshan, *Taiwan, China* **183** SIO
Kuantan, *Malaysia* **187** TIO
Kubachi, *Russ.* **157** UI6
Kuban', river, *Russ.* **138** HI2
Kuban Lowland, *Russ.* **138** GI2
Kubbum, *Sudan* **198** FIO
Kubenskoye, Ozero, *Russ.* **156** FIO
Kubokawa, *Japan* **185** R6
Kubonitu, Mount, *Solomon Is.* **217** MI8
Kuchaman, *India* **178** F4
Kuching, *Malaysia* **188** H9
Kuchinoerabu Jima, *Japan* **185** U4
Kuchino Shima, *Japan* **185** V3
Kuchnay Darvishan, *Afghan.* **177** Q4
Kuçovë, *Albania* **152** L9
Küçüksu, *Turk.* **169** GI6
Kud, river, *Pak.* **177** U5
Kudara, *Taj.* **176** JIO
Kudarebe, cape, *Aruba, Neth.* **121** QI6
Kudat, *Malaysia* **188** FI2
Kudgee, *N.S.W., Austral.* **211** XII
Kudremukh, peak, *India* **179** P4
Kudu Kyuyel', *Russ.* **159** JI7
Küē'ē Ruins, *Hawai'i, U.S.* **113** P2O
Kufra Oasis *see* Al Jawf, *Lib.* **197** EI6
Kufstein, *Aust.* **148** L9
Kugluktuk, *Nunavut, Can.* **82** FI2
Kugul'ta, *Russ.* **157** SI2
Kūhak, *Iran* **173** HI8
Kuh-e Sayyad, *Afghan.* **176** L4
Kuhgrat, peak, *Liech.* **160** N3
Kuhmo, *Fin.* **141** FI6
Kui Buri, *Thai.* **187** N8
Kuikui, Lae 'O, *Hawai'i, U.S.* **113** HI6
Kuikuina, *Nicar.* **115** LI8
Kuiseb, river, *Namibia* **202** H6
Kuitan, *China* **183** R6
Kuito, *Angola* **202** D7
Kuiu Island, *Alas., U.S.* **84** R7
Kuivaniemi, *Fin.* **141** FI5
Kuizhuang, *China* **182** D8
Kujang, *N. Korea* **182** DI2
Kuji, *Japan* **184** JI4
Kuju, peak, *Japan* **185** S5
Kūka'iau, *Hawai'i, U.S.* **113** K2O
Kukolu, island, *Solomon Is.* **217** JI8
Kukpowruk, river, *Alas., U.S.* **111** CI3
Kukui, *Hawai'i, U.S.* **113** M2I
Kukuihaele, *Hawai'i, U.S.* **113** K2O
Kukui'ula, *Hawai'i, U.S.* **112** C5
Kuku Point, *Wake I., U.S.* **216** F7
Kula, *Serb.* **152** E9
Kula, *Turk.* **168** F4
Kula Gangri, peak, *Bhutan, China* **178** FI2
Kūlagīno, *Kaz.* **174** E6
Kula Gulf, *Solomon Is.* **217** MI6
Kūlani, peak, *Hawai'i, U.S.* **113** M2I
Kulaura, *Bangladesh* **178** HI3
Kul'chi, *Russ.* **159** J2O
Kuldīga, *Latv.* **141** MI5
Kule, *Botswana* **202** H8
Kulebaki, *Russ.* **156** JII
Kulgera, *N. Terr., Austral.* **211** U8
Kulin, *W. Aust., Austral.* **211** X3
Kulkuduk, *Uzb.* **174** JIO
Kullorsuaq, *Greenland, Den.* **81** C2O
Kulm, *N. Dak., U.S.* **104** H6
Kulmbach, *Ger.* **148** G8
Kūlob, *Taj.* **176** J8
Kuloy, river, *Russ.* **138** BII
Kulp, *Turk.* **169** GI5
Kulu, *Turk.* **168** F8
Kūlua, Pu'u, *Hawai'i, U.S.* **113** M2O
Kulumadau, *P.N.G.* **213** E2I
Kulunda, *Russ.* **158** LII
Kuma, river, *Russ.* **157** SI4
Kumagaya, *Japan* **185** NI2
Kumai, *Indonesia* **188** KIO
Kumai, Teluk, *Indonesia* **188** KIO
Kumamoto, *Japan* **185** S4
Kumano, *Japan* **185** R9
Kumano Nada, *Japan* **185** R9

Kumanovo, *Maced.* **152** JII
Kuman Range, *Myanmar* **186** E7
Kumara Junction, *N.Z.* **213** NI7
Kumasi, *Ghana* **200** HIO
Kumawa, Pegunungan, *Indonesia* **213** CI4
Kumba, *Cameroon* **201** HI5
Kumbakale, *Solomon Is.* **217** KI5
Kumbakonam, *India* **179** R7
Kumbe, *Indonesia* **189** M2I
Kume Shima, *Japan* **185** YI
Kumo, *Nigeria* **201** FI5
Kumphawapi, *Thai.* **186** KIO
Kumta, *India* **179** P4
Kumukahi, Cape, *Hawai'i, U.S.* **113** M22
Kumukh, *Russ.* **157** UI5
Kumul *see* Hami, *China* **180** F9
Kumylzhenskaya, *Russ.* **157** PI2
Kumzār, *Oman* **173** HI5
Kunahandu, island, *Maldives* **179** W3
Kunashir, island, *Russ.* **159** K23
Kundapura (Coondapoor), *India* **179** P4
Kundar, river, *Afghan., Pak.* **177** Q8
Kundian, *Pak.* **177** P9
Kundu, *Solomon Is.* **217** MI5
Kunduz *see* Kondoz, *Afghan.* **176** K7
Kunene *see* Cunene, river, *Namibia* **202** F5
Kungsbacka, *Sw.* **140** MI2
Kungurtug, *Russ.* **159** MI4
Kunié *see* Pins, Île des, island, *New Caledonia, Fr.* **218** E9
Kunlon, *Myanmar* **186** F7
Kunlun Mountains, *China* **166** G8
Kunlun Shan, *China* **180** H4
Kunlun Shankou, *China* **180** J9
Kunming, *China* **180** NII
Kunnamkulam, *India* **179** R5
Kunu, island, *F.S.M.* **217** BI4
Kununurra, *W. Aust., Austral.* **211** Q6
Kuopio, *Fin.* **141** FI6
Kupa, river, *Croatia, Slov.* **152** E6
Kupang, *Indonesia* **189** NI4
Kūpikipiki'o Point (Black Point), *Hawai'i, U.S.* **112** EII
Kupino, *Russ.* **158** KII
Kupreanof Island, *Alas., U.S.* **III** M23
Kupupolo Heiau, *Hawai'i, U.S.* **112** DIO
Kup"yans'k, *Ukr.* **157** P9
Kuqa, *China* **180** F6
Kür (Kura), river, *Azerb.* **169** E22
Kura, river, *Asia* **166** F5
Kurakh, *Russ.* **157** VI6
Kūrān Dap, *Iran* **173** HI7
Kurashassaykiy, *Kaz.* **174** D8
Kurashiki, *Japan* **185** Q7
Kurayoshi, *Japan* **185** P7
Kurbağa Gölü, *Turk.* **168** GIO
Kürchatov, *Kaz.* **175** DI6
Kürdämir, *Azerb.* **169** D22
Kur Dili, cape, *Azerb.* **169** F23
Kurdistan, region, *Iran, Iraq, Turk.* **172** B9
Kurduna, *Pak.* **177** Q6
Kurduvadi, *India* **178** M4
Kürdzhali, *Bulg.* **153** KI5
Küre, *Turk.* **168** C9
Kure, *Japan* **185** Q6
Kure Atoll (Ocean Island), *Hawai'i, U.S.* **112** K2
Kure Beach, *N.C., U.S.* **96** KI2
Kuressaare, *Est.* **141** LI5
Kureyka, *Russ.* **159** GI3
Kurgan, *Russ.* **158** J9
Kurganinsk, *Russ.* **157** SII
Kuria Muria Islands *see* Khurīyā Murīyā, Jazā'ir, *Oman* **173** NI5
Kuri Bay, *W. Aust., Austral.* **211** Q5
Kurikka, *Fin.* **141** HI5
Kuril Basin, *Pac. Oc.* **238** D6
Kuril Islands *see* Kuril'skiye Ostrova, *Russ.* **166** DI4
Kuril'sk, *Russ.* **159** J23
Kuril'skiye Ostrova (Kuril Islands), *Russ.* **159** J23
Kuril Trench, *Pac. Oc.* **238** E7
Kurio, *Japan* **185** U4
Kurnool, *India* **179** N6
Kurobe, *Japan* **185** NIO
Kuroishi, *Japan* **184** JI3
Kuroiso, *Japan* **185** NI2
Kuro Shima, *Japan* **185** U3
Kurshskiy Zaliv, *Lith., Russ.* **141** NI5
Kursk, *Russ.* **156** M9

Kurşunlu, *Turk.* **168** D8
Kurtalan, *Turk.* **169** GI6
Kurtistown, *Hawai'i, U.S.* **113** M22
Kurtoğlu Burnu, *Turk.* **168** J4
Kuru, river, *Sudan* **198** GII
Kuruçay, *Turk.* **169** EI3
Kuruktag, desert, *China* **180** F7
Kuruman, *S. Af.* **202** K9
Kurume, *Japan* **185** R4
Kurunegala, *Sri Lanka* **179** T7
Kurun Uryakh, *Russ.* **159** HI9
Kuşadası, *Turk.* **168** G3
Kuşadası Körfezi, *Turk.* **168** G3
Kusaie *see* Kosrae, island, *F.S.M.* **216** Q9
Kusakaki Guntō, *Japan* **185** U3
Kus Gölü, *Turk.* **168** D4
Kushima, *Japan* **185** T5
Kushimoto, *Japan* **185** R9
Kushiro, *Japan* **184** FI5
Kushnīya, *Israel* **170** K6
Kushtia, *Bangladesh* **178** HI2
Kuskokwim, river, *Alas., U.S.* **III** JI3
Kuskokwim Bay, *Alas., U.S.* **110** KI2
Kuskokwim Mountains, *Alas., U.S.* **III** HI5
Kusŏng, *N. Korea* **182** DI2
Kussharo Ko, *Japan* **184** FI5
Kusur, *Russ.* **157** VI5
Kut, Ko, *Thai.* **187** PIO
Kütahya, *Turk.* **168** E5
K'ut'aisi, *Rep. of Georgia* **169** BI7
Kutanibong, *Indonesia* **188** G4
Kutch, Gulf of, *India* **178** JI
Kutchan, *Japan* **184** GI3
Kutina, *Croatia* **152** E6
Kutno, *Pol.* **149** EI5
Kutru, *India* **178** L7
Kutu, *Dem. Rep. of the Congo* **198** K8
Kutubdia, island, *Bangladesh* **178** JI3
Kutum, *Sudan* **198** EIO
Kutu-Puhi-Puhi, Pointe, *Fr. Polynesia, Fr.* **219** Q2O
Kuujjuaq, *Que., Can.* **83** KI9
Kuujjuarapik, *Que., Can.* **83** LI8
Kuuli-Mayak, *Turkm.* **174** K6
Kuusamo, *Fin.* **141** EI6
Kuvango, *Angola* **202** E6
Kuvshinovo, *Russ.* **156** H8
Kuwaé *see* Tongoa, island, *Vanuatu* **218** E3
Kuwait, *Asia* **167** U4
Kuwait City, *Kuwait* **172** GII
Kuybishevskiy, *Taj.* **176** J7
Kuybyshev, *Russ.* **158** KII
Kuybyshev Reservoir *see* Kuybyshevskoye Vodokhranilishche, *Russ.* **138** GIO
Kuybyshevskoye Vodokhranilishche, *Russ.* **156** JI5
Kuzey Anadolu Dağları, *Turk.* **168** C9
Kuznetsk, *Russ.* **156** LI4
Kuzumaki, *Japan* **184** KI3
Kv nangen, bay, *Nor.* **141** CI3
Kvaløy, island, *Nor.* **141** DI3
Kvarner, strait, *Croatia* **152** E4
Kvarnerić, strait, *Croatia* **152** F4
Kvikkjokk, *Sw.* **141** EI3
Kwa, river, *Dem. Rep. of the Congo* **198** L8
Kwadak, island, *Marshall Is.* **216** M5
Kwailibesi, *Solomon Is.* **217** MI9
Kwajalein, island, *Marshall Is.* **216** N5
Kwajalein Atoll, *Marshall Is.* **216** G4
Kwajalein Lagoon, *Marshall Is.* **216** L4
Kwale, *Kenya* **199** LI5
Kwangju *see* Gwangju, *S. Korea* **182** GI3
Kwango, river, *Angola, Dem. Rep. of the Congo* **194** L6
Kwanza, river, *Angola* **194** L6
Kwaos, *Indonesia* **189** KI7
Kwekwe, *Zimb.* **202** GII
Kwenge, river, *Dem. Rep. of the Congo* **198** M8
Kwethluk, *Alas., U.S.* **110** JI2
Kwidzyn, *Pol.* **149** CI4
Kwigillingok, *Alas., U.S.* **110** KI2
Kwilu, river, *Dem. Rep. of the Congo* **198** L8
Kwinana, *W. Aust., Austral.* **211** X2
Kwitaro, river, *Guyana* **129** FI4
Kwoka, peak, *Indonesia* **189** JI8
Kyaikkami, *Myanmar* **186** L7
Kyaikto, *Myanmar* **186** K6
Kyaukkyi, *Myanmar* **186** J6
Kyaukme, *Myanmar* **186** G7

Kyaukphyu, *Myanmar* **186** J4
Kyauktaw, *Myanmar* **186** H4
Kybartai, *Lith.* **141** NI6
Kyiv (Kiev), *Ukr.* **157** N6
Kyle, *Tex., U.S.* **103** QIO
Kyll, river, *Ger.* **160** HII
Kyllburg, *Ger.* **160** GII
Kynuna, *Qnsld., Austral.* **211** SII
Kyoga, Lake, *Uganda* **199** JI3
Kyōga Misaki, *Japan* **185** P8
Kyŏngju *see* Gyeongju, *S. Korea* **182** GI5
Kyŏngsŏng, *N. Korea* **182** BI4
Kyōto, *Japan* **185** Q9
Kyrenia (Keryneia, Girne), *Cyprus* **160** N8
Kyrgyz Range, *Kaz., Kyrg.* **176** EIO
Kyrgyzstan, *Asia* **167** U7
Kyshtovka, *Russ.* **158** JII
Ky Son, *Vietnam* **186** JII
Kythrea, *Cyprus* **160** N9
Kyubeyingde, *Russ.* **159** GI6
Kyūroku Jima, *Japan* **184** JI2
Kyushe, *Kaz.* **174** G8
Kyūshū, island, *Japan* **185** S5
Kyushu-Palau Ridge, *Pac. Oc.* **238** H5
Kyustendil, *Bulg.* **152** JI2
Kyzyl, *Russ.* **159** LI3
Kyzyl-Adyr, *Kyrg.* **176** E9
Kyzylkup, *Turkm.* **174** K6
Kyzyl-Kyya, *Kyrg.* **176** GIO
Kyzyl-Suu, *Kyrg.* **176** EI4

L

La Adela, *Arg.* **133** PIO
La Almunia de Doña Godina, *Sp.* **145** EI3
Laascaanood, *Somalia* **199** GI7
Laasqoray, *Somalia* **199** FI8
Laatzen, *Ger.* **148** D7
Lā'au Point, *Hawai'i, U.S.* **113** FI3
Laayoune, *W. Sahara, Mor.* **196** D6
La Banda, *Arg.* **132** GIO
La Bañeza, *Sp.* **144** C8
La Barca, *Mex.* **114** HIO
La Barge, *Wyo., U.S.* **106** J9
Labasa, *Fiji Is.* **218** G7
La Baule-Escoublac, *Fr.* **147** R5
Labé, *Guinea* **200** EI6
Labe, river, *Czech Rep.* **148** HI2
La Belle, *Fla., U.S.* **97** V9
Labinsk, *Russ.* **157** TII
Laborie, *St. Lucia* **121** LI4
Labota, *Indonesia* **189** KI4
Laboue, *Leb.* **170** H7
Labouheyre, *Fr.* **147** W6
Laboulaye, *Arg.* **132** LIO
Labra, *Neth. Antilles, Neth.* **121** QI8
Labrador, region, *Nfld. & Lab., Can.* **83** L2I
Labrador City, *Nfld. & Lab., Can.* **83** L2O
Labrador Sea, *Atl. Oc.* **236** D6
Lábrea, *Braz.* **130** F7
La Brea, *Trinidad & Tobago* **121** Q2I
Labrit, *Fr.* **147** W6
Labuan, island, *Malaysia* **188** GII
Labuk Bay, *Malaysia* **188** FI2
Labutta, *Myanmar* **186** L5
Lac, bay, *Neth. Antilles, Neth.* **121** RI9
La Calera, *Chile* **132** K6
Lacanau, *Fr.* **147** V6
Lacanau, Étang de, *Fr.* **147** V6
Lacanau-Océan, *Fr.* **147** V6
La Canourgue, *Fr.* **147** WII
La Capelle, *Fr.* **146** MII
Lacapelle-Marival, *Fr.* **147** V9
La Carlota, *Sp.* **144** JII
La Carolina, *Sp.* **144** JII
Lacaune, Montes de, *Fr.* **147** XIO
Laccadive Sea, *India* **179** P3
Lac du Flambeau, *Wis., U.S.* **98** G5
La Ceiba, *Hond.* **115** KI7
La Chambre, *Fr.* **147** UI4
La Chapelle-d'Angillon, *Fr.* **147** RIO
La Charité, *Fr.* **147** SIO
La Châtaigneraie, *Fr.* **147** S6
La Châtre, *Fr.* **147** T9
La Chaux-de-Fonds, *Switz.* **150** B2
Lachlan, river, *Austral.* **210** KI2
Lachyn, *Azerb.* **169** E2O
La Ciotat, *Fr.* **147** YI4
La Citadelle, site, *Haiti* **117** LI6
La Ciudad Encantada, *Sp.* **145** GI3
Lackawanna, N.Y., *U.S.* **94** J5
Lac La Biche, *Alta., Can.* **82** LII
La Clayette, *Fr.* **147** TI2

La Coche, island, Guadeloupe, Fr. 121 GI4
Lacon, Ill., U.S. 99 P5
La Condamine, Monaco 161 E2O
Laconia, N.H., U.S. 95 HI4
La Conner, Wash., U.S. 108 B4
Lacoochee, Fla., U.S. 97 T8
La Cordillera, islands, P.R., U.S. 120 M6
La Cortinada, Andorra 160 H3
Lacq, Fr. 147 X6
Lacre Punt, Neth. Antilles, Neth. 121 RI9
La Crosse, Kans., U.S. 105 T5
La Crosse, Wash., U.S. 108 D8
La Crosse, Wis., U.S. 98 K3
La Cruz, Costa Rica 115 MI8
La Cruz, Mex. 114 F8
La Cumbre, Volcán, Ecua. 128 Q8
La Cygne, Kans., U.S. 105 TIO
Ladakh, region, China, India 176 MI4
Ladakh Range, India 176 MI4
Ladd Seamount, Hawai'i, U.S. 112 K2
La Désirade, island, Guadeloupe, Fr. 121 EI7
La Digue, island, Seychelles 205 N2I
Ladik, Turk. 168 DII
Lādīz, Iran 173 GI7
Ladnun, India 178 F4
Ladoga, Lake, Russ. 138 C9
La Dogana, San Marino 161 GI6
La Dorada, Col. 128 E5
Ladozhskoye Ozero (Lake Ladoga), Russ. 156 E7
Ladrillero, Golfo, Chile 133 V6
Ladron Peak, N. Mex., U.S. 107 TII
Lady Ann Strait, Nunavut, Can. 83 DI6
Ladygin Yar, Russ. 159 FI3
Ladysmith, S. Af. 202 KII
Ladysmith, Wis., U.S. 98 G3
Ladyzhenka, Kaz. 175 DI3
Lae, P.N.G. 213 DI9
Laea, Indonesia 189 LI4
Lae Atoll, Marshall Is. 216 G3
Laem Ngop, Thai. 187 NIO
Laerdal Tunnel, Nor. 140 KIO
La Esmeralda, Venez. 128 FIO
Læsø, island, Den. 140 MII
La Esperanza, Cuba 116 G5
La Esperanza, P.R., U.S. 120 M3
Lafayette, Ala., U.S. 101 KI7
LaFayette, Ga., U.S. 96 K4
Lafayette, Ind., U.S. 99 Q4
Lafayette, La., U.S. 100 P8
Lafayette, Tenn., U.S. 101 EI6
La Fe, Cuba 116 H4
La Fe, Cuba 116 H6
La Felguera, Sp. 144 B9
La Fère, Fr. 147 NII
La Ferme, Mauritius 205 J2O
La Ferté-Macé, Fr. 147 P7
La Ferté-St.-Aubin, Fr. 147 R9
La Flèche, Fr. 147 R7
La Follette, Tenn., U.S. 101 EI8
Laga Bor, river, Kenya 199 JI5
La Gacilly, Fr. 147 R5
Lagan, river, Sw. 141 MI3
Laganá, Kólpos, Gr. 154 K7
Lagash (Telloh), ruin, Iraq 172 EIO
Lagdo Reservoir, Cameroon 201 GI7
Laggan Bay, Scot., U.K. 143 N7
Laghouat, Alg. 196 BII
La Gineta, Sp. 145 HI3
Lagoa, Azores 144 Q5
Lago Argentino see El Calafate, Arg. 133 V7
Lagodekhi, Rep. of Georgia 169 C2O
Lágos, Gr. 155 BI4
Lagos, Nigeria 200 HI2
Lagos, Port. 144 L5
Lagos de Moreno, Mex. 114 HIO
Lagosta see Lastovo, island, Croatia 152 H6
La Grand' Combe, Fr. 147 WI2
La Grande, Oreg., U.S. 108 F8
La Grande 2, Réservoir de, Que., Can. 83 LI8
La Grange, Ky., U.S. 101 BI7
La Grange, Mo., U.S. 105 RI3
La Grange, N.C., U.S. 96 HI2
La Grange, Tex., U.S. 103 QI2
La Grange, Wyo., U.S. 106 JI4
LaGrange, Ga., U.S. 96 M4
Lagrange, Ind., U.S. 99 NIO
Lagrange, W. Aust., Austral. 211 R4
La Gran Sabana, region, Venez. 128 EI2
La Grave, Fr. 147 VI4

La Grulla, Tex., U.S. 103 W9
La Guaira, Venez. 128 B9
Lagua Lichan, Puntan, N. Mariana Is., U.S. 216 A6
Laguépie, Fr. 147 W9
La Guerche, Fr. 147 Q6
Lagun, Neth. Antilles, Neth. 121 NI3
Laguna, N. Mex., U.S. 107 SII
Laguna Beach, Calif., U.S. 109 Y9
Laguna Blanca, Arg. 132 FI3
Laguna Dam, Ariz., Calif., U.S. 109 ZI3
Laguna de Perlas, Nicar. 115 MI9
Laguna Grande, Arg. 133 V8
Laguna Paiva, Arg. 132 JI2
Lagunas, Chile 132 C7
Lagunas, Peru 130 E3
Lagunillas, Bol. 130 K8
Lagwira, Mauritania 196 F4
Laha, China 181 CI6
La Habana (Havana), Cuba 116 G6
Lahad Datu, Malaysia 188 GI2
Lahaina, Hawai'i, U.S. 113 GI5
Laham, Indonesia 188 JII
Lahanás, Gr. 154 CII
La Harpe, Ill., U.S. 99 Q3
Lahat, Indonesia 188 K7
Lahīc, Azerb. 169 D22
Laḥij, Yemen 172 R9
Lāhījān, Iran 172 BI2
Lahi Passage, Tonga 218 HII
Lahn, river, Ger. 148 G6
Lahnstein, Ger. 148 G6
Lahontan Reservoir, Nev., U.S. 109 P7
Lahore, Pak. 177 QI2
Lahr, Ger. 148 K5
Lahri, Pak. 177 S7
Lahti, Fin. 141 JI6
Laï (Behagle), Chad 197 KI4
Laibin, China 183 RI
Lai Chau, Vietnam 186 GIO
Lāʻie, Hawai'i, U.S. 112 DII
Laifeng, China 182 L2
L'Aigle, Fr. 147 P8
Laïka, island, Vanuatu 218 E3
Laingsburg, S. Af. 202 M8
Laird, river, N. Amer. 80 E4
Lairg, Scot., U.K. 142 H9
Laisamis, Kenya 199 JI4
La Isleta, island, Canary Is. 204 Q6
Laiwu, China 182 G7
Laiyang, China 182 F9
Laizhou Wan, China 182 F8
Lajamanu, N. Terr., Austral. 211 R7
La Jara, Colo., U.S. 107 PI2
Lajas, P.R., U.S. 120 N2
Lajes, Azores 144 P3
Lajes, Braz. 130 NI2
Lajes das Flores, Azores 144 NI
Lajitas, Tex., U.S. 103 R2
La Jonquera, Sp. 145 CI8
La Junta, Colo., U.S. 107 PI5
Lakatoro, Vanuatu 218 D2
Lakaträsk, Sw. 141 GI3
Lake Andes, S. Dak., U.S. 104 M6
Lake Arthur, La., U.S. 100 P8
Lakeba, island, Fiji Is. 218 J9
Lakeba Passage, Fiji Is. 218 J9
Lake Butler, Fla., U.S. 97 R7
Lake Cargelligo, N.S.W., Austral. 211 XI3
Lake Charles, La., U.S. 100 P7
Lake Chelan National Recreation Area, Wash., U.S. 108 B6
Lake City, Colo., U.S. 107 PII
Lake City, Fla., U.S. 97 R7
Lake City, Iowa, U.S. 105 NIO
Lake City, Mich., U.S. 98 JIO
Lake City, Minn., U.S. 104 KI2
Lake City, S.C., U.S. 96 JIO
Lake Clark National Park and Preserve, Alas., U.S. 111 KI5
Lake Coleridge, N.Z. 213 PI7
Lake Crystal, Minn., U.S. 104 LIO
Lake District, Eng., U.K. 143 QIO
Lake Eyre Basin, Austral. 210 GIO
Lakefield, Minn., U.S. 104 LIO
Lake Geneva, Wis., U.S. 98 M6
Lake Grace, W. Aust., Austral. 211 X3
Lake Harbor, Fla., U.S. 97 V9
Lake Havasu City, Ariz., U.S. 107 S4
Lake Jackson, Tex., U.S. 103 SI4
Lake King, W. Aust., Austral. 211 X4
Lakeland, Fla., U.S. 97 U8
Lakeland, Ga., U.S. 97 Q6
Lake Linden, Mich., U.S. 98 E6
Lake Louise, Alta., Can. 82 MIO

Lake Mead National Recreation Area, Ariz., Nev., U.S. 109 UI3
Lake Meredith National Recreation Area, Tex., U.S. 102 G5
Lake Mills, Iowa, U.S. 104 MII
Lake Nash, N. Terr., Austral. 211 SIO
Lake Oswego, Oreg., U.S. 108 F3
Lakepa, Niue, N.Z. 219 B2I
Lake Placid, N.Y., U.S. 94 GII
Lake Preston, S. Dak., U.S. 104 K7
Lake Providence, La., U.S. 100 KIO
Lake Region, Fin. 138 C9
Lake Roosevelt National Recreation Area, Wash., U.S. 108 B8
Lakeside, Nebr., U.S. 105 N2
Lakeside, Oreg., U.S. 108 H2
Lake Stewart, N.S.W., Austral. 211 VII
Lakeview, Mich., U.S. 98 LIO
Lakeview, Oreg., U.S. 108 L6
Lake Village, Ark., U.S. 100 J9
Lakeville, Minn., U.S. 104 KII
Lake Violet, W. Aust., Austral. 211 V4
Lake Wales, Fla., U.S. 97 U8
Lakewood, Colo., U.S. 106 MI3
Lakewood, N.J., U.S. 94 PII
Lakewood, Ohio, U.S. 99 NI4
Lake Worth, Fla., U.S. 97 VIO
Lakhish, Tel, ruin, Israel 171 N5
Lakhpat, India 178 HI
Laki, Gr. 155 LI7
Lakin, Kans., U.S. 105 U3
Lakki, Pak. 177 P9
Lakkia, Cyprus 160 P8
Lakonikós Kólpos, Gr. 154 MIO
Lakota, N. Dak., U.S. 104 F7
Lakselv, Nor. 141 CI4
Lakshadweep, islands, India 179 R2
La Laguna, Canary Is. 204 Q5
Lala Musa, Pak. 177 PII
Lalara, Gabon 201 KI6
Lalbenque, Fr. 147 W9
L'Albera, Serra de, Sp. 145 CI8
La Leonesa, Arg. 132 GI3
La Libertad, Ecua. 128 K2
La Libertad, Guatemala 115 KI6
La Ligua, Chile 132 K6
Lalín, Sp. 144 C6
La Línea de la Concepción, Sp. 144 N9
Lalitpur, India 178 H6
Lalitpur (Patan), Nepal 178 FIO
Laluai Point, P.N.G. 217 KI4
La Lune, Trinidad & Tobago 121 Q22
La Maddalena, It. 150 L4
La Madrid, Arg. 132 G9
Lamag, Malaysia 188 GI2
La Malbaie, Que., Can. 83 N2O
Lamalou-les-Bains, Fr. 147 XII
La Manche see English Channel, Eur. 143 XI3
Lamap, Vanuatu 218 D2
Lamar, Colo., U.S. 107 NI5
Lamar, Mo., U.S. 105 UII
La Marmora, Punta, It. 151 N4
La Marque, Tex., U.S. 103 RI4
Lamas, Peru 130 F3
Lamas, Turk. 168 J9
La Massana, region, Andorra 160 H2
La Massana, Andorra 160 J3
Lamballe, Fr. 147 Q5
Lambaréné, Gabon 201 LI5
Lambay Island, Ire. 143 S7
Lambert Glacier, Antarctica 227 FI8
Lambert's Bay, S. Af. 202 L7
Lambertville, Mich., U.S. 99 NI2
Lámbia, Gr. 154 J9
Lambton, Cape, N.W.T., Can. 82 EII
Lame Deer, Mont., U.S. 106 EII
Lamentin, Guadeloupe, Fr. 121 EI4
La Mesa, Calif., U.S. 109 ZIO
La Mesa, N. Mex., U.S. 107 VI2
Lamesa, Tex., U.S. 102 L5
L'Ametlla de Mar, Sp. 145 EI6
La Meyze, Fr. 147 U9
Lamía, Gr. 154 GIO
Lamitan, Philippines 189 FI4
Lamlam, Mount, Guam, U.S. 216 DIO
Lamoille, Nev., U.S. 108 MII

Lamoni, Iowa, U.S. 105 QII
Lamont, Wyo., U.S. 106 JII
La Montaña, region, S. Amer. 126 F3
La Mothe-Achard, Fr. 147 S5
Lamotrek Atoll, F.S.M. 216 Q5
Lamotte-Beuvron, Fr. 147 R9
LaMoure, N. Dak., U.S. 104 H7
Lampang, Thai. 186 J8
Lampasas, Tex., U.S. 103 PIO
Lampertheim, Ger. 148 H6
Lampeter, Wales, U.K. 143 U9
Lamphun, Thai. 186 J8
Lampshoye, Russ. 156 L9
Lamu, Kenya 199 KI5
Lamutskoye, Russ. 159 C2O
Lāna'i, island, Hawai'i, U.S. 113 GI4
Lāna'i City, Hawai'i, U.S. 113 GI5
Lāna'ihale, peak, Hawai'i, U.S. 113 GI5
Lananibot, Puntan, N. Mariana Is., U.S. 216 B7
Lancang, China 180 PIO
Lancaster, Calif., U.S. 109 W8
Lancaster, Eng., U.K. 143 RII
Lancaster, Mo., U.S. 105 QI2
Lancaster, N.H., U.S. 95 FI4
Lancaster, Ohio, U.S. 99 RI3
Lancaster, Pa., U.S. 94 P8
Lancaster, S.C., U.S. 96 J9
Lancaster, Tex., U.S. 102 L2
Lancaster, Wis., U.S. 98 L4
Lancaster Sound, N. Amer. 80 C7
Lance Creek, Wyo., U.S. 106 HI3
Lanciano, It. 150 KII
Landau, Ger. 148 J6
Landay, Afghan. 177 R3
Landeck, Aust. 148 L8
Lander, river, Austral. 210 E8
Lander, Wyo., U.S. 106 HIO
Landerneau, Fr. 147 P3
Landivisiau, Fr. 147 P3
Land O'Lakes, Wis., U.S. 98 F5
Landor, W. Aust., Austral. 211 U2
Landquart, Switz. 150 B5
Landrum, S.C., U.S. 96 J7
Landsberg, Ger. 148 K8
Landsborough Creek, Austral. 210 FI2
Land's End, cape, Eng., U.K. 143 Y7
Lands End, cape, N.W.T., Can. 82 CI2
Landshut, Ger. 148 K9
Landskrona, Sw. 140 NI2
Lanett, Ala., U.S. 101 KI7
Langadás, Gr. 154 CII
Langádia, Gr. 154 K9
Langanes, cape, Ice. 140 E4
Langao, China 182 J2
Langar, island, F.S.M. 217 FI4
Langar, Taj. 176 KIO
Langdon, N. Dak., U.S. 104 E7
Langeac, Fr. 147 VII
Langenhangen, Ger. 148 D7
Langford, S. Dak., U.S. 104 J7
Langjökull, glacier, Ice. 140 F2
Langkawi, island, Malaysia 187 S8
Langlois, Oreg., U.S. 108 JI
Langøya, island, Nor. 140 DI2
Langres, Fr. 147 QI3
Langres, Plateau de, Fr. 147 RI2
Langsa, Indonesia 188 G5
Lang Son, Vietnam 186 GI2
Lang Suan, Thai. 187 Q8
Langting, India 178 GI4
Langtry, Tex., U.S. 103 R5
Langu, Thai. 187 S8
Languedoc, region, Fr. 147 XII
Lancang (Mekong), river, China 178 PIO
Lankao, China 182 H5
Länkäran, Azerb. 169 F22
Lannion, Fr. 147 P4
Lano, Wallis & Futuna, Fr. 218 BII
La Noix, Fr. 161 B22
Lanouaille, Fr. 147 U8
Lansdale, Pa., U.S. 94 P9
Lansdowne, W. Aust., Austral. 211 R6
Lansdowne House, Ont., Can. 83 MI6
L'Anse, Mich., U.S. 98 F6
L'Anse aux Meadows, Nfld. & Lab., Can. 83 L23
Lansing, Iowa, U.S. 104 LI3
Lansing, Mich., U.S. 98 MII

Lanusei, It. 151 P4
Lanxian, China 182 E4
Lan Yü (Orchid Island), Taiwan, China 183 SIO
Lanzarote, island, Canary Is. 204 P7
Lanzhou, China 180 JII
Laoag, Philippines 189 BI3
Lao Cai, Vietnam 186 GIO
Laoha, river, China 181 FI6
Laohekou, China 182 J3
Laojunmiao see Yumen, China 180 GIO
La Oliva, Canary Is. 204 Q7
Laon, Fr. 147 NII
Laona, Wis., U.S. 98 G6
La Orotava, Canary Is. 204 Q5
La Oroya, Peru 130 H3
Laos, Asia 167 WIO
Laoshan, China 182 G9
Laotougou, China 182 AI4
Lapalisse, Fr. 147 TII
La Palma, island, Canary Is. 204 Q3
La Palma, Pan. 115 N22
La Paloma, Uru. 132 LI5
La Paragua, Venez. 128 DII
La Paz, Arg. 132 JI2
La Paz, Arg. 132 K8
La Paz, Bol. 130 J7
La Paz, Mex. 114 F7
La Paz, Mex. 114 GII
Lape, Te Ava i te, Tuvalu 217 J23
La Pedrera, Col. 128 J8
Lapeer, Mich., U.S. 98 LI2
La Perouse Pinnacle, Hawai'i, U.S. 112 M6
La Perouse Strait, Russ., Japan 184 F5
Lâpseki, Turk. 168 D3
La Pine, Oreg., U.S. 108 H5
Lapinlahti, Fin. 141 GI6
Lapithos, Cyprus 160 N8
La Place, La., U.S. 100 PIO
La Plaine, Dominica 121 G2O
La Plaine, Reunion, Fr. 205 GI6
La Plaine des Cafres, Reunion, Fr. 205 HI6
Lapland, region, Fin., Russ., Sw. 141 EI3
La Plant, S. Dak., U.S. 104 J4
La Plata, Arg. 132 LI3
La Plata, Md., U.S. 96 DI3
La Plata, Mo., U.S. 105 RI2
La Pobla de Segur, Sp. 145 CI6
La Pola de Gordón, Sp. 144 B9
La Porte, Tex., U.S. 103 RI4
La Porte City, Iowa, U.S. 105 NI3
La Possession, Reunion, Fr. 205 GI5
Lappeenranta, Fin. 141 JI7
La Pryor, Tex., U.S. 103 S8
Laptev Sea, Arctic Oc. 242 C7
Lapthal, India 178 E7
Lapua, Fin. 141 HI5
La Puebla de Montalbán, Sp. 144 GIO
La Purísima, Mex. 114 E6
La Push, Wash., U.S. 108 B2
La Quiaca, Arg. 132 D9
L'Aquila, It. 150 K9
Lār, Iran 173 HI4
Laracha, Sp. 144 B5
Larache, Mor. 196 A8
Laramie, river, Wyo., U.S. 106 JI2
Laramie, Wyo., U.S. 106 KI2
Laramie Mountains, Wyo., U.S. 106 JI2
Laramie Peak, Wyo., U.S. 84 F9
Larantuka, Indonesia 189 MI4
Larat, island, Indonesia 189 MI8
Larche, Fr. 147 WI5
Laredo, Sp. 144 BII
Laredo, Tex., U.S. 103 U8
La Réole, Fr. 147 W7
Lares, P.R., U.S. 120 M2
Largo, Fla., U.S. 97 U7
Largo, Cayo, Cuba 116 H7
Larimore, N. Dak., U.S. 104 F7
La Rioja, Arg. 132 H8
Lárissa, Gr. 154 EIO
La Rivière, Reunion, Fr. 205 HI5
Larkana, Pak. 177 T7
Larnaka, Cyprus 160 P9
Larnaka Bay, Cyprus 160 P9
Larnakas, Cyprus 160 N8
Larne, N. Ire., U.K. 143 P7
Larned, Kans., U.S. 105 T6
La Robla, Sp. 144 C9
La Roca de la Sierra, Sp. 144 H7
La Rocca o Guaita, San Marino 161 JI5
La Roche, Fr. 147 TI4
La Rochefoucauld, Fr. 147 U8
La Rochelle, Fr. 147 T6

La Roche-sur-Yon, *Fr.* 147 S6
Larochette, *Lux.* 160 J10
La Roda, *Sp.* 144 H12
La Romana, *Dom. Rep.* 117 M20
La Ronge, *Sask., Can.* 82 L12
Larose, *La., U.S.* 100 Q10
La Rousse, *Fr.* 161 A22
Larrimah, *N. Terr., Austral.* 211 Q8
Lars Christensen Coast, *Antarctica* 227 F20
Larsen Bay, *Alas., U.S.* 111 M15
Larsen Ice Shelf, *Antarctica* 226 E5
La Rubia, *Arg.* 132 J11
Laruri, *India* 178 G15
Larvik, *Nor.* 140 L11
Larvotto, peninsula, *Monaco* 161 B23
Larvotto, *Monaco* 161 B22
Larvotto Beach, *Monaco* 161 B22
La Sagesse Bay, *Grenada* 121 L23
La Sal, *Utah, U.S.* 107 N9
La Salle, *Ill., U.S.* 99 P5
Lasan, *Indonesia* 188 H11
Las Animas, *Colo., U.S.* 107 N15
La Sarre, *Que., Can.* 83 N18
Las Cabezas de San Juan, *Sp.* 144 L8
Lascahobas, *Haiti* 117 M17
Lascano, *Uru.* 132 L15
Lascelles, *Vic., Austral.* 211 Y11
La Scie, *Nfld. & Lab., Can.* 83 L23
Las Cruces, *N. Mex., U.S.* 107 V12
Las Cuevas Bay, *Trinidad & Tobago* 121 N22
La Sènia, *Sp.* 145 F15
La Serena, *Chile* 132 J6
La Seu d'Urgell, *Sp.* 145 C16
La Seyne, *Fr.* 147 Y14
Las Flores, *Arg.* 132 M12
Lash-e Joveyn, *Afghan.* 177 Q2
Las Heras, *Arg.* 132 K8
Las Heras, *Arg.* 133 T8
Lashio, *Myanmar* 186 G7
Lashkar, *India* 178 G6
Lashkar Gah, *Afghan.* 177 Q4
Lashkari Bazar, ruin, *Afghan.* 177 Q4
Lasia, island, *Indonesia* 188 H4
La Sila, range, *It.* 151 P13
Las Lomitas, *Arg.* 132 F12
Las Martinas, *Cuba* 116 H4
La Sola, island, *Venez.* 119 N15
La Solana, *Sp.* 144 H11
La Sorcière, peak, *St. Lucia* 121 K14
La Souterraine, *Fr.* 147 T9
Las Palmas, *Canary Is.* 204 Q6
La Spezia, *It.* 150 G5
Las Piedras, *P.R., U.S.* 120 N5
Las Plumas, *Arg.* 133 R9
Lassen Peak, *Calif., U.S.* 109 N4
Lassen Volcanic National Park, *Calif., U.S.* 109 N5
Lassiter Coast, *Antarctica* 226 F7
Las Tablas, *Pan.* 115 P21
Las Toscas, *Arg.* 132 H12
Lastoursville, *Gabon* 201 L16
Lastovo (Lagosta), *Croatia* 152 H6
Lastovski Kanal, *Croatia* 152 H6
Las Tunas, *Cuba* 116 J12
La Suze, *Fr.* 147 R7
Las Varillas, *Arg.* 132 K11
Las Vegas, *N. Mex., U.S.* 107 R13
Las Vegas, *Nev., U.S.* 109 U12
Lata, *Samoa* 218 K2
Latacunga, *Ecua.* 128 J3
Latady Island, *Antarctica* 226 G5
Latady Mountains, *Antarctica* 226 F7
Latakia see Al Lādhiqīyah, *Syr.* 170 F6
Lata Mountain, *Amer. Samoa, U.S.* 218 P4
Latehar, *India* 178 H9
La Teste, *Fr.* 147 W6
Latheron, *Scot., U.K.* 142 H10
Lathi see Sakao, island, *Vanuatu* 218 C2
Latiano, *It.* 150 M15
Latina, *It.* 150 L9
Lato, ruin, *Gr.* 155 Q15
La Tortuga, Isla, *Venez.* 128 B10
Latouche Treville, Cape, *Austral.* 210 D4
La Tranche-sur-Mer, *Fr.* 147 T6
La Trinité, *Martinique, Fr.* 121 E23
Latta, *S.C., U.S.* 96 K11
La Tuque, *Que., Can.* 83 P19
Latur, *India* 178 L5
Latvia, *Eur.* 139 S8
Lau Basin, *Pac. Oc.* 238 M10
Laucala, island, *Fiji Is.* 218 G8
Laufen, *Switz.* 150 A2

Laughlan Islands, *P.N.G.* 213 E22
Laughlin Peak, *N. Mex., U.S.* 107 Q14
Lau Group, *Fiji Is.* 218 H9
Lauhkaung, *Myanmar* 186 E7
Laula Katan, Puntan, *N. Mariana Is., U.S.* 216 C5
Laulau, Bahia, *N. Mariana Is., U.S.* 216 C5
Lauli'i, *Samoa* 218 L3
Lauliituai, *Amer. Samoa, U.S.* 218 M8
Launceston, *Tas., Austral.* 211 Z16
La Unión, *Chile* 133 P6
La Unión, *Peru* 130 G3
La Unión, *Sp.* 145 K14
Laupāhoehoe, *Hawai'i, U.S.* 113 L21
Laura see Majuro, island, *Marshall Is.* 216 H10
Laura, *Marshall Is.* 216 G10
Laura, *Qnsld., Austral.* 211 Q13
Laurel, *Del., U.S.* 96 D15
Laurel, *Miss., U.S.* 100 M12
Laurel, *Mont., U.S.* 106 E10
Laurel, *Nebr., U.S.* 105 N8
Laurens, *Iowa, U.S.* 104 M10
Laurens, *S.C., U.S.* 96 K8
Laurentian Fan, *Atl. Oc.* 236 G6
Laurentian Scarp, *N. Amer.* 80 H8
Laurentide Scarp, *N. Amer.* 80 G9
Lauria, *It.* 151 N12
Lau Ridge, *Pac. Oc.* 238 N10
Laurie Island, *Antarctica* 226 A5
Laurinburg, *N.C., U.S.* 96 J11
Laurium see Lávrio, *Gr.* 155 K13
Laurium, *Mich., U.S.* 98 E6
Laurot Islands see Laut Kecil, Kepulauan, *Indonesia* 188 L11
Lausanne, *Switz.* 150 C1
Laut, island, *Indonesia* 188 G8
Laut, island, *Indonesia* 188 K12
Lautaro, Volcán, *Chile* 133 U6
Lauterbourg, *Fr.* 147 P16
Laut Kecil, Kepulauan (Laurot Islands), *Indonesia* 188 L11
Lautoka, *Fiji Is.* 218 H5
Lauvi Point, *Solomon Is.* 217 P19
Lava Beds National Monument, *Calif., U.S.* 108 L4
Lavaca, river, *Tex., U.S.* 103 R12
Lavaca Bay, *Tex., U.S.* 103 S13
La Vache Bay, *Trinidad & Tobago* 121 N22
Laval, *Fr.* 147 Q6
Lāvān, island, *Iran* 173 H14
Lavardac, *Fr.* 147 W7
Lavaur, *Fr.* 147 X9
L'Avedy, Cape, *P.N.G.* 217 J14
La Vega, *Dom. Rep.* 117 L18
Lavelanet, *Fr.* 147 Y9
Lavello, *It.* 150 M12
La Venta, ruin, *Mex.* 115 J14
La Verkin, *Utah, U.S.* 107 P6
Laverne, *Okla., U.S.* 102 E7
Laverton, *W. Aust., Austral.* 211 V4
La Veta, *Colo., U.S.* 107 P13
La Ville, Pointe, *St. Lucia* 121 K13
Lavina, *Mont., U.S.* 106 D10
Lavit, *Fr.* 147 X8
Lavonia, *Ga., U.S.* 96 K6
Lavoutte, Anse, *St. Lucia* 121 J14
Lavrentiya, *Russ.* 159 A21
Lávrio (Laurium), *Gr.* 155 K13
Lawa, river, *Fr. Guiana, Fr., Suriname* 129 F17
Lawdar, *Yemen* 172 Q10
Lawena, valley, *Liech.* 160 Q2
Lawit, peak, *Indonesia* 188 H10
Lawqah, *Saudi Arabia* 172 F9
Lawra, *Ghana* 200 F10
Lawrence, *Ind., U.S.* 99 R9
Lawrence, *Kans., U.S.* 105 S10
Lawrence, *Mass., U.S.* 95 J14
Lawrenceburg, *Ind., U.S.* 99 S11
Lawrenceburg, *Tenn., U.S.* 101 G14
Lawrenceville, *Ga., U.S.* 96 L5
Lawrenceville, *Ill., U.S.* 99 T7
Lawrenceville, *Va., U.S.* 96 F12
Lawton, *Okla., U.S.* 102 J4
Lawz, Jabal al, *Saudi Arabia* 172 G5
Laylá, *Saudi Arabia* 172 L10
Layou, river, *Dominica* 121 F19
Layou, *St. Vincent & the Grenadines* 121 K16
Laysan Island, *Hawai'i, U.S.* 112 L4

Layshi, *Myanmar* 186 E5
Layton, *Utah, U.S.* 106 K7
Laytonville, *Calif., U.S.* 109 P2
Lázaro Cárdenas, *Mex.* 114 J10
Lazo, *Russ.* 159 F18
Leachville, *Ark., U.S.* 100 F11
Lead, *S. Dak., U.S.* 104 K1
Lead Mountain, *Me., U.S.* 95 E18
Leadore, *Idaho, U.S.* 106 F6
Leadville, *Colo., U.S.* 106 M12
Leaf, river, *N. Amer.* 80 F8
Leakesville, *Miss., U.S.* 101 N13
Leakey, *Tex., U.S.* 103 R8
Leandro N. Alem, *Arg.* 132 G14
Leane, Lough, *Ire.* 143 U3
Learmonth, *W. Aust., Austral.* 211 T1
Leava see Sigavé, *Wallis & Futuna, Fr.* 218 E11
Leavenworth, *Kans., U.S.* 105 S10
Leavenworth, *Wash., U.S.* 108 C5
Lebak, *Philippines* 189 F15
Lebanon, *Asia* 167 T3
Lebanon, *Ind., U.S.* 99 R9
Lebanon, *Kans., U.S.* 105 R6
Lebanon, *Ky., U.S.* 101 C17
Lebanon, region, *Leb.* 170 J6
Lebanon, *Mo., U.S.* 105 U12
Lebanon, *N.H., U.S.* 95 H13
Lebanon, *Ohio, U.S.* 99 S11
Lebanon, *Oreg., U.S.* 108 G3
Lebanon, *Pa., U.S.* 94 P8
Lebanon, *Tenn., U.S.* 101 E16
Lebap, *Turkm.* 174 K10
Le Barcarès, *Fr.* 147 Y11
Le Barp, *Fr.* 147 W6
Le Beausset, *Fr.* 147 Y14
Lebec, *Calif., U.S.* 109 W7
Lebedyn, *Ukr.* 157 N8
Le Blanc, *Fr.* 147 S8
Lebombo Mountains, *Af.* 194 P9
Le Borgne, *Haiti* 117 L16
Lębork, *Pol.* 149 B13
Le Bouscat, *Fr.* 147 V6
Lebrija, *Sp.* 144 L8
Lebu, *Chile* 133 N6
Le Cap, *New Caledonia, Fr.* 218 D7
Le Carbet, *Martinique, Fr.* 121 E22
Le Caylar, *Fr.* 147 X12
Lecce, *It.* 151 N15
Lecco, *It.* 150 D5
Lecco, Lago di, *It., Switz.* 150 D4
Le Chambon-Feugerolles, *Fr.* 147 U12
Lechang, *China* 183 Q4
Lecompte, *La., U.S.* 100 N8
Le Creusot, *Fr.* 147 S12
Ledesma, *Sp.* 144 E8
Le Diamant, *Martinique, Fr.* 121 G22
Ledong, *China* 183 U1
Le Donjon, *Fr.* 147 T11
Le Dorat, *Fr.* 147 T8
Leduck Island, *Virgin Islands, U.S.* 120 N12
Ledyanaya, Gora, *Russ.* 159 C21
Lee, *Nev., U.S.* 109 N11
Leech Lake, *Minn., U.S.* 104 G10
Leedey, *Okla., U.S.* 102 F8
Leeds, *Ala., U.S.* 101 J15
Leeds, *Eng., U.K.* 143 R12
Leeds, *N. Dak., U.S.* 104 E6
Leek, *Neth.* 146 G14
Leer, *Ger.* 148 C6
Leesburg, *Fla., U.S.* 97 T8
Leesburg, *Va., U.S.* 96 C12
Lees Summit, *Mo., U.S.* 105 S11
Lee Stocking Island, *Bahamas* 120 E8
Leesville, *La., U.S.* 100 N7
Leeuwarden, *Neth.* 146 G13
Leeuwin, Cape, *Austral.* 210 L2
Leeward Islands, *Lesser Antilles* 119 G15
Le Faou, *Fr.* 147 Q3
Lefka, *Cyprus* 160 P7
Lefkáda, *Gr.* 154 G7
Lefkáda (Leucas), island, *Gr.* 154 G7
Lefkímmi, *Gr.* 154 F6
Lefkonoiko, *Cyprus* 160 N9
Lefkoşa see Lefkosia, *Cyprus* 160 N8
Lefkosia (Nicosia, Lefkoşa), *Cyprus* 160 N8
Le François, *Martinique, Fr.* 121 F23
Lefroy, Lake, *Austral.* 210 J4
Legan, island, *Marshall Is.* 216 M5
Legazpi, *Philippines* 189 D14
Legges Tor, *Austral.* 210 L16
Leggett, *Calif., U.S.* 109 P2
Leghorn see Livorno, *It.* 150 H6
Legionowo, *Pol.* 149 D16

Legnago, *It.* 150 E7
Legnano, *It.* 150 D4
Legnica, *Pol.* 148 F12
Le Grand-Lemps, *Fr.* 147 U13
Le Grau-du-Roi, *Fr.* 147 X12
Legune, *N. Terr., Austral.* 211 Q7
Leh, *India* 176 M14
Le Havre, *Fr.* 147 N7
Lehená, *Gr.* 154 J8
Lehr, *N. Dak., U.S.* 104 H6
Lehrte, *Ger.* 148 D8
Lehua, island, *Hawai'i, U.S.* 112 B3
Lehua, Pu'u, *Hawai'i, U.S.* 113 M19
Lehututu, *Botswana* 202 H8
Leiah, *Pak.* 177 Q9
Leiah, *Pak.* 177 Q9
Leicester, *Eng., U.K.* 143 T13
Leiden, *Neth.* 146 J12
Leigh, *N.Z.* 213 J19
Leigh Creek, *S. Aust., Austral.* 211 W10
Leikanger, *Nor.* 140 K10
Leimatu'a, *Tonga* 218 L11
Leine, river, *Ger.* 148 E7
Leinster, region, *Ire.* 143 S6
Leipzig, *Ger.* 148 F9
Leiria, *Port.* 144 G5
Leitchfield, *Ky., U.S.* 101 C16
Leiway, *Myanmar* 186 J6
Leiyang, *China* 183 P4
Leizhou, *China* 183 T1
Leizhou Bandao (Luichow Peninsula), *China* 183 T1
Leizhou Wan, *China* 183 T2
Le Kartala, peak, *Comoros* 205 M14
Lekeleka, island, *Tonga* 218 Q7
Lekitobi, *Indonesia* 189 K15
Leksula, *Indonesia* 189 K15
Lekunberri, *Sp.* 145 B13
Le Lamentin, *Martinique, Fr.* 121 F22
Leland, *Miss., U.S.* 100 J10
Lel'chytsy, *Belarus* 156 M5
Lele, *F.S.M.* 217 B19
Lele Harbor, *F.S.M.* 217 B19
Leleiwi Point, *Hawai'i, U.S.* 113 M22
Lélépa, island, *Vanuatu* 218 F3
Leli, island, *Solomon Is.* 217 M20
Lelingluang, *Indonesia* 189 M17
Lelintah, *Indonesia* 189 K17
Lêliogat, Île, *New Caledonia, Fr.* 218 D9
Le Lion-d'Angers, *Fr.* 147 R6
Le Locle, *Switz.* 150 B2
Le Lorrain, *Martinique, Fr.* 121 E22
Lelystad, *Neth.* 146 H13
Le Madonie, *It.* 151 S10
Le Maire, Estrecho de, *Arg.* 133 X10
Léman, Lac (Lake of Geneva), *Fr., Switz.* 147 T15
Lemanmanu, *P.N.G.* 217 J13
Le Mans, *Fr.* 147 Q7
Le Marin, *Martinique, Fr.* 121 G23
Le Mars, *Iowa, U.S.* 104 M9
Lemei Rock, *Wash., U.S.* 108 E4
Lemesos, *Cyprus* 160 Q7
Lemgo, *Ger.* 148 E7
Lemhi, river, *Idaho, U.S.* 106 F6
Lemhi Range, *Idaho, U.S.* 106 F6
Lemieux Islands, *Nunavut, Can.* 83 G19
Lemmer, *Neth.* 146 H13
Lemmon, *S. Dak., U.S.* 104 H3
Lemmon, Mount, *Ariz., U.S.* 107 V8
Lemnos see Límnos, island, *Gr.* 155 E14
Le Mont-Dore, *Fr.* 147 U10
Le Montet, *Fr.* 147 T11
Lemoore, *Calif., U.S.* 109 U6
Le Morne Brabant, cape, *Mauritius* 205 H19
Le Morne Rouge, *Martinique, Fr.* 121 E22
Lemotol, bay, *F.S.M.* 217 C14
Le Moule, *Guadeloupe, Fr.* 121 E16
Lempdes, *Fr.* 147 U11
Lemsid, *W. Sahara, Mor.* 196 D6
Lena, river, *Russ.* 166 C10
Lena, river, *Russ.* 159 F18
Lena Tablemount, *Antarctic Oc.* 245 D15
Lena Trough, *Arctic Oc.* 243 H14
Lencouacq, *Fr.* 147 W7
Lenger, *Kaz.* 175 J13
Lenghu, *China* 180 G9
Lengua de Vaca Point, *S. Amer.* 126 L4
Lenin, *Taj.* 176 J8
Leningrad see Sankt-Peterburg, *Russ.* 156 F6
Leningrad, *Taj.* 176 J8
Leningradskaya, *Russ.* 157 R10
Leninogorsk, *Russ.* 156 J16
Leninogorsk see Ridder, *Kaz.* 175 D18

Lenin Peak, *Kyrg., Taj.* 176 H10
Leninsk see Bayqongyr, *Kaz.* 174 G10
Leninskiy, *Russ.* 156 H13
Leninsk Kuznetskiy, *Russ.* 158 K12
Lennox, *S. Dak., U.S.* 104 M8
Lennox-King Glacier, *Antarctica* 227 L13
Lenoir, *N.C., U.S.* 96 H8
Lenoir City, *Tenn., U.S.* 101 F18
Lenora, *Kans., U.S.* 105 R5
Lenox, *Iowa, U.S.* 105 Q10
Lenox, *Mass., U.S.* 94 K12
Lens, *Fr.* 146 M10
Lensk, *Russ.* 159 J16
Lentekhi, *Rep. of Georgia* 169 B17
Lenti, *Hung.* 149 M13
Lentini, *It.* 151 T12
Lenya, *Myanmar* 187 P8
Léo, *Burkina Faso* 200 F10
Leoben, *Aust.* 148 L11
Léogâne, *Haiti* 117 M16
Leola, *S. Dak., U.S.* 104 J6
Leominster, *Mass., U.S.* 95 K14
Léon, *Fr.* 147 X6
León, *Mex.* 114 H10
León, *Nicar.* 115 M17
León, *Sp.* 144 C9
León, Montes de, *Sp.* 144 C8
Leon, *Iowa, U.S.* 105 Q11
Leon, river, *Tex., U.S.* 102 M10
Leonard, *Tex., U.S.* 102 K12
Leonard's, *Virgin Islands, U.K.* 120 Q6
Leonarisso, *Cyprus* 160 M10
Leonberg, *Ger.* 148 J6
Leonding, *Aust.* 148 K11
Leone, *Amer. Samoa, U.S.* 218 M7
Leone Bay, *Amer. Samoa, U.S.* 218 M6
Leongatha, *Vic., Austral.* 211 Z12
Leonídio, *Gr.* 154 L11
Leonora, *W. Aust., Austral.* 211 V4
Leopold and Astrid Coast, *Antarctica* 227 H21
Leopoldsburg, *Belg.* 146 K13
Léopoldville see Kinshasa, *Dem. Rep. of the Congo* 198 L7
Leoti, *Kans., U.S.* 105 T3
Lepanto, *Ark., U.S.* 100 F11
Lepe, *Sp.* 144 L6
Le Perthus, *Fr.* 147 Z10
Le Petit-Quevilly, *Fr.* 147 N8
Leping, *China* 182 M7
Lepontine Alpi, *It., Switz.* 150 C4
Le Porge, *Fr.* 147 V6
Le Port, *Reunion, Fr.* 205 G15
Le Prêcheur, *Martinique, Fr.* 121 E21
Lepsi, *Kaz.* 175 F17
Le Puy, *Fr.* 147 V12
Ler, *Sudan* 198 G12
Lercara Friddi, *It.* 151 S10
Léré, *Chad* 197 K14
Lerida, *Qnsld., Austral.* 211 T12
Lerik, *Azerb.* 169 F22
Lerma, river, *N. Amer.* 80 N5
Lerma, *Sp.* 144 D11
Le Robert, *Martinique, Fr.* 121 F23
Léros, island, *Gr.* 155 L17
Le Roy, *N.Y., U.S.* 94 J6
LeRoy, *Kans., U.S.* 105 T9
Lerwick, *Scot., U.K.* 142 D12
Leş, *Rom.* 152 C11
Les Abymes, *Guadeloupe, Fr.* 121 E15
Le St.-Esprit, *Martinique, Fr.* 121 F23
Les Amirante, islands, *Seychelles* 205 Q20
Les Anses-d'Arlets, *Martinique, Fr.* 121 G22
Les Avirons, *Reunion, Fr.* 205 H15
Les Bons, *Andorra* 160 J3
Les Borges Blanques, *Sp.* 145 D16
Lesbos see Lésvos, island, *Gr.* 155 F16
Les Cayes, *Haiti* 117 M15
Les Coteaux, *Trinidad & Tobago* 121 N17
Les Ecréhou, *Ch. Is.* 143 Z12
Les Escaldes, *Andorra* 160 J3
Leshan, *China* 180 L11
Leskovac, *Serb.* 152 H11
Les Landes, plain, *Fr.* 147 W6
Leslie, *Ark., U.S.* 100 F8
Lesmont, *Fr.* 147 Q12
Lesneven, *Fr.* 147 P3
Lesnoye, *Russ.* 156 G8
Lesosibirsk, *Russ.* 159 K13
Lesotho, *Af.* 195 Q21
Lesozavodsk, *Russ.* 159 L21
L'Esperance Rock, *Kermadec Is., N.Z.* 214 M9

Les Sables-d'Olonne, *Fr.* **147** T5
Les Saintes, islands, *Guadeloupe, Fr.* **121** G14
Lessay, *Fr.* **147** N6
Les Sept Îles, *Fr.* **147** P4
Lesser Antilles, islands, *N. Amer.* **80** N12
Lesser Caucasus, range, *Arm., Azerb., Rep. of Georgia* **169** C16
Lesser Khingan Range, *China* **166** E12
Lesser Slave Lake, *Alta., Can.* **82** K10
Lesser Sunda Islands, *Indonesia* **189** M13
Les Soeurs (The Sisters), islands, *Seychelles* **205** M21
Lesson, Point, *F.S.M.* **217** B18
Les Trois-Îlets, *Martinique, Fr.* **121** F22
Le Sueur, *Minn., U.S.* **104** K11
Lésvos (Lesbos, Mitilíni), *Gr.* **155** F16
Leszno, *Pol.* **149** E13
Le Tampon, *Reunion, Fr.* **205** H16
Letchworth, *Eng., U.K.* **143** U14
Letea, Ostrov, *Rom.* **153** E18
Le Teil, *Fr.* **147** W12
Lethbridge, *Alta., Can.* **82** N10
Lethem, *Guyana* **129** F14
Le Thuy, *Vietnam* **186** K13
Leti, Kepulauan, *Indonesia* **189** M16
Leticia, *Col.* **128** L8
Leting, *China* **182** D8
Letsôk-aw Kyun, *Myanmar* **187** P7
Leuca, *It.* **151** P16
Leucas *see* Lefkáda, island, *Gr.* **154** G7
Leucate, *Fr.* **147** Y11
Leucate, Étang de, *Fr.* **147** Y11
Leulumoega, *Samoa* **218** L3
Leuser, peak, *Indonesia* **188** G4
Leusoalii, *Amer. Samoa, U.S.* **218** P4
Levan, *Utah, U.S.* **106** M7
Levanger, *Nor.* **140** H11
Levant, Île du, *Fr.* **147** Y15
Levant Coast, *Asia* **166** F3
Levanto, *It.* **150** G5
Le Vauclin, *Martinique, Fr.* **121** F23
Levelland, *Tex., U.S.* **102** K4
Leveque, Cape, *Austral.* **210** C4
Levera Pond, *Grenada* **121** J23
Le Verdon-sur-Mer, *Fr.* **147** U6
Leverkusen, *Ger.* **148** F5
Levet, *Fr.* **147** S10
Levice, *Slovakia* **149** K14
Levídi, *Gr.* **154** K10
Levin, *N.Z.* **213** M19
Lévis, *Que., Can.* **83** P20
Lévitha, island, *Gr.* **155** L17
Levittown, *N.Y., U.S.* **94** N12
Levittown, *P.R., U.S.* **120** M4
Levittown, *Pa., U.S.* **94** P10
Levski, *Bulg.* **153** H14
Levuka, *Fiji Is.* **218** H7
Lewellen, *Nebr., U.S.* **105** P3
Lewes, *Del., U.S.* **96** C15
Lewes, *Eng., U.K.* **143** W14
Lewis, *Kans., U.S.* **105** U5
Lewis, river, *Wash., U.S.* **108** E4
Lewis, Isle of, *Scot., U.K.* **142** H6
Lewis and Clark National Historic Park, *Oreg., U.S.* **108** E2
Lewis and Clark Range, *Mont., U.S.* **106** C6
Lewisburg, *Tenn., U.S.* **101** F15
Lewisburg, *W. Va., U.S.* **96** E9
Lewis Pass, *N.Z.* **213** N17
Lewis Range, *Austral.* **210** E7
Lewis Smith Lake, *Ala., U.S.* **101** H14
Lewiston, *Idaho, U.S.* **106** D3
Lewiston, *Me., U.S.* **95** G16
Lewistown, *Ill., U.S.* **99** Q4
Lewistown, *Mont., U.S.* **106** C9
Lewistown, *Pa., U.S.* **94** N6
Lewisville, *Ark., U.S.* **100** J7
Lewisville Lake, *Tex., U.S.* **102** K11
Lexington, *Ky., U.S.* **101** B18
Lexington, *Miss., U.S.* **100** K11
Lexington, *Mo., U.S.* **105** S11
Lexington, *N.C., U.S.* **96** H10
Lexington, *Nebr., U.S.* **105** Q5
Lexington, *Oreg., U.S.* **108** F6
Lexington, *Tenn., U.S.* **101** F13
Lexington, *Va., U.S.* **96** E10
Lexington Park, *Md., U.S.* **96** D14
Leydsdorp, *S. Af.* **202** H11
Leyte, island, *Philippines* **189** E15
Leyte Gulf, *Philippines* **189** E15
Lezha, *Russ.* **156** G11

Lezhë, *Albania* **152** K9
L'gov, *Russ.* **156** M8
Lhasa, *China* **180** L8
Lhazê, *China* **180** L6
Lhokseumawe, *Indonesia* **188** G4
L'Hospitalet, *Fr.* **147** Z9
L'Hospitalet de Llobregat, *Sp.* **145** E17
Li, river, *China* **182** M3
Liamuiga, Mount, *St. Kitts & Nevis* **121** A17
Lian, river, *China* **183** Q4
Liancheng, *China* **183** Q7
Liancourt Rocks *see* Dokdo, *Japan* **184** M6
Liangbuaya, *Indonesia* **188** J12
Liangcheng, *China* **182** C4
Liangping, *China* **182** K1
Lianjiang, *China* **183** P8
Lianjiang, *China* **183** S2
Liannan, *China* **183** Q3
Lianping, *China* **183** Q5
Lianshan, *China* **183** Q3
Lianyun, *China* **182** H8
Lianyungang (Xinpu), *China* **182** H8
Liao, river, *China* **182** B11
Liaocheng, *China* **182** F6
Liaodong Bandao, *China* **182** D10
Liaodong Wan, *China* **182** C10
Liaodun, *China* **180** F8
Liaoyang, *China* **182** C11
Liaoyuan, *China* **182** A12
Liaozhong, *China* **182** C10
Liaquatpur, *Pak.* **177** S9
Liard, river, *N.W.T., Can.* **82** H10
Liari, *Pak.* **177** V5
Libby, *Mont., U.S.* **106** B4
Libenge, *Dem. Rep. of the Congo* **198** H8
Liberal, *Kans., U.S.* **105** V4
Liberec, *Czech Rep.* **148** G11
Liberia, *Af.* **195** H14
Liberia, *Costa Rica* **115** N18
Liberta, *Antigua & Barbuda* **121** B21
Libertador General San Martín, *Arg.* **132** E9
Liberty, *Mo., U.S.* **105** S10
Liberty, *N.Y., U.S.* **94** L10
Liberty, *S.C., U.S.* **96** J7
Liberty, *Tex., U.S.* **103** Q14
Lib Island, *Marshall Is.* **216** G3
Libni, Gebel, *Egypt* **171** P3
Liboi, *Kenya* **199** K15
Libourne, *Fr.* **147** V7
Libreville, *Gabon* **201** K15
Libya, *Af.* **195** E19
Libyan Desert, *Af.* **194** E8
Libyan Plateau, *Egypt, Lib.* **197** C16
Licantén, *Chile* **132** L6
Licata, *It.* **151** T10
Lice, *Turk.* **169** G15
Lichinga, *Mozambique* **203** D13
Lichtenfels, *Ger.* **148** G8
Lichuan, *China* **182** L2
Lichuan, *China* **183** N7
Licking, river, *Ky., U.S.* **101** B19
Licking, *Mo., U.S.* **105** U13
Ličko Lešće, *Croatia* **152** F5
Licosa, Punta, *It.* **151** N11
Lida, *Belarus* **156** K3
Lidgerwood, *N. Dak., U.S.* **104** H8
Lidköping, *Sw.* **140** L12
Lido di Jesolo, *It.* **150** D8
Lido di Ostia *see* Lido di Roma, *It.* **150** L8
Lido di Roma (Lido di Ostia), *It.* **150** L8
Liechtenstein, *Eur.* **160** D3
Liège, *Belg.* **146** L13
Lieksa, *Fin.* **141** G17
Lienz, *Aust.* **148** M9
Liepāja, *Latv.* **141** M15
Lier, *Belg.* **146** K12
Liestal, *Switz.* **150** A3
Liffey, river, *Ire.* **143** S6
Lifford, *Ire.* **143** P5
Lifou, Île (Lifu), *New Caledonia, Fr.* **218** C9
Lifu *see* Lifou, Île, island, *New Caledonia, Fr.* **218** C9
Lifuka, island, *Tonga* **218** P7
Ligneuville, *Belg.* **146** M14
Ligny-en-Barrois, *Fr.* **147** P13
Ligurian Sea, *It.* **150** H4
Liha Point, *Niue, N.Z.* **219** B21
Lihir, island, *P.N.G.* **213** C21
Lihir Group, *P.N.G.* **213** B21
Līhu'e, *Hawai'i, U.S.* **112** C6

L'Îlot, island, *Seychelles* **205** N21
Lijeron, island, *Marshall Is.* **216** L7
Lijiang, *China* **180** M10
Likasi, *Dem. Rep. of the Congo* **198** N11
Likiep Atoll, *Marshall Is.* **216** G4
Likoma Island, *Malawi* **203** D13
Liku, *Niue, N.Z.* **219** B21
Likuone Bay, *Tonga* **218** L12
Likupang, *Indonesia* **189** H15
Lilbourn, *Mo., U.S.* **105** V16
Lile, river, *China* **183** T1
Lilian, Point, *Austral.* **210** H6
Lilian Point, *Banaba, Kiribati* **217** D20
Liling, *China* **183** N4
Lille, *Fr.* **146** L10
Lillehammer, *Nor.* **140** K11
Lillesand, *Nor.* **140** M10
Lillie Glacier, *Antarctica* **227** Q14
Lillooet, *B.C., Can.* **82** L8
Lilongwe, *Malawi* **202** E12
Lilo Viejo, *Arg.* **132** G10
Lim, river, *Bosn. & Herzg., Serb.* **152** G9
Lima, *Mont., U.S.* **106** F7
Lima, *Ohio, U.S.* **99** Q11
Lima, *Peru* **130** H3
Lima, river, *Port.* **144** D5
Limarí, Río, *Chile* **132** J6
Liman, *Russ.* **157** R15
Liman Beren, lake, *Russ.* **157** R13
Lima Reservoir, *Mont., U.S.* **106** F7
Limari, Río, *Chile* **132** J6
Limavady, *N. Ire., U.K.* **143** P6
Limay, river, *S. Amer.* **126** N4
Limbara, Monte, *It.* **150** M4
Limbdi, *India* **178** J3
Limbé, *Haiti* **117** L16
Limbe, *Cameroon* **201** J15
Limburg, *Ger.* **148** G6
Limeira, *Braz.* **131** M13
Limenária, *Gr.* **155** C14
Limerick (Luimneach), *Ire.* **143** T4
Limestone, *Me., U.S.* **95** B18
Limfjorden, lake, *Den.* **140** N11
Limia, river, *Sp.* **144** D6
Limín *see* Thássos, *Gr.* **155** C14
Liminka, *Fin.* **141** F15
Limmen Bight, *Austral.* **210** B9
Límni, *Gr.* **154** G11
Límnos (Lemnos), island, *Gr.* **155** E14
Limoges, *Fr.* **147** U9
Limon, Den, *Zimb.* **202** F11
Limon, *Colo., U.S.* **106** M14
Limon, Mount, *Mauritius* **205** J20
Limone Piemonte, *It.* **150** F2
Limoux, *Fr.* **147** Y10
Limpopo, river, *Botswana, Mozambique, S. Af.* **202** H12
Limu, island, *Tonga* **218** Q7
Limufuafua Point, *Niue, N.Z.* **219** C20
Līnah, *Saudi Arabia* **172** G9
Lin'an, *China* **182** L9
Linapacan, island, *Philippines* **189** D13
Linares, *Chile* **132** M6
Linares, *Mex.* **114** F11
Linares, *Sp.* **144** K11
Linariá, *Gr.* **155** G14
Lincang, *China* **180** P10
Linchuan, *China* **183** N6
Lincoln, *Arg.* **132** L11
Lincoln, *Calif., U.S.* **109** Q5
Lincoln, *Eng., U.K.* **143** S13
Lincoln, *Ill., U.S.* **99** R5
Lincoln, *Kans., U.S.* **105** S7
Lincoln, *Me., U.S.* **95** E18
Lincoln, *Mich., U.S.* **98** J12
Lincoln, *N.H., U.S.* **95** G14
Lincoln, *Nebr., U.S.* **105** Q8
Lincoln City, *Oreg., U.S.* **108** F2
Lincoln Heights, *Eng., U.K.* **143** S13
Lincoln Island, *China* **188** B10
Lincoln Park, *Mich., U.S.* **98** M12
Lincoln Sea, *N. Amer.* **80** A7
Lincolnton, *Ga., U.S.* **96** L7
Lincolnton, *N.C., U.S.* **96** H8
Lind, *Wash., U.S.* **108** D8
Linda Downs, *Qnsld., Austral.* **211** T10
Lindale, *Ga., U.S.* **96** K4
Lindale, *Tex., U.S.* **102** L13
Lindau, *Aust.* **148** L7
Lindbergh Bay, *Virgin Islands, U.S.* **120** N8
Linden, *Ala., U.S.* **101** L14
Linden, *Guyana* **129** E14
Linden, *Tex., U.S.* **102** K15
Lindesnes, *Nor.* **140** M10
Lindi, *Tanzania* **199** N15

Lindisfarne *see* Holy Island, island, *Eng., U.K.* **143** N12
Lindo, river, *Parag.* **130** M10
Líndos, *Gr.* **155** N20
Lindsay, *Calif., U.S.* **109** U7
Lindsay, *Mont., U.S.* **106** C13
Lindsay, *Okla., U.S.* **102** H10
Lindsborg, *Kans., U.S.* **105** T7
Line Islands, *Kiribati* **214** G12
Linfen, *China* **182** F4
Lingao, *China* **183** T1
Lingbao, *China* **182** H3
Lingbi, *China* **182** J7
Lingchuan, *China* **183** P2
Lingen, *Ger.* **148** D6
Lingga, island, *Indonesia* **188** J7
Lingga, Kepulauan, *Indonesia* **188** J7
Lingle, *Wyo., U.S.* **106** J14
Lingqiu, *China* **181** G14
Lingshan, *China* **183** S1
Lingshui, *China* **183** V1
Lingtai, *China* **182** G1
Linguère, *Senegal* **196** G5
Lingui, *China* **183** Q2
Lingyuan, *China* **182** C8
Linhares, *Braz.* **131** L16
Linhe, *China* **182** C1
Linjiang, *China* **182** B13
Linköping, *Sw.* **141** L13
Linn, *Tex., U.S.* **103** V10
Linnhe, Loch, *Scot., U.K.* **142** L8
Linqing, *China* **182** F6
Linquan, *China* **182** J6
Linru, *China* **182** H4
Linstead, *Jam.* **120** J9
Lintao, *China* **180** J11
Linton, *Ind., U.S.* **99** S8
Linton, *N. Dak., U.S.* **104** H5
Lintong, *China* **182** H2
Linxi, *China* **182** A8
Linxi, *China* **182** D8
Linxian, *China* **182** E3
Linyi, *China* **182** F7
Linyi, *China* **182** G8
Linz, *Aust.* **148** K11
Lio Matoh, *Malaysia* **188** H11
Lion, Golfe du, *Fr.* **147** Y12
Lionel Town, *Jam.* **120** K9
Lions, Gulf of, *Fr.* **138** H4
Lions Den, *Zimb.* **202** F11
Liot Point, *N.W.T., Can.* **82** D12
Liouesso, *Congo* **201** K17
Lipa, *Philippines* **189** C13
Lipari, Isola, *It.* **151** R11
Lipari, Isole (Eolie), *It.* **151** R11
Lipetsk, *Russ.* **156** M10
Liping, *China* **183** P1
Lipno, *Pol.* **149** D14
Līpoa Point, *Hawai'i, U.S.* **113** F16
Lipova, *Rom.* **152** D11
Lipscomb, *Tex., U.S.* **102** F7
Lipsí, island, *Gr.* **155** L17
Lipsí, *Gr.* **155** L17
Liptovský Mikuláš, *Slovakia* **149** J15
Lipu, *China* **183** Q2
Lipu Lekh Pass, *China, India, Nepal* **178** E8
Liri, river, *It.* **150** L10
Līsakovsk, *Kaz.* **174** C10
Lisala, *Dem. Rep. of the Congo* **198** J9
Lisboa (Lisbon), *Port.* **144** H4
Lisbon, *N. Dak., U.S.* **104** H7
Lisbon *see* Lisboa, *Port.* **144** H4
Lisbon Falls, *Me., U.S.* **95** G16
Lisburn, *N. Ire., U.K.* **143** Q7
Lisburne, Cape, *Alas., U.S.* **110** C12
Liscannor Bay, *Ire.* **143** S3
Lishu, *China* **182** A11
Lishui, *China* **182** M9
Lisianski Island, *Hawai'i, U.S.* **112** L3
Lisieux, *Fr.* **147** P8
Liski, *Rom.* **153** D16
Liski, *Russ.* **156** N10
L'Isle-sur-la-Sorgue, *Fr.* **147** X13
Lismore, *N.S.W., Austral.* **211** W15
Lismore, island, *Scot., U.K.* **142** L8
Lissa *see* Vis, island, *Croatia* **152** H6
Lister, Mount, *Antarctica* **227** N14
Listowel, *Ire.* **143** T3
Listowel Downs, *Qnsld., Austral.* **211** U13
Litang, river, *China* **180** M10
Litang, *China* **183** R1
Litang, *China* **180** L10
Litani, river, *Fr. Guiana, Fr., Suriname* **129** F17

Lîtâni, river, *Leb.* **170** K6
Litchfield, *Ill., U.S.* **99** S5
Litchfield, *Minn., U.S.* **104** J10
Lit-et-Mixe, *Fr.* **147** W6
Lithgow, *N.S.W., Austral.* **211** X14
Líthino, Akrotírio, *Gr.* **155** R14
Lithuania, *Eur.* **139** S8
Litóhoro, *Gr.* **154** D10
Little, river, *La., U.S.* **100** M8
Little, river, *Okla., U.S.* **102** J14
Little, river, *Tex., U.S.* **103** P11
Little Abaco Island, *Bahamas* **120** A5
Little Andaman, island, *India* **179** R14
Little Barrier Island, *N.Z.* **213** J19
Little Bay, *Gibraltar, U.K.* **161** Q23
Little Belt Mountains, *Mont., U.S.* **106** D8
Little Bighorn, river, *Mont., Wyo., U.S.* **106** F11
Little Bighorn Battlefield National Monument, *Mont., U.S.* **106** E11
Little Bitter Lake *see* Murrat el Sughra, Buheirat, *Egypt* **171** Q1
Little Blue, river, *Nebr., U.S.* **105** R7
Little Cayman, island, *Cayman Is., U.K.* **116** L8
Little Chute, *Wis., U.S.* **98** J6
Little Coco Island, *Myanmar* **186** M4
Little Darby Island, *Bahamas* **120** D7
Little Dix Bay, *Virgin Islands, U.K.* **120** R8
Little Exuma, island, *Bahamas* **120** F9
Little Falls, *Minn., U.S.* **104** H10
Little Falls, *N.Y., U.S.* **94** J10
Littlefield, *Ariz., U.S.* **107** Q5
Littlefield, *Tex., U.S.* **102** J4
Little Fork, *Minn., U.S.* **104** E11
Littlefork, *Minn., U.S.* **104** E11
Littlehampton, *Eng., U.K.* **143** W13
Little Hans Lollik Island, *Virgin Islands, U.S.* **120** M9
Little Harbor, *Bahamas* **120** B7
Little Inagua Island, *Bahamas* **117** J16
Little Jost Van Dyke, island, *Virgin Islands, U.K.* **120** L11
Little London, *Jam.* **120** H6
Little Lost, river, *Idaho, U.S.* **106** G6
Little Marais, *Minn., U.S.* **104** F13
Little Mecatina, river, *Nfld. & Lab., Que., Can.* **83** L22
Little Missouri, river, *S. Dak., U.S.* **104** J1
Little Nicobar, island, *India* **179** T15
Little Powder, river, *Mont., Wyo., U.S.* **106** F13
Little Red, river, *Ark., U.S.* **100** F8
Little Rock, *Ark., U.S.* **100** G8
Little St. James Island, *Virgin Islands, U.S.* **120** N10
Little Salt Lake, *Utah, U.S.* **107** P6
Little San Salvador, island, *Bahamas* **117** E13
Little Sioux, river, *Iowa, U.S.* **105** N9
Little Snake, river, *Colo., U.S.* **106** L10
Little Sound, *Cayman Is., U.K.* **120** J2
Little Sound (Port Royal Bay), *Bermuda, U.K.* **120** C2
Little Suamico, *Wis., U.S.* **98** J7
Little Thatch Island, *Virgin Islands, U.K.* **120** R5
Little Tobago, island, *Trinidad & Tobago* **121** N19
Little Tobago Island, *Virgin Islands, U.K.* **120** L10
Littleton, *Colo., U.S.* **106** M13
Littleton, *N.H., U.S.* **95** G14
Little Wabash, river, *Ill., U.S.* **99** S6
Liucheng, *China* **183** Q1
Liuhe, *China* **182** B12
Liuwa Plain, *Zambia* **202** E9
Liuyang, *China* **183** N4
Liuzhai, *China* **180** N12
Liuzhou, *China* **183** Q1
Livadi, *Gr.* **155** L13
Livádia, *Gr.* **155** M18
Livadiá, *Gr.* **154** H11
Līvāni, *Latv.* **141** M17
Live Oak, *Fla., U.S.* **97** R7
Livermore, *Calif., U.S.* **109** S4
Livermore, *Ky., U.S.* **101** C15
Livermore, Mount, *Tex., U.S.* **103** P1
Liverpool, *Eng., U.K.* **143** S10
Liverpool, *N.S., Can.* **83** P22
Liverpool Bay, *N.W.T., Can.* **82** D11
Liverpool Range, *Austral.* **210** K14
Livingston, *Ala., U.S.* **101** L13

Livingston, *Mont., U.S.* 106 E8
Livingston, *Tenn., U.S.* 101 E17
Livingston, *Tex., U.S.* 103 P14
Lívingston, *Guatemala* 115 K16
Livingston, Lake, *Tex., U.S.* 103 P14
Livingstone, *Zambia* 202 F10
Livingston Island, *Antarctica* 226 C3
Livny, *Russ.* 156 M9
Livonia, *Mich., U.S.* 98 M12
Livorno (Leghorn), *It.* 150 H6
Livron, *Fr.* 147 V13
Līwā, region, *U.A.E.* 173 K14
Liwale, *Tanzania* 199 N14
Liwonde, *Malawi* 203 E13
Lixian, *China* 182 L3
Li Yubu, *Sudan* 198 H11
Lizard Point, *Eng., U.K.* 143 Y8
Lizarra *see* Estella, *Sp.* 145 C13
Ljubljana, *Slov.* 152 D4
Ljuboten, peak, *Kos.* 152 J11
Ljusdal, *Sw.* 141 J13
Llaima Volcano, *S. Amer.* 126 N4
Llamara, Salar de, *Chile* 132 D7
Llandrindod Wells, *Wales, U.K.* 143 U10
Llanes, *Sp.* 144 B10
Llano, river, *Tex., U.S.* 103 P8
Llano, *Tex., U.S.* 103 P9
Llanos, region, *S. Amer.* 126 B4
Llanquihue, Lago, *Chile* 133 Q6
Llavorsí, *Sp.* 145 C16
Lleida, *Sp.* 145 D15
Llerena, *Sp.* 144 J8
Lleyn Peninsula, *Wales, U.K.* 143 T8
Llica, *Bol.* 130 L6
Llívia, *Sp.* 145 C17
Llodio, *Sp.* 144 B12
Llorts, *Andorra* 160 H3
Llosa, river, *Sp.* 160 K5
Lloydminster, *Alta., Can.* 82 L11
Llucmajor, *Sp.* 145 G18
Lluidas Vale, *Jam.* 120 J9
Llyswen, *Wales, U.K.* 143 U10
Ló, Ponta do, *Sao Tome and Principe* 205 D20
Lo, river, *Vietnam* 186 G11
Loa, river, *Chile* 132 D7
Loa, *Utah, U.S.* 107 N7
Loaita Island, *Spratly Is.* 188 E11
Loʻaloʻa Heiau, *Hawaiʻi, U.S.* 113 H17
Lobamba, *Swaziland* 203 J11
Lobatse, *Botswana* 202 J10
Lobaya, river, *Cen. Af. Rep.* 194 J6
Lobería, *Arg.* 133 N12
Lobería, *Arg.* 133 Q10
Lobikaere, island, *Marshall Is.* 216 G11
Lobito, *Angola* 202 D5
Lobitos, *Peru* 130 E1
Lobo, *Indonesia* 189 K19
Lobos, *Arg.* 132 L12
Lobos, Cay, *Cuba* 116 H11
Lobos Islands, *S. Amer.* 126 E1
Lobuya, *Russ.* 159 D19
Locana, *It.* 150 D2
Locarno, *Switz.* 150 C4
Lochcarron, *Scot., U.K.* 142 J8
Lochearnhead, *Scot., U.K.* 142 L9
Lochgilphead, *Scot., U.K.* 142 M8
Lochmaddy, *Scot., U.K.* 142 J6
Lochsa, river, *Idaho, U.S.* 106 D5
Lochy, Loch, *Scot., U.K.* 142 K8
Lockesburg, *Ark., U.S.* 100 H6
Lockhart, *Tex., U.S.* 103 Q10
Lockhart River, *Qnsld., Austral.* 211 P12
Lock Haven, *Pa., U.S.* 94 M6
Lockney, *Tex., U.S.* 102 J5
Lockport, *N.Y., U.S.* 94 J5
Lockwood Terrace, *Guam, U.S.* 216 C10
Locminé, *Fr.* 147 Q4
Locri, *It.* 151 R13
Lod (Lydda), *Israel* 170 M5
Lodeynoye Pole, *Russ.* 156 E8
Lodge Creek, *Mont., U.S.* 106 A9
Lodge Grass, *Mont., U.S.* 106 E11
Lodgepole, *Nebr., U.S.* 105 P2
Lodgepole Creek, *Nebr., U.S.* 105 P1
Lodhran, *Pak.* 177 S10
Lodi, *Calif., U.S.* 109 R5
Lodi, *It.* 150 E5
Lodja, *Dem. Rep. of the Congo* 198 L10
Lodwar, *Kenya* 199 J14
Łódź, *Pol.* 149 E15
Loei, *Thai.* 186 K9
Lofanga, island, *Tonga* 218 P7
Lofoten, *Nor.* 140 E11
Lofty Range, *Austral.* 210 G3

Logan, *Iowa, U.S.* 105 P9
Logan, *Kans., U.S.* 105 R5
Logan, *N. Mex., U.S.* 107 R15
Logan, *Ohio, U.S.* 99 R14
Logan, *Utah, U.S.* 106 J7
Logan, *W. Va., U.S.* 96 E7
Logan, Mount, *Wash., U.S.* 108 A5
Logan, Mount, *Yukon, Can.* 82 F7
Logansport, *Ind., U.S.* 99 Q8
Logansport, *La., U.S.* 100 L6
Logashkino, *Russ.* 159 D18
Logone, river, *Cameroon, Chad* 194 H6
Logoniégué, *Burkina Faso* 200 F9
Logroño, *Sp.* 144 C12
Loh, island, *Vanuatu* 218 A1
Lohardaga, *India* 178 H8
Loharghat, *India* 178 G13
Lohne, *Ger.* 148 D6
Loi, island, *Marshall Is.* 216 N5
Loi Mwe, *Myanmar* 186 H8
Loire, river, *Fr.* 147 Q10
Loire, river, *Fr.* 147 R6
Loíza, *P.R., U.S.* 120 M5
Loja, *Ecua.* 128 L3
Loja, *Sp.* 144 L10
Loji, *Indonesia* 189 K16
Lojjairok, island, *Marshall Is.* 216 N5
Lojwa, island, *Marshall Is.* 216 G8
Lokhwabe, *Botswana* 202 J8
Lokitaung, *Kenya* 199 H14
Loknya, *Russ.* 156 H6
Lokoja, *Nigeria* 201 G14
Lokolama, *Dem. Rep. of the Congo* 198 K9
Lokomo, *Cameroon* 201 J17
Lokoro, river, *Dem. Rep. of the Congo* 198 K9
Loks Land, *Nunavut, Can.* 83 H19
Lokuru, *Solomon Is.* 217 M16
Lol, river, *Sudan* 198 G11
Lolland, island, *Den.* 140 P12
Lolo Pass, *Idaho, Mont., U.S.* 106 D5
Lolowaï, *Vanuatu* 218 C2
Lom, *Bulg.* 153 G13
Lom, *Nor.* 140 J10
Lomaloma, *Fiji Is.* 218 H9
Lomami, river, *Dem. Rep. of the Congo* 198 K10
Loma Mountains, *Guinea, Sierra Leone* 200 F6
Lomawai, *Fiji Is.* 218 J5
Lombadina, *W. Aust., Austral.* 211 R4
Lombez, *Fr.* 147 X8
Lomblen, island, *Indonesia* 189 M14
Lombok, island, *Indonesia* 188 M12
Lombok, Selat, *Indonesia* 188 M11
Lomé, *Togo* 200 H11
Lomela, river, *Dem. Rep. of the Congo* 198 K9
Lomela, *Dem. Rep. of the Congo* 198 K10
Lometa, *Tex., U.S.* 103 N9
Lomié, *Cameroon* 201 J17
Lomlom, island, *Solomon Is.* 217 P23
Lomond, Loch, *Scot., U.K.* 142 M9
Lomonosov, *Russ.* 156 F6
Lomonosov Ridge, *Arctic Oc.* 242 F8
Lomphat, *Cambodia* 186 M13
Lompoc, *Calif., U.S.* 109 W5
Łomża, *Pol.* 149 C17
Lon, Hon, *Vietnam* 187 N14
Lonauli, *India* 178 L3
Loncoche, *Chile* 133 P6
Loncopué, *Arg.* 133 N7
London, *Eng., U.K.* 143 V14
London, *Kiribati* 217 B22
London, *Ky., U.S.* 101 D18
London, *Ohio, U.S.* 99 R12
London, *Ont., Can.* 83 R18
London Bridge Island, *Grenada* 121 J23
Londonderry, *St. Lucia* 121 L14
Londonderry (Derry), *N. Ire., U.K.* 143 P6
Londonderry, Cape, *Austral.* 210 B6
Londonderry, Isla, *Chile* 133 Y8
Londrina, *Braz.* 130 M12
Lone Pine, *Calif., U.S.* 109 T8
Lonerock, *Oreg., U.S.* 108 F6
Longa, river, *Angola* 202 C6
Long Bay, *Barbados* 121 L19
Long Bay, *Virgin Islands, U.K.* 120 R5
Long Bay, *Virgin Islands, U.K.* 120 R5
Long Bay, *Jam.* 120 H5
Long Bay, *Jam.* 120 K8
Long Beach, *Calif., U.S.* 109 X8
Long Beach, *Miss., U.S.* 100 P12

Long Beach, *N.C., U.S.* 96 K12
Long Beach, *Wash., U.S.* 108 D2
Longboat Key, *Fla., U.S.* 97 V7
Long Branch, *N.J., U.S.* 94 P11
Long Cay (Fortune Island), *Bahamas* 117 H14
Longchuan, *China* 183 R5
Long Creek, *Oreg., U.S.* 108 G7
Longdenville, *Trinidad & Tobago* 121 P22
Long Eaton, *Eng., U.K.* 143 T12
Longeau, *Fr.* 147 R13
Longford, *Ire.* 143 R5
Longgglat, *Indonesia* 188 H12
Longhai, *China* 183 R7
Longhua, *China* 182 C7
Longido, *Tanzania* 199 L14
Longiram, *Indonesia* 188 J11
Long Island, *Antigua & Barbuda* 121 A21
Long Island, *Bahamas* 117 G14
Long Island, *N.Y., U.S.* 95 N13
Long Island, *Nunavut, Can.* 83 L17
Long Island, *P.N.G.* 213 C19
Long Island Sound, *Conn., N.Y., U.S.* 95 M13
Longjiang, *China* 181 C16
Longju, *India* 178 E14
Long Key, *Fla., U.S.* 97 Y10
Longkou, *China* 182 E9
Longlac, *Ont., Can.* 83 N16
Long Lake, *N. Dak., U.S.* 104 G5
Long Look, *Virgin Islands, U.K.* 120 Q7
Longmen, *China* 183 R5
Longmont, *Colo., U.S.* 106 L13
Longnan, *China* 183 Q5
Longnawan, *Indonesia* 188 H11
Longomapu, *Tonga* 218 L11
Long Pine, *Nebr., U.S.* 105 N5
Long Point, *Virgin Islands, U.S.* 120 N9
Long Point, *Virgin Islands, U.S.* 120 R2
Long Prairie, *Minn., U.S.* 104 H10
Longquan, *China* 183 N8
Long Range Mountains, *N. Amer.* 80 G10
Longreach, *Qnsld., Austral.* 211 T12
Longshan, *China* 182 L2
Longsheng, *China* 183 P2
Longs Peak, *Colo., U.S.* 106 L13
Longton, *Qnsld., Austral.* 211 S13
Longuyon, *Fr.* 160 L8
Longview, *Tex., U.S.* 102 L14
Longview, *Wash., U.S.* 108 E3
Longville, *La., U.S.* 100 P7
Longwy, *Fr.* 147 N13
Longxi, *China* 180 J12
Long Xuyen, *Vietnam* 187 P12
Longyan, *China* 183 Q7
Long'yugan, *Russ.* 158 G11
Lonoke, *Ark., U.S.* 100 G9
Lonquimay, *Chile* 133 N7
Lons-le-Saunier, *Fr.* 147 S13
Loogootee, *Ind., U.S.* 99 T8
Lookout, Cape, *N.C., U.S.* 96 J14
Lookout, Cape, *Oreg., U.S.* 108 F2
Lookout, Point, *Austral.* 210 H16
Lookout Mountain, *N. Mex., U.S.* 107 S10
Lookout Mountain, *Tenn., U.S.* 101 G17
Lookout Ridge, *Alas., U.S.* 111 C14
Loongana, *W. Aust., Austral.* 211 W6
Loop Head, *Ire.* 143 T2
Lop, *China* 180 G5
Lopatino, *Russ.* 156 L13
Lopatka, Cape, *Russ.* 166 C13
Lopatka, Mys, *Russ.* 159 G23
Lop Buri, *Thai.* 186 M9
Lopévi (Ulvéah), island, *Vanuatu* 218 E3
Lopez, Cap, *Gabon* 201 L14
Lopez Point, *Calif., U.S.* 109 U4
Lop Nur, *China* 180 G8
Lopphavet, *Nor.* 141 C13
Lora, Hamun-i-, *Pak.* 177 S4
Lorain, *Ohio, U.S.* 99 P14
Loraine, *Tex., U.S.* 102 M6
Loralai, *Pak.* 177 R7
Lorca, *Sp.* 145 K13
Lord Howe Atoll *see* Ontong Java Atoll, *Solomon Is.* 217 J18
Lord Howe Island *see* Tomotu Noi, *Solomon Is.* 217 Q22
Lord Howe Rise, *Pac. Oc.* 238 N8
Lord of the Sky *see* Khan Tängiri, peak, *Kaz., Kyrg.* 176 E15
Lordsburg, *N. Mex., U.S.* 107 V10
Lorentzweiler, *Lux.* 160 J10
Lorenzo, *Tex., U.S.* 102 K5

Loreto, *Bol.* 130 J7
Loreto, *Mex.* 114 E6
Loreto, *Braz.* 131 F14
Loretto, *Tenn., U.S.* 101 G14
Lorian Swamp, *Kenya* 194 J10
Lorica, *Col.* 128 C4
Lorient, *Fr.* 147 R4
Lorimers, *Turks & Caicos Is., U.K.* 117 H17
Loris, *S.C., U.S.* 96 K11
Lormes, *Fr.* 147 R11
Lormi, *India* 178 J8
Lorn, Firth of, *Scot., U.K.* 142 L7
Lorne, *Qnsld., Austral.* 211 U13
Lornel, Pointe de, *Fr.* 146 L9
Lörrach, *Ger.* 148 L5
Lorraine, region, *Fr.* 147 P13
Lorraine, *Qnsld., Austral.* 211 S10
Los Ángeles, *Chile* 133 N6
Los Alamos, *N. Mex., U.S.* 107 R12
Los Andes, *Chile* 132 K7
Los Angeles, *Calif., U.S.* 109 X8
Los Angeles Aqueduct, *Calif., U.S.* 109 V8
Losap Atoll, *F.S.M.* 216 Q6
Los Banos, *Calif., U.S.* 109 T5
Los Blancos, *Arg.* 132 E11
Los Cerrillos, *Arg.* 132 K9
Los Corrales, *Sp.* 144 B10
Los Cristianos, *Canary Is.* 204 Q4
Los Frailes, islands, *Venez.* 119 N14
Los Gatos, *Calif., U.S.* 109 S4
Losheim, *Ger.* 160 K12
Los Hermanos, islands, *Venez.* 119 N14
Lošinj, island, *Croatia* 152 F4
Los Lagos, *Chile* 133 P6
Los Llanos, *Canary Is.* 204 Q3
Los Loros, *Chile* 132 G7
Los Lunas, *N. Mex., U.S.* 107 S12
Los Mochis, *Mex.* 114 E7
Los Olmos Creek, *Tex., U.S.* 103 U10
Los Osos, *Calif., U.S.* 109 V5
Los Palacios, *Cuba* 116 G5
Lospalos, *Timor-Leste* 189 M16
Lossiemouth, *Scot., U.K.* 142 J10
Los Teques, *Venez.* 128 B9
Los Testigos, islands, *Venez.* 119 N15
Lostine, *Oreg., U.S.* 108 F9
Lost River Range, *Idaho, U.S.* 106 G6
Lost Trail Pass, *Idaho, Mont., U.S.* 106 E6
Losuia, *P.N.G.* 213 E21
Los Vilos, *Chile* 132 K6
Los Yébenes, *Sp.* 144 G10
Lot, river, *Fr.* 147 W8
Lot, *F.S.M.* 217 B18
Lota, *Chile* 133 N6
Lotagipi Swamp, *Kenya* 199 H14
Lot Harbor, *F.S.M.* 217 G14
Lotofaga, *Samoa* 218 L3
Lot's Wife *see* Sōfu Gan, island, *Japan* 184 K5
Lott, *Tex., U.S.* 103 N11
Lottin, Port, *F.S.M.* 217 B18
Lou, island, *P.N.G.* 213 B19
Louang-Namtha, *Laos* 186 H9
Louangphrabang, *Laos* 186 J10
Loubomo *see* Dolisie, *Congo* 201 M16
Loudéac, *Fr.* 147 Q4
Loudonville, *Ohio, U.S.* 99 Q14
Loudun, *Fr.* 147 S7
Loué, *Fr.* 147 Q7
Loufan, *China* 182 E4
Louga, *Senegal* 196 G4
Lougheed Island, *Nunavut, Can.* 83 C14
Louhans, *Fr.* 147 S13
Louisa, *Ky., U.S.* 101 B20
Louisburg, *N.C., U.S.* 96 G12
Louisburgh, *Ire.* 143 R3
Louisiade Archipelago, *P.N.G.* 213 E22
Louisiana, *Mo., U.S.* 105 S14
Louisiana, *U.S.* 100 L7
Louisiana Point, *La., U.S.* 100 Q6
Louis II Stadium, *Monaco* 161 F20
Louis Trichardt (Makhado), *S. Af.* 202 H11
Louisville, *Ga., U.S.* 96 M7
Louisville, *Ky., U.S.* 101 B16
Louisville, *Miss., U.S.* 100 K12
Louisville, *Nebr., U.S.* 105 Q9
Louisville Ridge, *Pac. Oc.* 238 P10
Louis-XIV, Pointe, *Que., Can.* 83 L17
Louj, island, *Marshall Is.* 216 G16
Loukouo, *Congo* 201 M17
Loulan Yiji, ruin, *China* 180 G8
Loulay, *Fr.* 147 T7
Loulé, *Port.* 144 L5

Loup, river, *Nebr., U.S.* 105 P7
Loup City, *Nebr., U.S.* 105 P6
Lourdes, *Fr.* 147 Y7
Lourdes-de-Blanc-Sablon, *Que., Can.* 83 L22
Lousã, *Port.* 144 F6
Louth, *Eng., U.K.* 143 S14
Louth, *N.S.W., Austral.* 211 W12
Loutrá Eleftherón, *Gr.* 155 C13
Loutrá Epidsoú, *Gr.* 154 G11
Loutráki, *Gr.* 154 F12
Loutráki, *Gr.* 154 J11
Loutrá Smokóvou, *Gr.* 154 G9
Louvet Point, *St. Lucia* 121 K14
Louviers, *Fr.* 147 N8
Lovango Cay, *Virgin Islands, U.S.* 120 M10
Lovea, *Cambodia* 187 N10
Lovech, *Bulg.* 153 H14
Loveland, *Colo., U.S.* 106 L13
Loveland Pass, *Colo., U.S.* 106 M12
Lovell, *Wyo., U.S.* 106 F10
Lovelock, *Nev., U.S.* 109 N8
Lovere, *It.* 150 D5
Loving, *N. Mex., U.S.* 107 V14
Lovington, *N. Mex., U.S.* 107 U15
Low, Cape, *Nunavut, Can.* 83 H16
Low Cay, *Bahamas* 120 F11
Lowell, *Mass., U.S.* 95 K14
Lowell, *Oreg., U.S.* 108 H3
Lowell, Lake, *Idaho, U.S.* 106 G3
Lower Belmont Bay, *Virgin Islands, U.K.* 120 M11
Lower Bogue, *Bahamas* 120 D5
Lower Guinea, region, *Af.* 194 K5
Lower Hutt, *N.Z.* 213 M19
Lower Lake, *Calif., U.S.* 108 M6
Lower Lough Erne, *N. Ire., U.K.* 143 Q5
Lower Matecumbe Key, *Fla., U.S.* 97 Y10
Lower Peninsula, *Mich., U.S.* 85 E16
Lower Post, *B.C., Can.* 82 H9
Lower Red Lake, *Minn., U.S.* 104 F10
Lower Tunguska, river, *Russ.* 166 D10
Lower Valley, *Cayman Is., U.K.* 120 J2
Lowestoft, *Eng., U.K.* 143 T16
Łowicz, *Pol.* 149 E15
Lowital, *Vanuatu* 218 H4
Lowkhi, *Afghan.* 177 Q3
Lowman, *Idaho, U.S.* 106 G4
Lowville, *N.Y., U.S.* 94 H9
Loyal, Loch, *Scot., U.K.* 142 H9
Loyalty Islands, *New Caledonia, Fr.* 214 K7
Loyauté, Îles (Loyalty Islands), *New Caledonia, Fr.* 218 D9
Loyew, *Belarus* 156 M6
Loyola, Punta, *Arg.* 133 W8
Loznica, *Serb. & Mont.* 152 F9
Lozova, *Ukr.* 157 P9
Luahiwa Petroglyphs, *Hawaiʻi, U.S.* 113 G15
Luahoko, island, *Tonga* 218 P7
Luama, river, *Dem. Rep. of the Congo* 198 L11
Luamotu, island, *Tuvalu* 217 L23
Luan, river, *China* 182 C7
Lu'an, *China* 182 K6
Luanco, *Sp.* 144 A8
Luanda, *Angola* 202 C5
Luang Prabang Range, *Laos* 186 J9
Luangwa, river, *Zambia* 202 E12
Luangwa, *Zambia* 202 E11
Luaniua, island, *Solomon Is.* 217 J18
Luaniva, island, *Wallis & Futuna, Fr.* 218 B12
Luanping, *China* 182 C7
Luanshya, *Zambia* 202 D11
Luanxian, *China* 182 D8
Luapula, river, *Dem. Rep. of the Congo, Zambia* 194 M9
Luarca, *Sp.* 144 A8
Luatefito, island, *Tonga* 218 M11
Luau, *Angola* 202 D8
Luba, *Eq. Guinea* 204 M7
Luba, Bahia de, *Eq. Guinea* 204 M7
Lubānas Ezers, lake, *Latv.* 141 M17
Lubang Island, *Philippines* 189 D13
Lubango, *Angola* 202 E5
Lubao, *Dem. Rep. of the Congo* 198 L11
Lubartów, *Pol.* 149 E17
Lübbenau, *Ger.* 148 E11
Lubbock, *Tex., U.S.* 102 K5
Lubec, *Me., U.S.* 95 E19
Lübeck, *Ger.* 148 B8
Lubero, *Dem. Rep. of the Congo* 198 K12

Lubéron, Montagne du, *Fr.* 147 XI3
Lubin, *Pol.* 148 FI2
Lublin, *Pol.* 149 FI7
Lubliniec, *Pol.* 149 GI4
Lubny, *Ukr.* 157 P7
Lubok Antu, *Malaysia* 188 HIO
Lubuagan, *Philippines* 189 BI3
Lubudi, *Dem. Rep. of the Congo* 198 NII
Lubuklinggau, *Indonesia* 188 K6
Lubumbashi (Elisabethville), *Dem. Rep. of the Congo* 198 NII
Lucas, *Kans., U.S.* 105 S6
Lucaya, *Bahamas* 120 F2
Lucca, *It.* 150 G6
Lucea, *Jam.* 120 H6
Lucedale, *Miss., U.S.* 101 NI3
Lucena, *Philippines* 189 CI4
Lucena, *Sp.* 144 LIO
Lucera, *It.* 150 LI2
Lucerne, Lake of *see* Vierwaldstätter See, *Switz.* 150 B4
Luchegorsk, *Russ.* 159 L2I
Luchuan, *China* 183 S2
Lucie, river, *Suriname* 129 FI5
Lucipara, Kepulauan, *Indonesia* 189 LI6
Lucira, *Angola* 202 E5
Lucknow, *India* 178 G8
Lucknow, *Qnsld., Austral.* 211 TII
Lucy Bay, *Scot., U.K.* 143 P8
Lucy Creek, *N. Terr., Austral.* 211 T9
Luda Kamchiya, river, *Bulg.* 153 HI6
Ludborough, *Eng., U.K.* 143 SI4
Lüdenscheid, *Ger.* 148 F6
Lüderitz, *Namibia* 202 J6
Ludhiana, *India* 178 D5
Ludington, *Mich., U.S.* 98 K9
Ludlow, *Calif., U.S.* 109 WII
Ludlow, *Vt., U.S.* 95 HI3
Ludogorie, region, *Bulg.* 138 J9
Ludogorsko Plato, *Bulg.* 153 GI6
Ludowici, *Ga., U.S.* 97 P8
Ludus, *Rom.* 153 CI3
Ludwigsburg, *Ger.* 148 J7
Ludwigshafen, *Ger.* 148 H6
Luebo, *Dem. Rep. of the Congo* 198 L9
Luena, *Angola* 202 D8
Lufeng, *China* 183 S6
Lufilufi, *Samoa* 218 L4
Lufkin, *Tex., U.S.* 103 NI4
Luga, *Russ.* 156 G6
Lugano, *Switz.* 150 D4
Luganville, *Vanuatu* 218 D2
Lugenda, river, *Mozambique* 203 DI4
Lugo, *It.* 150 F7
Lugo, *Sp.* 144 B7
Lugoj, *Rom.* 152 EII
Lugovoy, *Russ.* 158 HIO
Luhans'k, *Ukr.* 157 QIO
Lui, river, *China* 183 QI
Luiana, river, *Angola* 202 F8
Luichow Peninsula *see* Leizhou Bandao, *China* 183 TI
Luimneach *see* Limerick, *Ire.* 143 T4
Luing, island, *Scot., U.K.* 142 M8
Luino, *It.* 150 D4
Luitpold Coast, *Antarctica* 226 EIO
Luján, *Arg.* 132 LI2
Lujor, island, *Marshall Is.* 216 G8
Lukenie, river, *Dem. Rep. of the Congo* 198 L9
Lukeville, *Ariz., U.S.* 107 V6
Lukolela, *Dem. Rep. of the Congo* 198 K8
Lukovit, *Bulg.* 153 HI3
Łuków, *Pol.* 149 EI7
Lukulu, *Zambia* 202 E9
Lukunor Atoll, *F.S.M.* 216 Q7
Luleå, *Sw.* 141 FI4
Luleälven, river, *Sw.* 138 B8
Lüleburgaz, *Turk.* 168 C3
Lules, *Arg.* 132 G9
Lüliang Shan, *China* 182 F3
Luling, *Tex., U.S.* 103 RII
Lulonga, river, *Dem. Rep. of the Congo* 198 J9
Lulua, river, *Dem. Rep. of the Congo* 198 NIO
Lulu Fakahega, peak, *Wallis & Futuna, Fr.* 218 BII
Lumajangdong Co, *China* 180 J5
Luman, *Afghan.* 177 N6
Lumbala N'guimbo, *Angola* 202 E8
Lumber City, *Ga., U.S.* 97 N7
Lumberton, *Miss., U.S.* 100 NI2
Lumberton, *N.C., U.S.* 96 JII

Lumbo, *Mozambique* 203 EI5
Lumbrales, *Sp.* 144 E7
Lumbres, *Fr.* 146 L9
Lumding, *India* 178 GI4
Lumi, *P.N.G.* 213 CI8
Lumpkin, *Ga., U.S.* 97 N4
Lumu, *Indonesia* 189 KI3
Lumut, *Malaysia* 187 T9
Luna, *N. Mex., U.S.* 107 TIO
Lunavada, *India* 178 J4
Lund, *Nev., U.S.* 109 QI2
Lundazi, *Zambia* 202 DI2
Lundu, *Malaysia* 188 H9
Lundy Island, *Eng., U.K.* 143 W8
Lüneburg, *Ger.* 148 C8
Lüneburger Heide, region, *Ger.* 148 D8
Lunéville, *Fr.* 147 PI4
Lunglei, *India* 178 JI4
Lungwebungu, river, *Angola* 202 D8
Luni, river, *India* 178 G3
Luni, *India* 178 G3
Luning, *Nev., U.S.* 109 R8
Lunino, *Russ.* 156 LI3
Luninyets, *Belarus* 156 M4
Luntai, *China* 180 GI
Luo, river, *China* 182 G2
Luo, river, *China* 182 H4
Luobei, *China* 181 DI4
Luocheng, *China* 183 QI
Luoding, *China* 183 S3
Luohe, *China* 182 H5
Luonan, *China* 182 H3
Luoqing, river, *China* 183 QI
Luoshan, *China* 182 K5
Luoyang, *China* 182 H4
Luoyuan, *China* 183 P8
Lupanshui, *China* 180 NI2
Luperón, *Dom. Rep.* 117 LI8
Lupin, *Nunavut, Can.* 82 GI2
Lupog, *Guam, U.S.* 216 BI2
Luqa, *Malta* 161 L22
Luqu, *China* 180 JII
Luquillo, *P.R., U.S.* 120 M6
Luquillo, Sierra de, *P.R., U.S.* 120 N5
Luray, *Va., U.S.* 96 DII
Lure, *Fr.* 147 RI4
Lúrio, river, *Mozambique* 203 EI4
Lúrio, *Mozambique* 203 EI5
Lusaka, *Zambia* 202 EII
Lusambo, *Dem. Rep. of the Congo* 198 LIO
Lusancay Islands, *P.N.G.* 213 D2I
Lusanga, *Dem. Rep. of the Congo* 198 L8
Lushi, *China* 182 H3
Lushnjë, *Albania* 152 L9
Lushoto, *Tanzania* 199 LI5
Lüshun (Port Arthur), *China* 182 E9
Lusignan, *Fr.* 147 T7
Lusk, *Wyo., U.S.* 106 HI3
Lus-la-Croix-Haute, *Fr.* 147 VI4
Luso, *Port.* 144 F5
Lussac-les-Châteaux, *Fr.* 147 T8
Lustenau, *Aust.* 148 L7
Lüt, Dasht-e, *Iran* 173 EI6
Lüţak, *Iran* 173 FI7
Lü Tao, island, *Taiwan, China* 183 SIO
Lutcher, *La., U.S.* 100 QIO
Luti, *Solomon Is.* 217 LI5
Luton, *Eng., U.K.* 143 UI3
Łutselk'e, *N.W.T., Can.* 82 HI2
Lutsen, *Minn., U.S.* 104 FI4
Luts'k, *Ukr.* 157 N3
Lützow-Holm Bay, *Antarctica* 227 BI7
Luuq, *Somalia* 199 HI6
Luverne, *Ala., U.S.* 101 MI6
Luverne, *Minn., U.S.* 104 L9
Luvua, river, *Dem. Rep. of the Congo* 198 MII
Luxembourg, *Eur.* 160 C3
Luxembourg, *Lux.* 160 KIO
Luxeuil, *Fr.* 147 RI4
Luxi, *China* 182 M2
Luxi, *China* 180 NIO
Luyi, *China* 182 J3
Luxor, *Egypt* 197 EI9
Luxora, *Ark., U.S.* 100 FII
Luz, *Fr.* 147 Y7
Luz, *Braz.* 131 LI4
Luza, *Russ.* 158 F8
Luzaide, *Fr.* 147 Y6
Luzern, *Switz.* 150 B3
Luzhai, *China* 183 Q2

Luzhou, *China* 180 MI2
Luzon, island, *Philippines* 189 CI4
Luzon Strait, *Philippines* 189 AI3
Luzy, *Fr.* 147 SI2
L'viv, *Ukr.* 157 N2
Lyady, *Russ.* 156 G6
Lyakhovskiye Ostrova, *Russ.* 159 DI7
Lyaki, *Azerb.* 169 D2I
Lyckele, *Sw.* 141 GI3
Lycoming, *N.Y., U.S.* 94 H8
Lydda *see* Lod, *Israel* 170 M5
Lyddan Island, *Antarctica* 226 CIO
Lyepyel', *Belarus* 156 K5
Lyford, *Tex., U.S.* 103 WIO
Lyford Cay, *Bahamas* 120 BIO
Lyme Bay, *Eng., U.K.* 143 XIO
Lynch, *Ky., U.S.* 101 D2O
Lynch, *Nebr., U.S.* 104 M6
Lynchburg, *Va., U.S.* 96 FII
Lynden, *Wash., U.S.* 108 A4
Lyndhurst, *S. Aust., Austral.* 211 WIO
Lyndon, *W. Aust., Austral.* 211 U2
Lyndon B. Johnson National Historic Park, *Tex., U.S.* 103 Q9
Lyndonville, *Vt., U.S.* 95 FI3
Lynn, *Mass., U.S.* 95 KI5
Lynn Haven, *Fla., U.S.* 97 R3
Lynn Lake, *Man., Can.* 83 LI3
Lynton, *W. Aust., Austral.* 211 WI
Lyon, *Fr.* 147 UI3
Lyons, river, *Austral.* 210 G2
Lyons, *Ga., U.S.* 97 N7
Lyons, *Kans., U.S.* 105 T7
Lyons, *N.Y., U.S.* 94 J7
Lyons, *Nebr., U.S.* 105 P8
Lysi, *Cyprus* 160 P9
Lyskovo, *Russ.* 156 JI3
Lyss, *Switz.* 150 B2
Lysychans'k, *Ukr.* 157 PIO
Lytton, *B.C., Can.* 82 M8
Lyubertsy, *Russ.* 156 J9
Lyubim, *Russ.* 156 GII
Lyubimets, *Bulg.* 153 KI5
Lyuboml', *Ukr.* 156 M2
Lyubotyn, *Ukr.* 157 P8
Lyubytino, *Russ.* 156 G7
Lyucha Ongokton, Gora, *Russ.* 159 GI5
Lyudinovo, *Russ.* 156 L8

M

Māʻalaea, *Hawaiʻi, U.S.* 113 GI6
Māʻalaea Bay, *Hawaiʻi, U.S.* 113 GI6
Maale (Male), *Maldives* 179 U3
Maam Cross, *Ire.* 143 R3
Maʻan, *Jordan* 171 Q6
Maan Ridge *see* Maanselkä, *Fin., Russ.* 138 B9
Maanselkä, range, *Fin.* 141 EI6
Maʻanshan, *China* 182 K8
Maarianhamina *see* Mariehamn, *Fin.* 141 KI4
Maʻarrat an Nuʻmān, *Syr.* 170 E8
Maas, river, *Neth.* 146 JI3
Maastricht, *Neth.* 146 LI3
Maʻbar, *Yemen* 172 Q9
Mabaruma, *Guyana* 129 CI4
Mabiri, Cape, *P.N.G.* 217 KI4
MacAlpine Lake, *Nunavut, Can.* 83 GI3
Macapá, *Braz.* 130 CI2
Macaque, Morne, *Dominica* 121 FI9
Macará, *Ecua.* 128 L2
Macaroni, *Qnsld., Austral.* 211 QII
Macas, *Ecua.* 128 K3
Macau, *China* 183 S4
Macau, *Braz.* 131 EI7
Macaúba, *Braz.* 130 GI2
Macauley Island, *Kermadec Is., N.Z.* 214 L9
Macbride Head, *Falkland Is., U.K.* 133 WI3
Macclenny, *Fla., U.S.* 97 R8
Macclesfield Bank, *Ind. Oc.* 241 DI5
Macdonnell Ranges, *Austral.* 210 F8
Macedo de Cavaleiros, *Port.* 144 D7
Macedonia, *Eur.* 139 W8
Macedonia, region, *Gr.* 154 D8
Maceió, *Braz.* 131 GI8
Maceió, Ponta do, *Braz.* 131 EI7
Macenta, *Guinea* 200 G7
Macerata, *It.* 150 H9
Macgillycuddy's Reeks, *Ire.* 143 U2
Macgowen, Arrecife, *Ecua.* 128 RIO

Mach, *Pak.* 177 R6
Machagai, *Arg.* 132 GI2
Machakas, *Kenya* 199 KI4
Machala, *Ecua.* 128 L2
Machanao, Mount, *Guam, U.S.* 216 AII
Machault, *Fr.* 147 NI2
Machecoul, *Fr.* 147 S5
Macheng, *China* 182 K6
Macherla, *India* 179 N7
Machias, *Me., U.S.* 95 FI9
Machico, *Madeira* 204 M4
Machilipatnam (Bandar), *India* 179 N8
Machiques, *Venez.* 128 B6
Machu Picchu, ruin, *Peru* 130 H5
Machynlleth, *Wales, U.K.* 143 T9
Măcin, *Rom.* 153 EI7
Maçka, *Turk.* 169 DI4
Mackay, *Idaho, U.S.* 106 G6
Mackay, *Qnsld., Austral.* 211 TI4
Mackay, Lake, *Austral.* 210 E7
Mackenzie, river, *Austral.* 210 FI4
Mackenzie, *B.C., Can.* 82 K9
Mackenzie, river, *N.W.T., Can.* 82 FIO
Mackenzie Bay, *Yukon, Can.* 82 DIO
Mackenzie King Island, *N.W.T., Nunavut, Can.* 83 CI3
Mackenzie Mountains, *N.W.T., Yukon, Can.* 82 F9
Mackenzie Trough, *Arctic Oc.* 242 N5
Mackinac, Straits of, *Mich., U.S.* 98 GIO
Mackinac Island, *Mich., U.S.* 98 GII
Mackinaw City, *Mich., U.S.* 98 GIO
Macknade, *Qnsld., Austral.* 211 RI3
Mačkovci, *Slov.* 152 C6
Macksville, *Kans., U.S.* 105 U6
Macksville, *N.S.W., Austral.* 211 WI5
Maclear, *S. Af.* 202 LIO
Macleod, Lake, *Austral.* 210 GI
Macomb, *Ill., U.S.* 99 Q4
Macomer, *It.* 151 N3
Mâcon, *Fr.* 147 TI2
Macon, *Ga., U.S.* 96 M6
Macon, *Miss., U.S.* 101 KI3
Macon, *Mo., U.S.* 105 RI3
Macondo, *Angola* 202 D9
Macouba, *Martinique, Fr.* 121 E22
Macovane, *Mozambique* 203 HI3
Macpherson, Mount, *Austral.* 210 JI2
Macpherson's Strait, *India* 179 QI4
Macquarie, river, *Austral.* 210 JI3
Macquarie, Port, *Austral.* 210 KI5
Macquarie Island, *Austral.* 214 R6
Macquarie Ridge, *Pac. Oc.* 238 R7
Mac. Robertson Land, *Antarctica* 227 EI8
Macroom, *Ire.* 143 U4
Macurijes, Punta, *Cuba* 116 JIO
Macuro, *Venez.* 128 BI2
Macusani, *Peru* 130 H5
Mad, river, *Calif., U.S.* 109 N2
Mādabā, *Jordan* 170 M6
Madagascar, *Af.* 195 N24
Madagascar, island, *Ind. Oc.* 194 NII
Madagascar Basin, *Ind. Oc.* 240 L6
Madagascar Plateau, *Ind. Oc.* 240 M5
Madaʻin Şālih, *Saudi Arabia* 172 H6
Madalai, *Palau* 216 NII
Madalena, *Azores* 144 P3
Madalena, *Sao Tome and Principe* 205 D2O
Madan, *Bulg.* 153 KI4
Madang, *P.N.G.* 213 CI9
Madaripur, *Bangladesh* 178 JI3
Madawaska, *Me., U.S.* 95 AI8
Madayar, *Myanmar* 186 G6
Maddalena, Isola, *It.* 150 L4
Maddock, *N. Dak., U.S.* 104 F5
Madeira, island, *Atl. Oc.* 204 M3
Madeira, river, *Braz.* 130 E9
Madeira Islands, *Madeira* 204 C4
Madeleine, Îles de la, *Que., Can.* 83 N22
Madelia, *Minn., U.S.* 104 LIO
Madeline Island, *Wis., U.S.* 98 E4
Maden, *Turk.* 169 GI4
Madera, *Calif., U.S.* 109 T6
Madgaon, *India* 179 N4
Madhubani, *India* 178 GIO
Madidi, river, *Bol.* 130 H6
Madill, *Okla., U.S.* 102 JI2
Madimba, *Dem. Rep. of the Congo* 198 L7
Madīnat ash Shaʻb, *Yemen* 172 R9
Madīnat ath Thawrah, *Syr.* 170 EII
Madīnat Zāyid, *U.A.E.* 173 KI4
Madison, *Fla., U.S.* 97 Q6

Madison, *Ga., U.S.* 96 L6
Madison, *Ind., U.S.* 99 TIO
Madison, *Kans., U.S.* 105 T9
Madison, *Me., U.S.* 95 FI6
Madison, *Minn., U.S.* 104 J9
Madison, *N.C., U.S.* 96 GIO
Madison, *Nebr., U.S.* 105 P7
Madison, *S. Dak., U.S.* 104 L8
Madison, *W. Va., U.S.* 96 E8
Madison, *Wis., U.S.* 98 L5
Madisonville, *Ky., U.S.* 101 CI4
Madisonville, *Tex., U.S.* 103 PI3
Madiun, *Indonesia* 188 MIO
Madley, Mount, *Austral.* 210 F5
Mado Gashi, *Kenya* 199 JI5
Madoi, *China* 180 JIO
Madona, *Latv.* 141 LI7
Madrakah, Raʻs al, *Oman* 173 MI6
Madras *see* Chennai, *India* 179 P7
Madras, *Oreg., U.S.* 108 G5
Madre, Laguna, *Mex., U.S.* 103 WII
Madre, Sierra, *N. Amer.* 80 P6
Madre de Dios, river, *Bol., Peru* 130 H6
Madre de Dios, Isla, *Chile* 133 V6
Madre del Sur, Sierra, *Mex.* 114 JIO
Madre Lagoon *see* Madre, Laguna, *N. Amer.* 80 M5
Madre Occidental, Sierra, *Mex.* 114 D8
Madre Oriental, Sierra, *Mex.* 114 DIO
Madrid, *Iowa, U.S.* 105 PII
Madrid, *Sp.* 144 FII
Madridejos, *Sp.* 144 HII
Madrid Point, *S. Amer.* 126 H4
Madriu, river, *Andorra* 160 J4
Madura, island, *Indonesia* 188 MII
Madura, *W. Aust., Austral.* 211 X6
Madura, Selat, *Indonesia* 188 MII
Madurai, *India* 179 R6
Madurantakam, *India* 179 Q7
Madyan, *Pak.* 176 MIO
Maebashi, *Japan* 185 NII
Mae Hong Son, *Thai.* 186 J7
Mae Klong, river, *Thai.* 186 M6
Maentwrog, *Wales, U.K.* 143 T9
Mae Sariang, *Thai.* 186 K7
Mae Sot, *Thai.* 186 K7
Maestra, Sierra, *Cuba* 116 KI2
Maeva, Fr. Polynesia, *Fr.* 219 GI4
Maevatanana, *Madagascar* 203 FI7
Maéwo, island, *Vanuatu* 218 C3
Mafia Island, *Tanzania* 199 MI5
Maga, peak, *N. Mariana Is., U.S.* 216 B7
Magadan, *Russ.* 159 F2O
Magadi, *Kenya* 199 KI4
Magallanes, Estrecho de, *Chile* 133 X7
Magangué, *Col.* 128 C5
Magazine Mountain, *Ark., U.S.* 100 G7
Magdagachi, *Russ.* 159 KI8
Magdalena, *Bol.* 130 H8
Magdalena, river, *Col.* 128 D5
Magdalena, river, *N. Amer.* 80 L3
Magdalena, *N. Mex., U.S.* 107 TII
Magdalena, Bahía, *Mex.* 114 F6
Magdalena, Isla, *Chile* 133 S6
Magdalena, Isla, *Mex.* 114 E6
Magdalena, Llano de la, *Mex.* 114 E6
Magdalena Bay, *N. Amer.* 80 M3
Magdalena de Kino, *Mex.* 114 C7
Magdeburg, *Ger.* 148 E9
Magdelaine Cays, *Coral Sea Is. Terr., Austral.* 211 RI5
Magee, *Miss., U.S.* 100 MII
Magelang, *Indonesia* 188 M9
Magellan, Strait of, *S. Amer.* 126 R4
Magellan Rise, *Pac. Oc.* 238 JIO
Magellan Seamounts, *Pac. Oc.* 238 H7
Magens Bay, *Virgin Islands, U.S.* 120 M9
Magerøya, island, *Nor.* 141 BI4
Maggiore, Lago, *It., Switz.* 150 C4
Maggotty, *Jam.* 120 J7
Magina, peak, *Sp.* 144 KII
Maglić, peak, *Bosn. & Herzg., Serb. & Mont.* 152 H8
Maglie, *It.* 151 NI6
Magnitogorsk, *Russ.* 158 J8
Magnolia, *Ark., U.S.* 100 J7
Magnolia, *Miss., U.S.* 100 NIO
Mago, island, *Fiji Is.* 218 H9
Magpi, Puntan, *N. Mariana Is., U.S.* 216 A5
Magude, *Mozambique* 202 JI2
Magway, *Myanmar* 186 H5
Mahābād, *Iran* 172 BIO
Mahabharat Range, *Nepal* 178 F8
Mahabo, *Madagascar* 203 GI6

Mahad, *India* **178 M3**
Mahaena, *Fr. Polynesia, Fr.* **219 N17**
Mahaena, Passe de, *Fr. Polynesia, Fr.* **219 N17**
Mahagi, *Dem. Rep. of the Congo* **198 J12**
Mahaiatea, *Fr. Polynesia, Fr.* **219 P16**
Mahajamba, Baie de la, *Madagascar* **203 E17**
Mahajan, *India* **178 F4**
Mahajanga, *Madagascar* **203 E17**
Mahalapye, *Botswana* **202 H10**
Māhān, *Iran* **173 F15**
Mahana Bay, *Hawai'i, U.S.* **113 Q19**
Mahanadi, river, *India* **178 K9**
Mahanoro, *Madagascar* **203 G18**
Mahasamund, *India* **178 K8**
Mahaut, *Dominica* **121 F19**
Mahavavy, river, *Madagascar* **203 F17**
Mahbubnagar, *India* **178 M6**
Mahd adh Dhahab, *Saudi Arabia* **172 K7**
Mahdia, *Guyana* **129 E14**
Mahé, island, *Seychelles* **205 P20**
Mahébourg, *Mauritius* **205 G20**
Mahendraganj, *India* **178 G12**
Mahen dra Giri, peak, *India* **178 L9**
Mahenge, *Tanzania* **199 N14**
Maheno, *N.Z.* **213 Q16**
Mahere Honae, island, *Fr. Polynesia, Fr.* **219 K16**
Mahesana, *India* **178 H3**
Mahia Peninsula, *N.Z.* **213 L20**
Mahige, island, *Solomon Is.* **217 M18**
Mahilyow, *Belarus* **156 K6**
Mahina, *Fr. Polynesia, Fr.* **219 N16**
Mahina'akaka Heiau, *Hawai'i, U.S.* **113 N22**
Mahishadal, *India* **178 J11**
Mahitu, island, *Fr. Polynesia, Fr.* **219 K16**
Mahmud-e Raqi, *Afghan.* **176 M8**
Mahmudiye, *Turk.* **168 E6**
Mahnomen, *Minn., U.S.* **104 G9**
Mahoba, *India* **178 H7**
Māhoe, Pu'u, *Hawai'i, U.S.* **113 H17**
Mahón, *Sp.* **145 G20**
Mahri, *Pak.* **177 U6**
Mahu, *Fr. Polynesia, Fr.* **219 K20**
Mahuti, Baie de, *Fr. Polynesia, Fr.* **219 H14**
Mahuva, *India* **178 K2**
Maia, *Amer. Samoa, U.S.* **218 N4**
Maiao, island, *Fr. Polynesia, Fr.* **219 F16**
Maibong, *India* **178 G14**
Maicao, *Col.* **128 B6**
Maîche, *Fr.* **147 R15**
Maicuru, river, *Braz.* **130 C11**
Maida, *It.* **151 Q13**
Maidenhead, *Eng., U.K.* **143 V13**
Maiduguri, *Nigeria* **201 E16**
Maigualida, Sierra, *Venez.* **128 E10**
Maihar, *India* **178 H7**
Maikoor, island, *Indonesia* **189 L18**
Ma'ili, *Hawai'i, U.S.* **112 E10**
Mailly-le-Camp, *Fr.* **147 P12**
Mailsi, *Pak.* **177 R10**
Main, river, *Ger.* **148 H8**
Maina, island, *Cook Is., N.Z.* **218 Q11**
Main Channel, *Cayman Is., U.K.* **120 H2**
Mai-Ndombe, Lac, *Dem. Rep. of the Congo* **198 K8**
Maine, *U.S.* **95 E15**
Maine, Gulf of, *U.S.* **85 D22**
Maingkwan, *Myanmar* **186 D6**
Main Island (Bermuda Island), *Bermuda, U.K.* **120 B3**
Mainland, island, *Scot., U.K.* **142 D12**
Mainoru, *N. Terr., Austral.* **211 P9**
Main Ridge, *Trinidad & Tobago* **121 N18**
Maintirano, *Madagascar* **203 F16**
Mainz, *Ger.* **148 G6**
Maio, island, *Cape Verde* **205 D17**
Maipo Volcano, *S. Amer.* **126 L4**
Maiquetía, *Venez.* **128 B9**
Mairenui, peak, *Fr. Polynesia, Fr.* **219 Q17**
Maisí, *Cuba* **117 K15**
Maisí, Punta de, *Cuba* **117 K15**
Maiskhal, island, *Bangladesh* **178 K14**
Maitland, *N.S.W., Austral.* **211 X15**
Maitri, station, *Antarctica* **227 A14**
Maíz, Islas del, *Nicar.* **115 M19**
Maizuru, *Japan* **185 P8**
Majene, *Indonesia* **189 K13**
Majī, *Eth.* **199 H14**
Majorca see Mallorca, island, *Sp.* **145 G19**
Majuro, *Marshall Is.* **216 G12**

Majuro (Laura), island, *Marshall Is.* **216 H10**
Majuro Lagoon, *Marshall Is.* **216 G11**
Maka'ala, Pu'u, *Hawai'i, U.S.* **113 M21**
Mākaha, *Hawai'i, U.S.* **112 E10**
Makakilo City, *Hawai'i, U.S.* **112 E10**
Makale, *Indonesia* **189 K13**
Makaleha Mountains, *Hawai'i, U.S.* **112 B6**
Makalu, peak, *China, Nepal* **178 F11**
Makapala, *Hawai'i, U.S.* **113 K19**
Makapu Point, *Niue, N.Z.* **219 B20**
Makaroa, island, *Fr. Polynesia, Fr.* **219 R20**
Makarov, *Russ.* **159 J22**
Makarov Basin, *Arctic Oc.* **242 H8**
Makarovo, *Russ.* **159 K15**
Makar'yev, *Russ.* **156 G12**
Makassar (Ujung Pandang), *Indonesia* **189 L13**
Makassar Strait, *Indonesia* **188 K12**
Makatea, island, *Fr. Polynesia, Fr.* **219 E17**
Makawao, peak, *Hawai'i, U.S.* **113 G17**
Makefu, *Niue, N.Z.* **219 B20**
Make Jima, *Japan* **185 U4**
Makemo, island, *Fr. Polynesia, Fr.* **219 E19**
Mākena, *Hawai'i, U.S.* **113 H16**
Makeni, *Sierra Leone* **200 F6**
Makéone, *Vanuatu* **218 B2**
Makgadikgadi Pans, *Botswana* **202 G9**
Makhachkala, *Russ.* **157 U15**
Makhad, *Pak.* **177 N10**
Makhado see Louis Trichardt, *S. Af.* **202 H11**
Makhambet, *Kaz.* **174 E6**
Makhfar al Buşayyah, *Iraq* **172 F10**
Maki, *Indonesia* **189 K19**
Makīnsk, *Kaz.* **175 C13**
Makira Harbour, *Solomon Is.* **217 P20**
Makiyivka, *Ukr.* **157 Q10**
Makkah (Mecca), *Saudi Arabia* **172 L7**
Makkovik, *Nfld. & Lab., Can.* **83 K21**
Makó, *Hung.* **149 N16**
Makogai, island, *Fiji Is.* **218 H7**
Makokou, *Gabon* **201 K16**
Mākole'ā Point, *Hawai'i, U.S.* **113 L18**
Makoua, *Congo* **201 L17**
Makrá, island, *Gr.* **155 N16**
Makrakómi, *Gr.* **154 G10**
Makrana, *India* **178 G4**
Makran Coast Range, *Pak.* **177 V3**
Makrinítsa, *Gr.* **154 F11**
Makroníssi (Helena, Eléni), island, *Gr.* **155 K13**
Mākū, *Iran* **172 A10**
Makung, *Taiwan, China* **183 R8**
Makunudu Atoll (Malcolm), *Maldives* **179 T3**
Makura, island, *Vanuatu* **218 E3**
Makurazaki, *Japan* **185 T4**
Makurdi, *Nigeria* **201 G14**
Mâl, *Mauritania* **196 G5**
Malabar Coast, *India* **179 R4**
Malabo, *Eq. Guinea* **204 L7**
Malabuñgan, *Philippines* **188 E12**
Malacca, *Malaysia* **187 U10**
Malacca, Strait of, *Indonesia, Malaysia* **188 G5**
Malacky, *Slovakia* **149 K13**
Malad City, *Idaho, U.S.* **106 J7**
Maladzyechna, *Belarus* **156 K4**
Málaga, *Col.* **128 D6**
Málaga, *Sp.* **144 H10**
Malagón, *Sp.* **144 H10**
Malaita, island, *Solomon Is.* **217 N20**
Malakal, *Palau* **216 N11**
Malakal, *Sudan* **199 G13**
Malakal Harbor, *Palau* **216 N11**
Malakal Pass, *Palau* **216 P11**
Malakanagiri, *India* **178 M8**
Malakand, *Pak.* **176 M10**
Malake, island, *Fiji Is.* **218 H6**
Malakoff, *Tex., U.S.* **102 M13**
Malakula, island, *Vanuatu* **218 D2**
Malam, *F.S.M.* **217 B19**
Malang, *Indonesia* **188 M10**
Malanje, *Angola* **202 C6**
Malans, *Switz.* **160 Q2**
Malanville, *Benin* **200 E12**
Malao, *Vanuatu* **218 C1**
Malapo, *Tonga* **218 J11**
Malapu, *Solomon Is.* **217 P23**
Malar, *Pak.* **177 V4**
Mälaren, lake, *Sw.* **141 L14**

Malargüe, *Arg.* **132 M7**
Malaspina Glacier, *Alas., U.S.* **111 K20**
Malatya, *Turk.* **169 G13**
Mala Vyska, *Ukr.* **157 Q6**
Malawi, *Af.* **195 M22**
Malawi, Lake (Lake Nyasa), *Af.* **194 M10**
Malayagiri, peak, *India* **178 K10**
Malaya Vishera, *Russ.* **156 G7**
Malaybalay, *Philippines* **189 F15**
Malāyer, *Iran* **172 D11**
Malay Peninsula, *Malaysia, Thai.* **166 L10**
Malaysia, *Asia* **167 Y12**
Malbork, *Pol.* **149 B14**
Malbun, *Liech.* **160 Q3**
Malcolm see Makunudu Atoll, island, *Maldives* **179 T3**
Malcolm, *W. Aust., Austral.* **211 W4**
Maldegem, *Belg.* **146 K11**
Malden, *Mo., U.S.* **105 V15**
Malden Island, *Kiribati* **214 H12**
Maldive Islands, *Maldives* **179 U2**
Maldives, *Asia* **167 Y6**
Maldonado, *Uru.* **132 L14**
Maldonado, Punta, *Mex.* **114 K12**
Malè, *It.* **150 C6**
Male see Maale, *Maldives* **179 U3**
Maléas, Akrotírio, *Gr.* **154 M11**
Male Atoll, *Maldives* **179 U3**
Malebo, Pool, *Dem. Rep. of the Congo* **198 L7**
Malegaon, *India* **178 K4**
Malemba-Nkulu, *Dem. Rep. of the Congo* **198 M11**
Malessína, *Gr.* **154 H11**
Malevangga, *Solomon Is.* **217 K15**
Malgobek, *Russ.* **157 T14**
Malhão, Serra do, *Port.* **144 L6**
Malhargarh, *India* **178 H4**
Malheur, river, *Oreg., U.S.* **108 H9**
Malheureux, Cape, *Mauritius* **205 F20**
Malheur Lake, *Oreg., U.S.* **108 J7**
Mali, *Af.* **195 G15**
Mali, island, *Fiji Is.* **218 G7**
Mali, river, *Myanmar* **186 D7**
Mália, *Gr.* **155 Q15**
Mali Drvenik, *Croatia* **152 G6**
Mali Kyun, *Myanmar* **187 N7**
Malili, *Indonesia* **189 K13**
Malin, *Oreg., U.S.* **108 L5**
Malin Head, *Ire.* **143 N6**
Malin More, *Ire.* **143 P4**
Malinoa, island, *Tonga* **218 H11**
Malkapur, *India* **178 K5**
Malkara, *Turk.* **168 C3**
Malki, *Russ.* **159 F22**
Malko Tŭrnovo, *Bulg.* **153 J17**
Mallacoota, *Vic., Austral.* **211 Z14**
Mallawi, *Egypt* **197 D18**
Mallwil, island, *Malaysia* **188 F12**
Mallorca (Majorca), island, *Sp.* **145 G19**
Mallow, *Ire.* **143 U4**
Malmand Range, *Afghan.* **177 N3**
Malmberget, *Sw.* **141 E13**
Malmesbury, *S. Af.* **202 M7**
Malmö, *Sw.* **140 N12**
Malmok, cape, *Neth. Antilles, Neth.* **121 P18**
Malo, island, *Vanuatu* **218 D2**
Maloelap Atoll, *Marshall Is.* **216 G5**
Maloja, *Switz.* **150 C5**
Malolo, island, *Fiji Is.* **218 H5**
Malone, *N.Y., U.S.* **94 F10**
Maloshuyka, *Russ.* **158 E8**
Måløy, *Nor.* **140 J9**
Malozemel'skaya Tundra, *Russ.* **138 A11**
Malpaso, peak, *Canary Is.* **204 R3**
Malpelo Island, *S. Amer.* **126 C1**
Malportas Pond, *Cayman Is., U.K.* **120 J3**
Mäls, *Liech.* **160 Q2**
Malta, *Eur.* **160 E4**
Malta, island, *Malta* **161 K22**
Malta, *Mont., U.S.* **106 B10**
Maltahöhe, *Namibia* **202 J7**
Maltese Islands, *Medit. Sea* **138 L7**
Malton, *Eng., U.K.* **143 Q13**
Maluku see Moluccas, islands, *Indonesia* **189 J16**
Ma'lūlā, *Syr.* **170 J8**
Malung, *Sw.* **140 K12**
Maluu, *Solomon Is.* **217 M19**
Malvan, *India* **179 N3**

Malvern, *Ark., U.S.* **100 H8**
Malvern, *Iowa, U.S.* **105 Q9**
Malvern, *Jam.* **120 J7**
Malvinas, Islas see Falkland Islands, Falkland Is., U.K.* **133 W12**
Malyn, *Ukr.* **157 N5**
Malyye Karmakuly, *Russ.* **158 D11**
Malyy Lyakhovskiy, Ostrov, *Russ.* **159 D17**
Mamagota, *P.N.G.* **217 K14**
Māmala Bay, *Hawai'i, U.S.* **112 E11**
Mamalahoa Highway, *Hawai'i, U.S.* **113 L19**
Mamalu Bay, *Hawai'i, U.S.* **113 H17**
Mamberamo, *Indonesia* **189 K20**
Mamelles, islands, *Seychelles* **205 N20**
Mamer, *Lux.* **160 K9**
Mameyes (Palmer), *P.R., U.S.* **120 M5**
Mamfé, *Cameroon* **201 H15**
Mamiña, *Chile* **132 C7**
Mammoth, *Wyo., U.S.* **106 F8**
Mammoth Cave National Park, *Ky., U.S.* **101 D16**
Mammoth Spring, *Ark., U.S.* **100 E9**
Mamoiada, *It.* **151 N4**
Mamoré, river, *Bol., Braz.* **130 G7**
Mamoriá, *Braz.* **130 F7**
Mamou, *Guinea* **200 F6**
Mamou, *La., U.S.* **100 P8**
Mamoudzou, *Mayotte, Fr.* **205 P17**
Mampong, *Ghana* **200 G10**
Mamuju, *Indonesia* **189 K13**
Man, Côte d'Ivoire* **200 G7**
Mana, river, *Fr. Guiana, Fr.* **129 E17**
Mana, *Fr. Guiana, Fr.* **129 E17**
Mānā, *Hawai'i, U.S.* **112 B4**
Manacapuru, *Braz.* **130 D9**
Manacor, *Sp.* **145 G19**
Manado, *Indonesia* **189 H15**
Mañagaha Island, *N. Mariana Is., U.S.* **216 B4**
Managua, *Nicar.* **115 M18**
Managua, Lago de, *Nicar.* **115 M18**
Managua, Lake see Managua, Lago de, *N. Amer.* **80 Q7**
Manaia, *N.Z.* **213 L18**
Manakara, *Madagascar* **203 H17**
Manakau, peak, *N.Z.* **213 N18**
Manākhah, *Yemen* **172 Q9**
Mana La, *China, India* **178 D7**
Manam, island, *P.N.G.* **213 C19**
Manama see Al Manāmah, *Bahrain* **172 H12**
Manamadurai, *India* **179 R6**
Mananjary, *Madagascar* **203 H17**
Manaoba, island, *Solomon Is.* **217 M19**
Mānā Point, *Hawai'i, U.S.* **112 B4**
Manapouri, Lake, *N.Z.* **213 Q15**
Manas, *China* **180 E7**
Manas Hu, *China* **180 D7**
Manassas, *Va., U.S.* **96 D12**
Manatí, *Cuba* **116 J12**
Manatí, *P.R., U.S.* **120 M3**
Manaus, *Braz.* **130 D9**
Manavgat, *Turk.* **168 J6**
Manawai Harbour, *Solomon Is.* **217 N20**
Manbij, *Syr.* **170 D10**
Manchester, *Conn., U.S.* **101 L13**
Manchester, *Eng., U.K.* **143 S11**
Manchester, *Ga., U.S.* **96 M5**
Manchester, *Iowa, U.S.* **105 N13**
Manchester, *Ky., U.S.* **101 D19**
Manchester, *N.H., U.S.* **95 J14**
Manchester, *Tenn., U.S.* **101 F16**
Manchhar Lake, *Pak.* **177 V6**
Manchioneal, *Jam.* **120 J11**
Manchuria see Dongbei, region, *China* **181 D16**
Manchurian Plain, *China* **166 F12**
Manciano, *It.* **150 J7**
Mancos, *Colo., U.S.* **107 P10**
Mand, river, *Iran* **173 G13**
Mand, *Pak.* **177 V2**
Manda, *Tanzania* **199 N13**
Mandai, *Pak.* **177 R7**
Mandal, *Mongolia* **180 D12**
Mandal, *Nor.* **140 M10**
Mandal, *Virgin Islands, U.S.* **120 M9**
Mandala, Puncak, *Indonesia* **213 C17**
Mandalay, *Myanmar* **186 G6**
Mandalgovĭ, *Mongolia* **180 E12**
Mandalī, *Iraq* **172 D10**
Mandat see Sonid Zuoqi, *China* **182 A5**
Mandan, *N. Dak., U.S.* **104 G4**
Mandapeta, *India* **178 M8**

Mandara Mountains, *Cameroon, Nigeria* **201 F16**
Mandeb, Bab el, *Yemen* **172 R8**
Mandel, *Afghan.* **177 N2**
Mandera, *Kenya* **199 H16**
Manderscheid, *Ger.* **160 G12**
Mandeville, *Jam.* **120 J8**
Mandi, *India* **177 P14**
Mandi Burewala, *Pak.* **177 R10**
Mandimba, *Mozambique* **203 E13**
Mandioli, island, *Indonesia* **189 J16**
Mandla, *India* **178 J7**
Mándra, *Gr.* **154 J12**
Mandráki, *Gr.* **155 M18**
Mandritsa, *Bulg.* **153 K16**
Mandritsara, *Madagascar* **203 E18**
Mandsaur, *India* **178 H4**
Mandu, island, *Maldives* **179 V3**
Mandurah, *W. Aust., Austral.* **211 X2**
Manduria, *It.* **151 N15**
Mandvi, *India* **178 J1**
Manfredonia, *It.* **150 L12**
Manfredonia, Golfo di, *It.* **150 L13**
Manga, region, *Chad, Niger* **197 H13**
Manga, *Braz.* **131 G15**
Mangabeiras, Chapada das, *Braz.* **131 G14**
Mangaia, island, *Cook Is., N.Z.* **214 K12**
Mangalia, *Rom.* **153 G18**
Mangalore, *India* **179 Q4**
Mangareva, island, *Fr. Polynesia, Fr.* **219 Q20**
Mangarongaro, island, *Cook Is., N.Z.* **219 B17**
Mangeigne, *Chad* **197 K16**
Mangere, island, *Cook Is., N.Z.* **218 Q12**
Manggautu, *Solomon Is.* **217 Q18**
Mangghyystaū, *Kaz.* **174 H5**
Manghit, *Uzb.* **174 J9**
Mangnai, *China* **180 H8**
Mango, island, *Tonga* **218 Q6**
Mangoche, *Malawi* **203 E13**
Mangoky, river, *Madagascar* **203 H16**
Mangole, island, *Indonesia* **189 K15**
Mangqystaū Shyghanaghy, *Kaz.* **174 G5**
Mangrol, *India* **178 K2**
Mangrove Cay, *Bahamas* **120 D2**
Manguchar, *Pak.* **177 S6**
Manguinho, Ponta do, *Braz.* **131 G17**
Mangum, *Okla., U.S.* **102 H8**
Mangut, *Russ.* **159 M17**
Manhattan, *Kans., U.S.* **105 S8**
Manhattan, *Nev., U.S.* **109 R9**
Mani, peninsula, *Gr.* **154 M10**
Mania, river, *Madagascar* **203 G17**
Maniamba, *Mozambique* **203 D13**
Manica, *Mozambique* **202 G12**
Manicoré, *Braz.* **130 E9**
Manicouagan, Réservoir, *Que., Can.* **83 M20**
Manīfah, *Saudi Arabia* **172 H12**
Manifold, Cape, *Austral.* **210 F15**
Manihi, island, *Fr. Polynesia, Fr.* **219 D18**
Manihiki Atoll, *Cook Is., N.Z.* **214 H11**
Manihiki Plateau, *Pac. Oc.* **238 L12**
Manila, *Ark., U.S.* **100 F11**
Manila, *Philippines* **189 C13**
Manila, Utah, U.S.* **106 K9**
Manila Bay, *Philippines* **189 C13**
Manily, *Russ.* **159 D21**
Maningrida, *N. Terr., Austral.* **211 P9**
Manini, Motus, *Fr. Polynesia, Fr.* **219 J13**
Maninita, island, *Tonga* **218 M11**
Manipa, island, *Indonesia* **189 K16**
Manisa, *Turk.* **168 F3**
Manistee, river, *Mich., U.S.* **98 J9**
Manistee, *Mich., U.S.* **98 J9**
Manistique, *Mich., U.S.* **98 G9**
Manistique Lake, *Mich., U.S.* **98 F9**
Manitoba, *Can.* **83 L14**
Manitoba, Lake, *Man., Can.* **83 N13**
Manitou Island, *Mich., U.S.* **98 E7**
Manitou Islands, *Mich., U.S.* **98 H9**
Manitowoc, *Wis., U.S.* **98 K7**
Manizales, *Col.* **128 E4**
Manja, *Madagascar* **203 H16**
Manjra, river, *India* **178 M6**
Mankato, *Kans., U.S.* **105 R7**
Mankato, *Minn., U.S.* **104 L11**
Manley Hot Springs, *Alas., U.S.* **111 F16**
Manlleu, *Sp.* **145 D17**
Manly, *Iowa, U.S.* **104 M11**
Manmad, *India* **178 K4**
Mann, island, *Marshall Is.* **216 M5**
Manna, *Indonesia* **188 L6**

Mannar, Gulf of, *India, Sri Lanka* **179** S6
Mannheim, *Ger.* **148** H6
Manning, *Iowa, U.S.* **105** P10
Manning, *N. Dak., U.S.* **104** G2
Manning, *S.C., U.S.* **96** L10
Manning, Cape, *Kiribati* **217** A23
Manning Strait, *Solomon Is.* **217** L16
Mannington, *W. Va., U.S.* **96** C9
Mann Passage, *Marshall Is.* **216** M5
Mannu, *Malta* **161** K23
Manoa, *Bol.* **130** G7
Man of War Bay, *Trinidad & Tobago* **121** N18
Man-of-War Cay, *Bahamas* **117** G13
Manokotak, *Alas., U.S.* **111** L13
Manokwari, *Indonesia* **189** J19
Manono, *Dem. Rep. of the Congo* **198** M11
Manono, island, *Samoa* **218** L3
Manoron, *Myanmar* **187** P8
Mano Wan, *Japan* **185** M11
Man O'War Cay, *Bahamas* **120** B7
Man O'War Cay, *Bahamas* **116** C12
Manp'o, *N. Korea* **182** C12
Manra, island, *Kiribati* **214** H10
Manresa, *Sp.* **145** D17
Mansa, *Zambia* **202** D11
Mansehra, *Pak.* **176** M11
Mansel Island, *Nunavut, Can.* **83** J17
Mansfield, *Ark., U.S.* **100** G6
Mansfield, *Eng., U.K.* **143** S12
Mansfield, *La., U.S.* **100** G6
Mansfield, *Mo., U.S.* **105** V13
Mansfield, *Ohio, U.S.* **99** Q13
Mansfield, *Pa., U.S.* **94** L7
Mansfield, *Vic., Austral.* **211** Z12
Mansfield, Mount, *Vt., U.S.* **94** F12
Mansle, *Fr.* **147** U7
Manson, *Iowa, U.S.* **105** N10
Manta, *Ecua.* **128** J2
Mant'ap-san, peak, *N. Korea* **182** B14
Manteca, *Calif., U.S.* **109** S5
Manteo, *N.C., U.S.* **96** G15
Mantes-la-Jolie, *Fr.* **147** P9
Manti, *Utah, U.S.* **106** M7
Mantiqueira, Serra da, *S. Amer.* **126** J9
Mant Islands, *F.S.M.* **217** F14
Manton, *Mich., U.S.* **98** J10
Mantova, *It.* **150** E6
Mant Passage, *F.S.M.* **217** F14
Mantua, *Cuba* **116** H4
Manturovo, *Russ.* **156** G12
Mäntyluoto, *Fin.* **141** J15
Manú, *Peru* **130** H5
Manuae, island, *Fr. Polynesia, Fr.* **219** E14
Manua Islands, *Amer. Samoa, U.S.* **214** J10
Manuhangi, island, *Fr. Polynesia, Fr.* **219** F20
Manui, islands, *Fr. Polynesia, Fr.* **219** R20
Manui, island, *Indonesia* **189** K14
Manukau, *N.Z.* **213** J19
Manulu Lagoon, *Kiribati* **217** B23
Manus, island, *P.N.G.* **213** B19
Manvers, Port, *Nfld. & Lab., Can.* **83** J21
Many, *La., U.S.* **100** M7
Manych Gudilo, Ozero, *Russ.* **157** R12
Manych Guidilo, Lake *see* Manych Guidilo, Ozero, *Russ.* **138** G12
Many Farms, *Ariz., U.S.* **107** Q9
Manzai, *Pak.* **177** P8
Manzanares, *Sp.* **144** H11
Manzanar National Historic Site, *Calif., U.S.* **109** T8
Manzanilla Point, *Trinidad & Tobago* **121** P23
Manzanillo, *Cuba* **116** K11
Manzanillo, *Mex.* **114** J9
Manzanillo Bay, *Haiti* **117** L17
Manzano Mountains, *N. Mex., U.S.* **107** S12
Manzano Peak, *N. Mex., U.S.* **107** S12
Manzhouli, *China* **181** C15
Manzil, *Pak.* **177** S3
Mao, *Chad* **197** H14
Mao, *Dom. Rep.* **117** L18
Maoke, Pegunungan, *Indonesia* **189** L20
Maoke Mountains *see* Maoke, Pegunungan, *Indonesia* **166** L16
Maoming, *China* **183** S2
Map, island, *F.S.M.* **217** C18
Mapai, *Mozambique* **202** H12
Mapam Yumco, lake, *China* **180** K5

Mapi, *Indonesia* **189** M21
Mapia, Kepulauan (St. David Islands), *Indonesia* **189** J19
Mapimí, Bolsón de, *N. Amer.* **80** M4
Mapleton, *Iowa, U.S.* **105** N9
Mapleton, *Oreg., U.S.* **108** H2
Mapmaker Seamounts, *Pac. Oc.* **238** G8
Maprik, *P.N.G.* **213** C18
Mapuera, river, *Braz.* **130** C10
Maputo, *Mozambique* **202** J12
Maputo, Baía de, *Mozambique* **202** J12
Maqat, *Kaz.* **174** F7
Maqellarë, *Albania* **152** K10
Maqnā, *Saudi Arabia* **172** G5
Maqshūsh, *Saudi Arabia* **172** K6
Maquan, river, *China* **180** L6
Maquela do Zombo, *Angola* **202** B6
Maquinchao, *Arg.* **133** Q8
Maquoketa, *Iowa, U.S.* **105** N14
Mar, *Russ.* **159** H16
Mar, Serra do, *S. Amer.* **126** K8
Mara, *Guyana* **129** E15
Mara, *India* **178** F14
Maraã, *Braz.* **130** D7
Maraa, *Fr. Polynesia, Fr.* **219** P15
Maraa, Passe de, *Fr. Polynesia, Fr.* **219** P15
Marabá, *Braz.* **131** E13
Marabo, island, *Fiji Is.* **218** K9
Maracá, Ilha de, *Braz.* **130** B12
Maracaibo, *Venez.* **128** B7
Maracaibo, Lago de, *Venez.* **128** C7
Maracaibo Basin, *S. Amer.* **126** A3
Maracá Island, *S. Amer.* **126** C8
Maracaju, *Braz.* **130** L11
Maracaju, Serra de, *S. Amer.* **126** H7
Maracanã, *Braz.* **131** C14
Maracay, *Venez.* **128** B9
Maracayo, Punta, *P.R., U.S.* **120** M2
Marādah, *Lib.* **197** D15
Maradi, *Niger* **196** J11
Marāghah, Sabkhat, *Syr.* **170** E9
Marāgheh, *Iran* **172** B10
Maragogipe, *Braz.* **131** H16
Marahuaca, Cerro, *Venez.* **128** F10
Marajó, Ilha de, *Braz.* **131** C13
Marajó Bay, *S. Amer.* **126** D9
Marajó Island, *S. Amer.* **126** D8
Marakei, island, *Kiribati* **214** G8
Maralal, *Kenya* **199** J14
Maralinga, *S. Aust., Austral.* **211** W8
Maramasike, island, *Solomon Is.* **217** N20
Marambio, station, *Antarctica* **226** C4
Maran, *Malaysia* **187** U10
Marana, *Ariz., U.S.* **107** V7
Maranboy, *N. Terr., Austral.* **211** Q8
Maranchón, *Sp.* **144** E12
Marand, *Iran* **172** A10
Marang, *Malaysia* **187** T10
Maranges, *Sp.* **145** C17
Maranhão, Barragem do, *Port.* **144** H6
Marano, river, *It., San Marino* **161** J17
Marañón, river, *Peru* **130** E4
Marans, *Fr.* **147** T6
Marargiu, Capo, *It.* **151** N3
Mara Rosa, *Braz.* **131** H13
Mărăşeşti, *Rom.* **153** D16
Maratea, *It.* **151** N12
Marathon, *Fla., U.S.* **97** Y9
Marathon, battle, *Gr.* **155** J13
Marathon, *Tex., U.S.* **103** Q3
Marathónas, *Gr.* **155** J13
Marathus *see* 'Amrīt, ruin, *Syr.* **170** G7
Maraú, *Braz.* **131** J16
Maravae, *Solomon Is.* **217** M15
Marāveh Tappeh, *Iran* **173** B15
Maravillas Creek, *Tex., U.S.* **103** Q3
Maravovo, *Solomon Is.* **217** N18
Maraza, *Azerb.* **169** D22
Marbella, *Sp.* **144** M9
Marble Bar, *W. Aust., Austral.* **211** S3
Marble Canyon, *Ariz., U.S.* **107** Q7
Marble Falls, *Tex., U.S.* **103** P10
Marburg, *Ger.* **148** F6
Marcel, Anse, *St. Martin, Fr.* **121** A14
Marceline, *Mo., U.S.* **105** R12
Marchena, Canal de, *Ecua.* **128** P10
Marchena, Isla (Bindloe), *Ecua.* **128** P9
Marciana, *It.* **150** J5
Marckolsheim, *Fr.* **147** Q15
Marco, *Fla., U.S.* **97** X8
Marcola, *Oreg., U.S.* **108** H3
Marcos Juárez, *Arg.* **132** K11

Marcus *see* Minami Tori Shima, island, *Japan* **184** L8
Marcus Baker, Mount, *Alas., U.S.* **111** J17
Marcy, Mount, *N.Y., U.S.* **94** G11
Mardan, *Pak.* **176** M10
Mar del Plata, *Arg.* **133** N13
Mardin, *Turk.* **169** H15
Maré, island, *New Caledonia, Fr.* **214** K7
Maré, Île, *New Caledonia, Fr.* **218** D10
Marea del Portillo, *Cuba* **116** L12
Marecchia, river, *It.* **161** H13
Marechal Taumaturgo, *Braz.* **130** G4
Maree, Loch, *Scot., U.K.* **142** J8
Marenanuka, island, *Kiribati* **217** F17
Marengo, *Iowa, U.S.* **105** P13
Marennes, *Fr.* **147** U6
Marettimo, Isola, *It.* **151** S8
Mareuil, *Fr.* **147** U8
Marfa, *Tex., U.S.* **103** Q2
Marfa, Massif de, *Chad* **197** J16
Margaret River, *W. Aust., Austral.* **211** R6
Margarita, Isla de, *Venez.* **128** B11
Margat Castle *see* Marqab, al Qal'at, ruin, *Syr.* **170** F7
Margeride, Monts de la, *Fr.* **147** V11
Margherita di Savoia, *It.* **150** L13
Marghita, *Rom.* **152** B12
Margow Desert, *Afghan.* **177** R2
Marguerite Bay, *Antarctica* **226** F5
Marhanets', *Ukr.* **157** Q8
Mari, ruin, *Syr.* **170** G14
Marià, Pic del, *Andorra* **160** H5
Maria, island, *Fr. Polynesia, Fr.* **219** H22
Maria, Îles, *Fr. Polynesia, Fr.* **214** K12
Maria Bay, *Tonga* **218** H11
María Elena, *Chile* **132** D7
Maria Islands, *St. Lucia* **121** L14
Mariana Islands, *Pac. Oc.* **166** G16
Mariana Trench, *Pac. Oc.* **238** H6
Mariana Trough, *Pac. Oc.* **238** H6
Marianna, *Ark., U.S.* **100** G10
Marianna, *Fla., U.S.* **97** Q4
Marianne, island, *Seychelles* **205** M21
Mariánské Lázně, *Czech Rep.* **148** H10
Marias, river, *Mont., U.S.* **106** B8
Marías, Islas, *Mex.* **114** G8
Marías Islands *see* Marías, Islas, *N. Amer.* **80** N4
Maria van Diemen, Cape, *N.Z.* **213** G17
Ma'rib, *Yemen* **172** P10
Maricao, *P.R., U.S.* **120** N2
Maricopa, *Ariz., U.S.* **107** U7
Maricopa, *Calif., U.S.* **109** W7
Maridi, *Sudan* **198** H12
Marié, river, *Braz.* **130** C6
Marie Byrd Land, *Antarctica* **226** K7
Marie-Galante, island, *Guadeloupe, Fr.* **121** G16
Mariehamn (Maarianhamina), *Fin.* **141** K14
Mariel, *Cuba* **116** G6
Mariental, *Namibia* **202** J7
Marietta, *Ga., U.S.* **96** L5
Marietta, *Ohio, U.S.* **99** S15
Marietta, *Okla., U.S.* **102** J11
Marigot, *Dominica* **121** E19
Marigot, *Guadeloupe, Fr.* **121** F14
Marigot, *Haiti* **117** M16
Marigot, *Martinique, Fr.* **121** E22
Marigot, *St. Martin, Fr.* **121** B14
Marigot, Baie de, *St. Martin, Fr.* **121** B14
Marigot Harbour, *St. Lucia* **121** K13
Mariiru Point, *N. Mariana Is., U.S.* **216** E8
Marijampolė, *Lith.* **141** N16
Marília, *Braz.* **130** L12
Marillana, *W. Aust., Austral.* **211** T3
Marinduque, island, *Philippines* **189** D14
Marine City, *Mich., U.S.* **98** M13
Marineland, *Fla., U.S.* **97** R9
Marinette, *Wis., U.S.* **98** H7
Maringá, *Braz.* **130** M12
Maringa, river, *Dem. Rep. of the Congo* **198** J9
Marinha Grande, *Port.* **144** G5
Marino, *It.* **150** L8
Marino, *Vanuatu* **218** C3
Marion, *Ala., U.S.* **101** L14
Marion, *Ark., U.S.* **100** G11
Marion, *Ill., U.S.* **99** U6
Marion, *Ind., U.S.* **99** Q10
Marion, *Iowa, U.S.* **105** N13
Marion, *Kans., U.S.* **105** T8
Marion, *Ky., U.S.* **101** C13

Marion, *Mich., U.S.* **98** K10
Marion, *N.C., U.S.* **96** H8
Marion, *Ohio, U.S.* **99** Q13
Marion, *S. Dak., U.S.* **104** M7
Marion, *S.C., U.S.* **96** K11
Marion, *Va., U.S.* **96** G8
Marion, Lake, *S.C., U.S.* **96** L10
Marion Downs, *Qnsld., Austral.* **211** T11
Marionville, *Mo., U.S.* **105** V11
Maripa, *Venez.* **128** D10
Mariposa, *Calif., U.S.* **109** S6
Marisa, *Indonesia* **189** J14
Mariscal Estigarribia, *Parag.* **130** L9
Maritime Alps, *Fr., It.* **147** W15
Maritime Museum, *Bermuda, U.K.* **120** B2
Maritsa, river, *Eur.* **138** J9
Mariupol', *Ukr.* **157** R9
Marivan, *Iran* **172** C10
Mariyets, *Russ.* **156** H15
Marjayoûn, *Leb.* **170** J6
Marka (Merca), *Somalia* **199** J17
Markam, *China* **180** L10
Markandeh, ruin, *Afghan.* **176** M6
Marked Tree, *Ark., U.S.* **100** F11
Markermeer, bay, *Neth.* **146** H12
Markham, Mount, *Antarctica* **227** L13
Markham Bay, *Nunavut, Can.* **83** H18
Markit, *China* **180** G4
Markleeville, *Calif., U.S.* **109** Q6
Markópoulo, *Gr.* **154** J7
Markovo, *Russ.* **159** C21
Marks, *Miss., U.S.* **100** H11
Marks, *Russ.* **156** M14
Marksville, *La., U.S.* **100** N8
Mark Twain Lake, *Mo., U.S.* **105** S13
Marlborough, *Qnsld., Austral.* **211** T14
Marle, *Fr.* **147** N11
Marlette, *Mich., U.S.* **98** L12
Marlin, *Tex., U.S.* **103** N12
Marlinton, *W. Va., U.S.* **96** E10
Marlow, *Okla., U.S.* **102** H10
Marmande, *Fr.* **147** W7
Marmara, island, *Turk.* **168** D4
Marmara Denizi, sea, *Turk.* **168** D4
Marmaraereğlisi, *Turk.* **168** C4
Marmara Gölü, *Turk.* **168** F4
Marmarás, *Gr.* **154** D12
Marmári, *Gr.* **155** J13
Marmaris, *Turk.* **168** H4
Marmarth, *N. Dak., U.S.* **104** H1
Marmelos, river, *Braz.* **130** F8
Marmet, *W. Va., U.S.* **96** E8
Marmolada, peak, *It.* **150** C7
Marmolejo, *Sp.* **144** K10
Marne, river, *Fr.* **147** P12
Marne au Rhin, Canal de la, *Fr.* **147** P15
Maroa, *Venez.* **128** G9
Maroantsetra, *Madagascar* **203** E18
Marobee Range, *Austral.* **210** K13
Maroe, *Fr. Polynesia, Fr.* **219** H14
Maroe, Baie de, *Fr. Polynesia, Fr.* **219** G14
Marokau, island, *Fr. Polynesia, Fr.* **219** F19
Marol, *Pak.* **176** M13
Maromokotro, peak, *Madagascar* **203** E18
Maroni, river, *Fr. Guiana, Fr., Suriname* **129** E17
Marónia, *Gr.* **155** C15
Maroochydore, *Qnsld., Austral.* **211** V15
Maro Reef, *Hawai'i, U.S.* **112** L5
Marotiri (Îlots de Bass), *Fr. Polynesia, Fr.* **215** L14
Maroua, *Cameroon* **201** F17
Maro'u Bay, *Solomon Is.* **217** P20
Marovoay, *Madagascar* **203** F17
Marpi Point, *N. Mariana Is., U.S.* **216** A6
Márpissa, *Gr.* **155** L15
Marpo, Puntan, *N. Mariana Is., U.S.* **216** C8
Marqab, al Qal'at (Margat Castle), ruin, *Syr.* **170** F7
Marqaköl, lake, *Kaz.* **175** D19
Marquesas Fracture Zone, *Pac. Oc.* **239** L14
Marquesas Islands, *Fr. Polynesia, Fr.* **215** H14
Marquesas Keys, *Fla., U.S.* **97** Y8
Marquette, *Mich., U.S.* **98** F7
Marquis, *Grenada* **121** K23
Marquis, *St. Lucia* **121** J14
Marquis, Cape, *St. Lucia* **121** J14
Marquis Island, *Grenada* **121** K23
Marra, Jebel, *Sudan* **198** E10

Marrakech, *Mor.* **196** B8
Marra Mountains, *Sudan* **194** G8
Marrawah, *Tas., Austral.* **211** Y15
Marree, *S. Aust., Austral.* **211** W10
Marrero, *La., U.S.* **100** Q11
Marromeu, *Mozambique* **203** F13
Marrupa, *Mozambique* **203** D14
Marsa, *Malta* **161** K23
Marsá al Burayqah, *Lib.* **197** C15
Marsabit, *Kenya* **199** J14
Marsala, *It.* **151** S8
Marsalforn, *Malta* **161** H20
Marsaxlokk, *Malta* **161** L23
Marsaxlokk Bay, *Malta* **161** L23
Marsciano, *It.* **150** J8
Marseille, *Fr.* **147** Y13
Marsfjället, peak, *Sw.* **140** G12
Marshall, *Alas., U.S.* **110** H12
Marshall, *Ark., U.S.* **100** E8
Marshall, river, *Austral.* **210** F9
Marshall, *Ill., U.S.* **99** S7
Marshall, *Mich., U.S.* **98** M10
Marshall, *Minn., U.S.* **104** K9
Marshall, *Mo., U.S.* **105** S12
Marshall, *Tex., U.S.* **102** L15
Marshall Islands, *Pac. Oc.* **214** F8
Marshalltown, *Iowa, U.S.* **105** N12
Marshfield, *Mo., U.S.* **105** U12
Marshfield, *Wis., U.S.* **98** J4
Marsh Harbour, *Bahamas* **120** B6
Mars Hill, *Me., U.S.* **95** B18
Mars Hill, *N.C., U.S.* **96** H7
Marsh Island, *La., U.S.* **100** Q8
Marsland, *Nebr., U.S.* **105** N1
Mars-la-Tour, *Fr.* **147** P13
Marsugalt, island, *Marshall Is.* **216** K2
Mart, *Tex., U.S.* **103** N12
Martaban, Gulf of, *Myanmar* **186** K6
Martapura, *Indonesia* **188** K11
Martelange, *Lux.* **160** J8
Martha's Vineyard, island, *Mass., U.S.* **95** M15
Martí, *Cuba* **116** J11
Martigny, *Switz.* **150** C2
Martigues, *Fr.* **147** X13
Martin, *S. Dak., U.S.* **104** M3
Martin, *Slovakia* **149** J15
Martin, *Tenn., U.S.* **101** E13
Martin, Lake, *Ala., U.S.* **101** K16
Martínez, *Ga., U.S.* **96** L7
Martinez Lake, *Ariz., U.S.* **107** U4
Martinique, island, *Fr., Lesser Antilles* **119** K17
Martinique Passage, *Lesser Antilles* **119** J17
Martinsburg, *W. Va., U.S.* **96** C12
Martins Ferry, *Ohio, U.S.* **99** Q15
Martinsville, *Ind., U.S.* **99** S9
Martinsville, *Va., U.S.* **96** G10
Martos, *Sp.* **144** K10
Martuni, *Arm.* **169** E19
Martuni, *Azerb.* **169** E21
Maru, island, *Indonesia* **213** D14
Ma'ruf, *Afghan.* **177** Q6
Marum Volcano, *Vanuatu* **218** D3
Marutea, island, *Fr. Polynesia, Fr.* **219** E19
Marutea, island, *Fr. Polynesia, Fr.* **219** G22
Marvão, *Port.* **144** H6
Marv Dasht, *Iran* **173** F13
Marvel Loch, *W. Aust., Austral.* **211** X4
Marvine, Mount, *Utah, U.S.* **107** N7
Marvin Spur, *Arctic Oc.* **242** J10
Marwah, *Afghan.* **176** M3
Mary, *Turkm.* **174** M10
Maryborough, *Qnsld., Austral.* **211** U15
Maryland, *U.S.* **96** C12
Mary Point, *Virgin Islands, U.S.* **120** M11
Maryport, *Eng., U.K.* **143** P10
Marys, river, *Nev., U.S.* **108** M11
Marysvale, *Utah, U.S.* **107** N7
Marysville, *Calif., U.S.* **109** Q4
Marysville, *Kans., U.S.* **105** R8
Marysville, *Ohio, U.S.* **99** Q12
Marysville, *Wash., U.S.* **108** B4
Maryville, *Mo., U.S.* **105** R10
Maryville, *Tenn., U.S.* **101** F18
Marzo, Cabo, *Col.* **128** E3
Marzūq, *Lib.* **197** E14
Marzūq, Şahrā', *Lib.* **197** E13
Masada, ruin, *Israel* **171** N6
Masai Steppe, *Tanzania* **199** L14
Masallı, *Azerb.* **169** F22

Masalog, Puntan, *N. Mariana Is., U.S.* 216 B8
Masamba, *Indonesia* 189 KI3
Masan, *S. Korea* 182 GI4
Masasi, *Tanzania* 199 NI5
Masaya, *Nicar.* 115 MI8
Masbate, island, *Philippines* 189 DI4
Masbate, *Philippines* 189 DI4
Mascara, *Alg.* 196 AIO
Mascarene Basin, *Ind. Oc.* 240 J6
Mascarene Plain, *Ind. Oc.* 240 K6
Mascarene Plateau, *Ind. Oc.* 240 H7
Masefau Bay, *Amer. Samoa, U.S.* 218 L8
Masein, *Myanmar* 186 F5
Masela, island, *Indonesia* 189 MI7
Maseru, *Lesotho* 202 KIO
Masescha, *Liech.* 160 P2
Mash'abbe Sade, *Israel* 171 P5
Mashhad, *Iran* 173 CI6
Mashkai, river, *Pak.* 177 U5
Mashkel, river, *Pak.* 177 T3
Mashkel, Hamun-i-, *Pak.* 177 T2
Mashki Chah, *Pak.* 177 S2
Masi-Manimba, *Dem. Rep. of the Congo* 198 L8
Masin, *Indonesia* 189 M2I
Masira *see* Maşīrah, Jazīrat, island, *Oman* 173 LI7
Masira, Gulf of, *Oman* 166 J5
Maşīrah, Tur'at, *Oman* 173 LI7
Maşīrah, Jazīrat (Masira), *Oman* 173 LI7
Maşīrah, Khalīj, *Oman* 173 MI6
Masisea, *Peru* 130 G4
Masjed Soleymān, *Iran* 172 EI2
Mask, Lough, *Ire.* 143 R3
Maskanah (Meskéné), *Syr.* 170 EIO
Maskelynes Islands, *Vanuatu* 218 E2
Maslenica, *Croatia* 152 F5
Maslen Nos, *Bulg.* 153 JI7
Masoala, Presqu'île de, *Madagascar* 203 EI8
Mason, *Mich., U.S.* 98 MII
Mason, *Tex., U.S.* 103 P8
Mason Bay, *N.Z.* 213 RI5
Mason City, *Iowa, U.S.* 104 MI2
Mason Hall, *Trinidad & Tobago* 121 NI8
Masontown, *Pa., U.S.* 94 P3
Maspalomas, *Canary Is.* 204 R6
Masqaṭ (Muscat), *Oman* 173 KI6
Massa, *Congo* 201 MI7
Massachusetts, *U.S.* 94 KI2
Massachusetts Bay, *Mass., U.S.* 95 KI6
Massacre, *Dominica* 121 FI9
Massacre Bay, *Amer. Samoa, U.S.* 218 M7
Massafra, *It.* 150 MI4
Massakory, *Chad* 197 JI4
Massa Marittima, *It.* 150 H6
Massangena, *Mozambique* 202 HI2
Massawa *see* Mits'iwa, *Eritrea* 199 DI5
Massay, *Fr.* 147 S9
Mass City, *Mich., U.S.* 98 F6
Massena, *N.Y., U.S.* 94 FIO
Massenya, *Chad* 197 JI4
Masset, *B.C., Can.* 82 J7
Massiac, *Fr.* 147 VII
Massillon, *Ohio, U.S.* 99 PI4
Massinga, *Mozambique* 203 HI3
Masson Island, *Antarctica* 227 K2I
Mastābah, *Saudi Arabia* 172 L7
Maştağa, *Azerb.* 169 D23
Masterton, *N.Z.* 213 MI9
Mástiho, Akrotírio, *Gr.* 155 JI6
Mastuj, *Pak.* 176 LIO
Mastung, *Pak.* 177 R6
Mastūrah, *Saudi Arabia* 172 K6
Masty, *Belarus* 156 K3
Masuda, *Japan* 185 Q5
Masvingo, *Zimb.* 202 GII
Maşyāf, *Syr.* 170 F7
Mat, river, *Albania* 152 K9
Mataabé, Cape, *Vanuatu* 218 DI
Matacaw Levu, island, *Fiji Is.* 218 H5
Matadi, *Dem. Rep. of the Congo* 198 L7
Matador, *Tex., U.S.* 102 J6
Matagalpa, *Nicar.* 115 MI8
Matagami, *Que., Can.* 83 NI8
Matagorda, *Tex., U.S.* 103 SI3
Matagorda Bay, *Tex., U.S.* 84 NI2
Matagorda Peninsula, *Tex., U.S.* 103 SI3
Matah *see* Mataso, island, *Vanuatu* 218 E3
Matahiva *see* Mataiva, island, *Fr. Polynesia, Fr.* 219 DI7
Mataiea, *Fr. Polynesia, Fr.* 219 PI6

Mataigou *see* Taole, *China* 182 DI
Mataiva (Matahiva), island, *Fr. Polynesia, Fr.* 219 DI7
Matak, island, *Indonesia* 188 H8
Matala, *Gr.* 155 RI4
Matalaa, Pointe, *Wallis & Futuna, Fr.* 218 CII
Matale, *Sri Lanka* 179 T7
Matam, *Senegal* 196 G5
Matamoros, *Mex.* 114 FI2
Matane, *Que., Can.* 83 N2I
Matanzas, *Cuba* 116 G7
Mata Point, *Niue, N.Z.* 219 C2O
Matara, *Sri Lanka* 179 T7
Mataram, *Indonesia* 188 MI2
Mataranka, *N. Terr., Austral.* 211 Q8
Mataró, *Sp.* 145 DI8
Matasiri, island, *Indonesia* 188 LII
Mataso (Matah), island, *Vanuatu* 218 E3
Matatépai, Pointe, *Fr. Polynesia, Fr.* 219 M2O
Matatiele, *S. Af.* 202 LII
Matatula, Cape, *Amer. Samoa, U.S.* 218 L9
Mataura, *Fr. Polynesia, Fr.* 219 K2O
Mataura, Mouillage de, *Fr. Polynesia, Fr.* 219 K2O
Matâ'utu, *Wallis & Futuna, Fr.* 218 BII
Matautu, *Samoa* 218 L3
Mata-Utu, Baie de, *Wallis & Futuna, Fr.* 218 BI2
Matautulele Point, *Amer. Samoa, U.S.* 218 M7
Matauvau, Passe, *Fr. Polynesia, Fr.* 219 NI4
Matavai, Baie de, *Fr. Polynesia, Fr.* 219 NI6
Matavanu, Mount, *Samoa* 218 K2
Matavera, *Cook Is., N.Z.* 218 Q9
Matcha, *Taj.* 176 H8
Mateguá, *Bol.* 130 H8
Matehuala, *Mex.* 114 GII
Mateika, island, *Tuvalu* 217 L23
Mateika, Te Ava, *Tuvalu* 217 L23
Matelot, *Trinidad & Tobago* 121 N23
Matema, island, *Solomon Is.* 217 P22
Matera, *It.* 150 MI3
Matese, range, *It.* 150 LII
Mátészalka, *Hung.* 149 KI7
Matfors, *Sw.* 141 JI3
Mathematicians Seamounts, *Pac. Oc.* 239 HI7
Mather, *Calif., U.S.* 109 S6
Mathews, *Va., U.S.* 96 EI4
Mathis, *Tex., U.S.* 103 TIO
Mathráki, island, *Gr.* 154 E5
Mathura, *India* 178 F6
Mathurin Bay, *Mauritius* 205 J2O
Mati, *Philippines* 189 FI5
Matiere, *N.Z.* 213 KI9
Matinicus Island, *Me., U.S.* 95 GI7
Matira, Pointe, *Fr. Polynesia, Fr.* 219 LI4
Matlerjoch, pass, *Aust., Liech.* 160 P4
Matli, *Pak.* 177 W7
Matlock, *Eng., U.K.* 143 SI2
Matochkin Shar, *Russ.* 158 DII
Mato Grosso, *Braz.* 130 J9
Matopo Hills, *Zimb.* 194 N8
Matosinhos, *Port.* 144 E5
Maţraḩ, *Oman* 173 KI6
Maţrūḩ, *Egypt* 197 CI7
Matsu, island, *Taiwan, China* 183 P9
Matsubara, *Japan* 185 X2
Matsue, *Japan* 185 P6
Matsumoto, *Japan* 185 NII
Matsuyama, *Japan* 185 R6
Mattamuskeet, Lake, *N.C., U.S.* 96 HI4
Mattaponi, river, *Va., U.S.* 96 EI3
Mattawamkeag, *Me., U.S.* 95 DI8
Matterhorn, peak, *It., Switz.* 150 C3
Matterhorn, peak, *Nev., U.S.* 108 LII
Matthew, island, *Vanuatu* 214 K8
Matthews Peak, *Ariz., U.S.* 84 J7
Matthew's Ridge, *Guyana* 129 DI3
Matthew Town, *Bahamas* 117 JI5
Maţţī, Sabkhat, *Saudi Arabia, U.A.E.* 173 KI3
Mattili, *India* 178 L8
Mattinata, *It.* 150 LI3
Mattoon, *Ill., U.S.* 99 S6
Matu, *Malaysia* 187 UI6
Matua, *Indonesia* 188 K9
Matua, island, *Russ.* 159 H23
Matuku, island, *Fiji Is.* 218 K8
Matunga, island, *Cook Is., N.Z.* 219 BI7

Matunuck, *R.I., U.S.* 95 MI4
Matura, *Trinidad & Tobago* 121 P23
Matura Bay, *Trinidad & Tobago* 121 P23
Maturei Vavao, island, *Fr. Polynesia, Fr.* 219 G22
Maturín, *Venez.* 128 BI2
Maúa, *Mozambique* 203 EI4
Maubara, *Timor-Leste* 189 MI5
Maubeuge, *Fr.* 146 MII
Maud Rise, *Antarctic Oc.* 244 EII
Maués, *Braz.* 130 DIO
Maughold Head, *Isle of Man, U.K.* 143 Q9
Maug Islands, *N. Mariana Is., U.S.* 216 A2
Maui, island, *Hawai'i, U.S.* 113 GI7
Mauke, island, *Cook Is., N.Z.* 214 KI2
Maukme, *Myanmar* 186 H7
Maule, Rio, *Chile* 132 M6
Mauléon, *Fr.* 147 S6
Maullín, *Chile* 133 Q6
Maumee, river, *Ohio, U.S.* 99 PI2
Maumee, *Ohio, U.S.* 99 NI2
Maumusson, Pertuis de, *Fr.* 147 U6
Maun, *Botswana* 202 G9
Maunabo, *P.R., U.S.* 120 N5
Mauna Iki, peak, *Hawai'i, U.S.* 113 N2O
Mauna Kea, peak, *Hawai'i, U.S.* 113 L2O
Mauna Kea Adz Quarry, *Hawai'i, U.S.* 113 L2O
Mauna Kea Observatories, *Hawai'i, U.S.* 113 L2O
Mauna Loa, peak, *Hawai'i, U.S.* 113 NI9
Maunaloa, *Hawai'i, U.S.* 113 FI4
Mauna Loa Observatory, *Hawai'i, U.S.* 113 M2O
Mauna Ulu, peak, *Hawai'i, U.S.* 113 N2I
Maunalua Bay, *Hawai'i, U.S.* 112 EI2
Maungapu, peak, *Cook Is., N.Z.* 218 PII
Maungdaw, *Myanmar* 186 H4
Maunoir, Lac, *N.W.T., Can.* 82 FII
Maupihaa (Mopelia), island, *Fr. Polynesia, Fr.* 219 EI4
Maupin, *Oreg., U.S.* 108 F5
Maupiti, island, *Fr. Polynesia, Fr.* 219 EI5
Mau Ranipur, *India* 178 H7
Mauren, *Liech.* 160 M2
Maurepas, Lake, *La., U.S.* 100 PIO
Mauren, *Liech.* 160 M2
Maures, Monts des, *Fr.* 147 YI5
Mauriac, *Fr.* 147 VIO
Mauritania, *Af.* 195 FI4
Maurice, Lake, *Austral.* 210 H7
Mauritius, island, *Ind. Oc.* 204 H9
Mauritius Trench, *Ind. Oc.* 240 K6
Mauron, *Fr.* 147 Q5
Maury Bay, *Antarctica* 227 P2O
Maury Mountains, *Oreg., U.S.* 108 H6
Maury Seachannel, *Atl. Oc.* 236 E9
Mauston, *Wis., U.S.* 98 K4
Mautaro, Motu, *Fr. Polynesia, Fr.* 219 K2I
Mautau, Pointe, *Fr. Polynesia, Fr.* 219 M2O
Mauvezin, *Fr.* 147 X8
Maverick, *Ariz., U.S.* 107 T9
Mavinga, *Angola* 202 E8
Mavone, river, *It.* 161 GI5
Mavroli, *Cyprus* 160 P6
Mavrovouni Mine, *Cyprus* 160 P7
Mawarīd, 'Urūq al, *Yemen* 172 NI2
Mawlamyine, *Myanmar* 186 L7
Mawlite, *Myanmar* 186 F5
Mawlu, *Myanmar* 186 F6
Mawqaq, *Saudi Arabia* 172 H8
Mawshij, *Yemen* 172 Q8
Mawson, station, *Antarctica* 227 E2O
Mawson Coast, *Antarctica* 227 D2O
Mawson Escarpment, *Antarctica* 227 FI8
Mawson Peninsula, *Antarctica* 227 RI6
Max, *N. Dak., U.S.* 104 F4
Maxixe, *Mozambique* 203 HI3
Maxton, *N.C., U.S.* 96 JII
May, Cape, *N.J., U.S.* 85 G2O
May, Isle of, *Scot., U.K.* 142 MII
Mayabandar, *India* 179 TI4
Mayaguana Island, *Bahamas* 117 HI6
Mayaguana Passage, *Bahamas* 117 HI5
Mayagüez, *P.R., U.S.* 120 NI
Mayagüez, Bahía de, *P.R., U.S.* 120 NI
Mayāmey, *Iran* 173 CI5
Mayang, *China* 183 N2
Mayarí, *Cuba* 117 KI3
Mayaro Bay, *Trinidad & Tobago* 121 Q23
Maycock's Bay, *Barbados* 121 JI8

Maydān Ikbiz, *Syr.* 170 C8
Maydh, *Somalia* 199 FI7
Maydī, *Yemen* 172 P8
Mayenne, *Fr.* 147 Q7
Mayfa'ah, *Yemen* 172 QII
Mayfield, *Ky., U.S.* 101 DI3
Mayhill, *N. Mex., U.S.* 107 UI3
Maykop, *Russ.* 157 TII
Mayluu-Suu, *Kyrg.* 176 FIO
Mayno Gytkino, *Russ.* 159 C2I
Mayo, *Fla., U.S.* 97 R6
Mayo, *Trinidad & Tobago* 121 P22
Mayo, *Yukon, Can.* 82 F8
Mayo, Cerro, *Chile* 133 V7
Mayo Faran, *Nigeria* 201 GI6
Mayo Ndaga, *Nigeria* 201 GI6
Mayorga, *Sp.* 144 C9
Mayotte, Île de, *Fr., Mozambique Ch.* 203 DI6
May Pen, *Jam.* 120 J9
Mayreau, island, *St. Vincent & the Grenadines* 119 MI7
Maysville, *Ky., U.S.* 101 AI8
Maysville, *Mo., U.S.* 105 RII
Mayumba, *Gabon* 201 MI5
Maywood, *Nebr., U.S.* 105 Q4
Mazabuka, *Zambia* 202 FIO
Mazagan *see* El Jadida, *Mor.* 196 B8
Mazagão, *Braz.* 130 CI2
Mazamet, *Fr.* 147 XIO
Mazar, *China* 180 H4
Mazara del Vallo, *It.* 151 S8
Mazar-e Sharif, *Afghan.* 176 K6
Mazari Pass, *Pak.* 177 S3
Mazarrón, Golfo de, *Sp.* 145 LI3
Mazaruni, river, *Guyana* 129 DI3
Mazatán, *Mex.* 114 D7
Mazatenango, *Guatemala* 115 LI5
Mazatlán, *Mex.* 114 G8
Mazgirt, *Turk.* 169 FI4
Mazıdağı, *Turk.* 169 HI5
Mazirbe, *Latv.* 141 LI5
Mazotos, *Cyprus* 160 Q9
Mazowe, *Zimb.* 202 FII
Mazrub, *Sudan* 198 EI2
Mazyr, *Belarus* 156 P5
Mazzarino, *It.* 151 TIO
Mazzocco, river, *It.* 161 KI3
Mbabane, *Swaziland* 203 JII
Mbaïki, *Cen. Af. Rep.* 198 H8
Mbakaou Reservoir, *Cameroon* 201 HI6
Mbala, *Zambia* 202 CI2
Mbale, *Uganda* 199 JI3
Mbalmayo, *Cameroon* 201 JI6
Mbalo, *Solomon Is.* 217 PI9
Mbamba Bay, *Tanzania* 199 NI3
Mbandaka, *Dem. Rep. of the Congo* 198 K8
Mbang, Mount, *Cameroon* 201 GI7
Mbang Mountains, *Cameroon, Chad* 194 H6
Mbanika, island, *Solomon Is.* 217 NI8
M'banza Congo, *Angola* 202 B6
Mbanza-Ngungu, *Dem. Rep. of the Congo* 198 L7
Mbarara, *Uganda* 198 KI2
Mbari, river, *Cen. Af. Rep.* 198 HIO
Mbé, *Cameroon* 201 GI6
Mbéni, *Comoros* 205 MI4
Mbeya, *Tanzania* 199 NI3
M'Binda, *Congo* 201 MI6
Mbini, *Eq. Guinea* 201 KI5
Mborokua, island, *Solomon Is.* 217 NI7
Mbout, *Mauritania* 196 G6
Mbuji-Mayi, *Dem. Rep. of the Congo* 198 MIO
Mbulo, island, *Solomon Is.* 217 MI7
Mburucuyá, *Arg.* 132 GI3
Mbuyuni, *Tanzania* 199 MI4

McCormick, *S.C., U.S.* 96 L7
McCrory, *Ark., U.S.* 100 GIO
McDermitt, *Nev., U.S.* 108 L9
McDonald, *Kans., U.S.* 105 R3
McDonald Islands, *Antarctic Oc.* 245 GI6
McDonald Peak, *Mont., U.S.* 106 C6
McDouall Peak, *S. Aust., Austral.* 211 W9
McGehee, *Ark., U.S.* 100 J9
McGill, *Nev., U.S.* 109 PI2
McGrath, *Alas., U.S.* 111 HI4
McGregor, *Minn., U.S.* 104 GII
McGregor, *Tex., U.S.* 103 NII
McGuire, Mount, *Idaho, U.S.* 106 E5
Mchinji, *Malawi* 202 EI2
McIntosh, *Minn., U.S.* 104 F9
McIntosh, *S. Dak., U.S.* 104 H4
McKean Island, *Kiribati* 214 GIO
McKeesport, *Pa., U.S.* 94 N3
McKees Rocks, *Pa., U.S.* 94 N3
McKenzie, *Tenn., U.S.* 101 EI3
McKinlay, *Qnsld., Austral.* 211 SII
McKinley, Mount (Denali), *Alas., U.S.* 111 HI6
McKinleyville, *Calif., U.S.* 108 M2
McKinney, *Tex., U.S.* 102 KI2
McKinney, Lake, *Kans., U.S.* 105 U3
McKinnon, *Wyo., U.S.* 106 K9
McKittrick, *Calif., U.S.* 109 V6
McLaughlin, *S. Dak., U.S.* 104 H4
McLean, *Tex., U.S.* 102 G7
McLeansboro, *Ill., U.S.* 99 U6
McLean's Town (Self Town), *Bahamas* 120 E4
McLeod Bay, *N.W.T., Can.* 82 HI2
M'Clintock Channel, *Nunavut, Can.* 83 EI4
M'Clintock Inlet, *Nunavut, Can.* 83 AI6
McLoughlin, Mount, *Oreg., U.S.* 108 K4
M'Clure Strait, *N.W.T., Can.* 82 CI2
McMahon Line, *China, India* 178 FI4
McMinnville, *Oreg., U.S.* 108 F3
McMinnville, *Tenn., U.S.* 101 FI6
McMurdo, station, *Antarctica* 227 NI3
McMurdo Sound, *Antarctica* 227 NI4
McNary Dam, *Oreg., Wash., U.S.* 108 E7
McPherson, *Kans., U.S.* 105 T7
McRae, *Ga., U.S.* 97 N7
McVeigh, *Ky., U.S.* 101 C2O
McVille, *N. Dak., U.S.* 104 F7
Mdennah, region, *Alg., Mali, Mauritania* 196 E8
Mdina, *Malta* 161 K22
Mead, Lake, *Ariz., Nev., U.S.* 109 UI3
Meade, river, *Alas., U.S.* 111 CI4
Meade, *Kans., U.S.* 105 V4
Meade Peak, *Idaho, U.S.* 106 J8
Meadow, *Tex., U.S.* 102 K4
Meadow, *W. Aust., Austral.* 211 V2
Meadow Lake, *Sask., Can.* 82 LII
Meadow Valley Wash, *Nev., U.S.* 109 TI2
Mead Point, *Anguilla, U.K.* 120 RII
Mead's Bay, *Anguilla, U.K.* 120 RII
Meadville, *Pa., U.S.* 94 L3
Meandarra, *Qnsld., Austral.* 211 VI4
Meander River, *Alta., Can.* 82 JIO
Meares, Cape, *Oreg., U.S.* 108 F2
Mears, *Mich., U.S.* 98 K9
Meaux, *Fr.* 147 PIO
Mebane, *N.C., U.S.* 96 GII
Mecca, *Calif., U.S.* 109 YII
Mecca *see* Makkah, *Saudi Arabia* 172 L7
Mechanicsburg, *Pa., U.S.* 94 P7
Mechelen, *Belg.* 148 LI2
Mechol, *F.S.M.* 217 CI8
Mecitözü, *Turk.* 168 DIO
Meck, island, *Marshall Is.* 216 M5
Mecklenburger Bucht, *Ger.* 148 B9
Mecúfi, *Mozambique* 203 DI5
Mecula, *Mozambique* 203 DI4
Medan, *Indonesia* 188 G5
Médéa, *Alg.* 196 AII
Medellín, *Col.* 128 E4
Medford, *Okla., U.S.* 102 EIO
Medford, *Oreg., U.S.* 108 K3
Medford, *Wis., U.S.* 98 H4
Medgidia, *Rom.* 153 FI7
Media Luna, Cayo, *Cuba* 116 KII
Medical Lake, *Wash., U.S.* 108 C8
Medicine Bow, *Wyo., U.S.* 106 JI2
Medicine Bow Mountains, *Colo., Wyo., U.S.* 106 KI2
Medicine Bow Peak, *Wyo., U.S.* 106 KI2
Medicine Hat, *Alta., Can.* 82 NII
Medicine Lake, *Mont., U.S.* 106 BI3

Medicine Lodge, *Kans., U.S.* 105 V6
Medina, *N. Dak., U.S.* 104 G6
Medina, *N.Y., U.S.* 94 H5
Medina *see* Al Madīnah, *Saudi Arabia* 172 J7
Medina, *river, Tex., U.S.* 103 R9
Medina, *Tex., U.S.* 103 R8
Medinaceli, *Sp.* 144 E12
Medina del Campo, *Sp.* 144 E9
Medina de Pomar, *Sp.* 144 B11
Medina de Rioseco, *Sp.* 144 D9
Medina Lake, *Tex., U.S.* 103 R9
Medina Sidonia, *Sp.* 144 M8
Medinipur, *India* 178 J11
Mednogorsk, *Russ.* 158 J7
Mednyy, Ostrov, *Russ.* 159 E23
Médoc, *region, Fr.* 147 V6
Mêdog, *China* 180 L9
Medora, *N. Dak., U.S.* 104 G2
Medren, *island, Marshall Is.* 216 H9
Medvezh'i Ostrova (Bear Islands), *Russ.* 159 C19
Medvezh'yegorsk, *Russ.* 158 D7
Medyado, *island, Marshall Is.* 216 L8
Medyai, *island, Marshall Is.* 216 L8
Meekatharra, *W. Aust., Austral.* 211 V3
Meeker, *Colo., U.S.* 106 L10
Meerut, *India* 178 F6
Meeteetse, *Wyo., U.S.* 106 G10
Mega, *Indonesia* 189 J18
Mēga, *Eth.* 199 H15
Megálo Horió, *Gr.* 155 M18
Megalópoli, *Gr.* 154 K9
Mégara, *Gr.* 154 J12
Mēgham, *Vanuatu* 218 D3
Meghri, *Arm.* 169 F20
Megiddo, *Israel* 170 L5
Megion, *Russ.* 158 H11
Megísti (Kastellórizon), *Gr.* 155 N22
Mehadia, *Rom.* 152 F12
Mehamn, *Nor.* 141 B14
Mehar, *Pak.* 177 U6
Meharry, Mount, *Austral.* 210 F3
Meherrin, *river, Va., U.S.* 96 F12
Mehetia, *island, Fr. Polynesia, Fr.* 219 F17
Mehola, *W. Bank* 170 L6
Mehrīz, *Iran* 173 E14
Mehtar Lam, *Afghan.* 176 M8
Meichang, *China* 181 L16
Meiganga, *Cameroon* 201 G17
Meighan Island, *Nunavut, Can.* 83 B14
Meigs, *Ga., U.S.* 97 Q5
Meihekou, *China* 182 B12
Meiktila, *Myanmar* 186 H6
Meiningen, *Ger.* 148 G8
Meissen, *Ger.* 148 F10
Meizhou, *China* 183 R6
Mejatto, *island, Marshall Is.* 216 K1
Mejillones, *Chile* 132 E6
Mejillones del Sur, Bahía de, *Chile* 132 E7
Mejit Island, *Marshall Is.* 216 F5
Mékambo, *Gabon* 201 K17
Mek'elē, *Eth.* 199 E15
Mekerrhane, Sebkha, *Alg.* 196 D10
Mekhtar, *Pak.* 177 R8
Mekiro, *island, Fr. Polynesia, Fr.* 219 Q20
Meknès, *Mor.* 196 B8
Mekong, *river, Asia* 166 K11
Mekong River Delta, *Vietnam* 187 Q13
Mekoryuk, *Alas., U.S.* 110 P11
Melanesia, *islands, Pac. Oc.* 214 G4
Melbourne, *Fla., U.S.* 97 T10
Melbourne, *Vic., Austral.* 211 Z12
Melbourne, Mount, *Antarctica* 227 P14
Mele, Capo, *It.* 150 G3
Mélé Bay, *Vanuatu* 218 F3
Melegnano, *It.* 150 E4
Melekeok, *Palau* 216 N12
Melekeok Point, *Palau* 216 N12
Melenki, *Russ.* 156 J11
Melfi, *Chad* 197 J15
Melfi, *It.* 150 M12
Melfort, *Sask., Can.* 82 M12
Melgar de Fernamental, *Sp.* 144 C10
Melide, *Sp.* 144 B6
Meligalás, *Gr.* 154 L9
Melilla, *Sp.* 144 P11
Melinka, *Chile* 133 R6
Melipilla, *Chile* 132 L6
Melita *see* Mljet, *island, Croatia* 152 J7
Melitopol', *Ukr.* 157 R8
Mellansel, *Sw.* 141 H13

Melle, *Fr.* 147 T7
Melle, *Ger.* 148 E6
Mellen, *Wis., U.S.* 98 F4
Mellieha, *Malta* 161 J21
Mellieha Bay, *Malta* 161 J21
Mělník, *Czech Rep.* 148 G11
Melo, *Uru.* 132 K15
Melolo, *Indonesia* 189 N13
Melos *see* Mílos, *island, Gr.* 155 M13
Melrhir, Chott, *Alg.* 196 B12
Melrose, *Minn., U.S.* 104 J10
Melrose, *W. Aust., Austral.* 211 V4
Mels, *Switz.* 150 B5
Meltaus, *Fin.* 141 E14
Melton, *Vic., Austral.* 211 Z12
Meluan, *Malaysia* 188 H10
Melun, *Fr.* 147 Q10
Melvich, *Scot., U.K.* 142 G9
Melville, *Sask., Can.* 82 N12
Melville, Lake, *Nfld. & Lab., Can.* 83 K22
Melville Bay, *N. Amer.* 80 C8
Melville Hills, *N.W.T., Nunavut, Can.* 82 E11
Melville Island, *N. Terr., Austral.* 211 N7
Melville Island, *N.W.T., Nunavut, Can.* 83 D13
Melville Peninsula, *Nunavut, Can.* 83 F16
Melvin, *Tex., U.S.* 103 N8
Melvin, Lough, *Ire., U.K.* 143 Q5
Mé Maoya, *peak, New Caledonia, Fr.* 218 D7
Memba, *Mozambique* 203 E15
Memboro, *Indonesia* 189 N13
Memmingen, *Ger.* 148 K7
Memphis, *Mo., U.S.* 105 Q13
Memphis, *Tenn., U.S.* 100 G11
Memphis, *Tex., U.S.* 102 H7
Mena, *Ark., U.S.* 100 G6
Mena, *Ukr.* 156 M7
Menahga, *Minn., U.S.* 104 G10
Menai Strait, *Wales, U.K.* 143 S9
Ménaka, *Mali* 196 H10
Menard, *Tex., U.S.* 103 P8
Menard Fracture Zone, *Pac. Oc.* 239 Q15
Menasha, *Wis., U.S.* 98 J6
Mende, *Fr.* 147 W11
Mendebo Mountains, *Eth.* 194 H10
Mendeleev Plain, *Arctic Oc.* 242 J7
Mendeleev Ridge, *Arctic Oc.* 242 H6
Mendeleyevsk, *Russ.* 156 H16
Mendelssohn Seamount, *Pac. Oc.* 238 G12
Mendenhall, *Miss., U.S.* 100 M11
Mendi, *P.N.G.* 213 D18
Mendī, *Eth.* 199 F14
Mendip Hills, *Eng., U.K.* 143 W11
Mendocino, *Calif., U.S.* 109 P2
Mendocino, Cape, *Calif., U.S.* 84 E2
Mendocino Fracture Zone, *Pac. Oc.* 238 E12
Mendota, *Calif., U.S.* 109 T6
Mendota, *Ill., U.S.* 99 P5
Mendoza, *Arg.* 132 K8
Menehune Ditch, *Hawai'i, U.S.* 112 B5
Meneng, *region, Nauru* 217 F23
Meneng Point, *Nauru* 217 F23
Menetés, *Gr.* 155 P18
Meng, *river, Aust.* 160 P4
Menge, *island, Marshall Is.* 216 M8
Mengen, *Turk.* 168 D7
Mengene Daği, *Turk.* 169 G18
Menghai, *China* 180 Q10
Mengzi, *China* 180 P11
Meningie, *S. Aust., Austral.* 211 Y10
Menkere, *Russ.* 159 F17
Menno, *S. Dak., U.S.* 104 M7
Menominee, *Mich., U.S.* 98 H7
Menominee, *river, Mich., Wis., U.S.* 98 G7
Menomonee Falls, *Wis., U.S.* 98 L7
Menomonie, *Wis., U.S.* 98 H2
Menongue, *Angola* 202 E7
Menor, Mar, *Sp.* 145 K14
Menorca (Minorca), *Sp.* 145 G20
Men'shikova, Mys, *Russ.* 158 E11
Mentasta Lake, *Alas., U.S.* 111 H18
Mentawai, Kepulauan, *Indonesia* 188 K5
Mentawai Islands, *Indonesia* 166 M10
Menton, *Fr.* 147 X16
Mentor, *Ohio, U.S.* 99 N15
Menyamya, *P.N.G.* 213 D19
Menzies, *W. Aust., Austral.* 211 W4
Menzies, Mount, *Antarctica* 227 F18
Me'ona, *Israel* 170 K6

Meppel, *Neth.* 146 H13
Meppen, *Ger.* 148 D6
Mequinenza, Embalse de, *Sp.* 145 E15
Meramangye, Lake, *Austral.* 210 H8
Meramec, *river, Mo., U.S.* 105 T14
Merampit, *island, Indonesia* 189 G16
Merano, *It.* 150 C7
Merauke, *Indonesia* 189 N21
Merca *see* Marka, *Somalia* 199 J17
Mercan Dağları, *Turk.* 169 F14
Mercara, *India* 179 Q5
Merced, *Calif., U.S.* 109 S5
Mercedario, Cerro, *S. Amer.* 126 L4
Mercedes, *Arg.* 132 H13
Mercedes, *Arg.* 132 L12
Mercedes, *Arg.* 132 L9
Mercedes, *Tex., U.S.* 103 W10
Mercedes, *Uru.* 132 K13
Merceditas, *Chile* 132 H7
Mercherchar (Eil Malk), *island, Palau* 216 P11
Mercy, Cape, *Nunavut, Can.* 83 G19
Mercy Bay, *N.W.T., Can.* 82 D12
Meredith, Cape, *Falkland Is., U.K.* 133 W11
Meredith, Lake, *Tex., U.S.* 102 G5
Mereeg, *Somalia* 199 H17
Merefa, *Ukr.* 157 P9
Mergenevo, *Kaz.* 174 D6
Mergui Archipelago, *Myanmar* 187 N7
Meriç, *river, Turk.* 168 C2
Meriç, *Turk.* 168 C2
Mérida, *Mex.* 115 H16
Mérida, *Sp.* 144 H8
Mérida, *Venez.* 128 C7
Mérida, Cordillera de, *Venez.* 128 C7
Meriden, *Conn., U.S.* 94 M12
Meridian, *Idaho, U.S.* 106 G3
Meridian, *Miss., U.S.* 101 L13
Meridian, *Tex., U.S.* 102 M10
Mérig, *island, Vanuatu* 218 B2
Merimbula, *N.S.W., Austral.* 211 Z14
Merir, *island, Palau* 214 F2
Meritxell, *Andorra* 160 H4
Merizo, *Guam, U.S.* 216 E10
Merkel, *Tex., U.S.* 102 L7
Merkine, *Lith.* 141 P17
Meroe, *ruin, Sudan* 199 D13
Merowe, *Sudan* 199 D13
Merredin, *W. Aust., Austral.* 211 X3
Merrick Mountains, *Antarctica* 226 G7
Merrill, *Oreg., U.S.* 108 L4
Merrill, *Wis., U.S.* 98 H5
Merrillville, *Ind., U.S.* 99 P8
Merrimack, *river, N.H., U.S.* 95 J14
Merriman, *Nebr., U.S.* 104 M3
Merritt Island, *Fla., U.S.* 97 T10
Mer Rouge, *La., U.S.* 100 K9
Merryville, *La., U.S.* 100 N6
Mersa Fat'ma, *Eritrea* 199 E15
Mersch, *Lux.* 160 J10
Merseburg, *Ger.* 148 F9
Mersey River, *Eng., U.K.* 143 S10
Mersin *see* İçel, *Turk.* 168 J9
Mersing, *Malaysia* 187 U11
Merta Road, *India* 178 G4
Mertert, *Lux.* 160 J11
Merthyr Tydfil, *Wales, U.K.* 143 V10
Mértola, *Port.* 144 K6
Mertz Glacier, *Antarctica* 227 Q17
Mertz Glacier Tongue, *Antarctica* 227 R17
Mertzon, *Tex., U.S.* 103 N6
Méru, *Fr.* 147 N10
Meru, *Kenya* 199 K14
Merzifon, *Turk.* 168 D10
Merzig, *Ger.* 148 H5
Merz Seamount, *Antarctic Oc.* 244 B11
Mesa, *Ariz., U.S.* 107 U7
Mesabi Range, *Minn., U.S.* 85 C14
Mesach Mellet, *region, Lib.* 197 E13
Mesa Verde National Park, *Colo., U.S.* 107 Q10
Mescit Tepe, *Turk.* 169 D15
Meseong, *island, F.S.M.* 217 D15
Mese Shima, *Japan* 185 S2
Meskéné *see* Maskanah, *Syr.* 170 E10
Mesocco, *Switz.* 150 C4
Mesopotamia, *region, Iraq* 172 C8
Mesopotamia, *St. Vincent & the Grenadines* 121 K16
Mesquite, *Nev., U.S.* 109 T13

Mesquite, *Tex., U.S.* 102 L12
Messarás, Kólpos, *Gr.* 155 R14
Messene, *ruin, Gr.* 154 L9
Messina, *It.* 151 R12
Messina, *S. Af.* 202 H11
Messina, Stretto di, *It.* 151 R12
Messíni, *Gr.* 154 L9
Messiniakós Kólpos, *Gr.* 154 M9
Messolóngi, *Gr.* 154 H8
Mestá, *Gr.* 155 H16
Mestia, *Rep. of Georgia* 169 A17
Mestre, *It.* 150 D8
Mesudiye, *Turk.* 168 D12
Meta, *river, Venez.* 128 E8
Meta Incognita Peninsula, *Nunavut, Can.* 83 H19
Metairie, *La., U.S.* 100 Q11
Metalanim, *F.S.M.* 217 F14
Metalanim Harbor, *F.S.M.* 217 F14
Metaline Falls, *Wash., U.S.* 108 A9
Metallifere, Colline, *It.* 150 H6
Metán, *Arg.* 132 F9
Metaponto, *It.* 151 N14
Metaxádes, *Gr.* 155 B16
Meteora, *ruin, Gr.* 154 E9
Meteor Crater, *Ariz., U.S.* 107 S8
Meteor Seamount, *Atl. Oc.* 237 V14
Méthana, *Gr.* 154 K12
Methánon, *island, Gr.* 154 K12
Methóni, *Gr.* 154 M9
Metković, *Croatia* 152 H7
Metlakatla, *Alas., U.S.* 111 N24
Metlili Chaamba, *Alg.* 196 B11
Metolius, *Oreg., U.S.* 108 G5
Métoma, *island, Vanuatu* 218 A1
Metropolis, *Ill., U.S.* 99 V6
Metsovo, *Gr.* 154 E8
Metter, *Ga., U.S.* 97 N8
Mettlach, *Ger.* 160 K11
Mettur Dam, *India* 179 Q6
Metz, *Fr.* 147 P14
Meulan, *Fr.* 147 P9
Meuse, *river, Belg., Fr.* 146 M12
Mexia, *Tex., U.S.* 103 N12
Mexiana, Ilha, *Braz.* 131 C13
Mexicali, *Mex.* 114 A5
Mexican Hat, *Utah, U.S.* 107 Q9
Mexico, *Me., U.S.* 95 F15
Mexico, *Mo., U.S.* 105 S13
Mexico, *N. Amer.* 81 N17
Mexico, Gulf of, *N. Amer.* 80 M7
Mexico Basin, *Atl. Oc.* 236 K1
Mexico City, *Mex.* 114 J11
Meyanodas, *Indonesia* 213 D14
Meydan Shahr, *Afghan.* 176 M7
Meymaneh, *Afghan.* 176 L4
Meyrargues, *Fr.* 147 X13
Mezdra, *Bulg.* 153 H13
Mezen', *river, Russ.* 158 F9
Mezen', *Russ.* 158 E9
Mezen' Bay, *Russ.* 138 A11
Mezhdusharskiy, Ostrov, *Russ.* 158 E10
Mézidon-Canon, *Fr.* 147 P7
Mézin, *Fr.* 147 W7
Mezőtúr, *Hung.* 149 M16
Mezzolombardo, *It.* 150 C7
Mġarr, *Malta* 161 H20
Mġarr, *Malta* 161 K21
Miahuatlán, *Mex.* 115 K13
Miajadas, *Sp.* 144 H8
Miami, *Fla., U.S.* 97 X10
Miami, *river, N. Amer.* 80 K7
Miami, *Okla., U.S.* 102 E14
Miami, *Tex., U.S.* 102 G7
Miami Beach, *Fla., U.S.* 97 X10
Miamisburg, *Ohio, U.S.* 99 R11
Mianchi, *China* 182 H4
Miāndoāb, *Iran* 172 B10
Miandrivazo, *Madagascar* 203 G16
Miāneh, *Iran* 172 B11
Miani Hor, *bay, Pak.* 177 V5
Mianrud, *Pak.* 177 T3
Mianwali, *Pak.* 177 P9
Mianyang, *China* 180 L12
Miaodao, *island, China* 182 E9
Miaoli, *Taiwan, China* 183 Q9
Miarinarivo, *Madagascar* 203 G17
Miass, *Russ.* 158 J8
Michalovce, *Slovakia* 149 J17
Miches, *Dom. Rep.* 117 M20
Michigan, *U.S.* 98 F7
Michigan, Lake, *U.S.* 85 F16
Michigan City, *Ind., U.S.* 99 N8
Michurinsk, *Russ.* 156 L11
Micoud, *St. Lucia* 121 L14

Micronesia, *islands, Pac. Oc.* 214 E4
Midai, *island, Indonesia* 188 H8
Mid-Atlantic Ridge, *Atl. Oc.* 236 K7
Middelburg, *Neth.* 146 K11
Middelburg, *S. Af.* 202 L9
Middle Alkali Lake, *Calif., U.S.* 108 M6
Middle America Trench, *Pac. Oc.* 239 H18
Middle Andaman, *island, India* 179 Q14
Middle Bight, *Bahamas* 116 F11
Middlebury, *Vt., U.S.* 94 G12
Middlegate, *Norfolk I., Austral.* 217 F20
Middle Island, *St. Kitts & Nevis* 121 B17
Middle Loup, *river, Nebr., U.S.* 105 P5
Middlemarch, *N.Z.* 213 Q16
Middle Park, *Qnsld., Austral.* 211 S12
Middleport, *Ohio, U.S.* 99 S14
Middle Quarters, *Jam.* 120 J7
Middle River, *Minn., U.S.* 104 E9
Middlesboro, *Ky., U.S.* 101 D19
Middlesbrough, *Eng., U.K.* 143 Q12
Middleton, *Wis., U.S.* 98 L5
Middletown, *Conn., U.S.* 95 M13
Middletown, *N.Y., U.S.* 94 M10
Middletown, *Ohio, U.S.* 99 S11
Midelt, *Mor.* 196 B9
Midi, Canal du, *Fr.* 147 X9
Mid-Indian Basin, *Ind. Oc.* 240 H10
Mid-Indian Ridge, *Ind. Oc.* 240 G8
Midland, *Mich., U.S.* 98 K11
Midland, *S. Dak., U.S.* 104 L4
Midland, *Tex., U.S.* 102 M5
Midlothian, *Tex., U.S.* 102 L11
Mid-Pacific Mountains, *Pac. Oc.* 238 G7
Midu, *island, Maldives* 179 X3
Midway Islands, *U.S.* 112 K2
Midwest, *Wyo., U.S.* 106 H12
Midwest City, *Okla., U.S.* 102 G11
Midyat, *Turk.* 169 H16
Midžor, *peak, Bulg., Serb.* 152 H12
Międzyrzecz, *Pol.* 148 D12
Miélan, *Fr.* 147 X7
Mielec, *Pol.* 149 G16
Miercurea Ciuc, *Rom.* 153 D15
Mieres, *Sp.* 144 B9
Miguel Calmon, *Braz.* 131 H16
Migyaunglaung, *Myanmar* 186 M7
Mihalıççık, *Turk.* 168 E7
Mijas, *Sp.* 144 M9
Mijdaḩah, *Yemen* 172 Q11
Mijek, *W. Sahara, Mor.* 196 E6
Mijikadrek, *island, Marshall Is.* 216 G8
Mikhaylovka, *Russ.* 157 N12
Mikkeli, *Fin.* 141 H16
Míkonos, *island, Gr.* 155 K15
Míkonos, *Gr.* 155 K15
Mikrí Préspa, Límni, *Gr.* 154 C8
Mikun', *Russ.* 158 F8
Mikura Jima, *Japan* 185 R12
Milaca, *Minn., U.S.* 104 H11
Miladummadulu Atoll, *Maldives* 179 T3
Milagro, *Ecua.* 128 K2
Milan *see* Milano, *It.* 150 D4
Milan, *Mo., U.S.* 105 R12
Milan, *Tenn., U.S.* 101 F13
Milano (Milan), *It.* 150 D4
Milas, *Turk.* 168 H3
Milazzo, Capo di, *It.* 151 R12
Milbank, *S. Dak., U.S.* 104 J8
Milbridge, *Me., U.S.* 95 F18
Mildenhall, *Eng., U.K.* 143 T14
Mildura, *Vic., Austral.* 211 X11
Mile, *China* 180 P11
Mile and a Quarter, *Barbados* 121 J18
Mile Gully, *Jam.* 120 J8
Mil Entrance, *F.S.M.* 217 C18
Miles, *Qnsld., Austral.* 211 V14
Miles, *Tex., U.S.* 103 N7
Miles City, *Mont., U.S.* 106 D12
Mileto, *It.* 151 R13
Miletto, Monte, *It.* 150 L11
Miletus, *ruin, Turk.* 168 G3
Mileura, *W. Aust., Austral.* 211 V3
Milford, *Del., U.S.* 96 C15
Milford, *Iowa, U.S.* 104 M10
Milford, *Mass., U.S.* 95 K14
Milford, *Nebr., U.S.* 105 Q8
Milford, *Utah, U.S.* 107 N6
Milford Bay, *Trinidad & Tobago* 121 N17
Milford Haven (Aberdaugleddau), *Wales, U.K.* 143 V8
Milford Lake, *Kans., U.S.* 105 S8
Milford Sound, *N.Z.* 213 Q15
Milgarra, *Qnsld., Austral.* 211 R11
Milgun, *W. Aust., Austral.* 211 U3

Mili Atoll, *Marshall Is.* 216 H5
Miliés, *Gr.* 154 F11
Milikapiti, *N. Terr., Austral.* 211 N7
Mililani Town, *Hawai‘i, U.S.* 112 E11
Milingimbi, *N. Terr., Austral.* 211 P9
Milk, river, *Mont., U.S.* 106 B11
Milk, Wadi el, *Sudan* 198 D12
Mil'kovo, *Russ.* 159 F22
Milk River Bath, *Jam.* 120 K8
Millars Sound, *Bahamas* 120 B11
Millau, *Fr.* 147 W11
Mill City, *Oreg., U.S.* 108 G4
Milledgeville, *Ga., U.S.* 96 M6
Mille Lacs Lake, *Minn., U.S.* 104 H11
Millen, *Ga., U.S.* 96 M8
Millennium Island *see* Caroline Island, *Kiribati* 215 H13
Miller, *S. Dak., U.S.* 104 K6
Millerovo, *Russ.* 157 P11
Miller Peak, *Ariz., U.S.* 107 W8
Miller Point, *Solomon Is.* 217 R24
Millersburg, *Ohio, U.S.* 99 Q14
Millers Creek, *S. Aust., Austral.* 211 W9
Millevaches, Plateau de, *Fr.* 147 U9
Milligan Cay, *St. Vincent & the Grenadines* 121 L16
Millington, *Tenn., U.S.* 100 F11
Millinocket, *Me., U.S.* 95 D17
Mill Island, *Antarctica* 227 K21
Mill Island, *Nunavut, Can.* 83 H17
Millmerran, *Qnsld., Austral.* 211 V15
Mill Reef, *Antigua & Barbuda* 121 B21
Milltown, *Mont., U.S.* 106 D6
Milltown Malbay, *Ire.* 143 T3
Millungera, *Qnsld., Austral.* 211 S11
Millville, *N.J., U.S.* 94 Q10
Milly, *Fr.* 147 Q10
Milly Milly, *W. Aust., Austral.* 211 V2
Milnor, *N. Dak., U.S.* 104 H7
Milo, river, *Guinea* 200 F7
Milo, *Me., U.S.* 95 E17
Miloli‘i, *Hawai‘i, U.S.* 113 P18
Milord Point, *Virgin Islands, U.S.* 120 R3
Mílos, *Gr.* 155 M13
Mílos (Melos), *Gr.* 155 M13
Milpa, *N.S.W., Austral.* 211 W11
Milparinka, *N.S.W., Austral.* 211 W11
Milton, *Fla., U.S.* 97 Q2
Milton, *Pa., U.S.* 94 M7
Milton-Freewater, *Oreg., U.S.* 108 E8
Milton Keynes, *Eng., U.K.* 143 U13
Miltonvale, *Kans., U.S.* 105 S7
Milu, island, *Marshall Is.* 216 K4
Milu Pass, *Marshall Is.* 216 K4
Milwaukee, *Wis., U.S.* 98 L7
Mimizan-Plage, *Fr.* 147 W6
Mimot, *Cambodia* 187 N12
Mims, *Fla., U.S.* 97 T9
Min, river, *China* 183 P8
Min, river, *China* 180 K11
Mina, *Nev., U.S.* 109 R8
Mina Bazar, *Pak.* 177 Q8
Minahasa, region, *Indonesia* 189 H15
Minamata, *Japan* 185 S4
Minami Iwo To, *Japan* 184 L5
Minamitane, *Japan* 185 U4
Minami Tori Shima (Marcus Island), *Japan* 184 L8
Minas, *Cuba* 116 J11
Minas, *Uru.* 132 L14
Minatitlán, *Mex.* 115 K14
Minbu, *Myanmar* 186 H5
Minco, *Okla., U.S.* 102 G10
Mindanao, island, *Philippines* 189 F15
Mindelo, *Cape Verde* 205 B15
Minden, *Ger.* 148 D7
Minden, *La., U.S.* 100 K7
Minden, *Nebr., U.S.* 105 Q6
Minden, *Nev., U.S.* 109 Q6
Mindon, *Myanmar* 186 J5
Mindoro, island, *Philippines* 189 D13
Mindoro Strait, *Philippines* 189 D13
Mindouli, *Congo* 201 M17
Mine, *Japan* 185 Q3
Mineloa, *Tex., U.S.* 102 L13
Mineral'nyye Vody, *Russ.* 157 T13
Mineral Point, *Wis., U.S.* 98 L4
Mineral Wells, *Tex., U.S.* 102 L10
Minersville, *Utah, U.S.* 107 N6
Mineyama, *Japan* 185 P8
Minfeng (Niya), *China* 180 H6
Mingäçevir, *Azerb.* 169 D21
Mingäçevir Reservoir, *Azerb.* 169 D20
Mingan, *Que., Can.* 83 M21
Mingaora, *Pak.* 176 M10

Mingenew, *W. Aust., Austral.* 211 W2
Mingin, *Myanmar* 186 G5
Minglanilla, *Sp.* 145 H13
Mingo Cay, *Virgin Islands, U.S.* 120 M10
Mingteke, *China* 180 G3
Mingteke Pass, *China, Pak.* 178 A5
Mingulay, *Scot., U.K.* 142 K5
Minho, river, *Jam.* 120 J8
Minho, river, *Port.* 144 D5
Minicoy Island, *India* 179 S3
Minidoka, *Idaho, U.S.* 106 H6
Minidoka Internment National Monument, *Idaho, U.S.* 106 H6
Minigwal, Lake, *Austral.* 210 J5
Minilya, *W. Aust., Austral.* 211 U1
Minimarg, *Pak.* 176 M12
Minjilang, *N. Terr., Austral.* 211 N8
Minna, *Nigeria* 201 F13
Minneapolis, *Kans., U.S.* 105 S7
Minneapolis, *Minn., U.S.* 104 K11
Minnedosa, *Man., Can.* 83 N13
Minneola, *Kans., U.S.* 105 U5
Minneota, *Minn., U.S.* 104 K9
Minnesota, river, *Minn., U.S.* 104 K10
Minnesota, *U.S.* 104 H8
Minnewaukan, *N. Dak., U.S.* 104 E6
Miño, river, *Sp.* 144 C6
Minocqua, *Wis., U.S.* 98 G5
Minonk, *Ill., U.S.* 99 P6
Minorca *see* Menorca, island, *Sp.* 145 G20
Minot, *N. Dak., U.S.* 104 E4
Minqing, *China* 183 P8
Minsk, *Belarus* 156 K5
Minsk Mazowiecki, *Pol.* 149 E16
Minto, *N. Dak., U.S.* 104 E7
Minto, Lac, *Que., Can.* 83 K18
Minto, Mount, *Antarctica* 227 R14
Minto Inlet, *N.W.T., Can.* 82 E12
Minturno, *It.* 150 L10
Minwakh, *Yemen* 172 P11
Minxian, *China* 180 J11
Mio, *Mich., U.S.* 98 J11
Mir, *Belarus* 156 L4
Mira, *It.* 150 E8
Mira, *Port.* 144 F5
Mirabad, *Afghan.* 177 R2
Mirador, *Braz.* 131 F15
Miraflores, *Col.* 128 H7
Miragoâne, *Haiti* 117 M16
Miramar, *Arg.* 133 N13
Mirambeau, *Fr.* 147 U7
Mirambélou, Kólpos, *Gr.* 155 Q16
Miram Shah, *Pak.* 177 P8
Miran, *China* 180 G7
Miranda, river, *Braz.* 130 L10
Miranda, *Braz.* 130 L10
Miranda de Ebro, *Sp.* 144 C12
Miranda do Douro, *Port.* 144 D8
Mirandela, *Port.* 144 D7
Mirando City, *Tex., U.S.* 103 U9
Mirandola, *It.* 150 E6
Mirano, *It.* 150 D8
Mira Por Vos, island, *Bahamas* 117 H14
Mir Bacheh Kowt, *Afghan.* 176 M8
Mirbashir, *Azerb.* 169 D20
Mirbāţ, *Oman* 173 P15
Mirbāţ, Ra's, *Oman* 173 P15
Mirebalais, *Haiti* 117 M17
Mirebeau, *Fr.* 147 S7
Mirecourt, *Fr.* 147 Q14
Mirepoix, *Fr.* 147 Y9
Miri, *Malaysia* 188 G11
Miriam Vale, *Qnsld., Austral.* 211 U15
Mirik *see* Timiris, Cap, cape, *Mauritania* 196 F4
Mirim, Lagoa, *Uru.* 132 K15
Mírina, *Gr.* 155 E14
Mírtos, *Gr.* 155 R15
Mirnyy, station, *Antarctica* 227 J21
Mirnyy, *Russ.* 159 H16
Mirpur, *Pak.* 177 N11
Mirpur Khas, *Pak.* 177 V8
Mirpur Sakro, *Pak.* 177 W6
Mírtos, *Gr.* 155 R15
Mirzapur, *India* 178 H8
Misaki, *Japan* 185 R6
Misawa, *Japan* 184 J13
Misgar, *Pak.* 176 K12
Mish'āb, Ra's al, *Saudi Arabia* 172 G11
Mishawaka, *Ind., U.S.* 99 N9
Mi Shima, *Japan* 185 Q5
Misima, island, *P.N.G.* 213 E21
Miskitos, Cayos, *Nicar.* 115 L19

Miskitos, Costa de, *Nicar.* 115 M19
Miskolc, *Hung.* 149 K16
Misool, island, *Indonesia* 189 K17
Misquah Hills, *Minn., U.S.* 104 E14
Mişrātah, *Lib.* 197 C14
Mission, *S. Dak., U.S.* 104 M4
Mission, *Tex., U.S.* 103 W10
Mississippi, river, *U.S.* 85 K15
Mississippi, *U.S.* 100 M11
Mississippi Fan, *Atl. Oc.* 236 K2
Mississippi River, Source of the, *Minn., U.S.* 104 G9
Mississippi River Delta, *La., U.S.* 101 R13
Mississippi Sound, *Miss., U.S.* 100 P12
Mississippi State, *Miss., U.S.* 101 J13
Missoula, *Mont., U.S.* 106 D6
Missouri, river, *U.S.* 85 H14
Missouri, *U.S.* 105 T11
Missouri Valley, *Iowa, U.S.* 105 P9
Mistassini, *Que., Can.* 83 N19
Mistassini, Lac, *Que., Can.* 83 N19
Misterbianco, *It.* 151 S12
Misty Fiords National Monument, *Alas., U.S.* 111 M24
Misumi, *Japan* 185 Q5
Misurata, Cape, *Lib.* 194 D6
Mitai, *Japan* 185 S5
Mitchell, *Ind., U.S.* 99 T9
Mitchell, *Nebr., U.S.* 105 N1
Mitchell, *Oreg., U.S.* 108 G6
Mitchell, river, *Qnsld., Austral.* 211 Q12
Mitchell, *Qnsld., Austral.* 211 V14
Mitchell, *S. Dak., U.S.* 104 L7
Mitchell, Mount, *N.C., U.S.* 96 H7
Mitchell Lake, *Ala., U.S.* 101 K15
Mitchelstown, *Ire.* 143 U4
Mithankot, *Pak.* 177 S9
Mithi, *Pak.* 177 W8
Míthimna, *Gr.* 155 F16
Mitiaro, island, *Cook Is., N.Z.* 214 K12
Mítikas, *Gr.* 154 G8
Mitilíni (Mytilene), *Gr.* 155 F16
Mitilíni (Mytilene), *Gr.* 155 G17
Mitla, *Mex.* 115 K13
Mitla Pass, *Egypt* 171 Q2
Mito, *Japan* 185 N13
Mitre, peak, *N.Z.* 213 M19
Mitre Island *see* Fataka, *Solomon Is.* 214 J8
Mitrovica, *Kos.* 152 H10
Mitsamiouli, *Comoros* 205 L14
Mitsero, *Cyprus* 160 P8
Mitsio, Nosy, *Madagascar* 203 D18
Mits'iwa (Massawa), *Eritrea* 199 D15
Mitsoudjé, *Comoros* 205 M14
Mitsushima, *Japan* 185 Q3
Mittelland Canal, *Ger.* 138 F6
Mitú, *Col.* 128 H8
Mitumba Mountains, *Dem. Rep. of the Congo* 198 M11
Mitwaba, *Dem. Rep. of the Congo* 198 M11
Mityushikha, Guba, *Russ.* 158 D11
Mitzic, *Gabon* 201 K16
Miura, *Japan* 185 Q12
Mixian, *China* 182 H5
Miyake Jima, *Japan* 185 R12
Miyako, *Japan* 184 K14
Miyakonojō, *Japan* 185 T5
Miyazaki, *Japan* 185 T5
Miyazu, *Japan* 185 P8
Miyoshi, *Japan* 185 Q6
Miyun, *China* 182 C7
Mizdah, *Lib.* 197 C13
Mizen Head, *Ire.* 143 V2
Mizhi, *China* 182 E3
Mizil, *Rom.* 153 E16
Mizo Hills, *India* 178 H14
Mizusawa, *Japan* 184 K13
Mjøsa, lake, *Nor.* 140 K11
Mladá Boleslav, *Czech Rep.* 148 G11
Mladenovac, *Serb.* 152 F10
Mława, *Pol.* 149 C15
Mlima Bénara, peak, *Mayotte, Fr.* 205 P17
Mljet (Melita), island, *Croatia* 152 J7
Mljetski Kanal, *Croatia* 152 H7
Mmabatho, *S. Af.* 202 J10
Moa, *Cuba* 117 K14
Moa, river, *Guinea, Sierra Leone* 200 G6
Moa, island, *Indonesia* 189 M16
Moab, *Utah, U.S.* 107 N9
Moaco, river, *Braz.* 130 F6
Moala, island, *Fiji Is.* 218 J8

Moananui, island, *Cook Is., N.Z.* 219 B17
Moanda, *Gabon* 201 L16
Moapa, *Nev., U.S.* 109 T12
Moa‘ula Nui, Pu‘u ‘O, *Hawai‘i, U.S.* 113 H16
Mobayi-Mbongo, *Dem. Rep. of the Congo* 198 H9
Mobeetie, *Tex., U.S.* 102 G7
Moberly, *Mo., U.S.* 105 S13
Mobile, river, *Ala., U.S.* 101 N14
Mobile, *Ala., U.S.* 101 P13
Mobile Bay, *Ala., U.S.* 101 P14
Mobile Point, *Ala., U.S.* 101 P14
Mobridge, *S. Dak., U.S.* 104 J5
Moca, *Dom. Rep.* 117 L18
Moca, *P.R., U.S.* 120 M1
Mocajuba, *Braz.* 131 D13
Moçambique, *Mozambique* 203 E15
Moce, island, *Fiji* 218 J9
Moch, island, *F.S.M.* 217 B15
Mocha, Isla, *Chile* 133 N5
Mochenap, bay, *F.S.M.* 217 B16
Mochon Point, *N. Mariana Is., U.S.* 216 D8
Mochudi, *Botswana* 202 J10
Mocímboa da Praia, *Mozambique* 203 D15
Mocksville, *N.C., U.S.* 96 H9
Moclips, *Wash., U.S.* 108 C2
Mocoa, *Col.* 128 H4
Moctezuma, *Mex.* 114 C7
Mocuba, *Mozambique* 203 F14
Modane, *Fr.* 147 V15
Model, *Colo., U.S.* 107 P14
Modena, *It.* 150 F6
Modesto, *Calif., U.S.* 109 S5
Modica, *It.* 151 U11
Modugno, *It.* 150 M14
Moe, *Vic., Austral.* 211 Z12
Moen *see* Weno, island, *F.S.M.* 217 B15
Moengo, *Suriname* 129 E17
Moerai, *Fr. Polynesia, Fr.* 219 K23
Moerai, Baie de, *Fr. Polynesia, Fr.* 219 K23
Mogadishu *see* Muqdisho, *Somalia* 199 J17
Mogadouro, *Port.* 144 E7
Mogalo, *Dem. Rep. of the Congo* 198 J9
Mogán, *Canary Is.* 204 R5
Mogaung, *Myanmar* 186 E7
Mogi das Cruzes, *Braz.* 131 M14
Mogincual, *Mozambique* 203 E15
Mogocha, *Russ.* 159 K17
Mogoi, *Indonesia* 189 K18
Mogok, *Myanmar* 186 G6
Mogollon Rim, *Ariz., U.S.* 107 T8
Mogotes, Punta, *Arg.* 133 N13
Mohács, *Hung.* 149 N15
Mohala, *India* 178 K7
Mohall, *N. Dak., U.S.* 104 E4
Mohammad Agha, *Afghan.* 176 M8
Mohana, *India* 178 L9
Mohave, Lake, *Ariz., Nev., U.S.* 109 V12
Mohave, *Calif., U.S.* 109 W8
Mohawk, river, *N.Y., U.S.* 94 J10
Mohe, *China* 181 D17
Mohéli, island, *Comoros* 205 N15
Mohelnice, *Czech Rep.* 149 H13
Mohenjo Daro, ruin, *Pak.* 177 U7
Mohill, *Ire.* 143 R5
Mohns Ridge, *Arctic Oc.* 243 G17
Mohnyin, *Myanmar* 186 E6
Mohon Peak, *Ariz., U.S.* 107 S5
Mohotani (Motane), island, *Fr. Polynesia, Fr.* 219 N21
Mohyliv-Podil's'kyy, *Ukr.* 157 Q4
Moindou, *New Caledonia, Fr.* 218 D7
Moineşti, *Rom.* 153 C16
Mo i Rana, *Nor.* 140 F12
Moirang, *India* 178 H14
Moirans, *Fr.* 147 U13
Moisie, river, *Que., Can.* 83 M20
Moissac, *Fr.* 147 W8
Moïssala, *Chad* 197 K15
Moita, *Port.* 144 J5
Mojácar, *Sp.* 145 L13
Mojados, *Sp.* 144 E10
Mojave, river, *Calif., U.S.* 109 W10
Mojave, *Calif., U.S.* 109 W8
Mojave Desert, *Calif., Nev., U.S.* 109 V10
Mojave National Preserve, *Calif., U.S.* 109 V11

Mojokerto, *Indonesia* 188 M10
Mokdale, *Indonesia* 189 N14
Mokil Atoll, *F.S.M.* 216 Q8
Mokokchung, *India* 178 G15
Mokpo, *S. Korea* 182 G13
Mol, *Belg.* 146 K13
Mola di Bari, *It.* 150 M14
Moláoi, *Gr.* 154 M11
Molat, island, *Croatia* 152 F4
Moldavia, region, *Rom.* 153 B16
Molde, *Nor.* 140 J10
Moldova, *Eur.* 139 V10
Moldova, river, *Rom.* 153 B15
Moldova Nouă, *Rom.* 152 F11
Moldovearu, peak, *Rom.* 153 E14
Molepolole, *Botswana* 202 J10
Môle St.-Nicolas, *Haiti* 117 L15
Molesworth, *N.Z.* 213 N18
Mōlīlele, Heiau o, *Hawai‘i, U.S.* 113 Q19
Molina, *Chile* 132 L7
Molina de Aragón, *Sp.* 145 F13
Molina de Segura, *Sp.* 145 K14
Moline, *Ill., U.S.* 99 P4
Moline, *Kans., U.S.* 105 U9
Molinière Point, *Grenada* 121 K22
Molino, river, *San Marino* 161 J16
Moliterno, *It.* 151 N13
Mollendo, *Peru* 130 K5
Mollerussa, *Sp.* 145 D16
Molloy Hole, *Arctic Oc.* 243 H15
Moloa‘a Bay, *Hawai‘i, U.S.* 112 B6
Moloka‘i, island, *Hawai‘i, U.S.* 113 F14
Molokai Fracture Zone, *Pac. Oc.* 239 G14
Molopo, river, *Botswana, S. Af.* 202 J9
Moloundou, *Cameroon* 201 K17
Molsheim, *Fr.* 147 P15
Molson, *Wash., U.S.* 108 A7
Moltke, Cape, *P.N.G.* 217 K13
Molu, island, *Indonesia* 189 M17
Moluccas (Maluku), islands, *Indonesia* 189 H16
Molucca Sea, *Indonesia* 189 J15
Moma, *Mozambique* 203 F14
Moma, river, *Russ.* 159 E19
Mombasa, *Kenya* 199 L15
Mombetsu, *Japan* 184 E14
Mombetsu, *Japan* 184 G14
Momence, *Ill., U.S.* 99 P7
Momi, *Fiji Is.* 218 J5
Momote, *P.N.G.* 213 B20
Mompach, *Lux.* 160 J11
Mompós, *Col.* 128 C5
Møn, island, *Den.* 140 P12
Mona, Isla, *P.R., U.S.* 117 N21
Monach Islands, *Scot., U.K.* 142 J6
Monaco, *Eur.* 160 D3
Monaco, Port of, *Monaco* 161 D21
Monaco Railroad Station, *Monaco* 161 E20
Monaco-Ville, *Monaco* 161 F21
Monadhliath Mountains, *Scot., U.K.* 142 K9
Monaghan, *Ire.* 143 Q6
Monahans, *Tex., U.S.* 103 N3
Mona Passage, *Dom. Rep., P.R., U.S.* 117 M21
Monarch Pass, *Colo., U.S.* 107 N12
Mona Reservoir, *Utah, U.S.* 106 M7
Monari, *Afghan.* 177 P7
Moncada, *Sp.* 145 H14
Moncalieri, *It.* 150 E2
Monchegorsk, *Russ.* 158 D8
Mönchengladbach, *Ger.* 148 F5
Monchique, Serra de, *Port.* 144 L5
Moncks Corner, *S.C., U.S.* 96 L10
Monclava, *Mex.* 115 J15
Monclova, *Mex.* 114 E11
Moncton, *N.B., Can.* 83 P21
Mondego, river, *Port.* 144 F5
Mondego, Cabo, *Port.* 144 F5
Mondeodo, *Indonesia* 189 K14
Mondolfo, *It.* 150 G9
Mondoñedo, *Sp.* 144 A7
Mondorf, *Lux.* 160 K10
Mondovi, *It.* 150 F3
Mondovi, *Wis., U.S.* 98 J3
Mondragone, *It.* 150 M10
Mondy, *Russ.* 159 L15
Moneague, *Jam.* 120 H9
Monemvassía, *Gr.* 154 M11
Monessen, *Pa., U.S.* 94 P3
Monestier-de-Clermont, *Fr.* 147 V14
Monett, *Mo., U.S.* 105 V11
Monfalcone, *It.* 150 D9

Monforte, *Port.* 144 H6
Monforte de Lemos, *Sp.* 144 C7
Mongalla, *Sudan* 199 H13
Mongbwalu, *Dem. Rep. of the Congo* 198 J12
Mong Cai, *Vietnam* 186 G13
Mongers Lake, *Austral.* 210 J3
Möng Hsu, *Myanmar* 186 G7
Möng Küng, *Myanmar* 186 G7
Mongmong, *Guam, U.S.* 216 C11
Möng Nawng, *Myanmar* 186 G7
Mongo, *Chad* 197 J15
Mongolia, *Asia* 167 T10
Mongolian Plateau, *China, Mongolia* 166 F11
Mongororo, *Chad* 197 J16
Mongoy, *Russ.* 159 K17
Möng Pan, *Myanmar* 186 H7
Mongton, *Myanmar* 186 H8
Mongu, *Zambia* 202 E9
Moni, *Cyprus* 160 Q8
Monier, Mount, *St. Lucia* 121 J14
Monistrol-sur-Loire, *Fr.* 147 V12
Monito, island, *P.R., U.S.* 117 M21
Monitor Range, *Nev., U.S.* 109 Q10
Monkey Point see Mono Point, *N. Amer.* 80 Q8
Monkira, *Qnsld., Austral.* 211 U11
Monmouth, *Ill., U.S.* 99 P4
Monmouth, *Oreg., U.S.* 108 G3
Mono, island, *Solomon Is.* 217 L14
Mono, Punta, *Nicar.* 115 M19
Mono Lake, *Calif., U.S.* 109 R7
Monólithos, *Gr.* 155 N19
Monomoy Island, *Mass., U.S.* 95 L16
Monon, *Ind., U.S.* 99 Q8
Monona, *Iowa, U.S.* 104 M13
Monongahela, river, *Pa., W. Va., U.S.* 94 P3
Mono Point (Monkey Point), *N. Amer.* 80 Q8
Monopoli, *It.* 150 M14
Monreal del Campo, *Sp.* 145 F13
Mon Repos, *St. Lucia* 121 K14
Monroe, *Ga., U.S.* 96 L6
Monroe, *La., U.S.* 100 L8
Monroe, *Mich., U.S.* 99 N12
Monroe, *N.C., U.S.* 96 J9
Monroe, *Wash., U.S.* 108 B4
Monroe, *Wis., U.S.* 98 M5
Monroe City, *Mo., U.S.* 105 R13
Monroe Lake, *Ind., U.S.* 99 S9
Monroeville, *Ala., U.S.* 101 M14
Monrovia, *Liberia* 200 H6
Monschau, *Ger.* 148 G4
Mönsterås, *Sw.* 141 M13
Montagne, *Neth. Antilles, Neth.* 121 Q19
Montague, *Calif., U.S.* 108 L3
Montague Island, *Alas., U.S.* 111 K17
Montalbán, *Sp.* 145 F14
Montalegre, *Port.* 144 D6
Montalto di Castro, *It.* 150 K7
Montana, *Bulg.* 153 H13
Montana, *U.S.* 106 D7
Montanja, *Neth. Antilles, Neth.* 121 Q15
Montargil, Barragem de, *Port.* 144 H5
Montargis, *Fr.* 147 Q10
Montastruc-la-Conseillère, *Fr.* 147 X9
Montauban, *Fr.* 147 X9
Montauk Point, *N.Y., U.S.* 95 M14
Montbard, *Fr.* 147 R12
Montbéliard, *Fr.* 147 R15
Mont Belvieu, *Tex., U.S.* 103 Q14
Montblanc, *Sp.* 145 E16
Montbrison, *Fr.* 147 U12
Montceau-les-Mines, *Fr.* 147 S12
Montchanin, *Fr.* 147 S12
Mont-de-Marsan, *Fr.* 147 X7
Montdidier, *Fr.* 147 N10
Mont-Dore, *New Caledonia, Fr.* 218 E8
Monte, river, *Parag.* 130 M10
Monteagle, Mount, *Antarctica* 227 Q14
Montebelluna, *It.* 150 D8
Monte Carlo, *Monaco* 161 C21
Monte Carlo Beach Hotel, *Fr.* 161 A24
Monte Carlo Country Club, *Fr.* 161 A23
Monte Carlo Radio and Television Station, *Monaco* 161 D21
Monte-Carlo Sporting Club d'Eté, *Monaco* 161 B23
Monte Caseros, *Arg.* 132 J13
Montech, *Fr.* 147 X8
Montecito, *Calif., U.S.* 109 W7
Monte Comán, *Arg.* 132 L8
Monte Cristi, *Dom. Rep.* 117 L17

Montecristo, Isola di, *It.* 150 K5
Monte Dinero, *Arg.* 133 W9
Montefiascone, *It.* 150 J8
Monte Giardino, *San Marino* 161 K16
Montego Bay, *Jam.* 120 H6
Montego Bay, *Jam.* 120 H7
Montehermoso, *Sp.* 144 G8
Montejunto, Serra de, *Port.* 144 H4
Montelicciano, *It.* 161 L16
Montélimar, *Fr.* 147 W13
Montello, *Nev., U.S.* 108 M12
Montemaggio, *It.* 161 L14
Montemarciano, *It.* 150 G9
Montemayor, Meseta de, *Arg.* 133 R9
Montemorelos, *Mex.* 114 F11
Montemor-o-Novo, *Port.* 144 J5
Montemuro, peak, *Port.* 144 E6
Montendre, *Fr.* 147 V7
Montenegro, *Eur.* 139 W8
Montepescali, *It.* 150 J6
Monte Plata, *Dom. Rep.* 117 M19
Montepuez, *Mozambique* 203 D14
Monte Quemado, *Arg.* 132 F11
Montereau, *Fr.* 147 Q10
Monterey, *Calif., U.S.* 109 T4
Monterey, *Tenn., U.S.* 101 E17
Monterey Bay, *Calif., U.S.* 109 T4
Montería, *Col.* 128 C4
Monterotondo, *It.* 150 K8
Monterrey, *Mex.* 114 F11
Montesano, *Wash., U.S.* 108 D3
Monte San Savino, *It.* 150 H7
Monte Santu, Capo di, *It.* 151 N5
Montes Claros, *Braz.* 131 J15
Montescudo, *It.* 161 K18
Montese, *It.* 150 F6
Montevallo, *Ala., U.S.* 101 K15
Montevarchi, *It.* 150 H7
Montevideo, *Minn., U.S.* 104 K9
Montevideo, *Uru.* 132 L14
Monte Vista, *Colo., U.S.* 107 P12
Montezuma, *Ga., U.S.* 97 N5
Montezuma, *Iowa, U.S.* 105 P12
Montezuma, *Kans., U.S.* 105 U4
Montezuma Castle National Monument, *Ariz., U.S.* 107 S7
Montezuma Creek, *Utah, U.S.* 107 P9
Montfaucon, *Fr.* 147 V12
Montgenèvre, *Fr.* 147 V15
Montgomery, *Ala., U.S.* 101 L16
Montgomery, *W. Va., U.S.* 96 E8
Montgomery City, *Mo., U.S.* 105 S14
Monthey, *Switz.* 150 C2
Monti, *It.* 150 M4
Monticello, *Ark., U.S.* 100 J9
Monticello, *Fla., U.S.* 97 Q5
Monticello, *Ga., U.S.* 96 L6
Monticello, *Ill., U.S.* 99 R6
Monticello, *Ind., U.S.* 99 Q8
Monticello, *Iowa, U.S.* 105 N14
Monticello, *Ky., U.S.* 101 D17
Monticello, *Me., U.S.* 95 C18
Monticello, *Minn., U.S.* 104 J11
Monticello, *Miss., U.S.* 100 M12
Monticello, *N.Y., U.S.* 94 L10
Monticello, *Utah, U.S.* 107 P9
Montichiari, *It.* 150 E6
Montijo, *Port.* 144 J5
Montijo, *Sp.* 144 H7
Montilla, *Sp.* 144 L10
Montivilliers, *Fr.* 147 N7
Mont-Joli, *Que., Can.* 83 N20
Mont-Louis, *Fr.* 147 Z10
Montmarault, *Fr.* 147 T10
Montmédy, *Fr.* 160 K7
Montmirail, *Fr.* 147 P11
Monto, *Qnsld., Austral.* 211 U15
Montoro, *Sp.* 144 K10
Montoursville, *Pa., U.S.* 94 M7
Montpelier, *Idaho, U.S.* 106 J8
Montpelier, *Jam.* 120 H7
Montpelier, *Ohio, U.S.* 99 N11
Montpelier, *Vt., U.S.* 95 G13
Montpellier, *Fr.* 147 X12
Montpon-Ménestérol, *Fr.* 147 V7
Montréal, *Fr.* 147 Y10
Montréal, *Que., Can.* 83 P19
Montreal, *Wis., U.S.* 98 F4
Montreuil-Bellay, *Fr.* 147 S7
Montreux, *Switz.* 150 C2
Montrevault, *Fr.* 147 R6
Montrichard, *Fr.* 147 R8
Montrose, *Colo., U.S.* 107 N11
Montrose, *Scot., U.K.* 142 L11

Montsalvy, *Fr.* 147 V10
Montsec, Serra del, *Sp.* 145 D16
Montserrat, island, *U.K., Lesser Antilles* 119 G16
Montserrat, Monestir de, *Sp.* 145 D17
Monturull, Pic, *Andorra, Sp.* 160 K3
Monuafe, island, *Tonga* 218 H11
Monument, *Oreg., U.S.* 108 G7
Monument (Étarik), island, *Vanuatu* 218 E3
Monumental Buttes, *Idaho, U.S.* 106 C4
Monument Valley, *Ariz., Utah, U.S.* 107 Q9
Monveda, *Dem. Rep. of the Congo* 198 J9
Monywa, *Myanmar* 186 G5
Monza, *It.* 150 D4
Monze, *Zambia* 202 F10
Monzón, *Sp.* 145 D15
Moody, *Tex., U.S.* 103 N11
Mo'okini Heiau, *Hawai'i, U.S.* 113 J18
Moolawatana, *S. Aust., Austral.* 211 W11
Mooloogool, *W. Aust., Austral.* 211 U3
Moonless Mountains, *Pac. Oc.* 239 F14
Moora, *W. Aust., Austral.* 211 W2
Mooraberree, *Qnsld., Austral.* 211 U11
Moorcroft, *Wyo., U.S.* 106 G13
Moore, *Okla., U.S.* 102 G11
Moore, *Tex., U.S.* 103 S9
Moore, Lake, *Austral.* 210 J3
Moorea, island, *Fr. Polynesia, Fr.* 219 N14
Moorefield, *W. Va., U.S.* 96 C11
Moore Haven, *Fla., U.S.* 97 V9
Mooreland, *Okla., U.S.* 102 E8
Moore's Island, *Bahamas* 120 B5
Moore Town, *Jam.* 120 J11
Moorhead, *Minn., U.S.* 104 G8
Moorhead, *Miss., U.S.* 100 J10
Moorish Castle, *Gibraltar, U.K.* 161 N23
Moosehead Lake, *Me., U.S.* 95 D16
Moose Jaw, *Sask., Can.* 82 N12
Moose Lake, *Minn., U.S.* 104 H12
Mooselookmeguntic Lake, *Me., U.S.* 95 F15
Moosonee, *Ont., Can.* 83 N17
Mootwingee, *N.S.W., Austral.* 211 W11
Mopelia see Maupihaa, island, *Fr. Polynesia, Fr.* 219 E14
Mopti, *Mali* 196 H8
Moqor, *Afghan.* 177 P6
Moquegua, *Peru* 130 K5
Mor, Glen, *Scot., U.K.* 142 K8
Mora, *Minn., U.S.* 104 H11
Mora, *N. Mex., U.S.* 107 R13
Mora, *Sw.* 140 K12
Morača, river, *Mont.* 152 J9
Moradabad, *India* 178 F6
Móra d'Ebre, *Sp.* 145 E16
Mora de Rubielos, *Sp.* 145 F14
Moraleja, *Sp.* 144 G7
Moraleja del Vino, *Sp.* 144 E9
Moran, *Tex., U.S.* 102 L8
Moran, *Wyo., U.S.* 106 G8
Morane, island, *Fr. Polynesia, Fr.* 219 H22
Morant Bay, *Jam.* 120 J11
Morant Cays, *Jam.* 116 N13
Morant Point, *Jam.* 120 J12
Morar, Loch, *Scot., U.K.* 142 K7
Morava, river, *Czech Rep.* 149 H13
Moravia, region, *Czech Rep.* 149 H13
Morawhanna, *Guyana* 129 C14
Moray Firth, *Scot., U.K.* 142 J9
Morbi, *India* 178 J2
Morbihan, Golfe du, *Fr.* 147 R4
Mörbylånga, *Sw.* 141 N14
Morcenx, *Fr.* 147 W6
Mor Daği, *Turk.* 169 G18
Mordovo, *Russ.* 156 M11
Mordyyakha, *Russ.* 158 F11
Moreau, river, *S. Dak., U.S.* 104 J2
Morebeng, *S. Af.* 202 H11
Morecambe, *Eng., U.K.* 143 R11
Morecambe Bay, *Eng., U.K.* 143 R10
Morehead, *Ky., U.S.* 101 B19
Morehead City, *N.C., U.S.* 96 J14
Morehouse, *Mo., U.S.* 105 V16
Morelia, *Mex.* 114 J11
Morella, *Qnsld., Austral.* 211 T12
Morella, *Sp.* 145 F15
Morena, *India* 178 G6
Morena, Sierra, *Sp.* 144 K8
Moreni, *Rom.* 153 E15
Moreno Valley, *Calif., U.S.* 109 X9
Morere, *N.Z.* 213 L20
Moresby Island, *B.C., Can.* 82 K7

Moreton, *Qnsld., Austral.* 211 P12
Moreton Island, *Austral.* 210 H16
Moreuil, *Fr.* 147 N10
Morez, *Fr.* 147 T14
Morfou, *Cyprus* 160 N7
Morfou Bay, *Cyprus* 160 N7
Morgan, *S. Aust., Austral.* 211 X10
Morgan, *Utah, U.S.* 106 K7
Morgan City, *La., U.S.* 100 Q9
Morganfield, *Ky., U.S.* 101 C14
Morgan Hill, *Calif., U.S.* 109 T4
Morganito, *Venez.* 128 E9
Morganton, *N.C., U.S.* 96 H8
Morgantown, *W. Va., U.S.* 96 C10
Morgat, *Fr.* 147 Q2
Morges, *Switz.* 150 C1
Morgex, *It.* 150 D2
Mori, *Japan* 184 G12
Moriah, *Trinidad & Tobago* 121 N18
Moriah, Mount, *Nev., U.S.* 84 G6
Moriarty, *N. Mex., U.S.* 107 S12
Morioka, *Japan* 184 K13
Moriu, *Vanuatu* 218 E3
Morjärv, *Sw.* 141 F14
Mor Khun, *Pak.* 176 K12
Morkoka, river, *Russ.* 159 G16
Morlaas, *Fr.* 147 Y7
Morlaix, *Fr.* 147 P3
Mormanno, *It.* 151 P13
Mormon Lake, *Ariz., U.S.* 107 S7
Morne-à-l'Eau, *Guadeloupe, Fr.* 121 F15
Morne Raquette, *Dominica* 121 F18
Morne Seychellois, peak, *Seychelles* 205 N20
Mornington, *Qnsld., Austral.* 211 Q11
Mornington, Isla, *Chile* 133 V6
Mornington Island, *Qnsld., Austral.* 211 Q11
Moro, *Pak.* 177 U7
Morocco, *Af.* 195 D15
Morogoro, *Tanzania* 199 M14
Moro Gulf, *Philippines* 189 F14
Morombe, *Madagascar* 203 H16
Mörön, *Mongolia* 180 C11
Morón, *Arg.* 132 L12
Morón, *Cuba* 116 H10
Morona, river, *Peru* 130 E3
Morondava, *Madagascar* 203 G16
Morón de la Frontera, *Sp.* 144 L9
Moroni, *Comoros* 205 M14
Morotai, island, *Indonesia* 189 H16
Moroto, *Uganda* 199 J13
Morovis, *P.R., U.S.* 120 N4
Morozovsk, *Russ.* 157 Q12
Morpará, *Braz.* 131 H15
Morpeth, *Eng., U.K.* 143 N12
Morrill, *Nebr., U.S.* 105 N1
Morrilton, *Ark., U.S.* 100 G8
Morrinhos, *Braz.* 131 K13
Morris, *Ill., U.S.* 99 P6
Morris, *Minn., U.S.* 104 J9
Morris, *Okla., U.S.* 102 G13
Morris Jesup, Cape, *N. Amer.* 80 A7
Morrison, *Ill., U.S.* 99 N4
Morristown, *N.J., U.S.* 94 N10
Morristown, *N.Y., U.S.* 94 F9
Morristown, *S. Dak., U.S.* 104 H3
Morristown, *Tenn., U.S.* 101 E19
Morrisville, *Vt., U.S.* 95 F13
Morro Bay, *Calif., U.S.* 109 V5
Morrosquillo, Golfo de, *Col.* 128 C4
Morrumbene, *Mozambique* 203 H13
Morshansk, *Russ.* 156 L11
Morsi, *India* 178 K6
Mortagne, *Fr.* 147 Q8
Mortara, *It.* 150 E4
Morteau, *Fr.* 147 S14
Morteros, *Arg.* 132 J11
Mortlake, *Vic., Austral.* 211 Z11
Mortlock Islands, *F.S.M.* 216 Q7
Morton, *Ill., U.S.* 99 Q5
Morton, *Miss., U.S.* 100 L12
Morton, *Tex., U.S.* 102 K4
Morton, *Wash., U.S.* 108 D4
Mortyq, *Kaz.* 174 D8
Moruga, *Trinidad & Tobago* 121 Q22
Moruroa (Mururoa), island, *Fr. Polynesia, Fr.* 219 H21
Morvan, Monts du, *Fr.* 147 S12
Morven, *Qnsld., Austral.* 211 U13
Morven, peak, *Scot., U.K.* 142 K10
Morvern, peninsula, *Scot., U.K.* 142 L7
Mosal'sk, *Russ.* 156 K8
Moscos Islands, *Myanmar* 186 M7

Moscow, *Idaho, U.S.* 106 D3
Moscow, river, *Russ.* 138 E11
Moscow see Moskva, *Russ.* 156 J9
Moscow Canal, *Russ.* 156 J9
Moscow University Ice Shelf, *Antarctica* 227 N20
Mose, Cape, *Antarctica* 227 P19
Mosel see Moselle, river, *Ger.* 148 G5
Moselle, river, *Fr.* 138 G5
Moses Lake, *Wash., U.S.* 108 C7
Moses Lake, *Wash., U.S.* 108 D7
Moshi, *Tanzania* 199 L14
Mosinee, *Wis., U.S.* 98 J5
Mosjøen, *Nor.* 140 F12
Moskva, *Taj.* 176 J8
Moskva (Moscow), *Russ.* 156 J9
Moskva, river, *Russ.* 156 J8
Moso, island, *Vanuatu* 218 F3
Mosonmagyaróvár, *Hung.* 149 L13
Mosquero, *N. Mex., U.S.* 107 R14
Mosquitia, region, *Hond.* 115 K18
Mosquito Coast, *N. Amer.* 80 Q8
Mosquito Island, *Virgin Islands, U.K.* 120 Q9
Mosquito Lagoon, *Fla., U.S.* 97 S9
Mosquitos, Golfo de los, *Pan.* 115 N20
Mosquitos, Gulf of see Mosquitos, Golfo de los, *N. Amer.* 80 Q9
Moss, *Nor.* 140 L11
Mossaka, *Congo* 201 L18
Mossburn, *N.Z.* 213 Q15
Mossel Bay, *S. Af.* 194 R7
Mossel Bay, *S. Af.* 202 M8
Mossendjo, *Congo* 201 M16
Mossgiel, *N.S.W., Austral.* 211 X12
Mossoró, *Braz.* 131 E17
Moss Point, *Miss., U.S.* 101 P13
Moss Town, *Bahamas* 120 F8
Most, *Czech Rep.* 148 G10
Mosta, *Malta* 161 K22
Mostaganem, *Alg.* 196 A10
Mostar, *Bosn. & Herzg.* 152 H7
Mostardas, *Braz.* 130 Q12
Mosteiros, *Azores* 144 Q5
Móstoles, *Sp.* 144 F10
Mosul see Al Mawşil, *Iraq* 172 C9
Mota, island, *Vanuatu* 218 B2
Motaba, river, *Congo* 201 J18
Mota del Cuervo, *Sp.* 144 H12
Mota Khan, *Afghan.* 177 N7
Motala, *Sw.* 141 L13
Mota Lava, island, *Vanuatu* 218 B2
Motane see Mohotani, island, *Fr. Polynesia, Fr.* 219 N21
Motherwell, *Scot., U.K.* 142 M9
Motihia, Motu, *Fr. Polynesia, Fr.* 219 K21
Moto Piti Aau, island, *Fr. Polynesia, Fr.* 219 K14
Motopu, *Fr. Polynesia, Fr.* 219 N20
Motoyoshi, *Japan* 184 L13
Motril, *Sp.* 144 M11
Motru, river, *Rom.* 152 F12
Motru, *Rom.* 152 F12
Mott, *N. Dak., U.S.* 104 H3
Motta Misaki, *Japan* 184 G12
Motu, river, *N.Z.* 213 K20
Motueka, *N.Z.* 213 M18
Motu Iti see Tupai, island, *Fr. Polynesia, Fr.* 219 E15
Motukitiu, island, *Cook Is., N.Z.* 218 R12
Motu Ko, island, *Pukapuka, Cook Is., N.Z.* 218 R2
Motu Kotawa, island, *Pukapuka, Cook Is., N.Z.* 218 R2
Motul, *Mex.* 115 H16
Motuloa, island, *Tuvalu* 217 L22
Motupae, island, *Cook Is., N.Z.* 219 C14
Motupe, *Peru* 130 F2
Motupena Point, *P.N.G.* 217 K14
Moturakau, island, *Cook Is., N.Z.* 218 Q11
Moturiki, island, *Fiji* 218 J7
Motutapu, island, *Cook Is., N.Z.* 218 Q9
Motutapu, island, *Tonga* 218 H12
Motutunga, island, *Fr. Polynesia, Fr.* 219 E18
Motykleyka, *Russ.* 159 F20
Mouchard, *Fr.* 147 S13
Mouchoir Passage, *Turks & Caicos Is., U.K.* 117 J18
Moudjéria, *Mauritania* 196 G6
Moúdros, *Gr.* 155 E15
Mouila, *Gabon* 201 L15
Moulamein, *N.S.W., Austral.* 211 Y12
Mould Bay, *N.W.T., Can.* 83 C13
Moule a Chique, Cap, *St. Lucia* 121 L14

Mòulede Gaesa, *Eq. Guinea* **204** M7
Moulins, *Fr.* **147** T11
Moulins-la-Marche, *Fr.* **147** P8
Moulton, *Ala., U.S.* **101** H14
Moultrie, *Ga., U.S.* **97** P6
Moultrie, Lake, *S.C., U.S.* **96** L10
Mouly, *New Caledonia, Fr.* **218** C8
Mound Bayou, *Miss., U.S.* **100** J10
Mound City, *Ill., U.S.* **99** V5
Mound City, *Kans., U.S.* **105** T10
Mound City, *Mo., U.S.* **105** R10
Moundou, *Chad* **197** K14
Moundsville, *W. Va., U.S.* **96** B9
Moundville, *Ala., U.S.* **101** K14
Moʻungaʻone, island, *Tonga* **218** P7
Mounlapamôk, *Laos* **186** M12
Mountain, *Mo., U.S.* **105** V13
Mountainair, *N. Mex., U.S.* **107** S12
Mountain Brook, *Ala., U.S.* **101** J15
Mountain City, *Nev., U.S.* **108** L10
Mountain City, *Tenn., U.S.* **101** D21
Mountain Home, *Ark., U.S.* **100** E8
Mountain Home, *Idaho, U.S.* **106** H4
Mountain Lake, *Minn., U.S.* **104** L10
Mountain Nile *see* Jebel, Bahr el, river, *Sudan* **199** H13
Mountain View, *Ark., U.S.* **100** F9
Mountain View, *Hawaiʻi, U.S.* **113** M21
Mountain View, *Mo., U.S.* **105** V14
Mountain View, *Wyo., U.S.* **106** K8
Mountain Village, *Alas., U.S.* **110** H12
Mount Airy, *N.C., U.S.* **96** G9
Mount Arrowsmith, *N.S.W., Austral.* **211** W11
Mount Ayr, *Iowa, U.S.* **105** Q11
Mount Barker, *W. Aust., Austral.* **211** Y3
Mount Barnett, *W. Aust., Austral.* **211** R5
Mount Bellew, *Ire.* **143** S4
Mount Carmel, *Ill., U.S.* **99** T7
Mount Carmel, *Pa., U.S.* **94** N8
Mount Cavenagh, *N. Terr., Austral.* **211** U8
Mount Cook, *N.Z.* **213** P16
Mount Coolon, *Qnsld., Austral.* **211** T14
Mount Desert Island, *Me., U.S.* **95** F18
Mount Dora, *Fla., U.S.* **97** T8
Mount Dora, *N. Mex., U.S.* **107** Q15
Mount Douglas, *Qnsld., Austral.* **211** T13
Mount Ebenezer, *N. Terr., Austral.* **211** U8
Mount Elsie, *Qnsld., Austral.* **211** S13
Mount Enterprise, *Tex., U.S.* **102** M14
Mount Gambier, *S. Aust., Austral.* **211** Z11
Mount Hagen, *P.N.G.* **213** D18
Mount Hope, *N.S.W., Austral.* **211** X13
Mount Hope, *W. Va., U.S.* **96** E8
Mount House, *W. Aust., Austral.* **211** R5
Mount Ida, *W. Aust., Austral.* **211** W4
Mount Isa, *Qnsld., Austral.* **211** S11
Mount Jewett, *Pa., U.S.* **94** L5
Mount Keith, *W. Aust., Austral.* **211** V4
Mount Lofty Ranges, *Austral.* **210** K10
Mount Magnet, *W. Aust., Austral.* **211** V3
Mount Maunganui, *N.Z.* **213** K19
Mount Molloy, *Qnsld., Austral.* **211** R13
Mount Morris, *Ill., U.S.* **99** N5
Mount Morris, *Mich., U.S.* **98** L12
Mount Mulgrave, *Qnsld., Austral.* **211** Q12
Mount Murchison, *N.S.W., Austral.* **211** W12
Mount Olive, *Miss., U.S.* **100** M11
Mount Olive, *N.C., U.S.* **96** J12
Mount Pleasant, *Iowa, U.S.* **105** Q13
Mount Pleasant, *Mich., U.S.* **98** K10
Mount Pleasant, *Tenn., U.S.* **101** F14
Mount Pleasant, *Tex., U.S.* **102** K14
Mount Rainier National Park, *Wash., U.S.* **108** D4
Mount Riddock, *N. Terr., Austral.* **211** T9
Mount Rushmore National Memorial, *S. Dak., U.S.* **104** L2
Mount St. George, *Trinidad & Tobago* **121** N18
Mount St. Helens National Volcanic Monument, *Wash., U.S.* **108** E4
Mount Sanford, *N. Terr., Austral.* **211** R7
Mount Sarah, *S. Aust., Austral.* **211** U9
Mountʼs Bay, *Eng., U.K.* **143** Y8
Mount Shasta, *Calif., U.S.* **108** M3
Mount Sterling, *Ill., U.S.* **99** R3
Mount Sterling, *Ky., U.S.* **101** B18
Mount Stuart, *W. Aust., Austral.* **211** T2
Mount Vernon, *Ala., U.S.* **101** N14
Mount Vernon, *Ill., U.S.* **99** T6
Mount Vernon, *Ind., U.S.* **99** U7

Mount Vernon, *Ky., U.S.* **101** C18
Mount Vernon, *Mo., U.S.* **105** V11
Mount Vernon, *N.Y., U.S.* **94** N11
Mount Vernon, *Ohio, U.S.* **99** Q13
Mount Vernon, *Oreg., U.S.* **108** G7
Mount Vernon, *Tex., U.S.* **102** K14
Mount Vernon, *W. Aust., Austral.* **211** U3
Mount Vernon, *Wash., U.S.* **108** B4
Mount Wedge, *N. Terr., Austral.* **211** T8
Mount Willoughby, *S. Aust., Austral.* **211** V9
Mount Wynne Bay, *St. Vincent & the Grenadines* **121** K16
Mount Zion, *Ill., U.S.* **99** R6
Moura, *Braz.* **130** D8
Mourão, *Port.* **144** J6
Mourne Mountains, *N. Ire., U.K.* **143** Q7
Mouroubra, *W. Aust., Austral.* **211** W3
Mouse *see* Souris, river, *N. Dak., U.S.* **104** E4
Moussoro, *Chad* **197** J14
Moutiers, *Fr.* **147** U14
Moutsamoudou, *Comoros* **205** N16
Mouzáki, *Gr.* **154** F9
Moweaqua, *Ill., U.S.* **99** R5
Mowshkheyl, *Afghan.* **177** N7
Moÿ, *Fr.* **147** N11
Moyale, *Eth.* **199** H5
Moyo, *Uganda* **199** H13
Moyobamba, *Peru* **130** F3
Moyu, *China* **180** G5
Moyynqum, desert, *Kaz.* **175** H14
Moyynty, *Kaz.* **175** F15
Mozambique, *Af.* **195** N22
Mozambique Basin, *Ind. Oc.* **240** M4
Mozambique Channel, *Af.* **194** N10
Mozambique Escarpment, *Ind. Oc.* **240** N3
Mozambique Plateau, *Ind. Oc.* **240** M3
Mozarlândia, *Braz.* **130** J12
Mozdok, *Russ.* **157** T14
Mozdūrān, *Iran* **173** C17
Mozhaysk, *Russ.* **156** J8
Mozhga, *Russ.* **156** H16
Mpanda, *Tanzania* **198** M12
Mpandamatenga, *Botswana* **202** F10
Mpika, *Zambia* **202** D12
Mqabba, *Malta* **161** L22
Mrągowo, *Pol.* **149** B16
Mramani, *Comoros* **205** N16
Mrémani, *Comoros* **205** N16
Mrkojević, Zaliv, *Mont.* **152** K9
Msaken, *Tun.* **197** B13
Msida, *Malta* **161** K23
Mstsislaw, *Belarus* **156** K6
Mtʼa Didi Abuli, peak, *Rep. of Georgia* **169** C17
Mthatha, *S. Af.* **202** L11
Mtkvari (Kura), river, *Rep. of Georgia* **169** C18
Mtsensk, *Russ.* **156** L9
Mtsʼkhetʼa, *Rep. of Georgia* **169** C18
Mtwara, *Tanzania* **199** N15
Mua, *Wallis & Futuna, Fr.* **218** E12
Mua, *Wallis & Futuna, Fr.* **218** C11
Mua, Baie de, *Wallis & Futuna, Fr.* **218** C11
Muʼa, *Tonga* **218** J12
Mualama, *Mozambique* **203** F14
Muang Bèng, *Laos* **186** H9
Muang Gnômmarat, *Laos* **186** K11
Muang Kao, *Laos* **186** M13
Muang Khamkeut, *Laos* **186** J11
Muang Khoa, *Laos* **186** H10
Muang Meung, *Laos* **186** H9
Muang Ngoy, *Laos* **186** H10
Muang Paklay, *Laos* **186** K9
Muang Phin, *Laos* **186** L12
Muang Sing, *Laos* **186** H9
Muang Xianghon, *Laos* **186** J9
Muang Xon, *Laos* **186** H10
Muar, *Malaysia* **187** V10
Muaraaman, *Indonesia* **188** K6
Muarabungo, *Indonesia* **188** J6
Muaraenim, *Indonesia* **188** K7
Muarakumpe, *Indonesia* **188** J7
Muaramawai, *Indonesia* **188** J12
Muaratewe, *Indonesia* **188** J11
Mubi, *Nigeria* **201** F16
Mucajaí, river, *Braz.* **130** B8
Muchachos, Roque de los, *Canary Is.* **204** Q3
Muchea, *W. Aust., Austral.* **211** X2
München (Munich), *Ger.* **148** K8
Muchinga Mountains, *Zambia* **202** D12

Muchkapskiy, *Russ.* **156** M12
Muchot, Puntan, *N. Mariana Is., U.S.* **216** B4
Muck, island, *Scot., U.K.* **142** K7
Muckety, *N. Terr., Austral.* **211** R8
Muckle Flugga, island, *Scot., U.K.* **142** C12
Muckle Roe, island, *Scot., U.K.* **142** D12
Muconda, *Angola* **202** D8
Mucur, *Turk.* **168** F9
Mucuripe, Ponta de, *Braz.* **131** E17
Mucusso, *Angola* **202** F8
Muda, peak, *Canary Is.* **204** Q7
Mudamuckla, *S. Aust., Austral.* **211** X9
Mudan, river, *China* **181** D18
Mudanjiang, *China* **181** D18
Mudanya, *Turk.* **168** D5
Muḑayrib, *Oman* **173** K16
Muddy Gap, *Wyo., U.S.* **106** J11
Mudgee, *N.S.W., Austral.* **211** X14
Mudhol, *India* **179** N4
Mud Lake, *Idaho, U.S.* **106** G7
Mudurnu, *Turk.* **168** D7
Mueda, *Mozambique* **203** D15
Muéo, *New Caledonia, Fr.* **218** D7
Muertos Cays, *Bahamas* **116** F9
Mufulira, *Zambia* **202** D11
Mufu Shan, *China* **182** M5
Muga, Pico de la, *Sp.* **160** K5
Muganly, *Azerb.* **169** C20
Mughalzhar Taūy, range, *Kaz.* **174** E9
Muğla, *Turk.* **168** H4
Muglad, *Sudan* **198** F11
Muglad Basin, *Sudan* **198** F11
Mugu, *Nepal* **178** E8
Mūḩ, Sabkhat al, *Syr.* **170** H10
Muḩammad, Râs, *Egypt* **171** U4
Muhammad Qol, *Sudan* **199** C14
Muḩayy, *Jordan* **171** P6
Muhembo, *Botswana* **202** F8
Mühleholz, *Liech.* **160** P2
Muhlenfels Point, *Virgin Islands, U.S.* **120** N9
Mühlhausen, *Ger.* **148** F8
Mühlig-Hofmann Mountains, *Antarctica* **227** A13
Mui Hopohoponga, cape, *Tonga* **218** J12
Muine Bheag (Bagenalstown), *Ire.* **143** T6
Muir Woods National Monument, *Calif., U.S.* **109** R3
Muisne, *Ecua.* **128** H2
Mukacheve, *Ukr.* **157** P1
Mukah, *Malaysia* **188** H10
Mukawa, *Japan* **184** G13
Mukayris, *Yemen* **172** Q10
Mukeru, *Palau* **216** N11
Mukhtadir, *Azerb.* **169** B22
Mukinbudin, *W. Aust., Austral.* **211** W3
Muko Jima Rettō, *Japan* **184** K5
Mukomuko, *Indonesia* **188** K6
Mukry, *Turkm.* **174** M12
Muktinath, *Nepal* **178** F9
Mul, *India* **178** L7
Mula, river, *India* **178** L4
Muladu, island, *Maldives* **179** T3
Mulaku Atoll, *Maldives* **179** V3
Mulâtre, Pointe, *Dominica* **121** G20
Mulazzano, *It.* **161** H18
Mulberry, *Ark., U.S.* **100** F6
Mulberry Creek, *Tex., U.S.* **102** H6
Mulchatna, river, *Alas., U.S.* **111** K14
Muldraugh, *Ky., U.S.* **101** B16
Mulegé, *Mex.* **114** D6
Mule Peak, *N. Mex., U.S.* **107** U13
Muleshoe, *Tex., U.S.* **102** J4
Mulgildie, *Qnsld., Austral.* **211** U15
Mulhacén, peak, *Sp.* **144** L12
Mülheim, *Ger.* **148** E5
Mulhouse, *Fr.* **147** R15
Muli, *China* **180** M11
Mulifanua, *Samoa* **218** L3
Muling, *China* **181** D18
Mulinuʼu, Cape, *Samoa* **218** K1
Mulitapuili, Cape, *Samoa* **218** L3
Mulitefala, island, *Tuvalu* **217** J23
Mulka, *S. Aust., Austral.* **211** V10
Mull, Island of, *Scot., U.K.* **142** L7
Mull, Sound of, *Scot., U.K.* **142** L7
Mullan, *Idaho, U.S.* **106** C4
Mullen, *Nebr., U.S.* **105** N4
Mullens, *W. Va., U.S.* **96** E8
Mullet Peninsula, *Ire.* **143** Q3
Mullewa, *W. Aust., Austral.* **211** W2

Mullingar, *Ire.* **143** R6
Mullins, *S.C., U.S.* **96** K11
Mull of Galloway, cape, *Scot., U.K.* **143** Q8
Mulobezi, *Zambia* **202** F9
Mulroy Bay, *Ire.* **143** N5
Multan, *Pak.* **177** R9
Mulvane, *Kans., U.S.* **105** U8
Mumbai (Bombay), *India* **178** L3
Mumbwa, *Zambia* **202** E10
Mumra, *Russ.* **157** R15
Muna, island, *Indonesia* **189** L14
Muna, river, *Russ.* **159** G16
Munaba, *India* **178** G2
Munan Pass, *China, Vietnam* **186** G12
Munburra, *Qnsld., Austral.* **211** Q13
Muncie, *Ind., U.S.* **99** R10
Muncy, *Pa., U.S.* **94** M7
Munda, *Solomon Is.* **217** M16
Mundabullangana, *W. Aust., Austral.* **211** S3
Munday, *Tex., U.S.* **102** K8
Münden, *Ger.* **148** F7
Mundiwindi, *W. Aust., Austral.* **211** U3
Mundra, *India* **178** J1
Mundrabilla, *W. Aust., Austral.* **211** W6
Mundubbera, *Qnsld., Austral.* **211** U15
Mundul, *Afghan.* **176** L8
Munera, *Sp.* **144** H12
Mungana, *Qnsld., Austral.* **211** R13
Mungbere, *Dem. Rep. of the Congo* **198** J12
Mungeli, *India* **178** J8
Munger, *India* **178** H11
Mungindi, *N.S.W., Austral.* **211** W14
Munguba, *Braz.* **130** D12
Munia, island, *Fiji Is.* **218** H9
Munich *see* München, *Ger.* **148** K8
Municipal Administrative Center, *Monaco* **161** E21
Munising, *Mich., U.S.* **98** F8
Munku Sardyk, Gora, *Russ.* **159** L14
Münster, *Ger.* **148** E6
Munster, region, *Ire.* **143** U4
Muntok, *Indonesia* **188** K7
Munzur Dağları, *Turk.* **169** F14
Muong Te, *Vietnam* **186** G10
Muonio, *Fin.* **141** D14
Muping, *China* **182** F10
Muqdisho (Mogadishu), *Somalia* **199** J17
Mur, river, *Aust.* **148** M10
Muradiye, *Turk.* **169** F18
Murakami, *Japan* **184** L12
Murangʼa, *Kenya* **199** K14
Murashi, *Russ.* **158** G8
Murat, *Fr.* **147** V10
Murat, river, *Turk.* **169** F15
Murata, *San Marino* **161** K15
Murat Dağı, *Turk.* **168** F5
Muratlı, *Turk.* **168** C3
Muravera, *It.* **151** P4
Murazzano, *It.* **150** F3
Murça, *Port.* **144** E7
Murchison, river, *W. Aust., Austral.* **211** V2
Murcia, *Sp.* **145** K14
Mur-de-Bretagne, *Fr.* **147** Q4
Murdo, *S. Dak., U.S.* **104** L4
Mureş, river, *Rom.* **152** D11
Muret, *Fr.* **147** X9
Murfreesboro, *Ark., U.S.* **100** H7
Murfreesboro, *N.C., U.S.* **96** G13
Murfreesboro, *Tenn., U.S.* **101** F15
Murgap, river, *Turkm.* **174** N10
Murgha Kibzai, *Pak.* **177** R8
Murghob, river, *Taj.* **176** J11
Murghob, *Taj.* **176** J11
Murgoo, *W. Aust., Austral.* **211** V2
Murguz, peak, *Arm.* **169** D19
Muri, *Cook Is., N.Z.* **218** Q9
Murihiti, island, *Cook Is., N.Z.* **219** A14
Murilo Atoll, *F.S.M.* **216** Q6
Murimaora, Motu, *Fr. Polynesia, Fr.* **219** G14
Muritapua, island, *Cook Is., N.Z.* **218** Q12
Müritz, lake, *Ger.* **148** C10
Murjek, *Sw.* **141** F14
Murman Coast, *Russ.* **138** A10
Murmansk, *Russ.* **158** C9
Murmansk Rise, *Arctic Oc.* **243** D16
Muro, Capo di, *Fr.* **150** K3
Muro Lucano, *It.* **150** M12
Murom, *Russ.* **156** J11

Muroran, *Japan* **184** G13
Muros, *Sp.* **144** B5
Muros e Noia, Ría de, *Sp.* **144** B5
Muroto, *Japan* **185** R7
Muroto Zaki, *Japan* **185** R7
Murphy, *Idaho, U.S.* **106** H3
Murphy, *N.C., U.S.* **96** J6
Murphy, *N.C., U.S.* **96** J5
Murphysboro, *Ill., U.S.* **99** U5
Murrat el Kubra, Buheirat (Great Bitter Lake), *Egypt* **171** Q1
Murrat el Sughra, Buheirat (Little Bitter Lake), *Egypt* **171** Q1
Murray, river, *Austral.* **210** K11
Murray, river, *Austral.* **210** K2
Murray, *Ky., U.S.* **101** E13
Murray, Lake, *P.N.G.* **213** D17
Murray, Lake, *S.C., U.S.* **96** K8
Murray, Source of the, *Austral.* **210** L13
Murray Bridge, *S. Aust., Austral.* **211** Y10
Murray Fracture Zone, *Pac. Oc.* **238** F12
Murray River Basin, *Austral.* **210** K11
Murrayville, *Vic., Austral.* **211** Y11
Murrells Inlet, *S.C., U.S.* **96** L11
Murrenja Hill, *Austral.* **210** B7
Murrin Murrin, *W. Aust., Austral.* **211** V4
Murro di Porco, Capo, *It.* **151** T12
Murrumbidgee, river, *N.S.W., Austral.* **211** Y12
Murska Sobota, *Slov.* **152** C6
Mursko Središče, *Croatia* **152** C6
Murter, island, *Croatia* **152** G5
Murud, *India* **178** L3
Murud, Mount, *Malaysia* **188** G11
Murukta, *Russ.* **159** G14
Mururoa *see* Moruroa, island, *Fr. Polynesia, Fr.* **219** H21
Mürzzuschlag, *Aust.* **148** L12
Muş, *Turk.* **169** F16
Mûsa, Gebel (Mount Sinai), *Egypt* **171** T3
Musa Dağ, *Turk.* **168** K11
Musa Khel Bazar, *Pak.* **177** Q8
Musala, peak, *Bulg.* **153** J13
Musan, *N. Korea* **182** B14
Musandam, Raʼs, *Oman* **173** H15
Musa Qalʼeh, *Afghan.* **177** P4
Musaymīr, *Yemen* **172** R9
Muscat *see* Masqaţ, *Oman* **173** K16
Muscatine, *Iowa, U.S.* **105** P14
Muscle Shoals, *Ala., U.S.* **101** G14
Muse, *Okla., U.S.* **102** H14
Museum of Prehistoric Anthropology, *Monaco* **161** E20
Musgrave, Port, *Austral.* **210** A12
Musgrave Ranges, *Austral.* **210** G8
Mushie, *Dem. Rep. of the Congo* **198** L8
Mushuray *see* Wazah Khwah, *Afghan.* **177** P7
Musicians Seamounts, *Pac. Oc.* **238** F11
Muskegon, river, *Mich., U.S.* **98** K10
Muskegon, *Mich., U.S.* **98** L9
Muskegon Heights, *Mich., U.S.* **98** L9
Muskingum, river, *Ohio, U.S.* **99** R14
Muskogee, *Okla., U.S.* **102** F13
Muslimbagh, *Pak.* **177** R6
Muslimīyah, *Syr.* **170** D9
Musmar, *Sudan* **199** D14
Musoma, *Tanzania* **199** K13
Mussau, island, *P.N.G.* **213** B20
Mussau Islands, *P.N.G.* **213** B20
Musselburgh, *Scot., U.K.* **142** M10
Musselshell, river, *Mont., U.S.* **106** C10
Musselshell, *Mont., U.S.* **106** D10
Mussuma, *Angola* **202** E8
Mustafa-kemalpaşa, *Turk.* **168** D4
Mustahīl, *Eth.* **199** H17
Mustang, *Nepal* **178** E9
Musters, Lago, *Arg.* **133** S8
Mustique, *St. Vincent & the Grenadines* **119** L17
Muswellbrook, *N.S.W., Austral.* **211** X14
Mût, *Egypt* **197** E18
Mut, island, *Marshall Is.* **216** J8
Mut, *Turk.* **168** J8
Mutá, Ponta do, *Braz.* **131** J16
Mutalau, *Niue, N.Z.* **219** B20
Mutarara, *Mozambique* **203** F13
Mutare, *Mozambique* **202** G12
Mute, Motu, *Fr. Polynesia* **219** J14
Muting, *Indonesia* **189** M21
Mutki, *Turk.* **169** G16
Mutnovskaya Sopka, *Russ.* **159** F23
Mutok Harbor, *F.S.M.* **217** G14
Mutoray, *Russ.* **159** J14

Mutsu, *Japan* **184** HI3
Mutsu Wan, *Japan* **184** HI3
Muttaburra, *Qnsld., Austral.* **211** TI2
Muturi, *Indonesia* **189** KI8
Mu Us Shamo (Ordos), *China* **182** D2
Muxía, *Sp.* **144** B5
Müynoq, *Uzb.* **174** H9
Muzaffarabad, *Pak.* **176** MII
Muzaffargarh, *Pak.* **177** R9
Muzaffarnagar, *India* **178** E6
Muzaffarpur, *India* **178** GIO
Muztag, peak, *China* **180** H5
Mwaniwowo, *Solomon Is.* **217** Q2I
Mwanza, *Tanzania* **199** KI3
Mweka, *Dem. Rep. of the Congo* **198** L9
Mwene-Ditu, *Dem. Rep. of the Congo* **198** MIO
Mwenezi, *Zimb.* **202** GII
Mweru, Lake, *Dem. Rep. of the Congo, Zambia* **194** L8
Mwinilunga, *Zambia* **202** D9
Myaksa, *Russ.* **156** G9
Myanaung, *Myanmar* **186** J5
Myanmar (Burma), *Asia* **167** W9
Mycenae, ruin, *Gr.* **154** KIO
Myebon, *Myanmar* **186** H4
Myeik, *Myanmar* **187** N7
Myingyan, *Myanmar* **186** G6
Myitkyinä, *Myanmar* **186** E7
Myitta, *Myanmar* **186** M7
Mykolayiv, *Ukr.* **157** R6
Mymensingh, *Bangladesh* **178** HI3
Mynbulaq, *Uzb.* **174** JIO
Mynydd Preseli, peak, *Wales, U.K.* **143** U8
Myohaung, *Myanmar* **186** H4
Myoungmya, *Myanmar* **186** L5
Myrdal, *Nor.* **140** KIO
Mýrdalsjökull, glacier, *Ice.* **140** G2
Myrhorod, *Ukr.* **157** P7
Myrtle Beach, *S.C., U.S.* **96** LII
Myrtle Creek, *Oreg., U.S.* **108** J3
Myrtle Grove, *Fla., U.S.* **97** QI
Myrtle Point, *Oreg., U.S.* **108** J2
Myrtou, *Cyprus* **160** N7
Mysore, *India* **179** Q5
Mysovaya, *Russ.* **159** DI9
Mys Shmidta, *Russ.* **159** B2O
Mystic, *Conn., U.S.* **95** MI4
Mystic, *Iowa, U.S.* **105** QI2
Mys Zhelaniya, *Russ.* **158** DI2
Myszyniec, *Pol.* **149** CI6
My Tho, *Vietnam* **187** PI2
Mytilene *see* Mitilíni, *Gr.* **155** GI7
Mytishchi, *Russ.* **156** J9
Mzé Koukoulé Bandalankoua, peak, *Comoros* **205** NI5
Mzuzu, *Malawi* **202** DI2

N

Na, island, *F.S.M.* **217** GI4
Naafkopf, peak, *Aust., Liech., Switz.* **160** R3
Nä'älehu, *Hawai'i, U.S.* **113** P2O
Nabari, *Kiribati* **217** B2O
Nabatíyé et Tahta, *Leb.* **170** J6
Nabeina, *Kiribati* **217** FI7
Naberezhnyye Chelny, *Russ.* **156** HI6
Nabeul, *Tun.* **197** AI3
Nabire, *Indonesia* **189** KI9
Nablus *see* Näblus, *W. Bank* **170** L6
Näblus (Nablus), *W. Bank* **170** L6
Nabouwalu, *Fiji Is.* **218** H7
Nabq Bay, *Egypt* **171** U4
Nacala, *Mozambique* **203** EI5
Nacaome, *Hond.* **115** LI7
Naches, *Wash., U.S.* **108** D5
Nachingwea, *Tanzania* **199** NI5
Náchod, *Czech Rep.* **148** GI2
Nachu, island, *F.S.M.* **217** CI6
Nachvak Fiord, *Nfld. & Lab., Can.* **83** J2O
Nacimiento, Lake, *Calif., U.S.* **109** V5
Našice, *Croatia* **152** E8
Nacogdoches, *Tex., U.S.* **103** NI4
Nacozari de García, *Mex.* **114** C7
Nacula, island, *Fiji Is.* **218** H5
Nada *see* Danxian, *China* **183** UI
Nadale, island, *Maldives* **179** X3
Nadi, *Fiji Is.* **218** J5
Nadiad, *India* **178** J3
Nadi Bay, *Fiji Is.* **218** H5

Nadir, *Virgin Islands, U.S.* **120** N9
Nădlac, *Rom.* **152** DIO
Nadur, *Malta* **161** H2O
Naduri, *Fiji Is.* **218** G7
Nadvoitsy, *Russ.* **158** D8
Nadym, *Russ.* **158** GII
Náfpaktos, *Gr.* **154** H9
Náfplio, *Gr.* **154** KII
Nafúd ad Dahy, desert, *Saudi Arabia* **172** KIO
Nafúsah, Jabal, *Lib.* **197** CI3
Nag, *Pak.* **177** U4
Naga, *Indonesia* **189** MI3
Naga, *Philippines* **189** CI4
Naga Hills, *India* **178** GI5
Nagano, *Japan* **185** NII
Naganuma, *Japan* **184** MI2
Nagaoka, *Japan* **184** MII
Nagaon, *India* **178** GI4
Nagar Parkar, *Pak.* **177** W9
Nagasaki, *Japan* **185** S4
Nagato, *Japan* **185** Q5
Nagaur, *India* **178** F4
Nagêlê, *Eth.* **199** HI5
Nagercoil, *India* **179** S5
Nagir, *Pak.* **176** KI2
Nago, *Japan* **185** YI
Nagorno-Karabakh, region, *Azerb.* **169** E2O
Nagoya, *Japan* **185** QIO
Nagpur, *India* **178** K7
Nagqu, *China* **180** K8
Nag's Head, *St. Kitts & Nevis* **121** BI8
Naguabo, *P.R., U.S.* **120** N5
Nagykanizsa, *Hung.* **149** MI3
Naha, *Japan* **185** YI
Nahanni Butte, *N.W.T., Can.* **82** HIO
Nahari, *Japan* **185** R7
Nahma, *Mich., U.S.* **98** G8
Nahoe, *Fr. Polynesia, Fr.* **219** M2I
Nahuei Huapí, Lago, *Arg.* **133** Q7
Nailaga, *Fiji Is.* **218** H6
Naiman Qi, *China* **182** B9
Nain, *Nfld. & Lab., Can.* **83** K2I
Nā'in, *Iran* **173** EI3
Nainpur, *India* **178** J7
Nairai, island, *Fiji Is.* **218** J7
Nairiri, *Fr. Polynesia, Fr.* **219** PI6
Nairn, *Scot., U.K.* **142** J9
Nairobi, *Kenya* **199** KI4
Naitaba, island, *Fiji Is.* **218** H9
Naitonitoni, *Fiji Is.* **218** J6
Najafäbäd, *Iran* **173** EI3
Najd, region, *Saudi Arabia* **172** H8
Nájera, *Sp.* **144** CI2
Najin (Rajin), *N. Korea* **182** BI5
Najrän, oasis, *Saudi Arabia* **172** N9
Najrän, *Saudi Arabia* **172** N9
Naka, river, *Japan* **185** R7
Nakadöri Jima, *Japan* **185** R3
Nakagusuku Wan (Buckner Bay), *Japan* **185** YI
Naka Kharai, *Pak.* **177** W6
Näkälele Point, *Hawai'i, U.S.* **113** FI6
Nakamura, *Japan* **185** S6
Nakano, *Japan* **185** NII
Nakano Shima, *Japan* **185** P7
Nakano Shima, *Japan* **185** V3
Naka Shibetsu, *Japan* **184** FI6
Nakatane, *Japan* **185** U4
Nakatombetsu, *Japan* **184** EI4
Nakatsu, *Japan* **185** R5
Nakéty, *New Caledonia, Fr.* **218** D8
Nakfa, *Eritrea* **199** DI5
Nakhl, *Egypt* **171** Q3
Nakhodka, *Russ.* **159** M2I
Nakhon Phanom, *Thai.* **186** KII
Nakhon Ratchasima, *Thai.* **186** MIO
Nakhon Sawan, *Thai.* **186** L8
Nakhon Si Thammarat, *Thai.* **187** R8
Nakina, *Ont., Can.* **83** NI6
Nakło nad Notecią, *Pol.* **149** CI3
Naknek, *Alas., U.S.* **111** LI4
Nakodar, *India* **178** D5
Nakodu, *Fiji Is.* **218** H7
Nakuru, *Kenya* **199** KI4
Nal, *Pak.* **177** T5
Nal'chik, *Russ.* **157** TI3
Nalgonda, *India* **178** M7
Nallıhan, *Turk.* **168** D7
Nalogo, island, *Solomon Is.* **217** N22
Nälüt, *Lib.* **197** CI3
Namaite, island, *Fr. Polynesia, Fr.* **219** KI6
Namak, Daryäche-ye, *Iran* **173** DI3

Namakzar, Lake, *Afghan., Iran* **177** NI
Namakzär-e Shahdäd, desert, *Iran* **173** FI6
Namanga, *Kenya* **199** KI4
Namangan, *Uzb.* **175** KI4
Namapa, *Mozambique* **203** EI5
Namaram, *Vanuatu* **218** D3
Namatanai, *P.N.G.* **213** C2I
Nambour, *Qnsld., Austral.* **211** VI5
Nam Can, *Vietnam* **187** QII
Nam Dinh, *Vietnam* **186** HI2
Namekagon, river, *Wis., U.S.* **98** G3
Namelakl Passage, *Palau* **216** NI2
Namenalala, island, *Fiji Is.* **218** H7
Namgia, *India* **177** PI5
Namib Desert, *Namibia* **202** H6
Namibe, *Angola* **202** E5
Namibia, *Af.* **195** PI9
Namiquipa, *Mex.* **114** D8
Namlea, *Indonesia* **189** KI6
Nam Ngum Dam, *Laos* **186** JIO
Namoi, river, *Austral.* **210** JI4
Nämolokama Mountain, *Hawai'i, U.S.* **112** B5
Namoluk Atoll, *F.S.M.* **216** Q6
Namonuito Atoll, *F.S.M.* **216** P6
Namoren, island, *Marshall Is.* **216** K7
Namorik Atoll, *Marshall Is.* **216** H4
Nampa, *Idaho, U.S.* **106** G3
Nampala, *Mali* **196** H8
Namp'o, *N. Korea* **182** EI2
Nampö Shotö, *Japan* **184** J5
Nampula, *Mozambique* **203** EI4
Namsen, river, *Nor.* **140** GI2
Namsê Pass, *China, Nepal* **178** E8
Namsos, *Nor.* **140** GII
Namtsy, *Russ.* **159** GI8
Nam Tok, *Thai.* **186** M8
Namtu, *Myanmar* **186** G7
Namu Atoll, *Marshall Is.* **216** G4
Namuka-i-Lau, island, *Fiji Is.* **218** K9
Namukulu, *Niue, N.Z.* **219** B2O
Namuli, peak, *Mozambique* **194** MIO
Namur, *Belg.* **146** LI2
Namutoni, *Namibia* **202** G7
Namwön, *S. Korea* **182** GI3
Nan, river, *S. Amer.* **126** D3
Nan, *Thai.* **186** J9
Nanaimo, *B.C., Can.* **82** M8
Nänäkuli, *Hawai'i, U.S.* **112** EIO
Nanam, *N. Korea* **182** BI4
Nan'an, *China* **183** Q8
Nanao, *Japan* **185** NIO
Nanatsu Shima, *Japan* **184** MIO
Nanbu, *China* **180** LI2
Nanchang, *China* **182** M6
Nancheng, *China* **183** N6
Nanchong, *China* **180** LI2
Nancowry Island, *India* **179** SI5
Nancy, *Fr.* **147** PI4
Nanda Devi, peak, *India* **178** E7
Nanded, *India* **178** L6
Nandgaon, *India* **178** K4
Nandurbar, *India* **178** K4
Nandyal, *India* **179** N6
Nanfeng, *China* **183** N6
Nanga Parbat, peak, *Pak.* **176** LI2
Nangapinoh, *Indonesia* **188** JIO
Nangaraun, *Indonesia* **188** JIO
Nangatayap, *Indonesia* **188** J9
Nangin, *Myanmar* **187** P7
Nangiré, *Vanuatu* **218** C2
Nangis, *Fr.* **147** PIO
Nangnim Sanmaek, range, *N. Korea* **182** CI3
Nangong, *China* **182** F6
Nangtud, Mount, *Philippines* **189** DI4
Nanij, island, *Marshall Is.* **216** K8
Nanjing, *China* **182** K8
Nanjing, *China* **183** R7
Nankang, *China* **183** P5
Nankoku, *Japan* **185** R7
Nan Ling, *China* **183** Q4
Nanliu, river, *China* **183** SI
Nanmatol, island, *F.S.M.* **217** GI4
Nanmatol Islands, *F.S.M.* **217** GI4
Nanning, *China* **183** RI
Nannup, *W. Aust., Austral.* **211** Y2
Nanortalik, *Greenland, Den.* **81** D22
Nanpan, river, *China* **180** NI2
Nanping, *China* **183** P7
Nanri Dao, *China* **183** Q8
Nansan Dao, *China* **183** T2
Nansei Shotö *see* Ryukyu Islands, *Japan* **185** X3

Nansen Basin, *Arctic Oc.* **242** EIO
Nansen Sound, *Nunavut, Can.* **83** BI5
Nanshan Island, *Spratly Is.* **188** EII
Nansio, *Tanzania* **199** KI3
Nant, *Fr.* **147** XII
Nantes, *Fr.* **147** S6
Nanticoke, *Pa., U.S.* **94** M8
Nantong (Jinsha), *China* **182** K9
Nantou, *Taiwan, China* **183** R9
Nantucket, *Mass., U.S.* **95** MI6
Nantucket Island, *Mass., U.S.* **95** MI6
Nantucket Sound, *Mass., U.S.* **95** MI6
Nantulo, *Mozambique* **203** DI4
Nantwich, *Eng., U.K.* **143** SII
Nänu'alele Point, *Hawai'i, U.S.* **113** GI8
Nanukuloa, *Fiji Is.* **218** H6
Nanuku Passage, *Fiji Is.* **218** H8
Nanumanga, island, *Tuvalu* **214** H8
Nanumea, island, *Tuvalu* **214** H8
Nanuque, *Braz.* **131** KI6
Nanusa, Kepulauan, *Indonesia* **189** GI6
Nanutarra, *W. Aust., Austral.* **211** T2
Nanxian, *China* **182** M4
Nanxiong, *China* **183** Q5
Nanyang, *China* **182** J4
Nanzhang, *China* **182** K3
Nao, Cabo de la, *Sp.* **145** JI5
Nao Nao, island, *Fr. Polynesia, Fr.* **219** C23
Nao Nao, Passe, *Fr. Polynesia, Fr.* **219** C23
Naococane, Lac, *Que., Can.* **83** MI9
Naomid Plain, *Afghan.* **177** NI
Naonao, Motu, *Fr. Polynesia, Fr.* **219** KI6
Náousa, *Gr.* **154** CIO
Naozhou Dao, *China* **183** T2
Napa, *Calif., U.S.* **109** R3
Nä Pali Coast, *Hawai'i, U.S.* **112** B5
Naperville, *Ill., U.S.* **99** N7
Napia, island, *Kiribati* **217** B2O
Napier, *N.Z.* **213** L2O
Napier Mountains, *Antarctica* **227** CI9
Naples, *Fla., U.S.* **97** W8
Naples *see* Napoli, *It.* **150** MIO
Naples, *Tex., U.S.* **102** KI4
Napo, river, *S. Amer.* **126** D3
Napoleon, *N. Dak., U.S.* **104** H5
Napoleon, *Ohio, U.S.* **99** PII
Napoleonville, *La., U.S.* **100** QIO
Napoli (Naples), *It.* **150** MIO
Napoli, Golfo di, *It.* **150** MIO
Napuka, island, *Fr. Polynesia, Fr.* **219** D2O
Näpu'ukülua, peak, *Hawai'i, U.S.* **113** MI9
Nâqoûra, *Leb.* **170** K5
Nara, *Japan* **185** Q9
Nara, *Mali* **196** H7
Nara, river, *Pak.* **177** V8
Nara Canal, *Pak.* **177** U7
Naracoorte, *S. Aust., Austral.* **211** ZII
Narang, *Afghan.* **176** M9
Naranjito, *P.R., U.S.* **120** M4
Narao, *Japan* **185** S3
Narasannapeta, *India* **178** L9
Narathiwat, *Thai.* **187** S9
Nara Visa, *N. Mex., U.S.* **107** RI5
Narayanganj, *Bangladesh* **178** HI3
Narbonne, *Fr.* **147** YII
Narborough *see* Fernandina, Isla, island, *Ecua.* **128** Q7
Narcondam Island, *India* **179** PI5
Nardò, *It.* **151** NI5
Nardoo, *Qnsld., Austral.* **211** RII
Narembeem, *W. Aust., Austral.* **211** X3
Nares Plain, *Atl. Oc.* **236** K5
Naretha, *W. Aust., Austral.* **211** W5
Narew, river, *Pol.* **149** CI6
Narib, *Namibia* **202** H7
Nariva Swamp, *Trinidad & Tobago* **121** P23
Narlı, *Turk.* **168** HI2
Narmada, river, *India* **178** J4
Narmidj, island, *Marshall Is.* **216** K7
Narnaul, *India* **178** F5
Narndee, *W. Aust., Austral.* **211** W3
Narngulu, *W. Aust., Austral.* **211** W2
Narni, *It.* **150** J8
Narodnaya, peak, *Russ.* **166** C7
Narodnaya, Gora, *Russ.* **158** FIO
Narooma, *N.S.W., Austral.* **211** ZI4
Narovorovo, *Vanuatu* **218** C3
Narowal, *Pak.* **177** PI2
Narowlya, *Belarus* **156** M5
Narrabri, *N.S.W., Austral.* **211** WI4
Narragansett Pier, *R.I., U.S.* **95** MI4

Narrandera, *N.S.W., Austral.* **211** YI3
Narran Lake, *Austral.* **210** JI3
Narrogin, *W. Aust., Austral.* **211** X3
Narrows, *Va., U.S.* **96** F9
Narsarsuaq, *Greenland, Den.* **81** D22
Narsinghgarh, *India* **178** H5
Narsipatnam, *India* **178** M8
Nartës, Laguna e, *Albania* **152** M9
Nartkala, *Russ.* **157** TI3
Naruko, *Japan* **184** LI3
Naruto, *Japan* **185** Q8
Narva, *Est.* **141** KI7
Narvik, *Nor.* **140** DI2
Narvskoye Vodokhranilishche, *Russ.* **156** F5
Nar'yan Mar, *Russ.* **158** EIO
Naryilco, *Qnsld., Austral.* **211** VII
Naryn, river, *Kyrg.* **176** FIO
Naryn, *Kyrg.* **176** FI2
Naryn, *Russ.* **159** MI4
Naryn Khuduk, *Russ.* **157** SI4
Narynqol, *Kaz.* **175** HI8
Naryn Qum, desert, *Kaz.* **174** E5
Näs, *Sw.* **140** HI2
Nasarawa, *Nigeria* **201** GI4
Nasca, *Peru* **130** J4
Nasca Ridge, *Pac. Oc.* **239** M2O
Nashua, Iowa, *U.S.* **104** MI2
Nashua, *Mont., U.S.* **106** BI2
Nashua, *N.H., U.S.* **95** JI4
Nashville, *Ark., U.S.* **100** H6
Nashville, *Ga., U.S.* **97** P6
Nashville, *Ill., U.S.* **99** T5
Nashville, *Tenn., U.S.* **101** EI5
Nashwauk, *Minn., U.S.* **104** FII
Näsijärvi, lake, *Fin.* **141** HI5
Nasik, *India* **178** K4
Nasir, *Sudan* **199** GI3
Nasirabad, *India* **178** G4
Naso, *It.* **151** RII
Nassau, island, *Cook Is., N.Z.* **214** JII
Nassau, *Bahamas* **120** BII
Nassawadox, *Va., U.S.* **96** EI4
Nasser, Lake, *Egypt* **197** EI9
Nässjö, *Sw.* **141** MI3
Nastapoka Islands, *Nunavut, Can.* **83** KI8
Nata, *Botswana* **202** GIO
Natal, *Indonesia* **188** J5
Natal, *Braz.* **131** FI8
Natal Downs, *Qnsld., Austral.* **211** SI3
Natalia, *Tex., U.S.* **103** S9
Natal'inskiy, *Russ.* **159** C22
Natanz, *Iran* **173** DI3
Natara, *Russ.* **159** FI6
Natashquan, river, *Nfld. & Lab., Que., Can.* **83** L2I
Natashquan, *Que., Can.* **83** M22
Natchez, *Miss., U.S.* **100** M9
Natchitoches, *La., U.S.* **100** M7
Natewa Bay, *Fiji Is.* **218** G8
National City, *Calif., U.S.* **109** ZIO
National Museum of Fine Arts, *Monaco* **161** C2I
Natitingou, *Benin* **200** FII
Natividad, Isla, *Mex.* **114** D5
Natividade, *Braz.* **131** GI3
Natkyizin, *Myanmar* **186** M7
Natoma, *Kans., U.S.* **105** S6
Nattavaara, *Sw.* **141** EI4
Natuna Besar, island, *Indonesia* **188** G9
Natuna Besar, Kepulauan (Bunguran Utara), *Indonesia* **188** G8
Natuna Islands, *Indonesia* **166** LII
Natuna Selatan, Kepulauan (Bunguran Selatan), *Indonesia* **188** H9
Natural Bridges National Monument, *Utah, U.S.* **107** P9
Naturaliste, Cape, *Austral.* **210** K2
Naturaliste Plateau, *Ind. Oc.* **241** MI5
Naturita, *Colo., U.S.* **107** NIO
Naturno, *It.* **150** C6
Naubinway, *Mich., U.S.* **98** GIO
Naukot, *Pak.* **177** W8
Naungpale, *Myanmar* **186** J7
Nauroz Kalat, *Pak.* **177** S5
Nauru, *Pac. Oc.* **214** G7
Naushahra, *India* **177** NI2
Naushahro Firoz, *Pak.* **177** U7
Nausori, *Fiji Is.* **218** J7
Nauta, *Peru* **130** E4
Nautla, *Mex.* **115** HI3
Nauvoo, *Ill., U.S.* **99** Q3

Navabelitsa, *Belarus* 156 M6
Navadwip, *India* 178 J11
Navahrudak, *Belarus* 156 K4
Navai, *Fiji Is.* 218 H6
Navajo Mountain, *Utah, U.S.* 107 Q8
Navajo National Monument, *Ariz., U.S.* 107 Q8
Navajo Reservoir, *N. Mex., U.S.* 107 Q11
Navalmoral de la Mata, *Sp.* 144 G9
Navan (An Uaimh), *Ire.* 143 R6
Navapolatsk, *Belarus* 156 J5
Navarin, Cape, *N. Amer.* 80 P3
Navarin, Mys, *Russ.* 159 B21
Navarin, Cape, *Russ.* 166 A13
Navarino, Isla, *Chile* 133 Y9
Navarrenx, *Fr.* 147 Y6
Navasota, river, *Tex., U.S.* 103 N12
Navasota, *Tex., U.S.* 103 Q13
Navassa Island, *Greater Antilles* 117 M14
Navia, *Sp.* 144 A8
Navidad, river, *Tex., U.S.* 103 R12
Naviti, island, *Fiji Is.* 218 H5
Năvodari, *Rom.* 153 F18
Navoiy, *Uzb.* 174 L11
Navojoa, *Mex.* 114 E7
Navrongo, *Ghana* 200 F10
Navsari, *India* 178 K3
Navua, river, *Fiji Is.* 218 J6
Navua, *Fiji Is.* 218 J6
Nawá, *Syr.* 170 K7
Nawabshah, *Pak.* 177 V7
Nawada, *India* 178 H10
Nawah, *Afghan.* 177 P7
Nawalgarh, *India* 178 F5
Nawāşif, Ḥarrat, *Saudi Arabia* 172 L8
Naxçıvan, region, *Azerb.* 169 F19
Naxçıvan, *Azerb.* 169 F19
Náxos, island, *Gr.* 155 L15
Náxos, *Gr.* 155 L15
Naxos, ruin, *It.* 151 S12
Naxxar, *Malta* 161 K22
Nayau, island, *Fiji Is.* 218 J9
Nāy Band, *Iran* 173 E16
Nayoro, *Japan* 184 E14
Nay Pyi Taw, *Myanmar* 186 J6
Nazaré, *Port.* 144 G5
Nazaré, *Braz.* 131 H16
Nazareth *see* Naẕerat, *Israel* 170 L6
Nazareth, *Vanuatu* 218 C3
Nazareth Bank, *Ind. Oc.* 240 J7
Nazas, *Mex.* 114 F9
Naze, *Japan* 185 W3
Naẕerat (Nazareth), *Israel* 170 L6
Nāzīk, *Iran* 172 A10
Nazik Gölü, *Turk.* 169 F16
Nazilli, *Turk.* 168 G4
Nazimiye, *Turk.* 169 F14
Nazimovo, *Russ.* 159 J13
Naziya, *Russ.* 156 F7
Nazran', *Russ.* 157 U14
Nazrēt, *Eth.* 199 G15
Ndai *see* Dai, island, *Solomon Is.* 217 M19
N'dalatando, *Angola* 202 C6
Ndélé, *Cen. Af. Rep.* 198 G9
Ndendé, *Gabon* 201 M16
Ndeni *see* Nendo, island, *Solomon Is.* 217 Q22
N'Djamena, *Chad* 197 J14
Ndola, *Zambia* 202 D11
Nduindui, *Solomon Is.* 217 P18
Nduindui, *Vanuatu* 218 C2
Nea Epidavros, *Gr.* 154 K11
Neagh, Lough, *N. Ire., U.K.* 143 P7
Neah Bay, *Wash., U.S.* 108 B2
Neale, Lake, *Austral.* 210 F7
Néa Mihanióna, *Gr.* 154 D11
Nea Moni, *Gr.* 155 H16
Néa Moudaniá, *Gr.* 154 D11
Neápoli, *Gr.* 154 D8
Neápoli, *Gr.* 154 M11
Neapolis *see* Kavála, *Gr.* 155 C13
Near Islands, *Alas., U.S.* 110 L1
Néa Zíhni, *Gr.* 154 B12
Neba, Île, *New Caledonia, Fr.* 218 B6
Nebine Creek, *Austral.* 210 H13
Neblina, Pico da, *Braz., Venez.* 130 C7
Nebraska, *U.S.* 105 P2
Nebraska City, *Nebr., U.S.* 105 Q9
Nebrodi, Monti, *It.* 151 S11
Nécé, *New Caledonia, Fr.* 218 D10
Necedah, *Wis., U.S.* 98 K4
Neches, river, *Tex., U.S.* 103 N15
Neckar, river, *Ger.* 148 K6
Neckarboo Range, *Austral.* 210 K12

Necker Island, *Hawai'i, U.S.* 112 M7
Necker Ridge, *Pac. Oc.* 238 G11
Necochea, *Arg.* 133 N12
Nederland, *Tex., U.S.* 103 Q16
Needham's Point, *Barbados* 121 L18
Needles, *Calif., U.S.* 109 W12
Neenah, *Wis., U.S.* 98 K6
Neftçala, *Azerb.* 169 E23
Nefteyugansk, *Russ.* 158 H11
Negaunee, *Mich., U.S.* 98 F7
Negeribatin, *Indonesia* 188 L7
Negev, region, *Israel* 171 P5
Negoiul, peak, *Rom.* 153 E14
Negomane, *Mozambique* 203 D14
Negombo, *Sri Lanka* 179 T7
Negonego, island, *Fr. Polynesia, Fr.* 219 F20
Negotin, *Serb.* 152 G12
Negra, Laguna, *Uru.* 132 L15
Negre, Pic, *Andorra, Sp.* 160 K3
Negreira, *Sp.* 144 B5
Negreşti-Oaş, *Rom.* 153 B13
Negril, *Jam.* 120 H5
Negritos, *Peru* 130 E1
Negro, river, *Arg.* 133 P10
Negro, river, *Bol.* 130 J8
Negro, river, *Col., Venez.* 128 G9
Negro, river, *Guatemala* 115 L15
Negro, river, *Braz.* 130 D9
Negros, island, *Philippines* 189 E14
Negru Vodă, *Rom.* 153 G17
Nehbandān, *Iran* 173 E17
Nehe, *China* 181 C16
Néhoué, Baie de, *New Caledonia, Fr.* 218 C6
Nehus, Cape, *P.N.G.* 217 J14
Neiafu, *Tonga* 218 L11
Neiba, *Dom. Rep.* 117 M17
Neiba, Bahía de, *Dom. Rep.* 117 M18
Neiden, *Nor.* 141 C15
Neiges, Piton des, *Reunion, Fr.* 205 G16
Neihart, *Mont., U.S.* 106 D8
Neijiang, *China* 180 L12
Neillsville, *Wis., U.S.* 98 J4
Neilson Reef, *Pac. Oc.* 239 N13
Nei Mongol Gaoyuan, region, *China* 182 B2
Neiqiu, *China* 182 F5
Neiva, *Col.* 128 G5
Nekoosa, *Wis., U.S.* 98 J5
Neksø, *Den.* 141 P13
Nekurandu, island, *Maldives* 179 T3
Nelemnoye, *Russ.* 159 E19
Nelidovo, *Russ.* 156 J7
Neligh, *Nebr., U.S.* 105 N7
Nel'kan, *Russ.* 159 H19
Nell, island, *Marshall Is.* 216 L4
Nellore, *India* 179 P7
Nell Passage, *Marshall Is.* 216 L3
Nelson, *B.C., Can.* 82 M9
Nelson, *Eng., U.K.* 143 R11
Nelson, river, *Man., Can.* 83 L14
Nelson, *N.Z.* 213 M18
Nelson, *Nebr., U.S.* 105 R7
Nelson, *Nev., U.S.* 109 V12
Nelson, Cape, *Austral.* 210 M11
Nelson, Estrecho, *Chile* 133 W6
Nelson House, *Man., Can.* 83 L13
Nelson Island, *Alas., U.S.* 110 J11
Nelson Lagoon, *Alas., U.S.* 110 N12
Nelson Reservoir, *Mont., U.S.* 106 B11
Néma, *Mauritania* 196 G7
Neman *see* Nemunas, river, *Eur.* 138 E8
Neman, *Russ.* 156 J2
Nembrala, *Indonesia* 189 N14
Neméa, *Gr.* 154 J10
Nemiscau, *Que., Can.* 83 M18
Nemrut Dagh, ruin, *Turk.* 169 H13
Nemrut Gölü, *Turk.* 169 G16
Nemunas, river, *Lith.* 141 N16
Nemuro, *Japan* 184 F16
Nemuro Strait, *Japan* 184 E16
Nen, river, *China* 181 B16
Nenagh, *Ire.* 143 T4
Nenana, *Alas., U.S.* 111 G17
Nendeln, *Liech.* 160 N2
Nendo (Ndeni), island, *Solomon Is.* 217 Q22
Nenjiang, *China* 181 C16
Nenom, Mochun, *F.S.M.* 217 B14
Neoch, islands, *F.S.M.* 217 D15
Neodesha, *Kans., U.S.* 105 U9
Neola, *Utah, U.S.* 106 L9
Néos, *Gr.* 154 D12
Neosho, river, *Kans., Okla., U.S.* 85 H13

Neosho, *Mo., U.S.* 105 V11
Nepa, *Russ.* 159 J15
Nepal, *Asia* 167 V8
Nepalganj, *Nepal* 178 F8
Nepean, island, *Norfolk I., Austral.* 217 G20
Nephi, *Utah, U.S.* 106 M7
Nephin, peak, *Ire.* 143 Q3
Nepis, Mochun, *F.S.M.* 217 C15
Neptune Range, *Antarctica* 226 G10
Nèrassol, Pic de, *Fr.* 160 H6
Nerchinsk, *Russ.* 159 L17
Nerchinskiy Zavod, *Russ.* 159 L18
Nerekhta, *Russ.* 156 H10
Neretva, river, *Bosn. & Herzg., Croatia* 152 H7
Neretvanski Kanal, *Croatia* 152 H7
Neriquinha, *Angola* 202 F8
Néris, *Fr.* 147 T10
Nerja, *Sp.* 144 M10
Nero Seamount, *Hawai'i, U.S.* 112 K2
Nerpo, *Russ.* 159 J17
Nerva, *Sp.* 144 K7
Nesika Beach, *Oreg., U.S.* 108 K1
Neskaupstaður, *Ice.* 140 F4
Nespelem, *Wash., U.S.* 108 B7
Ness, Loch, *Scot., U.K.* 142 J9
Ness City, *Kans., U.S.* 105 T5
Néstos, river, *Gr.* 155 B13
Netanya, *Israel* 170 L5
Netherdale, *Qnsld., Austral.* 211 S14
Netherlands, *Eur.* 139 T5
Netherlands Antilles, islands, *Neth., Lesser Antilles* 118 L9
Nettilling Lake, *Nunavut, Can.* 83 G18
Netzahualcóyotl, *Mex.* 114 J12
Neuberg, *Ger.* 148 L12
Neubrandenburg, *Ger.* 148 C10
Neuchâtel, *Switz.* 150 B2
Neuchâtel, Lac de, *Switz.* 150 B1
Neuerburg, *Ger.* 160 H10
Neufchâteau, *Belg.* 146 M13
Neufchâteau, *Fr.* 147 Q13
Neumagen, *Ger.* 148 H5
Neumayer, station, *Antarctica* 226 A11
Neumünster, *Ger.* 148 B8
Neun, river, *Laos* 186 H11
Neunkirchen, *Aust.* 148 L12
Neunkirchen, *Ger.* 148 H5
Neuquén, river, *Arg.* 133 N7
Neuquén, *Arg.* 133 P8
Neuruppin, *Ger.* 148 D10
Neuschwanstein, site, *Ger.* 148 L8
Neuse, river, *N.C., U.S.* 96 H12
Neusiedler See, *Aust., Hung.* 149 L13
Neuss, *Ger.* 148 F5
Neustadt, *Ger.* 148 H6
Neustrelitz, *Ger.* 148 C10
Neu-Ulm, *Ger.* 148 K7
Neuve la Habay, *Belg.* 160 J8
Neuvic, *Fr.* 147 V8
Neuwied, *Ger.* 148 G5
Nevada, *Iowa, U.S.* 105 N11
Nevada, *Mo., U.S.* 105 U11
Nevada, *U.S.* 109 Q8
Nevada, Sierra, *N. Amer.* 80 J2
Nevada, Sierra, *Sp.* 144 L11
Nevada City, *Calif., U.S.* 109 Q5
Nevea, *Solomon Is.* 217 P22
Nevel', *Russ.* 156 J6
Never, *Russ.* 159 K18
Nevers, *Fr.* 147 S11
Nevinnomyssk, *Russ.* 157 T12
Nevis, island, *St. Kitts & Nevis* 121 C18
Nevis, Loch, *Scot., U.K.* 142 K8
Nevis Peak, *St. Kitts & Nevis* 121 C18
Nevşehir, *Turk.* 168 G10
New, river, *Guyana* 129 G15
New, river, *N.C., U.S.* 96 J13
New, river, *Va., U.S.* 96 F9
New Albany, *Ind., U.S.* 99 T9
New Albany, *Miss., U.S.* 100 H12
New Amsterdam, *Guyana* 129 D15
Newark, *Ark., U.S.* 100 F9
Newark, *Del., U.S.* 96 B14
Newark, *Eng., U.K.* 143 S13
Newark, *N.J., U.S.* 94 N11
Newark, *N.Y., U.S.* 94 J7
Newark, *Ohio, U.S.* 99 R13
Newaygo, *Mich., U.S.* 98 L9
New Bedford, *Mass., U.S.* 95 L15
Newberg, *Oreg., U.S.* 108 F3
New Bern, *N.C., U.S.* 96 J13

Newbern, *Tenn., U.S.* 100 E12
Newberry, *Fla., U.S.* 97 R7
Newberry, *Mich., U.S.* 98 F10
Newberry, *S.C., U.S.* 96 K8
Newbiggin by the Sea, *Eng., U.K.* 143 N12
New Bight, *Bahamas* 117 F13
New Boston, *Ohio, U.S.* 99 T13
New Boston, *Tex., U.S.* 102 K15
New Braunfels, *Tex., U.S.* 103 R10
New Britain, *Conn., U.S.* 94 L12
New Britain, island, *P.N.G.* 213 C21
New Brunswick, *Can.* 83 P21
New Brunswick, *N.J., U.S.* 94 N10
Newburg, *Mo., U.S.* 105 U13
Newburgh, *N.Y., U.S.* 94 M11
Newburgh, *Scot., U.K.* 142 K11
Newbury, *Eng., U.K.* 143 V12
New Caledonia *see* Nouvelle-Calédonie, island, *New Caledonia, Fr.* 218 D6
New Caledonia Basin, *Pac. Oc.* 238 N8
New Castle, *Ind., U.S.* 99 R10
New Castle, *Pa., U.S.* 94 M3
Newcastle, *Calif., U.S.* 109 Q5
Newcastle, *Eng., U.K.* 143 P12
Newcastle, *Jam.* 120 J10
Newcastle, *N.S.W., Austral.* 211 X15
Newcastle, *St. Kitts & Nevis* 121 B18
Newcastle, *Tex., U.S.* 102 K9
Newcastle, *Wyo., U.S.* 106 G14
Newcastle under Lyme, *Eng., U.K.* 143 S11
Newcastle Waters, *N. Terr., Austral.* 211 R8
Newcastle West, *Ire.* 143 T3
New City, *N.Y., U.S.* 94 M11
Newdegate, *W. Aust., Austral.* 211 X3
New Delhi, *India* 178 F6
Newell, *S. Dak., U.S.* 104 K2
New England, *N. Dak., U.S.* 104 G2
New England Range, *Austral.* 210 J15
New England Seamounts, *Atl. Oc.* 236 H5
Newenham, Cape, *Alas., U.S.* 110 L12
Newfoundland, Island of, *Nfld. & Lab., Can.* 83 M23
Newfoundland and Labrador, *Can.* 83 K21
Newfoundland Evaporation Basin, *Utah, U.S.* 106 K6
New Franklin, *Mo., U.S.* 105 S12
New Galloway, *Scot., U.K.* 143 P9
New Georgia, island, *Solomon Is.* 217 M16
New Georgia Group, *Solomon Is.* 217 M16
New Georgia Sound (The Slot), *Solomon Is.* 217 M17
New Glasgow, *N.S., Can.* 83 P22
New Grant, *Trinidad & Tobago* 121 Q22
New Guinea, island, *Indonesia, P.N.G.* 166 L10
New Hampshire, *U.S.* 95 J14
New Hampton, *Iowa, U.S.* 104 M12
New Hanover, island, *P.N.G.* 213 B21
New Harbor, *Me., U.S.* 95 G17
New Haven, *Conn., U.S.* 94 M12
New Haven, *Ind., U.S.* 99 P10
New Iberia, *La., U.S.* 100 Q9
New Ipswich, *N.H., U.S.* 95 J14
New Ireland, island, *P.N.G.* 213 C21
New Jersey, *U.S.* 94 P10
Newkirk, *N. Mex., U.S.* 107 S14
Newkirk, *Okla., U.S.* 102 E11
New Lexington, *Ohio, U.S.* 99 R14
New Lisbon, *Wis., U.S.* 98 K4
New Liskeard, *Ont., Can.* 83 P18
New London, *Conn., U.S.* 95 M13
New London, *Iowa, U.S.* 105 Q13
New London, *Wis., U.S.* 98 J6
New Madrid, *Mo., U.S.* 105 V16
Newman, *Calif., U.S.* 109 S5
Newman, *W. Aust., Austral.* 211 T3
Newman Grove, *Nebr., U.S.* 105 P7
New Market, *Va., U.S.* 96 D11
Newmarket, *Eng., U.K.* 143 U14
Newmarket, *Ire.* 143 U3
New Martinsville, *W. Va., U.S.* 96 C9
New Meadows, *Idaho, U.S.* 106 F4
New Mexico, *U.S.* 107 S10
Newnan, *Ga., U.S.* 96 L4
New Orleans, *La., U.S.* 100 Q11
New Philadelphia, *Ohio, U.S.* 99 Q15
New Plymouth, *N.Z.* 213 L18
Newport, *Ark., U.S.* 100 F10
Newport, *Eng., U.K.* 143 X13
Newport, *Jam.* 120 J8

Newport, *Ky., U.S.* 101 A18
Newport, *Me., U.S.* 95 F17
Newport, *Oreg., U.S.* 108 G2
Newport, *R.I., U.S.* 95 M14
Newport, *Tenn., U.S.* 101 E19
Newport, *Vt., U.S.* 95 E13
Newport, *Wales, U.K.* 143 V10
Newport, *Wash., U.S.* 108 B9
Newport Beach, *Calif., U.S.* 109 Y8
Newport News, *Va., U.S.* 96 F14
New Port Richey, *Fla., U.S.* 97 T7
New Prague, *Minn., U.S.* 104 K11
New Providence, island, *Bahamas* 116 E11
Newquay, *Eng., U.K.* 143 X8
New Richmond, *Wis., U.S.* 98 H2
New Roads, *La., U.S.* 100 N9
New Rochelle, *N.Y., U.S.* 94 N11
New Rockford, *N. Dak., U.S.* 104 F6
New Ross, *Ire.* 143 U6
Newry, *N. Ire., U.K.* 143 Q7
Newry, *N. Terr., Austral.* 211 Q7
New Salem, *N. Dak., U.S.* 104 G4
New Sandy Bay, *St. Vincent & the Grenadines* 121 J17
New Schwabenland, region, *Antarctica* 226 C12
New Siberian Islands *see* Novosibirskiye Ostrova, *Russ.* 159 D16
New Smyrna Beach, *Fla., U.S.* 97 S9
New South Wales, *Austral.* 211 W13
New Springs, *W. Aust., Austral.* 211 U3
New Stuyahok, *Alas., U.S.* 111 K14
Newton, *Ill., U.S.* 99 S6
Newton, *Iowa, U.S.* 105 P12
Newton, *Kans., U.S.* 105 U7
Newton, *Mass., U.S.* 95 K14
Newton, *Miss., U.S.* 100 L12
Newton, *Tex., U.S.* 103 P16
Newton Abbot, *Eng., U.K.* 143 X10
Newton Stewart, *Scot., U.K.* 143 P9
New Town, *N. Dak., U.S.* 104 F3
Newtown *see* St. Boswells, *Scot., U.K.* 143 N11
Newtown, *Wales, U.K.* 143 T10
Newtownabbey, *N. Ire., U.K.* 143 P7
Newtownards, *N. Ire., U.K.* 143 Q7
Newtownbarry *see* Bunclody, *Ire.* 143 T6
Newtownstewart, *N. Ire., U.K.* 143 P6
New Ulm, *Minn., U.S.* 104 K10
New Waverly, *Tex., U.S.* 103 P13
New York, *N.Y., U.S.* 94 N11
New York, *U.S.* 94 K6
New Zealand, *Pac. Oc.* 214 P8
Neya, *Russ.* 156 G12
Neyrīz, *Iran* 173 G14
Neyshābūr, *Iran* 173 C16
Nezperce, *Idaho, U.S.* 106 D4
Nez Perce National Historic Park, *Idaho, U.S.* 106 D3
Nez Perce Pass, *Idaho, Mont., U.S.* 106 E5
Ngabordamlu, Tanjung, *Indonesia* 213 D15
Ngain, island, *Marshall Is.* 216 K7
Ngajangel, island, *Palau* 216 K12
Ngake, island, *Cook Is., N.Z.* 218 B14
Ngake, Pukapuka, *Cook Is., N.Z.* 218 Q2
Ngala, *Cameroon* 201 E17
Ngalkol, *Palau* 216 Q10
Ngamegei Passage, *Palau* 216 L12
Ngami, Lake, *Botswana* 202 G9
Ngamring, *China* 180 L6
Ngangla Ringco, lake, *China* 180 K5
Nganglong Kangri, range, *China* 180 J5
Nganglong Range, *China* 166 H8
Ngaoundéré, *Cameroon* 201 G16
Ngaramasch, *Palau* 216 R9
Ngardmau, *Palau* 216 M12
Ngardmau Bay, *Palau* 216 M12
Ngaregur, island, *Palau* 216 L12
Ngarekeklau, island, *Palau* 216 L12
Ngaremediu, island, *Palau* 216 P11
Ngaruangl Passage, *Palau* 216 J12
Ngaruawahia, *N.Z.* 213 K19
Ngatangiia, *Cook Is., N.Z.* 218 Q9
Ngatik Atoll, *F.S.M.* 216 Q7
Ngauruhoe, Mount, *N.Z.* 213 L19
Ngcheangel *see* Kayangel Islands, islands, *Palau* 216 K12
Ngeaur *see* Angaur, island, *Palau* 216 R10
Ngemelis Islands, *Palau* 216 Q10
Ngerchelchuus, Mount, *Palau* 216 M12

Ngerchelong see Arekalong Peninsula, peninsula, Palau 216 M12
Ngeregong, island, Palau 216 Q11
Ngergoi, island, Palau 216 Q10
Ngertachebeab see Komebail Lagoon, lake, Palau 216 N11
Ngeruktabel see Urukthapel, island, Palau 216 P11
Ngesebus, island, Palau 216 Q10
Nggatokae, island, Solomon Is. 217 N17
Nggela Pile, island, Solomon Is. 217 N19
Nggela Sule, island, Solomon Is. 217 N19
Ngobasangel, island, Palau 216 P10
Ngoïla, Cameroon 201 J17
Ngoko, river, Cameroon, Congo 201 K17
Ngoring Hu, China 180 J10
Ngorongoro Crater, Tanzania 199 L14
Ngounié, river, Gabon 201 L15
Ngourti, Niger 197 H13
Nguigmi, Niger 197 H13
Nguiu, N. Terr., Austral. 211 P7
Ngukurr, N. Terr., Austral. 211 Q9
Ngulu Atoll, F.S.M. 216 Q2
Nguna, island, Vanuatu 218 E3
Nguru, Nigeria 201 E15
Nhamundá, Braz. 130 D10
Nha Trang, Vietnam 187 N14
Nhulunbuy, N. Terr., Austral. 211 P10
Niafounké, Mali 196 H8
Niagara, river, N.Y., U.S. 94 H5
Niagara, Wis., U.S. 98 G7
Niagara Falls, Can., U.S. 85 E19
Niah, Malaysia 188 G11
Niamey, Niger 196 J10
Niangara, Dem. Rep. of the Congo 198 H11
Niangua, river, Mo., U.S. 105 U12
Nianiau, Pu'u, Hawai'i, U.S. 113 G17
Nianzishan, China 181 C16
Nias, island, Indonesia 188 H4
Niau, island, Fr. Polynesia, Fr. 219 E17
Nibok, region, Nauru 217 E23
Nicaea see İznik, Turk. 168 D5
Nicaragua, N. Amer. 81 Q20
Nicaragua, Lago de, Nicar. 115 M18
Nicaragua, Lake see Nicar., Lago de, N. Amer. 80 Q8
Nicastro, It. 151 Q13
Nice, Fr. 147 X16
Nicephorium see Ar Raqqah, Syr. 170 E11
Niceville, Fla., U.S. 97 Q2
Nichinan, Japan 185 T5
Nicholas Channel, Bahamas, Cuba 116 F8
Nicholasville, Ky., U.S. 101 B18
Nicholls' Town, Bahamas 116 E11
Nicholson, W. Aust., Austral. 211 R7
Nicholson Range, Austral. 210 H2
Nickavilla, Qnsld., Austral. 211 U12
Nickerson, Kans., U.S. 105 T7
Nicobar Islands, India 179 S14
Nicopolis, ruin, Gr. 154 G7
Nicosia see Lefkosia, Cyprus 160 N8
Nicosia, It. 151 S11
Nicoya, Península de, Costa Rica 115 N18
Nicoya Peninsula see Nicoya, Península de, N. Amer. 80 Q8
Nida, Lith. 141 N15
Nidzh, Azerb. 169 C21
Nidzica, Pol. 149 C15
Niederanven, Lux. 160 J10
Niedere Tauern, Aust. 148 L11
Nienburg, Ger. 148 D7
Nieuw Amsterdam, Suriname 129 E16
Nieuw Nickerie, Suriname 129 E15
Nieuwpoort, Neth. Antilles, Neth. 121 Q15
Nieves, Pico da las, Canary Is. 204 R5
Nif, F.S.M. 217 D18
Nifiloli, island, Solomon Is. 217 P23
Niğde, Turk. 168 G10
Niger, Af. 195 G17
Niger, river, Af. 194 H5
Niger, Source of the, Guinea 194 H2
Niger Delta, Nigeria 201 J13
Nigeria, Af. 195 H17
Nightingale Island, Tristan da Cunha Is., U.K. 194 R2
Nigríta, Gr. 154 C12
Nihing, river, Pak. 177 V2
Nihiru, island, Fr. Polynesia, Fr. 219 E19
Nihoa, island, Hawai'i, U.S. 112 M8
Nihonmatsu, Japan 184 M13
Niigata, Japan 184 M11
Niihama, Japan 185 R7
Ni'ihau, island, Hawai'i, U.S. 112 C3
Niimi, Japan 185 Q7
Nii Shima, Japan 185 Q12
Nijmegen, Neth. 146 J13
Nikalap Aru, island, F.S.M. 217 G13
Nikao, Cook Is., N.Z. 218 Q9
Nikaupara, Cook Is., N.Z. 218 Q11
Níkea, Gr. 154 F10
Nikel', Russ. 158 C9
Nikiboko, Neth. Antilles, Neth. 121 Q19
Nikítas, Gr. 154 D12
Nikitin Seamount, Ind. Oc. 240 G10
Nikolai, Alas., U.S. 111 H15
Nikolayevsk, Russ. 157 N13
Nikolayevskiy, Russ. 159 J19
Nikolayevsk na Amure, Russ. 159 J21
Nikol'sk, Russ. 156 K13
Nikolski, Alas., U.S. 110 P8
Nikol'skoye, Russ. 157 Q14
Nikol'skoye, Russ. 159 E23
Nikopol', Ukr. 157 Q8
Nīk Pey, Iran 172 B11
Niksar, Turk. 168 D12
Nīk Shahr, Iran 173 H17
Nikšić, Mont. 152 J8
Nikumaroro, island, Kiribati 214 H10
Nil, Russ. 159 K18
Nilandu, island, Maldives 179 V3
Nilandu, island, Maldives 179 W3
Nilandu Atoll, Maldives 179 V3
Nile, river, Af. 194 E9
Nile, Sources of the, Burundi, Rwanda 194 K9
Nile River Delta, Egypt 194 D9
Niles, Mich., U.S. 99 N9
Niles, Ohio, U.S. 99 P15
Nilgiri Hills, India 179 Q5
Nimach, India 178 H4
Nimbahera, India 178 H4
Nimba Mountains, Côte d'Ivoire 200 G7
Nimbin, N.S.W., Austral. 211 W15
Nîmes, Fr. 147 X12
Nímos, island, Gr. 155 M19
Nimrod Glacier, Antarctica 227 L13
Ninati, Indonesia 189 L21
Nine Degree Channel, India 179 S3
Ninetyeast Ridge, Ind. Oc. 240 K11
Ninety Mile Beach, Austral. 210 M13
Ninety Mile Beach, N.Z. 213 H18
Nineveh, ruin, Iraq 172 C9
Ninfas, Punta, Arg. 133 R10
Ningbo, China 182 L10
Ningcheng, China 182 C8
Ningde, China 183 P8
Ningdu, China 183 P6
Ningguo, China 182 L8
Ningshan, China 182 H1
Ningwu, China 182 D4
Ningyuan, China 183 P3
Ninh Binh, Vietnam 186 H12
Ninh Hoa, Vietnam 187 N14
Ninigo Group, P.N.G. 213 B18
Ninilchik, Alas., U.S. 111 K16
Niniva, island, Tonga 218 P6
Ninnescah, river, Kans., U.S. 105 U7
Ninni, island, Marshall Is. 216 N5
Ninnis Glacier, Antarctica 227 Q16
Nīnole, Hawai'i, U.S. 113 L21
Nīnole, Hawai'i, U.S. 113 P20
Ninove, Belg. 146 L11
Nioaque, Braz. 130 L10
Niobrara, river, Nebr., U.S. 104 M5
Nioro du Sahel, Mali 196 H6
Niort, Fr. 147 T7
Nioumachoua, Comoros 205 N15
Nipawin, Sask., Can. 82 M12
Nipe, Bahía de, Cuba 117 K13
Nipigon, Ont., Can. 83 P16
Nipigon, Lake, Ont., Can. 83 N16
Nipton, Calif., U.S. 109 V12
Niquelândia, Braz. 131 J13
Niquero, Cuba 116 K11
Nīr, Iran 172 B11
Nirmal, India 178 L6
Niš, Serb. 152 H11
Nişāb, Saudi Arabia 172 G10
Nişāb, Yemen 172 Q10
Nišava, river, Serb. 152 H12
Nishikō, Japan 185 S4
Nishine, Japan 184 K13
Nishinoomote, Japan 185 U4
Nishino Shima, Japan 185 P6
Nishtūn, Yemen 173 P13
Nissi, Est. 141 K16
Níssiros, island, Gr. 155 M18
Nisswa, Minn., U.S. 104 H10
Niţā', Saudi Arabia 172 H11
Niterói, Braz. 131 M15
Nitra, Slovakia 149 K14
Nitro, W. Va., U.S. 96 D8
Niuafo'ou, island, Tonga 214 J9
Niuatoputapu, island, Tonga 214 J10
Niu Aunfo Point, Tonga 218 H11
Niue, island, N.Z., Pac. Oc. 214 K10
Niulakita, island, Tuvalu 214 J9
Niutao, island, Tuvalu 214 H9
Niutoua, Tonga 218 H12
Niutou Shan, China 182 M10
Nixon, Tex., U.S. 103 R10
Nixon's Harbor, Bahamas 120 C8
Niya see Minfeng, China 180 H6
Nizamabad, India 178 L6
Nizamghat, India 178 F15
Nizam Sagar, lake, India 178 M6
Nizao, Dom. Rep. 117 M19
Nizhnekamsk, Russ. 156 H16
Nizhneshadrino, Russ. 159 J13
Nizhneudinsk, Russ. 159 L14
Nizhnevartovsk, Russ. 158 H11
Nizhneyansk, Russ. 159 E17
Nizhniy Baskunchak, Russ. 157 Q14
Nizhniy Bestyakh, Russ. 159 G18
Nizhniy Lomov, Russ. 156 L12
Nizhniy Novgorod, Russ. 156 J12
Nizhniy Tagil, Russ. 158 H9
Nizhnyaya Tunguska, river, Russ. 159 H13
Nizhnyaya Tura, Russ. 158 H9
Nizhyn, Ukr. 157 N6
Nizip, river, Turk. 168 H12
Nizip, Turk. 168 H12
Nizwá, Oman 173 K16
Nizza Monferrato, It. 150 F3
Nizzana (El 'Auja), Israel 171 P4
Njegoš, peak, Mont. 152 H8
Njombe, Tanzania 199 N13
Nkhata Bay, Malawi 203 D13
Nkhotakota, Malawi 203 D13
Nkongsamba, Cameroon 201 H15
Nmai, river, Myanmar 186 D7
Noatak, river, Alas., U.S. 84 M3
Noatak, Alas., U.S. 111 D13
Noatak National Preserve, Alas., U.S. 111 D14
Nouans-les-Fontaines, Fr. 147 S9
Nobeoka, Japan 185 S5
Noblesville, Ind., U.S. 99 R9
Nobo, Indonesia 189 M14
Noboribetsu, Japan 184 G13
Nocera Terinese, It. 151 Q13
Nocona, Tex., U.S. 102 J10
Nodales, Bahía de los, Arg. 133 U9
Nodaway, river, Mo., U.S. 105 Q10
Nofre, Peña, Sp. 144 D7
Nogáles, Mex. 114 B7
Nogales, Ariz., U.S. 107 W8
Nogara, It. 150 E6
Nōgata, Japan 185 R4
Nogent-le-Rotrou, Fr. 147 Q8
Nogent-sur-Seine, Fr. 147 Q11
Noginsk, Russ. 156 J10
Nogoyá, Arg. 132 K12
Nogu Dabu, island, P.N.G. 217 H18
Nogueira, peak, Port. 144 D7
Nohar, India 178 E4
Noheji, Japan 184 J13
Nohili Point, Hawai'i, U.S. 112 B4
Nohona o Hae, peak, Hawai'i, U.S. 113 L19
Nohta, India 178 J7
Noia, Sp. 144 B5
Noire, Montagne, Fr. 147 X10
Noires, Montagnes, Fr. 147 Q3
Noirmoutier, Île de, Fr. 147 S5
Nojima Zaki, Japan 185 Q12
Noka, Solomon Is. 217 P22
Nokaneng, Botswana 202 G8
Nokia, Fin. 141 J15
Nok Kundi, Pak. 177 S2
Nokomis, Ill., U.S. 99 S5
Nokuku, Vanuatu 218 C1
Nola, Cen. Af. Rep. 198 H8
Noli, It. 150 F3
Nolinsk, Russ. 156 G15
Noma Misaki, Japan 185 T4
Nomans Land, island, Mass., U.S. 95 M15
Nome, Alas., U.S. 110 F12
Nomgon, Mongolia 180 F12
Nomoneas, island, F.S.M. 217 B15
Nomo Saki, Japan 185 S3
Nomuka, island, Tonga 218 Q6
Nomuka Group, Tonga 218 Q6
Nomuka Iki, island, Tonga 218 Q6
Nomwin Atoll, F.S.M. 216 Q6
Nonancourt, Fr. 147 P9
Nondalton, Alas., U.S. 111 K15
Nongjrong, India 178 G14
Nong Khai, Thai. 186 K10
Nonouti, island, Kiribati 214 G8
Nonpareil, Grenada 121 J22
Nonsuch Bay, Antigua & Barbuda 121 B21
Nonsuch Island, Bermuda, U.K. 120 B4
Nonthaburi, Thai. 186 M9
Nonume, Solomon Is. 217 Q22
Nonza, Fr. 150 J4
Noole, Solomon Is. 217 Q22
Noonan, N. Dak., U.S. 104 D2
Noord, Aruba, Neth. 121 Q16
Noordkaap, cape, Aruba, Neth. 121 Q17
Noordpunt, cape, Neth. Antilles, Neth. 121 N13
Noormarkku, Fin. 141 J15
Noorvik, Alas., U.S. 111 E13
Nóqui, Angola 202 B5
Nora, ruin, It. 151 Q4
Nora Hazel Point, Virgin Islands, U.K. 120 Q7
Norak, Taj. 176 J8
Norborne, Mo., U.S. 105 S11
Norcia, It. 150 J9
Nord, Greenland, Den. 81 A20
Nord, Baie du, Mauritius 205 J20
Nord, Pointe, Comoros 205 L14
Nord, Pointe, Wallis & Futuna, Fr. 218 E11
Nord, Pointe, St. Martin, Fr. 121 A15
Nordaustlandet, island, Norway 167 N7
Norden, Ger. 148 C6
Norderstedt, Ger. 148 C8
Nord Est, Grande Récif du, Mayotte, Fr. 205 N17
Nordeste, Azores 144 Q5
Nordfjordeid, Nor. 140 J10
Nordhausen, Ger. 148 F8
Nordhorn, Ger. 148 D5
Nordkapp, cape, Nor. 141 B14
Nordkjosbotn, Nor. 141 D13
Nordli, Nor. 140 G12
Nordoyar, island, Faroe Is., Den. 140 J6
Nore, river, Ire. 143 T5
Norfolk, Nebr., U.S. 105 N7
Norfolk, Va., U.S. 96 F14
Norfolk Island, Austral. 214 L7
Norfolk Ridge, Pac. Oc. 238 M8
Norfork Lake, Ark., U.S. 100 E9
Noril'sk, Russ. 159 F13
Normal, Ill., U.S. 99 Q6
Norman, Ark., U.S. 100 H7
Norman, river, Austral. 210 D11
Norman, Okla., U.S. 102 G11
Norman, Lake, N.C., U.S. 96 H9
Normanby Island, P.N.G. 213 E21
Normandy, region, Fr. 147 P6
Norman's Cay, Bahamas 120 G5
Norman's Pond Cay, Bahamas 120 E8
Normanton, Qnsld., Austral. 211 R11
Norman Wells, N.W.T., Can. 82 F10
Norna, Mount, Austral. 210 E11
Nornalup, W. Aust., Austral. 211 Y3
Ñorquincó, Arg. 133 Q7
Norris Lake, Tenn., U.S. 101 E18
Norristown, Pa., U.S. 94 P9
Norrköping, Sw. 141 L13
Norrsundet, Sw. 141 J13
Norseman, W. Aust., Austral. 211 X4
Norsk, Russ. 159 K19
Norsup, Vanuatu 218 D2
Nort, Fr. 147 R6
Norte, Cabo, Braz. 131 C13
Norte, Punta, Arg. 132 M13
Norte, Serra do, Braz. 130 G9
North, Cape, N.S., Can. 83 N22
North Adams, Mass., U.S. 94 J12
North Albanian Alps, Albania 152 J9
Northampton, Eng., U.K. 143 U13
Northampton, Mass., U.S. 95 K13
Northampton, W. Aust., Austral. 211 W2
Northampton Seamounts, Hawai'i, U.S. 112 L4
North Andaman, island, India 179 P14
North Aral Sea, Kaz. 174 G10
North Arm, N.W.T., Can. 82 H11
North Augusta, S.C., U.S. 96 L8
North Aulatsivik Island, Nfld. & Lab., Can. 83 J20
North Australian Basin, Ind. Oc. 241 J16
North Battleford, Sask., Can. 82 M11
North Bay, Ont., Can. 83 P18
North Belcher Islands, Nunavut, Can. 83 L17
North Bend, Oreg., U.S. 108 J2
North Bimini, island, Bahamas 120 B8
North Branch, Minn., U.S. 104 J12
North Branch Potomac, river, Md., W. Va., U.S. 96 C10
North Caicos, island, Turks & Caicos Is., U.K. 117 H17
North Canadian, river, Okla., U.S. 102 F9
North Cape, N.Z. 213 G18
North Cape see Nordkapp, Nor. 138 A8
North Cape, Kiribati 217 B20
North Carolina, U.S. 96 H7
North Cascades National Park, Wash., U.S. 108 A5
North Channel, Mich., U.S. 98 F12
North Channel, N. Ire., Scot., U.K. 143 N7
North Charleston, S.C., U.S. 96 M10
North Chicago, Ill., U.S. 98 M7
North China Plain, China 166 G11
Northcliffe, W. Aust., Austral. 211 Y3
North Comino Channel, Malta 161 H21
North Dakota, U.S. 104 F2
North Downs, Eng., U.K. 143 V14
North East, Pa., U.S. 94 K3
Northeast Cay, Jam. 116 P11
Northeast Pacific Basin, Pac. Oc. 238 D11
Northeast Pass, Marshall Is. 216 L8
Northeast Passage, Solomon Is. 217 R24
North East Point, Cayman Is., U.K. 116 L9
North East Point, Kiribati 217 B23
Northeast Point, Bahamas 117 G15
Northeast Point, Jam. 120 J11
Northeast Providence Channel, Bahamas 116 D12
Northeim, Ger. 148 E7
North Entrance, Palau 216 K12
Northern Cyprus, Cyprus 160 M8
Northern Dvina, river, Russ. 138 B11
Northern European Plain, Eur. 138 F5
Northern Ireland, U.K. 143 P6
Northern Karroo, region, Lesotho, S. Af. 194 Q7
Northern Light Lake, Minn., U.S. 104 E14
Northern Mariana Islands, U.S., Pac. Oc. 214 D4
Northern Perimeter Highway, Braz. 130 C10
Northern Range, Trinidad & Tobago 121 N22
Northern Sporades see Vóries Sporádes, islands, Gr. 155 F13
Northern Territory, Austral. 211 R8
Northern Uvals, Russ. 138 C12
Northfield, Minn., U.S. 104 K11
Northfield, Vt., U.S. 95 G13
North Fiji Islands Basin, Pac. Oc. 238 L9
North Fond du Lac, Wis., U.S. 98 K6
North Fork, Calif., U.S. 109 S7
North Fork Clearwater, river, Idaho, U.S. 106 D4
North Fork Flathead, river, Mont., U.S. 106 A5
North Fork Payette, river, Idaho, U.S. 106 F4
North Fork Red, river, Okla., Tex., U.S. 102 H8
North Fork Salt, river, Mo., U.S. 105 R13
North Friar's Bay, St. Kitts & Nevis 121 B18
North Frisian Islands, Ger. 148 A7
North Geomagnetic Pole 2005, Nunavut, Can. 83 B16
North Head, N.Z. 213 J18
North Island, N.Z. 213 K18
North Island, Seychelles 205 N19
North Korea, Asia 167 T12
North Lakhimpur, India 178 F14
North Land, islands, Russ. 166 B9
North Land see Severnaya Zemlya, Russ. 159 C14
North Las Vegas, Nev., U.S. 109 U12
North Little Rock, Ark., U.S. 100 G8
North Loup, river, Nebr., U.S. 105 N5
North Magnetic Pole 2006, N.W.T., Can. 83 A13
North Malosmadulu Atoll, Maldives 179 U3
North Manchester, Ind., U.S. 99 P9

North Mole, *Gibraltar, U.K.* **161** N22
North Myrtle Beach, *S.C., U.S.* **96** K12
North Naples, *Fla., U.S.* **97** W8
North Negril Point, *Jam.* **120** H5
North Olmsted, *Ohio, U.S.* **99** P14
North Palmetto Point, *Bahamas* **120** E6
North Pass, *Marshall Is.* **216** K4
North Perry, *Ohio, U.S.* **99** N15
North Pioa, peak, *Amer. Samoa, U.S.*
  218 M8
North Platte, river, *Nebr., U.S.* **105** P2
North Platte, *Nebr., U.S.* **105** Q4
North Point, *Barbados* **121** J18
North Point, *Cook Is., N.Z.* **219** A14
North Point, *Mich., U.S.* **98** H12
North Point, *Seychelles* **205** N2O
Northport, *Ala., U.S.* **101** K14
Northport, *Wash., U.S.* **108** A8
North Powder, *Oreg., U.S.* **108** F8
North Raccoon, river, *Iowa, U.S.* **105** P11
North Rock, *Bahamas* **120** A8
North Roe, *Scot., U.K.* **142** D12
North Ronaldsay, island, *Scot., U.K.*
  142 F11
North Saskatchewan, river, *Alta., Can.*
  82 L11
North Sea, *Eur.* **138** E5
North Sentinel Island, *India* **179** Q14
North Siberian Lowland, *Russ.* **166** C9
North Side, *Cayman Is., U.K.* **120** H3
North Slope, region, *Alas., U.S.* **111** C14
North Sound, *Virgin Islands, U.K.* **120** Q9
North Sound, *Cayman Is., U.K.* **120** J2
North Sound, *Ire.* **143** S3
North Sound Estates, *Cayman Is., U.K.*
  120 J2
North Springfield, *Pa., U.S.* **94** K3
North Stradbroke Island, *Austral.*
  210 H15
North Taranaki Bight, *N.Z.* **213** K18
North Tipalao, *Guam, U.S.* **216** C10
North Tonawanda, *N.Y., U.S.* **94** J5
North Truchas Peak, *N. Mex., U.S.*
  107 R13
North Uist, island, *Scot., U.K.* **142** J6
Northumberland, Cape, *Austral.* **210** M11
Northumberland Islands, *Austral.*
  210 E15
North Vanlaiphai, *India* **178** J14
North Vernon, *Ind., U.S.* **99** S1O
North Walsham, *Eng., U.K.* **143** T15
Northway Junction, *Alas., U.S.* **111** H19
North Waziristan, region, *Afghan.* **177** P8
Northwest Angle, region, *Minn., U.S.*
  104 D1O
Northwest Atlantic Mid-Ocean Canyon,
  Atl. Oc. **236** D6
North West Basin, *Austral.* **210** F1
North West Bay, *Seychelles* **205** N19
North West Cape, *Austral.* **210** F1
Northwestern Hawaiian Islands, *Hawai'i,*
  U.S. **112** K2
Northwest Hawaiian Ridge, *Pac. Oc.*
  238 F1O
Northwest Pacific Basin, *Pac. Oc.*
  238 E7
North West Point, *Cayman Is., U.K.*
  116 L7
North West Point, *Kiribati* **217** A22
Northwest Point, *Bahamas* **120** B1O
Northwest Providence Channel,
  Bahamas **116** C1O
North West River, *Nfld. & Lab., Can.*
  83 L21
Northwest Territories, *Can.* **82** G11
Northwich, *Eng., U.K.* **143** S11
North Wilkesboro, *N.C., U.S.* **96** G8
Northwind Escarpment, *Arctic Oc.*
  242 K6
Northwind Plain, *Arctic Oc.* **242** K6
Northwind Ridge, *Arctic Oc.* **242** K6
Northwood, *Iowa, U.S.* **104** L12
Northwood, *N. Dak., U.S.* **104** F7
North York Moors, *Eng., U.K.* **143** Q13
Norton, *Kans., U.S.* **105** R5
Norton, *Va., U.S.* **96** F7
Norton Bay, *Alas., U.S.* **111** F13
Norton Shores, *Mich., U.S.* **98** L9
Norton Sound, *Alas., U.S.* **110** G12
Norvegia, Cape, *Antarctica* **226** B1O
Norwalk, *Calif., U.S.* **109** X8
Norwalk, *Conn., U.S.* **94** M12
Norwalk, *Ohio, U.S.* **99** P13
Norway, *Eur.* **139** Q6
Norway, *Me., U.S.* **95** G15

Norway, *Mich., U.S.* **98** G7
Norway House, *Man., Can.* **83** M14
Norwegian Basin, *Arctic Oc.* **243** G18
Norwegian Bay, *Nunavut, Can.* **83** C15
Norwegian Sea, *Arctic Oc.* **243** G17
Norwich, *Conn., U.S.* **95** L13
Norwich, *Eng., U.K.* **143** T15
Norwich, *N.Y., U.S.* **94** K9
Norwood, *Colo., U.S.* **107** N1O
Norwood, *N.C., U.S.* **96** J1O
Norwood, *N.Y., U.S.* **94** F1O
Norwood, *Ohio, U.S.* **99** S11
Noshiro, *Japan* **184** J12
Nosivka, *Ukr.* **157** N6
Noşratābād, *Iran* **173** F17
Noss, Isle of, *Scot., U.K.* **142** D12
Nossob, river, *Botswana, S. Af.* **202** J8
Nosy-Varika, *Madagascar* **203** G17
Noteć, river, *Pol.* **149** D13
Noto, *It.* **151** T12
Noto, *Japan* **184** N1O
Noto, Golfo di, *It.* **151** U12
Noto Hantō, *Japan* **184** M1O
Notre Dame Bay, *Nfld. & Lab., Can.*
  83 L23
Nottaway, river, *Que., Can.* **83** N18
Nottingham, *Eng., U.K.* **143** S13
Nottingham Island, *Nunavut, Can.* **83** H17
Nottoway, river, *Va., U.S.* **96** F13
Nouadhibou (Port Etienne), *Mauritania*
  196 F4
Nouakchott, *Mauritania* **196** G5
Nouâmghâr, *Mauritania* **196** F4
Nouart, *Fr.* **147** N13
Nouméa, *New Caledonia, Fr.* **218** E8
Nouna, *Burkina Faso* **200** E9
Nouveau Québec, region, *Que., Can.*
  83 K19
Nouveau-Québec, Cratère du (Chubb
  Crater), *Que., Can.* **83** J18
Nouvelle-Calédonie (New Caledonia),
  island, *New Caledonia, Fr.* **218** C6
Novafeltria, *It.* **150** G8
Nova Friburgo, *Braz.* **131** M15
Nova Gorica, *Slov.* **152** D4
Nova Gradiška, *Croatia* **152** E7
Nova Iguaçu, *Braz.* **131** M14
Nova Kakhovka, *Ukr.* **157** R7
Novalukoml', *Belarus* **156** K5
Nova Mambone, *Mozambique* **203** G13
Nova Odesa, *Ukr.* **157** R6
Nova Olinda do Norte, *Braz.* **130** D9
Novara, *It.* **150** D4
Nova Scotia, *Can.* **83** P22
Nova Sofala, *Mozambique* **203** G13
Nova Xavantina, *Braz.* **130** J12
Novaya Sibir', Ostrov, *Russ.* **159** C17
Novaya Vodolaga, *Ukr.* **157** P8
Novaya Zemlya, island, *Russ.* **166** C7
Nova Zagora, *Bulg.* **153** J15
Novelda, *Sp.* **145** J14
Nové Zámky, *Slovakia* **149** K14
Novhorod-Sivers'kyy, *Ukr.* **156** M7
Novi Bečej, *Serb.* **152** E1O
Novi Ligure, *It.* **150** F4
Novi Pazar, *Bulg.* **153** H16
Novi Pazar, *Serb.* **152** H1O
Novi Sad, *Serb.* **152** E9
Novoaleksandrovsk, *Russ.* **157** S11
Novoanninskiy, *Russ.* **157** N12
Novo Aripuanã, *Braz.* **130** E9
Novobod, *Taj.* **176** H8
Novocherkassk, *Russ.* **157** R11
Novo Cruzeiro, *Braz.* **131** K15
Novo Hamburgo, *Braz.* **130** P12
Novohrad-Volyns'kyy, *Ukr.* **157** N4
Novoīshīmskīy, *Kaz.* **174** C12
Novokuybyshevsk, *Russ.* **156** L15
Novokuznetsk, *Russ.* **158** L12
Novolazarevskaya, station, *Antarctica*
  227 A14
Novo Mesto, *Slov.* **152** D5
Novomichurinsk, *Russ.* **156** K1O
Novomoskovs'k, *Ukr.* **157** Q8
Novomoskovsk, *Russ.* **156** K1O
Novopokrovskaya, *Russ.* **157** S11
Novorepnoye, *Russ.* **156** M15
Novorossiysk, *Russ.* **157** T9
Novorybnoye, *Russ.* **159** F15
Novorzhev, *Russ.* **156** H6
Novoshakhtinsk, *Russ.* **157** Q11
Novosibirsk, *Russ.* **158** K12
Novosibirskiye Ostrova (New Siberian
  Islands), *Russ.* **159** D16

Novotitarovskaya, *Russ.* **157** S1O
Novotroitsk, *Russ.* **158** J7
Novoukrayinka, *Ukr.* **157** Q6
Novouzensk, *Russ.* **157** N15
Novovolyns'k, *Ukr.* **157** N2
Novoye Ust'ye, *Russ.* **159** G2O
Novozybkov, *Russ.* **156** M6
Novvy Buh, *Ukr.* **157** Q7
Novyy Port, *Russ.* **158** F11
Novyy Urengoy, *Russ.* **158** G12
Nowabad-e Ish, *Afghan.* **176** J9
Nowa Nowa, *Vic., Austral.* **211** Z13
Nowa Sól, *Pol.* **148** E12
Nowata, *Okla., U.S.* **102** E13
Now Deh, *Afghan.* **177** P2
Nowood, river, *Wyo., U.S.* **106** G11
Nowra, *N.S.W., Austral.* **211** Y14
Nowrangapur, *India* **178** L8
Nowshak, peak, *Afghan.* **176** K1O
Nowshera, *Pak.* **177** N1O
Nowy Sącz, *Pol.* **149** H16
Nowy Targ, *Pol.* **149** H15
Now Zad, *Afghan.* **177** P4
Noxon, *Mont., U.S.* **106** B4
Noyabr'sk, *Russ.* **158** H11
Noyon, *Fr.* **147** N1O
Nozay, *Fr.* **147** R5
Nsukka, *Nigeria* **201** G14
Ntem, river, *Cameroon, Gabon* **194** J5
Ntingui, peak, *Comoros* **205** N16
Ntomba, Lac, *Dem. Rep. of the Congo*
  198 K8
Ntsaouéni, *Comoros* **205** M14
Nu (Salween), river, *China* **180** N1O
Nuapapo, island, *Tonga* **218** M11
Nuapapu, *Tonga* **218** L11
Nuatabu, *Kiribati* **217** F17
Nuba Mountains, *Sudan* **194** H9
Nubia, Lake, *Sudan* **198** C12
Nubian Desert, *Sudan* **199** C13
Nubledo, *Sp.* **144** A8
Nueces, river, *Tex., U.S.* **103** T9
Nueltin Lake, *Nunavut, Can.* **83** J14
Nuestra Señora, Bahía, *Chile* **132** F6
Nueva Gerona, *Cuba* **116** H6
Nueva Rosita, *Mex.* **114** E11
Nuevitas, *Cuba* **116** J11
Nuevo, Bajo, *Mex.* **115** H15
Nuevo, Golfo, *Arg.* **133** R1O
Nuevo Casas Grandes, *Mex.* **114** C8
Nuevo Laredo, *Mex.* **114** E11
Nuevo Rocafuerte, *Ecua.* **128** J5
Nuguria Islands, *P.N.G.* **213** C22
Nui, island, *Tuvalu* **214** H8
Nukapu, island, *Solomon Is.* **217** N22
Nuku, island, *Tonga* **218** H12
Nukuaeta, island, *Wallis & Futuna, Fr.*
  218 C11
Nuku'alofa, *Tonga* **218** H11
Nukubasaga, island, *Fiji Is.* **218** G9
Nukudamu, *Fiji Is.* **218** G8
Nukufetau, island, *Tuvalu* **214** H9
Nukufufulanoa, island, *Wallis & Futuna,*
  Fr. **218** A11
Nukufutu, island, *Wallis & Futuna, Fr.*
  218 A11
Nukuhifala, island, *Wallis & Futuna, Fr.*
  218 B12
Nuku Hiva, island, *Fr. Polynesia, Fr.*
  215 H14
Nukuira, island, *Fiji Is.* **218** G7
Nukulaelae, island, *Tuvalu* **214** H9
Nukuloa, island, *Wallis & Futuna, Fr.*
  218 A11
Nukumanu Islands, *P.N.G.* **217** H18
Nukumanu Islands, *Solomon Is.* **214** H6
Nukunonu, island, *Tokelau, N.Z.* **214** H1O
Nukuoro Atoll, *F.S.M.* **216** R7
Nukus, *Uzb.* **174** J9
Nukutapu, island, *Wallis & Futuna, Fr.*
  218 B11
Nukutavake, island, *Fr. Polynesia, Fr.*
  219 F21
Nukuteatea, island, *Wallis & Futuna, Fr.*
  218 B11
Nukutipipi, island, *Fr. Polynesia, Fr.*
  219 G19
Nulato, *Alas., U.S.* **111** F14
Nules, *Sp.* **145** G15
Nullagine, *W. Aust., Austral.* **211** T3
Nullarbor Plain, *Austral.* **210** J6
Num, island, *Indonesia* **189** K19
Numakawa, *Japan* **184** D13
Numan, *Nigeria* **201** F16

Numancia, Ruinas de, *Sp.* **144** D12
Numata, *Japan* **184** F13
Numata, *Japan* **185** N11
Numazu, *Japan* **185** Q11
Numbulwar, *N. Terr., Austral.* **211** P9
Num Co, *China* **180** L7
Numfoor, island, *Indonesia* **189** J19
Numila, *Hawai'i, U.S.* **112** C5
Numto, *Russ.* **158** G11
Nunap Isua (Cape Farewell), *Greenland,*
  Den. **81** D22
Nunavut, *Can.* **83** G14
Nuneaton, *Eng., U.K.* **143** T12
Nunivak Island, *Alas., U.S.* **110** J1O
Nunligran, *Russ.* **159** A21
Nuoro, *It.* **151** N4
Nupani, island, *Solomon Is.* **217** N22
Nuquí, *Col.* **128** E3
Nura, river, *Kaz.* **175** E14
Nuremberg see Nürnberg, *Ger.* **148** H8
Nur Gama, *Pak.* **177** T6
Nurina, *W. Aust., Austral.* **211** W6
Nurlat, *Russ.* **156** J15
Nurmes, *Fin.* **141** G16
Nürnberg (Nuremberg), *Ger.* **148** H8
Nurpur, *Pak.* **177** Q1O
Nurri, *It.* **151** P4
Nurse Cay, *Bahamas* **117** H13
Nusaybin, *Turk.* **169** H16
Nushki, *Pak.* **177** S5
Nuttal, *Pak.* **177** S7
Nutwood Downs, *N. Terr., Austral.*
  211 Q9
Nu'uanu Pali Overlook, *Hawai'i, U.S.*
  112 E11
Nuuk (Godthåb), *Greenland, Den.* **81** D21
Nu'ulua, island, *Samoa* **218** L4
Nuupere, Pointe, *Fr. Polynesia, Fr.*
  219 N14
Nuusilaelae, island, *Amer. Samoa, U.S.*
  218 N1
Nu'utele, island, *Samoa* **218** L4
Nuutele, island, *Amer. Samoa, U.S.*
  218 N1
Nuuuli, *Amer. Samoa, U.S.* **218** M7
Nuweiba', *Egypt* **171** S4
Nyagan', *Russ.* **158** G1O
Nyainqêntanglha Shan, *China* **180** L8
Nyala, *Sudan* **198** F1O
Nyalam, *China* **180** L6
Nyamlell, *Sudan* **198** G11
Nyandoma, *Russ.* **158** E7
Nyasa, see Malawi, Lake, *Af.*
  203 D13
Nyaunglebin, *Myanmar* **186** K6
Nybergsund, *Nor.* **140** K12
Nyborg, *Den.* **140** P11
Nyborg, *Nor.* **141** C15
Nyda, *Russ.* **158** G11
Nyeri, *Kenya* **199** K14
Nyerol, *Sudan* **199** G13
Nyeying, *India* **178** F15
Nyima, *China* **180** K7
Nyingchi, *China* **180** L8
Nyíregyháza, *Hung.* **149** K17
Nykarleby, *Fin.* **141** G15
Nyköbing, *Den.* **140** P12
Nyköping, *Sw.* **141** L13
Nymagee, *N.S.W., Austral.* **211** X13
Nymphaeum see Pínes, Akrotírio, cape,
  Gr. **155** D13
Nyngan, *N.S.W., Austral.* **211** X13
Nyoman, river, *Belarus* **156** K3
Nyoma Rap, *India* **177** N15
Nyon, *Switz.* **150** C1
Nyong, river, *Cameroon* **201** J15
Nyons, *Fr.* **147** W13
Nysa, *Pol.* **149** G13
Nysh, *Russ.* **159** J21
Nyssa, *Oreg., U.S.* **108** H9
Nyūdō Zaki, *Japan* **184** K12
Nyuksenitsa, *Russ.* **156** F12
Nyunzu, *Dem. Rep. of the Congo* **198** M11
Nyurba, *Russ.* **159** H16
Nzega, *Tanzania* **199** L13
Nzérékoré, *Guinea* **200** G7
N'zeto, *Angola* **202** B5

O

Oacoma, *S. Dak., U.S.* **104** L5
Oahe, Lake, *N. Dak., S. Dak., U.S.* **104** J5
O'ahu, island, *Hawai'i, U.S.* **112** D1O

Oak Bluffs, *Mass., U.S.* **95** M15
Oakdale, *Calif., U.S.* **109** S5
Oakdale, *La., U.S.* **100** N8
Oakes, *N. Dak., U.S.* **104** H7
Oakesdale, *Wash., U.S.* **108** C9
Oak Grove, *La., U.S.* **100** K9
Oak Harbor, *Wash., U.S.* **108** B4
Oak Hill, *Ohio, U.S.* **99** S13
Oak Hill, *W. Va., U.S.* **96** E8
Oakhurst, *Calif., U.S.* **109** S6
Oakland, *Calif., U.S.* **109** S3
Oakland, *Iowa, U.S.* **105** P9
Oakland, *Md., U.S.* **96** C1O
Oakland, *Nebr., U.S.* **105** P8
Oakland, *Oreg., U.S.* **108** J3
Oakland City, *Ind., U.S.* **99** T8
Oak Lawn, *Ill., U.S.* **99** N7
Oakley, *Idaho, U.S.* **106** J5
Oakley, *Kans., U.S.* **105** S4
Oak Park, *Ill., U.S.* **99** N7
Oak Ridge, *Tenn., U.S.* **101** E18
Oakridge, *Oreg., U.S.* **108** H3
Oakvale, *S. Aust., Austral.* **211** X11
Oakwood, *Qnsld., Austral.* **211** U13
Oamaru, *N.Z.* **213** Q17
Oaro, *N.Z.* **213** N18
Oatara, island, *Fr. Polynesia, Fr.* **219** B24
Oates Coast, *Antarctica* **227** R15
Oaxaca, *Mex.* **115** K13
Ob, Gulf of, *Russ.* **166** C8
Ob', river, *Russ.* **158** G11
Oba, *Ont., Can.* **83** P17
Obama, *Japan* **185** P9
Oban, *N.Z.* **213** R15
Oban, *Qnsld., Austral.* **211** S1O
Obanazawa, *Japan* **184** L13
O Barco, *Sp.* **144** C7
Ob' Bank, *Arctic Oc.* **243** J15
Ob' Bay, *Antarctica* **227** R14
Obelisk, site, *Vatican City* **161** Q17
Obelisk Island, *Solomon Is.* **217** N24
Obella, island, *Marshall Is.* **216** K4
Oberdrauburg, *Aust.* **148** M1O
Oberhausen, *Ger.* **148** E5
Oberlin, *Kans., U.S.* **105** R4
Oberlin, *La., U.S.* **100** P7
Oberlin, *Ohio, U.S.* **99** P14
Oberschan, *Switz.* **160** Q2
Oberursel, *Ger.* **148** G6
Obervellach, *Aust.* **148** M1O
Oberwart, *Aust.* **148** L12
Obi, island, *Indonesia* **189** K16
Obi, Kepulauan, *Indonesia* **189** K16
Óbidos, *Braz.* **130** D11
Obidos, *Port.* **144** H4
Obigarm, *Taj.* **176** H8
Obihiro, *Japan* **184** G14
Obilatu, island, *Indonesia* **189** J16
Obil'noye, *Russ.* **157** Q13
Obion, *Tenn., U.S.* **100** E12
Ob-Irtysh, Source of the, *China* **166** F9
Oblachnaya, Gora, *Russ.* **159** L21
Obluch'ye, *Russ.* **159** L2O
Obninsk, *Russ.* **156** K9
Obo, *Cen. Af. Rep.* **198** H11
Obome, *Indonesia* **189** K18
Oborniki, *Pol.* **149** D13
Obrenovac, *Serb.* **152** F1O
Obrovac, *Croatia* **152** F5
Obruk, *Turk.* **168** G8
Obshchiy Syrt, *Russ.* **138** E13
Obskaya Guba, *Russ.* **158** F12
Obstruccíon, Fiordo, *Chile* **133** W7
Ob' Tablemount, *Ind. Oc.* **240** R4
Oca, Montes de, *Sp.* **144** C11
Ocala, *Fla., U.S.* **97** S8
Ocaña, *Col.* **128** D6
Ocaña, *Sp.* **144** G11
Occidental, Cordillera, *S. Amer.* **126** B2
Occidental, Grand Erg, *Alg.* **196** C1O
Ocean Cay, *Bahamas* **116** D9
Ocean City, *Md., U.S.* **96** D15
Ocean City, *N.J., U.S.* **94** R1O
Ocean Falls, *B.C., Can.* **82** K7
Ocean Island see Kure Atoll, *Hawai'i, U.S.*
  112 K2
Ocean Island see Banaba, *Kiribati* **214** G7
Oceanographer Fracture Zone, *Atl. Oc.*
  236 H8
Oceanographic Museum, *Monaco*
  161 E21
Ocean Park, *Wash., U.S.* **108** D2
Oceanside, *Calif., U.S.* **109** Y9
Ocean Springs, *Miss., U.S.* **101** P13

Oceanview, Guam, U.S. 216 B11
O.C. Fisher Lake, Tex., U.S. 103 N7
Ocha, island, F.S.M. 217 D15
Ocha, Mochun, F.S.M. 217 D15
Och'amch'ire, Abkhazia 169 B16
Ochiishi, Japan 184 F16
Ochlockonee, river, Ga., U.S. 97 Q5
Ocho Rios, Jam. 120 H9
Ocilla, Ga., U.S. 97 P6
Ocmulgee, river, Ga., U.S. 97 N6
Ocmulgee National Monument, Ga., U.S. 96 M6
Ocna Mureş, Rom. 153 D13
Ocoa, Bahía de, Dom. Rep. 117 M18
Oconee, river, Ga., U.S. 97 N7
Oconee, Lake, Ga., U.S. 96 L6
Oconomowoc, Wis., U.S. 98 L6
Oconto, Wis., U.S. 98 H7
Oconto Falls, Wis., U.S. 98 H7
Ocracoke, N.C., U.S. 96 H15
Ocracoke Inlet, N.C., U.S. 96 J15
October Revolution Island, Russ. 166 B9
Ocumare del Tuy, Venez. 128 B10
Ōda, Japan 185 P6
Ŏdaejin, N. Korea 182 B14
Ōdate, Japan 184 J13
Odawara, Japan 185 P12
Odda, Nor. 140 K10
Odebolt, Iowa, U.S. 105 N10
Odem, Tex., U.S. 103 T11
Odemira, Port. 144 K5
Ödemiş, Turk. 168 G3
Odense, Den. 140 P11
Oder see Odra, river, Ger. 148 D11
Odesa, Ukr. 157 R6
Odessa, Mo., U.S. 105 S11
Odessa, Tex., U.S. 102 M4
Odessa, Wash., U.S. 108 C7
Odienné, Côte d'Ivoire 200 F7
O'Donnell, Tex., U.S. 102 L5
Odra see Oder, river, Pol. 148 D11
Odžaci, Serb. 152 E9
Oecusse see Pante Macassar, Timor-Leste 189 N15
Oeiras, Braz. 131 F15
Oelrichs, S. Dak., U.S. 104 M2
Oelwein, Iowa, U.S. 104 M13
Oeno Island, Pac. Oc. 215 K16
Oenpelli, N. Terr., Austral. 211 P8
Oeta, Mount see Oíti, Óros, Gr. 154 G10
Of, Turk. 169 D15
O'Fallon Creek, Mont., U.S. 106 D13
Offenbach, Ger. 148 G6
Offenburg, Ger. 148 K6
Office of Tourism, Monaco 161 C21
Offida, It. 150 J10
Oficina Rica Aventura, Chile 132 D7
Ofidoúsa, island, Gr. 155 M16
Ofolanga, island, Tonga 218 P7
Ofu, island, Amer. Samoa, U.S. 218 N2
Ofu, Amer. Samoa, U.S. 218 N1
Ofu, island, Tonga 218 M12
Ōfunato, Japan 184 K14
Oga, Japan 184 K12
Ogachi, Japan 184 L13
Ogadēn, region, Eth. 199 G17
Ōgaki, Japan 185 P9
Ogallala, Nebr., U.S. 105 Q3
Ogasawara Guntō see Bonin Islands, Japan 184 K5
Ogawara Ko, Japan 184 J13
Ogbomosho, Nigeria 200 G12
Ogden, Iowa, U.S. 105 N11
Ogden, Utah, U.S. 106 K7
Ogdensburg, N.Y., U.S. 94 F9
Ogea Driki, island, Fiji Is. 218 K9
Ogea Levu, island, Fiji Is. 218 K9
Ogeechee, river, Ga., U.S. 97 N8
Ogi, Japan 184 M11
Ogilvie Mountains, Yukon, Can. 82 E8
Oglesby, Ill., U.S. 99 P6
Oglethorpe, Ga., U.S. 97 N5
Ogmore, Qnsld., Austral. 211 T14
Ognev Yar, Russ. 158 J11
Ogoja, Nigeria 201 H14
Ogoki, river, Ont., Can. 83 N16
Ogoki, Ont., Can. 83 N16
Ogooué, river, Gabon 201 L15
Ogr, Sudan 198 F11
O Grove, Sp. 144 C5
Ogulin, Croatia 152 E5
Ohau, Lake, N.Z. 213 P16
Óhi, Óros, Gr. 155 J13
O'Higgins, Lago, Chile 133 U7
Ohio, river, U.S. 85 H15
Ohio, U.S. 99 Q12
Ohonua, Tonga 218 J12
Ohrid, Maced. 152 L10
Ohrid, Lake see Ohridsko Jezero, Albania, Maced. 152 L10
Ohridsko Jezero (Lake Ohrid), Albania, Maced. 152 L10
Ōi, river, Japan 185 P11
Oiapoque, river, Braz. 130 B12
Oiapoque, Braz. 130 B12
Oil City, Pa., U.S. 94 M4
Oildale, Calif., U.S. 109 V7
Oile, Turk. 168 C5
Oilton, Okla., U.S. 102 F12
Oise, river, Fr. 147 N10
Oistins, Barbados 121 L19
Ōita, Japan 185 R5
Oíti, Óros (Mount Oeta), Gr. 154 G10
Ojika, Japan 184 L13
Ojika Jima, Japan 185 R3
Ojinaga, Mex. 114 D9
Ojiya, Japan 184 M11
Ojo de Liebre, Laguna, Mex. 114 D5
Ojos del Salado, Cerro, Arg. 132 G8
Oka, river, Russ. 156 J12
Okaba, Indonesia 189 M21
Oka-Don Plain, Russ. 138 E12
Okahandja, Namibia 202 H7
Okak Islands, Nfld. & Lab., Can. 83 J21
Okanogan, river, Can., U.S. 84 B5
Okanogan, Wash., U.S. 108 B7
Okanogan Range, Wash., U.S. 108 A6
Okara, Pak. 177 Q11
Okau, F.S.M. 217 D18
Okaukuejo, Namibia 202 G6
Okavango, river, Angola, Namibia 202 F8
Okavango Delta, Botswana 202 G9
Okaya, Japan 185 P11
Okayama, Japan 185 Q7
Okazaki, Japan 185 Q10
Okeechobee, Fla., U.S. 97 V9
Okeechobee, Lake, Fla., U.S. 97 V9
Okeene, Okla., U.S. 102 F9
Okefenokee Swamp, Fla., Ga., U.S. 97 Q7
Okemah, Okla., U.S. 102 G12
Okha, Russ. 159 H21
Okhaldhunga, Nepal 178 F10
Okhotsk, Russ. 159 G20
Okhotsk, Sea of, Russ. 159 G22
Okhtyrka, Ukr. 157 N8
Okiep, S. Af. 202 K7
Okinawa, island, Japan 185 Y2
Okinawa Shotō, Japan 185 Y1
Okino Daitō Jima, Japan 184 L3
Okino Erabu Shima, Japan 185 X2
Okino Shima, Japan 185 Q4
Okino Shima, Japan 185 S6
Oki Shotō, Japan 185 N6
Oklahoma, U.S. 102 G8
Oklahoma City, Okla., U.S. 102 G11
Okmulgee, Okla., U.S. 102 G12
Okolona, Ky., U.S. 101 B16
Okolona, Miss., U.S. 101 J13
Okoppe, Japan 184 E14
Okoyo, Congo 201 L17
Okp'yŏng, N. Korea 182 D13
Okso' Takpochao, peak, N. Mariana Is., U.S. 216 B5
Oktyabr'sk, Kaz. 174 E8
Oktyabr'skiy, Russ. 157 Q13
Oktyabr'skiy, Russ. 158 H7
Oktyabr'skoy Revolyutsii, Ostrov, Russ. 159 D14
Ōkuchi, Japan 185 S4
Okulovka, Russ. 156 G7
Okushiri Tō, Japan 184 G12
Okwa, river, Botswana 202 H8
Okytyabr'skoye, Russ. 158 G10
Ola, Ark., U.S. 100 G7
Ólafsvík, Ice. 140 E1
Olancha Peak, Calif., U.S. 109 U8
Öland, island, Sw. 141 M14
Olary, S. Aust., Austral. 211 X11
Olathe, Kans., U.S. 105 S10
Olavarría, Arg. 132 M12
Oława, Pol. 149 F13
Olbia, It. 150 M4
Olbia, Golfo di, It. 150 M4
Old Bight, Bahamas 117 F13
Old Cork, Qnsld., Austral. 211 T11
Old Crow, Yukon, Can. 82 D9
Oldenburg, Ger. 148 C6
Old Forge, Pa., U.S. 94 M9
Old Fort Bay, Bahamas 120 B10
Oldham, Eng., U.K. 143 R11
Old Harbor, Alas., U.S. 111 M15
Old Man Bay, Cayman Is., U.K. 120 H3
Old Orchard Beach, Me., U.S. 95 H15
Old Road, Antigua & Barbuda 121 B20
Old Road Bluff, Antigua & Barbuda 121 C20
Old Road Town, St. Kitts & Nevis 121 B17
Old Stores, Cayman Is., U.K. 120 H1
Old Sugar Mill, Hawai'i, U.S. 112 D11
Old Town, Me., U.S. 95 E17
Olduvai Gorge, Tanzania 199 L14
Old Womans Point, Jam. 120 K8
Olean, N.Y., U.S. 94 K5
Olekma, river, Russ. 159 J17
Olekminsk, Russ. 159 H17
Oleksandriya, Ukr. 157 Q7
Olenegorsk, Russ. 158 D9
Olenek, river, Russ. 166 C10
Olenek, river, Russ. 159 F16
Olenek, Russ. 159 G15
Oleniy, Ostrov, Russ. 158 E12
Oléron, Île d', Fr. 147 U6
Oleśnica, Pol. 149 F13
Olga, Mount (Kata Tjuta), Austral. 210 G7
Olga Basin, Arctic Oc. 243 F14
Ölgiy, Mongolia 180 C8
Olhão da Restauração, Port. 144 L6
Olib, island, Croatia 152 F4
Olifantshoek, S. Af. 202 K8
Olimarao Atoll, F.S.M. 216 Q4
Ólimbos, Óros (Olympus), Gr. 154 D10
Olimbos, Gr. 155 P18
Olinda, Braz. 131 F18
Olio, Qnsld., Austral. 211 T12
Olite, Sp. 145 C13
Oliva, Arg. 132 K10
Olivenza, Sp. 144 J7
Olivet, Fr. 147 R9
Olivia, Minn., U.S. 104 K10
Olivo, Monte, It. 161 H17
Ölkeyek, river, Kaz. 174 E10
Olla, La., U.S. 100 M8
Olmedo, Sp. 144 E10
Olmos, Peru 130 F2
Olney, Ill., U.S. 99 T7
Olney, Tex., U.S. 102 K9
'Olomburi, Solomon Is. 217 N20
Olomouc, Czech Rep. 149 H13
Olongapo, Philippines 189 C13
Oloron, Fr. 147 Y6
Olorua, island, Fiji Is. 218 J9
Olosega, island, Amer. Samoa, U.S. 218 N2
Olosega, Amer. Samoa, U.S. 218 N2
Olotania Crater, Amer. Samoa, U.S. 218 P3
Olovyannaya, Russ. 159 L17
Olowalu, Hawai'i, U.S. 113 G16
Olpoï, Vanuatu 218 C1
Olsztyn, Pol. 149 B15
Olt, river, Rom. 153 G14
Olten, Switz. 150 A3
Olteniţa, Rom. 153 G16
Olton, Tex., U.S. 102 J5
Oltu, river, Turk. 169 D16
Oltu, Turk. 169 D16
Oluan Pi, cape, Taiwan, China 183 S9
Ólvega, Sp. 145 D13
Olympia, ruin, Gr. 154 K9
Olympia, Wash., U.S. 108 D3
Olympic National Park, Wash., U.S. 108 B3
Olympos, peak, Cyprus 160 P7
Olympus see Ólimbos, Óros, peak, Gr. 154 D10
Olympus, Mount see Ulu Dağ, Turk. 168 D5
Olympus, Mount, Wash., U.S. 108 B2
Olyutorskiy, Mys, Russ. 159 D22
Olyutorskiy, Cape, Russ. 166 B13
Olyutorskiy Zaliv, Russ. 159 D22
Ōma, Japan 184 H13
Omae Zaki, Japan 185 Q11
Ōmagari, Japan 184 K13
Omagh, N. Ire., U.K. 143 Q6
Omaha, Nebr., U.S. 105 P9
Omaha Beach, Fr. 147 N6
Omaja, Cuba 116 K12
Omak, Wash., U.S. 108 B7
Omak Lake, Wash., U.S. 108 B7
Oman, Asia 167 W4
Oman, Gulf of, Iran, Oman 173 J16
Omaok, Palau 216 Q10
Ōma Zaki, Japan 184 H13
Omba see Aoba, island, Vanuatu 218 C2
Omboué (Fernan Vaz), Gabon 201 L15
Ombu, China 180 K6
Omchak, Russ. 159 F20
Omdurman, Sudan 199 D13
Omega Gardens, Cayman Is., U.K. 120 J2
Omegna, It. 150 D3
Omelek, island, Marshall Is. 216 M5
Ometepec, Mex. 114 K12
Omihi, N.Z. 213 N17
Omin, F.S.M. 217 C18
Omodeo, Lago, It. 151 N4
Omoka, Cook Is., N.Z. 219 B17
Omolon, river, Russ. 159 D20
Omolon, Russ. 159 D20
Omoto, Japan 184 K14
Omsk, Russ. 158 K10
Omsukchan, Russ. 159 E20
Ōmu, Japan 184 E14
Omul, peak, Rom. 153 E15
Ōmuta, Japan 185 R4
Oña, Sp. 144 C11
Onaf, island, F.S.M. 217 A15
Onaga, Kans., U.S. 105 S9
Onalaska, Wis., U.S. 98 K3
Onamia, Minn., U.S. 104 H11
Onamue, island, F.S.M. 217 C14
Onancock, Va., U.S. 96 E14
Onaram, island, F.S.M. 217 C16
Onarga, Ill., U.S. 99 Q7
Onawa, Iowa, U.S. 105 N9
Onaway, Mich., U.S. 98 H11
Oncativo, Arg. 132 K10
Ondangwa, Namibia 202 F6
Ondjiva, Angola 202 F6
Ondo, Nigeria 201 G13
Ondor Sum, China 182 B5
One, Motu, Fr. Polynesia, Fr. 219 J14
One, Motu, Fr. Polynesia, Fr. 219 E14
One and Half Degree Channel, Maldives 179 W3
Oneata, island, Fiji Is. 218 J9
Onega, river, Russ. 158 E7
Onega, Russ. 158 E8
Onega, Lake see Onezhskoye Ozero, Russ. 138 C10
Onega Bay, Russ. 138 B10
Oneida, N.Y., U.S. 94 J9
Oneida, Tenn., U.S. 101 E18
Oneida Lake, N.Y., U.S. 94 J8
O'Neill, Nebr., U.S. 105 N6
Onekama, Mich., U.S. 98 J9
Onekotan, island, Russ. 159 H23
Onemak, island, Marshall Is. 216 L4
Onemak East Passage, Marshall Is. 216 L4
Onemak West Passage, Marshall Is. 216 L4
Oneonta, Ala., U.S. 101 J15
Oneonta, N.Y., U.S. 94 K10
Oneroa, island, Cook Is., N.Z. 218 Q9
Onevai, island, Tonga 218 H12
Onezhskoye Ozero, Russ. 156 E9
Ongarue, N.Z. 213 K19
Ongjin, N. Korea 182 E12
Ongniud Qi (Wudan), China 182 A8
Ongole, India 179 N7
Ongombua, Île, New Caledonia, Fr. 218 B6
Oni, Rep. of Georgia 169 B17
Onich, Scot., U.K. 142 L8
Onida, S. Dak., U.S. 104 K5
Onilahy, river, Madagascar 203 H16
Onima, Neth. Antilles, Neth. 121 Q19
Oniotto, island, Marshall Is. 216 K3
Onishika, Japan 184 E13
Onitsha, Nigeria 201 H14
Oniwaki, Japan 184 D13
Onnang, island, F.S.M. 217 C14
Ono, island, Fiji Is. 218 K6
Ōno, Japan 185 P9
Ono Channel, Fiji Is. 218 K6
Onoheha, Pass d', Fr. Polynesia, Fr. 219 N17
Ono-i-Lau, island, Fiji Is. 214 K9
Onomichi, Japan 185 Q7
Onon, Mongolia 181 C13
Onon, Mongolia 181 C13
Onon, river, Russ. 166 E11
Onsen, Japan 185 P8
Onslow, W. Aust., Austral. 211 T1
Ontario, Calif., U.S. 109 X9
Ontario, Can. 83 N16
Ontario, Oreg., U.S. 108 H9
Ontario, Lake, Can., U.S. 85 E19
Ontinyent, Sp. 145 J14
Ontonagon, Mich., U.S. 98 E5
Ontong Java Atoll (Lord Howe Atoll), Solomon Is. 217 J18
Ōnuma, Japan 184 H13
Ooa, island, Marshall Is. 216 N8
Oodnadatta, S. Aust., Austral. 211 V9
'Ō'okala, Hawai'i, U.S. 113 K21
Oologah Lake, Okla., U.S. 102 E13
Ooma, Banaba, Kiribati 217 E20
Oostende (Ostend), Belg. 146 K10
Oosterschelde, bay, Neth. 146 K11
Oostpunt, cape, Neth. Antilles, Neth. 121 Q15
'Ōpana Point, Hawai'i, U.S. 113 G17
Opava, Czech Rep. 149 H14
Opelika, Ala., U.S. 101 L17
Opelousas, La., U.S. 100 P8
Open Bay, P.N.G. 213 C21
Opheim, Mont., U.S. 106 A12
Ophir, Oreg., U.S. 108 K1
Ophthalmia Range, Austral. 210 F3
'Opihikao, Hawai'i, U.S. 113 N22
Opinaca, river, Que., Can. 83 M18
Opoa, Fr. Polynesia, Fr. 219 B23
Opochka, Russ. 156 H5
Opole, Pol. 149 G14
Oporto see Porto, Port. 144 E5
Opotiki, N.Z. 213 K20
Opp, Ala., U.S. 101 N16
Oppdal, Nor. 140 J11
Opportunity, Wash., U.S. 108 C9
Optima Lake, Okla., U.S. 102 E6
Opunake, N.Z. 213 L18
Opunohu, Baie d', Fr. Polynesia, Fr. 219 N14
Opuwo, Namibia 202 F6
Opyan, Puntan, N. Mariana Is., U.S. 216 D4
Or, river, Kaz. 174 D9
Or, Les Îles d' see Hyères, Îles de, Fr. 147 Y14
Oracabessa, Jam. 120 H9
Oracle, Ariz., U.S. 107 V8
Oradea, Rom. 152 C11
Orai, India 178 G7
Oral, Kaz. 174 C6
Oran, Alg. 196 A10
Orange, Fr. 147 W13
Orange, N.S.W., Austral. 211 X14
Orange, river, Namibia, S. Af. 202 K7
Orange, Tex., U.S. 103 Q16
Orange, Va., U.S. 96 D12
Orange, Cabo, Braz. 130 B12
Orange Bay, Jam. 120 H5
Orangeburg, S.C., U.S. 96 L9
Orange Cay, Bahamas 116 E10
Orange City, Iowa, U.S. 104 M9
Orange Grove, Tex., U.S. 103 T10
Orange Hill, St. Vincent & the Grenadines 121 J17
Orange Park, Fla., U.S. 97 R8
Orange Walk, Belize 115 J16
Oranienburg, Ger. 148 D10
Oranjemund, Namibia 202 K6
Oranjestad, Aruba, Neth. 121 Q16
Oranjestad, Neth. Antilles, Neth. 119 G15
Oraviţa, Rom. 152 E11
Orbe, Switz. 150 B1
Orbetello, It. 150 J7
Orbost, Vic., Austral. 211 Z13
Orcadas, station, Antarctica 226 A4
Orce, Sp. 144 K12
Orchard City, Colo., U.S. 107 N10
Orchid Island see Lan Yü, Taiwan, China 183 S10
Orchila, Isla, Venez. 128 A10
Ord, Nebr., U.S. 105 P6
Ord, river, W. Aust., Austral. 211 Q6
Ord, Mount, Austral. 210 D5
Orderville, Utah, U.S. 107 P6
Ordes, Sp. 144 B6
Ordino, region, Andorra 160 H3
Ordino, Andorra 160 H3
Ordos see Mu Us Shamo, China 182 D2
Ordot, Guam, U.S. 216 C11
Ord River, W. Aust., Austral. 211 R7
Ordu, Turk. 168 D12
Ordubad, Azerb. 169 F20
Ordway, Colo., U.S. 107 N14
Ordzhonikidze, Ukr. 157 Q7
Oreba, island, Marshall Is. 216 K1
Örebro, Sw. 141 L13

Oregon, *Ill., U.S.* **99** N5
Oregon, *Ohio, U.S.* **99** NI2
Oregon, *U.S.* **108** H3
Oregon Caves National Monument, *Oreg., U.S.* **108** L2
Oregon City, *Oreg., U.S.* **108** F3
Oregon Dunes National Recreation Area, *Oreg., U.S.* **108** H2
Orekhovo-Zuyevo, *Russ.* **156** JIO
Orel, *Russ.* **156** L9
Orellana, *Peru* **130** F4
Orellana, Embalse de, *Sp.* **144** H9
Orem, *Utah, U.S.* **106** L7
Ore Mountains, *Czech Rep., Ger.* **148** GIO
Ören, *Turk.* **168** H3
Orenburg, *Russ.* **158** J7
Orense *see* Ourense, *Sp.* **144** C6
Örenşehir, *Turk.* **168** FII
Oreor *see* Koror, island, *Palau* **216** NII
Orepuki, *N.Z.* **213** RI5
Orestiáda, *Gr.* **155** AI7
Oreti, river, *N.Z.* **213** RI5
Orfanoú, Kólpos, *Gr.* **154** CI2
Orford Ness, *Eng., U.K.* **143** UI6
Organ Pipe Cactus National Monument, *Ariz., U.S.* **107** V6
Organyà, *Sp.* **145** CI6
Orgaz, *Sp.* **144** GIO
Orgun, *Afghan.* **177** P8
Orhangazi, *Turk.* **168** D5
Orhei, *Mold.* **157** Q5
Orhon, river, *Mongolia* **180** CI2
Orick, *Calif., U.S.* **108** M2
Oricum *see* Orikon, ruin, *Albania* **152** M9
Orient, *Wash., U.S.* **108** A8
Oriental, Cordillera, *S. Amer.* **126** C2
Oriental, Grand Erg, *Alg.* **196** CII
Orientale, Baie, *St. Martin, Fr.* **121** BI5
Oriente, *Arg.* **133** NI2
Orihuela, *Sp.* **145** KI4
Orikhiv, *Ukr.* **157** R8
Orikon (Oricum), ruin, *Albania* **152** M9
Orinduik, *Guyana* **129** EI3
Orinoco, river, *Venez.* **128** CI2
Orinoco, Source of the, *S. Amer.* **126** C5
Orinoco River Delta, *S. Amer.* **126** A6
Oristano, *It.* **151** N3
Oristano, Golfo di, *It.* **151** P3
Oriximiná, *Braz.* **130** DII
Orizaba, Pico de, *Mex.* **114** JI2
Orjen, peak, *Bosn. & Herzg., Serb. & Mont.* **152** J8
Orkanger, *Nor.* **140** HII
Orkney Islands, *Scot., U.K.* **142** GII
Orland, *Calif., U.S.* **109** P4
Orlando, *Fla., U.S.* **97** T9
Orléans, *Fr.* **147** R9
Orleans, *Nebr., U.S.* **105** R5
Orleans, *Vt., U.S.* **95** FI3
Ormara, *Pak.* **177** W4
Ormara, Ras, *Pak.* **177** W4
Orménio, *Gr.* **155** AI6
Ormoc, *Philippines* **189** EI5
Ormond Beach, *Fla., U.S.* **97** S9
Ormos Stomíou, *Gr.* **154** QI2
Örnsköldsvik, *Sw.* **141** HI4
Orobie, Alpi, *It.* **150** C5
Orocovis, *P.R., U.S.* **120** N4
Orocué, *Col.* **128** F7
Orofino, *Idaho, U.S.* **106** D4
Oro Grande, *Calif., U.S.* **109** W9
Orohena, Mont, *Fr. Polynesia, Fr.* **219** PI6
Oroluk Atoll, *F.S.M.* **216** Q7
Oromahana, island, *Fr. Polynesia, Fr.* **219** A23
Oromia, region, *Eth.* **199** GI5
Orona, island, *Kiribati* **214** HIO
Orono, *Me., U.S.* **95** EI7
Oronsay, island, *Scot., U.K.* **142** M7
Orontes *see* Al ʻĀş, river, *Syr.* **170** F7
Oropesa, *Sp.* **144** G9
Oropuche Lagoon, *Trinidad & Tobago* **121** Q22
Orós, *Braz.* **131** FI7
Orosei, *It.* **151** N5
Orosei, Golfo di, *It.* **151** N5
Orosháza, *Hung.* **149** MI6
Orote Peninsula, *Guam, U.S.* **216** C9
Oroville, *Calif., U.S.* **109** P4
Oroville, *Wash., U.S.* **108** A7
Oroville, Lake, *Calif., U.S.* **109** P4
Orphan Knoll, *Atl. Oc.* **236** F7
Orr, *Minn., U.S.* **104** EI2

Orsa, *Sw.* **140** KI2
Orsha, *Belarus* **156** K6
Orshanka, *Russ.* **156** HI4
Orsk, *Russ.* **158** J8
Orsogna, *It.* **150** KIO
Orşova, *Rom.* **152** FI2
Orta, *Turk.* **168** D8
Ortaca, *Turk.* **168** H4
Orta Nova, *It.* **150** LI2
Ortegal, Cabo, *Sp.* **144** A6
Ortepah, *Afghan.* **176** L4
Orthez, *Fr.* **147** X6
Ortigueira, *Sp.* **144** A6
Ortisei, *It.* **150** C7
Ortles, range, *It.* **150** C6
Ortoire, river, *Trinidad & Tobago* **121** Q23
Ortón, river, *Bol.* **130** G7
Ortona, *It.* **150** KII
Ortonville, *Minn., U.S.* **104** J8
Orto Surt, *Russ.* **159** HI7
Orukuizu, island, *Palau* **216** PIO
Orūmīyeh, *Iran* **172** BIO
Orūmīyeh, Daryācheh-ye (Lake Urmia), *Iran* **172** BIO
Orune, *It.* **151** N4
Oruro, *Bol.* **130** K7
Oruzgan, *Afghan.* **177** P6
Orvieto, *It.* **150** J8
Oryakhovo, *Bulg.* **153** GI3
Os, river, *Andorra* **160** K2
Os, *Sp.* **160** J2
Osa, Península de, *Costa Rica* **115** PI9
Osage, *Iowa, U.S.* **104** MI2
Osage, river, *Mo., U.S.* **105** TI3
Osage Beach, *Mo., U.S.* **105** TI2
Osage City, *Kans., U.S.* **105** T9
Osaka, *Japan* **185** PIO
Ōsaka, *Japan* **185** Q9
Ōsaka Wan, *Japan* **185** Q8
Osakarovka, *Kaz.* **175** DI4
Osakis, *Minn., U.S.* **104** HIO
Osawatomie, *Kans., U.S.* **105** TIO
Osborne, *Kans., U.S.* **105** S6
Osborn Plateau, *Ind. Oc.* **240** JII
Oscar II Coast, *Antarctica* **226** D4
Osceola, *Ark., U.S.* **100** FII
Osceola, *Iowa, U.S.* **105** QII
Osceola, *Mo., U.S.* **105** TII
Osceola, *Nebr., U.S.* **105** Q7
Oschiri, *It.* **150** M4
Oscoda, *Mich., U.S.* **98** JI2
Oscura, Punta, *Eq. Guinea* **204** N6
Oscura Peak, *N. Mex., U.S.* **107** TI2
Ösel *see* Saaremaa, island, *Est.* **141** LI5
Osen, *Nor.* **140** GII
Osgood Mountains, *Nev., U.S.* **108** M9
Osh, *Kyrg.* **176** GIO
Oshawa, *Ont., Can.* **83** QI8
Ō Shima, *Japan* **185** S2
Ō Shima, *Japan* **184** HI2
Ō Shima, *Japan* **185** QI2
Ō Shima, *Japan* **185** R9
Oshkosh, *Nebr., U.S.* **105** P2
Oshkosh, *Wis., U.S.* **98** K6
Oshogbo, *Nigeria* **201** GI3
Oshta, *Russ.* **156** E8
Oshwe, *Dem. Rep. of the Congo* **198** L9
Osijek, *Croatia* **152** E8
Osimo, *It.* **150** H9
Oskaloosa, *Iowa, U.S.* **105** PI2
Oskarshamn, *Sw.* **141** MI3
Öskemen (Ustʼ Kamenogorsk), *Kaz.* **175** DI8
Oskoba, *Russ.* **159** JI4
Oslo, *Minn., U.S.* **104** E8
Oslo, *Nor.* **140** LII
Osmanabad, *India* **178** M5
Osmancık, *Turk.* **168** DIO
Osmaniye, *Turk.* **168** HII
Osnabrück, *Ger.* **148** D6
Osorno, *Chile* **133** Q6
Osorno, *Sp.* **144** CIO
Osorno, Volcán, *Chile* **133** Q6
Osprey, *Fla., U.S.* **97** V7
Óssa, Óros, *Gr.* **154** EIO
Ossa, Mount, *Austral.* **210** MI6
Ossabaw Island, *Ga., U.S.* **97** N9
Ossabaw Sound, *Ga., U.S.* **97** N9
Ossa de Montiel, *Sp.* **144** HI2
Osseo, *Wis., U.S.* **98** J3
Ossineke, *Mich., U.S.* **98** HI2
Ostashkov, *Russ.* **156** H7
Ostend *see* Oostende, *Belg.* **146** KIO
Østerdalen, valley, *Nor.* **140** JII

Osterholz-Scharmbeck, *Ger.* **148** C7
Östersund, *Sw.* **140** HI2
Östhammar, *Sw.* **141** KI4
Ostiglia, *It.* **150** E7
Ostrava, *Czech Rep.* **149** HI4
Ostróda, *Pol.* **149** CI5
Ostrogozhsk, *Russ.* **157** NIO
Ostrołęka, *Pol.* **149** CI6
Ostrov, *Russ.* **156** H5
Ostrowiec Świętokrzyski, *Pol.* **149** FI6
Ostrów Mazowiecka, *Pol.* **149** DI6
Ostrów Wielkopolski, *Pol.* **149** EI4
OʼSullivan Dam, *Wash., U.S.* **108** D7
Osŭm, river, *Bulg.* **153** HI4
Ōsumi Kaikyō, *Japan* **185** U4
Ōsumi Shotō, *Japan* **185** U4
Osuna, *Sp.* **144** L9
Oswego, *N.Y., U.S.* **94** H8
Oswestry, *Eng., U.K.* **143** TIO
Oświęcim (Auschwitz), *Pol.* **149** HI5
Ōta, *Japan* **185** NI2
Otaki, *N.Z.* **213** MI9
Otar, *Kaz.* **175** HI6
Otare, Cerro, *Col.* **128** G6
Otaru, *Japan* **184** FI3
Otavalo, *Ecua.* **128** H3
Otavi, *Namibia* **202** G7
Oʼtaʼ Downs, *N. Terr., Austral.* **211** Q9
Otepipi, island, *Fr. Polynesia, Fr.* **219** LI6
Oţelu Roşu, *Rom.* **152** EI2
Othello, *Wash., U.S.* **108** D7
Othoní, island, *Gr.* **154** E5
Othris, Óros, *Gr.* **154** GIO
Otish, Monts, *Que., Can.* **83** M2O
Otjiwarongo, *Namibia* **202** G7
Otobe, *Japan* **184** HI2
Otog Qi, *China* **182** D2
Otoineppu, *Japan* **184** EI4
Otradnoye, *Russ.* **159** G23
Otradnyy, *Russ.* **156** KI6
Otranto, *It.* **151** NI6
Otranto, Strait of, *Eur.* **138** K8
Otsego, *Mich., U.S.* **98** M9
Ōtsu, *Japan* **184** GI5
Ōtsu, *Japan* **185** Q9
Ōtsuchi, *Japan* **184** KI4
Ottawa, *Ill., U.S.* **99** P6
Ottawa, *Kans., U.S.* **105** TIO
Ottawa, *Ohio, U.S.* **99** PII
Ottawa, *Ont., Can.* **83** QI9
Ottawa, river, *Ont., Que., Can.* **83** PI8
Ottawa Islands, *Nunavut, Can.* **83** JI7
Ottenby, *Sw.* **141** NI4
Otter Rapids, *Ont., Can.* **83** NI7
Otter Tail Lake, *Minn., U.S.* **104** H9
Ottmarsheim, *Fr.* **147** QI5
Ottumwa, *Iowa, U.S.* **105** QI2
Otukpo, *Nigeria* **201** GI4
Otutéhé, *Fr. Polynesia, Fr.* **219** M2O
Otuzco, *Peru* **130** F2
Otztal Alps, *It.* **150** B6
Ou, river, *China* **183** N9
Ou, river, *Laos* **186** GIO
ʻOʼua, island, *Tonga* **218** Q6
Ouaco, *New Caledonia, Fr.* **218** C6
Ouadane, *Mauritania* **196** F6
Ouadda, *Cen. Af. Rep.* **198** GIO
Ouagadougou, *Burkina Faso* **200** EIO
Ouahigouya, *Burkina Faso* **200** DIO
Oualâta, *Mauritania* **196** G7
Oua-n-Ahaggar, Tassili, *Alg.* **196** FII
Ouanda Djallé, *Cen. Af. Rep.* **198** GIO
Ouani, *Comoros* **205** NI6
Ouargla, *Alg.* **196** CII
Ouarra, river, *Cen. Af. Rep.* **198** HII
Oubangui *see* Ubangi, river, *Dem. Rep. of the Congo* **198** J8
Oubatche, *New Caledonia, Fr.* **218** C6
Oudtshoorn, *S. Af.* **202** M8
Ouégoa, *New Caledonia, Fr.* **218** C6
Ouen, Île, *New Caledonia, Fr.* **218** E9
Ouessa, *Burkina Faso* **200** FIO
Ouessant, Île dʼ, *Fr.* **147** P2
Ouesso, *Congo* **201** KI8
Ouest, Baie de lʼ, *Wallis & Futuna, Fr.* **218** BII
Ouest, Pointe de lʼ, *Que., Can.* **83** M2I

Ouezzane, *Mor.* **196** A9
Oufrane, *Alg.* **196** DIO
Ouinné, Baie, *New Caledonia, Fr.* **218** D9
Oujda, *Mor.* **196** B9
Oujeft, *Mauritania* **196** F6
Oulainen, *Fin.* **141** GI5
Oullins, *Fr.* **147** UI3
Oulu, river, *Fin.* **138** B9
Oulu (Uleåborg), *Fin.* **141** FI5
Oulujärvi, lake, *Fin.* **138** C9
Oulujoki, river, *Fin.* **141** FI5
Oulx, *It.* **150** EI
Oum Chalouba, *Chad* **197** HI5
Oum Hadjer, *Chad* **197** JI5
Oumm ed Drous Telli, Sebkhet, *Mauritania* **196** E6
Ounianga Kébir, *Chad* **197** GI5
Ou Nua, *Laos* **186** G9
Our, river, *Belg., Ger., Lux.* **160** GIO
Ouranópoli, *Gr.* **155** DI3
Ouray, *Colo., U.S.* **107** PII
Ouray, *Utah, U.S.* **106** L9
Ourense (Orense), *Sp.* **144** C6
Ourinhos, *Braz.* **130** MI2
Ourique, *Port.* **144** K5
Ouse, river, *Eng., U.K.* **143** QI2
Ouse, *Tas., Austral.* **211** ZI6
Oust, *Fr.* **147** Y8
Outer Bailey, *Atl. Oc.* **236** DII
Outer Brass Island, *Virgin Islands, U.S.* **120** M8
Outer Hebrides, *Scot., U.K.* **142** J6
Outjo, *Namibia* **202** G6
Outokumpu, *Fin.* **141** GI7
Out Skerries, *Scot., U.K.* **142** DI2
Ouvéa, island, *New Caledonia, Fr.* **214** K7
Ouvéa, Baie dʼ, *New Caledonia, Fr.* **218** C8
Ouvéa, Île (Uvéa), *New Caledonia, Fr.* **218** C8
Ouyen, *Vic., Austral.* **211** YII
Ouzouer-le-Marché, *Fr.* **147** Q9
Ovacık, *Turk.* **168** J9
Ovaka, island, *Tonga* **218** MII
Ovalau, island, *Fiji Is.* **218** H7
Ovalle, *Chile* **132** J6
Ovamboland, region, *Namibia* **202** F6
Ovar, *Port.* **144** E5
Ovau, island, *Solomon Is.* **217** KI5
Overland Park, *Kans., U.S.* **105** SIO
Overland Village, *St. Vincent & the Grenadines* **121** JI7
Overstrand, *Eng., U.K.* **143** SI5
Overton, *Nev., U.S.* **109** TI2
Overton, *Tex., U.S.* **102** MI4
Ovgos, river, *Cyprus* **160** N7
Oviedo, *Dom. Rep.* **117** NI7
Oviedo, *Sp.* **144** B8
Ovoot, *Mongolia* **181** EI4
Ovruch, *Ukr.* **156** M5
Ow, island, *F.S.M.* **217** CI5
Owaka, *N.Z.* **213** RI6
Owando, *Congo* **201** LI8
Owase, *Japan* **185** R9
Owatonna, *Minn., U.S.* **104** LII
Owbeh, *Afghan.* **176** M3
Owego, *N.Y., U.S.* **94** L8
Owel, Lough, *Ire.* **143** R5
Owen, Mount, *N.Z.* **213** MI7
Owen Fracture Zone, *Ind. Oc.* **240** F6
Owens, river, *Calif., U.S.* **109** T8
Owensboro, *Ky., U.S.* **101** CI5
Owens Lake Bed, *Calif., U.S.* **109** U8
Owensville, *Mo., U.S.* **105** TI4
Owen Stanley Range, *P.N.G.* **213** E2O
Owensville, *Mo., U.S.* **105** TI4
Owia, *St. Vincent & the Grenadines* **121** JI7
Owl Creek Mountains, *Wyo., U.S.* **106** GIO
Owo, *Nigeria* **201** GI3
Owosso, *Mich., U.S.* **98** LII
Owyhee, river, *Idaho, Oreg., U.S.* **108** J9
Owyhee, *Nev., U.S.* **108** LIO
Owyhee, Lake, *Oreg., U.S.* **108** J9
Owyhee Mountains, *Idaho, U.S.* **106** H3
Oxford, *Ala., U.S.* **101** JI6
Oxford, *Eng., U.K.* **143** VI2
Oxford, *Kans., U.S.* **105** V8
Oxford, *Miss., U.S.* **100** HI2
Oxford, *N.Z.* **213** PI7
Oxford, *Nebr., U.S.* **105** R5
Oxford, *Ohio, U.S.* **99** SII
Oxford, *Pa., U.S.* **94** Q8
Oxiá, island, *Gr.* **154** H8
Oxnard, *Calif., U.S.* **109** X7

Oxus *see* Amu Darya, river, *Turkm.* **174** MII
Oyapok, river, *Fr. Guiana, Fr.* **129** FI8
Oyem, *Gabon* **201** KI6
Oyo, *Congo* **201** LI8
Oyo, *Nigeria* **200** GI2
Oyonnax, *Fr.* **147** TI3
Oyotung, *Russ.* **159** DI8
Oyster Bay, *Jam.* **120** H7
Oysterhaven, *Ire.* **143** V4
Oyster Pond, *St. Martin, Fr.* **121** BI5
Oysterville, *Wash., U.S.* **108** D2
Oytal, *Kaz.* **175** JI5
Oyyl, river, *Kaz.* **174** E7
Oyyl, *Kaz.* **174** E7
Özalp, *Turk.* **169** FI8
Ozark, *Ala., U.S.* **101** MI7
Ozark, *Ark., U.S.* **100** F7
Ozark, *Mo., U.S.* **105** VI2
Ozark National Scenic Riverways, *Mo., U.S.* **105** UI4
Ozark Plateau, *Mo., Okla., U.S.* **85** JI3
Ozarks, Lake of the, *Mo., U.S.* **105** TI2
Ózd, *Hung.* **149** KI6
Özen, *Kaz.* **174** H6
Ozernovskiy, *Russ.* **159** G23
Ozernoy, Mys, *Russ.* **159** E22
Ozernoy, Zaliv, *Russ.* **159** E22
Ozery, *Russ.* **156** KIO
Ozieri, *It.* **150** M4
Ozinki, *Russ.* **156** MI5
Ozona, *Tex., U.S.* **103** P6
Ōzu, *Japan* **185** R6
Ozurgetʼi, *Rep. of Georgia* **169** CI6

P

Paagoumène, *New Caledonia, Fr.* **218** C6
Paama, island, *Vanuatu* **218** E3
Paamiut, *Greenland, Den.* **81** D22
Paarden Bay, *Aruba, Neth.* **121** QI6
Paarl, *S. Af.* **202** M7
Paʻauhau, *Hawaiʻi, U.S.* **113** K2O
Paʻauilo, *Hawaiʻi, U.S.* **113** K2O
Paavola, *Fin.* **141** GI5
Pabbay, island, *Scot., U.K.* **142** J6
Pabbay, island, *Scot., U.K.* **142** K6
Pabianice, *Pol.* **149** EI5
Pabna, *Bangladesh* **178** HI2
Pacaraima, Serra, *S. Amer.* **126** C5
Pacasmayo, *Peru* **130** F2
Paceco, *It.* **151** S8
Pachia, island, *Gr.* **155** NI6
Pachino, *It.* **151** UI2
Pachuca, *Mex.* **114** HI2
Pachyammos, *Cyprus* **160** N6
Pacific-Antarctic Ridge, *Antarctic Oc.* **244** M9
Pacific Beach, *Wash., U.S.* **108** C2
Pacific City, *Oreg., U.S.* **108** F2
Pacific Grove, *Calif., U.S.* **109** T4
Pacy, *Fr.* **147** P9
Padam, *India* **177** NI4
Padang, *Indonesia* **188** H6
Padang, *Indonesia* **188** J5
Padang Endau, *Malaysia* **187** UII
Padangpanjang, *Indonesia* **188** J5
Padangsidempuan, *Indonesia* **188** H5
Padangtiji, *Indonesia* **188** G4
Padangtikar Maya, island, *Indonesia* **188** J9
Paden City, *W. Va., U.S.* **96** C9
Paderborn, *Ger.* **148** E7
Padeş, peak, *Rom.* **152** EI2
Padloping Island, *Nunavut, Can.* **83** FI9
Padma (Ganges), river, *Bangladesh* **178** HI2
Padmanabhapuram, *India* **179** S5
Padova (Padua), *It.* **150** E7
Padrauna, *India* **178** G9
Padre Island, *Tex., U.S.* **84** PI2
Padre Island National Seashore, *Tex., U.S.* **103** S9
Padua *see* Padova, *It.* **150** E7
Paducah, *Ky., U.S.* **101** DI3
Paducah, *Tex., U.S.* **102** J7
Paea, *Fr. Polynesia, Fr.* **219** PI5
Paektu-san, peak, *N. Korea* **182** BI3
Paeroa, *N.Z.* **213** JI9
Paestum, ruin, *It.* **151** NII
Paeu, *Solomon Is.* **217** R23

Paeua, island, Fr. Polynesia, Fr. 219 K17
Pafos, Cyprus 160 Q5
Pafúri, Mozambique 202 H12
Pag, island, Croatia 152 F5
Pagadian, Philippines 189 F14
Pagai Selatan, island, Indonesia 188 K5
Pagai Utara, island, Indonesia 188 K5
Pagan, island, N. Mariana Is., U.S. 216 B2
Paganico, It. 150 J7
Pagassitikós Kólpos, Gr. 154 F11
Pagatan, Indonesia 188 K11
Page, Ariz., U.S. 107 Q7
Page, N. Dak., U.S. 104 G7
Pageland, S.C., U.S. 96 J9
Paget Island, Bermuda, U.K. 120 A4
Pago, river, Guam, U.S. 216 C11
Pago Bay, Guam, U.S. 216 C11
Pagoda Point, Myanmar 186 L5
Pago Pago, Amer. Samoa, U.S. 218 M7
Pago Pago Harbor, Amer. Samoa, U.S. 218 M8
Pagosa Springs, Colo., U.S. 107 P11
Pagri, China 180 M7
Pagua Bay, Dominica 121 E20
Pagua Point, Dominica 121 E20
Pāhala, Hawaiʻi, U.S. 113 P20
Paharpur, Pak. 177 P9
Pāhoa, Hawaiʻi, U.S. 113 M22
Pahokee, Fla., U.S. 97 V10
Pahrump, Nev., U.S. 109 U11
Pahsimeroi, river, Idaho, U.S. 106 F6
Pahute Mesa, Nev., U.S. 109 S10
Pāʻia, Hawaiʻi, U.S. 113 G17
Paige, Tex., U.S. 103 Q11
Päijänne, lake, Fin. 141 H16
Paili, P.N.G. 213 E20
Pailin City, Cambodia 187 N10
Pailolo Channel, Hawaiʻi, U.S. 113 F16
Paine, Cerro, Chile 133 V7
Painesville, Ohio, U.S. 99 N15
Painted Desert, Ariz., U.S. 107 R7
Paint Rock, Tex., U.S. 103 N7
Paintsville, Ky., U.S. 101 B20
Paio, Motu, Fr. Polynesia, Fr. 219 K16
Païromé, New Caledonia, Fr. 218 B6
Paisley, Oreg., U.S. 108 K6
Paistunturit, Fin. 141 C14
Paita, New Caledonia, Fr. 218 E8
Paita, Peru 130 E1
Paja, Cerro, Ecua. 128 R9
Pajala, Sw. 141 E14
Pajares, Puerto de, Sp. 144 B9
Pajaro Point, Virgin Islands, U.K. 120 Q10
Pakālā, Hawaiʻi, U.S. 112 C5
Pakaraima Mountains, Braz. 130 A9
Pakbèng, Laos 186 H9
Pakin Atoll, F.S.M. 216 Q8
Pakistan, Asia 167 V6
Pakleni Otoci, Croatia 152 H6
Pak Nam Chumphon, Thai. 187 P8
Pakokku, Myanmar 186 G5
Pakpattan, Pak. 177 R11
Pak Phanang, Thai. 187 R8
Paks, Hung. 149 M15
Pakuru, island, F.S.M. 217 C15
Pakwach, Uganda 198 J12
Pakxan, Laos 186 J11
Pakxé, Laos 186 L12
Pal, Andorra 160 J2
Pala, Chad 197 K14
Pala, Myanmar 187 N7
Palace of Holy Office, Vatican City 161 R17
Palace of Justice, Monaco 161 E21
Palace of Monaco, Monaco 161 E21
Palace of the Tribunal, Vatican City 161 Q15
Palace Square, Monaco 161 E21
Palacios, Tex., U.S. 103 S13
Palafrugell, Sp. 145 D18
Palagruža (Pelagosa), island, Croatia 152 J6
Palaichori, Cyprus 160 P7
Palaiochóra, Gr. 154 Q12
Palaiseau, Fr. 147 P10
Palakkad, India 179 R5
Palalankwe, India 179 R14
Palamás, Gr. 154 F9
Palana, Russ. 159 E21
Palanga, Lith. 141 N15
Palangkaraya, Indonesia 188 K11
Palanpur, India 178 H3
Palaoa Point, Hawaiʻi, U.S. 113 H14
Palapye, Botswana 202 H10
Palatka, Fla., U.S. 97 R8
Palatka, Russ. 159 F20
Palau, Pac. Oc. 214 F2
Palauk, Myanmar 187 N7
Palauli Bay, Samoa 218 L2
Palau Trench, Pac. Oc. 238 J5
Palaw, Myanmar 187 N7
Palawan, island, Philippines 188 E12
Palawan Trough, Pac. Oc. 238 J3
Palazzolo Acreide, It. 151 T11
Paldiski, Est. 141 K16
Palékastro, Gr. 155 Q17
Palel, India 178 H15
Palembang, Indonesia 188 K7
Palencia, Sp. 144 D10
Paleokastritsa, Gr. 154 E6
Palermo, Calif., U.S. 109 P4
Palermo, It. 151 R9
Palestina, Chile 132 E7
Palestina, Virgin Islands, U.S. 120 M11
Palestine, region, Asia 170 J4
Palestine, Tex., U.S. 102 M13
Paletwa, Myanmar 186 G4
Pali, India 178 G4
Palian, Thai. 187 R8
Palikir, F.S.M. 217 F14
Palikir Passage, F.S.M. 217 F13
Palinuro, Capo, It. 151 N12
Palioúri, Gr. 154 E12
Palioúri, Akrotírio, Gr. 154 E12
Palisade, Nebr., U.S. 105 R4
Paliseul, Belg. 146 M13
Palk Bay, India 179 R7
Palkonda, India 178 L9
Palk Strait, India, Sri Lanka 179 R7
Pallasovka, Russ. 157 N14
Palliser, Cape, N.Z. 213 M19
Palma, Mozambique 203 C15
Palma, Badia de, Sp. 145 G18
Palma del Río, Sp. 144 K9
Palma de Mallorca, Sp. 145 G18
Palma di Montechiaro, It. 151 T10
Palmanova, It. 150 D9
Palmares, Braz. 131 G18
Palmas, Braz. 130 G13
Palmas, Braz. 130 N12
Palmas, Cape, Cote dIvoire, Liberia 194 J2
Palmas, Golfo di, It. 151 Q3
Palmas Altas, P.R., U.S. 120 M3
Palma Soriano, Cuba 117 K13
Palm Bay, Fla., U.S. 97 U10
Palm Beach, Aruba, Neth. 121 Q16
Palm Beach, Fla., U.S. 97 V10
Palm City, Cuba 116 H11
Palm Coast, Fla., U.S. 97 S9
Palmdale, Calif., U.S. 109 W8
Palmeira, Cape Verde 205 B17
Palmeira dos Índios, Braz. 131 G17
Palmeirinhas, Ponta das, Angola 202 C5
Palmer, Alas., U.S. 111 J17
Palmer, station, Antarctica 226 D4
Palmer see Mameyes, P.R., U.S. 120 M5
Palmer Archipelago, Antarctica 226 D3
Palmer Land, Antarctica 226 E5
Palmerston Atoll, Cook Is., N.Z. 214 K11
Palmerston North, N.Z. 213 M19
Palmer Valley, N. Terr., Austral. 211 U8
Palmerville, Qnsld., Austral. 211 Q12
Palmetto, Fla., U.S. 97 U7
Palmetto Point, Jam. 120 H10
Palmi, It. 151 R13
Palmira, Col. 128 F4
Palm Island (Prune Island), St. Vincent & the Grenadines 119 M17
Palmiste Bay, Grenada 121 K22
Palm Point, Nigeria 201 J13
Palm Springs, Calif., U.S. 109 X10
Palmyra, Mo., U.S. 105 R13
Palmyra, N.Y., U.S. 94 J7
Palmyra see Tadmur, Syr. 170 G10
Palmyra Atoll, Pac. Oc. 214 F11
Palmyras Point, India 178 K11
Palo Alto, Calif., U.S. 109 S4
Palo Alto Battlefield National Historic Site, Tex., U.S. 103 W11
Palo Duro Creek, Tex., U.S. 102 H4
Paloh, Indonesia 188 H9
Palomar Mountain, Calif., U.S. 109 Y10
Palopo, Indonesia 189 K13
Palos, Cabo de, Sp. 145 L14
Palo Seco, Trinidad & Tobago 121 Q22
Palouse, river, Wash., U.S. 108 D8
Palouse, Wash., U.S. 108 D9
Palpana, Cerro, Chile 132 D7
Palparara, Qnsld., Austral. 211 U11
Paltamo, Fin. 141 F16
Palu, Indonesia 189 J13
Palu, Turk. 169 F14
Palwal, India 178 F6
Pamiers, Fr. 147 Y9
Pamir, river, Afghan., Taj. 176 K10
Pamirs, range, Taj. 176 J10
Pamlico Sound, N.C., U.S. 96 H15
Pampa, Tex., U.S. 102 G6
Pampa del Castillo, region, Arg. 133 S8
Pampas, region, Arg. 132 M10
Pampas, Peru 130 H4
Pamplemousses, Mauritius 205 F20
Pamplona, Col. 128 D6
Pamplona (Iruña), Sp. 145 C13
Pamua, Solomon Is. 217 P20
Pamuk Imwintiati, island, F.S.M. 217 G13
Pamzal, India 176 M15
Pana, Ill., U.S. 99 S5
Panaca, Nev., U.S. 109 S12
Panacea, Fla., U.S. 97 R5
Panadura, Sri Lanka 179 T7
Panagyurishte, Bulg. 153 J14
Panahan, Indonesia 188 K10
Panaitan, island, Indonesia 188 M7
Panaji, India 179 N3
Panamá, Golfo de, Pan. 115 P21
Panama, N. Amer. 81 Q21
Panama, Okla., U.S. 102 G14
Panama, Gulf of see Panamá, Golfo de, N. Amer. 80 Q9
Panama, Isthmus of, N. Amer. 80 Q9
Panama Basin, Pac. Oc. 239 J20
Panama Canal, Pan. 115 N21
Panama City, Fla., U.S. 97 R3
Panama City, Pan. 115 N21
Panamint Range, Calif., U.S. 109 U9
Panay, island, Philippines 189 E14
Pancake Range, Nev., U.S. 109 Q11
Pančevo, Serb. 152 F10
Pančićev Vrh, peak, Serb. 152 H10
Pandharkawada, India 178 L6
Pandharpur, India 178 M4
Pandhurna, India 178 K6
Pandie Pandie, S. Aust., Austral. 211 U10
Paneri, India 178 G13
Panevėžys, Lith. 141 M16
Panfilovo, Russ. 157 N12
Pangai, Tonga 218 K12
Pangai, Tonga 218 P7
Pangaimoto, island, Tonga 218 L11
Pangaimotu, island, Tonga 218 H11
Pangalanes, Canal des, Madagascar 203 G18
Pangani, river, Tanzania 199 L14
Pangéo, Óros, Gr. 155 C13
Panggoe, Solomon Is. 217 L16
Pangi, Dem. Rep. of the Congo 198 L11
Pangkajene, Indonesia 189 L13
Pangkalpinang, Indonesia 188 K8
Pangnirtung, Nunavut, Can. 83 G19
Panguitch, Utah, U.S. 107 P6
Pangutaran Group, Philippines 189 F13
Panhandle, Tex., U.S. 102 G6
Panian, island, F.S.M. 217 G14
Pānīʻau, peak, Hawaiʻi, U.S. 112 C3
Panié, Mont, New Caledonia, Fr. 218 C7
Panj, river, Afghan., Taj. 176 J9
Panjakent, Taj. 176 H6
Panjang, island, Indonesia 188 H9
Panjgur, Pak. 177 U3
Panji Poyon, Taj. 176 K8
Panjshir, river, Afghan. 176 L8
Panna, India 178 H7
Pannawonica, W. Aust., Austral. 211 T2
Pano Lefkara, Cyprus 160 P8
Pano Panagia, Cyprus 160 P6
Pano Platres, Cyprus 160 P7
Panorama Point, Nebr., U.S. 105 P1
Pánormos, Gr. 155 K14
Panovo, Russ. 159 J15
Panruti, India 179 Q7
Panshi, China 182 A12
Pantà de Riba-roga, Sp. 145 E15
Pantanal, wetland, Braz. 130 K10
Pantelleria, It. 151 U7
Pantelleria, Isola di, It. 151 U8
Pante Macassar (Oecusse), Timor-Leste 189 N15
Panvel, India 178 L3
Panxian, China 180 N12
Panzhihua, China 180 N11
Pao, river, Thai. 186 L10
Paola, Kans., U.S. 105 T10
Paola, Malta 161 K23
Paoli, Ind., U.S. 99 T9
Paopao, Fr. Polynesia, Fr. 219 N14
Pápa, Hung. 149 L13
Papa, Samoa 218 K1
Pāpāʻaloa, Hawaiʻi, U.S. 113 L21
Pāpā Bay, Hawaiʻi, U.S. 113 P18
Papahānaumokuākea M.N.M., Hawaiʻi, U.S. 112 L5
Pāpā Heiau, Hawaiʻi, U.S. 113 F15
Papai, Mount, Mauritius 205 J20
Pāpāʻikou, Hawaiʻi, U.S. 113 L21
Papakura, N.Z. 213 J19
Papara, Fr. Polynesia, Fr. 219 P16
Papa Stour, island, Scot., U.K. 142 D11
Papau, island, Cook Is., N.Z. 218 Q12
Papa Westray, island, Scot., U.K. 142 F10
Papeari, Fr. Polynesia, Fr. 219 P17
Papeete, Fr. Polynesia, Fr. 219 N15
Papenburg, Ger. 148 C6
Papenoo, river, Fr. Polynesia, Fr. 219 N16
Papenoo, Fr. Polynesia, Fr. 219 N16
Papetoai, Fr. Polynesia, Fr. 219 N14
Papíkio, peak, Gr. 155 B15
Pāpōhaku Beach, Hawaiʻi, U.S. 113 F13
Papua, Gulf of, P.N.G. 213 E19
Papua New Guinea 213 D19
Papua Passage, Cook Is., N.Z. 218 Q9
Papun, Myanmar 186 K7
Papunya, N. Terr., Austral. 211 T8
Pará, river, Braz. 131 D13
Parabel', Russ. 158 J12
Paracas Peninsula, S. Amer. 126 G2
Paracatu, Braz. 131 K14
Paracel Islands see Xisha Qundao, China 188 B10
Parachilna, S. Aust., Austral. 211 W10
Parachinar, Pak. 177 N8
Parachute, Colo., U.S. 106 M10
Paraćin, Serb. 152 G11
Paracuru, Braz. 131 E17
Paradeep see Paradwip, India 178 K11
Paradera, Aruba, Neth. 121 Q17
Paradise, Calif., U.S. 109 P4
Paradise, Grenada 121 K23
Paradise, Mich., U.S. 98 F10
Paradise, Mont., U.S. 106 C5
Paradise Bay, Malta 161 J21
Paradise Island, Bahamas 120 B11
Paradise Point, Bahamas 120 B8
Paradise Valley, Nev., U.S. 108 L9
Paradwip (Paradeep), India 178 K11
Paragould, Ark., U.S. 100 E11
Paraguá, river, Bol. 130 J9
Paragua, river, Venez. 128 E11
Paraguaipoa, Venez. 128 B6
Paraguaná, Península de, Venez. 128 A8
Paraguay, S. Amer. 127 J18
Paraguay, river, S. Amer. 126 H6
Paraíso, Mex. 115 J14
Parakou, Benin 200 F12
Paralakhemundi, India 178 L9
Paralimni, Cyprus 160 P10
Param, island, F.S.M. 217 F14
Paramaribo, Suriname 129 E16
Paramera, Sierra de la, Sp. 144 F9
Paramithía, Gr. 154 F7
Paramushir, island, Russ. 159 G23
Paran, Israel 171 Q5
Paranã, Braz. 131 H13
Paraná, Arg. 132 K12
Paraná, river, S. Amer. 126 L6
Paraná, Source of the, S. Amer. 126 J9
Paranaguá, Braz. 131 N13
Paranaguá Bay, S. Amer. 126 J8
Paranaíba, river, Braz. 130 K12
Paranaíba, Braz. 130 K12
Paranésti, Gr. 155 B13
Paraoa, island, Fr. Polynesia, Fr. 219 F20
Parchim, Ger. 148 C9
Pardes Ḥanna-Karkur, Israel 170 L5
Pardo, river, Braz. 131 J16
Pardo, river, Braz. 130 L11
Pardo, river, Braz. 131 L13
Pardoo, W. Aust., Austral. 211 S3
Pardubice, Czech Rep. 148 H12
Parea, Fr. Polynesia, Fr. 219 H14
Parece Vela, island, Japan 214 D3
Parecis, Serra dos, Braz. 130 H9
Paredes de Nava, Sp. 144 D10
Paredón, Mex. 114 F11
Parem, island, F.S.M. 217 C15
Paren', Russ. 159 D21
Parepare, Indonesia 189 K13
Párga, Gr. 154 F7
Pargny, Fr. 147 P12
Pargo, Ponta do, Madeira 204 M2
Parguera, P.R., U.S. 120 N2
Parham Peninsula, Antigua & Barbuda 121 B21
Parham Town, Virgin Islands, U.K. 120 Q7
Paria, river, Utah, U.S. 107 P7
Paria, Gulf of, Trinidad & Tobago 119 P16
Pariaguánviche, Venez. 128 C11
Paria Peninsula, S. Amer. 126 A5
Parika, Guyana 129 D14
Parikkala, Fin. 141 H17
Parima, Serra, Braz., Venez. 128 F11
Parintins, Braz. 130 D10
Paris, Ark., U.S. 100 F7
Paris, Fr. 147 P10
Paris, Ill., U.S. 99 R7
Paris, Kiribati 217 B22
Paris, Ky., U.S. 101 B18
Paris, Mo., U.S. 105 S13
Paris, Tenn., U.S. 101 E13
Paris, Tex., U.S. 102 K13
Paris Basin, Fr. 138 G4
Parisot, Fr. 147 W9
Parit Buntar, Malaysia 187 T9
Parker, Ariz., U.S. 107 T4
Parker, S. Dak., U.S. 104 M8
Parker Dam, Ariz., Calif., U.S. 109 W13
Parker Ranch, Hawaiʻi, U.S. 113 K19
Parkersburg, W. Va., U.S. 96 C8
Parkes, N.S.W., Austral. 211 X13
Park Falls, Wis., U.S. 98 G4
Park Forest, Ill., U.S. 99 P7
Parkin, Ark., U.S. 100 G10
Parkland, Wash., U.S. 108 C4
Park Range, Colo., U.S. 106 L12
Park Rapids, Minn., U.S. 104 G10
Park River, N. Dak., U.S. 104 E7
Parksley, Va., U.S. 96 E15
Parkston, S. Dak., U.S. 104 M7
Park Valley, Utah, U.S. 106 J6
Parlatuvier, Trinidad & Tobago 121 N18
Parma, Idaho, U.S. 106 G3
Parma, It. 150 F6
Parma, Ohio, U.S. 99 P14
Parmakan, Afghan. 177 N2
Parnaguá, Braz. 131 G14
Parnaíba, river, Braz. 131 E15
Parnaíba, Braz. 131 D16
Parnamirim, Braz. 131 F16
Parnassós, peak, Gr. 154 H10
Parnassus, N.Z. 213 N18
Párnitha, Óros, Gr. 154 J12
Párnonas, Óros, Gr. 154 L10
Pärnu, Est. 141 L16
Paromay, Russ. 159 H21
Paroo, W. Aust., Austral. 211 U3
Paropamisus Range see Sefid Kuh Mountains, Afghan. 176 M3
Páros, island, Gr. 155 L15
Páros, Gr. 155 L15
Parottee Point, Jam. 120 J7
Parowan, Utah, U.S. 107 P6
Parraburdoo, W. Aust., Austral. 211 T2
Parral, Chile 132 M6
Parras, Mex. 114 F10
Parry, Cape, N.W.T., Can. 82 E11
Parry Channel, Nunavut, Can. 83 D13
Parry Islands, N.W.T., Nunavut, Can. 83 C13
Parshall, N. Dak., U.S. 104 F3
Parsons, Kans., U.S. 105 U10
Parsons, Tenn., U.S. 101 F13
Parsons, W. Va., U.S. 96 C10
Parsons Range, Austral. 210 B9
Partanna, It. 151 S9
Parthenay, Fr. 147 S7
Partizansk, Russ. 159 M21
Paru, river, Braz. 130 C11
Paru de Oeste (Cumina), river, Braz. 130 C10
Paruru, Solomon Is. 217 P19
Parvatipuram, India 178 L9
Pasa, island, F.S.M. 217 G13
Pasadena, Calif., U.S. 109 X8
Pasadena, Tex., U.S. 103 R14
Pasado, Cabo, Ecua. 128 J2
Pasaje, Ecua. 128 L2
P'asanauri, Rep. of Georgia 169 B18
Pasarseluma, Indonesia 188 L6
Pascagoula, Miss., U.S. 101 P13
Paşcani, Rom. 153 B16
Pasco, Wash., U.S. 108 E7

Pascua, Isla de (Easter Island), *Chile* 215 LI9
Pas de la Casa, *Andorra* 160 J5
Pasewalk, *Ger.* 148 CII
Pasighat, *India* 178 FI5
Pasinler, *Turk.* 169 EI6
Pasir Mas, *Malaysia* 187 SIO
Pasley, Cape, *Austral.* 210 K5
Pašman, island, *Croatia* 152 G5
Pasni, *Pak.* 177 V3
Paso de Indios, *Arg.* 133 R8
Paso de los Toros, *Uru.* 132 KI4
Paso Río Mayo, *Arg.* 133 S7
Paso Robles, *Calif., U.S.* 109 V5
Pasrur, *Pak.* 177 PI2
Passau, *Ger.* 148 KIO
Pass Christian, *Miss., U.S.* 100 PI2
Passero, Capo, *It.* 151 UI2
Passo Fundo, *Braz.* 130 PII
Passos, *Braz.* 131 LI4
Passu Keah, island, *China* 188 CIO
Pastavy, *Belarus* 156 J4
Pastaza, river, *Ecua.* 128 K4
Pastaza, river, *Peru* 130 E3
Pasto, *Col.* 128 H3
Pastora Peak, *Ariz., U.S.* 107 Q9
Pastos Bons, *Braz.* 131 FI5
Pasuruan, *Indonesia* 188 MIO
Patan, *India* 178 J7
Patan see Lalitpur, *Nepal* 178 FIO
Patanga, island, *Cook Is., N.Z.* 219 BI8
Patani, *Indonesia* 189 JI6
Patara Shiraki, *Rep. of Georgia* 169 C2O
Patchogue, *N.Y., U.S.* 94 NI2
Pate Island, *Kenya* 199 KI5
Paterna, *Sp.* 145 HI4
Paterson, *N.J., U.S.* 94 NII
Pathankot, *India* 177 PI3
Pathein, *Myanmar* 186 K5
Pathfinder Reservoir, *Wyo., U.S.* 106 JII
Patía, river, *Col.* 128 G3
Patiala, *India* 178 E5
Patillas, *P.R., U.S.* 120 N5
Patio, *Fr. Polynesia, Fr.* 219 A23
Pati Point, *Guam, U.S.* 216 BI2
Pativilca, *Peru* 130 G3
Pätkai Range, *Myanmar* 186 D6
Pátmos, island, *Gr.* 155 KI7
Pátmos, *Gr.* 155 LI7
Patna, *India* 178 GIO
Patnos, *Turk.* 169 FI7
Patos, *Braz.* 131 FI7
Patos, Isla de, *Venez.* 121 P21
Patos de Minas, *Braz.* 131 KI4
Patos Lagoon, *S. Amer.* 126 L8
Patquía, *Arg.* 132 H9
Pátra (Patrai), *Gr.* 154 J9
Patrai see Pátra, *Gr.* 154 J9
Patraïkós Kólpos, *Gr.* 154 H9
Patricio Lynch, Isla, *Chile* 133 U6
Patrick, Port, *Vanuatu* 218 H4
Patrington, *Eng., U.K.* 143 RI4
Patrot Hill, station, *Antarctica* 226 H9
Pattani, *Thai.* 187 S9
Patten, *Me., U.S.* 95 CI8
Patterson, *Calif., U.S.* 109 S5
Patterson, *La., U.S.* 100 Q9
Patterson, Port, *Vanuatu* 218 B2
Patteson Passage, *Vanuatu* 218 C3
Patti, *India* 178 D5
Pattoki, *Pak.* 177 QII
Patton Escarpment, *Pac. Oc.* 239 FI6
Patu, *Braz.* 131 FI7
Patuakhali, *Bangladesh* 178 JI3
Patuca, river, *Hond.* 115 KI8
Patuxent Range, *Antarctica* 226 HII
Patzau, *Wis., U.S.* 98 F2
Pátzcuaro, *Mex.* 114 JIO
Pau, *Fr.* 147 Y7
Pauini, *Braz.* 130 F6
Pauini, *Braz.* 130 F6
Pauktaw, *Myanmar* 186 H4
Paulatuk, *N.W.T., Can.* 82 EII
Paulding, *Ohio, U.S.* 99 PII
Paulhaguet, *Fr.* 147 VII
Paulhan, *Fr.* 147 XII
Paulistana, *Braz.* 131 FI6
Paulo Afonso, *Braz.* 131 GI7
Pauls Valley, *Okla., U.S.* 102 HII
Paungbyin, *Myanmar* 186 F5
Paungde, *Myanmar* 186 J6
Pauni, *India* 178 K7
Pausania, *It.* 150 M4

Pa'uwela, *Hawai'i, U.S.* 113 GI7
Pava, island, *Tuvalu* 217 J23
Pavagada, *India* 179 P5
Pavaiai, *Amer. Samoa, U.S.* 218 M7
Pavia, *It.* 150 E4
Pāvilosta, *Latv.* 141 MI5
Pavlikeni, *Bulg.* 153 HI5
Pavlodar, *Kaz.* 175 CI6
Pavlof Volcano, *Alas., U.S.* 110 NI2
Pavlovka, *Russ.* 156 LI4
Pavlovo, *Russ.* 156 JI2
Pavlovsk, *Russ.* 156 F6
Pavlovsk, *Russ.* 157 NII
Pavlovskaya, *Russ.* 157 SII
Pavuvu, island, *Solomon Is.* 217 NI8
Pawarenga, *N.Z.* 213 HI8
Pawhuska, *Okla., U.S.* 102 EI2
Pawleys Island, *S.C., U.S.* 96 LII
Pawnee, *Okla., U.S.* 102 FII
Pawnee City, *Nebr., U.S.* 105 R9
Paw Paw, *Mich., U.S.* 98 M9
Pawtucket, *R.I., U.S.* 95 LI4
Paxí, island, *Gr.* 154 F6
Paxí, *Gr.* 154 F6
Paxton, *Ill., U.S.* 99 Q7
Paxton, *Nebr., U.S.* 105 Q3
Payakumbuh, *Indonesia* 188 J6
Payer Mountains, *Antarctica* 227 BI4
Payette, river, *Idaho, U.S.* 106 G3
Payette, *Idaho, U.S.* 106 G3
Payette Lake, *Idaho, U.S.* 106 F4
Payne, Lac, *Que., Can.* 83 JI8
Paynes Find, *W. Aust., Austral.* 211 W3
Paynesville, *Minn., U.S.* 104 JIO
Payong, Tanjong, *Malaysia* 188 GIO
Paysandú, *Uru.* 132 KI3
Payshanba, *Uzb.* 174 LI2
Payson, *Ariz., U.S.* 107 T7
Pazar, *Turk.* 169 DI5
Pazar, *Turk.* 168 D8
Pazar, *Turk.* 168 EII
Pazarcık, *Turk.* 168 HI2
Pazardzhik, *Bulg.* 153 JI4
Pazin, *Croatia* 152 E4
Pčinja, river, *Maced.* 152 KII
Pea, river, *Ala., U.S.* 101 MI6
Pea, *Tonga* 218 JII
Peabody, *Kans., U.S.* 105 T8
Peace, river, *Alta., Can.* 82 JII
Peace, river, *Fla., U.S.* 97 V8
Peace River, *Alta., Can.* 82 KIO
Peach Springs, *Ariz., U.S.* 107 R5
Peacock Point, *Wake I., U.S.* 216 G8
Peak District, *Eng., U.K.* 143 SI2
Peaked Mountain, *Me., U.S.* 95 BI7
Peak Hill, *W. Aust., Austral.* 211 U3
Peale, Mount, *Utah, U.S.* 107 N9
Peale Island, *Wake I., U.S.* 216 F8
Peao, island, *Kiribati* 217 B2O
Peard Bay, *Alas., U.S.* 111 BI4
Pea Ridge National Military Park, *Ark., U.S.* 100 E6
Pearl, river, *La., Miss., U.S.* 85 LI5
Pearl, *Miss., U.S.* 100 LII
Pearl and Hermes Atoll, *Hawai'i, U.S.* 112 K3
Pearl City, *Hawai'i, U.S.* 112 EII
Pearl Harbor, *Hawai'i, U.S.* 112 EII
Pearl River see Zhu, *China* 183 S4
Pearls Rock, *Grenada* 121 K23
Pearsall, *Tex., U.S.* 103 S9
Pearson, *Ga., U.S.* 97 P7
Peary Channel, *Nunavut, Can.* 83 BI4
Peary Land, *N. Amer.* 80 A7
Pease, river, *Tex., U.S.* 102 J8
Pease Bay, *Cayman Is., U.K.* 120 J3
Peawanuk, *Ont., Can.* 83 LI6
Pebane, *Mozambique* 203 FI4
Pebas, *Peru* 130 D5
Pebble Island, *Falkland Is., U.K.* 133 VI2
Peć see Peja, *Kos.* 152 JIO
Pecan Island, *La., U.S.* 100 Q8
Pechora, river, *Russ.* 158 F9
Pechora, *Russ.* 158 FIO
Pechora Basin, *Russ.* 138 AI2
Pechora Bay, *Arctic Oc.* 243 AI6
Pechorskoy More, *Russ.* 158 EIO
Pecos, *N. Mex., U.S.* 107 RI3
Pecos, river, *N. Mex., Tex., U.S.* 84 MIO
Pecos, *Tex., U.S.* 103 N3
Pecos National Historic Park, *N. Mex., U.S.* 107 RI3
Pécs, *Hung.* 149 NI4
Pedálofos, *Gr.* 154 D8
Peddapalli, *India* 178 L7

Pedder, Lake, *Austral.* 210 MI6
Pedernales, *Dom. Rep.* 117 NI7
Pedernales, river, *Tex., U.S.* 103 Q9
Pedra Azul, *Braz.* 131 JI5
Pedra Lume, *Cape Verde* 205 BI7
Pedras Negras, *Braz.* 130 H8
Pedro Afonso, *Braz.* 131 FI3
Pedro Betancourt, *Cuba* 116 G7
Pedro Cays, *Jam.* 116 PII
Pedro de Valdivia, *Chile* 132 D7
Pedro Juan Caballero, *Parag.* 130 LIO
Pedro Luro, *Arg.* 133 PII
Pedro Osório, *Braz.* 130 QII
Pedro Point, *Jam.* 120 H6
Pedroso, Sierra del, *Sp.* 144 J8
Pedroso, Port. 144 E5
Peebles, *Ohio, U.S.* 99 SI2
Peedamulla, *W. Aust., Austral.* 211 T2
Peekskill, *N.Y., U.S.* 94 MII
Peel, *Isle of Man, U.K.* 143 Q9
Peel, river, *Yukon, Can.* 82 E9
Pe Ell, *Wash., U.S.* 108 D3
Peel Sound, *Nunavut, Can.* 83 EI5
Peetz, *Colo., U.S.* 106 KI5
Pegasus Bay, *N.Z.* 213 PI7
Pegeia, *Cyprus* 160 P5
Pego, *Sp.* 145 JII
Pehuajó, *Arg.* 132 MII
Peine, *Ger.* 148 D8
Peine, Pointe-à-, *Dominica* 121 F2O
Peipus, Lake (Chudskoye Ozero), *Est., Russ.* 141 KI7
Peixe, *Braz.* 131 HI3
Peja (Peć), *Kos.* 152 JIO
Pekalongan, *Indonesia* 188 M9
Pekan, *Malaysia* 187 UIO
Pekanbaru, *Indonesia* 188 J6
Pekelmeer, lake, *Neth. Antilles, Neth.* 121 RI9
Pekin, *Ill., U.S.* 99 Q5
Peking see Beijing, *China* 182 D7
Pelabuhanratu, Teluk, *Indonesia* 188 M8
Pelado, peak, *Sp.* 145 GI3
Pelagosa see Palagruža, island, *Croatia* 152 H7
Pelahatchie, *Miss., U.S.* 100 LII
Pelat, Mont, *Fr.* 147 WI5
Pelau, island, *Solomon Is.* 217 JI8
Peleaga, peak, *Rom.* 152 EI2
Pelée, Montagne, *Martinique, Fr.* 121 E22
Peleliu (Beliliou), island, *Palau* 216 QIO
Peleng, island, *Indonesia* 189 JI4
Pelham, *Ala., U.S.* 101 KI5
Pelham, *Ga., U.S.* 97 P5
Pelican, *Alas., U.S.* 111 L2I
Pelican Lake, *Minn., U.S.* 104 EI2
Pelican Point, *Bahamas* 120 E3
Pelican Point, *Namibia* 194 P6
Pelican Rapids, *Minn., U.S.* 104 G9
Péligre, Lac de, *Haiti* 117 MI7
Pelikaan Punt, *Neth. Antilles, Neth.* 121 RI4
Pelinéo, Óros, *Gr.* 155 HI6
Pelister, peak, *Maced.* 152 LII
Peljesac, peninsula, *Croatia* 152 H7
Pella, ruin, *Gr.* 154 CIO
Pella, *Iowa, U.S.* 105 PI2
Pellston, *Mich., U.S.* 98 GIO
Pelly, river, *Yukon, Can.* 82 G9
Pelly Bay, *Nunavut, Can.* 83 FI5
Pelly Crossing, *Yukon, Can.* 82 F8
Peloponnisos, peninsula, *Gr.* 154 K9
Pelotas, *Braz.* 130 QII
Pelotas, *Braz.* 130 QII
Pelusium, ruin, *Egypt* 171 NI
Pelvoux, Massif du, *Fr.* 147 VI4
Pematang, *Indonesia* 188 J6
Pematangsiantar, *Indonesia* 188 H5
Pemba, *Mozambique* 203 DI5
Pemba Bay, *Mozambique* 194 MII
Pemba Island, *Tanzania* 199 LI5
Pemberton, *W. Aust., Austral.* 211 Y3
Pembina, *N. Dak., U.S.* 104 D7
Pembroke, *Ga., U.S.* 97 N8
Pembroke, *Ont., Can.* 83 QI8
Pembroke, *Trinidad & Tobago* 121 NI8
Pembroke (Penfro), *Wales, U.K.* 143 V8
Pembroke Fort, *Malta* 161 K22
Pecos, river, *Tex., U.S.* —
Pen, *India* 178 L3
Peña, Sierra de, *Sp.* 145 CI4
Peña de Francia, Sierra de, *Sp.* 144 F8
Peñafiel, *Sp.* 144 DIO
Penal, *Trinidad & Tobago* 121 Q22
Peñalara, peak, *Sp.* 144 FIO
Peñalsordo, *Sp.* 144 J9

Penamacor, Port. 144 F7
Penambulai, island, *Indonesia* 189 MI9
Peñaranda de Bracamonte, *Sp.* 144 E9
Peñarroya, peak, *Sp.* 145 FI4
Peñarroya-Pueblonuevo, *Sp.* 144 J9
Peñas, Cabo de, *Sp.* 144 A8
Penas, Golfo de, *Chile* 133 T6
Peñas del Cache, peak, *Canary Is.* 204 P7
Pendan, *Malaysia* 188 HIO
Pendembu, *Sierra Leone* 200 G6
Pender, *Nebr., U.S.* 105 N8
Pendleton, *Oreg., U.S.* 108 F7
Pend Oreille, river, *Wash., U.S.* 108 B9
Pend Oreille, Lake, *Idaho, U.S.* 106 B4
Pendra, *India* 178 J8
Pendroy, *Mont., U.S.* 106 B7
Penedo, *Braz.* 131 GI7
Penfro see Pembroke, *Wales, U.K.* 143 V8
Pengcheng, *China* 181 HI4
Penghu (Pescadores), islands, *Taiwan, China* 183 R9
Penglai, *China* 182 E9
Pengshui, *China* 182 LI
Penha do Tapauá, *Braz.* 130 E7
Peniche, Port. 144 H4
Penicuik, *Scot., U.K.* 142 MIO
Peñíscola, *Sp.* 145 FI5
Penmarc'h, Pointe de, *Fr.* 147 Q3
Penna, Punta della, *It.* 150 KII
Penne, *It.* 150 JIO
Pennell Coast, *Antarctica* 227 RI4
Penner, river, *India* 179 P6
Penneshaw, *S. Aust., Austral.* 211 YIO
Penn Hills, *Pa., U.S.* 94 N3
Pennine Alpi, *Switz.* 150 C2
Pennington Gap, *Va., U.S.* 96 G6
Pennsylvania, *U.S.* 94 M3
Penn Yan, *N.Y., U.S.* 94 J7
Peno, *Russ.* 156 H7
Penobscot, river, *Me., U.S.* 85 C22
Penobscot Bay, *Me., U.S.* 95 FI7
Penola, *S. Aust., Austral.* 211 ZII
Penonomé, *Pan.* 115 N2I
Pénot, Mount, *Vanuatu* 218 D2
Penrhyn Atoll (Tongareva), *Cook Is., N.Z.* 214 HI2
Penrith, *Eng., U.K.* 143 PII
Pensacola, *Fla., U.S.* 97 QI
Pensacola Bay, *Fla., U.S.* 97 QI
Pensacola Mountains, *Antarctica* 226 GII
Pentakomo, *Cyprus* 160 Q8
Pentecost (Île Pentecote), *Vanuatu* 218 D3
Pentecote, Île see Pentecost, *Vanuatu* 218 D3
Penticton, *B.C., Can.* 82 M9
Pentland Firth, *Scot., U.K.* 142 GIO
Pentwater, *Mich., U.S.* 98 K9
Penuguan, *Indonesia* 188 K7
Penujok, Tanjong, *Malaysia* 187 TIO
Penwell, *Tex., U.S.* 103 N4
Penza, *Russ.* 156 LI3
Penzance, *Eng., U.K.* 143 Y7
Penzhinskaya Guba, *Russ.* 159 E2I
Peoples Creek, *Mont., U.S.* 106 BIO
Peoria, *Ariz., U.S.* 107 U6
Peoria, *Ill., U.S.* 99 Q5
Pepe'ekeo, *Hawai'i, U.S.* 113 L2I
Pepillo Salcedo, *Dom. Rep.* 117 LI7
Pepin, Lake, *Minn. Wis., U.S.* 98 J2
Pera, *Cyprus* 160 P8
Perabumulih, *Indonesia* 188 K7
Percival Lakes, *Austral.* 210 E5
Perdido, river, *Ala., U.S.* 101 PI4
Perdido, Monte, *Sp.* 145 CI5
Pereira, *Col.* 128 F4
Perelazovskiy, *Russ.* 157 PI2
Perelyub, *Russ.* 156 LI6
Peremul Par, island, *India* 179 Q2
Perenjori, *W. Aust., Austral.* 211 W2
Pereslavl' Zalesskiy, *Russ.* 156 HIO
Perga, ruin, *Turk.* 168 H6
Pergamino, *Arg.* 132 LI2
Perham, *Minn., U.S.* 104 G9
Peri, river, *Turk.* 169 FI5
Péribonka, river, *Que., Can.* 83 N2O
Perico, *Arg.* 132 E9
Perigot see Puamau, Baie, bay, *Fr. Polynesia, Fr.* 219 M2I
Périgueux, *Fr.* 147 V8
Perijá, Sierra de, *Col.* 128 C6
Peri Lake, *Austral.* 210 JI2

Perim see Barīm, island, *Yemen* 172 R8
Peristéra, island, *Gr.* 155 FI3
Perito Moreno, *Arg.* 133 T7
Perkins, *Okla., U.S.* 102 FII
Perky, *Fla., U.S.* 97 Y9
Perlé, *Lux.* 160 J9
Perlevka, *Russ.* 156 MIO
Perm', *Russ.* 158 H8
Pernambuco Plain, *Atl. Oc.* 237 P9
Pernik, *Bulg.* 152 JI2
Peron, Cape, *Austral.* 210 K2
Peronit Burnu, *Turk.* 169 CI5
Péronne, *Fr.* 146 MIO
Pérouges, *Fr.* 147 UI3
Perpetua, Cape, *Oreg., U.S.* 108 G2
Perpignan, *Fr.* 147 ZIO
Perranporth, *Eng., U.K.* 143 X8
Perry, *Fla., U.S.* 97 R6
Perry, *Ga., U.S.* 97 N6
Perry, *Iowa, U.S.* 105 PII
Perry, *Okla., U.S.* 102 FII
Perry Island, *Nunavut, Can.* 83 GI3
Perrysburg, *Ohio, U.S.* 99 NI2
Perryton, *Tex., U.S.* 102 E6
Perryville, *Alas., U.S.* 111 NI3
Perryville, *Mo., U.S.* 105 UI5
Persepolis, ruin, *Iran* 173 FI3
Perseverance Bay, *Virgin Islands, U.S.* 120 M8
Persian Gulf, *Asia* 166 G4
Pertek, *Turk.* 169 FI4
Perth, *Scot., U.K.* 142 LIO
Perth, *W. Aust., Austral.* 211 X2
Perth Basin, *Ind. Oc.* 241 MI5
Pertoúli, *Gr.* 154 F8
Peru, *Ill., U.S.* 99 P5
Peru, *Ind., U.S.* 99 Q9
Peru, *Nebr., U.S.* 105 Q9
Peru, *S. Amer.* 127 EI4
Peru Basin, *Pac. Oc.* 239 LI9
Peru-Chile Trench, *Pac. Oc.* 239 L2O
Perugia, *It.* 150 H8
Pervari, *Turk.* 169 GI7
Pervomays'k, *Ukr.* 157 Q6
Pervomaysk, *Russ.* 156 KI2
Pervomayskoye, *Russ.* 156 MI4
Pervoural'sk, *Russ.* 158 H8
Pervyy Kuril'skiy Proliv, *Russ.* 159 G23
Pesaro, *It.* 150 G9
Pescador, Punta, *Venez.* 121 R2I
Pescadores see Penghu, islands, *Taiwan, China* 183 R9
Pescara, *It.* 150 JIO
Peschici, *It.* 150 KI3
Peshawar, *Pak.* 177 N9
Peshawarun, ruin, *Afghan.* 177 Q2
Peshin Jan, *Afghan.* 177 NI
Peshkopi, *Albania* 152 KIO
Peshtera, *Bulg.* 153 KI4
Peshtigo, *Wis., U.S.* 98 H7
Pesmes, *Fr.* 147 RI3
Pessac, *Fr.* 147 V6
Pessons, Pic dels, *Andorra* 160 J4
Pestovo, *Russ.* 156 G8
Pesu, *India* 178 GI5
Petacalco, Bahía, *Mex.* 114 KIO
Petacalco Bay see Petacalco, Bahía, *N. Amer.* 80 P5
Petaẖ Tiqwa, *Israel* 170 M5
Petal, *Miss., U.S.* 100 NI2
Petalión, Kólpos, *Gr.* 155 JI3
Petaluma, *Calif., U.S.* 109 R3
Pétange, *Lux.* 160 K9
Petatlán, *Mex.* 114 KIO
Petén, region, *Guatemala* 115 KI6
Petenwell Lake, *Wis., U.S.* 98 J5
Peterborough, *Eng., U.K.* 143 TI4
Peterborough, *N.H., U.S.* 95 JI3
Peterborough, *Ont., Can.* 83 QI8
Peterborough, *S. Aust., Austral.* 211 XIO
Peterhead, *Scot., U.K.* 142 JII
Peter I Island, *Antarctica* 226 J4
Petermann Ranges, *Austral.* 210 G7
Peter Pond Lake, *Sask., Can.* 82 LII
Petersburg, *Alas., U.S.* 111 M23
Petersburg, *Ill., U.S.* 99 R4
Petersburg, *Ind., U.S.* 99 T8
Petersburg, *Tex., U.S.* 102 J5
Petersburg, *Va., U.S.* 96 FI3
Petersburg, *W. Va., U.S.* 96 CII
Petersfield, *Jam.* 120 H6
Petit Bois Island, *Miss., U.S.* 101 PI3
Petit-Bourg, *Guadeloupe, Fr.* 121 FI4
Petit-Canal, *Guadeloupe, Fr.* 121 EI5

Petit Cul-de-Sac Marin, bay, Guadeloupe, Fr. 121 F15
Petite Île, Reunion, Fr. 205 H16
Petite Rivière del' Artibonite, Haiti 117 L16
Petite Terre, Îles de la, Guadeloupe, Fr. 121 F17
Petite-Terre, island, Mayotte, Fr. 205 P17
Petit-Goâve, Haiti 117 M16
Petit Gravier, Mauritius 205 J21
Petitot, river, B.C., Can. 82 H10
Petit Piton, peak, St. Lucia 121 L13
Petit Savane Point, Dominica 121 G20
Petit Trou, cape, Trinidad & Tobago 121 P17
Petoskey, Mich., U.S. 98 H10
Petra, ruin, Jordan 171 Q6
Petrich, Bulg. 153 K13
Petrified Forest National Park, Ariz., U.S. 107 S9
Petrila, Rom. 153 E13
Petrinja, Croatia 152 E6
Petro, Pak. 177 U8
Petrolândia, Braz. 131 G17
Petrolia, Calif., U.S. 109 N1
Petrolia, Tex., U.S. 102 J10
Petrolina, Braz. 131 G16
Petropavlovsk, Kaz. 175 B13
Petropavlovsk-Kamchatskiy, Russ. 159 F23
Petrovac, Mont. 152 J8
Petrovaradin, Serb. 152 E9
Petrovgrad see Zrenjanin, Serb. 152 E10
Petrovsk, Russ. 156 L13
Petrovsk Zabaykal'skiy, Russ. 159 L16
Petrozavodsk, Russ. 158 E7
Petukhovo, Russ. 158 J9
Pevek, Russ. 159 C19
Peyrehorade, Fr. 147 X6
Peywar Kandaw, pass, Afghan., Pak. 177 N8
Pezinok, Slovakia 149 K13
Pfaffenhofen, Ger. 148 K8
Pforzheim, Ger. 148 J6
Phaestus, ruin, Gr. 155 R14
Phaeton, Port, Fr. Polynesia, Fr. 219 P17
Phagwara, India 178 D5
Phalodi, India 178 F3
Phaltan, India 178 M4
Phan, Thai. 186 J8
Phangan, Ko, Thai. 187 Q8
Phangnga, Thai. 187 R7
Phan Ly, Vietnam 187 P14
Phan Rang, Vietnam 187 P14
Phan Thiet, Vietnam 187 P13
Pharr, Tex., U.S. 103 W10
Pharus see Hvar, island, Croatia 152 H6
Phatthalung, Thai. 187 R8
Phayao, Thai. 186 J8
Phelps, Ky., U.S. 101 C20
Phelps Lake, N.C., U.S. 96 H14
Phenix City, Ala., U.S. 101 L17
Phetchabun Range, Thai. 186 L9
Phetchaburi, Thai. 187 N8
Phiafai, Laos 186 M12
Phichai, Thai. 186 K8
Phichit, Thai. 186 L8
Philadelphia see 'Ammān, Jordan 170 M7
Philadelphia, Miss., U.S. 100 K12
Philadelphia, Pa., U.S. 94 P9
Philip, S. Dak., U.S. 104 L3
Philippeville, Belg. 146 M12
Philippi, ruin, Gr. 155 B13
Philippi, W. Va., U.S. 96 C10
Philippi Glacier, Antarctica 227 H21
Philippine Islands, Philippines 166 J13
Philippines, Asia 167 W13
Philippine Sea, Pac. Oc. 166 H14
Philippine Trench, Pac. Oc. 238 H4
Philippolis, S. Af. 202 L9
Philippopolis see Plovdiv, Bulg. 153 J14
Philippopolis see Shahbā, Syr. 170 K8
Philipsburg, Mont., U.S. 106 D6
Philipsburg, Pa., U.S. 94 N5
Philipsburg, Neth. Antilles, Neth. 121 B14
Philip Smith Mountains, Alas., U.S. 111 D17
Phillip Island, Norfolk I., Austral. 217 G20
Phillips, Tex., U.S. 102 G6
Phillips, Wis., U.S. 98 G4
Phillipsburg, Kans., U.S. 105 R5

Phillips Inlet, Nunavut, Can. 83 A15
Philomath, Oreg., U.S. 108 G3
Philpots Island, Nunavut, Can. 83 D16
Phippsburg, Colo., U.S. 106 L12
Phitsanulok, Thai. 186 K8
Phnom Penh, Cambodia 187 P11
Phoenix, Ariz., U.S. 107 U7
Phoenix, Mauritius 205 G20
Phoenix Islands, Kiribati 214 H10
Phôngsali, Laos 186 G10
Phong Tho, Vietnam 186 G10
Phrae, Thai. 186 K8
Phrao, Thai. 186 J8
Phra Thong, Ko, Thai. 187 Q7
Phrom Phiram, Thai. 186 K8
Phu Cat, Vietnam 186 M14
Phuket, Thai. 187 R7
Phuket, Ko, Thai. 187 R7
Phulabani, India 178 K9
Phulad, India 178 G4
Phu Loc, Vietnam 186 L13
Phu My, Vietnam 186 M14
Phu Quoc, Dao, Vietnam 187 Q11
Phu Rieng, Vietnam 187 P13
Phu Tho, Vietnam 186 G11
Phyarpon, Myanmar 186 L6
Piacenza, It. 150 E5
Piamafua Mountain, Amer. Samoa, U.S. 218 N2
Pianguan, China 182 D4
Pianosa, Isola, It. 150 J5
Pianosa, Isola, It. 150 K12
Pianu, island, F.S.M. 217 C14
Pianu, Mochun, F.S.M. 217 C13
Piaseczno, Pol. 149 E16
Piatra Neamţ, Rom. 153 C15
Piave, river, It. 150 D8
Piazza Armerina, It. 151 T11
Piazza del Risorgimento, It. 161 N17
Piazza Pio XII, Vatican City 161 Q17
Pibor Post, Sudan 199 G13
Picara Point, Virgin Islands, U.S. 120 M9
Picardy, region, Fr. 146 M10
Picassent, Sp. 145 H14
Picayune, Miss., U.S. 100 P11
Pichanal, Arg. 132 E10
Picher, Okla., U.S. 102 D14
Pichilemu, Chile 132 L6
Pickens, Miss., U.S. 100 K11
Pickford, Mich., U.S. 98 E10
Pickle Lake, Ont., Can. 83 N15
Pickwick Lake, Ala., Miss., Tenn., U.S. 101 G13
Pico, island, Azores 144 P3
Pico, It. 150 L9
Picos, Braz. 131 F16
Picos, Punta dos, Sp. 144 D5
Pico Truncado, Arg. 133 T9
Pictured Rocks National Lakeshore, Mich., U.S. 98 F9
Picture Gallery, Vatican City 161 N15
Picúa, Punta, P.R., U.S. 120 M5
Pidarak, Pak. 177 V3
Piedmont, Ala., U.S. 101 J17
Piedmont, region, It. 138 H5
Piedmont, Mo., U.S. 105 U15
Piedmont, region, U.S. 85 J18
Piedra, Monasterio de, Sp. 145 E13
Piedras, river, Peru 130 G5
Piedras Blancas, Point, Calif., U.S. 109 V4
Piedras Negras, Mex. 114 D11
Pieksämäki, Fin. 141 H16
Pielinen, lake, Fin. 141 G17
Pieniężno, Pol. 149 B15
Pienza, It. 150 H7
Pierce, Nebr., U.S. 105 N7
Piéria, Óros, Gr. 154 D10
Pierre, S. Dak., U.S. 104 K5
Pierrelatte, Fr. 147 W12
Pierrot Island (Cat Island), Mauritius 205 K20
Piešt'any, Slovakia 149 K14
Pietarsaari see Jakobstad, Fin. 141 G15
Pieter Both, peak, Mauritius 205 G20
Pietermaritzburg, S. Af. 202 K11
Pietersburg see Polokwane, S. Af. 202 H11
Pietra-di-Verde, Fr. 150 K4
Pietrosu, peak, Rom. 153 C14
Pietrosul, peak, Rom. 153 B14
Pigailoe (West Fayu Atoll), F.S.M. 216 Q5
Pigeon, Guadeloupe, Fr. 121 F14
Pigeon, Mich., U.S. 98 K12

Pigeon Cay, Bahamas 120 B8
Pigeon Creek, Bahamas 120 F11
Pigeon Point, Trinidad & Tobago 121 N17
Piggott, Ark., U.S. 100 E11
Pigna Courtyard, Vatican City 161 N16
Pigs, Bay of see Cochinos, Bahía de, Cuba 116 H7
Pigüé, Arg. 133 N11
Piha Passage, Tonga 218 H12
Pihtipudas, Fin. 141 G15
Pi'ilanihale Heiau, Hawai'i, U.S. 113 G18
Piis-Panewu, island, F.S.M. 217 A15
Pijijiapan, Mex. 115 L14
Pikalevo, Russ. 156 F8
Pikelot, island, F.S.M. 216 Q5
Pikes Peak, Colo., U.S. 107 N13
Pikeville, Ky., U.S. 101 C20
Pikijin, island, Marshall Is. 216 L8
Piła, Pol. 149 C13
Pilão Arcado, Braz. 131 G15
Pilar, Parag. 130 N10
Pilar, Cabo, Chile 133 X6
Pilbarra Point, Vanuatu 218 G4
Pilcomayo, river, S. Amer. 126 J6
Pileni, island, Solomon Is. 217 P22
Pil'gyn, Russ. 159 B20
Píli, Gr. 154 F9
Pilibhit, India 178 F7
Pílio, Óros, Gr. 154 F11
Pilliga, N.S.W., Austral. 211 W14
Pillsbury Sound, Virgin Islands, U.S. 120 N10
Pilón, Cuba 116 L12
Pílos, Gr. 154 L9
Pilot Knob, Idaho, U.S. 106 E4
Pilot Peak, Nev., U.S. 109 R8
Pilot Point, Alas., U.S. 111 M13
Pilot Rock, Oreg., U.S. 108 F7
Pilot Station, Alas., U.S. 110 H12
Pilottown, La., U.S. 100 R12
Pilsen see Plzeň, Czech Rep. 148 H10
Pimba, S. Aust., Austral. 211 W9
Pimental, Dom. Rep. 117 L19
Pinaki 2, island, Fr. Polynesia, Fr. 219 F21
Pinang, island, Malaysia 187 T8
Pinangah, Malaysia 188 G12
Pınarbaşı, Turk. 168 F11
Pinar del Río, Cuba 116 G5
Piñas, Ecua. 128 L2
Pinas, Arg. 132 J9
Pinckneyville, Ill., U.S. 99 U5
Pinconning, Mich., U.S. 98 K11
Pindaré, river, Braz. 131 E14
Pinders Point, Bahamas 120 F1
Pindi Bhattian, Pak. 177 P11
Pindi Gheb, Pak. 177 N10
Pindos Óros see Pindus Mountains, Gr. 154 E8
Pindus Mountains, Albania, Gr. 138 K8
Pine Barrens, region, N.J., U.S. 85 F12
Pine Bluff, Ark., U.S. 100 H9
Pine Bluffs, Wyo., U.S. 106 K14
Pine City, Minn., U.S. 104 H12
Pine Creek, N. Terr., Austral. 211 P8
Pinedale, Calif., U.S. 109 T6
Pinedale, Wyo., U.S. 106 H9
Pinega, river, Russ. 138 B11
Pinegrove, W. Aust., Austral. 211 V2
Pine Hill, N. Terr., Austral. 211 T8
Pinehill, Qnsld., Austral. 211 T13
Pine Hills, Fla., U.S. 97 T9
Pinehurst, Idaho, U.S. 106 C4
Pinehurst, N.C., U.S. 96 J10
Pine Island Bay, Antarctica 226 K7
Pine Island Glacier, Antarctica 226 J7
Pineland, Tex., U.S. 103 N15
Pinellas Park, Fla., U.S. 97 U7
Pine Point, N.W.T., Can. 82 J11
Pine Ridge, S. Dak., U.S. 104 M2
Pine River, Minn., U.S. 104 G10
Pinerolo, It. 150 E2
Pínes, Akrotírio (Nymphaeum), Gr. 155 D13
Pinetop-Lakeside, Ariz., U.S. 107 T9
Pineville, Ky., U.S. 101 D19
Pineville, La., U.S. 100 N8
Piney Buttes, Mont., U.S. 106 C11
Ping, river, Thai. 186 L8
Pingdingshan, China 182 H5
Pingdu, China 182 F9
Pingelap Atoll, F.S.M. 216 Q8
Pingelly, W. Aust., Austral. 211 X3
Pinghe, China 183 R7

Pingjiang, China 182 M5
Pinglap, island, Marshall Is. 216 M7
Pingle, China 183 Q2
Pingli, China 182 J2
Pingliang, China 180 J12
Pinglu, China 182 D4
Pingluo, China 182 D1
Pingnan, China 183 R2
Pingquan, China 182 C8
Pingtan, China 183 Q9
Pingtung, Taiwan, China 183 S9
Pingxiang, China 183 N5
Pingxiang, China 180 P12
Pingyang, China 183 N9
Pingyao, China 182 F4
Pingyi, China 182 G7
Pingyin, China 182 F7
Pingyuan, China 183 Q6
Pinheiro, Braz. 131 D14
Pinhel, Port. 144 F7
Pini, island, Indonesia 188 J5
Piniós, river, Gr. 154 E10
Pinjan, Indonesia 189 H13
Pinjarra, W. Aust., Austral. 211 X2
Pinleibu, Myanmar 186 F6
Pinnacles National Monument, Calif., U.S. 109 T5
Pinnaroo, S. Aust., Austral. 211 Y11
Pinneberg, Ger. 148 C7
Pinos, Point, Calif., U.S. 109 T4
Pinos-Puente, Sp. 144 L11
Pins, Île des (Kunié), New Caledonia, Fr. 218 E9
Pinsk, Belarus 156 M4
Pinsk Marshes, Belarus 156 M4
Pinta, Canal de, Ecua. 128 N9
Pinta, Isla (Abingdon), Ecua. 128 N9
Pintados, Chile 132 C7
Pintharuka, W. Aust., Austral. 211 W2
Pinzón, Isla (Duncan), Ecua. 128 Q9
Pioche, Nev., U.S. 109 R12
Piombino, It. 150 J6
Pioneer Fracture Zone, Pac. Oc. 239 E13
Pioneer Mountains, Mont., U.S. 106 E6
Pioneer Tablemount, Hawai'i, U.S. 112 L4
Pioner, Ostrov, Russ. 159 D14
Pionsat, Fr. 147 T10
Piotrków Trybunalski, Pol. 149 F15
Pipanaco, Salar de, Arg. 132 H9
Pipar, India 178 G4
Piparia, India 178 J6
Pipéri, island, Gr. 155 F13
Piper Peak, Nev., U.S. 109 S8
Pipe Spring National Monument, Ariz., U.S. 107 Q6
Pipestone, Minn., U.S. 104 L8
Pipestone National Monument, Minn., U.S. 104 L8
Pipinas, Arg. 132 M13
Piplan, Pak. 177 P9
Pippu, Japan 184 F14
Piqua, Ohio, U.S. 99 R11
Piracicaba, Braz. 131 M13
Piracuruca, Braz. 131 E16
Pirae, Fr. Polynesia, Fr. 219 N16
Pirané, Arg. 132 F13
Piranhas, Braz. 130 J12
Pirapora, Braz. 131 K14
Pirássununga, Braz. 131 L13
Pireás, Gr. 154 J12
Pirgí, Gr. 155 J16
Pírgos, Gr. 154 K8
Pirimapun, Indonesia 189 M20
Pirin, range, Bulg. 153 K13
Piripiri, Braz. 131 E16
Pirmasens, Ger. 148 H5
Pirna, Ger. 148 F11
Pirot, Serb. 152 H12
Pir Panjal Range, India 177 N13
Pirsagat, river, Azerb. 169 D22
Pisa, It. 150 G6
Pisagua, Chile 132 C7
Pisamwe, island, F.S.M. 217 A15
Pisaras, island, F.S.M. 216 Q6
Piscaderabaai, bay, Neth. Antilles, Neth. 121 Q14
Pisciotta, It. 151 N12
Pisco, Peru 130 H3
Pisek, Czech Rep. 148 J11
Pisemew, island, F.S.M. 217 A15
Pishan (Guma), China 180 G4
Pishin, Pak. 177 R6

Pīshīn, Iran 173 H18
Pisininin, island, F.S.M. 217 A15
Pisinun, island, F.S.M. 217 C16
Pismo Beach, Calif., U.S. 109 V5
Piso Firme, Bol. 130 H8
Pissos, Fr. 147 W6
Pissouri, Cyprus 160 Q6
Pisticci, It. 151 N13
Pistoia, It. 150 G6
Pistol River, Oreg., U.S. 108 K1
Pisz, Pol. 149 C16
Pitaga, Nfld. & Lab., Can. 83 L20
Pitanga, Braz. 130 M12
Pitav, Afghan. 176 K8
Pitcairn Island, Pac. Oc. 215 L16
Piteå, Sw. 141 F14
Piteşti, Rom. 153 F14
Pit Gorodok, Russ. 159 J13
Pithagorio, Gr. 155 K18
Pithara, W. Aust., Austral. 211 W2
Piti, Guam, U.S. 216 C10
Piti U Tai, island, Fr. Polynesia, Fr. 219 K14
Piti U Uta, island, Fr. Polynesia, Fr. 219 L14
Pitlochry, Scot., U.K. 142 L10
Piton, peak, Wallis & Futuna, Fr. 218 F11
Pitons, Anse aux, St. Lucia 121 L13
Pitt, Punta, Ecua. 128 Q11
Pitti Island, India 179 R3
Pitt Island, island, N.Z. 214 P9
Pittsburg, Kans., U.S. 105 U10
Pittsburg, Tex., U.S. 102 L14
Pittsburgh, Pa., U.S. 94 N3
Pittsfield, Ill., U.S. 99 R3
Pittsfield, Mass., U.S. 94 K12
Pittsfield, Me., U.S. 95 F17
Pittston, Pa., U.S. 94 M9
Pittston Farm, Me., U.S. 95 D16
Piua Petrii, Rom. 153 F17
Piva, river, Mont. 152 H8
Pixian, China 182 H7
Pkulagalid, cape, Palau 216 M11
Pkulagasemieg, island, Palau 216 P11
Pkulngril, cape, Palau 216 M11
Pkurengel, cape, Palau 216 N11
Placentia Bay, Nfld. & Lab., Can. 83 M24
Placerville, Calif., U.S. 109 Q5
Placetas, Cuba 116 H9
Placida, Fla., U.S. 97 V8
Plain Dealing, La., U.S. 100 K6
Plainfield, Ind., U.S. 99 R9
Plainfield, N.J., U.S. 94 N10
Plains, Ga., U.S. 97 N5
Plains, Kans., U.S. 105 V4
Plains, Tex., U.S. 102 J5
Plains, Tex., U.S. 102 K4
Plainview, Minn., U.S. 104 K12
Plainview, Nebr., U.S. 105 N7
Plainview, Tex., U.S. 102 J5
Plainville, Kans., U.S. 105 S5
Plainwell, Mich., U.S. 98 M10
Plaisance, Haiti 117 L16
Pláka, Gr. 155 E15
Plakoti, Cape, Cyprus 160 M11
Plana Cays (French Cays), Bahamas 117 H15
Planken, Liech. 160 N3
Plankinton, S. Dak., U.S. 104 L6
Plano, Tex., U.S. 102 L12
Plantation, Fla., U.S. 97 W10
Plant City, Fla., U.S. 97 U8
Plaquemine, La., U.S. 100 P9
Plasencia, Sp. 144 G8
Plasstéikopf, peak, Liech. 160 Q3
Plata, Isla de la, Ecua. 128 K1
Plata, Río de la, Arg., Uru. 132 M14
Platamónas, Gr. 154 E10
Plate, River, S. Amer. 126 L6
Plateau Station, Antarctica 227 E15
Plato, Col. 128 C5
Platte, river, Mo., U.S. 105 R10
Platte, river, Nebr., U.S. 105 Q7
Platte, S. Dak., U.S. 104 M6
Platteville, Wis., U.S. 98 M4
Plattsburg, Mo., U.S. 105 S10
Plattsburgh, N.Y., U.S. 94 F12
Plattsmouth, Nebr., U.S. 105 Q9
Plauen, Ger. 148 G9
Plavsk, Russ. 156 L9
Playa Blanca, Canary Is. 204 Q7
Playa Dayaniguas, Cuba 116 H5
Playa de Guayanés, P.R., U.S. 120 N5
Playa de Guayanilla, P.R., U.S. 120 N2

Playa de Naguabo, *P.R., U.S.* 120 N6
Playa Girón, *Cuba* 116 H8
Playa Grandi, bay, *Neth. Antilles, Neth.* 121 N14
Playa Honda, *Canary Is.* 204 P7
Playas Lake, *N. Mex., U.S.* 107 W10
Play Ku (Pleiku), *Vietnam* 186 M13
Plaza Huincul, *Arg.* 133 P8
Pleasant, Lake, *Ariz., U.S.* 107 T6
Pleasant Bay, *Bahamas* 120 B10
Pleasant Grove, *Utah, U.S.* 106 L7
Pleasanton, *Kans., U.S.* 105 T10
Pleasanton, *Tex., U.S.* 103 S9
Pleasantville, *N.J., U.S.* 94 Q10
Pleasure Ridge Park, *Ky., U.S.* 101 B16
Pleiku see Play Ku, *Vietnam* 186 M13
Pléneuf, *Fr.* 147 P5
Plenty, river, *Austral.* 210 F9
Plenty, Bay of, *N.Z.* 213 M19
Plentywood, *Mont., U.S.* 106 A13
Plesetsk, *Russ.* 158 E8
Plestin, *Fr.* 147 P3
Plétipi, Lac, *Que., Can.* 83 M20
Pleubian, *Fr.* 147 P4
Pleven, *Bulg.* 153 H14
Plevna, *Mont., U.S.* 106 D13
Pljevlja, *Mont.* 152 H9
Ploče, *Croatia* 152 H7
Płock, *Pol.* 149 D15
Ploërmel, *Fr.* 147 Q5
Ploieşti, *Rom.* 153 E15
Plomári, *Gr.* 155 G17
Płońsk, *Pol.* 149 D15
Plouézec, *Fr.* 147 P4
Plouguerneau, *Fr.* 147 P2
Plovdiv (Philippopolis), *Bulg.* 153 J14
Plum, Pointe, *St. Martin, Fr.* 121 B13
Plummer, *Idaho, U.S.* 106 C3
Plumtree, *Zimb.* 202 G10
Plymouth, *Eng., U.K.* 143 X9
Plymouth, *Ind., U.S.* 99 P9
Plymouth, *Mass., U.S.* 95 L15
Plymouth, *Montserrat, U.K.* 121 B23
Plymouth, *N.C., U.S.* 96 H14
Plymouth, *N.H., U.S.* 95 H14
Plymouth, *Pa., U.S.* 94 M8
Plymouth, *Trinidad & Tobago* 121 N17
Plymouth, *Vt., U.S.* 94 H12
Plymouth, *Wis., U.S.* 98 K7
Plyusa, *Russ.* 156 G6
Plzeň (Pilsen), *Czech Rep.* 148 H10
Pniewy, *Pol.* 148 D12
Pô, *Burkina Faso* 200 E10
Po, river, *It.* 150 E6
Po, Foci del (Mouths of the Po), *It.* 150 E8
Po, Mouths of the see Po, Foci del, *It.* 150 E8
Pobeda, Gora, *Russ.* 159 E19
Pobedy, Pik see Jengish Chokusu, *China, Kyrg.* 176 E15
Pocahontas, *Ark., U.S.* 100 E10
Pocahontas, *Iowa, U.S.* 104 M10
Pocahontas, *Va., U.S.* 96 F8
Pocatello, *Idaho, U.S.* 106 H7
Pochep, *Russ.* 156 L7
Pochutla, *Mex.* 115 L13
Pocomoke City, *Md., U.S.* 96 D15
Poconé, *Braz.* 130 J10
Pocono Mountains, *Pa., U.S.* 94 M9
Poços de Caldas, *Braz.* 131 L13
Poddor'ye, *Russ.* 156 H6
Poděbrady, *Czech Rep.* 148 G11
Podgorica, *Mont.* 152 J9
Podil's'ka Vysochyna, *Ukr.* 157 N3
Podkamennaya Tunguska, river, *Russ.* 159 J14
Podkamennaya Tunguska, *Russ.* 159 J13
Podol'sk, *Russ.* 156 J9
Podporozh'ye, *Russ.* 156 E8
Podravska Slatina, *Croatia* 152 D7
Poggibonsi, *It.* 150 H6
Poggio Rusco, *It.* 150 E7
Poh, *Indonesia* 189 J14
P'oha, *N. Korea* 182 C14
Pōhakuea Point, *Hawai'i, U.S.* 113 H17
P'ohang, *S. Korea* 182 F15
Pohnpei (Ponape), island, *F.S.M.* 216 Q8
Pohnpei Harbor, *F.S.M.* 217 F14
Pohorje, range, *Slov.* 152 C5
Pōhue Bay, *Hawai'i, U.S.* 113 P19
Pohuerahi, peak, *Fr. Polynesia, Fr.* 219 H14
Poi, *Wallis & Futuna, Fr.* 218 E11
Poim, *Russ.* 156 L12

Poindimié, *New Caledonia, Fr.* 218 C7
Poinsett, Cape, *Antarctica* 227 M21
Point Arena, *Calif., U.S.* 109 Q2
Pointe a la Hache, *La., U.S.* 100 Q11
Pointe-à-Pitre, *Guadeloupe, Fr.* 121 F15
Point Michel, *Dominica* 121 G19
Pointe-Noire, *Congo* 201 N16
Pointe-Noire, *Guadeloupe, Fr.* 121 F14
Point Fortin, *Trinidad & Tobago* 121 Q21
Point Hope, *Alas., U.S.* 110 C12
Point Lake, *N.W.T., Can.* 82 G12
Point Lay, *Alas., U.S.* 111 C13
Point Pedro, *Sri Lanka* 179 R7
Point Pleasant, *N.J., U.S.* 94 N11
Point Pleasant, *W. Va., U.S.* 96 D7
Point Reyes National Seashore, *Calif., U.S.* 109 R3
Point Samson, *W. Aust., Austral.* 211 S2
Point Washington, *Fla., U.S.* 97 Q3
Po'ipū, *Hawai'i, U.S.* 112 C5
Poirino, *It.* 150 E3
Poissy, *Fr.* 147 P9
Poitiers, *Fr.* 147 T8
Poix, *Fr.* 147 N9
Pok, *F.S.M.* 217 G14
Pokataroo, *N.S.W., Austral.* 211 W14
Pokhvistnevo, *Russ.* 156 K16
Pokka, *Fin.* 141 D15
Poko, *Dem. Rep. of the Congo* 198 J11
Pola see Pula, *Croatia* 152 E4
Polacca, *Ariz., U.S.* 107 R8
Pola de Lena, *Sp.* 144 B8
Pola de Siero, *Sp.* 144 B9
Pola Island, *Amer. Samoa, U.S.* 218 L8
Polán, *Iran* 173 H17
Poland, *Eur.* 139 T8
Poland, *Kiribati* 217 B22
Polar Plateau, *Antarctica* 226 G12
Polatlı, *Turk.* 168 E7
Polatsk, *Belarus* 156 J5
Pol-e 'Alam, *Afghan.* 177 N7
Pol-e Khomri, *Afghan.* 176 L7
Polesella, *It.* 150 E7
Police, *Pol.* 148 C11
Police Point, *Seychelles* 205 P20
Políegos, island, *Gr.* 155 M14
Polígiros, *Gr.* 154 D12
Poligny, *Fr.* 147 S13
Polihale Heiau, *Hawai'i, U.S.* 112 B4
Polihnítos, *Gr.* 155 G16
Políkastro, *Gr.* 154 B10
Polink Point, *Jam.* 120 K9
Polis, *Cyprus* 160 P5
Polk, *Pa., U.S.* 94 M3
Pollino, Monte, *It.* 151 P13
Pollock, *S. Dak., U.S.* 104 H5
Polnovat, *Russ.* 158 G10
Poloa Bay, *Amer. Samoa, U.S.* 218 M6
Polohy, *Ukr.* 157 R9
Polokwane (Pietersburg), *S. Af.* 202 H11
Polson, *Mont., U.S.* 106 C5
Poltava, *Ukr.* 157 P8
Polvadera, *N. Mex., U.S.* 107 T12
Polyanovgrad see Karnobat, *Bulg.* 153 J16
Polyarnyy, *Russ.* 158 C9
Polynesia, islands, *Pac. Oc.* 214 D10
Polynesian Cultural Center, *Hawai'i, U.S.* 112 D11
Pom, *Indonesia* 213 B15
Pomabamba, *Peru* 130 G3
Pombal, *Port.* 144 G5
Pomene, *Mozambique* 203 H13
Pomerania, region, *Ger., Pol.* 148 C11
Pomeroy, *Ohio, U.S.* 99 S14
Pomeroy, *Wash., U.S.* 108 D9
Pomichna, *Ukr.* 157 Q6
Pomîrla, *Rom.* 153 A15
Pomona, *Calif., U.S.* 109 X9
Pomorie (Archilais), *Bulg.* 153 J17
Pomos Point, *Cyprus* 160 N6
Pompano Beach, *Fla., U.S.* 97 W10
Pompeii, ruin, *It.* 150 M11
Pompeiopolis, ruin, *Turk.* 168 J9
Pompeys Pillar National Historic Landmark, *Mont., U.S.* 106 E10
Ponape see Pohnpei, island, *F.S.M.* 216 Q8
Ponca City, *Okla., U.S.* 102 E11
Ponce, *P.R., U.S.* 120 N3
Ponce de Leon Bay, *Fla., U.S.* 97 X9

Ponchatoula, *La., U.S.* 100 P10
Poncin, *Fr.* 147 T13
Pond Creek, *Okla., U.S.* 102 E10
Pondicherry see Puducherry, *India* 179 Q7
Pondikónisí, island, *Gr.* 154 P12
Pondosa, *Calif., U.S.* 108 M4
Ponérihouen, *New Caledonia, Fr.* 218 C7
Pones, island, *F.S.M.* 217 C16
Ponferrada, *Sp.* 144 C8
Pong, *Thai.* 186 J8
Pongara, Pointe, *Gabon* 201 K15
Pongaroa, *N.Z.* 213 M19
Pongo de Manseriche, site, *S. Amer.* 126 E2
Poniya Point, *N. Mariana Is., U.S.* 216 E7
Ponnani, *India* 179 R5
Ponoy, *Russ.* 158 D9
Pons, *Fr.* 147 U7
Ponta Delgada, *Azores* 144 Q5
Ponta do Pargo, *Madeira* 204 M2
Ponta do Sol, *Madeira* 204 M3
Ponta Grossa, *Braz.* 130 M12
Pont-à-Mousson, *Fr.* 147 P14
Ponta Porã, *Braz.* 130 L10
Pontarlier, *Fr.* 147 S14
Pontaumur, *Fr.* 147 U10
Pont-Aven, *Fr.* 147 Q3
Pontchartrain, Lake, *La., U.S.* 100 P11
Pontchâteau, *Fr.* 147 R5
Pont-d'Ain, *Fr.* 147 T13
Pont-de-Salars, *Fr.* 147 W10
Ponteareas, *Sp.* 144 C5
Pontebba, *It.* 150 C9
Pontedecimo, *It.* 150 F4
Ponte de Lima, *Port.* 144 D5
Ponte-Leccia, *Fr.* 150 J4
Pontevedra, *Sp.* 144 C5
Pontevedra, Ría de, *Sp.* 144 C5
Ponte Vedra Beach, *Fla., U.S.* 97 R9
Pontiac, *Ill., U.S.* 99 Q6
Pontiac, *Mich., U.S.* 98 M12
Pontianak, *Indonesia* 188 J9
Pontifical Academy of Sciences, *Vatican City* 161 P15
Pontinia, *It.* 150 L9
Pontivy, *Fr.* 147 Q4
Pont-l'Evêque, *Fr.* 147 N7
Pontoise, *Fr.* 147 P9
Pontotoc, *Miss., U.S.* 100 H12
Pontremoli, *It.* 150 F5
Ponts, *Sp.* 145 D16
Pontypool, *Wales, U.K.* 143 V10
Ponza, Isola di, *It.* 150 M9
Ponziane, Isole, *It.* 150 M9
Poochera, *S. Aust., Austral.* 211 X9
Poofai, Baie de, *Fr. Polynesia, Fr.* 219 K14
Poole, *Eng., U.K.* 143 X12
Poolewe, *Scot., U.K.* 142 J8
Pooncarie, *N.S.W., Austral.* 211 X11
Poopó, *Bol.* 130 K7
Poopó, Lago, *Bol.* 130 K7
Popayán, *Col.* 128 G4
Poplar, river, *Man., Can.* 83 M14
Poplar, river, *Mont., U.S.* 106 B12
Poplar, *Mont., U.S.* 106 B13
Poplar Bluff, *Mo., U.S.* 105 V15
Poplarville, *Miss., U.S.* 100 N12
Popocatépetl, peak, *Mex.* 114 J12
Popondetta, *P.N.G.* 213 E20
Popovo, *Bulg.* 153 H15
Poprad, *Slovakia* 149 J16
Porali, river, *Pak.* 177 U5
Porangahau, *N.Z.* 213 M19
Porbandar, *India* 178 J1
Porcuna, *Sp.* 144 K10
Porcupine, river, *Alas., U.S.* 111 E18
Porcupine Bank, *Atl. Oc.* 236 E11
Porcupine Mountains, *Mich., U.S.* 98 F5
Porcupine Plain, *Atl. Oc.* 236 F11
Pordenone, *It.* 150 D8
Porea, island, *Cook Is., N.Z.* 219 C14
Poreč, *Croatia* 152 E3
Porga, *Benin* 200 F11
Porgy Bay, *Bahamas* 120 B8
Pori, *Fin.* 141 J15
Porirua, *N.Z.* 213 M19
Porlamar, *Venez.* 128 B11
Pornic, *Fr.* 147 S5
Porongurup, *W. Aust., Austral.* 211 Y3
Póros, island, *Gr.* 154 K12
Póros, *Gr.* 154 K12
Porpoise Bay, *Antarctica* 227 P19
Porrentruy, *Switz.* 150 A2

Porsangen, bay, *Nor.* 141 B14
Porsuk, river, *Turk.* 168 E6
Porta, *Fr.* 160 J6
Portadown, *N. Ire., U.K.* 143 Q7
Portage, *Ind., U.S.* 99 N8
Portage, *Mich., U.S.* 99 N10
Portage, *Wis., U.S.* 98 K5
Portage la Prairie, *Man., Can.* 83 N13
Portageville, *Mo., U.S.* 105 V16
Portal, *N. Dak., U.S.* 104 D3
Port Albert, *Vic., Austral.* 211 Z13
Portalegre, *Port.* 144 H6
Portales, *N. Mex., U.S.* 107 T15
Port Alfred, *S. Af.* 202 M10
Port Allegany, *Pa., U.S.* 94 L5
Port Allen, *La., U.S.* 100 P9
Port Angeles, *Wash., U.S.* 108 B3
Port Antonio, *Jam.* 120 J11
Port-à-Piment, *Haiti* 117 M15
Port Aransas, *Tex., U.S.* 103 U11
Port Arthur see Lüshun, *China* 182 E9
Port Arthur, *Tex., U.S.* 103 Q16
Port Augusta, *S. Aust., Austral.* 211 X10
Port-au-Prince, *Haiti* 117 M16
Port Austin, *Mich., U.S.* 98 K13
Port Beaufort, *S. Af.* 202 M8
Port Blair, *India* 179 Q14
Port Bolivar, *Tex., U.S.* 103 R15
Portbou, *Sp.* 145 C18
Port Broughton, *S. Aust., Austral.* 211 X10
Port Burwell, *Nunavut, Can.* 83 J20
Port-Cartier, *Que., Can.* 83 M21
Port Charlotte, *Fla., U.S.* 97 V8
Port Clinton, *Ohio, U.S.* 99 N13
Port-de-Paix, *Haiti* 117 L16
Port Douglas, *Qnsld., Austral.* 211 R13
Port Eads, *La., U.S.* 100 R12
Port Edward, *S. Af.* 202 L11
Porteira, *Braz.* 130 D10
Portel, *Port.* 144 J6
Portel, *Braz.* 130 D12
Port Elizabeth, *S. Af.* 202 M10
Port Elizabeth, *St. Vincent & the Grenadines* 119 L17
Port Ellen, *Scot., U.K.* 143 N7
Porté-Puymorens, *Fr.* 160 J6
Porterdale, *Ga., U.S.* 96 L5
Porter Point, *St. Vincent & the Grenadines* 121 J16
Porterville, *Calif., U.S.* 109 U7
Porterville, *S. Af.* 202 M7
Port Esquivel, *Jam.* 120 J9
Port Etienne see Nouadhibou, *Mauritania* 196 F4
Port Fairy, *Vic., Austral.* 211 Z11
Port-Gentil, *Gabon* 201 L14
Port Gibson, *Miss., U.S.* 100 M10
Port Graham, *Alas., U.S.* 111 L16
Port Harcourt, *Nigeria* 201 H14
Port Hardy, *B.C., Can.* 82 L7
Port Hawkesbury, *N.S., Can.* 83 P22
Port Hedland, *W. Aust., Austral.* 211 S3
Port Heiden, *Alas., U.S.* 111 M13
Port Henry, *N.Y., U.S.* 94 G12
Port Hope, *Mich., U.S.* 98 K13
Port Hope Simpson, *Nfld. & Lab., Can.* 83 L22
Port Howe, *Bahamas* 117 F13
Port Huron, *Mich., U.S.* 98 L13
Port-İliç, *Azerb.* 169 F22
Portimão, *Port.* 144 L5
Port Isabel, *Tex., U.S.* 103 W11
Port Jervis, *N.Y., U.S.* 94 M10
Port Kaiser, *Jam.* 120 K7
Port Kaituma, *Guyana* 129 D14
Port Láirge see Waterford, *Ire.* 143 U6
Portland, *Eng., U.K.* 143 X12
Portland, *Ind., U.S.* 99 Q10
Portland, *Me., U.S.* 95 H15
Portland, *Mich., U.S.* 98 L10
Portland, *N. Dak., U.S.* 104 F7
Portland, *Oreg., U.S.* 108 F3
Portland, *Tenn., U.S.* 101 E15
Portland, *Tex., U.S.* 103 T11
Portland, *Vic., Austral.* 211 Z11
Portland, Bill of, *Eng., U.K.* 143 X12
Portland Bight, *Jam.* 120 K9
Portland Cottage, *Jam.* 120 K9
Portland Point, *Jam.* 120 K9
Portland Rock, *Jam.* 116 P11
Port-la-Nouvelle, *Fr.* 147 Y11
Port Laoise, *Ire.* 143 S6
Port Lavaca, *Tex., U.S.* 103 S12

Port Lincoln, *S. Aust., Austral.* 211 Y9
Port Lions, *Alas., U.S.* 111 M15
Portloe, *Eng., U.K.* 143 Y8
Port Loko, *Sierra Leone* 200 F5
Port Louis, *Mauritius* 205 G20
Port-Louis, *Guadeloupe, Fr.* 121 E15
Port Macquarie, *N.S.W., Austral.* 211 X15
Port Mansfield, *Tex., U.S.* 103 V11
Port Maria, *Jam.* 120 H10
Port Mathurin, *Mauritius* 205 J20
Port-Menier, *Que., Can.* 83 M21
Port Morant, *Jam.* 120 J11
Portmore, *Jam.* 120 J10
Port Moresby, *P.N.G.* 213 E19
Portnacroish, *Scot., U.K.* 142 L8
Portnahaven, *Scot., U.K.* 143 N7
Port Neches, *Tex., U.S.* 103 Q16
Port Nelson, *Bahamas* 117 F14
Port Nolloth, *S. Af.* 202 K7
Port Norris, *N.J., U.S.* 94 R10
Porto, *Braz.* 131 E15
Porto, *Fr.* 150 K3
Porto (Oporto), *Port.* 144 E5
Porto, Golfe de, *Fr.* 150 K3
Porto Alegre, *Braz.* 130 P12
Porto Alegre, *Sao Tome and Principe* 205 E20
Porto Amboim, *Angola* 202 D5
Porto Artur, *Braz.* 130 H11
Porto Azzurro, *It.* 150 J6
Portobelo, *Pan.* 115 N21
Port O'Connor, *Tex., U.S.* 103 T12
Porto Covo, *Port.* 144 K5
Porto dos Gaúchos, *Braz.* 130 G10
Porto Esperidião, *Braz.* 130 J10
Portoferraio, *It.* 150 J5
Porto Franco, *Braz.* 131 F14
Port-of-Spain, *Trinidad & Tobago* 121 P22
Porto Garibaldi, *It.* 150 F8
Pórto Germenó, *Gr.* 154 J13
Porto Grande, *Braz.* 130 C12
Portogruaro, *It.* 150 D9
Porthéli, *Gr.* 154 L11
Pôrto Inglês, *Cape Verde* 205 D17
Porto Jofre, *Braz.* 130 J10
Portola, *Calif., U.S.* 109 P6
Porto Moniz, *Madeira* 204 M2
Porto Murtinho, *Braz.* 130 L10
Porto Nacional, *Braz.* 131 G13
Porto Novo, *India* 179 Q7
Porto-Novo, *Benin* 200 H12
Port Ontario, *N.Y., U.S.* 94 H8
Port Orange, *Fla., U.S.* 97 S9
Port Orchard, *Wash., U.S.* 108 C3
Porto Recanati, *It.* 150 H10
Port Orford, *Oreg., U.S.* 108 K1
Porto San Giorgio, *It.* 150 H10
Porto Santo, island, *Madeira* 204 L5
Porto Santo, *Madeira* 204 L5
Portoscuso, *It.* 151 Q3
Porto Seguro, *Braz.* 131 K16
Porto Tolle, *It.* 150 E8
Porto Torres, *It.* 150 M3
Porto-Vecchio, *Fr.* 150 L4
Porto-Vecchio, Golfe de, *Fr.* 150 L4
Porto Velho, *Braz.* 130 F8
Portoviejo, *Ecua.* 128 J2
Port Phillip Bay, *Austral.* 210 M12
Port Pirie, *S. Aust., Austral.* 211 X10
Port Royal, *Jam.* 120 J10
Port Royal, *S.C., U.S.* 97 N9
Port Royal Bay see Little Sound, *Bermuda, U.K.* 120 C2
Port Royal Sound, *S.C., U.S.* 97 N9
Port Said see Būr Sa'īd, *Egypt* 171 N1
Port St. Joe, *Fla., U.S.* 97 R4
Port St. Johns, *S. Af.* 202 L11
Port-St. Louis, *Fr.* 147 X13
Port St. Lucie, *Fla., U.S.* 97 V10
Port Salerno, *Fla., U.S.* 97 V10
Portsall, *Fr.* 147 P2
Port-Salut, *Haiti* 117 N15
Port Saunders, *Nfld. & Lab., Can.* 83 L22
Port Shepstone, *S. Af.* 202 L11
Portsmouth, *Dominica* 121 E18
Portsmouth, *Eng., U.K.* 143 W13
Portsmouth, *N.C., U.S.* 96 J14
Portsmouth, *N.H., U.S.* 95 J15
Portsmouth, *Ohio, U.S.* 99 T13
Portsmouth, *Va., U.S.* 96 F14
Port South East, *Mauritius* 205 J20
Portsoy, *Scot., U.K.* 142 J11
Port Sudan, *Sudan* 199 C14

Port Sulphur, *La., U.S.* 100 Q11
Port Talbot, *Wales, U.K.* 143 V10
Port Townsend, *Wash., U.S.* 108 B3
Portugal, *Eur.* 139 W1
Portuguesa, river, *Venez.* 128 C9
Port Vila, *Vanuatu* 218 F3
Port Vincent, *S. Aust., Austral.* 211 Y10
Port Warrender, *W. Aust., Austral.* 211 Q5
Port Washington, *Wis., U.S.* 98 L7
Porus, *Jam.* 120 J8
Porvenir, *Bol.* 130 G6
Porvenir, *Chile* 133 X8
Porvoo, *Fin.* 141 J16
Porzuna, *Sp.* 144 H10
Posadas, *Arg.* 132 G14
Poschiavo, *Switz.* 150 C5
Posio, *Fin.* 141 E16
Poso, *Indonesia* 189 J13
Posof, *Turk.* 169 C17
Possession Island, *Namibia* 202 K6
Possum Kingdom Lake, *Tex., U.S.* 102 L9
Post, *Tex., U.S.* 102 K5
Post Falls, *Idaho, U.S.* 106 C3
Post Office Barrel, *Ecua.* 128 R9
Postville, *Iowa, U.S.* 104 M13
Posušje, *Bosn. & Herzg.* 152 H7
Potamí, *Gr.* 155 B13
Potamós, *Gr.* 154 P11
Poteau, *Okla., U.S.* 102 G14
Poteet, *Tex., U.S.* 103 S9
Potenza, *It.* 150 M12
Poth, *Tex., U.S.* 103 S10
Potholes Reservoir, *Wash., U.S.* 108 D7
P'ot'i, *Rep. of Georgia* 169 B16
Potiskum, *Nigeria* 201 E15
Potlatch, *Idaho, U.S.* 106 C3
Pot Mountain, *Idaho, U.S.* 106 D4
Potnarvin, *Vanuatu* 218 G4
Potomac, river, *Md., Va., U.S.* 96 D13
Potosi, *Mo., U.S.* 105 T14
Potosí, *Bol.* 130 K7
Potrerillos, *Chile* 132 G7
Potsdam, *Ger.* 148 D10
Potsdam, *N.Y., U.S.* 94 F10
Pott, *Île, New Caledonia, Fr.* 218 B6
Potter, *Nebr., U.S.* 105 P1
Pottstown, *Pa., U.S.* 94 P9
Pottsville, *Pa., U.S.* 94 N8
Poudre d'Or, *Mauritius* 205 F20
Pouébo, *New Caledonia, Fr.* 218 C6
Pouembout, *New Caledonia, Fr.* 218 C7
Poughkeepsie, *N.Y., U.S.* 94 L11
Pougues, *Fr.* 147 S11
Pouilly, *Fr.* 147 R10
Poulaphouca Reservoir, *Ire.* 143 S6
Poulsbo, *Wash., U.S.* 108 C4
Poum, *New Caledonia, Fr.* 218 C6
Pouoanuu, Mont, *Fr. Polynesia, Fr.* 219 M20
Poutasi, *Samoa* 218 L3
Poutoru, *Fr. Polynesia, Fr.* 219 B23
Povai, *Fr. Polynesia, Fr.* 219 K14
Povoação, *Azores* 144 Q5
Póvoa de Varzim, *Port.* 144 D5
Povorino, *Russ.* 157 N12
Povungnituk, Baie de, *Que., Can.* 83 J17
Powder, river, *Mont., Wyo., U.S.* 106 D13
Powder, river, *Oreg., U.S.* 108 G9
Powder River, *Wyo., U.S.* 106 H11
Powell, *Wyo., U.S.* 106 F10
Powell, Lake, *Utah, U.S.* 107 Q7
Powell Butte, *Oreg., U.S.* 108 H5
Powell Point, *Bahamas* 120 F6
Powell River, *B.C., Can.* 82 M8
Powers, *Oreg., U.S.* 108 J2
Powers Lake, *N. Dak., U.S.* 104 E3
Poxoréo, *Braz.* 130 J11
Poya, *New Caledonia, Fr.* 218 D7
Poyang Hu, *China* 182 M6
Poygan, Lake, *Wis., U.S.* 98 K6
Poysdorf, *Aust.* 149 J13
Pozantı, *Turk.* 168 H10
Poza Rica, *Mex.* 114 H12
Poznań, *Pol.* 149 D13
Pozo Alcón, *Sp.* 144 K12
Pozo Almonte, *Chile* 132 C7
Pozoblanco, *Sp.* 144 J9
Pozzallo, *It.* 151 U11
Pozzuoli, *It.* 150 M10
Pracana, Barragem de, *Port.* 144 G6
Pracchia, *It.* 150 G6
Prachin Buri, *Thai.* 186 M9
Prachuap Khiri Khan, *Thai.* 187 P8

Pradelles, *Fr.* 147 V12
Prado, *Braz.* 131 K16
Prague *see* Praha, *Czech Rep.* 148 H11
Praha (Prague), *Czech Rep.* 148 H11
Praia, *Cape Verde* 205 D16
Praia da Vitória, *Azores* 144 P4
Prainha, *Braz.* 130 D11
Prainha, *Braz.* 130 F9
Prairie City, *Oreg., U.S.* 108 G7
Prairie Dog Creek, *Kans., U.S.* 105 R4
Prairie Dog Town Fork Red, river, *Tex., U.S.* 102 H6
Prairie du Chien, *Wis., U.S.* 98 L3
Prairie Grove, *Ark., U.S.* 100 E6
Pran Buri, *Thai.* 187 N8
Praslin, island, *Seychelles* 205 M20
Praslin, *St. Lucia* 121 K14
Prasonísi, island, *Gr.* 155 P19
Prato, *It.* 150 G6
Pratola Peligna, *It.* 150 K10
Prats, *Andorra* 160 H4
Prats-de-Mollo, *Fr.* 147 Z10
Pratt, *Kans., U.S.* 105 U6
Pratt Seamount, *Pac. Oc.* 239 B14
Prattville, *Ala., U.S.* 101 L15
Prazeres, *Madeira* 204 M2
Preau, *Trinidad & Tobago* 121 Q22
Précy-sous-Thil, *Fr.* 147 R12
Predazzo, *It.* 150 C7
Preguiça, *Cape Verde* 205 B15
Preguiça, *Cape Verde* 205 B17
Prehistoric Petroglyphs, ruin, *Afghan.* 176 K9
Premont, *Tex., U.S.* 103 U10
Premuda, island, *Croatia* 152 F4
Prentice, *Wis., U.S.* 98 G4
Prentiss, *Miss., U.S.* 100 M11
Prenzlau, *Ger.* 148 C10
Preobrazhenka, *Russ.* 159 J15
Preparis Island, *Myanmar* 186 M4
Preparis North Channel, *Myanmar* 186 L4
Preparis South Channel, *Myanmar* 186 M4
Přerov, *Czech Rep.* 149 H13
Prescott, *Ariz., U.S.* 107 S6
Prescott, *Ark., U.S.* 100 J7
Prescott, *Wash., U.S.* 108 E8
Presho, *S. Dak., U.S.* 104 L5
Presidencia Roca, *Arg.* 132 F12
Presidencia Roque Sáenz Peña, *Arg.* 132 G12
Presidente Dutra, *Braz.* 131 E15
Presidente Eduardo Frei, station, *Antarctica* 226 C3
Presidente Prudente, *Braz.* 130 L12
President Thiers Bank, *Pac. Oc.* 239 M13
Presidio, *Tex., U.S.* 103 R1
Prešov, *Slovakia* 149 J16
Prespa, peak, *Bulg.* 153 K14
Prespa, Lake *see* Prespansko Jezero, *Albania, Gr., Maced.* 152 L10
Prespansko Jezero (Lake Prespa), *Albania, Gr., Maced.* 152 L10
Presque Isle, *Me., U.S.* 95 B18
Presque Isle, *Mich., U.S.* 98 H12
Presteigne, *Wales, U.K.* 143 U10
Preston, *Eng., U.K.* 143 R11
Preston, *Idaho, U.S.* 106 J7
Preston, *Minn., U.S.* 104 L13
Preston, *Mo., U.S.* 105 U12
Prestonsburg, *Ky., U.S.* 101 C20
Pretoria (Tshwane), *S. Af.* 202 J10
Préveza, *Gr.* 154 G7
Pribilof Islands, *Alas., U.S.* 110 L9
Priboj, *Serb.* 152 G9
Priboj, *Serb.* 152 J11
Příbram, *Czech Rep.* 148 H11
Price, river, *Utah, U.S.* 106 M8
Price, *Utah, U.S.* 106 M8
Price, Cape, *India* 179 P14
Prichard, *Ala., U.S.* 101 N13
Prickly Bay, *Grenada* 121 L22
Prickly Pear Cays, *Anguilla, U.K.* 120 Q10
Prickly Pear Island, *Antigua & Barbuda* 121 A21
Prickly Pear Island, *Virgin Islands, U.K.* 120 Q9
Prickly Point, *Grenada* 121 L22
Priekule, *Latv.* 141 M15
Prieska, *S. Af.* 202 L9
Priest Lake, *Idaho, U.S.* 106 B3

Priestley Glacier, *Antarctica* 227 P14
Priest River, *Idaho, U.S.* 106 B3
Prieta, Peña, *Sp.* 144 B10
Prievidza, *Slovakia* 149 J14
Prijedor, *Bosn. & Herzg.* 152 E6
Prijepolje, *Serb.* 152 H9
Prilep, *Maced.* 152 L11
Primorsko Akhtarsk, *Russ.* 157 S10
Prince Albert, *S. Af.* 202 M8
Prince Albert, *Sask.* 82 M12
Prince Albert Mountains, *Antarctica* 227 N14
Prince Albert Peninsula, *N.W.T., Can.* 82 D12
Prince Albert Sound, *N.W.T., Can.* 82 E12
Prince Alfred, Cape, *N.W.T., Can.* 82 C12
Prince Charles Island, *Nunavut, Can.* 83 F17
Prince Charles Mountains, *Antarctica* 227 F18
Prince Edward Fracture Zone, *Ind. Oc.* 240 Q3
Prince Edward Island, *Can.* 83 N22
Prince Edward Islands, *Ind. Oc.* 204 K7
Prince George, *B.C., Can.* 82 K8
Prince Gustaf Adolf Sea, *Nunavut, Can.* 83 C14
Prince Harald Coast, *Antarctica* 227 B17
Prince Kūhiō Park, *Hawai'i, U.S.* 112 C5
Prince of Wales, Cape, *Alas., U.S.* 110 E11
Prince of Wales Island, *Alas., U.S.* 111 M23
Prince of Wales Island, *Nunavut, Can.* 83 E14
Prince of Wales Island, *Qnsld., Austral.* 211 N12
Prince of Wales Strait, *N.W.T., Can.* 82 D12
Prince Olav Coast, *Antarctica* 227 B18
Prince Patrick Island, *N.W.T., Can.* 83 C13
Prince Regent Inlet, *Nunavut, Can.* 83 E15
Prince Rupert, *B.C., Can.* 82 J7
Prince Rupert Bay, *Dominica* 121 E18
Princess Anne, *Md., U.S.* 96 D14
Princess Antoinette Park, *Monaco* 161 E20
Princess Astrid Coast, *Antarctica* 227 A14
Princess Charlotte Bay, *Austral.* 210 B12
Princess Grace Hospital Center, *Monaco* 161 E19
Princess Grace Rose Garden, *Monaco* 161 F21
Princess Martha Coast, *Antarctica* 226 C11
Princess Ragnhild Coast, *Antarctica* 227 B15
Princeton, *B.C., Can.* 82 M8
Princeton, *Ill., U.S.* 99 P5
Princeton, *Ind., U.S.* 99 T7
Princeton, *Ky., U.S.* 101 D14
Princeton, *Minn., U.S.* 104 J11
Princeton, *Mo., U.S.* 105 Q11
Princeton, *N.J., U.S.* 94 P10
Princeton, *W. Va., U.S.* 96 F8
Princeville, *Hawai'i, U.S.* 112 B5
Prince William Sound, *Alas., U.S.* 111 K17
Príncipe, island, *Sao Tome and Principe* 205 A20
Príncipe da Beira, *Braz.* 130 H7
Prineville, *Oreg., U.S.* 108 G5
Pringle, *S. Dak., U.S.* 104 L1
Prior, Cabo, *Sp.* 144 A6
Prishtina (Priština), *Kos.* 152 J11
Prislop, Pasul, *Rom.* 153 B14
Priština *see* Prishtina, *Kos.* 152 J11
Pritchett, *Colo., U.S.* 107 P15
Pritzwalk, *Ger.* 148 C9
Privas, *Fr.* 147 V12
Privol'noye, *Russ.* 159 G22
Privolzhsk, *Russ.* 156 H11
Privolzhskaya Vozvyshennost', *Russ.* 157 P13
Privolzhskiy, *Russ.* 156 M14
Prizren, *Kos.* 152 J10
Probolinggo, *Indonesia* 188 M10
Proctor, *Minn., U.S.* 104 G12
Prodromi, *Cyprus* 160 P5
Progreso Limitada, *Eq. Guinea* 204 M8
Progress, station, *Antarctica* 227 G20
Progress, *Russ.* 159 K20
Prokhladnyy, *Russ.* 157 T13

Prokhod Sveti Nikola, *Bulg., Serb.* 152 H12
Prokópi, *Gr.* 154 G12
Prokop'yevsk, *Russ.* 158 L12
Prokuplje, *Serb.* 152 H11
Proletarsk, *Russ.* 157 R12
Promírí, *Gr.* 154 F11
Pronsfeld, *Ger.* 160 G10
Prony, *New Caledonia, Fr.* 218 E9
Prony, Baie du, *New Caledonia, Fr.* 218 E9
Propriá, *Braz.* 131 G17
Propriano, *Fr.* 150 L4
Proserpine, *Qnsld., Austral.* 211 S14
Prospect, *Barbados* 121 K18
Prospect, *Cayman Is., U.K.* 120 J2
Prospect, *Oreg., U.S.* 108 K3
Prospect Point, *Jam.* 120 K11
Prossátsáni, *Gr.* 155 B13
Prosser, *Wash., U.S.* 108 E6
Prostějov, *Czech Rep.* 149 H13
Protection, *Kans., U.S.* 105 V5
Próti, island, *Gr.* 154 L8
Provadiya, *Bulg.* 153 H17
Provence, region, *Fr.* 147 X14
Providence, *Grenada* 121 L23
Providence, *Ky., U.S.* 101 C14
Providence, *R.I., U.S.* 95 L14
Providence, Atoll de, *Seychelles* 203 C19
Providence Mountains, *Calif., U.S.* 109 W12
Providencia, Isla de, *Col.* 115 L20
Providenciales, island, *Turks & Caicos Is., U.K.* 117 H16
Provideniya, *Russ.* 159 A21
Provincetown, *Mass., U.S.* 95 K16
Provo, *Utah, U.S.* 106 L7
Prudhoe Bay, *Alas., U.S.* 84 L4
Prudhoe Bay, *Alas., U.S.* 111 C17
Prudnik, *Pol.* 149 G13
Prüm, river, *Ger.* 160 G11
Prüm, *Ger.* 160 G11
Prune Island *see* Palm Island, *St. Vincent & the Grenadines* 119 M17
Pruszcz Gdański, *Pol.* 149 B14
Pruszków, *Pol.* 149 E16
Prut, river, *Mold., Rom.* 153 D17
Pružany, *Belarus* 156 L3
Prvić, island, *Croatia* 152 E5
Prydz Bay, *Antarctica* 227 F20
Pryluky, *Ukr.* 157 N7
Pryor, *Okla., U.S.* 102 E13
Pryor Creek, *Mont., U.S.* 106 E10
Pryp'yat', river, *Ukr.* 156 M3
Przemyśl, *Pol.* 149 H18
Przheval'sk *see* Karakol, *Kyrg.* 176 E14
Psahná, *Gr.* 154 H12
Psará, island, *Gr.* 155 F13
Psará, *Gr.* 155 H15
Psathoúra, island, *Gr.* 155 F13
Psérimos, island, *Gr.* 155 L18
Psiloreítis *see* Ídi, Óros, peak, *Gr.* 155 Q14
Pskov, *Russ.* 156 G5
Pskovskoye Ozero, *Est., Russ.* 141 L17
Ptolemaída, *Gr.* 154 D9
Ptuj, *Slov.* 152 C6
Pua, *Thai.* 186 J9
Puakō, *Hawai'i, U.S.* 113 L19
Puakonikai, *Banaba, Kiribati* 217 D20
Puamau, Baie (Perigot), *Fr. Polynesia, Fr.* 219 M21
Puán, *Arg.* 133 N11
Pua Pua, Te Ava, *Tuvalu* 217 L23
Pu'apu'a, *Samoa* 218 K2
Puaumu Nord, island, *Fr. Polynesia, Fr.* 219 Q20
Puava, Cape, *Samoa* 218 K1
Pubei, *China* 183 S1
Pubnico, *Russ.* 156 L15
Pucallpa, *Peru* 130 F4
Puca Urco, *Peru* 130 D5
Pucheng, *China* 183 S9
Pucheng, *China* 183 N8
Pucioasa, *Rom.* 153 E15
Puck, *Pol.* 149 A14
Pudasjärvi, *Fin.* 141 F15
Pudimoe, *S. Af.* 202 K9
Pudu, *Indonesia* 188 J6
Puducherry (Pondicherry), *India* 179 Q7
Pudukkottai, *India* 179 R6
Puebla, *Mex.* 114 J12
Puebla de Guzmán, *Sp.* 144 K6
Puebla de Sanabria, *Sp.* 144 D7

Pueblo, *Colo., U.S.* 107 N14
Pueblo Bonito, *N. Mex., U.S.* 107 R10
Puente-Genil, *Sp.* 144 L9
Pueo Point, *Hawai'i, U.S.* 112 C3
Pu'er, *China* 180 P10
Puerca, Punta, *P.R., U.S.* 120 N6
Puerco, river, *Ariz., U.S.* 107 S9
Puerto Acosta, *Bol.* 130 J6
Puerto Aisén, *Chile* 133 S6
Puerto América, *Peru* 130 E3
Puerto Ángel, *Mex.* 115 L13
Puerto Armuelles, *Pan.* 115 P19
Puerto Ayacucho, *Venez.* 128 E9
Puerto Ayora, *Ecua.* 128 Q9
Puerto Bahía Negra, *Parag.* 130 L10
Puerto Baquerizo Moreno, *Ecua.* 128 Q10
Puerto Barrios, *Guatemala* 115 K16
Puerto Belgrano, *Arg.* 133 N11
Puerto Berrío, *Col.* 128 E5
Puerto Cabello, *Venez.* 128 B9
Puerto Cabezas, *Nicar.* 115 L19
Puerto Carreño, *Col.* 128 E9
Puerto Chicama, *Peru* 130 F2
Puerto Coig, *Arg.* 133 V8
Puerto Colombia, *Col.* 128 B5
Puerto Cortés, *Hond.* 115 K17
Puerto Cumarebo, *Venez.* 128 B8
Puerto de la Cruz, *Canary Is.* 204 Q5
Puerto del Carmen, *Canary Is.* 204 P7
Puerto del Rosario, *Canary Is.* 204 Q7
Puerto de Luna, *N. Mex., U.S.* 107 S14
Puerto de Mazarrón, *Sp.* 145 L13
Puerto de Nutrias, *Venez.* 128 C8
Puerto Deseado, *Arg.* 133 T9
Puerto Etén, *Peru* 130 F2
Puerto Heath, *Bol.* 130 H6
Puerto Jiménez, *Costa Rica* 115 P19
Puerto La Concordia, *Col.* 128 G6
Puerto La Cruz, *Venez.* 128 B11
Puerto La Paz, *Arg.* 132 D11
Puerto Lápice, *Sp.* 144 H11
Puerto Leguízamo, *Col.* 128 J5
Puerto Libertad, *Mex.* 114 C6
Puerto Limón, *Costa Rica* 115 N19
Puertollano, *Sp.* 144 J10
Puerto Lobos, *Arg.* 133 Q10
Puerto López, *Col.* 128 F6
Puerto Madryn, *Arg.* 133 R10
Puerto Maldonado, *Peru* 130 H6
Puerto Manatí, *Cuba* 116 J12
Puerto Montt, *Chile* 133 Q6
Puerto Morelos, *Mex.* 115 H17
Puerto Natales, *Chile* 133 W7
Puerto Obaldía, *Pan.* 115 N22
Puerto Padre, *Cuba* 116 J12
Puerto Páez, *Venez.* 128 E9
Puerto Peñasco, *Mex.* 114 B6
Puerto Pinasco, *Parag.* 130 L10
Puerto Pirámides, *Arg.* 133 Q10
Puerto Plata, *Dom. Rep.* 117 L18
Puerto Portillo, *Peru* 130 G4
Puerto Princesa, *Philippines* 189 E13
Puerto Real, *P.R., U.S.* 120 N1
Puerto Rico, *U.S., N. Amer.* 81 N23
Puerto Rico, island, *N. Amer.* 80 N11
Puerto Rico Trench, *Atl. Oc.* 236 L5
Puerto San Carlos, *Chile* 133 U7
Puerto San Julián, *Arg.* 133 U9
Puerto Santa Cruz, *Arg.* 133 V8
Puerto Suárez, *Bol.* 130 K10
Puerto Tres Palmas, *Parag.* 130 L10
Puerto Vallarta, *Mex.* 114 H9
Puerto Velasco Ibarra, *Ecua.* 128 R9
Puerto Villamil, *Ecua.* 128 R8
Puerto Wilches, *Col.* 128 D5
Puerto Williams, *Chile* 133 Y9
Puetton Tanapag, bay, *N. Mariana Is., U.S.* 216 B4
Pueu, *Fr. Polynesia, Fr.* 219 P17
Pueyrredón, Lago, *Arg., Chile* 133 T7
Pugachev, *Russ.* 156 L15
Puget Sound, *Wash., U.S.* 84 B4
Puhi, *Hawai'i, U.S.* 112 C6
Puigcerdà, *Sp.* 145 C17
Puig Major, peak, *Sp.* 145 G18
Puigmal d'Err, peak, *Sp.* 145 C17
Pujehun, *Sierra Leone* 200 G6
Pujiang, *China* 182 M9
Pukaki, Lake, *N.Z.* 213 P16
Pukalani, *Hawai'i, U.S.* 113 G17
Pukapuka, island, *Fr. Polynesia, Fr.* 219 D21
Pukapuka, island, *Fr. Polynesia, Fr.* 215 J15

Pukapuka Atoll (Danger Islands), *Cook Is., N.Z.* **214** J11
Pukarua, island, *Fr. Polynesia, Fr.* **219** F22
Pukch'ŏng, *N. Korea* **182** C14
Pukp'yŏng-ni, *S. Korea* **182** E14
Pula, *It.* **151** Q4
Pula (Pola), *Croatia* **152** E4
Pula, Capo di, *It.* **151** Q4
Pulandian, *China* **182** D10
Pulap Atoll, *F.S.M.* **216** Q5
Pulaski, *N.Y., U.S.* **94** H8
Pulaski, *Tenn., U.S.* **101** G15
Pulaski, *Va., U.S.* **96** F9
Puławy, *Pol.* **149** F17
Puli, *Taiwan, China* **183** R9
Pulicat Lake, *India* **179** P7
Puliyangudi, *India* **179** S5
Puliyankulam, *Sri Lanka* **179** S7
Pull and be Damn' Point, *Virgin Islands, U.K.* **120** L11
Pullman, *Wash., U.S.* **108** D9
Pull Point, *Virgin Islands, U.S.* **120** Q3
Pulo Anna, island, *Palau* **214** F2
Pulog, Mount, *Philippines* **189** B13
Pülümür, *Turk.* **169** F14
Pulusuk, island, *F.S.M.* **216** Q5
Puluwat Atoll, *F.S.M.* **216** Q5
Pumpkin Creek, *Mont., U.S.* **106** E12
Puná, Isla, *Ecua.* **128** K2
Puna, region, *Hawai'i, U.S.* **113** N21
Punaauia, *Fr. Polynesia, Fr.* **219** P15
Punaauia, Pointe, *Fr. Polynesia, Fr.* **219** P15
Puna de Atacama, region, *S. Amer.* **126** J4
Punaeroa, Passe, *Fr. Polynesia, Fr.* **219** C23
Punakha, *Bhutan* **178** F12
Punalu'u, *Hawai'i, U.S.* **113** P20
Punan, *Indonesia* **188** H11
Puncak Jaya, peak, *Indonesia* **189** L20
Punch, *India* **177** N11
Pune, *India* **178** L4
Punitaqui, *Chile* **132** J6
Puno, *Peru* **130** J6
Punta, Cerro de, *P.R., U.S.* **120** N3
Punta Aguja, range, *Peru* **130** F1
Punta Alta, *Arg.* **133** N11
Punta Arenas, *Chile* **133** X8
Punta Coles, range, *Peru* **130** K5
Punta del Este, *Uru.* **132** L14
Punta Delgada, *Arg.* **133** R10
Punta Gorda, *Belize* **115** K16
Punta Gorda, *Fla., U.S.* **97** V8
Punta Negra, range, *Peru* **130** F1
Punta Pariñas, range, *Peru* **130** E1
Punta Prieta, *Mex.* **114** C5
Puntarenas, *Costa Rica* **115** N18
Punta Umbría, *Sp.* **144** L7
Puntland, region, *Somalia* **199** G18
Punto Fijo, *Venez.* **128** A8
Puntudo, Cerro, *Arg.* **133** U8
Punxsutawney, *Pa., U.S.* **94** M5
Puohine, *Fr. Polynesia, Fr.* **219** C23
Puqi, *China* **182** L5
Puquio, *Peru* **130** J4
Puranpur, *India* **178** F7
Purari, river, *P.N.G.* **213** D19
Purcell, *Okla., U.S.* **102** H11
Purcell Mountains, *Can., U.S.* **106** A4
Purdy Islands, *P.N.G.* **213** B19
Purgatoire, river, *Colo., U.S.* **107** P14
Puri, *India* **178** L10
Purmerend, *Neth.* **146** H12
Purna, river, *India* **178** K5
Purnia, *India* **178** G11
Pursat, *Cambodia* **187** N11
Purus, river, *Braz.* **130** E8
Purvis, *Miss., U.S.* **100** N12
Pusad, *India* **178** L6
Pusan *see* Busan, *S. Korea* **182** G14
Pushkin, *Russ.* **156** F6
Pushkino, *Russ.* **156** M14
Pusht-i-Rud, region, *Afghan.* **177** P3
Puta, *Azerb.* **169** D23
Putangaroa, island, *Cook Is., N.Z.* **219** C15
Putao, *Myanmar* **186** D7
Putian, *China* **183** Q8
Putilovo, *Russ.* **156** F12
Putina, *Peru* **130** H5
Puting, Tanjung, *Indonesia* **188** K10
Puto, *P.N.G.* **217** J13
Putorana, Plato, *Russ.* **159** G14

Putrachoique, Cerro, *Arg.* **133** R7
Puttalam, *Sri Lanka* **179** S7
Puttelange, *Fr.* **147** P15
Puttur, *India* **179** P7
Putumayo, river, *Col.* **128** K7
Putumayo, river, *Ecua., Peru* **128** H4
Pütürge, *Turk.* **169** G13
Pu'uanahulu, *Hawai'i, U.S.* **113** L19
Pu'uhonua o Hōnaunau National Historic Park (City of Refuge National Historic Park), *Hawai'i, U.S.* **113** N18
Pu'ukohola Heiau National Historic Site, *Hawai'i, U.S.* **113** K19
Pu'uwai, *Hawai'i, U.S.* **112** C3
Puwe, island, *F.S.M.* **217** B15
Puxian, *China* **182** F3
Puyallup, *Wash., U.S.* **108** C4
Puyang, *China* **182** G6
Puy de Sancy, peak, *Fr.* **147** U10
Puy-Guillaume, *Fr.* **147** U11
Puysegur Point, *N.Z.* **213** R14
Puzak, Hamun-e, *Afghan.* **177** Q2
Pweto, *Dem. Rep. of the Congo* **198** M12
Pya, Lake, *Russ.* **138** B9
P'yagina, Poluostrov, *Russ.* **159** F21
Pyasinskiy Zaliv, *Russ.* **159** E13
Pyatigorsk, *Russ.* **157** T13
P'yatykhatky, *Ukr.* **157** Q7
Pyay, *Myanmar* **186** J5
Pydna, battle, *Gr.* **154** D10
Pyeonghae, *S. Korea* **182** F14
Pyhäjoki, *Fin.* **141** G15
Pyhäselkä, lake, *Fin.* **141** H17
Pyinkayaing, *Myanmar* **186** L5
Pyinmana, *Myanmar* **186** J6
Pyin-U-Lwin, *Myanmar* **186** G6
Pymatuning Reservoir, *Ohio, Pa., U.S.* **99** N16
P'yŏng-sŏng, *N. Korea* **182** D12
P'yŏngyang, *N. Korea* **182** D12
Pyote, *Tex., U.S.* **103** N3
Pyramides, Pointe, *Wallis & Futuna, Fr.* **218** E11
Pyramid Lake, *Nev., U.S.* **109** P6
Pyramid Rock, *China* **188** B10
Pyramids and Sphinx, ruin, *Egypt* **197** C18
Pyrenees, range, *Eur.* **138** H4
Pýrgos, *Gr.* **155** R15
Pyryatyn, *Ukr.* **157** N7
Pytalovo, *Russ.* **156** H5
Pyu, *Myanmar* **186** J6

Q

Qabanbay, *Kaz.* **175** G18
Qabqa, *China* **180** J10
Qāḍub, *Yemen* **173** R14
Qā'emābād, *Iran* **173** E17
Qā'emshahr, *Iran* **173** C13
Qā'en, *Iran* **173** D16
Qagan Nur, *China* **182** A6
Qagan Nur, *China* **182** A5
Qagan Us *see* Dulan, *China* **180** J10
Qahar Youyi Houqi, *China* **182** B5
Qahar Youyi Zhongqi, *China* **182** C5
Qaidam Basin, *China* **166** G9
Qaidam Pendi, *China* **180** H9
Qairouan, *Tun.* **197** A13
Qala, *Malta* **161** H21
Qalamcheshmeh, *Afghan.* **177** N4
Qalansīyah, *Yemen* **173** R14
Qalat (Kalat), *Afghan.* **177** P6
Qal'at al Aẓlam, ruin, *Saudi Arabia* **172** H5
Qal'at Bīshah, *Saudi Arabia* **172** M8
Qal'eh Shahr, *Afghan.* **176** L5
Qal'eh-ye Fath, *Afghan.* **177** R2
Qal'eh-ye Gaz, *Afghan.* **177** P4
Qal'eh-ye Now, *Afghan.* **176** M3
Qal'eh-ye Sarkari, *Afghan.* **176** L6
Qalhāt, *Oman* **173** K17
Qallabat, *Eth.* **199** E14
Qamar, Ghubbat al, *Yemen* **173** P13
Qamdo, *China* **180** L9
Qamea, island, *Fiji Is.* **218** G8
Qamīnis, *Lib.* **197** C15
Qammieh Point, *Malta* **161** J21
Qamystybas, *Kaz.* **174** G10
Qandala, *Somalia* **199** F18
Qapshaghay, *Kaz.* **175** H16
Qapshaghay Reservoir, *Kaz.* **175** H17
Qarabutaq, *Kaz.* **174** D9

Qaraghandy, *Kaz.* **175** E14
Qaraghayly, *Kaz.* **175** E15
Qarah Bagh, *Afghan.* **177** N7
Qaraqoynn Köli, *Kaz.* **175** G13
Qaratal, river, *Kaz.* **175** G16
Qarataū, *Kaz.* **175** J14
Qarataū Zhotasy, range, *Kaz.* **174** H13
Qaratöbe, *Kaz.* **174** D7
Qaraton, *Kaz.* **174** F7
Qaraūyl, *Kaz.* **175** E17
Qarazhal, *Kaz.* **175** F14
Qarchi Gak, *Afghan.* **176** K6
Qardho, *Somalia* **199** F18
Qarokūl, lake, *Taj.* **176** H11
Qarqan, river, *China* **180** G7
Qarqaraly, *Kaz.* **175** E15
Qarqin, *Afghan.* **176** K5
Qarsaqbay, *Kaz.* **174** F12
Qarshi, *Uzb.* **174** L12
Qaryat al 'Ulyā, *Saudi Arabia* **172** H11
Qaryat az Zuwaytīnah, *Lib.* **197** C15
Qaṣr-e Qand, *Iran* **173** H17
Qaṣr Farāfra, *Egypt* **197** D17
Qaṣr Ḥamām, *Saudi Arabia* **172** L10
Qa'ṭabah, *Yemen* **172** Q9
Qaṭanā, *Syr.* **170** J7
Qatar, *Asia* **167** V4
Qattara Depression, *Egypt* **197** C17
Qaṭṭīnah, Buḥayrat, *Syr.* **170** G8
Qax, *Azerb.* **169** C20
Qayghy, *Kaz.* **174** D11
Qaynar, *Kaz.* **175** E16
Qazakh, *Azerb.* **169** C19
Qazaly, *Kaz.* **174** G10
Qazaq Shyghanaghy, *Kaz.* **174** J6
Qazi Deh, *Afghan.* **176** K10
Qazimämmäd, *Azerb.* **169** D22
Qazvīn, *Iran* **172** C12
Qeissan, *Sudan* **199** F13
Qele Levu, island, *Fiji Is.* **218** G9
Qena, *Egypt* **197** D19
Qeqertarsuaq (Godhavn), *Greenland, Den.* **81** C21
Qeqertarsuatsiaat, *Greenland, Den.* **81** D22
Qerqertarsuaq, island, *N. Amer.* **80** C8
Qeshm, island, *Iran* **173** H15
Qeshm, *Iran* **173** H15
Qeysar, *Afghan.* **176** L4
Qianjiang, *China* **181** L13
Qianxian, *China* **182** G1
Qianyang, *China* **182** G1
Qianyang, *China* **183** N2
Qidong, *China* **182** K10
Qidong, *China* **183** P3
Qiemo, *China* **180** G6
Qijiaojing, *China* **180** E8
Qikiqtarjuaq, island, *Nunavut, Can.* **83** H2O
Qikiqtarjuaq, *Nunavut, Can.* **83** F19
Qila Ladgasht, *Pak.* **177** T2
Qila Safed, *Pak.* **177** S1
Qila Saifullah, *Pak.* **177** R7
Qilian Shan, *China* **166** G9
Qimantag, range, *China* **180** H8
Qimen, *China* **182** L7
Qing, river, *China* **182** L3
Qingdao, *China* **182** G9
Qinghai Hu, *China* **180** H10
Qingjian, *China* **182** F3
Qingshuihe, *China* **182** D4
Qingtian, *China* **183** N9
Qingxu, *China* **182** E4
Qingyuan, *China* **182** B12
Qingyuan, *China* **183** R4
Qingzhou, *China* **182** F8
Qinhuangdao, *China* **182** D9
Qin Lin, range, *China* **166** G11
Qin Ling, *China* **182** H1
Qinxian, *China* **182** F4
Qionghai (Jiaji), *China* **183** U2
Qiongshan, *China* **183** U2
Qiongzhou Haixia, strait, *China* **183** T1
Qiqian, *China* **181** B15
Qiqihar, *China* **181** C16
Qiryat Shemona, *Israel* **170** K6
Qishn, *Yemen* **173** P13
Qitai, *China* **180** E8
Qitaihe, *China* **181** D18
Qixia, *China* **182** F9
Qiyang, *China* **183** P3
Qiyl, river, *Kaz.* **174** D7
Qizilaǧac Körfäzi, *Azerb.* **169** F22
Qizilqum, desert, *Uzb.* **174** J10
Qogir *see* K2, peak, *China, Pak.* **176** L13

Qom, river, *Iran* **172** D12
Qom, *Iran* **172** D12
Qomsheh *see* Shahrezā, *Iran* **173** E13
Qonaqkänd, *Azerb.* **169** C22
Qongyrat, *Kaz.* **175** F15
Qo'qon, *Uzb.* **175** K14
Qorakūl, *Uzb.* **174** L11
Qoraqalpog'iston, region, *Uzb.* **174** H8
Qormi, *Malta* **161** K22
Qosköl, *Kaz.* **174** E12
Qosshaghyl, *Kaz.* **174** F7
Qostanay, *Kaz.* **174** B11
Qowryah, *Afghan.* **177** Q4
Qrendi, *Malta* **161** L22
Quairading, *W. Aust., Austral.* **211** X3
Quakertown, *Pa., U.S.* **94** N9
Quamby, *Qnsld., Austral.* **211** S11
Quanah, *Tex., U.S.* **102** J8
Quan Dao Nam Du, island, *Vietnam* **187** Q11
Quanery, Anse, *Dominica* **121** F20
Quang Ngai, *Vietnam* **186** L14
Quang Tri, *Vietnam* **186** K13
Quannan, *China* **183** Q5
Quanshuigou, *China* **176** L15
Quanzhou, *China* **183** P3
Quanzhou, *China* **183** Q8
Quaraí, *Braz.* **130** P10
Quartier d'Orléans, *St. Martin, Fr.* **121** B15
Quartier du Colombier, *St. Martin, Fr.* **121** B14
Quartu Sant'Elena, *It.* **151** Q4
Quartzsite, *Ariz., U.S.* **107** T5
Quatre Bornes, *Mauritius* **205** G19
Quba, *Azerb.* **169** C22
Qūchān, *Iran* **173** B16
Qudaym, *Syr.* **170** G10
Queanbeyan, *N.S.W., Austral.* **211** Y14
Quebec, *Can.* **83** M2O
Québec, *Que., Can.* **83** P2O
Quebracho Coto, *Arg.* **132** F10
Quebradillas, *P.R., U.S.* **120** M2
Queen Adelaida Archipelago, *S. Amer.* **126** R4
Queen Alexandra Range, *Antarctica* **227** L13
Queen Charlotte Islands, *B.C., Can.* **82** J6
Queen Charlotte Sound, *B.C., Can.* **82** K7
Queen Elizabeth Islands, *Nunavut, Can.* **83** B15
Queen Elizabeth Range, *Antarctica* **227** L13
Queen Fabiola Mountains (Yamato Mountains), *Antarctica* **227** C17
Queen Ka'ahumanu Highway, *Hawai'i, U.S.* **113** L18
Queen Mary Coast, *Antarctica* **227** J21
Queen Maud Gulf, *Nunavut, Can.* **83** F14
Queen Maud Land, *Antarctica* **226** C11
Queen Maud Mountains, *Antarctica* **226** K12
Queensland, *Austral.* **211** T12
Queenstown, *N.Z.* **213** Q15
Queenstown, *S. Af.* **202** L10
Queenstown, *Tas., Austral.* **211** Z15
Queen Victoria's Profile, *Hawai'i, U.S.* **112** C6
Queets, *Wash., U.S.* **108** C2
Queiros, Cape, *Vanuatu* **218** C1
Quelimane, *Mozambique* **203** F14
Quellón, *Chile* **133** R6
Quemado, *N. Mex., U.S.* **107** T10
Quemado, *Tex., U.S.* **103** S6
Quemoy *see* Kinmen, island, *Taiwan, China* **183** R8
Quemú Quemú, *Arg.* **132** M10
Quequén, *Arg.* **133** N12
Quercy, region, *Fr.* **147** W9
Querétaro, *Mex.* **114** H11
Quesada, *Costa Rica* **115** N19
Queshan, *China* **182** J5
Quesnel, *B.C., Can.* **82** L8
Que Son, *Vietnam* **186** L13
Questa, *N. Mex., U.S.* **107** Q13
Quetta, *Pak.* **177** R6
Quetzaltenango, *Guatemala* **115** L15
Quezon City, *Philippines* **189** C13
Qufu, *China* **182** G7
Quibala, *Angola* **202** D6
Quibdó, *Col.* **128** E4
Quiberon, Presqu'île de, *Fr.* **147** R4
Quijotoa, *Ariz., U.S.* **107** V6

Quilá, *Mex.* **114** F8
Quilcene, *Wash., U.S.* **108** B3
Quillan, *Fr.* **147** Y10
Quillota, *Chile* **132** K6
Quilon *see* Kollam, *India* **179** S5
Quilpie, *Qnsld., Austral.* **211** V12
Quimilí, *Arg.* **132** G11
Quimper, *Fr.* **147** Q3
Quimperlé, *Fr.* **147** Q3
Quinault, river, *Wash., U.S.* **108** C2
Quinault, *Wash., U.S.* **108** C2
Quince Mil, *Peru* **130** H5
Quincy, *Calif., U.S.* **109** P5
Quincy, *Fla., U.S.* **97** Q5
Quincy, *Ill., U.S.* **99** R3
Quincy, *Mass., U.S.* **95** K15
Quines, *Arg.* **132** K9
Quinhagak, *Alas., U.S.* **110** K12
Qui Nhon, *Vietnam* **186** M14
Quinn, river, *Nev., U.S.* **108** L8
Quintanar de la Orden, *Sp.* **144** G11
Quinter, *Kans., U.S.* **105** S4
Quintin, *Fr.* **147** Q4
Quinto, *Sp.* **145** E14
Quintus Rocks, *Bahamas* **120** E5
Quipungo, *Angola* **202** E6
Quirindi, *N.S.W., Austral.* **211** X14
Quissanga, *Mozambique* **203** D15
Quissico, *Mozambique* **203** J13
Quitaque, *Tex., U.S.* **102** J6
Quitilipi, *Arg.* **132** G12
Quitman, *Ga., U.S.* **97** Q6
Quitman, *Miss., U.S.* **101** M13
Quito, *Ecua.* **128** J3
Quixadá, *Braz.* **131** E17
Qujiang, *China* **183** Q4
Qujing, *China* **180** N11
Qulan, *Kaz.* **175** J15
Qulandy, *Kaz.* **174** G9
Qulbān Banī Murrah, ruin, *Jordan* **171** Q8
Qullai Ismoili Somoni (Communism Peak), *Taj.* **176** H10
Qulsary, *Kaz.* **174** F7
Qundao, island, *China* **182** E9
Qŭnghirot, *Uzb.* **174** J8
Quobba, *W. Aust., Austral.* **211** U1
Quogue, *N.Y., U.S.* **95** N13
Qurayyāt, *Oman* **173** K16
Qŭrghonteppa, *Taj.* **176** J7
Quryq, *Kaz.* **174** H5
Qusar, *Azerb.* **169** C22
Quseir, *Egypt* **197** D19
Qusmuryn, *Kaz.* **174** C11
Qusmuryn Köli, *Kaz.* **174** C11
Quwo, *China* **182** G4
Quxian, *China* **180** L12
Qüxü, *China* **180** L7
Quy Chau, *Vietnam* **186** J11
Quyang, *Kaz.* **175** G15
Quyghan, *Kaz.* **175** G15
Quy Hop, *Vietnam* **186** J11
Quzhou, *China* **182** F6
Quzhou, *China* **182** M8
Qvareli, *Rep. of Georgia* **169** B19
Qyzan, *Kaz.* **174** G6
Qyzylorda, *Kaz.* **174** H11

R

Raahe, *Fin.* **141** G15
Raas, island, *Indonesia* **188** M11
Raasay, island, *Scot., U.K.* **142** J7
Raasay, Sound of, *Scot., U.K.* **142** J7
Rab, island, *Croatia* **152** E4
Raba, *Indonesia* **189** M13
Rabacca, *St. Vincent & the Grenadines* **121** K17
Rabastens, *Fr.* **147** X7
Rabat *see* Victoria, *Malta* **161** H20
Rabat, *Malta* **161** K22
Rabat, *Mor.* **196** B8
Rabaul, *P.N.G.* **213** C21
Rabga Pass, *China, Nepal* **178** F11
Rabi (Rambi), island, *Fiji Is.* **218** G8
Rábida, Isla (Jervis), *Ecua.* **128** Q9
Rābigh, *Saudi Arabia* **172** K7
Racale, *It.* **151** N15
Răcari, *Rom.* **153** F15
Racconigi, *It.* **150** E2
Raccoon Cay, *Bahamas* **117** H13
Raccoon Point, *La., U.S.* **100** R10
Race, Cape, *Nfld. & Lab., Can.* **83** M24
Raceland, *La., U.S.* **100** Q10

Rachaïya, *Leb.* 170 J6
Rach Gia, *Vietnam* 187 Q11
Racine, *Wis., U.S.* 98 M7
Raco, *Mich., U.S.* 98 F10
Rădăuți, *Rom.* 153 A15
Radcliff, *Ky., U.S.* 101 C16
Radford, *Va., U.S.* 96 F9
Radhanpur, *India* 178 H3
Radisson, *Que., Can.* 83 M18
Radix, Point, *Trinidad & Tobago* 121 Q23
Radnevo, *Bulg.* 153 J15
Radom, *Pol.* 149 F16
Radomsko, *Pol.* 149 F15
Radomyshl', *Ukr.* 157 N5
Radviliškis, *Lith.* 141 N16
Raḍwá, Jabal, *Saudi Arabia* 172 J6
Radzyń Podlaski, *Pol.* 149 E17
Rae Bareli, *India* 178 G8
Raeford, *N.C., U.S.* 96 J11
Rae Isthmus, *Nunavut, Can.* 83 G16
Rae Lakes, *N.W.T., Can.* 82 G11
Raeside, Lake, *Austral.* 210 H4
Raetihi, *N.Z.* 213 L19
Rāf, Jabal, *Saudi Arabia* 172 G7
Rafaela, *Arg.* 132 J11
Rafaḥ, *Gaza Strip* 171 N4
Rafaï, *Cen. Af. Rep.* 198 H10
Raffadali, *It.* 151 T10
Rafḥā', *Saudi Arabia* 172 F9
Rafina, *Gr.* 155 J13
Rafsanjān, *Iran* 173 F15
Raga, *Sudan* 198 G11
Ragachow, *Belarus* 156 L6
Ragged, Mount, *Austral.* 210 K5
Ragged Island, *Bahamas* 117 H13
Ragged Island, *Me., U.S.* 95 G17
Ragged Point, *Barbados* 121 K20
Ragusa *see* Dubrovnik, *Croatia* 152 J8
Ragusa, *It.* 151 T11
Raha, *Indonesia* 189 L14
Raḥeb, Ras ir, *Malta* 161 K21
Rahimyar Khan, *Pak.* 177 T9
Raiatea, island, *Fr. Polynesia, Fr.* 219 E15
Raijua, island, *Indonesia* 189 N14
Rainbow Bridge National Monument, *Utah, U.S.* 107 Q8
Rainbow City, *Ala., U.S.* 101 J16
Rainbow Falls, *China* 180 L9
Rainbow Falls, *Hawai'i, U.S.* 113 M21
Rainier, *Oreg., U.S.* 108 E3
Rainier, Mount, *Wash., U.S.* 108 D4
Rainy, river, *Minn., U.S.* 104 E10
Rainy Lake, *Minn., U.S., Ont., Can.* 104 E11
Raipur, *India* 178 K8
Rairakhol, *India* 178 K9
Rairik, island, *Marshall Is.* 216 H12
Ra'īs, *Saudi Arabia* 172 K6
Raisinghnagar, *India* 178 E4
Raita Bank, *Hawai'i, U.S.* 112 L5
Raititi, Pointe, *Fr. Polynesia, Fr.* 219 K14
Raivavae (Vavitu), island, *Fr. Polynesia, Fr.* 219 J17
Raiwind, *Pak.* 177 Q12
Raja, Ujung, *Indonesia* 188 G4
Rajahmundry, *India* 178 M8
Rajampet, *India* 179 P6
Rajang, river, *Malaysia* 188 H11
Rajang, *Malaysia* 188 H10
Rajanpur, *Pak.* 177 S9
Rajapalaiyam, *India* 179 S6
Rajgarh, *India* 178 F5
Rajin *see* Najin, *N. Korea* 182 B15
Rajkot, *India* 178 J2
Raj Nandgaon, *India* 178 K8
Rajpura, *India* 178 E5
Raj Samund, *India* 178 H4
Rakahanga Atoll, *Cook Is., N.Z.* 214 H11
Rakaia, *N.Z.* 213 P17
Rakaposhi, peak, *Pak.* 176 L12
Rakhiv, *Ukr.* 157 N2
Rakhman Qaynary, *Kaz.* 175 D20
Rakhshan, river, *Pak.* 177 U4
Rakhyūt, *Oman* 173 P14
Rakiraki, *Fiji Is.* 218 H6
Rakops, *Botswana* 202 G9
Rakvere, *Est.* 141 K16
Raleigh, *Miss., U.S.* 100 M12
Raleigh, *N.C., U.S.* 96 H11
Ralik Chain, *Marshall Is.* 216 G3
Ralls, *Tex., U.S.* 102 K5
Ramah, *N. Mex., U.S.* 107 S10
Rām Allāh, *W. Bank* 170 M5
Raman, *Thai.* 187 S9

Ramanum, island, *F.S.M.* 217 B14
Ramat Gan, *Israel* 170 M5
Rambi *see* Rabi, island, *Fiji Is.* 218 G8
Rambu, *Indonesia* 189 J14
Rambutyo, island, *P.N.G.* 213 B20
Rameshki, *Russ.* 156 H9
Ramgarh, *India* 178 F2
Ram Head, *Virgin Islands, U.S.* 120 N11
Ramla, *Israel* 170 M5
Ramnagar, *India* 178 E7
Râmnicu Vâlcea, *Rom.* 153 E14
Ramona, *Calif., U.S.* 109 Y10
Ramos Island, *Solomon Is.* 217 M19
Rampart, *Alas., U.S.* III F16
Rampur, *India* 178 D6
Rampur, *India* 178 F7
Rampur Hat, *India* 178 H11
Ramree, *Myanmar* 186 J5
Ramree Island, *Myanmar* 186 J4
Ramsay, *Mich., U.S.* 98 F5
Ramsey Island, *Wales, U.K.* 143 V8
Ramu, *Bangladesh* 178 K14
Ramu, river, *P.N.G.* 213 C18
Ramvik, *Sw.* 141 J15
Ranchester, *Wyo., U.S.* 106 F11
Ranchi, *India* 178 J10
Rancho Cordova, *Calif., U.S.* 109 R5
Rancione, river, *San Marino* 161 H16
Ranco, river, *San Marino* 161 H15
Ranco, Lago, *Chile* 133 P6
Randazzo, *It.* 151 S11
Randers, *Den.* 140 N11
Randolph, *Nebr., U.S.* 105 N7
Randolph, *Utah, U.S.* 106 K8
Randolph, *Vt., U.S.* 95 G13
Rangahoe, island, *Cook Is., N.Z.* 219 B13
Rangamati, *Bangladesh* 178 J14
Rangeley, *Me., U.S.* 95 E15
Rangely, *Colo., U.S.* 106 L10
Ranger, *Tex., U.S.* 102 L9
Rangiroa, island, *Fr. Polynesia, Fr.* 219 D17
Rangitaiki, river, *N.Z.* 213 K20
Rangkasbitung, *Indonesia* 188 L8
Rangoon *see* Yangon, *Myanmar* 186 K6
Rangpur, *Bangladesh* 178 G12
Rangsang, island, *Indonesia* 188 H6
Raniganj, *India* 178 J11
Ranikhet, *India* 178 E7
Ranikot, ruin, *Pak.* 177 V7
Rankin, *Tex., U.S.* 103 N5
Rankin Inlet, *Nunavut, Can.* 83 H15
Rannoch, Loch, *Scot., U.K.* 142 L9
Rann of Kutch, wetland, *India* 177 X8
Ranong, *Thai.* 187 Q7
Ranongga (Ganongga), island, *Solomon Is.* 217 M15
Rans, *Switz.* 160 P2
Ransiki, *Indonesia* 189 J19
Rantau, island, *Indonesia* 188 J6
Rantauprapat, *Indonesia* 188 H5
Rantekombola, peak, *Indonesia* 189 K13
Rantoul, *Ill., U.S.* 99 Q7
Ranwas, *Vanuatu* 218 D3
Raohe, *China* 181 C19
Raoping, *China* 183 R7
Raoul Island (Sunday), *Kermadec Is., N.Z.* 214 L9
Rapa, island, *Fr. Polynesia, Fr.* 215 L14
Rapallo, *It.* 150 F4
Rapa Passage, *Kiribati* 217 B20
Rapar, *India* 178 H2
Raper, Cape, *Nunavut, Can.* 83 E18
Rapid, river, *Minn., U.S.* 104 E10
Rapid City, *S. Dak., U.S.* 104 L2
Rapid River, *Mich., U.S.* 98 G8
Rapota, island, *Cook Is., N.Z.* 218 Q11
Rappenstein, peak, *Liech.* 160 Q3
Rápulo, river, *Bol.* 130 H7
Raquette Lake, *N.Y., U.S.* 94 G10
Raraka, island, *Fr. Polynesia, Fr.* 219 E18
Raroia, island, *Fr. Polynesia, Fr.* 219 E19
Rarotonga, island, *Cook Is., N.Z.* 214 K12
Rasa, Punta, *Arg.* 133 Q11
Ra's al 'Ayn, *Syr.* 170 C13
Ra's al-Khaimah, *U.A.E.* 173 J15
Ra's an Naqb, *Jordan* 171 Q6
Rasa Point, *S. Amer.* 126 N6
Rashad, *Sudan* 198 F12
Rashīd (Rosetta), *Egypt* 197 C18
Rasht, *Iran* 172 B12
Raška, *Serb.* 152 H10
Ras Koh Range, *Pak.* 177 S4
Raso, Cabo, *Port.* 144 J4

Rason Lake, *Austral.* 210 H5
Ra's Shamrah (Ugarit), ruin, *Syr.* 170 F6
Rasshua, island, *Russ.* 159 H23
Rasskazovo, *Russ.* 156 L11
Rasua Garhi, *Nepal* 178 F10
Ratak Chain, *Marshall Is.* 216 F5
Ratangarh, *India* 178 F4
Rathdrum, *Idaho, U.S.* 106 B3
Rathenow, *Ger.* 148 D9
Rathlin Island, *N. Ire., U.K.* 143 N7
Ráth Luirc (Charleville), *Ire.* 143 U4
Rätikon, range, *Switz.* 150 B5
Ratingen, *Ger.* 148 F5
Ratisbon *see* Regensburg, *Ger.* 148 J9
Rat Island, *Alas., U.S.* 110 M3
Rat Islands, *Alas., U.S.* III M2
Ratlam, *India* 178 J4
Ratnagiri, *India* 178 M3
Ratnapura, *Sri Lanka* 179 T7
Ratodero, *Pak.* 177 T7
Raton, *N. Mex., U.S.* 107 Q14
Raton Pass, *N. Mex., U.S.* 107 Q14
Rattlesnake Creek, *Oreg., U.S.* 108 K9
Rattlesnake Hills, *Wash., U.S.* 108 D6
Rattlesnake National Recreation Area, *Mont., U.S.* 106 C6
Rau, island, *Indonesia* 189 H16
Raub, *Malaysia* 187 T9
Rauch, *Arg.* 132 M12
Raudal Yupurari (Devils Cataract), *Col.* 128 H7
Raufarhöfn, *Ice.* 140 E4
Raukotaha, island, *Cook Is., N.Z.* 219 C14
Rauma, *Fin.* 141 J15
Raurkela, *India* 178 J10
Rausu, *Japan* 184 E16
Rausu Dake, *Japan* 184 E16
Ravahere, island, *Fr. Polynesia, Fr.* 219 F19
Rāvar, *Iran* 173 E15
Ravena, *N.Y., U.S.* 94 K11
Ravenna, *It.* 150 F8
Ravenna, *Nebr., U.S.* 105 Q6
Ravenna, *Ohio, U.S.* 99 P15
Ravensburg, *Ger.* 148 K7
Ravenshoe, *Qnsld., Austral.* 211 R13
Ravensthorpe, *W. Aust., Austral.* 211 X4
Ravenswood, *Qnsld., Austral.* 211 S13
Ravenswood, *W. Va., U.S.* 96 D8
Ravi, river, *Pak.* 177 Q11
Ravnina, *Turkm.* 174 M10
Rāwah, *Iraq* 172 D8
Rawaki, island, *Kiribati* 214 H10
Rawalpindi, *Pak.* 177 N11
Rawa Mazowiecka, *Pol.* 149 E15
Rawandoz, *Iraq* 172 B10
Rawḍah, dry lake, *Syr.* 170 F14
Raẉhah, *Saudi Arabia* 172 M8
Rawi, Ko, *Thai.* 187 S8
Rawicz, *Pol.* 149 F13
Rawlinna, *W. Aust., Austral.* 211 W6
Rawlins, *Wyo., U.S.* 106 J11
Rawson, *Arg.* 133 R10
Rawu, *China* 180 L9
Ray, *N. Dak., U.S.* 104 E2
Ray, Cape, *Nfld. & Lab., Can.* 83 N22
Raya, point, *Indonesia* 188 J10
Rayachoti, *India* 179 P6
Raychikhinsk, *Russ.* 159 L19
Rayda' plain, *Saudi Arabia* 172 M11
Raymond, *Alta., Can.* 82 N10
Raymond, *Calif., U.S.* 109 S6
Raymond, *Wash., U.S.* 108 D2
Raymond Terrace, *N.S.W., Austral.* 211 X15
Raymondville, *Tex., U.S.* 103 W10
Ray Mountains, *Alas., U.S.* 84 N4
Rayne, *La., U.S.* 100 P8
Rayner Glacier, *Antarctica* 227 C18
Rayoke, island, *Russ.* 159 H23
Rayong, *Thai.* 187 N9
Raysūt, *Oman* 173 P14
Rayville, *La., U.S.* 100 L9
Raz, Pointe du, *Fr.* 147 Q2
Razelm, Lacul, *Rom.* 153 E18
Razgrad, *Bulg.* 153 G16
Razlog, *Bulg.* 153 K13
Razmak, *Pak.* 177 P8
Razzaza Lake, *Iraq* 172 E9
Ré, Île de, *Fr.* 147 T6
Re, river, *San Marino* 161 J14
Reading, *Eng., U.K.* 143 V13
Reading, *Jam.* 120 H6

Reading, *Pa., U.S.* 94 P8
Realicó, *Arg.* 132 L10
Réalmont, *Fr.* 147 X10
Ream, *Cambodia* 187 P11
Reao, island, *Fr. Polynesia, Fr.* 219 F22
Rebecca, Lake, *Austral.* 210 J4
Rebiana Sand Sea, *Lib.* 194 E7
Rebola, *Eq. Guinea* 204 L8
Rebun Tō, *Japan* 184 D13
Rebun Tō, *Japan* 184 D13
Recey, *Fr.* 147 R12
Recherche, Archipelago of the, *Austral.* 210 K5
Rechytsa, *Belarus* 156 M6
Recife, *Braz.* 131 G18
Recife, Cape, *S. Af.* 202 M10
Récifs, Île aux, *Seychelles* 205 N21
Recklinghausen, *Ger.* 148 E5
Reconquista, *Arg.* 132 H12
Recreo, *Arg.* 132 H9
Rector, *Ark., U.S.* 100 E11
Red, river, *China, Vietnam* 166 J10
Red *see* Red River of the North, river, *Man., Can.* 83 N14
Red, river, *U.S.* 85 L14
Redang, island, *Malaysia* 187 S10
Redange sur Attert, *Lux.* 160 J9
Red Bank, *Tenn., U.S.* 101 G17
Red Bay, *Ala., U.S.* 101 H13
Red Bay, *Cayman Is., U.K.* 120 J2
Red Bluff, *Calif., U.S.* 109 N4
Red Bluff Lake, *Tex., U.S.* 102 M2
Red Butte, *Ariz., U.S.* 107 R7
Red Cliff, *St. Kitts & Nevis* 121 C18
Redcliffe, Mount, *Austral.* 210 H4
Red Cloud, *Nebr., U.S.* 105 R6
Red Deer, *Alta., Can.* 82 M10
Red Devil, *Alas., U.S.* III J14
Redding, *Calif., U.S.* 109 N3
Redfield, *S. Dak., U.S.* 104 K6
Red Hills, *Kans., U.S.* 105 U5
Red Hook, *Virgin Islands, U.S.* 120 N10
Redig, *S. Dak., U.S.* 104 J2
Red Lake, *Minn., U.S.* 104 F10
Red Lake, *Ont., Can.* 83 N14
Red Lake, *W. Aust., Austral.* 211 X4
Red Lake Falls, *Minn., U.S.* 104 F8
Redlands, *Calif., U.S.* 109 X9
Red Lodge, *Mont., U.S.* 106 F9
Redmond, *Oreg., U.S.* 108 H5
Red Mountain, *Mont., U.S.* 106 C7
Red Oak, *Iowa, U.S.* 105 Q10
Redon, *Fr.* 147 R5
Redonda, island, *Antigua & Barbuda* 119 G16
Redonda, Roca, *Ecua.* 128 P7
Redondo, *Port.* 144 J6
Redoubt Volcano, *Alas., U.S.* III K15
Red River of the North, *Minn., N. Dak., U.S.* 104 F8
Red Rock, river, *Mont., U.S.* 106 F7
Red Rocks Point, *Austral.* 210 J6
Redruth, *Eng., U.K.* 143 X8
Red Sea, *Af., Asia* 166 G2
Red Springs, *N.C., U.S.* 96 J11
Redwater, river, *Mont., U.S.* 106 C12
Red Wing, *Minn., U.S.* 104 K12
Redwood Empire, region, *Calif., U.S.* 108 L2
Redwood Falls, *Minn., U.S.* 104 K10
Redwood National Park, *Calif., U.S.* 108 L2
Ree, Lough, *Ire.* 143 R5
Reed City, *Mich., U.S.* 98 K10
Reeder, *N. Dak., U.S.* 104 H2
Reedley, *Calif., U.S.* 109 T7
Reeds, Plain of, *Vietnam* 187 P12
Reedsburg, *Wis., U.S.* 98 K4
Reedsport, *Oreg., U.S.* 108 H2
Reedville, *Va., U.S.* 96 E14
Reedy Glacier, *Antarctica* 226 K11
Reef Bay, *Virgin Islands, U.S.* 120 N11
Reef Islands, *Solomon Is.* 217 P22
Reef Islands (Rowa Islands), *Vanuatu* 218 B2
Reefton, *N.Z.* 213 N17
Reese, river, *Nev., U.S.* 109 N9
Refahiye, *Turk.* 169 E13
Reform, *Ala., U.S.* 101 J14
Refugio, *Tex., U.S.* 103 T11
Regensburg (Ratisbon), *Ger.* 148 J9
Reggane, *Alg.* 196 D10
Reggio di Calabria, *It.* 151 R12
Reggio nell'Emilia, *It.* 150 F6
Reghin, *Rom.* 153 C14
Régina, *Fr. Guiana, Fr.* 129 F18

Regina, *Sask., Can.* 82 N12
Rehoboth, *Namibia* 202 H7
Rehoboth Beach, *Del., U.S.* 96 C15
Reid, *W. Aust., Austral.* 211 W7
Reid River, *Qnsld., Austral.* 211 S13
Reidsville, *Ga., U.S.* 97 N8
Reidsville, *N.C., U.S.* 96 G10
Reigate, *Eng., U.K.* 143 W14
Reims, *Fr.* 147 N12
Reina Adelaida, Archipiélago, *Chile* 133 W6
Reinosa, *Sp.* 144 B10
Reisdorf, *Lux.* 160 H10
Reitoru, island, *Fr. Polynesia, Fr.* 219 F19
Rekareka *see* Tehuata, island, *Fr. Polynesia, Fr.* 219 E19
Rekata Bay, *Solomon Is.* 217 L17
Reliance, *N.W.T., Can.* 82 H12
Reliance, *Wyo., U.S.* 106 K9
Remada, *Tun.* 197 C13
Remanso, *Braz.* 131 G15
Remedios, *Cuba* 116 H9
Remer, *Minn., U.S.* 104 G11
Remeshk, *Iran* 173 H16
Remich, *Lux.* 160 K11
Rémire, *Fr. Guiana, Fr.* 129 E18
Remiremont, *Fr.* 147 Q14
Remontnoye, *Russ.* 157 R13
Ren, island, *Marshall Is.* 216 K7
Rendezvous Bay, *Virgin Islands, U.S.* 120 N11
Rend Lake, *Ill., U.S.* 99 U6
Rendova, island, *Solomon Is.* 217 M16
Rendsburg, *Ger.* 148 B7
Rengat, *Indonesia* 188 J6
Reni, *Ukr.* 157 S4
Renmark, *S. Aust., Austral.* 211 X11
Rennell, island, *Solomon Is.* 217 Q19
Rennes, *Fr.* 147 Q5
Rennick Glacier, *Antarctica* 227 Q14
Reno, *Nev., U.S.* 109 P6
Renovo, *Pa., U.S.* 94 M6
Rensselaer, *Ind., U.S.* 99 P8
Renton, *Wash., U.S.* 108 C4
Renville, *Minn., U.S.* 104 K9
Repetek, *Turkm.* 174 M10
Republic, *Mich., U.S.* 98 F7
Republic, *Wash., U.S.* 108 A7
Republican, river, *Nebr., U.S.* 105 R6
Repulse Bay, *Austral.* 210 E14
Repulse Bay, *Nunavut, Can.* 83 G16
Requena, *Peru* 130 E4
Requena, *Sp.* 145 H14
Requin Bay, *Grenada* 121 L23
Reşadiye, *Turk.* 168 D12
Researcher Ridge, *Atl. Oc.* 236 L7
Reserve, *La., U.S.* 100 P10
Reserve, *N. Mex., U.S.* 107 T10
Resia, *It.* 150 B6
Resistencia, *Arg.* 132 G12
Reşiţa, *Rom.* 152 E11
Resolute, *Nunavut, Can.* 83 D15
Resolution Island, *N.Z.* 213 R14
Rest, *Jam.* 120 J8
Restinga, Punta, *Canary Is.* 204 R3
Réthimno, *Gr.* 155 Q13
Reti, *Pak.* 177 T8
Réunion, island, *Fr., Ind. Oc.* 204 H9
Reus, *Sp.* 145 E16
Reutlingen, *Ger.* 148 K7
Reva, *S. Dak., U.S.* 104 J2
Reval *see* Tallinn, *Est.* 141 K16
Revda, *Russ.* 158 ...
Revelstoke, *B.C., Can.* 82 M9
Revigny, *Fr.* 147 P13
Revillagigedo, Islas, *Mex.* 114 H5
Revillagigedo Island, *Alas., U.S.* III M23
Revillagigedo Islands *see* Revillagigedo, Islas, *N. Amer.* 80 N2
Revsbotn, *Nor.* 141 C14
Rewa, river, *Fiji Is.* 218 J6
Rewa, *India* 178 H8
Rexburg, *Idaho, U.S.* 106 G7
Rexford, *Mont., U.S.* 106 A5
Rexton, *Mich., U.S.* 98 F10
Rey, *Iran* 173 C13
Rey, Isla del, *Pan.* 115 N21
Rey Bouba, *Cameroon* 201 G17
Reyes, *Bol.* 130 H6
Reyes, Point, *Calif., U.S.* 84 G2
Reyhanlı, *Turk.* 168 J11
Reykjanes, cape, *Ice.* 138 A3
Reykjanes Ridge, *Atl. Oc.* 236 D9
Reykjavík, *Ice.* 140 F2

Reynosa, *Mex.* 114 F12
Rēzekne, *Latv.* 141 M17
Rgotina, *Serb.* 152 G12
Rhame, *N. Dak., U.S.* 104 H2
Rheine, *Ger.* 148 D6
Rhiconich, *Scot., U.K.* 142 H8
Rhine *see* Rhein, Rhin, river, *Eur.* 138 F5
Rhine, Sources of the, *Switz.* 138 H6
Rhinelander, *Wis., U.S.* 98 G5
Rhinns of Kells, region, *Scot., U.K.* 143 P9
Rhino Camp, *Uganda* 198 J12
Rhinocolura *see* El 'Arīsh, *Egypt* 171 N3
Rhir, Cape, *Mor.* 194 D2
Rhiy di-Irīsal, cape, *Yemen* 173 R15
Rho, *It.* 150 D4
Rhode Island, *U.S.* 95 L14
Rhodes *see* Ródos, island, *Gr.* 155 N20
Rhodes *see* Ródos, *Gr.* 155 M20
Rhodes Peak, *Idaho, U.S.* 106 D5
Rhodope Mountains, *Bulg., Gr.* 138 J9
Rhône, river, *Fr., Switz.* 138 H5
Rhône au Rhin, Canal du, *Fr.* 147 R15
Rhum, Sound of, *Scot., U.K.* 142 K7
Rhydargaeau, *Wales, U.K.* 143 U9
Rhyl, *Wales, U.K.* 143 Q4
Rhynie, *Scot., U.K.* 142 K10
Riaba, *Eq. Guinea* 204 M7
Riaba, Bahia de, *Eq. Guinea* 204 M7
Riachão, *Braz.* 131 F14
Rialb, river, *Andorra* 160 G3
Riang, *India* 178 F14
Riaño, *Sp.* 144 B9
Riasi, *India* 177 N12
Riau, Kepulauan, *Indonesia* 188 J7
Riaza, *Sp.* 144 E11
Ribadeo, *Sp.* 144 A7
Ribáuè, *Mozambique* 203 E14
Ribeira Afonso, *Sao Tome and Principe* 205 D20
Ribeira Brava, *Madeira* 204 M3
Ribeira da Cruz, *Cape Verde* 205 A14
Ribeira Grande, *Azores* 144 Q5
Ribeira Grande, *Cape Verde* 205 A14
Ribeirão Preto, *Braz.* 131 L13
Ribera, *It.* 151 S9
Riberalta, *Bol.* 130 G7
Ribes de Freser, *Sp.* 145 C17
Ribewon, island, *Marshall Is.* 216 J8
Riblah, *Syr.* 170 H8
Rib Lake, *Wis., U.S.* 98 H4
Rib Mountain, *Wis., U.S.* 98 H5
Ribniţa, *Mold.* 157 Q5
Ribnitz-Damgarten, *Ger.* 148 B9
Riccione, *It.* 150 G8
Rice Lake, *Wis., U.S.* 98 G3
Richards Bay, *S. Af.* 202 K12
Richardson Highway, *Alas., U.S.* III H18
Richardson Mountains, *N.W.T., Yukon, Can.* 82 E9
Richardton, *N. Dak., U.S.* 104 G3
Richey, *Mont., U.S.* 106 C13
Richfield, *Utah, U.S.* 107 N7
Richford, *Vt., U.S.* 95 E13
Rich Hill, *Mo., U.S.* 105 T11
Richland, *Ga., U.S.* 97 N4
Richland, *Mo., U.S.* 105 U13
Richland, *Oreg., U.S.* 108 G9
Richland, *Wash., U.S.* 108 E7
Richland Center, *Wis., U.S.* 98 L4
Richland Chambers Reservoir, *Tex., U.S.* 102 M13
Richlands, *Va., U.S.* 96 F8
Richlands Springs, *Tex., U.S.* 103 N9
Richmond, *Calif., U.S.* 109 R3
Richmond, *Ind., U.S.* 99 R10
Richmond, *Jam.* 120 H10
Richmond, *Ky., U.S.* 101 C18
Richmond, *Me., U.S.* 95 G16
Richmond, *Mo., U.S.* 105 S11
Richmond, *N.S.W., Austral.* 211 Y14
Richmond, *Qnsld., Austral.* 211 S12
Richmond, *S. Af.* 202 L9
Richmond, *St. Vincent & the Grenadines* 121 K16
Richmond, *Tex., U.S.* 103 R13
Richmond, *Utah, U.S.* 106 J7
Richmond, *Va., U.S.* 96 E13
Richmond Hill, *Bahamas* 120 E8
Richmond Peak, *St. Vincent & the Grenadines* 121 K16
Rich Square, *N.C., U.S.* 96 G13
Richton, *Miss., U.S.* 100 N12
Richwood, *W. Va., U.S.* 96 E9
Rico, *Colo., U.S.* 107 P10

Ricobayo, Embalse de, *Sp.* 144 D8
Ridā', *Yemen* 172 Q9
Ridanna, *It.* 150 B7
Ridder (Leninogorsk), *Kaz.* 175 D18
Riddle, *Idaho, U.S.* 106 J3
Riddle, *Oreg., U.S.* 108 J2
Ridgecrest, *Calif., U.S.* 109 V9
Ridgefield, *Wash., U.S.* 108 E3
Ridgeland, *S.C., U.S.* 96 M9
Ridgway, *Colo., U.S.* 107 N11
Ridgway, *Pa., U.S.* 94 M5
Riding Point, *Bahamas* 120 E3
Riding Rocks, *Bahamas* 116 D10
Riesa, *Ger.* 148 F10
Rieti, *It.* 150 K9
Rieumes, *Fr.* 147 X8
Rieupeyroux, *Fr.* 147 W10
Riez, *Fr.* 147 X14
Rifle, *Colo., U.S.* 106 M11
Rifstangi, cape, *Ice.* 138 A4
Rīga, *Latv.* 141 M16
Riga, Gulf of, *Est., Latv.* 141 L16
Rīgān, *Iran* 173 G16
Rigby, *Idaho, U.S.* 106 G7
Rigestan, desert, *Afghan.* 177 R5
Riggins, *Idaho, U.S.* 106 E4
Riglos, *Sp.* 145 C14
Rigo, *P.N.G.* 213 E20
Rigolet, *Nfld. & Lab., Can.* 83 K22
Rig Rig, *Chad* 197 H14
Riiser-Larsen Ice Shelf, *Antarctica* 226 B10
Riiser-Larsen Peninsula, *Antarctica* 227 B17
Rijeka (Fiume), *Croatia* 152 E4
Rijeka Crnojevića, *Mont.* 152 J8
Rikitea, *Fr. Polynesia, Fr.* 219 Q20
Rikubetsu, *Japan* 184 F15
Rikuzentakata, *Japan* 184 L14
Rila, range, *Bulg.* 153 J13
Riley, *Kans., U.S.* 105 S8
Rilly, *Fr.* 147 P12
Rimã', Jabal ar, *Jordan* 170 L8
Rimah, Wādī ar, *Saudi Arabia* 172 H8
Rimatara, island, *Fr. Polynesia, Fr.* 215 K13
Rimavská Sobota, *Slovakia* 149 K15
Rimini, *It.* 150 G8
Rîmnicu Sărat, *Rom.* 153 E16
Rimouski, *Que., Can.* 83 N20
Rincón, *P.R., U.S.* 120 N4
Rincón, Bahía de, *P.R., U.S.* 120 P4
Rincón, *Neth. Antilles, Neth.* 121 Q19
Rincon, *Ga., U.S.* 97 N9
Rinconada, *Arg.* 132 D9
Rincón de la Victoria, *Sp.* 144 M10
Rincón del Bonete, Lago, *Uru.* 132 K14
Ringbu, *Nor.* 140 J11
Ringdom Gompa, *India* 176 M13
Ringdove Passage, *Solomon Is.* 217 Q23
Ringgold, *La., U.S.* 100 L7
Ringgold Isles, *Fiji Is.* 218 G12
Ringkøbing, *Den.* 140 N10
Ringling, *Okla., U.S.* 102 J10
Ringling, *Mont., U.S.* —
Ringvassøy, island, *Nor.* 141 C13
Ringwood, *N. Terr., Austral.* 211 T9
Rinía, island, *Gr.* 155 K15
Rio, *Gr.* 154 H9
Riobamba, *Ecua.* 128 K3
Rio Branco, *Braz.* 130 G6
Río Bueno, *Jam.* 120 H8
Río Bueno, *Chile* 133 P6
Rio Canario, *Neth. Antilles, Neth.* 121 P14
Río Cauto, *Cuba* 116 K12
Rio Claro, *Trinidad & Tobago* 121 Q23
Río Cuarto, *Arg.* 132 K10
Rio de Janeiro, *Braz.* 131 M15
Rio Dell, *Calif., U.S.* 109 N1
Rio do Ouro, *Sao Tome and Principe* 205 C20
Río Gallegos, *Arg.* 133 W8
Rio Grande, river, *Mex., U.S.* 84 N11
Rio Grande, *Arg.* 133 X9
Rio Grande, *Braz.* 130 Q11
Rio Grande City, *Tex., U.S.* 103 W9
Rio Grande Rise, *Atl. Oc.* 237 S8
Rio Grande Wild and Scenic River, *Tex., U.S.* 103 Q4
Ríohacha, *Col.* 128 B6
Rio Hondo, river, *N. Mex., U.S.* 107 U13
Riom, *Fr.* 147 U11
Río Mulatos, *Bol.* 130 K7
Río Muni, region, *Eq. Guinea* 201 K15
Rioni, river, *Rep. of Georgia* 169 B17

Rio Nuevo, *Jam.* 120 H9
Rio Peñasco, river, *N. Mex., U.S.* 107 U14
Rio Puerco, river, *N. Mex., U.S.* 107 S12
Rio Rancho, *N. Mex., U.S.* 107 S12
Rio Tejo, Foz do, *Port.* 144 J4
Río Verde, *Chile* 133 W8
Río Verde, *Mex.* 114 H11
Rio Verde, *Braz.* 130 K12
Rio Verde de Mato Grosso, *Braz.* 130 K11
Rio Vouga, Foz do, *Port.* 144 F5
Rioz, *Fr.* 147 R14
Ripley, *Calif., U.S.* 109 Y13
Ripley, *Miss., U.S.* 100 G12
Ripley, *Ohio, U.S.* 99 T12
Ripley, *Tenn., U.S.* 100 F12
Ripley, *W. Va., U.S.* 96 D8
Ripoll, *Sp.* 145 C17
Ripon, *Eng., U.K.* 143 Q12
Ripon, *Wis., U.S.* 98 K6
Risāfe *see* Ar Ruşāfah, ruin, *Syr.* 170 F11
Riscle, *Fr.* 147 X7
Rishikesh, *India* 178 E6
Rishiri Tō, *Japan* 184 D13
Rishon LeZiyyon, *Israel* 170 M5
Rising Star, *Tex., U.S.* 102 M9
Rison, *Ark., U.S.* 100 H8
Risør, *Nor.* 140 L11
Rita Blanca Creek, *Tex., U.S.* 102 F4
Ritchie's Archipelago, *India* 179 Q14
Ritidian Point, *Guam, U.S.* 216 A11
Ritscher Upland, *Antarctica* 226 B11
Ritzville, *Wash., U.S.* 108 C8
Riva, river, *San Marino* 161 K16
Riva del Garda, *It.* 150 D6
Riva di Tures, *It.* 150 B8
Rivas, *Nicar.* 115 M18
Rivadavia, *Chile* 132 J7
Rive-de-Gier, *Fr.* 147 U12
Rivera, *Uru.* 132 J14
River Cess, *Liberia* 200 H7
Riverdale, *N. Dak., U.S.* 104 F4
Riverhead, *N.Y., U.S.* 95 N13
Riverina, region, *Austral.* 210 L12
Riverina, *W. Aust., Austral.* 211 W4
Riverside, *Calif., U.S.* 109 X9
Riverside, *Wash., U.S.* 108 B7
Riverside, *Wyo., U.S.* 106 K11
Riversleigh, *Qnsld., Austral.* 211 R10
Riverton, *Man., Can.* 83 N14
Riverton, *Wyo., U.S.* 106 H10
Rivesaltes, *Fr.* 147 Y10
Riviera, *Fr., It.* 138 H5
Rivière des Anguilles, *Mauritius* 205 H20
Rivière-du-Loup, *Que., Can.* 83 N20
Rivière du Rempart, *Mauritius* 205 F20
Rivière Noire, Piton de la, *Mauritius* 205 G19
Rivière-Pilote, *Martinique, Fr.* 121 F23
Rivière-Salée, *Martinique, Fr.* 121 F23
Rivne, *Ukr.* 157 N3
Rivoli, *It.* 150 E2
Riwoqê, *China* 180 L9
Riyadh *see* Ar Riyaḍ, *Saudi Arabia* 172 J10
Rize, *Turk.* 169 D15
Rizhao, *China* 182 G8
Rizokarpaso, *Cyprus* 160 M11
Rizzuto, Capo, *It.* 151 Q14
Ro, *New Caledonia, Fr.* 218 D10
Ro (Ágios Geórgios), island, *Gr.* 155 N22
Roa, *Sp.* 144 D10
Road Bay, *Anguilla, U.K.* 120 R11
Road Bay, *Virgin Islands, U.K.* 120 Q6
Road Town, *Virgin Islands, U.K.* 120 Q6
Roan Cliffs, *Colo., Utah, U.S.* 84 G7
Roanne, *Fr.* 147 T12
Roanoke, *Ala., U.S.* 101 K17
Roanoke, river, *N.C., Va., U.S.* 96 G13
Roanoke, *Va., U.S.* 96 F10
Roanoke Island, *N.C., U.S.* 96 G15
Roanoke Rapids, *N.C., U.S.* 96 G12
Roan Plateau, *Colo., U.S.* 106 M10
Roaringwater Bay, *Ire.* 143 V3
Robāt-e Khān, *Iran* 173 D15
Robat-e Khoshk Aveh, *Afghan.* 177 P2
Robāţ-e Posht-e Bādām, *Iran* 173 D15
Robe, *S. Aust., Austral.* 211 Z10
Robersonville, *N.C., U.S.* 96 H13
Robert Glacier, *Antarctica* 227 D19
Robert Lee, *Tex., U.S.* 102 M7
Roberts, *Idaho, U.S.* 106 G7
Roberts Butte, *Antarctica* 227 Q15

Roberts Creek Mountain, *Nev., U.S.* 109 P10
Robert S. Kerr Reservoir, *Okla., U.S.* 102 G14
Roberts Mountain, *Alas., U.S.* 84 Q1
Robertsport, *Liberia* 200 G6
Robeson Channel, *Nunavut, Can.* 83 A17
Robinson, *Ill., U.S.* 99 S7
Róbinson Crusoe, Isla, *S. Amer.* 126 M2
Robinson Range, *Austral.* 210 G3
Robinson River, *N. Terr., Austral.* 211 Q10
Robinvale, *Vic., Austral.* 211 Y11
Robokaere, island, *Marshall Is.* 216 G11
Roboré, *Bol.* 130 K9
Rob Roy, island, *Solomon Is.* 217 L16
Robson, Mount, *B.C., Can.* 82 L9
Robstown, *Tex., U.S.* 103 U11
Roby, *Tex., U.S.* 102 L7
Roca Partida, Isla, *Mex.* 114 H6
Roca Partida Island *see* Roca Partida, Isla, *N. Amer.* 80 N3
Rocas, Atol das, *S. Amer.* 126 E12
Rocas Brazil, Atol das, *Braz.* 131 E18
Roccadaspide, *It.* 151 N12
Rocca San Casciano, *It.* 150 G7
Roccastrada, *It.* 150 H7
Rocha, *Uru.* 132 L15
Rochdale, *Eng., U.K.* 143 R11
Rochedo, *Braz.* 130 K11
Rochefort, *Belg.* 146 M13
Rochefort, *Fr.* 147 T6
Rochelle, *Ga., U.S.* 97 N6
Rochelle, *Ill., U.S.* 99 N5
Rocheservière, *Fr.* 147 S6
Roches Noires, Mouillage des, *Fr. Polynesia, Fr.* 219 J20
Rochester, *Eng., U.K.* 143 N11
Rochester, *Eng., U.K.* 143 V15
Rochester, *Ind., U.S.* 99 P9
Rochester, *Minn., U.S.* 104 L12
Rochester, *N.H., U.S.* 95 H15
Rochester, *N.Y., U.S.* 94 J6
Rock, river, *Ill., U.S.* 99 N5
Rockall, island, *Atl. Oc.* 236 D11
Rockaway, *Oreg., U.S.* 108 F2
Rock Creek, *Mont., U.S.* 106 E9
Rock Creek Butte, *Oreg., U.S.* 108 G8
Rockdale, *Tex., U.S.* 103 P11
Rockefeller Plateau, *Antarctica* 226 L9
Rock Falls, *Ill., U.S.* 99 N5
Rockford, *Ill., U.S.* 98 M5
Rockhampton, *Qnsld., Austral.* 211 T15
Rockhampton Downs, *N. Terr., Austral.* 211 R9
Rock Hill, *S.C., U.S.* 96 J9
Rockingham, *N.C., U.S.* 96 J10
Rockingham, *W. Aust., Austral.* 211 X2
Rockingham Bay, *Austral.* 210 D13
Rock Island, *Ill., U.S.* 99 P4
Rock Lake, *N. Dak., U.S.* 104 E6
Rockland, *Me., U.S.* 95 G17
Rockland, *Mich., U.S.* 98 F6
Rocklea, *W. Aust., Austral.* 211 T2
Rockledge, *Fla., U.S.* 97 T9
Rockly Bay, *Trinidad & Tobago* 121 N17
Rockmart, *Ga., U.S.* 96 K4
Rock Port, *Mo., U.S.* 105 Q9
Rockport, *Calif., U.S.* 109 P2
Rockport, *Ind., U.S.* 99 U8
Rockport, *Tex., U.S.* 103 T11
Rock Rapids, *Iowa, U.S.* 104 M9
Rock River, *Wyo., U.S.* 106 J12
Rock Sound, *Bahamas* 120 F6
Rock Sound, *Bahamas* 120 F6
Rock Springs, *Mont., U.S.* 106 D12
Rock Springs, *Wyo., U.S.* 106 K9
Rocksprings, *Tex., U.S.* 103 Q7
Rockton, *Ill., U.S.* 98 M6
Rockville, *Ind., U.S.* 99 R8
Rockville, *Md., U.S.* 96 C13
Rockwell City, *Iowa, U.S.* 105 N10
Rockwood, *Me., U.S.* 95 D16
Rockwood, *Tenn., U.S.* 101 F18
Rocky Ford, *Colo., U.S.* 107 N14
Rocky Mount, *N.C., U.S.* 96 H12
Rocky Mount, *Va., U.S.* 96 F10
Rocky Mountain National Park, *Colo., U.S.* 106 L12
Rocky Mountains, *N. Amer.* 80 F3
Rocky Point, *Bahamas* 120 C6
Rocky Point, *Norfolk I., Austral.* 217 G20
Rocky Point, *Bahamas* 120 E11
Rodanthe, *N.C., U.S.* 96 H15
Roddickton, *Nfld. & Lab., Can.* 83 L23

Rodeo, *Arg.* 132 J7
Rodeo, *N. Mex., U.S.* 107 W10
Rodez, *Fr.* 147 W10
Rodinga, *N. Terr., Austral.* 211 U9
Ródos (Rhodes), island, *Gr.* 155 N20
Ródos (Rhodes), *Gr.* 155 M20
Rodrigues, island, *Ind. Oc.* 204 H10
Rodrigues Fracture Zone, *Ind. Oc.* 240 K7
Roebourne, *W. Aust., Austral.* 211 S2
Roebuck Bay, *Austral.* 210 D4
Roebuck Plains, *W. Aust., Austral.* 211 R4
Roermond, *Neth.* 146 K13
Roeselare, *Belg.* 146 L11
Roes Welcome Sound, *Nunavut, Can.* 83 H16
Rogagua, Lago, *Bol.* 130 H7
Rogers, *Ark., U.S.* 100 E6
Rogers, *Tex., U.S.* 103 P11
Rogers, Mount, *Va., U.S.* 96 G8
Rogers City, *Mich., U.S.* 98 H11
Rogers Lake, *Calif., U.S.* 109 W9
Rogerson, *Idaho, U.S.* 106 J5
Rogersville, *Tenn., U.S.* 101 E19
Roggan, river, *Que., Can.* 83 L18
Rogliano, *Fr.* 150 J4
Rogliano, *It.* 151 Q13
Rognan, *Nor.* 140 E12
Rogue, river, *Oreg., U.S.* 108 K2
Rogue River, *Oreg., U.S.* 108 K3
Roguron, island, *Marshall Is.* 216 G10
Rohrbach, *Aust.* 148 K10
Rohri, *Pak.* 177 T7
Rohtak, *India* 178 F5
Roi, *F.S.M.* 217 G14
Roi Anchorage, *Marshall Is.* 216 K4
Roi Et, *Thai.* 186 L11
Roi-Namur, island, *Marshall Is.* 216 K4
Rojas, *Arg.* 132 L12
Rojhan, *Pak.* 177 S8
Rojo, Cabo, *P.R., U.S.* 120 P1
Rokera, *Solomon Is.* 217 N20
Rokiškis, *Lith.* 141 M17
Rôlas, Ilhéu das, *Sao Tome and Principe* 205 E19
Rolette, *N. Dak., U.S.* 104 E5
Rolla, *Mo., U.S.* 105 T13
Rolla, *N. Dak., U.S.* 104 D5
Rolleston, *N.Z.* 213 P17
Rolleston, *Qnsld., Austral.* 211 U14
Rolletown, *Bahamas* 120 F9
Rolleville, *Bahamas* 120 E8
Rolling Fork, *Miss., U.S.* 100 K10
Rollins, *Mont., U.S.* 106 B5
Rolvsøya, island, *Nor.* 141 B14
Roma, *Qnsld., Austral.* 211 V14
Roma (Rome), *It.* 150 K8
Romain, Cape, *S.C., U.S.* 96 M11
Romaine, river, *Que., Can.* 83 M21
Roma-Los Saenz, *Tex., U.S.* 103 W9
Roman, *Rom.* 153 C16
Romanche Fracture Zone, *Atl. Oc.* 237 N11
Romanche Gap, *Atl. Oc.* 237 N10
Romang, island, *Indonesia* 189 M16
Români, *Egypt* 171 N1
Romania, *Eur.* 139 V9
Romanija, peak, *Bosn. & Herzg.* 152 G8
Romano, Cape, *Fla., U.S.* 97 X8
Romano, Cayo, *Cuba* 118 M17
Romanovka, *Russ.* 159 L16
Romans, *Fr.* 147 V13
Romanshorn, *Switz.* 150 A5
Romanzof, Cape, *Alas., U.S.* 84 P1
Rombo, Ilhéus do *see* Secos, Ilhéus, *Cape Verde* 205 D15
Rome, *Ga., U.S.* 96 K4
Rome *see* Roma, *It.* 150 K8
Rome, *N.Y., U.S.* 94 J9
Romilly, *Fr.* 147 Q11
Rommani, *Mor.* 196 B8
Romney, *W. Va., U.S.* 96 C11
Romny, *Ukr.* 157 N7
Romodanovo, *Russ.* 156 K13
Romorantin-Lanthenay, *Fr.* 147 R9
Romsey, *Eng., U.K.* 143 W12
Rona, island, *Scot., U.K.* 142 F7
Ronan, *Mont., U.S.* 106 C5
Roncador, Serra do, *Braz.* 130 H12
Roncador Cay, *N. Amer.* 80 P9
Ronceverte, *W. Va., U.S.* 96 E9
Ronda, *Sp.* 144 M9
Ronde, Point, *Dominica* 121 E18
Ronde Island, *Grenada* 121 H24
Rondônia *see* Ji-Paraná, *Braz.* 130 G8

Rondonópolis, *Braz.* 130 J11
Rondu, *Pak.* 176 L12
Rong, Koh, *Cambodia* 187 P10
Rong'an, *China* 183 P1
Rongcheng, *China* 182 F10
Ronge, Lac la, *N. Amer.* 80 G5
Rongelap Atoll, *Marshall Is.* 216 F3
Rongerik Atoll, *Marshall Is.* 216 F3
Rongjiang, *China* 183 P1
Rongxian, *China* 183 R2
Ronkiti, *F.S.M.* 217 G14
Ronkiti Harbor, *F.S.M.* 217 G14
Rønne, *Den.* 141 P13
Ronne Entrance, *Antarctica* 226 G6
Ronne Ice Shelf, *Antarctica* 226 F8
Ronse, *Belg.* 146 L11
Roodhouse, *Ill., U.S.* 99 S4
Roof Butte, *Ariz., U.S.* 107 Q9
Roonui, Mont, *Fr. Polynesia, Fr.* 219 Q17
Roorkee, *India* 178 E6
Roosendaal, *Neth.* 146 K12
Roosevelt, *Utah, U.S.* 106 L9
Roosevelt, Mount, *B.C., Can.* 82 J9
Roosevelt Island, *Antarctica* 226 M11
Roosevelt Roads Naval Station, *P.R., U.S.* 120 N6
Root, river, *Minn., U.S.* 104 L13
Roper, river, *N. Terr., Austral.* 211 Q9
Roper Valley, *N. Terr., Austral.* 211 Q9
Ropesville, *Tex., U.S.* 102 K4
Roquefort, *Fr.* 147 W7
Roques, Islas Los, *Venez.* 128 A10
Roquetas de Mar, *Sp.* 144 M12
Roraima, Mount, *S. Amer.* 126 B6
Røros, *Nor.* 140 J11
Rorschach, *Switz.* 150 A5
Rørvik, *Nor.* 140 G11
Rosa, Lake, *Bahamas* 117 J15
Rosa, Monte, *It., Switz.* 150 D3
Rosal de la Frontera, *Sp.* 144 K7
Rosalia, *Wash., U.S.* 108 C9
Rosalie, *Dominica* 121 F20
Rosalie Bay, *Dominica* 121 F20
Rosário, *Braz.* 131 D15
Rosario, *Arg.* 132 K12
Rosario, *Mex.* 114 G9
Rosario, *Parag.* 130 M10
Rosario, Cayo del, *Cuba* 116 H7
Rosario de la Frontera, *Arg.* 132 F9
Rosario de Lerma, *Arg.* 132 F9
Rosarno, *It.* 151 R13
Roscoe, *S. Dak., U.S.* 104 J6
Roscoe, *Tex., U.S.* 102 L7
Roscommon, *Ire.* 143 R5
Roscommon, *Mich., U.S.* 98 J11
Roscrea, *Ire.* 143 S5
Rose, Pointe de la, *Martinique, Fr.* 121 F23
Rose Atoll, *Amer. Samoa, U.S.* 214 J10
Roseau, river, *Dominica* 121 G19
Roseau, *Dominica* 121 G19
Roseau, river, *Minn., U.S.* 104 D8
Roseau, *Minn., U.S.* 104 D9
Roseau, river, *St. Lucia* 121 K14
Rose Belle, *Mauritius* 205 G20
Rosebery, *Tas., Austral.* 211 Z15
Rosebud, *Mont., U.S.* 106 D12
Rosebud, *Tex., U.S.* 103 P11
Rosebud Creek, *Mont., U.S.* 106 E12
Roseburg, *Oreg., U.S.* 108 J3
Rosedale, *Miss., U.S.* 100 J10
Rosedale, *Qnsld., Austral.* 211 U15
Rose Hall, *Jam.* 120 G7
Rose Hill, *Mauritius* 205 G20
Rose Island, *Bahamas* 120 B12
Rosenbach, *Aust.* 148 M10
Rosenberg, *Tex., U.S.* 103 R13
Rosenheim, *Ger.* 148 L9
Rose Peak, *Ariz., U.S.* 107 U9
Rosepine, *La., U.S.* 100 N7
Roses, *Bahamas* 117 G14
Roses, *Sp.* 145 C18
Roses, Golfe de, *Sp.* 145 C18
Rosetown, *Sask., Can.* 82 M11
Rosetta see Rashîd, *Egypt* 197 C18
Roseville, *Calif., U.S.* 109 Q5
Rosholt, *S. Dak., U.S.* 104 H8
Rosht-Kala, *Taj.* 176 K9
Rosia Bay, *Gibraltar, U.K.* 161 Q22
Rosiclare, *Ill., U.S.* 99 V6
Roşiori de Vede, *Rom.* 153 G14
Roslavl', *Russ.* 156 K7

Roslyatino, *Russ.* 156 F12
Roslyn, *Wash., U.S.* 108 C5
Rosporden, *Fr.* 147 Q3
Rosport, *Lux.* 160 J11
Ross, *N.Z.* 213 N16
Ross, Mount, *N.Z.* 213 M19
Ross, Point, *Norfolk I., Austral.* 217 G20
Rossano, *It.* 151 P14
Rossan Point, *Ire.* 143 P4
Ross Barnett Reservoir, *Miss., U.S.* 100 L11
Rosscarbery, *Ire.* 143 V3
Ross Dam, *Wash., U.S.* 108 A5
Rossel, Cap, *New Caledonia, Fr.* 218 C8
Rossel Island, *P.N.G.* 213 F22
Ross Ice Shelf, *Antarctica* 226 M12
Ross Island, *Antarctica* 227 N13
Ross Lake, *Wash., U.S.* 108 A5
Ross Lake National Recreation Area, *Wash., U.S.* 108 A5
Rosslare Harbour, *Ire.* 143 U7
Rosslau, *Ger.* 148 E9
Rosso, *Mauritania* 196 G5
Rosso, Capo, *Fr.* 150 K3
Ross of Mull, peninsula, *Scot., U.K.* 142 L7
Rossosh', *Russ.* 157 N10
Ross River, *N. Terr., Austral.* 211 T9
Ross River, *Yukon, Can.* 82 G8
Ross Sea, *Antarctica* 226 P11
Røssvatnet, lake, *Nor.* 140 F12
Rossville, *Ill., U.S.* 99 Q7
Rossville, *Qnsld., Austral.* 211 Q13
Røst Bank, *Arctic Oc.* 243 F19
Rostaq, *Afghan.* 176 K8
Rostock, *Ger.* 148 B9
Rostov, *Russ.* 156 H10
Rostov na Donu, *Russ.* 157 R11
Rostrenen, *Fr.* 147 Q4
Roswell, *Ga., U.S.* 96 K5
Roswell, *N. Mex., U.S.* 107 U14
Rota, island, *N. Mariana Is., U.S.* 216 D2
Rota see Songsong, *N. Mariana Is., U.S.* 216 E7
Rota, *Sp.* 144 M7
Rotan, *Tex., U.S.* 102 L7
Rotenboden, *Liech.* 160 P2
Roth, *Ger.* 148 J8
Roth, *Ger.* 160 H10
Rothera, station, *Antarctica* 226 E4
Rotherham, *Eng., U.K.* 143 S12
Rothschild, *Wis., U.S.* 98 H5
Rothschild Island, *Antarctica* 226 F4
Roti, island, *Indonesia* 189 N14
Roto, *N.S.W., Austral.* 211 X12
Roto, Pukapuka, *Cook Is., N.Z.* 218 Q2
Rotondella, *It.* 151 N13
Rotorua, *N.Z.* 213 K19
Rotterdam, *Neth.* 146 J12
Rottumeroog, island, *Neth.* 146 G14
Rottumerplaat, island, *Neth.* 146 G14
Rotuma, island, *Fiji* 214 J8
Roubaix, *Fr.* 146 L11
Rouen, *Fr.* 147 N8
Rouge, Baie, *St. Martin, Fr.* 121 B14
Rouge, Pic de la, *Fr., Sp.* 160 G2
Rough Point, *Virgin Islands, U.K.* 120 Q6
Round Island see Yalewa Kalou, *Fiji Is.* 218 G6
Round Island, *Mauritius* 205 E20
Round Island Passage, *Fiji Is.* 218 G6
Round Mountain, *Nev., U.S.* 109 Q9
Round Rock, *Bahamas* 120 C8
Round Rock, *Tex., U.S.* 103 P10
Roundstone, *Ire.* 143 S3
Roundup, *Mont., U.S.* 106 D10
Roura, *Fr. Guiana, Fr.* 129 E18
Rousay, island, *Scot., U.K.* 142 F10
Rouses Point, *N.Y., U.S.* 94 E12
Rouyn-Noranda, *Que., Can.* 83 P18
Rovaniemi, *Fin.* 141 E15
Rovereto, *It.* 150 D6
Rovieng, *Cambodia* 187 N11
Rovigo, *It.* 150 E7
Rovinj, *Croatia* 152 E3
Rovuma see Ruvuma, river, *Tanzania* 199 N15
Rowa Islands see Reef Islands, *Vanuatu* 218 B2
Rowd-e Lurah, river, *Afghan.* 177 P6
Rowena, *N.S.W., Austral.* 211 W14
Rowland, *N.C., U.S.* 96 K11
Rowley Island, *Nunavut, Can.* 83 F17
Roxas, *Philippines* 189 D14
Roxas, *Philippines* 189 E13
Roxboro, *N.C., U.S.* 96 G11

Roxborough, *Trinidad & Tobago* 121 N18
Roy, *Mont., U.S.* 106 C10
Roy, *N. Mex., U.S.* 107 R14
Royale, Isle, *Mich., U.S.* 98 D6
Royal Island, *Bahamas* 120 D5
Royal Oak, *Mich., U.S.* 99 M12
Royal Society Range, *Antarctica* 227 N14
Royan, *Fr.* 147 U6
Roy Hill, *W. Aust., Austral.* 211 T3
Royston, *Ga., U.S.* 96 K6
Roznov, *Rom.* 153 C16
Rrogozhinë, *Albania* 152 L9
Rt Kamenjak, cape, *Croatia* 152 E4
Rua, island, *Marshall Is.* 216 L7
Ruacaná Falls, *Angola* 202 F6
Ruahara, island, *Cook Is., N.Z.* 219 A17
Ruapehu, Mount, *N.Z.* 213 L19
Ruapuke Island, *N.Z.* 213 R15
Ruatoria, *N.Z.* 213 K20
Ruawai, *N.Z.* 213 J18
Rub al Khali, desert, *Saudi Arabia* 166 H4
Rubicone, river, *It.* 150 G8
Rubtsovsk, *Russ.* 158 L11
Ruby, *Alas., U.S.* 111 G15
Ruby, river, *Mont., U.S.* 106 E7
Ruby Dome, *Nev., U.S.* 84 F5
Ruby Mountains, *Nev., U.S.* 109 N11
Rudan, *Iran* 173 H16
Rudbar, *Afghan.* 177 R2
Rudder Cut Cay, *Bahamas* 120 D7
Rüdnyy, *Kaz.* 174 C6
Rudolf, Lake see Turkana, Lake, *Eth., Kenya* 199 H14
Rudolph, Ostrov, *Russ.* 158 C12
Rudong (Juegang), *China* 182 K10
Rudyard, *Mich., U.S.* 98 F11
Rue, *Fr.* 146 M9
Ruffec, *Fr.* 147 T7
Rufiji, river, *Tanzania* 199 M14
Rufino, *Arg.* 132 L11
Rufisque, *Senegal* 196 H4
Rugby, *N. Dak., U.S.* 104 E5
Rugeley, *Eng., U.K.* 143 T12
Rügen, island, *Ger.* 148 B10
Ruggell, *Liech.* 160 M2
Ruhnu Saar, island, *Est.* 141 L16
Ruhr, river, *Ger.* 148 F6
Ru'i, *Afghan.* 176 L7
Rui'an, *China* 183 N9
Rui Barbosa, *Braz.* 131 H16
Ruiché, *Eq. Guinea* 204 M7
Ruidosa, *Tex., U.S.* 103 Q1
Ruidoso, *N. Mex., U.S.* 107 U13
Ruijin, *China* 183 P6
Ruille, Pic de, *Fr.* 160 G5
Ruivo, Pico, *Madeira* 204 M3
Ruj, peak, *Bulg., Serb.* 152 H12
Rujen, peak, *Bulg., Maced.* 152 J12
Rukuruku Bay, *Fiji Is.* 218 G7
Rukwa, Lake, *Tanzania* 199 M13
Rule, *Tex., U.S.* 102 K7
Ruleville, *Miss., U.S.* 100 J10
Rum, island, *Scot., U.K.* 142 K7
Ruma, *Serb.* 152 E9
Rumaylah, 'Urūq ar, *Saudi Arabia* 172 M10
Rumbalara, *N. Terr., Austral.* 211 U9
Rumbek, *Sudan* 198 G12
Rum Cay, *Bahamas* 117 F14
Rumelange, *Lux.* 160 K9
Rumford, *Me., U.S.* 95 F15
Rumia, *Pol.* 149 A14
Rumoi, *Japan* 184 F13
Rum Point, *Cayman Is., U.K.* 120 H2
Rum Point Channel, *Cayman Is., U.K.* 120 H2
Rumung, island, *F.S.M.* 217 C18
Runanga, *N.Z.* 213 N17
Runaway, Cape, *N.Z.* 213 K20
Runaway Bay, *Jam.* 120 H8
Runde, river, *Zimb.* 202 G12
Rundeng, *Indonesia* 188 H4
Rundu, *Namibia* 202 F8
Runge, *Tex., U.S.* 103 S10
Rungwa, river, *Tanzania* 199 M13
Rungwa, *Tanzania* 199 M13
Runit, island, *Marshall Is.* 216 H8
Running Water Draw, *Tex., U.S.* 102 H4
Runu, *F.S.M.* 217 C18
Ruo, island, *F.S.M.* 217 B16
Ruoqiang, *China* 180 G7
Rupat, island, *Indonesia* 188 H6

Rupert, *Idaho, U.S.* 106 H6
Rupert, Rivière de, *Que., Can.* 83 M19
Ruppert Coast, *Antarctica* 226 N9
Rupununi, river, *Guyana* 129 F14
Rurrenabaque, *Bol.* 130 J6
Rurutu, island, *Fr. Polynesia, Fr.* 219 H15
Rusanovo, *Russ.* 158 E10
Ruse, *Bulg.* 153 G15
Rushan, *Taj.* 176 J9
Rush City, *Minn., U.S.* 104 J12
Rushden, *Eng., U.K.* 143 U13
Rushford, *Minn., U.S.* 104 L13
Rush Springs, *Okla., U.S.* 102 H10
Rushville, *Ill., U.S.* 99 R4
Rushville, *Ind., U.S.* 99 R10
Rushville, *Nebr., U.S.* 104 M2
Rusk, *Tex., U.S.* 102 M14
Ruskin, *Fla., U.S.* 97 U7
Russas, *Braz.* 131 E17
Russell, *Kans., U.S.* 105 S6
Russell Cave National Monument, *Ala., U.S.* 101 G16
Russell Islands, *Solomon Is.* 217 N18
Russellville, *Ala., U.S.* 101 H14
Russellville, *Ark., U.S.* 100 F7
Russellville, *Ky., U.S.* 101 D15
Rüsselsheim, *Ger.* 148 G6
Russi, *It.* 150 F8
Russia, *Asia* 167 Q6
Russian, river, *Calif., U.S.* 109 Q2
Russian Fort Elizabeth, *Hawai'i, U.S.* 112 C5
Russian Mission, *Alas., U.S.* 110 H12
Russkaya Gavan', *Russ.* 158 D12
Russkaya Polyana, *Russ.* 158 K10
Rust'avi, *Rep. of Georgia* 169 C19
Ruston, *La., U.S.* 100 L8
Rutaki Passage, *Cook Is., N.Z.* 218 Q9
Rute, *Sp.* 144 L10
Ruteng, *Indonesia* 189 M13
Ruth, *Nev., U.S.* 109 P12
Rutherfordton, *N.C., U.S.* 96 J8
Rutland, *Vt., U.S.* 94 H12
Rutland Island, *India* 179 Q14
Rutog, *China* 180 J4
Ruvuma see Rovuma, river, *Mozambique* 203 D15
Ruwāq, Jabal ar, *Syr.* 170 H9
Ruwenzori, peak, *Dem. Rep. of the Congo, Uganda* 198 J12
Ruwer, *Ger.* 160 J12
Rüzaevka, *Kaz.* 174 C12
Ruzayevka, *Russ.* 156 K13
Ružomberok, *Slovakia* 149 J15
Rwanda, *Af.* 195 K21
Ryan, *Okla., U.S.* 102 J10
Ryan, Loch, *Scot., U.K.* 143 P8
Ryazan', *Russ.* 156 K10
Ryazhsk, *Russ.* 156 L10
Rybachiy, *Russ.* 156 J2
Rybinsk, *Russ.* 156 G10
Rybinskoye Vodokhranilishche, *Russ.* 156 G10
Rybnik, *Pol.* 149 H14
Rye, *Colo., U.S.* 107 P13
Ryegate, *Mont., U.S.* 106 D9
Rye Patch Reservoir, *Nev., U.S.* 109 N8
Ryl'sk, *Russ.* 156 M8
Ryōtsu, *Japan* 184 M11
Ryōtsu Wan, *Japan* 184 M11
Rypin, *Pol.* 149 C15
Rysy, peak, *Pol., Slovakia* 149 J15
Ryukyu Islands (Nansei Shotō), *Japan* 185 Y2
Ryukyu Trench, *Pac. Oc.* 238 G4
Ryzhovo, *Russ.* 159 E19
Rzeszów, *Pol.* 149 G17
Rzhev, *Russ.* 156 J8

S

São Marcos Bay, *S. Amer.* 126 D10
Sa, *Thai.* 186 J9
Sa'a, *Solomon Is.* 217 P20
Sa'ādatābād, *Iran* 173 G15
Saale, river, *Ger.* 148 G9
Saalfeld, *Ger.* 148 G8
Saarbrücken, *Ger.* 148 H5
Saaremaa (Ösel), island, *Est.* 141 L15
Saba, island, *Neth. Antilles, Neth.* 119 F15
Sab 'Ābār, *Syr.* 170 J9
Šabac, *Serb.* 152 F9
Sabadell, *Sp.* 145 D17

Sabah, region, *Malaysia* 188 G12
Saba Island, *Virgin Islands, U.S.* 120 N8
Sabana, Archipiélago de, *Cuba* 116 G8
Sabana de La Mar, *Dom. Rep.* 117 L19
Sabana Grande, *P.R., U.S.* 120 N2
Sabanalarga, *Col.* 128 B5
Sabaneta, *Dom. Rep.* 117 L17
Sabaneta, Puntan, *N. Mariana Is., U.S.* 216 A5
Sabang, *Indonesia* 189 J13
Şabanözü, *Turk.* 168 D8
Sabaya, *Bol.* 130 K6
Şāberī, Hāmūn-e, *Afghan., Iran* 177 Q1
Sabetha, *Kans., U.S.* 105 R9
Şabḩā, *Jordan* 170 L7
Sabhā, *Lib.* 197 D14
Sabidana, Jebel, *Sudan* 194 F10
Sabinal, *Tex., U.S.* 103 R8
Sabinal, Cayo, *Cuba* 116 H11
Sabiñánigo, *Sp.* 145 C14
Sabinas Hidalgo, *Mex.* 114 E11
Sabine, river, *La., Tex., U.S.* 100 N6
Sabine, *Tex., U.S.* 103 Q16
Sabine Lake, *La., Tex., U.S.* 100 Q6
Sabinosa, *Canary Is.* 204 R3
Sable, Cape, *Fla., U.S.* 97 Y9
Sable, Cape, *N.S., Can.* 83 Q22
Sable, Île de, *New Caledonia, Fr.* 218 A6
Sable Island, *N.S., Can.* 83 P23
Sables, Île aux (Sandy Island), *Mauritius* 205 J19
Sabres, *Fr.* 147 W6
Sabrina Coast, *Antarctica* 227 N20
Sabtang, island, *Philippines* 189 A14
Sabugal, *Port.* 144 F7
Sabunçu, *Azerb.* 169 D23
Sabura, *Pak.* 177 Q6
Şabyā, *Saudi Arabia* 172 N8
Sabzak Pass, *Afghan.* 176 M3
Sabzevār, *Iran* 173 C15
Sacaca, *Bol.* 130 K7
Sacajawea Peak, *Oreg., U.S.* 108 F9
Sac City, *Iowa, U.S.* 105 N10
Sacedón, *Sp.* 144 F12
Săcel, *Rom.* 153 B14
Săcele, *Rom.* 153 E15
Sachigo, river, *Ont., Can.* 83 L15
Sachs Harbour, *N.W.T., Can.* 82 D11
Sacile, *It.* 150 D8
Sackets Harbor, *N.Y., U.S.* 94 G8
Saco, *Me., U.S.* 95 H15
Saco, *Mont., U.S.* 106 B11
Sacramento, river, *Calif., U.S.* 109 N4
Sacramento, *Calif., U.S.* 109 R4
Sacramento Mountains, *N. Mex., U.S.* 107 V13
Sacramento Valley, *Calif., U.S.* 84 F3
Sacred Falls see Kahuwa'a, *Hawai'i, U.S.* 112 D11
Sacristy and Treasury, *Vatican City* 161 Q16
Sada, *Mayotte, Fr.* 205 P17
Şa'dah, *Yemen* 172 P9
Saddle Hill, *St. Kitts & Nevis* 121 C18
Saddle Mountain, *Idaho, U.S.* 106 G6
Saddle Mountains, *Wash., U.S.* 108 D6
Saddle Peak, *India* 179 P14
Saddle Road, *Hawai'i, U.S.* 113 L19
Şadh, *Oman* 173 N15
Sadiqabad, *Pak.* 177 T8
Sadiya, *India* 178 F15
Sadlers, *St. Kitts & Nevis* 121 A17
Sado, island, *Japan* 184 L11
Sado, river, *Port.* 144 J5
Sadon, *Myanmar* 186 F6
Sadovoye, *Russ.* 157 Q13
Sae Islands, *P.N.G.* 213 B19
Saelices, *Sp.* 144 G12
Şafājah, region, *Saudi Arabia* 172 H7
Safata Bay, *Samoa* 218 L3
Saffar Kalay, *Afghan.* 177 R3
Säffle, *Sw.* 140 L12
Safford, *Ariz., U.S.* 107 U9
Safi, *Mor.* 196 B7
Şāfītā, *Syr.* 170 G7
Safonovo, *Russ.* 156 K7
Safranbolu, *Turk.* 168 C8
Saga, *China* 180 L6
Saga, *Japan* 185 R4
Sagae, *Japan* 184 L12
Sagaing, *Myanmar* 186 G6
Sagami Nada, *Japan* 185 Q12
Sagar, *India* 178 H6
Sagar, *India* 179 P4

Sagarejo, *Rep. of Georgia* **169** C19
Sage, Mount, *Virgin Islands, U.K.* **120** R6
Sage Creek, *Mont., U.S.* **106** A8
Sag Harbor, *N.Y., U.S.* **95** N13
Saghyz, river, *Kaz.* **174** E7
Saghyz, *Kaz.* **174** E7
Saginaw, *Mich., U.S.* **98** L11
Saginaw Bay, *Mich., U.S.* **98** K12
Saglek Bay, *Nfld. & Lab., Can.* **83** J20
Sagone, *Fr.* **150** K3
Sagone, Golfe de, *Fr.* **150** K3
Sagra, peak, *Sp.* **144** K12
Sagres, Ponta de, *Port.* **144** L4
Sagu, *Myanmar* **186** H5
Saguache, *Colo., U.S.* **107** N12
Sagua de Tánamo, *Cuba* **117** K13
Sagua la Grande, *Cuba* **116** G8
Saguaro National Park, *Ariz., U.S.* **107** V8
Sagunto-Sagunt, *Sp.* **145** G15
Saḥāb, *Jordan* **170** M7
Sahagún, *Sp.* **144** C9
Şaḥam, *Oman* **173** J15
Sahamalaza, Baie de, *Madagascar* **203** E17
Sahara, desert, *Af.* **194** F2
Sahara, *Japan* **184** G13
Saharan Atlas, range, *Alg., Mor.* **194** D4
Saharanpur, *India* **178** E6
Saharsa, *India* **178** G11
Sahel, plain, *Af.* **194** G3
Sahiwal, *Pak.* **177** P10
Sahiwal, *Pak.* **177** R11
Sahl Rakbah, plain, *Saudi Arabia* **172** K8
Sahuaripa, *Mex.* **114** D7
Sai, *Japan* **184** H13
Sai Buri, *Thai.* **187** S9
Saïda, *Alg.* **196** B10
Saïda (Sidon), *Leb.* **170** J6
Sa'īdābād *see* Sīrjān, *Iran* **173** F15
Saidapet, *India* **179** Q7
Saidor, *P.N.G.* **213** C19
Saidu, *Pak.* **176** M10
Saignes, *Fr.* **147** V10
Saigon *see* Ho Chi Minh City, *Vietnam* **187** P12
SaihanTal *see* Sonid Youqi, *China* **182** A5
Saijō, *Japan* **185** R6
Saiki, *Japan* **185** S5
Sailolof, *Indonesia* **189** J17
Saimaa, lake, *Fin.* **141** H17
Saimbeyli, *Turk.* **168** G11
Sain, Chenal, *Wallis & Futuna, Fr.* **218** E12
Saindak, *Pak.* **177** S1
St. Abb's Head, *Scot., U.K.* **142** M11
St.-Agrève, *Fr.* **147** V12
St.-Aignan, *Fr.* **147** S9
St. Albans, *Eng., U.K.* **143** V14
St. Albans, *Vt., U.S.* **94** F12
St. Albans, *W. Va., U.S.* **96** D8
St.-Amand, *Fr.* **146** M11
St.-Amand-Montrond, *Fr.* **147** S10
St.-Amans-Soult, *Fr.* **147** X10
St.-Ambroix, *Fr.* **147** W12
St. André, Cap, *Madagascar* **194** M11
St.-André, *Reunion, Fr.* **205** G16
St. Andrew Bay, *Fla., U.S.* **97** R3
St. Andrews, *N.Z.* **213** Q17
St. Andrews, *Scot., U.K.* **142** L10
St. Andrews Bay, *Grenada* **121** K23
St. Annabaai, bay, *Neth. Antilles, Neth.* **121** Q14
St. Ann's Bay, *Jam.* **120** H9
St. Anthony, *Idaho, U.S.* **106** G7
St. Anthony, *Nfld. & Lab., Can.* **83** L23
St. Anthony's Peak, *St. Kitts & Nevis* **121** B18
St. Arnaud, *Vic., Austral.* **211** Y12
St.-Aubin-d'Aubigne, *Fr.* **147** Q6
St.-Aubin-du-Cormier, *Fr.* **147** Q6
St.-Augustin, *Que., Can.* **83** L22
St. Augustin Bay, *Madagascar* **194** P11
St. Augustine, *Fla., U.S.* **97** R9
St. Austell, *Eng., U.K.* **143** X8
St. Austell Bay, *Eng., U.K.* **143** X8
St.-Avold, *Fr.* **147** N14
St.-Barthélemy, island, *Lesser Antilles* **119** F15
St. Bees Head, *Eng., U.K.* **143** Q10
St.-Benoît, *Reunion, Fr.* **205** G17
St. Boswells (Newtown), *Scot., U.K.* **143** N11
St.-Brieuc, *Fr.* **147** P4
St.-Cannat, *Fr.* **147** X13
St. Catherine, Mount, *Grenada* **121** K23

St. Catherine Point, *Bermuda, U.K.* **120** A3
St. Catherines Island, *Ga., U.S.* **97** P9
St.-Cernin, *Fr.* **147** V10
St. Charles, *Idaho, U.S.* **106** J7
St. Charles, *Mich., U.S.* **98** L11
St. Charles, *Minn., U.S.* **104** L13
St. Charles, *Mo., U.S.* **105** S15
St. Charles' Church, *Monaco* **161** C22
St.-Chély-d'Apcher, *Fr.* **147** V11
St. Christoffelberg, peak, *Neth. Antilles, Neth.* **121** N13
St. Christopher *see* St. Kitts, island, *St. Kitts & Nevis* **121** A17
St. Clair, river, *Mich., U.S.* **98** L13
St. Clair, *Mich., U.S.* **98** L13
St. Clair, *Mo., U.S.* **105** T14
St. Clair, Lake, *Can., U.S.* **85** E17
St. Clair Shores, *Mich., U.S.* **98** M13
St.-Claude, *Fr.* **147** T14
St.-Claude, *Guadeloupe, Fr.* **121** G14
St. Clears, *Wales, U.K.* **143** V9
St. Cloud, *Fla., U.S.* **97** T9
St. Cloud, *Minn., U.S.* **104** J10
St. Combs, *Scot., U.K.* **142** J11
St. Croix, river, *Me., U.S.* **95** E19
St. Croix, river, *Minn., Wis., U.S.* **98** H1
St. Croix, island, *Virgin Islands, U.S.* **119** F13
St. Croix Falls, *Wis., U.S.* **98** G2
St. Croix Island International Historic Site, *Me., U.S.* **95** E19
St. Croix National Scenic Riverway, *Minn., Wis., U.S.* **98** G2
St. David Islands *see* Mapia, Kepulauan, *Indonesia* **189** J19
St. David's, *Grenada* **121** L23
St. David's Head, *Wales, U.K.* **143** U8
St. David's Island, *Bermuda, U.K.* **120** B4
St. David's Lighthouse, *Bermuda, U.K.* **120** A4
St. David's Point, *Grenada* **121** L23
St.-Denis, *Fr.* **147** P10
St.-Denis, *Fr.* **147** T6
St.-Denis, *Reunion, Fr.* **205** F16
St.-Dié, *Fr.* **147** Q15
St.-Dizier, *Fr.* **147** P13
Ste.-Anne, *Guadeloupe, Fr.* **121** F15
Ste.-Anne, *Martinique, Fr.* **121** G23
Ste. Dévote's Church, *Monaco* **161** D21
St. Edward, *Nebr., U.S.* **105** P7
Ste. Genevieve, *Mo., U.S.* **105** T15
St. Elias, Mount, *Alas., U.S., Yukon, Can.* **111** K19
St. Elias Mountains, *Alas., U.S.* **111** J19
St. Elias Mountains, *B.C., Yukon, Can.* **82** G7
St.-Éloy-les-Mines, *Fr.* **147** T10
Ste.-Luce, *Martinique, Fr.* **121** G23
Ste.-Marguerite, *Guadeloupe, Fr.* **121** E15
Ste. Marie, Cap, *Madagascar* **203** J16
Ste. Marie, Nosy, *Madagascar* **203** F18
Ste.-Marie, *Guadeloupe, Fr.* **121** F15
Ste.-Marie, *Martinique, Fr.* **121** E23
Ste.-Marie, *Reunion, Fr.* **205** F16
Ste.-Maxime, *Fr.* **147** X15
Ste.-Rose, *Guadeloupe, Fr.* **121** E14
Ste.-Rose, *Reunion, Fr.* **205** G17
Saintes, *Fr.* **147** U6
Ste.-Suzanna, *Guadeloupe, Fr.* **205** F16
Ste. Suzanne, *Fr.* **147** Q7
St.-Étienne, *Fr.* **147** U12
St.-Étienne-du-Rouvray, *Fr.* **147** N8
St. Eustatius, island, *Neth. Antilles, Neth.* **119** G15
St.-Fargeau, *Fr.* **147** R11
St. Finan's Bay, *Ire.* **143** U2
St.-Firmin, *Fr.* **147** V14
St.-Florent, Golfe de, *Fr.* **150** J4
St.-Florentin, *Fr.* **147** Q11
St.-Flour, *Fr.* **147** V11
St. Francis, river, *Ark., Mo., U.S.* **85** J15
St. Francis, *Kans., U.S.* **105** R3
St. Francis, *Me., U.S.* **95** A17
St. Francis, *S. Dak., U.S.* **104** M4
St. Francis Bay, *S. Af.* **194** R8
St.-François, *Guadeloupe, Fr.* **121** E16
St Gallen, *Switz.* **150** A5
St. George, *Bermuda, U.K.* **120** A3
St. George, *Qnsld., Austral.* **211** V14
St. George, *S.C., U.S.* **96** L9
St. George, *Utah, U.S.* **107** Q5
St. George, Cape, *Fla., U.S.* **97** S4
St. George, Cape, *P.N.G.* **213** C21
St. George, Point, *Calif., U.S.* **108** L1

St. George Island, *Alas., U.S.* **110** L9
St. George Island, *Fla., U.S.* **97** R4
St. George's, *Grenada* **121** L22
St. George's Bay, *Malta* **161** K23
St. George's Channel, *India* **179** T15
St. George's Channel, *Ire., U.K.* **143** U7
St. George's Channel, *P.N.G.* **213** C21
St. George's Harbour, *Grenada* **121** L22
St. George's Island, *Bermuda, U.K.* **120** A3
St.-Germain, *Fr.* **147** P9
St.-Germain-des-Vaux, *Fr.* **147** N5
St.-Gildas, Pointe de, *Fr.* **147** S5
St. Giles Islands, *Trinidad & Tobago* **121** M18
St.-Gilles-les-Bains, *Reunion, Fr.* **205** G15
St.-Girons, *Fr.* **147** Y8
St.-Guénolé, *Fr.* **147** Q4
St. Helena, island, *U.K., Atl. Oc.* **204** G4
St. Helena, *Calif., U.S.* **109** R3
St. Helena Bay, *S. Af.* **202** L7
St. Helena Sound, *S.C., U.S.* **97** N10
St. Helens, *Eng., U.K.* **143** S11
St. Helens, *Oreg., U.S.* **108** E3
St. Helens, Mount, *Wash., U.S.* **108** E4
St. Helier, *Ch. Is.* **143** Z12
St.-Hillaire-du-Harcouët, *Fr.* **147** P6
St.-Hippolyte, *Fr.* **147** R15
St. Hubert, *Belg.* **160** H7
St.-Hyacinthe, *Que., Can.* **83** P20
St. Ignace, *Mich., U.S.* **98** G10
St. Ignatius, *Mont., U.S.* **106** C5
St. Ives Bay, *Eng., U.K.* **143** X8
St. James, *Cayman Is., U.K.* **120** J2
St. James, *Minn., U.S.* **104** L10
St. James, *Mo., U.S.* **105** T13
St.-Jean, Lac, *Que., Can.* **83** N20
St.-Jean-d'Angély, *Fr.* **147** U7
St.-Jean-de-Losne, *Fr.* **147** S13
St.-Jean-de-Luz, *Fr.* **147** X5
St.-Jean-de-Maurienne, *Fr.* **147** U14
St.-Jean-de-Monts, *Fr.* **147** S5
St.-Jean-Pied-de-Port, *Fr.* **147** Y6
St. Joe, river, *Idaho, U.S.* **106** C4
St. John, *Kans., U.S.* **105** U6
St. John, river, *Me., U.S.* **95** B16
St. John, *N. Dak., U.S.* **104** D5
St. John, *N.B., Can.* **83** P21
St. John, island, *Virgin Islands, U.S.* **120** N11
St. John, *Wash., U.S.* **108** D9
St. John's, *Antigua & Barbuda* **121** B20
St. John's, *Montserrat, U.K.* **121** B23
St. John's, *Nfld. & Lab., Can.* **83** M24
St. Johns, *Ariz., U.S.* **107** T9
St. Johns, river, *Fla., U.S.* **97** R8
St. Johns, *Mich., U.S.* **98** L11
St. Johnsbury, *Vt., U.S.* **95** F13
St. John's Church, *Barbados* **121** K19
St. John's Harbour, *Antigua & Barbuda* **121** B20
St. Jona Island *see* Iony, Ostrov, *Russ.* **159** H20
St. Jorisbaai, bay, *Neth. Antilles, Neth.* **121** Q15
St. Joseph, *Dominica* **121** F18
St. Joseph, river, *Ind., U.S.* **99** P10
St. Joseph, *La., U.S.* **100** M9
St. Joseph, *Mich., U.S.* **99** N9
St. Joseph, *Mo., U.S.* **105** R10
St. Joseph, *Trinidad & Tobago* **121** Q23
St. Joseph, Lake, *N. Amer.* **80** G7
St.-Joseph, *Martinique, Fr.* **121** F22
St.-Joseph, *New Caledonia, Fr.* **218** C8
St.-Joseph, *Reunion, Fr.* **205** J16
St. Joseph Bay, *Fla., U.S.* **97** R4
St. Joseph's Church, *Fr.* **161** C22
St. Julian's, *Malta* **161** K22
St.-Junien, *Fr.* **147** U8
St. Kitts (St. Christopher), island, *St. Kitts & Nevis* **121** A17
St. Kitts and Nevis, *N. Amer.* **81** N24
St.-Laurent du Maroni, *Fr. Guiana, Fr.* **129** E17
St. Lawrence, *Barbados* **121** L19
St. Lawrence, river, *N. Amer.* **80** G9
St. Lawrence, *Tex., U.S.* **103** N5
St. Lawrence, Gulf of, *Atl. Oc.* **236** F5
St. Lawrence, Gulf of, *Que., Can.* **83** N22
St. Lawrence Island, *Alas., U.S.* **110** G10
St. Lawrence Islands National Park, *N.Y., U.S.* **94** F9
St.-Leu, *Reunion, Fr.* **205** H15

St.-Lô, *Fr.* **147** P6
St. Louis, *Mich., U.S.* **98** L11
St. Louis, river, *Minn., U.S.* **104** G12
St. Louis, *Mo., U.S.* **105** T15
St.-Louis, *Fr.* **147** R15
St.-Louis, *Guadeloupe, Fr.* **121** G16
St.-Louis, *New Caledonia, Fr.* **218** E8
St.-Louis, *Reunion, Fr.* **205** H15
St.-Louis, *Senegal* **196** G4
St.-Louis du Nord, *Haiti* **117** L16
St.-Loup, *Fr.* **147** Q14
St. Lucia, *N. Amer.* **81** P24
St. Lucia, island, *N. Amer.* **80** N12
St. Lucia, Lake, *S. Af.* **202** K12
St. Lucia Channel, *Lesser Antilles* **119** K17
St.-Lys, *Fr.* **147** X8
St. Magnus Bay, *Scot., U.K.* **142** D11
St.-Maixent, *Fr.* **147** T7
St.-Malo, *Fr.* **147** P5
St.-Malo, Golfe de, *Fr.* **147** P5
St.-Marc, *Haiti* **117** L16
St.-Marc, Canal de, *Haiti* **117** M16
St.-Marcel, Mont, *Fr. Guiana, Fr.* **129** G18
St. Marie, Kaap, *Neth. Antilles, Neth.* **121** P13
St. Maries, *Idaho, U.S.* **106** C3
St. Mark Bay, *Grenada* **121** J22
St. Marks, *Fla., U.S.* **97** R5
St. Martin, island, *Lesser Antilles* **119** F15
St.-Martin, *Fr.* **147** X11
St.-Martin, Cap, *Martinique, Fr.* **121** E22
St. Martin's, island, *Eng., U.K.* **143** Y7
St. Martin's Gardens, *Monaco* **161** F21
St. Martinville, *La., U.S.* **100** P9
St. Mary's, island, *Eng., U.K.* **143** Y7
St. Marys, river, *Fla., Ga., U.S.* **97** Q8
St. Marys, *Ga., U.S.* **97** Q8
St. Marys, *Kans., U.S.* **105** S9
St. Marys, *Ohio, U.S.* **99** Q11
St. Marys, *Pa., U.S.* **94** M5
St. Marys, *Tas., Austral.* **211** Z16
St. Marys, *Trinidad & Tobago* **121** Q22
St. Marys, *W. Va., U.S.* **96** C8
St. Mary's Bay, *Nfld. & Lab., Can.* **83** M24
St. Mary's City, *Md., U.S.* **96** D14
St. Mary's Loch, *Scot., U.K.* **143** N10
St.-Mathieu, *Fr.* **147** U8
St.-Mathieu, Pointe de, *Fr.* **147** Q2
St. Matthew Island, *Alas., U.S.* **110** H9
St. Matthews, *S.C., U.S.* **96** L9
St.-Maurice, river, *Que., Can.* **83** P19
St.-Méen-le-Grand, *Fr.* **147** Q5
St. Michael, *Alas., U.S.* **110** G12
St. Michael's Caves, *Gibraltar, U.K.* **161** Q23
St. Michielsbaai, bay, *Neth. Antilles, Neth.* **121** P14
St.-Nazaire, *Fr.* **147** R5
St.-Omer, *Fr.* **146** L10
St.-Palais, *Fr.* **147** Y6
St. Patrick's, *Montserrat, U.K.* **121** C23
St. Paul, island, *Ind. Oc.* **240** N10
St. Paul, *Minn., U.S.* **104** K12
St. Paul, *Nebr., U.S.* **105** P6
St.-Paul, *Reunion, Fr.* **205** G15
St.-Paul, Île, *Ind. Oc.* **204** K10
St.-Paulien, *Fr.* **147** V11
St. Paul Island, *Alas., U.S.* **110** L9
St. Paul's, *St. Kitts & Nevis* **121** A17
St. Paul's Bay, *Malta* **161** J21
St. Paul's Bay, *Malta* **161** J22
St. Paul's Islands, *Malta* **161** J22
St. Paul's Point, *Pitcairn I., U.K.* **219** Q23
St.-Péray, *Fr.* **147** V13
St. Peter, *Minn., U.S.* **104** K11
St. Peter and St. Paul Rocks, *Atl. Oc.* **204** F2
St. Peter Port, *Ch. Is.* **143** Z11
St. Peter's Basilica, *Vatican City* **161** Q16
St. Petersburg, *Fla., U.S.* **97** U7
St. Petersburg *see* Sankt-Peterburg, *Russ.* **156** F6
St. Peter's Square, *Vatican City* **161** Q17
St.-Philippe, *Reunion, Fr.* **205** H17
St. Pierre, *Mauritius* **205** G20
St. Pierre, *Trinidad & Tobago* **121** N22
St.-Pierre, *Martinique, Fr.* **121** E22
St.-Pierre, *Reunion, Fr.* **205** H16
St.-Pierre and Miquelon, islands, *Fr.* **83** N23
St.-Pierre-de-Chignac, *Fr.* **147** V8
St. Pierre Island, *Seychelles* **203** C18

St.-Pierre-le-Moûtier, *Fr.* **147** S11
St. Pölten, *Aust.* **148** K12
St.-Pons, *Fr.* **147** X10
St.-Quay-Portrieux, *Fr.* **147** P4
St.-Quentin, *Fr.* **146** M11
St.-Quentin, Pointe de, *Fr.* **146** M9
St.-Raphaël, *Fr.* **147** X15
St. Rogatien Bank, *Hawai'i, U.S.* **112** M6
St. Roman, *Monaco* **161** A23
St.-Savin, *Fr.* **147** T8
St.-Sernin, *Fr.* **147** X10
St.-Servan, *Fr.* **147** P5
St.-Sever, *Fr.* **147** X6
St. Simons Island, *Ga., U.S.* **97** P8
St. Stanislas Bay, *Kiribati* **217** B22
St. Stephen, *S.C., U.S.* **96** L10
St. Thomas, *N. Dak., U.S.* **104** E7
St. Thomas, island, *Virgin Islands, U.S.* **120** N8
St. Thomas Bay, *Virgin Islands, U.K.* **120** R8
St. Thomas Harbor, *Virgin Islands, U.S.* **120** N9
St. Truiden, *Belg.* **146** L13
St. Tudwal's Islands, *Wales, U.K.* **143** T9
St. Veit, *Aust.* **148** M11
St. Vincent, *Minn., U.S.* **104** D8
St. Vincent, island, *N. Amer.* **80** P12
St. Vincent, Cape, *Madagascar* **194** N11
St. Vincent, Cape, *Port.* **138** J1
St. Vincent, Gulf, *Austral.* **210** K10
St. Vincent and the Grenadines, *N. Amer.* **81** P24
St. Vincent Island, *Fla., U.S.* **97** R4
St. Vincent Passage, *Lesser Antilles* **119** L17
St. Vith, *Belg.* **146** M14
St.-Vivien, *Fr.* **147** U6
St. Wendel, *Ger.* **148** H5
St. Willebrordus, *Neth. Antilles, Neth.* **121** P14
Saipan, island, *N. Mariana Is., U.S.* **216** C2
Saipan Channel, *N. Mariana Is., U.S.* **216** D4
Saipan Harbor, *N. Mariana Is., U.S.* **216** B4
Sairang, *India* **178** H14
Saito, *Japan* **185** S5
Saivomuotka, *Sw.* **141** D14
Sajama, Nevado, *Bol.* **130** K6
Sajyang Pass, *China* **180** N10
Sakai, *Japan* **185** Q8
Sakaide, *Japan* **185** Q7
Sakaiminato, *Japan* **185** P7
Sakākah, *Saudi Arabia* **172** F7
Saka Kalat, *Pak.* **177** U4
Sakakawea, Lake, *N. Dak., U.S.* **104** F3
Sakami, river, *Que., Can.* **83** M18
Sakami, *Que., Can.* **83** M18
Sakami, Lac, *Que., Can.* **83** M18
Sakania, *Dem. Rep. of the Congo* **198** P11
Sakao (Lathi), island, *Vanuatu* **218** C2
Sakarya, river, *Turk.* **168** D6
Sakarya, *Turk.* **168** D6
Sakata, *Japan* **184** L12
Sakçagöze, *Turk.* **168** H12
Sakhalin, island, *Russ.* **166** D13
Sakhalin, Ostrov, *Russ.* **159** J21
Sakhar, *Afghan.* **177** N5
Şäki, *Azerb.* **169** C21
Sakishima Shotō, *Japan* **184** L2
Sakon Nakhon, *Thai.* **186** K11
Sakrand, *Pak.* **177** V7
Saky, *Ukr.* **157** S7
Sal, island, *Cape Verde* **205** B17
Sal, Cay, *Bahamas* **116** F8
Sal, Cayo de, *Venez.* **118** N11
Sala, *Sw.* **141** K13
Sala Consilina, *It.* **151** N12
Salada, Laguna, *Mex.* **114** B5
Saladas, *Arg.* **132** G13
Saladillo, *Arg.* **132** M12
Salado, river, *Arg.* **132** H11
Salado, river, *Arg.* **132** M13
Salado, river, *Arg.* **132** M9
Salaga, *Ghana* **200** G10
Sala'ilua, *Samoa* **218** K2
Salal, *Chad* **197** H14
Salala, *Sudan* **199** C14
Salālah, *Oman* **173** P14
Salamanca, *Chile* **132** K7
Salamanca, *Mex.* **114** H11
Salamanca, *N.Y., U.S.* **94** K5
Salamanca, *Sp.* **144** E8

Salamat, Bahr, Chad 197 K15
Salamína, Gr. 154 J12
Salamis, Gr. 154 J12
Salamis, ruin, Cyprus 160 N10
Salamīyah, Syr. 170 G8
Salang Tunnel, Afghan. 176 L7
Salani, Samoa 218 L4
Salapaly Bay, Madagascar 194 P11
Salas, Sp. 144 B8
Salas de los Infantes, Sp. 144 D11
Salatiga, Indonesia 188 M9
Salavan, Laos 186 L12
Salavat, Russ. 158 J7
Salaverry, Peru 130 G2
Salawati, island, Indonesia 189 J17
Sala-y-Gómez, island, Chile 215 L19
Sala y Gómez Ridge, Pac. Oc. 239 M18
Salazie, Reunion, Fr. 205 G16
Salbris, Fr. 147 R9
Salda Gölü, Turk. 168 H5
Saldaña, Sp. 144 C10
Saldanha, S. Af. 202 M7
Sale, Vic., Austral. 211 Z13
Salebabu, island, Indonesia 189 G16
Salée, strait, Guadeloupe, Fr. 121 E15
Saleimoa, Samoa 218 L3
Salekhard, Russ. 158 F11
Salelologa, Samoa 218 K2
Salem, Ark., U.S. 100 E9
Salem, Ill., U.S. 99 T6
Salem, Ind., U.S. 99 T9
Salem, India 179 Q6
Salem, Mass., U.S. 95 K15
Salem, Mo., U.S. 105 U14
Salem, Montserrat, U.K. 121 B23
Salem, N.H., U.S. 95 J14
Salem, Ohio, U.S. 99 P15
Salem, Oreg., U.S. 108 G3
Salem, S. Dak., U.S. 104 L7
Salem, Va., U.S. 96 F10
Salem, W. Va., U.S. 96 C9
Salemi, It. 151 S9
Salerno, It. 150 M11
Salerno, Golfo di, It. 151 N11
Salez, Switz. 160 M2
Salford, Eng., U.K. 143 S11
Salgótarján, Hung. 149 K15
Salgueiro, Braz. 131 F16
Salibea, Trinidad & Tobago 121 N23
Salibia, Dominica 121 E20
Salida, Colo., U.S. 107 N12
Salies-du-Salat, Fr. 147 Y8
Şalīf, Yemen 172 P8
Salihli, Turk. 168 F4
Salihorsk, Belarus 156 L4
Salima, Malawi 203 E13
Salina, Kans., U.S. 105 T7
Salina, Utah, U.S. 107 N7
Salina, Isola, It. 151 R11
Salina Bay, Malta 161 J22
Salinas, river, Calif., U.S. 109 U5
Salinas, Calif., U.S. 109 T4
Salinas, Ecua. 128 K1
Salinas, P.R., U.S. 120 N4
Salinas, Bahía, P.R., U.S. 120 P1
Salinas Peak, N. Mex., U.S. 107 U12
Salinas Pueblo Missions National Monument (Gran Quivira), N. Mex., U.S. 107 T12
Saline, river, Ark., U.S. 100 J8
Saline, river, Kans., U.S. 105 S5
Saline Bay, Trinidad & Tobago 121 N23
Saline di Volterra, It. 150 H6
Salines, Étang des, Martinique, Fr. 121 G23
Salines, Cap de ses, Sp. 145 H18
Salines, Point, Grenada 121 L21
Salinópolis, Braz. 131 C14
Salins, Fr. 147 S14
Salisbury, Dominica 121 F18
Salisbury, Eng., U.K. 143 W12
Salisbury, Guam, U.S. 216 B12
Salisbury, Md., U.S. 96 D15
Salisbury, Mo., U.S. 105 S12
Salisbury, N.C., U.S. 96 H9
Salisbury, Ostrov, Russ. 158 C12
Salisbury Island, Nunavut, Can. 83 H17
Salisbury Plain, Eng., U.K. 143 W12
Salish Mountains, Mont., U.S. 106 B5
Şalkhad, Syr. 170 L8
Sallent, Sp. 145 D17
Sallfelden, Aust. 148 L10
Sallisaw, Okla., U.S. 102 G14
Salluit, Que., Can. 83 H18
Salmās, Iran 172 B10
Salmon, river, Idaho, U.S. 106 E5
Salmon, Idaho, U.S. 106 F6
Salmon Bank, Hawai'i, U.S. 112 K2
Salmon Gums, W. Aust., Austral. 211 X4
Salmon Peak, Tex., U.S. 103 R7
Salmon River Canyon, Idaho, U.S. 106 E5
Salmon River Mountains, Idaho, U.S. 106 F5
Salò, It. 150 D6
Salo, Fin. 141 J15
Salobelyak, Russ. 156 H14
Salome, Ariz., U.S. 107 T5
Salomon, Cap, Martinique, Fr. 121 F22
Salon, Fr. 147 X13
Salonga, river, Dem. Rep. of the Congo 198 K9
Salonica see Thessaloníki, Gr. 154 C11
Salonta, Rom. 152 C11
Salou, Cap de, Sp. 145 E16
Salpaus Ridge see Salpausselkä, Fin. 138 D9
Salpausselkä, range, Fin. 141 J16
Salqīn, Syr. 170 E8
Sal Rei, Cape Verde 205 C17
Sal'sk, Russ. 157 R12
Salsomaggiore Terme, It. 150 F5
Salt, river, Ariz., U.S. 107 U7
Salt, Sp. 145 D18
Salta, Arg. 132 F9
Saltash, Eng., U.K. 143 X9
Saltburn by the Sea, Eng., U.K. 143 Q13
Salt Cay, Bahamas 120 B12
Salt Cay, Turks & Caicos Is., U.K. 117 J18
Salt Cay, Virgin Islands, U.S. 120 M7
Salt Desert see Kavīr, Dasht-e, Iran 173 D14
Saltee Islands, Ire. 143 U6
Saltfjorden, bay, Nor. 140 E12
Salt Fork Arkansas, river, Okla., U.S. 102 E9
Salt Fork Brazos, river, Tex., U.S. 102 K6
Salt Fork Red, river, Tex., U.S. 102 H6
Saltillo, Mex. 114 F11
Salt Lake City, Utah, U.S. 106 L7
Salto, Uru. 132 J13
Salton Sea, Calif., U.S. 84 K5
Salt Range, Pak. 177 P10
Salt River, Jam. 120 K9
Salt River Bay, Virgin Islands, U.S. 120 Q2
Salt River Range, Wyo., U.S. 106 H8
Saltville, Va., U.S. 96 G8
Saluafata Harbour, Samoa 218 L4
Saluda, river, S.C., U.S. 96 K8
Saluda, S.C., U.S. 96 K8
Salûm, Egypt 197 C17
Salûm, Gulf of, Egypt, Lib. 194 D8
Saluzzo, It. 150 F2
Salvación, Bahía, Chile 133 V6
Salvador (Bahia), Braz. 131 H17
Salvador, Lake, La., U.S. 100 Q11
Salvador, Port, Falkland Is., U.K. 133 V12
Salvage Islands, Canary Is. 194 D1
Salwá, Saudi Arabia 172 J12
Salween, river, Asia 166 J10
Salyan, Azerb. 169 E22
Salyersville, Ky., U.S. 101 C19
Salzbrunn, Namibia 202 J7
Salzburg, Aust. 148 L10
Salzgitter, Ger. 148 E8
Salzwedal, Ger. 148 D8
Samā'il, Oman 173 K16
Samaipata, Bol. 130 K8
Samalaeulu, Samoa 218 K2
Samâlût, Egypt 197 D18
Samaná, Dom. Rep. 117 L20
Samaná, Bahía de, Dom. Rep. 117 L19
Samaná, Cabo, Dom. Rep. 117 L20
Samana Cay (Atwood), Bahamas 117 G15
Samandağı (Seleucia), Turk. 168 K11
Samangan (Aybak), Afghan. 176 L7
Samani, Japan 184 G14
Samar, island, Philippines 189 D15
Samara, river, Russ. 138 E13
Samara, Russ. 156 K15
Samarai, P.N.G. 213 E21
Samaria Gorge, Gr. 155 Q13
Samarinda, Indonesia 188 J12
Samarqand, Uzb. 174 L12
Sāmarrā', Iraq 172 D9
Samar Sea, Philippines 189 D15
Samarskoe, Kaz. 175 D18
Samba, India 177 P12
Sambalpur, India 178 K9
Sambava, Madagascar 203 E18
Sambir, Ukr. 157 N2
Samboja, Indonesia 188 J12
Samborombón, Bahía, Arg. 132 M13
Samborombón Bay, S. Amer. 126 M7
Samburg, Russ. 158 G12
Samcheok, S. Korea 182 E14
Samdari, India 178 G3
Same, Tanzania 199 L14
Samer, Fr. 146 L9
Sámi, Gr. 154 H7
Sami, Pak. 177 V3
Samina, river, Aust., Liech. 160 N3
Saminatal, valley, Liech. 160 P3
Sam Lord's Castle, Barbados 121 K20
Samnangjin, S. Korea 182 G14
Samo, P.N.G. 213 C21
Samoa, Pac. Oc. 214 J10
Samoa Islands, Pac. Oc. 214 J10
Samokov, Bulg. 153 J13
Sámos, island, Gr. 155 J17
Sámos, Gr. 155 J18
Samothrace see Samothráki, island, Gr. 155 D15
Samothráki (Samothrace), island, Gr. 155 D15
Samothráki, Gr. 155 D15
Sampacho, Arg. 132 K10
Sampit, Indonesia 188 K10
Sampwe, Dem. Rep. of the Congo 198 N11
Sam Rayburn Reservoir, Tex., U.S. 103 N15
Samrong, Cambodia 186 M10
Sam Son, Vietnam 186 J12
Samson, Ala., U.S. 101 N16
Samsun, Turk. 168 C11
Samu, Indonesia 188 K11
Samui, Ko, Thai. 187 Q8
Samundri, Pak. 177 Q11
Samur, Afghan. 177 Q1
Samur, river, Russ. 157 V16
Samut Prakhan, Thai. 186 M9
Samut Songkhram, Thai. 187 N8
San, river, Cambodia 186 M13
San, Japan 185 X2
San, Mali 196 H8
San, river, Pol. 149 G17
Şan'ā' (Sanaa), Yemen 172 P9
Sana, river, Bosn. & Herzg. 152 E6
Sanaa see Şan'ā', Yemen 172 P9
San Adrián, Cabo, Sp. 144 A5
SANAE IV, station, Antarctica 226 A12
Şanāfīr, island, Egypt 171 U4
Sanaga, river, Cameroon 194 J5
San Agustín, Col. 128 G4
San Agustin, Cape, Philippines 189 F15
Sanak Islands, Alas., U.S. 110 P11
Sanām, Saudi Arabia 172 K9
San Ambrosio, Isla, S. Amer. 126 K2
Sanana, island, Indonesia 189 K15
Sanandaj, Iran 172 C11
San Andés Tuxtla, Mex. 115 J13
San Andreas, Calif., U.S. 109 R5
San Andrés, Isla de, Col. 115 M20
San Andrés del Rabanedo, Sp. 144 C9
San Andres Mountains, N. Mex., U.S. 107 U12
San Andros, Bahamas 116 E11
San Angelo, Tex., U.S. 103 N7
San Antonio, Chile 132 L6
San Antonio, N. Mex., U.S. 107 T12
San Antonio, N. Mariana Is., U.S. 216 C4
San Antonio, river, Tex., U.S. 103 S11
San Antonio, Tex., U.S. 103 R9
San Antonio, Cabo, Arg. 132 M13
San Antonio, Cabo de, Cuba 116 H4
San Antonio, Cape see San Antonio, Cabo de, N. Amer. 80 N8
San Antonio, Mount, Calif., U.S. 109 X9
San Antonio, Punta, Mex. 114 C5
San Antonio Bay, Tex., U.S. 103 T12
San Antonio de los Cobres, Arg. 132 E9
San Antonio de Ureca, Eq. Guinea 204 N7
San Antonio Missions National Historic Park, Tex., U.S. 103 R9
San Antonio Oeste, Arg. 133 Q10
Sanat, island, F.S.M. 217 C16
San Augustine, Tex., U.S. 103 N15
Sanāw, Yemen 173 N13
Sanawad, India 178 J5
San Benedetto del Tronto, It. 150 J10
San Benedicto, Isla, Mex. 114 H6
San Benedicto Island, N. Amer. 80 N3
San Benito, Tex., U.S. 103 W11
San Bernardino, Calif., U.S. 109 X9
San Bernardino Strait, Philippines 189 D15
San Bernardo, Chile 132 L7
San Blas, Mex. 114 E8
San Blas, Archipielago de, Pan. 115 N22
San Blas, Cape, Fla., U.S. 97 R4
San Blas, Punta, Pan. 115 N21
San Borja, Bol. 130 J7
San Candido, It. 150 B8
San Carlos, Arg. 132 F9
San Carlos, Ariz., U.S. 107 U8
San Carlos, Philippines 189 E14
San Carlos, Venez. 128 C7
San Carlos, Gran Caldera Volcánica de, Eq. Guinea 204 M6
San Carlos de Bariloche, Arg. 133 Q7
San Carlos de Bolívar, Arg. 132 M11
San Carlos de Río Negro, Venez. 128 G9
San Carlos Reservoir, Ariz., U.S. 107 U8
Sánchez, Dom. Rep. 117 L19
Sanchor, India 178 H3
Sanchung, Taiwan, China 183 Q10
Sanchursk, Russ. 156 H13
San Clemente, island, Calif., U.S. 109 Z8
San Clemente, Calif., U.S. 109 Y9
San Clemente, Sp. 144 H12
San Cristóbal, Arg. 132 J11
San Cristóbal, Cuba 116 G5
San Cristóbal, Dom. Rep. 117 M19
San Cristóbal, Venez. 128 D6
San Cristóbal, Isla (Chatham), Ecua. 128 Q11
San Cristobal, island, Solomon Is. 217 Q20
San Cristóbal de Las Casas, Mex. 115 K15
San Cristoforo, Monte, San Marino 161 L15
Sancti Spíritus, Cuba 116 H9
Sand, Nor. 140 L10
Sanda Island, Scot., U.K. 143 N8
Sandakan, Malaysia 188 G12
Sandal, Baie de, New Caledonia, Fr. 218 C9
San Daniele del Friuli, It. 150 C9
Sanday, island, Scot., U.K. 142 F11
Sand Bluff, Cayman Is., U.K. 120 J4
Sand Cay, India 179 Q2
Sanders, Ariz., U.S. 107 S9
Sanderson, Tex., U.S. 103 Q4
Sandersville, Ga., U.S. 96 M7
Sandes, Nor. 140 L10
Sand Hills, Nebr., U.S. 105 N3
Sandia Crest, N. Mex., U.S. 107 S12
San Diego, Calif., U.S. 109 Z9
San Diego, Tex., U.S. 103 U10
San Diego, Cabo, Arg. 133 X10
San Diego de los Baños, Cuba 116 G5
Sandıklı, Turk. 168 F6
Sand Island, Hawai'i, U.S. 112 K2
Sand Island, Solomon Is. 217 P22
Sand Island, Wis., U.S. 98 E4
Sandness, Scot., U.K. 142 D11
Sandoa, Dem. Rep. of the Congo 198 N10
Sandomierz, Pol. 149 G17
San Donà di Piave, It. 150 D8
Sandon Iwa, island, Japan 185 W3
Sandovo, Russ. 156 G9
Sandown-Shanklin, Eng., U.K. 143 X13
Sandoy, island, Faroe Is., Den. 140 J6
Sand Point, Alas., U.S. 110 N12
Sandpoint, Idaho, U.S. 106 B4
Sandray, island, Scot., U.K. 142 K6
Sandspit, B.C., Can. 82 K7
Sand Springs, Mont., U.S. 106 C11
Sand Springs, Okla., U.S. 102 F12
Sandstone, Minn., U.S. 104 H12
Sandstone, W. Aust., Austral. 211 V3
Sandur, Faroe Is., Den. 140 J6
Sandusky, Mich., U.S. 98 L13
Sandusky, Ohio, U.S. 99 P13
Sandviken, Sw. 141 K13
Sandwich, Ill., U.S. 99 N6
Sandwich Bay, Nfld. & Lab., Can. 83 K22
Sandy, Utah, U.S. 106 L7
Sandy Bay, Gibraltar, U.K. 161 P23
Sandy Bay, Jam. 120 H6
Sandy Cape, Austral. 210 G16
Sandy Cay, Virgin Islands, U.K. 120 L11
Sandy Creek, Tex., U.S. 103 R12
Sandy Ground Village, Anguilla, U.K. 120 R11
Sandy Hill Bay, Anguilla, U.K. 120 R12
Sandy Island, Grenada 121 J24
Sandy Island see Sables, Île aux, Mauritius 205 J19
Sandykgaçy, Turkm. 174 N10
Sandy Lake, Ont., Can. 83 M15
Sandy Point, Bahamas 120 C6
Sandy Point, India 179 R14
Sandy Point, Virgin Islands, U.S. 120 R1
Sandy Point Town, St. Kitts & Nevis 121 A17
Saneku, Japan 185 W3
San Esteban de Gormaz, Sp. 144 D11
San Felice Circeo, It. 150 L9
San Felipe, Chile 132 K7
San Felipe, Col. 128 G9
San Felipe, Mex. 114 B5
San Felipe, Venez. 128 B8
San Felipe, Cayos de, Cuba 116 H5
San Félix, Isla, S. Amer. 126 K2
San Fernando, Calif., U.S. 109 X8
San Fernando, Chile 132 L7
San Fernando, Mex. 114 F12
San Fernando, Sp. 144 M8
San Fernando, Trinidad & Tobago 121 Q22
San Fernando de Apure, Venez. 128 D9
San Fernando de Atabapo, Venez. 128 F9
Sanford, Fla., U.S. 97 T9
Sanford, Me., U.S. 95 H15
Sanford, N.C., U.S. 96 H11
San Francique, Trinidad & Tobago 121 Q21
San Francisco, Arg. 132 J11
San Francisco, Arg. 132 K9
San Francisco, Calif., U.S. 109 S3
San Francisco, river, N. Mex., U.S. 107 U10
San Francisco Bay, Calif., U.S. 84 G3
San Francisco de Paula, Cabo, Arg. 133 V9
San Francisco del Oro, Mex. 114 E9
San Gabriel, Ecua. 128 H3
San Gabriel, river, Tex., U.S. 103 P11
Sangamner, India 178 L4
Sangamon, river, Ill., U.S. 99 R5
Sangan, Kuh-e, Afghan. 177 N4
Sangar, Russ. 159 G17
Sangareddi, India 178 M6
Sang Bast, Iran 173 C16
Sang Bor, Afghan. 176 M2
Sangeang, island, Indonesia 189 M13
Sang-e Masheh, Afghan. 177 N6
Sanger, Calif., U.S. 109 T7
Sanger, Tex., U.S. 102 K11
San Germán, P.R., U.S. 120 N2
Sanggan, river, China 182 D5
Sanggou Wan, China 182 F10
Sangha, river, Cameroon, Congo 201 K18
Sanghar, Pak. 177 V7
Sangihe, island, Indonesia 189 H15
Sangihe, Kepulauan, Indonesia 189 H15
San Gil, Col. 128 E6
Sangin, Afghan. 177 P4
San Giovanni, San Marino 161 K15
San Giovanni in Fiore, It. 151 Q14
San Giovanni in Persiceto, It. 150 F7
San Giovanni Valdarno, It. 150 H7
Sangkulirang, Indonesia 188 J12
Sangli, India 178 M4
Sangmélima, Cameroon 201 J16
Sangola, India 178 M4
Sangolquí, Ecua. 128 J3
San Gorgonio Mountain, Calif., U.S. 109 X10
Sangowo, Indonesia 189 H16
Sangre de Cristo Mountains, Colo., N. Mex., U.S. 107 P13
San Gregorio, Uru. 132 K14
Sangre Grande, Trinidad & Tobago 121 P23
Sang Sang, Nicar. 115 L18
Sangüesa, Sp. 145 C13
Sanguinet, Fr. 147 W6
Sangvor, Taj. 176 H9
Sangzhi, China 182 L2
Sanhe, China 181 B15
Sanibel Island, Fla., U.S. 97 W8
San Ignacio, Arg. 132 G14
San Ignacio, Bol. 130 J9
San Ignacio, Mex. 114 D6
Saniquellie, Liberia 200 G7
San Javier, Arg. 132 J12
San Javier, Sp. 145 K14
Sanjiang, China 183 P2
San Joaquin, river, Calif., U.S. 109 T6

San Joaquín, *Bol.* **130** H7
San Joaquín, Cerro, *Ecua.* **128** Q10
San Joaquin Valley, *Calif., U.S.* **84** G3
San Jon, *N. Mex., U.S.* **107** S15
San Jorge, Golfo, *Arg.* **133** T9
San Jorge Island, *Solomon Is.* **217** M18
San José, *Costa Rica* **115** N19
San José, *Guatemala* **115** LI5
San José, *Golfo, Arg.* **133** Q10
San José, Laguna, *P.R., U.S.* **120** M5
San José, *Calif., U.S.* **109** S4
San Jose, *N. Mex., U.S.* **107** R13
San Jose, *N. Mariana Is., U.S.* **216** C4
San Jose, *N. Mariana Is., U.S.* **216** C8
San José, Isla, *Mex.* **114** F7
San José de Amacuro, *Venez.* **129** C13
San José de Comondú, *Mex.* **114** E6
San José de Jáchal, *Arg.* **132** J8
San José de Las Lajas, *Cuba* **116** G6
San José del Guaviare, *Col.* **128** G6
San José de Mayo, *Uru.* **132** L14
San José de Ocuné, *Col.* **128** F7
San Juan, *Arg.* **132** J8
San Juan, *Dom. Rep.* **117** M18
San Juan, *P.R., U.S.* **120** M4San Juan, *Peru* **130** J4
San Juan, *Trinidad & Tobago* **121** P22
San Juan, river, *Utah, U.S.* **107** P8
San Juan, Cabezas de, *P.R., U.S.* **120** M6
San Juan, Cabo, *Arg.* **133** X10
San Juanbaai, bay, *Neth. Antilles, Neth.* **121** P13
San Juan Bautista, *Calif., U.S.* **109** T4
San Juan Bautista, *Parag.* **130** N10
San Juan Capistrano, *Calif., U.S.* **109** Y9
San Juan del Norte, *Nicar.* **115** M19
San Juan del Sur, *Nicar.* **115** M18
San Juan Islands, *Wash., U.S.* **108** A3
San Juan Mountains, *Colo., N. Mex., U.S.* **107** P11
San Juan y Martinez, *Cuba* **116** H5
San Julián, Bahía, *Arg.* **133** U9
San Julián, Gran Bajo de, *Arg.* **133** U8
San Just, Sierra de, *Sp.* **145** F14
San Justo, *Arg.* **132** J12
San Justo, *Arg.* **132** L13
Sankeshwar, *India* **179** N4
Sankt-Peterburg (St. Petersburg, Leningrad), *Russ.* **156** F6
Sankuru, river, *Dem. Rep. of the Congo* **198** L9
San Lázaro, Cabo, *Mex.* **114** E6
Şanliurfa (Edessa), *Turk.* **169** H13
San Lorenzo, *Arg.* **132** K12
San Lorenzo, *Ecua.* **128** H3
San Lorenzo, *P.R., U.S.* **120** N5
San Lorenzo, Cabo, *Ecua.* **128** J1
San Lorenzo de El Escorial, *Sp.* **144** F10
San Lorenzo de la Parrilla, *Sp.* **144** G12
San Luis, *Arg.* **132** K9
San Luis, *Ariz., U.S.* **107** V4
San Luis, *Colo., U.S.* **107** P13
San Luis, *Cuba* **117** K13
San Luis, *Guatemala* **115** K16
San Luis, Lago de, *Bol.* **130** H8
San Luis de Palenque, *Col.* **128** E7
San Luis Obispo, *Calif., U.S.* **109** V5
San Luis Potosí, *Mex.* **114** G11
San Luis Reservoir, *Calif., U.S.* **109** T5
San Luis Río Colorado, *Mex.* **114** B6
Sanluri, *It.* **151** P3
San Marcos, *Col.* **128** C5
San Marcos, *Tex., U.S.* **103** Q10
San Marino, *Eur.* **160** D4
San Marino, river, *It., San Marino* **161** J14
San Marino, *San Marino* **161** J15
San Martín, station, *Antarctica* **226** B5
San Martín, *Arg.* **132** K8
San Martín, river, *Bol.* **130** H8
San Martín, *Col.* **128** F6
San Martín, Cape, *Calif., U.S.* **109** U4
San Martín, Lago, *Arg.* **133** U7
San Martín de los Andes, *Arg.* **133** P7
San Mateo, *Calif., U.S.* **109** S3
San Mateo, *N. Mex., U.S.* **107** S11
San Matías, Golfo, *Arg.* **133** Q10
Sanmen Wan, *China* **182** M10
Sanmenxia, *China* **182** G3
San Miguel, river, *Bol.* **130** J8
San Miguel, island, *Calif., U.S.* **109** X5
San Miguel, *El Salv.* **115** L17

San Miguel Bay, *Philippines* **189** C14
San Miguel Creek, *Tex., U.S.* **103** S9
San Miguel de Cozumel, *Mex.* **115** H17
San Miguel de Huachi, *Bol.* **130** J7
San Miguel de Huachi, *Bol.* **130** J7
San Miguel del Monte, *Arg.* **132** M12
San Miguel de Tucumán, *Arg.* **132** G9
Sanming, *China* **183** P7
San Miniato, *It.* **150** G6
Sannat, *Malta* **161** H20
Sannicandro Garganico, *It.* **150** K12
San Nicolás, *Arg.* **132** K12
San Nicolas, island, *Calif., U.S.* **109** Y7
Sannikova, Proliv, *Russ.* **159** D17
Sannohe, *Japan* **184** J13
Sanok, *Pol.* **149** H17
San Pablo, *Philippines* **189** C13
San Pedro, *Arg.* **132** E9
San Pedro, *Arg.* **132** L12
San Pedro, river, *Ariz., U.S.* **107** V8
San Pedro, *Parag.* **130** M10
San Pedro, Sierra de, *Sp.* **144** H7
San Pedro de las Colonias, *Mex.* **114** F10
San Pedro de Macorís, *Dom. Rep.* **117** M20
San Pedro Sula, *Hond.* **115** K17
San Pietro, island, *It.* **151** N14
San Pietro, Isola di, *It.* **151** Q3
Sanpoil, river, *Wash., U.S.* **108** B7
San Quintín, *Mex.* **114** B5
San Rafael, *Arg.* **132** L8
San Rafael, *Bol.* **130** J9
San Rafael, *Calif., U.S.* **109** R3
San Rafael, Cabo, *Dom. Rep.* **117** L20
San Rafael del Yuma, *Dom. Rep.* **117** M20
San Remo, *It.* **150** G2
San Roque, *N. Mariana Is., U.S.* **216** B5
San Roque, *Sp.* **144** N9
San Saba, river, *Tex., U.S.* **103** P8
San Saba, *Tex., U.S.* **103** N9
San Salvador, *El Salv.* **115** L16
San Salvador (Watling), island, *Bahamas* **117** F14
San Salvador, Isla (Santiago, James), *Ecua.* **128** P9
San Salvador de Jujuy, *Arg.* **132** E9
Sansanné-Mango, *Togo* **200** F11
San Sebastián, *P.R., U.S.* **120** M2
Sansepolcro, *It.* **150** H8
San Severo, *It.* **150** L12
Sansha, *China* **183** P9
Sanshui, *China* **183** R4
San Simeon, *Calif., U.S.* **109** V5
San Simon, *Ariz., U.S.* **107** V9
Sanski Most, *Bosn. & Herzg.* **152** F6
San Sosti, *It.* **151** P13
Sans Souci, *Trinidad & Tobago* **121** N23
Sansui, *China* **183** N1
Santa Ana, *Bol.* **130** H7
Santa Ana, *Calif., U.S.* **109** X9
Santa Ana, *El Salv.* **115** L16
Santa Ana, *Philippines* **189** B14
Santa Ana, island, *Solomon Is.* **217** Q21
Santa Anna, *Tex., U.S.* **103** N8
Santa Bárbara, *Chile* **133** N6
Santa Bárbara, *Mex.* **114** E9
Santa Bárbara, peak, *Sp.* **144** L12
Santa Barbara, island, *Calif., U.S.* **109** Y7
Santa Barbara, *Calif., U.S.* **109** W6
Santa Barbara Channel, *Calif., U.S.* **109** X6
Santa Catalina, island, *Calif., U.S.* **109** Y8
Santa Catalina, island, *Solomon Is.* **217** Q21
Santa Catalina, Gulf of, *Calif., U.S.* **109** Y8
Santa Catarina, *Sao Tome and Principe* **205** D19
Santa Catharina, *Neth. Antilles, Neth.* **121** P15
Santa Clara, *Calif., U.S.* **109** S4
Santa Clara, *Cuba* **116** H9
Santa Clara, *Oreg., U.S.* **108** H3
Santa Clotilde, *Peru* **130** D4
Santa Coloma, *Andorra* **160** J2
Santa Comba, *Sp.* **144** B5
Santa Cruz, *Neth. Antilles, Neth.* **121** N13
Santa Cruz, river, *Arg.* **133** V8
Santa Cruz, river, *Ariz., U.S.* **107** W8

Santa Cruz, *Bol.* **130** K8
Santa Cruz, island, *Calif., U.S.* **109** X6
Santa Cruz, *Calif., U.S.* **109** T4
Santa Cruz, *Canary Is.* **196** C5
Santa Cruz, *Madeira* **204** M3
Santa Cruz, *Sao Tome and Principe* **205** D20
Santa Cruz, *Braz.* **131** F18
Santa Cruz, Isla (Chaves, Indefatigable), *Ecua.* **128** Q9
Santa Cruz Cabrália, *Braz.* **131** J16
Santa Cruz da Graciosa, *Azores* **144** P3
Santa Cruz das Flores, *Azores* **144** N1
Santa Cruz de la Palma, *Canary Is.* **204** Q3
Santa Cruz del Norte, *Cuba* **116** G7
Santa Cruz del Sur, *Cuba* **116** K11
Santa Cruz de Mudela, *Sp.* **144** J11
Santa Cruz de Tenerife, *Canary Is.* **204** Q5
Santa Cruz do Sul, *Braz.* **130** P11
Santa Cruz Islands, *Solomon Is.* **214** H7
Santa Elena, *Venez.* **129** E13
Santa Elena, Cabo, *Costa Rica* **115** N18
Santa Elena Peninsula, *S. Amer.* **126** D1
Santa Eugenia, *Sp.* **144** C5
Santa Eulalia del Río, *Sp.* **145** H17
Santa Fé, *Sp.* **144** L11
Santa Fe, Canal de, *Ecua.* **128** Q10
Santa Fe, *Arg.* **132** J12
Santa Fe, *N. Mex., U.S.* **107** R12
Santa Fe, Isla (Barrington), *Ecua.* **128** Q10
Santa Helena, *Braz.* **130** E10
Santa Inés, Isla, *Chile* **133** X7
Santa Inês, *Braz.* **131** E14
Santa Isabel, *Arg.* **132** M9
Santa Isabel, island, *Solomon Is.* **217** L17
Santa Isabel, *P.R., U.S.* **120** P4
Santa Isabel, island, *Solomon Is.* **217** L17
Santa Isabel, Pico de, *Eq. Guinea* **204** M7
Santa Isabel do Rio Negro, *Braz.* **130** C7
Santa Lucía, *Arg.* **132** H12
Santa Lucía, *Arg.* **132** J8
Santa Lucía, *Cuba* **116** G5
Santa Lucía, *Uru.* **132** L14
Santa Lucia Range, *Calif., U.S.* **109** U4
Santa Luzia, *Azores* **144** P3
Santa Luzia, island, *Cape Verde* **205** B15
Santa Maddalena Vallalta, *It.* **150** B8
Santa-Manza, Golfe de, *Fr.* **150** L4
Santa Margarita, Isla, *Mex.* **114** F6
Santa Maria, island, *Azores* **144** R5
Santa Maria, *Calif., U.S.* **109** W5
Santa Maria, *Cape Verde* **205** B17
Santa Maria, *Neth. Antilles, Neth.* **121** P14
Santa Maria, *Switz.* **150** C6
Santa Maria, island, *Vanuatu* **218** B2
Santa María, *Arg.* **132** G9
Santa María, *Peru* **130** D4
Santa Maria, *Braz.* **130** D9
Santa Maria, *Braz.* **130** P11
Santa Maria, Cabo de, *Angola* **202** E5
Santa Maria, Cabo de, *Port.* **144** L6
Santa Maria, Cape, *Bahamas* **117** F13
Santa María, Cayo, *Cuba* **116** G10
Santa María, Isla (Floreana, Charles), *Ecua.* **128** R9
Santa Maria Bay, *Virgin Islands, U.S.* **120** M8
Santa Maria da Vitória, *Braz.* **131** H15
Santa María de Huerta, *Sp.* **144** E12
Santa María de Nanay, *Peru* **130** E4
Santa Maria di Leuca, Capo, *It.* **151** P16
Santa Maria, Col. **128** B5
Santa Martabaai, bay, *Neth. Antilles, Neth.* **121** P13
Santa Marta de Ortigueira, Ría de, *Sp.* **144** A6
Santa Marta Grande, Cabo de, *Braz.* **131** P13
Santa Monica, *Calif., U.S.* **109** X8
Santa Monica Mountains National Recreation Area, *Calif., U.S.* **109** X7
Sant Ana, *Sao Tome and Principe* **205** D20
Santana, *Madeira* **204** M3
Santana, *Braz.* **131** H15
Santana do Livramento, *Braz.* **130** P11
Santander, *Sp.* **144** B11
Santander, Bahía de, *Sp.* **144** B11
Santander Jiménez, *Mex.* **114** F12

Sant'Andrea Apostolo dello Ionio, *It.* **151** R13
Santanilla, Islas, *Hond.* **115** J19
Sant'Antioco, Isola di, *It.* **151** Q3
Sant Antoni de Portmany, *Sp.* **145** H16
Santa Olalla del Cala, *Sp.* **144** K8
Santa Paula, *Calif., U.S.* **109** X7
Santa Pola, *Sp.* **145** K14
Santaquin, *Utah, U.S.* **106** L7
Santarém, *Port.* **144** H5
Santarém, *Braz.* **130** D11
Santaren Channel, *Bahamas* **116** F9
Santa Rita, *Guam, U.S.* **216** D10
Santa Rita, *Venez.* **128** B7
Santa Rita do Weil, *Braz.* **130** D6
Santa Rosa, *Arg.* **132** K9
Santa Rosa, *Arg.* **132** M10
Santa Rosa, *Bol.* **130** G6
Santa Rosa, island, *Calif., U.S.* **109** X6
Santa Rosa, *Calif., U.S.* **109** R3
Santa Rosa, *Neth. Antilles, Neth.* **121** Q15
Santa Rosa, *Ecua.* **128** Q9
Santa Rosa, *Hond.* **115** L16
Santa Rosa, *N. Mex., U.S.* **107** S14
Santa Rosa, *Peru* **130** G5
Santa Rosa, *Peru* **130** J5
Santa Rosa, *Braz.* **130** G5
Santa Rosa, Mount, *Guam, U.S.* **216** B12
Santa Rosa and San Jacinto Mountains National Monument, *Calif., U.S.* **109** Y11
Santa Rosa Beach, *Fla., U.S.* **97** Q3
Santa Rosa Island, *Fla., U.S.* **97** Q2
Santa Rosalía, *Mex.* **114** D6
Santa Rosa Range, *Nev., U.S.* **108** L9
Santa Severina, *It.* **151** Q14
Santa Teresa, *N. Terr., Austral.* **211** T9
Santa Teresa, Embalse de, *Sp.* **144** F9
Santa Victoria, *Arg.* **132** D11
Santa Vitória do Palmar, *Braz.* **130** Q11
Santa Ynez, *Calif., U.S.* **109** W6
Santa Ynez Mountains, *Calif., U.S.* **109** W6
Sant Carles de la Ràpita, *Sp.* **145** F16
Santee, river, *S.C., U.S.* **96** L11
San Telmo Point, *N. Amer.* **80** P4
Sant'Eufemia, Golfo di, *It.* **151** Q13
Santhià, *It.* **150** E3
Santiago, island, *Cape Verde* **205** D16
Santiago, *Chile* **132** K7
Santiago, *Dom. Rep.* **117** L18
Santiago *see* San Salvador, Isla, island, *Ecua.* **128** P9
Santiago, *Pan.* **115** P20
Santiago, Punta, *Eq. Guinea* **204** N7
Santiago de Baney, *Eq. Guinea* **204** L8
Santiago de Compostela, *Sp.* **144** B5
Santiago de Cuba, *Cuba* **117** K13
Santiago del Estero, *Arg.* **132** G10
Santiago do Cacém, *Port.* **144** K5
Santiago Ixcuintla, *Mex.* **114** G9
Santiago Papasquiaro, *Mex.* **114** F9
Santiago Peak, *Tex., U.S.* **103** Q2
Santigi, *Indonesia* **189** H13
Sant Jordi, Golf de, *Sp.* **145** F16
Sant Julià de Lòria, region, *Andorra* **160** K3
Sant Julià de Lòria, *Andorra* **160** K2
Santo André, *Braz.* **131** M13
Santo Ângelo, *Braz.* **130** P11
Santo Antão, island, *Cape Verde* **205** A14
Santo António, *Cape Verde* **205** D17
Santo António, *Sao Tome and Principe* **205** A21
Santo Antônio do Içá, *Braz.* **130** D6
Santo Corazón, *Bol.* **130** K9
Santo Domingo, *Dom. Rep.* **117** M19
Santo Domingo, Cay, *Bahamas* **117** J13
Santo Domingo de Silos, *Sp.* **144** D11
Santo Domingo Pueblo, *N. Mex., U.S.* **107** R12
Santop, Mount, *Vanuatu* **218** G3
Santopitar, peak, *Sp.* **144** M10
Santoríni *see* Thíra, island, *Gr.* **155** M15
Santos, *Braz.* **131** M14
Santos, Sierra de los, *Sp.* **144** K9
Santos Plateau, *Atl. Oc.* **237** R7
Santo Tirso, *Port.* **144** E5
Santo Tomás, *Peru* **130** J5
Santo Tomás, Volcán, *Ecua.* **128** Q8
Santo Tomé, *Arg.* **132** H14
San Valentín, Monte, *Chile* **133** T6

San Vicente, *N. Mariana Is., U.S.* **216** C5
San Vicente de Alcántara, *Sp.* **144** H7
San Vicente de Barakaldo, *Sp.* **144** B12
San Vincente del Caguán, *Col.* **128** G5
Sanya, *China* **183** V1
Sanyuan, *China* **182** G2
São Bento do Norte, *Braz.* **131** E18
São Borja, *Braz.* **130** P10
São Cristóvão, *Braz.* **131** H17
São Félix do Xingu, *Braz.* **130** F12
São Filipe, *Cape Verde* **205** E15
São Francisco, river, *Braz.* **131** J15
São Francisco, Ilha de, *Braz.* **131** N13
São Gabriel, *Braz.* **130** P11
São Gabriel da Cachoeira, *Braz.* **130** C6
São Gens, peak, *Port.* **144** J6
São João da Aliança, *Braz.* **131** J13
São João da Madeira, *Port.* **144** E5
São João del Rei, *Braz.* **131** L14
São Jorge, island, *Azores* **144** P3
São José de Anauá, *Braz.* **130** C8
São José de Ribamar, *Braz.* **131** D15
São José do Rio Preto, *Braz.* **126** H20
São José dos Campos, *Braz.* **131** M14
São Leopoldo, *Braz.* **130** P12
São Lourenço, Ponta de, *Madeira* **204** M4
São Lourenço do Sul, *Braz.* **130** Q12
São Luís, *Braz.* **131** D15
São Luís, Ilha de, *Braz.* **131** D15
São Mamede, Pico, *Port.* **144** H6
São Manuel *see* Teles Pires, river, *Braz.* **130** F10
São Martinho do Porto, *Port.* **144** G4
São Mateus, *Azores* **144** P3
São Mateus, *Braz.* **131** K16
São Miguel, island, *Azores* **144** Q5
São Miguel do Araguaia, *Braz.* **130** H12
Saona, Isla, *Dom. Rep.* **117** M20
Saonek, *Indonesia* **189** J17
Saoner, *India* **178** K6
São Nicolau, island, *Cape Verde* **205** B16
São Paulo, *Braz.* **131** M13
São Paulo de Olivença, *Braz.* **130** D6
São Raimundo Nonato, *Braz.* **131** G15
São Romão, *Braz.* **130** E6
São Roque, Cabo de, *Braz.* **131** F18
São Sebastião, *Azores* **144** P4
São Sebastião, Ponta, *Mozambique* **203** H13
São Sebastião Island, *S. Amer.* **126** J9
São Teotónio, *Port.* **144** K5
São Tiago, *Cape Verde* **205** D16
São Tomé, island, *Sao Tome and Principe* **205** D19
São Tomé, *Sao Tome and Principe* **205** C20
São Tomé, Cabo de, *Braz.* **131** M15
São Tomé, Pico de, *Sao Tome and Principe* **205** D20
Sao Tome and Principe, *Af.* **204** F5
Saoute, Wādī, *Syr.* **170** L9
São Vicente, island, *Cape Verde* **205** B14
São Vicente, *Madeira* **204** M3
São Vicente, Cabo de, *Port.* **144** L4
Sapanca, *Turk.* **168** D6
Sapanjang, island, *Indonesia* **188** M11
Sapele, *Nigeria* **201** H13
Sapelo Island, *Ga., U.S.* **97** P9
Sápes, *Gr.* **155** B15
Şaphane Dağı, *Turk.* **168** F5
Sapiéntza, island, *Gr.* **154** M9
Saposoa, *Peru* **130** F3
Sapphire Mountains, *Mont., U.S.* **106** D6
Sappho, *Wash., U.S.* **108** B2
Sapporo, *Japan* **184** G13
Sapri, *It.* **151** N12
Sapudi, island, *Indonesia* **188** M11
Sapulpa, *Okla., U.S.* **102** F12
Saqqez, *Iran* **172** C10
Sara Adasy, island, *Azerb.* **169** F22
Sarāb, *Iran* **172** B11
Saraburi, *Thai.* **186** M9
Saraféré, *Mali* **196** H8
Saraguro, *Ecua.* **128** L3
Sarahs, *Turkm.* **174** N9
Sarajevo, *Bosn. & Herzg.* **152** G8

Sarakhs, *Iran* **173** BI7
Saranac Lake, *N.Y., U.S.* **94** GII
Saranac Lakes, *N.Y., U.S.* **94** GIO
Sarandë, *Albania* **152** N9
Sarangani Islands, *Philippines* **189** GI5
Sarangpur, *India* **178** J5
Saransk, *Russ.* **156** KI3
Sarapul, *Russ.* **156** HI6
Sarapul, *Russ.* **158** H8
Sarasota, *Fla., U.S.* **97** V7
Sarasota Bay, *Fla., U.S.* **97** V7
Saratoga, *Wyo., U.S.* **106** KII
Saratoga Springs, *N.Y., U.S.* **94** JII
Saratov, *Russ.* **156** MI3
Sarāvān, *Iran* **173** GI8
Sarawak, region, *Malaysia* **188** HII
Saray, *Turk.* **168** C4
Saray, *Turk.* **169** FI8
Sarayköy, *Turk.* **168** G4
Sar Banader, *Afghan.* **177** R3
Sarbāz, *Iran* **173** HI7
Sarbīsheh, *Iran* **173** EI7
Sarcelle, Passe de la, *New Caledonia, Fr.* **218** E9
Sardar Chah, *Pak.* **177** T4
Sardegna (Sardinia), island, *It.* **151** N3
Sardinia *see* Sardegna, island, *It.* **151** N3
Sardis, *Miss., U.S.* **100** HII
Sardis, ruin, *Turk.* **168** F4
Sardis Lake, *Miss., U.S.* **100** HII
Sar-e Howz, *Afghan.* **176** L4
Sareiserjoch, *Liech.* **160** Q4
Sar-e Pol (Sari Pol), *Afghan.* **176** L5
Sargans, *Switz.* **160** RI
Sargent, *Nebr., U.S.* **105** P5
Sargo Plateau, *Arctic Oc.* **242** H6
Sarh, *Chad* **197** KI5
Sarhadd, *Afghan.* **176** KII
Sāri, island, *Gr.* **155** PI8
Sarigan, island, *N. Mariana Is., U.S.* **216** B2
Sarıgöl, *Turk.* **168** G4
Sarıkamış, *Turk.* **169** DI7
Sarina, *Qnsld., Austral.* **211** TI4
Sariñena, *Sp.* **145** DI5
Sarinleey, *Somalia* **199** JI6
Sari Pol *see* Sar-e Pol, *Afghan.* **176** L5
Sarīr Tibasti, region, *Lib.* **197** EI4
Sariwŏn, *N. Korea* **182** EI2
Sarıyar Baraji, *Turk.* **168** E7
Sarıyer, *Turk.* **168** C5
Sarız, *Turk.* **168** GII
Sarjektjåkko, peak, *Sw.* **141** EI3
Sark, island, *Ch. Is.* **143** ZII
Sarkari Tala, *India* **178** F2
Şarkîkaraağaç, *Turk.* **168** G7
Şarkışla, *Turk.* **168** FII
Şarköy, *Turk.* **168** D3
Sarles, *N. Dak., U.S.* **104** D6
Sarmansuyu, *Turk.* **169** GI7
Sarmi, *Indonesia* **189** K2O
Sarmiento, *Arg.* **133** S8
Särna, *Sw.* **140** JI2
Sarnano, *It.* **150** H9
Sarny, *Ukr.* **156** M4
Saroma Ko, *Japan* **184** EI5
Saronikós Kólpos, *Gr.* **154** JI2
Saronno, *It.* **150** D4
Saros Körfezi, *Turk.* **168** D3
Sarowbi, *Afghan.* **176** M8
Sarowbi, *Afghan.* **177** P8
Sarpa, Ozero, *Russ.* **157** QI4
Sar Passage, *Palau* **216** PII
Sarqan, *Kaz.* **175** GI7
Sarracín, *Sp.* **144** CII
Sarrebourg, *Fr.* **147** PI5
Sarreguemines, *Fr.* **147** NI5
Sarria, *Sp.* **144** B7
Sarrión, *Sp.* **145** GI4
Sarteano, *It.* **150** J7
Sartène, *Fr.* **150** L4
Sarthe, river, *Fr.* **147** Q7
Sarti, *Gr.* **155** DI3
Sarufutsu, *Japan* **184** DI4
Saruna, *Pak.* **177** V6
Sarupsar, *India* **178** E4
Särur, *Azerb.* **169** EI9
Sarych, Mys, *Ukr.* **157** T7
Saryesik-Atyraū Qumy, *Kaz.* **175** GI6
Sarygamysh Köli, *Turkm. Uzb.* **174** J8

Saryköl, *Kaz.* **174** BII
Saryözek, *Kaz.* **175** HI7
Saryqamys, *Kaz.* **174** G7
Saryqopa Köli, *Kaz.* **174** DII
Sarysay, *Kaz.* **174** E9
Saryshagan, *Kaz.* **175** GI5
Sarysū, river, *Kaz.* **175** EI3
Sary-Tash, *Kyrg.* **176** GIO
Saryzhal, *Kaz.* **175** DI7
Sasalaguan, Mount, *Guam, U.S.* **216** DIO
Sasamungga, *Solomon Is.* **217** LI5
Sasaram, *India* **178** H9
Sasebo, *Japan* **185** R3
Saseno *see* Sazan, island, *Albania* **152** M9
Saskatchewan, *Can.* **82** LI2
Saskatchewan, river, *N. Amer.* **80** G5
Saskatoon, *Sask., Can.* **82** MI2
Sason, *Turk.* **169** GI6
Sasora, *Indonesia* **189** K2O
Sasovo, *Russ.* **156** KII
Sassafras Mountain, *S.C., U.S.* **96** J7
Sassandra, *Côte d'Ivoire* **200** H8
Sassari, *It.* **150** M3
Sassnitz, *Ger.* **148** BIO
Sassofeltrio, *It.* **161** LI7
Sasstown, *Liberia* **200** H7
Sassuolo, *It.* **150** F6
Sasykoli, *Russ.* **158** J5
Sasyqköl, lake, *Kaz.* **175** FI8
Sata, *Japan* **185** T4
Satadougou, *Mali* **196** J6
Satala, ruin, *Turk.* **169** EI4
Sata Misaki, *Japan* **185** U4
Satanta, *Kans., U.S.* **105** U4
Satara, *India* **178** M4
Sataua, *Samoa* **218** KI
Satawal, island, *F.S.M.* **216** Q5
Satawan Atoll, *F.S.M.* **216** Q6
Sätbaev, *Kaz.* **174** FI2
Satbarwa, *India* **178** H9
Satilla, river, *Ga., U.S.* **97** P6
Satipo, *Peru* **130** H4
Satkania, *Bangladesh* **178** JI4
Satna, *India* **178** H7
Sato, *Japan* **185** T3
Šator, peak, *Bosn. & Herzg.* **152** F6
Sátoraljaújhely, *Hung.* **149** KI7
Satpura Range, *India* **178** K4
Satteins, *Aust.* **176** M4
Satulung, *Rom.* **153** BI3
Satu Mare, *Rom.* **152** BI2
Satun, *Thai.* **187** S8
Satupa'itea, *Samoa* **218** L2
Sauce, *Arg.* **132** JI3
Sauda, *Nor.* **140** LIO
Saudárkrókur, *Ice.* **140** E3
Saudi Arabia, *Asia* **167** U3
Saugatuck, *Mich., U.S.* **98** M9
Saugerties, *N.Y., U.S.* **94** LII
Sauk Centre, *Minn., U.S.* **104** JIO
Sauk City, *Wis., U.S.* **98** L5
Saukorem, *Indonesia* **189** JI8
Sauk Rapids, *Minn., U.S.* **104** JII
Saulieu, *Fr.* **147** R9
Sault Ste. Marie, *Mich., U.S.* **98** FII
Sault Ste. Marie, *Ont., Can.* **83** PI7
Saūmalköl, *Kaz.* **174** BI2
Saumlaki, *Indonesia* **189** MI7
Saumur, *Fr.* **147** R7
Saunders Coast, *Antarctica* **226** NIO
Saupon Point, *Guam, U.S.* **216** CII
Saura, *Kaz.* **174** H5
Saurimo, *Angola* **202** C8
Sausalito, *Calif., U.S.* **109** S3
Sauteurs, *Grenada* **121** J23
Sauteurs Bay, *Grenada* **121** J23
Sauveterre, *Fr.* **147** X6
Sava, river, *Bosn. & Herzg., Croatia, Slov.* **152** F9
Savage, *Mont., U.S.* **106** CI3
Savai'i, island, *Samoa* **218** K2
Savalou, *Benin* **200** GI2
Savana Island, *Virgin Islands, U.S.* **120** N7
Savane des Pétrifications, site, *Martinique, Fr.* **121** G23
Savaneta, *Aruba, Neth.* **121** RI7
Savanna, *Ill., U.S.* **99** N4
Savannah, *Cayman Is., U.K.* **120** J2
Savannah, *Ga., U.S.* **97** N9
Savannah, river, *Ga., S.C., U.S.* **96** M8
Savannah, *Mo., U.S.* **105** RIO
Savannah, *Tenn., U.S.* **101** GI3

Savannah Bay, *Virgin Islands, U.K.* **120** Q8
Savannah Sound, *Bahamas* **120** E6
Savannakhét, *Laos* **186** LII
Savanna-la-Mar, *Jam.* **120** H6
Savanna Point, *Jam.* **120** HIO
Savaştepe, *Turk.* **168** E3
Save, river, *Mozambique* **202** HI2
Sāveh, *Iran* **172** CI2
Savenay, *Fr.* **147** R5
Saverne, *Fr.* **147** PI5
Savigliano, *It.* **150** F2
Savignac-les-Églises, *Fr.* **147** V8
Savignone, *It.* **150** F4
Savissivik, *Greenland, Den.* **81** C2O
Savo, island, *Solomon Is.* **217** NI8
Savona, *It.* **150** F3
Savonet, *Neth. Antilles, Neth.* **121** NI3
Savonlinna, *Fin.* **141** HI7
Savoonga, *Alas., U.S.* **110** FIO
Savukoski, *Fin.* **141** DI5
Savur, *Turk.* **169** HI5
Savusavu, *Fiji Is.* **218** G7
Savusavu Bay, *Fiji Is.* **218** H7
Savu Sea, *Indonesia* **189** NI4
Sawada, *Japan* **184** MII
Sawah, *Indonesia* **188** HII
Sawahlunto, *Indonesia* **188** J6
Sawai Madhopur, *India* **178** G5
Sawankhalok, *Thai.* **186** K8
Sawa-i-Iau, island, *Fiji Is.* **218** H5
Sawatch Range, *Colo., U.S.* **107** NI2
Sawda, Jabal, *Saudi Arabia* **172** N8
Sawdā', Jabal as, *Lib.* **197** DI4
Sawe, *Indonesia* **188** H4
Sawi, *Thai.* **187** Q8
Sawkanah, *Lib.* **197** DI4
Şawqirah, *Oman* **173** NI5
Şawqirah, Ghubbat, *Oman* **173** NI6
Sawtooth Mountains, *Minn., U.S.* **104** FI3
Sawtooth National Recreation Area, *Idaho, U.S.* **106** G5
Sawtooth Range, *Idaho, U.S.* **106** G4
Sawu, island, *Indonesia* **189** NI4
Sax, *Switz.* **160** MI
Saxby Downs, *Qnsld., Austral.* **211** SI2
Saxony, region, *Ger.* **148** FIO
Say, *Niger* **196** JIO
Saya de Malha Bank, *Ind. Oc.* **240** H7
Sayanogorsk, *Russ.* **159** LI3
Sayhūt, *Yemen* **173** QI3
Saylac, *Somalia* **199** FI6
Saynshand, *Mongolia* **181** EI3
Sayötesh, *Kaz.* **174** H6
Sayram Hu, *China* **180** E6
Sayre, *Okla., U.S.* **102** G8
Sayre, *Pa., U.S.* **94** L8
Sayville, *Mich., U.S.* **98** K9
Saywūn, *Yemen* **172** PII
Sayylyk, *Russ.* **159** EI8
Saza'i Kalan, *Afghan.* **176** L5
Sazan (Saseno), island, *Albania* **152** M9
Sazin, *Pak.* **176** LII
Sbaa, *Alg.* **196** DIO
Scafell Pike, peak, *Eng., U.K.* **143** QIO
Scalpay, island, *Scot., U.K.* **142** J7
Scalpay, island, *Scot., U.K.* **142** K7
Scammon Bay, *Alas., U.S.* **110** HII
Scandia, *Kans., U.S.* **105** R7
Scandinavia, region, *Eur.* **138** D7
Scanzano Ionico, *It.* **151** NI4
Scapa Flow, bay, *Scot., U.K.* **142** GIO
Scaraben, peak, *Scot., U.K.* **142** HIO
Scarba, island, *Scot., U.K.* **142** M7
Scarborough, *Eng., U.K.* **143** QI3
Scarborough, *Trinidad & Tobago* **121** NI7
Scarinish, *Scot., U.K.* **142** L6
Scarp, island, *Scot., U.K.* **142** H6
Scarriff, *Ire.* **143** T4
Scatterbreak Channel, *Fiji Is.* **218** G8
Šcedro, island, *Croatia* **152** H6
Schaan, *Liech.* **160** N2
Schaanwald, *Liech.* **160** N3
Schefferville, *Que., Can.* **83** L2O
Schell Creek Range, *Nev., U.S.* **109** QI2
Schellenberg, *Liech.* **160** M3
Schenectady, *N.Y., U.S.* **94** JII
Schertz, *Tex., U.S.* **103** RIO
Schiermonnikoog, island, *Neth.* **146** DI2
Schio, *It.* **150** D7
Schleswig, *Ger.* **148** A7

Schoelcher, *Martinique, Fr.* **121** F22
Schofield, *Wis., U.S.* **98** H5
Schofield Barracks, *Hawai'i, U.S.* **112** DIO
Schönberg, peak, *Liech.* **160** P3
Schönebeck, *Ger.* **148** E9
Schooner Cays, *Bahamas* **120** F6
Schottegat, bay, *Neth. Antilles, Neth.* **121** QI4
Schouten Islands, *P.N.G.* **213** CI8
Schrems, *Aust.* **148** JII
Schroeder, *Minn., U.S.* **104** FI3
Schuckmannsburg, *Namibia* **202** F9
Schulenburg, *Tex., U.S.* **103** RI2
Schull, *Ire.* **143** V3
Schuyler, *Nebr., U.S.* **105** P8
Schwabach, *Ger.* **148** J8
Schwäbische Alb, *Ger.* **148** K7
Schwäbisch Hall, *Ger.* **148** J7
Schwaz, *Aust.* **148** L9
Schwechat, *Aust.* **149** KI3
Schwedt, *Ger.* **148** DII
Schweich, *Ger.* **160** JI2
Schweinfurt, *Ger.* **148** G8
Schwerin, *Ger.* **148** C9
Schwyz, *Switz.* **150** B4
Sciacca, *It.* **151** S9
Scilla, *It.* **151** RI2
Scilly, Isles of, *Eng., U.K.* **143** Y6
Scioto, river, *Ohio, U.S.* **99** SI3
Scipio, *Utah, U.S.* **106** M7
Scobey, *Mont., U.S.* **106** AI2
Scofield Reservoir, *Utah, U.S.* **106** M8
Scooba, *Miss., U.S.* **101** KI3
Scotch Bonnet, cape, *St. Kitts & Nevis* **121** BI8
Scotia Sea, *Antarctic Oc.* **244** D8
Scotland, *S. Dak., U.S.* **104** M7
Scotland, *U.K.* **142** K9
Scotland Neck, *N.C., U.S.* **96** GI3
Scott, Mount, *Oreg., U.S.* **108** J4
Scott Base, station, *Antarctica* **227** NI3
Scott City, *Kans., U.S.* **105** T4
Scott City, *Mo., U.S.* **105** UI6
Scott Coast, *Antarctica* **227** NI4
Scott Glacier, *Antarctica* **227** K2I
Scott Islands, *B.C., Can.* **82** L7
Scott Point, *Mich., U.S.* **98** G9
Scottsbluff, *Nebr., U.S.* **105** NI
Scotts Bluff National Monument, *Nebr., U.S.* **105** NI
Scottsboro, *Ala., U.S.* **101** GI6
Scottsburg, *Ind., U.S.* **99** T9
Scottsdale, *Ariz., U.S.* **107** U7
Scotts Head, *Dominica* **121** GI9
Scottsville, *Ky., U.S.* **101** DI6
Scottville, *Mich., U.S.* **98** K9
Scotty's Junction, *Nev., U.S.* **109** S9
Scranton, *Pa., U.S.* **94** M9
Scribner, *Nebr., U.S.* **105** P8
Scrubby Creek, *Qnsld., Austral.* **211** PI2
Scrub Island, *Anguilla, U.K.* **120** QI2
Scunthorpe, *Eng., U.K.* **143** RI3
Scuol, *Switz.* **150** B6
Scurdie Ness, *Scot., U.K.* **142** LII
Scutari *see* Shkodër, *Albania* **152** K9
Scutari, Lake *see* Skadarsko Jezero, *Albania, Mont.* **152** J9
Scyros *see* Skíros, island, *Gr.* **155** GI3
Sea Club, *Monaco* **161** B23
Sea Cow Bay, *Virgin Islands, U.K.* **120** N6
Seadrift, *Tex., U.S.* **103** TI2
Seaford, *Del., U.S.* **96** DI4
Seaford, *Eng., U.K.* **143** WI4
Seaforth, *Jam.* **120** JII
Seaforth, Loch, *Scot., U.K.* **142** H7
Sea Grape, *Bahamas* **120** FI
Seagraves, *Tex., U.S.* **102** L4
Seaham, *Eng., U.K.* **143** PI2
Sea Island, *Ga., U.S.* **97** P9
Sea Islands, *Ga., U.S.* **85** LI9
Seal, river, *Man., Can.* **83** KI4
Seal, Cape, *S. Af.* **202** M9
Sea Lake, *Vic., Austral.* **211** YII
Seal Cay, *Bahamas* **117** GI3
Seal Cays, *Turks & Caicos Is., U.K.* **117** JI7
Sealevel, *N.C., U.S.* **96** JI4
Seal Islands, *Anguilla, U.K.* **120** QII
Sealy, *Tex., U.S.* **103** RI3
Searchlight, *Nev., U.S.* **109** VI2
Searcy, *Ark., U.S.* **100** G9
Searles Lake, *Calif., U.S.* **109** V9

Seaside, *Oreg., U.S.* **108** E2
Seaside Park, *N.J., U.S.* **94** PII
Seaton Glacier, *Antarctica* **227** CI9
Seatons, *Antigua & Barbuda* **121** B2I
Seattle, *Wash., U.S.* **108** C4
Sebago Lake, *Me., U.S.* **95** GI5
Sebakor, Teluk, *Indonesia* **213** CI4
Sebastian, *Fla., U.S.* **97** UIO
Sebastian, Cape, *Oreg., U.S.* **108** KI
Sebastián Vizcaíno, Bahía, *Mex.* **114** D5
Sebastián Vizcaíno Bay, *N. Amer.* **80** L3
Sebastopol, *Calif., U.S.* **109** R3
Sebatik, island, *Indonesia, Malaysia* **188** GI2
Sebeka, *Minn., U.S.* **104** GIO
Seben, *Turk.* **168** D7
Sebeş, *Rom.* **153** DI3
Sebewaing, *Mich., U.S.* **98** KI2
Sebezh, *Russ.* **156** H5
Şebinkarahisar, *Turk.* **169** EI3
Sebring, *Fla., U.S.* **97** U9
Sebuyau, *Malaysia* **188** HIO
Sechura, Bahía de, *Peru* **130** FI
Sechura Desert, *S. Amer.* **126** EI
Secica, *Slovakia* **149** JI3
Second Cataract, *Sudan* **198** CI2
Secondigny, *Fr.* **147** S7
Second Mesa, *Ariz., U.S.* **107** R8
Secos, Ilhéus (Ilhéus do Rombo), *Cape Verde* **205** DI5
Secretary Island, *N.Z.* **213** QI5
Sécure, river, *Bol.* **130** J7
Securé, river, *S. Amer.* **126** G5
Security, *Colo., U.S.* **107** NI3
Sedalia, *Mo., U.S.* **105** TI2
Sedan, *Fr.* **147** NI2
Sedan, *Kans., U.S.* **105** V9
Seddon, *N.Z.* **213** NI8
Sedeh, *Iran* **173** DI6
Sedom, *Israel* **171** P6
Sedona, *Ariz., U.S.* **107** S7
Sedro Woolley, *Wash., U.S.* **108** A4
Seeheim, *Namibia* **202** K7
Sées, *Fr.* **147** P7
Seevetal, *Ger.* **148** C8
Seferihisar, *Turk.* **168** F2
Sefid Kers, range, *Afghan.* **176** J9
Sefid Kuh Mountains (Paropamisus Range), *Afghan.* **176** M3
Seg, Lake, *Russ.* **138** CIO
Segamat, *Malaysia* **187** UIO
Segbana, *Benin* **200** FI2
Segesta, ruin, *It.* **151** S9
Segezha, *Russ.* **158** D8
Seghe, *Solomon Is.* **217** MI6
Ségou, *Mali* **196** H7
Segovia, *Sp.* **144** EIO
Segré, *Fr.* **147** R6
Seguam Island, *Alas., U.S.* **110** P7
Séguéla, *Côte d'Ivoire* **200** G8
Seguin, *Tex., U.S.* **103** RIO
Seguntur, *Indonesia* **188** HI2
Segura, river, *Sp.* **145** KI4
Segura, Sierra de, *Sp.* **144** KI2
Sehwan, *Pak.* **177** V7
Seikan Submarine Tunnel, *Japan* **184** HI2
Seil, island, *Scot., U.K.* **142** L8
Seiling, *Okla., U.S.* **102** F9
Seinäjoki, *Fin.* **141** HI5
Seine, river, *Fr.* **147** P9
Seine, Baie de la, *Fr.* **147** N7
Sekikawa, *Japan* **184** MI2
Sekondi-Takoradi, *Ghana* **200** HIO
Sek'ot'a, *Eth.* **199** EI5
Sekseūil, *Kaz.* **174** FIO
Selah, *Wash., U.S.* **108** D6
Selaru, island, *Indonesia* **189** MI7
Selatan, Bunguran *see* Natuna Selatan, Kepulauan, *Indonesia* **188** H9
Selawik, *Alas., U.S.* **111** EI3
Selawik Lake, *Alas., U.S.* **111** EI3
Selayar, island, *Indonesia* **189** LI3
Selby, *Eng., U.K.* **143** RI3
Selby, *S. Dak., U.S.* **104** J5
Selden, *Kans., U.S.* **105** S4
Seldovia, *Alas., U.S.* **111** KI6
Selendi, *Turk.* **168** F4
Selenga, river, *Mongolia, Russ.* **166** EIO
Selenga, river, *Russ.* **159** LI6
Selenge, river, *Mongolia* **180** CI2
Sélestat, *Fr.* **147** QI5

Seleucia see Salandağı, Turk. 168 KII
Selfoss, Ice. 140 F2
Selfridge, N. Dak., U.S. 104 H4
Self Town see McLean's Town, Bahamas 120 E4
Sélibaby, Mauritania 196 H6
Seliger, Ozero, Russ. 156 H7
Seligman, Ariz., U.S. 107 S6
Selima Oasis, Sudan 198 CI2
Selinus, ruin, It. 151 S9
Selkirk, Scot., U.K. 143 NIO
Selkirk Mountains, Idaho, U.S. 106 A3
Sellheim, Qnsld., Austral. 211 SI3
Sellières, Fr. 147 SI3
Sells, Ariz., U.S. 107 V7
Selma, Ala., U.S. 101 LI5
Selma, Calif., U.S. 109 T6
Selma, N.C., U.S. 96 HI2
Selmer, Tenn., U.S. 101 GI3
Selongey, Fr. 147 RI3
Selsey Bill, Eng., U.K. 143 XI3
Seltz, Fr. 147 PI6
Selvas, region, S. Amer. 126 E3
Selway, river, Idaho, U.S. 106 D5
Selwyn, Qnsld., Austral. 211 SII
Selwyn Mountains, N.W.T., Yukon, Can. 82 F9
Selwyn Strait, Vanuatu 218 D3
Semarang, Indonesia 188 M9
Sembé, Congo 201 KI7
Şemdinli, Turk. 169 HI9
Semenov, Russ. 156 HI2
Semeru, peak, Indonesia 188 MIO
Semey (Semipalatinsk), Kaz. 175 DI7
Semichi Islands, Alas., U.S. III L2
Semiluki, Russ. 156 MIO
Seminoe Dam, Wyo., U.S. 106 JII
Seminoe Reservoir, Wyo., U.S. 106 JII
Seminole, Okla., U.S. 102 GI2
Seminole, Tex., U.S. 102 L4
Seminole, Lake, Fla., Ga., U.S. 97 Q4
Semipalatinsk see Semey, Kaz. 175 DI7
Semipalatinsk Nuclear Test Range, Kaz. 175 DI6
Semisopochnoi Island, Alas., U.S. IIO N3
Semnān, Iran 173 CI4
Semporna, Malaysia 188 FI2
Sen, river, Cambodia 186 MII
Seña, Slovakia 149 JI7
Senaja, Malaysia 188 FI2
Senaki, Rep. of Georgia 169 BI6
Sena Madureira, Braz. 130 G6
Senanga, Zambia 202 F9
Senatobia, Miss., U.S. 100 HII
Sendai, Japan 184 LI3
Sendai, Japan 185 T4
Sendhwa, India 178 K4
Senduruhan, Indonesia 188 J9
Seneca, Kans., U.S. 105 R9
Seneca, Oreg., U.S. 108 H7
Seneca, S.C., U.S. 96 K6
Seneca Falls, N.Y., U.S. 94 J7
Sénégal, river, Mauritania, Senegal 196 H5
Senegal, Af. 195 GI3
Senftenberg, Ger. 148 FII
Sengiley, Russ. 156 KI5
Senhor do Bonfim, Braz. 131 GI6
Senigallia, It. 150 G9
Senj, Croatia 152 E5
Senja, island, Nor. 140 DI2
Senkaku Shotō (Diaoyu Islands), China 183 PII
Senlis, Fr. 147 NIO
Senmonorom, Cambodia 187 NI3
Sennar, Sudan 199 EI3
Sennecey-le-Grand, Fr. 147 SI3
Sennen, Eng., U.K. 143 Y7
Senneterre, Que., Can. 83 PI8
Sennwald, Switz. 160 L2
Senorbi, It. 151 P4
Sens, Fr. 147 QII
Sensuntepeque, El Salv. 115 LI6
Senta, Serb. 152 DIO
Šentilj, Slov. 152 C6
Sentinel, Okla., U.S. 102 G8
Sentinel Range, Antarctica 226 H8
Senyavin Islands, F.S.M. 216 Q8
Seogwipo, S. Korea 182 JI3
Seoni, India 178 J7
Seosan, S. Korea 182 FI3
Seoul, S. Korea 182 EI3
Sepasu, Indonesia 188 JI2

Sepi, Solomon Is. 217 MI8
Sepik, river, P.N.G. 213 CI8
Sept-Îles, Que., Can. 83 M2I
Sepúlveda, Sp. 144 EII
Sepupa, Botswana 202 G8
Sequim, Wash., U.S. 108 B3
Sequoia National Park, Calif., U.S. 109 T8
Seraing, Belg. 146 LI3
Serang, Indonesia 188 L8
Serasan, island, Indonesia 188 H9
Serbia, Eur. 139 W8
Serdobsk, Russ. 156 LI3
Serebryansk, Kaz. 175 DI8
Sered', Slovakia 149 KI4
Seredka, Russ. 156 G5
Şereflikoçhisar, Turk. 168 F9
Seremban, Malaysia 187 U9
Serena, Embalse la, Sp. 144 H9
Serengeti Plain, Tanzania 199 KI3
Séres, Gr. 154 BI2
Sergach, Russ. 156 JI3
Sergeya Kirova, Ostrova, Russ. 159 DI3
Sergino, Russ. 158 GIO
Sergiyev Posad, Russ. 156 J9
Serian, Malaysia 188 H9
Sérifos, island, Gr. 155 LI3
Sérifos, Gr. 155 LI3
Sérignan, Fr. 147 YII
Serik, Turk. 168 H6
Seringa, Serra da, Braz. 130 FI2
Seriole, river, San Marino 161 LI5
Serkovo, Russ. 159 GI3
Sermata, island, Indonesia 189 MI6
Sermata, Kepulauan, Indonesia 189 MI6
Sernur, Russ. 156 HI4
Seroczyn, Pol. 149 EI7
Seroe Colorado, Aruba, Neth. 121 RI7
Serov, Russ. 158 H9
Serowe, Botswana 202 HIO
Serpa, Port. 144 K6
Serpentine Lakes, Austral. 210 H7
Serpent Island, Mauritius 205 E2I
Serpent's Mouth, strait, Trinidad & Tobago 121 R2I
Serpukhov, Russ. 156 K9
Serra do Navio, Braz. 130 CI2
Serra Nevada de Santa Marta, S. Amer. 126 A3
Serravalle, San Marino 161 HI6
Serre-Ponçon, Lac de, Fr. 147 WI4
Serrera, Pic de la, Andorra, Fr. 160 G4
Serres, Fr. 147 WI4
Serrezuela, Arg. 132 J9
Serrières, Fr. 147 UI3
Serrinha, Braz. 131 HI6
Sersale, It. 151 QI4
Sertã, Port. 144 G6
Sertão, region, S. Amer. 126 FIO
Serti, Nigeria 201 GI5
Serui, Indonesia 189 KI9
Sérvia, Gr. 154 D9
Sesfontein, Namibia 202 G5
Sesheke, Zambia 202 F9
Sesimbra, Port. 144 J4
Sesklí, island, Gr. 155 MI9
Sessa Aurunca, It. 150 LIO
Sestri Levante, It. 150 F4
Sestri Ponente, It. 150 F4
Sestroretsk, Russ. 156 F6
Setana, Japan 184 GI2
Sète, Fr. 147 XII
Sete Lagoas, Braz. 131 KI4
Sete Quedas Falls, S. Amer. 126 J7
Sétif, Alg. 196 B8
Seto, Japan 185 PIO
Setouchi, Japan 185 W3
Settat, Mor. 196 B8
Setté Cama, Gabon 201 MI5
Settimo Torinese, It. 150 E3
Settlement, Marshall Is. 216 N5
Settlement, Wake I., U.S. 216 F8
Setúbal, Port. 144 J5
Setúbal, Baía de, Port. 144 J5
Seul, Lac, Ont., Can. 83 NI5
Seul Choix Point, Mich., U.S. 98 G9
Sevan, Arm. 169 D8
Sevana Lich, lake, Arm. 169 DI9
Sevastopol', Ukr. 157 T7
Sevelen, Switz. 160 P2
Seven Islands Bay, Nfld. & Lab., Can. 83 J2O

Seven Stones, islands, Eng., U.K. 143 Y7
Severn, river, Ont., Can. 83 LI6
Severn, S. Af. 202 J9
Severnaya Dvina, river, Russ. 158 F8
Severnaya Zemlya (North Land), Russ. 159 CI4
Severnyy, Russ. 158 FII
Severobaykal'sk, Russ. 159 KI6
Severodvinsk, Russ. 158 E8
Severo Kuril'sk, Russ. 159 G23
Severomorsk, Russ. 158 D9
Severo Sibirskaya Nizmennost', Russ. 159 FI3
Sevi, Russ. 159 LI3
Sevier, river, Utah, U.S. 106 M6
Sevier Desert, Utah, U.S. 106 M6
Sevier Lake, Utah, U.S. 107 N6
Sevilla, Col. 128 F4
Sevilla (Seville), Sp. 144 L8
Sevilla Nueva, site, Jam. 120 H9
Seville see Sevilla, Sp. 144 L8
Sevlievo, Bulg. 153 HI4
Seward, Alas., U.S. III KI6
Seward, Nebr., U.S. 105 Q8
Seward Peninsula, Alas., U.S. IIO FI2
Sewell, Chile 132 L7
Seweweekspoortpiek, peak, S. Af. 194 Q7
Seychelles, Af. 204 F9
Seychelles Group, Seychelles 205 P2O
Seydi, Turkm. 174 LIO
Seydişehir, Turk. 168 H7
Seydisfjördur, Ice. 140 F4
Seyfe Gölü, Turk. 168 F9
Seyhan, river, Turk. 168 HIO
Seyhan Barajı, Turk. 168 HIO
Seyitgazi, Turk. 168 E6
Seylla Glacier, Antarctica 227 EI9
Seymchan, Russ. 159 E2O
Seymour, Ind., U.S. 99 S9
Seymour, Iowa, U.S. 105 QI2
Seymour, Tex., U.S. 102 K8
Seymour, Vic., Austral. 211 ZI2
Seymour, Wis., U.S. 98 J6
Seymour, Isla, Ecua. 128 Q9
Seyne, Fr. 147 WI4
Sézanne, Fr. 147 PII
Sfakia, Gr. 155 QI3
Sfântu Gheorghe, Rom. 153 DI5
Sfântu-Gheorghe, Ostrov, Rom. 153 EI8
Sfax, Tun. 197 BI3
Sferracavallo, Capo, It. 151 P5
's Gravenhage (The Hague), Neth. 146 JI2
Sha, river, China 183 P7
Shabla, Nos, Bulg. 153 GI8
Shabwah, Yemen 172 QII
Shache, China 180 G4
Shackleton Coast, Antarctica 227 LI3
Shackleton Ice Shelf, Antarctica 227 K2I
Shackleton Range, Antarctica 226 EII
Shadehill Reservoir, S. Dak., U.S. 104 H2
Shaduzup, Myanmar 186 E6
Shafter, Nev., U.S. 108 MI2
Shafter, Tex., U.S. 103 QI
Shagedu, China 182 D3
Shageluk, Alas., U.S. III HI3
Shaghan, river, Kaz. 174 F8
Shaghan, Kaz. 175 DI7
Shag Rocks, S. Amer. 126 R9
Shahbā' (Philippopolis), Syr. 170 K8
Shahbandar, Pak. 177 X7
Shahdadkot, Pak. 177 T7
Shahdadpur, Pak. 177 V7
Shahdol, India 178 J8
Shahgarh, India 178 F2
Shaḥḥāt (Cyrene), Lib. 197 BI6
Shahjahanpur, India 178 F7
Shah Juy, Afghan. 177 P6
Shah Malan, Afghan. 177 Q4
Shah Maqsud Range, Afghan. 177 P5
Shahpur, India 178 M5
Shahpur, Pak. 177 PIO
Shahpur Chakar, Pak. 177 V7
Shahr-e Bābak, Iran 173 FI4
Shahrezā (Qomsheh), Iran 173 EI3
Shahrig, Pak. 177 R6
Shahrisabz, Uzb. 174 LI2
Shāhrūd, Iran 173 CI4
Shaighalu, Pak. 177 Q7

Shajapur, India 178 J5
Shakhbuz, Azerb. 169 EI9
Shakhtakhty, Azerb. 169 FI9
Shakhtersk, Russ. 159 J2I
Shakhty, Russ. 157 QII
Shakhun'ya, Russ. 156 GI3
Shaktoolik, Alas., U.S. III GI3
Shali, Russ. 157 UI4
Shallowater, Tex., U.S. 102 K5
Shalqar, Kaz. 174 F9
Shalqar Köli, Kaz. 174 D6
Shām, Jabal ash, Oman 173 KI6
Shamattawa, Man., Can. 83 LI5
Shambe, Sudan 198 GI2
Shamkhor, Azerb. 169 D2O
Shammar, Jabal, Saudi Arabia 172 G7
Shamokin, Pa., U.S. 94 N8
Shamrock, Tex., U.S. 102 G7
Shamva, Zimb. 202 FI2
Shandan, China 180 HII
Shandong Bandao, China 182 F9
Shandur Pass, Pak. 176 LIO
Shangcai, China 182 J5
Shangcheng, China 182 K6
Shangchuan Dao, China 183 S4
Shangdu, China 182 B5
Shanghai, China 182 KIO
Shanghang, China 183 Q6
Shangnan, China 182 H3
Shangombo, Zambia 202 F8
Shangqiu, China 182 H6
Shangrao, China 182 M7
Shangxian, China 182 H2
Shangyi, China 182 C5
Shangyou, China 183 Q4
Shaniko, Oreg., U.S. 108 G5
Shannon, Ire. 143 T4
Shannon, River, Ire. 143 T3
Shantar Islands, Russ. 166 DI2
Shantarskiye Ostrova, Russ. 159 H2O
Shantou (Swatow), China 183 R6
Shanxian, China 182 H6
Shanyang, China 182 H2
Shanyin, China 182 D5
Shanyincheng, China 182 D5
Shaoguan, China 183 Q4
Shaowu, China 183 N7
Shaoxing, China 182 L9
Shaoyang, China 183 N3
Shap, Eng., U.K. 143 QII
Shapa, China 183 S3
Shapinsay, island, Scot., U.K. 142 FIO
Shaqrā', Saudi Arabia 172 JIO
Shaqrā', Yemen 172 RIO
Shar, Kaz. 175 DI7
Shār, Jabal, Saudi Arabia 172 G5
Sharan, Afghan. 177 N7
Sharâtîb, Râs, Egypt 171 T2
Sharbaqty, Kaz. 175 CI6
Sharbatāt, Oman 173 NI5
Sharbatāt, Ra's ash, Oman 173 NI5
Sharhulsan, Mongolia 180 EI2
Shari, Japan 184 EI6
Sharjah, U.A.E. 173 JI5
Sharkan, Russ. 156 GI6
Shark Bay, W. Aust., Austral. 211 VI
Sharlawuk, Turkm. 174 L7
Sharm el Sheikh, Egypt 171 U4
Sharon, Pa., U.S. 94 M3
Sharon Springs, Kans., U.S. 105 S3
Sharpe, Lake, S. Dak., U.S. 104 L5
Sharqī, Al Jabal ash (Anti-Lebanon), Leb., Syr. 170 H7
Sharuhen, ruin, Israel 171 N4
Sharwayn, Ra's, Yemen 173 QI3
Shar'ya, Russ. 156 GI3
Shashe, river, Botswana, Zimb. 202 HII
Shashi, China 182 L4
Shasta, Mount, Calif., U.S. 108 M4
Shasta Lake, Calif., U.S. 108 M4
Shatskiy Rise, Pac. Oc. 238 F7
Shatt al Arab, river, Iran, Iraq 172 FII
Shattuck, Okla., U.S. 102 F7
Shaumyan, Azerb. 169 D2O
Shaumyani, Rep. of Georgia 169 CI8
Shaunavon, Sask., Can. 82 NII
Shaw, Miss., U.S. 100 JIO
Shawano, Wis., U.S. 98 J6
Shawinigan, Que., Can. 83 PI9
Shawnee, Kans., U.S. 105 SIO
Shawnee, Okla., U.S. 102 GII
Shaxian, China 183 P7
Shaybārā, island, Saudi Arabia 172 J6
Shay Gap, W. Aust., Austral. 211 S3
Shaykh 'Uthmān, Yemen 172 R9

Shayman, Taj. 176 JI2
Shchekino, Russ. 156 K9
Shchigry, Russ. 156 M9
Shchūchīnsk, Kaz. 175 CI3
Shebar Pass, Afghan. 176 M7
Shebekino, Russ. 157 N9
Shebelē, Wabē, Eth. 199 HI6
Sheberghan, Afghan. 176 K5
Shebir, Kaz. 174 G6
Sheboygan, Wis., U.S. 98 K7
Sheboygan Falls, Wis., U.S. 98 K7
Sheelin, Lough, Ire. 143 R6
Sheep Haven, Ire. 143 N5
Sheep Mountain, Colo., U.S. 106 LII
Sheep Range, Nev., U.S. 109 TI2
Sheerness, Eng., U.K. 143 VI5
Shefar'am, Israel 170 K5
Sheffield, Ala., U.S. 101 GI4
Sheffield, Eng., U.K. 143 SI2
Sheffield, Tex., U.S. 103 P5
Shekhupura, Pak. 177 QII
Shelbina, Mo., U.S. 105 RI3
Shelburne, N.S., Can. 83 Q22
Shelby, Mich., U.S. 98 K9
Shelby, Miss., U.S. 100 JIO
Shelby, Mont., U.S. 106 B7
Shelby, N.C., U.S. 96 J8
Shelby, Ohio, U.S. 99 PI3
Shelbyville, Ill., U.S. 99 S6
Shelbyville, Ind., U.S. 99 S9
Shelbyville, Ky., U.S. 101 DI4
Shelbyville, Tenn., U.S. 101 FI5
Sheldon, Iowa, U.S. 104 M9
Sheldon Point, Alas., U.S. IIO HII
Shelikhova, Zaliv, Russ. 159 E2I
Shelikhov Gulf, Russ. 166 BI2
Shelikof Strait, Alas., U.S. III LI5
Shell Beach, Guyana 129 CI4
Shelley, Idaho, U.S. 106 H7
Shell Lake, Wis., U.S. 98 G2
Shellman, Ga., U.S. 97 P5
Shelter Cove, Calif., U.S. 109 NI
Shelton, Nebr., U.S. 105 Q6
Shelton, Wash., U.S. 108 C3
Shemakha, Azerb. 169 D22
Shemonaïkha, Kaz. 175 DI8
Shemya Island, Alas., U.S. III L2
Shenandoah, Iowa, U.S. 105 Q9
Shenandoah, Pa., U.S. 94 N8
Shenandoah, Va., U.S. 96 DII
Shenandoah National Park, Va., U.S. 96 DII
Shenchi, China 182 D4
Shendam, Nigeria 201 GI5
Shengxian, China 182 M9
Shenmu, China 182 D3
Shennongjia, China 182 K3
Shenqiu, China 182 J6
Shenyang, China 182 BII
Shenzhen, China 183 S5
Sheoganj, India 178 H3
Sheopur, India 178 G5
Shepetivka, Ukr. 157 N4
Shepherd, Ill., U.S. 99 R9
Shepherd Islands, Vanuatu 218 E3
Shepparton, Vic., Austral. 211 YI2
Sheppey, Isle of, Eng., U.K. 143 VI5
Sherbo Island, Sierra Leone 200 G5
Sherbrooke, Que., Can. 83 P2O
Sherburn, Minn., U.S. 104 LIO
Shereiq, Sudan 199 CI3
Sheridan, Ark., U.S. 100 H8
Sheridan, Wyo., U.S. 106 FII
Sheridan, Cape, Nunavut, Can. 83 AI7
Sheringham, Eng., U.K. 143 SI5
Sherkaly, Russ. 158 GIO
Sherkin Island, Ire. 143 V3
Sherlovaya, Russ. 159 LI7
Sherman, Tex., U.S. 102 KI2
Sherman Mills, Me., U.S. 95 DI8
Sherman Peak, Idaho, U.S. 84 E7
Sherobod, Uzb. 174 MI2
Sherridon, Man., Can. 83 LI3
's Hertogenbosch, Neth. 146 KI3
Sherwood, N. Dak., U.S. 104 D4
Sherwood Forest, Eng., U.K. 143 SI3
Shetland Islands (Zetland), Scot., U.K. 142 CI2
Shetpe, Kaz. 174 H6
Shexian, China 182 M8
Sheyang (Hede), China 182 H9
Sheyenne, river, N. Dak., U.S. 104 F7
Sheyenne, N. Dak., U.S. 104 F6
Shiant Islands, Scot., U.K. 142 J7
Shiashkotan, island, Russ. 159 H23

Shibām, *Yemen* 172 P11
Shibata, *Japan* 184 M12
Shibecha, *Japan* 184 F15
Shibetsu, *Japan* 184 E14
Shibetsu, *Japan* 184 F16
Shibushi Wan, *Japan* 185 T5
Shicheng, *China* 183 P6
Shidao, *China* 182 F10
Shidler, *Okla., U.S.* 102 E12
Shiel, Loch, *Scot., U.K.* 142 L8
Shiel Bridge, *Scot., U.K.* 142 K8
Shīeli, *Kaz.* 174 H12
Shiguai, *China* 182 C3
Shiḥan, *Yemen* 173 N13
Shihezi, *China* 180 E7
Shijiazhuang, *China* 182 E5
Shikarpur, *India* 178 G9
Shikarpur, *Pak.* 177 T7
Shikine Shima, *Japan* 185 Q12
Shikoku, island, *Japan* 185 R7
Shikotan, island, *Russ.* 159 K23
Shikotsu Ko, *Japan* 184 G13
Shildon, *Eng., U.K.* 143 P12
Shīli, *Kaz.* 174 D10
Shiliguri, *India* 178 G11
Shilik, *Kaz.* 175 H17
Shiliu *see* Changjiang, *China* 183 U1
Shilka, *Russ.* 159 L17
Shilla, peak, *India* 177 P15
Shillong, *India* 178 G13
Shiloh National Military Park, *Tenn., U.S.* 101 G13
Shilou, *China* 182 F3
Shilovo, *Russ.* 156 K11
Shimabara, *Japan* 185 S4
Shimada, *Japan* 185 Q11
Shima Hantō, *Japan* 185 Q10
Shimanovsk, *Russ.* 159 K19
Shimen, *China* 182 L3
Shimizu, *Japan* 184 F14
Shimizu, *Japan* 185 Q11
Shimoda, *Japan* 185 Q11
Shimoga, *India* 179 P4
Shimokoshiki, *Japan* 185 T3
Shimonoseki, *Japan* 185 R5
Shimono Shima, *Japan* 185 Q3
Shin, Loch, *Scot., U.K.* 142 H9
Shinapaaru, *N. Mariana Is., U.S.* 216 D8
Shināṣ, *Oman* 173 J15
Shindand, *Afghan.* 177 N2
Shiner, *Tex., U.S.* 103 R11
Shingbwiyang, *Myanmar* 186 D6
Shingphel, *Bhutan* 178 F13
Shingū, *Japan* 185 R9
Shinjō, *Japan* 184 L12
Shinkay, *Afghan.* 177 Q6
Shinkay Hills, *Afghan.* 177 P7
Shinkolobwe, *Dem. Rep. of the Congo* 198 N11
Shinnston, *W. Va., U.S.* 96 C9
Shinonoi, *Japan* 185 N11
Shinoússa, island, *Gr.* 155 M15
Shinyanga, *Tanzania* 199 L13
Shiono Misaki, *Japan* 185 R9
Shiping, *China* 180 P11
Ship Island, *Miss., U.S.* 100 P12
Shippensburg, *Pa., U.S.* 94 P6
Ship Rock, *N. Mex., U.S.* 107 Q10
Shiprock, *N. Mex., U.S.* 107 Q10
Shipu, *China* 182 M10
Shiquan, *China* 182 J1
Shiquanhe, *China* 180 J4
Shirakami Misaki, *Japan* 184 H12
Shirase Coast, *Antarctica* 226 M10
Shirase Glacier, *Antarctica* 227 C17
Shīrāz, *Iran* 173 F13
Shire, river, *Malawi* 203 F13
Shireet, *Mongolia* 181 E14
Shiren, *China* 182 B13
Shiretoko Misaki, *Japan* 184 E16
Shiriya Zaki, *Japan* 184 H13
Shir Khan, *Afghan.* 176 K7
Shīr Kūh, peak, *Iran* 173 H14
Shirley, Cape, *Antigua & Barbuda* 121 C21
Shiroishi, *Japan* 184 M13
Shirone, *Japan* 184 M11
Shirshov Ridge, *Pac. Oc.* 238 B9
Shishaldin Volcano, *Alas., U.S.* 110 N11
Shishmaref, *Alas., U.S.* 110 E12
Shishou, *China* 182 L4
Shitai, *China* 182 L7
Shiv, *India* 178 G2
Shivpuri, *India* 178 H6

Shivta, ruin, *Israel* 171 P4
Shivwits Plateau, *Ariz., U.S.* 107 R5
Shixian, *China* 182 A14
Shiyan, *China* 182 J3
Shíza, island, *Gr.* 154 M9
Shizhu, *China* 182 L1
Shizuishan, *China* 182 D1
Shizunai, *Japan* 184 G14
Shizuoka, *Japan* 185 Q11
Shkin, *Afghan.* 177 P8
Shkodër (Scutari), *Albania* 152 K9
Shkumbin, river, *Albania* 152 L9
Shmidta, Ostrov, *Russ.* 159 C14
Shoals, Isles of, *Me., N.H., U.S.* 95 J15
Shoghot, *Pak.* 176 L10
Sholapur, *India* 178 M5
Shollar, *Azerb.* 169 C22
Shonian Harbor, *Palau* 216 P11
Shonzhy, *Kaz.* 175 H17
Sho'rchi, *Uzb.* 174 M12
Shoreham by Sea, *Eng., U.K.* 143 W14
Shorkot, *Pak.* 177 Q10
Shorobe, *Botswana* 202 G9
Shortland, island, *Solomon Is.* 217 L14
Shortland Islands, *Solomon Is.* 217 L14
Shosambetsu, *Japan* 184 E13
Shoshone, *Calif., U.S.* 109 U10
Shoshone, *Idaho, U.S.* 106 H5
Shoshone, river, *Wyo., U.S.* 106 F10
Shoshone Falls, *Idaho, U.S.* 84 E6
Shoshone Lake, *Wyo., U.S.* 106 G8
Shoshone Mountain, *Nev., U.S.* 109 T10
Shoshone Mountains, *Nev., U.S.* 109 Q9
Shoshone Range, *Nev., U.S.* 109 N10
Shoshoni, *Wyo., U.S.* 106 H10
Shostka, *Ukr.* 156 M7
Shotor Khun Pass, *Afghan.* 176 M4
Shoval, *Israel* 171 N5
Shōwa, *Japan* 184 K12
Show Low, *Ariz., U.S.* 107 T9
Shpola, *Ukr.* 157 P6
Shreveport, *La., U.S.* 100 L6
Shroud Cay, *Bahamas* 116 E12
Shū, river, *Kaz.* 175 H14
Shū, *Kaz.* 175 H15
Shū'ab, Ra's, *Yemen* 173 R14
Shuangcheng, *China* 181 D17
Shuangchengzi, *China* 180 G10
Shuangliao, *China* 182 A11
Shuangyang, *China* 182 A12
Shuangyashan, *China* 181 C18
Shubarqudyq, *Kaz.* 174 E8
Shucheng, *China* 182 K7
Shugozero, *Russ.* 156 F8
Shukpa Kunzang, *India* 176 M15
Shule, river, *China* 180 G9
Shulgareh, *Afghan.* 176 L6
Shumagin Islands, *Alas., U.S.* 110 N12
Shumanay, *Uzb.* 174 J9
Shumen (Kolarovgrad), *Bulg.* 153 H16
Shumerlya, *Russ.* 156 J13
Shumshu, island, *Russ.* 159 G23
Shunchang, *China* 183 P7
Shungay, *Kaz.* 174 E4
Shungnak, *Alas., U.S.* 111 E14
Shuozhou, *China* 182 D4
Shupenzë, *Albania* 152 K10
Shuqualak, *Miss., U.S.* 101 K13
Shuraabad, *Azerb.* 169 C23
Shūrāb, *Iran* 173 D15
Shurakian, *Afghan.* 177 P4
Shūr Gaz, *Iran* 173 G16
Shurma, *Russ.* 156 H15
Shur Tappeh, *Afghan.* 176 K6
Shurugwi, *Zimb.* 202 G11
Shūsf, *Iran* 173 E17
Shūshtar, *Iran* 172 E11
Shuya, *Russ.* 156 H11
Shuyak Island, *Alas., U.S.* 111 L15
Shuyang, *China* 182 H8
Shwebo, *Myanmar* 186 G6
Shwedaung, *Myanmar* 186 J5
Shwegu, *Myanmar* 186 F6
Shwegyin, *Myanmar* 186 K6
Shweli, river, *Myanmar* 186 F7
Shymkent, *Kaz.* 175 J13
Shyngghyrlau, *Kaz.* 174 D7
Shyok, *India* 176 M15
Shyok, river, *Pak.* 176 L13
Sia, *Indonesia* 189 M19
Siahan Range, *Pak.* 177 U4
Sialkot, *Pak.* 177 P12
Siantan, island, *Indonesia* 188 H8

Siapa, river, *Venez.* 128 G11
Siargao, island, *Philippines* 189 E15
Siátista, *Gr.* 154 D9
Siau, island, *Indonesia* 189 H15
Šiauliai, *Lith.* 141 M16
Sibari, *It.* 151 P13
Sibay, *Russ.* 158 J8
Šibenik, *Croatia* 152 G6
Siberia, region, *Russ.* 166 D8
Siberut, island, *Indonesia* 188 J5
Siberut, Selat, *Indonesia* 188 J5
Sibi, *Pak.* 177 S7
Sibidiro, *P.N.G.* 213 E18
Sibigo, *Indonesia* 188 H4
Sibiti, *Congo* 201 M16
Sibiu, *Rom.* 153 D13
Siboa, *Indonesia* 189 J13
Sibolga, *Indonesia* 188 H5
Sibsagar, *India* 178 F15
Sibu, *Malaysia* 188 H10
Sibuco, *Philippines* 189 F14
Sibut, *Cen. Af. Rep.* 198 H9
Sibutu Passage, *Malaysia, Philippines* 189 G13
Sibuyan, island, *Philippines* 189 D14
Sibuyan Sea, *Philippines* 189 D14
Sicasica, *Bol.* 130 K6
Sichon, *Thai.* 187 Q8
Sichuan Basin, *China* 166 H10
Sicié, Cap, *Fr.* 147 Y14
Sicilia (Sicily), island, *It.* 151 S10
Sicily *see* Sicilia, island, *It.* 151 S10
Sicily, Strait of, *It.* 151 T7
Sicuani, *Peru* 130 J5
Sidári, *Gr.* 154 E6
Sidas, *Indonesia* 188 J9
Siddhapur, *India* 178 H3
Siddipet, *India* 178 M6
Side, ruin, *Turk.* 168 J6
Síderos, Akrotírio, *Gr.* 155 Q17
Sîdi Barrâni, *Egypt* 197 C17
Sidi Bel Abbès, *Alg.* 196 A10
Sidi Ifni, *Mor.* 196 C7
Sidirókastro, *Gr.* 154 B12
Sidlaw Hills, *Scot., U.K.* 142 L10
Sidmouth, *Eng., U.K.* 143 X10
Sidmouth, Cape, *Austral.* 210 B12
Sidney, *Iowa, U.S.* 105 Q9
Sidney, *Mont., U.S.* 106 C13
Sidney, *N.Y., U.S.* 94 K9
Sidney, *Nebr., U.S.* 105 P2
Sidney, *Ohio, U.S.* 99 Q11
Sidney Lanier, Lake, *Ga., U.S.* 96 K5
Sidon *see* Saïda, *Leb.* 170 J6
Sidorovsk, *Russ.* 158 G12
Sidra, Gulf of, *Lib.* 197 C14
Siedlce, *Pol.* 149 E17
Siegen, *Ger.* 148 F6
Siemiatycze, *Pol.* 149 D17
Siem Pang, *Cambodia* 186 M12
Siem Reap, *Cambodia* 187 N11
Siena, *It.* 150 H7
Sieradz, *Pol.* 149 E14
Sierck, *Fr.* 160 L11
Sierpc, *Pol.* 149 D15
Sierra Blanca, *Tex., U.S.* 103 V3
Sierra Blanca Peak, *N. Mex., U.S.* 107 U13
Sierra Colorada, *Arg.* 133 P8
Sierra Leone, *Af.* 195 H14
Sierra Mojada, *Mex.* 114 E10
Sierra Nevada, range, *Calif., U.S.* 109 P5
Sierra Vista, *Ariz., U.S.* 107 W8
Sierre, *Switz.* 150 C2
Sífnos, island, *Gr.* 155 L14
Sigatoka, *Fiji Is.* 218 J5
Sigavé (Leava), *Wallis & Futuna, Fr.* 218 E11
Sigave, Anse de, *Wallis & Futuna, Fr.* 218 E11
Sigean, *Fr.* 147 Y10
Siġġiewi, *Malta* 161 L22
Sighetul Marmatiei, *Rom.* 153 A13
Sighişoara, *Rom.* 153 D14
Sighnaghi, *Rep. of Georgia* 169 C19
Siglufjördur, *Ice.* 140 E3
Signal Hill, *Gibraltar, U.K.* 161 P23
Signal Peak, *Ariz., U.S.* 107 U5
Sigourney, *Iowa, U.S.* 105 P13
Sigri, *Gr.* 155 F16
Sigüenza, *Sp.* 144 E12
Siguer, Pic de, *Andorra, Fr.* 160 G3
Siguer, Port de, *Andorra, Fr.* 160 G3
Siguiri, *Guinea* 200 E7

Sihanoukville, *Cambodia* 187 P11
Sihora, *India* 178 J7
Sihui, *China* 183 R4
Siirt, *Turk.* 169 G16
Siis, island, *F.S.M.* 217 C15
Sikar, *India* 178 F5
Sikasso, *Mali* 196 J7
Sikeston, *Mo., U.S.* 105 V16
Sikhote Alin' Range, *Russ.* 166 E13
Síkinos, island, *Gr.* 155 M14
Síkinos, *Gr.* 155 M15
Siki Rangi Passage, *Cook Is., N.Z.* 219 A17
Sil, river, *Sp.* 144 C7
Silat, *Indonesia* 188 J10
Silba, island, *Croatia* 152 F4
Silchar, *India* 178 H14
Siler City, *N.C., U.S.* 96 H10
Silesia, region, *Pol.* 148 F13
Silet, *Alg.* 196 F11
Silgarhi, *Nepal* 178 E8
Silhouette, island, *Seychelles* 205 N19
Silifke, *Turk.* 168 J9
Siling Co, *China* 180 K7
Silisili, Mount, *Samoa* 218 K2
Silistra, *Bulg.* 153 G16
Silivri, *Turk.* 168 C4
Siljan, lake, *Sw.* 141 K13
Silkeborg, *Den.* 140 N11
Silla, *Sp.* 145 H14
Sillon de Talbert, *Fr.* 147 P4
Siloam Springs, *Ark., U.S.* 100 E6
Silogui, *Indonesia* 188 J5
Silopi, *Turk.* 169 H16
Silsbee, *Tex., U.S.* 103 P15
Silum, *Liech.* 160 P3
Silvan, *Turk.* 169 G15
Silvânia, *Braz.* 131 J13
Silvassa, *India* 178 K3
Silver Bay, *Minn., U.S.* 104 F13
Silver Bell, *Ariz., U.S.* 107 V7
Silver City, *Idaho, U.S.* 106 H3
Silver City, *Mich., U.S.* 98 E5
Silver City, *N. Mex., U.S.* 107 U10
Silver City, *Nev., U.S.* 109 Q6
Silver Creek, *Oreg., U.S.* 108 H6
Silver Hill, *Montserrat, U.K.* 121 A23
Silver Lake, *Oreg., U.S.* 108 J5
Silver Peak, *Nev., U.S.* 109 S9
Silver Plains, *Qnsld., Austral.* 211 P12
Silver Spring, *Md., U.S.* 96 C13
Silverton, *Colo., U.S.* 107 P11
Silverton, *Oreg., U.S.* 108 F3
Silverton, *Tex., U.S.* 102 H6
Silves, *Braz.* 130 D10
Silvies, river, *Oreg., U.S.* 108 H7
Sima, *Comoros* 205 N16
Simansih, *Indonesia* 188 K5
Simao, *China* 180 P10
Şīmareh, river, *Iran* 172 D11
Simav, river, *Turk.* 168 D4
Simav, *Turk.* 168 F5
Simbo, island, *Solomon Is.* 217 M15
Simcoe, Lake, *Ont., Can.* 83 Q18
Simdega, *India* 178 J9
Simeria, *Rom.* 152 D12
Simeulue, island, *Indonesia* 188 H4
Simferopol', *Ukr.* 157 S7
Sími, island, *Gr.* 155 M19
Sími, *Gr.* 155 M19
Simikot, *Nepal* 178 E8
Simi Valley, *Calif., U.S.* 109 X8
Simla, *Colo., U.S.* 106 M14
Simla, *India* 178 D6
Şimleu Silvaniei, *Rom.* 152 B12
Simms Point, *Bahamas* 120 B10
Simonsbaai *see* Simson Bay, *Neth. Antilles, Neth.* 121 B14
Simon's Point, *Bahamas* 120 F9
Simontornya, *Hung.* 149 M14
Simpang, *Indonesia* 188 J7
Simpson Desert, *N. Terr., Austral.* 211 U9
Simpson Peninsula, *Nunavut, Can.* 83 F15
Simrishamn, *Sw.* 141 N13
Simson Baai, *Neth. Antilles, Neth.* 121 B14
Simson Bay (Simsonbaai), *Neth. Antilles, Neth.* 121 B14
Simson Bay Lagoon, *St. Martin, Fr.* 121 B14
Simushir, island, *Russ.* 159 H23
Sinai, peninsula, *Egypt* 171 R3
Sinai, region, *Egypt* 197 C19

Sinai, Mount *see* Mûsa, Gebel, *Egypt* 171 T3
Sinai, Mount, *Grenada* 121 L22
Sinan, *China* 182 M1
Sinbang-ni, *N. Korea* 182 C13
Sinbaungwe, *Myanmar* 186 J5
Sincelejo, *Col.* 128 C4
Sinclair, *Wyo., U.S.* 106 J11
Sinclair, Lake, *Ga., U.S.* 96 M6
Sinclair's Bay, *Scot., U.K.* 142 G10
Sin Cowe Island, *Spratly Is.* 188 E11
Sındırgı, *Turk.* 168 E4
Sindoa, Mont, *New Caledonia, Fr.* 218 D8
Sinegorskiy, *Russ.* 157 Q11
Sines, *Port.* 144 K5
Sines, Cabo de, *Port.* 144 K5
Singa, *Sudan* 199 E13
Singapore, *Asia* 167 Y11
Singapore, *Singapore* 188 H7
Singapore Strait, *Indonesia, Singapore* 188 H7
Singaraja, *Indonesia* 188 M11
Singavi, Mont, *Wallis & Futuna, Fr.* 218 E11
Sing Buri, *Thai.* 186 M8
Singen, *Ger.* 148 K6
Singida, *Tanzania* 199 L13
Singkaling Hkāmti, *Myanmar* 186 E6
Singkawang, *Indonesia* 188 J9
Singkep, island, *Indonesia* 188 J7
Singleton, *N.S.W., Austral.* 211 X14
Sinh Ho, *Vietnam* 186 G10
Siniscola, *It.* 150 M5
Sini Vrükh, peak, *Bulg.* 153 K14
Sinj, *Croatia* 152 G6
Sinjai, *Indonesia* 189 L13
Sinjār, *Iraq* 172 C8
Sinkat, *Sudan* 199 C14
Sinkiang, region, *China* 180 F5
Sinnamary, *Fr. Guiana, Fr.* 129 E17
Sinnar, *India* 178 L4
Sînnicolau Mare, *Rom.* 152 D10
Sinó, Ponto do, *Cape Verde* 205 B17
Sinoe, Lacul, *Rom.* 153 F18
Sinop, *Braz.* 130 H11
Sinop (Sinope), *Turk.* 168 C10
Sinop Burnu, *Turk.* 168 B10
Sinope *see* Sinop, *Turk.* 168 C10
Sinp'o, *N. Korea* 182 C14
Sinsheim, *Ger.* 148 H6
Sintang, *Indonesia* 188 J10
Sint Nicolaas, *Aruba, Neth.* 121 R17
Sinton, *Tex., U.S.* 103 T11
Sinŭiju, *N. Korea* 182 D11
Sinzig, *Ger.* 148 G5
Siófok, *Hung.* 149 M14
Sion, *Switz.* 150 C2
Siorapaluk, *Greenland, Den.* 81 B19
Sioux Center, *Iowa, U.S.* 104 M9
Sioux City, *Iowa, U.S.* 105 N8
Sioux Falls, *S. Dak., U.S.* 104 L8
Sioux Lookout, *Ont., Can.* 83 N15
Sioux Rapids, *Iowa, U.S.* 104 M8
Sipapo, Cerro, *Venez.* 128 E9
Siparia, *Trinidad & Tobago* 121 Q22
Siping, *China* 182 A11
Sipiwesk, *Man., Can.* 83 L14
Siple, Mount, *Antarctica* 226 M7
Siple Coast, *Antarctica* 226 L11
Siple Island, *Antarctica* 226 M7
Sipura, island, *Indonesia* 188 K5
Sira, *India* 179 P5
Siracusa (Syracuse), *It.* 151 T12
Şiran, *Turk.* 169 E14
Sirdaryo, *Uzb.* 175 K13
Sir Edward Pellew Group, *Austral.* 210 C10
Siret, river, *Rom.* 153 E17
Siri, Gebel, *Egypt* 194 F9
Sirīk, *Iran* 173 H15
Sirik, Tanjong, *Malaysia* 188 H10
Sīrjān (Sa'īdābād), *Iran* 173 F15
Sirkka, *Fin.* 141 D14
Sirmaur, *India* 178 H8
Sírna, island, *Gr.* 155 N17
Şırnak, *Turk.* 169 H17
Síros, island, *Gr.* 155 K14
Sirsa, *India* 178 E5
Sir Thomas, Mount, *Austral.* 210 G7
Sirsi, *India* 178 L4
Sirur, *India* 178 L4
Şirvan, *Turk.* 169 G16
Sisak, *Croatia* 152 E6
Sisaket, *Thai.* 186 L11
Sisian, *Arm.* 169 E20

Siskiyou Mountains, *Calif., Oreg., U.S.* 108 L2
Sisophon, *Cambodia* 186 M10
Sisseton, *S. Dak., U.S.* 104 J8
Sissonne, *Fr.* 147 N11
Sīstān, region, *Iran* 173 E17
Sīstān, Daryācheh-ye, *Iran* 173 F17
Sister Bay, *Wis., U.S.* 98 H8
Sisteron, *Fr.* 147 W14
Sisters, *Oreg., U.S.* 108 G4
Sistersville, *W. Va., U.S.* 96 C8
Sistine Chapel, *Vatican City* 161 P16
Sitapur, *India* 178 F7
Sitges, *Sp.* 145 E17
Sithonía, peninsula, *Gr.* 154 D12
Sitía, *Gr.* 155 Q16
Sitian, *China* 180 F9
Sitio da Abadia, *Braz.* 131 J14
Sitka, *Alas., U.S.* III M22
Sitka National Historic Park, *Alas., U.S.* III M22
Sittard, *Neth.* 146 L13
Sittee, *Gr.* 154 NII
Sittwe (Akyab), *Myanmar* 186 H4
Siufaalele Point, *Amer. Samoa, U.S.* 218 P3
Siufaga, *Amer. Samoa, U.S.* 218 P3
Siulagi Point, *Amer. Samoa, U.S.* 218 N3
Siuri, *India* 178 H11
Siuslaw, river, *Oreg., U.S.* 108 H2
Sivac, *Serb.* 152 E9
Sivas, *Turk.* 168 E12
Siverek, *Turk.* 169 H14
Sivers'kyy Donets', river, *Ukr.* 157 P9
Sivrihisar, *Turk.* 168 E7
Sīwa, *Egypt* 197 D17
Siwalik Range, *India, Nepal* 178 C5
Siwan, *India* 178 G9
Sixaola, *Costa Rica* 115 N19
Six Feet, island, *Pitcairn I., U.K.* 219 Q23
Sixian, *China* 182 J7
Six Men's Bay, *Barbados* 121 J18
Sixth Cataract, *Sudan* 199 D13
Siyäzän, *Azerb.* 169 C22
Siziwang Qi, *China* 182 B4
Sjælland, island, *Den.* 140 P12
Sjenica, *Serb.* 152 H9
Skadarsko Jezero (Lake Scutari),
  Albania, Mont. 152 J9
Skagafjördur, *Ice.* 140 E3
Skagen, *Den.* 140 M11
Skagerrak, strait, *Den., Nor.* 140 M11
Skagit, river, *Wash., U.S.* 108 B5
Skagway, *Alas., U.S.* III K21
Skála, *Gr.* 154 M10
Skalistyy Golets, *Russ.* 159 K17
Skandzoúra, island, *Gr.* 155 G13
Škarda, island, *Croatia* 152 F4
Skardu, *Pak.* 176 L13
Skarżysko-Kamienna, *Pol.* 149 F16
Skawina, *Pol.* 149 H15
Skeena, river, *B.C., Can.* 82 J8
Skegness, *Eng., U.K.* 143 S14
Skeleton Coast, *Namibia* 202 G5
Skellefteå, *Sw.* 141 G14
Skellefteälven, river, *Sw.* 141 G13
Skerries, *Ire.* 143 R7
Skerryvore, island, *Scot., U.K.* 142 L6
Skíathos, island, *Gr.* 154 G12
Skíathos, *Gr.* 154 G12
Skiatook, *Okla., U.S.* 102 E12
Skidmore, *Tex., U.S.* 103 T11
Skídra, *Gr.* 154 C10
Skien, *Nor.* 140 L12
Skierniewice, *Pol.* 149 E15
Skikda, *Alg.* 196 A12
Skipton, *Eng., U.K.* 143 R11
Skíros, *Gr.* 155 G13
Skíros (Scyros), island, *Gr.* 155 G13
Skive, *Den.* 140 N11
Skokholm Island, *Wales, U.K.* 143 V8
Skokie, *Ill., U.S.* 99 N7
Skomer Island, *Wales, U.K.* 143 V8
Skomv r, island, *Nor.* 140 E11
Skópelos, island, *Gr.* 154 G12
Skópelos, *Gr.* 154 G12
Skopin, *Russ.* 156 L10
Skopje, *Maced.* 152 K11
Skopunarfjørdur, bay, *Faroe Is., Den.* 140 J6
Skouriotissa, *Cyprus* 160 P7
Skövde, *Sw.* 140 L12
Skovorodino, *Russ.* 159 K18

Skudeneshavn, *Nor.* 140 L9
Skunk, river, *Iowa, U.S.* 105 P13
Skvyra, *Ukr.* 157 P5
Skye, Island of, *Scot., U.K.* 142 K7
Skykomish, *Wash., U.S.* 108 C5
Slantsy, *Russ.* 156 F5
Slater, *Mo., U.S.* 105 S12
Slatina, *Rom.* 153 F14
Slaton, *Tex., U.S.* 102 K5
Slave, river, *Alta., Can.* 82 J11
Slave Coast, *Af.* 194 J4
Slavgorod, *Belarus* 156 L6
Slavonia, region, *Croatia* 152 E7
Slavonska Požega, *Croatia* 152 E7
Slavonski Brod, *Croatia* 152 E8
Slavuta, *Ukr.* 157 N4
Sławno, *Pol.* 148 B12
Slayton, *Minn., U.S.* 104 L9
Sleaford, *Eng., U.K.* 143 S13
Sleat, Sound of, *Scot., U.K.* 142 K7
Sleeper Islands, *Nunavut, Can.* 83 K17
Sleeping Bear Dunes National
  Lakeshore, *Mich., U.S.* 98 H9
Sleepy Eye, *Minn., U.S.* 104 K10
Sleetmute, *Alas., U.S.* III J14
Slessor Glacier, *Antarctica* 226 E11
Slide Mountain, *N.Y., U.S.* 94 L10
Slidell, *La., U.S.* 100 P11
Sliema, *Malta* 161 K23
Slieve Aughty Mountains, *Ire.* 143 S4
Slieve Gamph (The Ox Mountains), *Ire.* 143 Q4
Sligo, *Ire.* 143 Q4
Sligo Bay, *Ire.* 143 Q4
Slippery Rock, *Pa., U.S.* 94 M3
Slite, *Sw.* 141 M14
Sliven, *Bulg.* 153 J16
Sljeme, peak, *Croatia* 152 D6
Sloan, *Nev., U.S.* 109 U12
Slobozia, *Rom.* 153 F16
Slonim, *Belarus* 156 L3
Slough, *Eng., U.K.* 143 V13
Slovakia, *Eur.* 139 U8
Slovenia, *Eur.* 139 V7
Slov''yans'k, *Ukr.* 157 P9
Słupsk, *Pol.* 149 B13
Slutsk, *Belarus* 156 L4
Slyudyanka, *Russ.* 159 L15
Smackover, *Ark., U.S.* 100 J8
Smallan, *Pak.* 177 R7
Smallwood Reservoir, *Nfld. & Lab., Can.* 83 L21
Smalyavichy, *Belarus* 156 K5
Smara, *W. Sahara, Mor.* 196 D6
Smederevo, *Serb.* 152 F10
Smederevska Palanka, *Serb.* 152 F10
Smeïda see Taoudenni, *Mali* 196 E8
Smerwick Harbour, *Ire.* 143 U2
Smethport, *Pa., U.S.* 94 L5
Smidovich, *Russ.* 158 D11
Smidovich, *Russ.* 159 K20
Smila, *Ukr.* 157 P6
Smiltene, *Latv.* 141 L17
Smith see Sumisu Jima, island, *Japan* 184 J5
Smith, river, *Mont., U.S.* 106 C8
Smith Arm, *N.W.T., Can.* 82 F10
Smith Bay, *Alas., U.S.* III B15
Smith Bay, *Nunavut, Can.* 83 C16
Smith Center, *Kans., U.S.* 105 R6
Smithers, *B.C., Can.* 82 K8
Smithfield, *N.C., U.S.* 96 H12
Smithfield, *Utah, U.S.* 106 J7
Smithfield, *Va., U.S.* 96 F14
Smith Glacier, *Antarctica* 226 L7
Smith Island, *Nunavut, Can.* 83 J17
Smith Mountain Lake, *Va., U.S.* 96 F10
Smith River, *B.C., Can.* 82 H9
Smith River, *Calif., U.S.* 108 L2
Smith Sound, *Nunavut, Can.* 83 C16
Smithville, *Tex., U.S.* 103 Q11
Smoke Creek Desert, *Nev., U.S.* 109 N6
Smoky, river, *Alta., Can.* 82 L9
Smoky Bay, *S. Aust., Austral.* 211 X8
Smoky Hill, river, *Kans., U.S.* 105 T6
Smoky Hills, *Kans., U.S.* 105 S6
Smoky Mountains, *Idaho, U.S.* 106 G5
Smøla, island, *Nor.* 140 H10
Smolensk, *Russ.* 156 K7
Smolensk-Moscow Upland, *Belarus, Russ.* 138 E10
Smólikas, peak, *Gr.* 154 D8
Smolyan, *Bulg.* 153 K14

Smyley Island, *Antarctica* 226 G6
Smyrna, *Del., U.S.* 96 C14
Smyrna, *Ga., U.S.* 96 L5
Smyrna, *Tenn., U.S.* 101 E15
Smyrna see İzmir, *Turk.* 168 F3
Snaefell, peak, *Isle of Man, U.K.* 143 Q9
Snake, river, *U.S.* 84 C5
Snake, river, *Yukon, Can.* 82 F9
Snake City, *Bahamas* 120 B6
Snake Point, *Anguilla, U.K.* 120 Q12
Snake Range, *Nev., U.S.* 109 Q13
Snake River Plain, *Idaho, U.S.* 106 H6
Snåsa, *Nor.* 140 G11
Sneads, *Fla., U.S.* 97 Q4
Sneek, *Neth.* 146 G13
Sneeuberg, peak, *S. Af.* 194 Q8
Snezhnogorsk, *Russ.* 159 G13
Sněžka, peak, *Czech Rep., Pol.* 148 G12
Snihurivka, *Ukr.* 157 R7
Snina, *Slovakia* 149 J17
Snøhetta, peak, *Nor.* 140 J11
Snohomish, *Wash., U.S.* 108 B4
Snoqualmie, *Wash., U.S.* 108 C4
Snoqualmie Pass, *Wash., U.S.* 108 C5
Snowdon, peak, *Wales, U.K.* 143 S9
Snowflake, *Ariz., U.S.* 107 T9
Snow Hill, *Md., U.S.* 96 D15
Snow Hill Island, *Antarctica* 226 C4
Snowville, *Utah, U.S.* 106 J6
Snowy, river, *Austral.* 210 M13
Snowy Mountain, *N.Y., U.S.* 94 H10
Snug Corner, *Bahamas* 117 H15
Snuol, *Cambodia* 187 N12
Snyder, *Okla., U.S.* 102 H9
Snyder, *Tex., U.S.* 102 L6
Soala see Sokolo, *Mali* 196 H7
Soalala, *Madagascar* 203 F16
Soanierana-Ivongo, *Madagascar* 203 F18
Soap Lake, *Wash., U.S.* 108 C7
Soay, island, *Scot., U.K.* 142 K7
Sobinka, *Russ.* 156 J10
Sobolevo, *Russ.* 156 L16
Sobradinho Reservoir, *S. Amer.* 126 F10
Sobral, *Braz.* 131 E16
Soča, river, *Slov.* 152 C4
Sochaczew, *Pol.* 149 E15
Sochi, *Russ.* 157 T11
Society Islands, *Fr. Polynesia, Fr.* 219 D14
Socompa, *Chile* 132 E8
Socorro, *Col.* 128 E6
Socorro, *N. Mex., U.S.* 107 T12
Socorro, *Tex., U.S.* 103 U2
Socorro, Isla, *Mex.* 114 H6
Socorro Island see Socorro, Isla,
  N. Amer. 80 N3
Socotra see Suquṭrá, island, *Yemen* 173 R14
Soc Trang, *Vietnam* 187 Q12
Soda Lake, *Calif., U.S.* 109 V11
Sodankylä, *Fin.* 141 E15
Soda Springs, *Idaho, U.S.* 106 H7
Soddy-Daisy, *Tenn., U.S.* 101 G17
Södertälje, *Sw.* 141 L14
Sodiri, *Sudan* 198 E12
Sodo, *Eth.* 199 G14
Sofádes, *Gr.* 154 F9
Sofia see Sofiya, *Bulg.* 153 J13
Sofiya (Sofia), *Bulg.* 153 J13
Sōfu Gan (Lot's Wife), island, *Japan* 184 K5
Sog, *China* 180 K8
Sogamoso, *Col.* 128 E6
Soganlı, river, *Turk.* 168 C8
Sognefjorden, bay, *Nor.* 140 K9
Sogo Nur, *China* 180 F11
Sohâg, *Egypt* 197 D18
Sohano, *P.N.G.* 217 J13
Soheuksando, island, *S. Korea* 182 H12
Soignies, *Belg.* 146 L11
Soissons, *Fr.* 147 N11
Sojat, *India* 178 G4
Sokcho, *S. Korea* 182 E14
Söke, *Turk.* 168 G3
Sokhumi (Sukhum), *Abkhazia* 169 A15
Sokodé, *Togo* 200 F11
Sokol, *Russ.* 156 F10
Sokol, *Russ.* 159 E16
Sokol, *Russ.* 159 F20

Sokółka, *Pol.* 149 C18
Sokolo (Soala), *Mali* 196 H7
Sokolov, *Czech Rep.* 148 G9
Sokołów Podlaski, *Pol.* 149 D17
Sokoto, river, *Nigeria* 200 E12
Sokoto, *Nigeria* 201 E13
Sol, Costa del, *Sp.* 144 M10
Sol, Ponta do, *Cape Verde* 205 C17
Sola, *Cuba* 116 J11
Solander Island, *N.Z.* 213 R15
Solano, Punta, *Col.* 128 E3
Sol de Julio, *Arg.* 132 H10
Soldeu, *Andorra* 160 H4
Soldotna, *Alas., U.S.* III K16
Soledad, *Calif., U.S.* 109 U4
Soledad, *Col.* 128 B5
Solenzara, *Fr.* 150 K4
Solhan, *Turk.* 169 F15
Soligalich, *Russ.* 156 F11
Solikamsk, *Russ.* 158 G9
Solimões (Amazonas), river, *Braz.* 130 D7
Solingen, *Ger.* 148 F5
Solitary Islands, *Austral.* 210 J15
Sollefteå, *Sw.* 141 H13
Sol'Iletsk, *Russ.* 158 J7
Solnechnogorsk, *Russ.* 156 J9
Solo, island, *Fiji Is.* 218 J7
Solok, *Indonesia* 188 J6
Solomon, river, *Kans., U.S.* 105 S7
Solomon, *Kans., U.S.* 105 S7
Solomon Islands, *Pac. Oc.* 214 H6
Solomon Sea, *P.N.G.* 213 D21
Solon Springs, *Wis., U.S.* 98 F3
Solor, island, *Indonesia* 189 M14
Solothurn, *Switz.* 150 A2
Solov'yevsk, *Russ.* 159 K18
Solsona, *Sp.* 145 D16
Šolta, island, *Croatia* 152 H6
Soltānābād, *Iran* 173 C16
Soltan Bagh, *Afghan.* 177 N7
Soltan-e Bakva, *Afghan.* 177 P3
Sol'tsy, *Russ.* 156 G6
Solunska Glava, *Maced.* 152 K11
Soluntum, ruin, *It.* 151 S10
Solvay, *N.Y., U.S.* 94 J8
Solway Firth, *Eng., Scot., U.K.* 143 P10
Solwezi, *Zambia* 202 D10
Solyanka, *Russ.* 156 M16
Solyplayas, *Canary Is.* 204 Q7
Soma, *Turk.* 168 E3
Sōma, *Japan* 184 M13
Somain, *Fr.* 146 M11
Somali, region, *Eth.* 199 G16
Somalia, *Af.* 195 J24
Somali Basin, *Ind. Oc.* 240 G6
Somaliland, region, *Somalia* 199 F17
Somali Peninsula, *Af.* 194 H12
Somaloma, Rochers, *Wallis & Futuna, Fr.* 218 E11
Sombor, *Serb.* 152 D9
Sombrero, island, *Anguilla, U.K.* 119 E15
Sombrero Channel, *India* 179 S15
Somers, *Mont., U.S.* 106 B5
Somerset, *Bermuda, U.K.* 120 B1
Somerset, *Colo., U.S.* 107 N11
Somerset, *Ky., U.S.* 101 D18
Somerset, *Pa., U.S.* 94 P4
Somerset Island, *Bermuda, U.K.* 120 B1
Somerset Island, *Nunavut, Can.* 83 E15
Somersworth, *N.H., U.S.* 95 H15
Somerton, *Ariz., U.S.* 107 V4
Somerville, *Tenn., U.S.* 100 G12
Somerville, *Tex., U.S.* 103 Q12
Someş, river, *Rom.* 152 B12
Sommariva, *Qnsld., Austral.* 211 V13
Somme, river, *Fr.* 146 M9
Somme, Baie de la, *Fr.* 146 M9
Somosomo, *Fiji Is.* 218 G8
Somosomo Strait, *Fiji Is.* 218 G8
Somuncurá, Meseta de, *Arg.* 133 Q9
Son, river, *India* 178 H9
Sōnbong, *N. Korea* 182 B15
Sŏnch'ŏn, *N. Korea* 182 D12
Sonda, *Pak.* 177 W7
Sondar, *India* 177 N10
Sønderborg, *Den.* 140 P11
Sondershausen, *Ger.* 148 F8
Sondrio, *It.* 150 C5
Song, *Malaysia* 188 H10
Song Cau, *Vietnam* 186 M14
Songea, *Tanzania* 199 N14
Songeons, *Fr.* 147 N9
Songhua, river, *China* 181 C18
Songhua Hu, *China* 182 A13

Songjiang, *China* 182 L10
Sŏngjin see Kimch'aek, *N. Korea* 182 C14
Songkhla, *Thai.* 187 R9
Song Ma, *Vietnam* 186 H10
Songnim, *N. Korea* 182 E12
Songsong (Rota), *N. Mariana Is., U.S.* 216 E7
Songxi, *China* 183 N8
Songxian, *China* 182 H4
Songzi, *China* 182 L3
Son Ha, *Vietnam* 186 L14
Son Hoa, *Vietnam* 187 N14
Sonid Youqi (SaihanTal), *China* 182 A5
Sonid Zuoqi (Mandalt), *China* 182 A5
Sonkovo, *Russ.* 156 H9
Son La, *Vietnam* 186 H11
Sonmiani, *Pak.* 177 V5
Sonmiani Bay, *Pak.* 177 W5
Sonneberg, *Ger.* 148 G8
Sonoma, *Calif., U.S.* 109 R3
Sonora, *Calif., U.S.* 109 R6
Sonora, *Tex., U.S.* 103 P6
Sonoran Desert, *Ariz., Calif., U.S.* 84 K6
Sonoran Desert National Monument, *Ariz., U.S.* 107 U6
Sonqor, *Iran* 172 D11
Sonseca, *Sp.* 144 G10
Sonsón, *Col.* 128 E5
Sonsonate, *El Salv.* 115 L16
Sonsorol Islands, *Palau* 214 F2
Soperton, *Ga., U.S.* 97 N7
Sophia-Antipolis, *Fr.* 147 X15
Sopot, *Pol.* 149 B14
Sopron, *Hung.* 149 L13
Sopur, *India* 176 M12
Sopwer, Mochun, *F.S.M.* 217 A15
Sopweru, island, *F.S.M.* 217 A15
Sora, *It.* 150 L10
Sorah, *Pak.* 177 U7
Soran, *Kaz.* 175 E14
Sorazocco, *San Marino* 161 J16
Sorbas, *Sp.* 144 L12
Soresina, *It.* 150 E5
Sorezaru Point, *Solomon Is.* 217 L15
Sorgono, *It.* 151 N4
Sorgues, *Fr.* 147 W13
Sorgun, *Turk.* 168 E10
Soria, *Sp.* 144 D12
Sorkh Ab, *Afghan.* 177 P3
Sorkh Kowtal Temple, ruin, *Afghan.* 176 L7
Sørkjosen, *Nor.* 141 C13
Sørli, *Nor.* 140 G12
Sorobon, *Neth. Antilles, Neth.* 121 R19
Soroca, *Mold.* 157 Q4
Sorocaba, *Braz.* 131 M13
Sorong, *Indonesia* 189 J17
Soroti, *Uganda* 199 J13
Sørøya, island, *Nor.* 141 C13
Sør Rondane Mountains, *Antarctica* 227 B15
Sorsele, *Sw.* 141 F13
Sorso, *It.* 150 M3
Sortavala, *Russ.* 158 D7
Sørvágur, *Faroe Is., Den.* 140 J5
Sosanjaya Bay, *N. Mariana Is., U.S.* 216 E7
Sosanlagh Bay, *N. Mariana Is., U.S.* 216 E7
Sosna, *Russ.* 159 J15
Sosnogorsk, *Russ.* 158 F9
Sosnovka, *Russ.* 156 H14
Sosnovka, *Russ.* 156 H15
Sosnovka, *Russ.* 156 L11
Sosnovo, *Russ.* 156 E6
Sosnovo Ozerskoye, *Russ.* 159 L16
Sosnowiec, *Pol.* 149 G15
Soso Bay, *Fiji Is.* 218 K6
Sos'va, *Russ.* 158 G10
Sos'va, *Russ.* 158 H9
Soto, *Neth. Antilles, Neth.* 121 P13
Souanké, *Congo* 201 K17
Soubré, *Côte d'Ivoire* 200 H8
Soucis, *St. Lucia* 121 K14
Soudan, *N. Terr., Austral.* 211 S10
Souflí, *Gr.* 155 B16
Soufrière, peak, *Guadeloupe, Fr.* 121 F14
Soufrière, *St. Lucia* 121 K13
Soufrière Bay, *St. Lucia* 121 K13

Soufriere Hills, *Montserrat, U.K.* 121 B23

Soufrière Mountains, *St. Vincent & the Grenadines* 121 JI6

Souillac, *Fr.* 147 V9

Souillac, *Mauritius* 205 H2O

Soúnion, ruin, *Gr.* 155 KI3

Soûr (Tyre), *Leb.* 170 K5

Sourdeval, *Fr.* 147 P6

Soure, *Braz.* 131 CI3

Souris (Mouse), river, *N. Dak., U.S.* 104 E4

Sour Lake, *Tex., U.S.* 103 QI5

Soúrpi, *Gr.* 154 GII

Sousa, *Braz.* 131 FI7

Sousel, *Port.* 144 H6

Sous le Vent, Îles, *Fr. Polynesia, Fr.* 219 EI4

Sousse, *Tun.* 197 AI3

South Africa, *Af.* 195 Q2O

South Alligator, river, *Austral.* 210 B8

South Ambo Channel, *Marshall Is.* 216 M5

Southampton, *Eng., U.K.* 143 WI2

Southampton, *N.Y., U.S.* 95 NI3

Southampton, Cape, *Nunavut, Can.* 83 JI6

Southampton Island, *Nunavut, Can.* 83 HI6

South Andaman, island, *India* 179 QI4

South Aulatsivik Island, *Nfld. & Lab., Can.* 83 K2I

South Australia, *Austral.* 211 V9

South Australian Basin, *Ind. Oc.* 241 NI7

South Australian Plain, *Antarctic Oc.* 245 PI7

Southaven, *Miss., U.S.* 100 GII

South Baldy, peak, *N. Mex., U.S.* 107 TII

South Bay, *Fla., U.S.* 97 VIO

South Bend, *Ind., U.S.* 99 N9

South Bend, *Wash., U.S.* 108 D2

South Bimini, island, *Bahamas* 120 C8

South Boston, *Va., U.S.* 96 GII

South Branch Potomac, river, *W. Va., U.S.* 96 CII

South Caicos, island, *Turks & Caicos Is., U.K.* 117 JI7

South Cape, *Fiji Is.* 218 H8

South Cape see Ka Lae, *Hawai'i, U.S.* 85 RI6

South Carolina, *U.S.* 96 K9

South Cay, *Jam.* 116 PII

South Channel, *Marshall Is.* 216 J8

South Charleston, *W. Va., U.S.* 96 E8

South China Sea, *Asia* 166 KI2

South Comino Channel, *Malta* 161 J2I

South Dakota, *U.S.* 104 K2

South Downs, *Eng., U.K.* 143 WI3

Southeast Indian Ridge, *Ind. Oc.* 240 PIO

Southeast Pacific Basin, *Pac. Oc.* 239 QI9

Southeast Pass, *Marshall Is.* 216 M8

South East Point, *Kiribati* 217 C24

Southeast Point, *Kiribati* 217 EI7

South East Range, *St. Kitts & Nevis* 121 BI7

South End, *Sask., Can.* 83 LI3

Southend, *Scot., U.K.* 143 N7

Southend-on-Sea, *Eng., U.K.* 143 VI5

Southern Alps, *N.Z.* 213 PI6

Southern Bight, *Bahamas* 116 FII

Southern Bug, river, *Ukr.* 138 GIO

Southern Cross, *W. Aust., Austral.* 211 W3

Southern Indian Lake, *Man., Can.* 83 KI4

Southern Pines, *N.C., U.S.* 96 JII

Southern Uplands, *Scot., U.K.* 143 NIO

Southesk Tablelands, *Austral.* 210 E6

Southfield, *Jam.* 120 J7

South Fiji Islands Basin, *Pac. Oc.* 238 M9

South Fork Owyhee, river, *Idaho, Nev., U.S.* 108 LIO

South Fork Shenandoah, river, *Va., U.S.* 96 DII

South Fork Solomon, river, *Kans., U.S.* 105 S5

South Friar's Bay, *St. Kitts & Nevis* 121 BI8

South Fulton, *Tenn., U.S.* 100 EI2

South Geomagnetic Pole, *Antarctica* 227 JI6

South Georgia, island, *S. Amer.* 126 R9

South Grand, river, *Mo., U.S.* 105 TII

South Haven, *Mich., U.S.* 98 M9

South Henik Lake, *Nunavut, Can.* 83 JI4

South Hill, *Va., U.S.* 96 FI2

South Indian Basin, *Antarctic Oc.* 245 LI5

South Island, *N.Z.* 213 QI7

South Korea, *Asia* 167 TI3

South Lake Tahoe, *Calif., U.S.* 109 Q6

South Loup, river, *Nebr., U.S.* 105 P5

South Magnetic Pole, *Antarctica* 227 RI9

South Male Atoll, *Maldives* 179 V3

South Malosmadulu Atoll, *Maldives* 179 U3

South Milwaukee, *Wis., U.S.* 98 L7

South Mole, *Gibraltar, U.K.* 161 P22

South Nahanni, river, *N.W.T., Can.* 82 G9

South Negril Point, *Jam.* 120 H5

South Orkney Islands, *Antarctica* 226 A4

South Ossetia, *Rep. of Georgia* 169 BI8

South Palmetto Point, *Bahamas* 120 E6

South Pass, *Marshall Is.* 216 N5

South Passage, *Kiribati* 217 B22

South Pittsburg, *Tenn., U.S.* 101 GI6

South Platte, river, *Colo., U.S.* 106 LI4

South Point, *Barbados* 121 LI9

South Point see Kalae, *Hawai'i, U.S.* 113 QI9

South Point, *Marshall Is.* 216 N8

South Ponte Vedra Beach, *Fla., U.S.* 97 R9

Southport, *N.C., U.S.* 96 KI2

South Portland, *Me., U.S.* 95 HI6

South Ronaldsay, island, *Scot., U.K.* 142 GIO

South Sandwich Trench, *Antarctic Oc.* 244 D9

South San Francisco, *Calif., U.S.* 109 S3

South Saskatchewan, river, *Alta., Sask., Can.* 82 MII

South Shetland Islands, *Antarctica* 226 C3

South Shore, *Ky., U.S.* 101 AI9

South Sioux City, *Nebr., U.S.* 105 N8

South Sound, *Virgin Islands, U.K.* 120 Q9

South Sound, *Ire.* 143 S3

South Sound Bluff, *Virgin Islands, U.K.* 120 Q9

South Taranaki Bight, *N.Z.* 213 LI8

South Tasman Rise, *Pac. Oc.* 238 Q6

South Uist, island, *Scot., U.K.* 142 K6

South Waziristan, region, *Afghan.* 177 P8

Southwest Anchorage, *Virgin Islands, U.S.* 120 R2

South West Bay, *Bahamas* 120 BIO

South West Bay, *Vanuatu* 218 E2

South West Cape, *Austral.* 210 MI5

Southwest Cape, *Virgin Islands, U.S.* 120 RI

Southwest Cay, *Jam.* 116 PII

Southwest Indian Ridge, *Ind. Oc.* 240 Q3

Southwest Pacific Basin, *Pac. Oc.* 238 MII

Southwest Pass, *Marshall Is.* 216 M7

Southwest Passage, *Marshall Is.* 216 H7

South West Point, *Cayman Is., U.K.* 120 JI

South West Point, *Kiribati* 217 B22

South West Point, *Bahamas* 120 FII

Southwest Point, *Bahamas* 120 D6

Southwest Rift, *Hawai'i, U.S.* 113 NI9

Southwest Rock, *Jam.* 116 PIO

Southwold, *Eng., U.K.* 143 TI6

South Yolla Bolly Mountains, *Calif., U.S.* 109 N3

Souvannakhili, *Laos* 186 LI2

Souvigny, *Fr.* 147 TII

Sovata, *Rom.* 153 CI4

Sovetsk, *Russ.* 156 GI4

Sovetsk, *Russ.* 156 J2

Sovetskaya Gavan', *Russ.* 159 K2I

Sovetskiy, *Russ.* 158 GIO

Sovetskoye, *Russ.* 157 QI3

Soweto, *S. Af.* 202 JIO

Sōya, *Japan* 184 DI3

Sōya Misaki, *Japan* 184 DI3

Soyo, *Angola* 202 B5

Spa, *Belg.* 146 LI3

Spaansebaai, bay, *Neth. Antilles, Neth.* 121 QI5

Spaansewater, bay, *Neth. Antilles, Neth.* 121 QI5

Spaatz Island, *Antarctica* 226 G6

Spain, *Eur.* 139 W3

Spalatum see Split, *Croatia* 152 G6

Spalding, *Eng., U.K.* 143 TI4

Spalding, *Nebr., U.S.* 105 P6

Spaldings, *Jam.* 120 J8

Spánda, Akrotírio, *Gr.* 154 PI2

Spanish Fork, *Utah, U.S.* 106 L7

Spanish Peak, *Oreg., U.S.* 108 G6

Spanish Point, *Bermuda, U.K.* 120 B2

Spanish Rock, *Bermuda, U.K.* 120 B3

Spanish Town, *Virgin Islands, U.K.* 120 R8

Spanish Town, *Jam.* 120 J9

Spanish Wells, *Bahamas* 120 D5

Sparkman, *Ark., U.S.* 100 J8

Sparks, *Nev., U.S.* 109 P6

Sparta, *Ga., U.S.* 96 L7

Sparta see Spárti, *Gr.* 154 LIO

Sparta, *Ill., U.S.* 99 U5

Sparta, *Tenn., U.S.* 101 FI7

Sparta, *Wis., U.S.* 98 K4

Spartanburg, *S.C., U.S.* 96 J8

Spartel, Cap, *Mor.* 144 N8

Spárti (Sparta), *Gr.* 154 LIO

Spartivento, Capo, *It.* 151 SI3

Spearfish, *S. Dak., U.S.* 104 KI

Spearman, *Tex., U.S.* 102 F6

Speedwell Island, *Falkland Is., U.K.* 133 WI2

Speightstown, *Barbados* 121 KI8

Spello, *It.* 150 J8

Spelonk, *Neth. Antilles, Neth.* 121 QI9

Spencer, *Idaho, U.S.* 106 G7

Spencer, *Ind., U.S.* 99 S8

Spencer, *Iowa, U.S.* 104 MIO

Spencer, *N.C., U.S.* 96 H9

Spencer, *Nebr., U.S.* 104 M6

Spencer, *W. Va., U.S.* 96 D8

Spencer, Cape, *Austral.* 210 L9

Spencer Gulf, *S. Aust., Austral.* 211 Y9

Spercheiós, river, *Gr.* 154 GIO

Sperrin Mountains, *N. Ire., U.K.* 143 P6

Spétses, island, *Gr.* 154 LII

Spétses, *Gr.* 154 LII

Speyside, *Trinidad & Tobago* 121 NI8

Spezand, *Pak.* 177 R6

Spicer Islands, *Nunavut, Can.* 83 FI7

Spiddal, *Ire.* 143 S3

Spiess Seamount, *Antarctic Oc.* 244 CII

Spiez, *Switz.* 150 B3

Spíli, *Gr.* 155 QI4

Spilsby, *Eng., U.K.* 143 SI4

Spinazzola, *It.* 150 MI3

Spin Buldak, *Afghan.* 177 Q5

Spirit Lake, *Idaho, U.S.* 106 B3

Spirit Lake, *Iowa, U.S.* 104 MIO

Spiro, *Okla., U.S.* 102 GI4

Spišská Nová Ves, *Slovakia* 149 JI6

Spitsbergen, island, *Norway* 167 N7

Spitsbergen Bank, *Arctic Oc.* 243 FI6

Spittal, *Aust.* 148 MIO

Spittal of Glenshee, *Scot., U.K.* 142 LIO

Split (Spalatum), *Croatia* 152 G6

Split Lake, *Man., Can.* 83 LI4

Splügen, *Switz.* 150 C4

Spokane, river, *Wash., U.S.* 108 B8

Spokane, *Wash., U.S.* 108 C9

Spolaíta, *Gr.* 154 G8

Spoleto, *It.* 150 J8

Spoloshino, *Russ.* 159 JI6

Spoon, river, *Ill., U.S.* 99 P5

Spooner, *Wis., U.S.* 98 G3

Sporting Club, *Monaco* 161 D2I

Spotts, *Cayman Is., U.K.* 120 J2

Sprague, river, *Oreg., U.S.* 108 K5

Sprague, *Wash., U.S.* 108 C8

Sprague Lake, *Wash., U.S.* 108 C8

Sprague River, *Oreg., U.S.* 108 K4

Spratly Island, *Spratly Is.* 188 FIO

Spratly Islands, *S. China Sea* 188 EII

Spray, *Oreg., U.S.* 108 G6

Spree, river, *Ger.* 148 EII

Spremberg, *Ger.* 148 FII

Springbok, *S. Af.* 202 L7

Spring City, *Bahamas* 120 B6

Spring Creek, *W. Aust., Austral.* 211 R7

Springdale, *Ark., U.S.* 100 E6

Springdale, *Wash., U.S.* 108 B8

Springer, *N. Mex., U.S.* 107 QI4

Springfield, *Colo., U.S.* 107 PI5

Springfield, *Fla., U.S.* 97 R3

Springfield, *Ill., U.S.* 99 R5

Springfield, *Ky., U.S.* 101 CI7

Springfield, *Mass., U.S.* 95 LI3

Springfield, *Minn., U.S.* 104 KIO

Springfield, *Mo., U.S.* 105 UI2

Springfield, *Ohio, U.S.* 99 RI2

Springfield, *Oreg., U.S.* 108 H3

Springfield, *S. Dak., U.S.* 104 M7

Springfield, *Tenn., U.S.* 101 EI5

Springfield, *Vt., U.S.* 95 HI3

Spring Grove, *Minn., U.S.* 104 LI3

Spring Hill, *Tenn., U.S.* 101 FI5

Springhill, *La., U.S.* 100 K7

Spring Mountains, *Nev., U.S.* 109 UII

Springsure, *Qnsld., Austral.* 211 UI4

Spring Valley, *Ill., U.S.* 99 P5

Spring Valley, *Minn., U.S.* 104 LI2

Springview, *Nebr., U.S.* 104 M5

Springville, *N.Y., U.S.* 94 K5

Spruce Knob, *W. Va., U.S.* 96 DIO

Spruce Mountain, *Nev., U.S.* 109 NI2

Spruce Pine, *N.C., U.S.* 96 H7

Spulico, Capo, *It.* 151 NI4

Spur, *Tex., U.S.* 102 K6

Spurn Head, *Eng., U.K.* 143 RI4

Squillace, Golfo di, *It.* 151 QI4

Squinzano, *It.* 151 NI5

Srebrenica, *Bosn. & Herzg.* 152 G9

Sredinnyy Khrebet, *Russ.* 159 F22

Sredne Sibirskoye Ploskogor'ye, *Russ.* 159 FI4

Sredniy, *Russ.* 159 F2I

Śrem, *Pol.* 149 EI3

Sremska Mitrovica, *Serb.* 152 F9

Sretensk, *Russ.* 159 LI7

Sriharikota Island, *India* 179 P7

Srikakulam, *India* 178 M9

Sri Kalahasti, *India* 179 P7

Sri Lanka, *Asia* 167 Y7

Sri Lanka, island, *Ind. Oc.* 166 L8

Srinagar, *India* 176 MI2

Srivardhan, *India* 178 M3

Stack Skerry, *Scot., U.K.* 142 G9

Stade, *Ger.* 148 C7

Städjan, peak, *Sw.* 140 JI2

Stadlandet, *Nor.* 140 J9

Stadskanaal, *Neth.* 146 GI4

Stadtallendorf, *Ger.* 148 F7

Staffa, island, *Scot., U.K.* 142 L7

Stafford, *Eng., U.K.* 143 TII

Stafford, *Kans., U.S.* 105 U6

Staithes, *Eng., U.K.* 143 QI3

Staked Plain see Estacado, Llano, *N. Amer.* 80 L5

Stalingrad see Volgograd, *Russ.* 157 PI3

Stalowa Wola, *Pol.* 149 GI7

Stambaugh, *Mich., U.S.* 98 G6

Stamford, *Conn., U.S.* 94 MII

Stamford, *N.Y., U.S.* 94 KIO

Stamford, *Tex., U.S.* 102 L8

Stamford, Lake, *Tex., U.S.* 102 L8

Stamps, *Ark., U.S.* 100 J7

Stamsund, *Nor.* 140 EI2

Stanberry, *Mo., U.S.* 105 RIO

Stancomb-Wills Glacier, *Antarctica* 226 DII

Standish, *Mich., U.S.* 98 KII

Stanford, *Ky., U.S.* 101 CI7

Stanford, *Mont., U.S.* 106 C9

Staniard Creek, *Bahamas* 116 EII

Stanley, *Falkland Is., U.K.* 133 WI3

Stanley, *Idaho, U.S.* 106 G5

Stanley, *N. Dak., U.S.* 104 E3

Stanley, *Tas., Austral.* 211 YI5

Stanley, *Wis., U.S.* 98 H4

Stanley, Port, *Vanuatu* 218 D2

Stanleyville see Kisangani, *Dem. Rep. of the Congo* 198 JIO

Stanovaya, *Russ.* 159 DI9

Stanovoye Nagor'ye, *Russ.* 159 KI6

Stanovoy Khrebet, *Russ.* 159 JI8

Stanovoy Range, *Russ.* 166 DII

Stanton, *N. Dak., U.S.* 104 F4

Stanton, *Nebr., U.S.* 105 P8

Stanton, *Tex., U.S.* 102 M5

Stanwood, *Wash., U.S.* 108 B4

Staples, *Minn., U.S.* 104 HIO

Stapleton, *Nebr., U.S.* 105 P4

Stara Pazova, *Serb.* 152 FIO

Staraya Russa, *Russ.* 156 G7

Stara Zagora, *Bulg.* 153 JI5

Starbuck, *Minn., U.S.* 104 J9

Starbuck, *Wash., U.S.* 108 D8

Starbuck Island, *Kiribati* 214 HI2

Star City, *Ark., U.S.* 100 J9

Stargard Szczeciński, *Pol.* 148 CII

Staritsa, *Russ.* 156 J8

Starke, *Fla., U.S.* 97 R8

Starkville, *Miss., U.S.* 100 JI2

Starobil's'k, *Ukr.* 157 PIO

Starobin, *Belarus* 156 L4

Starodub, *Russ.* 156 M7

Starogard Gdański, *Pol.* 149 BI4

Starokostyantyniv, *Ukr.* 157 N4

Starorybnoye, *Russ.* 159 FI4

Staroshcherbinovskaya, *Russ.* 157 RIO

Starozhynets', *Ukr.* 157 Q3

Start Point, *Eng., U.K.* 143 YIO

Starve Gut Bay, *Jam.* 120 J7

Staryy Oskol, *Russ.* 157 N9

State College, *Pa., U.S.* 94 N6

Stateline, *Nev., U.S.* 109 Q6

Staten Island see Estados, Isla de los, *Arg.* 133 XIO

Staten Island, *N.Y., U.S.* 94 NII

Statesboro, *Ga., U.S.* 97 N8

Statesville, *N.C., U.S.* 96 H9

Staunton, *Ill., U.S.* 99 S4

Staunton, *Va., U.S.* 96 EII

Stavanger, *Nor.* 140 LIO

Stavropol', *Russ.* 157 SI2

Stavropol' Plateau, *Russ.* 138 GI3

Stavrós, *Gr.* 154 CI2

Stavrós, *Gr.* 154 H7

Stavroúpoli, *Gr.* 155 BI4

Stawell, *Vic., Austral.* 211 ZII

Stayton, *Oreg., U.S.* 108 G3

Steamboat Springs, *Colo., U.S.* 106 LII

Stebbins, *Alas., U.S.* 110 GI2

Steele, *N. Dak., U.S.* 104 G5

Steele Point, *Virgin Islands, U.K.* 120 R5

Steels Point, *Norfolk I., Austral.* 217 F2O

Steelton, *Pa., U.S.* 94 P7

Steelville, *Mo., U.S.* 105 TI4

Steenbergen, *Neth.* 146 KI2

Steens Mountain, *Oreg., U.S.* 108 K8

Steenwijk, *Neth.* 146 HI3

Steese Highway, *Alas., U.S.* III FI7

Stefansson Island, *Nunavut, Can.* 83 DI4

Steffen, Cerro, *Arg.* 133 S7

Steg, *Liech.* 160 P3

Steinbach, *Man., Can.* 83 NI4

Steinfort, *Lux.* 160 J9

Steinhatchee, *Fla., U.S.* 97 R6

Steinhort, *Liech.* 160 P3

Steinkjer, *Nor.* 140 HII

Steinsel, *Lux.* 160 JIO

Stella Maris, *Bahamas* 117 FI3

Stendal, *Ger.* 148 D9

Stepanakert (Xankändi), *Azerb.* 169 E2O

Step'anavan, *Arm.* 169 DI8

Stephen, *Minn., U.S.* 104 E8

Stephens, *Ark., U.S.* 100 J7

Stephens, Port, *Falkland Is., U.K.* 133 WII

Stephenson, *Mich., U.S.* 98 H7

Stephenson, Mount, *Antarctica* 226 F5

Stephenville, *Nfld. & Lab., Can.* 83 M23

Stephenville, *Tex., U.S.* 102 MIO

Stepnogorsk, *Kaz.* 175 CI4

Steps Point, *Amer. Samoa, U.S.* 218 N7

Sterling, *Colo., U.S.* 106 LI5

Sterling, *Ill., U.S.* 99 N5

Sterling, *Kans., U.S.* 105 T6

Sterling, *N. Dak., U.S.* 104 G5

Sterling City, *Tex., U.S.* 102 M6

Sterling Heights, *Mich., U.S.* 98 MI2

Sterling Highway, *Alas., U.S.* III KI6

Sterlitamak, *Russ.* 158 J7

Stettiner Haff (Zalew Szczeciński), *Ger., Pol.* 148 CII

Stettler, *Alta., Can.* 82 MIO

Steubenville, *Ohio, U.S.* 99 QI6

Stevenson, *Wash., U.S.* 108 E4

Stevens Point, *Wis., U.S.* 98 J5

Stevens Village, *Alas., U.S.* III FI6

Stevensville, *Mont., U.S.* **106** D5
Steventon, *Bahamas* **120** E8
Stewart, *B.C., Can.* **82** J8
Stewart, *Nev., U.S.* **109** Q6
Stewart, *Isla, Chile* **133** Y8
Stewart Island, *N.Z.* **213** R15
Stewart Town, *Jam.* **120** H8
Steyr, *Aust.* **148** K11
Stickney, *S. Dak., U.S.* **104** L6
Stigler, *Okla., U.S.* **102** G14
Stikine, *river, B.C., Can.* **82** H8
Stiles, *Tex., U.S.* **103** N5
Stillwater, *Minn., U.S.* **104** J12
Stillwater, *Okla., U.S.* **102** F11
Stillwater Range, *Nev., U.S.* **109** P8
Stilo, *It.* **151** R13
Stilo, Punta, *It.* **151** R14
Stilwell, *Okla., U.S.* **102** F14
Stinnett, *Tex., U.S.* **102** F5
Stintino, *It.* **150** M3
Štip, *Maced.* **152** K12
Stíra, *Gr.* **155** J13
Stiring-Wendel, *Fr.* **147** N15
Stirling, *Scot., U.K.* **142** M9
Stirling City, *Calif., U.S.* **109** P4
Stirling Island, *Solomon Is.* **217** L14
Stjørdalshalsen, *Nor.* **140** H11
Stobi, *ruin, Maced.* **152** K11
Stockdale, *Tex., U.S.* **103** R10
Stockerau, *Aust.* **148** K12
Stockholm, *Sw.* **141** L14
Stocking Island, *Bahamas* **120** F9
Stockport, *Eng., U.K.* **143** S11
Stocks Seamount, *Atl. Oc.* **237** Q9
Stockton, *Calif., U.S.* **109** R5
Stockton, *Ill., U.S.* **98** M4
Stockton, *Kans., U.S.* **105** S5
Stockton, *Mo., U.S.* **105** U11
Stockton Lake, *Mo., U.S.* **105** U11
Stockton-on-Tees, *Eng., U.K.* **143** Q12
Stoke on Trent, *Eng., U.K.* **143** S11
Stokes, *Bahía, Chile* **133** X7
Stokes, Mount, *N.Z.* **213** M18
Stolberg, *Ger.* **148** F4
Stolbovoy, Ostrov, *Russ.* **159** D17
Stolin, *Belarus* **156** M4
Stonehaven, *Scot., U.K.* **142** K11
Stonehenge, *Eng., U.K.* **143** W12
Stonehenge, *Qnsld., Austral.* **211** U12
Stones River National Battlefield, *Tenn., U.S.* **101** F15
Stonewall, *Miss., U.S.* **101** L13
Stonewall, *Okla., U.S.* **102** H12
Stony, *river, Alas., U.S.* **111** J14
Stony Rapids, *Sask., Can.* **82** J12
Stora Lulevatten, *lake, Sw.* **141** E13
Storavan, *lake, Sw.* **141** F13
Støren, *Nor.* **140** H11
Storkerson Bay, *N.W.T., Can.* **82** D12
Storlien, *Sw.* **140** H11
Storm Lake, *Iowa, U.S.* **105** N10
Stornoway, *Scot., U.K.* **142** H7
Storr's Lake, *Bahamas* **120** E11
Storsjön, *lake, Sw.* **140** H12
Storuman, *Sw.* **141** G13
Story, *Wyo., U.S.* **106** F11
Story City, *Iowa, U.S.* **105** N11
Stoughton, *Wis., U.S.* **98** L5
Stoyba, *Russ.* **159** K19
Strabane, *N. Ire., U.K.* **143** P6
Strahan, *Tas., Austral.* **211** Z15
Stralsund, *Ger.* **148** B10
Stranda, *Nor.* **140** J10
Strangford Lough, *N. Ire., U.K.* **143** Q8
Strangways, *S. Aust., Austral.* **211** V9
Stranorlar, *Ire.* **143** P5
Stranraer, *Scot., U.K.* **143** P8
Strasbourg, *Fr.* **147** P15
Strasburg, *N. Dak., U.S.* **104** H5
Strasburg, *Ohio, U.S.* **99** Q14
Strasburg, *Va., U.S.* **96** C11
Strassen, *Lux.* **160** K10
Strata Florida, *Wales, U.K.* **143** U9
Stratford, *Tex., U.S.* **102** F5
Stratford upon Avon, *Eng., U.K.* **143** U12
Strathalbyn, *S. Aust., Austral.* **211** Y10
Strathcona, Mount, *Antarctica* **227** K21
Strathmore, *valley, Scot., U.K.* **142** L10
Stratobowl, *site, S. Dak., U.S.* **104** L2
Stratton, *Colo., U.S.* **106** M15
Stratton, *Me., U.S.* **95** E15
Stratton, *Nebr., U.S.* **105** R3
Straubing, *Ger.* **148** J9

Strawberry Mountain, *Oreg., U.S.* **108** G7
Strawberry Reservoir, *Utah, U.S.* **106** L8
Strawn, *Tex., U.S.* **102** L9
Streaky Bay, *S. Aust., Austral.* **211** X9
Streator, *Ill., U.S.* **99** P6
Streeter, *N. Dak., U.S.* **104** G6
Streich Mound, *Austral.* **210** J5
Strelka, *Russ.* **159** F20
Strezhevoy, *Russ.* **158** H11
Stříbro, *Czech Rep.* **148** H10
Strickland, *river, P.N.G.* **213** D18
Strimónas, *river, Gr.* **154** C12
Stringtown, *Okla., U.S.* **102** H12
Stroma, *island, Scot., U.K.* **142** G10
Stromboli, Isola, *It.* **151** Q12
Stromeferry, *Scot., U.K.* **142** K8
Stromness, *Scot., U.K.* **142** G10
Stromsburg, *Nebr., U.S.* **105** Q7
Strömstad, *Sw.* **140** L11
Strömsund, *Sw.* **140** H12
Strongíli (Ypsili), *island, Gr.* **155** N22
Stronsay, *island, Scot., U.K.* **142** F11
Stroud, *Eng., U.K.* **143** V11
Stroud, *Okla., U.S.* **102** F12
Stroudsburg, *Pa., U.S.* **94** N9
Strovolos, *Cyprus* **160** P8
Struga, *Maced.* **152** L10
Struis, *Maced.* **152** K11
Struma, *river, Bulg.* **153** K13
Strumica, *Maced.* **152** K12
Struy, *Scot., U.K.* **142** J9
Stryy, *Ukr.* **157** P2
Stuart, *Fla., U.S.* **97** V10
Stuart, *Nebr., U.S.* **105** N6
Stuart, *Va., U.S.* **96** G9
Stuart Island, *Alas., U.S.* **84** P2
Stuart Lake, *B.C., Can.* **82** K8
Stuart Range, *Austral.* **210** H9
Stubbs, *St. Vincent & the Grenadines* **121** L16
Stuhr, *Ger.* **148** C7
Stump Lake, *N. Dak., U.S.* **104** F7
Stumpy Point, *N.C., U.S.* **96** H15
Stung Treng, *Cambodia* **186** M12
Stupino, *Russ.* **156** K9
Sturgeon Bay, *Wis., U.S.* **98** J8
Sturgis, *Ky., U.S.* **101** C14
Sturgis, *Mich., U.S.* **99** N10
Sturgis, *S. Dak., U.S.* **104** K2
Sturt Stony Desert, *Austral.* **210** G11
Stuttgart, *Ark., U.S.* **100** H9
Stuttgart, *Ger.* **148** J7
Stykkishólmur, *Ice.* **140** E2
Suai, *Timor-Leste* **189** N15
Suakin, *Sudan* **199** C14
Suakin Archipelago, *Sudan* **194** F10
Suao, *Taiwan, China* **183** Q10
Subaşı Dağı, *Turk.* **169** G16
Subay', 'Urūq, *Saudi Arabia* **172** L9
Subei, *China* **180** G9
Subi, *island, Indonesia* **188** H9
Sublette, *Kans., U.S.* **105** U4
Subotica, *Serb.* **152** D9
Suceava, *Rom.* **153** B15
Sucia, Bahía, *P.R., U.S.* **120** P1
Sücka, *Liech.* **160** P3
Sucre, *Bol.* **130** K7
Sud, Canal du, *Haiti* **117** M16
Sud, Pointe, *Comoros* **205** M14
Sud, Récif du, *Mayotte, Fr.* **205** P17
Sudak, *Ukr.* **157** T8
Sudan, *Af.* **195** G21
Sudan, *Tex., U.S.* **102** J4
Suday, *Russ.* **156** F11
Sudbury, *Ont., Can.* **83** P18
Sudd, *wetland, Sudan* **194** H9
Suddie, *Guyana* **129** D14
Sud-Est, Passe du, *Fr. Polynesia, Fr.* **219** R21
Sudeten, *range, Czech Rep., Pol.* **148** G12
Sud-Ouest, Passe du, *Fr. Polynesia, Fr.* **219** R20
Sudr, *Egypt* **171** R1
Suðuroy, *island, Faroe Is., Den.* **140** J6
Sue, *river, Sudan* **198** G11
Sueca, *Sp.* **145** H15
Suez *see* El Suweis, *Egypt* **171** Q1
Suez *see* El Suweis, *Egypt* **197** C19
Suez, Gulf of, *Egypt* **171** R1
Suez Canal, *Egypt* **171** N1

Suffolk, *Va., U.S.* **96** F14
Sugar Land, *Tex., U.S.* **103** R13
Sugar Loaf, *island, Grenada* **121** J23
Sugarloaf Key, *Fla., U.S.* **97** Y9
Suğla Gölü, *Turk.* **168** H7
Suhai Hu, *China* **180** G9
Suhar, *Oman* **173** J15
Şuḩār, *Oman* **173** J15
Suhl, *Ger.* **148** G8
Suichang, *China* **182** M8
Suichuan, *China* **183** P5
Suide, *China* **182** E3
Suining, *China* **182** H7
Suining, *China* **183** P2
Suining, *China* **180** L12
Suippes, *Fr.* **147** P12
Suir, *river, Ire.* **143** U5
Suixi, *China* **182** H7
Suixi, *China* **183** S2
Suizhong, *China* **182** C9
Suizhou, *China* **182** K4
Sujawal, *Pak.* **177** W7
Sukabumi, *Indonesia* **188** M8
Sukadana, *Indonesia* **188** J9
Sukagawa, *Japan* **184** M13
Sükh, *Uzb.* **175** L14
Sukhinichi, *Russ.* **156** K8
Sukhona, *river, Russ.* **156** E12
Sukhothai, *Thai.* **186** K8
Sukhum *see* Sokhumi, *Abkhazia* **169** A15
Sukkur, *Pak.* **177** T7
Sukumo, *Japan* **185** S6
Sula, *river, Ukr.* **157** N7
Sula, Kepulauan, *Indonesia* **189** K15
Sulaiman Range, *Pak.* **177** R8
Sulanheer, *Mongolia* **181** F13
Sula Sgeir, *island, Scot., U.K.* **142** F7
Sulawesi (Celebes), *island, Indonesia* **189** K13
Sulei, *island, Solomon Is.* **217** M18
Sule Skerry, *island, Scot., U.K.* **142** F9
Süleymanlı, *Turk.* **168** G11
Sulima, *Sierra Leone* **200** G6
Sulina, *Rom.* **153** E19
Sullana, *Peru* **130** E2
Sulligent, *Ala., U.S.* **101** J13
Sullivan, *Ill., U.S.* **99** R6
Sullivan, *Ind., U.S.* **99** S7
Sullivan, *Mo., U.S.* **105** T14
Sulmona, *It.* **150** K10
Sulphur, *La., U.S.* **100** P7
Sulphur, *Okla., U.S.* **102** H11
Sulphur, *river, Tex., U.S.* **102** K14
Sulphur Cone, *Hawai'i, U.S.* **113** N19
Sulphur Springs, *Tex., U.S.* **102** K13
Sulphur Springs Draw, *Tex., U.S.* **102** L4
Sultan Dağları, *Turk.* **168** G7
Sultanhanı, *Turk.* **168** G9
Sultanpur, *India* **178** G8
Sulu Archipelago, *Philippines* **189** G13
Sulu Basin, *Pac. Oc.* **238** J3
Sülüklü, *Turk.* **168** F8
Sülüktü, *Kyrg.* **176** G8
Suluova, *Turk.* **168** D11
Sulu Sea, *Philippines* **189** E13
Sumampa, *Arg.* **132** H10
Sumas, *Wash., U.S.* **108** A4
Sumatra, *island, Indonesia* **166** L10
Sumaúma, *Braz.* **130** F9
Sumba, *Faroe Is., Den.* **140** J6
Sumba, *island, Indonesia* **189** N13
Sumbawa, *island, Indonesia* **188** M12
Sumbawa Besar, *Indonesia* **188** M12
Sumbawanga, *Tanzania* **198** M12
Sumbe, *Angola* **202** D5
Sumisu Jima (Smith Island), *Japan* **184** J9
Summer Lake, *Oreg., U.S.* **108** K5
Summerland Key, *Fla., U.S.* **97** Y9
Summersville, *W. Va., U.S.* **96** D9
Summerville, *Ga., U.S.* **96** K4
Summerville, *S.C., U.S.* **96** M10
Summit, *Miss., U.S.* **100** N10
Summit Mountain, *Nev., U.S.* **109** P10
Summit Peak, *Colo., U.S.* **107** P12
Sumner, *Iowa, U.S.* **104** M13
Šumperk, *Czech Rep.* **149** H13
Sumprabum, *Myanmar* **186** D7
Sumpter, *Oreg., U.S.* **108** G8
Sumqayıt, *Azerb.* **169** D23
Sumrall, *Miss., U.S.* **100** M12
Sumter, *S.C., U.S.* **96** K10
Sumy, *Ukr.* **157** N8

Sun, *river, Mont., U.S.* **106** C7
Sunagawa, *Japan* **184** F13
Sunart, Loch, *Scot., U.K.* **142** L7
Sunbaron Roads (Tinian Harbor), *N. Mariana Is., U.S.* **216** C7
Sunburst, *Mont., U.S.* **106** A7
Sunbury, *Pa., U.S.* **94** N7
Sunbury, *Vic., Austral.* **211** Z12
Sunchales, *Arg.* **132** J11
Suncheon, *S. Korea* **182** G13
Sunch'ŏn, *N. Korea* **182** D12
Sun City, *Ariz., U.S.* **107** T6
Sunda, Selat, *Indonesia* **188** L8
Sundance, *Wyo., U.S.* **106** F13
Sundar, *Malaysia* **188** G11
Sundarbans, *wetland, Bangladesh, India* **178** J12
Sundargarh, *India* **178** J9
Sunday *see* Raoul Island, *island, Kermadec Is., N.Z.* **214** L9
Sunderland, *Eng., U.K.* **143** P12
Sundi, *Sao Tome and Principe* **205** A20
Sündiken Dağ, *Turk.* **168** E6
Sundown, *Tex., U.S.* **102** K4
Sundsvall, *Sw.* **141** J13
Sunflower, Mount, *Kans., U.S.* **105** S3
Sungaianyar, *Indonesia* **188** K12
Sungaibatu, *Indonesia* **188** J9
Sungai Kolok, *Thai.* **187** S9
Sungaipenuh, *Indonesia* **188** K6
Sungai Petani, *Malaysia* **187** S9
Sung Men, *Thai.* **186** K8
Sungurlu, *Turk.* **168** E9
Sunland Park, *N. Mex., U.S.* **107** V12
Sunnyside, *Wash., U.S.* **108** E6
Sunnyvale, *Calif., U.S.* **109** S4
Sun Prairie, *Wis., U.S.* **98** L5
Sunray, *Tex., U.S.* **102** F5
Sunset Beach, *Hawai'i, U.S.* **112** D10
Sunset Crater Volcano National Monument, *Ariz., U.S.* **107** S7
Suntar, *Russ.* **159** G19
Suntar Khayata, Khrebet, *Russ.* **159** G19
Suntsar, *Pak.* **177** V2
Sunwu, *China* **181** B17
Sunyani, *Ghana* **200** G10
Suomen Ridge *see* Suomenselkä, *Fin.* **138** C9
Suomenselkä, *Fin.* **141** H15
Suonenjoki, *Fin.* **141** H16
Supai, *Ariz., U.S.* **107** R6
Superior, *Ariz., U.S.* **107** U7
Superior, *Mont., U.S.* **106** C5
Superior, *Nebr., U.S.* **105** R7
Superior, *Wis., U.S.* **98** E2
Superior, Lake, *Can., U.S.* **85** C15
Süphan Dağı, *Turk.* **169** F17
Supiori, *island, Indonesia* **213** B15
Support Force Glacier, *Antarctica* **226** E11
Supu, *Indonesia* **189** H16
Sup'ung Reservoir, *N. Korea, China* **182** C12
Suqutrá (Socotra), *island, Yemen* **173** R14
Şūr, *Oman* **173** K17
Sur, Point, *Calif., U.S.* **109** U4
Sur, Punta, *Ecua.* **128** R9
Sura, *river, Russ.* **156** J13
Surab, *Pak.* **177** T5
Surabaya, *Indonesia* **188** M10
Sürak, *Iran* **173** J16
Surakarta, *Indonesia* **188** M10
Suramana, *Indonesia* **189** J13
Surat, *India* **178** K3
Surat, *Qnsld., Austral.* **211** V14
Surat Thani, *Thai.* **187** Q8
Sûre, *river, Ger., Lux.* **160** J11
Sürétiméat, Mount, *Vanuatu* **218** B2
Surf City, *N.C., U.S.* **96** K13
Surgères, *Fr.* **147** T6
Surgidero de Batabanó, *Cuba* **116** G6
Surgut, *Russ.* **158** H11
Surigao, *Philippines* **189** E15
Surin, *Thai.* **186** M10
Suriname, *S. Amer.* **127** B19
Surin Nua, Ko, *Thai.* **187** Q7
Sürmene, *Turk.* **169** D14
Surprise, Île de la, *New Caledonia, Fr.* **218** A5
Surrey, *B.C., Can.* **82** M8
Sursee, *Switz.* **150** B3
Surskoye, *Russ.* **156** K14
Surt, *Lib.* **197** C14

Surtanahu, *Pak.* **177** V8
Surtsey, *island, Ice.* **140** G2
Suruç, *Turk.* **169** J13
Suruga Wan, *Japan* **185** Q11
Surulangun, *Indonesia* **188** K6
Sušac, *island, Croatia* **152** H6
Süsah (Apollonia), *Lib.* **197** B16
Susak, *island, Croatia* **152** F4
Susaki, *Japan* **185** R7
Susamyr, *Kyrg.* **176** J11
Susanville, *Calif., U.S.* **109** N5
Suşehri, *Turk.* **169** E13
Susitna, *river, Alas., U.S.* **111** H17
Susoh, *Indonesia* **188** G4
Susquehanna, *river, Pa., U.S.* **94** N7
Susquehanna, *Pa., U.S.* **94** L9
Susques, *Arg.* **132** E9
Susubona, *Solomon Is.* **217** M18
Susuman, *Russ.* **159** F20
Susunu, *Indonesia* **213** C15
Susupe, *N. Mariana Is., U.S.* **216** C4
Susurluk, *Turk.* **168** E4
Sutak, *India* **177** N14
Sütçüler, *Turk.* **168** H6
Sutherland, *Nebr., U.S.* **105** P4
Sutherland, *S. Af.* **202** L8
Sutherlin, *Oreg., U.S.* **108** J3
Sutlej, *river, Pak.* **177** S10
Sutton, *Nebr., U.S.* **105** Q7
Sutton, *river, Ont., Can.* **83** L16
Sutton, *W. Va., U.S.* **96** D9
Sutton on Sea, *Eng., U.K.* **143** S14
Suttsu, *Japan* **184** G12
Sutwik Island, *Alas., U.S.* **111** M14
Su'u, *Solomon Is.* **217** N19
Suva, *Fiji Is.* **218** J6
Suvadiva Atoll (Huvadu), *Maldives* **179** W3
Suvorov, *Russ.* **156** K9
Suwa, *Japan* **185** P11
Suwałki, *Pol.* **149** B17
Suwannaphum, *Thai.* **186** L11
Suwannee, *river, Fla., U.S.* **85** M18
Suwannee, *Fla., U.S.* **97** S6
Suwanose Jima, *Japan* **185** V3
Suwarrow Atoll, *Cook Is., N.Z.* **214** J11
Suwayqīyah, Hawr as, *Iraq* **172** E10
Suwon, *S. Korea* **182** F13
Suyutkino, *Russ.* **157** T15
Suzhou, *China* **182** J7
Suzhou, *China* **182** K9
Suzu, *Japan* **184** M10
Suzuka, *Japan* **185** Q9
Suzu Misaki, *Japan* **184** M10
Svalbard, *archipelago, Nor.* **167** P7
Svartisen, *glacier, Nor.* **140** F12
Svatove, *Ukr.* **157** P10
Svay Rieng, *Cambodia* **187** P12
Sveg, *Sw.* **140** J12
Svendborg, *Den.* **140** P11
Sverdrup Channel, *Nunavut, Can.* **83** B15
Sverdrup Islands, *Nunavut, Can.* **83** B15
Svetac (Sveti Andrija), *island, Croatia* **152** H5
Sveti Andrija *see* Svetac, *island, Croatia* **152** H5
Svetlograd, *Russ.* **157** S12
Svetogorsk, *Russ.* **158** D7
Svilengrad, *Bulg.* **153** K16
Svir', *river, Russ.* **138** C10
Sviritsa, *Russ.* **156** E7
Svishtov, *Bulg.* **153** G15
Svobodnyy, *Russ.* **159** K19
Svolvær, *Nor.* **140** E12
Svyataya Anna Fan, *Arctic Oc.* **242** F12
Svyataya Anna Trough, *Arctic Oc.* **242** D12
Svyatoy Nos, Mys, *Russ.* **159** D17
Svyetlahorsk, *Belarus* **156** L5
Swain Reefs, *Austral.* **210** F15
Swainsboro, *Ga., U.S.* **96** M7
Swains Island, *Amer. Samoa, U.S.* **214** J10
Swakop, *river, Namibia* **202** H6
Swakopmund, *Namibia* **202** H6
Swan, *river, Austral.* **210** K2
Swan, *river, Man., U.S.* **106** C6
Swanlinbar, *Ire.* **143** Q5
Swan Peak, *Mont., U.S.* **106** C6
Swanquarter, *N.C., U.S.* **96** H14
Swan River, *Man., Can.* **83** M13
Swansboro, *N.C., U.S.* **96** J13

Swansea (Abertawe), *Wales, U.K.* 143 V9
Swansea Bay, *Wales, U.K.* 143 V9
Swans Island, *Me., U.S.* 95 G18
Swanton, *Vt., U.S.* 94 E12
Swan Valley, *Idaho, U.S.* 106 H8
Swatow *see* Shantou, *China* 183 R6
Swaziland, *Af.* 195 Q21
Sweden, *Eur.* 139 R7
Sweeney Mountains, *Antarctica* 226 F7
Sweetgrass, *Mont., U.S.* 106 A7
Sweet Home, *Oreg., U.S.* 108 G3
Sweeting's Cay, *Bahamas* 120 E4
Sweetwater, *Tenn., U.S.* 101 F18
Sweetwater, *Tex., U.S.* 102 L7
Sweetwater, river, *Wyo., U.S.* 106 J10
Sweetwater Lake, *N. Dak., U.S.* 104 E6
Swellendam, *S. Af.* 202 M8
Swetes, *Antigua & Barbuda* 121 B21
Świdnica, *Pol.* 149 G13
Świdnik, *Pol.* 149 F17
Świdwin, *Pol.* 148 C12
Świebodzin, *Pol.* 148 E12
Świecie, *Pol.* 149 C14
Swift Current, *Sask., Can.* 82 N11
Swilly, Lough, *Ire.* 143 N5
Swindon, *Eng., U.K.* 143 V12
Swinford, *Ire.* 143 R4
Świnoujście, *Pol.* 148 B11
Switzerland, *Eur.* 139 V5
Syamzha, *Russ.* 156 F11
Syava, *Russ.* 156 G13
Sychevka, *Russ.* 156 J8
Sydney, *N.S., Can.* 83 N23
Sydney, *N.S.W., Austral.* 211 Y14
Sydney Bay, *Norfolk I., Austral.* 217 G20
Sydney Point, *Banaba, Kiribati* 217 E20
Syeri, *Indonesia* 189 K19
Syktyvkar, *Russ.* 158 F8
Sylacauga, *Ala., U.S.* 101 K16
Sylhet, *Bangladesh* 178 H13
Sylt, island, *Ger.* 148 A7
Sylva, *N.C., U.S.* 96 J6
Sylvania, *Ga., U.S.* 96 M8
Sylvania, *Ohio, U.S.* 99 N12
Sylvester, *Ga., U.S.* 97 P5
Sylvester, *Tex., U.S.* 102 L7
Sylvester, Lake, *Austral.* 210 D9
Synel'nykove, *Ukr.* 157 Q8
Synya, *Russ.* 158 F10
Syowa, station, *Antarctica* 227 B17
Syracuse *see* Siracusa, *It.* 151 T12
Syracuse, *Kans., U.S.* 105 U3
Syracuse, *N.Y., U.S.* 94 J8
Syracuse, *Nebr., U.S.* 105 Q9
Syr Darya, river, *Kaz.* 166 F6
Syria, *Asia* 167 T3
Syrian Desert, *Asia* 166 F3
Syrian Gates, *Turk.* 168 J11
Sysy Basa, *Russ.* 159 H18
Syumsi, *Russ.* 156 G15
Syutkya, peak, *Bulg.* 153 K13
Syzran', *Russ.* 156 L15
Szczecin, *Pol.* 148 C11
Szczecinek, *Pol.* 149 C13
Szczytno, *Pol.* 149 C16
Szeged, *Hung.* 149 N16
Székely, *Hung.* 149 K17
Székesfehérvár, *Hung.* 149 L14
Szekszárd, *Hung.* 149 N15
Szentes, *Hung.* 149 M16
Szolnok, *Hung.* 149 L16
Szombathely, *Hung.* 149 L13

T

Taakoka, island, *Cook Is., N.Z.* 218 Q9
Taapuna, *Fr. Polynesia, Fr.* 219 N15
Taapuna, Passe de, *Fr. Polynesia, Fr.* 219 N15
Taatioe, Mont, *Fr. Polynesia, Fr.* 219 K23
Tâba, *Egypt* 171 R5
Tabago, *P.N.G.* 217 K14
Ţābah, *Saudi Arabia* 172 H8
Tabalo, *P.N.G.* 213 B20
Tabaquite, *Trinidad & Tobago* 121 P22
Tabar Islands, *P.N.G.* 213 B21
Ţabas, *Iran* 173 D15
Ţabas, *Iran* 173 D17
Tabelbala, *Alg.* 196 C9
Tabernacle, *St. Kitts & Nevis* 121 A17
Tabernas, *Sp.* 144 L12
Tabiang, *Banaba, Kiribati* 217 D20
Tabiang, *Kiribati* 217 G17
Tabik, island, *Marshall Is.* 216 K1
Tabik Channel, *Marshall Is.* 216 K2
Tabiteuea, island, *Kiribati* 214 G8
Tabiteuea, *Kiribati* 217 G18
Tablas, island, *Philippines* 189 D14
Table, Pointe de la, *Reunion, Fr.* 205 H17
Table Mountain, *S. Dak., U.S.* 104 H1
Table Rock Lake, *Mo., U.S.* 105 V11
Tabontebike, *Kiribati* 217 E17
Tábor, *Czech Rep.* 148 J11
Tabor, *Russ.* 159 D18
Tabora, *Tanzania* 199 L13
Tabor City, *N.C., U.S.* 96 K11
Tabou, *Côte d'Ivoire* 200 H7
Tabrīz, *Iran* 172 B10
Tabu, Motu, *Fr. Polynesia, Fr.* 219 M23
Tabuaeran (Fanning Island), *Kiribati* 214 F12
Tabūk, *Saudi Arabia* 172 G6
Tabunifi, *F.S.M.* 217 D18
Taburiente, Caldera de, *Canary Is.* 204 Q3
Tacheng, *China* 180 D6
Tacloban, *Philippines* 189 D15
Tacna, *Peru* 130 K6
Tacoma, *Wash., U.S.* 108 C4
Tacuarembó, *Uru.* 132 K14
Tacutu, river, *S. Amer.* 126 C6
Tad, *Pak.* 177 V3
Tademaït, Plateau du, *Alg.* 196 D10
Tadine, *New Caledonia, Fr.* 218 D10
Tadjmout, *Alg.* 196 E11
Tadjoura, Gulf of, *Djibouti* 194 G11
Tadmur (Palmyra), *Syr.* 170 G10
Tadoule Lake, *Man., Can.* 83 K14
Tadoussac, *Que., Can.* 83 N20
Tadpatri, *India* 179 N6
Taean, *S. Korea* 182 F13
Taedong, *N. Korea* 182 C12
Taejŏn *see* Daejeon, *S. Korea* 182 F13
Taenarum *see* Ténaro, Akrotírio, *Gr.* 154 N10
Taenga, island, *Fr. Polynesia, Fr.* 219 E19
Tafahi, island, *Tonga* 214 J10
Tafalla, *Sp.* 145 C13
Tafassasset, Oued, *Alg.* 196 E12
Tafelberg, peak, *Neth. Antilles, Neth.* 121 Q15
Tafí Viejo, *Arg.* 132 G9
Tafonsak, *F.S.M.* 217 A18
Taft, *Calif., U.S.* 109 V7
Taft, *Tex., U.S.* 103 T11
Taftān, Kūh-e, *Iran* 173 G17
Taga, *Samoa* 218 L2
Taganrog, *Russ.* 157 R10
Taganrogskiy Zaliv, *Russ., Ukr.* 157 R10
Tagant, region, *Mauritania* 194 F2
Tagawa, *Japan* 185 R4
Taghaz, *Afghan.* 177 R3
Tagliamento, river, *It.* 150 C9
Tagounit, *Mor.* 196 C8
Tagtabazar, *Turkm.* 174 N10
Taguatinga, *Braz.* 131 H14
Tagula, island, *P.N.G.* 213 F22
Tagum, *Philippines* 189 F15
Tagus *see* Tajo, river, *Sp.* 144 G8
Tagus *see* Tejo, river, *Port.* 144 H5
Tahaa, island, *Fr. Polynesia, Fr.* 219 E15
Tahan, peak, *Malaysia* 187 T10
Tahanea, island, *Fr. Polynesia, Fr.* 219 E18
Tahat, Mount, *Alg.* 196 E11
Ţaherī, *Iran* 173 H13
Tahueia, Mouillage de, *Fr. Polynesia, Fr.* 219 J21
Tahgong, Puntan, *N. Mariana Is., U.S.* 216 A7
Tahi, cape, *Fr. Polynesia, Fr.* 219 K14
Tahiti, island, *Fr. Polynesia, Fr.* 219 P16
Tahlab, river, *Pak.* 177 T2
Tahlab, Dasht-i-, *Pak.* 177 S2
Tahlequah, *Okla., U.S.* 102 F14
Tahoe, Lake, *Calif., Nev., U.S.* 109 Q6
Tahoe City, *Calif., U.S.* 109 Q6
Tahoka, *Tex., U.S.* 102 K5
Taholah, *Wash., U.S.* 108 C2
Tahoua, *Niger* 196 H11
Tahtalı Dağ, *Turk.* 168 F11
Tahtalıdaği, peak, *Turk.* 168 J6
Tahuata, island, *Fr. Polynesia, Fr.* 219 N20
Tahueia, *Fr. Polynesia, Fr.* 219 K21
Tahulandang, island, *Indonesia* 189 H15
Tahuna, *Indonesia* 189 G15
Tai'an, *China* 182 G7
Taiarapu, Presqu'île de, *Fr. Polynesia, Fr.* 219 P18
Taiaro, island, *Fr. Polynesia, Fr.* 219 E18
Taibei *see* Taipei, *Taiwan, China* 183 Q10
Taibus Qi (Baochang), *China* 182 B6
Taichung, *Taiwan, China* 183 R9
Taígetos, Óros, *Gr.* 154 L10
Taigu, *China* 182 E4
Taihang Shan, *China* 182 F5
Taihape, *N.Z.* 213 L19
Taihe, *China* 183 P5
Tai Hu, *China* 182 K9
Taihu, *China* 182 L6
Taiki, *Japan* 184 G15
Tailai, *China* 181 D16
Tailem Bend, *S. Aust., Austral.* 211 Y10
Tain, *Fr.* 147 V13
Tainan, *Taiwan, China* 183 S9
Taining, *China* 183 P7
Taiof, island, *P.N.G.* 217 J13
Taipei (Taibei), *Taiwan, China* 183 Q10
Taiping, *Malaysia* 187 T9
Taipingot, peak, *N. Mariana Is., U.S.* 216 E7
Tairapa, Passe, *Fr. Polynesia, Fr.* 219 K17
Taira Shima, *Japan* 185 V3
Taishan, *China* 183 S4
Taita, Mont, *Fr. Polynesia, Fr.* 219 K21
Taitao, Península de, *Chile* 133 T6
Taitung, *Taiwan, China* 183 S10
Taivalkoski, *Fin.* 141 F16
Taiwan, China, *Asia* 167 V13
Taiwan, island, *Taiwan, China* 183 R10
Taiwan Strait, *China, Taiwan, China* 183 S8
Taiyuan, *China* 182 E4
Taizhou, *China* 182 J9
Taizhou (Jiaojiang, Haimen), *China* 182 M10
Ta'izz, *Yemen* 172 R9
Tajarḩī, *Lib.* 197 E14
Tajikistan, *Asia* 167 U7
Tajima, *Japan* 184 M12
Taj Mahal, site, *India* 178 G6
Tajo (Tagus), river, *Sp.* 144 G8
Tak, *Thai.* 186 K8
Taka, island, *Marshall Is.* 216 M7
Taka Atoll, *Marshall Is.* 216 F4
Takāb, *Iran* 172 C11
Takahe, Mount, *Antarctica* 226 L7
Takaiu, *F.S.M.* 217 F14
Takaka, *N.Z.* 213 M17
Takamatsu, *Japan* 185 Q7
Takamori, *Japan* 185 S5
Takaoka, *Japan* 185 N10
Takapau, *N.Z.* 213 L19
Takapoto, island, *Fr. Polynesia, Fr.* 219 D18
Takara Jima, *Japan* 185 V3
Takaroa, island, *Fr. Polynesia, Fr.* 219 D18
Takasaki, *Japan* 185 N11
Takatik, island, *F.S.M.* 217 F14
Tā-kaw, *Myanmar* 186 H7
Takayama, *Japan* 185 P10
Takefu, *Japan* 185 P9
Takengon, *Indonesia* 188 G4
Takeo, *Cambodia* 187 P11
Takeo, *Japan* 185 R4
Take Shima, *Japan* 185 U4
Takeshima *see* Dokdo, island, *Japan* 184 M6
Tākestān, *Iran* 172 C12
Taketa, *Japan* 185 S5
Takfon, *Taj.* 176 H7
Takhiatosh, *Uzb.* 174 J9
Takhtakŭpir, *Uzb.* 174 J9
Takhteh Pol, *Afghan.* 177 Q5
Taki, *P.N.G.* 217 K14
Takikawa, *Japan* 184 F13
Taklimakan Desert, *China* 166 G8
Taklimakan Shamo, *China* 180 G5
Taksimo, *Russ.* 159 K17
Takuan, Mount, *P.N.G.* 217 K14
Takua Pa, *Thai.* 187 Q7
Takum, *India* 178 F14
Takume, island, *Fr. Polynesia, Fr.* 219 E19
Takuua, island, *Cook Is., N.Z.* 219 B18
Takuua Passage, *Cook Is., N.Z.* 219 B18
Tal, *Pak.* 176 L10
Talagang, *Pak.* 177 P10
Talaimannar, *Sri Lanka* 179 S7
Talamanca, Cordillera de, *N. Amer.* 80 Q8
Talangbatu, *Indonesia* 188 L7
Talara, *Peru* 130 E1
Talas, *Kyrg.* 176 E10
Talaud, Kepulauan, *Indonesia* 189 G16
Talavera de la Reina, *Sp.* 144 G9
Talbot, Cape, *Austral.* 210 B6
Talbot Inlet, *Nunavut, Can.* 83 C16
Talbotton, *Ga., U.S.* 96 M5
Talca, *Chile* 132 M6
Talcahuano, *Chile* 132 M6
Taldora, *Qnsld., Austral.* 211 S11
Taldyqorghan, *Kaz.* 175 G17
Talhar, *Pak.* 177 W7
Talia, *S. Aust., Austral.* 211 X9
Taliabu, island, *Indonesia* 189 K15
Talihina, *Okla., U.S.* 102 H14
Tali Post, *Sudan* 198 H12
Taliwang, *Indonesia* 188 M12
Talkeetna, *Alas., U.S.* 111 H16
Talkeetna Mountains, *Alas., U.S.* 111 J17
Talladega, *Ala., U.S.* 101 J16
Tall 'Afar, *Iraq* 172 C9
Tallahassee, *Fla., U.S.* 97 Q5
Tall al Abyaḑ al 'Atiq, *Syr.* 170 D11
Tall al Aḩmar (Til Barsip), *Syr.* 170 D10
Tallapoosa, river, *Ala., U.S.* 101 L16
Tallapoosa, *Ga., U.S.* 96 L4
Tallard, *Fr.* 147 W14
Tallassee, *Ala., U.S.* 101 L16
Tall Birāk, *Syr.* 170 D14
Tall Ḩalaf, ruin, *Syr.* 170 C13
Tallinn (Reval), *Est.* 141 K16
Tall Kalakh, *Syr.* 170 G7
Tall Tamir, *Syr.* 170 D13
Tallulah, *La., U.S.* 100 L10
Tall Ya'rūbīyah, *Syr.* 170 C16
Talmont-St. Hilaire, *Fr.* 147 T5
Talnakh, *Russ.* 159 F13
Tal'ne, *Ukr.* 157 P6
Talodi, *Sudan* 198 F12
Talofofo, *Guam, U.S.* 216 D10
Talofofo Bay, *Guam, U.S.* 216 D11
Taloga, *Okla., U.S.* 102 F9
Talok, *Indonesia* 189 H13
Taloqan, *Afghan.* 176 K8
Talorha, *Mauritania* 196 F6
Talos Dome, *Antarctica* 227 Q15
Taloyoak, *Nunavut, Can.* 83 F15
Talparo, *Trinidad & Tobago* 121 P23
Talshand, *Mongolia* 180 E10
Talsi, *Latv.* 141 M16
Taltal, *Chile* 132 F7
Tama, *Iowa, U.S.* 105 N12
Tamakautonga, *Niue, N.Z.* 219 B20
Tamale, *Ghana* 200 F10
Tamana, island, *Kiribati* 214 G8
Tamanoura, *Japan* 185 S2
Tamanrasset (Fort Laperrine), *Alg.* 196 F11
Tamarin, *Mauritius* 205 G19
Tamatoa, *Fr. Polynesia, Fr.* 219 K21
Tamazunchale, *Mex.* 114 H12
Tambacounda, *Senegal* 196 H5
Tambalan, *Indonesia* 188 H11
Tambelan, Kepulauan, *Indonesia* 188 H8
Tambisan, *Malaysia* 189 G13
Tambo, *Qnsld., Austral.* 211 U13
Tambov, *Russ.* 156 L11
Tambura, *Sudan* 198 H11
Tamch, *Mongolia* 180 D9
Tamchekkeţ, *Mauritania* 196 G6
Tame, *Col.* 128 E7
Tâmega, river, *Port.* 144 D6
Tamel Aike, *Arg.* 133 U7
Tamiahua, *Mex.* 114 H12
Tam Ky, *Vietnam* 186 L14
Tammerfors *see* Tampere, *Fin.* 141 J15
Tamotoe, Passe, *Fr. Polynesia, Fr.* 219 P17
Tampa, *Fla., U.S.* 97 U7
Tampa Bay, *Fla., U.S.* 97 U7
Tampere (Tammerfors), *Fin.* 141 J15
Tampico, *Mex.* 114 G12
Tampin, *Malaysia* 187 U10
Tampok, river, *Fr. Guiana, Fr.* 129 F17
Tam Quan, *Vietnam* 186 M14
Tamsagbulag, *Mongolia* 181 D15
Tamshiyacu, *Peru* 130 E4
Tamu, *Myanmar* 186 F5
Tamuning, *Guam, U.S.* 216 C11
Tamworth, *N.S.W., Austral.* 211 X14
Tana, river, *Fin., Nor.* 141 C15
Tana, river, *Kenya* 199 K15
Tana, *Nor.* 141 B15
Tanabe, *Japan* 185 R8
Tanacross, *Alas., U.S.* 111 H18
Tanaga Island, *Alas., U.S.* 110 N4
Tanagomba Harbor, *Solomon Is.* 217 M18
T'ana Hāyk', *Eth.* 199 F14
Tanahbala, island, *Indonesia* 188 J5
Tanahgrogot, *Indonesia* 188 K12
Tanahjampea, island, *Indonesia* 189 M13
Tanahmasa, island, *Indonesia* 188 J5
Tanahmerah, *Indonesia* 189 M21
Tanami, *N. Terr., Austral.* 211 S7
Tanami, Mount, *Austral.* 210 E7
Tanami Desert, *N. Terr., Austral.* 211 R8
Tanana, river, *Alas., U.S.* 111 G16
Tanana, *Alas., U.S.* 111 F16
Tanapag, *N. Mariana Is., U.S.* 216 B5
Tanaunella, *It.* 150 M5
Tanavuso Point, *Fiji Is.* 218 H6
Tancheng, *China* 182 H8
Tanch'ŏn, *N. Korea* 182 C14
Tăndărei, *Rom.* 153 F17
Tandil, *Arg.* 133 N12
Tandil, Sierra del, *S. Amer.* 126 M6
Tandlianwala, *Pak.* 177 Q11
Tando Adam, *Pak.* 177 V7
Tando Allahyar, *Pak.* 177 V7
Tando Bago, *Pak.* 177 W7
Tando Muhammad Khan, *Pak.* 177 W7
Tandur, *India* 178 L7
Tanega Shima, *Japan* 185 U4
Tanen Range, *Myanmar, Thai.* 186 J8
Tanezrouft, region, *Alg., Mali* 196 E9
Ţanf, Jabal aţ, *Syr.* 170 J11
Tanga, *Tanzania* 199 L15
Tangail, *Bangladesh* 178 H12
Tanga Islands, *P.N.G.* 213 C22
Tanga Langua, *Grenada* 121 J23
Tanganyika, Lake, *Af.* 194 L9
Tange Promontory, *Antarctica* 227 B19
Tanger (Tangier), *Mor.* 196 A8
Tanggu, *China* 182 D7
Tanggula Range, *China* 166 H9
Tanggula Shan, *China* 180 K7
Tanghe, *China* 182 J4
Tangi, *India* 178 L10
Tangier *see* Tanger, *Mor.* 196 A8
Tango, *Japan* 185 P8
Tangorin, *Qnsld., Austral.* 211 T12
Tangra Yumco, lake, *China* 180 K6
Tangse, *Indonesia* 188 G4
Tangshan, *China* 182 D8
Tanguisson Point, *Guam, U.S.* 216 B11
Tanimbar, Kepulauan, *Indonesia* 189 M17
Tanimbar Islands, *Indonesia* 166 L15
Tanimbili, *Solomon Is.* 217 Q23
Tanjore *see* Thanjavur, *India* 179 R6
Tanjungbalai, *Indonesia* 188 H5
Tanjungbatu, *Indonesia* 188 H12
Tanjungkarang-Telubketung, *Indonesia* 188 L7
Tanjungpandan, *Indonesia* 188 K8
Tanjungpinang, *Indonesia* 188 J7
Tanjungredep, *Indonesia* 188 H12
Tank, *Pak.* 177 P9
Ta-n-Kena, *Alg.* 196 D12
Tankovo, *Russ.* 159 J13
Tanna, island, *Vanuatu* 218 H4
Tännäs, *Sw.* 140 J12
Tannu Ola, Khrebet, *Russ.* 159 M13
Tannur, ruin, *Jordan* 171 P6
Tanobato, *Indonesia* 188 J5
Tanot, *India* 178 F2
Tânout, *Niger* 196 H12
Tanowrah, *Afghan.* 177 N2

Ṭanṭa, *Egypt* 197 CI8
Tan-Tan, *Mor.* 196 C7
Tanumbirini, *N. Terr., Austral.* 211 Q9
Tanzania, *Af.* 195 L22
Tao, *river, China* 180 JII
Tao, Ko, *Thai.* 187 Q8
Tao'er, *river, China* 181 DI6
Taojiang, *China* 182 M3
Taonan, *China* 181 DI6
Taole (Mataigou), *China* 182 DI
Taongi Atoll, *Marshall Is.* 216 E4
Taos, *N. Mex., U.S.* 107 QI3
Taoudenni (Smeïda), *Mali* 196 E8
Taouz, *Mor.* 196 C9
Taoyuan, *China* 182 M3
Taoyüan, *Taiwan, China* 183 QIO
Tapa, *Est.* 141 KI6
Tapachula, *Mex.* 115 LI5
Tapajós, *river, Braz.* 130 EIO
Tapak, *island, F.S.M.* 217 FI4
Tapan, *Indonesia* 188 K6
Tapana, *island, Tonga* 218 MII
Tapanahoni, *river, Suriname* 129 FI6
Tapauá, *river, Braz.* 130 E7
Tapawera, *N.Z.* 213 MI7
Taphan Hin, *Thai.* 186 L9
Tapi, *river, India* 178 K4
Tapiche, *river, Peru* 130 F4
Tapini, *P.N.G.* 213 DI9
Tapirapecó, Sierra, *Venez.* 128 GII
Tapita, *Liberia* 200 H7
Tapiwa, Banaba, *Kiribati* 217 D2O
Taplejung, *Nepal* 178 FII
Tapora, Passe, *Fr. Polynesia, Fr.* 219 PI7
Tappahannock, *Va., U.S.* 96 EI3
Tapu, Motu, *Fr. Polynesia, Fr.* 219 KI3
Tapuaenuku, *peak, N.Z.* 213 NI8
Tapuaetai, *island, Cook Is., N.Z.* 218 QI2
Tapuamu, *Fr. Polynesia, Fr.* 219 A23
Tapueraha, Passe de, *Fr. Polynesia, Fr.* 219 QI7
Tapul Group, *Philippines* 189 GI3
Tapunui, *island, Cook Is., N.Z.* 219 AI7
Taputapu, Cape, *Amer. Samoa, U.S.* 218 M6
Taputimu, *Amer. Samoa, U.S.* 218 N7
Ṭāqah, *Oman* 173 PI4
Taquari, *river, Braz.* 130 KIO
Tar, *river, N.C., U.S.* 96 HI2
Tara, *Qnsld., Austral.* 211 VI4
Tara, *Russ.* 158 JIO
Tara, *river, Mont.* 152 H9
Tara, Hill of, *Ire.* 143 R6
Ṭarābulus (Tripoli), *Lib.* 197 BI3
Tarakan, *island, Indonesia* 188 HI2
Tarakan, *Indonesia* 188 HI2
Tarakite Iti, *island, Cook Is., N.Z.* 219 CI4
Taranaki, Mount (Mt. Egmont), *N.Z.* 213 LI8
Tarancón, *Sp.* 144 GII
Taransay, *island, Scot., U.K.* 142 H6
Taranto, *It.* 151 NI4
Taranto, Golfo di, *It.* 151 NI4
Tarapacá, *Col.* 128 K8
Tarapaina, *Solomon Is.* 217 N2O
Tarapoto, *Peru* 130 F3
Taraqu, *ruin, Afghan.* 177 RI
Tarara, *P.N.G.* 217 KI4
Tarare, *Fr.* 147 UI2
Tarasa Dwip, *island, India* 179 SI5
Tarascon, *Fr.* 147 Y9
Tarata, *Peru* 130 K6
Taratai, *island, Kiribati* 217 FI7
Taratai, *Kiribati* 217 FI7
Tarauacá, *river, Braz.* 130 F5
Tarauacá, *Braz.* 130 F5
Taravai, *island, Fr. Polynesia, Fr.* 219 Q2O
Taravai, *Fr. Polynesia, Fr.* 219 Q2O
Taravao, *Fr. Polynesia, Fr.* 219 PI7
Taravao, Baie de, *Fr. Polynesia, Fr.* 219 PI7
Taravo, *river, Fr.* 150 K4
Tarawa (Bairiki), *Kiribati* 217 GI7
Tarawera, Mount, *N.Z.* 213 KI9
Taraz, *Kaz.* 175 JI4
Tarazit Massif, *Niger* 194 F5
Tarazona, *Sp.* 145 DI3
Tarazona de la Mancha, *Sp.* 145 HI3
Tarbagannakh, Gora, *Russ.* 159 GI9
Tarbaghatay Zhotasy, *Kaz.* 175 FI8
Tarbat Ness, *Scot., U.K.* 142 J9

Tarbert, *Scot., U.K.* 142 J6
Tarbert, *Scot., U.K.* 142 M8
Tarbes, *Fr.* 147 Y7
Tarboro, *N.C., U.S.* 96 HI3
Tarbrax, *Qnsld., Austral.* 211 SI2
Tarcoola, *S. Aust., Austral.* 211 W9
Tardun, *W. Aust., Austral.* 211 W2
Taree, *N.S.W., Austral.* 211 XI5
Ṭarfā, Ra's aṭ, *Saudi Arabia* 172 N8
Tarfaya, *Mor.* 196 C6
Tarfside, *Scot., U.K.* 142 KIO
Targhee Pass, *Idaho, Mont., U.S.* 106 F8
Târgu Mureş, *Rom.* 153 CI4
Tari, *P.N.G.* 213 DI8
Ṭarīf, *U.A.E.* 173 KI4
Tarifa, *Sp.* 144 N8
Tarifa, Punta de, *Sp.* 144 N8
Tarija, *Bol.* 130 L7
Tarikere, *India* 179 P5
Tariku-Taritatu Plain, *Indonesia* 189 K2O
Tarim, *river, China* 180 F6
Tarim Basin, *China* 166 G8
Tarim Pendi, *China* 180 F5
Tarin Kowt, *Afghan.* 177 P5
Taritatu, *river, Indonesia* 213 CI7
Tarkastad, *S. Af.* 202 LIO
Tarkhankut, Mys, *Ukr.* 157 S7
Tarkio, *Mo., U.S.* 105 Q9
Tarko Sale, *Russ.* 158 GI2
Tarkwa, *Ghana* 200 HIO
Tarlac, *Philippines* 189 CI3
Tarma, *Peru* 130 H4
Tarn, *river, Fr.* 147 X9
Tärnaby, *Sw.* 140 FI2
Tarnak, *river, Afghan.* 177 Q5
Tarnobrzeg, *Pol.* 149 GI7
Tarnogskiy Gorodok, *Russ.* 156 EI2
Tarnów, *Pol.* 149 GI6
Ṭārom, *Iran* 173 GI5
Taroom, *Qnsld., Austral.* 211 UI4
Tarpon Springs, *Fla., U.S.* 97 U7
Tarpum Bay, *Bahamas* 120 E6
Tarpum Bay, *Bahamas* 120 F6
Tarquinia, *It.* 150 K7
Tarra, *N.Z.* 213 QI6
Tarras, *N.Z.* 213 QI6
Tarsia, *It.* 151 PI3
Tarsus, *Turk.* 168 JIO
Tarta, *Turkm.* 174 K6
Tartagal, *Arg.* 132 DIO
Tartas, *Fr.* 147 X6
Tartu, *Est.* 141 KI7
Ṭarṭūs (Tortosa), *Syr.* 170 G7
Taruia Passage, *Cook Is., N.Z.* 219 BI7
Tarutao, Ko, *Thai.* 187 S8
Tarutung, *Indonesia* 188 H5
Tasek Dampar, *lake, Malaysia* 187 UIO
Taseyevo, *Russ.* 159 KI4
Tashanta, *Russ.* 158 MI2
Tash Gozar, *Afghan.* 176 K6
Tashk, Daryācheh-ye, *Iran* 173 FI4
Tashkent *see* Toshkent, *Uzb.* 175 KI3
Tash-Kömür, *Kyrg.* 176 FIO
Tasiilaq, *Greenland, Den.* 81 C22
Tasikmalaya, *Indonesia* 188 M9
Tasiusaq, *Greenland, Den.* 81 C2O
Taskan, *Russ.* 159 F2O
Taskesken, *Kaz.* 175 FI8
Taşköprü, *Turk.* 168 C9
Tasman, *N.Z.* 213 MI8
Tasman Bay, *N.Z.* 213 MI8
Tasman Fracture Zone, *Antarctic Oc.* 245 NI4
Tasmania, *island, Austral.* 210 MI6
Tasmania, *Austral.* 211 ZI5
Tasman Peninsula, *Austral.* 210 MI6
Tasman Plain, *Pac. Oc.* 238 P7
Tasman Sea, *Pac. Oc.* 238 P7
Tăşnad, *Rom.* 152 BI2
Taşova, *Turk.* 168 DII
Tassialouc, Lac, *Que., Can.* 83 KI8
Tas Tumus, *Russ.* 159 GI7
Tasure, *Solomon Is.* 217 LI5

Tataacho Point, *N. Mariana Is., U.S.* 216 D7
Tatabánya, *Hung.* 149 LI4
Tatafa, *island, Tonga* 218 P7
Tatakoto, *island, Fr. Polynesia, Fr.* 219 E2I
Tatamba, *Solomon Is.* 217 MI8
Tatarbunary, *Ukr.* 157 S5
Tatarsk, *Russ.* 158 KII
Tatarskiy Proliv, *Russ.* 159 J2I
Tatar Strait, *Russ.* 166 DI3
Tate, *Ga., U.S.* 96 K5
Tateyama, *Japan* 185 QI2
Tathlina Lake, *N.W.T., Can.* 82 HIO
Tathlith, *Saudi Arabia* 172 M9
Tatkon, *Myanmar* 186 H6
Tatnam, Cape, *Man., Can.* 83 LI5
Tatoosh Island, *Wash., U.S.* 107 SII
Tatry, *range, Pol., Slovakia* 149 JI5
Tattershall, *Eng., U.K.* 143 SI4
Tatui, *Braz.* 131 MI3
Tatum, *N. Mex., U.S.* 107 UI5
Tatvan, *Turk.* 169 GI6
Tau, *island, Amer. Samoa, U.S.* 218 P3
Tau, *Amer. Samoa, U.S.* 218 P3
Tau, *island, Tonga* 218 HI2
Tauá, *Braz.* 131 FI6
Tauak Passage, *F.S.M.* 217 FI3
Tauanap, Mochun, *F.S.M.* 217 BI4
Taubaté, *Braz.* 131 MI4
Tauenai Channel, *F.S.M.* 217 GI3
Tauere, *island, Fr. Polynesia, Fr.* 219 E2O
Taugarau, *island, Fr. Polynesia, Fr.* 219 KI8
Tauhunu, *island, Cook Is., N.Z.* 219 BI3
Tauhunu, *Cook Is., N.Z.* 219 BI3
Tauhunu Landing, *Cook Is., N.Z.* 219 BI3
Taula, *island, Tonga* 218 MII
Taulaga, *Amer. Samoa, U.S.* 218 R3
Taumako, *island, Solomon Is.* 217 N24
Taumarunui, *N.Z.* 213 LI9
Taumatawhakatangihangakoauauota-
mateapokaiwhenuakitanatahu, *peak, N.Z.* 213 MI9
Taum Sauk Mountain, *Mo., U.S.* 105 UI5
Taunga, *island, Tonga* 218 MII
Taunggok, *Myanmar* 186 J5
Taunggyi, *Myanmar* 186 H6
Taungoo, *Myanmar* 186 J6
Taungup Pass, *Myanmar* 186 J5
Taunsa, *Pak.* 177 R9
Taunton, *Eng., U.K.* 143 WIO
Taunton, *Mass., U.S.* 95 LI5
Taupo, *N.Z.* 213 KI9
Taupo, Lake, *N.Z.* 213 LI9
Taupo Tablemount, *Pac. Oc.* 238 N7
Tauragė, *Lith.* 141 NI6
Tauranga, *N.Z.* 213 KI9
Taurere, Pointe, *Fr. Polynesia, Fr.* 219 LI4
Taurus *see* Toros Dağları, *range, Turk.* 168 J8
Taūshyq, *Kaz.* 174 G5
Tauste, *Sp.* 145 DI3
Tautama, *island, Pitcairn I., U.K.* 219 Q23
Tautau, *island, Fr. Polynesia, Fr.* 219 A23
Tautira, *Fr. Polynesia, Fr.* 219 PI7
Tautu, *Cook Is., N.Z.* 218 QII
Tautua, *island, Cook Is., N.Z.* 219 BI8
Tauu Islands, *P.N.G.* 217 HI6
Tavaerua, *island, Cook Is., N.Z.* 218 QI2
Tavai, *Wallis & Futuna, Fr.* 218 EII
Tavan Bogd Uul *see* Youyi Feng, *peak, China, Mongolia* 180 C8
Tavannes, *Switz.* 150 A2
Tavas, *Turk.* 168 G4
Tavda, *Russ.* 158 H9
Taverna, *It.* 151 QI4
Taverner Bay, *Nunavut, Can.* 83 GI8
Tavernes, *Fr.* 147 XI4
Tavernes de la Valldigna, *Sp.* 145 HI5
Tavernier, *Fla., U.S.* 97 YIO
Taveuni, *island, Fiji Is.* 218 H8
Tavropoú, Límni, *Gr.* 154 F9
Tavşanlı, *Turk.* 168 E5
Tavua, *Fiji Is.* 218 H6
Tavu-Na-Sici, *island, Fiji Is.* 218 J9
Tawai, *India* 178 FI3
Tawake, *Fiji Is.* 218 G8
Tawakoni, Lake, *Tex., U.S.* 102 LI3
Tawang, *India* 178 FI3

Tawas City, *Mich., U.S.* 98 JI2
Tawau, *Malaysia* 188 GI2
Tawi Tawi, *island, Philippines* 189 GI3
Tawu, *Taiwan, China* 183 S9
Taxco, *Mex.* 114 JII
Taxkorgan, *China* 180 G4
Tay, Firth of, *Scot., U.K.* 142 LII
Tay, Loch, *Scot., U.K.* 142 L9
Tayan, *Indonesia* 188 J9
Tayandu, Kepulauan, *Indonesia* 189 LI8
Ṭāybād, *Iran* 173 CI7
Taygonos, Poluostrov, *Russ.* 159 E2I
Taylakova, *Russ.* 158 JII
Taylor, *Mich., U.S.* 98 MI2
Taylor, *Tex., U.S.* 103 PII
Taylor, Mount, *N. Mex., U.S.* 107 SII
Taylor Glacier, *Antarctica* 227 NI4
Taylor Highway, *Alas., U.S.* III GI9
Taylorsville, *Miss., U.S.* 100 MI2
Taylorville, *Ill., U.S.* 99 S5
Taymā', *Saudi Arabia* 172 G6
Taymyr, Lake, *Russ.* 166 C9
Taymyr, Ozero, *Russ.* 159 EI4
Taymyr, Poluostrov, *Russ.* 159 EI4
Taymyr Peninsula, *Russ.* 166 C9
Tay Ninh, *Vietnam* 187 PI2
Taypaq, *Kaz.* 174 E6
Tayshet, *Russ.* 159 KI4
Taytay, *Philippines* 189 EI3
Tayynsha (Krasnoarmeysk), *Kaz.* 175 BI3
Taz, *river, Russ.* 158 GI2
Taza, *Mor.* 196 B9
Tazawa Ko, *Japan* 184 KI3
Tazawako, *Japan* 184 KI3
Tazewell, *Va., U.S.* 96 F8
Tāzirbū, *Lib.* 197 EI6
Tazovskiy, *Russ.* 158 GI2
Tazovskiy Poluostrov, *Russ.* 158 FI2
Tba P'arvani, *lake, Rep. of Georgia* 169 CI8
Tbilisi (Tiflis), *Rep. of Georgia* 169 CI8
Tchabal Gangdaba, *range, Cameroon* 201 GI6
Tchad, Lac *see* Chad, Lake, *Af.* 197 JI3
Tchibanga, *Gabon* 201 MI6
Tchin-Tabaradène, *Niger* 196 HII
Tczew, *Pol.* 149 BI4
Teaehoa, Pointe, *Fr. Polynesia, Fr.* 219 N2O
Te Afualiku, *island, Tuvalu* 217 J23
Teague, *Tex., U.S.* 103 NI2
Teahupoo, *Fr. Polynesia, Fr.* 219 QI7
Teaiti Point, *Cook Is., N.Z.* 218 Q9
Teakava, *island, Fr. Polynesia, Fr.* 219 Q2I
Te Anau, *N.Z.* 213 QI5
Te Anau, Lake, *N.Z.* 213 QI5
Teaoraereke, *Kiribati* 217 GI7
Tearinibai, *Kiribati* 217 FI7
Tea Tree, *N. Terr., Austral.* 211 T8
Teava Moa, Passe, *Fr. Polynesia, Fr.* 219 B24
Teavanui, Passe, *Fr. Polynesia, Fr.* 219 KI3
Teavapiti, Passe, *Fr. Polynesia, Fr.* 219 B23
Teavaraa, Passe de, *Fr. Polynesia, Fr.* 219 PI6
Teavaro, *Fr. Polynesia, Fr.* 219 NI4
Teberda, *Russ.* 157 UI2
Tébessa, *Alg.* 196 BI2
Tebingtinggi, *Indonesia* 188 H5
Techirghiol, *Rom.* 153 GI8
Techla, *W. Sahara, Mor.* 196 E5
Tecka, *Arg.* 133 R7
Tecomán, *Mex.* 114 J9
Tecpan, *Mex.* 114 KII
Tecuala, *Mex.* 114 G9
Tecuci, *Rom.* 153 DI6
Tecumseh, *Mich., U.S.* 98 NII
Tecumseh, *Nebr., U.S.* 105 R9
Tecumseh, *Okla., U.S.* 102 GII
Teec Nos Pos, *Ariz., U.S.* 107 Q9
Teel, *Mongolia* 180 DII
Tefala, *island, Tuvalu* 217 L22
Tefarerii, *Fr. Polynesia, Fr.* 219 HI4
Tefé, *river, Braz.* 130 E7
Tefé, *Braz.* 130 D7
Tefenni, *Turk.* 168 H5
Tegal, *Indonesia* 188 M9
Teglio, *San Marino* 161 LI4

Tégua, *island, Vanuatu* 218 AI
Tegucigalpa, *Hond.* 115 LI7
Teguise, *Canary Is.* 204 P7
Tehachapi, *Calif., U.S.* 109 V8
Tehachapi Mountains, *Calif., U.S.* 109 W8
Tehachapi Pass, *Calif., U.S.* 109 V8
Te Hapua, *N.Z.* 213 GI7
Tehek Lake, *Nunavut, Can.* 83 HI4
Tehoohaivei, Cap, *Fr. Polynesia, Fr.* 219 M2I
Tehrān, *Iran* 173 CI3
Tehuacán, *Mex.* 114 JI2
Tehuantepec, *Mex.* 115 KI3
Tehuantepec, Golfo de, *Mex.* 115 LI4
Tehuantepec, Gulf of *see* Tehuantepec, Golfo de, *N. Amer.* 80 P6
Tehuantepec, Isthmus of *see* Tehuantepec, Istmo de, *N. Amer.* 80 P6
Tehuantepec, Istmo de, *Mex.* 115 KI4
Tehuata (Rekareka), *island, Fr. Polynesia, Fr.* 219 EI9
Teide, Pico de, *Canary Is.* 204 Q4
Teignmouth, *Eng., U.K.* 143 XIO
Teiko, Motu, *Fr. Polynesia, Fr.* 219 R2O
Tejen, *Turkm.* 174 M9
Tejenstroy, *Turkm.* 174 N9
Tejo (Tagus), *river, Port.* 144 H5
Tekamah, *Nebr., U.S.* 105 P9
Te Karaka, *N.Z.* 213 K2O
Tekax, *Mex.* 115 HI6
Tekeli, *Kaz.* 175 GI7
Tekirdağ, *Turk.* 168 C3
Tekirova, *Turk.* 168 J6
Tekkali, *India* 178 L9
Tekman, *Turk.* 169 EI6
Teknaf, *Bangladesh* 178 KI4
Tekoa, *Wash., U.S.* 108 C9
Tekokota, *island, Fr. Polynesia, Fr.* 219 EI9
Tekopua, *island, Cook Is., N.Z.* 218 QI2
Te Koutu Point, *Cook Is., N.Z.* 218 QII
T'elavi, *Rep. of Georgia* 169 BI9
Tel Aviv-Yafo, *Israel* 170 M5
Telde, *Canary Is.* 204 R6
Telebekelel Ngerael, *Palau* 216 KII
Telefomin, *P.N.G.* 213 C17
Telegraph Creek, *B.C., Can.* 82 H8
Telekitonga, *island, Tonga* 218 R7
Telekivavau, *island, Tonga* 218 Q7
Telele, *island, Tuvalu* 217 L23
Telén, *Arg.* 132 M9
Telescope Peak, *Calif., U.S.* 109 U9
Telescope Point, *Grenada* 121 K23
Teles Pires (São Manuel), *river, Braz.* 130 FIO
Teljo, Jebel, *Sudan* 194 G8
Tell Atlas, *Alg., Tun.* 194 C4
Tell City, *Ind., U.S.* 99 T9
Teller, *Alas., U.S.* 110 FII
Tellicherry *see* Thalassery, *India* 179 Q4
Telloh *see* Lagash, *ruin, Iraq* 172 EIO
Tell Tayinat, *ruin, Turk.* 168 JII
Telluride, *Colo., U.S.* 107 PII
Telsen, *Arg.* 133 R9
Telšiai, *Lith.* 141 NI6
Telukbutun, *Indonesia* 188 G9
Telukdalem, *Indonesia* 188 J4
Teluk Intan, *Malaysia* 187 T9
Tema, *Ghana* 200 HII
Te Manga, *peak, Cook Is., N.Z.* 218 Q9
Tematagi, *island, Fr. Polynesia, Fr.* 219 H2O
Tembagapura, *Indonesia* 189 L2O
Tembenchi, *Russ.* 159 HI4
Témbi, *range, Gr.* 154 EIO
Temerin, *Serb.* 152 E9
Temerloh, *Malaysia* 187 UIO
Teminabuan, *Indonesia* 189 JI8
Teminikov, *Russ.* 156 KI2
Temirtaū, *Kaz.* 175 DI4
Temoe (Timoe), *island, Fr. Polynesia, Fr.* 219 H23
Temora, *N.S.W., Austral.* 211 YI3
Tempe, *Ariz., U.S.* 107 U7
Tempio, *It.* 150 M4
Temple, *Okla., U.S.* 102 JIO
Temple, *Tex., U.S.* 103 PII
Temple Bay, *Austral.* 210 BI2
Temryuk, *Russ.* 157 S9
Temryukskiy Zaliv, *Russ.* 157 S9
Temse, *Belg.* 146 KI2
Temuco, *Chile* 133 P6
Temuka, *N.Z.* 213 PI7
Tena, *Ecua.* 128 J3

Tenali, *India* 179 N7
Tenao, *Monaco* 161 B22
Tenararo, island, *Fr. Polynesia, Fr.* 219 G22
Ténaro, Akrotírio (Taenarum), *Gr.* 154 N10
Tenarunga, island, *Fr. Polynesia, Fr.* 219 G22
Tenasserim, region, *Myanmar* 186 M7
Tenasserim, *Myanmar* 187 N8
Tenby, *Wales, U.K.* 143 V8
Tende, *Fr.* 147 W16
Ten Degree Channel, *India* 179 R14
Tendō, *Japan* 184 L13
Tendürek Dağı, *Turk.* 169 F18
Ténéré, region, *Niger* 196 F12
Tenerife, island, *Canary Is.* 204 Q5
Tengako, island, *Tuvalu* 217 J24
Tengasu, island, *Tuvalu* 217 L22
Tengchong, *China* 180 N10
Te Nggano, *Solomon Is.* 217 R19
Tengiz, oil field, *Kaz.* 174 G7
Tengiz, Lake, *Kaz.* 166 E7
Tengiz Köli, *Kaz.* 175 D13
Tengxian, *China* 182 G7
Tengxian, *China* 183 R2
Tenino, *Wash., U.S.* 108 D3
Tenjo, Mount, *Guam, U.S.* 216 C10
Tenkasi, *India* 179 S5
Tenke, *Dem. Rep. of the Congo* 198 N11
Tenkiller Ferry Lake, *Okla., U.S.* 102 F14
Tenkodogo, *Burkina Faso* 200 E11
Tennant Creek, *N. Terr., Austral.* 211 S9
Tennessee, river, *Tenn., U.S.* 101 E14
Tennessee, *U.S.* 101 F13
Tennessee Pass, *Colo., U.S.* 106 M12
Tennille, *Ga., U.S.* 96 M7
Tenoka, island, *Fr. Polynesia, Fr.* 219 Q20
Ténos, Pointe, *Martinique, Fr.* 121 E22
Tenos see Tínos, island, *Gr.* 155 K15
Tenosique, *Mex.* 115 K15
Tensaw, river, *Ala., U.S.* 101 N14
Ten Sleep, *Wyo., U.S.* 106 G11
Ten Thousand Islands, *Fla., U.S.* 97 X9
Teófilo Otoni, *Braz.* 131 K15
Teoho Ote Papa, Pointe, *Fr. Polynesia, Fr.* 219 N23
Teohotepapa, Pointe, *Fr. Polynesia, Fr.* 219 M21
Teora, *It.* 150 M12
Tepa, *Wallis & Futuna, Fr.* 218 B11
Tepaeture, Pointe, *Fr. Polynesia, Fr.* 219 Q20
Tepako, Pointe, *Wallis & Futuna, Fr.* 218 B12
Tepa Point, *Niue, N.Z.* 219 B20
Tepati, *Fr. Polynesia, Fr.* 219 Q17
Tepé, *Eq. Guinea* 204 L8
Tepe, peak, *Kosovo* 152 J11
Tepe Musyan, ruin, *Iran* 172 E11
Tepic, *Mex.* 114 G9
Tepu, *Fr. Polynesia, Fr.* 219 K20
Te Puka, island, *Cook Is., N.Z.* 219 B13
Tepuka, island, *Tuvalu* 217 J22
Tepuka, Te Ava, *Tuvalu* 217 J22
Tepuu, Pointe, *Fr. Polynesia, Fr.* 219 K20
Téra, *Niger* 196 H9
Terae, island, *Cook Is., N.Z.* 219 B17
Teraina (Washington Island), island, *Kiribati* 214 F12
Teramo, *It.* 150 J10
Teratak, *Indonesia* 188 J9
Tercan, *Turk.* 169 E15
Terceira, island, *Azores* 144 P4
Tereai, island, *Fr. Polynesia, Fr.* 219 K15
Terek, river, *Russ.* 138 G13
Terekhovka, *Belarus* 156 M6
Terekli Mekteb, *Russ.* 157 T14
Terekty, *Kaz.* 175 E19
Terenos, *Braz.* 130 L11
Teresina, *Braz.* 131 E15
Terhazza, ruin, *Mali* 196 E8
Terihi, island, *Fr. Polynesia, Fr.* 219 N21
Termas de Río Hondo, *Arg.* 132 G9
Terme, *Turk.* 168 D12
Termini Imerese, *It.* 151 S10
Termini Imerese, Golfo di, *It.* 151 S10

Términos, Laguna de, *Mex.* 115 J15
Términos Lagoon see Términos, Laguna de, *N. Amer.* 80 P6
Termita, *Russ.* 157 S14
Termiz, *Uzb.* 174 M12
Termoli, *It.* 150 K11
Ternate, *Indonesia* 189 J16
Terneuzen, *Neth.* 146 K11
Terni, *It.* 150 J8
Ternitz, *Aust.* 148 L12
Ternopil', *Ukr.* 157 P3
Terrace, *B.C., Can.* 82 K8
Terracina, *It.* 150 L9
Terralba, *It.* 151 P3
Terrassa, *Sp.* 145 D17
Terrebonne Bay, *La., U.S.* 100 R10
Terre-de-Bas, island, *Guadeloupe, Fr.* 121 G14
Terre-de-Bas, *Guadeloupe, Fr.* 121 G14
Terre-de-Haut, island, *Guadeloupe, Fr.* 121 G14
Terre-de-Haut, *Guadeloupe, Fr.* 121 G14
Terre Haute, *Ind., U.S.* 99 S7
Terreiro Velho, *Sao Tome and Principe* 205 B21
Terrell, *Tex., U.S.* 102 L12
Terre Rouge, *Mauritius* 205 F20
Terry, *Mont., U.S.* 106 D12
Tersakan Gölü, *Turk.* 168 G8
Terschelling, island, *Neth.* 146 G13
Tertenia, *It.* 151 P4
Teru, *Pak.* 176 L10
Teruel, *Sp.* 145 F14
Teseney, *Eritrea* 199 E14
Teshekpuk Lake, *Alas., U.S.* 111 C15
Teshikaga, *Japan* 184 F15
Teshio, river, *Japan* 184 E13
Teshio, *Japan* 184 E13
Teshio Sanchi, *Japan* 184 E14
Tesiyn, river, *Mongolia* 180 C10
Teslić, *Bosn. & Herzg.* 152 F7
Teslin, *Yukon, Can.* 82 G8
Tesovo Netyl'skiy, *Russ.* 156 G6
Tessalit, *Mali* 196 F10
Tessaoua, *Niger* 196 H12
Testa del Gargano, *It.* 150 K13
Tetas, Punta, *Chile* 132 E6
Te Tautua, *Cook Is., N.Z.* 219 B18
Tete, *Mozambique* 202 F12
Tetepare, island, *Solomon Is.* 217 M16
Tetere, *Russ.* 156 J15
Teteven, *Bulg.* 153 H14
Tetford, *Eng., U.K.* 143 S14
Tetiaroa, island, *Fr. Polynesia, Fr.* 219 E16
Tetlin, *Alas., U.S.* 111 H19
Teton, river, *Mont., U.S.* 106 C8
Teton Range, *Wyo., U.S.* 106 G8
Tétouan, *Mor.* 196 A9
Tetovo, *Maced.* 152 K10
Tetufera, Mont, *Fr. Polynesia, Fr.* 219 P16
Tetutu, Pointe, *Fr. Polynesia, Fr.* 219 N23
Tetyushi, *Russ.* 156 J14
Teuaua (Hat), island, *Fr. Polynesia, Fr.* 219 N23
Teuco, river, *Arg.* 132 F12
Teulada, *It.* 151 Q3
Teulada, Capo, *It.* 151 Q3
Teuri Tō, *Japan* 184 E13
Teutonic College, *Vatican City* 161 Q16
Tevahavaha, island, *Cook Is., N.Z.* 219 C14
Tevai, island, *Solomon Is.* 217 R24
Tevaro, island, *Fr. Polynesia, Fr.* 219 K17
Teveiroa, island, *Fr. Polynesia, Fr.* 219 K13
Tevere (Tiber), river, *It.* 150 J8
Teverya (Tiberias), *Israel* 170 K6
Tewantin, *Qnsld., Austral.* 211 V15
Texarkana, *Ark., U.S.* 100 J6
Texarkana, *Tex., U.S.* 102 K15
Texas, *U.S.* 103 N4
Texas City, *Tex., U.S.* 103 R14
Texas Point, *Tex., U.S.* 103 Q16
Texel, island, *Neth.* 146 G12
Texhoma, *Okla., U.S.* 102 E5
Texico, *N. Mex., U.S.* 107 S15
Texline, *Tex., U.S.* 102 E3
Texoma, Lake, *Okla., U.S.* 102 J12
Texon, *Tex., U.S.* 103 N5

Teykovo, *Russ.* 156 H10
Teylan, *Afghan.* 176 L4
Teywarah, *Afghan.* 177 N4
Tezpur, *India* 178 G14
Tfaritiy, *W. Sahara, Mor.* 196 D7
Thabana Ntlenyana, peak, *Lesotho* 202 K11
Thabaung, *Myanmar* 186 K5
Thabazimbi, *S. Af.* 202 J10
Thaga Pass, *China, India* 178 D7
Thagyettaw, *Myanmar* 186 M7
Thai Binh, *Vietnam* 186 H12
Thai Hoa, *Vietnam* 186 J12
Thailand, *Asia* 167 X10
Thailand, Gulf of, *Asia* 166 K10
Thai Nguyen, *Vietnam* 186 G12
Thal, *Pak.* 177 N9
Thalabarivat, *Cambodia* 186 M12
Thalassery (Tellicherry), *India* 179 Q4
Thal Desert, *Pak.* 177 Q10
Thale Luang, lake, *Thai.* 187 R8
Thamarīt, *Oman* 173 N14
Thames, River, *Eng., U.K.* 143 V15
Thamūd, *Yemen* 172 N12
Thana, *Pak.* 177 S3
Thandaung, *Myanmar* 186 J6
Thane, *India* 178 L3
Thanet, cape, *Eng., U.K.* 143 V16
Thangool, *Qnsld., Austral.* 211 U15
Thanh Hoa, *Vietnam* 186 J12
Thanh Tri, *Vietnam* 187 Q12
Thanjavur (Tanjore), *India* 179 R6
Thanlwin (Salween), river, *Myanmar* 186 G7
Tharabwin, *Myanmar* 187 N8
Thar Desert see Great Indian Desert, *India, Pak.* 177 T9
Thargomindah, *Qnsld., Austral.* 211 V12
Tharros, ruin, *It.* 151 N3
Tharthār, Lake, *Iraq* 172 D9
Tha Sala, *Thai.* 187 Q8
Thássos, island, *Gr.* 155 C14
Thássos (Limín), *Gr.* 155 C14
Thatch Cay, *Virgin Islands, U.S.* 120 M10
Thaton, *Myanmar* 186 K7
Thatta, *Pak.* 177 W7
Thau, Bassin de, *Fr.* 147 X11
Thaungdut, *Myanmar* 186 F5
Thayawthadanngyi Kyun, *Myanmar* 187 N7
Thayer, *Mo., U.S.* 105 V14
Thayet, *Myanmar* 186 J5
The Alley, *Jam.* 120 K8
The Barony, *Scot., U.K.* 142 F10
The Baths, *Virgin Islands, U.K.* 120 R8
Thebes, ruin, *Egypt* 197 E19
Thebes see Thíva, *Gr.* 154 H11
The Bight, *Bahamas* 120 B5
The Bluff, *Bahamas* 120 D5
The Bottom, *Neth. Antilles, Neth.* 119 F15
The Brothers, islands, *Bahamas* 117 H14
The Brothers see Al Ikhwān, islands, *Yemen* 173 R14
The Caves, *Qnsld., Austral.* 211 T15
The Cheviot, peak, *Eng., U.K.* 143 N11
The Cockpit Country, *Jam.* 120 H7
The Cow, island, *Ire.* 143 V2
The Crane, *Barbados* 121 L20
The Dalles, *Oreg., U.S.* 108 F5
The Deeps, bay, *Scot., U.K.* 142 D12
Thedford, *Nebr., U.S.* 105 N4
Theebine, *Qnsld., Austral.* 211 V15
The Everglades, wetland, *Fla., U.S.* 97 X9
The Ferry Settlement, *Bahamas* 120 F9
The Galleries, *Gibraltar, U.K.* 161 N23
The Hague see 's Gravenhage, *Neth.* 146 J12
The Heads, cape, *Oreg., U.S.* 108 K1
The Isles Lagoon, *Kiribati* 217 B23
The Little Minch, strait, *Scot., U.K.* 142 J6
Thelon, river, *N.W.T., Can.* 83 H13
The Lynd, *Qnsld., Austral.* 211 R13
The Marls, islands, *Bahamas* 120 B6
The Minch, strait, *Scot., U.K.* 142 H7
The Moors, plateau, *Scot., U.K.* 143 P8
The Narrows, strait, *Bermuda, U.K.* 120 A3
The Narrows, strait, *Virgin Islands, U.K., U.S.* 120 M11

The Narrows, strait, *Bahamas* 120 B12
The Narrows, strait, *St. Kitts & Nevis* 121 B18
The Naze, cape, *Eng., U.K.* 143 U15
The North Sound, *Scot., U.K.* 142 F10
Theodore, *Qnsld., Austral.* 211 U14
Theodore Roosevelt, river, *Braz.* 130 F9
Theodore Roosevelt Lake, *Ariz., U.S.* 107 T8
Theodore Roosevelt National Park (Elkhorn Ranch Site), *N. Dak., U.S.* 104 F2
Theodore Roosevelt National Park (North Unit), *N. Dak., U.S.* 104 F2
Theodore Roosevelt National Park (South Unit), *N. Dak., U.S.* 104 G2
Theológos, *Gr.* 155 C14
The Ox Mountains see Slieve Gamph, *Ire.* 143 Q4
The Pas, *Man., Can.* 83 M13
The Pennines, range, *Eng., U.K.* 143 Q11
Thera, ruin, *Gr.* 155 N15
The Remarkables, peak, *N.Z.* 213 Q15
Thermaïkós Kólpos, *Gr.* 154 D11
Thérmo, *Gr.* 154 H9
Thermopolis, *Wyo., U.S.* 106 G10
Thermopylae, battle, *Gr.* 154 G10
The Rope, island, *Pitcairn I., U.K.* 219 Q23
The Rosses, region, *Ire.* 143 P5
The Salt Ponds, *Jam.* 120 K11
The Sisters, islands, *Grenada* 121 H23
The Sisters see Les Soeurs, islands, *Seychelles* 205 M21
The Sisters, islands, *Trinidad & Tobago* 121 N18
The Skerries, islands, *Wales, U.K.* 143 S9
The Slot see New Georgia Sound, bay, *Solomon Is.* 217 M17
The Smalls, islands, *Wales, U.K.* 143 V7
The Snares, islands, *N.Z.* 214 Q7
The Solent, strait, *Eng., U.K.* 143 X12
The Sound, *Bahamas* 120 A8
Thessalon, *Ont., Can.* 83 Q17
Thessaloníki (Salonica), *Gr.* 154 C11
Thessaly, region, *Gr.* 154 F10
The Steppes, *Kaz.* 174 E8
Thetford, *Eng., U.K.* 143 T15
The Triangle, region, *Myanmar* 186 D7
The Twins, *S. Aust., Austral.* 211 W9
The Valley, *Anguilla, U.K.* 120 R11
The Wash, bay, *Eng., U.K.* 143 S14
The Weald, region, *Eng., U.K.* 143 W14
The Wolds, region, *Eng., U.K.* 143 R13
Thíamis, river, *Gr.* 154 E7
Thiaucourt, *Fr.* 147 P13
Thibodaux, *La., U.S.* 100 Q10
Thief River Falls, *Minn., U.S.* 104 E9
Thielsen, Mount, *Oreg., U.S.* 108 J4
Thiene, *It.* 150 D7
Thiers, *Fr.* 147 U11
Thiès, *Senegal* 196 H4
Thika, *Kenya* 199 K14
Thímena, island, *Gr.* 155 K17
Thimphu, *Bhutan* 178 F12
Thingeyri, *Ice.* 140 E2
Thinkèo, *Laos* 186 J10
Thio, *New Caledonia, Fr.* 218 D8
Thíra, *Gr.* 155 N15
Thíra (Santoríni), island, *Gr.* 155 M15
Thirassía, island, *Gr.* 155 M15
Third Cataract, *Sudan* 198 C12
Thirsk, *Eng., U.K.* 143 Q12
Thiruvananthapuram (Trivandrum), *India* 179 S5
Thisted, *Den.* 140 N11
Thistilfjördur, bay, *Ice.* 140 E4
Thitu Island, *Spratly Is.* 188 D11
Thíva (Thebes), *Gr.* 154 H11
Thjórsá, river, *Ice.* 140 F2
Tho Chu, Dao, *Vietnam* 187 Q10
Thoen, *Thai.* 186 K8
Thohoyandou, *S. Af.* 202 H11
Thomas, *Okla., U.S.* 102 F9
Thomaston, *Ga., U.S.* 96 M5
Thomaston, *Me., U.S.* 95 G17
Thomasville, *Ala., U.S.* 101 M14
Thomasville, *Ga., U.S.* 97 Q5
Thomasville, *N.C., U.S.* 96 H10
Thompson, river, *Iowa, U.S.* 105 Q11
Thompson, *Man., Can.* 83 L14

Thompson Falls, *Mont., U.S.* 106 C4
Thompson Springs, *Utah, U.S.* 107 N9
Thompson Town, *Jam.* 120 J8
Thomson, river, *Austral.* 210 F12
Thomson, *Ga., U.S.* 96 L7
Thongwa, *Myanmar* 186 K6
Thonon, *Fr.* 147 T14
Thonze, *Myanmar* 186 K6
Thoreau, *N. Mex., U.S.* 107 S10
Thórisvatn, lake, *Ice.* 140 F3
Thorndale, *Tex., U.S.* 103 P11
Thorne Bay, *Alas., U.S.* 111 M23
Thornhill, *Scot., U.K.* 143 N8
Thornton, *Colo., U.S.* 106 L13
Thorntonia, *Qnsld., Austral.* 211 S10
Thorp, *Wash., U.S.* 108 D5
Thorp, *Wis., U.S.* 98 H4
Thorpe, *Barbados* 121 K18
Thórshöfn, *Ice.* 140 E4
Thouars, *Fr.* 147 S7
Thrace, region, *Gr.* 155 B15
Three Forks, *Mont., U.S.* 106 E7
Three Gorges Dam, *China* 182 K3
Three Kings Islands, *N.Z.* 213 G17
Three Lakes, *Wis., U.S.* 98 G6
Three Pagodas Pass, *Myanmar, Thai.* 186 L7
Three Points, Cape, *Ghana* 200 H10
Three Rivers, *Mich., U.S.* 99 N10
Three Rivers, *Tex., U.S.* 103 T10
Three Sisters, peak, *Oreg., U.S.* 108 H4
Three Sisters Islands, *Solomon Is.* 217 P20
Thrissur, *India* 179 R5
Throckmorton, *Tex., U.S.* 102 K8
Throssell, Lake, *Austral.* 210 H5
Thuin, *Belg.* 146 M12
Thuir, *Fr.* 147 Z10
Thule Air Base, *Greenland, Den.* 81 C19
Thun, *Switz.* 150 B3
Thunder Bay, *Mich., U.S.* 98 H12
Thunder Bay, *Ont., Can.* 83 P15
Thuner See, *Switz.* 150 B3
Thung Song, *Thai.* 187 R8
Thunkar, *Bhutan* 178 F13
Thurles, *Ire.* 143 T5
Thurmont, *Md., U.S.* 96 C12
Thurso, *Scot., U.K.* 142 G10
Thurston Island, *Antarctica* 226 K5
Thusis, *Switz.* 150 B5
Thylungra, *Qnsld., Austral.* 211 U12
Tiamahana, Passe, *Fr. Polynesia, Fr.* 219 B23
Tianjin (Tientsin), *China* 182 D7
Tianjun, *China* 180 H10
Tianlin, *China* 180 P12
Tianmen, *China* 182 L4
Tianqiaoling, *China* 182 A14
Tian Shan, *Asia* 166 J7
Tianshan see Ar Horqin Qi, *China* 182 A9
Tianshifu, *China* 182 C11
Tianshui, *China* 180 J12
Tianshuihai, *China* 176 L15
Tianzhu, *China* 183 N1
Tiarei, *Fr. Polynesia, Fr.* 219 N17
Tiaret, *Alg.* 196 A10
Tiari, *New Caledonia, Fr.* 218 C6
Tiaro, *Qnsld., Austral.* 211 U15
Tiaro Bay, *Solomon Is.* 217 N18
Ti'avea, *Samoa* 218 L4
Tibagi, river, *Braz.* 130 M12
Tibati, *Cameroon* 201 H16
Tibé, Pic de, *Guinea* 200 F7
Tiber see Tevere, river, *It.* 150 K8
Tiber Dam, *Mont., U.S.* 106 B8
Tiberias see Teverya, *Israel* 170 K6
Tibesti Mountains, *Chad* 197 F15
Tibet, region, *China* 180 K5
Tibet, Plateau of, *China* 180 J6
Tibiri, *Niger* 196 J11
Tiboku Falls, *Guyana* 129 E14
Tibooburra, *N.S.W., Austral.* 211 W11
Tibrikot, *Nepal* 178 F9
Tibugá, Golfo de, *Col.* 128 E3
Tiburón, Isla, *Mex.* 114 D6
Tichît, *Mauritania* 196 G7
Ticonderoga, *N.Y., U.S.* 94 G12
Ticul, *Mex.* 115 H16
Tiddim, *Myanmar* 186 F4
Tidjikdja, *Mauritania* 196 G6
Tidore, *Indonesia* 189 J16
Tidra, Île, *Mauritania* 196 F4
Tiel, *Neth.* 146 J13

Tièl, *Senegal* 196 H5
Tieling, *China* 182 BII
Tielongtan, *China* 176 LI6
Tielongtan, *China* 180 H5
Tientsin *see* Tianjin, *China* 182 D7
Tierra Amarilla, *Chile* 132 G7
Tierra Amarilla, *N. Mex., U.S.* 107 QI2
Tierra Blanca Creek, *Tex., U.S.* 102 H4
Tierra del Fuego, island, *S. Amer.* 126 R5
Tieyon, *S. Aust., Austral.* 211 U8
Tiffin, *Ohio, U.S.* 99 PI2
Tiflis *see* T'bilisi, *Rep. of Georgia* 169 CI8
Tifristós, peak, *Gr.* 154 G9
Tifton, *Ga., U.S.* 97 P6
Tiga, *Île, New Caledonia, Fr.* 218 CIO
Tiger Bay, *Angola* 194 N6
Tigray, region, *Eth.* 199 EI4
Tigre, river, *Ecua.* 128 K4
Tigre, river, *Peru* 130 D3
Tigris, river, *Asia* 166 F4
Tigyaing, *Myanmar* 186 F6
Tîh, Gebel el, *Egypt* 171 R3
Tihamah, region, *Saudia Arabia, Yemen* 166 H3
Tihāmat ash Shām, range, *Saudi Arabia, Yemen* 172 L7
Tiheró, *Gr.* 155 BI6
Tijuana, *Mex.* 114 A5
Tikamgarh, *India* 178 H6
Tikanlik, *China* 180 F7
Tikapai, island, *Cook Is., N.Z.* 219 BI4
Tikchik Lakes, *Alas., U.S.* III KI3
Tikehau, island, *Fr. Polynesia, Fr.* 219 DI7
Tikei, island, *Fr. Polynesia, Fr.* 219 DI8
Tikhoretsk, *Russ.* 157 SII
Tikhvin, *Russ.* 156 F8
Tikopia, island, *Solomon Is.* 214 J7
Tikrīt, *Iraq* 172 D9
Tiksi, *Russ.* 159 EI6
Tiladummati Atoll, *Maldives* 179 T3
Til Barsip *see* Tall al Aḥmar, *Syr.* 170 DIO
Tilbooroo, *Qnsld., Austral.* 211 VI2
Tilburg, *Neth.* 146 KI2
Til-Châtel, *Fr.* 147 RI3
Tilden, *Nebr., U.S.* 105 N7
Tillabéri, *Niger* 196 HIO
Tillamook, *Oreg., U.S.* 108 F2
Tillamook Head, *Oreg., U.S.* 108 E2
Tillanchang Dwip, island, *India* 179 SI5
Tillia, *Niger* 196 HII
Tilloo Cay, *Bahamas* 116 CI2
Tílos, island, *Gr.* 155 MI8
Tilpa, *N.S.W., Austral.* 211 WI2
Timan Ridge *see* Timanskiy Kryazh, *Russ.* 138 AII
Timanskiy Kryazh, *Russ.* 158 F9
Timaru, *N.Z.* 213 PI7
Timashevo, *Russ.* 156 KI6
Timashevsk, *Russ.* 157 SIO
Timbalier Bay, *La., U.S.* 100 RII
Timbalier Island, *La., U.S.* 100 RIO
Timbaúba, *Braz.* 131 FI8
Timbedgha, *Mauritania* 196 G7
Timber Creek, *N. Terr., Austral.* 211 Q7
Timber Lake, *S. Dak., U.S.* 104 J4
Timbío, *Col.* 128 G4
Timbuktu *see* Tombouctou, *Mali* 196 G8
Timbun Mata, island, *Philippines* 189 GI3
Timfi, Óros (Gamila), *Gr.* 154 E7
Timimoun, *Alg.* 196 CIO
Timiris, Cap (Mirik), *Mauritania* 196 F4
Timiryazevskiy, *Russ.* 158 KI2
Timiš, river, *Rom.* 152 EII
Timişoara, *Rom.* 152 DII
Timiti's Crack, cape, *Pitcairn I., U.K.* 219 Q23
Timmiarmiut, *Greenland, Den.* 81 D22
Timmins, *Ont., Can.* 83 PI7
Timmonsville, *S.C., U.S.* 96 KIO
Timms Hill, *Wis., U.S.* 98 H4
Timoe *see* Temoe, island, *Fr. Polynesia, Fr.* 219 H23
Timor, island, *Indonesia, Timor-Leste* 189 NI5
Timor-Leste (East Timor), *Asia* 167 ZI4
Timor Sea, *Indonesia* 189 NI6

Timote, *Arg.* 132 LII
Timpanogos Cave National Monument, *Utah, U.S.* 106 L7
Timpson, *Tex., U.S.* 102 MI5
Timsâh, Buheirat el (Lake Timsah), *Egypt* 171 PI
Timsah, Lake *see* Timsâh, Buheirat el, *Egypt* 171 PI
Tims Ford Lake, *Tenn., U.S.* 101 GI6
Tîna, Khalîg el, *Egypt* 171 NI
Tinaca Point, *Philippines* 189 GI5
Tinajo, *Canary Is.* 204 P7
Tinakula, island, *Solomon Is.* 217 P22
Tindouf, *Alg.* 196 D7
Tindouf, Sebkha de, *Alg.* 196 D8
Tineo, *Sp.* 144 B8
Tinggoa, *Solomon Is.* 217 RI9
Tingmerkpuk Mountain, *Alas., U.S.* 84 M2
Tingo María, *Peru* 130 G3
Tingri, *China* 180 L6
Tinharé, Ilha de, *Braz.* 131 HI6
Tinhosa Grande, island, *Sao Tome and Principe* 205 B2O
Tinhosa Pequena, island, *Sao Tome and Principe* 205 B2O
Tinhosas, Pedras, *Sao Tome and Principe* 205 B2O
Tinian, island, *N. Mariana Is., U.S.* 216 C2
Tinian Harbor *see* Sunbaron Roads, *N. Mariana Is., U.S.* 216 C7
Tinnenburra, *Qnsld., Austral.* 211 VI3
Tinogasta, *Arg.* 132 G8
Tínos, *Gr.* 155 KI5
Tínos (Tenos), island, *Gr.* 155 KI5
Tiñoso, Cabo, *Sp.* 145 LI4
Tinrhert, Hamada de, *Alg., Lib.* 196 DI2
Tinsukia, *India* 178 FI5
Tintamarre, Île, *St. Martin, Fr.* 121 AI5
Tintigny, *Belg.* 147 NI3
Tintina, *Arg.* 132 GII
Tintinara, *S. Aust., Austral.* 211 YII
Ti-n-Zaouâtene, *Alg.* 196 FIO
Tioga, *N. Dak., U.S.* 104 E2
Tioga, *Pa., U.S.* 94 L7
Tioman, island, *Malaysia* 187 UII
Tipp City, *Ohio, U.S.* 99 RII
Tipperary, *Ire.* 143 T4
Tipperary, *N. Terr., Austral.* 211 P7
Tipton, *Calif., U.S.* 109 U7
Tipton, *Ind., U.S.* 99 Q9
Tipton, *Iowa, U.S.* 105 PI4
Tipton, *Mo., U.S.* 105 TI2
Tipton, *Okla., U.S.* 102 H8
Tipton, Mount, *Ariz., U.S.* 107 R5
Tiptonville, *Tenn., U.S.* 100 FI2
Tiputa, *Fr. Polynesia, Fr.* 219 KI6
Tiputa, Passe de, *Fr. Polynesia, Fr.* 219 KI6
Tiracambu, Serra do, *Braz.* 131 EI4
Tîrān, island, *Egypt* 171 U4
Tîrān, Strait of, *Egypt* 171 U4
Tirana *see* Tiranë, *Albania* 152 L9
Tirana, *Qnsld., Austral.* 211 TI2
Tiranë (Tirana), *Albania* 152 L9
Tiraspol, *Mold.* 157 R5
Ţirbîl, *Iraq* 172 E7
Tire, *Turk.* 168 G3
Tirebolu, *Turk.* 169 DI3
Tiree, island, *Scot., U.K.* 142 L6
Tîrgovişte, *Rom.* 153 FI5
Tîrgu Frumos, *Rom.* 153 BI6
Tîrgu Jiu, *Rom.* 153 EI3
Tîrgu Lăpuş, *Rom.* 153 BI3
Tîrgu Neamţ, *Rom.* 153 BI5
Tîrgu Ocna, *Rom.* 153 DI6
Tîrgu Secuiesc, *Rom.* 153 DI5
Tirich Mir, peak, *Pak.* 176 LIO
Tîrna Mare, *Rom.* 152 AI2
Tîrnăveni, *Rom.* 153 DI3
Tírnavos, *Gr.* 154 EIO
Tir Pol, *Afghan.* 176 MI
Tirso, river, *It.* 151 N3
Tiruchchendur, *India* 179 S6
Tiruchchirappalli, *India* 179 R6
Tirunelveli, *India* 179 S6
Tirupati, *India* 179 P7
Tiruppattur, *India* 179 R6
Tiruppur, *India* 179 R5
Tiruvannamalai, *India* 179 Q6
Tiryns, ruin, *Gr.* 154 KII
Tisa, river, *Serb.* 152 DIO
Tisaiyanvilai, *India* 179 S6
Tishomingo, *Okla., U.S.* 102 JI2

Tisis, *Aust.* 160 M3
T'is Isat Fwafwatê (Blue Nile Falls), *Eth.* 199 FI4
Tista, river, *Bangladesh, India* 178 GI2
Tisza, river, *Hung.* 149 MI6
Tiszafüred, *Hung.* 149 LI6
Tiszaújváros, *Hung.* 149 KI6
Titan Dome, *Antarctica* 226 JI2
Titano, Monte, *San Marino* 161 JI5
Titicaca, Lago, *Bol., Peru* 130 J6
Titikaveka, *Cook Is., N.Z.* 218 Q9
Titule, *Dem. Rep. of the Congo* 198 JII
Titusville, *Fla., U.S.* 97 T9
Titusville, *Pa., U.S.* 94 L4
Tiva, *Fr. Polynesia, Fr.* 219 A23
Tivaru, island, *Fr. Polynesia, Fr.* 219 KI5
Tiverton, *Eng., U.K.* 143 WIO
Tiverton, *R.I., U.S.* 95 LI5
Tiverau, island, *Cook Is., N.Z.* 219 AI7
Tivoli, *Grenada* 121 K23
Tivoli, *It.* 150 K9
Tiyâs, *Syr.* 170 G9
Tizimín, *Mex.* 115 HI6
Tizi Ouzou, *Alg.* 196 AII
Tiznit, *Mor.* 196 C7
Tlemcen, *Alg.* 196 BIO
Tmassah, *Lib.* 197 EI4
Tmiet, island, *Marshall Is.* 216 L9
Toa Baja, *P.R., U.S.* 120 M4
Toachel Mlengui (West Passage), *Palau* 216 MII
Toadlena, *N. Mex., U.S.* 107 RIO
Toagel Mid Passage, *Palau* 216 NII
Toahotu, *Fr. Polynesia, Fr.* 219 PI7
Toamaro, island, *Fr. Polynesia, Fr.* 219 B23
Toamaro, Passe, *Fr. Polynesia, Fr.* 219 B23
Toamasina, *Madagascar* 203 FI8
Toano, *Va., U.S.* 96 HI3
Toatoratara, Pointe, *Fr. Polynesia, Fr.* 219 L23
Toau, island, *Fr. Polynesia, Fr.* 219 EI8
Toay, *Arg.* 132 MIO
Tobago, island, *S. Amer.* 126 A6
Tobago, island, *Trinidad & Tobago* 119 NI8
Toba Kakar Range, *Pak.* 177 Q7
Tobarra, *Sp.* 145 JI3
Toba Tek Singh, *Pak.* 177 QIO
Tobermorey, *N. Terr., Austral.* 211 TIO
Tobermory, *Qnsld., Austral.* 211 VI2
Tobi, island, *Palau* 214 G2
Tobin, Mount, *Nev., U.S.* 109 N9
Tobi Shima, *Japan* 184 KI2
Toboali, *Indonesia* 189 JI3
Tobol, river, *Russ.* 166 E7
Tobol'sk, *Russ.* 158 JIO
Tobolski, *Jam.* 120 H8
Tobona, island, *Solomon Is.* 217 MI7
Tobruk *see* Ţubruq, *Lib.* 197 CI6
Tobyl, river, *Kaz.* 174 BII
Tobyl, *Kaz.* 174 CIO
Tocal, *Qnsld., Austral.* 211 TI2
Tocantínia, *Braz.* 131 GI3
Tocantinópolis, *Braz.* 131 FI3
Tocantins, river, *Braz.* 131 DI3
Toccoa, *Ga., U.S.* 96 K6
Toco, *Chile* 132 D7
Toco, *Trinidad & Tobago* 121 N23
Tocón, Punta, *P.R., U.S.* 120 PI
Toconao, *Chile* 132 E8
Tocopilla, *Chile* 132 D7
Todi, *It.* 150 J8
Todmorden, *S. Aust., Austral.* 211 V9
Todoga Saki, *Japan* 184 KI4
Todos os Santos Bay, *S. Amer.* 126 GII
Todos Santos, *Mex.* 114 F7
Todos Santos, Bahía, *Mex.* 114 B5
Tofino, *B.C., Can.* 82 M7
Tofte, *Minn., U.S.* 104 FI3
Tofua, island, *Tonga* 218 P6
Toga, island, *Vanuatu* 218 AI
Tōgane, *Japan* 185 PI3
Togiak, *Alas., U.S.* 110 KI2
Togian, Kepulauan, *Indonesia* 189 JI4
Togo, *Af.* 195 HI6
Togtoh, *China* 182 C4
Togyz, *Kaz.* 174 F9
Tohatchi, *N. Mex., U.S.* 107 RIO
Tohiea, Mont, *Fr. Polynesia, Fr.* 219 NI4
Tohma, river, *Turk.* 168 FI2
Tohopekaliga, Lake, *Fla., U.S.* 97 T9
Toi, *Japan* 184 HI3

Toi, *Niue, N.Z.* 219 B2O
Toibalawe, *India* 179 RI4
Toili, *Indonesia* 189 JI4
Toi Misaki, *Japan* 185 T5
Toiyabe Range, *Nev., U.S.* 84 G5
Tok, *Alas., U.S.* III HI8
Tokachi Dake, *Japan* 184 FI4
Tōkamachi, *Japan* 185 NII
Tokar, *Sudan* 199 DI4
Tokara Kaikyō, *Japan* 185 U4
Tokara Rettō, *Japan* 185 V3
Tokarevka, *Kaz.* 175 DI4
Tokat, *Turk.* 168 EII
Tŏkch'ŏn, *N. Korea* 182 DI2
Tokelau, islands, *N.Z., Pac. Oc.* 214 HIO
Tokerau, island, *Cook Is., N.Z.* 219 AI7
Toki, *Japan* 185 PIO
Toki Point, *Wake I., U.S.* 216 F8
Tokmak, *Ukr.* 157 R8
Tokmok, *Kyrg.* 176 DI2
Toko, *Russ.* 159 JI9
Tokomaru Bay, *N.Z.* 213 K2O
Tokoro, river, *Japan* 184 FI5
Tokoroa, *N.Z.* 213 KI9
Toksook Bay, *Alas., U.S.* 110 JII
Toksun, *China* 180 F7
Toktar, *Afghan.* 176 L5
Toktogul, *Kyrg.* 176 EIO
Tokung, *Indonesia* 188 JII
Tokuno Shima, *Japan* 185 NII
Tokunoshima, *Japan* 185 X2
Tokushima, *Japan* 185 R8
Tokuyama, *Japan* 185 R5
Tōkyō, *Japan* 185 PI2
Tōkyō Wan, *Japan* 185 PI2
Tol, island, *F.S.M.* 217 CI4
Tôlañaro, *Madagascar* 203 JI7
Tolarno, *N.S.W., Austral.* 211 XII
Tolbo, *Mongolia* 180 C8
Tolchin, Mount, *Antarctica* 226 HII
Töle Bī, *Kaz.* 175 HI5
Toledo, *Iowa, U.S.* 105 NI2
Toledo, *Ohio, U.S.* 99 NI2
Toledo, *Oreg., U.S.* 108 G2
Toledo, *Sp.* 144 GIO
Toledo, *Wash., U.S.* 108 D3
Toledo, Montes de, *Sp.* 144 HIO
Toledo Bend Reservoir, *La., Tex., U.S.* 100 MI6
Toli, *China* 180 D6
Toliara, *Madagascar* 203 HI6
Tolitoli, *Indonesia* 189 HI3
Tol'ka, *Russ.* 158 HI2
Tollya, Zaliv, *Russ.* 159 DI4
Tolmezzo, *It.* 150 C9
Tolo, Teluk, *Indonesia* 189 KI4
Tolob, *Scot., U.K.* 142 EI2
Tolosa, *Sp.* 145 BI3
Toltén, *Chile* 133 P6
Tolti, *Pak.* 178 B5
Tolú, *Col.* 128 C4
Toluca, *Mex.* 114 JII
Tolyatti, *Russ.* 156 KI5
Tomah, *Wis., U.S.* 98 K4
Tomahawk, *Wis., U.S.* 98 H5
Tomakomai, *Japan* 184 GI3
Tomanivi, peak, *Fiji Is.* 218 H6
Tomar, *Port.* 144 G5
Tomar, *Braz.* 130 C8
Tomari, *Japan* 184 HI3
Tomasjów Lubelski, *Pol.* 149 GI8
Tomaszów Mazowiecki, *Pol.* 149 EI5
Tomatin, *Scot., U.K.* 142 K9
Tombador, Serra do, *Braz.* 130 GIO
Tombe, *Solomon Is.* 217 MI6
Tombigbee, river, *Ala., U.S.* 101 LI3
Tombouctou (Timbuktu), *Mali* 196 G8
Tombstone, *Ariz., U.S.* 107 W8
Tombua, *Angola* 202 E5
Tomé, *Chile* 132 M6
Tomea, island, *Indonesia* 189 LI5
Tomil, *F.S.M.* 217 DI8
Tomil Harbor, *F.S.M.* 217 DI8
Tomini, Teluk, *Indonesia* 189 JI3
Tomintoul, *Scot., U.K.* 142 KIO
Tomman, island, *Vanuatu* 218 E2
Tommot, *Russ.* 159 HI8
Tomo, river, *Col.* 128 E8
Tomorit, Maja e, *Albania* 152 LIO
Tomotu Noi (Lord Howe Island), *Solomon Is.* 217 Q22

Tompa, *Russ.* 159 KI6
Tompkinsville, *Ky., U.S.* 101 DI6
Tom Price, *W. Aust., Austral.* 211 T3
Tomsk, *Russ.* 158 KI2
Tomsyu, *Russ.* 159 EI8
Tomtor, *Russ.* 159 FI7
Tomtor Tasa, Gora, *Russ.* 159 FI6
Tom White, Mount, *Alas., U.S.* III JI8
Tonalá, *Mex.* 115 KI4
Tonami, *Japan* 185 NIO
Tonantins, *Braz.* 130 D6
Tonasket, *Wash., U.S.* 108 A7
Tonbridge, *Eng., U.K.* 143 WI4
Tønder, *Den.* 140 PII
Tondou, Massif du, *Cen. Af. Rep.* 198 GIO
Tonga, *Pac. Oc.* 214 KIO
Tonga, *Sudan* 198 FI2
Tonga Islands, *Tonga* 214 KIO
Tong'an, *China* 183 Q7
Tongareva *see* Penrhyn Atoll, island, *Cook Is., N.Z.* 214 HI2
Tongariki, island, *Vanuatu* 218 E3
Tongatapu Group, *Tonga* 214 KIO
Tongcheng, *China* 182 K7
Tongchuan, *China* 182 G2
Tongdao, *China* 183 P2
Tongde, *China* 180 JII
Tongeren, *Belg.* 146 LI3
Tongguan, *China* 181 JI3
Tonghua, *China* 182 BI2
Tongjiang, *China* 181 CI8
Tongliao, *China* 182 AIO
Tongling, *China* 182 L7
Tonglu, *China* 182 L9
Tongo, *N.S.W., Austral.* 211 WI2
Tongoa (Kuwaé), island, *Vanuatu* 218 E3
Tongoy, *Chile* 132 J6
Tongren, *China* 183 NI
Tongshi, *China* 183 UI
Tongtian, river, *China* 180 J9
Tongue, river, *Mont., U.S.* 106 EI2
Tongue, *Scot., U.K.* 142 H9
Tongue, Kyle of, *Scot., U.K.* 142 G9
Tongue of the Ocean, bay, *Bahamas* 116 FII
Tongue River Reservoir, *Mont., U.S.* 106 FII
Tongxin, *China* 180 HI2
Tongzhou, *China* 182 D7
Tonj, *Sudan* 198 GI2
Tonk, *India* 178 G5
Tonkawa, *Okla., U.S.* 102 EII
Tonkin, Gulf of, *China, Vietnam* 166 JII
Tonle Sap, lake, *Cambodia* 187 NII
Tonneins, *Fr.* 147 W7
Tonnerre, *Fr.* 147 RI2
Tōno, *Japan* 184 KI3
Tonoas (Dublon), island, *F.S.M.* 217 CI5
Tonopah, *Nev., U.S.* 109 R9
Tønsberg, *Nor.* 140 LII
Tonto National Monument, *Ariz., U.S.* 107 U8
Tonumea, island, *Tonga* 218 R6
Tonya, *Turk.* 169 DI4
Toodyay, *W. Aust., Austral.* 211 X2
Tooele, *Utah, U.S.* 106 L7
Toomaru, Mont, *Fr. Polynesia, Fr.* 219 B23
Toompine, *Qnsld., Austral.* 211 VI2
Toopua, island, *Fr. Polynesia, Fr.* 219 KI3
Toopua Iti, island, *Fr. Polynesia, Fr.* 219 KI3
Toora Khem, *Russ.* 159 LI4
Toowoomba, *Qnsld., Austral.* 211 VI5
Top, Lake, *Russ.* 138 B9
Topaze, Baie, *Mauritius* 205 J2O
Tope de Coroa, peak, *Cape Verde* 205 BI4
Topeka, *Kans., U.S.* 105 S9
Topliţa, *Rom.* 153 CI4
Topock, *Ariz., U.S.* 107 S4
Topol'čany, *Slovakia* 149 KI4
Topolobampo, *Mex.* 114 E7
Toppenish, *Wash., U.S.* 108 E6
Topsail Beach, *N.C., U.S.* 96 KI3
Top Springs, *N. Terr., Austral.* 211 Q8
Tor, *Sp.* 160 HI
Tora Bora, site, *Afghan.* 176 M8
Torbalı, *Turk.* 168 G3
Torbat-e Ḥeydarīyeh, *Iran* 173 CI6

Torbat-e Jām, *Iran* 173 C17
Torbay, *Eng., U.K.* 143 X1O
Torbay, *W. Aust., Austral.* 211 Y3
Torbert, Mount, *Alas., U.S.* 111 J15
Torch Lake, *Mich., U.S.* 98 H1O
Töre, *Sw.* 141 F14
Torello, *It.* 161 H13
Torez, *Ukr.* 157 Q1O
Torghay, river, *Kaz.* 174 E1O
Torghay, *Kaz.* 174 E11
Torgo, *Russ.* 159 J17
Torhout, *Belg.* 146 L1O
Torino (Turin), *It.* 150 E2
Tori Shima, *Japan* 185 Y1
Tori Shima, *Japan* 185 U13
Torixoreu, *Braz.* 130 J12
Torkestan Mountains, *Afghan.*
    176 L4
Tornal'a, *Slovakia* 149 K16
Torneå see Tornio, *Fin.* 141 F15
Torneälven, river, *Sw.* 138 B8
Torneträsk, *Sw.* 141 D13
Torngat Mountains, *Nfld. & Lab., Can.*
    83 J2O
Tornillo, *Tex., U.S.* 103 V2
Tornimparte, *It.* 150 K9
Tornio (Torneå), *Fin.* 141 F15
Torniojoki, river, *Fin., Sw.* 141 E14
Tornquist, *Arg.* 133 N11
Tōro, *Japan* 184 F15
Toro, *Sp.* 144 D9
Toro, Cerro del, *Arg.-Chile* 132 H7
Torokina, *P.N.G.* 217 K14
Törökszentmiklós, *Hung.* 149 L16
Torom, *Russ.* 159 J2O
Toronto, *Kans., U.S.* 105 U9
Toronto, *Ohio, U.S.* 99 Q16
Toronto, *Ont., Can.* 83 Q18
Toropets, *Russ.* 156 H7
Tororo, *Uganda* 199 J13
Toros Daği, *Turk.* 168 H9
Toros Dağları, *Turk.* 168 H7
Torquemada, *Sp.* 144 D1O
Torrance, *Calif., U.S.* 109 X8
Torran Rocks, *Scot., U.K.* 142 M7
Torre, *It.* 150 M11
Torre Astura, *It.* 150 L8
Torre de Moncorvo, *Port.* 144 E7
Torredonjimeno, *Sp.* 144 K15
Torrejón de Ardoz, *Sp.* 144 F11
Torrelavega, *Sp.* 144 B1O
Torremaggiore, *It.* 150 L12
Torremolinos, *Sp.* 144 M1O
Torrens, Lake, *S. Aust., Austral.*
    211 W1O
Torrent, *Sp.* 145 H14
Torreón, *Mex.* 114 F1O
Torre San Giovanni, *It.* 151 N15
Torres Islands, *Vanuatu* 218 A1
Torres Strait, *Austral.* 210 A12
Torres Vedras, *Port.* 144 H4
Torrevieja, *Sp.* 145 K14
Torriana, *It.* 161 G13
Torrijos, *Sp.* 144 G1O
Torrington, *Conn., U.S.* 94 L12
Torrington, *Wyo., U.S.* 106 J14
Torrutj, *Marshall Is.* 216 M5
Torsby, *Sw.* 140 K12
Tórshavn, *Faroe Is., Den.* 140 J6
Tortola, island, *Virgin Islands, U.K.*
    119 F14
Tortona, *It.* 150 E4
Tortosa, *Sp.* 145 F15
Tortosa see Ṭarṭūs, *Syr.* 170 G7
Tortosa, Cap de, *Sp.* 145 F16
Tortue, Île de la, *Haiti* 117 K16
Tortuga, Isla, *Ecua.* 128 R9
Tortuga Island, S. *Amer.* 126 A5
Tortuguero, Laguna, *P.R., U.S.*
    120 M3
Tortum, *Turk.* 169 E16
Ṭorūd, *Iran* 173 C14
Torugart, *Kyrg.* 176 G12
Torul, *Turk.* 169 D14
Toruń, *Pol.* 149 D14
Tõrva, *Est.* 141 L17
Tory Island, *Ire.* 143 N5
Torzhok, *Russ.* 156 H8
Tosa del Braidal, *Andorra* 160 J4
Tosashimizu, *Japan* 185 S6
Tosa Wan, *Japan* 185 R7
Tosca, *S. Af.* 202 J9
Toscano, Arcipelago, *It.* 150 J6
To Shima, *Japan* 185 Q12
Toshka Lakes, *Egypt* 197 E18

Toshkent (Tashkent), *Uzb.* 175 K13
Tostado, *Arg.* 132 H11
Tosters, *Aust.* 160 M3
Tosu, *Japan* 185 R4
Tosya, *Turk.* 168 D9
Totana, *Sp.* 145 K13
Totegegie, island, *Fr. Polynesia, Fr.*
    219 Q21
Toteng, *Botswana* 202 G9
Tôtes, *Fr.* 147 N8
Totia, island, *Cook Is., N.Z.* 219 C15
Totiw, island, *F.S.M.* 217 C15
Tot'ma, *Russ.* 156 F11
Totness, *Suriname* 129 E16
Toto, *Angola* 202 B6
Totokafonua, island, *Tonga* 218 M11
Totolom, peak, *F.S.M.* 217 G14
Totora, *Bol.* 130 K7
Totoya, island, *Fiji Is.* 218 K8
Tottan Hills, *Antarctica* 226 C11
Tottori, *Japan* 185 P7
Totu Tofari, island, *Fr. Polynesia, Fr.*
    219 K14
Toubkal, Jebel, *Mor.* 196 C8
Toucy, *Fr.* 147 R11
Tougan, *Burkina Faso* 200 E9
Touggourt, *Alg.* 196 B12
Touho, *New Caledonia, Fr.* 218 C7
Toul, *Fr.* 147 P13
Touliu, *Taiwan, China* 183 R9
Toulon, *Fr.* 147 Y14
Toulouse, *Fr.* 147 X9
Toummo, *Libya* 197 F14
Toungo, *Nigeria* 201 G16
Touques, river, *Fr.* 147 P7
Touriñán, Cabo, *Sp.* 144 B5
Tournai, *Belg.* 146 L11
Tournavista, *Peru* 130 G4
Tournay, *Fr.* 147 Y7
Touros, *Braz.* 131 E18
Tours, *Fr.* 147 R8
Toury, *Fr.* 147 Q9
Touside, Pic, *Chad* 194 F6
Touwsrivier, *S. Af.* 202 M8
Tovarkovskiy, *Russ.* 156 L1O
Tovuz, *Azerb.* 169 D19
Towada, *Japan* 184 J13
Towada, *Japan* 184 J13
Towada Ko, *Japan* 184 J13
Towanda, *Pa., U.S.* 94 L8
Tower see Genovesa, Isla, island, *Ecua.*
    128 P1O
Tower, *Minn., U.S.* 104 F12
Towner, *N. Dak., U.S.* 104 E5
Town Hall, *Monaco* 161 E21
Town Hill, *Bermuda, U.K.* 120 B3
Townsend, *Mont., U.S.* 106 D8
Townsend, *Va., U.S.* 96 F14
Townsville, *Qnsld., Austral.* 211 S13
Towot, *Sudan* 199 H13
Towraghondi, *Afghan.* 176 L2
Towrzi, *Afghan.* 177 R5
Towson, *Md., U.S.* 96 C13
Toyah, *Tex., U.S.* 103 N2
Toyahvale, *Tex., U.S.* 103 P2
Tōya Ko, *Japan* 184 G13
Toyama, *Japan* 185 N1O
Toyama Wan, *Japan* 185 N1O
Toyohashi, *Japan* 185 Q1O
Toyooka, *Japan* 185 P8
Toyotomi, *Japan* 184 D13

Transantarctic Mountains, *Antarctica*
    226 F11
Trans-Canada Highway, *Can.* 82 M8
Transdniestria, region, *Mold.* 157 R5
Transylvania, region, *Rom.* 152 C13
Transylvanian Alps, *Rom.* 152 E12
Trapani, *It.* 151 S8
Trapper Peak, *Mont., U.S.* 106 E5
Traralgon, *Vic., Austral.* 211 Z13
Trarza, region, *Mauritania* 194 F1
Trasimeno, Lago, *It.* 150 H8
Traun, *Aust.* 148 K11
Traunreut, *Ger.* 148 K9
Traverse, Lake, *Minn., S. Dak., U.S.*
    104 J8
Traverse City, *Mich., U.S.* 98 J1O
Travis, Lake, *Tex., U.S.* 103 Q1O
Travnik, *Bosn. & Herzg.* 152 F7
Trayning, *W. Aust., Austral.* 211 X3
Treasure Beach, *Jam.* 120 J7
Treasure Cay, *Bahamas* 120 B6
Treasure Island, *Solomon Is.*
    217 N24
Treasurers Island, *Solomon Is.*
    217 N24
Treasury Islands, *Solomon Is.* 217 L14
Třebíč, *Czech Rep.* 148 J12
Trebinje, *Bosn. & Herzg.* 152 J8
Trebisacce, *It.* 151 P13
Trebišov, *Slovakia* 149 J17
Třeboň, *Czech Rep.* 148 J11
Trégastel, *Fr.* 147 P4
Tregrosse Islets, *Coral Sea Is. Terr.,*
    Austral. 211 R15
Tréguier, *Fr.* 147 P4
Treignac, *Fr.* 147 U9
Treinta y Tres, *Uru.* 132 K15
Trelew, *Arg.* 133 R9
Trelleborg, *Sw.* 140 P12
Tremadoc Bay, *Wales, U.K.* 143 T9
Tremblant, Mount, *N. Amer.* 80 H8
Tremiti, Isole, *It.* 150 K12
Tremonton, *Utah, U.S.* 106 J7
Trenary, *Mich., U.S.* 98 F8
Trenčín, *Slovakia* 149 J14
Trenque Lauquen, *Arg.* 132 M11
Trento, *It.* 150 C7
Trenton, *Mich., U.S.* 99 N12
Trenton, *Mo., U.S.* 105 R11
Trenton, *N.J., U.S.* 94 P1O
Trenton, *Nebr., U.S.* 105 R4
Trenton, *Tenn., U.S.* 100 E12
Trepassey, *Nfld. & Lab., Can.* 83 M24
Tres Arroyos, *Arg.* 133 N12
Tres Esquinas, *Col.* 128 H5
Treshnish Isles, *Scot., U.K.* 142 L7
Três Lagoas, *Braz.* 130 L12
Tres Montes, Golfo, *Chile* 133 T6
Tres Montes, Península, *Chile* 133 T5
Tres Picos, Cerro, *Arg.* 133 R7
Tres Puntas, Cabo, *Arg.* 133 T9
Tres Zapotes, ruin, *Mex.* 115 J13
Treviso, *It.* 150 D8
Trevose Head, *Eng., U.K.* 143 X8
Trgovište, *Serb.* 152 J11
Triabunna, *Tas., Austral.* 211 Z16
Triàngulos, Arrecifes, *Mex.* 115 H15
Tribal Areas, region, *Afghan.* 177 N9
Tribulation, Cape, *Austral.* 210 C13
Tribune, *Kans., U.S.* 105 T3
Tricarico, *It.* 150 M13
Tricase, *It.* 151 N16
Trie, *Fr.* 147 Y7
Trier, *Ger.* 148 H5
Triesen, *Liech.* 160 Q2
Triesenberg, *Liech.* 160 P2
Trieste, *It.* 150 D1O
Triglav, peak, *Slov.* 152 C4
Trigueros, *Sp.* 144 L7
Trihonida, Límni, *Gr.* 154 H9
Tríkala, *Gr.* 154 F9
Tríkeri, *Gr.* 154 G11
Trikomo, *Cyprus* 160 N1O
Trikora, Puncak, *Indonesia* 213 C16
Trincomalee, *Sri Lanka* 179 S8
Třinec, *Czech Rep.* 149 H14
Trinidad, *Bol.* 130 J7
Trinidad, *Calif., U.S.* 108 M2
Trinidad, *Colo., U.S.* 107 P14
Trinidad, *Cuba* 116 H9
Trinidad, island, *Trinidad & Tobago*
    119 P17
Trinidad, Golfo, *Chile* 133 V6
Trinidad, Isla, *Arg.* 133 P11
Trinidad and Tobago, *N. Amer.* 81 P24
Trinidad Head, *Calif., U.S.* 108 M1

Trinitapoli, *It.* 150 L13
Trinity, river, *Calif., U.S.* 108 M2
Trinity, river, *Tex., U.S.* 103 P14
Trinity, *Tex., U.S.* 103 P14
Trinity Bay, *Nfld. & Lab., Can.* 83 M24
Trinity Beach, *Qnsld., Austral.* 211 R13
Trinity Hills, *Trinidad & Tobago*
    121 Q23
Trinity Islands, *Alas., U.S.* 111 N14
Trinity Peninsula, *Antarctica* 226 C4
Trinity Range, *Nev., U.S.* 109 N8
Trinkat Island, *India* 179 S15
Triolet, *Mauritius* 205 F2O
Trion, *Ga., U.S.* 96 K4
Trionto, Capo, *It.* 151 P14
Triora, *It.* 150 G2
Tripoli see Trâblous, *Leb.* 170 H7
Tripoli see Ṭarābulus, *Lib.* 197 B13
Trípoli, *Gr.* 154 K1O
Tripolitania, region, *Lib.* 197 C13
Tripp, *S. Dak., U.S.* 104 M7
Tristaina, river, *Andorra* 160 G3
Tristaina, Pic de, *Andorra* 160 G2
Tristan da Cunha Group, *Atl. Oc.*
    204 J4
Tristan da Cunha Island, *Tristan da*
    Cunha Is., U.K. 194 R2
Tristão, Ponta do, *Madeira* 204 M2
Tristao, Îles, *Guinea* 200 E4
Trivandrum see Thiruvananthapuram,
    India 179 S5
Trnava, *Slovakia* 149 K13
Trobriand Islands, *P.N.G.* 213 E21
Trofors, *Nor.* 140 G12
Trois Fourches, Cap des, *Mor.* 144 P11
Trois Pitons, Morne, *Dominica* 121 F19
Trois-Rivières, *Guadeloupe, Fr.* 121 G14
Trois-Rivières, *Que., Can.* 83 P2O
Troisvierges, *Lux.* 160 G9
Troitsk, *Russ.* 158 J8
Troitskoye, *Russ.* 157 R13
Troja, *Jam.* 120 H9
Trojanów, *Pol.* 149 E17
Troll, station, *Antarctica* 227 B13
Trollhättan, *Sw.* 140 M12
Trombetas, river, *Braz.* 130 C1O
Tromelin, island, *Ind. Oc.* 240 J6
Tromsø, *Nor.* 141 D14
Trona, *Calif., U.S.* 109 V9
Tronador, Monte, *Arg.-Chile* 133 Q7
Trondheim, *Nor.* 140 H11
Trondheimsfjorden, *Nor.* 140 H11
Troodos Mountains, *Cyprus* 160 P7
Troon, *Scot., U.K.* 143 N9
Trostyanets', *Ukr.* 157 N8
Trou d'Eau Douce, *Mauritius*
    205 G2O
Trou Gras Point, *St. Lucia* 121 K14
Troumaka, *St. Vincent & the Grenadines*
    121 K16
Troup, *Tex., U.S.* 102 M14
Trout Creek, *Utah, U.S.* 106 M5
Trout Lake, *N.W.T., Can.* 82 H1O
Trout Lake, *Ont., Can.* 83 N14
Trout Peak, *Wyo., U.S.* 106 F9
Trout River, *Nfld. & Lab., Can.*
    83 M23
Troy, *Ala., U.S.* 101 M16
Troy, *Jam.* 120 H7
Troy, *Kans., U.S.* 105 R1O
Troy, *Mo., U.S.* 105 S14
Troy, *Mont., U.S.* 106 B4
Troy, *N.C., U.S.* 96 H1O
Troy, *N.Y., U.S.* 94 J11
Troy, *Ohio, U.S.* 99 R11
Troy, *Oreg., U.S.* 108 E9
Troy, ruin, *Turk.* 168 D2
Troyes, *Fr.* 147 Q12
Troy Peak, *Nev., U.S.* 109 R11
Trübbach, *Switz.* 160 Q2
Trubchevsk, *Russ.* 156 M7
Truckee, *Calif., U.S.* 109 Q6
Truckee, river, *Nev., U.S.* 109 P6
Trujillo, *Hond.* 115 K18
Trujillo, *Peru* 130 G2
Trujillo, *Sp.* 144 G8
Trujillo, *Venez.* 128 C7
Trujillo Alto, *P.R., U.S.* 120 M5
Truk Islands see Chuuk, *F.S.M.*
    216 Q6
Truk Lagoon see Chuuk Lagoon, *F.S.M.*
    217 B15
Trumann, *Ark., U.S.* 100 F11
Trumbull, Mount, *Ariz., U.S.* 107 Q6

Truro, *Eng., U.K.* 143 X8
Truro, *N.S., Can.* 83 P22
Truth or Consequences, *N. Mex., U.S.*
    107 U11
Trutnov, *Czech Rep.* 148 G12
Tryavna, *Bulg.* 153 H15
Trzebnica, *Pol.* 149 F13
Tsada, *Cyprus* 160 Q6
Tsagaan Bogd Uul, peak, *Mongolia*
    180 F1O
Tsagaannuur, *Mongolia* 180 C8
Tsagan Aman, *Russ.* 157 Q14
Ts'ageri, *Rep. of Georgia* 169 B17
Tsagveri, *Rep. of Georgia* 169 C17
Tsahir, *Mongolia* 180 D1O
Tsaile, *Ariz., U.S.* 107 R9
Tsaka La, *India* 178 C7
Tsalka, *Rep. of Georgia* 169 C18
Tsangpo Canyon see Yarlung Zangbo
    Canyon, *China* 180 L9
Tsao see Tsau, *Botswana* 202 G8
Tsarevo, *Bulg.* 153 J17
Tsau (Tsao), *Botswana* 202 G8
Tschida, Lake, *N. Dak., U.S.* 104 G3
Tsenhermandal, *Mongolia* 181 D13
Tsentral'nyy, *Russ.* 159 G2O
Tses, *Namibia* 202 J7
Tsetsegnuur, *Mongolia* 180 D9
Tsetserleg, *Mongolia* 180 D11
Tshabong, *Botswana* 202 J8
Tshane, *Botswana* 202 H8
Tshela, *Dem. Rep. of the Congo* 198 L7
Tshikapa, *Dem. Rep. of the Congo*
    198 M9
Tshofa, *Dem. Rep. of the Congo*
    198 L1O
Tshootsha, *Botswana* 202 H8
Tshuapa, river, *Dem. Rep. of the Congo*
    198 K1O
Tshwane see Pretoria, *S. Af.* 202 J1O
Tsiigehtchic, *N.W.T., Can.* 82 E9
Tsil'ma, river, *Russ.* 138 A12
Tsimlyanskoye Vodokhranilishche, *Russ.*
    157 Q12
Tsimlyansk Reservoir, *Russ.* 138 F12
Tsiombe, *Madagascar* 203 J16
Tsipanda, *Russ.* 159 H19
Ts'khinvali, *S. Ossetia* 169 B18
Tsna, river, *Russ.* 156 K11
Tsnori, *Rep. of Georgia* 169 C2O
Tsu, *Japan* 185 Q9
Tsubame, *Japan* 184 M11
Tsuchiura, *Japan* 185 P12
Tsugaru Kaikyō, *Japan* 184 H13
Tsuma, *Japan* 185 N7
Tsumeb, *Namibia* 202 G7
Tsuruga, *Japan* 185 P9
Tsuruga Wan, *Japan* 185 P9
Tsuruoka, *Japan* 184 L12
Tsushima, island, *Japan* 185 Q3
Tsushima Strait, *Japan* 185 R3
Tsutsu, *Japan* 185 Q3
Tsuyama, *Japan* 185 Q7
Tsyurupyns'k, *Ukr.* 157 R7
Tuahora, Pointe, *Fr. Polynesia, Fr.*
    219 K14
Tuakau, *N.Z.* 213 J19
Tual, *Indonesia* 189 L18
Tuam, *Ire.* 143 R4
Tuamotu Archipelago, *Fr. Polynesia, Fr.*
    219 D18
Tuan Giao, *Vietnam* 186 G1O
Tuangku, island, *Indonesia* 188 H4
Tu'anuku, *Tonga* 218 L11
Tuapa, *Niue, N.Z.* 219 B2O
Tuapse, *Russ.* 157 T1O
Tuaran, *Malaysia* 188 F12
Tuasivi, *Samoa* 218 K2
Tuasivi, Cape, *Samoa* 218 K2
Tuatapere, *N.Z.* 213 R15
Tuauru, river, *Fr. Polynesia, Fr.*
    219 N16
Tubac, *Ariz., U.S.* 107 W7
Tuba City, *Ariz., U.S.* 107 R7
Ṭubah, Qaṣr aṭ, *Jordan* 171 N7
Tubarão, *Braz.* 131 P13
Tübingen, *Ger.* 148 J6
Tubmanburg, *Liberia* 200 G6
Tubou, *Fiji Is.* 218 J9
Ṭubruq (Tobruk), *Lib.* 197 C16
Tubuai, island, *Fr. Polynesia, Fr.*
    219 H16
Tubuai Islands see Austral Islands, *Fr.*
    Polynesia, Fr. 219 H16
Tucacas, *Venez.* 128 B9

Tucavaca, river, *Bol.* **130** K9
Tuckerman, *Ark., U.S.* **100** F10
Tucker's Town, *Bermuda, U.K.* **120** B3
Tuckerton, *N.J., U.S.* **94** Q10
Tucson, *Ariz., U.S.* **107** V8
Tucumcari, *N. Mex., U.S.* **107** S15
Tucumcari Mountain, *N. Mex., U.S.* **107** S15
Tucupita, *Venez.* **128** C12
Tucuruí, *Braz.* **131** E13
Tudela, *Sp.* **145** D13
Tuen, *Qnsld., Austral.* **211** V13
Tuensang, *India* **178** G15
Tuffé, *Fr.* **147** Q8
Tufi, *P.N.G.* **213** E20
Tufts Plain, *Pac. Oc.* **239** D13
Tufuone, *Wallis & Futuna, Fr.* **218** B11
Tufu Point, *Amer. Samoa, U.S.* **218** P4
Tufuvai, *Tonga* **218** K12
Tugela Falls, *S. Af.* **194** Q8
Tug Fork, *Ky., W. Va., U.S.* **101** C20
Tūghyl, *Kaz.* **175** E19
Tuguegarao, *Philippines* **189** B14
Tugur, *Russ.* **159** J20
Tui, *Sp.* **144** C5
Tuineje, *Canary Is.* **204** Q7
Tukangbesi, Kepulauan, *Indonesia* **189** L14
Tukao, *Cook Is., N.Z.* **219** A14
Tukchi, *Russ.* **159** H20
Tukosméra, Mount, *Vanuatu* **218** H4
Tūkrah, *Lib.* **197** C15
Tuktoyaktuk, *N.W.T., Can.* **82** D10
Tukums, *Latv.* **141** M16
Tula, *Mex.* **114** G11
Tula, *Russ.* **156** K9
Tulaghi, island, *Solomon Is.* **217** N19
Tulak, *Afghan.* **177** N3
Tulare, *Calif., U.S.* **109** U7
Tulare Lake Bed, *Calif., U.S.* **109** U6
Tularosa, *N. Mex., U.S.* **107** U12
Tulcán, *Ecua.* **128** H3
Tulcea, *Rom.* **153** E18
Tul'chyn, *Ukr.* **157** P5
Tulelake, *Calif., U.S.* **108** L4
Tuli, *Zimb.* **202** H11
Tulia, *Tex., U.S.* **102** H5
Tulit'a, *N.W.T., Can.* **82** F10
Ţulkarm, *W. Bank* **170** L5
Tullah, *Tas., Austral.* **211** Z15
Tullahoma, *Tenn., U.S.* **101** F16
Tullamore, *Ire.* **143** S5
Tullamore, *N.S.W., Austral.* **211** X13
Tulle, *Fr.* **147** V9
Tully, *Qnsld., Austral.* **211** R13
Tulsa, *Okla., U.S.* **102** F12
Tuluá, *Col.* **128** F4
Tulun, *Russ.* **159** L14
Tulu Welel, peak, *Eth.* **199** G14
Tum, *Indonesia* **189** K17
Tumacacori National Historic Park, *Ariz., U.S.* **107** W7
Tumaco, *Col.* **128** H3
Tumaco, Ensenada de, *Col.* **128** H3
Tumbes, *Peru* **130** E2
Tumby Bay, *S. Aust., Austral.* **211** X9
Tumd Youqi, *China* **182** C3
Tumd Zuoqi, *China* **182** C4
Tumen, *China* **182** A14
Tumen, river, *China, N. Korea* **182** B14
Tumeremo, *Venez.* **129** D13
Tumkur, *India* **179** P5
Tummel, Loch, *Scot., U.K.* **142** L9
Tumon Bay, *Guam, U.S.* **216** B11
Tumucumaque, Serra de, *S. Amer.* **126** C7
Tumu Mountain, *Amer. Samoa, U.S.* **218** N2
Tumu Point, *F.S.M.* **217** F13
Tumwater, *Wash., U.S.* **108** D3
Tunapuna, *Trinidad & Tobago* **121** P22
Tunas de Zaza, *Cuba* **116** J9
Tunbridge Wells, *Eng., U.K.* **143** W14
Tunceli, *Turk.* **169** F14
Tunchang, *China* **183** U1
Tundubai, *Sudan* **198** E10
Tunduma, *Tanzania* **199** N13
Tunduru, *Tanzania* **199** N14
Tundzha, river, *Bulg.* **153** J16
Tungabhadra, river, *India* **179** N6
Tunga Pass, *China, India* **178** E14
Tungkang, *Taiwan, China* **183** S9
Tungua, island, *Tonga* **218** Q6
Tunguskhaya, *Russ.* **159** G17
Tunica, *Miss., U.S.* **100** G11

Tunis, *Tun.* **197** A13
Tunis, Gulf of, *Tun.* **194** C6
Tunisia, *Af.* **195** D18
Tunja, *Col.* **128** E6
Tununak, *Alas., U.S.* **110** J11
Tunuyán, *Arg.* **132** L8
Tuo, river, *China* **180** L12
Tuolumne, river, *Calif., U.S.* **109** S5
Tup, *Kyrg.* **176** D14
Tupã, *Braz.* **130** L12
Tupai (Motu Iti), island, *Fr. Polynesia, Fr.* **219** E15
Tupelo, *Miss., U.S.* **101** H13
Tupelo National Battlefield, *Miss., U.S.* **101** H13
Tupi, *Philippines* **189** F15
Tupinier, Cape, *F.S.M.* **217** B18
Tupiza, *Bol.* **130** L7
Tupper Lake, *N.Y., U.S.* **94** G10
Tüpqaraghan Tübegi, *Kaz.* **174** H6
Tupungato, Cerro, *S. Amer.* **126** L4
Túquerres, *Col.* **128** H3
Tura, *India* **178** G12
Tura, *Russ.* **159** H14
Turabah, *Saudi Arabia* **172** L8
Turakh, *Russ.* **159** E16
Turan Lowland, *Asia* **166** F6
Ţurāq al 'Ilab, range, *Syr.* **170** H10
Ţurayf, *Saudi Arabia* **172** E7
Turbaco, *Col.* **128** B5
Turbat, *Pak.* **177** V2
Turbo, *Col.* **128** D4
Turda, *Rom.* **153** D13
Turégano, *Sp.* **144** E10
Tureia, island, *Fr. Polynesia, Fr.* **219** G21
Turek, *Pol.* **149** E14
Turfan *see* Turpan, *China* **180** F8
Turghan Pass, *Afghan.* **176** K9
Tŭrgovishte, *Bulg.* **153** H16
Turgut, *Turk.* **168** F7
Turgutlu, *Turk.* **168** F3
Turhal, *Turk.* **168** D11
Türi, *Est.* **141** K16
Turi, peak, *Fr. Polynesia, Fr.* **219** G14
Turia, river, *Sp.* **145** G14
Turiaçu, *Braz.* **131** D14
Turin *see* Torino, *It.* **150** E2
Turka, *Ukr.* **157** P2
Turkana, Lake (Lake Rudolf), *Eth., Kenya* **199** H14
Türkeli, island, *Turk.* **168** D3
Turkey, *Asia* **167** S3
Turkey, river, *Iowa, U.S.* **104** M13
Turkey, *Tex., U.S.* **102** J6
Turkey Creek, *W. Aust., Austral.* **211** R6
Türkistan, *Kaz.* **175** J13
Türkmenabat (Chärjew), *Turkm.* **174** L10
Türkmen Aylagy, *Turkm.* **174** L6
Türkmenbaşy, *Turkm.* **174** K6
Türkmenbaşy Aylagy, *Turkm.* **174** K6
Türkmen Dağı, *Turk.* **168** E6
Turkmenistan, *Asia* **167** T5
Turks and Caicos Islands, *U.K., Greater Antilles* **117** J17
Turks Island Passage, *Turks & Caicos Is., U.K.* **117** J17
Turks Islands, *Turks & Caicos Is., U.K.* **117** J18
Turku (Åbo), *Fin.* **141** K15
Turkwel, river, *Kenya* **199** J14
Turlock, *Calif., U.S.* **109** S5
Turnagain, Cape, *N.Z.* **213** M19
Turner, *Mont., U.S.* **106** A10
Turner Hole, *Virgin Islands, U.S.* **120** Q4
Turnhout, *Belg.* **146** K12
Turnu Măgurele, *Rom.* **153** G14
Turnu Roşu, Pasul, *Rom.* **153** E13
Turpan (Turfan), *China* **180** F8
Turpan Depression, *China* **166** F9
Turpan Pendi, *China* **180** F8
Turquino, Pico, *Cuba* **116** K12
Tursunzoda, *Taj.* **176** J7
Turt, *Mongolia* **180** B11
Türtkül, *Uzb.* **174** K9
Turtle *see* Vatoa, island, *Fiji Is.* **218** L10
Turtle Crawls, *Cayman Is., U.K.* **120** J2
Turtle Lake, *N. Dak., U.S.* **104** F4
Turtle Mountain, *N. Dak., U.S.* **104** D5
Turtle Rocks, *Bahamas* **120** C8

Turugart Pass, *China* **180** F4
Tuscaloosa, *Ala., U.S.* **101** K14
Tuscarora, *Nev., U.S.* **108** M10
Tuscola, *Ill., U.S.* **99** R6
Tuscola, *Tex., U.S.* **102** M8
Tuscumbia, *Ala., U.S.* **101** G14
Tuskegee, *Ala., U.S.* **101** L16
Tuskar Rock, *Ire.* **143** U7
Tutak, *Turk.* **169** E17
Tutayev, *Russ.* **156** G10
Tuticorin, *India* **179** S6
Tuting, *India* **178** E15
Tutira, *N.Z.* **213** L20
Tutoko, Mount, *N.Z.* **213** Q15
Tutrakan, *Bulg.* **153** G16
Tuttle Creek Lake, *Kans., U.S.* **105** S8
Tuttlingen, *Ger.* **148** K6
Tutu, island, *Fiji Is.* **218** G7
Tutu, *Virgin Islands, U.S.* **120** N9
Tutuala, *Timor-Leste* **189** M16
Tutuila, island, *Amer. Samoa, U.S.* **218** M7
Tutumu, *Solomon Is.* **217** N19
Tuvalu, *Pac. Oc.* **214** H9
Tuvuca, island, *Fiji Is.* **218** H9
Ţuwayq, Jabal, *Saudi Arabia* **172** J10
Tuwayq Mountains, *Saudi Arabia* **166** H3
Tuxpan, *Mex.* **114** G9
Tuxpan, *Mex.* **114** H12
Tuxtla Gutiérrez, *Mex.* **115** K14
Tuyen Hoa, *Vietnam* **186** K12
Tuyen Quang, *Vietnam* **186** G11
Tuy Hoa, *Vietnam* **187** N14
Tūyserkān, *Iran* **172** D11
Tuz Gölü, *Turk.* **168** F8
Tuzigoot National Monument, *Ariz., U.S.* **107** S7
Tuzla, *Bosn. & Herzg.* **152** F8
Tuzla Gölü, *Turk.* **168** F11
Tuzluca, *Turk.* **169** E18
Tveitsund, *Nor.* **140** L11
Tver', *Russ.* **156** H8
Tvøroyri, *Faroe Is., Den.* **140** J6
Tweed Heads, *N.S.W., Austral.* **211** V15
Twentynine Palms, *Calif., U.S.* **109** X11
25 de Mayo, *Arg.* **133** N8
26 Baky Komissary, *Azerb.* **169** E23
Twin Bridges, *Mont., U.S.* **106** E7
Twin Buttes Reservoir, *Tex., U.S.* **103** N7
Twin City, *Ga., U.S.* **96** M8
Twin Falls, *Idaho, U.S.* **106** H5
Twin Peaks, *Idaho, U.S.* **106** F5
Twin Valley, *Minn., U.S.* **104** G8
Twisp, *Wash., U.S.* **108** B6
Twizel, *N.Z.* **213** P16
Two Butte Creek, *Colo., U.S.* **107** P15
Two Buttes, *Colo., U.S.* **107** P16
Two Harbors, *Minn., U.S.* **104** G13
Two Rivers, *Wis., U.S.* **98** K7
Tyab, *Iran* **173** H15
Tybee Island, *Ga., U.S.* **97** N9
Tychy, *Pol.* **149** G15
Tygda, *Russ.* **159** K19
Tyler, *Minn., U.S.* **104** K9
Tyler, *Tex., U.S.* **102** L14
Tylertown, *Miss., U.S.* **100** N11
Tymvou, *Cyprus* **160** P9
Tynda, *Russ.* **159** K18
Tyndall, *S. Dak., U.S.* **104** M7
Tyndaris, ruin, *It.* **151** R11
Tyndrum, *Scot., U.K.* **142** L8
Tynemouth, *Eng., U.K.* **143** P12
Tyonek, *Alas., U.S.* **111** J16
Tyre *see* Soûr, *Leb.* **170** K5
Tyrnyauz, *Russ.* **157** U13
Tyrol, region, *Aust., It.* **150** C6
Tyrone, *Okla., U.S.* **102** E6
Tyrone, *Pa., U.S.* **94** N5
Tyrrell, Lake, *Austral.* **210** L11
Tyrrhenian Sea, *It.* **150** L6
Tyuguyuren, *Russ.* **159** E18
Tyukalinsk, *Russ.* **158** J10
Tyumen', *Russ.* **158** J9
Tywyn, *Wales, U.K.* **143** T9
Tzaneen, *S. Af.* **202** H11
Tziá *see* Kéa, island, *Gr.* **155** K13

U

U, *F.S.M.* **217** F14
Uaboe, region, *Nauru* **217** E23

Ua Huka, island, *Fr. Polynesia, Fr.* **215** H14
Ua Pu, island, *Fr. Polynesia, Fr.* **215** H14
Uaroo, *W. Aust., Austral.* **211** T2
Uatio, Île, *New Caledonia, Fr.* **218** E9
Ubá, *Braz.* **131** L15
Ubangi *see* Oubangui, river, *Congo* **201** K18
Ubauro, *Pak.* **177** T8
Ube, *Japan* **185** R5
Úbeda, *Sp.* **144** K11
Uberaba, *Braz.* **131** K13
Uberlândia, *Braz.* **131** K13
Ubierna, *Sp.* **144** C11
Ubon Ratchathani, *Thai.* **186** L11
Ubundu, *Dem. Rep. of the Congo* **198** K11
Üçajy, *Turkm.* **174** M10
Ucar, *Azerb.* **169** D21
Ucayali, river, *Peru* **130** F4
Uch, *Pak.* **177** S9
Uchiura Wan, *Japan* **184** G13
Uchiza, *Peru* **130** G3
Uchquduq, *Uzb.* **174** J11
Udachnyy, *Russ.* **159** G16
Udaipur, *India* **178** H4
Udayagiri, *India* **178** L9
Uddevalla, *Sw.* **140** M12
Uderolal, *Pak.* **177** V7
Udgir, *India* **178** L5
Udhampur, *India* **177** N12
Udine, *It.* **150** D9
Udintsev Fracture Zone, *Pac. Oc.* **238** R12
Udipi, *India* **179** P4
Udon Thani, *Thai.* **186** K10
Udot, island, *F.S.M.* **217** C15
Udskaya Guba, *Russ.* **159** J20
Udu Point, *Fiji Is.* **218** G8
Uebonti, *Indonesia* **189** J14
Ueda, *Japan* **185** N11
Uele, river, *Dem. Rep. of the Congo* **198** H10
Uelen, *Russ.* **159** A21
Uelzen, *Ger.* **148** D8
Ufa, river, *Russ.* **138** C14
Ufa, *Russ.* **158** H8
Ufra, *Turkm.* **174** K6
Ugab, river, *Namibia* **202** G6
Uganda, *Af.* **195** J21
Ugarit *see* Ra's Shamrah, ruin, *Syr.* **170** F6
Uglich, *Russ.* **156** H9
Ugljan, island, *Croatia* **152** F5
Ugljane, *Croatia* **152** G6
Uglovoye, *Russ.* **159** K19
Ugol'nyye Kopi, *Russ.* **159** B21
Ugum, river, *Guam, U.S.* **216** D10
Uherské Hradiště, *Czech Rep.* **149** J13
Uhrichsville, *Ohio, U.S.* **99** Q15
Uig, *Scot., U.K.* **142** H6
Uig, *Scot., U.K.* **142** J7
Uige, *Angola* **202** C6
'Uiha, island, *Tonga* **218** Q7
'Uiha, *Tonga* **218** Q7
Uinta, river, *Utah, U.S.* **106** L9
Uinta Mountains, *Utah, U.S.* **106** L8
Uiseong, *S. Korea* **182** F14
Uitenhage, *S. Af.* **202** M9
Uithuizen, *Neth.* **146** G14
Ujae Atoll, *Marshall Is.* **216** G3
Ujajiivan, island, *Marshall Is.* **216** L4
Ujelang Atoll, *Marshall Is.* **216** G1
Uji Guntō, *Japan* **185** T3
Ujiie, *Japan* **185** N12
Ujjain, *India* **178** J5
Ujung Pandang *see* Makassar, *Indonesia* **189** L13
Uke Shima, *Japan* **185** W3
Ukhiya, *Bangladesh* **178** K14
Ukhrul, *India* **178** G15
Ukhta, *Russ.* **158** F9
Ukiah, *Calif., U.S.* **109** Q2
Ukiah, *Oreg., U.S.* **108** F7
Uki Ni Masi Island, *Solomon Is.* **217** P20
Ukmergė, *Lith.* **141** N17
Ukraine, *Eur.* **139** U10
Uku, *Japan* **185** R3
Ukulahu, island, *Maldives* **179** U3
Uku Shima, *Japan* **185** R3
Ula, *Turk.* **168** H4
Ulaanbaatar (Ulan Bator), *Mongolia* **180** D12

Ulaangom, *Mongolia* **180** C9
Ulaga, *Russ.* **159** F17
Ulan Bator *see* Ulaanbaatar, *Mongolia* **180** D12
Ulan Erge, *Russ.* **157** R13
Ulanhad *see* Chifeng, *China* **182** B8
Ulanhot, *China* **181** D16
Ulan Khol, *Russ.* **157** S15
Ulansuhai Nur, *China* **182** C2
Ulan Ude, *Russ.* **159** L16
Ulaş, *Turk.* **168** F12
'Ula'ula, Pu'u, *Hawai'i, U.S.* **113** H17
Ulawa, island, *Solomon Is.* **217** N20
Ulawun, Mount, *P.N.G.* **213** C21
Uldz, river, *Mongolia* **181** C14
Uldz, *Mongolia* **181** C13
Uleåborg *see* Oulu, *Fin.* **141** F15
Uleguma, island, *Maldives* **179** T3
Ulen, *Minn., U.S.* **104** G8
Uliastay (Javhlant), *Mongolia* **180** D10
Ulingan, *P.N.G.* **213** C19
Ulithi Atoll, *F.S.M.* **216** P3
Uljin, *S. Korea* **182** F14
Uljma, *Serb.* **152** E11
Ülken Borsyq Qumy, *Kaz.* **174** F9
Ullapool, *Scot., U.K.* **142** J8
Ulleungdo (Dagelet), island, *S. Korea* **182** E15
Ulm, *Ger.* **148** K7
Ulmarra, *N.S.W., Austral.* **211** W15
Ulsan, *S. Korea* **182** G15
Ulster, region, *Ire., U.K.* **143** Q6
Ulu, *Russ.* **159** H18
Ulubat Gölü, *Turk.* **168** D4
Uluborlu, *Turk.* **168** G6
Ulu Dağ (Mount Olympus), *Turk.* **168** D5
Ulufala Point, *Amer. Samoa, U.S.* **218** P4
Uliutu, island, *Wallis & Futuna, Fr.* **218** A11
Ulukışla, *Turk.* **168** H9
Ulul, island, *F.S.M.* **216** Q5
Ulundi, *S. Af.* **202** K11
Ulungur Hu, *China* **180** D7
Uluru *see* Ayers Rock, peak, *Austral.* **210** G7
Ulus, *Turk.* **168** C8
Ulva, island, *Scot., U.K.* **142** L7
Ulvéah *see* Lopévi, island, *Vanuatu* **218** G3
Ulverston, *Eng., U.K.* **143** Q10
Ul'yanovsk, *Russ.* **156** K14
Ulysses, *Kans., U.S.* **105** U3
Ulytaū, range, *Kaz.* **174** E12
Um al Dami, Jabal, *Jor.* **171** S6
Uman, island, *F.S.M.* **217** C15
Uman', *Ukr.* **157** P5
Umari, *Indonesia* **189** L19
Umaria, *India* **178** J7
Umarkot, *Pak.* **177** V8
Umatac, *Guam, U.S.* **216** D10
Umatac Bay, *Guam, U.S.* **216** D10
Umatilla, river, *Oreg., U.S.* **108** F8
Umatilla, *Oreg., U.S.* **108** E7
Umba, *Russ.* **158** D8
Umboi, island, *P.N.G.* **213** C20
Umbriatico, *It.* **151** P14
Umbukul, *P.N.G.* **213** B20
Umeå, *Sw.* **141** G14
Umeälven, river, *Sw.* **141** G13
Umfors, *Sw.* **140** F12
'Umikoa, *Hawai'i, U.S.* **113** L20
Umm al Arānib, *Lib.* **197** E14
Umm al-Qaiwain, *U.A.E.* **173** J15
Umm as Samīm, dry lake, *Oman, Saudi Arabia* **173** L15
Umm Lajj, *Saudi Arabia* **172** J6
Umm Qaşr, *Iraq* **172** F11
Umm Urūmah, island, *Saudi Arabia* **172** H5
Umnak Island, *Alas., U.S.* **110** P9
Umpqua, river, *Oreg., U.S.* **108** J2
Umred, *India* **178** K7
Umuahia, *Nigeria* **201** H14
Umuna, island, *Tonga* **218** L12
Una, river, *Bosn. & Herzg., Croatia* **152** E6
Unadilla, *Ga., U.S.* **97** N6
Unai Obyan, peninsula, *N. Mariana Is., U.S.* **216** D5
Unai Pass, *Afghan.* **176** M7
Unalakleet, *Alas., U.S.* **111** G13
Unalaska, *Alas., U.S.* **110** P9

Unalaska Island, *Alas., U.S.* 110 P9
'Unayzah, *Saudi Arabia* 172 H9
'Unayzah, Jabal, *Iraq, Jordan, Saudi Arabia* 170 M12
Uncía, *Bol.* 130 K7
Uncompahgre Peak, *Colo., U.S.* 107 P11
Uncompahgre Plateau, *Colo., U.S.* 107 N10
Underwood, *N. Dak., U.S.* 104 F4
Undurhaan, *Mongolia* 181 D13
Unecha, *Russ.* 156 L7
Ungama Bay, *Kenya* 194 K10
Ungava Bay, *Que., Can.* 83 J19
Ungava, Péninsule d', *Que., Can.* 83 J18
Ungava Peninsula see Ungava, Péninsule d', *N. Amer.* 80 F8
União da Vitória, *Braz.* 130 N12
Unije, island, *Croatia* 152 F4
Unikar, Mochun, *F.S.M.* 217 C16
Unimak Island, *Alas., U.S.* 110 N11
Unimak Pass, *Alas., U.S.* 110 N10
Unini, river, *Braz.* 130 D8
Union, *Grenada* 121 J23
Union, *Miss., U.S.* 100 L12
Union, *Mo., U.S.* 105 T14
Union, *Oreg., U.S.* 108 F8
Union, *S.C., U.S.* 96 J8
Union, island, *St. Vincent & the Grenadines* 119 M17
Unión, Bahía, *Arg.* 133 P11
Union City, *Ohio, U.S.* 99 Q11
Union City, *Pa., U.S.* 94 L3
Union City, *Tenn., U.S.* 100 E12
Union Point, *Ga., U.S.* 96 L6
Union Springs, *Ala., U.S.* 101 L16
Uniontown, *Ala., U.S.* 101 L14
Uniontown, *Pa., U.S.* 94 P3
Unionville, *Mo., U.S.* 105 Q12
Unionville, *Nev., U.S.* 109 N8
United Arab Emirates, *Asia* 167 V4
United Estates, *Bahamas* 120 E12
United Kingdom, *Eur.* 139 S4
United States, *N. Amer.* 81 K18
Unity, *Oreg., U.S.* 108 G8
University Park, *N. Mex., U.S.* 107 V12
Unnao, *India* 178 G7
Unst, island, *Scot., U.K.* 142 C12
Ünye, *Turk.* 168 D12
Unzha, *Russ.* 156 G12
Uoleva, island, *Tonga* 218 P7
Upata, *Venez.* 128 C12
Upemba, Lake, *Dem. Rep. of the Congo* 194 L8
Upernavik Kujalleq, *Greenland, Den.* 81 C20
Upham, *N. Dak., U.S.* 104 E4
Upington, *S. Af.* 202 K8
Upolu, island, *Samoa* 218 L3
'Upolu Point, *Hawai'i, U.S.* 113 J19
Upper Arlington, *Ohio, U.S.* 99 R13
Upper Bogue, *Bahamas* 120 D5
Upper Darby, *Pa., U.S.* 94 P9
Upper Guinea, region, *Af.* 194 H3
Upper Hutt, *N.Z.* 213 M19
Upper Kama Upland, *Russ.* 138 C13
Upper Klamath Lake, *Oreg., U.S.* 108 K4
Upper Lake, *Calif., U.S.* 108 L6
Upper Lough Erne, *N. Ire., U.K.* 143 Q5
Upper Manzanilla, *Trinidad & Tobago* 121 P23
Upper Missouri River Breaks National Monument, *Mont., U.S.* 106 C10
Upper Peninsula, *Mich., U.S.* 98 F6
Upper Red Lake, *Minn., U.S.* 104 E10
Upper St. Clair, *Pa., U.S.* 94 N3
Upper Sandusky, *Ohio, U.S.* 99 Q12
Uppsala, *Sw.* 141 K14
Upshi, *India* 178 C6
Upton, *Wyo., U.S.* 106 G13
'Uqayribāt, *Syr.* 170 F9
Ur, ruin, *Iraq* 172 F10
Urabá, Golfo de, *Col.* 128 D4
Urad Houqi, *China* 182 B1
Urad Qianqi, *China* 182 C2
Urad Zhongqi, *China* 182 B2
Urakawa, *Japan* 184 G14
Ural, river, *Kaz., Russ.* 166 E5
Ural, river, *Russ.* 158 J8
Uralla, *N.S.W., Austral.* 211 W15
Ural Mountains, *Russ.* 166 D7
Urana, *N.S.W., Austral.* 211 Y13

Urandangi, *Qnsld., Austral.* 211 S10
Urania, *La., U.S.* 100 M8
Uranium City, *Sask., Can.* 82 J12
Uranu, island, *F.S.M.* 217 B14
Uraricoera, river, *Braz.* 130 B8
Uraricoera, *Braz.* 130 B9
Uravan, *Colo., U.S.* 107 N10
Urawa, *Japan* 185 P12
Urbana, *Ill., U.S.* 99 R7
Urbana, *Ohio, U.S.* 99 R12
Urbandale, *Iowa, U.S.* 105 P11
Urbano Noris, *Cuba* 116 K12
Urbett, island, *Marshall Is.* 216 K7
Urbino, *It.* 150 G8
Urbión, Picos de, *Sp.* 144 D12
Urdos, *Fr.* 147 Y6
Uren', *Russ.* 156 G13
Uréparapara, island, *Vanuatu* 218 A2
Urganch, *Uzb.* 174 K9
Urgut, *Uzb.* 174 L12
Uriah, Mount, *N.Z.* 213 N17
Uribia, *Col.* 128 A6
Uriondo, *Bol.* 130 L7
Uritskoye, *Russ.* 159 H17
Urla, *Turk.* 168 F2
Urlaţi, *Rom.* 153 E15
Urlins, *Antigua & Barbuda* 121 B20
Urmia, Lake see Orūmīyeh, Daryācheh-ye, *Iran* 172 B10
Uroševac see Ferizaj, *Kos.* 152 J10
Üroteppa see Istaravshan, *Taj.* 176 G7
Urt Moron, *China* 180 H8
Uruana, *Braz.* 131 J13
Uruapan, *Mex.* 114 J10
Urubamba, river, *Peru* 130 H5
Urucará, *Braz.* 130 D10
Uruçuí, *Braz.* 131 F15
Uruçuí, Serra do, *S. Amer.* 126 F9
Urugi, *Japan* 185 P10
Uruguai, river, *Braz.* 130 N11
Uruguaiana, *Braz.* 130 P10
Uruguay, *S. Amer.* 127 L19
Uruguay, river, *S. Amer.* 126 K7
Urukthapel (Ngeruktabel), island, *Palau* 216 P11
Ürümqi, *China* 180 E7
Uruno Point, *Guam, U.S.* 216 B11
Urup, island, *Russ.* 159 J23
Uryupinsk, *Russ.* 157 N12
Ürzhar, *Kaz.* 175 F18
Urzhum, *Russ.* 156 G15
Urziceni, *Rom.* 153 F16
Usa, *Japan* 185 R7
Usa, river, *Russ.* 138 A12
Uşak, *Turk.* 168 F5
Usakos, *Namibia* 202 H6
Usarp Mountains, *Antarctica* 227 Q15
Usedom, island, *Ger.* 148 B11
Useldange, *Lux.* 160 J9
Ushakova, Ostrov, *Russ.* 159 C13
Ushakovskoye, *Russ.* 159 B19
Üsharal, *Kaz.* 175 F18
Ushibuka, *Japan* 185 S4
Ushi Point, *N. Mariana Is., U.S.* 216 A8
Üshtöbe, *Kaz.* 175 G17
Ushuaia, *Arg.* 133 X9
Ushumun, *Russ.* 159 K19
Usinsk, *Russ.* 158 F10
Usman', *Russ.* 156 M10
Usol'ye Sibirskoye, *Russ.* 159 L15
Usove, *Ukr.* 156 M4
U.S. Range, *Nunavut, Can.* 83 A16
U.S.S. Arizona Memorial, *Hawai'i, U.S.* 112 E11
Ussel, *Fr.* 147 U10
Ussuri, river, *China, Russ.* 166 E12
Ussuriysk, *Russ.* 159 M21
Uster, *Switz.* 150 A4
Ustica, *It.* 151 R9
Ustica, Isola di, *It.* 151 R9
Ust' Ilimpeya, *Russ.* 159 H15
Ust' Ilimsk, *Russ.* 159 K15
Ustí nad Labem, *Czech Rep.* 148 G11
Ustka, *Pol.* 149 B13
Ust'-Kamchatsk, *Russ.* 159 E22
Ust' Kamenogorsk see Öskemen, *Kaz.* 175 D18
Ust' Kamo, *Russ.* 159 J14
Ust' Kut, *Russ.* 159 K15
Ust' Labinsk, *Russ.* 157 S11
Ust' Maya, *Russ.* 159 G19
Ust' Mil', *Russ.* 159 H19
Ust' Nera, *Russ.* 159 F19
Ust' Olenek, *Russ.* 159 E16

Ust' Omchug, *Russ.* 159 F20
Ust' Ordynskiy, *Russ.* 159 L15
Ust' Usa, *Russ.* 158 F10
Ust' Yansk, *Russ.* 159 E17
Ust' Yudoma, *Russ.* 159 H19
Ustyurt Plateau, *Kaz., Uzb.* 174 H7
Ustyuzhna, *Russ.* 156 G9
Usu, *China* 180 E7
Usuki, *Japan* 185 R5
Usumacinta, river, *N. Amer.* 80 P6
Usvyaty, *Russ.* 156 J6
Uta, *Russ.* 159 R7
Utah, *U.S.* 106 M6
Utah Beach, *Fr.* 147 N6
Utah Lake, *Utah, U.S.* 106 L7
Utara, Bunguran see Natuna Besar, Kepulauan, *Indonesia* 188 G8
Ute Creek, *N. Mex., U.S.* 107 Q14
Utete, *Tanzania* 199 M15
Uthai Thani, *Thai.* 186 L8
Uthal, *Pak.* 177 V5
Utiariti, *Braz.* 130 H10
Utica, *N.Y., U.S.* 94 J9
Utiel, *Sp.* 145 H14
Utirik Atoll, *Marshall Is.* 216 F4
Utkela, *India* 178 L9
Utnur, *India* 178 L6
Utopia, *N. Terr., Austral.* 211 T9
Utraula, *India* 178 G8
Utrecht, *Neth.* 146 J12
Utsunomiya, *Japan* 185 N12
Utta, *Russ.* 157 R14
Uttaradit, *Thai.* 186 K8
Utuado, *P.R., U.S.* 120 N3
Utuloa, *Wallis & Futuna, Fr.* 218 B11
Utupua, island, *Solomon Is.* 217 Q23
Uturoa, *Fr. Polynesia, Fr.* 219 B23
Utva, river, *Kaz.* 174 D7
Utwa, *F.S.M.* 217 B18
Uummannaq, *Greenland, Den.* 81 C21
Uusikaupunki, *Fin.* 141 J15
Uva, *Russ.* 156 G16
Uvalde, *Tex., U.S.* 103 R8
Uvarovo, *Russ.* 156 M12
Uvéa see Ouvéa, Île, island, *New Caledonia, Fr.* 218 C8
Uvea, island, *Wallis & Futuna, Fr.* 218 B11
Uvinza, *Tanzania* 198 L12
Uvol, *P.N.G.* 213 D21
Uvs Nuur, *Mongolia* 180 C9
Uwajima, *Japan* 185 R6
'Uwayriḍ, Ḥarrat al, *Saudi Arabia* 172 H6
'Uweinat, Jebel, *Sudan* 198 C11
Uxin Qi (Dabqig), *China* 182 E2
Uxmal, ruin, *Mex.* 115 H16
Uyar, *Russ.* 159 K13
Uyuni, *Bol.* 130 L7
Uyuni, Salar de, *Bol.* 130 L7
Uzbekistan, *Asia* 167 T6
Uzbel Shankou, *China, Taj.* 176 H11
Uzerche, *Fr.* 147 U9
Uzès, *Fr.* 147 W12
Uzhhorod, *Ukr.* 157 P1
Užice, *Serb.* 152 G9
Uzlovaya, *Russ.* 156 K9
Üzümlü, *Turk.* 168 H4
Uzunköprü, *Turk.* 168 C3
Uzynköl, *Kaz.* 174 B11

V

Vaal, river, *S. Af.* 202 K10
Vaals, *Neth.* 146 L13
Vaasa, *Fin.* 141 H14
Vác, *Hung.* 149 L15
Vacaville, *Calif., U.S.* 109 R4
Vache, Île à, *Haiti* 117 N15
Vacía Talega, Punta, *P.R., U.S.* 120 M5
Vacoas, *Mauritius* 205 G20
Vadodara, *India* 178 J3
Vadsø, *Nor.* 141 C15
Vaduz, *Liech.* 160 P2
Vaduz Castle, *Liech.* 160 P2
Værøy, island, *Nor.* 140 E11
Vaga, river, *Russ.* 138 C11
Vágar, island, *Faroe Is., Den.* 140 J5
Vaghena, island, *Solomon Is.* 217 L16
Vagthus Point, *Virgin Islands, U.S.* 120 R3
Váh, river, *Slovakia* 149 J14

Vahanga, island, *Fr. Polynesia, Fr.* 219 G22
Vahdat (Kofarnihon), *Taj.* 176 J7
Vahitahi, island, *Fr. Polynesia, Fr.* 219 F21
Vahituri, island, *Fr. Polynesia, Fr.* 219 L17
Vaiaau, *Fr. Polynesia, Fr.* 219 B23
Vaiau, Passe, *Fr. Polynesia, Fr.* 219 Q17
Vaiden, *Miss., U.S.* 100 K11
Vaiea, *Niue, N.Z.* 219 B20
Vaiere, island, *Cook Is., N.Z.* 219 C17
Vaigalu, *Samoa* 218 L4
Vailala, *Wallis & Futuna, Fr.* 218 B11
Vailoa, *Samoa* 218 K2
Vailoatai, *Amer. Samoa, U.S.* 218 N7
Vaimalau, *Wallis & Futuna, Fr.* 218 B11
Vaini, *Tonga* 218 J11
Vaionifa, Passe, *Fr. Polynesia, Fr.* 219 P18
Vaipae, *Cook Is., N.Z.* 218 Q11
Vaipaee, *Fr. Polynesia, Fr.* 219 N23
Vaipeka, *Cook Is., N.Z.* 219 P11
Vairaatea, island, *Fr. Polynesia, Fr.* 219 F21
Vairo, *Fr. Polynesia, Fr.* 219 Q17
Vaitahu, *Fr. Polynesia, Fr.* 219 N20
Vaïtape, *Fr. Polynesia, Fr.* 219 K14
Vaitoare, *Fr. Polynesia, Fr.* 219 B23
Vaitogi, *Amer. Samoa, U.S.* 218 N7
Vaitupu, island, *Tuvalu* 214 H9
Vaitupu, *Wallis & Futuna, Fr.* 218 B11
Vai'utukakau Bay, *Tonga* 218 L11
Vaka'eitu, island, *Tonga* 218 M11
Vakfıkebir, *Turk.* 169 D14
Vakhan, region, *Afghan.* 176 K10
Vakhrushev, *Russ.* 159 J22
Vakhsh, river, *Taj.* 176 H9
Vakhtan, *Russ.* 156 G13
Valamaz, *Russ.* 156 G15
Valcheta, *Arg.* 133 Q9
Valdagno, *It.* 150 D7
Valdahon, *Fr.* 147 S14
Valdai Hills, *Russ.* 138 D10
Valdayskaya Vozvyshennost', *Russ.* 156 J7
Valdepeñas, *Sp.* 144 J11
Valderrobres, *Sp.* 145 F15
Valdes, Península, *Arg.* 133 R10
Valdez, *Alas., U.S.* 111 J18
Valdez, *Ecua.* 128 H2
Valdivia, *Chile* 133 P6
Valdivia, *Col.* 128 D4
Valdivia Fracture Zone, *Pac. Oc.* 239 P19
Valdosta, *Ga., U.S.* 97 Q6
Vale, *Oreg., U.S.* 108 H9
Valea lui Mihai, *Rom.* 152 B11
Valença, *Port.* 144 D5
Valença, *Braz.* 131 H16
Valence, *Fr.* 147 V13
Valence, *Fr.* 147 W8
Valencia, *Sp.* 145 H14
Valencia, *Venez.* 128 B9
Valencia, Golfo de, *Sp.* 145 H15
Valencia, Lake, *S. Amer.* 126 A4
Valenciennes, *Fr.* 146 M11
Valentia Island, *Ire.* 143 U2
Valentine, *Nebr., U.S.* 104 M4
Valentine, *Tex., U.S.* 103 P1
Valenza, *It.* 150 E4
Valera, *Venez.* 128 C7
Valga, *Est.* 141 L17
Valguarnera Caropepe, *It.* 151 S11
Valier, *Mont., U.S.* 106 B7
Valinco, Golfe de, *Fr.* 150 L4
Valira, river, *Andorra* 160 J3
Valira del Nort, river, *Andorra* 160 J3
Valira d'Orient, river, *Andorra* 160 H4
Valjevo, *Serb.* 152 F9
Valka, *Latv.* 141 L17
Valkeakoski, *Fin.* 141 J15
Valkenswaard, *Neth.* 146 K13
Valkyrie Dome, *Antarctica* 227 D15
Valladolid, *Mex.* 115 H16
Valladolid, *Sp.* 144 D10
Valle de la Pascua, *Venez.* 128 C10
Valledupar, *Col.* 128 B6

Valle Fértil, Sierra del, *Arg.* 132 J8
Valle Formozo, *Sao Tome and Principe* 205 D20
Vallegrande, *Bol.* 130 K8
Vallehermoso, *Canary Is.* 204 Q4
Vallejo, *Calif., U.S.* 109 R3
Vallenar, *Chile* 132 H6
Valletta, *Malta* 161 K23
Valley Center, *Kans., U.S.* 105 U7
Valley City, *N. Dak., U.S.* 104 G7
Valley Falls, *Kans., U.S.* 105 S9
Valley Falls, *Oreg., U.S.* 108 K6
Valley Mills, *Tex., U.S.* 103 N11
Valley Station, *Ky., U.S.* 101 B16
Vallo della Lucania, *It.* 151 N12
Vallorbe, *Switz.* 150 B1
Valls, *Sp.* 145 E16
Valmeyer, *Ill., U.S.* 99 T4
Valmiera, *Latv.* 141 L17
Valmy, *Fr.* 147 P12
Valona see Vlorë, *Albania* 152 M9
Valozhyn, *Belarus* 156 K4
Valparaíso, *Fla., U.S.* 97 Q2
Valparaiso, *Ind., U.S.* 99 P8
Valparaíso, *Chile* 132 K6
Valparaíso, *Mex.* 114 G10
Vals, Tanjung, *Indonesia* 213 D16
Valsad, *India* 178 K3
Valüna, valley, *Liech.* 160 Q3
Valuyevka, *Russ.* 157 R13
Valuyki, *Russ.* 157 N10
Valverde, *Canary Is.* 204 R3
Valverde del Camino, *Sp.* 144 K7
Van, *Turk.* 169 G17
Van, Lake, *Turk.* 166 F4
Vana, *Solomon Is.* 217 R23
Vanadzor, *Arm.* 169 D18
Van Alstyne, *Tex., U.S.* 102 K12
Vanavana, island, *Fr. Polynesia, Fr.* 219 G21
Vanavara, *Russ.* 159 J15
Van Blommestein Meer, *Suriname* 129 E16
Van Buren, *Ark., U.S.* 100 F6
Van Buren, *Me., U.S.* 95 A18
Vanceboro, *Me., U.S.* 95 D19
Vanceboro, *N.C., U.S.* 96 H13
Vanceburg, *Ky., U.S.* 101 A19
Vancouver, *B.C., Can.* 82 M8
Vancouver, *Wash., U.S.* 108 F3
Vancouver Island, *B.C., Can.* 82 L7
Vandalia, *Ill., U.S.* 99 S5
Vandalia, *Mo., U.S.* 105 S14
Vandalia, *Ohio, U.S.* 99 R11
Vanderbilt, *Mich., U.S.* 98 H11
Vanderford Glacier, *Antarctica* 227 M20
Van Diemen, Cape, *Austral.* 210 A7
Van Diemen Gulf, *Austral.* 210 A8
Vänern, lake, *Sw.* 140 L12
Vangaindrano, *Madagascar* 203 H17
Van Gölü, *Turk.* 169 G17
Vangunu, island, *Solomon Is.* 217 M17
Vangunu, Mount, *Solomon Is.* 217 M16
Vangviang, *Laos* 186 J10
Van Horn, *Tex., U.S.* 103 N1
Vanikolo, island, *Solomon Is.* 217 R23
Vanikolo Islands, *Solomon Is.* 217 R23
Vanimo, *P.N.G.* 213 B17
Vanino, *Russ.* 159 K21
Vanj, *Taj.* 176 J9
Vankarem, *Russ.* 159 A20
Vännäs, *Sw.* 141 G14
Vannes, *Fr.* 147 R4
Van Ninh, *Vietnam* 187 N14
Vannøy, island, *Nor.* 141 C13
Vanoise, Massif de la, *Fr.* 147 U15
Vanrhynsdorp, *S. Af.* 202 L7
Vanrook, *Qnsld., Austral.* 211 R12
Vansbro, *Sw.* 140 K12
Vansittart Island, *Nunavut, Can.* 83 G16
Van Tassell, *Wyo., U.S.* 106 H14
Vanua, island, *Fiji Is.* 218 H9
Vanua Lava, island, *Vanuatu* 218 B2
Vanua Levu, island, *Fiji Is.* 218 G7
Vanua Masi, island, *Fiji Is.* 218 J9
Vanuatu, *Pac. Oc.* 214 K8
Vanua Vatu, island, *Fiji Is.* 218 J9
Vanuca, island, *Fiji Is.* 218 J6
Van Wert, *Ohio, U.S.* 99 Q11
Vao, *New Caledonia, Fr.* 218 E9
Vao, Nosy, *Madagascar* 203 F16

Varadero, *Cuba* 116 G7
Varanasi (Banaras), *India* 178 H9
Varangerfjorden, bay, *Nor.* 141 C15
Varangerhalvøya, peninsula, *Nor.* 141 B15
Varano, Lago di, *It.* 150 K12
Varas, *Afghan.* 177 N4
Varaždin, *Croatia* 152 D6
Varazze, *It.* 150 F3
Varberg, *Sw.* 140 M12
Vardar, river, *Maced.* 152 K12
Vardø, *Nor.* 141 B15
Varéna, *Lith.* 141 N17
Varennes, *Fr.* 147 N13
Varese, *It.* 150 D4
Varilhes, *Fr.* 147 Y9
Varkaus, *Fin.* 141 H16
Varna, *Bulg.* 153 H17
Varnavino, *Russ.* 156 H12
Varnenski Zaliv, *Bulg.* 153 H17
Varnensko Ezero, *Bulg.* 153 H17
Varnville, *S.C., U.S.* 96 M9
Varosha, *Cyprus* 160 P10
Varto, *Turk.* 169 F16
Värts Järv, *Est.* 141 L17
Varungga Point, *Solomon Is.* 217 L16
Varzob, *Taj.* 176 H7
Varzy, *Fr.* 147 R11
Vasafua, island, *Tuvalu* 217 K22
Vasiliko, *Cyprus* 160 Q8
Vasil'yevo, *Russ.* 156 J14
Vaskess Bay, *Kiribati* 217 B22
Vaslui, *Rom.* 153 C17
Vassar, *Mich., U.S.* 98 L12
Vassiliki, *Gr.* 154 H7
Vassilikós, *Gr.* 154 K8
Vassilítsa, Óros, *Gr.* 154 E8
Västerås, *Sw.* 141 K13
Västervik, *Sw.* 141 M13
Vasto, *It.* 150 K11
Vasyl'kiv, *Ukr.* 157 N6
Vasyugan'ye, wetland, *Russ.* 166 E8
Vatan, *Fr.* 147 S9
Vaté, Île see Éfaté, *Vanuatu* 218 F3
Vatersay, island, *Scot., U.K.* 142 K6
Vathí, *Gr.* 154 H12
Vathý see Itháki, *Gr.* 154 H7
Vatia, *Amer. Samoa, U.S.* 218 M8
Vatia Bay, *Amer. Samoa, U.S.* 218 L8
Vatia Point, *Fiji Is.* 218 H6
Vatican City, *Eur.* 160 D4
Vatican Gardens, *Vatican City* 161 P15
Vatican Library, *Vatican City* 161 P16
Vatican Museums, *Vatican City* 161 N16
Vaticano, Capo, *It.* 151 R13
Vatican Radio, *Vatican City* 161 Q14
Vatili, *Cyprus* 160 P9
Vatnajökull, glacier, *Ice.* 140 F3
Vatneyri, *Ice.* 140 E2
Vatoa, island, *Fiji Is.* 214 K9
Vatoa (Turtle), island, *Fiji Is.* 218 L10
Vatra Dornei, *Rom.* 153 B14
Vättern, lake, *Sw.* 141 L13
Vatuki, island, *Fiji Is.* 218 G7
Vatukoula, *Fiji Is.* 218 H6
Vatulele, island, *Fiji Is.* 218 J6
Vatu Vara, island, *Fiji Is.* 218 H8
Vaughn, *Mont., U.S.* 106 C7
Vaughn, *N. Mex., U.S.* 107 S13
Vaupés, river, *Col.* 128 H7
Vauvilliers, Île, *New Caledonia, Fr.* 218 C9
Vauvilliers, Point, *F.S.M.* 217 B17
Vav, *India* 178 H3
Vavara, Motu, *Fr. Polynesia, Fr.* 219 G14
Vava'u, island, *Tonga* 218 L12
Vava'u Group, *Tonga* 214 K10
Vavitu see Raivavae, island, *Fr. Polynesia, Fr.* 219 J17
Vavla, *Cyprus* 160 Q8
Vavuniya, *Sri Lanka* 179 S7
Vawkavysk, *Belarus* 156 L3
Växjö, *Sw.* 141 M13
Vayegi, *Russ.* 159 C21
Vaygach, Ostrov, *Russ.* 158 E11
Veblen, *S. Dak., U.S.* 104 H7
Vecchia, river, *San Marino* 161 J16
Vedea, river, *Rom.* 153 G15
Vedeno, *Russ.* 157 U14
Veendam, *Neth.* 146 G14
Vega, island, *Nor.* 140 G11
Vega, *Tex., U.S.* 102 G4
Vega Baja, *P.R., U.S.* 120 M4

Vegadeo, *Sp.* 144 A7
Veghel, *Neth.* 146 K13
Vegorítida, Límni, *Gr.* 154 C9
Vegreville, *Alta., Can.* 82 L11
Veharnu, island, *P.N.G.* 217 H14
Veio, ruin, *It.* 150 K8
Vejer de la Frontera, *Sp.* 144 N8
Vekai, island, *Fiji Is.* 218 H9
Velarde, *N. Mex., U.S.* 107 R12
Velas, *Azores* 144 P3
Velay, Monts du, *Fr.* 147 V11
Velbert, *Ger.* 148 F5
Velden, *Aust.* 148 M10
Velé, *Wallis & Futuna, Fr.* 218 E11
Velé, Pointe, *Wallis & Futuna, Fr.* 218 E12
Velebit, range, *Croatia* 152 F5
Velenje, *Slov.* 152 C5
Veles, *Maced.* 152 K11
Velestíno, *Gr.* 154 F11
Vélez, *Col.* 128 E5
Velež, peak, *Bosn. & Herzg.* 152 H8
Vélez de la Gomera, Peñón de, *Sp.* 144 P10
Vélez-Málaga, *Sp.* 144 M10
Velhas, river, *Braz.* 131 K14
Velia, ruin, *It.* 151 N12
Velika, river, *Serb.* 152 F11
Velika Ljubuša, peak, *Bosn. & Herzg.* 152 G7
Velika Plana, *Serb.* 152 F10
Velikaya, river, *Russ.* 138 E9
Veliki Drvenik, island, *Croatia* 152 G6
Veliki Snežnik, peak, *Slov.* 152 D4
Veliki Troglav, peak, *Bosn. & Herzg.* 152 G6
Velikiye Luki, *Russ.* 156 J6
Velikiy Novgorod, *Russ.* 156 G7
Velikonda Range, *India* 179 N7
Veliko Türnovo, *Bulg.* 153 H15
Vélingara, *Senegal* 196 H5
Velingrad, *Bulg.* 153 K13
Velizh, *Russ.* 156 J6
Vella Gulf, *Solomon Is.* 217 M15
Vella Lavella, island, *Solomon Is.* 217 L15
Velletri, *It.* 150 L9
Vellore, *India* 179 Q6
Velopoúla, island, *Gr.* 154 L12
Vel'sk, *Russ.* 158 F7
Velva, *N. Dak., U.S.* 104 F4
Vema Fracture Zone, *Atl. Oc.* 236 M7
Vema Fracture Zone, *Ind. Oc.* 240 H8
Vema Seamount, *Atl. Oc.* 237 S14
Véna, *Gr.* 155 B15
Venable Ice Shelf, *Antarctica* 226 H6
Venado Tuerto, *Arg.* 132 L11
Venango, *Nebr., U.S.* 105 Q3
Vendas Novas, *Port.* 144 J5
Vendôme, *Fr.* 147 R8
Vendôme, *Grenada* 121 K22
Veneta, Laguna, *It.* 150 E8
Venetie, *Alas., U.S.* 111 E17
Venétiko, island, *Gr.* 154 M9
Venezia (Venice), *It.* 150 E8
Venezuela, *Neth. Antilles, Neth.* 121 Q18
Venezuela, *S. Amer.* 127 B17
Venezuela, Golfo de, *Venez.* 128 B7
Vengurla, *India* 179 N3
Veniaminof, Mount, *Alas., U.S.* 111 N13
Venice, *Fla., U.S.* 97 V7
Venice see Venezia, *It.* 150 E8
Venice, *La., U.S.* 100 R12
Venice, Gulf of, *It.* 150 E9
Venkatapuram, *India* 178 M7
Venlo, *Neth.* 146 K14
Vennesund, *Nor.* 140 G11
Venosa, *It.* 150 M12
Venray, *Neth.* 146 K13
Vent, Îles du, *Fr. Polynesia, Fr.* 219 F16
Ventimiglia, *It.* 150 G2
Ventnor City, *N.J., U.S.* 94 Q10
Ventoso, *San Marino* 161 H15
Ventotene, Isola, *It.* 150 M9
Ventoux, Mont, *Fr.* 147 W13
Ventry see Ceann Tra, *Ire.* 143 U2
Ventspils, *Latv.* 141 M15
Ventuari, river, *Venez.* 128 F10
Ventura, *Calif., U.S.* 109 X7

Vénus, Pointe, *Fr. Polynesia, Fr.* 219 N16
Venus, Bahía de, *Eq. Guinea* 204 L7
Vera, *Arg.* 132 H12
Vera, *Sp.* 145 L13
Vera, Bahía, *Arg.* 133 R10
Veracruz, *Mex.* 115 J13
Veraval, *India* 178 K2
Verbania, *It.* 150 D4
Vercelli, *It.* 150 E3
Verçinin Tepesi, *Turk.* 169 D15
Verdalsøra, *Nor.* 140 H11
Verde, river, *Ariz., U.S.* 107 T7
Verde, Cape, *Senegal* 194 G1
Verde, Cay, *Bahamas* 117 H13
Verde, Península, *Arg.* 133 P11
Verdigre, *Nebr., U.S.* 105 N7
Verdigris, river, *Kans., Okla., U.S.* 85 J13
Verdun, *Fr.* 147 N13
Vereeniging, *S. Af.* 202 J10
Verga, Cap, *Guinea* 200 F4
Vergara, *Uru.* 132 K15
Vergato, *It.* 150 F6
Vergennes, *Vt., U.S.* 94 G12
Vergina, ruin, *Gr.* 154 D10
Vergt, *Fr.* 147 V8
Véria, *Gr.* 154 D10
Verín, *Sp.* 144 D7
Verkhneimbatsk, *Russ.* 159 H13
Verkhneye Penzhino, *Russ.* 159 D20
Verkhnyaya Amga, *Russ.* 159 H18
Verkhovazh'ye, *Russ.* 156 E11
Verkhov'ye, *Russ.* 156 L9
Verkhoyanskiy Khrebet, *Russ.* 159 F17
Verkhoyansk Range, *Russ.* 166 C11
Vermelharia, Ponta da, *Cape Verde* 205 B15
Vermelho, river, *Braz.* 130 J12
Vermenton, *Fr.* 147 R11
Vermilion, *Alas., U.S.* 111 J13
Vermilion Bay, *La., U.S.* 100 Q8
Vermilion Cliffs National Monument, *Ariz., U.S.* 107 Q7
Vermilion Lake, *Minn., U.S.* 104 F12
Vermilion Range, *Minn., U.S.* 104 F13
Vermillion, *S. Dak., U.S.* 104 M8
Vérmio, Óros, *Gr.* 154 C9
Vermont, *St. Vincent & the Grenadines* 121 K16
Vermont, *U.S.* 94 G12
Vernadsky, station, *Antarctica* 226 D4
Vernal, *Utah, U.S.* 106 L9
Verneuil, *Fr.* 147 P8
Vérno, Óros, *Gr.* 154 C8
Vernon, *Ala., U.S.* 101 J13
Vernon, *Fr.* 147 P9
Vernon, *Tex., U.S.* 102 J8
Vernonia, *Oreg., U.S.* 108 E3
Vernou, *Guadeloupe, Fr.* 121 F14
Vero Beach, *Fla., U.S.* 97 U10
Verona, *It.* 150 E6
Verona, *Miss., U.S.* 101 H13
Verraco, Punta, *P.R., U.S.* 120 P2
Versailles, *Fr.* 147 P10
Versailles, *Ky., U.S.* 101 B17
Versailles, *Mo., U.S.* 105 T12
Verte, Pointe, *Wallis & Futuna, Fr.* 218 E12
Vertientes, *Cuba* 116 J10
Verucchio, *It.* 161 G14
Verzy, *Fr.* 147 P12
Vescovato, *Fr.* 150 J4
Veselyy, *Russ.* 159 J17
Vesoul, *Fr.* 147 R14
Vesterålen, *Nor.* 140 D12
Vestfjorden, *Nor.* 140 E12
Vestmanna, *Faroe Is., Den.* 140 J6
Vestmannaeyjar (Westman Islands), *Ice.* 140 G2
Vestraumen Glacier, *Antarctica* 226 C11
Vestvågøy, island, *Nor.* 140 E12
Vesuvio, Monte, *It.* 150 M11
Vesuvius see Vesuvio, Monte, peak, *It.* 138 J7
Ves'yegonsk, *Russ.* 156 G9
Veszprém, *Hung.* 149 M14
Vétaounde, island, *Vanuatu* 218 A2
Vetapalem, *India* 179 N7
Vetavuua, island, *Fiji Is.* 218 G9
Vetluga, river, *Russ.* 138 C12
Vetralla, *It.* 150 K8
Veules-les-Roses, *Fr.* 146 M8

Vevaru, island, *Maldives* 179 V3
Vezhen, peak, *Bulg.* 153 J14
Vezirköprü, *Turk.* 168 D10
Viacha, *Bol.* 130 J6
Viana do Bolo, *Sp.* 144 C7
Viana do Castelo, *Port.* 144 D5
Vianden, *Lux.* 160 H10
Viangchan (Vientiane), *Laos* 186 K10
Viareggio, *It.* 150 G5
Viborg, *Den.* 140 N11
Vibo Valentia, *It.* 151 Q13
Vibraye, *Fr.* 147 Q8
Vic, *Sp.* 145 D17
Vic, Étang de, *Fr.* 147 X12
Vic-en-Bigorre, *Fr.* 147 X7
Vicente Guerrero, *Mex.* 114 B5
Vicenza, *It.* 150 D7
Vic-Fézensac, *Fr.* 147 X7
Vichada, river, *Col.* 128 E9
Vichuga, *Russ.* 156 H11
Vichy, *Fr.* 147 T11
Vici, *Okla., U.S.* 102 F8
Vicksburg, *Mich., U.S.* 99 N10
Vicksburg, *Miss., U.S.* 100 L10
Vicksburg National Military Park, *Miss., U.S.* 100 L10
Vicovu de Sus, *Rom.* 153 A15
Victor, Mount, *Antarctica* 227 C16
Victor Harbor, *S. Aust., Austral.* 211 Y10
Victoria, *Austral.* 211 Z12
Victoria, *B.C., Can.* 82 M8
Victoria, *Chile* 132 C7
Victoria, *Chile* 133 N6
Victoria, *Grenada* 121 J22
Victoria, *Kans., U.S.* 105 S6
Victoria, river, *N. Terr., Austral.* 211 Q7
Victoria, *Seychelles* 205 N20
Victoria, *Tex., U.S.* 103 S11
Victoria, *Va., U.S.* 96 F12
Victoria (Rabat), *Malta* 161 H20
Victoria, Lake, *Kenya, Tanzania, Uganda* 199 K13
Victoria, Mount, *Myanmar* 186 H5
Victoria, Mount, *P.N.G.* 213 E20
Victoria Falls, *Zambia, Zimb.* 202 F10
Victoria Falls, *Zimb.* 202 F10
Victoria Island, *N.W.T., Nunavut, Can.* 83 E13
Victoria Land, *Antarctica* 227 R14
Victoria River Downs, *N. Terr., Austral.* 211 Q7
Victoria Sports Centre, *Gibraltar, U.K.* 161 N23
Victorica, *Arg.* 132 K12
Victorica, *Arg.* 132 M9
Victorin, Mount, *St. Lucia* 121 L14
Victorville, *Calif., U.S.* 109 W9
Victory Peak see Jengish Chokusu, *China, Kyrg.* 176 E15
Vicuña, *Chile* 132 J7
Vidalia, *Ga., U.S.* 97 N7
Vidalia, *La., U.S.* 100 M9
Videle, *Rom.* 153 F15
Vidigueira, *Port.* 144 J6
Vidin, *Bulg.* 152 G12
Vidor, *Tex., U.S.* 103 Q16
Vidzy, *Belarus* 156 J4
Viedma, *Arg.* 133 Q10
Viedma, Lago, *Arg.* 133 V7
Vieille Case, *Dominica* 121 D19
Vielha, *Sp.* 145 C15
Vienna see Wien, *Aust.* 148 K12
Vienna, *Ga., U.S.* 97 N6
Vienna, *Ill., U.S.* 99 V6
Vienna, *W. Va., U.S.* 96 C8
Vienne, *Fr.* 147 U13
Vientiane see Viangchan, *Laos* 186 K10
Viento, Punta, *P.R., U.S.* 120 P5
Vieques, island, *P.R., U.S.* 120 N6
Vieques see Isabel Segunda, *P.R., U.S.* 120 N6
Vieques Sound, *P.R., U.S.* 120 N6
Vierge Point, *St. Lucia* 121 L14
Vierwaldstätter See (Lake of Lucerne), *Switz.* 150 B4
Vierzon, *Fr.* 147 S9
Vieste, *It.* 150 K13
Vietnam, *Asia* 167 X11
Viet Tri, *Vietnam* 186 H12
Vieux-Boucau, *Fr.* 147 X5
Vieux-Bourg, *Guadeloupe, Fr.* 121 E15

Vieux Fort, *St. Lucia* 121 L14
Vieux-Fort, *Guadeloupe, Fr.* 121 G14
Vieux-Fort, Pointe du, *Guadeloupe, Fr.* 121 G14
Vieux-Habitants, *Guadeloupe, Fr.* 121 F14
Vigan, *Philippines* 189 B13
Vigía Chico, *Mex.* 115 H17
Vignemale, Pic de, *Fr.* 147 Y7
Vigo, *Sp.* 144 C5
Vigo, Ría de, *Sp.* 144 C5
Vihari, *Pak.* 177 R10
Viipuri see Vyborg, *Russ.* 156 E6
Vijayawada, *India* 179 N7
Vík, *Ice.* 140 G2
Vikenara Point, *Solomon Is.* 217 M18
Vikhorevka, *Russ.* 159 K14
Vikhren, peak, *Bulg.* 153 K13
Vikna, *Nor.* 140 G11
Vila Bela da Santíssima Trindade, *Braz.* 130 H9
Vila Bittencourt, *Braz.* 130 D6
Vila da Ribeira Brava, *Cape Verde* 205 B15
Vila de Moura, *Port.* 144 K6
Vila de Sagres, *Port.* 144 L4
Vila do Bispo, *Port.* 144 L4
Vila do Conde, *Port.* 144 E5
Vilafranca del Penedès, *Sp.* 145 E17
Vila Franca do Campo, *Azores* 144 Q5
Vilagarcía de Arousa, *Sp.* 144 C5
Vila Murtinho, *Braz.* 130 G7
Vila Nova de Gaia, *Port.* 144 E5
Vila Nova de Milfontes, *Port.* 144 K5
Vilanova i la Geltrú, *Sp.* 145 E17
Vila Real, *Port.* 144 E6
Vila-real de los Infantes, *Sp.* 145 G15
Vilar Formoso, *Port.* 144 F7
Vila Velha, *Braz.* 130 B12
Vila Velha (Espírito Santo), *Braz.* 131 L16
Vila Velha de Ródão, *Port.* 144 G6
Vilhelmina, *Sw.* 141 G13
Vilhena, *Braz.* 130 H9
Viljandi, *Est.* 141 L16
Vil'kitskogo, Proliv, *Russ.* 159 D14
Villa Ahumada, *Mex.* 114 C9
Villa Alberdi, *Arg.* 132 G9
Villa Ángela, *Arg.* 132 G12
Villa Atuel, *Arg.* 132 L8
Villablino, *Sp.* 144 B8
Villa Cañás, *Arg.* 132 L11
Villacarrillo, *Sp.* 144 K11
Villacastín, *Sp.* 144 F10
Villach, *Aust.* 148 M10
Villacidro, *It.* 151 P3
Villa Dolores, *Arg.* 132 K9
Villafranca de los Barros, *Sp.* 144 J8
Villafranca di Verona, *It.* 150 E6
Village, *Fr. Polynesia, Fr.* 219 K17
Villa Grove, *Ill., U.S.* 99 R7
Villaguay, *Arg.* 132 K12
Villa Guillermina, *Arg.* 132 H12
Villahermosa, *Mex.* 115 J14
Villa Krause, *Arg.* 132 J8
Villalba, *P.R., U.S.* 120 N3
Villalba, *Sp.* 144 B6
Villalonga, *Arg.* 133 P11
Villamar, *It.* 151 P4
Villa María, *Arg.* 132 K10
Villa Martín, *Bol.* 130 L6
Villamartín, *Sp.* 144 M8
Villamontes, *Bol.* 130 L8
Villa Nueva, *Arg.* 132 K8
Villanueva, *Mex.* 114 G10
Villanueva de Córdoba, *Sp.* 144 J10
Villanueva del Fresno, *Sp.* 144 J7
Villanueva de los Infantes, *Sp.* 144 J11
Villa Ocampo, *Arg.* 132 H12
Villa Regina, *Arg.* 133 P9
Villarosa, *It.* 151 S10
Villarrica, *Chile* 133 P6
Villarrica, Lago, *Chile* 133 P6
Villarrobledo, *Sp.* 144 H12
Villasalto, *It.* 151 P4
Villasimius, *It.* 151 Q4
Villatobas, *Sp.* 144 G11
Villa Unión, *Arg.* 132 H8
Villa Unión, *Mex.* 114 G8
Villavicencio, *Col.* 128 F6
Villaviciosa, *Sp.* 144 A9
Villazón, *Bol.* 130 L7
Villedieu-les-Poêles, *Fr.* 147 P6
Villefranche, *Fr.* 147 T12

Villefranche-de-Lauragais, Fr. 147 X9
Villefranche-de-Rouergue, Fr. 147 W9
Villemaur, Fr. 147 Q11
Villena, Sp. 145 J14
Villeneuve-St. Georges, Fr. 147 P10
Villeneuve-sur-Lot, Fr. 147 W8
Ville Platte, La., U.S. 100 N8
Villers devant Orval, Belg. 160 K7
Villerupt, Fr. 147 N13
Villeurbanne, Fr. 147 U13
Villingen-Schwenningen, Ger. 148 K6
Villisca, Iowa, U.S. 105 Q10
Villupuram, India 179 Q7
Vilnius, Lith. 141 N17
Vilyuy, river, Russ. 166 D10
Vilyuysk, Russ. 159 H17
Vilyuyskoye Vodokhranilishche, Russ. 159 H16
Vimoutiers, Fr. 147 P7
Vina, Calif., U.S. 109 P4
Viña del Mar, Chile 132 K6
Vinalhaven, Me., U.S. 95 G17
Vinarós, Sp. 145 F15
Vincennes, Ind., U.S. 99 T7
Vincennes Bay, Antarctica 227 M21
Vincent, Point, Norfolk I., Austral. 217 F20
Vindelälven, river, Sw. 141 G13
Vindeln, Sw. 141 G14
Vindhya Range, India 178 J4
Vindrey, Russ. 156 K12
Vineland, N.J., U.S. 94 Q10
Vinh, Vietnam 186 J12
Vinhais, Port. 144 D7
Vinh Chau, Vietnam 187 Q12
Vinh Long, Vietnam 187 P12
Vinita, Okla., U.S. 102 E13
Vinkovci, Croatia 152 E8
Vinnytsya, Ukr. 157 P5
Vinson Massif, Antarctica 226 H8
Vinton, Iowa, U.S. 105 N13
Vinton, La., U.S. 100 P6
Vinukonda, India 179 N7
Vipiteno, It. 150 B7
Viqueque, Timor-Leste 189 M15
Vir, island, Croatia 152 F5
Vir, Taj. 176 J10
Virac, Philippines 189 C15
Virachei, Cambodia 186 M13
Viranşehir, Turk. 169 H14
Virawah, Pak. 177 W9
Virden, Ill., U.S. 99 S5
Virden, Man., Can. 83 N13
Vire, Fr. 147 P6
Vîrfurile, Rom. 152 D12
Vírgenes, Cape, S. Amer. 126 R5
Virgin, river, Ariz., Nev., U.S. 109 T13
Virgin Gorda, island, Virgin Islands, U.K. 119 F14
Virgin Gorda Peak, Virgin Islands, U.K. 120 Q9
Virgin Islands, U.S., Lesser Antilles 119 E13
Virginia, Ill., U.S. 99 R4
Virginia, Minn., U.S. 104 F12
Virginia, U.S. 96 F10
Virginia Beach, Va., U.S. 96 F14
Virginia City, Mont., U.S. 106 E7
Virginia City, Nev., U.S. 109 Q6
Virginia Falls, N.W.T., Can. 82 H9
Virgin Islands, Lesser Antilles 119 F14
Virgin Islands National Park, Virgin Islands, U.S. 120 N11
Viroqua, Wis., U.S. 98 K3
Virovitica, Croatia 152 D7
Virrat, Fin. 141 H15
Virton, Belg. 160 K8
Virtsu, Est. 141 L16
Virú, Peru 130 G2
Virudunagar, India 179 R6
Vis (Lissa), island, Croatia 152 H6
Visalia, Calif., U.S. 109 U7
Visayan Sea, Philippines 189 D14
Visby, Sw. 141 M14
Viscount Melville Sound, Nunavut, Can. 83 D13
Višegrad, Bosn. & Herzg. 152 G9
Viseu, Port. 144 F6
Vişeu de Sus, Rom. 153 B14
Vishakhapatnam, India 178 M9
Viški Kanal, Croatia 152 H6
Viso, Monte, It. 150 F2

Viso del Marqués, Sp. 144 J11
Visp, Switz. 150 C3
Vista, Calif., U.S. 109 Y9
Vista Alegre, Braz. 130 E6
Vistula see Wisła, river, Pol. 138 F8
Vit, river, Bulg. 153 G14
Viterbo, It. 150 J8
Vitichi, Bol. 130 L7
Vitigudino, Sp. 144 E8
Viti Levu, island, Fiji Is. 218 J6
Viti Levu Bay, Fiji Is. 218 H6
Vitim, river, Russ. 166 E10
Vitim, Russ. 159 J16
Vítor, Peru 130 J5
Vitória, Braz. 130 D12
Vitória, Braz. 131 L16
Vitória da Conquista, Braz. 131 J16
Vitoria-Gasteiz, Sp. 144 C12
Vitória Seamount, Atl. Oc. 237 R8
Vitré, Fr. 147 Q6
Vitry-le-François, Fr. 147 P12
Vitsyebsk, Belarus 156 J6
Vittangi, Sw. 141 E14
Vittorio Veneto, It. 150 D8
Vivario, Fr. 150 K4
Viveiro, Sp. 144 A7
Vivi, river, Russ. 159 H14
Vivi, Russ. 159 H14
Vivian, La., U.S. 100 K6
Viwa, island, Fiji Is. 218 H5
Vizcaíno, Desierto de, Mex. 114 D6
Vize, Turk. 168 C4
Vize, Ostrov, Russ. 159 D13
Vizianagaram, India 178 M9
Vizzini, It. 151 T11
Vjosë, river, Albania 152 M9
Vlădeasa, peak, Rom. 152 C12
Vladikavkaz, Russ. 157 U14
Vladimir, Russ. 156 J10
Vladīmīrovka, Kaz. 174 B11
Vladivostok, Russ. 159 M21
Vlasenica, Bosn. & Herzg. 152 G8
Vlasinje, Bosn. & Herzg. 152 F7
Vlieland, island, Neth. 146 G12
Vlorë (Valona), Albania 152 M9
Vlorës, Gjiri i, Albania 152 M9
Vltava, river, Czech Rep. 148 J11
Vöcklabruck, Aust. 148 K10
Vod Ab, Afghan. 176 J9
Voe, Scot., U.K. 142 D12
Vogelsberg, range, Ger. 148 G7
Voghera, It. 150 E4
Voh, New Caledonia, Fr. 218 C7
Vohemar see Iharaña, Madagascar 203 D18
Voiron, Fr. 147 U13
Voitsberg, Aust. 148 M11
Vojvodina, region, Serb. 152 E9
Volborg, Mont., U.S. 106 E12
Volcano, Hawai'i, U.S. 113 N21
Volcano Islands (Kazan Rettō), Japan 184 L5
Volda, Nor. 140 J10
Volga, river, Russ. 157 R15
Volga, S. Dak., U.S. 104 K8
Volga, Source of the, Russ. 138 D10
Volga-Baltic Waterway, Russ. 156 F9
Volga-Don Canal, Russ. 157 P13
Volga River Delta, Russ. 138 G14
Volga Upland, Russ. 138 E12
Volgodonsk, Russ. 157 Q12
Volgograd (Stalingrad), Russ. 157 P13
Volgograd Reservoir see Volgogradskoye Vodokhranilishche, Russ. 138 F13
Volgogradskoye Vodokhranilishche, Russ. 157 N14
Volímes, Gr. 154 J7
Volissós, Gr. 155 H16
Volkhov, river, Russ. 138 D10
Volkhov, Russ. 156 F7
Völklingen, Ger. 148 H5
Volksrust, S. Af. 202 K11
Volna, Gora, Russ. 159 E20
Volnorez, Gora, Russ. 159 E13
Volnovakha, Ukr. 157 Q9
Volodarsk, Russ. 156 J12
Vologda, Russ. 156 F10
Vólos, Gr. 154 F11
Vol'sk, Russ. 156 M14
Volta, Lake, Ghana 200 G11
Volta, Pointe de, Wallis & Futuna, Fr. 218 F12
Voltaire, Cape, Austral. 210 B5
Volturno, river, It. 150 L10
Vólvi, Límni, Gr. 154 C12

Volx, Fr. 147 X14
Volyn-Podolian Upland, Ukr. 138 G9
Volzhsk, Russ. 156 J14
Volzhskiy, Russ. 157 P13
Vonavona, island, Solomon Is. 217 M16
Vónitsa, Gr. 154 G7
Vopnafjördur, Ice. 140 F4
Vóras, Óros, Gr. 154 C9
Vóries Sporádes (Northern Sporades), islands, Gr. 155 F13
Vórios Evvoïkós Kólpos, Gr. 154 H11
Vorkuta, Russ. 158 F11
Vormsi, island, Est. 141 K16
Voronezh, Russ. 156 M10
Voronin Trough, Arctic Oc. 242 D11
Vorontsovka, Russ. 159 J16
Vorukh, Taj. 176 G9
Võru, Est. 141 L17
Vostochnaya, Russ. 159 E13
Vostochnyy (Vrangel'), Russ. 159 M21
Vostochnyy Sayan, Russ. 159 L14
Vostok, station, Antarctica 227 K16
Vostok Island, Kiribati 215 H13
Votice, Czech Rep. 148 J11
Votkinsk, Russ. 156 G16
Votkinsk, Russ. 158 H8
Votlo, Vanuatu 218 E3
Voulx, Fr. 147 Q10
Voúrnios, Óros, Gr. 154 D9
Voúxa, Akrotírio, Gr. 154 P12
Vouziers, Fr. 147 N12
Vovchans'k, Ukr. 157 N9
Voyageurs National Park, Minn., U.S. 104 E11
Voyampolka, Russ. 159 E21
Voyvozh, Russ. 158 F9
Voza, Solomon Is. 217 K15
Vozhe, Ozero, Russ. 156 E10
Vozhega, Russ. 156 E10
Vozhgora, Russ. 158 F9
Voznesens'k, Ukr. 157 Q6
Vozvyshennost' Lavruska, Russ. 159 H15
Vrachíonas, peak, Gr. 154 J7
Vrahnéika, Gr. 154 J9
Vrang, Taj. 176 K10
Vrangel' see Vostochnyy, Russ. 159 M21
Vrangelya, Ostrov (Wrangel Island), Russ. 159 B19
Vranica, peak, Bosn. & Herzg. 152 G7
Vranje, Serb. 152 J11
Vranov, Slovakia 149 J17
Vransko Jezero, Croatia 152 G5
Vratsa, Bulg. 153 H13
Vrbas, river, Bosn. & Herzg. 152 F7
Vršac, Serb. 152 E11
Vryburg, S. Af. 202 K9
Vryheid, S. Af. 202 K11
Vuagava, island, Fiji Is. 218 K9
Vučitrn see Vushtrria, Kos. 152 J10
Vulcano, Isola, It. 151 R11
Vulci, ruin, It. 150 K7
Vunaniu Bay, Fiji Is. 218 J6
Vung Tau, Vietnam 187 P13
Vunindawa, Fiji Is. 218 J6
Vunisea, Fiji Is. 218 K6
Vunivutu Bay, Fiji Is. 218 G7
Vushtrria (Vučitrn), Kos. 152 J10
Vyatka, river, Russ. 138 D12
Vyatskiye Polyany, Russ. 156 H15
Vyazemskiy, Russ. 159 K21
Vyaz'ma, Russ. 156 K8
Vyazniki, Russ. 156 J11
Vyborg (Viipuri), Russ. 156 E6
Vychegda, river, Russ. 138 B12
Vychegda Lowland, Russ. 138 B12
Vyerkhnyadzvinsk, Belarus 156 J5
Vyg, Lake, Russ. 138 C10
Vyksa, Russ. 156 J11
Vylkove, Ukr. 157 S5
Vym', river, Russ. 138 B12
Vyritsa, Russ. 156 F6
Vyshniy Volochek, Russ. 156 H8
Vyškov, Czech Rep. 149 J13
Vysokaye, Belarus 156 L2
Vysokovsk, Russ. 156 J9
Vytegra, Russ. 158 E7

W

Wa, Ghana 200 F10
Waar, island, Indonesia 189 K19
Wabao, Cape, New Caledonia, Fr. 218 D10
Wabasca, river, Alta., Can. 82 K11
Wabash, river, Ill., Ind., U.S. 99 T7
Wabash, Ind., U.S. 99 Q9
Wabasha, Minn., U.S. 104 K13
Wabasso, Fla., U.S. 97 U10
Wabeno, Wis., U.S. 98 H6
Wabowden, Man., Can. 83 L14
Wabuk Point, Ont., Can. 83 L16
Waco, Tex., U.S. 103 N11
Waco Lake, Tex., U.S. 103 N11
Wad, Pak. 177 U5
Waddenzee, bay, Neth. 146 G13
Waddington, Mount, B.C., Can. 82 L8
Wadena, Minn., U.S. 104 H10
Wadena, Sask., Can. 82 M12
Wädenswil, Switz. 150 B4
Wadesboro, N.C., U.S. 96 J10
Wadeye, N. Terr., Austral. 211 P7
Wadi Halfa, Sudan 198 B12
Wadley, Ga., U.S. 96 M7
Wad Medani, Sudan 199 E13
Wadomari, Japan 185 X2
Wadsworth, Nev., U.S. 109 P7
Wadsworth, Ohio, U.S. 99 P14
Wadu, island, Maldives 179 T3
Waelder, Tex., U.S. 103 R11
Waeshe, Mount, Antarctica 226 M8
Wafangdian, China 182 D10
Wager Bay, Nunavut, Can. 83 G15
Wagga Wagga, N.S.W., Austral. 211 Y13
Wagin, W. Aust., Austral. 211 X3
Wagner, S. Dak., U.S. 104 M7
Wagoner, Okla., U.S. 102 F13
Wagontire Mountain, Oreg., U.S. 108 J6
Wągrowiec, Pol. 149 D13
Wahai, Indonesia 189 K17
Waha'ula Heiau, Hawai'i, U.S. 113 N22
Wah Cantonment, Pak. 177 N10
Wahiawā, Hawai'i, U.S. 112 D11
Wahoo, Nebr., U.S. 105 P8
Wahpeton, N. Dak., U.S. 104 H8
Waħx, Ras il, Malta 161 J21
Wai, India 178 M4
Wai, Indonesia 189 K16
Wai, Koh, Cambodia 187 Q10
Waiakoa, Hawai'i, U.S. 113 G17
Wai'ale'ale, peak, Hawai'i, U.S. 112 B5
Waialua, Hawai'i, U.S. 113 G16
Waialua Bay, Hawai'i, U.S. 112 D10
Wai'anae Range, Hawai'i, U.S. 112 E10
Waiau, river, N.Z. 213 R15
Waibeem, Indonesia 189 J18
Waigama, Indonesia 189 K17
Waigeo, island, Indonesia 189 J17
Waihe'e, Hawai'i, U.S. 113 G16
Waiheke Island, N.Z. 213 J19
Waikabubak, Indonesia 189 N13
Waikahalulu Bay, Hawai'i, U.S. 113 H16
Waikapū, Hawai'i, U.S. 113 G16
Waikapuna Bay, Hawai'i, U.S. 113 P20
Waikato, river, N.Z. 213 K19
Waikawa, N.Z. 213 R16
Waikīkī Beach, Hawai'i, U.S. 112 E11
Waikoloa, Hawai'i, U.S. 113 L19
Waikouaiti, N.Z. 213 Q16
Wailagi Lala, island, Fiji Is. 218 G9
Wailea, Hawai'i, U.S. 113 H16
Wailua, Hawai'i, U.S. 112 B6
Wailua, Hawai'i, U.S. 113 G17
Wailuku, Hawai'i, U.S. 113 M21
Wailuku, Hawai'i, U.S. 113 G16
Waimānalo Beach, Hawai'i, U.S. 112 E12
Waimarama, N.Z. 213 L20
Waimate, N.Z. 213 Q17
Waimea, Hawai'i, U.S. 112 C5
Waimea, Hawai'i, U.S. 112 D10
Waimea (Kamuela), Hawai'i, U.S. 113 K19
Waimea Canyon, Hawai'i, U.S. 112 B5
Wainaworasi, Solomon Is. 217 Q20
Waingapu, Indonesia 189 N13
Wainunu Bay, Fiji Is. 218 H7
Wainwright, Alas., U.S. 111 B14
Wai'ōhinu, Hawai'i, U.S. 113 P19
Waiohonu Petroglyphs, Hawai'i, U.S. 113 H18

Wai'oli Mission, Hawai'i, U.S. 112 B5
Waipa, river, N.Z. 213 K19
Waipahi, N.Z. 213 R16
Waipahu, Hawai'i, U.S. 112 E11
Waipi'o Bay, Hawai'i, U.S. 113 K20
Waipi'o Valley, Hawai'i, U.S. 113 K19
Waipu, N.Z. 213 H18
Waipukurau, N.Z. 213 L19
Wairokai Harbor, Solomon Is. 217 N20
Waïsisi, Vanuatu 218 H4
Waïsisi Bay, Vanuatu 218 H4
Waitsburg, Wash., U.S. 108 E8
Wajima, Japan 184 M10
Wajir, Kenya 199 J15
Wakasa Wan, Japan 185 P9
Wakatipu, Lake, N.Z. 213 Q15
Wakaya, island, Fiji Is. 218 H7
Wakayama, Japan 185 Q8
WaKeeney, Kans., U.S. 105 S5
Wakefield, Eng., U.K. 143 R12
Wakefield, Jam. 120 H7
Wakefield, Kans., U.S. 105 S8
Wakefield, Mich., U.S. 98 F5
Wakefield, Nebr., U.S. 105 N8
Wake Forest, N.C., U.S. 96 H12
Wake Island, Wake I., U.S. 216 F8
Wakema, Myanmar 186 L5
Wakhan Mountains, Afghan. 176 K10
Wakhjir Pass, Afghan., China 176 K12
Wakkanai, Japan 184 D13
Wakuach, Lac, Que., Can. 83 K20
Wakunai, P.N.G. 217 J14
Wakuya, Japan 184 L13
Wala, New Caledonia, Fr. 218 B6
Walachia, region, Rom. 153 F14
Wałbrzych, Pol. 148 G12
Walcott, Lake, Idaho, U.S. 106 H6
Walden, Colo., U.S. 106 L12
Waldkraiburg, Ger. 148 K9
Waldo, Ark., U.S. 100 J7
Waldo Lake, Oreg., U.S. 108 H4
Waldorf, Md., U.S. 96 D13
Waldport, Oreg., U.S. 108 G2
Waldron, Ark., U.S. 100 G6
Walea, Selat, Indonesia 189 J14
Wales, Alas., U.S. 110 E11
Wales, U.K. 143 U10
Wales Island, Nunavut, Can. 83 G16
Walferdange, Lux. 160 J10
Walgreen Coast, Antarctica 226 K6
Walhalla, N. Dak., U.S. 104 D7
Walhalla, S.C., U.S. 96 J6
Walikale, Dem. Rep. of the Congo 198 K11
Walkaway, W. Aust., Austral. 211 W2
Walker, Minn., U.S. 104 G10
Walker Lake, Nev., U.S. 109 Q8
Wall, S. Dak., U.S. 104 L3
Wallabadah, Qnsld., Austral. 211 R12
Wallaby Island, Austral. 210 C11
Wallaby Plateau, Ind. Oc. 241 K14
Wallace, Idaho, U.S. 106 C4
Wallace, N.C., U.S. 96 J12
Wallace, Nebr., U.S. 105 Q4
Wallal Downs, W. Aust., Austral. 211 S3
Wallam Creek, Austral. 210 H13
Wallara, N. Terr., Austral. 211 U8
Wallaroo, S. Aust., Austral. 211 X10
Walla Walla, Wash., U.S. 108 E8
Wallibou, St. Vincent & the Grenadines 121 K16
Wallilabou, St. Vincent & the Grenadines 121 K16
Wallis, Îles, Pac. Oc. 214 J9
Wallis and Futuna, Fr., Pac. Oc. 214 J9
Wallops Island, Va., U.S. 96 E15
Wallowa, Oreg., U.S. 108 F9
Wallowa Mountains, Oreg., U.S. 108 F9
Walls, Scot., U.K. 142 D11
Wallsend, Eng., U.K. 143 P12
Walney, Isle of, Eng., U.K. 143 R10
Walnut Canyon National Monument, Ariz., U.S. 107 S7
Walnut Cove, N.C., U.S. 96 G10
Walnut Ridge, Ark., U.S. 100 E10
Walong, India 178 F16
Walsall, Eng., U.K. 143 T12
Walsenburg, Colo., U.S. 107 P13

Walsh, Colo., U.S. 107 P16
Walsrode, Ger. 148 D7
Walterboro, S.C., U.S. 96 M9
Walter F. George Reservoir, Ala., Ga., U.S. 101 M17
Walters, Okla., U.S. 102 J9
Walters Shoal, Ind. Oc. 240 M4
Walton, N.Y., U.S. 94 K9
Walvis Bay, Namibia 202 H6
Walvis Ridge, Atl. Oc. 237 S13
Walyahmoning Rock, Austral. 210 J3
Wama, Afghan. 176 M9
Wamba, river, Dem. Rep. of the Congo 198 M8
Wamba, Dem. Rep. of the Congo 198 J11
Wamego, Kans., U.S. 105 S9
Wamena, Indonesia 189 L20
Wami, river, Tanzania 199 M15
Wamsasi, Indonesia 189 K15
Wamsisi, Indonesia 189 K16
Wamsutter, Wyo., U.S. 106 K10
Wana, Pak. 177 P8
Wanaaring, N.S.W., Austral. 211 W12
Wanaka, N.Z. 213 Q16
Wanaka, Lake, N.Z. 213 Q16
Wan'an, China 183 P5
Wanapa, Neth. Antilles, Neth. 121 R19
Wanchese, N.C., U.S. 96 G15
Wanderer Bay, Solomon Is. 217 N18
Wanding, China 180 P9
Wando, S. Korea 182 H13
Wandoan, Qnsld., Austral. 211 V14
Wangal, Indonesia 213 D15
Wanganui, river, N.Z. 213 L19
Wanganui, N.Z. 213 L19
Wangaratta, Vic., Austral. 211 Y13
Wangary, S. Aust., Austral. 211 Y9
Wangdu, China 182 E6
Wangerberg, Liech. 160 Q2
Wangiwangi, island, Indonesia 189 L14
Wang Kai, Sudan 198 G12
Wangpan Yang, China 182 L10
Wangqing, China 182 A14
Wanigela, P.N.G. 213 E20
Wanione, Solomon Is. 217 P21
Wankaner, India 178 J2
Wanlaweyn, Somalia 199 J17
Wanlockhead, Scot., U.K. 143 N9
Wanning, China 183 U2
Wanow, Afghan. 177 P5
Wanxian, China 182 K1
Wanyuan, China 182 J1
Wanzai, China 183 N5
Wapakoneta, Ohio, U.S. 99 Q11
Wapato, Wash., U.S. 108 D6
Wapello, Iowa, U.S. 105 P14
Wappapello, Lake, Mo., U.S. 105 V15
Wapsipinicon, river, Iowa, U.S. 105 N13
War, W. Va., U.S. 96 F8
Waranga Basin, Austral. 210 L12
Warangal, India 178 M7
Waraseoni, India 178 K7
Waratah, Tas., Austral. 211 Z15
Warbreccan, Qnsld., Austral. 211 U12
Warburg, Ger. 148 F7
Warburton, W. Aust., Austral. 211 U6
Warden, Wash., U.S. 108 D7
Ward Hunt Island, Nunavut, Can. 83 A16
Wardija Point, Malta 161 H19
Waren, Ger. 148 C10
Waren, Indonesia 189 K19
Ware Shoals, S.C., U.S. 96 K7
Warialda, N.S.W., Austral. 211 W14
Warlubie, Pol. 149 C14
Warmbad, Namibia 202 K7
Warminster, Eng., U.K. 143 W11
Warm Springs, Ga., U.S. 96 M4
Warm Springs, Nev., U.S. 109 R10
Warm Springs, Va., U.S. 96 E10
Warm Springs Reservoir, Oreg., U.S. 108 H8
Warner Mountains, Calif., Oreg., U.S. 108 L6
Warner Robins, Ga., U.S. 96 M6
Warner Valley, Oreg., U.S. 108 K6
Waroona, W. Aust., Austral. 211 X2
Warora, India 178 K6
Warrabri, N. Terr., Austral. 211 S9
Warrawagine, W. Aust., Austral. 211 S4
Warrego, river, Austral. 210 H13

Warren, Ark., U.S. 100 J8
Warren, Mich., U.S. 98 M13
Warren, Minn., U.S. 104 E8
Warren, Ohio, U.S. 99 P15
Warren, Pa., U.S. 94 L4
Warrender, Cape, Nunavut, Can. 83 D16
Warrenpoint, N. Ire., U.K. 143 Q7
Warrensburg, Mo., U.S. 105 T11
Warrenton, Ga., U.S. 96 L7
Warrenton, Oreg., U.S. 108 E2
Warrenton, S. Af. 202 K9
Warrenton, Va., U.S. 96 D12
Warri, Nigeria 201 H13
Warrina, S. Aust., Austral. 211 V9
Warrington, Eng., U.K. 143 S11
Warrington, Fla., U.S. 97 Q1
Warrnambool, Vic., Austral. 211 Z11
Warroad, Minn., U.S. 104 D9
Warsa, Indonesia 189 J19
Warsaw, Ind., U.S. 99 P9
Warsaw, N.C., U.S. 96 J12
Warsaw see Warszawa, Pol. 149 E16
Warsaw, Va., U.S. 96 E13
Warszawa (Warsaw), Pol. 149 E16
Warta, river, Pol. 148 D12
Waru, Indonesia 189 K17
Warwick, Eng., U.K. 143 U12
Warwick, Qnsld., Austral. 211 V15
Warwick, R.I., U.S. 95 L14
Wasado, peak, Indonesia 213 C15
Wasaka, Vanuatu 218 B2
Wasam, Pak. 176 K10
Wasatch Range, Utah, U.S. 106 K7
Wasco, Calif., U.S. 109 V7
Wasco, Oreg., U.S. 108 F5
Waseca, Minn., U.S. 104 L11
Washap, Pak. 177 U3
Washburn, Me., U.S. 95 B18
Washburn, N. Dak., U.S. 104 F4
Washburn, Wis., U.S. 98 F4
Washburn, Mount, Wyo., U.S. 106 F8
Washington, Neth. Antilles, Neth. 121 Q18
Washington, D.C., U.S. 96 C13
Washington, Ga., U.S. 96 L7
Washington, Ill., U.S. 99 Q5
Washington, Ind., U.S. 99 T8
Washington, Iowa, U.S. 105 P13
Washington, Kans., U.S. 105 R8
Washington, Mo., U.S. 105 T14
Washington, N.C., U.S. 96 H13
Washington, Pa., U.S. 94 P3
Washington, U.S. 108 C3
Washington, Utah, U.S. 107 Q5
Washington, Wis., U.S. 98 H8
Washington, Cape, Antarctica 227 P13
Washington, Cape, Fiji Is. 218 K6
Washington, Mount, N.H., U.S. 95 G14
Washington Court House, Ohio, U.S. 99 R12
Washington Island see Teraina, Kiribati 214 F12
Washington Island, Wis., U.S. 98 H8
Washita, river, Okla., Tex., U.S. 102 H11
Washougal, Wash., U.S. 108 F4
Washtucna, Wash., U.S. 108 D8
Washuk, Pak. 177 T4
Wasilla, Alas., U.S. 111 J16
Wasior, Indonesia 189 K19
Waskaganish, Que., Can. 83 M18
Wasserbillig, Lux. 160 J11
Waswanipi, Lac, Que., Can. 83 N18
Watampone, Indonesia 189 L13
Waterbury, Conn., U.S. 94 L12
Water Cay, Bahamas 120 E2
Water Cays, Bahamas 116 F11
Wateree Lake, S.C., U.S. 96 K9
Waterford (Port Láirge), Ire. 143 U6
Waterford Harbour, Ire. 143 U6
Water Ground, Cayman Is., U.K. 120 H1
Water Island, Virgin Islands, U.S. 120 N9
Waterloo, Ill., U.S. 99 T4
Waterloo, Iowa, U.S. 105 N12
Waterloo, N. Terr., Austral. 211 Q7
Waterloo, Trinidad & Tobago 121 P22
Waterman, Isla, Chile 133 Y8
Watersmeet, Mich., U.S. 98 F6
Waterton-Glacier International Peace Park, Mont., U.S. 106 A6

Waterton Lakes National Park, Alta., Can. 106 A6
Watertown, N.Y., U.S. 94 G9
Watertown, S. Dak., U.S. 104 K8
Watertown, Wis., U.S. 98 L6
Water Valley, Miss., U.S. 100 H12
Waterville, Kans., U.S. 105 R8
Waterville, Me., U.S. 95 F16
Waterville, Minn., U.S. 104 K11
Waterville, Wash., U.S. 108 C6
Watford, Eng., U.K. 143 V13
Watford City, N. Dak., U.S. 104 F2
Watkins Glen, N.Y., U.S. 94 K7
Watling see San Salvador, island, Bahamas 117 F14
Watling's Castle, Bahamas 120 F11
Watonga, Okla., U.S. 102 F9
Watrous, N. Mex., U.S. 107 R13
Watsa, Dem. Rep. of the Congo 198 J12
Watseka, Ill., U.S. 99 Q7
Watson, S. Aust., Austral. 211 W8
Watson Lake, Yukon, Can. 82 H9
Watsonville, Calif., U.S. 109 T4
Watt Mountain, Dominica 121 G19
Watts Bar Lake, Tenn., U.S. 101 F17
Wattwil, Switz. 150 A4
Watubela, Kepulauan, Indonesia 189 L18
Wau, P.N.G. 213 D19
Wau, Sudan 198 G11
Waubay, S. Dak., U.S. 104 J7
Wauchope, N. Terr., Austral. 211 S9
Wauchula, Fla., U.S. 97 U8
Waukarlycarly, Lake, Austral. 210 E4
Waukegan, Ill., U.S. 98 M7
Waukesha, Wis., U.S. 98 L6
Waukon, Iowa, U.S. 104 M13
Wauneta, Nebr., U.S. 105 Q3
Waupaca, Wis., U.S. 98 J6
Waupun, Wis., U.S. 98 K6
Waurika, Okla., U.S. 102 J10
Wausa, Nebr., U.S. 105 N7
Wausau, Wis., U.S. 98 H5
Wauseon, Ohio, U.S. 99 N11
Wautoma, Wis., U.S. 98 K5
Wauwatosa, Wis., U.S. 98 L7
Wave Hill, N. Terr., Austral. 211 R7
Waverly, Iowa, U.S. 104 M12
Waverly, N.Y., U.S. 94 L8
Waverly, Nebr., U.S. 105 Q8
Waverly, Ohio, U.S. 99 S13
Waverly, Tenn., U.S. 101 E14
Waverly, Va., U.S. 96 F13
Wawa, Ont., Can. 83 P17
Wāw al Kabīr, Lib. 197 E14
Waxahachie, Tex., U.S. 102 L12
Waxweiler, Ger. 160 G11
Waya, island, Fiji Is. 218 H5
Wayamli, Indonesia 189 H16
Waycross, Ga., U.S. 97 P7
Wayne, Nebr., U.S. 105 N8
Waynesboro, Ga., U.S. 96 M8
Waynesboro, Miss., U.S. 101 M13
Waynesboro, Pa., U.S. 94 Q6
Waynesboro, Tenn., U.S. 101 F14
Waynesboro, Va., U.S. 96 E11
Waynesburg, Pa., U.S. 94 P3
Waynesville, Mo., U.S. 105 U13
Waynesville, N.C., U.S. 96 H6
Waynoka, Okla., U.S. 102 E9
Wazah, Afghan. 177 N8
Wazah Khwah (Mushuray), Afghan. 177 P7
Wazirabad, Pak. 177 P12
Wé, New Caledonia, Fr. 218 C9
We, island, Indonesia 188 F3
Weatherford, Okla., U.S. 102 G9
Weatherford, Tex., U.S. 102 L10
Weaverville, Calif., U.S. 108 M3
Webb City, Mo., U.S. 105 V11
Weber Basin, Ind. Oc. 241 H18
Webster, Mass., U.S. 95 L14
Webster, S. Dak., U.S. 104 J7
Webster City, Iowa, U.S. 105 N11
Webster Groves, Mo., U.S. 105 T15
Webster Springs, W. Va., U.S. 96 D9
Weda, Indonesia 189 J16
Weda, Teluk, Indonesia 189 J16
Weddell Island, Falkland Is., U.K. 133 W11
Weddell Plain, Antarctic Oc. 244 E10
Weddell Sea, Antarctica 226 D7
Wedemark, Ger. 148 D7
Weed, Calif., U.S. 108 M3

Weeki Wachee, Fla., U.S. 97 T7
Weeping Water, Nebr., U.S. 105 Q9
Weert, Neth. 146 K13
Węgorzewo, Pol. 149 B16
Wei, river, China 182 H2
Wei, river, China 181 H15
Wei, river, China 180 J12
Weichang, China 182 B7
Weiden, Ger. 148 H9
Weifang, China 182 F8
Weihai, China 182 F10
Weilheim, Ger. 148 L8
Weimar, Ger. 148 F8
Weimar, Tex., U.S. 103 R12
Weinan, China 182 H2
Weinsberger Wald, Aust. 148 K11
Weipa, Qnsld., Austral. 211 P12
Weir, river, Austral. 210 H14
Weirton, W. Va., U.S. 96 B9
Weiser, river, Idaho, U.S. 106 F3
Weiser, Idaho, U.S. 106 F3
Weishan, China 182 H7
Weishan Hu, China 182 H7
Weissenburg, Ger. 148 J8
Weissenfels, Ger. 148 F9
Weiss Lake, Ala., Ga., U.S. 101 H17
Weiswampach, Lux. 160 G10
Weite, Switz. 160 Q2
Weixi, China 180 M10
Wejherowo, Pol. 149 A14
Welbourn Hill, S. Aust., Austral. 211 V9
Welch, W. Va., U.S. 96 F8
Welch Point, Cayman Is., U.K. 120 J2
Weldiya, Eth. 199 F15
Weldon, N.C., U.S. 96 G13
Welford, Qnsld., Austral. 211 U12
Weligama, Sri Lanka 179 T7
Welker Seamount, Pac. Oc. 239 C14
Welkom, S. Af. 202 K10
Wellesley Islands, Austral. 210 C11
Wellin, Belg. 146 M13
Wellington, Colo., U.S. 106 L13
Wellington, Kans., U.S. 105 V7
Wellington, N.Z. 213 M18
Wellington, Nev., U.S. 109 Q7
Wellington, Tex., U.S. 102 H7
Wellington, Isla, Chile 133 V6
Wellington, Lake, Austral. 210 M13
Wellington Bay, Nunavut, Can. 83 F13
Wells, Me., U.S. 95 H15
Wells, Minn., U.S. 104 L11
Wells, Nev., U.S. 108 M12
Wells, Tex., U.S. 103 N14
Wells, Lake, Austral. 210 G5
Wellsboro, Pa., U.S. 94 L7
Wellston, Ohio, U.S. 99 S13
Wellsville, N.Y., U.S. 94 K6
Wellsville, Ohio, U.S. 99 Q16
Wellton, Ariz., U.S. 107 U5
Wels, Aust. 148 K10
Welsh, La., U.S. 100 P7
Welshpool, Vic., Austral. 211 Z12
Welshpool, Wales, U.K. 143 T10
Wemyss Bight, Bahamas 120 F6
Wenatchee, Wash., U.S. 108 C6
Wenchang, China 183 U2
Wencheng, China 183 N9
Wenchi, Ghana 200 G10
Wendeng, China 182 F10
Wendesi, Indonesia 189 K19
Wendover, Nev., U.S. 108 M13
Wendover, Utah, U.S. 106 K5
Wengyuan, China 183 R5
Wenling, China 183 N10
Wenman see Wolf, Isla, island, Ecua. 128 N7
Weno, F.S.M. 217 B15
Weno (Moen), island, F.S.M. 217 B15
Wenshan, China 180 P11
Wensu, China 180 F5
Wentworth, N.S.W., Austral. 211 X11
Wenzhou, China 183 N9
Werdau, Ger. 148 G9
Werder, Ger. 148 E10
Werdēr, Eth. 199 G17
Weri, Indonesia 213 C14
Werris Creek, N.S.W., Austral. 211 X14
Weser, river, Ger. 148 C7
Weskan, Kans., U.S. 105 S3
Weslaco, Tex., U.S. 103 W10

Wesley, Dominica 121 E19
Wesleyville, Pa., U.S. 94 K3
Wessel Islands, Austral. 210 A9
Wessex, region, Eng., U.K. 143 W11
Wessington, S. Dak., U.S. 104 K6
Wessington Springs, S. Dak., U.S. 104 L6
Wesson, Miss., U.S. 100 M11
West, Tex., U.S. 102 M11
West Allis, Wis., U.S. 98 L7
West Antarctica, region, Antarctica 226 K9
West Bank, occupied territory, Asia 170 M6
West Bay, Cayman Is., U.K. 120 J1
West Bay, Cayman Is., U.K. 120 H1
West Bay, Fla., U.S. 97 R3
West Bay, La., U.S. 100 R12
West Bend, Wis., U.S. 98 L7
West Branch, Iowa, U.S. 105 P13
West Branch, Mich., U.S. 98 J11
Westbrook, Me., U.S. 95 H15
Westbrook, Tex., U.S. 102 M6
West Burra, island, Scot., U.K. 142 E12
Westby, Wis., U.S. 98 K4
West Caicos, island, Turks & Caicos Is., U.K. 117 J16
West Cape Howe, Austral. 210 L3
West Caroline Basin, Pac. Oc. 238 J5
West Cay, Virgin Islands, U.S. 120 M8
West Chester, Pa., U.S. 94 P9
Westcliffe, Colo., U.S. 107 N13
West Columbia, Tex., U.S. 103 R13
West Des Moines, Iowa, U.S. 105 P11
West End, Virgin Islands, U.K. 120 R5
West End, Bahamas 120 E1
West End Point, Virgin Islands, U.K. 120 L10
West End Point, Cayman Is., U.K. 116 L8
West End Village, Anguilla, U.K. 120 R11
Westerhall Bay, Grenada 121 L22
Westerhall Point, Grenada 121 L22
Westerland, Ger. 148 A7
Westerly, R.I., U.S. 95 M14
Western, river, Nunavut, Can. 83 G13
Western Australia, Austral. 211 T3
Western Beach, Gibraltar, U.K. 161 N22
Western Desert, Egypt 197 D17
Western Dvina, river, Eur. 138 E9
Western Ghats, range, India 178 L3
Western Plateau, Austral. 210 F4
Western Sahara, Af. 195 E14
Western Sayan Mountains, Russ. 166 E9
Western Soverign Base Area see Akrotiri Sovereign Base Area, Cyprus 160 Q7
Westerschelde, Neth. 146 K11
Westerville, Ohio, U.S. 99 R13
West Falkland, island, Falkland Is., U.K. 133 W11
Westfall, Oreg., U.S. 108 H8
West Fayu Atoll see Pigailoe, F.S.M. 216 Q5
Westfield, Mass., U.S. 94 L12
Westfield, N.Y., U.S. 94 K4
West Fork Poplar, river, Mont., U.S. 106 B12
West Fork Trinity, river, Tex., U.S. 102 K10
West Frankfort, Ill., U.S. 99 U6
West Frisian Islands, Neth. 146 G12
West Glacier, Mont., U.S. 106 B6
West Grand Lake, Me., U.S. 95 E18
West Helena, Ark., U.S. 100 H10
Westhope, N. Dak., U.S. 104 D4
West Ice Shelf, Antarctica 227 H21
West Indies, N. Amer. 80 N7
West Islet, Coral Sea Is. Terr., Austral. 211 T16
West Lafayette, Ind., U.S. 99 Q8
West Landing, Marshall Is. 216 G10
West Liberty, Iowa, U.S. 105 P14
West Liberty, Ky., U.S. 101 B19
Westman Islands see Vestmannaeyjar, Ice. 140 G2
West Mariana Basin, Pac. Oc. 238 H5
West Memphis, Ark., U.S. 100 G11
Westminster, Md., U.S. 96 B13
Westminster, S.C., U.S. 96 K6
West Monroe, La., U.S. 100 L8

Westmoreland, Qnsld., Austral. 211 R10
Westmorland, Calif., U.S. 109 Y11
West Nicholson, Zimb. 202 G11
Weston, Mo., U.S. 105 S10
Weston, W. Va., U.S. 96 C9
Weston Point, Kiribati 217 B20
Weston super Mare, Eng., U.K. 143 V11
West Palm Beach, Fla., U.S. 97 V10
West Passage see Toachel Mlengui, Palau 216 M11
West Plains, Mo., U.S. 105 V13
West Point, Austral. 210 K9
West Point, Ga., U.S. 96 M4
West Point, Marshall Is. 216 M7
West Point, Ky., U.S. 101 B16
West Point, Miss., U.S. 101 J13
West Point, N.Y., U.S. 94 M11
West Point, Nebr., U.S. 105 P8
West Point, Va., U.S. 96 E13
West Point Lake, Ga., U.S. 96 M4
Westport, Calif., U.S. 109 P2
Westport, Ire. 143 R3
Westport, N.Z. 213 N17
Westport, Wash., U.S. 108 D2
Westpunt, Neth. Antilles, Neth. 121 N13
Westray, island, Scot., U.K. 142 F10
Westray Firth, Scot., U.K. 142 F10
West Siberian Plain, Russ. 166 D8
West Spit, Marshall Is. 216 H7
West Union, Iowa, U.S. 104 M13
West Valley City, Utah, U.S. 106 L7
West Virginia, U.S. 96 C9
Westwego, La., U.S. 100 Q11
Westwood, Calif., U.S. 109 N5
Westwood Downs, N.S.W., Austral. 211 W11
West Wyalong, N.S.W., Austral. 211 X13
West Yellowstone, Mont., U.S. 106 F8
West York Island, Spratly Is. 188 E11
Wetar, island, Indonesia 189 M15
Wetaskiwin, Alta., Can. 82 L10
Wetumka, Okla., U.S. 102 G12
Wetumpka, Ala., U.S. 101 L16
Wetzlar, Ger. 148 G6
Wewahitchka, Fla., U.S. 97 R4
Wewak, P.N.G. 213 C18
Wewoka, Okla., U.S. 102 G12
Wexford, Ire. 143 U6
Wexford Harbour, Ire. 143 U7
Weyburn, Sask., Can. 82 N12
Weyer, Aust. 148 L11
Weymouth, Eng., U.K. 143 X11
Weymouth, Cape, Austral. 210 B12
Whakapunake, peak, N.Z. 213 K20
Whakatane, N.Z. 213 K20
Whale Cay, Bahamas 116 D11
Whale Cove, Nunavut, Can. 83 J15
Whaler Anchorage, Kiribati 217 B20
Whalsay, island, Scot., U.K. 142 D12
Whangamata, N.Z. 213 J19
Whangarei, N.Z. 213 H18
Wharton, Tex., U.S. 103 R13
Wharton Basin, Ind. Oc. 241 K13
Wheatland, Wyo., U.S. 106 J13
Wheatland Reservoir, Wyo., U.S. 106 J12
Wheaton, Minn., U.S. 104 J8
Wheeler, Tex., U.S. 102 G7
Wheeler Lake, Ala., U.S. 101 H15
Wheeler Peak, N. Mex., U.S. 107 Q13
Wheeler Peak, Nev., U.S. 84 G6
Wheeling, W. Va., U.S. 96 B9
Wheelwright, Ky., U.S. 101 C20
Whidbey, Point, Austral. 210 K9
Whiddy Island, Ire. 143 V3
Whim Creek, W. Aust., Austral. 211 S2
Whiskeytown Shasta-Trinity National Recreation Area, Calif., U.S. 108 M3
Whitby, Eng., U.K. 143 Q13
White, river, Ark., U.S. 100 H10
White, river, Colo., U.S. 106 L10
White, river, Ind., U.S. 99 T17
White, river, Nev., U.S. 109 Q12
White, river, S. Dak., U.S. 104 L5
White, S. Dak., U.S. 104 K8
White, river, Tex., U.S. 102 K6
White, Lake, Austral. 210 E7
White Bay, Virgin Islands, U.K. 120 L11
White Bird, Idaho, U.S. 106 E4
White Butte, N. Dak., U.S. 104 H2
White Cliffs, N.S.W., Austral. 211 W12
White Cloud, Mich., U.S. 98 K9

White Deer, Tex., U.S. 102 G6
Whitefish, Mont., U.S. 106 B5
Whitefish Bay, Mich., U.S. 98 F10
Whitefish Point, Mich., U.S. 98 F10
Whitefish Point, Mich., U.S. 98 F10
White Hall, Ark., U.S. 100 H9
White Hall, Ill., U.S. 99 S4
Whitehall, Mich., U.S. 98 L9
Whitehall, Mont., U.S. 106 E7
Whitehall, N.Y., U.S. 94 H12
Whitehall, Ohio, U.S. 99 R13
Whitehall, Wis., U.S. 98 J3
Whitehaven, Eng., U.K. 143 Q10
Whitehorse, Yukon, Can. 82 G8
White Horses, Jam. 120 J11
Whitehouse, Jam. 120 J6
White Island, Antarctica 227 C19
White Island, Nunavut, Can. 83 G16
White Lake, La., U.S. 100 Q8
White Mountains, Alas., U.S. 110 F12
White Mountains, Calif., U.S. 109 S8
White Mountains, N.H., U.S. 95 F14
White Mountains National Recreation Area, Alas., U.S. 111 F17
White Nile see Abyad, El Bahr el, river, Sudan 199 F13
White Pine, Mich., U.S. 98 F5
White Plains, N.Y., U.S. 94 M11
White River, S. Dak., U.S. 104 L4
Whiteriver, Ariz., U.S. 107 T9
White River Junction, Vt., U.S. 95 H13
White Salmon, Wash., U.S. 108 E5
White Sands National Monument, N. Mex., U.S. 107 U12
Whitesboro, Tex., U.S. 102 K11
Whitesburg, Ky., U.S. 101 D20
White Sea, Arctic Oc. 243 B18
White Sea-Baltic Canal, Russ. 138 B10
White Sulphur Springs, Mont., U.S. 106 D8
White Sulphur Springs, W. Va., U.S. 96 E9
Whitetail, Mont., U.S. 106 A12
Whiteville, N.C., U.S. 96 K11
Whiteville, Tenn., U.S. 100 F12
White Volta, river, Af. 194 G3
Whitewater, Mont., U.S. 106 B11
Whitewater, Wis., U.S. 98 M6
Whitewater Baldy, N. Mex., U.S. 107 U10
Whitewood, Qnsld., Austral. 211 S12
Whitewright, Tex., U.S. 102 K12
Whithorn, Scot., U.K. 143 P9
Whitman, Nebr., U.S. 105 N3
Whitman Mission National Historic Site, Wash., U.S. 108 E8
Whitmire, S.C., U.S. 96 K8
Whitmore Mountains, Antarctica 226 J10
Whitney, Lake, Tex., U.S. 102 M11
Whitney, Mount, Calif., U.S. 109 T8
Whittier, Alas., U.S. 111 K17
Wholdaia Lake, N.W.T., Can. 82 J13
Whyalla, S. Aust., Austral. 211 X10
Wialki, W. Aust., Austral. 211 W3
Wiay, island, Scot., U.K. 142 J6
Wibaux, Mont., U.S. 106 C13
Wichita, Kans., U.S. 105 U7
Wichita, river, Tex., U.S. 102 J9
Wichita Falls, Tex., U.S. 102 J9
Wichita Mountains, Okla., U.S. 102 H9
Wick, Scot., U.K. 142 H10
Wickenburg, Ariz., U.S. 107 T6
Wickepin, W. Aust., Austral. 211 X3
Wickett, Tex., U.S. 103 N3
Wickiup Reservoir, Oreg., U.S. 108 H4
Wickliffe, Ky., U.S. 100 D12
Wicklow, Ire. 143 S7
Wicklow Head, Ire. 143 T7
Wicklow Mountains, Ire. 143 T6
Wide Bay, P.N.G. 213 C21
Widnes, Eng., U.K. 143 S11
Wieleń, Pol. 148 D12
Wieluń, Pol. 149 F14
Wien (Vienna), Aust. 148 K12
Wiener Neustadt, Aust. 148 L12
Wieprz, river, Pol. 149 E17
Wiesbaden, Ger. 148 G6
Wigan, Eng., U.K. 143 R11
Wiggins, Miss., U.S. 100 N12
Wight, Isle of, Eng., U.K. 143 X12

Wigtown Bay, Scot., U.K. 143 P9
Wikieup, Ariz., U.S. 107 S5
Wil, Switz. 150 A4
Wilberforce, Cape, Austral. 210 A9
Wilburton, Okla., U.S. 102 H13
Wilbur, Wash., U.S. 108 C7
Wilcannia, N.S.W., Austral. 211 W12
Wilczek, Zemlya, Russ. 158 C12
Wildcat Peak, Nev., U.S. 109 Q10
Wildespitze, peak, Aust. 148 M8
Wildrose, N. Dak., U.S. 104 E2
Wildwood, Fla., U.S. 97 S8
Wildwood, N.J., U.S. 94 R10
Wilhelm, Mount, P.N.G. 213 C19
Wilhelm II Coast, Antarctica 227 J21
Wilhelmina Gebergte, Suriname 129 F15
Wilhelmina Mountains, S. Amer. 126 B7
Wilhelmshaven, Ger. 148 C6
Wilkes-Barre, Pa., U.S. 94 M9
Wilkes Island, Wake I., U.S. 216 F8
Wilkes Land, Antarctica 227 Q17
Wilkins Coast, Antarctica 226 E5
Willacoochee, Ga., U.S. 97 P6
Willamette, river, Oreg., U.S. 108 G3
Willapa Bay, Wash., U.S. 108 D2
Willapa Hills, Wash., U.S. 108 D3
Willard, Ohio, U.S. 99 P13
Willard, Utah, U.S. 106 K7
Willcox, Ariz., U.S. 107 V9
Willemstad, Neth. Antilles, Neth. 121 Q14
Willeroo, N. Terr., Austral. 211 Q8
William, Mount, Austral. 210 L11
William "Bill" Dannelly Reservoir, Ala., U.S. 101 L15
William Cay, Bahamas 120 E8
William Creek, S. Aust., Austral. 211 V9
Williams, Ariz., U.S. 107 S7
Williams, Calif., U.S. 109 Q4
Williams, Minn., U.S. 104 E10
Williams, W. Aust., Austral. 211 X3
Williamsburg, Ky., U.S. 101 D18
Williamsburg, Va., U.S. 96 F13
Williamsfield, Jam. 120 J8
Williams Island, Bahamas 116 E10
Williams Lake, B.C., Can. 82 L8
Williamson, W. Va., U.S. 96 E7
Williamson Glacier, Antarctica 227 M20
Williamsport, Pa., U.S. 94 M7
Williamston, N.C., U.S. 96 H13
Williamston, S.C., U.S. 96 K7
William's Town, Bahamas 120 F9
Williamstown, Ky., U.S. 101 A18
Williamstown, W. Va., U.S. 96 C8
Willikies, Antigua & Barbuda 121 B21
Willis, Tex., U.S. 103 P14
Willis Islets, Coral Sea Is. Terr., Austral. 211 R15
Williston, N. Dak., U.S. 104 E2
Williston, S.C., U.S. 96 L8
Williston Lake, B.C., Can. 82 J9
Willits, Calif., U.S. 109 P2
Willmar, Minn., U.S. 104 J10
Willoughby Bay, Antigua & Barbuda 121 B21
Willow City, N. Dak., U.S. 104 E5
Willowlake, river, N.W.T., Can. 82 G10
Willowra, N. Terr., Austral. 211 S8
Willows, Calif., U.S. 109 P4
Willow Springs, Mo., U.S. 105 V13
Wills Point, Tex., U.S. 102 L13
Wilmington, Del., U.S. 96 B14
Wilmington, Ill., U.S. 99 P7
Wilmington, N.C., U.S. 96 K12
Wilmington, Ohio, U.S. 99 S12
Wilmington, S. Aust., Austral. 211 X10
Wilmore, Ky., U.S. 101 C17
Wilmot, Ark., U.S. 100 K9
Wilmot, S. Dak., U.S. 104 J8
Wilsall, Mont., U.S. 106 E8
Wilson, Ark., U.S. 100 F11
Wilson, Kans., U.S. 105 T6
Wilson, N.C., U.S. 96 H12
Wilson, Okla., U.S. 102 J11
Wilson, Tex., U.S. 102 K5
Wilson, Mount, Colo., U.S. 107 P10
Wilson, Mount, Oreg., U.S. 108 F4
Wilson Creek, Wash., U.S. 108 C7
Wilson Hills, Antarctica 227 R15
Wilson Lake, Ala., U.S. 101 G14
Wilson Lake, Kans., U.S. 105 S6

Wilson's Creek National Battlefield, Mo., U.S. 105 V12
Wilsons Promontory, Vic., Austral. 211 Z12
Wilson Strait, Solomon Is. 217 M15
Wilton, N. Dak., U.S. 104 G4
Wiltz, river, Lux. 160 H9
Wiltz, Lux. 160 H9
Wiluna, W. Aust., Austral. 211 V4
Winamac, Ind., U.S. 99 P8
Winchester, Eng., U.K. 143 W12
Winchester, Idaho, U.S. 106 D3
Winchester, Ind., U.S. 99 R10
Winchester, Ky., U.S. 101 B18
Winchester, Tenn., U.S. 101 G16
Winchester, Va., U.S. 96 C12
Winchester Bay, Oreg., U.S. 108 H2
Wind, river, Wyo., U.S. 106 H9
Wind, river, Yukon, Can. 82 E9
Windber, Pa., U.S. 94 P5
Winder, Ga., U.S. 96 K6
Windhill Beach, Gibraltar, U.K. 161 Q23
Windhoek, Namibia 202 H7
Windom, Minn., U.S. 104 L10
Windorah, Qnsld., Austral. 211 U12
Window Rock, Ariz., U.S. 107 R10
Wind River Range, Wyo., U.S. 106 H9
Windsor, Colo., U.S. 106 L13
Windsor, Conn., U.S. 95 L13
Windsor, Eng., U.K. 143 V13
Windsor, Mo., U.S. 105 T11
Windsor, N.C., U.S. 96 G13
Windsor, Ont., Can. 83 R17
Windsor, Vt., U.S. 95 H13
Windsor Forest, Ga., U.S. 97 N9
Windward Islands, Lesser Antilles 119 L16
Windward Passage, Cuba, Haiti 117 K15
Winfield, Ala., U.S. 101 J14
Winfield, Kans., U.S. 105 V8
Wini, Indonesia 189 N15
Winifred, Mont., U.S. 106 C9
Wininen, island, F.S.M. 217 C16
Winion, Mochun, F.S.M. 217 C16
Winipirea, island, F.S.M. 217 B15
Winipiru, island, F.S.M. 217 C14
Winisk, river, Ont., Can. 83 L16
Wink, Tex., U.S. 103 N3
Winkelman, Ariz., U.S. 107 U8
Winlock, Wash., U.S. 108 D3
Winneba, Ghana 200 H10
Winnebago, Minn., U.S. 104 L11
Winnebago, Lake, Wis., U.S. 98 K6
Winnemucca, Nev., U.S. 108 M9
Winnemucca Lake, Nev., U.S. 109 N7
Winner, S. Dak., U.S. 104 M5
Winnfield, La., U.S. 100 M8
Winnibigoshish, Lake, Minn., U.S. 104 F10
Winnipeg, Man., Can. 83 N14
Winnipeg, Lake, Man., Can. 83 M14
Winnipegosis, Man., Can. 83 M13
Winnipegosis, Lake, N. Amer. 80 G5
Winnipesaukee, Lake, N.H., U.S. 95 H14
Winnsboro, La., U.S. 100 L9
Winnsboro, S.C., U.S. 96 K9
Winnsboro, Tex., U.S. 102 L14
Winona, Kans., U.S. 105 S3
Winona, Minn., U.S. 104 L13
Winona, Miss., U.S. 100 J11
Winseler, Lux. 160 H9
Winsen, Ger. 148 C8
Winslow, Ariz., U.S. 107 S8
Winslow, Me., U.S. 95 F16
Winston-Salem, N.C., U.S. 96 H10
Winter Garden, Fla., U.S. 97 T8
Winter Haven, Fla., U.S. 97 U8
Winter Park, Fla., U.S. 97 T9
Winters, Calif., U.S. 109 R4
Winters, Tex., U.S. 102 M7
Winterset, Iowa, U.S. 105 P11
Winterswijk, Neth. 146 J14
Winterthur, Switz. 150 A4
Winthrop, Me., U.S. 95 F16
Winthrop, Minn., U.S. 104 K10
Winthrop, Wash., U.S. 108 B6
Winton Heights, Bahamas 120 B12
Wippra, Ger. 148 F8
Wirrulla, S. Aust., Austral. 211 X9
Wisas, island, F.S.M. 217 C16
Wisbech, Eng., U.K. 143 T14
Wiscasset, Me., U.S. 95 G16

Wisconsin, U.S. 98 J3
Wisconsin, river, Wis., U.S. 98 J5
Wisconsin Dells, Wis., U.S. 98 K5
Wisconsin Rapids, Wis., U.S. 98 J5
Wiseman, Alas., U.S. 111 E16
Wishek, N. Dak., U.S. 104 H5
Wishram, Wash., U.S. 108 F5
Wisła, river, Pol. 149 B14
Wismar, Ger. 148 B9
Wisner, La., U.S. 100 M9
Wisner, Nebr., U.S. 105 N8
Wissembourg, Fr. 147 N16
Witchcliffe, W. Aust., Austral. 211 Y2
Witham, Eng., U.K. 143 U15
Witten, S. Dak., U.S. 104 M5
Wittenberg, Ger. 148 E10
Wittenberge, Ger. 148 D9
Wittenoom, W. Aust., Austral. 211 T3
Wittlich, Ger. 148 G5
Wittlich, Ger. 160 H12
Wittstock, Ger. 148 C10
Wittstock, Ger. 148 C9
Witu Islands, P.N.G. 213 C20
Włocławek, Pol. 149 D14
Włodawa, Pol. 149 E18
Wöbbelin, Ger. 148 C9
Woburn Bay, Grenada 121 L22
Wodonga, Vic., Austral. 211 Y13
Wohlthat Mountains, Antarctica 227 B14
Wojejairok, island, Marshall Is. 216 L4
Wojejairok Pass, Marshall Is. 216 L4
Wokam, island, Indonesia 189 L19
Wokingham, Eng., U.K. 143 V13
Wolauna, island, F.S.M. 217 G13
Wolcott, N.Y., U.S. 94 J7
Woleai Atoll, F.S.M. 216 Q4
Wolf, river, Wis., U.S. 98 H6
Wolf, Isla (Wenman), Ecua. 128 M7
Wolf, Volcán, Ecua. 128 P8
Wolf Creek, Mont., U.S. 106 D7
Wolf Creek, Oreg., U.S. 108 K2
Wolf Creek, Tex., U.S. 102 F7
Wolf Creek Pass, Colo., U.S. 107 P11
Wolfeboro, N.H., U.S. 95 H14
Wolfe City, Tex., U.S. 102 K12
Wolfen, Ger. 148 E9
Wolfenbüttel, Ger. 148 E8
Wolfforth, Tex., U.S. 102 K5
Wolf Point, Mont., U.S. 106 C12
Wolfsberg, Aust. 148 M11
Wolfsburg, Ger. 148 D8
Wollaston, Islas, Chile 133 Y9
Wollaston Lake, Sask., Can. 83 K13
Wollaston Peninsula, N.W.T., Nunavut, Can. 82 E12
Wollogorang, N. Terr., Austral. 211 R10
Wollongong, N.S.W., Austral. 211 Y14
Wolo, Indonesia 189 K13
Wolverhampton, Eng., U.K. 143 T11
Wondai, Qnsld., Austral. 211 V15
Wongan Hills, W. Aust., Austral. 211 W2
Wongawal, W. Aust., Austral. 211 U4
Wonju, S. Korea 182 F14
Wŏnsan, N. Korea 182 D13
Wonthaggi, Vic., Austral. 211 Z12
Wonti, Indonesia 213 B16
Woodall Mountain, Miss., U.S. 101 G13
Woodbine, Ga., U.S. 97 Q8
Woodbridge, Eng., U.K. 143 U15
Woodbridge, Va., U.S. 96 D13
Woodbridge Bay, Dominica 121 G19
Woodburn, N.S.W., Austral. 211 W15
Woodburn, Oreg., U.S. 108 F3
Woodbury, N.J., U.S. 94 Q9
Wood Cay, Bahamas 120 A5
Woodcock, Mount, Austral. 210 D9
Woodenbridge, Ire. 143 T7
Woodford, Grenada 121 K22
Wood Lake, Nebr., U.S. 105 N5
Woodlake, Calif., U.S. 109 U7
Woodland, Calif., U.S. 109 Q4
Woodland, Me., U.S. 95 E19
Woodland, Wash., U.S. 108 E3
Woodland Park, Colo., U.S. 106 M13
Woodlark, island, P.N.G. 213 E21
Wood River, Ill., U.S. 99 S4
Wood River, Nebr., U.S. 105 Q6
Wood River Lakes, Alas., U.S. 111 K13
Woodruff, S.C., U.S. 96 J8
Woodruff, Utah, U.S. 106 K8
Woods, Lake, Austral. 210 D8
Woods, Lake of the, Can., U.S. 85 B13
Woodsboro, Tex., U.S. 103 T11

Woodsfield, Ohio, U.S. **99** R15
Woods Hole, Mass., U.S. **95** L15
Woodstock, Qnsld., Austral. **211** S12
Woodstock, Va., U.S. **96** D11
Woodstown, N.J., U.S. **94** Q9
Woodsville, N.H., U.S. **95** G13
Woodville, Miss., U.S. **100** N9
Woodville, N.Z. **213** M19
Woodville, Tex., U.S. **103** P15
Woodward, Okla., U.S. **102** E8
Woody Head, Austral. **210** J15
Woomera, S. Aust., Austral. **211** W10
Woonsocket, R.I., U.S. **95** L14
Woonsocket, S. Dak., U.S. **104** L7
Woorabinda, Qnsld., Austral. **211** U14
Wooramel, W. Aust., Austral. **211** V1
Wooster, Ohio, U.S. **99** P14
Worbab, island, Marshall Is. **216** N5
Worcester, Eng., U.K. **143** U11
Worcester, Mass., U.S. **95** K14
Worcester, S. Af. **202** M7
Worden, Mont., U.S. **106** E10
Workai, island, Indonesia **189** M19
Workington, Eng., U.K. **143** P10
Worland, Wyo., U.S. **106** G10
Wormeldange, Lux. **160** K11
Worms, Ger. **148** H6
Worth, Lake, Tex., U.S. **102** L11
Wortham, Tex., U.S. **102** M12
Worthing, Barbados **121** L19
Worthington, Minn., U.S. **104** L9
Wosi, Indonesia **189** J16
Wotho Atoll, Marshall Is. **216** F3
Wotje Atoll, Marshall Is. **216** G5
Wotje Atoll, Marshall Is. **214** F8
Wowoni, island, Indonesia **189** L14
Wragby, Eng., U.K. **143** S13
Wrangel Island see Vrangelya, Ostrov, Russ. **159** B19
Wrangel Island, Russ. **166** A11
Wrangell, Alas., U.S. **111** M23
Wrangell, Cape, Alas., U.S. **110** K1
Wrangell Mountains, Alas., U.S. **84** P5
Wrangell-St. Elias National Park and Preserve, Alas., U.S. **111** J19
Wrangel Plain, Arctic Oc. **242** G8
Wrath, Cape, Scot., U.K. **142** G8
Wray, Colo., U.S. **106** L16
Wreck Hill, Bermuda, U.K. **120** C1
Wreck Point, S. Af. **194** Q6
Wrecks, Bay of, Kiribati **217** B23
Wrens, Ga., U.S. **96** M7
Wrexham, Wales, U.K. **143** S10
Wright, Wyo., U.S. **106** G12
Wright Brothers National Memorial, N.C., U.S. **96** G15
Wright Patman Lake, Tex., U.S. **102** K15
Wrightsville, Ga., U.S. **96** M7
Wrightsville Beach, N.C., U.S. **96** K13
Wrigley Gulf, Antarctica **226** N7
Wrocław, Pol. **149** F13
Września, Pol. **149** E13
Wu, river, China **183** N1
Wu, river, China **181** M13
Wu'an, China **182** F5
Wubin, W. Aust., Austral. **211** W2
Wubu, China **182** E3
Wuchang, China **181** D17
Wuchuan, China **182** C4
Wuchuan, China **182** M1
Wuchuan, China **183** S2
Wuda, China **182** D1
Wudan see Ongniud Qi, China **182** A8
Wudaoliang, China **180** J9
Wudi, China **182** E7
Wudinna, S. Aust., Austral. **211** X9
Wufeng, China **182** L3
Wugang, China **183** N2
Wuhai, China **182** C1
Wuhan, China **182** L5
Wuhe, China **182** J7
Wuhu, China **182** K8
Wukari, Nigeria **201** G15
Wular Lake, India **176** M12
Wulian, China **182** G8
Wuliaru, island, Indonesia **213** D14
Wum, Cameroon **201** H15
Wundowie, W. Aust., Austral. **211** X2
Wuning, China **182** M5
Wunlah, Indonesia **189** M17
Wuntho, Myanmar **186** F6
Wupatki National Monument, Ariz., U.S. **107** R7

Wuping, China **183** Q6
Wuppertal, Ger. **148** F5
Wuqi, China **182** F2
Wuqia, China **180** F4
Wuqing, China **182** D7
Wurarga, W. Aust., Austral. **211** V2
Wurung, Qnsld., Austral. **211** R11
Würzburg, Ger. **148** H7
Wushan, China **182** K2
Wusi, Vanuatu **218** C1
Wust Seamount, Atl. Oc. **237** T12
Wusuli (Ussuri), river, China **181** C19
Wutai, China **182** E5
Wutongqiao, China **180** L11
Wuvulu Island, P.N.G. **213** B18
Wuwei, China **182** K9
Wuwei, China **180** H11
Wuxi, China **182** K2
Wuxi, China **182** K9
Wuxue, China **182** L6
Wuyiling, China **181** C17
Wuyi Shan, China **183** P6
Wuyuan, China **182** C2
Wuyuan, China **182** M7
Wuzhai, China **182** D4
Wuzhen, China **182** K4
Wuzhong, China **180** H12
Wuzhou, China **183** R3
Wyandot Seamount, Atl. Oc. **237** T15
Wyandra, Qnsld., Austral. **211** V13
Wye, river, Eng., Wales, U.K. **143** U11
Wyk, Ger. **148** A7
Wylie Lake, N.C., S.C., U.S. **96** J9
Wyloo, W. Aust., Austral. **211** T2
Wymore, Nebr., U.S. **105** R8
Wynbring, S. Aust., Austral. **211** W8
Wyndham, W. Aust., Austral. **211** Q6
Wyndmere, N. Dak., U.S. **104** H8
Wynne, Ark., U.S. **100** G10
Wynnewood, Okla., U.S. **102** H11
Wynniatt Bay, N.W.T., Can. **82** E13
Wyoming, Mich., U.S. **98** L9
Wyoming, U.S. **106** H9
Wyoming Range, Wyo., U.S. **106** H8
Wyszków, Pol. **149** D16
Wytheville, Va., U.S. **96** F8
Wyville Thomson Ridge, Atl. Oc. **236** D12

X

Xaafuun, Somalia **199** F19
Xàbia see Jávea, Sp. **145** J15
Xaçmaz, Azerb. **169** C22
Xaghra, Malta **161** H2O
Xaignabouri, Laos **186** J9
Xainza, China **180** K7
Xai-Xai, Mozambique **202** J12
Xalapa, Mex. **115** J13
Xalin, Somalia **199** G18
Xamba see Hanggin Houqi, China **182** C1
Xangdin Hural, China **182** A3
Xangongo, Angola **202** F6
Xankändi see Stepanakert, Azerb. **169** E2O
Xánthi, Gr. **155** B14
Xanthus, ruin, Turk. **168** J4
Xapuri, Braz. **130** G6
Xarardheere, Somalia **199** H18
Xar Moron, river, China **182** A9
Xàtiva, Sp. **145** H14
Xau, Lake, Botswana **202** G9
Xayar, China **180** F6
Xèng, river, Laos **186** H10
Xenia, Ohio, U.S. **99** R12
Xépôn, Laos **186** K12
Xérxis Canal, Gr. **154** D12
Xewkija, Malta **161** H2O
Xi, river, China **183** R4
Xiachuan Dao, China **183** S3
Xiajiang, China **183** N5
Xiamen (Amoy), China **183** Q7
Xi'an, China **182** H2
Xianfeng, China **182** L2
Xiang, river, China **183** P3
Xianggang see Hong Kong, China **183** S5
Xianghuang Qi (Xin Bulag), China **182** B5
Xiangkhoang, Laos **186** J10
Xiangning, China **182** G3
Xiangshan (Dancheng), China **182** M1O

Xiangtan, China **183** N4
Xiangxi, China **182** K3
Xiangyin, China **182** M4
Xiangyunn, China **180** N1O
Xianju, China **182** M9
Xiantao, China **182** L4
Xianyou, China **183** Q8
Xiaogan, China **182** K5
Xiao Hinggan Ling, China **181** B17
Xiaojiang, China **183** N9
Xiaoshan, China **182** L9
Xiaoyi, China **182** F4
Xiapu, China **183** P9
Xichang, China **180** M11
Xifeng, China **182** B11
Xifeng, China **182** F1
Xigazê, China **180** L7
Xilaganí, Gr. **155** C15
Xiliao, river, China **182** A1O
Xilinhot, China **182** A7
Xilókastro, Gr. **154** J1O
Ximiao, China **180** G1O
Xin Barag Youqi, China **181** C14
Xin Barag Zuoqi, China **181** C15
Xinbin, China **182** B12
Xin Bulag see Xianghuang Qi, China **182** B5
Xincai, China **182** J5
Xinfeng, China **183** Q5
Xinfeng, China **183** R5
Xinfengjiang Shuiki, China **183** R5
Xing'an, China **183** P2
Xingcheng, China **182** C9
Xinghai, China **180** J1O
Xinghe, China **182** C5
Xinghua, China **182** J9
Xinghua Wan, China **183** Q8
Xingkai Hu see Khanka, Ozero, China **181** D19
Xingning, China **183** R6
Xingshan, China **182** K3
Xingtai, China **182** F5
Xingu, river, Braz. **130** D12
Xinguara, Braz. **131** F13
Xingxian, China **182** E3
Xingxingxia, China **180** F9
Xingyi, China **180** N12
Xingzi, China **182** M6
Xinhe, China **182** F6
Xinhua, China **183** N3
Xinhuang, China **183** N1
Xinhui, China **183** S4
Xining, China **180** J11
Xinji, China **182** E6
Xinjiang, China **182** G3
Xinmin, China **182** B1O
Xinning, China **183** P2
Xinpu see Lianyungang, China **182** H8
Xinshao, China **183** N3
Xinwen, China **182** G7
Xinxiang, China **182** G5
Xinxing, China **183** S3
Xinyang, China **182** K5
Xinye, China **182** J4
Xinyi, China **182** H8
Xinyi, China **183** S2
Xinyuan, China **180** E6
Xinzhou, China **182** E4
Xinzo de Limia, Sp. **144** D6
Xique Xique, Braz. **131** G15
Xisha Qundao (Paracel Islands, Hoàng Sa), China **188** B1O
Xishui, China **182** L6
Xiushan, China **182** M1
Xiushui, China **182** M5
Xiuyan, China **182** C11
Xiuying, China **183** T2
Xixian, China **182** J5
Xixiang, China **182** J1
Xorkol, China **180** G8
Xuan'en, China **182** L2
Xuanhan, China **182** K1
Xuanhua, China **182** C6
Xuan Loc, Vietnam **187** P13
Xuanwei, China **180** N11
Xuanzhou, China **182** L8
Xuchang, China **182** H5
Xuddur, Somalia **199** H16
Xudun, Somalia **199** G17
Xulun Hoh see Zhenglan Qi, China **182** B7
Xun, river, China **183** R2
Xunke, China **181** B17

Xunwu, China **183** Q6
Xunyi, China **182** G2
Xupu, China **183** N2
Xuwen, China **183** T2
Xuyong, China **180** M12
Xuzhou, China **182** H7
Xylofagou, Cyprus **160** P1O

Y

Yaak, Mont., U.S. **106** A4
Ya'an, China **180** L12
Yabbenohr, island, Marshall Is. **216** L3
Yablonovyy Khrebet, Russ. **159** L17
Yablonovyy Range, Russ. **166** E11
Yabrūd, Syr. **170** H8
Yabucoa, P.R., U.S. **120** N5
Yabucoa, Puerto, P.R., U.S. **120** N5
Yacata, island, Fiji Is. **218** H8
Yachats, Oreg., U.S. **108** G2
Yacimiento Río Turbio, Arg. **133** W7
Yacuiba, Bol. **130** L8
Yacyretá Dam, Parag. **130** N1O
Yadgir, India **178** M5
Yadkin, river, N.C., U.S. **96** G9
Yadong, China **180** M7
Yadua, island, Fiji Is. **218** G6
Yafi, Indonesia **189** K21
Yagasa, island, Fiji Is. **218** K9
Yağca, Turk. **168** H6
Yaguajay, Cuba **116** H9
Yahyalı, Turk. **168** G1O
Yaita, Japan **185** N12
Yakacık, Turk. **168** J11
Yakapinar, Turk. **168** J1O
Yakeshi, China **181** C15
Yakima, river, Wash., U.S. **108** D6
Yakima, Wash., U.S. **108** D6
Yakishiri Jima, Japan **184** E13
Yakmach, Pak. **177** S3
Yakoma, Dem. Rep. of the Congo **198** H1O
Yakossi, Cen. Af. Rep. **198** H1O
Yaksha, Russ. **158** G9
Yaku Shima, Japan **185** U4
Yakutat, Alas., U.S. **111** K2O
Yakutat Bay, Alas., U.S. **111** K2O
Yakutsk, Russ. **159** H18
Yala, Sri Lanka **179** T8
Yala, Thai. **187** S9
Yale, Mich., U.S. **98** L13
Yale, Okla., U.S. **102** F11
Yalewa Kalou (Round Island), Fiji Is. **218** G6
Yalgoo, W. Aust., Austral. **211** V2
Yallahs, Jam. **120** J1O
Yalleroi, Qnsld., Austral. **211** U13
Yallock, N.S.W., Austral. **211** X12
Yalong, river, China **180** M11
Yalova, Turk. **168** D5
Yalta, Ukr. **157** T7
Yalu, river, N. Korea, China **182** C11
Yalvaç, Turk. **168** G6
Yamada, Japan **184** K14
Yamagata, Japan **184** L12
Yamaguchi, Japan **185** Q5
Yamal, Poluostrov, Russ. **158** F11
Yamal Peninsula, Russ. **166** C8
Yamas, Indonesia **189** K21
Yamato Glacier, Antarctica **227** C16
Yamato Mountains see Queen Fabiola Mountains, Antarctica **227** C17
Yamba, N.S.W., Austral. **211** W15
Yambio, Sudan **198** H11
Yambol, Bulg. **153** J16
Yamdena, island, Indonesia **189** M17
Yamethinn, Myanmar **186** H6
Yamm, Russ. **156** G5
Yammaw, Myanmar **186** E7
Yamma Yamma, Lake, Austral. **210** G11
Yampa, river, Colo., U.S. **106** L1O
Yamzho Yumco, lake, China **180** L7
Yana, river, Russ. **166** C11
Yana, Gulf of, Arctic Oc. **242** C6
Yanagawa, Japan **185** R4
Yanai, Japan **185** R6
Yan'an, China **182** F2
Yanbu' al Baḥr, Saudi Arabia **172** J6
Yancannia, N.S.W., Austral. **211** W12
Yanchang, China **182** F3
Yancheng, China **182** J9

Yanchi, China **182** E1
Yanchuan, China **182** F3
Yandé, Île, New Caledonia, Fr. **218** B6
Yandina, Solomon Is. **217** N18
Yandoon, Myanmar **186** K6
Yangbajain, China **180** L7
Yangchun, China **183** S3
Yangi Qal'eh, Afghan. **176** J8
Yangi Qal'eh, Afghan. **176** L4
Yangjiang, China **183** S3
Yangon (Rangoon), Myanmar **186** K6
Yangquan, China **182** E5
Yangshan, China **183** Q4
Yangshuo, China **183** Q2
Yangtze see Chang Jiang, Jinsha, river, China **181** L13
Yangtze, Mouth of the, China **182** K1O
Yangtze, Source of the, China **180** K7
Yangtze Gorges, China **182** K2
Yangxian, China **182** H1
Yangxin, China **182** L5
Yangyang, S. Korea **182** E14
Yangyuan, China **182** D5
Yangzhou, China **182** J8
Yanhe, China **182** M1
Yanji, China **182** A14
Yankeetown, Fla., U.S. **97** S7
Yankton, S. Dak., U.S. **104** M7
Yanling, China **183** P4
Yano-Indigirskaya Nizmennost', Russ. **159** E17
Yano-Oymyakonskoye Nagor'ye, Russ. **159** F18
Yanqi, China **180** F7
Yanshan, China **182** E7
Yanshan, China **183** N7
Yanskiy, Russ. **159** F17
Yanskiy Zaliv, Russ. **159** E17
Yantabulla, N.S.W., Austral. **211** W12
Yantai, China **182** F1O
Yantra, river, Bulg. **153** H15
Yanuca, island, Fiji Is. **218** G8
Yao, Japan **185** Q9
Yaoundé, Cameroon **201** J16
Yaoxian, China **182** G2
Yap, island, F.S.M. **217** D18
Yapen, island, Indonesia **189** K19
Yapen, Selat, Indonesia **189** K19
Yapero, Indonesia **189** L2O
Yap Islands, F.S.M. **216** P2
Yap Trench, Pac. Oc. **238** I7
Yaqaqa, island, Fiji Is. **218** G7
Yaqeta, island, Fiji Is. **218** H5
Yaqui, river, Mex. **114** D7
Yaquina Head, Oreg., U.S. **108** G2
Yara, Cuba **116** K12
Yaraka, Qnsld., Austral. **211** U12
Yaralıgöz, peak, Turk. **168** C9
Yaransk, Russ. **156** G14
Yardımcı Burnu, Turk. **168** J6
Yardymly, Azerb. **169** F22
Yaren, Nauru **217** F23
Yarí, river, Col. **128** H6
Yarım, Yemen **172** Q9
Yaring, Thai. **187** S9
Yarkant, river, China **180** F5
Yarle Lakes, Austral. **210** J8
Yarlung Zangbo (Brahmaputra), river, China **180** L8
Yarlung Zangbo (Tsangpo) Canyon, China **180** L9
Yarma, Turk. **168** G8
Yarmouth, N.S., Can. **83** Q21
Yaroslavl', Russ. **156** H1O
Yaroua, island, Fiji Is. **218** H9
Yarozero, Russ. **156** E1O
Yarraden, Qnsld., Austral. **211** Q12
Yarraloola, W. Aust., Austral. **211** T2
Yartsevo, Russ. **156** K7
Yartsevo, Russ. **159** J13
Yarumal, Col. **128** D4
Yasawa, island, Fiji Is. **218** G6
Yasawa Group, Fiji Is. **218** H5
Yashkul', Russ. **157** R14
Yasin, Pak. **176** K11
Yasinza'i Kalay, Afghan. **177** Q4
Yasothon, Thai. **186** L11
Yasun Burnu, Turk. **168** D12
Yasur Volcano, Vanuatu **218** H4
Yata, river, Bol. **130** G7
Yatağan, Turk. **168** H4
Yatakala, Niger **196** H9
Yaté, New Caledonia, Fr. **218** E9

Yates Center, *Kans., U.S.* 105 U9
Yathkyed Lake, *Nunavut, Can.* 83 JI4
Yato, *Pukapuka, Cook Is., N.Z.* 218 Q2
Yatsushiro, *Japan* 185 S4
Yauca, *Peru* 130 J4
Yauco, *P.R., U.S.* 120 N2
Yaupi, *Ecua.* 128 K3
Yavatmal, *India* 178 K6
Yaviza, *Pan.* 115 N22
Yawatahama, *Japan* 185 R6
Yawri Bay, *Sierra Leone* 200 G5
Yayladağı, *Turk.* 168 KII
Yaynangyoung, *Myanmar* 186 H5
Yazd, *Iran* 173 EI4
Yazdān, *Iran* 173 DI7
Yazılıkaya, *Turk.* 168 F6
Yazlıca Dağı, *Turk.* 169 HI7
Yazman, *Pak.* 177 SIO
Yazoo, river, *Miss., U.S.* 85 KI5
Yazoo City, *Miss., U.S.* 100 KII
Ye, *Myanmar* 186 L7
Yebyu, *Myanmar* 186 M7
Yecheng (Kargilik), *China* 180 G4
Yecla, *Sp.* 145 JI4
Yeeda, *W. Aust., Austral.* 211 R5
Yefremov, *Russ.* 156 L9
Yegua Creek, *Tex., U.S.* 103 QI2
Yeguas, Punta, *P.R., U.S.* 120 N5
Yei, *Sudan* 198 HI2
Yekaterinburg, *Russ.* 158 H9
Yekateriny, Proliv, *Russ.* 159 K23
Yelabuga, *Russ.* 156 HI6
Yela Island, *P.N.G.* 217 QI3
Yelan', *Russ.* 157 NI2
Yelan Kolenovskiy, *Russ.* 157 NII
Yelets, *Russ.* 156 MIO
Yélimané, *Mali* 196 H6
Yelizavety, Mys, *Russ.* 159 H2I
Yell, island, *Scot., U.K.* 142 DI2
Yellandu, *India* 178 M7
Yellow *see* Huang, river, *China* 181 GI3
Yellow, river, *Fla., U.S.* 97 Q2
Yellow, Source of the, *China* 166 G9
Yellowknife, *N.W.T., Can.* 82 HII
Yellow River, Mouth of the, *China* 182 E8
Yellow Sea, *Asia* 166 GI2
Yellowstone, river, *Mont., U.S.* 106 DII
Yellowstone Lake, *Wyo., U.S.* 106 F8
Yellowstone National Park, *Wyo., U.S.* 106 F8
Yell Sound, *Scot., U.K.* 142 DI2
Yellville, *Ark., U.S.* 100 E8
Yelm, *Wash., U.S.* 108 D3
Yelverton Bay, *Nunavut, Can.* 83 AI5
Yelwa, *Nigeria* 201 FI3
Yemanzhelinsk, *Russ.* 158 J8
Yemassee, *S.C., U.S.* 96 M9
Yemen, *Asia* 167 W3
Yenakiyeve, *Ukr.* 157 QIO
Yen Bai, *Vietnam* 186 GII
Yendi, *Ghana* 200 FII
Yeniçağa, *Turk.* 168 D7
Yenice, river, *Turk.* 168 GII
Yenice, *Turk.* 168 F8
Yeniceoba, *Turk.* 168 F8
Yenişehir, *Turk.* 168 D5
Yenisey, river, *Russ.* 166 C8
Yenisey-Angara, Source of the, *Mongolia* 166 F9
Yenisey Gulf, *Russ.* 166 C8
Yeniseysk, *Russ.* 159 KI3
Yeniseyskiy Zaliv, *Russ.* 159 FI3
Yen Minh, *Vietnam* 186 FII
Yenyuka, *Russ.* 159 JI7
Yeola, *India* 178 K4
Yeongdeok, *S. Korea* 182 FI4
Yeosu, *S. Korea* 182 GI4
Yeovil, *Eng., U.K.* 143 WII
Yeppoon, *Qnsld., Austral.* 211 TI5
Yerbogachen, *Russ.* 159 JI5
Yerema, *Russ.* 159 JI5
Yerevan, *Arm.* 169 EI8
Yergeni Hills, *Russ.* 138 GI3
Yerilla, *W. Aust., Austral.* 211 W4
Yerington, *Nev., U.S.* 109 Q7
Yerköy, *Turk.* 168 E9
Yermak Plateau, *Arctic Oc.* 243 HI4
Yermo, *Calif., U.S.* 109 WIO
Yeroẖam, *Israel* 171 P5
Yershov, *Russ.* 156 MI5
Yeşilhisar, *Turk.* 168 GIO

Yeşilırmak, river, *Turk.* 168 DII
Yeşilkent, *Turk.* 168 JII
Yeşilova, *Turk.* 168 H5
Yessentuki, *Russ.* 157 TI2
Yessey, *Russ.* 159 GI4
Yetman, *N.S.W., Austral.* 211 WI4
Ye-u, *Myanmar* 186 G6
Yeu, Île d', *Fr.* 147 S5
Yevlax, *Azerb.* 169 D2I
Yevpatoriya, *Ukr.* 157 S7
Yexian, *China* 182 F9
Yeysk, *Russ.* 157 RIO
Ygatimí, *Parag.* 130 MII
Yi, river, *China* 182 G9
Yi, river, *Uru.* 132 KI4
Yialias, river, *Cyprus* 160 P8
Yibin, *China* 180 MI2
Yichang, *China* 182 L3
Yicheng, *China* 182 K4
Yichuan, *China* 182 F3
Yichun, *China* 183 N5
Yichun, *China* 181CI7
Yigo, *Guam, U.S.* 216 BII
Yijun, *China* 182 G2
Yilan, *China* 181 CI8
Yıldız Dağları, *Turk.* 168 B4
Yıldızeli, *Turk.* 168 EII
Yiliang, *China* 180 NII
Yinan, *China* 182 G8
Yinchuan, *China* 182 DI
Yindarlgooda, Lake, *Austral.* 210 J4
Yindi, *W. Aust., Austral.* 211 W5
Ying, river, *China* 181 KI5
Yingcheng, *China* 182 K5
Yingde, *China* 183 R4
Yingshan, *China* 182 K5
Yingshang, *China* 182 J6
Yingxian, *China* 182 D5
Yining (Gulja), *China* 180 E6
Yin Shan, *China* 182 B2
Yirga 'Alem, *Eth.* 199 GI5
Yirol, *Sudan* 198 GI2
Yirrkala, *N. Terr., Austral.* 211 PIO
Yishan, *China* 183 QI
Yishui, *China* 182 G8
Yitong, *China* 182 AI2
Yitulihe, *China* 181 BI5
Yiwu, *China* 182 M9
Yiwu, *China* 180 F9
Yixian, *China* 182 C9
Yixing, *China* 182 K9
Yiyang, *China* 182 M4
Yiyuan, *China* 182 G8
Ylig Bay, *Guam, U.S.* 216 CII
Ylivieska, *Fin.* 141 GI5
Ÿnderbor, *Kaz.* 174 E6
Yoakum, *Tex., U.S.* 103 RII
Yobe, river, *Niger, Nigeria* 194 G6
Yogyakarta, *Indonesia* 188 M9
Yoichi, *Japan* 184 FI3
Yokadouma, *Cameroon* 201 JI7
Yokkaichi, *Japan* 185 Q9
Yoko, *Cameroon* 201 HI6
Yokoate Shima, *Japan* 185 W3
Yokohama, *Japan* 184 HI3
Yokohama, *Japan* 185 PI2
Yokote, *Japan* 184 KI3
Yola, *Nigeria* 201 FI6
Yolöten, *Turkm.* 174 MIO
Yom, river, *Thai.* 186 K8
Yomra, *Turk.* 169 DI4
Yona, *Guam, U.S.* 216 CII
Yonago, *Japan* 185 P7
Yonezawa, *Japan* 184 MI2
Yong'an, *N. Korea* 182 BI4
Yongchun, *China* 183 Q8
Yongdeng, *China* 180 HII
Yongfu, *China* 183 Q2
Yonggyap Pass, *China, India* 178 EI5
Yŏngjŏ, *N. Korea* 182 BI3
Yongkang, *China* 182 M9
Yongshun, *China* 182 M2
Yongtai, *China* 183 P8
Yongxin, *China* 183 N5
Yongxing, *China* 183 P4
Yongxiu, *China* 182 M6
Yongzhou, *China* 183 P3
Yonkers, *N.Y., U.S.* 94 NII
Yonne, river, *Fr.* 147 RII
York, *Ala., U.S.* 101 LI3
York, *Eng., U.K.* 143 RI3
York, *Nebr., U.S.* 105 Q7
York, *Pa., U.S.* 94 P7
York, *S.C., U.S.* 96 J8

York, Cape, *Austral.* 210 AI2
York, Cape, *N. Amer.* 80 C7
Yorke Peninsula, *Austral.* 210 KIO
Yorkton, *Sask., Can.* 83 NI3
Yorktown, *Tex., U.S.* 103 SII
Yorktown, *Va., U.S.* 96 FI4
Yoron Jima, *Japan* 185 X2
Yoro Shima, *Japan* 185 W3
Yortan Tepe, ruin, *Turk.* 168 F3
Yosemite National Park, *Calif., U.S.* 109 S7
Yoshii, river, *Japan* 185 Q7
Yoshkar Ola, *Russ.* 156 HI4
Yos Sudarso *see* Dolak, island, *Indonesia* 189 M2O
Yotvata, *Israel* 171 R5
You, river, *China* 180 PI2
Youghal, *Ire.* 143 U5
Youghal Bay, *Ire.* 143 U5
Young, *N.S.W., Austral.* 211 YI3
Young, Mount, *Austral.* 210 C9
Young Island, *Bahamas* 120 E7
Young's Rock, *Pitcairn I., U.K.* 219 Q23
Youngstown, *Ohio, U.S.* 99 PI6
Youth, Isle of *see* Juventud, Isla de la, *Cuba* 116 J5
Youxian, *China* 183 N4
Youyang, *China* 182 MI
Youyi Feng (Tavan Bogd Uul), peak, *China, Mongolia* 180 C8
Yovan, *Taj.* 176 J7
Yovkovo, *Bulg.* 153 GI7
Yovo, island, *P.N.G.* 217 HI4
Yozgat, *Turk.* 168 EIO
Ypé Jhú, *Parag.* 130 MII
Ypres *see* Ieper, *Belg.* 146 LIO
Ypsilanti, *Mich., U.S.* 98 MI2
Ypsilí *see* Strongílí, island, *Gr.* 155 N22
Yreka, *Calif., U.S.* 108 L3
Yrghyz, river, *Kaz.* 174 E9
Yrghyz, *Kaz.* 174 EIO
Ysabel Channel, *P.N.G.* 213 B2O
Ysyk Köl, lake, *Kyrg.* 176 EI3
Ysyk-Köl *see* Balykchy, *Kyrg.* 176 EI2
Ytterån, *Sw.* 140 HI2
Ytyk Kyuyel', *Russ.* 159 GI8
Yuan, river, *China* 182 M3
Yuan (Red), river, *China* 180 PII
Yuan'an, *China* 182 K3
Yuanbaoshan, *China* 182 B8
Yüanli, *Taiwan, China* 183 Q9
Yuanling, *China* 182 M2
Yuanqu, *China* 182 G4
Yuba, river, *Calif., U.S.* 109 Q4
Yuba City, *Calif., U.S.* 109 Q4
Yūbari, *Japan* 184 FI4
Yuben', *Taj.* 176 KIO
Yūbetsu, *Japan* 184 EI5
Yucatan Channel, *Cuba, Mex.* 80 N7
Yucatán Peninsula, *Mex.* 115 HI6
Yucca, *Ariz., U.S.* 107 S5
Yucca Flat, *Nev., U.S.* 109 TII
Yucca Valley, *Calif., U.S.* 109 XIO
Yucheng, *China* 182 F7
Yuci, *China* 182 E4
Yudino, *Russ.* 156 JI4
Yuendumu, *N. Terr., Austral.* 211 T8
Yueqing, *China* 183 N9
Yueyang, *China* 182 M4
Yugan, *China* 182 M7
Yugorenok, *Russ.* 159 GI9
Yugorskiy Poluostrov, *Russ.* 158 FII
Yuhuan Dao, *China* 183 NIO
Yukagir, *Russ.* 159 EI7
Yukagirskoye Ploskogor'ye, *Russ.* 159 DI9
Yukon, river, *N. Amer.* 80 CI
Yukon, *Can.* 82 F8
Yukon, *Okla., U.S.* 102 GIO
Yukon-Charley Rivers National Preserve, *Alas., U.S.* III FI8
Yukon Delta, *Alas., U.S.* 110 GI2
Yukon Flats, *Alas., U.S.* 84 N4
Yukon Plateau, *N. Amer.* 80 D3
Yüksekova, *Turk.* 169 HI8
Yulara, *N. Terr., Austral.* 211 U7
Yuleba, *Qnsld., Austral.* 211 VI4
Yüli, *Taiwan, China* 183 RIO
Yuli, *China* 180 F7
Yulin, *China* 182 E3
Yulin, *China* 183 R2
Yuma, *Ariz., U.S.* 107 U4
Yuma, *Colo., U.S.* 106 LI5

Yumbi, *Dem. Rep. of the Congo* 198 K8
Yumen (Laojunmiao), *China* 180 GIO
Yumenzhen, *China* 180 GIO
Yumrukaya Burnu, *Turk.* 168 BIO
Yumurtalık, *Turk.* 168 JIO
Yunan, *China* 183 R3
Yunaska Island, *Alas., U.S.* 110 P8
Yuncheng, *China* 182 G3
Yungas, region, *S. Amer.* 126 G5
Yunhe, *China* 181 LI6
Yunotsu, *Japan* 185 P6
Yunta, *S. Aust., Austral.* 211 XIO
Yunxi, *China* 182 J3
Yunxian, *China* 182 J3
Yunxiao, *China* 183 R7
Yunyang, *China* 182 K2
Yuribey, *Russ.* 158 FI2
Yurimaguas, *Peru* 130 F3
Yur'yevets, *Russ.* 156 HI2
Yur'yev Pol'skiy, *Russ.* 156 HIO
Yü Shan, *Taiwan, China* 183 RIO
Yushan, *China* 182 M8
Yushu, *China* 180 K9
Yuste, Monasterio de, *Sp.* 144 G8
Yusufeli, *Turk.* 169 DI6
Yutian, *China* 182 D7
Yutian, *China* 180 H5
Yuxi, *China* 180 PII
Yuxian, *China* 182 D6
Yuxian, *China* 182 E5
Yuza, *Japan* 184 LI2
Yuzawa, *Japan* 184 KI3
Yuzha, *Russ.* 156 HII
Yuzhno Sakhalinsk, *Russ.* 159 K22
Yuzhnyy, *Kaz.* 174 DIO
Yuzhnyy, *Russ.* 157 SI4
Yuzhnyy, Mys, *Russ.* 159 F2I
Yverdon, *Switz.* 150 BI
Yvetot, *Fr.* 147 N8

Z

Za, river, *China* 180 K9
Zaanstad, *Neth.* 146 HI2
Zabaykal'sk, *Russ.* 159 LI7
Zabbar, *Malta* 161 K23
Zabīd, *Yemen* 172 Q8
Zābol, *Iran* 173 EI7
Zābolī, *Iran* 173 HI8
Zabrze, *Pol.* 149 GI4
Zacapa, *Guatemala* 115 LI6
Zacatecas, *Mex.* 114 GIO
Zadar (Zara), *Croatia* 152 F5
Zadoi, *China* 180 K9
Zafóra, island, *Gr.* 155 NI7
Zafra, *Sp.* 144 J7
Żagań, *Pol.* 148 FI2
Zagorá, *Gr.* 154 FII
Zagora, *Mor.* 196 C8
Zagoria, range, *Gr.* 154 E7
Zagreb, *Croatia* 152 D6
Zagros, Kūhhā-ye (Zagros Mountains), *Iran* 172 DII
Zagros Mountains *see* Zagros, Kūhhā-ye, *Iran* 172 EII
Zaháro, *Gr.* 154 K9
Zāhedān, *Iran* 173 FI7
Zahirabad, *India* 178 M6
Zaḥlé, *Leb.* 170 J7
Zaḥrān, *Saudi Arabia* 172 N9
Zaječar, *Serb.* 152 GI2
Zakamensk, *Russ.* 159 MI5
Zakataly, *Azerb.* 169 C2O
Zakho, *Iraq* 172 B9
Zakhodnyaya, river, *Belarus* 156 J6
Zákinthos, *Gr.* 154 J7
Zákinthos (Zante), island, *Gr.* 154 K7
Zakopane, *Pol.* 149 HI5
Zákros, *Gr.* 155 QI6
Zalaegerszeg, *Hung.* 149 MI3
Zalantun, *China* 181 CI6
Zalău, *Rom.* 152 CI2
Zalewo, *Pol.* 149 BI5
Zalew Szczeciński *see* Stettiner Haff, *Ger., Pol.* 148 CII
Zalim, *Saudi Arabia* 172 K8
Zamakh, *Yemen* 172 PII
Zambeze *see* Zambezi, river, *Angola, Mozambique* 202 D9
Zambeze River Delta, *Mozambique* 203 GI3

Zambezi *see* Zambeze, river, *Zambia* 202 F9
Zambezi, *Zambia* 202 E9
Zambezi, Source of the, *Zambia* 194 M8
Zambia, *Af.* 195 M2I
Zamboanga, *Philippines* 189 FI4
Zambrów, *Pol.* 149 CI7
Zamindavar, region, *Afghan.* 177 Q3
Zamora, *Ecua.* 128 L3
Zamora, *Sp.* 144 D8
Zamość, *Pol.* 149 FI8
Zanaga, *Congo* 201 MI7
Zanda, *China* 180 K4
Zanderij, *Suriname* 129 EI6
Zanesville, *Ohio, U.S.* 99 RI4
Zangla, *India* 177 NI4
Zanguinasso, *Côte d'Ivoire* 200 F8
Zanjān, *Iran* 172 CII
Zante *see* Zákinthos, island, *Gr.* 154 K7
Zanthus, *W. Aust., Austral.* 211 W5
Zanzibar, island, *Tanzania* 199 MI5
Zanzibar, *Tanzania* 199 MI5
Zaouatallaz, *Alg.* 196 EI2
Zaoyang, *China* 182 K4
Zaozhuang, *China* 182 H7
Zapadna Morava, river, *Serb.* 152 GIO
Zapadnaya Dvina, *Russ.* 156 J7
Zapadno Sibirskaya Ravnina, *Russ.* 158 HII
Zapala, *Arg.* 133 P7
Zapata, *Tex., U.S.* 103 V8
Zapata, Peninsula de, *Cuba* 116 H7
Zapiga, *Chile* 132 C7
Zapiola Ridge, *Atl. Oc.* 237 U7
Zaporizhzhya, *Ukr.* 157 Q8
Zara *see* Zadar, *Croatia* 152 F5
Zara, *Turk.* 168 EI2
Zarafshon, *Uzb.* 174 KII
Zarafshon Range, *Taj.* 176 H7
Zaragoza, *Sp.* 145 DI4
Zarand, *Iran* 173 FI5
Zaranj, *Afghan.* 177 Q2
Zarautz, *Sp.* 144 BI2
Zaraysk, *Russ.* 156 KIO
Zaraza, *Venez.* 128 CIO
Zard, Kūh-e, *Iran* 172 EI2
Zaria, *Nigeria* 201 FI4
Zárkos, *Gr.* 154 FIO
Zărneşti, *Rom.* 153 EI4
Zaruma, *Ecua.* 128 L2
Żary, *Pol.* 148 EII
Zaskar Mountains, *India* 177 NI5
Zatish'ye, *Russ.* 159 D2O
Zatobyl, *Kaz.* 174 BII
Zatoka, *Ukr.* 157 S5
Zavolzhsk, *Russ.* 156 HII
Zawiercie, *Pol.* 149 GI5
Zāwiyat Masūs, *Lib.* 197 CI5
Zawr, Ra's az, *Saudi Arabia* 172 HI2
Zayaki Jangal, *Pak.* 177 T5
Zaysan, *Kaz.* 175 EI9
Zaysan Köli, *Kaz.* 175 EI9
Zayü, *China* 180 M9
Zdolbuniv, *Ukr.* 157 N3
Zealand, island, *Den.* 138 E6
Zebbuġ, *Malta* 161 H2O
Zebbuġ, *Malta* 161 K22
Zeča, island, *Croatia* 152 E4
Zednes, peak, *Mauritania* 196 E6
Zeeland, *Mich., U.S.* 98 M9
Zefat, *Israel* 170 K6
Zeil, Mount, *Austral.* 210 F8
Zeist, *Neth.* 146 JI3
Zejtun, *Malta* 161 L23
Zelee, Cape, *Solomon Is.* 217 P2O
Zelenchukskaya, *Russ.* 157 TI2
Zelenodol'sk, *Russ.* 156 JI4
Zelenoe, *Kaz.* 174 E6
Zelenogorsk, *Russ.* 156 E6
Zelenogradsk, *Russ.* 156 JI
Zelenokumsk, *Russ.* 157 TI3
Železná Ruda, *Czech Rep.* 148 JIO
Železnik, *Serb.* 152 FIO
Zelzate, *Belg.* 146 KII
Zemetchino, *Russ.* 156 LI2
Zemio, *Cen. Af. Rep.* 198 HII
Zemongo, *Cen. Af. Rep.* 198 GIO
Zencirli, site, *Turk.* 168 HII
Zenica, *Bosn. & Herzg.* 152 F7
Zeni Su, island, *Japan* 185 RII
Zenobia, ruin, *Syr.* 170 EI2
Žepče, *Bosn. & Herzg.* 152 F8
Zereh Depression, *Afghan.* 177 R2

Zerf, Ger. 160 KI2
Zermatt, Switz. 150 C3
Zernez, Switz. 150 B5
Zernograd, Russ. 157 RII
Zestap'oni, Rep. of Georgia 169 BI7
Zetland see Shetland Islands, islands,
 Scot., U.K. 142 CI2
Zeya, Russ. 159 KI9
Zgharta, Leb. 170 H7
Zgierz, Pol. 149 EI5
Zgorzelec, Pol. 148 FII
Zhalpaqtal, Kaz. 174 D5
Zhaltyr, Kaz. 175 DI3
Zhanatal, Kaz. 174 GIO
Zhangaly, Kaz. 174 F5
Zhangaözen, Kaz. 174 H6
Zhanga Qazan, Kaz. 174 E5
Zhangaqorghan, Kaz. 174 HI2
Zhangatas, Kaz. 175 HI3
Zhangbei, China 182 C6
Zhangguangcai Ling, China 181 DI8
Zhangjiakou, China 182 C6
Zhangping, China 183 Q7
Zhangpu, China 183 R7
Zhangshu, China 183 N6
Zhangwu, China 182 BIO
Zhangye, China 180 GII
Zhangzhou, China 183 Q7
Zhangzi, China 182 G4
Zhanhua, China 182 E8
Zhanjiang, China 183 T2
Zhanyi, China 180 NII
Zhao'an, China 183 R7
Zhaoqing, China 183 R3
Zhaosu, China 180 E6
Zhaotong, China 180 MII
Zhaoxian, China 182 E6
Zhapo, China 183 S3
Zhaqsy, Kaz. 174 CI2
Zharkamys, Kaz. 174 F8
Zharkent, Kaz. 175 HI8
Zharma, Kaz. 175 EI7
Zharmysh, Kaz. 174 H6
Zhashui, China 182 H2
Zhaslyk, Uzb. 174 H8
Zhayrang, Kaz. 175 FI3
Zhayylma, Kaz. 174 DIO
Zhayyq (Ural), river, Kaz. 174 E6
Zhdanov, Azerb. 169 E2I
Zhecheng, China 182 H6
Zhelezĭnka, Kaz. 175 BI5
Zheleznodorozhnyy, Russ. 158 F9
Zheleznogorsk, Russ. 156 M8
Zheleznovodsk, Russ. 157 TI3
Zhem, river, Kaz. 174 F8
Zhemgang, Bhutan 178 FI3
Zhenba, China 182 JI
Zhenghe, China 183 N8
Zhenglan Qi (Xulun Hoh), China
 182 B7
Zhengxiangbai Qi, China 182 B6
Zhengzhou, China 182 H5
Zhenjiang, China 182 K8
Zhenlai, China 181 DI6
Zhenping, China 182 J2
Zhenyuan, China 182 GI
Zhenyuan, China 183 NI
Zhenyuan, China 180 PIO
Zherdevka, Russ. 156 MII
Zhetiqara, Kaz. 174 CIO
Zhexi Shuiki, China 183 N3
Zhezqazghan, Kaz. 174 FI2
Zhicheng, China 182 L3
Zhidan, China 182 F2
Zhigansk, Russ. 159 GI7
Zhigulevsk, Russ. 156 KI5
Zhijiang, China 183 N2
Zhilaya Kosa, Kaz. 174 F6
Zhil'gur, Russ. 159 HI8
Zhilinda, Russ. 159 FI5
Zhlobin, Belarus 156 L6
Zhmerynka, Ukr. 157 P4
Zhob, river, Pak. 177 Q8
Zhob, Pak. 177 Q8
Zhokhova, Ostrov, Russ. 159 CI7
Zhongba, China 180 L5
Zhongdian, China 180 MIO
Zhongning, China 180 HI2
Zhongshan, station, Antarctica
 227 G2O
Zhongshan, China 183 Q3
Zhongwei, China 180 HI2
Zhongxian, China 182 LI
Zhongxiang, China 182 K4
Zhosaly, Kaz. 174 GII

Zhoukou, China 182 J5
Zhoushan, China 182 LIO
Zhoushan Dao, China 182 LIO
Zhoushan Qundao, islands, China
 182 LIO
Zhovtneve, Ukr. 157 R6
Zhu (Pearl River), river, China
 183 S4
Zhuanghe, China 182 DIO
Zhucheng, China 182 G8
Zhuji, China 182 L9
Zhukovka, Russ. 156 L7
Zhuolu, China 182 C6
Zhuozhou, China 182 D6
Zhuozi, China 182 C4
Zhuozi Shan, China 182 CI
Zhupanovo, Russ. 159 F23
Zhuryn, Kaz. 174 E8
Zhushan, China 182 J2
Zhuzhou, China 183 N4
Zhympity, Kaz. 174 D6
Zhytomyr, Ukr. 157 N5
Zi, river, China 182 M3
Ziarat, Pak. 177 R6
Zibak, Afghan. 176 K9
Zibo, China 182 F8
Zicavo, Fr. 150 K4
Zichang, China 182 F2
Zielona Góra, Pol. 148 EI2
Zigana Geçidi, pass, Turk. 169 DI4
Zigar, Taj. 176 J8
Zigey, Chad 197 HI4
Zigong, China 180 LI2
Ziguinchor, Senegal 196 H4
Zile, Turk. 168 EII
Žilina, Slovakia 149 JI4
Zillah, Lib. 197 DI5
Zima, Russ. 159 LI5
Zimbabwe, Af. 195 N2I
Zimnicea, Bulg. 153 GI5
Zimnicea, Rom. 153 GI5
Zimovniki, Russ. 157 RI2
Zinder, Niger 196 HI2
Zinjibār, Yemen 172 RIO
Zion, Ill., U.S. 98 M7
Zion, St. Kitts & Nevis 121 CI8
Zion National Park, Utah, U.S.
 107 P6
Žirje, island, Croatia 152 G5
Zirndorf, Ger. 148 H8
Zittau, Ger. 148 GII
Živinice, Bosn. & Herzg. 152 F8
Ziway Hāyk', Eth. 199 GI5
Zixi, China 183 N7
Zixing, China 183 P4
Ziyang, China 182 JI
Ziyuan, China 183 P2
Zizhou, China 182 E3
Zlarin, island, Croatia 152 G5
Zlatoust, Russ. 158 J8
Zlatoustovsk, Russ. 159 J2O
Zlín, Czech Rep. 149 JI4
Złotów, Pol. 149 CI3
Zmari Sar, peak, Afghan. 177 Q5
Zmeica, Lacul, Rom. 153 FI8
Zmeinogorsk, Russ. 158 LII
Zmiyev, Ukr. 157 P9
Zmiyinyy, Ostriv, Ukr. 157 S5
Znamenka, Kaz. 175 DI7
Znamensk, Russ. 156 J2
Znam'yanka, Ukr. 157 Q7
Znojmo, Czech Rep. 148 JI2
Zoetermeer, Neth. 146 JI2
Zofar, Israel 171 Q5
Zofingen, Switz. 150 A3
Zogang, China 180 L9
Zolochiv, Ukr. 157 N3
Zolochiv, Ukr. 157 N8
Zolotaya Gora, Russ. 159 KI8
Zolotonosha, Ukr. 157 P6
Zomba, Malawi 203 EI3
Zongo, Dem. Rep. of the Congo
 198 H8
Zonguldak, Turk. 168 C7
Zonza, Fr. 150 K4
Zor Dağ, Turk. 169 EI8
Zorkol Lake, Afghan., Taj. 176 JII
Zorritos, Peru 130 E2
Zouar, Chad 197 FI4
Zoushi, China 182 M3
Zouxian, China 182 G7
Zrenjanin (Petrovgrad), Serb. 152 EIO
Zubayr, Jazā'ir az, Yemen 172 Q8
Zubovo, Russ. 156 F9
Zubtsov, Russ. 156 J8

Zuera, Sp. 145 DI4
Z̧ufār, region, Oman 173 NI4
Zug, Switz. 150 B4
Zugdidi, Rep. of Georgia 169 BI6
Zugspitze, peak, Aust., Ger. 148 L8
Zululand, region, S. Af. 202 KI2
Žumberačka Gora, Croatia, Slov.
 152 D5
Zumberge Coast, Antarctica 226 G7
Zumbo, Mozambique 202 EII
Zunhua, China 182 D8
Zuni, river, Ariz., U.S. 107 S9
Zuni Pueblo, N. Mex., U.S. 107 SIO
Zunyi, China 180 MI2
Zuoz, Switz. 150 C5
Zürich, Switz. 150 A4
Zur Kowt, Afghan. 177 N8
Zurrieq, Malta 161 L22
Zuru, Nigeria 201 EI3
Žut, island, Croatia 152 G5
Zutphen, Neth. 146 JI4
Zuwārah, Lib. 197 BI3
Zvenyhorodka, Ukr. 157 P6
Zvishavane, Zimb. 202 GII
Zvolen, Slovakia 149 JI5
Zvornik, Bosn. & Herzg. 152 F9
Zwettl, Aust. 148 KII
Zwickau, Ger. 148 G9
Zwolle, La., U.S. 100 M6
Zwolle, Neth. 146 HI3
Zygi, Cyprus 160 Q8
Zyrya, Azerb. 169 D23
Zyryanka, Russ. 159 EI9
Zyryanovo, Russ. 159 HI3
Zyryanovsk, Kaz. 175 DI9

Moon Index

LUNAR EQUIVALENTS

Lacus .... lake
Mare .... sea
Montes .... range
Oceanus .... ocean
Palus .... marsh
Rupes .... scarp
Sinus .... bay
Vallis .... valley

All other entries are craters.

A

Abel, 249 M18
Abulfeda, 249 K14
Aestuum, Sinus, 248 G12
Agrippa, 249 H13
Aitken, 250 K12
Albategnius, 249 K13
Al-Biruni, 250 F6
Alden, 250 L7
Aliacensis, 249 L13
Almanon, 249 K14
Alpes, Montes, 248 D12
Alpes, Vallis, 249 D13
Alphonsus, 248 K12
Altai, Rupes, 249 K14
Amundsen, 249 R13
Anaxagoras, 248 B12
Anaximenes, 248 B11
Anders, 251 M15
Anderson, 250 G12
Anguis, Mare, 249 F18
Ansgarius, 249 K19
Antoniadi, 251 P13
Apenninus, Montes, 248 G12
Apianus, 249 L13
Apollo, 251 M14
Appleton, 250 E11
Archimedes, 248 F12
Aristarchus, 248 F9
Aristillus, 249 E13
Aristoteles, 249 D14
Arnold, 249 C14
Artamonov, 250 F7
Arzachel, 248 K12
Atlas, 249 D15
Australe, Mare, 250 N7
Avicenna, 251 D18
Avogadro, 250 C12
Azophi, 249 K14

B

Baade, Vallis, 248 N8
Babbage, 248 C10
Babcock, 250 H6
Baillaud, 249 B14
Bailly, 248 Q10
Balboa, 248 F6
Balmer, 249 L18
Banachiewicz, 249 H19
Barocius, 249 M14
Barringer, 251 L15
Barrow, 249 C13
Bel'kovich, 249 B16
Bell, 251 F19
Bellingshausen, 251 P13
Belyaev, 250 F10
Berosus, 249 E17
Bettinus, 248 P11
Billy, 248 K8
Birkhoff, 251 C14
Blancanus, 248 P12
Blanchard, 251 P16
Boguslawsky, 249 Q14
Boltzmann, 251 P16
Bond, W., 249 C13
Borman, 251 M15
Bose, 251 N13
Boussingault, 249 Q14
Bragg, 251 D17
Brianchon, 251 B14

Bridgman, 250 D10
Brouwer, 251 M16
Buffon, 251 M16
Bullialdus, 248 K11
Busching, 249 M14
Byrd, 249 B13
Byrgius, 248 L8

C

Cabannes, 251 P13
Cabeus, 248 Q12
Campbell, 250 D11
Cannizzaro, 251 C16
Cantor, 250 E8
Capuanus, 248 M11
Carnot, 251 D14
Carpatus, Montes, 248 G10
Carpenter, 248 B11
Casatus, 248 Q12
Cassini, 249 E13
Catharina, 249 K15
Caucasus, Montes, 249 E13
Chaffee, 251 M14
Chamberlin, 250 Q9
Chandler, 250 E12
Chaplygin, 250 J10
Chapman, 251 C17
Chappell, 251 D13
Charlier, 251 E16
Chebyshev, 251 M16
Chretien, 250 N11
Clairaut, 249 N13
Clavius, 248 N12
Cleomedes, 249 F17
Cockcroft, 251 F14
Cognitum, Mare, 248 J10
Colombo, 249 K16
Compton, 250 C9
Comstock, 251 F17
Condorcet, 249 G18
Copernicus, 248 H11
Cordillera, Montes, 248 L7
Coriolis, 250 H12
Coulomb, 251 C16
Crisium, Mare, 249 G17
Cruger, 248 K7
Curie, 250 L6
Curtius, 249 P13
Cyrano, 250 K11
Cyrillus, 249 K15

D

Daedalus, 250 J12
D'Alembert, 250 D12
Dante, 251 F13
Darwin, 248 L7
Davisson, 251 M13
Debye, 251 D13
Delambre, 249 J14
DeLaRue, 249 C15
Dellinger, 250 J9
Demonax, 249 Q14
Desargues, 248 B10
De Sitter, 249 B13
Deslandres, 248 L12
Dobrovol'skij, 250 K8
Doppelmayer, 248 L9
Doppler, 251 K14
Drygalski, 248 Q11

E

Eddington, 248 F7
Einstein, 248 F6
Elvey, 251 G19
Emden, 251 C13
Endymion, 249 D15
Englehardt, 251 H14
Eotvos, 250 M9
Epidemiarum, Palus, 248 L10
Eratosthenes, 248 G12

Erro, 250 H6
Esnault-Pelterie, 251 D15
Euctemon, 249 B13
Eudoxus, 249 E14
Euler, 248 F10
Evershed, 251 E14

F

Fabricius, 249 M15
Fabry, 250 D8
Fecunditatis, Mare, 249 J17
Fermi, 250 L8
Fersman, 251 G17
Firmicus, 249 H18
Fitzgerald, 251 F13
Fizeau, 251 P15
Flammarion, 248 J12
Fleming, 250 G7
Fontenelle, 248 C12
Fowler, 251 E15
Fracastorius, 249 K15
Fra Mauro, 248 J10
Franklin, 249 E16
Freundlich, 250 F12
Frigoris, Mare, 249 D13
Furnerius, 249 M17

G

Gadomski, 251 E15
Gagarin, 250 K10
Galois, 251 K15
Gamow, 250 C11
Gartner, 249 C14
Gassendi, 248 K9
Gauricus, 248 L12
Gauss, 249 D17
Geminus, 249 E16
Gemma Frisius, 249 L14
Gerard, 248 D8
Gerasimovich, 251 L17
Gibbs, 249 L19
Gilbert, 249 J18
Goddard, 249 G19
Goldschmidt, 249 B13
Green, 250 H8
Grimaldi, 248 J7
Grissom, 251 N15
Gruemberger, 248 P12
Gutenberg, 249 J16
Guyot, 250 G7

H

Haemus, Montes, 249 G13
Hagecius, 249 P15
Hahn, 249 E18
Hansteen, 248 K8
Hartmann, 250 H9
Hase, 249 M17
Hausen, 248 Q9
Hayn, 249 B15
Heaviside, 250 J12
Hecataeus, 249 L18
Helberg, 251 F18
Helmholtz, 249 Q15
Henyey, 251 G15
Hercules, 249 D15
Hermite, 248 A12
Herodotus, 248 F9
Herschel, J., 248 C11
Hertz, 250 G7
Hertzsprung, 251 H17
Hess, 250 N12
Hevelius, 248 H7
Heymans, 251 B14
Hilbert, 250 K7
Hipparchus, 249 J13
Hirayama, 250 J6
Houzeau, 251 K17
Hubble, 249 F19
Humboldt, 249 L18

Humboldtianum, Mare, 249 C16
Humorum, Mare, 248 L9

I

Icarus, 251 J13
Imbrium, Mare, 248 E11
Ingenii, Mare, 250 M11
Inghirami, 248 N9
Ioffe, 251 K17
Iridum, Sinus, 248 D10

J

Jackson, 251 F14
Jansky, 249 G19
Janssen, 249 N15
Jarvis, 251 M15
Joliot, 250 E6
Joule, 251 F15
Jules Verne, 250 M10
Julius Caesar, 249 H14
Jura, Montes, 248 D10

K

Kane, 249 C14
Karpinskiy, 250 B12
Kastner, 249 J19
Keeler, 250 J11
Kekule, 251 G16
Kepler, 248 H9
Kibal'chich, 251 H15
King, 250 H8
Kircher, 248 P11
Klaproth, 248 P11
Kohlschutter, 250 G10
Kolhorster, 251 G18
Komarov, 250 F10
Kondratyuk, 250 K7
Konstantinov, 250 G11
Korolev, 251 J14
Kostinskiy, 250 G8
Kovalevskaya, 251 E16
Krafft, 248 G7
Krasovskiy, 251 H13
Kugler, 250 P9
Kurchatov, 250 E10

L

La Caille, 249 L13
Lagrange, 248 M8
Lamarck, 248 L7
Lamb, 250 N8
Lame, 249 K18
Landau, 251 D16
Langemak, 250 J8
Langrenus, 249 J18
La Perouse, 249 K18
Larmor, 251 F13
Lavoisier, 248 D7
Lebedev, 250 N8
Lebedinskiy, 251 H14
Leeuwenhoek, 251 L13
Legendre, 249 M18
Le Gentil, 248 Q11
Leibnitz, 250 M12
Lemaitre, 251 P14
Letronne, 248 J9
Leuschner, 251 H18
Levi-Civita, 250 L9
Licetus, 249 M13
Lilius, 249 N13
Lomonosov, 250 E7
Longomontanus, 248 N11
Lorentz, 251 E18
Lucretius, 251 J17
Lyman, 250 P12
Lyot, 249 P17

M

Mach, 251 G15
Macrobius, 249 F16
Maginus, 248 N12
Maksutov, 251 M13
Mandel'shtam, 250 H11
Manzinus, 249 P13
Marconi, 250 J10
Marginis, Mare, 249 G19
Marginis, Mare, 250 G6
Marius, 248 G8
Markov, 248 C9
Maunder, 251 K19
Maurolycus, 249 M14
Maxwell, 250 E7
McAuliffe, 251 L15
McLaughlin, 251 C17
McMath, 251 G14
McNair, 251 M15
Medii, Sinus, 248 H12
Mee, 248 N10
Meitner, 250 K7
Mendel, 251 N16
Mendeleev, 250 H9
Mercurius, 249 D16
Mersenius, 248 L9
Messala, 249 D17
Metius, 249 M15
Mezentsev, 251 B14
Michelson, 251 H17
Milankovic, 250 B12
Millikan, 250 D9
Milne, 250 M8
Minkowski, 251 N14
Minnaert, 250 P12
Mitra, 251 G14
Mohorovicic, 251 K14
Moretus, 248 P12
Mortis, Lacus, 249 D14
Moscoviense, Mare, 250 F10
Murakami, 251 L15
Mutus, 249 P14

N

Nansen, 250 B12
Nassau, 250 L12
Nectaris, Mare, 249 K15
Neper, 249 G19
Nernst, 251 D18
Neujmin, 250 L8
Newton, 248 Q12
Niepce, 251 B14
Nother, 251 B15
Nubium, Mare, 248 K11
Numerov, 251 P13

O

Oken, 249 N17
Olbers, 248 H7
Olcott, 250 F8
Omar Khayyam, 251 C16
Onizuka, 251 M14
Oppenheimer, 251 M13
Oresme, 250 M12
Orientale, Mare, 251 L19
Orontius, 248 M12
Ostwald, 250 G8

P

Pallas, 248 H12
Palmieri, 248 L9
Papaleksi, 250 H11
Paracelsus, 250 L11
Parenago, 251 F17
Pascal, 248 B11
Paschen, 251 K16
Pasteur, 250 K7
Patsaev, 250 K9
Pauli, 250 N10

Pavlov, 250 L10
Perepelkin, 250 J8
Petavius, 249 L17
Petermann, 249 B14
Petropavlovskiy, 251 E17
Petzval, 251 P15
Phillips, 249 L18
Philolaus, 248 B12
Phocylides, 248 P9
Piccolomini, 249 L15
Pilatre, 248 Q9
Pingre, 248 P9
Pitatus, 248 L11
Pitiscus, 249 N14
Pizzetti, 250 M8
Planck, 250 P10
Planck, Vallis, 250 P10
Plaskett, 251 B13
Plato, 248 D12
Playfair, 249 L13
Plinius, 249 G14
Plutarch, 249 F18
Poincare, 250 N11
Poinsot, 251 B13
Polzunov, 250 F8
Poncelet, 248 B11
Pontecoulant, 249 P16
Posidonius, 249 F15
Poynting, 251 G16
Prandtl, 250 P11
Procellarum, Oceanus, 248 E8
Proclus, 249 G16
Ptolemaeus, 248 J12
Purbach, 248 L12
Putredinis, Palus, 249 F13
Pyrenaeus, Montes, 249 K16
Pythagoras, 248 B10

R

Racah, 250 K12
Raimond, 251 G14
Rayleigh, 249 E18
Razumov, 251 E17
Reinhold, 248 H11
Resnik, 251 M15
Rheita, 249 M16
Rheita, Vallis, 249 M16
Riccioli, 248 J6
Riemann, 249 D18
Riphaeus, Montes, 248 J10
Robertson, 251 F18
Roche, 250 M10
Rontgen, 251 E18
Rook, Montes, 248 L6
Roris, Sinus, 248 D9
Rosenberger, 249 P15
Rowland, 251 D13
Rozhdestvenskiy, 251 B13
Rumford, 251 L14
Russell, 248 E7

S

Sacrobosco, 249 L14
Saha, 250 J6
Scaliger, 250 L7
Scheiner, 248 P11
Schickard, 248 N9
Schiller, 248 N10
Schlesinger, 251 D15
Schliemann, 250 J10
Schluter, 248 J6
Schneller, 251 E14
Schomberger, 249 Q13
Schrodinger, 250 Q11
Schrodinger, Vallis, 250 Q10
Schuster, 250 H10
Schwarzchild, 250 B11
Scobee, 251 L15
Scott, 249 Q13
Seares, 250 B12
Sechenov, 251 J16
Segner, 248 P10
Serenitatis, Mare, 249 F14
Seyfert, 250 F8
Sharonov, 250 G12
Shayn, 250 F12
Short, 248 Q12
Sierpinski, 250 L11
Sirsalis, 248 K8
Sklodowska, 250 L6

Smith, 251 L15
Smoluchowski, 251 B16
Smythii, Mare, 249 H19
Snellius, 249 L17
Sommerfeld, 251 C13
Somni, Palus, 249 G16
Somniorum, Lacus, 249 E15
Spencer Jones, 250 G11
Spitzbergensis, Montes, 248 E12
Spumans, Mare, 249 H18
Stebbins, 251 C14
Stefan, 251 D16
Sternberg, 251 G17
Sternfeld, 251 L15
Stevinus, 249 M16
Stiborius, 249 M15
Stofler, 249 M13
Stormer, 250 C11
Strabo, 249 C15
Struve, 248 F7
Subbotin, 250 L9
Szilard, 250 E7

T

Taurus, Montes, 249 F16
Teneriffe, Montes, 248 D12
Theaetetus, 249 E13
Theophilus, 249 J15
Thomson, 250 L12
Tikhov, 250 C12
Timocharis, 248 F11
Tranquillitatis, Mare, 249 H15
Trumpler, 250 F12
Tsander, 251 H15
Tsiolkovskiy, 250 K9
Tycho, 248 M12

U

Undarum, Mare, 249 H18

V

Valier, 250 H12
Van de Graaff, 250 L12
Van der Waals, 250 N9
Van Rhijn, 250 D10
Van't Hoff, 251 C15
Vaporum, Mare, 249 G13
Vasco da Gama, 248 G6
Vavilov, 251 J16
Vendelinus, 249 K17
Vening Meinesz, 250 H11
Vernadskiy, 250 F9
Vesalius, 250 J7
Vestine, 250 E7
Vieta, 248 L8
Vlacq, 249 N15
Volkov, 250 K8
Volta, 248 C9
Von der Pahlen, 251 L16
Von Karman, 250 M12
Von Neumann, 250 E11
Von Zeipel, 251 E15

W

Walther, 249 L13
Wargentin, 248 N9
Waterman, 250 L9
Wegener, 251 D17
Wells, 250 D9
Werner, 249 L13
Weyl, 251 G17
White, 251 N14
Wiechert, 250 Q12
Wiener, 250 E10
Wilhelm, 248 M11
Wilsing, 251 K15
Wilson, 248 Q11
Wrottesley, 249 L17
Wyld, 250 J6

Y

Yablochkov, 250 C10
Yamamoto, 250 C12

Z

Zach, 249 P13
Zagut, 249 L14
Zeeman, 251 Q14
Zhukovskiy, 251 H14
Zsigmondy, 251 C16
Zucchius, 248 P10

SPACECRAFT LANDING OR IMPACT SITES

Apollo 11 (Tranquillity Base) 249 H15
Apollo 12 248 J11
Apollo 14 248 J11
Apollo 15 249 F13
Apollo 16 249 J14
Apollo 17 249 G15
Luna 2 249 F13
Luna 5 248 J10
Luna 7 248 H9
Luna 8 248 H7
Luna 9 248 H7
Luna 13 248 F8
Luna 15 249 G17
Luna 16 249 J17
Luna 17 248 E10
Luna 18 249 H17
Luna 20 249 H17
Luna 21 249 F15
Luna 23 249 G17
Luna 24 249 G18
Lunar Prospector 249 R13
Orbiter 1 250 H11
Orbiter 2 250 H6
Orbiter 3 251 G19
Orbiter 5 248 J6
Ranger 4 251 K17
Ranger 6 249 G14
Ranger 7 248 J11
Ranger 8 249 H15
Ranger 9 248 K12
Surveyor 1 248 J9
Surveyor 2 248 H12
Surveyor 3 248 J11
Surveyor 4 248 H12
Surveyor 5 249 H14
Surveyor 6 248 H12
Surveyor 7 248 M12

Printed in Verona, Italy

Acknowledgments

WORLD THEMATIC SECTION

Introduction   pp. 14–15
CONSULTANTS
John Morrison
World Wildlife Fund (WWF)

GRAPHICS
ECOREGIONS: Terrestrial Ecoregions of the World were developed by D.M. Olson, E. Dinerstein, E.D. Wikramanayake, N.D. Burgess, G.V.N. Powell, E.C. Underwood, J.A. D'Amico, I. Itoua, H.E. Strand, J.C. Morrison, C.J. Loucks, T.F. Allnutt, T.H. Ricketts, Y. Kura, J.F. Lamoreux, W.W. Wettengel, P. Hedao, K.R. Kassem, World Wildlife Fund. Marine Ecoregions of the World (MEOW) were developed by the MEOW Working Group, co-chaired by The Nature Conservancy and the World Wildlife Fund (Mark Spalding, Helen Fox, Gerald Allen, Nick Davidson, Zach Ferdana, Max Finlayson, Ben Halpern, Miguel Jorge, Al Lombana, Sara Lourie, Kirsten Martin, Edmund McManus, Jennifer Molnar, Kate Newman, Cheri Recchia, James Robertson).

Structure of the Earth   pp. 22–23
CONSULTANTS
Laurel M. Bybell
U.S. Geological Survey (USGS)

Robert I. Tilling
U.S. Geological Survey (USGS)

GRAPHICS
CONTINENTS ADRIFT IN TIME: Christopher R. Scotese/PALEOMAP Project
CUTAWAY OF THE EARTH: Tibor G. Tóth
TECTONIC BLOCK DIAGRAMS: Susan Sanford
PLATE TECTONICS: *National Geographic Atlas of the World*, 8th ed. Washington, D.C.: The National Geographic Society, 2005
GEOLOGIC TIME: National Geographic Books

Earth's Rocky Exterior   pp. 24–25
CONSULTANTS
Jon Spencer
Arizona Geological Survey

Robert I. Tilling
U.S. Geological Survey (USGS)

GRAPHICS
ROCK CYCLE AND READING EARTH HISTORY: Chapel Design & Marketing and XNR Productions
GLOBAL DISTRIBUTION OF ROCK TYPES: Global distribution of surface rock from *The National Geographic Desk Reference*. Washington, D.C.: The National Geographic Society, 1999. Age of oceanic crust from Simkin et al., *This Dynamic Planet: World Map of Volcanoes, Earthquakes, Impact Craters, and Plate Tectonics*, 3rd ed. Washington, D.C.: USGS, 2006

PHOTOGRAPHS
PAGE 24, (UP) R.D. Griggs, USGS; (CT) Sharon Johnson; (LO) David Muench
PAGE 25, Raymond Gehman/NGS Image Collection

Landforms   pp. 26–29
CONSULTANTS
Sharon Johnson
University of California, Berkeley

Mike Slattery
Texas Christian University

GRAPHICS
FICTIONAL LANDFORMS: *National Geographic World Atlas for Young Explorers*. Washington, D.C.: The National Geographic Society, 2003
DUNES: Chapel Design & Marketing
RIVERS: Steven Fick/Canadian Geographic
GLACIAL LANDFORMS: Steven Fick

SATELLITE IMAGES
MISSISSIPPI RIVER DELTA: Centre National d'Etudes Spatiales (CNES)

PHOTOGRAPHS
PAGE 26, (LE) Joel Sartore/www.joelsartore.com; (CT) Science Photo Library/CORBIS; (UP RT) George F. Mobley; (LO RT) James D. Balog
PAGE 27, (UP LE) Wolfgang Kaehler/CORBIS; (UP CT) Lyle Rosbotham; (UP RT) Adriel Heisey; (LO LE) Marc Moritsch/NGS Image Collection; (LO CT) Peter Essick; (LO RT) Sam Abell, NGS
PAGE 28, (LE) Peter Essick; (CT) Douglas R. Grant; (RT) Tom and Pat Leeson
PAGE 29, (UP CT) Rob Brander; (UP RT) George Veni and James Jasek; (LO LE) Sharon Johnson; (LO RT) Douglas R. Grant/Parks Canada

Surface of the Earth   pp. 30–31
CONSULTANTS
Peter W. Sloss
NOAA National Geophysical Data Center (NGDC)

SATELLITE IMAGES
EARTH SURFACE ELEVATIONS AND DEPTHS, A SLICE OF EARTH, AND HYPSOMETRY: Peter W. Sloss, NOAA National Geophysical Data Center
SNOW DEPTH AND SEA ICE: Data provided by NASA/Goddard Space Flight Center (GSFC), Don Cavalieri, Dorothy Hall, and Gene Carl Feldman
CLOUD COVER: Data provided by NASA/Goddard Institute for Space Studies (GISS), William B. Rossow, and Gene Carl Feldman
DAY AND NIGHT TEMPERATURE DIFFERENCE: Data provided by NASA/GSFC, Joel Susskind, and Gene Carl Feldman
VEGETATION COVER : Data provided by NASA/GSFC, Compton J. Tucker, and Gene Carl Feldman

Land Cover   pp. 32–33
CONSULTANTS
Paul Davis
The Global Land Cover Facility, University of Maryland

SATELLITE IMAGES
GLOBAL LAND COVER COMPOSITION: M. Hansen, R. DeFries, J.R.G. Townshend, and R. Sohlberg. 1998. "Global land cover classification at 1km spatial resolution using a classification tree approach." 1 Km Land Cover Classification Derived from AVHRR; College Park, Maryland: The Global Land Cover Facility. (Note: Data were derived from NOAA AVHRR and NASA Landsat imagery.)

PHOTOGRAPHS
PAGE 32, (UP LE) Tom and Pat Leeson/Photo Researchers; (UP RT) Michael Nichols/NGS Image Collection; (LO LE) Stephen J. Krasemann/Photo Researchers; (LO CT LE) Rod Planck/Photo Researchers; (CT LE) Jim Steinberg/Photo Researchers; (CT RT) Matthew C. Hansen, University of Maryland; (LO CT RT) Gregory G. Dimijian/Photo Researchers; (LO RT) Sharon Johnson
PAGE 33, (LE) Georg Gerster/Photo Researchers; (LO CT LE) Rod Planck/Photo Researchers; (LE CT) Jim Richardson; (RT CT) George Steinmetz; (LO CT RT) Steve McCurry; (RT) B. and C. Alexander/Photo Researchers

Climate   pp. 34–37
CONSULTANTS
William Burroughs

H. Michael Mogil
Certified Consulting Meteorologist (CCM)

Vladimir Ryabinin
World Climate Research Programme

GRAPHICS
TOPOGRAPHY: Chapel Design & Marketing and XNR Productions
GLOBAL AIR TEMPERATURE CHANGES, 1850–2000: Reproduced by kind permission of the Climatic Research Unit.

SATELLITE IMAGES
Images originally created for the GLOBE program by NOAA's National Geophysical Data Center, Boulder, Colorado, U.S.A.
CLOUD COVER: International Satellite Cloud Climatology Project (ISCCP); National Aeronautics and Space Administration (NASA); Goddard Institute for Space Studies (GISS)
PRECIPITATION: Global Precipitation Climatology Project (GPCP); International Satellite Land Surface Climatology Project (ISLSCP)
SOLAR ENERGY: Earth Radiation Budget Experiment (ERBE); Greenhouse Effect Detection Experiment (GEDEX)
TEMPERATURE: National Center for Environmental Prediction (NCEP); National Center for Atmospheric Research (NCAR); National Weather Service (NWS)

PHOTOGRAPHS
PAGE 35, Sharon Johnson

Weather   pp. 38–39
CONSULTANTS
Gerry Bell
National Oceanic and Atmospheric Administration (NOAA)

H. Michael Mogil
Certified Consulting Meteorologist (CCM)

GRAPHICS
WATER CYCLE, AIR MASSES, JET STREAM, WEATHER FRONTS, CLOUD TYPES: Chapel Design & Marketing

SATELLITE IMAGES
HURRICANE IMAGE: NASA Goddard Space Flight Center (GSFC), data from NOAA
EL NIÑO IMAGE SEQUENCE: Courtesy Robert M. Carey, NOAA
LIGHTNING IMAGE: NASA Marshall Space Flight Center Lightning Imaging Sensor (LIS) Instrument Team, Huntsville, Alabama

Biosphere   pp. 40–41
CONSULTANTS
Manuel Colunga-Garcia (Entomology), **Patrick J. Webber** (Plant Biology), **David T. Long** (Geological Sciences), **Stuart H. Gage** (Entomology), **Craig K. Harris** (Sociology)
Earth Systems Science Education Program, Michigan State University

Jane Robertson Vernhes
World Network of Biosphere Reserves, UNESCO

GRAPHICS
BIOSPHERE DYNAMICS: Earth Systems Science Education Program, Michigan State University, and Chapel Design & Marketing
EARTH SYSTEM DYNAMICS: Edward Gazsi
SIZE OF THE BIOSPHERE: The COMET Program and Chapel Design & Marketing
BIOSPHERE OVER TIME: Earth Systems Science Education Program, Michigan State University

SATELLITE IMAGES
BIOSPHERE FROM SPACE: SeaWiFS, NASA/Goddard Space Flight Center, Gene Carl Feldman and ORBIMAGE

Biodiversity   pp. 42–43
CONSULTANTS
Craig Hilton-Taylor
International Union for Conservation of Nature and Natural Resources (IUCN)

Mike Hoffmann
Conservation International

John Morrison
World Wildlife Fund (WWF)

GENERAL REFERENCES
Conservation International: www.biodiversityhotspots.org
International Union for Conservation of Nature and Natural Resources (IUCN): www.iucnredlist.org

GRAPHICS
THE NATURAL WORLD, SPECIES DIVERSITY, AND PROJECTED BIODIVERSITY: Biodiversity. NG Maps for *National Geographic* magazine, February 1999

Population   pp. 44–47
CONSULTANTS
Carl Haub
Population Reference Bureau

Gregory Yetman
Center for International Earth Science Information Network (CIESIN), Columbia University

GENERAL REFERENCES
Center for International Earth Science Information Network (CIESIN), Columbia University: www.ciesin.org
World Migrant Stock: The 2005 Revision Population Database. New York: United Nations Population Division
Population Reference Bureau: www.prb.org
World Urbanization Prospects: The 2007 Revision. Population Division of the Department of Economic and Social Affairs of the United Nations Secretariat. New York: United Nations, 2008

GRAPHICS
POPULATION DENSITY: Center for International Earth Science Information Network (CIESIN), Columbia University, and Centro Internacional de Agricultura Tropical (CIAT), 2005. Gridded Population of the World Version 3 (GPWv3): Population Density Grids—World Population Density, 2005 [map]. Palisades, New York: Socioeconomic Data and Applications Center (SEDAC), Columbia University. Available at http://sedac.ciesin.columbia.edu/gpw.

SATELLITE IMAGES
LIGHTS OF THE WORLD: Composite image: MODIS imagery; ETOPO-2 relief; NOAA/NGDC and DMSP lights at night data

Languages   pp. 48–49
CONSULTANTS
Bernard Comrie
Max Planck Institute for Evolutionary Anthropology

GRAPHICS
VOICES OF THE WORLD, HOW MANY SPEAK WHAT?, VANISHING LANGUAGES, MAJOR LANGUAGE FAMILIES TODAY: *National Geographic Atlas of the World*, 8th ed. Washington, D.C.: The National Geographic Society, 2005
EVOLUTION OF LANGUAGES: *National Geographic Almanac of Geography*. Washington, D.C.: The National Geographic Society, 2005

Religions   pp. 50–51
CONSULTANTS
William M. Bodiford
University of California, Los Angeles

Todd Johnson
Center for the Study of Global Christianity, Gordon-Conwell Theological Seminary

GENERAL REFERENCES
World Religion Database: Institute on Culture, Religion and World Affairs (CURA) at Boston University. www.brill.nl/wrd

PHOTOGRAPHS
PAGE 50, (LE) Jodi Cobb, National Geographic Photographer; (RT) James L. Stanfield
PAGES 50–51, Tony Heiderer
PAGE 51, (LE) Thomas J. Abercrombie; (RT) Annie Griffiths Belt

Health and Education
pp. 52–53

CONSULTANTS

Carlos Castillo-Salgado
Pan American Health Organization (PAHO)/
World Health Organization (WHO)

George Ingram and Annababette Wils
Education Policy and Data Center

Margaret Kruk
United Nations Millennium Project and
University of Michigan School of Public Health

Ruth Levine
Center for Global Development

GENERAL REFERENCES

2008 Report on the Global AIDS Epidemic. World Health Organization and the Joint United Nations Programme on HIV/AIDS, 2008

Education Policy and Data Center: www.epdc.org

Global Burden of Disease Estimates. Geneva: World Health Organization, 2004

Human Development Report, 2007/2008. New York: United Nations Development Programme (UNDP), 2008

UN Millennium Development Goals: www.un.org/millenniumgoals

The State of the World's Children 2008. Table 5: Education. New York: UNICEF, 2008

The World Health Report 2006. Annex table 5. Selected national health accounts indicators. Geneva: World Health Organization, 2006

World Bank list of economies, 2008. Washington, D.C.: World Bank

World Health Statistics, 2008. World Health Organization: www.who.int

National Literacy Rates for Youths (15–24) and Adults (15+)
New York: UNESCO Institute for Statistics, 2008

GRAPHICS

ACCESS TO IMPROVED SANITATION: Adapted from *WHO Water Supply and Sanitation Monitoring Mid-Term Report, 2004.*
DEVELOPING HUMAN CAPITAL: Adapted from Human Capital Projections developed by Education Policy and Data Center.

Conflicts
pp. 54–55

CONSULTANTS

Barbara Harff
Genocide Prevention Advisory Network (www.gpanet.org)

Monty G. Marshall
Center for Systemic Peace and Center for Global Policy, George Mason University

Christian Oxenboll
United Nations High Commissioner for Refugees (UNHCR)

GENERAL REFERENCES

Global Security.org: www.globalsecurity.org

Global Statistics. Internal Displacement Monitoring Centre (iDMC). 2008: www.internal-displacement.org

Monty G. Marshall, Jack A. Goldstone, and Benjamin R. Cole. *Global Report 2009: Conflict, Governance, and State Fragility.* Center for Systemic Peace and Center for Global Policy, George Mason University, 2009.

Proliferation News and Resources. Carnegie Endowment for International Peace. www.carnegieendowment.org/npp

United Nations High Commissioner for Refugees (UNHCR): www.unhcr.org

United Nations Peacekeeping: www.un.org/Depts/dpko/dpko/

Economy
pp. 56–57

CONSULTANTS

William Beyers
University of Washington

Michael Finger
World Trade Organization (WTO)

Richard R. Fix
World Bank

Susan Martin
Institute for the Study of International Migration

GENERAL REFERENCES

CIA World Factbook: www.cia.gov

International Monetary Fund: www.imf.org

International Telecommunication Union: www.itu.int

International Trade Statistics, 2008. Geneva, Switzerland: World Trade Organization

UNESCO Institute for Statistics: www.uis.unesco.org

World Development Indicators, 2008. Washington, D.C.: World Bank

Note: GDP and GDP (PPP) data on this spread are from the IMF.

GRAPHICS

LABOR MIGRATION: *National Geographic Atlas of the World,* 8th ed. Washington, D.C.: The National Geographic Society, 2005

Trade
pp. 58–59

CONSULTANTS

Peter Werner and Michael Finger
World Trade Organization (WTO)

United Nations Conference on Trade and Development (UNCTAD)

GENERAL REFERENCES

International Trade Statistics, 2008, Geneva, Switzerland: World Trade Organization

United Nations Conference on Trade and Development: www.unctad.org

World Trade Organization: www.wto.org

GRAPHICS

GROWTH OF WORLD TRADE: World Trade Organization

Food
pp. 60–61

CONSULTANTS

Food and Agriculture Organization of the United Nations (FAO)

Kate Sebastian
The International Food Policy Research Institute (IFPRI)

Dirk Zeller
The Sea Around Us Project, University of British Columbia

GENERAL REFERENCES

Food and Agriculture Organization of the United Nations (FAO) Statistics Division: faostat.fao.org/faostat

GRAPHICS

CROPLANDS OF THE WORLD: IFPRI 2007, derived from cropland and pasture intensity data (Ramankutty 2002 & 2005) and FAO/IIASA (2000) climate data. Unpublished data.
GLOBAL CATCH FIGURES: Adapted and updated from Pauly, D., V. Christensen, S. Guénette, T.J. Pitcher, U.R. Sumaila, C.J. Walters, R. Watson, and D. Zeller. 2002. Towards sustainability in world fisheries. *Nature* 418: 689–695.
WORLD CAPTURE FISHERIES AND AQUACULTURE PRODUCTION: Data from The Sea Around Us Project, www.seaaroundus.org.

Energy
pp. 62–63

CONSULTANTS

Connie Brooks
Sandia National Laboratories

George Douglas, Dennis Elliott, Donna Heimiller, Gary Schmitz, Thomas Stoffel
National Renewable Energy Laboratory (NREL)

Jean-Yves Garnier
International Energy Agency

Michael Grillot
U.S. Energy Information Administration

Elena Nekhaev
World Energy Council

Simon Walker
Independent Editorial and Technical Services

GENERAL REFERENCES

Bertani, Ruggero. December 2005. World Geothermal Power Generation in the Period 2001–2005. *Geothermics,* Volume 34, Number 6: p. 651–690

BP Statistical Review of World Energy 2005

Energy Information Administration, U.S. Department of Energy: www.eia.doe.gov

Global Wind Report 2008, GWEC (Global Wind Energy Council): www.gwec.net

http://pvresources.com

National Renewable Energy Laboratory: www.nrel.gov

Power Reactor Information System. International Atomic Energy Agency: www.iaea.org/programmes/a2/index.html

Survey of Energy Resources: Biomass. World Energy Council: www.worldenergy.org

The LNG industry. Groupe International des Importateurs de Gaz Naturel Liquefie, 2004

GRAPHICS

FOSSIL FUEL EXTRACTION: Chapel Design & Marketing and XNR Productions

PHOTOGRAPHS

PAGE 63, (UP) Jim Richardson; (UP CT) Mark C. Burnett/Photo Researchers; (CT) Courtesy National Renewable Energy Laboratory; (LO CT) Mick Roessler/CORBIS (LO) Ryan Pyle/CORBIS

Minerals
pp. 64–65

CONSULTANTS

Philip Brown
University of Wisconsin—Madison

Nelson Fugate
Mineral Information Institute

W. David Menzie and J. Michael Eros
USGS Minerals Information Team

GENERAL REFERENCES

USGS Minerals Information: minerals.usgs.gov/minerals

PHOTOGRAPHS

PAGE 64, (UP LE) Philip Brown; (CT LE) Philip Brown; (LO LE) Philip Brown; (UP CT) Phillip Hayson/Photo Researchers; (CT) Mark A. Schneider/Photo Researchers; (LO CT) Steven Holt/Stockpix.com; (UP RT) Mineral Information Institute/www.mii.org; (CT RT) Russ Lappa/Photo Researchers; (LO RT) Russ Lappa/Photo Researchers
PAGE 65, (UP LE) U.S. Geological Survey; (CT LE) E.R. Degginger/Photo Researchers; (LO LE) U.S. Geological Survey; (UP CT) U.S. Geological Survey; (CT) Mineral Information Institute/www.mii.org; (LO CT) U.S. Geological Survey; (UP RT) Kenneth W. Larsen, Courtesy Smithsonian Institution, NMNH; (CT RT) Kenneth W. Larsen, Courtesy Smithsonian Institution, NMNH; (LO RT) Philip Brown

Environmental Stresses
pp. 66–67

CONSULTANTS

Jane E. Barr
Associate, International Institute for Sustainable Development (IISD)

Christian Lambrechts
Division of Early Warning and Assessment (DEWA), United Nations Environment Programme (UNEP)

GENERAL REFERENCES

Acidification and eutrophication of developing country ecosystems. Swedish University of Agricultural Sciences (SLU), 2002

Centre of Documentation, Research and Experimentation on Accidental Water Pollution (Cedre): www.le-cedre.fr

EM-DAT: The OFDA/CRED International Disaster Database. Université Catholique de Louvain, Brussels. Belgium: www.emdat.be

Energy Information Administration. U.S. Department of Energy: www.eia.doe.gov

Global Environment Outlook: Environment for Development (GEO-4). United Nations Environment Programme, 2007.

Global Forest Resources Assessment. Forestry Department of the Food and Agriculture Organization of the United Nations, 2005

Natural Resources Conservation Service: www.nrcs.udsa.gov

United Nations Environment Programme-World Conservation Monitoring Centre (UNEP-WCMC): www.unep-wcmc.org

GRAPHICS

CARBON EMISSIONS GRAPHS (MAIN MAP): *Carbon Dioxide Emissions—Total (UNFCCC-CDIAC), 2007.* United Nations Framework Convention on Climate Change and Carbon Dioxide Information Analysis Center (UNFCCC and CDIAC). GEO Data Portal, http://geodata.grid.unep.ch/
GLOBAL CLIMATE CHANGE/CARBON EMISSIONS BY REGION: *Global Environment Outlook: environment for development (GEO-4).* United Nations Environment Programme, 2007, p. 61. http://www.unep.org/geo/geo4/media/
LAND DEGRADATION AND DESERTIFICATION: *The challenge of degraded land and its remediation,* Fig. 1.1 (after Oldeman et al. 1990, FAO-AGL 2000). Genske, Dieter, ETH-Zurich. Via www.contaminated-land.org
HUMAN FOOTPRINT: Wildlife Conservation Society

SATELLITE IMAGES

DEPLETION OF THE OZONE LAYER: Ozone Processing Team at NASA/Goddard Space Flight Center

Protected Areas
pp. 68–69

CONSULTANTS

Simon Blyth
UNEP World Conservation Monitoring Centre (UNEP-WCMC)

UNESCO World Heritage Centre

GENERAL REFERENCES

Antarctic Protected Areas Information Archive: http://cep.ats.aq/cep/apa/index.html

Protected areas map and statistics produced from the World Database on Protected Areas (WDPA) in March 2006 by UNEP World Conservation Monitoring Centre (WDPA custodian) (www.unep-wcmc.org), Cambridge, UK

UNEP-WCMC: www.unep-wcmc.org

UNESCO World Heritage Centre: whc.unesco.org

PHOTOGRAPHS

PAGE 69, (UP) James P. Blair; (LO LE) Art Wolfe/Getty Images; (LO CT) Richard Nowitz/NGS Image Collection; (LO RT) Sarah Leen

Acknowledgments

Globalization
pp. 70–71

CONSULTANTS
Samantha King and Janet Pau
Global Business Policy Council, A.T. Kearney, Inc.

Shang-Jin Wei
Columbia Business School

GENERAL REFERENCES
Airports Council International: www.airports.org

Amiti, Mary, and Shang-Jin Wei, December 2004. "Demystifying Outsourcing." *Finance & Development*, pp. 36–39.

International Telecommunication Union: www.itu.int

"Measuring Globalization." *Foreign Policy*, May/June 2005: 52–60. Globalization Index is developed by A.T. Kearney, Inc. and Foreign Policy (Carnegie Endowment for International Peace).

World Investment Report, 2007. Geneva, Switzerland: United Nations Conference on Trade and Development.

GRAPHICS
TRANSNATIONAL CORPORATIONS: *World Investment Report, 2007*. Geneva, Switzerland
EXTREMES OF GLOBALIZATION: 2007 Globalization Index, A.T. Kearney, Inc.
GLOBALIZATION STATUS: 2007 Globalization Index, A.T. Kearney, Inc.
ECONOMIC INTEGRATION: UNCTAD FDI database, 2007; 2007 Globalization Index, A.T. Kearney, Inc.
PERSONAL CONTACT: *World Telecommunications Indicators, 2006*, International Telecommunication Union; 2007 Globalization Index, A.T. Kearney, Inc.; Airports Council International: www.airports.org
TECHNOLOGICAL CONNECTIVITY: *World Telecommunications Indicators, 2006*, International Telecommunication Union; 2007 Globalization Index, A.T. Kearney, Inc.
POLITICAL ENGAGEMENT: Balance of Payments CD-ROM, International Monetary Fund, 2007; 2007 Globalization Index, A.T. Kearney, Inc.
IMPORTS IN BUSINESS SERVICES AS A SHARE OF GDP: Adapted and updated from Amiti, Mary, and Shang-Jin Wei, December 2004. "Demystifying Outsourcing." *Finance & Development*, pp. 36–39.

Technology and Communication
pp. 72–73

CONSULTANTS
Tim Kelly
Strategic Planning Unit,
International Telecommunication Union

Sarah Parkes
Media Works Creative

GENERAL REFERENCES
International Telecommunication Union: www.itu.int

GRAPHICS
CENTERS OF TECHNOLOGICAL INNOVATION: *Human Development Report 2001*, United Nations Development Programme (source data updated by Human Development Report Office in 2006) and World Intellectual Property Organization.
MILESTONES IN TECHNOLOGY: Adapted from *Human Development Report 2001*, United Nations Development Programme.
THE DIGITAL DIVIDE: NG Maps. Source data provided by TeleGeography Research, a division of PriMetrica, Inc. (www.telegeography.com) and the International Telecommunication Union. The Fuller Projection map design is a trademark of the Buckminster Fuller Institute © 1938, 1967, and 1992. All rights reserved.

Internet
pp. 74–75

CONSULTANTS
Josh Polterock and Brad Huffaker
Cooperative Association for Internet Data Analysis (CAIDA)

GENERAL REFERENCES
Cooperative Association for Internet Data Analysis (CAIDA): www.caida.org

International Telecommunication Union: www.itu.int

GRAPHICS
All images provided by the Cooperative Association for Internet Data Analysis (CAIDA), located at the San Diego Supercomputer Center (SDSC). CAIDA is a research unit of the University of California at San Diego (UCSD). URL: www.caida.org. Sponsors of this work include CAIDA Members, Cisco Systems, Department of Homeland Security (DHS, award NBCHC-040159), National Science Foundation (NSF, awards OCI-0137121, CNS-0433668, and CCR-0311690), and WIDE. Images copyright © 2006 The Regents of the University of California.

MAPPING THE SPREAD OF A COMPUTER VIRUS: Cooperative Association for Internet Data Analysis (CAIDA) "Nyxem Virus Analysis." Copyright © 2006 The Regents of the University of California. All rights reserved. Used by permission.
GLOBAL INTERNET CONNECTIVITY: Cooperative Association for Internet Data Analysis (CAIDA) "Skitter" Internet Map, 2005. Copyright © 2005 The Regents of the University of California. All rights reserved. Used by permission.
WORLDWIDE DISTRIBUTION OF INTERNET RESOURCES: Cooperative Association for Internet Data Analysis (CAIDA) "BGP Geopolitical Analysis Visualization." Copyright © 2006 The Regents of the University of California. All rights reserved. Used by permission.

ADDITIONAL CONSULTANTS

Regional Thematic Maps
Carl Haub
Population Reference Bureau

W. David Menzie and J. Michael Eros
USGS Minerals Information Team

Freddy Nachtergaele
Food and Agriculture Organization of the United Nations (FAO)

Gregory Yetman
Center for International Earth Science Information Network (CIESIN), Columbia University

Flags and Facts
Carl Haub
Population Reference Bureau

Whitney Smith
Flag Research Center

Antarctica
pp. 222–229
Graham Bartram
The Flag Institute

Scott Borg
National Science Foundation (NSF)—Antarctic Division

Mark R. Drinkwater
European Space Agency

Kenneth Jezek
Byrd Polar Research Center, Ohio State University

Tony K. Meunier
USGS Polar Program

Whitney Smith
Flag Research Center

David G. Vaughan
Bedmap Consortium, British Antarctic Survey

Roland Warner
Antarctic Cooperative Research Centre and Australian Antarctic Division

Oceanography
pp. 232–233
Eric J. Lindstrom
National Aeronautics and Space Administration (NASA)

Keelin Kuipers
National Oceanic and Atmospheric Administration (NOAA)

Bob Molinari
NOAA

Bruce Parker
NOAA/National Ocean Service (NOS)

Richard A. Schmalz, Jr.
NOAA

Limits of the Oceans and Seas
pp. 234–235
Adam J. Kerr
International Hydrographic Management Consulting

Space
pp. 246–261
Alexei V. Filippenko
Department of Astronomy, University of California, Berkeley

Sanjay S. Limaye and Rosalyn A. Pertzborn
Space Science and Engineering Center, University of Wisconsin—Madison

Stephen P. Maran

Robert E. Pratt
National Geographic Maps

The Moon
pp. 248–251
Paul D. Spudis
Lunar and Planetary Institute, Houston, Texas

Mars
pp. 252–253
Damond Benningfield
StarDate radio series

The Solar System
pp. 254–255
Lucy McFadden
University of Maryland, College Park

The Planets
pp. 256–257
Henry Kline
NASA Jet Propulsion Laboratory (JPL)

The Universe
pp. 258–259
Todd J. Henry
Harvard-Smithsonian Center for Astrophysics

Edmund Bertschinger
Massachusetts Institute of Technology

Donald P. Schneider
Pennsylvania State University

Marc Postman
Space Telescope Science Institute (STScI)

Christopher D. Impey
University of Arizona

R. Brent Tully
University of Hawai'i

August E. Evrard
University of Michigan

Geographic Comparisons
pp. 264–265
John Kammerer
National Geospatial-Intelligence Agency (NGA)

George Sharman
NOAA/NESDIS/NGDC

Peter H. Gleick
Pacific Institute for Studies in Development, Environment, and Security

R.L. Fisher
Scripps Institution of Oceanography

Philip Micklin
Western Michigan University

Political Entities and Status
pp. 266–269
Leo Dillon
Department of State, Office of the Geographer

Carl Haub
Population Reference Bureau

Whitney Smith
Flag Research Center

Special Flags
pp. 270–271
Whitney Smith
Flag Research Center

Glossary
pp. 282–284
Rex Honey
University of Iowa

Bernard O. Bauer
University of Southern California

PHYSICAL AND POLITICAL MAPS

Bureau of the Census,
  U.S. Department of Commerce

Bureau of Land Management,
  U.S. Department of the Interior

Central Intelligence Agency (CIA)

National Geographic Maps

National Geospatial-Intelligence
  Agency (NGA)

National Park Service,
  U.S. Department of the Interior

Office of the Geographer and Global Issues,
  U.S. Department of State

U.S. Board on Geographic Names (BGN)

U.S. Geological Survey,
  U.S. Department of the Interior

PRINCIPAL REFERENCE SOURCES

Columbia Gazetteer of the World. Cohen, Saul B., ed. New York: Columbia University Press

Encarta World English Dictionary. New York: St. Martin's Press and Microsoft Encarta

Human Development Reports. New York: United Nations Development Programme (UNDP)

International Trade Statistics. Geneva, Switzerland: World Trade Organization

McKnight, Tom L. *Physical Geography: A Landscape Appreciation*. 5th ed. Upper Saddle River, New Jersey: Prentice Hall, 1996

National Geographic Atlas of the World, 8th ed. Washington, D.C.: The National Geographic Society, 2005

Strahler, Alan and Arthur Strahler. *Physical Geography: Science and Systems of the Human Environment*. 2nd ed., John Wiley & Sons, Inc, 2002

Tarbuck, Edward J. and Frederick K. Lutgens. *Earth: An Introduction to Physical Geology*. 7th ed. Upper Saddle River, New Jersey: Prentice Hall, 2002

World Development Indicators, Washington, D.C.: World Bank

The World Factbook. Washington, D.C.: Central Intelligence Agency

The World Health Report. Geneva: World Health Organization

World Investment Report. New York and Geneva: United Nations Conference on Trade and Development

Cambridge Dictionaries Online
dictionary.cambridge.org

Central Intelligence Agency
www.cia.gov

CIESIN
www.ciesin.org

Conservation International
www.conservation.org

Energy Information Agency
www.eia.doe.gov

Food and Agriculture
Organization of the UN
www.fao.org

International Monetary Fund
www.imf.org

Merriam-Webster OnLine
www.m-w.com

National Aeronautics and
Space Administration
www.nasa.gov

National Climatic Data Center
www.ncdc.noaa.gov

National Geophysical Data
Center
www.ngdc.noaa.gov

National Oceanic and
Atmospheric Administration
www.noaa.gov

National Park Service
www.nps.gov

National Renewable Energy
Laboratory
www.nrel.gov

Population Reference Bureau
www.prb.org

United Nations
www.un.org

UN Conference on Trade and
Development
www.unctad.org

UN Development Programme
www.undp.org

UN Educational, Cultural,
and Scientific Organization
www.unesco.org

UNESCO Institute for Statistics
www.uis.unesco.org

UNEP-WCMC
www.unep-wcmc.org

UN Millennium
Development Goals
www.un.org/millenniumgoals

UN Population Division
www.unpopulation.org

UN Refugee Agency
www.unhcr.org

UN Statistics Division
unstats.un.org

U.S. Board on
Geographic Names
geonames.usgs.gov

U.S. Bureau of Economic
Analysis
www.bea.gov

U.S. Census Bureau
www.census.gov

U.S. Geological Survey
www.usgs.gov

World Bank
www.worldbank.org

World Health Organization
www.who.int

World Trade Organization
www.wto.org

WWF
www.worldwildlife.org

SATELLITE IMAGES

CONTINENTAL SATELLITE IMAGES: NASA/Jet Propulsion Laboratory (JPL)/California Institute of Technology/Advanced Very High Resolution Radiometer (AVHRR) Project/Cartographic Applications Group (CAG)

The Cartographic Applications Group manipulated more than 500 NOAA weather satellite images acquired by the AVHRR instrument to create satellite coverages at one-kilometer resolution (one pixel of data equals one kilometer on the Earth). Using hundreds of multidate NOAA AVHRR satellite scenes and imaging in the visible and near-infrared wavelengths, the mosaics were created in a rapid fashion using semiautomated software procedures based on JPL's VICAR/IBIS image processing and GIS software.

FRONT JACKET, BACKGROUND: ETOPO-2 relief; Digital Chart of the World

FRONT JACKET, SMALL GLOBE (PACIFIC OCEAN): Image created using NASA Aqua satellite mission, MODIS Sensor data, provided by NASA Goddard Space Flight Center, NASA Ocean Biology Processing Group

TITLE PAGE (PAGE 2), Peter Sloss, NOAA (National Geophysical Data Center)

PAGE 29, MISSISSIPPI RIVER DELTA: Centre National d'Etudes Spatiales (CNES)

PAGES 32–33, GLOBAL LAND COVER CLASSIFICATION AT 1KM SPATIAL RESOLUTION USING A CLASSIFICATION TREE APPROACH: M. Hansen, R. DeFries, J.R.G. Townshend, and R. Sohlberg. 1998. 1 Km Land Cover Classification Derived from AVHRR. College Park, Maryland: The Global Land Cover Facility (Note: Data were derived from NOAA AVHRR and NASA Landsat imagery.)

PAGE 34, *Images created originally for the GLOBE program by NOAA's National Geophysical Data Center, Boulder, Colorado, U.S.A.*
CLOUD COVER: International Satellite Cloud Climatology Project (ISCCP); National Aeronautics and Space Administration (NASA); Goddard Institute for Space Studies (GISS). **PRECIPITATION:** Global Precipitation Climatology Project (GPCP); International Satellite Land Surface Climatology Project (ISLSCP). **SOLAR ENERGY:** Earth Radiation Budget Experiment (ERBE); Greenhouse Effect Detection Experiment (GEDEX). **TEMPERATURE:** National Center for Environmental Prediction (NCEP); National Center for Atmospheric Research (NCAR); National Weather Service (NWS).

PAGE 38, HURRICANE IMAGE: NASA Goddard Space Flight Center (GSFC), data from NOAA

PAGE 39, EL NIÑO IMAGE SEQUENCE: Courtesy Robert M. Carey, NOAA; **LIGHTNING IMAGE:** NASA Marshall Space Flight Center Lightning Imaging Sensor (LIS) Instrument Team, Huntsville, Alabama

PAGE 40, BIOSPHERE FROM SPACE: SeaWiFS, NASA/Goddard Space Flight Center, Gene Carl Feldman and ORBIMAGE

PAGE 44, LIGHTS OF THE WORLD: Composite image: MODIS imagery; ETOPO-2 relief; NOAA/NGDC and DMSP lights at night data

PAGE 66, DEPLETION OF THE OZONE LAYER: Ozone Processing Team at NASA/Goddard Space Flight Center

PAGE 228, SURFACE ELEVATION: Byrd Polar Research Center, Ohio State University. **ICE SHEET THICKNESS:** Bedmap Project. **ICE FLOW VELOCITY:** Roland Warner, Antarctic Cooperative Research Centre and Australian Antarctic Division. **SEA ICE MOVEMENT AND WIND FLOW: SEA ICE VELOCITY DATA:** Mark R. Drinkwater and Xiang Liu, Jet Propulsion Laboratory/California Institute of Technology. **SURFACE WINDS:** Based on data from David H. Bromwich, Ohio State University, and Thomas R. Parish, University of Wyoming.

PAGES 246–247, HELIX NEBULA: NASA, ESA, C.R. O'Dell (Vanderbilt University), M. Meixner and P. McCullough (STScI)

PAGES 249 AND 251, CLEMENTINE TOPOGRAPHIC MAP OF THE MOON: Courtesy of the Lunar and Planetary Institute, Houston, Texas

PAGES 252–253, MARS EXPLORATION: NASA/JPL-Caltech; **VASTITAS BOREALIS IMPACT CRATER:** ESA/DLR/FU Berlin (G. Neukum)

PAGES 256 AND 257, THE PLANETS: Courtesy of NASA/JPL-Caltech

PAGE 384, ETOPO-2 relief; Digital Chart of the World

PHOTOGRAPHS

Front Jacket
(LE) Jodi Cobb/NGS Image Collection
(CT LE) Julien Grondin/iStockphoto
(CT RT) Olivier Lantzendörffer/iStockphoto
(RT) George F. Mobley/NGS Image Collection

Interior
PAGE 24, (UP) R.D. Griggs, USGS
PAGE 24, (CT) Sharon Johnson
PAGE 24, (LO) David Muench
PAGE 25, Raymond Gehman/NGS Image Collection
PAGE 26, (LE) Joel Sartore/www.joelsartore.com
PAGE 26, (CT) Science Photo Library/CORBIS
PAGE 26, (UP RT) George F. Mobley
PAGE 26, (LO RT) James D. Balog
PAGE 27, (UP LE) Wolfgang Kaehler/CORBIS
PAGE 27, (UP CT) Lyle Rosbotham
PAGE 27, (UP RT) Adriel Heisey
PAGE 27, (LO LE) Marc Moritsch/NGS Image Collection
PAGE 27, (LO CT) Peter Essick
PAGE 27, (LO RT) Sam Abell, NGS
PAGE 28, (LE) Peter Essick
PAGE 28, (CT) Douglas R. Grant
PAGE 28, (RT) Tom and Pat Leeson
PAGE 29, (UP CT) Rob Brander
PAGE 29, (UP RT) George Veni and James Jasek
PAGE 29, (LO LE) Sharon Johnson
PAGE 29, (LO RT) Douglas R. Grant/Parks Canada
PAGE 32, (UP LE) Tom and Pat Leeson/Photo Researchers
PAGE 32, (UP RT) Michael Nichols/NGS Image Collection
PAGE 32, (LO LE) Stephen J. Krasemann/Photo Researchers
PAGE 32, (LO CT LE) Rod Planck/Photo Researchers
PAGE 32, (CT LE) Jim Steinberg/Photo Researchers
PAGE 32, (CT RT) Matthew C. Hansen, University of Maryland
PAGE 32, (LO CT RT) Gregory G. Dimijian/Photo Researchers
PAGE 32, (LO RT) Sharon Johnson
PAGE 33, (LE) Georg Gerster/Photo Researchers
PAGE 33, (LO CT LE) Rod Planck/Photo Researchers
PAGE 33, (LE CT) Jim Richardson
PAGE 33, (RT CT) George Steinmetz
PAGE 33, (LO CT RT) Steve McCurry
PAGE 33, (RT) B. and C. Alexander/PhotoResearchers
PAGE 35, Sharon Johnson
PAGE 50, (LE) Jodi Cobb/National Geographic Photographer
PAGE 50, (RT) James L. Stanfield
PAGES 50–51 Tony Heiderer
PAGE 51, (LE) Thomas J. Abercrombie
PAGE 51, (RT) Annie Griffiths Belt;
PAGE 61, (LE) Steven L. Raymer/NGS Image Collection
PAGE 61, (CT) Richard Olsenius/NGS Image Collection
PAGE 61, (RT) Jim Richardson
PAGE 63, (UP) Jim Richardson
PAGE 63, (UP CT) Courtesy National Renewable Energy Laboratory
PAGE 63, (LO CT) Mick Roessler/CORBIS
PAGE 63, (LO) Ryan Pyle/CORBIS
PAGE 64, (UP LE) Philip Brown
PAGE 64, (CT LE) Philip Brown
PAGE 64, (LO LE) Philip Brown
PAGE 64, (UP CT) Phillip Hayson/Photo Researchers
PAGE 64, (CT) Mark A. Schneider/Photo Researchers
PAGE 64, (LO CT) Steven Holt/Stockpix.com
PAGE 64, (UP RT) Mineral Information Institute/www.mii.org
PAGE 64, (CT RT) Russ Lappa/Photo Researchers
PAGE 64, (LO RT) Russ Lappa/Photo Researchers
PAGE 65, (UP LE) U.S. Geological Survey
PAGE 65, (CT LE) E.R. Degginger/Photo Researchers
PAGE 65, (LO LE) U.S. Geological Survey
PAGE 65, (UP CT) U.S. Geological Survey
PAGE 65, (CT) Mineral Information Institute/www.mii.org
PAGE 65, (LO CT) U.S. Geological Survey
PAGE 65, (UP RT) Kenneth W. Larsen, Courtesy Smithsonian Institution, NMNH
PAGE 65, (CT RT) Kenneth W. Larsen, Courtesy Smithsonian Institution, NMNH
PAGE 65, (LO RT) Philip Brown
PAGE 69, (UP) James P. Blair
PAGE 69, (LO LE) Art Wolfe/Getty Images
PAGE 69, (LO CT) Richard Nowitz/NGS Image Collection
PAGE 69, (LO RT) Sarah Leen
PAGES 76–77, Ron Watts/CORBIS
PAGE 79, W.E. Garrett/NGS Image Collection
PAGES 122–123, Skip Brown/NGS Image Collection
PAGE 125, L. Scott Shelton
PAGES 134–135, George F. Mobley/NGS Image Collection
PAGE 137, Winfield I. Parks, Jr.
PAGES 162–163, J. Yip/Imagestate/Panoramic Images
PAGE 165, Steve McCurry/NGS Image Collection
PAGES 190–191, Beverly Joubert/NGS Image Collection
PAGE 193, David Boyer/NGS Image Collection
PAGES 206–207, Theo Allofs/CORBIS
PAGE 209, Pam Gardner/Frank Lane Picture Agency/CORBIS
PAGES 222–223, Paul A. Souders/CORBIS
PAGE 225, Maria Stenzel

KEY TO FLAGS AND FACTS

The National Geographic Society, whose cartographic policy is to recognize de facto countries, counted 194 independent nations in the spring of 2009. Within this atlas, fact boxes for independent nations, most dependencies, and U.S. states are placed on or next to regional maps that show the areas they represent. Each box includes the flag of the political entity, as well as important statistical data. Boxes for some dependencies show two flags—a local flag and the flag of the administering country. Since Paraguay and the state of Oregon have different designs on the obverse and reverse sides of their flags, their fact boxes show both sides of their flags.

The statistical data provide highlights of geography, demography, and economy. These details offer a brief overview of each entity; they present general characteristics and are not intended to be comprehensive studies. The structured nature of the text results in some generic collective or umbrella terms. The industry category, for instance, includes services in addition to traditional manufacturing sectors. Space limitations dictate the amount of information included. For example, the only languages listed for the U.S. are English and Spanish, although many others are spoken.

Fact boxes are arranged alphabetically by the conventional short forms of the country or dependency names (except for the Oceania, Islands of Africa, and Europe's Smallest Countries fact boxes, where country and dependency boxes are grouped separately). The short-form names for dependencies are followed by the name of the administering country in parentheses. The short-form names for Côte d'Ivoire, Myanmar, and Timor-Leste are followed by alternate, commonly referred to names in parentheses. The conventional long-form names of the country or dependency appear within colored stripes below the short-form names; if there are no long forms, the short forms are repeated. This policy has two exceptions: For U.S. states, nicknames are shown inside the colored stripes, and for French overseas departments, the words "Overseas Department of France" appear inside the colored stripes. These departments of France are the equivalent of states in the United States, and thus not considered dependencies. NA indicates that data are not available or not applicable.

AREA accounts for the total area of a country, U.S. state, or dependency, including all land and inland water delimited by international boundaries, intranational boundaries, or coastlines.

In the POPULATION category, the figures for U.S. state populations are from the U.S. Census Bureau's 2008 midyear estimates. Two population figures are listed for the CAPITAL and LARGEST CITY of each state. The city-proper figure, from data provided by the U.S. Census Bureau, shows the estimated number of people who lived within the incorporated city limits on July 1, 2007. The larger metro-area figure represents the number of people who live within a U.S. Office of Management and Budget-defined metropolitan statistical area—a broader designation that includes both a city proper and the surrounding urbanized region. These July 1, 2007, estimates are from the U.S. Census Bureau's table of Annual Estimates of the Population of Metropolitan and Micropolitan Statistical Areas. Metropolitan statistical areas and their geographic boundaries can cross state borders and are defined on the basis of population as well as other factors. Some state capitals with small populations are not defined as part of a metropolitan statistical area and thus do not have a metro-area figure.

POPULATION figures for independent nations and dependencies are mid-2008 figures from the Population Reference Bureau in Washington, D.C. Next to CAPITAL is the name of the seat of government, followed by the city's population. Capital city populations for both independent nations and dependencies are 2007 United Nations estimates and represent the population of the city's urban agglomeration, which usually includes both city proper and adjacent suburbs. Both POPULATION and CAPITAL population figures for countries, dependencies, and U.S. states are rounded to the nearest thousand.

Under RELIGION, the most widely practiced faith appears first. "Traditional" or "indigenous" connotes beliefs of important local sects, such as Maya in Middle America. Under LANGUAGE, the most widely spoken language is listed first. Both RELIGION and LANGUAGE are in rank ordering, taken from the 2009 CIA World Factbook.

LITERACY generally indicates the percentage of the population above the age of 15 who can read and write. There are no universal standards of literacy, so these estimates (from the 2009 CIA World Factbook) are based on the most common definition available for a nation. LIFE EXPECTANCY (from 2008 Population Reference Bureau data) represents the average number of years a group of infants born in the same year can be expected to live if the mortality rate at each age remains constant in the future.

GDP PER CAPITA is gross domestic product (GDP) based on purchasing-power parity (PPP) in current international dollars divided by midyear population estimates. GDP per capita estimates, rounded to the nearest hundred, are from the International Monetary Fund's World Economic Outlook Database, October 2008, and are supplemented by the 2009 CIA World Factbook. Gross domestic product is the value of all final goods and services produced within a region in a given year. These estimates are calculated using the purchasing-power parity (PPP) conversion factor designed to equalize the purchasing powers of different countries. For U.S. states, equivalent measurements to GDP on the intranational level have been used. 2007 PCPI, or Per Capita Personal INCOME, figures from the U.S. Bureau of Economic Analysis are presented; PCPI divides the total personal income of all residents of a state by midyear population.

Individual income estimates such as GDP PER CAPITA and PCI are among the many indicators used to assess a nation's well-being. As statistical averages, they hide extremes of poverty and wealth. Furthermore, they take no account of factors that affect quality of life, such as environmental degradation, educational opportunities, and health care.

ECONOMY information for the independent nations and dependencies is divided into three general categories: Industry, Agriculture, and Exports. Because of structural limitations, only the primary industries (IND), agricultural commodities (AGR), and exports (EXP) as listed in the 2009 CIA World Factbook are reported. Agriculture serves as an umbrella term not only for crops but also for livestock, products, and fish. In the interest of conciseness, agriculture for the independent nations presents, when applicable but not limited to, four major crops, followed by leading entries for livestock, products, and fish. For the other two categories, the leading industries and export products are listed as data and space limitations allow. The information provided for each category is listed in rank order, starting with the largest by value or importance.

NATIONAL GEOGRAPHIC
Family
REFERENCE
THIRD EDITION
Atlas
OF THE
WORLD

Published by the National Geographic Society

John M. Fahey, Jr.	*President and Chief Executive Officer*
Gilbert M. Grosvenor	*Chairman of the Board*
Tim T. Kelly	*President, Global Media Group*
John Q. Griffin	*Executive Vice President; President, Publishing*
Nina D. Hoffman	*Executive Vice President, President, Book Publishing Group*

Prepared by the Book Division

Barbara Brownell Grogan	*Vice President and Editor in Chief*
Marianne R. Koszorus	*Director of Design*

Staff for this Atlas

Carl Mehler	*Project Editor and Director of Maps*
Nicholas P. Rosenbach	*Supervisor of Map Edit*
Timothy J. Carter, Laura Exner, Steven D. Gardner, Thomas L. Gray, Joseph F. Ochlak	*Map Editors*

Sam Chernawsky, Matt Chwastyk, Sven M. Dolling, Steven D. Gardner, Gregory Ugiansky, and XNR Productions *Map Research and Compilation*

Matt Chwastyk, Gregory Ugiansky *Map Production Managers*

Sven M. Dolling, Steven D. Gardner, James Huckenpahler, Michael McNey, Kyle T. Rector, Martin S. Walz, and XNR Productions *Map Production*

David B. Miller *Contributing Geographer*

Rebecca Lescaze; Principal, Carolinda E. Averitt, Laura Exner, Judith Klein, K. M. Kostyal, Jane Sunderland *Text Editors*

Elisabeth B. Booz, Patrick Booz, Philip Brown, William Burroughs, Carlos Castillo-Salgado, Manuel Colunga-Garcia, Byron Crape, Ellen Ficklen, Michael Finger, Richard Fix, Stuart H. Gage, Matthew C. Hansen, Craig K. Harris, Mike Hoffmann, Tim Kelly, K. M. Kostyal, Ruth Levine, Eric Lindstrom, David T. Long, Enrique Loyola-Elizondo, Stephen P. Maran, Carl Mehler, W. David Menzie, H. Michael Mogil, John Morrison, Rhea Muchow, Ted Munn, Margaret Murray, Sarah Parks, Janet Pau, Josh Polterock, Antony Shugaar, Brad Singer, Peter W. Sloss, Whitney Smith, Paul D. Spudis, Robert Tilling, Simon Walker, Patrick J. Webber, Joe Yogerst *Contributing Writers*

Sam Chernawsky, Elizabeth B. Booz, Victoria Garrett Jones, Rhea Muchow, Joseph F. Ochlak, Anne E. Withers *Text Researchers*

Marty Ittner, Principal; Jennifer Christiansen, Megan McCarthy, Susan K. White *Book Design*

ChrisOrr.com, Tibor G. Tóth *Art and Illustrations*

Dana Chivvis, Sadie Quarrier *Photo Editors*

Abby Lepold, Meredith C. Wilcox *Photo Assistants*

Jennifer A. Thornton *Managing Editor*

R. Gary Colbert *Production Director*

Manufacturing and Quality Control

Christopher A. Liedel	*Chief Financial Officer*
Phillip L. Schlosser	*Vice President*
Chris Brown	*Technical Director*
Nicole Elliott, Rachel Faulise	*Managers*

Reproduction by Quad/Graphics, Alexandria, Virginia

Printed and Bound by Mondadori S.p.A., Verona, Italy

RUSSIA

Alaska
110

Greenland

ICELAND

CANADA
82

UNITED
KINGDOM

BRITAIN AND IRELAND
142

IRELAND

FRANCE AND THE LOW COUNTRIE

PORTUGAL

NORTH AMERICA **76-121**

UNITED STATES
84-113

IBERIAN PENINSULA
144

MOROCC

Hawai'i
112

MEXICO

CUBA

BAHAMAS

BAHAMAS AND
GREATER ANTILLES
116

DOMINICAN
REPUBLIC

Western
Sahara

MEXICO AND
CENTRAL AMERICA
114

JAMAICA

HAITI

BELIZE

HONDURAS

Puerto
Rico

LESSER ANTILLES
118

ST. KITTS AND NEVIS
ANTIGUA AND BARBUDA

DOMINICA

MAURITANIA

CAPE
VERDE

SENEGAL

GUATEMALA
EL SALVADOR

NICARAGUA

ST. LUCIA

BARBADOS

GAMBIA

GRENADA ST. VINCENT AND THE GRENADINES

GUINEA-BISSAU

GUINEA

PANAMA

TRINIDAD AND TOBAGO

SIERRA LEONE

CÔ
D'IVO

COSTA RICA

VENEZUELA

GUYANA

LIBERIA

PACIFIC OCEAN
238

NORTHERN
SOUTH AMERICA
128

SURINAME

French Guiana

COLOMBIA

WEST-CENT
AFR

KIRIBATI

ECUADOR

B R A Z I L

ATLANTIC
OCEAN
236

American
Samoa

OCEANIA
214-221

PERU

CENTRAL
SOUTH AMERICA
130

SAMOA

French Polynesia

BOLIVIA

SOUTH AMERICA **122-133**

TONGA

PARAGUAY

CHILE

URUGUAY

ARGENTINA

SOUTHERN
SOUTH AMERICA
132

Falkland
Islands

ROCKY
MOUNTAINS
106

NORTHERN
PLAINS
104

GREAT
LAKES
98

NORTHEAST
94

MAINE

WASHINGTON

MONTANA

NORTH DAKOTA

MINNESOTA

VT.

N.H.

OREGON

IDAHO

WYOMING

SOUTH DAKOTA

WISCONSIN

MICHIGAN

NEW
YORK

MASS.

R.I.
CONN.

WEST
COAST
108

NEVADA

UTAH

COLORADO

NEBRASKA

IOWA

ILLINOIS

IND.

OHIO

PA.

NEW
JERSEY

DELAWARE
MARYLAND
WASHINGTON, D.C.

CALIFORNIA

KANSAS

MISSOURI

KENTUCKY

W. VA.

VA.

ARIZONA

NEW
MEXICO

OKLAHOMA

ARKANSAS

TENNESSEE

N.C.

S.C.

TEXAS

MISS.

ALABAMA

GEORGIA

SOUTH
ATLANTIC
96

LA.

FLORIDA

TEXAS AND
OKLAHOMA
102

MIDDLE
SOUTH
100